Historic Homes and Institutions and Genealogical and Personal Memoirs of Worcester County, Massachusetts, With a History of Worcester Society of Antiquity

GEORGE F. HOAR

HISTORIC HOMES AND INSTITUTIONS

AND

GENEALOGICAL AND PERSONAL MEMOIRS

OF

WORCESTER COUNTY

MASSACHUSETTS

WITH A HISTORY OF

WORCESTER SOCIETY OF ANTIQUITY

PREPARED UNDER THE EDITORIAL SUPERVISION OF

ELLERY BICKNELL CRANE

Librarian of the Worcester Society of Antiquity, and Editor of its Proceedings,
Author of "The Rawson Family Memorial," "Crane
Family," two vols, Etc

"Knowledge of kindred and the genealogies of the ancient families deserveth the highest praise Herein consisteth a part of the knowledge of a man's own self It is a great spur to virtue to look back on the work of our lines"—*Lord Bacon*

"There is no heroic poem in the world but is at the bottom the life of a man"—*Sir Walter Scott*

VOL. I ~~4340A.195~~

ILLUSTRATED

NEW YORK CHICAGO
THE LEWIS PUBLISHING COMPANY
1907

INTRODUCTORY

WORCESTER COUNTY

The history of Massachusetts—civil, political and military—has been written by various authors and at various times, each succeeding writer adding a new chapter of annals, or treating his subject from a different viewpoint. Such history, however, splendid narrative that it is, is principally concerned with what has been accomplished by the people in a mass, and takes little note of individuals, except those so pre-eminent as leaders as to come under the full glare of fame.

Hence it follows that genealogical and family memoirs are of peculiar importance, including, as they do, the personal annals of those who make heroes and heroism possible—those who have marched in the ranks of progress, bearing the heat and burden of the day,—portraying the spirit which actuated them, and holding up their effort for an example to those who come afterward. As was written by Martineau, "To have forefathers renowned for honorable deeds, to belong by nature to those who have bravely borne their part in life and refreshed the world with mighty thoughts and healthy admiration, is a privilege which it were mean and self-willed to despise. It is a security given for us of old, which it were false-hearted not to redeem; and in virtues bred of a noble stock, mellowed as they are by reverence, there is often a grace and ripeness wanting to self-made and brand-new excellence. Of like value to a people are heroic national traditions, giving them a determined character to sustain among the tribes of men, making them familiar with images of great and strenuous life, and kindling them with faith in glorious possibilities."

PRESCOTT HOMESTEAD, AT PEPPERELL

The home of Col. William Prescott, second son of Benjamin Prescott, and the grandfather of William H. Prescott, the distinguished historian. Col. Prescott was born in Groton, and settled on a large tract of land previously owned by his father, located in what was called the "Gore," later included in the town of Pepperell. He served as a Lieutenant in the expedition sent in 1755, to remove the French Neutrals from Nova Scotia; and as colonel of the Minute Men enrolled in and about Groton in 1774. At the battle of Bunker Hill, June 17, 1775, he occupied the distinguished position of Commander of the American forces. He died October 13, 1795, aged sixty-nine years, having been born February 20, 1726. His widow died October 21, 1821, aged eighty-eight years; both buried at Pepperell.

The county of Worcester affords a peculiarly interesting field for a study of family traits, individual character and personal achievements. It is rich in historical associations, and its soil has been the scene of events of the utmost importance to the entire nation. To it came a sturdy people, men and women, too, of brawn and brain and conscience, their hearts fervent in reverence of God and love for religious and political liberty. They came up out of great tribulations. They were of that overflow of Pilgrim and Puritan stock which traversed an unbroken wilderness to make homes where were savages, and to conquer primeval nature. They builded better than they knew.

> "For Good is not a shapely mass of stone,
> Hewn by man's hand, and worked by him alone.
> It is a seed God suffers him to sow—
> Others will reap, and, when the harvests grow,
> He giveth increase through all coming years,
> And lets men reap in joy, seed that was sown in tears."

ISAIAH THOMAS, LL. D.
Founder of "Massachusetts Spy," and American Antiquarian Society, born July 30, 1749, died April 4, 1831, in Worcester.

Simple and clean in their lives, as were these early settlers, the homes which they builded were humble, but they were the seat of all the virtues that constitute ideal manhood and womanhood. The courage, fortitude and activity displayed by these hardy pioneers was most remarkable, and, when the struggle for national independence came, the sons and daughters of these illustrious sires were not wanting in patriotism and devotion, freely sacrificing comfort, life and property, that they might bequeath to the generations that should follow them a free liberal government "of the people, by the people, and for the people." They were, from the beginning, prime movers in every patriotic movement, and in all looking to the elevation of humanity. In 1775, in convention assembled, they expressed their abhorrence of human slavery, and that, whenever opportunity should present, they would use their influence toward the emancipation of the negro. From here, their birthplace, marched Captain (later known as Colonel) Timothy Bigelow and Captain Benjamin Flagg—with their companies of minute-men on that memorable 19th of April, 1775, and here, in the city of Worcester, the Declaration of Independence was first read in Massachusetts. Here, too, was the home of General Artemas Ward, the trusted friend and chief lieutenant of the great Washington. In Worcester was set up, by Isaiah Thomas, the first printing press in an inland town in Massachusetts, and the journal which was printed from it was one which was unparalleled in its influence upon the minds of the common people in their ready espousal of the cause of independence from British tyranny. Here entered upon his illustrious career Levi Lincoln, one of the giants in those days—a great lawyer, jurist and statesman. Here lived and labored representatives of the famous Prescott, Curtis, Allen, Washburn and Devons families and here was born George Bancroft, the historian. Here, too, were heard, at various periods, Webster, Sumner, Lincoln, Henry Wilson and Henry Ward Beecher, and, in the yet later

FARNUM HOUSE, UXBRIDGE
Built by Moses Farnum in 1766, and stands in the southerly part of the town of Uxbridge.

Worcester Art Museum, Salisbury Street, Worcester

days, the lamented Senator George F. Hoar, all eloquent proclaimers of liberty and pleaders for humanity. And, in the Civil war, the grandsons of the men of Bunker Hill fought at Gettysburg, and on many another glorious field, that the Union might be preserved.

There were not only patriots among the settlers of Worcester county, but men of special note in various fields of industry. Perhaps no spot of the same area on this continent has produced so many of superior mechanical genius, or those who have given to the world mechanisms of such great utility and advantage to the progress of civilization. Senator Hoar, in a speech made before the United States Senate, on January 6, 1903, said; "Within twelve miles of the spot where I live, was born Eli Whitney, the inventor of the cotton gin, who doubled the value of every acre of land in this country on which cotton can grow. Six miles in another direction was born Erastus Bigelow, the inventor of the carpet machine. Six miles in another direction lived Blanchard, the inventor of the machine for turning irregular forms, perhaps the most important single mechanical invention that has been made in the country down to this time. Eight miles another way was born Whittemore, inventor of the card clothing machine. Twelve miles another way was born and lived Elias Howe, inventor of the sewing machine. When the Civil war broke out, Mr. Howe enlisted as private. When, in its embarrassment, in the summer of 1861, the government could not pay its soldiers, this private soldier drew his check for all the arrears due his regiment of a thousand men, for some months. * * * All around me there are homesteads, some bordering my own, owned by inventors, foremen and skilled workmen, who have acquired fortunes in this honorable service, so beneficent to mankind and so honorable to this country."

Major-General Artemas Ward

Chief Justice of the Court of Common Pleas, October 27. 1774; General in the Continental army; Commander-in-Chief of the Massachusetts forces, May 19, 1775. Born in Shrewsbury, Massachusetts, November 26. 1727, son of Nahum and Martha (Howe) Ward. As Major took part in the campaign of 1755 against the French, near Lake Champlain, attaing the rank of colonel. Member of the Massachusetts Legislature for sixteen years; Speaker of that body 1785; Member of Congress 1791-95; died in Shrewsbury October 27, 1800.

The founders of the olden time, who laid the foundations for the development of the present, left not only a splendid posterity on this their own soil, but they gave a pregnant interpretation to the words of Bishop Berkley: "Westward the course of the empire takes its way," for from them came an overflow which was destined to continue until it reached the far-off Pacific—men and women to carry forth and perpetuate that plain, sturdy, personal character of manhood and womanhood for which the people of Massachusetts have gained a large degree of renown. Wherever they planted their homes, there the church and the school house are found as monuments of their personality. Nor is this all, they prided themselves in thrift, and the reward that comes as the fruit of honest toil and endeavor; and, wherever placed, have proved a power for ideal citizenship and good government, for that righteousness which exalteth a nation.

In each generation and at every stage of progress, the people of Worcester county have had the service of men of the loftiest character and highest capability—in arms, in the arts of peace, in statesmanship, in affairs, and in letters. It is to connect the active progressive men of the present generation with their illustrious ancestry, that the present volumes were undertaken, in the conviction that

"It is indeed a blessing when the virtues
Of noble races are hereditary,
And do derive themselves from imitation
Of virtuous ancestors."

The honorable ancestry which belongs to the people of Worcester county is a noble heritage, and the story of its achievements is a sacred trust committed to its descendants, upon whom devolves the perpetuation of their record. History is constantly making, and that of yesterday and today is as important in its place as that of the centuries past. Throughout the country are those who are memorialized in its pages, through whose sagacity, determination and philanthropy, states and communities have been benefited in material ways, and in religious, educational and political affairs—in all that stands for progress and improvement.

GOVERNOR LEVI LINCOLN

Continued in the office of Governor for nine successive re-elections, until, declining to be a candidate for re-election, retired from the office on the induction of his successor, in January, 1834. Chosen member of 24th Congress. Both Harvard and Williams college conferred upon him the degree of LL. D. He was born October 25, 1782; died May 28, 1868.

It was the consensus of opinion of leading men in Worcester county—men well informed and loyal to the memories of the past, who were consulted with reference to the matter—that the editorial supervision of Mr. Ellery Bicknell Crane in the preparation of the work, would insure the best results attainable in these deeply interesting channels. For fifteen years the President of the Worcester Society of Antiquity, and the present librarian of that body and the editor of its "Proceedings," he has long been deeply interested in the pursuit of genealogical information in the county of Worcester, and his wide knowledge and the ample material at his command in the library of the above mentioned society have afforded to the local writers upon this work a rich mine of information along the lines prescribed, and through his instrumentality, also, they have had access to the wealth of historical and genealogical records in the archives of the American Antiquarian Society, through the courtesy of its librarian, Mr. Edmund M. Barton. Mr. Crane has also contributed to these pages a historical sketch of the Worcester Society of Antiquity, including a brief notice of the American Antiquarian Society. The publishers have given all possible care with reference to the family and personal narratives. If, in any case, one should be found incomplete or faulty, the shortcoming is ascribable to the paucity of data furnished by the subscriber, or to be obtained from public record, many families being without exact records in their family line; while,

BANCROFT HOUSE, WORCESTER

The home of Rev. Aaron Bancroft, in Worcester, Massachusetts. Here was born George Bancroft, the Historian, October 3, 1800, son of Rev. Aaron and Lucretia (Chandler) Bancroft.

Views of Polytechnic Institute, Worcester

in c ses, various representatives of a family are at disagreement as to names and dates of . their forbears. In all cases the sketch has been submitted to the subject or his rep tive, and upon him, in case of error, must rest the ultimate responsibility

s believed that the present work will prove a real addition to the mass of literatur rning the families of historic old Worcester county and that, without it, much valuable information contained therein would be inaccessible to the general reader, or irretrievably lost, owing to the passing away of many custodians of family records, and the consequent disappearance of material in their possession

THE PUBLISHERS

WORCESTER SOCIETY OF ANTIQUITY

WORCESTER SOCIETY OF ANTIQUITY

On the third day of May, 1775, was issued the first copy of the *Massachusetts Spy*, printed in Worcester, by Isaiah Thomas, since which date this town (now city), the heart of the Commonwealth, has been a prominent news center.

Worcester has also been a great book publishing center, "The Royal Standard English Dictionary" (Perry's), the first dictionary published in America, was printed here by Mr. Thomas, as was also the first music books printed from types, music having been previously printed from engraved plates. Various editions of dictionaries, lexicons, Bibles, medical works, law books and standard works in history and general literature, were printed and kept on sale here. The Koran was printed here in 1806, a Greek Lexicon in 1808; Plutarch's Lives, in six volumes (1802); Josephus, in six volumes (1794). A folio edition of the Bible published in 1791, illustrated with fifty copper-plate engravings, furnishes a fine specimen of the work of Mr. Thomas. Almanacs, sermons, school books, broadsides and works on nearly every branch of literature of that period, came from the press (or, rather, presses) of Mr. Thomas.

Thus were the people of Worcester early given special opportunity to learn the use and value of books, acquiring more or less an honest desire for them, and to appreciate the benefits of the knowledge to be gained through their use. The addresses and patriotic utterances distributed among the people of New England through the circulation of the *Massachusetts Spy*, had much to do with stimulating the spirit and feeling of resistance to the arbitrary measures inaugurated by the government of Great Britain. And, after the contest was over, and the independence of the United States secured, the influence of the editor and publisher of that organ was exerted for the establishment of a society that should bring together and preserve the mementoes of that heroic struggle, and also become an institution that should take its place among the prominent historical societies in England, France and other countries of Europe.

With that object in view, the *American Antiquarian Society* was formed in the year 1812. Its membership included representative men from the various States in the Union. The printer, and founder of the society, Isaiah Thomas, LL. D., was its first president. The first home or hall of this Society was a brick building, with a main upright part two stories in height, and a wing extending out on the north and also one on the south side. The main or center portion of this building was dedicated on August 24, 1820, and the two wings added about eleven years later. This home, known as Antiquarian Hall, stood on the easterly side of Summer street, near the corner of Belmont street, and was built at the expense of Mr. Thomas, on a lot of land which he owned and subsequently gave, by will, to the Society. In 1852 it was found necessary to have more commodious quarters to accommodate the needs of the American Antiquarian Society, and land was given by Honorable Stephen Salisbury, father of the late Honorable Stephen Salisbury, as a site for their *new building*, which now stands at the corner of Highland street and Main street, next north of the Court House, and is the present home of this most popular *national* institution.

In the year 1820, of the eighty-three names on the membership roll, twenty-four were residents of Massachusetts, ten of whom resided in Worcester, the remainder of the number were scattered throughout twenty-one other states of the Union In 1880, thirty-nine members were residents of Worcester, forty-four from Massachusetts, outside of Worcester, sixty-two from other states of the Union, and seventeen from foreign countries At present the membership in America of this (the American Antiquarian Society) is limited to one hundred and forty In 1893 there were twenty-six from Worcester, forty-three from Massachusetts, at large, sixty-two from other states in the Union, and thirty-two from foreign countries, total membership, one hundred and sixty-three.

Since its organization it has been co nucting a noble and most important work It came into the field so soon after the birth of our national government that special and most favorable opportunities have been found for the accumulation of books, pamphlets, papers and manuscripts treating of historical events, not alone of America, but of various other nations—a service to which it was early commissioned Its sphere of labor was, and is, world-wide, special attention being given to the subject of Archæology, including a study of the antiquities of this American continent, and every measure was to be adopted that should "make the Society appear respectable as a National Institution," and the American Antiquarian Society has not fallen short of accomplishing its mission, and is recognized as one of the leading Societies of its class in the world Its voluminous library contains a collection of Americana of rare value, while its stock of original manuscripts may be counted of much more than ordinary interest But as the population of Worcester increased, and the good influence of this parent society was felt among the citizens, there sprang up a desire for *another organization*, that should give opportunity for other citizens of Worcester and vicinity to engage in historical study and research, and also to provide a suitable place for preserving and placing on exhibition relics of the past, especially those bearing upon the history of the City and County of Worcester, including their people and institutions, preserving, for he benefit of future generations, such books, pamphlets and documents of every description as would furnish account of and portray the habits, life and character of the people that came to reclaim this wilderness and plant the institutions from whence so many benefits are at present derived, and to foster and encourage an interest in the history of this special locality

A number of conferences were held in the printing office of Messrs Tyler and Seagrave, then on Main street, opposite the City Hall. At these preliminary meetings there were present Samuel E. Staples, Franklin P. Rice, John G Smith, Daniel Seagrave and Albert Tyler As a result of these deliberations, notices were issued for a meeting to be held at the home of Samuel E. Staples, Number 1, Lincoln Place, January 24, 1875. Besides Mr Staples, there were present at this meeting John G Smith, Franklin P Rice, and Richard O'Flynn It was here decided to proceed with the formation of a society, and arrangements were made for drafting a constitution, which was submitted at a meeting held January 30th, and, after slight changes, was adopted at the third meeting, held February 13th The first regular meeting held under the constitution came on March 2, 1875, at which time the organization was completed by the election of the following named officers Samuel E Staples, president, Henry D Barber, vice-president, Daniel Seagrave, secretary, Henry F. Stedman, treasurer, and John G Smith, librarian For more than two years meetings were held at the homes of the members, where occasionally a paper was read on some historical subject But usually the time was passed in sociability and examining the collection of books and relics in the possession of the member with whom the meeting was called.

The infant society soon came into favor and was received by the citizens of Worcester with open arms, and grew with such rapidity that it became necessary to clothe it with a charter, that was secured in the month of March, 1877, Honorable Clark Jillson having been chosen by a vote of the Society, at its annual meeting, held January 2d of that year, to secure such an act The names of the charter members were Samuel E Staples, Clark Jillson, Ellery B Crane, Daniel Seagrave, Franklin P Rice, James A Smith, Albert A. Lovell and Albert Tyler.

The organization of the corporation took place at the meeting held on March 6, 1877, at the home of Edward I Cornius, on Wellington street, Worcester, at which time the following officers were elected President, Samuel E Staples, vice-presidents, Clark Jillson and Ellery B Crane, treasurer, James A Smith, clerk, Daniel Seagrave These officers constituted the executive committee and Albert A Lovell, Franklin P Rice with Charles R Johnson, were chosen to serve as the committee on nominations Thus was the organization set in motion and started on its errand of usefulness. Good moral character and an interest in the pursuit of historical studies, with the agreement to contribute five dollars each year, and also pay such other assessments, not exceeding one dollar, levied at any one time, as the society might elect, was the early test of qualification requisite for membership At the annual meeting January 4, 1876, twelve names constituted the membership roll The next year saw the number increased to thirty names, and at the meeting held January 2, 1877, the librarian reported four bound volumes and four pamphlets as the extent of the Society's library

The first book given the Society was entitled "Worcester in the Revolution," presented by the author, Albert A Lovell, at a meeting held September 12, 1876, at the home of Ellery B Crane. There was no special effort put forth for rapidly increasing the membership Some care was, however, given to securing workers in the cause that would enable the organization to make a showing sufficient to attract the attention of other persons of similar desires, and, if possible, secure their co-operation, and it is the belief that in this direction the efforts advanced were not futile

In the year 1878 the Society counted sixty-nine names upon its roll, fifty-two of them classed as active, two as life members and fifteen as honorary members Among the latter class were men occupying exalted places as literary men and writers of history, all of whom, we regret to note, have now passed away, and gone to their eternal reward At this writing not one of these fifteen gentlemen is left

The monthly reports made by members of their additions to their private collections stimulated the work of collecting, and helped to create interest in all matters of a historical nature, with the result that, when the time came for forming the Society's Collection, there was a generous response from those private sources, making it possible to create a commendable showing within a comparatively brief period of time. That the handful of books and pamphlets which by gift had become the property of the Society might receive proper care, and the secretary have a place for his books and papers, some kind of a repository was needed for their safe keeping, and the secretary purchased for one dollar and a half the Society's first book case. For want of a better place it was temporarily set up in the printing office of Messrs. Tyler and Seagrave

But the institution was growing, and June 19, 1877, steps were taken toward securing a room in which to hold business meetings and deposit the Society's treasures, and on the fourth of September a vote was passed instructing the Treasurer to hire a room in the Bank Block, Foster street, and the first meeting of the Society was held there in room Number Six, up one flight of stairs, on Tuesday evening, October 2, 1877, twenty-one members being present This was a notable meeting in the life of the young organization. More than two hundred and forty gifts of books and pamphlets with a few pictures were presented that evening, many of them being of special value. Honorable Clark Jillson's contribution included a large folio volume of Cicero's Orations, printed in the year 1472, a fine specimen of early printing. Four honorary members and three active members were voted in at that meeting, and Elihu Burritt, "the learned blacksmith," was proposed for honorary membership, and notice of the death of Harvey Dwight Jillson, M D , of Fitchburg, was given, it being the first death within the Society.

For more than thirteen years the designation painted on the door of room Number Six announced to the visitor or the passer-by that it was the home of the Worcester Society of Antiquity, and many pleasant hours were passed within those walls by the little band of faithful and constant workers who, by common consent, met there not only on the first Tuesday evening in each month, but on every Tuesday evening, unless absent from the city or detained by sickness, for all Tuesday evenings were consecrated to the interest of this Society Not all who met there then are now within the sound of the human voice. But their influence and their works abide, and the memories of those pleasant, fascinating, edifying social gatherings linger in the minds of those living today, who can, perhaps, more fully appreciate the value of those social conclaves in bringing together and centralizing the forces out of which this Society has been evolved, and also the words uttered by a member of that circle who has gone hence, one who in those days was a tower of strength, a giant among the weaklings, and possibly did more at the critical moment to put this Society in a condition to stand alone, than any other man. These are his prophetic words "Our mission is not one that changes with the seasons When we become weary with the labor it imposes and seek other employments, the places we leave will be filled by zealous laborers from a new generation, but the corner stone laid by our hands will continue to support the superstructure, though the sound of the builders' hammer may ring through its arches for centuries to come "

Before the close of the year 1877, members of the Society were greatly encouraged in their work, as well as in the future prospects of the organization, by the kindly, stimulating words received from certain gentlemen prominent in historical and literary circles, in reply to notices sent them by the secretary, informing them of their having been elected to honorary membership in the young Society Among those who responded with special reference to what had been accomplished, and the future outlook, were Benjamin J. Lossing, Rev. Adin Ballou, Rev Abijah Marvin, John G Metcalf, M D., Holmes Ammidown, Elihu Burritt, William S. Barton, Esq., Dr. Guilermo Rawson, and Rev. Carlton A. Staples Of these, at this writing, not one remains

During the life of the Society, there has been no step taken that apparently produced more beneficial results, and brought the Society into more popular favor, than printing and disseminating its transactions and literature Thus was attention called to the valuable work being performed, and the publications of the Society soon found a demand which to this moment has continued to increase. Among the early tasks assumed was copying and printing the inscriptions upon the tombstones in the ancient cemetery in Worcester, known as the Mechanic Street Burial Ground And, before the summer of 1877 was ended, much had been done in securing inscriptions from burial grounds in Lancaster, Lunenburg, Mendon, Shrewsbury and three of the ancient cemeteries in Worcester, while some progress had been made in copying those from the burial grounds in Brookfield, Leicester, Rutland, Southbridge and Sturbridge. This initial effort awakened fresh interest throughout the community in the preservation of both public and private records, and, through persistent exertions of members of this Society, and the co-operation of friends, the early records of Worcester were published, from the earliest date down to the adoption of the city charter in 1848, including the vital records, all of which have been assembled within the covers of the Society's publications, and constitute a part of the historical work accomplished through its members

At the close of the year, 1879, the librarian, Albert Lovell, reported that the Society's library contained thirteen hundred and twenty-five bound volumes and four thousand three hundred and forty-two pamphlets and in the spring of 1881 it became necessary to add another room to Number Six, the latter being used for meetings, while the second room was for the accommodation of the rapidly increasing library and a small collection of relics. It was thought, with this addition, ample room had been provided for some time to come. But in June, 1885, came a substantial increase to the library, of a gift from Mrs. Charlotte Downes, of a collection of books and pamphlets, once the property of her late husband, John Downes, Esq , of Washington, D C It was a pleasant surprise, and caused no slight enthusiasm throughout the membership of the Society, for they fully appreciated the value of the gift.

On the thirty-first day of March, 1883, occurred the death of Rev. George Allen He had been a frequent visitor at the meetings, and much interested in the work of the Society. During his lifetime he had accumulated a large library. A short time before his death, a considerable portion, however, had been sold at public auction in Boston, but there still remained at the time of his decease about three thousand volumes, and, through contributions of money from members and their friends, this collection of books and pamphlets was added to the Society's library

The next red-letter day was the observance of the tenth anniversary of the organization The exercises were held in the Old South meeting-house, then standing on the common on the site of the present City Hall. It was held on the twenty-seventh day of January, 1885. Rev Carlton A Staples delivered the principal address The proper date came the twenty-fourth, but as that fell on Saturday, it was decided to celebrate on the following Tuesday There was a large attendance at the meeting in the church, after which there was a banquet served at the Bay State House Alfred S Roe was toastmaster, and it was after midnight when the end came to the good things that were said there Not long after this event, Honorable Stephen Salisbury, one of Worcester's prominent philanthropists, who had been watching the growth and conduct of this institution, offered to assist in providing a home for it by contributing a lot of land on which to erect a building, and also to give a certain sum of money toward a building fund His offer was accepted with most grateful acknowledgments, committees were chosen for carrying the work forward, and in due time the Society came into possession of a substantial, commodious, brick building, well adapted to the needs of the Society, and through the exertion of its members and their friends, chief among them the late Stephen Salisbury, it is the possessor of a property valued at fifty thousand dollars, not including its valuable library of twenty thousand bound volumes, thirty-five thousand pamphlets, and an interesting museum containing over six thousand relics of Indian, Colonial, Revolutionary, Civil and Domestic life, many articles of which it would be exceedingly difficult to duplicate, all debts paid, and eleven thousand dollars of invested funds. Truly a remarkable showing

The home of this *Worcester Society of Antiquity* is located at Number Thirty-nine Salisbury street, Worcester, Massachusetts, and was dedicated on the afternoon of November 24, 1891

WORCESTER COUNTY

HON GEORGE FRISBIE HOAR No more popular and truly meritorious family name comes to the mind in writing of the many celebrated family circles of Worcester county than that to which the late lamented United States senator, George F Hoar, belonged Others have attained to high eminence in local, state and national fame, but to recite the history of their accomplishments is an easier task than to pick from a vast collection of important data the facts from which a sketch suitable in length for a work of this character can be compiled and do justice to the memory of him for whom it is written Senator Hoar was born at Concord, Massachusetts, August 29, 1826, and passed from earthly scenes September 30, 1904—seventy-eight eventful, well spent years

His ancestors from the early day "Massachusetts Bay Colony," were men of great courage and activity One writer says 'They were in advance of the times in which they lived and were leaders to a higher and better sphere, both in social and political sense" The earliest of his male ancestors in this country was John Hoar, one of three brothers who came with their sister and mother from Gloucester, England The husband and father, Charles Hoar, was sheriff of Gloucester and died before his family came to America His wife, Joanna, died at Braintree, 1661 They had three sons and two daughters The sons were Daniel, who returned to England in 1653, Leonard, who graduated at Harvard College, 1650, and was president of that institution from 1672 to 1675, when he died, and John (See Hudson's "History of Lexington," page 104, Genealogical Register)

(II) John Hoar, son of the first family who located in New England by this name, was a lawyer, distinguished for bold, manly independence He resided in Scituate, Massachusetts, from 1643 to 1655 It was about 1660 when he settled in Concord and died April 2, 1704 His wife Alice died June 5, 1697 Their children included Elizabeth, who in December, 1675, married Jonathan Prescott, Mary, married Benjamin Graves, October 21, 1668, and Daniel, who married (first) Mary Stratton, (second) Mary Lee The Hoar family were among the early bay colonists and some true conception of their character may be had by referring to a matter of New England history, wherein it is recorded that after the Indian massacre at Lancaster at the time of King Philip's war, John Hoar, at the request of the colonial authorities, followed the Indian band far into the wilderness, and after great hardship and the exercise of great ingenuity, recovered by ransom Mrs Rowlandson, a lady captive from Lancaster Her account of her ransom is published The rock where she was redeemed is situated in ————, close by the base of Wachusett Mountain, and has been marked by the senator with a suitable inscription

(III) Daniel Hoar, son of John, born about 1655, married, July 19, 1677, Mary Stratton, and October 16, 1717, Mary Lee By these marriages the following children were born John, October 24, 1678, Leonard, a captain, died April, 1771, aged eighty-seven years, in Brainfield, where a part of the descendants now reside—some having taken the name of Homer, Daniel, 1680, married Sarah Jones, Jonathan, died at the Castle, October 26, 1702, Joseph died at sea, 1707, Benjamin, Mary, March 14, 1689, died June 10, 1702, Samuel, April 6, 1691, David, November 14, 1698, Isaac, May 18, 1695 Elizabeth, February 22, 1701

(IV) Daniel Hoar, son of Daniel (3) and great-grandson of the ancestor, born 1680, married Sarah Jones, daughter of John and Sarah Jones, December 20, 1705, lived in southeastern part of Concord, where he died February 8, 1773, aged ninety-three years Their children were John, born January 6, 1707, he was twice married Jonathan, born January 6, 1707 (twin brother of John), graduated at Harvard College, 1740, was an officer in the provincial service during the war of 1744 to 1763. In 1755 he went as a major to Fort Edward, the next year was a lieutenant-colonel in Nova Scotia, and an aide to Major-General Winslow at Crown Point After the peace of 1763 he went to England and was appointed governor of Newfoundland and neighboring provinces, but unfortunately died on his passage thither, aged fifty-two years Daniel, entered Harvard College, 1730, but did not graduate, he married Rebecca Brooks, November 2, 1743, and removed to Westminster, where he died, leaving two sons and two daughters Lucy, married John Brooks Elizabeth, married a Mr Whittemore of West Cambridge Mary, married Zachariah Whittemore

(V) John Hoar, born January 6, 1707, married in Lexington, June 13, 1734, Esther Pierce, by whom he had two children She died and he married, August 21, 1740, in Watertown, Elizabeth Cooledge He died in Lincoln, Massachusetts, May 16, 1786, and his widow died March 20, 1791 He lived successively in Lexington, Watertown and again in Lexington and Lincoln It is not quite clear when he first came to Lexington He was taxed for a personal and realty in 1729, and had a seat assigned him in the meeting house in 1731, when they reseated the house He was a member of the school committee in 1743 He subsequently filled the offices of constable, assessor and selectman His home was in that part of Lexington set off to Lincoln in 1754 His children were Rebecca, born in Lexington, July 1, 1735, married, May 6, 1755, Joseph Cutler, Esther, born in Watertown, January 28, 1739, married Edmond Bowman, 1760, John, born in Lexington, July 14, 1741, died young, Samuel, born at Lexington, August 23, 1743, Elizabeth, born in Lexington, October 14, 1746, Mary, born in Lexington, October 5, 1750, died young, Sarah, born in Lincoln, June 9, 1755 married Nehemiah Abbot, Leonard, born in Lincoln, June 29, 1758, was twice married, Rebecca, born in Lincoln, October 18, 1761, married Joseph White, Lancaster, Mary, born June 17, 1764, married Thomas Wheeler, March 27, 1788, Joseph, born July 30, 1767

(VI) Samuel Hoar, son of John (5), born in Lexington, Massachusetts, August 23, 1743, was an important man in Lincoln, he frequently represented his town in the house of representatives, and was a state senator from Middlesex county, Massachusetts, from 1813 to 1816 He married Susanna Pierce, by whom he had ten children—five of each sex

(VII) Samuel Hoar, eldest son of Samuel (6), born May 18, 1778, graduated at Harvard College, 1802, received the degree of LL D, 1838 He taught school in Virginia two years, and was admitted to the Massachusetts bar in 1805 He was an eminent lawyer, contemporary with Choate, Mason and Daniel Webster He frequently represented the town of Lincoln in the Massachusetts legislature, was a senator from the county of Middlesex from 1813 to 1816, and was elected to congress for the years 1835-37-41 The legislature of Massachusetts sent him to South Carolina to test the constitutionality of certain acts authorizing the imprisonment of free colored persons held as prisoners in that state By order of the governor of South Carolina, he was forcibly ejected from the state and compelled to leave before fulfilling his mission, but acquitted himself manfully throughout the entire case He was a man of marked character and standing He died at Concord, Massachusetts, November 2, 1856 He married Sarah, youngest daughter of Roger Sherman of Connecticut, who was one of the signers of the Declaration of Independence, one of the framers of the United States Constitution, judge, and later United States senator, and mayor of New Haven until his death The children of Samuel and Sarah (Sherman) Hoar were Elizabeth, born July 14, 1814, Ebenezer Rockwood, February 21, 1816, Sarah Sherman, November 9, 1817, Samuel Johnson, February 4, 1820, died 1821, Edward Sherman, December 22 1823 graduate of Harvard College, 1844, George Frisbie, August 29, 1826

(VIII) Ebenezer Rockwood Hoar, eldest son of Samuel and Sarah (Sherman) Hoar, born February 21, 1816, graduated at Harvard College, 1835, and in 1839 began the practice of law in Concord, Massachusetts, and aside from representing his native county in the state senate was in 1840 made judge of the court of common pleas In 1850 he was appointed a justice of the supreme court of Massachusetts, and in General U S Grant's administration was appointed attorney general of the United States in March, 1869 In 1871 he was high commissioner of the Washington treaty, and a member of congress from Massachusetts from 1873 to 1875

(VIII) George Frisbie Hoar, son of Samuel and Sarah (Sherman) Hoar, born in Concord Massachusetts, August 29, 1826 The scenes of his boyhood were cast in pleasant places, midst fine influences, all calculated to unfold the germ of the true life to be enacted After his common school days at Concord he entered Harvard College, graduating in 1846 He chose the honorable profession of law for his calling in life, fitting himself in Harvard Law School and in the law office of Judge Thomas in Worcester He was admitted to the bar in 1849 and at once began the practice of his profession in Worcester, which city has ever since claimed him as one of her most honored citizens Among his legal associates were Hon Emery Washburn and later with Hon Charles Devens and J Henry Hill, Esq Mr Hoar rapidly rose to a very eminent rank in his profession The native genius of his mind, well disciplined by a thorough educational training, and augmented by an uncommon energy, he steadily moved forward and became a recognized leader In 1869, when he entered congress, after twenty years at the bar, his legal practice was the largest of any west of Middlesex county and the most valuable in a financial point of view

It was in 1849 when George F Hoar first entered the political arena as the chairman of the Free-Soil party for Worcester county, where the party was the best organized of any county in the United States When he was twenty-five years of age, in 1851, he was elected as a representative to the general court of Massachusetts He was the youngest member in that body, but became the leader of the constitution in law matters and to him was given the task of drawing resolutions protesting against the compromise measures of the National government in 1850 He had so far advanced in political life that he could have succeeded Hon Charles Allen in congress, but he would not listen to the call made by his friends to enter congress as it would be to put politics ahead of law—his chosen profession Had he at that time entered the congressional field, he would no doubt have been among the foremost in civil war and reconstruction periods He would not go to congress, but did not refuse to serve in the state legislature, which was pressed upon him In 1857 he was a member of the senate and chairman of the judiciary committee In that body he made a masterly report He was always ready to make campaign speeches, and but few advanced more thorough, extended and logical arguments

In 1868 Mr Hoar was elected a representative in congress (Republican) as the successor of the late Hon John D Baldwin In this, the forty-first congress, he was a member of the committee on education and labor and his chief work was the preparation and advocacy of the bill for national education The bill did not pass in that session, and Mr Hoar reported it in the next, and finally in the forty-third congress it passed by the house but failed in the senate In the same congress he vindicated General Howard and supported Sumner in his opposition to General Evarts' scheme of annexation of Santo Domingo As a member of the election committee in the forty-second congress, he drew the bill and had much to do along this line In the following congress he made his famous eulogy on Senator Sumner He was instrumental in passing the Lad's jetty bill, and thus was opened up the New Orleans ocean commerce line But perhaps of more importance than all was his connection with the electorial commission bill, he being associated with General Garfield Judge Abbott, of Massachusetts, and Payne, of Ohio In 1872 and again in 1874 Mr Hoar had made known his desire to retire to private life, but each time felt his duty was in serving, because his state demanded it

In 1876 his resolve to not be a candidate again for re-election was announced as final, and the people elected his successor, but the next Massachusetts legislature chose Mr Hoar to succeed Mr Boutwell as United States senator, and he took his seat March 4, 1877, at the beginning of President Hayes' administration Here he rapidly rose in the scale and dignity of a true American diplomat and statesman He became chairman of many important committees, including that of privileges and claims and on judiciary He was author of the bill for distributing the balance of the Geneva Award, the Lowell bankruptcy bill, the presidential succession bill, tenure of office act, bureau of labor statistics and many others The most of his time in the house and United States senate was spent in working for bills, laws and measures of large scope and wide range, leaving others less competent than himself to discharge their duties in matters of not so much real importance to the great and growing nation

In 1883 and 1889, he was re-elected to his seat in the senate To have been elected by the legislature so many times by a unanimous vote of its members was a new record for Massachusetts, and only bespoke of merit for him of whom this brief memoir is compiled, giving him a rank along with Charles Sumner and Daniel Webster, who were in the same office, and as a cotemporary with Samuel Hoar, his father His voice has been heard in the national halls of legislation for thirty-five years, and he served as United States senator twenty-seven years of this period, his service being as long if not longer than any American of our time

Mr Hoar has four times served as the chairman of the Massachusetts Republican State Convention In 1880 he was president of the National Convention at Chicago, by which General Garfield was made presidential nominee In his deliberations upon that occasion he proved his masterly fitness as a leader of great bodies of great men in exciting, eventful history-making times In 1898 President McKinley tendered him the ambassadorship to London, but on account of his extreme age and desiring to further serve in the senate, he respectfully declined He enjoyed travel, especially in Europe From his first visit to England in 1860, he has made trips as follows 1860-68-71-92-96-99 He was a member of the Worcester Fire Society for fifty years This society was formed in 1793, and was limited to a membership of thirty persons, it has come to be a social and historical body of much interest

In 1903 Senator Hoar wrote and had published what is known by its title, "Autobiography of Seventy Years" It is a neat and well written detailed account of his own life It embraces two volumes, and is dedicated to his wife and children—"a record of a life which they made happy," he says in its dedication One paragraph in his introduction of this work reads "The lesson I have learned in life, which is impressed more deeply as I grow old, is the lesson of Good Will and Good Hope I believe that to-day is better than yesterday and that tomorrow will be better than to-day I believe that in spite of so many errors and wrongs and even crimes, my countrymen of all classes desire what is good and not what is evil"

While much of his time for more than one-third of a century has been in Washington, yet has Worcester felt the touch of his influence and life He was the prime mover in establishing a free public library in this city He materially aided in placing the Polytechnic Institute on solid foundation He was a great friend and help to Clark University He was trustee of the Leicester Academy and first president of St Wulstan Society, at Worcester He also was instrumental in founding the Worcester Art Society and Worcester Club He was an honorary member of the Worcester Mechanics' Association He was the oldest member at the time of his decease of any save two of the American Antiquarian Society, and was an honorary member of the Worcester Society of Antiquity, as well as active in the Massachusetts Historical Society He was chairman of the public preservation committee of Massachusetts, and helped to mark permanently the old revolutionary landmarks by proper stones, tablets, etc He bought the old house in which had lived General Rufus Putnam, at Rutland, and made it a permanently preserved historic relic of revolutionary times

That the effect of his noble impulses and the care and consideration he always gave to the helpless and oppressed be not lost sight of, it should here be given as an illustration of this marked trait of his character, what relates to the early abolition days, when he, a young lawyer practicing in Worcester, helped to defend a person from mob violence It was the case wherein a slave "kidnapper" during the fifties" was arrested and tried in Worcester, but finally allowed to depart, with the promise of never returning Many colored people here and many more radical abolitionists felt justice had not been meted out to him, and had it not been for young George F Hoar and his associates he would have been violently mobbed While Mr Hoar was a life long friend and helper of the colored race, he did not believe in the theory of mob law He ever took deep interest in the freedmen of the south and gave liberally toward their educational institutions, believing, as he did, that education would sooner or later solve the race problem

One more recent act of his great kindness was seen in securing the discharge of two small Assyrian girls, who accompanied their mother to this country from Assyria in 1901 to be with the head of the family who had been here several years and declared his intention of becoming a citizen in Worcester Before landing at Boston harbor the officers discovered that one of the little girls was afflicted with a disorder of the eye known as trachoma and considered incurable in adults and contagious They under the law, were ordered not to land on our shores and to return at once to their native country The family was poor, the father a hard working citizen of Worcester, and the mother was to be thus ruthlessly torn from the two idols of her heart The various officials tried in vain to evade the existing law, but were thwarted The steamer which was to take the little girls back was to sail the next day, but through the interposition of Senator Hoar, whose son Rockwood made the facts known to him, finally through a touching telegram to President Roosevelt, secured a peremptory order of release of the children, and they were brought to Worcester, cared for and soon cured When the kindhearted president visited Worcester, a few months later, he wished to see them and they met him at Senator Hoar's residence, where all parties were pathetically touched by the scene It is small deeds that introduce to us great characters and tender hearts, such as was that of both Senator Hoar and President Roosevelt Soon thereafter Senator Hoar had the law so amended that such a proposed hardship could not again exist in this country through "red tape"

While he of whom we write had his political enemies—and within his own party—perhaps no other man has been in public life so many years and made so few enemies, and even those who opposed his position were at all times personally his friends In the part he took in opposing the action of the present Republican administration policy regarding the Philippine Island questions—one where he crossed swords politically with many of our brainiest statesmen—all, even President McKinley himself, knew of and respected his manly independent stand as against popular opinion McKinley was of a different opinion regarding a vexed question, but personally was one of Senator Hoar's warmest friends In Mr Hoar's Autobiography, he says 'It has been my ill fortune to differ with my party many times" One such occasion was when he bluntly said to McKinley, you cannot maintain a Despotism in Asia and a Republic in America" The man with no opposers has accomplished little and has made but few friends, but he who in the pride and spirit of his manhood advocates the right, as he sees the right, and not from policy, is sure to accomplish what is demanded of a well rounded character, whether in politics, social or private life Senator Hoar was broad-minded, scholarly and patriotic in all he said and sought to accomplish

Of his domestic relations it may be stated that in 1853 he married Mary Louisa Spurr, daughter of Samuel D Spurr, who conducted a dry goods house in Worcester, kept in a large two-story brick block on the north corner of Main and Central streets Near it stood a large two-story frame house, which was the residence of Mr Spurr Mrs Hoar at her death left two children, a daughter Mary, and a son Rockwood, who graduated from Harvard College in 1876, and was elected district attorney for Worcester county in 1899, serving until January 1, 1905 In the autumn of 1904 he was elected to a seat in congress as the nominee of the Republican party for his district For his second wife Senator Hoar married Ruth Ann, daughter of the late Henry W Miller, of Worcester She died about a year in advance of her husband Finally the end came and he who had been styled 'the grand old man" was claimed by the death messenger and the spirit took its flight at his home in Worcester, September 30, 1904 He was a firm believer in the Unitarian faith, and was identified with that church many years His funeral was attended by one of the largest concourse of people ever seen in the commonwealth on such a sad occasion His remains now repose in Sleepy Hollow cemetery, at the place of his birth

ROCKWOOD HOAR, late congressman from the third congressional district, was the only son of the late Senator George F Hoar While the best wishes of the friends of the honored sire always followed the son, while the ability and character of the father seemed to be in large measure inherited by the son, Mr Hoar won his own spurs He gained his election because he had evinced the capacity essential to represent this district in congress, because he was one of the most accomplished lawyers in his native city, because his record as district attorney deserved endorsement and commendation He demonstrated an unprecedented popularity when a candidate for office His vote for district attorney showed increasing strength at the polls every time he ran His friends took an unqualified pride in his career

Rockwood Hoar was born in Worcester, August 24 1855, and always lived there He fitted for college in the Worcester public schools He graduated at Harvard College in the class of 1876 and entered the law school He received the degree of LL. B in 1878 and A M in 1879 He was admitted to the bar in 1879 and immediately began to practice in the law office of his father, which was then shared by Colonel A George Bullock, president of the State Mutual Life Insurance Company, at present, and the Hon Thomas L Nelson, late justice of the United States district court In 1884 he was appointed assistant district attorney for the middle district of Massachusetts, a district which includes the city and county of Worcester He was assistant while Colonel W S B Hopkins was district attorney until 1888 In 1899 he was elected district attorney of the middle district and served until January, 1905 He was thus closely identified with the administration of justice in this county for twenty years He had an excellent general practice, but his reputation as a lawyer and public official depended chiefly on his record in the district attorney's office as assistant and as chief It would be difficult to find anywhere a man who had shown more sympathy for the unfortunate, combined with absolute faithfulness to his duty as prosecuting officer No district attorney of Worcester county showed more discriminating judgment in performing his office His ideal seemed to be, not the one of securing convictions at any cost, but to see justice done and the spirit of the law executed in good faith

The detective officers of the district have a high reputation for intelligence and thoroughness in the performance of their duties By a careful and systematic preparation and supervision of important criminal cases, Mr Hoar was able to thoroughly master the questions at issue and to ascertain in advance what disposition should be made of them He rarely lost cases in which he went to trial The counsel for defendants soon learned that his recommendations to the court were carefully considered by the presiding judge and that they could obtain the best results for their clients by submitting to his careful and sympathetic judgment and to his recognition and frank endorsement of all that could fairly be said in favor of the defendant The first trial in Massachusetts upon an indictment for murder in the second degree was conducted by him and the indictment sustained by the supreme judicial court The murder trials conducted by him were held without the expensive relays of stenographers, which had so largely increased the expense of these trials in earlier days His cases were promptly and vigorously presented

Shortly after he was elected district attorney he became convinced that the probation system was in line with modern methods and a means of making the law more efficient In 1900 he secured the appointment of Colonel James M Drennan as probation officer for the superior court Under this system about one hundred cases annually are taken on probation by Colonel Drennan That means about a third of the cases presented to the court that would eventually come to trial This policy gives the first offender a chance to reform and avoid a criminal career The harsh and indiscriminate treatment of criminals has been found to defeat the very purpose of criminal law, and manufacture and harden criminals rather than to teach them a lesson First offenders in all the more serious crimes, as for instances boys who have committed theft, burglary or embezzlement, have been put in the care of the probation officer Of the four hundred and twenty-five cases put on probation during Mr Hoar's term as district attorney, only a very few have proved to be second offenders The probation system is not only humane and reasonable, but it is a Christian and philosophical way to teach men who have erred to keep straight, to demonstrate that the law of our times is not provided as an instrument of vengeance, but merely to protect society and to correct the criminal himself What *The Worcester Spy* said of Mr Hoar when he was elected district attorney is very fitting at the close of his service as he enters upon a new career in the public service "In all his official acts, Mr Hoar has been scrupulously painstaking, no matter what degree of importance was attached to them and his tenure of the office of assistant district attorney was characterized by a measure of success that augurs well for a satisfactory administration of the department with him as chief"

He held many other positions of honor and trust He was a member of the common council in

Rockwood Hoar

Worcester from 1887 to 1891, inclusive, being president the last-named year These were important years in the municipal history of Worcester, and Mr Hoar was always useful and energetic He was a private in the Massachusetts Concord Artillery Company, Company C, Fifth Regiment, Massachusetts Volunteer Militia, from 1875 to 1878 He was appointed aide-de-camp on the staff of Governor Oliver Ames and served from 1887 to 1890 with the rank of colonel He was appointed judge advocate general on the staff of Governor Roger Wolcott in 1897 and served four years, acting as president of the military board of officers, having charge of the equipment of the Massachusetts troops in the war of 1898 with Spain He had the rank of brigadier-general He was known by all the prominent men of the state, and well liked by his associates in office He was a director of the Worcester Trust Company He was formerly a director of the Washburn & Moen Manufacturing Company before it was absorbed by the American Steel & Wire Co He was a trustee of Clark University He was for twenty years a trustee of the Worcester Insane Hospital, having in charge also the Worcester Insane Asylum, both institutions being a part of the state system for the care and cure of the insane He received his appointments from successive governors He always took great personal interest in the development and conduct of these hospitals

He was a member of the Grafton Country Club, Tatnuck Country Club and the Worcester Club, but too busy to take advantage of his privileges often His recreations were golfing, driving and hunting He was a lover of good horses He took an occasional hunting trip in New Hampshire, but he followed in a general way the old fashioned devotion to his home and his office more closely than most of his professional brethren He was a member of the parish committee of the Church of the Unity, of which his mother was a charter member, and which his father attended from the time of his coming to Worcester till his death He was one of the most prominent laymen in the Unitarian church in the state, and an active and enthusiastic participant in all concerning the welfare of the Church of the Unity Mr Hoar occupied the modest house at Washington which his father purchased about a year before he died

He would have been an interesting figure among the new congressmen, partly because of the prominence of his father, partly because of his having redeemed the third congressional district by a substantial majority His was a district where a Democrat was elected to congress for three successive terms and in a year when a Democratic governor was elected in Massachusetts (1904), he was elected to congress, the vote of his district standing Rockwood Hoar, Republican, 17,796, John B Ratigan, Democrat, 10,617, John W Brown, Socialist, 733 Incidentally it may be noted that never before in the history of the government has a father in the senate been followed upon his death by a son in the house of representatives His grandfather, Samuel Hoar, his uncle, Judge E Rockwood Hoar, and Judge Hoar, son of Sherman Hoar, were prominent Massachusetts congressmen

He married, June 1, 1893, Christine Rice, daughter of William E Rice, of Worcester, Massachusetts (See Sketch of Rice Family and William E Rice) Mrs Hoar is well fitted for her social duties at Washington by training and personal attractiveness At the recent visit of President Roosevelt to Worcester he was the guest of Mr and Mrs Hoar, at their charming home at 16 Hammond street Their children are Frances Helen, born November 24, 1895, Louisa Ruth, born August 22 1898

At the close of the last session of congress he came home greatly fatigued and almost immediately started on a European trip in search of rest, accompanied by members of his immediate family, and although the trip proved restful, the severe strain to which he had been subjected, had laid the foundations for a disease of the brain which finally terminated his life Soon after reaching Worcester on his return from Europe, he placed himself under the care of his family physician, and all that was possible for human hands to do, was done to save his life, but he passed away on Thursday evening, November 1, 1906, at his home, No 34 Oak avenue, Worcester, in the same house in which his father died

SALISBURY FAMILY The earliest record of the Salisbury family goes back into the history of Great Britain, and it is very likely that the family had ancestors in Wales From family records and those of Suffolk county, Massachusetts, it is clear that John Salisbury, who came to Boston between 1630 and 1640, was the founder of the family in America But little can be learned of his history either on this side or beyond the seas It is certain that he was a Boston taxpayer in Suffolk county, Massachusetts, in 1689, that he was among 'The List of Inhabitants in Boston," 1695, and that he died in 1702

(I) John Salisbury, earliest known at Boston, married first, Annabel ———, and (second) Bridget Williams, from whom were children, including Nicholas and James (twins), born August 20, 1694, Nicholas was baptized in the Second Church of Boston, John was styled in the Suffolk county probate records as 'late of Boston, a marriner," generally understood in those early days to mean a sea captain

(II) Nicholas Salisbury, son of John and Bridget (Williams) Salisbury (1), born August 20, 1694, was a mere boy at the time of his father's death Little of positive record can be had of the career of Nicholas, who was described as a 'Merchant' in the Boston records, but that he grew to manhood and married Martha Saunders, and to them were born Elizabeth, Sarah and Stephen The date of the marriage of Nicholas and Martha was October 1, 1724, and tradition says he fell in love with her at first sight at the Old South Church in Boston" Her father was Josiah Saunders, who in the records was described as "Marriner" (sea captain) Martha's mother was Rebekah Eldridge whose brother John left a legacy of eight thousand pounds sterling to 'My Sister and all her daughters and their children in New England" In the will of Nicholas Salisbury, April 4 1748, he is called 'shopkeeper" He gave three hundred pounds sterling to his son Stephen, and the balance of his estate left at the time of his wife's decease He also gave My beloved brother Benjamin' one hundred pounds sterling or its equivalent Viewed in the light of what was the true fact, and what transpired in later years in connection with the Salisburys' standing and worth as men of means and integrity of character, the following copied from the proceedings of the selectmen of Boston, at a meeting held July 9, 1711, is amusing Ordered that Nicholas Salisbury, who belongs to Charlestown and came lately to our Town to dwell, be notified to appear before the Selectmen with security or depart out of our Town" In explanation of this it should be stated that it was then the law and custom in New England to require security of all newcomers, this being for a twofold purpose, first, to insure the town against people who might be paupers or liable to be a financial burden and second, to make sure of the religious and political loyalty of the newcomer before admitting him as a citizen who should have their protection, and who should walk and live in harmony with them

(III) Stephen Salisbury came to Worcester in 1767 to establish a branch house for Samuel and Stephen Salisbury, of Boston, his partner being an elder brother He was born in Boston, September 25, 1746, the son of Nicholas and Martha (Saunders) Salisbury The above firm were importers of hardware and kindred goods from England and the West Indies Worcester proved a favorable centre for a large country trade, then numbering about one thousand people The Salisburys imported their own merchandise, and hence could afford to sell almost as cheaply in Worcester as in Boston When Mr Salisbury first moved to Worcester, political affairs were engaging the attention of the people, and the trouble with the mother country was becoming more and more serious Here controversies had become more acute than in most places, for here lived numbers of obstinate Tories, as well as many who were fearless defenders of the colonial rights Mr Salisbury early took his stand with the patriots He accepted no office, but his name frequently appears in town records as being on committees to prepare resolutions against some act of tyranny He bought a large farm to the northward of the city, and his place of business was at Lincoln Square To the east of the front door of his "mansion' was the counting-room and salesroom Until well advanced in life his mother presided over his household January 31, 1797, after his mother s death, he married Elizabeth Tuckerman, daughter of Edward and Elizabeth Tuckerman, of Boston By this marriage one son was born—Stephen, March 8, 1798 A daughter, Elizabeth T, was born in 1800, died in 1803, and a son, Edward Tuckerman, born in 1803, died in 1809 Mr Salisbury died May 11, 1829, eighty-four years of age 'His figure was slight and very graceful, and it is said that his face was very handsome, and he retained a complexion of youthful freshness until the end of his life" His pastor and friend, Rev Dr Aaron Bancroft, described him as a 'just man ' He was an original member of the famous Worcester Fire Society, organized January 21, 1793, and continued an associate until July 6, 1801 A part of the above facts have been gleaned from writings of his contemporaries, each and all plainly verifying all that is here claimed as to the sterling qualities of his manly character

(IV) Stephen Salisbury was born at Lincoln Square, in the city of Worcester, Massachusetts, March 8, 1798, at the old Salisbury mansion, erected by his father Stephen, who came from Boston to Worcester in 1767 and built the above residence in 1770, in which he dwelt for the remainder of his days Stephen Salisbury obtained his primary education at the Old Centre district school, prepared for college at the Leicester Academy, and graduated with honors from Harvard University in the class of 1817, celebrated for what its members accomplished after they went forth to the actual work of their lives Among them were Hon George Bancroft, Hon Caleb Cushing, Professor Alva Woods and George B Emerson He studied law under Hon Samuel M Burnside, and was admitted to practice at the Massachusetts bar, but owing to his extensive local interests never entered actively into the practice of the legal profession, though a well read and highly capable attorney His own business interests kept his time fully occupied, but his legal schooling was of lasting benefit to him in after life While he never sought office, he yielded to the calls of his fellow-citizens and served in various prominent positions all of which he filled with a most thorough completeness Among the places of trust thus accepted by him were those of selectman, 1839, representative in the general court of Massachusetts, 1838-39, senator, 1846-47, and alderman during the first year Worcester was an organized city, 1848 In 1860 and again in 1872 he was elected presidential elector from his state As early as 1840 the records show he was an active member of the American Antiquarian Society, a member of its council from October, 1853, and president in 1854, continuing as such for more than thirty years He was the third president of the Worcester Free Public Library, and served from 1864 to 1865, and again from 1868 to 1872, inclusive He generously contributed toward the reading rooms connected with this library He was also a member of the Massachusetts Historical Society The degree of Doctor of Laws was conferred on him by Harvard University in 1875 He was overseer of the University for two full terms from 1871 to 1883 He was also a conspicuous figure in the history of the Worcester Free Institute, now the Polytechnic Institute, was its first president, an office which he held until his death in 1884, he gave the valuable land on which the buildings stand, and contributed liberally to the support of the institution

In reviewing his many responsible financial trusts it is found that from 1845, when Hon Daniel Waldo died, for more than thirty-nine years he served as president of the Worcester Bank, and was for fifty-two years one of the directors, being first elected in 1832 He also held the office of president of the Worcester County Institution for Savings for a quarter of a century, resigning in 1871 He was made a director of the Worcester & Nashua Railroad at the date of its organization in 1845, and was its president from 1850 to 1851 At Lincoln Square he built the factory long known as "Court Mills," for the manufacture of farm implements, and when the site was needed for other purposes he built for the Ames Plow Company (which had succeeded to the business of the earlier partnership), a large factory on Prescott street He built the first wire-mill on Grove street, and enlarged the works to adapt them to the expanding business, finally selling the site to the Washburn & Moen Manufacturing Company He built other large factories on Union street

While busy with a multitude of cares, he neglected not the weightier matters He was identified as a member of the Second Parish Unitarian Church, in which he ever took a deep interest In all of his relations he was every inch a man, honored and trusted by a wide circle of friends throughout the commonwealth Whether he be viewed from a social, religious, civic or financial point of view, he always showed a full, well rounded character—a genuine type of American citizenship His personal manner was genial, courteous and obliging to a marked degree His own interests were always gauged by the best interests of his friends and neighbors He was a well-read gentleman, deeply versed in historical and antiquarian lore, art and literature, in which he took great delight, with the added years of his busy, eventful life

During his latter years he accomplished much for the substantial improvement of the northern portion of his home city, aiding very materially in building up a great manufacturing centre He built the spacious business block on Lincoln Square, and in 1837 his residence on Highland street His father s ancient 'mansion" in which he was born, presents at this writing about the same homelike appearance that it did a century ago, when it was occupied by a trustworthy loyal revolutionary patriot

Stephen Salisbury.

Stephen Salisbury

Stephen Salisbury

Of his domestic relations it may be said that no more affectionate husband or loving parent ever graced a Massachusetts home and fireside His first wife, to whom he was married November 7, 1833, was Rebekah Scott Dean, of Charlestown, New Hampshire, who died July 24, 1843, leaving as their only child, Stephen Salisbury, Jr He next married Nancy Hoard, widow of Captain George Lincoln, who died September 4, 1852 In 1855 he married Mary Grosvenor, widow of Hon Edward D Bangs, former secretary of state for Massachusetts, she died September 25, 1864 He died August 24, 1884, in his eighty-seventh year In the language of one who had long known him, 'He was a considerate gentleman of the old school type, a model of which this generation has none too many imitators" At his funeral the Rev Andrew P Peabody, DD, LL D, used for his text, 'We all do fade as a leaf" With his demise a generous property passed to his only child, Stephen Salisbury, Jr, a considerable portion of this property being composed of farm lands lying in close proximity to the business portion of the city of Worcester The son, with wise business discretion, erected many dwellings, factories and business blocks thereon, thereby contributing greatly to the growth and prosperity of the city, and a proportionate increase in valuation to the estate

(V) Hon Stephen Salisbury is one whose name is familiar to every citizen of Worcester, who has any knowledge of the city and its principal institutions His local pride has been evidenced by his many generous acts for the public welfare, and it is justly to be said that scarcely any undertaking of magnitude has been attempted during recent years without his co-operation, directly or indirectly

The only son of Stephen and Rebekah Scott (Dean) Salisbury, he was born March 31, 1835, in Worcester, in one of the brick houses near the end of Main street, opposite the court house He began his education in an infant school taught by Mrs Levi Heywood, on Main street When six years old he passed the winter of 1841-42 with his parents in Savannah, Georgia In the latter year he attended the private school of Mrs Jonathan Wood, at the corner of Main and School streets, Worcester, Massachusetts, and for a short time in 1844 was a pupil in Miss Bradford's school in Boston In 1845 he was a student in the grammar school under Warren Lazell, later kept by C B Metcalf, until 1848, when he entered the Worcester High School, then in charge of Nelson Wheeler He matriculated in Harvard College in 1852 and graduated therefrom in 1856 after completing the four years' course After his graduation he went to Berlin and became a student in the Frederick William University During the spring of 1857 he attended lectures at the Ecole de Droit, in Paris He spent the summer and autumn with his classmates Rice and Kinnicutt in England, Scotland and Ireland and late in the year visited Turkey, Asia Minor and Greece, including a month's tour on horseback, accompanied by a guide This trip gave him much interesting and valuable information concerning the country and customs of Greece Afterward he resumed his studies at Berlin, then re-visiting Paris, and set out with his father's family upon a tour covering portions of Italy, England, Scotland, Ireland and Wales In December, 1858, after an absence of more than two years, he returned to Worcester, and took up bookkeeping for a time as a special study He subsequently entered the law office of Dewey and Williams as a student of law, and in 1859 entered Harvard Law School Two years later he received the degree of Bachelor of Laws, and was admitted to the bar in Worcester in October, 1861 During the following winter months he visited David Casares, a college classmate, in Yucatan, where he made a study of the Maya Indians' ruins and monuments In 1885 he traveled through the same country and other portions of Mexico and Cuba, re-examining some of the ruins which he had seen on his former visit In 1888 he again visited Europe, his tour including France, Belgium, Holland and Spain In Spain, especially, he found much to interest him, as also in portions of Portugal He was also an extensive traveler in his own country and with his taste for the study of history and natural history became possessed of a large fund of useful knowledge, a review of which he has given to American societies of historical investigation

Mr Salisbury early entered into the responsibilities of business life In 1863 he became a trustee of the State Mutual Life Assurance Company of Worcester In 1865 he was chosen a director of the Worcester National Bank, and after the death of his father (in 1884) succeeded him in the presidency In 1877 he became a trustee and member of the board of investment of the Worcester County Institution for Savings, of which his father had been president, and in 1882 he succeeded the late Governor Alexander H Bullock as its president He was also a director of the old Worcester & Nashua and of the Boston, Barre & Gardner Railroads He also gave much attention to public affairs, In 1864, 1865 and 1866 he was a member of the common council of Worcester, and president of the board during his last term In 1889 he was made one of the commissioners of the sinking funds of the city, and served in that capacity to the time of his death, November 16, 1905 As a Republican he represented the first Worcester district in the state senate in 1893, 1894 and 1895, serving as chairman of the committees on education, banks and banking, and the committee on the treasury In all these various positions he displayed the qualities of the well equipped man of affairs, and discharged every trust with scrupulous fidelity

Mr Salisbury was conspicuously active and useful in his relation to many educational, historical and charitable institutions, devoting to them not only his service, but liberally of his means He was a prominent member of the Worcester Lyceum and Natural History Association, vice president of the Worcester Agricultural Society, a director of the State Mutual Life Assurance Company, a trustee of Clark University from its founding in 1887 until his death, and was at one time its treasurer He was also a trustee of Leicester Academy, and for ten years served as treasurer of the Music Hall Association, as well as one of its directors He was a trustee of the City Hospital at its incorporation in 1872, and secretary for eighteen years, trustee of the Memorial Hospital and secretary for ten years, and vice president of St Vincent Hospital He was also a trustee of Rural Cemetery, and secretary of Hope Cemetery Mr Salisbury became a member of the American Antiquarian Society in 1863, a member of its council in 1874 vice-president in 1884 and in 1887 was elected president, a position which he occupied to the time of his death, and by his will this society received about two hundred and fifty thousand dollars and his library In 1884 he was elected a trustee of the Worcester Polytechnic Institute and president in 1895, to which institution he recently gave three hundred thousand dollars He was a member of the faculty of the Peabody Museum of Archaeology connected with Harvard University a member of the Massachusetts Historical Society, to which institution by his will he gave five thousand dollars, a member of the Worcester County Horticultural Society, and formerly its president, the American Geographical Society, the New England Historic Genealogical Society, the Sociedad Mexicana de Geografia y Estadistica and the Conservatorio Yucateco In all of these he ever maintained a deep and intelligent interest His writings include important papers on the people of Yucatan and their arts, which he contributed to the American Antiquarian Society He also translated several valuable papers from the German of Dr Valentine on the same and kindred subjects In 1888 he prepared and read an exhaustive paper on "Early Books and Libraries" Mr Salisbury was an accomplished linguist, and enjoyed a good speaking knowledge of the Spanish and other languages

Mr Salisbury's public spirit was shown not only by his interest in municipal and state affairs, but his more tangible works show him to have had at heart the beauty and convenience of the city Among his public benefactions may be further mentioned a building for the City Hospital, a laboratory and electrical station for the Worcester Polytechnic Institute, eighteen acres of land bordering on Salisbury Pond given to the city in 1887, and by him named Institute Park, a lot of land to the Worcester Society of Antiquity and contributions to their building fund, and by will another lot of land and five thousand dollars In 1896 he gave land for the Worcester Art Museum, and contributed with other citizens funds for the erection of a museum building and for the endowment of the corporation, and by his will made that institution his residuary legatee In 1899 he gave land for a building for the Worcester Woman's Club, which has been recently erected In 1900 Mr Salisbury built on the summit of Bancroft Hill, one of the most prominent elevations in Worcester, a gateway of rough stone, known as Bancroft Tower, which affords an excellent opportunity for observation This has been opened to the public, together with the grounds surrounding it

It is unusual in any family for one generation to succeed another during so long a period of time as that between John Salisbury in 1640 and his representative of the present day without degeneration in some instance Of the Salisbury family it is to be said that from the emigrant ancestor down the name has been a synonym for industry, integrity, public-spirit, and civic duties ably and faithfully performed Each bearer of the name, in his own generation, has shown the faculty of making his work bear fruits beneficial to the general welfare of his fellow-citizens, and in no instance has he hesitated to devote himself, intellect and means to these ends

The late Mr Salisbury never married The value of his estate at the time of his decease, which at this writing has not been settled has been by estimate fixed at from three to four millions of dollars

WASHBURN FAMILY This name is derived from two simple words—wash, which imples a swift current of a stream and burne (or bourne), signifying a brook or small stream It has been said of this family, whose origin is in England carrying a coat-of-arms, that the posterity of John Washburn, who was the first emigrant to locate in New England in 1632, will seldom find occasion to blush upon looking back upon the past lives of those from whom they have descended Fortunate indeed, may the generations now in being, esteem themselves, if they can be sure to bequeath to their posterity an equal source of felicitation"

In this illustrious family have been found some of our nation's greatest characters, in public and private life, including great lawyers, statesmen and military men in all of the American wars Maine, Vermont, Massachusetts and Wisconsin have each had governors from this Washburn family, and three brothers served as congressmen from three states at the same time, and all with much ability Authors and college graduates may be found to a score or more, who have left their impress upon the world As manufacturers, they have excelled, and wherever wire goods and wire fencing are known, there is found the name Washburn as being pioneers in this line

(I) John Washburn, the original immigrant, who settled at Duxbury, Massachusetts, in 1632, married Margery ————, and by her was born a son named John, of Bridgewater, who married in 1645 Eliza Mitchell His father was secretary of the Massachusetts Bay Colony, and he, with his two sons, John and Philip, were able to bear arms in 1643 The immigrant and his son John were among the original fifty-four persons who became proprietors of Bridgewater, Massachusetts, in 1645 They bought the lands of the old Sachem Massasoit, for seven coats of one and a half yards each, nine hatchets, eight hoes, twenty knives, four moose skins, ten and a half yards of cotton cloth The transfer was signed by Miles Standish, Samuel Nash and Constant Southworth

(II) John Washburn was born in England, 1621, and his brother Philip at the same place in 1624 He died unmarried John (II) and his wife Eliza Mitchell had these children John married Rebecca Lepham, Thomas, married (first) Abigail Leonard and (second) Deliverance Packard, Joseph, married Hannah Latham, Samuel, married Deborah Packard, Jonathan, married Mary Vaughan, Benjamin, died on the Phipps expedition to Canada, Mary, married Samuel Kingsley, Elizabeth, married (first) James Howard and (second) Edward Sealy, Jane, married William Orcutt, James, married Mary Bowden, Sarah, married John Ames

(III) Samuel Washburn, son of John (2) called 'Sergeant" was born in 1651 at Duxbury, Massachusetts He married Deborah Packard, by whom he had six children, including Israel

(IV) Israel Washburn, born at Bridgewater, 1684, married Waitstill Sumner in 1708, and had four children—one named Israel

(V) Israel Washburn, who settled at Raynham, was born August 11, 1718, and married Leah Fobes He was committeeman of "Inspection and Safety" and captain of a train band, 1774, and served a short time in the revolutionary war His son was Israel

(VI) Israel Wahburn son of Israel Washburn (5), was born in 1775, and married a Miss King in 1783 He served in the revolution and was at the Lexington alarm He served in the general court and was a member of the constitutional convention He talked but little and made but one speech in public life He died at Raynham, 1841 Of his ten children Israel (VII) was one

(VII) Israel Washburn, son of Israel (6), was born at Raynham, Massachusetts, November 18, 1784 died at Livermore Maine, September 1, 1876 He went to Maine in 1806 and taught school for a time and then engaged in ship and boat building He removed to Livermore in 1809 and bought a farm, store and goods, and continued in trade until 1829 This farm was later and is still known as the "Norlands" He represented his "district of Maine" before it had been set off from Massachusetts which was in 1820 He served in 1815, 1816, 1818 and 1819 Toward the end of his life he was afflicted by blindness and his friends used to read the news to him, of which he never tired He was great in cheerfulness, rivaled Lincoln in story-telling and could remember events well It is said he could name all congressmen and give the district to which they belonged, when he himself had three sons in congress

His noble son, Hon Elihu B, of Illinois fame, wrote from Paris, when Minister to France, as follows

"This is the eighty-sixth birthday of my father All hail to the glorious, great hearted, great headed, noble old man! In truth, the noblest Roman of them all How intelligent, how kind, how genial, how hospitable, how true!"

This same worthy son had carved on his father's monument at death, 'He was a kind father and an honest man" Passers by to-day, may see this in the cemetery overlooking the family place, 'The Norlands"

(VIII) Hon Elihu B Washburne, the only member who still clung to the final "e" on his name, was the son of Israel (7), born at Livermore, Maine, September 23, 1816, and died at Chicago, Illinois, October 22, 1887, aged seventy-one years In his early manhood, he taught school for ten dollars per month and "boarded round" In 1836 he entered Kents Hill Seminary, and in 1839 the Cambridge Law School In 1840 he moved to Illinois, practicing law at Galena In 1852 he was elected to a seat in congress, continuing sixteen years, and upon retirement was known as the "Watch Dog of the U S Treasury" and also as "Father of the House" He swore into office Schuyler Colfax and James G Blaine as speakers To him and William Seward alone did Abraham Lincoln confide the secret of the running of his train from Philadelphia to Washington, March, 1861, when Washburne had the telegraph wires cut fearing trouble would ensue en route Both Seward and Washburne agreed to meet him at the depot in Washington, but Washburne was the only friend who did in fact meet him He was a constituent and admirer of General Grant, who owed to him promotion to high office In 1869 Grant offered him a place in his cabinet as secretary of state, which he soon resigned and accepted the office of Minister to France, and was there during the trying days of the siege and commune, coincident with the Franco-Prussian war He remained there nearly nine years, and longer than any predecessor During the Andrew Johnson impeachment trial, he was chairman of the house committee

He married in 1845, Adele Gratiot, granddaughter of Stephen Hemstead, of Connecticut, a soldier of the revolutionary war She died March, 1887, aged sixty, her husband only surviving her until October 22 Their son, Gratiot Washburne, was graduated from the Highland Military Academy of Worcester and from the Naval Academy at Newport, Rhode Island He was secretary of the United States legation under his father in France, and was one of four upon whom the French government bestowed the Cross of Legion of Honor for services performed during the siege of Paris He was secretary of the American Exposition at London in 1886, and died suddenly in Kentucky

(VIII) Governor Israel Washburn, son of Israel (7), was born at Livermore, Maine, June 6, 1813 He was admitted to the bar in 1823 He was in the legislature in 1842 and congressman from Maine in the thirty-second, thirty-third, thirty-fourth, thirty-fifth and thirty-sixth United States congresses He was first a Whig and later a Republican He was elected governor of Maine in 1860, and Lincoln made him collector of the port of Portland in 1863 He was a literary man and also lectured much He married (first) Mary M Webster and (second) Robina Naper Brown, of Boston, in 1876 He died May 12, 1883, at Philadelphia, Pennsylvania His son Israel was an officer in the Sixteenth Maine Regiment during the civil war period

(VIII) General C C Washburn, ex-Governor of Wisconsin, was fully named Cadwallader Colden Washburn He was the son of Israel, born at Livermore, Maine, 1818 He was a land surveyar, went to Illinois in 1839, and settled at Mineral Point, Wisconsin He practiced law, and in 1859 moved to La Crosse, Wisconsin He was elected to congress, serving from 1856 to 1862 He was delegate to the peace convention in 1861, and raised a cavalry regiment the same year and was made colonel During 1862 he was promoted to brigadier-general and then to major-general, and was at Vicksburg with Grant and under General Banks in Louisiana In 1867 he was elected to a seat in congress from Wisconsin, serving until 1871, when he was chosen governor of Wisconsin

(VII) Governor Emory Washburn, of Massachusetts, descended from the original immigrant thus 1 John and Margery, 2 John and Elizabeth Mitchell, 3 Joseph and Hannah Latham, 4 Joseph and Hannah Johnson, 5 Seth and Mary Harrod, 6 Joseph and Ruth Davis, 7 Governor Emory, who was born in Leicester, Worcester county, Massachusetts, 1800, and graduated at Williams College, 1817 In 1826 and 1827 we find him in the general court of Massachusetts, and in 1841 and 1842, state senator, in 1844 judge of the court of common pleas, from which bench he resigned in 1847, and in 1853 he became governor of the state he had so faithfully served He was made a professor in law at Harvard College in 1856, continuing until March 18, 1877, when death claimed him He was a noted author of many law works, genealogy and general historical books and papers, including the excellent 'History of Leicester," his native place He married Marianna C Giles, who bore him three children

(V) John Washburn, son of John (4), was born in 1699, married Abigail Johnson, and had these children John, born 1730, married Lydia Prince, Abigail, born 1732, Mary, born 1734, Mercy, born 1736, Seth, born 1738, married (first) Faer Howard, (second) Ann Fullerton (third) Deborah Churchill, Phillip, Thankful born 1742

(VI) Seth Washburn, born 1738, married as above three wives and his children were Fear, born 1766, Perris, Abigail, Seth born 1769, married Sarah Adams, Ichabod, Anna (by second wife), Ephraim (by third wife)

(VII) Captain Ichabod Washburn son of Seth (6), was born about 1771, and in 1793 married Sylvia Bradford, whose ancestors came in the "Mayflower," through the following line Governor William Bradford, who came on that ship, had a son, William, whose son, Samuel, had a son, Gamaliel, whose son, Gamaliel, Jr, had a son named Peabody, whose daughter, Sylvia, was the wife of Captain Ichabod Washburn, who was a sea captain and lost his life while off the coast at Portland Maine, helping to care for his brother seamen who were sick with yellow fever He died at twenty-eight years of age leaving three children Ichabod (VIII) and Charles (twins), who subsequently came to Worcester, and a daughter Pamelia

(VIII) Ichabod Washburn, the founder of the great wire industry in Worcester, which is now a prominent factor in the American Steel and Wire Company, son of Ichabod and Sylvia (Bradford) Washburn, was born August 11 1798, at Kingston, Massachusetts His father died when he was but an infant, and his mother was left to support herself and little ones by working at her loom and spinning wheel When nine years of age Ichabod

Washburn went to live with a harness maker in Duxbury, Massachusetts, where he did chores and learned to stitch harness, attending school during the winter terms After five years experience at Duxbury, he returned to Kingston and worked for a time in a small cotton factory At the age of sixteen years he was employed as an apprentice to learn the blacksmith's trade with Jonathan and David Trask of Leicester After a service of two years the firm dissolved partnership and young Washburn found employment with Nathan Muzzy at the same trade, engaging to work for two years, to receive fifty dollars for his services, be allowed twelve weeks schooling and furnished with board and clothing Mr Muzzey at the end of a year left Leicester for the adjoining town of Auburn Washburn accompanying him, continuing until his twentieth birthday In the winter of 1817 and 1818 he went to Millbury to work as journeyman, but within a few weeks the news came that a position as clerk in Mr Warren's grocery store in Portland, Maine, was awaiting him his sister having become in the meantime Mrs Warren A brief trial at clerking in his brother-in-law's store convinced him that he was better adapted to mechanical than mercantile pursuits, and he returned to Millbury and began making ploughs on his own account He had no funds, but, though a stranger, came to Worcester and presented his case to Mr Daniel Waldo, a man of means, who heard his story and upon his own note gave him money with which to operate This was his start financially In 1819 he worked in an armory making ramrods, and in the autumn of that year came to Worcester

In 1820 he engaged in business with William H Howard, manufacturing woolen machinery and lead pipe, and soon thereafter purchased Mr Howard's interest in the business In 1822 he took as a partner Benjamin Goddard and with the increase of business they employed thirty workmen They made the first condenser and long-roll spinning-jack that was made in the county During the winter of 1830 and 1831, while on School street, he experimented in the manufacture of wooden screws Later he and Goddard sold their business and moved to Northville, where the manufacture of wire and wooden screws began, the wire being made by Washburn & Goddard and the screws by C Reed & Company, associates They also made card-wire Some in 1836-37 the screw business was removed to Providence, and finally merged into the 'American Screw Company" In January, 1835 he dissolved with Goddard at Northville and continued the wire business in a building erected for him by Stephen Salisbury, on Mill brook, which furnished the power for driving the crude and experimental machinery then in use This building was forty by eighty feet three stories high In 1835 his twin brother Charles came from Harrison, Maine, where he had been practicing law, and formed a partnership with his brother, which terminated in January, 1838, but soon after the substitution of the 'wire-block' by Ichabod Washburn which revolutionized the industry, the business began rapidly to multiply, and in 1842 they again associated themselves as partners, the firm name being I & C Washburn

In 1847 the two Washburns put in a rolling mill of their own at Quinsigamond, and soon the firm of Washburn, Moen & Company was formed The same, however, was dissolved in 1849 the business going to Henry S Washburn a member of the firm The firm of I & C Washburn that same year was dissolved and a division of the plant made, Charles taking the part at Quinsigamond April 1 1850, Philip L Moen became a partner of Ichabod Washburn, the style of the firm being I Washburn and Company Ichabod Washburn spent much time in experimenting in the tempering of wire that it might be put to various uses, and at the suggestion of Mr Chickering, of Boston, he produced samples of piano string wire, an article which hitherto had been brought from England That branch of the business has been conducted with success up to the present time, as well as other musical instrument wires In July, 1859, Ichabod Washburn employed one hundred and twenty men and made three tons of wire per day In 1863 he and his partner built a cotton-mill, which they operated about ten years, producing sufficient yarn to cover four tons of tempered crinoline wire per day January, 1865, Ichabod Washburn and Mr Moen changed the firm name to I Washburn and Moen Iron Works'—capital stock, five hundred thousand dollars In 1868 it became the Washburn-Moen Manufacturing Company, with one million dollars capital In 1889 the plant was operated by three thousand workmen A few years since the whole business was merged into the American Steel & Wire Company

Ichabod Washburn married (first) Ann G Brown, October 6, 1823 She was the daughter of Mrs David Brown, with whom he boarded in Worcester One son was born to them, December 1, 1824, but survived only a few days Two daughters were born to them Eliza Ann born June 4, 1826, married Philip L Moen, and died at the age of twenty-six years, and Lucy Pamelia, born March 8, 1832, who died when twenty-two years old The mother and little granddaughter soon passed from earth, leaving Mr Washburn alone in the world He founded the Worcester Memorial Hospital to the fond memory of his two daughters For his second companion he married Elizabeth B Cheever

Of his political standing, let it be recorded that he was a strong anti-slavery advocate and gave of his means abundantly, and urged by a petition to President Lincoln the emancipation of the colored race After the formation of the Republican party, he ever voted and worked and paid for the principles it advocates He believed that capital and labor should alike be busy and ever put to producing for the world He was state senator in 1860 and performed his part faithfully and well

He was a life-long Christian and did very much to aid the church He was one of the first four deacons of the Union Church, and assisted materially in building that church He was treasurer of the Church Anti-Slavery Society in 1859 From his own funds, he erected the Mission Chapel on Summer street, Worcester Space in this volume precludes the enumeration of but few of the benevolent causes and benevolent industries to which he gave most lavishly, believing as he did that money was made to use and to use for mankind He was a systematic giver and in proportion to his income He felt it a duty to donate, and like Peabody, his business multiplied on his hand by liberal giving to worthy causes hence he headed all subscription papers with a Christianlike pleasure From him came twenty-five thousand dollars to further on the building of the Mechanics Hall so appreciated today and for the past decades used for great audiences, religious and political He also was one of the original promoters of the 'Bay State House' He despised intoxicating drinks and tobacco giving time and wealth for their suppression When he built his first lumber house, he would not ask men to help 'raise' it, if they asked to have liquor, as was customary, but preferred to pay cash to men who would do it without intoxicants, furnishing instead lemonade and 'small beer" Among his benefactions should not be forgotten the large amounts he gave toward the erection and support of educational and

Charles F. Washburn

religious institutions Home for the Aged (eighty-five thousand dollars), Memorial Hospital, the Freedmen's Cause, the Home and Foreign Missions, Orphans' Home, etc, scattered from Maine to Georgia But even the lives of the truly great and good must cease Seized by a stroke of paralysis in February, 1868, he lingered on until death came December of the same year His last words were spoken to a brother, "It is all right," and thus Worcester and the world lost one of her noblest sons, a self-made, wealthy, devoted Christian

(VIII) Hon Charles Washburn, twin brother of Ichabod Washburn, was born in Kingston, Massachusetts, August 11, 1798 He selected as his vocation the profession of a lawyer, and after receiving the advantages of a common school education entered Brown University, from which institution he was graduated with the class of 1820 He was admitted to the bar, and in 1823 was practicing his profession in Otisfield, Maine The following year he removed to Harrison, same state, where he continued to labor in his chosen profession, gaining special distinction as a lawyer During the years 1830 and 1833 he served his district in the Maine legislature In 1835 he came to Worcester, Massachusetts, to join his brother Ichabod in the wire industry, and in 1842 the firm of I & C Washburn was formed and two years later the rolling-mill at Quinsigamond was built In 1849, through a dissolution of the firm and a division of the property, the plant at Quinsigamond came into the hands of Charles Washburn, who was actively engaged in conducting this branch of the wire business, which he continued until the year 1868, when the Washburn and Moen Manufacturing Company was formed, this industry becoming a part of the great business plant. As early as 1849 Mr Washburn served as a member of the school committee, in 1849 and 1850 he was chosen a member of the common council, having been president of the same for three years, in 1851 was a member of the Massachusetts legislature, and in 1854 served in the board of aldermen Mr Washburn retained an interest in the firm of the Washburn & Moen Manufacturing Company, and was a member of the board of directors up to the time of his death, October 27, 1875

Mr Washburn married Zibeah Cary Blake, daughter of Grenfill Blake, of Otisfield, Maine, November 30, 1826, she died August 12, 1845 Their children were Charles F (IX), born August 23, 1827, Grenfill B May 16, 1829, Lucia B, October 29, 1730, Grenfill H, April 20, 1833, George I, May 26, 1835, Henry B, November 10, 1837, Maurice B, July 25, 1839, Zibeah C, April 15, 1844, Maurice, August 9, 1845 Charles Washburn married for his second wife Anna F Brown, February 2, 1847 There were three children of this marriage—a son John, and two daughters, Ellen and Anna

(IX) Charles Francis Washburn, son of Hon Charles Washburn, having acquired an excellent education in the schools of Worcester and Leicester Academy, from which he graduated, was prevented by illness from attending college, but he added to his academical knowledge a liberal store of general information from his personal reading and observation After an extended trip to Europe he entered his father's rolling mills, and from the beginning gave evidence of that mechanical skill and business sagacity that characterized him in his later career He mastered every detail of the industry, working in all departments, and gaining perfect mastery of them In 1857 he was admitted to partnership with his father under the firm name of Charles Washburn & Son The business expanded rapidly as new methods made possible new products, and the Quinsigamond plant was finally incorporated, in 1869, with that on Grove street as the Washburn & Moen Manufacturing Company, and grew to operate a capital of $1,000,000, and gave direct employment to some four thousand people Originally restricted to the manufacture of wire for card teeth and other similar purposes, the factories began the making of telegraph wire as soon as the Morse invention had demonstrated its practicability, and in 1850 was begun the making of piano wire, in which the product of the Washburn mills soon superseded the English make in the markets of the United States The company met every necessity as it arose where wire could be used—wire for hoop skirts between 1860 and 1870, and after that the great demand for all varieties of barbed wire for fencing During the last ten years it has produced vast quantities of iron and steel cables and ropes, spiral springs, etc, and, following the introduction of electric energy for heating, light and power, thousands of tons of wire annually for these purposes The yearly output of steel is about 40,000 tons, and of all products about 100,000 tons In 1891 the company also established works at Waukegan, Illinois, with wire capacity nearly equal to that of the parent establishment

In the capacity of secretary, director and vice-president of the corporation, Mr Washburn continually took a leading part in the administration of its business, and to his perseverence and sagacity was largely due the great advancements which were made from time to time in the development of its usefulness and importance a signal attestation of this fact being found in his securing to his company the conrol of the barbed wire patents

Deeply absorbed in his business Mr Washburn held aloof from public concerns, except in one instance where he served the city as a member of the common council He was deeply interested, however, in benevolent and philanthropic works, and rendered zealous and useful service to two of the most notable and praiseworthy institutons of his city, acting as vice-president of the governing board of the Memorial Hospital, founded by his uncle, Ichabod Washburn, and as president of the Home for Aged Women Of a sincere, christian temperament he was a communicant of All Saints' Protestant Episcopal Church He was a warm advocate of free-soil principles in his early days, was an original member of the Republican party, and affiliated with it earnestly and effectually during the remainder of his life He was a man of culture and refinement, delighting in healthful and ennobling literature, and devoted his leisure hours to his home and library He died July 20, 1893, leaving behind him to his family and the community the fragrant memories which cling to a noble and useful life in those broad ways where such an unselfish man can make his every act a benediction upon the thousands who surround him

Mr Washburn married, October 10 1855 Mary, the eldest daughter of James M Whiton, of Boston, Massachusetts Eight children were born to them, all sons except one and all excepting one son survived their honored parent The children were Charles G, born January 28 1857, James M, died in infancy December 27, 1858, Philip, born August 2, 1861, died October 6, 1898, Miriam born July 12, 1864, Robert M, born January 4, 1868, Henry B, born December 2, 1869, Reginald, born October 13, 1871, Arthur, born May 27 1877 Reginald Washburn married August 26, 1903 Dorcas daughter of Hon Edward S Bradford, of Springfield, Massachusetts Philip Washburn married, June 5, 1883, Miriam Phillips, youngest daughter of Rev R S Storrs, D D, of Brooklyn, New York He had five daughters, two of whom died in infancy

(X) Robert Morris Washburn, son of Charles Francis and Mary Elizabeth Washburn, was born in Worcester, January 4, 1868 He was educated in the public schools, and was graduated at the Worcester high school in 1886 He received the degree of A B from Harvard University in 1890 He then studied law for one year in the office of Rice, King & Rice He was then admitted a member of the second-year class at the Harvard law school, where he remained for one year, and in November, 1892, was admitted to the Worcester county bar He is a practicing lawyer at 314 Main street, Worcester He is unmarried, living at the homestead estate, 42 Elm street He is a member of the Republican city committee, 1906, and a vice-president of the Republican club of Massachusetts, and a member of the Republican Club of Worcester He is also a member of the Worcester Club, and Quinsigamond Boat Club

(X) Hon Charles Grenfill Washburn, son of Charles Francis and Mary E (Whiton) Washburn, was born in Worcester January 28, 1857 He began his education in the public schools of his native city, was graduated from the Worcester Polytechnic Institute in 1875, and from Harvard University in 1880 He subsequently took up the study of law and was admitted to the Suffolk bar in 1886 He has been constantly identified with the manufacturing interests of the city In 1880 he established the business now conducted by the Wire Goods Company, with which he is still connected In 1882 he became treasurer and manager of the Worcester Barbed Fence Company, which was subsequently absorbed by the Washburn & Moen Manufacturing Company, and from 1884 to 1891 was a member of the last named corporation, and during a part of that period served in the capacity of director and executive officer

A Republican in politics, Mr Washburn was a member of the Massachusetts house of representatives in 1897-98, in which body he served the first year on the committee on mercantile affairs, and the second year as chairman of the committee on taxation On the expiration of his term in the lower branch he was elected to the state senate from the first district of Worcester, serving two terms—1899 and 1900 In 1902 he was a member of the committee to revise the corporation laws of Massachusetts He was a delegate to the Republican national convention in Chicago, and the Massachusetts member of the committee appointed to notify Theodore Roosevelt of his nomination He was elected November 6, 1906, to the sixtieth congress from the Third Massachusetts District He is a trustee and president of the Worcester Polytechnic Institute He married, April 25, 1889, Caroline Vinton Slater, daughter of Horatio N Slater, of Webster Their children were Elizabeth, born 1892, died in infancy, Slater, born August 5 1896, Charles Francis born May 10, 1898, died December 19, 1902, Philip, born October 4, 1899, Esther Vinton, born August 10, 1902

Mrs Washburn is a great-granddaughter of Samuel Slater, founder of the town of Webster, and a manufacturer of much importance in his day He was a native of Derbyshire England, and when fourteen years of age was apprenticed to Jedediah Strutt, a partner of Arkwright, the celebrated pioneer in cotton manufacture The offer of a premium for the introduction of the Arkwright machinery into the United States brought him to America at the close of his apprenticeship He arrived in New York about December 1, 1790, and established at Pawtucket, Rhode Island, a manufactory for cotton yarn In 1812 in partnership with Bela Tiffany, of South Brimfield Massachusetts, under the firm name of Slater & Tiffany, he began the erection at Webster, Massachusetts, of mills for the manufacture of cotton yarn During the war of 1812 the firm also engaged in the manufacture of broadcloth In 1816 Mr Slater purchased the interest of his partner, and afterwards associated with himself Edward Howard, a practical cloth maker In 1829 Howard sold his interest to Samuel Slater and his sons—George B and Horatio N Slater—who conducted business under the firm name of Samuel Slater & Sons From 1835, the year of the death of the senior Slater, the sons conducted the business until 1843, when occurred the death of George B Slater and Horatio N Slater succeeded to the sole management, in which he continued until his death, in 1888, when his nephew and namesake, the father of Mrs Charles G Washburn, became the owner and manager The business after the death of H N Slater, Jr, was incorporated as S Slater & Sons Samuel Slater, the emigrant, was twice married First, October 2, 1791, to Hannah, daughter of Oziel Wilkinson She died about 1812, and about 1817 he married Esther, daughter of Robert Parkinson, of Philadelphia His first wife bore him nine children, of whom the seventh was Horatio Nelson Slater

(VII) Hon William Barrett Washburn, son of Asa and Phebe (Whitney) Washburn, and grandson of Colonel Elijah Washburn and Captain Phineas Whitney, was born in Winchendon, January 31, 1820 He fitted for college at the Westminster and Hancock Academies, and was graduated from Yale College in 1844 He clerked three years and then engaged in the manufacture of doors, chairs and wooden-ware at Erving In 1857 he moved to Greenfield, where he lived at the time of his death, October 5 1887 He was a member of the house of representatives in 1850 and of the senate in 1854 He was a member of congress from 1863 to January 1, 1872, when he resigned to be inaugurated governor of Massachusetts April 17, 1874, he resigned as governor to fill the unexpired term of Hon Charles Sumner in the United States senate, holding the office until March 4 1875 For many years he was president of the Greenfield Bank and one of the trustees of Yale College and an overseer of Amherst College He married, September 6, 1847, Hannah Sweetster by whom were born two sons and four daughters

(IX) General Francis Washburn, son of John M Washburn, was born July, 1838, at Lancaster, his parents having the April previous removed from Boston From the academy of his native town at the age of sixteen years, he went to serve a regular term in the Lawrence Machine Company's shop He next went to the Scientific School of Mining and Engineering at Freiburg Saxony When in 1860-1861 the civil war cloud darkened our fair national sky, he wrote, "I *must* hasten my return If the war comes, I shall sail at once" In December, 1861, he was given a commission in the army, which he used as soon as he waited to see his father pass from earth He was mustered in as second lieutenant in the First Massachusetts Cavalry, the history of which is well known in the war department He became captain, lieutenant-colonel, and in February, 1865, commissioned as colonel, which he held at the time of his death He was mortally wounded in the brilliant engagement at High Bridge, Virginia, April 6, 1865 His bravery was noted by the then Lieutenant-General Grant, at whose request he was commissioned brigadier-general Here men fought hand to hand, an uncommon occurence He fell from saber stroke and pistol shot He was brought home to the house of his brother, Hon John D Washburn, where he

C. G. Washburn

shortly gave up his young life, being but twenty-six years of age He was called the 'White Knight of Modern Cavalry"

(IX) Hon John D Washburn, born in Boston, March 27, 1833, was the eldest son of John Marshall and Harriet (Kimball) Washburn His parents removed to Lancaster when he was five years old and there his youth was spent amid those beautiful surroundings In 1853 he was graduated from Harvard College, entering the law, first studying with Hon Emory Washburn and Hon George F Hoar in 1854, finally receiving a diploma from the Harvard School in 1856 He practised in Worcester with Hon H C Rice He made for himself a place of importance among insurance circles, as legal adviser Later he succeeded Hon Alexander H Bullock as general agent and attorney of the insurance companies in 1866 Through this association he became connected with Governor Bullock as chief of the staff from 1866 to 1869, receiving a colonel's commission From 1871 to 1881 he was trustee of the Worcester Lunatic Hospital, and from 1875 to 1885 filled a similar place in the School for Feeble Minded He was a member of the house of representatives from 1876 to 1879, and a senator from Worcester in 1884 From 1866 to 1880 he was a director of the Citizens' National Bank He was also a member of the board of investment for the Worcester County Institution for Savings, also trustee and treasurer of the Memorial Hospital In 1883 he became president of the Merchants' and Farmers' Insurance Company For many years he was the councilor and secretary of the American Antiquarian Society During the latter years of his life he was appointed as minister to represent this country in Switzerland

He married in 1860 Mary F Putnam Their daughter Edith, in 1884, married Richard Ward Greene, of Worcester He died April 4, 1903, leaving a record in itself, a royal legacy to any community He was one of nature's own noblemen Even to the most humble of his constituents, he would grant a personal favor and special attention It is believed that exposure to the hot sun, while visiting in Paris, affected his head and that from this was traced his lingering illness and final death

(VIII) William Ansel Washburn, deputy sheriff of Worcester, was born in Paxton, Massachusetts, August 14, 1837 He was the son of John and Nancy (Bemis) Washburn His grandfather was Francis Washburn, born in Brockton, 1769, died 1844, the great-grandfather being Jacob Washburn, born in the same place

John Washburn, William Ansel Washburn's father, was born in Leicester, November 14, 1800, and died in 1867 He was a shoemaker and blacksmith and drove the stage many years between Boston and Worcester He married Nancy Bemis in 1831 Their children were Delia, William A and Alice (twins), and Julia

William Ansel was reared to farm life and then learned the trade of shoemaker with his father When eighteen he left home and came to Worcester, securing employment in the Hospital for the Insane for four years Then he clerked for a time, but soon began as a nail-maker in the factory of Prouty & Allen He was finally appointed a patrolman on the police force in 1865, and two years later was made assistant-marshal, holding the same from 1873 to 1880, again in 1883, and from 1886 to 1893 In 1893, he, by appointment, was made deputy sheriff and deputy jailer Like many another modern man, he is closely identified with civic societies, including the Masonic and Odd Fellows orders He is a Knight Templar Politically he affiliates with the Republican party In his religious belief he adheres to that of the Universalist faith November 29, 1860, he married Emily Delano, of Provincetown, Massachusetts

(VII) Hon Peter Thatcher Washburn, once governor of Vermont, was born in Lynn, Massachusetts, September 7, 1814, and died at Woodstock, Vermont, February 7, 1870 He was the son of Reuben and Hannah Washburn The father was born in Leicester, Massachusetts, December 30, 1781 When Mr Washburn was but three years of age his father removed to Cavendish, Vermont He graduated at Dartmouth College in 1835, and began law practice in 1838 at Ludlow, Vermont He became one of the most marked political figures in the state For eight years, from 1844 to 1852, he held the office of supreme court reporter In 1853-54, he was in the legislature, and when the rebellion broke out he raised troops and entered the service as lieutenant-colonel of the First Regiment from Vermont, being stationed at Fortress Monroe He only remained in the service about three months, and in 1861 was appointed inspector-general of Vermont September, 1869, he was elected governor of Vermont He was active with his pen, and in 1844 published a 'Digest of Vermont Reports" and many other works of value

BARTON FAMILY Hon Ira Moore Barton was a gentleman of unusual qualities as a scholar, jurist and judge He was born in Oxford, Massachusetts, October 25, 1796, and was of the fifth generation from Samuel Barton, of Salem, Massachusetts, 1693, and of Sutton, 1718 After preparation by a private tutor and at Leicester Academy, he entered Brown University and was graduated from that institution in 1819 He began the study of law with Samuel W Bridgham, of Providence, continuing his legal education with Sumner Barstow, of Sutton, and Hon Levi Lincoln, of Worcester, from whose office he entered the Harvard Law School, graduating in 1822 He immediately established an office in Oxford, where his recognized ability and skill as a legal adviser and advocate soon brought him a large practice

For three years (1830-31-32) he represented the town of Oxford in the state legislature, and in 1833-34 represented the county of Worcester in the state senate, serving for a time as commissioner for the revision of the statutes He removed to Worcester in 1834, and two years later was appointed by Governor Edward Everett judge of probate for the county of Worcester As the duties of the office did not require his entire time, he continued his practice in other courts In 1844 he resigned as judge of probate to devote his entire time to his growing practice In 1840 he was chosen presidential elector, and in 1846 represented the town of Worcester in the house of representatives in the state legislature He rendered efficient service in behalf of his constituents and the state, exerting himself earnestly in favor of an act to extend the equity and jurisdiction of our highest court In 1844 Judge Barton took as law partner Peter C Bacon, also of Oxford, and two years later William Sumner Barton, eldest son of the judge, was taken into the firm

In 1849 Judge Barton went to Europe, where he passed nearly two years, enjoying a much needed rest On his return he resumed his practice in the firm He was a member of the American Antiquarian Society, and one of its councillors He died July 18, 1867 and the librarian of that institution, Samuel F Haven, LL D, in his council report of October of that year says of Judge Barton—"In every station public or private, he was distinguished for ability, sterling integrity, and earnest devotion to the fullest performance of every duty." He was an accomplished lawyer, an upright magistrate, an enlightened patriotic citizen. His widow died in Worcester, November 24, 1883, aged eighty-three years. Their children were: William Sumner, born September 30, 1824, died July 13, 1899; Hannah Maria, born April 21, 1826, died December 13, 1906; Artemas Bullard, born August 12, 1828, died June 21, 1831; Charles Henry, born April 10, 1830, died February 16, 1885; Artemas Bullard, born December 5, 1831, died April 17, 1837; Lucy Ann, born July 24, 1834, died September 25, 1905; Francis Augustus, born October 24, 1836, died January 29, 1898; Edmund Mills, born September 27, 1838; George Edward, born July 30, 1841, died May 29, 1878.

William Sumner Barton, eldest son of Judge Barton, was born in Oxford, September 30, 1824, and came when ten years of age with his parents to Worcester. He attended the common schools and also the Worcester Academy, was graduated from Brown University in 1844, and later received the degree of A. M. After studying law in the office of his father and law partner, Peter C. Bacon, and attending the Harvard Law School, he was admitted to the bar in 1846, and became a partner in his father's firm, the style of the firm being Barton, Bacon & Barton. In June, 1854, he accepted a position in the Bank of Commerce, Boston, where he remained until January, 1872, when he was elected treasurer and collector of taxes for the city of Worcester. From 1876 until his death he was treasurer of the sinking funds, and also from 1872 treasurer of all the trust funds of the city. Mr. Barton was a genial, courteous gentleman, prompt and accurate, thoroughly competent to discharge the duties of his office—an ideal public official. He inaugurated a new and modern system of arranging and keeping accounts, which greatly facilitated and simplified the work of the department. He was fond of historical study and research, and among the articles from his pen are, "Sketch of the Bullard Family," "Sketch of the Life of the Duchess of Orleans and her Sons, the Comte de Paris, and the Duc de Chartres," and "Epitaphs from the Cemetery on Worcester Common, with occasional notes, references and an index." After a faithful, honorable service as city treasurer for twenty-seven years, he died July 13, 1899.

He married April 4, 1849, Anne Elizabeth, daughter of Samuel and Mary Gould (Ellery) Jennison, of Worcester. He married for his second wife, November 22, 1870, Katharine Almy, daughter of William and Jane Byron Ellery, of New York city. His widow and five children survive him; three daughters by the first marriage, and a son and daughter by the second.

Edmund Mills Barton was born in Worcester, Massachusetts, September 27, 1838, the son of the late Hon. Ira Moore Barton and his wife, Maria Waters (Bullard) Barton. She was born January 25, 1800, in the town of Northbridge, daughter of Artemas Bullard, M. D., and his wife Lucy, eldest daughter of Deacon Jesse and Anna Mason White, of Northbridge. Dr. Bullard was a successful practitioner, who acquired an extensive practice, and as a citizen was greatly respected and beloved. He was appointed by Governor Strong surgeon of the local infantry regiment, and was in 1814 elected a fellow of the council of the Massachusetts Medical Society. Mr. Barton's great-grandfather, Asa Bullard, of Holliston, Massachusetts, answered the Lexington Alarm, serving in Captain Stapels Chamberlain's company, Colonel Samuel Bullard's regiment.

Mr. Barton's boyhood days were chiefly spent in Worcester. After passing through the various graded schools, he took a course at the Valentine school in Northborough. The opening scenes of the civil war found him at home, assisting in the care of his invalid father. In May, 1863, he went to the headquarters of the Army of the Potomac, visiting hospitals on the way, and laboring in the field hospitals after the battle of Chancellorsville. He then visited the headquarters of General John A. Dix, at Fortress Monroe, and accompanied him upon his expedition to Bottom's Bridge, near Richmond. The battle of Gettysburg called him to that field for hospital work, and there he was commissioned field relief agent of the United States sanitary commission, under the authority of the secretary of war, and was assigned to the Fifth Army Corps of the Army of the Potomac. This position he held at the front until the end of the war and the final review at Washington. (See Marvin's "Worcester in the war of the Rebellion" for further details.)

After Mr. Barton's return from the war, July 1, 1865, he spent a few months in travel and on April 1, 1866, became assistant librarian of the American Antiquarian Society, Worcester. Upon the death of the eminent librarian, Dr. Samuel Foster Haven, he was unanimously elected on April 24, 1883, to succeed him in the important office. It was a most fitting recognition of the services of a zealous, painstaking efficient officer, who has at all times given the best at his command to further the good service of that remarkably well equipped institution. For Mr. Barton's literary productions, reference is made to Ford's partial bibliography of published works of members of the American Historical Association, of which Mr. Barton is an original life member of the American Library Association, of which he was for some years a councillor; life member of the American Antiquarian Society; life member of the Massachusetts Library Club, and at one time a vice-president; member of the Worcester High School Association, and its president in 1894; also a member

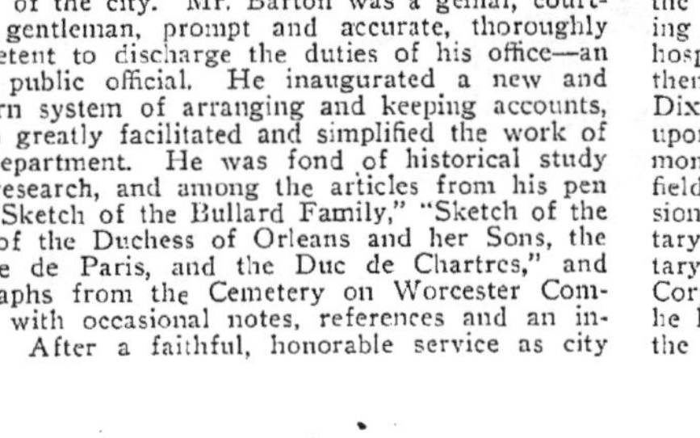

BULLARD HOUSE, WEST SUTTON

The Bullard house was built by Ebenezer Waters in 1767, who sold it to Mr. Hunt, of whom Dr. Artemas Bullard purchased it about the year 1805. Here Mrs. Henry Ward Beecher was born, courted and married. In the parlor at the left as you enter the house, in which Mr. and Mrs. Beecher were married, is a painting of Boston Common, on the panel over the fire place, and in the chamber overhead is a painting of the Boston Tea Party, in a panel over the fireplace there.

John Woodcock

of various historical military, and benevolent societies and church clubs

He married, September 6, 1871, Abigail Twycross Blake daughter of the Rev Samuel Paine Blake, and they have one daughter and three sons Lydia Maud, born August 2, 1872, Edmund Blake, born October 30, 1874, Frederick MacDonald, born June 19 1880, and Harold Bullard, born December 21, 1885

WOODCOCK FAMILY We find from "Historical Collections" that the first settlement in Attleborough was commenced by a John Woodcock and his sons, about 1669 He built a public house on the Bay road, and laid out about three hundred acres of land for his farm He took up in several parts of the town six hundred acres, some on his own shares and the rest on rights that he purchased His house was occupied for a garrison, and was licensed in 1670 Woodcock was a man of some consequence in those days, his name often appearing in town offices and on committees In 1691 he was chosen deputy to the general court from Rehoboth, and at several other times He was shrewd, hardy and brave, a strong and implacable enemy to the Indians He died in 1701, at an advanced age After his death seven bullet holes were counted in his body He had two wives Sarah, died May 10 1676, and Joanna, who survived him His children were 1 John, married Sarah Smith, 1673 2 Israel 3 Nathaniel 4 Jonathan 5 Thomas, and three daughters

In August, 1894, the following item appeared in the *Boston Journal* "The grave of Nathaniel Woodcock who was killed by the Indians, and who was the first white settler in Attleborough, has probably been located The discovery promises to be of much historical importance A few days ago, while workmen were grading at the 'Old North Burying Ground,' a grave-stone was ploughed up At present all that can be traced without acids is 'In Memory of N—— W——, died March, 1665'" Nathaniel Woodcock is known to have been killed by Indians in March, 1665

Nathan Woodcock, the great-grandfather of our subject proper, Theodore E, was married in Easton, Massachusetts, September 26, 1765, to Elizabeth Stone

John Woodcock, their son, was born in Easton, Massachusetts, October 14, 1775, and died in Leicester in 1814 He was educated in the common schools of his neighborhood, and was a man of keen intellect, shrewd and practical with a warmhearted nature He was endowed with the gift of inventive genius and in 1809 he received United States Letters Patent for a machine, still much in use, for splitting leather, and which at that time was of great value He is mentioned by Governor Washburn in his "History of Leicester," as a very "ingenious mechanic," for whose valuable invention the town owes a debt of gratitude which ought not to be forgotten He lived but fourteen years after coming to Leicester, falling a victim to consumption but in those years he had built up, in connection with his partner, a valuable business, known as the manufacture of card clothing, which in the hands of descendants and their associates, continued many years He married, in Easton, December 15, 1796 Ruth Mehurin, of Easton, Massachusetts, and was at the time of marriage of Rutland, Massachusetts He left three sons and two daughters whose lives were all passed in Leicester, "usefully and honorably " Hannah married Benjamin Conklin, 1826 Ruth, married Dwight Bisco, Esq, January 8, 1826 John Josephus Lucius

John Woodcock son of John (4), was born in Rutland, Massachusetts July 23, 1800, and died in Leicester, August 26, 1880 He obtained a common school education, and true to the best traditions of New England life, as well as to the education he had received, he entered early, at the age of seventeen upon a course of business industry He took service with James and John A Smith, who were his father's successors in business In 1825 he became, with Hiram Knight, Esq, partner in the same firm, later known as Woodcock & Knight, and in 1848 Theodore E Woodcock and Dexter Knight, sons of seniors, came to the firm under the name of Woodcock, Knight & Company He retired from business in 1867 During his life, he gave a good share of his time to the public service, was a selectman, and in other town offices, and in the legislature two years He was always a stanch Republican, was a director of the Leicester Bank from 1836 to the time of his death, a period of forty-four years, and a trustee of the Savings Bank from its beginning He was for ten years chairman of the directors of the Public Library of the town in which he took a warm interest, and to which he made many donations of valuable books He was known as a man of intelligence, and of sound, practical judgment, of a memory remarkably exact both of persons and events

Mr Woodcock was married, in 1823, to Anna Jenkins, born in Cambridge, New York, daughter of Joshua and Remember Bowen Jenkins, who were both stanch Quakers Reared in this faith, the daughter Anna retained the gentle, loving nature so characteristic of the Society of Friends, ever ready to lend a helping hand to the sick and unfortunate, of affable and pleasing manner, her many fine qualities endeared her to a large circle of friends Three children were the result of this marriage Theodore Earle, Ann Eliza, married Dr William H Brown, of Bangor, Maine, in 1851, and died in 1889, Ruth Mehurin, married William W Caldwell, Esq, of Newburyport, Massachusetts, September 21, 1848 Mrs Woodcock died in 1856 Mr Woodcock married (second) in 1858, Ellen L Burnett, of North Brookfield, Massachusetts, a lady of culture, who cared for him most tenderly in his declining years, and still survives him His home was always the happy resort of children and grandchildren, his spirit ever affectionate and generous

Theodore Earle Woodcock, son of John (5), was born in Leicester, Massachusetts, February 19, 1825 He obtained his education in the schools of his native town and in Leicester Academy He commenced at an early age working in his father's card factory, learning the business, and in 1848 was admitted as a partner in the card clothing manufacturing with his father, the firm known for many years as Woodcock Knight & Company, Mr Woodcock retiring in 1881, the company dissolving by mutual consent, having had a high reputation in one form or another since 1802 when the business was established by Winthrop Earle and John Woodcock grandfather of Theodore E, the subject proper of this sketch

Mr Woodcock was chosen director of the Leicester Bank in 1869 serving until 1904, when the bank went into liquidation is second vice-president of the Leicester Savings Bank, also a member of the finance committee, he has served as selectman in his town, and was a director of the Public Library for many years Mr Woodcock is a man of quiet tastes home-loving and fond of reading Although residing in Worcester, he is still loyal to his native town Leicester, and retains his legal residence there, and is also a regular attendant at the John Nelson Memorial Church of that place

In 1850 he was married to Miss Ellen Caldwell, daughter of John Caldwell, Esq, of Newburyport, Massachusetts, a most estimable lady of pleasing manner, but who was unfortunately an invalid for several years, and died in 1873 By this union, three children were born, viz Anna Ruth, Ellen Orne, died in 1873, aged seventeen years, John, died in infancy Anna Ruth married, April 28, 1875, George Richardson, of the firm of Clark, Sawyer Co, of Worcester They have two children, and reside in Worcester, Massachusetts

HON THOMAS H DODGE Among the noted and praiseworthy types of manhood whose career has brightened and blessed his fellowmen, none rises to a more truly noble and lofty attitude than an honored son of the "Green Mountain" state, of whom the subjoined notice and genealogical sketch is written With such an abundance of real facts from which to draw, one scarcely knows which to select for record use and which to leave unemployed The subject of which we write is

Thomas H Dodge, who has been an active, brainy, never-stand-still character, whose career, now well nigh spent by the coming-on of old age, will for generations yet to come be kindly remembered for the work he had so intelligently wrought out with his own brains and willing hands While some men achieve great names by military fame, some by statesmanlike lives, others by money-making traits alone, this gentleman has made for the world a true pattern for any young man who wishes to improve his time and make good use of the opportunities with which he finds himself environed, upon his advent into the world In this man one finds a study, which to fully comprehend needs to be re-enforced by a knowledge of his noble ancestry—noble not in a sense of handed-down "royalty," but of that sturdy self-making, self-denying, painstaking sort of which most truly great men are produced

Concerning the genealogy of Mr Dodge, let it be said that he is of English origin, and what people have been felt more for their intellect and virtues than the Anglo-Saxon race? The Dodges have a history known somewhat of as far back as 1306 A D, when members of the family held lands in Stockport, England But as the object of this volume is to begin with the American ancestry, as a rule, and trace the descendants to the present time, such facts as might be had concerning the English family will not be attempted to be reproduced herein

In the course of researches for this family history only two main branches have been found, one descended from William, or Richard, of Beverly, Massachusetts, and the other from Tristram Dodge, who settled on Block Island, Rhode Island, in 1660 April 25, 1629, there sailed from Gravesend, on the Thames, two boats—one the "Talbot," a vessel of three hundred tons, and the "Lion's Whelp" a neat ship of one hundred and twenty tons They reached Yarmouth, Isle of Wight, May 8 The journal kept by Reverend Francis Higginson, of the "Talbot," has been preserved and gives clue to the origin of all American Dodges That record says that the "Lion's Whelp" had forty planters from Dorchester, many mariners, eight pieces of ordnance, provisions, and four goats Both vessels sailed from Yarmouth, May 11, 1629, and arrived at Salem June 29, the same year

William Dodge settled in that location now called Beverly, but in early times known as Bass-River-Side, being separated from Salem by the bay Tradition states he was tall, with black hair and a dark complexion He became a freeman April 17, 1637, and received a grant of land containing sixty acres in September that year William Dodge came to Salem nine years earlier than Richard, hence he has been called the "father of American Dodges" The records, however, show the descendants of Richard outnumber his, probably on account of the fact that the former had but two sons, while Richard had five

Richard Dodge, brother of William (1), was received as an inhabitant in October, 1638, and was granted ten acres by the town of Salem He was admitted into the church at Salem May 5, 1644 In 1671 he helped to establish the First Church at Beverly Richard died in June, 1671, leaving a will by which it appears that he left a brother Michael, the will of Richard, in connection with the will of his father, John Dodge, renders the origin of Salem Dodges quite clear Records in the register's office of Essex county also show that William Dodge, senior, had a nephew William Dodge (Coker William or William Coker), son of Michael, to whom by a deed dated May 12, 1685, he gave sixteen acres of land where now stands the Beverly reservoir On the same date he also imposed a duty upon his son Captain William Dodge of Beverly, to "pay my brother," "if he came to New England and dwell in this town of Beverly, five pounds per annum, so long as he shall dwell here"—referring to his brother in England—doubtless Michael Sprague, then his only brother, Richard having died in 1671

The Dodges for at least four generations rarely engaged at anything besides farming They wanted to possess and improve the soil They were hard workers and seldom irreligious, rarely office seekers, and were a temperate set of people With the expansion of population they pushed forth for new homes, to subdue other lands, and have been found on the wild frontiers, through the northern states, and today count their descendants by the hundreds if not thousands all the way from New England to the waters of the Pacific Men of note and national fame may be found here and there from out their ranks of workers They are found among the philanthropic, military, literary, clergy, medical, legal and college professorships and callings—ever ready to do and to dare

To come now direct to the line of genealogy in this country it may be said first, that John Dodge (1) and wife Margery, of Somersetshire, England, had these children 1 William came to America, 1629, died between 1685 and 1692 He was probably born about 1604 2 Richard, appeared in Salem 1637 died June, 1671 probably born 1602 3 Michael lived and died in Somerset county, England and had five children 4 Mary, died in England and had one son—John

(II) William Dodge, eldest son of John (1), born about 1604, came to Salem, Massachusetts, in 1629 A tradition was handed down by Col Robert Dodge to his son Francis, of Georgetown, D C, that "farmer William" came to America when about twenty-one years of age, to see how he liked it, and returned to England, telling his father that he had determined to settle in America and asked him for some present His father said, "get married and I will give it" William is said to have had two refusals but finally succeeded married, and for his "present" his father gave him a pair of bulls "Farmer William," as he was styled, became a prominent factor in his new home in the New World He was elected to many local offices and served in courts as juryman, helped construct roads bridges churches and was an extensive farmer In 1685 he sold his real estate conveying the homestead to his son Captain William His

children were 1 Capt William, born September, 1640, died 1720 2 Hannah, born 1642, married Samuel Porter, who died 1660, married Thomas Woodberry Josiah Dodge killed in the Narragansett war in 1675, may have been another son

(II) Richard Dodge, son of John Dodge (1), the English ancestor, and a brother to William above named, married in England, and had a son John, who died there His wife was baptized as Edith It is quite certain that Richard and wife joined the New England colony in 1638, and as the King at that time was not allowing emigration, it is possible that he left England without royal sanction He settled in "Dodge Row," North Beverly, where he built a house that was occupied and kept in the family for more than two hundred years He and his wife Edith were members of the Wenham Church, but the most of his time and talent seems to have been spent in farm improvements, not paying any special attention to church work His wife outlived him seven years, dying June 27, 1678, at the age of seventy-five years Their children were John, Mary, Sarah, Richard, Samuel, Edward, Joseph

(III) Joseph Dodge, son of Richard (2), born in Beverly, 1651, died August 10, 1716, married Sarah Eaton, of Reading, 1671 He was a farmer in Beverly, near his father, on Dodge Row He was one of the executors of his father's estate, receiving a liberal joint share with his brother Edward The children born to Joseph and his wife were Abigail, Joseph, Noah, Prudence, Abigail, Jonah, Sarah, Elisha, Charity, Nathaniel

(IV) Elisha Dodge, son of Joseph (3), born January, 1687, died January 17, 1755 With his brother Jonah he shared his father's real estate holdings In his will he gave his wife Mary two cows four sheep and other property, and to his son Elisha all real and personal estate He left to his wife a negro woman, Bathsheba, who was to belong to his daughters Lois and Mary on the death of their mother His realty was appraised at 380 pounds and personal at 114 pounds He married Mary Kimball, of Wenham, October, 1709, and the children born to them were Jerusha, Lois, Elisha Mary, Elisha

(V) Elisha Dodge, son of Elisha (4), born in Beverly, May 17, 1723, died after 1777, in New Boston, married, first, to Eleanor Dodge, secondly, to Sarah Foster, of Wenham, 1748, who died August, 1768, and in 1769 he married Mrs Deborah Lovett He lived in Beverly until 1777, when he moved his family to New Boston, New Hampshire, where he died His children were Sarah, Jerusha, Elisha, Noah, Malachi, Abigail, Ella, Enoch, Mehitable, Mary

(VI) Enoch Douglas, son of Elisha (5), born May 1762, in Beverly, died December 27, 1834, in Eden, Vermont, married, December 18, 1787, Jael Cochran, born in New Boston, New Hampshire, 1768, died at Eden, Vermont, April 6, 1844 They moved to New Boston in 1788 Their children were 1 Malachi Foster, born New Boston, New Hampshire, August 20 1789 2 Elizabeth, born March 28, 1792, died February 22, 1793 3 Betsey, born January 17, 1794, died July 22 1802 4 Enoch, born December, 1795, died Crete, Illinois, March 4, 1873 5 Elisha, born February 18, 1798, died July, 1802 6 Jane, born January 25, 1800, died February 1844, married Daniel Cornish 7 Nathaniel C, born May, 1802, lived at Jeffersonville, Vermont 8 Joseph born March 31, 1804, died June, 1864 9 Mary, born June 24, 1806, died 1880 10 Hiram, born June 25, 1808, died May 13, 1859 11 John, born December, 1810, died March, 1814

(VII) Malachi F Dodge, son of Enoch (6), born August 20, 1789, in New Boston, New Hampshire, died October 13, 1865, in Nashua, New Hampshire He married Jane Hutchins, January 9, 1812, at Belvidere, Vermont They first resided in Belvidere and next in Lowell, Vermont, whence they removed in 1837 to Nashua, New Hampshire Their children were 1 Priscilla D, born May 1813, died August 12, 1861, married William H Huntley 2 Malachi F, born January 8, 1815 3 Elisha C, born September 27, 1816, died February, 1825 4 Sarah Jane, born July 6, 1818, married, November 18, 1845, Frederick Plummer Bixby, both deceased 5 Daniel Darling, born June 28, 1820, married Miss Wyman, both deceased 6 Thomas Hutchins, born September 27, 1823, married Eliza Daniels 7 Abbie R, born June, 1825, married Rodney M Rollins, both deceased 8 Elisha E, born November 17, 1827, married Martha E Fernald, both deceased 9 Mary Harding, born November 20, 1829, married Mason Boyd, he is deceased, she resides in New Hampshire 10 Emeline A, born July, 1832, died October 26, 1865

(VIII) Malachi F Dodge, Jr, son of Malachi F (7), born January 8, 1815, at Eden, Vermont, married, May, 1838, Charlotte A Ober, of Hopkinton, New Hampshire, first, and after her death he married Hannah P Edwards Both are now deceased They resided at Manchester, New Hampshire, and had following children 1 Infant son, died in 1841 2 Edward O, born February, 1844, married Ellen L Dearborn, deceased 3 Thomas F, born October, 1846 4 Willy H, born November, 1851, deceased 5 James E, born March, 1854, resides in Manchester, New Hampshire, and although a Republican in politics has been city auditor for many years under the administration of both parties 6 Frank E, born September, 1863, deceased

(VIII) Having brought down from the English ancestor, the line of descendants to which our chief subjects belonged, it should here be stated that he of whom we write, Hon Thomas H Dodge (8), was born September 27, 1823, in the town of Eden, Lamoille county, Vermont He is the fourth son of Malachi F Dodge (7), and wife Jane Hutchins Thomas H had the early advantages of good district schools, as his father was a well-to-do farmer The family later moved to the town of Lowell, Vermont, residing on a farm until he was about fourteen years of age, when his eldest brother secured a good position with a manufacturing concern at Nashua New Hampshire and the family removed there Here he applied himself to his school duties and became a great admirer of Judge Edmund Parker, who was his Sabbath school superintendent The Dodge family there were members of the Olive St Congregational Church Through the influence of Judge Parker, young Dodge resolved on becoming a lawyer and manufacturer He proposed to his parents to bear his own expenses and thus showing what he could accomplish, agreeing to pay to his father a sum for the remainder of his time, as he had not yet reached his majority He decided on learning the cotton manufacturing business, hence commenced at the bottom as a roll carrier giving him a chance to understand all about the raw product and its preparation for spinning All this time he was reading books on this subject After earning sufficient money in the factory he entered Gymnasium Institute at Pembroke, New Hampshire, where he rapidly advanced, and at the commencement delivered his first oration, "The Canadian Patriot's Address before his Execution" Learned state lawyers and jurists were present and he made a great impression upon all One judge made the remark, "That lad has a bright and eventful future before him' And true it was But little did they dream that within a third of a century this lad would stand so high as a manufacturer and inventor as well at the forefront as an advocate and jurist in a special branch of law He returned to the cotton mills, and in 1850 published his famous review of the "Rise, Progress and Importance of Cotton Manufactures of the United States" He was a close student in many branches of natural philosophy and chemistry He was a born inventor, and knew to succeed he must needs be fully posted, hence his extra training along all mechanical lines occupied his time for years Among his numerous inventions was his printing press patented to him by the United States Patent Office, November 18, 1851 From the use of this and other inventions he received a large income at a time in his career of research and activities when most needed to send him up higher Now having the funds—the product of his own brains—he decided to fit himself for law, and in 1851 he entered the office of Hon George Y Sawyer and Col A F Stevens, of Nashua, New Hampshire Having given three years close study, he was admitted to the bar at Manchester, New Hampshire In 1854 he opened an office at Nashua He was then thirty-one years of age Aside from his own position as a lawyer he had gained prominence as a manufacturer and inventor of no small skill By reason of these things Hon Charles Mason then United States Commissioner of Patents, was attracted toward this rising genius, and tendered him the position in the examining corps of the United States Patent Office He was first assistant but soon his peculiar ability and fitness caused him to be made an examiner-in-chief As long as Commissioner Mason was at the head of the Patent Office the advice and opinion of Mr Dodge were constantly sought after He was finally admitted to practice in the United States supreme court, and had very many large patent cases, some involving millions of dollars, in which he was eminently successful His clients came from one ocean to the other and from the forests of Maine to the cotton belt of the far away Southland In the forepart of 1864, Mr Dodge took up a residence in Worcester He had an office and was a third owner of the Union Mowing Machine Company, at Worcester, which plant employed many men and made goods for all parts of the country In 1881, while still in an extensive law practice, he in connection with Charles G Washburn, organized the Barbed Fence Company, of Worcester of which Mr Dodge was president This was but the commencement of what has become an immense barbed wire industry In 1883 the long years of brain work caused a serious break in his usual good health, and he was compelled to retire from the active routine of business cares to which he had subjected himself for so many years

In a work such as this it is impossible to give space sufficient to give at length even an outline, of all of interest connected with this man's career, but in closing this sketch, a brief review of some of the more important acts in both his private and public life will be noted He started out in life with a high aim He worked his own way through school He invented several cotton cloth-making appliances by which hundreds of dollars were saved each month by each cotton mill He invented a printing press in the fifties, which principle carried out has given the world its great continuous roll printing presses He improved the manner of making mowing machines whereby over a million men's work is saved each haying season He discovered the safety valve defect and has taught the world much about the cause of steam boiler explosions He was a chief examiner and chairman of the board of appeals in the United States Patent Office, being appointed by Judge Holt, chairman, who succeeded Judge Mason as Commissioner of Patents The latter office Mr Dodge resigned in the fall of 1858 Some idea of the esteem in which Mr Dodge's services were held may be gained from the fact that the venerable editor-in-chief of the *National Intelligencer* of Washington said that no other public officer had ever received such a genuine and high tribute as that which Commissioner Holt bestowed upon Mr Dodge, which was as follows

United States Patent Office
November 3 1858

Sir —I have received with emotions of unmingled sorrow your letter of yesterday resigning the office of examiner the duties of which you have for years discharged with such distinguished honor to yourself and advantage to the public interest It would have been to me a source of high gratification could I have enjoyed for the future that zealous support which you have so kindly afforded me in the past While however I feel that your retirement will be a severe loss to the service as it will be a personal affliction to myself I cannot be insensible to the weight of the considerations which have determined you to seek another and more attractive field of labor I shall ever recall with the liveliest satisfaction the pleasant social and official relations which have marked our intercourse and in accepting your resignation I beg to offer to you my heartfelt thanks alike for your personal friendship and for the high loyal and most effective co-operation which in the midst of circumstances of difficulty and embarrassment you have constantly extended to me in the administration of this office In whichever of the varied paths of life it may be your fortune to tread be assured that you will bear with you my warmest wishes for your success and happiness

Most sincerely your friend
J Holt

Mr Thomas H Dodge

He was instrumental in bringing about a change in the United States Postal Department at Washington, by which letters not called for, it containing a return card, would find their way back to the writer, without the long, expensive routine of going through the Dead Letter office He has been an eminently successful patent attorney, handling intricate cases, wherein many millions of money have been at stake He has been connected with vast mower and barb wire manufacturing industries at Worcester He has given "Dodge Park" to the city—a gift royal in and of itself He has, together with his truly estimable wife, been a faithful church and Sabbath school worker They have donated large sums of money from time to time toward the building of church edifices in Worcester and other places, including Trinity Methodist Episcopal Church, and Union and Piedmont Congregational Churches He has given to the Odd Fellows of Massachusetts the charming grounds upon which stands the State Odd Fellows' Home in Worcester, and then gave beautiful grounds adjacent known as Dodge Park These were unselfish gifts because he is not a member of this great order He wrote a twenty page genealogy of one branch of the Dodge family in 1880 He was true and loyal to the Union cause in the dark and trying days of the civil war He lived in Washington, D C, and has home was ever open to those disposed to care for the sick and wounded soldiers Both he and his truly good companion gave of their means and distributed delicacies of food, both in and outside the regular hospitals At no time did this far-seeing man ever doubt the final triumph which came to the Union cause Not able himself to enter the army, he furnished a substitute at a cost of one thousand dollars—a young French Canadian, who served with great credit, and rose to the rank of a commissioned officer

Mr Dodge was married June 29, 1843, to Eliza Daniels of Brookline New Hampshire and to her he attributes much of his success in life, as she

ODD FELLOWS PROCESSION

Passing Residence of Thomas H. Dodge after dedicating Odd Fellows' State Home, June 22, 1892

has ever cheered and encouraged his undertakings The deep interest they have both taken in church work and the support of the same, with their interest in the Natural History Camp and the Summer schools for boys and girls, give the readers to know the tendencies of their minds May 18, 1905, Mr and Mrs Dodge each donated five hundred dollars to the cause

Mr Dodge is a man of distinguished presence, dignified yet genial His has been a life of great usefulness He is noted for liberality of mind and kind hospitality The warm place he holds in the affections of the people, in a community in which he has done so much good work, and spent so large a portion of his useful and honorable life, is the best evidence of his work as a citizen whom all Massachusetts may well be proud to own

AUGUSTUS GEORGE BULLOCK Richard Bullock, (I) the emigrant ancestor of A George Bullock, of Worcester, settled in Rehoboth, Mass, in 1643 He was a man of some prominence in the town Among other positions he held was that of town clerk in 1659 He married (first), August 4, 1647, Elizabeth Ingraham, probably daughter of Richard Ingraham a settler of Rehoboth, he married (second) Elizabeth Billington, September 21, 1660 His children were Samuel, born August 19, 1648, Elizabeth, October 9, 1650, Mary, February 16, 1652 Mehitable April 4 1655, Abigail, August 29 1657, Hopestill December 26 1659, Israel, July 15, 1661, Mercy, March 13, 1662, died March 19, 1663 John May 19 1664 Richard, March 15, 1666-7

(II) Samuel Bullock son of Richard (1) and Elizabeth (Ingraham) Bullock, was born at Rehoboth, Massachusetts, August 19, 1648 He was a farmer and lived at Rehoboth His name appears in the list of proprietors of Rehoboth in 1689 He was a contributor to the fund raised for defence in King Philip's war in 1675 He married (first) Mary Thurber, November 12, 1673 He married (second) Thankful Rouse, May 26, 1675 Their children were Mary, born October 4, 1674, Ebenezer, February 22, 1676, Thankful, June 26, 1681, Samuel, November 7, 1683, Israel, April 9, 1687, Daniel 1689, Richard, July 1, 1692, Seth, September 26, 1693

(III) Ebenezer Bullock, son of Samuel Bullock (2), was born at Rehoboth, Massachusetts February 22 1676 He married Sarah Moulton, March 29, 1698 They resided at Rehoboth Their children were Mary, born June 6, 1699, Mehitable, April 1, 1701, Samuel, November 17, 1703, Hugh, April 1, 1706, Aaron, 1707, Squier, March 4, 1709, Miriam September 30, 1711, Thankful, May 23, 1714, Katherine died December, 1707, James, August 21, 1716

(IV) Hugh Bullock, son of Ebenezer Bullock (3) was born at Rehoboth, Massachusetts, April 1, 1706 He married (first) Anna Cole, 1733 (second) Mehitable——————— He resided at Rehoboth His children were James, born December 17, 1734, Alethea, March 12, 1736, Ebenezer, June 30, 1739, Sarah, August 17, 1741, Moulton, November 5, 1743, Prudence, May 6, 1746, Hugh, August 12 1751, Barnet (records give Barnard), June 20, 1773

(V) Hugh Bullock, son of Hugh Bullock (4) and Anna Cole, was born August 12 1751, at Rehoboth Massachusetts His brother Moulton removed to Royalston, Massachusetts before the revolution and settled there Moulton's farm was owned in 1865 by Jason Fisher Hugh went to Royalston during the revolution Hugh Bullock's farm was north of his brother's After his sons were grown up and engaged in other business he built a house on the common, west of his son Barnet's house This house was occupied in 1865 by C H Newton Hugh died in this house in 1837, at the age of eighty-five His wife, Rebecca (Davis) Bullock, died 1809, aged fifty years Hugh Bullock was one of the company that started for Saratoga to repel the invasion of Burgoyne He was in Captain Peter Woodbury's company, Colonel Job Cushing's regiment, which reinforced General Stark at Bennington, Vermont The children of Hugh Bullock (5) were Rufus, born September 23, 1779, Calvin, Moulton, born 1787, died 1865, Barnet born 1798, died 1884, Candace, was living in Royalston 1865

Christopher, Ebenezer, Nathan, and David Bullock also settled in Royalston about this time The history of Royalston states that they were cousins of Hugh and Deacon Moulton Bullock They were all stalwart men David being the tallest man in town Their stay in town was short When they had their places well cleared and were in the full vigor of manhood they went westward, following the tide of settlers from the Atlantic states inland after the revolution

(VI) Rufus Bullock son of Hugh Bullock (5), was born at Royalston, Massachusetts, September 23, 1779 He was perhaps the most distinguished man who spent his life in the town of Royalston He died there January 10, 1858 With small means he laid the foundation of a good education and became an acceptable school teacher before he was of age He taught school several winters and worked out at farming in the summers He was clerk in the country store, and finally opened a store on his own account on the common The business prospered and he led the life of a country merchant the remainder of his days, accumulating a fortune for his day and enjoying to a remarkable degree the respect and confidence of the people of the vicinity Mr Bullock made it a rule to expand his business as his means increased, never going beyond but always using fully what he had He always gave every detail of his varied business interests his personal supervision He began to manufacture at his mill in South Royalston, which was very successful He always conducted a farm and took time to work in the fields himself, notwithstanding the demands of his store and factory He seemed to find recreation in the variety of his interests

Mr Bullock often served the town in public office He was town clerk in 1812 and 1813 He was selectman in 1811-12-13 He represented Royalston and his district for five years in the general court He was in the state senate 1831-32 He was delegate to the constitutional conventions in 1820 and 1852 and was once chosen a presidential elector He left $5,000 in his will to the Congregational church, in which he always took a profound interest he gave $2,500 to the Baptist Society, $2,500 to the Second Congregational Church at South Royalston, $5,000 to the town of Royalston for schools A significant proviso of the last named bequest was that the town must keep the cemetery in repair or forfeit the money The condition of the old graveyards of Massachusetts at times has been a reproach to civilization in this state Mr Bullock's bequest will doubtless save the graves of Royalston from desecration and neglect Mr Bullock was a trustee of Amherst College and presented the telescope for the observatory

He married May 4 1808, Sarah Davis, of Rindge, New Hampshire The history of Royalston says of her "She still survives (1865) and lives among us, the same industrious and cheerful matron of the olden type, whose wisdom and energy helped to build the house, and who is still spared to enjoy it, when builded, and still to attract the children and the children's children to the ancient homestead" Of Mr Bullock it says 'He was a patriot of the early type—a gentleman of the olden school—a friend to be trusted, a man whose principles bore the test of intimate acquaintance and inspection, and whose influence, unobtrusive but potent, has been eminently useful" Their children were Maria Louisa, born October 14, 1809, Emily, born September 10, 1811, married W D Ripley, died May 1, 1904, Rebecca, born April 28, 1814, married Nelson Wheeler, Alexander Hamilton, born March 2, 1816, died January 17, 1882, Charles Augustus, born 1818, died August 25, 1882, Rufus Henry, born January 9, 1821

(VII) Alexander Hamilton Bullock, son of Rufus Bullock (6), was born at Royalston, Massachusetts, March 2, 1816 He entered Amherst College in 1832, was a diligent student and on his graduation, in 1836, delivered the salutatory oration at commencement In the catalogue of his contemporaries at college are found the names of Rev Richard S Storrs, Rev Henry Ward Beecher, Bishop Huntington and other famous men After graduating he taught school for a short time at Princeton, N J, and then partly at the wish of his father and partly on account of his own inclination entered the Harvard Law School After leaving the law school he spent a year in the office of the well known lawyer, Emory Washburn, of Worcester, where he gained a good knowledge of the details of legal practice, and in 1841 was admitted to the bar Senator Hoar said of Mr Bullock "He disliked personal controversy While he possessed talents which would have rendered him a brilliant and persuasive advocate, the rough contests of the court house could never have been congenial to him He was associated with Judge Thomas as junior counsel in one important capital trial, in which he is said to have made an eloquent opening argument He had a considerable clientage for a young man, to whom he was a safe and trustworthy adviser But he soon established a large business as agent of important insurance companies and withdrew himself altogether from the practice of law"

From early manhood Mr Bullock took a decided interest in politics The prominence of his father in political circles may have increased a natural taste for public life He was particularly well versed in constitutional law and that tact, together with the well defined convictions he held gave him in debate and in administration great advantages He was originally a Whig Step by step he advanced to the highest position in the commonwealth He was a member of the house of representatives for eight years, first in 1845 last in 1865 In 1862-63-64-65, during the civil war, all legislative positions were of extraordinary importance and involved great responsibility He was exceedingly popular among his colleagues He was a state senator in 1849, judge of the Worcester county court of insolvency for two years—1856-8, having served as commissioner of insolvency since 1853 He was mayor of Worcester in 1859 The greatest event of his public career was his service as governor of the commonwealth in 1866-67-68 At his first election he received nearly 50,000 votes more than his opponent Governor Bullock had many opportunities to serve in high positions in the national government Among other places that he declined was the mission to England offered him by President Hayes

In financial, humane and all reformatory movements Governor Bullock was active and efficient He was president of the State Mutual Life Assurance Company, and of the Worcester County Institution of Savings, director of the Worcester National Bank, chairman of the finance committee of the trustees of Amherst College, and a life member of the New England Historic-Genealogical Society While editor and publisher of the *Daily Aegis* (now *The Gazette*) he displayed marked ability as a writer and newspaper man He received the honorary degree of LL D from Amherst and Harvard Colleges He was a great friend of learning, interested in all educational institutions

In 1869 he visited Europe with his family Upon his return the following year he was received with a public demonstration to welcome him home and give evidence of the respect and love of his townsmen Governor Bullock was an orator of great power A volume of his addresses was published Senator Hoar, who made a special study of orators, said of Governor Bullock's speeches 'Above all, he possessed, beyond any of his living contemporaries, that rare gift of eloquence which always has been and always will be a passport to the favor of the people where speech is free' His eulogy of President Lincoln in Worcester in 1865 was one of many notable public addresses that he delivered He delivered the commemorative oration at the centennial of the incorporation of his native town of Royalston

Governor Bullock married, 1844, Elvira Hazard, daughter of Colonel A G Hazard, of Enfield, Connecticut, founder of the Hazard Gunpowder Manufacturing Company Their children were Augustus George, born at Enfield, Connecticut, Isabel, married Nelson S Bartlett, of Boston, Fanny, married Dr William H Workman, of Worcester

(VIII) A George Bullock, son of the late Alexander H (7) and Elvira (Hazard) Bullock, was born June 2, 1847, at Enfield, Connecticut His life has been spent from infancy, however, in the city of Worcester He attended the Highland Military Academy and graduated there in 1862 After two years of preparation under Professor E G Cutler he entered college in 1864 Professor Cutler, his tutor, was afterward professor of English literature at Harvard In 1868 Mr Bullock graduated at Harvard College Soon afterward he began the study of law in the offices of the late Judge Thomas L Nelson and the late Senator George F Hoar He was admitted to the bar and entered upon the practice of his profession His career as a lawyer closed with his election to the presidency of the great insurance company, although a legal training is perhaps most essential in the education of the executive head of such a corporation Certainly Mr Bullock's legal experience increased his efficiency and augmented his success in developing the business of the State Mutual Company His predecessor in the presidency was Philip L Moen, who completed the year to which Mr Bullock's father, Alexander H Bullock, had been elected in January, 1882, his death two weeks later making a vacancy In the following year A George Bullock was elected New methods were introduced and the company grew amazingly This company began its business in Worcester in 1845 Its first first president, John Davis, its third president, Alexander H Bullock, and its vice-president, Emory Washburn, were at various times elected governor of the commonwealth The second president of the company, Isaac Davis, was almost as prominent in public affairs as his uncle who preceded him He was president twenty-nine years A vice president and one of the organizers was John Milton Earle, who was editor of *The Spy* for so many years In

Alex. H. Bullock

A. G. Bullock

recent years, under the present management, the business of the company has increased phenomenally The company has among its assets one of the attractive office buildings of Boston and the most valuable office building by far in Worcester, containing two hundred and one offices

Mr Bullock's other interests are extensive He is president of the Norwich & Worcester Railroad Company, vice-president of the Worcester Consolidated Street Railroad Company, president of the Worcester Railways and Investment Company, trustee and member of the board of investment of the Worcester County Institution for Savings, director of the Providence & Worcester Railroad Company, director of the Boston & Albany Railroad Company, director of the Worcester Gaslight Company, director of the Worcester National Bank, director of the Worcester Trust Company, director of the Railways and Lighting Company of Boston, director of the State Street Trust Company of Boston, director of the American Loan and Trust Company of Boston He was a commissioner at large to the Columbian exposition at Chicago in 1893, appointed by the president of the United States He has been chairman of the directors of the Public Library He was formerly trustee of the State Lunatic Hospital at Worcester He is a member of the American Antiquarian Society and of The Worcester Society of Antiquity He is a member of the Tatnuck Country Club, Commonwealth Club, Worcester Club, Harvard Club of New York, University Club of New York Somerset Club of Boston and of the Union Club of Boston He attends the First Unitarian church He is a Republican He resides in a handsome brownstone house at 48 Elm street, built by Governor Bullock By a singular coincidence the former residence of Governor Lincoln is directly across Elm street Mr Bullock has a beautiful country home near Mt Wachusett, in the town of Princeton

He married Mary Chandler, daughter of Dr George and Josephine (Rose) Chandler, of Worcester, October 4, 1871 Their children, all of whom were born in Worcester, were Chandler, born August 24, 1872, Alexander Hamilton, November 7, 1875, Augustus George, Jr, April 20, 1880, died April 29, 1880, Rockwood Hoar, August 21, 1881

(IX) Chandler Bullock married, October, 1900, Mabel Richardson, daughter of George Richardson, of Worcester Their children are Margaret, born in Worcester, December 22, 1901, Josephine Rose, born June 21, 1904 He is a lawyer practicing in Worcester

(IX) Alexander Hamilton Bullock married Florence Armsby, widow of ——— McClellan, June, 1902 His wife has a daughter Beulah by her first marriage He is a lawyer practicing in Worcester

(IX) Rockwood Hoar Bullock married Elizabeth Bliss Dewey, daughter of Francis H Dewey, of Worcester, June 8, 1905

Barnet Bullock was the fifth generation from Richard Bullock, the emigrant ancestor He was born in the west part of Royalston, June 9, 1798, and during his active life followed the business of a merchant in that town He held for a long time the commission of justice of the peace, doing most of the public business in that line in the town for many years, besides filling various responsible town offices He was town clerk from 1837 to 1847, selectman 1840, 1844 and 1845, and representative to the general court in 1843 and 1844 One of the oldest and most prominent citizens of Royalston, he died September 1, 1884, being the last survivor of the four sons of Hugh Bullock, who came from Rehoboth and settled in Royalston during the revolution He married November 27, 1828, Lucy Newton, daughter of Nathan Brigham Newton Their children were Calvin, born September 21, 1829 died March 5, 1870, Brigham Newton, born April 6, 1831, died February 20, 1906, Barnet Ellis, born March 22, 1833, Lucy Lee, born May 25, 1835 died September 18, 1882, Elizabeth Candace, born October 16, 1838, died March 24, 1843, Charles Stuart, born January 20, 1841, James Frederick, born July 21, 1842, died May 28, 1870, Mary Elizabeth, born December 18, 1847, died March 21, 1869

Brigham Newton Bullock was the second son of Barnet Bullock, and was born in Royalston, April 6, 1831 He spent his early life in his native town, where he attended the common schools February 24, 1847, at the age of sixteen, he started out in life by entering the employment of Joseph Estabrook, who kept a country store and the postoffice He remained with Mr Estabrook until the fall of 1851, when for a short time he attended the fall term of the high school, kept by Crandall Bros On October 20 of the same year he left Royalston and the high school to enter the passenger department of the office of the Vermont & Massachusetts Railroad in Fitchburg, where he remained until January, 1874 He then went to Boston where he was cashier of the Boston, Hartford & Erie Railroad from March, 1874, until August, 1874 From there he went to the Home Savings Bank, Boston August 6, 1874, as treasurer, and remained until February 27 1882 when he returned to Fitchburg and entered the Fitchburg National Bank as cashier, holding that office until he was made president in 1888, and as an active working president he served the bank for the remainder of his life Under his administration its affairs were conducted with great success, and its resources largely increased

His acknowledged ability as a financier led the trustees of the Fitchburg Savings Bank to secure his services as treasurer, when a vacancy occurred in that office in July, 1894, and he remained treasurer, to their great satisfaction, until the law separating national and savings banks went into effect in 1904, when he was chosen chairman of the board of investment, and in that capacity was able to give to the bank the benefit of his valuable oversight and experience while he lived In addition to the responsibilities of the conduct of these two large financial institutions, to which he gave most of his time and attention he served as a director in the Fitchburg Railroad Company, in the Fitchburg Mutual Fire Insurance Company, in the Grant Yarn Company and in the Simonds Manufacturing Company of Fitchburg He was a member of the First (Unitarian) Parish

Mr Bullock was not only a successful financier, but a man of sterling character and to all the responsibilities which he assumed he honestly and faithfully devoted himself His 'word was as good as his bond" He would have nothing superficial The whole structure of every institution which he managed must be thoroughly sound and strong from its very foundation, and so he left them Not only was he a strong practical man of business, firm in his convictions, and just in all his dealings, but he also had a heart sensitive to all needs of humanity and the beautiful in art and nature He was a devoted husband and father, and a faithful friend and a genial companion to all who enjoyed his intimate acquaintance He always retained his affection for his native town of Royalston, and spent a portion of each summer in that beautiful hill town of Massachusetts He was of the best product of the New England country town

Brigham N Bullock married November 13, 1888,

Flora Belle Ripley, of Fitchburg She survives her husband who died in Boston, February 20 1906 Their only child is Richard Bullock, born May 3, 1892

THE GREEN FAMILY (I) Thomas Green was the ancestor of the Green family of Worcester, to which belong Samuel Swett Green, librarian of the Free Public Library, Martin Green, a civil engineer and contractor, and James Green, a lawyer, of Worcester, Oliver Bourne Green a civil engineer and contractor, of Chicago, Dr John Green and Dr John Green, Jr, both oculists, of St Louis, the late Andrew Haswell Green Father of Greater New York," and many others, both of the surname of Green and of other surnames

Thomas Green was born in England in about the year 1600, according to a deposition which he made August 16, 1662 A Thomas Green who probably was his son, came over to Massachusetts, at the age of fifteen, in the "Planter," which sailed from England April 2, 1635 The same name and age appear also in the "Hopewell," which sailed the next day, and are believed to represent the same Thomas Green Jr Preceding the list of passengers in the 'Planter," is a certificate which states that Thomas Green came from St Albans, Hertfordshire It seems likely that Thomas Green, senior, came to New England at the same time or a little earlier, and settled at Lynn and Ipswich He was living at Lady Moody's farm at Lynn about 1646 The Green 'Genealogical Sketch" which was published before some of these facts were discovered in the records, states that he probably removed from Ipswich to Malden in 1649 or 1650 He was certainly in Malden October 28, 1651, when his wife Elizabeth and his daughter Elizabeth signed a petition to the general court He had a farm of sixty-three acres in the northern part of Malden He was one of the leading citizens serving repeatedly on the grand jury, and in 1658 as a selectman of Malden

When the 'Genealogical Sketch of the Descendants of Thomas Green(e) of Malden Mass by Samuel S Green of Providence R I," was written, there were "reasons for supposing that Thomas Green senior came from Leicestershire but no proofs of the fact" If the suggestion that Thomas Green who came over in the "Planter' was his son is well grounded the home of the family would seem to have been at St Albans

The first wife of Thomas Green senior, Elizabeth whom he married in England was the mother of all his children She died August 22 1658 He married secondly Frances Cook September 5 1659 She was born in 1608 married first to Isaac Wheeler secondly to Richard Cook, who died October 14, 1658 She had children by the first two husbands none by the third Thomas Green Thomas Green (I) died December 19 1667 His will dated November 12 1667 was proved January 15 1667-8 In it he mentions five sons five daughters and his wife The homestead was situate in that part of Malden which is now included in Melrose and Wakefield The children of Thomas and Elizabeth Green were

1 Elizabeth born about 1628

2 Thomas born in 1620 (if it is true as the ship-records say that he was fifteen years old when he sailed [in 1635] but ages in these lists of emigrants are not to be relied on) He married Rebecca Hills 1653 [See his sketch later, "Thomas (II)"]

3 John born in England about 1632 according to the Genealogy married to Sarah Wheeler, December 18, 1660 (Church records give birth of John son of Thomas, Sr, January 25, 1658)

4 Mary, born in England about 1633, married before 1656 to Capt John Waite, who was selectman seven years and representative to the general court 1666 to 1684

5 William, born about 1635, married first to Elizabeth Wheeler, married secondly to Isabel (Farmer) Blood

6 Henry, born 1638 married January 11, 1671-2

7 Samuel, born March 1645, married first, 1666, to Mary Cook, secondly, to Susanna ———

8 Hannah born 1647, married November 5, 1666, to Joseph Richardson of Woburn Mass She died May 20 1721

9 Martha, born 1650

10 Dorcas, born in Malden, May 1 1653 married January 11, 1671-2, to James Barrett of Malden, who was born April 6, 1644 She died 1682, he died 1694

(II) Thomas Green son of Thomas Green (1), was born in England 1620,—if the record of the list of passengers of the ship Planter' which sailed April 2 1635, or the "Hopewell" which sailed the next day, is correct He claimed to be fifteen years old then He married in 1653, or before Rebecca Hills daughter of Joseph Hills of Malden later of Newbury, Massachusetts (See sketch Joseph Hills family in this work) Rebecca's mother was Rose Dunster a sister of Rev Henry Dunster, first president of Harvard College Thomas Green (2) settled in Malden He was a farmer, was admitted a freeman May 31, 1670, and died February 13, 1671-2 His will was dated the same day, and proved April 2, 1672 His widow, Rebecca, died June 6 1674 The inventory of her estate was filed March 4, 1674-5, by her son-in-law, Thomas Newell The children of Thomas and Rebecca Green were

1 Rebecca, born 1654, married to Thomas Newell of Lynn 1674

2 Thomas, born February, 1655-6, died April 15 1674

3 Hannah, born October 16, 1658, died March 25, 1650

4 Hannah born February 24 1659-60, married August 26 1677 to John Vinton, of Malden, and later of Woburn, Massachusetts

5 Samuel, born October 5, 1670, married to Elizabeth Upham about 1692

(III) Captain Samuel Green, the only son of Thomas (2) and Rebecca Hills Green who came to full age was born October 5, 1670 He was one of the principal men in Leicester or Strawberry Hill where he settled in 1717 The town was granted February 10 1713-14 and Capt Samuel Green was on the committee with Col William Dudley of Roxbury and others to settle it He owned three lots of forty acres each and two of thirty each, in the town of Leicester, and was highly respected and very influential The vicinity of his old homestead, now a village, is called after him, Greenville He built a house grist mill and saw mill At the first town meeting of which there is any record he was elected moderator first selectman and grand juror, and he held like offices in the town of Leicester the remainder of his life Governor Washburn in his history calls him a prominent man, and he is honored as one of the pioneers He also owned land in Hardwick, Massachusetts He was always called Captain a rank he won at Malden, and he was the first captain of the Leicester company of militia Capt Samuel Green married Elizabeth daughter of Lieut Phinehas Upham of Worcester a son of Deacon John Upham, who had arrived from England, September 2 1635, settled at Weymouth, Massachusetts, moved to Malden about 1650, and was one of the original proprietors of Quinsigamond His son Phinehas Upham settled in Worcester in April, 1675 After the Indians had destroyed the first white settlements at Mendon, Brookfield and Worcester, Lieut Upham fought bravely in the battle of Narraganset Fort, December 19 1675, where he was mortally wounded Capt Samuel Green died January 2, 1735-6 His will was made at Malden just before he came to Leicester to settle April 18 1717, and it was proved February 5, 1735-6 His wife died at Leicester, probably in 1761 Their children were

1 Elizabeth, born April 4, 1693, married to Thomas Richardson of Malden

2 Rebecca, born April 4 1695, married to Samuel Baldwin (According to Malden records the first two were twins, born April 4, 1695)

3 Ruth, married to Joshua Nichols

4 Thomas born 1699 married to Martha Lynde in Malden, January 13, 1725-6

5 Lydia, married to her cousin, Abiathar Vinton of Malden, April 30, 1723 He resided in Braintree a year or two after his marriage then settled in Leicester, where he lived until his death in 1740 His widow Lydia married secondly, January 15, 1746 Samuel Stower, of Leicester, a native of Malden

6 Bathsheba married to Elisha Nevins

7 Abigail married to Henry King

8 Amy (Anna?), married to Ebenezer Lamb

(IV) Dr Thomas Green son of Capt Samuel Green (3), was born in Malden in 1699 He married January 13, 1725-6 Martha Lynde, daughter of Capt John Lynde by his third wife, Judith Worth, widow of Joses Bucknam of Malden Martha Lynde was born July 6 1700 Before Capt Samuel Green removed his family to Leicester, in 1717, he and his son Thomas had driven some cattle from Malden to the site of their new home, preparatory to moving the family Thomas was left at Leicester in charge of the cattle, while his father returned to Malden While there alone the boy was attacked with fever and became very ill In his weak state he lay in a sort of cave made by an overhanging rock on a little stream, and secured food by milking a cow which he induced to come to him frequently by tying her calf to a tree near the cave At length two of his former neighbors at Malden who had come on horseback to look after their cattle found him, but refused to take him home They notified his father however, who went at once to his relief, and got him home on horseback after a painful journey of four days

Thomas Green s attention was early turned to the study of medicine His impluse in this direction is said to have come from two English ship-surgeons—it is even said they were pardoned buccaneers—who lived in his father's house at Leicester, taught young Thomas with interest and lent him medical books He grew to be friendly with the Indians and learned from them the curative properties of native herbs As the settlement grew his medical practice extended over a wider field and even into Rhode Island and Connecticut Many young men came to him for instruction in medicine he is said to have taught one hundred and twenty-three medical students The very slight facts which have come down to us about Dr Thomas Green's study and practice of medicine show him to have been the most prominent practitioner of the country doctors of his time, but these facts are especially interesting because he was the first of a long line of famous physicians and surgeons His son, grandson and great-grandson, each named John Green, were each of them the most distinguished physician in Worcester county, while Dr John Green of St Louis, the descendant of Thomas in the next generation, is now the foremost eye-surgeon in the Mississippi Valley, and his son Dr John Green, Jr, also of St Louis, is already a prominent and successful practitioner in the same specialty of medicine Five generations of Dr John Greens go back to Dr Thomas Green as their progenitor and their forerunner in the noble art of improving the health of man

Dr Thomas Green (4) joined the First Baptist Church at Boston, November 7, 1731 But in 1735 he was dismissed from that church to take part in forming another church at Sutton, the parent-church of his denomination in Worcester county, and the fourth Baptist church in the Province of Massachusetts Bay On September 28 1737 he and Benjamin Marsh were ordained as pastors of this Sutton church One year later to a day the Leicester families of the congregation erected a church of their own at Greenville (in Leicester), the eighth Baptist church in Massachusetts and Dr Thomas Green who was a charter member of both the Sutton and the Leicester church, was chosen the first pastor of the new church, and he remained its pastor for almost thirty-five years In a historical discourse delivered at the Greenville church in 1888, on the 150th anniversary of its foundation, the Rev Hiram C Estes, D D its pastor, says of the church-building, "that Dr Green was the principal proprietor of the house, that its grounds were given by him, and its frame was raised and covered at his expense" "While he was preaching on Sunday," said Hon Andrew H Green on the same anniversary, 'at his home across the way the pot was kept boiling to supply the needed sustenance to the little flock which came from all directions to attend upon his ministrations" During his ministry in Leicester he baptized more than a thousand persons In "Rippon's Register" he is spoken of as 'eminent for his useful labors in the gospel ministry" His preaching was not confined to his own parish, he was widely known as Elder Green In 1756 Rev Isaac Backus, the Baptist Annalist in New England held a meeting with Mr Green's church, and made the following entry in his diary "I can but admire how the Doctor (Thomas Green) is able to get along as he does, having a great deal of farming business to manage, multitudes of sick to care for several opportunities to instruct in the art of physic and a church to care for and watch over yet in the midst of all he seems to keep religion uppermost—to hold his mind bent upon divine things—and to be very bold in Christian conversation with all sorts of people" Dr Estes said in his discourse above quoted that 'Dr Green lived three lives and did the work of three men in one He was a man of business active energetic and successful * * * He was also a noted physician * * * and was a preacher of the gospel quite as eminent in this as in his other spheres of life"

Dr Green s homestead was next beyond the river from the Baptist Church on the road to Charlton, where his grandson Samuel Green, afterwards kept a tavern He died August 19, 1773, at the age of seventy-four years His wife Martha died June 20 1780 They were buried in the church-yard at Greenville but their remains were removed to the Rural Cemetery in Worcester, by Dr John Green (7), a descendant, where the graves are suitably marked The children of Thomas and Martha Green were

1 Samuel, born in Leicester 1726, married to Zeruiah Dana, married secondly to Widow Fish

2 Martha, born at Leicester April 23 1727, married about 1753 to Robert Craig (born December 10, 1726, he died October 13, 1805), she died September 17 1801, Craig studied medicine under Dr Thomas Green, but returned to the manufacture of spinning wheels instead of practicing, they had nine children

3 Isaac, married to Sarah Howe

4 Thomas L, born 1733, married to Hannah Fox, married secondly to Anna Hovey

5 John, born in Leicester August 14, 1736, married to Mary Osgood, and secondly to Mary Ruggles

6 Solomon, married to Elizabeth Page

7 Elizabeth, married first, to Daniel Hovey, married secondly, January 16, 1776 to Rev Benjamin Foster (Yale 1774, Brown DD 1792), who succeeded Rev Thomas Green as pastor of the Baptist church at Leicester, removed to Newport, Rhode Island thence to Gold Street Church, New York city, where he died of yellow fever in 1798

"Dr Thomas Green," says Samuel S Green in his biography of the late Andrew H Green, "bought the homestead in Worcester which forms the nucleus of the extensive and beautifully situated estate on Green Hill, lately owned by Andrew H Green This is one of the finest gentlemen's places in that neighborhood, contains over five hundred acres of field and forest and water, and has lately become a part of the park system of the City of Worcester The deed was given by Thomas Adams to Thomas Green of Leicester, dated May 28, 1754, in consideration of 330 pounds" His son John appears to have married and gone to Green Hill to live, about the year 1757 when he came of age The tradition of the family is that Thomas located his son on this hill remote from Worcester village that he might be protected by distance from the temptations of the town At Dr Thomas Green's death, August 19 1773, his entire estate passing through the probate office was appraised at 4,495 pounds, equivalent very nearly to $22,477, an estate said to have been larger than any that had been entered at the probate office in Worcester previous to his death

(V) Dr John Green fifth child of Dr and Rev Thomas Green (4), was born in Leicester, Massachusetts August 14 1736 He married first, Mary Osgood, of Worcester, apparently just as he came of age, in 1757 She was born August 31, 1740, and died September 5 1761 He married secondly apparently in 1762, Mary Ruggles, daughter of Brig Gen Timothy Ruggles of Sandwich, afterwards of Hardwick, Massachusetts Mary was born in Sandwich, on Cape Cod, in 1740 and died in Worcester, June 16, 1814, aged seventy-four years

Dr John Green studied medicine with his father, in company with many other students On coming of age he moved to Worcester and built his house upon the eminence at the north end of Worcester which came to be known as Green Hill Here he lived for his whole life He was very successful from the first He adopted the practice of watching over his patients like a nurse day and night, if required He became even more famous as a physician and surgeon than his distinguished father His son grandson great-grandson and great-great-grandson all of the same name and title of Dr John Green have also attained unusual eminence in the same profession No better evidence of inherited aptitude and skill in medicine and surgery could be shown Dr John Green instructed many students, as his father had done At first he had his office at the house on Green Hill, but later in a small wooden structure on Main street, on the original site of the Five Cent Savings Bank building At that time there were but seven houses on Main street between the Common and Lincoln Square William Lincoln, in his "History of Worcester," writing in 1836, says "Tradition bears ample though very general testimony to his worth Fortunate adaptation of natural capacity to professional pursuits gave an extensive circuit of employment and high reputation Habits of accurate observation, the action of vigorous intellect, and the results of experience, seem to have supplied the place of that learning deriving its acquirements from the deductions of others through the medium of books Enjoying great esteem for skill and fidelity, hospitality and benevolence secured personal regard" Dr Samuel B Woodward writes of Dr Green "An earnest patriot he was in 1773 a member (and the only medical member) of the American Political Society, which was formed 'on account of the grievous burdens of the times,' and did so much to bring about that change of public sentiment which expelled the adherents of the Crown He took a prominent part in all the Revolutionary proceedings, and in 1777 was sent as representative to the general court In 1778 and 1779 he was town treasurer and in 1780 one of the selectmen, the only physician who ever held that office" in Worcester

The father of Dr Green's second wife, Gen Timothy Ruggles, of Hardwick, was a distinguished lawyer, judge statesman and soldier He was opposed, however, to the Revolution, and is called by historians "Massachusetts' great loyalist" Hon Andrew H Green of New York, a descendant, had a biography of Gen Ruggles published

Dr John Green died in Worcester, October 29, 1799, at the age of sixty-three All his children were born on Green Hill Worcester, the first three being the children of Mary Osgood Thomas's first wife, and the last ten being the children of Mary Ruggles his second wife

1 John, born April 1, 1758, died September 20, 1761

2 Mary, born November 27, 1759, died February 15 1759-60

3 Thomas born January 3 1761, married October 8, 1782, to Salome Barstow of Sutton

4 John, born March 18, 1763, married to Nancy Barber of Worcester [See sketch of his life later]

5 Timothy, born January 9, 1765, married to Mary Martin of Providence, Rhode Island

6 Samuel, born May 10, 1767 married to Widow Tillinghast, married secondly, to —— Waring

7 Elijah Dix, born July 4 1769 never married he was a graduate of Brown, 1792, practiced medicine at Charleston, South Carolina, died September 21, 1795

8 Mary, born April 30, 1772, never married, she died at the house of her brother, Samuel, in Columbia South Carolina, September 24, 1824

9 Elizabeth born July 31, 1774, unmarried, she died at Green Hill February 3, 1854 aged eighty lived chiefly with her brother Timothy, in New York city

10 William Elijah born January 31, 1777 [See his sketch later]

11 Meltiah, born July 28 1779, died unmarried December 1800 of yellow fever at St Bartholomew West Indies was a resident of Jamaica

12 Bourne born December 15, 1781, died un-

married, August, 1806, at sea, was engaged in commerce

13 Isaac, born September 4, 1784, died September 9, 1807, while a member of the Sophomore class of Columbia College, New York

(VI) Dr John Green, son of Dr John Green (5) and Mary (Ruggles) Green, was born at Worcester, on Green Hill, March 18, 1763 He studied medicine with his father and began to practice at the age of eighteen He inherited the skill and ability of his father and grandfather Particularly skilled in surgery his services were in constant demand, "while daily could be seen," says Charles Tappan, "Dr Green and his half-dozen students mounted on horesback and galloping through the streets as if some one or more were in peril" He lived at first in the little wooden office-building of his father on Main street Later he built a house just south of it He was, we are told by the "Genealogy," "of industrious habits, patient, persevering, in his manners, urbane and obliging, in his judgments, discriminating, and always reliable, a man of great powers of observation, he had an extensive practice in Worcester and the surrounding region He combined with accurate practice as a physician, rare skill as a surgeon" Hon Oliver Fiske his biographer, said of him "From his childhood the natural bias of his mind led him to that profession which through life was the sole object of his ardent pursuit To be distinguished as a physician was not his chief incentive To assuage the sufferings of humanity by his skill was the higher motive of his benevolent mind Every duty was performed with delicacy and tenderness With these propensities, aided by a strong, inquisitive and discriminating mind, he attained to a pre-eminent rank among the physicians and surgeons of our country" He was tall, strong and attractive in person He died August 11, 1808, at the age of forty-five years, having practiced, however, for twenty-seven years, for the last nine of which he was practically the only physician in the town The *Worcester Spy* reported that "To his funeral came the largest concourse of people from this and neighboring towns ever known to be collected here on a similar occasion" "It has been the high privilege of few of our community to enjoy so much confidence and respect, to be so loved while living and so mourned when dead"

He married Nancy Barber granddaughter of Robert Barber of Northville, who was among the Presbyterians who fled from the religious persecutions in his native land and sought refuge in Ireland, whence he came to America, and made the Barber estate near Barber's Crossing, in Northville, Massachusetts The children were

1 John, born April 19, 1784, married to Dolly Curtis of Worcester They had no children [See sketch of his life later]

2 Eunice, born April 29 1786 married to Leonard Burbank, (Brown 1807) They had four children 1 John Green, graduated at West Point, first in his class He served in the Seminole and Mexican wars, and was killed in the battle of Molino del Rey where he had volunteered upon a forlorn hope He was never married, but was engaged to Anna M, daughter of Gen Belknap, of the Regular Army, a contemporary of Gen Scott 2 Ann Elizabeth married to Joseph Gardner, of Fitchburg They had one child, Elizabeth who lived and died in Fitchburg unmarried Ann Elizabeth is now dead 3 George G married to Lydia O Whiting, of Worcester No child was born to them, but they adopted one under the name of Caroline Amelia Burbank George and Lydia are dead 4 James Leonard, married to Persis S Wood, of Grafton They had one child only, Emma Jourdan James I is now dead Emma J married Frank Richard Macullar, of Worcester, son of Addison Macullar They had one child, Margaret Burbank, now living Frank R Macullar is now dead

3 Mary, born March 14, 1788, died unmarried, September 16, 1817

4 Nancy, born August 28, 1790, married to Dr Benjamin F Heywood of Worcester, (Dartmouth, 1812) [See the sketch of the Heywood Family later]

5 Samuel, born March 21, 1792, died August 24, 1796

6 Sarah, born August 22, 1794, died August 23, 1796

7 Samuel B, born April 11, 1797, died July 20, 1822

8 Frederick William, born January 19 1800, he settled in Columbia, South Carolina, married Sarah Briggs of Columbia, they had thirteen children and are both dead

9 James, born December 23, 1802, he married Elizabeth Swett of Dedham [See his sketch, later, "James Green (VII)"]

10 Meltiah Bourne born July 16, 1806, he married Mary Stone Ward [See his sketch, later, "M B Green (VII)"]

11 Elizabeth R born September 26, 1808, she married Dr Benjamin F Heywood, who had also married her sister Nancy [See Heywood Family sketch]

(VI) William Elijah Green, son of Dr John and Mary (Ruggles) Green, (5), was born on Green Hill January 31, 1777, and died there July 27, 1865, aged eighty-eight years He was graduated at Brown University in 1798 He succeeded his father in the ownership of the homestead on Green Hill, comprising then two hundred acres He studied law under Judge Edward Bangs, with whom and with whose son, Edward D Bangs, he was associated in practice for some years afterwards He was an original member of the First Baptist Society of Worcester but late in life became identified with the Universalists He will be remembered for the earnest work he did for temperance and the Public schools of Worcester He was for many years captain of the Worcester Light Infantry, and was a volunteer in the War of 1812 He was one of the foremost promoters of the Blackstone Canal, and never lost an opportunity to help advance the interests of his native town It has been said of him that he was a man of great geniality and cheerfulness affable to men of all conditions, highly respected and very popular In his later years William E Green withdrew from the practice of the law and spent his time in the development of his estate on Green Hill While this estate has been brought to its present perfection by his sons, Andrew H Green and Martin Green—the latter one of whom resided there for thirty-two years—Green Hill has been for one hundred and fifty years an attractive spot a gentleman's estate, suggesting the old English homes rather than the farms of New England The original house, to which Andrew H Green added a fine modern structure by cutting the old house in two and putting a new section between the front and rear is approached by Green Lane an old county road It had a museum of family heirlooms and relics In itself it is one of the choicest inheritances of the early settlers of Worcester What is called the Green Hill Book originated September 15 1861, when the ten children of William E Green the old "Squire," met together for the first time since their childhood, and this meeting proved also the last gathering of the family as a whole At that time Oliver B Green came from Chicago, John P Green was at home on a visit from Copiapo, Chili, where he lived forty years, Mary R, Lucy M and Andrew H came from New York, and Martin from Peshtigo, Wisconsin Some interesting portrait groups of the family were taken and are preserved in the Green Hill Book a large folio record book, in which an account of this reunion was entered, and in which records of interest to the family, including notices of visits have since been kept It is illustrated with photographs of several generations of the family, has clippings from newspapers containing obituaries and other family items

Mr Green died July 27, 1865, in the same room at Green Hill in which he was born,—at the age of eighty-eight years He was married four times, first to Abigail Nelson, daughter of Josiah Nelson, of Milford, who bore him one child, William Nelson Green secondly to Lucy Merriam, daughter of Deacon Joseph Merriam of Grafton, who bore him one child, Lucy Merriam Green, thirdly to Julia Plimpton daughter of Oliver Plimpton Esq, of that part of Sturbridge now known as Southbridge Massachusetts She had nine children and fourthly, to Elizabeth D Collins, a widow From this marriage there was no child The children of William E Green were

1 William Nelson, born at Milford Massachusetts, February 23, 1804 died December 6 1870 He was judge of the police court of Worcester [See his sketch, later]

2 Lucy Merriam, born at Grafton, November 12, 1810 She was for a great many years the joint owner with her sister Mary Ruggles Green, of a young ladies' school at No 1 Fifth avenue, New York city, which they made famous, unmarried, her brother, Andrew H Green a bachelor, lived with these two sisters and helped them conduct their business affairs she died May 8, 1893, at Worcester

3 Mary Ruggles, born in Worcester June 29, 1814 she married Carl W Knudsen who was born in Denmark 1818 and died in South Norwalk, Connecticut February 27 1894 She was a teacher and joint proprietor with her sister Lucy M of the young ladies' school at No 1 Fifth avenue, New York city She died March 17, 1894

4 Julia Elizabeth, born in Worcester, February 2 1816 she lived at home with her parents, was a teacher never married and died August 5, 1880

5 Lydia Plimpton, born at Worcester, August 4, 1817 died August 27, 1818

6 John Plimpton, born in Worcester January 19 1819 he became a physician, practiced in New York and lived in China and South America He died ———

7 Andrew Haswell born in Worcester October 6 1820 a prominent lawyer in New York city, associated in practice with Hon Samuel J Tilden, president of the Board of Education commissioner of Central Park and comptroller of New York city [See a sketch of his life, later.—"A H Green (VII) "]

8 Samuel Fiske born in Worcester, October 10 1822 a physician and missionary in Ceylon

9 Lydia Plimpton born at Worcester March 18 1824 she lived at the old home on Green Hill, and died there September 7 1869

10 Oliver Bourne born at Worcester January 1 1826 he married August 28 1855 Louisa Pomeroy of Stanstead Canada, a prominent civil engineer at Chicago Illinois [See a sketch of his life, later, —"O B Green (VII) "]

11 Martin born at Worcester, April 24, 1828, for many years a civil engineer engaged in important work, now resident at Worcester [See a sketch of his life, later.— Martin Green (VII) "]

(VII) Dr John Green son of Dr John Green (6), was born in Worcester, April 19 1784 He was graduated at Brown University in 1804, and began to practice medicine in Worcester in 1807, a year before the death of his father and eight years after that of his grandfather, Dr John Green of Revolutionary fame He seems destined to be remembered longer than either, for he will be known to future generations as the founder of the Free Public Library of Worcester Having early decided to devote a liberal portion of his fortune to the founding of such an institution, he was engaged for many years in collecting books, which in 1859 he presented to the city, adding continually to the number afterward and leaving in his will funds of $35,000 for the library, with a provision for further accumulation The funds amounted, November 30, 1905 to $61 403

He studied medicine with his father, succeeded to his father's practice at his death and for half a century was the acknowledged leader of his profession in this section of the state He was a good student gentle and sympathetic with his patients, especially with women and children, but quite inflexible when it seemed to him necessary, very cautious and also very daring but his most valuable professional quality was the keenest possible observation

Although this third Dr John Green is likely to be best known hereafter as the founder of Worcester's Public Library contemporary physicians and his own patients generally believed him to be the greatest physician and surgeon of the three who under the name of Dr John Green had cared for this community for ninety-eight years He was the last Dr Green of the four in this continuous family line who had served this neighborhood medically for over one hundred and thirty-five years without a break He was given the degree of M D by Harvard College in 1815 and in 1826 by his Alma Mater Brown University He was treasurer of the District Medical Society three years, vice-president five years, and president seven, vice-president of the American Medical Society in 1854 the first president of the Worcester County Horticultural Society, a councillor of the Massachusetts Medical Society and of the American Antiquarian Society He was an early and constant patron and supporter of the Worcester Natural History Society On account of age and failing health he retired from practice about 1855 He died in his eighty-second year, at Worcester, October 17 1865 He married Dolly Curtis, daughter of David Curtis of Worcester and aunt of the late George William Curtis the distinguished author and orator They had no children

(VII) James Green, son of Dr John Green (6) was born in Worcester December 23 1802, less than six years before the death of his father who died at the early age of forty-five years, and left a family of nine children surviving him The oldest son John (7) had already received his collegiate and medical education and had started in 1826 by his Alma Mater Brown University He practice but James had to go to work at the age of twelve, after very little schooling This calamity made him very eager afterwards to give his own children the best education he could He lived all his life in Worcester and married, May 1 1833, Elizabeth Swett, daughter of Samuel Swett of Boston and Dedham Massachusetts a merchant engaged in foreign trade They lived at

12 Harvard street, in Worcester, for about twenty-eight years just preceding his death on June 10, 1874 All their children were born in Worcester The widow Elizabeth continued to live in the same house until she died, May 7, 1901, leaving her three sons surviving Their children were

1 James, born February 15, 1834, died February 17, 1834

2 John, born April 2, 1835, graduated at Harvard College, 1855, M D Harvard, an eminent ophthalmologist and leader of his profession in St Louis, Missouri [See sketch of his life later,—Dr John Green (VIII)"]

3 Samuel Swett, born February 20, 1837, A B, Harvard, 1858, Harvard Divinity School, 1864, Harvard A M, 1870 [See a sketch of his life later,—"Samuel S Green, VIII"]

4 Elizabeth Sprague, born April 19, 1839, she died at St Louis at the home of her brother John, January 9, 1870

5 James, born March 2, 1841, Harvard A B, 1862, LL B, 1864, A M, 1865 [See sketch of his life later,—"James Green, VIII"]

(VII) Meltiah Bourne Green, son of Dr John Green (6), was born in Worcester, July 16, 1806 He married Mary Stone Ward, daughter of Artemas Ward of Worcester Massachusetts He lived in Worcester, and died there May 24, 1888 His wife died at Worcester, January 7, 1896 Their children were:

1 Meltiah, born August 27, 1838, died August 29, 1838

2 Mary Caroline, born December 13, 1839, died August 13, 1840

3 Meltiah Bourne, born January 3 1843, A B Trinity, 1865, LL B Harvard, 1867 He died at Geneva, Switzerland, December 27, 1877

(VII) William Nelson Green, son of William E Green (6), was born in Milford, Massachusetts, where his father lived and practiced law for a time, February 23, 1804 He was educated in the public schools of Worcester He studied law in the office of Samuel M Burnside in Worcester, and was admitted to practice in 1827 From 1833 to 1836 he was the editor of the *National Aegis*, a Worcester newspaper, distinguished more for the excellence of its editing and the greatness of some of its editors after they left the paper, than for any degree of financial success attained Somebody has said that half the lawyers in Worcester in the early days served their time as editor of the *Aegis* He was for a time a school teacher He will be remembered best for his high-minded and efficient service as the first judge of the city court When Worcester was incorporated as a city in 1848, the new charter established a police court, of which he became the justice Judge Green was undoubtedly the best qualified among the justices of the peace who had hitherto administered the criminal law in the town of Worcester He was not only the first but the last and only judge of the Worcester police court When, after a faithful service of twenty years, Judge Green retired the municipal court was established and the police court abolished to meet new needs of the city Judge Green loved nature and was very fond of hunting He died December 6 1870, two years after retiring from the judgeship He married February 23 1839 Sarah Munroe (Ball) Staples, who was born in Northboro and was a widow when he married her They had five children born in Worcester

1 William Nelson, (8), born January 10, 1843 He enlisted in the 25th Massachusetts Regiment and was promoted for gallantry in the battle of Roanoke to be second lieutenant in the 102d New York Regiment He was in the battle of Cedar Mountain and was a prisoner in Libby Prison He received special mention for brave conduct in the battle of Chancellorsville, and a commission as lieutenant-colonel in the 173d New York Regiment He was shot at Pleasant Hill, Louisiana, during a battle, and died May 13 1864, from the wound

2 Timothy Ruggles, born June 22, 1844 He lived many years in New York with his uncle Andrew H Green, and after his uncle's death returned to Worcester, where he now resides

(VII) Andrew Haswell Green son of William E Green (6) was born in Worcester, Massachusetts October 6, 1820 The best account of the life and achievements of "the Father of Greater New York" is that written by his cousin and friend, Samuel Swett Green, librarian of the Free Public Library of Worcester, and read at the semi-annual meeting of the American Antiquarian Society, April 27, 1904 From that account the writer of this sketch has drawn most of the facts and in many cases has quoted freely from it

At the age of fifteen Mr Green left school His early education was obtained at the old Thomas street school at the corner of Summer street He went to work in New York city, whither he journeyed by stage and steamboat He was employed first at the munificent salary of fifty dollars a year in the store of Hinsdale & Atkins as errand boy His next position was clerk in the store of Lee, Savage & Co, wholesale cloth merchants and importers, where he steadily advanced until he had reached nearly the head position when the firm failed After a severe illness and return to Green Hill for some months during convalescence and recuperation, he entered the employ of Wood, Johnston & Barritt, linen importers, Exchange Place, New York Then he went to the house of Simeon Draper At the age of twenty-one he went to Trinidad, where he spent a year on the sugar plantation of Mr Burnley, a friend of the family While there he became interested in the cultivation of sugar cane, the manufacture of sugar and molasses and tried without success to introduce some improvement in the methods and processes in use He gave up the attempt returned to New York and entered the law office of a relative, John W Mitchell He began the practice of law in the office of Samuel J Tilden, "whose political principles he shared," to quote his own words "and with whom he sustained confidential and trusted relations throughout life"

He was elected trustee of the schools in the fourth ward of New York, and afterward school commissioner and member of the board of education He was made president of the board, which consisted of forty four members, in 1855 Two years later he was appointed a commissioner of Central Park and became treasurer of the board of commissioners, president and executive officer of the board, and for ten years comptroller of the park He had complete supervision of the engineers, landscape architects gardeners and the whole force of laborers amounting at times to three thousand men The office of comptroller of the park was created especially for Mr Green It happened that in the first years of the park there was constant friction between the commissioners and the Tweed ring, then being formed, and the commissioners were quite willing to leave the work to anyone who would attend to it So Mr Green was made both president and treasurer As the park was developed and grew in popularity some member of the board intimated that it was not right for one man to hold both offices, and Mr Green was elected treasurer, to which the salary, which the legislature had authorized the commissioners to pay either to the president or treasurer, was to be paid But Mr Green promptly declined to serve in the salaried position, whereupon another member was elected treasurer and he was elected president without salary The new treasurer failed to give satisfaction and in a few months the office of comptroller of parks was created and Mr Green elected to fill the position The nominal president of the board had the duty of presiding at meetings but all the executive and administrative work devolved on the comptroller, who was likewise the treasurer He served in this very important and honorable position for ten years, when the Tweed charter of 1870 removed the members of the board from office and turned Central Park over to a department of the city government appointed by A Oakey Hall, mayor Although Mr Green was appointed a member of the new board the conditions were such that he resigned in 1872

Chancellor MacCracken of New York University, in speaking of Mr Green, said that "by his care for Central Park he was led to care for related enterprises, such as the Museum of Art, the Museum of Science and the Zoological Garden" He was constantly alive to the work of beautifying the city, whether by individual effort or as a member of one or another organization A recent address declared that his thoughtfulness was woven into the structure and visible aspect of New York Here we see it in a reserved acre of greensward, there in the curve of a graceful line, like the beautiful span of Washington Bridge and somewhere else in a sweet sounding name, like Morningside "Mr Green had a rare combination of qualities," said Samuel Swett Green "to fit him to do the great work which he did in laying out and developing Central Park He had an eye for the picturesque and beautiful and a fondness and aptitude for the kind of practical service needed He had too a passion for having everything done thoroughly"

Mr Green was naturally appointed a member of the original board of commissioners on the Niagara reservation and held the position until his death being president most of the time An island formerly known as Bath Island has been named for Mr Green Several years ago the state of New York established a commission with the title "Trustees of Scenic and Historical Places and Objects in the State of New York" The name has twice been changed and is now American Scenic and Historic Preservation Society Mr Green was the founder and enthusiastic president of this society from its organization until his death

In 1865 the legislature imposed upon the commissioners of Central Park the duty of laying out that portion of the island lying north of One Hundred and Fifty-fifth street It was while he was directing the work of laying out Central Park and Upper New York that Mr Green first called attention in a serious and deliberate manner to the desirability of the union of the towns and cities now popularly known as the Greater New York The first result of Mr Green's recommendation of the consolidation was the annexation in 1873 of Morrisania West Farms and Kingsbridge Mr Green presented to the legislature of New York in 1890 a notable brief advocating consolidation A referendum in 1894 resulted in a favorable vote in all the four counties concerned The commission to draft the charter was appointed by the state June 9 1896 with Mr Green as chairman The charter as drafted became a law November 4 1897 The new city was established January 1, 1898 and May 22, 1898, Mr Green appeared before the legislature by invitation to receive congratulations for his work in forming the Greater New York A thoughtful address was given by him A medal was struck off as a memorial and presented to Mr Green October 6, 1898, and by general consent also he has come to be known as "The Father of Greater New York"

Mr Green's connection with the New York library system is interesting history He was one of the executors of the will of his law partner, the late Samuel J Tilden, and was one of the original trustees, three in number, appointed in the will to add to their number and establish a great free library in New York Mr Green's efforts resulted in saving much of the property for the libraries when all was involved in contests and litigations It was his scheme to bring about the union of some of the great libraries in New York, and he quietly secured the legislation necessary with the final result of consolidating the Astor, Lenox and Tilden foundations in the formation of the New York Public Library, which, Mr S S Green says, "through the assiduous and valuable labors of its well known and accomplished librarian, Dr John S Billings, by means of subsequent consolidations and aided by a munificent gift from Mr Andrew Carnegie and by city appropriations bids fair to become one of the most important institutions in New York"

Mr Green first became prominent in the whole country of which New York is the metropolis by his work in the office of comptroller in behalf of good government during the exposure of the frauds of the Tweed ring This office he held for five years, till in 1876, he became executor of the will of William B Ogden, the railroad king of New York and Chicago Had Mr Tilden been declared president of the United States Mr Green would undoubtedly have been in the cabinet He was one of the original trustees of the New York and Brooklyn Bridge In 1890 the legislature appointed him a commissioner to locate and approve the plan of the great railroad bridge across the Hudson river which is to join Manhattan Island with the rest of the country He was elected to the constitutional convention in 1894

He was a member of the New York Historical Society, the New York Genealogical and Biographical Society and many other societies devoted to geography, history, the fine arts, science and philanthropy He became a member of the American Antiquarian Society in October 1889, and left that society $5,000 in his will He also bequeathed $5,000 to Clark University in Worcester, and $1,000 to the Isabella Heimath, a home for aged women in New York In politics he was a Democrat, although he was not in agreement with the majority of his party in his position on the tariff He was a Protectionist He was killed November 13, 1903, by a crazy man just as he was entering his home in New York He never married, but lived in his own home Park avenue, New York

He was the owner of the old homestead on Green Hill, where he made large purchases of land destined it seems to benefit the city of Worcester, where he was born, as greatly as his service in the Park Board of New York benefited the city of his adoption He enlarged the old house by cutting it in two, moving back the rear portion and building between the front and back of the old building a fine mansion, thus securing in the middle of the house large and higher rooms on the lower floor and suits of apartments for himself, his brothers and sisters upstairs Later a spacious porch and veranda were added in front His deep affection for his family and reverence for his ancestors were frequently shown He always carried his brothers and sisters and their children and grandchildren in his heart," writes Mr S S Green, and no one of them ever suffered for the lack of a home or the comforts of life Mr Green placed a mural bronze tablet in the interior of the church at Greenville in remembrance of its first pastor (his ancestor), Thomas Green Had I given him encouragement to believe that it was fitting to single out one from the thousands of young men who did service in the civil war for especial and lavish commemoration he would, I am sure, have engaged St Gaudens, or another sculptor as distinguished to have made a statue of his nephew, William Nelson Green, Jr, to be placed in an appropriate position in Worcester"

It should be said of Mr Green, as of his brothers to whom reference is made elsewhere, that they were descended from the Bournes of the Cape, from Governor Dudley, of the Massachusetts Bay colony, and from Rev John Woodbridge, a brother of Benjamin Woodbridge, whose name stands first on the roll of graduates of Harvard College He was also descended from the three Tillies and John Howland, passengers on the 'Mayflower"

His character has been described by the *New York Tribune*, which said of him at the time he was appointed deputy comptroller "Incorruptible, inaccessible to partisan or personal considerations, immovable by threats or bribes, and honest by the very constitution of his own nature" and as fitted for the office by "long experience in public affairs, strict sense of accountability and thorough methods of doing business" Hon Seth Low, mayor of New York at the time of Mr Green's death, said of him "It may truthfully be said that to no one man who has labored in and for the city during the last fifty years is the city under greater and more lasting obligations than to Andrew H Green The city itself, in some of its most beautiful and enduring features, is the monument of his love, and the city may well cherish his honored name with the undying gratitude that is due to a citizen who has made it both a greater and better city than it was"

(VII) John Plimpton Green, son of William E Green (6), was born in Worcester, January 19, 1819 He studied medicine in New York and practiced there for a time He removed to Whampoa, China, thence to Copaipo in Chile South America, where he spent most of his mature years, practicing medicine He died January 6 1892, at Green Hill

(VII) Samuel Fisk Green son of William E Green (6) was born at Green Hill, Worcester, October 10 1822, died there May 28, 1884 He studied medicine and practiced for a time, but when a young man went to Batticotta in the Island of Ceylon as a missionary physician for the American Board of Commissioners for Foreign Missions He spent almost a quarter of a century in ministering personally to the wants of both the bodies and souls of the Tamil population of the Island After his return to Green Hill, he continued to translate medical treatises into the Tamil language until his death Besides practicing medicine in Ceylon he established there a medical school, and his pupils were very numerous He is given the credit of creating the medical literature of the Tamil language He married May 22 1862 Margaret Phelps Williams Since his death his family has been occupying the mansion at Green Hill His children were Julia E, born January 1, 1864, Lucy Maria, February 26, 1865, Mary Ruggles September 22, 1867, Nathan Williams, March 13 1871

(VII) Oliver Bourne Green, son of William E Green (6), was born January 1, 1826 He and his brother, Martin Green, of Worcester are the only survivors among the eleven children of Squire Green His early education was received in the school house at the corner of Thomas and Summer streets For a few winters he taught school, but the building of steam railroads attracted him and he obtained a position as rodman on trench survey for the New York & Erie Railroad, and for a few weeks assisted in the preliminary surveys What he himself calls his first position, however, was on the Worcester & Nashua Railroad, where, beginning as rodman, he learned the art and science of civil engineering in the way it was then taught, by experience He next went to the Hudson River Railroad and took part in the survey of what has since become one of the greatest railroads in the country He was particularly strong in field work and he obtained more than his share of that part of the engineering After the Hudson River job, he became resident engineer in charge of part of the construction of the Baltimore & Ohio Railroad He was stationed in West Virginia in the section containing the Welling tunnel one of the longest on the road It is about thirty miles from the Ohio line He stayed there two years and a half until the road was completed and in operation He was occupied for a time in the survey for the Cincinnati, Lebanon & Xenia Railroad, only part of which was built at the time He accepted the difficult task of engineer of a division on the Mississippi Central Railroad, of which his brother, Martin Green, was later the chief engineer He spent the years 1853-54-55 in the south In 1857 he was engaged in the dredging and contracting business with his brother, Martin Green, and later for over thirty years on his own account He did much of the construction along the Lake front, more than any other contractor He had many city contracts for breakwaters and in the park system of Chicago He built a mile of the Lake Shore drive One of his best known jobs was done in 1877 for the Sturgeon Bay Canal Company He constructed the canal which connects Green Bay with Lake Michigan and saved all the lumber vessels that enter Green Bay at least two hundred miles on their round trip

Since 1867 Mr Green has lived at 403 LaSalle avenue, Chicago His house was burned there in the 'great fire," but he rebuilt later He continued in active business until 1898, when he turned his business over to his son Andrew Hugh Green Mr Green is a member of the Western Society of Civil Engineers and is one of the oldest members He is a member of the New England Congregational Church of Chicago He is a Democrat in politics with a belief in the Republican principle of protection that made him what he calls an Eclectic

He married, August 28 1855, and in 1905 celebrated his golden wedding in the mansion on Green Hill It was a notable event socially, from the gathering of the relatives and several old schoolmates and other friends who had not met for years

His wife, Louise Pomeroy was the daughter of Hazen and Lois Pomeroy She was born in Stanstead, Canada, and he met her while making the survey of the Mississippi Central Railroad She was a school teacher there Their children are Mary Pomeroy, born April 26, 1857, lives with her parents Olivia born December 10, 1859, married Wyllis W Baird and they have two children Warner Green Baird, a student in Cornell, Katharine L Baird Andrew Hugh, born November 26, 1860 graduated at Harvard University in 1892, and at the Massachusetts Institute of Technology, in 1896 He took over his father's business, with which he was thoroughly familiar, and having introduced some of the newest methods and latest machinery, sold it in 1901 to advantage, and has been traveling since then

(VII) Martin Green, son of William E Green (6), was born in Worcester, April 24 1828 The room in which he was born in the homestead at Green Hill is the same in which his father was born and died and in which his ten brothers and sisters were born He received his schooling in the old school at the corner of Summer and Thomas streets when Warren Lazell was the teacher of the English department and Charles Thurber of the Latin department He took a course at Little Blue Seminary at Farmington Maine His father intended to have him go to college but he was attracted to the profession in which his brother Oliver was making good progress and he started his career as civil engineer as chainman in the survey for the Hudson River Railroad where his brother was also employed He was promoted rapidly and became a proficient civil engineer When the survey was completed to Greenbush he returned to the old home at Green Hill, but went to work for the Worcester & Nashua Railroad Company When the work was done on the Nashua road he accepted a position with the Pennsylvania Coal Company Railroad He was occupied here for three years in surveying and building gravity railroads in Luzerne county Pennsylvania When the work was done he was offered the superintendency of the road He returned to Worcester but was called to take the position of division engineer on the New York & Harlem Railroad He was in charge of the construction of the line from Millerton to Copake When the work was done he was selected as chief engineer for the Lebanon Springs Railroad Company This road was to run from Chatham, New York to Bennington Vermont, through a rough and hilly country and presented some difficult engineering problems The work was left unfinished on account of the financial troubles of the railroads involved in the great frauds of Robert Schuyler who had been president of sixteen railroad companies

Mr Green was then appointed chief engineer of the Mississippi Central Railroad, which had been begun all along the two hundred and sixty-seven miles of its length, and was left by his predecessor in the greatest disorder and confusion Some sections he found built a one-fourth mile out of the proper course so that it taxed his resources to build curves and schemes to save the work already done He found the engineering force grossly incompetent When he left this railroad was substantially complete but so anxious were the planters who were directors of the road, and the president to keep him that they offered him what was at that time a very large salary $20000 a year to remain And after he had actually left, they sent a delegation to New York to see him and mother to Chicago to try to persuade him to come back No stronger testimony to the value of his work as a railroad engineer need be cited To his natural gift for this kind of work he added great physical strength and vigor and he gave all his energy to the performance of the work whatever it might be that he had in hand The Mississippi Central is now a part of the Illinois Central Railroad As first constructed by Mr Green it ran from the junction with the Memphis & Charleston Railroad six miles north of the Tennessee line to Canton and Jackson Mississippi It was a very important railroad in the southern interests He had the honor to run the first locomotive ever run in the state of Mississippi

Although Mr Green received offers of positions as chief engineer from three other railroads, he persisted in his purpose when leaving Mississippi and went to Chicago, where he was employed first to study the question of a tunnel under the Chicago river, to gather statistics and make plans He proceeded with the work of building the Chicago tunnel and remained with the work until the coffer dams were built He then went into business on his own account as contractor and dredger At that time one of the prime necessities of commercial Chicago was the widening and deepening of Chicago river and the construction of proper wharves for shipping He had the contracts for the dredging of the river from the lake to the old Rush street bridge He took out the old government light houses and government barracks and the old fort The river was made about five times its original width He also improved the north branch of the river as far as Ward's rolling mill, and the south branch for about twelve miles He was in Chicago in its first great period of development, and of that work he took a large and important part In 1867 he sold his Chicago business and went to Peshtigo, Wisconsin, for the Peshtigo Lumber Company, in which William B Ogden was interested with whom Mr Green was associated during much of his active business life This company owned one hundred and seventy-six thousand acres of lumber land As manager of this vast property he had to erect saw mills and grist mills and build two large ships for the lumber trade He was in Peshtigo three years He built the ship canal at Benton Harbor, Michigan This canal gave steamships access to Benton in the heart of the peach country He owned a line of boats and when the work was completed his line took during the season forty thousand baskets to Chicago every night Besides his steamship line he built and owned saw and grist mills at Benton Harbor

Before the great fire in Chicago he returned and was interested with his brother in the contracting business The fire caused him to over-work and break down On May 23, 1872 by advice of his physician he returned to Green Hill, Worcester, Massachusetts to rest and recuperate The life in Worcester attracted him and he remained here, developing the Green Hill estate to its present state He removed, November 13 1905, to No 974 Pleasant street, where he has since lived Mr Green has never cared to join secret societies and clubs He is a member of Central Congregational church, Worcester He served three years on the Worcester park board and for about three years on the board of trustees of the State Lunatic Asylum at Westboro Massachusetts

He married December 25 1859 Mary Frances Stewart of the New York Stewart family She was born in New York city, December 25 1821, and died at 4 Melville street Worcester April 20, 1905 Their children are William Ogden born in Chicago, September 26 1860, Samuel Martin born at Benton Harbor Michigan April 13, 1864

(VIII) John Green, of St Louis Missouri, son of James Green (7), was born in Worcester, Massachusetts April 2 1835 He was fitted for college at the Worcester Classical and English high school entered Harvard College, 1851, was graduated A B 1855 S B 1856 A M 1859 M D, 1866 He studied medicine at Cambridge, Massachusetts under the direction of Profs Morrill and Jeffries Wyman also at the Massachusetts Medical College in Boston, and from 1858 to 1860 in London Paris, Berlin and Vienna He was admitted a Fellow of the Massachusetts Medical Society, on examination in 1858 He was elected a member of the Boston Society of Natural History in 1856,

Martin Green

Samuel Swett Green.

and member of the council, as curator of Comparative Anatomy, in 1857, in the latter year he accompanied Prof Jeffries Wyman on a scientific expedition to Surinam (Dutch Guiana) He began the practice of medicine in Boston in 1861 He was a member of the Boston Medical Association, the Suffolk District Medical Society, of which he was elected secretary in 1865, and of the Boston Society for Medical Observation He was appointed a delegate to the American Medical Association, from Boston, in 1864 and 1865 He held successively the positions of attending physician and attending surgeon at the central office of the Boston Dispensary During 1862 he was in the medical service of the Western Sanitary Commission and of the United States Sanitary Commission, and was for several months acting assistant surgeon in the Army of the Tennessee

In 1865 he went again to Europe for the purpose of continuing studies in ophthalmology, in London Paris, and Utrecht In 1866 he removed to St Louis, Missouri, where he has since resided and practiced his profession He is a member of the American Ophthalmological Society, elected 1866, one of the original members of the American Otological Society, founded 1868, and a member of the International Ophthalmological Congress since 1872 He was a member by special appointment of the International Medical Congress held in Philadelphia in 1876, and was secretary of the section of Ophthalmology In 1867 he was appointed lecturer on Ophthalmology in the St Louis Summer School of Medicine, in 1868, professor of Ophthalmology and Otology in the St Louis College of Physicians and Surgeons, which position he held during the two years of existence of that institution, in 1871 lecturer on Ophthalmology in the St Louis Medical College, in 1872 ophthalmic surgeon to the St Louis Eye and Ear Infirmary, and consulting ophthalmic surgeon to the St Louis City Hospital, and, in 1874 ophthalmic surgeon to St Luke's Hospital In 1886 he was elected professor of Ophthalmology in the St Louis Medical College (later the Medical Department of Washington University St Louis Missouri) He is president of the St Louis Ophthalmological Society He is a member of the St Louis Academy of Science, of which he was president in 1895, member of the board of trustees of the Missouri Botanical Garden (Shaw's Garden), since 1895, member of the Missouri Historical Society, member of the American Antiquarian Society, member (and first vice-president) of the St Louis Society of the Archaeological Institute of America, etc He has contributed scientific papers to leading medical journals, to the "Transactions of the American Ophthalmological Society," "Transactions of the American Otological Society," "Proceedings of the International Ophthalmological Congress" (London 1872, and New York, 1876), "Reference Handbook of the Medical Sciences" etc The honorary degree of LL D was conferred upon him by Washington University in 1905 and by the University of Missouri in 1906 He is a charter member of the University Club of St Louis member of the St Louis Club the (discontinued) Germania Club, the Liederkranz Club, of the Round Table Club and member (president from 1890 to 1906 now honorary president) of the Harvard Club of St Louis He is also a member of the Society of the Sons of the Revolution, and of the Society of Colonial Wars

Dr Green married October 23 1868 Harriet Louisa Jones daughter of George Washington and Caroline (Partridge) Jones, of Templeton Massachusetts of this marriage two children, John (born at Templeton Massachusetts, August 2, 1873), and Elizabeth (born in St Louis December 3, 1878), are living in St Louis His home is at 2670 Washington avenue, St Louis, Missouri

(VIII) Samuel Swett Green, was born in Worcester, Massachusetts, February 20, 1837 He is a son of the late James Green (7), and a nephew of Dr John Green (7) the principal founder of the Free Public Library, of Worcester

His descent from Thomas Green (I), who came to this country early in the seventeenth century, has been described already, and an account of his ancestors in the line of the Greens has been given above Mr Green's mother was the late Elizabeth Green daughter of Samuel Swett, of Boston and Dedham Through her mother, a daughter of Dr John Sprague, of Boston she and the subject of this sketch are descended from an even earlier resident of the Massachusetts Bay Colony than Thomas Green, namely, Ralph Sprague, who came to Charlestown in 1629 from Upway, Devonshire, England Through his great-great-grandfather, Gen Timothy Ruggles, of Hardwick, Mr Green is also descended from Rev John Woodbridge, one of the earliest settlers of Newbury, and from Mr Woodbridge's wife's father, Thomas Dudley, the second governor of the colony of Massachusetts Bay Rev John Woodbridge was the brother of Rev Dr Benjamin Woodbridge, whose name stands first on the list of graduates of Harvard College Through the same ancestor, Mr Green is descended from John Tilley, his wife and his daughter, Elizabeth, wife of John Howland These four ancestors came to this country in the "Mayflower"

The first school attended by Samuel S Green was that of Mrs Levi Heywood Her school was discontinued, however, before long, and he was sent for several years to another infant school, kept by the late Miss Sarah B Wood, afterward a resident of Chicago, the wife of Jonathan Wood From that private school he passed, upon examination, into the public grammar school on Thomas street, which, during his studies there was under the charge of Mr Caleb B Metcalf Going next to the high school, he graduated from that institution in 1854, and immediately entered Harvard College Among his classmates there, were two other graduates of the Worcester high school, namely, Eugene Frederick Bliss who has been for most of his life, since graduation, a citizen of Cincinnati, Ohio, and the late Lieut Thomas Jefferson Spurr, who was mortally wounded at the battle of Antietam Mr Green graduated from Harvard College in 1858 In the early part of the summer of 1859 he sailed from Boston for Smyrna as a passenger in the barque "Race Horse," and before returning home in the same vessel visited Constantinople Remaining two years in Worcester on account of ill-health, he resumed his studies at Harvard University in the autumn of 1861, and graduated from the divinity school connected with that institution in 1864 He visited Europe again in 1877 1902, 1903 1904 and 1906 and added in 1905 to extensive travels previously made in this country a visit to Alaska During the civil war and while in the divinity school Mr Green was drafted for service in the army but was debarred from entering it by delicate health He took the degree of Master of Arts at Harvard University in 1870, and June 28 1877, was chosen an honorary member of the Phi Beta Kappa society by the chapter of the order connected with the same university

In 1864 Mr Green became bookkeeper in the Mechanics National Bank of Worcester, and in the course of a few months teller in the Worcester National Bank The latter position he held for several years He was offered the position of cashier of the Citizens National Bank, to succeed the late Mr John C Ripley, but declined it, as he also declined at about the same time, a place in the Worcester County Institution for Savings

Mr Green became a director of the Free Public Library January 1 1867, and four years later, January 15 1871, librarian of the same institution The latter position he still holds, having been elected for the thirty-sixth year of service January 2, 1906 The library has grown rapidly in size and use under his care It contained, December 1, 1905, 153,176 volumes The use of its books in the year ending with that date was 366,935 A feature in that use is the remarkably large proportion of books that are employed for study and purposes of reference Mr Green is regarded as an authority among librarians in respect to matters relating to the use of libraries as popular educational institutions, and in respect to the establishment of close relations between libraries and schools He was a pioneer in the work of bringing about inter-library loans and in a large use of photographs and engravings in supplementing the value of books He has for a few years past set the example of having, in a library, talks about books on specified subjects, and is now conducting some interesting experiments in bringing the users of the circulating department and the children's room under the influence of the best works of art

Mr Green was one of the founders of the American Library Association, and is a life fellow of the society He was for several years the chairman of the finance committee of that body and its vice-president for 1887-9 and 1892-3 In 1891 Mr Green was chosen president of the association, and presided at the annual meeting held that year in San Francisco He was in 1896 the first president of the council He is an original Fellow of the Library Institute, founded in 1905, an organization supposed to be composed of a limited number of the most distinguished librarians of the country Mr Green was a delegate of the American Library Association to the International Congress of Librarians held in London in October, 1877, was a member of the council of that body, and took an active part in the discussions carried on in its meetings Before the close of the Congress, the Library Association of the United Kingdom was formed Mr Green was chosen an honorary member of that association, in July, 1878 He presided for a day over the World's Congress of Librarians held in Chicago in 1903 and at a meeting of the American Library Association held at Chicago University the same year Mr Green was a vice-president of the International Congress of Librarians held in London in 1897 In 1890 he was appointed by the governor of Massachusetts an original member of the Free Public Library Commission of the Commonwealth and was reappointed in 1894, 1899 and 1904 Mr Green was one of the founders and the original first vice-president of the Massachusetts Library Club He was for many years a member of the committee of the overseers of Harvard University to make an annual examination of the library of the university occupied a similar position in connection with the Boston Public Library for a single year, and began in 1887, to deliver annual courses of lectures as lecturer on "Public libraries as popular educational institutions" to the students of the School of Library Economy connected with Columbia College New York city He has also lectured at the Library School since it became an institution of the state of New York and was chosen a member of a committee to examine the school in both places

As librarian of the Free Public Library, Mr Green has gained for himself and his library a wide reputation In "The Worcester of 1898" it is said of him that his purpose has been from the first to make the Public Library an instrument for popular education and a practical power in the community To this end he has written and spoken much during the past twenty years, and his efforts and advice have influenced, in no slight degree, library methods and administration throughout the United States The library methods of Worcester have been studied in the Department of the Seine, in which the city of Paris is situated Mr Green's advice has been sought by the Educational Department of the English government The Free Public Library of Worcester has recently been described at great length by a German scholar as an example worthy to be followed in that country, in advocating the introduction of popular libraries, such as we have in the United States, into Germany" There is a picture of the interior of the children's room of the Free Public Library in a recent Danish pamphlet written by Andr Sch Sternberg, of the Free Public Library Commission of Denmark Mr Green was chosen a Fellow of the Royal Historical Society of Great Britain, May 8, 1879, and on April 28, 1880, a member of the American Antiquarian Society Since October 22, 1883, he has been a member of the council of the latter organization He was also elected a member of the American Historical Association immediately after its formation He was an early member of the Colonial Society of Massachusetts and of the American organization known as the Descendants of Colonial Governors Mr Green is a life member of the New England Historic-Genealogical Society, and was for several years a member of the Archaeological Institute of America, and of the committee on the School for Classical Studies at Rome He is a corresponding member of the National Geographical Society and of the Historical Society of Wisconsin He is a member of the Bunker Hill Monument Association, and was for several years a fellow of the American Geographical Society, and a member of the American Social Science Association He has been a manager of the Sons of the Revolution, and was a charter member and the first lieutenant-governor of the Society of Colonial Wars in Massachusetts, presiding at its first general court and the dinner which followed it Mr Green is a member of the Society of Mayflower Descendants, and of the Old Planters Society He has been a member of the University Club, Boston, from its organization and was an original member of the Worcester Club, the St Wulstan Society, and the Worcester Economic Club He is also a member of the old organization the Worcester Association for Mutual Aid in Detecting Thieves October 12, 1882, Mr Green was chosen a member of the board of trustees of Leicester Academy, to fill the vacancy caused by the resignation of Rev Edward H Hall, on his removal from Worcester to Cambridge In 1886 he assisted in the formation of the Worcester High School Association and was chosen its first president and re-elected to the same position in 1887 In the summer of 1886 he was chosen president of the Worcester Indian Association and held the office for two years

Mr Green has been president of the Worcester Art Society He was a member of a committee of three asked by the late Mr Salisbury to consult with him about arrangements for starting the Worcester Art Museum and to help him in the choice of the list of corporators When the Museum was organized, he was offered a position as trustee, but declined to accept it Mr Green has been, from the beginning of the organization, secretary of the Art Commission of the St Wulstan Society He has been treasurer of the Worcester Public School Art League since its establishment in 1895 He has been very influential in promoting interest in the fine arts in Worcester by means of exhibitions which he started in the Public Library building and by the installation in the library of a large collection of the best photographs of the old and more modern masterpieces in painting and sculpture

Mr Green was also, at two different times and for several years, treasurer of the Worcester Natural History Society, and has been for many years a trustee of the Worcester County Institution for Savings In 1903 Mr Green was made second vice-president of the Worcester Harvard Club (which not long before he had helped to form), and in 1904 first vice-president For several years he has been a member of the corporation for the administration of the Home for Aged Men Mr Green formerly wrote constantly for the *Library Journal,* sending an article to the first number, and has made many contributions to the proceedings of the American Antiquarian Society He has also written papers for the *American Journal of Social Science,* the *Sunday Review* of London and other periodicals Two books by him were published by the late Frederick Leypoldt of New York, namely "Library Aids' and "Libraries and Schools" Both were printed in 1883 The former work, in a less complete form, had been previously issued by the United States Bureau of Education as a circular of information At the request of the secretary of the Board of Education of Massachusetts, Mr Green wrote an appendix to his forty-eighth annual report on "Public Libraries and Schools" The essay was afterwards printed as a separate pamphlet A paper by him on "The use of pictures in the public libraries of Massachusetts" was printed as an appendix to the eighth report of the Free Public Library Commission of Massachusetts Mr Green has made many addresses and read a number of papers on library and other subjects Among the earliest of these are "Personal Relations Between Librarians and Readers" a paper which was presented to a meeting of librarians who came together in Philadelphia in October, 1876, and formed the American Library Association (of this paper two editions have been printed and exhausted) It was made the subject of editorials in several Boston and New York newspapers and the plans of conducting a library described in it, were regarded at the time of its appearance as novel and admirable, "Sensational Fiction in Public Libraries," a paper read July 1 1879 at one of the of the sessions of the meetings of the American Library Association held in Boston that year (this paper was also printed in pamphlet form and widely distributed) "The Relations of the Public Library to the Public Schools," a paper read before the American Social Science Association, at Saratoga, in September, 1880 (this address was printed in the form of a pamphlet and has been widely read and very influential in awakening an interest in work similar to that described in it in America and abroad) papers and an address on subjects similar to the one last mentioned read or delivered at meetings of the American Library Association in Cincinnati and Buffalo at Round Island one of the Thousand Isles in the St Lawrence river in San Francisco and at a meeting of the Library Section of the National Educational Association at a meeting in Washington Other important papers by Mr Green on questions in library economy are "The Library in its relation to persons engaged in industrial pursuits" "Opening Libraries on Sundays," "The duties of trustees and their relations to librarians," Address as President of the American Library Association," 'Interlibrary loans in reference work," 'Adaptation of libraries to constituencies," printed in vol I of the report of the United States Commissioner of Education for 1892-3, 'How to encourage the foundation of libraries in small towns,' and three closely connected papers entitled Discrimination regarding 'open shelves' in libraries," "What classes of persons, if any, should have access to the shelves in large libraries' and "Lead us not into temptation" Addresses have been printed in pamphlet form that were made at the opening of library buildings in Newark, New Jersey, Rindge, New Hampshire, North Brookfield and Oxford, Massachusetts *

Mr Green made remarks at the library school in Albany and in two or three Massachusetts towns favoring the purchase of books for grown-up immigrants in the languages to which they have been accustomed He wrote "A History of the Public Libraries of Worcester" for the Worcester of 1898," and earlier for Hurd's 'History of Worcester County" He was *chairman of a committee to supervise the portion of* that history relating to the town and city of Worcester

The first account of the methods introduced by Mr Green in the conduct of the Free Public Library in Worcester, which was printed in pamphlet form, was presented as an appendix to his annual report as librarian for the year 1874-5 copies of which were sent to the Exposition in Philadelphia in 1876 It was afterwards reprinted at the request of the directors of the Free Public Library for distribution In the fourth report of the Free Public Library Commission of Massachusetts, Mr Green wrote on "Libraries and Schools," in the fifth report, on 'Loaning reference books to small libraries," in the seventh report, "On the use of libraries by children" and as stated above, in the eighth report, 'On the use of pictures in libraries" He also wrote portions of the reports of the Free Public Library of Worcester while a director and has written nearly the whole of the reports (excepting the presidents' reports) while librarian He wrote sketches of the lives of such librarians as William Frederick Poole and John Fiske for the American Antiquarian Society's proceedings The more elaborate historical papers which have been prepared by Mr Green are 'Gleanings from the Sources of the History of the Second Parish, Worcester, Massachusetts," read at a meeting of the American Antiquarian Society, held in Boston, April 25, 1883 and 'The Use of the Voluntary System in the Maintenance of Ministers in the Colonies of Plymouth and Massachusetts Bay during the earlier years of their existence," an essay which formed the historical portion of the report of the Council of the American Antiquarian Society, which Mr Green presented to that society at its meeting in Boston, April 28, 1886 Both of these papers have been printed in a form separate from the proceedings of the society for which they were written The latter was highly praised by the distinguished student of early ecclesiastical history in Massachusetts the late Rev Dr Henry Martyn Dexter Other interesting and valuable historical papers by Mr Green are "Bathsheba Spooner," "The Scotch-Irish in America," "The Craigie House," and "Some Roman Remains in Britian"

*The address of welcome at the dedication in 1901 of the building of Clark University Library was printed in the 'Publications" of the library

He has also written for the American Antiquarian Society, and the Colonial Society, elaborate sketches of the lives of Pliny Earle Chase, George Bancroft, Edward Griffin Porter, Andrew Haswell Green and Benjamin Franklin Stevens Mr Green was invited by the late Justin Winsor to write a chapter in his "Narrative and Critical History of the United States," but had to decline the invitation for lack of time and strength

(VIII) James Green, a counsellor-at-law in the City of Worcester, was born March 2, 1841, at Worcester Massachusetts His parents were James (7) and Elizabeth (Swett) Green He studied in the Worcester public schools, and graduated at Harvard College in 1862 The college course held pretty strictly then to the classics, mathematics and philosophy, and he was particularly interested in Greek and history and English composition In the social life of the college, he was a member of the Institute of 1770, the Hasty Pudding Club, the Haidee Boat Club, etc His college rank was sufficient to give him a "Detur" (a prize for the work of the freshman year), and parts at the junior and senior exhibitions At the time of his graduation, in the summer of 1862, the civil war was going on, and the fortunes of the Northern side were discouraging He tried to enter the army, against the medical advice of his uncle, who had always cared for him professionally, and he actually signed the enlistment roll, but his company was not filled in time to be accepted He had entered the law office of Hon Dwight Foster, at Worcester, before commencement, and in the spring of 1863 he entered the Harvard Law School; and was a proctor in the college, and he received his Harvard degrees of LL B in 1864, and A M in 1865 He passed the year 1864-5 in law offices in New York city, especially in the office of Miller Peet & Nichols, and was admitted to the New York bar on examination in 1865 Most of the year 1865-6, he was traveling in the western states, and in the latter year he was admitted to the Worcester bar He has been in practice in Worcester ever since In January, 1872, he went to Europe on account of threatened ill health, and spent two years and a half in traveling on the continent, and largely in Italy, studying the languages wherever he went, and also architecture, painting and sculpture and modern history He traveled also in Greece, and journeyed as far as to Constantinople and Smyrna Upon his father's death on June 10, 1874, he returned at once to Worcester Since that time he has busied himself a good deal in the care of real estate as well as at the law In 1877-8 he traveled another year in France and Spain and England

On June 2, 1881, he married Miss Mary A Messinger, of Worcester daughter of David Sewell and Harriet (Sawyer) Messinger and they have lived ever since at 61 Elm street Worcester They have had two children Mary Sprague and Thomas Samuel Green, who both attended the public schools of Worcester and are now living After graduating at the Classical High School the daughter attended Miss Baldwin's school at Bryn Mawr, and the son entered Harvard College in 1905

James Green's tastes have always been in the direction of literary study, and he has interested himself a good deal in modern languages and modern history, but his life has been too much occupied with the details of business, and handicapped by a defective eyesight and a too sensitive constitution to allow him to follow out his tastes freely He became very much interested in the late war between the British and the Boers in South Africa, and, feeling that the British cause was grossly misrepresented in the United States, he wrote a lecture on this subject which he delivered before the Society of Antiquity in Worcester and afterwards issued as a pamphlet The ground that he covered had been very little touched by other pamphleteers, for he tried to show, in contradiction of what was often said in American papers, that the British were fighting for the very same principles for which the American colonists fought a century before, and that the Boers, in their anger at the British policy of emancipating the blacks, were as illiberal and false toward the British colonists in South Africa as King George's ministers had been toward our ancestors in America This pamphlet was circulated widely in the United States, and was declared by many thoughtful critics to be one of the very best short statements of the subject that had been printed Upon the unsolicited recommendation of a high official at Washington, to the Imperial South African Association in London, to reprint this pamphlet and circulate it freely in all English-speaking countries, it was republished by the association for free distribution, and the distinguished Quaker philanthropist, John Bellows, of Gloucester, England, reprinted the book for the association at his own expense Mr Green has also printed various other pamphlets and biographical notices from time to time in his own name and anonymously, and among them an address to his college classmates at an anniversary dinner, a notice of a new edition of Aristotle's Musical Problems that had been brought out by certain Dutch scholars, and a tribute to the memory of his associate and friend at the bar, Hon David Manning etc Mr Green was an early member of the St Botolph Club, and the Massachusetts Reform Club, of Boston, and of various local organizations including the Worcester Club, the Shakespeare Club, the Gesang Verein Frohsinn, the Twentieth Century Club, and the Economic Club, all of Worcester, and also of clubs for reading and conversation in French and German He was brought up in the historic First Unitarian Church of Worcester, to which he still belongs The earlier pages of these Memoirs show his descent from four of the Pilgrims of the "Mayflower," and from Thomas Dudley, second governor, and other early Puritans of Massachusetts Bay, and his connection with Henry Dunster, first president, and Benjamin Woodbridge, first-named graduate, of Harvard College

(IX) John Green, Jr, of St Louis, Missouri, was born August 2 1873, at Templeton, Massachusetts, the son of Dr John Green (8), and Harriet L (Jones) Green He was fitted for college in St Louis, and also with Mr Charles W Stone in Boston, and entered Harvard College in September, 1891, from which he was graduated A B in June, 1894 He entered the Medical Department of Washington University (St Louis) in October, 1895, and was graduated M D in April, 1898 receiving the Gill prize in Diseases of Children He entered the St Louis City Hospital on competitive examination, and served as junior assistant from June to December, 1898 Since November 1899, he has been engaged in the practice of ophthalmology in the city of St Louis He is a member of the St Louis Medical Society the Medical Society of City Hospital Alumni, the Missouri State Medical Association the American Medical Association, the St Louis Medical Library Association and the American Academy of Ophthalmology and Oto-Laryngology He has been secretary vice-president and president of the Medical Society of City Hospital Alumni He is also a member of the Society of the Sons of the Revolution and the Civic League of St Louis

James Green.

Dr Green has published the following pamphlets "The General Practitioner and Ophthalmology," "Treatment of Ophthalmia Neonatorum," "Double Optic Neuritis occurring during Lactation," "Ocular Examination as an aid to the early diagnosis of Multiple Sclerosis, with report of a Case" (with Dr S I Schwab), "Juvenile Glaucoma Simplex associated with Myasthenia Gastrica et Intestinalis," "A case of Cerebro-spinal Rhinorrhoea with Retinal Changes" (with Dr S I Schwab), "Treatment of Certain External Diseases of the Eyes by the X-ray," "Ocular Signs and Complications of Diseases of the Accessory Sinuses of the Nose," Report on Progress in Ophthalmology for the years 1903, 1904, 1905 and 1906," and "The Control of Municipal Medical Institutions, with special reference to the City of St Louis," etc He is editor of the Department of Ophthalmology of *The Interstate Medical Journal*, visiting ophthalmic surgeon to the Jewish Hospital Dispensary of St Louis, and consulting ophthalmic surgeon to the St Louis Female Hospital

He married, October 29, 1902, Miss Lucretia Hall Sturgeon, of St Louis, Missouri Their children are Helen Celeste, born November 23, 1903, and Harmon, born July 3, 1905 His office address in 1906 is 225 Vanol building, corner of Vandeventer avenue and Olive street, St Louis, Missouri

(VIII) William Ogden Green son of Martin Green (7), was born in Chicago, Illinois, September 26, 1860 He was educated at the Worcester Polytechnic Institute He went to work first in an electric light factory at New Britain, Connecticut, then for the Merrick Thread Company, Holyoke, Massachusetts From there he went as a manager for a silk mill at Bethlehem, Pennsylvania He put it into first class condition and left it highly prosperous to take charge of the Peshtigo Lumber Company in Wisconsin, for which his father was manager years before Andrew H Green, as trustee of the estate of the late William B Ogden, represented the owners, but Mrs Ogden herself made frequent visits to the property and paid Mr Green high compliments on the reformation he brought about and the improvement effected By his advice the property was sold and he wound up its complicated affairs in a manner so pleasing to the directors that they made him a present of $10,000 at their last meeting as a testimonial of their satisfaction He is a member of the American Society of Mechanical Engineers He is now a member of the firm of Ogden, Sheldon & Company, one of the most important real estate broker firms in Chicago

He married October 20 1891, Josephine Poole Giles at Bethlehem Pennsylvania Their children, all of whom were born in Chicago, are William Stewart born November 7, 1893, Andrew Haswell, born May 10, 1896, Lucretia Poole, born June 19, 1899

(VIII) Samuel Martin Green son of Martin Green (7), was born at Benton Harbor, Michigan, April 13, 1864 He was graduated at the Worcester Polytechnic Institute His first position was with Frederick E Reed, the manufacturer of machinery, Worcester Massachusetts, for whom he designed and draughted various tools He also designed the interlocking switches on the railroad viaduct in Worcester He next went to Buffalo to work for Noyes & Company, millers When his brother, William Ogden Green, left the Merrick Thread Company, where he was the engineer in charge of the plant the management desired him to remain but took the younger brother in his place on his recommendation Although young and inexperienced Samuel Green made good He successfully completed the big mill, one hundred and twenty-five by five hundred feet He remained with the Merrick Thread Company until the trust was formed, when he was chosen engineer-in-chief for the new management, the American Thread Company He has charge of all the changes and new construction of the company At the present time, at Ilion, New York, he is reconstructing and building a two million dollar plant, and the old mills are all receiving modern equipment of machinery and power He has recently constructed at Waukegan, Illinois, a large factory for the United States Envelope Company His chief office is at Holyoke, Massachusetts, and his residence is at Springfield, Massachusetts He is at present rebuilding the cartridge factory at Bridgeport, Connecticut He is a member of the American Society of Mechanical Engineers

He married, at Holyoke, June 18, 1890, Ida McKown, of that city Their children are Mildred, born September 27, 1895, in Holyoke, Lydia, born June 2, 1902, in Holyoke

HENRY F HARRIS From the best obtainable evidence, which includes recorded data, it is certain that the Harris family, as represented in Worcester, Massachusetts, is descended from Thomas Harris who came with his brother William and Roger Williams in the ship "Lion" from Bristol, England, to Lynn, Massachusetts, as early as 1630 The line of descent is traced as follows

(I) Thomas Harris married Elizabeth ———, and they were the parents of Thomas Mary and Martha As a friend and follower of Roger Williams he was imprisoned and otherwise illtreated in Boston, Massachusetts, in 1658

(II) Thomas Harris, son of Thomas the emigrant, married Elnactrau Tew, and they were the parents of eight children

(III) Thomas Harris, son of Thomas (2), was born in 1665 and died in 1741 He married Phoebe Brown, and they were the parents of eight children

(IV) Charles Harris son of Thomas (3) and Phoebe (Brown) Harris was born in 1709 He married Mary Hopkins, March 19 1748, at North Scituate, Rhode Island, and they were the parents of ten children

(V) Gideon Harris, son of Charles (4), and Mary (Hopkins) Harris, married Rhoda Smith widow of his brother Henry, and of this marriage seven children were born

(VI) Henry Harris, son of Gideon (5) and Rhoda (Smith) Harris, was born August 2, 1787 He married Bernice Randall, and (second) Waty Smith Of his second marriage were born the following children 1 Alsaide 2 Linus Monroe 3 Gideon 4 Mary Smith 5 Charles Morris, see forward 6 Thomas Henry 7 Otis Braddock 8 Whipple Burlingame Gideon and Otis B passed away prior to 1880, Mary S, widow of Alfred Whiting died in Worcester in the spring of 1904, Thomas H resides at Canada Mills Holden Massachusetts Whipple B resides in Three Rivers Palmer Massachusetts The father of this family died at the age of thirty years, leaving his family without means His wife was a remarkable type of true New England womanhood, possessing a strong mind and noble character, and gave to her children an excellent rearing

(VII) Charles Morris Harris, fifth child and third son of Henry (6) and Waty (Smith) Harris, was born in Providence Rhode Island, August 3, 1822 Through his mother he was a grandson of Captain Jonathan Smith of Revolutionary fame, who tradition says stood fully six feet in height, and commanded a company each of whom was of that or greater stature Mr Harris was also a descendant of that John Smith, of Dorchester, who was banished for his divers dangerous opinions, and who removed from the Massachusetts Bay Colony to Rhode Island at the request of Roger Williams, who wanted him as a miller and he was ever afterward known as Smith the miller

Shortly after his birth, the parents of Charles Morris Harris removed to Scituate, Rhode Island, where he was reared Until he was thirteen years old he attended the common schools for eight weeks in summer and a like term in winter and later attended two short winter terms, completing his schooling when he was fifteen years old From the age of six to fourteen years his time out of school was given to labor in the Richmond cotton mills, twelve to fourteen hours daily at the pitiful wage of one cent an hour One dollar and a quarter a week was the highest wages he received until he was almost of age, when he was paid six dollars and fifty cents a week During this period he had gone from the Richmond mills to the Sprague mills at Smithfield, Rhode Island thence to the Blackstone mills at Mendon Washington, and to Woonsocket, Rhode Island, and was thoroughly and practically conversant with every detail of the cotton milling industry, capable of conducting every process from the handling of the raw material to the final finishing of the product

In the spring of 1842, when he was twenty-two years old, he engaged in thread manufacturing on his own account, in partnership with David S Wilder In the autumn of the same year they removed to West Boylston and purchased a small mill at Central Village, where they began the manufacture of satinet warps They also leased a mill at Lovellville in the Town of Holden, which they also operated in connection with that at Central Village In 1845 he became associated in a business partnership with his brothers, Linus M and Gideon and a brother-in-law, Alfred Whiting, who had bought the Holt mill, at what was then called Holt s Village, but later Harrisville Under the firm name of L M Harris & Co they engaged in the manufacture of cotton cloth, and built up a thriving business The factory was destroyed by fire about 1851, but rebuilding was begun within thirty days after the disaster, and in less than a year the new factory was in successful operation and with increased capacity In 1857 Mr Harris bought an interest in a cotton mill at Poquonnock, Connecticut His beginning was inauspicious The first year he lost six thousand dollars, but he only redoubled his effort, and with such success that two years later he had made good his loss and was worth twelve thousand dollars more in addition Early in 1860 he sold his Connecticut interests and bought an interest in a factory at Savage, Howard county, Maryland, where he remained nearly two years In the fall of 1861 he returned to the factory of L M Harris & Co remaining until 1863 In that year he and his brother Linus M Harris, bought one-half of the stock of the West Boylston Manufacturing Company at Oakdale This was then as it is to-day, one of the most important manufacturing institutions in the state In 1814 it received from the commonwealth of Massachusetts a special charter under which it was authorized to "manufacture 'cotton and woolen clothes and fine wire ' On coming into this corporation Mr Harris became general manager and treasurer, and he served as such with such conspicuous ability for a period of twenty-six years, ending with his death, April 24 1889, in Boston

Mr Harris married Miss Emily Dean on Thanksgiving Day, 1848 She was born in Sterling, Massachusetts, November 9, 1823, and at the time of her marriage was residing in West Boylston She was a direct descendant of Thomas Dudley, second governor of the Massachusetts Bay Colony To Mr and Mrs Harris were born three children 1 Henry Francis, of whom further 2 Charles Morris, Jr, for several years prior to his father s death superintendent of the West Boylston Manfg Co mills, he died November 10 1892, aged forty-one years, leaving a widow, two sons and three daughters 3 Emily Armilla died March 11, 1892, aged thirty-five years, she was twice married, by her first husband, Lyman P Goodell, she had one son, Roscoe Harris Goodell now banker in Chicago and married to Helen Peabody, daughter of Frederick F Peabody, of Evanston, Illinois, by her second husband, Alonzo R Wells she had a son Ray Dean Wells Mrs Harris, the mother of these children, died August 6, 1892

(VIII) Henry Francis Harris eldest child of Charles Morris (7) and Emily Dean Harris, was born in Harrisville, West Boylston, Massachusetts, August 19, 1849 He fitted for college in the Green Mountain Institute at South Woodstock, Vermont, in Worcester Academy and Lancaster Academy, attending the latter institution two years In 1867 he entered Tufts College, from which he was graduated in 1871 at the head of his class He then entered the Harvard Law School, and after a six months' course further prosecuted his legal studies for about a year in the office of Hon Hartley Williams, of Worcester He subsequently entered the Boston University Law School, from which he was graduated in the first class from that institution in 1873 He was for some time following in the office of John A Loring, of Boston, and was admitted to the bar in that city in December, 1873 January 1 of the following year he entered upon a professional practice at Worcester Aside from attending to the demands of a constantly increasing legal practice he has been prominently interested in the manufacture of cotton goods, succeeding his father in 1889 as treasurer of the West Boylston Manufacturing Company, whose valuable plant, having been purchased by the Metropolitan Water Commission was relocated at Easthampton Massachusetts and doubled in size and capacity He has served as such until the present time He was also president of the L M Harris Manufacturing Company Mr Harris is a member of the board of directors of the Worcester Trust Company, the Worcester Safe Deposit and Trust Company, and is solicitor for that corporation He was a director of the First National Insurance Company is a member of the board of trustees of the Worcester City Hospital, and was a member of the school board, serving on various important committees of that body Mr Harris is a public-spirited gentleman, and among the various organizations with which he is conspicuously associated is that of Free Masons He is a man of sound judgment, a safe counsellor in matters public and private, and enjoys the confidence and respect of the community where he resides

May 17, 1883 Mr Harris married Emma Frances Dearborn daughter of William F and Mary J (Hurd) Dearborn, of Worcester She is a lady of culture and an accomplished musician She graduated from the Worcester High School in 1878 and subsequently studied vocal music under Madam Capianna Possessor of a sweet and cultivated voice, she was for many years a member of the

Francis H. Dewey.

choir of the Universalist church, and its director during much of that time

Mr and Mrs Harris have two living children Rachel, born December 11, 1887, and Dorothy, born March 22, 1890 They lost an infant son by death

DEWEY FAMILY From among the various branches of the Dewey family have come many distinguished celebrities, including the eminent Judge Francis H Dewey, and the famous Admiral George Dewey, who attained fame at Manila Bay, in the Spanish-American war The family is of royal descent, with coat-of-arms going back many generations in England In America all trace to the common ancestor,

(I) Thomas Dewey, who came to the Massachusetts Bay Colony from Sandwich, Kent, England, with Rev John Warham and his little band of one hundred and forty passengers, who formed a church before leaving England, and sailed in the "Mary and John," and became the first settlers at Dorchester, Massachusetts, arriving at Nantucket, May 30, 1630, a month earlier than the Winthrop colony On June 6, the following Sunday after they arrived, services of gratitude and praise were held under the open sky After being a pioneer in that section, the church and the above emigrants mostly removed to Windsor, Connecticut Thomas Dewey married the widow of Joseph Clark and had five children 1 Thomas, born 1640 2 Josiah, born 1641, he was the Dewey from whom descended Admiral George Dewey 3 Ann, born 1643 4 Israel, born 1645 5 Jedediah, born 1647

(II) Jedediah Dewey, son of Thomas, the emigrant, born 1647, and died 1721

(III) James Dewey, fifth son of Jedediah, born 1692, and died 1756

(IV) Daniel Dewey son of Stephen, had a son Daniel, who became judge

(VI) Judge Daniel Dewey, son of Daniel, was born in Sheffield, Massachusetts, and moved to Williamstown He was a distinguished man of his day, was a lawyer of note, and for many years a judge of the supreme court of Massachusetts, and was also a member of congress

(VII) Judge Charles Augustus Dewey, son of Judge Daniel Dewey, was born March 13, 1793, in Williamstown, Massachusetts, died in 1866 He became a lawyer, was elected district attorney, and was appointed judge of the supreme court of Massachusetts, in which important position he served for the long period of thirty years He married first Frances Aurelia, daughter of Hon Samuel and Martha (Hunt) Henshaw, of Northampton, Massachusetts She died at Williamstown July 20, 1821 He married second, July 28, 1824, Caroline Hannah Clinton, daughter of General James and Mary (Little) Clinton, of Newburg, New York, and a sister of Gov De Witt Clinton, of New York Among the eight children born to Judge Dewey, Sr, were Francis H, Charles A, Mary Clinton, wife of Judge H B Staples, of Worcester, and Maria Noble, of Worcester

(VIII) Francis Henshaw, oldest son of Judge Charles Augustus and Frances A (Henshaw) Dewey, was born in Williamstown, July 12, 1821 His career in public and professional life was so brilliant that the outline of it must be here preserved as an important part of the family history His mother died when he was an infant, but he was tenderly cared for by his stepmother, Caroline H Clinton, who married his father when he was three years old Francis H Dewey graduated from Williams College in 1840, at the early age of nineteen years, studied law at Yale and Harvard, and was admitted to the bar at Worcester in 1843 He soon became the partner of Hon Emory Washburn who was made justice of the common pleas bench the following year, and from that time the legal business of the office was thrown upon Mr Dewey, who had a very large practice For more than twenty years he was recognized as the leader of the bar in Worcester county While not elegant in diction he was possessed of what all termed 'common sense,' and dealt practically and energetically with whatever matters were entrusted to him He was very successful in the conduct of cases before juries He was appointed to the bench of the supreme court in February, 1869, and resigned in 1881

Judge Dewey came to Worcester when the inhabitants numbered only eight thousand, and he lived to see this number multiplied ten times over He was active in all public offices, church matters and charitable enterprises He seemed born for diplomacy, and was the embodiment of tact and skill, combining with these qualities the abilities of the thoroughly equipped and entirely practical man of affairs He was a leading spirit in the organization of various railroad companies and manufacturing and financial corporations, and was an official in and counsel for many of the same Up to the time of his death he was president of the Norwich & Worcester Railroad, president of the Mechanics' Saving Bank, a director in the Mechanics' National Bank, and a director and one of the heaviest stockholders in the Washburn & Moen Manufacturing Company, attending to a great amount of its legal business He was deeply interested in educational and the higher moral concerns of the community He was a trustee of his alma mater, Williams College, from 1869 to the time of his death a period of eighteen years He was also until his death president of the board of trustees of the Worcester Public Library, president of the board of trustees of the Old Men's Home, a trustee of the Washburn Memorial Hospital, president of the Rural Cemetery Corporation, president of the Worcester County Horticultural Society, and a trustee of the Young Men's Christian Association He was inclined to business more than office holding, but at the request of friends in his party he served in the two branches of the city government, and two terms in the state senate He died in the full vigor of his manhood, December 16, 1887, while devoting his strength to the many public interests with which he was connected

Judge Dewey married, November 2, 1846 Frances Amelia Clarke, only daughter of John and Prudence (Graves) Clarke, of Northampton, Massachusetts Her father was the founder of Clarke Institution for Deaf Mutes Judge Dewey married (second) April 26, 1853 Sarah Barker Tufts, only daughter of Hon George A and Azuba Boyden (Fales) Tufts, she was born January 31, 1825, at Dudley, Massachusetts and is now (April, 1905) living in Worcester By his first marriage Judge Dewey had a daughter, Fannie, born September 17, 1849, died the following day His children by his second wife were 1 Fanny Clarke, born February 1, 1854, died July 28, same year 2 Caroline Clinton, born December 18, 1854, died December, 1878, married, 1877, Charles L Nichols, and had Caroline Dewey 3 Francis Henshaw, to be further mentioned 4 John Clarke, born May 19, 1857, who is a lawyer He married his second cousin, Sarah B Dewey, and their children are John Clarke, Jr, and Daniel 5 George Tufts, born September 12, 1858 who is a lawyer, he married Mary L Nichols and their children are Mary Linwood, George Tufts, Jr, and Charles Nichols 6 Sarah Frances, born September

15, 1860, died, married Oliver Hurd Everett, and their children were Caroline Dewey and Francis Dewey 7 Charles Augustus, born and died April, 1863

(IX) Francis Henshaw Dewey, son of Hon Francis H and Sarah B (Tufts) Dewey, was born March 23, 1856, in Worcester, Massachusetts He was reared in his native city and there attended the private schools, after which he spent two years at a primary school and four years at St Mark's School in Southborough, preparatory for college In 1872 he entered Williams College, graduating therefrom four years later among the six highest of his class He was a member of the Phi Beta Kappa Society, where membership is based on scholarship In 1879 he received the degree of Master of Arts from his alma mater After reading law in the office of Messrs Staples and Goulding, of Worcester, he entered Harvard Law School, from which he graduated in 1878 with the degree of Bachelor of Laws In February, 1879, he was admitted to the bar, and has since been actively engaged in practice, and his prominence in his profession is attested by his election in 1897 to the vice-presidency of the Worcester County Bar Association In 1880 he became solicitor for the Worcester Mechanics' Savings Bank and the Mechanics' National Bank, and on the death of his honored father, in 1887, he succeeded him as a trustee and director in these institutions, respectively In April, 1888, he was elected president of the Mechanics, National Bank, which office he still holds One of his most important trusts is the presidency of the Worcester Consolidated Street Railway Company, to which he was elected in May, 1898, having been a director since 1893, and under his supervision and management a system of about forty miles of track confined principally to the city of Worcester has been extended to one hundred and sixty miles, and connects eighteen cities and towns, together with frequent service, carrying nearly thirty millions of passengers in a year For many years he has been a director in the Norwich & Worcester Railroad Company, the Worcester Gas Light Company, the Worcester Traction Company, the Worcester Theatre Association, of which he is also treasurer, he is president and treasurer of the Bay State House, and a director in many business corporations He is a trustee of the Worcester Railways and Investment Company He has also had charge of the settlement of many large estates in the capacity of trustee and executor, and possesses unusual business qualifications

Mr Dewey has ever taken a deep interest in educational and charitable work, and is actively identified with many of the most important institutions in these lines He is a trustee and vice-president of Clark University, and of Clark College, and has long been vice-president of the Art Museum and a member of the American Antiquarian Society He is a director of the Associated Charities, chairman of the Commission of City Hospital Funds, and a trustee of the Memorial Hospital He is a member of the Board of Trade, of which he was for several years a director, vice-president of the Massachusetts Street Railway Association, and a member of the Worcester Fire Society and many social organizations For many years he has been prominent in the First Unitarian Parish, and has been superintendent of the Sunday school and chairman of the parish committee He is a stanch Republican in politics

December 12, 1878, Mr Dewey married Miss Lizzie Davis, daughter of the late Harrison Bliss, and of this union were born two children Elizabeth Bliss Dewey, July 19, 1883, and Francis Henshaw Dewey, May 19, 1887

EDWIN BROWN John Brown (1), or Browne, the progenitor of Edwin Brown, of Worcester, was associated with the Pilgrims at Plymouth While he was travelling in his youth he became acquainted with Rev John Robinson, pastor of the Pilgrims, and through him met many of his people in the same way that Governor Winslow and Captain Miles Standish came to join the Pilgrims He did not come in the "Mayflower," however It was not until March, 1629, that he reached New England He landed at Salem Two years earlier, however, March 19, 1627, the council for New England approved a patent for trade soil and planting on which a Royal charter was obtained March 4, 1628, to certain patentees and their associates, among whom were John Browne, John Saltonstall, and others who became well known in the colonies He was elected to Governor John Endicott's council, April 3, 1629, with Francis Higginson, Samuel Skelton, Francis Bright, Samuel Browne, Thomas Graves and Samuel Sharp He went from Salem to Plymouth and later to Taunton with his son, James In 1643 John Brown and his sons, John and James, were residents of Taunton, but next year they settled at Rehoboth, Massachusetts There John Browne, Sr, and John Brown, Jr, stayed and were among the first settlers, but James Browne being a Baptist was forced to leave town in 1663 and with others of his sect founded the town of Swansey, Massachusetts The designation Mr given him in the records always shows that he was counted among the gentry His sons and grandsons were leaders in civic, judicial and military affairs John Brown was appointed one of the townsmen (an office) in Rehoboth, March 16, 1645, and again in 1650-51 He served the town on important commissions He was on the prudential committee He was for seventeen years from 1636 to 1653 one of the governor's assistants or magistrates In 1638 the following were the governor's assistants William Bradford, Edward Winslow, Captain Miles Standish, John Alden, John Jenny and John Browne He was one of the commissioners of the United Colonies of New England (which foreshadowed the later confederation) from 1644 to 1655 In the governor's court June 4, 1652, he won a notable suit for damages for defamation against Samuel Newman, the judgment being for one hundred pounds and costs Mr Browne waived the judgment, however, and let Newman off on payment of the costs Mr Browne was a friend of Massasoit, and the proof of their friendship was shown when the life of his son James was spared by King Philip, son of Massasoit, when he came on a mission from the governor to the Indians Colonel Church in his narrative says "that the Indians would have killed Mr Browne, who with Mr Samuel Gorton and two other men bore the letter, but Philip prevented them, saying that his father had charged him to show kindness to Mr Browne" It is said in his honor that he was the first magistrate to raise his voice against the coercive support of the ministry, taking the stand that all church support should be voluntary and backed his precepts by liberal example He was a man of abilities, intellect, piety and patriotism, and was buried with civic and military honors in 1662 His wife Dorothy died in 1674 His eldest son died the same year as he (1662) His other son, James, was afterwards in the magistracy His grandson, John Browne, became useful and eminent In 1685 John Browne was one of the first associate justices of the court of common pleas in the county of Bristol In 1699, during the administration of Lord Bellamont, he was again appointed a justice John Browne, Sr, was born in 1505 and died April 10, 1662 His wife died at Swansey, Massachusetts, January 27, 1673 The children of John Browne (I) were Ensign John, Jr, born in England, died last of March, 1662, (settled in Rehoboth and had these children John, born last Friday in September, 1650, Lydia, August 5 or 6, 1656, Annah, January 29, 1657, Joseph, April 9, 1658, Nathaniel, June 9, 1661, Major James, of Swansey, born in England 1623, died 1710, Mary, born in England, married, July 6, 1636, Captain Thomas Willett, of Plymouth, the first English mayor of New York city, who was twice elected to that office William, resided in Salem, not mentioned in will and not proved to be son of John Browne (I)

(II) Major James Brown, son of John Browne (1), born in England in 1623, was in Taunton in 1643 with his father, the assistant, and went with him to Swansea, Massachusetts He was said to be a Baptist and preacher He was chosen an assistant in 1665 He married Lydia Howland, daughter of John Howland, who came over in the "May flower," and all his descendants are likewise descended from Mayflower ancestry He died October 29, 1710, aged eighty-seven years Their children were James, born at Rehoboth, Massachusetts, May 4, 1655, died at Barrington, Rhode Island, 1725, Dorothy, born at Swansey, Massachusetts, August 29, 1666, married ——— Kent, Jabez, born July 9, 1668, at Swansey, Massachusetts

(III) James Brown, son of Major James Brown (2), born at Rehoboth, May 4, 1655 (or May 21), died April 15, 1718, aged fifty-nine years, (probably should be sixty-two), married Margaret Denison, June 5, 1678 She died May 5, 1741, aged eighty-four years He was a sergeant in the militia All his children were born in Swansey They were, as recorded Lydia, born January 23, 1678-9, died February 1, 1678-9, Mary, September 11, 1680, Margaret (given by Savage), June 28, 1682, Lydia, July 28, 1684, James, September 7, 1685, Mary, July 5, 1687, Peleg, February 28, 1688, William, June 2, 1690, Dorothy, May 7, 1694

(IV) William Brown, son of James Brown (3), was born June 2, 1690 He married (first) Elizabeth ———, about 1710 She died April 27, 1725, aged twenty-seven years He married (second) Rebecca Follett, October 27, 1725 He died February 26, 1731-2 He settled at Rehoboth, where all his children are recorded except William As the records clearly show that the son is William, Jr, he must be the eldest son of William, there being no other William at Rehoboth or Swansey at the time The children of William Brown were William, born about 1710, Consider, September 8, 1711, Amos, May 28, 1714, Elizabeth, June 14, 1716, Bethiah, July 8, 1718, Jerusha, August 27, 1720, Ezra, August 18, 1722, Rebecca, April 17, 1725, Noah, August 7, 1726, Isaac, August 24, 1728, Ann, March 13, 1729, died October 27, 1731, Ann, January 8, 1731-2

(V) William Brown, son of William Brown (4), was born about 1710 at Rehoboth Massachusetts He married at Rehoboth, Ruth Walker, October 10, 1728 The births of their eleven children are all recorded at Rehoboth He was commissioned a cavalry officer Ruth Walker was born December 2, 1710, and died March 6, 1790 She was descended from Widow Walker, one of the original settlers of Rehoboth, Massachusetts Widow Walker was born about 1620 Her son Philip Walker, married in 1654 Jane ———, and died in 1679, leaving sons, Samuel, and Philip Walker

Samuel Walker, son of Philip Walker (2), was born 1655, died 1712 He served in King Philip's war under Major Bradford He married Martha Ide (born 1654, died 1700), daughter of Nicholas Ide, who also served in King Philip's war under Major Bradford His son, Samuel Walker (4), was born in 1682 and died in 1712 He married Ruth Bliss, who was born 1687 Their daughter, Ruth Walker (born December 2, 1710, died March 6, 1790), married William Brown, Jr, as already stated October 10, 1728 William Brown, Jr, settled at Rehoboth Their children were Ruth, born September 10, 1729, Lucy, October 26, 1731, Sarah, November 6, 1733, William, November 22, 1735, Sarah, December 4, 1737, Samuel, March 25, 1740, Molly, April 18, 1742, John, July 10, 1745, Deborah, August 29, 1747, Chloe, October 1, 1749, Huldah, December 4, 1751

(VI) Lieutenant Samuel Brown, son of William Brown, Jr (5), was born at Rehoboth, Massachusetts, March 25, 1740 He married (first) Esther Bucklin, January 5, 1764 She died about 1777 He married (second) Polly Luther, of Warren, August 23, 1778 She died in 1782 He married (third) Huldah Hunt, January 16, 1783

The children of Samuel Brown (6) were Samuel, born March 2, 1765, married Polly Brown, March 11, 1801, Josiah, October 18, 1767, Lucy, October 20, 1770, Esther, October 16 1772, Mollie (probably a twin of preceding), October 16, 1772 (1774 on records, obviously an error), Theophilus, April 9, 1774, Abigail, February 12, 1780, Elizabeth, October 22, 1781, Luther, July 21, 1782, Joseph, March 2, 1787, Ira, January 15, 1791, Peter Hunt, January 13, 1793

(VII) Samuel Brown, son of Samuel Brown (6), born at Rehoboth, Massachusetts, March 2, 1765, died in 1820 He married Ada Hardy, died 1847, daughter of Samuel and Betsey (Walker) Healy, of Seekonk Betsey Walker was born in 1753 and died in 1839, daughter of Nathaniel Walker, of North Providence (born 1703, died 1783), who married, 1727, Anna Sweeting (born 1707, died 1772) Nathaniel Walker was son of Philip Walker (born 1661, died 1739), who married Sarah Bowen daughter of William Bowen (born 1671, died 1739) This Philip Walker was son of Philip and grandson of Widow Walker, already mentioned in this sketch Samuel Brown settled at Rehoboth Children of Samuel and Ada (Healy) Brown 1 William, born August 19, 1797, married Louisa Gladding, of Providence 2 Mary (on Rehoboth records) born, March 17, 1801 3 Albert, born (date given in Rehoboth records) March 20, 1804 4 Elizabeth Walker, (record from her grandson, Appleton L Clark) born September, 1813, died November, 1891, married Appleton Purdy Lesure (born May 13, 1814, died August 4, 1865) 5 Abby, married A R Marsh, resided in Boston (birth not recorded at Rehoboth) 6 Theophilus, born September 12, 1811, married Sarah Ann Knowlton

(VIII) Albert Brown, son of Samuel Brown (7), born at Seekonk, Massachusetts, March 20, 1804, married, 1828, Mary Blair Eaton (See Eaton Family, also Rice Family) Mary Blair Eaton was a descendant of Adonijah Rice, the first white child born in Worcester Albert Brown learned the tailor's trade and located first in Providence He came to Worcester about 1825 and opened an "Emporium of Fashion" as he called his shop, on Main street, opposite Central street He took into partnership his brother William Brown, and under the firm name of W & A Brown they were the first merchant tailors located in Worcester At the death of Albert Brown September 29, 1854, the surviving partner took his brother Theophilus Brown into the firm, and at present the firm is conducted by W T Brown, son of Theophilus Albert Brown was a well known citizen of Worcester He represented his ward in the common council He went to England with the Peace Commission, and his descendants treasure a Bible given to him by Richard Cobden, with whom he formed an acquaintance there He was to some extent an owner of shipping He was a member of the Mutual Fire Society of Worcester Children of Albert and Mary Blair (Eaton) Brown 1 Albert Samuel, born Worcester, February 22, 1829, of whom later, 2 Henry William, born Worcester June 21, 1831 married Harriet B Rathbone 3 James Stewart, born January 12, 1834, of whom later 4 Mary Eaton born April 15, 1835, died April 29, 1843 5 James Stewart, born September 12, 1837, married first, Fanny Emma Childs of Worcester, married (second) Elizabeth Johonnot, is treasurer of the Worcester Five Cents Savings Bank, veteran of the civil war, prominent in business and financial circles in Worcester 6 Sarah Dean, born in Worcester, February 13, 1840, married George Wilson Ryerson of New York 7 Emily, born January 24 1842, married John Stanton Baldwin, formerly editor and publisher of *Worcester Daily Spy* (See sketch Baldwin Family) 8 Edwin, born in Worcester, March 24, 1844, married, June 12 1872 Mariana Mifflin Earle, daughter of Timothy K and Nancy (Hacker) Earle of Worcester 9 Charles Eaton, born January 23, 1847 10 Mary Louisa, born June 1, 1849, married Stephen C Earle, the well known architect of Worcester 11 Ada, born September 29, 1852, died February 3, 1869

(IX) Albert Samuel Brown, son of Albert Brown (8), was born in Worcester, Massachusetts, February 22, 1829 He attended the public schools of his native town until he was sixteen years old, when he entered a wholesale woolen house in Boston After a short time he took a position in Collamore's crockery store in Boston He finally returned to Worcester to enter business with his father in the store and tailor shop In 1853 he made a trip to Europe, partly for business and partly for pleasure When he returned home he worked for a time in a Worcester crockery store In 1860 he bought out J P Hale's crockery store and began business on his own account The store was located at 181 Main street He added wall paper to his line of goods and later moved to 284 Main street In 1880 he sold his store to E G Higgins, the wall paper dealer, whose business grew to be the largest of its kind in New England, Mr Brown retired from active business life after selling his store He loved travel and spent two years in Europe He made his home in Worcester until his death, September 14, 1900

Mr Brown stood well as a citizen and business man He was highly esteemed for his manly character and many good qualities He was a member of the First Unitarian Church and later of the Church of the Unity and was a teacher in the Sunday school In politics he was a Republican He served the city in the common council He was a member of no secret orders or military organizations

He married November 28, 1860 Ellen M Morse daughter of Mason H and Maria (Bigelow) Morse of Worcester Mason H Morse was a carpenter and builder He served on the building committee when the Church of the Unity to which he belonged erected the present edifice on Elm street Ellen M Morse, as well as Mr Brown, was a descendant of the first white child born in Worcester She was born March 22, 1837 Maria Bigelow was the daughter of Lewis and Sophia Bigelow, and was born in Worcester, April 1, 1815 and married May 24, 1836 (See sketch of Bigelow family) Mr and Mrs Brown had no children Mrs Brown resides at her home in Worcester, 21 Elm street

(IX) Henry William Brown, son of Albert Brown (8), born in Worcester, June 21, 1831, died February 21, 1900, at Daytona, Florida, where he was spending the winter He married Harriet B Rathbone, of Providence, Rhode Island He graduated from Harvard College in 1852, and from Harvard Divinity School in 1857 He preferred teaching to the ministry, and from 1875 to 1896, a period of twenty-one years, was an instructor in the State Normal School of Worcester His services in the school are best told by quoting the words of Principal E Harlow Russell

> Coming to the school so soon after its beginning, he had much to do with shaping its policy and in establishing the department which he maintained with so much efficiency and distinction A graduate of Harvard College and later of the Harvard Divinity School in his early years he was a clergyman but left that profession for the more congenial one of teaching He may certainly be said to have given the best years of his life to the service of the Worcester school He was always thoroughly in sympathy with the aims and purposes of its administration loyal to its principal appreciative of its excellencies, and considerate to a marked degree of its defects With his fellow teachers his relations were most friendly They felt the strength that he brought to the faculty and always regarded him with affectionate admiration While not an ambitious man as the word is ordinarily used his standard of excellence was high and he gave to his professional work the best that was in him He was a ripe scholar with a thorough command of the classical languages and literatures but he never ceased to be a diligent student with a genuine taste for knowledge of all sorts in the lines of science as well as of literature His most conspicuous service to the cause of education was probably his translation from the German of Prof Preyer's famous books 'The Mind of the Child' and 'Mental Development in the Child' Mr Brown's intimate acquaintance with German acquired during two periods of residence in Germany together with his command of a clear idiomatic English style, render these translations of the highest authority and value The work was published by D Appleton & Co New York in their *International Education Series* and the translation received the highest commendation from the editor of the series Dr William T Harris United States Commissioner of Education
>
> Mr Brown was a man of unusual refinement of lofty ideals and of warm affections These qualities combined with his ample intellectual equipment made him a teacher of rare breadth and power The graduates of this school will bear unanimous testimony to the quality and permanence of the influence he exerted upon growing minds an influence appreciated by them more and more with the lapse of time Although his standard was high his dealings with individual pupils were always felt to be just and humane and in his classes there was no tyranny and no friction It may be truly said that among the hundreds of young people who have come under his instruction here there was not one who did not feel toward him not only profound respect but warm esteem And his attachment to the graduates was shown by his manifest pleasure in meeting them on their visits to the school and his genial speeches to them at their annual reunions The graduates have a permanent memorial of him which they greatly prize in the shape of a reunion song composed for them by him some years ago and which is sung yearly to the tune of 'Fair Harvard' at their annual gatherings When Mr Brown was in Worcester last autumn he was invited by a committee of graduates to sit for his portrait for the graduates' room of the school This he did and the result a large photograph by Notman of Boston proved a most satisfactory likeness and is now of priceless value To the large body of graduates who for a score of years have enjoyed Mr Brown's instructions as well as to the circle of his more intimate friends the news of his death will come with a sense of personal loss '

He had one son, Conway Rathbone who died while a student and undergraduate at Harvard at the age of twenty-three years

(IX) J Stewart Brown son of Albert Brown (8), was born in Worcester, Massachusetts September 12, 1837 He was educated in the public and high schools of Worcester, and began the active duties of life by entering the employ of Henry W Miller, proprietor of a hardware store with whom he remained several years later he established a house-furnishing business of his own which he continued until the breaking out of the civil war At that time he was sergeant of the old Worcester Light Infantry, and was made sergeant of his company in the famous Sixth Massachusetts Regiment, which was mustered out August 2, 1861, and which was attacked while marching through the streets of Baltimore to Washington, District of Columbia. In the fall of 1861 he went to the front with a committee of relief, with between eleven and twelve hundred dollars contributed for the Worcester soldiers. In November, 1862, he was commissioned adjutant of the Fifty-first Regiment, Massachusetts Infantry, participated in the battles of Kinston, Whitehall and Goldsboro, North Carolina, and was mustered out July 2, 1863. Later he entered the commissary department with the Ninth Army Corps and remained until the close of the war, receiving his honorable discharge April 16, 1865. Upon his return to civil life Mr. Brown again entered the employ of Mr. Miller, remaining two years. He then engaged in business on his own account, manufacturing braid and shoe laces, and after conducting the same for four years disposed of the business in order to accept the office of water registrar of the city of Worcester, which he filled to the satisfaction of the various administrations, and to the people of the city, until his resignation in 1883, when he accepted the treasurership of the Worcester Five Cents Savings Bank, to which he had been elected. For nearly twenty-five years he has been the executive head of this large and prosperous savings institution, which, judged from every standard, is one of the most successful of its kind in the city. It has shown a wonderful growth in the total deposits and investments. He is a director of the Merchants' and Farmers' Fire Insurance Company, of Worcester, rendering faithful service in that capacity. Upon the organization of George H. Ward Post, No. 10, Grand Army of the Republic, he was appointed the first adjutant, and he has been a constant and earnest worker for the best interests and welfare of the post ever since. He has also been an officer of his regimental association since its organization. In the war play, "The Drummer Boy of Shiloh," which has been given for many years annually in the Worcester theatre, he took, for a number of years, the part of Frank Rutledge, and his achievements in this part will never be forgotten by his comrades and those who attended the performances. The excellence of the cast originally had much to do with the perennial popularity of this grand old war play in Worcester. The Grand Army of the Republic has netted a considerable income every year from the week's performances of the "The Drummer Boy," as it is commonly called. Mr. Brown is a member of the Unitarian church. In politics he is a Republican.

He married (first), September 26, 1872, E. Fannie Childs, born at Hartford, Connecticut, April 29, 1845, died in Worcester, Massachusetts, May 13, 1894, daughter of Gardner and Fannie (Goulding) Childs, of Worcester. The children of this union were: Albert, born November 2, 1877, educated at the Worcester public and high schools, and a graduate of the American Academy of the Stage, which he attended for three years; he has made a very promising start in his first professional engagement on the stage. Helen Elizabeth, born in Worcester, July 21, 1886, attended the Worcester public schools, and was a graduate of the class of 1904 of Prospect hill school, at Greenfield, Massachusetts. He married (second), June 11, 1896, Harriet E. Johonnot, born September 3, 1848, at Boston, Massachusetts, daughter of Ambrose E. and Elizabeth (Gaffield) Johonnot, of Boston.

(IX) Edwin Brown, son of Albert Brown (8), was born in Worcester, March 24, 1844. He attended the Worcester public schools, leaving the high school in 1860 to accept a position in the City Bank, afterwards the City National Bank, absorbed in 1903 by the Worcester Trust Company. At the age of eighteen he enlisted in Company C, Fifty-first Regiment, and served in the campaigns in North Carolina and Maryland. He returned to Worcester with his regiment in 1863, and became book-keeper at the City Bank, but after two years was called to the Worcester National Bank, where he became teller, remaining in that position for one year, when he was called back to the City National Bank as teller and assistant cashier. He continued there until 1871, when he went into business with his father-in-law, Timothy K. Earle, becoming a member of the firm of T. K. Earle & Co., whose factory for the manufacture of machine card clothing for cotton and woolen mills was located on Grafton street, Worcester. In 1880 a stock company was formed under the name of the T. K. Earle Manufacturing Company, with Mr. Brown as treasurer and manager. Mr. Earle died in 1881, and Mr. Brown continued the business for the company until 1890. At that time there was a consolidation of the various card clothing factories of the country under the name of the American Card Clothing Company. Mr. Brown was treasurer of the new corporation, and he held that position until 1905, when the company was liquidated.

Mr. Brown is a vice-president of the Worcester Five Cents Savings Bank. He was one of the founders of the Quinsigamond Boat Club in 1857, and in his younger days was the stroke oar of the crack crew of that club, which formerly held the championship of the lake, and which rowed on the Hudson river at Troy, New York, October 9, 1867, in the first national amateur regatta in the United States. Mr. Brown has always taken an interest in healthful athletics and sports. He was a charter member of the Worcester Club, and is a member of the old Worcester Fire Society, a veteran member of George H. Ward Post, 10, G. A. R., a life member of the Worcester County Mechanics Association, a member of the Worcester Natural History Society, the Worcester Society of Antiquity, the Tatnuck Country Club, and was formerly a member of the Commonwealth Club, the Grafton Country Club, and the Worcester County Musical Association. He is a Republican. He belongs to the First Unitarian Church.

He married, June 12, 1872, Mariana Mifflin Earle, daughter of Timothy K. and Nancy (Hacker) Earle. Their children are: 1. Earle, born in Worcester, August 15, 1873, graduated Harvard University 1895, was in business two years, went to Spanish-American war in the First Rhode Island Regiment, then went to Harvard Law School, is practicing law in Worcester, 314 Main street. 2. Edwin Hacker, born Worcester, July 29, 1875, graduated Harvard University 1896, and at Worcester Polytechnic Institute 1898, is a mechanical engineer with the Minneapolis Steel and Machinery Company of Minneapolis, Minnesota, and is now (1905) at Nome, Alaska, on his fourth trip as engineer for gold mining companies. 3. Caspar Mifflin, born in Worcester, October 13, 1878, graduated at Harvard University 1900, with Graton & Knight Manufacturing Company of Worcester, and has had charge of their exhibits at St. Louis, Missouri, and Portland (Oregon) Expositions; while in college he was a member of the Hasty Pudding Club, president of the Varsity Banjo Club, and was on his class crews and football teams. 4. Lloyd Thornton, born August 20, 1880, graduated at Harvard University 1903, now in Harvard Medical School, was president of the Varsity Mandolin Club and a member of the Hasty Pudding and other clubs while in college.

(IX) Charles Eaton Brown, son of Albert Brown (8), was born in Worcester, January 23, 1847 He graduated from the Worcester High School in 1863, and from the United States Naval Academy at Annapolis in 1867 He was one of the officers of the U S navy who were with the first embassy ever received at the court of the Tycoon of Japan, and, when Minister De Long was received, the Americans were entertained with barbaric splendor The Tycoon had some selected executions of criminals, and even some crucifixions to entertain and honor his guests The U S gunboat "Oneida," of which he was an officer, was sunk in the harbor of Yokohama, January 23, 1870, by the British steamship 'Bombay," and one hundred and twenty officers and men lost their lives The body of Ensign Brown was recovered and brought home to Worcester for interment He was unmarried

THE SPRAGUE FAMILY, descended from good old English stock, have an honorable history covering a period of nearly three hundred years in America The late Hosea Sprague published in 1828 a genealogy of the Spragues in Hingham to the fourth generation He lived at Hingham, Massachusetts, and his personal knowledge of the family aided him in making a compilation of the records, and from it we glean many points invaluable in this connection

Edward Sprague, of England, was a resident of Upway, county of Dorset, where he died in 1614 He was a fuller by trade He married Christiana (family name not given in the record) by whom he had six children Ralph, Alice, Edward, Richard, Christopher, William Ralph, Richard and William arrived at Naumkeag (Salem) in 1628, coming over in the interest of the Massachusetts Bay Company, who decreed that "none but honest and godly men should go over to settle" In "Prince's Chronology" we read 'Among those who arrived at Naumkeag are Ralph Sprague, with his brothers Richard and William, who with three or four more were by Governor Endicott employed to explore and take possession of the country westward They traveled through the woods to Charlestown, on a neck of land called Mishawum, between Mystic and Charles rivers, full of Indians named Aberginians, with whom they made peace" Hon Edward Everett in his address commemorative of the bi-centennial of the arrival of Winthrop at Charlestown, said 'Ralph, Richard and William Sprague are the founders of the settlement in this place, and were persons of substance and enterprise, excellent citizens, generous public benefactors, and the head of a very large and respectable family of descendants"

Ralph Sprague was about twenty-five years of age when he came to this country He had four sons, John, Richard, Samuel and Phineas, and a daughter Mary, who married Daniel Edmands on September 28 1630 John and Richard were born in England Ralph was one of a jury impaneled which seems to have been the first jury in Massachusetts Ralph Sprague was a lieutenant in the train band In 1631 Captain Richard Sprague commanded a company of the train band, and on Friday of each week exercised his command at a convenient place near the Indian wigwams February 10, 1634, the famous order creating a board of selectmen was passed, Richard and William Sprague signed the order Richard Sprague left no posterity His sword which is named in his brother William's will was preserved in one of the old Sprague houses in Hingham in 1828

(I) William Sprague, son of Edward, of England, was born in England He married, 1635, Millesaint, daughter of Anthony Eames She died February 8, 1696 He remained in Charlestown until 1636 His wife was admitted into the church in Charlestown in 1635, and the eldest son was baptized there May, 1636 He came to Hingham in the same year in a boat which landed on the east side of the cove, on a tract afterward granted to him by the town, and became one of the first planters, the name Bare Cove having been changed to Hingham, September 2, 1635 William Sprague's house lot was said to be the pleasantest in Hingham Many parcels of land were granted to him from 1636 to 1647 These gifts show the esteem in which he was held by his fellow townsmen January 30, 1645, he was one of seven men chosen in town meeting to order the prudential affairs of the town In 1662 he was disbursing officer for the town, and also constable and fence viewer, etc February 21, 1673, he deeded to his son Anthony certain lands for six and thirty pounds of lawful money of New England, and nine pounds in merchantable corn He died October 26, 1675 The children of William and Millesaint Sprague were 1 Anthony, born September 2, 1635, married Elizabeth Bartlett, daughter of Robert Bartlett, of Plymouth He was a large landowner of Hingham His house was burned by Indians, April 19, 1676 He died September 3, 1719 2 John, baptized April, 1638, married Elizabeth Holbrook, December 13, 1666 Sprague Island was given to him by his father He died in Mendon, 1690 3 Samuel, baptized May 24, 1640 He removed to Marshfield, Massachusetts, where he became secretary of the colony and register of deeds before 1692 He was the great-grandfather of Hon Seth Sprague, of Duxbury 4 Elizabeth, baptized May 2, 1641 5 Jonathan, baptized March 20, 1642, died July 4, 1647 6 Perses, baptized November 12, 1643, married John Doggett 7 Joanna, baptized December, 1644, married Caleb Church, December 16, 1667 8 Jonathan, born May 28, 1648, moved to Providence, Rhode Island 9 William, born May 7, 1650, married Deborah Lane, daughter of Andrew Lane, December 13 1674 At a later date he removed to Providence, Rhode Island 10 Mary, baptized May 25, 1652, married Thomas King 11 Hannah baptized February 26, 1655, died March 31, 1658

(II) Jonathan Sprague, born in Hingham, May 28, 1648, son of William (1), married Mehitabel, daughter of William and Elizabeth Holbrook, and in 1672 removed to Mendon, Massachusetts In 1675 his father died and left to him sixty acres of land in Providence, Rhode Island, where he settled before 1680' He aided in surveying the eastern line of the colony His was a strong, manly character He was a member of the house of deputies for sixteen years between 1695 and 1714, speaker of the house, 1703, and member of the town council eight years from 1705 to 1712, clerk of the assembly in 1707 In 1703, with two others, he was appointed to draw up the methods and proceedings of the court of common pleas The 'Annals of Providence" says he was a decidedly religious man, professed the Baptist faith, and preached as an exhorter He died in 1741 The children of Jonathan and Mehitabel Sprague were 1 Jonathan, a resident of Providence and Smithfield, Rhode Island, married Bethiah Mann, November 28, 1699 She was born March 12 1683, and died April 6, 1712 For his second wife he married Hannah Hawkins, widow of Stephen Hawkins He died April 22, 1764 2 William, born February 2, 1691, was a resident of Providence, and also of Smithfield, Rhode Island Smithfield was set off from Providence and organized as a town in 1730 He died in Smithfield, 1768 He bore the rank of captain in the

A. B. R. Sprague

second militia regiment of Providence in 1732 The "History of Woonsocket, Rhode Island," says "For upwards of a century the Spragues were prominent actors in the religious and political history of old Smithfield" He deeded much land to one cause and another, and large tracts to his children 3 Patience, married William Jenks, and they had ten children 4 Joanna, married John Teft, who died in 1762 She died in 1757 They had eleven children 5 Mary, married Daniel Brown, and they had six children 6 A daughter whose name is unknown, married Ebenezer Cook

(III) Captain William Sprague, son of Jonathan (2), born 1691, married September 16, 1714, Ales Browne, who was born May 31, 1691 Their children were 1 Nehemiah, born January 5, 1717, married, 1738, Mary Brown 2 Ales, born October 2, 1720 3 Sarah, born February 10, 1722, married William Sly 4 Samuel, born September 12, 1724 5 Jetter, born September 19, 1726 6 Joshua, born July 3, 1729, married Abigail Wilber

(IV) Nehemiah Sprague, son of Captain William Sprague (3), married April 16, 1738, Mary Brown, and had Elias, born in Smithfield, Rhode Island, June 16, 1744, Nehemiah, born January 20, 1750, who died there in June, 1796 These brothers were farmers, and members of the Society of Friends

(V) Elias Sprague, son of Nehemiah (4), was born in Smithfield, Rhode Island, June 16, 1744, and died in Douglass, Massachusetts, February 15, 1799 He married Mercy, daughter of Joseph Bassett, August 5, 1764, she was sister of Alice, who became the wife of Nehemiah (5) Elias moved to Douglass, Massachusetts, not later than 1788, at which date he deeded his homestead in Smithfield, Rhode Island, for three hundred and ninety pounds silver money The children born to Elias and Mercy Sprague were 1 Jonathan, born December 9, 1765 2 Theodate, born January 4, 1768 3 Amy, born October 6, 1769 4 Benjamin, born April 10, 1771 5 Lavinia, born August 12, 1773 6 Stephen, born November 18, 1775, married Olive Seagrave 7 Preserved, born October 17, 1777, married Joanna Trask 8 Thankful, born October 19, 1779 9 William, born June 3, 1782 10 Alice, born August 29, 1784 11 Elias, born ——— 12 Lucina, born —— 13 Unnamed

(VI) Jonathan Sprague, son of Elias Sprague (5), born at Smithfield, Rhode Island, December 9, 1765, was twice married His first wife was Patience, daughter of Robert Pixley (or Pidgeley), of New Grafton, Massachusetts She was born in 1765 They were married in Smithfield by Peleg Arnold, justice of the peace, August 12, 1785 Their children were 1 Sarah, born in Smithfield, Rhode Island, December 3, 1785 2 Nehemiah, born in Smithfield, Rhode Island, June 17, 1787 3 Mercy, born in Douglas, Massachusetts, January 17, 1789 4 Federal Constitution, born in Douglas, Massachusetts, October 16, 1790 5 Amy born in Douglas, October 14, 1792 6 Daniel, born in Douglas, August 4, 1794 7 Preserved, born in Douglas, April 4, 1796, died in childhood 8 Lee, born in Douglas, February 7, 1798 9 Patience, born in Douglas, March 1, 1800 10 Jonathan, Jr, born in Douglas, October 6, 1801

The father, Jonathan Sprague, died in Thompson, Connecticut, October 29, 1815 Patience, his wife, died December 14, 1801 They were buried in the Friends' burying-ground at South Douglas, Massachusetts Jonathan Sprague married (second) Kezia, daughter of Daniel and Kezia Torrey, of Sutton Massachusetts She was born there April 19, 1770, and died in Douglas, Massachusetts, May 10, 1844 Their children were Almira, Philinda, Elias and Emeline In all, Jonathan Sprague had ninety-seven grandchildren

(VII) Lee Sprague, son of Jonathan (6), and Patience Sprague, was born in Douglas, Massachusetts, February 7, 1798 He married (first) Olive How Williams, May 21, 1821, who was born in Pomfret, Connecticut, November 27, 1803 She died in Ware, Massachusetts, November 11, 1822 The second wife of Lee Sprague was Lucia Snow, born April 28, 1805, daughter of Deacon Eli Snow and Alice Alden, she being in the sixth generation from John Alden of the "Mayflower" The father of Lucia Snow was in the fifth generation from Nicholas Snow, who came to Plymouth in the ship "Ann," in 1623, and married Constance Hopkins, a "Mayflower" pilgrim Lucia Snow was married in Ware, Massachusetts, to Lee Sprague, September 8, 1824, and died in Worcester, Massachusetts, December 4, 1864 Lee Sprague married for his third wife Mary A Bradley, born in 1808, married May 8, 1866, deceased The children of Lee and Lucia Sprague were 1 Olive Williams, born in Ware, Massachusetts, June 12, 1825, died in East Douglas, Massachusetts, December 23, 1840 2 Augustus B R, born in Ware, Massachusetts, March 7, 1827 3 Caroline Florella, born in Ware, Massachusetts, July 1, 1829, died in East Jaffrey, New Hampshire, August 7, 1863 4 Francis Henry, born in Ware, Massachusetts, June 3, 1833, died April 13, 1834 5 William Wirt, born in Ware, Massachusetts, February 8, 1835, died August 20, 1837, in East Douglas 6 William Lee, born in East Douglas, Massachusetts, November 9, 1839, died January 23, 1841

Lee Sprague, the father of these children, died in Worcester, Massachusetts, September 9, 1877

(VIII) Caroline Florella Sprague, daughter of Lee and Lucia Sprague, born in Ware, Massachusetts, July 1, 1829, died in East Jaffrey, New Hampshire, August 7, 1863 She married Rev Franklin D Austin, at Worcester, Massachusetts, January, 1853 Their children were 1 Frank Lee, born in Tolland, Massachusetts, March 16, 1855, became a civil engineer, a graduate of Worcester Polytechnic Institute, 1877, died in April, 1897 2 Flora Lucia, born in East Jaffrey, New Hampshire, December 27, 1857, graduated at Mt Holyoke, Massachusetts, died in St Paul, Minnesota, January 5, 1900 3 Caroline Sprague, born in East Jaffrey, New Hampshire, July 29, 1863, graduated at Smith's College, Massachusetts

GENERAL AUGUSTUS BROWN REED SPRAGUE was born in Ware, Massachusetts, March 7, 1827, son of Lee and Lucia (Snow) Sprague He is a lineal descendant in the seventh generation from William Sprague, who came from England in 1628 with Endicott in the interest of the Massachusetts Bay Company to prepare for a new colony His maternal grandmother, Alice Alden, was a descendant in the fifth generation from John Alden, and his grandfather, Eli Snow, in the same generation, from Constance Hopkins, another "Mayflower" pilgrim

General Sprague obtained his education in public and private schools in Ware and East Douglas, and was fitting for college when home circumstances compelled a change of plan, and in 1842 he came to Worcester At first a clerk, he soon engaged in mercantile business for himself, and was so occupied from 1846 to 1861, when at the outbreak of the rebellion he gave his services to his country He was well prepared for the emergency, being already a well drilled soldier He had joined the Worcester

Guards at the age of seventeen, and had served as private, non-commissioned and commissioned officer, as adjutant of the Eighth Regiment, and major and inspector on the staff of the commander of the Fifth Brigade, Third Division, Massachusetts Volunteer Militia, which latter position he was holding at the time of the attack upon Fort Sumter Under the call of President Lincoln for the first seventy-five thousand men, Major Sprague was unanimously elected to the captaincy of the Worcester City Guards, designated as Company A, Third Rifle Battalion, commanded by Major Charles Devens, Jr This body left for the seat of war April 20, 1861 Early in July Major Devens was called to the command of the Fifteenth Regiment Massachusetts Volunteers, and Captain Sprague, by virtue of seniority, commanded the battalion until its muster-out on August 3d, its term of service having expired Upon his return home he at once identified himself with the organization of the Twenty-fifth Regiment, Massachusetts Volunteers, in which he was commissioned lieutenant-colonel On his solicitation several who had served with him in the Third Battalion were commissioned in this regiment, among them being Major McCafferty, Adjutant Harkness, and Captains Pickett, Moulton, O'Neil and Atwood Before the regiment left its rendezvous for the front Colonel Sprague was presented with a magnificent sword and belt by the members of his old company Later his Worcester friends presented him with a valuable horse and equipments, Hon Alexander H Bullock making the presentation address on behalf of the donors Colonel Sprague served with his regiment until November 11, 1862, taking part in all the skirmishes and battles in which it participated, including the famous Burnside Expedition and he was officially commended by his superior officer "for bravery and efficiency in the battles of Roanoke Island and Newberne" He was promoted, on the date which marked his separation from the Twenty-fifth Regiment, to the colonelcy of the Fifty-first Massachusetts Regiment By special request of Major General John G Foster, the department commander, Colonel Sprague was ordered with his new regiment back to North Carolina, where he participated in the battles of Kinston, Whitehall and Goldsboro The names of these engagements were subsequently by order of Major General Foster inscribed upon the regimental colors which had been presented by the ladies of Worcester

When General Lee led the Confederat army on the campaign which found its disastrous ending at historic Gettysburg, Colonel Sprague's regiment, with others, was ordered from Newberne to reinforce General John A Dix at White House, on the Pamunky river, after which it returned to Fortress Monroe for transportation to Massachusetts, its term of service having expired Learning, however, that the rebel army was yet north of the Potomac river, Colonel Sprague telegraphed to Edwin M Stanton, Secretary of War an offer of his regiment for further service This patriotic proffer was gladly accepted, and the regiment was ordered to Baltimore, and thence to the Army of the Potomac at Williamsport, Maryland, and only left the field when Lee's army was well out of reach on its retreat into Virginia The return of the Fifty-first Regiment to Worcester was a notable event in the history of the city glad hearts, and the sorrowful ones as well, joining in the glad welcome to the returning heroes, and making a day long to be remembered July 27 the regiment was mustered out of service

Colonel Sprague, however, was not to remain long inactive Soon after the disbandment of his regiment he was requested by Governor John A Andrew to recruit and command the Fifty-seventh Regiment, but illness in his family constrained him to decline Later he again offered his service to his state, and as there were then no new regiments being raised, he was offered by Governor Andrew a commission as lieutenant-colonel in either one of two regiments then in the field—the Fourth Cavalry and the Second Heavy Artillery His warm personal regard and soldierly admiration for a young man well remembered in Worcester county, Francis Washburn, who had made a brilliant record as a captain in the First Massachusetts Cavalry Regiment and was well deserving of promotion, moved him to decline the first of these offers in favor of his friend, and he accepted the latter He was commissioned February 1, 1864, and at once joined his regiment, with which he served in some of the most momentous campaigns which marked that stirring period He commanded his regiment in its field service in southern Virginia and North Carolina, and formed a part of General Schofield's column in its march to open up communication at Goldsboro, North Carolina, with the army of Major General William T Sherman, which, having come thus far from Savannah after its "March to the Sea," was now moving against the confederate General Joseph E Johnston These operations, combined with those of General Ulysses S Grant against the rebel army under Lee, worked the downfall of the Confederacy, and soon afterward the regiment was sent to the mouth of Cape Fear river to dismantle Fort Fisher and repair Fort Caswell, and later assembled at Galloupe Island, in Boston Harbor, where it was discharged from service September 20, 1865, previous to which he was commissioned colonel of the regiment He was brevetted brigadier-general to date from March 13, 1865, "for gallant and meritorious services during the war" His entire service covered the long period of three years and nine months, and ever received the warmest commendation of his superior officers

Returning to civil life, General Sprague was soon called to important civil service, which marked the beginning of a period of more than a quarter of a century of public life In February, 1867, he was appointed collector of internal revenue of the Eighth Massachusetts District On the death of Hon J S C Knowlton, sheriff of the county of Worcester, General Sprague was appointed his successor, in July, 1871, and he acquitted himself with such conspicuous ability that he was elected to the position at the next election, and successively re-elected until his tenure of office was extended to six terms of three years each, continuing until January, 1890 Soon after entering upon his duties the Worcester prison was greatly enlarged, and after its completion General Sprague gave to all the details of prison management his close personal attention entering upon a work which was justly regarded as a public benefit, and a pronounced advance in the improvement of modern prisons He revised the entire system of accounts keeping, and introduced innovations which at once conduced to the comfort of the prisoners and awoke in them a sense of gratitude to him and respect for themselves which found additional fruits in improved morale and more efficient discipline In both prisons under his control (at Fitchburg as well as at Worcester) he did away with the shaving of heads and the wearing of parti-colored garments, believing them to be unnecessary indignities imposed upon short-term prisoners Food of better quality, in greater variety, and prepared under the best hygienic methods was provided, and at less cost than that of an inferior quality Better clothing and bedding were provided,

Wm E. Rice

and the library was largely increased with carefully selected books. General Sprague's efforts, many of them innovations, were so highly appreciated by the commissioners of prisons that they gave warm expressions to their commendation in their annual reports, pronouncing the Worcester county prisons the model prisons of the commonwealth. Additional appreciation was expressed by Governor Long, who urged General Sprague to accept the appointment of warden of the state prison, but he was so interested in his work in the Worcester county prison that he declined.

General Sprague has also rendered useful service in both branches of the municipal government. In December, 1895, he was elected mayor of Worcester, and was re-elected the following year, his term of office being thus extended to January, 1898. His administration was particularly distinguished as the one during which was erected the new city hall, a building of notable beauty and utility, and from the beginning of the work until it was practically completed, he was an ex-officio member of the building commission, and gave his oversight to the work of construction. At the present time General Sprague is president of the Worcester Electric Light Company, and of the Worcester Mechanics Savings Bank. General Sprague maintains a deep interest in the various military bodies with which he is connected, and in which he is most widely and favorably known. A. B. R. Sprague Post No. 24, G. A. R., of Grafton, was named in his honor. In 1868 he was commander of the Massachusetts Department of that order, and in 1873-74 was quartermaster-general on the staff of the national commander, General Charles Devens. He is a charter member of the Massachusetts Commandery, Military Order of the Loyal Legion of the United States, and in 1868 was its junior vice-commander. He aided in the formation of the Fifty-first Massachusetts Regiment Association, of which he has been for many years president. In 1889 that body presented to him a beautiful and valuable diamond studded Grand Army badge, and in 1903 it paid him the high compliment of causing his war-time portrait to be painted and presented to the Worcester County Mechanics Association, which placed it upon the wall of their hall. He is also a member of the Society of Mayflower descendants, of the Masonic fraternity, and of numerous other social and beneficial organizations.

General Sprague married, December 23, 1846, Elizabeth Janes, daughter of Samuel and Eliza Shepard Rice, who was born January 25, 1826, and died February 20, 1889. Their children, all born in Worcester, Massachusetts, were: Samuel Augustus, born June 17, 1847, died May 12, 1848. William Augustus, born May 11, 1850, died April 9, 1857. Josephine Elizabeth, born December 19, 1851, married, October 16, 1872, Edward H. Knowlton, and died in Worcester, December 7, 1879. She left one son, Howard Sprague Knowlton, born March 4, 1878. He was graduated at the Worcester Polytechnic Institute, class of 1898, and married, October 17, 1901, Alice Frances Conant. Carrie Lee, born April 17, 1858, died August 28, 1877. Fred Foster, born October 24, 1864, married, April 12, 1892, Adaline Estelle Sprague. He died July 16, 1906. General Sprague married (second), October 23, 1890, Mary Jennie, daughter of William C. and Martha Kimball Barbour, of Worcester. She was born September 24, 1857, and was at the time of her marriage assistant librarian of the Free Public Library of Worcester. Their only child, Alice Alden, was born September 11, 1893.

WILLIAM ELLIS RICE, son of William and Emeline (Draper) Rice, was born at Ware, Massachusetts, August 6, 1833.

He is from colonial stock, being in the seventh line from his first American ancestor, Deacon Edmund Rice, who, born in 1594, came from Berkhamstead, Hertfordshire, England, and settled in Sudbury, Massachusetts, in 1638. His genealogical descent is through Thomas, born 1611, Ephraim, born 1655, John, born 1704, Peter, born 1755, William, born 1803. His grandfather, Peter Rice, born at Sudbury, Massachusetts, June 25, 1755, moved to Spencer, Massachusetts, and married Olive, daughter of Major Asa Baldwin, of Spencer, an officer in the revolutionary army. Peter Rice was a soldier in the revolutionary war, a member of Captain Seth Washburn's company that marched from Leicester, and was one of those actually in the fight at Bunker Hill, June 17, 1775. William, son of Peter, and the youngest of thirteen children, all born at Spencer, was the father of William Ellis. He died at Worcester, November 18, 1882.

On the maternal side his grandfather, Hon. James Draper, born at Spencer, February 26, 1778, was the sixth of that name in direct descent from James Draper, who, born 1618, came from Halifax, Yorkshire, England, and settled in Roxbury, Massachusetts. He was born in Spencer and died there in 1868, in his ninety-first year, having served his native town in many capacities, such as town clerk, chairman board of selectmen, town treasurer, overseer of the poor, town agent, etc. He was also a county commissioner, a member of the general court for thirteen years, a senator, a magistrate for over fifty years, and the author of Draper's "History of Spencer," published in 1841.

His mother, the eldest daughter of James and Lucy (Watson) Draper, of Spencer, was a woman of unusual dignity of character, intelligent, kind-hearted and sympathetic. She died in 1854. The parents of Mr. Rice were residing at his birth in Ware, where his father with his father's eldest brother were proprietors of the general store of the town, some years later his parents took up their residence in Worcester.

The subject of this sketch was given such education as was considered necessary to fit for commercial business, including a year or so at the high school and about the same time at Leicester Academy. In 1852, at the age of eighteen he obtained the position of clerk and book-keeper in the counting room of Ichabod Washburn & Co., in Worcester, at that time the principal drawers and finishers of the finer grades of iron wire in this country. He remained with this firm about seven years, acquiring a general knowledge of business and of the manufacture of wire, and then relinquished his position and engaged in similar business in a smaller way on his own account, in partnership with Mr. Dorrance S. Goddard, under the firm name of William E. Rice & Co. Business was started in leased premises in Connecticut, and shortly after moved to Holyoke, Massachusetts, where a large modern plant was erected by them, and the venture made successful and prosperous.

In 1865, at the solicitation of Mr. Ichabod Washburn, whose confidence and favor Mr. Rice possessed, this business was joined with Mr. Washburn's larger business, then incorporated under the title of I. Washburn & Moen Wire Works. Concurrently Mr. Rice became a stockholder, director and executive officer in this corporation. From this merger Mr. Rice's influence and activity in the further development in Worcester of its greatest industry, the manufacture of wire, began He was in hearty accord with Mr Washburn in the belief that the business could be greatly expanded with beneficial results Closely following this connection, a plant in the village of Quinsigamond was purchased and a company incorporated under the title of the Quinsigamond Iron and Wire Works, for the manufacture of wire-rods and wire, with Mr Rice as its treasurer and general manager This company was very successful in business, and was merged with the I Washburn & Moen Wire Works, under the corporate title of Washburn & Moen Manufacturing Company, in 1868 This merger marked an epoch in the enlargement of the wire industry in Worcester, and was the occasion of the purchase of the manufacturing site on Grove street, at that time occupied in part, under lease, by the I Washburn & Moen Wire Works, and the erection, under a comprehensive plan, of substantial mill buildings and power plants and the installation of the continuous rod-rolling system for producing rods of small gauge and in longer lengths than was at the time practiced in this country This practice was introduced from England, where it was reported upon by Mr Rice during his visit to the manufacturing districts there in 1867 This system, modified and greatly improved by Worcester engineers has been a potent factor in promoting the growth of the wire industry in Worcester Mr Rice, who was a director in the corporation and its treasurer, was influential and active in the expansion, as well as in the general conduct of the business which has resulted in adding so noticeably to the population and to the property of Worcester

In 1870 Mr Rice visited the iron manufacturing districts of Sweden, and arranged for the manufacture of special bars for the continuous rolling system, acquiring for his company the distinction in Sweden of being the first consumer in this country to import rolled iron direct from Swedish manufacturers In 1877 Mr Rice organized the Worcester Wire Company, for the general manufacture of wire, with a plant at South Worcester This also, became an exceedingly successful company In 1899 Mr Rice as president of the Worcester Wire Company, which office he took in 1877, and of the Washburn & Moen Manufacturing Company, which office he took in 1891, was instrumental in behalf of the stockholders in effecting a sale and transfer of all the shares of the above mentioned corporations, and in merging the business affairs of both in the American Steel & Wire Co The successful conclusion of this important negotiation permitted the much desired withdrawal of Mr Rice from the business affairs upon which his attention had so long been concentrated and his general relinquishment of business pursuits Mr Rice has filled numerous fiduciary positions of importance, and been connected in matters of consequence with many corporate and other organizations

Mr Rice married January 11 1866, Frances Helen daughter of Thomas L and Margaret (Bartlett) Randlett of Newburyport Massachusetts who died May 3 1879 December 15 1881, he married Lucy Draper daughter of Moores M and Sophia A (Draper) White of the city of New York He has two children Christine the wife of Hon Rockwood Hoar, M C, and Albert White A M Harvard 1905 now a student in the Harvard Law School

WHITNEY FAMILY John Whitney the emigrant ancester of George C Whitney and the late Edward Whitney of Worcester settled in Watertown Massachusetts in 1635 He was born about 1589 His wife, Elinor, was born about 1599 With seven children they embarked at Ipswich, England, in April, 1635 They have a very large posterity in America Another John Whitney settled in Connecticut and founded an equally large family

John Whitney bought the sixteen acres homestall of John Strickland at what is now Waltham, in Watertown then, situated on what is now Belmont and East Common streets Strickland went to Wethersfield, Connecticut, to live John Whitney was admitted a freeman March 3, 1635-6 He was a constable in 1641 and a selectman from 1638 to 1655 inclusive He was town clerk in 1655 His wife Elinor died May 11, 1659, said to be fifty-four years old, though other records would make her about sixty He married (second), September 29, 1669, Judah Clement He died June 1, 1673, said to be seventy-four years old The ancestry of John Whitney is given with the Whitney Family elsewhere in this work

The children of John and Elinor Whitney were Mary, baptized in England, May 23, 1619, died young John baptized in England, 1620, Richard, baptized in England, 1626, married Martha Coldam, Nathaniel baptized in England, 1627, Thomas, baptized in England 1629, married Mary Kedall (Kettell), Jonathan baptized in England 1634, married Lydia Jones, Joshua, baptized in England, July 5, 1635, married Lydia ———, Mary ———, and Abigail Tarbell, Caleb, born in Watertown, July 12, 1640, Benjamin, born in Watertown, June 6, 1643, married Jane ——— and Mary Poor

(II) John Whitney, son of John Whitney (1) was born in England in 1620 He settled in Watertown, Massachusetts He married, 1642, Ruth Reynolds, daughter of Robert Reynolds, of Wethersfield, Watertown and Boston John Whitney lived on a three acre lot on the east side of Lexington street on land granted to E How, next the homestall of the Phillips (q v) Family Whitney was admitted a freeman May 26, 1647, at the age of twenty-three He was selectman from 1673 to 1680 inclusive He was a soldier in 1673, and was in King Philip's war He died October 12, 1692

The children of John and Ruth (Reynolds) Whitney were John, born September 12, 1643, married Elizabeth Harris, Ruth, born April 15, 1645, married, June 20 1664, John Shattuck, son of the emigrant William Shattuck, John was drowned while crossing the Charlestown Ferry, September 14 1675, he was in the Squakeag fight September 4, 1675, and was on his way to Boston to report the disaster to his company Nathaniel born February 1 1646 married Sarah Hagar Samuel, born July 26 1648 married Mary Bemis, Mary, born April 29, 1650, died unmarried after 1693, Joseph, born January 15, 1651, married Martha Beach, Sarah born March 17, 1653, married October 18, 1681, Daniel Harrington, she died June 8, 1720 he married (second), October 25, 1720 Elizabeth Bridge, widow of Captain Benjamin Garfield, Elizabeth born June 9 1656 married, December 19 1678 Daniel Warren, Hannah, Benjamin born June 28, 1660, married Abigail Hagar and Elizabeth ———

(III) Benjamin Whitney, son of John Whitney (2) was born in Watertown Massachusetts, June 28 1660 He married March 30 1687, Abigail Hagar, daughter of William and Mary (Benis) Hagar He married (second) Elizabeth ——— He died in 1736 His children were Abigail, born in Watertown March 3 1688 married March 18, 1717 Richard Sawtel, Benjamin, baptized July 10, 1698 married Rebecca ——— Ruth baptized July 10 1698, married, July 7, 1715, John Bond, baptized November 23 1690 removed to Worcester

EDWARD WHITNEY

before 1752, John, born June 15, 1694, married (first) Susan ———, (second) Bethia Cutter and (third) Mrs Beriah (Bemis) (Child) Pierce, David, born June 16, 1697, Daniel, born July 17, 1700, married Dorothy Tainter

(IV) Ensign David Whitney, son of Benjamin Whitney (3), was born in Watertown, Massachusetts, June 16, 1697 He married, 1720, Rebecca Fillebrown, born in Cambridge, Massachusetts, November 6, 1695, and died 1749 He was one of the proprietors of land at Paris, Maine, in 1736 He died in 1745 He resided in Watertown and Waltham, Massachusetts Their children were Rebecca, born November 2, 1721, married, July 18, 1845, Thomas Stowell, David, September 25, 1723, married Mary Merriam, Anna, August 8, 1725, married, June 4, 1752, Samuel Merriam, Nathan, born March 12, 1726, Ruth, February 23, 1728, died April 23, 1757, Josiah, November 22, 1730, married Sarah Lawrence, Jonas, June 25, 1733, married Sarah Whittemore, Jonathan, February 10, 1735, died April 9, 1757

(V) Nathan Whitney, son of David Whitney (4), was born March 12, 1726-7 He married Tabitha Merriam He settled in Westminster, Massachusetts He bought of Benjamin Brown, December 26, 1750, a lot of ninety acres of land in the southern part of the town, part of this land is still owned by his descendants and used as the summer home of George C Whitney and the family of Edward Whitney, of Worcester He also bought of Thomas Merriam, his father-in-law, the southeast ends of the adjoining lots, 83 and 84, on which he built his first temporary house His framed house which was built later forms the older part of the present structure on the old homestead He brought his bride to Westminster in 1752 or 1753 His struggle with the soil and misfortune almost discouraged him In the epidemic of 1756 both their children were taken Again in 1764 their four children died of the epidemic Out of nine children only three lived to maturity

Nathan Whitney was a persevering and enterprising man and at length he prospered He became one of the leading men of the town, and had an honorable military record He was corporal in Captain Daniel Hoar's company in 1759 From 1771 to 1776 he held a commission from George III as captain He sided with the colonists against the king, resigned his commission and took what part his age and health permitted in the revolution In 1776 he was in charge of the Hessian prisoners from the British army stationed at his old homestead in Westminster He died August 10, 1803 aged seventy-six His wife Tabitha died December 26, 1822, aged ninety years Mr Whitney was one of the largest property holders on the Westminster tax list of 1798

The children of Nathan and Tabitha (Merriam) Whitney were Tabitha, born June 29, 1753, Nathan, May 16, 1755 died August 28, 1756, Tabitha, July 6, 1757, died January 27, 1764, Nathan, April 9 1760, died July 2 1764, Jonathan, May 14, 1761, died June 21, 1764, Ruth, April 17, 1763, died July 7 1764 Nathan, July 1 1765, David, August 10, 1767, John, October 13, 1769

(VI) John Whitney, son of Captain Nathan Whitney (5), was born in Westminster, Massachusetts He married Elizabeth Stearns, daughter of Josiah and Abigail (Emerson) Stearns December 31, 1793 He settled on the first lot bought by his father, No 90 and built the house now in use as a summer home by the Whitney family of Worcester He died at the early age of thirty-two years, June 25 1802 His widow married James Walker, who died without issue She married (third) Luke Warren, of Hibbardston, by whom she had four children She died October 30, 1838, aged sixty-eight years The children of John and Elizabeth (Stearns) Whitney were John, born January 15, 1795, died February 22, 1796, John, February 20, 1797, Betsy, May 3, 1799, married April 30, 1829, Thomas Merriam, and resided at Westminster, had three children, died July 15, 1888

(VII) John Whitney, son of John Whitney (6), was born in Westminster, Massachusetts He succeeded to his father's estate and lived upon it all his life He married Lydia Allen, daughter of Deacon Ephraim Allen, of Hubbardston (published September 30), 1821 They had a family of eight children, all of whom were of excellent character and reputation He was greatly interested in the education of his children, fitted up a school room in his house, and maintained a private school, the advantages of which were shared by many children besides his own He became a Baptist in middle life and joined the church Later he was chosen deacon In 1843-4 typhoid fever struck down all the members of the household The father, mother and one child died The date of his death was March 15, 1844, aged forty-seven, of his wife December 19, 1843, aged forty-one

Their children were J Emerson, born September 13 1822, married twice, resided at Grafton, Massachusetts, Sumner A, June 27, 1824, married Lura Clarke, had three children, he died August 29, 1861, Ephraim, July 6, 1826, died June 20, 1850, Mary, October 23, 1829, married Charles M Imley, had three daughters, she died February 25, 1859, Harriet, May 29, 1832, married twice, resided in Worcester and Minnesota, had two children, Edward, August 12, 1834, Francis S, March 25, 1840, died January 16, 1844, George Clarkson, September 19, 1842

(VIII) Edward Whitney son of John Whitney (7), was born on the old Whitney homestead in Westminster, Massachusetts, August 12, 1834 He obtained his elementary education in the public schools of his native town In 1852, at the age of eighteen, he went to New York to strike out in business for himself There he remained for four years, holding a position of trust in the Metropolitan Bank In 1856 he came to Worcester, joining his elder brother, Sumner A Whitney, in the stationery business which was carried on in the Butman block for a few years His brother died in 1861 and he continued the business alone He removed soon after to the Bowen block at the corner of Main and Mechanic streets, where he remained for about twenty years Early in the eighties he removed to the present location of the business at 112 Front street Shortly before his death Mr Whitney admitted to partnership his two sons, Edward Cutting Whitney and Harry Sumner Whitney, and they have succeeded to the business which is carried on under the same name The firm does a large wholesale trade in paper and stationery, blank books, manila paper and paper bags, all over New England Mr Whitney occupied a high position in the business community His sterling character was the foundation of the great business success of his business

During the last few years of his life he turned his business cares over to his sons and spent some time in foreign travel visiting various sections of America Europe and the Holy Land, in which he took especial interest He was an active and efficient worker in church and Sunday school When he first came to Worcester he joined the Union Congregational Church and was superintendent of its Sunday school for more than ten years He was also deacon for many years. About 1892 he transferred his membership to the Plymouth Congregational Church. He was president of the Worcester Young Men's Christian Association for two years. He was for several years chairman of the executive committee of the Young Men's Christian Association of Massachusetts. He was president of the Worcester Congregational Club for two years. He was a trustee of the Home for Aged Men. Few men have done more for the religious interests of the city than Mr. Whitney. He never cared for politics to any extent and never considered public office. It has been said of him that he was "interested in whatever was conducive to human welfare and he did much to promote the better life of his adopted city and to lift the world to a higher level." Mr. Whitney died February 5, 1897. He married, November 26, 1857, Susan Louise Cutting, born August 29, 1838, died January 1, 1880. He married (second), October 27, 1886, Emma Louise Rice, who survives him; she is the daughter of William Rice. The children of Edward and Susan Louise (Cutting) Whitney were: Lillie Marie, born in Worcester, June 19, 1867, died August 24, 1868; Edward Cutting, born July 19, 1869; Harry Sumner, born June 1, 1873, married Alice Wright Gibson, of Germantown, Philadelphia, daughter of Alfred C. Gibson, of Germantown; they have one daughter, Louise, born March 30, 1905.

GROUT FAMILY. Of English descent, we find the first representative in this country to be Captain John Grout (I), of Watertown and Sudbury, Massachusetts. He came from England with his gun in his hand and first settled at Watertown. His date of settlement was about 1640, and in 1662 he was granted leave to practice as a "Chirurgeon." A few years later it is found that he moved to Sudbury, where for thirty years he served as selectman. He acquired the title of Captain and was given charge of defending the settlements at Sudbury. May 14, 1648, he testified that, about 1642, Tacomus, an Indian Sagamore or chief man among the Indians at Chapnacunco, came to Boston with his sons and received sundry gifts and favors from Governor John Winthrop. In return he proposed to give Winthrop some land up in his country (Nipmug). John Grout, with others, went to take possession of the land. His eldest son kneeled down on the ground, and Tacomus made his mark to the deed on his son's back, then the father signed it on his father's back, and so one, with all the other sons, the same way, thus abandoning all right of succession to the land. John Grout was recognized as a man of great courage and much wisdom. For forty years he was in charge of the train bands or militia of Sudbury. He was twice married. His second wife was Sarah Busby, widow of Captain Thomas Cakebread. By his first wife Mary he had children: John, born 1641; Sarah, 1643; Joseph, 1649; Abigail, 1655; Jonathan, 1658; Mary, 1661; Susannah, 1664; and Elizabeth.

(II) Jonathan Grout, born 1658, married Abigail Dix, sister of John Dix, grandfather of Dr. Elijah, of Worcester and Dixmont, Maine. Their children: 1. Jonathan, born February 9, 1702. 2. Josiah, born 1703. 3. John, born 1704. 4. Abigail, born 1708. 5. Sarah, born 1711. 6. Patience, born in 1714. 7. Peter, born 1715.

(III) Jonathan Grout, son of Jonathan (2), born February 9, 1702, married Hannah Hurd, June 6, 1743, and purchased the farm referred to and removed from Sudbury to Worcester with his wife and one child in 1744. He died 1748, leaving his widow with three children: 1. Jonathan, born June 2, 1744. 2. Silence, born November 8, 1745, married Josiah Gates, February 20, 1771. 3. Priscilla, born August 13, 1747.

(IV) Captain Jonathan Grout, son of Jonathan (3), born June 2, 1744, when sixteen years of age returned to Worcester, assuming charge of his father's estate, left him by his father. He rendered valuable service during the revolutionary war. He married March 2, 1769, Anna Harrington, who died August 25, 1827. He died October 17, 1828, leaving children: 1. Jonathan, born February 14, 1772. 2. Anna, born September 16, 1774. 3. Francis, born October 30, 1777. 4. Hannah, born May 7, 1781.

(V) Captain Francis Grout, second son of Captain Jonathan Grout (4), born October 30, 1777, remained on the old homestead and became a farmer. True to the loyalty of the Grout family, in early life he enrolled in the Massachusetts militia, April 20, 1804, became sergeant of a company in First Regiment, March, 1809, was made ensign, and a year later lieutenant, and promoted to captain in 1811. He married Aumah Davis, of Templeton, and their children were: Julia Aumah, Sarah, Jonathan Davis. Captain Francis Grout died in Worcester, October 31, 1864, aged eighty-seven years. His youngest child and only son was:

(VI) Jonathan Davis Grout, who succeeded to the old homestead, and married Adeline S. Washburn, 1850, and died, leaving two sons: 1. Francis, born 1851. 2. Charles Henry, born 1854. The latter became a popular music teacher of Worcester, where he still resides. Francis W. inherited the home farm. He was selected a member of the city government, serving as Alderman in 1891-92-93-94.

Jonathan Grout ("Master"), son of Jonathan (4), born 1772, after gaining the advantages of the Worcester schools, entered Leicester Academy and there fitted himself for a teacher. Success as a teacher gave him the title far and near of "Master" Grout. He mastered the book-binding trade as well, and became an extensive dealer in books and stationery in Millbury. He also became a noted author of school text-books, including "The Pupil's Guide to Practical Arithmetic," published in 1802, the first work on mathematics published in this country. His books had a wide sale, as his work was a great improvement over the old hand-written "lessons" and rules on mathematics, which together with his book, are now among the antiquarian relics of the Worcester Society of Antiquity. It is said of him that "he was a Puritan through and through except their faults." He married Sally De Wolfe, of Lyme, Connecticut, and had children: 1. Edwin, born August 4, 1812. 2. Jonathan, born September 24, 1815. 3. Sarah Ann, born February 13, 1820.

(VI) Jonathan Grout, son of Jonathan (5), born September 24, 1815, became a popular book seller and owned Grout's block, coming to Worcester from his native town, Millbury, in 1841. He first started in a small way. After twelve years of remarkable business success, in 1852 he sold his business to John Keith. Other changes occurred in the business, he having it again, but in 1876 it was sold to Putnam & Davis. Mr. Grout built several fine business houses in Worcester and was a well-to-do man. He died April 4, 1882. His grandfather settled in 1744 upon the Grout estate on Vernon street, Worcester, which has remained in one branch of the family ever since. The subject of this notice was the fifth of the same name (Jonathan) in direct line of succession from the progenitor in this country, Captain John Grout of Watertown, 1640. Jonathan Jr. was interested in the making of copying presses, perforated paper, etc., and indirectly through pecuniary investment in the enterprise of Dr. Rus-

John W. Groat.

Jonathan Grout

sell L Hawes, who invented the machines for and produced the first envelopes in the world, which were put upon the market by Mr Grout He was a man of great business tact, energy and sagacity, quick to decide and act His capacity for taking in large transactions was wonderful It was in 1860 that he went in company with L H Bigelow and built another business block He found time from out all his business concerns to devote some happy hours in the cultivating of his finer instincts He loved art and good pure literature He loved nature and was an admirer of birds, trees and flowers in their state of freedom Also, in horticulture and floriculture he took great delight He was a Whig and Republican in politics, but no office seeker He married Mary J Smith, by whom he had children 1 Charles Edwin died in infancy 2 Ellen Mandeville, married George H Gould, D D, who died May 8, 1899, and she then married Rev William S Smith 3 John William, born July 25 1843 4 Mary Elizabeth, married Hiram R Adams

(VII) Lieutenant John W Grout, only son of Jonathan Grout (6), born July 25 1843, was barely old enough to claim a man's standing when he fell a voluntary sacrifice on the altar of his country, in the civil war period He was fine and manly in his features and with elastic vigor, and the "crimson glow of health" he seemed every inch a soldier His was a rare combination of qualities He was an accomplished pianist, was also proficient in mathematics and had an art for drawing, to which he added some knowledge of the French language and of ancient classics In early youth he exhibited signs of military genius A treasured specimen is a whittled dagger with a Union shield on it, now doubly prized He entered the military department of Caleb B Metcalf's Highland school at Worcester and became an expert in tactics This peculiarly fitted him, when the Rebellion opened up, for active, useful service Upon the organization of the Fifteenth Massachusetts Regiment he was welcomed to Company D as its second lieutenant, and he drilled the company until it went to the front True to his retiring nature he chose some secluded spot in which to drill his men

The story of Leesburg (Balls Bluff), October 21, 1861, is familiar to many, and is a matter of war department record but we wish here to make mention of the fact enacted by him of whom we write The Fifteenth Massachusetts Regiment was in the thickest of the fight and suffered great loss Lieutenant Grout was found adequate to his duties His coolness and self-possession astonished all of his men In the terrific showers of leaden hail, Providence shielded him from harm Upon the foe, who would bayonet a wounded soldier, he executed summary wrath Every blow of his own sword told in hand-to-hand contest He declared he would never surrender alive Compelled to retreat, his coolness was still maintained Driven to the bank of the river, he still forgot himself, in the service being rendered to make good the escape of his command With inadequate means for transportation he crossed the stream with the wounded men and returned again the frail boat was filled to its capacity and he remained upon the shore, but he had risked too much for his own safety The remainder were now reduced to the last extremity, and when the young lieutenant went up to his superior, with the calm but heroic enquiry, "Is there anything more I can do?" the reply of Colonel Devens was, 'Nothing but take care of yourself" And when the Colonel cried to his brave men "I shall never surrender!" and with benediction, God be with you all," gave the final order,' Every man for himself," Lieutenant Grout had done his duty, and nobly justified the highest expectations of his admirers After waiting for the first faint glimpse of the rising moon, he threw his incumbrances beyond recovery, and with a few companions plunged into the stream, but before he could reach the opposite shore, the fatal ball of the barbarous assassin left him only time and strength to exclaim Tell Company D that I should have escaped, but I am shot" He was lost in the dark rolling waters of the Potomac, but after some time the river yielded up the treasure and under the flag of his heroic love he was borne from the paternal mansion to the house appointed for all living" We are indebted for the facts here given to a memorial written by Rev E Cutler, soon after the gallant soldier was killed, and it is a priceless gem among the family possessions, and they have thus had it inserted in this volume to further perpetuate the pathetic story of one who gave up his young life to save his comrades—and his country as well

This sketch of the Grout family would be incomplete without a few lines to place upon record some of the accomplishments of a sister of this deceased hero Lieutenant John William Grout Ellen Mandeville Grout was born in the town of Princeton, Massachusetts, at the foot of Mount Wachusett, in the year 1840 Her father soon removed from Princeton, and while prosecuting successful business enterprises in Worcester, the daughter attended the graded schools there, and also attended the Oread Collegiate Institute that famous school founded by Hon Eli Thayer for the education of girls In October, 1862, she was married to Rev George H Gould who two years later was settled as pastor over the old Center Church in Hartford, Connecticut About the year 1870 Dr Gould returned to Worcester, Massachusetts, and for several years was pastor of Piedmont Church He was a very popular and gifted preacher and distinguished for his brilliant oratory He died May 8, 1899 and his widow married for her second husband the Rev William S Smith, of Auburndale Mrs Smith is greatly interested in the subject of conchology, and is the possessor of a large and valuable collection of shells, many of them rare and very beautiful She has given much time to the study of conchology, and has lectured in Boston, Worcester and other places on that subject, illustrating her addresses with selections from her stock of beautiful shells, also with fine water-color designs She presents her subject not so much in a scientific as in a popular way quoting from literature, history and geology She has published a volume of Dr Gould's sermons, which is entitled 'In what Life Consists and Other Sermons," and has written articles for the papers and magazines Mrs Smith has traveled extensively in this country and in Europe

WELLINGTON EVARTS PARKHURST

The family of which Wellington E Parkhurst, who was born January 19, 1835, in Framingham, Massachusetts, is a member, is of ancient English origin, the name appearing as early as A D 1000 The signification of the name is seen in its construction, 'Park" meaning a public ground, and "Hurst" a grove or wood The history of the Isle of Wight mentions a royal park called "Parkhurst Forest" Two centuries ago a colony of Parkhursts migrated from Parkhurst, on that island, to Surrey county, in England from which branch of the family the Americans of this name are supposed to have descended Bishop Parkhurst, of Norwich, England, who died in 1574 is supposed to have been the grandfather of the great-grandfather of George Parkhurst the first settler in America

The descent of the American families from the George mentioned above, was as follows I George living in Watertown, Massachusetts, in 1643 II George, Jr, born in 1618, lived in Watertown III John born in 1644 also resided in Watertown IV John Jr, deacon, born in 1671, lived in Weston V Josiah, born in 1706, also resided in Weston VI Josiah, Jr born in 1736 first settled in Weston and in 1762 removed to Framingham, building a house near "Cutler Mills," later a part of the town of Ashland VII Ephraim born in Framingham, January 16, 1765, a farmer died at the homestead, January 29, 1850 VIII Charles F W, of whom later IX Wellington Evarts, of whom later

Charles F W Parkhurst (father) was born March 5, 1808, in Framingham, Massachusetts, a son of Ephraim Parkhurst a farmer, also the teacher of district schools for twenty-one successive winters Charles F W was educated in the town schools and at Framingham Academy In 1853 he removed to Clinton, Massachusetts, and for twenty-one years was paymaster of the Clinton Wire-Cloth Company also for a part of the time served as clerk at Parker's Machine Works He served as first town clerk of Ashland Massachusetts also several years as a member of the school committee a justice of the peace, chorister of the village choir, and teacher in penmanship During his residence in Clinton, he also served as a member of the school committee board a portion of which time he acted as chairman He was a member of the Congregational church, and served several years as deacon Originally he was an Abolitionist in politics, but later became a Republican On November 8 1832, Mr Parkhurst married Mary Goodale, born in Marlboro Massachusetts, November 18, 1807, and prior to her marriage was a school teacher Mr Parkhurst died February 9 1878, his wife passed away March 15 1887

Wellington Evarts Parkhurst attended the public schools and Framingham Academy In May, 1853, at the age of eighteen, he went to Clinton, taking a position in the office of the Bigelow Carpet Company Later he was paymaster at the Lancaster Quilt Company's mill, and afterwards assistant treasurer of the Clinton Savings Bank He held the office of town clerk six years and for fifteen years was a member of the school board, he also has filled the office of town treasurer, library director and assessor, and for four years was the superintendent of the Congregational Sunday school He represented the Worcester thirteenth district four years in the legislature in the sessions of 1890 91-92 and '93 serving as house chairman of the joint committee on education of public charitable institutions also as house chairman of the state legislative delegation to the Chicago World's Fair visiting in the "Massachusetts House," June 17 1893

For a time during the civil war Mr Parkhurst filled the position of city editor of the *Worcester Daily Spy* and was subsequently promoted to take the chief editorial chair but declined on account of ill health In 1865 he assumed the editorial management of the Clinton *Weekly Courant* which position he still fills, after a continuous service of about forty-one years In 1893 he also became the editor of the Clinton *Daily Item* having served to the present date, a period of about thirteen years On the occasion of a vacancy on the board of trustees of the State Sanitarium for Consumptives, at Rutland Massachusetts, Governor Wolcott, in 1897 appointed him to the position, which he still holds by a reappointment in 1902 At the semi-centennial of the incorporation of the town of Clinton in 1900, he officiated as chairman of the reception committee, and as chairman on the occasion of the public exercises in the town hall In 1904 he was elected by the Republican convention of the fourth Massachusetts district a delegate to the national convention held in Chicago Mr Parkhurst is a member of the Masonic Order, lodge, chapter and commandery A member of the Odd Fellows Order A member of the Massachusetts Press Association, of which he was one of the original members A member of Pomona and Lancaster Granges A member of Clinton Historical Society, of which he was one of the organizers and for ten years the treasurer A member of the Clinton board of trade

On September 13, 1866, Mr Parkhurst married Miss Hattie F Fairbank, of West Boylston, who died December 13, 1885 On August 9, 1887, Mr Parkhurst married Miss Georgiana B Warren, a daughter of George and Pamelia (Eames) Warren, of Framingham, Massachusetts Mr Parkhurst has one sister, Miss Helen Adelaide, for many years a teacher of music and of day schools, also two brothers Rev Charles H Parkhurst, D D, for the past twenty-five years pastor of the Madison Square Presbyterian Church of New York city, and Professor Howard E Parkhurst, organist at the same church, also a teacher of music, a resident of Englewood, New Jersey

GENERAL JOSIAH PICKETT The record of Worcester is no exception to that of other cities in this great Republic, but the reader has only to glance at the long roll of names of patriotic men who, during those trying days of the civil war, responded to the call of President Lincoln and went forth from this city to strengthen the hands of the government and help to preserve the Union, to in some measure appreciate the service her citizen soldiery rendered the country from the spring of 1861 to the close of the war Among those names representing that honored list appears that of General Josiah Pickett, who was born at Beverly, Massachusetts, November 21, 1822 and after attending the common schools of his native town was apprenticed to learn a mechanical trade which he in reasonable time acquired and in the prosecution of which for a number of years he found remunerative employment The prevailing gold excitement induced him in 1852 to make a trip to California, via the Lake Nicaragua route, where after a sojourn of nearly three years, and in the meantime a satisfactory trial at mining, he returned to Massachusetts, and in the early spring of 1855 found a home in the city of Worcester

His military experience began in July, 1840, as a member of Company F, Sixth Infantry Massachusetts Volunteer Militia, and within three years was advanced to a lieutenancy Soon after his arrival in Worcester he became a member of the city guards, and in 1850 was elected a lieutenant of the company When the call for troops came in April, 1861 he was among the first to offer his services and to encourage others to do likewise, and as first lieutenant he left Worcester April 20 with his company then assigned to the Third Battalion of Rifles Major Charles Devens, Jr commanding The battalion reported at Annapolis then proceeded to Fort McHenry, Maryland, where Lieutenant Pickett rendered valuable service during a three months' campaign Returning to Worcester in August he became actively interested in organizing the Twenty-fifth Massachusetts Infantry receiving a commission as captain in September This regi-

Josiah Pickett

ment left Worcester October 29, 1861 and was assigned to General Burnside's forces for service in North Carolina, sailing from Annapolis Maryland, January 9 1862, and after a perilous experience at sea reached the scene of the battle of Roanoke Island in season to receive their baptismal fire on that eighth day of February, Captain Pickett being among the first to effect a landing, and was highly commended for gallantry in this engagement

The battle and capture of Newberne followed, on March 14 and on the 20th he was promoted to be major, in which capacity he commanded the regiment during the Tarboro and Goldsboro expedition, and, upon the resignation of Colonel Upton, on October 29 received a commission as colonel of the regiment Colonel Pickett gave abundant evidence of his courage and capability as an officer and soldier He brought his regiment to a high standard of discipline, rendering conspicuous service in all the subsequent battles and military operations in North Carolina, commanding also with signal ability, the forces and defences at Plymouth, and of the sub-military district of the Pamlico at Washington, North Carolina, receiving honorable mention for such services upon his departure for Virginia to rejoin his regiment in December, 1863

Early in 1864 the Twenty-fifth Regiment was assigned to Heckman's brigade of the Eighteenth Army Corps for service in the Army of the James, and, with his brave and loyal veterans in a new field of operations, Colonel Pickett won further distinction in the severe engagements that followed, notably his gallant repulse of the charging Confederate lines at the battle of Arrowfield Church, May 9 Again in the battle of Drury's Bluff, May 16 at the critical moment in the fight, the intrepid and decisive action of Colonel Pickett saved the Union right from irretrievable disaster In this instance the First Brigade was being severely pressed by the enemy General Heckman, Colonel Lee, with Captain Belger and a portion of his battery had fallen into the hands of the enemy and were prisoners The brigade was in a most critical and serious plight, when the command fell to Colonel Pickett, whose self possession served him at this moment as it had on former occasions He quickly rallied what was left of the brigade, formed a new line of battle and succeeded in holding the enemy in check, thereby protecting the base of supplies at Bermuda Hundred from possible capture

June 3 1864 at the battle of Cold Harbor Virginia, in a most heroic charge upon the enemy's works, the Twenty-fifth losing two hundred and nineteen out of three hundred and two men taken into action Colonel Pickett was severely wounded while leading his brave men through that "Valley of death" and not since the famous charge of the brigade at Balaklava, immortalized in story and in song has greater heroism been displayed So says the Confederate General Bowles in his official report of the battle For his distinguished gallantry upon this and previous occasions during the war he received a commission as brevet brigadier-general to date from June 3 1864, the recommendation for this commission being signed by Brevet-Major-General George J Stannard and endorsed by Major General A E Burnside Major General John G Foster, U S A and Brevet Brigadier General A B R Sprague U S V Disabled from further active service in consequence of his wound and deeply regretting his inability to continue with his brave comrades until the final victory, he reluctantly retired after a service of nearly four years, on January 10 1865 having won the respect and confidence not only of his entire command, but that of his superior officers as well It is not the purpose of this sketch to present to the reader incidents associated with all of the various engagements during the civil war in which General Pickett took part, but merely to mention those in which his conduct as a soldier and military tactician called for the special commendation from his associates in arms and from others knowing the facts and competent to pass judgment upon his patriotic and praiseworthy service

After returning to his home in Worcester, and suffering severely for nearly a year from the wound in his hip the ball was finally extracted, and in October, 1865, General Pickett accepted a position in the Boston Custom House Within a year (namely in September 1866) he received the appointment as postmaster of Worcester, a compliment most satisfactory to her citizens With his characteristic promptness and foresight for the accommodation of the public, he sought new and more commodious quarters, and the postoffice was removed from the old Exchange building to Pearl street, and for twenty years he was the efficient and progressive postmaster of Worcester All reforms that seemed to him necessary for the best interests of the service he adopted, and the capacity of the office grew with public demand, and the present efficient postmaster of Worcester (Mr Hunt) was educated from a boy of sixteen in the Worcester postoffice while it was under the management of the subject of this sketch In fact it may be said that other valuable assistants in that department were also early brought under the same care and training and still continue in service In 1889 he was appointed by Governor Ames a member of the State Armory Commission This choice was made by the governor at a time when it was proposed to erect at the expense of the state of Massachusetts a number of buildings to be used as headquarters for the militia of the state, and the stately structures with their convenient appointments, that may be seen in Worcester, Boston, Fall River Lowell Springfield and other cities within the state attest the good judgment and wisdom of that commission of which General Pickett is still (1905) a member and for the service on which board he possesses special qualifications To the military associations that originated through service performed in behalf of the country General Pickett has given most cordial support While no attempt is made to mention the list it was noted that he is a charter member of the Massachusetts Commandery of the Military Order of the Loyal Legion a member of the Grand Army of the Republic president of the Twenty-fifth Massachusetts Veteran Regiment Association and has been treasurer of Post 10 Relief Fund from its organization In 1894 Hon Henry A Marsh mayor of Worcester selected him to serve as a member of the License Commission and in the discharge of the perplexing duties devolving upon that board his integrity has never been questioned

Since the day of General Josiah Pickett's retirement from the army the citizens of Worcester have sought to do him honor in various ways It was the accepted belief that no street parade of any considerable magnitude either of civic or military nature could be handled in the streets of Worcester without General Pickett as chief marshal in command and it is but fair to say that from the military procession July 4 1865 when the war regiments returned and were received by the citizens of Worcester together with the many subsequent military and civic processions under his direction as chief marshal including the ceremony of laying the corner stone of the new city hall, September 12, 1896 there was no confusion in the line, all moving on time with promptness and military precision

But the latest perhaps the most deserving and lasting compliment paid this quiet thoughtful, modest loyal citizen and soldier, was the placing of his portrait upon the walls of Mechanical Hall, that famous forum of Worcester, the walls of which have echoed and re-echoed during the past half century as works of patriotism fell from the lips of Andrews, Philips, Sumner, Bullock, Devens, Hoar, and others And upon those walls may be seen as companion pictures portraits of Washington, Lincoln, Garfield, Andrews, General Ward, Sergeant Tom Plunkett and many others The presentation speech was made October 30, 1902, by General A B R Sprague, a comrade thoroughly familiar with the military life of General Pickett, and the portrait was received by ex-Alderman Edward M Woodward president of the Worcester County Mechanics Association Both addresses were of high order, and in eloquent language expressed the high estimation in which the subject of this sketch is held by both his comrades and fellow citizens—the man who from the impulse of the hour performed his duty as he saw it, without thought of reward and on account of such service was promoted from lieutenant to a brevet-brigadier-general is certainly worty of respect and special mention The ancestral line of General Pickett has been traced to Nicholas Pickett, who was born about 1649, and an inhabitant of Marblehead, Massachusetts as early as 1670, then a young man about twenty-one years of age He married a daughter of John Northey Of his connection with other families of the same name, or from whence he came to Massachusetts, the records are silent It is believed that by occupation he was a mariner He was living in 1692 He had children Henry born about 1676, Nicholas born about 1678 died 1825, John born about 1680 died May 1763 Dorothy, born about 1682 married Thomas Stevens

(II) John Pickett, born about 1680 died May, 1763 was a fisherman and later a shoreman, residence Marblehead February 16 1727 he bought for 250 pounds a tract of land near the southerly end of the town of Peter Levally He married January 17, 1704, Elizabeth Kelley, a daughter of John and Grace Kelley Elizabeth died 1720 July 22 1737, he bought the mansion house once the homestead of his deceased father-in-law John Kelley John Pickett married (second) October 31 1721 Elizabeth Savory By his will dated April 1 1763 we learn that he was owner of the schooner called the Pelican and one-half of the sloop called the Lizard in which his son John carried on the coasting business The will also mentions a silver tankard Children were John, baptized February 27, 1708-9 Grace baptized July 17, 1709 died young William baptized July 27, 1712 died December 1761, Joseph baptized October 10 1714, died April 11 1775 Elizabeth baptized July 27, 1717, died young Thomas, baptized July 17, 1719-20, died about 1753 Sylvester baptized March 25, 1722 died young, Elizabeth baptized May 17 1724, married Thomas Swan, Jr, living 1763, Nicholas, baptized November 6 1726 died before 1762

(III) Thomas Pickett was a mariner, and was lost at sea about 1753 He married Sarah, daughter of Richard Trevett, Jr, and wife whose maiden name was Elizabeth Ingalls She died 1803 Her great-grandfather Henry Trevett is reported as the earliest resident of Marblehead bearing that family name Their children Sarah, baptized August 23 1743 died young Sarah baptized July 2, 1749 died unmarried, Thomas, born June 27 1750, died July 10, 1819, Elizabeth, baptized July 1, 1753, died prior to 1763

(IV) Thomas Pickett, born June 27, 1750 He removed to Beverly about 1775 where he died July 10, 1819 He was by occupation a sailmaker and married Miriam daughter of Samuel and Mary Striker April 18, 1775 She died in Beverly, August 23, 1839 March 8 1788, he purchased a house and lot of William Abbott, and other real estate transactions were recorded in his name later Their children were all born in Beverly, but baptized in the old Second Church in Marblehead, the parents taking them over the river in a small boat, there being no bridge over which to cross the harbor at that time Their children were Thomas, born December 10 1775, died July 4, 1817, Miriam born May 22 1777, died October 17, 1818, married Moses Howard Martha Trevett, born January 25, 1779, died February 14 1811, married Nehemiah Roundy, Richard born November 8 1780 died December 29 1864, John born July 20 1782 died June 13, 1800, Sarah, born June 22 1784, died February 24, 1809, Samuel Striker born March 8 1786, died November 24 1854, Margaret, born May 31 1788, was the second wife of Nehemiah Roundy, Charles, born April 15 1790 died August 8, 1812 Hannah, born July 9 1792 died December 5, 1818 married Amos Stickney Josiah, born February 19 1795, died February 11 1860, Polly, born March 6 1797

(V) Josiah Pickett born in Beverly February 19 1795 died February 11 1860, married February 10 1822 Mary daughter of John and Mary (Batchelder) Creesy She was born September 12, 1799, and died in 1879 He served in the United States navy, war of 1812 was taken prisoner and confined in Dartmoor prison England After returning home was for some years a seafaring man but finally adopted his former occupation—that of sailmaking Children Josiah, born November 21, 1822 John William, born December 30 1824, shoemaker married Susan H Tucker, Charles born December 12 1826 was a mason in Salem and resided in Beverly Mary Howard born February 3, 1829 died September 25 1833, Sarah Frances born December 25 1830 married Dewing Southwick, Mary Elizabeth born November 13 1832 married Samuel Bell Martha born November 26 1834, married James H Kendall, George Augustus born September 10 1836 married Agnes G Munsey, Hepzibah Ann born June 28, 1843 married (first) Charles L Woodbury, (second) Charles Friend

(VI) Josiah Pickett, born in Beverly, November 21 1822 at the age of thirteen years left his home to carve out his own success in life He married, December 2, 1847, Elizabeth, daughter of Jacob and Anna Burnham born March 4, 1827 Since March, 1855, the family home has been in Worcester, Massachusetts (See sketch) Their children Frank Lewis born January 25 1849 died November 9 1852, William A, born October 12, 1857

The foregoing closes the ancestral record of this branch of the Pickett family to date of July, 1905 There was a John Pickett, who landed at Salem, with Governor Endicott's company in 1628, who removed to New London, Connecticut and subsequently married Ruth, daughter of Jonathan Brewster, and granddaughter of Elder William Brewster of Mayflower celebrity Their descendants are still living in that section of the state The family name also appears among the earliest legislative official and historical records of Virginia and North Carolina and among the conspicuous descendants of more recent date is the Confederate general George E Pickett, of Gettysburg fame in the civil war Descendants of these early settlers are found in many of the southern states

WILLIAM SEDLEY DOGGETT Thomas Doggett (1), the immigrant ancestor of William Sedley Dogget of Clinton Massachusetts, was born in England in 1607 His name is spelled also Dogged Doged and Daggett and many of his descendants have adopted the latter form of the name He sailed for New England in May, 1737, from Yarmouth in the Mary Ann," William Goose, master He was registered as servant to Thomas Oliver of Norwich England, for some unknown reason, perhaps for lack of funds Many of the emigrants who came here to better their fortunes worked out their passage after coming He settled first at Concord, Massachusetts, removed to Marshfield then to Weymouth He was planter and town officer, both at Weymouth and Marshfield In the latter town he was selectman He was fined six pence for being an hour late at town meetings May 18, and August 13 1657 He took the oath of fidelity in 1657 His farm at Marshfield that he occupied in 1659 was adjoining that of Peregrine White, famous as the first child of English parents born in New England The cellar of his house is believed to be in the field back of the house now or lately owned by Asa Sherman, of Marshfield He was a constable in 1660, on the grand jury May 28, 1666 and his name is constantly on the records in various public services and as holding minor offices for many years

He died at Marshfield, August 18. 1692 His first wife died at Concord, August 23. 1642 He married (second) Elizabeth Fry widow of William Fry of Weymouth, and daughter of Jonas and Frances Humphrey, of Dorchester She was probably born in England and died 1652, at Weymouth He married at Marshfield, August 17, 1654 Joane Chillingsworth, widow of Thomas Chillingsworth of Marshfield She was born in England died September 4, 1684 at Marshfield His children John born at Concord 1642, see forward Hannah, born at Weymouth, 1646, married ——— Blancher, Sarah born 1650, married ——— Sherman, Samuel, born 1652 Rebecca, born July 29, 1655, married ——— Wilder

(II) John Doggett, son of Thomas Doggett (1), was born in Concord in 1642 and died at Marshfield 1718 He resided at Marshfield most of his life but in 1662 was at Hingham where he lived for a time His father gave him half the home farm April 20, 1672 and he settled at Marshfield, where he was admitted townsman May 13, 1672 He was constable in 1682 and highway surveyor in 1684 He bought some adjoining land of Justus Eames April 1 1686 for ten pounds, and one of the witnesses was Peregrine White John Doggett and his brother Samuel hired the flats on the South river of the town, probably to cut the salt hay He was admitted a freeman in June 1680 He was on the grand jury, May 18, 1691 and highway surveyor 1692 He held the office of tithingman and other places of responsibility and trust in the town He was admitted to the church May 30, 1697, and was on the jury at Plymouth as late as December 13, 1708

He married (first) at Hingham, 1673 Persis Sprague, daughter of William and Milicent (Eames) Sprague of Hingham She was born there November 12 1643, and died at Marshfield, 1684 He married (second), at Marshfield, September 3 1691, Mehitable Truant daughter of Maurice and Jane Truant of Duxbury He married (third), at Newbury, June 22 1697, Rebecca Brown, widow of Isaac Brown of Newbury, daughter of ——— Bailey She was born 1640 and died at Newbury, August 25 1731 Children of John and Persis Doggett were John, born at Marshfield June 28, 1674, died March 1, 1678-79, Thomas, born 1676, see forward, John, born February 26, 1674, probably died unmarried Children of John and Mehitable were Isaac, born June 7, 1692, died September 21, 1692, Hannah, born December 28, 1693

(III) Thomas Doggett, son of John Doggett (2), was born at Marshfield, Massachusetts, 1676, and died there January 5 1736-37 He gave his son Thomas part of the homestead, February 27, 1701 He was a juror at Plymouth May 10, 1708, field driver, March 21, 1708-09, on the grand jury, January 10, 1710, highway surveyor, hogreeve, etc He was a farmer and prominent in town affairs He married (first), at Marshfield, January 18, 1698-99 by Rev Edward Thompson, Experience Ford, daughter of William Ford, of Marshfield She was born 1676 and died there October 25, 1728 He married (second), Sarah Phillips He died January 5 1736-37 and is buried in Cedar Grove cemetery, alongside the grave of his first wife Both graves are marked with stones His second wife married, at Pembroke, September 7, 1737, Joseph Ford, of that town The will of Thomas Doggett was dated April 19, 1736 The children William, born October 30 1699 died February 16, 1699-1700 John, born 1702, Persis born 1704 Thomas, born 1706 see forward, Sarah, born 1709, died unmarried, September 30, 1745 Experience, born 1714, died at Lebanon, Connecticut 1730

(IV) Thomas Doggett son of Thomas Doggett (3), was born at Marshfield Massachusetts 1706, and died at Middleborough Massachusetts August 11 1788 He married at Marshfield December 11, 1728, by Rev Joseph Gardner Joanna Fuller a descendant of Samuel Fuller, of the 'Mayflower" So all their descendants are eligible to the Mayflower Society Thomas was a yeoman of Marshfield and Middleborough He was executor of his father's estate and was part owner of the sloop Middleborough" in 1732 He sold the homestead March 6 1741, at Marshfield, and bought at Marlboro May 7 1741, settling there before September 7 His will was dated August 30 1785 and proved October 6 1788 Their children, all born at Marshfield were John born 1729 Thomas, born 1731, died young Mark born 1733 died young, Jabez, born March 3, 1734 Seth, born February 15, 1736 Simeon, born January 4, 1738 see forward Experience, born May 1 1740, baptized April 23, 1741 died at Middleborough, 1830, Joanna, born March 16 1742

(V) Simeon Doggett son of Thomas Doggett (4) was born at Marshfield January 4 1738 and died at Middleborough May 6 1823 He and his brother Jabez served in the French and Indian war under Captain Benjamin Pratt being at Oneida Station, New York, September 28, 1758 He was a carpenter by trade, as well as a farmer In the revolution he did not think it right for the colonies to rebel, and as a consequence he was forbidden by the town authorities to leave his farm He and a neighbor who was suffering from the same cause, used to meet daily to talk it over each remaining religiously on his own farm He was a stanch Episcopalian in religion He built his house on the highway from Taunton to Plymouth in the town of Middleboro and it was occupied for many generations by his descendants He married, February 28 1760 Abigail Pratt daughter of David Pratt who was a native of North Carolina The children Thomas born at Middleboro, April 14, 1761 Elkanah born October 27 1762, Simeon born March 6 1765 see forward, Abigail, born March 4, 1775

(VI) Rev Simeon Doggett, son of Simeon Doggett (5), was born in Middelboro, Massachusetts, March 6, 1765, and died at Raynham, Massachusetts, March 20 1852 His early associations were those of an orderly, industrious and pious Puritan home His mother was a native of North Carolina and had brought with her from her southern birthplace the prepossessions of an Episcopal training, and she took care to indoctrinate the mind of her son with the tenets of the English church The sterner influences of Calvinism in his home were softened by the grace of the Arminian liturgy, and while a heretical bias was thus given to the faith of the child an attachment to the English ritual was fostered which no length of years, no change of opinions, no constant use of other methods could weaken His father, though not rich, was in easy circumstances and able to prepare and send his son to college Simeon entered Brown University, where he was graduated in 1788 at the age of twenty-three He taught school for a year at Charlton, Massachusetts His mind was directed to theology, and after being refused admission to one Congregational church, he was admitted by Rev Dr Hitchcock's church at Providence and he began to study He lived six months in a planter's family in Virginia In 1790 he went to live in the family of the celebrated Dr West, of Dartmouth, and studied divinity under this eccentric but able teacher He became a tutor in Boston University in 1791 and held the position five years In May, 1792, he was licensed to preach by the Rhode Island Convention of Congregational ministers and began immediately to supply pulpits and preach at every opportunity One of his early sermons was printed and it was one of the first published in the United States which openly defended Unitarian views

In 1796 Bristol Academy in Taunton was formally opened with Mr Doggett as first preceptor, and his address was another milestone in theological emancipation in New England He accepted a call to settle at Mendon, Massachusetts, and was ordained January 17, 1813 He resigned his position at the academy, but remained on the board of trustees The Mendon church was large influential and supposedly orthodox yet it called him knowing his Unitarian views, unanimously and did not rescind the call when he required a change of the church creed before he became minister After a notable pastorate he was dismissed January 4, 1830 at his own request and settled at Raynham, where he wished to spend his declining years His means placed him above the fear of want, he had a good library and at Raynham leisure to enjoy it He visited the southern states in 1834-35, and preached the sermon at the dedication of the Unitarian church at Savannah He retired from the ministry at Raynham in 1845 His eighty-seventh birthday was celebrated by his townsmen and friends very elaborately and pleasantly He died March 20, 1852 He and his wife made a joint will

He married October 29, 1797 Nancy Fobes, daughter of Rev Perez Fobes, LL D, and Prudence (Wales) Fobes She was born at Raynham, Massachusetts September 8, 1769 and died there December 14, 1854 Their children John Locke, born at Taunton September 9 1798, Samuel Wales born at Taunton, July 9 1800 Simeon born at Taunton, November 11 1802 died in Georgia, July 21 1826. Prudence Wales, born at Raynham September 30, 1804 died at Raynham December 27, 1854 Perez Fobes born at Taunton Massachusetts, June 2, 1806 see forward Theophilus Pipon born at Taunton January 20 1810 Abigail, born at Taunton, November 8, 1812, William Paley, born June 29, 1814, died at Raynham, November 25, 1836

(VII) Dr Perez Fobes Doggett, son of Simeon Doggett (6), was born in Taunton, Massachusetts, June 2, 1806, and died at Wareham, Massachusetts, January 28, 1875 In early life he lived on the farm and his education was obtained largely through his father s excellent library He spent two years in Florida, working for his brother in mercantile business He decided at length that he would study medicine and began in the office of Dr Usher Parsons a distinguished physician at Providence He attended the Jefferson Medical School at Philadelphia for three years, and was graduated at the age of twenty-five years He began immediately to practice in Wareham, Massachusetts, and was fortunate from the outset in winning the confidence of his patients He had a good practice "For forty-four years he went in and out among his friends, neighbors and patrons in his own and surrounding towns, meeting with the success which a man may command who is well equipped for his business" He died suddenly, falling in the street just after making a professional call in apparently full possession of his physical and mental health He was sixty-nine years old

"Dr Doggett was not a brilliant man and in some directions he was as simple-minded as a child, but it is believed that few men bring to the study and practice of their profession more of those peculiar and varied mental and physical qualifications which help to make up the true physician and surgeon"

"Timid and slow in some departments of life, in everything relating to his profession he was always alert quick to see, prompt to act Proving himself the well trained, patient, conscientious physician, whose judgment was not often at fault, he also demonstrated by delicate operations skillfully performed that a brilliant surgeon was only concealed by his narrow field and lack of opportunity"

He married, November 26, 1832, at Wareham, Lucy Maria Fearing, daughter of William and Elizabeth (Nye) Fearing She was born at Wareham, August 27, 1807, and died there October 2 1885 Their children, all born at Wareham, were Charles Seymour, born March 9 1836, resides Brookline, Massachusetts, William Sedley, born November 9, 1837, see forward Anna Maria, born November 5, 1839, married in Sandwich Massachusetts, November 25, 1858, by Rev Nathan P Philbrook, to Walter Danforth Burbank, son of Samuel Burbank, she died March 16, 1870, he was born in Sandwich, 1834 and resided at Wareham, died 1893

(VIII) William Sedley Doggett, son of Perez Fobes Doggett, MD (7), was born at Wareham, Massachusetts, November 9, 1837 He was educated in the public schools of his native town He chose a mercantile career and began as clerk in a Boston dry goods establishment, in which he was employed five years He then went to Glastonbury Connecticut, was associated with his brother in the manufacture of woolen goods and remained in that business for some years He left there to conduct a general store at Warren, New Hampshire, where he remained eight years, doing a modest but prosperous business He removed to Clinton, Massachusetts, and engaged in the dry goods business After a long, honorable and very successful career there, for a period of twenty years he retired in 1897 Mr Doggett has taken an interest in the affairs of Clinton and has invested largely in real estate there He built one of the finest business buildings in the town known as the Doggett Block He is a Republican and has been steadfast in his support of the principles of his party He has never cared for public office He is a member of Clinton Lodge of Odd Fellows, and has been its treasurer for many years

Mr Doggett married, at Auburn, New York, June 21, 1866, Frances Pomeroy Willson, who was born at Auburn, July 5, 1842, the daughter of Harvey and Fanny (Pomeroy) Willson Her father was a merchant at Auburn Their children are Lucy Fearing, born at Auburn, August 7, 1867, married Ernest Silberburg and they have four children, Anna Frances, born at Warren, New Hampshire, May 3, 1871, married Edward Page and they have one child, Amy Willson, born at Clinton, August 31, 1884

MOEN FAMILY The Moen family, for more than a half century prominently identified with the manufacturing interests of the city of Worcester, and whose members have borne a most useful part in promoting the development of its various institutions, financial, educational and religious, is of French origin

Louis Moen and his wife, Madeleine D'Arquienne, came from France about 1808, and settled in the village of Wilna, Jefferson county, New York A son of Louis Moen by a former marriage remained in France, and his descendants still reside in Paris

Augustus René Moen son of Louis and Madeleine (D'Arquienne) Moen, was born in Paris, France, September 1, 1799, and was nine years old when he accompanied his parents to the United States He was educated in Wilna, New York About the year 1830, having made the acquaintance of S H Collins, the famous ax manufacturer of Collinsville, Connecticut Mr Moen removed to that place to accept a position as his business agent, or salesman He subsequently conducted a hardware business on his own account in the city of New York, with residence in Brooklyn, Long Island He afterward made his home in Stamford, Connecticut, where he died, August 24, 1867, after enjoying the entire confidence and esteem of a wide circle of friends He was married, in Utica, New York, October 7, 1823, to Sophie Anne Le Clanche, who was also born in Paris, France, August 30, 1803, daughter of Nicholas and Maria (Pint) Le Clanche, the latter born in Treves, a city of Rhenish Prussia Sophie Anne Moen survived her husband nearly a score of years, dying January 30, 1887 Their children were

1 Philip Louis, see forward

2 Mathilda Louisa born July 11, 1826, in Wilna, New York, married Lewis R Hurlbutt, April 11, 1854 and died January 25, 1881

3 Augustus M, born May 22, 1830, died in infancy

4 Cornelia Ann born October 3, 1832, in Collinsville, Connecticut, married, November 21, 1855, William W Rice, Esq of Worcester, Massachusetts, afterward mayor of that city and member of congress from that district She died June 16 1862

5 Henry A R born September 30 1838, in Brooklyn, New York, married Mary Biddle, of Philadelphia, Pennsylvania and died in London, England November 10, 1887

6 Edward A, born May 31, 1841, in Brooklyn, New York, married Mary Sophia Cram, of Portland Maine, and died, 1903

Philip Louis Moen, eldest child of Augustus Rene and Sophie Anne (Le Clanche) Moen, was born in Wilna New York, November 13, 1824 He began his studies in the town of his birth, and later in turn attended schools in Carthage, New York, Collinsville, Connecticut, and Brooklyn, New York His studies in the later city were preparatory to a course in Columbia College, New York, but an eye ailment necessitated his discontinuance, and he turned his attention to commercial affairs setting himself to learn the details of the hardware trade, the occupation of his father While thus occupied he made the acquaintance of Ichabod Washburn, of Worcester, Massachusetts, whose manufacturing interests required an occasional visit to the city of New York, where he marketed a portion of the product of his mills In the year 1846 the anniversary of the American Board of Foreign Missions was held in Brooklyn, and as delegate to that assembly the elder Mr Washburn, accompanied by his daughter, was assigned for the session to the home of Augustus R Moen, where a friendly acquaintance was formed which later resulted in young Philip Moen coming to Worcester to claim the daughter as his bride

Philip L Moen was first associated with his father-in-law, Ichabod Washburn, at his Grove street works, and later with Messrs Henry S and Charles Washburn in the rolling mill at Quinsigamond village This firm was dissolved January 12, 1849, and April 1, 1850, Mr Moen became a partner with his father-in-law in the wire-drawing industry, where he filled a much needed place, assuming the financial conduct of the business, while Mr Washburn directed the mechanical operations Under the new firm the business prospered and increased in volume and from that modest beginning grew until many acres were covered with the great structures from which went out thousands of tons of wire to assist in the forwarding of civilization throughout the world Mr Moen had the satisfaction of living to enjoy the fruits of his energy and financial ability, coupled with the technical knowledge of such an expert mechanic as Ichabod Washburn At the death of Mr Washburn in 1868, Mr Moen succeeded to the presidency of the corporation, a position which he retained up to the time of his decease

The same characteristics which made Mr Moen so successful in the world of business would also have rendered him a most valuable public official, but the demands of his life occupation were too pressing for many interludes In 1854 and 1855 he was a member of the city school committee, and in 1885, as a presidential elector from the Tenth District he cast an unsuccessful ballot for James G Blaine Mr Moen was always a Republican in politics and ever ready to assist in advancing the principles of his party In his religious affiliations he was a member of the Union Congregational Church and for many years one of its deacons There was nothing relating to the good of humanity that did not receive his hearty and generous support He was a zealous advocate and liberal supporter of the Young Men's Christian Association, was president of its board of trustees, and as a life member he was the second largest contributor toward the construction of the elegant home of the Association now standing in Elm street, in the city of Worcester As an earnest advocate of higher education he lent his efforts in behalf of the Worcester Polytechnic Institute, and was one of its trustees from its founding until his death, a portion of the time serving as treasurer of the corporation He was a director of the Central National Bank president of the board of trustees of the Memorial Hospital director of the State Mutual Life Insurance Company trustee of the People's Savings Bank trustee of the Home for Aged Women director of the Free Public Library, president of the Worcester County Mechanics Association and a member of the Worcester Agricultural Society

Mr Moen was a man of commanding presence, genial, courteous, conscientious, with frank open manners, bearing all the marks of a gentleman of the old school His loss from the social as well as the business world was deeply felt throughout the city, county, and even far beyond their bounds, wherever he was known He died at his home in Lincoln street, Worcester, April 23, 1891

Mr Moen married (first) November 17, 1846, Eliza Ann, daughter of Ichabod and Ann G (Brown) Washburn Their only child, Annie Eliza, died in her third year, March 21, 1854 The mother died January 25, 1853, in her twenty-seventh year Mr Moen married (second) March 26, 1856, Maria Sloan Grant, of Chelsea, Vermont, a lineal descendant of Mathew Grant, one of the first settlers of Windsor, Connecticut Their children were Philip Washburn, of whom further, Sophie, who resides in Boston, Cornelia, died in infancy, Alice, married Arthur Edward Childs, whose home is in Boston

Philip Washburn Moen, eldest child of Philip L and Maria Sloan (Grant) Moen, was born in Worcester, Massachusetts, April 28, 1857 After receiving his early educational training at home, he accompanied his parents during a European tour, and on their return after a final year in the high school, he entered Yale University, where he took the academic course, graduating with honors in 1878 After his graduation he studied for two years in Sweden, after which he spent a year in travel on the continent He then returned home and entered upon his business career, in May 1881, joining the firm of Washburn & Moen, becoming first a director, later the treasurer, and in 1888 added to the latter duties those of general manager, remaining in that twofold position until 1899, when the American Steel and Wire Trust Company purchased the business and plant, Mr Moen being retained as one of the vice-presidents As an executive officer he was ready and decisive, with thorough knowledge of the great industry which was developed to larger proportions under his management Four years after the property was acquired by the American Steel and Wire Trust Company he relinquished connection with it to busy himself with his personal affairs He held positions as a director of the Worcester Trust Company the Worcester Consolidated Street Railway Company the People's Savings Bank, the Worcester Electric Light Company, and trustee of the Massachusetts Lighting Company and the Boston and Worcester Electric Company He was vice-president of the Massachusetts Home Market Club, and a member of the Boston University and Union Clubs also of the University and Yale Clubs of New York city Although a Republican in politics, he seldom accepted public trusts but was a liberal contributor to all legitimate expenses of the party and might have held the office of mayor of the city of Worcester had he been willing to accept a nomination He was from boyhood a member of the Union Congregational Church of which he became a trustee and chairman of the building committee The Memorial Chapel, now a part of the church property was a tribute from him, with his mother and sisters, to the memory of his father, Philip L Moen who was for many years identified with all its interests To the Young Men's Christian Association of Worcester he lent his personal aid and followed his father as chairman of its board of trustees

Mr Moen was married, in Edinburg, Scotland June 5, 1890 to Margaret Brown, daughter of Thomas and Elizabeth (Leishman) Struthers, of that city, her father being a retired manufacturer These parents are now deceased After his retirement from business Mr Moen took special delight in amplifying and beautifying his summer home in the hill-town of Shrewsbury To this attractive country seat was given the name of Ard-na-Clachan, suggested perhaps from his associations with Scottish life and localities Here he erected upon a most sightly outlook a charming residence, where, surrounded by the broad acres of a beautiful farm, he passed more than half his time in superintending the cultivation of fields and the growing of choice varieties of fancy domestic animals in which he took special interest, and which he delighted in exhibiting to the many friends who visited him At the New England Fair, in connection with the Worcester Agricultural Society, in September, 1904, as a member of the committee of arrangements and the reception committee, and also as a department superintendent, he was constant and untiring in his efforts to make the occasion a triumphant success Immediately after the close of the fair, although greatly fatigued, he went on business to Toronto, Ontario returning home September 11th, and on the night of the following day (September 12th) was stricken with apoplexy and passed away His death was deeply felt by the citizens of Worcester That such a generous-hearted broad-minded, public-spirited man with high aspirations, guided as he was by a noble purpose, should be so suddenly removed from his place of usefulness, brought a sharp pang of regret to the community, and called forth the most profound sympathy

COES FAMILY John Coes (1) was born in 1748, probably in Scotland There is evidence that he came from a family of Scotch that lived near the southern boundary, and some of the same name are living in Glasgow now The name is distinct from the family of Coe in this country, at any rate During the Revolution several soldiers by the name appear on the Massachusetts rolls The name was apparently spelled Coas and Coose at times, and incorrectly Samuel Coes, of Marblehead was a soldier in the Revolution Joshua Coes, of Bridgewater (spelled Coesse) and William Coas, of Cape Ann, were soldiers also It is possible that William Coes (or Coose), of East Greenwich Rhode Island, was a relative of the Worcester settler

John Coes settled in Worcester before the Revolution He was a farmer His seven children were born here, and so far as is known all of the Coes in this country are descended from him and his wife Rebecca He died in Worcester June 24, 1827 aged seventy-nine years His children were 1 Daniel born December 10 1776 2 Simeon born July 9 1781 died March 3 1833 He married Sabra, and their children were William, married Lucy H Green April 30, 1835, Simeon Sibley born May 22, 1811, died September 22, 1847, John Green, born July 24 1814 Levi Charles born July 15, 1819 married Charlotte McFarland, November 1, 1846 Mary Augustus born January 22, 1823 died July 8, 1838 3 William, born February 19 1786, died April 17, 1829 He married Jemima Chapin, September 14 1809 Their children were Nancy Chapin born September 10, 1810 Leonard Chapin, born July 7, 1812 William Seth born August 9 1814, Rebecca Salome born December 24, 1816 school teacher at Worcester, married James E Budlong of Providence December 15 1843, William Seth Leonard born May 29 1820 Luther Draper, born October 13 1822 4 Sally, born January 23 1787 married John Pratt, of Fitchburg, Massachusetts, December

Loring Laes

29, 1811 5 Mary, born November 28, 1791, died September 12, 1831 6 Levi, born October 28, 1793, married Kezia 7 Elijah, born May 19, 1795

(II) Daniel Coes, son of John Coes (1), was born and brought up on his father's farm in what is now called New Worcester, December 19, 1776, and died January 26 1838 He married, October 26, 1808 Roxana, or Roxlany (as the records have it) Gates (See Gates Family Sketch) Their children were 1 Sally, born February 22 1810, died February 16, 1832, Loring, born April 22, 1812, Albert, born September 29, 1813, died February 13, 1837, Aury Gates (name originally was Horatio Gates) born January 22, 1816

(III) Aury Gates Coes son of Daniel Coes (2), was born in Worcester, Massachusetts, January 22, 1816, and died December 2, 1875 He married Nancy Maynard, who was born in 1815, and died December 1 1842 He married Ann S Cutting, May 29, 1845 He married (third) a Miss Gibson He married (fourth) a Miss Winch His children were John Henry, born in Springfield Massachusetts, September 25, 1840, Frederick Lewis, Anna Rebecca, born March 25, 1847, Mary, bursar of Radcliffe College, Cambridge, Massachusetts, Stella, died in Dresden, Bavaria and body was lost at sea The business career of the late Aury G Coes is given with that of Loring Coes herewith

Loring Coes, third in line from John, the founder, is the son of Daniel Coes, and was born in Worcester, Massachusetts, April 22, 1812 He has been for many years the nestor of Worcester manufacturers, the most wonderful instance of mental and physical capacity in the history of Worcester, if not of the country At the date of writing he is the active head of the business that he established in 1836, and at the age of ninety-four years is as alert and active as the majority of men are at sixty

Mr Coes spent his boyhood on his father's farm in New Worcester, where he was born He attended the district school in the winter months, but his education has been attained largely outside the schoolroom He is a self-educated, as well as a self-made man At the age of fourteen years he was apprenticed to Anson Braman, of Worcester a carpenter to learn his trade and served with him three years He then worked for Mr Salmon Putnam until he was of age Afterwards he worked for various manufacturers of Worcester, constructing the wooden parts of woolen machinery then in use He had a contract with Henry Goulding and employed six or eight men Among others whom he and his brother worked for was the firm of Kimball & Fuller makers of woolen machinery, and in 1836 they bought the business, forming the co-partnership of L & A G Coes Originally this business was carried on at the mill privilege owned by the Coes interests for so many years, but in 1835, just before the Coes took possession it had been removed to Court mills, where L & A G Coes continued in business until October 1839, when the Court mills were destroyed by fire

This disaster impaired their capital so much that they were unable to continue the business and they went to Springfield to work for Laurin Trask as pattern makers in his foundry While there they invented a new and very convenient form of wrench There were at that time two styles of wrenches in common use, one an English patent the other known as the Merrisk or Springfield wrench Both hands had to be used to adjust either of these kinds of wrenches The Coes wrench could be adjusted by the same hand using it leaving the other hand of the workman free In order to obtain a patent on the device they returned to Worcester and sold the patterns of their spinning machinery, that had been saved from the fire, to Samuel Davis, a manufacturer of woolen machinery With this money they secured a patent, issued to Loring Coes, April 16, 1841

The firm of L & A G Coes proceeded to manufacture wrenches under the patent They were assisted by the late Henry Miller, a hardware dealer and prominent citizen of Worcester He fitted up a shop in the northwest end of Court mill with the necessary machinery and tools, of which he retained the ownership, and he sold for the firm all of the wrenches they made Early in 1843 the firm had paid for its plant, was employing three machinists, and had a contract with Calvin Foster & Co to handle their product The next winter L & A G Coes moved to the shop of Albert Curtis in New Worcester

At the close of their contract with C Foster & Co, April 1, 1848, they entered into a contract with Ruggles, Nourse & Mason to handle their product for the next five years They bought for $5 500 the old woolen mill at New Worcester in which they had worked in their youth With the mill they got two houses and four acres of land, besides the water privilege The famous Captain Daniel Gookin was its first owner, and from him the great-grandfather of Loring and Aury G Coes purchased it, and built a saw mill at the upper privilege where there had been previously a beaver dam When they moved to New Worcester they were employing from twelve to fifteen men, and making from five hundred to six hundred wrenches a month They repaired and raised the mill and put in new machinery and a new water wheel Their contract with Ruggles, Nourse & Mason expired April 1, 1853 and after that L & A G Coes sold their own goods They had made many improvements in the wrenches, and in the special machines used in constructing them

On July 21, 1853 with Levi Hardy the firm purchased from Moses Conant his shop machinery and business, that of the manufacture of shear blades and knives for hay cutting machines The co-partnership continued until May 2 1864 after which the business was conducted by the firm of L & A G Coes, who bought the interests of Levi Hardy In 1865 a dam was built half a mile above their mill privilege to form a reservoir and next year a new shop was built at the reservoir, and devoted exclusively to the manufacture of shear blades, hay cutting knives and similar goods In 1867 a new dam was built a hundred rods below the reservoir The two brothers dissolved the partnership and divided the business Loring Coes had the upper privilege with the knife business, Aury G Coes having the lower one with the wrench business At that time the annual product had increased to ten thousand wrenches or more

In 1871 Loring Coes began to manufacture wrenches also the patents having expired He erected the building at Coes Square for the purpose At the outlet of the upper pond Loring Coes carried on an extensive business in the manufacture of die stock for cutting sole leather and other purposes as well as many kinds of blades

Aury G Coes formed the firm of A G Coes & Co in partnership with his two sons and continued to carry on the very prosperous wrench business until his death in 1875 The sons continued under the same firm name until April 1 1888 when the two Coes firms were consolidated under the name of Coes Wrench Co The officers were President Loring Coes treasurer John H Coes, and secretary, Frederick L Coes The factory was then turning out about fifteen hundred wrenches a day An important patent was issued to Loring Coes in 1880, on the "Knife Handle" or scaled and riveted handle, also his invention, replacing the old round handle made of a single block This model was very successful and was one of the causes that united the wrench business of the Coes family in one concern, as it is to-day Improvements and inventions have followed, and improved models were adopted in 1895 and again in 1901 and 1903 A little more than a month before his ninetieth birthday, Loring Coes bought out the interests of his partners, John H and Frederick L Coes, sons of his former partner, Aury G Coes, and assumed the sole ownership of the wrench business In June, 1902, he consolidated with it the corporation of Loring Coes & Co, Incorporated, making the capital stock of the Coes Wrench Co $150,000 The knife business is conducted as part of the corporation under the name of Loring Coes & Co, Incorporated, Department

The knife business of the Coes family is hardly less famous than the wrench business It has a reputation of producing steel goods of unsurpassed quality and merit Mr Coes has always followed as his maxim in business "Make the best only,—Quality first, Price afterwards" and his reputation is literally world-wide There is not a country in the world where the Coes Wrench is not in use Even in the Levant there is a demand for this indispensable tool Mr Coes not only attends to his business in person, daily, but continues to make improvements and secure patents The business has never been more prosperous than at present

In 1903 a new factory was completed, fifty by one hundred and fifty feet, with an ell fifty by fifty feet and with new machinery and equipment the product of the company was doubled The capacity of the knife shop within a few years has also been increased one hundred and fifty per cent At the present time the Coes factories produce three hundred dozens of wrenches daily about three thousand six hundred, and four and one-half tons of wrenches are completed every day the shop runs The pay-roll includes one hundred and ninety hands, mostly machinists and mechanics of skill and experience The Coes wrench shop is the largest wrench shop in the world

Mr Coes was representative in the general court in 1864 and 1865 He has served the city in both branches of the council, and was for more than thirty years a director of the City National Bank He is a director of the Worcester Electric Light Company For some years he has been the oldest living manufacturer engaged in the hardware trade He is fond of fishing and has for many years made a fishing trip to Maine during the season

The present officers of the corporation are President Loring Coes, vice-president and clerk, Frank Loring Coes, treasurer, Loring Coes, directors Fred W Blackmer and Frederick Searle Mr Blackmer is counsel for Mr Coes (See sketch elsewhere in this work) Mr Searle is a native of St Austel Cornwall England and for fifteen years has been superintendent of the works He is also the master mechanic He worked in the copper mines in Vermont and machine shops in Fitchburg Massachusetts, before coming to Worcester

Loring Coes married Harriet Newell Read, daughter of Russell Read of Attleboro Massachusetts January 14 1835 She died in 1902 Their children were 1 Francis Russell born June 9 1837 2 Ellen Stanley born October 1, 1839, married Melvin O Whittier who was born in Mercer, Maine, May 13 1834, and came to work at the Coes shop at the age of seventeen, worked up until he was superintendent of the manufacturing department in 1865, and became partner of Loring Coes, his father-in-law, when L & A G Coes dissolved Mr Whittier sold out to Mr Coes in 1887 and returned to Maine to live, where he died in 1905 His daughter, Mabel Ella Whittier, married George Churchill, and they have a daughter, Hildegarde Churchill 3 Anna Read, born November 12, 1842, died May 13, 1845 4 Chester E B, lives with his father, never in business

(IV) Frank Loring Russell Coes, son of Loring Coes (3), was born June 9, 1837, in Worcester, Massachusetts He received his early education in the school of his native town Later he attended Leicester Academy and Middleboro Academy Early in life he showed an inclination for the military, and at the age of nineteen was a lieutenant in the city guards When the civil war broke out he took an early opportunity to enlist in the Twenty-fifth Massachusetts Volunteers and served with honor until nearly the close of the war, when by reason of disability he was compelled to return home (For his business relations with the Coes firm and his father's business, see the sketch of Loring Coes preceding)

He married in 1867, Persis J Putnam, daughter of Salmon Putnam (See Putnam Family Sketch) The death of Mr Coes in 1871, at the early age of thirty-four, was doubtless hastened, it not directly due to exposure in the army He left one child, Frank Loring born August 30, 1872

(V) Frank Loring Coes, son of Frank Loring Russell Coes (4), was born in Worcester, Massachusetts, August 30, 1872 He attended the Worcester public and high schools, and took a course at Worcester Academy He also attended a private school at Northboro, Massachusetts At the age of seventeen he went into the shops of the Coes Wrench Co to learn the business He worked in every department and learned the trade thoroughly He was placed in charge of the knife factory in 1892 When Loring Coes bought out his partners in 1902, he was put in charge of the main office He is a member of the Commonwealth Club, the Worcester Golf Club, and the Hardware Club of New York In politics he is a Republican On July 11, 1891, he married Cora Braman, daughter of Charles Braman of Providence Rhode Island Her mother was Priscilla Braman nee Wright, born in Northboro Massachusetts The children of Frank Loring Coes are Loring, born September 17, 1892, Russell Read born August 26, 1894

EDWARD A GOODNOW In 1632 twelve years after the landing of the Pilgrims at Plymouth Rock, three Goodnow brothers sailed from England to join the enterprise beyond the stormy Atlantic They shared the hardships of those who laid the foundations of the Commonwealth of Massachusets Among the three brothers who came to these shores was Thomas, who settled at Sudbury

(II) Thomas Goodnow, son of the English branch, married Jane ————, and had a son named Samuel

(III) Samuel Goodnow, son of Thomas (2), born February 28 1646, married Mary ———— by whom a son Samuel was born

(IV) Samuel Goodnow, son of Samuel (3), born November 30, 1675, died about 1720, married Sarah Brigham, and they had a son Thomas

(V) Thomas Goodnow, son of Samuel (4), born March 18, 1709, married Persia Rice, of Marlboro April 17, 1734, and they had a son Edward

(VI) Edward Goodnow, son of Edward (5),

GOODNOW MEMORIAL LIBRARY, PRINCETON

(Given by E. A. Goodnow, of Worcester)

born October 30, 1742, married Lois Rice, and they had a son Edward.

Edward (6) removed from Sudbury to Princeton, Massachusetts, and in 1786 built the old Goodnow homestead, still standing and owned by his grandson, William B Goodnow, the brother of our subject proper

(VII) Edward Goodnow, son of Edward (6), born December 1776, married Rebecca Beaman He inherited his father's estate Rebecca Beaman took her turn with other girls in going to Worcester, thirteen miles, to get the mail She went on horseback and the trail was through the woods, her only guide being the "blazed" trees To Edward and Rebecca Goodnow were born six sons and two daughters, all were born in Princeton, and with one exception grew to manhood and womanhood These children were Erastus D, Edward A, Jonas B, Franklin, William B, Harriet E Louis R and Abel The father died in 1852, and the mother in 1870, both in Princeton

(VIII) Edward Augustus Goodnow, son of Edward and Rebecca (Beaman) Goodnow, was born at the old homestead, Princeton, July 16, 1810 Although the New England boy of his time had much hard work to perform, yet the people believed in the value of a good education To this lot he of whom we write was no exception to that rule His boyhood days were spent for the most part on his father's farm After attending the district school he attended three terms at Hadley Academy With this schooling he went forth to meet and to do battle with the practical side of life's career In 1823 when he was thirteen years old his parents opened an inn at their homestead on the Connecticut and Boston road So well was the house kept that it soon became famous Teamsters and stock men were only too glad to reach its homelike rooms and sit around its bountiful tables This inn was kept open twenty-seven years Young Edward mingled with the travelers and merchants who stopped there and here he first acquired his taste for mercantile pursuits When twenty years of his life had passed, he left the scenes of farm life and began clerking in the store of his older brother Erasmus Goodnow, in Princeton It was soon discovered that he had sought and found the calling for which he was especially adapted So well did he succeed in his new role that at the end of two years service, he was admitted as a partner in the business Quick to observe the trend and fashion of the times, this firm soon improved their golden opportunities and commenced the manufacture of palm-leaf hats, in connection with the general merchandise business the junior partner performing much of the outside work His early farm life fitted him well to care for such matters, including the teaming for the firm For several seasons he might have been seen rising at two o'clock in the morning and driving to Boston a distance of forty-five miles There he would sell such commodities as his load from his country home was made up of and reload with goods and supplies bought in exchange, to be used in the general store at home Much of the time consumed by such long and frequent trips was made while others slept But it was a good schoolmaster to him Antagonism is the law of development and hence these early hardships proved but stepping stones to a marked and prosperous career

Like many other sensible and thoughtful young business men, Mr Goodnow sought out a loving wife in the person of Harriet Bagg of Princeton After five years of married life the angel of death called her from his side Subsequently he married her sister, Augusta, by whom one son was born, Henry Bagg Goodnow, who died in infancy Affliction again settled down on the household of Mr Goodnow and death claimed the second companion Later he married Catherine B Goodnow, who journeyed with him for a quarter of a century and who was an active member of the Congregational church for about twenty-five years, when she passed from earthly scenes

In 1836, after four years of partnership, the business was expanded by admitting another member to the firm, with the view of manufacturing shoes The new firm relations existed eleven years, when Mr Goodnow realized that the domain of Princeton was limited as a trade center for the carrying out of his plans, so, after having been in trade in his native town fifteen years in all, he went to Shelburne Falls in 1847, where he formed a partnership with the great cutlery establishment of Lamson, Goodnow & Company, but soon finding the damp air of Deerfield Valley did not agree with him he removed to Eaton, central New York, remained there for a time, and finally returned to New England and located at Worcester, in 1852, when the city had but 18,000 people Being familiar with the shoe business Mr Goodnow opened a retail shoe store, which he pursued for four years, and then changed to the wholesale trade in the same line of goods To him belongs the honor of opening the first jobbing house in Worcester Success crowned his efforts, and sales ran from one hundred thousand to four hundred thousand dollars per annum Integrity in his business methods was the key to his success After a successful business of fourteen year in Worcester, Mr Goodnow retired from active mercantile life

Concerning the political belief of Mr Goodnow it should be said that he was one of the stanch Abolitionists, when it meant something to advocate such a cause He was one of eight persons to adopt the principles of the Free-soil party, and subscribe to the principles, "We inscribe on our banner, 'Free soil, free speech, and free men' and under it we will fight on fight ever until triumphant victory shall reward our exertions" When gun number one sounded the alarm from Fort Sumter in 1861, he was not surprised More than a dozen clerks from his own place of business, one after another, marched to the battlefield, all were aided by him, and one of the brave number was under full pay by him during the entire time of his military service and his business place open for him upon his return from the Southland when victory was for the Union When Governor Andrew proposed to raise a colored regiment and equip it for the field, he gave five hundred dollars for its expenses, heading the subscription paper for that amount When the war cloud was darkest and the finances of the country were in peril he subscribed liberally for the first bond issued He thoughtfully erected marble tablets to the memory of fifteen high school students who gave their young lives on the altar of their native land As an object lesson to the youth of the city, he placed a bust of General Grant in the high school Among other benefactions was a life sized oil portrait of President Garfield, to be hung in the hall of the Mechanics' Association The following resolution was passed by the Association

Resolved That the Worcester County Mechanics Association hereby tenders a note of thanks to Mr Edward A Goodnow for his public spirited liberality in presenting to the association a full length portrait of James A Garfield late president of the United States Attest

WILLIAM A SMITH Clerk

A few years later he presented the same association with a portrait of Henry Wilson

Mr Goodnow was never an office seeker, but did hold the position of trustee of the State Reform School, under appointment of Governor Andrew and by re-appointment by Governor Bullock, serving in all seven years Upon retirement from business, he spent two years in leisure, but that was enough to convince him that man is happiest when employed, so he accepted the position of president of the First National Bank, tendered by a unanimous vote Here Mr Goodnow was not a figure-head, but the real head All the paper passed through his hands He took some risks that more timid men would not have dared to take He secured large deposits by a liberal attitude toward patrons of the bank When he took the office, the bank stock was quoted at one hundred and ten, but under his good management, the par value was doubled So much was his business sagacity appreciated by the stock-holders, that a set of complimentary resolutions were passed thanking him and giving him the credit for building up a great banking business—second to none in the Commonwealth While Mr Goodnow was a busy man of affairs, he found pleasure in spending much of his means in way of magnificent gifts of a philanthropic and truly charitable nature He gave not to be seen of men, but where good could be accomplished—where the condition of his fellow men could be bettered The list of such generous acts is indeed too lengthy to insert in a work of this character but a few will here be noticed briefly Beginning with his native town, Princeton, he gave a library building known as the Goodnow Memorial Building," which consists of a library, reading-room, two school rooms, with desks for forty scholars each, together with an endowment of five thousand dollars This is indeed a magnificent memorial, a thing of beauty is a joy forever" To educational institutions, he has ever been more than generous Among such instances may be named the Female Seminary at Mount Holyoke in way of scholarship, parks and other matters, all amounting to twenty-five thousand dollars He gave to the Iowa College at Grinnell ten thousand dollars to replace buildings destroyed by a terrible cyclone Subsequently he gave five thousand dollars for the erection of a cottage named the Mary Grinnell Mears, in honor of the wife of Rev D O Mears, D D To the Wellesley College and the Moody School at Northfield he gave each five thousand dollars His anti-slavery sentiments were expressed by the gift of five thousand dollars to Washburn College in Kansas, to found a John Brown professorship The colored race has not been overlooked by the philanthropist, for he has repeatedly been a contributor toward the erection of buildings for the colored school at Hampton, Virginia, also at Oberlin, Ohio, Berea College, Kentucky, and Lincoln College, Pennsylvania Not content with the donating of his wealth on this side of the seas, he was the first man to erect a building on the continent of Africa for the education of women Thus he commenced the laudable work of Christianity and civilization among the female portion of "Darkest Africa" This is in connection with the Huguenot Seminary, Wellington, Cape of Good Hope, Africa The building known as Goodnow Hall was constructed after Mr Goodnow's plans and then shipped to Africa ready to be erected The expense was over fifteen thousand dollars

In connection with his church benefactions it should be here recorded that he was long associated with the Plymouth Congregational Church of Worcester, to which he was a very generous donator as the years and decades rolled by Among these benefactions must not be forgotten the superb chime of bells which each week sounds from the belfry of this church edifice The same was given in memory of his late wife, Catherine B Goodnow, also, as a memorial of his only son, Henry B Goodnow, who died in infancy, he gave an organ to this church, the total expense being ten thousand dollars In 1887 he gave five thousand dollars toward the Catherine B Goodnow Fund of the Young Women s Christian Association of Worcester Toward the completion of this magnificent building he gave not less than thirty thousand dollars

Although having lived four score and three years, until recently he of whom we write saw with undimmed eye, and was exceptionally robust for one so far advanced on the journey of life He was a constant attendant at the church of his choice Indeed, the life of Mr Goodnow was one of marked success and of such noble characters the world has none too many He died February 1, 1906, after an illness of only two days, and a large concourse of sorrowing friends followed him to his last resting place

SAMUEL R HEYWOOD In sketching the useful and eventful career of Samuel R Heywood, founder of one of the most enterprising and successful manufacturing establishments of the city of Worcester, it is to be noted that his influence has touched almost every branch of trade and public interest in his community within the period of more than a half century He has not only been one of the principal factors in making Worcester an important manufacturing center, but a leader in the promotion of various other enterprises—financial, commercial, transportation, etc He has rendered valuable service to the public in various official stations, and has liberally aided with his influence, personal effort and means, all that goes to make up the higher life of the community—the churches, schools of all degree, and those beneficent institutions which minister to the needs of the suffering and afflicted In all the relations of life he has so acquitted himself as to receive sincere recognition as an ideal citizen

Mr Heywood was born at Princeton, Worcester county, Massachusetts, November 24 1821, and was reared upon a farm, where he developed attributes of a model manhood—a splendid physique, which enabled him to carry into his octogenarian years the ambitions and abilities which in ordinary men wane in the sixties, and those habits of industry and persistency which were to form the foundations of a career of unusual usefulness and success As a lad he attended the ordinary country schools, and was for two terms a student in the Westminster Academy, defraying his expenses with the earnings from his own labors When about twenty years old he entered upon a business life as an employe of E D and E A Goodnow, of Princeton, manufacturers of boots and shoes, and proprietors of an extensive general store In August, 1848, he located in Hubbardstown, as senior member of the firm of Heywood & Warren, general merchants, bringing to the business a small amount of capital of his own earning, and a character which afforded him all the credit he desired In the course of three years he purchased the interest of his partner, and carried on the business until January, 1855 This experience marks the end of his preparation for the larger enterprises upon which he was now to enter He had not only acquired considerable means, but he had developed his business abilities to such a degree as to justify him in seeking a wider field for his effort, and he decided to remove to Worcester Here he became a partner of one of his first employers, E A Goodnow, under the style of Goodnow & Heywood, in the wholesale and retail boot and shoe trade This partnership was dissolved in the following year, Mr Heywood taking the retail trade, in which he continued until 1864 He at once engaged in the manufacture of boots and shoes, extending his operations from time to time, constantly reaching out into larger and more distant markets, and introducing new goods as experience demonstrated their worth and acceptability The Heywood boot soon came to be known as the best product in its line, from what was for many years the leading city in the country in this class of manufacture Later, as a more cultivated taste warranted the making of a lighter and more dressy style of foot wear, he turned his attention to the manufacture of that style of goods At whatever stage, his house maintained its high reputation by its use of only the very best obtainable materials, the most finished workmanship, and strictly honorable business dealings To the present time the product of the Heywood factory is the standard in men's high-grade foot wear, stylish, perfect fitting and durable made in all the leading styles and shapes, and in sizes and widths to fit any foot Aside from the great and constantly increasing demand for the Heywood goods from every part of the United States, for fifteen years past they have been extensively sold in Canada, England, Honolulu Havana, Buenos Ayres, Cape Town, and other foreign markets The constant development of this industry necessitated various enlargements of the factory and changes in the managerial force In 1879 Mr Heywood erected the Wachusett building on Winter street which was then one of the largest and best equipped boot and shoe factories in the country This establishment, after repeated enlargements, now occupies a frontage of one hundred and forty feet on Winter street eighty-five feet on Harding street, and a wing ninety-one feet in depth at the east end, near Grafton street, all the principal buildings being five stories in height The plant is equipped with the latest and most improved machinery, and is a model one in every respect At whatever stage of the development of this gigantic enterprise, Mr Heywood has given to it his close personal attention maintaining a close oversight of every detail—the selection of material, the operation of the machinery at every step of manufacture besides keeping a close touch with the market, its conditions and possibilities and introducing innovations in style of goods, seeking new outlets for his product, and, in short ever maintaining for his house a position of leadership which was unquestioned throughout the country As they came of proper age, Mr Heywood introduced his sons to the business, as will appear in connection with their respective names In 1884 the Heywood Boot and Shoe Company was incorporated with Mr Heywood as president, a position which he has occupied to the present time abating nothing of his deep personal interest, and exercising general managerial powers

While thus busied with the building-up and conduct of a great establishment which would seemingly tax the abilities of any one man, Mr Heywood has given his aid to various enterprises having a large place in the business life of the city In 1865 he became a director in the Central National Bank of Worcester serving as such until February 1903, when that institution was absorbed by the Worcester Trust Company In 1864 he was also a charter member of the People's Saving Bank, and a member of its board of trustees and finance committee from that time until July, 1884, when he became president, in which position he still continues He has also for many years been a director in the Cotton and Woolen Mutual Insurance Company of Boston In all these various positions he has displayed the same high ability and conscientiousness which have characterized him in his personal concerns He has besides, rendered inestimable service to the community and commonwealth in various important positions where he labored with rare sagacity and unfailing devotion to the interests committed to his keeping He was a member of the common council in 1859 and of the board of aldermen for two years following In 1873 and 1874 he was again elected to the common council, and in the latter year was president of that body In 1875 he represented the city of Worcester in the Massachusetts house of representatives, and was re-elected for the two succeeding years, serving on the railroad committee each year He was an ardent admirer of that splendid old-school statesman (and his intimate personal friend) Hon George F Hoar, was an early and efficient advocate of his election to the United States senate for his first term and as a member of the legislature was largely instrumental in effecting a result which gave to the country the services of one of its grandest men A man of strong convictions and unflinching moral courage, Mr Heywood has never allowed considerations of personal popularity or expediency to govern his conduct as a citizen He was an original "Free Soiler," and cast his first vote for James G Birney for president, and labored in his behalf as zealously as though defeat were not foreordained Mr Heywood aided in the organization of the Republican party in 1856, and was ever a vigorous upholder of its principles In his political conduct he only regarded legitimate and honorable ends to the good of the nation and community regardless of all personal considerations That he held office from time to time was in no instance due to his self-seeking but to the estimation in which he was held in the community as a man well equipped in heart and brain for the service of his fellows His well known interest in education and his broad humanitarianism led to his being called to connection with the system of state charities of the commonwealth In 1877 he was appointed by the governor a trustee of the State Reform School at Westboro and he was one of the seven trustees retained by that executive out of the entire number (twenty-one) when in 1879 the state schools at Monson Lancaster and Westboro were by act of the legislature consolidated under one management He held this position until 1888 giving to its duties much thought and labor, marked with a genuine feeling of sympathy for unfortunate youths, and a spirit of genuine helpfulness toward them He has always been among the foremost in the establishment and maintenance of the ennobling institutions of this city, and one of his most highly appreciated acts was the creation of the much needed library at the Memorial Hospital His example and precept have ever been recognized as a power for practical temperance Without pretension to oratorical powers, he possesses the faculty of impressing his hearers through his evident sincerity A Congregationalist in religion, he was formerly with the Salem Street Church, and with Plymouth Church from its organization He was prominent in its creation, active in all pertaining to its interests especially in connection with the erection of its edifice and the extinguishment of its building debt His personal benefactions are ever liberal being freely bestowed for legiti-

Obadiah B Hadwen

mate religious, moral and charitable work abroad as well as at home His personal character is best discerned by considering the relations which have ever subsisted between himself and his hundreds of employees, who recognize in him a appreciative personal friend as well as a just and kind employer A half century of uninterrupted business life is a record made by but few men of large affairs, yet today, thanks to his native vigor of mind and body, pure life and equable disposition, he maintains an active interest in the great business with which his name will ever be associated, and in all the varied community interests which have engaged his attention during his entire career

In June, 1856, Mr Heywood married Harriet Butler Milliken, daughter of Z T and Anna B Milliken, of Chelsea, Massachusetts, natives of Franklin county, Maine Of this marriage were born five children, three of whom were sons, two coming to maturity, one passing away in infancy and one still remains to share with his father the duties and responsibilities of his large concerns The children were

1 George Ezra, born January 26, 1859, died the following month

2 Frank Everett Heywood, born April 20, 1860 He was most promising from his youth When seventeen he graduated from the Worcester Classical High School, and was then for a year a student at Easthampton He entered Harvard University, where he was not only a close student, displaying a special interest in chemistry, but was prominent in athletic sports He graduated with the class of 1882, and the same year was admitted to partnership with his father as a member of the firm of S R Heywood & Company At the incorporation of the Heywood Boot and Shoe Company in 1884 he became vice-president and treasurer, and served in that twofold capacity until his death, October 25 1899 He was also a director in the Citizens' National Bank of Worcester He was a man of excellent business ability, and admirable personal character—qualities which marked him as, in the course of events, the fit successor of his honored father in the headship of the Heywood Company He died universally mourned, and it was noted by a local chronicler that seldom had the city seen evidence of such sincere and general grief as that which followed him to his untimely grave December 18, 1884, he married Harriet Dodd Jennings, born December 4, 1864 daughter of Horace N and Maria (Dodd) Jennings, of East Orange, New Jersey His widow resides in Worcester, with her children Chester Dodd, born October 12, 1887, Philip Butler, born March 24 1889, Florence Blair, born May 18, 1893 Richard, born May 8, 1897

3 Caroline Louise Heywood, born September 13, 1862, died September 16 1866

4 Henrietta Butler Heywood, born May 15 1865, died November 25, 1868

Albert Samuel Heywood, only surviving son of Samuel R Heywood, was born May 31, 1867 He was fitted for college in Worcester High school and Worcester Academy He was graduated from the Massachusetts Institute of Technology with the class of 1892 He became connected with the General Electric Company of New York, and was winning distinction in the world of electrical science when occurred the death of his brother, Frank Everett Heywood and this untoward event made it desirable that he should abandon a calling in which he was deeply interested in order to share the burdens of the father He accordingly resigned his position January 1, 1900, and became vice-president and treasurer of the Heywood Company the positions which had been rendered vacant by the death of his brother Taking up his new duties methodically and with cheerful alacrity, he has proven himself an earnest and devoted man of affairs and a worthy companion as well as son to his honored parent September 28, 1899, he married Laura Chester Foute, of Atlanta, Georgia, who was born in Adairsville, Georgia, October 30, 1873, daughter of William Edward and Eliza (Houston) Roberts Foute Their children are Edward Foute Heywood, born July 17, 1900, Harriet Butler Heywood, born August 16, 1901, Dorothy Heywood, born October 5, 1902

OBADIAH BROWN HADWEN, who enjoys national reputation as a scientific horticulturist and pomologist, is a native of Rhode Island, born in Providence, August 2, 1824, son of Charles and Amy Sherman (Brownell) Hadwen He comes of sturdy English ancestry, descending from John Hadwen, of Rochdale, England, who was a settler in Newport, Rhode Island, in early colonial days His great-aunt was the wife of Obadiah Brown, who was prominent as a pioneer in the cotton-spinning industry in America Charles Hadwen, father of Obadiah B Hadwen, was a resident of Providence, Rhode Island, where he was a leading manufacturer and merchant In 1835 he retired from these occupations and removed to Worcester, Massachusetts, and purchased and located upon the Wing Kelley farm, near Tatnuck

Obadiah Brown Hadwen attended in turn the Friends' Schools in Providence, Rhode Island, the Clinton Grove Institute in Ware, New Hampshire where he was a student for four winters' terms and the Worcester (Massachusetts) Manual Labor School, where he remained for one term The principal preparation for his peculiarly useful life work however, was obtained upon the parental farm near Tatnuck, where he developed those tastes and capabilities which marked his career In 1844, the year before attaining his majority, he came into possession of a portion of the home farm which he has since occupied for the long period of sixty-two years For forty years of this time he followed market gardening, and a nursery and dairy business Meantime he greatly enhanced the value of the property by the erection of new buildings But his principal delight was practical and scientific agriculture and horticulture, and in these lines his deep knowledge and sound judgment found general acknowledgment He adorned his grounds with trees of his own planting, in great profusion, of the most beautiful specimens of their kind, many which were unknown in that region until introduced by him, and which have attracted the admiring attention of horticulturists from every part of the United States Amid the changes incident to the great expansion of a thriving industrial city, the rural surroundings of his farm have been almost entirely obliterated, but his immediate home and the grounds pertaining to it have been preserved intact—a veritable *rus in urbe*

Mr Hadwen's accomplishments as a horticulturist found early recognition and for more than half a century he has been known as the leading exponent of those interests which he has labored so earnestly and usefully to promote He early became connected with the famous Massachusetts Agricultural Club, organized April 4, 1840, and was for many years its president and is now a most active member, and he was long vice-president of the Worcester County Agricultural Society, of which he is yet a trustee His unusual abilities also found legislative recognition and he was for many years a trustee of the Agricultural College at Amherst, where, under his direction in the capacity of chairman of the board, many important additions and salutary innovations were made He became a member of the Worcester County Horticultural Society in 1847, serving that body as trustee, vice-president and president, and he was re-elected to the latter office in 1895, after a period of twenty years from his first incumbency and has since been re-elected no less than twelve times He has also long been a prominent member of the Massachusetts Horticultural Society and the American Pomological Society In 1867 he was made one of the commissioners in charge of the public parks of Worcester, and the great value of his services in that capacity is evidenced by his continuous reappointment For several years he was chairman of the parks commission, and he still holds membership in that board This brief epitomization of his life work sets him forth among the most valuable members of the community—one who, in love of nature, delightedly holds communion with her visible forms, and brings her refining and uplifting influences to bear upon all about him, conveying the lesson that contentment and peace and most real happiness comes to him who nestles closest to nature's heart And so it is not strange that in religion he adheres to the tenets of the Society of Friends He was originally a Whig in politics, and his abhorrence of human slavery led him to identify himself with the Republican party on its organization, and he cast his vote for its first presidential candidate, General (then Captain) John C Fremont An ardent Unionist and an appreciative admirer of Abraham Lincoln, he was a firm upholder of that great statesman in his struggle for the vindication of the national authority and the re-establishment of the Union His natural tastes and habits of mind forbade him taking an active part in political affairs, but he suffered himself on one occasion to be elected to the common council of Worcester, and was a valued and efficient member of that body in 1868-69

Mr Hadwen married, December 25, 1845, Harriet Page, of Westminster, Vermont, a descendant of an honored revolutionary family of that state Three children were born of this marriage A son, William E Hadwen, is deceased, and another, Charles Hadwen, is a prominent produce merchant in Chicago, Illinois A daughter, Amy, is the wife of John H Coes, of the Coes Wrench Company of Worcester, Massachusetts

CHANDLER FAMILY William Chandler (1), the immigrant ancestor of one of the foremost families of Worcester county, to which John Greene Chandler, of Lancaster belonged, was born in England and settled early in Roxbury Massachusetts. He was there in 1637 and was one of the proprietors He was admitted a freeman May 13, 1640 His homestead consisted of twenty-two acres The following, from the Roxbury records, gives a contemporary opinion of him "He lived a very religious and godly life among us and fell into a consumption to which he had a long time been inclined, he lay near a year sick in all which time his faith, patience and holiness and contentation so shined that Christ was much glorified in him He was a man of Weake parts but Excellent faith and holiness, he was a Very thankful man, & much magnified God's goodness He was poor but God prepared the hearts of his people to him that he never wanted that which was (at least in his esteem) Very plentiful and Comfortable to him he died about in the yeare 1641 & left a sweet memory behind him" Rev John Eliot wrote "A Christian, Godly brother" He was buried January 19, 1641-2

His widow Annis married (second), July 21, 1643, John Dane, of Barkhamstead and Bishop's Stortford, Hertfordshire England, and Ipswich and Roxbury, in New England Dane died at Roxbury and was buried September 14, 1658 She married (third), at Roxbury, August 9, 1660, John Parmenter, of Sudbury, a prominent man there, selectman 1641

The children of William Chandler were 1 Hannah, born about 1629 in England, married, December 12, 1646, George Abbot, (second), 1690, Rev Thomas Dane 2 Thomas, born about 1630, married Hannah Brewer 3 William, born in England, married (first), August 5 or 18, 1658, Mary Dane, of Ipswich, married (second), October 8, 1679, Bridget Henchman, widow of James Richardson 4 John, born February 16 1658 married Elizabeth Douglas 5 Sarah, born at Roxbury, married (first), November 4 1659 William Cleaves, (second) —— Wilson, (third), October 11, 1688, Ephraim Stevens, (fourth) ——— Allen

(II) Deacon John Chandler, son of William Chandler (1), was born about 1635 He married, February 16, 1658, Elizabeth Douglas, of Woodstock, Connecticut She died in New London Connecticut, July 23, 1705 She was born in England about 1610 the daughter of William and Anna (Mattle) Douglas He and his wife were admitted to the church May 28, 1665 He was active in the settlement of Woodstock and served on important committees He had first choice of a home lot and he took one situated on the brook on the highway at the north end He was selectman of Woodstock in 1693, 1694, and also moderator in 1694 He was on the committee to build a meeting house on Plaine hill, nearly in front of the Bowen Mansion He was one of six who bought the Moshamoquet Purchase of James Fitch, of Norwich Deacon Chandler died April 5, 1703, aged sixty-eight years By his side in the graveyard at Woodstock are buried a number of his descendants His will was dated June 1, 1702

The children of Deacon John and Elizabeth Chandler, all born in Roxbury, before their removal to Woodstock, were 1 John, born March 4, 1659, died young, and his gravestone bears the earliest date of death of any of the family in America as recorded by gravestones 2 Elizabeth, born February 20, 1661, married, November 18 1680 Robert Mason, of Roxbury 3 John, born April 16, 1665. 4 Joseph, born April 3 1667 died in Roxbury, September 29 1668 5 Hannah born September 18, 1669, married July 7, 1685 Moses Draper, of Roxbury 6 Mehitable, born August 24, 1673, baptized June, 1673, married, June 25, 1695, John Coit, of New London 7 Sarah born November 19, 1676, died July 3, 1711 married (first), June 9, 1697, William Coit, of New London (second) September 2 1708 John Gardiner, of Gardiner's Island 8 Joseph born June 4 1683 married, June 29, 1708, Susannah Perrin, of Roxbury

(III) Hon John Chandler, son of Deacon John Chandler (2), was born at Roxbury, Massachusetts, April 16, 1665 He married November 10, 1692, Mary Raymond, of Woodstock who was born March 12, 1671-2 the fifth child of Deacon John Raymond, who married December 10, 1652, Elizabeth Smith, daughter of Nehemiah Smith Deacon Joshua Raymond was the eldest son of Richard and Judith Raymond of Salem Mrs Chandler died April 8 1711 aged thirty-nine years, and is buried on Plain hill Woodstock There is an interesting tradition in the family of Mrs Joshua Raymond and Captain Kidd whom she had entertained at her house for some time It is said but not universally believed that when the blithesome pirate left her hospitable roof he filled her apron full of gold, jewelry and costly plunder Mr Chandler married (second), November 14 1717, Esther Butman, widow of Palgrave Alcock

John Chandler was town clerk of Woodstock in 1690, 1691 1692 and 1694, and selectman in 1693 and 1694 He resided several years at New London, where four of his children were born In 1698 he had a tavern license there He returned to Woodstock to live and was surveyor of the town in 1703 deputy to the general court in 1711, Woodstock then being in Massachusetts When the county of Worcester was established he was appointed judge of probate He held the first probate court in the meeting house of Worcester July 13, 1731 He also held the court of common pleas and general sessions August 10, following The county was organized April 2, 1731 Judge Chandler's son John was appointed clerk of the courts Judge Chandler held his position as judge of these two tribunals until his death One of his sons, John, Jr, succeeded him on the bench, while another, Thomas Chandler, became a judge in Vermont, where he had settled Judge Chandler was for forty years a commissioner of the peace and was seven years in his Majesty's council He died at Woodstock, August 10, 1743, in his seventy-ninth year

The children of John and Mary Chandler, born at Woodstock or New London, were John, born at New London, October 18, 1693, of whom later, Joshua, born February 9 1695-6, married Elizabeth Cutler, William, born November 3, 1698, married Jemima Bradbury Mary, born April 30, 1700, married John McCoy, Elizabeth born May 13, 1702, married Joseph Frizzell, Samuel, born January 5, 1703-4, married Dorothy Church, Sarah, born October 11, 1705 died March 7, 1721-2, Mehitable, born at Woodstock August 10, 1707, married, 1747, Thomas Buckminster, of Brookfield, Thomas, born July 23, 1709, married Elizabeth Eliot, Hannah, born March 27, 1711 died May 23, 1711

(IV) John Chandler, son of John Chandler (3), was born at New London, Connecticut, October 18, 1693 He married, October 23, 1716, Hannah Gardiner, on the Isle of Wight, off Long Island She was born December 11, 1699, and died January 5 1738-9, in Worcester, and was buried on the Worcester common Her grave with the others has been covered from sight, and the stones covered, for some inscrutable reason She was descended from Lion Gardiner who came over in 1635 and married Mary Williams, daughter of Dericke Williams and Hachim Bastians Williams; he bought the Isle of Wight, better known, perhaps, as Gardiner's Island (east of Long Island) His son, David Gardiner, married Mary ——, his grandson, John Gardiner, son of David, married Mary King and three other wives and was the father of Hannah Gardiner, who married Judge Chandler According to the Chandler Genealogy Gardiner's Island was entailed The attempts to entail estates in Massachusetts failed in every case The old English law of primogeniture was broken down effectually John Chandler married (second) Sarah Clark, widow of Hon Nathaniel Paine, of Bristol, Rhode Island

He was a surveyor by profession and was appointed to plot Pomfret Connecticut, and later he surveyed the line agreed upon between Massachusetts and Connecticut June, 1714 He was coroner for Suffolk county before the county of Worcester was established He removed to Worcester when the county was formed, and was moderator of the town meeting in 1733 He represented Woodstock in the general court and also Worcester in 1732-35-38-39-52-53 He was a selectman of the town of Worcester in 1733-34-35-37-39-40-42-43 to 1753 inclusive, town treasurer 1741 to 1752 inclusive, first clerk of the county courts 1731 to 1754 inclusive, sheriff from 1751 to 1754 inclusive (while Mr Chandler was sheriff Timothy Paine was associate clerk with him), register of probate from the organization of the county until 1754, register of deeds until 1762 In May, 1754, he was appointed judge succeeding his father, and in May, 1757, he was made chief judge with three associates He was one of the delegates of the American colonies who met at Albany, New York, delegates of the Five Nations of Indians, and were partly successful in making allies of them An interesting character in Judge Chandler's family was a colored slave "Aunt Sylvia," who lived to be one hundred and seven years old

Of Judge Chandler the historian of Worcester, Lincoln wrote 'On the decease of his father he succeeded to the higher office of judge, colonel and councillor His talents were brilliant and showy, rather than solid and profound With manners highly popular he possessed a cheerful and gay disposition, indulging in jest and hilarity and he exercised liberal hospitality While Judge of Probate he kept open table for the widows and orphans who were brought to his tribunal by the concerns of business" He was made a member of the Ancient and Honorable Artillery Company in 1734, and was elected commander in 1737 He died August 10, 1762, and is buried on the Worcester common

The children of Hon John and Hannah Chandler were Mary born at New London, September 9 1717 married, February 7, 1736-7, Benjamin Greene, Esther born May 23 1719, married, May 9 1745 Rev Thomas Clapp, John, of whom later, Gardner, born at Woodstock September 18, 1723, married Hannah Greene, married (second), August 2 1767, Anne Leonard, Sarah, born January 11, 1725, married, 1749, Timothy Paine, Hannah, born February 1 1727-8, married, May 17, 1750, Samuel Williams, Lucretia, born July 18, 1728, married, September 1, 1761, John Murray, of Rutland, Elizabeth, born January 5, 1732-3, married, September 20 1751, Hon James Putnam, Katherine, born March 28, 1735 married Levi Willard, a son, born and died January 5, 1737-8

(V) Hon John Chandler son of Hon John Chandler (4), was born at Woodstock, Connecticut, February 26, 1720-1 He married Dorothy Paine, of Worcester, March 5 1740 She was the daughter of Colonel Nathaniel Paine, of Bristol, Rhode Island, and Worcester, Massachusetts Colonel Paine's wife, her mother, was Sarah Clark, daughter of Timothy Clark, of Boston Colonel Paine removed to Worcester in 1738 and had land near Lincoln street Mrs Dorothy Paine died October 5 1745 He married (second), June 11, 1746 Mary Church daughter of Charles Church, of Bristol, Rhode Island, sheriff, who died December 31, 1746, aged sixty-four years Her sister Dorothy Church, married Samuel Chandler Their father, Colonel Charles Church, was son of Colonel Benjamin Church, born in Duxbury, 1639, and wife Alice, the daughter of Constant Southworth, of Plymouth (See sketch of Southworth family)

John Chandler resided on the east side of Main street near the present site of Clark's block, formerly the site of Mower's Tavern and of the United States Hotel He followed in the footsteps of his father and grandfather, both prominent servants of the Crown He was town treasurer from 1753 to

1760, inclusive, town clerk from 1764 to 1768, inclusive county treasurer from 1762 to 1775, inclusive, sheriff from 1751 to 1762, judge of probate from 1762 to 1774 Colonel Chandler marched to the relief of Fort William Henry, August, 1757 John Adams who was then living in Worcester, afterwards president of the United States wrote "At the time Fort William Henry was besieged Colonel Chandler had occasion to send expresses often and while keeping school in Worcester I offered my services and was sent to the Governor of Rhode Island"

He inherited the traits of character as well as the offices of his father and grandfather He was cheerful and engaging in manner, hospitable as a citizen, friendly and kind as a neighbor, industrious and enterprising as a merchant To a chivalrous sense of loyalty to the British government he sacrificed during the revolution property valued at over 36,000 pounds In his own schedule presented to the British government after he had left his country, he reduced these figures which were probably about right, to 17,000 pounds, including 6000 for loss of income from his offices So just and moderate was this compensation ascertained to be at a time when extravagant claims were presented by others that his claims were allowed in full and he was called in England "The Honest Refugee His portrait is to be seen at the foot of the stairs in the front hall of the American Antiquarian Hall at Worcester Colonel Chandler had a pew in Old South Church

After the revolution broke out and Colonel Chandler left Worcester to affiliate with the Tories and British he never returned His estate was confiscated and he was named with his brother-in-law, Hon James Putnam, and others of his family on the list of six who were banished and forbidden to return under penalty of death Two of his sons, Rufus and William were among the proscribed, and his nephew, Dr William Paine The son William Chandler and Dr Paine, were permitted later to return home, and Dr Paine regained the confidence and esteem of the community Col Chandler died in London, September 26 1800, and was buried at Islington His son Rufus was buried in the same grave The spot is marked by a simple stone suitably inscribed

The children of John and Dorothy Chandler were John, born March 3 1742, of whom later, Gardner born December 1 1743 died December 16 1743, Clark born December 1 1743 Dorothy, born September, 1745, married December 26, 1767, Samuel Ward, of Lancaster The children of John and Mary Chandler were Rufus, born May 18, 1747, married, November 18, 1770, Eleanor Putnam, Gardner born January 27, 1749 married in 1772 Elizabeth Ruggles Nathaniel born November 6, 1750 William born December 7, 1752 Charles, born January 22 1755 married November 18, 1796, Sally Mower Samuel, born February 25 1757, Sarah born December 14 1758, married September 14 1780 William Sever Jr Benjamin born August 15, 1761, died December 16 1775 Francis born July 28 1763 died December 16 1775 the two latter were drowned together in the mill pond in South Worcester, Lucretia born June 9 1765 married October 24 1786, Rev Aaron Bancroft Thomas born January 11, 1768, married September 25 1802 Eliza Davis widow of William Denny Elizabeth, born February 20, 1770, married, December 2, 1786 Ebenezer Putnam of St John, New Brunswick where the family lived after the expatriation

(VI) John Chandler son of Colonel John Chandler (5), was born in Worcester, March 3, 1742, the eldest child, married, April 4, 1766, Lydia Ward, who was born in 1732 and died July 30, 1794, aged sixty-two years She was descended from Deacon William Ward, who came over with his second wife Elizabeth, from Yorkshire, and settled in Sudbury, dying in Marlboro, formerly part of Sudbury, aged eighty-seven years His son, William Ward, born in Sudbury in 1640, married Hannah Johnson, daughter of Solomon Johnson, widow of Gershom Amee His son, Colonel Nahum Ward, of Shrewsbury, was born 1684, and married Martha How, daughter of Daniel and Elizabeth (Kerby) How They were the parents of Nahum Ward, Jr, of Shrewsbury who married Lydia Stearns, was a merchant died when about twenty-five years old, leaving two daughters one of whom Lydia, married a Mr Chandlee

John Chandler was an enterprising merchant of Petersham, Massachusetts His home was about a mile from the center and is still remembered for the deer park in which he indulged His deer escaped finally from the enclosure and he lost them all He was successful in business He committed suicide during a fit of despondency and melancholy to which he was subject, in 1794, aged fifty-two years

The children of John and Lydia Chandler were John born July 23, 1667, married, June 5 1800, Elizabeth Greene Lydia born August 28, 1768 married Joseph Head Clark, born April 19, 1770, married July 14 1791, Nancy Lyon, Nathaniel, born February 3, 1772, died August 19, 1772, Nathaniel, of whom later

(VII) Nathaniel Chandler, youngest child of John Chandler (6), was born in Petersham, Massachusetts, October 6, 1673 married, August 17, 1802, Dolly Greene, of Lancaster She was born in Stafford, Connecticut, February 25, 1783, died July 30, 1869 the tenth child of John Greene, son of Nathaniel, who was born in Surinam South America, December 10, 1736 John's wife was Azubah Ward, born at Woodstock, Connecticut November 11, 1737, daughter of Major Daniel Ward by his wife Mary, daughter of Nathaniel Stone and widow of Henry Coggin Major Daniel Ward was a son of Obadiah and Hannah (Harrington) Ward, grandson of Richard Ward and wife Mary, daughter of John and Elizabeth Moore, and great-grandson of the Sudbury immigrant, 1639, William Moore (See Moore family sketch)

Nathaniel Chandler graduated from Harvard College in 1792 He settled in Petersham and managed the Petersham branch of the business of John Chandler & Brothers Afterwards he removed to Lancaster to assume the estate of his uncle-in-law there Samuel Ward Esq He was representative to the general court in 1807 Although troubled with an affliction that kept him under the care of Dr George Chandler and Dr S B Woodward during the last years of his life Dr Chandler wrote of him 'He was of medium height and size, his complexion light and features regular and marked He retained his intelligence shrewdness wit and dry humor his dignity of person and character, his marked courtesy and gentlemanly bearing to the last' He died in Worcester, June 4 1852, aged seventy-eight years

The children of Nathaniel and Dolly Chandler were Samuel Ward born July 12 1803 married, November 18 1830 Eliza Fales Richmond Catherine Amory, born April 18 1805 married May 7 1833 Theophilus Parsons Esq, Charles born September 7 1807 married March 25 1834 Sarah Whitney, John Greene of whom later, Mary Greene, born

May 23 1818, married February 25, 1862, Dr John Ware son of Rev Henry Ware, of Harvard College (See sketch of Charles E Ware and family of Fitchburg George Frederick, born March 12, 1822, married, April 22, 1847, Susan Buss

(VIII) John Greene Chandler, fourth child of Nathaniel Chandler (7), was born in Petersham, Massachusetts, December 18, 1815 He was brought up on the farm in Lancaster and attended school there Having a natural aptitude for drawing he learned the art of wood engraving, and became one of the most proficient artists in this line of his day After residing in various places Mr Chandler returned to Lancaster in 1869 and spent the remainder of his life there In religion he was an earnest Unitarian

He married, June 5, 1850, Sarah Ann Guild, who was born October 26, 1817, the daughter of Samuel Guild president of the People's Bank of Roxbury Her father was born in Walpole, March 18, 1777, and died January 12, 1862, married, 1806, Sarah Means, daughter of James Means, Jr Her grandfather Nathaniel Guild, married, 1733 Mary Boyden of Wrentham, he was the son of Samuel and Sarah (Hartshorn) Guild, the grandson of Samuel and Mary (Woodcock) Guild Mary Woodcock was the daughter of Samuel and Ann Woodcock The immigrant ancestors were John and Elizabeth (Crook) Guild of Dedham The children of John Greene and Sarah Ann Chandler were Alice Greene born July 18, 1851, who resides in Lancaster, Miss Chandler has been connected with the Lancaster town library since 1872 For eighteen years she was librarian and is now advisory librarian and trustee Fanny Guild, born July 10, 1857, died July, 1901

CHARLES FRAZER, a prominent business man of Worcester county, was born in Glasgow, Scotland April 7 1838 the son of the late Charles and Margaret (Bruce) Frazer, both natives of Scotland

Charles Frazer obtained his education in the common schools of his native place, and in 1849 emigrated to this country with his parents, landing at New York, proceeding to South Hadley Falls, Massachusetts His father was an expert mill hand, and was engaged in the mill business at Hadley Falls where he died in August 1850, after which the family removed to Clinton and Charles was there employed in the Lancaster mills He also was employed with his father in the mill at Hadley Falls He later learned the trade of a bricklayer, being thus engaged for some time Subsequently he formed a partnership with Mr Fairbanks, and conducted a contracting and building business with considerable success In 1879 Mr Frazer engaged in the coal business in Clinton Massachusetts, which he has since conducted with the most flattering success During the war of the rebellion Mr Frazer enlisted, in 1861, in Company C, Fifteenth Massachusetts Infantry He participated in the various engagements that made that company famous, and distinguished himself for his bravery and fearlessness on the field of action He entered the service as a private and was mustered out a lieutenant

Mr Frazer's political affiliations are with the Republican party and he has served as assessor and road commissioner for his party He is a member of the Masonic order and a member of the commandery He is an enthusiastic member of the G A R Clinton Post, a member of the Odd Fellows and is also treasurer of the Sterling Worsted Mills Mr Frazer is pre-eminently a self-made man, and enjoys the confidence and respect of the entire community In matters of religion he and his family attend the Unitarian church

On September 6, 1858, Mr Frazer was united in marriage to Mary Barr, a daughter of Robert Barr, of Jamestown, Scotland, and their children were Charles R married Bertha Eager, and they have two children Robert B and Bertha A Etta M married James Charnock, and two children were born to them Sydney T and Harold Irving Frederick E, married Helen Smith and has three children Etta F Helen and Jeannette B Charles R, died June 8, 1906

EZRA GREEN James Green (1), immigrant ancestor of the late Ezra Green, of Fitchburg Massachusetts was born in England about 1620 He came to Charlestown, in New England, before 1647, and was admitted a freeman there May 26, 1647 He removed to Malden, the Mystic side, in 1647 and was one of the petitioners for a division of the town in 1648 He was interested in church affairs, and he appears prominent in various church matters He married Elizabeth ——— Their house lot was on land bought of Richard Harrington in 1656 and remaining in the possession of his family until 1765 It was situated on Green hill and the house is still preserved on what is now Appleton street James Green served on a committee to lay out a highway in June, 1671 He was a citizen of influence in Malden He died there March 29 1687 aged seventy-seven years His will was dated September 2 1682, and probated May 5, 1687 It mentions his wife and two sons mentioned below, viz John "of the Hill," died 1709, of whom later, James resided in Malden

(II) John Green "of the Hill" as he was called from his place of residence to distinguish him from the other John Greens of Malden, was son of James Green (I), and born perhaps in England about 1645 He was a mariner in 1673 He was admitted a freeman in 1683 and died March 22, 1709 He married Mary ——— It is obviously difficult to distinguish him from the others of the name in some instances The children of John and Mary were Mary born December 1668, Samuel only son of whom later, Elizabeth, Hannah All were born in Malden

(III) Samuel Green, only son of John Green (2) was born in 1679 He settled at Malden and became a prominent citizen He was deputy to the general court in 1742 and selectman in 1743 He bought the dwelling and five acres of land of Rev David Parsons after he had removed to Leicester He ranked high socially as he was called "Mr" on various records He died February 21, 1761, aged eighty-two years His will dated January 30, 1752, was proved March 23, 1761 His wife, Martha Green, daughter of Samuel Green, died May 29 1754 aged seventy-two years He married about 1700 His wife was granddaughter of Thomas Green (I) of Malden so that the children of Samuel Green are descended from both the immigrant Greens of Malden

(I) Thomas Green, the grandfather of Mrs Samuel Green was born in England 1606, and came to this country in 1635 or 1636 He was probably in Ipswich until 1649 or 1650, and then settled in Malden Massachusetts He was selectman in 1658 He died December 19 1667 and his will is dated November 12 1667 He married (first) Elizabeth ——— and (second) Frances Cook widow of Richard Cook, and previously widow of Isaac Walker (See further facts in sketch of the Green Family of Leicester and Worcester) Ex-Mayor Green of New York was a descendant

The children of Thomas and Elizabeth Green were Elizabeth, born in England, about 1628, Thomas, born in England, about 1620 (See Pope's Pioneers of Massachusetts), married Rebecca Hills, John, born about 1632, married Sarah Wheeler, Mary, born about 1633, married Captain John Waite, William, born 1635, married Elizabeth Wheeler, and (second) Isabel (Farmer) Blood, Henry, born 1638, married Esther ———, Samuel, of whom later, Hannah, born 1647, married Joseph Richardson, Martha, born 1650, Dorcas, born May 1 1653 married James Barrett

(II) Samuel Green, father of Martha, who married Samuel Green (III), was the son of Thomas Green (I), mentioned above He was born March 1645, married, 1666, Mary Cook sister of Frances Cook, whose third husband was Thomas Green (I) Mary died November 24, 1715, and Samuel (II), married (second) Susanna ———, who survived him

Samuel Green (II) lived in Malden and was known as Samuel, Sr He bought, October, 1670, of his brother William half of his father's farm and occupied the old mansion house He bought the other half June 13, 1684 He died October 31, 1724, aged seventy-nine years, seven months His will was dated January 3, 1721 The children of Samuel (II) and Mary Green were Samuel, born January, 1667-8, married Mary Wheeler, Thomas, born 1669, married Hannah Vinton, John, born April 1, 1672, William, born August, 1674, married Elizabeth Farmer, Mary, born about 1677, married her cousin, John Green, Jonathan, born February 2, 1679-80 married Lydia Buchmann, Martha, of whom later, David, born 1685, married Martin Pratt, Elizabeth, born November 16, 1687, married David Gould, Isaac, born May 20, 1690, married Mary Pratt

The children of Samuel Green (son of John (II)) and his wife Martha Green, daughter of Samuel Green (son of Thomas (I) Green) were James, born November 22, 1702, selectman of Malden 1751, Martha, born January 18, 1703-4, married John Sweetser, October 2 1722, John, born August 11, 1707, resided in Carlisle, Timothy, born October 10, 1709, removed to Lancaster, Ezra, of whom later, Mary, born December 28, 1717, Sarah, born April 24, 1721, Samuel born April 14 1724

(IV) Ezra Green, fifth child of Samuel Green (3), was born in Malden Massachusetts, February 31, 1714-5 He was deacon of the Malden Church, and very prominent in town affairs He was selectman in 1753-57-63-68 deputy to the general court 1760-61-62, town clerk and for many years justice of the peace and magistrate He died April 28, 1768, aged fifty-four years

He married (first) Sarah Hutchinson, February 12, 1740 She died July 7, 1741, aged twenty-six years, without issue He married (second) Eunice Burrill daughter of Hon Eben Burrill of Lynn She died October 2 1760 He married (third) April 29 1762, Mary (Green) Vinton, daughter of Isaac Green, and widow of Benoni Vinton The children of Deacon Ezra and Eunice Green were Dr Ezra, born June 17, 1746, graduate of Harvard 1765, surgeon in the revolution, settled at Dover New Hampshire, and died there July 25 1847 aged one hundred years, twenty-eight days, Bernard, of whom later The children of Deacon Ezra and Mary were Mary born March 22, 1763, Aaron born January 22 1765

(V) Bernard Green, second child of Ezra Green (4) was born in Malden Massachusetts January 14 or 15, 1752 He was one of the most distinguished and influential men of his day in the town He was in the battles of Lexington, Bunker Hill and White Plains, Trenton and Princeton, New Jersey He was a corporal in Captain Blaney Shirley's company at Lexington He was first sergeant in Captain John Walton's company, Colonel Brooks's regiment, in 1776, and was at White Plains, Trenton and Princeton battles He was lieutenant in Colonel Thatcher's regiment of Middlesex militia in 1778, and later was captain of the Malden company After the revolution he was deputy to the general court, and for thirty years justice of the peace and magistrate Much of the early history and especially the oral traditions were preserved owing to his interest in them He is described as a man of towering frame and colossal mind His son was the orator at the two hundredth anniversay celebration of the foundation of the town of Malden He died at Malden, July 15, 1834, aged eighty-two years

He married (second) Lois Diman, daughter of Rev James Diman, minister of the East Church at Salem, Massachusetts, June 7, 1789, and she died February 22, 1839, aged eighty-one years The children of Bernard Green were Bernard, born December 30, 1783, Mary Anne, born August 5, 1791, died young, Eunice Burrill, born October 21, 1792, Ezra of whom later, Mary Orne, born August 22, 1796 James Dimon, born October 8, 1798, graduate of Harvard 1817, pastor Third Church, Cambridge, mayor of Cambridge, 1653, orator at the Malden bi-centennial

(VI) Ezra Green, fourth child of Bernard Green (5), was born at Malden, Massachusetts, February 11, 1795 He was educated there in the public schools and at Phillips Academy Exeter, New Hampshire He thought he preferred to follow the sea to studying at the academy and without permission of the constituted authorities he shipped before the mast and brought his school days abruptly to an end. Upon his return home he worked on the farm until 1858, succeeding his father on the homestead at Malden He was a Whig in politics and a Unitarian in religion He was interested in public affairs and wrote several books of travel He was a man of sturdy character, broad views and unusual general intelligence He removed from Malden to Lancaster in 1858 and died there in 1862 He had a handsome home in Lancaster, in which his widow has since resided She is a bright and interesting woman notwithstanding her great age She was born in 1819 the daughter of Ralph and Abigail (Childs) Richardson, of Vermont

Bernard Green married Elmina Richardson, 1842 Their children were Bernard Richardson, born December 28, 1843, married Julia Lincoln, and they have four children Elmina Minerva, born August 28, 1845, married H T Harwood, and they have eight children, Sarah Elizabeth, born April 1, 1847 married Charles Wilder, and they have one child, James D, born December 25, 1848, married Elizabeth Damon, George Ezra, born September 17, 1850, died young, Abby F, unmarried, Marion, unmarried They were born in Malden Two others died young

JAMES LOGAN The •Logan family, represented by James Logan, a prominent Massachusetts manufacturer, of Worcester, originated in Ayrshire Scotland The genealogy of James Logan is traced as follows from the middle of the eighteenth century

(I) David Logan, of Brouchallmuir, in the parish of Dunlop, in Ayrshire, Scotland, married Elizabeth Muir

(II) James Logan, son of David and Eliza-

James Logan

beth (Muir) Logan was born in the village named above, July 18, 1778 and died March 26, 1860, aged eighty-one years, eight months and eight days He married, December 25, 1801, Margaret, daughter of Archibald and Janet (Gibson) Thompson, of Corbert, parish of Kilbarchan, Renfrewshire, Scotland, she was born in November, 1782, died August 28, 1825 Their children were Janet, born November 3, 1802, died August 23, 1855, married John Allison David, September 1, 1805, died July 23, 1818, Elizabeth, July 31, 1807, died September 30, 1824, Mary, March 30, 1809, died February 27, 1829, married Alexander Reid, Margaret Thompson, June 15, 1811 died October 27, 1812, Archibald Thompson, July 22 1813 died January 4, 1886, Margaret Thompson, August 2, 1816, died December 2, 1835, David (see forward), Agnes Logan, July 24 1822, married William Robb

(III) David Logan, eighth child and third son of James and Margaret (Thompson) Logan, was born in Lochwinnoch, Renfrewshire, Scotland, December 5, 1818 He married Mary Kennedy, born in Paisley, Scotland, January 25, 1816 With their children two sons and two daughters, they sailed in 1852 from Greenock, Scotland, in the ship "Isabella," and arrived in the United States after a voyage of seven weeks David Logan first settled in Connecticut whence he soon removed to Worcester Massachusetts He found employment with the Norwich & Worcester Railroad serving as watchman for several years and subsequently located on a farm in Cherry Valley, near Worcester, Massachusetts He died in Cherry Valley, Massachusetts, March 20, 1893 His wife died in Cherry Valley, Massachusetts September 20, 1888 Of his children, four were born in Scotland, and two in Worcester, Massachusetts David, born August 16 1840, in Paisley, Scotland died in Brewster, New York, October 10, 1902, Margaret, August 2 1848, in Paisley Scotland died at North Woodstock Connecticut February 2, 1902, Annie Kennedy, born September 7, 1850 in Paisley, Scotland, became the wife of Lendall Houghton, James, see forward; Oscar Alva, born January 24, 1854, in Worcester, Massachusetts, John Kennedy, born December 14, 1855 in Worcester Massachusetts

(IV) James Logan fourth child and second son of David and Mary (Kennedy) Logan was born in Glasgow, Scotland May 6, 1852 and was a babe three months old when his parents came to the United States His life was one of arduous labor from his very boyhood, and his education was in greater part eked out at spare times As was the custom then in both Great Britain and the United States boys became bread winners as soon as they were large enough, and at the age of ten years young Logan found employment in the Parkhurst Woolen Mill at Valley Falls a village near Worcester Massachusetts Labor began at five in the morning, the operatives working for two and a half hours before breakfast the entire mill day being extended to fourteen hours The machinery was clumsy even when working at its best the pace was slow, and there were frequent stoppages on account of breakdowns and want of water that being before the day of steam engines These delays were of great advantage to the young workman He had attended school some little before and he now devoted his hours of enforced relief from work to further improving his mind The teacher at the Valley Falls school was Mary E D King a noble woman whose entire life was given to school work in Worcester, and whose memory is revered by hundreds of men and women as the friend of their youth, the faithful guide who inspired them to apply themselves to study, and to fit themselves for the active duties of life Upon young Logan she left a strong impress, and he ever regarded her with peculiar affection and gratitude She induced a half-dozen mill lads to come to the school to recite in the odd hours when the mill was shut down, for want of water power, and at noon hour, when the work was more continuous, she heard them recite their lessons Of this company young Logan alone persisted in continuing his studies and recitations, and the fact is significant as showing his determination to procure an education which should enable him to enter upon a larger career than that of a mere laborer When about eleven an accident indirectly further advanced him on the highway to success His arm was caught in a machine and was broken in three places, being almost torn off at the wrist, and leaving a frightful scar for life While his arm had lost some of its power and usefulness, he was not incapacitated, and he resumed mill work At fifteen he was taken ill, and on his recovery, after a period of six months, was able to perform only light mill labor, and the fact that his left arm was weak turned his mind toward bookkeeping In his sixteenth year he entered B G Howe's Business College, which then occupied quarters in the building where the Park theatre now stands, and while attending that school assisted for a short time as billing clerk in the office of S R Heywood & Co, the veteran shoe manufacturer The next year after completing his commercial course, he took temporary employment with the First National Fire Insurance Company, then in the building now occupied by Green's drug store, at the corner of Main and Pleasant streets he soon obtained a position as bookkeeper with A Y Thompson & Co, dry goods dealers, in the Flagg block on Main street Here he remained for about two years receiving $150 for his first year's work, and sleeping on the counter, as was the custom in those days in order to serve as a watchman over the store His course now was one of gradual but substantial advancement After leaving Mr Thompson he returned to the woolen mill of G N and J A Smith, Cherry Valley (now operated by their nephew, Channing Smith), in which he had previously worked as a mill boy, and in which he now served for about two years in the capacity of bookkeeper In 1873 he became bookkeeper for Sanford & Company book sellers and stationers at the corner of Main and Maple streets, one of the two book stores then in the city, and now conducted by the Sanford-Putnam Company Finding that his office duties did not require all his time he volunteered to sell goods in the store in addition to his office duties and developed unusual ability as a salesman In 1878 he received an offer from David Whitcomb of G Henry Whitcomb & Company, envelope manufacturers (established since 1864 to enter their employ The salary was considerably less than he had been receiving but he saw an opportunity for a more extended field of usefulness and he accepted Mr Logan soon gained an accurate practical knowledge of all the processes of manufacture, the marketing of the product, and the details of the business, gaining the entire confidence of his employers His services as a salesman were of particular advantage and he contributed in marked degree to the extension of the business

In December 1882 Mr Logan associated with himself George H Lowe of Boston under the name of the Logan & Lowe Envelope Company A factory was established in the Stevens block on Southbridge street, Leader machines were installed, and the business was inaugurated most promisingly In

July, 1883. Mr Logan received a flattering offer to return to the Whitcomb Company, and the firm of Logan & Lowe Envelope Company, was dissolved, Mr Lowe returning to Boston to become a partner in the wholesale paper house of Carter, Rice & Company Mr Logan's stay was short, and in January, 1884, he with Henry D Swift, D Wheeler Swift and John S Brigham (all formerly connected with the Whitcomb Company) formed the Logan, Swift & Brigham Envelope Company, for the manufacture of envelopes A factory was established at 16 Union street and operations were begun with Leader and Reay machines, which were soon superseded by a new equipment designed by the Swifts, who were the mechanical experts of the enterprise, and who were the inventors of all the envelope folding machinery in the Whitcomb Company With the advantage of the more rapid production made possible by improved machinery, and Mr Logan's splendid ability for marketing the goods, the success of the firm was phenominal, and it was of world-wide fame as the most extensive, most completely equipped and most profitable of any in its line in the United States In 1898 the business was consolidated with that of the Whitcomb Company, the Hill Envelope Company and seven other large envelope manufacturing firms under the corporate title of the United States Envelope Company, with Mr Logan as first vice-president and general manager, positions which he has occupied to the present time To the complex duties thus devolved upon him, with new problems and new conditions continually arising, he has brought tireless energy and abilities of the highest order, his grasp extending from the initial process through all the stages of manufacture, the continual improvement of the equipment, and the great responsibilities connected with the marketing of the immense product of the factories At the present time nearly two thousand operatives are constantly employed Much of the success attending the practical work of the establishment is due to D Wheeler Swift, the chief mechanical engineer, Of the original Logan Swift & Brigham Company, Mr Brigham died February 19, 1897, and Henry D Swift has retired from business

Mr Logan occupies much of his time in the general offices in Springfield Massachusetts, and makes his home in Salisbury street, Worcester, where he occupies a handsome residence He has always taken a deep and active interest in community affairs He was formerly a trustee of the Worcester County Institute for Savings, served for several years as president of the Worcester County Mechanics' Association, was a director of the board of trade, was a member of the grade crossing commission of 1898, and would at that time probably have been elected to the mayoralty, had he been willing to accept a nomination, but having agreed to accept the office of general manager of the Consolidating Envelope Company, did not feel he would be able to give to the service of the city the time which he believed a mayor ought to give He has ever been particularly interested in the educational and benevolent institutions of the city He has long been a trustee of the Worcester Polytechnic Institute is a trustee of the Bancroft Scholarship, charged with the use of a fund by George Bancroft the historian in aiding Worcester young people to a collegiate education, and is a trustee of the Worcester City Hospital, in which he takes an active and efficient interest He was one of the chief promoters and has always been among the principal supporters of the Young Men's Christian Association in Worcester which he has served in the capacity of president, and is at the present time one of the trustees and it is largely through his effort that this beneficent institution has been preserved from financial embarrassment He is also a member of the state executive committee of the Young Men's Christian Association of Massachusetts and Rhode Island He is a member of the Central Congregational Church and of its board of deacons He is an active member of the Congregational Club, of which he has been president, and of the Worcester Society of Antiquity He is a member of various Masonic bodies—Montacute Lodge, Eureka Royal Arch Chapter, and Hiram Council He is one of the thirty members of the Civic Federation of New England, representing the manufacturers of the state of Massachusetts in that body Mr Logan gave to the town of Leicester a park adjoining the cemetery at Cherry Valley (where he began his life as a school and mill boy) known as Towtaid Park, the Indian name for that locality He is one of the lecturers upon business topics at Dartmouth College in the Tuck School of Administration and Finance, and in 1904 received the degree of Master of Arts from that institution

James Logan married in 1879 Annie D, daughter of Levi Johnson, of Worcester, who for many years was proprietor of the jewelry store in the Bay State House at the corner of Main and Exchange streets Mr Johnson is now (1905) living in Worcester at his home, 12 John street, having retired from business several years ago He was born in 1819 The children of James and Annie D Logan are Oscar Johnson, born September 23, 1880 died August 28, 1881 Donald Brigham, November 8, 1881, graduated from Dartmouth College in 1904 taking the degree of Bachelor of Laws, after spending another year in the Tuck School of Administration and Finance he received in 1905 the degree of Master of Commercial Science, Alice, born August 29, 1887, Ruth, born April 20, 1889

CHACE FAMILY Bartholomew Chace (1), one of the first settlers of Rhode Island, was probably the immigrant ancestor of Mrs Maria A (Chace) Haskell, of Clinton, Massachusetts The Chace family of Rhode Island has been distinguished for ability and worth Most of the descendants spell the name *Chace* in distinction from the numerous descendants of Aquila *Chase* and his brother, Thomas Chase, of northern Massachusetts and of New Hampshire

(II) Joseph Chace, perhaps a grandson of the immigrant, Bartholomew Chace, was born about 1680 He settled in Warwick, Rhode Island His wife Abigail died there November 25, 1730 Their children born in Warwick, were Gideon, born December 22, 1712, Ebenezer, January 17, 1715, Paul May 22, 1716, Mome, July 23, 1718, Arbra, July 1, 1720, Joseph, January 13, 1723, died young, Abigail, January 13, 1723 (twin), died young, Mary, June 18, 1726 David The children of Joseph and Mary Chace, born at North Kingston, Rhode Island, were Joseph, William settled in Bellingham, Massachusetts, and had Isabel, born May 12, 1758 married Seth Hayward, Joseph, born August 16, 1764, and others

(III) Joseph Chace, Jr son of Joseph Chace (2), was born at North Kingston, Rhode Island, February 16, about 1740 Among the children of Joseph was Charles, born in Rhode Island about 1765 Joseph appears to have been a soldier in the revolution from Bellingham and his brother William settled there permanently

(IV) Charles Chace, son of Joseph Chace, Jr (3), was born in Rhode Island about 1762 He was at Cumberland, Rhode Island, November 5,

1786, when he married Abigail Ide, daughter of Timothy Ide, of a well known old family He lived there a few years, then was at Bellingham, where his father lived at one time and where his uncle made his home He married (second), also at Cumberland Rhode Island, December 28, 1794, Ruth Jencke of Wrentham Charles and his wife's brother, William Jencke, of Wrentham, bought the Tucker house and farm on what is now known as Chace street in the spring of 1798 of Major Merrick Rice As Major Rice was one of the lawyers of Lancaster and as the property had come into his hands from Benjamin Houghton and Josiah Cooldge, who had it two years before from Thomas Tucker, it is probable that the estate had passed from the hands of the Tucker family on account of the hard times at the close of the eighteenth century The house, like that of William Gould on the Mill road and that of Elias Sawyer at what is now Lancaster Mills, had been begun, but through lack of funds had never been finished It remained for Mr Chace to complete it, a large square New England mansion, still standing on the original site between Chace street and the Nashua river The farm contained about one hundred and fifty acres, or some thirty-five more than in the old Tucker place The price paid was two housand dollars In 1802 Mr Jenks (as the name is now spelled) released his part in the ownership to Mr Chace

Mr Chace was not only a farmer but also a tanner currier and shoemaker He bought directly from the neighboring farmers whenever they slaughtered cattle and tanned the hides in vats to the north and south of his house Some two years after he bought a skin he had it ready for use as leather His currying and shoemaking were done in a shop one story high, eighteen by thirty feet six rods or so west of the house The sides of leather were hung on the sides of this building to dry On one side of the shop the drying and dressing were done, on the other the boots and shoes were made by Mr Chace and his hands and apprentices He had simple tools and all the work was by hand His two eldest sons probably learned the whole business of their father, but in later life Alanson confined his activity to shoemaking while the other son Charles became a tanner Mr Chace's home life is thus described in the Clinton history "The family life was that of the ideal New England home, as it existed in the early part of the century (nineteenth) There was great earnestness of religious belief, but no austerity Mr Chace belonged to the Rhode Island family of Chaces and brought with him from his old home the Baptist belief Although the members of the family attended public worship at the old church at Lancaster Center still they clung to their own form of faith and gathered their neighors to worship with them, and thus became the originators of the Baptist organization in the town When John Burdett settled in Clinton, they found in him an equally devoted worker Something of the beautiful home life of the family can be surmised from this extract from a letter written by the youngest son to his mother on his thirty-sixth birthday "This day reminds me anew of the untold, unpaid, and unpayable debt of gratitude which every son is under to a good mother, and for which the only return he can make is to show her that he is not insensible of it Frequently when not otherwise occupied, does my mind wander back to the days of my early childhood, when it was so sweet to pillow my head upon my mother's knee, when her lap was my home, the safe refuge to which I flew from every childish grief and trouble And there are moments when my spirit, worn and soiled by the cares of life, has lost its freshness and its hope, in which I would fain be that little boy over again and nestle in my mother's bosom and find it as secure a retreat from the trials of manhood as I did then from the trials of infancy"

Mr Chace died in 1852, aged ninety years In his will, which was proved in 1852, he mentioned his nephew, Timothy Ide Crowninshield, and his four surviving children Alanson, Charles, Jr, George Ide and Diana The children of Charles and Abigail (Ide) Chace were 1 Timothy Ide, born March 6, 1787, at Cumberland, Rhode Island, died Sptember 12, 1789 2 Sally, born November 7, 1789 married —— Crowninshield The children of Charles and Ruth (Jenks) Chace 3 Alanson, see forward 4 Charles, Jr, built the old part of the house at No 1 Green street, he was a tanner, settled at Stillriver (Harvard) and became deacon of the church there in August, 1819, and served for more than seventy years 5 William J, died young 6 George Ide, who gained a world-wide reputation, prepared for college at Lancaster Academy, graduated as valedictorian of his class at Brown University in 1830, he was for a year principal of a classical school at Waterville, Maine, then returned to Brown in 1831, as tutor in mathematics, in 1833 became adjunct professor of mathematics and applied philosophy, in 1836 professor of chemistry, geology and physiology, and filled that chair for thirty-one years, was well known as a public lecturer, traveled in Canada, Nova Scotia and Central America, as well as the western portion of his own country in his capacity as mining expert, in 1867 he was acting president of the University, resigned as professor in 1872 and traveled abroad, returned to Providence and during the remainder of his life devoted himself to the interests of his city and state, chiefly as the chairman of the Rhode Island State Board of Charities and Correction, a volume of his essays published in 1886, reveals his scholarship and ability President Andrews said of him after his death, April 29, 1885 "Professor Chace had the keenest analytical power of any thinker whom I ever heard discourse * * * and he joined with this a hardly less remarkable faculty for generalization" 7 Diana 8. Amia Ann

(V) Alanson Chace, son of Charles Chace (4), was born in Cumberland, Rhode Island, October 22, 1795 He came to South Lancaster, now Clinton, with his father when he was very young and was educated there in the common schools He learned the trades of tanner and shoemaker of his father In 1818 he and his brother, Charles Chace, Jr, probably with the aid of their father, bought of Seth Grout one acre of land and of James Pitts one acre of land and one twentieth of the water power at the dam now controlled by the Lancaster Mills, they erected a small tannery between the spot where the present machine shop stands and the river He settled on the homestead at Clinton and as his father was old took charge of the farm and of the shoe making about 1828 he sold his house, shop and water rights to James Pitts He served the district as member of the Lancaster school committee, as one of five representing Clintonville in the division of property when the town of Clinton was incorporated, and was a selectman in the new town of Clinton He was one of the organizers and most devoted supporters of the Baptist church in Clinton He built the Chace mansion formerly on Prescott street, now removed to Cedar street He was, in fact, one of the most honored and trusted as well as among the most public-spirited men of the town of Clinton in its early days He died February 13, 1875, at Clinton He married Maria Harris and they had two children Charles H, born February 19 1826, see forward Maria A, married W H Haskell, see forward

(VI) Charles H Chace, son of Alanson Chace (5), was born February 19, 1826, died January 9, 1904 He succeeded his father in possession of the old homestead He took contracts for cellars and excavating in the early fifties In 1858 he went into business with his brother-in-law, W H Haskell In 1861 he continued to run the grocery business and erected an addition to the store building which he occupied at that time on Mechanic street He is a Baptist in religion He had been selectman of the town He married, April 11, 1850, Caroline M Ball, of Boylston, now deceased They left three living children A Alanson, Addie Eliza and Emma Chace

(VI) Maria A Chace, daughter of Alanson Chace (5), was born at Clinton, Massachusetts, February 1, 1833 She married October 20, 1855, William H Haskell, who was born in Rochester, Massachusetts, October 20, 1824 the son of Seth and Unice (Hammond) Haskell, a native of Mattapoisett, Massachusetts He spent his boyhood and early manhood in Rochester, acquired his education there in the public schools and academy He entered the general store kept by his father and subsequently managed a store at North Abington, Massachusetts About 1850 he went to Clinton to work for his brother, David Haskell, who was seven years older than he, and who had already a store on Mechanic street on the lot afterward occupied by the C H Chace building He soon became a partner and the business was conducted under the firm name of Haskell Brothers The elder brother David was the victim of a dreadful accident, September 5, 1854 He was returning some "burning fluid" to a barrel when it took fire from a lantern, exploded, and the cellar of the store was filled with flame He died from his injuries the next day The home of David Haskell was on Water street in the brick house built by Asahel Harris For more than three years William H Haskell continued the business alone, but in August, 1858, he advertised groceries and dry goods at the old stand in partnership with D W Kilburn In the same year Charles H Chace succeeded Mr Kilburn in the firm In August, 1861, the firm was dissolved and the business divided, Mr Haskell keeping the dry goods and Mr Chace the grocery Mr Haskell finally sold his business to Mr Chace He had a store for a short time at the rear of his residence on Chestnut street During the closing years of the civil war he was in the grocery business in the basement of Burdett & Fiske's block on the corner of Union and High streets In 1868 he erected the block at the corner of Union and Walnut streets, where he continued in the grocery business until his death, December 2, 1878 He was a leading member of the Congregational church of Clinton, and his wife is still active in the church He was a worthy citizen and highly respected

The children of William H and Maria A (Chace) Haskell were 1 Harriet M born June 29 1858, married Clarence H Bowers, D D S, of Clinton, and they have three children—George I H, Alice D, and Caroline A 2 Alice C, born June 23, 1861, died in childhood 3 Elnathan, born December 14, 1863, died young 4 Minnie Eliza, born October 28, 1865, died in infancy 5 William David, born July 9, 1867, died July 17, 1887 6 Mary Agnes, born February 22, 1873, died in infancy

WILLIAM H BLOOD Richard Blood (1), the immigrant ancestor of William H Blood, of Lancaster, Massachusetts, was one of several brothers who came to New England among the early settlers Some of them owned land in Ruddington, Nottinghamshire, England, and it is thought they all hailed from that neighborhood

James Blood, whom good authority calls brother of Richard, was a yeoman and sergeant at Concord, proprietor of the town and was admitted a freeman June 2, 1641 He was one of the commissioners to lay out the Hough grant of four hundred acres in 1650, commissioner to end small causes at Chelmsford in 1660 He deposed March 30, 1660, that he was about fifty-five years old, he died September 17, 1683, and his will makes no mention of Richard or his other brothers His wife Ellen died August 1, 1674

John Blood settled in Lynn and he was living there in 1647, but removed to Concord where James Blood was living, his brother, Robert Blood, administered his estate by appointment dated September 27, 1692

Robert Blood, probably younger than John and James, was a yeoman and planter at Lynn before 1647 He and John Blood, his brother, sold a moiety of one tenement and half an ox gang in Ruddington, mentioned above, to William Crafts, of Lynn He married, April 8, 1653, Elizabeth Willard, daughter of Major Simon Willard, he died October 22, 1701

These four immigrants are ancestors of all of the name, or nearly all Richard Blood, Robert Blood, Joseph Blood and James Blood were among the original proprietors of Groton, Massachusetts Richard and Robert were petitioners for the plantation

Richard Blood was on the first board of selectmen and served for several years afterward He was town clerk in 1668 and for years was the largest taxpayer He is called the chief among the original proprietors He died December 7, 1783, at Groton He married Isabel —— Their children were Mary, died April 19, 1662, James, of whom later, Nathaniel, of Groton, married, June 13, 1670, Hannah Parker, daughter of James Parker, Elizabeth, married Thomas Tarbell, Joseph, probably the proprietor mentioned above

(II) James Blood, son of Richard Blood (1), was born perhaps in England before his parents came over, about 1640 He was a prominent citizen of Groton, where he was killed by the Indians September 13, 1692 He married, September 7, 1669, Elizabeth Longley, daughter of William Longley She died before 1687 He married (second) Abigail —— The children of James and Elizabeth Blood were Richard, born May 29, 1670, died July 8, 1670, Mary, born September 1, 1672, Elizabeth, born April 27, 1675, Hannah, died January 6 1675 The children of James and Abigail Blood were James, Jr, born August 12, 1687, John, born March 16 1689, of whom later, Martha, born October 20, 1692

(III) John Blood, sixth child of James Blood (2), was born in Groton, Massachusetts, March 16, 1689, and died August 23 1758, in his seventieth year He settled also in Groton He married there, July 13, 1712, Joanna Nutting, of one of the old families Their children, all born at Groton, were John, born February 18 1713-4, Elizabeth, born March 19, 1715-6, David, born September 28, 1718, Lydia, born September 28, 1720, William, born December 9, 1722, Moses, born November 25 1724, Hannah, born July 7 1727, Oliver, born July 9, 1729 Caleb born November 23, 1734, of whom later

(IV) Caleb Blood, youngest child, of John Blood (3), was born November 23, 1734, at Groton, Massachusetts, and died there December 9, 1804, aged seventy years His grave is marked by a stone in the old graveyard He was a soldier in the revolution, in Captain Longley's company, Colonel Asa Whitcomb's regiment in 1775, and also helped with funds contributed to carry on the war

He married, November 1, 1753, Hannah Holden, daughter of John and Sarah (Davis) Holden He married (second), March 3, 1774, Elizabeth Farnsworth, who died September 1, 1773 She was a daughter of Isaac and Anna (Green) Farnsworth The children of Caleb and Hannah Blood were Caleb, Jr, born at Groton, October 24, 1755, served all through the revolution and it is difficult to distinguish his record from that of his father of the same name, Hannah, born September 23, 1757, John, born September 6, 1759, David (twin), born July 8, 1762, Samuel (twin), born July 8, 1762 The children of Caleb and Elizabeth Blood were Timothy, born March 8, 1775, died January 13, 1777, Thomas, born August 31, 1776, of whom later, Timothy, born September 8, 1778, Elizabeth, born August 25, 1780, Levi, born September 14, 1782, died September 29, 1782, Sally, born August 31, 1783, Luther, born October 1, 1785, Nancy, born May, 1787

(V) Thomas Blood, son of Caleb Blood (4), was born August 31, 1776, at Groton, Massachusetts, and died there October 13, 1835, aged fifty-nine years The following inscription is copied from his gravestone

"Canst thou by faith survey with joy
The change before it comes?
And say 'let death this house destroy,
I have a Heavenly home'"

Thomas Blood was brought up in Groton and educated there in the common schools He was well-read, a student of public questions and an influential citizen of his native place He was captain of the militia company He was a prosperous farmer of this city

He married Sarah Fitch Their children were Roxy, Millie, Betsy, Alfred, Mary, Nancy, Thomas F Gilman

(VI) Thomas F Blood, son of Thomas Blood (5), was born in Groton, Massachusetts, January 10 1814, and died at Lancaster, January 23, 1884, aged seventy years, according to his gravestone He succeeded to the homestead of his father at Groton and resided on it until 1845, when he removed to Lancaster, where he built a substantial house on the farm now owned by his son William H Blood In politics he was a Whig and he took a lively interest in public affairs He was an active member of the Congregational church

He married January 30, 1840, Caroline E Parker, daughter of Charles Parker, of Groton Their children were Charles Edwin, born at Groton, April 2, 1842, served in civil war for two years in Company H Thirty-fourth Massachusetts Regiment, William Henry born September 21, 1843 of whom later, Angelo P, born December 26, 1845, Caroline E, born October 25, 1847, Ellen F born November 27, 1849, Lucius M, born February 24, 1856

(VII) William Henry Blood, son of Thomas F Blood (6), was born in Groton, Massachusetts, September 21, 1843 He removed to Lancaster with his parents when he was but two years old and has lived there ever since His education was acquired in the public and high schools of Lancaster, and he followed in the footsteps of his ancestors, working on the homestead of his father at Lancaster When he was twenty-three he purchased his present farm of twenty-seven acres and later added many acres to his farm He is one of the most successful general farmers in his locality For a number of years he was connected with the Lancaster Creamery, which produced a large quantity of excellent butter He has an extensive dairy department on his farm He has acquired a competence from his farm and is counted among the most substantial citizens of the town In politics he is a Republican and has frequently been chosen to positions of trust and responsibility He was tax collector in 1868-69-70, was road commissioner four years, superintendent of streets fifteen years, was on the board of water commissioners for seven years, was on the board of selectmen from 1879 until 1898 He is on the parish and church committees of the Lancaster Congregational Church, and he and his family are active in church work

Mr Blood married May 31, 1866, Mary E Priest, daughter of Levi Priest, of Harvard, Massachusetts She was born February, 1845 Her mother was Eliza (Hartwell) Priest, of Groton The children of William H and Mary E Blood are Alice M, born May 18, 1867, married Sereno Goodnow, who is an assistant on the Thayer estate and they have three children Ellen, Edith, Grace Goodnow, George H, born July 26, 1869, is engaged in the oil business married Florence McCloud and they have three children Mabel, Ada, George Blood, Arthur W, born April 7, 1872, married Sadie Israel, resides in Lancaster, their children are Walter R, and Harold William Blood, Frankie, died in infancy, Walter died young, Nellie E, born September 22, 1884, Horace, died young, Edgar Nelson, born October 1, 1900

MANNING FAMILY William Manning (1), the founder of his family in America, came to the colony of Massachusetts Bay at an early date He came (from best evidence) from Essex county, England The first nine or ten weeks—he said himself—he lived at Roxbury, Massachusetts, after landing here He then removed to Cambridge where documents were first signed by him the date not later than about 1634 possibly several years before He was on the list of landholders in February 1635 An old church record says 'Payd our brother Manninge for a bellrope" This was dated 1648, when he was engaged in "A business laudable and commendable" He had doubtless been a merchant in England In 1638 he bought "foure acres of Swamp ffield of planteing grounde, Charles Towne East" His son William was a journeyman in Middlesex county, 1652 William Manning (1) was a freeman (church member and voter) 1640 His wife Susannah died 1650, and later he removed to Boston and there united with the church in 1664 Susannah was his second wife, of the first nothing is known His third wife was Elizabeth, who outlived him He died in 1665 or 1666 He was probably born in 1592 It is not quite clear, but from the best present obtainable evidence it seems that his children were William born about 1614, in England and Hannah

(II) William Manning son of the first to locate on American soil, born about 1614, in England, came in or before 1634 to the Massachusetts Bay Colony and lived in Cambridge the remainder of his days He purchased lands and engaged in business as a merchant He also owned a warehouse, boathouse on a canal to which boats had free access and constructed with his own hands a wharf by his boathouse He was elected highway surveyor 1651 also a 'gauger' of casks and constable, 1652-53 In 1652, 1666, 1670 he was selectman, also for the years 1672-75-81-83—a total of fifteen years He was a member of the grand jury in 1686, 1688 As a selectman he was on a committee to inspect into the families "that there be no bye drinking or any misdemeanor whereby sin is committed, and persons from their houses unseasonably" His wife was Dorothy, and their children were Hannah, Samuel Sarah, John, Mary all born and baptized in the church In 1668 he was sent to England to procure another minister and in 1671 Rev Urian Oakes was received and ordained through their visit abroad Oakes remained pastor until his death, and was also president of Harvard College In 1670 Mr Manning was appointed "to catechise the youth" of his town The most important act of his life was in connection with Harvard College, he having been selected, with Deacon John Cooper, to replace the old college building with a new one, and to receive and disburse funds for that purpose This was in 1672 and his work extended until 1684 This college was then nearer the people's hearts than any institution since It was established by the general court (legislature) sixteen years after the landing of the "Mayflower" It was the pride and hope of the people who cast their fortunes in the New World In 1639 it received the name of Harvard College William Manning (2) had much to do with the starting of this great educational school The bodies of William and Dorothy Manning were buried in the cemetery of Harvard Square, and the headstones, still well preserved show that he died March 14 1690, and his wife July 26, 1692 He died full of years and honors—a merchant, selectman and held many other offices, aside from being a rebuilder of Harvard College Their children were 1 Hannah born 1642 2 Samuel, born 1644 3 Sarah born 1645 4 Abigail born 1647 5 John born 1649 6 Mary, born 1651 7 Timothy, born 1653

(III) Samuel Manning son of William (2) and Dorothy, born 1644 was reared in his native town and educated in the midst of the good school surroundings of Cambridge His handsome penmanship and easy style of composition showed him much superior to his associates When eighteen years of age he and other associates were summoned before the court and reproved for firing off their guns at night to cause an alarm They belonged to a militia company and the real object of the alarm was to give the impression that Indians had attacked the town, but even the court was not disposed to look too sternly upon the boyish prank He married at about that date (1666) and removed to Billerica twenty miles distant He was in the true sense a pioneer When he settled only forty-six years had elapsed since the "Mayflower" landed on the 'stern and rock-bound coast" The Indians were still strong on all sides—friendly one day and hostile the next King Philip's war was in 1675, and twice his new home was assailed by savages While they lived beyond the Concord river they were greatly exposed to danger, conflagration and death In 1696 his new house became a 'garrison" He was made a corporal in 1682 sergeant in 1684 and ensign in 1699 He followed farm life and endured great hardship to subdue his lands In 1668 he was surveyor of highways, sealer of weights and measures, 1675-1700, constable, 1677, trial juryman, 1679, assessor, 1694 1698 1702, tithing man, 1679-82-97, 1704-9, town clerk seven years, selectman eighteen years, and representative, 1695-97 The town records are full of commissions to him At various times between 1677 and 1700 he was connected with repairing "the great bridge" over the Concord river He followed surveying a quarter of a century In 1692 he was paid fourteen shillings for writing fourteen pages in the 'town book" In 1693 he superintended the erection of a meeting house In 1670 he was made a freeman of the colony He was a large real estate holder His will was made February 21, 1710 The children by his two wives are as follows By Elizabeth: Samuel, born 1695 and John By Abiel Timothy, born 1673, Hannah, William, Mary, Sarah, Dorothy, Isaac, Ephraim, Elizabeth, Timothy, Eliphalet, Abiel

(IV) William Manning, son of Samuel (3), born June 27, 1677, at Billerica, where he always resided He inherited the old homestead He was one of nineteen men out of one hundred and fifty who were dignified by the title of "Mr" and one of ten who occupied the best or "fore seat below," as it was termed in church pews He was prominent in the militia, being an ensign in 1723 He married Elizabeth French, born 1679, died 1736, when he married Mary Shed Ensign Manning died 1764 His children were Elizabeth, born 1701, Esther, born 1703, Mary, 1705, William, 1707, Jacob, 1710, Sarah, 1711, Rachel, 1714, Martha, 1718, Hannah, 1719

(V) Jacob Manning, son of William Manning (4), born March 27, 1710, at Billerica, Massachusetts, always resided in his native place He received a portion of his father's farm by deed, or gift His rate to the church in 1755 was 7 shillings, 11 pence. He was a journeyman in the second session of court, and surveyor in 1741-48-54, also a constable He died 1762 He married Martha Beard, and had the following named children 1 Jacob, born 1739 2. Mary, born 1741 3 Isaac, born 1743 4 Jesse, born 1745 5 Thomas, born 1747 6 David, born 1749. 7 Martha, born 1750 8 David, born 1753 9. Esther, born 1756

(VI) Jesse Manning, son of Jacob (5), born at Billerica, Massachusetts, August 18, 1845, was a soldier of the Revolution, and marched on the Lexington Alarm, April 19, 1775, in Col Green's regiment He was a farmer After his father died he bought a portion of the old homestead December 2 1766 he was married to Anne Carleton, she died in 1779 and he married Elizabeth Abbott of Andover, Massachusetts For his third companion he married (1802) Abigail Baldwin, who died in 1825 Jesse Manning died in the autumn of 1825 His children were 1 Mercy, born 1768 2 David, born 1751 3 Elizabeth, born 1773 4 Jesse, born 1776. 5 Julia, born 1778

(VII) Jesse Manning, son of Jesse (6), born at Billerica, Massachusetts, July 12, 1776 He resided first in his native place and then removed to Sutton, New Hampshire and later to Paxton Massachusetts, where his latter days were spent In New Hampshire he was engaged in the lumber business and had a mill in connection therewith At Paxton he was a carpenter He married Mary Kilbridge at Tewksbury in 1796 He died at Paxton July 28 1852 having married for his second wife Mary Durah (or Durren) His children by his first wife were 1 Jesse born 1797 2 Nancy, born 1800 The children by Mary Durah were 1 Elizabeth, born 1810 2 David, born 1812. 3 Mary Jane born 1814 4 Elmira born 1816 5. Samuel Stillman born 1818, at Lexington

(VIII) David Manning son of Jesse (7), born at Sutton New Hampshire, April 14, 1812, lived at Paxton, Leicester and Worcester, Massachusetts, he died at the last named place April 15, 1890 He

DAVID MANNING

married Lucy B Grosvenor, who died in 1896 Their children were 1 Betha, married Joseph A Titus 2 George G 3 Theodore 4 David 5 Charles W 6 Joseph Avery 7 Frederick During the rebellion he was a member of the Freedom Club, a loyal organization, and was one of three of its business committee

(IX) Joseph Avery Manning, son of David and Lucy B (Grosvenor) Manning, born February 19, 1851, at Worcester He married Ella Amsden, and their children were 1 Joseph Nelson, born June 30, 1879 2 Frances G, born April 21, 1883 3 Edward Avery, born September 14, 1894

(IX) Charles Walter Manning, son of David and Lucy B (Grosvenor) Manning, born August 2, 1848, married Eva W Parker and had 1 Walter Webster, born May 24, 1875 2 Frank Grosvenor, born January 1, 1877, died May 6, 1879 3 Earl G, born January 9, 1881

(IX) George G Manning, son of David and Lucy B (Grosvenor) Manning, born October 20, 1842, married Ellen Moore, and had one son Roger, born February 21, 1879

(IX) Theodore Manning, son of David and Lucy B (Grosvenor) Manning, born in Paxton, Massachusetts, October, 1844, became a member of the Manning Shoe and Rubber Company, and for more than forty years resided at Worcester When twenty years of age he came to Worcester, in 1856 He completed his education in the public schools and acquired his good business training with E A Goodnow, wholesale boot and shoe dealer, after which he became a member of the S R Heywood & Company, as a shoe manufacturer In 1870 he associated himself with his brother George G and B W Childs The latter withdrew from the concern and the two brothers continued until 1896, when he was transferred to Boston, being consolidated with that of J A Manning, thus forming the Manning Shoe and Rubber Company Our subject's health failed and on April 28, 1898, he passed from earthly scenes He married Caroline E Woods, of Hardwick, Massachusetts, and left eight children Frederick, Charles S, Grace W, Florence, David R, Robert H, Harold G, and Clarence W Charles S resides in Ohio, the others at Newton He was a regular attendant of the Plymouth church from the time of its formation He had a wide circle of personal friends

(IX) Hon David Manning, son of David and Lucy B (Grosvenor) Manning, was born August 29, 1846 The first ten years of his life was spent in Leicester, to which place his parents had moved from Paxton, Massachusetts, when he was an infant After 1856 Worcester was his home He was proud of his ancestry, tracing family ties back to Samnel Adams David, the father of our subject, was one of six children, all of with the exception of Joseph Manning, member of the shoe jobbing firm of Boston, known as Manning Brothers, are dead The others were George C, Theodore Walter and Mrs Joseph A Titus

Mr Manning was educated in the public schools, graduating in 1865 from the Worcester high school, where he was awarded prizes for efficiency in different branches In the autumn of 1865 he entered Yale College, from which he graduated in high rank in 1869 He then entered Harvard Law School, but failing health compelled him to leave the confinement of college life, but he entered the law office of Col Joseph A Titus, his brother-in-law, and H O Smith In 1872 he was admitted to the practice of his chosen profession Soon after he accepted a position in the law office of Rice & Blackmer, where he gained wide experience in bankruptcy proceedings In 1880 he left this firm, and associated himself for a time with Burton W Potter but soon opened an office of his own He was regarded by his fellow associates at the bar as among the most prominent in the county Taking much interest in public affairs he was elected as a representative from Ward No 7 in 1887 and in 1899, the record time, and there became prominent through his service on the judiciary committee In 1900 he was elected to the state senate, serving two years Prior to having served in the legislature he was an associate justice of the Central district court from 1881 to 1887, when he resigned He was a member of the state central committee in 1888, 1897, 1898, and was frequently urged to become a candidate for mayor of Worcester, but declined the honor He aspired to be a congressman in 1902, but was defeated in nomination by Rufus B Dodge Mr Manning, who died Thursday, January 5, 1905, was a great lover of home life A devoted husband and father, he spent all possible time at his own home circle, finding supreme happiness in the quiet of the sacred precincts of his own affairs He was not a secret society man, and did not believe in some respects in secret organizations, but was in sympathy with the great principles of the benevolent features of such institutions He was an honored member of the Commonwealth and Tatnuck Clubs He was an active member and supporter of Unity Church, being the chairman of the pastoral committee The year 1878 marked a new era in Mr Manning's life, in his marriage to Elizabeth, daughter of Alexander Bigelow and wife, born January 16, 1849 Mrs Manning and one son, Alexander Bigelow Manning, survive him Shortly after their marriage Mr and Mrs Manning toured abroad, returning in the autumn of that year One of his most intimate associates, Charles R Johnson, remarked upon hearing of his sudden death from apoplexy "I shall never meet a better man He stood for honesty, integrity and reliability and the highest sense of honor He was indeed the most high-minded man I ever met" He disliked to take a case that he did not believe in, but when his heart was in the case he was an antagonist to be legally feared He would fight a case to the bitter end if he believed he was right, his client's cause in such instance becoming his own He was well read in philosophy as well as law, and was made up of the most sterling qualities He was laid to rest in Hope Cemetery As an exponent of law, a radical temperance advocate, a conscientious citizen, a loving home companion and an indulgent father, no better, truer type of manhood ever graced the city of Worcester

PERLEY PIERCE COMEY, M D David Comey (1) was the emigrant ancestor of Dr Perley Pierce Comey, of Worcester He was in Woburn as early as 1663 and was doubtless the first of the name in this country Family tradition says that he was born in Scotland His son John married the daughter of a Scotchman, and the district in which he lived in Concord later was known as Scotland The name is spelled Comee by part of the descendants In the earlier days it was spelled in various ways, Comv Come, Com, Comay and Coomy

About 1664 David Comey removed from Woburn, where he first settled, and made his home in Concord, Massachusetts, and there he lived the remainder of his days He was killed while a soldier in King Philip s war in the Sudbury fight, described elsewhere in this work, April 21, 1676 There is a pathetic petition on file in the archives of the general court wherein the widow recites her woes after the loss of her husband He was a young man, born about 1640, and when he was killed the widow had six small children including a baby six weeks old and four children of the first marriage to care for. The estate amounted to only eighty-seven pounds, fifty of which was represented by the house and land and the rest by clothing and furniture. She had to give away the children. In the petition she prayed that Captain Timothy Wheeler be named guardian for the purpose. The records fail to tell us how the orphans of the soldier fared later.

David Comey married (first) Elizabeth, who died at Concord, May 4, 1671, leaving four children. He married (second) Esther ———. His widow married (second), November 7, 1682, Samuel Parry. The children of David and Elizabeth Comey were: Elizabeth, married, March 29 1691, John Kendall, born 1646, died 1732, of Woburn, where she died December, 1701 (See Kendall Sketch); Mary, born January 30, 1663, married, May 24, 1688, Joshua Kibby, of Sherburn and died July 9, 1712, he died 1731; John, of whom later; David, born November 14, 1666, died before 1676; Sarah. The children of David and Esther Comey were two daughters, one of whom was Esther, born February 14, 1676.

(II) John Comey, third child of David Comey (1), was born in Concord, Massachusetts, October 18, 1665. He was a farmer. He removed from Concord to Cambridge Farms, as Lexington was then called, in 1689. He died in Lexington, 1729, aged sixty-four years. The date 1723 given in the Cambridge history is incorrect.

He married, June 21, 1688, Martha Munroe, who was born November 2, 1667, the eldest daughter of William Munroe, a Scotch soldier sent over a prisoner of war by Cromwell. (See Sketch of Munroe Family.) Their first four children were baptized February 26, 1699. Their children were: John, born at Concord, April 8, 1687, died young probably; Hannah, died unmarried May 26, 1720; Martha, died July 9, 1713; David, of whom later; Elizabeth, born January 29, 1701, at Lexington; Abigail, baptized October 26, 1707, married, January 4 1728, Jonas Pierce, and died at Westminster, Massachusetts.

(III) David Comey, fourth child of John Comey (2), was born in Lexington, Massachusetts, January 11, 1696. If family tradition is correct he died in 1800 at the age of one hundred and four years. In 1729 he was called a yeoman. In 1736 he was an inn-holder.

He married (first) Ruhama Brown, daughter of Joseph and Ruhamah Brown. She was born in Watertown July 15, 1701, died June 3, 1730. He married (second) Sarah ———. There were five or six children by the first marriage, who died young. Only two of the children of David and Ruhamah (Brown) Comey survived, viz: John, baptized September 28, 1725; Joseph, baptized August 4, 1728. The children of David and Sarah Comey were: Benjamin, born November 15, 1733; Sarah, September 11, 1735; Mary, April 11, 1738; Ezekiel, April 27, 1740; Ruhama, April 15 1742; David, April 21, 1744; Jonathan, April 4, 1746.

(IV) Jonathan Comey, youngest child of David Comey (3), was born in Lexington, Massachusetts, April 4 1746. When he was a young boy he went to Foxboro, where some of his elder brothers settled, and while still a young man removed to Holliston, Massachusetts, where he lived with Samuel Messinger. After he married he went to live in the west part of Hopkinton on the west side of Whitehall Pond. At the Lexington Alarm April 19, 1775 he turned out with the minute men. He served in the revolution in Captain John Holmes company, Colonel Samuel Bullard s regiment. His name was spelled Jno Commey on the rolls.

He married Elizabeth Wells about 1768. Their children were: Parmelia, married Nathaniel Chamberlain, of Holliston, and settled in Wardsboro, Vermont; Royal, of whom later; Betsey, married Joshua Mellen, and resided in Westboro, Massachusetts, their only son was Judge Edward Mellen, of Worcester, they had four daughters; Polly (Mary), married Jonathan Fairbanks, and lived in Holden; Nellipee, married John Wheelock, of Vermont, she died at the birth of her son John, who was brought up by ——— Adams; Hannah, married Abner Prentiss, of Hopkinton.

(V) Royal Comey, second child of Jonathan Comey (4), was born in Hopkinton, Massachusetts, January 29, 1772. He died in Hopkinton, October 1853, aged eighty years. He was a well-to-do farmer. He always lived in his native town of Hopkinton. His place was on the east side of Whitehall pond, and he also owned a large tract on the western side and also an island in the pond, now known as Comey's island.

He married Polly Andrews, of Millford, who died August 29, 1873, aged eighty-eight years, eight months, eight days. The children of Royal and Polly (Andrews) Comey were: Hiram, born July 18, 1806, married, 1832, Emily Gibbs; Elbert, August, 1806, married twice and had seven children; Elbridge Gerry, of whom later; Dexter, February 21, 1814, died in Westboro, November 8, 1892; Martha Ann, August 19, 1817, married William B Wales of Hopkinton, who died April 13, 1845, leaving one child, Mary Ann; Mary, July 12, 1823, died July, 1844.

(VI) Elbridge Gerry Comey, third child of Royal Comey (5), and father of Dr Perley P Comey (VII), was born in Hopkinton, Massachusetts, November 11, 1811. He married Abigail J Pierce. He was a farmer. He settled first in Holliston, but in 1860 returned to his native town, Hopkinton, Massachusetts, to live. He was a man of sterling character and exemplary life. He died in Hopkinton, ——, 1868. They had children: Amanda Ann, born December 20 1832 died November 10, 1856, educated at Mt Holyoke Female Seminary; Aratus, born October 27, 1837; Henry Newton, born March 4, 1840; Manlius, born March 18, 1843; Mary Abby, born November 28, 1845 married, July 15, 1868, George S Gibson, of Hopkinton, Massachusetts, has five children, resides in Clinton Massachusetts; and Perley P, of whom later.

(VII) Dr Perley Pierce Comey, youngest son of Elbridge Gerry Comey (6), was born in Holliston, Massachusetts, January 14 1852. He removed to Hopkinton with the family when eight years old. He spent his boyhood and youth helping his father on the farm when he was not attending the district schools of Holliston and Hopkinton. In 1868, after his father died he was sent to the Oread high school in Worcester, a classical school connected with the Oread Institute at that time. He afterward learned the business of a druggist and pharmacist in Worcester. He began to study medicine in the office of Dr A P Richardson, of Boston. He graduated from the Harvard Medical School in 1878. In the following August he began to practice his profession in Clinton, Massachusetts. Almost from the start he received liberal patronage and soon had a very extensive practice, not only in Clinton but in all the adjoining towns. Ever ready to sympathize and advise the afflicted and suffering, he became popular wherever he was known. He was not only a successful physician and skillful surgeon, but his tact and excellent judgment were quickly rec-

O. Willis Rugg

ognized by his patients He removed to the larger field of Worcester about 1897, though still retaining much of his county practice He resides at 63 Lincoln street, and his office is at 61 Lincoln street Dr Comey stands high in the estimation of his fellow practitioners in Worcester, and in hospital and private practice has been singularly fortunate in recent years He is a member of the Massachusetts Medical Society He is a prominent Free Mason and Odd Fellow

He married, in 1873 Marion L Jones, daughter of John O Jones, of Boston, and granddaughter of the late Colonel James Estabrook, of Worcester, with whom she lived They have three children, viz 1 Effie M, born in Clinton, a graduate of Smith College, married D E Manson, of Brookline, Massachusetts, manager of the Westinghouse Electric Company of Boston, they have two children Marian and John I , Gertrude J, born in Clinton, a graduate of Smith College, resides at home, Clifton J, born in Clinton, a graduate of Worcester Academy, class of 1905, now (1906) a student in Boston

OLIVER WILLIS RUGG John Rugg was the emigrant ancestor of Oliver Willis Rugg and Arthur P Rugg, of Worcester, and probably of all the families of that surname in this vicinity He came to this country about 1650 and settled at Watertown, but soon removed and was one of the first settlers of Lancaster, Massachusetts Rugg is an ancient family in Norfolk county, England, and Lord Braybrooke says that two men of this branch of the family were aldermen of Norwich One report states that John Rugg was born in Sowerby, Halifax parish, England, March 11, 1632 John Rugg was in Lancaster in 1652 He married first, in 1654, Martha Prescott, and (second) Hannah Prescott, both daughters of Jonathan and Mary (Platts) Prescott He was very active in town affairs He was admitted a freeman in 1669 His wife Martha died May 4, 1660, after having had two children, both of whom died young John Rugg died at Lancaster in 1696 His widow was killed by the Indians at Lancaster, September 22, 1697 His children were 1 ——— died January 18 1655-6 2 John, born January 17, 1655-6, died January 29, 1655-6 3 John born June 4 1662, died 1712 had i John ii Samuel, settled at Hadley iii Nathaniel iv David v Jonathan vi Benjamin vii Mary viii Abigail 4 Mary, born July 11, 1664 5 Thomas, born September 15 1666 resided at Lexington, Massachusetts, married Elizabeth ———, and had i Thomas, born December 6 1691 ii William, born November 19, 1693 iii Elizabeth born January 20 1695 iv Hannah, born April 26, 1697 v Abigail, born March 13, 1699 vi Sarah, born February 12, 1702 vii Mary born May 30, 1703 viii Ruth, born September, 1706 ix Tabitha, born September 10, 1708 x Milicent born November 11 1710 xi Martha, born November 10 1713 6 Joseph, born December 15 1668 (Joseph his wife and three children and his mother Hannah were murdered by the Indians at their home in Lancaster, September 22, 1697 The others killed at that time were Rev Mr Whiting Daniel Hudson, his wife and two daughters Ephraim Roper wife and daughter, John Skait and wife, Jonathan Fairbank, Widow Wheeler, Mary Glazier and a son of each of Ephraim Roper John Skait and Joseph Rugg Most of these families were in South Lancaster Peace had already been declared between Great Britain and France when this attack was made) 7 Hannah, born January 2, 1671 married John Bell, 1690 8 Rebecca, born May 16, 1673 married Nathaniel Hudson 9 Daniel, born November 15, 1678 10 Jonathan, born February 10, 1681, settled in Marlborough, Massachusetts, married Sarah, daughter of John Newton, removed to Framingham Massachusetts, married (second) Hannah Singletary, married (third) Elizabeth ———, who was living when he died, December 25, 1753

(II) Daniel Rugg, son of John Rugg (1), lived in that part of Lancaster that is now Sterling He was born September 15, 1678, at Concord, while the family was away from Lancaster He died at Sterling, June 23 1758 He was constable in 1718, and always prominent in church affairs at South Lancaster or Sterling He lived near the Sawyers, Fairbanks, Samuel Prescott, John Harris and Rev Andrew Gardner They served together in the same garrison by order of the general court at Mr Gardner s house on the west side of the Nashua river Daniel Rugg saw much service during the Indian troubles He married Elizabeth daughter of Reuben Priest, of Sterling, March 10, 1730 He died June 23 1758 His wife died December 3, 1754 He joined the church March 3, 1716-17, she joined April 1, 1716-17 Both had been members of the Lancaster church Daniel Rugg signed the covenant in 1708 at Lancaster Children of Daniel and Elizabeth Rugg 1 Captain Daniel 2 Reuben, born at Sterling, married Lydia Ross 3 Amos, born December 17 1716, baptized January 20, 1717 4 Nathan, born April 13 1718 5 Isaac, baptized April 3 1720 6 Sarah baptized July 21, 1728 7 Mary (full communion), May 6, 1733

(III) Amos Rugg, son of Daniel Rugg (2), was born at Sterling, December 17, 1716, married December 29, 1741 Mary Burpee, and settled in Sterling He was a farmer Children of Amos and Mary (Burpee) Rugg 1 Amos, born January 6, 1744-45 died September 11 1746 2 Amos, (2d), born March 1747, married Sarah Willard 1769 intentions recorded February 8, 1769 3 Mary born May 7, 1750 4 Stephen born October 30, 1751, died October 19, 1756 5 Solomon born March 17, 1754, died November 5 1756 6 Phebe, born June 5 1756 7 Olive born April 6 1760 8 Pamelia, born April 12, 1762 9 Hannah born June 22, 1764 10 Luther born April 12, 1770

(IV) Luther Rugg son of Amos Rugg (3), was born at Sterling, then the western part of Lancaster April 12 1770, and died in Sterling October 20, 1863 He was prominent in town affairs an active and useful citizen He was elected a member of the committee on laying out roads in 1817, as assessor six years, 1818-27, served on the school committee five years 1818-25, on board of overseers of poor 1820 and 1821, on board of officers to preserve order in public worship, in 1820 1824, 1826 and 1827 elected field driver 1825 and 1832, and member of committee on gift of the Jacob Conant farm to the town in 1839 He married June 22 1800, Ruth Jewett daughter of Amos Jewett, who was born in Lancaster, March, 1747 died at Lancaster, April 15, 1781, married, October, 1768 Sarah Willard Amos Jewett was a soldier in the Continental army during the revolutionary war in the campaign about Boston Ruth was born January 16, 1776, and died September 20, 1864 Their children 1 Harriet born March 30 1801, died August 23, 1892, married Spencer Wilder 2 Mason, born September 16 1802, died September 7, 1804 3 Luther Warren, born August 24, 1804, died December 14 1859 4 Amos Willard born February 23 1806 died June 2 1866 5 Ruth Eliza, born February 13, 1808 died April 19 1836 married Charles Powers 6 John Abbot, born June 19,

1810, died June 25, 1814 7 Adolpha born December 15, 1812, died September 24, 1861, married William Crowell, 1850 8 Augustus Kendall born February 17, 1815 died August 7, 1843 9 Prentice Mason, born July 22 1817 died February 25, 1885

(V) Prentice Mason Rugg, son of Luther Rugg (4) born at Sterling July 22, 1817, died in Boston, February 25 1885 He carried on a farm at Sterling and taught school in the winter for many years in Lancaster and Sterling For twenty-one winters in succession he taught school, and later four years more He was frequently honored by his fellow citizens He served as assessor nineteen years, from 1855 to 1881 as member of school committee, nine years from 1847 to 1860 as moderator of town meetings, eight years from 1869 to 1879 as selectman, as juryman eight terms from 1868 to 1882, as highway surveyor four years from 1843 to 1869, as trustee of the Conant fund three years from 1868 to 1870 and other various committees He married, June 15, 1847, Cynthia Ross She was born in Bakersfield Vermont, December 17, 1825, daughter of Willis and Mary (Taylor) Ross Both of her parents were born in Sterling and removed to Bakersfield The children of Prentice Mason and Cynthia (Ross) Rugg were 1 John Mason born June 6, 1848, died in Sterling, August 28, 1866, was educated in common schools of Sterling and was fitted for college in the Lancaster Academy under W A Kilburn, principal He taught the South Lancaster grammar school during the winter term of 1865 and 1866 2 Oliver Willis born March 24 1850 3 Carrie Hannah born February 7, 1852, married Herbert R Sylvester, who was born in Newton Massachusetts, and is principal of the Claflin School of Newton Carrie Hannah was educated in the public schools and at the State Normal School at Salem, class of 1873 She taught school at Lancaster and Sterling Wellesley and Newton They reside at Newtonville 4 Arthur Prentice, born August 20 1862, married Florence Belcher, of Worcester has had four children 5 Mary Taylor born September 4 1864, died September 1, 1866

(VI) Oliver Willis Rugg, son of Prentice Mason Rugg (5) was born at Sterling, March 24, 1850 His early days were spent on the farm in that town He attended the district schools of Sterling and later spent two terms at the Lancaster Academy under W A Kilburn, principal He taught the Chocksett district school during the winter term of 1868-69 and later substituted in Sterling for his sister Carrie H so that she might accept a better position which had been offered her after she had been engaged at Sterling He entered the Worcester Polytechnic Institute in September, 1869 graduating in 1872 in the second class graduated from that Institute Among his classmates were Parkman T Denny, of Leicester, A W Woods of Worcester George H Scott of the Morgan Spring Company of Worcester Solon Davis and Jonathan Moore of Holden, Herbert S Rice, of Barre S C Heald Jr of Jamaica Plains, and M B Smith of Lowell During the vacation of 1871 he worked with William A Smith, engineer in charge of the water supply for the city of Fitchburg In September 1872 he went to work for George Raymond who was engineer in charge of the preliminary surveys for the introduction of water into the town of Leominster also into the city of Springfield, engineer for the Vermont & Massachusetts Railroad Company and engineer for the Fitchburg Railroad Company While in his employ Mr Rugg made estimates for the Leominster water supply surveys and estimates for the Springfield water supply and did much of the engineering for the Vermont & Massachusetts Railroad Company, and some for the Fitchburg Railroad Company Mr Raymond was elected city engineer of Fitchburg the first year it was incorporated as a city, and he gave into the hands of Mr Rugg the engineering for the street department of that city After leaving Mr Raymond, Mr Rugg worked for a time on his own account at Clinton and other places It was at this time that he substituted in the school at Sterling for his sister He was elected a member of the school committee about this time and served for many terms In 1878 he formed a partnership with his classmate A W Woods, as civil engineers and surveyors and they opened an office at 44 Front street, Worcester Three years later they moved to the Rogers Block, at the corner of Pleasant and Main streets, and still later to the J H Walker building at the corner of Barton Court and Main street This firm had all the work of the Washburn & Moen Manufacturing Company until they established an office of their own They also had the work of George Crompton for many years The firm made a preliminary survey to Marlboro for H H Bigelow who planned to extend the line he had built to the Lake They also made an accurate survey and very artistic plan of Lake Quinsigamond for Mr Bigelow They did the preliminary surveying for the Grafton Upton & Milford Railroad and carried out the construction of a part of that road Mr Rugg, for the firm, made the plans and superintended the construction of the first electric railroad in Worcester, the Worcester, Leicester & Spencer Electric Street Railway The firm were the engineers for the Worcester & Millbury Electric Street Railway Company In 1893 they made preliminary surveys for electric railways from Worcester to Southbridge, Webster, Northbridge, via the Blackstone Valley, and to Marlboro This was done by order of the late Samuel Winslow, who was then president and one of the promoters of the Worcester, Leicester and Spencer Electric Railway None of these roads however, were built under these franchises Mr Rugg and his partner dissolved in 1894 and Mr Rugg opened his office in the Day building, on Main street After that building was destroyed by fire in March, 1897 he moved to his present office Room 824 State Mutual Building He has been occupied much of the time with street railway work, although his office has had a large variety of work for individuals and corporations in Worcester county He engineered the relocation of the Worcester Leicester & Spencer Electric Street Railway to conform to the state highway, made preliminary surveys for an electric railway from Pen Yan to Branchport, in the state of New York, on which he was afterward the constructing engineer was constructing engineer for the Worcester & Clinton Street Railway Company, relocated and constructed a part of the Worcester & Webster Street Railway was constructing engineer for the Worcester & Southbridge Street Railway Company made preliminary surveys for an electric railway from Washington Junction to Castine in the state of Maine a distance of about forty miles this road however has never been built He has also made preliminary surveys plans and estimates for a railroad to connect at Millbury with the Worcester Consolidated Street Railway and run to Singletary Lake, a railroad from Fiskdale to Palmer an extension of the Southbridge & Sturbridge Street Railway, and one from Whitinsville to Providence, an extension of the Blackstone Valley Street Railway but these likewise were never built He has in the past few years done practically all of

Arthur P. Rugg.

the engineering for the Worcester Consolidated Street Railway Company Plans and estimates have been prepared for the abolition of grade crossings in the towns of Webster and Winchendon under his supervision Mr Rugg is a member of Athelstan Lodge, A F and A M, of Hiram Council, of Worcester Chapter, of the Worcester County Commandery, Knights Templar, and he has taken all the degrees to and including the thirty-second in the Scottish Rite He is Republican in politics and a member of the Board of Trade

He married May 14 1902, Maud Edith Thresher, daughter of Harrison O and Mary Lizzie (Hinckley) Thresher of Hardwick, Massachusetts Their children are 1 Oliver Willis, Jr, born October 28 1903 2 Alma Beatrice, born April 6, 1905, both born at Worcester

ARTHUR PRENTICE RUGG (6), son of Prentice M Rugg (5), was born at Sterling, Massachusetts, August 20, 1862 (For ancestery see sketch of his brother, O Willis Rugg)

Arthur P Rugg passed his youthful days at home in his native town, where he attended the district schools, and later prepared for college at Lancaster high school, from which institution he was graduated in 1879 He entered Amherst College was graduated *cum laude* in 1883, and immediately began the study of law, entering the Boston University Law School In 1886 he received his degree of Bachelor of Laws *magna cum laude*, was admitted to the bar the same year, and was selected to serve as class orator at the commencement exercises Worcester having been chosen as the central field for his work he entered into a law partnership with John R Thayer, recently representative in congress from the third Massachusetts district The firm of Thayer & Rugg in 1886 had their offices in the Walker building but the present spacious offices of the firm are to be found on the eighth floor of the State Mutual building, where they located shortly after the completion of the building

Mr Rugg s professional career has been very active and successful He has won many notable victories for his firm, having few equals as a trial lawyer and no superior in the preparation of cases He has confined himself to no special line of practice, and though not generally known as a criminal lawyer has had an extended experience in the criminal courts, having in 1893 and 1894 served as assistant district attorney *pro tempore* and in April, 1895 was appointed assistant district attorney by Herbert Parker He was chosen city solicitor July 5 1897, to succeed William S B Hopkins, and has been annually re-elected since that year a fact which testifies to his sterling integrity and qualifications for office This is one of the most important positions of the kind in the state and his excellent service rendered in behalf of the public during his term of office has won for him the complete confidence of the citizens and taxpayers of the city He was admitted to practice in the supreme court of the United States, November 28, 1904 for the purpose of arguing writs of error in the famous cases of the City of Worcester *vs* the Worcester Consolidated Street Railway in relation to conditions in location for tracks He has devoted himself exclusively to the work of his profession avoiding political office and other interests that he felt would conflict with the requirements of his chosen vocation His services as counsel for various towns in the county when involved in litigation have been often sought He is counsel for many corporate interests and has a large clientage among all classes In recent years he has been called upon to serve on many important commissions to abolish grade crossings and to determine apportionments in the Metropolitan district Mr Rugg had a brief service in the common council of Worcester, representing his ward in 1894-95 and during his second year was president of the board He has been a trustee of the Worcester Mechanics Savings Bank since 1897, and was a director of the First National Bank from 1900 to 1903, when the bank went into voluntary liquidation He is a member of Athelstan Lodge, Ancient, Free and Accepted Masons, Hiram Council, Worcester Chapter, Worcester County Commandery, Knights Templar He is a member of the Worcester Club, Commonwealth Club, American Bar Association, Appalachian Club of Boston, American Forestry Association, Worcester Board of Trade, Worcester County Horticultural Society, Worcester County Agricultural Society, and the Worcester Society of Antiquity He is president of the Amherst College Alumni Association (1906), a trustee of the School of Expression, Boston, an active member of the Church of the Unity (Unitarian), of Worcester, a member of the parish committee and a Republican in politics

Mr Rugg has met with uncommon success in the prosecution of his chosen profession because of the elements of success within him He is studious, thoughtful, quick to comprehend, has in store a generous fund of practical knowledge, and is a gentleman and a man of honor Aside from his extensive yet rapidly increasing legal practice, he has found time to respond to invitations to deliver various addresses, among which might be named a memorial address at Sterling, Massachusetts, on the death of the late President McKinley, and "Colonial Farm Life in Colonial New England," delivered before the Worcester Society of Antiquity He has also delivered Memorial Day addresses before various Grand Army Posts, also on other public occasions, some of which may be found in print He has also been called upon to act on various commissions and boards of arbitrations when questions of law were involved

As these pages were undergoing revision, Mr Rugg was paid the high compliment of having been selected by Governor Guild to fill the vacancy occasioned by the resignation of Hon John Lathrop and was accordingly commissioned associate justice of the supreme court and took his seat on the bench, in the court house at Worcester, on October 1 1906

Mr Rugg married, in Worcester, Massachusetts April 10, 1889 Florence May Belcher, daughter of Charles and Esther (Jewett) Belcher, of Worcester Their children are Charles Belcher, born January 20, 1890, Arthur Prentice, Jr, born August 22 1893 Esther Cynthia, born September 5 1896 Donald Sterling, born August 18, 1898, died February 22 1899

ANDREW J BANCROFT Lieutenant Thomas Bancroft (1) son of John and Jane Bancroft was born in England in 1622 He was the immigrant ancestor of Andrew J Bancroft of Lancaster Massachusetts His father also came over but died in Lynn in 1637 His mother, Jane Bancroft had land assigned to her in Lynn where the family first settled in New England She was living in Lynn in 1638

Thomas Bancroft was living in Dedham Massachusetts in 1647 and was admitted to townsman in 1648 He removed in 1652 or 1653, when his name first appears on the church records of Reading Massachusetts but there is no proof that he ever lived within the limits of that town but he certainly lived in that vicinity the remainder of his days He hired a five hundred acre farm of Samuel Bennett in what is now Saugus, an adjacent town, and the Reading church was the nearest to his home, so he belonged to that parish The town lines in that neighborhood seem to have been indefinite He was not a proprietor of the town of Reading, but his son Thomas lived in Reading and became a very prominent citizen there

The home of Lieutenant Thomas Bancroft was just south of the Straits, a narrow roadway through the rocky hills leading from Reading to Saugus It is still known as the Bancroft place The survey of the line between Lynn and Charlestown made about 1670 mentions the house that was Ensign Bancroft's" About that time he bought seventy acres of land at Lynnfield, three miles from Reading church which was still the nearest to his home In 1678 the deed of the adjoining Holyoke farm recites "that it had been for some time in possession and improvement of Thomas Bancroft and a half acre with building thereon was reserved and deeded to Bancroft"

Lieutenant Bancroft died in Lynn, August 19, 1691 The inventory of his estate was filed November 24, 1691 by his son Ebenezer It shows that he owned land at Reading and Lynn, etc An agreement for a division of the property was made by the widow, Elizabeth, sons Thomas, John and Ebenezer, Joseph Brown, husband of the daughter Elizabeth, and Sarah Bancroft, the youngest daughter The widow died May 1, 1711

He married (first) Alice Bacon daughter of Michael Bacon, of Dedham, Massachusetts, March 31, 1647-8 She died March 29, 1648 He married (second) Elizabeth Metcalf, daughter of Michale and Sarah Metcalf She was admitted to the church December 14, 1651, at Dedham, and November 22, 1669, at Reading, by letter from Dedham The only child of Lieutenant Thomas and Alice was Thomas born 1648, of whom later The children of Thomas and Elizabeth were Elizabeth, born and died 1650, John, born February 3 1651-2, married Elizabeth Bacon, Elizabeth, born at Reading, December 7 1653 married Joseph Brown, Sarah, born 1660, died 1661, Raham, born 1662, died 1683, Sarah born 1665, married John Woodward, Ebenezer, born 1667, married Abigail Eaton and resided at Lynnfield Mary, born 1670

(II) Thomas Bancroft son of Lieutenant Thomas Bancroft (1), was born in Dedham Massachusetts in 1648 or 1649 He settled in Reading, Massachusetts, and became one of the most prominent citizens there He was an officer in King Philip's war, selectman for several years He resided in the western part of Reading where the old Bancroft homestead is to be seen at present His was the fourth house built in the west parish, it was near what is now called the Abraham Temple place

He married in 1673, Sarah Poole daughter of Jonathan and Judith Poole Their children were Thomas of whom later, Jonathan, born and died 1675 Sarah born 1676, married Abraham Bryant, Mehitable, born 1678 married ——— Parker, Jonathan born 1681 married Sarah ———, died in 1702 Raham born 1684 Judith, born 1688 married ——— Parker Samuel, born 1691, died 1692, Samuel born 1693, Elizabeth, born 1696, married 1713

(III) Captain Thomas Bancroft, son of Thomas Bancroft (2) was born in Reading Massachusetts 1673 He also settled in Reading He married Mary Webster Their children were Thomas, born in Reading about 1705, Benjamin, of whom later, Jonathan, married Mary Pierpont, Joshua, married Mary Lamson, resided in Reading and Worcester

(IV) Captain Benjamin Bancroft, son of Captain Thomas Bancroft (3), was born in Reading, Massachusetts, 1701 or 1702, died at Groton, July 21, 1787 He settled first in the adjoining town of Charlestown and later at Groton, Massachusetts. He joined the church at Charlestown November 3, 1728 He bought his house there in 1723 of John Allum He was a tanner by trade He was captain of militia and probably served in the colonial wars He married Anna Lawrence, daughter of John Lawrence, of Lexington, and a descendant of John Lawrence, of Watertown (See Lawrence pedigree with A B Lawrence sketch, Fitchburg, in this work) The children of Captain Benjamin and Anna Bancroft were Benjamin, Jr, of whom later, Edmund, born at Charlestown, Massachusetts November 23, 1726, settled at Pepperell, formerly part of Groton, was treasurer, deputy to the general court, and captain, Anna, born December 20, 1728, at Groton, died November, 1806, Mary, born April 4, 1731, died December 1, 1732, Joseph, born September 5, 1733 died November 24, 1737, Mary, born February 6, 1735, died November 25, 1737, Joseph, born August 1, 1738, died November 2, 1745, Sarah, born November 2, 1740, died November 2, 1745, Jonathan, born January 27, 1743, died October 26, 1745

(V) Deacon Benjamin Bancroft, son of Captain Benjamin Bancroft (4), was born in Charlestown, Massachusetts, September 29, 1724, and died at Groton, October 27, 1804, aged eighty years He followed his father's trade, a tanner, and like his father became captain of the militia company In the revolution his son Benjamin was a soldier He seems to have served also at Rutland, guarding British prisoners in Captain Nathaniel Harrington's company, Colonel Abijah Stearns's regiment, in 1778 He was treasurer of the town and deacon of the church at Groton

He married, October 18, 1749, Alice Tarbell, of Groton She died November 29, 1781 Their children were Benjamin, Jr, born August 7, 1750, at Charlestown or Groton, Abel, born at Groton, May 28, 1752, Thaddeus, born April 12, 1754, William, born May 2, 1756, lieutenant in the revolution, married 1782 Agnes Edes, Joseph, born July 3, 1760, Samuel, of whom later, Sarah, born July 29, 1767 John born January 28, 1771

(VI) Samuel Bancroft son of Deacon Benjamin Bancroft (5) was born at Groton, Massachusetts July 6, 1764 He settled in Groton He married, May 7, 1789, Abigail Child He was educated in the common schools and learned the trade of stone mason, which he followed all his life He was also a farmer His children were Isaac, born November 6, 1789, Tarbell, May 19, 1792, Edmund, May 23, 1794, Abigail, October 23, 1796, Stowell, April 11, 1799, George W, August 11, 1801, Eliza, July 14 1803

(VII) Stowell Bancroft son of Samuel Bancroft (6), was born in Groton Massachusetts, April 11 1799 He was educated in the district schools and learned the trade of his father, a stone mason, and followed it as a business during his active life In politics he was an active Whig for many years He resided in Lancaster, Massachusetts, and in Mount Vernon New Hampshire He married (first) Mary Heywood, December 3 1822, she died January 3, 1825 She was born February 7, 1796, daughter of Joseph and Elizabeth (Perkins) Trow He married (second) Martha D Trow, July 3, 1825 she died December 15, 1876 He died March

14, 1883 Of his children one was by the first marriage and five by the second The child of Stowell and Mary was Mary Elizabeth, born December 17, 1824. The children of Stowell and Martha Bancroft were Emily Heywood, born July 19, 1826, died December 29, 1875, Andrew Jackson, born April 28, 1829, Sabrina Francis, born August 28, 1831, William Henry Child, born August 10, 1833, Charles Bainbridge, born September 4, 1838, died June 2 1903

(VIII) Andrew J Bancroft, son of Stowell Bancroft (7), and Martha Dodge (Trow) Bancroft, was born in Dunstable, Massachusetts, April 28, 1829 He removed to New Hampshire with his parents when he was a young boy and attended the district schools there He settled in Mount Vernon, New Hampshire where he engaged in the business of lumbering and farming achieving more than ordinary success In 1856 he removed to Lancaster, Massachusetts, and settled there on a farm For the past few years Mr Bancroft has led a retired life In politics Mr Bancroft is a Republican He has taken a leading part in town affairs in Lancaster and for over thirty years has been on the board of assessors He has also served the town as road commissioner, overseer of the poor and selectman He is an active attendant of the Congregational church and one of its most liberal supporters Mr Bancroft inherits the executive ability and strength of character that have made the Bancrofts for many generations leaders and men of prominence He has given to his fellow citizens the utmost satisfaction in the various positions of trust and responsibility that he has filled

He married, October, 1856, Mary A Clough, daughter of James and Sarah (Sargent) Clough, of Orange, New Hampshire Their children are Edwin E, born September 10, 1858, married Josephine Given and they have three children, William L, born February 20 1862 married Agnes White and they have had two children George A, born July 1, 1865 married Edith R Worcester, Charles G, born December 3, 1867 married Blanche Hight and they have two children, Martha S, born November 2, 1871

WHITNEY FAMILY John Whitney (1), the immigrant ancestor of Anna Henshaw Whitney, of Lancaster, Massachusetts was born in England in 1659 He settled early in Watertown, Massachusetts, where he was living in June, 1635 He married in England, Elinor ——— who was born in 1599 and died at Watertown, May 11, 1659 He married (second) in Watertown, September 29, 1659 Judith Clement, who died before him He died June 1, 1673 (Something of his ancestry and more of his early history will be found under the sketch of the Whitney family of Worcester, Massachusetts, in this work)

The children of John and Elinor Whitney were Mary, baptized in England May 23 1619, died young, John, of whom later, Richard, born in England 1626 married Martha Coldam, Nathaniel born in England, 1627, Thomas, born in England 1629 married Mary Kettell, Jonathan, born in England, 1634, married Lydia Jones Joshua, born in Watertown, July 5 1635, married Lydia ———, (second) Mary ———, (third) Abigail Tarbell, Caleb born at Watertown, July 12 1640, buried July 12, 1640, Benjamin, born at Watertown, July 6, 1643 married Jane —— and (second) Mary Poor

(II) John Whitney, son of John Whitney (1), was born in England, 1620 He settled in Watertown He married Ruth Reynolds, daughter of Robert Reynolds, of Watertown, Weathersfield and Boston John Whitney's estate was administered by his widow and sons, John and Benjamin The inventory dated October 26, 1692, included eighteen parcels of land amounting to two hundred and ten acres His will was dated February 27, 1685, it was not proved His homestall was a three-acre lot on the east side of Lexington street on land granted first to E How, bought by him in 1643, the lot next south of the homestead of the Phillips family and probably the same lot occupied by his grandson, Bradshaw Whitney He was a soldier in King Philip's war under Captain Hugh Mason He died October 12, 1692

The children of John and Ruth Whitney were John born September 17, 1643, married Elizabeth Hinds, Ruth, born April 15, 1645 married, June 20 1664, John Shattuck, who was in the Squakeag fight September 4 1675 and was drowned soon afterward at Charlestown Ferry, Nathaniel, born February 1 1646 married Sarah Hagar, Samuel, born July 26, 1648, married Mary Bemis, Mary, born April 29 1650, Joseph born January 15 1651 married Martha Beach Sarah, born March 17, 1653, married, October 18, 1681, Daniel Harrington Elizabeth born June 9, 1656, married, December 19, 1678, Daniel Warren Hannah, Benjamin, born June 28, 1660, married Abigail Hagar

(III) John Whitney, son of John Whitney (2), was born in Watertown, September 17, 1643, married in 1669, Elizabeth Harris who was born November 9, 1644, daughter of Robert Harris She owned the covenant in the Roxbury church March 30, 1671 He was admitted a freeman in May, 1684 He was a member of the Second Church of Roxbury, November 2 1712, and doubtless had belonged to the First Church there His house lot, containing nine acres, was situated on Pond street, in that part of Roxbury called Jamaica Plain He was a soldier in King Philip's war in 1676, and owned the covenant in the church at Roxbury in February 1684 He was a tailor by trade His will is dated September 1718 and was proved March 13 1726-7 He died March 4, 1726 The children of John and Elizabeth Whitney were Daniel born December 3 1681 married Susanna Curtis, Timothy, born April 16, 1678, married Margaret Bacon, Elizabeth, born September 9 1670, Ruth, born at Roxbury, baptized August 31, 1674, married April 22 1701, Joseph Adams, resided in Brookline, Sarah, baptized August 2, 1684, died July 4 1689, John born April 1, 1672 died young

(IV) Daniel Whitney, eldest son of John Whitney (3), was born in Roxbury, Massachusetts, December 3 1681 He lived at Roxbury He married, June 21, 1704, Susanna Curtis Their children were John born May 23 1705 inherited land of his grandfather Whitney at Woodstock, Connecticut, then in Massachusetts, Elizabeth born February 4, 1706 Susanna, born February 21, 1708, Daniel born March 26, 1711, Anna, born April 30, 1713, Elijah of whom later, Ruth, born December 5, 1718, Elisha, born October 5, 1722, Esther, born July 11, 1726, married, March 8, 1745, John White

(V) Elijah Whitney, son of Daniel Whitney (4) was born at Roxbury, Massachusetts January 15 1715 He married Hannah ——— They settled in Warwick Massachusetts where in 1776 he served on the committee of safety and correspondence Their children, born at Roxbury, were Elijah, born September 23 1744, Elisha, born October 6, 1747, of whom later, John, born November 29 1749 married May Payson, Hannah, born June 13 1756 baptized at Roxbury same year, Daniel, married Sarah Gay

(VI) Elisha Whitney, son of Elijah Whitney (5), was born at Roxbury, October 6, 1747 He married in Newton, Massachusetts, June 4, 1769, Abigail Dana He was a lieutenant in the revolution His picture painted by Stuart is owned by his grandson, Benjamin D Whitney He resided at West Roxbury Massachusetts The children of Lieutenant Elisha and Abigail Whitney were Experience, born February 1776, died September 17, 1777. Abigail born April 10, 1778, married, November 17, 1799, Joseph Staver, of Boston, Elisha born February 4, 1780, married Sarah Heath, Asa of whom later Pedy, born July 20 1784, married in Roxbury, 1801, Colonel Joseph Dudley, who was born October 16 1780, he owned and occupied the old Dudley homestead in Roxbury, he was a farmer strict in principles, generous with his fortune, he gave a site for a townhouse in Roxbury, William born June 17, 1788, died unmarried, Elizabeth, born March 3, 1793, died unmarried

(VII) Asa Whitney, son of Elisha Whitney (6), was born in Boston, May 18, 1782 He married at Pomfret, Connecticut, December 31, 1805, Mary Hammond, who was born December 7, 1787, and died 1845 He died March 4 1826 He resided at Pomfret, Roxbury, Cambridge and Boston

The children of Asa and Mary Whitney were 1 Benjamin Duick, born November 6, 1807, married (first) Elizabeth Williams and (second) Charlotte Genella 2 Daniel H, born October 7, 1809, died October 6 1817 3 Sarah Hammond, born May 23 1812, died June 23 1817 4 Mary, born March 5 1815, married Professor Cornelius C Felton of Harvard University who was born in West Newbury Massachusetts November 6, 1807, and died in Chester, Pennsylvania, February 26, 1862 He graduated from Harvard in 1827, taught school two years at Geneseo, New York, was appointed Latin tutor at Harvard in 1829, became Greek tutor in 1830, college professor of Greek in 1832, and in 1834 was chosen Eliot professor of Greek literature He was for many years regent of the college, in 1860 he was elected president and continued in the office until his death He was a member of the Massachusetts Board of Education and one of the regents of the Smithsonian Institute He was one of the most profound and enthusiastic classical scholars in the country He edited and translated a number of important works He wrote "Greece Ancient and Modern"—and other important books 5 Emily, born September 27 1817, married Dr Joseph Sargent of Worcester (See sketch of Dr Sargent and his family in this work) 6 Asa H of whom later 7 Sarah born July 13, 1822, married Frederick W Gale of Worcester both lost on the steamer "Arctic," September 27, 1854 8 Catherine Dean, born December 17, 1824 married May, 1849 Dr Henry Sargent (See Sargent family of Worcester and Leicester)

(VIII) Asa Hammond Whitney, son of Asa Whitney (7) was born in Boston June 17 1819 He married October 3 1842 Laura Leffingwell Henshaw, who was born June 23 1820 at Warren, Ohio, and died April 20 1886 He prepared for college in Boston schools and was graduated at Harvard College in 1838 After leaving college he made a voyage to the Mediterranean for his health and subsequently went to Rio Janiero as supercargo On his return he became the junior partner of the firm of Henshaw & Whitney wholesale druggists, Boston He resided in Cambridge, later he became interested in railroad business and removed to Norfolk Virginia where he managed the financial affairs of the Seaboard & Roanoke Railroad Company, as its treasurer He was a man of great energy and earnestness of character He resided late in life at Vicksburg, Mississippi, where he died October 7 1858

The children of Asa Hammond and Laura Leffingwell Whitney were 1 Laura L, born June 15 1843, died January 24 1870 2 Anna Henshaw, of whom later 3 Richard Sullivan, born June 19 1846, died August 23, 1847 4 Catherine Dean, born June 17, 1849, married Robert George Lawton, of Hudson New York, on the English frigate "Narcissus," off Havana Cuba, May 31 1871 He was born August 12, 1839, and died December 2, 1904 was a resident of Havana, member of the banking firm of Lawton Brothers Their children were Robert Henshaw Lawton, born in Havana, April 3 1872, died at Lancaster, Massachusetts, December 10 1881 Sydney Allen Lawton, born at Lancaster, November 2 1873, graduate of Harvard University, 1895 now with the firm of Wrenn Brothers, brokers, New York city, married, June 20 1901, Harriet Sheldon Lawton, of Hudson New York, and they reside at Rye, New York, and have two children—Sarah, born October 19, 1902, and Katharine born October 14 1904, Ethel Whitney Lawton, born at Lancaster, October 4, 1875, married Chester Parker, of South Lancaster, Massachusetts, at New York city October 5, 1899, resides in Lancaster and they have had three children—Chester Parker, Jr, born September 29 1900, Felton Parker, born January 14 1902 died March 21, 1902, and Lydia Parker born November 4, 1903 Richard Henshaw Lawton, born in Lancaster, March 23, 1888 resides in Rye, New York 4 Hammond Moore, born at Norfolk Virginia, June 28, 1851, resides in Brookline Massachusetts, married at Boston, November 13, 1879, Catherine Howard Reed, and their children are—Catherine, born at Longwood, Massachusetts, September 28 1881 married September 30, 1903 Theodore W Little, at Cohasset Massachusetts, they reside in Brookline, Margaret born at Longwood Massachusetts December 28 1886 resides at Longwood 5 Emily Stark born at Norfolk, Virginia, July 10, 1854 resides at Lancaster

(IX) Anna Henshaw Whitney, daughter of Asa Hammond Whitney (8), was born in Cambridge, Massachusetts, November 30 1844 She attended school there and in Norfolk, Virginia In 1855 she was sent to a boarding school at Keene New Hampshire with her elder sister, Laura L Whitney In 1858 they entered Lasell Seminary at Auburndale, Massachusetts, graduating in 1860 During the next two years she was a teacher in Lasell Seminary and in the year following she taught for a year in a private school in Worcester In February, 1864 she accepted a position as teacher in the academy at Lancaster, which shortly became the Lancaster high school With the exception of one year, 1880-1, spent abroad she continued to teach there until 1888

Miss Whitney has served several three-year terms on the school committee of Lancaster, and is at present secretary of the board She is also secretary of the board of trustees of the Public Library

Since giving up her work as teacher in the public schools she has taught drawing and painting to private pupils and in the public schools at times Miss Whitney has an attractive home at Lancaster and pursues agriculture at her farm "Few Acres," as one of her avocations For many years she kept kennels of St Bernards and pug dogs for pleasure and profit and has officiated as judge of these and various other breeds at the leading bench shows in the United States and Canada beginning soon after her return from Europe and continuing to the present time

EZRA BURTON The Burton family from which Ezra Burton of Lancaster, Massachusetts, is descended, settled in Essex county The progenitor was probably Boniface Burton, of Salem, who died June 13, 1669, at the age of one hundred and thirteen years He was one of the first settlers, being made a freeman May 6, 1635 He removed to Reading, Massachusetts, in 1644 His wife was Frances The Burtons settled in New Hampshire where Mahlon Burton, grandfather of Ezra Burton, was born He is remembered as a man of fine physique and a public speaker of some distinction He lived at Wilton, New Hampshire, where many of the descendants of the old Burton family are to be found today In this section of southern New Hampshire the family has lived for five or more generations Some of them went to Vermont after the revolution when a new state was carved out of the wilderness by the sons of Massachusetts and New Hampshire Among the children of Mahlon Burton was a son named for him, Mahlon Burton, Jr

Nahum Burton spent his youth on his father's farm He attended school at Wilton and became a farmer He too went to Vermont and settled at Weston, where he lived and died He was a Whig and like most of the pioneers extremely patriotic He married (first) Charlotte Pettingill After her death he married her sister, Lucinda Pettingill Their father was in the revolutionary war at the battle of Bunker Hill, and died in Weston, New Hampshire, May 16, 1859 She was born in New Hampshire She was a woman of exceptional beauty of character Among her children was a son, Ezra, who was born at Weston, March 6, 1827

Ezra Burton lived the typical life of a Vermont farmer's son in the early part of the nineteenth century He remembers the introduction of the steam railroads and the gradual extinction of the stage coach and other former methods of transportation He saw the industrial birth of the new era in America He attended such schools as were within his reach at his Vermont home There were eight children and each in turn had to do his share in helping run the farm The pioneers who went to Vermont saw their children and grandchildren drift away In this family Ezra was the fourth son to leave the old homestead and start life in Boston The brothers were in the trucking business and at first he worked for them At length he went into the business of brush making with one of his brothers, and he followed this business until he retired For thirty years he was salesman of the firm and spent much of his time travelling in the United States He began when there were few railroads, when the stage covered more ground than the steam cars He was successful in building up a large business and the firm established a reputation second to none for their product He moved to Lancaster, Massachusetts, in 1868, and since then occupied the residence in which he now resides He still retains an interest in the brush factory, although he retired from active business in 1895 He is a Republican in politics He attends the Unitarian church at Lancaster

He married April 7, 1863 Sarah Elizabeth Brace, daughter of Thomas Brace, of Salem Massachusetts Thomas Brace was a sea captain of a vessel in trade with China Their children were Linda, died young, Edward O, Maude E, married David Hinckley, Ruth O

SUMNER FAMILY From the best obtainable evidence it is believed that Roger Sumner, of Bicester, Oxford county, England died December, 1608 and buried in St Edbury churchyard was the progenitor of the Sumner family in America, at least the New England and especially the Worcester county branches He married Joan Franklin, November 2, 1601, and by this union one son was born, William (1), who became the American ancestor William was baptized at Bicester church, Oxford county, England, January 2, 1602, and in 1625 married Mary West, and by her had two sons, born in England Roger, baptized August, 1632, and George baptized March, 1633 The family then emigrated to New England, settling at Dorchester, Massachusetts, about 1635, and from this family, it is believed, have sprung all the New England Sumners, including Governor Increase, Gen W H Sumner, and our great statesman, Hon Charles Sumner, of congressional fame

(II) William Sumner, son of William (1) and Mary, was probably born in Massachusetts He married Elizabeth Clement, daughter of Augustine Clement, of Dorchester He was a mariner

(II) Roger Sumner, born in England, son of William (1), married the daughter of Thomas Joslin, an early settler at Hingham Roger was admitted to the church at Dorchester, 1656, but moved to Lancaster and there remained until that town was destroyed by the Indians, when he moved to Milton, Massachusetts, where he was deacon of the first church His children were Abigail Samuel and Ebenezer Another son, William, was the father of Seth Sumner, and he the father of Job Sumner, who had a son Job, born at Milton January 20, 1776, and changed his name to Charles Pinckney The last named was high sheriff of Suffolk county, Massachusetts, and married Relief Jacobs, by whom he had children, including Hon Charles Sumner, born at Boston, January 6 1811, who became the great and eloquent American anti-slavery statesman, and who was brutally assaulted in his seat in congress by Brooks, a pro-slavery member

(II) George Sumner, son of William (1), was born in England, February 14, 1634, made a freeman, 1637, married Mary Baker He lived on Brush hill, Milton, and was deacon of the church there His children were Mary, George, Samuel, William, Ebenezer, Edward, Joseph, Benjamin

(III) George Sumner, son of George (2) and Mary (Baker) Sumner, married Ann Tucker of Roxbury Their children were Samuel, born November 13, 1695 died February 8 1782, George, Ann, Mary, William, Susanna, Elizabeth, Josiah, Abigail

(IV) Samuel Sumner, son of George (3), and Ann (Tucker) Sumner married Elizabeth Griffin, daughter of Joseph Griffin, of Roxbury They settled at Pomfret Elizabeth was born February 2, 1700 and died November 13 1772 She was esteemed a woman of exemplary piety Their children were Ann, Samuel, Elizabeth, George Joseph born January 19, 1740, died December 9, 1824, Sarah

(V) Joseph Sumner, son of Samuel (4), and Elizabeth (Griffin) Sumner was born July 19 1740 at Pomfret, Connecticut He became a member of Yale College, and from that institution received high honors He early devoted his life to the ministry, and in June, 1762, when twenty-three years of age, commenced preaching During all the trials and conflicts of his life he was noted for cheerfulness, and other social graces Not easily provoked he knew what was due to his character and he secured respect from all Soon after he commenced preaching, says Aaron Bancroft, D D (father of the historian George Bancroft) in a tribute-sermon on Mr Sumner "In the contest between the parent country and the American provinces, he proved himself an efficient patriot and during the Revolutionary struggle he suffered the inconveniences and privations to which men of his profession were exposed from the state of public affairs, and all these trials he bore with patience and equanimity His constitution was vigorous, through all his life he was blessed with good health During the period of sixty-two years he was never absent from the stated communion of his church, and till bodily infirmity rendered him unable to officiate, the public exercises of the Sabbath in this place were suspended only seven times, on account of his indisposition, or his journeyings His method of preaching was evangelistic, he dwelt not on controversy, but, well instructed in the essential truths of revelation, kept back nothing profitable to his people An advocate for Christian liberty, and supporting the Protestant principles of the sufficiency of Scripture as the rule of faith and practice he endeavored to secure the harmony of the church by inspiring Christian brethren with unity of spirit, and binding them together in the bond of peace" As an illustration of his broad, liberal views, it is related that at a meeting of the Worcester Association of Ministers as was usual, Dr Bancroft applied for admission to membership Opposition was made by some of the members, and the subject was put over to the next meeting, and at that time a majority appeared against Dr Bancroft's admission On this result, Dr Sumner of Shrewsbury, and Mr Avery of Holden arose and declared that they would not belong to a body which passed so illiberal a vote as that rejecting Dr Bancroft and that the Association might meet when and where they would but they would no longer be considered members of it In consequence of this withdrawal the Association was broken up Dr Sumner, of whom this memoir is written married Lucy Williams, of Pomfret, Connecticut, June 8, 1763 Their children were Sarah Samuel, Joseph, Joanna, Lucy, Elizabeth Dorothy, Erastus

(V) Increase Sumner, governor of Massachusetts, son of Increase (4), was born in Norfolk county, Massachusetts November 27, 1746 The first rudiments of his education were taught him by Judge William Cushing of the supreme judicial court who was preceptor of the public grammar school in Roxbury in 1752 His father believed that the life of an honest hard-working farmer was the best for his son but afterward many importuned him to educate his son and namesake to fill higher places of public trust All obstacles having been surmounted he entered college in 1763 and graduated 1767 He spent the next two years in teaching at Roxbury He studied law under barrister Samuel Quincy, and was admitted to the bar in 1770, opening his office at Roxbury, in the house in which his mother continued to reside until her death In 1776, a period of great difficulty, Mr Sumner was chosen a member of the general court, serving until 1780, and was then elected senator from Suffolk county Massachusetts

It was September 30, 1779, when he formed a connection of much importance in every well-rounded man's career, by his marriage with Elizabeth Hyslop of Boston, a lady of rare intelligence, and remarkable for her amiable disposition During the same year he was chosen a member of the convention for forming a state constitution In June 1782 he was chosen a member of congress by the Massachusetts legislature, in place of Timothy Danielson who resigned but Sumner never took his seat in that body August of the same year he was made associate justice of the supreme judicial court In 1797 he was elected governor, and was re-elected, and his able, firm and patriotic administration won for him a lasting place in the great heart of the commonwealth In 1799 he was made governor by an almost unanimous vote Out of three hundred and ninety-three towns in the state, including the 'District of Maine,' one hundred and eighty were unanimous for Sumner But at the commencement of the political year he was bedridden, and June 7, 1799 in his fifty-third year, his career ended 'No death,' says one biographical writer of that day, except Washington's (which took place six months later) was ever more deeply deplored in Massachusetts" Personally, it should here be added of Governor Sumner, that he was a devoted son a loving and attentive husband, a kind and affectionate father and friend The purity of his morals was never once questioned He was a practical farmer and enjoyed the cultivation of the soil He was a lover and owner of fine horses In horticulture, he found great delight and with his own hands grafted his whole orchard In early life he made a public profession of Christianity, becoming a member of the Congregational Society and church The only child of Governor Increase Sumner and his wife Elizabeth Hyslop was William Hyslop, born July 4, 1780

(VI) William Hyslop, only son of Governor Increase Sumner (5), was born, 'on the night of July 4, 1780' He graduated from Harvard College, 1799, was aide-de-camp to Governors Strong and Brooks, to the former 1810-16, and to the latter 1816-48, when he was appointed adjutant-general by Governor Brooks He held that position under Brooks, Eustis, Lincoln and Davis, till 1834, when he resigned For eleven years from 1808 he was one of the representatives of Boston September 10 1814, he was appointed by Governor Strong executive agent to repair to "the District of Maine (then invaded by the enemy) and promptly provide every practicable means for defense of that part of the state" In December, 1814, he was appointed by the Board of War to borrow money of the banks and pay off the troops which had been called out in Maine In 1816 he was agent with Hon James Lloyd to present the Massachusetts militia claim to the United States government for its services In November, 1826 he was appointed by the secretary of war, a member of the board of army and militia officers of which Major General Scott was president, to report a plan for the organization of the militia and a system of cavalry tactics He first married Mary Ann Perry, October 4, 1826 She was the widow of Raymond H Perry, brother of Commodore O H Perry Mr Sumner died July 14, 1834

(VI) Samuel Sumner, son of Joseph (5), and Lucy (Williams) Sumner, was born at Shrewsbury, September 24 1765 He was graduated at Dartmouth College, 1776, and appointed English preceptor of the Leicester Academy, July, 1788 After leaving Leicester he studied theology with his father, and was ordained over the church and society at Southboro June, 1791 In 1797 he was dismissed by letter to St Albans Vermont He next moved to Bakersfield Vermont, and became pastor The peculiar circumstances under which he was ordained are thus given "The region of the country about Bakersfield was, in the beginning of the last century, an almost unbroken wilderness Indeed, it is said Mr Sumner's first approach to its wild domain was by a path designated by blazed trees As the place was so difficult to cross, Dr Sumner arranged that the ceremonies of installation should be held in his own church in Shrewsbury, where they were performed after the approved orthodox man-

Geo Sumner

ner, the only peculiarity being the absence of the minister installed" He afterward removed to Troy, Vermont, where he died at the home of his son, in 1837, aged seventy-two years He is said to have often expressed himself, that in selecting the pulpit for his sphere of duty, he mistook his calling

(VI) Sarah Sumner, eldest daughter of Joseph (5), and Lucy (Williams) Sumner, married William Jennison, of Worcester, in 1788

(VI) Joanna Sumner, second daughter of Joseph (5) and Lucy Sumner, married, September 6, 1806, Edward Sumner, of Roxbury He was a cousin of Governor Increase Sumner

(VI) Lucy Sumner, third daughter of Joseph (5) and Lucy Sumner, born at Shrewsbury, December 2, 1771, married Joseph Wheeler, of Worcester, January 13, 1793 In 1803 they moved to Dixfield, Maine, then a part of Massachusetts, and known as 'the District of Maine" Dixfield was then known as Township No 1, on Androscoggon River, District of Maine,' and letters were so addressed to Mr Wheeler

(VI) Erastus Sumner, youngest child of Joseph (5) and Lucy (Williams) Sumner, born February 10, 1783, married Lavinia Boyd, of Marlboro, July 12, 1805 Their children were L Caroline, born January 7, 1807 2 Lucy, born August 14, 1809 3 Lydia Ann, born November 8, 1814 5 Jane Augusta, born November 18, 1817 6 George, born March 22, 1819, died September 19, 1821 7 Catherine Whipple, born July 8, 1822 8 George, born July 25 1824, died 1893

(VII) George Sumner, son of Erastus (6) and Lavinia (Boyd) Sumner, was born July 25, 1824, and died 1893 He was the grandson of Rev Dr Joseph Sumner His first entrance into mercantile life was at the age of fifteen years, in the store of Bigelow & Goodnow, in the 'Old Tavern House," in Shrewsbury After two years of training there he came to Worcester as a clerk for Henry H Chamberlain, founder of the house of Barnard, Sumner & Putnam Co His ability rapidly advanced him until he was made a partner in the growing business and continued at its head throughout his life, and his son Edward P is still an active partner in the concern Before his marriage he made his home with Allen Rice and was thrown into the company of men who have left footprints on the business and social ways of Worcester, including the "Sixteen Associates,' a society of social and literary character He was an active member of the Worcester City Guards, as well as of the old State Guards in time of the civil war In the financial circles of the city his judgment was often appealed to He became a director in the Worcester Safe Deposit and Trust Company, and vice-president of the Five Cents Savings Bank He was a regular attendant of the Church of Unity He had no taste for political preferment, but had deep concern for the business welfare of the city He was a liberal contributor to the Library and Museums of the Worcester Society of Antiquity In 1888 he published a work entitled "Memorials of the Rev Joseph Sumner, D D, Minister of Shrewsbury, 1762-1824" The man who could say "George Sumner is my friend" had a friend indeed He was a lover of the beautiful in both art and nature, but no painter himself

One of the rules of the society of "Associates," all being single men at the time, was "He who marries first shall provide a supper for the Club" Mr Sumner married, in 1854 Sarah E Richardson daughter of Charles and Mary Richardson of Manchester, New Hampshire, and he carried out the obligation taken under the above named club rule, in a royal manner To Mr and Mrs George Sumner were born 1 George R, born May 30, 1861, married Louisa Ford of Portland, Maine, had one child, George Sumner 2 Mary Locke, born February 5, 1863, married William D Sewall of Bath, Maine, had four children—Arthur, Margaret, Dorothy and Sumner 3 Edward Prentiss, born January 18, 1866, married Pertha Perry, of Worcester, had two children, Catherine and Frances 4 Caroline Allen, born April 12, 1867, married Albert G Liscomb, of Worcester

REV GEORGE MURILLO BARTOL John Bartol (1), who lived and died in Crewkerne, Somersetshire, England, was the father of the immigrant ancestor of the Bartol family of America, to which Rev George Murillo Bartol, of Lancaster, belongs He was a glover by trade He married at Crewkerne, March 17, 1598, Agnes Williams Among their children was John Bartol, of whom later John Bartol, Sr, died at Crewkerne and was buried there February 20, 1639-40

(II) John Bartol, son of John Bartol (1) was born at Crewkerne, and baptized there April 26 1601 He married Parnell ——— His father died probably soon after he left England and he inherited the estate in England, which Thomas Letchford, a Boston attorney, conveyed to Henry Hazzard, of Bristol, England, mariner, consisting of house and garden at Crewkerne, July 25, 1641 He was plaintiff in a civil suit in 1640 and again in 1644 He lived at Salem a short time before settling in Marblehead He was selectman of the latter town in 1649-56-57-58-64 He was called a planter in the records, but was probably also a mariner He was found drowned and the inquest was held October 1 1664 His estate was administered in the Essex county court November 29, 1664 Many of his descendants have lived in Marblehead The children of John and Parnell Bartol were William, born 1629 (aged thirty-two in 1662, another record), John, Jr, born 1631, aged forty-two in 1673 Mary, born at Marblehead, February 1, 1642 Probably others died young

(III) William Bartol, son of John Bartol (2), was born in England in 1629 He died in 1690, having five sons and three daughters

(IV) Robert Bartol, son of William Bartol (3), was born in Marblehead Massachusetts, about 1660, married, March 16, 1681, Sarah Beckett He died in 1708 They had four children

(V) William Bartol, son of Robert Bartol (4), was born in Marblehead in 1691 He married, May 4, 1718, Mary Felt (One of this name was born at Casco Bay, October 12, 1687) They had four children

(VI) George Bartol, youngest son of William Bartol (5), was born in 1721 died at Freeport Maine in 1788 He settled there and his children were born there and his grandchildren to the number of thirty-one He died there and was buried with his wife and children in the old burying ground on the hill that overlooks the town and Casco Bay He died January 21, 1788 Mrs Hannah Bartol died April 4, 1784, aged sixty-five years He married (second) Hannah Allen at Falmouth (now Maine), April 17, 1746 Their children were William, born 1747, died 1843, married Elizabeth Grant, who was born in 1749 and died 1833, George, of whom later, John baptized July 21, 1734, married Mary Carter, Samuel, born 1753 died 1786, married Mary Soule The children of the first marriage were Mary, baptized May 25, 1746, married ——— Winslow, Deborah baptized May 29, 1743, died young, Deborah, baptized June 10, 1750

(VII) John Bartol, son of George Bartol (6), was born in North Yarmouth, Maine, July, 1734

He bought a place of his father containing fifty acres at Havaseeket He married Mary Carter Their children were John, born 1779, died 1805, Daniel, born 1781, married Mary Lowe, Solomon, born 1782, Desire born 1784, died 1806, Jacob, born 1786, died 1804, Dorcas, born 1788, Ephraim, born 1791, Reuben, born 1793, married ——— Chase, and had Reuben and Joseph, Ammi born 1795, Miriam, born 1797, died 1809, Alfred born 1801, married ——— Coffin and had Ansyl, Melinda, George, John and Martha, George, born 1803

(VII) William Bartol, another son of George Bartol (6), was born 1747, and died 1843 He married Elizabeth Grant, who was born in 1749 and died in 1833 Their children were David, of whom later, Hannah, Elizabeth married ——— Trott, Susan, married ——— Trott, Sarah, Esther, married ——— Douglass, Samuel, married Sarah Weston, and had Samuel and Sarah Trott, Lucretia, married ——— Denison, Jane, married ——— Stetson

(VII) George Bartol, son of George Bartol (6) and brother of the two preceding, was born about 1750 and died 1796 He married, January 12, 1775, Jane Soule, daughter of Barnabas Soule, of Freeport She was born 1756 and died January 24, 1833 Her second husband was Captain James Bacon Her ancester, George Soule, came over on the "Mayflower" on the first voyage He married about 1623 Mary Beckett, who came to Plymouth in 1621 They settled at Duxbury and had eight children Their son, John Soule, born 1632, died 1707, married Hester Dewsbury, born 1638, died 1738, and they had nine children Their fifth son, Moses Soule, died in 1751, leaving nine children The third son of Moses was Barnabas Soule, born 1705, died 1780, married Jane Bradbury She was born 1718, and Jane who married George Bartol (VII) was one of her nine children

The children of George and Jane (Soule) Bartol were Solomon, born 1775, died September 23, 1781, Barnabas, born 1777, of whom later, George, of whom later, ancestor of Rev George Bartol, Jane, born 1781, married ——— Fields, Phebe, born 1784, died 1876, married (first) ——— Veazie, (second) ——— Soule, Sarah, born 1787, married ——— Latchfield, Patience, born 1789, died 1871, married ——— Lufkin, Samuel, born 1791, died 1817, married Mary Chandler, Elizabeth, born 1793, married ——— Staples, Polly, born 1796-8

(VIII) David Bartol, son of William Bartol (7), was born 1781 and died 1849 His children were Sarah, married ——— Trott, Benjamin, born 1810, married ——— Blanchard, George, born 1812, married Betty Mitchell, William, born 1814, died 1842, Jane, born 1816, married ——— Merrill, Elizabeth, born 1821, died 1840, Mary, born 1824

(VIII) George Bartol, son of George Bartol (7), was born August 8, 1779, and died April 6, 1855 He is the father of Rev George M Bartol and also the late Rev Dr Cyrus A Bartol Like his father, he was a merchant He kept the leading general store at Freeport, Maine, for many years

He married Ann Given, March 27, 1809 Her father was a soldier in the revolution The children of George and Ann Bartol were Samuel Veazie born December 29, 1809, died February, 1810, Horace Veazie, born April 23, 1811, died January 6, 1881 Cyrus A (Rev Dr) born April 30, 1813 married, February 7, 1838, Elizabeth Howard, died December 16, 1900, leaving one child Elizabeth Howard, born January 14, 1842, Samuel Lewis, born July 23, 1817, died September, 1818, George Murillo, of whom later, Mary, born December 12, 1822, died June 21, 1902

(IX) Rev George Murillo Bartol, son of George Bartol (8), was born in Freeport, Maine, September 18, 1820 He attended the public schools of Portland, where the family lived during his youth He prepared for college at Phillips Academy, Exeter, New Hampshire He was graduated in regular course from Brown University, Providence in 1842 He studied for the ministry in the Harvard Divinity School at Cambridge from which he was graduated in 1845 He began immediately to preach He occupied the pulpit of the First Unitarian Church of Chicago for several months He preached for some time in various other towns

His first accepted call was to Lancaster to the pastorate that for nigh sixty years he filled with ability and success Under date of June 19, 1847, he wrote in reply to the call of the Society at Lancaster "I have given to the proposal of the Unitarian Society in Lancaster, by you their committee, my most serious consideration I beg that you will not deem me wanting in a proper sensibility to this mark of confidence and esteem on the part of those you represent I return my warmest thanks for the invitation and for the flattering terms with which it was accompanied I am happy to accept it and hereby very respectfully do so With fervent prayers that the grace of our Lord Jesus Christ, and the love of God, and the fellowship of His Holy Spirit may be with you all, I remain, my brethren, in the truth and affection of the Gospel, ever your friend and servant"

The committee in charge consisted of John M Washburn, Ezra Sawyer and Luke Bigelow Twenty churches were represented at the ordination, August 4, 1847 The council met in Lancaster House and organized with Rev Joseph Allen, of Northboro, moderator and Rev T P Allen, of Sterling, scribe When the certificates as to Mr Bartol's education and Christian standing were read, Rev Edward Everett Hale, then pastor of the Church of the Unity at Worcester, made the formal motion "that we are satisfied with the above testimonials and that we are ready to proceed with the ordination" Among the clergymen who took part that day Dr Hale and Mr Bartol alone survive The sermon was preached by Rev Cyrus A Bartol, brother of the candidate The Scriptures were read by Dr Hale The others who took part in the service were Rev Joseph Allen, Rev C T Thayer, of Beverly, Rev Alonzo Hill, of Worcester, Rev Mr Frothingham, of Salem

Mr Bartol came to what his friend Rev Mr Marvin called a "wealthy and respectable" congregation and the passing years have surely enhanced both those qualities The history of the First Church of Christ of Lancaster dates to 1653 when the ministry of Rev Joseph Rowlandson began His pastorate was terminated by the destruction of the town by the Indians in King Philip's war, 1675 Rev John Whiting, who was minister from 1690 to 1697, met his death at the hands of hostile Indians, and his successor, who was pastor from 1701 to 1704, met a similar fate Rev John Prentice began to preach in 1705 and died in 1748, the year he was succeeded by Rev Timothy Harrington, whose ministry continued until 1795 Rev Nathaniel Thayer was his colleague about two years and his successor as minister His remarkable record as minister, lasting until the summer of 1840, is told in a sketch of his life elsewhere in this work The next pastor and predecessor of Mr Bartol was

Rev Edmund H Sears, who was installed December 23, 1840, but was obliged to resign on account of ill health, and his work in the parish ended April 1, 1847

The present church edifice was erected in 1816 The architect was Charles Bulfinch, who is known the world over as the designer of the Massachusetts State House and of the Capitol at Washington Rev A P Marvin, who was for some years the orthodox minister at Lancaster, wrote of Mr Bartol many years ago 'The present pastor, living in times of change, has seen, with rare exceptions every pulpit, of every denomination, in the region round, occupied by successive ministers, whose power for usefulness has been, in many cases, weakened by the fickleness of the people The record is honorable to the church, and to the parish and the town with which it has been connected, during nearly seven generations of men The church was in connection with the town as a parish from 1653 till the Second Parish was formed, when the church and the First Precinct were united When Sterling became a town, Lancaster resumed its parochial functions, which continued till near the close of the ministry of Dr Thayer"

At the close of twenty-five years, August 4, 1872, the anniversary of his pastorate, a reception was given Mr Bartol and his wife in the town hall and was largely attended not only by his own parishioners but by all his townspeople and many from neighboring towns and the distance Among the speakers were Rev A P Marvin, the pastor of the Evangelical Church, Rev E H Sears, the predecessor of Mr Bartol, the venerable Rev B Whittemore and Mr Bartol himself An even more elaborate celebration of his fortieth anniversary was held August 4, 1887 When Mr Bartol completed his fiftieth year he was given such an ovation and greeting by the people of his parish, town and of the whole denomination as few men ever live to receive As Dr Hale said, and Dr Hale was one of the central figures of the celebration because he himself was one of the ministers in charge of Mr Bartol's ordination fifty years before, "there were more hydrangeas in the church today than there were in the whole state of Massachusetts fifty years ago" Mr and Mrs Bartol were given a most delightful and hearty reception in the Thayer Memorial Chapel after the more formal services in the church Dr Edward A Horton was one of the speakers Among the gifts lavished upon the good minister that day were a silver loving cup from past and present members of the Worcester Ministerial Association, of which he was a veteran member, and a magnificent silver service, suitably engraved, from his parish A poem for the occasion was written by Mrs Julia A Carney, of Galesburg, Illinois On this occasion the Springfield *Republican* said "While extremely liberal in his religious views, Dr Bartol's singularly cordial and sincere nature has won the loving regard of the ministers of all other denominations The old Unitarian Church designed by Charles Bulfinch is one of the landmarks of Worcester county People of all denominations filled it in Dr Bartol's honor"

Of Mr Bartol's service to the public Mr Henry S Nourse, the historian, said 'His power for good has not been limited by parish confines, nor restricted to the stated religious teachings of his order The clergy in Lancaster had ever been held the proper supervisors of the schools, and upon his coming Mr Bartol was at once placed in the school board and was annually re-chosen, until, having given faithful service, usually as chairman of the board, during twenty-one years, he felt constrained to ask relief from this onerous duty

'From the establishment of the public library, he has always stood at the head of the town's committee, entrusted with its management, and in its inception and increase, his refined taste, rare knowledge of books and sound literary judgment have been invaluable With talent and scholarship that invited him to a much wider field of service, he has clung lovingly to his quiet country parish, making it the centre of his efforts and aspirations He is an enthusiastic lover of nature in all her moods, a discriminating admirer of beauty in art, earnest in his soul convictions, although averse to sectarian controversy—and so tender of heart as to seem charitable to all human weakness, save that he is intolerant of intolerance"

It was Mr Bartol who expressed the unanimous sentiments of the people of Lancaster by the following resolution adopted at a legal town meeting May 20, 1865 "Whereas, on the fifteenth day of April, 1865, Abraham Lincoln, the venerated and beloved president of the United States, was by an assassin, suddenly assaulted and slain, the blow by which he fell being aimed not only at his life, but through him at the life of the nation

"Resolved, that in recording our tribute to the memory of the late president with profound sorrow for his loss, we do all beyond all party pre-possessions, own and bless in him an unselfishness in disposition and singleness of purpose, a gentleness, humanity and benevolence under great provocation, with an honesty of intention, an ardent patriotism, a fidelity to duty, and a growing mastery of the circumstances of his position, which enabled him with the blessing of God, to fulfill and bring to a successful completion, a work almost unprecedented for difficulty, that in his removal at the moment in which his labors were being crowned with the triumph of national authority and the evident approach of the blessings of peace, we see the completion of a career which the nation will ever look back to with thankfulness, and hold in tender and affectionate remembrance"

One of the most interesting homes in a town where all the homes are interesting and some remarkable for artistic and beautiful features, is the low, quaint, rambling structure in which Mr Bartol lives It stands back modestly from the highway, shielded by trees and shrubbery, with ample grounds where the flowers seem to delight in adding to the decorations of a fascinating place Inside the house there are treasures of art and literature, birds and flowers

Mr Bartol is a Republican in politics He belongs to few organizations outside the church He has been since graduation a member of the scholars' fraternity, the Phi Beta Kappa He received the degree of D D from his alma mater (Brown University) in 1892

He married, June, 1856, Elizabeth Washburn, the daughter of John M Washburn, of Lancaster Their children are George, born May 16, 1857, married January 12, 1898, Nellie Holt, and they have two children Eleanor, born October 31, 1901, Elizabeth, born November 7, 1902, Anna, born May 5, 1859, died at Manchester, Massachusetts, August, 1880, Elizabeth Washburn, born April 10, 1861, married, July 29, 1884, Harold Parker, and they have three children—Bartol Parker, born June 7, 1885, Elizabeth Parker, born September, 1886, Cornelia Conway Parker, born May 21, 1894 (See sketch of Parker family of Lancaster) Dr John Washburn, born January 10, 1864, graduate of Harvard College,

1887, married, October 2, 1900, Charlotte Hemenway Cabot, and they have three children Janet, born July 13, 1902, Dorothy, born December 15, 1903, Ann, born December 21, 1905, Mary Washburn, born August 2, 1867, resides at home with her parents, Dr Edward Francis Washburn, born in Manchester, September 5, 1874, graduate of Harvard, 1896

CHARLES AUGUSTUS CHASE William Chase (1), from whom Charles Augustus Chase, of Worcester, is directly descended, came from England with Winthrop in 1630 The surname Chase is undoubtedly derived from the French *Chasser* (to hunt) The ancestral seat in England was at Chesham in Rockinghamshire, through which runs a rapidly flowing brook or river, the Chess

Thomas Chase and Aquila Chase, who settled at Hampton, New Hampshire, in 1639, were brothers, and were perhaps cousins of William Chase, the first comer The record of Rev John Eliot, the Indian Apostle, of 'such as adjoyned themselves to this church," the First Church of Roxbury, has this entry "William Chase, he came with the first company, bringing with him his wife Mary and his son William" The maiden name of his wife is not known The son William was about seven years old at the time of migration The father applied for admission as a freeman, October 19, 1630 He was a town officer at Roxbury He served against the Narragansetts in 1645 He removed to Yarmouth, Massachusetts, in 1638, and died there His will, dated May 4, 1659, states that he was aged It was proved May 13, 1659, hence his death occurred in May of that year He bequeathed to his wife Mary and two sons, Benjamin and William (see N E Hist Reg V 388) His daughter Mary was buried at Barnstable, Massachusetts, October 28, 1652 The early records of the town of Yarmouth were destroyed by fire, so that it is impossible to give the dates of birth and death of all the children

(II) William Chase, son of William Chase (1), was born in England about 1623, if he was seven at the time of the migration He removed with his father's family to Yarmouth in 1638 He died there in 1685 It is impossible to give the name of his wife or the dates of birth of his children, it is known, however, that he had eight children, of whom William was the eldest

(III) William Chase, eldest son of William Chase (2), was born in Duxbury, Massachusetts He married for his first wife Hannah Sherman, of the stock to which Roger Sherman and General W T Sherman belonged His second wife was Priscilla Perry By the first marriage he had five children of whom the third was Isaac

(IV) Isaac Chase, third child of William Chase (3), married (first), February 10, 1704 Elizabeth Blethen of Salem, by whom he had five children, married (second) Mary Fowler, by whom he had seven

(V) Isaac Chase third son of Isaac Chase (4) married, November 13 1729, Amy Anthony, married (second) Elizabeth ———, who survived him Isaac and Amy Chase had eight children, of whom the eldest was Anthony Chase

(VI) Anthony Chase, son of Isaac Chase (5), was born at Swanzey Massachusetts February 21 1832 married (first) Katherine, daughter of Timothy and Bridget Sewell and lived at Mendon, Massachusetts He died May 3, 1817, leaving a widow Mary Chase Anthony and Katherine Chase had eight children, of whom the seventh was Israel

(VII) Israel Chase, son of Anthony Chase (6), was born September 13, 1760, married February 1, 1787, (Caroline) Matilda Butterworth, daughter of Noah and Dorcas Butterworth, of Smithfield, Rhode Island They lived in Mendon, Paxton and Worcester and had six children, of whom Anthony was the third

(VIII) Anthony Chase, third son of Israel Chase (7), was born at Paxton, Massachusetts, June 16, 1791, married (first), June 2, 1819, Lydia Earle, daughter of Pliny and Patience Earle, of Leicester (See Ralph Earle and his descendants, p 215) Married (second), April 19, 1854, Hannah Greene, daughter of Daniel and Phebe Greene, of East Greenwich, Rhode Island In early youth Mr Chase lost his father, and in 1816 entered into mercantile business in Worcester with John Milton Earle, his future brother-in-law, and became one of the owners of the *Massachusetts Spy*, continuing as such from 1823 to 1835 In 1829 he was agent for the Worcester & Providence Boating Company, formed to operate the newly opened Blackstone canal, and was soon afterward appointed collector of the canal revenue In March, 1831, he was elected county treasurer and held the office for thirty-four years In 1832 Mr Chase was chosen secretary of the Worcester Mutual Fire Insurance Company, and in 1852 was its president, an office which he held until his death, August 4, 1879 He was one of the founders and the first secretary of the Worcester Lyceum in 1829, and shaped the Worcester County Mechanics' Association in its infancy, drawing up its constitution and by-laws with his own hand in 1841, was one of the corporators of the Central Bank of Worcester on 1828, was for many years treasurer of the Worcester Agricultural Society, and for a long period director in the Citizens Bank of Worcester, was trustee and vice-president of the Worcester County Institution for Savings

Mr Chase took great interest in the public schools, often serving on the school committee, and was an alderman in the early days of the city, but frequently declined public offices on account of the confining nature of his regular vocation He gave his three sons an education at Harvard College He was a member of the Society of Friends, holding the office of elder in that body Most of the children of his ancestor, William Chase (II), joined the Society of Friends, and their descendants in great measure have been members of that religious body Some of the family in Rhode Island and southeastern Massachusetts began about a century ago to write the name Chace, but Chase is the accepted spelling He died August 4 1879, aged eighty-eight years

Lydia Earle was descended from Ralph Earle of whom a sketch is given elsewhere in this work The children of Anthony and Lydia (Earle) Chase all born in Worcester, were Pliny Earle born August 18, 1820, Lucy, December 1 1822, Thomas June 16, 1827, Eliza Earle, October 8, 1829, Charles Augustus, see forward, Sarah E May 29 1836 The children of Anthony and Hannah (Greene) Chase were Emily G, married Joseph Russell Marble (see sketch of George Russell Marble of Webster), Frederick Anthony died young

(IX) Charles Augustus Chase, fifth child of Anthony Chase (8) was born in Worcester Massachusetts September 9 1833 in a house on Salisbury street where the armory now stands His education began with the infant school, in a small building that stood at the northerly end of Summer street He graduated from the Thomas street grammar school in 1845 into the 'Classical and English High School' where he remained five years, taking a post-graduate course in mathematics While in the high school he printed a juvenile paper, "The

Humble Bee" In 1851 he entered Harvard College and was graduated from that institution in 1856, receiving the degree of A M in 1858 He joined the staff of the *Boston Daily Advertiser* in 1855, and filled the position of reporting the various departments and of office editor for seven years In 1862 he made a five months' tour of Europe and upon his return again took up his residence in Worcester, and in the autumn of 1864 was elected treasurer of Worcester county, succeeding his father, who had held the office for a third of a century He was re-elected and served altogether eleven years as treasurer In 1875 was elected on an independent ticket as register of deeds, serving in 1876 —centennial year—was soon afterward elected secretary of the board of trade, and in 1879 was treasurer and manager of the Worcester Telephone Company

Mr Chase has for more than twenty-five years been one of the pricipal officers of the largest savings bank in Massachusetts outside of Boston, having been elected November 10, 1879, treasurer of the Worcester County Institution of Savings, and succeeding Hon Stephen Salisbury in 1904 as its president This savings bank was incorporated February 8, 1828 Samuel Jennison the cashier of the Worcester Bank, was the first treasurer, and until recently the president of the Worcester Bank has also been president of the Worcester County Institution for Savings The interests of the two banks were mutual The second treasurer of the Institution was Charles A Hamilton whom Mr Chase succeeded At the time Mr Chase became president of the bank, the deposits amounted to about $20,000,000 In 1905 the bank bought the lot at the corner of Main and Foster streets, and began to build its own home, a handsome and artistic structure It should be stated also that these two institutions the Worcester Bank and the Worcester County Institution for Savings were the pioneer banking institutions of Worcester county Mr Chase was a director of the Citizens National Bank from 1880 to 1889, has been a director of the Worcester National Bank since January, 1888, of the (Worcester) Merchants and Farmers Fire Insurance Company since 1883 and was vice-president of the Worcester Art Society Mr Chase was secretary of the Worcester Lyceum Association from 1863 to 1866 vice-president 1862-8, on the lecture committee from 1866 to 1880 and was a director of the Free Public Library of Worcester from 1866 to 1874 He has been for several years treasurer of the Memorial Hospital and recording secretary of the American Antiquarian Society and is a member of the New England Historic Genealogical Society, the Colonial Society of Massachusetts, the Bunker Hill Monument Association and the Worcester Society of Antiquity He is also vice-president of the Home for Aged Men, president of the North End Street Railway Company and president of the Worcester Harvard Club

Mr Chase has written many papers and pamphlets relating to the history of Worcester In 1879 Mr Chase wrote under contract with C F Jewett & Company of Boston a history of Worcester for their history of Worcester county in which much valuable matter, the result of original research was preserved For the "History of Worcester County," published by J W Lewis & Company in 1889 Mr Chase contributed a chapter on the newspaper press He also prepared an historical sketch of the Worcester Bank which was published in book form to celebrate the centennial of that institution in 1904

He married in April 1863, Mary Theresa Clark, of Boston and they had two children Mary Alice, married Thomas Hovey Gage, Jr, of Worcester, and Maud Eliza, who lives with her father

HENRY SALEM PRATT The subject of the following sketch is of one of Worcester's up-to-date business factors His financial success has been remarkable and the element entering into his life and general business career are indeed possessed by many another man, but rarely applied and managed to the success he has wrought out by them

Mr Pratt, the eldest son of Salem and Sally (Hobbs) Pratt, was born November 18, 1836, at Charlton, Massachusetts By referring to his family genealogy it is learned that his grandfather, Captain Joseph Pratt, was an officer in the war of 1812 Captain Pratt's grandfather was a full blooded Indian of Maine, traces of whose noble blood run down through the generations, giving courage and honor to the descendants Mr Pratt traces his genealogy through his mother, Sally Hobbs, whose mother was an Adams, to the famous Adams family, from which President John Adams and President John Quincy Adams were descended, and through them the ancestry has been traced back to the Emperor Charlemagne This noble strain has never died out, and Sally Hobbs embodied the noblest qualities of womanhood, and was a supporter and guiding influence to their children as long as she lived She has recently died at the age of eighty-seven July 8, 1904

When Henry S Pratt was quite young his parents removed to Charlton where he remained and attended the schools of his neighborhood until he was sixteen years of age working a part of the time with his father at bottoming boots and shoes In 1853 we find him coming to Worcester and at first he worked in a shoe store for his board, but such a character could not long remain at the bottom of life's ladder After two years clerking in a dry goods store, he in 1855 became salesman in the clothing store of A P Ware The years roll by and we find him a partner in the concern In 1866 there was a branch house formed, under style of Ware & Pratt, which today have one of the most complete clothing stores in the commonwealth In 1857 they commenced to manufacture clothing for the retail trade and it has come to be among the most extensive in the state William W Johnson became a partner after Mr Ware's retirement in 1870 also Edward T Wardwell, and January 1, 1888 a stock company was organized with Mr Johnson as president Mr Pratt as treasurer and Charles E Black as clerk The firm of Ware & Pratt conducted business until January 1 1869, when it was changed to Ware Pratt & Co, and remained so until January 1, 1888 when it was changed to a stock company

Aside from his interests in this good business firm he became interested in numerous financial institutions In 1887 he became a director in the Citizens' National Bank and in 1891 its vice-president Upon the decease of Hon Samuel Winslow the president in the autumn of 1894, Mr Pratt was chosen to fill the vacancy and he served to the satisfaction of the stockholders until the bank was merged with the Worcester Trust Company He is also connected with the Mechanics Savings Bank of Worcester and is one of its trustees He bought the Hillcroft farm, where he has erected a charming residence The view is among the most romantic of any within the varied and extensive as well as historic environments of Worcester city He also built the "Chadwick Block" on Main street the same deriving the name from the maternal side of

Mr Pratt's wife's people It should here be added that this block stands on the exact spot where Mr Pratt commenced his career by working for his board until some better opening presented itself to him

Like every other good American citizen, Mr Pratt appreciates the right of suffrage, and believing the Republican party comes the nearest to maintaining a good form of government he casts his vote with it While he is a strong party man yet he prefers others to hold the public offices, while he labors in other fields and remains a law-abiding citizen of the best type In religious belief he is a Unitarian and attends the First Church

His friends are legion He has belonged to various societies, including the Hancock and Commonwealth Clubs, where he was a popular and highly esteemed member He is the active manager of the Ware-Pratt Company Not unlike other well rounded characters, Mr Pratt established for himself a home influence by marrying Melora Fletcher, December 24, 1857, and to her he acknowledges much of the happiness of his life The career of such a man should be a model for the rising young men of Worcester, who may be sons of parents unable to start them in business Mr Pratt commenced unaided, and by virtue of industry and economy steadily made his way to the front rank in the business circle of Worcester men He is kind genial, temperate and progressive, all essential elements in a successful life

WILLIAM H HOBBS Josiah Hobbs (1), the pioneer ancestor of William H Hobbs and Horace Hobbs of Worcester, is also the progenitor of practically all the families in New England of this surname He was born in England, in 1649 and came to America in the 'Arabella," Richard Sprague, master leaving Gravesend, May 27, 1671, arriving in Boston in July For the next eighteen years he was a resident of Boston In 1690 he removed to Lexington Massachusetts, then the west precinct of Cambridge and there he lived during the remainder of his life, except for two years spent in Woburn, in the western part, now Burlington, Massachusetts In 1691 he was a subscriber to the building fund of the first meeting house in Lexington In 1692-3 he was among the contributors to the support of Rev Mr Esterbrook, the first minister there He and his wife, Tabitha, were baptized in August 1699 In September of the same year their children Josiah, Tabitha and Mary Hobbs were baptized, in October, 1700, Matthew and Susan Hobbs were baptized, January 8 1710, Ebenezer was baptized and April 13, 1712, Tabitha Of his seven children none had families according to the records, except Josiah Josiah Hobbs (father) died May 30 1741, aged ninety-two years He married in 1683

(II) Josiah Hobbs, son of Josiah Hobbs (1), was born in Boston in 1684, and moved to Lexington with his parents in 1690 He resided there until 1705, when he was twenty-one, he then returned to Boston and settled there In 1708 he married Esther Davenport, of Dorchester and resided on a farm at the north end of Boston According to his own statements he used to drive cows to pasture from the North End to Muddy river, now Brookline and to Roxbury now a part of Boston He told his grandchildren that he had hoed corn on Cornhill Boston He and his wife joined Rev Cotton Mather's church (the New North) and their children were christened there He purchased a farm at Weston of a man named Cheney and removed there He joined the Weston church and was a very devot man, of strict Puritan views He died February 27, 1779, aged ninety-four His wife died November 29, 1778, aged eighty-eight years Children of Josiah Hobbs and his wife, Esther Davenport Hobbs 1 Ebenezer, born in Boston, 1709, married Eunice Garfield, of Lancaster, 1734 died of injuries received October 19, 1762 2 Josiah (twin), born at Governor's Island, in Boston Harbor, 1721, married Mary Huntington, of Weston, she died 1804, was a soldier in the revolution and deacon of the church, he died 1802, aged eighty-one years 3 John (twin), born on Governor's Island, 1721, married Beulah Warren, of Weston, was a deacon and soldier in the revolution, was present at the taking of Burgoyne, he and his twin brother bought farms in Brookfield, then called Podunk, he died from a cold taken while he was in the service in 1777, leaving a large family of children, from some of whom are descended many of the Hobbs families of Worcester, and other towns of the county 4 Esther, born in Boston, October 22, 1722, married ——— Gibbs, settled in Framingham, Massachusetts 5 Sarah, born May 10, 1724, married ——— Stone, of Weston, settled in Vermont and had son, Joseph 6 Dorcas born 1726, married ——— Parks, settled in Lincoln, Massachusetts 7 Hannah, born January 25, 1729, married Jeremiah Wetmore, of Weston, settled in Middleton Connecticut, ancestors of the well known Wetmore family of Boston 8 Nathan born in Weston in 1731, married Elizabeth Fiske and had ten children

(III) Ebenezer Hobbs son of Josiah Hobbs (2), was born in Boston, 1709, married Eunice Garfield of Lincoln, 1734 He died of injuries received October 19, 1762 His widow died October 4, 1776, aged sixty-eight years Children were Isaac, born 1735, married Mary Sanderson, of Waltham, 1757 had several children who died in infancy he died September 30 1813, Ebenezer, born 1736, died October 28, 1756, unmarried, Elisha, born 1843, married Lois Hastings, of Waltham, 1764 Susannah died young Hepsibath died young, Mathew, born 1745, married Lydia Wesson, of Lincoln, in 1760, she died in 1782, aged thirty-five years, he married (second) Lucy Holmes, of Boston, who died 1812, he was a soldier in the revolution, was at Lexington April 19 1775 and followed the retreating British as far as West Cambridge, where he was relieved and returned to Concord, served under Captain Jonathan Fiske, was captain of his company in 1780, Elizabeth, born 1748, married Phineas Gregory, who settled in Princeton in 1767, Samuel, born 1751, married Lucy Monroe, of Lexington who died in 1812, aged sixty years he was one of the party who threw the tea overboard in Boston Harbor, settled in Sturbridge, died May 1823 Esther, 1753 married Captain Bowker, of Sudbury removed to western New York

(IV) Elisha Hobbs, son of Ebenezer Hobbs (3), was born in 1743 He married Lois Hastings of Waltham in 1764 He settled in Princeton before the revolutionary war and spent the remainder of his days there He was deacon of the church His wife died September 22 1807, aged sixty-four years He died December 16, 1816, aged seventy-four years. Children were Lois, born May 10 1765, married, 1783 John Mirick of Princeton, where she died 1843, Elisha January 29 1768 Micah, November 22 1770, died October 29, 1775 Jonas, August 31, 1772 went to Vermont early, Susanna, May 20, 1774 Micah September 29, 1776 died at Hope Maine, February 2 1842 aged sixty-six years, had two sons Josiah and Henry John, July 21, 1779, married Betsey Bailey, of Sterling, William, August 30, 1781, married Nancy Gill, of Princeton, had three sons William, born 1809, resided in Worcester, and Elisha lived on the homestead in Princeton Moses, October 24, 1783 married Mercy Gill, of Princeton, was killed in Hubbardston at the raising of a barn, 1823

(V) John Hobbs son of Elisha Hobbs of Princeton (4), was born in Princeton Massachusetts, July 21, 1779 He married Betsey Bailey, of Sterling Their children were Betsey, born March 10, 1800, John, June 17, 1801, resided in Yonkers, New York, Micah, February 22, 1804, married a daughter of Moses Hobbs and resided in Princeton, George, May 16, 1806, resided in Worcester, Henry, November 4, 1808, died 1840, Susan June 2, 1811, Isaac, June 13, 1813, removed to Hope, Maine, Samuel, January 29, 1816, at Princeton, Bailey, October 8, 1818, resided in Yonkers, New York

(VI) George Hobbs major-general, son of John Hobbs (5), was born in Princeton, Massachusetts, May 16, 1806 He died in Worcester, November 3, 1872 He married Calista Beaman, 1829 He settled in Sterling, where he kept a hotel in the days when the country tavern was at the height of its prosperity He also managed an extensive stage business there General Hobbs removed to Worcester in 1838 and kept the Eagle Hotel, at the corner of Main and Thomas streets He is still remembered by the older citizens of Worcester as a manufacturer of brick He had kilns on Lincoln street, and continued to manufacture bricks until his health failed, a few years before his death He invested in real estate and built many brick buildings in various parts of the city He left a valuable estate He was one of the few Worcester men who attained the rank of major-general, he became commander of the City Guards in 1840, and he rose through the various ranks in the state militia to that position He resigned in 1856, but always retained an interest in the military affairs of the state He had two sons, prominent officers in Worcester regiments in the civil war He was highly respected as a citizen as well as a soldier For several years he was chief of the Worcester fire department He served the city of Worcester in 1861-63-64 as alderman He was an assessor for several years During the last years of his life he was in feeble health, for a year was confined to the house

The *Worcester Gazette* said of him at the time of his death He was deeply interested in the military branch of the public service, and the spirit and efficiency of the militia in his time were largely due to his influence and example * * * In all positions of public trust he was faithful and energetic"

Children of George and Calista (Beaman) Hobbs Ann born 1830, at Sterling, married George S Howe, she resides at present in The Aurora, Worcester Horace, September 2, 1831, at Sterling, Martha, at Sterling, 1834, Catherine or Kate Rust, born 1836, George Webster, March 22, 1839, at Worcester, William Harrison, April 28, 1841, at Worcester

(VII) Horace Hobbs son of General George Hobbs (6) was born in Sterling, Massachusetts, September 2 1831 He attended the Worcester public schools He learned the profession of civil engineering and surveying and followed it for about seven years He was a strong anti-slavery man, and when Eli Thayer organized the movement for Free Kansas Mr Hobbs was one of the first to enlist as a pioneer When he reached Kansas he found the feeling at fever heat In fact he participated in the first practical and effective resistance against slavery He was in a cavalry company in the town of Lawrence at the time of the Border Ruffian Invasion from Missouri, and he remained in Kansas until hostilities ceased He was there thirteen months He worked at brick making, with his father, for about five years in all When the civil war broke out he enlisted early In 1863 he was commissioned captain of Company H, Fifty-first Regiment

Captain Hobbs lived for a time in Auburn, a town adjoining Worcester He was town treasurer there for five years He was deacon of the Congregational church for a number of years, treasurer, and also superintendent of the Sunday school All his life he has been known as an earnest and consistent supporter of the temperance movement in its various forms In politics he has always been a Republican, and has been satisfied with the straight ticket He has never voted for a Democrat Since 1876 he has been examiner of titles at the Worcester county registry of deeds His careful, painstaking work there is known to members of the bar all over the state He and his brother have made a specialty of searching titles, and have won a high reputation for excellent work He is a member of George H Ward Post No 10, G A. R and of the Loyal Legion He is also a member of the Congregational Club and the board of trade

He married (first) Mary P Parker He married (second) Maria K Knowles, daughter of Elisha and Eunice (Huntington) Knowles, of Auburn The children of Horace and Mary P (Parker) Hobbs Horace B, died at the age of eighteen months, Cora Louise, a clerk in the office of the register of deeds, William H, attended the Worcester high school a graduate of Worcester Polytechnic Institute, then took a course at Harvard University at Johns Hopkins, and at Heidelberg University, Germany (where he studied again in 1905), for some years professor of geology in Wisconsin State University at Madison Wisconsin, he married Sarah Kimball, has one child Winnifred B, born 1900 Children of Horace and Maria K (Knowles) Hobbs Howard K, was in the Second regiment at the battle of Santiago is sergeant of the Worcester Light Infantry and treasurer of the company, also treasurer of Willie Grout Camp, Sons of Veterans, treasurer of the Sunday school, graduate of Worcester high school, associated with his father and uncle as examiner of titles at the court house Alice M, graduate of Wheaton Seminary

(VII) George Webster Hobbs son of General George Hobbs (6), was born in Worcester March 22, 1839 He was educated in the public schools of his native city and at Norwich University, Vermont He studied law with Colonel E B Stoddard He was admitted to the bar and commenced to practice in 1860, at Uxbridge He was a lieutenant in the Worcester Light Infantry For many years he was one of the most prominent and influential citizens of Uxbridge He was interested in historical subjects and wrote extensively He married Chloe E Taft daughter of David Taft, of Uxbridge

(VII) William Harrison Hobbs, youngest son of General George Hobbs (6) was born in Worcester, Massachusetts, April 28, 1841 in the hotel at the corner of Main and Thomas streets, which at that time was kept by his father He first attended school in the old school house on Main street, then in the Thomas street school in the various grades He also attended the Worcester Academy, the Highland Military Academy and the Worcester high school In 1855 he joined the Worcester Light Infantry and was with his company in the famous march through Baltimore at the beginning of the civil war, April 19, 1861 This company was part of the Sixth Massachusetts Regiment He was one of those detailed by Captain Harrison W Pratt to notify the members of the company to be at the armory for active service He still has the written order, viz

"Private W H Hobbs You are hereby ordered to warn, and give immediate verbal notice, to the non-commissioned officers and privates of the company under my command, and whose names are specified in roll annexed, to appear at their armory at four o'clock in the forenoon of Wednesday, the seventeenth day of April, current, uniformed and equipped as the law directs for military duty and active service

HARRISON W PRATT,
"Commanding Company B, Third Battalion Infantry"

He was mustered out of service, with the rank of corporal, at the expiration of his enlistment After his return from the service Mr Hobbs went into the business of brick-making with his father, and continued until the death of his father in 1872 In the following year he went to Haverhill and started in the brick business, but on account of the financial troubles and hard times of that period, he sold out in 1874 He returned to Worcester and entered the real estate and conveyancing business He had an office in the building on the present site of the Chadwick until 1883, when he went into the registry of deeds, working with his brother Horace in examining titles He has continued in this business ever since At present he is the head of the Hobbs Title Company, and his associates are Samuel H Longley and Howard K Hobbs, his nephew Mr Hobbs is well known, especially among the lawyers of the county, and is highly esteemed He is regarded as one of the leading experts in real estate matters in Worcester county He is a Republican in politics, but not an active one He belongs to George H Ward Post, No 10, G A R, and has been a member of the auditing committee for the past three years, a member of the Independent Order of Odd Fellows Quinsigamond Lodge No 48, and trustee of the Independent Order of Odd Fellows' Mutual Benefit Association for several years, also a member of the Veteran Independent Order of Odd Fellows' Association, having been an Odd Fellow for twenty-five years Mr Hobbs married, November 26, 1865, Martha Lydia Holt, daughter of Lucius K and Rebecca (Miles) Holt They have two children, both living Charles H, resides at New Orleans, educated at Worcester Academy, Katharine, lives with her parents, 146 Main street, Worcester

(I) Nicholas Holt, the pioneer ancester of Mrs William H Hobbs, was born in England, in 1602 He came from Romsey, England, in the ship "James," William Cooper, master, sailing April 6, and landing in Boston June 3, 1635 He was one of the first settlers at Newbury and Andover, Massachusetts At Newbury he was husbandman, proprietor and town officer He made a long journey with others to take the freeman's oath May 17, 1637, and vote against Sir Harry Vane He was a tanner as well as a farmer He removed to Andover in 1644 He sold his Newbury land November 14, 1652 He is called a plate-turner (woodworker) in some records He married (first) Elizabeth —— She died at Andover, November 9 1656 He married (second), June 20, 1658, Hannah (Bradstreet) Rolfe, widow of Daniel Rolfe and daughter of Humphrey Bradstreet She died June 20, 1665 He married (third) Mrs Martha Preston, widow of Roger Preston, May 21, 1666 She died March 21, 1703, aged eighty years He died January 30, 1685, aged eighty-three years Children of Nicholas and Elizabeth Holt Hannah, born in England, married Robert Gray, Elizabeth, born at Newbury, March 30, 1636, Mary, born at Newbury, October 6, 1638, Samuel, October 6, 1641, Henry, born 1644, of whom later, Nicholas, 1647, James, 1651, Priscilla, June 20, 1653 Children of Nicholas and Hannah Holt were Rebecca, born November 14, 1662, John, January 14, 1663-4

(II) Henry Holt, fifth child of Nicholas Holt (1), was born in Newbury, Massachusetts, 1644 He married, February 24, 1669, Sarah Ballard, daughter of William Ballard She died at Andover, November 25, 1733 He died January 17, 1719, aged seventy-five years They joined the church June 3, 1716 He was prominent in town affairs In 1686 he owned a mill on Ladle brook Children were Elizabeth, born in Andover, Massachusetts, December 29, 1670, Oliver, January 14, 1671, Henry, January 24, 1673, James, see forward, George, March 17, 1677, Sarah, August 17, 1678, Josiah, December 13, 1679, Dinah, May 23, 1681, Paul, February 7, 1684, William, February 3, 1687, Zerviah, March 24, 1689, Keturah, December 15, 1690, Humphrey, September 22, 1693, Benjamin, July 8, 1696

(III) James Holt, fourth child of Henry Holt (2), born in Andover, Massachusetts, September 3, 1675, married, May 24, 1705, Susannah Preston She died February 20, 1741-2 He died November 25, 1751, aged seventy-six Their children Abigail, born in Andover, Massachusetts, March 20, 1705, died 1716, James, 1707, Zerviah, 1712, Barzillai see forward, Abigail, died February 20, 1756

(IV) Barzillai Holt, fourth child of James Holt (3), born in Andover, Massachusetts, October 25, 1715, married (first) August 27, 1738, Elizabeth Goss, married (second), February 22, 1759, Lois Allena, and settled in Marlboro, Massachusetts, in the part later set off as Shrewsbury He was one of the first settlers in West Boylston about 1720 He died at Boylston in 1774, aged fifty-eight years Children of Barzillai and Elizabeth (Goss) Holt Abel, see forward, Barzillai May 12, 1745, James, June 6, 1746, Elizabeth, August 29, 1753, Silas, born in Marlboro, Levi, May 6, 1760, Abiel, May 11, 1763, Jotham, January 10, 1765

(V) Abel Holt, eldest child of Barzillai Holt (4), born in Marlboro, Massachusetts, June 14, 1740, married October 21, 1765 or February 27, 1766, Eunice Keyes, daughter of Henry Keyes, of Shrewsbury, born April 19, 1745 died October 21, 1840, aged ninety-five years and six months He died February 18, 1815, aged seventy-five years He was a soldier in the revolution Children were Lois, born in Shrewsbury, Massachusetts, May 11, 1767, married William Drury, of Holden, Amasa born in Boylston, April 24, 1772, married, 1798, Nabby Nourse, of Berlin, Asa, born in Boylston, June 26, 1776, Abel, June 26, 1776, married Hannah Wright, Jonas, October 22, 1779, Eunice, October 21, 1782, Henry Keyes, July 2, 1788, married, November 16, 1813, Lydia Fairbanks, see forward, Tyler, September 21, 1791, married, October 1, 1812, Arethusa Fairbanks, she died August 16, 1837 He died November 8 1866 at West Boylston

(VI) Henry Keyes Holt, seventh child of Abel Holt (5), born in Boylston, Massachusetts, July 2, 1788, married, November 16, 1813, Lydia Fairbanks, a descendant of Jonathan Fairbanks, of Dedham, in the following line Lydia (VI), Seth (V),

Jonathan (IV), Jabez (III), Jonas (II), Jonathan (I) He died September 8, 1828, from injuries received in a fall His widow married (second), September 25, 1844, Nathaniel Davenport Children of Henry Keyes and Lydia (Fairbanks) Holt Henry Fairbanks, born in South Berwick, Maine, November 26, 1816, married, December 22, 1841, Martha Levina Wood, daughter of Merritt Wood, Lucius Keyes, see forward

(VII) Lucius Keyes Holt, youngest child of Henry Keyes Holt (6), born in Sterling, Massachusetts, married, October 10, 1843, Rebecca Frost, of Marlboro, Massachusetts They resided in Lancaster, Massachusetts Children were Martha Lydia, born in Shirley, Massachusetts, November 24, 1845, see forward, Henry Keyes, born in Lancaster, March 5, 1850, died August 4, 1857, drowned at Holyoke, Massachusetts, Frank E, born in Holyoke, December 17, 1856, married Nellie Hastings, resides at Bayonne, New Jersey, superintendent of the Singer Sewing Machine Company factory at Elizabeth, New Jersey, they have one child, Olive, born 1893, Lucius M, born in Lancaster, July 13, 1859, deceased

(VIII) Martha Lydia Holt, eldest child of Lucius Keyes Holt (7), born at Shirley, Massachusetts, November 24, 1845 In early life she lived with her parents and went to school in Clinton, Massachusetts During the civil war the family lived at Easthampton She attended Williston Seminary and Worcester Academy She is a member of the Fairbanks Association and as indicated above is descended in the same line as Vice-President Fairbanks, who is her cousin She married William Harrison Hobbs (See sketch above)

ARTHUR LANE SAFFORD Thomas Safford (1), the immigrant ancestor of Arthur Lane Safford, of Lancaster, Massachusetts, was born in England and settled in New England at Ipswich before 1641 He was on the list of proprietors of the town April 6, 1641, and was admitted a freeman December 19, 1648 He bought a farm at Ipswich, thirty-two acres, of Henry Kingsbury, February 8, 1648 He was a subscriber to Denison's allowance in 1640 and had a share and a half in Plum Island He died in February, 1666-7 His will was dated February 20, 1666-7, and proved March 26, 1667 He gave his farm to his son Joseph on condition of his care of the father and mother and paying certain amounts to daughters Elizabeth, Mary and Abigail

He married Elizabeth ——, who died March 4, 167, at Ipswich Their children were Joseph, born 1631 or 1632, (he deposed March 29, 1692, that he was about fifty-nine or sixty years old,) was admitted a freeman 1682, married, March 6, 1660, Mary Baker, John, of whom later, Elizabeth, Mary, Abigail (One of the daughters married —— Kilum)

(II) John Safford, son of Thomas Safford (1), was born about 1633, probably in England He settled in Ipswich, Massachusetts He had a share of Plum Island He gave land to his son Thomas for the maintenance of his wife and daughter by deed dated September 5, 1698 The children of John and Sarah Safford were John Jr, of whom later, Sarah, born July 14, 1664, died July 21, 1712, Margaret, February 28, 1665-6, Rebecca, August 30, 1667, Mercy or Mary, born February 26, 1669-70, Elizabeth, February 27 1670-1, Thomas, October 16, 1672, married, October 7, 1698, Eleanor Shatswell or Setchwell, widow of Richard Setchwell and daughter of Daniel Cheney, married (second) at Rowley, June 29, 1725, Sarah Scott, their son Joseph was a pioneer at Hardwick, where many of his descendants live, Joseph, March 12, 1674-5

(III) John Safford, Jr, son of John Safford (2), was born about 1660 He took the oath of allegiance in 1683 at Ipswich He was administrator of the estate of his father-in-law, Thomas Newman, March 5, 1691 He married, September 15, 1685, Hannah Newman, daughter of Thomas Newman He married (second), June 28, 1702, Abigail Martin He resided at Ipswich The children of John, Jr, and Hannah Safford were John Jr, born February 28, 1687-8, Hannah, September 24, 1691, Sarah, December 25, 1694, Mary, March 5, 1697, Elizabeth, January 24, 1700 The children of John, Jr and Abigail Safford were Mary, April 24, 1703, Joseph, January 18, 1705, Gideon, March 24, 1709, of whom later

(IV) Gideon Safford, son of John Safford, Jr, (3), was born in Ipswich, Massachusetts, March 24, 1709 He lived in Ipswich He married there, January 13, 1731-2, Elizabeth Hill Their children were Mary, born September 1, 1732, Thomas, October 15, 1735, of whom later, Elizabeth, September 17, 1737, Thankful, October 15, 1739, Amy, January 25, 1742, Lucy, April 3, 1744, Samuel January 2, 1748, Pagy, May 10 1750, Anne, July 12, 1752, Gideon, Jr, November 4, 1754

(V) Thomas Safford, son of Gideon Safford (4), was born in Ipswich, Massachusetts, October 15, 1735 He was a soldier in the French and Indian war and was in Captain Jonathan Brown's company at Lake George in 1758 During the revolution he was living at or near Watertown, and he enlisted July 2, 1778, with others to serve as guards over the powder magazine for six months He continued to serve on this duty until August 2, 1779 He was called "corporal" in some of the records He married at Watertown, July 31, 1764, Sarah Kettell, of Medford, his residence being given as Dedham His wife joined the Dedham church, March 23, 1766 The only record of birth of children born to Thomas and Sarah is found in Dedham records Thomas, baptized at Dedham, August 24, 1766, by Rev Mr Townsend

(VI) Thomas Safford, Jr, son of Thomas Safford (5), of Dedham and Watertown, was baptized at Dedham, August 24, 1766 He lived at Dedham, Watertown and Concord He learned the trade of baker He removed from Concord to Lancaster in 1795 He bought of Joseph Willington Page of Lancaster for one thousand and ninety pounds his estate in Lancaster, including land on the Berlin road, land known as the Rugg Intervale, formerly of Isaac Rugg's estate, and land on the Harvard road by deed dated April 22, 1795 This deed gives his residence as Concord, but he must have removed immediately afterward, as his son Thomas was baptized at Lancaster, September 6, 1795

He married (first) Elizabeth Stetson, who died at Lancaster, March 11, 1818, aged forty-nine years He married (second), 1819, Anna Brigham Elizabeth Stetson was the daughter of Ebenezer Stetson, who married in Watertown, July 1, 1765, Lucy Ruggles Ebenezer Stetson died in 1809 and the children of Thomas and Elizabeth (Stetson) Safford were named among his heirs, Thomas Safford being appointed guardian of the minor children, September 26, 1809 The second wife was of Marlboro, Massachusetts The children of Thomas and Elizabeth Safford, all except George, born or baptized in Lancaster were George, of whom later, Thomas, baptized September 6, 1795, Catherine, baptized April 23, 1797, died July 4, 1798, Joseph Collis, baptized December 6, 1798, Francis Augustus, baptized August 3, 1800, died August 3, 1801, Caroline, born May 30, 1802, died August 31, 1803, Catherine born December 9, 1804, died February 14, 1807, Henry, born March 1 1807, Susan Palmer, born February 19 1809, Adeline, born January 13 1811, Elizabeth, (guardian appointed at her father's death)

(VII) George Safford, eldest son of Thomas Safford (6), was born about 1794, probably in Concord Massachusetts He was brought up in Lancaster and attended school there He was a farmer He married Mary (Polly) Stevenson, July 8, 1816, daughter of Martin Stevenson, of Lancaster She died February 19, 1831, aged thirty-six years He was guardian of their children who were heirs of their grandfather Stevenson, who owned forty acres on George Hill The children of George and Polly Safford were Charles, born September 14 1817, of whom later, George Fosdick, born March 19, 1819, had children George and Helen Shortly, Roby Ruel, born December 12, 1821, Augustus, born January 9, 1825, Henry, of Fitchburg, Mary E George Safford married again and had Fred, whose children are George Safford and Lizzie Snyder of Troy, New York George Safford married a third wife

(VIII) Charles Safford, son of George Safford (7), was born in Lancaster, September 14, 1817 He resided in Lancaster, where he carried on the business of cabinet making, painting, etc He was for many years the town undertaker He died in 1879 aged sixty-nine years He married, May 16, 1843, Julia A D Carter, than aged twenty-four years Their children were A daughter, died young, Charles Ethan, born October 17, 1845, married twice, one son, Clarence, was killed in the destruction of the Maine at Havana, Sarah Julia, February 16, 1847, died June 22, 1847, Ellen Frances, June 1, 1848, married Frank Havard, of Bolton, they have two sons and two daughters, Frank, a painter by trade, died unmarried at Lancaster, Henry, a painter by trade, married Carrie Divoll, has had five children, two of whom are living, Arthur Lane, of whom later, William P is in the employ of his brother in the general store at Lancaster married Lillian Wilder, daughter of William G Wilder, of Clinton, they have one daughter Mabel

(IX) Arthur Lane Safford son of Charles Safford (8), was born at Lancaster, Massachusetts, August 15, 1856 He attended the public and high schools of his native town At the age of sixteen he began to work in the general store at Lancaster The store changed hands several times, but he remained in the employ of the various proprietors until December, 1879, when in partnership with Benjamin Kingsbury Gallup he became proprietor of the store himself The firm name was Gallup & Safford and they had an excellent business In 1891 Mr Safford bought out his partner and since then has conducted the business alone He has a high grade general store, groceries dry goods hardware, agricultural implements and the usual stock of the large country store He also deals in grain flour, etc His former partner is now manager for the Swift concern of a branch at Trenton, New Jersey

In politics Mr Safford is a Republican He was for seven years town treasurer and tax collector but declined to serve after his partner withdrew from the business He is at present trustee of the town's charity funds, held under various bequests, for the benefit of the poor of the town He is a Free Mason, member of Trinity Lodge of Clinton He is a member of the Lancaster Lodge of Odd Fellows

He married Marian Adams Fuller, daughter of Edward M Fuller, brother of Eben S Fuller, of Clinton (See sketch of Fuller family in this work) Their children were Edith Marie, born June, 1891, Edward, May 6, 1895

ELI JONES WHITTEMORE The genealogy of the Whittemore family to which Eli Jones Whittemore, of Worcester, belongs, has been traced back in England to the twelfth century Mr Whittemore has the result of the researches of D J Whittemore, chief engineer of the Chicago, Milwaukee & St Paul Railroad, which were carried on for a number of years in England at considerable expense and infinite pains to secure accuracy A vast amount of information that he collected should be edited A brief abstract only can be used here It will serve to correct some of the errors in the Whittemore and Whitmore genealogies The name is commonly spelled Whitmore in England, while some descendants of the original stock spell their name Wetmore

(I) The Whitmores of Staffordshire, England, were originally termed de Boterel The name of the father of William de Boterel (1100-1135) and his brother, Peter de Botrel, is unknown William had a son William (1158-1163)

(II) Peter de Botrel, of Staffordshire, had a son Radulph or Ralph

(III) Ralph de Botrel (1152-1171) married twice His son William by the first wife married Avisa de Whitmore (1179) William (IV) (1174) had a son Reginald (V) (1204-16), who had a son Robert (VI) (1238), who had a son Robert (VII) (1260) This is not the American line That descends from the second wife, by her son Ralph de Botrel and not by Rad Fitz Wetmore (1220-40), an illegitimate son Rad had a son Will le Burgvyllon (1242-54)

(IV) Ralph de Botrel had a son, Sir John

(V) Sir John de Whitmore married Agnes (1252-76) and had at least three sons John, Lord of Whitmore, founder of what the genealogists call the Caunton line, William, married Alice Fenners, had son Philip (VII), founded what is called the Claverly branch, Ralph (VI)

(VI) John Whitmore, son of Sir John Whitmore married Margerie (1270-1301)

(VII) Richard of Whitmore married Susannah Draycote, daughter of Sir Philip Draycote of Painesley, knight, and had Jane, married John Blunt Mary, married John Gifford, Beatrix married John Chetwind, Christina married Richard Fleetwood, Philip

(VIII) Philip Whitmore, married Thomasine, daughter of Richard Oliver (?), and had a son, Richard Whitmore

(IX) Richard Whitmore, son of Philip Whitmore (8) married (first) a daughter of Sir Ralph Bagot, married (second) daughter of Richard Devereux married (third) a daughter of Simon Harcourt probably of Ellenhall, Staffordshire and by his third wife had son Nicholas

(X) Nicholas Whitmore son of Richard Whitmore (9) married Annie Aston daughter of Thomas Aston of Tixall Staffordshire, and had Mary, married William Lusone, Anthony

(XI) Anthony Whitmore son of Nicholas Whitmore (10) married Christina Vaux daughter and heir of Nicholas Vaux, and had Joan William

(XII) William Whitmore son of Anthony Whitmore (11), had a son John

(XIII) John Whitmore of Caunton, second son

Eli J. Whittemore

of William Whitmore (12), in the reign of Henry VI, married Alice Blyton, daughter and heir of Robert Blyton of Caunton, county Notts, married (second) Catherine Compton, daughter and heir of Robert Compton, of Hawton (Visitation of York 1563), and had William, Robert, who was the heir

(XIV) Robert Whitmore, son of John Whitmore (13), of Caunton, married Catherine Claye, daughter of George Claye, of Finningly, county Notts (Visitation of Yorkshire), and had son William, the heir, who married a daughter of John Ridley William of Rotterham died in 1568 Robert Whitmore married (second) Alice Atwoode, of Harlington, Bedfordshire He died at Caunton in 1540 By this marriage the children were Richard died without issue, 1559, John, living in 1545, Charles, died 1568, Thomas, living in 1559, probably died about 1603, Edmund living in 1559, Rowland, living in 1591, James, Randall, and three daughters Thomas Whitmore, Sr, of Hitchin, was the son of Edmund or Rowland, sons of Robert Hitchin is the parish where the emigrant Thomas Whitmore was born, and he was the son of another Thomas Whitmore as will be seen later

(XV) Charles Whitmore son of Robert Whitmore (14), died in 1568 He lived at Tuxforth, county Notts His children were William, died 1582 in county Notts, John, supposed to have lived in Staffordshire and died 1571, Robert, died 1608, Richard, died 1578, James died 1614, Thomas, the elder, died 1649 Roger, of Hitchin, Christopher of county Beds, died 1640, four daughters, and a posthumous child supposed to be George Three of the sons spelled the name Whittamore, three spelled it Watmore and one Whitmore, the spelling that has prevailed in England

(XVI) Thomas Whitmore, son of Charles Whitmore (15), lived at Hitchin, county of Hertford, England He married Mary ——— His two sons emigrated to New England Thomas to Malden Massachusetts, and John to Stamford Connecticut Thomas, of Malden is the ancestor of most of the American Whittemores John Whitmore, of Stamford had a daughter Elizabeth and son John Whittemore who was of age in 1649, lived at Stamford and Middletown Connecticut

(XVI) Roger Whitmore son of Charles Whitmore (15), and brother of Thomas Whitmore, of Hitchin, was the father of Nicholas Whitmore, Nicholas was the father of two sons also who emigrated to New England Francis Whitmore to Boston and Thomas Whitmore to Middletown Connecticut From these are descended the American Whitmores Their father was a first cousin of the Malden emigrant, Thomas Whittemore

(XVII) Thomas Whittemore son of Thomas Whittemore (16), was born at Hitchin, Hertfordshire England He came to New England prior to 1640 for at that time he was in Charlestown, Massachusetts, on the Mystic side which later was the town of Malden and signed a petition with neighbors for better privileges in 1640 He bought land there of Mr John Cotton in 1645 This lot adjoined his home lot and is now in the city of Everett Massachusetts It remained in the Whittemore family until May 1 1845 over two hundred years after he bought it The site of the first dwelling house is known

He married (second) Sarah Deardes, April 14, 1623, in England She was buried November 17, 1628 He married (third) Hannah ———, who according to her deposition in 1662 was born in 1612 She married (second) Benjamin Butterfield June 3 1663 at Chelmsford Massachusetts Thomas Whittemore died at Malden, May 25, 1661 His will was proved June 25, 1661 Children of Thomas Whittemore were Sarah, baptized April 14, 1616, Mary, baptized May 12, 1624, Thomas, baptized October 6, 1626, lived in England, Daniel, baptized July 31, 1633, married Mary Mellins, daughter of Richard Mellins, of Charlestown, March 7, 1662, John, baptized April 27, buried 29, 1635, Nathaniel, baptized May 1, 1636, married Mary Knower left no male descendants, John, baptized February 11, 1638-9, at Hitchin, England, as were also all the preceding, settled in Cambridge, Massachusetts had fifteen children and has many descendants, Elizabeth, Benjamin, married Elizabeth Bucknam, who died July 18, 1726, he died July 16, 1726, Thomas (one of the few cases where there are two sons of exactly the same name living at the same time The elder Thomas Whittemore was in England and never came over) married Elizabeth Peirce, of Woburn, November 9 1666, and had son Thomas, born August 14 1667, Samuel, married Hannah ———, removed to Dover, New Hampshire, thence to Somerville, Massachusetts, and died September 15, 1726, both he and his wife buried at Cambridge, Massachusetts, Peletiah, Abraham, served in the army in King Philip's war in 1676, died January 14, 1690-1

(XVIII) Daniel Whittemore son of Thomas Whittemore (17) was born in Hitchin Hertfordshire, England and baptized there July 31, 1633 He married Mary Mellins, daughter of Richard Mellins, of Charlestown, March 7, 1662 Richard removed from Charlestown to Weymouth where he was admitted a freeman September 7 1639 He inherited the homestead from his father and settled on it He bequeathed the homestead to his sons Daniel and John, the latter being the father of John Whittemore, of Leicester The will was noncupative and was not proved till nearly two years after his death His widow Mary was the administrator Children of Daniel Whittemore were Daniel born April 27, 1663, resided in Charlestown and Malden died September 21, 1756 aged ninety-four, left the homestead to his son Daniel John February 12, 1664-5 died 1730 Thomas, March 5, 1667, Mary, February 15 1668-9 Nathaniel, February 7 1670 Peletiah 1680 James

(XIX) John Whittemore son of Daniel Whittemore (18), married Ruth Bassett She and her sister, Lydia Bassett who married his brother Daniel Whittemore were daughters of Joseph Bassett son of the emigrant William Bassett, who came over in the "Fortune" in 1621 lived at Duxbury, Massachusetts, in 1637, was deputy to the general court in 1640-41-42-43-44 Bassett joined Governor Bradford and others in the purchase of Dartmouth Massachusetts and removed to Bridgewater where he died in 1667 John Whittemore died in 1730 His wife Ruth was appointed administratrix April 3 1730 His whole estate was appraised at five hundred and three pounds Children of John and Ruth Whittemore were John born September 12, 1694, settled in Leicester, Jeremiah (q v) Benjamin, married Sarah Kendall 1723 Patience married Timothy Lamson David born April 6 1706, married Alice Kendall, of Bedford Massachusetts March 11 1730-31 resided at Boston Deborah, born March 1, 1707-8 Peletiah, born October 30 1710 resided at Dunstable

(XX) Jeremiah Whittemore son of John Whittemore (19) was born in Malden Massachusetts 1695 He married in Boston March 15 1722 Patience Reed, seventh daughter of Israel and Mary (Kendall) Reed of Woburn Massachusetts She was born December 3 1699 She was received in the Weston Church from the church in Chelsea, February 26, 1726-7, and died in Weston, October 24, 1745, aged forty-seven years, ten months, twenty-one days They were then living in Weston He married (second), May 10, 1746, Abigail Wooley, of Concord He died in Concord, Massachusetts, March 31, 1783, aged eighty-eight years His children were by the first wife

Children of Jeremiah and Patience (Kendall) Reed were Jeremiah, born in Concord, August 16, 1723, of whom later, Isaac, born in Weston, Massachusetts, November 15, 1726, married May 9, 1751, Ruth Bullard, who died October 10, 1764, he married (second) (published July 6), 1765, Elizabeth Graves, of Sudbury, Massachusetts, he had seven children, Patience, born January 20, 1729-30, married, May 28, 1754, John Flagg, Israel, born July 10, 1732, married, May 1, 1755, Abigail Brown, had seven children, Asa, born August 7, 1736, died April 12, 1746

(XXI) Jeremiah Whittemore, son of Jeremiah Whittemore (20), was born in Concord, Massachusetts, August 16, 1723, and died at Spencer, Massachusetts, May 14, 1803 aged seventy-eight years He went from Weston to settle in Spencer in 1760 Some of his children were born before he moved, some afterward He married Mary Carter Their children were Amos, died 1751, Asa born November 10, 1749, married Lucy Muzzey, March 2, 1765, removed from Spencer to the south part of Leicester, Massachusetts, died 1821, she died 1822, (Otis Whittemore now or lately living in Leicester is a grandson, as is also Eber Whittemore Their father was Amos Mrs H D Edwards daughter of Asa's son Charles is now or was lately living in Leicester Massachusetts), Reuben, born April 29 1754, Mary born in Weston married Nathan Wright, October 26, 1779, Tamar born June 18 1756, married Robert Watson, Sybil, born January 17, 1758, married Reuben Underwood, February 1, 1779, Aaron, born in Spencer, March 1, 1762, married Sally ——, Esther born in Spencer December 28, 1764 died unmarried Jeremiah, born in Spencer, February 21, 1766 married February 21 1792, Polly Washburn, of Paxton Sarah, born in Spencer, March 16, 1768, married Ebenezer Kingsbury

(XXII) Reuben Whittemore, son of Jeremiah Whittemore (21), born April 29, 1754, at Weston, Massachusetts died at Spencer April 19 1832 He married Abigail Watson, March 2, 1794 He settled at Spencer, Massachusetts Their children were Betsey born at Spencer June 15 1780, married James Browning Amos born at Spencer September 7 1782 resided in Hartford Connecticut, married Sally (Barnard) Hotchkiss, July 18, 1813, he died July 3, 1854, she died August 13 1853, had six children, Thankful born February 6, 1785, died August 22, 1838 Daniel born at Spencer, April 28, 1787, married Fanny Prouty, daughter of Joshua Prouty March 4, 1815 he died October 5 1872 aged eighty-five she died November 21, 1843 aged fifty-four, Roswell born October 3, 1789 Rhuben, born in Spencer February 5 1795 married Salome Clark November 30 1810, born September 5, 1795 died January 22, 1869, he died January 17 1861 had eight children Oliver, born February 11 1797 of whom later, Caroline born December 14, 1798, married Samuel M Hobbs, William born July 7, 1801, died April 4 1841, unmarried Abigail born in Spencer November 20, 1803 married Augustus Rider, of Spencer, had one son Alfred

(XXIII) Oliver Whittemore son of Reuben Whittemore (22) was born in Spencer, Massachusetts February 11 1797, died March 29 1830 He married Lydia Jones, June 26, 1823 He was a farmer His children were Eli Jones, born April 30, 1824, Harriet Susannah, born March 8, 1826, married, April 19, 1853, Phineas Jones, of Spencer, Massachusetts, removed later to Newark, New Jersey where he was in partnership in the wheelwright business with Eli J Whittemore, she died March 6, 1866, had one son, Frederick Augustus, born August 21, 1868, Oliver Augustus, born March 2, 1828, married in Denver, Colorado, ————, no children

(XXIV) Eli Jones Whittemore, son of Oliver Whittemore (23), was born April 30, 1824, in Spencer, Massachusetts He was educated in the district schools of his native town and at Leicester Academy, at Leicester, Massachusetts His father died when he was only six years old He worked on a farm until he was sixteen, when he entered the wheelwright shop of S G Reed at Spencer He became a partner of Mr Reed some years afterward and succeeded him in the business there Mr. Whittemore manufactured carriages and wagons and developed a substantial business in which he acquired a competence In 1866 he removed to Newark, New Jersey, where he entered partnership with Phineas Jones, who married his sister, Harriet L Whittemore The firm name was Phineas Jones & Company and they did a general wheelwright business and manufactured carriages and wagons The firm still does a prosperous business there Mr Whittemore sold his interests to Mr Jones, his partner, in 1874 and retired The present owner of the business is Henry P Jones, son of Phineas, the original partner with Mr Whittemore

Mr Whittemore returned to Worcester county when he retired from business and settled in Worcester In 1877 he moved to the handsome house on Main street, which he now occupies While in Spencer he served four years as postmaster under President Lincoln, as assessor for two years and selectman for three years He is one of the appraisers of the Mechanics' Savings Bank of Worcester In politics he is a Republican He was formerly a member of the Worcester County Mechanics' Association and the Agricultural Society

He married (first), April 13, 1858, Maria I Pope, at Spencer, Massachusetts She died in 1862 at Spencer He married (second) Elizabeth M Hamblett of Manchester, New Hampshire, at that city, May 3 1866 She died February 19, 1901 He had two children by the second marriage, namely Eric Hamblett born July 30, 1867, Emma Lizzie, February 23, 1869, resides with her father in Worcester

(XXV) Eric Hamblett Whittemore, son of Eli Jones Whittemore (24), was born in Newark, New Jersey, July 30 1867 He married Jennie Black, of Medford, Massachusetts He was educated in the Worcester schools graduating from the Worcester high school He is engaged in the manufacture of paper boxes in Fitchburg a business which he started and built up himself His children are Elizabeth Hamblett, born October 7, 1897, Ruth Bailey, July 2, 1905

DR KENDALL EMERSON The Emerson Family, which has been prominent in New England since the first settlement originated in England and numbers among its members many distinguished and able men The first to use the name Emerson in England was Johannes Emeryson, of Brancepeth parish Durham county, England who was born before 1300 From him the various branches of the English family are descended, though the line cannot be traced perfectly The coat of arms was borne by the American branches of the family as well as the English

(I) Thomas Emmerson, the first English ancestor to whom the pedigree of Dr Emerson, of Worcester, can be traced definitely, was born some time before 1540 in England He was a resident of Great Dunmow, county Essex, where his three children are registered He was probably son of Ralf of Foxton, who received arms in 1535 His children were Robert, baptized at Great Dunmow, October 25, 1561, Joan, baptized 1562, John, baptized 1565

(II) Robert Emerson, son of the preceding Thomas Emerson (1), was born in Great Dunmow and baptized there October 25, 1561 He may be identical with Robert Emerson, of Bishop's Stortford, who married there November 24, 1578, Susan Crabb, who was buried there November 20 1626, aged seventy years Robert was buried at Bishop's Stortford, January 6 1620 His children were Alice, baptized at Bishop's Stortford, November 22, 1579, Margaret, baptized February 21, 1581-2, Thomas, see forward, Anne, Robert, baptized April 12, 1596, John

(III) Thomas Emerson son of the preceding Robert Emerson (2), was baptized at Bishop's Stortford July 26, 1584 In the church warden's book of St Michael's he is recorded as a collector for the poor in 1636 He married Elizabeth Brewster, July 1, 1611, at Bishop's Stortford, and the genealogist of the English Emersons suggests that she was the daughter of the postmaster of Scrooby and the elder of the colony at Plymouth The children of Thomas Emerson as recorded in the baptismal registry of St Michael's church at Bishop's Stortford Herts, were Robert baptized May 24, 1612 Benjamin, baptized October 2, 1614, Ralfe, baptized October 19, 1615, killed by falling tree June, 1626 James, baptized February 16, 1617, Joseph, baptized June 25, 1620, settled in Mendon, Massachusetts Elizabeth baptized June 14 1623, John baptized February 26, 1625 settled in Gloucester, Massachusetts, Thomas, see forward, Nathaniel, baptized July 18, 1630, settled Ipswich, Massachusetts, Susan, baptized March 17, 1632, may have died on the voyage

(IV) Thomas Emerson, son of the preceding Thomas Emerson (3), was the emigrant ancestor of Dr Emerson He died in Ipswich, Massachusetts, May 1, 1666 His wife Elizabeth was named executrix of his will 1653 She survived him They settled in Ipswich They came according to family tradition in the ship 'Elizabeth Ann" in 1635 He had a grant of land there in 1638 The children of Thomas Emerson were Elizabeth, married John Fuller, Thomas, died 1653, before his father, Joseph, see forward, John 1625, died December 2, 1700 James, resided in England, Nathaniel, 1629, Sarah, died August 12, 1640

(V) Joseph Emerson third child of Thomas Emerson (4), the emigrant, was born in England, about 1620-1 and died at Concord, Massachusetts, January 3 1680 Through his son Joseph he was the ancestor of that most illustrious American, Ralph Waldo Emerson Ralph Waldo (9) William (8), Joseph (7), Edward (6), Joseph (5), He married, 1646 Elizabeth Woodmansey, daughter of Robert and Margaret Woodmansey, schoolmaster of Boston They resided at Ipswich, Massachusetts York, Maine and Milton Massachusetts Joseph Emerson was a Puritan minister said to have been educated in England He may have studied at Harvard He was at Ipswich as early as 1638 He was admitted freeman there December 19, 1648 He preached at York Maine, the same year In 1653 he was a resident of Wells and took the freeman's oath there July 4, 1653 He signed a petition to Cromwell while of Wells, asking the Protector to confirm the jurisdiction of Massachusetts over the inhabitants of Wells About 1664 he left Wells, where he seemed to have a turbulent lot of parishioners and where the church, after he left, had to disband About 1664 he became minister at Milton, Massachusetts December 1, 1669, he settled in Mendon, Massachusetts, where he remained until the town was destroyed by the Indians, when he retired to Concord, where he died He married (second), December 7, 1665, Elizabeth Bulkeley, daughter of Rev Edward Bulkeley, of Concord, Massachusetts granddaughter of Rev Peter Bulkeley first minister of Concord She was born in 1638 and died September 4 1693, having married Captain John Brown, of Reading, Massachusetts The children of Rev Joseph Emerson were (by the first wife) Joseph, Mary, (by second wife the following) Lucian, born October 2 1667, married, May 15 1683 Thomas Damon, of Reading (see Damon family), Edward, April 26, 1670, married Rebecca Waldo, Peter, see forward Ebenezer, Daniel married May 19, 1709, Jane Armitage

(VI) Peter Emerson son of Rev Joseph Emerson (5), was born in Mendon, Massachusetts, 1673 and died 1749 He married, November 11, 1696, Anna Brown who was born in Reading, 1678, daughter of Captain John and Anna (Fiske) Brown, of Reading Captain John Brown had married Peter's mother They resided in the first parish of Reading, now South Reading, on the farm inherited from Captain Brown Peter Emerson was a farmer The children of Peter and Anna (Brown) Emerson were Anna born July 6, 1697, died August 11, 1697, Elizabeth February 20, 1699, Anna, March 9 1701 resided in Hollis, New Hampshire, Brown, April 16, 1704, Lucy, 1706, Sarah, November 8, 1708 Jane, March 11, 1711, resided at Hollis, Mary December 20, 1713, resided at Salisbury, Massachusetts Rev Daniel, May 20, 1716 (see forward) resided in Hollis, Catherine, December 2, 1718

(VII) Rev Daniel Emerson ninth child of Peter Emerson (6), was born at Reading Massachusetts, May 20, 1716, died at Hollis, New Hampshire, September 30 1801 He married November 7, 1744, Hannah Emerson daughter of Rev Joseph and Mary (Moody) Emerson of Malden, Massachusetts She was born at Malden December 3 1722, died at Hollis February 28, 1812 They resided at Hollis. Mr Emerson was graduated at Harvard College, 1739 and immediately prepared himself for the work of the ministry In 1741 he was called to be the first minister of Hollis New Hampshire, then the west precinct of Dunstable, Massachusetts He continued minister until November 27, 1793, when Rev Eli Smith who married his granddaughter, was elected as his colleague In 1755, during the old French war, he was chaplain to the famous rangers of which Robert Rogers and John Stark were the officers He was considered the ranking officer because of his family arms bearing three lions He kept a journal during his service and it has been preserved He was chaplain again in 1758 in Colonel Hart's regiment One of his letters to his wife dated at Crown Point in 1755 was brought to Hollis by his dog, which he had trained for the purpose He taught school and fitted his students for college He gave the land on which the meeting house was built He was one of the ablest advocates of the "New Light" doctrine and for many years was the leading and most influential minister in his section of the country Professor Churchill said of him "He was a kind of Congregational Bishop in his region" His dwelling house, built and occupied while he was minister in Hollis, is in good repair and habitable The children of Rev Daniel and Hannah (Emerson) Emerson were Hannah, born September 30, 1745, Daniel, December 15 1746 (see forward), Mary, September 19, 1748, Peter, November 9, 1749, Lucy, October 29, 1751, Mary, November 14, 1753, Elizabeth, May 5, 1755, Ebenezer, August 14, 1757, Joseph, September 28, 1759 (H C 1779), Ralph, March 4, 1761, Rebecca, July 5, 1762, Samuel, September 6, 1764, William December 11, 1765

(VIII) Daniel Emerson second child of Rev Daniel Emerson (7), was born at Hollis New Hampshire, December 15, 1746, died there October 4, 1820 He married, November 17, 1768, Ama Fletcher, daughter of Joseph and Elizabeth (Underwood) Fletcher She was born April 7, 1746, died November 22, 1797 They resided at Hollis He was a leading citizen, the wealthiest taxpayer and deacon of the church He was one of the eighteen proprietors of New Ipswich New Hampshire, preached there occasionally and had his tax refunded for that reason He was one of the thirty-two proprietors of the New Ipswich Academy in 1787, and was a trustee from the time of its incorporation in 1789 until his death In the revolutionary war Captain Emerson was active As a minute man he marched at the head of his company for Ticonderoga in 1776, reaching the Connecticut river He started a second time and reached Cavendish, Vermont He was captain of the first company in Colonel Nichol's regiment and of the fifth company in Colonel Mooney's regiment He served in the Rhode Island campaign in 1778-9 He was a member of the governor's council in 1787, and representative to the legislature nineteen terms, 1780-1812 He was coroner and high sheriff of Hillsboro county, New Hampshire, town clerk of Hollis, 1780-81, selectman twelve years, and town treasurer 1774-79 and 1798 and 1799 Mrs Emerson inherited besides the Fletcher blood that of Adams and Underwood, founders of Chelmsford, Massachusetts Her father settled in Dunstable when it was a wilderness, and lived there fifty years a prominent and respected citizen Family gatherings were held twice yearly until their children and grandchildren numbered above sixty in the Fletcher homestead at Dunstable The children of Daniel and Ama (Fletcher) Emerson were Ama born August 20, 1769 died August 4 1860, married Rev Eli Smith Daniel see forward, Hannah, December 7, 1773 Joseph October 13 1777, Ralph, August 18, 1787, Samuel, November 9 1791, William, November 9 1791 (twin of preceding) Daniel Emerson married (second) Hannah Mosier, widow who survived him and died August 20 1831

(IX) Daniel Emerson second child of Daniel Emerson (8) was born at Hollis, New Hampshire, July 15 1771, died at Dartmouth Massachusetts, November 16 1808 He married December 3 1797 Esther Frothingham a daughter of Major Benjamin Frothingham She was born in Charlestown, Massachusetts, 1770 died in Hollis New Hampshire March 14 1849 They resided at Charlestown, in Maryland in Virginia in New Hampshire and at Dartmouth Mr Emerson was graduated at Harvard 1794 He was a student at law with Samuel Dexter He was a merchant in Charlestown in Maryland in Virginia and Hollis, New Hampshire He sold out to his partner, Bixby, who did not pay the firm's debts as agreed and he ruined himself in paying them He was ordained in 1806 and settled as minister at South Dartmouth, Massachusetts, where he remained until his death His widow returned to Hollis and for many years kept the village store, driving to Boston at regular intervals in her own chaise to make purchases She thus supported and educated her large family The children of Daniel and Esther (Frothingham) Emerson were Daniel, born August 8, 1798, Elizabeth, July 29, 1800, died October 4, 1870, married, August 26, 1823, William S Bradbury, resided at Westminster, Massachusetts, Edward, October 1, 1802, died April 21, 1851, married, November 13, 1844, Hannah Pierce, resided at Hollis and at Allegan, Michigan, Charles, April 9, 1805, died July 6, 1805, Benjamin Frothingham, see forward, Joseph, September 4, 1808, died July 21, 1885, married (first) Sarah H Davis, (second) October 16, 1858, Martha A Howard, resided at Andover

(X) Benjamin Frothingham Emerson fifth child of Daniel Emerson (9), was born at Hollis, New Hampshire, July 3, 1806, died at Nashua, New Hampshire, September 6, 1884 Mr Emerson entered Dartmouth College in 1826 and studied two years, he was graduated from Union College in 1830 He attended the law school at Cambridge the next year, then taught school in the west He practiced law in Nashua from 1836 to 1873, and was intrusted with the settlement of many of the largest estates of that region He married, November 29 1842, Elizabeth Kendall, daughter of Nathan and Elizabeth (Thompson) Kendall She was born at Bedford, New Hampshire, October 7, 1812 died at Nashua, September 26, 1870 They resided a Nashua He married (second), October 9, 1872, Caroline Carlton (Frye) Rankin, widow of James Henry Rankin, and daughter of Samuel and Mary (Hoyt) Frye, of Danville, Vermont, where she was born February 8, 1817 She died March 1, 1886 The children of Benjamin Frothingham and Elizabeth (Kendall) Emerson were Benjamin Kendall, see forward, Charles Edward, born October 11, 1846, graduate of the Chandler Scientific School at Hanover, New Hampshire, 1870, a civil engineer of Nashua, New Hampshire

(XI) Professor Benjamin Kendall Emerson, eldest child of Benjamin Frothingham Emerson (10), was born at Nashua New Hampshire, December 20 1843 He married, April 2, 1873, Mary Annette Hopkins a daughter of Erastus and Charlotte Freylinghuysen (Allen) Hopkins She was born at Northampton, Massachusetts, April 2, 1848, died at Amherst, Massachusetts, July 31, 1897 They resided at Amherst Mr Emerson was graduated valedictorian of the class of 1865 of Amherst College He studied at Gottingen and took his Ph D there in 1869 He was assistant in the German geological survey in 1869 and made geological studies in Switzerland, Saxony, Bohemia and Norway He became professor of geology and zoology at Amherst College in 1870 He is the author of the genealogy, The Emerson Family, an excellent work He is a member of the German Geological Society, the Appalachian Club the American Philosophical Society the American Academy of Arts and Sciences, the Society of Naturalists of Eastern United States the National Geographic Society He was vice-president in 1896 of the American Association for the Advancement of Science vice-president in 1897 of the Geological Congress at St Petersburg first vice-president in 1898 of the Geological Society of America assistant geologist of the United States Geological Survey since 1887 and is now geologist (1905) He is the author of monograph xxvii, United States Geological Survey, entitled Geology of Old Hampshire county or Franklin, Hampshire and Hampden counties, in Massachusetts He wrote bulletin No 126, United States Geological Survey, entitled A Mineral Lexicon of Franklin, Hampshire and Hampden counties, in Massachusetts He wrote the United States Geological Survey bulletin, entitled The Geology of Southwestern Berkshire, and also the United States geological survey folios, which contain geological maps and descriptions of Eastern Berkshire, Franklin, Hampshire, Hampden and Worcester counties in Massachusetts He has written many articles for the scientific journals

Mrs Emerson's father was the Hon and Rev Erastus Hopkins, of an ancestry noted in the New England ministry Her great-great-grandmother was Esther Edwards, sister of Rev Jonathan Edwards Her grandfather on her mother's side was Rev William Allen, D D, president of the ephemeral Dartmouth University and later of Bowdoin College She was also descended from Eleazar Wheelock, founder of Dartmouth College from Rev Thomas Allen, of Pittsfield, the renowned "fighting parson" of the American revolution, and also in the eighth generation from William Bradford, the second governor of Plymouth colony Of her the *Springfield Republican*, August 6, 1897, said

"The college circle at Amherst feels itself sadly stricken by the recent unlooked for death of Mrs Annette Hopkins Emerson, wife of Professor B K Emerson Her life seemed so abounding in health and joyousness that her friends cannot realize that it is ended It was Mrs Emerson's rare and happy fortune to radiate sunlight in the world through her bright and fervent personality None who came within the range of its influence failed to feel its cheering effect Nor was its characteristic merely negative loveliness There was a fire, a sparkle, an intellectual stimulus in Mrs Emerson's presence and conversation that were fairly exhilirating So clever and charming and genuine a woman did not fail to receive recognition as a leader in the social life of Northampton which became her home after marriage Though her attention was largely occupied in her later years by the absorbing domestic interests which belong to the rearing of a large family, she kept well in touch with the progress of the intellectual world She had a decided literary interest and could herself write brightly and forcefully when occasion offered She had hoped to go with her husband to the congress of geologists at St Petersburg this summer, and had planned to describe her experiences and impressions in letters to the *Republican* and other journals, but she was obliged to forego this great pleasure It is hard to submit to the termination of a life so strong, so rich, so healthful, but solace and inspiration come with the thought of its accomplishment, its wholesome and helpful influence"

The children of Professor Benjamin Kendall and Mary Annette (Hopkins) Emerson were Charlotte Frelinghuysen, born January 3, 1874 graduate of Smith College, (Benjamin) Kendall, see forward, Edward Hopkins, born September 18, 1877, graduate of Amherst, 1899, Annette Hopkins, born September 3 1879, Malleville Wheelock, born August 28, 1887, Caroline Dwight, born March 14, 1891

(XII) Dr Benjamin Kendall Emerson or Kendall Emerson, as he is known having dropped his first name, son of Professor Benjamin Kendall Emerson (11), was born in Northampton, Massachusetts, June 27, 1875 He attended the public schools of Amherst in early life He entered Amherst College in 1893 and graduated in 1897 He is a member of the Phi Beta Kappa of Amherst He was graduated from Harvard Medical School in 1901, and after some hospital practice settled in Worcester and began the practice of his profession, in which he has made good progress and has acquired an excellent practice He married October 1, 1903, Josephine Devereux Sewall, born in Watertown, New York, October 14, 1875 She is a graduate of Smith College, 1897 They have one child, Sewall, born at Worcester, October 13, 1904 They reside at 72 West street, Worcester Dr Emerson's office is on Pearl street

HENRY H STOWE John Stowe or Stow (1), was the progenitor in New England of Henry H Stowe, of Lancaster, Massachusetts He came with his wife Elizabeth and six children in one of Winthrop's companies and settled in Roxbury, Massachusetts He arrived May 7, 1634 The children were Thomas, Elizabeth John, Nathaniel, Samuel and Thankful He was admitted a freeman September 3 1634 He was a proprietor of the colony and a delegate to the general court in 1639 He was elected in 1638 a member of the Ancient and Honorable Artillery Company

He married Elizabeth Biggs, daughter of Mrs Rachel Biggs, who came to Dorchester in 1635 with her daughter, —— Foster The Foster and Stowe children received valuable legacies from their uncles, John and Smalhope Biggs, of Cranbrook and Maidstone, Kent county, England His wife, Elizabeth, a very godly woman, was buried August 24, 1636 All his children were probably born in England They were Thomas, resided at Concord, Massachusetts, and Middletown, Connecticut Elizabeth, married Henry Archer John Samuel, born about 1620, graduated from Harvard College in 1645, the second class to graduate, the year 1644 having no graduates (The Harvard quinquennial catalogue states that he had the A M degree There had been but thirteen graduates before he had his degree There were seven graduates in 1645) He was a clergyman at Middletown, Connecticut He died in 1704 Nathaniel, resided at Ipswich, was born according to a deposition he took there in 1622 Thankful, married John Pierpoint, of Roxbury, Massachusetts

(II) Thomas Stowe, son of John Stowe (1), was born in England, probably Lincoln or Middlesex county, where the families of Stowe were numerous about 1610 He was in Concord, Massachusetts, before 1640, and had a family of at least three children Samuel, Thomas and Nathaniel He and his brother Nathaniel owned six hundred acres of land between Fairhaven Pond and the Sudbury Line Thomas Stowe sold his rights in 1660 to Thomas Gobble and David Dam, he having moved to Connecticut He probably left Concord about 1650 and moved to Middletown, then part of Hartford, Connecticut The town of Stow, Massachusetts, was near Marlboro and Sudbury where this land of the Stowe brothers was located but the Stowe family seems to have had no part in establishing the town It was incorporated in May, 1683, but the history shows no Stowe active as a pioneer In fact the whole family seems to have been in Connecticut about this time and the Stowes do not appear as of the town of Stow until much later Still the town was probably named in some way for a member of the family or by a friend of the Stowes

The children of Thomas Stowe were Samuel who became the progenitor of the Marlboro and Stow families after his return to Massachusetts,

Nathaniel, Thomas, born 1650, settled in Middletown, Connecticut

(III) Samuel Stowe, son of Thomas Stowe (2), was born in Concord, Massachusetts, before his father went to Middletown, Connecticut, probably about 1648 He was a soldier in King Philip's war Immediately afterward he became interested in the new settlement at Marlboro His name is on a petition for the plantation in 1677 and he was probably there some months before, perhaps directly after peace was established and the settlers in towns like Sudbury and Marlboro were able to work their plantations once more In 1684 he bought of Waban and James Atchuit, two Indians of Natick, Massachusetts, for six pounds in money and six pounds in corn—twenty acres of land in Marlboro He was also one of the proprietors of the Ockoocangansett plantation purchased by the Indians He was prominent as a proprietor and citizen of the new town

His children were Samuel, born May 2, 1680, married, December 19, 1704, Sarah Snow, Thomas, born December 27, 1682, married, January 20, 1713, Hannah Johnson, Mary, born July 18, 1685, married, June 13 1706, Jonathan Morse, Thankful, born October 8, 1687, married March 29, 1710, Samuel Stevens Rachel, born February 21, 1690, married December 14, 1715 Luke Rice, John, born March 30, 1696 married April 25, 1722, Elizabeth Brigham All three sons left large families of children and have numerous descendants in Marlboro and central Massachusetts

(IV) Thomas Stowe, son of Samuel Stowe (3), was born probably at Marlboro (where it was recorded), December 27, 1782 He married, January 20, 1713 Hannah Johnson, daughter of William and Hannah Johnson She died June 15, 1789 He died August 28 1765 His will proved October 8, 1765, mentions his sons Benjamin, Thomas, Samuel Stephen and David and Experience Newton, deceased also son Josiah who is required to provide for the support of his mother, Hannah

Their children were Comfort, born July 16, 1716 died 1716 Thomas, born September 8, 1717, died 1717 Benjamin born August 25 1718 David, born October 14 1719 died young, Thomas, born October 15, 1720 married June 3 1752 Elizabeth Newton, Charles born December 31 1721, died young, Samuel born December 26 1723 married, April 28 1748 Rebecca Howe, Stephen, born December 15, 1724 married, May 23, 1753 Abigail Smith, Josiah, born December 8, 1725, died young, Hannah, born December 9 1726 died young Experience, born February 24, 1728, married —— Newton, David, born April 29, 1729 Josiah born July 5, 1730, married 1760 Ruth Howe Hannah, born September 8 1731, Sabella, born September 4, 1732, died 1752, Silas born October 20 1734 All the sixteen children seem to have been by one wife an unusual family even for those prolific days She was evidently over ninety, the mother when she died

(V) Stephen Stowe son of Thomas Stowe (4), was born at Marlboro Massachusetts, December 15, 1724 He married, May 23 1753, Abigail Smith Two of their children were born at Marlboro They removed to Stow Massachusetts probably about 1758 where for several generations their descendants lived He was a soldier in the revolutionary war

Their children were Lydia born in Marlboro, March 24 1754 Silas born in Marlboro, April 26, 1756 Ichabod born about 1758 (and others probably) on the old homestead in Stow Massachusetts

(VI) Ichabod Stowe, son of Stephen Stowe (5) was born in Stow, Massachusetts 1759 He married Ruth Whitney November 29 1781 He was a soldier in the revolutionary war He settled in Stow and conducted the old farm He had a son Moses and other children, namely Ichabod, Abraham, Levi, Luke

(VII) Moses Stowe son of Ichabod Stowe (6), was born on the old Stowe homestead at Stow, Massachusetts, in 1803 He died in Lancaster, Massachusetts, in 1883 He attended the schools in Stow He went to work first on the old farm, but later decided to learn the wheelwright's trade He followed this business all his active life He settled in Lancaster where he spent his last years In politics he was originally an "old line Whig" and was deeply interested in his party, for which he worked earnestly and faithfully He married Eliza W Jones, January 1, 1829 They had two children Franklin, born October 16, 1829 died September 23, 1817 and Henry H, born March 29, 1841

(VIII) Henry H Stowe, son of Moses Stowe (7) was born in Lancaster, Massachusetts, March 29 1841 He was educated there in the public schools and then for a time worked at the wheelwright's trade with his father He succeeded to his father's business and conducted it successfully He was able to retire a few years ago and enjoy life quietly and comfortably at his pleasant home in Lancaster Massachusetts Mr Stowe has always taken an interest in political affairs and at times has been an active worker in the Republican party He has been overseer of the poor of Lancaster for several years He belongs to the local branch of the Red Men and is active in the order He is an active member of the Lancaster Unitarian church As a conservative but successful man in his own business, as a man of high personal character, of simple manly virtues he has the respect and confidence of his neighbors He married in 1863 Lydia A Robbins of Ashby, Massachusetts Their children are Mabel G, born at Lancaster, Massachusetts December, 1873, resides at home, Cora R, born at Lancaster August 29, 1877, stenographer for Boston Mutual Life Insurance Company, 141 Milk street, Boston, Massachusetts

JOHN HENRY COES, a retired business man of Worcester, Massachusetts formerly serving in the capacity of treasurer of the Coes Wrench Company, one of the leading industrial enterprises of that city was born in Springfield Massachusetts, September 25 1840 a son of Aury Gates and Nancy (Maynard) Coes grandson of Daniel and Roxana or Roxalana (Gates) Coes and great-grandson of John Coes, who settled in Worcester, Massachusetts, prior to the revolutionary war So far as is known all the Coes in this country are descended from this John Coes and his wife Rebecca John Coes died in Worcester, June 24, 1827, aged seventy-nine years

Daniel Coes (grandfather) was born on his father's farm in Massachusetts, in that part of Worcester formerly known as New Worcester, December 19, 1776 was reared thereon, and died January 26 1838 He married, October 26, 1808, Roxana (Roxalana or Roxalana) Gates, and their children were Sally born February 22, 1810, died February 16 1832 Loring born April 22, 1812, Albert, born September 20 1813 died February 13 1837, Aury Gates born January 22 1816 The Gates family is mentioned at length hereinafter

Aury Gates Coes (father) was born in Worcester Massachusetts January 22, 1816, and died December 2 1875 Among the firms for which he worked during his early life was that of Kimball & Fuller makers of woolen machinery, and in 1836 Aury Gates and his brother Loring purchased the

John H. Coes

business, forming the copartnership of L & A G Coes Aury Gates Coes also took an active part in politics, wielding a potent influence in behalf of the principles of the Republican party During the years 1870-71 he served in the house of representatives and was a member of several important committees He was an active and leading member of the Union Congregational Church in Worcester, Massachusetts He married Nancy Maynard, born 1815, died December 1, 1842, who bore him one child John Henry, mentioned at length hereinafter He married (second) May 29, 1845, Anna S Cutting, who bore him two children Anna Rebecca, born March 25, 1847, and Frederick Lewis, born January 9 1849 He married (third) Mrs Lucy Gibson, nee Wyman, a widow, born in Fitchburg, who bore him two daughters Estella, born September 25, 1858 died in Dresden, January 3, 1883, unmarried, and Mary born March 24, 1861, she is a graduate of Radcliffe College, class of 1887, and received the degree of Master of Arts from the same institution in 1897 She was assistant to the secretary of the college from 1888 to 1894, and from the latter year to the present time (1905) has served in the capacity of secretary Mr Coes married (fourth) Abigail Winch, no issue

John Henry Coes, whose name appears at the head of this sketch, received his elementary education in the public schools of Worcester, to which city his parents removed from Springfield during his early lifetime The knowledge thus acquired was supplemented by attendance at Leicester Academy and Wilbraham Academy He began the practical duties of life by entering the office of the firm of L & A G Coes, manufacturers of wrenches his father and uncle comprising the company and there mastered every detail of the business When the partnership between Loring and Aury Gates Coes was dissolved in 1869, the latter formed the firm of A G Coes & Company, admitting his son John Henry to partnership and continued the manufacture of wrenches in Worcester This connection continued until the death of the senior member of the firm, December 2, 1875, after which the business was carried on under the same firm name by John H Coes and his brother, Frederick L Coes In 1888 the firm of A G Coes & Co and that of Loring Coes & Co were incorporated under the laws of Massachusetts with a capitalization of $100 000 as the Coes Wrench Company and its officers were Loring Coes, president John H Coes, treasurer Frederick L Coes, clerk In 1902 the two brothers—John H and Frederick L—sold their stock and interest in the company to their uncle, Loring Coes, and retired from the business

John H Coes is a director of the Worcester Trust Company and member of its executive committee also vice-president and a member of the finance committee of the Mechanics Savings Bank, of Worcester and the duties of these two responsible positions occupy the greater portion of Mr Coes' business hours He holds membership in the Commonwealth Club, Worcester Club, Tatnuck Country Club, Massachusetts Agricultural Club of Boston and the Sons of the Revolution, being eligible to membership in the latter named through Simon Gates, the fifth in line of descent on the maternal side Mr Coes was at one time quite active in Masonic circles He is a member of Montacute Lodge, Worcester Royal Arch Chapter, Hiram Council and Worcester County Commandery, Knights Templar Mr Coes married February 5, 1874 Annie Brownell Hadwen born in Worcester Massachusetts November 4, 1846 daughter of Obadiah B Hadwen (see sketch) They have one child Mary Maynard Coes born March 14, 1876 The family reside at No 1058 Main street, Worcester

GATES FAMILY Stephen Gates was an emigrant ancestor of John H Coes, of Worcester For biographical sketch and children of Stephen Gates, see elsewhere in this work This line is traced through his son Simon

(II) Simon Gates son of Stephen Gates (1), was born in 1645 died April 21, 1693, at Brockton, Massachusetts He married Margaret ——, of Cambridge Massachusetts They resided in Cambridge, Lancaster and Brookline, Massachusetts He inherited his father's estate at Cambridge The children of Simon and Margaret Gates were 1 Abigail, born August 14, 1671, died 1771, aged one hundred years, at Brighton, Massachusetts, married (first) Nathaniel Sparhawk, Jr, who died November 8, 1734, married (second), 1735, Josiah Mayo, of Roxbury, Massachusetts 2 Simon, born September 1, 1673 died January 2, 1675-76 3 Simon, born January 5, 1675-76, died March 10, 1735, aged sixty years married, May 29, 1710, Sarah Wood, daughter of John and Lydia Wood of Marlboro, Massachusetts, they settled in Marlboro, where she died in 1751 4 George, born April 6 1678, died May 23, 1679 5 Amos, born 1681, died 1754, married, May 19, 1703, Hannah Oldham, daughter of Samuel and Hannah (Dana) Oldham, whose birth occurred October 10, 1681 6 Jonathan born June 22, 1683, died February 7 1755-56 at Worcester, Massachusetts, married Persis Shepard, daughter of John and Persis (Pierce) Shepard of Charlestown, Massachusetts and granddaughter of Thomas and Hannah (Ensign) Shepard, of Malden Massachusetts She was born 1691 died July 12 1776 7 Samuel born August 11 1685 said to have settled somewhere in Connecticut, but no descendants known 8 Margaret, born August 13 1689, married James How or John How

(III) Simon Gates son of Simon Gates (2), was born January 5 1675-76, died March 10, 1735, aged sixty years married May 29 1710, Sarah Wood daughter of John and Lydia Wood, of Marlboro Massachusetts They settled in Marlboro, where she died in 1751 The children of Simon and Sarah (Wood) Gates were 1 Simon, born December 11, 1710 died April 11 1777 aged sixty-six years married, 1749 Sarah How, who died September 30 1800, aged seventy-five years 2 Sarah born October 15, 1712, died at Hubbardston Massachusetts married February 3 1736, Ephraim Church of Rutland Massachusetts 3 Susannah, born December 19, 1714, died at Hubbardston, married Captain John Phelps, of Rutland Massachusetts 4 Stephen born August 20, 1718, died October 5 1773 aged fifty-five years at Rutland married February 4 1742-43 Damaris How, born August 12, 1725 at Marlboro, Massachusetts, died December 3 1809 aged eighty-three years at Rutland, Massachusetts, whence they removed in 1749 5 Solomon born May 14, 1721 died March 2, 1761 aged forty years at Worcester, married November 10, 1748 Mary Clark, and resided at Worcester 6 Samuel born February 28 1722 married Caroline How he was a soldier in the revolution 7 Silas born February 3, 1727, died August 25, 1793, aged sixty-six years, at Marlboro married May 9 1754 Elizabeth Bragg, who died March 20 1806 aged seventy-four years 8 John, born January 27, 1729

(IV) Simon Gates son of Simon Gates (3), was born December 11, 1710 died April 11 1777, married, 1749 Sarah How who died September 30,

1800, aged seventy-five years They resided in Worcester, Massachusetts The children of Simon and Sarah (How) Gates were 1 Rebecca, born in Worcester, 1752, died October 13, 1834, married, May 5, 1778, David Richards, who died January 29, 1829, aged seventy-eight years 2 Simon, Jr, born at Worcester, 1752, died February 2, 1849, married Sarah Edgerton, daughter of S N Edgerton, she died August 19, 1843, aged eighty-five years 3 Asa, born in Worcester January 29, 1757, died November 21, 1835, married, February 15, 1786, Fanny Field 4 Sarah, born in Worcester, April 2, 1761, died November 21, 1819, married, May 15, 1783, John Sargent, who died February 7, 1829 5 John, born 1764, died May 20, 1786 6 Mary, born 1768, died December 24, 1809, married William Moore 7 Katherine, born April 22 1772 married Phineas Jones, he died March 22, 1814, aged sixty-six years 8 Levi, born May 21, 1776, died October 6, 1837, buried at Ashland, Ohio, married, 1791, Chloe Sumner, daughter of Josiah Sumner, born 1769, died October 4, 1828 They resided at Charlton Massachusetts, and thence went to Shoreham, Vermont

(V) Simon Gates son of Simon Gates (4), was born January 6, 1756, in Worcester, Massachusetts He died February 2, 1849, aged ninety-three years, in Worcester He married Sarah daughter of S N Edgerton and her death occurred August 19, 1843 aged eighty-five years He responded to the Lexington call to arms in 1775 entered Captain Hubbard's company before Boston, and served in the battle of Bunker Hill He also served in Captain Stone's company in the battle of Bennington, campaign of 1777 also in Captain Cushing's company in the fall of 1777 He was a revolutionary war pensioner Mr Gates was a very domestic man, and was never away from home but two or three nights in his life except while in the service He died in the same room in the same house in which he was born The children of Simon and Sarah (Edgerton) Gates were 1 Olive born August 28 1784 married ——— Hayward of Mercer Maine 2 Roxalany born May 10 1786, see forward 3 John born June 10, 1789 married Letitia Burr 4 Levi born May 7, 1790 died at Claquato Lewis county Washington married Hannah Paine of Worcester February 20 1820 5 Mary born October 10 or 11, 1792, married Erastus Tucker October 5 1810 6 Sarah born September 9 1794 7 David R born March 31, 1799 died at Worcester, married (first) Eliza Fessenden, February 11, 1824, married (second) Sarah N Britton, born November 24 1809 at Spencer Massachusetts, died February 8 1893 8 Horatio born September 4, 1801, died 1852 married Fidelia A Hall 1825, married (second) Hannah Head born 1799, died 1893

(VI) Roxalany or Roxalana Gates, daughter of Simon Gates (5), was born May 10 1786, at Worcester Massachusetts She married, October 26, 1808 Daniel Coes aforementioned in this narrative as the grandfather of John H Coes and their children were 1 Sally born February 22 1810 2 Loring born April 22 1812, see Coes Family 3 Albert born September 29, 1813 4 Aury Gates, born January 22, 1826 aforementioned as the father of John H Coes

PAUL BEAGARY MORGAN Miles Morgan (I) the emigrant ancestor of Charles H Morgan, of Worcester and his son Paul Beagary Morgan, was born probably in 1615 in Llandorff, Glamorgan county Wales and removed to Bristol, England, a few years before he emigrated to America He came to Boston in April 1636, with two brothers The eldest, James settled in New London, Connecticut, John went to Virginia and Miles joined the colonists and became one of the founders of Springfield Massachusetts These colonists were organized at Roxbury, Massachusetts, now part of Boston John Morgan is the ancestor of General David Morgan, of rangers' fame in the revolution, and of famous members of this family in the southern states James Morgan, of Connecticut, also has many prominent men among his descendants

Miles Morgan drew land for his home lot on the south side of Ferry Lane At present the site of the original Morgan dwelling house is occupied by the repair shop of the Connecticut River Railroad Having prepared his first home, Miles Morgan married about 1643 Prudence Gilbert The following quaint story of his courtship and marriage is taken from the Morgan Genealogy On his passage from England he formed an acquaintance with a young woman who belonged to a family which on their arrival settled in Beverly, Massachusetts To her he determined to prefer his suit This he did by letter in which he proposed to her to become his wife and the sharer of his dubious fortunes in the wilderness To this frank proposition she with equal frankness (for coquetry it seems was not then the fashion) wrote him an explicit answer and avowed her willingness to comply with his wishes Her suitor it appears was resolved to prosecute the affair like a man of business On receiving an answer so favorable to his inclinations he immediately engaged two of his friends and an Indian to attend him in his matrimonial expedition and departed with all convenient speed' taking with them an old horse for the purpose of conveying the household stuff of the intended bride to her future habitation and their muskets with which they might put to flight the 'armies of the aliens' who might perchance molest them in their pilgrimage to and from the land of the people of the east Prosperity attended the journey and the hymeneal torch was kindled on his arrival The matrimonial contract having been satisfied in due form the old pack horse received his destined burden, the bridegroom and his companions shouldered their muskets and thus escorted the bride to Springfield, who walked with them on foot the whole distance from Beverly to that place viz 130 miles"

In 1675 during King Philip's war the Morgan House was attacked by the Indians but so bravely was it defended by Miles Morgan and his sons that the Indians retired after an unsuccessful siege Peletiah Morgan, one of these sons, was killed in this war in the following year at what is now Chicopee, Massachusetts

Among other prominent descendants of Miles and Prudence Morgan are J Pierpont Morgan and his late father, Junius S Morgan the bankers The line of descent is Miles (I) Nathaniel (II), Joseph (III), Captain Joseph (IV), Joseph (V), Junius Spencer (VI), J Pierpont (VII) Morgan The Worcester family traces its descent from David, son of Miles (II)

The genealogy of the Morgan family has recently been traced by George T Clark, Antiquary, from remote Welsh ancestors He gives sixteen generations of Morgan ancestors of Miles Morgan, of Springfield It is so seldom that English and American genealogies can be so successfully united that American Morgans may well take some satisfaction in their Welsh ancestry

(I) Cadivor-Fawr, married Elen, daughter and heir to Llwch Llawen and had

(II) Bleddri third son witnessed a Berkerolles grant of Bassalleg to Glastonbury and was probably a land owner in those parts He bore "Argent, 3 bulls' heads cabossed sable" The ordinary coat of the Morgans has long been "Or, a griffin segreant sable," but some branches have used Cadivor and others Bleddri Morgans of Pencoyd bore 'Argent, a lion rampant gardant sable between two cantons, the dexter, Or, a griffin segreant sable,' the sinister, Bleddri'" The Llantarnam Morgans bore the griffin on a field argent The descendants of Ivor Howel used Bleddri, but inserted a chevron between the Bulls' heads The Lewises of St Pierre used the Cadivor lion, and the Griffin for a crest Bleddri is said to have married Clydwen, daughter of Griffith ap Cydrich ap Gwaethfoed-fawr, and had

(III) Ivor, who married Nest, daughter of Caradoc ap Modoc ap Idnerth ap Cadwgan ap Elystan Gloddrydd, and had

(IV) Llewelyn, who married Lleici, daughter of Griffith ap Beli, and had

(V) Ivor, who married Tanglwst, daughter of Homel Sais ap Arglwydd Rhys They had

(VI) Llewelyn Lleia, married Susan, daughter of Howel ap Howel Sais, a first cousin They had

(VII) Ivor, father of

(VIII) Llewelyn ap Ivor of Tredegar, Lord of St Clear, married Angharad, daughter of Sir Morgan ap Meredith, from the Welsh lords of Caerleon, ap Grifhth ap Meredith ap Rhys, who bore "Argent a lion rampant sable" Sir Morgan died 1332, when Angharad was aged thirty-two years They had 1 Morgan 2 Ivor Hael, whence Morgan of Gwern-y-Cleppa 3 Philip whence Lewis of St Pierre

(IX) Morgan of Tredegar and St Clear, married Maud daughter of Rhun ap Grono ap Llwarch, Lord of Cibwr He died before 1384 Issue Llewelyn Philip whence Morgan of Langstone, John father of Gwenllian, married David Goch ap David Christian, married Jevan ap Jenkin Kemeys, Ann married David Gwilim David, of Rhiwperra Margaret, married Traherne ap Meyric of Merthyr A daughter married Thomas ap Gwillim of Carnllwyd, Elenor, married Grono ap Howel Bennet

(X) Llewelyn ap Morgan of Tredegar and St Clear, living 1387, married Jenet, daughter and heir of David-vychan ap David of Rhydodyn, 1384-87 Issue Jevan, Christy, married Madoc ap Jevan of Gelligaer, ———, married Roger ap Adam of St Mellon's, ——— married Madoc of Bassalleg, ——— married Thomas Llewelyn, Ann married John ap Jenkin, ———, married ———, of Raglan, ——— married ——— Builth

(XI) Jevan Morgan, 1415-48, married Denise or Elizabeth, daughter of Thomas ap Llewelyn-vychan of Llan gattog-on-Usk Issue John, David, 1442-48 Jenkin 1454

(XII) Sir John Morgan, Knight of the Sepulchre 1448 stewart of Gwentlloog, married Jenet, daughter and co-heir of John ap David Mathew of Llandaff Issue Morgan, Thomas, whence Morgan of Machen and Tredegar, John, whence a branch, Lewis, 1491, William Morgan, coroner, 1501 father of John of Newport, died 1541, father of William, 1541-1559, Philip 1491, Elizabeth, married John Fiennes Lord Clinton and Say, Jane, married William David Powel, Mary, married Thomas Llewelyn-vychan of Rhiwperra, Isabella, married James Kemeys of Began, died 1591

(XIII) Thomas Morgan, second son of Sir John Morgan was of Machen esquire of the body to Henry VII, living 1538, married Elizabeth, daughter of Roger Vaughan, of Porthaml Issue Rowland Reynold, whence Morgan of Llanvedw, John, whence Morgan of Bassalleg, Edmond, whence Morgan of Penllwyn-Sarth Margaret, married (first) John Kemeys (second) William Edmunds, Barbara, married Sir Henry Seymour, Maud, married John ap Rosser, Jane, married (first) William Gunter, (second) Richard ap Jenkins, (third) William Vaughan, of Magor, Constance, married William Jones, of Treowen, Mary, married (first) Edward Williams, (second) Richard Herbert, Elizabeth, married Edward James

(XIV) Rowland Morgan, of Machen, 1517-77, married Blanch, daughter of John Thomas, of Llanarth Settlement, November 11, 1517, sheriff, 1557 Issue Thomas, Henry, whence Morgan of St Mellon's, Catherine, married (first) Thomas Mathew, (second) Miles Morgan, (third) Henry Jones, Ann, married Philip Morgan, of Gwern-y-Cleppa, Mary, married Thomas Lewis, of Rhiwperra, Elizabeth, married Edward Kemeys, of Cefn Mably

(XV) Thomas Morgan, of Machen and Tredegar and of the Middle Temple, 1567-77, sheriff, 1581, M P for county in 1589, will, 1603, married Elizabeth Bodenham, daughter Roger Bodenham Issue Sir William, Edward, 1586, married Elizabeth Thomas, daughter of Richard Thomas, of Bertholley, Sir John, died before 1610, married Florence Morgan, daughter and eventual heir of William Morgan of the Friars They had William Morgan of the Friars, 1663, mayor of Newport, 1667 father of Lewis Morgan, died about 1690, father of Lewis died 1729 who sold to the Friars He was father of Blanch and Catherine David Morgan, whence a branch, Blanch married Edward Lewis of Van, settlement 1585, Catherine, married William Herbert, of Coldbrook, Elizabeth, married William Jones, of Abergavenny Jane, married Rowland Morgan, of Bassalleg, Elizabeth, married William Blethyn of Dynham, Ann, Margaret, married Henry Williams of Mathern

(XVI) Sir William Morgan of Tredegar knighted 1633 M P for the county 1623-25, will made 1650, proved 1653, sheriff 1612 aged ninety-three at death he received Charles I at Tredegar July 16 and 17, 1645 married (first) Elizabeth Winter daughter of Sir William Winter of Lidney, (second) Bridget Morgan, daughter of Anthony Morgan of Heyford county Northampton, widow of Anthony Morgan of Llanvihangel Crucorney Issue by first wife Thomas, Edward of Kilfengan, will dated April 4 1660, proved February, 1661, married Elizabeth James daughter and heir of Charles James of Llandewi Rhydderch, had Elizabeth daughter and heir married Henry Chambre of Court Morgan William, whence Morgan of Rhymny Rowland of Risca, will dated December 19, 1660 proved February 1661, married Honora ——— and had Colonel William Morgan, buried at Bassalleg, October 27 1679 John of the Temple in 1652, coel Mary, married George Lewis of St Pierre Blanch married John Carne of Ewenny Frances, married Charles Williams, of Llangibby Mary, single, will 1687 Elizabeth married William Morgan, of Dderw, she died 1638 he died 1649 By Sir William's second wife Sir Anthony of Kilfengan s p His widow was alive in 1673 Mary, married Peter Farmer, of London, who died 1691 They had Margaret daughter and heir, married John More, who sold Kilfengan in 1707

(XVII) Elizabeth Morgan daughter of Sir William of Tredegar (16), married William Morgan, merchant of Diveru, went to Bristol, England, in 1616 Elizabeth died 1638 William died 1648, both buried in Bristol (See Great Orphan Book and Book of Wills of Bristol) Issue MILES MORGAN, born 1616 named perhaps after Miles Morgan, captain British army who perished with Sir Humphrey Gilbert, half brother of Sir Walter

Raleigh, who sailed 1576 under a patent to occupy any heathen lands not actually possessed ot any Christian prince or people" The only other Miles I find (than Capt Miles supra) is Miles Morgan or Morgan Miles, son of William Miles of Cabalva

(XVIII) Miles Morgan was next to Col Pynchon the most important and useful of the Springfield Colony He was made second in command, though he was the youngest of the company He was the only pioneer in tact who was less than twenty-one years of age when admitted He was a brave and intrepid Indian fighter in the frequent conflicts on the frontier He was a wise counsellor and a sturdy tiller of the soil In civil life Col Pynchon was the grocer and Morgan was the butcher A handsome monument was erected at Springfield in 1879 in testimony of the services of Miles Morgan in settling the town, governing the colony, fighting the Indians in 1675 when Springfield was sacked and burned and many of the little colony killed

Miles Morgan married Prudence Gilbert 1636 Issue 1 Mary, born December 14 1644 2 Jonathan, born September 16, 1646 3 David, born July 23, 1648 4 Peletiah, born May 17 1650 killed by the Indians 1675, died unmarried 5 Isaac, born March 12, 1652 6 Lydia, born February 8, 1654 7 Hannah, born February 11, 1656 8 Mercy, born May 18, 1658 Prudence Gilbert Morgan died November 14, 1660 Miles married February 15, 1669 (2) Elizabeth Bliss By her he had issue 1 Nathaniel, born June 14, 1671 Miles Morgan died May 28 1699, aged eighty-four years

(XIX) David Morgan son of Miles Morgan (18), was born at Springfield, Massachusetts, July 23, 1648 He married Mary Clark of Springfield, January 16, 1672 They lived at Springfield He died May 30, 1731 Issue 1 Peletiah born March, 1676 2 David, born February 18, 1679 3 John, born October 7 1682 4 Jonathan, born September 13, 1685 5 Mary, born December 24 1686 6 Benjamin, born May 2, 1695, married Mary Graves, June 4, 1718 Issue 1 Benjamin, born November 26, 1719 2 Stephen, born May 4, 1722 3 Aaron, born November 7, 1724 4 Mary born August 4, 1727

(XX) Deacon David Morgan, son of David Morgan (19), was born in Springfield, Massachusetts February 18 1679 He married Deborah Colton, daughter of Ephraim Colton, 1703 He died September 11 1760 See Colton family annexed David Morgan and his son Joseph were among the original proprietors of Brimfield Massachusetts, drawing respectively grants number 46 and 25 in the distribution of land to the first settlers in 1732 and the family went to Brimfield about that time Descendants of David are still living in the town He was town clerk in 1731

The standing of Deacon Morgan's family is shown by the report of the seating committee September 12 1757 when the widow of Mr Morgan is given a post of honor in the first pew with such well known men as John Sherman Esq Captain Leonard Hoar Mr Nathan Collins and their wives The daughters of Deacon David Morgan married into the Hoar and Sherman families His children were 1 David 2 Joseph born August 19 1705 3 Mary, born 1706, married Leonard Hoar Jr, May 6 1736 4 Elizabeth married Phineas Sherman December 12 1738 5 Jonathan, born 1740 6 Deborah married Nathaniel Collins 1763 7 Mercy born 1741 died 1745 8 Isaac born 1747

(XXI) Sergeant Joseph Morgan son of Deacon David Morgan (20) was born at Springfield August 19, 1705, and died January 28, 1798 He was a sergeant, in the troops sent from New England, at the second seige of Louisburg in 1758, and although seventy years of age he responded to the call April 19, 1775, and went to Lexington, under Capt Sherman and Col Pynchon He married Margaret Cooley, December 25, 1729 She died July 17, 1754 He married (second) Rachel Dada, August 11, 1759 She died March 27, 1810 He was a cabinet maker by trade and his son Joseph continued the business after his death

Their children were 1 Margaret, born April 20, 1730, married John Mighell, February 2, 1749 2 Joseph, Jr, born April 17, 1733 3 Mary, born February 28, 1735, died 1736 4 Mary, born June 15, 1737, married Capt Ebenezer Hitchcock May 7, 1761 5 Benjamin, born July 24, 1739 6 Miriam, born May 7, 1742 8 David, born January 25, 1745 8 Keziah, born January 26, 1747, married Benjamin Cady, December 31, 1767 9 Aaron, born March 16, 1749 10 Elijah, born May 31, 1758 11 Enoch, born August 3, 1763

(XXII) Sergeant Aaron Morgan, son of Sergt Joseph (21), and Margaret Morgan, was born at Brimfield, Massachusetts, March 16, 1749, and died there August 30, 1825 He responded to the Lexington Alarm April 19, 1775, in Capt Thompson's company, Col Danielson's regiment He was in Gates Army in the north 1777 in Capt Capen's company, Col Woodbridge's regiment He had other service also to his credit He was a prominent man in Brimfield town affairs He was moderator in 1807, 1810, 1811, 1812, 1813 1814, 1815, he was town clerk from 1784 to 1797, selectman in 1798, 1799, 1800 1801, 1802, 1803 1804, assessor 1775, 1776 1780, 1781, 1783 1785, to 1793 1795, 1796, 1798 to 1804 inclusive He married Abigail Sherman November 26, 1772 She died October 23, 1828 See Sherman family annexed Their children were 1 Lucy born January 20, 1774 married James Moore, December 19, 1793 2 Justin, born March 8, 1777 3 Aaron Jr, born December 6 1779 4 Calvin, born May 27, 1782 5 Thomas born April 7, 1788, married Orra Morgan, October 27, 1816 6 Sally, born June 30, 1790 married Harris Sherman, April 28, 1814

(XXIII) Calvin Morgan son of Sergt Aaron Morgan, was born at Brimfield, Massachusetts, May 27, 1782, and died June 13, 1832 He married Polly Forbush of Grafton, Massachusetts, March 10, 1803, she died January 12, 1868

Their children were 1 Hiram born August 1, 1803 died June 29 1866 2 Dexter, born June 2, 1805 died March 17, 1818 3 Margaret F, born September 23 1806 married G W Dinsmore, September 23 1829 4 Calvin Jr born April 4, 1808 married Susannah P Lane, died October 31, 1835 5 Mary Ann born December 28, 1809, married Joseph B Parker October 15 1833 6 Abigail T, born June 13 1811 married Heman S Jackson May 20 1859 7 Enoch Melvin born June 2, 1813 died December 9 1813 8 Sarah B, born March 26 1815, married Luther Bigelow, June 11, 1835 died September 17 1840 9 Malvina F, born April 12 1817 married Andrew J Copp, July 2, 1839 died June 27, 1841 10 Francis Dexter, born April 24, 1810, married Elizabeth Phelps, November 25, 1841, died 1846 11 Harriet N, born September 28 1821 12 Cordelia born October 20, 1825, died February 14 1842

(XXIV) Hiram Morgan son of Calvin Morgan (23), was born at Brimfield, Massachusetts, August 1 1803 died June 29, 1866 He married Clarissa Lucina Rich daughter of Dr Noah Rich Hiram was a mechanic skillful in wood turning

Children were as follows 1 Charles Hill, born January 8, 1831 2 Francis Henry, born September 23, 1833 3 Hiram Dexter, born July 27, 1836, died in infancy 4 Cyrus Rich born July 4, 1838, married Adelaide Fisher 5 Harriet Eaton, born March 27 1845 died in infancy

(XXV) Charles Hill Morgan, son of Hiram Morgan (24), was born at Rochester, New York, January 8, 1831 His parents moved to Clinton, Massachusetts when he was an infant He attended the Clinton schools and Lancaster Academy At the age of fifteen he began to learn the machinist's trade in his uncle's shop He developed a love for mechanical drawing and acquired a thorough knowledge of mechanics as well as much technical skill In 1852 when he was twenty-one years of age he had acquired sufficient knowledge of chemistry to take charge of the dye house of the Clinton Mills Mr Morgan was for a time draughtsman for the Lawrence Machine Company and for Erastus B Bigelow He went to Philadelphia in 1860 and for a short time was associated in business there with his brother Returning to Worcester in 1864 he accepted the position of general superintendent of the wire mills of Washburn & Moen, where he remained for twenty-three years during eleven of which he was a director of the corporation While with the Washburn & Moen Co he designed the first hydraulic elevator introduced in New England He made seven trips to Europe to visit the steel and wire mills of England, Belgium, Germany, France and Sweden He studied the new patents, read the trade journals and kept his mill well to the front in the development of new methods and machines An advance step in the wire business was an improvement of the continuous rolling mill designed and constructed in Manchester, England, in accordance with the designs of George Bedson This continuous rolling was a great improvement in methods but production was limited by the imperfections of the ordinary hand reel Mr Morgan's first improvement was a reel operated by steam power, the second was the invention and construction of a continuous train of rolls having only horizontal axles Experience has shown that this mill consisting of a series of horizontal rolls with intermediate twistings or turning guides between the rolls, giving the metal one quarter or a turn in its passage from one pair of rolls to the next, was far superior to a mill with alternate horizontal and vertical rolls Nine years after the building of the Bedson mill another mill from new designs furnished by Mr Morgan was built on the Belgian and continuous plan and was known as the Combination mill In 1886 Mr Morgan patented automatic reels with vertically moving platform

Mr Morgan became consulting engineer for the American Wire Company of Cleveland in 1887 and introduced new and valuable inventions In 1889 he completed and put in operation at Dollar Bay, Michigan a large copper mill for the Tamarack mine one of the mines producing the famous lake copper

Mr Morgan began the manufacture of rolling mill machinery etc in 1888 and three years later incorporated the business under the name of The Morgan Construction Co The capital stock of the company is $100 000 Mr Morgan is president and his son Paul B Morgan, treasurer The executive office and the mill is at 11 to 21 Lincoln street Worcester Branch offices are located in New York city and Brussels Belgium The company manufactures rolling mill machinery for steel billets merchant shapes, rods, cotton ties and barrel hoops also wire drawing and hydraulic machinery A specialty of the company is the equipment of entire plants from boilers to special devices made to order complete Business has developed steadily and a large export trade has been built up The company has valuable patents for machinery used in modern mills

Chas H Morgan is also the president and owner to a large extent of the Morgan Spring Company which was incorporated in 1881 It is capitalized at $700 000 The business developed to its present proportions by steady but rapid growth Mr Morgan began the manufacture of springs at the Morgan mills on Lincoln street In 1896 the extensive plant at Barber's Crossing was constructed and has been enlarged to allow for the increase in business This location is ideal for the purposes of the company The works are at the junction of the Fitchburg and Nashua Railroads, making shipping facilities admirable In 1905 the Morgan Spring Company purchased an extensive plant at Struthers Ohio where rod rolling and wire making machinery has been installed The company manufactures wire rods, the best grade of oil-tempered steel wire, also spiral and flat springs of all kinds many special designs being made for agricultural and other machinery There are departments for wire drawing tempering and spring making

Mr Morgan's connection with the Washburn Shops of the Worcester Polytechnic Institute gives him a high place among the benefactors of that institution In March 1886, Ichabod Washburn made his gift to establish the machine shop and working mechanical department of the Worcester Polytechnic Institute The idea of Mr Washburn was unique Mr Morgan more than any other man deserves credit for the successful development of the plan made by the founder The shop is at the same time a laboratory and trade school for the Institute and a business concern self-supporting Mr Washburn recommended Mr Morgan as a suitable trustee knowing his great mechanical skill and large experience Mr Washburn died before the shop was completed Mr Morgan was elected a trustee of the Institute March 27, 1886 and at the request of the dying founder of the institution Mr Morgan took charge of the construction and equipment of the shops Mr Morgan at the request of Mr Washburn selected the first superintendent Milton P Higgins a graduate of the Chandler Scientific School at Hanover, New Hampshire From the first Mr Morgan co-operated with Mr Higgins to set a high standard of efficiency The success of the experiment in technical education has made the Worcester Polytechnic Institute famous and its shops are the model for the whole country Mr Washburn's idea as worked out by Mr Morgan Mr Higgins and their associates has been a new triumph in American industrial education and progress

Mr Morgan has been an active member of the Plymouth Congregational Church and was one of the its founders and deacons he has been director of the Y M C A and member of the Congregational Club of Worcester He was a director of the First National Bank

He married in 1852 Harriet C Plympton of Shrewsbury In 1862 his wife died He married second August 4 1863 Rebecca A Beagary, of Philadelphia, Pennsylvania

His children were 1 C Henry Morgan, born February 1, 1854 married Jessie Bradbury, resides in Worcester 2 Hiram Plympton, born ———— — 1862 died in infancy 3 Harriet L, born June 9 1864 married Dr Winthrop D Mitchell of East Orange New Jersey (They have one child Beatrice Mitchell, born June 6, 1891) 4 Charlotte, born July 10, 1866, married Frederick M McFadden of Philadelphia, Pennsylvania 5 Paul Beagary born May 7, 1869, married June 15, 1893, Lessie Louise Maynard 6 Ralph Landers, born September 5, 1872 married Alice Sawyer

(XXVI) *Francis Henry Morgan, son of Hiram* (24), was born September 23, 1833, and died June 19 1899 He married Ellen A Wright who died, and he married second Caroline Augusta Smith, October 1, 1868 He resided in Worcester, being from the time of the founding of Morgan Spring Company to the date of his death, the treasurer and general manager of that company His children are Harry Wallis, born September 26, 1869, died August 13 1870 2 Mary Colchester born June 28, 1874 3 Charles Francis, born June 23, 1877 4 Ray born August 6, 1883, died November 28 1888

(XXVII) Paul Beagary Morgan son of Charles Hill Morgan (25) and Rebecca A (Beagary) Morgan was born in Worcester, May 7, 1869 He attended the Worcester schools leaving the high school after three years to enter Worcester Academy He graduated from the Academy in 1887 and from Worcester Polytechnic Institute in 1890 He completed his education abroad with a year in Sweden studying the iron industry taking a special course in metallurgy and chemistry in the Royal School of Mines at Stockholm He had practical experience in the celebrated Munkfors Works of Uddeholm Company Upon his return he went into business with his father and has had in recent years a large share in the management and responsibility for the business established by his father He is treasurer of the Morgan Spring Company and of the Morgan Construction Company and president of the Heald Machine Company

He has won a reputation among business men for his integrity prudence and common sense He was in 1904 elected a director of the Worcester National Bank He is a trustee of the Peoples Savings Bank and of Memorial Hospital He has accepted the honor and trying duties of the presidency of the Worcester County Musical Association This organization gives the annual Musical Festival for which the name of Worcester is celebrated in the musical world

Mr Morgan is a member of the Plymouth Congregational Church, of the Worcester Y M C A and of the Congregational Club He is an ex-president of the Alumni Association of the Worcester Polytechnic Institute vice president of the Alumni of Worcester Academy He is interested in public affairs, a Republican, an honorary member of George H Ward Post G A R and a member of the Sons of the American Revolution He is a member of the Worcester Club the Quinsigamond Boat Club, the Tatnuck Country Club the Worcester Automobile Club the Youngstown (Ohio) Club and the Engineers Club (New York)

He married Lessie Louise Maynard daughter of William and Mary (Adams) Maynard June 15, 1893 at Worcester, Massachusetts His wife is a descendant of the Maynard family of Marlboro, for which the town of Maynard Massachusetts, is named Their children are 1 Philip Maynard, born April 13 1896 2 Charles Hill 2d born September 19 1902 3 Paul Beagary, Jr, born June 11 1904 4 Vincent, born February 2, 1906

(I) John Maynard, the emigrant ancestor of Mrs Paul B Morgan of Worcester was one of the petitioners for the grant of Marlborough, Massachusetts He was in Sudbury in 1638 and was one of the forty-seven who shared in the division of Sudbury meadows in 1639 He was selectman of Sudbury He removed to Marlborough soon after the grant in 1657 He married Mary Gates He died December 22, 1711 His children were 1 Elizabeth, born May 26, 1649, died young, 2 Hannah, born September 30, 1653, 3 Mary, born August 3, 1656, 4 John, born January 7, 1661, married Lydia Ward, 5 Elizabeth, born April 2, 1664, 6 Simon, born June 15, 1666, married Hannah ——— 7 David born December 21, 1669, married Hannah ———, 8 Zachariah, born October 27, 1672, 9 Sarah, born May 15, 1680, married June 9, 1705, Joseph Johnson, 10 Lydia, born August 29, 1682, married April 7, 1703, Thomas Haggate, 11 Joseph, born August 27 1685, married Elizabeth Prue and had Benjamin born May 7, 1721

(II) Simon Maynard, son of John Maynard (1), was born in Marlborough, June 15, 1666, married Hannah ——— He died January 19, 1748 She died April 5, 1748 Their children were 1 Hannah, born June 9, 1694 married April 21, 1714, Joseph Crosby, 2 Simon, born March 4, 1696, married November 18, 1718, Sarah Church, 3 Elizabeth, born September 26 1698, married 1723, Robert Horn 4 Tabitha, born February 2, 1701, died April 7 1724, 5 Elisha born March 20, 1703, 6 Eunice, born November 17 1705 married Nathaniel Falkner, 7 Ephraim, born October 17, 1707 married Sarah ——— and Mary Balcom, 8 Benjamin, born December 1, 1709, died 1711

(III) Ephraim Maynard son of Simon Maynard (2) was born at Marlborough, Massachusetts, October 17, 1707 He married first Sarah ——— who died May 21 1742 second January 3 1743, Mary Balcom Their children were 1 Tabitha, born July 21 1738, died May 24, 1742, 2 Ephraim, born March 7, 1740 died May 10, 1742 Sarah, born November 6 1743 4 Ephraim, born August 29, 1745 married September 14 1773 Eunice Jewell, 5 Simon born June 5, 1748 married Silence Priest, 6 Joseph born December 31, 1750, married November 14 1777 Lovina Barnes, 7 Benjamin, born March 10, 1753, 8 Eunice, born February 7, 1757

(IV) Simon Maynard son of Ephraim Maynard (3) was born at Marlborough Massachusetts, June 5, 1748 He married Silence Priest He died November 15, 1818 Their children were 1 Isaac, born December 3, 1779, married 1803, Lydia Howe, 2 Hannah, born December 28, 1782, married January 31, 1802, Peace Peters 3 John Priest, born June 2, 1791, married 1812, Betsey Weeks, daughter of John Weeks

(V) Isaac Maynard, son of Simon Maynard (4), was born at Marlborough, Massachusetts, December 7, 1779, married in 1803, Lydia Howe, daughter of Artemas Howe She married second Isaac's children were 1 Amory, born February 28, 1804, married Mary Priest, daughter Benjamin Priest, 2 Lydia, born November 16, 1805, married Joel Wilkins

(VI) Amory Maynard, son of Isaac Maynard (5), was born at Marlborough, Massachusetts, February 28, 1804 He married Mary Priest, daughter of *Benjamin Priest of Marlboro* Among their children was William

(VII) William Maynard son of Amory (6), Maynard, was born May 6 1833, at Marlboro He married Mary Adams Their children were 1 Lessie Louise, born June 23, 1868

(VIII) Lessie Louise Maynard daughter of William Maynard (7), was born June 23, 1868 She married Paul Beagary Morgan (27) See Morgan sketch

(XXVIII) Ralph Landers Morgan son of Charles H Morgan (25), was born at Worcester,

Walter H. Blodget

Massachusetts, September 5, 1872 He married, October 12, 1897, Alice Sawyer, daughter of William H Sawyer, the lumber merchant of Worcester He was educated at Worcester Academy and W P I After leaving school he was associated with the firm of Flint, Eddy & Co, of New York He was president of the Morgan Motor Company, the business of which has been discontinued He was for a year manager of the automobile department of the American Bicycle Co, at Toledo, Ohio At present he is a consulting engineer, and is interested in a number of local and foreign enterprises He is a member of Plymouth Church, Worcester, Quinsigamond Boat Club and Engineers Club of New York

(XXIX) Charles Francis Morgan, son of Francis Henry Morgan (26), was born June 23, 1877 He married Edith Jeanette Norcross (daughter of Orlando W Norcross), October 5, 1904 He is active in the management of Morgan Spring Company holding the office of assistant treasurer and clerk of the corporation He is a member of the Winter Club

THE COLTON FAMILY from which Paul B Morgan is descended, originally came from Sutton Coldfield, Warwick county, England George Colton the emigrant, settled at Springfield Massachusetts before 1644 Removed from Hartford He did important service in King Philip's war He was representative to the General Court in 1669, 1671 and 1677 By his wife Deborah Gardner, of Hartford Connecticut, he had Isaac Colton born November 21 1646, died September 3 1670

(II) Isaac Colton, son of George (1), was born November 21 1646, married Mary Cooper, daughter of Thomas Cooper, June 30, 1670 She was born November 15 1651 She married second Edward Stebbins. October 18, 1701, she died August 29, 1742

(III) Deborah Colton daughter of Isaac Colton (2) married Deacon David Morgan, of Springfield

COOLEY FAMILY (I) Benjamin Cooley of Springfield a proprietor in 1645, was born in England about 1615, married Sarah ——— He died August 17, 1684 She died August 23, 1684

(II) Daniel Cooley, son of Benjamin Cooley (1), was born at Springfield May 2 1651 died February 9, 1727, married Elizabeth Wolcott daughter of Simon Wolcott, December 8, 1680 See Wolcott sketch

(III) Benjamin Cooley, son of Daniel Cooley (2) was born October 28, 1681, married January 31 1701 Margaret Bliss daughter of Samuel Bliss Jr and wife Sarah Benjamin They removed to Brimfield, Massachusetts

(IV) Margaret Cooley, daughter of Benjamin Cooley (3) was born January 30, 1710, married Joseph Morgan

THE SHERMAN FAMILY (I) Edmund Sherman the emigrant, came from Dedham, Essex county England and settled at Watertown, Massachusetts, about 1632 He married Judith Angin, 1611

(II) Rev John Sherman, son of Edmund Sherman (1), was baptized January 14, 1614, married Abigail ———

(III) James Sherman, son of Rev John Sherman (2), was born 1645, died March 3, 1718, married May 13 1680, Mary Walker

(IV) Capt and Dr John Sherman son of James Sherman (3), was born about 1683, died March 9 1772, married Abigail Stone, who was born February 13 1680

(V) Thomas Sherman son of Capt John Sherman (IV), was born September 6, 1722, died November 22, 1803, married Anna Blodgett, September 12, 1751 She died December 10, 1808 He was in the revolution

(VI) Abigail Sherman, daughter of Thomas Sherman (V), was born January 11, 1752, married Aaron Morgan, November 26, 1772 See Morgan sketch

BLODGETT FAMILY (I) Thomas Blodgett, came from England in 1635, and settled at Cambridge, Massachusetts, married Susanna ———

(II) Samuel Blodgett son of Thomas Blodgett (1), was born 1633, died July 3, 1687, married about December 13, 1655, Ruth Ingleden

(III) Thomas Blodgett, son of Samuel Blodgett (2), was born 1660, removed to Lexington, Massachusetts, about 1699, married Rebecca Tidd, November 11, 1684

(IV) Joseph Blodgett, son of Thomas Blodgett (3), was born September 17, 1696, married Sarah Stone, who was born at Lexington, November 7, 1700 She died May 6 1755, married second Sarah Ingersoll, June 29, 1738

(V) Anna Blodgett daughter of Joseph Blodgett (4), was born April 10, 1824, married Thomas Sherman See Sherman sketch

THE TIDD FAMILY (I) John Tidd embarked May 12, 1637 at Yarmouth, England aged nineteen years, married Margaret, who died 1651 He died April 24 1657

(II) John Tidd, Jr, son of John Tidd (1), was born in England, married April 14, 1650, Rebekah Wood

(III) Rebekah Tidd daughter of John Tidd (2), was born ———, married Thomas Blodgett November 11 1685

THE STONE FAMILY (I) Gregory Stone was born in England 1590, married there 1618, Mary Ganda

(II) Deacon John Stone son of Gregory Stone (1), was born August 31, 1644, died 1719, married Mary Ward who was born about 1647 She died June 10, 1703

(III) Abigail Stone daughter of Deacon John Stone (2) was born February 13, 1680 married Dr John Sherman of Springfield, Massachusetts

WARD FAMILY (I) William Ward of Sudbury was representative to General Court in 1644 and several other years He was chairman of the selectmen He served in King Philip's war He died at Marlborough, August 10, 1687, married Elizabeth ———

(II) Mary daughter of William Ward (1), married Daniel Stone See Stone sketch

WOLCOTT FAMILY (I) Henry Wolcott was born in 1577, died 1655 He was the son of John Wolcott, of Tolland Somersetshire, England married January 19 1606 Elizabeth, daughter of Thomas Saunders of Tolland

(II) Simon Wolcott son of Henry Wolcott (1), was born September 11 1624 married second Martha Pitkin sister of William (parents of Roger the governor) She married second Daniel Clark, died October 13, 1719

(III) Elizabeth Wolcott, daughter of Simon (2) and Martha married December 8, 1680, Daniel Cooley See Cooley sketch

HON WALTER H BLODGET, the present mayor of Worcester comes from a New York family The grandfather Jesse Blodget, was the first male settler in what is now known as Denmark New York He was born in 1764 and died in 1848 He was a man of great energy and known as one of the leading factors of that town for many years By occupation he was a farmer He married and the lady of his choice was the first woman to settle in Denmark, New York They were the parents of several children, including among the number Harrison, the father of Walter H Blodget Harrison Blodget was the first male child born in Denmark He was born in 1801 and died in 1899 He was educated in the common schools of his day and worked in spare hours, assisting his father, as best he could He finally chose law for a profession and soon became one of the foremost attorneys of the state He was active in local and state politics, being a staunch Democrat He became a member of the general assembly and was instrumental in the passage of several important bills He was later appointed as associate judge of Lewis county, New York, filling the position with credit He married Diantha Dewey of Leyden, New York, born October, 1806, and died in 1890 By this union the following children were born Philander, Irene L, Charles D, Francis A, Florence C, and Walter H

Walter H Blodget was born at the old homeplace erected by his grandfather, in Denmark, New York, November 2, 1850 He was educated in the common schools and in the Ives Seminary and then attended a business college in New York state, where he fitted himself for the activities of a business career On finishing his education he entered a small store in his home town, where he clerked for a time and later became agent for a warehouse on the Black river canal After following this for a time he decided to go into business for himself and opened up a small store at Lowville, New York, in which he dealt in butter, cheese and produce generally Success attended him from the start He remained there until 1881 when he came to Worcester and engaged in the produce business He associated with him A C Boshart and chose as a location the Warren block at present (1906) is located at 65 to 77 Park street under the name of Blodget & Boshart Later on Mr Boshart retired from the firm selling to Mr Blodget It was in 1898 that the firm of W H Blodget & Co was formed and incorporated with Mr Blodgett as president and his son, Walter H Jr as vice-president The firm also opened a large place of business at Boston Their annual sales are immense In 1904 they were more than one million dollars

Soon after arriving in Worcester Mr Blodget became identified with many business associations here and in Boston He became a member of the local board of trade of which he was president two years 1902-03 He served on the railroad committee of this body of which he became chairman, and in all their offices proved himself equal to the emergencies which came up for speedy action and final solution He is a member of the Fruit and Produce Exchange of Boston He is one of the regular speakers of the Farmers' Institute and is registered as such in Washington and vice-president of the Massachusetts state board of trade He also is vice-president of the advisory board of the Philadelphia Museum Politically he differs from his forefathers and has ever been a progressive Republican, and he fully believes in the great principles of that political party He was elected to the office of mayor of Worcester in 1903, and re-elected in 1904 proving a highly satisfactory official ever guarding the interests of all the people While absorbed in actual business affairs and official duties he forgets not to care for the higher and more sacred trusts of life He is active in church work and was one of the organizers of the Adams Square Church and has served at the superintendent of the Sabbath school from the first He is a person of rare judgment As a speaker, he has no little notoriety As a toast-master at banquets and public gatherings, he has a remarkable tact His benevolent spirit is manifested toward the unfortunate poor and suffering within his community

In December, 1873 Mr Blodget was united in marriage to Miss Lotta J Boshard, daughter of Garrett Boshard, of New York She died in 1882 By this union one son was born—Walter H, Jr, born in New York in 1882 He was educated in the schools of the Empire state and Worcester, Massachusetts, and is now vice-president of his father's company In 1883 Mr Blodget, Sr, married Miss Mary F Spaulding, daughter of M W and Verrila (Arsbury) Spaulding Mr Spaulding was a merchant and county clerk of Canton, New York Mr and Mrs Spaulding had nine children Mr and Mrs Blodget are the parents of four children as follows Bertha, born April 20, 1889, Chester, born May 27, 1892, Anna D, born July 24, 1894, Jesse M, born October 16, 1900 Mr Blodget still retains the old homestead at Denmark, New York, which is used as the summer home for his family He also has considerable property interests in Worcester county

DICKINSON FAMILY Eleven centuries ago a soldier of fortune made his appearance at the court of Halfdan Huilbein, King of Norway His name was Ivar He had been a shepherd and had been captured by the Northmen and carried to sea He drifted into a life of adventure He became a favorite at the Norwegian Court The King made him general of his army and in 725 gave him his daughter Eurithea in marriage He was called Prince of Uplands When the King died the son of Ivar became heir to the throne and during his minority Ivar was regent This son Eystein, reigned until 755 He was succeeded by his son, Harold Harfager Rollo, a Prince of this line, overran Normandy in 910 His sixth and youngest son Walter received the castle and town of Caen as an inheritance His great-grandson, Walter de Caen accompanied William, the Norman to England at the time of the Conquest To this nobleman the line of Dickinsons descended from the first American pioneer Nathaniel, may be traced Nathaniel is the fifteenth in line as follows

(I) Walter de Caenm later Walter de Kenson, taking the name from his manor in Yorkshire

(II) Johnne Dykonson freeholder of Kingston upon Hull, Yorkshire married 1260 Margaret Lambert died 1316

(III) William Dykenson freeholder as above, died 1330

(IV) Hugh Dykensonne freeholder as above, died 1376

(V) Anthoyne Dickensonne, freeholder as above married 1376, Catheryne De La Pole he died 1396

(VI) Richard Dickerson, freeholder as above married 1399, Margaret Cooper died 1441

(VII) Thomas Dickinson, freeholder as above, married 1470 Margaret Lambert alderman first ward Hull 1443-4 mayor 1444-5, died 1475

(VIII) Hugh Dickinson freeholder as above married 1431 Agnes Swillington removed 1475 to Kenson Manor, Yorkshire, died 1509

(IX) William Dickinson, freeholder of Kenson Manor married 1475 Isabel Langton died 1546

(X) John Dickinson settled in Leeds Yorkshire married in 1499 Elizabeth Danby alderman 1525-54 died in 1554

(XI) William Dickinson, settled Brindley Hall, Staffordshire, married in 1520, Rachel Kinge, died 1580

(XII) Richard Dickinson, of Bradley Hall, married, 1540 Elizabeth Bagnall, died 1605

(XIII) Thomas Dickinson, clerk in the Portsmouth navy yard 1567 to 1587, removed to Cambridge 1587, married 1567, Judith Carey, died 1590

(XIV) William Dickinson, settled in Ely, Cambridge, married, 1594, Sarah Stacey, of Ely, died 1628

(XV) Nathaniel Dickinson, son of William Dickinson (14), was born in Ely, Cambridge, in 1600 He married, January, 1630 at East Bergolat, Suffolk Anna Gull, widow of William Gull They came to Wethersfield, Connecticut, in 1636 or 1637 He was one of the leaders in the colony He was town clerk in 1645, representative to the general court in 1646 and 1647 He removed to Hadley, Massachusetts in 1659, and was admitted a freeman there in 1661 He was chosen deacon of the church and first recorder of the town He was selectman assessor and town magistrate He was a member of the Hampshire Troop and on the first board of trustees of Hopkins Academy He resided a few years at Hatfield He died at Hadley, June 16 1676 He married (first) in England, (second) Anne ———, when he went to Hadley The children of Nathaniel and Hannah (Gull) Dickinson were John, born 1630 killed in King Philip's war. Joseph, 1632, killed by Indians, 1675, Thomas, 1634, Anna or Hannah, 1636 married John Clary and Enos Kingsley of Northampton, Samuel, see forward, Obadiah April 15, 1641, Nathaniel, August, 1643. Nehemiah, about 1644, Hezekiah, February, 1645-6, Azariah October 4 1648, killed in swamp fight, August 25 1675

(XVI) Samuel Dickinson, fifth child of Nathaniel Dickinson (15), was born in Hatfield, Massachusetts, July 1638 He was admitted a freeman in 1690 and served in the war in 1675-6 He died November 30, 1711 aged seventy-three He married January 4, 1668, Martha Bridgeman daughter of James Bridgeman, of Springfield and Northampton Massachusetts She was born November 2, 1649 and died July 16, 1711, aged sixty-one years Their children were Samuel born August 17, 1669 ———, December 12 1671. Nathaniel, February 10 1672 Sarah November 5, 1675, Azariah, February 2, 1681, Ebenezer see forward, Ann, December 17, 1683, Joseph, August 3, 1686 Hannah April 4 1689

(XVII) Ebenezer Dickinson sixth child of Samuel Dickinson (16), was born in Hatfield, February 2 1681 He settled there He married, June 27 1706 Hannah Frary He died March 16, 1730 Their children were Editha, born August 23, 1707, Elizabeth, August 2 1709, Nathan, see forward, Hannah February 17, 1715 Reuben, August 2, 1717 Samuel (twin) October 14, 1718 Mary (twin) October 14 1718, died unmarried 1754, Ebenezer January 5 1724

(XVIII) Nathan Dickinson third child of Ebenezer Dickinson (17), was born in Hatfield May 3 1712 He removed from Hatfield to Amherst Massachusetts an adjoining town, in 1742, and died there August 7, 1796 aged eighty-four He married (first) Thankful Warner, (second) Joanner Leonard of Springfield, (third) Judith Hosmer His children were Nathan, see forward Ebenezer January 3 1741 Irene, July 13, 1743 died March 28, 1834 aged ninety, Enos, March 28 1746 Azariah March 6 1752, Elihu, October 14 1753, Shelah September 20, 1755 soldier in revolution, died April 30, 1777, Thankful, March 15, 1758, Lois baptized August 5, 1759, Asa, baptized May 10, 1761, Levi, Joanna, baptized April 6 1766 The following children were by the second wife Stephen, baptized July 6, 1770, Judith, married Daniel Heath

(XIX) Nathan Dickinson, eldest child of Nathan Dickinson (18), was born in Hatfield, Massachusetts October 19 1835 He was a soldier in the revolution He served in Lieutenant Noah Dickinson's company in 1775 and in Captain Reuben Dickinson's company in 1777-78 He resided in Amherst Massachusetts, where he died at the age of ninety, August 3 1825 He married (first), January 15 1761, Esther Fowler, who died March 15, 1803 aged sixty-three He married (second), March 19 1804 Jerusha Blodgett, widow, who died October 17 1818 Children of Nathan and Esther (Fowler) Dickinson all born in Amherst, were Timothy, born 1761, Perez, March 26, 1763, Ezekiel, May 25, 1765, Esther, May 3 1767, Esther, December 14, 1768, Irene, December 30 1770, Samuel Fowler, see forward Anna, April 15, 1780

(XX) Samuel Fowler Dickinson, seventh son of Nathan Dickinson (19), was born in Amherst, Massachusetts October 9, 1775 He received his early education in that town He fitted himself for college and entered Dartmouth from which he was graduated in 1795 Upon completing his college course he returned to his father's home in Amherst and entered the law office of Judge Simeon Strong, where he studied until he was admitted to the bar He became one of the ablest lawyers in western Massachusetts He was a natural leader of men and quite naturally became prominent in politics He served his district in the general court in the house and senate for twelve years He was town clerk of Amherst for many years His public career was brilliant and he became well known throughout the state He was an influential Whig leader Perhaps his greatest public service was the part he took as founder of Amherst Academy and Amherst College For the college he sacrificed his property, his time and his professional opportunities, and he was held in the highest regard by the friends and alumni of that institution and his memory is cherished there for his generous and distinguished service to the college He was for many years the college treasurer He was prominent in the church as well as the state At the age of twenty-one he was elected deacon of the Congregational church, to which he belonged, and he was a church officer all his active life In 1833 he removed from his old home in Amherst to Cumberland, Ohio where he maintained his prominence as a citizen He practiced law there, but became interested in Lane Seminary and acted as its steward Later he filled the office of steward for the Western Reserve University He exercised his benevolence here repeatedly in helping deserving boys through college His memory is cherished at Western Reserve University with the same affectionate regard and honor as at Amherst He helped both institutions in the trying days of their early life He died at Hudson Ohio April 23 1838

He married, March 21, 1802 Lucretia Gunn, born October 3, 1775, of Montague Massachusetts Their children were 1 Edward born January 1 1803, graduate of Yale College, 1823, married, May 6, 1828 Emily Norcross, daughter of Joel Norcross, of Monson, Massachusetts, he was representative and senator in the general court of Massachusetts, member of the governor's council, congressman, he died in Boston 2 William, see forward 3 Lucretia born December 16 1806, married Rev Asa Bullard of Cambridge, Massachusetts, where she died 4 Mary, born February 10, 1809, died in New York city March 31, 1852, married Mark H Newman, of New York 5 Samuel Fowler, Jr, born August 16, 1811, died in Richmond, Virginia, his home was at Macon, Georgia, he married in the south 6 Catherine, born February 17, 1814, died in New York city, married Artemattus Sweetser, son of Joseph Sweetser, of New York 7 Timothy, born March 11, 1816, died in Griffin, Georgia, married January 10, 1838, Hannah Dickinson, daughter of Ezekiel Dickinson 8 Frederick, born August 13, 1818 (or August 31 1819, Hadley History) graduate of Amherst College, 1837, died in Billerica, Massachusetts, married, February 17, 1846, Mary Richardson, of Billerica, leaving three sons 9 Elizabeth, born May 29, 1823, died in Worcester, married Augustus N Currier, and had three children

(XXI) William Dickinson, second child of Samuel Fowler Dickinson (20), was born in Amherst, Massachusetts, September 7, 1804 He attended the Amherst district schools and Amherst Academy until fifteen years of age His education was shaped to fit him for a business career He went to work first as a clerk in a dry goods store in Boston, where he remained several years and learned the essentials of business He came to Worcester and worked in the grocery store of Mr Butman in the old Brinley block on the corner of Main and Elm streets After some time in this business he started in business for himself in the manufacture of paper at Hardwick, Massachusetts After a few years he sold out his mill and returned to Worcester, in 1836, and was elected cashier of the Central National Bank, then the Central Bank and since 1903 part of the Worcester Trust Company He filled the position of cashier with signal ability, and after fourteen years in that office resigned to become the treasurer of the State Mutual Life Assurance Company He was well fitted for the great trust and responsibility of this position It proved congenial to him and he remained in it for nearly forty years He held a prominent position in the financial life of Worcester for many years He was treasurer also of the Merchants' and Farmers' Insurance Company for about forty years He was a director in the Quinsigamond Bank, later the Quinsigamond National Bank merged in 1905 with the Worcester Trust Company He was also director in the Providence & Worcester Railroad, now leased by the New York, New Haven & Hartford Railroad Company

In 1863 Mr Dickinson began the manufacture of paper making machinery, with others, and was interested in this business for eight years He subsequently manufactured felt, a business in which his son Samuel F Dickinson, was interested with him The factory was in a large block which he built on Foster street

Mr Dickinson was a man of unusual business ability He took advantage of his opportunities and made a large fortune for his day He invested largely in real estate He was the owner of the Dickinson Block and many other valuable parcels of real estate in the city and county He was always interested in public affairs, especially in municipal matters He was originally a member of the Whig party but like a large majority of that party turned to the Republican party when the Whig party was dissolved He was never a strong partisan, however He served the city for several years in the common council and in the board of aldermen He was nominated for mayor against Charles B Pratt the Democratic nominee but failed of election He was a member of the school board for three years He was the donor of the bell on the Walnut street high school and also of the fountains in front of the school buildings He was a director of the Free Public Library and member of the Worcester Society of Antiquity Although not a college graduate he was always, like his father, a liberal supporter of colleges and institutions of learning and profoundly interested in the public schools and educational matters He was appointed by Governor Benjamin F Butler, of whom Mr Dickinson was a warm admirer, on the board of trustees of the State Lunatic Hospital at Worcester He was an attendant at Union Congregational Church

Mr Dickinson married (first) October 31, 1831, at Andover, Massachusetts, Eliza Hawley, of Andover, Massachusetts He married (second) October 26, 1852, Mary Louisa Whittier, of Andover, daughter of Noah and Hannah (Hawley) Whittier, of Andover Mr Whittier was a department superintendent of railroad bridges and road bed He was captain of the Andover militia company The only child of William and Eliza (Hawley) Dickinson was William Hawley, born in Hardwick, October 22, 1832, deceased, married Ellen Bike, of New York city Children of William and Mary Louisa (Whittier) Dickinson were Helen Whittier, born in Worcester, March 5, 1855, married Thomas L Shields, of Sewickley, Pennsylvania, they have two children William Dickinson, a student in Cornell University, and Mary Whittier, Samuel Fowler, born in Worcester, March 14, 1857, married Nellie Goodnow, of Worcester, George Stuart, born in Worcester, October 22, 1863, married Mabel Marshall, daughter of Frank Marshall, of Worcester, he is a graduate of Yale University

GILBERT JONES RUGG, for many years prominently identified with the manufacturing interests of the city of Worcester, and who has served the community usefully in various responsible positions of a public nature, is a descendant of one of the first settlers of Lancaster, Massachusetts The immigrant ancestor and founder of his family in America was John Rugg, who came from Somerby, England, landing March 11, 1632 His wife was the ill-fated Hannah Prescott, who was cruelly killed by the Indians, September 11, 1696 She was a daughter of John Prescott, the first settler at Lancaster, Massachusetts To John and Hannah (Prescott) Rugg were born eleven children, all of whom settled in Lancaster and became the ancestors of various branches of the Prescott family, now widely dispersed throughout the United States John Rugg died in Lancaster November 24, 1655 Descended from him was Abel Rugg, who died February 14, 1843, aged ninety-two years, and whose wife, Catherine Frost, died November 2, 1843, the same year with her husband, at the age of eighty-six years They were the parents of Abel Warner Rugg, born March 17, 1797 He married Hannah Jones, and they were the parents of eight children

Gilbert Jones Rugg, son of Abel Warner and Hannah (Jones) Rugg, was born in Lancaster, Massachusetts March 27, 1836 He was reared upon the parental farm, and was early habituated to industry, frugality and perseverance—traits which were the strongest characteristics of the sturdy people of that day He received a practical education in the neighborhood schools, common and private, his school studies concluding with his seventeenth year, when he went to Worcester to procure employment and learn a trade, purposes which he pursued with all the ardor of youth and the wise judgment of mature years, not only laboring industriously to master his chosen calling but at the same time improving his mind through carefully chosen

E D Buffington

books and intercourse with persons of broad knowledge and wide experience At the early age of seventeen he became an apprentice in the machine shops of Willard Williams & Co, with whom he remained after the expiration of his term of service, eight years in all, and only leaving his employers to accept the foremanship of the Ball & Williams manufactory of planers and other wood-working machinery, a position for which he was eminently qualified With well established reputation for skill as a mechanic and business qualifications of a high order, in 1864 he entered into partnership with Luke B Witherby and Seneca Merrill Richardson for the manufacture of wood-working machinery, and created an establishment which for a third of a century has been one of the conspicuous industrial institutions of the city of Worcester For thirty years the business was conducted under the firm name of Witherby, Rugg & Richardson After the death of his partners Mr Rugg procured (in 1901) the incorporation of the business under the title of the Witherby, Rugg & Richardson Company, thus perpetuating the names of those with whom he had been most pleasantly associated during a long and peculiarly useful period Mr Rugg became president of the corporation, and continued to act in that capacity until March 1, 1903, when he made a sale of his stock to the Hobbs Manufacturing Company

While giving close attention to the affairs of the company before referred to—watching with painstaking care the practical operations of the works as well as the office affairs, and keeping constantly in touch with the manufacturing world with constantly developing business as a result—Mr Rugg at the same time gave careful and intelligent interests to many concerns of a public nature, and contributive to the advantage of the community at large As vice-president of the Worcester Five Cents Savings Bank and a member of its investing committee he rendered service of a peculiarly useful nature In 1871 he was elected a member of the Worcester board of aldermen, for a term of two years, was made a member of the common council of 1875-76, and again was elected to the board of aldermen in 1885 In the latter period he rendered exceptionally meritorious service on the city highway committee, and in all his official conduct acquitted himself most usefully and with conscientious devotion to the trusts committed to him At the election in November, 1904, he was elected a representative to the general court, and in that body served efficiently upon the street railway committee Aside from official relations he has always borne a full share in all movements contributing to the interests of the city, whether in material, moral or educational lines He is affiliated with various Masonic bodies—Morning Star Lodge, A F and A M, Eureka Chapter, R A M, Hiram Council, R and S M, and Worcester Commandery K T

Mr Rugg married Miss Susan M Earle, who died in 1896 He married (second) Celia A Williams, widow of Beman A Lovell, of Worcester His children were by his first marriage, 1 Florence E Rugg, born April 24, 1865, married Robert A Mason, of Worcester 2 Clara Emily Rugg, born August 10, 1871, died in 1896, married Charles A Rogers, and they had one child, Hazel R 3 Alice Gertrude Rugg, born November 24, 1873, married Irvin W Howard, of a prominent Worcester family Mr Rugg resides at 809 Main street, Worcester, where has been his home since 1871 when he first occupied it

ELISHA DEWEY BUFFINGTON Thomas Buffington (1), said to be from Scotland, came to America soon after 1650 probably, and settled at Salem, where he married Sarah Southwick, December 30, 1671 As he married the daughter of a Quaker and the granddaughter of one, it is likely that he led a very quiet life at Salem on his farm He was not in public life or in military companies and seems to have escaped persecution and publicity as well His wife, Sarah Southwick, was daughter of John and Sarah Southwick Her mother was the widow of Samuel Tidd The father of John Southwick was Lawrence Southwick, of Salem Lawrence Southwick was a glassman, proprietor of Salem He was admitted a freeman September 6, 1639 His wife Cassandra was received in the church at Salem 1639, and Elizabeth Southwick September 1, 1650 They were Quakers His will, dated August 10, 1659, at the house of Nathaniel Sylvester, at Shelter Island, proved in Essex court, November 29, 1660, mentions sons Daniel Southwick and John Burnell, daughters, Provided Southwick and Mary, wife of Henry Traske, Deborah and Josiah Southwick, Ann Potter, Henry Traske's children—Mary, Sarah and Hannah, Samuel (born February 19, 1658), and Sarah, children of John Southwick, son deceased probably before 1659

Besides Thomas Buffington there was a John Buffington in Salem about the same time that Thomas first appears in the records There seems to be no record of any descendants, nor of his relationship to Thomas The name is more commonly spelled by the descendants of Thomas Buffington without the "g," but Mr Buffington of Worcester preferred this spelling The name was found sometimes in the records spelled Bovington The Commoners' Record recently published showed Thomas Buffington, Sr, a landowner 1702 and as late as 1723 when, if living he must have been seventy-five and perhaps older Savage gives three children, but it is probable that the third is a child of his son's (See Abigail, born July 25, 1695, under Thomas Buffington (2) Thomas and Benjamin are unquestionably his sons Joseph Buffington, whose son Joseph married at Swansea in 1734, was probably another son Children of Thomas and Sarah (Southwick) Buffington 1 Thomas, born in Salem March 1, 1672, married Hannah Ross there, and had a family in Salem, is probably the ancestor of the Salem branch of the family, many of whom were interested in the shipping business in Salem His children were Abigail, born in Salem July 25, 1695 (Savage makes her daughter of Thomas, Sr) Hannah, born in Salem May 11, 1701, married Eleazer Pope, who died August 2, 1734, leaving son Stephen and others, James (?), perhaps father of Captain Zadock Buffington, prominent in Salem many years, incorporator of Acqueduct, 1798, Mary (?), baptized an adult in Salem, March 31 1728 2 Benjamin, see forward 3 Joseph (?), had son Joseph who married at Swansea, Abigail son of Samuel and Martha Shearman, December 11 1734 James Buffington, who with his wife Elizabeth joined the Congregational church at Salem was probably the James son of Thomas Buffington (2) mentioned above His children Betty, Mary, Hannah and James, all baptized when their parents were by Rev Benjamin Prescott at the church now of South Danvers, July 27, 1740 They probably had been Quakers until then

(II) Benjamin Buffington, son of Thomas Buffington (1), born July 24, 1675, at Salem, married Hannah ——— They were Quakers, and the records indicate that he removed soon after marriage about 1700 to Swansea, where the Quakers and Baptists persecuted elsewhere lived peaceably side by side The family tradition states that some fifty families from Salem went to Swansea and bought titles to their lands from the Indians, as was their custom, in addition to getting the grant from the government Benjamin Buffington had a deed, which is now in possession of the family, and shows he bought three hundred acres of land of ——— Marcy, who was the only one of the settlers not a Quaker The homestead has been in the possession of the Buffington family about two hundred years The Buffingtons have all been Quakers down to E D Buffington of Worcester," writes a member of the family, "and he was a thorough Quaker in principle, although a few years before his death he joined the Unitarian church, to which his wife belonged" The family records indicate that Benjamin Buffington, the settler at Swansea, had seven children From the records of Salem, Savage's Dictionary, and the more recently published Vital Records of Rhode Island, in which the records of the Friends' church at Swansea are given, partial records of six have been discovered The records of William Buffington, the son from whom Elisha D Buffington is descended, are preserved in his old homestead at Swansea, and have been copied for use here Children of Benjamin and Hannah 1 Benjamin, born Salem, May 9, 1699, probably died young (Savage mentions two others not named, presumably born in Salem 2 Benjamin, born April 9, 1701, died June 9, 1760 at Swansea, Massachusetts, married Isabel, daughter of Joseph and Sarah Chase (given in another Rhode Island record as daughter of Eben and Mary Chase), she was born July 6, 1705 at Swansea, and died June 6, 1791, both buried in the Friends' yard at Swansea, their children Benjamin, Moses, Stephen, Elizabeth, Hannah 3 William, see forward 4 Esther, born in Swansea probably, married Stephen Chase (or Chace), son of Joseph and Sarah November 11, 1728 5 Hannah, married Silas Chase, December 20, 1733 6 Jonathan, married Sarah, daughter of James and Martha Luther, April 12, 1735

(III) William Buffington, son of Benjamin Buffington (2), born probably in Swansea, Massachusetts, possibly Salem, fifth day of week October 9, 1703, married Susanna, daughter of Samuel and Sarah Chase, all of Swansea, July 25, 1726 Susanna was born fifth day of week, April 7, 1704 They had nine children born at Swansea 1 William, born December 20, 1726, third day of week, married Phebe, daughter of James and Martha Luther, February 5, 1746-7 2 Elizabeth, born February 9, 1729, first day of week, married Ezekiel Chase 3 Susanna, born June 9, 1731, fourth day of week, married William Luther June 16, 1748 4 Sarah, born May 1, 1735, fifth day 5 Phebe, born May 29 1739, first day 6 Samuel, see forward 7 Hannah, born March 5, 1741, seventh day 8 Martha, born September 22, 1744, first day of week 9 Benjamin, born September 7, 1747, second day of week, married Hannah ———, had son William, married Mary Lawton, March 11, 1770

(IV) Samuel Buffington, son of William Buffington (3), born Swansea, Massachusetts, July 26, 1740, married ——— ———, born March 13, 1739, died February 2, 1809 They settled on the homestead at Swansea Their children 1 Elisha, see forward 2 Samuel, born about November, 1770, died February 16, 1816, aged forty-five years, four months 3 Susanna, born October 23 1773, died July 30, 1827, aged fifty-three years, nine months and seven days 4 Elizabeth, born 1775, died April 7, 1807

(V) Elisha Buffington, son of Samuel Buffington (4), born Swansea, June 8, 1767 died April 17, 1858, aged ninety years, ten months and eleven days, married Sara Chase, born July 19, 1762, daughter of John Chase, who died March 27, 1786, aged sixty-five years, three months, and whose wife died May 19, 1805, aged seventy-eight years, three months Sara died December 13, 1841, aged seventy-nine years, five months Peace Chase, her sister, died November 27, 1788, aged thirty-nine years, six months Jonathan Chase, her brother, died July 25, 1824, about seventy-eight years old Martha, her sister, died March 15, 1826, aged seventy-two years, twelve days Children of Elisha and Sara (Chase) Buffington 1 Susanna, born March 13, 1794, died April 8, 1818 2 Martha, born October 27, 1795, married Peleg Gardner, she died April 19, 1842. 3 John, born April 16, 1798, died June 28, 1816, in Havana, Cuba 4 Frances, born December 10, 1800 5 Phebe, born January 7, 1803 6 Samuel, see forward

(VI) Samuel Buffington, son of Elisha Buffington (5), was born in Swansea, Massachusetts, on the old homestead there October 3, 1806 He was a man of influence and a Quaker He carried on the farm He married Eliza Ann Mason, born June 7, 1810, died 1881 He died October 26, 1871 Their children were John H, born August 13, 1829, Sarah E, born February 3, 1834, died July 30, 1835, Elisha Dewey, born in Swansea, November 4, 1836, Samuel L, born October 7, 1839, lives on the old homestead, married Augusta Wood, and their children are Mabel, Raymond W, Julia S Durand, Elisha L, Elizabeth, Paul, Carl, all living on the old homestead, Frank Benton, born January 9, 1842, died April 14, 1855

(VII) Elisha Dewey Buffington, son of Samuel (6), was born in Swansea, Massachusetts, November 4, 1836 He was brought up on the old Buffington homestead which has been in the family from the time of King Philip, of whom it was bought

Elisha Buffington when a boy attended school at Warren Rhode Island, in the winter, and worked on his father's farm in the summer At the age of eighteen, in 1854, he went to California, by way of the Isthmus He stayed in California, but a short time, and then returned by way of Lake Nicaragua For a short time he taught school in Lansing, Michigan Afterward he walked from Michigan to Pike's Peak and back Although the party had a wagon and perhaps some horses, there were always too many sick to admit of the well ones riding He returned to Massachusetts and entered a druggist's shop in Fall River, where he learned the business, which he found congenial, and in which he was to achieve success He started for himself in Worcester in 1862, buying the drug store of William H Goulding, where Buffington's store is at present Very soon after he started, he added the manufacture of homœopathic remedies, and later the wholesale department, which soon became the most important part of the business When the Day building was burned the store was located in the Flagg building, the next block, but was removed to the new Day building as soon as it was completed Soon afterward the business was incorporated as the Buffington Pharmacy Company, by whom it has been carried on since his death The original officers of the company were Mr Buffington and some of his clerks in the store

Mr Buffington was always an enthusiastic sportsman and traveler In 1893 he was appointed a member of the Massachusetts State Fish and Game Commission and was very active in propagating and preserving fish and game, not only in Worcester county but throughout the state He was a member of the Oquosic Angling Club, composed of enthusiastic and regular anglers in the Rangeley Lakes.

He was practically the founder of the hatchery of the Fish Commission at Wilkinsville, and had an earnest desire to have Lake Quinsigamond properly stocked with fish He was serving his third term on the Fish and Game Commission at the time of his death He had a taste for travel and means to gratify it, made many trips abroad, and brought home many artistic and interesting souvenirs of his travels His house is filled with treasures that he collected when abroad He was a liberal contributor to the Worcester Art Museum Corporation, of which he was a member and was a member of the Society of Antiquity, the Home Market Club of Boston, the Tatnuck Country Club, the Worcester Club, and the Commonwealth Club He was a director of the Worcester Safe Deposit and Trust Company He attended the First Unitarian Church In politics he was a stanch Republican His grandfather on his mother's side was Squire Mason who was a member of Governor Lincoln s staff when it contained but three members Mr Buffington died November 19, 1900, after a short illness at his home, 33 Chestnut street He married, November 4 1867, Charlotte Eaton Walker, daughter of Benjamin and Charlotte (Eaton) Walker Her father was born in Greenfield, Massachusetts, but lived most of his life in Worcester Her mother belonged to the Eaton family, one of the best of the old Worcester families, her grandfather was Nathaniel Eaton Mr Buffington had no children

There could be no better and more appreciative tribute to the character of Mr Buffington than that sent to the editor of the *Worcester Spy* by Colonel E B Stoddard, one of his dearest friends, who has himself passed away since then It was published November 20, 1900, as follows

He belonged distinctly to that class of men, who, without early advantages of education, have by their own native intelligence and energy made their way to recognized positions of prominence and influence in the community Mr Buffington began at the bottom of the ladder, so far as worldly advantages are concerned, but was not destined to stay there He was gifted with rare common sense and quick insight, and easily took in the essential conditions of any situation Success was no accident with him He saw the path to it, and followed it with the necessary self-denial and persistence to accomplish his object Whether in the accumulation of property or the keeping of it by judicious investment, his judgment was always of the soundest But though he thus acquired a large competence, he was by no means a mere money getter He knew not only how to get it, but how to spend it He always looked upon money as a means, not as an end He had a large range of interests, and was constantly engaged in making investigations into many subjects His knowledge of nature, of plants and animals especially, was wide and accurate Perhaps no man in this community had a better command of everything relating to game, not only the haunts and habits, but the game laws and usages and the best method of propagation and protection He had also a genuine interest in art, not merely of American and European art and artists, but various forms of art in the Fast where he traveled extensively and observed intelligently His large collection contains not only pictures of unusual merit and high value, but also tapestries, ceramics and other objects of rare excellence His taste in this direction was fully shared and greatly assisted by his accomplished wife Even in his recreations, as whist and chess, he was not content with any superficial practice of the game, but always wanted to go to the bottom of it and find its underlying mathematical principles Above all, Mr Buffington was a steadfast friend and genial companion, and it is his cheerful, loyal and affectionate disposition that will be longest remembered by those who knew him best"

THEODORE P BROWN James Brown (1) was the emigrant ancestor of Theodore P Brown, of Worcester, Massachusetts, the manufacturer of the Simplex Piano Player He was born in Scotland about 1720-30 There is a tradition in the family that he was wealthy, having with him a chest of gold Owing to a storm or shipwreck the gold was lost Besides the gold it is said he had twenty fine linen shirts that were also lost on the journey over He was a tailor by trade He married Hannah Blanchard, of Dunstable, Massachusetts, and their descendants have been numerous in the vicinity Dunstable is now Nashua, New Hampshire The Blanchards were among the pioneers there Thomas Blanchard, her emigrant ancestor, came to America from the vicinity of Andover, England, in the ship Jonathan in 1639 He settled first at Braintree His son George was with him He bought of Rev John Wilson, February 12, 1650-1, house and land in the south part of Malden, Massachusetts (Pope says he came from Penton, Hants, England) He married first in England His wife died there He married (second) Agenes (Bent) Barnes, widow, a sister of John Bent She died on the passage over He married (third) Mary ——— He died May 21, 1654 His will is dated May 16, and was proved June 20, 1654 He made bequests to his wife Mary, to children George, Thomas, Samuel, Nathaniel, to grandson Joseph, and to the church at Malden He provided that Benjamin Thompson should be fitted for the University (Harvard) if his parents consent Benjamin was son of Deacon John Blanchard Benjamin does not appear in the list of Harvard graduates, however His estate was administered by his widow, appointed June 3, 1656

(II) Deacon John Blanchard, son of Thomas Blanchard, the emigrant, was one of the pioneers at Dunstable Massachusetts, now Nashua, New Hampshire He was admitted a freeman in 1649 He was one of the founders of the Dunstable Church in 1685 Children were Joseph, Thomas, Hannah, born January 6 1659, Benjamin, James, Sarah, Mary, Nathaniel

(III) Thomas Blanchard, son of Deacon John Blanchard, and grandson of Thomas Blanchard, the emigrant, was born about 1670 and must have been a young child when his father went to Dunstable He married Tabitha ——— She died November 29, 1696 He married (second) Ruth Adams, of Chelmsford Massachusetts, October 4, 1698 He died March 9 1727 In the possession of Mrs Charles F Wheelock, 8 Cottage street, Worcester, is a deed from Thomas to his son Thomas, dated 1721, of land in Dunstable Children of Thomas and Tabitha Blanchard were Abigail, born May 5 1694, John, May 20, 1696 Children of Thomas and Ruth (Adams) Blanchard were Thomas (see forward), William, born 1701, Ruth, April 1, 1703

(IV) Thomas Blanchard, son of Thomas Blanchard, and grandson of Deacon John Blanchard, of Dunstable, was born August 12, 1699 He served in the Indian wars and was taken prisoner in September, 1724 He was a prominent man in Dunstable, and held various town offices Mrs Wheelock has the original tax warrant for the year 1738, for the old town of Dunstable, issued to Thomas Blanchard as collector of taxes It shows the results of his work It contains a full list of the taxpayers of the town Joseph Blanchard, son of Captain Joseph Blanchard who was uncle of Thomas Blanchard, heads the list

Hannah Blanchard, born about 1740 daughter of Thomas, married James Brown, the emigrant He died in 1778 A copy of his will, dated October 10, 1778, is owned by Mrs Wheelock It is a certified copy made soon after the will was proved in the Nashua court It should be noted that James Brown of Dunstable, was a lieutenant in the battle of Bunker Hill, according to the history of Dunstable and no other James Brown of the right age and description is to be found

The children of James and Hannah (Blanchard) Brown were John, James, settled in Waterford, Ohio, (Mrs Wheelock has a letter written by him in which he mentions the death of his first wife in 1798 and his second marriage), Phebe, Hannah, Isaac, Daniel, Samuel, Aaron, (see forward) The will indicates that all but Samuel and Aaron were of age, as it specifies that the others receive their bequests, and the two youngest receive theirs when they become of age

(II) Aaron Brown, son of James Brown (1), was born in Dunstable or Nashua, New Hampshire, November 17, 1773 He was a soldier in the war of 1812 He married, September 5, 1797, Hannah Proctor, daughter of Reuben Proctor, of Merrimac, New Hampshire She was born July 13, 1778 He lived in Nashua and died April 24, 1844, in Canton, Maine, where he removed about 1815 He was a charter member of the Livermore Falls, Maine, Lodge of Free Masons and was a prominent man in the order The children of Aaron and Hannah (Proctor) Brown were James (see forward), Nancy, born at Dunstable, December 28, 1799 married Rev ——— Bartlett, Larned Small, born in Dunstable, March 18, 1801, John, (see forward), Reuben Proctor, born in Wilton, Maine, January 28, 1805, Jefferson, born in Wilton, Maine, September 22, 1806, Arthur, born in Wilton, Maine, October 15 1807, Rebecca Proctor, born in Wilton, February 5, 1810, Abigail Bigelow, born at Jay, Maine, March 29, 1812, Susannah Carpenter, born in Jay, Maine, July 16, 1815, Hiram, born February 9, 1817, at Jay now Canton, Maine, Orin, born October 20, 1818 at Jay, now Canton, died in Texas, Belinda Bartlett born in Canton, Maine, July 1, 1821

(III) James Brown, son of Aaron Brown (2) born in Dunstable, Massachusetts, or Nashua, New Hampshire, August 5, 1798, died April 8, 1881, at Grafton, Maine Married (first) Mary Thompson July 4, 1824 She died April 19, 1833, married (second) Ruth Stewart, October 28 1838, she died February 4, 1901 The children of James and Mary (Thompson) Brown were James Monroe, (see forward), Arthur, born September 24 1827, died October 15, 1857, Ira Bisbee, born April 5 1829, died March 12, 1831 Ira Bisbee, born June 10, 1831, died July 19, 1831, William Thompson, born January 16, 1833, married Esther H Swan, June 10, 1859, he died April 28, 1861 The children of James and Ruth (Swan) Brown were Mary (see forward), George Miller, born August 16, 1844 married Ella M Briggs, March, 1864, Euthalius Irving born November 14 1848, married Freda W Small

(III) John Brown, son of Aaron Brown (2) born in Wilton, Maine, December 29 1802, he married Huldah Gardner When he was a young boy the family removed to Livermore, Maine He was a house carpenter and farmer His children were John Quincy, married Lucia Littlefield, resides at Portland, Joanna Allen, married Seth L Davis, a farmer at Errol, New Hampshire, Hannibal Gardner, married Mary Parlin, resides at West Parish Maine, Aaron, (see forward), Bartlett Jackson married, resides in Hyde Park, Massachusetts, has been in the same house for thirty-five years, Maria Lunice, dressmaker, Tremont street, Boston, Orin Hutchinson, born 1838, married, was a soldier in the civil war, prisoner in Libby for months, and came home and died at his brother Hannibal's, at Patten, Maine, was in a cavalry regiment

(IV) Aaron Brown, son of John Brown (3), born in Livermore, Maine, July 29, 1832, died in Lawrence, Massachusetts, 1903 He married Ella M Ratcliffe, born March 26, 1829 He was a cabinet maker by trade He became an architect and followed his profession in Boston and various towns in Maine and New Hampshire He was a man of great mechanical skill and his son Theodore evidently inherits some of his inventive genius from his father The children of Aaron and Ellen M (Ratcliffe) Brown were Arabella, died in infancy, Wendell Phillips, Theodore Parker, born at Malden, Massachusetts, October 2, 1860

(IV) James Monroe Brown, son of James Brown (3), born November 15, 1825, died September 11, 1895, married Eunice E Frost, November 15, 1849 They were the parents of Mrs Charles E Wheelock, of Worcester, Massachusetts

(IV) Mary T Brown, daughter of James Brown (3), born August 22, 1839, married George H Otis, October 10, 1863 Their children are Frances Lillian, married Fred Decker, of Burlington, New Hampshire, Arthur Monroe, Jennie M, married Harvey C Philbrook, of Bethel, Maine, Will Howe

(V) Theodore Parker Brown, son of Aaron Brown (4), was born in Malden, Massachusetts October 2, 1860 When he was two years old the family moved to Sterling, Massachusetts When he was five years old the family moved again to Lisbon, New Hampshire, where he attended the public schools He came to Worcester with his parents at the age of thirteen He began work in the shoe factory of Hon Joseph H Walker, and remained with him for nine years He is known by the general public and all over the world among dealers in musical instruments, as the inventor and manufacturer of the Simplex Piano Player He began to manufacture this instrument at 9 May street, Worcester, when piano players were a novelty, and looked upon by the people generally as toys He developed and perfected the instrument until it ranks first among the piano players in the opinion of competent judges It has won prizes at the Expositions It has been a very popular instrument The general recognition of the value of piano players, and the very promising future for the business, has made the Simplex Player an article of which the citizens of Worcester take a peculiar pride on account of its production here The success of Mr Brown in the business world has been very gratifying to his friends He is especially popular in the Masonic bodies to which he belongs He is a member of Montauck Lodge, of Lawrence Chapter, of Hiram Council and the Worcester County Commandery, Knights Templar, the Consistory thirty-second degree, the Commonwealth Club, of which he is president, and to the Tatnuck Country Club He is a Republican in politics and was a member of the city council, Worcester, in 1892, and president of that body in 1893

He married, January 13, 1881, Alice J Daniels, born April 26 1863, daughter of Horace and Ann M (Inman) Daniels, of Paxton, Massachusetts She was educated in the public schools of Paxton and at the Friends school, Providence, Rhode Island The children of Theodore Parker and Alice J (Daniels) Brown were Barbara, born May 5 1884,

Theodore C. Bates

graduate of Worcester high school and is taking a four years' course at the Museum of Fine Arts in Boston, Marjorie, died young, Dorothy, died young

ELDRED FAMILY The late Frederick Augustus Eldred, of Worcester, traced his descent from Jehoshaphat Eldred, who came from England in 1731 He bought of Isaac Green land at North Falmouth, it being the fourteenth and fifteenth lots of the allotment, and is spoken of in history as a yeoman His son, Lemuel Eldred, born November 5, 1751 in Falmouth, died July 24, 1842, in the ninety-first year of his age

William Eldred, son of Lemuel Eldred, was born Sepember 25, 1780, in Falmouth (Quisset), and received his education in the schools of that town He was a farmer, and it was from his farm that the first shipment of Cape Cod cranberries was obtained He was also a salt manufacturer, having on his land salt works where he evaporated sea-water During the war of 1812 he served in the militia as a member of Colonel Dimmick's regiment, and participated in the defense of Falmouth The British sailed into the harbor, and under cover of night tried to land in their smaller boats, but were repulsed by Captain Eldred's company, who were concealed behind the sand hills along the beach The British finally sailed to North Falmouth, where they burned much shipping Captain Eldred and others of the townspeople were joint owners of some of these vessels, and appealed to congress for reimbursement under the French spoliation act, but Captain Eldred, losing his claim papers, abandoned the case and never received his share of the indemnity In politics he was first a Whig and later a Republican He was a member of the Congregational church, in which he held various offices, and to the work of which he was sincerely and earnestly devoted Mr Eldred was twice married His first wife was Miss Fessenden, and their children were 1 Cornelius, born in Falmouth, as were all the others 2 Edwin, married Elizabeth Knowlton, of Williamstown, Massachusetts, and had several children among them Lucian, recently died in Worcester 3 Lorenzo, married, 1845, Mercy F Grew, of Falmouth 4 William Henry, lost at sea 5 Frederick Augustus (see forward), 6 Patience, married William Eldred, of another branch of the family, and had children Edwin, married Hannah Lovell, of Worcester, William Henry married Harriet McFarland, of Worcester, and has two children, Arthur Warren, a dentist in Worcester and preceptor at the Harvard Dental College of Boston, Marion Frederica, wife of Charles Minckler, of Worcester, and mother of two children—Ralph Eldred and Glen Canon 7 Elizabeth, married Robert Tobey, of Sandwich Massachusetts 8 Susan wife of Stephen Davis of Falmouth, their children Deborah Patience, Salome, Alom Hyde, John William, and Robert Franklin 9 Hannah wife of Benjamin Franklin Hatch The mother of these children died and Mr Eldred married, when seventy years of age, Miss Worthington of Boston By this marriage there were no children When about sixty years old Mr Eldred's mind became unsettled and did not recover its tone for ten years after which his reason was undisturbed for the remainder of his life, his death occurring November 26, 1859 on the homestead where he had been born and had always lived

Frederick Augustus Eldred, son of William Eldred was born in Falmouth (Quisset), and was educated in the common schools of his native town When about eighteen years old he went to New Bedford where he served an apprenticeship of three years to a carriage-maker Later he entered into partnership with Lyman Drury, of Worcester, in the manufacture of refrigerators, and after carrying on the business for several years sold his interest to Mr Drury Not long after he purchased the hat store of Mr Barker, on Main street, and conducted the business for a number of years In 1861 or '62 he associated with himself N S Liscomb, under the firm name of Eldred & Liscomb The connection remained unbroken until the close of Mr Eldred's life, after which Mr Liscomb continued the business until a few years ago, when he also died Mr Eldred was a good citizen, but always avoided public life He was a Republican in politics, and an earnest member of the Congregational church, twice serving as superintendent of the Sunday school

Mr Eldred married, October 2, 1848, Mary A, daughter of Albert Gallitan and Mary Cunningham (Stott) Liscomb, of Fair Haven, Massachusetts, and sister of N S Liscomb, mentioned above Mr Liscomb, the father, was a ropemaker of Fair Haven, and during the gold era went to California, taking with him his small stock of machinery He there worked very successfully at his trade for three years, at the end of which time he returned to Fair Haven Mr and Mrs Eldred had no children The death of Mr Eldred, which occurred in 1872, deprived the community of a good man and a worthy citizen

HON THEODORE C BATES The ancestors of Clement Bates, who was the first to come to the United States of America, are traceable for five (5) generations before the Pilgrims came to New England

Thomas Bates, of Lydd, parish of All Hallows, county of Kent, England, who died in 1485, had a son, John Bates, who died at Lydd, England in 1522 leaving a son, Andrew Bates, who died at Lydd England, in 1533, leaving a son, James Bates, who died at Lydd England, in 1614, whose three sons Clement Edward and James embarked at London, England, for New England, April 6 1635 in the ship Elizabeth," William Stagg, master

Edward Bates settled at Weymouth, Massachusetts, James at Dorchester, Massachusetts, and Clement in Cohasset, Massachusetts Clement Bates brought with him in 1635—he then being forty years of age—his wife Anna, also aged forty, and his five children, as follows James, aged fourteen, Clement, aged twelve, Rachel, aged eight, Joseph, aged five, Benjamin, aged two, and two servants, and there was born to them in Massachusetts a son Samuel March 24 1639 On September 18, 1635, Clement Bates received a grant of five acres of land on Town street—now called South street, Cohasset, which land has been in the possession of the original grantee and his descendants for two and a half centuries

Joseph Bates, born in England, 1630 married in Hingham, Massachusetts, January 9, 1657, Esther Hilliard, was selectman in 1671 and later He died April 30 1706 She died June 3, 1709 They had nine children, all born in Hingham, Massachusetts Joseph, September 28, 1660, Esther, August 29, 1663, Caleb, March 30, 1666, Hannah, October 31, 1668, Joshua, August 14 1671, Bathsheba, January 26, 1674, Clement September 22, 1676, Ellenor, August 25, 1679, Abigail, October 16, 1780

(III) Joseph Bates, son of Joseph (2), born September 28 1660 married Mary daughter of Samuel and Martha Lincoln He died November 3, 1714 She died March, 1752, aged ninety years

They had six children Mary, Joseph, Jonathan, Rachel, Susanna and Hester

(IV) Joseph Bates, son of Joseph (3), born in Hingham, Massachusetts, March 6, 1687, married Deborah, daughter of Samuel and Hannah (Gill) Clap He died in 1750 He was a deacon in the church They had five children, all born in Hingham, Massachusetts Joseph, May 6, 1714, Deborah, April 2, 1716, Samuel, March 25, 1718, Jonathan, March 27, 1720, Mary, April 10, 1723

(V) Samuel Bates, son of Joseph (4), born March 25, 1718, in 1737 married Mercy Beal He died, aged seventy-one, in 1789 They had twelve children, all born in Hingham Mordecai, June 29, 1738, Hannah, March 11, 1740, Joseph, June 11, 1742, Samuel, November 15, 1744, Mercy, February 15, 1747, Adna, November 14, 1749, Mary, 1752, Mary, February 15, 1755, Susanna, March 11, 1756, Jonathan, May 5, 1757, Mary, April 30, 1760, Thomas, January 12, 1763

(VI) Samuel Bates, son of Samuel (5), born November 15, 1744, married Martha, daughter of Jonathan and Priscilla (Lincoln) Beal, who died in 1905 He died November 3, 1801, was drowned off Cohassett Rocks They had nine children, all born at Cohassett, Massachusetts Deborah, December 9 1765, Eliza, January 20, 1767, Obadiah, August 20, 1769, Bela, May 10, 1772, Laban, April 3, 1774 Sarah, January 26, 1777 Newcomb, April 17, 1779 Samuel, January 1, 1783, Sybil, February 1, 1786

(VII) Obadiah Bates, son of Samuel (6), born August 20, 1769, was a private in Captain Peter Lothrop's company of (Cohassett) Massachusetts militia in the war of 1812, he married Hannah Beal, of Cohassett He died October 20, 1831, aged sixty-two years She died November 11, 1841, aged seventy years They had six children, all born at Cohassett Elijah, April 25, 1796, Martha, December 25, 1797, Hannah Loring, August 10, 1799, Mary, May 5, 1802, Ann Beal, December 12, 1803, Joseph, April 12, 1805

Theodore C Bates, youngest son of Elijah and Sarah Fletcher Bates, is third in descent from Obadiah Bates, who was a private in Captain Peter Lothrop's company, (Cohassett) Massachusetts militia, in the war of 1812

He is third in descent from Ensign Ebenezer Beal Jr, who was ensign of Captain Thomas Jones fourth company of Hingham militia in Colonel Josiah Quincy's regiment January 21, 1762

He is fourth from Captain Ebenezer Beal Sr, of Hingham, Massachusetts, who was captain of the Hingham company in Colonel Benjamin's company in the Third Suffolk regiment, which marched to the relief of Fort William, August 15, 1757

He is fifth from Lazarus Beal, of Hingham, Massachusetts who was a representative to the Massachusetts Bay Colony or general court in 1719 and 1720

He is sixth in descent from Lieutenant Jeremiah Beal, of Hingham, Massachusetts, who was an ensign of the Hingham Foot Company May 11, 1681, and a lieutenant, March 30, 1683, and a representative to the Massachusetts Bay Colony or general court in 1691, 1692 and 1701

He is seventh in descent from Lieutenant John Beal, of Hingham, Massachusetts who was a deputy in the Massachusetts Bay Colony or general court from 1649 to 1659

He is sixth from Captain Thomas Andrews, who was captain of the Hingham company in 1690

He is seventh in descent from Joseph Andrews, who was a deputy in the Massachusetts Bay Colony or general court from 1636 to 1638

He is sixth from Samuel Clapp, son of Thomas Clapp, of Hingham, Massachusetts, who was a deputy from Scituate to Plymouth from 1680 to 1686, from 1690 to 1691, from 1692 to 1696, from 1699 to 1703, 1705 to 1709 and 1714 and 1715, making twenty years

He is seventh from Thomas Clapp, who was a deputy to Plymouth court in 1649

He is eighth in descent from Edmund Hobart, of Hingham, Massachusetts, who was a deputy in the Massachusetts Bay Colony or general court in 1639, 1640 and 1642

He is sixth in descent from Lieutenant James Lewis, of Barnstable, Massachusetts, who was lieutenant of the militia company in Barnstable (1678)

He is fifth in descent from Lieutenant Benjamin Loring, of Hull, who was ensign of the militia in Hull from 1713 to 1715 He was a deacon in the church He held many town offices—town treasurer 1709, town clerk, 1717

He is third in descent from Major Daniel Fletcher, of Concord, Massachusetts, who was born in Concord, Massachusetts, October 18, 1718

He is second in descent from Captain Jonathan Fletcher, who was born in Acton, Massachusetts, January 21, 1757

He is fourth in descent from Lieutenant Jonathan Hartwell, of Littleton, Massachusetts (1692-1778)

He is fifth in descent from John Hartwell of Concord, Massachusetts, who was a soldier in Captain Thomas Wheeler's company at the Indian ambuscade and siege of Brookfield, August, 1675, in King Philip's war

He is sixth in descent from William Hartwell, of Concord, Massachusetts, who was a corporal of Concord company and quartermaster of Captain Thomas Wheeler's company, October 15, 1673

He is fifth in descent from Cornet Samuel Fletcher, of Concord, Massachusetts, who was bugler in Concord company, and in Captain Thomas Wheeler's company in 1675, and was with Captain Thomas Wheeler's company at the Indian attack in Brookfield, Massachusetts

He is fifth in descent from Ensign Thomas Wheeler, Jr, of Concord, Massachusetts, son of Captain Thomas Wheeler, and ensign of the Concord company, which was commanded by his father, Captain Thomas Wheeler, in King Philip's war at Brookfield, Massachusetts, in 1675 At the time of this battle or Indian ambuscade and siege, Captain Thomas Wheeler was severely wounded and his horse killed whereupon Ensign Wheeler, his son, placed his father on his own horse, and took his father out of danger, and in doing so was twice severely wounded in the attempt to rescue his father from the perilous position and pursuit by the Indians, during the retreat of the ambuscade, in which so many of Captain Thomas Wheeler's men were killed and wounded, he kept close beside his father until he caught a horse whose rider had been killed by the Indians he then with Captain Thomas Wheeler, and the few soldiers who were escaping and being closely pursued by the Indians, was by the aid of two friendly Indians, brought back by a circuitous route, unknown to the soldiers, to the fortified house at Brookfield, arriving there just before the several hundred savages came and laid siege to the fortified house so fiercely and destroyed and burnt the houses of the town

He is sixth in descent from Captain Thomas Wheeler, of Concord, Massachusetts, who was in command of the Colonial soldiers and the inhabitants when attacked by the Indians at Brookfield, when the town was destroyed and so many of its inhabitants killed in 1675 The narrative of Captain

Thomas Wheeler regarding the attack on Brookfield by the Indians in August, 1675, is one of the most interesting of official records of the state archives of the hardships endured by the early settlers of Massachusetts and in King Philip's war

He is sixth in descent from Lieutenant Simon Davis, of Concord, Massachusetts, who served under Captain Thomas Wheeler at the Brookfield ambuscade and siege August, 1675 in King Philip's war, and who, after Captain Wheeler's wounds became so serious, was one of those who was by Captain Wheeler placed in command of the soldiers at Brookfield in the fortified house

There were five ancestors of Theodore C Bates with Captain Thomas Wheeler at the ambuscade by the Indians and the siege of the fortified house, or fort, at Brookfield, Massachusetts, August 5, 1675, namely

Captain Thomas Wheeler, Ensign Thomas Wheeler, Jr, Lieutenant Simon Davis, Cornet Samuel Fletcher, John Hartwell

(VIII) Elijah Bates, son of Obadiah Bates (7), born April 25, 1796, married Sarah Fletcher, youngest daughter of Jonathan and Lucretia Emerson Fletcher Sarah Fletcher was born in Boston, Massachusetts, May 3, 1799, and died in Worcester, Massachusetts, September 28, 1890 Jonathan Fletcher, her father, was born in Acton, Massachusetts, January 21, 1758, and died in Boston, January 16, 1807 Lucretia Emerson, wife of Captain Jonathan Fletcher, was born in Acton, Massachusetts, August 4, 1764 She married Jonathan Fletcher, May 20, 1782 Lucretia Emerson Fletcher died in Thomaston, Maine, July 7, 1800 They had four children Francis, Susan, Lucretia, and Sarah

Elijah Bates was born in Cohasset, Massachusetts, April 25, 1796, died in North Brookfield, Massachusetts, September 6, 1863 He was a furniture manufacturer in Boston, Massachusetts, where he gave seven years to learn his trade He moved with his wife and only child to North Brookfield, Massachusetts, in 1820 Then Brookfield was the largest town between Boston and Springfield, on the Connecticut river He was the first of his name in the town For many years, in addition to manufacturing furniture, he did an extensive business manufacturing large wooden boxes for shipping boots and shoes, for several large boot and shoe manufacturers in North Brookfield and the adjoining towns He was a successful business man and although he was unfortunate in meeting several heavy losses by fire, having no insurance on his property destroyed, no man ever lost a dollar by dealing with him He held many different town offices, having been selectman and assessor for many years He took a deep interest in the old 'Liberty Party" and the Anti-Slavery agitation, and when the war of the rebellion came, he encouraged his sons to offer their services for the Union cause, and one of them, Thomas, was the first person to enlist from North Brookfield

THE FLETCHER FAMILY "The Fletchers are supposed to be of Norman descent, and to have come over with William the Conquerer, as there was a family of their name in the Southern part of Normandy," so says Bentham in his "Baronetage of England" The family name of Fletcher has always been an honorable one in England, and there are three Fletchers holding Baronetcies, and many others have high offices in the army and navy, and also in civil life

The first of that name known to have come to this country was Robert Fletcher, who was born in Oxford, England in 1592, as shown by the records of his death found in the town records of Concord, Massachusetts He settled in Concord, Massachusetts, in 1630, being thirty-eight years of age when he came to America He brought with him his wife and two sons, named Luke and William, and a daughter named Carey, also a brother William, who afterward settled in Middletown, Connecticut Robert Fletcher was a wealthy and influential man He died in Concord, Massachusetts, April 3, 1677, aged eighty-five years He had five children Luke, William, Carey, Samuel and Francis

Francis Fletcher, the fifth child of Robert Fletcher, was born in Concord, Massachusetts, in 1636, and married, August 1, 1656, Elizabeth, daughter of George and Catharine Wheeler He remained with his father in Concord, and became, like his two older brothers who settled in the adjoining towns, a great land owner He was reported in full communion with ye Church" in Concord in 1677, and was admitted a freeman the same year His wife Elizabeth died June 14, 1704 They had eight children, viz Samuel, Joseph, Elizabeth, John, Sarah Hezekiah, Hannah and Benjamin

Samuel Fletcher, oldest son of Francis Fletcher, was born August 6, 1657, and married Elizabeth Wheeler, April 15, 1682 He was a selectman of Concord many years, and town clerk from 1705 to 1713 He died October 23, 1744, and his wife lived but three days after his death They had eleven children, all born in Concord, Massachusetts, viz Samuel (who died young), Joseph, Elizabeth, Sarah, John Hannah, Ruth, Rebecca, Samuel, Benjamin and Timothy

Joseph Fletcher, second son of Samuel Fletcher, was born in Concord Massachusetts March 26, 1686 He married for his first wife, Elizabeth Carter, December 20, 1704, and married, as his second wife, Hepzibah Jones, July 11, 1711 He was made a deacon of the church in Acton Massachusetts, in 1738 and was a member of the committee to apportion the land to be set off from Concord as 'Concord Village" in 1723, afterwards called Acton in 1736 He died September 11 1746 He lived on the site where his grandfather, Robert Fletcher first settled By his first wife he had three children Lucy Abigail and Lydia By his second wife he had five children Lucy, Elizabeth, Daniel, Charles Elijah and Ruth

Daniel Fletcher fifth child and first son of Deacon Joseph Fletcher, was born in Concord, Massachusetts, October 18, 1718 He was a lieutenant in Captain David Melvin's company from March to September, 1747, and was stationed at Northfield He was captain of a company in 1755 in His Majesty's service coming from Acton, Massachusetts, and served from September 10 to December 30, 1755 fifteen weeks and six days, as signed by Daniel Fletcher Boston Massachusetts March 4 1756 (See Vol 94, p 70, on Muster Roll of the Company in State Archives at Boston Mass)

In Vol 95 p 320, "The Alarm List" whereof Samuel Davies was captain Daniel Fletcher's name appears also as captain This list included those who were held in reserve such as clergymen deacons in the church etc 1757 Again in the Massachusetts Archives Vol 136 p 504 is an account for billetting soldiers on their return from Lake George in 1758 On March 133 1758, Daniel Fletcher enlisted in Colonel Ebenezer Nichols' regiment in the Canada Expedition, in which expedition he was wounded and taken prisoner He enlisted at that time from March 13 to November 28 1758 as appears in Vol 96 pp 416 and 418, upon a Muster Roll of a Company of Foot in His Majesty's service in the French war, under the command of Captain Daniel Fletcher, in a regiment raised by the Province of Massachusetts Bay for the reduction of Canada, under Colonel Ebenezer Nichols In Vol 98, pp 157 and 158, upon the Muster Roll of a Company in His Majesty's service, under the command of Captain Daniel Fletcher, it appears that he rendered service in the capacity of captain from November 2, 1759, to August 1, 1760 In Vol 98, p 452, upon a Muster Roll of Officers and Men in Captain Daniel Fletcher's company, in Colonel Frye's regiment, in the service of the Province of Nova Scotia, he served as captain from January 1, 1760, to the time of their discharge, August 1, of the same year In 1768, Captain Daniel Fletcher was a member of the Honourable House of Representatives of His Majesty's Province of the Massachusetts Bay in New England, begun and held at Boston, county of Suffolk, on Wednesday, the 25th day of May, Anno Domini, 1768 (See the Journal of Massachusetts Bay, May, 1768, to April, 1770, No 16, p 4, Captain Daniel Fletcher acting member) In 1772 Captain Daniel Fletcher was appointed on a committee of public affairs On June 26, 1776, under Field Officers of the Regiment raising for Quebec, New York and Ticonderoga, John Cummings, Esq was elected brigadier-general of the forces destined to Canada (See Vol 26, p 277) On June 5, of the same year, James Brickett, Esq, was elected in the room of John Cummings, who declined to be colonel of the regiment to be raised in Middlesex county Jonathan Reed colonel, Benjamin Brown, lieutenant-colonel, Daniel Fletcher, major (See Brooks' Militia Officers, 6-months Men, Continental Balances, Vol 28, p 28 red mark, and p 72) (See also Vol 26, p 277, Roll and Abstract of the File, and Staff Officers as proposed in the Spring of 1776, Col Reed's Regiment, in the Northern Army in the Service of the United States of America, Jonathan Reed to be Colonel from Littleton, Mass , Benjamin Brown to be Lieutenant-Colonel, from Reading, Mass , Daniel Fletcher to be Major, from Littleton Mass William Emerson to be Chaplain, from Concord, Mass , John Porter to be Adjutant, from Littleton, Mass Edmund Monroe to be Quartermaster, from Lexington, Mass , David Taylor to be Sergeant, from Charlestown, Mass , Ezekiel Brown to be Sergeant's Mate, from Concord Mass) At the same time, his son, Jonathan Fletcher, was in the revolutionary war as a private in Captain Samuel Reed's company of Minute Men in Colonel William Prescott's regiment, as is demonstrated by the fact that the name of Jonathan Fletcher is on file of the Revolutionary Rolls of Massachusetts among the names "For the Muster Roll of Captain Samuel Reed's Company of Minute Men in Colonel William Prescott's Regiment who, on and after the 19th day of April last (1775), did march in consequence of the Alarm on that day," dated at "Littleton February 19, 1776" (See Vol 56 Coat Rolls) He served as a Minute Man at the Lexington Alarm six days from April 19 to 24, 1775

Major Daniel Fletcher was elected by the Massachusetts assembly June 26, 1776, or after the revolutionary war had commenced, as a major in the Third battalion destined to Canada (See Vol 26, p 277 Revolutionary Rolls at State House)

Major Daniel Fletcher died in Acton Massachusetts December 15, 1776 in the fifty-ninth year of his age, and was buried in Woodlawn Cemetery at Acton about one mile east from the center of the town

Major Daniel Fletcher first son of Deacon Joseph Fletcher was born in Concord Massachusetts, October 18 1718 He married Sarah Hartwell, of Westford Massachusetts, the intention of marriage having been entered November 12, 1741 They had nine children, all born in Acton, Massachusetts Daniel, Charles (who died young), Peter, Sarah, Ruth, Joseph Charles, Jonathan and Betsey

Jonathan Fletcher eighth child and sixth son of Major Daniel and Sarah Hartwell Fletcher, was born in Acton Massachusetts, January 21, 1757 Major Daniel Fletcher, father of Captain Jonathan Fletcher was connected with the Revolutionary war very early in the struggle, of which fact there is abundant evidence Jonathan Fletcher enlisted April 24, 1775 in Captain Abijah Wyman's company, Colonel William Prescott's regiment, as from Littleton, although his father, Major Daniel Fletcher, was a citizen of Acton (See Vol 16, p 76, Massachusetts Revolutionary Rolls) He was in the battle of Bunker Hill in which battle Colonel Prescott's regiment suffered such severe loss of life He served eight months or more in the revolutionary army at the siege of Boston under General Washington (See Vol 56, Coat Rolls, p 66, October 3, 1775, also Vol 16, p 76) Vol 57 contains Jonathan Fletcher's autograph Under figure seven of indexes of that volume in Captain Abijah Wyman's company, is the receipt of Jonathan Fletcher for supplies, dated November 14, 1775 On January 15, 1776 his name appears on the roll of Captain David Wheeler's company in Colonel Nixon's regiment, as a fifer from Acton, Massachusetts (See Vol 24 p 73, Massachusetts Revolutionary Rolls) In 1777 he was a private in Captain George Minot's company Colonel Samuel Bullard's regiment (See Vol 21 p 79 Massachusetts Revolutionary Rolls) Jonathan Fletcher is recorded as a lieutenant, February 27, 1778 and was on the pay roll of Captain Jacob Haskin's company, Colonel John Jacob's regiment (See Vol 2, p 83, Massachusetts Revolutionary Rolls) How much before that time he was commissioned as a lieutenant, we are unable to find by the records From the pay rolls, it is thought it must have been nearly or quite a year He served five months and twenty days from February 27, 1778 as a lieutenant in this company (See Vol 2, p 83 Massachusetts Revolutionary Rolls) (Vol 46 p 162, shows Lieutenant Jonathan Fletcher's accounts from December 1, 1778 to January 1, 1779) He was in continuous service as a lieutenant, until we find that he had been commissioned as captain in the Ninth Company of the Seventh Regiment, on July 27, 1780. (See Vol 28, p 66, Massachusetts Revolutionary Rolls)

On November 1 1781, the town of Fitchburg was required to pay certain soldiers who had not been paid for service, among them was Captain Jonathan Fletcher, who received from the selectmen of Fitchburg, one hundred and five pounds and mileage for seventy-five miles to each of his men by order of the general court The soldiers constituting his company came from the towns of Lexington, Acton Westminster and Fitchburg (See Vol 33, p 535, Massachusetts Revolutionary Rolls) He remained as Captain until the close of the war, so that from the time he was commissioned as lieutenant, made him in continuous service as lieutenant or captain nearly or quite six years, and as private or officer from the very commencement of the revolutionary war, April 19, 1775 (being then but eighteen years of age), in the battle of Lexington to its final termination in 1783 Captain Jonathan Fletcher had a very elegant sword presented to him by the soldiers of his company at the close of the war which sword was destroyed at the time the Bates family residence at North Brookfield was burned in 1844 There was also destroyed at that time a large family Bible, prepared by Captain Jonathan Fletcher, and containing a perfect and full record of the Fletcher family, extending back through many generations and branches

Captain Jonathan Fletcher was a warm personal friend of Paul Revere and also of General Henry Knox After the close of the war General Knox became a very large owner of real estate in St George's, Maine, and went there to live in 1795, afterwards removing to Thomaston, Maine, where he died on October 25, 1806 Captain Jonathan Fletcher accompanied General Knox to Maine and remained there near or with him, for several years, until the death of his wife, Lucretia Emerson Fletcher, who died in Thomaston, July 7, 1800 Captain Jonathan Fletcher went to Boston, Massachusetts, and died there January 16, 1807, and was buried in Copp's Hill burial grounds, near the Old North Church, with Masonic honors He was a member of Saint Andrew's Lodge, Ancient Free and Accepted Masons, of Boston Massachusetts

Thus it is clearly shown that both Major Daniel Fletcher and his son, Captain Jonathan Fletcher, were very patriotic soldiers in the colonial and revolutionary wars, especially is this true of Jonathan, who at the early age of sixteen years entered the service as a private in the minute men of 1775, and who merited and received several promotions, and remained in the revolutionary army until the close of the war, during six years of which he served as a commissioned officer, the first three being as a lieutenant, the last three as a captain

Captain Jonathan Fletcher, son of Major Daniel and Sarah Hartwell Fletcher, was born in Acton, Massachusetts, January 21, 1757 He was married on May 20, 1782, in Acton, to Lucretia Emerson She was born in Acton, August 4, 1764, and died in Thomaston, Maine, July 7, 1800 Captain Jonathan Fletcher died in Boston, Massachusetts, January 16, 1807

Sarah Fletcher, fourth and youngest daughter of Captain Jonathan and Lucretia Emerson Fletcher, was born in Boston, Massachusetts, May 3, 1799 She was married on August 2, 1818, in Boston, Massachusetts, to Elijah Bates, born in Cohasset, Massachusetts, April 25, 1796 They were married by the Rev John Murray, of Boston Elijah Bates died in North Brookfield, Massachusetts, September 6, 1863 Sarah Fletcher died in Worcester, Massachusetts, September 28, 1890

BERRY FAMILY Joseph Berry (1), ancestor of Russell Woodward Berry, late of Worcester, Massachusetts, was born before 1700 While the record of his birth has not been found, it is believed that he came from a Boston family Ambrose Berry and wife Hannah were living in Boston from 1686 and probably earlier, and in 1697 and probably later They had a son Joseph, born July 11, 1693, died July 24 1693 and there are reasons for believing that Joseph Berry (1), may be a son born after they left Boston Ambrose Berry was at Saco, Maine, in 1636, perhaps the father of Ambrose Berry, of Boston, and died May 3, 1661

Other members of the Berry family, of Boston, were Thomas and Grace Berry, who had a son John, born March 3, 1664, and a daughter Grace born June 1, 1669 Thaddeus and Hannah Berry had 1 Elizabeth, born December 2, 1665, married Joseph Townsend 2 Samuel, June 20, 1667 3 Hannah, August 12, 1668 4 Thomas, September 20, 1670 Thomas and Margaret Berry, of Boston, had Margaret, June 26, 1692, and Thomas, March 19, 1694 Oliver and Gartright Berry, of Boston, had Sarah, born January 28, 1678, Abigail, May 10, 1688, Oliver, February 26, 1693, John, February 4, 1696 To some of these families it seems certain that Joseph Berry belonged, and it is believed that all of them were related closely

Joseph Berry settled in Framingham, Massachusetts, and married there Thankful Shears, January 27, 1719-20 She was the daughter of John Shears, of Framingham

John Shears (3), son of Samuel Shears (2), was born in Wrentham, Massachusetts, 1666, and went to Framingham, Massachusetts, to settle His farm was on Doeskin Hill where he was living in 1693 He was a town officer in 1724 He married, April 9, 1688, Alice Mitchleson, of Cambridge, Massachusetts Their children were 1 Thomas, born January 9, 1708 2 Thankful, married January 17, 1719-20, Joseph Berry, before mentioned

Samuel Shears (2), son of Jeremiah Shears (1), was born in 1627, in England, and probably came to Dedham, Massachusetts, with his father He married Mary ——— and settled in Wrentham, which was originally part of Dedham, Massachusetts He died in 1691, aged sixty-four years His wife died April 26, 1704 Their children were 1 Mary, born 1664 2 John, 1666, before mentioned 3 Mehitable, February 1, 1668 4 Solomon, February 20, 1669, died at the age of nineteen years 5 Grace, February 29, 1672 6 Judith, July 17, 1675

Jeremiah Shears (1), was an emigrant and pioneer of Dedham, Massachusetts He was probably from Yorkshire in England He married (probably for his second wife) Susanna Green, widow of Nicholas Green He died in 1664 It is presumed that he was the father of the preceding, though little is known of him

Joseph Berry married (second) Hepzibah Benjamin He owned the farm later owned by Ezekiel Howe, whose father bought it of Berry His widow administered his estate in 1757 Children of Joseph and Thankful (Shears) Berry were 1 Alice, born 1721, baptised June 18, 1721, at Framingham 2 Abijah, baptised July 14, 1723, died young 3 Shears, (see forward) 4 Thomas, March 16, 1726-7, was in Sudbury 1760 5 Benjamin, April 14, 1733, settled in Framingham, fought in the Concord fight, April 19, 1775, died at Oakham, Massachusetts, March 1, 1800 6 Thankful, October 14, 1735, married General John Nixon, February 7, 1754, one of the most prominent officers of Central Massachusetts in the revolution, his family came from New York and the South 7 Mary, May 29, 1737, married Amos Parmenter 8 Abijah, December 5, 1738, died, unmarried, at Marlboro about 1810 9 Lydia, April 5 1739, married Joel Newton, June 3, 1862, in Southboro (One of the two latter dates of birth is obviously erroneous, but is according to record—Ed)

(II) Shears Berry, third child of Joseph Berry (1), the preceding, born in Framingham, Massachusetts, December 25, 1725, married June 15, 1750, Esther Woodward, of Holden He settled in the West Wing of Rutland about the time of his marriage, and his children were born there In 1766 he bought a farm of Samuel Gordon at Oakham, and removed to that town He and his son Joseph were associated in the ownership of considerable land in the vicinity He was a soldier in the revolution He was in Captain Barnabas Shears' company in 1776, and in the Continental army, in Colonel Converse's regiment, in 1777 He enlisted for three years in 1777 in Captain Wheeler's company Colonel Nixon's regiment He was also a private in Captain Abel Holden's company, same regiment, and was at Peekskill in 1779, in Captain Timothy Paige's company, Colonel John Rand's regiment, and in 1780 was at West Point with his company

After the revolution it seems that Shears and Joseph Berry left Oakham and settled in Salem, New York, as stated in a deed dated March 24, 1788, and recorded in 1797, in which land in Oakham is deeded to them by John Powers, of Oakham They also bought land in common from George Caswell, February 4, 1789, when they were both living in Oakham About 1797 the family moved to Vermont, where Shears probably died Some of them located at Guildhall, Vermont Children of Shears or Sheers (as the records have it) Berry were 1 Eunice, born in Rutland, June 22, 1751 2 Joseph, born in Rutland December 29, 1752 3 Ephraim, born in Rutland, November 25, 1754 4 Esther, born in Rutland, December 5, 1757, married Elias Marsh, August 1, 1776 5 Lydia, born at Rutland, September 9, 1760, married at Oakham (intentions August 23) 1789 6 John, born at Oakham, April 4, 1772 7 Woodward (see forward) 8 Benjamin, baptised August 17, 1777, at Rutland

(III) Captain Woodward Berry, seventh child of Shears Berry (2), born in Oakham September 2, 1774, baptised October 1, 1775 He married Nancy The family removed to Vermont and resided at Guildhall, where most of the children were born He was captain in the militia and served, it is said, in the war of 1812

Joseph Berry, brother of Captain Woodward Berry, was also a very prominent man, a lawyer, in 1799 one of the seven founders of the Guildhall Church, chief judge of the court in 1822, in the governor's council in 1819-20-21-22-23-24, state's attorney in 1811-12-15-16-17-18-21-23-24, representative to the state legislature of Vermont in 1816, removed to Newbury, Vermont, thence to Iowa where he died, his wife was Sarah Perhaps Woodward Berry went West also The date of his death and place are not known His wife returned with the family to her old home in Oakham, Massachusetts, about 1830 She lived to an advanced age and died in the eighties, in Worcester, at the home of her son Russell Woodward Berry, Chatham street

Children of Captain Woodward and Nancy Berry were 1 Joseph Austin, born in Oakham, July 7, 1807, died young (probably the Joseph who died January 7, 1839, at Oakham, though his age is given wrongly as twenty-two instead of thirty-two) 2 Sarah, born in Vermont, 1811 died December 28 1839, at Oakham 3 Sophronia, born in Vermont about 1812, died October 19, 1842, married Captain Russell Ripley, December 13, 1832 at Oakham Captain Ripley was the son of Lieutenant Zenas and Sarah Ripley and was born at Oakham February 22, 1804 4 Russell Woodward (see forward) 5 Deacon Zebina E (see forward) 6 Isaac, settled in Vermont, married Emily Copeland and had two children Hortense, who married James W Rand, of Weymouth Massachusetts and had children, Nancy, who married David G Tapley of Worcester and they have two children Walter married living in Washington District of Columbia, and Ella, married ——— Robinson and resides with her parents at 110 Austin street

(IV) Russell Woodward Barry (Berry) son of Captain Woodward Berry, born in Guildhall Vermont died in Worcester in 1891 He went to school in Vermont When a young boy he returned with his mother to Oakham Massachusetts, but soon afterward came to Worcester to learn his trade He had little schooling but having a taste for books, managed to acquire a good education He learned the carpenter's trade and followed it all his life in Worcester He built his own house at 42 Chatham street, where his widow now resides During his active life he worked for the leading contractors and helped construct many of the important buildings that rank among the landmarks of Worcester

Mr Berry was a good citizen, modest, quiet and domestic in his tastes, belonging to no secret orders He was for many years a member of the Worcester County Mechanics Association In poltics he was a Republican, but never cared for public office He attended the Congregational church He married October 5, 1843, Harriet Gage, daughter of Eben and Sally (Stone) Gage, of Leicester, Massachusetts Eben Gage was a farmer He lived for a time also at Orford, New Hampshire He was colonel of a regiment of New Hampshire militia No children were born to Russell Woodward Berry

(IV) Deacon Zebina E Berry, son of Captain Woodward Berry (3), was born in Guildhall, Vermont He was educated there and worked on the farm of his father there until 1831, when he returned with the family to Massachusetts, and went to work in Worcester He was then twenty-five years of age He was employed first by Carter & Tobey, builders, and helped to build the first part of the old Lunatic Asylum on Summer street, and worked on other large structures built at that time He retained the spelling, Berry, while his brother Russell preferred Barry At the time of his death he was one of the oldest and best known carpenters and builders in Worcester He died in 1889, at the home of his daughter Mrs Alonzo W Cole, 12 Maywood street He was very active in church work Soon after coming to Worcester he joined the First Baptist Church, and was one of forty baptized November, 1831, in Fox's Pond near Green street, and in 1836 he was elected deacon He served until 1848 In his later years he was a member of the South Baptist Church because of his residence in that section of the city

He married (first) November 3, 1836, Lucretia H Culver, daughter of Joshua and Susan (Teed) Culver, of Somers, New York, married (second) a sister of his first wife, Susan Augusta Culver, September 4, 1849 Children of Deacon Zebina E and Lucretia H (Culver) Berry were 1 Susan Augusta, September 16, 1838, deceased 2 Sarah Louisa, July 22, 1840, deceased 3 Ella Lucretia, (see forward) 4 Susan Culver, January 9, 1846, married Charles Amidon, of Worcester

(V) Ella Lucretia Berry, third child of Deacon Zebina E Berry (4), born in Worcester, Massachusetts, March 6, 1843, married August 6, 1867, Alonzo W Cole a native of Orleans, Massachusetts They reside on Maywood street, Worcester They have one child, Arthur Williams Cole, born February 17, 1875, married January 23, 1903, Emma Louise Taylor daughter of Robert C Taylor, formerly of Webster, Massachusetts (See sketch of Alonzo W Cole and the Cole Family in this work)

THE KNOWLES FAMILY, as represented in Worcester county, is from Eastham, (the Nauset of the aborigines) Barnstable county, that portion of Massachusetts known as Cape Cod, where for more than a hundred and fifty years the ancestors of L J and F B Knowles lived, and were known as exemplary, wise and industrious farmers

Richard Knowles who had lived in Plymouth and there married Ruth Bower August 15 1639 was at Eastham as early as 1653, according to Freeman the trustworthy historian of Cape Cod (Vol II, p 393, noted) At least three of his children were born in the former town Mercy, married Ephraim Doane, February 5, 1668, John, Samuel, born September 17, 1651 It would appear that Mehitable, born in 1655, and Barbara, born September 28, 1656, were born in Eastham Samuel married, December, 1679, Mercy Freeman, and Barbara, June 13, 1677, married Thomas Mayo The complete genealogy of the Knowles family would reveal marriages with all the names early represented in Eastham, so that it was nearly or remotely related with all the dwellers in that township

John Knowles, son of Richard, married, December 28, 1670, Apphia, daughter of Edward Bangs, one of the first comers and a very important man in the community Apphia and her twin sister Mercy, born October 15, 1651, were married on the same day, the latter to Stephen Herrick John Knowles was one of nineteen men Eastham furnished for the King Philip war, and was one of the slain, as appears in the action of the colony government in providing for his widow Freeman (vol I, p 280) says, "and provision was especially made for Apphia, widow of John Knowles, of Eastham, lately slain in the service" From a note at the foot of p 366, vol II, the conclusion is drawn that he was killed near Taunton, June 3d, 1675 (i e 3d day, 4th month, O S) John and Apphia Knowles had three children Edward, November 7, 1671, John, July 10, 1673, Deborah, March 2, 1675 When the father died no one of his children was old enough to appreciate their deprivation Edward older son, married (first) Ann Ridley, and (second) the widow Sarah Mayo, and was the father of six children He was known in town annals as Deacon Knowles, and died November 16, 1740 The widow of John Knowles later married Joseph Atwood, and the appearance of a Bangs Atwood in a later generation of the Atwoods would indicate that she bore children by her second husband The son John, of the third generation in the Knowles family, married Mary ———, of whom no record is found In an old burial burial ground of Eastham, near the shores of the town cove, the bodies of the brothers are buried Quite likely many more of the family lie there also, but if so their memorials long ago disappeared Side by side are two ancient slates, each having the winged skull, that of the wife with the traditional crossed bones, and inscriptions as follows Here Lyes Buried the Body of Mrs Mary Knowles, wife of Colnl John Knowles Died Nov ye 7th, 1745, in the 73d Year of Her age." "Here lies buried the body of Colnl John Knowles who departed this life Nov 3d, 1757, in the 85th Year of His Age" When he bore the title of captain, John Knowles was a member of general court Very likely his military appellations came from service in the militia Colonel John and Mary Knowles had Joshua, born 1696, John, 1698, Seth, 1700, Paul, 1702, James, 1704, Jesse, 1707, Mary, 1709

Joshua, eldest child of Colonel John and Mary Knowles, apparently followed the vocation of his father, farming, with possibly an occasional venture at fishing The metes and boundaries of the town assignments of land to the successive generations of the family indicate nearness to the center of the town of Eastham, and the burial of their dead in the cemeteries near that part bears out the supposition Joshua Knowles was married to Sarah Paine, March 13, 1717-18, by Nathaniel Freeman, Esq She was born April 14, 1699 daughter of John and Bennet Paine, another of the oldest families in the township, one that later gave a signer of the Declaration of Independence to the country The wife died July 12, 1772, and the husband, May 27, 1786 Their children were Jesse, born April 13, 1723, Rebecca, May 23, 1726, Sarah, March 10, 1727-28, Joshua, April 27, 1730, Josiah, May 24, 1735, Simeon, August 11, 1737, Susanah, March 9, 1740

Simeon, youngest son of Joshua and Sarah Knowles, appears as follows in the Eastham records "August 12, 1758, then entered the intentions of Simeon Knowles and Eunis Mayo boath of Eastham to proseed in marriage, Recorded Thomas Knowles, town clk" The foregoing is nearest the date of marriage thus far found The wife was a representative of another long placed Eastham family, the prime ancestor, John Mayo, having been the first minister in the town From Simeon comes whatever claims his descendants have on revolutionary memories from the name of Knowles The state rolls have under his name the following entry Simeon Knowles, Private Captain Israel Higgins Co, Major Zenas Winslow's Regiment, Sept 9 to Sept 13, 1778, 4 days, on an alarm at Falmouth' Roll endorsed, 'on alarm att Bedford" It is possible that Simeon died in Eastham, before the moving of the family to Hardwick, certainly Paige, historian of the latter town, makes no mention of his death His wife died in Hardwick, April 5, 1819, aged seventy-nine years The eldest and possibly all the children were born in Eastham, Simeon, August 17, 1766, Elisha, about 1769, died August 14, 1859, Phebe, died, unmarried, April 7, 1824 and others The family had remained in Eastham or in adjoining towns for considerably more than one hundred years, but now comes the migratory spirit It is said that the disposition of people from the Cape to seek better homes in northern Worcester county arose from the locating there of the Rev Timothy Ruggles, father of his more famous son, who was a loyalist in the revolution Having lived and preached in towns near Barnstable county, he drew upon some of his acquaintances for recruits to the settlements in the northwest

Simeon, eldest child of Simeon and Eunis (Mayo) Knowles, married Priscilla Doane, their marriage intentions having been published November 10, 1787, in Eastham The Doanes were also among the long established dwellers in the town Their children were Bangs, born in Eastham, March 9, 1789, died September 17, 1806, Simeon, born Eastham, June 22, 1791, Leonard, Edward, Harriet and perhaps others From the above facts it would seem reasonable that the second Simeon was the real migrant, and that his mother and brethren accompanied him He died August 22, 1823 while his widow survived until February 5, 1839, dying at the age of seventy-five years

Simeon, second child of Simeon and Priscilla (Doane) Knowles, was the first of the family in nearly two centuries to marry outside the Old Colony He married, March 14 1814 Lucetta Newton, of Hardwick, daughter of Silas and Naomi (Washburn) Newton The Newton lineage of Lucetta born January 2, 1792, began in Sudbury in the person of Richard, whose son, Moses of Marlboro, transmitted the name to Josiah and he to Timothy a farmer, who lived on the road from Hardwick to Barre All of these men were prominent in their day and generation Timothy, born February 28 1728, married Sarah Merrick was a soldier in the French and Indian war, and died July 10 1811 His son Silas, born February 11 1766, was a Hardwick farmer and the father of Simeon's wife Lucetta The latter died in Warren, August 23, 1868 aged seventy-six years Simeon Knowles died in Warren April 9, 1860 The children of

Simeon and Lucetta (Newton) Knowles were Laura Loraine, born October 10, 1816, married Rufus Washburn, Jr, of Johnstown, New York, February 21, 1837, Lucius James, born July 2, 1819, Harriet Evaline, July 24, 1821, married Lorin Brown, Fitchburg, October 1, 1844, Francis Bangs, November 29, 1823 The family resided about three miles northerly from the common in Hardwick

Francis B, youngest child of Simeon and Lucetta (Newton) Knowles, was twice married, (first), December 23 1845, to Ann Eliza Poole of Gloversville, New York The children by this marriage were Eliza Evaline, born January 5 1848, in Gloversville, married September 2, 1873, C Henry Hutchins, of Worcester, long identified with the Knowles Loom Works and now president of the corporation Their children are Arthur Knowles and Helen Mabel Mrs Hutchins died February 13, 1898, and Frank Poole born February 1, 1853, in Gloversville, married, October 2, 1879, Alice J, daughter of George C and Eleanor J (Doane) Bigelow, of Worcester, their children are George Francis, Marion and Lillian The mother died February 24, 1865, soon after the removal to Warren Mr Knowles's second marriage, April 23, 1867, was to Hester A, daughter of John Reynolds and Fanny (Wightman) Greene, of Worcester Their children are Mabel, married June 15 1893, Dr Homer Gage, of Worcester They have one child, Homer Gage, Jr Frances, married April 23, 1900, George Eddy Warren, of Boston, a business man Lucius James, married, April 6, 1904, Laura, daughter of John R McGinley, of Pittsburg, Pennsylvania Their son, Lucius James, Jr was born in London, England Both sons of Francis B Knowles are directly connected with the great business established by father and uncle The names of "Frank" and "Lucius" are still heard in the works and, from the names in the latest generations, the famous appellations bid fair to obtain for years to come

Mrs Knowles comes of an old Rhode Island family, descended from John Greene, surgeon, of Gillingham, England, who came to America in 1635 and settled in Warwick, Rhode Island, where through successive generations the family resided The line from the first John Greene included Peter, Peter, Elisha Elisha, Stephen, William, who married Abigail Reynolds, thus becoming the father of John Reynolds Greene, the father of Mrs Knowles He was for many years a Worcester merchant, and a warden of All Saints' Church He was born in Warwick, Rhode Island, December 22, 1811, and died April 1, 1873 Well educated he was highly successful in business, and deeply interested in church work His children were Byron W, Hester A, Stephen E, Mary, Fannie and Abbie

So blended were the lives of the brothers L J and F B Knowles, it were much easier to write of them together than separately Their characteristics supplemented each other perfectly, and never did men better exemplify the scriptural words "Behold how good and how pleasant it is for brethren to dwell together in unity" There were only two sons in the family of Simeon Knowles and they appeared to have little affiliation for the life so long pursued by their ancestors, for we see them in due order leaving the hills of Hardwick determined to win their way by other means than those employed by the fathers To the younger brother had been given the rather unusual name, for those days, of Francis with another, still more uncommon, but recalling an uncle, Eastham born, who had died in his early manhood As a Christian name, Bangs suggester a long line of ancestral facts and no doubt the father, Simeon, in thus naming his boy had in mind a tribute to the 'Cape Cod Folks,' whose memory to him was especially dear However, as the years went by and the boy advanced to manhood his double name was seldom used in its entirety Indeed among his immediate friends he was more often known as "Frank," while for signature purposes the initials, F B, were found to be all he had time to write

After securing whatever of educational aid the common schools of Hardwick could afford, with some higher attainments at Leicester Academy, he early essayed the role of schoolmaster himself, in this capacity serving in Dana, and possibly in other nearby towns While still four years away from his majority he was permitted to leave the farm and to undertake the task of shifting for himself His older sister Laura had married in Johnstown, New York, and it is possible that this fact accounts for her brother's presence, when nineteen years old, as a teacher in the neighboring village of Gloversville He had not assumed the profession as a lifelong occupation, but rather a makeshift till some better way appeared The place where he thus found himself was noted then, as it is now, for its manufacture of kid and buckskin gloves and mittens, leading in this particular all other places in the country What more natural than that this enterprising resourceful New England boy should speedily see a chance for himself to better his condition, by forsaking the schoolroom for the mart of trade At any rate ere long he became a salesman for one of the great glove making companies of the town and, going upon the road, he speedily familiarized himself with a large part of the eastern portion of the country April 1, 1845, he entered upon the making of gloves himself, continuing in this occupation till he embarked in the clothing business, and this was his vocation when in 1883 came the call from his brother to come back to Massachusetts

He, therefore, came to Warren, Worcester county, to bear a hand in the development of the inventions which were taking shape in the fertile brain of Lucius J, and from that time onward his interests were largely in this part of the Commonwealth Though L J Knowles was conducting a great business in his making of steam pumps in his Warren factory, he was not satisfied, but desired rather to enter upon the manufacture of looms, upon whose improvement his mind had been dwelling Accordingly the advent of the younger brother followed and with expected pleasing results We are told that the first loom was constructed in the pump works of Warren, but the advantages of Worcester soon became so obvious that in 1866 the loom works were transferred to this city and first established in Allen court, the name of F B Knowles appearing in a Worcester directory for the first time in 1867 The older brother continued his residence in Warren

Though constantly growing, the business remained in Allen court until 1879, when it took a move to the southward and expanded into the so-called Junction shops Progress, however, knows no boundaries and the capacity of this location was soon overtaxed In 1890, having been erected near the Boston & Albany Railroad on the corner of Grand and Tainter streets, the most extensive plant of its kind in the country, the business was removed for the third time into quarters seemingly ample for years of development, yet in 1892, before the blight of the Wilson Bill had struck the nation, enlarged area was again in urgent demand During all these years of growth and prosperity, the younger of the Knowles Brothers was constantly at his post,

F. B. Knowles

an invaluable factor in all the many features of the vast enterprise Of the older brother, it is said that he never sold a machine, gave little heed to the purely business details of the enterprise, but busied himself with the endless possibilities in the mechanism of loom making On the contrary, F B had no mechanical tastes nor talent, could not drive a nail, but the pushing of the manufactured articles into public sight and favor was his delight The financial side of the work he could and did handle marvelously well, till at his death he could truthfully say, had he cared to do so, that the Knowles Loom Works were the most extensive in the country, if not in the world

The limitations of human strength and energy speedily appear in the strenuous life which the ardent Americans lead and, long before the Knowles Brothers had reached the age at which their fathers were still doing long and arduous days' work on their respective farms, these princes of mechanical industry found it necessary to abate somewhat the intensity of their labors, but they did not begin early enough Both of them were wont to seek rest and recuperation during the winter months in various ways Florida, long the fabled possessor of the fountain of youth, had been a resort for Francis B, and he was with his brother when, in the spring of 1884, the latter passed away at the Riggs House, in Washington, a victim of that specially characteristic ailment of Americans, another name for overwork, "Heart Failure," a fate that a few years later was to fall to the lot of F B himself, whose physical breaking down began with his arduous labors at the Centennial Exposition in 1876 through his determination to make the Knowles loom succeed The loom became a wonderful success, but at what a cost

Recognizing the advisableness of a yearly respite Mr Knowles had several years before interested himself in Florida investments and had become the owner of extensive areas there In Winter Park he was the principal owner of the Seminole Hotel, and was the president of the development company, and here a large part of the year, at any rate during the cold weather, but he was wont to remain It was at the end of his annual stay that, in the spring of 1890, with his family he started homeward For six weeks, by slow stages, they were working northward, that he might the better adapt himself to the climate The month of May found them in Washington and, while friends were expecting their early return, there came to his older son the startling dispatch that the father had suddenly died of angina pectoris The news thus sent came from Postmaster General John Wanamaker, a personal friend of many years standing There followed the sad completion of the homeward journey, the services at Piedmont Church, of which he had been so long a pillar, and the final resting place in beautiful Rural cemetery

The smile which ever lighted the face of Francis B Knowles was an excellent index of his nature, and perhaps this very look had much to do with the success that attended him "The world shall be better for my having passed through it" is said to have been a sentiment close to whose truth he he tried to live How well he succeeded a grateful community has repeatedly borne testimony From friends, acquaintances, and employees there came one common statement, that he merited all the success that he achieved, that he was a faithful friend the kindest of employers and in every way the best of citizens

In these hurrying days, it is a sad fact that the most admirably equipped men cannot afford the time for political preferment The degree to which machinery and enterprises are speeded, demands every bit of strength that a man possesses and ever the call is for more Though a lifelong Republican in his political affiliations and a liberal supporter of campaign expenses, Mr Knowles never saw the day in his Worcester life that he could give to serving his fellow citizens in any official capacity Had he been able to accept there can be no doubt as to the positions in which he would have shone through the suffrages of those who knew so well his sterling worth Whatever diversion he took from business was found in religious lines For years he conducted Sunday school institutes through Worcester county, and in the labors of the Young Men's Christian Association he was indefatigable

With so long a lineage, including so many names of sterling worth, there need be no surprise that Mr Knowles was a devoted member of the Congregational church His advent to Worcester was in the days when that denomination was beginning its career of expansion He was here early enough to give hearty aid and comfort to the proposition to establish Plymouth Church, but that was located somewhat distant from the part of the city in which his interests chiefly lay, hence he was ready to help forward the new Piedmont venture and here was his church home for the remainder of his days He was an early Sunday school superintendent here and one of the most beloved deacons from the beginning Still he was not at all confined in his giving, and when Pilgrim Church was taking shape, along with his sister-in-law, Mrs Helen C Knowles, he gave the site for the edifice and was in addition a liberal giver to the enterprise all the way along He was a generous donor towards every good cause, and Knowles Hall, an edifice in the plant of Rollins College at Winter Park Florida, attests his interests in the educational development of the new south To the same institution he gave a further sum of money for the endowment of scholarships No good cause ever appealed to him in vain He was the third largest giver toward the edifice of the Young Men's Christian Association and had long been a life member The last check drawn by him was for $5 000 in behalf of the Young Women's Christian Association of Worcester

His home life was an ideal one There he surrounded himself with all that wealth and culture could provide, and the same was a favorite resort for those who delighted in art and literature Mrs Knowles, having traveled extensively at home and abroad, is an excellent judge of art and, with ample means at her command, has made a collection of paintings larger than that afforded by some public galleries The only regret that one can have in contemplating so admirable a career is that to the successful manufacturer, the faithful friend, good citizen and Christian gentleman there had not been granted greater length of days for the enjoyment of the fruitage of wise planting and judicious culture

For more than twenty-five years the name of Lucius J Knowles, of Worcester, was a synonym for the business enterprise and integrity His name with that of his brother, though only the initials were usually employed, became known as far as the necessity of looms extended, and that means the limits of the civilized world From a long line of industrious Cape Cod farmers, he and the other children of Simeon Knowles were the first to enjoy the luxury of double names, but the easily pronounced combination, Lucius James, was quite too long for his busy life and it was generally abbreviated, especially when written, to the first letters only The student of genealogy may find interest in the fact that his Christian appellations do not appear in the long line of ancestral names Evidently Simeon, the third, intended to begin a new series Hardwick, as an agricultural town, though a great improvement on Eastham, so long the home of the Knowles family, did not present attractions sufficient to hold the older son of Simeon and Lucetta Evidently, like so many New Hampshire people, he thought his native town a good one to emigrate from It is easy to fancy his boyhood on the country farm, getting what he could out of the district school, meanwhile dreaming dreams of the great outside world in which he early determined to play a conspicuous part

One of his early schoolmasters was his maternal uncle, John C Newton, for many years a resident of Worcester, and thereafter he was privileged to add several terms at Leicester Academy, then one of the best secondary schools in the Commonwealth In a word, though by no means liberally educated, he was well equipped for the work on which he was about to enter Before he was twenty-one years old we find him in Shrewsbury, a clerk in the store of W W Pratt In 1838, when only nineteen years of age, he formed a partnership with his Uncle Newton, his former teacher, and together they conducted a general store in the same village On the retirement of his uncle in 1841, he took in as partner, his first employer, W W Pratt, and so continued till 1844 During these days, the young merchant has married and, in a small way, prospered, but he is very far from the goal which in vision attracts him In these days the public begins to hear of the accomplishments of Daguerre, the Frenchman, in his experiments with light on sensitized silver, and L J Knowles is the very first man in Worcester to undertake a realization of this wonderful discovery His studio was on Main street, near the old location of the Quinsigamond Bank, or just north of Central street It is possible to find in the city today several specimens of his early work Indeed, the very first exposure made for pay is still a cherished possession of the subject But photography did not satisfy and he next engaged in spooling cotton thread in New Worcester In 1847 he is making cotton warp in the town of Spencer and two years later in Warren There he busied himself with both cotton and woolen mills and engaged in the manufacture of the steam pump which he had invented This was eminently successful and its development would have satisfied any ordinary man but he had not yet reached the vocation which he deemed specially his own All successful men have pet schemes or plans, some of which if they are persistent, they realize During all these years Mr Knowles, who was a mechanic by nature, had fancied improvement in looms for the making of fabrics His first invention in this line was in 1856 By the aid of one wood workman and two machinists, the first loom was set up in the pump works An inspection of the inventions made by this Hardwick farmer's son, with a realization of the consideration each one involved leads us to wonder where he found any leisure for diversion We are told that when in Shrewsbury he made improvements in organs and other reed instruments and that here he began his studies in the safety steam boiler feed regulator" As early as 1840 he was working on appliances for the application of electricity as a motor anticipating in this respect the invention of later years for he made several engines to be thus propelled Apparently there was very little time when he was not devising some way of improving an old machine or of making an entirely new one In fine, more than one hundred inventions issued by him stand to his credit in the Washington patent office

Of the calling of his younger brother in 1863 mention has been made in the sketch of the latter's life, and of the development of the loom manufacture, the second greatest industry in Worcester, the story is briefly told in that chapter Were it desirable to extend the story in any way it would be only to note the character of the workmen that the loom works demand Skilled mechanics are ever the boast of New England and few enterprises ever drew together a greater number of men, every one of whom was able to successfully conduct great enterprises of his own An inspection of the intelligent faces seen in the great shops on Grand and Tainter streets can not but impress the beholder with the *nobility of labor* The overalled, dusty workmen are members of the city government, leaders in the political parties of the state deacons and Sunday school superintendents in their respective churches and, in nearly all cases, among the most respected men in the community

While a resident of Warren, Mr Knowles enjoyed the distinction of representing the district to which his town belonged in the general court in 1862, and again in 1865, thus having the privilege of assisting in upholding the hands of John A Andrew in the trying days of the civil war In 1869, his senatorial district sent him as its choice to Boston as one of the forty senators for that term That he was painstaking, faithful public servant need not be affirmed He was one of the most public-spirited citizens in Warren and his departure was considered a great loss to the township, but the demands of his investment in Worcester were too strong to be resisted However, he left in the town so long his abode and so loyal to him, substantial tokens of his reward, for in his will he devised the sum of $5,000 as a fund for the support and maintenance of the free public library of that town, also the sum of one thousand dollars for the perpetual care of his lot in the cemetery, where rest the remains of his parents and those of his brother's wife

As a resident of Worcester, the directory for 1871 has his name for the first time and thence for *thirteen years he was an embodiment of zeal and* energy for every good cause and work in the city's development Not alone was he devoted to the improvement and advancement of the industry with which his name was linked, but also the best interests of the city were his In 1873 he held a seat in the common council and gladly would his fellow citizens have kept him there longer had his time and other duties permitted The dominance of business robs the public of the very best services which *might otherwise be employed* He was a director in the Central National Bank and in the State Mutual Life Insurance Company was president of the People's Savings Bank and of the Board of Trade and was a prominent figure in the management of other financial interprises of a public or semi-public character It was a pleasant recognition of his life-long labors, intellectually as well as physically, that Williams College in 1869 gave him the honorary degree of A M Many a wearer of such honors secured in regular course, never merited them half so much as this self-taught mechanic and manufacturer of Worcester The college was honored in his acceptance of the proffered recognition

When a young man in Shrewsbury, Mr Knowles married May 13, 1841, Eliza Ann Adams, of that town, and for more than twenty years she was his faithful companion as he strove for success. She died at the age of fifty-six years, February 17, 1873. Some time afterwards he was married to Mrs. Helen C. Hayward, of Boston, daughter of Alexander and Cornelia (Goodnow) Strong. Possessed of similar tastes, theirs was a singularly happy life during the remainder of his earthly work. The collection of paintings which they made and with which they adorned their beautiful Main street residence was one of the largest and best in Central Massachusetts. Mrs. Knowles, who did not long survive her husband, dying November 5, 1884, when fifty-one years old, signalized her devotion by leaving the sum of $25,000 for the furtherance of art study in Worcester. The income of this sum, at present in the care of the St. Wulstan's Society, is the prime source for the maintenance of the Art Museum, one of Worcester's most cherished institutions.

While usually enjoying a high degree of health, Mr. Knowles was conscious of serious impairment of the same through his excessive labors in the care of his wife during a visit made by them to Europe some two years before his death. Realizing somewhat the limitations of energy and strength, he had begun to abate the incessant strain to which he had so long subjected himself. It was with this thought in mind that with his wife he had visited Fortress Monroe in the winter of 1884, and coming northward had met in Washington his brother and wife. Here at the Riggs House he was taken violently ill with the same ailment which carried off Charles Sumner and so many other hard workers, viz. angina pectoris, and after a brief period of agony died February 25. His body was brought home for interment and with that of his brother sleeps in Rural cemetery.

From the day that he found himself possessed of anything to give, Lucius J. Knowles was a generous giver. To his church, to public measures, to everything that seemed good and needy he was charitable. The Lord loving a cheerful giver, must have had an unusual liking for the Knowles Brothers. He was long a mainstay in Union Church and for many a year one of its cherished deacons. While a Congregationalist in his first allegiance, few churches ever went to him for aid without getting it. Though he has passed on to another world several thousands of his estate went towards the building of the beautiful edifice of the Young Men's Christian Association, of which he was a life member. While his home was in the southern part of the city, on Main street, and he had a just and proper liking for his vicinage, he was not cribbed nor confined by narrow boundaries. In everything his progress was on the very broadest lines possible. Worcester's most prosperous days have been seen under the developing care and assistance of such men as the brothers' Knowles, men whose interests and affections were here not spread over a section so extended that little thickness was possible. Constant, determined, honest, progressive, would that Worcester had more of their kind and character.

ALONZO WILLIAMS COLE. In the Cole family to which Alonzo Williams Cole, of Worcester, belongs, the tradition of three emigrant brothers is confirmed by sufficient proof. John, Job and Daniel Cole came to New England in the employ of William Collier, a London merchant, in 1633. John Cole died in Plymouth, in 1637, and in his will mentioned Master Collier's men in describing his brothers to whom he made bequests.

(I) Daniel Cole, the youngest of the trio, first appears on the records April 6, 1640, when he owned fifty acres of upland granted then. He was reported as able to bear arms at Yarmouth in 1643, and was made a freeman June, 1645, at Yarmouth. He was one of the jury that tried Alice Bishop for infanticide in 1648. He was a tailor by trade. He sold land at Marshfield June 8, 1649. He removed to Eastham in 1652. He was a deputy to the general court in 1654-57-61-67-89. He was constable in 1664 and selectman in 1668-70-71-72-81.

He died December 21, 1694, aged eighty years. His wife Ruth died December 15, 1694, aged sixty-six years. Administration was granted to his son Israel, on Daniel Cole's estate, January 15, 1695, and later an agreement was signed by all the heirs, as given in the following list of his children: 1. John, see forward. 2. Timothy, born September 4, 1646. 3. Hepsebah, April 16, 1649, married Daniel Doane. 4. Ruth, April 15, 1651, married John Young. 5. Israel, January 8, 1653. 6. James, November 3, 1655. 7. Mary, March 10, 1658, married Joshua Hopkins. 8. William, September 15, 1663. 9. Daniel. 10. Esther or Hester, married Medad Atwood.

(II) John Cole, eldest child of Daniel Cole (1), was born in Yarmouth, July 16, 1644. He moved to Eastham with his parents and lived there during most of his active life. He married Ruth Snow, daughter of Nicholas Snow, December 12, 1666. He was at Groton in 1672, but returned to Eastham when the settlers had to abandon their homes in 1675-76 in King Philip's war. He was living in Eastham again in 1695. His wife died June 27, 1717. He died June 6, 1725. Their children, most of whom were born in Eastham were: 1. Ruth, born March 11, 1668, married William Twining. William (2), William (1). 2. John (see forward). 3. Hepsibah, June 20, 1672. 4. Hannah, March 27, 1675, died June 11, 1677. 5. Joseph, June 11, 1677. 6. Mary, October 27, 1679. 7. Sarah, June 10, 1682.

(III) John Cole, second child of John Cole (2), born in Eastham, Massachusetts, March 6, 1670, married Mary ———, who died February 17, 1731-2. He died December 13, 1746. Their children were: 1. Jonathan, born October 4, 1694. 2. John, October 14, 1696. 3. Mary, August 25, 1698. 4. James, October 23, 1700. 5. ———, January 21, 1703. 6. Joshua, March 20, 1705. 7. Moses, July 22, 1707. 8. Phebe, October 29, 1709. 9. Thankful, October 20, 1712, died young. 10. Joseph, (see forward). 11. Thankful, October 19, 1716.

(IV) Joseph Cole, tenth child of John Cole (3), was born in Eastham, Massachusetts, October 13, 1714. He died in the south parish of Eastham in 1800. The records of his children are not at hand and that of Jesse, presumed to be his son, is not recorded.

(V) Jesse Cole, believed to be the son of Joseph Cole (4), born in Eastham, Massachusetts, February 4, 1755, married January, 1772, Bethia Young, of Eastham, of one of the pioneer families there. She was born September 21, 1752. Jesse Cole was a soldier in the revolution, in Captain Solomon Higgins' company of Eastham, enlisted July 12, 1775, and served six months, four days in defence of the seacoast. He died in the south parish of Eastham in 1803.

The record of his children is not complete. Among them were: 1. Jesse, Jr., who died in 1800. 2. Elisha, (see forward).

(VI) Elisha Cole, the grandfather of Alonzo Williams Cole, of Worcester, Massachusetts, born in Orleans, Massachusetts, June 4, 1784, died there April 6, 1865. He was educated in the common schools of Orleans and at an early age studied navigation and followed the sea. For many years he was a sea captain, but finally abandoned this occupation and bought large tracts of land in and near Orleans, where he conducted a farm and salt works. He raised sheep and cattle and was one of the leading men of his day in the town. He continued to run his farm up to the time of his death. He was a selectman in 1828 and representative to the general court 1833. He was a Universalist in religion and a Republican, in his later years, in politics. He was greatly interested in public questions and his one great desire in his last years was that he might live until Richmond was taken. His wish was gratified.

He married January 5, 1804, Keziah Doane, daughter of Azariah and Polly Doane, and descendant of the emigrant John Doane (1), through Daniel Doane (2), Joseph Doane (3), Joshua Doane (4) father of Azariah Doane (5). She died at Orleans, September 20, 1869. Children were: 1 Jesse, born September 30, 1804, died March 16, 1806. 2 Bethiah, December 4, 1806, died October 10, 1808. 3 Meriel, December 25, 1808. 4 Alonzo (see forward). 5 Dorinda, January 19, 1814. 6 Keziah Doane, July 1, 1817. 7 Elisha, June 12, 1820. 8 Mary Doane, July 16, 1822. 9 Sally, April 8, 1825. 10 Mark, November 12, 1826, died July 21, 1849. 11 Benjamin, February 10, 1830.

(VII) Alonzo Cole, fourth child of Elisha Cole (6), was born at Orleans, Massachusetts, March 4, 1812. He received a common school education in the schools of his native town. He shipped before the mast when very young and followed the sea for many years. He was captain of various vessels. He was part owner of his last vessel, a barque, the Clara C. Bell. His wife wished to accompany him on one of his voyages, and against the wishes of her parents and friends she went with him on a voyage south, taking with her their only child, Alonzo Williams. While in port at Charleston, South Carolina, she was stricken with yellow fever and died. He determined to bury the body of his wife in Orleans. He succeeded in evading the quarantine officers until he reached Boston, where some of the crew informed the authorities and he was fined for evading the quarantine laws. But he succeeded finally in getting the body buried in the old graveyard in Orleans after much difficulty. It cost him fully a thousand dollars to carry out his purpose.

Mr. Cole was a Universalist in religion and a Republican in politics. He was a Free Mason. He married August 20, 1839, Melissa Smith, daughter of William and Abigail (Doane) Smith, of Orleans. William Smith was also a sea captain. Their only child was Alonzo Williams Cole (see forward).

(VIII) Alonzo Williams Cole, only child of Alonzo Cole (7), was born in Orleans, Massachusetts, March 13, 1844. He attended the common schools at Orleans until seventeen, when he went to East Somerville, Massachusetts, and lived with his aunt while attending the Somerville high school. He returned to Orleans, but after a short time removed to Worcester, where he lived with another aunt, Mrs. A. E. Peck, for about three years and worked in the art store of his uncle at first. Then he decided to learn the trade of machinist and entered the Loom works of George Crompton for that purpose. After a year and a half he went to work for L. W. Pond as a machinist. He was working there during the war. He left the shop to enlist July 12, 1864, in Company E, Forty-second Massachusetts Infantry. The company was on guard duty in the city of Washington and vicinity. They were stationed at Great Falls, Maryland. He was mustered out November 11, 1864.

Upon his return home, he went to work again for L. W. Pond and became a journeyman machinist in about a year and a half. He accepted a position at Piedmont, West Virginia, as mechanic for the Baltimore & Ohio Railroad, but after a year there his health obliged him to give up the work. He became foreman for Richardson & Merriam, and later for McIver Bros., who succeeded the former firm. He remained in a responsible relation to this firm for twenty-five years. He worked for Marcus Mason & Co., makers of plantation machinery, and the Stowe Shoe Machinery Company for three years. He has been for several years tool-maker for the A. Burlingame Company, manufacturers of engines. He ranks well among the expert mechanics and skilled machinists of a city that has few rivals in this respect. Mr. Cole is a man of retiring disposition, greatly attached to his home and business interests. He is highly respected in the church and community that knows him. He is an active member and one of the trustees of the Trobridge Memorial Methodist Church. In politics he is a Republican.

He married Ellen Lucretia Berry, August 6, 1867, at Worcester, Massachusetts. She was the daughter of Zebina and Lucretia H. (Culver) Berry, of Worcester. They have one child, Arthur Williams Cole, born in Worcester, February 17, 1875, married January 23, 1903, Emma Louise Taylor, daughter of Robert C. Taylor, formerly of Webster, Massachusetts. He was educated in the Worcester schools, graduate of the high school, also the Worcester Polytechnic Institute, is at present professor in the State University of Maine, near Bangor.

CYRENUS ALDRICH. George Aldrich (I) was the emigrant ancestor of Cyrenus Aldrich of Worcester, Massachusetts. He came in 1631 from Derbyshire, England, to America, and settled first in Dorchester in New England. In 1640 he was in Braintree, and in 1663 he was among the first seven to arrive in the town of Mendon. He married in England September 3, 1629, Katherine Seald. She was born in 1610 according to a deposition made in 1670. He died March 1, 1683. His will was dated at Mendon, November 2, 1682, and was proved April 26, 1683. The children of George and Katherine Aldrich were: Abel, Joseph, Mary, Miriam, Experience, John, Sarah, married a Mr. Bartlett; Peter, Mercy, married a Mr. Randall; Jacob, see forward; Martha, married a Mr. Dunbar.

(II) Jacob Aldrich, son of George Aldrich (1), was born February 28, 1652. He married November 3, 1675, Huldah Thayer. He died February 22, 1695. Their children were: Jacob, Abel, Seth, Huldah, Rachel, Sarah, David, see forward; Peter, John, Moses, Mercy and Rachel.

(III) David Aldrich, seventh child of Jacob Aldrich (2), was born in Mendon, Massachusetts, May 3, 1685. He married (first) Hannah Capron, who died February 20, 1732. He married (second) Mehitable ———. The children of David and Hannah (Capron) Aldrich were: David, Edward, Elizabeth, Jonathan, Peter, Jonathan, Margaret, Abner, Levi, see forward; and Ichabod. David Aldrich died March 15, 1771.

(IV) Levi Aldrich, ninth child of David Aldrich (3), was born in Mendon, Massachusetts, December 10, 1729. He married February 7, 1745, Abigail Hunt. He died December 22, 1795. Their children were: Rufus, Nathan, Levi, Nathaniel, Amasa, see forward; Chloe, Phineas, Abigail, Luther, Calvin and David.

(V) Amasa Aldrich, fifth child of Levi Aldrich (4), was born in Mendon, Massachusetts, June 13,

1760 He married, November 1, 1780, Urana Paine She was born September 17, 1763, and died February 11, 1843 He died December 2, 1813 His widow married (second) Gen Philemon Whitcomb, of Swanzey, New Hampshire Amasa Aldrich went from Mendon to Swanzey after the revolution The children of Amasa and Urana (Paine) Aldrich were Marmaduke, born August 13, 1781, Mary, May 27, 1783, Urana, March 3, 1785, Phineas, May 20, 1787, Amasa, March 18, 1789, Paine, see forward, Rufus, January 20, 1793, died 1798, Otis, July 6, 1795, died 1798, David September 6, 1797, Anna, August 31, 1799, Paul Fisher, December 26, 1801, Jacob, March 3, 1804, died 1804, John Langdon, March 27, 1805, Jethro, May 14, 1807, died 1807, William, October 20, 1808

(VI) Paine Aldrich, sixth child of Amasa Aldrich (5), was born in Swanzey, New Hampshire, January 4, 1791 He married (first), February 18, 1813, Sarah (Sally) Hammond, daughter of Joseph Hammond She was born June 17, 1793 Paine Aldrich was brought up in his native town and attended the schools there After his marriage he removed to Richmond, New Hampshire, where he bought the Cook Mills at North Richmond and repaired and built them over While there he invented the turntable for railroads, and in 1830 he came to Worcester to manufacture turntables During the early period of railroad building in the United States and in fact from the thirties until the time of his death Mr Aldrich had a large demand for his contrivance for turning around locomotives, cheaply and quickly He built his shop first where the Aldrich House stands near Aldrich Place He associated with him in the business his son Cyrenus Aldrich He invested largely in Worcester real estate He bought pasture land in the vicinity of Pleasant street and on both sides of High street between Pleasant and Chatham streets He built brick houses on the street opposite his works For a time he lived in a house on the site of the present Hotel Newton Later he built a fine house on the present site of Hotel Adams He owned large tracts of land on Chatham, Clinton and Irving streets, and in that section of the city which became very valuable as the period of rapid growth which made the town a city came in the forties, and they became in time some of the most valuable residential property in the city He died August, 1871, and the business ceased to exist soon afterward Another patent iron turntable took the place of the Aldrich design, but at that time there was practically no railroad in the country that did not have the Aldrich turntable in use They were built in Worcester and shipped in sections to all parts of the country and exported to foreign lands Mr Aldrich acquired large wealth for his day and invested it wisely

Mr Aldrich was modest and retiring in disposition, notwithstanding his material successes and his position in the business world and was highly esteemed and respected in the community During his last years he was in feeble health and was confined to his bed for a year before he died He attended the First Universalist Church and later the Salem Square Congregational Church while Rev Mr Richardson was pastor In politics he was a Whig later a Republican but never active in party affairs and never sought office He was a member of no secret societies He was a member of the Worcester County Mechanics Association He married (second) Sophia Capron, widow, who survived him The children of Paine and Sarah (Hammond) Aldrich were Harriet see forward, Cyrenus, see forward

(VII) Harriet Aldrich, daughter of Paine Aldrich (6), was born in Swanzey, New Hampshire She married Erastus Metcalt, of Rindge, New Hampshire, and they afterwards lived in Fitzwilliam, New Hampshire, where she died June 2 1865 The children of Erastus and Harriet (Aldrich) Metcalf were 1 Elizabeth, born November 13 1835, married Benoni Fullam, son of Judge Fullam, of Ludlow, Vermont 2 Sarah Jane, born February 9 1838, married James F Kettell, of Worcester, and had four children Jennie Maria, born October 2, 1863, married George F Hutchins, of Worcester, and had one child, Richard, born April 28, 1881, Henry James Kettell, born April 19, 1869, married Mary Goodwin, of Worcester, and had two children James, born August 23, 1898, and Katherine Kettell, born July 25, 1905 John Frederick Kettell, born November 29, 1865, deceased, Frank Kettell, born January 26, 1873, married Maud Barnes, no children 3 Melissa Metcalf, born February 8, 1840, married George W Davis, of Hudson, Massachusetts, and had two children George Fred Davis, unmarried, Fannie Melissa Davis, married Ralph Joslyn, of Hudson Massachusetts, and has three children Ralph Davis Joslyn, Mary Joslyn, and James Metcalf Joslyn 4 Hammond Cyrenus Metcalf, born January 9, 1842, unmarried 5 Helen Sophia Metcalf born February 21, 1846, married Henry F Smith, of Woburn, Massachusetts and had three children Henry, Caroline and Ralph

(VII) Cyrenus Aldrich, only son of Paine Aldrich (6), was born in Swanzey, New Hampshire, September 24, 1815 He attended the schools of that town He was raised on the old farm in the same town with "Joshua Whitcomb," and worked with his father on the homestead, in the mill and in the turntable business The firm of Paine Aldrich & Son was formed when Cyrenus was still a young man The junior member of the firm superintended the construction of the turntables and set them up for the railroads They were made in Worcester and shipped in sections As his father's health began to fail in the sixties he gradually assumed charge of the entire business At the close of the civil war his father retired from business on account of his health and he also discontinued the business The last three turntables were made and set up in New Brunswick, for European and North American Railroad

Mr Aldrich retired from active business and gave his time to his investments, and property He attended the old Pleasant Street Baptist Church which stood where the present Lothrop's Opera House stands He was a quiet and unassuming, amiable and democratic in his disposition He devoted all his time to his business and his home He was a Republican after the party was organized He was a member of the Worcester County Mechanics Association and of the old Worcester Light Infantry and later of the Veteran Association He married February 25, 1845 Sarah Patch daughter of William W and Sarah (Willard) Patch, of Worcester William Patch was a prosperous farmer He was the son of Joseph and Hannah (Flagg) Patch of Worcester, and was born January 1 1794 (See sketch of Hartshorn Family for his ancestry) Both Willard and Patch families date from the early settlement of New England

The children of Cyrenus and Sarah (Patch) Aldrich were 1 Eldora Metella born September 16 1846 is living at the homestead, 22 High street Worcester unmarried 2 William Paine, born December 18 1848 married Charlotte Gibb of New York city October 16 1876 and had four children Grace Eldora Aldrich born November 9

1877, married William Sumner Radway, of Richmond, Virginia, and they have two children, Albert Beverly Radway, born July 12, 1902, and Charles Aldrich Radway, born December 4, 1903 William Paine Aldrich, Jr, born July 26, 1879, unmarried, Sarah Alice Aldrich, born September 26, 1881, died April, 1883, Edith Marion Aldrich born July 24 1885, unmarried William Paine is the proprietor of a large cloth printing business plant located at Passaic, New Jersey, and an office in New York city, also a bleaching and dyeing plant at Delawanna, New Jersey 3 Frank Edgar, born May 20, 1854, was associated with his brother in the cloth printing business in New York city, died December 2, 1903, married Louise M Love, of Providence, Rhode Island, and had one child, Roger Cyrenus Aldrich born February 13, 1879, who married May Locke, of Brooklyn, but now living at Reading Pennsylvania They have two children Roger Williams, born October 12, 1902, and Harold Locke, born November 12, 1905 Cyrenus Aldrich died January 12, 1889

GEORGE FARNUM HEWETT William Hewett (I) great-grandfather of George F Hewett, of Worcester is believed to be a descendant of Thomas Hewett who was a proprietor of Hingham, Massachusetts, 1647, settled in Uxbridge among the pioneers of that town bought land in Sutton, February 25 1779 and other parcels later, and resided in Sutton the latter part of his life He bought land in Ward (now Auburn) in 1803 of Eliphalet and Tamar Holman, and his sons Daniel and William Hewett lived there several years He married Patience ——— Their children were 1 William Jr, see forward 2 Daniel 3 Phinehas 4 Alanson 5 Henry 6 A daughter, married a Cummings, and had Sabrina and Abel Cummings 7 Hammond Jewett 8 Patience, married ——— Blackman 9 Rhoda, married Hammond 10 Eli, residuary legatee

(II) William Hewett, son of William Hewett (1), born in Sutton, now Northbridge, Massachusetts August 1, 1778 died at Grafton, Vermont, 1850 married in Uxbridge, January 14 1802, Lurany Leonard Paine, born in Uxbridge, January 1, 1777, died at Northbridge, February 29, 1806 He married (second) Nabby (or Abigail), daughter of Francis and Sally Holman, of Millbury, before December 15, 1808 He had one son, Elbridge, by the first marriage, see forward His other children were Lurania, born in Sutton, March 13, 1809 recorded in Auburn Sally born in Northbridge (recorded in Auburn), June 11 1811, Francis Holman born in Auburn, May 29 1814

(III) Elbridge Hewett, son of William Hewett, Jr (2), born in Sutton now Northbridge Massachusetts, August 11 1804 died in Worcester, March 17, 1877 married in Grafton February 20, 1827, Nancy Wadsworth He resided in Grafton where he owned a farm About the time of his marriage he removed to Worcester and opened a store at the corner of Central and Summer streets He kept a general store including West India goods and later added a lumber yard on Central street near the Blackstone canal, which was then in full operation He dealt extensively in lumber and wood in the adjoining towns He owned the last canal boat which ran on the Blackstone canal His son, George F Hewett, has an interesting oil painting showing the location of the store and vicinity seventy-five years ago before the railroads had begun to alter the map of Worcester The great industries of Worcester started in the very neighborhood of this store and many of them have outgrown the locality The brick factories and mills in this neighborhood are among the oldest landmarks of the city Mr Hewett had the contract with merchants to water the streets of Worcester when conditions warranted it He had a farm at Northville, in Worcester About 1860 he removed his store from Central street to the corner of Glue and Hanover streets, where later his son erected a brick block Children of Elbridge and Nancy (Wadsworth) Hewett 1 Andrew Fuller, died unmarried 2 Mary L, married John Wheeler, resided in Grafton, where she now lives, a widow, he was a shoe manufacturer 3 Caroline, died in Grafton, unmarried 4 George Farnum, see forward

(IV) George Farnum Hewett, son of Elbridge Hewett (3), was born in Worcester, Massachusetts, July 5, 1836 He was educated in Worcester in the public schools, the high school and Worcester Academy, where he studied several terms He worked for a time in his father's store, but in 1854 decided to follow the advice of Horace Greeley, went west and found employment on the Cleveland & Toledo Railroad, now the Michigan Southern, beginning as a brakeman, and was promoted to various positions during the six years he remained with the company About 1857, when serving as station agent at a new railroad junction first called Clay Junction, he had the privilege of naming the town that sprang up there He called it Millbury, and it has since grown into a thriving town of considerable importance It is about eight miles from Toledo, Ohio Mr Hewett built a saw mill there In the fall of 1859 Mr Hewett left the railroad business and returned to Worcester He was associated with his father for a time but in 1860 started in business for himself, laying the foundation for the extensive interests of which he has since been the head He began with a shop on Front street, in the rear of a store in the Front Street Theatre building. Three years later he took the store now occupied by Hall & Lyon, druggists, and extended his business to the wholesale and retail liquor trade He removed a few years later to a large store on the corner of Foster and Waldo streets, near the present location In 1899 the business was removed to the present location at 41, 43 and 45 Waldo street, to a building especially erected for Mr Hewett by the heirs of Dwight Foster It has a frontage of one hundred feet on Waldo street and a depth of one hundred and twenty-five feet extending through to Commercial street, having a height of four stories in front and five at the rear The building and plant was constructed from plans designed specially to handle the business to the best advantage The product of the George F Hewett Company bottling works is the largest of any in New England, and the plant and equipment is the largest and best The George F Hewett Company deals in ales, lager and porter bottled at the shop, also in the leading brands of bourbon and rye whiskies, imported wines and cordials, and Continental gin The business of bottling gives employment to a hundred men Already the spacious quarters are overtaxed, and an addition is being built The business was incorporated in 1891 as the George F Hewett Company, with a capital of $50,000, George F Hewett president and treasurer

Mr Hewett has not allowed business to engross his time completely He is one of the best known Free Masons of Worcester, having taken all the degrees in the Scottish Rite, and having held the chairs in all the degrees He is a member of Quinsigamond Lodge Hiram Council St Andrews Chapter the Boston Commandery, Knights Templar, and was at the head of the Worcester Lodge of

George F. Hewitt

Perfection for five years He holds the rank of captain in the Ancient and Honorable Artillery Company of Boston, and having been over twenty-five years a member is on the veteran list He was one of the charter members of the Worcester Continentals He is a member of the Worcester Elks the Royal Arcanum and the Red Men In politics he has always been a Democrat, except from 1896 to 1900 when he voted against Bryanism and free silver He was in the board of aldermen one year and the common council for eight years He represented Ward 3 in the council and Ward 7 in the board of aldermen, served on the finance committee, and was deeply interested in the City Hospital, of which he was a trustee Mr Hewett married, 1858, at Painesville, Ohio, Maria L Knox, whose mother married (second) Elbridge Hewett, at Stafford Springs, Connecticut They have had one child Mabel E, born September, 1860, married Charles F Bigelow, of Worcester, lately deceased, and had one daughter, Helen Bigelow, now living in Worcester with her mother at her home, 69 Cedar street Mr Hewett resides at the Standish Hotel, 767 Main street, Worcester

WADSWORTH FAMILY Christopher Wadsworth (I), one of the early settlers of Cambridge, Massachusetts, was an emigrant ancestor of George Farnum Hewett, of Worcester, through his mother's line Christopher Wadsworth is believed to have been the son of Thomas Wadsworth, from the records in a Bible he brought with him and which is now owned by the Cowles family in Hartford, Connecticut He was born in England, and is believed to have come in the same ship with William Wadsworth, who may have been his brother William came in the ship "Lion," which sailed Sunday, September 16, 1632, with one hundred and twenty-three passengers, of which fifty were children After a twelve weeks voyage the ship touched at Cape Ann, and five days later landed in Boston William settled in Cambridge, and in 1636 removed to Hartford Christopher lived and died at Duxbury He was a prominent citizen in a town where such prominent men as Miles Standish, Elder Brewster and John Alden lived He married Grace Cole He was the first constable, then an office of more importance relatively than the sheriff is now, was deputy to general court, selectman and highway surveyor at various times The first record mentioning his name at Duxbury is under date of 1633 In 1638 he drew land in Holly Swamp and the site of his house is west of Captain's Hill, near the new road to Kingston, his lands ran clear to the bay, on what was formerly known as Morton's Hole The homestead remained in the family until 1855 when it was sold The will of Christopher, dated July 31 1677 was filed September, 1678 Of his four children, Joseph and John lived and died in Duxbury, Captain Samuel removed to Milton and was killed by the Indians in the fight at Sudbury, 1676 The children were 1 Mary married —— Andrews 2 John born 1638, died 1700, married Abigail Andrews, 1667, she died 1723, he lived on the old homestead of Christopher, was deacon of the church at Duxbury many years, had eleven children 3 Joseph, born 1636, died 1689 married Abigail Wait 1655 second wife was Mary, six children 4 Samuel probably the eldest son

(II) Captain Samuel Wadsworth, son of Christopher Wadsworth (1), probably born 1630, lived at Bridgewater then Duxbury plantation where he was a taxpayer in 1655 to 1665 About 1655 he married Abigail Lundall, of Duxbury He occupied the land at Bridgewater owned by his father, and had a sixty-fourth interest in the township His son Timothy succeeded his grandfather as owner in 1686 Captain Samuel and his brother Joseph Wadsworth owned land at Bridgewater longer than any others of the early settlers after they moved away from the town Captain Samuel bought a beautiful tract of land in Dorchester in what is now Milton, about 1660 The farm was between the Blue Hills, Milton, and Boston Some of this property is now or was recently owned by descendants, having been in the family ever since the first settlement Captain Samuel was a man of means and influence, active in church and state His descendants of the name of Wadsworth are more numerous than those of any of his brothers He had six sons He was a soldier in King Philip's war, in command of the Milton company In April, 1676, he was ordered to Marlboro with fifty men to strengthen the garrison in that town On the way thither his command passed through Sudbury, where the Indians were in hiding After Captain Wadsworth reached Marlboro he learned that the Indians had attacked the settlement at Sudbury and burned the houses on east side of the Sudbury river The Watertown soldiers under Captain Hugh Mason checked the enemy, but Wadsworth hurried to his relief without waiting for his men to rest, though they had marched all day and all night before Captain Brocklebank went with the company and some of the Marlboro garrison Captain Wadsworth and his men were ambushed by about five hundred Indians, with the usual war-whoops and savage attack After a desperate struggle for five hours Wadsworth had lost five men, the Indians had lost more than a hundred But as night approached the Indians set fire to the dry grass, the smoke blinding the colonists and they were obliged to abandon their sheltered position and were literally cut to pieces Captain Wadsworth, covered with wounds, it is said, was one of the last to fall Thirty men, including Captain Brocklebank, Captain Wadsworth and two other officers were slain, and were buried in one grave The twenty who escaped found refuge in a mill that had been fortified and were rescued by Captain Prentice and Captain Crowell Five or six were taken prisoners and tortured to death by fire The date of this fight was April, 1676 some authorities giving the 18th, others the 21st Captain Wadsworth is described as "that resolute, stout-hearted soldier, one worthy to live in our history under the name of a good man" The first monument to him and his comrades in arms buried on the battle field at Sudbury was erected by his son, President Wadsworth, of Harvard College On November 27 1852, a monument built by the joint action of the commonwealth of Massachusetts and the town of Sudbury was dedicated At that time the twenty-nine bodies were all found, the marks of the wounds showing in some cases after a lapse of nearly two hundred years Children of Captain Samuel Wadsworth 1 Christopher, born 1661 died 1687 (his grave is marked by the oldest stone in the graveyard at Milton) 2 Ebenezer, see forward 3 Timothy born 1662 4 Joseph born 1667 5 Benjamin, born 1670 6 Abigail, born 1672, married A Boardman 7 John, born 1674, died 1734

(III) Ebenezer Wadsworth, son of Captain Samuel Wadsworth (2), was among the early settlers of Milton, Massachusetts, where he was born, 1660, died 1717 He married Mary ——, and their children were 1 Mary born 1684, married —— Simpson 2 Samuel born 1685, was lieutenant in Milton company died 1754 married Ann Withington 3 Recompense, see forward 4 George, born 1698, in Milton died 1778, married Hannah Pitcher, was farmer and miller at Stoughton, Massachusetts, ensign in Captain Goffe's company in French war, had seven children

(IV) Recompense Wadsworth, son of Ebenezer Wadsworth (3), born at Milton, 1688, died 1729, married Sarah Morey, their children 1 Sarah, born 1715, died 1728 2 Mary, born 1718, married Jeremiah Tucker 3 David, see forward 4 Jonathan, born 1722 at Roxbury, removed from Milton about 1755, died 1798 (gored to death by a bull), married 1742, Rebecca Davenport, of Milton, born in Roxbury, 1723, ten children

(V) David Wadsworth, son of Recompense Wadsworth (4) born in Milton, 1720, died December 5 1749, in Grafton, Massachusetts, where he removed and settled, married Hannah Paul, their children 1 David, see forward 2 Ebenezer born August 20, 1745, in Milton married Lucy —— and Patience Swift 3 Samuel, born September 28, 1747, at Grafton died 1842, married Margery Hutchinson, seven children 4 Sarah, married Joseph Merriam

(VI) David Wadsworth, son of David Wadsworth (5), born at Grafton, 1741, died 1821, married Elizabeth Whipple, born 1744, died October 31, 1827, their children 1 Susannah, born at Grafton September 13, 1765, married Peter Farnum 2 David, born July 5, 1767, scythe manufacturer at Barre, Massachusetts married Virtue Willard 3 Jonathan, see forward 4 John, born July 18, 1771, settled at Barre, died 1833, married Lois Warren, twelve children 5 Jacob, born August 24 1773, died April 11, 1774 6 Samuel born June 18, 1775, died 1812, married Elizabeth Barnes 7 Ebenezer, born June 24, 1777, died August 5 1777 8 Moses, born October 30, 1778, married Elizabeth Tisdale, and removed to Walpole, Massachusetts 9 Paul, born February 9, 1781 died December 16, 1783 10 Joseph born March 29 1784 scythe manufacturer at Auburn, New York, married Anna Barnes, died 1854

(VII) Jonathan Wadsworth, son of David Wadsworth (6), born at Grafton in the section now called Farnumsville, May 23 1769, died 1850 He married in Grafton, 1790, Tabitha, born in Grafton May 8 1772 died in 1853, daughter of Captain Joseph Warren (See Warren Family) Children of Jonathan and Tabitha (Warren) Wadsworth 1 Mary born November 19, 1790 married James Martin died June 15 1833 2 Sally, born August 24, 1794 married Paul Farnum, died April 9 1829, Boston 3 Nancy see forward 4 David, born 1800 died young 5 David, born October 20, 1803, South Boston, married, December 8, 1825, Caroline Metcalf nine children 6 Eliza Ann, born June 9, 1806, married Zephaniah Frost 7 Lucina, born May 5 1808 married Adolphus Fowler 1829 8 Susan born June 3 1810 married Calvin Taft 1834, died October 23 1837 9 Jonathan, born October 30 1816 died June 3, 1833

(VIII) Nancy Wadsworth daughter of Jonathan Wadsworth (7), born March 11 1798 died December 29 1830 married Elbridge Hewett

WARREN FAMILY John Warren (I) was an emigrant ancestor of George Farnum Hewett, of Worcester, through his mother's mother's line John Warren came to America in 1630 at the age of forty-five He was born in England therefore, in 1585 He settled in Watertown, Massachusetts where he was made freeman May 18, 1631 In 1635 he and Abraham Browne were appointed to lay out highways and see that they were repaired His homestall of twelve acres drawn 1642, was bounded by the homestalls of William Hammond, John Biscoe and Isaac Sterne, and he had seven other lots, amounting in all to one hundred and seventy-six acres He sympathized with the Quakers, and was at odds with the Puritan church In October, 1651, he and Thomas Arnold were fined for an offense against the laws concerning baptism He was warned March 14, 1658-9, for not attending church, and later fined for neglecting to go to church fourteen Sabbaths, at the rate of twenty shillings each May 27 1661, his house was searched for Quakers His neighbor Hammond was also suspected of harboring the persecuted Quakers His wife Margaret died November 6 1662 He died December 13, 1667, aged eighty-two His will, dated November 30, 1667, was proved December 17, 1667 His children, all born in England were 1 John, see forward 2 Mary, born in England, married, October 30, 1642, John Bigelow 3 Daniel, born 1628, took the oath of fidelity, 1652 4 Elizabeth, married about 1654 James Knapp

(II) Captain John Warren, son of John Warren (1), was born in England 1622 He took a prominent part in town affairs at Watertown, was selectman in 1676 during the war His will is dated January 12, 1702-3, and proved February 22 same year He married, July 11, 1667, Michal widow of Richard Bloys and daughter of Robert Jennison She died July 14 1713 Their children 1 Margaret, born May 6 1668 died unmarried, 1703 2 Sarah, born January 25 1670-1 3 Elizabeth born July 8, 1673, married October 18 1705 Daniel Harrington 4 Mary, born May 25 1675, married December 30, 1698 Joseph Peirce 5 John born May 21, 1678 6 Grace born May 12 1679-80, died unmarried, January, 1703 7 Samuel, born January 23 1683, married Lydia Cutting he died November 13, 1759, she died July 15 1766

(III) John Warren son of Captain John Warren (2), settled in Weston He married first, Abigail Hastings died July 19, 1710, second May 14, 1711, Lydia Fiske His estate was administered by his wife Lydia, appointed July 29 1726 She married (second) in Watertown June 17, 1730, Benjamin Harrington Children of John and Abigail (Hastings) Warren were 1 John born April 3, 1701, a blacksmith at Marlboro 2 Sarah, born September 20 1702 married, October 29, 1725, Samuel Harrington 3 Samuel, see forward 4 Thomas, born March 11 1705-6, married, 1727, Lydia Mixer 5 David born June 22 1708 married, June 22, 1733, Martha Coolidge 'Jr" 6 Lydia born 1712 7 Benjamin, born April 4 1715 8 David, born January 5 1716-7 9 Abigail, born October 28, 1719 10 Lucy born October 26, 1721 11 William, born October 21, 1723, died 1739 12 John, baptized 1725

(IV) Captain Samuel Warren, son of John Warren (3) born March 18 1703-4, died January 26, 1775 Captain Samuel Warren came to Grafton from Weston in 1730 He was one of the original members of the church there His daughter Sarah was the first white child born in the town of Grafton His house was a log cabin at first nearly opposite Chapin's Lane He was captain of a company that marched to the relief of Fort William Henry, March 25, 1757 He married, at Weston, Massachusetts August 26 1728, Tabitha, born 1702, died April 21 1765 daughter of Joseph and Sarah (Waite) Stone Their children 1 Samuel born April 20 1730 married May 29 1754 Eunice Corbet of Mendon 2 Sarah, born December 24, 1731, married Phineas Leland 3 Rebecca, born April 16, 1733 4 Abigail, born April 29, 1735 5 John born

August 8, 1736, died September 8, 1755 6 Tabitha, born August 6 1738, died September 7, 1754 7 William born May 29, 1740, removed to Conway 8 David, born March 24, 1742, married Prudence Whipple 9 Joseph, see forward 10, Martha born May 31, 1747

(V) Captain Joseph Warren, son of Captain Samuel (4), born April 22, 1743, died July 19, 1808, married, March 28, 1765, Lois Lyon born 1746, died February 7, 1816 In February, 1763, he was a private in Captain Ebenezer Cox's regiment in His Majesty's service He was sergeant in Captain Luke Drury's company He responded to the Lexington call In April, 1776, he was made second lieutenant in Captain Nathaniel Sherman's company, Colonel John Goulding's regiment He marched August 1, 1777, with his company to the relief of Bennington Children of Captain Joseph Warren 1 Samuel, born December 7, 1765, married —— Stow, and (second) Widow Crowninshield, removed to Wethersfield, Connecticut 2 John, born November 28, 1767, married Polly Chapin and Susannah Grout 3 Sally, born November 30 1769, married Gardner Brown, of Sutton November, 1791 4 Tabitha, see forward 5 Lois, born June 14, 1779, married, November 12, 1797, John Wadsworth 6 Phila, born February 21 1783, married March 12, 1801, Nathaniel Whipple 7 Delphia, born November 3 1786, died 1869 unmarried

(VI) Tabitha Warren daughter of Captain Joseph Warren (5), married Jonathan Wadsworth She was the mother of Mrs Elbridge Hewett, mother of George F Hewett (See Wadsworth Family and George F Hewett)

PAINE FAMILY Stephen Paine (1), from whom so many of the families of the name in America traces their descents, was an emigrant ancester of George Farnum Hewett, of Worcester through his father's mother, Mrs William Hewett The substance of the following account of the family is taken from a sketch written some years ago by Nathaniel Paine, vice-president of the Worcester Trust Company, who also wrote the history of the Paine family in Worcester

Stephen Paine was descended from a family of Great Ellingham, a parish in the Hundred of Shropham, near Hingham, Norfolk county, England He was a miller by trade He came to New England with a large party from Hingham and vicinity in 1638, in the ship "Diligent," John Martin, master, with a family consisting of his wife, three sons and four servants There are records subsequently of only two sons, however One died early or returned to England Paine settled at Hingham, in Plymouth Colony where he had land grants He was admitted a freeman in 1639, and elected a deputy to general court 1641 In 1641-2 he and four others obtained leave of general court to settle Seekonk, and he removed to that place, which was afterward called Rehoboth in 1643-4 There he became prominent, holding many offices of honor and trust, was made a townsman, an office of some importance, 1644, in 1645 he was again sent to the general court and continued to represent Seekonk, until 1660 also held various town offices until 1671 He became a founder of the town of Attleboro, Massachusetts in 1661, he and his sons Stephen and Nathaniel being among those who bought Attleboro of the Indians They also owned the tract which includes the present town of Swansea, Massachusetts and Barrington, Rhode Island

Stephen Paine died in August, 1679, outliving both his sons His first wife died January 20, 1660 He married (second) Alice, widow of William Parker of Plymouth and Taunton Massachusetts She died December 5 1682 His children Nathaniel and Stephen both born in England

(II) Stephen Paine, son of Stephen Paine (1), born 1629, in Norfolk county, England, was nine years old when he came to New England with his folks He settled with them at Hingham, and removed with them to Rehoboth in 1643-4 He became a prominent citizen there, taking the oath of fidelity in 1657 He was a tanner by trade He was active in town affairs and held a number of offices He may have resided a few years at Swansea, where he and his father owned land He was active in King Philip's war under Major William Bradford, as a soldier and also as a contributor to the war fund He died at Rehoboth, January 1677-8 His wife Anne married (second) Thomas Metcalf, of Rehoboth Children of Stephen and Ann Paine 1 Stephen, born September 29, 1651, married Elizabeth, daughter of Rev Ebenezer Williams, of Taunton, married (second) Mary Brintnall, August 12, 1707, was deputy to general court 1694 and 1703 2 Rebecca, born October 20, 1656, married, December 24, 1673, Peter Hunt, Jr , married (second) Samuel Peck, November 21, 1677 3 John, born April 3, 1658, resided at Swansea, 1683, surveyor of highways there 1686, married Elizabeth Belcher and had large family 4 Mary, born May 11, 1660 married October 29 1678-9, Enoch Hunt, of Reboboth 5 Samuel, born, at Rehoboth, May 12, 1662, married Anne Peck, of Rehoboth, December 16, 1685, married (second) Mrs Abigail Fussell of Woonsocket, removed 1708 from Rehoboth to Woonsocket, Rhode Island 6 Elizabeth, born August 27, 1664, married February 10 1685 Jacob Pepper 7 Sarah born October 12, 1666, died April 17, 1711, married, November 23, 1688, Daniel Alden 8 Nathaniel born September 20, 1667, married May 1, 1694, Dorothy Chaffee

(III) Samuel Paine, son of Stephen Paine (2), born at Rehoboth, August 12, 1662, married December 16, 1685, Anne Peck, born December 22, 1667, at Rehoboth, daughter of Deacon Samuel and Sarah (Hunt) Peck Sarah Hunt was daughter of Peter Hunt, Sr., and granddaughter of Enoch Hunt, the emigrant Joseph Peck, grandfather of Anne, came over in the "Diligent" with Stephen Paine from old Hingham Norfolk county, England, with his family and servants Anne (Peck) Paine died February 26, 1703, soon after the birth of Daniel her last child Samuel married second (intentions January 18, 1708-9), Abigail, daughter of —— Bartholomew, widow of Joseph Frizzell She was admitted in full communion in the church May 5 1728, died January 13, 1752, aged seventy-nine Samuel died May 11, 1735 The graves of Samuel and his wives are marked by stones in the old graveyard at East Providence, Rhode Island Children of Samuel 1 Samuel, born September 13, 1686 removed to Pomfret, Connecticut, 1705-6, married Ruth, daughter of Abraham and Sarah Perrin, she was born March 30, 1688, probably at Rehoboth, both admitted to church at Pomfret, September, 1719, was on petition for town charter, held office, wife died June 5, 1725, he died February 15, 1725 2 Anne, born September 15 1688, married, March 13, 1717, Peter Hunt, his second wife 3 Seth, born August 20 1690, married Mary Morris, removed to Connecticut 4 Judith, born February 18, 1695, married January 5 1719, Ichabod Peck, of Rehoboth, brother of Ensign Daniel Peck, nine children 5 Noah, born May 28, 1696, married January 13, 1732, Mehitable Storrs, born March 30, 1709 6 Daniel, born February 22, 1702-3 7 Rebecca, born 1710, married, July 4, 1744, Deliverance Cleveland, of Canterbury, Connecticut, where she died 1784 8 Ebenezer, see forward

(IV) Ebenezer Paine, son of Samuel Paine (3), was born 1711 His mother was a granddaughter of John Grosvenor, of Roxbury, who died September 27, 1691 (The only gravestone in the Roxbury, Massachusetts graveyard bearing a coat-of-arms is that of John Grosvenor) He was a tanner and town constable, had property in Pomfret, where his children went in 1700 with his widow She died 1738, aged eighty-seven Ebenezer Paine settled in Woodstock, Connecticut He owned the covenant in 1740, served on several important church committees for the town, admitted freeman 1749, served as constable He died March 29, 1789, aged seventy-eight years, his wife died May 23, 1758 Their children 1 Mary, born at West Woodstock, Connecticut (where all the children were born), September 23, 1737, married May 2, 1769, Moses Perrin, of Woodstock (the records tell us that she died of the bite of a skunk) 2 Ebenezer, Jr, born December 16, 1739, married 1766, Esther, born May 2, 1743, daughter of Samuel Child and Keziah Hutchins of Killingly, Connecticut, mason, removed from Woodstock to Hartland Vermont, where he died April 9, 1795, wife died March 6, 1839, aged ninety-six 3 Leicester, see forward 4 Asa, born September, 1744, married a daughter of Samuel and Keziah Child, settled in Pomfret, Vermont, four sons 5 Stephen, born September 17, 1749, married, May 19, 1795, Martha, daughter of Dr Parker Morse, of Woodstock, Connecticut, held many offices of honor and trust, in 1788 was member Connecticut state convention to ratify federal consitution and voted no, represented Woodstock in legislature and was generally called Deputy Paine, died June, 1820, his wife died January 5, 1825 6 Hannah, born December 23, 1753

(V) Leicester Paine, son of Ebenezer Paine (4), born at West Woodstock, Connecticut, May 11, 1742, removed to Uxbridge, Massachusetts, about 1780, married Elizabeth, daughter of David Draper, who built the house generally known as the Draper House, at Uxbridge He died July 7 1821, aged seventy-nine, she died November 6 1830, aged eighty Children of Leicester Paine 1 Lurana Leonard, see forward 2 Mary Grosvenor born November 19, 1781, Woodstock died unmarried 1832 3 David Draper, born July 26, 1788, married October 23, 1822, Jemima French, of Uxbridge, born 1800 died April 23 1859, joiner by trade, also school teacher, prominent man selectman, assessor, deacon Baptist church, died November 18 1854 eight children

(VI) Lurana Leonard Paine, daughter of Leicester Paine (5), born Woodstock, Connecticut, January 1, 1777, married January 14, 1802, at Uxbridge, Massachusetts, William Hewett Jr He was born August 1, 1770, at Gloucester, Rhode Island His father was William Hewett, of Sutton, Massachusetts Lurana died at Sutton, February 29 1807 Her children, all born at Northbridge, Massachusetts formerly Sutton 1 Elias P Hewett, born 1802, died 1803 2 Elbridge Hewett, born August 11 1804 married, February 20 1828, Nancy Wadsworth, of Grafton Massachusetts, who died 1869, he died March 17, 1777 at Worcester Massachusetts Children 1 Andrew Fuller Hewett born August 29 1829 2 Mary Lurana, born July 16, 1831, married John Wheeler, of Grafton, who died 1881 3 Caroline Hewett, born January 16, 1833; teacher in public schools of Worcester, Massachusetts, many years 4 George Farnum, born July 5, 1836, married Maria L Knox

THAYER FAMILY The original American ancestor of one branch of the Thayer family in New England was Thomas Thayer, who settled in Braintree, Massachusetts, coming from Thornbury, England He married Margery Wheeler, who died December 11, 1672 He died April, 1672 Thomas (1) was a shoemaker, as shown by his will made September 13, 1665 The children of Thomas and Margery were Thomas, Jr, Ferdinando and Shadrach

(II) Ferdinando Thayer, son of Thomas Thayer (1), married Huldah Hayward, of Braintree and settled at Mendon about 1668 where he reared his large family, and died there March 28, 1713 and his wife Huldah, 1690 He had been at Mendon before the King Philip war and his name appears in the minutes of the first town meeting, June, 1667, as selectman Among the lands set off and surveyed for him was one tract in January, 1674, and then after the Indians burned the town, it seems he went back again and re-located and took lands, including a forty acre house-lot, May 26, 1686 They had twelve children about half of them born in Braintree and the latter ones at Mendon Their names were—Sarah, Huldah, Jonathan David died 1674 Naomi, Thomas, Samuel, Isaac Josiah, Ebenezer, Benjamin and David

(III) Benjamin Thayer, son of Ferdinando Thayer (2), born in Mendon, December 20 1712, married (first) Sarah Haywood, (second) Hannah Haywood Youngest child was Aaron, born November 11 1715

(IV) Aaron Thayer, son of Benjamin Thayer (3), married Jemima Cook, in 1738, and they had thirteen children, including one named Benjamin

(V) Benjamin Thayer, born April 16, 1744, son of Aaron Thayer (4), married Sarah Bosworth, of Bellingham July 9, 1767, and they had seven children, including one named Caleb

(VI) Caleb Thayer, son of Benjamin Thayer (5), born January 31, 1770, married Elizabeth Thayer, April 7, 1791, and they had five children including Caleb

(VII) Caleb Thayer, son of Caleb Thayer (6) born January 5 1803 married Hannah Gaskill, May 20, 1827, and they had Adin, born December 5, 1828, Elias Ellis, born April 21, 1832, died 1840 Elizabeth, born June 11 1836

(VIII) Judge Adin Thayer, son of Caleb Thayer (7), was born December 5 1828 His was but a limited educational opportunity He attended the common district schools and later the Worcester Academy Thinking he might follow teaching for a profession, he took a thorough course of training at the Westfield Normal school He had not long tested his fitness and liking for steady school room life, when he decided that the best channel for his success would be that of the legal profession, so he began the study of law with Henry Chapin whom he finally succeeded on the bench. It was in 1854 that Mr Thayer commenced his legal practice at Worcester His judgment being of the soundest type, marked by the plain, practical, common sense he soon rose to a man of more than ordinary importance in Massachusetts While he was an eminent lawyer, his most brilliant work was in the arena of politics and within this field he was pre-eminent Early allied with the Free Soil party, he was eager and earnest in opposition to the en-

croachments of the slave power, and despised the proceedings under the Fugitive Slave Law, as it affected his own native state His relatives were intimate with Hon Charles Sumner and John Andrew He was unselfish and consistent in his devotion to the principles which he believed should actuate and predominate in his state and nation While he might have appreciated high office, he never sulked or faltered because another was chosen to hold such honorable places He became an invaluable adviser among the early day leaders within the Republican party In the truest, best sense he was a strong partisan Believing as he did in justice to all men, he threw himself into the canvass spirited like a brave warrior, determined that the cause should not fail by reason of any neglect upon his part He was a great political organizer and the campaigns he directed were complete in every detail He seldom appeared as a speaker, but when he did his arguments were logical and convincing He held but few offices Under President Lincoln he was internal revenue collector and re-appointed by General Grant Two years he served as state senator In 1878, as chairman of the state committee of the Republican party, he rendered great service The bench was vacated by the death of Judge Chapin in 1878, and Mr Thayer was appointed to succeed him in probate court, and faithfully discharged his duty for ten years In his death in 1888 Massachusetts lost a stanch defender

(IX) Charles Martin Thayer, only child of Judge Adin and Caroline W (Kendrick) Thayer, was born in Worcester, December 4 1866 He was educated in the public schools and Harvard University graduating from the latter institution in 1889 He then entered Harvard Law School, graduating therefrom in 1892, studied law in the office of Hopkins & Bacon, was admitted to the bar in Suffolk county in 1891, and took up his practice in the city of Worcester He is a member of the Worcester County Bar Association He is a director of the Worcester Trust Company at the present time (1905), the Peoples Savings Bank, Crompton & Knowles Loom Works, and the Merchants and Farmers Insurance Company He is the trustee of several large estates He was chairman of the school committee for a period of three years He is the Worcester county attorney for the Boston & Maine Railroad He is a Republican in politics

(VIII) Frederick Thayer, son of Caleb and Hannah (Gaskill) Thayer (7), and the brother of the eminent judge and jurist of Massachusetts, Hon Adin Thayer, was born in Blackstone, Massachusetts He completed his school studies at the academies at Wilbraham and Greenwich He then engaged in teaching for a season and then embarked in trade, a member of the Worcester firm of Thayer & Taft He soon became manager of the Worcester Company of Capitalists, who purchased the mill and power privilege at Blackstone, formerly owned by A T Stewart, of New York Mr Thayer became one of the largest dealers in shoddy and satinet in New England While at Blackstone he represented his district in the general court, two terms—1879-80 For his first wife he married Adelia L. Greene related to General Nathaniel Greene, of revolutionary fame His second wife was a sister of his former companion—Carrie D Greene

(III) Isaac Thayer, son of Ferdinando and Huldah Thayer (2), married (first) Mercy Ward, (second) Mary —, and had eleven children born to him

(IV) Joseph Thayer, son of Isaac Thayer (3), married (first) Sarah Balcome, and (second) Rachel Richardson To Joseph were born twelve children, including John, the fifth child

(V) John Thayer, son of Joseph Thayer (4), married Dasa Richardson, in 1776, and they were the parents of six children, including one named John, Jr

(VI) John Thayer, Jr, son of John Thayer (5) born in 1787, married Ruth Mowry, in 1810, and had three children—Mowry Richardson, Charles Dexter and Aurilla

(VII) Mowry Richardson Thayer, eldest son of John Thayer (6), was born April 27, 1811 Like most farmer boys at that time he received only an ordinary common school education He devoted his life to farming and cutting and marketing wood and timber He was also widely known as a trader, mostly in cattle and horses, and was an excellent judge of both He held many town offices and was by nature highly endowed with practical common sense Had he received a college education he would probably have taken high rank among the prominent men of the state His natural attainments were of a high order, and his opinions and judgment were much sought by his fellow townspeople May 1, 1838, he married Harriet Morse and to them were born three children Chester M, Lucy A, and John Randolph The last named is referred to in a following narrative

(VIII) Hon John Randolph Thayer, ex-congressman, was born in Douglas, Massachusetts, March 9, 1845, son of Mowry Richardson and Harriet (Morse) Thayer (7), and grandson of John and Ruth (Mowry) Thayer Of this line of the Thayer family for three generations down to himself he was the first to choose a professional life

He was left an orphan at the age of fifteen, to which time his school days were passed in his native town At the age of sixteen he became a student at Nichols Academy in Dudley, where he fitted for college In 1865 he entered Yale College, at New Haven, Connecticut, and graduated four years later with far above average standing in his class While at college he took much interest in athletics, and rowed in his class crew He belonged to various college societies, and was quite a favorite among the students

Immediately after his graduation Mr Thayer came to Worcester and at once began the study of law with the law Judge Henry Chapin, and in 1871 was admitted to the bar During his early practice he was associated first with Judge Hartley Williams later with W A Williams and afterward formed a partnership with Charles S Chapin, the firm being styled Thayer & Chapin In 1885 he formed a partnership with Arthur P Rugg, which co-partnership has continued under the name of Thayer & Rugg to the present time From the beginning of his professional life Mr Thayer has enjoyed a lucrative practice and has tried many important cases, including six capital cases Some lawyers succeed best before juries but fail when addressing their argument to the judge alone, but not so with him of whom we write for before the highest courts where strictly legal questions are involved, he has achieved signal success A logical reasoner and well read in law, he commands the attention and respect of the justices of the highest courts Of late years his special practice has been in civil cases

Not unlike other fellow attorneys he early took a deep interest in political affairs He has been in great demand as a campaign speaker for the last thirty years and more, and, gifted by nature as an interesting and impressive orator ever holds the closest attention of his audiences

As an indication of the admiration in which he is held for his manliness of character, it need only be remarked that whenever he has been a candidate for public position, his majorities have been much larger than his party vote would have promised. If one trait be stronger than another in his well-balanced make-up, it is his earnest belief in the civil equality of all men, and their everyday rights, whether as laborer or capitalist. His friendship when once made becomes part of his life, and unfailing as it is strong. His is a true friendship, a genuine fraternal regard not often found among the politicians of modern times.

For four years Mr. Thayer served as a member of the common council in the city of Worcester, and the same number of years on the board of aldermen. For two terms (1880-81) he was a representative in the general court, serving on the judiciary committee, one of the most important in that body. His work was effective among the leaders of the house in both sessions. The people set a high value upon his services, and in 1890 and 1891 he was elected to the state senate, although the senatorial district was naturally Republican by more than two thousand plurality. He ranked among the most active and influential leaders of the senate during both terms of his service. Another evidence of his strong hold upon the regard of his fellow townsmen is afforded in the fact that notwithstanding his city is strongly of another political belief than that which he advocates, when he was nominated for mayor of Worcester he received the largest vote ever given up to that time to a Democratic candidate for that position. When he was put forward as the candidate of his party for a seat in congress, in 1892, against Hon. J. H. Walker, he wanted only seven hundred and eighty-four votes of being elected, while at the same election the Democratic candidate for president ran three thousand behind the Republican nominee in that congressional district. His party friends felt such encouragement that they believed his election to congress could be accomplished, and in 1898 he became a candidate against Mr. Walker, who had held his seat for ten years, and this time Mr. Thayer was elected by a plurality of one hundred and sixty-seven votes, while the Democratic candidate for governor ran more than eight thousand votes behind the Republican candidate in the district.

His conduct while representing his district in congress was not only above reproach, but he acquitted himself so capably and with such integrity as to win the admiration of both political parties. Elected as he was from a Republican district, he never shirked the labors and responsibilities of looking after the best interests of the district at large and of the entire people, and made many personal friends even among his political opponents. His courtesy was extended in behalf of every constituent, regardless of his political affiliations. In brief, the important district which he had the honor to represent in congress enjoyed the services of a clean, honorable, progressive, painstaking and capable advocate during the six years he occupied his seat, he being re-elected twice, the last time with a majority of nearly eight hundred, which was five times the majority he received at his first election. He voluntarily retired at the expiration of his third term, though strongly urged by leading representatives of both political parties to accept another nomination. He was succeeded by Hon. Rockwood Hoar, son of the late lamented Senator George F. Hoar. Mr. Thayer is recognized as one of the most forceful Democratic leaders in Massachusetts, and while he takes much pride in tracing his Democracy through three generations, he is one of the most independent thinkers and actors in public life at the present time.

Mr. Thayer possesses a strong and magnetic personality, and with it great will power, but controlled by a most kindly tempered disposition, enabling him to make and retain the constant friendship of a wide circle of his fellow-men. While his brain is ever active, and his mental powers find constant exercise, he is wise in that he takes occasion to turn from his multiplied duties and care for his physical manhood by interesting himself in various sports and amusements. For twelve years he was president of the Worcester Sportsmen's Club, which comprises in its membership about one hundred and eighty sportsmen who give their attention principally to fox hunting. It cannot be affirmed that he is a society man, for aside from his college fraternities he has never connected himself with any of the many civic, military or secret organizations of his day.

Mr. Thayer is happy in the possession of a most interesting family. He married, January 30, 1872, Charlotte D. Holmes, daughter of Pitt and Diana (Perrin) Holmes. Their six children are: Henry Holmes, born November 25, 1873; John Mowry, January 4, 1875; Charlotte Diana, May 8, 1879; Marguerite Elizabeth, February 2, 1881; Mary Perrin, February 7, 1885; Edward Carrington, October 2, 1893.

(III) Benjamin Thayer, son of Ferdinando (2), by wife Hannah Haywood, had among other children:

(IV) Aaron Thayer, who married Jemima Cook, in 1738. Their son:

(V) Benjamin Thayer, born April 16, 1744, married first Sarah Bosworth, in 1767, and second Ruth Alden, in 1793.

(VI) Cushman Thayer, son of Benjamin Thayer (5), married Miranda Pond in 1818, by whom several children were born.

(VII) Hon. Eli Thayer, son of Cushman Thayer (6), born in Mendon, Massachusetts, June 11, 1819. He is sixth in descent from John Alden, who came in the 'Mayflower,' through Ruth, daughter of Rev. Noah Alden, of Bellingham, who married his grandfather, Benjamin Thayer.

Eli obtained his early education in the old fashioned common schools of Mendon and at Bellingham high school. Later he attended the academy at Amherst and the Manual Labor school, now the Worcester Academy. In 1835-6 he taught a school in Douglas, and the next four years clerked in his father's store in Millville. In 1840 he entered the Manual Labor school to fit for Brown University, and entered as a student there in the autumn of that year. In 1842 he taught school at Hopkinton, Rhode Island. In September, 1844, he took charge of the boys' high school at Providence, receiving $600 for the balance of that year. It had been an unruly school, but he became complete master of every pupil. He graduated from Brown University in 1845, second in his class. He immediately came to Worcester to accept a position in the Academy and soon became its principal. The same year he bought land on what was styled Goat Hill at $150 per acre, and began the erection of the building called the Oread, which was completed in 1852. Here he established the famous school for young women, which he conducted with much success until he entered upon his well-known work as congressman. He served in the legislature in 1853-54, when he introduced a bill to incorporate the Bank of Mutual Redemption It was in 1854 that Mr Thayer accomplished the great and historic act of his life, in originating the plan which saved Kansas and other territories to freedom and settled the destiny of the nation, for had the southern leaders then secured this territory for slavery, it would have held it long years and no rebellion would have followed and the slave would not have been free, at least for many decades It was at a meeting to protest against the repeal of the Missouri Compromise, held in the old city hall at Worcester, March 11, 1854, that Mr Thayer announced his celebrated 'Plan of Freedom" He at once secured an act to incorporate the Massachusetts Emigrant Aid Company, and prior to the repeal of the Missouri Compromise, he hired a hall in Boston and began speaking day and night, to further his course of sending emigration to Kansas, but it was difficult to arouse enthusiasm and make up the first Kansas Colony He traveled much, addressed many thousands of people, but soon after the departure of the first colony in 1854, there was no trouble, and the south soon awoke to the fact that it had a power to contend with The border war in Kansas began and the powers at Washington abandoned the fight at the close of 1856

In the fall of 1856 Mr Thayer was elected to a seat in congress from the Worcester district, and at once took a leading place in national matters He was ever a great advocate of colonization of the colored men, whom he divided to be set off in Central America, or other localities, thus freeing our own republic of the curse entailed upon us by the slave trade His speeches on "Suicide of Slavery" and on the admission of Oregon brought great fame to him In 1860, after a most exciting canvass, he failed of re-election by a narrow majority

The south end of Worcester owes much to him for the matter of developing its domain, for manufacturing purposes It was nearly fifty years ago that he was instrumental in the erection of the large shops called the Adriatic mills He laid out streets and improved several tracts in that neighborhood He was the author of 'The Kansas Crusade," a graphic, valuable historic work He also wrote much for newspapers and magazines, concerning the great times which tired men's souls

(V) Benjamin Thayer and wife Sarah Bosworth Their seventh child

(VI) Benjamin Thayer, married Rachel Wales, 1802 settled in Mendon, Massachusetts Their eighth child

(VII) Davis Thayer, born October 13, 1817, in Mendon, married April 15 1843, Sarah, daughter of Jonathan and Sarah Grout Mrs Thayer was born February 13, 1820 They had one son and two daughters Mr Thayer died in Worcester, April 13 1895

(VIII) Charles Davis Thayer son of Davis Thayer and grandson of Benjamin Thayer, was born in Worcester, July 7, 1850, his father being buried on his fiftieth wedding anniversary day For many years he was the private gardener for Colonel Isaac Davis, mayor of Worcester For a quarter of a century he conducted a market garden In 1869 he sold out and settled on Pleasant street, continuing his agricultural pursuits for pleasure April 15, 1845, he married Sarah A Grout Three children were born of this union, one of whom, Idella Grout, died May 2 1870, aged about seven years The others were Charles D and Anna E

Charles Davis Thayer was educated at Worcester, graduating from Highland University Military Academy, July 9, 1869, where for two years he had been an officer in the corps He drilled and was an honorary member of the Worcester Light Infantry He clerked for his uncle, Jonathan Grout, bookseller, a short time, and when nineteen years old engaged in his present business agriculture, horticulture and florist He began without capital, indeed had to borrow a thousand dollars, paying more than seven per cent interest He at once began his greenhouse work For a short time he employed his father, a man of experience, to assist him Today his greenhouse is among the most extensive of any in the great commonwealth From time to time he had added to his real estate, including a part of the Greendale estate, also the "Liberty Farm" of seventy acres, known as the Abby Kelly Foster property The latter he converted into a dairy farm, selling milk to city customers His possessions are now wide and valuable He is a member of the Worcester County Agricultural Society and Horticultural Society, the Worcester Grange, of which he has been chaplain He has also been commander of Cavalry, Commandery H and I Order, Knights of Malta, and first lieutenant of Company A of the Worcester Continentals Politically he uniformly supports the principles of the Republican party

Mr Thayer married, December 9, 1874 Nellie Wyman, who was born in Newburyport, Massachusetts, but reared in Worcester Her father was a thriving flour merchant in Worcester He was a noted Abolitionist in his younger days and later a strong Republican He died June, 1895 aged seventy-eight years Mr and Mrs Thayer are the parents of seven children, of whom two died young Willie, second-born, died when he was seven years old, and Leon in infancy The others were Alfred D, Joseph F, Mary W, Charles D, Jr and Sarah G

(V) Benjamin Thayer and second wife, Ruth Alden, had four children, one of them,

(VI) Alden Thayer, born December 27, 1796, brother of Cushman, married Silance McNama, April 6, 1821 Their son,

(VII) Alden Thayer born February 3, 1826, married Martha C Knowles, in 1850

Alden Thayer, Jr, son of Alden Thayer, Sr, was born February 3, 1826, at Mendon, Massachusetts, where he spent his boyhood days completing his education at Worcester Baptist School, taking the civil engineering course On leaving school he found employment as surveyor's assistant in making surveys for the Boston & Worcester Railway He gave this up and clerked in his father s store in Worcester, he having recently removed from his farm at Mendon and engaged in business in 1850 he bought a business of his own, which increased, and he sought better and more spacious quarters from time to time, and finally became a leader among Worcester merchants When his son became of age he was admitted as a partner The entire business was sold in 1884 when Alden Thayer retired to a beautiful home at Tatnuck and there spent the remainder of his days He was ever known as a man of correct habits and conscientious and one who made few mistakes Being a foremost Baptist he aided in building up the Dewey Street Church He died in 1889 Martha C Knowles became his wife in 1850 Their children were Ida, Walter L, George A Charles Austin, Sarah Maud Isadore Grace, and Lucius

George Alden Thayer, son of Alden and Martha C (Knowles) Thayer, was born in Worcester March 11, 1856 His father was a merchant at old

Boylston, but later came to Worcester and engaged in trade He died in 1889 at Tatnuck, possessed of the esteem of all who knew him George Alden passed his youth in Worcester, attending the public schools He then spent seven years as bookkeeper for a pork-packing house and three years more at Swift & Company's branch at Ithaca, New York, as resident manager We next find him associated with his father at Worcester, who then conducted the largest grocery in the city This business was sold in 1884, when George Alden engaged in the meat and provision business, conducting the same until 1890, when his real estate interests demanded his whole time and he sold out

In 1884 he married Eliza A Rice, by whom were born Ida May, Ralph T, Helen and Carl A Mr Thayer died February 13, 1893 Of a genial, warm-hearted nature, he easily made friends, and had the happy trait of keeping them his admirers When very young he united with the Baptist church and was ever a devout Christian Like his father he was a great Bible student

RODNEY HAYWARD DAVIS Dolor Davis (I), the emigrant ancestor of Rodney Hayward Davis, of Worcester, was one of the prominent pioneers in both colonies His posterity is very numerous and among them have been some very distinguished men, namely Hon John Davis, governor and United States senator, and Hon John D Long, governor, congressman, and secretary of the navy He married, in County Kent, England, March 29, 1624, Margery Willard, daughter of Richard Willard, of Horsemonden, County Kent, yeoman She was baptized at Horsemonden, November 7, 1602, and died before 1667 Dolor Davis, accompanied by his wife three children, and Simon Willard, his wife's brother, came from England to New England and settled prior to August 4, 1634, in Cambridge, Massachusetts Simon Willard was one of the founders of Concord, he was captain of foot in 1646, major in 1654 and at his death in 1673 "the colony lost one of its most distinguished members" Dolor Davis was a carpenter and master builder He rereceived first grant of land in Cambridge, June 4 1635, and others later He removed to Duxbury, August 5, 1638-39, was admitted a freeman, and was granted land there in 1640 He was a resident of Barnstable in 1643, and was admitted a freeman there, June 2, 1646 He was honored in Barnstable with various public offices, including those of highway surveyor and constable He and his wife were dismissed from the Duxbury to the Barnstable church, August 27, 1648 In 1656 he left Plymouth colony and returned to Massachusetts Bay, and purchased in Concord one hundred and fifty acres with a house thereon In 1666, however, he returned to Barnstable and died there, in June, 1673 His will was made September 13 1672, and proved July 2, 1673 It mentions sons Simon and Samuel as already having their portions, eldest son John, son-in-law Lewis and Mary his wife, and daughter Ruth Hall

Children of Dolor and Margery (Willard) Davis were John born in England about 1626 to whom was bequeathed the Concord homestead, Mary, born in England about 1631, Elizabeth, Lieutenant Simon, see forward, Samuel, settled in Concord and Bedford, Ruth, born in Barnstable, March 24 1645

(II) Lieutenant Simon Davis, son of Dolor and Margery (Willard) Davis, was born in America, and died in Concord June 14 1713 aged seventy-seven years His will was proved July 3, 1713 His homestead was near his father's house on a farm given him by his father He was one of Captain Thomas Wheeler's troopers in the expedition of 1675 to the Nipmuck country, and he took command when the captain was wounded He received his commission as lieutenant, July 2, 1689 He was admitted a freeman, March 21, 1699 He was deputy to the general court in 1689-90-92-1705 He married December 12, 1660, Mary Blood, daughter of James and Eleanor Blood, born at Concord, July 12, 1640 Their children were Dr Simon, see forward, Mary, born October 3, 1663, married Deliverance Wheeler, of Stow, Sarah, March 11 or 15, 1666, married Thomas Wheeler, James, January 19, 1668, Eleanor, October 22 1672, Ebenezer, June 1, 1676, Hannah, April 1, 1679, married Samuel Blood

(III) Dr Simon Davis, eldest son of Lieutenant Simon and Mary (Blood) Davis, was born in Concord Massachusetts, October 12, 1661 He settled in Concord and was one of the distinguished physicians of his day The children of Dr Simon Davis were Dr John, see forward, Simon, born September 7 1692, married June 1 1719, Hannah Bacon, Henry, February 23, 1694, Elizabeth, March 28, 1695 died November 15, 1706, Mary, November 8, 1701, Samuel March 6 1703, see forward, Eleanor, March 4, 1705-06, Peter, September 25, 1707, probably removed to Rutland

(IV) Dr John Davis, eldest son of Dr Simon Davis, lived in Concord and Acton He was born in Concord, Massachusetts, November 19, 1689 and died November 16 1762 He married, December 17, 1713, Abigail Dudley, and their children were John, born July 15, 1714, died young, Ezekiel see forward, Micah, February 15, 1720, Isaac, October 24, 1723, Abigail, March 22, 1726-27, Samuel, April 23, 1730, resided at Acton, John, June 1 1735 of Acton Dr John Davis was the grandfather of Captain Isaac Davis, who was killed in the Concord fight In order to show the relationship with the Worcester family the line will be continued

(V) Ezekial Davis, or as the old records almost invariably give the name down to the last century (1800) Davies son of Dr John and Abigail (Dudley) Davis, was born in Concord, Massachusetts, June 8, 1717 He settled in Acton He married his third cousin, Mary Gibson, daughter of Abraham Gibson (4), granddaughter of Deacon Timothy Gibson (3), great-granddaughter of John Gibson Jr (2), and great-great-granddaughter of John Gibson (1) The children of Ezekial and Mary (Gibson) Davis were Isaac see forward, Mary, born November 21, 1746 Sarah, married Stephen Hosmer, brother of Abner Hosmer, who was killed in the Concord fight, Ruth, February 19 1751, Sergeant Ezekial born in Acton June 8 1753, was in his brother's company in the fight at Concord, Josiah June 14 1755, was a revolutionary soldier in Captain Israel Heald's company, Colonel Eleazer Brooks' regiment, Rebecca, September 11, 1757, Lois April 7, 1760 Abraham, February 10, 1764, Olive, October 29, 1765

(VI) Captain Isaac Davis, eldest son of Ezekial and Mary (Gibson) Davis was born at Acton Massachusetts, February 23, 1744-45 and was killed at the fight at North Bridge (Concord) April 19 1775 at the head of his company the first officer killed in the revolution He joined the church, February 10 1765 His old homestead is or was lately owned by Charles Wheeler It is located about eighty rods southwest of the present site of Deacon W W Davis's house Two fine old elms that were planted by Captain Davis still mark the location, on the opposite side of the road from where the house stood in which the Acton company gathered to go to Lexington, and in which the funeral of the three victims was held Captain Davis, the man who headed the first column against the King's troops in the revolutionary war, was early on the ground with thirty-eight Acton minute men, and in the hesitancy of older officers to attack the British regulars drew his sword and said "I am not afraid, I haven't a man that's afraid to go" He led two companies from Concord, two from Bedford, and one from Lincoln besides his own They advanced to the bridge to the tune of "The White Cockade" He was the first to fall The other two victims of the fight were friends, neighbors and relatives Abner Hosmer, son of Deacon Jonathan Hosmer, was twenty-two years old, and engaged to be married. Sarah Davis married his brother, Stephen Hosmer James Hayward son of Deacon Samuel Hayward, was killed after the battle, near Fiske Hill, on the road from Concord to Lexington He lived eight hours after he was shot A monument was erected by the town and state jointly in 1851 to the memory of Captain Davis and his two soldiers, Hosmer and Hayward, and their remains were placed under the memorial Captain Davis married October 24, 1764, Hannah Brown, born in 1746

(III) Lieutenant Simon Davis son of Samuel Davis (2), grandson of Dolor Davis (1), was the progenitor of many of the Rutland and Holden Davis families

(IV) Samuel Davis, sixth child of Dr Simon Davis (3), was born in Concord, Massachusetts, March 6, 1703, died in Acton, July 4, 1800 He removed to Acton when a young man and was already there when the town was incorporated in 1735 His homestead was on the Stow and Carlisle road, in 1735 He married Sarah —— who died in Acton, April 13, 1801, and their children were Elijah, see forward, David, settled in Acton Rev Nathan, see forward, a son, lived in Boston, Sarah, born October, 1741 in Acton, probably others Rev Nathan Davis, third child was born in Cambridge, Massachusetts, November 30, 1737 He graduated from Harvard College, 1759, and became minister at Dracut, November 20, 1765 He was dismissed at his own request in 1785 and removed to Boston He was chaplain at Ft Independence, also review officer He died March 4, 1803, aged sixty-five years In the Harvard catalogue his name is spelled Davies He received the degree of Master of Arts

(V) Elijah Davis, son of Samuel (4) and Sarah Davis, was born in Acton, Massachusetts, May 21, 1753 died May 7, 1832, aged seventy-nine years He was a private in Captain Israel Heald's company, Colonel Eleazer Brooks' regiment, and was on guard duty at Cambridge in 1776 Later in the year he was in Captain John Minot's company, Colonel Dike's regiment at Dorchester He married Elizabeth Hayward a relative of James Hayward who gave his life in the fight at Concord, and they settled in Acton, in which town all their children were born The names of their children were as follows Betsey, lived in Townsend, Samuel, died young Mary, died young, Sarah, died young, Elijah died in Worcester, March 24, 1844, aged forty-seven years, Sarah, married Benjamin Peabody, of Dracut, Samuel, see forward, Nathan, lived in Townsend, Massachusetts

(VI) Samuel Davis seventh child of Elijah (5) and Elizabeth (Hayward) Davis, was born in Acton, Massachusetts, December 18, 1806, died in Worcester, Massachusetts November 1, 1892 He learned the carpenter trade in Acton After serving his apprenticeship he worked in Lowell, Massachusetts, and Saco, Maine He came to Worcester, Massachusetts, 1828, and entered the employ of Washburn & Goddard making woolen machinery on School street He afterwards bought out Washburn & Goddard, and conducted the business himself for a number of years Afterwards he sold this business to Henry Goulding, and then entered the firm of Nourse, Mason & Company, agricultural manufacturers at Court Mills, which is now the Ames Plow Company He held a number of public offices In 1847 he was town surveyor, was one of the last three selectmen before Worcester was made a city, was a member of the house of representatives in 1848 and an alderman of the city under Mayor Richardson He was interested in the early development of real estate in Worcester being instrumental in making State street Harvard street, Exchange street, Oak avenue and other streets in the thickly settled parts of Worcester

He declared his intentions of marriage December 3, 1829, and married, December 30, 1829 in Millbury, Massachusetts Selina E Stockwell born in Sutton, Massachusetts, February 24, 1809, died in Worcester, Massachusetts, January 22, 1889, daughter of John and Elizabeth (Walker) Stockwell, of Sutton Their children were Rodney Hayward, born April 2, 1831, died October 2, 1852, he was drowned at sea between San Francisco and China he was an officer in the clipper ship "Shooting Star," Frances Emily, born February 25, 1833, died August 26, 1833, Samuel Everard, see forward, Selina Elizabeth, born November 23, 1841, died October 13, 1884

(VII) Samuel Everard Davis, third child of Samuel (6) and Selina E (Stockwell) Davis, was born in Worcester, Massachusetts, November 20, 1838, died in Worcester, July 14 1893 As a boy he attended the Sumner and Thomas street schools in Worcester After leaving these schools he went to Berlin Academy, and from there to Norwich University, Vermont He spent two years in France, and upon his return to Worcester, Massachusetts, entered the employ of Nourse Mason & Company, agricultural manufacturers at Court Mills He later went to Boston with the Frank Holbrook Company, dealers in agricultural implements, where he remained until he moved back to Worcester in 1878 With Dorrance S Goddard and Charles S Hall he bought forty acres of land on Belmont street, near Eastern avenue, which they developed for building purposes He was interested in this work at the time of his death

He married, at Dorchester, Massachusetts (Boston) June 16, 1864 Hannah Caroline Robinson, born in Dorchester January 29, 1836, a graduate of the Dorchester high school, 1855

Hannah Caroline (Robinson) Davis traces her ancestry to James Robinson (1), who came from England about 1660 and settled in Dorchester, Massachusetts He married Mary Alcock From them the line is traced to John Robinson (2), who married Ruth Burt John Robinson Jr (3), who married Susannah Williams James Robinson (4) a soldier in the revolution in Captain Ebenezer Withington's company of Dorchester married Sarah Breck Stephen Robinson (5), who married Hannah Withington Stephen Augustus Robinson (6), who married Mary Capen of Canton, Massachusetts, and they were the parents of Hannah Caroline, aforementioned as the wife of Samuel E Davis Children of Samuel Everard and Hannah Caroline (Robinson) Davis, all born in Dorchester, Massachusetts, are as follows Rodney Hayward born September 15 1867, chief draughtsman for the Webb Granite and Construction Company, Caroline Eliza, born August 23, 1868, was a music teacher by profession, married, June 27 1904 John M Kendall, and resides at No 111, Beacon street (see Kendall family sketch in this work), George Robinson, born March 20, 1870 married November 19, 1895 Helen Aileen Kennedy, he is a clerk at Logan, Swift & Brigham's branch of the United States Envelope Company, Grove street Worcester, Cornelia Vinson, born July 26 1872 graduate of the Worcester high school, Worcester State Normal school, a teacher in the Ash street public school, she resides with her mother, Charles Stephen born January 10, 1876, died August 8, 1877 Mrs Davis, the mother of these children, who survives her husband, resides at No 11 Orne street, Worcester

FRANKLIN BAKER WHITE Thomas White (1), the emigrant ancestor of Franklin Baker White, of Worcester, was in Weymouth, Massachusetts and a proprietor there as early as 1643 He probably came from England in 1635 He was admitted a freeman, of Weymouth, March 3, 1636 He represented the town in the general court in 1636-37-57-70 He was born in 1599 according to an affidavit he made in 1659 He died August, 1679 His will was dated July 5, and proved August 28, 1679 He bequeathed to sons, Joseph, Samuel, Thomas, Ebenezer and daughter, Hannah, grandchildren Lydia, Mary and Ebenezer White and Hannah Baxter, pastor Samuel Torrey and Elder Edward Bate Children of Thomas White were 1 Joseph, (see forward) 2 Samuel, married Mary Dyer 3 Thomas 4 Hannah, married June 24, 1660, John Baxter 5 Ebenezer

(II) Joseph White, eldest child of Thomas White (1), was born about 1635, perhaps in England He married Lydia Rogers She died March 8, 1727, at Mendon, Massachusetts He is the founder of an important branch of the White family in Worcester county He was an early settler in Mendon, with others of his friends and relatives, and was a leading man there He had ten children, some of whom were born in Mendon, others in towns where the family took refuge during the Indian war The children of Joseph and Lydia (Rogers) White were 1 Joseph, born December 16, 1662, removed to Mendon with the family when a year old 2 Samuel, February 14, 1667 3 Ebenezer 4 Experience, married Ephraim Miller 5 Hannah, married Samuel Warfield, July 22, 1701 6 Thomas, (see forward) 7 Ann, married Trask 8 Joseph 9 Lydia, married ——— Cook 10 Mary, married ——— Hill

(III) Thomas White, sixth child of Joseph White (2), was born in Mendon probably about 1665 He married Mehitable ———, who died September 27, 1704 Captain Thomas White, who was a very prominent man in Mendon, in church, town and militia, died March 23, 1706, in the prime of life Their children, all born in Mendon, were 1 Mehitable, born January 20, 1688-9, married Benjamin Darling 2 Thomas, (see forward) 3 Thankful, August 3, 1693 4 Joseph, August 28, 1695, married Abigail Skinner, of Oxford, April 15, 1718 5 John, March 12, 1698 6 Samuel, September 21, 1700 7 Ebenezer, February 4, 1703-4, died August 27, 1726

(IV) Thomas White, son of Thomas (3), born in Mendon Massachusetts April 15, 1691, married Deborah ——— There were descendants of the Plymouth family of White in the same region, and there may have been some relationship to account for the fact that the eldest son of Thomas White was named Peregrine Children, all born in Mendon, Massachusetts, were 1 Peregrine, September 11, 1711 2 Seth, September 22, 1712 3 Lydia, January 16, 1715-6 4 Hopestill, July 15, 1717 5 Samuel, May 17, 1719 6 Deborah, February 10, 1722 7 Josiah, (see forward)

(V) Josiah White, youngest child of Thomas White (4), born in Mendon, Massachusetts, April 29, 1723, married (first) January 2, 1746, Hannah Gardner, he married (second), November 28, 1751, Lucy Whipple He settled in Sutton, where he was called Josiah, Jr, to distinguish him from a relative of the same name some ten years older All his children were born in Sutton, but it is thought that late in life he removed to Dudley where his son lived

Children of Josiah and Hannah (Gardner) White were 1 Hannah, born July 20, 1747 2 Beatrice, March 6, 1749 Children of Josiah and Lucy (Whipple) White were 3 Ebenezer, (see forward) 4 Abel, April 23, 1754 5 Jeptha, December 26, 1755 6 Josiah, March 9, 1758 7 Elias, December 13, 1759 8 Noah, November 6, 1761 9 Lucy, April 16, 1764 10 Job, March 6, 1766

(VI) Ebenezer White, third child of Josiah White (5), was born in Sutton, September 25 1752 He was the great-grandfather of Franklin B White He was brought up on the farm in Sutton and went to school there When he attained his majority he went to Dudley, where he married in 1773, and where his children were born, except perhaps the two youngest He left Dudley in 1788, and soon afterward bought a farm and settled in Charlton, Massachusetts He was a man of considerable means, as the administration of his estate in 1827 discloses He was very active in town affairs in Dudley He was fence-viewer in 1776-87. He was tithingman in 1777-82 He was highway surveyor in 1781-84 He was on the school committee in 1787-88 He was also active in Charlton (There was another Ebenezer White in Charlton who must not be confused with this one in searching records He was called Junior, and his wife was Christian) Ebenezer White (6) married, December 16, 1773, Lydia Davis, daughter of Ebenezer and Lydia (Dana) Davis She was born in Oxford, May 5, 1754 Children of Ebenezer and Lydia (Davis) White were 1 Lydia, born September 7, 1774, married October 30, 1792, Abraham McIntire, of Charlton, and moved to New York state 2 Sylvanus, (see forward) 3 Zilpha, April 9, 1779, married Aaron Dresser (intentions recorded February 29), 1804 4 Dorcas, January 28, 1781, married Willrad Albee (intentions recorded April 6), 1801 5 Betty, November 15, 1783, died November 5, 1811, unmarried 6 Tammy, May 16, 1785, married Ebenezer Baker (intentions recorded March 7), 1806 7 Althusa, born about 1790, married Lemuel Waldron, of Dudley, (intentions recorded December 3), 1815 8 Polly, married Asa Davis, of Charlton, September 7, 1817 9 Ebenezer, Jr, born 1794, married March 24 1822, Sylvia Partridge, daughter of Benjamin and Milcah Partridge, of Charlton Their children were 1 Horace D, born 1822 2 Moses P, April 11, 1826 3. Betsey Ann, January 17, 1828 4 Mary Ann, November 28, 1832, died January 6, 1838 5 Amelia, December 22 1836 died January 6 1837 6 Sylvia Jane, March 19 1838, died December 28, 1854 7 Harriet Eliza, October 22, 1840, married Albert Marcy

(VII) Sylvanus White, second child of Ebenezer White (6), grandfather of Franklin B White, born in Charlton, Massachusetts, October 9, 1776, died there May 8, 1854 He was brought up there and learned the trade of cooper, which he followed for many years He lived with his father until about twenty-five, when he began farming on his own account as well as carrying on the cooper's trade during the seasons He was a man of sturdy character and strong principles He was deemed a man of sound judgment, well-read and of sterling honesty He was one of the most prosperous and substantial men of the town

He married Lucy Baker, born March 5 1781, died January 13, 1859 She was the daughter of Joseph Capen Baker, of Charlton The marriage intentions were recorded March 2, 1801 Children of Sylvanus and Lucy (Baker) White were 1 Ziba, born August 13, 1802, married Eloise Davis, of Dudley 2 Hosea, (see forward) 3 Sylvia, November 7, 1807, died January 7, 1833, married Almon Platt 4 Harvey, May 18, 1810 5 Harriet, November 18, 1812, married April 12, 1835, Francis W Winn, of Sutton, Massachusetts 6 Julia Ann, April 26, 1816, died December 26, 1849, unmarried 7 Clarissa Jane, July 21, 1819, died June 22, 1862, married Elijah Hanson 8 Chandler, December 25, 1822 9 Mary Lucy, April 18, 1826, died August 31, 1857 married ——— Gulliver

(VIII) Hosea White, second child of Sylvanus White (7), was born in Charlton, Massachusetts, May 30, 1804 He received his early education in that town, working at the same time with his father on the homestead When about twenty-two years of age, he started to learn the trade of wool dyer, but owing to a disabled arm he had to change his occupation He became a spinner and worked at that trade for about eight years in the mill at Globe Village in Southbridge, Massachusetts He worked also at Merino Village in Webster for a time He was overseer of a spinning room in an Uxbridge mill He finally returned to the home of his youth and bought a farm He sold it to good advantage and later bought another, remaining a farmer the rest of his days He died May 23, 1888

He was a member of the Universalist church and an active worker He was a strong advocate of temperance He was a leader in the Sons of Temperance organization which was very active fifty years ago He took part in various temperance movements In his early days he was a Whig, later a Republican in politics He married Lucina Hammond, who was born in West Wardsboro, Vermont, September 24, 1811 She died September, 1849, in Southbridge He married (second) Elmira Stone, daughter of John Stone, a farmer, of Charlton Children of Hosea and Lucina (Hammond) White were 1 Franklin Baker, (see forward) 2 Alfred, deceased Children of Hosea and Elmira (Stone) White were 3 Henry Wilson 4 Cynthia

(IX) Franklin Baker White, eldest son of Hosea White (8), was born in Dudley, Massachusetts November 3, 1837 He received his earliest education in the district schools of his native town, soon removing with his parents to Southbridge, where he again attended school, afterward attending Wilbraham Academy at Wilbraham, Massachusetts When he finished school he began work at shoemaking and farming, like a large percentage of the men of mechanical ability in eastern Massachusetts at that time He came to Worcester in 1863, and worked for the Bay State Shoe and Leather Company on High street five years In 1868 he entered the employ of D & C P Stevens, dealers in doors, sash and blinds, as bookkeeper (See sketch of Stevens Family for history of this business) In January, 1872, Mr White was admitted as an equal partner in the firm, and was manager and bookkeeper until 1888, when Daniel Stevens, the senior partner, died He then bought out the other interests in the business, and has continued as sole proprietor since then The business continues, however, under the old firm name of D & C P Stevens Under Mr White's ownership the business has continued to grow and develop This house has a large business throughout New England The location at 24 Southbridge street has been the same for many years, dating from the building of the block

Mr White has been prominent in church and public affairs He is a member of the Church of the Unity (Unitarian) and has been on the parish committee for many years He is interested in music and has served on the music committee of this church several years In politics he is a Republican He was a representative to the general court from Ward Six in 1890-91 He was on the Worcester school board in 1875-76-77-78 He is president of the board of directors of the Worcester Protective Union Grocery Company, one of the most successful co-operative companies in the state, maintaining the best grocery store in the city for a long period of years He is a member of the Worcester County Mechanics' Association, and has served as trustee for three years He is a Free Mason, a member of Montacute Lodge, since May 25, 1868

He married Emma Cornelia Stevens, June 15 1870 She is the daughter of Daniel and Hannah Jane (Adams) Stevens, of Worcester Her father was senior partner of the firm of D & C P Stevens, now owned by Mr White (See Stevens Family sketch) Their children are Florence Emma, born December 6, 1872, Josephine L born May 14, 1877.

HAMMOND FAMILY Thomas Hammond (1), immigrant ancestor of Franklin B White, was one of the early settlers of Newton, Massachusetts He was the son of William and Mary Hammond, of Melford, England, and grandson of John and Agnes Hammond, of Lavenham, England He was baptized at Melford, county of Suffolk, England, with his twin brother, John Hammond, September 2, 1603 He was first cousin of William Hammond who settled in Watertown, Massachusetts, in 1630

Thomas Hammond married in Lavenham, England, November 12, 1623, Elizabeth Cason, who was born in Great Whelhetham, a few miles north of Lavenham, before 1604, the daughter of Robert and Prudence (Hammond) Cason She was a granddaughter of Robert and Elizabeth Hammond, of Great Whelhetham Thomas Hammond was one of the first settlers of Hingham, Massachusetts He had land granted to him there in 1636, and was admitted a freeman March 9 1836-7 He served on the grand jury in 1637 His two younger children were baptized in Hingham, the elder children were born in England With several other Hingham pioneers Hammond removed to a locality near the boundary line of what are now Newton and Brookline, Massachusetts Five of them settled in the vicinity Hammond's homestead in Newton was near the pond, afterwards known as Hammond's Pond Hammond became one of the wealthiest men of his day He died in 1675, leaving an unsigned will, which was admitted to probate His estate according to the inventory amounted to nearly eleven hundred and forty pounds

An interesting relic of Elizabeth (Cason) Hammond is a silver coin, in the possession of George W Hammond, of Yarmouthville, Maine, in 1902, which she herself was allowed to coin when visiting the Mint in England, when a young girl (See Jackson's history of Newton page 299)

Children of Thomas and Elizabeth (Cason) Hammond were 1 Thomas, (see forward) 2 Elizabeth, born about 1633-4 3 Sarah, baptized September 13, 1640 4 Nathaniel, baptized March 12, 1643

(II) Thomas Hammond, eldest child of Thomas Hammond (1), born in England about 1630, died in Newton, Massachusetts, October 20, 1678, of smallpox He married, December 17, 1662, Elizabeth Stedman, (probably a sister of Nathaniel Stedman who married his sister, Sarah Hammond) She died in Newton in 1715 Thomas Hammond cultivated the farm he inherited from his father in Newton His estate was administered by his widow, it amounted to four hundred and sixty-eight pounds Their children were 1 Elizabeth, born Nov 3 1664 2 Thomas, born December 16, 1666 3 Isaac (twin) and 4 Sarah (twin), born December 20, 1668 5 Nathaniel, February 3, 1671, probably died young 6 John, April 30, 1674 7 Eleazer, (see forward)

(III) Eleazer Hammond, son of Thomas Hammond (2), born in Newton, Massachusetts, November 13 1677, died there in 1760, married April 29, 1703, Hannah Harrington, who was born August 9 1682, died in 1775, the daughter of John and Hannah (Winter) Harrington, of Watertown, Massachusetts He was selectman of Newton in 1741 His will was dated May 1, 1760, and mentions his children and others His widow's will was dated April 4 1764 Their children were 1 Hannah, born 1704, married Bartholomew Green 2 Eleazer, October 1, 1705, died young 3 Elizabeth, January 12, 1707 4 Eleazer, May 26, 1711, settled in Connecticut 5 Abigail, January 31, 1712-3 6 Patience, September 8, 1717, married Eleazer Chamberlain 7 Ephraim, (see forward) 8 Susanna, 1722 9 Lydia, February 5, 1726, married John Hammond

(IV) Ephraim Hammond, seventh child of Eleazer Hammond (3), born in Newton, Massachusetts March 15 1719-20 married 1741, Martha Steel Their children were 1 Hannah born August 8, 1742 2 Martha December 9 1743 3 Ephraim, December 31 1745 4 Thankful, 1747 5 Samuel, February 2, 1748 6 Hannah, September 20, 1749 7 Edward, September 20, 1752 8 Catherine 9 Henry, July 27, 1757 10 Patience, married, 1778, Nathaniel Parker 11 Elizabeth 12 Jemima

(V) Samuel Hammond, fifth child of Ephraim Hammond, (4), born in Newton, Massachusetts, February 2, 1748, died at Wardsboro, Vermont, January 4, 1742, married (first), 1770, Mary Rogers, daughter of John Rogers She was born January 28, 1752 He was one of the party of patriots who threw the tea overboard in Boston Harbor He was a private in Captain Hopestill Hall's company, Colonel Lemuel Robinson's regiment, January 31, 1776 He was then living in Roxbury, according to the roll He was also in Captain Amariah Fuller's company, Colonel William McIntosh's regiment, in 1778, stationed at Roxbury After the revolution he removed to Wardsboro, Vermont, where he was one of the first settlers The family erected mills at what is now West Wardsboro, then called Hammond's Mills

Children of Samuel and Mary (Rogers) Hammond were 1 Samuel born May 25, 1772 2 Mary 3 Peter, April 9 1776 4 Joel July 13, 1778 5 Jemima 1780 6 Artemas April 3, 1782 7 Nathaniel, August 14 1784 Peter Hammond (7), son of Samuel lived to be one hundred and two years of age When his parents went to Wardsboro Vermont in 1791 he was seventeen years old He was left with his grandparents in Newton for a time, and his mother returned for him on horseback, a distance of one hundred and twenty-five miles, and the boy walked back with her In later years he owned the Hammond Mills and was by far the most prominent and influential man in the town, was justice of the peace and postmaster for nearly twenty-five years He cast his first vote for John Adams, and lived to be a Republican during and after the civil war He removed to Geneseo, Illinois, with his son in 1856, and for several years prior to his death had made his home with his daughter, Mrs Martha H Taylor He died the very day he was one hundred and two years old, and was taken to Wardsboro to be buried Stewart Lodge of Free Masons in Geneseo presented him with a gold-headed cane when he was one hundred years old He was made a Mason in 1799 He had seven children

(VI) Joel Hammond, son of Samuel Hammond (5), was born in Newton, Massachusetts July 13, 1778 (See page 708, Vol 2, of Hammond Genealogy, for facts given before For the following records, which are not in the genealogy, we are indebted to the town clerk of Wardsboro, (1906) D C Dexter) Joel married (first), Hannah Moon (Moore?) and had seven children, he married (second), Sena Higgins and had one daughter, Elmira He is said to have removed late in life to Oneonta, New York His children were 1 Beri, married Benjamin Converse and had one daughter and two sons, Asa and Henry Converse, the daughter married Sylvester Johnson and lived in West Dover, Vermont, where their children are now living (1906), Asa Converse is dead, Henry resides in Malden 2 Lucina, born September 24 1811 3 Lovina, probably died young 4 William, June 20, 1816, died in Boston, September 23, 1897, married Mary Isabel Mason, who died February 24 1889, daughter of Ephraim Balker and Mary T (Spearr) Mason Their children were William Henry, born May 29, 1850 married Ella Maria Curtis, Grace, February 12, 1853, Albert Ballard, December 31, 1855, Mary Alice 5 Joel 6 Artemas, resided in Boston in 1868, his daughter Josephine married a Guild (?) 7 George, married Louisa Higgins and settled in Wardsboro Their children were Lovina, who married Rodney Watson, and live West, Flora, married Leroy Webster and lives in West Jamaica Vermont, Zella died unmarried, Herbert, a school teacher in the West 8. Elmira, married ——— Shepardson, and resides in Warwick, Massachusetts (The genealogy gives also 9 Elmore, a son, born June 6, (probably 1810 instead of 1811) died at Candor, Tioga county, New York, married, 1834 Caroline Cooke, who was born March 20, 1816, daughter of Samuel and Diadama (Green) Cook, of Tioga county, New York He was a farmer at Oneonta, where his father died, and at Candor His children were 1 Rebecca born October 12, 1838 2 Mary, November, 1840 3 Eliza, November, 1842 4 Seth G, March 18, 1845 5 Lois D April 2 1847, died July 7, 1899 6 A DeWitt, November 5, 1850 7 Frances L, March 12 1852, died August, 1895 8 Emma, July 5 1857 9 Edmund, September 23 1860 10 Polly (sic) born at Wardsboro, married Joseph Guile of Orwell, Vermont, and died at Mount Holly, Vermont Their children were George, Andrew, shoemaker at Sandy Hill, New York, DeWitt G Asenath married ——— Richmond, of Orwell Vermont, Orange S

(VII) Lucina Hammond, daughter of Joel Hammond (6), born in West Wardsboro, Vermont September 24 1811, married Hosea White, father of Franklin B White, of Worcester (See sketch of this White family)

DR JOHN MERRICK BEMIS Joseph Bemis (1) was the immigrant ancestor of Dr John Merrick Bemis, of Worcester, Massachusetts Not all of the Bemis families of America can be traced to him, but most of them have been He was born in England in 1619, and came to Watertown, Massachusetts, as early as 1640, when he was about twenty-one He died in Watertown, August 7, 1684 There is some evidence to show that he married in England before emigrating here, and that his wife Sarah came over with him Their first child, however, was born at Watertown, Massachusetts, in 1642, and they may have been married in Watertown or, as the birth is on the Boston records, in Boston, Massachusetts It is known that Joseph Bemis was the son of John Bemis, who was born in Dedham, Essex county, England, as early as 1550 The will of John Bemis was proved June 28, 1604 His children were Isaac, Luke, Mary, James, Susan, Joseph, and Abraham Joseph and his sister Mary came together to Watertown Perhaps others of the family also came Mary married William Hagar March 20, 1644-45, died December, 1695 Her husband died January 10, 1683-4 They had ten children and have a host of descendants

Joseph Bemis was a quiet, hard-working man, a blacksmith and farmer He served the town of Watertown as hayward," collector of taxes, member of the school committee, constable and selectman He was on the board of selectmen in 1648-73-75 There was an amusing case before the magistrate where he was fined for having one disorderly hog" Truly New England has always taxed her ingenuity to invent crime! On another occasion he was fined three pounds for cutting trees on the common land without the formal permission of the constituted authorities Most of the fine was remitted As his biographer says, otherwise than this he was apparently a good and law-abiding citizen He was fairly well-to-do, leaving an estate valued at over two hundred pounds His will was made the day of his death, August 7, 1684, and proved October 7, 1684 The widow administered the estate She died 1712, and the estate was divided among the heirs November 18, 1712, except those parts already given to the eldest son Joseph, and daughter Martha The children of Joseph Bemis were 1 Sarah, born January 15, 1642-3, married at Watertown, October 2, 1694 John Bigelow, born in England, 1617, died in Watertown July 14, 1703, blacksmith, freeman in 1652, selectman in 1665-70-71, married, before, Mary Warren (this was the first marriage recorded in Watertown, Massachusetts), who died October 19, 1691, Sarah being, it is said, his third wife 2 Mary, born September 10, 1644, died before 1730, married February 16, 1683-4, Samuel Whitney, son of John, Jr, and Ruth (Reynolds) Whitney, of Watertown, born in Watertown, July 23, 1648, died there 1730 John Whitney was born in England 1624, and died in Watertown October 12, 1692 Samuel Whitney was a soldier from Groton or Watertown in King Philip's war He had a large family of children and has many descendants 3 Joseph, Jr, (twin) born October 28, 1647 4 Ephraim (twin), born October 28, 1647, died a few days later, buried November 4, 1647 5 Martha born March 24, 1649, died unmarried, was admitted to the church February 25 1697-8 6 Joseph, Jr, 2d, born December 12 1651 died at Westminster, Massachusetts, August 7 1684 7 Rebecca, born April 17, 1654, married (first) at Watertown, April 11, 1684, John White, born at Watertown February 25 1648-9, died there (killed by a bull) May 30, 1684, the son of Anthony White, who was born in England 1607, died at Watertown March 28 1686, and who embarked from Ipswich, England, for New England, April, 1634, with his wife, Grace (Hall) White, married (second) at Watertown, April 1, 1686, Thomas Harrington, born at Watertown, April 20, 1665, died there March 29 1712, the son of George and Susannah Harrington, of Watertown leaving by this second marriage a large family of children 8 Ephraim, 2d, born August 25, 1656, was living 1738, at Windham, Connecticut 9 John, (see forward)

(II) John Bemis son of Joseph Bemis (1), born at Watertown, Massachusetts, August, 1659, died there October 24, 1732, married (first) at Watertown, 1680, Mary Harrington, daughter of George and Susannah Harrington, born January 12, 1663-4, died at Watertown September 8, 1716, married (second) January 1, 1716-7, Mrs Sarah (Holland) Phillips, widow of Jonathan Phillips and daughter of Nathaniel Holland Her mother was Sarah (Hosier) Holland, second wife of Nathaniel Sarah (Holland) Bemis was born at Watertown, November 30, 1662, died there prior to 1726, married (third) at Watertown, May 30, 1726, Mrs Judith (Jennison) Barnard, born at Watertown, August 13, 1667, died there She was the daughter of Ensign Samuel and Judith (Macomber) Jennison and widow of James Barnard, who was born at Watertown, January 14, 1666-7, died there January 23, 1726 Ensign Jennison was born at Watertown 1645, died there October, 1701 His wife, Judith Macomber, died at Watertown, March 1, 1722-3

John Bemis sold April 26, 1701, for fifty-six pounds, a half of the quarter of Alcock's farm of nine hundred acres in Marlboro With his son-in-law, Daniel Child, he bought, April 6, 1702, of Nathaniel Saltonstall (Fellow of Harvard College) one hundred and sixty acres of land in Watertown, Lot No 30, origanally granted to Sir Richard Saltonstall Here the home of John Bemis was established and the property remained in the Bemis family for some generations

John Bemis was a farmer He was corporal in the militia company He served the town of Watertown as tithing-man, as a member of the school board, as highway surveyor, as selectman, and on important special committees He was one of the leading citizens of his time Children were Beriah, born June 23, 1681, died at Watertown about 1768, married (first) at Watertown, February 10, 1701-2, Daniel Child, baptized June 5, 1687 After the second marriage of his mother he died in Watertown, January 29, 1723-4, son of John Child, (born 1636, died October 15, 1676) and Mary (Warren) Child, (born November 29, 1651, died May 12, 1734), married (second) August 12, 1736 Joseph Pierce, born at Watertown, October 2, 1669, died at Weston, March 13, 1753, son of Joseph and Martha Pierce, of Watertown, married (third) John Whiting, born at Watertown, June 15 1694, died at Westford, Massachusetts, 1776, son of Benjamin Whiting, (born at Watertown, June 28 1660, died there 1736), and Abigail (Hagar) Whiting, daughter of William and Mary (Bemis) Hagar, Beriah had many children and has many descendants, she is buried in the old graveyard at Watertown 2 Susanna, born December 24 1682, died November 15 1703, married at Watertown, November 2, 1702, John Hastings, (died prior to 1747), son of John Hastings, (born March 1, 1653-4, died March 28, 1718), and Abigail (Hammond) Hastings, (born June 21, 1659, died April 7 1718), had no children 3 Joseph, born November 17, 1684 died 1738 4 John born October 6 1686 5 Mary, born September 24 1688, married at Watertown, October 26, 1708, Isaac Stearns born December 31, 1674, died

1737, son of Samuel Stearns of Watertown (born April 24 1638, died August 3 1683), and Hannah (Manning) Stearns (born June 21 1642 died February 26 1723-4) had large family of children and has many descendants 6 Samuel, born 1690, died at Spencer, Massachusetts, August, 1776, founder of the well known Spencer branch of the Bemis family 7 Lydia born 1692, married April 10 1716 Jonathan Fiske, baptized at Watertown, December 8, 1680 son of John Fiske (born at Watertown, November 20 1655 died at Watertown 1709-18), and Abigail (Parks) Fiske, (born at Watertown, March 3, 1758-9), left a large family of children and other descendants 8 Hannah born October 9, 1694, died October, 1700 9 Isaac, born 1696 10 Jonathan, born April 30, 1699, probably died young 11 Jonathan, 2d, born November 17, 1701 12 Abraham born November 26 1703 13 Susanna, 2d, (twin) born December 3, 1705, died November 25 1785, married July 2, 1731, John Viles (Vilas), of Waltham, Massachusetts, who died at Waltham, February 4, 1774, had many children 14 Hannah, (twin) born December 3 1705, married (first) April 11 1724 John Flagg born September 21, 1700, killed accidentally March 14 1733-4, son of John Flagg, (born November 6, 1677, died prior to 1755), and Anna Flagg, (died prior to 1712) married (second) July 23, 1734, Captain John Brown, born April 19, 1705, died at Weston Massachusetts, 1804 son of Captain Abraham Brown (born August 26 1671, died November 27, 1729), and Mary (Hyde) Brown, (born June 21, 1673, died November 29 1723) Hannah Bemis was his second wife Captain Brown was selectman of Watertown 1744-45-46-47-48-52, representative to the general court in 1748 He was an innholder, and a man of uncommon energy and enterprise He removed to Weston in 1761, lived at Newton 1770 to 1778 and returned to Weston 1779 They had a large family of children

(III) John Bemis son of John Bemis (2) born October 6 1686, at Watertown, Massachusetts, married (first) May 8, 1710 Hannah Warren born January 25 1690-91, died prior to 1713, daughter of Daniel Warren (born October 6 1653), and Elizabeth (Whitney) Warren (born June 9 1756) married (second) April 2 1713 Anna Livermore born 1690, daughter of Samuel Livermore (born about 1640, died 1690), and Anna (Bridge) Livermore (born 1646 died August 28, 1727) After John Bemis died his widow married (second) December 5, 1769, Josiah Smith John Bemis was a constable in Watertown 1730 selectman in 1735 His children were 1 John, born February 11 1711 2 Anna, born April 29 1714 died at Waltham, Massachusetts, a widow, January 9 1793 married (first) February 26, 1734 Samuel Fiske born January 4 1709, died March 29 1761, son of William Fiske (born February 23 1663-4 died 1742), and Hannah (Smith) Fiske (born December 27 1672, died December 7 1728), married (second) April 26 1763 Hopestill Bent, of East Sudbury Massachusetts and had a large family of children by each husband 3 Josiah born February 29 1715-6 4 Abraham born December 27, 1717 5 Grace born November 5 1719 married and had many children 6 Lydia born April 5 1721 married Jonas Dix born May 21, 1721, died August 30 1783 He was captain in the militia, civil magistrate for the trial of small causes selectman for twenty-one years, assessor eighteen years, representative to the general court from 1764 to 1783 inclusive He was the son of John Dix and Martha (Lawrence) Dix They had many children and have many descendants 7 Abijah born March 16 1722, died at Paxton June 19, 1790 8 Elisha, born March 20, 1725 9 Elizabeth, born March 23, 1727-8 10 Nathaniel, born May 6 1730 11 Susanna, born April 3, 1732, married November 15, 1753, Elisha Garfield, son of Lieutenant Thomas Garfield, of Weston, and Mercy (Bigelow) Garfield, and had many children 12 Phinehas born March 24, 1734

(IV) Abijah Bemis son of John Bemis (3), born at Watertown, Massachusetts, March 16 1722 23, died at Paxton, Massachusetts, June 19 1790, was the founder of what is generally known as the Paxton branch of the Bemis family He went from Weston, Massachusetts, to Paxton about 1751, married January 29, 1751, Dinah Hagar, of Waltham, born in 1728, baptized May 5, 1728, died January 19, 1792, at Paxton, daughter of William Hagar, of Waltham, and Mary (Flagg) Hagar born December 7, 1690 Dinah Hagar was a direct descendant of Mary Bemis, sister of Joseph Bemis, the immigrant She was descended through her mother from John Livermore, the ancestor of all of that name in this country All his children were probably born at Paxton The children were 1 Abijah, born 1753, died December 6 1829 2 Daniel 3 Dinah, married July 15 1788 David Cutting of Brookfield 4 Beulah married November 11 1784 John Pike, born November 10 1762 son of John and Mehitable Pike of Sturbridge Massachusetts John and Beulah Pike moved to Marshfield, Vermont, in 1806 They had seven children 5 Lydia married January 25, 1788, Francis Pike 6 John (see forward) 7 Ruth married at Spencer, April 7, 1785, John Pike, of Paxton 8 Alpheus

(V) John Bemis, son of Abijah Bemis (4), born at Paxton, Massachusetts, 1767, died at Brookfield, Massachusetts August 8, 1852, married (first) July 1, 1793, Grizel Livermore, married (second) July 5 1796 Mary Flagg married (third) Jemima Adams born at Brookfield, 1779 died there March 27 1861, daughter of Eleazer Adams He had one child by his first wife, three by the second, and the rest by the third wife His children were 1 Celicia born September 4 1794, died at Brookfield January 23 1875, married, at Warren, Michael Walsh 2 Samuel Flagg (see forward) 3 Catherine, born 1797 died at Warren Massachusetts March 3 1878 married at Sturbridge, April 2 1822, Charles Goodell 4 Mary, died young 5 Mary died at Sturbridge, July 19 1851, married Thomas Kellogg 6 John, born September 24 1803 died at Brookfield, April 7, 1871, married at Brookfield Mary Newton 7 David Adams born March 16 1805 died at Warren, Massachusetts April 30, 1886 8 Charles born at Spencer Massachusetts, March 9 1807 died at Warren, December 18, 1891, married at Warren Lucinda Reed 9 Eleazer Adams born at Spencer, September 30 1810 died at Brookfield, June, 1886, married at Brookfield, Sarah Harwood 10 Addison born at Spencer, Massachusetts March 17, 1812, died March 7 1895 11 Eliza A, born at Paxton 1817 died at Sherburne Vermont March 7, 1895 married (first) at Brookfield January 1, 1837 Hiram Gleason, married (second) at Brookfield April 1851, Lyman H Hodgman 12 Sophronia born 1818 married at Brookfield Austin Woodward, died at Brimfield, Massachusetts, May 30 1901 13 Waldo (twin) born at Brookfield, October 13 1820, died there November 24 1856 14 William (twin) born October 13 1820, married (first) at Stafford, Connecticut September 9 1848, Frances A Daniels, died at Oxford Massachusetts, March 1905 15 Austin F, born at Sherburne, Vermont, November, 1863

(VI) Samuel Flagg Bemis, son of John Bemis (5) born March 1 1795 died at Brookfield Massa-

Merrick Bemis

chusetts, November 10, 1869, married Betsey Barrett, of Charlton, Massachusetts, born November 28, 1796, died at Brookfield, April 15, 1842, daughter of Philip and Elizabeth (Barrett) Bigelow, of Charlton. Their children were 1 Merrick, see forward 2 Freeland, born December 9, 1821, died January, 1880, married at Enfield, Massachusetts, Mary A Underwood 3 Fitz Henry, born November 9, 1823 4 Ann Elizabeth, born November 15, 1826, married at Brookfield, Massachusetts, May 30, 1851, Eli Truxton, born at Sturbridge, March 27, 1821, died there January 3, 1897, son of Benjamin Brooks (born at Warren, Massachusetts, February 7, 1769, died at Sturbridge 1852), and Esther (Fink) Brooks (born at Wellington, Connecticut, 1780, died at Sturbridge 1863), had several children 5 Samuel Flagg, Jr, born November 15, 1828 at Sturbridge, married Hannah Blodgett 6 Maria Louisa, born October 3, 1831, died 1863 married at Sturbridge, Henry C Storrs 7 Francis Emily, born June 21, 1832, at Sturbridge, Massachusetts, married March 13, 1855, Marvin Clark, born at Southbridge, Massachusetts, February 3, 1816, son of Marvin Clark, of Woodstock, and Nancy (Carpenter) Clark of Ashford, Connecticut had five children 8 Daniel Webster born in Charlton, Massachusetts, April 21, 1835, married (second) Maria T Woods

(VII) Dr Merrick Bemis, son of Samuel Flagg Bemis (6), born at Sturbridge, Massachusetts, May 4, 1820, died October 3, 1904 He was one of the most eminent physicians that ever resided in Worcester He practiced his profession for fifty-six years Almost to the day of his death he retained his faculties and health It was often said of him during the last score of years that he practiced, that he was one of the most active aged men of Worcester, carrying on a business that would tax the energies of a man of fifty Through his entire period of practice Dr Bemis confined his study and attention to his specialty, nervous and mental diseases, and he was for many years recognized as one of the leading alienists of the country The wide range of knowledge and experience in cases of insanity, coming under his observation and care during his long connection with large institutions for the insane, gave him an advantage over most of the specialists in this line of study He was called often as an expert in consultation, and by the courts His record of twenty-five years of continuous service in the State Insane Asylum, at Worcester, was in itself a remarkable record, and evidence of his ability and powers of endurance

His parents moved from Sturbridge to Charlton when he was quite young He was brought up on a farm, getting what educational advantages the district schools of his day afforded He sought a higher education and worked his way through Dudley Academy He walked each way every week from his home to the academy, a distance of twelve miles He taught school in winter to pay his way in the academy He went to Amherst Academy for two years with the expectation of going to Amherst College A long and severe illness caused him to abandon his plans for a college education, and for several years he taught school in Brookfield, Massachusetts He began to study medicine when he was twenty-two years old, and entered the office of Dr Winslow Lewis as a student, but continued to pay his way by teaching school in the winters He attended medical lectures at Pittsfield, Massachusetts, Medical College, where he received the first half of his medical education He then changed to Castleton Medical College, of Vermont, where, in 1848, he received his degree of M D He came to Worcester November 14 1848, to take the place, temporarily, of one of the physicians in the lunatic asylum, and soon afterward received an appointment as assistant physician to Dr George Chandler, the superintendent When, eight years later, in 1855, Superintendent Chandler resigned, the attention of the trustees was at once turned to Dr Bemis as the most capable man for the position, and he was elected to the office Being given a leave of absence for the purpose of travel and study in Europe, he made an extended tour, lasting eight months He returned to Worcester in the summer of 1857, and took charge He began immediately to put into operation the reforms and new methods he had learned For seventeen years he filled the position of superintendent to the satisfaction of the state authorities, and developed the institution until it stood among the foremost American hospitals for the insane Radical changes in the methods of treating insanity were made during his administration One of the innovations due to Dr Bemis was the employment of competent female physicians in lunatic asylums It is difficult to understand now how these institutions got along without women physicians The custom has now become general One of his last and most important duties in the state institution was the establishment of the hospital at Bloomingdale, the land for which was bought during the last years of his superintendency of the Summer street institution He submitted plans for the buildings and again visited Europe in 1868, to inspect hospitals for the insane and study the treatment of lunatics The Massachusetts institution was kept in the front rank of progress The example set by this Commonwealth has been exceedingly useful and beneficent because it has been followed in other states, and by private institutions generally in this country

Dr Bemis resigned his position in 1872 to establish a private hospital for the care and treatment of patients afflicted with the various forms of mental and nervous diseases He located the hospital on Salisbury street, Worcester The main building is the mansion built in 1857, by Rev Nathaniel Bent, for a young ladies seminary This property, which includes ten acres of land is very favorably located for its purpose The hospital is known as Herbert Hall The large, handsome mansion is cheerful, airy and well furnished There are spacious verandas surrounding the buildings The view from the hall is one of the most picturesque in a country abounding in fine scenery There are attractive walks under the stately old shade trees in the spacious grounds, and altogether it is an ideal place for an invalid and convalescent It has been successfully conducted ever since its foundation, first by Dr Merrick Bemis then by him and his son Dr John M Bemis, and since the founder's death by his son alone No mention of Dr Bemis's professional career would be complete without referring to his prominence as a specialist in psychiatry He was frequently consulted both by medical brethren and by the courts in difficult cases of insanity or alleged insanity He wrote many monographs upon hospital work among the insane and on the general subject of insanity He was a man of large heart and generous impulses He gave freely to charities Few have equalled him in proportion to his means in the number of gifts judiciously distributed among a variety of worthy objects His patriotic service during the civil war deserves special mention When in 1861 the president's proclamation calling for a force of 75,000 men to take the field immediately, was made Dr Bemis earnestly desired to enter the service He was unable to pass the physical examination, however but he gave freely of his means to support the Union cause He organized and equipped a company and sent it to the front He took an active interest in their welfare while they were in the field, and contributed freely to the support of the families of the boys in that company while the war continued It was due largely to his efforts that the public subscription to purchase the organ for Mechanics Hall was successful In 1864 the organ, which cost $9.000, was dedicated, and it has proved to be one of the finest instruments of its kind It has been one of the factors in making the Musical Festivals there so successful, from a musical point of view

Dr Bemis collected one of the most valuable and interesting private libraries in the state Much of the library is, of course, devoted to medical works, and some of the volumes are very old and rare He found some time to devote to public affairs and was a member of the Worcester board of aldermen in 1861-62-63 serving at the same time on the school board This was a particularly important period during the early and darker years of the civil war He was a director of the Mechanics National Bank, a member of the Worcester Horticultural Society, the Worcester Society of Antiquity, the Natural History Society, of which he was president till his death the Massachusetts and Worcester District Medical Societies, the American Medical Association, the New England Psychological Society and the American Medico-psychological Association He was connected with various Masonic bodies He was a member of the Church of the Unity, and a life member of the American Unitarian Association He was for about fifteen years one of the state trustees of the Baldwinville Hospital Cottages for Children, in the management and development of which he had taken a leading part, and was president of the corporation at the time of his death He was the first American physician to take a stand for the division of hospital buildings for the insane into separate cottages or pavilions He married January 1, 1856 Caroline A Gilmore, whose father was for thirty years a successful practitioner at Brookfield, Massachusetts In his office, in fact, Dr Bemis received his first lessons in medicine, and was started on his professional career while a school teacher at Brookfield They had one child John Merrick, (see forward)

(VIII) Dr John Merrick Bemis, son of Dr Merrick Bemis (7), born at Worcester, Massachusetts February 14, 1860 The life work of Dr Bemis has been so completely merged and identified with that of his father for the past twenty years, at Herbert Hall, that what has been said as to the attainments of the father as a physician and specialist applies equally well to the son He was educated from the start as a specialist, and had unusual opportunities for practice and hospital study He attended the Worcester schools Before graduating he left the high school to prepare for college at Phillips Andover Academy, but was obliged, by poor health at that time, to leave the academy, and he studied at home for three years under private tutors He attended medical lectures at the Harvard Medical College in Boston and at the Burlington University (Vermont) Medical Department where he received his diploma in 1893 He had been an active assistant to his father at Herbert Hall for some years, before and after graduation he returned to the hospital where he has been actively engaged in the management and treatment of patients ever since He has continued his studies with the intention of keeping up the times. He has studied at Harvard and Clark universities from time to time and written papers for various learned societies His specialty, of course, has been mental diseases Herbert Hall, of which he is now, since his father's death, owner and manager, is the only private hospital in the state devoted to insane patients exclusively, except the McLean Hospital, which is in a class by itself Herbert Hall is chartered by the state and under the state supervision. It ranks high among the institutions of its kind

Dr Bemis has devoted his time almost exclusively to the hospital He is trustee of the Baldwinville Hospital Cottages for Children He is on the education committee of the Highland Military Academy, of Worcester, a member of the Massachusetts Medical Society, the Worcester Medical Society, the American Psychological Society and the New England Psychological Society In religion he is an Episcopalian He married June 25, 1887, Fannie Bishop Brown of Andover, Massachusetts, daughter of John Brown, for many years druggist at Andover, Massachusetts He was born at Newburyport in 1809, died at Andover in 1886 Her mother was Emily Fiske, daughter of Eben Fiske, born at Roxbury, Massachusetts, June 24, 1819 resided many years at New Orleans, Louisiana. She is living (1905), remarkably active and well for her years She is related to the Willards, celebrated as clockmakers in the colonial days Children of Dr Bemis are 1 Annie Merrick, born October 1, 1888 2 Caroline Gilmore, born May 25, 1891

Daniel Webster Bemis, son of Samuel Flagg Bemis, and brother of Dr Merrick Bemis, late of Worcester, was born in Charlton, Massachusetts, April 21, 1835 He obtained his early education in the public schools of Brookfield, Massachusetts After leaving school he entered the employ of the Hospital for the Insane on Summer street, Worcester, of which Dr Merrick Bemis was the superintendent He was appointed steward and filled this position for twenty years For seven years he was also treasurer of the hospital In the early seventies he bought a farm in Shrewsbury, and having resigned his position at the hospital devoted his attention to farming since then With a natural aptitude for agriculture and horticulture Mr Bemis has lived quietly and enjoyably upon his farm in the picturesque old town of Shrewsbury He has an excellent farm well stocked and well conducted

Mr Bemis represented Worcester in the general court in his younger days and assisted in the passage of the bill to locate the Hospital for the Insane at Bloomingdale in Worcester The site has proved an ideal place for an institution of this kind, which has grown very rapidly and for which there is ample opportunity for growth Mr Bemis was prominent in Masonic circles when a citizen of Worceser He has taken the Blue Lodge, the Royal Arch chapter the council and the commandery degrees in the York Rite degrees He was elected to take the Scottish Rite degrees also in Worcester He has been high priest of the chapter and held all the elective offices in that body Since living in Shrewsbury, Mr Bemis has served the town for twenty years on the school committee He is deeply interested in educational matters, has taken an active part in town affairs, and served three years on the board of assessors and has been a selectman He is an active member of the Congregational church and Sunday school, and has for a number of years been a deacon He is a Republican in politics No citizen in Shrewsbury is more highly esteemed than Mr Bemis In every walk of life he has taken his part modestly and capably As a friend, neighbor and citizen he is popular In private life and public office alike his integrity and common sense have been appreciated

Mr Bemis married (first) Jennie Learned, of Underhill, Vermont She lived only about a year He married (second) Maria T Wood, daughter of Joel Fay Wood, of Grafton Their children are 1 Agnes L, graduate of the Worcester high school, and State Normal school, teacher in the Castine Normal school and elsewhere, and for some time superintendent of the domestic department at Mt Holyoke College 2 Leigh Jannette, a graduate of Mt Holyoke College, 1894, married Rev Frank B Doane, an Amherst graduate of Amherst College and of the New Haven Divinity School, now pastor of the Congregational church at Cheney, Washington 3 Mabel G, a graduate of the high school, married Ned Wesley Parker, foreman for John L Parker & Co, ferule manufacturers, 70 School street, Worcester, they reside with Mr Bemis in Shrewsbury

PARKER FAMILY Thomas Parker (1), was the immigrant ancestor of Edmund L Parker and Ned Wesley Parker, of Worcester He belonged to an old English family of which something has been written for this work He was about thirty years of age when he embarked from London, England, March 11, 1635, on the ship "Susan and Ellen" He settled at Lynn where he was a proprietor in 1638 He was admitted a freeman there May 17, 1637 He may have about 1635, married his wife Amy there He removed to Reading between 1638 and 1640 and was founder and deacon of the church there He died in Reading, August, 12, 1683 His wife Amy died in Reading, January 15, 1690 His will was dated August 3, 1683, and proved December 18, of that year He bequeathed to wife Amy, to sons John, Thomas, Nathaniel and Hananiah, daughters Mary and Martha, grandchildren Samuel and Sarah Parker, to John, "a great Bible that Boniface Burton gave me" Children were 1 Thomas, born in Lynn, 1636, died July 17, 1699, married Deborah —— 2 Lt Hananiah, born about 1638, died at Reading, March 10, 1724, married (first) Elizabeth Browne of Reading, September 30, 1663, married (second) Mary (Bursham) Bright, December 12, 1700 3 Sergeant John, born in Reading, 1640, died 1698 4 Joseph, born 1642, died 1644 5 Joseph, born 1645, died 1646 6 Mary, born December 12, 1647, died 1705, married Samuel Dodge 7 Martha, born March 14, 1649 8 Nathaniel (see forward) 9 Sarah, born September 30, 1653, died October 26, 1656 10 Jonathan, born May 18, 1656, died at Reading, June 10, 1680 11 Sarah, born May 23, 1658 12 Deborah, (given by Pope)

(II) Nathaniel Parker, eighth child of Thomas Parker (1), born at Reading, Massachusetts, May 16, 1651, died there 1737, married Bethiah Polly of Roxbury, Massachusetts, September 24 1677, daughter of John and Bethiah (Gowdrey) Polly, baptized 1659 He was ensign of the Reading Company Children were 1 Bethiah, born 1678, died young 2 Nathaniel, born 1679, married Elizabeth, 1702 3 Stephen born 1684, died young 4 Bethiah, born 1685, died 1715, married Ebenezer Emerson 1707 5 Susannah, born 1687 married Joseph Underwood, 1707 6 Ebenezer, born 1689, married Mercy Damon 1714 7 Stephen, born 1692, married Elizabeth Batchelder, 1713 8 Caleb, born 1694 9 Timothy born 1696 10 Obadiah, born 1698 11 Abigail, born 1699 12 Amy, born 1701, died young 13 Amy, born 1702, married Stephen Richardson, of Billerica, 1728 14 Phineas (see forward)

(III) Phineas Parker, youngest and fourteenth child of Nathaniel Parker (2), born at Reading, Massachusetts, September 27, 1704, died at Pepperell, August 28, 1787, married Martha ——, who died at Pepperell, January 31, 1793, aged eighty-three years Their children were 1 Edmund, (see forward) 2 Martha, born February 5, 1735, married Captain Jonas Richardson, July 27, 1756 3 Elizabeth born June 18, 1737, married —— Nagle 4 Phineas (Captain), born July 9, 1739 5 Lydia, born February 17, 1742, died at Pepperell, August 31, 1822, married Reuben Shattuck, of Pepperell, November 25, 1773 6 Abijah, born 1745, died at Pepperell, December 4, 1811, married January 21, 1772, Sarah Lawrence 7 John, January 8, 1748 8 Mary, May 4, 1751, died November 12 1752, at Reading, all the foregoing were born at Reading, Massachusetts

(IV) Edmund Parker, eldest child of Phineas Parker (3), born in Reading, Massachusetts, February 7, 1731, died in Pepperell, Massachusetts, August 13, 1813, married (first) Lydia Varnum, in Pepperell, July 22, 1755 She died August 4, 1756 married (second) in Pepperell, April 13, 1757, Elizabeth Sheple, widow of James Green, Jr, of Groton, daughter of John and Elizabeth (Boyden) Sheple, Jr, of Groton, born there May 22, 1730, died at Pepperell, November 21, 1812, aged eighty-two years

There was one child born to Edmund and Lydia (Varnum) Parker 1 Lydia, born in Pepperell, July 30, 1756, and probably died at Pepperell, February 10, 1774 Children of Edmund and Elizabeth (Sheple) (Green) Parker were 2 Edmund, born in Townsend, May 23, 1761, died at Norridgewock, Maine, November 18, 1838, married Mary Shepley, of Pepperell, March 11, 1783 3 Asa born at Pepperell, December 29, 1763, married Sibbel White, of Pepperell December 6, 1792 4 Jonas, (see forward) 5 James, born in Pepperell, April 19, 1769, died at Brookline, New Hampshire, January 14, 1826, married Sally Boynton, of Pepperell, October 11, 1792 6 John, born in Pepperell, October 3, 1774 married Sally Tarbell, of Pepperell, October 3, 1797 6 Elizabeth born at Pepperell, January 26 1778, married David Shed, Jr, of Pepperell, December 27, 1797

Elizabeth Sheple or Shepley was the daughter of John Shepley, Jr, (born April 1, 1703, married February 16, 1725-6, Elizabeth Boyden) and granddaughter of John Shepley (born probably at Wenham, died September 4, 1736, resided at Groton) and wife Lydia, probably great-granddaughter of John or Nathaniel Shepley, sons of the emigrant John Shepley, Shipley or Shapleigh, was born in England about 1587, and settled before or in 1636 in Salem, removed to Wenham, Massachusetts

Elizabeth Boyden, before mentioned, was born March 10, 1707, the daughter of Jonathan and Elizabeth Boyden, and descendant of Thomas Boyden, the immigrant, who settled in Watertown

(V) Jonas Parker, fourth child of Edmund Parker (4) born in Pepperell, July 16, 1766, died at Pepperell, December 7 1849, married (first) Ruth Farmer in Pepperell, December 18, 1788, daughter of Nathaniel and Hannah (Fessenden) Farmer, of Lexington, Massachusetts born in Lexington, August 15, 1765, died at Pepperell, February 5, 1828, married (second) Mrs Mehitable S Frost, widow of Lemuel Parker, of Pepperell, January 18, 1829

Nathaniel Farmer, father of Ruth, born January 29, 1725, died September 3, 1778, son of John

Farmer (born September 18, 1703) and Hannah Woods, of Groton John Farmer, Jr was the son of John Farmer (born August 19 1671, died September 9, 1736), of Billerica and his wife, Abigail Shed (born 1679, died at Tewksbury, Massachusetts, March 20, 1754, aged seventy-five), daughter of Daniel Shed John Farmer was the son of Edward Farmer, the emigrant, who came to New England between 1660 and 1670, born in England 1640, died May 27, 1727, and his wife, Mary, born 1642-3, died at Billerica, March, 1719, about seventy-eight years of age

Hannah Fessenden, mother of Ruth Farmer, born in Lexington, Massachusetts, August 9, 1736, died December 20, 1782, married May 28, 1755, daughter of Thomas Fessenden, Jr, (born December 9, 1709 died July 22, 1768), of Lexington and his wife, Hannah Prentice, married June 19, 1735, of Cambridge, Massachusetts

Thomas Fessenden was the son of Thomas Fessenden (born August 12, 1684, died March 6, 1738), of Lexington, and his first of three wives, Abigail Poulter, daughter of Jonathan and Elizabeth Poulter (she was born September 5, 1692, died April 25, 1719, married 1708) Thomas Fessenden was the son of Nicholas Fessenden (the emigrant, born in England 1650, died February 24, 1719), of Cambridge, and Margaret Cheney, born 1755, died December 10, 1717

Nathaniel Farmer, father of Ruth (Farmer) Parker, was a member of Captain Parker's company and was in the battle on Lexington common April 19, 1775 He received a severe wound that morning, the bullet struck his right arm and fractured the bone, so that he was disabled for a long time The general court granted him fifteen pounds, fifteen shillings for loss of labor and expense of surgical attendance

The children of Nathaniel and Hannah (Fessenden) Farmer were 1 John, born July 18, 1757, married Lucy Read, March 27, 1783 2 Hannah, January 28, 1760, married Jacob Kilburn, of Lancaster 3 Isaac, October 8, 1762, died young 4 Ruth, before mentioned 5 Abigail, November 1, 1768 6 Sally, December 19, 1771, married Samuel Pierce, of Groton 7 Rebeckah, December 19, 1771 8 Thomas Shattuck, September 10, 1775, 9 Isaac, December 31, 1779

(VI) John Parker, fourth child of Jonas Parker (5), was born at Pepperell Massachusetts, December 18, 1795 He spent his younger days at Pepperell and Lancaster, but during most of his active years he was engaged in the shipping business at Cohasset, in partnership with Laban Souther under the firm name of Souther & Parker He was an officer in the Lancaster company in the war of 1812 and was on duty in Boston He was a member of the Cohasset Unitarian church He was for many years a neighbor and personal friend of Daniel Webster He died March 26, 1868, at Cohasset He married November 15, 1822 Mary Oakes Lawrence, then only fifteen years of age, born May 1, 1807, at Cohasset, daughter of Deacon Thaddeus and Joa Lawrence They lived at Pepperell for a time after they were married and the first four children were born there, the others at Cohasset

Children were 1 Caroline Willard born October 2, 1823 2 Mary Elizabeth March 3 1826 died young 3 Harriet Maria, March 13, 1828 4 John Loring see forward 5 Louisa Frances August 22, 1832 6 James Henry, December 3, 1834 7 Mary Elizabeth, October 21, 1837 8 George Odion, February 9, 1840 9 Sophronia Lawrence, February 18, 1842 10 Charles Oakes, October 18 1844 11 Edmund Lawrence (see forward) 12 Frank Lewis, Jan 11 1849 Of these two, John L and Edmund L lived in Worcester

(VII) John Loring Parker, fourth child of John Parker (6), born at Pepperell, Massachusetts, August 11, 1830, removed when very young to Cohasset, where he attended the common schools, and was graduated from the high school in 1848 He went to Pepperell after leaving school and served an apprenticeship in the machine shop of Blake & Co, manufacturers of paper machinery Later he married Marrinda C Blake, the daughter of the senior partner of the firm, Henry Blake He worked as journeyman and foreman and finally became superintendent of the factory During the civil war he secured a contract for the manufacture of swords, and as partner of the firm of Roby & Company carried on this business in a shop at West Chelmsford His partners were Christopher Roby and Charles Blake At the close of the war he accepted a position as superintendent of the shoe factory of Gevernor Baldwin, at Detroit, Michigan He returned to Worcester to take the position of superintendent of the loom works of L J Knowles & Brother, and set up the first Knowles loom made in Worcester in 1866 He went into business for himself a few years later, manufacturing ferules, etc, at 209 Union street He bought the business of White & Emerson, manufactures of iron and steel pressed goods, and carried on the business until his death At first the business was located on Foster street In 1879 it was moved to the present location on School street in order to get larger quarters At first George S Barton was a silent partner in the firm of John L Parker & Co In 1876 the interests of Mr Barton were purchased by Edmund L Parker, brother of the senior partner and the business was continued under the same name

The firm was prosperous and after the death of the senior partner the business continued under the original name In recent years some fifty hands were employed, and goods made for the foreign as well as the home trade All the products of this shop were patented and made for the consumers The company makes parts for manufacturers of agricultural machinery, cotton machinery, cutlery shoe last manufacturers and a large variety of concerns using pressed metal For a time Mr Parker was interested in the manufacture of cutlery at Natick, Massachusetts, in partnership with Joel Allen and his brother James H Parker

He was a Free Mason, was a member of the Coral Street Methodist Church and was superintendent of the Sunday school He died December 20, 1887 Children were 1 Herbert Lawrence, (see forward) 2 Nellie Gertrude, married Elmer W Lewis of Boston, he is with Kidder, Peabody & Co, bankers, they have two children, Arthur G and Thelma 3 Harry Strickland, married Edith Gross, he is a graduate of the Peekskill, New York Military Academy, and one of the confidential men of F S Bowser & Co of Boston and Indianapolis 4 Ned Wesley, (see forward)

(VIII) Herbert Lawrence Parker, son of John Loring Parker (7), born in Worcester, was educated in the public schools of Worcester and at the Worcester Polytechnic Institute After graduation he went to Mexico as the general agent of the Atchison Topeka & Santa Fe Railroad Company He lived at Juarez Mexico, for a year, and in the city of Mexico for two years and a half he then went to San Francisco In 1896 he bought a controlling interest and has since been the president and manager of the Emerson Electric Manufactur-

Edmund L. Parker

ing Company of St Louis The business of this concern has been very prosperous under his ownership

He married Emily King Their children are King Herbert, Katherine, Elizabeth

(VIII) New Wesley Parker, son of John Loring Parker (7), was born in Worcester May 22, 1870 When he was two years old his parents removed to Shrewsbury, Massachusetts, where he began his education in the common schools He graduated from the high school at the age of eighteen and entered the business which his father established in Worcester In 1888, shortly after his father's death, he removed with the rest of the family to Cohasset, and while living there he took a course in the business college of Bryant & Stratton in Boston In 1889 he returned to Worcester and entered the manufactory of John L Parker & Co, in which his father had been the senior partner and which his uncle, Edmund L Parker, the junior partner He learned the business thoroughly, and for nearly twenty years was superintendent of the manufacturing end of it Since 1905, when the business was incorporated as the John L Parker Company, under the laws of Massachusetts, he has been a director The other officers of the company are President, Frank R Jones, secretary, John M Kendall, director, Sanford C Kendall Mr Parker lives in Shrewsbury where he has a handsome residence He is a Methodist in religion, although he attends the Shrewsbury Congregational church In politics he is a Republican He is active in town affairs and is chief of the local fire department He was formerly a member of the Shrewsbury Grange Patrons of Husbantry, and was a charter member of the Hancock Club of Worcester He married June 4 1892, Mabelle G Bemis, daughter of Daniel W Bemis a sketch of whom will be found elsewhere in this work (See the Bemis Family under sketch of Dr J M Bemis) Her mother was Maria (Wood) Bemis Children are Winifred Agnes, born December 30, 1895, Lawrence Bemis born August 19, 1901

(VII) Edmund Lawrence Parker, son of John Parker (6), born at Cohasset Massachusetts, February 8 1847, died August 17, 1906 He received his education at the Cohasset schools and at Wilbraham Academy Was a graduate of high school in 1865 After leaving school he became a clerk in the Second National Bank of Boston In 1870 he became a member of the firm of Caverly Parker & Young of Lynn Massachusetts In 1876 he came to Worcester and became a partner with his brother in the firm of John L Parker & Co in the manufacture of pressed metal goods After the death of his brother he carried on the business under the same name until 1905 when the business was incorporated and he retired The business was very prosperous and Mr Parker was one of the best known manufacturers of the city He built a handsome residence at 15 Massachusetts avenue in 1905 and there enjoyed a well earned rest from active business He enjoyed travel and had been abroad many times He was a Republican and prominent in city affairs He served four years in the common council from 1887 to 1890, inclusive and was an alderman in 1891-92 He was a diligent and effective worker for the welfare of the city, and was counted among the best men that have served in the city council in recent years His common-sense and good judgment won the respect and confidence of his associates He was always an active and consistent advocate of temperance reform As a candidate it has been noted that he received the highest number of votes on the ticket and he would have been kept in the city council longer had he not declined to be re-elected His name was frequently urged as Republican candidate for mayor He was in every sense a self-made man He was one of the organizers of the Hancock club of Worcester, was a member of the Worcester board of trade and a director in the Eastern Bridge Construction Company of Worcester, the Equity Corporation Bank, of Worcester, the Fidelity Mercantile Agency Company, of Worcester, the West Side Land Company, of Worcester, the Worcester Real Estate Company, of Worcester the Toadvine Lumber Company, of Elizabeth City, North Carolina He was a well known Free Mason, a member of Athelstan Lodge, Eureka Chapter and the Worcester County Commandery Knights Templar He was a member of St John's Episcopal Church and for fifteen years was warden

He married October 6, 1869, Eva Sarah Jones, daughter of William and Rachel Jones, of Lynn, Massachusetts Their only child is Dr Ernest L Parker, born February 13, 1878, graduated from Phillips Academy at Andover, Massachusetts, in 1898, and from the Harvard Medical school in 1903 after which he took a post graduate course at the medical school He then received a two-year appointment in the Boston city hospital, from which he graduated and served five months on its executive board He was elected on the staff of the Worcester city hospital in 1905, at the time he began to practice his profession in Worcester His office is at 11 Elm street He married, October 8, 1906, Sally Leeds Bufford, of Dorchester, Massachusetts

CHRISTOPHER COLUMBUS STONE Deacon Simon Stone (1), the immigrant ancestor of Hon Christopher Columbus Stone, of Clinton, Massachusetts, with his younger brother, Gregory Stone, of whom a sketch appears elsewhere in this work were early settlers at Watertown, Massachusetts and are progenitors of most of the old New England families of this surname Simon Stone, husbandman, aged fifty years with his wife Joan aged thirty-eight years, and children, Frances, aged sixteen Ann aged eleven Simon, aged four, Marie aged three and John, aged five weeks sailed in the ship Increase," April 15, 1635, from Ipswich, Robert Lea master He was admitted a freeman May 25, 1636 He was selectman for seven years between 1637 and 1656, and was deacon of the church

He died at Watertown, September 22, 1665 His will was proved October 3, 1665 by his brother, Gregory Stone and Stephen Day He bequeathed to sons Simon and John daughters Frances and Mary Johanna and Nathaniel Green children of Frances and her husband Thomas Greene, kinsmen John and Daniel Warner (Warren?) and Thomas Wells His wife died and he married (second), 1654 Sarah Lumpkin widow of Richard Lumpkin, of Ipswich Massachusetts who came from Boxtead, Essex county England Her will was dated March 25 1663 and proved October 6 following Deacon Stone was eighty years old at the time of his death and fifty years old when he emigrated Hence his birth year was 1585 Children of Simon and Joan (or Jane) Stone were Frances, born in England 1619 married Thomas Green and had children Joanna and Nathaniel, Ann born in England, 1624 Simon Jr, born in England, 1631, see forward, Marie born in England, 1632 died unmarried June 25 1691, John born in England, baptized August 15 1635 at Watertown Elizabeth born April 5, 1639

(II) Simon Stone Jr, son of Deacon Simon

Stone (1), was born in England in 1631 and came to America with his parents and their family in 1635 He settled in Watertown, where he was a distinguished citizen He was often elected town clerk, indicating that he was a man of some education, and selectman, indicating that he was a man of some force of character and of property He was deputy to the general court in 1678-79-80-81-82-83-84-86-89-90 and during those years was one of the foremost men of the town He died February 27, 1707-08, aged seventy-seven years

He married Mary Whipple who died June 2, 1720 aged eighty-six years Their children Simon, Jr born August 18, 1656, see forward, John, July 23, 1658 Matthew, February 6, 1659-60, of Lancaster, 1693 of Sudbury and in 1697 was deacon of the Sudbury church, married Mary ——, Nathaniel, February 22, 1661-62, died February 24, same year, Ebenezer, February 27, 1662 admitted freeman March 26, 1690 Mary, January 6 1664-65 Nathaniel 1667 graduate of Harvard, 1690 died 1755, aged eighty-eight years minister at Harwich, Elizabeth October 9 1670, admitted to full communion in church February 13 1697-98, married November 6 1706 John Maddock, of Boston, David October 19 1672, admitted to church December 12 1697 married December 12 1710, Mary Rice he died October 7 1750 aged seventy-eight years blind for fifty-six years, infant, born and died August 1674, Susannah, November 6, 1675, married, June 1697, Edward Goddard, Jonathan, December 26, 1677 died January 7, 1754

(III) Deacon Simon Stone son of Simon Stone (2) was born at Watertown Massachusetts, August 18 or 19, 1656 He died December 10, 1741, at Groton He and his brother John settled in Groton Massachusetts John had a son John, Jr born September 23 1699 and son James, born January 23, 1701, and probably Joseph, all three of whom settled in Groton and had families there

Dr Green says of Simon Stone "This has been a common name for nearly two centuries and the families bearing it have lived in the south part of the town Deacon Simon Stone was an original proprietor, owning an eighteen-acre right He was the eldest of the children of Deacon Simon and Mary (Whipple) Stone, of Watertown Perhaps he was the person referred to by Mather's (Magnalia (VII 74), who was severely wounded by the Indians July 4, 1690, at Exeter" The story of the wounds as told in the Magnalia seem incredible He was wounded by bullets in nine places and left for dead When the Indians came to strip his body they struck him with a hatchet twice to cut off his head but the British soldiers were heard coming and he was left unscalped When his fellow-soldiers found him he was not dead so they placed him in a canoe and took him to a safe place where he finally recovered fully Simon was often chosen town officer and on important committees of the church and served as deacon for many years He was often selectman The epitaph on Deacon Stone's gravestone is "Here lies the body of Deacon Simon Stone who departed this life December 19 A D 1741 aged eighty-five years three months and eleven days Died 1741" He married Sarah —— and all their children were born at Groton except the first two Simon and John Their children John, born 1690 Simon Jr about 1692 Susanna October 23, 1694 Isaac May 4, 1697, see forward, Benjamin, August 12 1706 Hannah, died September 27, 1723, Lydia died September 30 1723

(IV) Simon Stone Jr son of Simon Stone (3) was born in Watertown, probably in 1692, and removed when an infant with his parents to Groton, Massachusetts, where he lived all the remainder of his days, although his section of the town was set off as Harvard, and he was a prominent citizen of the new town He was the leader in the movement to have Harvard set of, and the general court recognized him as the first citizen of the town by ordering him to summon the first town meeting, June 30, 1732 He was at that meeting elected moderator and a member of the first board of selectman He served the new town in many offices and on many committees He was on the committee to build the meeting house in 1729 and to invite the minister to settle—Rev John Seccomb He was one of the first deacons of the church with Joseph Fairbanks, Jonathan Whitney and Joseph Haskell He died in 1746, leaving an estate valued at 508 pounds The history of Harvard calls him "the foremost citizen" In the long list of his chattels the history notes some showing the character of household goods at that time, viz Silver cup, an oval table—unwonted luxuries in those days—also a loom and tackling, a lanthorn, a looking glass, wheels and cards, flax-combs, sheep shears, warming pan, skillets, a fire slice, trammels, keelers, a razor, two swarms of bees, a pigeon net and a cyder mill He married Sarah —— All their children are recorded at Groton until 1732 and the two youngest are recorded at Harvard, probably all born on the old homestead, located in what is now Harvard, formerly Groton Children Simon, Jr, born September 10 1714, settled at Harvard married Eunice ——, Ephraim, January 2, 1715-16, Oliver, January 20, 1719-20, Sarah, January 27, 1721-22, Isaac, February 17 1723-24 see forward, Hannah, April 18, 1726 Elias, April 2, 1728, Amos, September 9, 1729, Solomon, September 3, 1732, Micah, April 10, 1735

(V) Isaac Stone son of Simon Stone (4), was born at Groton, Massachusetts, February 17, 1723-24 The farm on which he lived was set off in the territory of the new town of Harvard, where he was brought up He was assigned a seat in the Harvard church in 1750 He was a soldier in the French and Indian war, corporal in Captain Israel Taylor's company Colonel Oliver Wilder's regiment in 1757 and in Judah Clark's company in 1755 He or his son Isaac served in the revolution in Captain Joseph Whitcomb's company of Lancaster, Captain James Reed's company in Colonel Timothy Ruggles's regiment He resided at Boylston for many years, but died at Lancaster, September 14 1816, aged ninety-three years He married (first) Keziah Pierce April 16, 1744, at Harvard He married (second), May 3, 1765, at Boylston, Massachusetts by Rev Mr Morse, Rachel Fiske, of Shrewsbury She died at Boylston, July 12, 1824 aged ninety years After the death of his first wife he removed to Shrewsbury Children of Isaac and Keziah Stone were Ephraim, born at Harvard January 22, 1745-46, Isaac, January 26, 1746-47 resided at Boylston, married Abigail Moore Sarah Moore, 1808, and Abigail Green, 1824 Dinah August 3 1749, Daniel, July 10, 1754, Jacob, July 25, 1756, died young, infant born and died December 16, 1758, Keziah, April 6, 1760, Sarah March 30 1762 Abigail, February 19 1765 Children of Isaac and Rachel Stone, all born at Shrewsbury were Esther, May 30, 1766, Elizabeth October 21 1767 Jacob, August 25, 1770, see forward Annis, March 4, 1772, married —— Robinson

(VI) Jacob Stone son of Isaac Stone (5), was born in Shrewsbury, Massachusetts, August 25 1770 He settled in the north district of Shrewsbury, Boylston and at Lancaster, where the births of his children are recorded, though all may not have been born there. About 1796 Jacob Stone purchased of Ephraim Bennett three hundred acres of land along the old country road from Lancaster to Worcester. He was a carpenter by trade and for many years was the leading builder in that section. He employed a large force of carpenters at times. He did the carpenter work of the brick church in Lancaster in 1816. Both he and his sons were very skillful in framing and raising houses. He built a large two-story house for himself before his first marriage and he lived in it more than forty years, but late in life he met with reverses and had to give up the place to creditors. He then moved to the Fitch place in Sterling, where he died July 8, 1847.

He married (first), September 23, 1793, Martha Barnes. She died March 23, 1795. He married (second) Anna Barnes, of Boylston, May 11, 1796, and she died at Lancaster, April 12, 18—. Jacob married (third) April 14, 1819, Isabelle Bennett, daughter of Asa Bennett, of Lancaster. The children of Jacob and Martha Stone were: Twins, died in infancy. The children of Jacob and Anna Stone were: Joseph, born February 19, 1797; James, August 29, 1799, see forward; Martha, June 29, 1801; Jacob, March 6, 1803, died October 9, 1830; Anna, February 9, 1805, died September 30, 1842; Achsah, April 18, 1806, died October 21, 1843; Abel, April 6, 1808, died June 11, 1856; Betsy, March 11, 1810, died September 30, 1813; Captain Oliver, January 16, 1812, father of Louis L. Stone; Betsy, March 3, 1814, died December 23, 1853; Tamar, born December 30, 1815, died May 19, 1836; Maria, born March 23, 1818, died September 11, 1845. The children of Jacob and Isabelle Stone were: one child which died in infancy.

(VII) James Stone, son of Jacob Stone (6), was born in Lancaster, August 29, 1799. He lived all his life at Lancaster. He was a carpenter and farmer. He held the office of prudential agent, whose duty it was to hire the district school teachers, in 1839. He married, February 15, 1827, Eliza Burditt. Their children: Christopher Columbus, born November 27, 1829, see forward; Ellen Eliza, February 15, 1827, Eliza Burditt. Their children: see forward. Ellen Eliza, February 19, 1836; Harriet Elizabeth (twin), January 23, 1839; Caroline Louisa (twin), January 23, 1839; infants died October 11, 1842, and in 1846.

(VIII) Christopher Columbus Stone, son of James Stone (7), was born in Lancaster in that part of the town set off as Clinton, November 27, 1829. He attended the district schools of Clintonville and took a course at the Lancaster Academy. He learned the carpenter trade, which his father and grandfather had followed successfully, and for twenty years was a carpenter and builder in Clinton. Then he decided to study law. He had all his life been a student and had obtained a liberal education from private reading and study. He studied law in the office of Hon. C. G. Stevens, a lawyer of high repute and attainments who practiced in Worcester and Clinton. He did not apply for admission to the bar, as he received the appointment of trial justice at Clinton in 1871 and remained in this position until the formation of the second district court of eastern Worcester, when he was appointed associate justice, but on retirement of the presiding judge, Mr. Stevens, became his successor and has ever since filled this position with rare judgment and ability.

In his younger days Mr. Stone was active in the militia and when the civil war broke out he was major of the Ninth Regiment, to which the Light Guard of Clinton belonged. He was one of the directors of a drill club organized August 11, 1861, that did good work for the cause. Throughout the war he was active in support of the government and in recruiting soldiers. Judge Stone became active in the temperance movement in its early days. In 1850, when the order of the Sons of Temperance was flourishing, he was among the worthy patriarchs. He is a member of Clinton Lodge of Odd Fellows, the order of Red Men and the Free Masons. He has attained the Knight Templar degree in Masonry. He is president of the First National Bank of Clinton, member of the board of investment of Clinton Savings Bank, and a leader in financial circles. He is vice-president of the Hospital Association and vice-president of the Clinton Historical Society. Judge Stone has conducted for a long time the iron foundry in Clinton in which his sons and son-in-law are now interested. In politics Judge Stone has been for many years one of the leading Republicans of that section.

He married (first), September 30, 1854, Elizabeth A. Whitcomb, of Stow, Massachusetts. She died April 2, 1870. He married (second), December 25, 1880, Anna Hunt, who died June 17, 1887. He married (third), February 13, 1890, Mary L. Holman. Children of Christopher C. and Elizabeth A. Stone were: Elsie, born July 16, 1855, died October 2, 1871; Henrietta L., born June 6, 1857; Anna C., born January 31, 1859; James A., born February 2, 1861, died February 5, 1861; Jerome E., born February 22, 1862; George C., born March 31, 1864; Walter A., born December 28, 1867.

(IX) George Stone, son of Hon. Christopher C. Stone (8), was born in Clinton, Massachusetts, March 31, 1864. He was educated in the public and high schools of his native town, graduating in 1880. He learned the trade of machinist in the shop of the J. B. Parker Company. After he became a journeyman he went to work in his father's foundry in Clinton, became a member and officer of the company, and at present has exclusive charge of the machine shop connected with the foundry. In politics Mr. Stone is a Republican. He is a member of the Clinton Council, Royal Arcanum, the order of Red Men and Odd Fellows. He attends the Unitarian church. Mr. Stone ranks high among the younger manufacturers of the town. He married, September, 1900, Henrietta Johnstone, of Clinton, daughter of Charles Johnstone. Their children are: Walter C., born in Clinton, 1892; Charles Clifford, born in Clinton, 1898.

(IX) Walter A. Stone, son of Hon. Christopher C. Stone (8), was born in Clinton, Massachusetts, December 28, 1867. He was educated in the Clinton schools and graduated from the High school in 1884. He became associated with his father in the foundry and machine shop. Later he worked in the Locomotive Works at Providence, Rhode Island, and became superintendent. He was superintendent of large foundries at New Bedford and Springfield, Massachusetts. In 1896 he returned to Clinton and took charge of the foundry which his father owned there, in association with his brother and Gerton A. Beam, his brother-in-law, who took charge of the machine shop. The firm have built up a large and growing business. Mr. Stone is a skillful mechanic as well as a capable business man. In politics he is an active Republican, especially during campaigns. He is a member of the Order of Odd Fellows and of the Order of Red Men. He attends the Episcopal church. He married, July 31, 1902, Helena Oakley, daughter of Samuel and Elizabeth (Boyd) Oakley, natives of England.

They have one child, Margery A., born at Clinton, Massachusetts.

ARTHUR C. HAWKINS. Colonel Nathaniel Hawkins (1), the immigrant ancestor of Arthur C. Hawkins, of Lancaster, was born in England and came to this country during the French and Indian war with the British army, in which he was an officer. He came with the troops in 1761 and took part in the first battle of Quebec. For his valor and intrepidity on the field of action he was awarded a medal suitably inscribed.

He settled first in America at South Kingston, Rhode Island, but during the American revolution settled in Charlestown, Massachusetts, in April, 1779. He was living in Charlestown in 1789 with children: Nathaniel, Christopher, Sarah and Samuel. Mitty Flagg was also a member of his family. In 1783 he bought a lot of land in Charlestown of Thomas Robbins. He bought and sold land at Charlestown often afterward. He died at Charlestown, October 3, 1817, aged sixty-nine years. That would make his birth year 1748, and he must have been very young to have served in the army at Quebec. Possibly there is an error in the record of his age, at death. His estate was administered by P. Tufts, Jr., appointed November 13, 1817.

He married Sarah Kent, who died April 17, 1785, aged thirty-two years. Her gravestone is to be seen at Charlestown. He married (second), February 12, 1788, Rebecca Kent, who died February 23, 1827, aged eighty years, according to her gravestone. The children of Colonel Nathaniel and Sarah Hawkins, born probably in South Kingston, Rhode Island, or vicinity were: 1. Nathaniel, Jr., settled in Richmond, Virginia, where he was living at the time of his father's death; he deeded land in which he had rights at Charlestown. 2. Christopher, married Eunice ——, and had children—Christopher, Catherine, Hannah, Eunice, Sarah K., Rebecca K. Christopher, Nathaniel and Sarah joined in selling land formerly of their father, Nathaniel Hawkins. 3. Guy Carlton, of whom later. 4. Samuel, settled in Henrico, Virginia, where he was living at the time of his father's death, signed deed with Guy Carlton in 1819. 5. Elizabeth, married Robert Long Jr. 6. Sarah K., married Henry Adams.

(II) Guy Carlton Hawkins, son of Colonel Nathaniel Hawkins (1), was born probably in South Kingston, Rhode Island, about 1785. He joined with his brother, Samuel Hawkins, in a deed to Sarah R. Hawkins, of Charlestown, Massachusetts, the house on Cambridge avenue with ten acres of land, 1819. He was a farmer and settled in Charlestown. He married Eliza Miller, of that town. Among their children was Nathaniel C., of whom later.

(III) Nathaniel C. Hawkins, son of Guy Carlton Hawkins (2), was born in Charlestown, Massachusetts, now Boston, September 9, 1827. He was educated there in the common schools. He engaged in business in Boston for many years, and when he retired removed to Lancaster, Massachusetts, where he bought a farm and has since lived. In politics Mr. Hawkins is a Democrat. He was selectman of the town of Somerville, where he lived in his younger days.

He married, 1849, Amelia Magoun, daughter of John C. Magoun. She died in 1887. Their children were: Ida A., Eleanor C., died young, Edward C., Arthur C., of whom later, Annie E., Guy C., died young, Everett M., Alice M., died young, Frank W., who is a banker at Seattle, Washington.

(IV) Arthur Calvin Hawkins, son of Nathaniel C. Hawkins (3), was born at Somerville, Massachusetts, where his parents were then living, November 28, 1855. He was only four years old when the family removed to Lancaster. He attended the public schools, and when a young man engaged in the poultry business, which he has followed for thirty years. He is the proprietor of one of the largest and most prosperous poultry farms in the state of Massachusetts. He is especially prominent among the poultry men of the country. He is a member of the National Poultry Association, of the New England Plymouth Rock Association, of the American Buff Plymouth Rock Association, of the New England White Wyandotte Association, and is a director of the American Poultry Association. At the "Riverview" stock farm in Lancaster, Mr. Hawkins breeds for the market many fancy trotting and carriage horses.

Mr. Hawkins is a Unitarian in religion and a member of the parish committee of the Lancaster Unitarian church. In politics he is a Republican. He is a member of the board of water commissioners of the town of Lancaster. He commands the respect and confidence of his fellow citizens. He is earnest, industrious and successful in his business.

He married, 1881, Minnie M. Brockway, daughter of Henry and Mary (Martin) Brockway, of Lawrence, Massachusetts. Their children are: Mary Louise, Helen M., Evelyn A., Nathaniel Carlton.

CAPTAIN EDWARD WILLIAM WHEELER. Obadiah Wheeler (1), pioneer settler of Concord, Massachusetts, was the emigrant ancestor of Captain Edward William Wheeler, of Worcester, Massachusetts. Obadiah Wheeler was born in England, 1608. He came to New England and settled in Concord as early as 1638. He was made a freeman June 2, 1641. He owned land in the centre of the town and lived for a time near the eastern end of the burying ground. He also had land in Meadow Brook. His wife Susannah died in 1649. He died in Concord, October 29, 1671. Of their nine children the first was born in England and the remainder in Concord; the youngest was killed by the Indians in Sudbury, Massachusetts. His will is dated October 6, 1671, bequeathing to his six children: Joshua, Obadiah, Samuel, John, Josiah and Susannah. Administration was granted December 19, 1671, to his kinsman, Thomas Wheeler, and John, son of the deceased.

The children of Obadiah Wheeler were: Joshua, born in England, married Elizabeth ——; John, born January 29, 1640, died young; Ruth, April 23, 1642; a son, November 25, 1643, died November 29, 1643; Samuel, February 22, 1644-5, married Mary Perry; John, 1647; Susannah, March 16, 1649, married —— Shipley; Obadiah, 1651-2; Josiah, died April 21, 1676, killed by the Indians at Sudbury.

(II) Obadiah Wheeler, son of Obadiah Wheeler (1) and second wife, was born in 1651-2 in Concord, Massachusetts. He was a farmer and lived in Concord, where all his children were born. He married Elizabeth White, the daughter of Resolved White. Her father was son of William and Susanna (Fuller) White, who came over in the "Mayflower." Their son, Peregrine White, was the first child of the Pilgrims born in New England. Peregrine was born in the ship "Mayflower" while at anchor in Cape Cod Harbor, November 20, 1620. William White was the son of Bishop John White and brought with him on the "Mayflower" the celebrated Breeches Bible. He died during the first winter at Plymouth, February 21, 1621-2, and his widow married Governor Edward Winslow, May 12, 1621. So the two boys, Resolved, who was five years old when his father died, and Peregrine, who was

Capt. Edward W. Wheeler

an infant, were raised in the family of Governor Winslow.

Resolved White, born at Leyden, Holland, 1615, died between 1690 and 1694. He settled at Scituate but later removed to Salem, and married his second wife there August 5, 1674. She was Abigail Lord, widow of William Lord. His first wife was Judith Vassall, born 1619-20, died April 13, 1670, daughter of William Vassall, one of the assistants of the Massachusetts Bay Colony, settled at Scituate and Marshfield, finally removing to the Barbadoes. His wife was Ann King, born in England 1593, and she had six children. The children of Resolved White were: William, born April 10, 1642, at Marshfield; John, March 11, 1644, at Scituate; Samuel, March 13, 1646; Resolved, born at Scituate; Anna, June 2, 1649, at Scituate; Elizabeth, June 4, 1652; Josiah, born at Scituate, baptized October 14, 1654; Susannah, born at Scituate, baptized November 9, 1656.

Obadiah Wheeler settled on his father's farm in the southwesterly part of Concord until 1715, when he disposed of his lands and no trace has yet been found of his whereabouts after that. His family consisted of eight sons and one daughter, all of whom were married and settled in adjoining towns, most of them in what was then Lancaster. Numerous descendants are still found in Bolton and Berlin. Two of them however, Obadiah and Joseph, received from their father his farm lands in equal shares and probably retained possession of them for a time. Samuel Wheeler, his son, married Joanna Walcott, and settled in Carlisle. Uriah Wheeler went to Sudbury and married Abigail Rice. His descendants have been numerous.

The children of Obadiah and Elizabeth (White) Wheeler were: Obadiah, born September 21, 1673, married Hannah Fletcher, daughter of Moses Fletcher; Josiah, October 22, 1675, died at Lancaster, December 8, 1738, married Martha ——, born 1679, died May 21, 1748, married (second) Captain Peter Joslin, of Lancaster; Uriah, April 13, 1678, died December 9, 1750, married, December 29, 1704, Abigail Rice, of Sudbury, where they settled, she died June 10, 1754; Samuel Wheeler, January 23, 1680-81, married Joanna Walcott, settled in Carlisle; Jonathan, July 28, 1683, died about 1747, married Mary ——, settled in Lancaster and left many descendants; Elizabeth, February 7, 1685-6; Joseph, March 7, 1690-91; Benjamin, September 29, 1693, died 1759, at New Marlboro, married Hannah ——, born 1698, had five children; Joshua, April 9, 1696, died April 11, 1778, married about 1720 Annah ——, who died October 26, 1761, had four children.

(III) Joseph Wheeler, son of Obadiah Wheeler (2), was born at Concord, Massachusetts, March 7, 1690-91, died February 29, 1780, in Lancaster, Massachusetts. He married, March 2, 1726-7 (first) Abigail Butterfield, daughter of Jonathan and Ruth (Wright) Butterfield, of Menotomy (Arlington). She was born May 11, 1702, died October 2, 1764. Jonathan Butterfield was son of Benjamin Butterfield, who was in Woburn as early as 1638. He was also in Charlestown, where he was admitted a freeman May 10, 1643. He removed from Woburn to Chelmsford. He died March 2, 1688. His will, dated May 8, 1677, proved at Boston, June 7, 1688, mentions wife and children. He married Hannah Whittemore for his second wife. The wife of Jonathan Butterfield (II) was Ruth Wright, who is descended from Deacon John Wright, one of the first settlers of Woburn, Massachusetts, and she died 1754.

Joseph Wheeler settled on the old homestead in Concord until he followed several of his brothers to Lancaster, and in 1742 purchased a farm of sixty acres on Chestnut Hill about two miles south of the present town of Lancaster. He sold this farm in 1753 and next year bought another at a place now known as Pratt's Crossing in Lancaster. A mill pond and grist mill were included in the purchase and the mill dam and the farm house are still standing or were recently. He bought other parcels of land. His last residence was on George Hill in Lancaster, where he died in 1780. His wife Abigail died in 1764. Two years later he married Sarah Allen, daughter of Ebenezer Allen, of Lancaster. He was eighty-eight when he made his will and ninety when he died. His son Joseph was his executor.

The children of Joseph and Abigail Wheeler were: Phebe, born January 11, 1727-8, married, March 3, 1746, Jotham Wilder, of Lancaster, born in 1710, had six children. Wilder was a descendant of Thomas Wilder, of Shiplake, Berkshire, England; Reuben, December 3, 1729, died July 29, 1763, of small pox while in the military service of George III in Ireland, was unmarried; Rachel, September 15, 1731, died May 15, 1790, in Lancaster, unmarried; Joseph, March 13, 1735; Abigail, March 13, 1737, died October 25, 1817, married (first) July 23, 1758, Louis Conqueret, mariner, had one child, Mary, married (second) Joseph Rogers, of Lancaster.

(IV) Joseph Wheeler, son of Joseph Wheeler (3), was born March 13, 1735, died February 10, 1793, in Worcester. He married (first), January 8, 1761, Mary Greenleaf, daughter of Dr. Daniel and Silence (Nichols) (Marsh) Greenleaf, of Bolton. Dr. Daniel Greenleaf was born in Cambridge, November 2, 1702, and died 1795. He was a descendant of Edmund Greenleaf, born in the parish of Brixham, Devonshire, near Torbay, England, about 1600, came to America in 1635 with his family and settled in Newbury, Massachusetts. He was a dyer by trade, was admitted a freeman March 13, 1638-9, kept a tavern 1639, magistrate-commissioner to end small causes in 1642, captain of the militia company. His will was made December 22, 1668, and proved April 12, 1671. Silence Nichols was born in Hingham, July 4, 1702, died in Bolton, May 13, 1761. She was the daughter of Israel and Mary (Sumner) Nichols and widow of David Marsh. Mary Sumner was a descendant in the third generation from William Sumner. Senator Charles Sumner was descended in the same line the seventh generation.

Joseph Wheeler was under the care of his grandmother after he was three years of age. He went to school at the age of fifteen to prepare for college and entered Harvard at the age of eighteen. He graduatd in the class of 1757 and studied divinity with Rev. Mr. Woodward, of Weston. He taught school in the town of Weston. In 1759 he was approbated to preach and "ordained to the pastoral care of the Church of Christ in Harvard" December 12, 1759. Two years later he married Mary Greenleaf. Her father Dr. Daniel and her grandfather Dr. Daniel were both physicians. The latter became a minister of the Gospel. Dr. Daniel Greenleaf, Jr., was at first at Hingham, where he married and afterward removed to Bolton, Massachusetts, in which town he practiced living to the age of ninety-three years. His second wife was Dolly, widow of Josiah Richardson. His children numbered ten, of whom Mary was the ninth. She was eighteen and a half years old when she married and had ten children when she died at the age of forty-one Dr Greenleaf's grandfather was Captain Stephen, distinguished in the Indian wars, deputy to general court a prominent citizen

Rev Joseph Wheeler erected a house in Harvard soon after his settlement there This house is well preserved and is now (or was recently) occupied by William H Savage He left the ministry July 28, 1768, but continued to reside in Harvard and was prominent in all the affairs of the town He was an ardent patriot and was elected to various positions of trust and honor He was a member of the local committee of safety and correspondence and attended the convention of committees at Worcester, August 9, 1774 He was a member of the provincial congress held at Salem, October 7, 1774, and at Watertown, July 19, 1775 In these assemblies he served at the head of important committees He represented Harvard in the session of the general court held at Watertown, July 19, 1775 At the Lexington alarm he marched as a private in Captain Joseph Fairbanks' company, Colonel Asa Whitcomb's regiment He spent several weeks at Washington's headquarters and tradition says that he was chaplain to Washington Another tradition is that he assisted in laying out the fortifications at Bunker Hill There is no proof of this except a cane and cannon ball treasured in the family as mementoes The cannon ball was fired at a group of men on the slope of the hill from a British man of war in the harbor It cut a sucker from the appletree under which the group was standing and it lodged in the earth near by Mr Wheeler secured both ball and stick from which he made a cane

Mr Wheeler was appointed register of probate for Worcester county in 1775, but continued to reside at Harvard until 1781, when he purchased an acres and a half of land on Main street, Worcester, nearly opposite the present site of the court house, and erected there a house which report says that he brought from Harvard Not long afterward he built the house long known as the Wheeler mansion This estate remained in the family a hundred years He held various offices in Worcester and continued in the office of register until his death in 1793 His wife died in 1783 and the following year he married Mrs Margaret Jennison, widow of Captain Israel Jennison, of Worcester She was the thirteenth child of Antoine and Mary Sigourne, French Huguenots, and her maiden name was Marguerita Olivier She was born at Annapolis, Nova Scotia, and was married in 1746 to Joseph Coolidge a distinguished merchant of Boston, by whom she had seven children one of whom, Margaret became the wife of Jacob Sweetser, of Lancaster Mr Coolidge died in 1771, and she married in 1775 Captain Israel Jennison She survived her third husband, died at the age of ninety and was buried in the tomb of her son, Joseph Coolidge, in King's Chapel burying ground, Boston

The estate of Rev Joseph Wheeler in Worcester, on which he resided, contiguous to those of Joseph Lynde and Judge Edward Bangs, extended eastward several hundred feet equally with the others These grounds were well cultivated and stocked with choice fruits and flowering shrubs This unique garden is described by a relative as follows "In the rear of these mansions were extensive gardens of equal size, across the lower part flowed a purling stream and rare fruits and choice flowers, fountains and the more common embellishments were the result of the industry taste and skill of the younger branches of the families Near the centre of each garden was an arbor covered with vines and furnished with seats and also a closet, a deposit for such books and luxuries as might by chance find their way there Or as another description has it "liberally stocked with all the edibles and delicacies that a company of merry young people would enjoy on a moonlight evening They entertained each other with music and similar enjoyments that made the occasions life-long memories of vanished joys"

The children of Rev Joseph and Mary (Greenleaf) Wheeler were 1 Elizabeth, born December 31, 1761, died July 18, 1782, unmarried 2 Mary born April 7, 1863, died at Kingston, Jamaica, of yellow fever, May 4, 1799, married, March 24, 1790, Ezra Waldo Weld, son of Rev Ezra and Anna (Weld) Weld, of Braintree 3 Theophilus, born December 22, 1764, died at Worcester, August 14, 1840, married Elizabeth Lynde, daughter of Joseph and Mary (Lemmon) Lynde, of Worcester, who came to Worcester from Charlestown after it was destroyed by the British Theophilus Wheeler was register of probate at Worcester forty-three years, town clerk five years, treasurer two years, overseer of schools, overseer of house of correction, director of the Worcester Bank eighteen years, served as soldier against the Shays insurgents 4 Joseph, born August 27,* 1766, died at Dixfield, Maine, January 21, 1852 married, January 13 1793, Lucy Sumner, daughter of Rev Joseph and Lucy (Williams) Sumner, of Shrewsbury Rev Joseph Sumner was a descendant of George Sumner, born in England, February 14, 1634, later settled at Milton, Massachusetts 5 Daniel Greenleaf, born March 14, 1768, died December 10, 1847, married, September 23, 1799, Elizabeth Dupee Sweetser, daughter of Jacob and Margaret (Coolidge) Sweetser, of Lancaster, she died December 15 1800 He married (second), November 14, 1802, Elizabeth Grosvenor, daughter of Rev Ebenezer and Elizabeth Grosvenor, she died August 18, 1803 He married (third), 1805, Nancy Clapp, daughter of William and Priscilla (Otis) Clapp, of Scituate 6 John, born May 17, 1770, died at Dover, New Hampshire, April 3 1840, married (first), March 12, 1793 Rebecca Harris, daughter of Captain William and Rebecca (Mason) Harris, and sister of Rev Thaddeus Mason Harris, of Dorchester, she was of Malden, born April 17, 1770, died January 28, 1804 John was an apothecary, postmaster twenty-six years representative to the general court, associate justice court of common pleas, founder of the Cocheco Manufacturing Co, first president of the Strafford Bank 7 Moses, born April 4, 1772, died at Boston, March 27, 1838, married (first), November 8 1807, Elizabeth Porter, daughter of John and Elizabeth (Lamb) Porter of Malden 8 Clarissa, born February 1, 1774, died at Medford May 26 1844, unmarried 9 Abigail born February 29, 1776, died at Andover, Massachusetts, February 21, 1846, married, October, 1799, Rev Leonard Woods son of Samuel and Abigail Whitney (Underwood) Woods He was born at Princeton, June 19 1774 died at Andover, August 24 1854 He married (second) Lucia J, widow of Dr Ansel G Ives, of New York (H C 1796), professor in Andover Theological Seminary thirty-eight years 10 Levi, born October 22, 1779, died at Worcester March 8 1781 11 Sophia born at Worcester, January 20, 1782, died at Danvers, October 8, 1831, married, May 17 1807, Rev Samuel Walker, of Danvers, born at Haverhill January 27, 1779, died at Danvers, July 7, 1826 (D C 1802), pastor of Danvers Church from 1805 till his death

(V) Joseph Wheeler, son of Joseph Wheeler (4), was born in Harvard Massachusetts, August 27 1766, died at Dixfield Maine January 21 1852 He married January 13 1793 Lucy Sumner, daughter of Rev Joseph and Lucy (Williams) Sumner, of Shrewsbury She was born December 24, 1771, died April 10, 1863

Rev Joseph Sumner was a descendant of William Sumner, of Dorchester, Massachusetts, who was born at Bicester, Oxfordshire, England, and baptized January 27, 1604-5, son of Roger and Joan (Franklin) Sumner He married Mary West, October 22, 1625, was admitted freeman May 17, 1637, was deputy to the general court, town officer, commissioner to try small causes His son George, through whom descent is traced, was born in England, February 14, 1634, settled at Milton, Massachusetts Rev Joseph was the son of Samuel and Elizabeth (Griffin) Sumner

The children of Joseph and Lucy (Sumner) Wheeler were Lucy Williams, born at Worcester, September 14, 1793, died 1881, at Rumford, Maine, married David Kimball, had twelve children, Dorothy Sumner, born in Worcester, September 5, 1795, died in Worcester, 1865, married (first) Benjamin Doyen, (second) Elisha Hayden, Sarah Danielson, born at Princeton, June 19, 1798, died in Dixfield, Maine, April 12, 1843, unmarried, Eunice Russell, born at Princeton, February 17, 1801, died in Dixfield, Maine, 1886, married Daniel Sumner Libby, born January 17, 1837, Joseph Sumner, born at Dixfield, Maine, May 9, 1803, died 1870, married Phebe Cole Gleason, had nine children, Erastus Williams, born at Dixfield, Maine, June 17, 1805, died in Worcester, January 17, 1893, married, October 5, 1842, Sarah Pollard, daughter of Stephen and Betsey (Hastings) Pollard, of Berlin, Elizabeth Sumner, born at Dixfield, Maine, February 22, 1809, died at Worcester, July 12, 1879, married, January 29, 1850, Edwin Conant, of Worcester, son of Jacob Conant, of Sterling His first wife was Maria E Estabrook, daughter of Joseph Estabrook, of Royalton, married 1832

(VI) Erastus Williams Wheeler, son of Joseph Wheeler (5), was born at Dixfield, Maine, June 17, 1805, died in Worcester, January 17, 1893, married, October 5, 1842, Sarah Pollard, daughter of Stephen and Betsey (Hastings) Pollard, of Berlin Their children were Joseph Pollard, born July 28, 1843, Henry Theophilus, June 25, 1845, died in Florence, Alabama, October 16, 1864 in a Rebel prison, Edwin Wallace, November 13, 1848, married, April, 1872, Clara A Black, daughter of Edward B and Matilda A (Freeman) Black, of Salem, Nova Scotia, William Jennison, September 13 1851, married, February 14, 1877, Ida Stratton, daughter of Samuel and Isabelle (Brimhall) Stratton, has one child Lotta Belle, born January 1, 1883

(VII) Edwin Wallace Wheeler, son of Erastus William Wheeler (6), was born in Worcester, Massachusetts, November 13 1848 He is a farmer in Worcester, a member of the Worcester Grange, Patrons Husbandry He inherited his father's farm on Forest street He married, April 4, 1872, Clara A Black, daughter of Edward B and Matilda A (Freeman) Black, of Salem, Nova Scotia Their children are Edward William, born May 1, 1873, Henry Clifford, April 19, 1875, Sarah Matilda May 9, 1877, died January 22, 1892, Alice Abbie, June 10, 1888, Wallace Sumner, April 30 1893

(VIII) Edward William Wheeler, son of Edwin Wallace Wheeler (7), was born May 1, 1873 He was educated in the Worcester public schools and at Highland Military Academy at Worcester His father expected him to assist on the farm but he thoroughly disliked farming and left home He went to work for Fuller & Delano, architects, in Worcester, and found the business to his tastes He studied architecture and remained with Fuller & Delano for five years He was with the Webb Granite and Construction Company for six months He went into business with Albert E Scoville in the contracting and building business The firm name is Scoville & Wheeler They have offices in the Knowles building, 518 Main street They have had a large variety of contracts and have been successful It is one of the most promising firm of builders in Worcester

Some of the work of the firm is as follows The Howe Memorial Library in Shrewsbury, the women's and men's wards and the administration building in the State Colony for the Insane at Gardner, Massachusetts, two modern school houses at Gardner, the postoffice building at Gardner, owned by the Heywood estate, buildings and additions to the plant of Heywood Bros & Wakefield Co at Gardner Massachusetts, residence of John S Gould, German street, Worcester, residences in Worcester for Fred A Mann, Lenox street, for Samuel D Spurr, Dean street, Mrs W J Wheeler, nee Stratton, Forest street, for her daughter, Mrs Lotta Tracey, residences of L E Carlton, president of the Heywood Bros & Wakefield Co, at Gardner, costing twenty thousand dollars, residence for E L Thompson, the chair manufacturer of Baldwinville, and a number of handsome residences and stables in Westboro and Gardner

Captain Wheeler is best known perhaps for his excellent record in the militia But for his energy and persistent work to maintain the standard of efficiency at a critical time, this organization in which the citizens of Worcester take great pride and which has maintained a long and honorable record, would have been disbanded He enlisted January 21, 1891, and has been in the militia ever since He was made a corporal September 9, 1892, and was promoted to sergeant January 18, 1894, having charge of one of the gatling guns then in the possession of Battery B, to which he belonged When the guns were transferred to another branch of the service he became a guidon corporal He was again appointed sergeant June 1, 1895, and first sergeant June 4, 1902 His promotion to second lieutenant came March 18, 1903 Just a year later, May 19 1904, he received his commission as captain of the battery in which he had been for thirteen years of continuous service The title of his command in full is Battery B First Battalion, Light Artillery, Massachusetts Volunteer Militia The celebration of the thirty-fifth anniversary of the battery was observed October 18, 1904 There was a parade, a banquet in the drill shed and a drill at the Fair Grounds The speeches of Congressman Thayer, Mayor Blodgett, Representative Mark N Skerrett, General Robert H Chamberlain, Captain E G Barrett, Rev Dr Willard Scott, President W H Brody and General F W Wellington showed the esteem in which the organization is held and the credit due the commanding officer while lieutenant in maintaining the efficiency of the battery The inspection of the battery April 12, 1905, was a source of satisfaction to the officers and men, who were complimented on their work

Captain Wheeler is a prominent Free Mason, being a member of Athelstan Lodge, Eureka Royal Arch Chapter and the Worcester County Commandery, Knights Templar He is equally active in the Independent Order of Odd Fellows being a member of Quinsigamond Lodge, and Mt Vernon Encampment also of the Patriarchs Militant, Grand Canton, of Worcester He is assistant adjutant general with the rank of major on the staff of Brigade Commander Daniel Harrington He is a member of the

Commonwealth Club, the Tatassit Canoe Club, Worcester County Mechanics Association, Worcester County Agricultural Society, Worcester Grange, Patrons of Husbandry

BLACK FAMILY William Black (1) was the emigrant ancestor of the mother of Edward W Wheeler, of Worcester William Black was born in Paisley, Scotland, in 1727 His father was a public officer and possessed an independent fortune His leisure was largely employed in the chase and he kept a good pack of hounds, and until William his son, was of age, he made hunting his chief amusement His first occupation was in the position of traveling salesman for a large manufacturing establishment In one of his business trips he met an English lady in Huddersfield, England, whom he subsequently married Her name was Elizabeth Stocks He engaged in the business of linen and woolen drapery

By the chance misspelling of the name Stokes for Stocks in the will of her brother, Thomas Stocks, a fortune of twenty thousand pounds intended for her went to a maiden lady named Elizabeth Stokes, a relative of Mrs Black Mrs Black received only fifteen hundred pounds from the estate Mrs Black was a woman of fashion in her day, and when she came to Nova Scotia with her husband she brought her scarlet riding habit and the cap she used to wear in the hunts, also dresses of embroidered white satin and other rich garments for which she found little use in the life of a pioneer William Black was attracted by the movement to settle Nova Scotia after the expulsion of the French from Arcadia There were rich agricultural districts untenanted since 1755 In 1758 Governor Lawrence, of Nova Scotia, had given invitations to the inhabitants of New England to settle these lands Liberal terms were given and freedom of conscience and worship was guaranteed by a proclamation Various religious sects were persecuted by the Puritans in Massachusetts and there were vexatious restrictions in religious worship in New York Virginia and other colonies A small Baptist church emigrated en masse from Massachusetts to Sackville, then Nova Scotia, now New Brunswick, in 1763

Michael Franklin, then lieutenant governor of Nova Scotia, engaged several families to emigrate from Yorkshire, England, to Nova Scotia, in 1772 and others in 1773 and 1774 Mr Black went to Halifax in 1774 to see the country He concluded to try the new country and purchased an estate at Amherst, a part of which is occupied or was recently occupied by his descendants He returned to his home in England in the fall and in the following April chartered a vessel in which he brought his wife, four sons and a daughter A nurse girl who came with the family later married a son of one of the settlers Mrs Black was injured while embarking at Hull and this accident probably hastened her death a year later When Mr Black made his home in America Halifax had been settled about twenty-five years and had a population of three thousand There were twelve thousand souls in the whole province at that time Most of these settlers were Methodists and William Black, his wife four sons and daughter joined that church in 1779 One son, William Black, became a Methodist preacher another John Black, a local preacher in the Methodist church Thomas S Black, another son, joined the Baptist church later Mr Black was justice of the peace for Cumberland and in 1779 was appointed judge of the common pleas He was one of three trustees of the court house grounds for the county

Many of the New England settlers in Nova Scotia were in sympathy with the revolution in the other colonies in 1775 and in 1776, by the influence of disaffected persons in the county and vicinity, the garrison at Fort Cumberland was besieged by a force from Machias They disarmed those who were loyal to the British government and forbade them to stir off their farms under penalty of imprisonment or death The British forces finally appeared in such large numbers that Nova Scotia revolutionists were subdued

The names of the children of William and Elizabeth (Stocks) Black who came from England with their parents were John, William, Richard Thomas Stocks and Sarah He married soon after his wife's death Elizabeth Abber, by whom he had seven children After his second marriage he purchased a large estate in Dorchester, New Brunswick, where he spent the latter part of his life with his son Joseph He died in 1820 at the advanced age of ninety-three years His wife died some years before At the age of eighty-eight he was strong and active and rode thirty miles on horseback to pay a visit to his sons in Amherst Some of his descendants are or recently were living on the old place at Dorchester

The children of William Black (I) were 1 John, married Barbara Donkin, and settled at River Philip, was a Methodist local preacher, justice of the peace had six sons and five daughters 2 William, born in Huddersfield, England, in 1760, and removed with his father's family to Cumberland in 1775 became a Methodist preacher and converted many to that faith in his itinerant preaching, he was called Bishop Black and the Father of Methodism in Nova Scotia and New Brunswick, as he was the pioneer itinerant of Methodism in the three lower provinces where Methodism has been very strong in later years He preached for seven years and a half before he was ordained In 1789 among the first to be ordained in America he was ordained at a conference in Philadelphia, and was soon afterward appointed to succeed Dr Coke as superintendent of the Methodist organization in Nova Scotia, New Brunswick and Newfoundland Rev William Black married Mary Gay, daughter of Martin Gay, of Westmoreland, and had five children His wife died in 1827, aged seventy-three He married (second), in 1828, Mrs Calkins, widow of Elisha Calkins, of Liverpool, Nova Scotia He died 1834, aged seventy-four years 3 Richard born in England, 1762 was thirteen when he arrived with the family at Amherst, Cumberland 4 Thomas Stocks, born in England, came to America with his father married Mary Freeze, whose father also came from England, settled at Amherst on a farm of five hundred and forty acres which has since been owned by him and his descendants and greatly improved In 1806 he left the Methodist church to join the Baptist and was later elected deacon, an office he held until his death in 1850, aged eighty-four years, his wife died 1842 aged sixty-six years had seven sons and five daughters 5 Sarah, born in England, married John Chapman, who also came from England with his father, settled at Dorchester on what is now very valuable farm land, was justice of the peace at Dorchester, had six children 6 Elizabeth, married Joshua Freeman, who settled on a farm in the centre of Amherst, about 1816 he sold the farm and removed to Hamilton now Ontario taking his large family with him, they had twelve children 7 Mary, born in Nova Scotia married John Weldon whose father was one of the first emigrants from England to Dorchester, removing thence from Hillsboro, New Brunswick, was a farmer had five children 8 Nancy, born in Nova

Scotia, married Cyprian Killam, of Nova Scotia, whose parents came from England, settled in Dorchester on a farm, had seven sons and four daughters 9 Jane, married John Fawcett, of Sackville, New Brunswick, where they settled and engaged in farming, had five children 10 James, married Elizabeth Etter, of Halifax, settled on a portion of the farm of his father at Dorchester, had nine children 11 Joseph A, inherited a portion of his father's farm just above the bend in the Memramcook river and overlooking the river to its mouth, married Margaret Ryan, had eight children 12 George Mason, settled on part of his father's estate at Dorchester, where he followed his trade of cabinet and carriage maker, married (first) Emily Freeman, daughter of Samuel Freeman, of Amherst, married (second) Sarah Smith, daughter of Gideon Smith, of Memramcook, had five children by the first wife and fourteen by the second

(II) Richard Black, son of William Black (1), was born in England in 1762 and was thirteen years of age when he arrived with his father at Amherst, Cumberland He first settled at River Philip, where he bought five hundred acres of land from Roger Robinson and remained for several years, moving later to Amherst to settle on the farm that his father bought on his first visit to Cumberland in 1774 Here he lived the remainder of his life His youngest son inherited the homestead and his grandsons also owned it The family still owns the farm or did recently About 1804 Richard Black, his brother, and Thomas S and Samuel Holsted bought a large tract of land at Amherst Richard was an earnest Methodist and late in life, when his hearing failed, sat in the pulpit with the preacher in order to hear He married Sally Chapman, who also came from Yorkshire in England They had eleven children besides two who died young and all were particularly strong and well built The smallest of the seven boys was when grown six feet tall and weighed one hundred and eighty-five pounds Richard Black died in 1834, aged seventy-two years His first wife died in 1820, aged fifty-three years He married (second) Elizabeth Smith, of Parrsboro, and she died in 1861, aged eighty-four years

The children of Richard Black were 1 William, married Mary Bent, daughter of John Bent, of Amherst, settled on a farm in what is now called Salem, then called Sugarwood Hill, had six children, he died 1829, aged forty-six years 2 Thomas, settled on a new farm in Salem and by persevering industry turned the woodland into fruitful fields and left a valuable property to his sons, died in 1838, aged fifty-three years, married Phebe Purdy, of Westchester, then called Cobequid Mountains, his widow married (second) Daniel MacNutt Thomas had twelve children 3 Maria, married Thomas Gray, who came from England and taught school in the provinces for several years, had five children 4 Richard, Jr, married Arathusa Oxley, daughter of George Oxley, of Wallace, settled near River Philip on a farm that his brother Joseph left when he went to Prince Edward Island, and he improved it until it became a valuable property, he died 1873, aged seventy-five years, she died 1871 aged seventy-three years, had nine children 5 Joseph, the third son, married Sarah Canfield, of Wallace, lived several years near River Philip and moved thence to Prince Edward Island where for many years he was high sheriff of Prince county, had nine children 6 Sarah, the second daughter, married Joshua Heustis of Wallace where they settled, he was justice of the peace and for several years was custos of the county and postmaster at Wallace, had six children 7 Asher, the fifth son, owned and resided on part of his father's farm, a portion of which his grandfather bought before removing his family to this country, was justice of the peace, a very ingenious and useful citizen Married Eleanor Archibald, of Truro daughter of James Archibald, Esq, and had eight children, he died in 1863, aged sixty-three, his wife died in 1876, aged seventy-three years 8 John Chapman, sixth son, married Tabitha Pugsley of Maccan, settled in Amherst and cleared a farm where he lived until 1861, when his wife died aged fifty-six and his son-in-law took the farm, he had three children 9 Ann, married Charles Carter, of Onslow, who settled at Amherst and was a carpenter, he had three children, he died 1831, aged thirty-four years, his widow married (second) James Mageney, and she had six children by the second marriage, she died in 1880 aged seventy-five years 10 George, youngest son, married Jane Coates, of Amherst, who owned and lived upon part of the old homestead—a portion of which his grandfather owned and occupied first after he came to America, had nine children 11 Mary G, married Elisha Gourley, a native of Colchester county but lived for some years at Amherst, where after his marriage he built a house lately occupied by Peter Etter and lived in it several years, he removed later to his native county, and settled at Truro, they had six children and many descendants

(III) William Black, son of Richard Black (2), was born in Amherst, 1783, died 1829 He married Mary Bent, daughter of John Bent, of Amherst They settled upon a farm in what is now called Salem, then called Sugarwood Hill from the rock maples with which it was originally covered They had one daughter and five sons Their children were 1 Maria, married William Sharp, son of Matthew Sharp, of Maccan, settled in Amherst and have three daughters, he died 1848, aged thirty-seven years Their children are Mary Jane Sharp, married Robert C Sharp, of Amherst, where they lived and had four children, Selina Sharp, married Joseph Cove, and resided in Amherst until 1881, when they removed to Boston, had eight children Emma Sharp, youngest daughter, married William Cove a physician who lived and practiced at Spring Hill, had several children, only two of whom grew up 2 Edward of whom later 3 Luther married Jane Gibson, of Shinimcas, Cumberland, where they purchased a farm and lived, had seven children 4 Ezra, married Mary Ann Carter, daughter of James Carter, of Amherst owned and occupied half of his father's homestead in Salem, had five children 5 Daniel, married Jane Embree, of Salem, lived at Leicester, Cumberland, and had five children, four of whom died young of diphtheria 6 Rufus, the youngest son, when a young man went to Canaan Queens county New Brunswick, where he married Jane Price, they had seven children

(IV) Edward Black, son of William Black (3), was born in Salem, Nova Scotia, married Matilda Freeman, daughter of William Freeman of Amherst They owned and lived on half of his father's homestead at Salem They had five sons and six daughters Their children were Sarah married Hazen Goodwin, lived at Point de Bute, New Brunswick, and had one child who died young, Clifford, died in 1869, aged twenty-four years, Bessie married Joseph Black, of Amherst, they have three daughters, Clara Maud Jane and Sarah, another died young, they live on a portion of the first farm of William Black, bought in 1774 Clara A, of whom later, Alice, married Arthur Walker, resides at Cambridge, Vermont, J Avard, Margaret, Fred, Walter, Amelia, Cyrus

(V) Clara A Black, daughter of Edward Black (4), was born at Salem, Nova Scotia, October 12, 1850, married Edwin W Wheeler, of Worcester, April 4, 1872 (See Wheeler family sketch under Captain Edward W Wheeler)

THE FREEMAN FAMILY William Freeman (1), who came from England about 1765 and settled in Nova Scotia, was an emigrant ancestor of Captain E W Wheeler, of Worcester His posterity is very numerous throughout the Dominion and particularly at the head of the Bay of Fundy He was probably in Nova Scotia before the main body of English or those families allied with the Blacks from Yorkshire He married Jerusha Yeomans about the time of their arrival in America They had five sons and nine daughters, of whom one son died in infancy, and the others were Sarah, William and Jerusha (twins), Samuel, Joshua, Elizabeth, Dorothy, Martha, Philip, Hannah, Ann, Charlotte, Rebecca The daughter Sarah married ——— Weatherhead, and had nineteen children

(II) William Freeman, son of William Freeman, married Desire Newcomb, of Horton They had one son and seven daughters Mrs Freeman died in 1811 He married (second) Sarah Dimock, sister of Rev Joseph Dimock, and had three sons and three daughters The two youngest sons, Joseph and G William Freeman, inherited the farm and lived there George William Freeman was an inventor Their children were Rufus, a merchant, died when a young man, built part of the Lamy Hotel, Pamelia, Olivia, Mary, Charlotte, Eunice, Margaret, Desire, Jane, Daniel, Joseph, Matilda, George William, Elizabeth

(III) Matilda Freeman, daughter of William Freeman (2), married Edward Black (3), and they were the parents of Mrs Edwin W Wheeler, of Worcester, mother of Captain Edward W Wheeler

CHAPMAN FAMILY William Chapman, an early settler in Nova Scotia, was an ancestor of Captain E W Wheeler, of Worcester, Massachusetts He came from England and settled at Point de Bute His children were William, married a daughter of Charles Dixon and settled at Ft Lawrence, Thomas, settled at Ft Lawrence, John, married Sarah Black, Henry, married ——— Seaman, of Wallace, Mary, married George Taylor, of Memramcook, now Rockland, Sally, married Richard Black, ancestor of Captain Wheeler through his mother's family, Nancy, married (first) Thomas Robinson, (second) James Roberts, Jane, married John Smith, who came from England when a young man and lived at Ft Lawrence, had nine athletic sons, and one daughter who married Israel Embree

THOMAS HARLOW REED William Reed (1), of Woburn, was the emigrant ancestor of Thomas Harlow Reed, of Worcester, Massachusetts He was born in England in 1587 He came to New England at the age of forty-eight in the ship "Defence" in July, 1635, bringing with him his wife Mabel, aged thirty, and three children George aged six, Ralph, aged five, and Justus, aged eighteen months He settled first in Boston where he was admitted a freeman September 2, 1635 He lived also at Dorchester and Scituate, Massachusetts He was a constable in the latter town in 1644 While living there his wife rode on horseback to Dorchester with an infant in her arms to have the child baptized in the church to which Reed belonged In 1648 they were living in Muddy River (Brookline), Massachusets He finally settled in Woburn Massachusetts in 1648, on land bought of Nicholas Davis July 7, 1648 It is said that the cellar hole where his house was located in Woburn can be discerned in what has been called in late years the Baldwin pasture on the road to Kendall's mills

He married Mabel Kendall in England They returned to England after their children were grown up and he died there at Newcastle on Tyne, in 1656, aged sixty-nine years His will was probated in London, England, October 31, 1656, and letters of administration were granted by the Protector, Oliver Cromwell, himself, to the widow She returned to New England and married (second) November 21, 1660, Harry Summers, Sr, of Woburn She died at the home of her son, George Reed, June 5, 1690, at the age of eighty-five

The children of William Reed were George, see forward, Ralph, Justus, Michael, Israel, Abigail, married Francis Wyman, Bethia, married, 1657, Sarah, married Samuel Walker, Jr, 1662, Rebecca, married Ensign Joseph Winn, 1664

(II) George Reed, son of William Reed (1), was born in England in 1629 He was a child of six years when he was brought to New England by his parents He settled after his marriage in Woburn, Massachsetts, where the committee, November 9 1653, laid out for him a six-acre home lot in place of one previously granted to him He was admitted a freeman there in 1684 He married, October 4 1652, Elizabeth Jennison, daughter of Robert Jennison, of Watertown She died February 26, 1664-5 He married (second), November 9, 1665, Hannah Rockwell, of Charlestown, Massachusetts He died February 21, 1705-6, aged sixty-seven years

The children of George and Elizabeth (Jennison) Reed were born in Woburn, viz Elizabeth, born July 29, 1653, twin sons, born and died November 14, 1654, Samuel, born April 29, 1656, Abigail, June 27, 1658, George, September 14, 1660, William, see forward, Sarah, February 12, 1664-5 The children of George and Hannah (Rockwell) Reed were Hannah, February 18, 1669-70, John, March 18, 1672, Mary, June 15, 1674, Timothy, October 20, 1678, Thomas, July 15, 1682

(III) William Reed seventh child of George Reed (2), was born in Woburn, Massachusetts, September 22, 1662 He married Abigail Kendall, May 24, 1686, by whom was introduced a singular characteristic of the Kendall family of Woburn, an inherited tendency to an extra number of fingers and toes William Reed was a prominent man in the town and colony He was captain of the Lexington militia company, and is the progenitor of the Lexington Reed family Captain Reed was a justice of the peace and magistrate there for many years He was a selectman and represented the town repeatedly in the general court He was one of the original members of the Lexington church The historian of Lexington goes out of his way to remark of the descendants of Captain Reed that no family of early settlers has sustained its standing through all the periods of town history better than the Reed family" His homestead was in the northwest part of the town, near Bedford street He acquired a large estate and was able to leave a valuable farm to each of his sons Some of this land is still held in the family At one time his home was in the most populous part of the village

He died May 12, 1718 aged fifty-six His wife died October 12, 1734 Their children, all born in Lexington, Massachusetts, were Abigail, born May 29, 1687, William, see forward, Mary, April 8, 1695, Benjamin, October 22, 1699, Joshua June 20, 1702 Hepsibah December 10, 1705

(IV) William Reed second child of William Reed (3), was born July 18, 1693, at Lexington,

Massachusetts He married, about 1719, Sarah Poulter, daughter of John Poulter Like his father he became an active and efficient citizen of Lexington He was justice of the peace and magistrate for many years and became widely known as Squire Reed He was prominent in the church as well as the town He was selectman eleven years and a representative to the general court for the extraordinary period of seventeen years He was popular as well as influential He was captain of the militia company of the town and during the French war was in the service with part of his company, in 1755 His homestead was the house lately occupied by Christopher Reed on Bedford street, Lexington He died there February 11, 1778, aged eighty-five years His wife died November 25, 1769 Their children, all born in Lexington, were William, born January 1, 1720, Samuel, see forward, Sarah, June 3, 1725, Mary, March 10, 1728, Oliver, March 25, 1730, John, May 28, 1731, Hammon, April 26, 1734, Eliot, April 28, 1737, Hannah, October 21, 1740, Nathan, November 9, 1743

(V) Samuel Reed, second child of William Reed (4), was born in Lexington, Massachusetts, May 4, 1722 He settled in Burlington, Massachusetts, and became a prominent man there and was for many years deacon of the church He married Eunice Stone, of Lexington She was born July 2, 1724, and died April 25, 1809 He died April 28, 1809 The children of Samuel and Eunice (Stone) Reed were born in Burlington, Massachusetts, viz Samuel, born August 6, 1744, died February 23, 1798, Micah, see forward, Moses, born May 31, 1749, married, April 23, 1770, Sarah Whittemore, of Lexington, where he settled and became prominent, Frances, May 3, 1751, Eunice, November 17, 1753, died February 19, 1754, Abigail, born August 13, 1757, died April 16, 1795, Lucy, October 12, 1759, died November 21, 1801, Sarah, December 31, 1762, Mary, August 11, 1767

(VI) Micah Reed, second child of Samuel Reed (5), was born in Burlington, Massachusetts, September 28, 1746 About 1780 he removed to Hardwick, Massachusetts, and later to New Braintree He married Elizabeth Paige, daughter of John Paige, of Bedford, Massachusetts She was born August 2, 1748, and died March 21, 1838, aged ninety years He died March 1, 1804, at New Braintree, Massachusetts He was in the third Woburn company in the revolution under Captain Timothy Winn in 1775, and Captain Eleazer Brooks in 1777 His death was caused by a fall from a scaffolding on which he was working The children of Micah and Elizabeth (Paige) Reed, born in Hardwick and New Braintree, were Micah, see forward, Elizabeth, born January 2, 1777, died October 17, 1778, Elizabeth, February 25, 1779, Samuel, June 11, 1783, died at Burlington, Vermont, May 5, 1846, Eunice, January 13, 1787, married James Barr, of New Braintree, and (second) Perley Granger

(VII) Colonel Micah Reed, eldest son of Micah Reed (6), was born October 17, 1773, in Burlington, probably He came to Hardwick when a young boy with his parents He spent most of his active life, however, in the neighboring town of New Braintree, where he died August 3, 1825 His homestead was in that part of New Braintree known as Ditch Meadow, and he kept a tavern as well as a farm He was prominent in the military affairs of the state for a long period, and was colonel of a Worcester county regiment He was a man of large influence and high standing

He married Deborah Thurston, daughter of Samuel Thurston, of Hardwick She was born September 23, 1778, and died June 30, 1828 He died August 3, 1823 Their children, all born in New Braintree, were 1 Arminley, born September 22, 1798, never married 2 Rebecca Paige, July 6, 1801, died January 5, 1848 3 Abel Wheeler, January 5, 1805, died 1874, married Elizabeth Scovil, of East Haddam, Connecticut, and had a daughter Nellie, deceased 4 Micah Thurston, see forward 5 Samuel Gardner, May 21, 1809, died 1884, married thrice, (first) Fannie Louise Tilton, of West Boylston, and had Sarah Elizabeth, died young, Charles Gardner, born April 22, 1835, died December 21, 1899, married (first) Lucella P Ware, of Worcester, and had two children Charles Arthur, who died young, and Frank Theodore, married (second) Elizabeth P Fielding, of Worcester, and had one child, Karl Beagary Reed, unmarried, married (third) Hannah W Whitcomb, Henry Wheeler, born March 11, 1843, married Annie Lindsay, of Greensboro, North Carolina, and have four children Fannie Louise, who married Herbert D Bartlett, of Worcester, and has one child, Herbert Davis Bartlett, Jr, living in Seattle, Washington, Samuel Gardner, Robert Lindsay, Elizabeth Begeary, of Seattle, Mary Frances, born May 13, 1845, married George Henry Taft, of Worcester, and has three children Arthur Reed Taft, born January 28, 1877, died June 2, 1904, Maria Elizabeth Taft, born in Paris, France, May 9, 1881, Philip Newell Taft, born October 19, 1884 Abbie Jane, born January 31, 1850, married William Northam Taft, of Worcester, and has two children Elizabeth Northam Taft, born December 15, 1882, died November 6, 1903, Donald Reed Taft, born November 7, 1886 The only child of Samuel Gardner Reed and his second wife, Cleora Eager Harlow, of Shrewsbury, was Rev George Harlow, of Concord, Massachusetts, who married Virginia W Dean, of Taunton, Massachusetts, and has one child, Margaret Dean The only child of Samuel Gardner and Eliza Bowman (Currier) Reed (the third wife) was Arthur Currier, deceased 6 Hammond, born August 7, 1811 7 Sumner, born March 29, 1813, married Jane Henshaw, of Charlton, Massachusetts 8 Rebecca, born December 2, 1815, married James B Bardwell, of New Braintree, Massachusetts, and has three children Everett J Bardwell, Frederick Bardwell, deceased, Alice R Bardwell, deceased 9 Dwight, born August 25, 1817, married Susan Vaughn, of East Brookfield, Massachusetts, and had two children Susan Ella, married Dr C P Lawton, of Webster, Massachusetts, and has one child, lieutenant Dwight Lawton, of the United States army, Mary Emma, unmarried

(VIII) Micah Thurston Reed, fourth child of Colonel Micah Reed (7), was born in New Braintree, Massachusetts, May 21, 1807 He received his early education in the schools of his native town He worked with his father on the homestead until he was about sixteen Then he learned the trade of mason and plasterer He removed from his father's home at New Braintree to North Brookfield about 1834 and followed his trade there During all the active years of his life until about 1875 he was in business connected with his trade of mason He was for a time interested with his son in a tinshop and stove store, which the son managed He retired from active business in 1875 and died at his home in North Brookfield, Massachusetts, January 11, 1885 He was a devout member of the First Congregational Church of North Brookfield, took a great interest in all its affairs, and served the church on several important building committees He was a stanch Republican, but never cared for public office He served in the militia in his younger days and was active in his company at New Braintree for several years He was in Captain John Barnard's company

He married, September 16, 1834 Abigail Harlow, of Shrewsbury, Massachusetts She was a daughter of Thomas and Thankful (Bannister) Harlow, of Shrewsbury He was a farmer and deacon of the Congregational church there Their only child was Thomas Harlow Reed, see forward

(IX) Thomas Harlow Reed, only child of Micah Thurston Reed (8), was born in North Brookfield, Massachusetts, September 14, 1835 He attended the public schools of his native town When seventeen years of age he and his father purchased the stove store and tin shop of C J Boynton, of North Brookfield Mr Reed carried on the business, his father being a silent partner but after ten years, in 1863, the store was burned He sold what was saved from the fire and came to Worcester where he bought the stove store of Mordacai Carey on Main street, nearly opposite Elm street, where he carried on his business until the building was torn down when he removed to No 2 Pleasant street, where he continued in business for some ten years Since then he has worked for S R Leland & Co and for John W Green, the plumber at Lincoln square, where he is at present the bookkeeper Mr Reed is a member of Union Congregational Church, which he served three years as treasurer In politics he is a Republican He is a member of Morning Star Lodge, A F and A M, of Worcester

He married Mary Frances Whiting, June 11, 1862 She was the daughter of Louis and Fannie (Parks) Whiting, of North Brookfield Her father was a shoemaker, employed in the Bacheller shop in that town and later a farmer He died August, 1881 The children of Thomas Harlow and Mary Frances (Whiting) Reed are 1 Nellie Frances born October 21, 1865, married, July 16, 1896, Rev Henry Walker of Boulder, Colorado, and has three children Helen Frances Walker, born May 27 1897, Florence Hammersley Walker, born August 13, 1899, Margaret Walker, born November 6, 1902 2 Florence Harlow Reed, born November 22, 1868 living in Boulder, Colorado 3 Lewis Thurston born September 5 1870 pastor First Congregational Church, Canandaigua, New York married Isabelle Dwight, October 25 1899 4 Fannie Whiting, born December 4 1879 lives with parents, graduate of the high school teacher in the public schools of Amherst, Massachusetts Mr Reed lives at No 134 Elm street, Worcester

GEORGE MASON FOSKETT, M D, son of Samuel Waters Foskett, was born October 26, 1856 He attended the public schools of Charlton and Webster, and prepared for college at the Nichols Academy in Dudley, and entered Amherst College, from which he graduated with the degree of Bachelor of Arts in 1878, and in 1881 he received from the same institution the degree of Master of Arts After leaving college he taught school in Webster from 1878 to 1880, and at the same time studied medicine under the preceptorship of Dr F D Brown, of that town He graduated from the medical department of the University of Vermont in 1882, and shortly after located in North Dana, where he practiced his profession for eight years After two years spent in post graduate studies in New York hospitals he came to Worcester, where he has since resided having established a large and lucrative practice He maintains his office and residence at No 491 Pleasant street He is a member of the Worcester District Medical Society, the Massachusetts Medical Society, the American Academy of Medicine, and the American Medical Association He is a member of Trinity Methodist Episcopal Church, and in politics is a Republican He has attained high rank in the Masonic order, and affiliated with Athelstan Lodge, December 7, 1892 He received the royal arch degree in Eureka Chapter, Royal Arch Masons, April, 1894, the cryptic degrees in Hiram Council, Royal Scottish Masons, May 24, 1894, was knighted in Worcester County Commandery, Knights Templar, August 15, 1895, and has taken the fourteenth, sixteenth and eighteenth degrees of Ancient and Accepted Scottish Rite Masonry He is a member of Alepo Temple Nobles of the Mystic Shrine, of Boston In Odd Fellowship he is a member of Anchoria Lodge, No 142, of Mount Vernon Encampment, No 53, and of Worcester Canton, No 3 He is also a member of Regulus Lodge, Knights of Pythias, and of the Hancock Social Club, of Worcester

Dr Foskett married (first) at North Dana, June 5, 1885, Harriet Ella Linsey, who was there born August 28, 1851, daughter of Silas Foster and Maria (Hale) Linsey She died November 28, 1898 Dr Foskett married (second), November 28, 1903, Miss Carrie Gilmore, daughter of Henry E and Sarah E Gilmore, of Worcester

CYRUS G WOOD Among the men who have made their mark in the business life of Worcester county we find the name of Cyrus Grout Wood He was born November 16, 1819, in the town of Uxbridge, Massachusetts, where several generations of his ancestry had spent their lives, leaving behind them the indelible impress of their industry, frugality and uprightness He was the son of Reuben and Sally Grout Wood

His father, who died in 1857, was an industrious farmer, and young Cyrus passed his early life at work upon the farm and in the mill, for Uxbridge was not only an agricultural town but a manufacturing town as well His early education was acquired in attending the schools of his native village On attaining his majority he took the little sum of money that by patient toil and strict economy he had saved, and after adding to it one hundred dollars borrowed money, started in the sale of boots, shoes and dry goods, following the style of the usual country store, later adding a line of furniture, being the first person in the town to embark in that branch of trade His business grew under his management and proved quite successful But still it did not fully satisfy his ambition, and with Charles C Capron as a partner, he began the making of shoddy, and dealing in woolen waste, etc After a trial of three years Mr Wood retired from the firm, leasing a mill in the southern part of the town and continued in the same line of business As time went on and success attended his efforts, he added other mills, even as far away as the state of Rhode Island In the year 1876 Mr Wood purchased the mill at Quinapoxet, in the town of Holden, he having had an interest there for two or more years previous to that date, the mill being operated by Wood & Ward This same year he also purchased the Lovell Woolen Company's mill in Holden, and for many years operated both mills, combining them as one plant About two hundred hands were employed and over one hundred and twenty-five thousand yards of satinet was manufactured each month at this plant In February, 1882, a postoffice was established at Quinapoxet, with Cyrus Grout Wood as postmaster

Thus from a small beginning we have followed the career of the subject of this sketch onward and upward That he experienced trials and met with

C. G. Wood

QUAKER MEETING HOUSE

Uxbridge. Built 1770. It stands in the South part of the town, and cost of building was £206-8-1. It was located "near Moses Farnums" at the junction of the roads from Millville and Ironstone, to Uxbridge Center.

many obstacles that seemed to stand across his pathway, there can be no doubt, but by strict fidelity to business, genuine courage, perseverance and natural ability, he overcame them all and at last found himself with a comfortable fortune Although Mr Wood was never prominent in politics he was chosen to represent his native town in the legislature in 1854 He was an all round citizen, thoughtful, broadminded, public-spirited and more than an ordinary reader Naturally of a quiet disposition, not a leader except in business, there he was at home, and he put his mind and strength into it He must have approved machinery, and his personal attention was given to every detail in running his plant Of the welfare of his employees he was ever thoughtful From experience he knew that by fair and honorable treatment he would gain sympathy and co-operation In all his dealings with them he applied the principle of doing unto others as you would be done by, and that was the spirit in which he conducted all his business, and as a neighbor and friend his greeting and friendship was of the real old fashioned New England type, genuine in every particular Labor strikes at his mills were unheard of

In the spring of 1880 Mr Wood changed his residence from Uxbridge to Worcester, locating at No 21 Harvard street, in order to shorten the distance between the home and his factory in Holden, and also to gain the advantages of Worcester schools for the younger members of his family We have called attention to the fidelity with which Mr Wood applied himself to business that no branch of it might suffer from neglect, yet he found much time to devote to his family, the associations of which he fully appreciated and of which he was very fond He also enjoyed the society of men of broad and high aims In religion he was a Unitarian, and with his family attended the Church of the Unity, where almost from their immediate arrival in Worcester they took a prominent part in helping forward the work of the parish He was a charter member of the Uxbridge Lodge of Odd Fellows, one of the directors of the Citizens' National Bank of Worcester, and a member of the Board of Trade, also of the Worcester Society of Antiquity, being very much interested in historical studies, especially the annals of his native town, and when that society passed their field-day at Uxbridge in 1894, no speaker present was more entertaining than Mr Wood as he recited his early business experiences when a young man in that town He always deemed it a special pleasure when privileged to visit the home of his boyhood, and once he took his Quinapoxet employees to Uxbridge, where he entertained them throughout the day, pointing out the scenes of his early life and relating to them how step by step he felt his way along amid trials and disappointments, until at last by patient honest toil he had reached the point of success

Mr Wood was twice married, first to Lucetta, daughter of Joseph Day, of Uxbridge, who was a manufacturer and much respected citizen of that place She died in 1854, and he married (second) in 1858, Mary U F, daughter of Jonathan F and Chloe (Holbrook) Southwick The Southwicks were Quakers, and among the first Quakers of Salem, Massachusetts, and whom Whittier immortalized in his poem "Cassandra Southwick"

Mr Southwick was a son of Royal and Phoebe (Farnum) Southwick of Uxbridge, and in the sixth generation from Lawrence and Cassandra Southwick, who came from Lancashire England, and settled in Salem By occupation he was a tanner and currier a trade which he learned of his father Being a prosperous business man, he became a large owner of real estate, including the Ironstone factory property The old mill having been consumed by fire, he built a new one, and sold the property to Messrs Fairbanks and Messenger He also owned the mill below on the same stream, which he sold to J C Keith & Co He was a public-spirited citizen, giving special attention to educational matters, in his native town, where he was recognized as one of the substantial and representative men of the place He was much interested in temperance movements He married, November 14, 1822, Chloe Holbrook, a most estimable person, a kind and affectionate mother to their six children, including Mary Urania Farnum Southwick, born May 31, 1833 The children of Cyrus G Wood and Mary U F Southwick were 1 John Franklin, married Mary Leonard, resides at Quinapoxet He and his brother are continuing the business left by their father Their children are 1 Marion, born October 17 1897 2 Ernest Henry a graduate of Harvard University, married Adelaide Wyman, and resides at No 69 West street, Worcester Their children are Cyrus W, born January 31, 1900, Austen, born May 25, 1903, Daniel, born September 7, 1904, a daughter, born October 27, 1905 3 Gertrude S 4 Sarah Louise Mr Wood died at his home in Worcester, March 3, 1898

The ancestry of this branch of the Wood family we trace as follows

(I) Thomas Wood, married Ann Hunt of Ipswich, April 7, 1654, settled in Rowley, Massachusetts, where he died and was buried, September 12, 1667 She died December 29, 1714 Their children were Mary, John, Thomas, Ann, Ruth, Josiah, Elizabeth, Samuel, Elithrop, Solomon, Ebenezer and James

(II) Solomon, born May 17, 1669, married Mary Haseltine, October 15, 1690 She died February 20, 1749 He died January 13, 1752 For a time their home was in Bradford, Massachusetts, where many if not all of their children were born, after which they removed to that part of Mendon now Uxbridge Their children were David, Dorcas, Joshua, Mary, Solomon, James, Ezekiel, Obediah, Daniel and Betsey (See sketch Pliny W Wood ancestry)

(III) Obediah, born May 28, 1709, married Esther Hayward, and settled in Uxbridge Their children were 1 Warfield, born and died 1733-4 2 Eliza, born August 4, 1735 3 Obediah, May 9, 1737 4 Sarah, August 18, 1739 5 Esther, August 11, 1741 6 Solomon, May 25, 1744 7 David, August 11, 1748 Both the youngest sons, Solomon and David were soldiers in the revolutionary war

(IV) David, born August 11, 1748, served in the American army and was with Ethan Allen when he demanded the surrender of Ticonderoga He married Molly Farnum and lived in a house he built near his father's home in Uxbridge Their children were 1 Phebe, born January 8, 1769 2 Chloe, 1770 3 Farnum and 4 Keith (twins), born December 22 1772 5 Oliver, March 19 1775 6 Howard C, born January 3, 1777 7 Polly, January 27, 1779 8 Eunice, January 4 1781 9 Amos, December 23, 1783 10 Sally, March 15, 1785, drowned 11 Nancy February 6, 1787 12 Sally born March 29, 1789 married (first) Cyrus Grout, who died, and she then married (second) Reuben Wood 13 Dorinda, born March 6, 1791 14 David, born November 6, 1792 15 Clarissa, born December 27, 1797

KENDALL FAMILY Prominent among the early representatives of the Kendall family in England was John Kendall sheriff of Nottingham, who was killed in the Battle of Bosworth in 1485, fighting in the army of Richard III Francis Kendall, of a much later generation, was banished to the Barbadoes in the year 1687 by Bloody Judge Jeffreys, for participating in the Monmouth rebellion He is believed to have been a near relative of Francis Kendall, the emigrant ancestor, who came to America before 1640

Francis Kendall was the pioneer ancestor of Sanford C Kendall, Charles D Kendall, Frederick H Kendall and John M Kendall, of Worcester, Massachusetts, and also of other Kendall families in Worcester county In fact, he is believed to be the common ancestor of all families in America bearing this surname In December, 1658, he deposed that his age was about thirty-eight years On April 2, 1662, he deposed that his age was about forty-eight years Possibly the date of his birth was between the two dates indicated by these statements, say 1618 He came from England before 1640 With thirty-one others he signed the town orders of Woburn, December 18, 1640 He had been living in Charlestown, of which Woburn was then a part and where he was a taxpayer in 1645 He had a brother, Thomas Kendall, living in Reading Massachusetts, where he was a proprietor, in 1644 Thomas Kendall had ten daughters, and while he doubtless has a large posterity, none are named Kendall in direct line The father of Thomas and Francis is believed by some writers to be John Kendall

Francis Kendall married, December 24 1644, Mary Tidd, daughter of John Tidd In the record he is called Francis Kendall, alias Miles There are several explanations of this record It was common with emigrants to America to take assumed names to avoid vexatious laws, and there is a tradition that Kendall left England against the wishes of his family, using the name of Miles until he was settled in this country His brother Thomas seems not to have used any other name Francis Kendall was admitted a freeman May 10, 1648 Sewall says of him "He was a gentleman of great respectability and influence in the place of his residence" He served the town at different times for eighteen years on the board of selectmen, and on important committees, such as those for distributing grants to the pioneers, and on building the meeting house He was tithingman in 1676 He was not entirely in accord with the Puritan church, and was fined for some infraction of church rules about infant baptism, or attendance at communion, or attending meetings of the Anabaptists He was a miller by trade and owned a corn mill, which he left to his sons Samuel and John Samuel was the ancestor of the Worcester families John Kendall's grandson, Amos, also has descendants in Worcester county This corn mill, at Woburn has been in the possession of the family down to the present time The mill now, or lately, on the Kendall place, is one built by Samuel Kendall soon after 1700, and is some distance from the location of the first mill

He died, in 1708 at the age of eighty-eight according to the record, corroborating the affidavit of 1658 His wife Mary died in 1705 His will was dated May 9, 1706 His sons, Thomas and John, were the executors Children of Francis and Mary (Tidd) Kendall John, born July 2, 1646, Thomas, January 10, 1648-9, Mary, January 20, 1650-1, married Israel Reed, about 1669, Elizabeth, January 15, 1652-3, married (first) Ephraim Winship, (second) James Pierce, Hannah, January 26, 1654-5, married William Green Jr, as his second wife Rebecca, March 2, 1657, married Joshua Eaton, December, 1706, Samuel, March 8, 1659, Jacob, January 25, 1660-1, Abigail, April 6, 1666, married William Reed, May 24, 1686

(II) Samuel Kendall, son of Francis Kendall (2), born in Woburn, Massachusetts, March 8, 1659-60, married, November 13, 1683, Rebekah, daughter of Isaac Mixer She died October 25, 1691 He married (second), March 30, 1692, Mary Locke, daughter of William Locke He removed to Lancaster, probably in 1742, as he was taxed in Woburn January 28, 1741-2, but not the following years He was constable and collector in Woburn in 1726-27 He was a carpenter by trade His will was dated December 6, 1742, and proved 1749 He died in 1749 at the age of ninety years Children of Samuel and Rebecca (Mixer) Kendall Samuel, born August 13, 1684, married Prudence ———, about 1710, Isaac, September 1686, married, October 9, 1706, Hannah Walker, settled in Ashford, Connecticut, Joshua, March 14, 1689, married May 23, 1710, Susanna Harrington, settled in Watertown, Massachusetts, and Ashford, Connecticut, Rebecca, July 6, 1691, died November 25, 1691 Children of Samuel and Mary (Locke) Kendall were. Mary, February 3, 1693, died August 14, 1727, unmarried, Rebecca, January 26, 1694-5, died July 26, 1791, married Samuel Russell, Abigail, March 31, 1697, married William Nichols, of Reading, January 14, 1720, Ebenezer, May 16, 1700, married Hannah Thompson about 1731, Ruth, April 23, 1703, married Raham Bancroft, Tabitha, born January 22, 1706-7, married Nathan Richards, July 3, 1729, died November 25 1739

(III) Samuel Kendall, son of Samuel Kendall (2), born August 13, 1684, at Woburn, Massachusetts He settled in Lancaster, Massachusetts, where he died in 1743 His will mentions his wife Prudence and three children Children of Samuel and Prudence were Samuel, born September 4, 1711, Rebecca, August 27, 1714, Stephen, March 10, 1717

(IV) Samuel Kendall, son of Samuel Kendall (3), was born in Lancaster (?), Massachusetts, September 4, 1711 He married Phebe Brintain, September 23, 1736 They settled in what is now Sterling, possibly on the homestead of his father, as Samuel and wife, Phebe, joined the Chocksett (Sterling) church soon after the father's death February 3, 1744-5 Chocksett became the town of Sterling in 1781 The church was organized in the December preceding (1744)

Samuel Kendall was in the expedition to Canada, in 1759, under Colonel Oliver Wilder, of Lancaster, as was also his brother, Stephen Kendall Children of Samuel and Phebe (Brintain) Kendall, baptized in the Chocksett church by the pastor, Rev Mr Mellen Samuel, baptized February 17, 1745, Rebecca, February 17, 1745, Abigail, July 20, 1746, Caleb, May 15, 1748, probably died young, Bartholomew, February 18, 1749, Caleb, March 24, 1750, Bartholomew February 28, 1753, William, October 13, 1754, Phebe, July 3, 1757, Lucy, February 10, 1760, Lucinda, November 14, 1762

(V) Caleb Kendall, son of Samuel Kendall (4), born in Sterling, then Chocksett, Massachusetts, a part of Lancaster, and baptized March 24, 1750, married (first), December 8, 1773, Priscilla Townsend daughter of Joshua Townsend, in Shrewsbury, Massachusetts He resided in Shrewsbury several years, and then removed to Ashburnham, where his cousin Amos, son of Francis and grandson of John Kendall (brother of his great-grandfather Samuel Kendall) was living He went there some time before 1787 While living at Ashburnham he married (second) at Lancaster, April 15, 1788 Lucy (Baldwin) Kendall widow of Thomas Kendall, of Lancaster In 1792 he removed to Winchendon, Massachusetts, but his son Samuel, born in 1792, was baptized in Boylston, and the records show that Caleb settled in Boylston in that year, also Boylston was the north district of Shrewsbury, so he merely returned to his old home Caleb Kendall was a soldier in the revolution He was in Captain John Maynard s company and Colonel Job Cushing's regiment, which marched August 21, 1777, to Hadley, on the Bennington Alarm He was also in Captain Inglesby s company, Colonel Cushing s regiment, in the Rhode Island campaign He was also in Captain Ezra Beaman s company in Shrewsbury June 6, 1777 He was a housewright He bought his home in Shrewsbury of Jotham Flagg, and from time to time other lots The first deed is dated January 7, 1773 He died 1807 The eleven children signed the partition deeds September 2, 1807 Lucy, widow of Caleb Kendall, died at Boylston, November 22, 1745, aged eighty-five Children of Caleb and Priscilla (Townsend) (sketch in Boylston centennial gives her name Savory, but the town records in several places give it Townsend) Kendall Priscilla, born January 20, 1777, at Shrewsbury, married Thaniel Cutting, Caleb, at Shrewsbury, January 25, 1779, (Holden records say January 27) settled in Holden, Massachusetts, married, June 24, 1803, Dolly Sawyer, Zippora, Joshua, 2d, married Patty Sawyer, died in Boylston 1813 Children of Caleb and Lucy (Baldwin) Kendall Lucy, baptized June 14, 1789, probably born in Ashburnham, married Joseph Sawyer, David, born March 12, 1791, baptized at Boylston, May 29, 1791, Samuel, born October 11, 1792, in Winchendon and recorded there, baptized at Boylston, Hannah, married Phineas Moore, Elmira or Myra, married Jotham Howe, Emily or Emilia, married Jonas Hastings (court papers indicate that she is older than Myra), William, married Susan Hartshorn

(VI) David Kendall, son of Caleb Kendall (5), was born in Ashburnham, Massachusetts His father removed to Boylston when he was about a year old, and he resided there most of his life It has been said of him that "to him manual labor seemed more like a pastime than a task" He married Polly Wellington, April 2, 1812 His wife was also known as Molly (See John Kendall) Children of David and Molly (Wellington) Kendall Elizabeth Temple, born March 19, 1814, married, September 8, 1844, Rev A Stowell, Sanford M (name was originally Joshua and was altered by general court), March 6, 1816, Horace, June 21, 1821, died April 27, 1827, Mary, July 18, 1823, died August 13, 1824, Mary, July 9, 1825, married Fisk B Temple, March 8, 1848, Horace, August 28, 1827, John, November 6, 1829, Lyman P, February 9, 1832, Sophia Brooks, April 27, 1834, died May 9, 1834, Olive S, May 4, 1836, died August 11, 1839 David Kendall married (second) at Greenfield, Massachusetts

(VII) Elizabeth Temple Kendall, daughter of David Kendall (6), born in Boylston, Massachusetts, March 19, 1814, married, September 8, 1844, Rev A Stowell, of Erving, Massachusetts Their children are Mary E, born March 28, 1847, died February 9, 1893, unmarried, was a teacher in Bridgewater School for the Blind to the time of her death, S Louise, born July 10, 1853, married Clinton J Smith, of Keene, New Hampshire, and they have two children Ralph and Alice

(VII) Horace Kendall, son of David Kendall (6), was born in Boylston, Massachusetts, August 28, 1827 He married, April 4, 1854, Sarah A Maynard, of Boylston, Massachusetts He married (second) Fanny Buck, of Worcester, January 1, 1874 She died August 22, 1881 He married (third) Hattie S Hagan, who survives him He removed to Worcester with his family in 1871, and engaged in the furniture business He was a well known auctioneer, and prominent merchant in Worcester for thirty years His store was in the Mechanics building Children of Horace and Sarah A (Maynard) Kendall Charles D, November 10, 1854, married Kate E Lindsay, of Grafton, Massachusetts, Sanford Clayton, born in Boylston, October 6, 1856, married Jennie Bruce, December 24, 1877 The only child of Horace and Fanny (Buck) Kendall was Frederick H, born January 20, 1875

(VIII) Charles David Kendall, son of Horace Kendall (7), was born in Boylston, Massachusetts, November 10, 1854 He attended the district schools of Boylston In 1871, when his father moved to Worcester, he went to work in the store In 1880 he went to Grafton to work In 1888 he returned to Worcester and entered the furniture business, again with his father After his father s death the three sons were in partnership for a time Sanford C Kendall, in 1903, bought the interests of Charles D and Frederick H Kendall, and has since carried on the business under the firm name of Kendall Furniture Company Charles D and Frederick H bought an interest in the Warren Leather Goods Company, of Worcester, in July, 1903 The business of this concern is the manufacture of suit cases and traveling bags of every description, and various fancy goods of leather The company has a large factory at 80 Austin street, employing about two hundred hands The company was incorporated in 1902 with a capital of thirty thousand dollars The business was formerly that of J J Warren The present officers of the corporation are President, Thomas T Hickey, of Shrewsbury, vice-president, Charles D Kendall, secretary, W H Hayden, treasurer, Frederick H Kendall

Mr Kendall is a Congregationalist In politics he is a Republican He married Kate Elizabeth Lindsay, of Grafton, June 26, 1884 She was born January 16, 1860, daughter of Ira and Mary (Estabrook) Lindsay Her mother was born January 18, 1830, at Princeton, and married, June 11, 1857, Ira Lindsay, at Princeton Children of Ira and Mary (Estabrook) Lindsay Ellen F, born May 6, 1858, Kate E, January 16, 1860, married, June 26, 1884, Charles David Kendall, Joseph J, September 21 1864, married, October 8, 1883

The children of Charles David and Kate Elizabeth (Lindsay) Kendall Horace Clayton, born in Grafton, Massachusetts, September 26, 1885, graduate of English high school, Worcester, in 1904, is in Worcester Polytechnic Institute, class of 1907, Herbert Lindsay, born in Worcester, June 22, 1889, Charles Donald, born in Worcester, August 14, 1899 Mr Kendall resides at 5 Barnard road, Worcester

(VIII) Sanford Clayton Kendall, son of Horace Kendall (7), was born in Boylston, Massachusetts, October 6 1856 He received a common school education in his native town With his parents he removed to Worcester in 1871, and went to work in his father's store He was associated with his father in the furniture and auctioneer business until his death in 1899 The store at 319 Main street is well known to Worcester people, especially to lovers of antiques and colonial furniture During the last years of his father's life he was manager of the business After the death of the father, the three sons became partners in the Kendall Furniture Company In 1902 Mr Kendall became the sole owner His two brothers withdrew to enter the Warren Leather Goods Company Since then Mr Kendall has conducted the business at the old stand He has been prominent in city affairs He is a Republican He was elected to the common council from ward two in 1895, and served until he was elected an alderman In the council he served on the committees on charities, street lighting, military affairs and the joint special committee on central workshop In the board of aldermen he was chairman of the committees on charities, and lighting streets, and member of the committees on fire department and ordinances, and of the aldermanic committees on elections and returns He married, December 24, 1877, Jennie Bruce They have one child, Clayton

(VIII) Frederick H Kendall, son of Horace Kendall (7), was born in Worcester, January 20, 1875 He was educated in the Worcester public schools and at Cushing Academy, Ashburnham, where he graduated in 1894 in about a year He went into the furniture business with his father, and later he became a partner with his two brothers, after their father's death, in the Kendall Furniture Company He sold his interest in the business in February, 1902, and in the following July bought an interest and became the treasurer of the Warren Leather Goods Company, which was formed to take over the business of the J J Warren Company His brother, Charles D Kendall, also entered the Warren Leather Goods Company, and is the vice-president Mr Kendall is treasurer of the concern He is an attendant of the Congregational church, a member of the Lakeside Boat Club, and a Republican in politics He married, December 7, 1900, Fanny F Chambers, daughter of Calvin M and Frances (Keyes) Chambers, of Redwing, Minnesota They have a daughter Eleanor, born April 17, 1904 Mr Kendall resides at 730 Pleasant street

(VII) John Kendall, son of David Kendall (6), was born in Boylston, Massachusetts, November 6, 1829 He began his schooling in Boylston, but did not continue long, for at the age of twelve years he became highly incensed at what he felt was an unprincipled act on the part of the teacher toward a pupil So he broke away from the yoke of school life and hired out at farming to Squire Aaron White, of Boylston, who was at that time, it is said, the richest farmer in the county He remained with the Squire until 1847, when he became clerk in the country store at Boylston, kept by a Mr Hathaway, for whom he worked a year In 1848 he came to Worcester and began to learn the fur business with J H Knight, where he remained until 1862, when Mr Knight died He and William H McClennen formed a partnership and bought the business The business was conducted under the firm name of Kendall & McClennen until 1875, when Mr McClennen sold his interest to his partner, and Mr Kendall continued alone The store at that time was at 163 Main street Their stock included hats, caps and men s furnishings as well as furs In 1888 Mr Kendall took into partnership David Boyden, who continueed with him until he died in 1895, he then admitted his son, John M Kendall, to partnership The firm was in business until 1897, when he retired from active life He was a prosperous and successful merchant and knew the fur business in every branch His favorite sport was fishing and he was known all over the county among the disciples of Izaac Walton He died July 14,1903 He was a member of the Old South Congregational Church, and a Republican in politics He was a member of the Worcester County Mechanics Association He belonged to no secret societies He married, August 10, 1852, Mary T Knight, daughter of Erastus and Theodamia (Cushman) Knight, of Chesterfield, Massachusetts Her father was a farmer in Chesterfield Children of John and Mary (Knight) Kendall were Olive Cushman, born in Worcester, July 16, 1862 (1855 in Genealogy), is living in Worcester, John Melvin (see forward)

(VIII) John Melvin Kendall, son of John Kendall (7), born in Worcester, Massachusetts, March 5, 1866, received his early education in the public schools of this native city, where he passed through the grammar schools and graduated from the Classical high school in 1883 He entered Amherst College in the fall in the class of 1887, but after a year he returned home at the desire of his father and entered the store He became his father s partner in 1895 and remained in the business until 1897, when his father and the firm retired from business He then entered the employ of the Denholm & McKay Company as expert buyer of furs and manager of the fur department He continued in this position eight years In 1905 he withdrew to become the treasurer of the John L Parker Company, manufacturers of sheet metal goods, having become a part owner of the business He is a member of St John s Episcopal Church, and has been treasurer, vestryman and superintendent of the Sunday school

He has taken an active part in Republican politics, frequently serving his party as delegate to the county and state conventions He served the city in the common council for four years, 1902-3-4-5 He has been a trustee of the City Hospital since 1903, and is one of the overseers of the poor He is a member of Regulus Lodge, Knights of Pythias, No 71, of Worcester, and of the Hancock Club Mr Kendall is a musician of distinction and has written several successful operas He is a clever writer and is regarded as an authority in baseball matters In years past he has written much for *The Spy* on dramatic and sporting subjects He is an earnest, capable business man, and stands high in the estimation of the entire community in which he has lived all his life He married June 27, 1904, Caroline Eliza Davis, daughter of Samuel E and Hannah E (Robinson) Davis, of Boston She was born August 23, 1868 Her father was a woolen manufacturer (See sketch of Samuel E Davis)

DR JEREMIAH FISKE The family of Fiske flourished for centuries in England in the county of Suffolk As early as the reign of King John in 1208 we find the name of Daniel Fisc, of Laxfield, appended to a document issued by the king confirming a grant of land in Digneveton Park, made by the Duke of Loraine to the men of Laxfield, May 1, 1208 There was the seat of the family for a long period The ancient coat of arms is Chequey, argent and gules upon a pale, sable, three mullets, pierced, or

(I) Lord Symond Fiske, to whom the English and American line is traced, was the progenitor of Dr Jeremiah Fiske, of Clinton, Massachusetts It is believed that he was grandson of Daniel Fiske, the first mentioned in the records of the locality, he was Lord of the manor of Stadhaugh, parish of Laxfield county of Suffolk, England, from 1399 to 1422 He married (first) Susannah Smyth and (second) Katherine —— His will was dated December 22 1463 and was probated at Norwich, February 26 1463-4 He bequeathed 'his soul to God, the Virgin Mary and all the Saints in Heaven" He named each of his sons, William, Jeffrey, John and Edmund and daughter, Margaret Dowsing His wife Katherine son John and Nichols Nolock were the executors He died February, 1464 The chil-

Jeremiah Fröke

dren William married Joanne Lynne, Jeffrey, married Margaret ——, John, Edmund, married Margery ——, Margaret, married Dowsing or Dowling

(II) William Fiske, son of Lord Symond Fiske (1), was born at Stadhaugh, county Suffolk, England, and died 1504 He married Joan Lynne, of Norfolk Her will was dated July 15, 1504, proved February 28 1505 It mentions her sons John, Augustine, Simon, son's wife Anne, daughters Margery and Margaret Sir John Fiske and her sons John Fiske and son Simon were executors The children Thomas, married Anne ——, William, married Joan ——, Augustine, married Joan ——, Simon, see forward, Robert, married Joan ——, John, Margery, Margaret

(III) Simon Fiske, son of William Fiske (2), was born in Laxfield He married Elizabeth ——, who died at Halesworth, June, 1558 They resided at Laxfield His will was dated July 10, 1536, and proved July 13, 1538 He was buried in the chancel at the end of the church of All Saints, Laxfield, next his father and other members of his family He died June 1538 The children Simon, see forward, William, Robert, married Alice ——, Joan, married —— Iverton, Jeffrey, Gelyne, married —— Warner Agnes, Thomas, Elizabeth, John

(IV) Simon Fiske, son of Simon Fiske (3), was born in Laxfield, England His will was dated January 25, 1505 The children Robert, see forward John, married Thomasin Pinchard, George, married Anne ——, Nicholas, married Joan Crispe, Jeffrey, Jeremy, William, Richard, married Agnes Crispe, Joan, Gelvne, Agnes

(V) Robert Fiske son of Simon Fiske (4), was born in England, 1525 He married Mrs Sybil (Gould) Barber For some time he was of the parish of St James, South Elmham, England Sybil was in great danger of religious persecution at the time her sister Isabella was confined for her religious opinions in Castle Norwich The children William, born 1566, see forward Jeffrey, married Sarah Cooke, Thomas, married Margery ——, Eleazer, died at Metfield, Elizabeth, married Robert Barnard

(VI) William Fiske son of Robert Fiske (5), was born at Laxfield, England 1566 He married Anna Anstyle, daughter of Walter Anstyle, of Tibbenham, Long Row, Norfolk He married (second) Alice —— He lived in St James parish, South Elmham He and his father had to leave the country on account of their Puritan ideas His will was dated November 25, 1616, and proved May 17, 1623 His children John born at South Elmham, married Anne Lantersee Nathaniel born at South Elmham see forward, Eleazer born at South Elmham, settled in Norwich, Eunice, unmarried, Hannah, married William Candler, and their son Rev Mathias Candler was author of the celebrated Candler manuscript in the British Museum, Hester, married John C Chalke of Rednall Mary, married Anthony Fisher, ancestor of the Fisher emigrants at Dedham, Massachusetts (See sketch of Fisher families in this work)

(VII) Nathaniel Fiske, son of William Fiske (6) was born in England He was named in the wills of his father, his uncle Eleazer, and cousin Eleazer of Weybred, England He married Mrs Alice (Henel) Leman The children Nathaniel, see forward Sarah, married Robert Rogers

(VIII) Nathaniel Fiske son of Nathaniel Fiske (7), was born at Weybred, Suffolk county England He married Dorothy Symonds, of Wendham, daughter of John Symonds The children John, born 1619 married Sarah Wyeth Nathan see forward, Esther, born in England, Martha married Martin Underwood weaver, settled in Watertown, Massachusetts died November 17, 1672

(IX) Nathan Fiske, son of Nathaniel Fiske (8) was born in England, 1615 and died June 21, 1676 He settled at Watertown, Massachusetts, as early as 1642, and was admitted a freeman May 10 1643 He bought land there September 10, 1643 He was a selectman in 1673 His homestall was on the north side of the road to Sudbury granted first to R Frake His will was dated June 19, 1676, and he died two days later He mentioned his five children as named below Children Nathan, born October 17, 1642, see forward, John, born August 25, 1647, David, born April 29, 1650 married Elizabeth Reed, Nathaniel, born July 12, 1653, married Mrs Mary (Warren) Child Sarah, born 1656, married, September 3, 1673, Abraham Gale, son of Richard Gale, the immigrant, of Watertown

(X) Lieutenant Nathan Fiske, son of Nathan Fiske (9), was born in Watertown, Massachusetts, October 17, 1642 He married Elizabeth Fry who died May 15, 1696 He bought two hundred and twenty acres of land in Weston, October 1, 1673, of Thomas Underwood and wife Magdalen for ten pounds He was selectman in 1684-88-91 His widow Elizabeth was appointed administratrix December 10, 1694 His estate was divided November 23, 1696 He died October 11, 1694 , The children Nathan born February 9, 1665, died December 9, 1668, Elizabeth born January 19, 1667 married, January 16, 1693 James Ball, weaver, born March 7, 1670, died February 22, 1729, Martha, born January 12, 1670 married, March 13, 1694, Edward Park, born April 8 1661 son of Thomas and grandson of Richard of Cambridge, Nathan, see forward, Susanna, born April 7, 1674 died at Shrewsbury, April 28, 1752, unmarried, Abigail, born February 18, 1675, married August 15 1695, John Mixer, son of Isaac Mixer Jr William, born December 5, 1677, died 1677, William, born November 10, 1678 married Eunice Jennings, Anna, died July 13, 1683

(XI) Deacon Nathan Fiske, son of Nathan Fiske (10), was born at Watertown Massachusetts, January 3 1672, married, October 14, 1696 Sarah Coolidge, who was born about 1678, daughter of Ensign John Coolidge of Watertown She died November 27, 1723 and he married (second) May 22, 1729, Mrs Hannah (Coolidge) Smith, who was born December 7, 1671 and died October 4, 1750, the daughter of Simon Coolidge and widow of Daniel Smith Jr Nathan Fiske was deputy to the general court 1727-28-29-32, selectman 1711-14-17-19-20-22-23-24-26-27, treasurer 1720-22-23, town clerk 1724-28-30 He was elected deacon as early as 1717 The will of his wife Hannah was dated September 12 and proved October 22 1750 it mentions various relatives in the Coolidge family Deacon Nathan died January 26 1741 The children Sarah born 1697, died November, 1713, Elizabeth died aged seven years, Nathan, born February 25, 1701, married Anne Warren and Mary Fiske of Sudbury Josiah, born October 10 1704 see forward, Henry born January 24, 1706 married Mary Stone, Daniel, born August 19 1709, married Deliverance Brown and Jemima Shaw Samuel, born February 16, 1711, married Lydia Bond, Grace, born May 9 1714 married, September 25 1733, Benjamin Goddard, of Shrewsbury she died at Hopkinton, October 28, 1803, aged ninety years, Hannah, born May 19 1719 married, February 15 1743, William Smith, Jr, of Weston, born May 23 1721, she died September 2, 1813 aged ninety-four years

(XII) Deacon Josiah Fiske, son of Deacon Nathan Fiske (11) was born at Watertown, October 10 1704, married Sarah Lawrence born June 20, 1708 daughter of John and Anne (Tarbell) Lawrence, of Lexington died 1798 He was selectman 1749-50 assessor 1743-44 48 He was dismissed to the Groton church May 13, 1753, and settled in Pepperell, where the births of his children (born in Waltham) were recorded He was deacon of the church and leading citizen in that part of Groton set off later as Pepperell He was town clerk of Groton and first town clerk of Pepperell, holding that office twenty years His will was dated September 1, 1778, and proved January 23, 1779 He died October 27, 1778 Children David born January 28, 1727, died October 28, 1729, Sarah, born August 7, 1729, died May 1 1731, David, born December 16 1731, died February 1, 1766, killed by an apple thrown from the church window at the ordination service at Lunenburg. Josiah born February 12, 1733, see forward. Sarah born October 7, 1736, married, April 14, 1756, Simon Gibson, Amos, born May 10, 1739, married Mary Whitney, Daniel, born May 18, 1742, married Elizabeth Varnum, Anna, born February 16 1744 died February 12, 1745, Anna born December 16, 1747, married, March 3 1768 Dr Ephraim Lawrence a physician of Pepperell, Pennsylvania she died June 12, 1774, Abel, born May 28 1752, married Anna Spaulding and (second) Sarah Putnam

(XIII) Josiah Fiske, son of Josiah Fiske (12) was born at Waltham, February 12, 1733, married Sarah Colburn, of Dracut, born 1737, died 1825 His estate was administered by his widow Sarah appointed April 11, 1767 He had a good education and taught school for several years He was only thirty-three years old when he died beloved by all" His widow married (second) Levi Blood, of Groton, who died April 14, 1766 His children Josiah, born September 3 1755 see forward, David, born 1756, Sarah born about 1760, Phinehas, born January 29, 1765, died young, Submit, (posthumous) born 1767

(XIV) Josiah Fiske, son of Josiah Fiske (13), was born at Pepperell September 3, 1755, married there November 25 1779, Mary Caldwell, of Cambridge, who was born April 20, 1755, died December 25, 1834 He was a soldier in the revolution, joined the company of Captain Dow, of Hollis, New Hampshire He took part in the battle of Bunker Hill and was afterward a fifer in the army at Saratoga At Bunker Hill he took a register from the pocket of a British officer This article and his old fife are treasured as keepsakes by his descendants In 1782 he moved from Pepperell to Temple, New Hampshire and settled on the Searles farm In 1787 he purchased the Lieutenant Jonathan Marshall farm, immediately north of the other place His son Jeremiah afterward occupied the place Josiah was highly esteemed He was very pious and never was known to omit family worship from the time of his marriage to that of his death, May 29 1832 His widow died December 25 1834 Children Josiah, born November 14 1781, married Betsey Kimball, Sarah born April 19 1784, and died August 27, 1784, Polly, born October 12, 1785, married William Patterson, who died at Francestown, New Hampshire, May 13, 1832 she died at Nashua, New Hampshire January 6, 1854, Sally, born February 25, 1788, married 1809 Earl Boynton resided at New Ipswich, born April 20, 1788 died August 26, 1881, and had ten children, Jeremiah, born August 17, 1790, see forward Artemas born September 11, 1792 married Lucy Jones, David born May 12 1795, died July 10 1795 David, born January 12, 1797, married Milly Sheldon lived in Oxford New York Seth H born September 20 1800 married (first) Lydia Putnam in Marblehead November 1, 1827, (second) Hannah Miles in Oxford New York 1833, and (third) Mrs Fanny Pollock December 1, 1870

(XV) Jeremiah Fiske, son of Josiah Fiske (14), was born in Temple, New Hampshire, August 17, 1790 He married Sarah Heald, born 1798, died March 23 1858, daughter of James Heald, born in Temple, November 28 1777, and Sarah Walker, and granddaughter of Deacon Peter Heald and Rebecca Russell, of Townsend He married (second) Mrs Cemma Monroe, who died November, 1895 Jeremiah Fiske was one of the most successful farmers of the county He settled on the homestead After retiring from business he traveled extensively He was the largest real estate owner in Temple, and among his holdings was what was formerly Cummings Hill, upon which large bonfires are built every year as they can be seen at a great distance, and a large tract called Fiske Hill He died October 9, 1882 He was a Republican in politics He was interested in the family genealogy and well posted in it His children were well educated and at one time six of them were public school teachers The children James born March 16, 1816, died 1878, unmarried Sarah Ann, born January 20, 1817, married, December 1, 1842, Captain Charles Walton resided at New Ipswich, she died in Temple, 1885 Lois, born March 21, 1819, died July 29 1836 Josiah, born November 6, 1820, died December 11, 1904, married March 5 1848, Rebecca Flint, who died December 16 1852, married (second) Mary Wood, May 12, 1865 Charlotte born July 9 1822, married May 14, 1846, Dr Thomas Palmer, an expert dental surgeon of Fitchburg Jeremiah, born February 10, 1824, see forward Alvah, born November 4 1825, died January 31, 1854, at Indianapolis Martin H, born May 10 1827, graduate of Dartmouth, 1853, principal of seminary at Paris Tennessee, elected in 1854 president Paducah College, Kentucky married Henrietta F Breed, born September 27, 1827 died January 29, 1901, at Old Fiske homestead Temple, New Hampshire Emily, born May 8 1829 died at Abington, Massachusetts, July 29, 1902 married June 2, 1856 Daniel Lamson, of East Weymouth, killed in the battle of Fredericksburg, December, 1862 Rebecca Davis, born February 20, 1831, married, March 1865, Thomas Fessendon and she and her son a Presbyterian minister, the Rev Alvah Grant Fessendon, reside at Los Angeles Charles F born December 2 1832, married Emma Bailey, she died at Milford December 2, 1894, he is practicing his profession of dentistry at Milford, New Hampshire

(XVI) Dr Jeremiah Fiske son of Jeremiah Fiske (15), was born at Temple, New Hampshire, February 10, 1824 His maternal great-grandfather was the first settler in Temple, New Hampshire, and his son, Peter Heald, the first male child born in the town He attended the public schools, the Appleton Academy of New Ipswich, and the Hancock Academy He worked on his father's farm until he was of age On account of an injury which unfitted him for farm labor, he left home and found employment in Boston in a market Afterward he began the study of dentistry with his brother-in-law, Dr Thomas Palmer, at Fitchburg In 1849 he went to Clintonville then a part of the town of Lancaster then without a dentist and began to practice his profession there As the town grew rapidly his practice grew large and for a period of fifty years he was the leading dentist of the vicinity The town of Clinton was formed and grew to the proportions of a city in that period His first office was in the Ford block, which block he owned for several years in company with the late Dr G W Burdett in a front room over what is now Sargent's jewelry store After a few years he moved into a larger front room in the same building, over what is now Hubberd's dry goods store, and this room is still used as a dentist's office being occupied by Dr Harris During his practice eight of our prominent dentists were pupils in his office. During the civil war he was in partnership for a time with Dr D B Ingalls

Dr Fiske formerly took much interest in the Congregational parish, assisting materially in the building of two additions to the old church, also in building the parsonage He was on the building committee He was one of ten who contributed the fund for the clock on the old church His family are all members of the Congregational church and his daughter has been the leading contralto in the choir for the past seven years In politics Dr Fiske is a prohibitionist and was the first to cast a vote for the Prohibition ticket in the town of Clinton Like most of his party, he voted for President McKinley, but has otherwise always been a steadfast third party man Before the civil war he was an anti-slavery man and not a few runaway slaves received assistance from him He entertained and kept over night an escaped follower of Captain John Brown when there was a thousand dollar reward offered for his arrest It was very interesting to hear this man tell of his many narrow escapes He and five others including two sons of John Brown, passed through Clinton on their way north and a reward of a thousand dollars had been offered for the capture of each of them Dr Fiske has always taken much interest in the Lancaster Lodge of Odd Fellows of which he is a member He is also a member of the Grand Lodge and Encampment and the Grand Assembly of the Rebekahs In 1850 Dr Fiske was a member of a division of the Sons of Temperance, one of the most active temperance societies that ever existed in Clinton, consisting of one hundred and twenty members, all men, including many of the leading men of the town The society was a terror to the illicit rum seller, and did excellent work for many years Dr Fiske had in his keeping a beautiful silk banner presented to this society by the ladies of Clinton which he presented to the Historical Society to adorn the walls of a room in the new Historical building The donor of this beautiful building was a member of this once famous division of the Sons of Temperance

Dr Fiske has seen many changes during the fifty-seven years he has lived in Clinton He is now one of the oldest persons in the town The population has grown from twenty-five hundred to thirteen thousand Only two persons are now living on High street who lived there when he came to town When he built his house with the eleven gables in 1857 there were only three dwelling houses in the neighborhood In front of his house, where Dr Otis's house, the town house, the Unitarian Church and Central Park are now, was then a swamp Most of the land east of Chestnut street and north of Church street was then covered with a forest His house is now half surrounded with public buildings

On grounds of Dr Fiske stands an English walnut tree which is probably the only one in Worcester county It was first planted in Salem by the daughters of General Miller and was brought from Temple, New Hampshire, and planted where it now is by Dr Fiske It is about fifty feet high and over a foot in diameter, and bears nuts every year of a superior quality

He married February 17 1853 Caroline Elizabeth Bailey of Greenfield New Hampshire She was born February 10 1830 daughter of Leonard and Betsey (Hardy) Bailey of Greenfield Their children Ella Athelia, born December 15 1853, who for more than a score of years has conducted successfully a private school in Clinton, for several years she has conducted her father's business as collector of rents and care of real estate, under a power of attorney, she is a member of the Runaway Brook Golf Club Carrie Novella, born July 5, 1860, an artist of more than ordinary note, has won many prizes for her work married, October 28, 1891, Willard Forrest Hallett, they reside at 804 Lafayette street, Bridgeport, Connecticut

DADMUN FAMILY Samuel Dadmun (1), the immigrant ancestor of William Slocomb Dadmun, of Worcester, and probably of all of this surname in this section of the country, was said to be of Scotch birth and family He was born about 1690, and the first record found in which his name is mentioned is that of his marriage at Framingham, Massachusetts, May 27, 1714, to Martha Jennings, daughter of Stephen Jennings Her father came to Framingham in 1690, married at Sudbury, January 11, 1685, Hannah Stanhope, he died September 3, 1701, and Hannah, his widow, bought, January 6, 1702-03, of James Brewer and Caleb Johnson part of the Appleton farm lying between Lake Cochituate and Cochituate brook where her descendants lived until after the revolution The place is known as the Luther Eaton place Martha (Jennings) Dadmun and her children were living there with her mother in 1718 Samuel probably died in 1717 or 1718 Their children were Samuel, see forward, and a daughter who married ——— Wadsworth The name is spelled also Deadman and Dedman

(II) Samuel Dadmun, son of Samuel Dadmun (1), was born in Framingham, Massachusetts, about 1715 He settled in Framingham near Stone's Mills and died in 1794 In 1761 he bought of Hezekiah Stone fifty acres on Square Meadow brook, afterwards called also Dadmun brook, and this farm has been known since then as the Dadmun place He was sergeant in a company of militia under the command of Captain Henry Emmes in the French and Indian war, 1757 He married Lois Pratt, born June 7, 1726, died 1808, daughter of Daniel Pratt (IV), granddaughter of Thomas Pratt (III), of Watertown and Framingham, great-graddaughter of Thomas Pratt (II), of Sudbury, son of Thomas Pratt (I), the immigrant Children of Samuel and Lois Pratt were Nathan, born March 7, 1742, died young, Daniel, March 27, 1744, Nathan, see forward, Timothy, baptized March 25, 1750, Martha, born in Framingham, baptized March 25, 1752, died unmarried July 26, 1833, Elijah, baptized October 19, 1755, Samuel, married, October, 1757, Dorcas Stone, of Framingham settled in Princeton and died 1821 in Templeton Jonathan, Lois, baptized May 20, 1764, married Isaac How, of Framingham, Susannah, born February 5 1769 married Ezra Belcher

(III) Nathan Dadmun, son of Samuel Dadmun (2), was born at Framingham, Massachusetts June 16, 1747 He lived on the Lemuel Jones farm in that part of Framingham now Ashland He died February 16, 1827 He was a soldier in the revolution, a minute man of Captain Simon Edgell's company on the Lexington Alarm, April 19, 1775 His brother Elijah also marched to Concord and Lexington Nathan also served later under Captain Edgell, in 1776 marching to Ticonderoga He was a corporal and his company was in Colonel Samuel Brewer's regiment He married Hannah Sanger, daughter of David Sanger She died November 19, 1821 Their children were Joseph, born May 14 1774, Jeduthan, December 23, 1775, see forward, Eleanor, March 18, 1777, married Elias Grout, Sarah, January 10, 1779, married Eli Eames, of Holliston, Hannah, January 11, 1781, married William Clark, Bathsheba, December 26, 1782, married, July 14, 1807, Jacob Prescott of Westford, Massachusetts, Nathan, March 29, 1785, married Barrodell Jackson, Mary, March 31, 1787, married John Clark

(IV) Jeduthan Dadmun, son of Nathan Dadmun (3), was born in that part of Framingham now Ashland, December 23, 1775 Most of the family lived in that locality He bought in 1804 a house and seven acres of land north of his father's farm, and he also was a farmer He died February 14, 1825 He married, December 18 1801, Lois Jones, daughter of Nathaniel Alden Jones, granddaughter of Anthony Jones, who resided in Hopkinton, but was of Framingham in 1796 Nathaniel Alden Jones married Lois Chapin in 1770 and lived in the Parson Swift house in Framingham His father was Colonel John Jones Anthony Jones married Elizabeth Alden, daughter of Nathaniel Alden, a lineal descendant of John Alden, who came over in the 'Mayflower' Hence all the Dadmuns of Worcester, descended as noted below, are eligible for the Mayflower Society Colonel John Jones removed to Framingham from Boston in 1715, was a cordwainer by trade, justice of the peace, town officer, owned slaves—James, Tom and Bacchus He married, May 12, 1713, Elizabeth Simpson, daughter of Samuel Simpson Lois (Jones) Dadmun died April 14, 1822 Children of Jeduthan and Lois Dadmun were Louisa, born June 18, 1802, married Abijah Claflin, John Jones, October 23, 1804, Henry J, January 10, 1807, married, February 22, 1832, Esther G Allard, settled in Ashland and died there November 13 1879, Hannah J, May 8, 1809, Elizabeth S, November 25, 1811, married Bradford Belknap, Sarah, July 5, 1814, Jeduthan, October 13, 1816 see forward, Lucy A P, July 21, 1819, Izanna E, December 23, 1821

(V) Jeduthan Dadmun, Jr, son of Jeduthan Dadmun (4), was born at Ashland, Massachusetts, October 13, 1816 He was brought up on his father's farm until he was ten, when he was apprenticed to learn the trade of shoemaker in Hopkinton He had the usual common school education of that period When he came of age he went to Worcester and obtained a position in a general store, where he worked for several years He left Worcester to take a position in Holliston at his trade of shoemaker for the custom trade After five or six years he removed to Lunenburg and worked two years there at his trade About 1855 he was appointed agent of a union grocery store at Grafton, and he remained in charge of this concern for the stockholders until 1863, when the store was destroyed by fire He then went into business for himself as a grocer in Grafton, remaining for a year or two He then started a grocery store in Springfield, Massachusetts, in company with Henry F Putnam, under the firm name of Dadmun & Putnam, located on State street From there he went to Boston and worked at his trade of shoemaker for a number of years His last years were spent in Worcester where he made his home with his son, William S Dadmun, and died September 21, 1884 In religion Mr Dadmun was a Unitarian and in politics a Republican He married September 29, 1839, Lucy Davis, born at Rutland Massachusetts, September 24, 1811, daughter of Isaac and Betsey (Rice) Davis, of Rutland She died January 14 1878 Her father Isaac was a blacksmith and farmer The children of Jeduthan and Lucy (Davis) Dadmun were 1 George Lyman, born July 29, 1840, at Holden, died at East Winthrop, Maine, April 4, 1842 2 Frances, born August 21, 1842 at Worcester, died September 18, 1843 3 Frank Jones, born January 3, 1844, at Worcester, died September 4, 1898, married (first) October 9, 1867, Mary E Dudley, of Sutton born January 22, 1847, died January 13, 1878, and they have one child Mary Florence, born July 31, 1868, who married William E Hartwell, of Providence, Rhode Island Frank Jones married (second) October 14, 1880, Mary E Chase, of Sutton, born November 17, 1853, died June 24, 1906, and they have one child, Frank Abram, born born May 3, 1882 4 Hiram Davis, born February 5 1846, at Worcester, died April 10, 1902, married January 14, 1867, Emily F Gardner, of Worcester, and they have one child, Harry Lincoln, who married Anna Howe, of Worcester 5 William Slocomb, born at Holliston, August 20, 1848, married December 31, 1868, Lydia P Lathrop, resides in Worcester 6 Lucy Ellen, born at Holliston, February 9, 1850 7 Georgianna Frances, born April 4, 1852 married February 24, 1875, Arthur J Marble, of Worcester, and they have one child, Georgie Alice, who married (first) Anson Blenus and (second) J William Patstone

Isaac Davis, father of Mrs Jeduthan Dadmun, mentioned above was born November 16, 1779, probably at Rutland, where many of his family lived, all descendants of Dolor Davis (see sketch of Davis family elsewhere in this work) He was of Rutland when he married, May 8, 1803, Betsey Rice, born November 25, 1781, daughter of John and Lydia Rice Her father, John Rice was born November 7, 1745, son of Captain Edward Rice and descendant of the immigrant, Edmund Rice, of Sudbury, Massachusetts (See sketch of various Rice families) Betsey (Rice) Davis died at Rutland, December 10, 1824, aged forty-three years, fifteen days Isaac Davis was a blacksmith by trade, a farmer and handy at various other trades He bought land in Rutland with John Rice, Jr, his brother-in-law, November, 1808, and April, 1809 He bought land of Benjamin Rice in Rutland, June 22, 1809 He bought, November 10, 1805, of Silas and Lydia Merrill, in Rutland, a tract of three-fourths of a mile He sold land to Taylor Estabrook, November 2, 1808 He was master of Thompson Lodge of Free Masons, Rutland He died March 26, 1833, aged fifty-three years, five months and ten days His will dated April 19, 1832, was disapproved May 1, 1833, and his son Lyman was appointed administrator May 27, 1833 Rufus Putnam was the guardian of his children after the death of their grandmother, Lydia Rice, in 1825, until he resigned April 8, 1836

The children were Mary, born September 25, 1803, died at Worcester August 11, 1852, John, born August 27, 1805, died at West Rutland, aged sixty-seven years, seven months and thirteen days, Eliza, born August 1, 1807, died July 11 1836, Lyman, born November 28, 1809, died June 29, 1834, Lucy, born September 24, 1811, died January 14, 1878, married Jeduthan Dadmun, who died September 21, 1884, mentioned above, Hiram, born August 27, 1813, died December 20, 1814, Hiram, born January 4, 1815, died November 6, 1846, James, born September 8, 1817 died April 9, 1860 Sarah, born June 8, 1818, died February 10, 1905, Charles, born February 22, 1820, killed in civil war, George, born September 12, 1823 killed in civil war

(VI) William Slocomb Dadmun, son of Jeduthan (5), was born at Holliston, Massachusetts

Samuel Warren

August 20, 1848 At the age of five years he moved with his parents to Lunenburg, where they lived for some time, removing thence to Grafton, where he received his education in the common schools He left the high school before graduating and removed with his father to Springfield, where for several months he worked in his father's grocery store He worked a year in the dry goods store of L J Holt, and then went to Worcester, Massachusetts, to work in the store of Simeon Clapp later Clapp & Haven, and later died and Mr C Haven bought the store and Mr Dadmun remained with the new proprietor for six years He left this concern to start in business for himself In partnership with James H Howland, he was the senior member of the firm of Dadmun & Howland, dealers in shoes, etc At the end of two years Mr Dadmun's brother Frank J Dadmun, bought the interests of Mr Howland and the name of the firm for two years was Dadmun Brothers Then the firm was dissolved and William S Dadmun entered the employ of J O Bemis, shoe dealer, Worcester Twenty months later he started in the shoe business again, under his own name, at 349 Main street After two years Henry E Putnam was admitted a partner and the firm name became Dadmun & Putnam Charles H Heywood represented Mr Putnam's interests in the business When the business was moved to the basement of the old city hall, Mr Heywood was admitted as a partner and the firm name became Dadmun, Heywood & Company When the city hall was torn down, after the new building was erected, the firm removed to its present location, 520 Main street In the meantime the Putnam interests had been acquired by the other partners and the firm name changed to Dadmun & Heywood The present store is very prosperous and gives evidence of constant growth It is one of the most spacious and best appointed in the city

Mr Dadmun attends the First Universalist church He is a Republican in politics He is one of the most prominent Free Masons of the city He was made a Master Mason in Athelstan Lodge, June 1, 1870, received his Royal Arch degree in Eureka Chapter, April 9, 1872, received the Cryptic degree in Hiram Council, June 12, 1873, received his Templar degree in Worcester County Commandery, September 4, 1874, and has been the recorder without interruption since 1876, a period of thirty years He is a member of the Scottish Rite bodies up to the Eighteenth degree, and trustee of Masonic fraternity He is a member of Aletheia Grotto, Mystic Order of Veiled Prophets, and the Worcester County Mechanics' Association, of which he was a trustee for three years He is a director of the Home Co-operative Bank

He married, December 31, 1868, Lydia Lathrop, of Worcester She was born April 1, 1845, daughter of Samuel and Julia Ann (Wheelock) Lathrop Their children are Alice Gertrude, born December 9, 1869, died November 29, 1871, Wilton Wells, born December 27, 1872, married Alice W Gifford, of Worcester, and they have one child—Chester Gifford, born September 5, 1897, Walter Robbins, born August 23, 1878.

WARREN FAMILY Peter Warren (1), the immigrant ancestor of Waterman G Warren and his family, of Holden Massachusetts, was probably born in England No connection can be established between him and John Warren, of Watertown, who came over in 1630, and he was certainly not son of John Warren as one writer states Neither can any relationship be shown between Peter and Abraham Warren, who settled in Salem in 1635, with Arthur Warren, who settled in Weymouth before 1637, with Richard Warren, who came on the "Mayflower" in 1620 There were other early settlers of the name, and the Warren families were numerous at an early date The name is ancient and distinguished also in England, where all these early immigrants were born In fact the family dates back to a Baron of the name who came over with William the Conqueror, and fought in the battle of Hastings in 1066 He was high in the confidence of the king and was one of two guardians left in charge of England when William returned to Normandy for a visit William, the Earl of Warren, held the fief of Warrenne and many surnames were adopted from the locality, so that perhaps not all of the family are descended from the Earl. The place of birth of Peter Warren is unknown and his English ancestry untraced He was born in 1628, and bought land in Boston, March 8, 1659, of Thomas Atkinson He was a seafaring man The nature of his business prevented him from figuring much in public records or holding publice office

He married (first) Sarah Tucker, of Dorchester, daughter of Robert Tucker, August 1, 1660 He married (second) Hannah —— and (third) Esther Woodward Children of Peter and Sarah Warren were John, born September 8, 1661, Joseph, February 19, 1663, father of Joseph who was the father of General Joseph Warren, of Bunker Hill fame, Benjamin, July 25, 1665, Elizabeth, January 4, 1667, Robert, December 14, 1670, Ebenezer, February 1, 1672-73, see forward, Peter, born and died 1675, Peter, April 20, 1676 Children of Peter and Hannah Warren were Hannah, May 19, 1680, Mary, November 25, 1683, Robert, December 27, 1864

(II) Ebenezer Warren, son of Peter Warren (1), was born in Boston, February 11, 1672 He settled in that part of Dorchester, now Milton, Massachusetts, a section now of Boston He married, June 2, 1697, Mary Ryder, of Milton Their children, all born at Milton, were Mary, born June 9, 1700, Ebenezer, March 30 1702, see forward, Elizabeth, June 1, 1704, Jonathan, March 9, 1706, Hannah, August 11, 1708 Their are no further records of children at Milton and none of the children settled in Milton

(III) Ebenezer Warren, Jr, son of Ebenezer Warren (2), was born at Milton, Massachusetts, formerly Dorchester and now Boston, March 30, 1702 He settled in Medford and removed thence to Leicester in 1744, when he bought the tannery now or lately owned by Edward Warren He paid one hundred and twelve pounds ten shillings Besides the tannery he bought with it a house, bark-house, mill-house, beam-house and land The house was a primitive affair and he built a good house in 1780 The homestead descended to his son Elijah whose son Henry Elijah took down the old house in 1860 Ebenezer died in Leicester in 1800 He married Lydia Harrington, of Brookfield She died 1795 Their children were 1 Lydia, born November 24 1746, died August 7, 1748 2 Ebenezer, born December 27, 1748, died February 13, 1753 3 Jonathan born November 27, 1750, see forward 4 Lydia, born December 6, 1752 married March 31, 1774, Abner Dunbar born April 9, 1753 whose son Ebenezer was born March 29 1777, and died October 28, 1877 over one hundred years old, the grandfather of John D Clark Malcolm G Clark and Mrs F A Blake of Rochdale (See Clark sketch) 5 Ebenezer born June 9 1754 6 Esther, married, 1782, Daniel Newhall, of Brookfield, resided at Alstead, New Hampshire, and had children—John,

Sally and others 7 Hannah, married, 1781, Levi Chilson, resided in Leicester and had children—Lydia, Warren, Edward, Humes, Ebenezer, Samuel, Basineth 8 Elijah, born 1758 9 Sally, married, 1786, Thaddeus Upham, of Watertown, and they had—Lewis (or Lois), Otis, Mary, Sally Upham

(IV) Jonathan Warren, son of Ebenezer Warren (3), was born at Leicester, Massachusetts, November 27, 1750 He married (first), January 3, 1775, Martha Bemis, of Spencer, Massachusetts In 1796 his wife fell in a faint into the fireplace, containing a large bed of burning tanbark, and was fatally burned He married (second) Lucy How, who died June 11, 1831 He resided where Horace Warren lately lived, and a portion of his house is part of the present structure In 1797 he bought a half interest in the old tanyard with his brother Elijah He died January 26, 1827

The children of Jonathan and Martha Warren were Sally, born August 13, 1775, married John Beers, Joshua, July 25, 1777, settled in Vermont, Samuel, July 31 1779, see forward Jonathan, December 2, 1782, Polly, June 16, 1785, died 1800, Persis, March 5, 1788, married, April 1, 1818, Aaron Sibley, died June 24, 1819, having one child, Warren Sibley born February 19, 1819, resided at Auburn, Amasa, born November 16 1790, Jesse Smith, March 18, 1794 Children of Jonathan and Lucy Warren were Eliza born February 16 1799, married —— Parker, Sarah, March 11, 1801, married —— Curtis

(V) Samuel Warren, son of Jonathan Warren (4), was born in Leicester, Massachusetts, September 10, 1779 He was a tanner by trade He settled in Auburn, Massachusetts, a town adjoining Leicester and Worcester, and became a prominent citizen there He was a very active and zealous Baptist in religion He was baptized in 1810 joined the church in 1814 He and his father-in-law erected the meeting house on their farm, then a church was organized at Auburn and a pastor settled Samuel Warren was deacon of the church at the time of his death, September 10, 1832 He married, 1806, Sally Goulding, daughter of Captain Jonah Goulding Their children, all born at Auburn were Waterman Goulding, born May 16 1807, see forward, Elbridge Gerry March 27 1810 Jonah Goulding September 11, 1812, Samuel October 31, 1816 John November 27, 1819, Sarah Jane April 10, 1825 died March 26, 1843, George, December 9 1831

Captain Jonah Goulding was born November 25 1753, son of Colonel John Goulding who resided in the northeast part of Grafton and was a tanner by trade Late in life he was excessively corpulent He was a soldier in the revolution from Grafton, under Captain Luke Drury and General Ward in 1775 He was conspicuous in "Shays Rebellion" after the revolution and commanded a company under Shays led his men to Worcester and helped prevent Judge Artemas Ward from opening court He was imprisoned after the collapse of the rebellion "forty days and forty nights" according to his own account of it and was, of course, in serious danger of hanging But the participants in the rebellion escaped with light punishments the grievous conditions making leniency the wisest course Captain Goulding was an honored and respected citizen, returned to the militia and served faithfully rising to the rank of colonel in command of his regiment Colonel John Goulding married (first), February 22, 1753 Lucy Brooks born September 30 1733 Colonel Jonah Goulding married (first) April 1777 Grace Knowlton daughter of Jonah Knowlton He married (second) Widow Sarah Leland

(VI) Waterman Goulding Warren, son of Deacon Samuel Warren (5), was born on the Warren homestead in that part of the town of Ward (now Auburn) known as West Auburn May 16, 1807 He was the eldest of six sons The opportunities for schooling in his day were very limited He attended the old district school for a few weeks during the winter term In summer he worked on his father's farm and in the tannery He learned the trade of tanner He was twenty-five years old when his father died in 1832, and he inherited the tannery which Jonah Goulding bought of Nathaniel Southworth when he moved from Grafton to Auburn Mr Warren conducted the tanning business with varying success until 1839, when he removed to Holden and entered partnership with his brother Samuel in the tannery which John P Maynard built about 1825, at Eagleville then called Brick City, in the year 1840 The partnership was dissolved in the spring of 1850, when Waterman G Warren bought the Edward Richardson tannery This tannery with seventeen acres of land was sold by John Watson to Heman Richardson, December 23, 1789 for one hundred and twenty pounds sterling It is located a half mile from Holden Centre The exact date of the building of the tanyard is unknown The old tannery was enlarged and greatly improved, and the business successfully conducted by Mr Warren alone and later in partnership with his son Samuel, for a quarter of a century

In 1874, while continuing the business at the old stand in partnership with his eldest son Samuel, Mr Warren formed a new firm with his son Berthier as partner, under the name of B Warren & Co, and this firm commenced business in the brick tannery near Holden Centre built by Berthier Warren This new tannery, in its character and equipment, its facilities for producing the kind of leather which is its specialty card leather, probably is unsurpassed by any in the state In 1882 the two firms became one, Samuel Warren, Berthier Warren and H W Warren all became partners with their father under the firm name of W G Warren & Sons and a prosperous business was conducted by this firm until the death of the senior partner and father, August 7 1886 at the age of seventy-nine years During these years there had been a steady growth of business from the tanning of about fifteen hundred sides of leather in 1845 to twenty thousand in 1886 After Mr Warren's death the business was continued by his three sons under the firm name of W G Warren's Sons

One who knew Mr Warren well has written "He was a devoted husband and father, kind-hearted and charitable A man of good common sense, sound judgment and strictest integrity and enjoyed the fullest confidence of all in his business and other relations He had marked peculiarities and his strong personality impressed itself upon all with whom he came in contact He was the relentless foe of the liquor traffic The cause of temperance and all the moral reforms of his day received from him a liberal and hearty support In his early life in the palmy days of slavery, he was an Abolitionist, a follower of Gerritt Smith Garrison and Phillips He boldly proclaimed his sentiments in favor of liberty for the oppressed when such action meant hardship, scorn and persecution (such was the unpopularity of the abolition movement even in New England) After the enactment of the Fugitive Slave Law, he was zealous and active in all movements in behalf of the fugitive and made his home on a place of refuge for the bondmen a station on the Underground Railroad to freedom—thus earning the honor due to those who have the courage of their convictions, and

Henry W. Warren

The Lewis Publishing Co

the daring of their duty" In his later years he was a stanch Republican He and his wife were both attendant and active and liberal supporters of the Baptist church of Holden

He married, April 22, 1830, Mary Eddy, born February 7, 1806, daughter of Samuel and Sarah (Hart) Eddy, of Auburn Her father was a farmer They celebrated their golden wedding in 1880 Mrs Warren died September 3, 1887 The children of Waterman Goulding and Mary (Eddy) Warren were 1 Ann Eliza, born February 13, 1831, married Rev Lester Williams, of Holden, who was born at West Springfield, Massachusetts, July 24, 1823, now deceased, she resides in Holden, their only child was Waterman Lester Williams, born August 10, 1867, graduate of Amherst College, 1891 2 Susan Ellen, born at Auburn Massachusetts, May 27, 1833, resides at Holden, unmarried 3 Samuel, born at Auburn, October 15, 1834, see forward 4 Berthier, born October 22, 1836, married Eunice Boyden, of Holden see forward 5 Henry Waterman, born March 18, 1838, see forward

(VII) Samuel Warren, son of Waterman Goulding Warren (6), was born at Auburn, Massachusetts, October 15, 1834 He was five years old when the family removed to Holden He attended the public schools of Holden, various private schools, Worcester Academy and graduated in 1858 from the State Normal school at Westfield, Massachusetts He then became associated with his father in the tanning business and in 1867 was taken in partnership under the firm name of W G Warren & Son At the end of ten years the tannery was sold to Michael McLoughlin, a former employee of the firm, who died not long after starting in business The plant was bought back by the Warrens from McLoughlin's widow When the business was sold to McLoughlin in 1881, the two firms of which Waterman G Warren was the head became one and all three sons were members under the name of W G Warren & Sons Since the death of their father the three sons have been in business under the firm name of W G Warren's Sons and have been very successful Mr Samuel Warren, the head of the firm, has done his full share to maintain the high standing of the firm and develop its business Berthier Warren died in February 1905, and his share was purchased by the surviving members of the firm, which continues under the same name Of late much of the leather produced in the Warren tannery has been made for Howard Brothers of Worcester for the manufacture of card clothing, etc The hides used in the tannery came principally from Ohio and the west After his father's death Samuel bought out the other heirs in 1888 and became the owner of the homestead

He attends the Congregational church of Holden He has been active in the Republican party organization, serving frequently as delegate to the Republican state convention and other nominating conventions He was on the Holden school committee from 1862 to 1865 and from 1883 to 1886 He was assessor of the town of Holden in 1868-69-87-88 He was a representative to the general court in 1867, and selectman in 1872-73 He has held many other positions of trust and honor He is a member of the Holden Farmers' and Mechanics' Club Mr Warren assisted materially in getting the new electric railroad built from Worcester to Holden and has considerable stock in the company In business and town affairs for many years Mr Warren has been a leader his judgment has been trusted and his business ability widely recognized He stands high in the estimation of his townsmen

He married May 13, 1869, Marion Elizabeth Lakin, born June 27, 1845, at Paxton, daughter of George Shipley and Nancy (Hubbard) Lakin Her father was a manufacturer of boots and shoes at Paxton and was prominent in town affairs, holding many town offices at various times, he died in 1875 and his wife died in 1883 Mrs Warren was the only surviving child Mrs Warren was elected a member of the Holden school committee in 1887, one of the first women holding this office in Massachusetts, and she has served with great credit to herself and to the distinct advantage of the public schools of the town The children of Samuel and Marion E Warren were Herbert Lakin, born August 24, 1870, graduate of Amherst College, 1893. Arthur Kirke, born December 13, 1871, George Waterman born December 3, 1882

(VII) Berthier Warren, son of Waterman Goulding Warren (6), was born at Auburn, Massachusetts, October 22, 1836 He removed to Holden with the family in 1840 and attended the public schools there Later he was a student at Wilbraham Academy, the Williston Seminary at Easthampton, Massachusetts, and the Claverack (New York) Academy Just after the close of the civil war, in 1866, he and his brother Henry purchased a cotton plantation in Leake county, Mississippi, and he lived there for nine years In 1874 he returned to Holden, went into the tannery business, built the brick tannery and commenced business with his father as a partner under the name of B Warren & Co, and later took in his brothers, under the firm name of B & H W Warren & Co Later the two Warren firms were consolidated and the new plant, built by Berthier Warren was used by the new firm of W G Warren & Sons The chief product of the tannery has been card leather for card clothing Mr Berthier Warren was an active and important factor in the business until his death He was a man of unusual ability and good judgment, successful in business and devoted to the interests of his firm, yet never a slave of his material interests He died at his home 744 Main street, Worcester, February 15, 1905

He was liberal in his religious views In politics he was a Republican While he was in Mississippi he served on the board of registration one year, and was clerk of the chancery court three years He was interested in town affairs, but never cared for public office He was a charter member of the Worcester Driving Club, which for several years furnished the main racing events in Worcester He was a member of the Worcester Agricultural Society, and was a member of the Commonwealth Club In Holden he organized the Young Men's Club, and he had a strong and wholesome influence on the young men of that town

Mr Warren married September 4, 1871, Eunice Chace Boyden, born June 18, 1841, daughter of Comfort and Silence (Dryden) Boyden, of Holden Her father was a carpenter and millwright Children of Berthier and Eunice Chace (Boyden) Warren were 1 Mary Silence, born January 24, 1875, married, October 12, 1897, Dr Walter Herbert Richardson, and they have one son, Berthier Warren Richardson, born August 20, 1900 2 Henry Lester, born April 9, 1880 died April 15, 1881

(VII) Henry Waterman Warren, son of Waterman Goulding Warren (6), was born in Auburn, Massachusetts March 18, 1838 He obtained his education in the public schools of Holden, at the Worcester Academy, the State Normal school at Westfield Williston Seminary at Easthampton Massachusetts, where he prepared for college, and at Yale, where he was graduated in the class of 1865, having an oration appointment at the junior examination and at commencement He taught school six months at Nashville, Tennessee In 1866, with his brother Berthier Warren he went to Leake county, Mississippi, and engaged in business as a cotton planter He remained there ten years and was active in public affairs during the trying and difficult period of reconstruction He was appointed judge of probate of Leake county in 1867 by General Adelbert Ames, acting governor of the state He was elected a member of the constitutional convention of the state, although the whites outnumbered the negroes two to one in that county He was elected to the legislature in 1870 and 1871, and was speaker of the house of representatives of the state of Mississippi in 1871 He was the chief clerk of the legislature for four years afterward He was appointed by Governor Powers levee commissioner, whose duty it was to collect and disburse the funds for the payment of the old levee debt and to dispose of the tax lands held by the state for that purpose He was a delegate to the Republican National Convention held at Chicago in 1868, when General Grant was first nominated, and also to the national convention at Cincinnati in 1876, when General Rutherford B Hayes was nominated

He returned to Holden in 1876 and has since then been actively interested in the tannery business At present he and his elder brother Samuel are the only surviving partners of the well known firm of W G Warren's Sons, tanners Mr Warren has shared in the prosperity of the Warren business for the past thirty years and is one of the prominent men of the state in his line He has been distinguished in public affairs as well as in business In politics he has been active in the Republican party, a delegate to the various congressional conventions and other nominating conventions of the Republican party He has been constantly called to positions of trust and honor in the town and state He represented his district in the general court in 1882 and 1885, and served on important committees He was on the board of overseers of the poor in 1890, has been town treasurer for nine years was selectman in 1878-79-80-85-1902-03-04, and for several years was chairman of the board, has been water commissioner two years, and supervised the installation of the Holden water works Mr Warren is an active attendant of the Baptist church in Holden and has been on the prudential committee He has been president of the Holden Village Improvement Society for many years He is a member of the famous old Skull and Bones Society at Yale, and of the Holden Farmers' and Mechanics Club In 1905 he was elected president of the Worcester & Holden Street Railway Company, of which he has been a director from the organization of the company

He married, November 8, 1877 Dora Louise Howe, born October 23, 1847, daughter of Deacon William and Mary Ann (Jefferson) Howe, of Holden and granddaughter of Thomas Howe son of Jotham and Dorothy Howe Mrs Warren's father engaged in the manufacture of woolen goods in partnership with Theron E Hall at the village now known as Jeffersonville, in Holden, and later with M V B Jefferson, as Howe & Jefferson, which was the name of the firm for twenty-six years Mr Howe was deacon of the Baptist church, of which he was a member over sixty years He was for eleven years selectman of the town of Holden and in 1887 was representative to the general court (See sketch of Howe family) Children of Henry Waterman and Dora Louise Warren are William Howe, born September 28, 1879, resides at home with his parents, Blanche Louise, born July 11, 1881, married April 3, 1906, Rev Alfred Edward Alton, of Rome, New York, Helen Goulding, born November 7, 1883, Waterman Goulding, born November 16, 1890

INGRAHAM FAMILY Genealogists begin the record of the Ingraham family with Randolph, the son of Ingel'ram or Ing'ram, who was sheriff of Nottingham and Derby in the reign of Henry II (1133-1189), as were his sons, Robert and William

Robert Ingram, Knight, whose arms are painted at Temple Newsam (or Newsham), England, was of such eminence in the reign of Henry III, that the Prior and Convent of Lenton granted to him a yearly rent out of their lands, in Sheynton and Nottingham, in recognition of his military services in their defense Temple Newsam, an immense estate, six miles in length and four in width, situated about four and a half miles east of Leeds, England, now called the "Ingram Estate" was first a settlement of Knights Templar in the twelfth and thirteenth centuries After their dispersion, it was granted by Edward III to Sir John Darcy, and descended to Lord Thomas Darcy, who was beheaded by Henry VIII The estate was then forfeited to the Crown It was afterward granted by the same monarch (1554) to Mathew Earl of Lennox, and here was born his son, Henry Darnley, who later became the husband of Mary, Queen of Scots The estate descended to their son James I of England, and from him to his kinsman, Esme Stuart, Duke of Lennox from whom it passed to Sir Arthur Ingram, the first of the Lords Viscount Irwin, one of the conditions being that the room in which Lord Darnley was born should remain unaltered This room is still called the "King's Chamber"

Sir Arthur, who is supposed to have been born about 1570, was celebrated for his valor as a cavalier He was a near relative of Wentworth, the celebrated Earl of Stafford He was twice married first to Eleanor daughter of Sir Henry Slingsby, of the Red House" Second to Lady Katherine, daughter of Thomas Lord Viscount Fairfax, of Gilling Sir Arthur died in 1655 His sons were Henry and Arthur (The portraits of Sir Arthur in cavalier costume, of the First Viscount Irwin in full armor, and of Henry, the second Viscount Irwin in half armor, all nearly full length, were in the collection of the Bishop of California, William Ingraham Kip, DD LL D, who died in 1894)

Henry, the eldest son of Sir Arthur Ingram, born between 1595 and 1600, was, at the time of the Restoration, six years after the death of his father, created a Peer of Scotland by Charles II, with the title of Viscount Irwin, by letters patent, dated May 23, 1661, as a recompense to the family for their loyalty He married Anne, daughter of Montacute, Earl of Manchester, a leader in parliament The male branch in England as descended from Sir Henry, the second Viscount Irwin, became extinct with Charles Ingram ninth Viscount Irwin, who died in 1778 (Burke's Extinct Peerage) His daughter, the Marchioness of Hertford, and Lady William Gordon successively inherited Temple Newsam, and from them it passed to their sister, Mrs Hugo Maynell, whose son took the name of Ingram, and his descendants are the present owners of the family estate

Arthur Ingram, of Barrowby second son of Sir Arthur, was born between 1595 and 1600 He married a daughter of Sir John Mallory about 1615, and genealogists agree that from him is descended the Ingraham family in the United States

Edward Ingraham, the first of the name to come to America, was born in 1617 At the age of eighteen years, in July, 1635, he sailed in the ship "Blessing," and settled in Salem, Massachusetts, where he was a proprietor as early as 1638 His occupation was farming

Richard Ingram, as he apparently preferred to spell his name, came to America between 1638 and 1642 He settled in Rehoboth, Massachusetts, where in 1645 he was a proprietor Some years later he removed to Northampton, Massachusetts, where in 1668, late in life, he married (probably not his first marriage) Joan Rockwell Baker, daughter of William Rockwell, and widow of Jeffrey Baker, of Windsor, Connecticut He contributed a sum at the time of the general subscription for the support of Harvard College, in 1672-3 He died in August, 1683 and his widow died September 16, 1683, both at Northampton, Massachusetts

Jared Ingraham, who settled first at Boston, also went to Rehoboth, where Richard lived, and had several children born in Swansea, near Rehoboth, between 1665 and 1671 He left descendants in that vicinity

Since genealogists agree that the Ingraham family in America are descended from Arthur Ingram, of Barrowby, the second son of Sir Arthur Ingram, it is quite probable that Edward Ingraham, who came to America in 1635, and Richard Ingram, who came between 1638 and 1642, were brothers, and were sons of Arthur of Barrowby Also that Jared Ingram, of Boston, Rehoboth and Swansea, and John Ingram, of Boston and Hadley, were sons of Richard, as indicated by the fact that they spelled the name Ingram, and were located at various times near Richard

(I) John Ingram, presumably a son of Richard Ingram, mentioned above, and the pioneer ancestor of Edward Payson Ingraham, was born in England about 1642 He came to New England when a young man, and settled first in Boston, Massachusetts He removed to Hadley, Massachusetts, with two others in 1661, and was admitted a freeman in 1863 He was a member of Joseph Kellogg's company of Hadley, under Captain William Turner, and was engaged in the fight at Turner's Falls, during King Philip's war, May 19, 1676 He died June 22, 1722

He married, in 1664, Elizabeth Gardner, daughter of Samuel and Elizabeth Gardner, of Hadley, Massachusetts She died November 29, 1684 Their children were John, born June 29, 1665, Jadiah, August 16, 1668, Samuel, October 8, 1670, Ebenezer, February 3, 1673, Nathaniel, of whom later, Jonathan, 1676, Elizabeth, May 1, 1679, Abigail, January 12, 1683

(II) Nathaniel Ingram, fifth son and child of John (1), and Elizabeth (Gardner) Ingram, was born at Hadley, Massachusetts, October 8, 1674 He and his son Nathaniel had a grant of land at South Hadley, which the Ingraham family retained and occupied one hundred and seventy-five years This land was sold in the spring of 1904

Nathaniel Ingram married, October 20 1696, Esther Smith, born March 31, 1674, daughter of Chileab and Hannah (Hitchcock) Smith, of Hadley Massachusetts Their children were Esther born July 23, 1697, Elizabeth, April 6, 1699, Abigail August 24, 1700, Mercy, April 15, 1702, Ebenezer, November 18, 1703, Nathaniel, of whom later, Hannah, April 14, 1711, Jonathan, June 5, 1713, Sarah, October 2 1717

(III) Nathaniel Ingram second son and sixth child of Nathaniel (2) and Esther (Smith) Ingram, was born at Hadley, Massachusetts, May 18, 1708 The original house built by him at South Hadley stands today as the ell to the house that his son Nathaniel built in the year 1800

He married November 11, 1742, Martha Kellogg born May 21 1720, daughter of Joseph and Abigail (Smith) Kellogg, of Hadley The children were Nathaniel, of whom later Sarah, born September 18, 1745 Martha, November 23, 1747

(IV) Nathaniel Ingram eldest child of Nathaniel (3) and Martha (Kellogg) Ingram was born at South Hadley, Massachusetts, August 23, 1743 He was a prominent and prosperous citizen of his native town He was a farmer, and built the house mentioned above on the old Ingram place He was one of the two largest growers of grain in that vicinity He was a minute-man a private in the company of Captain Noah Goodwin, which marched on the alarm at Lexington, April 19, 1775 He was also in Lieutenant Martin White's company, Colonel Ruggles Woodbridge's regiment, in the northern department, under General Gates, and marched on the alarm at Bennington, August 17, 1777

He married, December 12, 1769, Hannah Warren, born August 25, 1745, died July 8, 1838, daughter of Daniel and Martha (Coolidge) Warren, of Marlboro, Massachusetts She was a direct descendant of Richard Warren, the twelfth signer of the compact in the "Mayflower" The children of Nathaniel and Hannah (Warren) Ingram were Esther, born April 19 1770, Hannah, February 16, 1772, died March 15, 1797, Ebenezer, November 3, 1774 died February 19, 1844, Martha, February 2, 1777, died October 21, 1869, Nathaniel, of whom later, Esther (second), April 19, 1781, Abigail, July 2, 1784, Artemas, March 11, 1787, died 1830, Alpheus, October 31, 1789 died June 24, 1862, Warren, October 31, 1792, died May 2, 1839

(V) Nathaniel Ingram second son and fifth child of Nathaniel (4) and Hannah (Warren) Ingram, was born at South Hadley, Massachusetts, March 26, 1779, and died September 19, 1817 He was a prosperous farmer and held various town offices in South Hadley

He married, March 5, 1807, Ruth B Burnett, born June 27, 1787, died April 14 1838 daughter of Jonathan and Mehitable (Dickinson) Burnett of South Hadley Their children were Mary, born November 13 1808, died September 15 1885 she married June 7, 1834, Lucius Horton Cowles, who was born December 11, 1796, and died April 3 1860, Dexter, of whom later, Lewis Burnett May 13, 1813, died September 2, 1846 married, October 28, 1834, Sophia U Graves who was born February 24 1813, and died May 10 1850, Nathaniel, May 10 1815 a physician of Pelham, Massachusetts died January 11, 1840 Ruth, August 2, 1817, died July 7, 1889, married Emery Tilton, who was born April 24 1817, and died January 1, 1880

(VI) Dexter Ingraham, second child and eldest son of Nathaniel (5) and Ruth B (Burnett) Ingram, was born at South Hadley Massachusetts, April 29 1810 and died June 9, 1892 His education was acquired in the common schools of that town He was but seven years old when his father died He learned the trade of carpentering, and followed this for a number of years He also taught singing schools in various places in the Connecticut valley and was choir director of the old First Church at South Hadley for twenty-seven years Most of his active years, however were spent in farming in South Hadley In religious belief he was a Congregationalist and in politics, first a Free Soil Advocate and later a Republican He was the first

Republican representative to the general court from South Hadley, was a selectman, and assessor for a number of years

He married (first), April 30, 1834, Lucina Ball, who was born January 31, 1810, daughter of Abraham and Martha (Field) Ball, of Amherst, Massachusetts Abraham Ball was a farmer, born September 14, 1783, died April 16, 1837 Martha (Field) Ball was born October 6, 1785, died March 3 1857 Dexter Ingraham married (second), December 25, 1869, Elizabeth M Butts, of South Hadley, who was born April 30, 1818, and died April 22 1895 The children of Dexter and Lucina (Ball) Ingraham were Emery Dexter, of whom later, Albert Wellington, of whom later, Nathaniel Hoyt of whom later, William Field, of whom later, Mary Lucina of whom later, Edward Payson, born March 8, 1852, died September 16, 1853

(VII) Emery Dexter Ingraham, eldest child of Dexter (6) and Lucina (Ball) Ingraham, was born at South Hadley, Massachusetts, February 6, 1835 His education was received in the public schools of the town He very early displayed marked musical ability and commenced the study of music under the able tuition of his father While still a youth he played in the orchestras and bands of the vicinity At the age of seventeen he was instructor and director of several military bands As very little music was published in those days, the repertoire of bands was almost wholly manuscript It was therefore very necessary that the director should have a thorough knowledge of instrumentation, harmony and composition Previous to the spring of 1859 he moved to Haydenville, Massachusetts where he assumed the leadership of the band He soon went to Bath, Maine where he accepted a position as bookkeeper for a firm of ship builders, and took charge of the Bath band He enlisted August 22, 1861 as the regimental bandmaster of the Seventh Maine Regiment This regiment was at Baltimore for eight weeks, going thence to Kalaramo Heights, and from there to winter quarters at Lewinsville, Virginia, where it remained until March, 1862 At that time this band together with many others was disbanded He was discharged in August, 1862, and came to Boston He enlisted in the navy at Charlestown, Massachusetts, August 13 1864 receiving his discharge August 26, 1865 He then joined the celebrated P S Gilmore Band of Boston, in which he had played for a time before enlisting in the navy He enlisted in the navy for the second time in April, 1867, and served until March 31, 1868, after which he was again affiliated with the Gilmore Band until 1870 when he became leader of the National Band at Taunton, Massachusetts He retained this position for two years He served various engagements with the Gilmore Band while he was still in the navy, while at Taunton, and from 1872 to 1874, when he came to Worcester to take the leadership of the National Band his brother Albert having retired Two years later he was made leader and manager of the organization now known as "Battery B Band" of Worcester Massachusetts At that time Colonel Fred W Wellington was in command of the battery Few military bands have maintained so high a standard of excellence as this organization and its engagements have extended throughout New England the Middle States, and Canada Mr Ingraham attends the Piedmont Congregational Church He is a Republican in politics, and a member of the George H Ward Post, No 10, Grand Army of the Republic

He married June 26 1856, Martha Jane Preston, who was born at South Hadley Massachusetts September 14 1835 daughter of Joel and Mabel (Smith) Preston, of South Hadley Joel was born December 23, 1801, and died September 19, 1883 He was a farmer Mabel (Smith) Preston was born April 1 1806, and died October 17, 1869 The children of Emery Dexter and Martha Jane (Preston) Ingraham are Louis Albert, of whom later, Edward Payson, of whom later

(VIII) Louis Albert Ingraham, eldest child of Emery Dexter (7) and Martha Jane (Preston) Ingraham, was born in South Hadley, Massachusetts, June 23, 1857, died September 16, 1906 When about six years of age he removed with his parents to Boston, receiving his education in the public schools of that city and in Taunton He began the study of the piano and cornet while still attending school, and became proficient as a cornetist Coming to Worcester in 1874, he went to work in the tuning department of the Taylor & Farley Organ Company, having previously served an apprenticeship with his uncle, N H Ingraham, in New Haven, Connecticut He entered into an engagement with the Vocalion Organ Company, about 1887, and retained this position up to his decease He was connected with several musical organizations and was a prominent member of the Battery B Band and orchastra, which he joined in 1880

He married (first) Mary E Sampson, of Worcester They had one child, Charlena Louise, born March 25, 1880, died April 11, 1888 He married (second) Alice Clapp, of Worcester They had one child, Nina D, born March 10, 1883, died September 7, 1897

(VIII) Edward Payson Ingraham, second and youngest child of Emery Dexter (7) and Martha Jane (Preston) Ingraham, was born in Haydenville, Massachusetts, April 27, 1859 At the age of four years he removed with his parents to Boston He was educated in the public schools of Boston and Taunton He came to Worcester in 1874 and began his business career as clerk in the Central National Bank He was steadily advanced until 1878, when he resigned his position on account of illness For a time after this he continued the study of music, in which he had been interested since his childhood and for the next few years he made the playing and teaching of the piano and violoncello his profession In 1883 he entered the fire insurance business, associating himself with Edwin G Field, of Worcester, under the firm name of Field & Ingraham In 1885 he retired from the firm, having bought an interest in the fire insurance agency of Loren C Parks, and in 1888 he acquired Mr Parks' interest and afterward conducted the business in his own name He was elected secretary of the Worcester Board of Underwriters in 1889 which position he held in connection with his insurance business In 1895 he sold his insurance business to Alexander C Munroe, of Worcester and thereafter devoted his entire attention to the interests of the Worcester Board of Underwriters until January 1, 1903 when he resigned his position to enter into partnership with Mr Munroe, the firm name being A C Munroe & Ingraham The agency is one of the largest and best known in Worcester county Mr Ingraham is a director of the Home Co-Operative Bank and the Thule Music Hall Association Mr Ingraham is a Republican and a member of the Piedmont Congregational Church and parish He is also a member of the following organizations The Congregational Club, Commonwealth Club, and the Worcester County Mechanics Association

He married June 23 1884 Rose Eva Field, born in Sunderland Massachusetts, August 25 1858, daughter of Edwin Graves and Nancy S (Clark) Field of Worcester Edwin Graves Field was born in Leverett Massachusetts, March 24, 1823, died August 22 1899 Nancy S Clark Field was born in Sunderland, Massachusetts, November 5, 1822, died May 14, 1885 The children of Edward Payson and Rose Eva (Field) Ingraham were Winifred Rose, born March 17, 1889, a student in the Worcester high school, Richard Edward, born February 27, 1902, died March 22 1903, Roger Emory, born May 6, 1904, died February 25, 1905

(VII) Albert Wellington Ingraham, second child and son of Dexter (6) and Lucina (Ball) Ingraham was born at South Hadley, Massachusetts, November 22, 1838 He was educated in the common schools of the town until the age of nineteen years, when he went to Hazardville, Connecticut, to take charge of the brass band at that place He remained there until the spring of 1860, when he went to Newburyport Massachusetts, to take the leadership of the band there and to teach music He enlisted in August, 1861, as musician in the band, Seventh Maine Infantry, under the leadership of his brother, Emery D Ingraham After the band was discharged from the service, in the spring of 1862, he returned to his old home at South Hadley He went to Newbern, North Carolina, in 1863, in charge of the Forty-fourth Regiment Band, returning home with the regiment in June He went to Worcester in 1867 to tune organs for the Taylor & Farley Organ Company then located on Herman street, and was connected with this company for twenty years He was also the leader of the National Brass Band from the time he came to Worcester until 1874, when he resigned and was succeeded by his brother In 1886 he entered the employ of the Vocalion Organ Company, Summer street, under Bailey Hamilton the English inventor of the vocalion, and remained after the business was bought by Mason & Risch, in 1889, until 1894, when he accepted a position with the Taber Organ Company as head tuner, which position he held for eight years When the Taber business was sold he returned to the Vocalion Organ Company, where he has since been employed He was formerly the director of the Worcester Orchestral Union, and a member of the Schumann Club He attends the Piedmont Congregational Church and is a Republican He is a member of George H Ward Post, No 10 Grand Army of the Republic

He married (first) November 29, 1860, Sarah Louisa Preston, born May 9, 1840, died March 19 1874 daughter of Gardner and Amanda (Smith) Preston, of South Hadley Gardner Preston was born March 31 1798 and died January 24, 1876 He was a farmer and was selectman and assessor of the town of South Hadley Amanda (Smith) Preston was born January 7, 1805 and died September 24, 1878 Mr Ingraham married (second), January 4, 1882, Caroline Lucinda Nutting, connected for many years with Worcester church choirs She was born at Brimfield, Massachusetts, April 18, 1850, and was the daughter of Calvin Ward and Mary (Poland) Nutting, of North Brookfield Mr Nutting was born July, 11, 1817, died September 7, 1896 he was a farmer and shoemaker, and as "Deacon Nutting" was well known for fifty years Mrs Nutting was born April 20 1822 and died January 18 1906 The only child of Albert Wellington and Sarah Louise (Preston) Ingraham is Nellie Louise, born December 10, 1863 She is a pianist of note Was a pupil of G Arthur Adams, B J Lang and Edward Mac Dowell

(VII) Nathaniel Hoyt Ingraham third son and child of Dexter (6) and Lucina (Ball) Ingraham, was born at South Hadley Massachusetts, June 4, 1841 He received his education in the common schools of that place, finishing at the age of nineteen in the high school He then went to New York city and took charge of a dormitory in the New York Juvenile Asylum, a position which he held until January 1, 1862 when he returned to South Hadley In the following August he enlisted in Company F, Forty-fourth Regiment, Massachusetts Volunteers under Colonel Francis E Lee, and was attached with his regiment to the Eighteenth Army Corps He went to Newbern, North Carolina, where he was in the service for nine months He was in engagements at Goldsboro, Whitehall, Plymouth and Little Washington, and was mustered out June 18, 1863 Upon his return to Boston he found employment in the organ factory of Mason and Hamlin, and learned the trade of 'tuner" After three and a half years with this Boston firm he came to Worcester to work for the Taylor & Farley Organ Company, where he remained for two and a half years He went to New Haven in 1868 to work for the New Haven Organ Company, and remained with that company six years He finally returned to Worcester and entered into partnership with William B Taber to manufacture organs under the name of the Worcester Organ Company, later the Taber Organ Company The product of this firm is known all over the country, their chapel and parlor organs ranking among the best The Taber Organ Company was established in 1872 as the Worcester Organ Company Shortly afterward Mr Taber bought the business and Mr Ingraham became his partner The Taber Organ Company was organized in 1877, and for many years Mr Ingraham was president and William N Taber was treasurer Mr Ingraham resides at No 4 Woodbine street, and since the organ business was sold a few years ago, has managed a manufacturing company on Keese street He has been connected with many musical organizations, and was a member of the old Worcester Orchestral Union and the Schumann Club He is a member of George H Ward Post, No 10, Grand Army of the Republic He attends a Congregational church and in politics is a Republican

He married, September 15 1868, Martha A Putnam, born June 21, 1849, daughter of Ephraim and Harriet (Speare) Putnam, of Boston Mr Putnam was for many years a stage carpenter at the Boston Theatre The children of Nathaniel Hoyt and Martha A (Putnam) Ingraham are Rena May, born August 2, 1869, married George J Legasey, of Worcester, he is station agent at Lincoln Square, and they have one child, Ruth Geraldine, William Field, of whom later, Blanche Nathalie, born October 31, 1873, married Frank Robbins, Myrtie Dexter, born October 29, 1879, Nathaniel, born July 26, 1888, died July 29, 1888.

(VIII) William Field Ingraham, second child and eldest son of Nathaniel Hoyt (7) and Martha A (Putnam) Ingraham, was born in New Haven, Connecticut, November 6 1870 He removed to Worcester, Massachusetts, with his parents, in 1874 His education was acquired in the public schools of Worcester, and after graduating from the high school he began his business career as clerk for a firm conducting a fire insurance business Later he was appointed a special agent for the Phoenix Assurance Company of England for the state of New Jersey, and he resides in New York city He married, January 25, 1898, Maud N Hayford, of Worcester, Massachusetts

(VII) William Field Ingraham fourth son and child of Dexter (6) and Lucina (Ball) Ingraham, was born in South Hadley, Massachusetts, August 26 1843 He was educated in the common and high schools of that town Early in life he began the study of music, and soon displayed unusual musical talent He became proficient in playing the piana, violoncello and organ and gave instruction on those instruments When he was but fourteen years of age he was the organist of the Old First Congregationalist Church of South Hadley This position he resigned when he enlisted in the spring of 1861 in Company F, Fourty-fourth Massachusetts Volunteers While still in the service he died in the hospital at Newbern, North Carolina, after a brief illness, January 24 1863 He was unmarried In a family of exceptional musical ability he is pronounced by general consent to have been the most gifted of all

(VII) Mary Lucina Ingraham fifth child and only daughter of Dexter (6) and Lucina (Ball) Ingraham, was born at South Hadley Massachusetts, November 16, 1845 She received her education in the public schools of South Hadley, and at the age of seventeen years began the study of music She was a pupil of Madame Anna Bishop, of New York city, and later of Madame Rudersdorff, of Boston She was the leading soprano in various churches in Boston, Worcester, Norwich and New Haven, has now retired from active work and is living in Worcester Massachusetts

She married (first), May 18 1875, George Arthur Adams born November 13 1848, died October 28, 1889 He was a gifted musician and a noted organist was the son of Hon Charles Adams, Junior, and his wife, Eliza Cummings, of North Brookfield Massachusetts She married (second), October 3 1893, Charles W Delvey, of Worcester, born January 13 1848, died April 29, 1903 The children of George A and Mary Lucina (Ingraham) Adams were Arthur Ingraham Adams born November 26 1883 died June 29, 1905 Mabel Cummings Adams born May 9, 1886, died March 8, 1888

JOHN WILSON BISHOP, of Worcester Massachusetts, whose name has been identified for thirty years with some of the largest building operations in the United States and Canada, was born in Prince Edward's Island May 29 1846 His father was William Bishop, a ship carpenter, who migrated from Plymouth England, in 1819, and was for many years employed in the dockyards at St John's, cultivating also a small farm at White Sands in the south of the island He married, March 27, 1838, Sarah Hooper, daughter of William Hooper who was also of English birth They had nine children Rachael born February 12, 1839, married, June 30, 1861, W M White resides at Attleboro Massachusetts, Elizabeth born December 8 1840, died in infancy, Elizabeth, born July 14 1842, died 1857, Anne born June 1, 1844 married Jonathan Davison resides at Lonsdale Rhode Island John Wilson, born May 29, 1846, Sarah, born May 5 1843 unmarried, resides at Lonsdale, Rhode Island William born August 17, 1850, resides at Lonsdale Rhode Island, Maria born July 20 1852, married Daniel Andrews, resides at East Providence, Rhode Island Nathaniel Smart born November 29 1854, married Annie Tucker of Smithfield, Rhode Island, resides at Providence

In 1857 the family removed to Lonsdale a mill village in Rhode Island where following the custom of the times John was put to work in the cotton mills Here he worked until his fourteenth year when he left the mill to learn the carpenter's trade He was first with Ezra Bliss of Pawtucket with whom he spent two years Later he went to Providence and worked a year for John and Charles Hull, contractors of that city During this time his opportunities for schooling were very slight, altogether he had not more than a year's regular instruction But with the same tireless energy and perseverance which in later years characterized all his great operations he applied himself evenings and during every spare moment to laying the foundations for that remarkable fund of practical knowledge and information which was to win for him a place among the most successful organizers and projectors of his generation

Mastering his trade Mr Bishop began to look about him for a more promising field and in 1867 decided to make Worcester his home There his first employer was H W Eddy, whose shop was on Norwich street Later he worked for George and Amos Bigelow, for William Sibley and for Thomas G Learned and George S Clough, both while they were partners and for each afterwards In the fall of 1874 Mr Bishop went into business for himself His shop was on Central street, and here he took his first contract, which was to build brick stables for Harrington Brothers on Central street Next he built a residence for Thomas Eaton on Boynton street and one for C S Goddard and W B Fay on Irving street The business was successful from the start and in 1879 he entered into partnership with George H Cutting under the firm name of Cutting & Bishop For fourteen years this firm stood among the foremost in Massachusetts in the extent of its operations In May, 1893, the partnership was dissolved and Mr Bishop continued in business alone under the name of J W Bishop & Co In 1899 the business had assumed proportions which induced Mr Bishop to incorporate it the better to handle the wide territory over which he was now operating, and under the corporate name of the J W Bishop Co the business has since been conducted with offices in Worcester, Providence, Boston and New York

The rapid growth of great business enterprises in America during the past fifty years has become so common as to be accepted as a matter of course But it is a mistake to overlook the fundamental truths which govern success, and the career of John W Bishop contains a valuable lesson as illustrating that individual effort and individual worth must, after all remain its true basis A business such as he is the head of today can never owe its upbuilding to anything but the personal factor What it is he made it He worked hard and he worked late, and he never ceased to learn and apply He learned from his triumphs and he learned from his defeats, and his lessons became a part of his capital for the future In like manner he capitalized his rare judgment of men his foresight, his faculty of quick and unerring decision all his own ability and the abilities of those he gathered around him he made a working force of and directed it steadily at the objective point Thus in one word, the secret of his business is effectiveness and the secret of its effectiveness is its organization and here his powers are at their highest Whenever he undertakes a great building project he first organizes it in every department and detail until the whole becomes an engine with its potentiality centered under his hand He reduces every detail to a science and then studies it in its relation to every other detail, and thus mastering them all comes to know and understand the whole as a man knows and understands the five fingers of his hand and how to use them

Although he has devoted thirty years to business and has reached the age of sixty success has not abated Mr Bishop's efforts nor has its rewards spoiled his energy He gives to his business today the same constant care and attention as in the early years when he was struggling for recognition Then

J. W. Bishop

the success of his first undertaking, though amounting to but a few thousand dollars, meant the good or bad beginnings of his reputation, and it is only too natural that the young contractor should have exerted himself to the utmost, but today with a business running annually into the millions he is as jealous of the maintenance of that reputation as he was thirty years ago of its building up, and to that end the successful man of sixty feels himself as much bound by his business and his obligations to his clients as he was as a struggling beginner A recognized expert in matters of construction Mr Bishop's opinion and judgment are naturally widely sought, and many of the best known architects and engineers in the country are glad to supplement their technical knowledge with his wide and practical experience, and in the exercise of this high responsibility, as in all his dealings, Mr Bishop's opinions have never been known to be influenced by private motives

While Mr Bishop's opportunities to become interested in various enterprises have naturally been numerous during the many years of his active business life, it has been his rule to confine his activities almost wholly to his own business or to industries closely connected thereto He has organized at different times a number of subsidiary companies to engage in the manufacture of products used in his own business, and these have been without exception highly successful He is treasurer of The Clason Architectural Metal Works, president of the Rhode Island Brownstone Works and of the Rhode Island Machine Co, Providence enterprises, and is also interested in a number of Worcester's leading industries, though not actively He is well known among Masons and Odd Fellows, belonging to Athelstan Lodge, A F and A M, and to Eureka Chapter, R A M He is a member of Worcester Lodge, I O O F, and of Wachusett Encampment He is a member of the Worcester County Mechanics' Association and also of the Worcester Board of Trade He and his family attend the Pilgrim Congregational Church

Mr Bishop married January 4, 1870, Sarah A Foster, daughter of Thomas R and Sarah Jane (Fales) Foster, of Holden, Massachusetts Their children are Mina, born January 24, 1871, died in infancy, William Thomas, January 25, 1872, Frederick Herbert, November 19, 1874, died in infancy, Florence Jane, August 24 1875, Marion Edith, August 16, 1877, married, March 4, 1897, Thomas H Coe of Worcester, they have three children, Dorothy, John Bishop and Thomas Hamilton, John Warren, January 14, 1880, Sarah Adelaide, July 6, 1881, Alice Maria, July 7, 1884, died in infancy, Nathaniel Smart January 31, 1886, died April 13, 1904 Mr Bishop and his family reside at 1212 Main street William T and John W, Jr, are associated with their father in business, William T being vice-president of the company He is likewise prominent in Masonic circles being a member of Athelstan Lodge A F and A M, Worcester Chapter, R A M and Hiram Council, R and S M Florence J has taught in the public schools at Providence, Rhode Island, but is now residing with her parents

The J W Bishop Co's offices and mill are located at 107 and 109 Foster street Here all the wood and ornamental iron work is gotten out, while the structural iron and stone work is gotten out at the Providence plants The Providence office is located at 417 Butler Exchange and is in charge of O D Purington The Boston office is in the Essex building at 683 Atlantic avenue and is in charge of Heywood S French The New York office is at 353 Fifth avenue, and is in charge of Robert F Brown The present officers of the company are J W Bishop, president, William T Bishop, first vice-president, H S French, second vice-president, Herbert N Leach, treasurer, and Robert F Brown, secretary

The monuments to John W Bishop's long and successful career as a builder are numerous and enduring The costly palaces of Newport and Lenox, the great government, state and municipal buildings throughout the country which he has erected, will represent to the next generation both his genius and its reward, but as enduring will be the story of his rise from humble beginnings to a foremost place in the business world, a story which will worthily add to a record of achievement in which the history of industrial progress in America is peculiarly rich, and the lesson of it will remain an incentive and an influence for good so long as pluck, ability and success are recognized and admired by the youth and manhood of America

FALES FAMILY James Fales (1), was the emigrant ancestor of Mrs John W Bishop, daughter of Thomas R and Sarah J (Fales) Foster James Fales, or Vales as the name was often spelled, came from England to Dedham, Massachusetts, in the year 1650 There in 1654, he married Ann Brock They had seven children, three sons and four daughters Their sons were James, born July 4, 1656, settled at Walpole, married Dorothy Fisher and has many descendants there, John, October 6, 1658, married Eunity Hawes, settled at Wrentham, where his descendants still live, Ebenezer, February 1, 1661, settled on the old homestead at Dedham

(II) Nehemiah Fales, son of Ebenezer Fales (1), was born at Dedham in 1695 He married Mary Carew, of Dedham, January 31, 1720 Their recorded children are Nehemiah, died November 9, 1720, Nehemiah born November 8, 1724

(III) Nehemiah Fales, son of Nehemiah (2), born November 8, 1724, married Susanna Searles, at Dedham, June 27, 1745 Their children were Lemeul, born August 19, 1747, Nehemiah, February 1, 1749, married Sarah Whiting, October 10, 1772, Ebenezer, died April 20, 1761, an infant

(IV) Lemuel Fales, son of Nehemiah Fales (3), settled at Holden, Massachusetts, about 1786 and died there February 14 1826 His wife Elizabeth died February 4, 1838 Their children were Sarah, born in Dedham, June 16, 1775, Eleanor, born in Dedham, December 16, 1777, married Joel Johnson of Pelham, Massachusetts, February 7 1808 Betsey, born in Dedham, June 4, 1779, married David Kimball, at Holden, Massachusetts, December 26 1804, Ambrose, born in Dedham, December 28 1780, married Amy Newell, March 8, 1804, Hannah born in Dedham, September 7, 1782, Lemuel born in Dedham, March 11, 1785, settled in Alburg, Vermont, Anna, born in Holden, April 14, 1787, married Hugh Johnson, of Henderson New York December 5, 1815, Samuel Damon, born in Holden, June 15, 1789, David, born in Holden, May 17 1791, John born in Holden, May 28, 1793, Leonard born in Holden, March 16 1798, married Sarah Gray, April 17, 1834, settled in Holden, died February 21, 1839

(V) Ambrose Fales, son of Lemeul Fales (4), married Amy Newell and had six children Sarah Jane, born at Holden, Leonard, married Sally Gray, Ira, married Adaline King, settled at Monson, Massachusetts, Mary married Porter Tower, removed to Minnesota, died there, Susan, died young Sarah Jane, born November 18, 1827, married

Thomas R Foster, December 24, 1845, they were the parents of Mrs John W (Foster) Bishop

Lemuel Fales, of Dedham, Massachusetts, was a private in Captain Joseph Guild's company of minute men in Colonel Greaton's regiment, which assembled on the Lexington alarm April, 1775 He was also in Captain George Gould's company, Colonel Paul Sargent's regiment, August 1, 1775 He was in Captain Joseph Lewis company, Colonel William McIntosh's regiment in 1776 He was a corporal in Captain Timothy Stow s company, Colonel Ephraim Wheelock's regiment at Ticonderoga, 1776 He was in Captain Robert Smith's company Lieutenant-Colonel Symmes' regiment in 1778

FOSTER FAMILY Hon Samuel Foster, who was born in England in 1619 and settled in Dedham, Massachusetts, was the progenitor of the Fosted family to which Mrs John W Bishop belongs He married in Dedham, Massachusetts, May 30 1647 Esther Kemp daughter of Edward Kemp, of Wenham She died April 16, 1702 He removed to Wenham in 1650, and afterwards to Chelmsford, which town he represented in the general court in 1679 While in Wenham he was a member of the Rev John Fiske s church there He was one of the petitioners for the incorporation of the new town on the west side of the Concord river, afterwards called Chelmsford, and when the church was organized there he was chosen its first deacon The Foster homestead was on the lower edge of the northeast corner of Robbins Hill not far from the center of the village, now or lately the home of George A Parkhurst, the town clerk He also had other grants of land In 1666 he was styled lieutenant In that year he was appointed with two others to lay out land and to view fences He and his son Samuel and his grandson Samuel purchased of Jonathan Tyng in 1675 his interest in five hundred acres of land in Wamesit on the Concord and Merrimac rivers, twenty acres of which they gave to encourage the erection of Hale s mill In 1675, in King Philip's war, the whites in reprisal butchered the old men left at home by the Indians Deacon Foster opposed this act and sought to have it punished, but without success He died July 10, 1702, aged eighty-three

The children of Samuel and Esther (Kemp) Foster were Hannah, born 1649, married, June 18, 1705, Benjamin Barrett, of Chelmsford, Samuel, 1650, married Sarah Keyes, Eli, 1653, married Judith Keyes, Edward, April 30, 1657, Esther, November 1, 1659, married, July 1, 1681, Abraham Foster, of Andover, Massachusetts, Andrew, April 30, 1662, died December 20, 1671, Abraham, October 27, 1664, died December 7, 1671, Nathaniel, October 14, 1667, married Frances Lovejoy, John, September 28, 1671, died December 13, 1671

(II) Samuel Foster, son of Samuel Foster (1), was born at Wenham in 1650 He married, May 28, 1678, Sarah Keyes, daughter of Solomon Keyes She was born in 1657 and died in 1738 He died July 21, 1730 Their children were Anna, born December 3, 1684, Joseph November 14, 1686, died January 29, 1689, Edward, January 29, 1689, married Remembrance Fletcher, Moses October 4, 1692, Sarah August 14, 1694, Andrew, March 28, 1695, married Mary Blodgett, Jean, October 28, 1696, married, April 8, 1717, John Senter, one of the proprietors of the Scotch-Irish town of Londonderry, New York, she died there in 1765, Samuel, died December 17, 1698, Samuel, died February 18, 1718, Joseph married Thankful Walker, Elizabeth, spinster, made Robert Foster, son of her brother Joseph her heir, November 11, 1734

(III) Joseph Foster, son of Samuel Foster (2), married Thankful Walker She was born October 11, 1698, died January 8, 1750 He died May 4, 1741 Their children were Robert born January 4, 1735, died April 14, 1737, Leonard (twin), July 12, 1738, married Esther Blodgett, Robert (twin), July 12, 1738, married Mary Emery, Benoni, January 23, 1733, died young, Sampson, March 16, 1736, died young, Abigail, July 6, 1741, married October 17, 1761, Charles Barron

(IV) Robert Foster, son of Samuel Foster (3), was born at Chelmsford, July 12, 1735 He married, November 8, 1764, Mary Emery, born May 1, 1740, died June 21, 1787 He died September 16, 1784. Their children were Thankful, born March 9, 1764, Joseph, March, 1766, married Mary Adams, Jacob, May 1, 1768, died September 8, 1791, Noah, November 3, 1778, Samuel Emery, March 19, 1781, married Mary Byam

(V) Joseph Foster, son of Robert Foster (4), was born at Chelmsford March 4, 1766 He married there August 22, 1789, Mary Adams Their children were Moses, born February 14, 1790, Mary, May 9, 1792, Adams, May 6, 1794, Sarah, May 3, 1796, Franklin, November 6, 1798, Rufus, January 31, 1801, Almira, September 13, 1803, Calvin, December 6, 1805

(VI) Rufus Foster, son of Joseph Foster (5), was born at Chelmsford, January 31, 1801 He married Nancy Torrey, daughter of Abner and Sarah (Hobart) Torrey and granddaughter of Abner and Lydia Beal Torrey, of Weymouth Her great-grandfather, Jonathan Torrey, was born October 29, 1711, at Weymouth, died April 9, 1784 Abner Torrey, Sr, was a corporal in the French and Indian wars Abner Torrey, Jr, was a private in Captain Edward Cobb's company, Colonel Edward Mitchell's regiment in 1775 Rufus Foster and his wife went to Alabama to live and their three children were born there After his death his wife married John S Haven (June, 1828), and had two children, Ann Maria and Elmira She married the third time in 1839 H B Brewster She was born in 1800 and died in 1843 The children of Rufus Foster were Rufus, Sarah and Thomas R

(VII) Thomas R Foster, son of Rufus Foster (6), was born in Mobile, Alabama, May 16, 1822 He returned to the north and married there Sarah Jane Fales, of Holden, Massachusetts Their children were Sarah Ann, born September 18, 1849, Elmira Jane September 9, 1857, died 1869

(VIII) Sarah A Foster, daughter of Thomas R Foster (7), was born September 18, 1849 She married, January 4, 1870, John Wilson Bishop, of Worcester, Massachusetts

SAMUEL WATERS FOSKETT Ebenezer Foskett, son of Samuel and Sarah (Hunt) Foskett, was born in Charlton, Massachusetts, March 8, 1787 He was a farmer and spent his whole life on the old Foskett homestead in Charlton, where Ebenezer Foskett, of Stoneham, settled in 1739, and where Dan Foskett lives now (1905) He died in Charlton, October 14, 1860 He married in West Sutton, July 4, 1820, Anna Waters (See sketch of Waters family) She was born in West Sutton, May 20, 1791, and continued to live on the old place after the death of her husband until her death, September 23, 1875, in Charlton Their children were 1 Harriet, born April 3 1821, died at Webster, June 17, 1894, married, 1851, Reuben T Eddy, son of Joel and Sally (Thurston) Eddy, born in Oxford, December 7, 1811 He had a meat market in Webster, died in Webster, July 3, 1876 Married (first), May 24, 1837, Dulcinea

Converse, of Spencer, who died March 10, 1846, had three children Anna Maria, Byron Edgar, Lewis Elmer 2 Samuel Waters born December 29, 1823 3 Tamma, born August 15, 1825 died at Charlton, April 30, 1855, married, 1853, Whitman B Potter, a Charlton farmer, he went west in 1856, settled in LaCrescent, Minnesota, had by this his first marriage Amelia Tamma, born at Charlton, March 24, 1855, married, 1872, George Martin 4 Mercy, born June 25, 1826, engaged in sale of millinery and fancy goods at Southbridge, Massachusetts, in 1858 removed to Worcester, unmarried 5 John, born March 28, 1828, died at Webster, June 6, 1898, married, 1869, Betsey A Dockham, he was a farmer at Charlton, removed to Lake Village, New Hampshire, 1872, lived at Webster again later and died there, his children were Annie Augusta, Harrison Brown, John Waters, Herbert 6 Samantha born November 1, 1829, for some years had a millinery store at Webster, later kept house for her brother John and brought up his children, removed 1902 to North Wilmington, Massachusetts, unmarried 7 Dan, born February 11, 1833, married in Worcester, September 26, 1862, Millia Antoinette Davis, daughter of Samuel and Chloe (Simpson) Davis, who was born in Paxton, February 14 1843, is the fifth Foskett in direct line to occupy the old homestead of Ebenezer Foskett, bought in 1734, has twelve children 13 Eliza, born April 26, 1835, taught school some years and afterward was a nurse in Webster and Lowell, removed in 1896 to Worcester, where she lived with her sister Mercy and died there October 30, 1902

Samuel Waters Foskett, son of Ebenezer Foskett, was born in Charlton, Massachusetts, December 29, 1823 He went to school in his native town and at Nicholls Academy in Dudley For seventeen years he taught school in winter and among other schools in which he taught were those of Sutton street, Southbridge, Dudley and Charlton At the time that daguerreotypes came in vogue, some sixty years ago, he went to Boston and learned the process For three years he made photography his business It was the custom at first for the photographer to move from town to town, much as the itinerant picture saloon man was doing a few decades ago and is doubtless still doing in some sections Mr Foskett was located in Framingham, South Framingham and Charlton Doubtless the daguerreotypes that he took in those years are the treasured possessions of many families to-day The old silver plates are as fresh and good now as when first taken There was not much money in the business and most of the early photographers took up some other line of work before the later processes made photography cheap enough to be popular Mr Foskett had learned the trade of carpenter and had a natural aptitude for the use of tools He liked wood-working and eventually entered the business He moved to Webster in 1869 He went to work for Palmer & Kent, manufacturers of sash and blinds John D Putnam subsequently bought the shop and Mr Foskett worked for him nine years He was a first-class mechanic and wood worker He built a house at Webster Mr Foskett stood well in the estimation of his neighbors He was elected member of the school committee while in Charlton In 1888 he removed to Worcester and has since resided there He has built several houses in Worcester, but has not been in active business or employment there He is a Republican in politics and is a member of Trinity Methodist Episcopal Church He married in Charlton, December 8, 1855 Georgianna Mason daughter of Ephraim Hubbard and Prudence (Hills) Mason, born in Putney, Vermont, May 9, 1830, and died in Worcester, January 27, 1892 Their children, all born in Charlton, were 1 Dr George Mason, born October 26, 1856 2 Ann, born December 8, 1860, taught for many years in the public schools of Worcester, was later a music teacher, married, July 29, 1905, Charles R Stobbs, of Webster, Massachusetts 3 Eben, born January 14, 1864

Dr Eben Foskett, son of Samuel Waters Foskett, was born in Charlton, Massachusetts, January 14, 1864 He was educated at Webster high school and Nicholls Academy, Dudley He learned the printer's trade and for several years was assistant foreman of the *Worcester Evening Gazette* composing room While working at his trade he qualified himself to enter the medical school of New York University, from which he graduated M D in 1894, and after two years service as interne at Bellevue Hospital began the practice of his profession in New York city, where he has been located since He is at present instructor in diseases of women at the University and Bellevue Hospital Medical School in connection with his extensive surgical practice He married in Worcester, October 14, 1897, Flora Gertrude Fay, adopted daughter of Winthrop Baxter and Elizabeth (Watson) Fay She was born in Jamaica Plain, Boston, March 10, 1868 Their children, born in New York city, are Winthrop Fay, born February 4, 1899, Elizabeth, February 8, 1900, Eben Maxwell, June, 1904

(I) Richard Waters, who came to Salem in 1636, was the emigrant ancestor of Stephen Waters Foskett, of Worcester He was the second son and third child of James and Phebe (Manning) Waters He was born in St Botolph, without Aldgate, London, and baptized March 3, 1604 His father, James Waters, was an iron-monger in St Botolph His will was proven in 1617 His mother, Phebe Manning, was the daughter of George Manning, gent, of Downe, Kent county, and descended from the sister of Geoffrey Chaucer, the poet His father was buried February 2, 1617, and the widow married, February 23, 1618, William Plasse, a gunsmith Richard Waters was also a gunsmith Richard Waters came to Salem, Massachusetts, in 1636, with his mother and her second husband He was admitted a freeman May 22, 1639 He was a proprietor of the town His wife Joyce was admitted to the church May 23, 1641 He had a tavern in Salem in 1668 The town of Salem voted to buy Roger Conant's house and land for William Plasse because they wished him to stay and follow his trade of gunsmith in that town This place is opposite Derby square and the Town Hall Plasse, or Place, as the name is spelled now, died April 15, 1646 Waters made his will July 16, 1676, and it was proved November 28, 1677 The children of Richard Waters were Mary, married Clement English, August 27, 1667, James born in England, married Mary Stalworth, March 24, 1669-70, William, Martha (daughter recorded born November 27, 1640), John, married Sarah Tompkins, August 1, 1663 Elizabeth or Eliza, baptized February 26, 1642-3, died unmarried February 4, 1662-3, Abigail, baptized May 18, 1645, married William Punchard, October 4, 1669, Ezekiel, baptized April 9, 1647, Susanna, baptized April 1, 1649, married Benedict Pulsifer, February, 1673, Hannah, baptized January 30, 1652-3, married Joseph Striker, April 10, 1673, Sarah, married, February 26, 1651, Joshua Ray, Phebe, married, October 11, 1658, Thomas West, she died April 16, 1674

(II) John Waters, son of Richard Waters (1), was born in Salem, baptized there November 13, 1669 He lived in North Field now North Salem He was a farmer and owned land on Royal Side, now Beverly

He died in Salem, February, 1707 He married, June 1, 1663, Sarah Tompkins, daughter of John and Margaret Tompkins of Salem probably granddaughter of Ralph Tompkins, of Salem She was baptized November 1, 1642, and died in Salem He made his will February 14, 1706-7, and it was proved March, 1707-8 His children were Richard and John (twins), born the last of September 1664, and died within two weeks, John, born July 4, 1665, married Mary ———, Sara, born August 30, 1667, married John Symonds, March 3, 1689-90, Richard born November 13, 1669 married Martha Read, March 3, 1697-8, Nathaniel, born February 6, 1671, married, December 12, 1699, Elizabeth King, Samuel, born March 29, 1674, died aged five weeks, Samuel, born May 6, 1675 probably died young, Elizabeth, born January 10, 1677-8, administration granted on her estate to brother John November 13 1734, Abigail, baptized May 6, 1683, married, April 6, 1704, John Jacobs

(III) Richard Waters, son of John Waters (2) was born in Salem, November 13 1669, died at Oxford while on a visit, February, 1725-6 He removed in 1720 from Salem to Sutton, Massachusetts With Samuel Rich, of Bellingham he purchased, December 8, 1720, a tract of land at Sutton of about one thousand acres of William Taylor of Dorchester, Massachusetts, executor of the Stoughton estate This tract, annexed to the town of Sutton in 1724, is now known as West Sutton and two-thirds of it belonged to Waters Waters bought more land near Manchaug pond of Ezekiel Lewis, William Dudley and Nathaniel Byfield He built a house at the northeast corner of Sutton street and Millbury road The old well remains in use the house has long since disappeared He was "desired" by the church in Oxford to become a member and deacon but did not comply He probably joined the Sutton church by letter He made his will then living adjacent to Oxford, county of Suffolk (now Worcester county), and it was proved February 17, 1725-6 He then owned land in Salem He married March 3, 1697-8, Martha Read, of Salem His children all born at Salem, were Hannah, born March 4 1699, Richard, November 22, 1700 married Anna Holman daughter of Solomon Holman of Newbury, Abigail August 1 1702, married Samuel Dudley, of Littleton, Samuel, September 1 1704, married November 13, 1729 Rachel Holman of Newbury Mercy baptized July 24 1707 Ebenezer baptized July 10, 1709, died in Cuba while taking part in the expedition of Admiral Vernon in 1742 Mary, baptized September 30, 1711, Lois baptized May 16 1714, married Thomas Chamberlain, of Littleton, Amos born June 9, 1717

(IV) Richard Waters son of Richard Waters (3), was born at Salem Massachusetts November 22, 1700 He had a part of his father's large farm at Sutton and built a house on the site now occupied by Bullard's farmhouse in West Sutton The present house was built by Elezer Waters his son in 1767 and was standing as late as 1903 He was admitted to the First Congregational Church in Sutton by letter from Salem between 1724 and 1728 and was an active and useful church member and citizen of Sutton during a long life He died there May 7 1787 He married at Sutton, July 12, 1732 Anne Holman daughter of Solomon and Mary (Barton) Holman She was probably born in Newbury Massachusetts 1715 and died in West Sutton February 20 1788 Their children were Mary married Anthony Sigourney of Boston Stephen born April 13, 1735 Ebenezer, born July 3 1739 Abraham born April 3 1743, Ruth, born January 6, 1746, married Thomas Kendall, Samuel, born November 21, 1750, Hannah, born August 5, 1754, married ——— Marsh

(V) Stephen Waters, son of Richard Waters (4), was born in West Sutton, Massachusetts, April 13, 1735 His father, Richard, set off to him a portion of the old homestead property southeast of his house In 1757 Stephen erected upon it the house to which he brought his bride five years later, and which has been the Waters home from that day to this (1903) and now or recently owned by his great-grandson, Samuel Nathan Waters Stephen and his father made many trips to Boston to sell produce The best road led through Grafton by the house of Eleazer Flagg, where they often stopped for rest and food Here he met Eleazer's daughter, whom he married He had extensive orchards and manufactured cider in considerable quantities His apple trees are still in evidence on the old place He died at West Sutton, January 10 1819 He married, May 19, 1762, Huldah Flagg, daughter of Eleazer Flagg She was born in Grafton, December 14 1732 She was an invalid for many years in the latter part of her life and became blind She died in West Sutton, January 24, 1825 Their children were Anna born March 30, 1763 died at West Sutton, October 22, 1790, unmarried, John, born October 23 1764, died at West Sutton, October 19 1847 married (first) Huldah Howard, David, born February 2, 1767, died young, Nathan, born May 18, 1769 died aged about twenty-one, Huldah born August 11, 1771, died at Providence Rhode Island March 6 1833, married, 1802, Daniel Hunt Rebecca born May 25 1775, probably died young

(VI) John Waters son of Stephen Waters (5), was born in West Sutton October 23, 1764 From his father he inherited a large farm and devoted himself even more extensively to fruit, so that he is said to have had the largest orchards in that section of the state He made much cider He divided the farm between his sons Nathan and Richard He died in West Sutton, October 19 1847 He married first at Sutton November 25 1790, Huldah Howard daughter of Captain John and Huldah (Sibley) Howard She was born in Oxford, June 23, 1768, and died in West Sutton, September 26 1795 He married (second) at Sutton, December 15, 1796 Hannah Putnam daughter of Nathan and Betty (Buffington) Putnam She was born in West Sutton, March 13, 1763 and died there October 28, 1818 He married (third) at Millbury, August 10 1819, Hitty Kidder daughter of Jonathan and Susanna (Dwinnel) Kidder She was born in Oxford, March 18, 1778, died July 17, 1866 at West Sutton He had four children by each wife They were 1 Anna, born May 20, 1791, died at Charlton September 23, 1875, married, 1820 Ebenezer Foskett 2 Lucy, born September 7, 1792, died at Charlton, October 15 1830, married 1812 David Carpenter, farmer in Sutton, born in Sutton January 9, 1794 died in Worcester, May 28, 1886, married (second) Abigail Rich, who died October 5, 1873 David and Lucy had five children 3 Lydia born December 24, 1793, died at Webster, April 19, 1872, married, 1820, Elkanah McIntire, farmer and printer in Charlton born in Charlton, March 16, 1782, died there August 9, 1853 married (first) Polly Chase, Elkanah and Lydia had six children 4 Huldah, born September 24, 1795 died at Oxford, December 14, 1843, married 1814 Jesse Bigelow farmer in Sutton and west part of Oxford and Webster, born in Douglas March 7, 1792, died in Webster, March 14 1877, married (second), about 1844 Esther M Simpson, of Webster, Jesse and Huldah had five children

5 Stephen, born August 6, 1797, died at West Sutton, September 22, 1850, married Matilda Carpenter 6 Nathan, born May 24, 1799, died at West Sutton, May 8, 1878, married, 1832, Ulvah A Putnam, had seven children, he received half the paternal estate and the old house, he manufactured cider, he was selectman and justice of the peace, he settled many estates, he was one of the main supports of the Baptist church His wife was the daughter of Cornelius and Abigail (Bigelow) Putnam, she was born in Sutton, January 18, 1811, died in West Newton, August 26, 1893 7 Richard, born November 1, 1802, died at West Sutton, March 29, 1876, married, 1837, Julia A Torrey, he was a farmer and had immense apple orchards, his wife was daughter of Lewis and Betsey (Titus) Torrey, born in Sutton, April 7, 1816, died in Worcester September 5, 1881, had five children 8 Betsey, born January 17, 1804, died at Rochester, Minnesota, November 5, 1863, married, 1832, Tyler Carpenter, born in Sutton, October 8, 1805, removed to Rochester, Minnesota, 1856, and later to Marshall, Minnesota, where he died March, 1884 He had seven children born in Sutton

(VII) Anne Waters, daughter of John Waters (VI), was born in Sutton, Massachusetts, May 20, 1791 She married, 1820, Ebenezer Foskett (q v)

(I) Thomas Flagg or Flegg as the name is still spelled commonly in England, who came to New England with *Richard Carver in 1637*, was an ancestor of Samuel Waters Foskett, of Worcester He was son of Bartholomew and Alicia Flagg, baptized at Whinbergh, Norfolk county, England, in 1615 He embarked at Scratby when emigrating to America He settled in Watertown as early as 1641, when he had a homestall of six acres and other land He was selectman there in 1671-72-73-74-75-76-78-81-85-86-87 He is ancestor of all the American Flagg families, it is believed He died February 6, 1697-8 His wife Mary died December 30, 1702 Their children were 1 Gershom, born at Watertown, April 16, 1641, was a tanner, removed to Woburn about 1668, held a commission as lieutenant in King William's war and was killed by the Indians in a skirmish at Wheelwright's pond, Lee, New Hampshire, July 6, 1690, married, 1668, Hannah Leffingwell, had ten children 2 John, born in Watertown, June 14, 1643, settled there, died February, 1696-7, married, 1670, Mary Gale, three children 3 Bartholomew, born at Watertown, February 23, 1644, served in Captain Moseley's company in King Philip's war, 1675, probably died before 1697 4 Thomas, born April 28 1646, settled at Watertown, died there 1719, married Rebecca Dix, had six children 5 William, born in 1648, soldier on guard at Lancaster in King Philip's war and killed by the Indians in the massacre August 22, 1675 6 Michael, born at Watertown, March 23 1650-1, settled there, one of the first proprietors of the attempted settlement of Worcester in 1674, served in King Philip's war, died in Watertown, October 16, 1711, married (first), 1674, Mary Bigelow, (second) Mary (Lawrence) Earle, had six children 7 Eleazer, born at Watertown, May 14, 1653, see forward 8 Elizabeth, born at Watertown, March 22, 1654-5, died August 9, 1729, married, 1676, Joshua Bigelow 9 Mary born at Watertown, January 14, 1656-7, died September 7, 1720, married, 1674, Samuel Bigelow 10 Rebecca born at Watertown, September 5, 1660, married, 1679, Deacon Stephen Cook 11 Benjamin, born at Watertown, June 25, 1652, removed to Worcester at the time of the third and successful attempt to settle in 1718 and was very prominent among the early settlers, died at Worcester, May 3, 1741, married, 1689 or 1690, Experience Child, had nine children 13 Allen, born at Watertown, May 16, 1665, settled there, died November 11, 1711, married, 1684-5, Sarah Ball, had nine children

(II) Eleazer Flagg, son of Thomas Flagg (1), was born at Watertown, Massachusetts, May 14, 1653 He removed to Concord, was a tanner Like at least three of his brothers he served in the King Philip war, being in Captain Samuel Appleton's company in the Narragansett expedition in 1675 He was admitted a freeman March 20, 1690, and held town offices He died in Concord, May 1, 1722 He married at Concord, October 10, 1676, Deborah (Wright) Barnes, widow of John Barnes, who was killed by the Indians in the Sudbury fight March 31, 1676 She may have been daughter of Edward and Elizabeth Wright, of Concord Their children were Deborah, born at Concord, October 9, 1677 Abigail, born at Concord, March 9, 1679-80, died there August 11, 1680, Eleazer, born about 1687, Priscilla, married, 1705, Joseph Wheat, of Concord, Joseph, married, 1713, Mary Tompkins, of Salem, had eight children

(III) Eleazer Flagg, son of Eleazer Flagg (2), was born at Concord about 1687 He lived in Concord and was constable and surveyor of highways He was one of the forty original purchasers of Hassanamisco, later called Grafton On the various divisions of the land among the proprietors 1728-*1744 he received parcels aggregating* about one hundred and fifty acres There is no evidence that he himself ever lived in the new town, but he deeded his land to his three sons, Eleazer, Robert and Nathaniel Eleazer Flagg was also a petitioner for the Narragansett townships, as eldest male heir of his father, and on the setting apart of these lands by the general court in 1733 his name is found as a grantee in Narragansett No 6 (Templeton) and he received lot 94 in the division of the township in 1735 He died in Concord, March 28, 1745 in his fifty-ninth year He married at Concord, January 26, 1708-9, Deborah Tompkins, daughter of John Tompkins, Jr and Rebecca Knight, born in Salem January 8, 1688-9, died in Grafton December 16 1753 Their children were 1 Eleazer, born in Concord October 23, 1709, married Huldah Chandler 2 Nathan, settled in Concord bought land in Grafton, left no issue 3 Robert, born at Concord, August 25, 1713, removed to Grafton about 1735, married Miriam ——— and had seven children 4 Nathaniel, born at Concord, May 21, 1716, received a gift of land in Grafton from his father and removed to that town, was a soldier at Crown Point 1755, died before 1786, married Elizabeth ——— and had nine children 5 Deborah, born at Concord, February 13, 1718-9, died before 1757 married at Concord, October 19, 1749, Jacob Whittemore, of Concord 6 James, born at Concord, May 3, 1723, removed to Upton about 1750 and to Wilmington, Vermont, 1783, died 1807 married Anna Morse, of Cambridge, had eight children 7 Jonathan, born at Concord, February 3 1725-6, died at Bolton, September 26, 1747 8 Abigail, born at Concord, January 25, 1728-9, married Jonathan Rolf, of Westboro 9 Elizabeth (twin), born at Concord, January 25, 1728-9, married ——— Nelson

(IV) Eleazer Flagg, son of Eleazer Flagg (3), was born at Concord, Massachusetts, October 23, 1709 He removed to Grafton probably in 1728, the year of the purchase from the Indians He settled first on his father's land In 1831 he received a lot by deed of gift from his father, comprising forty-two acres of the eighteenth lot of the first division and a part of the thirty acres of the second division This estate was situated in the

Merriam district, east of the centre of the town, occupying part of the eastern slope of Chestnut Hill and meadow land beyond There is now on exhibition at the museum of the Worcester Society of Antiquity a large wooden bowl hewn from a tree on this hill by Eleazer Flagg in 1732, four years after the original settlement In 1745 a substantial dwelling house was built, which was torn down in 1845 He was one of the charter members of the church in 1731 He was appointed deputy sheriff in 1746 by Sheriff Benjamin Flagg a cousin of Eleazer Flagg (III), who was a very prominent man in Worcester He married at Concord, September 28, 1731, Huldah Chandler, daughter of Samuel and Dorcas (Buss) Chandler, who was born in Concord, July 5, 1709 She was received in full communion by the Grafton Church, February 20, 1742 She died January 27, 1765, he died 1771 Their children were Huldah, born December 14, 1732, died at West Sutton, January 24 1825, married 1762, Stephen Waters, Eleazer, born November 12, 1734, died at Grafton, February 10, 1767, married 1763, Sarah Chandler, Simon, born May 25, 1736 died at Grafton May 26, 1736, John born August 2, 1737, probably died young, Mary, born March 19, 1740 died April 6 1724, married, 1763, Benjamin Goddard (See Goddard Family), Samuel, born December 5, 1741, died at Grafton, October 17, 1822 married, 1769 Lydia Rockwood, Submit, born September 5, 1744, died at Berlin, Vermont, March 14, 1839, married, 1773, Daniel Hayden

(V) Huldah Flagg, daughter of Eleazer Flagg (4), was born at Grafton, December 14 1732 married, May 19 1762 Stephen Waters (See Waters Family sketch in this work)

(I) Roger Chandler, one of a company of twenty from Plymouth Colony who settled Concord about 1658, was an ancestor of Samuel W Foskett and most of the Worcester county Waters and Flagg families He was admitted a freeman May 24 1682 He died at Concord, January 11, 1716-7, aged about eighty, according to his gravestone He married at Concord, April 25 1671, Mary Simons of Concord, probably daughter of William and Judith (Phippen) Simonds, born December 9, 1647, died in Concord August 29, 1728 Their children were Mary, born at Concord, January 7, 1671-2, died there August 14 1759 married, 1690, Lieutenant John Heald, Samuel, born at Concord, March 23 1673-4, Joseph, born at Concord, October 7 1678, died there November 14 1679, Abigail, born at Concord, May 31 1681 died there March 29, 1766, married Eleazer Brown of Concord, Hepzibath married (first) Ephraim Jones, married (second), 1711, Joseph Fletcher, of Concord and Acton, who died 1746, married (third) ——— Stow

(II) Samuel Chandler, son of Roger Chandler (1), was born in Concord Massachusetts, March 23, 1673-4 He was a prominent citizen of Concord, serving as selectman in 1718-19-20-21-22-23-24-30-31-32-33-34-35-36-39, town treasurer from 1723 to 1727, inclusive, and representative in the general court from 1729 to 1736, inclusive, and again in 1739 He was active in the purchase of Grafton township from the Indians in 1728, being one of the forty proprietors • was also an early petitioner for the grant of the Narragansett townships to survivors of King Philip's war in the right of his father-in-law John Buss, who had been a member of Captain Nathaniel Davenport's company in that war In the records of Narragansett No 6 now Templeton granted by the general court in 1733 His name also occurs in the drawing of lots among the proprietors in 1735 He probably never gave up his residence in Concord however He died there April 27 1743 He married in Concord, December 11, 1695, Dorcas Buss, daughter of Joseph and Elizabeth (Jones) Buss, born in Concord, January 26, 1672-3, died January 13, 1757 The children of Samuel Chandler were 1 Elizabeth, born October 6, 1696, died October 18, 1712 2 Mary, born September 22, 1699 died before 1773, married (first), 1718, Joseph Dudley, married (second), 1752, Judah Clark, of Lexington 3 Joseph, born October 11, 1701, died at Concord, January 31, 1746 4 Samuel, born October 19, 1704, was a farmer in Concord, will proved November 17, 1754, married about 1730 Dinah ———, had nine children 5 John, born January 11, 1706-7, died at Concord, May 3, 1730 6 Huldah, born July 5, 1709, married Eleazer Flagg, (III) 7 Rebecca, born December 2, 1709, married, 1731, Eleazer Davis, of Bedford 8 James, born August 28, 1714, was on committee of safety and correspondence in 1774, and the military stores the seizure of which was one of the objects of the British expedition to Concord April 19, 1775, were in part in his care at that time, he died December 8, 1792, married (first) Mary Wright, (second) Mary Flagg, daughter of Joseph and Mary Tompkins Flagg, married (third) Mary Whittaker, of Carlisle, daughter Sarah married Eleazer Flagg (5)

(III) Huldah Chandler, daughter of Samuel Chandler (2), was born July 5, 1709, married Eleazer Flagg (4) (See Flagg Family Also Waters and Foskett families)

RUFUS BENNETT FOWLER Philip Fowler (1), the emigrant ancestor of Rufus Bennett Fowler, was a cloth worker and was probably born in Marlborough, Wiltshire, England, about 1590 He sailed from England on the ship 'Mary and John" the 24th day of March 1633-4, and arrived in New England in May Owing to misrepresentation of the activities and intentions of the colonists in New England ships sailing to that place were subjected at that time to a rigid scrutiny, the passengers were compelled to take the Oathes of Allegiance and Supremicie and the master to give bond to perform the services of the Church of England during the voyage On his arrival in New England Philip settled in Ipswich Essex county Massachusetts, and the Fowler place in that town on which he lived is still occupied by a Fowler He received grants of other lands in and near Ipswich during his life, and performed the duties of a respected and honored citizen of the town of Ipswich He died in 1679, having reached the age of eighty-nine He was twice married first to Mary Winslow in England Of this marriage there were seven children Margaret, Samuel Hester, Joseph and Thomas all of whom except Thomas were born in England Mary Fowler died in 1659 and in 1660 Philip married Mary Norton by whom he had no children

(II) Samuel Fowler was born in England in 1618 and came to Ipswich with his parents in the ship Mary and John" The record of Samuel (2) is confused but it is probable he lived in Portsmouth New Hampshire, until 1668, when he moved to Salisbury Massachusetts He was a shipwright He was probably a Quaker and there is a record of his being brought before the court in 1675 for travelling on Sunday He married twice his first wife's name being unknown He married as his second wife about 1675 Margaret, the widow of Robert Morgan He died in Salisbury, January, 1710-11 at the age of ninety-two His children probably by his first wife, were William, Mary, Sarah and Samuel

(III) Samuel Fowler was born in Portsmouth, New Hampshire and came to Salisbury with his father in 1668 He was a laborer and lived in Salisbury until his death in 1737-8 In 1693 his father Samuel (2) transferred all his property to his son Samuel (3) in return for the care of him and his wife Margaret during their old age At his death Samuel (3) was possessed of considerable property for that time He married in 1684 Hannah Worthen, and their children were Samuel Hannah, Susanna, Jacob, Mary, Sarah, Ann, Ezekiel, Robert, Abraham, Thomas, Lydia and Judith

(IV) Ezekiel Fowler was born at Salisbury, 1697-8 He lived at Salem and married, in 1722, Martha Chase, of Bristol county, Rhode Island He died at Salem in 1735 The record of his children is incomplete He had however a son Samuel

(V) Samuel Fowler was a cordwainer and was born probably about 1730 His place of birth is unknown He married Hannah Bowen of Swansea Rhode Island, in 1752, and lived there until 1753 He moved to Warren Rhode Island, in the following year, and about 1764 moved to Northbridge, then a part of Uxbridge, settling in the easterly part of the town Like his father and grandfather he was a Quaker His children were Sarah Ezekiel, Mary, Isaac, Olive, Bernard John, Martha, Elizabeth, Hannah Peace and Phebe

(VI) Bernard Fowler was born in Warren, Rhode Island, in 1762, and came to Northbridge with his father in the following year He married his first wife, Rebecca Mowry of Smithfield Rhode Island, in 1790 she died in 1805 In 1810 Bernard (6) married Abigail Steere, of Gloucester, Rhode Island Bernard (6) died in 1843, at the age of eighty-one He was a farmer His children by his first marriage were Mary, Robert, Willis, Phebe, Caleb and Samuel and by his second marriage Thomas Rebecca, Charles and Nancy

(VII) Charles Fowler was born at Northbridge in 1815 He was a farmer and lived in Northbridge until about 1890 He married, February 9, 1841, Susan Frost Bennett, of Northbridge She was the daughter of Rufus Bennett, known as "Father" Bennett, a farmer in Northbridge and member of the legislature from that town for a number of years He was ordained a Methodist minister in the early days before the Methodists settled and became salaried preachers, and he refused to accept such a settlement He continued to minister without pay to all who required his services since as he said, "The Grace of God is free" All the country side was his parish in which he solemnized marriages and attended funerals and no gathering of the citizens was complete without the presence and advice of 'Father" Bennett Charles (7) died in Worcester, in 1895, at the age of eighty, surviving his wife but three days He was born a Quaker He had three children Rufus Bennett, named for his maternal grandfather, Charles Thomas and Mary Abby

(VIII) Rufus Bennett Fowler was born at Northbridge, Massachusetts December 5, 1841 He graduated at the Barre Academy Barre Vermont, in 1861 After his graduation he became assistant superintendent of the Uxbridge woolen mill He later took a course in the Eastman Business College at Poughkeepsie New York, the first to adopt actual business methods in its course of instruction and at that time at the height of its popularity, having about fourteen hundred students At the close of his course Mr Fowler accepted the position of superintendent and instructor of the banking department of the Eastman College In this department two banks and a clearing house illustrated in a practical way the functions of banks in business life In addition to his duties as instructor and superintendent Mr Fowler also studied law In 1864-5 he became lecturer on commercial law at the United States College of Business in New Haven, Connecticut This college was an ambitious undertaking of Mr Thomas H Stevens, for many years teacher in the Claverack Institute, New York, to broaden the instruction in schools of this class From 1865 to the time of the great fire, Mr Fowler was engaged in the wholesale business in Chicago, gradually drifting into mechanical pursuits and patent law, urged both by his natural ability and his inclination in that direction His services as an expert in such matters were in constant demand In 1872 he returned to the east and was for some time engaged in designing special machinery in Worcester He also at this time completed an invention of a ribbon loom

He married in 1875 Helen M Wood of Barre Vermont, and after his marriage lived in Stafford Springs, Connecticut, where he conducted the manufacture of narrow wares by means of looms of his own invention In 1881 he returned to Worcester where he now lives and took up the profession of patent attorney and expert in patent causes The nature of his profession is such that a comparatively few become acquainted with his merits and ability, and although he ranks high in his profession he is better known through his connection with various organizations devoted to public service

He was president of the Worcester Board of Trade in 1900 and 1901 his natural fitness and ability for the position and his public spirit and interest in the welfare of Worcester directing attention to him and he was recognized as a very capable and efficient president While at the head of the board of trade there was a spontaneous movement to run Mr Fowler for mayor of Worcester, and he could have had the Republican nomination with the support of all the newspapers but he declined it on account of the pressure of his private business The only public office he has accepted is that of park commissioner of Worcester which he now holds He is a member of the Worcester Society of Antiquity the Worcester Economic Club the Public Education Association of Worcester, the Worcester County Musical Association, the Massachusetts Civic League, the National Municipal League, the American Forrestry Association and the National Geographic Society He is an honorary member of the Worcester Continentals, a trustee of the Worcester County Institution for Savings and a director in several manufacturing corporations Although he was reared as a Quaker he and his family have attended Central Congregational Church His children are Henry Wood born in 1876, and Susan Bennett born in 1885, died in 1892

WOODWARD FAMILY Thomas Woodward (1), seems to be the first person of this family of which there can now be any positive knowledge He married Elizabeth Tynen in Childwell parish Lancashire England May 23 1592 Five children were born to them two of whom John born April 10 1504 and Henry, born March 22 1607, emigrated to America in the company that followed Rev Richard Mather They landed in Dorchester Massachusetts, from the ship 'James" Captain Taylor, August 16 1635

(II) Henry Woodward above named, remained in Dorchester until 1660 when he went to Northampton on the founding of the church there, where he became one of the seven pillars" He died April 7 1685 aged seventy-eight years His wife, Elizabeth died August 13 1690

(III) John Woodward son of Henry (2), was born in Dorchester 1649 went to Northampton with his father and married in 1685 He was among the first party to settle Northfield and five years later, on the desertion of this northern post, came back and went to Westfield, from which town his wife came Before 1700, he removed to Lebanon, Connecticut, where his name appears as one of the fifty-one grantees to the "five mile purchase" He died in Lebanon about 1718 He married Anna Dewey, at Westfield, May 18, 1671 Of their six children the second John was born April 2, 1674

(IV) John Woodward son of John (3), born in Northampton, accompanied his father on his many migrations and was thus one of the original proprietors of Lebanon He was a constable in 1703, selectman in 1717-19-25-26 again from 1731-35 He was a deputy to the general court of the province of Connecticut from 1720 to 1731 A justice of the peace for Windham county from 1725 to 1743 He was a deacon in the church and a member of the council He died September 19 1743, aged sixty-nine years He married Experience Baldwin June 2 1703 They had three children, of whom Israel, the second was born June 5, 1707

(V) Israel Woodward, son of John and Experience Woodward, born in Lebanon, lived on the old place until after the death of his father In 1747 he bought a farm in Watertown, Connecticut He died August 17, 1800, aged ninety-three years In October, 1744 he was commissioned captain of a train band and was ensign in May, 1749 He served in the French and Indian war as captain of the Sixth Company of the First Regiment, Connecticut Line and was at Fort Edward, Ticonderoga and Crown Point He married Abigail Baird, of Huntington Connecticut, March 31, 1730 His wife died December 27 1803, aged ninety-six years Of the ten children all but one who died in infancy, were present at their mother's funeral the oldest being seventy-one years and th youngest fifty-three

(VI) Samuel Woodward son of Israel Woodward, the youngest of the family was born October 25 1750 He was apprenticed to his brother to learn the tanners trade and remained with him until he was of age He taught school for five years and entered Yale College in 1776 In 1779 the college was broken up by an attack of the British and he decided to study medicine After due training he began the practice of medicine in Torringford, Connecticut where he remained until his death, January 26 1835, at the age of eighty-four For twenty years he was a member of the legislature, and for a long period the "father of the House" He was the unsuccessful Democratic candidate for Congress from 1800 to 1810 He married Mary Griswold, daughter of Captain Shubael Griswold, February 10, 1782 There were eight children born of this marriage

(VII) Samuel Bayard Woodward, M D, the eldest son of Samuel and Mary (Polly) (Griswold) Woodward was born in Torringford Connecticut, June 10, 1787 His mother was a daughter of a captain in the French and Indian and the revolutionary wars Her brother was a state senator for fifty sessions Another brother, Stanley was secretary of the territory of Michigan and its governor under Jefferson's administration Later he became United States senator from Ohio Samuel Bayard Woodward with three brothers, studied medicine under his father who was a physician with a large practice in Torringford and educated many students in his profession In 1809 he received a license to practice in Connecticut He remained with his father one year and in 1810 removed to Wethersfield, Connecticut began practice for himself and there remained until he came to Worcester in 1832 In 1822 he received the honorary degree of Doctor of Medicine from Yale College He was instrumental in founding the Retreat for the Insane at Hartford While working up this project he traveled over a large part of Connecticut in his gig From 1827 to 1832 he was physician to the Connecticut State Prison, and here became familiar with the cases of the insane poor, to which he was to devote the best years of his manhood

The Massachusetts State Lunatic Hospital at Worcester, the first public institution of the kind in America for the care of criminal and pauper insane, had meanwhile been established through the unceasing exertions of Horace Mann and was being built Dr Woodward was made first superintendent He began in December, 1832, and served until June, 1846 and during this period made the Worcester Hospital a model for the entire country for the successful treatment of the insane poor The report of the trustees in 1846 says "The success of the hospital is due to the professional skill personal address, and energy conscientious fidelity and pure ardent philanthropy of Dr Woodward" In accepting his resignation they add "We feel that we are bound to bear our unqualified testimony to the justice of your claims to be recognized and remembered as one of the most distinguished benefactors of the Commonwealth" After resigning he retired to a beautiful estate in Northampton, where he received a few private patients, but he never recovered his impaired health and passed from earthly scenes, January 3, 1850, aged fifty-three years

Hon Stephen Salisbury describes his personal appearance and character as follows "His person was a rare model of strength and manly beauty On his brow sat courtesy and command in entire harmony, and it is no exaggeration to say that his form and carriage were majestic His stature was six feet four inches and without the deformity of obesity, his weight was two hundred and sixty pounds His temper was benevolent, liberal, sanguine, decided and persevering He understood readily the character of men had great power over their feelings and easily gained their confidence and love His mind was of a practical character"

He married in 1815 Miss Maria Porter, of Hadley, Massachusetts a lineal descendant of Jonathan Edwards She died in Worcester, October 10, 1873, at the home of her son Samuel By her he had twelve children Charles born April 17, 1816, Urania B, born June 16 1817, died October 7, 1857, Rufus, born October 3 1819, mentioned below, Stanley Griswold, born June 5 1821, Henry, born September 2, 1822, mentioned below, Samuel born January 11, 1825, Maria Porter, born August 3, 1826, Edwin born June 9, 1828 died 1829 Catherine Todd, born March 30 1831, died 1849, Edwin Porter, born July 16, 1832, Algernon Sidney, born June 6 1835, died February, 1836 Of these children Dr Rufus, Samuel and Henry bore well their part in the history of Worcester

To better fix the reader's mind on the wonderful skill and capacity of this man it may be summed up by the subjoined review of his work He studied with his father, practiced twenty years at Wethersfield, Connecticut, was elected secretary of the Connecticut Medical Society, was one of the examiners of the Medical College, six years physician of the Connecticut State Prison, was a prime mover in the formation of the Retreat for the Insane at Hartford, served fourteen years as superintendent of the Insane Asylum at Worcester in 1832 represented the Hartford district in the legislature as senator became a Fellow of the Albany Medical College, was the first president of the Association of Insane Asylum

Superintendents and the founder of the society, a member of the Ohio State Medical Society and Ohio Historical Society, he wrote extensively for medical works and scientific journals

(VIII) Samuel Woodward son of Dr Samuel B Woodward and father of Samuel B Woodward, was born at Wethersfield, Connecticut January 11, 1825, and came to Worcester with his father He attended the Worcester schools and from school soon went into the Worcester postoffice as a clerk under Mr Fisher, postmaster, after one year of faithful work there he entered the employ of the leading hardware store of the city at that date—Kinnicutt & Rice, in 1846 was admitted to the firm as partner 1847 After the death of Mr Rice he still continued in the firm of which he and Mr Kinnicutt were active members In 1887 he retired Though many times tendered office he always declined to accept, preferring rather to attend to his own matters and support other capable fellow-citizens for the various offices For a number of years he was a director in the Citizens' Bank of Worcester, also connected officially with the Worcester Gas Company He held an important business trust as member of the board of sinking fund commissioners, which place he held at the time of his death, which took place December 30, 1888, at the age of sixty-four years September 14, 1852, he married L E R Treadwell, of Ipswich, by whom one child was born—Samuel B, August 24, 1853 Mrs Woodward died March, 1857

(VII) Edwin Woodward, son of Samuel Woodward (VI), was born July 16, 1832, at Wethersfield In 1861 he entered the service of his country as lieutenant in Captain Studley's company, Fifteenth Massachusetts Regiment of Infantry, and was subsequently detailed to serve in the signal corps, where he remained until the close of the war After the close of the war he engaged in the drug business at Worcester in partnership with David Scott, and later went to New York and engaged in the brokerage business He now lives a retired life at Summit, New Jersey He married Helen M Musgrave, five children Thomas N, born July 8 1863, died July 27, 1864, Helen M, born December 8, 1864, died January 9, 1870, Martha G born July 6, 1867, William S, born October 17, 1869, died 1890, Anna T, born September 17, 1871

(IX) Dr Samuel B Woodward son of Samuel Woodward (8), born August 24 1853 In Worcester, his native city, he attended the common schools, in 1870 entered Harvard College, graduating in the class of 1874, and the Harvard Medical School in 1878 He began his active medical practice at Worcester in 1881, and is to-day among the leaders in his profession Dr Woodward has descended from a line of eminent medical practitioners—his grandfather and great-grandfather being such in their day and generation, also his uncle and others Dr Woodward is a Republican, and in church relations affiliates with the Unitarians Among the offices held by this gentleman are that of surgeon of the Memorial Hospital, consulting surgeon of City and St Vincent's Hospital, trustee of the Worcester Insane Hospital and Worcester Insane Asylum Has been president of the Worcester District Medical Society, director of Worcester Gas Light Company, trustee for Worcester County Institution for Savings and one of its investment board

He married, September 16, 1884 Margaret Perley, of New Hampshire, daughter of the late chief justice of that state

(VIII) Henry Woodward, son of Dr Samuel B Woodward (7) was born in Wethersfield Connecticut, September 2, 1822 He came with his parents to Worcester when he was only seven years old, and his early education was received in the common and high schools there When he was in the high school his father gave him his choice of studying art or a college education, and he chose art He had a gift for drawing and painting and he studied under good masters While he never made painting his exclusive occupation it has been an absorbing avocation He has been prominent among the artists of Worcester for many years He has frequently sold his pictures and exhibited in various exhibitions for many years He was one of the organizers of the Worcester Art Students' Club and has been president of that interesting organization When a young man he taught drawing and painting at Holy Cross College and at one time had a studio in the business section of the town For the most part he has worked in his studio at his residence, 43 West street, Worcester He devoted virtually all his time not claimed by business to painting pictures, and in spite of ill health is still at work with the palette and brush at every opportunity Mr Woodward is an artist by nature He loved nature and art alike and many of his pictures were out-door scenes along the sea shore or in the fields He did not confine himself to scenery, however, but painted many and varied subjects

Mr Woodward is known to many who are not interested in art as an excellent business man For many years he was an active factor in the financial life of Worcester He began his business career in Boston as clerk in the dry goods store of Henry Pettis, who was a relative After a few years he returned to Worcester to accept a position as secretary to his father, who was the superintendent of the Worcester Insane Hospital on Summer street After a few years he entered the Worcester Mechanics' Savings Bank where for forty-nine years he was the treasurer The Mechanics' Savings Bank was the second in Worcester It was chartered May 15, 1851, with Isaac Davis as president and Parley Hammond as treasurer In 1854 Mr Woodward became treasurer, and at the end of a half century retired from active work at the bank He was the oldest and best savings bank official of the state While Mr Woodward divided his time between banking and painting he had few other interests He is a member of the Worcester Horticultural Society and of the Worcester Agricultural Society In politics he is a Republican

He married (first), May, 1853, Mary Hunt, daughter of Eben and Mary (Abbey) Hunt She died January 24 1872 She was born in Milford, Massachusetts He married (second) Mrs Amelia (Gerry) Wells, of Boston, December 21 1875 She was the widow of Benjamin Wells of Boston The children of Henry and Mary (Hunt) Woodward were Henry, died young, Catherine Burns, died young, Alice Hunt, resides at home, Maria Philips, resides at home, Harry Andrews, graduate of the Classical high school, married Lottie Benson, daughter of Mr and Mrs James K Comstock, Harry Andrew is with Goldman & Sachs brokers, in New York city, he has one son, James Henry Woodward, Norman Porter graduate of the Classical high school, is with Samuel Ward & Co, stationers, Boston, as traveling salesman, resides in Boston, Mary Hunt teacher of kindergarten at the Winslow street public school Mr Woodward is a member of the Church of the Unity of Worcester, being one of its early members when its first pastor was Edward Everett Hale, and he has taken great interest in its building up

FOX FAMILY Thomas Fox (1), who settled in Cambridge, Massachusetts, as early as March 1631, was the emigrant ancestor of Mrs C W Hamilton and Dr Lemuel F Woodward through their mother's line He was evidently one of the earliest political reformers in New England and a man of great moral courage, for the very first record of Thomas Fox is an account of the proceedings in the general court which punished him for suggesting that the court had taken bribes in the Bratcher case That was in March, 1630-31 He was evidently a man of influence He was admitted a freeman in March, 1637-8, and was then thirty years of age, showing that he was born in 1607-08 and probably came over when he was twenty-one, in 1630 It is said that he came from London and that he was the son of Dr Thomas Fox, a physician of that city He seems to have been an apprentice to Governor Craddock, who had a farm in Medford A tradition that has more than the usual claim for credence states that he emigrated from England in anger and disgust at the injustice done him in a law suit, which he believed was decided against him because he was a grandson of John Fox, the author The suit was about a lease for three lives on seventeen houses in London, and as it happened in the reign of Charles I, when Puritans were persecuted at every opportunity, Fox had good reason, perhaps, to doubt the justice of the English courts

Thomas Fox was one of the original proprietors of Cambridge, Massachusetts He dealt in real estate and was executor and administrator of many estates He was selectman in 1658 and repeatedly afterwards elected to that office He was an esteemed and enterprising citizen and stood well in the church The name of his first wife was Rebecca ——— She died May 11, 1647 He married (second) Ellen Green, widow of Percival Green, May 24, 1650 She died May 27, 1682, aged eighty-two years He married (third), April 24, 1683, Elizabeth Chadwick, widow of Charles Chadwick She died in 1685, aged seventy-one years He married (fourth) Rebecca Wyeth widow of Nicholas Wyeth, December 16, 1685 He died April 25, 1693, aged eighty-five years

The house at Cambridge owned by Thomas Fox, sometimes called the Holmes house, stood originally on the north side of the college grounds but is now owned by the college In the early days of the colony the place belonged to Mrs Ellen Green, the second wife of Fox The house was repaired by their grandson, Jabez Fox, who owned it, and his son Thomas Fox, of Woodstock, Connecticut, sold it to Rev John Fox of Woburn, Massachusetts General Ward, of Shrewsbury, made this house his headquarters while in command of the American forces in Cambridge in 1775, and he was there at the time of the battle of Bunker Hill Dr Abiel Holmes, while he was chaplain to the college, and Dr Oliver Wendell Holmes, his son, was born in this house The house was torn down in 1890, and the site is suitably marked It is near the law school

The daughter of Mrs Rebecca Fox by a former husband, Thomas Andrews, was a victim of the witchcraft craze, and there is on record a pathetic letter written by Mrs Fox in 1692 to the general court, asking for the release of her daughter who was crazed, distracted and broken in mind and had been so these twelve years and upwards She had then been in prison for six months Her husband was a fugitive to avoid the same fate, and she had four young children, one a baby left to the mercy of neighbors Not until the following January was she tried acquitted and released By that time the delusion had passed and the persecution ceased abruptly

Thomas Fox had one son, Jabez, baptized at Concord, Massachusetts, and possibly Thomas Fox who married, December 13, 1647, Hannah Brooks

(II) Rev Jabez Fox, son of Thomas Fox (1), was born in Concord in 1647 and baptized there He was educated at Harvard College, where he graduated in 1665 On taking his second degree there, three years later, his public address consisted of a few lines of Latin verse He served one year as assistant of Rev Mr Carter, pastor of the Woburn church, and November 5, 1679, he was called to be minister there The house which the town built for him was on Pleasant street, near the site of the public library, and was occupied by Mr Fox and his son, who succeeded him as minister, for seventy-six years He died of smallpox, February 26, 1702, in the city of Boston, and was buried in Woburn, where in the oldest burying ground his grave stone may be seen

He married Judith Rayner, daughter of Rev John Rayner, minister of Plymouth, Massachusetts, and Dover, New Hampshire His widow married (second) Colonel Jonathan Tyng, of Boston, formerly member of the council of Sir Edmund Andros, governor Colonel Tyng died January 19, 1723 His widow died June 5, 1736, in her ninety-ninth year The children of Rev Jabez and Judith Fox were John, born at Woburn, May 10, 1678, Thomas, born at Woburn, November 6, 1680, died July 10, 1730, Thomas, born at Woburn, November 13, 1681, Jabez, born at Woburn, December 2, 1684, Judith, born at Woburn, June 19, 1690, died 1703 of smallpox

(III) Jabez Fox, son of Jabez Fox (2), was born at Woburn, Massachusetts, February 25, 1705 He was a merchant tailor and maker of woolen cloth He married Hannah Burroughs, daughter of Rev George Burroughs, March 8 1705 Their children were Thomas, born in Boston, December 6, 1706, Hannah, born in Boston, June 27, 1708, Judith, born in Boston, August 19, 1711, Rebecca, born in Boston, 1714

(IV) Thomas Fox, son of Jabez Fox (3), was born in Boston, Massachusetts December 7, 1706 He married Mercy ——— They settled at Woodstock Connecticut, among the first settlers, where he followed the trade of fuller, manufacturing and dressing woolen cloth He resided in a two-story frame house near the famous Putnam wolf cave The old house was destroyed by fire in 1850 He died in 1796 His children were Hannah, born April 27, 1731, Thomas, born April 27, 1731, Thomas, born September 7, 1732, Maria, born April 23, 1735, John, born March 10 1737, Mary, born March 10, 1740, Jabez, born May 6, 1745, Fanny, born November 17, 1749, Rebecca, born July 9, 1753 It is said that there were seven daughters while the names of only five are known It is said also that one of these daughters married ——— Parmenter

(V) Sergeant Jabez Fox, son of Thomas Fox (4), was born at Woodstock, Connecticut, May 6 1745 He married Mary Strobridge, September 28, 1769, at Woodstock She was born August 10 1749, at Middleborough, Massachusetts He was a draper and had a fulling mill at Ketch brook He was the first in this country to make Scotch plaids He was an ardent patriot and was actively engaged in the revolution Sergeant Fox raised a company of men to defend the coast at the time General Arnold the traitor, was attacking Connecticut Sergeant Fox and twelve men were attacked by a largely superior force of British and Tory cavalry The Americans were stationed in a brick school house, where they defended themselves desperately, killing six of the attacking party Then ammunition became exhausted and they attempted to escape through the back window to a swamp in the rear Sergeant Fox, the last to leave the building, was overtaken by the Tory leader, Captain Finch, a man who Fox knew and to whom he appealed for quarter Finch called him a damned Rebel and cut him down with his sabre The sword, coat and hat of Sergeant Fox were preserved in the Boston Atheneum He was killed May 20, 1780, and July 1, 1780, his widow gave birth to a daughter (Hannah) The children of Sergeant Jabez and Mary (Strobridge) Fox were Thomas, born May 12 1770, Polly, born June 20, 1772, William born March 19, 1773, Jabez, born December 13, 1774, died in infancy, Asa, born March 23, 1776, died at City Point, Virginia, of yellow fever, Jabez, born August 5, 1777, Betsey, born February 4 1779, Hannah, born July 1, 1780 The widow of Sergeant Fox married (second) William Spear, by whom she had a daughter Miriam, who married Marvin Mudge and had ten children

(VI) Thomas Fox, son of Sergeant Jabez Fox (5), was born at East Windsor, Connecticut May 22, 1770, and was but ten years old when his father was killed He learned the same trade that his father and grandfather had followed He had a fulling mill first at Westfield, Massachusetts, and later at Tolland, Connecticut He married Chloe Bradley, of Tolland He died of malignant fever November 1, 1811, probably in Ulster county, New York His wife died at Crystal Lake, Henry county, Illinois, aged seventy-two years Their children were William Bradley, born in Scotland, Connecticut, in 1795, Chauncy Johnston, born at Tolland, Connecticut, August 21, 1797, Pliny L, born at Tolland, Connecticut, 1799, Mary, born at Tolland, probably in 1802, Eliza, born at Tolland, Harriet, born at Tolland

(VII) William Bradley Fox, son of Thomas Fox (6), was born in Scotland, Hartford county, Connecticut, in 1795 At the time of his father's death he was only sixteen years of age He was apprenticed to the fuller's trade that had been followed for at least four generations by his ancestors After serving his apprenticeship he married Eliza Ingalls in 1819, and three years later went to Worcester, where he established himself in the business he had learned From a modest fulling mill he developed a large industry He owned the well known Fox's mills and became wealthy He died in 1860 His children were 1 Lemuel Ingalls, born at Tolland Connecticut, January 23, 1821 2 William Bradley, Jr, born at Tolland, Connecticut, April 16, 1823 3 Nancy Jane, born February 10, 1825, married Dr Rufus Woodward, she died December 8, 1905 4 Charles, born in Worcester, June 7, 1827, married Jennett Hyde in 1855, he died 1891, no children 5 Ann Rebecca Sumner, born December 16, 1829 6 Thomas, born February 29, 1832 died young 7 Eliza, born March 23, 1834, married, 1859, C Willard Hamilton, of Worcester, a tape manufacturer, who died Oct 3, 1901, she resides at 37 Oak avenue, Worcester, with her daughter, Fanny Maria, born March 9, 1865, unmarried 1905 8 Thomas, born in Worcester, May 24, 1835, married Mary Feel in 1863, he died 1875, no children 9 Maria Peabody, born in Worcester, September 30 1837, died young 10 Maria, born January 22, 1841, died 1886, unmarried

(VIII) Nancy Jane Fox, daughter of William B Fox (7), was born in Worcester, February 10, 1825, married Dr Rufus Woodward (q v)

(VIII) Rufus Woodward, M D, son of Dr Samuel B Woodward (7) and father of Dr Lemuel F Woodward, was born in Wethersfield, Connecticut, October 3, 1819 He was fitted in the Worcester schools for Harvard College, which he entered in 1837 After his graduation in 1841 he began the study of medicine with Dr Joseph Sargent, and in 1842 entered the Harvard Medical School, from which he graduated in 1845 For three years he was assistant physician at the State Lunatic Hospital, of which his father was the first superintendent Then he spent two years in study in Europe devoting much attention to insanity with the intention of assisting his father in a private asylum at Northampton, Massachusetts His plans were changed by the sudden death of his father in 1850, and on his return home, soon afterward, he began to practice his profession in Worcester His first office was at No 2 Elm street Later he built the house at 52 Pearl street, now occupied by Dr Lemuel F Woodward or "Doctor Lem" as he is universally known to distinguish him from his cousin, Doctor Sam" Woodward This house was built in 1870 For thirty-three years he devoted himself to his profession, seeing patients on the very day of his own sudden death, December 30, 1885, at the age of sixty-six

He was a member of the local and state medical societies During the civil war he was examining surgeon for volunteers, and in 1862 volunteer surgeon under the sanitary commission From 1863 to 1866 he was city physician, and on the formation of the board of health in 1877 was induced to accept the position again He was city physician the remainder of his life and was chairman of the board of health, of which ex-officio he was a member From 1871 to 1880 he was visiting surgeon to the city hospital He was consulting surgeon to the Washburn Dispensary from 1874 till his death He was physician to the House of Correction and to the Orphans' Home For twelve years he was a member of the school board He was elected a member of the American Antiquarian Society in 1861 He was a member of the Harvard Natural History Society and always greatly interested in botany and natural history He was one of the founders of the Worcester Natural History Society, an organization that has shown much activity recently He was president of it for many years Much of Dr Woodward's leisure time was spent in his garden Perhaps nobody in Worcester knew more about the flora of this vicinity than he He was a member of the famous old Worcester Fire Society

He married Nancy Jane Fox, daughter of William B and Eliza Fox She was born in Worcester, February 10, 1825 Her father came to Worcester about 1825 and was the proprietor of the Fox mills at Vernon square He formerly lived at Tolland Connecticut His children were Dr Lemuel F, Rufus S, Ralph, Jane, (see Woodward Family sketch and Dr Samuel B Woodward sketch elsewhere in this work)

(IX) Dr Lemuel F Woodward, son of Dr Rufus Woodward (8), was born in Worcester, April 26, 1857 He attended the public schools of his native city and the high school, preparing for college at the latter institution He graduated from the Lawrence scientific school at Harvard University in 1878 He went to Harvard Medical School where he took his degree of M D in 1882 He spent two years in the Boston City Hospital and the Lying-in Hospital in Boston He began to practice medicine in Worcester, at 49 Pearl street, but soon afterward his father died and he succeeded to his practice and has since occupied his father's offices at 52 Pearl street The medical library alone is exceedingly valuable and interesting from a historical point of view The medical works date back in some cases two centuries and are the collections of four generations of Doctors Woodward The father, grandfather and great-grandfather of Dr Woodward were all noted doctors in their day He has a group of portraits of the three in his office Their libraries and apparatus have descended directly to him With this inheritance of three generations of education and training, of practice and skillfulness, Dr Woodward could scarcely help taking the leading position he has among the surgeons of Worcester His great-grandfather was Dr Samuel Woodward, his grandfather and father have been mentioned here Further history of the family will be found elsewhere in this work

Dr Lemuel F Woodward succeeded his father as city physician of Worcester and held the position until 1893 when he resigned and was succeeded by Dr W T Clark, the present city physician Dr Woodward was the first out-patient surgeon at the City Hospital, when that department was established For the past nine years he has been house surgeon at the City Hospital He has been on the staff of the Memorial Hospital since it was organized This institution was endowed by Ichabod Washburn and incorporated in 1871 A dispensary was opened in 1874 and the hospital in 1888 It is devoted exclusively to the treatment of diseases of women and children He is orthopedic surgeon at St Vincent's Hospital, Worcester He is a member of the Worcester District Medical Society, the Massachusetts Medical Society, the Worcester Natural History Society, of which he is a director, the Worcester Club, the Quinsigamond Boat Club, the Tatassit Canoe Club the Tatnuck Country Club, All Saints' Protestant Episcopal Church In politics he is a Republican

While Dr Woodward has had a general practice in Worcester, he has made surgery a specialty He is called upon to perform a large number of the major operations in the hospitals and ranks among the best and most successful surgeons in this section of the state His personalty helps him win the confidence of his patients His work as city physician among the poorer classes has made him generally popular and his professional skill is recognized by physicians and surgeons as universally as by the public Dr Woodward lived for many years at 52 Pearl street with his mother, who died December 8, 1905 He is unmarried

(IX) Rufus S Woodward, second child of Rufus (8) and Mary Jane (Fox) Woodward, and brother of Dr Lemuel F Woodward, was educated in the public schools of Worcester and Amherst College, from which institution he was graduated with the class of 1881 He was employed by his uncle, Samuel B Woodward, in the hardware firm of Kinnicutt & Co until 1886, and from that time until 1889 by Jerome, Marble & Co From 1889 until 1904 he was a member of the last named firm, which then became the J Russel Marble Company, with which he became identified and with which he continues to be connected He attends All Saints' Protestant Episcopal Church, and in politics is a Republican He is a member of the Quinsigamond Boat Club, of which he was a former president In 1894 he married, at Newburg New York Stella Brooks, daughter of Colonel T Benton and Hannah (Hulse) Brooks Her father was breveted colonel of the First Regiment, New York Engineers, for gallant and meritorious conduct at the siege of Fort Pulaski in Charleston Harbor during the war of the rebellion He is a distinguished geologist and mining engineer Mrs Woodward was educated chiefly in German private schools Mr and Mrs Woodward are the parents of four children, all born in Worcester Rufus Stanley, Jr, born in 1895, Hildegard Hulse, in 1898, Katherine Fox, in 1900, Stella Brooks, born July 2, 1905

ELIAS HARLOW RUSSELL Robert Russell (1) was the emigrant ancestor of Principal E Harlow Russell, of the Worcester State Normal school

Robert Russell is said to have come from Scotland He settled in Andover, Massachusetts and from the strength of his characteristics, or something, the district in which he had his home was called the Scotland District He was there probably in 1677, perhaps earlier He took the oath of fidelity February 11, 1678 He was one of the proprietors in 1681, and doubtless earlier He married Mary Marshall July 6, 1659 He was admitted a freeman in 1691, died December, 1710, in the eightieth year of his age He was the first person buried in the South Parish graveyard His homestead is now, or was recently, owned by a lineal descendant, Dr Ammon Russell

The children of Robert Russell (1) were 1 Robert, died in military service, in war, May 27, 1689 2 Thomas, died 1731, aged sixty-eight 3 Benjamin 4 John, (see forward) 5 James, and perhaps daughters

(II) John Russell, son of Robert Russell (1), born about 1682, at Andover, probably, died 1778 aged ninety-six years four months He married Sarah Chandler and settled in Andover Among his children were John, Joseph

(III) John Russell, son of John Russell (2), was born in Andover, Massachusetts, settled there, and married Hannah Foster Among their children were two who removed to Bethel, Maine 1 Benjamin, born January 27, 1737 married Mary Favor 2 Abraham married Abigail Swan, resided at Bethel, Maine

(IV) Benjamin Russell, son of John Russell (3), born in Andover, Massachusetts, January 27, 1737, married, October 7, 1762, Mary Favor, born March 1, 1739 He removed from Andover and became one of the early settlers at Fryeburg, Maine, in 1767 There he became a leading citizen, serving the town as chairman of the board of selectmen In March 1777, he removed to Bethel, Maine, where he was, in 1779, the first town clerk He performed the duties of magistrate under his commission of justice of the peace His records indicate that he was well educated His penmanship was excellent He was one of the most prominent citizens for many years He died November 23, 1802 His children were 1 Benjamin, Jr, born July 28, 1763, married Mehitable Abbott 2 Mary, born October 15, 1764, married Nathaniel Segar 3 Theodore, born December 6 1765 married Abigail Abbott, of Andover Massachusetts 4 William (see forward) 5 John born at Andover, Massachusetts married Susie Twitchell

(V) William Russell, son of Benjamin Russell (4), born at Andover, Massachusetts, in 1766, removed with his parents to Fryeburg and later to Bethel, Maine, where he died suddenly about 1846 He was a farmer He married Mehitable Kilgore, of Bethel Maine Children were 1 Mehitable born January 4, 1792, married Sebra Dunham of Paris Maine 2 Cynthia born December 20 1793; married William Bent, of Paris 3 Elsie, born

March 8, 1796, married William Bartlett 4 William, born March 12, 1798 5 Elias, (see forward) 6 Samuel, born March 9, 1802, married Hannah Dustin 7 Henry, born February 15, 1804, resided at Newburyport, Massachusetts 8 Mary, born June 13, 1806, married Paul Pearson 9 Theodore, born August 1, 1808, removed from Bethel early 10 Sophia, born August 8, 1811, married Rodney Cole 11 Palmer, born August 1, 1813, removed from Bethel early

(VI) Elias Russell, son of William Russell (5), was born in Bethel, Maine, March 28, 1800 He learned the shoemaker's trade and divided his time between that and farming He settled in Sanbornton, New Hampshire, when a young man, and married, September 29, 1825, Comfort Rundlett, a resident of Sanbornton, though they were married at Northfield, New Hampshire He died January 31, 1868 Their children, all born at Sanbornton, were 1 John Simons born March 30, 1826 2 William Rundlett, born August 7, 1827 3 Mehitable Ann, born December 31, 1828 4 Cynthia Eliza, born July 22, 1832 5 Elias Harlow, (see forward)

(VII) Elias Harlow Russell, son of Elias Russell (6), was born in Sanbornton, New Hampshire, November 27, 1836 His early education was received in the district schools of his native town Like every New Hampshire boy he had more farm work than school in his boyhood He attended the Woodman Sanbornton Academy and the Literary and Biblical Institution at New Hampton, New Hampshire In 1853, while he was still a student at the last named institution, he began to teach school, but continued his study and preparation for his profession and went to the New England Normal Institute at Lancaster, Massachusetts, of which Professor William Russell was the principal This was an admirable school in its day and the principal was an exceptionally gifted teacher and scholar It is now extinct In 1856 Mr Russell taught school again At that time he determined to study medicine and he began to study under the direction of Professor Albert Smith, M D, who was a member of the faculty of Dartmouth College Before completing his course in the Medical school, however, he desired to follow his original purpose to teach, and in 1859 he went back to teaching He was instructor for three years in the teachers' institutes of Grafton and Coos counties, New Hampshire Then he taught in a number of academies and private schools His subject was chiefly elocution Among other institutions he taught in the Highland Military Academy, Worcester, at Eaton's Business College, the predecessor of Hinmann's, in the Board of Trade building, Professor Bushee's Private school in the Walker building, a boarding school in the old Salisbury mansion, Lincoln square For two years and a half he taught in Nichols Academy, Dudley, Massachusetts During the same years, 1861-62-63, he gave three courses of lectures on elocution in the Divinity school of Harvard University In 1864 he accepted the position of principal of the Leroy Academy at Leroy, New York, a non-sectarian school of high character and reputation, and he held this position for ten years In 1894 he was unanimously invited by the State Board of Education to become principal of the Worcester Normal school, then about to be established He accepted, and from that time to the present has been identified with the institution

The Worcester Normal school was established by a Resolve of the general court which went into effect June, 1871 The State Board of Education was authorized and required to establish a State Normal school in Worcester, and the trustees of the Worcester Lunatic Hospital, a state institution, were authorized and required to convey for the purpose a tract of land, of not more than five acres, for a site, to be designated by the governor and his council The site chosen is ideal From the hill on which the Normal school was built the city and surrounding country, with its green hills and orchards, the smoking factory chimneys in the foreground, the picturesque buildings of the city around and about them, spread out like a great panorama below The tract of land was a part of what had been called Hospital Grove The stone for the building was quarried on and near the land where the structure was built The building is massive and dignified The architecture is well suited to the purposes of the building The interior arrangements, designed by Mr Russell for the purposes he had in view, have been found admirably suited to the needs of the institution Another building has been added to the school, for the purpose of a gymnasium It is a valuable adjunct to the institution The Normal school was opened September 15, 1874, and for thirty-one years Mr Russell has been the principal He laid out the general plan in the first place, he has developed the school year by year till its reputation now is second to none among the normal schools of the country

He has always cut loose from stereotyped methods, not so much for the sake of novelty as to develop in the students the special talents or abilities of the individual The graduates of this school begin their teaching with the idea of reaching each of their pupils in different ways, in dealing with each individual according to his needs, and the graduates of the Worcester Normal school have proved the value of Mr Russell's methods during the past thirty years

An apprentice system, developed by the principal along original lines, has been one of the most popular and attractive features of the school The little folks like to go there to school The parents are eager to send their children there for instruction and the students at the school find the training for school work, with real pupils there and in the Worcester schools, extremely valuable This apprentice system accounts in large measure for the high standing of the graduates of this institution compared with those of other schools, where actual experience and practice in the art of teaching is not given

To quote from the school announcement "The design of the Normal school is strictly professional, that is to prepare in the best possible manner the pupils for the work of organizing, governing and teaching the public schools of the Commonwealth It is made a special aim to seize every opportunity to give the pupils the benefit of whatever tends to fit them for the work of teaching The spirit of this endeavor pervades the whole school The knowledge demanded is in great part knowledge of the material to be operated on, and of the conditions and limitations under which the work must be carried on The government of the school is not a government of rules, not even of laws The school is not without law, but the pupils are led by suggestion, encouragement and admonition to become a law unto themselves"

Of course, the primary purpose of the Worcester Normal school is filled when it educates teachers for the public schools About half of the teachers in the Worcester city schools are trained in this school, and many of the graduates find employment in the county There is a very harmonious arrangement between the school and the city school authorities The pupils in the Normal school are given the opportunity to serve in the schools of the city under the direction of the Normal school teachers and the teachers in charge It is an open question whether the city needs the school more than the school needs the city to maintain its present efficiency

Mr Russell was a pioneer in the child study movement and must be reckoned among the foremost investigators of the subject He was one of the earliest to study the child after modern scientific methods, and his was the first Normal school systematically engaged in child-study which has been taken up everywhere in America and Europe in the past twenty years The school work under his direction began in 1884 For twenty years he has been investigating reading, studying, writing papers and making addresses on this subject of Child-Study He has remained at his post at the Normal school, notwithstanding offers of more lucrative positions in other cities He could have been president of the Massachusetts Agricultural College at Amherst He was offered the principalship of the State Normal school at Providence, Rhode Island, and of the Swain Free school, of New Bedford He was offered an attractive place in the faculty of Washington University at St Louis He was on two different occasions offered a vacancy on the board of school supervisors in Boston And when Clark University established its collegiate department he was offered the presidency, and unanimously elected before he had made his decision This great compliment on the part of an institution located in the very city in which his life's work has been largely accomplished was a source of great satisfaction, and he very reluctantly decided finally to adhere to his determination to stay at the Normal school He resigned the post of college president to continue his labors in the Normal school This incident reveals one of the most noticeable characteristics of the man He believes in drilling in one hole, in persisting in a good course once begun It shows, too, how little financial considerations have influenced him in continuing to serve Worcester and the Commonwealth as the principal of the Normal school Everyone of these positions, it is learned, carried with them larger salaries than that of the principalship of this school, some of them very much larger In thirty years Mr Russell seems not to have lost a particle of the enthusiasm and abounding magnetism with which he influences his pupils He seems to have carried into effect the notion of President Eliot, that with the proper training, care and development a man's intellectual and mental powers should improve year after year, regardless of age, unless health fails There is a suggestion of youth and cheerfulness in Mr Russell's words and manner very encouraging and stimulating to all who meet him

He has written a number of papers, printed in the New England Historic-Genealogical Society among them a sketch of a very intimate friend, the late Senator George F Hoar He has written extensively on educational topics, and twice has read papers before the National Educational Association, in Chicago in 1893, and in St Louis in 1904 He has several papers published in the proceedings of the American Antiquarian Society, of which he is a member, and for a number of years member of the council Few literary honors in America are more highly appreciated than honors in the American Antiquarian Society Mr Russell has delivered lectures at the Summer schools of Clarke University, and for two years he was a lecturer in the Harvard University Summer school

He has been a member of the St Wulstan Society, since its organization by the leading scholars and most gifted men of the city He is at present its vice-president He is a member of the Colonial Society, of Massachusetts, of the Friday Evening Club, of Boston, of the Worcester Art Museum corporation, of the State Teachers' Association, of the New Hampshire Forestry Association, of the Appalachian Mountain Club he was formerly a member of the famous old Worcester Fire Society He is a trustee of Leicester Academy He was formerly a member and president of the board of directors of the Free Public Library of Worcester He has been elected honorary member of the Phi Beta Kappa in Massachusetts, notwithstanding the fact that he holds no college degree

He married, November 11, 1862, Harriet Thurston Lee, daughter of George W and Laura (Sanford) Lee, a native of Lancaster, Massachusetts, where they were married She died October 22, 1900 Their children were 1 Lee, born at Leroy, New York, January 8, 1865, graduate of the Worcester Polytechnic Institute, member of the faculty of the State Normal school, married Alice L B Woodworth July 4, 1894, and had Ralph, born January 14, 1900, Helen, born October 28, 1901, Walter, born April 1 1905 2 Olive, born at Leroy, New York, March 23 1867, kindergartner graduate of the State Normal school 3 Philip, born July 24, 1869, died September 16, 1895, at Worcester, unmarried 4 Ernest, born at Leroy, New York, September 28, 1871, clerk in the Worcester County Institution of Savings, married July 9 1897, Ella G Price, daughter of William B and Rebecca E Price Their children are Robert Price, born July 16 1898 Elizabeth, born May 9, 1903, Sidney Lee, born in Worcester, February 1, 1905

DR WESLEY DAVIS was born in Waitsfield, Vermont (now called Northfield), September 5 1841, the son of Horace Atkins and Harriet (Bradley) Davis His grandfather was John B Davis His ancestral line runs as follows

(I) Thomas Davis, of Amesbury married Deborah Martin December 15 1709 Their children were 1 Abigail, born October 6 1710 2 Thomas, born February 28 1711-12 3 Mary, born January 17, 1713-14 4 Sarah, born January 20, 1715 5. Amos, born November 28, 1718 6 Meribah, born January 21, 1719 7 Moses, born January 16. 1721, married Mary Whittier 8 Timothy, born March 1, 1723

(II) Amos Davis, son of Thomas (1), born November 28, 1718, at Amesbury, Massachusetts He was in Newton New Hampshire 1758 in Upson, New Hampshire, 1765, in Danville, New Hampshire, 1767, in Bradford Vermont, between 1768 and 1784, and died at Warner, New Hampshire, 1803, leaving a widow His son John, of Warner, New Hampshire, was his administrator Amos Davis married (first) Alice Carrier and had 1 Allis, born April 9, 1748 2 Abigail born March 22, 1750, married (second) Hannah Blank ——— and had 1 Amos born October 26 1752 2 Benjamin, born October 24, 1754 3 Hannah born November 8, 1756 4 John born August 12, 1758

(III) Benjamin Davis son of Amos (2), born October 24, 1754 at Newton New Hampshire He was in Bradford, Vermont from 1768 to 1793 served in the revolutionary war as private under Captain Frye Braley and Colonel Peter Olcott, one month and four days from September 23 1777, receiving three pound sterling for service in two hundred and seventy miles travel and must have been present at the surrender of Burgoyne In 1781 he served for

Wm. E. Fyfe
Clinton Mass

a short period on scouts under Captain Joseph Huber and Major John Barton. In 1786 he was elected petit juror and in 1788 was a grand juror. In 1790 he was second constable and collector, and in 1792 lister. In 1793 he was petit juror, trustee of schools and lister. April 4, 1793, he sold his homestead in Bradford to his brother-in-law Stephen Jenkins, and moved with his family to Duxbury, Vermont. In 1794 he was elected town representative, being the first one ever elected by the town of Duxbury. In 1795 and in 1805 he also served as town representative. He died October 13, 1830, in Duxbury, and his gravestone inscription reads, "Captain Benjamin Davis," the title doubtless coming from his militia service. He married Betsey Jenkins and they had: 1. Abigail, born May 28, 1774. 2. Amos, born December 17, 1775. 3. Betsey, born April 18, 1778. 4. Hannah, born April 14, 1783. 5. Pally, born May 18, 1785. 6. Elijah, born November 6, 1787. 7. John Barron, born October 2, 1790. 8. Lydia Styles, born August 29, 1792. 9. Andrew (date not known). The mother, Betsey (Jenkins) Davis, died April 28, 1814, aged sixty years.

(IV) John Barron Davis, son of Benjamin Davis (3), born October 2, 1790, married (first) Nancy Atkins, daughter of (6), John (5), John (4), Josiah (3), Josiah (2), William (1). Their children were: Azro, Charles, Chandler, Mary, Ellen, Horace. The mother died March 6, 1834, and Mr. Davis married (second) Lucius Cobb, and had: Nancy, Laura, John.

(V) Horace Atkins Davis, son of John (4), born June 20, 1819, in Duxbury, Massachusetts, married Harriet Newell Braley (6), Silas (5), John (4), Roger (3), Roger (2), Roger (1). Children were: 1. Wesley, born at Northfield, Vermont, September 15, 1841. 2. George Washington, born at same place, March 26, 1847. 3. Lydia Ann, born at Duxbury, Vermont, June 11, 1849.

(VI) Dr. Wesley Davis, son of Horace Davis (5), born September 15, 1841, was educated in the academy of his native town and at the University of Vermont. He graduated from the Pittsfield Medical school in 1866, and began the practice of his chosen profession at Westport, New York. In 1869 he came to Worcester, where he practiced his profession. He was for twenty-one years visiting physician of the city hospital. He was the owner of the five story Adams apartment house—a family hotel at number 1 High street, Worcester, where he had his office.

November 1, 1866, he married Cynthia H. Adams, daughter of Daniel Adams, of Parton, Vermont, for whom Adams Ferry was named. Three sons were born to them: George A., September 16, 1868; Nellie Harriatt, June 14, 1872, died September 14, 1872; Edwin H., November 2, 1874; Daniel A. W., April 5, 1882.

FYFE FAMILY. The family to which William E. Fyfe, deceased, of Clinton, Massachusetts, belonged was from William Fyfe, the first American ancestor, who emigrated from Fifeshire, Scotland, and early in 1700 settled upon a tract of land in Bolton, Massachusetts. This William (I) had a son named William (II), who married and had among his children a son named William (III). The line runs thus:

(I) William Fyfe, the Scotch immigrant, came to Bolton about 1700.

(II) William Fyfe, son of William (1).

(III) William Fyfe, son of William (2).

(IV) William Fyfe, son of William (3), born August 10, 1837.

(II) William Fyfe, grandfather of the late William E. Fyfe, of Clinton, succeeded to the farm which had been cleared and improved by his father, and devoted the years of his life to agriculture. He was one of the best farmers of Bolton and took a leading part in public matters in his town. He died at the age of seventy-six years.

(III) William Fyfe, father of the late William E. Fyfe, of Clinton, was reared on the old homestead farm. When a young man he engaged in teaming and transporting produce to the Boston market. He later returned to the old farm and married, but eventually settled on another farm in the same neighborhood and there spent the remainder of his days. His wife's maiden name was Sally Carruth; she was born in Spencer, Massachusetts. He was her second husband. By her union with Mr. Fyfe, she had three children, of whom William E. was one. The father, William Fyfe, died at the age of sixty-four years. She died at the age of sixty-three. They attended the Unitarian and Baptist churches, respectively.

(IV) William E. Fyfe, son of William and Sally (Carruth) Fyfe, was born in Bolton, Massachusetts, August 10, 1837, on the old Fyfe homestead. He received his education at the common schools of his native place, but only remained in school until thirteen years of age, when his services were needed on his father's farm. He there found employment as a mill operator and in a shoe shop. When seventeen years of age, he went to Cambridge, where for two years he drove a bread-cart and later a wagon for the Kennedy Cracker Co. for four years. He clerked for a short time in a grocery, and then opened a grocery store of his own, conducting the same for two years and met with good success. He finally disposed of his business and purchased a bakery, which he conducted in connection with the grocery business. This he followed eight years, when he sold out and removed to Clinton, Massachusetts, where he engaged in the real estate business and erected a handsome residence known as the "Fyfeshire" on the Bolton Hills. After three years he sold this property and bought a sixty-two acre farm, and for five years devoted his time and energy to the raising of garden produce. He then sub-divided his place, reserving a large share for himself and sold many lots upon which to-day may be seen many dwellings. His real estate business proved one of success and he was financially rewarded.

For two years he carried on the bakery business at Clinton and was for twelve years interested in a large comb factory, being the director and purchasing agent. For eight years he was engaged as a partner with B. L. Nowell & Co., of Montreal, in the horn-glue stock and Canada ash business. Not many years since he formed a partnership with E. L. Plummer for the purpose of carrying on the butter business. This firm later was consolidated with that of C. M. Fay, and in April, 1895, moved to the new and spacious quarters in a business house erected for them by Mr. Fyfe. This firm was known as Fyfe, Fay and Plummer, who carried on an extensive retail and wholesale grocery and produce business. Mr. Fyfe was also a director in the Clinton Wall Trunk Co. Politically Mr. Fyfe was a Republican. He served as road commissioner for five years. Both he and his wife were members of the Baptist church.

In 1861 Mr. Fyfe married Josephine Carruth, born in Cambridgeport, Massachusetts, June 25, 1839, daughter of C. Edward Carruth, a grocer of that city. By this marriage one daughter was born, Dora I., who married Edward L. Plummer, her father's business associate. They have three children—Helen L., Josephine Fyfe and George Fyfe Plummer.

Mr Fyfe was an extensive traveler, both in this country and in Europe and Canada The beautiful residence he erected was built in the most thorough manner and contains every modern improvement In his estate was a thirty-two acre tract of land, being part of the old Fyfe homestead This land has been greatly improved and it should be recorded as a part of the original tract granted by the king It is now a beautiful park and has a small lake He, in his lifetime, provided that it should go to a charitable institution, and be forever known as the "Fyfeshire" in honor of its ancestral history, coming as it did, direct from the king In the midst of life surrounded by all that tended to give him pleasure, in the enjoyment of the handsome fortune he had accumulated by industry, when all bid fair for many more years, both he and his estimable daughter were killed by a railway train, upon a crossing in Lancaster, June 23 1899 The funeral was among the largest attended of any in the country, showing in what esteem they were held

CHARLES B GATES The Worcester family of descendants of the emigrant Stephen Gates has been traced elsewhere in this work in detail The line of descent of Charles B Gates, of Worcester, is as follows

(I) Stephen Gates descendant in England from Thomas Gates of Higheaster and Thurseubie, Essex county 1327 through William, Peter, Geoffrey, Geoffrey, Sir Geoffrey, William, Sir Geoffrey William and Thomas Gates He was the son of Thomas Gates of Norwich Norfolk county, England, and came to Hingham, Massachusetts, in 1638, removed to Lancaster, then to Cambridge, Massachusetts He died at Cambridge in 1662 His children were Elizabeth, Mary, Stephen, Thomas, Simon, Isaac, and Rebecca

(II) Simon Gates, son of Stephen Gates was born 1645 died April 21, 1693, at Brockton Massachusetts He married Margaret —— and they resided at Cambridge Lancaster and Brookline, Massachusetts Their children were Abigail Simon, Simon 2d George Amos Jonathan, Samuel, Margaret

(III) Simon Gates, son of Simon Gates (2), born January 5, 1675-6, died March 10 1735, married May 29 1710 Sarah Wood, and settled in Marlboro Their children were Simon, Sarah, Susannah, Stephen, Solomon, Samuel, Silas, John

(IV) Solomon Gates son of Simon Gates (3), born May 14 1721 died March 2, 1761, at Worcester, Massachusetts married Mary Clark and lived at Worcester Their children were Sarah, Samuel, Mary Paul Silas and James

(V) Samuel Gates, son of Solomon Gates (4), born at Worcester, Massachusetts, January 1, 1750-1, died December 19, 1831, married Lucy Chadwick He was a soldier in the revolution His children were 1 Joel, born March 7, 1782 2 Polly, born October 12 1783 3 Joshua, born June 19 1787 4 Willard, born October 15, 1793 5 Henry Brazer, born August 1 1797 6 Nahum born June 10, 1801 All the foregoing were born at Worcester, Massachusetts

(VI) Joel Gates son of Samuel Gates (5) born at Worcester, Massachusetts, March 7 1782, died in Worcester 1856 married Joanna Stearns May 17 1805 at Worcester They settled on the old Gates farm at Bloomingdale now in large part occupied by the state hospital for the insane The old house is owned by A Frank Gates Later in life he resided on Prospect street He married (second) —— Wood All his children were by the first wife The children were according to Worcester records 1 Leonard born January 3 1805 2 John, born March 1 1807 3 Charles Emory, born April 13 1806 4 Harriet Porter, born April 17, 1810 5 Lucy Chadwick, born June 22 1813 6 Samuel, born December 19, 1817 7 Mary Walker, born October 27 1818

(VII) John Gates, son of Joel Gates (6), born in Worcester, March 1, 1806, died at Worcester December 12, 1877 He was raised on the old Gates homestead at Bloomingdale, and educated in the Worcester schools He learned the carpenter's trade and worked at it in Worcester for a number of years About 1831 he began business as an undertaker with an office and shop on School street, adding the lumber business in a small way in 1835, and continued to deal in lumber until his death He sold the undertaking business to his partner, W G Maynard, about 1845, and bought the place on Union street where the lumber yard of John Gates and of John Gates Sons has since been located Before starting for himself he had been in partnership for a time with Henry Golding in the manufacture of woolen machinery Golding subsequently sold his business to R B Wetherbee Mr Gates carried on an extensive lumber business with marked success He was one of the substantial business men of the old school in Worcester

He married Betsey W Allen, of Plymouth, Massachusetts Their children, all born in Worcester, were 1 George Allen, born January 7, 1833, now associated with his brother Charles B Gates, proprietor of the business conducted as John Gates' Sons lumber dealers at 179 Union street, Worcester 2 Harriet Davis, born January 8, 1836 3 John Bradford, born April 16, 1839 4 Mary Elizabeth, born March 3 1841 5 Albert Holmes, born July 14 1842 6 Albert Stearns, born January 21 or 23, 1844 7 Emory Winslow, born June 22, 1848 8 Charles B, born September 12, 1851

(VIII) Charles B Gates, son of John Gates, was born in Worcester, Massachusetts, September 12, 1851 His early home was on Central street He attended the public schools, Worcester Academy and Leicester Academy He entered the University of Michigan as a special student, and graduated there from the Law Department in 1874 with the degree of LL B He practiced law in Michigan for a short time, then returned to Worcester He was admitted to the Worcester county bar in 1875, and opened an office in Fitchburg Massachusetts Two years before his father died the lumber business on Union street was closed out In November, 1877, Charles B Gates and his brother Emory W Gates decided to revive the business A partnership was formed under the firm name of John Gates' Sons The taste for a business life was stronger in Mr Gates than the love of a professional career as a lawyer, so he abandoned law to take up his father's business as a lumber merchant Unfortunately his brother died at the very outset of the new firm's career in 1880, and Charles B Gates has carried the business on alone really building it up to its present proportions The name of his firm stands well among business men The central location has perhaps given the business some advantages for retail trade Mr Gates simply buys and sells every kind of lumber according to the demand He has no mill and manufactures none of his stock As a business man he ranks high He has tended pretty closely all his life to his business interests and has not entered politics or other business He is well known in Masonic circles He is a member of Athelstan Lodge, of Eureka Chapter of Hiram Council Lawrence Chapter of Rose Croix Worcester County Commandery, and has taken the thirty-second degree in the Scottish Rite

N. H. Fairbanks

in Masonry He is a member of the college fraternity Phi Delta Phi, which is especially strong in the western colleges He is a Republican

He married February 2, 1881, Ida Evelina Noble, at Ann Arbor, Michigan She was the daughter of Charles E Noble and Jerusha P (Crosman) Noble Her mother was born at St Johnsbury, Vermont, 1824, and removed in 1830 to Michigan, where the family settled Her father was in the railroad business, and during the last years of his life was general eastern agent of the Michigan Central and Great Western Railroad with offices in the Astor House, New York city He died in New York, 1873 Her mother is living (1905) at the age of eighty-one She was born November 22, 1851, at Detroit where the family was then located They have two children, both born in Worcester 1 Burton Noble, born December 19, 1881, spent two years in Cornell University, graduated at Clark College, Worcester, in 1905, and will take graduate courses in Clark University next year His specialty in college has been biology 2 Aleene Crosman, born September 28, 1886, graduate of the South high school at Worcester, now a student in the Burnham Preparatory school at Northampton, Massachusetts

JOSEPH CHARLOTLE DAPPER, artist, of Worcester, was born in Rhine, Hessen, Germany, April 12, 1861, a son of Matthew and Emilie (Miller) Dapper, who were born in Mayennce, on the Rhine, Germany Matthew Dapper (father) served in the capacity of judge They were the parents of three other children, all of whom reside in Germany and are married, namely Eugenia, Ludwig, who serves as judge in a high court, and Franz, a district attorney in Metz

Joseph C Dapper pursued a course of study in art at the Royal Academy in Munich under the famous painter, Carl von Piloty, who for the greater part of his life, was a member and professor of the Munich Academy He began his studies in 1878 and continued up to 1883, a period of five years In 1884 he came to the United States, locating in New York city, and for a time was engaged in the practice of his profession with several artists Later he opened a studio in the building on the southwest corner of Fifth avenue and Fourteenth street, New York city, where he remained for a number of years In 1899 he took up his residence in Worcester, Massachusetts, and opened a studio in the Dexter building, No 540 Main street He makes a specialty of portrait work, in which line he is highly proficient

In the city of New York, September 2, 1891, Mr Dapper was united in marriage to Miss Alexandria C Enig, who was born in Roeskilde, Denmark, January 5, 1868, a daughter of Andreas Enig, a musician Their children are May W, Alice E, Harry H, and Helen E Their residence is at No 80 Merrick street, Worcester

WILLIAM HENRY FAIRBANKS Jonathan Fairbanks (1), the immigrant ancestor of William Henry Fairbanks, of Clinton, Massachusetts was born in England before 1600 and came to Boston with his family in 1633, remained there about three years, and then settled in Dedham, where he was one of the pioneers He was a singer of the famous Dedham Covenant His house is still standing at Dedham and is now owned by the family association, having been occupied to the present time by Jonathan and his lineal descendants He was admitted to the church August 14, 1646, and was a town officer He married Grace Lee, who died December 28, 1673 He died at Dedham, December 5, 1668, and his will was proved January 26 following The children John, died November 13, 1684, George, died January 10, 1682-3, Mary, born April 18, 1622, married Michael Metcalf, Susan, married October 12, 1647, Ralph Day, of Dedham, Jonas, see forward, Jonathan, Jr, died January 28, 1711-2

(II) Jonas Fairbanks, son of Jonathan Fairbanks (1), was born in England, and came to Dedham with his parents He signed the covenant in 1657, and March 7, 1659, became one of the fathers of the town He was a farmer and believed to be a carpenter also In 1652 he was fined for wearing great boots, not being worth two hundred pounds, the amount of wealth prescribed by the laws of the colony in 1651 to suffice for men who could lawfully wear great boots He removed to Lancaster in 1657 There he met his death in the assault by King Philip and fifteen hundred warriors, February 10, 1675-6 Some fifty persons were slain that day, including Joshua Fairbanks, son of Jonas

Jonas Fairbanks married, May 28, 1658, Lydia Prescott, daughter of John Prescott, who came from Sowerby, Halifax, England, the same place that the Fairbanks came from Lydia was born in Watertown, August 15, 1641 After Fairbanks was killed she married (second) Ellis Barron, of Watertown, Groton and Lancaster The children of Jonas Fairbanks Marie, born June 20, 1659, Joshua, April 6, 1661, killed by Indians, Grace, November 15, 1663, Jonathan, October 7, 1666 Hasadiah, February 28, 1668, married John Moore of Concord, January 1, 1698, Jabez, January 8, 1670-1, see forward, Jonas, May 6, 1673, was of Watertown, 1695-6, when he sold to brother Jabez land of their father Jonas, died September 13, 1697 and is buried in his brother Jonathan's lot

(III) Captain Jabez Fairbanks, son of Jonas Fairbanks (2), was born at Lancaster, January 8 1670-1, and he settled there after the war He died March 2, 1758, aged eighty-seven He was a very efficient soldier and officer in the Indian war, and was no doubt incited to heroic exploits by the massacre of his father and brother in 1676 and of his only surviving brother in 1697 during a raid on the town At the time his brother Jonathan and one of his children were killed, Captain Jabez was the means of saving a garrison and perhaps many lives including that of his own little son Joseph Twenty-one persons were killed in this raid, two were wounded and six carried off captives, of whom five were ransomed later, including the wife of Jonathan Fairbanks In 1700 Jabez had lands laid down to him on both sides of Dane's brook above Thomas Sawyer's saw mill This site was the homestead of Jabez and his descendants for a hundred years He was deputy to the general court in 1714-21-22-23

He married Mary Wilder, daughter of Thomas and Mary (Houghton) Wilder, who died February 21, 1718, in her forty-third year He married (second), March 25, 1719, Elizabeth Whitcomb, who died May 11, 1755, aged about eighty years The children of Jabez and Mary were Joseph, born 1693, see forward, Jabez, Elizabeth, married Deliverance Brown, December 24, 1718, Jonas, Thomas, Abigail, married Major Henry Willard, of Ashburnham, descendant of Major Simon Willard, Jonathan baptized June 18, 1710, Grace, baptized February 27, 1712, married Joseph Brown, March 27, 1733, Joshua, baptized March 28, 1714, Anna, baptized November 18, 1716, married, April 5, 1738, Simon Butler

(IV) Deacon Joseph Fairbanks, son of Jabez Fairbanks (3), was born in Lancaster, Massachusetts, 1693, and died at Harvard, December 6

1772, in his seventy-fourth year The section of Lancaster in which he lived was set off in the new township of Harvard in 1732, and he was dismissed from the First Church at Lancaster to the new church at Harvard, September 9, 1733 He was selectman of Harvard in 1733-35-43-45-52, and was town treasurer from 1736 to 1740 He was the first deputy to the general court from the town, sent in 1740, but he declined and Peter Atherton served instead He was a prominent citizen for many years and was on most of the town committees appointed to protest against and resist British aggression The old homestead at Harvard is owned by Andrew Fairbanks It was built about the year 1720

Deacon Joseph Fairbanks married, April 21, 1718, Mary Brown, who died November 14, 1791, aged ninety-one years, eleven months and six days Their children Phineas born April 8, 1719, Mary, October 17, 1721, died October 22, 1721 Joseph, November 4, 1722, Mercy, February 6, 1724-5 died February 17, 1724-5, Cyrus, May 23, 1726, died September 3, 1736, Mary, January 19, 1729, married, October 12, 1748, John Priest, Lydia, August 16, 1731, married, February 18, 1756, Manasseh Sawyer, Elizabeth, May 1, 1734, died November 19, 1736, Amos, April 21, 1737, Relief, December 31, 1739, married December 31, 1760, Caleb Sawyer

(V) Captain Amos Fairbanks, son of Deacon Joseph Fairbanks (4), was born in Harvard, Massachusetts, April 21, 1737 He was a farmer He was a soldier in the French war, a private in the foot company from Harvard commanded by Captain Israel Taylor, of Harvard, Colonel Oliver Wilder's regiment, in 1757 He was an ensign in the oldest military company in 1774 was lieutenant when the company responded to the Lexington call, April, 1775 and captain in the miscellaneous service during the revolution He was on the committee of safety and correspondence in Harvard, 1780 He was deacon of the church, elected November 28, 1786 resigned November 4, 1798 He died January 4, 1809, aged seventy-one years, eight months and twenty-three days

He married (first), April 23, 1760, Lucy Gates, who died November 12, 1767, aged twenty-eight years, twelve days He married (second) Rhoda Sawyer, who died February 23, 1813, aged seventy-two years Children of Captain Amos and Lucy Fairbanks were Jacob, born June, 1761, died young, Jacob, May 6, 1762, Lucy, March 24, 1764, married Reuben Whitney, Mercy, March 28, 1766 The children of Captain Amos and Rhoda Fairbanks Amos, born September 5, 1769, see forward, Noah, June 23, 1771, Rhoda, June 15, 1774, married Josiah Haskell, Jr , Joseph, February 19, 1776, Daniel, October 20, 1778, died March 10, 1779, Mary, February 24, 1781

(VI) Amos Fairbanks, son of Captain Amos Fairbanks (5), was born at Harvard, Massachusetts, September 5, 1769 died March 28, 1837 He settled at Harvard, on the old farm He married, April 27, 1794, Rebecca Whitney, born April 13 1777, daughter of Israel and Hannah (Mead) Whitney, of Harvard She died at Charlestown, Massachusetts, October 15, 1763 at the home of her daughter Eliza Seymour, aged eighty-six years Their children all born at Harvard, were Horace, October 15, 1795, resided at Boston married Amelia Dodge July 13, 1818, Amos, November 27 1799, Clark, February 13, 1802 died May 7, 1885, Israel W November 1, 1804 Zopher October 20 1806 resided at Duxbury married Harriet C Longley, December 31 1833 died December 14 1879, Rebecca, August 5, 1808, married, February 23, 1836, Edmund Sawyer, of Warner, New Hampshire, Henry, June 11, 1811, see forward, William, May 4, 1813, died 1817, Eliza, September 6, 1718, married, October, 1844, Friend Seymour, and lived at Charlestown

(VII) Henry Fairbanks, son of Amos Fairbanks (6), was born at Harvard, Massachusetts, June 11, 1811, on the old homestead He received a common school education in his native town and learned the butcher s trade He was in business in Princeton and Sterling, and drove a market wagon to Boston from 1850 to 1870 About 1870 he removed to Sudbury and subsequently returned to Sterling, where he died January 18, 1897, in the eighty-sixth year of his age He married Martha Conant, who died August 25, 1858, in Princeton, and is buried in Acton, Massachusetts He married (second) Sarah A Moore, of Sudbury, who died in Sterling and was buried in Sudbury He married (third) Lucinda Brown, died in Sudbury. The children of Henry and Martha Fairbanks were William Henry, born at Littleton, November 7, 1841, see forward, Martha Ann born at Littleton, died aged eight years, Ellen Maria, died December 9, 1897, Albert Conant, born September 5, 1852, married Emma T Sprague, Curtis Albio, born September 27, 1855, died 1871 Albert Conant Fairbanks is a successful manufacturer of musical instruments, and wood rims for bicycles and other vehicles, the patent for which is his His company has a large plant for manufacturing the wooden rims in England and also at Tonawanda, New York He was a member of the city council of Somerville, Massachusetts, in 1893-94

(VIII) William Henry Fairbanks, son of Henry Fairbanks (7), was born at Littleton, Massachusetts, November 7, 1841 He was educated in the public schools of the neighboring towns of Sterling and Acton He became associated with his father in the meat business In 1865 he started in business on his own account in South Lancaster In 1867 he removed to Hudson, Massachusetts, and carried on the meat and provision business there for three years From 1870 to 1875 he was in the manufacturing business in Boston, making rubber syringes and other goods He settled in Clinton in 1875 and since then has been engaged in the meat and provision business there He has also dealt extensively in cattle and horses, buying his stock in the west by the carload He has been successful in business and commands the esteem and confidence of his townsmen He is a Republican in politics, but has never cared for public office

He married, at Sterling, Mary Jennie Bailey, born at Northborough, Massachusetts, March 3, 1840, died September 5, 1895, daughter of Charles M and Mary (Rice) Bailey Her father was a tanner by trade The children May Bailey, born May 30, 1871, formerly a teacher in the Clinton public schools, now residing at home, Harry Conant, born October 23, 1881, now a partner in his father's business

LAWRENCE WILLMORE PENNINGTON. Arthur Pennington (1), father of Lawrence Willmore Pennington, of Worcester, Massachusetts, was born in Birmingham, England He married Sarah Shaw, daughter of William Shaw, of Birmingham, England They were married at Birmingham and lived there He was a tool maker and chain maker by trade After making ready to go to America twice they finally started in March, 1854, with their son Lawrence • Arthur Pennington died on the voyage over His widow remained in Boston for about two years and then returned to her old home in Birmingham, England, with her two children, the younger having been born on the voyage to America A few years later she married William Empson, and had several children, only one of whom is now living, Emma, who married John Asbury, and now or recently was living in Providence, Rhode Island Sarah Shaw, mother of Lawrence W Pennington, was the only daughter among thirteen children borne by her mother Her father married twice and had in all twenty-five children (She died in Birmingham in 1869) The children of Arthur Pennington were Lawrence Willmore, born at Birmingham, England, February 26, 1852, Arthur, born on the voyage from England to America, March, 1854, returned to England, came to Providence, Rhode Island, after he was grown up, but soon returned to his native place, where he married Julia Howland

(II) Lawrence Willmore Pennington, son of Arthur Pennington (1), was born in Birmingham, England, February 26, 1852 He came to America first with his parents when two years old and returned a few years later to England with his mother and brother He was brought up and educated in Birmingham He is a graduate of Midland Institute, receiving in 1873 the degree of Master of Arts He had specially good training in draughting and designing, for which he early showed a special aptitude

He learned the trade of manufacturing jeweler and followed his trade in England for a time In 1870 and 1871 he was designer and pattern maker for Joseph Josephs & Son St Paul s Square, Birmingham, England, who had at that time the reputation of making the highest grade and most costly diamond and precious stone jewelry of any makers in England In 1871 he patented his first invention, a reversible "E" ring top, and sold forty-three designs at considerable profit In 1872 he patented a scarf stud and sold sixty-one designs In 1873 he patented eighteen designs used in the jewelry trade, a window curtain pulley, a new suspender buckle, a separable cuff button, patented in the United States, and sold to George Mason In 1873 he came to the United States and located at Providence, Rhode Island, where he worked as foreman for a number of the large manufacturing establishments, such as Thomas Quail's Mehm & Hutchins, and here he invented his method of iridescent coloring of metals, which was a great money maker for him He also had a secret process for straight and for basket coloring that was in great demand He invented about this time a contrivance for bending scrolls and another for setting stones and pearls In 1874 he returned to England and stayed about three years, and while there patented several more valuable patents, one of which netted him for some time a hundred pounds a week He made a machine for cutting joints for bracelets and lockets

He returned to the United States in 1878 After working a short time at Newark, New Jersey, he returned to Providence Rhode Island Here he taught the workmen of Dity Wilcox the trade of diamond ring manufacturing He opened his own shop on Peck street, Providence, in 1878, and began to manufacture jewelry Much of his work, however, was applying his process of coloring and lapping to the work of other Providence jewelry manufacturers For Rice, Allen & Mason alone he did contract work to the amount of seventy-five dollars a day profit Twice he enlarged his shop, moving first to Dyer street then to Eddy street In 1887 he transferred his business to Worcester In 1879 he sold George Mason his process for inlaying and producing colors on metals From 1878 to the time of his removal to Worcester he produced a series of valuable inventions, used by manufacturers of jewelry, most of which are of too technical a nature to be described here

His first location in Worcester was at 81 Mechanic street, where he made all kinds of jewelers' goods to order He developed a large business, designing all kinds of jewels, diamond settings, designing and making emblems, badges and insignia of all sorts He made goods for retail jewelers in all parts of the state He had to move soon to better quarters on Main street, at the corner of Mechanic He continued to experiment, invent and patent new devices In 1886 he invented a method of soldering metal to glass, in 1891 he brought out his process for soldering aluminum, in 1891, after he had become interested in pyrography, he invented a poker for the work, and in 1894 devised the electric pencil, for permanent writings and drawings on glass, china and all delicate surfaces, in 1896 he invented a new process for casting gold and silver hollow It is doubtful if any man in his line of work has produced more useful and numerous inventions than Mr Pennington He continues to experiment as he has the opportunity

He opened a retail store at 6 Elm street in connection with his manufacturing business In 1904 he removed to No 377 Main street, where he is now located Mr Pennington has made many famous designs He made the Ten Eyck charm and pin, and the Prince Henry souvenir, consisting of the Worcester city seal wrought in ivory and silver, presented to Prince Henry of Prussia, March 6, 1902, by the citizens of Worcester As far back as 1869 he took a queen's prize for pencil drawing of his teacher In 1870 he took a prize for a bronze design He has a burnt wood picture in the Dublin Art Gallery and a portrait of President Roosevelt in the White House

It is as an artist in burnt wood that Mr Pennington has made himself famous He was a few years ago conceded to be the best artist in burnt wood in this country Pyrography has become in the last few years the most attractive and popular form of art among all classes and ages The beautiful and skillful work of Mr Pennington has done as much to inspire the devotion to this form of art as anything else His exhibitions have interested many to learn how to do burnt wood pictures When Mr Pennington began to burn pictures on wood he found the art in a crude state He broke away from the conventional scrolls and designs and attempted successfully pictures requiring delicate shading and coloring He was probably the first artist to make a distinctly successful picture of nude figures in burnt wood The first large production which is now famous, is the "Diana s Hunting Party," owned by J F Regan, of Worcester This picture brings out in elaborate detail thirteen figures over fifteen inches in height, while the effect of foliage and water is produced very naturally and effectively This picture is as large as the original painting, eight feet long and forty-two inches in width The original painting by Hans Makart in the Metropolitan Art Museum of New York is one of the best known productions of any artist At the time Mr Pennington made this beautiful specimen of his art, it was pronounced the largest, most elaborate and artistic specimen of pyrography ever produced

Mr Pennington has made many hundreds of pictures since he began to study burnt wood art He has been a prize winner in exhibitions in New York, Chicago and Boston, besides numerous exhibitions in smaller cities One collection of his pictures was exhibited in London and Germany Among his best are Reveries' and 'The Golden Age" While much of his work is original in design, he has made very artistic reproductions of many famous paintings, such as Rosa Bonheur's Head of a Lion' Paul Potter's "Head of a Bull and Cow," 'Lion in His Cage," and Words of Comfort," which is a specially fine piece of work representing an aged woman reading to her husband, sick in bed Another large production of Mr Pennington's is the Battle of Newbern," which is forty-four inches in length and fourteen in width, containing four hundred and thirty different figures He made for Nathan I Durlech, of New York, a reproduction of 'Nymphs and Satyr" a well known painting Another specimen of his best work is 'Bacchante Awakening," a life size nude figure, beautifully drawn and colored It is fifty-four inches by seventy-two inches in size It is a copy of the painting by Frederick Kraus Another large work is a reproduction of Le Quesne's 'The Daughters of Menistho," four feet five and three-fourth inches by six feet, one inch The 'Nymphs and Satyr" picture was the largest of all, being six feet by nine and a half One of his most successful collections of burnt etchings consisted of portraits of members of the Mitchell family of London, made from photographs It is impossible to give an adequate idea of the extent and variety of Mr Pennington's work with poker and aluminum pencil He received much assistance from his daughter, Lavinia, who was also a clever artist Mr Pennington has never joined any secret orders and is not a club man Most of his burnt wood pictures were produced at home evenings For the past thirteen years he has resided at No 13 June street, Worcester

He married September 6 1871 Selma Cashmore, daughter of Edward and Elizabeth Cashmore, at Birmingham England Her father is still living in that city at an advanced age She died January, 1898 He married (second) Lucy Chaffee daughter of James H and Laura Chaffee of Berkshire Vermont June 20 1905 at Worcester The children of Lawrence W and Selma (Cashmore) Pennington were Lawrence, born at Birmingham, England, February 24, 1873 married Lillian Wheeler, of Grafton, has one daughter, Selma Lavinia, born January 16 1876 married at Worcester, January 29 1904, Dr Nicholas William Hoffman of Dubuque, Iowa, dean of the N A R D. resides in Worcester

Arthur H Hioms professor of Electro-Metallurgy in the Midland Institute at Birmingham England, married Elizabeth Cashmore sister of Mrs Pennington His text books known as "Mixed Metal and Metallic Alloys," 'Elementary Metallurgy," "Iron and Steel Manufacturing' and 'Practical Metallurgy and Assaying'—are used in this country by most all the teachers of that line in the colleges, and his works are accepted as authority on the various subjects

THE STEWART BOILER WORKS of Worcester, well known throughout the New England states and which stands high among the leading industries of the city of Worcester sustaining a reputation for thorough workmanship and honorable dealing has since September, 1888 been under the ownership of James C, John C and Charles M Stewart sons of Charles Stewart a native of Glasgow Scotland who learned his trade in England Upon his arrival in Worcester, Massachusetts Charles Stewart began manufacturing boilers for Bellows & Whitcomb who were at that time engaged in building portable steam engines

The firm comprising the three gentlemen above named was founded in 1865 by Charles Stewart and David M Dillon under the original firm name of Stewart & Dillon, and the first shop was on Manchester street, but was later removed to Cypress street In December, 1869 Mr Dillon retired from the firm and Mr Stewart continued the business alone until 1872, when William Allen became his partner, the style changing to Stewart & Allen, and this partnership continued for a period of three years Prior to that time (1871) Mr Stewart purchased the boiler business of Rice, Barton & Fales, machine and iron company, which they carried on in connection with their business of paper-making machinery Upon the dissolution of the partnership, in 1875, Mr Allen established the firm of William Allen & Sons, which has continued in business in the city of Worcester since, and Mr Stewart in 1878 admitted his son James C Stewart to partnership, changing the name of the firm to that of C Stewart & Son In 1888 Charles Stewart retired and his three sons, above mentioned, have continued the business up to the present time (1906)

In September 1889, the works were moved to new shops at the present location, Albany street The plant is extensive, covering a space of nearly two acres of land located a half mile east of the Union station and on the line of the Boston & Albany Railroad and easily accessible from all parts of the city of Worcester by means of the electric cars The main building is sixty by three hundred and seventy feet, and there are a number of smaller buildings for various purposes, all admirably equipped with machinery There is a spur track running alongside the works and with a powerful electric hoisting crane gives excellent facilities for receiving and shipping goods The firm manufactures locomotive, marine and tubular boilers tanks for oil water and general purposes, smoke stacks, penstocks, and heavy plate iron work of all kinds They also attend to repairs of boilers in mills, etc They employ on an average seventy-five men, many of whom have served at the works for a long period of time

JOSEPH McGOWN The pioneer ancestor of the American branch of the McGown family was Joseph McGown (grandfather), who emigrated thither from his native land—Scotland—landing in New York city Prior to his emigration to America he married and among the children born to him was a son Henry McGown

Henry McGown (father) was born at Paisley, an important manufacturing town in Scotland, was reared and educated there and by giving close attention to his studies and by pursuing a course of reading good literature became a well informed man on a number of subjects After his marriage to Elizabeth Bizland of Paisley, Scotland, about 1842 he came to the United States locating first at Unkersville Connecticut where he was employed at his trade of weaver After a residence of one year there he moved to Mason Village New Hampshire, where he served as foreman for the Columbia Manufacturing Company's mill for about thirty years, and later he removed to High Bridge same state, where he continued to act as foreman for the same company In 1871 he took up his residence in Clinton Massachusetts, and engaged in the grocery business this proving a most lucrative enterprise The following named children were born to Mr and Mrs McGown Joseph of whom later Elizabeth, John, Henry, William W and Jean Henry McGown (father) died January 1874, his wife passed away August 1874

Joseph McGown eldest son of Henry and Elizabeth (Bizland) McGown, was born in Paisley Scot-

land, November 13, 1840 When eighteen months old he was brought to this country by his mother, his father having preceded them, and after a tedious and perilous voyage on a sailing vessel was landed safely in New York city He received his education in the schools of New Ipswich and Mason Village, New Hampshire, and when five years old accompanied his parents to High Bridge, New Hampshire, where he was employed for a number of years in the mill operated by his father Upon the removal of the family to Clinton, Massachusetts, he followed the trade of machinist for a short period of time, and then entered into partnership with his father in the grocery business, established by the latter this connection continuing until the death of Mr McGown, Sr, since which time the son has conducted the business alone and is now in receipt of an extensive and lucrative patronage only exceeded by establishments in the large cities Mr McGown has accumulated considerable real estate in his adopted town, and ranks among the prosperous and influential citizens Although repeatedly requested by the leaders of the Republican party in his community to accept political office, he has always declined the honor but is willing to aid the party otherwise to the best of his ability He is an active and interested member of the Masonic Order, also the Independent Order of Odd Fellows

Mr McGown married January 1, 1863, Miss Clementine E Baxter, a daughter of Anson Baxter, of Central Falls, Rhode Island and their children are Henry A, married Grace Buttrick, and their family consists of three children Margery, Mary J, and Ellenoir Joseph E, who married Jean McGown, and the issue of this marriage were three children Edith Muriel, and one who died young George, deceased who married May Barden, and one children was born to them, Pauline Andrew B, who married Mary Morgan now deceased, and their children are Dorothy Virginia John L, who married Nellie Jenkins Isabelle C, who became the wife of John Sparks, issue Donald, and one who died young Esther, unmarried, resides at home The family attend the Congregational church of Clinton

CHARLES BASSETT EATON The Eaton family of which Charles Bassett Eaton is a representative in the present generation, is lineally descended from Jonas Eaton

(I) Jonas Eaton came from England and purchased land in Watertown Massachusetts, where he had a residence in 1643 He with his brother William, also of Watertown Massachusetts, were among the first settlers of Reading, Massachusetts Jonas and wife Grace were recorded among the members of the church at Reading as early as September 29, 1648 He died there February 24, 1674 and his widow married November 18 1680 Henry Sillsbee of Lynn Jonas and Grace Eaton had children Mary born February 8, 1643-4 died 1731, John, born September 10, 1645 Jonas born September 28 1647, died October 14 1647, Jonas born September 24 1648, Sarah born 1650, Joseph, born January 5, 1651, Joshua, born December 4 1653, Jonathan, born December 6 1655, David, born September 22, 1657, died October 7 1657

(II) John Eaton born September 10, 1645, married November 26 1674 Dorcas Green, and lived in Reading He died there May 25, 1691 Their children were Jonas, born March 13, 1676-7, died March 28 1676-7 Grace born January 12 1677-8, married John Boutelle Noah, born January 26 1678, died in 1701, Thomas born June 22, 1679 died November 30, 1679, Jonas, born May 18, 1680, married and settled in Framingham, Joseph, born April 18, 1681, died April 29 1681, Benjamin, born January 16, 1683-4 died February 2, 1683-4, Joseph, settled in Reading, Benjamin, settled in Roxbury, Dorcas, born July 26, 1688 died young, Stephen, born August 11, 1689, died August 25, 1689, Phoebe, born August 25, 1690, married Jonathan Nichols

(III) Jonas Eaton, born May 18, 1680, was a carpenter and bricklayer, settled in Framingham, Massachusetts and married Grace, daughter of John Gould He purchased March 10, 1705-6, the east half of what was known as the "Half Mile Square," and died there August 13 1727 His children were Mehitable born February 17, 1706-7, Noah, born July 22 1708, John, born September 3, 1710 settled in Killingly, Connecticut, Phebe, born October 22, 1714, Jonas, born October 22, 1714, Joseph, born March 12, 1716, Mary born March 12, 1718 Joshua, born July 1, 1721, settled in Voluntown, Connecticut, Benjamin, born October 9, 1723, Ebenezer, born September 2, 1727, cordwainer

(IV) Noah Eaton, born July 22, 1708 married Hannah Vinton of Stoneham, and resided in Framingham He died October 8, 1791, she died March 8, 1795 Their children are Hannah, born November 8, 1731, married John Cheney, Noah, born August 7, 1733, Abigail, born February 1, 1735, married Daniel Gregory, Jonas, born January 29, 1737, John, born July 30, 1740, Mehitable, born April 21, 1743, married Deacon Samuel Dakin, Ruth, born February 16, 1744, married Peter Parker, Maltiah, born January 15, 1747, Silas, born December 1, 1750, Mary, born May 11, 1753, married Simon Goddard, of Phillipston

(V) Maltiah Eaton, born January 15, 1747, in Framingham, Massachusetts, married Huldah Haynes, of Sudbury, December 31, 1778, who died in 1816 In the year 1773 he purchased a tract of land in the township of Gerry, now Phillipston, Massachusetts somewhat later removing his goods from Framingham to that place on a one-horse litter made of two wooden poles serving as thills extending back of the horse to the ground, across which short poles were fastened to support a platform to hold the freight the horse dragging the poles along, after the Indian style of transporting camp fixtures He died August 17 1831 His children were Amy born 1780, married Daniel Crossman, Huldah born April 19, 1785, died unmarried, July 4, 1849, in Winchester, New Hampshire, Avery, born February 2, 1789 Maltiah, died in infancy

(VI) Avery Eaton, born February 2, 1789, in Phillipston, married January 22, 1818, Lydia Brown born in Lexington, Massachusetts, January 18 1793 Lydia Brown was a descendant from Deacon Joseph Brown, who came from England and located in Lexington Massachusetts, where his son Benjamin was born June 30, 1720 He married Sarah Read December 23, 1742, and died March 4 1802 Their son Nathan, born September 5 1766, married Lydia Muzzy, December 25 1788 and were the parents of Lydia Brown wife of Avery Eaton She died in Springfield Massachusetts, July 14 1881 Avery Eaton built a house just back of his father's on the old homestead at Phillipston and resided there until his father's death In 1844 the place passed into the hands of the eldest son William Avery Eaton who resided there about thirty years, when he built a house in Athol and removed there, subsequently selling the farm The children of Avery Eaton were William Avery born October 5 1818, Lydia Samantha born October 15 1820, Caroline Huldah born October 12 1822, Harriet Relief, born November 9 1824 married April 7, 1847, Lorenzo Blanchard, of Petersham Almira J, born May 27,

1827, died July 27, 1827 John Osgood, born September 2 1828, died July 6, 1832, Charles Bassett, born June 20, 1831, Mary Augusta, born July 18, 1835, married George P King, of Barre, Massachusetts

(VII) Charles Bassett Eaton, seventh child of Avery and Lydia (Brown) Eaton, was born in Phillipston, Massachusetts, June 20, 1831, on the original homestead of seventy-five acres that his grandfather Maltiah Eaton, purchased November 11, 1773 Here upon this farm were spent the first twelve years of his life, attending the village school, building windmills, sleds, wagons and water-wheels in the old shed chamber (the latter used in driving a miniature saw mill constructed on the brook near the house), while his sisters braided palm leaf hats At the death of the grandfather the farm became the property of his father Avery and his Aunt Huldah Later they sold the place to their brother William, and in April, 1844, removed to a farm of forty-five acres with cottage house and barn upon it in Winchester township, New Hampshire, about three miles south of the center In the fall of 1845 young Eaton, at the age of fourteen, entered the employ of Mr Belding in a cotton factory in West Winchester Within a few weeks this mill with a woolen factory standing near it were consumed by fire, and the lad found employment as chore boy for Mr Murdock, who owned a woolen mill in the town and boarded his help at the house During winters the lad usually went home to attend the town school In 1847 he was engaged in painting pails in South Orange, Massachusetts, for Mr Washburn (afterwards governor of the state), and the following season performed the same work at a pail factory in Winchester, New Hampshire Here he gained great proficiency in the work but found it quite injurious to health for on entering Edwin Kendall's high school at Petersham in September, 1848, he found his strength greatly impaired This however, returned to him and those school days in Petersham have ever been to him a source of pleasant recollections, for it was at that time that he made the acquaintance of Mary Caroline Cheney, who afterward became his wife and who for more than fifty years has been a true helpmate

After returning to Winchester and giving a little further attention toward obtaining an education, he began looking for a situation as clerk and visiting the store of B B Murdock at Northfield, Massachusetts in the midst of a severe snow storm made such a favorable impression that within a few days he received a letter asking him to call again when the contract was closed to accept a clerkship in his store one year for one hundred dollars and his board It was a very large country store, and the associations between employer and employed proved to be of the most pleasant character In the fall Mr Murdock sold the business to Messrs Hastings and Fay, who desired Mr Eaton to remain with them but wishing to be among his acquaintances at Petersham he entered the employ there of Wetherell & Mudge, making a contract to remain with them three years, and continued at the store and postoffice until disabled by a severe attack of rheumatism which made him almost helpless for several months As soon as he was able to leave his home at Winchester whither he had gone when unable to attend to his duties with Wetherell & Mudge he again returned to Petersham and engaged to clerk in the store of George A Rogers, who after a time sold out to Messrs Hawes & Tolman, Mr Eaton continuing with them about two years

In 1849 E D Cheney, father of Mary Caroline (before mentioned) removed from Petersham to Worcester, and Mr Eaton followed them there, engaging with B L Hardon & Company, dealers in dry goods, with store on Main street, Worcester, the members of the firm being B L Hardon, Stephen Sawyer and William Cary After his clerkship here, he was with Warren & Emerson, who kept a country store in Royalston, but in September, 1852, he entered the store of Lee & Bassett, in Athol, who carried on a large general store business, also having an extensive palmleaf hat trade, and a tailoring department, where a large number of girls found employment Here Mr Eaton remained nearly three years, much of the time having a large share of responsibility in the conduct of the business November 14, 1854, he married Mary Caroline Cheney, and began housekeeping in Athol, at the same time making a home for his widowed mother who for more than thirty years received his generous and kindly ministrations of help and support Mr Eaton was now enjoying the full confidence of his employers, and business was prosperous, but there existed an undercurrent which in time changed the course of events Mrs Eaton was an only daughter, and her parents were arriving at the conclusion that she must have a home near them All the inducements Messrs Lee & Bassett could offer and the earnest appeals from other friends in Athol failed to check the tidal wave rolling toward Worcester, and there the young couple arrived in April, 1855 Mr Eaton soon found employment with Mr E H Sanford who had opened a store in Flagg's block for the sale of fancy dry goods, and here made himself so useful that within a few months he was given a substantial increase in salary, and within a year was allowed to take a third interest in the business This agreement was continued for six years, when (in 1862) Mr Eaton rented a store in Brinley Hall block and began for himself, at first in a small way, but business grew as time went, and in 1870, for the purpose of securing more room he removed to the old Butman store, on the site of the present State Mutual building Here he continued the fancy dry goods business until October, 1877, when he sold to Hebbard & Shepherd The following year he engaged in the galvanized iron and sheet metal business That not proving satisfactory, he relinquished it and in 1879 went to work in the store of Sanford & Dixon, dealers in paper and stationery, soon purchasing Mr Sanford's interest, and with Mr Dixon removed the stock to No 505 Main street, and for two years business was conducted under the firm name of Eaton & Dixon After purchasing Mr Dixon's interest the business was continued under the style of C B Eaton & Company Harry H Browning holding an interest about two years At that time Mr Eaton sold one-half interest in the business to Will W Lewis, who had been a clerk in the store a number of years, but November 1, 1892, Mr Eaton sold his half interest to W B Emerson, since which time Mr Eaton has been engaged in the real estate business and caring for the large property interests now in the possession of the family

Mary Caroline (Cheney) Eaton, wife of Charles Bassett Eaton, was a granddaughter of Ebenezer Cheney born in Milford, Massachusetts, April 14, 1782 He was by trade a blacksmith, and married Mary Daniels of Holliston Their son Edson Daniels Cheney born in Milford October 16, 1810, married Sarah B Shattuck, of Barre, April 11 1833 She was daughter of Asa Shattuck born in Hancock New Hampshire March 26 1789 and his wife Abigail Conant of Oakham, Massachusetts, born there November 16, 1791 This Asa Shattuck was son of Ezekiel of Groton, Massachusetts and his wife Sarah Bullard Edson Daniels Cheney came to Worcester in 1849, and was engaged in the manufacture of carriages, in Petersham, Massachusetts, until he came to Worcester Then for six years he carried on carpentering and house building, and in 1860 opened a flour and grain store, and after a period of seventeen years retired with a well earned competency and the reputation of a successful, honest business man He died in Worcester, April 13, 1894 His daughter, Mary Caroline Cheney, wife of Charles Bassett Eaton, was born in Barre, Massachusetts, February 23, 1834

The children of Charles Bassett and Mary Caroline (Cheney) Eaton, born in Worcester, were Alice Carrie, born March 8, 1859, Cora Belle, born October 15, 1870, Grace Cheney, born August 12, 1876, died August 12, 1877

(VIII) Alice Carrie Eaton, eldest child of Charles Bassett and Mary Caroline (Cheney) Eaton married Frederick Norton Cooke, February 9 1881 He is a native of Norwich Connecticut, born September 12, 1854, a telegrapher Their home is with the parents Their children are Cheney Eaton Cooke, born November 13 1882 died January 31, 1884, Frederick Norton Cooke, born August 12, 1884

(VIII) Cora Belle Eaton, second child of Charles Bassett and Mary Caroline (Cheney) Eaton, married William H Nelson August 16, 1893 Their children are Charles Winthrop born June 8, 1894, Madeline born June 19 1900, died August 21, 1900, William Earl born April 25, 1903

(VII) William Avery Eaton, eldest brother of Charles B, married Emily Johnson, of Petersham, May 2 1843 They had three children Lucy Caroline, Emily Elvira, and Martha Fidelia He died June 12 1895

(VII) Lydia Samantha Eaton his eldest sister, married, April 23, 1844, Uri Twichell, of Athol, a farmer They had four daughters and one son She died August 31, 1854

(VII) Caroline Huldah another sister married, January 3, 1853, William Hutchins of Winchester, New Hampshire, a farmer, who died September 6, 1860 She married (second), July 4, 1863, Edwin M Cooper, also of Winchester They had no children She died August 17, 1901

WILLIAM HERBERT INMAN, senior member of the firm of Pratt & Inman conducting an extensive steel business in Worcester, Massachusetts, is a native of Rhode Island, born in Burrillville, March 15, 1845 His parents were Francis Henry and Hannah (Marsh) Inman His mother was a daughter of John and Lucy Marsh, of Slatersville, Rhode Island His paternal grandparents were James and Nancy Inman, of the same town

William H Inman was four years old when his parents took up their residence in Worcester, Massachusetts He was educated in the public schools of that city, and after leaving his studies entered the office of his father May 8, 1864, when nineteen years of age From that time he has been continuously connected with the business to which he was then introduced, and which is worthy of somewhat extended notice

The keeping of bar iron and steel for sale as a special business in Worcester was commenced by Joseph Pratt and Samuel Hathaway, under the firm name of J Pratt & Co, in May 1829 At that time the only modes of transportation to Worcester were by horse or ox teams from Boston, or by the Blackstone canal from Providence The business gradually developed in importance, and was continued by the firm above named until 1832, when occurred the death of Mr Hathaway It was then continued without change of name by Mr Pratt with Isaac Davis as a partner, until 1835, when Edward Earle succeeded Mr Davis and the style of the firm was changed to that of J Pratt & Earle This was continued until 1848, when Elbridge G Pratt, brother of Joseph Pratt, purchased the interest of Edward Earle, and the firm again took the designation of J Pratt & Company Elbridge G Pratt died that year, and the business was continued without change of firm name until 1853, when Francis H Inman, who had entered the house as a clerk in 1849, was admitted to partnership and the firm name was changed to that of Pratt & Inman which has been its form to the present time In 1871 William H Inman, who had entered the employ of the house in May 1864, was admitted to partnership In 1874 Mr Pratt retired from the firm This excellent man who was born in 1800 lived to the remarkable age of ninety-five years, dying in 1895 Mr Francis H Inman continued his connection with the business until his death in 1898, after which the business was continued by William H Inman until 1903, when his son Albert H Inman who had been with the establishment since 1887, was admitted to partnership The firm fully maintains the prestige enjoyed by its predecessors, through so many years and its house is recognized as one of the substantial and important enterprises of Worcester distributing its goods through a wide territory and supplying many of the largest manufacturing establishments throughout the East

October 3, 1867 William H Inman married Mary E Cheney, a granddaughter of Charles Davis, who was for many years connected with the Washburn & Moen firm of Worcester Two children were born of this marriage Albert Henry and Edith Loraine

Albert H Inman, son of William H Inman married January 1 1891, Effie B Moore a daughter of Charles F Moore, of Worcester, and to them have been born two children, Chester M and Marjorie Mr Inman is a member of the Masonic fraternity affiliated with Quinsigamond Lodge and Worcester Royal Arch Chapter

THE GODDARD FAMILY has had for several generations some very distinguished representatives in Worcester and Worcester county It is one of the finest old families of English lineage The emigrant ancestor was William Goddard Some of his descendants especially those who are ancestors of the Worcester families are here given

(I) William Goddard was born about 1630 in London England He was a grocer In 1650 he married Elizabeth Miles They had six children before coming to America, three of whom died when infants and they had six more in Watertown Massachusetts, where they settled in 1666 He came over the year before and prepared a home for his family Of the American born children three died in infancy and three sons survived as happened with the six born in England The second son born in Watertown was Benjamin

(II) Benjamin Goddard son of William Goddard (1) was born at Watertown Massachusetts, in 1668 He married Martha Palfrey, of Cambridge, Massachusetts about 1700 and died in Cambridge October 21 1730 Their children were Nathaniel, born in Charlestown about 1702 died in Weston 1780 Benjamin born in Charlestown 1705, died in Grafton Massachusetts 1759 John, born in Charlestown 1709 died in Cambridge May 12, 1751 Thomas born in Charlestown, died in Cambridge 1768 Martha born in Charlestown, died in Cambridge 1770

(III) Benjamin Goddard, son of Benjamin Goddard (2) born 1705 married Mary Kidder, of Grafton in that town about 1730 Their children were Nathaniel born in Grafton, Massachusetts about 1732, Josiah about 1735, Benjamin, November 15, 1737 died in Grafton March 11, 1806, James, April 24 1740 died in Athol, February 22, 1809, Samuel, December 27, 1742, died in Royalston, Massachusetts, August 16, 1806. Elizabeth, died in Petersham, Massachusetts, 1820, Hannah, settled in Worcester, New York Mary, married Thomas Gregg of Sutton

(IV) Samuel Goddard, son of Benjamin (3) and Mary Goddard, was born December 27, 1742, married Elizabeth King, of Sutton in that town (Rev D Ball), and second Catherine Parker Parks, nee Gerry, a widow, of Petersham, June 28, 1790 He had twenty-three children, including four sons that his second wife had by her first marriage Some of his children were Henry, born in Sutton, February 25, 1770, died in Royalston, February, 1848, Samuel born in Sutton, July 6, 1772, died in Norwich, Vermont November 14, 1844, Elizabeth, born in Sutton February 2, 1774 died in Montpelier, Vermont, October 4 1834, Salmon, born January 26, 1776, died young, Ashahel, born in Sutton, September 25, 1777 died in Belfast, Maine, November 11, 1806 Salmon, born in Royalston, Massachusetts, January 6 1783 James, born in Royalston, July 5, 1784, died in Royalston, February 9, 1841, a son, born in Royalston, March 15 1786 died the same day and was buried with his mother, Benjamin, born in Royalston, May 5 1791, died in Worcester, September 1, 1867, Catherine, born in Royalston, March 5, 1793, died March 6, 1793, Tamar, born in Royalston, February 5, 1795, died in Minneapolis, Minnesota, May, 1888, Nathaniel, born in Royalston, February 7, 1797, died in Millbury, Massachusetts, after 1890, a son, born in Royalston, April 8, 1799 died 1799, Catherine, born in Royalston, November 4 1800, died 1800, Danford born in Royalston November 8, 1801, died 1804, Danford, born in Royalston, March 7, 1804, died in Valparaiso, South America, February 2, 1859 Two infants by the first wife died unnamed

(V) Benjamin Goddard, son of Samuel (4) and Catherine Goddard, was born May 5 1791, married Sarah (Stockwell) Sibley, widow of Dorrance Sibley, of Sutton, at Millbury February 7, 1822 He died in Worcester, September 1, 1867 Their children were Henry, born in Worcester October 4, 1823, died in Worcester, January 12, 1904, Harriet, born in Worcester, October 11, 1825 died in Dowagiac Michigan, December 3, 1869, Catherine Parker, born in Worcester, November 2, 1827, died in Worcester, August 18, 1843, Dorrance Sibley born in Worcester October 11, 1829, Delano Alexander born in Worcester, August 27, 1831, was editor of the *Worcester Spy* and the *Boston Advertiser*, died in Boston January 11 1882

(VI) Henry Goddard, eldest son of Benjamin (5) and Sarah (Stockwell) Goddard, was born in Worcester, October 4 1823 During his entire business life he was intimately identified with the progress of the manufacture of wire With the exception of a single attempt in Walpole, all the earliest efforts at wire drawing in this country were made in Worcester and two or three neighboring towns Prior to 1831 the hardware dealers of Worcester county imported all their wire from England and Germany, and it is stated on good authority that shortly before that the entire output of wire in England did not exceed one four horse load weekly In 1843 or 1844 he entered the mill of the Washburn & Moen Company where his father was manager, later was employed as a wire drawer, and continued in that company's service uninterruptedly for more than fifty years Upon the death of his father he became manager of the South Worcester mill Shortly after this building was destroyed by fire, and he was transferred to the larger mill of the company on Grove street, returning the following year to take charge of the new mill at the old location In 1869 this mill was closed and Mr Goddard went again to the Grove street works, where he remained as foreman of the wire drawing and nail department until poor health and the arrival of his seventy-fifth birthday induced him to give up active work He finally severed his connection with the company in December, 1898 After that date he was not actively engaged in any business

His withdrawal from this service was marked with many tokens of the esteem and affection of those who for so many years had been associated with him or served under him The directors of the corporation testified upon their records to his faithful and intelligent leadership, his unvarying devotion to the company's interest and the great respect inspired in all who knew him by his uprightness of character and kindly disposition No other person had been so long and so prominently identified with the business which, during his connection with it, had grown from what was almost a mere handicraft to a leading place among the great industries

Mr Goddard married April 7, 1849, Eugenia D C Ball, a native of Holden but living with her parents in Worcester at the time of their marriage Of this union two children survive him, Julius Goddard and Mrs Willietta Goddard Ball, both of whom now reside in Massachusetts

His naturally retiring disposition and his fidelity to the interests of his employers hindered to some extent his active participation in the burdens of public office He was always deeply interested, however in public matters, jealous of the reputation of his city keenly alive to its best interests, and for a long time influential in its affairs He served as a member of the common council in 1860-62-73-74, and as alderman in 1865-68-69

There was perhaps no place in Massachusetts where the Morgan or anti-Masonic excitement was greater or attracted a larger percentage of the leading business and professional men than Worcester county, where it actively interferred with the affairs of both church and state Mr Goddard's father, being naturally a man of positive conviction and great earnestness, and sustaining an important relation to one of the leading industries having adopted a position hostile to the Fraternity, was prominent and outspoken in his opposition, and after a bitter contest, was elected to the general court upon the anti-Masonic issue It is, however, worthy of note that his son Henry never sympathized with his father's attitude, and was among the earliest to ally himself with the Fraternity in the Masonic revival, which followed this great excitement This act seemed to completely upset his father's antagonism to the Order From the moment that he knew of his son's connection with it he never uttered another word against Freemasonry Others who had been hostile to the Fraternity were heard to say that if all its members were like Henry Goddard there was much to be said for it and nothing against it

He received the first three degrees in Morning Star Lodge in 1847 the orders of Knighthood in Worcester County Commandery in 1855 and was its eminent commander in 1866-67-68 On September 7 1871, the Commandery elected him to honorary membership In 1863 he received the Scottish Rite in Boston Consistory, was subsequently a deputy

Durrana S Goddard

master of Worcester Lodge of Perfection and was the first senior warden of Lawrence Chapter of Rose Croix which was instituted June 17, 1870

When the Masonic bodies in Worcester first occupied their present halls in 1866, Mr Goddard was one of those most actively interested in securing them, and was a generous contributor in preparing them to suitably accommodate the Fraternity He was made a member of the board of directors of Masonic Apartments at its organization, and up to the time of his death was active in the management of that body and its successor, the present trustees of the Masonic Fraternity

Few men in Worcester had a larger personal acquaintance and none more highly respected Modest and unassuming, he never sought preferment, but when it came he faithfully performed the duties it imposed In his relations with his fellowmen, he exemplified the principles of charity and brotherly love, and by his many amiable qualities made himself beloved by men of every station His deep sympathy with any one who was in trouble was continually manifested by his kindly acts To such he gave freely and gladly, never grudgingly He was thoroughly devoted to his business, proverbially honest and his great simplicity and purity of character were recognized and prized by all who knew him Departing, he has left the record of an upright and honorable citizen a kind and genial man, a true and sympathizing friend Mr Goddard died at his home in Worcester, January 12, 1904

(VI) Dorrance Sibley Goddard, son of Benjamin (5) and Sarah S Goddard, was born October 11, 1829 married Mary Howe Williams of Hubbardston, in that town, March 25, 1855 Their children were Gertrude, born in Worcester March 20 1856, married Henry Brannon see sketch elsewhere in this work Alice, born in Worcester, August 28, 1857, married John Sackville West, of Tiverton, Rhode Island, June 19, 1890, no children Emma, born in Holyoke November 25, 1859, see sketch of C S Hall Dwight, born in Worcester, December 27, 27, 1861 Harry Williams, born in Holyoke, September 14 1863 Winthrop, born in Worcester, July 16 1866 died April 10, 1868 Mary, born in Worcester, October 3, 1869, married Archibald N Goddard, in Worcester, August 1, 1900 Their children, born in Worcester, are Eloise Olive born January 28, 1902, Miriam, April 19, 1903, Emmons, August 10, 1904

Dorrance Sibley Goddard was educated in the Worcester public schools and at Worcester Academy After completing his studies he went back to the home and for three years lived the strenuous life of a New England farmer Then he decided that he preferred manufacturing and he apprenticed himself in the Washburn & Moen wire mills at South Worcester where he learned the trade of wire drawer He learned the business of wire making thoroughly and rose step by step to the superintendence of the mill, a position that he filled for many years Dorrance S Goddard followed in his father's footsteps in entering the wire business It is fair to count Benjamin Goddard as one of the founders of the great wire business now owned by the American Steel and Wire Company operated in Worcester The Washburn & Moen Manufacturing Company started in 1831 in Northville in a small wooden building The owners were Benjamin Goddard and Ichabod Washburn The building was occupied in part by C Read & Co, manufacturers of wooden screws and it was in connection with the making of screws that the first wire making machinery was developed Wire was drawn by hand when Washburn & Goddard began operations, most of the wire being imported from England The business grew rapidly, but in 1835 Mr Goddard withdrew and Mr Washburn established the first wire mill on the Grove street location It was natural then for his son Dorrance to enter the business that had developed during his youth by consolidation and growth to the point where it became the largest wire manufactory in the world Mr Goddard has the distinction probably of having seen more of the progress and development of this the greatest of Worcester industries than any other living man, possibly more than any other one man He has the satisfaction too of seeing his son Harry W Goddard, president of a great wire making institution The Spencer Wire Company making the third generation of the family prominent in the manufacturer of wire and wire goods After the firm of Washburn & Goddard was dissolved, Benjamin Goddard at first manufactured wool machinery in the Northville mill where the wire works were started After he gave up this business, however, the mill passed into the hands of Mr Washburn, his former partner, and Mr Goddard again entered the business of wire making there under contract for Mr Washburn In 1840 Benjamin Goddard took charge of the wire mill established by Mr Washburn at South Worcester on the site later occupied by the Worcester Wire Company and its successor, The American Steel and Wire Company Benjamin continued in charge of this mill until his son succeeded him He died in 1867 His son, Henry Goddard, worked here and became the head of an important department for The Washburn & Moen Manufacturing Co Delano A Goddard, another son, making three of them in all, worked under his father in the South Worcester mill Delano was a man of culture and great intellectual powers He went on the editorial staff of *The Spy* and later to Boston, where he made a brilliant record as editor of *The Advertiser* The South Worcester mill was a one-story structure about thirty by fifty feet Coarse wire was drawn there and then taken to the Grove street mill to be finished The old mill at Northville was burned February 13, 1845 and the mill at South Worcester was also burned July 7, 1867, but rebuilt immediately In February 1868, the various companies were consolidated under the name of Washburn & Moen Manufacturing Co with a capital of one million dollars In the capacity of superintendent of the Quinsigamond works of this great company Dorrance S Goddard spent his life until he retired some years ago

For a time Mr Goddard was in the wire business at Holyoke, Massachusetts In 1862 he formed a partnership with William E Rice, of Worcester, and started a mill at Holyoke This firm continued in the business of wire making until 1866, when a favorable proposition to sell to the Washburn & Moen Company was accepted and both Mr Rice and Mr Goddard became identified with the Quinsigamond works of the Washburn & Moen Manufacturing Company, Mr Rice being president and Mr Goddard superintendent of the wire department The mill and real estate at Holyoke were sold to the Whiting Paper Company

Mr Goddard loves travel and has taken advantage of his opportunities to see much of his own country Soon after the discovery of gold in California he made his first trip across the continent That was in 1851 when the journey was slow difficult and dangerous He has been an interested observer of the development of the railroad system that now makes travel to California an attraction for the pleasure seeker and a brief vacation outing for the business man of the east

He has kept a journal of his travel that should be of public interest as well as record for his friends and family He has crossed the continent twelve times, and returned nine times by land and thrice by water He has made three trips to Alaska, the first in 1885, when the country was isolated from the rest of the world and difficult of access He crossed the Isthmus of Panama three times while the French companies were trying to dig the canal Now that the American government is pushing the work in a workmanlike way he is following the progress made with great interest and plans a visit to Panama shortly Mr Goddard's interest in this great undertaking is not only that of a business man with a love for the solution of mechanical and engineering problems, but of a very earnest American citizen who believes that the completion of this canal will add immensely to the future prosperity and wealth of the American people Mr Goddard is an active man in spite of his years and is fully able to enjoy travel He loves books and thoroughly enjoys his home life at his beautiful residence at South Worcester

In his religious views he is liberal He belongs to no secret societies He relates that his father was much opposed to all secret orders and when one of the sons became a Mason he was greatly shocked Somewhat to the surprise of his son, however, the subject was never mentioned between them Mr Goddard has been a Republican since the party was organized He has been a member of the school board, of the board of aldermen for four years and representative to the general court one year

When the First Co-operative Bank was organized in Worcester Mr Goddard was a charter member and its first president and served seven years, when he resigned

(VII) Dwight Goddard, eldest son of D S Goddard (6), was born December 27, 1861 He graduated from the Worcester Polytechnic Institute, class of 1881, as mechanical engineer, and from that year up to 1884 was superintendent of the Massachusetts Screw Company, at Holyoke From 1884 to 1887 he was assistant mechanic of the Washburn & Moen Manufacturing Company, and from 1888 to 1891 was treasurer of the Goddard Machine Company, at Holyoke He then entered the Hartford Theological Seminary, from which he was graduated in 1894 For five years, from 1895 to 1900, he served as missionary of the American Board at Foochow, China, and during the years 1900 and 1901 served as minister at Lancaster, Massachusetts, and associate pastor of the Tabernacle Church, Chicago, Illinois In the latter named year he returned to his former vocation, mechanical engineer, becoming connected with the firm of Wyman & Gordon, manufacturers of drop forgings, and at the present time (1905) is the manager of their Cleveland office Mr Goddard is a member of the Worcester Central Conference of Congregational Ministers, and of the American Society of Mechanical Engineers He is the author of a series of biographies of Engineers and Inventors

Mr Goddard married, October 22, 1889, Harriet M Webber, of Holyoke, Massachusetts who died May 17, 1890 Mr Goddard married (second), November 27 1893, Frances E Nieberg M D, of St Marys, Ohio Their children are Dorrance born October 4, 1897, Theodore N, May 18, 1902 Mr Goddard is at present a resident of Cleveland, Ohio

(VII) Harry Williams Goddard son of Dorrance S Goddard (6), was born September 14, 1863, at Holyoke, Massachusetts, where his father was in business for a few years His father returned to Worcester when he was an infant and both father and son have subsequently lived there or at Spencer Harry attended the public schools of Worcester and entered the high school After two years in the high school he left to work in the wire mills of the Washburn & Moen Manufacturing Company at Quinsigamond, Worcester He began as a scale boy, weighing the wire After two years in the wire mill, he spent a year at Wilbraham Academy The wire business had its attractions for him, as his father and grandfather were prominent figures in the wire industry and it was natural that he should inherit a liking for the business and an aptitude for it At seventeen he left the academy and started in the Spencer Wire Company at Spencer, Massachusetts, literally at the foot of the ladder He did all kinds of work, and became familiar with each department as a matter of course Without design or expectation of advancement he gained a thorough insight and understanding of the business, so that almost as a matter of course he was made superintendent of the mills when he was twenty-one years old Mr Sugden, who was at that time the president of the corporation, had been his own superintendent The Spencer Wire Company was an old and somewhat conservative concern It had grown from a small beginning in 1828 to considerable importance In 1884, when Mr Goddard was made superintendent, about seventy-five hands were employed and an extensive property at Spencer had been acquired Mr Goddard was secretary of the company as well as superintendent of the mills for several years

When the president of the Spencer Wire Company, Mr Sugden, died in 1895, Mr Goddard took his place At that time he bought of the heirs of Mr Sugden the latter's interests in the corporation which gave him the control of the capital stock Mr Goddard has remained the chief owner of the company since then For many years the business had not been extended much, the proprietors being satisfied with quiet progress Not until 1900 was any great change made The facilities of the company were then increased by the addition of a new and model plant in Worcester Four acres of land at the corner of Webster and Jacques streets were acquired and substantial brick buildings erected there The general offices were moved to the new plant and the business has been rapidly developed in the past five years The company has now five and a quarter acres of floor space devoted to manufacturing and has over four hundred acres of land for yard, storage and other purposes of the business There are forty separate buildings in the plant at Spencer The company makes all kinds of uncovered steel iron and copper wire, besides hundreds of specialties, and employs at present about four hundred hands

Mr Goddard has become interested in other corporations to some extent He is the treasurer of the Hobbs Manufacturing Company, which makes paper box machinery at its factory near Lincoln Square, Worcester He was for ten years president of the Springfield Drop Forging Company He is president of the New England Anchor Fence Company, the Worcester Color Company and the Central Grocery Company, a co-operative grocery organized in 1905

The energy and executive ability that have made him so successful in his business brought him into prominence in the board of trade, and in 1903 when President Blodget became mayor of Worcester, Mr Goddard was elected president of the Wor-

H. W. Goddard

cester Board of Trade He was re-elected the following year His administration is conceded to be one of the best in the history of the board The activity of the organization was increased and its usefulness greatly extended With the co-operation of an exceptionally able secretary Mr Goddard has maintained the record of the past and maintained gratifying progress in the organization When Secretary of War Taft came to Worcester in 1905 to speak at the annual banquet of the board of trade, Mr Goddard had the pleasant duty of entertaining Judge Taft at his beautiful home on Salisbury street

Mr Goddard is a director of the Mechanics' National Bank of Worcester, and a trustee of the People's Savings Bank He is a member of the Maine Coast Club, the Quinsigamond Boat Club, the Commonwealth Club and of the Tatnuck Country Club He is an earnest Republican and has been at times active in the party management He and his family attend Piedmont Church Mr Goddard easily ranks among the leading captains of industry in a city where hundreds of men have achieved success in manufacturing He belongs to a group of young men who are building their fortunes under the new and complicated conditions of modern business, young men who have been fitted by education, inherited gifts and early training to carry their burdens easily and keep the industries of Worcester in the front ranks

He married, December 14, 1887, Grace Watson, daughter of George and Eleanor Watson, of Spencer Their children are Eleanor Grace, born March 25, 1889, Marion Williams, August 29, 1893

DELANO ALEXANDER GODDARD, youngest son of Benjamin Goddard (5), was born in Worcester, August 27, 1831 His early education was obtained in the Worcester schools His father had hoped to send all his boys to college, but owing to financial reverses the older sons had to forego the benefits of a liberal education When Delano reached the age when his preparation for college examinations should begin, the father felt his circumstances improved enough to warrant the expense of a college education for the youngest son and the one perhaps most attracted by learning and study Benjamin Goddard was a man of broad sympathy, but rather taciturn He was a strong anti-slavery man, a man of firm integrity in business, but seldom given to the expression of his feelings He had the characteristic habit of the old Yankee stock of hiding his sentiments and emotions One day as Delano was standing at his machine in the wire mill, where his half holidays were industriously spent, his father stopped at his side and said abruptly "Delano, do you want to go to college?" The reply came without hesitation "Yes, sir!" Apparently the father expected this decision, for he said "Go home, change your clothes and go to the academy to be examined" There was no more talk The boy went home That interview was characteristic of both Delano graduated from Worcester Academy with honor, delivering the valedictory of his class He entered Brown University in 1849, but the following year entered the sophomore class at Yale College and graduated in 1853

He left Worcester and sought his opportunity in the west He began his career as an editor in a humble way on the local weekly, *The Herald*, at Painesville, Ohio A year later he returned to his native city He was on the staff of *The Chronicle* a Boston daily, in 1856 Early in 1857 he became the associate editor of *The Worcester Transcript*, a daily newspaper, but soon became the editor of *The Spy*, under the Hon John D Baldwin, a post filled afterward by Captain J Evarts Greene, late postmaster of Worcester While writing the editorials of *The Spy* Mr Goddard served the city in the legislature in 1861 and in 1867 in the house of representatives He was for about a year trustee of the public library In April, 1868, he became editor of the *Daily Advertiser* of Boston and filled this position with unsurpassed intelligence and ability, till his death, January 11, 1882 In 1876 he took a sea voyage for his health and spent a few weeks in England and the Isle of Wight In 1880 he made an extended trip through the southern and western states

He was specially interested in the American Indians and perhaps no work of his pen was undertaken with more intense earnestness than his pleas for the nation's wards He wrote little except for his newspaper He contributed in 1880 a paper on "Newspapers and Newspaper Writers in New England, 1787-1815" to the New England Historic-Genealogical Society and a number of other papers to learned societies to which he belonged and also some magazine articles He was a member of the council of the Massachusetts Historical Society, and member of the American Antiquarian Society He took the degree of A M in regular course at Yale College in 1856 Hon Robert C Winthrop, president of The Massachusetts Historical Society at the time of Mr Goddard's death, said in a tribute at the society meeting next day "Amiable, intelligent accomplished, he had entered heartily into our work I often met him here and never without a renewed sense of the variety of his information, of the candor of his judgment, of the kindness of his heart, and of that singular modesty which sometimes threatened to conceal his sterling abilities" Charles C Smith the author of a memoir published by the Historical Society of Mr Goddard, said of him "Mr Goddard's character was such that no one who was brought into anything like intimate relations with him could help being attached to him as by hooks of steel Those who were connected with him in his daily duties felt for him an affectionate regard which he called loyalty to the paper—apparently not suspecting that it was a personal relationship to their chief" Rev Edward Everett Hale took occasion to speak of the editor's duty toward history "In a word," he concluded his eulogy, "with fresh memory for the loss which this society and the press of this country have both sustained, I should say that we could in no way draw better the distinction between the two schools of journalism—that which is bad through and through, because it is sensational, and that which is good through and through, because it aims at truth—than by saying of the two that the editor in the first school fails because he is false to the claims of history, and that the editor of the upright school triumphs because to history he is true" These are but brief selections from the tributes paid to the deceased When the history of journalism in Massachusetts is written for the Nineteenth Century the name of Delano A Goddard, of Worcester, will take a place among the foremost editors of his generation

HARVEY BRADISH WILDER Nicholas Wilder (1), to whom the ancestry of Harvey Bradish Wilder is traced, settled on Sulham estate in Berkshire county England in April, 1497, when the property was given him by Henry VII The property is now or was at last accounts still in the Wilder family Four of the line have been rectors of the parish Nicholas Wilder was a chief in the army of the Earl of Richmond at the battle of Bosworth, 1485 When he was given the Sulham estate he was also given a coat of arms which may be found in Burke or the Genealogy He had but one son, John

(II) John Wilder, son of Nicholas Wilder (1), inherited his father's estates in 1525 His children were John, see forward, Agnes, died 1580

(III) John Wilder, son of John Wilder (2), and grandfather of Thomas Wilder, who emigrated to New England, married the only daughter and heiress of Thomas Keats, who built Sulham House It was given in 1582 by entail to William Wilder, their son During the nineteenth century it was greatly improved and the church was restored and repaired by the owner, John Wilder, D D, who was also rector Since 1777 Purley Hall has been the residence of the inheritors of the estate It is about two miles north of Sulham Thomas Wilder, the fourth son, received the entailed Wilder estate The sons John and Thomas were also provided for in his will Their children were John, Nicholas, William, Thomas, Eleanor, Joan, Alice

(IV) Thomas Wilder, son of John Wilder (3), was born in Sulham, England He settled in Shiplake, Oxford county, but was proprietor of the Sulham estate He was born and died in Shiplake, however He married Martha ——— He died in 1634 and she went to New England where two of her sons, Edward and Thomas, settled She came on the ship Confidence' in 1638 with her daughter Mary She settled near her son Edward in Hingham, where she was a proprietor in 1638 She died April 20, 1652 Some authorities spell the name Shiplake, Shiplock The children of Thomas and Martha Wilder were John, heir to his father's estates, died in 1688, Thomas, see forward, Elizabeth, born 1621, married Thomas Ensign, Edward, married Elizabeth Ames, settled in Hingham, Massachusetts, died October 28, 1690, Mary, came to Hingham also

(V) Thomas Wilder, son of Thomas Wilder (4), was born in Shiplock, England, in 1618 He settled in Charlestown, New England, where he was a proprietor as early as 1638 He was admitted a freeman June 2, 1641 He bought land in Charlestown, October 27, 1643 He was selectman in 1660 and 1667 and held other offices He removed to Lancaster in 1659 He married Ann ——— in 1641 She died June 10, 1692 She was admitted to the church May 7, 1650 He died October 23, 1667 He may have been born later than the date given as he deposed June 17, 1654, that he was thirty-three years of age His will was dated January 22, 1667-8 and proved March 4, 1667-8 He bequeathed to his wife and six children named below The children of Thomas and Ann Wilder were Mary, born June 30, 1642, in Charlestown, Thomas, born September 14, 1644, John, born 1646, Elizabeth, born 1648, Nathaniel see forward, Ebenezer

(VI) Nathaniel Wilder, son of Thomas Wilder (5), was born in Charlestown, November 3, 1650, died July, 1704 He married Mary Sawyer, of Lancaster, daughter of Thomas Sawyer and his wife Mary and was born July 4, 1652 (See sketch of Sawyer Family) He settled in Lancaster, was lieutenant in the company, and was killed by the Indians The children of Nathaniel and Mary (Sawyer) Wilder were Nathaniel, born 1675, settled in Petersham, Ephraim, born August 16, 1678, of Lancaster, representative in general court, Mary, born May 13, 1679, Elizabeth born April 20, 1685, died 1707 Jonathan, born 1686, married, and was killed by the Indians 1707, Dorothy, born 1686, married Samuel Carter, Oliver, see forward

(VII) Oliver Wilder, youngest son of Nathaniel Wilder (6), was born in 1694 He married 1713, Mary Fairbanks daughter of Jonathan Fairbanks, who served in Captain Champney's company under Sir William Phipps in the Canada Expedition, and was a grandson of the emigrant, Jonathan Fairbanks, of Dedham (See sketch) She was born in 1692 and died June 15, 1745 When he was sixteen years old he was working on his father's farm with his brother Nathaniel, when they were attacked by Indians Three years before their brother Jonathan had been brutally tortured to death by the Indians and their brother Ephraim severely wounded Oliver and Nathaniel managed to escape to the garrison, but the Indian servant who was working with them was killed Oliver was an ensign in the service August 23, 1725, and at that time was living at Turkey Hills In 1726 he refused to accept the office of constable and declined to pay the five pound fine which the law imposed as a penalty for refusing to take office He rose through the various grades to the rank of colonel At the age of sixty-three he turned out with his regiment at the Fort William alarm in 1757 and marched as far as Springfield, Massachusetts He was in the Crown Point expedition in 1759 He often served the town as moderator and selectman He owned a mill privilege His home was at South Lancaster and his house is now or was lately standing The place is now known as the Heald place He was a cousin of Judge Joseph Wilder, another very prominent Worcester county man Colonel Oliver Wilder died March 16, 1765 There are stones suitably inscribed marking the graves of Colonel Wilder and his wife

The children of Colonel Oliver and Mary (Fairbanks) Wilder were Hannah born January 15, 1716, died November 23, 1723, Mary, December 24, 1717, Oliver, see forward, Tilley, June 23, 1722, Keziah, February 27, 1725, Tamar, May 23, 1727, Phinehas, April 24, 1730, married, 1780, Lois Boies, Lois April 20, 1733, Moses, May 4, 1736, married Submit Frost, Abigail December 16, 1740

(VIII) Oliver Wilder, third child of Colonel Oliver Wilder (7), was born May 17, 1720, at Lancaster, Massachusetts. He settled in that part of Lancaster set off as Sterling He was justice of the peace and captain of the militia company there He became one of the leading citizens He served in the Indian wars He married (first), June 6, 1739, Sarah Townsend She died 1743 He married (second), 1745, Ruth ——— The children of Oliver and Sarah (Townsend) Wilder were Ezra, born May 27, 1741, died 1816, Oliver and Sarah (twins), born November 7, 1743, Samuel, born January 13, 1746 The only child of Oliver and Ruth Wilder was Tamar, born May 27, 1748

(IX) Samuel Wilder, fourth child of Oliver Wilder (8), was born in Lancaster, Massachusetts, January 13, 1746 He settled in Sterling He died October 22, 1824, aged seventy-nine years He was a sergeant in Captain Benjamin Houghton's company, Colonel John Whitcomb's regiment in the revolution at the Lexington Alarm in 1775 Later he was a lieutenant He married January 15, 1772, Martha Rugg The children of Lieutenant Samuel Wilder or Mr Wilder as he is designated usually on the records were Calvin, see forward, Alice, baptized April 10, 1774, David, baptized April 6, 1777, Daniel, baptized April 4, 1779, Polly, baptized November 18, 1779, John, baptized August 26, 1781, Josiah, baptized October 26, 1783, Luke, baptized October 2 1785, Dolly, baptized May 25, 1788 (Five children of Samuel, Jr, recorded as baptized 1794 to 1808 may be his also)

(X) Calvin Wilder, eldest child of Samuel

Wilder (9), was born in Lancaster, Massachusetts, October 30, 1772, and was baptized in the Lancaster church, November 11 following He died April 5, 1832, aged sixty years He married, December 17, 1795, Susanna Celandine or Solendine, of Lancaster They settled in Lancaster He was selectman of the town in 1812-15-24-25 He served the town in other offices and committees He was one of the leading citizens His only son was Alexander Hamilton Wilder, born July 20, 1804, see forward

(XI) Alexander Hamilton Wilder, only son of Calvin Wilder (10), was born in Lancaster, Massachusetts, July 20, 1801 He married, November 10, 1835, Harriet Eaton, of Philadelphia She was the daughter of Nathaniel and Eunice (Wilder) Eaton Her mother was from another branch of the Lancaster Wilder family Her parents were married in 1792

Alexander H Wilder received his early education in the schools of Lancaster He came to Worcester at the age of nineteen in 1823 and entered the office of the register of deeds under Artemas Ward, Esq When twenty years old he suffered an attack of rheumatic fever that crippled him for life, but did not interfere seriously with his duties in the register's office He was a clerk and assistant to Mr Ward for twenty-three years He succeeded him as register June 17, 1846, and was elected and re-elected to this office until his death From 1823 to 1874 he was continuously in the register's office as clerk and chief More than half of the business of the office, from the establishment of the county in 1731 to the day of his death, was performed under his administration His name first appears as register in book No 409 and is signed for the last time in book No 945 During the latter years of his service he had no opponent at the polls, both parties honoring him with a nomination The *Spy* said at the time of his death "Probably no one who habitually transacts business with that office can remember the time when Mr Wilder was not employed in it, and the experience of very few goes back to the time of the register who preceded him His unfailing courtesy and patience, his quiet and systematic business methods, his absolute rectitude and accuracy, made him a model official whose service and example have been of inestimable value to the community" He was a man of deep religious feeling He was for many years member of the Central Congregational Church, but joined the Plymouth Church when it was formed He was generous in his charity He was a man of many friends Few men were better known or more highly esteemed in the county He died December 12, 1874 The children of Alexander Hamilton and Harriet (Eaton) Wilder were Harvey Bradish, see forward, Alexander E, born August, 1839, died September 29, 1839

(XII) Harvey Bradish Wilder, only surviving son of Alexander Hamilton Wilder (11), was born in Worcester, Massachusetts, October 12, 1836 He attended the Worcester public schools, the Thetford (Vermont) Academy and the Leicester Academy He began the business of life in the office of the register of deeds, under his father's administration, in 1853 In April, 1855, he accepted a clerkship in the book store of Ticknor & Fields, in Boston, but in August, 1856, he was called back to Worcester, Massachusetts, to become chief clerk in the register's office In 1875 he served as register, having been appointed by the county commissioners to fill the unexpired term of Alexander H Wilder He resigned this office at the expiration of a year, and Mr Charles A Chase was elected and served during the year 1876 At the election in 1876 Mr Wilder and Mr Chase were both candidates, and Mr Wilder was elected It is a notable fact that Mr Wilder was connected with this office as clerk for his father, and as register for a period of forty-four years, until his retirement January 1, 1901 His successor was Daniel Kent, the present register Mr Wilder was recognized as a model officer The Worcester registry is the third largest in the state, being exceeded in volume of business done only by the registry offices of Suffolk county and Middlesex county, both older and larger Worcester held its rank even after the towns of Fitchburg, Leominster, Lunenburg, Ashburnham and Westminster were taken to form a new registry in August, 1884 (See Merriam family of Fitchburg, Massachusetts) The office is looked upon as showing the highest efficiency and accuracy Since the new quarters were occupied in the new court house the registry has had the best modern appliances and conveniences, as well as fireproof rooms Since his retirement Mr Wilder has lived at his home in Worcester, No 12 Walnut street, having no active business He is a charter member of Quinsigamond Lodge of Free Masons He is a member of the Ancient and Honorable Artillery Company of Massachusetts He was a member of Worcester City Guards from 1856 to 1861 He was appointed adjutant of the Third Battalion of Rifles, Fifth Brigade, Third Division, Massachusetts Volunteer Militia, January 18, 1861, and March 2, 1861, was appointed on the staff of Brigadier-General George H Ward, Fifth Brigade, Third Division, Massachusetts Volunteer Militia, with rank of captain He was first sergeant of Artillery in the Ancient and Honorable Artillery Company in 1877, and second lieutenant in 1880 He is a member of the Commonwealth Club

He married, October 21, 1862, Anna F Chapman, of Ossipee, New Hampshire She died November 12, 1864 He married (second), June 14, 1870, Mary J, daughter of Dr Jefferson Pratt, of Hopkinton, Massachusetts, and they have one son, Charles Pratt Wilder, born in Worcester, April 3, 1873

NELSON R SCOTT The name Scott is obviously of Scotch origin The families bearing that name are now scattered all over the world Before the year 1200 there were well established lines in the counties of Peebles, Fife, Forfair, Roxbury, Dumfries, Selkirk, Kincardine, etc Members of the Scott family have held the dukedoms of Buccleuch and Queensbury, the marquisate of Dumfrieshire, the earldoms of Buccleuch, Deloraine, Drumlanrig, Sanquahar and Tarras, the viscounties of Hermitage, Nith Torthorwald and Ross Alexander Scott was in the Scotch Parliament in 1473, and throughout its history the Parliament, frequently if not always, had members of this family among its membership

The branch of the Scott family that went to the north of Ireland at the instance of the Protestant rulers of England to settle in the place of dispossessed Roman Catholic Irish have still some representatives there, though many of the Scotch-Irish branch have come to America In 1890 there were born in the whole of Ireland only one hundred and ninety-six persons of the name of Scott Of this number one hundred and forty-seven were in the Ulster counties of Antrim Down and Londonderry, indicating a population of about seven thousand

(I) John Scott, the pioneer ancestor of Nelson R Scott, of Worcester, was from the Scotch Covenanters of Ulster He came among the first Scotch-Irish emigrants in 1718, or soon before He must have brought with him more than most of the settlers, for he soon became one of the heaviest taxpayers of the town of Leicester, Massachusetts, where he bought land and made his home His wife Martha and five or more children came with him He bought his first land of the original proprietors of the town of Leicester The original homestead which he settled upon remained in the hands of his descendants until 1850 It has been known to the present generation as the Grosvenor farm The farm is situated in Auburn, formerly Ward, formerly Leicester

John Scott was on the ministerial tax list dated December 7, 1727, as owning thirteen hundred and three acres of land, the largest amount of any person on the list He paid the largest tax in 1735 and subsequent years In his will he bequeaths a coat of armor, an indication that some ancestor had been a knight some generations before His will is dated 1753, and it was allowed May 15 following Before he died he deeded lands to his son Matthew, December 29, 1743-4, to his 'beloved son' Nathaniel, August 1, 1749 Thomas received the homestead in the will The children were Matthew, born 1712, died at Leicester, November 25, 1797, aged eighty-eight, according to town records, married Martha Lockard, January 2, 1745-6, Nathaniel, was captain in the revolutionary war, married Eunice Woods (intention dated January 2, 1762), Elizabeth, married Hugh Cunningham, Thomas (see forward), Rebecca, married James Browning, of Rutland, January 15, 1756, Jane, married ——— Thomson

(II) Thomas Scott, son of John Scott (1) was born about 1720-30 He came with the family to Leicester and worked with his father to clear the land and subdue the soil He inherited the homestead on the death of his father in 1753 He bought land first of Thomas Denny, November 20, 1760, in Leicester, and then December 3, 1760, of Caleb Nichols, a piece of land adjoining the other He deeded his farm and buildings to his son Thomas Scott, Jr, January 10, 1791 Nine of his ten children were living, and most of them married, in 1803, when he made his will The will is filed May 19, 1803 He died April 23, 1803, age not given, in Ward, Massachusetts, now Auburn

He married Mary Livermore, January 3, 1766 She was born in 1743 He must have been much older Their children were Asa, born August 23, 1767, Thomas, Jr, March 13, 1769, Elizabeth, January 6, 1771, married ——— Eddy, Reuben, December 29, 1772, Nancy, December 27, 1774, died September 17, 1787, Catherine (twin), January 18, 1777, married ——— Phillips, the preceding are recorded in Auburn as born in Ward, the following were born in Ward David, November 1, 1779, Mary, February 4, 1781, Jerusha, April 17, 1783, married ——— Gale

(III) David Scott, eighth child of Thomas Scott (2), was born in Auburn, Massachusetts, November 1, 1779 He inherited the old homestead He was a farmer He married (first), August 30, 1820, Chloe Ryan, of Charlton, Massachusetts, who was born April 13, 1796, and died at Auburn July 31, 1823, leaving two children, married (second), March 13, 1825, Betsey (Sprague) Trask, who died at Auburn August 25, 1840, married (third) Elmira (Watson) Crosby, widow, of Brookfield, June 25 or 24, 1841, she died at Auburn July 28, 1845, married (fourth) the sister of his first wife, April 2, 1849, Ruth (Ryan) Sibley, of Spencer She survived him Children of David and Chloe (Ryan) Scott were David, Jr, (see forward), Nelson Ryan, (see forward) Child of David and Betsey (Trask) Scott was Elizabeth Sprague, born in Auburn Massachusetts, April 16, 1827, lived and died in Worcester, unmarried

(IV) David Scott, Jr, eldest son of David Scott (3), born June 7, 1821, married, October 14, 1846 Lucinda H Fay, of Princeton, Massachusetts, who was born March 8, 1823 He came to Worcester when a young man, learned the drug business and opened a drug store For many years he was successful in business His store was on the north corner of Main and Mechanic streets, Worcester, and he was the owner of the land and building in which his store was located The block is still owned by his heirs Mr Scott was a prominent Free Mason and was a member of the Worcester County Commandery, Knights Templar He died March 16, 1878 Children were Frank, born January 5, 1850, died young, Fred, June 13, 1852, was a physician, died at Terre Haute, Indiana, unmarried, Alice, December 16, 1854 All the foregoing were born in Worcester

(IV) Nelson Ryan Scott, second child of David Scott (3), was born at Auburn, Massachusetts, July 23, 1823 His mother died when he was but a week old His mother's sister, Ruth W, then the wife of Deacon Sibley, of Spencer, took him to her home and brought him up After the death of Deacon Sibley, she became the fourth wife of David Scott and step-mother to Nelson Ryan Scott He attended the district and high schools at Spencer, and Leicester Academy, and worked at farming until he was seventeen, when he went to his father's home in Auburn and helped his father with the farm work there In order to induce him to remain on the old homestead his father deeded to him an undivided half of the farm, provided he would remain on it and care for him the rest of his life But farm life was distasteful to him and in March, 1849, he gave up the deed and followed his elder brother to Worcester, and went to work for him in his drug store He learned the business thoroughly and remained there until 1852

He formed a partnership with the late Charles Sibley, the deputy sheriff and court crier for many years afterwards The firm name was Sibley & Scott They began business May 22, 1852, in the store at the south corner of Main and Sudbury streets The partnership was dissolved in 1854 Mr Scott entered into a new partnership with Thomas Pierce, his father-in-law, for the purpose of manufacturing boots and shoes Their factory was on Main street opposite the foot of Chatham street The firm managed to pull through the financial panic of 1857 with severe losses, but without failure In 1858, however, Mr Scott retired from the shoe business and went to work again for his brother David, May 1, 1858 He remained with him until December 1, 1866, when he started to build Scott's block at the junction of Main and Southbridge streets, on a triangular lot, from which it is generally called the Flatiron Building ' When the building was completed he opened a drug store in the north store July 4, 1867, and this store has been conducted successfully there by Mr Scott, and since his death by his son, George T The store was favorably located and Mr Scott took rank among the most successful merchants of the city

He found much pleasure in genealogical and antiquarian research He collected antiques, coins, medals, Indian implements of stone, etc He had a very large and valuable collection which after his death was presented to the Worcester Society of Antiquity, of which he was an active and interested member Among other things of special value in this collection are the pewter platters He loved travel and knew his own country thoroughly He went to California when trips for pleasure to that state were rare He went by steamer by way of the

Isthmus of Panama, and he brought back with him, after a stay of five months, an exceedingly interesting collection of natural curiosities, such as pebbles, mosses, chemicals, etc He spent the last year of his life in Europe, a country that fascinated him with its antiquities and historical researches

Mr Scott was well known in Masonic circles He was a member of Montacute Lodge, of which he was the Worshipful Master in 1871, declining a re-election, a member of Worcester Chapter, Royal Arch Masons, of Worcester County Commandery, Knights Templar, and of the Worcester Lodge of Perfection, to which he was exalted September 13, 1863 He was a charter member of the Worcester Continentals and remained an active member until his last trip to Europe, when he was made an honorary member He was also a member of Stella Chapter, order of the Eastern Star, Hopewell Council, Legion of Honor, the Worcester Council, Royal Arcanum, the Worcester County Mechanics' Association, the Worcester Art Students' Club, the American Pharmaceutical Association, the Massachusetts College of Pharmacy, and the Worcester Pharmaceutical Association, of which he was the first president He was a regular attendant of the Salem Street Congregational Church from the time he came to Worcester until he left for his last trip abroad, when he deeded his pew to the society He sat under the preaching and pastorates of Rev George Bushnell, Rev Merrill Richardson and Rev Charles M Lamson

He was of a cheerful, self-sacrificing disposition, ready and willing to extend a helping hand in case of need He was unwilling to mar the pleasure of others, a characteristic that was shown even during the last few weeks of his life when, rather than detain the party with which he was travelling at Cairo in Egypt, he decided, only two weeks before his death to push on up the River Nile with them On his arrival at Luxor he was so exhausted that he had to be carried by two natives to the hotel When questioned within three days of his death whether he would remain at Luxor or return with the party to Cairo, he replied "I will return with you to Cairo, so as to be nearer my Heavenly home" He was unconscious when the boat arrived at Cairo and died three days afterward February 19, 1883, aged fifty-nine years, seven months, seven days His wife died January 17, 1904

He married (first) June 15, 1845, Maria E Crosby, of Brookfield, daughter of his father's third wife She had one son, Charles Nelson, born at Auburn April 6, 1846 She died at the age of twenty-four years, July 27, 1847 He married (second) Julia A Pierce, daughter of Major Thomas and Maria (Mason) Pierce, May 6, 1851 She had one son, George T, born October 30, 1853 She died at Boston January 17, 1904

(V) Charles N Scott, eldest son of Nelson Ryan Scott (4), was born in Auburn, Massachusetts, April 6, 1846 He was educated in the public and high schools of the city and at the Highland Military Academy He entered the United States navy as midshipman He was in the United States Naval Academy during the war when it was located at Newport, and later when it was back in the old home at Annapolis He was in the same class with Commodore Richard T Wainright, with Adolph Marix, who was judge advocate at the hearing on the Maine disaster, and with Seaton Shroeder, ex-governor of Guam Mr Scott suffered a severe attack of malaria and was pronounced by a medical board physically unfit for naval service He resigned before graduating and returned to his home in Worcester When the drug store was opened he entered upon an apprenticeship in pharmacy After three years in the drug business he was obliged to leave to take charge of the property of his late father-in-law, Benjamin Goddard, who died suddenly Mr Goddard was the owner of a large jewelry business which was continued by Mr Scott in partnership with Frank A Knowlton, under the firm name of Benjamin Goddard & Co In 1876 Mr Knowlton purchased the interests of the Goddard estate and the partnership was dissolved The jewelry store of Mr Goddard was for a long time located at the corner of Main and Walnut streets In July, 1876, he opened a jewelry store on Main street, opposite Foster street He removed later to the Butman block, corner of Elm and Main streets Then he removed to the south store of Scott's block, where he was in business for about five years In 1888 he retired from the jewelry business, and with the exception of three years, when he was in the brokerage business with an office in the Taylor building, opposite the city hall, he has not been engaged in any active business He is a member of Montacute Lodge of Free Masons, of Eureka Royal Arch Chapter, and of Worcester County Commandery, Knights Templar He is a Republican in politics He attends Plymouth Congregational Church

Mr Scott has had the same love of travel and interest in genealogy, archaeology and antiquities that characterized his father He spent many winters in the tropics and is quite familiar with Jamaica, Cuba and the West Indies He was in Cuba when the war broke out, and crossed the island under a guard of Spanish soldiers on his way home

He married, May 3, 1869, Ella Frances Goddard, daughter of Benjamin and Martha (Dolliver) Goddard Benjamin Goddard was born May 15, 1813, in Philadelphia Martha Dolliver was born in Worcester, July 8, 1814 The children of Charles N and Ella Frances (Goddard) Scott are Arthur Nelson, born in Worcester, January 29, 1870, died August 12, 1886, drowned while bathing in Coe's Pond, just after entering Massachusetts Institute of Technology at the age of fifteen with honors in French and English, Ralph Goddard born at Worcester, November 10, 1884, died October 24, 1890, Chester Francis, born in Worcester, October 20, 1887, graduate of the English high school

(V) George T Scott, youngest son of Nelson Ryan Scott (4), was born in Worcester, Massachusetts, October 30, 1853 He received his early education in the Worcester public schools He also attended the academy at Easthampton, Massachusetts He then entered the drug store of his father and learned the business, for which he showed a natural aptitude He became a skillful pharmacist and soon assumed the burden of the business His father took him into partnership in 1875 After his father's death he became the sole owner of the business which he has carried on successfully to the present time His drug store has held its rank as one of the leading stores of its line in the city He is a prominent Free Mason, a member of Athelstan Lodge, Eureka Chapter, Hiram Council, Worcester County Commandery of Knights Templar, and received the thirty-second in the Massachusetts Consistory He is also a member of the Worcester Pharmaceutical Association, the American Pharmaceutical Association, Conquest Council, Royal Arcanum, and the Worcester County Mechanics' Association

He married, October 28, 1879, Emma E Longley, of Worcester, who was born December 26, 1856, died September 18, 1903, daughter of James O and Caroline E Longley James O Longley was born in Boylston, September 11, 1830 Caroline (Lawrence) Longley was born in West Brookfield July 30, 1833 Their children are Harry Longley, born in Worcester, February 5, 1882, associated with his father in the drug store, Nelson Theo, born in Worcester February 7, 1884, associated with his father in the drug store, Sidney Mason, born in Worcester June 4, 1889, student in the South high school, Forrest L, born September 9, 1890, died December 21, 1891

HENRY BRANNON, manufacturer of Worcester, is a striking example of a self-made man, one who, favored by no stroke of luck or family heritage, has carved out his own career and achieved conspicuous success entirely through the exercise of unflagging industry indomitable resolution and wise judgment

He is a native of England, born in Nottingham, March 7, 1850 a son of John and Margaret E Brannon The father was a trunk maker in that city He came to the United States in the year in which his son was born and the following year sent for his wife and child who joined him in Boston In 1857 Mr Brannon bought a farm in Princeton, Massachusetts, and was engaged in its cultivation during the remainder of his life He was a Republican in politics, and his first vote after his naturalization was cast for Abraham Lincoln at the first election of that immortal man Mrs Brannon died in 1892 and her husband five years afterwards, in 1897 They had ten children of whom two died in infancy the oldest being Henry, of whom further, Margaret E, James H, William E, Katie M, died aged eleven years, Charles F Sarah B, and A Gertrude

Henry, eldest child of John and Margaret E Brannon was less than a year old when his parents arrived in the United States He received his education in the common schools of Princeton, Massachusetts, and at the early age of sixteen years went to work devoting his earnings to assist his father in liquidating a mortgaged indebtedness on the farm which he had purchased Young Brannon's first employment was in the Crompton Loom Works in Worcester, where he remained for five years He then worked for some years in Taylor & Farley's organ factory in the same city In 1874, at the age of twenty-four, having acquired a little money by dint of energetic labor and careful economy, he purchased the turning and cabinet shop of J M Goodell in Worcester and has been the proprietor of that establishment ever since Mr. Brannon has developed a business of considerable proportions one of the first in its particular line His product includes all descriptions of doors sash and blind work door and window screens, and fine house finishing wood work A specialty for which his factory is widely famed is artistic bank office, store and other fine hardwood cabinet work made to order and after special designs The establishment is equipped with the most modern machinery and employs seventeen operatives throughout the year

Mr Brannon is actively identified with various institutions of a semi-public nature, and which largely enter into the life of the community He is a member of the directorate of the Worcester Co-operative Bank, and has served as trustee of the City Hospital, a trustee of the Mechanics' Association and a director and treasurer of the Young Men's Christian Association Political honors have been bestowed upon him and he has served with tact judgment and efficiency for four terms as a member of the board of aldermen from the fifth ward and in his last term honorably filled the position of president of the board, the most important in the gift of the citizens, next to that of mayor He served in the Old State Guard with the rank of orderly sergeant and is an honorary member of the Worcester City Guards, in which he served four years He is a member of the Union Congregational Church of Worcester has been treasurer of the church and parish, and on the standing committee of the church for many years He is a member of the Congregational Club, Worcester Society of Antiquity, Worcester Board of Trade, and Home Market Club of Boston Mr Brannon is also connected with the local lodge of Odd Fellows In Masonry he is a Knight Templar, and a trustee of the permanent fund of the Commandery, also a trustee of the Masonic Fraternity and vice-president of the Masonic Charity and Educational Society In politics he is an unswerving Republican He is deeply interested in all things affecting the community, and has rendered efficient aid in behalf of municipal improvements as well as religious, educational and benevolent institutions

Mr Brannon is a man of sterling business integrity His word is as good as his bond, and that has been rated AA in the first grade among financial agencies for many years The popularity of Mr Brannon among his fellow citizens was demonstrated some time ago when he had a unanimous request from the prominent Republicans of his ward to be their nominee for the position of representative to the legislature His probity of character, companionable disposition and genius as a master workman have all tended to place him in an enviable position among his fellow citizens He has taken his own full share in the duties of a public-spirited citizen, and all the interests that have engaged his attention included in the organizations already mentioned, particularly has he rendered invaluable service to the church in which he is an honored member and also in the Y M C A in which organization he has received signal honors and done yeoman service for the young men of the city

February 14, 1878, Mr Brannon was united in marriage to Gertrude Goddard, oldest daughter of Dorrance S Goddard, who for many years was connected with the wire industry in Worcester, and whose sketch appears in this work By this marriage were born these children Alice M, a graduate of the high school and Smith College, and is a school teacher Mildred I a graduate of the school of Domestic Science of Boston Olive G, a high school graduate, and bookkeeper in her father's office Henry G who is completing his course in the high school Roger W, Dorothy W, Edna L, and two who died in infancy

HARRISON GRAY OTIS The Otis family has had many men of distinction from colonial times to the present and all are of the same family, all descendants of the same progenitor, John Otis, or as the name is spelled otherwise Attis, Oates Oatise The English family has a coat of arms

(I) John Otis the emigrant ancestor of Harrison Gray Otis John P K Otis and Mary Elizabeth Otis of Worcester, Massachusetts was born in Barnstable England in 1581 He settled in Hingham in New England He was there at the time of the first division and drew land in 1635 Most of the early settlers in Hingham Massachusetts were from Hingham England and it is thought that Otis lived in Hingham for a time before coming to New England His homestead was on Otis Hill in the southwest part of Hingham, Massachusetts He had numerous grants of land between 1635 and 1647 He was admitted a freeman March

Henry Brannon

3, 1635-6 He was a town officer His buildings burned March 15, 1645-6 He removed about 1655 to Weymouth Massachusetts

He married (first) Margaret ——— in England She died in Hingham, June 28, 1653 He married (second) and his widow drew land in Weymouth in 1663 He died in Weymouth, May 31, 1657, aged seventy-six His will was dated the day before his death and was proved July 28, 1657 He bequeathed to his wife, to son John, who was made executor, to daughter Margaret Burton and her three children, to daughter Hannah Gile, to Mary and Thomas Gile, Jr, to daughters Anne and Alice His widow Elizabeth made will September 12, 1672, proved July 17, 1676, and bequeathed to son John Streme, daughter Elizabeth and son-in-law, Lieutenant John Holbrook The children of John Otis were John, see forward, Richard, went to Weymouth in 1654 settled in Dover, New Hampshire, in 1662, killed by the Indians 1689 with his son Stephen, wife and child captured and sold to the French, his widow married a Frenchman in Canada, but after his death she returned to her old home and married (third) Captain Thomas Baker, Margaret, married Thomas Burton, of Hingham, Hannah married Thomas Gile, Ann, Alice

(II) John Otis, eldest son of John Otis (1), was born in Barnstable, Devonshire, England, in 1620 He came to New England with his parents and lived on Otis Hill in Hingham He held land in Hingham in 1668-9 In 1661 John Otis removed to Scituate, where John Otis was buried May 8, 1611 It seems likely that John Otis, who died there and of whom all record is lacking, may be father of John Otis (I) and grandfather of John Otis (II), who went to Scituate twenty years later to live He probably had land there He bought a house of Deacon Thomas Robinson, south of Coleman's hill Otis also bought of John Hatherly twenty-three shares of the Conihasset partnership of forty shares This Conihasset tract was three miles square and included parts of the present towns of Hanover and Abington He was admitted a freeman at Hingham 1662, and at Barnstable, Massachusetts, in 1678 He settled in Barnstable on the Otis farm, opposite Hinkley lane, near the marshes in the West Parish He left his son John there and returned to Scituate, where he died January 16, 1683 There is a stone on his grave in the old burying ground in the meeting house land a mile south of the harbor, but the inscription is not legible

He married (second) Mary Jacob daughter of Nicholas Jacob, who came over in 1633 His children were Mary, baptized 1653, married John Gowan, Elizabeth married (first) Thomas Allyn, (second), David Loring, John, born in Hingham, 1657, married Mercy Bacon, captain, deputy to general court chief justice of the court of common pleas first judge of probate member of His Majesty's council, Hannah (probably), born 1660, Stephen see forward, James, 1663, settled at Weymouth, Joseph 1665, judge of court of common pleas, deputy general court, etc, Job, 1667, settled at Scituate

(III) Stephen Otis fifth child of John Otis (2), was born at Hingham Massachusetts, 1661 He was captain of the company and prominent in town affairs He was a tanner by trade He built a new house about 1691 He died May 26, 1733 His grave is marked in the old burying ground near the harbor His will was made in 1729 He married Hannah Ensign, of Scituate, 1685 She was the daughter of John Ensign and granddaughter of Thomas Ensign, one of the Conihasset partners in 1646 She was born in 1669 Her father fell in the Pawtucket fight, March 26, 1676 The estate which came from the Ensign family went to Ensign Otis, her son, and was owned by three of the name, Ensign Otis, in successive generations The children of Captain Stephen and Hannah (Ensign) Otis were Ensign, born 1691, John, 1694 selectman of Boston, Hannah, 1696, Mary, 1697, Dr Isaac, see forward, Stephen, 1707, died in Scituate, 1755, Joseph, 1709, settled in Boston and was keeper of the jail there, Joshua 1711, settled in Scituate

(IV) Dr Isaac Otis, fifth child of Stephen Otis (3), was born in 1699 He married 1718 Deborah Jacobs daughter of Deacon David Jacobs and his wife Sarah Cushing, daughter of John Cushing Deacon Jacobs was grandson of Nicholas Jacobs, of Hingham, whose daughter, Mary Jacobs, married John Otis (2) Isaac Otis was the first regularly bred and educated physician in Scituate He settled there and began to practice in 1719, when the town voted a settlement of a hundred pounds to encourage him to remain there He was a man of uncommon accomplishments of person and mind He died in 1786 The children of Dr Isaac and Deborah (Jacobs) Otis were Isaac, born in Scituate 1719, graduate of Harvard College, 1738, Josiah, 1721, died young, Josiah, 1725, died young William, 1726, married, died without issue, Stephen 1728, settled in Hanover, see forward, James, 1732 died young, James, 1734, married Lucy Cushing granddaughter of Rev Jeremiah Cushing, he was third physician in Scituate, was in French war Thomas, 1736, died young, Thomas, 1738, died young

(V) Stephen Otis fifth child of Dr Isaac Otis (4), was born in Scituate, Massachusetts in 1728 died early in life He married Elizabeth Wade, They settled at Hanover, a neighboring town Their children were Charlotte, born 1763, Deborah 1765 William January 16, 1768, Paul, born 1771, see forward, a daughter, married ——— Howard

(VI) Paul Otis, fourth child of Stephen Otis (5), was born in 1771 He married (first) Penelope Nichols November 5, 1791 She was born April 15 1769, died April 24 1792 He married (second) Lucy Bailey, August 1795 She was born March 9 1776, died August 21, 1805 He married (third) Mabel Litchfield February 15, 1806 She was born October 12 1784 and survived him In 1792 he lost three children by small pox, during an epidemic His children were Elizabeth, born April 25, 1792, died November 25 1792 Henry, July 18, 1796, died February 10, 1834 Benjamin Bailey, July 11 1799 see forward Harvey, September 19 1802 settled in Kingston, New York William April 16, 1807 married Mary Boynton and lived at Hubbardston Massachusetts, and Claremont, New Hampshire, Lucy Bailey, May 22 1809, married William Ross of Worcester, Mary F, October 25 1811, married ——— Mussey, of Leominster, Silas D, June 26 1814, married and settled in Lowell Massachusetts Roland L, September 11 1816 married Elizabeth Thompson and settled in Leominster Massachusetts, Paul October 18 1818, settled in Worcester married there, October 13 1840 Laura M Knight

(VII) Benjamin B Otis third child of Paul Otis (6), was born in North Scituate, Massachusetts on the old homestead He married Mary Carter 1822 She was the daughter of John Carter of Lancaster Massachusetts Mr Otis started for himself in Worcester in the shoe and leather business His store was on Main street, between School and Thomas streets which in the thirties and forties was the business centre of the town Mr Otis was a prominent business man in his day and was active in town affairs He was constable for many years

He was a member of the First Unitarian Church (Second Parish) of Worcester during the pastorate of Rev Alonzo Hill, who was appointed colleague of the first minister, Dr Aaron Bancroft Mr Otis died in Lancaster, Massachusetts, his wife also died in Lancaster

Their children, all born in Worcester except the eldest, were Mary Elizabeth born April 23, 1823, in Lancaster, Massachusetts, died in Worcester June 26, 1824, John Carter, see forward. Benjamin Franklin January 27, 1827, lives in West Newton and is auditor of the city of Newton, Massachusetts. George Henry, March 10, 1829, Nancy Carter, July 10, 1831, died October 10, 1832, Mary Jane born September 3 1833 married, November 29 1865, Hon Phinehas Ball who was mayor of Worcester, etc (See sketch of Ball Family), Harrison Gray, see forward, Ann Eliza, March 19, 1838, Lucy Maria, July 30, 1840, Edwin Augustus, March 16, 1843, Ellen Louisa, March 31, 1846

(VIII) John Carter Otis eldest son and second child of Benjamin B Otis (7), was born in Worcester, Massachusetts, March 12, 1825 He received his education in the public schools At the age of fifteen he entered the employ of Samuel B Scott, who kept a shoe store in Worcester, and also went to live in his employer's family, after the custom of the times He remained in this position for about five years, when he went to work for his father, who was a manufacturer and dealer of boots, shoes and leather in Worcester In 1844 he went to St Louis, Missouri, where his mother's brother resided, and was employed about three years as clerk He returned to Worcester in 1848 and was in partnership with his father until 1850, when he formed with C H Fitch the firm of Fitch & Otis for the manufacture of boots and shoes, occupying first a shop on Front street and later part of the Bangs block on Main street The financial troubles of 1857 caused a suspension of their business in common with that of many others

In 1861 Mr Otis was employed for a time in the office of the city treasurer, and the following year entered the Quinsigamond Bank as teller, and during the absence of the cashier on account of illness served as assistant cashier He held this position for ten years and retired, greatly to the regret of the directors, to devote himself exclusively to the duties of the treasurership of the Union Water Meter Company, an office to which he had been elected in 1868, when the company was formed by his brother-in-law, Hon Phinehas Ball, and Abram and Benajah Fitts, for the manufacture of the Ball & Fitts water meter At the death of Mr Ball in 1894 Mr Otis was elected president, and the two positions he held until his death March 11, 1900

Mr Otis was vice-president of the Worcester Five Cents Savings Bank, member of the Worcester County Mechanics' Association, of which he was vice-president and for twelve years a trustee, an active member of the Worcester Society of Antiquity From early childhood he was a member of the First Unitarian church, and was elected deacon in 1863 He was a life member and for several years was a director of the American Unitarian Association, and he served twenty-five years from 1866 as treasurer of the Worcester County Conference of Unitarian Churches, of which he was later vice-president He was a man of upright character generous and kindly in disposition and highly esteemed in social as well as business circles

Mr Otis married, April 18 1849, Mary E Kettell, daughter of John P and Maria (Vose) Kettell She died February 2, 1894 He died March 11 1900 They had three children John Pierce Kettell, born March 9, 1853, succeeded his father in business; Mary Elizabeth, born April 27, 1857, James Franklin, born May 19, 1861, died March 8, 1884

(IX) John P K Otis, son of the late John C Otis (8) and grandson of B B Otis (7), was born in Worcester March 9, 1853 He attended the public schools of Worcester, leaving the high school in his second year He was in the city engineer's office from 1869 to 1871, when he entered the Worcester Free Institute, now the Worcester Polytechnic Institute, and was graduated as a civil engineer in 1873 He was assistant engineer of the Springfield (Massachusetts) Water Works from 1873 to 1876, and engineer of the Portland (Maine) Water Company from 1876 to 1878 During the three years from 1878 to 1880 he was an instructor in civil engineering in the Worcester Polytechnic Institute. He became manager of the Union Water Meter Company, with which his father and uncle were connected in 1880 When his father died in March, 1900 he was elected president and treasurer of the company

The Union Water Meter Company was organized November 9, 1868, and re-organized in 1875 with a capital of $75000 The first building occupied by the company was a one-story wooden structure in the rear of 31 Hermon street In 1872 a four-story brick building forty by one hundred feet was added to the plant The first meter made by the company was the Ball & Fitts reciprocating piston meter, the joint invention of the Hon Phinehas Ball and Benajah Fitts In 1876 the company bought the Union rotary piston meter of Benajah Fitts, and in 1892 the company bought the Columbia pattern meter of Phinehas Ball This meter was especially designed and adapted for measuring water carrying sediment or tending to corrode or form deposits in meters The company has been among the leaders in its line of business for many years and it is one of the unique industries in which all Worcester takes pride. Besides the manufacture of water meters the company makes water, steam air and gas pressure regulators, steam fire gongs, chronometer governor valves hydraulic valves, cement testing machines, cement lining presses, hand feed drills and special hydraulic machinery The products of the company are used in every state and territory of the country and largely exported Mr Otis was a member of the Worcester County Mechanics Association, the Worcester Board of Trade, the Worcester Society of Civil Engineers, the Worcester Society of Antiquity and the Commonwealth Club

Mr Otis married October 19, 1874, Isabelle C. Stratton, daughter of Charles T and Jane M (Griffin) Stratton, of Worcester Charles T Stratton was a machinist Mr and Mrs Otis have five children Albert Stratton born November 23, 1875; Emma Heywood, born January 30, 1880, married John Wilson of Bangor, Maine their child Caroline, born July 26 1905, Edward King, born October 6, 1884, Donald Kettell, born March, 1892, Mary Elizabeth born October 14, 1895

(VIII) Harrison Gray Otis, seventh child of Benjamin B Otis (7), was born in Worcester, Massachusetts, September 18, 1835 He received his early education in the public schools of his native town and at Worcester Academy After leaving school he went to work for Fitch & Otis shoe manufacturers His brother, John C Otis (VIII), was the junior partner He was first a leather cutter then traveling salesman for the firm From 1859 to 1863 he was assistant door-keeper at the state house in Boston during the time that Hon Alexander H Bullock, of Worcester was speaker of the house When Mr Bullock was elected governor he offered

Mr Otis the position of governor's messenger During these years Mr Otis was a law student in Mr Bullock's office He returned to the shoe business, and for twenty years was associated with Smyth Brothers, shoe manufacturers, and Charles H Fitch & Co, boot and shoe manufacturers

In 1887 Mr Otis was elected an assessor of the city of Worcester and was at once chosen chairman of the board He served the city in this important office, giving the taxpayers the utmost satisfaction until 1899, when he was appointed to his present position as deputy tax commissioner of Massachusetts, a position to which his experience as an assessor and long business training admirably fitted him Mr Otis has made a thorough study of taxation and is one of the leading experts in this subject today He was one of the founders of the Association of Massachusetts Assessors, and was for four years its president and for many years chairman of its legislative committee He is known to all the assessors and legislators of the state and his intelligent and courteous co-operation with the managers of the corporations of the state in getting them to conform to the statutes, in making their reports and adjusting their taxes, is thoroughly appreciated Mr Otis is an ideal public officer having the tact, common sense and integrity that his responsible position requires Mr Otis is a Congregationalist He was for many years member of the Salem Street Congregational Church and treasurer of its society He is now a member and trustee of Union Congregational Church He is a member of the Worcester Society of Antiquity and of the Congregational Club

He married, April 29, 1858, Olive Haywood Fitch, daughter of James Harvey Fitch Their children are Charles H, born in Worcester, July 7, 1859, died 1880, Edward F, born September 29 1867 Annie Louise, resides at home with her parents, is clerk in the city treasurer's office, Worcester, Harry Benjamin, clerk in the city treasurer's office Mr Otis resides at 41 Harvard street All the children live at home

BENJAMIN WILLIS CHILDS Samuel Childs (1), the emigrant ancestor of Benjamin Willis Childs, of Worcester, was an early settler at Plymouth, New England He came from England and was probably the first emigrant of this name in New England He was related in some way to the families of this name at Roxbury Savage gives Richard Childs as his brother Freeman states that he was slain by the Indians at Rehoboth, March 25, 1675 He has many descendants in western Massachusetts Vermont and in the west Another line of his descendants is to be found in Maine The family genealogy gives Richard, of Barnstable, as the son of Samuel Childs (1)

(II) Richard Childs, son of Samuel Childs (1), was born in 1624 He married Mary Linnett, October 15, 1648 She was of Barnstable They had one son, Richard, and probably other children

(III) Richard Childs son of Richard Childs (2), was born in Barnstable, Massachusetts March, 1653 He married about 1678, Elizabeth Crocker, daughter of John Crocker She was born October 7, 1660, died January 15, 1716 He married (second) Hannah ——— He was a prominent citizen of Barnstable and was the honored deacon of the church there He died January 15 1716 The children of Richard and Elizabeth (Crocker) Childs were Samuel, born November 6 1679 see forward, Elizabeth, January 25 1681, Thomas, January 10 1682 Hannah, 1684, Timothy September 22, 1686, Ebenezer, 1691, married Hope ———, born 1690 who died in Barre where her son and other relatives lived May 3, 1783, Elizabeth, June 6 1692, James, November 6 1694, Mercy, May 7, 1697, Joseph, March 5, 1699, Thankful, August 15, 1702

(IV) Deacon Samuel Childs, son of Richard Childs (3), was born in Barnstable, Massachusetts, November 6, 1678 He married (first), July 7, 1709, Hannah Barnard She died May 16, 1727 He married (second), about 1729, Experience ——— She died May 25, 1744 He married (third), June 25, 1750 Sarah Philip (Mattoon) Field, widow of Zachariah Field, of Northfield, Massachusetts She died March 21, 1752, aged sixty-three years He died March 18, 1756, aged seventy-seven years He removed from Barnstable to Deerfield when a young man He was a man of character and influence He was deacon of the Northfield church He was a blacksmith by trade His children were born in Deerfield, viz Hannah, born July 8, 1710, Samuel, Jr September 20, 1712 Asa, January 3, 1715, David (twin), March 23, 1718, Jonathan (twin), March 23 1718 see forward, Ebenezer, November 11, 1720, Elizabeth August 5 1724, Experience, June 7, 1730

(V) Jonathan Childs, twin son of Deacon Samuel Childs (4), was born in Deerfield, Massachusetts, March 23 1718 He married, about 1739, Rebecca Scott, who was born January 9 1707 He removed from Deerfield to Hardwick, Worcester county, Massachusetts, where he died March 18, 1793, aged seventy-three years Rebecca, it is said, was a woman of marvellous strength and health She lived to the age of one hundred and one years Tradition in the family tells us that she met the good old-fashioned test of physical prowess—She could lift a barrel of cider from the cart and carry it to the door unaided She died at Hardwick in 1809 The children of Jonathan and Rebecca (Scott) Childs were Jesse born October, 1740, Hannah, September 17 1742, Ebenezer, see forward, Joseph, March 2 1746 Jonathan Jr, October 13 1748, died young, Elizabeth, November 29, 1750, Moses, April 3 1752 Sarah, April 2, 1755, Jonathan October 24, 1756 Rebecca, October 8, 1758, David, November 16 1760, Sarah, April 22, 1763

(VI) Ebenezer Childs, third child of Jonathan Childs (5), was born January 25, 1744 He married (intentions dated November 15), 1769, Abigail Willis He removed from New Salem to Barre about 1775, thence to Hardwick, Massachusetts about 1785 He died at Hardwick, March 7, 1809 His wife died December 25, 1810 Their children were Betsey, born at New Salem, Massachusetts, May 27, 1772, died 1870, Benjamin Willis, born in Barre, October 5, 1774 see forward Moses, July 6, 1777, Ebenezer, born in Hardwick, March 21, 1784, died March 7, 1786, Ebenezer, born in Hardwick, July 2, 1787, married (first) Hannah Lowell, (second) Pede Johnson (third) Mary Bullen, Anna, married Lionel Tenney, of Barre

(VII) Deacon Benjamin Willis Childs, second child of Ebenezer Childs (6), was born October 5, 1774, in Barre Massachusetts He married, about 1798, Anna Washburn who was born May 21, 1780, died October 1844 She was the daughter of Eliphalet Washburn Deacon Childs lived for several years in Barre, but spent most of his life in Hardwick, where he was deacon of the Congregational church, and a successful farmer and school teacher He died at Hardwick January 13, 1838 The children of Benjamin Willis and Anna (Washburn) Childs were Benjamin Willis Jr, see forward, Tryphena August 13, 1801, married Eli Cooley, Aurelia June 28, 1803, married William Burnap, Elvira May 28, 1805 died January 31, 1842, Franklin L. September 10, 1807, married Margaret Marsh, Tyler June 18, 1809, married Nancy Williams,

Martin Luther, June 2, 1811, married, January 6, 1840, Mercy Holmes Chapin, Ann W, May 26 1813, married (first), October 18, 1832, Lyman Hawkes, married (second) 1840 Elias Ayers, Julia Ann, April 5, 1815 married, October, 1828, Rev Gideon Dana of Amherst, Alexander Hanson, February 26, 1817, married Phebe Stevens William Allen, June 2, 1820, married, October 29, 1845 Olive Hinckley, Elizabeth Hoyt, January 21, 1826, died 1850

(VIII) Benjamin Willis Childs, eldest son of Benjamin Willis Childs (7), and father of Benjamin Willis Childs (IX), of Worcester, was born in Barre, November 6, 1799 He married, January 24, 1827, Elizabeth Southworth See account of her ancestry forward He was a mason by trade He came to Worcester about 1833 and after a few years moved to Oxford, where he spent most of the active years of his life following his business of mason and builder While in Worcester he was lieutenant in the Worcester Light Infantry in the early thirties He died in Oxford, December 31, 1866 His wife died August 7, 1853

The children of Benjamin Willis and Elizabeth (Southworth) Childs were 1 Anne Elizabeth born at Granby, Massachusetts, December 19 1827, died in Worcester, Massachusetts, July 30, 1888, unmarried 2 William Lee, born June 7, 1830 died August 28 1830 3 Frances Maria, born March 21, 1834, in Worcester, married November 26, 1863 Bernard Barton Vassall, of Oxford, Massachusetts, who was born October 10, 1835, died in Worcester March 23, 1894 He was the son of Vester and Sarah (Barton) Vassall, and grandson of Benjamin and Polly (Stone) Vassall He enlisted in Company F, Fifteenth Massachusetts *Infantry, in the civil war*, May 4, 1861, and was commissioned second lieutenant He was taken prisoner at the battle of Ball's Bluff and confined in a prison in Richmond for six months He was promoted to the rank of first lieutenant but resigned and was honorably discharged December 20 1862 After the war he served the government in the post office department, reorganizing the service in North and South Carolina He was for many years special agent of the postal department for New England He was connected with the juvenile department of the State Board of Charities for several years as agent He was a prominent member of the *Grand Army* He made his home in Worcester after the war, and his widow resides at 247 Park avenue Worcester They had no children 4 Benjamin Willis, Jr, see forward

(IX) Benjamin Willis Childs, youngest child of Benjamin Willis Childs (8), and the third in direct line of this name, was born in Oxford, Massachusetts, January 15 1839 He received his early education in the district schools of Oxford At the age of fourteen he went to the Berlin (Massachusetts) Academy when Mr Bride was the principal He began his business career as clerk in the general store of Erastus Ormsbee, of Oxford where he worked for four years Then was a student at Wilbraham and Dudley Academies At the age of nineteen he bought the store of Mr Ormsbee and began business on his own account His affairs prospered and after ten years he sold his store in Oxford, which is at the present time owned by Leonard E Thayer and entered upon a larger field in Worcester He became the senior partner of the firm of Childs & Manning Brothers, wholesale dealers and jobbers of boots and shoes His partners were George G Manning and Theodore Manning Their place of business was on Pleasant street and they began to do business in 1869 In 1874 Mr Childs sold his interests to his partners, who continued the business Mr Childs started in business again on Mechanic street at the present location of Polis Theatre He was associated with Irving W Tourtelotte under the firm name of B W Childs & Co After six months Henry E Smith was admitted to the firm and the name became Childs, Smith & Co The business grew rapidly and became the largest in this section of the state Mr Childs continued in business until 1890, when he sold to his partner, Colonel Henry E Smith, and retired from active business He has for many years been prominent in the banking circles of the city From 1880 to 1896 he was a director of the Citizens' National Bank, and from 1885 to 1889 was the president Since 1896 he has been a director of Merchants' National Bank of Worcester His business judgment and knowledge of banking and business and his sterling common sense are appreciated by his associate directors

Mr Childs has always taken an interest in political affairs He was a Republican until 1884 but having always advocated a tariff for revenue only," supported Grover Cleveland for president, and he has since been allied with the Democratic party He was elected as a Republican to represent ward eight in the common council in 1882 and 1883 He was an active member of the Republican city committee and could have had other positions had he cared for public office Since he has been a Democrat he has occasionally been drafted by his party He was their candidate for mayor, senator and other offices Mr Childs has been a member of the Church of the Unity of Worcester since 1888, and has served as member and chairman of the parish committee for several years He is a trustee by appointment of the governor of Westboro Insane Hospital and has served since 1892 on the board He has been one of the park commissioners of Worcester since 1899

He married September 20 1865, Olive Maria Chamberlin, of Templeton, Massachusetts, who was born there January 5 1843 the daughter of Moses and Charlotte (Miller) Chamberlin Their children are 1 Thomas Southworth, born in Oxford, Massachusetts August 13, 1866, married, December 29, 1897, Eliza Porter Prescott, of Rockville Connecticut, they have two children Prescott, born at Holyoke Massachusetts December 2, 1898, Benjamin Willis, fourth of this name, born at Holyoke, May 14, 1903 Thomas S is a graduate of Philips Academy at Exeter He was formerly in business with his father, but since 1888 has been in the shoe business in Holyoke 2 Frances Maria, born in Oxford, January 3, 1868 died at Templeton, Massachusetts, August 30, 1896, unmarried 3 Alice Louise, born in Worcester August 23, 1873 graduate of Smith College, 1896, now assistant registrar of Smith College 4 Mabel Willis born in Worcester November 12 1875 died January 2, 1885 5 Agnes Chamberlin born in Worcester, September 29 1877, graduate of Smith College, 1901, teacher of physics at Smith College 6 Gertrude born in Worcester, March 6 1883 graduate of Bradford (Massachusetts) Academy lives with her parents 7 Breta Willis, born in Worcester, February 10, 1888, student in Worcester high school

THE SOUTHWORTH FAMILY (I) Edward Southworth was the progenitor of the American families in Southworth He was born in England about 1590 and died there about 1621 He married, May 28, 1613, Alice Carpenter, born About 1590 died in Plymouth Massachusetts March 26, 1670 She was the daughter of Alexander Carpenter, of Wrington England which is in Somersetshire He was a silk worker in Leyden one of the Pilgrim exiles who formed Rev John Robinson's church He was descended from the Southworths of Samlesbury Hall in Lancashire, where the family was established in the thirteenth century His widow married Governor William Bradford, of Plymouth Tradition has is that Alice Carpenter and Bradford were lovers before either married and that her parents selected Edward Southworth because of his higher social rank After Bradford's wife Dorothy was drowned in Provincetown Harbor, Governor Bradford wrote to the widow in England and she came over in the ship "Ann" in 1623 to marry him Her two sons, Thomas and Constant, came with her or soon followed She died March 27, 1670, aged eighty years The children of Edward and Alice (Carpenter) Southworth were Constant, born in Leyden, Holland, 1615, died in Duxbury, Massachusetts March 10, 1678-9, Thomas, born in Leyden, Holland, 1616, died in Plymouth, Massachusetts, December 8, 1669

(II) Constant Southworth, son of Edward Southworth (1), was born in Leyden, 1615 He was brought up in the family of his step-father, Governor William Bradford, at Plymouth, Massachusetts He was admitted a freeman 1636-7 He was in the service against the Indians in the troubles of 1637 In 1646 he was color bearer for the Duxbury company He was of the council of war in 1653 He was a deputy to the general court and assistant to the governor He was treasurer of the colony, 1659 to 1673 He owned land in Tiverton and Little Compton as well as Duxbury He married, November 2, 1637 Elizabeth Collier, of Duxbury, daughter of William Collier, a London merchant, who assisted the Plymouth colonists and in 1633 himself made his home in Plymouth, where he died in 1670 Constant Southworth died March 10, 1679 His children were Mercy, born about 1638, Edward, Alice, 1646, married Benjamin Church, the celebrated Indian fighter, Nathaniel, see forward, Mary, probably about 1650 married David Alden son of John and Priscilla Alden, Pilgrims, Elizabeth, Priscilla, William 1659

(III) Nathaniel Southworth, son of Constant Southworth (2), was born in Plymouth, Massachusetts, 1648 died in Middleboro, Massachusetts, January 14 1710-11 He married, January 10, 1671-2, Desire Gray, born November 6, 1651, died at Plymouth, December 4, 1690, daughter of Edward and Mary (Winslow) Gray He lived at first in Plymouth later in Middleboro Massachusetts He was surveyor of highways in Plymouth in 1673, constable there in 1668, selectman 1689 and 1691, and ensign 1694 and 1695 He owned land in Tiverton, Rhode Island The children of Nathaniel and Desire (Gray) Southworth were Constant, born August 12 1674 Mary, April 3, 1676 Ichabod, March, 1678-9, Elizabeth, 1682, Nathaniel, May 18, 1684 Edward see forward

(IV) Edward Southworth youngest child of Nathaniel Southworth (3) was born in Plymouth, Massachusetts 1688 died in Bridgewater, Massachusetts, April 26 1748 He married in Hull, June 25 1711, Bridget Bosworth of Hull He removed with his family to the north parish of Bridgewater during its early settlement The children of Edward and Bridget (Bosworth) Southworth were Constant born July 25 1712 see forward, Bridget, April 15 1714 Ebenezer August 13, 1716, Edward, December, 1718 Theophilus February 10, 1720, revolutionary soldier Sarah January 16 1723, Lemuel, April 27 1728 (twin), Benjamin (twin), April 27, 1728 Mary January 2 1732

(V) Constant Southworth eldest child of Edward Southworth (4), was born July 25, 1712, died 1775 He married (first), April 18, 1734, Martha Keith, daughter of Joseph and Elizabeth (Fobes) Keith He married (second), January 6, 1770, Mrs Hannah Shaw, of Raynham She married (second), September 29 1780, Robert Keith Constant Southworth and wife joined the church in 1741 He was a loomer by trade He resided at Bridgewater where all his children were born He was in the militia in 1762, and in 1775 was ensign in Captain Abiel Packard's company (Sixth Bridgewater), Colonel Thomas Clapp's regiment He died from disease contracted while working on the Continental fortifications of Dorchester Heights The children of Constant and Martha (Keith) Southworth were Betsy, born January, 1735, Nathaniel, see forward, Ezekiel, March 10, 1738, revolutionary soldier, Martha, April 18, 1741, Mary (twin of preceding), April 18, 1741, Desire, September 7, 1742, Jedediah, January 6, 1745, Constant, January 29, 1747, Sarah, December 9, 1749, Ichabod, June 9, 1751

(VI) Nathaniel Southworth, second child of Constant Southworth (5), was born February 16, 1737, in Bridgewater He married (first), January 15, 1762, Katherine Howard, daughter of David Howard, son of David (III), son of Ephraim (II), son of John (I) Howard, a pioneer at Duxbury Nathaniel married (second), March 18, 1777, Janet or Jenny Brett, daughter of Simeon and Mehitable (Packard) Brett, of North Bridgewater She married (second), April 20, 1789, Ephraim Groves He resided at North Bridgewater, where his children were born The children of Nathaniel and Katherine (Howard) Southworth were Martha, born 1764, died young, Simeon, July 17, 1766, see forward, Nathaniel, April 6, 1769, David, 1773 The child of Nathaniel and Janet (Brett) Southworth was Catherine, 1777, married Ambrose Keith

(VII) Simeon Southworth, second child of Nathaniel Southworth (6), was born in North Bridgewater Massachusetts, July 17, 1766, died July 1 1820, in Lyme, New Hampshire He married, December 24, 1789, Elizabeth Anderson, born 1768, died August 28 1795 He married (second), April 30, 1798, Anna Stone, of Oxford (North Gore) born February 1, 1770, died October 28, 1834, in Worcester She is buried at North Oxford She was the daughter of Uriah and Lois (Stone) Stone He was a carpenter, born in Bridgewater removed to Ward now Auburn, Massachusetts, and later to Lyme, New Hampshire, where his six youngest children were born The children of Simeon and Elizabeth (Anderson) Southworth were Alva, born 1791, Justin, 1793, child, died young The children of Simeon and Anna (Stone) Southworth were Elizabeth, see forward, Nancy, April 24, 1801, died January 20, 1881, at Hardwick, Massachusetts unmarried, Sarah, September 17, 1803, died April 5 1824, unmarried, Louisa, November 29, 1806, died in Oxford January 8, 1870, married (first) Benjamin Vassall, probably a descendant of Hon William Vassall, who settled in Scituate among the Pilgrims, (Vester Vassall, see above, was his son by a previous marriage) James M, January 2, 1809, died September 19 1816, Alvah, August 15 1812, died January 19 1872, in Hardwick, married, 1843, Fanny Hunter, representative to general court, 1851, farmer, Constant March 15 1814 died December 5, 1877

(VIII) Elizabeth Southworth fourth child of Simeon Southworth (7) was born in Auburn, Massachusetts July 12 1799 died in Oxford, August 7, 1853 She married Benjamin Willis Childs (VIII), and was the mother of Benjamin Willis Childs (IX), see above

WILLIAM ARTHUR KILBOURN Thomas Kilburn (1) the immigrant ancestor of William Arthur Kilbourn of Lancaster, Massachusetts was born in Wood Ditton, Cambridgeshire England, in 1578 and baptized there May 8, that year In 1613 he received a bequest in the will of Agatha Borrowdale He was a member of the Church of England in good standing and seems not to have been a Puritan like most of the immigrants of the first half century of the settlement of New England He was warden of his parish in 1632 In April, 1635 with part of his family, he sailed in the ship "Increase," Robert Lea, master, and settled in Wethersfield, Connecticut He died there before 1639, she about 1650 He married in England Frances ——— Their children were Margaret baptized at Wood Ditton, England, September 23 1607, married Richard Law, prominent magistrate of Connecticut, Thomas baptized November 30, 1609 came over with wife Elizabeth, aged thirty, in the ship Elizabeth of Ipswich sailing April 30, 1634 from England, may have returned to England, George, of whom later, Elizabeth, baptized May 12, 1614, did not emigrate, Lydia, baptized July 14, 1616, married Robert Howard of Windsor, Connecticut and had five children, Mary, born 1619, married John Root, Sr. resided at Farmington Connecticut, he died August 1684, Frances, baptized September 4, 1621, married Thomas Ufford of Stratford, Connecticut, John, baptized at Wood Ditton, September 2, 1624, prominent citizen, sergeant in militia, representative to general court, etc

(II) George Kilburn son of Thomas Kilburn (1) was baptized at Wood Ditton, England, February 12, 1612 He came to Roxbury in New England as early as 1638 and was a member of John Eliot's church there He removed to Rowley, where he became a proprietor He was admitted a freeman there May 13 1640 He married Elizabeth Barker, sister of James Barker He died October 14, 1685 The inventory of his estate was returned by his widow Elizabeth November 20 1685 The children of George and Elizabeth Kilburn were Mary born at Rowley May 3, 1640, Joseph March 2 1652-3 married Mary Trumball, May 3, 1678, Jacob December 1, 1654, soldier in the Indian wars in 1680, Samuel of whom later Isaac January 20, 1659 married July 24 1684 Mary Cheney, he died December 19 1713, was a deaf mute, Elizabeth, February 1 1663

(III) Samuel Kilburn, fourth child of George Kilburn (2) was born in Rowley, Massachusetts, January 9 1656 He settled at Rowley Married Mary Foster, November 12 1682, died April 22, 1722, leaving a will in the court at Ipswich Their children were Hannah, born October 2, 1683, married, April 5 1701, Judah Clark, Samuel July 20, 1687, married Mary Lovell, December 7 1734, David, of whom later Maria July 21, 1696, died September 24, 1710, Jedediah April 20, 1699, married Susannah Fisher, of Ipswich, March 22 1724, died February 4, 1759, Dr Eliphalet, 1706, married Jane Frazer, widow of Nathan Prime, widow of Mark Prime, he died June 4, 1752

(IV) David Kilburn, third child of Samuel Kilburn (3), was born in Rowley Massachusetts, March 12 1689 He settled in Rowley also He married, January 25 1724 Elizabeth Fiske, of Ipswich She died April 17 1731 He married (second) November 5, 1731 Ruth Fiske of Andover The children of David and Ruth Kilburn were David, born at Rowley October 10 1733 died aged three months, David November 22 1734 died aged two years, Jonathan, November 15 1737, married Elizabeth Nelson, July 22, 1760 removed to Lunenburg, 1767, and died there 1806 leaving a son David, David, March 2 1738-9, Ruth, June 15, 1740, died 1746, Samuel, April 12 1742 died 1747, William, 1743, of whom later Lydia May 22, 1746, became a Shaker at Shirley, Ruth February 24 1747-8, married Thomas Houghton after he died she joined the Shakers, Samuel, November 10 1749, removed to Lunenburg in 1767, married Sarah Cook he joined the Shakers in 1785 son Samuel settled in Fitzwilliam, New Hampshire

(V) William Kilburn seventh child of David Kilburn (4) was born in Rowley, March 9, 1743-4 He removed with others of the family in 1767 to Lunenburg, in Worcester county, Massachusetts He was a soldier in the revolution in 1779-80 in the Tenth Massachusetts Regiment He married Mercy Smith He died in Fitchburg in the home of his son William August 14 1832 aged eighty-eight years Their children were William of whom later, Jeremiah died young, Ilmous died young, Mercy, born in Lunenburg married Ezra Cowdrey of Lunenburg, and had twelve children, Betsey, married William Tamtor of Leominster had nine children, son John graduated at Brown University, she died at Charlestown, June 1843, aged forty-three years, Ruth, married Josiah Burrage and had thirteen children

(VI) William Kilburn, son of William Kilburn (5), was born in Lunenburg, Massachusetts July 16, 1773 He settled there and married Mary Mace or Macy, January 12, 1796 He removed to the adjoining town of Fitchburg in 1802, and to Groton, Massachusetts, in 1840 He was a shoemaker by trade and also carried on a farm until his death in 1857 Their children were Deacon Jeremiah of whom later Mary born April 8, 1800, married, 1830, Stephen Stickney, William, June 12, 1802, was a physician and surgeon, Elbridge Gerry Fitchburg, February 25, 1808 attended Brown University, but left in senior year before graduating, married November 1840 Elizabeth A Hall, Martha Fitchburg, March 18 1810, married Avery Stockwell, 1830, Sarah June 26 1819 married Asa L Kendall June, 1842 resided at Groton Massachusetts

(VII) Deacon Jeremiah Kilbourn, eldest child of William Kilburn (6), was born at Lunenburg, Massachusetts January 24, 1797 He settled in Groton where his parents moved in 1840 He became deacon of the Groton Unitarian Congregational Church there He was a hatter by trade He died in Groton in 1862, aged sixty-five years He married April 7 1818, at Fitchburg Patty Flint, daughter of John Flint of Concord, Massachusetts Her father was a prosperous farmer Their children Martha Augusta born 1818, died August 17, 1841 Jemima Flint 1820 died in Fitchburg while visiting in 1826, Mary E, 1822, Josiah Burrage, Groton March 15 1824, married Mary F Farnsworth, daughter of Dr Amos Farnsworth, of Boston, December 9, 1851, member of the firm of French, Wells & Company, dealers in crockery, etc, Milk street, Boston director of the Grocers' Bank, Boston, Ann Maria, 1826, Frances Jane 1829 married James E Wellington, William Arthur, 1838, George Wells 1844

(VIII) William A Kilbourn seventh child of Jeremiah Kilbourn (7), was born in Groton, Massachusetts, July 16 1838 He was educated there in the common schools at Lawrence Academy at Groton Philips Academy at Exeter, New Hampshire, where he fitted for college and at Harvard University where he was graduated in the class of 1858 For the fifteen years following he was engaged in educational work He taught school at Framingham Academy five years and in the Lancaster Acad-

H A Kilbourne

 emy In 1873 he accepted the position of manager of the country place and farm at Lancaster of Nathaniel Thayer and he has filled that responsible position with eminent success ever since He is well known among the agriculturists and horticulturists of the state He is an expert in his line and the farms of which he has charge are famous throughout the country for their fruits vegetables and stock their cattle and horses Mr Kilbourn was for many years secretary of the Worcester East Agricultural Society and a member of the State Board of Agriculture of Massachusetts for sixteen years He is past master of Lancaster Grange and Worcester East Pomona Grange, Patrons of Husbandry, and he has accomplished much to better the lot of the Massachusetts farmer and to make farming more attractive and profitable

He is highly esteemed and honored by his fellow citizens For more than twenty years he served on the board of overseers of the poor of Lancaster He was on the school committee and for nearly twenty years served as moderator of the town meetings He is the treasurer of the water board of the town and has served on many important special committees of the town He is a Republican in politics In religion he is a Unitarian

He married (first) Ellen Levingston of Keene, New Hampshire, 1862 He married (second) Abbie F Goss daughter of Jonas and Abbie (Fletcher) Goss of Lancaster The children of William A and Ellen Kilbourn were Robert B born April 29, 1863 Nellie October 22, 1865 died February 21, 1901, leaving two children, Eben C Mann and Maud K Manning The children of William A and Abbie Kilbourn were Martha, born December 8, 1871, married George L Willard, of Somerville, Massachusetts, William born August 14 1873 died February 25, 1873, Elizabeth F born December 28, 1874, Arthur Goss born August 19, 1876, Mary, born April 25, 1880, Alice Maud, born January 10, 1882, Anna Goss, born August 23 1883, Flint, died in infancy Ruth B, born February 23 1888, Walton Goss born May 18, 1891

GEORGE ALEXANDER BIGELOW John Bigelow (1), proprietor of Watertown, in New England, as early as 1642, was the pioneer ancestor of George Alexander Bigelow, of Worcester, and, in fact of all the American families of that surname He bought a house and lot in Watertown in 1649 and took the oath of fidelity in 1652 He was a blacksmith by trade He acquired considerable real estate and carried on a farm His homestall was bounded by those of Richard Ambler, William Parker, Thomas Straight and Miles Ives For further details of John Bigelow, see sketches of other branches of the Bigelow family of Worcester county in this work He was a town officer

He married (first), October 30, 1642, Mary Warren She died October 19, 1691 He married (second) October 2, 1694, Sarah Bemis, daughter of Joseph Bemis, of Watertown Mr Bigelow died July 14, 1703, aged eighty-six years His will was made January 4 1703, and proved July 23, 1703 The children of John and Mary Bigelow were John, born October 27, 1643, Jonathan, born December 11 1646, Mary, born March 14 1648, married Michael Flagg, ancestor of the Worcester county Flaggs, Daniel, born December 1, 1650, resided in Framingham, Samuel, mentioned below, Joshua, born November 5, 1655 resided in Watertown and Weston, Elizabeth, born June 15 1657, married Lieutenant John Stearns, Sarah, born September 29, 1659, married Isaac Learned, of Sherborn near Framingham, James lived in Watertown, Martha, born April 1 1662, Abigail born February 4 1664, married Benjamin Harrington, Hannah, born March 4, 1666, died young, a son, born and died December 18, 1667

(II) Samuel Bigelow, fifth child of John Bigelow (1), was born in Watertown, Massachusetts, October 28, 1653 He married Mary Flagg, daughter of Thomas and Mary Flagg, who was born January 14, 1658, died September 7, 1720 He was a prominent citizen of Watertown He was an innholder from 1702 to 1716 He represented the town in the general court in 1708, 1709 and 1710 His will, dated September 30, 1720, mentions his children, as given below, and some of his grandchildren The children of Samuel and Mary Bigelow were John, born May 9, 1675, Mary, September 12, 1677, Samuel, September 18, 1679, Sarah, October 1, 1681, married Josiah Howe, Thomas mentioned below, Mercy, April 4, 1686, (Martha in some accounts) married Lieutenant Thomas Garfield, son of Captain Benjamin Garfield (see Garfield family sketch), Abigail, May 7, 1687, married, August 1, 1710, Jonathan Cutler, of Killingly, Connecticut, Hannah, May 24, 1711, married Daniel Warren a soldier in the French war

(III) Thomas Bigelow, fifth child of Samuel Bigelow (2), was born in Watertown, Massachusetts, October 24, 1683, married, July 12, 1705, Mary Livermore of Watertown He settled in Marlborough, Massachusetts, where he lived until 1720, when he removed to Waltham, where he died October 6, 1755 His wife died August 14 1753 The children of Thomas and Mary Bigelow were Thomas, born April 26, 1706, resided in Marlboro, Mary, September 2, 1707 Grace, February 7, 1709, Uriah, July 15, 1711, killed accidentally at Marlboro, March 5, 1734, Abraham, March 5 1713 resided in Weston, Isaac, September 1, 1716, Jacob, September, 1717, Sarah, May 15, 1720, married Lieutenant Elisha Livermore, who was prominent in Waltham, Josiah, mentioned below

(IV) Lieutenant Josiah Bigelow, youngest child of Thomas Bigelow (3), was born in Waltham Massachusetts, July 30, 1730 He married, July 27, 1749, Mary Harrington, daughter of Jonas and Abigail (Stearns) Harrington, born March 8 1730 He was prominent, like his brothers, Jacob and Abraham, in town affairs He was lieutenant of the Weston Artillery Company and turned out on the Lexington Alarm, April 19, 1775 He died at Waltham, July 15, 1810, aged eighty years His children, all born in Weston or Waltham, were William born October 11, 1749, Anna, August 23, 1751, Uriah, November 30, 1753, Converse, January 20, 1755, Mary, March 3, 1756, Alpheus, November 4 1757, Eunice, married, April 24 1788, Joseph Morse, and settled in Templeton, Massachusetts, and Eaton, New York, had eight children Uriah, March 15 1766, Thomas August 11 1768, Sarah, July 31, 1773, married, July 8, 1790, Hezekiah Morse

(V) William Bigelow eldest child of Lieutenant Josiah Bigelow (4) was born in Weston, October 11, 1749, married, March 25, 1772, Hepsibah Russell who was born September 12 1758 at Weston They lived a few years at Weston and then removed in 1778 to Natick, Massachusetts, an adjoining town where he spent the remainder of his life He died March 25, 1813, and his widow died October 31, 1830 He served in the revolution in Captain Samuel Lamson's company at the Lexington call He was the original character described by Harriet Beecher Stowe in her "Old Town Folks" as "Deacon Badger" and his wife Hepsibah was described as Grandmother Badger Those who remembered Mr and

Mrs Bigelow at the time the story was written declared that the characters were very accurately drawn William Bigelow, their eldest son, was described as Uncle Bill" Hepsibah, the mother of Professor Calvin E Stowe, husband of the author was known as 'Susy" while Eunice figured as "Aunt Lois" and Abigail as "Aunt Keziah"

Their first three children were born at Weston, the remainder in South Natick The children 1 William, born September 21, 1773, married Margaret Lander 2 Mary, born August 16, 1775, died October 17, 1823 3 Isaac, born October 2, 1777, married Fanny Jackson 4 Hepsibah, born December 15, 1779, married, March 16, 1797, Samuel Stowe, of Natick, and resided in Natick (Their second child was Calvin Ellis Stowe, born April 26, 1802, married Harriet Beecher, daughter of Dr Lyman Beecher She was the famous author of Uncle Tom's Cabin, he wrote many theological works) 5 Abigail, born February 15, 1782, died October 30, 1844, unmarried 6 Josiah, born March 16, 1784, died April 13, 1794 7 Eunice, born April 10, 1786, died April 15, 1831, unmarried 8 Abraham, mentioned below 9 Susanna, born May 20, 1790, married, 1817, Alexander Thayer, mother of A W Thayer, for twenty-five years consul at Trieste, Austria, a well known writer, author of life of Beethoven, she was mother also of Dr Henry Thayer, she died June 12, 1845 10 Mehitable, born August 18, 1792, married Hon Chester Adams, a native of Bristol, Connecticut, resided at Natick, was colonel in the war of 1812, town clerk of Natick for twenty-seven years, representative to the general court five years, to the state senate four years, she died November 10, 1877, he died 1856, aged seventy-one years

(VI) Colonel Abraham Bigelow, youngest child of William Bigelow (5), was born at Natick Massachusetts, March 15, 1788 He married, March 15, 1814, Louisa Train, who was born at Weston, June 6, 1794, and died in Natick, December 23, 1874 Colonel Bigelow was prominent in the militia and became colonel of a regiment of mounted militia He was commander of the Ancient and Honorable Artillery Company of Boston in 1827 and 1828 He was colonel of the Artillery when Rev John Pierpont delivered his election sermon in which he made a strong protest against the military in so offensive a way that it was noticed in the records of the organization He died at Natick, October 16, 1873, aged eighty-five years

The children of Colonel Abraham and Louisa Bigelow were 1 Alexander, mentioned below 2 Louisa Fiske, born May 14, 1816, married, October 6, 1840, James W Locke, who was born at Fitzwilliam, New Hampshire, October 6 1813, and died March 4, 1844, resided at Batesville, Arkansas 3 Margaret L, born September 21, 1817, married, November 29, 1843, Farnum White, of Holden, resided at Hudson, New York, where he died 1854, she died at Natick, July 6, 1886 4 Lucy Train, born April 8, 1819, married, May 15, 1845, Jonathan B Mann, he resided for many years in Washington, D C She wrote often for the newspapers on historical subjects, he died 1905 5 Marshall Train, born January 28, 1821, died August 16, 1822 6 Marshall Field, born October 5, 1822, married Caroline Warland 7 Francis Oliver, born February 6, 1823, died February 25, 1862, resided at Medford Massachusetts 8 Mary, born March 8, 1825, died July 30, 1827 9 Mary Elizabeth, born January 5, 1828, died November 30, 1846 10 Martha Greenwood, born February 8, 1830, married Samuel S Richardson, and settled in Terre Haute, Indiana 11 Ellen Maria born November 14, 1831, married, April 12, 1859, Isaac De Forest White, resided at Buffalo, New York, he died October 12, 1873 12 William Perkins, born July 29, 1834, married Martha Mansfield 13 Abby Frances, born in Holden, Massachusetts, September 29, 1836, married, February 22, 1855, Isaac Gale

(VII) Alexander Bigelow, eldest child of Abraham Bigelow (6), was born in Natick, Massachusetts, December 12, 1814 His educational advantages were limited to the common schools When he was fifteen he went into a woolen mill to work, and after he learned the trade of woolen manufacturing in its various branches, came to Worcester and started in business for himself in partnership with George Barber about 1850 The firm was Bigelow & Barber and their location was the present site of the carpet mills of M J Whittall at South Worcester In 1853 Bigelow & Barber bought the mill and privilege at Hopeville on the Middle river, below the power station They built a new mill, were twice burned out, but rebuilt In 1870 Mr Barber withdrew from the business and Mr Bigelow formed a stock company with E D Thayer to continue the mill The name of the corporation is the same as that under which the business has since been conducted to the present time, the Hopeville Manufacturing Company Mr Thayer was president, Mr Bigelow treasurer and Edward Gould, a director After ten years Mr Bigelow bought the other interests and remained until his death the sole owner

Mr Alexander Bigelow started with nothing and acquired a very creditable competence, he built up a prosperous business and ranked among the most respected and esteemed of the manufacturers of his day in Worcester The industries of Worcester of which the Hopeville Manufacturing Company is an example have been developed by the energy and ability of men like Mr Bigelow His woolen mill is the best memorial of his prudence, economy and thrift, his business sagacity and indefatigable industry Mr Bigelow was a member of the Church of the Unity (Unitarian) In politics he was a Republican, but never cared for public office himself

He married, April 5, 1845, Adeline Stockwell, daughter of Cyrus Stockwell She died at Worcester, December 24, 1879 He married (second) October 18, 1881, Sarah M Goodwin She resides in Worcester Mr Bigelow died January 22, 1887 The children of Alexander and Adeline Bigelow were 1 Elizabeth, born in Worcester, married in Worcester, July 16, 1878, David Manning, Jr, a prominent lawyer, he was representative to the general court, state senator two terms, he died January 5, 1905, leaving one son, Alexander Bigelow Manning (see sketch of Manning family) 2 George Alexander, mentioned below

(VIII) George Alexander Bigelow, younger child of Alexander Bigelow (7), was born in Worcester, July 19, 1853 He attended the public schools of his native place After three years in the Worcester high school he left to accept a position in the Central National Bank He was advanced to various positions in the bank, where he worked in all for four years He then entered partnership with George W Coombs in the firm of Hyatt, Coombs & Company, dealers in wool, 184 Front street Joseph Hyatt, who was interested in the firm, lived at Delaware, Ohio After three or four years the headquarters of the business was removed to the Boston office on Federal street, and the firm name was changed to Coombs & Bigelow After seven years Mr Bigelow withdrew from the business in order to take charge of the Mechanical Refrigerating Company on North street, Boston, the controlling interest of which was owned by his father and brother Mr Bigelow managed this business until it was bought by the Quincy Market Cold Storage Company

In 1894 Mr Bigelow returned to Worcester to take charge of his father's mill Since then he has been president and treasurer of the Hopeville Manufacturing Company For some years his brother-in-law, David Manning, was an officer of the corporation and devoted some attention to its affairs At present Mr Bigelow's son, Edward A Bigelow, is the clerk of the company During the past ten years the capacity of the plant has been doubled and the product correspondingly increased The chief product of the mill is woolen cloth for men's and boys' clothing Mr Bigelow is a member of the Commonwealth Club, and the Worcester County Mechanics' Association He is a member of the South Unitarian Church In politics he is a Republican

He married, October 10, 1877, Dora L. Tucker, daughter of James and Ellen (Walbridge) Tucker, of Norwich, Connecticut Their children are 1 Adelaide, born in Norwich, July 27, 1878 2 Helen Louise, born in Worcester, August 5, 1880 3 Edward Alexander, born in Worcester, May 5, 1885, attended the Worcester public schools and the Lowell Textile School and now with the Hopeville Manufacturing Company 4 Dorothy Elizabeth, born in Worcester, September 10, 1891

WALTER FREDERIC BROOKS Captain Thomas Brooks (1) was the emigrant ancestor of Walter Frederic Brooks, of Worcester, Massachusetts, and a large part of the Brooks families in this country It is claimed by some authority he came from Suffolk, England He settled first at Watertown, where he had a lot assigned him in 1631 He was admitted a freeman December 7, 1636, but very soon afterward removed to Concord and settled In Watertown he was one of "the townsmen then inhabiting" to whom the general court granted certain plow lands along Beaver brook in 1636

He was elected by the general court constable of Concord, December 4, 1638 He was a deputy to the general court seven years, representing the town of Concord He was captain of the Concord company He held various other offices He was an assessor, or "appraiser of horses, cattle, etc, for the purpose of taxing" He was appointed a special officer to prevent drunkenness among the Indians He purchased of the general court the right to carry on the fur trade at Concord for the sum of five pounds. In his day he was a leading citizen, both in civil affairs and in the military

His wife Grace died May 12, 1664 He died intestate, May 21, 1667 An agreement among his heirs on file at the probate office made June 17, 1667, was signed by the eldest son, Joshua Brooks, Captain Timothy Wheeler, husband of Mary Brooks, Caleb Brooks and Gershom Brooks, also sons of Captain Thomas The children of Captain Thomas Brooks were 1 Mary, married Captain Timothy Wheeler, of Concord He died July 10, 1687, she died October 4, 1693 2 Hannah, married, December 13, 1647, Thomas Fox 3 Joshua, of whom later 4 Caleb, born 1632, married, April 10, 1660, Susannah Atkinson (daughter of Thomas Atkinson), born 1641 and died 1669, married (second) Hannah, sister of his first wife, born 1643, removed from Concord to Medford in 1670 5 Gershom, married March 12, 1666-7, Hannah Eckles, daughter of Richard and Mary Eckles, of Cambridge, had sons Daniel and Joseph, and four daughters There may have been other children of Captain Thomas Brooks

(II) Joshua Brooks, son of Captain Thomas Brooks (1), was born about 1630, probably in England He married, October 17, 1653, Hannah Mason, daughter of Captain Hugh Mason He was a tanner by trade He settled in that part of Concord later made the town of Lincoln, where many of his family and his descendants have since lived Three generations of his descendants in the direct male line have successively held the office of deacon of the Lincoln Church He was the ancestor of nearly all the name since in Concord and Lincoln He inherited one-half the Medford property, but there is no account of its disposition except that in January, 1708 He learned his trade as furrier and tanner from Captain Mason, and subsequently married his daughter He was admitted as freeman May 26, 1652 The children of Joshua Brooks were Hannah, married Benjamin Pierce, of Watertown, John, died May 18, 1697, Noah, born 1657, died February 1, 1738-9, married Dorothy Wright, daughter probably of Edward Wright, of Concord Grace born at Concord, March 10, 1660-1, died 1753, married Judah Potter, Daniel, born at Concord, November 15, 1663, of whom later, Thomas, born May 5, 1666, died September 9, 1671, Esther, born July 4, 1668, died 1742, married, August 17, 1692, Benjamin Whittemore, born 1669, died 1734, son of John and Mary (Upham) Whittemore, Joseph, born September 16, 1671, married (first) Abigail Bateman, (second) Rebecca Blodgett, Elizabeth, born December 16, 1672, Job, born July 26, 1675, died May 18, 1697, Hugh, born January 1, 1677-8, died January 17, 1746-7, married, March 9, 1701-2, Abigail Barker, born 1683, daughter of John and Judith (Simonds) Barker, Thomas (possibly), married Elizabeth

---

(III) Daniel Brooks, son of Joshua Brooks (2), was born at Concord, Massachusetts, November 15, 1663 He was known as Daniel Brooks Sr, or Ensign Daniel Brooks He died October 18, 1733 He married, August 9, 1690, Ann Meriam She died January 24, 1757, and was daughter of John and Mary (Cooper) Meriam His will is dated January 6, 1728-9 It mentions 'my brother Joseph,' wife Anna, daughters Anna Jones and Mary Wheeler, sons Samuel and Job and no others The children of Daniel Brooks were Daniel, born June 5, 1693, died young, Samuel, born May 5, 1694, married in Weston, September 6, 1738, Elizabeth Garfield, Hannah or Anna, born February 21, 1695-6, married, 1716, John Jones, who died March 12, 1762, aged seventy-two years, she died in 1753, she had five children, Job, baptized 1698, (he was the father of John Brooks, and the grandfather of Hon Eleazer Brooks), married, January 26, 1721, Elizabeth Flagg, Mary, born March 2, 1699-1700, married Thomas Wheeler, John, born February 12, 1701-2

(IV) Deacon John Brooks, son of Daniel Brooks (3), was born February 12, 1701-2, in Concord He married Lydia Barker, daughter of John and Elizabeth Barker, and born June 18, 1711 He was deacon of the First Church in Acton, where he died March 6, 1777 Issue, four children recorded at Concord, the remainder at Acton John, born December 17, 1728, Samuel March 16, 1729-30, Charles, April 6, 1732, Lydia, May 7, 1734, Ephraim, August 5, 1736, Daniel October 24 1738, Nathaniel February 17, 1740-1, Jonas, March 18, 1742-3, died March 15, 1746, Peter, March 29, 1745, Jonas, July 31, 1747

(V) Captain Samuel Brooks, son of Deacon John Brooks (4), was born in Concord Massachusetts March 16, 1729-30 He married Mrs Hannah Brown, of Carlisle, Massachusetts, March 14,

1755 Her maiden name was Hannah Davis, and she was a daughter of Simon and Hannah (Brown) Davis, of Concord, Massachusetts, where she was born June 9, 1724 Captain Samuel Brooks settled in Worcester, Massachusetts, about 1752, the first of the name in that town, and where many of his descendants have lived and are living He was on the jury list as early as 1760 He was elected field driver in 1762, highway surveyor in 1764 town warden in 1766, tythingman in 1768, juror of the superior court, highway surveyor in 1770, surveyor of boards, shingles, etc, and special committee to perambulate the town line between Shrewsbury and Worcester in 1771, juror in 1772, tythingman, school committee and special committees 1773 In 1774, with many of the most wealthy and influential men of Worcester, he signed a protest against the acts and agitation of the committee of safety and correspondence He apparently wished to avoid war and separation from the mother country, but when the war came he worked and fought against the crown He was sent to the general court from Worcester in 1786 and 1787 He was a selectman from 1783 to 1793 He was captain in the militia He died in Worcester, June 29, 1817, aged eighty-seven years Hannah, his widow, died at Worcester, December 6, 1819, at the advanced age of ninety-five years The child of Captain Samuel Brooks was Samuel, born at Worcester, Massachusetts, June 10, 1755

(VI) Deacon Samuel Brooks, son of Captain Samuel Brooks (5), was born in Worcester Massachusetts, June 10, 1755 He removed from Worcester, Massachusetts, to Haverhill New Hampshire, at about the close of the revolution and settled there He went to Haverhill to open a store at the "Corner" He was also the owner of an oil mill on the brook, but was not very successful in these ventures Later he went to Quebec in Canada, and contracted with the governor of the provinces for a tract of land in the town of Chester, then in an unbroken wilderness and two of his brothers began lumbering in the forest A year or two later, in 1812, he took his family to Canada but owing to a change of governors in the provinces the plans he had marked out were defeated, and he left Chester to settle Stanstead Canada, where he lived to the close of his life Deacon Brooks was, while in Haverhill, the History of Haverhill says, one of the most influential citizens of the town He took part in all public affairs He was a representative to the general court, selectman of the town and filled many other positions of honor and trust For many years he was the register of deeds for Grafton county, New Hampshire He was a man of genial manners very ingenious and skillful

He married Ann Bedel Butler, March 8, 1789 She was the daughter of Colonel Timothy Bedel who was prominent in the revolutionary war She was the widow of Dr Thaddeus Butler Their daughter Hannah married for her first husband Captain William Trotter of Bradford Vermont and for her second husband Colonel William Barron, of the same town Both it is said were famous in their day for their fondness for the chase and they had access to hunt for deer back of Mt Gardner Barron was a gentleman of the old school, somewhat slightly built and very dignified and commanding in person and in speech Another daughter of Deacon Samuel Brooks married Asa Low of Bradford, Vermont and a third, Judge Nesmith, of Franklin New Hampshire The Haverhill history says these women were of great excellence of character and ornaments of home, society and church Other children were Nathaniel, born in Haverhill, New Hampshire October 3 1797, resided at Worcester, Massachusetts Samuel Edwin, George Washington, had twenty children The old Brooks house where the Deacon lived in Haverhill stood on the South Park near where the pump now or was recently The house and barn were afterward moved to Court street It was remodeled and was recently occupied by Judge Westgate, and later by Mrs Barstow Samuel Brooks, son of Samuel Brooks (6), was born in 1793 at Haverhill, New Hampshire He married Eliza Fowle of Haverhill They lived a short time at Newbury Vermont, then removed to Canada, where he became a prominent merchant at Stanstead, later at Lennoxville, where he was a farmer and trader In 1837 he was appointed a delegate to go to London to interest capital in developing Canada He formed the British Land Company, and became the manager He removed to Sherbrooke He was manager there of a branch of the Montreal Bank He was a promoter of the Grand Trunk Railroad His sons William and Charles resided in Chicago Another son Dr Samuel Brooks (Dartmouth 1874 McGill M D) resides at St Johnsbury Vermont Edward Brooks, son of Samuel (VII) is also a graduate of Dartmouth is a lawyer has been senator and judge of the Canadian courts Edwin Brooks son of Samuel Brooks (VI), was a lawyer in New York, removed to California where he was living in 1888

(VII) Nathaniel Brooks son of Samuel Brooks (6) was born at Haverhill New Hampshire, October 3 1797 His parents removed from Haverhill with a large family of children and settled finally at Stanstead Canada where they both died At the age of twenty-one Nathaniel Brooks came to Worcester where his grandfather Brooks died in 1817, the year before His grandfather had been in his day one of the leading citizens He soon took a leading part in the affairs of the town of Worcester He was selectman and filled various other town offices He represented the town in the general court in 1843-44 He was deacon of the old South Church the last fourteen years of his life and was highly esteemed for his many excellent qualities as a neighbor and citizen

He married April 9 1822 Mary Chadwick who was a member of the family for which Chadwick Square was named was born in Worcester July 3 1791 She died August 31, 1876 He died November 3 1850 They had eight children all born in Worcester as follows John Adams born April 10, 1823, died July 17 1832 Charles Edwin August 15 1824, Elizabeth Fisk June 8 1826 married George Prichard, of Bradford Vermont June 5, 1844 Nathaniel Newton November 27 1828 (twin) Mary Chadwick, November 27, 1828 (twin) married John Anderson of Anderson Heath and Company, of Boston Massachusetts and is the last survivor of the family, Horace Earle, March 1, 1834 was in the civil war and died October 22 1870 Frederic Barron, July 11, 1838 (twin), died April 11, 1839, Francis Lowe born July 11, 1838 (twin), died April 11, 1839

(VIII) Charles Edwin Brooks son of Nathaniel Brooks (7), was born at Worcester Massachusetts, August 15, 1824 He was educated in the Worcester schools and at Worcester Academy When a young man he left the farm to enter mercantile life After a service of four years in the office of the *Daily Spy*, he entered the grocery business as a member of the firm of Brooks and Stearns, whose store was at 8 Front street He was in business there for about twelve years During a part of the civil war he served as commissary at Newbern, North Carolina Upon his return to this city he

THE PARKER HOMESTEAD, LANCASTER, MASS.

became associated with his brother Horace and his brother-in-law, David H Fanning, in the Worcester Skirt Company, the name of which was afterward changed to the Worcester Corset Company He was treasurer and librarian of the Worcester County Horticultural Society from 1879 until his death, which occurred December 22, 1890

He married, December 2, 1851, Elizabeth Capron Fanning Her father, Henry Willson Fanning, was of the sixth generation in descent from Edmund Fanning, who settled at what is now Groton, Connecticut, in 1653 (See sketch of Fanning family and D H Fanning in this work) Her mother was of the well known Hale family of Connecticut The children of Charles Erwin and Elizabeth Capron (Fanning) Brooks were 1 Ella Brooks, died at the age of four 2 Arthur Anderson, born in Worcester, December 25, 1856, was graduated at the Worcester high school, fitted for college He graduated from Harvard College in the class of 1879, and from the Divinity School in 1884 He was ordained and installed in 1885 minister of the Third Congregational Society (Unitarian) at Greenfield, Massachusetts He resigned this charge December, 1896, and went abroad for study and recreation He resides in Boston, Massachusetts 3 Walter Frederic, born in Worcester Massachusetts, January 13, 1859

(IX) Walter Frederic Brooks, son of Charles Edwin Brooks (8), was born in Worcester, Massachusetts, January 13, 1859 He was educated in the Worcester schools and fitted for college He graduated from the high school in the class of 1877 He preferred to enter business at once rather than go to college, and he entered the office of George Crompton, loom manufacturer, where he worked for two years He was associated with William H Morse for eleven years in the banking business In 1891, in partnership with Mr J F Rock, he leased the Worcester Theatre and they managed it for three years He was elected treasurer of the Worcester Corset Company in December, 1895 and since then has been identified with this concern, which is the largest, best equipped one of the most famous corset factories in the country The present corporation is the Royal Worcester Corset Company, of which he is the treasurer The plant is located on Wyman, Hollis and Grand streets, Worcester, and is one of the finest manufacturing buildings in the city During Mr Brooks' connection with the business, it has been growing very rapidly and has greatly prospered

Mr Brooks is a well known Mason, having taken all the degrees to the commandery He is a member of the Worcester County Commandery, Knights Templar He is a member of the Worcester Society of Antiquity, and of the New England Historic Genealogical Society as well as other societies He is a Republican He resides at 54 Queen street, Worcester, with his aged mother, Elizabeth Fanning Brooks He is author and compiler of "History of the Fanning Family," published in two volumes in 1905

PARKER FAMILY Since that memorable nineteenth day of April, 1775, when Captain John Parker stood in command of his company of minutemen lined up on Lexington Green confronting the progress of Major Pitcairn and his eight hundred British regulars, the name of Parker has occupied a prominent place in the early annals of the United States of America But members of this family have not only become distinguished for services upon the battle field, but as divines, doctors of medicine and of surgery, judges, members of congress, journalists, artists, lawyers, civil engineers and in fact in all the various walks of life In this monograph, however, we design to present to the reader in brief outline some of the incidents and professional undertakings of George Alanson Parker and three of his sons, Harold, Herbert and Chester

George Alanson Parker was born in Concord, New Hampshire, May 8 1821, son of Joseph and Esther (Chapman) Parker His childhood days were spent in Concord, and from experience in the schools of that town he developed a strong desire for a classical education and with that object in view fitted for entrance to Harvard College But the fates led in another direction, and he entered the office of Loammi Baldwin, a noted civil engineer, where he prepared himself for a lifework that proved not only congenial, but in the prosecution of which he was highly successful

In 1842 he, in company with Samuel M Felton, became the successors of Loammi Baldwin at Mr Baldwin s death and for many years they were the most successful firm of civil engineers in New England Among the public works in which he was engaged during this time were the surveys of the Fitchburg Peterboro and Shirley and Sullivan roads, and the building of the Sugar River and Bellows Falls bridges About 1855 he established a home in Lancaster which was occupied as a summer residence mainly until his business permitted him to make it his permanent abode He was chief engineer of Philadelphia, Wilmington & Baltimore Railroad during and after the war, and built while chief engineer of that road the then famous bridge across the Susquehanna river at the head of Chesapeake Bay This undertaking was particularly difficult owing to the depth of water, the insecure bottom and the immense bodies of ice that annually descended the river The successful completion of this structure brought Mr Parker in national reputation as a constructing engineer He was one of a board to examine and report upon the proposed bridge across the Mississippi at St Louis

He was for a time acting president of the Philadelphia, Wilmington & Baltimore Railroad and was offered the office permanently He, however, preferred a more independent life than the duties of such a position would permit

During the civil war he was engaged by the United States government to supply the rolling stock for the various roads used by the war department He built many railroad lines in Delaware, Virginia, the eastern shore of Maryland and later the Zanesville & Ohio River Railway, and for many years was consulting engineer for the Baltimore and Ohio Railroad corporation He was also interested in railroads in Mississippi and Texas

Mr Parker was a special admirer of nature therefore found enjoyment in out-door life and recreation, and in selecting a home for himself and family in which to take the comfort and leisure due as a reward for an active strenuous, successful business life, located in the ancient but charming residential town of Lancaster And here he entered heartily into the duties as a citizen, serving on various committees for the improvement of the highways and the building of substantial bridges, a work for which by large experience he was specially well fitted He was also chosen to represent his district in the state legislature, serving in that capacity for three years, 1870-71-72, and when Memorial Hall was ready for occupancy he gave liberally toward furnishing it with fixtures and a valuable collection of books and works of art With his natural taste for rural life Mr Parker took great delight at his Lancaster home and gave much time to beautifying it with trees, choice shrubs, and plants, and the entertaining of his friends and neighbors upon his premises was an additional pleasure, for he was held in high esteem by the people of Lancaster He was among the first to recognize the consequences of the destruction of our forests and believed that it was a wise business proposition for every farmer who owned even a small territory to plant trees to take the place of those annually cut down He exemplified his views by himself planting many thousands of forest trees in plantations, distinct from ornamental planting and now the practical value of his views is demonstrated by the valuable timber growing upon sandy hillsides and fields otherwise valueless, within the limits of his Lancaster estate

Mr Parker married Harriet N, daughter of Cornelius C Felton and Anna Morse his wife She was a sister of Samuel M Felton, Mr Parker's first associate in civil engineering in Charlestown, Massachusetts and in the seventh generation from Nathaniel Felton, who came from England to Salem in 1633, when seventeen years of age, and later married Mary Skelton, daughter of Rev Samuel Skelton, the first minister of Salem George Alanson Parker died April 20, 1887 His children were Edith, born in Charlestown, August 2 1848, George A, May 22 1852, died February 18, 1853, Harold, June 17 1854, Herbert, March 2, 1856, Bertha, March 16, 1858, Felton, October 8, 1860, Chester, born in Chester, Pennsylvania, August 10, 1862

Harold Parker, born in Charlestown, Massachusetts, June 17, 1854, received his early education in the public schools at Lancaster, and by private tutor Subsequently he attended a private school in the city of Philadelphia, Pennsylvania, and then entered the Lancaster Academy, then a popular and highly successful institution Here he prepared to enter Exeter Academy and there fitted to enter Harvard College, after a year and a half he left Cambridge and between the years 1871 and 1899 was engaged in engineering, manufacturing and railroad work in many parts of the United States, and for most of that period maintained an engineering office in Clinton, but has always had his home in Lancaster He represented the twelfth district in the legislature and has held continued town office for many years He was appointed by Governor Crane commissioner of Wachusett Mt State Reservation in 1899 and re-appointed by Governor Bates He was appointed by Governor Crane a commissioner of state highways and has been re-appointed by successive governors to the present time He has been engaged in the cutting and manufacture of lumber in Massachusetts and Connecticut, and in the construction and operation of street railways and other enterprises And as a token that he is competent, and that the people have confidence in him, Mr Parker has frequently been selected as arbiter where differences were to be adjusted and where property rights came in question He has served as road commissioner and water commissioner in his home town, and the Lancaster people have honored him with other public positions, all of which he has filled with credit to himself and profit to the community

He married, July 29 1884 Elizabeth W, daughter of Rev Dr George M Bartol, of Lancaster, which place has for many years been his home Mr Parker is a member of the famous Hasty Pudding Club of Cambridge, president of the Chaffee Manufacturing Company and a director in several street railway companies In politics he is a Republican, and an active worker in whatever he undertakes Public-spirited and like his father is fond of outdoor exercise, appreciating to the full his beautiful home in Lancaster Their children are Bartol, born 1885 a student at Harvard, Elizabeth, 1887, Cornelia, 1894

Herbert Parker, son of George Alanson Parker, was born in Charlestown, Massachusetts, March 2, 1856 He received his early instruction in private schools in Philadelphia, Pennsylvania, and after fitting for college with private tutors entered Harvard in 1874, from whence he graduated with high honors in 1878 Because of ill health he did not complete the academic course but was later given his degree of A B He read law in the office of the late United States senator, George F Hoar, and in 1883 was admitted to the bar of Massachusetts, and commenced the practice of his profession in Worcester the following year Attracted by his special qualities, Senator Hoar engaged him to act as his private secretary at Washington, where his associations with leading legislators of the country gave opportunity for the young lawyer to add materially to his already generous stock of knowledge At the conclusion of his duties as private secretary for Senator Hoar, he again opened a law office in Worcester, but later located in Clinton, forming a copartnership with the late Judge Corcoran He became a member of the law firm of Norcross, Baker & Parker in Fitchburg, Massachusetts, later opening an office in Worcester, where the practice of his profession was continued until he was appointed assistant district attorney for the county of Worcester in 1886, the district attorney being the Hon Francis A Gaskill, and upon Mr Gaskill's retirement to go upon the superior court bench, he became district attorney by appointment of Governor Greenhalge, and was later elected to the same office, the duties of which he discharged with ability and professional skill

In 1901 he was elected attorney general for the state of Massachusetts and re-elected until 1905, when he declined a renomination for the purpose of conducting his private practice During his term as attorney general it devolved upon him to try many important cases, in all of which he displayed remarkable foresight, care and wisdom, and especially was he congratulated for the manner in which he conducted the trial of the murderer of Mable Page and its successful issue, in obtaining the conviction of the guilty party In 1905 Tufts College conferred upon him the honorary degree of L L D Mr Parker is a gentleman of many gifts, learned thoughtful witty, has a good command of language and knows how to use it effectively He is a member of the Union Club, the St Botolph, and the Tatcum Club of Boston, also of the Boston Press Club and of the Worcester Club of Worcester He resides in Lancaster, Massachusetts

He married in 1886, Mary C Vose, a daughter of Josiah H and Caroline C (Forbes) Vose, of Clinton, Massachusetts Their children are George A, born in 1887, Katherine Vose, 1888, Edith, September, 1894, Haven, April, 1899, Mary C, June 1903, Harriet Felton April, 1905

Chester Parker, son of George Alanson Parker, born in Chester, Pennsylvania, August 10, 1862, was educated in the schools in Lancaster, Massachusetts, a private school in Worcester and at Exeter Academy, New Hampshire, remaining two years at the latter place He then entered into the real estate business in Boston, and has continued in that with great success as a real estate broker with offices in Devonshire Building and 15 Exchange street, Boston He resides at Lancaster, Massachusetts, upon the old Parker homestead He is a member of the board of real estate arbitration in Boston, also a member of the Real Estate Exchange in that city He is a Republican in politics but, like his brothers, not a seeker for public office He is a gentleman whose opinions are greatly respected, and whose judgment on values of real estate are in frequent demand

He married, October, 1899, Ethel Whitney Lawton, daughter of Robert G Lawton, of Havana, Cuba Their children are Chester, born September, 1900, Felton, 1902, died the same year, Lydia B F, November, 1904

In tracing out the emigrant ancestor of this family we have not been confined to the narrow limits of the three brothers," but found on investigation that choice must be made from at least three dozen Parkers, who were launched upon our New England shores prior to the year 1630 To the uninitiated it might appear that where there are so many to select from, the choice might be the more easily made, but experience teaches otherwise We have after careful research taken as the progenitor of this New England family

(I) Joseph Parker, who located in the town of Newbury, Massachusetts, as early as 1642, when in May of that year his son Joseph was born Three years later he was of Andover, where he helped to form the first church there His children were Joseph, Stephen, John and Samuel Joseph, the father, died 1678

(II) Joseph Parker, born at Newbury, May 15, 1642, resided in Andover subsequently to 1645, and had a son Joseph

(III) Joseph Parker, born about 1660, married Elizabeth Bridges, lived in Andover, Massachusetts, and had sons Joseph and Peter

(IV) Joseph Parker, born February 27, 1682, married, February 6, 1712, Abigail Mitchell, and made their home in Andover, Massachusetts Had son Joseph and perhaps others

(V) Joseph Parker, born November 12, 1712, in Andover, married Elizabeth Martin, April 26, 1757 He was one of the very early settlers of Pembroke, New Hampshire As early as 1737 a vote was passed that the ferryboat at Suncook be kept against Joseph Parker's house lot, which was No 14 He also bought lot No 20 of Eleazer Allen about 1760, which he sold to James Knox, May 8, 1776 He signed the "Association Test" in summer of 1776 "We the subscribers do hereby solemnly engage and promise that we will to the utmost of our power at the risk of our lives and fortunes with arms oppose the hostile proceedings of the British fleets and armies against the United American Colonies" Their children were John, born August 15, 1760, Molly, born September 7, 1766, Dorcas, born February 12, 1769, and perhaps others

(VI) John Parker, born August 15, 1760, married Martha Lovejoy, May 21, 1781 He purchased a tract of wild land in North Pembroke and there built a log house and lived with his father until he could build a better one He was a member of the first militia company of the town, and with others signed a petition December 30, 1777, to have this company annexed to Colonel Stickney's regiment July 1, 1780, he enlisted to serve for three months He died May 27, 1825, having merited the military title of colonel Children were Joseph, born November 3, 1781, Caleb, February 28, 1784, Abigail, June 29, 1787, John Ladd, 1789, Ezra, September 12, 1791, Obidiah, 1793, James, 1794, Mehitable Lovejoy, April 17, 1800, Charlotte, April 30, 1803, Martha, 1805

(VII) Joseph Parker, born November 3, 1781, married Esther Chapman He went to Concord, New Hampshire, about the year 1821, and for several years was employed on the Granite Ledge, and later was the first overseer of the alms house and town farm He was a much respected and useful citizen He left Concord in 1834 Children were Lucretia born May 4 1807, Martha, November 30, 1808, Caleb September 8, 1810, Lyman, January 2, 1812 Horace April 5 1814, Joseph, April 30, 1817 Horace August 15, 1819, George Alanson, May 8, 1821, Mary Esther, July 10, 1823, Lucy Ann, March 9 1826, Lucretia, August 19 1829

(VIII) George Alanson Parker, born in Concord, New Hampshire, May 8, 1821

HENRY WILLIAM EDDY Rev William Eddy (1), of Cranbrook, Kent county, England, was the father of the two emigrants of the name who settled in New England in 1630 He was the progenitor of Henry William Eddy of Worcester The sons were John, born about 1595, Samuel, was in Plymouth in 1632, and probably came with his brother in 1630 he was admitted a freeman at Plymouth in 1633 reported able to bear arms 1643, his wife was Elizabeth, and they had a large family and resided in the Plymouth colony

(II) John Eddy, son of Rev William Eddy (1), was born in Cranbrook, Kent county, England, in 1595, according to his oath made December 15, 1673, when at the age of seventy-seven he asked to be excused from training' John Eddy came to Plymouth in New England in the ship "Handmaid," arriving October 29 1630 He removed to Watertown Governor Bradford wrote of him "A Godly man, now and then a little distempered" He was admitted a freeman in Watertown, September 3, 1634 He served the town in various town offices He married (first) Amy ———, and (second) Joanna ———, who died August 25 1683, at the age of eighty years The children of John and Amy Eddy were Pilgrim, born August 25, 1634, John, born February 16, 1636-7, Benjamin, buried in 1639, Samuel, born September 30, 1640, Abigail, born October 11, 1643

John Eddy died October 12, 1684, at the age of ninety years His will dated January 11, 1677, and probated December 16, 1684, bequeathed to sons Samuel and John, sons-in-law John Miriam (Merriam) and Thomas Orton, and daughters Mary Orton Sarah Miriam, Pilgrim Steadman and Ruth Gardner, wife to have according to their marriage contract

(III) Samuel Eddy son of John Eddy (2), was born in Watertown, Massachusetts, September 30, 1640 He was a farmer, settled at Watertown He married Sarah Mead, November 31 (sic 31 9), 1664 She was the daughter of Gabriel Mead, of Dorchester, Massachusetts He was admitted a freeman there May 2, 1638 Her mother, Joanna, was admitted to the church there about 1638 Gabriel Mead died May 12, 1666 aged about seventy-seven and his will was proved July 17, 1667 His four daughters, Lydia, Experience Sarah and Patience, were all minors at the time The children of Samuel and Sarah (Mead) Eddy were all born in Watertown viz Samuel, born June 4, 1668, Benjamin born September 16, 1673

(IV) Samuel Eddy, son of Samuel Eddy (3), was born in Watertown, Massachusetts, June 4 1668 He married, December 13 1693, Elizabeth Woodward, of an old Watertown family He died August 6, 1746 She died August 7, 1753 The children of Samuel and Elizabeth (Woodward) Eddy were John born at Watertown, May 6, 1696, settled in Oxford Massachusetts, Elizabeth, born in

Watertown, May 28, 1697, died young, Sarah, born in Watertown, May 9, 1700, settled in Oxford, married June 1, 1730 Peter Hurd, Samuel, born in Watertown, August 18, 1701, Elizabeth, born in Watertown, July 29, 1703, Ebenezer, born in Watertown, January 9, 1705 settled in Oxford, Benjamin, born in Watertown, November 30, 1707, married, 1733, Elizabeth Truesdell, he was a tailor, settled in Winchendon or Royalston where he died aged ninety years

(V) Samuel Eddy, son of Samuel Eddy (4), was born in Watertown, Massachusetts August 18, 1701 He settled in Oxford Massachusetts He married, January 30, 1727, Elizabeth Bellows, of Marlboro, Massachusetts His farm was in that part of Oxford later set off as Ward, now Auburn He died there August 4 1762 The inventory of his estate was five hundred and seventy-eight pounds The deed of his farm was dated May 20, 1724 when Abraham Skinner of Colchester Connecticut, sold him sixty acres on Prospect Hill He was selectman and held other offices The children of Samuel and Elizabeth (Bellows) Eddy were Elizabeth, born November 24, 1728, at Oxford, Samuel, born 1731 died 1736 Ruth, born in Oxford, October 23, 1733 married (intentions dated July 10), 1762 John Hart, of Leicester, Jonathan born in Oxford, December 23 1735, soldier in the French war, died at Fort Edward unmarried, Samuel, born July 31, 1738, Abigail, born in Oxford, December 5 1740, married January 2 1759 Joshua Merriam, of Oxford North Gore, Levi, born in Oxford, April 27, 1745, married (intentions dated June 28) 1766, Sarah Stone (Smith?) of Charlton The Eddy genealogy gives also John died in French and Indian war

(VI) Samuel Eddy, son of Samuel Eddy (5), was born in Oxford July 31 1738 He married March 13, 1760 Susannah Merriam, of Oxford North Gore, and settled on the Eddy homestead He was a man of prominence He served in the French war, 1757 At the close of the war in 1763 he was lieutenant of the second company, Joseph Phillips, captain In 1776 with William Campbell and Amos Shumway he was on the Oxford committee of safety and correspondence He was captain of the militia and served in the revolution He was selectman in 1771 and 1773 He served the town as constable and in other capacities He died July 4 1798 His wife died January 17, 1803 aged sixty-six years The children of Samuel and Susanna (Merriam) Eddy were Isabella, born March 27, 1761, Samuel, born July 11, 1764, John born May 31, 1768, Rufus born April 6 1772, Susanna, Ruth All of the foregoing are mentioned in their father's will dated June 5, 1793, excepting Isabella

(VII) Samuel Eddy son of Samuel Eddy (6), was born in Oxford, Massachusetts July 11 1764 He married Sarah Hart and settled in Oxford He died May 11, 1813, she died October 17 1838 aged seventy years He was deputy sheriff for many years and well known all over the county The children of Samuel and Sarah (Hart) Eddy were Lines Samuel born July 19 1796 settled on the homestead, Lewis born February 16 1801 Leonard Lydia, married Daniel P, son of Reuben Eddy, Sarah married (first) Thomas Baird, married (second) Swan Knowlton, Susan, Mary, married W I Warren resided at Holden Massachusetts

(VIII) Lewis Eddy son of Samuel Eddy (7), was born in Oxford Massachusetts February 16 1801 He married May 14 1823 Almira Smith, daughter of Samuel Smith of Oxford Massachusetts He settled on a farm in Auburn and also owned a farm in Fitchburg Massachusetts He was a carpenter and builder, also a leading citizen of Oxford He and his brother Samuel were both captains of the militia company and both represented the town in the general court, Samuel of Oxford, Lewis of Auburn Lewis Eddy was assessor and selectman in Auburn, and a prominent member of the Congregational church He sold both farms some years before his death and moved to Worcester, where he died June 14, 1875 His wife died June 5, 1867, also in Worcester The children of Lewis and Almira (Smith) Eddy were 1 Eliza N, born April 16, 1824 married, December 22, 1847, Levi Eddy, settled in Worcester, he died December 5, 1870, she died 1888 2 Henry William, born October 17, 1826, married January 3, 1850, Julia Foster, of Fitchburg, married (second) Nancy M Merrill 3 Amelia L, born April 1, 1829, married, April 10, 1849, William H Richards, married (second), June 24 1869, David B Galloupe, of Salem, no children 4 Emily S, born November 24, 1831, married December 11, 1856, Charles A Bowker, she died January 15, 1852 5 Lewis M, born June 9 1834 married, April, 1871, V Adelaide Libby, of Rockland, Maine, resided in Boston 6 Mary F, born February 10 1836, married, December 29, 1859, John N Peters, of Westboro, resided in Worcester 7 Samuel S, born April 27, 1838, married, January 1 1857, Susan W Carry married, (second), October 14, 1880, Franc O Webster, of Rochester, New York, second lieutenant Fifty-first Regiment Massachusetts Volunteer Militia in the civil war and very efficient, raised in Worcester, Company F, Forty-second Regiment, of which he was made captain, removed in 1867 to Rochester, New York, where he became colonel of the Fifty-fourth Regiment, New York National Guard, manufacturer and trader 8 Lucian A, born March 5, 1842, married, June, 1863, Caroline A Haskell, of North Brookfield, Massachusetts, resides in Syracuse, New York 9 Albert M, born March 22, 1843 married, December, 1869, Caroline M Hervey, resides in St Louis, Missouri 10 Alfred Theodore, born February 28, 1845 married, July 12 1864, Elizabeth S Cummings, of Nashua, New Hampshire, she died April 1, 1878, he was in the civil war, the Forty-second and Fifty-first Massachusetts Regiments 11 Herbert, born 1849, died 1850

(IX) Henry William Eddy, son of Lewis Eddy (8) was born in Auburn Massachusetts, October 17, 1826 He attended the district schools of his native town and Leicester Academy After leaving school he learned the trade of carpenter of his father, who was a contractor in Auburn When he was twenty-one years old he came to Worcester and worked at his trade for Captain Lamb After a year he went into business for himself in Worcester, and his first shop was on Southbridge street He began in a small way, but in 1849 when he started as a builder Worcester was growing into cityhood and he soon became one of the leading builders of the place When he started Worcester had a population of only 8,500 It has now 130,000 He was in business until he was seventy years old a period of nearly fifty years, while his active life was much longer But in those fifty years Mr Eddy took a large share in the development of Worcester, in building the shops, business blocks homes and public buildings that comprise the tangible city of today, that will comprise a substantial part of Worcester for hundreds of years in part, for the monument of a builder's work lasts longer than the work of most craftsmen

Among the buildings that Mr Eddy constructed in the course of his business career are the following The People's Savings Bank building on Main street, a fine type of modern office building, the Fawcett building adjoining the People's Bank building, the Five Cents Savings Bank building, another fine office building, the Dean and Salisbury buildings at Lincoln square, the Vaill building, Loring & Blake's building, the National Wire Goods building and other shops on Union street He built the Whitcomb Envelope factory on Salisbury street, the Logan Swift & Brigham Envelope factory and the Ames Plow Company works on Prescott, the Chase building and others for Ransom C Taylor on Front street, the Foster building on Foster street, the stone freight house of the Boston & Maine Railroad, formerly the Worcester & Nashua Railroad, near Lincoln square, the Grout building, Main street, Dr Henry Clarke's building, Waldo street, the Sargent building, the Sumner Paratt building, Front street He re-built the Central Exchange building, now next to the best and largest office building in the city He has constructed more than two hundred dwelling houses in Worcester, some of them among the finest in this section He built the home of Charles F Washburn on Elm street, Mrs William Dickinson on Cedar street, Major L J White on Harvard street, the Bowker house on Cedar place, the residence of the late Lucius J Knowles and that of William H Burns

His place of business was first on Southbridge street Then he removed to the Paine-Aldrich shop on High street, and later to 6 Norwich street, where he was located for some forty years In 1865 he began the manufacture of small parts of boot and shoe machinery in Lynn The name of the firm was Tripp, Eddy & Co Later the firm removed to Boston and bought the business of A L Perkins & Co, a firm in the same line, and continued in business until 1900, when the firm sold to the trust, the United Shoe Manufacturing Company Since retiring from business Mr Eddy has lived at his handsome home, 7 Ashland street, Worcester

He married, 1848, Julia Ann Foster, of Fitchburg He married (second), 1884, Mrs Nancy M Merrill a widow daughter of ——— Lord The children of Henry W and Julia Ann (Foster) Eddy were 1 Frank Foster, born in Worcester, he is a manufacturing dentist with places of business at 172 Tremont street, Boston, and at the Franklin building, New York city, married and has one daughter 2 Charles H, born in Worcester, general manager and treasurer of the Chickering Piano Company of Boston

FRANK AUGUSTUS ATHERTON has been identified with the business life of Worcester since the close of the civil war His boyhood was spent in his native town of Harvard, in Worcester county In 1864, when he was only fifteen years of age, he enlisted in Company E, of the Sixth Massachusetts Regiment, one of the famous Worcester county regiments, and served for three months At the close of his term of service the war was approaching an end, and he returned to his home in Harvard where for a year and a half he worked in a sawmill, and acquired a knowledge of wood manufacturing that was essential to his success in his subsequent business In 1865 he purchased his father's business, which he still conducts He has a large mill, one hundred and sixty-three feet in length, at 183-5-7 Park avenue, in Worcester, equipped with modern machinery for the manufacture of refrigerators, store fixtures and other cabinet making For forty years he has taken an active interest in city affairs He is a Republican, and in 1889, 1890-91-92 represented his ward in the common council He was a member of the committees on sewers and highways He is and has been for twelve years (1905) an overseer of the poor of the city He is a member of the Masonic order in Massachusetts, having taken all the degrees, including the thirty-second, is also a member of Morning Star Lodge His home is at 5 Hall street, Worcester, Massachusetts

Mr Atherton's ancestry is extremely interesting It runs back in the Atherton line to James Atherton, probably a brother of Governor and Major General Humphrey Atherton The Athertons came to Lancaster, Massachusetts, in 1653, and some of the Atherton family still reside on the original farm Harvard, Massachusetts, where Frank A Atherton and several generations before him were born, was part of the same settlement

(I) James Atherton was born in England, probably in Lancaster, where for a thousand years the Athertons have been an important family, having a manor and of course bearing arms He was born in 1626, he died in Sherborn, Massachusetts, at the home of his daughter, Deborah, wife of Captain Samuel Bullard, August 6, 1710 His wife died also at Sherborn, December 29, 1713 Children were 1 Hannah and 2 James, (twins), born March 13, 1654 3 Joshua, born March, 1656 4 Hannah, born November 10, 1657 5 Mary, born November 17, 1660 6 Elizabeth, born June 10, 1665, died September 6, 1666 7 Deborah, born June 1, 1669 8 Joseph, (see forward)

(II) Joseph Atherton, son of James (1) and Hannah Atherton, born May 28, 1672, at Lancaster, Massachusetts, married Hannah Rogers, at Lancaster, January 9, 1720 Children, born at Harvard, Massachusetts, were 1 Oliver, born August 1, 1721 2 Mary, born May 8, 1722-3 3 Joseph, (see forward) 4 Elizabeth, born May 5, 1727 5 Elizabeth, born September 7, 1729 6 Hannah, born May 16, 1731 7 Patience, born August 15, 1735

(III) Joseph Atherton, son of Joseph (2) and Hannah (Rogers) Atherton, his wife, was baptised October 26, 1729, born about 1725, married Sarah Hutchins in 1752 Children, born at Harvard, were 1 David, born July 31, 1753, died young 2 Sarah, born May 25, 1755 3 David, born September 17, 1757 4 Jonathan, born November 11, 1759 5 Abigail, born November 2, 1762 6 Joseph, born May 12, 1768

(IV) David Atherton, son of Joseph (3) and Sarah Atherton, born September 17, 1757, married Esther Atherton He lived in the house built by Joshua (2) Atherton It stood under a great elm and was one of the familiar land marks for nearly two hundred years It was destroyed in 1852 It had a great central chimney, part of stone, part of brick laid in clay mortar Joshua Atherton died there His son, Peter, who was a prominent man in the town of Harvard, representing the town in the general court and serving as its first town clerk, occupied the house David Atherton was its fourth owner In 1805, while gathering nuts, he fell from a tree, and as a result of his injuries his legs and the lower part of his body were paralyzed He lived for twenty-five years, working at the shoemaker's trade which he learned after his misfortune His children were 1 Silence, born May 29, 1785 2 Louisa, born May 11, 1787 3 Ebon, born March 1, 1789 4 Charles, born February 22, 1792 5 Martin, born July 2, 1793 6 Emily, born July 31, 1795 7 George, born January 21, 1798 8 Mary, born March 2, 1801

(V) Ebon Atherton, son of David (4) and Esther Atherton, born March 1, 1789, at Harvard and lived there He had a son Alfred, born at Harvard

(VI) Alfred Atherton, son of Ebon Atherton

(5), was born at Harvard and learned the carpenter's trade He established the business in Worcester now carried on by his son, Frank A Atherton He married Abbie M (Adams) Stacy, born in Harvard about 1822 She was a daughter of Jonathan and Alice (Whitney) Adams, a descendant of Henry Adams, of Braintree, Massachusetts, who was the progenitor of John Adams, John Quincy Adams and many other famous men Her father died at the age of forty-seven She is the youngest and only survivor of a family of ten children and was obliged, at the age of thirteen, to earn her own living She went to work in a cotton mill at Lowell, where she was employed till her marriage, in her twentieth year, to George W Stacy, who died before the birth of her first child This daughter, Georgianna, is now the wife of Francis Merrifield, of Worcester The children of Alfred Atherton and his wife, Abbie, were 1 Frank Augustus (see forward) 2 Edward Herbert, born at Harvard, February 11, 1856, graduated at Harvard College 1879, teacher of foreign languages in Boston Latin School 3 Walter E. Atherton, born May 16, 1860, a resident of Worcester, married Ethel Muzzy and had Leroy, born August, 1880, Dora, born September 27, 1885, Carl, born June, 1886 The widow of Alfred Atherton is still living (1905) in Worcester He died there in 1892

(VII) Frank Augustus, son of Afred Atherton (6), born February 15, 1849, married November 5, 1873, Inez L Adams, daughter of John Quincy and Harriet L (Bottom) Adams, born at Woodstock, Connecticut, a descendant of President Adams Their children are 1 Ralph, (see forward) 2 Bessie F, (see forward) 3 Philip Hyde, born May 27, 1888 4 Ruth Eveline, born March 5, 1890 5 Laura Inez, born June 11, 1892

(VIII) Ralph Edward Atherton, son of Frank A Atherton (7), born August 18, 1878, was educated in the Worcester schools He graduated from the Worcester Polytechnic Institute and is now a district inspector for the American Bell Telephone Company, at Chicago, Illinois

(VIII) Bessie F Atherton, daughter of Frank A Atherton (7), born September 17, 1885, graduated from the Worcester high school in 1903

GEORGE HENRY CLEMENCE Richard Clemence (1), from whom George Henry Clemence is descended, emigrated from England about 1782 He was born November 12, 1757, and died in Brookfield, Massachusetts, March 5, 1813 He married Anne Ainsworth November 22, 1781 She was born in England May 4, 1762, and died April 20, 1832 Eight children were born to them

(II) Henry Clemence, son of Richard Clemence (1), born October 14 1795, was a hatter by trade, and located in Brookfield, Massachusetts He settled in Hubbardston, Massachusetts, about 1814, and was made a Master Mason April 27, 1830, in the Templeton Lodge of Templeton, Massachusetts

He married, November 27, 1820, Harriet W Waite of Hubbardston, Massachusetts, born February 26, 1802, at Hubbardston, died there December 11, 1824 He died in Hubbardston, January 30, 1863 Two children were born to them

(III) Richard Henry Clemence, son of Henry Clemence (2), born at Hubbardston, September 28, 1821, died September 17, 1868 in Worcester Massachusetts He was a carpenter by trade, and lived in Fitchburg a number of years He came to Worcester where he entered the employ of the Washburn & Moen Manufacturing Company, and in 1863 went to New York city for the company Before the close of the civil war he returned to Worcester and opened there a grocery and provision store He was a member of Masonic bodies He married Mrs Eva L Kendall (born Osgood), November 27, 1862 She was born January 9, 1831, at Hartland, Vermont, and died December 21, 1904, at Worcester, Massachusetts

(IV) George Henry Clemence, son of Richard Henry Clemence (3), was born at Worcester, Massachusetts, January 13 1865 He attended the Worcester public schools, afterward preparing under private tutors for entrance to the Massachusetts Institute of Technology, which he entered in the year 1886, taking the special course in architecture He entered the employ of Stephen C Earle, architect, of Worcester, in 1882, severing his connections with him in 1890, he entered the employ of Darling Brothers, general building contractors, of Worcester, and remained with them two years In 1892 he began the practice of his profession, taking offices in the Walker building, Worcester, Massachusetts, where he has remained to date His practice has steadily increased, resulting in placing his reputation with those of the leaders of the profession in Worcester A large number of residences, public buildings, business premises, etc, attest his capacity and industry in his profession

He married at Worcester, Massachusetts, October 9, 1889, Anna Eliza McDonald She was born in Worcester November 27, 1865, and is a graduate of the Classical high school, class of 1883 They have one child, Hazel, born at Worcester, Massachusetts, August 28, 1890 Mr Clemence is a member of local Masonic bodies and of the order of Odd Fellows, also a member of Hancock Club He is a fellow of the American Institute of Architects, and of Worcester Chapter, American Institute of Architects

LYMAN JOSIAH TAFT Robert Taft (1), the first emigrant of this surname, who is the progenitor of so many of the Taft families of Worcester county where the name is more common than in any other section of the country was the ancestor of Lyman Josiah Taft, late of Worcester Under the heading of other Taft families a pretty complete record of the life of Robert Taft in New England, gathered largely from the researches of the late Judge Alphonso Taft, father of the Secretary of War, may be found in this work

Robert Taft was a native of Scotland He appears to have come to New England in 1677 or 1678 and settled in Braintree, now Quincy, Massachusetts, near Boston It was just after the disastrous King Philip's war In 1678 and 1679 the colonists who had been driven away from the frontier towns by the Indians were making plans for re-settling their farms Robert Tait and Savill Simpson joined in the purchase of Colonel William Crowne's farm at Mendon for which they paid ninety pounds August 15 1679 They sold their place in Braintree, November 18 1670 and doubtless moved to Mendon with others from Braintree in the spring of 1680 The land was divided by deed dated July 29, 1680 Half the property which was on one side the road was known as Pondfield and that went to Simpson, while the land on the opposite side of the road known as Fortfield from an old fort built long before the days of King Philip as shown by the name in earlier deeds went to Robert Taft and became the nucleus of the Taft homestead Taft was acquisitive He got land in one way and another until he owned all about the pond which was in the earlier days known as Taft Pond Alanson Taft, of Mendon, lately owned the original home site besides owning for two miles and a half from his home a tenth

Lyman J. Taft

interest in what became the town of Sutton Massachusetts, in 1703 In rebuilding the town of Mendon Taft was an important factor He was on the first board of selectmen He and his sons built the first bridge over the Blackstone river He served during all his active life on important town committees and in other offices of trust and honor He was for his day a citizen of wealth and distinction, and he founded a family than which there is none in Worcester county with a more honorable record or with a greater number of distinguished men The children of Robert and Sarah Taft were Thomas, born 1671, Robert, Jr, 1674, Daniel, 1677, Joseph, 1680, and Benjamin

(II) Daniel Taft, third son of Robert Taft (1), was born probably in Braintree, Massachusetts, but possibly in England in 1677 He died August 24, 1761, as stated on his gravestone in the Mendon burying ground at the age of eighty-four years He settled on part of the Fortfield farm given him at the time of his marriage by his father It is the farm occupied some years ago by Samuel H Taft He had five sons who became enterprising farmers in the vicinity After his wife Lydia died in 1758 he went to live with his son Daniel on what is now known as the Southwick farm in Mendon where he died in 1761 He was a lawyer as well as farmer He was legal adviser to his brothers and to the town He was town treasurer many years and moderator of the town meetings He was the leading citizen for some years He was a delegate to negotiate for a new county and Mendon and Uxbridge were transferred from Suffolk county to the new county of Worcester He gave the town the site for a burying ground in Mendon He represented the town in the general court in 1728 and other years, and was justice of the peace and conveyancer for his section Mr Taft married (first), 1702-03, Hannah ——, who died August 8, 1704, leaving an infant son Daniel, who died soon afterward He married (second), December 5, 1706, Lydia Chapin, daughter of Captain Josiah Chapin The child of Daniel and Hannah Taft was 1 Daniel, born August 4, 1704 The children of Daniel and Lydia (Chapin) were 2 Abigail, born September 24, 1707 3 Josiah see forward 4 Lydia April 13, 1713 5 Daniel, April 29, 1715 6 Ephraim, May 25, 1718 7 Japhet, March 3 1721-22 8 Caleb 1724

(III) Josiah Taft, third child of Daniel Taft (2), was born April 2, 1709, and died 1756, aged forty-seven years His father gave him his farm by deed It was on the west side of the Blackstone and passed to his son Bazaleel He was captain of the militia In 1732 he became a resident of the town of Uxbridge where he became as prominent as his father had been in Mendon He held the various town offices Among his children were Caleb, died at Harvard College in 1756, Bazaleel, a prominent citizen soldier in the revolution, Joel, born 1747-48 see forward

(IV) Joel Taft son of Captain Josiah Taft (3), was born in Uxbridge, Massachusetts, in 1747-48, and settled there Among his children was Joel

(V) Joel Taft, son of Joel Taft (4), was born on the old homestead at Uxbridge, Massachusetts, in 1766 He married Chloe Fisher in 1789, and they had among others a son John, born June 22 1797

(VI) John Taft, son of Joel Taft (5), was born in Uxbridge, Massachusetts June 22, 1797 He received a good education in the public schools and in New Salem Academy He married, April 18, 1826, Lurenza Newton daughter of Josiah Newton a resident of Hubbardston Massachusetts John Taft died at Petersham in 1834 leaving a widow and two sons Mrs Taft married (second) Captain Sewall Moulton, of Hubbardston The children of John and Lurenza (Newton) Taft were Alonzo, and Lyman Josiah, see forward

(VII) Lyman Josiah Taft, son of John Taft (6), was born in Petersham Massachusetts, October 10, 1829, and died in Worcester, February 24, 1878 His father died when he was very young and after his mother married again his stepfather and he did not get along well together The boy had a taste for books and study, the stepfather expected him to be content with a single term in the district school of Hubbardston, and when the boy studied at home by candle light the stepfather interfered and forbade him the use of candles He then resorted to pine knots for light and the woods for his school room Here he was not molested, but the strain on his eyes weakened them and later probably caused them to fail him He went to the Westminster Academy and offered to work for his tuition He made the arrangement and then his mother saw to it that each week when he came home he should take a week's supply of provisions back with him He made rapid progress in his studies, especially in the classics, but after two years his eyes failed him and were so bad that he had to stay in a darkened room to save them He gave up further study and was never able to read much afterward This misfortune made a prosperous business man out of a promising scholar

First Mr Taft decided to follow the example of Richard H Dana, who was a common sailor for two years when a young man, and who detailed his adventures in a fascinating book "Two Years before the Mast" Mr Taft went to sea He made voyages to South America and the Pacific and accepted every chance to study navigation His progress was so rapid that when at the end of two years the ship's captain and mate both died in New Orleans, he was able to assume command and he brought the ship to its home port in safety He visited his mother at Hubbardston and then came on foot to Worcester to look for work He got a position in a railroad restaurant not being able to take employment requiring much strain on the eyes He found the work congenial and made many friends among the traveling public as well as in Worcester He decided to follow this business on his own account He established a restaurant and became a prosperous business man in Worcester He soon acquired a competence His partners were Charles H Rice and Frank Harrington, and their store at 233 Main street was run under the name of Taft, Rice & Harrington He extended his business to include the railroad restaurant in the Union station He built a five-story building in which he located his business, he purchased other real estate in Worcester and invested his money to advantage In 1868 he was able to retire from active business leaving his business interests in the hands of partners At that time he was one of the foremost citizens of Worcester He traveled extensively in the South and elsewhere In 1876 he sold out all his business interests and two years later died as universally regretted as any man of his day in Worcester He was still in the prime of life and had reason to expect many more years of life Although his career would probably have been professional if his eyes had been stronger, he found much to occupy his mental gifts in his business career The purity of his life and the nobility of his character were an example to all about him The following resolution passed by some of his associates expresses the esteem and appreciation for him "To an unusual degree Mr Taft mingled devoutness of spirit with strong practical good sense Modest and retiring to a fault yet he was never afraid nor ashamed to speak out the faith that was in him when occasion called As a Christian man he merited and received the respect of all who knew him Kind to the poor a helper of the needy in their distress, ever ready to respond according to the measure of his ability to calls for help, he failed not to adorn the doctrines of Christ in all things He rests from his labors and his works do follow him" He was brought up in the Congregational church, but later joined the Episcopal church when it was located in Pearl street He was a vestryman and helped build the present edifice of All Saints Church He married Mary Augusta Roper daughter of Ephraim and Eunice (Richardson) Roper of Templeton, Massachusetts She was born at Templeton October 21, 1832 married December 12, 1854

Ephraim Roper was the son of Manasseh and Lucy (Livermore) Roper, born at Sterling Massachusetts, September 17, 1790 married at Sterling, July 10, 1821 Eunice Swan Richardson born Barre, Vermont, May 30 1799, daughter of Asa and Mary (Stuart) Richardson and granddaughter of Captain Benjamin Richardson Ephraim Roper settled in Templeton He was the first overseer of the town farm He had eight children Manasseh Roper, father of Ephraim, was born in Sterling May 26, 1752 He married at Princeton, November 25, 1790, Lucy Livermore, born Weston November 25, 1760 He was a soldier in the revolution He lived on the homestead in Sterling He had seven children

Ephraim Roper, father of Manasseh Roper, was born in Sudbury Massachusetts October 21 1716 He married April 8, 1748 Michal daughter of Benjamin and Zerviah Houghton She was born June 22 1725, and died December 31, 1816 He died December 5, 1793 They had eleven children Mr Roper was the founder of the Sterling branch of the Roper family

Ephraim Roper, father of the preceding Ephraim Roper, was born in Sudbury, Massachusetts, about 1714 He married Sybilla Moore, who was born in Sudbury September 2 1694 He was captive among the Indians 1697-9 He lived in Sudbury and Worcester Massachusetts where he was a farmer He was accidentally killed in the woods February 16, 1730 He had ten children the records of only two being known—Ephraim and Daniel, who founded the Rutland family of his name

Ephraim Roper father of the preceding Ephraim Roper was born in Dedham Massachusetts, December 23 1644 He married (first) Priscilla —— He was a farmer and settled in Lancaster His eldest daughter, Priscilla the only child born in Dedham, and his wife Priscilla were killed by the Indians February 10 1676 He married (second) at Concord, November 20 1677, Mrs Hannah Goble of Concord Both husband and wife were killed in the second massacre at Lancaster, September 11 1697 and also the third daughter He was the father of six children, the last five being born in Concord

John Roper, father of the preceding Ephraim Roper was born probably in Buckingham England, 1611 He married Alice —— born 1614 They probably came on the ship "Rose" of Yarmouth He was admitted a freeman at Dedham Massachusetts, June 2, 1641 He resided in Charlestown and Lancaster and was selectman in the latter place He was massacred by the Indians March 26 1676 Alice his widow married (second) at Charlestown April 12 1681 John Dickinson and resided at Salisbury, Massachusetts She married (third) 1684 William Allen She died there April 1, 1687 John and Alice Roper had eight children

John Roper, father of the preceding John Roper, lived in New Buckingham, Norfolk county, England, born about 1588 He sailed with his family to New England in 1637, and settled in August of that year in Dedham, Massachusetts Two of the children are known John Jr, mentioned above, and Walter, born 1614 married Susan ——

Mrs Taft came from a sturdy race Her ancestors fought in the early wars and many of them lost their lives Mrs Taft lives at 2 Congress street, where she has lived for over forty years

The children of Lyman Josiah and Mary Augusta (Roper) Taft were Marion Lurenza, born October 23, 1855 died May 4, 1879, Ella Lillie January 17 1858, married in 1900 Archibald Blinn, they reside in Mavilette, Nova Scotia, Frank Wilfred January 11 1862, died April 6, 1864, Walter Stuart November 17 1863, died April 9 1864, Georgia Frances February 1 1867, died August 28, 1867, Charles Lyman January 9 1870 died July 25 1888, at Pigeon Cove, Massachusetts

CLARENCE WHITMAN HOBBS Jeremiah Hobbs (1), born in Hopkinton, Massachusetts, June 14 1747, removed to Norway, Maine, with the first settlers Eight children and his wife came also soon afterward Part of the town of Norway was formerly called Rustfield from the fact that the land was owned by Henry Rust, of Salem Massachusetts In 1786 five settlers came to form a colony at Norway They were Jeremiah Hobbs Amos Hobbs, his brother, Joseph Stevens Jonas Stevens and George Lessley (Leslie), all from the town of Gray, Maine The records do not show that they stayed at Gray for any length of time They felled trees and cleared land in what they supposed was the Rust land By mistake Jeremiah Hobbs cleared a lot in the Cummings purchase, which was later incorporated in the town of Norway, however His lot is east of the present location of the Congregational Church The five pioneers built their little houses next spring each of these houses were of the same style sixteen by twenty-seven feet They were clapboarded with pine rift clap-boards, nailed on the studding and the roofs were covered with long shingles similar to those still used in some remote places in New England and the provinces The chimneys were topped out with what was called 'Catting"—laying up split sticks cob-house fashion in clay mortar mixed with straw chopped fine to make it adhere The floors were of bass wood planks, hewed out with axes Each of the five had a board sawed at Jackson's saw mill in Paris Maine, out of which to make a door Most of the window panes were made of paper oiled to make it weather-proof and translucent The houses were occupied in the spring of 1787 as soon as they were ready The families stayed that winter at Shepardsfield, now Hebron, and Oxford to be nearer their new homes where the men were preparing the land and houses

Jeremiah Hobbs moved his wife and eight children to Norway about September 1, 1787 Amos Hobbs had moved June 1, in the same year The first marriage in the town of Norway Maine was that of Miriam Hobbs, daughter of Jeremiah Hobbs, to Nathan Foster, May 17 1791, and the third was another daughter Olive Hobbs to Joel Stevens one of the pioneers Lydia Hobbs the only child of Jeremiah Hobbs, the pioneer, to be born in Norway was one of the first children born in the town

Jeremiah Hobbs married about 1770, Anna Fowler who was born in Kittery, Maine October 20, 1746 died June 18 1821 He died June 17, 1814. Their children were Olive born May 30, 1771, married Joel Stevens third wife Miriam July 17, 1772, married May 17, 1791, Nathan Foster,

Wealthy, February 10, 1774, died April, 1845, married John Daniels, Jr, of Paris, Maine, Anna, March 15, 1776 died 1849, married Deacon John Horr, Daniel, September 17, 1778, was on list of those coming to Norway in 1797, probably had lived there most of the time, married Sarah Noyes, daughter of Bela Noyes, William, April 2, 1780, died February 19, 1845, settled in Norway in 1802, married Catherine Wetherby, kept a general store at Norway, Sally, January 8, 1782, died February 15, 1850, married Nathan Foster, Jeremiah, January 17, 1785 died February 15, 1850, married Anna Frost, Lydia, born in Norway, Maine, August 20, 1789, died April 25, 1813 (In 1807 Jeremiah Hobbs Jr, and Jeremiah Hobbs, 3d, are mentioned as coming to Norway They were probably Jeremiah, Jr, here mentioned and a son of Amos Hobbs, named Jeremiah, about the same age)

Amos Hobbs, mentioned above, the brother of Jeremiah, was born in Hopkinton Massachusetts, in 1761, and came to Norway, Maine, with the first settlers He married Lucy Robinson, who died in Norway, September 7, 1848, aged eighty-nine years They had eight children and have many descendants

(II) William Hobbs, son of Jeremiah Hobbs (1), was born probably in Maine April 2, 1780 died February 19, 1845 He married, June 7, 1808, Catherine Wetherbee or Weterby He settled in Norway and kept one of the first general stores in that town, his place was near what is now the centre of the village He was a prominent man in the vicinity, and active in town affairs His children were Charlotte Sophronia, born October 29 1808, married Dr Nathaniel Grant removed to Ossipee, New Hampshire, William Whitman May 20, 1810, married Sarah Farrington Merrill, daughter of Ezekiel Merrill, first settler of Andover, Maine said to be from Andover, Massachusetts, Jeremiah Wellington June 8 1814, married Fanny O Greenleaf, Charles Leslie June 10, 1816, died May 16, 1834 Henry Hill, March 13, 1821, married Sarah Moulton, Milton Wilkins April 30, 1823 married Mrs Louisa Mudgett, resided in Boston, Cornelius Washington, June 5 1826 married Lucy J Hobbs, daughter of Robinson Hobbs

(III) William Whitman Hobbs, son of William Hobbs (2), was born at Norway Maine, May 20, 1810 He received a good education at first class schools and an academy, and for several years devoted himself to teaching, for which he had a special aptitude He taught schools at Paris Hill, Augusta, Andover and others places in Maine, and with invariable success While teaching at Andover, Maine, he first met Sarah Farrington Merrill, whom he married June 17, 1840 She was the daughter of Deacon Ezekiel Merrill, who was the oldest son of the first settler of the town of Andover, Maine Mr Hobbs settled at Norway after his marriage and conducted a farm there In 1849 Mr Hobbs caught the gold fever and was captain of a company which crossed the continent He remained in the gold fields of California about two years When he returned he settled on the old homestead in Norway and greatly improved it He was selectman in 1850 and representative in the legislature in 1865 For many years he was deputy sheriff in his county, and he was well known to all the lawyers jurors and others attending the courts at Paris, the county seat He was appointed to a department position in Washington, but after two years resigned on account of his dislike for Washington life He moved to Minnesota and engaged in business there He was liberally endowed physically and mentally, and had great energy and public spirit He died in Minnesota in 1876

The children of William Whitman and Sarah F (Merrill) Hobbs were Adele Sophronia, born July 12, 1842, married April 18 1867, John Milton Adams, of Portland, Maine, and settled at Deering, Maine, their children are Susan Merrill, Sarah Whitman, John Milton, Adele, Charles, Martha Ellen, born July 4, 1844, married, December 2, 1872, Alvin S Wilcox and have one son Roger Merrill Wilcox Sarah Frances born June 11, 1847, died September 10, 1851, Clarence Whitman, born June 27, 1852

(IV) Clarence Whitman Hobbs, son of William Whitman Hobbs (3), was born in Norway, Maine, January 27, 1852 He was educated in the schools of his native town He began his business life in the office of the *Daily Eastern Argus* of Portland, Maine, in 1870 He soon afterward entered the First National Bank as clerk and filled various positions there for two years This experience has been extremely valuable to him in his subsequent career as a manufacturer and man of business He started in business at Lynn, Massachusetts, manufacturing paper boxes in 1883 The business was run under the name of the New England Paper Box Co and proved successful He sold his interests in 1888 and removed to Boston In 1891 he went to Worcester and organized the Hobbs Manufacturing Company with Richard Sugden and Harry W Goddard, of the Spencer Wire Company In 1894 Mr Sugden died The Hobbs Manufacturing Company started on Union street to make paper box machinery the value of which Mr Hobbs had seen in his business in Lynn In 1895 the Hobbs Manufacturing Company was incorporated, and in 1903 bought the business of Wintherby, Rugg & Richardson and their factory at 26 Salisbury street (See sketches in this work of Seneca M Richardson and Gilbert J Rugg for history of the firm) Another large brick building was constructed The president of the corporation is Mr Hobbs the treasurer Harry W Goddard and the other director is J Philip Bird Besides the paper box machinery and the wood working machinery made by the company some envelope making machinery is built With the four story addition on Prescott street the company now has sixty-five thousand feet of floor space The new building is one hundred and twenty-five by sixty feet, four stories high and adjoins the old building

There has been a systematic and very successful effort made for the past fifteen years to improve the machinery turned out by this concern New patents and devices have added to the simplicity and efficiency of the machines The paper box machines of 1891 are crude affairs compared with those of the present day These machines find a market in all parts of the world They are made to be as nearly automatic as possible and capable of many adjustments for various sizes and styles of paper boxes The Hobbs Manufacturing Co has the reputation among those in the business of bringing out new machines ahead of all their competitors The experimentation goes on constantly In the summer of 1906 Mr Hobbs says there are no less than six new machines in preparation for the paper box making business The regular force at present is about one hundred and thirty hands and the business of the company gives the best of promises for future growth and expansion

Mr Hobbs belongs in the list of Worcester manufacturers who have built up new industries by his shrewdness and energy He has made two paper boxes grow where only one was used before his time His company is turning out better woodworking machinery than ever before Mr Hobbs has devoted himself almost exclusively to his business, which has naturally made great demands upon him He is a member of the Commonwealth Club and of the Knights of Pythias He is a Republican in politics He is a member of Central Congregational church, Worcester

He married, June 13, 1877, Marion Blanchard Twitchell, daughter of Samuel B and Malvina A (Chapman) Twitchell, of Bethel, Maine Their children are 1 Clarence Whitman, Jr, born October 1, 1878, educated in the Worcester schools and at Harvard College, graduated 1902, from the law school in 1904, practicing law in Worcester 2 Samuel Twitchell, born in Portland, Maine, October 29, 1880, a graduate of Harvard College, 1903, Master of Arts, 1904, salesman for Hobbs Manufacturing Co Both sons live at home, 12 Westland street

THE WHITMAN FAMILY John Whitman (1), one of the earliest settlers of the town of Weymouth, Massachusetts, is an emigrant ancestor of Clarence Whitman Hobbs, of Worcester, and of nearly all bearing the name of Whitman in this country, as well as an equal number, at least, bearing others names, in this country

He came from England, but from what particular part of it has not been ascertained He may have come from Holt in the county of Norfolk The name of Whitman or Whiteman was common there, and he may have been attracted to a colony in New England where old friends were to be found Governor Winthrop and his company came from the vicinity of Holt and settled Weymouth, Massachusetts Mr Whitman probably came to New England some years prior to 1638 He was made a freeman March 13, 1638-9, was a town officer of Weymouth in 1643, and was appointed an ensign by the governor in 1645 He was probably the first military officer in the town of Weymouth At the same time, May 14, 1645 he was made the magistrate of the town, a commissioner to end small causes, as the office was termed He was also deacon of the church there probably from its foundation, and until his death, November 13, 1692

He was probably nearly ninety when he died, as the youngest of his nine children was born in 1644 and the eldest son was born in 1629, while some of the daughters may have been older It is supposed that he was married in England about 1625 The family did not follow the father to Weymouth until 1641 He had a brother Zachariah who emigrated at the time he did or soon afterward and settled in Milford, Connecticut, as early as 1639 His estate at Milford was bequeathed to Rev Zechariah Whitman, son of his brother John Whitman, of Weymouth The records according to Pope's Pioneers show that Zachariah aged forty came with his wife Sarah, aged thirty-five and child Zachariah, aged two and one-half in the "Elizabeth" from Weymouth England, April 11, 1635

Robert Whitman aged twenty from the parish of Little Minories England, came in the "Abigail" in June 1635 and settled at Ipswich It is not known that he was a relative The fact that Zachariah and Robert Whitman came in 1635 makes it probable that John came also in that year

John Whitman owned and lived upon a farm adjoining the north side of the highway leading by the north side of the meeting house of the north parish of Weymouth and directly against it and extending to Weymouth river His dwelling house was near the middle of the farm and a part of the house now on the place was built about 1680 if this date is correct it was occupied by the emigrant ancestor The farm until 1830 was owned by a descendant He had many grants of land and must have become by purchase and otherwise the largest land-holder or one of the largest in the town He held the office of ensign until March 16, 1680 May 15, 1664, he was appointed a messenger to the Indians and held other positions of trust in the colony

The children of John Whitman (1) were Thomas, born about 1629, died 1712, married Abigail Byram, settled at Bridgewater, Massachusetts John, died February 1, 1713 Zechariah, born 1644, died November 5, 1726, married Ruth Reed, settled at Weymouth Abiah, born 1646, died January 28, 1727-8, inherited the homestead, admitted freeman October 12, 1681, married Mary Ford daughter of Andrew Ford, had seven children Sarah married about 1653, Abraham Jones son of Thomas Jones, the tailor, of Hingman, she was probably the eldest child, they lived together sixty-five years lacking a month or two she died June 11, 1718, they resided at Hull Mary, born 1634, died July 10 1716, married, November 22, 1656, John Pratt Elizabeth, died February 2, 1720, married, May, 1657, Joseph Green Hannah, born August 24, 1641 married September 9, 1660, Stephen French Judith, married Philip King

(II) Rev Zechariah Whitman, son of John Whitman (1), was born in Weymouth, Massachusetts, 1644 He graduated at Harvard University in 1668, and was ordained September 13, 1670, as the first minister of Point Alderton, Nantasket or Hull, with the munificent salary of forty pounds per annum Marmaduke Matthews had been preaching at Hull, but for "several erroneous expressions" was admonished by the government which would not grant the desire of his people to have him return

The young minister, soon after his ordination married Sarah Alcock, twin of Anna daughter of Dr John Alcock (H U 1646) of Roxbury The contract of marriage was dated October 26, 1670 He was admitted a freeman in May, 1673 At the death of his uncle Zachariah Whitman, of Milford, Connecticut, in 1666, he inherited the property and in the right of his wife had a considerable property at Stow, Massachusetts Mr Whitman continued minister of the Hull church until his death, though November 24 1725 he had a colleague Ezra Carpenter (H U 1720) ordained Mr Whitman died November 5, 1726 The preceding August the town voted to pay to his children twenty-five pounds a year for his maintenance while he lived and did not preach His wife died April 3, 1715, aged sixty-five years, according to her gravestone

Mr Whitman was a good scholar and penman and wrote most of the wills and legal papers in Hull According to the *Boston News Letter* in which his obituary was published December 15, 1726 "he was well esteemed for his natural and acquired accomplishments but especially for steady piety, diligent zeal and faithfulness in the discharge of his pastoral office the exemplariness of his conversation and his patience and submission to the will of God under his afflictions" By his will, made June 12, 1725, and proved December 16 1726 he confirms the grants of land already made to his sons and daughters and names various heirs His children were Zechariah, born 1672, died 1752, aged eighty, married (first) January 6, 1702-3 Mrs Sarah Fitch who died November 27, 1705 he married (second) Damaris Carmen who died November 27, 1705-6, married (third) Hannah —— he received from his father the Milford estate and he removed to Milford about 1700 John, born 1674 died February 22 1684 his gravestone was evidently inscribed by Rev Zechariah his father and is the oldest stone in the graveyard Joanna, born at Hull, married Ephraim or John Hunt, and resided in Boston

Rev Samuel, born 1677, died July 31, 1751 aged seventy-five years, graduated at Harvard in 1696 and is said to have been a tutor there for a short time He occasionally preached at Lancaster, Massachusetts, between 1697-1701 In 1699 he was the teacher of the grammar school at Salem, later the minister at Farmington, Connecticut, at that time one of the largest towns in Connecticut Ordained December 10, 1706 He married, March 19, 1707, Sarah Stoddard, daughter of Rev Solomon and Esther (Warham) Stoddard, of Northampton, by whom he had a large family He was a fellow of Yale College in 1726, a position he retained for more than twenty years, he died July 31, 1751 Sarah, married (first) —— Cocks, (second) Lieutenant Robert Gould, Sr, of Hull, his third wife She lived with and took care of her father until his death, he having deeded her his homestead, to take effect upon his decease, she died at Hull, September 29, 1784 Elizabeth died at Hull, November 19, 1708 John, born 1688, died August 3, 1772, aged eighty-five years Mary, married, October 22, 1713, Nathaniel Jacobs, of Hull Eunice, born April 10, 1696, died October 5, 1734

(III) John Whitman, son of Rev Zechariah Whitman (2), was born in 1688, married Mary Graves, of Charlestown She died November 24, 1716, aged seventeen years nine months He married (second) Dorcas Chitty, widow of Thomas Chitty and daughter of Captain Jacob Green, of Charlestown Massachusetts She died October 18, 1718, aged thirty-four He married (third) Margaret Damon, widow of John Damon, of Charlestown and daughter of Rev John Clark She died October 16, 1758, aged sixty-six years He was a magistrate, deacon of the church and one of the wealthiest and most influential men of the town He received by deed and inheritance from his father a large tract of land at Stow, Massachusetts, and settled there He also received from his second wife and her brother a considerable property He died August 3 1772, aged eighty-four By his will dated October 15 1757, proved September 8, 1772, he made his son Charles Whitman, residuary legatee and sole executor, directing him to support and manumit a negro servant named Boston His children were 1 Jacob, born November 16, 1716, died May 10, 1802 aged eighty-six, married Hannah Hartshorn, daughter of Jacob and Martha Hartshorn, of Boston, he settled at Bristol, Rhode Island about 1745, he was a blacksmith by trade and especially skilled in making iron work for ships, was thrice elected deputy to the general assembly of Rhode Island, was member of the town council from 1769 to 1773, was appointed in 1778 by the general assembly general sealer of weights and measures within and throughout the state He left a large and valuable estate, some of which is now or recently was owned by his descendants he subscribed toward the building fund for the college edifice and president's house of Brown University He had thirteen children 2 John, born September 21, 1717, died September 12, 1763, married February 6, 1747, Mary Foster, daughter of Rev Mr Foster, of Stafford, Connecticut He went to Nova Scotia in June, 1761, with forty-five others in the sloop "Charming Molly" but he died before the settlers received their grants of land, his share being distributed among his sons He was deacon of the church at Stow, and left considerable real estate He had eleven children His widow married (second) Samuel Bancroft, brother of Rev Aaron Bancroft of Worcester, and is said to have several children by this marriage 3 Lucy, born January 1, 1718-9 married —— Harris 4 Thomas, born March 18, 1720, was a physician, died unmarried before his father 5 Zechariah, born November 18, 1722, died January 14, 1793, married Elizabeth Gates, settled upon a part of his father's lands, and had fifteen children, all of whom survived their parents and were married 6 Jean, born November 25, 1724 probably died without issue before her father 7 Charles, born 1731, died December 10, 1807, aged seventy-six

(IV) Dr Charles Whitman, son of John Whitman (3) was born at Stow, Massachusetts, 1731 He studied medicine settled in his native town and practiced his profession for nearly fifty years His first wife was Anna Stevens, a direct descendant of Pocahontas She died in 1785 and the next year he married Mrs Catherine Davis Swift, widow of the Rev Dr Swift, of Billerica, Massachusetts He died December 10, 1807, aged seventy-six His widow died September 28, 1834, aged eighty-seven He had eleven children, all by his first wife He was a man of great dignity of manner and fastidious about his dress He always wore a long dark green coat with silver buttons, silver knee buckles, his cue tied with ribbons three yards and a half in length He was a man of great influence and much respected in the vicinity

The children of Dr Charles Whitman were 1 Isaac, born August 13, 1758, died October 24, 1758 2 Isaac, born February 16, 1760, died August 15, 1791, aged thirty-one married July 1, 1781, Susanna Gates 3 Catherine, born April 30, 1761 4 Eunice, born November 30, 1762, died March 11, 1811, and married John Russell, Jr, son of John and Abigail (Hildreth) Russell, married (second), November 2, 1801 Dr Martin Howe, son of Adonijah and Lydia (Church) Howe who practices in Barre and Boston, the Russell homestead was at Princeton, Massachusetts 5 Lois, born May 17, 1765, died October 17, 1778 6 Dorcas, born April 7, 1767, died July 11, 1844, aged seventy-seven years, married, April 20, 1788 Dr Isaiah Whitney, who settled at Rindge New Hampshire, had ten children, she was drowned by the upsetting of a coach near Burlington, Vermont 7 Hannah, born February 11, 1769, died June 23, 1784 8 Jane, born April 8, 1771, died December, 1858, aged eighty-seven years, married, September 25 1794, Captain Moses Todd, a farmer and inn-holder, first postmaster of Rindge, New Hampshire, often town officer, removed to Fitchburg, Massachusetts, in 1833, had nine children 9 Charles (twin) born April 28 1773 died September 24, 1846, married, 1798, Charlotte Wood, who died June 8 1836, married (second), March 26 1840 Lydia Whitnay, daughter of Jacob and Esther Whitnay, studied medicine with Dr Eldridge, father of the first husband of "Fanny Fern" he inherited a large estate and his father's professional practice, he represented the town in the general court six years, in 1802 was appointed surgeon to the Second Regiment of militia, had six children 10 Betty (twin) born April 28, 1773, died October 6, 1778 11 Anna, born December 12 1787 died November 21, 1868, married, August 30, 1805, Benjamin Hapgood, of Marlboro Massachusetts where they resided for fifteen years, then settled in Stow she married (second), December 20 1842 Deacon Josiah Whitman son of Deacon John and Abigail (Whitman) Whitman removed to Bridgewater, Massachusetts where she died November 21, 1868 aged eighty years, had ten children by first marriage

(V) Catherine Whitman daughter of Charles Whitman (4) was born April 30 1761 She married June 10 1780 Judah Wetherbee, son of Silas and Betsey Wetherbee He was born in Stow about April 13, 1755 died in Stow about December, 1835

They resided for a time in Stow, then removed to Waterford, Maine She died in Boston about 1843 Their children were 1 Charles Wetherbee, born November 30, 1781, said to have married and died in New York city about 1825 2 Betsey Wetherbee, born March 8, 1783, died about 1833 unmarried at Marlboro 3 Amelia Wetherbee, born December 4, 1784, married, September 17, 1810, Darius Wilkins, born February 26, 1774, died November 23, 1858, she died June 23, 1843, resided at Norway, Maine, had five children 4 Catherine Wetherbee, born May 26, 1787, married William Hobbs 5 Charlotte Wetherbee, born June 20, 1789, married Henry Hill, died at Providence, Rhode Island 6 Jane Whitman Wetherbee, born January 28, 1791, married at Norway, Maine, March 16, 1813, David Fowler, son of John Fowler, of Ipswich, Massachusetts, deputy sheriff, she died August 16, 1866, aged seventy-five years, had four children 7 Judah Wetherbee, born at Stow, Massachusetts, July 19, 1794, married (first), January 4, 1821, Miranda Russell, married (second) at Dedham, Massachusetts, November 28, 1833, Mary Draper Kingsbury, daughter of Dr Ezekiel, and Mary (Draper) Kingsbury, he served in the war of 1812, resided till 1803 in Stow, then removed to Charlestown, provision dealer in Quincy market, Boston, also milk dealer, died in Charlestown, January 7, 1869, widow died after 1889, had ten children 8 Isaac Wetherbee, born July 17, 1797, married, September, 1818, Sophia Greene, daughter of Barnabas and Mary Greene, he died at Lawrence, Massachusetts, July 18, 1868, she was living in 1889, at Lawrence 9 Jacob Wetherbee, born August 19, 1798, died young 10 Ann S Wetherell, born November 17, 1799, married in Stow about 1827 Charles Newell, resided in Florida, she died in Nashville, Tennessee, December 8, 1872 11 Mary Wetherbee, born August 12, 1803, married (first) John Hunter, married (second), 1837, Charles Whitman Hapgood, son of Benjamin and Anna (Whitman) Hapgood, she died August, 1850

(VI) Catherine Wetherbee, daughter of Judah and Catherine (Whitman) Wetherbee (5), was born May 26, 1787 She married, January 17, 1807, William Hobbs, son of Jeremiah and Anne (Fowler) Hobbs He was born April 2, 1781, and died February 19, 1843 They settled at Norway, Maine She died in 1864 Their children were all born in Norway Maine (See sketch of Hobbs Family)

JAMES EDWIN WESSON John Wesson (1), of Salem, Massachusetts, the earliest American ancestor of James Edwin Wesson, of Worcester, was the progenitor of many if not all the Massachusetts families of that name, as well as of those known as Weston, the patronymic appearing in both these forms The family originated in England, whither came its founder with William the Conqueror, from whom he received valuable estates in Staffordshire and elsewhere in England

John Wesson was born in 1630 or 1631, in Buckinghamshire, England, and died about 1723, aged over ninety years About 1644, when only thirteen years old, his father being dead, he sailed as a stowaway in a ship bound for America He settled in Salem, Massachusetts, where in 1648, at the age of eighteen, he was a member of the First church About 1653 he removed to that part of Reading now known as Wakefield, and accumulated one of the largest estates in the town, his lands adjoining the Meeting House square and extending southerly He was a Puritan very earnest in his piety, and his gravestone in the Reading graveyard shows that he was one of the founders of the church there He served in King Philip's war In 1653 he married Sarah, daughter of Zachariah Fitch, of Reading, and this is the first marriage there of which record exists He had at least eight children, four sons among them, each of whom became the head of a family, and has many descendants in all parts of the country His children were 1 Sarah, born July 15, 1656, baptized May 10, 1657 2 Mary, born May 25, 1659, probably died young 3 John, born March 8, 1661, baptized August 29, 1661, married Mary Bryant, 1684, and had twelve children, lived at Reading, Massachusetts 4 Elizabeth, born at Reading, baptized October, 1663 5 Samuel, (see forward) 6 Stephen, born 1667, was a pious, industrious man, had a farm in Reading where he died in 1753, aged nearly ninety (Stephen, his son, became the owner of a farm in Wilmington, Massachusetts, deacon of the church and a leading citizen, died 1776, aged eighty-one years, left many descendants) 7 Thomas, born 1670, married Sarah Townsend, and is the ancestor of the Weston families in New Hampshire The facts herein given with reference to John Wesson are from a manuscript record left by his son John

(II) Samuel Wesson, son of John Wesson (1), was born at Reading, Massachusetts, 1665 His name usually appears as Weston He married Abigail ——— about 1688 and settled at Reading Their children were Abigail, born 1689, Samuel, (see forward)

(III) Samuel Wesson, son of Samuel Wesson (2), was born in Reading, Massachusetts, in 1690, and went to Framingham, in 1711, when he was twenty-one years old, and there married, May 7, 1711, Martha, daughter of Nathaniel Haven, granddaughter of Richard Haven, of Lynn, who came over in 1645 In 1713 Samuel died, and his widow married Isaac Cousins, of Sherborn, Massachusetts, January 12, 1745-46, she died the following year, at her home in Sherborn The one child of Samuel and Martha (Haven) Wesson was John (see forward)

(IV) John Wesson, born in Framingham, Massachusetts, December 1, 1711 He married Ruth Death, of Sherborn, Massachusetts, an adjoining town, January 22, 1740 She was born April 20, 1711, daughter of Henry and Rachel (Leland) Death, her father being the son of John, who came from Natick to Sherborn in 1677-78 John Wesson probably lived at Framingham until after the death of his mother in 1746 He moved to Grafton, Massachusetts, near the Sutton and Worcester lines as early as 1749 He bought of John Gould nine acres in Sutton in 1749, and several other tracts of land in the neighborhood, owning land in Grafton, Worcester, and Sutton, in that part now Millbury, but part of which was annexed to Worcester in 1785, called the Gore" He was a revolutionary soldier in the Framingham company He was in Captain Joseph Winch's company, Colonel Samuel Bullard's regiment in 1777, and was in the campaign under General Gates that ended in the surrender of Burgoyne He married (second) Rebecca Daniel, August 24, 1757 The children of John and Ruth Wesson were 1 Samuel, born at Sherborn, July 14, 1741, he became a revolutionary soldier, married Rebecca ———, died 1776 2 Levi 3 Joel 4 John, Jr, married Mehitable Elliott 5 Abel, married Sarah Drury 6 Silas, he was one of twelve soldiers who joined with Major Timothy Bigelow, of Worcester, and marched to Canada, where Silas was killed at the attack on Quebec, December 31, 1775

(V) Joel Wesson, son of John Wesson (4), was born probably about 1746, at Framingham He married Hannah Bigelow, born in Worcester, July

James Edwin Nisson

3, 1748, daughter of Joshua and Lydia Bigelow They lived for a few years, in the seventies, in Brookfield, but for the greater part of their lives in Worcester He held much real estate, and paid one of the largest taxes in that town He was a juror in 1785 and on the school committee in 1787 He was a plow-maker by trade and was in Framingham in 1789 plying his trade there Hannah, his widow, died December 29, 1829, aged eighty-two years Their children were 1 Hulda, married Lewis Witherby, of Shrewsbury 2 Hannah, married ——— Bartlett 3 Mary, married Charles Warren, November 16, 1808, she was called Polly 4 Sewell 5 Joel, Jr, born April 7, 1775 at Brookfield, Massachusetts, married Thankful Newton, in Shrewsbury, September 15, 1796, she was born January 4, 1778, they had two sons David, married Anna Burbank, of Worcester, November 1, 1827, and Andrew, born November 14, 1808 at north parish of Sutton, now Millbury, who had a son Frank B, now (1905) of New York city 6 Rufus, (see forward)

Joel Wesson and his brothers were the owners of a large part of 'the Gore," which was claimed by both Worcester and Grafton Joel was considered an inhabitant of Grafton until 1785, when the title of Worcester to the section was acknowledged formally A very important deed in tracing this genealogy is recorded at Worcester Joel Wesson and his brother Levi Wesson deeded to their brothers, John, Jr and Samuel, October 24 1777, certain lands in "the Gore," and the deed gives the names of the children of John and Ruth (Death) Wesson Joel sold his farm in North Brookfield to his brother, John Wesson, June 25, 1789

(VI) Rufus Wesson, son of Joel Wesson (5), was born in 1786, in Worcester, on the old homestead at "the Gore" He was a farmer, and acquired much real estate, and bought what is known as the Wesson place near Lake Quinsigamond, March 7, 1814, of Lewis Baird He was also a plow-maker He was a highway surveyor and collector of taxes in 1825, fence viewer in 1816, and served in the militia in the Grafton company He married, at Worcester, September 18, 1808, Betsey Baird She was of a family well known in Worcester The Bairds were from the west of England, and of earlier date from Scotland The English and Scotch pedigrees have been carefully kept (See Vol 1, Proceedings of the Worcester Society of Antiquity) Of the children of Rufus and Betsey Wesson, nine are recorded in Worcester 1 Cornelia, born January 28, 1810, married to H H Harrington, of Shrewsbury, 1833, of her children were Gilbert H Harrington, late of Harrington & Richardson Arms Company (See sketch of Gilbert H Harrington elsewhere in this work) Mrs Cornelia (Wesson) Harrington lived to the age of upwards of ninety years 2 Martin, married Abigail H Green, of Grafton, at Marlboro, January 6, 1840 He was a shoe manufacturer in Springfield 3 Edwin, born December 13, 1811, married at Marlboro, Nancy H Harrington, of Grafton, June 10, 1838 He was a rifle manufacturer, and operated a factory at Northboro, and afterward in Hartford, Connecticut He died at the age of thirty-nine years 4 Betsy, born January 26, 1814, married W H H Conner, of Grafton, October 17, 1844 5 Rufus, Jr, (see forward) 6 Charlotte born September 3, 1819 7 Jane, born May 8, 1823 8 Daniel B (see forward) 9 Franklin, born November 8, 1828, at Worcester, Massachusetts He went to California in 1851 built the first brick building in Shasta, and there carried on a large business, being an expert rifle-maker 10 Frances, born August 8, 1830

(VII) Daniel Baird Wesson, who made for himself world-wide fame as an inventor of the revolver which bears his name, was a son of Rufus Wesson (6) He was born at Worcester, Massachusetts, May 18, 1825 At the age of seventeen, while yet at school, he began to devote his evenings to making firearms in Northborough Massachusetts, under the direction of his brother Edwin, who died in 1850, and whose interests he took in charge, and it was this establishment which turned out the Wesson rifle, the leading favorite with hunters at that time Subsequently, at Norwich, Connecticut, he formed a partnership with Horace Smith, under the name of Smith & Wesson, and they established a factory and made the "volcanic" rifle, a repeater Mr Wesson also invented a metallic cartridge About 1855 the firm sold their patent rights to the Volcanic Repeating Arms Company, now the Winchester Rifle Company Mr Wesson remained for a time as superintendent, but in 1857 joined Horace Smith again, under the firm name of Smith & Wesson and began to manufacture revolvers in Springfield, Massachusetts They began in a small shop with about seventy-five men, making a few thousand arms a year, but the business grew very rapidly, especially after the breaking out of the civil war, and became enormous The Smith & Wesson works are in some respects the largest and most complete of the kind in the world The buildings and equipment are especially substantial and complete, and an average force of five hundred men have been employed for many years The Smith & Wesson revolvers are famous all over the world, and are the favorite weapon in some of the foreign armies, as they are in that of the United States They received the highest award, against the competition of the whole world, at the Exposition in Paris, 1867, Moscow, 1872, Vienna, 1873, Philadelphia, 1876, Australia, 1880, and at many of the numerous exhibitions more recently Mr Smith retired from the firm in 1874 Mr Wesson admitted to partnership, January 1, 1882, his son, Walter H, and later his son Joseph and these two are now the active managers of the business

Mr Wesson has also been actively identified with with various other business interests, being a director in the First National Bank of Springfield, Massachusetts, and the Bigelow-Cheney Wire Company, and was an officer in the water companies of Leadville Colorado, and Independence, Iowa He has borne a prominent part in local affairs, and has generously contributed of his means to various enterprises of public worth He is president of the Oak Grove Cemetery Association and a charter member and vice president of the Hampden County Horticultural Society His broad, public spirit is manifest in various splendid gifts With James Kirkland and Joshua D Sackett he purchased the magnificent estate out of which Edgewood Park was made and opened to the public, and he gave to the city of Springfield the beautiful Wesson Fountain, designed by Gilbert and Thompson In politics he is a Republican, and has been an active and influential advocate of its principles and policies Mr Wesson married May 26, 1847, Cynthia M Hawes of Northboro Some years ago he built on the place where his wife was born within sight of the little shop in which he learned to make arms a residence costing it is said $300 000 The children of Daniel Baird and Cynthia M (Hawes) Wesson were 1 Sarah Jeanette, married George J Bull 2 Walter Herbert 3 Frank Luther 4 Joseph Hawes

(VII) Rufus Wesson, Jr, son of Rufus Wesson (6), was born May 17, 1815, at Worcester, Massachusetts He began work with his father on the farm, making plows In 1844 he engaged in the manufacture of shoes in South Shrewsbury, cutting out the stock and distributing it among farmer-shoemakers for miles about, as was then the custom He built up a large demand for his goods, and in 1848 established his factory on Front street, Worcester Prosperity there attended him, but he decided to locate in the west, and in 1851 removed to Peoria, Illinois, where he engaged in shoe manufacturing Suffering financial reverses, in 1854 he returned to Worcester and made a new beginning as a shoe manufacturer, opening a shop on Waldo street, nearly opposite the police station, where he carried on a successful business until 1870, when he retired, just before the great change in shoe manufacture, whereby the shoes were made in large factories by machinery, operated by steam power He married Miriam Harrington, July 23, 1840, daughter of Colonel Daniel and Zillah Harrington, of Shrewsbury, where they were married She died in Chicago in 1851 There were two children by this marriage 1 James Edwin, (see forward) 2 Charlotte Miriam, born April 18, 1845, at Shrewsbury, Massachusetts, married Charles T Sherer, the dry goods dealer, and has a son, Joseph F Sherer, and several daughters Mr Wesson married, in 1851, Mrs Jennie (Burtnett) Kendrick, of Kenosha, Wisconsin, who died in 1856 without issue He married (third) in 1858, Sophia Goddard, daughter of Deacon Nathaniel Goddard, of Millbury, who is now (1905) living in Worcester Their children were 1 Alfred, born July 18, 1863, married Ella Daniels, and has two sons, is manager for the Woodbury-Carlton Engraving Company, Walnut street, Worcester 2 Walter Gale, (see forward)

(VIII) James Edwin Wesson, son of Rufus Wesson, Jr, (7), was born in Grafton, Massachusetts, June 14, 1841 He was educated in the public schools of Springfield and Worcester, Massachusetts, but at the age of fourteen, at the time of his father's financial reverses, left school and went to work with him to build up their fortunes anew, and the two were thus associated until the son attained his majority, and learned the shoe manufacturing business thoroughly as it was then conducted The father was conservative and disposed to let well-enough alone, but the son, recognizing the impending revolution in the shoe business, established in a small way a business on his own account, in a small room in the same building owned by his father on Waldo street It was his purpose, as soon as possible, to install the most modern machinery and make shoes entirely at the factory In a few years, however, all manufacturers were driven to choose between the large shop and an elaborate equipment of machinery, or retirement from business The senior Wesson retired, and the son, James E Wesson, fitted up a larger and more completely equipped shop in the C C Houghton building, 105 Front street, Worcester He had made an auspicious beginning on Waldo street, and after five years at the Front street location he moved (in 1874) into a building at 31 Mulberry street, owned by Samuel Winslow, where he remained for six or seven years Finding these quarters inadequate to the increased demands he leased of Charles Bigelow the building at 10 Mulberry street, where he continued business for five years Again the business had outgrown his facilities, and he again made a removal (in 1889), this time to the present factory, corner of Asylum street, then owned by Samuel Winslow, but which he subsequently purchased from the Winslow Trust In 1905 Mr Wesson received into partnership his brother, Walter Gale Wesson, who had been associated with him in the business and had resided with him for many years The factory is one of the few shoe factories of Worcester which have been uniformly successful, and has constantly extended its business The building is 40x100 feet, four stories with basement, and in recent years has employed two hundred operatives or more, with a daily capacity of fifteen hundred pairs of shoes An interesting memento of the earlier days of the industry is to be seen at the factory, a shoe made in 1854 by Rufus Wesson, Jr

Mr Wesson married, January 1, 1865, at Clinton, Massachusetts, Anna Endora Stoneberger (See forward) They reside at 7 Linden street, in a house which was erected by Mr Wesson's father One of the pleasant reminiscences of the family life in the old mansion was the entertaining at dinner, on the fortieth wedding anniversary of Mr and Mrs James Edwin Wesson, the same company that was entertained by his father and mother, on that New Year's eve forty years before, with the exception that, the father having died, his place was occupied by his youngest son, Walter Gale Wesson Otherwise the personnel of the company was exactly the same Mr Wesson is a man of domestic tastes, and has but few interests outside his home, his only society connection being with Morning Star Lodge, Ancient Free and Accepted Masons, the Worcester Club, and the Tatnuck County Club

Mrs James Edwin Wesson, daughter of Adam and Harriet Newell (Mason) Stonebarger, was born in Dayton, Ohio The early representatives were called Steinberger and are of Austrian origin The founder of the American branch came to this country in 1767, settling in Frankfort township, Cumberland county, Pennsylvania

Peter Stonebarger (3), grandfather of Mrs Wesson, went from Harrisburg, Pennsylvania, to Dayton, Ohio, and was among the early settlers of that place He was architect and builder of the first bridge built across the Miami river at Dayton, before the days of railway construction, cutting the timbers for it in the Alleghany mountains and floating them down the river to their destination When the old bridge was torn down in 1904 it was seen that the timbers were all hewn out by hand, he also designed and built the first Roman Catholic Church in Dayton, and Leon Beaver, his grandson, was supervising architect of the present cathedral built on the old site, the original church having been torn down Adam Stonebarger, son of Peter Stonebarger (3), after being associated with his father for a time, went into business for himself as a dealer in paints and oils in western Pennsylvania He married Harriet Newell Mason, born in Southbridge, Massachusetts, the daughter of Lemuel and Lydia (Adams) Mason whose ancestors (Adams, Harthaway and Mason) came from early Puritan stock

(VIII) Walter Gale Wesson, son of Rufus Wesson (7), was born at Worcester, Massachusetts, October 14, 1865 He attended the Worcester schools and the Worcester Polytechnic Institute, from which he graduated in 1886 Directly after graduating he accepted a position in the school department of Washington, District of Columbia, to organize and take charge of a manual training course in the high schools The next year he held a position with the Baltimore & Ohio Railroad Company at Baltimore, Maryland After a year at Baltimore, he spent three years in Philadelphia, organizing the manual training department in a private school for boys At a later day he was similarly occupied for three years at Menomonie, Wisconsin, as principal of an industrial school established there by Senator Stout along the lines of a technical institute

When manual training was introduced into the public schools of Worcester, Mr Wesson was chosen to organize the work He has won high praise from those competent to judge, and from the families of the boys and girls who have taken the manual training courses in the past few years The manual training idea with its natural development into the industrial school is by far the most useful and important thing recently adopted in the American system of public education, and the inherited mechanical skill and fine technical training of Mr Wesson admirably fitted him for the pioneer work of organizing such schools Mr Wesson left the Worcester schools in 1904, and became associated with his brother, J Edwin Wesson in the manufacture of shoes, and in 1905 became a member of the firm

KINNICUTT FAMILY Roger Kennicutt (I) (in the first deed, 1680, spelled Kennecut) came from Devonshire, England, about the middle of the seventeenth century, and settled in Malden, Massachusetts He married, 1661, Johanna Shepardson, born March 13, 1642, the third daughter of Daniel and Johanna Shepardson Daniel Shepardson came to America from England in 1632, and settled in Charlestown, Massachusetts, where he died July 26, 1644 January 30, 1679, Roger Kennicutt sold his estate in Malden, consisting of a house, land in the limits of Charlestown, known as Molton Island, south and southwest, to Lieutenant J Smith He moved with his family to Swansea, Rhode Island, and bought, May 19, 1680, of John and James Brown, a tract of land bounded on one side by Kikemut Creek He died about 1696 Roger and Johanna Kennicutt had three children Johanna, born January, 1664, Lydia, born January, 1667, John, born October, 1669

(II) John Kennicutt, son of Roger and Johanna (Shepardson) Kennicutt, born in Malden, October, 1669, moved with his father to Swansea, Rhode Island, 1680 He married Elizabeth Luther, daughter of Hezekiah Luther, of Swansea The exact date is not known He died August 23, 1722

(III) John Kennicutt, son of John and Elizabeth (Luther) Kennicutt, born in Swansea, 1700, married Anna Eddy, 1725, who died December 8, 1735 Two years after her death, May 30, 1737, he married Hannah Gorham, daughter of Jabez Gorham, of Bristol, and great-great-granddaughter of John Howland, one of the "Mayflower" passengers He died in March, 1782 He was town clerk of Warren, Rhode Island, and a noted Tory at the outbreak of the revolution He was a "firm Episcopalian" "His usual practice was to catechise his children every Sunday morning and then prepare for church They attended St Michael's, Bristol, distant six miles His daughters rode on horseback and the sons walked on foot" Records "Historical Discourse, St Mark's Church, Warren, Rhode Island, November 10, 1878" Providence Press Company, printers, 1879

(IV) Shubael Kinnicutt, son of John and Hannah (Gorham) Kennicutt, born Swansea, March 28, 1732, married Elizabeth, daughter of Simon Burr, of Rehoboth, July 3, 1766 He died in Swansea, August 13, 1810

(V) Thomas Kinnicutt, son of Shubael and Elizabeth (Burr) Kinnicutt, born Swansea, August 13, 1768, married Amey, daughter of Deacon Samuel Wightman, of Rehoboth, June 14, 1794 He died in Seekonk, August 28, 1820

(VI) Francis Harrison Kinnicutt, son of Thomas and Amey (Wightman) Kinnicutt, was born in Seekonk, Rhode Island, April 27, 1812 He came to Worcester, Massachusetts, in 1828, and in 1830 became a clerk in the hardware store of George T Rice, Main and Walnut streets He was soon admitted as a partner, and after a few years, with his brother, Thomas Kinnicutt, he purchased the interest held by Mr Rice, who took up cloth manufacturing Samuel Woodward took the place of Thomas Kinnicutt, who was a lawyer by profession, and in later years assumed the active management, giving Mr Kinnicutt time to attend to other important duties The above named were all honorable members of the Worcester Fire Society Francis H Kinnicutt from his coming to Worcester took up and bore well his part in the functions connected with the social life of the then small town, and his name appears in connection with many of the early-day balls and other assemblies held each winter, especially in court time The man of affairs of today is often so absorbed in the details of his business that he does not show the world the better side of his nature In the last years of Mr Kinnicutt's life, relieved from care, his geniality of disposition became known to a wider circle He maintained his interest in the prosperity of the city to the last His great sympathy for young men to whom he took a liking was frequently manifested in a practical manner

He was made director of the Citizens' Bank in 1842, and was its president from 1860 until his death, September 12, 1885 He was also a director of the Worcester & Nashua Railroad from 1855, and its president from 1866 to 1881, when he surrendered his trust For nearly a quarter of a century he was a member of the board of investment of the Worcester County Institution for Savings, and in each and every position of trust evinced fidelity and good management He held few if any public offices, but took an interest and supported every means calculated to make better his city, county and commonwealth He married Elizabeth, the second daughter of Hon Leonard Moody Parker, of Shirley Mrs Kinnicutt was the granddaughter of the first Levi Lincoln and great-granddaughter of the first Daniel Waldo

(VII) Rebecca Newton Kinnicutt, daughter of Francis H and Elizabeth Waldo (Parker) Kinnicutt, born September 17, 1838, married Dr George E Francis, of Worcester, June 23, 1868 She had two children Elizabeth and George Kinnicutt

(VII) Elizabeth Waldo Kinnicutt, daughter of Francis H and Elizabeth Waldo (Parker) Kinnicutt, born August 18, 1840, married Dr William H Draper, of New York, October 15 1861, died December 19 1869 She had three children William, Martha and Robert Watts

(VII) Julia Burling Kinnicutt, daughter of Francis H and Elizabeth Waldo (Parker) Kinnicutt, born July 1, 1843, married John M Barker, of Worcester, no issue

(VII) Frank Parker Kinnicutt son of Francis H and Elizabeth Waldo (Parker) Kinnicutt, born July 13, 1846, married Eleanor Kissel, of New York, November 19, 1875 He engaged in medical practice They had two children Frank Harrison, and Gustave Herman Kissel

(VII) Lincoln Newton Kinnicutt, son of Francis H and Elizabeth Waldo (Parker) Kennicutt, born March 14 1849 was educated in the public schools and completed his education abroad At the age of seventeen he entered the hardware house of his father, and upon attaining his majority was admitted as a partner In 1877 he retired from this business and entered the office of George T Rice a banker, and in 1884 formed a partnership with Alexander Dewitt, and the firm of Kinnicutt & Dewitt, bankers, was founded which is today the largest private banking house in Worcester Mr Kinnicutt has been actively connected with many of the institutions of Worcester, serving in the capacity of treasurer of the Worcester Art Museum since its organization, trustee and treasurer of the Worcester Polytechnic Institute, trustee of the Worcester County Institution of Savings, and as a director of the Citizens' National Bank, Worcester National Bank, Worcester Consolidated Street Railway, Worcester Trust Company, and the Boston Tow Boat Company He is also an active factor in the following charitable institutions of Worcester, namely The Children's Friend Society, the Worcester Employment Society, and the Old Men's Home He is a Republican in politics, but has never taken any active part in public affairs He married, October 10, 1878, Edith Perley, daughter of Judge Perley, of Concord, New Hampshire They have one son, Roger, born at Worcester, February 12, 1880 He is a graduate of Harvard, and is now attending the Harvard Medical School

(VII) Leonard Parker Kinnicutt D Sc, son of Francis H and Elizabeth Waldo (Parker) Kinnicutt, was born in Worcester, May 22, 1854 He married Louisa Hoar Clarke, daughter of Dr Henry Clarke, June 4, 1885, who died January 22, 1892 He married (second) Frances Ayres Clarke, daughter of Josiah H Clarke, July 9, 1898, no issue He is professor of chemistry in the Worcester Polytechnic Institute

The Parker and Kinnicutt families, together with the families into which they have married and intermarried, have been of much importance and associated with many of the historic events during the period covered by the last two centuries

(I) James Parker was living in Woburn, Massachusetts, in 1640 He married Elizabeth Long, daughter of Robert Long, of Charlestown, May 23, 1643, by whom he had one son She died and in his old age he married Mrs Eunice Carter, widow of Samuel Carter, who was the son of the Rev Thomas Carter, by whom a daughter was born thirty years after any of her father's other children There are no records of his children except his son James, to be further written of in this narrative

He came to Groton about the date of its organization, and was the first and largest proprietor The town was divided into "acre rights," each one of which entitled its owner to nearly fifty acres Mr Parker had fifty of these "rights," and his landed estates were increased until he became the largest land owner, if not the richest man within the territory during its early history He was an influential man, a deacon in the church, a sergeant, and so on up to captain, in the military service, a selectman at the town organization in 1662, holding the position more than thirty years, and was also town clerk and usually moderator of the meetings and chairman on all important committees, appointed to locate roads lay off lands, and establish bounds In later life he was appointed to represent the town in the general court His home was far out from the present village, near Martin's Pond, somewhat removed from the highway, in a shaded secluded spot with at present no house to mark the spot where dwelt the chief original proprietor His son,

(II) James Parker, Jr, was born in Woburn, April 15 1652 He married Mary Parker, December 11 1678 lived at Groton, and had five children He was killed by the Indians, July 27, 1694, and his family carried into captivity His second son was,

(III) Phineas Parker, born 1684, at Groton, where he died August 13, 1744 He was twice married, first to Abigail ——, who died February 4, 1721, and second to Elizabeth —— Of the eight children of Phineas Parker, his second son was

(IV) Leonard Parker, born at Groton, June 3 1718, married Abigail ——, and had ten children, the third of whom was

(V) James Parker, born at Groton, November 26, 1744 He came to Shirley soon after he reached his majority, and settled upon the farm for many years in the possession of the Parker family He married Sarah Dickenson and had ten children For one year he was a selectman, and later held a justice's commission, but never exercised the function of his office He lived in the trying days of the revolution, but took no active part except to enroll with the eighty volunteers called out by the alarm of April 19, 1775 His life was mainly spent in the discharge of his personal business his lands were kept under good cultivation, and he thus became wealthy In 1802 he resigned his farm to his eldest son and removed to the centre village where he died September 29, 1830 His wife Sarah preceded him to the grave, her death occurring November 22, 1829 He had ten children Sarah, James, Lovey, Henrietta, Rhoda Abigail, Daniel, David, Lydia and Leonard Moody

(VI) Leonard Moody Parker, son of James and Sarah (Dickenson) Parker, was born in Shirley, January 9, 1789 At the age of fourteen he was sent to Groton Academy then under the preceptorship of Caleb Butler, Esq, and in 1804 entered Dartmouth College from which he was graduated in 1808 with high honors He studied law two years in the office of the Hon Abijah Bigelow, of Leominster and one year in the office of Hon Levi Lincoln, of Worcester, and in 1811 commenced the practice of law in Charlestown Massachusetts In 1812, upon the declaration of war against Great Britain, Mr Parker was appointed army judge advocate attached to military district No 1, and held that office until the reduction of the army, after peace was declared During his life he was an ardent and consistent politician of the Democratic school, and repeatedly held seats in both branches of the state legislature He held the office of commissioner, and was a member of the national convention of 1820 But politics did not absorb the active life of Mr Parker He was a life member of the Boston Society of Natural History, an honorary member of the Northern Academy of Arts and Sciences, of Hanover, New Hampshire, and a corresponding member of the North Eastern Historical and Genealogical Society In 1830 he received from President Johnson the appointment of naval officer for the Port of Boston and Charlestown in which he continued for four years, when he retired to his native place, the pleasant and quiet town of Shirley, where he passed the residue of his days He married, March 22 1814 Martha, daughter of Governor Levi Lincoln (senior), by whom he had three children Martha, Elizabeth and Sarah Mrs Parker died at Charlestown April 26, 1822 Mr Parker died in Shirley, August 25 1854 In his will he bequeathed the sum of four thousand dollars to constitute a fund for the endowment and support of a high school for the benefit of all the youth of the town, and his books were given to the town for the beginning of a library

(VII) Elizabeth Waldo Parker, daughter of Leonard Moody Parker (6), was born in Charlestown May 9, 1817 married Francis H Kinnicutt, of Worcester, October 26 1837 and is the mother of six children Rebecca Newton Elizabeth Waldo, Julia B, Frank Parker, Lincoln N, Leonard Parker

(VII) Sarah Rebecca Parker daughter of Leonard Moody Parker (6), born March 6 1822, married Joseph Mason, of Worcester November 10, 1846 One child was born of this union, Joseph P, at Worcester September 15 1848 married A Wright, of New York city, November 13 1877

FREDERICK SUMNER PRATT The Pratt family, of which Frederick S Pratt is a representative traces its ancestry to Thomas Pratt, who took the oath of fidelity in Watertown Massachusetts, in the year 1652, and who was there as early as 1647 He is reported to have come to America about that date from London, England About the year 1679 he purchased of Thomas Eames thirty acres of land in Framingham and settled in that town By his wife Susanna he had the following children Thomas, Abial married Daniel Bigelow, Ebenezer, Joseph, John, Philip, Ephraim, Nathaniel, Jonathan David, and Jabez

(II) Jonathan Pratt married Sarah, daughter of John Gale, of Framingham, and first resided on a portion of his father's place in Framingham, then removed to Oxford and was a selectman of Oxford in 1723 Administration on his estate was granted in 1735 His children were Jonathan born April 21, 1701, Abraham, Sarah, married Oliver Shumway, Joseph Lydia, married Jedediah Barton, Micah Jonas, and Susanna, married Jonas Coller

(III) Jonathan Pratt, born April 21, 1701, received from his father a deed of sixty acres of land in Oxford, in 1723, and November 18 1725 married Lydia daughter of Theophilus Phillips, of Watertown He built the house afterward known as the Deacon Stone place, which was standing in 1892 and then considered to be the oldest house in Oxford His wife died in May, 1729 and he married (second), May 28, 1730 Ruth Eddy, who died April 1, 1731, and he married (third), December 15 1731, Deborah, daughter of Deacon John Coolidge, of Watertown He died July 25, 1788 and his wife died February 9 1793, aged eighty-three years He was a selectman of Oxford in 1740-41-51-56 His children were Keziah born March 18, 1727, married Moses Holmes, Lydia, born 1728, died 1729, Ruth, born 1731, died 1746, Mellison, born 1733, died 1746, Lydia, born 1736, died 1746, Huldah born March 1, 1739 married Isaac Town, Jonathan, born August 15, 1741 Elias born November 7, 1743, Elisha, born July 15, 1747 Esther, born June 6, 1752 Deborah, born July 15 1754, married Jesse Merriam

(IV) Elias Pratt, born in Oxford, November 7, 1743, married August 6 1767 Lydia, daughter of Jonathan Hill of Billerica She was born March 25 1746 He settled near the old homestead in Oxford, and was one of the men who marched in Captain John Town's company in answer to the alarm, April 19 1775 They went to Roxbury and served fourteen and three-quarter days September 25 1778, he was commissioned captain of the Fifteenth Company, Fifth Worcester County Regiment, Colonel Jonathan Holman, commanding He again served as captain, from April 11, 1779 to July 1, 1779, a period of two months and twenty days, his company being stationed at Rutland He was a selectman of Oxford from 1785 to 1794 He died March 14, 1816 and his wife died March 10, 1820, in Sutton Their children were Lydia, born 1768, died the same year, Jerusha born September 18, 1769, married Thomas Davis Lydia and Ruth (twins), born September 25, 1771, married brothers, Ambrose and William Stone Elias and Elijah (twins) born March 4 1773, Zadock, born November 17, 1775, Jeremiah, born September 20, 1779, Sylvanus and Sylvester (twins), born August 20, 1781 and Amasa, born May 7, 1787

(V) Elias Pratt born in Oxford, March 4, 1773, married Sally, daughter of Dr Ezra Conant of Oxford November 15, 1801 He first settled upon the old family homestead in Oxford, but about 1817 removed to the neighboring town of Sutton, where, in 1825, he purchased the Hathaway place, known later as the Pratt house, and afterward as the Rufus King house He made this farm his home for a number of years, but finally removed to Worcester, where he died September 2, 1854 In Oxford he served on the board of selectmen 1808-09-17, and was captain of militia His children were Sally, born 1802 died 1804, Ezra, born October 6, 1804, died October 9 1805, Serena, born August 14 1806, married Charles King, Sarah, born January 29, 1808 married Joshua O Lewis, Sumner, born September 30 1809, Emeline, born December 14, 1812, married Leonard Woodbury, and Amanda, born August 11, 1815, died May 22, 1837 The mother of these children, Sally (Conant) Pratt, was a lineal descendant of Roger Conant often called the first Colonial governor of Massachusetts She was born in Warwick, Massachusetts, May 15, 1777, and died in Worcester, December 4, 1852

(VI) Sumner Pratt was born in Oxford Massachusetts, September 30, 1809, upon the farm which was the home of his ancestors for three generations and there his school days and early manhood were passed His business career began with the manufacture of loom shuttles in 1831 In 1843 he was engaged in manufacturing cotton thread in Worcester This continued for two years when he established an agency for cotton and wool machinery and mill supplies in that city He was very successful in this business which grew extensively in the course of years, and he maintained an active interest in the firm which bore his name until a short time before his death, which occurred January 6, 1887 He was respected as a high-minded and public-spirited citizen and was held in esteem by all his associates for his sound judgment and nobility of character In his social and family life he was beloved for personal qualities of an uncommon order He served the city as a member of the common council in 1869-70-71-72, and of the board of aldermen in 1876-77 He was a trustee of the Worcester County Institution for Savings, vice-president of the People's Savings Bank, a director of the Worcester Safe Deposit and Trust Company, and at one period president of the Board of Trade During his life in Worcester he attended All Saints' Church (Protestant Episcopal), holding the offices of vestryman and warden for a long period In politics he was first a Whig and then a Republican

Sumner Pratt was twice married His first wife, whom he married May 10, 1836, was Serena daughter of Caleb Chase, of Sutton and who died June 19, 1848 By her he had two children Frederick Sumner, born September 21 1845 and Emma Amanda born May 8, 1848 His second wife whom he married August 5 1850 was Abby Curtis daughter of Ebenezer Read, of Worcester and who died April 29, 1896 By her he had one child, Edward Read born May 1 1851 died October 31, 1880

(VII) Frederick Sumner Pratt was born in Worcester, Massachusetts September 21, 1845 He was educated in the schools of Worcester, graduating from the high school in 1862 After four years of service in the Worcester Bank he entered the business of his father soon after becoming a member of the firm of Sumner Pratt & Co In 1896 he retired from this firm in order to confine his attention to portrait and landscape painting, a work which for some years had been of exceeding interest to him. This interest, although dating from art studies pursued in early life, received a fresh impulse from the visit of John Sargent to Worcester in the year 1890, when a most friendly and helpful intercourse with that distinguished master was brought about. Naturally his advice and criticism proved an invaluable aid to the Worcester artist. There are many portraits bearing Mr. Pratt's signature now in Worcester homes and others, and he has been an occasional exhibitor at the art galleries of national reputation. He is a trustee of the Worcester County Institution for Savings and an officer of the Worcester Art Society and the Worcester Art Museum, as well as a member of several clubs. He is a parishioner and warden of All Saints' Church (Protestant Episcopal) and a Republican in politics.

Frederick Sumner Pratt married, January 19, 1871, at Worcester, Sarah McKean Hilliard, who was born in Boston and was a daughter of Judge Francis Hilliard and Catharine Dexter Haven (daughter of Judge Samuel Haven, of Dedham, Massachusetts). She died in Worcester, December 27, 1897. Their children are: Francis Hilliard, born in Worcester, November 3, 1871, died November 4, 1871. Frederick Haven, A. M., M. D., born in Worcester, July 19, 1873, a graduate of Harvard College and of the Harvard Medical School, who has published papers on scientific and educational subjects, and is engaged in physiological research. He is a member of the American Association for the Advancement of Science, the Boston Society of Medical Sciences and of the St. Botolph Club, Boston. Katherine Chase, born in Worcester, December 29, 1875. She became the wife of Dr. Alfred Lindsay Shapleigh, of Boston, June 2, 1896, and they both went to China as missionaries in 1896 and again in 1904. In February, 1905, her husband and only children (Samuel Brooks and Stephen) died from smallpox at Ngankin, a third son (Frederick Gordon), having died in 1900 at Worcester. With rare courage and devotion she resolved to continue her work in China and is now (1906) at Yang Chow. Robert Gage, born in Worcester, October 17, 1877, a graduate of Harvard College, class of 1900, and now (1906) holds a responsible position in the Crompton & Knowles Loom Works. He married, July 9, 1906, Edythe McCord Coleman, of Morristown, New Jersey. Elizabeth Hilliard, born in Worcester, July 27, 1882, married Dr. William Irving Clark, of New York, June 23, 1906.

PETER WOOD. Thomas Wood (1), great-grandfather of Peter Wood of Worcester, Massachusetts, was born and brought up in Yorkshire, England. He came of an old English family not quite generally scattered over Ireland as well as England. Few surnames had a larger representation among the early settlers and pioneers of New England. Thomas Wood left England when a young man to make a home in Ireland and establish himself in business there. He bought a farm in Castle Bleyney, county Monaghan, Ireland, established a woolen mill and manufactured woolen cloth. His son John, grandfather of Peter Wood, of Worcester, succeeded him in business.

(II) John Wood, son of Thomas Wood (1), was born in Castle Bleyney, county Monaghan, Ireland. He followed his father in the manufacture of woolen goods in his native town. He left his business to three of his sons, Bernard, James and William. In fact, the woolen mill established a hundred years ago by Thomas Wood is still owned and operated by his descendants. The children of John Wood were: James, Thomas, William, Bernard, father of Peter Wood; Catherine, married —— Markey. All the children were born in Castle Bleyney, Ireland.

(III) Bernard Wood, son of John Wood (2), was born about 1798 in Castle Bleyney, Ireland, died there in 1848. He was a farmer and manufacturer, owning with his two brothers the woolen mill of his father and grandfather. He married Anne Cummesky. She died 1880, aged about seventy-eight years. The children of Bernard and Anne (Cummesky) Wood were: Catherine, resides on the old homestead in Ireland; Mary, died unmarried at the age of nineteen in her native place; Patrick, millwright, resides in Bleyney, has a family; Margaret, died in 1900 in Albany, New York, four of her children are living in New York state, viz: Anne, John, Patrick and Bernard; Owen, died in Ireland unmarried; Bernard, a bleacher by trade, resides in Brookfield, Massachusetts, married Anne Shevlin; Peter, born March 18, 1845; James, died young in Ireland.

(IV) Peter Wood, son of Bernard Wood (3), was born in Castle Bleyney, county Monaghan, Ireland, March 16, 1845. He obtained a common school education in the national schools of his native parish. He went to work in the dyeing establishment of Alexander Reid & Son in the city of Glasgow, Scotland, and there learned the trade of dyeing and bleaching. In 1868, at the age of twenty-three years, he came to this country. He was engaged at his trade for four years and saw something of the country, working in various places in the United States. In 1872 he came to Worcester and since then he has lived there. He went to work first in the dye-shop of Orr & Walker at the corner of Gardner and Southgate streets. Two years later he bought an interest in the business of Mr. Walker and became a partner with Mr. Orr of the original firm. The firm name was the Worcester Bleach and Dye Works, with shops at 110 Grove street. In 1894 Peter Wood sold his interest in the company. The Worcester Bleach and Dye Works are now located at 61 Fremont street, near Webster. James E. Orr is treasurer of the company, which was incorporated in 1891. This company bleaches and dyes cotton yarns and warps, braids, threads and tapes.

Mr. Wood established his present business in the following year. He formed a corporation known as the Peter Wood Dyeing Company, with capital of $20,000. The original officers were Peter Wood, Walter Delano and Robert Ruddy. The present works were built at the foot of Holmes street, South Worcester, in 1895 and Mr. Wood began business there in 1896. At present the officers of the company are: President and treasurer, Peter Wood; directors, Robert Wood, his son, and Ira C. Davis. Robert Wood is the boss bleacher. Another son, Peter Wood, Jr., is superintendent of the works. The company bleaches and dyes cotton yarns and warps, threads, tapes, braids, etc., largely for the cotton mills, employing thirty or more hands regularly. Mr. Wood has interests in several other successful Worcester enterprises. In 1887 Mr. Wood, Robert Ruddy and Robert Redford started the thread factory on Manchester street under the firm name of Ruddy Thread Company. It developed into an excellent business, but in 1899 it seemed advisable to sell out to the trust—The American Thread Company. But Mr. Wood and his associates did not stay out of the thread business long. Mr. Wood bought the shop of the Worcester Steam Heating Company at 116 Gold street. Mr. Wood, James Montgomery, Charles Dolan, Charles Hall and James

Geo H. Coates

Ruddy became the directors of the Wachusett Thread Company, which for several years has conducted a profitable and growing business in the manufacture of thread Mr Wood is president, Mr Dolan superintendent of the mill and Mr Montgomery treasurer The business in 1905 amounted to $360,000 Mr Dolan has demonstrated the fact that he has good judgment and business ability The industries that he has established have been creditable to the city as well as to him, and there is every prospect that the business has a great future in Worcester Mr Wood is a member of the Worcester Lodge of Elks, No 243, Alhambra Lodge, Knights of Columbus, and of the Frohsinns He belongs to the Roman Catholic Church of St Peter's parish, Worcester In politics he is a Republican

He married (first), November 24, 1875, Anne McKenna, daughter of Terence and Anna (Hughes) McKenna, at Worcester, Massachusetts He married (second), July 31, 1895, at Worcester, Agnes Mitchinson, daughter of Joseph and Ellen (Pilkenton) Mitchinson the children of Peter and Anne (McKenna) Wood were Catherine, born October 12, 1876, resides at Albany, New York, Owen, born October 12, 1878, plumber by trade, resides in Schenectady, New York, Robert, born December 17, 1879, attended the Worcester schools, entered the dye shop and learned the business, is now boss bleacher for the Peter Wood Dyeing Co, Peter, Jr, born March 1, 1881, attended the Worcester schools, went into the dyeshop and learned the business, is now superintendent, unmarried, lives with parents at 24 Cambridge street, Anne, born March 28, 1882, lives at home with her parents The children of Peter and Agnes (Mitchinson) Wood were Mildred, born May 10, 1896, William, born July 31, 1897, Agnes, born March 10, 1898 All the children were born in Worcester, Massachusetts

GEORGE HENRY COATES, son of Henry Moss and Orra Natalia (Cone) Coates, was born in Windsor, Vermont, June 23, 1849 For his mother's family see sketch of Cone family She is living, 1905, with her son in Worcester at the age of eighty-four There were twelve children born to her parents and six of them are now living Mrs Coates, H S Cone, Ascutneyville, Vermont, aged eighty-seven, Mrs Lucy Marston, Marshall, Michigan, aged seventy-nine, James M Cone, Keene, New Hampshire, aged seventy-three, Mrs Ellen M Putnam, Manchester, New Hampshire, aged seventy-one In her immediate family there was not a death until the oldest child was sixty-two years old There were ten of the twelve alive in 1901, when the youngest was sixty-six years old The family has an unusual record for longevity Henry M Coats, as his name was formerly spelled was a blacksmith by trade He was the son of Prescott and Lydia (Penniman) Coates

George H Coates was educated in the public schools and at Windsor Academy He had some mechanical knowledge and doubtless much inherited skill in mechanics He came to Worcester at the age of eighteen to learn tool making and mechanical engineering He started to work for the Ethan Allen Fire Arms Company and learned the business thoroughly He had charge of the construction of the first self-cocking fire arms He was foreman at Allen's for about eight years

In 1877 he established the business in which he has been so successful and with which his name is associated the world over, the manufacture of the Coates Clipper When he invented the adjustable clipper in 1876 all clippers were imported from England and France Mr Coates had made a specialty of repairing these imported instruments It required a mechanic of exceptional skill to insert new teeth in these instruments, temper them anew and grind them Mr Coates did considerable work of this kind for McCoy & Saunders of New York city He naturally came to devise a vastly better article than the one then made abroad He showed his patent to McCoy & Saunders and received at once an order for five hundred These were the adjustable hair clippers, and doubtless many of the first made are still in use in barber shops Mr Coates had no machine shop, but the price he had been quoted by Forchand & Wadsworth for the manufacture of his machine caused him to buy a small plant and start to manufacture his own goods Step by step he advanced until he has a very extensive plant and an extremely successful business His first machinery was bought in Boston of Hill, Clark & Company, and he has bought a great deal of machinery of that firm since After a year in the little basement of a house on Dewey street, Mr. Coates was able to build a shop forty by fifty feet on the present location, 237 Chandler street He had only a five horse power engine to run his machinery His first engine and boiler was bought of William Allen & Son His Chandler street shop was built in 1878 and was but one story high He soon had to build an addition forty feet long In 1884 he raised the building to two stories and added fifty feet, making the building six times its original size The business increased with proportionate rapidity The clippers found a market all over the world The power was increased to one hundred and fifty horse Another addition of seventy-five feet on the Dewey street end of the building was erected in 1903 At present the factory has over an acre of floor space

Mr Coates was not satisfied with his first invention and he has from time to time improved on his own work and added new devices He has taken out more than forty patents He says that in his experimenting and designing he has been greatly indebted to the education received at the night school in mechanical drawing at the Worcester Polytechnic Institute soon after he came to Worcester He studied under Professor Alden and Superintendent Higgins, who are now the owners of the Norton Emery Company and the Plunger Elevator Company He won several prizes at exhibitions of mechanical drawings in Boston, and received the highest reward of merit there for a colored drawing of a Corliss engine The business is now a corporation The officers are President and treasurer, George H Coates, vice-president and manager, B Austin Coates These two own the business The additions have been made as their means would permit Mr Coates has shown a rare combination of inventive genius and shrewd business ability He has made his own fortune without outside assistance from the outset

The Coates Clipper Manufacturing Company is known all over the world for ingenious and useful machinery The selling agents are John H Graham & Co, 113 Chambers street, New York The London place of business is at 14 Thavies Inn, Holborn Circus, the continental headquarters in Copenhagen The latest patterns of clippers are models of artistic work They have ball bearings, the teeth are beautifully cut and hardened, and each blade is ground with diamond dust These clippers, for the use of amateur and professional barbers, are sold from $2 50 to $3 50 each A Worcester man who returned recently from a visit to Australia told Mr Coates that he found the Coates clipper the only kind on the market in Australia, where he and many others used it to keep their beards trimmed close

The power clipper equipped with the Coates patent flexible non-heating shaft is the best instrument yet devised for clipping horses and shearing animals It is the only gearless machine on the market Special sheep shearing machines are built The ordinary horse clipper is run by hand power, but some very fine instruments run by electric motors are made A number of other specialties are made by the Coates Clipper Mfg Co The Coates grooming brush is operated by power and is warranted to groom perfectly twenty-five horses in an hour This company makes an ingenious machine to grind the caulks on horses' shoes without having the expense and trouble of taking the shoes off when they get dull

The flexible shaft which Mr Coates invented is one of the most important devices recently used in the mechanical world They are made large enough to transmit twenty horse power or more and small enough for the most delicate dentist machinery The Coates Company has recently built some dentists machinery, using this shaft which never breaks like the coiled wire flexible shafts in general use The flexible shafting has been found extremely useful by some manufacturers of automobiles and launches In some forms of grinders used in the manufacture of machinery this device is a wonderful time saver It is believed that Mr Coates has in this shaft an even more valuable patent than that of the clippers In all of the Coates manufacture the greatest pains is taken to make all parts interchangeable and to test fully everything made in the shop

Another important department of the Coates Company is the manufacture of the Coates housed gear breast drills and the Coates drill press An ingenious device is a combination of the Coates flexible shaft, an electric motor for power and a magnetic hold-on with a Coates drill for use in marine work, bridge work and in other places difficult to reach by ordinary drills It is easily portable, is used under water and it is said to be a great time saver for all kinds of drilling The Coates angle drive is a device to transmit power at right angles The Coates screw driver is used by chair builders and others having to insert a large number of screws It is operated with a flexible shaft and works very rapidly There is hardly a day but some new use for this flexible shafting develops It has been tried successfully in transmitting one hundred and fifty horse power The possibilities of the device are incalculable

A biography of a man like Mr Coates, who has made his business what it is, must be something of a catalogue of the products of his factory Those products represent his life work and thought They represent an important contribution to civilization and progress Mr Coates has made some tremendous contributions to the labor-saving machinery of the world Every successful device means labor-saving for the whole human race, in other words means that each man's labor should bring him a little more of the fruits of human toil, more of what is generally described as wealth While Mr Coates is one of the inventors who has gained some return financially from his invention, he has given to the world devices that will always be useful and labor-saving

Mr Coates is fortunate in his partner His son, B Austin Coates, was born June 2, 1879 He graduated from the Worcester high school in 1896 and from the Worcester Polytechnic Institute in 1900 Since then he has been associated in business with his father He married Louisa Boyden Coe, daughter of S Hamilton Coe, June 5, 1901 He is a member of the Commonwealth Club, the Worcester Automobile Club, Quinsigamond Lodge, Ancient Free and Accepted Masons, Eureka Royal Arch Chapter, Hiram Council, Lawrence Chapter of Rose Croix, Worcester County Commandery, Knights Templar He has taken all the degrees in the Scottish Rite He attends St Mark's Protestant Episcopal Church

George H Coates has taken all the degrees of Free Masonry in the Scottish Rite, and is a member of the Quinsigamond Lodge, Hiram Council, the Chapter and Worcester County Commandery He is a Shriner He is also a member of the Economic Club, the Worcester Automobile Club, the Worcester County Agricultural Society, the Worcester County Mechanics' Association, the Home Market Club of Boston

He married, June 23, 1872, Adelaide Long, daughter of William Long, an expert machinist of Biddeford Maine They were married in Worcester in what was then a first class neighborhood on Mechanics street Their only son is B Austin Coates, mentioned above George H Coates was himself an only son

(I) Daniel Cone, who was of Connecticut before 1657, was the first known ancestor of Mrs Henry M Coates, mother of George H Coates, of Worcester Massachusetts, and of a large number of descendants now scattered widely throughout the United States He was probably the first of the name in this country The first mention of Daniel Cone was March 2, 1657, when Governor John Winthrop of the Connecticut made a requisition on Governor Peter Stuyvesant of New York for the return of one James Parker, for whom Daniel Cone was a bondsman, and on whose complaint the action was brought In the spring of 1662 he appears as one of twenty-eight persons who received from the Connecticut Colony a grant of land situated on both sides of the Connecticut river about thirty miles above its mouth This land had been in the possession of the Wangunk tribe of Indians from time immemorial The Indians deeded to them a tract of land six miles east and west and from Middletown to Chester, Connecticut The consideration was thirty red coats, which may have been worth a hundred dollars The colony granted the land to these twenty-eight settlers and later the general court confirmed their title The town was called Haddam after a town in England of that name Daniel Cone received his allotment of four acres on the town site, on the west side of the river, with land in the meadow and timbered land adjoining in 1662, and removed to the new town in that year Previous to this change of location he had married Mehitable Spencer, fourth daughter of Jared and Alice Spencer, then of Hartford, Connecticut Jared Spencer settled at Newtown (Cambridge), Massachusetts in 1634 removed to Lynn, Massachusetts, in 1637, to Hartford, Connecticut, in 1660, and to Haddam, Connecticut in 1662, being also one of the founders of that town Mehitable Spencer was born in Lynn in 1642 and died in Haddam in 1691

Daniel Cone married (second) Rebecca Walkley, widow of Richard Walkley, of Haddam Connecticut No record of her death has been found He resided in Haddam until 1680, when he removed to the east side of the river to the vicinity of Machi-Moodus About 1695 he returned to Haddam where he died October 24 1706, aged eighty years He was commissioner for his town in 1669 and held other town offices A few months before he died he deeded his land on the west side of the river at

Haddam to his youngest son, Caleb The children of Daniel Cone (I) were Ruth, born January 7, 1662, place of birth unknown, Hannah, born April 6, 1664, in Haddam, Connecticut, Daniel, born January 21, 1666, married Mary Gates, died June 25, 1725, Jared, born January 7, 1668, married Elizabeth ——, he died April 11, 1718, Rebecca, born February 6, 1670, Ebenezer, born in Haddam, baptized, March 25, 1673, Nathaniel, born in Haddam, baptized June 4, 1675, married Sarah Hungerford, he died about 1730, Stephen, born at Haddam, baptized March 26, 1678, married Mary Hungerford, he died December 1, 1756, Caleb, baptized March 19, 1682, married (first) Elizabeth ——, married (second) Elizabeth Cunningham, he died September 25, 1743

(II) Caleb Cone, youngest child of Daniel Cone (1), was born at Haddam, Connecticut, in 1679, and baptized in the Middletown Congregational Church, March 19, 1682 He married in Haddam, December 16, 1701, Elizabeth ——, who died there November 14, 1714 He married (second) Elizabeth Cunningham September 6, 1723 He was born, lived and died on the homestead where his father originally settled in Haddam He was buried within sight of the old home, his grave being marked by a stone suitably inscribed He was a representative of his district in the general court in 1731-32-33-34-35-39 He held the commission of captain in the colonial troops for many years He held other offices in the town

The children of Caleb Cone were Caleb, born September, 1702, married (first) Hannah ——, (second) Sybil Bailey, he died February 27, 1790, Joseph, born January 26 1704, married Susannah Wells, he died 1779, Noah born July 14, 1707, married Hannah —— he died August 5, 1757, Elisha born September 11, 1709, married Hannah Hubbard, he died March 6, 1809, Joshua, born July 4, 1714, died young, Simon, born June 11 1724, died 1756, Daniel, born December 22, 1725 married Susannah Hurlburt, he died July 12 1762, Beriah, born September 12, 1727, had son Beriah, Abigail born July 2, 1730, married Elisha Knowles, Mary, born March 23, 1732, married Richard Knowles she died October 8, 1796, Lydia, born January 29, 1735 married Joseph Tyler, died 1823

(III) Daniel Cone, son of Caleb (2) and Elizabeth (Cunningham) Cone, was born in Haddam, Connecticut December 22 1725 He married, May 12, 1750, Susannah Hurlburt, daughter of Daniel and Esther (Hamlin) Hurlburt who was born in Middletown, Connecticut They settled in Middletown and most of their children were born there She was born November 19, 1729, died May 15, 1774 He died in Middletown, July 12, 1762 Their children were Esther, born August 11, 1751, Daniel II, born July 16, 1753 married Elizabeth Atkins, he died April 17, 1841, William, born April 6, 1755, married Abiah Atkins, he died 1834, Joshua born September 1 1757, married Mehitable Blinn, Robert, born December 16, 1759, married Margaret Paget, he died May 19 1804 Thomas born probably in Middletown, baptized February 8, 1763, married Mehitable Lyman, he died April 12 1854

(IV) Thomas Cone, son of Daniel Cone (3), was baptized at Middletown, Connecticut, February 8 1763 At the age of twenty-one and just at the close of the revolutionary war he left his home and started up the Connecticut valley in search of work He was a tailor by trade He located first at Northampton, Massachusetts, where he worked for two years He married there, March 13 1786 They started immediately on horseback to make a home for themselves in Vermont Their wedding trip was through the wilderness to the little town of Winchester, in western Vermont, where they settled and spent the remainder of their lives He became one of the most prominent citizens of the town His wife was born November 17, 1764, died October 11, 1827 He died April 12, 1854, at the age of ninety-one years Their children, all born at Winchester, Vermont, were Thomas, born May 5, 1787, married Olive Lane, he died January 22, 1858, Robert, born November 27, 1788, married Fanny Royce, he died December 30, 1814, Morris, born October 6, 1790, married Lydia Farrington, he died March 29, 1846, Laura, born March 13, 1793, married (first) Cyrus Jones, married (second) James Swinton, she died February 13, 1879, Theodore, born October 11, 1795, married Eliza Wooley, he died August 25, 1852, John, born October 7, 1797, married Lucinda Rand, he died June 2, 1879, James, born October 7, 1797, married Catherine Cuyler, he died October 24, 1861, Stephen, born February 2, 1800, married Sally Pratt, he died November 1, 1884, Charles, born March 4, 1802, married Martha Dean, he died November 7, 1870, Eliza, born December 13, 1805, married Lyman Haywood, she died 1848

(V) Thomas Cone, son of Thomas (4), and Mehitable (Lyman) Cone, was born at Westminster, Vermont, May 5, 1787 He married Olive Lane, daughter of Samuel Lane, in 1808. She was born at Claremont, New Hampshire, March 4, 1790, died May 6, 1852 He was a tailor by occupation He settled first at Swanton, Vermont, near his birthplace, removed 1816 to West Claremont, New Hampshire, where he died January 22, 1858 He was held in high esteem by his neighbors He was a man of excellent character and standing in the community His children were Curtis E, born January 17, 1809, married Celia S Judd, he died July 17, 1873, Julia Ann, born September 17, 1811, married John Mercer, she died December 6, 1902, Narcissa M, born February 9, 1814, married (first) Elias Lovell, (second) Abel Camp, she died February 8, 1885, Fannie E, born October 13, 1815, married John L Seaver, she died May 3, 1900, Harley S, born December 28, 1817, married Estella J Adams, lived at Ascutneyville, Vermont, Charles E, born June 2, 1820, married Luthera E Sturtevant, died October 12, 1900, Natalia O, born March 18, 1822, married Henry W Coates, lives at Worcester, Massachusetts, with her son, George H Coates, Lucy E, born April 6, 1824, married Lorenzo Marston, lives at Marshall, Michigan, Robert L, born September 2, 1826, married Mary S Maynard, no children, died May 21, 1900, Lyman H, born January 22, 1829, married Lucia Judd, resided at Windsor, Vermont, James Monroe, born June 28, 1831, married Harriet C Richardson, lives at Keene, New Hampshire, Ellen M, born March 2, 1834, married Orrin Putnam, lives at Manchester, New Hampshire

(VI) Natalia Ora Cone, daughter of Thomas Cone (5), was born at Claremont, New Hampshire, March 18, 1822 She married March 18, 1847, Henry Moses Coates, son of Prescott and Lydia (Penniman) Coates She resides with her son, George H Coates, Worcester, Massachusetts See George H Coates sketch which precedes this in the work

CHARLES HOMER PERRY, M D John Perry (1), the first American ancestor of Dr Charles H Perry of Worcester, was born in England in 1613 He was in Watertown, Massachusetts, in 1674, when his age was sixty-one years That is about all that is known of him He came late in life and Bond surmises that he was the brother of William Perry, of Watertown, who was born in England in 1606, a tailor by trade, who came over before 1642

Another John Perry lived in Roxbury and had three children there Elizabeth, born January 25, 1637, John, born September 7, 1639, Samuel, born March 1, 1640 But this John Perry, Sr, died September, 1642, leaving his house and land to his wife to bring up his three children Curiously enough we are told that John Perry, Jr, had a brother and a sister Obviously, however, the John Perry, Sr, who died in 1642 was not the same one that was in Watertown in 1674

(II) John Perry, son of John Perry (1), was born in London, England, according to the generally accepted story, in 1644, and came to America in 1660 He married Sarah Clary, daughter of John Clary, of Cambridge, where she was born October 10, 1649 They settled in Watertown In 1701 he was in North Brookfield for a year and Perry's pond there was named for him He died in 1724, before December 23 Children of John and Sarah Perry were John, Joanna, born November 8, 1672, Sarah, born July 11, 1675, Elizabeth, Josiah, see forward, Joseph, born January 17, 1690

(III) Josiah Perry, son of John Perry (2), was born in Watertown, Massachusetts, November 28, 1684, married, January 12, 1708, Bethia Cutler, daughter of John Cutler, of Watertown She was born November 26, 1684, and died September 16, 1767 He married (second) Elizabeth Harrington The children of Josiah and Bethia Perry, all born in Watertown, were Jonathan, born January 7, 1710, Lydia, December 8, 1711, married John Ball, Josiah, Jr, February 7, 1714, Ephraim, November 1, 1715, Nathan, of whom later, Bethia, January 31, 1719, Mary, February 13, 1721, Israel, February 6, 1723, Dorcas, December 2, 1727, Sarah, 1728

(IV) Nathan Perry, fifth child of Josiah Perry (3), was born in Watertown, Massachusetts, May 2, 1718 He was a weaver by trade He came with his father April, 1751, and settled in Worcester and was for twenty-three years deacon of the church (Old South) from 1783 until he died, February, 1806, aged eighty-eight years He succeeded John Chandler as county treasurer He was town treasurer and selectman for ten years from 1780 to 1790 His homestead was on what is now Vernon street, the Elijah Hedge estate, which he bought when he came to Worcester He married, at Watertown, May 1, 1745, Hannah Fiske, daughter of Deacon Nathan Fiske She was born in 1719 and died in 1813, aged ninety-four years Their children were Hannah, born in Watertown, 1747, died 1749, Hannah, born 1749, in Watertown, Nathan, Jr, born March 30, 1751, in Watertown, the following children were born in Worcester Sarah, born November 29, 1752, Josiah, see forward, Mary, born March 1, 1759, Deacon Moses, born February 16, 1762, father of Deacon Samuel Perry and ancestor of many of the Worcester Perrys

(V) Josiah Perry, son of Deacon Nathan Perry (4), was born in Worceser, March 9, 1755 died March 12, 1842 He married (first) Lydia Flagg, April 3, 1777, (second) Prudence Harrington, July 6 1780, (third) Sarah Metcalf, November 22 1790 The only child of Josiah and Lydia was Lydia born February 20, 1778 The children of Josiah and Prudence Perry were Nathan, see forward, Mindwell February 7, 1783, Josiah, October 16, 1784, Sophia, October 3, 1786, William, April 22, 1789 The children of Josiah and Sarah Perry were Sarah, October 20, 1797, Prudence, January 31, 1803

(VI) Nathan Perry, second child of Josiah Perry (5), was born in Worcester, Massachusetts March 24, 1781 He conducted a farm and had a grist mill on the old homestead He married Anna Galen, daughter of Elisha Galen, she died February 1, 1845, aged seventy years He died October 3, 1837 Their children, all born in Worcester, were Sereno Haven, born December 26, 1802, Loring Fish, June 17, 1804, died August 8, 1848, Louisa, May 15, 1806, Miranda, May 18, 1808, Josiah Galen, see forward, Julia, June 12, 1812, Dexter Harrington, June 4, 1814, married, December 17, 1839, Elizabeth A Baker, born September 21, 1815, daughter of James Baker and sister of Charles and William J Baker, the lumber merchants of Worcester, he died March 16, 1872, and she died April 19, 1877, Frank D Perry, the contractor, is their son, Sophronia, February 27, 1816, Nancy, October 5, 1819, Harriet, February 22, 1822, died August 2, 1848, unmarried

(VII) Josiah Galen Perry, fifth child of Nathan Perry (6), was born in Worcester, June 15, 1810 He lived on the homestead at Quinsigamond village He carried on a grist mill with his brother, Dexter H Perry, until 1855 The partnership was dissolved in 1862 and the property divided He married Martha Homer, born in Hopkinton, Massachusetts Their children were Charles H, see forward, Louisa Emerett, born February 24, 1839, Mary Aurelia, December 28, 1841, a child, born August 11, 1845, a child, born March 15, 1848

(VIII) Dr Charles Homer Perry, son of Josiah Galen Perry (7), was born in Worcester, Massachusetts, March 17, 1835 He was educated in the public schools of Worcester and at Worcester Academy, where he fitted for college He was graduated from Brown University in 1859 He studied medicine at the University of Pennsylvania in Philadelphia and Bellevue Hospital and received his medical degree in medical college there He was connected with Bellevue Hospital in New York city when the civil war broke out, and he entered the service in 1861 as assistant surgeon, United States navy, and served through the war He served under Admiral Farragut for twenty-six months and also under Admiral Porter Served as surgeon on United States gunboat 'Kenebec" twenty-six months, United States receiving ship "Ohio" six months, United States ship "Susquehanna" nine months, under Admiral Porter At the close of the war he returned to Bellevue to complete his studies He began the practice of his profession in Medway, Massachusetts, but after a short time settled in Worcester, where he has been practicing since 1874 He has been fortunate in his practice and ranks high in the medical fraternity He is a member of the Massachusetts Medical Society, the Worcester Medical Society, and the American Academy of Medicine He was a charter member of a G A R post at West Medbury, this post is no longer in existence Is a member of Worcester Post, No 10, G A R Member of Montague Lodge, F and A M

He married, 1868, Clara T Thayer, daughter of Eli Thayer, the great anti-slavery leader of Massachusetts They have no children

CHARLES AUGUSTUS VAUGHAN John Vaughan (1), the pioneer ancestor of Charles Augustus Vaughan, of Worcester, Massachusetts, was born in England, probably about 1615 He settled in Providence, although he seems to have lived in Watertown, Massachusetts Bay, for a few years John Vaughan was in Watertown in 1633, and a proprietor in 1636, but John Vaughan, of Providence, had a case in court in Providence March 4, 1634 The only other early settler of this family was William Vaughan, a proprietor of Springfield, who leased his land January 10, 1644, for a period of six years, and perhaps returned to England John Vaughan was accepted as an inhabitant in good standing at Newport, May 20, 1638, and was admitted a freeman, which meant also membership in the church, 1655 He was granted forty-two acres of land at a place called the Hermitage in 1639, and May 22, 1662, had an eighty-acre lot laid out to him He deeded eight acres to his son, John, by deed of gift April 16, 1673, and a farm July 23, 1680, to his son Daniel, of Newport He died 1687, at Newport, where he lived during most of his active life Children were 1 John, born April 19, 1644, settled in Newport 2 David, born July 19, 1646, settled at Portsmouth 3 George, (see forward) 4 Daniel, born April 27, 1653, married Susan Grimes and settled in Newport 5 Mary, born July 3, 1658

(II) George Vaughan, son of John Vaughan (1), born October 20, 1650, died May 7, 1704 He lived at Newport, Rhode Island, and later at East Greenwich He was a blacksmith by trade He had a grant, with others, of five thousand acres of land at East Greenwich, October 31, 1677 He was deputy to the general assembly in 1684-98-99, and was on the grand jury in 1698 He commanded a cavalry company in 1687 His will was dated April 11, 1699, and was proved May 25, 1704 His wife Mary and son George, Jr, were the executors He mentioned his smith's tools in the will He married, July 26, 1680, Margaret Spink, daughter of Robert and Alice Spink She died 1704 Their children were 1 George, Jr, born April 19, 1682, married Jane Nichols 2 David, born April 29, 1683, married Mary Pearce 3 Mary, born February 23, 1685 4 Christopher, (see forward) 5 Abigail, born February 24, 1689, married John Hall 6 Robert, born March 7, 1691, married Joanna Sweet

(III) Christopher Vaughan, fourth child of George Vaughan (2), born in Newport, Rhode Island, April 29, 1686 He was admitted a freeman 1707, and settled in East Greenwich, on the land granted to his father He died there October 11, 1751, and his will was proved August 29, 1752 It mentions a loom, showing that Christopher was probably a weaver as well as a planter His executor was Christopher, Jr, to whom he left the homestead for life, and to his grandson Christopher after him His estate was valued at two thousand, six hundred and forty-eight pounds He married, June 26, 1709, Deborah Nichols, born February 17, 1688, daughter of Thomas and Mercy (Reynolds) Nichols Their children, all born at East Greenwich, were 1 Christopher, Jr, born July 6, 1710 2 Benjamin, born July 2, 1713 3 Mary, born May 8, 1715, married ——— Nichols 4 Deborah, born July 13, 1719, married ——— Weaver 5 Ruth, born August 12, 1729, married ——— Spencer

(IV) Christopher Vaughan, Jr, son of Christopher Vaughan (3), born July 6, 1710, at East Greenwich, Rhode Island, died there April 23, 1758 He had the homestead of his grandfather He married (first) Hannah ——— and (second) Elizabeth (?) ——— The children of Christopher and Hannah Vaughan, all born at East Greenwich, were 1 Christopher, Jr, born April 22, 1735, settled in East Greenwich 2 Benjamin, born September 6, 1744, settled in Vermont and was in the revolution, (he seems to be the Benjamin Vaughan who finally settled at Danby, Vermont, though the statement of his English birth there is evidently wrong, being confused apparently with the earlier ancestor, John) Benjamin lived also at Tinmouth, Vermont In the revolution he was in the same company with John and James Vaughan, his brothers (See the record of John) 3 Abigail, born September 6, 1744 The only child on record of Christopher and Elizabeth, born at East Greenwich, was Alice, born October 25, 1754 Other children were 5 James, soldier in the Vermont companies with John and Benjamin Vaughan 6 John, (see forward)

(V) John Vaughan, son of Christopher Vaughn (4), born about 1760 Benjamin, John and James Vaughan were all soldiers together in the revolution Benjamin Vaughan was the first to enlist in the Shoreham (Vermont) company, Captain Ebenezer Allen's, April, 1778, probably about the time that the Vaughan family went to Vermont In 1780 Benjamin and James Vaughan were in Captain Gideon Ormsby's company, Colonel Ira Allen's regiment In 1781 Benjamin, James and John Vaughan were in the same regiment, Colonel Ira Allen's, under Captain Jacob Odell The only other Vaughans in the revolution, from Vermont, were Charles, Obadiah and Jabesh, whose relationship has not been traced

John Vaughan settled in Shoreham, in the western part of Vermont, named evidently from Shoreham, Rhode Island Some of the settlers came from Danby where Benjamin Vaughan settled There were only six families in Shoreham before 1775 The Vaughan family came during the revolution It is related in the town history that Major Nathan Smith, who settled there with three brothers from Nine Partners, New York, was, with Benjamin Vaughan, the first to scale the breastworks in pursuit of the enemy at the battle of Bennington According to family tradition John Vaughan sold supplies from his farm to the soldiers at the battle of Bennington in 1777 John Vaughan married Achsah Hill, the daughter of David Hill Among their children was George Pike Vaughan, (see forward)

(VI) George Pike Vaughan, son of John Pike (5), was born in Shoreham, Vermont, about 1813 For many years he was engaged in farming in the neighborhood of his birthplace, but later in life changed his abode to Thetford, Vermont, where he died He married, October 29, 1845, Mary Moore Palmer, born August 21, 1823 She is still living with her family Her father was Jared Palmer

Jared Palmer was born January 18, 1795, at Orford, New Hampshire, and died May 23, 1886, his wife died 1867 Their children were 1 Mary Moore Palmer, before mentioned 2 James M Palmer, a real estate agent in Lowell, Massachusetts, where he died 3 Charles Palmer, lived in Thetford, was an invalid all his life, from an accident early in childhood 4 Caroline Palmer, married Wilson Farnsworth, of Thetford, Vermont, they were missionaries for fifty years in Turkey, representing the American Board 5 Helen Palmer, married William Slade, who was a farmer and judge in Thetford, Vermont, and has four children William, Congregational clergyman, Maria, married Fred Garey, a carpenter, of Thetford, and they have four children Nellie, school teacher in Gloucester, Massachusetts, Mary, married Leon Turner, resides in Vermont

The children of George Pike and Mary Moore (Palmer) Vaughan all born at Shoreham, Vermont, were 1 George Leslie, born July 1846, married Emma Lyman, of Thetford, is a farmer, they have five children Lyman, Elizabeth, Raymond, Christine, Charles 2 Charles Augustus (see forward) 3 Mary E, married Warren C Jewett, of Worcester (See sketch of Jewett) 4 David Albert, married A Emily King, resides in Metcalf, Massachusetts, they have four children Mabel, Ethel, Irving Justin (twin of preceding) 5 Frank M, married and has two children, resides at Cambridge,

Massachusetts 6 Arthur J, a carpenter and builder, resides in Worcester, married Clara Davis and they have two children 7 Octavia H teaches school in the Adams square public school, Worcester 8 Henry, married Cora Dakin, died leaving one child, Florence

(VII) Charles Augustus Vaughan, second child of George Pike Vaughan (6), born at Shoreham, Vermont, August 19, 1847 His education was acquired in the common schools and academy of Thetford, Vermont, whither his parents removed during the early years of his life, and at the age of fifteen he left school to work on the farm with his father Three years later he came to Worcester, Massachusetts, to learn the trade of carpenter, of H & A Palmer, for whom he worked ten years In 1875 he started in business for himself as carpenter and builder, and has since been engaged successfully in this business Among the many fine residences and buildings that he has built are the following L D Thayer's residence, Main street, Gilbert Harrington's, Main street, T B Brown's and Henry Taylor's, Richards street, William H Sawyer's, Lincoln street, Fred S Taylor's, Institute road, John D Baldwin's, Cedar street, George F Blake's, Judge William T Forbes's, Trowbridge road, George Moore's, George Heywood's, Gardner, Massachusetts, Andrew J Bates's, Webster, Massachusetts, Mr Sibley's country house, Spencer, Massachusetts, Mann Brothers', Leicester, The Armsby Block, Main street, Worcester, Whitinsville public school, a number of churches in Worcester county

Mr Vaughan was for two years president of the Builders' Exchange, of Worcester He has been active in public affairs in Worcester and prominent in public life He is a leading Republican, serving the city in the board of aldermen in 1899, 1900-01-02, from Ward one He is an active member of Union Church, was a member of the building committee, and has been a trustee since 1897 He is a member of the Worcester Board of Trade and of the Vermont Association, a trustee of the Worcester County Mechanics' Association, a director of the Young Men's Christian Association and director of the Merchants' and Farmers' Insurance Company of Worcester He married (first) October 6, 1869, Ann E Morse, daughter of Willis and Maria M Morse, of Southbridge, Massachusetts, a descendant of Samuel Morse, one of the pioneer settlers of Massachusetts, and one of the leading families She died December 19, 1889 He married (second) September 19, 1896, Adele Fairbanks, daughter of William H and Ellen (Williams) Fairbanks, of Holden, Massachusetts She is a descendant of Jonathan Fairbanks, of Dedham, the progenitor of all of that name in this country

The children of Charles Augustus and Ann E Vaughan were 1 Charles Albert, born October 7, 1871, now a resident of Minneapolis, Minnesota, of the firm of Bull & Vaughan, builders and contractors he was a corporal in Company C, Light Infantry, of Worcester, and served in the Spanish war, in Cuba, married, in 1900, Isabella Cundall, of Worcester, and they have had two children Isabel and Edward Cundall Vaughan 2 Robert Henry, born October 27, 1876, married, 1899, Elizabeth Cundall, sister of Isabella (Cundall) Vaughan, and they have four children Charles Augustus born October 3 1900, Jessie, born August 7, 1902, Marian, born October 29, 1904, Willard Cundall, born January, 1906 3 Louis Edgar, born March 9, 1880, graduate of the Boston Technical school 4 Ralph Donald, born January 28, 1884, student at Cornell University, class of 1907, making a specialty of architectural engineering 5 Catherine May, born May 24, 1887 The children of Charles Augustus and Adele (Fairbanks) Vaughan were 6 George Fairbanks, born January 30, 1897 7 Margaret, born July 16, 1902 8 Barbara, born August 21, 1904

CLAFLIN FAMILY Robert Claflin (1), or Mackclothlan, was the immigrant ancestor of Charles Winslow Claflin, late of Hopkinton, and his daughter, Mrs Arthur Osgood Young, of Worcester, and in fact all of the name in this vicinity, including Governor Claflin and the late H B Claflin, the great dry goods merchant of New York This name was particularly difficult for our forefathers to spell, it is found rendered in fourteen different ways in Scotch records and about as many in the early American records The first of the name was probably Norse or Scandinavian, and the name means without the Mac, lake-land, the first of the name doubtless taking his name from some locality Mac means simply "son of" in Scotch and Irish names The name is found in Ireland as McLaughlin at present

The family tradition supports the belief that Robert McLaughlin was a soldier in the Scottish army, taken prisoner by Cromwell at the battle of Dunbar Many of these prisoners were sent to New England and sold for a term of years to the colonists Robert settled in Essex county and was admitted or accepted as a townsman November 4, 1661, in Wenham He received a grant of land in 1669 in Wenham and sold some land in 1673 He was surveyor of highways there His house or part of it is still standing and the old well is still in use The place was owned lately by a family named Richards Robert Claflin married Joanna Warner, October 14, 1664 She was probably a daughter of John Warner, an early settler at Ipswich and later at Brookfield, Massachusetts He died shortly before September 19, 1690 when the inventory of his estate was filed by Thomas Fiske, administrator The children of Robert and Joanna Claflin all born at Wenham except the second, were Joanna, born August 12, 1665, Robert probably born at Brookfield, Elizabeth, May 18, 1670, Priscilla, August 22, 1672 Daniel, January 25, 1674, of whom later, Abigail, March 19, 1676, Mary, February 22, 1678, Antipas, 1680

(II) Daniel Claflin, son of Robert Claflin (1), was born in Wenham, Massachusetts January 25, 1674 He was a tanner by trade and lived in Wenham until after May 25, 1722, when he sold to Emerson Cogswell, of Ipswich, for eighty pounds his home, bark, mill tan vat and material for carrying on the trade of tanner He had three acres of land He then removed to Hopkinton, Massachusetts He was probably attracted to this town by the large number of Scotch Presbyterians who located there among the first settlers The town was incorporated December 24, 1715 It was bought with a legacy of eight hundred pounds given by Governor Edward Hopkins, of Connecticut, "for the breeding up of youth in the way of learning for the public service of the country in future time" and "for the upholding and promotion of the kingdom of the Lord Jesus Christ in New England" The income from the rentals of the land owned by the trustees of the estate was paid to Harvard College Claflin was one of the most prominent of the early settlers He was selectman in 1727 and town treasurer in 1729 and several years after that

He married, March 11, 1701, Sarah Edwards, probably daughter of Rice Edwards, who was in Salem in 1643 and removed to Wenham, where he died in 1683 Sarah died January 6, 1743, at Hop-

William H. Dexter

kinton, and Claflin died at Framingham, the adjoining town, 1775, calling himself in his will "old and decrepid" The children of Daniel and Sarah Claflin, born at Wenham, were Daniel, born February 19, 1702, Sarah, April 27, 1703, Mesheck, November 4, 1705, died June 3, 1706, Joshua, June 8, 1707, Caleb, December 11, 1708, Cornelius, February 2, 1711, Robert, August 16, 1714, Ebenezer, July 2, 1716, of whom later

(III) Ebenezer Claflin, son of Daniel Claflin (2), was born in Wenham, Massachusetts, July 2, 1716, and died at Hopkinton in 1793 His wife was received into the church at Hopkinton, September 10, 1731, by letter from the Ipswich Church He served in the second Hopkinton company, under Captain John Jones, and was later on the trainband and alarm list of the town of Hopkinton He married in Hopkinton, May 22, 1739, Hannah Smith, daughter of Nathaniel and Elizabeth Smith Their children, all born at Hopkinton, were Hannah, April 26, 1741, Ebenezer, September 14, 1742, Dolly, 1744, died July 1, 1839, unmarried, Isaac, of whom later, John, July 5, 1750, Aaron, 1753

(IV) Isaac Claflin, son of Ebenezer Claflin (3), was born at Hopkinton, Massachusetts, 1748, and died there May 19, 1831 He was a soldier in the revolution in Captain John Holman's company, Colonel Samuel Bullard's regiment, and responded with his company on the Lexington alarm, April 19, 1775 He married Mary Stimpson, daughter of Stephen and Hannah (Haven) Stimpson His wife died at Hopkinton, July 27, 1825, aged sixty-nine years Their only child was James, born at Hopkinton, July 4, 1790

(V) James Claflin, son of Isaac Claflin (4), was born at Hopkinton, Massachusetts, July 4, 1790, and died there May 25, 1851 He settled at Hopkinton also He married, August, 1812, at Barre Massachusetts, Susannah Wadsworth, and she died January 9, 1890, aged ninety-eight years Their children, all born at Hopkinton, were Thomas Jefferson, born August 21, 1813, Mary Wadsworth, September 7, 1816, Charles Winslow, April 4, 1820, of whom later, Martha Wadsworth, April 15, 1823, Isaac, June 13, 1826, Susannah, January 28, 1828, James Fitzgerald, March 25, 1834

(VI) Charles Winslow Claflin, son of James Claflin (5), was born at Hopkinton, April 4, 1820, and died October 13, 1884 He was the founder of the business still bearing his name in Boston and Worcester He was one of the most successful coal merchants of New England He married April 18, 1844, Ann Maria Valentine, who was born December 23, 1819 Their children, born at Hopkinton, were Emma Francis, born February 21, 1845, Charles Leslie, of whom later, Mary Valentine, November 3, 1855, of whom later

(VII) Mary Valentine Claflin, daughter of Charles Winslow Claflin (6), was born at Hopkinton, Massachusetts, November 3, 1855 She married, January 16, 1890, Arthur Osgood Young, of Worcester, son of Stephen Young Mr Young has been a member of the firm of C W Claflin & Company for many years The business was in charge of Charles L Claflin, son of C W Claflin, when started in Worcester, in 1875, and later an office was opened in Boston The business at present is a partnership and is owned by the Charles L Claflin estate of Hopkinton, Arthur O Young, of Worcester, and Edward W Pierce, of Brookline The wholesale department in Boston is in charge of Mr Pierce, and the Worcester business, wholesale and retail, is in charge of Mr Young The main office in Worcester is at 375 Main street The firm has extensive yards at 5 Grafton street, 301 Shrewsbury street, and at Ludlow street, opposite the station at Jamesville Mr Young's home is at 26 Institute road, Worcester

The children of Arthur Osgood and Mary Valentine Young are Charles Claflin, born December 5, 1893, Margaret Valentine, February 1, 1897, Arthur Osgood, Jr, November 5, 1898

DEXTER FAMILY The following family to which William H Dexter business factor and philanthropist, belongs, descended from Gregory Dexter, of Rhode Island, one of the companions of Roger Williams, when he founded Providence plantation in 1636-1674

William H Dexter, was born in Charlton, Massachusetts, January 11, 1823 He is the son of John B and Lucinda (McIntyre) Dexter The father was born in Marlboro, Massachusetts, June 24, 1795; died at Worcester, November 24, 1867 He married Lucinda McIntyre, February 12, 1818, a native of Charlton, born April 8, 1793, died at Worcester, January 5, 1866 William H attended the schools of his native town, entering his father's store when but fourteen years of age Later he clerked at Burrillville, Rhode Island, but returned to Charlton and re-entered his father's store, where he remained for a time, and then spent five years clerking in Boston, three years in a hotel with Pardon Stevens and two years in a general merchandise house His various clerkships imbued him with the notion of becoming a merchant himself In 1846, having acquired a good knowledge of business and sufficient capital he came to Worcester, opening the first grocery store off of Main street Here he operated five years with much success He then started in business as a wholesale and retail flour and grain merchant Here he laid well the foundation of his future business career, which proved more than usually successful Three years later, 1854, he bought land of Judge Charles Allen, on Franklin square, and erected a fine four-story block, moving his business to the ground floor He paid one dollar per foot for the land and many thought he paid more than it was worth, but he looked ahead and had faith in the location and prosperity which finally came to Worcester The same land he sold in 1893 at thirteen dollars per foot He kept pushing ahead in his operations and became easily the largest grain and flour merchant of his city, at the same time building up for himself a good and lasting business reputation over a large area of country

In 1873 he retired from the flour business by selling to Curtis & Company He then gave his attention to the development of Franklin square, which he so named Dexter s name adorns the five-story blocks on the square and another block was erected by him on the northeast corner of Main street and Allen court The Franklin building, erected by Mr Dexter in 1872, stands near the postoffice building, and was at that time one of the largest building blocks in the city It has has an imposing brown stone front, contains numerous offices and fine stores, and has paid on the investment good returns for thirty years Mr Dexter has always been noted for his rare good judgment in real estate matters

From 1873 to 1878 inclusive, he was a valued member of the city council and was for three years a member of the school board He has never been especially interested in holding office, being too much absorbed in his own affairs He was an originator of the First National Fire Insurance Company, of which he was a director for twenty-four years, and three years vice-president and manager resigning to look after his real estate business While this worthy gentleman has been an active business factor in Worcester, and has amassed a goodly fortune, he has not become sordid and miserly, but on the contrary, has been a benefactor second to none His religious life has ever been consistent with his profession He has been identified with the Main Street Baptist Church for about fifty years, and has rendered invaluable aid to the Worcester (Baptist) Academy, as a trustee and treasurer, having had charge of the endowment fund for nearly a quarter of a century He has been a great force in the upbuilding of this institution, having accomplished more, perhaps, than any other man In 1892 he gave the United States government five thousand dollars to help purchase the site for the new post office building, and many thousands toward the erection of Dexter hall, Worcester Academy This structure, named for him is among the finest up-to-date dormitories in this country, East or West Half of his time has been spent in behalf of the institution He has encouraged study and research among the students, by giving valuable prizes to them for merit, hence is revered ever as a father by the whole faculty and students roll One of the supreme pleasures of his life has been to aid struggling young men, many of whom have made their mark in the world

In 1848 he was married to Eliza A Foss, of Livermore, Maine Their only child, a daughter, died in infancy January 11, 1905, Mr Dexter and his friends celebrated his eighty-second birthday He is robust for one of four-score and two years He preaches and practices the gospel of pure air and sunshine Summer and winter, when the weather is at all suitable both he and his good wife take their usual ride about the city

To enumerate the many benefactions of his life would not be practical in such a sketch, but the chief, in addition to those above referred to are these He gave, but a short time ago, the Worcester Academy a block on Main street, Newton Seminary five thousand, five hundred dollars, Dexter hall, to Worcester Academy, statute in memory of the soldiers of the civil war to the town of Charlton Charlton was his native town where he attended school and spent his childhood days and hence the tender regard for her people Recently he gave that place a town hall and public library, costing over thirty thousand dollars It is a fine brick structure complete in every detail To the Methodist church of Charlton he gave an organ Mrs Dexter gave a handsome dormitory to the young ladies' Colby College at Waterville Maine, costing nearly fifty thousand dollars Through the associations of Oread school in Worcester she became an intimate friend of Mrs John D Rockefeller and her younger day associates

In sketching the life of this busy man, one is impressed with the value of good training and a consistent religious life, for in such cases the results of a business career become potent factors for the common good of mankind

GEORGE F BLAKE William Blake (1) was the emigrant ancestor of George F Blake, of Worcester, Massachusetts His father was William Blake, of Pitminster England where he was baptized July 10 1594 He married there, September 23, 1617, Agnes Band, widow, whose maiden name has not been ascertained Some recent investigations however suggest that she may have been the widow of Richard Band and daughter of Hugh Thorne of Pitminster baptized January 12 1594 In the same parish in England four of the children of William Blake were baptized but from 1624 to 1636 his place of residence is unknown It is believed that he came to America in the fall of 1635 or early in 1636 and remained at Dorchester or Roxbury making the acquaintance there of William Pynchon and others who were considering a plan of settlement in the Connecticut valley At any rate he was with Pynchon and his associates on May 14 and 16, 1636, when they drew up and signed the articles of association at Agawam now Springfield, and he was one of five to assign the lots and manage affairs of the colony He drew land there but apparently decided to return to Dorchester and settle He drew land in South Boston in March, 1637-8 He was made a freeman of the colony March 14, 1638-9 He was a man of integrity and ability He was constable in 1641, selectman in 1645-7 and 1651 on the committee to build the new meeting house In 1656 he was elected town clerk and "clerk of the writs for the county of Suffolk," and these offices he held till within six weeks of his death, which occurred October 25 1663 He was also the clerk of the train band In his will he made a bequest for the repairing of the burying ground Soon after his death his widow Agnes removed to Boston, probably to live with her son, John, or her only daughter, Anne Leager She died in Dorchester His estate was appraised at two hundred and twenty-four pounds His children were John baptized baptized at Pitminster September 6, 1620, died at Boston January 25, 1688-9 Anne baptized at Pitminster, August 30 1618, died at Boston, July 12, 1681 in the sixty-third year of her age. William, baptized at Pitminster, September 6, 1620, died at Milton Massachusetts, September 3, 1703, at the age of eighty-three years, James, baptized at Pitminster, April 27, 1624 died at Dorchester, June 28, 1700, aged seventy-six years, Edward, supposed to be the youngest child, died at Milton, Massachusetts, September 3, 1692

(II) James Blake son of William Blake (1), was born in Pitminster England, baptized April 27, 1624 He came to New England with his father He married about 1651 Elizabeth Clap, daughter of Deacon Edward and Prudence (Clap) Clap, who died in Dorcester January 16, 1693-4 in the sixty-first year of her age He married (second) in Rehoboth September 17, 1695, Elizabeth (Smith) Hunt, widow of Peter Hunt and daughter of Henry and Judith Smith from county Norfolk England Mr Blake lived in the north part of Dorchester His house built about 1650, was of such substantial character that the town voted to model the parsonage after it in 1669 and it remained in the Blake family until 1825 In 1895 it was removed from the original location on Cottage street to Richardson Park and the Dorchester Historical Society secured possession of it and have fitted it up for their purposes Mr Blake was a busy man From 1658 to 1685 there is scarcely a year that he did not serve the town in some official capacity He was selectman thirteen years, later constable deputy to the general court clerk of the writs, recorder sergeant of the militia company He was deacon of the Dorchester church for fourteen years and ruling elder for the same period He was often called upon as administrator and in other capacities in the settlement of estates He died June 28, 1700 leaving a will dated June 26 1700 His estate was appraised at four hundred and seventy-three pounds He and his wife are buried in the old graveyard in Dorchester and the stones that mark their graves are in excellent condition

Their children were 1 James born August 15 1652 married (first) Hannah Macey February 6, 1681 and married (second) Ruth Bachellor July 8 1684 2 John, born March 16, 1656-7, inherited property of his uncle John in Boston, but remained in Dorchester, deacon, married Hannah ———, who had four children, she died May 16, 1729, he died March 2, 1718 3 Elizabeth, born October 3, 1658, married Jeremiah Fuller 4 Jonathan, born July 12, 1660, died November 10 1660 5 Sarah, born February 28, 1665 died May 22, 1666 6 Joseph, born August 27, 1667, married Mehitable Bird, who died April 15 1751, he died February 1, 1738-9, eleven children lived at Dorchester

(III) James Blake, son of James Blake (2), was born at Dorchester, Massachusetts August 15, 1652 He married (first) February 6, 1681, Hannah Macey, daughter of George and Susannah Macey, of Taunton, who died June 1, 1683 aged twenty-three years He married (second) July 8, 1684, Ruth Bachellor who was born in Hampton, New Hampshire, May 9 1662, daughter of Nathaniel and Deborah (Smith) Bachellor She died in Dorchester, January 11, 1752, aged ninety years

There has long been a tradition in the family that the first house upon Dorchester Neck (now South Boston) was erected by James Blake An investigation made a few years ago brought to light evidence that Captain James Foster had a dwelling there as early as 1676, but Blake's house was without doubt the second built on the peninsula about 1681 Although isolated from the village of Dorchester the house was beautifully situated to command a view of the harbor and shore It was on the road to Castle William, later Fort Independence, and at times it became a sort of house of entertainment for the English officers at the fort His new house was almost entirely destroyed by the British troops, February 13 1776 Mr Blake was a farmer He was deacon of the Dorchester church twenty-three years He died October 22, 1732, at the age of eighty years

His children were 1 Hannah, born September 16, 1685, died October 2, 1686 2 James, born April 29, 1688, married Wait Simpson, daughter of Jonathan and Wayte (Clap) Simpson, born in Charlestown, March 30, 1685, died in Dorchester, May 22, 1753, town clerk twenty-four years author of Blake's Annals the original of which is deposited with the New England Historic Genealogical Society, he died December 4, 1750, at Dorchester, had seven children 3 Increase, born June 8, 1699, married, July 23, 1724, in Boston, Anne Gray

(IV) Increase Blake, son of James Blake (3), was born at Dorchester, Massachusetts, June 8, 1699 He married in Boston, July 23 1724, Anne Gray, daughter of Edward and Susanna (Harrison) Gray who was born in Boston March 16 1704-5, and died there June 20 1751 Mr Gray was a rope maker and became wealthy One of his sons, Harrison Gray was prominent in public life and treasurer of the province Another, Rev Ellis Gray, was pastor of the Second Church of Boston, and these names, Ellis Gray and Harrison Gray, have been retained among the descendants of their sister even to the present generation

Increase Blake shared with his only brother James in his father's estate in 1732, but soon afterward sold all his share of the real estate He resided in Boston where all his sixteen children were born, probably in the vicinity of Milk and Batterymarch streets He was a tin plate worker, and his trade was followed by several of his sons and grandsons He did not appear in public life as much as his brother He was an inn-holder on Merchants row in 1740 From 1734 to 1748 he was sealer of weights and measures, an office appropriately connected with his trade In 1737 he leased of the town of Boston one of the shops at the town dock at an annual rental of thirty pounds and in 1744 requested a renewal He died probably in 1770 It is stated that he was buried in the Gray and Blake tomb, No 74, at the Granary burying ground

His children were 1 Ann born May 8 1725, married, November 6 1746, Thomas Andrews, housewright, died in Boston, June 2, 1752, aged thirty-five years (Granary burying ground inscription) 2 Increase, born October 28, 1726, married April 18 1754, Ann Crafts, and married (second), December 7, 1762, Elizabeth Bridge 3 Edward born July 9 1728 married, October 24, 1751, Rebecca Hallowell 4 James, born March 20, 1730, living 1774 5 Harrison, born September 10 1731 6 William, born September 14, 1732, married in Boston, March 26, 1770, Dorcas Ward 7 Hannah born September 9 1733, married 1752 Colonel Thomas Dawes 8 Susannah, born October 14, 1734, married, 1755, Captain Caleb Prince 9 John, born June 22, 1736 married in Boston, June 28, 1757, Anne Clarage, was a tinplate worker 10 Thomas, born January 14 1737-8 11 Benjamin, born May 9, 1739, married, August 17, 1763, Elizabeth Harris 12 Joseph born July 5, 1740, married, December 3, 1761, Sarah Dawes 13 Nathaniel, born September 28, 1741, died October 15 1741 14 Ellis Gray, born September 9, 1743 married, August 23 1778, Jane Cook 15 Mary, born August 17 1745, married, March 1, 1770 in Boston, Simon Whipple, had three children 16 Sarah born August 18 1746 married Joseph Bachelder, of Chelsea, Massachusetts

(V) Increase Blake, son of Increase Blake (4), was born in Boston, October 28, 1726, married there, April 18 1754, Anne Crafts, daughter of Thomas and Anne (White) Crafts, who was born in Boston, January 10, 1734 and died March 21, 1762, aged twenty-eight A few years ago a grave stone inscribed with her name and date of death was found on Boston Common He married (second), December 7, 1762, Elizabeth Bridge, perhaps daughter of Ebenezer and Mary Bridge of Boston born 1731 She died of small pox in Worcester, November 22, 1792, aged sixty-one years, and was buried in a pasture in the northern part of the city near what is now Nelson place An obituary notice in the *Spy* of December, 1792, refers to her as "one of the noblest women earth was ever blessed with A living Christian"

Mr Blake was a tinplate worker in Boston, having a shop on King street, now State street, near the old State House He is said to have supplied the Provincial troops with canteens, cartridge boxes and the like, but refusing to make them for the British troops was driven from town His wife was equally patriotic Her bible, which is in possession of Mrs E A Knowlton of Rochester, Minnesota gives evidence of an encounter she had with a British soldier One day when sitting in front of her door reading her Bible she was asked by a soldier as he passed what she was reading She replied "the story of the cross" upon which he answered that he would fix her Bible so she would always remember the cross and with his sword he made a deep cut across the page through many leaves The story has several forms as it has been handed down, but the Bible the cut and the sword of the British soldier are undoubted realities When forced to leave Boston just after the Battle of Bunker Hill, he removed his wife and seven children to Worcester sacrificing nearly all of his Boston property He opened a shop in Worcester at Lincoln square and worked at his trade In 1780 and for a number of years he was jailer or gaoler He died in Worcester February 28 1795 His estate was appraised for forty-two pounds and proved to be insolvent The claims amounted to $91 49, the net assets were only eleven shillings, six and a half pence—$1 92—to be divided Twelve of his children were born in Boston, the thirteenth at Worcester

His children by his first wife were Anne, born August 9, 1755, died December 6, 1760, Thomas, born December 20, 1756, died in infancy, William, born March 12, 1758, died September 7, 1759, Elizabeth, died March 7, 1760, James, died January 22, 1762, James, born January 29, 1762, married, July 14, 1784, Rebecca Cunningham The children of his second wife were Mary, born November 5, 1763, married, September 15, 1797, Andrew Tufts, Persis, born March 31, 1765, married, December 8, 1790, Samuel Case, Thomas Dawes, born October 23, 1768, married, January 3, 1802, Martha Norton, Ebenezer, born May 31, 1771, supposed to have been lost at sea, Sarah, born November 25, 1772, living 1795, Susanna, born April 4, 1774, married, August 3, 1800, George Anson Howes, Dorothy, born June 15, 1781, in Worcester, no further record of her

(VI) Dr Thomas Dawes Blake, son of Increase Blake (5), was born in Boston, October 23, 1768 He married, January 3 1802, Martha Norton, daughter of Cornelius and Lydia (Claghorn) Norton, of Vineyard Haven, Massachusetts, who was born there May 1, 1786, and died September 30, 1873, at Farmington, Maine Mr Blake spent his early days in Worcester and attended Dr Payson's celebrated school, from which he graduated with the highest honors of his class He practiced for a short time as a physician at Petersham, Massachusetts, but in 1799 settled at Farmington Falls, Maine He was a ripe scholar and to quote the history of Farmington, possessed of those strong virtues acquired during the troublous times in which his early life was spent" He died in Farmington, Maine, November 20, 1849

His children, all born at Farmington, were Cordelia, born April 19, 1804, died May 24, 1808, Adeline, born September 16, 1806, married, April 9, 1835, John F W Gould, Martha, born November 12, 1808 married, April 27, 1828, David C Morrill son of David and Lucinda (Woods) Morrill, who was born December 4, 1804 and died June 12, 1877, she died January 22, 1895, lived at Farmington, Thomas Dawes born February 4, 1811, married, May 13, 1841, Hannah D Norton, Increase, born December 8, 1812, married, September 26, 1844, Sarah Farnsworth, Cornelius N, born February 8, 1815, died August 29, 1827, Ebenezer Norton, born July 30, 1817, married, February 16, 1843, Harriet Cummings, George Fordyce, born May 20, 1819, married (first), January 1, 1845, Sarah S Skinner, married (second) December 24, 1857, Martha J Skinner, Jotham Sewall, born February 6, 1821, died March 5, 1881, Freeman Norton, born June 1, 1822, married Helen S Baker

(VII) George Fordyce Blake son of Dr Thomas Blake (6), was born May 20, 1819, at Farmington, Maine He married (first) at Lynnfield, Massachusetts, January 1, 1845, Sarah Silver Skinner, daughter of William and Lucy (Aborn) Skinner, who was born at Lynnfield June 18, 1821, and died in Boston, October 14, 1856 He married (second) at North Sandwich, Massachusetts, December 24, 1857, Martha J Skinner, sister of his first wife, who was born at Lynnfield, June 24, 1835, and died in Boston, June 2, 1897

Mr Blake began his business career at an early age and before he was thirty he held a responsible position as mechanical engineer at the Cambridge brick yards His mechanical skill led him to devise several useful inventions, among which was a water meter which brought his name into public prominence His greatest achievement, however, was the Blake steam pump, which he devised originally for use in his own business This pump was so successful that he devoted most of his energies to its manufacture and improvement He must be counted as one of the great mechanical inventors of the nineteenth century Unlike many of them he reaped richly of the fruit of his invention The Blake pump is now manufactured by a corporation known as the George F Blake Manufacturing Company Mr. Blake made his home at various times in Cambridge, Medford, Belmont and lastly in Boston, where he died July 22, 1905 He had two children by his first wife and four by his second

His children were Thomas Dawes, born October 25, 1847, at Cambridge, Massachusetts, married, May 18, 1870, Susan P Symounds, four children, Sara Augusta, born December 6, 1853, at Cambridge, Massachusetts, married, October 21, 1885, at Belmont, Massachusetts, Roland H Boutwell, son of Rodney C and Nancy J Boutwell, she died at Belmont, February 27, 1891, no children, George Fordyce, born February 9, 1859, at Medford Massachusetts married, April 29, 1885, Carrie H Turner, Grace Bertha, born August 30, 1863, at Medford, died there February 29, 1868, Jennie Maria born April 29, 1869, at Medford married at Boston, April 17 1895 Arthur Stoddard Johnson, son of Samuel and Mary (Stoddard) Johnson who was born in Boston, June 4, 1863, has three children, Alice Norton, born July 6, 1872, at Belmont, resided at Boston, Massachusetts, married James M Newell, June 6, 1901, one child

(VIII) George Fordyce Blake, son of George Fordyce Blake (7), was born at Medford, Massachusetts, February 9, 1859 He was educated in the public schools of his native town He attended the Warren Academy at Woburn where he prepared for admission to the Massachusetts Institute of Technology, and entered in the class of 1879 He made a trip around the world in 1880 During the next four years he was a draughtsman in the office of the Blake Manufacturing Company, of which his father was the president He was also connected with the Knowles pump works as draughtsman His father was also president of this company

He engaged in business on his own account February 28, 1884, when he formed a partnership under the firm name of Blake, Boutwell & Co to deal in iron and steel at Worcester, Massachusetts In October 1891, the firm became George F Blake, Jr. & Company In May, 1893, the business of the company was extended by the addition of an iron mill at Wareham Massachusetts, and a store in Boston Mr Blake has numerous other interests and connections Since 1896 he has been the senior partner in the firm of Blake, Sampson & Co dealers in wood and coal in Worcester He is a director of the Worcester Trust Company, the State Mutual Life Assurance Company, and the Callahan Supply Company He was a director of the Central National Bank, which was absorbed by the Worcester Trust Company He is a trustee of the Worcester County Institution for Savings He was for three years a director of the Providence & Worcester Railroad now owned by the New York, New Haven & Hartford Railroad Company He is a trustee of the Worcester Insane Asylum and Hospital, appointed by Governor Bates to fill out the unfinished term of Philip W Moen, a director and vice-president of the Worcester Cold Storage Company He is a member of the Worcester Board of Trade, the Home Market Club, the Worcester Club, the Commonwealth Club the Quinsigamond Boat Club, of which he was for two years president, the Tatnuck Country Club, the Exchange Club, Boston, the Technology Club, Boston, the Calumet Club, New York, and Grafton Country Club Mr Blake's home is on Lincoln street, Worcester, and he has a beautiful summer place on Salisbury street, Worcester, where he indulges a taste for farm life at its best He has traveled extensively both for business and for pleasure

He married, April 29, 1885, at Newton, Massachusetts Carrie Howard Turner, daughter of Job A Turner, treasurer of the George F Blake Manufacturing Company and of the Knowles Pump Works Her mother was Vesta Howard Mrs Blake was born April 19, 1861, in Boston Their children are Fordyce Turner, born February 10, 1889, Vesta Carolyn, born March 31, 1896

COLLEGE OF THE HOLY CROSS The College of the Holy Cross, founded in the year 1843, by the Rt Reverend Benedict Joseph Fenwick second Bishop of Boston is the oldest Catholic College in New England The most cherished wish of Bishop Fenwick was to establish in his diocese an institution which should furnish a secular education of the highest grade and at the same time thoroughly imbue its students with the principles of the Catholic faith He was aided in his first steps to realize this desire by the generosity of the Rev James Fitton, of Boston who in 1840. had erected on Pakachoag Hill, or Hill of the Pleasant Springs, near Worcester, the Seminary of Mount St James This building, with nearly sixty acres of land Father Fitton presented to the Bishop in 1842 The fact that the site was given for the purpose was not the only consideration that induced the Bishop to erect his college there The location is ideal for an institution of this kind There is a magnificent view of the city of Worcester to the north Beyond the city is Mount Wachusett, amid the clustering hills of Central Massachusetts, and in every direction the scenery is the finest that nature affords It is true that from the Bancroft Tower from the summit of Newton Hill or from Green Hill one gets equally beautiful scenery, but none better There could be no more picturesque site to display the architectural simplicity of Holy Cross, there could be no location in Worcester offering more natural beauty to the eye of teacher and student

The Bishop organized the first classes in the Seminary of Mount St James November 2, 1843 He had called the Fathers of the Society of Jesus to take care of the new college The college building was completed and occupied January 13 1844 The cornerstone was laid June 21, 1843, by Bishop Fenwick The first annual exhibition was held July 29 1844 Bishop Fenwick died August 10, 1846, just as his great work was fairly under way At his own request he was buried in the college cemetery A few days before his death he gave to the Fathers in charge of the college the legal title to the property

On the afternoon of July 14, 1852, eight days before Commencement fire broke out in the main building, and it was burned down This disaster was so serious that the very existence of the college was threatened, but Rt Rev John B Fitzpatrick, the Bishop of Boston, determined that the institution, which had been established by his predecessor, should not perish He began the work of rebuilding and October 3, 1853, a larger and better college building was ready for the students, and the college resumed its functions as before A class of students who had entered in 1843 and 1844 had advanced to Philosophy, by which name the senior year was then known, and were ready for graduation in 1849 The college authorities, therefore, applied to the legislature to be incorporated Their petition was not granted, and it was not until the close of the civil war, which effectually eliminated the sectarian prejudices at Beacon Hill, in 1865, that the charter was granted by the general court While the action of the Massachusetts legislature prevented the conferring of degrees that had been rightfully earned at Holy Cross, an arrangement was made, so that Georgetown College in the District of Columbia conferred the degrees earned at the Worcester institution until the Act of Incorporation was passed in 1865 How the faculty and students bore their disappointment at this time may be judged from the testimony of His Excellency Alexander H Bullock, who said at the Commencement in 1868 that he had been deeply impressed by the manner in which the friends of the college hid all signs of their disappointment in failing to get the charter, and exhibited a patience which under such circumstances, he should hardly have dared to expect from many Christian denominations It was during the civil war that the college, besides having become dear to the Catholics of New England, attracted the favorable notice and support of many of their non-Catholic brethren Gov John A Andrew visited and inspected the college during the school term of 1862, and presided at the annual Commencement that year On that occasion he spoke in the highest terms of the college, and the sincerity of his praise was shown by his constant friendship for the college at every opportunity The charter was signed by the governor March 24, 1865 It gave the college the right to confer such degrees as are conferred by other colleges in the state, except medical degrees and placed Holy Cross on an equal footing in the statutes of the Commonwealth with Harvard, Amherst, Williams Tufts and other colleges Perhaps the Holy Cross degrees mean more to the graduate now than they would if the charter had not been withheld for a time In this connection the college acknowledges its indebtedness to the late Hon Alexander H Bullock, of Worcester, who, while Speaker of the House, offered to present the petition for a charter, and while governor of the state presided at three successive Commencements

The college buildings have been vastly improved and greatly enlarged in the past twenty-five years In 1875 the east wing of the main building was raised and extended This wing, which was the only part of the building not destroyed by the fire of 1852, gave place in time to a structure one hundred and twelve feet long with an easterly frontage of ninety feet On the first story is the refectory, on the second the study hall, on the upper floor the chapel Adjoining this wing on the southeast corner is the infirmary A later and more modern structure, known as the O'Kane building was completed in 1895, and formally opened in September of that year It contains the gymnasium, 50x139 feet one of the largest and most complete in New England On the third floor is Fenwick hall, an auditorium for public lectures, debates, meetings, assemblies of students, etc A new dormitory building alumni hall with one hundred rooms for students was completed in the fall of 1905

The system of education is the one in use in all the colleges of the Society of Jesus, and is guided b the principles laid down in the famous "Ratio Studiorum" This body of rules and suggestions has been elaborated by centuries of experience, and has been judged worthy of attentive study and hearty approbation by the ablest scholars The college announces that instead of abolishing prescribed studies and increasing elective courses it advocates a wise deliberate and prudent selection by men whose profession is education, and not an unwise, sudden and rash choice by inexperienced youths just entering on the process of education 'It is not a system of ever-changing theory and doubtful experiment but one on which have been built the characters of the world's best scholars and statesmen for centuries It meets the demand for modern improvement by wise adaptation and readjustment The natural sciences and modern languages are by no means overlooked or neglected in this system, but the ancient languages and their literatures are still retained as prescribed studies and, with mathematics and philosophy, form the 'essential trinity of courses' which Professor Ladd of Yale considers 'absolutely necessary for a truly liberal education'"

The college has an excellent library In every department the college has grown rapidly in the past few years Nearly a thousand bachelors of arts have been graduated in the college of the Holy Cross In the athletic world Holy Cross more than holds her own with colleges of her size The present officers of the college are President, Rev Joseph F Hanselman vice-president, Rev Joseph H Hann, chaplain, Rev Albert R Peters, treasurer, Rev Patrick A McQuillan, prefect of studies, Rev Thomas E Murphy, prefect of discipline, Rev Fernand A Rousseau There are sixteen instructors in the college and thirty in the preparatory department besides the faculty

REV JOSEPH FRANCIS HANSELMAN (I) Henry Hanselman, father of Rev Joseph Francis Hanselman, of the Society of Jesus, and president of the College of the Holy Cross at Worcester, was born in the Canton of St Gall, Switzerland, October 16, 1828 He was a paper manufacturer, and in 1847 came to this country, in the interests of his firm, to establish a paper mill, first in Philadelphia and then in New York city but the undertaking was not successful Later he engaged in various commercial enterprises successfully in Brooklyn and New York city The later years of his life he was engaged in the real estate business in Brooklyn, where he won the respect and confidence of his fellow citizens He was interested in public affairs and held various offices in the city government of Brooklyn Shortly before he died he was tendered the nomination for city auditor but his health was failing and he had to decline the honor He was a Democrat He was originally a Protestant in his religious beliefs and affiliations but was converted to Catholicism after he came to America While in search of the same sect to which he belonged in Switzerland, he found such a conflicting array of various denominations in America that he began to doubt whether God's truth which ought to be the same everywhere, could consistently be found in all the sects alike His investigations led him into the Catholic Church He died October 17, 1884 in Brooklyn New York

He married Margaret Jacobs She was born near Treves in Rhenish Prussia, November 30, 1830 She emigrated to this country in 1849, and lived before as well as after her marriage in New York city and Brooklyn She died December 28, 1904

(II) Joseph Francis Hanselman son of Henry Hanselman (I) was born in Brooklyn New York, October 28 1856 He received his early education in the parochial school He studied the classics under private tutors and fitted for college He entered St Vincent's College near Latrobe, Pennsylvania where he was a student for two years He completed his collegiate education at St Francis Xavier's College, in New York city and was graduated with the degree of A B in the class of 1877 He studied theology in the Grand Seminary, Montreal in 1877 and 1878 On September 7, 1878 he entered the novitiate of the Society of Jesus at Manresa, West Park, New York In 1880 he went to Frederick, Maryland, to review his classical studies at the Jesuit Normal school He spent three more years at Woodstock, Maryland in the study of philosophy From 1884 to 1888 inclusive he was professor of the classics at St Peter's College, Jersey City, New Jersey, and during the college year, 1888-9 he taught philosophy and mathematics in St John's College, Fordham, New York city After three years more of study at Woodstock, Maryland he was ordained there in June 1892, but remained in the study of theology until 1893 During the years 1893 to 1897, inclusive, he was prefect of studies and discipline at Holy Cross, Worcester Then he spent another year at Frederick in the study of ascetic theology He returned to the College of the Holy Cross and was prefect of discipline in 1898-99, 1900-01 He became president of the college, August 24, 1901, and has since held the position During his administration the college has enjoyed the utmost prosperity It has been difficult to accommodate all the students who have sought admission

WILLIAM PHINEHAS SEARLS Robert Searls (I), the pioneer ancestor of William Phinehas Searls, late of Worcester, Massachusetts, and of a number of families in Massachusetts and Connecticut, was born in England, in Dorchester if the family tradition is correct The date of his birth was about 1640 He married in 1660, Deborah ———, and about the same time came to this country, settling in Dorchester, Massachusetts Other Searles or Searle pioneers preceded him Many of the Searles families are descended from John Searles, of Springfield, Massachusetts, who was there as early as 1637, and from Philip Searl of Roxbury, Massachusetts The name is variously spelled in the early records, but the descendants of Robert Searls, of Dorchester, Massachusetts, have maintained the spelling, Searls, in all the generations, except for occasional variations of individuals

Robert Searls was admitted an inhabitant of Dorchester June 9, 1662 His wife died March 2, 1713-4, at Dorchester The town record of his death notes that he was "town clerk for many years" Doubtless the completeness of the early records in Dorchester, relating to the Searls family, is due to the fact that for sixteen years he himself kept the record as town clerk He died at Dorchester, February 7, 1717 He signed the Dorchester petition to the King in 1664 He owned twelve acres in the 'Great Lots' in 1668 The children of Robert and Deborah Searls were Nathaniel, born in Dorchester, June 9, 1662, baptized there April 5 1668, married 1694, Sarah daughter of John Rogers and Elizabeth Peabody, and great-granddaughter of Thomas Rogers of the "Mayflower", Salter (a peculiar family name found in almost every family of Robert Searls' descendants There were several pioneers of this name William Salter, of Boston, left a large family of children and was in Boston as early as 1638), born June 26, 1664, died April 8 1690 baptized at Dorchester Church, April 5, 1668, Esbon (given Edna in some accounts), born February 24, 1669, died young, Robert, (see forward), Esbon, born March 18, 1674, Deborah born April 4, 1677, Jabez, born March 13 1679, married Thankful Topliff, April 9 1702, at Dorchester, and had a large family of children there, she died May 1, 1747, he died July 31, 1724

(II) Robert Searls, son of Robert Searls (I), born in Dorchester Massachusetts July 2, 1671, married there December 4 1695, by Rev Mr Danforth Rebecca Evans He settled in Dorchester

Joseph F. Hanselman, S.J.

and died there July 13 1752, of smallpox "being," the town records tell us, the fourth person that had it in the town in the year 1752, and the only person that died of it in the town of Dorchester, though such numbers had it in Boston and surrounding towns, and hundreds died of it there" His widow, Rebecca, died May 17, 1761, in her eighty-fifth year Both were buried in Dorchester, and their graves are marked with headstones The children of Robert and Rebecca (Evans) Searls were Salter, baptized December 6, 1696, died at Dorchester, May 15, 1753 (headstone at Dorchester), Rebecca (twin), born February 15, 1700, Deborah, (twin), born February 15, 1700, died January 20, 1755 unmarried. Mary, born December 21, 1701, died unmarried October 12, 1765, Robert, (see forward)

(III) Robert Searls, son of Robert Searls (2), born in Dorchester, Massachusetts, July 3, 1705, settled in Dorchester and married Sarah Maudsley, who was of an old Dorchester family, January 6, 1731 He was known generally as Robert Searls, Jr Children, all born in Dorchester, were Elizabeth, born December 17, 1732, Rebecca, May 26, 1734, Elijah, March 28, 1736, John, May 17, 1738, settled in Dorchester and raised a family there, Salter, (see forward)

(IV) Salter Searls, son of Robert Searls, Jr (3), was born in Dorchester, Massachusetts, June 15, 1741 When a young man he removed to Brooklyn, the county seat of Windham county, Connecticut He died there May 25, 1808 He served on the school committee and in other offices He married Alice Cady, of Brooklyn, Connecticut, born February 23, 1747, died October 24, 1819 Their seven sons and one daughter all settled in Windham county in the towns of Plainfield, Brooklyn, Hampton, and Pomfret The children were Daniel, Sarah Phinehas, (see forward), Elijah, Joel, John, Richard, Bela

(V) Phinehas Searls, son of Salter Searls (4), was born April 26, 1773, died May 30, 1856, married (first) Althea Brown, born in Brooklyn, Connecticut, April 11, 1786, died February 15, 1825 She was the daughter of Alpheus and Sarah Brown, married (second) Mary Witter Paine, born January 30, 1785, died January 5, 1857

The children of Phinehas and Althea (Brown) Searls were Harriet, born May 28 1805, died July 8 1805, William (see forward), Charles, July 5, 1815, died October 18, 1892, Althea, October 27, 1819, died January 24, 1824, Henry, March 18, 1821, died July 13, 1821, Almary, August 12, 1822, died April 8, 1856, Daniel, February 15, 1825, died June 29, 1866 The children of Phinehas and Mary Witter (Paine) Searls were Martha Ann, November 29, 1826, died February 15, 1829, Lewis, September 2, 1828, died December 19, 1902

(VI) William Searls son of Phinehas Searls (5) and father of William P Searls, was born in Plainfield, Connecticut, (now called Wauregan) on the Quinebaug river, January 26, (?) 1811, died January 11, 1900 He married Catherine Jane Backus, of New York city, May 27, 1841 She was the twin daughter of Simon and Eunice Alice (Linus) Backus, of a family of ten children She was born in New York city December 8, 1822, died in Worcester, April 20, 1905 She was the great-great-granddaughter of Rev Timothy Edwards, her father's grandmother being a sister of the famous Rev Jonathan Edwards The record of the Linus family was destroyed in a fire some years ago, when the old homestead at Bridgeport, Connecticut was destroyed The family was of English and French descent

Mr Searls removed from Plainfield, with his parents, to Brooklyn, Connecticut, when he was a young boy The Searls place at Brooklyn is the farm now owned there by Frank Weaver The family occupied the place forty-seven years He began life as clerk in the country stores at Brooklyn and Plainfield, Connecticut From there he went to Hartford, Connecticut, where he held a position in a dry goods establishment He went to New York to take a responsible position in one of the largest dry goods store there Eventually he went to Wall street and became one of the leading brokers of his day With his brother Charles he became associated with several of the most prominent operators of Wall street Both were members of the New York Stock Exchange for many years William Searls was elected president of the Stock Exchange in 1868 At the end of his term he retired from active life For thirty years he enjoyed his retirement, occupied only with the cares of his investments He resided in Brooklyn, New York He became a member of the Clinton Avenue Congregational Church of that city May 1, 1850

Children were Catherine Isabelle, born in New York city, June 2, 1842, died July 26, 1842, Florence Amelia, born in Brooklyn Heights, New York, June 29, 1848, educated in private schools and at the Parker Collegiate Institute, has lived in recent years in Worcester, at the home of her brother, William P Searls, 105 Burncoat street, William Phinehas, (see forward)

(VII) William Phinehas Searls, son of William Searls (6), was born in Brooklyn, June 3, 1851, died November 20, 1904 His early education was obtained at private schools and at the Brooklyn Polytechnic Institute For a time he was with his father on Wall street in the brokerage business Later he was associated with Hatch & Foote, bankers and brokers, and with the Tiffany jewelry establishment He went to Chicago, where he was connected with the grocery business of J W Doane Returning to New York, he married September 12, 1882, Kate Robinson, daughter of John R Robinson His father-in-law was interested in Mexican silver mines and Mr Searls for a time managed a mine for him at Chihuahua, Mexico He was in the real estate business until 1890, when he came to Worcester to live on account of the health of his daughter Florence He made his home at 105 Burncoat street, in an attractive portion of the suburbs of the city Soon after coming to Worcester he became interested in the North End Street Railway Company When the company was organized in 1892 he became its first president While his company was fighting for its franchise and locations he was called upon many times to appear before the Board of Aldermen at hearings in opposition to the powerful Consolidated Street Railway Company, of Worcester He won for his company and the line was constructed from Greendale to Washington Square and it was operated by the North End Street Railway Company until it was leased to the Consolidated August 1, 1895, for a term of ninety-nine years The North End Street Railway Company is still in existence as a corporation It was the intention of the company from the first to extend its lines to Clinton He was also interested for a time in the Drapery Fixture and Wood Carving Company, and during the last years of his life was interested in the Worcester Manufacturing Company which conducted extensive experiments with compressed air motors etc

He was one of a committee of seven appointed to recommend a plan for the investment of the funds obtained by the Worcester Agricultural Society from the sale of its grounds His committee reported in favor of the purchase of the present grounds at Barbers' Crossing At a meeting in Horticultural Hall it was voted to accept the recommendation and to negotiate the purchase of the tract, also to locate and lay out a regulation racing track, much to the satisfaction of horsemen generally Mr Searls was an ardent Republican He represented Ward Two in the general court in 1893-94-95 He was on the committee on election laws in 1894, and chairman of the committee on finance and house chairman of the committee on expenditures in 1895 He was a man of attractive personality He made friends readily and kept them He was a shrewd man of business The only child of William Phinehas and Kate (Robinson) Searls was Florence, born on West End avenue, New York city, November 3, 1888

DANIEL KINSLEY Richard Montague (1) was the emigrant ancestor of Daniel Kinsley, of Worcester, and of many others in Worcester county and Western Massachusetts His pedigree is traced in England back to 1066 An abstract of the line of descent is as follows Beginning with William Montague, who was born about 1500 William Montague, of Boveney Parish, Burnham, Buckinghamshire, England Robert Montague, married Margaret Cotton, daughter of Roger Cotton, of Wardville, Berkshire William Montague, married Margaret Malthouse, daughter of John Malthouse, of Binfield, Berkshire William Montague of Boveney, M A, Fellow of Kings College, Cambridge, left Eton College and succeeded to his estate at Boveney, 1585, living in 1634 He married Richard Burn's daughter Elizabeth Their children were William, Peter, was in Virginia in 1634, Richard, Robert, Elizabeth, Anne, Margaret

Richard Montague was born about 1614 in Boveney, where for generations his ancestors had lived When he came to New England is not known The first record is 1646, when he removed with his wife from Wells, Maine, to Boston, Massachusetts It is believed that he went to Wells in 1637 from Boston He married Abigail Downing, daughter of Rev Dr Downing, of Norwich, England The Downing family in England has a well established pedigree in the Montague genealogy, but some of the links connecting Rev Dr Downing with the pedigree seem to lack proof, though probably correctly guessed

In 1651 Richard Montague removed to Wethersfield, Connecticut, taking with him a letter from Emanuel Downing, of Salem, his wife's cousin, to Governor Winthrop, of Connecticut He was one of the original fifty-nine citizens who signed the agreement April 18, 1659, at Goodman Ward's house in Hartford to settle at Hadley, Massachusetts He held various town offices in Hadley and was selectman in 1671 and 1677 In March, 1681, he was made clerk of writs He died December 14, 1681 His wife died November 8, 1694 Their children were Mary, born about 1642, probably in Wells, Maine, Sarah, born June 15, 1646, in Boston, died June 19, 1646, in Boston, Martha, born June 16, 1647, in Boston, Peter, born July 8, 1651, probably in Wethersfield, Connecticut, Abigail, born 1653, in Wethersfield, John, born probably 1655, in Wethersfield

(II) John Montague, son of Richard Montague (1), was born probably in 1655 or 1656, in Wethersfield Connecticut He removed with his parents to Hadley, Massachusetts, in 1659 or 1660 He married, March 23 1681, in Hadley, Hannah Smith, daughter of Chileab and Hannah (Hitchcock) Smith, granddaughter of Luke and Elizabeth (Gibbons) Hitchcock, of Wethersfield She was born July, 1662 The grave-stones of her parents are of interest They read 'Ens Chileab Smith d March 7, 1731, aged 96 years, and Hannah his wife d Aug 31, 1733, aged 88 years It is a worthy memorial they lived in marriage state 70 years" John Montague was a selectman in 1697 He lived on the original homestead at Hadley until his death about 1732, as stone shows The children of John Montague were John, born December 31, 1681, Richard, born March 16, 1684, Hannah, born August 8, 1687, died November, 1688, Hannah, born March 21, 1689, died April 19, 1689, Peter, born May, 1690, William, born December 16, 1692, Samuel, born April 2, 1695, Hannah, born May 28, 1697, Luke, born October 4, 1699, Nathaniel, born October 6, 1704

(III) Deacon Samuel Montague, son of John Montague (2), was born in Hadley, Massachusetts, April 2, 1695 He married, January or June 24, 1716, Elizabeth White, daughter of Deacon Nathaniel White, of Hadley She died October 15, 1753, aged fifty-seven years He married (second), June 13, 1754 Mary Billings, widow of Jonathan Billings, and daughter of Joseph Root He was one of the first forty settlers in Sunderland, Massachusetts His home lot, which he received from his Uncle Peter, was No 14 and this land is now or was recently owned by his descendants He was a man of energy, activity and good judgment, and in the course of his long life filled almost every office in the gift of his fellow citizens The records indicate the order or rank of certain offices He is designated as lieutenant, then deacon, then captain, showing the rank of deacon in the estimation of the people was higher than lieutenant but lower than captain He was selectman also He died January 31, 1779, aged eighty-four years The children of Deacon Samuel Montague were Samuel, born June 30, 1720, John, born January 10, 1723, died February 15, 1748, unmarried, Daniel, born January 13, 1725, Giles, born January 29, 1727, Richard, born May 7, 1729, Caleb, born July 27, 1731, Giles, born December 16 1733, died September 10 1734, Elizabeth, born September 18, 1735, died September 17, 1743, Nathaniel, born February 13, 1739, slain in battle at Lake George, August 7, 1757, Ebenezer, born October 1, 1741, died September 28, 1743

(IV) Samuel Montague, son of Samuel Montague (3), was born in Sunderland, Massachusetts, June 30, 1720 He married in 1742, Elizabeth Montague (his cousin), daughter of Peter and Mary (Hubbard) Montague, of South Hadley, Massachusetts He resided in Sunderland many years and there his children were born He was one of a number of Separatists who were excommunicated from the church at Sunderland, September 24, 1753 He removed to Bennington, Vermont, in 1761, and was moderator of the first town meeting there Some of the Kinsley family, among them John Kinsley, were also among the early settlers of Bennington The church at Bennington was founded by the Separatists In 1773-4 he removed to Pittsford, Vermont, but returned to Bennington, where he died of smallpox, January 17, 1777 His widow married Rev James Smith a Baptist minister She died January 31, 1816, in Pittsford, aged ninety-five years, three months He was a weaver by trade His sons settled on the land he owned in Pittsford His children were Samuel, born in Sunderland, as were all the other children, January 15, 1743, Elizabeth, born October 4, 1744, Mary, born November 25 1746, baptized February 1, 1747, at Amherst Martha, born November 21, 1748, Persis, born February 13, 1751, Azubah, born February 14,

1753, Experience, born May 14, 1755, Adonijah born April 11, 1757, Nathaniel, born June 4, 1759, died in Oneida, New York, Rufus, born October 28, 1762

(V) Samuel Montague, son of Samuel Montague (4), was born in Sunderland, Massachusetts, January 15, 1743 He married, 1764, in Bennington, Vermont, Lucy Safford, daughter of Joseph and Ann (Bottom) Safford, of Ipswich, Massachusetts, and Norwich, Connecticut She was born June, 1748, and removed with her parents to Bennington They resided in Bennington until eight of their children were born He removed in July, 1784, to Cambridge, Vermont, when there was no road and the trail was blazed They were among the first settlers in Cambridge He died March 27, 1826, in Cambridge, Vermont She died April 4, 1828, aged eighty-one The children of Samuel and Lucy (Safford) Montague were Lucy, born February 12, 1765, Darius, born April 18, 1767, died of smallpox, Anna, born October 2, 1769, Elizabeth, born February 11, 1771, Samuel, born April 23, 1775, Celinda, born November 28, 1777, Child, born April 3, 1779, died April 27, 1780, Joseph, born July 6, 1781, Solomon, born April 15, 1785, Challis, born November 18, 1788

(VI) Lucy Montague, daughter of Samuel Montague (5), was born in Bennington, Vermont, February 12, 1765 She married Daniel Kinsley (See Kinsley Family)

KINSLEY FAMILY (I) Stephen Kinsley was the emigrant ancestor of Daniel Kinsley, of Worcestor The records show that his descendants have followed this way of spelling the name without a "G" wherever they have settled The emigrant was in Braintree, first in 1637 John Kingsley, of Dorchester, is believed to be a brother Stephen was a proprietor of the town of Braintree and was admitted a freeman May 13, 1640 He removed to Dorchester and bought half of the Hutchinson farm, February 23, 1656 He returned to Braintree and sold land in Milton, May 11, 1670 He was an elder of the church and deputy to the general court His will was dated at Milton May 27, 1673, and proved July 3, 1673, in which he mentions his family His children were Samuel, John, a daughter who married Henry Crane, a daughter who married Anthony Golliver, a daughter who married Robert Mason, Mary, born August 30, 1640, at Braintree

(II) Samuel Kinsley, son of Stephen Kinsley (1), was born probably in England He married Hannah ——— He died before 1673, when his father's will was made He probably lived at Milton His children were Samuel, born 1662, and two daughters

(III) Samuel Kinsley, son of Samuel Kinsley (2), was born in 1662, at Dorchester He married Mary Washburn, in 1694 She was the daughter of John Washburn They settled at South Bridgewater, Massachusetts, and bought the Jeduthan Robbins place, adjoining Thomas Washburn's His children, except Daniel, who is believed to belong here, are given by the Bridgewater history See also Easton, Massachusetts, history The children Samuel, born 1720, died 1773, at Worcester, John, married Thankful Washburn, daughter of William Washburn, 1746, Nathan, married Betty Dunbar, daughter of James Dunbar, Benjamin, born March 16, 1701, married (first) Priscilla Manley, died March 13, 1759, Easton married (second) Widow Perkins, Mary, married Thomas Willis, 1716, Sarah, married Josiah Hayward, 1715, Benjamin, Bethia, married William Brett, 1732, Susanna, married Samuel Packard, 1729, Daniel, born 1720-30, (need proof of this connection) (Samuel (IV) died in Worcester on his way from Deerfield to his family in Bridgewater, September 25, 1773, aged fifty-three His son Samuel went to Charlemont, Massachusetts, where Daniel Kinsley settled His son Martin settled at Hardwick, Massachusetts His son Caleb at Montague, Massachusetts He married Sophia White, about 1742)

(IV) Daniel Kinsley, son of Samuel Kinsley (3), of Bridgewater, probably, was born about 1720-30 He removed to western Massachusetts and was one of the prominent settlers of Charlemont in Hampden county His brother, Samuel Kinsley, had sons settle in Charlemont and other towns in the vicinity Samuel died at Worcester on his way home from Deerfield to his home in Bridgewater, as the inscription on his stone tells He was buried in Worcester He must have been one of the early settlers at Charlemont, as his son Daniel was born there in 1764, and in 1770 he was one of the three largest property owners as shown by the tax list The others were Othniel Taylor from Deerfield, and Aaron Rice, brother of the founder, Moses Rice He married Eunice ——— The following list of children is probably incomplete Daniel, born at Charlemont, Massachusetts, April 22, 1764, John, settler at Bennington before 1775, Stephen, who drew lot 47 in Cambridge at the same time Daniel, Sr, and Daniel, Jr, drew land there in 1783 (The records show that the family was in Bennington, Vermont, before coming to Cambridge and the adjoining town of Fletcher, Vermont)

(V) Daniel Kinsley, son of Daniel Kinsley (4), both in battle of Bennington, Vermont, was born at Charlemont, Massachusetts, April 22, 1764 He removed with his father to Bennington, Vermont, about 1780 He and his father drew land in Cambridge, Vermont, together, August 28, 1783 Daniel, Sr, had lot No 1, Daniel, Jr, lot No 44, Stephen Kinsley lot 47

Daniel Kinsley married, November 22, 1788, Lucy Montague (q v), daughter of Samuel Montague (V) This was the first marriage in the town of Cambridge, Vermont (Date from family record differs from that in Montague Genealogy) He died in Fletcher, Vermont, September 27, 1828, she died February 10, 1850 in Fletcher Their children, all born in Cambridge, were Clarissa, born August 9, 1789, died at North Hero January 22, 1820, married Moses Haynes, of North Hero, March 31, 1805, Eunice, born August 23, 1790, died at Cambridge, Hannah, born January 21, 1792, married Elihu Parks, of Russelton, Canada, January 31, 1812, Lucretia, born January 19, 1794, lived at Brasher, New York, died there 1871, married Melzar E Buck, at Russelton, Canada, January 6, 1812, Ben Alvah, born January 11, 1796, died at Lowell, Vermont, December 6, 1870, Elvira born January 5, 1798, died at Fletcher, Vermont, July 3, 1859, Guy, born May 8, 1800, married Emily Scott Fletcher, July 4, 1826, Earl, born in North Hero, Vermont, August 4, 1802, died at Grand Isle, June 29, 1868, Nancy, born December 17, 1804, married Jefferson Scott, at Fletcher, May 8, 1828, Samuel, born May 29, 1807, died at North Hero, October 5, 1808, Chellis, born July 19, 1809, married March 12, 1837, Almira Hubbard, at North Hero, Calista, born in Russelton, Canada, April 20, 1812, died in North Hero, August 8, 1847

(VI) Ben Alvah Kinsley, son of Daniel Kinsley (5), was born in Cambridge, Vermont, January 11, 1796 In 1812 he served six months in the New York state militia He enlisted April 27, 1813, in the Second Company, Thirtieth Vermont Volunteers, and served a year in the army commanded by General Wade Hampton The sufferings and privations of this campaign were terrible He was slightly wounded by a bullet in the battle of LaCole Mill, Odelltown, Canada He had a narrow escape from death crossing the ice from Butler's Island to North Hero, which is related in Vol 2, page 200 of the Vermont Gazeteer He married, February 26, 1824 Catherine Montague, daughter of Rufus Montague, granddaughter of Samuel Montague (q v) above, a second case of marriage of cousins in the line She was crippled several years before her death, February 15, 1849 He married (second) Lucy or M P Blair, of Fletcher He was the author of the history of Fletcher in the Vermont Gazeteer He was said to be a man of good judgment, deep feeling and excellent religious principles He was original in his ways and thought His biographer terms some of his ideas eccentricities Five of his sons, Rufus, Jason, Edgar, William and Alonzo, were soldiers in the civil war and all passed through the service After the war a very interesting family reunion was held at which all the children were present He died December 6, 1870, at Lowell, Vermont

The children of Ben Alvah Kinsley, all born in Fletcher, Vermont, were Guy, born February 12, 1825, married, March 14, 1853, Lucinda Ellsworth, resides at Council Hill Clayton county, Iowa, has had eleven children Lucretia, born February 13, 1827 Daniel born June 13, 1829 Rufus, born October 9, 1831, printer by trade, married, April 10, 1872, at Cambridge, Ella L Bingham, daughter of Judge Royal T Bingham, of Fletcher, has seven children Jason, born October 25, 1833, served in First Iowa Cavalry throughout civil war, teacher, died at McGregor, Iowa, October, 1903 Alonzo, born February 3, 1836, served in Company H, wounded in breast by minie ball July 16, 1861, farmer at Cambridge, Vermont married, January 6, 1869, at Johnson, Vermont, Emma Alsie Brown, daughter of Dexter W Brown, of Waterville, Vermont, has four daughters Edgar, born August 16, 1837, adopted by his uncle, Rufus Montague, and name changed by act of legislature, married, March, 1860 Louise Sherwood, daughter of Zalmon Sherwood, of Fletcher, married (second) Annette Blair, daughter of Charles Blair, of Fletcher, was a soldier in the civil war has had six children William Lyon, born March 12 1844, died September 24, 1901, carried a ball in his elbow received in the battle of Cold Harbor, married Ellen Lucretia Whittle, in Lowell Vermont has one son Ross

(VII) Daniel Kinsley, son of Ben Alvah Kinsley (6), was born in Fletcher, Vermont, June 13, 1829 He spent his boyhood in his native town, working on a farm and attending the district school He came to Massachusetts when he was seventeen, as many Vermont boys did about that time, hoping to save money enough to buy a farm and settle in Fletcher He went to work for Bonum Nye, of North Brookfield, one of the county commissioners, and he became acquainted with the other county commissioners in the course of business When a vacancy occurred in the messenger's office at the court he was the unanimous choice of the board He was elected June 21, 1853 as messenger of the courts and held the position for fifty years His duties at first included work now done by the janitor and others Time has worked many changes in the court house and the courts of Worcester county One interesting souvenir of the early days of his work for the county is the magnificent elm, known as the Kinsley elm, between the court house and the Unitarian church It was a seedling in the year he began as custodian of the court house, and next year he transplanted it to its present location It is as large as many elms of twice its age and nowhere is to be found a more graceful and beautiful tree

Hon Alfred S Roe in an article in the Worcester Magazine, October, 1903, just after Mr Kinsley had completed his fifty years of service at the court house, reviewed briefly the history of those years "In these fifty years," he said, Mr Kinsley saw no less than thirty-three different men sit upon the supreme bench and, had he been a note-taker, what a volume of reminiscences he might have prepared He has followed the entire existence of the superior court, for he had been six years on duty when it was established and each one of the more than fifty judges left his own distinct impression on the mind of the messenger He saw the progress of distinguished and elequent lawyers from their places as counsel to those of judges and two, Gray and Holmes, he saw promoted to the highest judicial positions attainable in the United States, viz seats in the supreme court of the nation He was present when Charles Devens exchanged his pen for the the sword and went out to do battle for his country "

Mr Kinsley returned to Fletcher to marry an old schoolmate, August 24, 1854 His wife was Harriet Newell Mudgett, daughter of Jesse Mudgett, of Cambridge Mrs Kinsley died March 4, 1900 Mr Kinsley is now retired He resides at the rear of the Court House at 15 Court street, this being a portion of the Isaiah Thomas estate, which Mr Kinsley purchased in 1883 and upon which he built two apartment houses He is a member of Plymouth Congregational Church, although formerly a member of Central Church He was one of the early promoters of the Y M C A His children are Catherine Montague, born in Worcester, June 23, 1855, married 1878 Charles A Reed They have had ten children Josephine E, born September 1, 1880, wife of Rev Tyler E Gale, Henry D, born September 4, 1881, died August 16, 1882, Millicent E, born January 30, 1883, Horace B, born July 8, 1884, Karl, born March 11, 1886, died in infancy, Margaret K born May 19 1887, Katherine Montague, born May 6 1889, died June 2, 1900, Frank H, born July 27, 1891, Maybelle, born August 22, 1893, Raymond, born June 11, 1897, died January 31, 1898 Fanny Amelia, born September 10, 1857, died January 17, 1863 Florence Josephine, born October 26, 1860, resides at home Carrie Carleton, born March 26, 1864, is a public school teacher Sumner Alvah born April 8, 1868, married Maybelle Pierce, in 1893, they have two children Katherine Montague, born October 9, 1896, and Mildred, born September 7, 1901 He (Sumner Alvah) is with the Woodbury-Carlton Engraving Company of Worcester, Massachusetts Edward William, born January 12, 1871, married, December, 1905, Edith Lancaster He is a member of the banking house of Kinsley & Adams of Worcester

SHATTUCK FAMILY William Shattuck (1), the progenitor of the Shattucks, of Worcester, and of most of the name in this country, was born in England in 1621 or 1622, and died at Watertown, Massachusetts, August 14 1672 He was a young boy when he came to America, and his name does not appear in the records until 1642, when he was twenty years old That same year he married Susanna ——— After the death of Shattuck she married Richard Norcross who survived her She died December 1, 1686 Shattuck was a farmer and weaver In 1853 one of his descendants, Lemuel

Shattuck, had a monument erected on his grave and suitably inscribed It is in the old graveyard on the road from Cambridge to Watertown west of Mount Auburn Their children were 1 Susanna, born 1643, married J Morse and J Fay 2 Mary, born August 25, 1645, married Jonathan Brown 3 John, born February 11, 1647, married Ruth Whitney 4 Philip, born 1648, married D Barstow and R Chamberlain 5 Joanna, died April 4, 1673, unmarried 6 William (see forward) 7 Rebecca, born 1655, married Samuel Church 8 Abigail, born 1657, married J Morse and J Parker 9 Benjamin, died in his twentieth year 10 Samuel, born February 28, 1666, married Abigail ———

(II) William Shattuck, son of William (1) and Susanna Shattuck, born 1653 at Watertown, in the old homestead in the easterly parish on the highway to the pond, where he lived all his life and died October 19, 1732, at the ripe old age of seventy-nine Like his father he was a weaver, but like the versatile neighbors about him he did other things, such as farming and brick-making, as the season called him He was a prominent man and held several town offices He married Susanna Randall in 1678 She died May 8, 1723 Her father, Stephen Randall, married Susanna Barron He died February 26, 1708 Susan Barron was the daughter of Ellis Barron, who died at Watertown, October 30, 1676, and sister of Moses Barron, born March 1, 1643, who married Mary Learned, settled in Chelmsford and was ancestor of Lucy Barron, wife of Dr Benjamin Shattuck, (see forward) The children of William and Susanna Shattuck were 1 Susanna, married Samuel Holden 2 Joanna, married Isaac Holden 3 Elizabeth, born November 23, 1684, married R Goddard and others 4 William, born 1686, married Hepzibah Hammond 5 Benjamin, (see forward) 6 Mary, baptized April 13, 1690, married William Greenleaf 7 Abigail, married Joseph Holden 8 Joseph, born October 9, 1694, died October 15, 1694 9 Jonathan, born October 16, 1695, married Elizabeth Stearns 10 Robert, born January 1, 1698, married Mary Pratt 11 Moses, born November 11, 1703, died at Boston, May 31, 1724, unmarried

(III) Rev Benjamin Shattuck, son of William (2) and Susanna Shattuck, born at Watertown, July 30, 1687 He graduated at Harvard College in 1709 and engaged soon afterward as teacher of the public school at Littleton, at the princely salary of thirty pounds a year The town engaged to build for him a new school house During the next six years he studied for the ministry while he taught the youth of Littleton, and he was so well liked there that he was called to preach, and became the first minister of Littleton He preached for fifteen years, then resigned, but spent the rest of his life in the same town He died August 30, 1730 He married Martha Sherman, baptized September 1, 1689, the daughter of Joseph Sherman, blacksmith and prominent citizen of Watertown This Joseph Sherman married Elizabeth, daughter of Edward Winship, of Cambridge, and was the father of William Sherman, shoemaker, of Watertown, and grandfather of Roger Sherman, signer of the Declaration of Independence The father of Joseph Sherman was Captain John Sherman, a distinguished citizen, born 1613 at Dedham, Essex county, England who came to America in 1634 The children of Rev Benjamin Shattuck were 1 Stephen, born February 10 1710, married Elizabeth Robbins 2 Martha, born January 7, 1712, married Samuel Tuttle 3 Benjamin, (see forward) 4 Timothy, married Desire Hall 5 William, born January 1, 1718, married Abigail Reed 6 Sarah December 13 1719, married Jonathan Dix 7 Ebenezer, born February 22, 1722 8 Susanna, born April 8 1724, married Caleb Taylor 9 Elizabeth, born February 13, 1726, married Elias Taylor 10 Jonathan, born July 1728, died February 19 1745 11 Moses, born June, 1732, died December 13, 1737

(IV) Dr Benjamin Shattuck, son of Rev Benjamin (3) and Martha (Sherman) Shattuck, born in Watertown, December 8, 1713, was a physician at Littleton, but removed shortly before his death to live with his son at Groton, where he died October, 1790 He married, November 13, 1740 Dinah Hunt of Littleton, probably a descendant of William Hunt, one of the early settlers of Concord, Massachusetts She was buried at Littleton, January 17, 1791 Their children were 1 Moses, born August 10, 1741, keeper of general stage house at Portland, Maine, where he died February 1, 1801 He married Hannah, widow of Joseph Golding, daughter of John Waite of Newbury, Massachusetts She died December 22, 1800 Edmund, born July 20, 1744, married Abigail Chamberlain 3 Jonathan, (see forward) 4 Somers, born July 6, 1749, married Esther Rogers 5 Arthur, born November 29, 1751, probably lost at sea

(V) Jonathan Shattuck, son of Dr Benjamin (4) and Dinah Shattuck, born in Littleton, August 9, 1746 In 1776 he bought of John Earle a farm in Oxford In 1781, he removed to Chesterfield, New Hampshire and in 1787 to Townshend, Vermont, where he died April, 1821 He married September 15, 1767, Huldah Curtis, born at Dudley, Massachusetts 1748 After his death she removed to Bakersfield, Vermont, where she died November 1, 1821 Their children were 1 Jonathan, born September 20, 1768, married Mehitable Fairbanks 2 Huldah born March 24, 1770, married Hiram Davis, a blacksmith of Townshend, Vermont, died October, 1805 3 Arethusa, born August 15, 1772, married James Saunders, of Chesterfield, New Hampshire 4 Elizabeth, born April 6, 1774, married Amos Coburn, farmer of Champion, New York, died July, 1851 5 Moses, born November 20, 1776, married Hannah Brigham 6 Phebe, born June 27, 1778, married Winslow Wheelock, settled in LeRoy, New York 7 Josiah, (see forward) 8 John, born September 11, 1786, resided at Brandon New York 9 Benjamin, born March 20, 1789, married Lydia Jackman 10 Hepsibah, born May 16, 1793, married Ezekiel Cady, chair-maker, of Wilmington, Vermont, married (second) John Smith, farmer of the same town died August, 1850

(VI) Josiah Shattuck son of Jonathan Shattuck (5) born in Chesterfield New Hampshire October 20 1781, died, 1858 He was a farmer at Bakersfield Vermont He married, October 25, 1810, Susan B Boutelle, born at Leominster Massachusetts, February 9 1792, daughter of William and Tabitha Boutelle, died 1877 Their children were 1 Harriet S, born March 4, 1812, died December 2, 1812 2 William B, (see forward) 3 Harriet A, born February 9 1818, married March 5 1837, James Maynard, a farmer of Bakersfield 4 Jason L, born May 5, 1820, married, May 1, 1844 Lucy R Farnsworth who was a farmer at Bakersfield, Vermont 5 Noel K, born May 9 1822, married July 12, 1853 Emily A Purdy, school teacher in Moundsville Loudon county, Vermont 6 Ora L, and 7 Orrilla L, born October 9 1824 died 1855, unmarried 8 Laura A, born November 3, 1826, married December, 1849 Horace H Farnsworth, carpenter, teacher 9 Henry and 10 Henrietta, born February 9 1829, Henrietta died August 16, 1845

11 Lydia S, born October 3, 1831, married William H Drake, born in New London, Connecticut, machinist, resided in Bellows Falls, Vermont

(VII) William Boutelle Shattuck, son of Josiah (6) and Susan Shattuck, born January 18 1816, died December 9, 1893, married Emily M, daughter of Simon and Phoebe (Bowen) Maynard of Bakersfield, Vermont, formerly of Leominster, Massachusetts She was born in 1813 and died April 8, 1879 Their children were 1 James Harlan (see forward) 2 William Oscar, born April 3, 1847, in Burlington, Vermont 3 Raymond B, born May 26, 1856, died December 13, 1893

(VIII) James Harlan Shattuck, son of William B (7) and Emily M (Maynard) Shattuck, was born May 25, 1844, at Bakersfield, Vermont, where his early years were spent His education was obtained in the common schools of his native town and in Bakersfield Academy At the age of twenty he came to Worcester, after a short stay in Boston, and started in the fruit and commission business, building up a large and successfull business After twenty years of mercantile life he retired, and has since lived in the city of his adoption In 1865 he enlisted for service on the frontier but on account of a full quota he was not called upon to serve

Mr Shattuck is a Republican He is a member of St Mark's Episcopal Church He married, April 20, 1874 Anne Emerson Perley, daughter of Anderson and Edith Emerson Perley, of Enosberg, Vermont, born June 3, 1843 They have no children

FREDERICK E REED Reed, Read, Reede, and Rede were all derived from the word Rehea, which had its origin in Phoenicia and Greece The mode of spelling used by the Puritan ancestors was usually Reede and Reade There are many accounts of the race of Reeds fighting against the Romans They are to be found in England, Scotland, Ireland, and America About fourteen hundred or fifteen hundred years before the Christian era, in the great western emigration, the Reed families emigrated to the present England and Scotland, and Prince Reda, their chief, and his knights put to flight the Romans in 180, A D The Reads or Reeds are directly descended from these conquerors, who settled in the region now forming the barony of Redesdale The present Baron of Redesdale is a relative and a prominent member of the House of Lords The scenes in Scott's novels and poetical works are laid in this territory, rich in monuments of the past, and some of the present names of towns and parishes are derived from Reed, Redsford, for Reidsfors, Radham for Reedham and Riddle for Redesdale

As the line of England and Scotland was constantly changing according to the valor and the strength of parties, the Reeds have become mixed with both nations, and the barony of Redesdale, being on the border, the Reeds had the advantage of distinguishing themselves and consequently were promoted in civic government, and they were connected with the royal family of England long before the days of William the Conqueror There was Withred, King of Kent in the seventh century Ethelred or Read the Good, in 866 Alfred, or Reed the Shrewd, in 871 Eldred, or Reed the Elder in 946 Eethelred the Second, in 978

When William the Conqueror took possession of the English throne, the legal heir to the throne was the brother-in-law of the King of Scotland William's heir married the legal heiress, the daughter of Edward the Confessor, who was Ethelred the Second's own son So both houses became merged into one family The Reeds are among the reigning princes of Northumberland, Kent, Wessex and Mercia, and all are politically allied Many ruins of castles and fortifications are to be found in England and Scotland along rivers, valleys, and highlands, and there are still some splendid castles occupied by the Reed descendants at the present time, as Chipchase Castle at the junction of the Reed and Tyne rivers, which is now occupied by Sir Christopher Reed, and owned by Sir Christopher's son, who is deputy lieutenant of the county, also Ewellgrove, Ipsden House, Ashmans in Suffolk, Wood Parks in Galway, Rossenara in Kilkenny

Brianus De Rede, 1139, living in Morpeth on Mensbach river, in the northern part of England, had Robert, of Rede William, bishop of Chichester, Thomas, of Redydale William's grandson, Golfrinus had William, Thomas, of Redydale, Robert Thomas, of Redydale, had Thomas and John John, mayor of Norwich, 1388, had an only son, who married Isiod Stanley, and they had John, Bothomomew, Robert William William Reade, S T P, had a son, Sir William, whose son married Revecca, daughter and co-heir of Menis, whose first child, Mathew, married Alice daughter of Andrew Wood, whose son William married Lucy Henage who had Elias John and William William sailed from Gravesend, county of Kent, in the "Assurance de London" in 1635, of which Isaac Bromwell and George Percy were masters There were on this vessel at the time of sailing two hundred and twenty-one persons, the average age of whom was about twenty-five years The vessel sailed July 24 1635, and probably landed about a month later in Boston whence Reade proceeded to Weymouth and settled there

It is supposed that he came from Maidstone, near London On March 9, 1636-7, he purchased from the estate of Zachery Bicknell his house and farm, which was located on the west side of Middle street The old house stood on the knoll opposite the junction of Middle and Charles streets The premises were recently owned by James Clapp They passed out of the family in 1769 William Reade was among the first settlers of Weymouth, which was made a plantation May 8, 1635 He was admitted a freeman September 2, 1635, and was elected deputy to the general court, December 7, 1636, and again September 6, 1638 Rev Joseph Hull and his company came to Weymouth in the spring of 1635, shortly before Reade settled there and this band of very worthy settlers established one of the most noted colonies of the early days of the New England Puritans In the same month that Mr Reade left England another ship containing his future wife sailed Avis Deacon was on the "Alice," of which Richard Orchard was the master, and which sailed July 13, 1635, from Gravesend with thirty-two passengers, most of whom were young men and women Her twin brother, Thomas Deacon, came on the boat with Reade Avis Deacon married William Reade probably soon after her arrival in New England Reade was allotted land in the first division at Weymouth and he acquired considerable real estate later

The children of William and Avis (Deacon) Reade were Margaret, born 1636, died July 6, 1659, married, May 11, 1651, John Vining, Hannah, born 1637, married, April 2, 1658, Nicholas Whitmarsh William, born October 15, 1639, married, 1675, Esther Thompson, Esther, born May 8, 1641, Ruth, born 1642, died 1663, married, December 19, 1662, John Whitman, Thomas, born 1645, died November 14, 1719, married, in 1670, Sarah Bicknell, Mary, born 1647, died 1655, unmarried, John, born 1649, died January 13, 1720, married Bethiah Frye, James, died July 21, 1726, married, April 18, 1683, Susanna Richmond There is considerable difficulty

T. E. Reed.

in tracing the children of William Reade of Weymouth and the authorities differ In this sketch it has been thought best to follow the genealogy written by John L Reed, published in 1901

(II) William Reed, son of William Reed (1), was born October 15, 1639, at Weymouth, Massachusetts, and died in 1706 He was constable of Weymouth in 1675 and selectman in 1681 He was an extensive dealer in land His will, dated October 26, 1705, was proved September 12, 1706 He lived on Pleasant street on the southwesterly side In 1888 a part of the old house was still standing, having been remodeled and occupied by Palmer Loud The old dam which Reed built across the river in 1680 or before 1690 is near the house He owned all the land on both sides of the street from Hingham line to Ragged plain and from the river to a point westerly from the house owned by William Dyer He built a double house later on the site that had been occupied by William Dyer's house, and also a house between that and his own residence

Esther Thompson, his wife, was the daughter of Lieutenant John Thompson, who was born in Wales and was only six years old when he landed in Wesson's company in May, 1622 He married, December 6, 1645, Mary Cook, daughter of Francis Cook, who came in the Mayflower to Plymouth She was born in Plymouth in 1626, died March 21, 1715 He settled thirteen miles west of Plymouth and built a log house there The site is now in Halifax or Middleboro He lived there until his house was burned by the Indians While living there he or his wife walked to the church at Plymouth every Sunday John Thompson died June 16, 1696 He and his wife are buried at Middleboro, Massachusetts After his death the widow removed to Abington Mr Thompson was a private in Lieutenant Edward Oaks' company, April 26, 1676, in King Philip s war He removed to Weymouth and settled on land bought of John Raue, whose house had been burned by the Indians in King Philip s war Some of the timbers of the original house are in the house now standing on the property In 1900 the Thompson place at Halifax was sold to John Lynberg and passed out of the hands of the Thompson family, which had owned it from the first settlement

In 1669-70 William Reed was fence viewer of Weymouth He was elected a selectman November 28, 1681, and in 1682 perambulated the Hingham line with Corporal French He was again selectman in 1686 and 1687, 1695, 1696 and 1697 He also served the town on important special committees at various times His will names his children They were John, born October 21, 1680, died young, William, born May 24, 1682, died June 3, 1753, married, 1703, Alice Nash, John, born July 10, 1687, married (first) Sarah Hersey, married (second) Mary Whitmarsh, Jacob, born November 6, 1691, died 1766, married (first) Sarah Hersey, married (second) Hannah Noyes, widow, Bushna, married Nicholas Porter, Mercy, born at Weymouth, married ——— Whitmarsh, Mary, born at Weymouth, Hester, Sarah, born March 21, 1694, married Hezekiah King

(III) William Reed, son of William Reed (2), was born at Weymouth, May 24, 1682, died June 3, 1753 He married, 1703, Alice Nash She died December 5, 1751 She was a daughter of Lieutenant Jacob Nash, the son of James Nash, who settled in Weymouth, in 1628 William Reed moved to Abington in 1708 At the first town meeting held in Abington he was elected town clerk and selectman He was fence viewer in Weymouth in 1707, and served that town as a member of many important committees Rev Mr Dodge in his journal June 3, 1753, says of William Reed "Attended the funeral of the aged Capt Reed, the largest I have ever seen in town Ten at least of his descendants in the male line have been liberally educated Of these two have been members of Congress, viz his grandson, the late Rev Dr John Reed, of West Bridgewater and his son, Hon John Reed, or Yarmouth, now a member After the expiration of his present term he will have been in Congress twenty-two years—eighteen in succession"

The children of William Reed (3) were Alice, born in Boston, October 19, 1703, died October 24, 1703, William, born December 15, 1704, died November 21, 1724, Obadiah, born March 14, 1707, died November 4, 1753, married, October 19, 1731, Mary Nash, Ebenezer, born July 13, 1709, married, February 21, 1732, Hannah Thompson, Alice, born April 4, 1711, died September 29, 1724, Daniel, born December 6, 1713, died April 5, 1781, married (first) September 15, 1739, Ruth White, married (second), February 7, 1776, Sarah Hamlin, James, born March 3, 1716, died aged thirty-seven years, married, May 10, 1739, Abigail Nash, Solomon, born October 22, 1719 died 1785, married (first), in 1748, Abigail Stoughton, of Connecticut, married (second) Sarah Reed, widow of Elijah Reed, Jacob, Moses, born January 15, 1723, married Phebe ———, Alice, born April 19, 1725, married, December 1, 1748, Jacob Reed

(IV) Rev Solomon Reed, son of Captain William Reed (3), was born October 22, 1719, at Weymouth, Massachusetts He died in the spring of 1785, aged sixty-six years He married (first), in 1748, Abigail Stoughton, of Connecticut, married (second), Sarah Reed, the daughter of Jacob Reed, his father's youngest brother

He graduated at Harvard College in 1739 He was ordained as minister of the Second Congregational Church in Framingham in 1746, and remained there until 1756, when he was installed as minister of Titicut, a parish in the northwestern part of Middleboro and the southwest part of Bridgewater His health failed in 1684 and he died in the spring of 1685, at little past sixty-five years of age He seems to have been a very earnest and pious minister of the church There are a few of his manuscript sermons in the archives of the Pilgrim Society at Plymouth, written in a fine clear hand, and showing decided ability as a writer There is also a manuscript journal for the period from October 3, 1743, to January 9, 1745 During this period Rev Mr Whitefield was preaching in this country and laying the foundations of many churches

In his will he mentions by name all his children except Sarah His children were Sarah, born 1750, John, born November 11, 1751, married (first), in 1780, Hannah Sampson, married (second), in 1822, Mrs Phebe Sampson Paddock, Solomon, born March 18, 1753, died February 2 1808, married, March 14, 1781, Susannah Willard, Samuel, born 1754, died July 13, 1812, married, 1780 Anna Shaw, Timothy, born 1756, married, 1788, Hannah Kingman

(V) Rev Samuel Reed, son of Rev Solomon Reed (4), was born probably at Framingham, Massachusetts, where his father was then pastor He died July 13, 1812, aged fifty-seven, and in the thirty-third years of his ministry He married, 1780, Anna Shaw, of Warwick, Massachusetts He graduated at Yale College in 1777 and was ordained over the church and society at Warwick, Massachusetts, in 1779 He was said to be a man of sound sense, a devoted Christian and much beloved by his people and the community generally The inscription on the monument erected by his parishioners at Warwick is as follows "Rev Samuel Reed, second minister at Warwick died July 13th, 1812, aged 57 He had strong powers of mind, was bold in the defense of truth, severe against wickedness, mild towards the humble, pitiful to the distressed, affectionate towards his friends Frank and sincere in all his professions, rational and fervent in his piety, faithful in his pastoral duties

"He taught the Christian doctrine in its simplicity and truth, he maintained the freedom of the human mind, the unchangeable obligations of moral duty, the impartial justice of God and future retribution

Under the vital impression of this faith he felt, and communicated the cheering entertainments of life, and enjoyed the richest solace and triumph in death"

The children of the Rev Samuel Reed were Samuel, born March 23, 1781, died young, Anna, born April 19, 1784, died 1835, in Warwick, married, December, 1813, Deacon Joseph Wilson, Abigail, born February 17, 1786, married, December, 1805, Joel Mayo, Samuel, born April 25, 1788, married Melinda Wheelock, Stephen, born November 5, 1790, died 1847, married Jerusha Moor, Timothy, born July 10, 1793, died 1854, married Susan Kingsley

(VI) Samuel Reed, son of Rev Samuel Reed, (5), was born at Warwick, Massachusetts, April 25, 1788 He married Melinda Wheelock They settled in Greenfield, Massachusetts He died very suddenly and was buried in Warwick, Massachusetts, where his widow afterward resided His children were John, born February 26, 1820, married Delia Winter, Melinda A, born October 12, 1824

(VII) John Reed, son of Samuel Reed, was born in Greenfield, Massachusetts, February 26, 1820 He married Delia Winter They resided first at Croyden, Sullivan county, New Hampshire, where their son, Frederick E Reed, was born They removed to Worcester about 1850 John Reed was a teacher of music and later foreman of one of the departments of one of the largest and best equipped machine shops in New England at that time He continued in the machinist business after coming to Worcester He retired from active work in 1883 He resided after that at Shrewsbury and Worcester He died in Holden, Massachusetts, December, 1902, at the advanced age of eighty-two He was a member of the First Church of Christ His children were Frederick E, born in Croyden, New Hampshire, March 1, 1847, Ella E, born in Worcester, Massachusetts, August 7, 1856

(VIII) Frederick E Reed, son of John Reed (7), was born in Croyden, New Hampshire, March 1, 1847 He came to Worcester with his parents when very young, and was educated in the Worcester schools At seventeen he went into the machine shop and learned the trade of machinist After two years he returned to school and took a course at Worcester Academy and at Howe s Business College in Worcester While attending school he also kept books for the Wood & Light Machine Co, the concern with which his father was for many years connected This business was established in 1848 They made iron working machinery did mill work, dealing in shafting, pulleys and hangers He was bookkeeper five years for this company He rested for a year on account of his health, and then went into the draughting department and had charge of the draughting and designing of the company for five years He studied in the drawing school of the Worcester County Mechanics' Association This school was established in 1864 and is said to be the first of its kind in the country It gave practical instruction in architectural and mechanical drawing and daughter Drawing was later introduced into the public schools, and when it was finally taught in the evening schools of the city the school of the Mechanics' Association was discontinued Mr Reed was active in the promotion and support of the school during the time when it was needed in the city

Mr Reed went into business for himself in 1875 at 54 Hermon street under the firm name of A F Prentice & Co He manufactured an improved upright drill, also hand and foot power lathes, slide rests, milled machine screws and made to order special machinery of all kinds He makes a specialty of machine tools, of engine lathes, hand lathes and foot lathes of all kinds He built the first building on the present site in 1883 at 120 Gold street The business has been very successful and the plant has grown from a small beginning to large proportions The present name of the company is F E Reed Company The original shop at the Gold street location had 2262 feet of floor space In 1905 the shops of the F E Reed Co had two and three-tenths acres of floor space The first building in 1883 was two stories high, 55 by 183 feet The second, built in 1888, was 50 by 58 feet A large building was erected in 1889, another in 1890, another 93 by 107 was erected in 1896, another 50 by 131 in 1899, another 30 by 107 in 1901 and another in 1904, 40 by 53 feet The later buildings are four stories in height and all are well constructed brick buildings of modern design When Mr Reed began he employed six men The average pay roll lately has contained over three hundred names of employees He is the chief owner of a number of other important enterprises in Worcester The Matthew Manufacturing Company at 104 Gold street was organized in 1894 with Mr Reed as president and A T Matthews as general manager They manufacture metal goods and employ one hundred and fifty hands They make a specialty of drawn sheet steel work, stove trimmings, steam pipe collars, bicycle fittings, ferules, and other sheet metal specialties Mr Reed is a partner in the Reed & Curtis Machine Screw Company, which employs one hundred and fifty hands He is the proprietor of the Reed Foundry Company at 95 Gold street, iron foundaries, employing one hundred and twenty-five hands He is treasurer of the Worcester Lawn Mower Company, employing sixty hands Mr Reed has been one of the most successful manufacturers in Worcester He has built up a very large business and has shown himself possessed of business ability of a high order He has been devoted to his business career and has cared for no outside interests He is counted among the leaders of industry in Worcester Mr Reed's summer home at Thompson, Connecticut, is a model of its kind

SOUTHGATE FAMILY Richard Southgate, the pioneer of the American branch of the family, came with Daniel Denny from Coombs, Suffolk, England in 1715 The following year he went back for his family, brought then over in July, 1717 and with them his brother James In March, 1718, the Southgates and Daniel Denny removed to Leicester and settled there, but what circumstances led to their selecting that spot is not known Mr Southgate became an extensive landowner in the town, and is one of the grantees in the settlers' deed, lots Nos 35, 41, and 42 were conveyed to him by that deed In 1737 he was the owner of seven hundred and seventy acres in the town He was the first treasurer of the town, and was much employed as a surveyor of lands, being a skillful and trustworthy person

Richard Southgate was born in 1671, a son of

John Southgate In October, 1700, he married Elizabeth Steward, they had six children, all born in England, five of whom came to Leicester, Massachusetts Steward, born 1703, Elizabeth, 1705, died 1791, unmarried, Hannah, 1709, married Nathaniel Waite, of Leicester, 1737, and died 1754, Mary, 1712, married Daniel Livermore, of Weston, 1732, Richard, 1714 Richard Southgate (father) died in 1758, aged eighty-eight years, his wife died in 1751, in the eighty-eighth years of her age They are said to be the ancestors of all of the name in New England

Steward Southgate, son of Richard and Elizabeth (Steward) Southgate, married Elizabeth Scott, of Palmer, then called the "Elbow," in 1735, while he was living there About 1740 he returned to Leicester, and spent the remainder of his days there Their children were John, born 1738, Robert, 1741, was a physician, removed to Scarboro, Maine, and is noticed in this work, Margaret, 1743, Sarah, 1744, married Azariah Dickinson, of Hadley, Steward, 1748

Steward Southgate, son of Steward and Elizabeth (Scott) Southgate, married and removed to Hardwick He was a soldier in the revolution, and after the close of the war went to Barnard, Vermont, where in 1795 he lost five children by the canker-rash within a few days of each other For his second wife, Mr Southgate married Elizabeth, daughter of Nathaniel Potter, and their children were Amos, born 1751, died in Boston, 1775, he married and had a daughter born after his death, who became the wife of Jonah Earle, Rebekah, born 1754, died 1756, Ruth, born 1758, died in Boston, 1777, Moses, born 1761, died in Boston, 1777 Mr Southgate was at first a member of the Congregational church, but became a zealous and leading member of the Society of Friends, to which society his second wife's father belonged prior to 1732 He must have been well educated for his day, and seems to have possessed a clear head, strong purpose, and withal great sensibility and Christian resignation He had a commanding influence among his religious brethren, and the memoranda that he left alludes in terms of deep emotion to the afflictions through which he was called to pass He did in 1765, and his second wife died in 1748

John Southgate, son of Steward Southgate, married Eleanor Sargent, daughter of Jonathan Sargent, 1776, and their children were Sally, born 1777, died unmarried, John, born 1778, died 1804, unmarried, as related in this work, William, born 1782, died 1811, unmarried He was rather a skillful and talented painter, he had cultivated his taste under several masters, among others, Ralph Earle, to whom he was remotely related, and Gilbert Stuart The department of art to which he devoted his attention was that of portraits, in which he would have probably attained a distinguished reputation had he diligently devoted himself to it as a profession Harriet, born 1792, died 1841, unmarried, Eliza, born 1796, married Jacob Bigelow, then of Montreal, where she died, leaving one son, Dr George F Bigelow, of Boston George W, born 1800 Mrs Southgate died in 1825

Richard Southgate, youngest son of Richard and Elizabeth (Steward) Southgate, the pioneer ancestors, came with his father from England He married Eunice Brown, daughter of Samuel Brown 1741, and their children were Richard born 1742, removed to Bridgewater, Vermont, Isaac, 1744, Samuel, 1747, resided in various places and died in Scarborough, 1773, Elijah, 1751 married Patty Hastings, died in Shrewsbury, 1837, aged eighty-seven years, without children, Jonas, 1753, married Mary Whitney, of Grafton, 1782, and died 1784, Eunice, 1757, died unmarried, Judah, 1761, married Susannah Taylor, of Spencer, 1798, and died 1799, Mercy, died unmarried Mr Southgate was known as "Elder," and was a Baptist preacher He held meetings in the schoolhouse when it stood where the brick factory now stands, opposite to where Esquire Rawson lived He resided in the southeast part of the town, near the line of Spencer, and was a farmer

Isaac Southgate, son of Richard and Eunice (Brown) Southgate, married Rebekah Brown, daughter of John Brown, 1769, and they were the parents of one daughter, Rebekah, born 1770, married a Mr Hodges, of the state of New York Mr Southgate married for his second wife, Eunice White, 1771, and their children were Asa, born 1772, Betsey, 1774, married Nathan Beers, 1790, Samuel, 1776, married Hannah Waite, 1801, and they reared a family of children in Leicester, one of their sons, John P, died 1882, in Worcester, and another, Samuel, died in 1874, in Leicester, Eunice, 1779, married Sylvanus Earle, removed to Ohio, and died in 1835, Isaac, 1782, married Maria Webb, daughter of Peter Webb, Esq, and granddaughter of Thomas Denny, Sr Mr Southgate died in 1800, aged fifty-six years He was one of the active business men and public-spirited citizens of the town, for many years a manufacturer of cards He represented the town in the legislature, served as trustee of the Worcester County Agricultural Society, and took an active part in promoting the interests of that important association

James Southgate, who came with his brother Richard Southgate, from England, as above stated, became a proprietor of the settlers' half of the town, as owner of lot No 30 At the first town meeting he was chosen one of the selectmen and surveyor of highways He with his brother and several other inhabitants of Leicester addressed a letter to the governor, in 1725 asking for soldiers to guard the town from the Indians He was a deacon of the church, and took an active part in settling Mr Parsons in 1720 His wife's name was Mary, and they had one son, James, born 1718, who married Dorothy Lincoln, in 1741, and they were the parents of one daughter, Dorothy, born 1746 His house was located a little north of Mr Morton's, in the east part of the town There is no trace of the family after that period

John P Southgate, son of Samuel and Hannah (Waite) Southgate, above referred to, was born in Leicester, Massachusetts, July 29, 1804 died February 7, 1882, in the seventy-eighth year of his age Samuel Southgate (father) was also born in Leicester, 1776, and probably attended the schools of that town During the latter years of his life he engaged in the manufacture of cards and continued the same until his decease, February, 1882 John P Southgate learned the trade of a cabinet maker of Deacon Murdock then town sexton in Leicester, and after attaining his majority in 1825 worked at his trade a few years in Worcester, and then returned again to Leicester where he changed his business to brush making and in 1834 removed again to Worcester, where he opened a shop for brush making in a building which stood on the site of the present Horticultural Hall on Front street In 1837 he removed to the north corner of Main and Mechanic streets where he went in company with James H Wall in the boot shoe and leather rade and was burned out in 1841 He then removed to the building which then stood on the site of Piper's Block, next south of the old United States Hotel, where he was alone two or three years, and in 1844 went in partnership with Thomas M Rogers in the leather and shoe findings trade, the firm being Southgate & Rogers In 1850 they removed to the north corner of Main and Pleasant streets, in the block on the site of the one now owned by Mr Rogers Mr Southgate retired from this business in 1855, with a handsome competence, and engaged for a few years in some real estate operations which resulted very unfortunately for him in the sudden collapse of 1857 and '58, which proved disastrous to so many From 1860 to 1880 he was engaged in manufacturing on a limited scale in Auburn, but during the last year or two, since the decease of his wife, he had resided in this city with one of his sons Mr Southgate was a man of sound practical judgment and strict business integrity, and universally respected Always taking a lively interest in public affairs, he was a member of the common council in 1850 and 1851, and alderman in 1855 and 1856, ever faithful and prompt in attention to the duties assigned him

Mr Southgate married May 21, 1829, Sarah Swan, of Leicester, and their children were John Frederick, born June 13. 1831, died 1858, Reuben H, born December 8, 1833, mentioned hereinafter, Frank White, born February 10, 1840, now a resident of Worcester, James Stewart, born October 8, 1842, died November 22, 1899

Reuben H Southgate, second son of John P and Sarah (Swan) Southgate, was born in Leicester, Massachusetts, December 8, 1833 In 1835 he was brought by his parents to Worcester, Massachusetts, attended the common and high schools of that town and for a short time the Baptist Academy, now Worcester Academy Shortly after attaining the age of eighteen years he engaged in business with his father, who was associated with Thomas M Rogers, they being dealers in shoe findings In 1855 Mr Southgate, Sr, retired from active pursuits, his son, Reuben H, succeeding him, and under the name of Rogers & Southgate they conducted a store at the corner of Pleasant and Main streets until 1873 In that year Mr Southgate bought out the interest of his partner, Mr Rogers, and moved to Franklin Square, where he remained until April 1, 1888, when he retired from business Since then he has devoted his time to travel in foreign countries, visiting Asia, Africa, Europe, and in fact all parts of the globe, gaining thereby a vast store of useful and interesting knowledge and pleasure He has always adhered to the principles of the Republican party, and he cast his first presidential vote for J C Fremont

Mr Southgate married, June 8, 1864, Anna J Wood, daughter of Ichabod and Anna (Warren) Wood, of Watertown, the latter named now leading a retired life at Asheville, North Carolina, aged ninety years Their children are Louis Warren, born February 25, 1865, married, June 8, 1892, Clara Brigham, daughter of L L Brigham, of Worcester, and they are the parents of one child, Richard Brigham, born May 5 1893 Philip Wood, born May 10, 1868, died December 7, 1905 Both Louis Warren and Philip Wood Southgate graduated at Worcester Technical School and Columbia Law School of Washington Both spent three years in the patent office in Washington, D C Under the firm name of Southgate & Southgate they were engaged as patent attorneys in Worcester, where they conducted an extensive and lucrative business They were admitted to practice in the supreme and district courts in all the states of the Union

FRANCIS A GASKILL Many persons in the United States bearing the name of Gaskill may trace their lineage to Edward, the ship carpenter of Salem, Massachusetts As early as 1636 his name appears among those in the list of proprietors of lands in that old historic town The name is variously spelled in the early records as Gaskin, Gasking, Gascoyne, Gascoins, Gaskell, Gaskill and Gaskil

(I) Edward Gaskill, the ship carpenter, owned in 1636 the right to twenty acres of land in Salem, and by his wife Sarah had children Samuel, baptized August 7, 1639, Daniel, born October 10, 1640, Sarah, born May 14, 1643, married Peter Joy, May 24, 1661, Hannah, born March 1, 1646, Edward, born April 30, 1648

(II) Samuel Gaskill, born 1639, married Provided Southwicke, 30th day, 10th month, 1662 In the Registry of Deeds, book 9, leaf 29, date of October 13, 1690, we find that Thomas Maul of Salem, merchant, for forty-five pounds conveyed to "Josiah and Daniel Southwicke, Samuel Gaskin, Caleb Buffum, Christopher Foster, and Sarah Stone, all of Salem, in New England, Samuel Collins of Lynn, and several others of ye people called Quakers, in ye county of Essex in New England, a small tract or parcel of land containing about four rods or poles, be it more or be it less, being situate in ye town of Salem aforesaid, bounded easterly and southerly by said Maul, westerly by land in possession John Richards of Salem, northerly by the main broad street or highway just as it lies and is now fenced together, with a meetinghouse which stands upon said land, for the use of the above named and several other of ye people commonly called Quakers, to worship and serve God in" The before mentioned meeting house was the first Quaker meeting house in Salem, and the Samuel Gaskill mentioned is without doubt the son of Edward, who married Provided Southwick, and was punished for attending the Quaker meeting In 1716 they sold this meeting house and the land to Thomas Maul, of Salem, for twenty-five pounds, and two years later Daniel Southwick, Samuel Gaskill, Caleb Buffum and Samuel Collins having bought another lot on the other side of the way, more commodious for setting a meeting house, and erected a meeting house thereon, etc (See deed recorded November 18, 1718, vol xxxii, p 202, Registry of Deeds) This was the second Quaker meeting house in Salem The children of Samuel Gaskill and Provided Southwick Samuel, born 23, 11th month, 1663, Edward, born October 23, 1667, Hannah, born January 2, 1669, Provided, born April 22, 1672

(III) Samuel Gaskill, born 23, 11th month, 1663, married Bethiah Gardner, daughter of Thomas Gardner, Jr, and his wife Hannah, February 18, 1723-4 Mr Gaskill owned four rights to common land in the two lower parishes of Salem By his will dated September 1, 1725, we find the names of several of his children 1 Samuel 2 Nathan 3 Jonathan, married Alice Pickering, of Salem, and had Jonathan, married Hannah Estes, November 30, 1761 4 Hannah, married David Nichols 5 Content, and 6 Sarah, both unmarried, also four other daughters, names not given, ten children in all Nathan had, January 18, 1726, eighty acres of land in Mendon, and Jonathan had eighteen acres laid out to him in the same town in February, 1737-8

(IV) Samuel Gaskill married Sarah ——, and was living in Salem in 1722, a shipwright by occupation April 8, 1736, he purchased of Stephen Swett a large farm which was formerly the property of John Cass, situated in the south parish of

Mendon (now Blackstone) whither he removed, and where he died in September 1761. In his will dated December 5, 1758, his son Ebenezer was named executor. An inventory of the estate was filed October 28, 1761. His children were: Samuel, died prior to December 5, 1758; Ebenezer, Joseph, Stephen, Benjamin, Sarah, married Richard Estes; Huldah, married Benjamin Cook; Elizabeth.

(V) Ebenezer Gaskill married Hannah Girdler (or Gurley), July 15, 1745. He resided in the south parish of Mendon, now Blackstone. Their children were: George, married Sarah Read, November 5, 1767; David, Peter, Joseph, Samuel, married (first) Olive Cook, May 27, 1784, and had Hannah, Naum and Sarah.

(VI) Peter Gaskill, born 1763, died May 17, 1846, married, January 20, 1790, Hannah Thompson, of Mendon, who was the mother of his children. She died July 1, 1809, in the forty-seventh year of her age. He married (second) Esther Scott, widow of David Metcalf. He resided in the south parish of Mendon, now Blackstone. He was a very thrifty farmer, and left a large estate for his time. His will was dated November 24, 1830, in which he provided for the care of his wife Esther, gave each of his six daughters one thousand dollars, and named his son Peter sole executor. He also mentioned the following children: 1. Lebbeus. 2. Elisha. 3. Dianna, married Daniel Aldrich. 4. Sally, married William Metcalf. 5. Asenath, married Joseph Aldrich. 6. Mariah, married Thomas Aldrich. 7. Hannah, married Caleb Thayer, Jr. 8. Anne, married Samuel Verry. 9. Peter, died unmarried, September 18, 1846, before his father's will had been approved. This Peter Gaskill left a will dated September 17, 1846, by which he bequeathed the farm where he lived to Albert and David Gaskill, sons of his brothers, Lebbeus and Elisha. By an inventory of the Peter Gaskill estate, dated October 10, 1846, and returned October 27, same year, we learn that the value of the estate was $21,097.83.

(VII) Lebbeus Gaskill married Susan DeWitt. He was by occupation a farmer, and called of Cumberland, Rhode Island, but was the proprietor of lands in Mendon, south parish. His will was dated December 23, 1861, and the inventory was returned March 16, 1863. He died February 9, 1863, aged sixty-nine years, seven months and ten days. The widow, Susan Gaskill, then of Smithfield, Rhode Island, made her will October 15, 1867. Their children were: Albert, born April 9, 1821; Warren, born August 31, 1822.

(VIII) Albert Gaskill married Anna Smith Comstock, December 30, 1840, Rev. Adin Ballou performing the ceremony. Mr. Gaskill was a farmer and an extensive dealer in real estate. His children were: 1. Alice K., attended Oread Institute, Worcester, 1869 and 1870, married Charles Wilson, who is deceased, and they have one child, also deceased. 2. Francis Almon.

(IX) Judge Francis Almon Gaskill was born January 3, 1846, at the family home in that part of Mendon now known as Blackstone. He attended the schools in his native town and after taking a course at the Woonsocket High School entered Brown University, from which institution he graduated in 1866 at the age of twenty years. For a year he served as private tutor for a family in Newport, and at the close of this engagement entered the Harvard Law School, remaining there a year and a half, when he came to Worcester and continued the study of law in the office of Hon. George F. Verry, one of the most noted and accomplished lawyers in central Massachusetts. After being admitted to the bar in 1869 an association was formed for the practice of law under the style of Verry & Gaskill, resulting in a most successful business career, and which was brought to a close by the death of Mr. Verry in 1883. In 1875 and 1876 Mr. Gaskill served the city of Worcester as a member of the common council. After the death of Hon. George F. Verry, Mr. Gaskill became associated with a stepson, Horace Verry, Esq. For ten years this firm continued, and during this time Mr. Gaskill was district attorney for the middle district of Massachusetts, holding that office from 1887 to 1895, when he was appointed by Governor Greenhalge associate justice of the superior courts of Massachusetts, an office which he now holds.

Judge Gaskill has served the city of Worcester as a director of the Free Public Library for several years, and as president of the board in 1888, and as trustee of both Brown University and Worcester Academy. His fondness for books, of which he possesses a rare assortment, brings him into the circle of various literary and social bodies, notably the Club of Odd Volumes of Boston, also the University Club of that city, the Worcester Club and the Tatnuck Country Club. He is vice-president of the People's Savings Bank, and director of the State Mutual Life Assurance Company. Brown University in 1899 gave him the degree of LL. D., and recently paid him an honor by placing him upon its Board of Fellows. In politics Judge Gaskill is a strong Republican, and at various times has given valuable aid to the promotion of the principles of that party upon the political platform, being a forcible and polished speaker.

Judge Gaskill married (first), 1869, Katherine M., daughter of A. B. and Ann Eliza Whittaker, of Providence, Rhode Island, where Mr. Whittaker was a prominent merchant. She died in 1889, having borne to her husband two children: Mary M., and George A. Gaskill. Judge Gaskill married (second) Josephine L., daughter of Joseph and Phebe Abbott, of Providence, Rhode Island. No children have been born of this marriage. Judge Gaskill attends the First Baptist Church in Worcester.

George A. Gaskill, only son of Judge Francis Almon and Katherine M. (Whittaker) Gaskill, was born in Worcester, June 4, 1877. He graduated from Worcester Academy, class of 1894, and from Brown University, A. B., 1898. He attended Harvard Law school two years, was admitted to the bar 1901, and has since practiced law in Worcester in the office of Herbert Parker, attorney general of Massachusetts. He was elected a trustee of Worcester Academy, 1905. He married, June 1, 1905, Caroline Dewey Nichols, daughter of Dr. Charles L. Nichols, and granddaughter of Judge Francis H. Dewey.

ROBINSON FAMILY OF DORCHESTER. James Robinson (1), the immigrant ancestor of Hannah Caroline (Robinson) Davis of Worcester, was born in England and came to this country about 1660, when a young man. There is no proof that he was related to any of the numerous other immigrants of this surname among the early settlers, nor is there any clue yet discovered whereby his birthplace in England could be discovered. This difficulty in tracing the family in England is of course the rule with all the Puritan fathers, and the difficulties are enormously increased in the case of a family bearing a surname like Robinson because of the great number of persons of the same name at the same time.

James Robinson settled in Dorchester and was admitted a freeman there in 1669. He died here

April 18 1694 His name appears in the seating of the church March 17, 1693-94, in the 'fourth men's below" His wife was admitted to the church February 15 1673-74, and a month later on the strength of her membership her four children were baptized—James Thomas, Samuel and Mary He married September 27, 1664, Mary Alcock, daughter of Thomas Alcock, now generally spelled Olcott She died March 13, 1718 aged seventy-three years Children of James and Mary Robinson were 1 James, born November 8, 1665 was soldier in the Canada expedition in 1690 under Captain John Withington there is no record of his having any family at Dorchester 2 Thomas born April 15 1668 3 Samuel born September 4, 1670 4 Mary, born March 17, 1673, died young 5 John, born April 17, 1675, see forward (Many of the early writers have followed excellent authority in calling this John the Rev John Robinson, who became the minister at Duxbury in 1701 and preached there until dismissed in 1738 but it has been shown that he was the son of Samuel Robinson of Dorchester, possibly a brother or some relative of James he died at Lebanon Connecticut, 1745, aged seventy-four years making him several years older than John son of James Robinson (1) mentioned above) 6 Henry born June 21 1678 died young 7 Ebenezer, born January 5, 1682, killed at Port Royal, May 27 1707, while fighting with the Americans and British against the French

(II) John Robinson son of James Robinson (1) was born in Dorchester Massachusetts, April 17 1675 He seems to have been a quiet citizen like his father He joined the church October 15 1699 and owned the covenant February 22, 1701-02 He died at Dorchester February 6, 1742-43 He married Mary —— who died at Dorchester December 22 1713 He married (second), January 20, 1714-15 Ruth Burt Only two children were recorded at Dorchester viz 1 James born May 19 baptized May 21 1704 2 John, Jr, born March 20, 1706-07 see forward

(III) John Robinson Jr son of John Robinson (2) of Dorchester was born there March 20 1706-07 He seems to have been a prominent citizen of Dorchester and is called Major doubtless serving in the Colonial wars He died in 1767 He married Susannah Williams born 1706 and died 1804 Their children all born at Dorchester, were John born July 28 1728, probably captain in the revolution, Mary born January 12 1730-31, Captain James, see forward, Ebenezer born March 25 1735 died young Ruth born December 19, 1737 Ebenezer, born September 27 1741, Stephen born January 4 1748

(IV) Captain James Robinson, son of John Robinson Jr (3), was born in Dorchester, Massachusetts January 30, 1732, and died there March 14, 1808 He seems to have been a soldier in the revolution in Captain Ebenezer Withington's company, Colonel John Robinson's regiment April 19, 1775, at the battle of Lexington Later he became captain of the militia and commanded a company in the regiment of Colonel Ezra Bedlam during Shays's Rebellion' in 1787 He was one of the signers of the Suffolk Resolves He was on a committee with a number of other Dorchester men to remonstrate with the general court against the annexation of Dorchester Neck to Boston January 23 1804 He married Sarah Breck born in 1736 and died 1797 They lived at Dorchester and their children all born there were 1 Stephen see forward, 2 James, born July 17 1756 3 Edward born December 26, 1758 4 John born November 27 1761 5 John, born July, 1763 6 Joseph, born June 18, 1766 7 Sarah Breck, February 2, 1769 8 Susanna, born June 8, 1771

(V) Lieutenant Stephen Robinson, eldest son of Captain James Robinson (4), was born in Dorchester, Massachusetts, August 23, 1776, and died there October 24, 1852 He was lieutenant of the First Brigade of Artillery, First Division, in 1806 He married April 11, 1805, at Dorchester Hannah Withington, daughter of Ebenezer Withington, who was a soldier in the revolution, a minute man at Lexington The children of Stephen and Hannah Robinson were Stephen Augustus, see forward, James Ebenezer, born December 16, 1810, James Withington, February 21, 1812, Hannah Withington, July 10, 1814, John Flavel January 29, 1817, Mary Withington, April 30, 1819, Edward Breck, May 29, 1821

(VI) Captain Stephen Augustus Robinson, eldest child of Stephen Robinson (5), was born at Dorchester, Massachusetts, May 3, 1806 (family record May 5), and died there June 9, 1863 He settled at Dorchester and married Mary Capen, daughter of Joseph Capen, of Canton, Massachusetts

CHARLES FREEMAN READ Esdras Read (1), the immigrant ancestor of Charles Freeman Read, of Worcester, was born in England, the son of Mathew Read The name Esdras is sometimes found Ezra A tract of land was granted him by the town of Boston of which he was a proprietor as early as 1638 His place was at Muddy river, now Brookline, but he removed that year to Salem and was a proprietor of the town He was admitted to the Salem church, May 10, 1640, and his wife Alice December 29, 1640, when Rev John Fiske was pastor, and went with him and his church to Wenham then called Enon, meaning much water," in 1643 He was deputy to the general court from Wenham in 1648 and also in 1651 He was sent in 1655 by Rev Mr Fiske and his church to look out for a more commodious settlement and he selected Chelmsford The next spring Rev Mr Fiske, Mr Read and a majority of the church members removed to that place While at Wenham he was deacon of the church In 1658 he was again admitted an inhabitant of Boston, where he died in 1680, and his gravestone is now standing in Copps Hill cemetery He was a tailor by trade and owned considerable property on Copps Hill at the time of his death Administration was granted December 17, 1680, to his son, Obediah Read, of Boston Esdras Read married Alice Ward

(II) Obediah Read, son of Esdras Read (1), was born about 1639 He married Anna Swift, of Boston She died September 13, 1680 The record of his death is on his gravestone in Copps Hill cemetery, Boston, as February 19, 1721 He was a carpenter by trade The children of Obediah and Anna Read Thomas born 1665 see forward, Rebecca, 1668, Elizabeth 1669 Sarah, 1671, Anna, 1672, Obediah Jr 1677, James 1679

(III) Thomas Read, son of Obediah Read (2), was born in Boston in 1665 He went back to Chelmsford and had a grant of land from the town The name of his first wife is not known He married (second) Hannah —— His children by the first wife were Thomas born 1687 see forward, Jonathan, William, Esdras John The children of Thomas and Hannah Benjamin Timothy

(IV) Thomas Read son of Thomas Read (3), was born at Chelmsford, Massachusetts, 1687, and married Sarah Fletcher He was a prominent man in the town of Chelmsford and held the office of justice of the peace He died December 24, 1773,

Chas. F. Read

aged eighty-six years The Reads were the first settlers in that part of Chelmsford, now Westford The children of Thomas and Sarah Sarah, born 1712 Timothy, 1714, see forward, Eleazer, 1731, Benjamin 1732

(V) Timothy Read, son of Thomas Read (4), was born at Chelmsford, Massachusetts, March 21, 1714 He married, November 10, 1732, Mary Cummings He moved from Chelmsford to Dunstable, Massachusetts, when that town included the present towns of Dunstable, Nashua, Nashville, Hollis and parts of the towns of Pelham, Londonderry, Hudson, Merrimac and Townsend, some now of New Hampshire some of Massachusetts, having an area of two hundred square miles For many years Dunstable was on the frontier and the early settlers were exposed to Indian attack frequently Many outrages were committed there by the Indians and many deeds of valor and heroism by the white men The children of Timothy and Mary Read Elizabeth, born 1733 Mary 1734, Timothy, Jr, 1736 Eleazer 1749

(VI) Eleazer Read son of Timothy Read (5), was born in Dunstable, Massachusetts, February, 1749 He was a soldier in the revolutionary war and fought in the battle of Bunker Hill He married Rachel Cummings Their children Rachel born January 4 1770, Rhoda, November 26, 1772, Caleb, August 7 1775 see forward, Leonard, 1777, Rebecca 1779 Betsey, December 17 1780

(VII) Caleb Read son of Eleazer Read (6), was born in Dunstable Massachusetts August 7 1775 died November 28, 1838 He was a captain in the militia and served as such in the war of 1812 He married Sarah Richardson and their children were Calvin, see forward, James, born in 1799 Rachel, Abigail

(VIII) Calvin Read, son of Caleb Read (7), was born in Dunstable Massachusetts, January 20, 1798 He was educated in the common schools He was a farmer during his active life In religion he was a Universalist, in politics a Democrat He was a very skillful fifer and used to play a great deal for parades and military occasions He married Catherine Baxter, born December 30, 1799 in Hawley Massachusetts Their children Sarah Richardson born in Hawley January 4 1821 Calvin Dwight, born at Ashfield, February 28 1824 William Eleazer, born in Hawley June 25 1828, Caroline Rathbone born in Hawley, December 19, 1829, Calista Blood, born in Hawley July 13, 1831 Anna Eliza, born in Dunstable February 8 1833, Charles Freeman, see forward James Alonzo, born at Dunstable November 9 1839 Emily Etta born in Lennox, New York, September 2, 1844 All deceased except Calista, Charles F James A and Emily E

(IX) Charles Freeman Read son of Calvin Read (8) was born in Dunstable, Massachusetts August 7 1835 He received his early education in the public and high schools working when not in school, on the homestead He went with his father's family to Lennox Madison county New York, in 1841 and worked with his father on the farm there until 1852 He then went to Fitchburg Massachusetts, and attended the high school He began his career in business at Gardner where he became clerk in a general store February 21 1853 He remained in this store as clerk and bookkeeper for five years He then entered the employ of Greenwood & Wright, chair manufacturers of Gardner as shipping clerk and bookkeeper Later he became a member of the firm and was for many years identified with the chair manufacturing business of Gardner He retired from business and removed to Worcester in 1896 His home there is on Burncoat street corner Marie avenue Mr Read has always been a Republican in politics He was elected to various positions of honor and trust in Gardner He was town auditor, assessor, and member of the school committee During the civil war he served three years in the cavalry At the expiration of his term of enlistment he was mustered out as first sergeant in "Read's" company, Third Massachusetts Cavalry, Second Division, Nineteenth Army Corps He served under Generals Banks, Butler and Sheridan He was in the Department of the Gulf and in Shenandoah Valley He was at the battle of Cedar Creek. He saw Sheridan's famous ride

Mr Read joined the Evangelical Congregational church in Gardner, Massachusetts, in 1858 That church afterward merged into and became a part of the First Congregational Church of Gardner He remained in that church until 1896 when removing to Worcester, he changed his membership to the First Congregational (Old South) church, Worcester Since 1902 he has been parish clerk of Old South While at Gardner he was superintendent of the Sunday school for a number of years In 1865 he joined Hope Lodge, A F and A M, of which he was master in 1876 and of which he is at present an honorary member He was commander of D G Farragut Post, No 116, G A R, in 1880 and 1881 He was a member of the Massachusetts staff of the national commander, G A R, in 1895 He is a member of George H Ward Post, No 10, G A R of Worcester, and served for four years on the library committee He was elected quartermaster of the post March 15 1906

Mr Read married, at Gardner, Massachusetts, December 15, 1858, Catherine Augusta Wright born April 9 1839 daughter of David and Elizabeth (Gay) Wright, granddaughter of Joseph Wright, who came from Sterling to Gardner, settled on Wright Hill, married Rebecca Nichols Of the children of Joseph Wright Rebecca born June 25 1791, married Walter Greenwood, Martha, born July 12, 1802, married Levi Heywood, the chair manufacturer; and Emily, born December 24, 1814 married Seth Heywood the chair manufacturer, all of Gardner David Wright was one of the pioneers in the manufacture of cane and wooden seat chairs He was one of a family of eleven children and lived to the advanced age of ninety-one years He was born in Gardner October 25 1808 Catherine was educated in the public and high schools and academy and taught school for some time before marriage She was eligible for membership in the Daughters of the American Revolution through her maternal ancestors She died at Gardner April 10, 1889

Mr Read married (second), at Worcester, January 1 1896, Oella Elizabeth Stone She is eligible to membership in the Daughters of the American Revolution through her great-grandfather, Jeduthan Stone, son of Nathan and Mary Stone born January 13 1748 served in the revolutionary army under Captain Thomas Eusts marching from Rutland to Cambridge April 19 1775 Jeduthan married January 11, 1773 Elizabeth Howe, who bore him seven children Mrs Read's grandfather was Augustus Stone and her father, Joseph Stone who married Martha E Maynard Oella was educated in the public schools and at Worcester Academy The children of Charles Freeman and Catherine Augusta Read Ettie Elizabeth born in Gardner, March 11, 1860, died 1884 married A F Knowlton had one son Stanley Read Knowlton Charles Clarence, born in Gardner January 2, 1862 graduate of the Gardner high school, commercial traveler selling chairs and furniture, married Annie Hurlbut and they have three daughters—Katherine, Alice, and Esther Gertrude Wright born in Gardner, August

26, 1866, died 1901, married A. F. Knowlton, whose first wife was her sister Ettie E.; their three children—Dorothy, Henry Hazel, David Wright, born in Gardner, November 27, 1874, died aged three years and two months.

JAMES ATKINSON NORCROSS. The emigrant ancestor, Jeremiah Norcross (1), came from England to America in the year 1638, and from "Bond's History and Genealogies of Watertown, Massachusetts," we learn that he was a proprietor in that place, as early as 1642, his family then consisting of wife Adrean and three children, Nathaniel, Richard and Sarah. The original homestead in Watertown covered about twenty-six acres, the title to which was held within the family for more than one hundred and sixty years. A portion of this estate was later purchased by the United States government, and is now the location of the Watertown arsenal. The senior Mr. Norcross, in 1654, when arranging to visit England, executed a will in which the various members of his family are mentioned, leaving at his death the greater part of his estate to his son Richard. The brother Nathaniel received the degree of A. B. at "Catherine Hall College," Cambridge, 1636-37, was called to become the minister at Lancaster, and signed with others a petition to the general court to plant a settlement there. But there being so much delay in preparing for the settlement and building the early houses, that his attention was called in another direction, he is said to have returned to England in 1646. His father died in England in 1657.

(II) Richard Norcross, born in England, 1621, was the possessor of a small estate at Watertown in 1642. He was chosen to act as the first schoolmaster in that town, and from 1651 to about the year 1700 followed the occupation of a school teacher, and for nearly a quarter of a century was the only person in the town to fill that office. He married (first) Mary Brooks, daughter of Captain Thomas Brooks. She died in 1671, and he married (second) Susanna, widow of William Shattuck. Mr. Norcross died in 1709, leaving six children, the eldest, Mary, having died in 1661.

(III) Nathaniel Norcross, born in Watertown, December 18, 1665, was a shoemaker, and resided in Watertown and Sudbury. He married (first) Mehitable Hagar. She died April 5, 1691, and he married (second) Susanna, daughter of Dr. Philip Shattuck, of Watertown. She died in Sudbury, February 15, 1711-12. He died in 1717, leaving a family of four children.

(IV) Philip Norcross, born March 5, 1698, married, in 1721, Sarah, daughter of Edward Jackson, of Newton, and settled in that town, their home being on the site of the present Eliot meeting house. Philip Norcross died in 1748, leaving nine children.

(V) Jonathan Norcross, born February 7, 1734-35, the fifth child of Philip Norcross, was a soldier in the French and Indian war, and at Lake George in 1758. Two years later he removed to Georgetown, Maine, where he married Martha, daughter of James Springer. In 1775, he was a resident of Readville, Maine, but we have no record of his death. His wife died in 1809, and was buried at Hollowell, Maine.

(VI) Jonathan Norcross, Jr., born 1767, married Jane Atkinson, of Lancaster, England, and resided during the greater portion of his life in Wayne, Maine, where he owned a farm. It is believed at his death he was buried in Winthrop, Maine. His widow died and was buried in Salem, Massachusetts.

(VII) Jesse Springer Norcross, son of Jonathan Norcross, Jr., was born in Wayne, Maine, in 1800. He was a carpenter and builder, also proprietor of the "Norcross Mills," at Winslow, Maine. He married, in 1826, Margaret Ann Whitney, of Westboro, Massachusetts. They resided in various places in the state of Maine, among them the towns of Clinton and Winslow. In 1843 he removed to Salem, Massachusetts, where he continued to ply his occupation as carpenter and builder. In the year 1849 he joined the great concourse of seekers for gold in California. He died the following year and was buried at Benicia, in that state. His widow, Margaret Ann (Whitney) Norcross, was the daughter of Jonah and Anna (Rider) Whitney. The father of Jonah was Thomas Whitney, a revolutionary soldier from the town of Shrewsbury, Thomas being in the fifth generation from the emigrant ancestor, John Whitney, who settled in Watertown, Massachusetts, and was admitted freeman there in 1635-36. The children of Jesse Springer and Margaret Ann (Whitney) Norcross were: Rosina C., Julia and James A., twins, Elizabeth, Orlando W., William, died at sea, when nineteen years of age, Leander, who died an infant, and Charles Henry, died when four years of age. As the business career of the two brothers, James Atkinson, born March 24, 1831, and Orlando Whitney, born October 25, 1839, appears so closely interwoven, it seems highly proper that they should be reviewed together.

James Atkinson Norcross, eldest son of Jesse Springer and Margaret Ann (Whitney) Norcross, born March 24, 1831, in Kennebec county, Maine, was a mere lad when the family removed to Salem, Massachusetts. The early death of his father placed upon his shoulders heavy responsibilities. Having inherited in a large degree the mechanical genius of his father, he learned the trade of a carpenter, which he followed at Salem a number of years. In 1864, upon the return of his brother Orlando from his three years service in the war of the rebellion, the two formed a partnership which continued until the year 1897. The style of the firm was Norcross Brothers, and their business career was started in Essex county, Massachusetts, in the city of Salem, but they soon removed to the city of Worcester to gain a larger field in which to labor. The Leicester Congregational Church was their first large contract. The excellent manner in which that contract was filled gave the firm an enviable reputation among building contractors, and from that date onward they were awarded a large share of the contracts given out for expensive structures erected within their immediate locality. As their facilities for executing work, and the quality of their workmanship became known to the public, demand for their services came not only from the various cities and towns in the New England states, but far and near throughout the United States, until there was scarcely a city among those most prominent in the Union but what contained a sample of their handiwork.

During the thirty-three years of most unprecedented business prosperity, James A. Norcross attended to the clerical and financial part, while Orlando Norcross gave attention to directing the men in their employ, an arrangement which proved to ensure signal success. They erected factories, equipped with the latest improved machinery, where they manufacture doors, sash and all necessary finish required by their contracts, and the firm soon became conspicuous for reasonable prices, promptness, and the skillful way in which all of their contracts were met. Scores of magnificent structures erected by this firm may be found noted in the personal sketch of

Mrs James A Norcross

J A Norcross

the brother partner, Orlando, which follows at the conclusion of the notice of James A, who retired from the firm in 1897 for the purpose of enjoying some of the ease and comfort to which a lifetime of labor and steady brain work entitled him For years he had resided in an elegant mansion on Claremont street, Worcester, built of Longmeadow sandstone, but he sought better and more roomy surroundings, and after purchasing a tract of land containing several acres, situated on May street, a short distance west from his Claremont street home, upon a beautiful eminence, furnishing a commanding view of the surrounding country, he reared his "Fairlawn," and passed the remainder of his days within this home of beauty and luxury, into which he with his family removed in July, 1895 After his retirement from business he visited various portions of the United States for the purpose of inspecting rare and choice specimens of work produced by his craft, and in February, 1892, in company with his wife, visited the Old World, passing considerable time in England, France, Holland, and Italy, enjoying the scenes and meditating on the contrast between the New and the Old World

James A Norcross was not a seeker of public office although he served the city one term as a member of the common council in 1877 He was a member of the Worcester Board of Trade, the Commonwealth Club, the Sportsman and Continental Clubs, also the Worcester County Mechanics' Association In the building of the South Unitarian Church he was one of the most liberal contributors In this society he took an active interest, and within its circle found his religious home He was a man of charitable disposition, and his kindliness was often evinced by his many acts of charity He died at his home, August 4, 1903, and was survived by his widow, who was Mary Ellen Pinkham, and their children, as follows

1 Julia Ellen, born October 14, 1851, married, June 8, 1871, at Worcester, Thomas Seymour Osborne, of Nova Scotia, and had children John Seymour, born February 28, 1872, died an infant, Mary Gertrude, May 5, 1873, married Alfred Merrifield, of Worcester, Florence Elizabeth, born April 27, 1875, died July 9, 1902 She married, 1892, Fred A Corey, of Worcester, and had children Charles E, died August 29, 1893, James Earle, born April 27, 1896, Fred, born September 10, 1900 Rosie Winifred, born April 5, 1878, married, January 18, 1899 Harry E Mayo, of Worcester, and had one child, Virginia, born June 3, 1899 John Edwin Norcross, born August 24 1880, married Nellie Billings James William Thomas, born July 24, 1882, married Ethel Comstock, and have Lawrence Wilmot Arthur Wilmot born February 7, 1888, died January 18, 1889 Ellen, born September 28, 1890 David Benjamin, born July 7, 1894

2 James Ephraim, born 1853, in Salem, died 1855

3 James Franklin Norcross, born in Salem, Massachusetts, January 8, 1856 He attended the common schools there, and in South Adams and Worcester, in turn He left school at the early age of fourteen years to enter the employ of Norcross Brothers and took up carpentering, in which he continued almost three years He then went to East Longmeadow, Massachusetts, to learn quarrying and stone cutting After ten years he was made superintendent of all this business for Norcross Brothers and served in that capacity until April 1, 1897 when he resigned, and later engaged in the same line of business on his own account After a year he sold his plant and on December 1, 1898, removed to Springfield, Massachusetts, where he has since resided He was engaged in caring for his father's business and arranging his own affairs until 1901, when he bought an interest in the Westfield Marble and Sandstone Company, a corporation doing business in Westfield, Massachusetts, where their quarries are located He was vice-president and manager from the time he entered the company until 1906, when his widowed mother, desiring his assistance in the management of her affairs, he resigned the position of manager, but has retained to the present time, that of vice-president While in East Longmeadow, Mr Norcross attended the Congregational church, and served as a member of its parish committee, and was also for one year secretary of the school board In 1882 he joined Hampden Lodge No 27, I O O F, of Springfield, Massachusetts, of which he is yet a member In politics he is a Republican He married, March 7, 1878, Sarah Etta Robinson, born in East Longmeadow, Massachusetts, July 13, 1857, a daughter of Jonas and Martha (Bradbury) Robinson, her father is a leading stone cutter and setter To Mr and Mrs Norcross were born two children Jonas Walter, May 23, 1879, and Mary Etha, August 21, 1882

4 Arthur Warren, born at Salem, Massachusetts, July 27, 1861 He received his education in the Worcester public schools, graduating from Woodland grammar school in June 1878 In the fall of that year he entered the Classical High School, where he continued his studies for a time, subsequently taking a course in Bryant & Stratton's Business College at Boston In 1881 he entered the employ of Norcross Brothers, contractors and builders, where he remained about a year, subsequently removing to New York city, Baltimore, Cleveland and other cities in the employ of the firm until about 1897, when he became a partner in the firm of Norcross & Cleveland, contractors and builders, of Boston This firm built the present Brewer building on Front street, Worcester Mr Norcross, since the dissolution of Norcross & Cleveland, continued as contractor until recently, and is at present superintendent of a large building concern in New York city He was an attendant of the First Universalist Church at Worcester, and is a Republican in politics He married, December 18, 1888, Alice Willard Warren, born in Worcester, adopted daughter of Otis and Caroline E Warren, of Worcester One child was born to them, Pauline, born September 12, 1890, died February 10, 1892

5 Rosa Minerva, born in Salem, June 2, 1863, died April 5, 1877

6 William Ephraim, born at Salem, Massachusetts, May 11, 1866 At the age of three years he removed with his parents to Worcester, where he attended the public schools at Woodland street, from which he graduated, taking a year's course in the Classical High School He then entered the employ of Norcross Brothers, where he was paymaster of the outside help for two years, after which time he entered the shipping department as head shipper, continuing for three years Subsequently he entered the office of the draughting department where he remained for two and a half years About a year before the dissolution of partnership of Norcross Brothers, he became interested in the affairs of "Fairlawn," the estate of his father, where he assumed charge of the farm and has remained in charge of affairs to the present day In 1898 he built his residence at "Fairlawn," adjoining the home of his father, where he resided until the death of his father August 4 1903, when he came to live with his family at "Fairlawn" Mr Norcross is an attendant of the South Unitarian Memor-

ial Church in which he has served as treasurer and clerk. He is a Republican in politics and a member of the Worcester Automobile Club, he was a member for two years of the Lakeside Boat Club and for three years of the Commonwealth Club. He married November 23, 1890, Lillian Mabel Blenus, born at South Dedham, Massachusetts, June 17, 1867, daughter of Charles W. and Vesta (Gates) Blenus, of Worcester, Massachusetts. Charles W. Blenus was a piano case maker, a veteran of the civil war, and a member of Post No. 10, G. A. R. The children of Mr. and Mrs. Norcross are: Hazel, born August 19, 1893; Rosemary, born November 26, 1899.

7. Mary Elizabeth, born at South Adams, Massachusetts, October 31, 1868, married September 20, 1892, William Lorin Davis, of Millbury, Massachusetts, a brick manufacturer. One child, Margaret, born at Worcester, Massachusetts, January 10, 1896.

8. Florence A., born in Worcester, 1871, died July 9, 1871.

9. Jesse Orlando, born at Worcester, Massachusetts, December 1, 1875. He received his education in the Woodland street grammar school, the private school of John Dalzell on West street, where he remained two years. He then entered the employ of Norcross Brothers as clerk and bookkeeper in his father's office. Here he remained about two years and then entered the employ of his brother, who was of the firm of Norcross & Cleveland. In the latter position he began to learn the trade of carpenter, and later became a journeyman in the business. He remained about two years in their employ. In 1901 he purchased an eleven acre farm on Millbury avenue just over the line in Millbury, where he built an elegant mansion and engaged in the poultry business for some time; he still resides at this place. In January, 1905, the firm of Norcross & Shiland under Massachusetts laws was incorporated with quarters at 214 Summer street, for the sale of automobiles. Jesse O. Norcross is the president and director, H. E. Shiland secretary, S. Norcross, clerk of the corporation. Mr. Shiland retired from the company six months later. In February, 1906, the company moved to more commodious quarters at the corner of Foster and Commercial street, the firm name having changed to that of Norcross Automobile Company, agents for the "Packard," "Peerless," and "Auto Car." Mr. Norcross is an attendant of the South Unitarian Memorial Church, a Republican in politics, a member of Worcester Grange, No. 22, Patrons of Husbandry, the Worcester Automobile Club and was formerly a member of the Lakeside Boat Club. He was a charter member of Wellington Rifles, Company H, Second Regiment, Massachusetts Volunteer Militia, enlisting as private at its organization May 2, 1894, serving three years. He married, December 16, 1896, Maud Marie Smith, born July 13, 1877, daughter of Marcus M. and Ann Elizabeth (Butterfield) Smith, of Keene, New Hampshire. Marcus M. Smith has been connected with the foundry department of the Crompton & Knowles Company.

Mrs. Mary Ellen Norcross, widow of James Atkinson Norcross, was born January 8, 1835, in Peabody, Massachusetts, daughter of Hicks and Mary B. Pinkham. Her father was born October 6, 1806, in New Hampshire and died December 23, 1849; he was a contractor and carpenter; his wife, the mother of Mrs. Norcross, was born in Massachusetts December 16, 1806, and died January 21, 1850. Mrs. James A. Norcross is possessed of like charitable and philanthropic traits of character with her lamented husband. Like him she has always been deeply attached to the South Unitarian Church of Worcester, to which, since her husband's death, she has presented the sum of $20,000 for the liquidation of its debt. Her benefactions have been constantly extended to all worthy purposes.

CHARLES ANDREW FLETCHER. Robert Fletcher (1) was the emigrant of Charles Andrew Fletcher of Worcester. The family name is doubtless of French origin, signifying archer. While some genealogists state that the family came to England first at the time of William the Norman, others believe that the first of the name was Jean de la Flechiere, who came to England with the Duke of Savoy in the thirteenth century. He came from Burgundy, now the Canton de Vaud of Switzerland. His son Henry and other descendants were prominent in English and Scotch history.

Robert Fletcher, the emigrant, was born as shown by the record of his death in 1592. Family tradition has it that he was from Yorkshire, England. He settled in Concord, Massachusetts, early. He is said to have come to New England in 1630. He was appointed the constable of the town of Concord by the general court, November 2, 1637. He removed to Chelmsford and joined with William Fletcher and others in 1654 in inviting Mr. John Fiske and the Wenham Church to remove to Chelmsford. His will was made February 4, 1672, "aged about fourscore," as the will has it. He commits his wife to the care of his son Francis and his wife and bequeaths also to sons, Francis, William and Samuel. The inventory was dated May 12, 1677. He died April 3, 1677, at Concord, at the age of eighty-five years. He was counted among the most influential and wealthy men of the vicinity. The children of Robert Fletcher were: Luke, born in England, died in Concord May 21, 1665, probably unmarried; William, born in England, 1622, settled in Chelmsford, Massachusetts; Cary, married —— Kebby; Samuel, see forward; Francis, born in Concord, Massachusetts, 1636, settled there.

(II) Samuel Fletcher, son of Robert Fletcher (1), was born in Concord, Massachusetts, in 1632. He was admitted a freeman March 21, 1689-90. He settled in that part of Chelmsford now Westford, Massachusetts. He married Margaret Hailston, October 10, 1659. He died December 9, 1697, and his grave is in the Middle Chelmsford cemetery. The inscription on the headstone reads: "Here lyes ye body of Samuel Fletcher aged 65 years died December 9, 1697." The children of Samuel and Margaret (Hailston) Fletcher were: Samuel, born in Concord, Massachusetts, 1661, married Mary Cotton; Sarah, born August 24, 1663; Hannah, born September 26, 1669; William, see forward.

(III) William Fletcher, youngest son of Samuel Fletcher (2), was born in Chelmsford, Massachusetts, January 1, 1671. He married there December 10, 1701, Mary ——. He died about 1743. His will (Vol. 21, Page 205, Middlesex) names his living children. His children, all born in Chelmsford, were: William, born 1702, at what is now Westford in Chelmsford, died September 22, 1781; Samuel (captain), born 1707, had fifteen children at Westford; Oliver (H. C. 1735), selectman 1758-61, died December 1, 1771; Thomas, born January 15, 1711; Robert, born April 20, 1713, resided near what is now the Lowell city farm; Benjamin, see forward; Mary, born January 1, 1718; Lydia, born June 1, 1724.

(IV) Benjamin Fletcher, sixth child of William Fletcher (3), was born in Chelmsford, now Westford, Massachusetts, February 22, 1715, died 1774. He lived in Chelmsford and vicinity. He was a prominent man and wealthy for his day, as the inventory of his estate in the possession of Charles A Fletcher shows He was collector of taxes in Chelmsford in 1754 He held other offices His children were Benjamin see forward, Eleazer

(V) Benjamin Fletcher son of Benjamin Fletcher (4) was born probably in Chelmsford, Massachusetts, about 1750 He married, December 4, 1770, Rachel Spaulding, of Chelmsford, and they settled in that town Among their children was Benjamin William or William Benjamin see forward

(VI) Benjamin William Fletcher, as his name is given in the Weare New Hampshire, history son of Benjamin Fletcher (5), was born November 1, 1772, in Chelmsford, Massachusetts He settled in Weare New Hampshire, about a mile north of the Oil Mill village He was a farmer He appears as a taxpayer of Weare as early as 1820 and as late as 1840 and probably lived all his active life in Weare He married Sarah Ballard, and their children were William, removed to Vermont, Harriet Sarah remained in Weare, Susan Benjamin, see forward, Charles B, Beulah, Mary Grace

(VII) Benjamin Franklin Fletcher, son of Benjamin William Fletcher (6) was born in Weare New Hampshire, January 7 1811 died at Manchester, New Hampshire June 18 1886 He married Elvira Adams Wilson of the well known Scotch-Irish Wilson family whose progenitor was among the settlers of Londonderry New Hampshire in 1718 She was a native of New Boston New Hampshire He resided at Manchester, New Hampshire, was a house carpenter and contractor His wife was born April 24 1812 in New Boston, New Hampshire and died in Manchester, September 25, 1886 The children of Benjamin F and Elvira Adams (Wilson) Fletcher were 1 James Franklin Wilson born April 9 1843 died November 13 1902, was a house carpenter, served through the whole civil war in Company E Eighth New Hampshire Regiment he enlisted as a private and was discharged as first lieutenant he resided in Manchester and Nashua where he died never married 2 Eben Harris born in Manchester July 5 1845, died at Manchester, New Hampshire September 5 1868 resided at Manchester New Hampshire and Salem, Massachusetts where he was editor of the *Salem Enterprise*, was captain of a militia company in Manchester, never married 3 Mary Maria married George Warren Currier he is deceased and she resides in Bedford New Hampshire, with her son Allen Fletcher Currier who conducts the farm 4 Sarah Elizabeth married John Milton Todd resides at New Boston New Hampshire, their son Samuel Herbert Todd resides at home 5 Laura A born January 7 1850 died June 1 1853 6 Charles Andrew, born July 17 1851 see forward

(VIII) Charles Andrew Fletcher president of the Clark-Sawyer Company of Worcester was born in Manchester New Hampshire July 17 1851 He was the son of Benjamin Franklin and Elvira Adams (Wilson) Fletcher His mother came from a well known Scotch-Irish family that settled in 1718 in Londonderry New Hampshire Mr Fletcher attended the Manchester public schools After graduating from the grammar school he accepted a clerkship in the crockery store of Charles A Smith in Manchester New Hampshire where he gained his first experience and knowledge of the business in which he has been engaged ever since After a year and a half later he came to Worcester in November, 1869 and went to work for Clark Sawyer & Company then as now the leading store in the crockery, glassware and housefurnishing trade Except for two periods of two years each Mr Fletcher has remained in the Clark-Sawyer store ever since he came to Worcester, serving in various capacities from clerk to president In 1874-75-76 Mr Fletcher was in business in Fitchburg In 1884 he left the company again and established at Gardner, Massachusetts, the Central Oil and Gas Stove Company After two years he was induced by the Clark-Sawyer Company to return and take charge of the house furnishing department The business was incorporated at this time and Mr Fletcher became a director and clerk of the company The company became a Massachusetts corporation in 1890 with a capital of $100,000 The officers for the past few years have been President, Charles A Fletcher, treasurer, George Richardson, secretary, Stephen Sawyer Mr Fletcher has been president since 1897 and during these years the company has enjoyed a season of great growth and prosperity The Clark-Sawyer Company stores occupy 30,000 square feet of floor space in the best business section of Worcester The wholesale department has become the larger and more important end of the business The company has commercial travelers all over New England and they make a specialty of foreign novelties, having their own buyers in the markets abroad every season A characteristic of the house is to take hold of a new invention of an attractive novelty, a specialty for instance having been made of refrigerators Mr Fletcher has for many years given personal attention to the imported goods of the house The holiday trade has grown to enormous proportions in both wholesale and retail departments, owing largely to the attractive line of toys and bric-a-brac of both foreign and domestic manufacture sold there The markets of England Germany, France, Italy, Austria and Bohemia are visited every season The Clark-Sawyer Company carries the largest line of wholesale novelties in New England It is the largest retail house furnishing store in New England and outside of Boston also the largest crockery house

Mr Fletcher is a member of the Commonwealth Club and of the Worcester Society of Antiquity He is a Republican On account of the pressure of business he has in late years withdrawn from most of the clubs and societies to which he formerly belonged

He married October 1, 1874 Helen Maria Shattuck, daughter of Samuel F Shattuck of Worcester They have had two children Helen Esther, born July 1876 married Edward Marcus Dodge (See sketch elsewhere in this work), Charles Shattuck, born July 21 1878 died September 13, 1903, while a junior at Harvard College

STILLMAN HOUGHTON FAMILY Sir Richard Houghton (1) bart, of Houghton Towers, Lancashire England, father of Ralph Houghton, of Lancaster was a progenitor of the Houghton family of Worcester county to which the late Stillman Houghton belonged Sir Richard fought against King Charles although the rest of the family fought for the king If tradition is correct then and John Houghton of Lancaster was cousin of Ralph son of Sir Richard the two men came for opposite reasons to America one because he was against the king the other because he was not That is not important The two cousins seem to have lived amiably side by side in Lancaster the son and nephew of Sir Richard Houghton The Houghton ancestors are traced to Roger de Bushi, one of the followers of William the Conqueror

(II) Ralph Houghton son of Sir Richard Houghton (1) born in England in 1633 died April 15 1705 in Lancaster He is believed to have emigrated to New England in 1635 He was in Lancaster in 1647, and was one of the founders of that town with five others Edward Breck Nathaniel Hadlock William Kerley, Thomas Sawyer John Prescott He was the first town clerk, and the writing of the early records in his hand show that he was not only a good penman but well educated His home was on the Neck He was town clerk for many years was admitted a freeman in 1668, and was deputy to the general court in 1673-89 He was one of the leaders, and was identified with the organization of the town and its government until his death He had to abandon his home with the others at the time of King Philip's war in 1675 In 1682 he settled in Milton He returned to his Lancaster home in 1685 but was again in Milton in 1690 and built a homestead there in which seven generations of descendants have been born He married Jane ——, who was born 1626, in England, and died January 10, 1700-1 Their children were 1 Mary, born January 4 1654 2 John, born April 28, 1655 3 Joseph, born July 6 1657 settled in Milton 4 Experience, born October 1 1659, married May 22, 1784 Ezra Clapp of Dorchester 5 James (see forward) 6 Sarah born February 17 1664 Ralph Houghton, of Dorchester (Milton later), was lost at Port Royal June 7 1782 aged twenty-eight, in the earthquake

(III) James Houghton, son of Ralph Houghton (2) born in Lancaster, in 1661 (This date is given in the American Ancestry) It is stated by some writers that he was born before the family came to Lancaster Ralph Houghton's family was among the first to come and was doubtless living there by 1650 James Houghton settled first on the Neck but removed to Still river before the massacre in 1697 with his brother-in-law, Caleb Sawyer, and built upon lands given him by his father Ralph Houghton He had eight children The second son, Ralph was a soldier in the Acadian expedition to Canada and died in 1710, in the service His brother James was his administrator

James Houghton died in 1711 His will was proved September 11, 1711 His widow was the Widow Mary Houghton mentioned in the list of those in the garrison house in 1711 The garrison house of James Houghton has descended from father to son for five generations, and has been occupied the longest of any in old Lancaster, continuously in the same family The present house is a capacious farm house including at least three structures, all ancient The west end is the original garrison house which sheltered the families of the neighborhoods from Indian raids It was built from 1692 to 1704 The first chimney was of stone, and the huge foundations still fills half the cellar It was early replaced by the present many-flued brick pile, with eight fire places, ovens, cupboards and smoke closet where there is room enough to cure simultaneously the hams and shoulders of a dozen swine Many of the little windows remain though the sash has been renewed at nearly double the height now thought convenient The walls are filled with brick and stone so as to be bullet proof The huge oak beams and plates show for a third of their length below plaster and laths These timbers are 12x14 inches Once when it became necessary to remove some of the panels of the wainscoting, during renovations the wood was found to be unpainted soft pine without knot or check of excellent workmanship thought to be from the hand of James Houghton himself a carpenter and builder of his own house The house passed to Thomas Houghton his son also ancestor of Stillman Houghton It passed to his son Elijah to his son Thomas to his son Cephas and then to his son now or lately the owner, Edward Warren Houghton, of Harvard, Massachusetts, as that section of Lancaster is now known

Children of James and Mary Houghton were: 1 James, born 1690, married Sarah —— (called James Houghton Sr, to distinguish him from James Houghton, son of Jonas Houghton, a younger man) 2 Ralph, died in service in Canada, his brother James administered his estate 3 John 4 Thomas (see forward) 5 Edward (see Houghton family under Knapp family) 6 Ephraim, joined in deed, with Edward and James to Jonas 7 Hannah 8 Experience In 1723 Ephraim, Edward, Thomas and John, sons of James, lived in the vicinity of the old house in Harvard James Houghton, who married Sarah, was not there at that time

Caleb Sawyer was grandson of John Prescott, the founder of Lancaster, and fifth son of Thomas Sawyer, one of the first proprietors, who married Mary Prescott Caleb Sawyer was born in Lancaster, April 20, 1659, married Sarah, daughter of Ralph Houghton December 28, 1683 He had a special grant of thirty acres on the east side of Bare Hill where he built his house some time after the massacre of 1697 The well known "rendezvous" tree was near his house He died February 13, 1755

(IV) Thomas Houghton, son of James Houghton (3), born in Lancaster, Massachusetts, about 1690-1700, married Maria or Moriah Moor and settled on the homestead in Harvard He was a farmer Children were 1 Hanah, born December 16, 1728-9 2 Thomas, born October 9, 1731 3 Moriah (as Maria was then spelled by the family), born September 5 1736 4 Elijah (see forward)

(V) Elijah Houghton son of Thomas Houghton (4), born in Harvard, or what is now Harvard, then Lancaster Massachusetts, June 2, 1739, married Mercy Whitney and settled in Harvard Their children were 1 Thomas, born January 11, 1767 2 Elijah, born October 23, 1769 3 Abraham, born January 23, 1771 4 Moriah, born November 7, 1772 5 Mercy, born September 27 1774 6 Abraham (2d), born April 26, 1777 7 Elizabeth, born December 3 1779 8 Hanah born April (?), 1781 9 Alice born February 22, 1784 10 Hannah, born April 22, 1786 11 Sally, born September 22 1788.

(VI) Abraham Houghton son of Elijah Houghton (5) born in Harvard, Massachusetts April 26, 1777 He settled in Harvard Massachusetts, and died there He married Elizabeth Parks They had six children Betsey, Maria, Andrew, Martha, William, Thomas Stillman

(VII) Stillman Houghton, son of Abraham Houghton (6), born in Harvard, Massachusetts, June 19 1820, died April 26 1889 He was raised on the farm in Harvard and attended school there He learned the machinist trade and started the first loom for the Clinton Wire mill, where he was employed for a number of years He came to Worcester to associate himself with D H Fanning who in 1861 started the manufacture of hoop skirts in Worcester The company was called the Worcester Skirt Company Out of it grew the Worcester Corset Company at the head of which Mr Fanning has continued Mr Houghton was engaged in the manufacturing of skirts and corsets for many years For a time he was in business for himself in the manufacture of pocketbooks He retired some years before his death His widow now lives in their old home 19 Oak avenue Worcester He died April 26 1889 in Worcester He was a Republican in politics

He married 1845 Mercy Randall Weatherbee, daughter of Silas and Mary (Taylor) Weatherbee, born in Boxboro, Massachusetts November 8, 1824

Stephen Sawyer

Her father was born in Boxboro, her mother in Harvard, Massachusetts She was one of fourteen children Her grandfather was Simeon Weatherbee

Children of Stillman and Mercy Randall (Weatherbee) Houghton were 1 Evander, born 1847, died 1853 2 Herbert O (see forward) 3 Lilla, born February 12, 1861, married Albert C Marble and had Ralph L., born, 1898

(VIII) Herbert O Houghton, son of Stillman Houghton (7), born in Clinton, Massachusetts, October 22, 1850 He was educated in the Worcester schools and is in the city directory business He resides at 19 Oak avenue, Worcester He married Carrie L Stockwell, daughter of Deacon Leander and Julia (Lealand) Stockwell of Grafton Children are 1 Arthur S, born February 17, 1879, attorney in Worcester 2 Mabel S, born July 18, 1881 3 Cecil F, born September 20, 1883, is a teacher in Sharon, Connecticut 4 Louis H (twin), born May 14 1887, is now on training ship Enterprise 5 Louise M (twin), born May 14, 1887

STEPHEN SAWYER Thomas Sawyer, one of the founders of Lancaster, Massachusetts, was the emigrant ancestor of Stephen Sawyer, of Worcester, Massachusetts

(II) Thomas Sawyer, born in England about 1616, settled first at Rowley, Massachusetts, about 1643 He removed to Lancaster in 1647, when there were but three permanent settlers there John Prescott, Richard Linton and Lawrence John Ball had apparently left the settlement after being there for some time in behalf of the proprietors In May, 1653, Thomas Sawyer was appointed by general court one of the prudential managers of the town They had full powers to allot land, govern the town and admit freemen The other members of the board were Edward Breck, Nathaniel Hadlock, William Kerley, John Prescott and Ralph Houghton Thomas Sawyer was admitted a freeman 1654 and was a proprietor of Lancaster 1648 Naturally he became one of the leading men He was a blacksmith by trade His farm was on the present grounds of the Seventh Day Adventists, between South Lancaster and Clinton There is a stone to mark his grave in the old graveyard in Lancaster He died September 12, 1706 about ninety years of age

There is little of interest on the records about Thomas Sawyer until 1676, when King Philip's war was raging and Lancaster suffered greatly His son Ephraim Sawyer was killed by the Indians at Prescott's Garrison now in Clinton Sawyer's house was one of the garrisons, and he was in command there It was just behind the house now or lately owned by John A Rice, of Lancaster It is interesting to note that other heads of Worcester county families of note, written about in this work, were in the same garrison In 1704 the garrison was at the house of Thomas Sawyer, Jr, the aged father in command Sawyer had nine men under him Andrew Gardner Thomas Sawyer, Jr, Mr Gardner Jabez Fairbanks, ancestor of the vice-president, Nathaniel, another son of Thomas Sawyer, John Harris, Daniel Rugg ancestor of Arthur P Rugg and most of the Worcester county Ruggs, Samuel Prescott ancestor of the historian and of Worcester families of the name These families all lived on the west side of the Nashua river, at what is now called South Lancaster In the following year Thomas Sawyer, Jr was taken captive, as will be related later Thomas Sawyer Sr lived with his daughter, Mary Wilder, while Thomas was a captive in Canada

Thomas Sawyer, Sr married 1648, Mary, daughter of John Prescott of Watertown and Lancaster (See Prescott family) His will is dated March 6, 1705-6, proved April 12, 1720 The children of Thomas Sawyer and Mary (Prescott) Sawyer were: 1 Thomas, born July 2, 1649 2 Ephraim, born January 16 1650-1 3 Marie born January 4, 1652-3, married —— Wilder 4 Elizabeth, born January, 1654 5 Joshua, born March 13 1655 6 James, born March 22, 1657 7 Caleb, born April 22, 1659 8. John, born April, 1661 9 Nathaniel, born November, 1670, mentioned in father's will, three of foregoing not living at time father's will was made—Ephraim John and Elizabeth

(II) Thomas Sawyer son of Thomas Sawyer (1), was born in Lancaster, Massachusetts, July 2 1649, the first white child born there His capture by the Indians forms one of the most familiar stories of the colonial period in Massachusetts He was a man of fifty-five when the event took place and was living in the garrison as described above Queen Anne's war was making the lives of the colonists unsafe especially on the frontier Indians made frequent attacks and massacred men, women and children On October 16, 1705 Thomas Sawyer, Jr his son Elias, and John Bigelow, of Marlboro, were at work in his saw mill when they were surprises and captured by Indians The Indians took their captives back to Canada and turned Bigelow and young Sawyer over to the French to ransom The Indians kept the other Thomas Sawyer to put to death by torture Sawyer proposed to the French governor that he should build a saw mill on the Chamblay river in consideration of saving his life from the Indians and giving the three captives their freedom The French needed the mill and were glad of the opportunity But the Indians had to be reckoned with They insisted on burning Thomas Sawyer at the stake They knew him and knew he was a brave man not afraid of torture and death The crafty French governor defeated their purpose by a resort to the church When Sawyer was tied to the stake a French friar appeared with a key in his hand, and so terrible did he paint the tortures of purgatory, the key of which he told them he had in his hand ready to unlock, that they gave up their victim Indians fear the unseen more than real dangers and doubtless the friar took care not to specify just what he would do in case the *auto-de-fe* was carried on Sawyer built the mill successfully, the first in Canada it is said He and Bigelow came home after seven or eight months of captivity Elias Sawyer was kept a year longer to run the mill and teach others to run it The captives were well treated after the French found them useful to them

Thomas Sawyer married three times First, Sarah ——, 1670, second, Hannah ——, 1672, and third, Mary White 1718 He died at Lancaster, and his grave there is marked by a stone He died September 5, 1736, in the eighty-ninth year of his age (so said), but was probably eighty-seven, if the records are correct His will mentions four sons and two daughter He bequeathed twelve pounds to purchase a communion vessel for the Lancaster church Children of Thomas Sawyer were 1 William 2 Joseph 3 Bazalies 4 Elias 5 Mary, married Joshua Rice of Marlboro 6 Hannah married Jonathan Moore of Bolton 7 (perhaps) Sarah married Rev Nathaniel Whitman, of Deerfield Massachusetts

(III) William Sawyer son of Thomas Sawyer (2) was born in Lancaster, where the family located during Indian troubles He married, 1700, Hannah daughter of John Houghton 2d They settled in Lancaster in what is now the village of Bolton, in the southerly part Their garrison assignment near the centre was with John Moore, near Fryeville He owned land in other places—a hundred acres on the west slope of Gates Hill, now called Sawyer Hill, and one hundred and twenty acres on the east slope of the hill

Deacon Josiah Sawyer, son of William Sawyer (3), born in Lancaster, 1714, married Sarah Fairbanks a descendant of the Lancaster branch of he descendants of Jonathan Fairbanks of Dedham (See Fairbanks) She was the daughter of Jabez Fairbanks of Bolton granddaughter of the famous Indian fighter, and brother of Esquire Ephraim Fairbanks of Berlin Massachusetts, whose home in 1738 was on Wheeler Hill Josiah Sawyer was one of the charter members of the Berlin church and its deacon His Bible and the stand on which it rested during his daily family devotions have been preserved by his descendants The Indians were still a menace to the inhabitants of Worcester county towns when he was a young man In 1735 he was living with his father at Bolton, but was clearing the land on Sawyer Hill and was preparing to make his home there While returning home one evening afoot, as was his custom, an Indian waylaid him, just as he was descending the hill north of Quaker meeting house Sawyer dodged the upraised tomahawk and took to his heels Fortunately for him he was a good runner, for he was unarmed The savage soon saw that he was outclassed and gave up the pursuit By measurement next day it was found that one of the leaps, as the foot prints showed, was sixteen feet That lean is famous in Berlin history

He married Sarah ——, who died 1762 He married (second) Mary Tooker The Tooker family preceded the Chase family on the Acre in Clinton She died March 25, 1799, aged seventy-one years He died July 3, 1805 aged ninety-one years He was deacon of the church from 1770 to 1799 The children of Deacon Josiah and Sarah Sawyer were 1 Josiah born November 24 1738 died young 2 William born March 5 1740 3 Hannah born June 25 1743 married —— Cuttis, of Harvard 4 Rebecca born February 15 1745 married —— Wilder of Putney, Vermont 5 Sarah born February 6, 1747 married William Wilder of Putney Vermont 6 Aholiab born 1749 6 Josiah, born November 8 1752 The children of Josiah and Mary were 7 Levi, born November 10 1764, died young 8 Silas, born July 5, 1766 9 Thomas, born March 9, 1770, died 1771

(V) Josiah Sawyer son of Deacon Josiah Sawyer (4) was born in Berlin Massachusetts, November 8 1752 He married Bathsheba Moore, of Putney Vermont He had the homestead in Berlin which he left to his daughter Lucinda Her son Daniel H Carter inherited it The place is now or was lately owned by Willard G Bruce Josiah was a farmer Bathsheba his wife died March 17, 1778 He married (second) Persis Baker daughter of Samuel Baker She died 1785, and he married (third) Prudence Johnson, of Leominster, Massachusetts January 4 1786 The children of Josiah and Bathsheba (Moore) Sawyer were 1 Alvan born October 30 1770 2 Eunice born November 10 1774 married Ephraim Babcock 3 Bathsheba born May 9 1778 died young The children of Josiah and Persis (Baker) Sawyer were 4 Susannah born November 19 1781, married Caleb Houghton 5 Bathsheba born 1784, died young The children of Josiah and Prudence (Johnson) Sawyer were 6 Ira born October 1, 1787 7 Lucinda born April 20, 1789 married Amory Carter and Cummings Moore 8 Rufus born September 22 1790 9 George born February 6 1793 10 Asa born September 3 1795 11 Persis born June 18, 1798, married Loring Howe of Marlboro 12 Sarah, born July 12 1800, married Lewis Carter, died February 26 1895 Josiah Sawyer was a soldier in the revolution in Captain Benjamin Hasting's company, Col John Whitcomb's regiment in 1775, and also served in Captain Jonathan Houghton's company and Captain David Nourse's company He served at Fishkill New York, and at the Bennington alarm in 1778

(VI) Alvan Sawyer, son of Josiah Sawyer (5), was born in Lancaster, (now Berlin), October 30, 1700 He married February 13 1794, Sarah, daughter of James Goddard, Sr He settled in Berlin on the farm previously owned by Thomas Bride and now or lately by Leonard W Brewer His wife Sarah died November 14 1806 and he married (second) Sally Newton, of Marlboro, 1808 The children of Alvin and Sarah (Goddard) Sawyer were 1 Lucy, born March 16, 1795, married Amory Sawyer 2 Zilpah born February 3 1797, died October 11 1775, unmarried 3 Levi born April 7, 1799 died unmarried, 1837 4 Eli, born January 7 1801 5 Alvan, born September 8, 1803, married Lucy Bigelow, of Lowell, who died May 18 1831, married (second) Jerusha A W Tarleton, of Nashua, he died in Cuba 1856 The children of Alvan, Sr, and Sally (Newton) Sawyer were 6 Josiah born March 25 1810 7 George W, born October 11, 1811 8 Stephen, born February 11 1813 9 Sally Newton, born 1815, married Julius L Clarke, son of Rev Eber L Clarke, resided in Worcester and Newton, Massachusetts, has been state auditor and commissioner of insurance 10 Susan, born 1819, married Edward L Brigham, of Worcester, in 1844, she died 1871

(VII) Stephen Sawyer, son of Alvan Sawyer (6), was born in Berlin, Massachusetts, February 11, 1813 He worked on the farm in summer and went to school in the winter, and obtained an excellent education At an early age he began to teach school, but preferred a mercantile life and went to work in the general store of Haman Hunt in Berlin After a year there the outlook did not seem to him wide enough to accord with his aspirations Most of his youthful friends elected to settle in their native town Against much sincere and kindly advice he concluded that a larger field would be more promising to his hopes In accordance with this conclusion, which he has called an inspiration, he left Berlin in 1831 and came to Worcester, he at once found employment in the dry goods house of H B Claflin & Co there

At that time H B Claflin & Co's was the liveliest business house in the commonwealth outside of Boston A few years later, when Mr Claflin sought the larger field for business afforded by New York Mr Sawyer was retained as salesman by the succeeding firm of Hardon Hunt & Brown, which was soon reconstructed under the title of B L Hardon & Co with Mr Sawyer as one of the partners Through his connection with this well known business Mr Sawyer became well known in mercantile circles, his ability was generally recognized, and he acquired a thorough knowledge of business that must have been a large factor in his greater successes in later life He was a member of the firm for fifteen years, retiring in 1856 on account of ill health Like many others who have lived to an advanced age and won large successes in the business world, he met ill health in middle life and retired built up his health and strength, and went back to work with renewed vigor and courage He re-entered business in Worcester with T H Clark and E W Ball in 1866 under the well known firm name of Clark Sawyer & Co They bought the stock of crockery, glassware, etc, of

John Firth & Co, and rented the store, their predecessors had occupied in the Flagg building, Main street The business prospered and they soon outgrew their quarters, and they rented two large stores in R C Taylor's building on Main street, opposite the Worcester Common A few years later Mr Ball retired and George Richardson took his place in the firm They had to increase their store space again, and moved to their present stores at 478 to 482 Main street No mercantile house in the city has shown a greater and steadier rate of growth They have constantly added to their store by taking rooms in the building above and adjoining and occupy more floor room and transact a larger wholesale and retail trade than any other house of the kind outside of Boston in Massachusetts Besides all kinds of glassware, silverware and crockery, the firm deals in a multitude of housefurnishing articles, and has for years had a practical monopoly of the business in Worcester They import extensively staple goods and novelties, toys, etc

Mr Sawyer devoted himself zealously to business As head of the firm, for most of the time he was responsible directly for its great success He enjoyed his material advantages modestly He was elected a trustee of the Worcester Five Cents Savings Bank in 1867, and vice-president in 1876 His position in the business world was shown soon after the firm of Clark, Sawyer & Co was formed, by his election in January, 1867, as a director of the Mechanics' National Bank, a position that he filled until his death in 1904 He was a director of the Worcester Mutual Fire Insurance Company of Worcester, elected December 8, 1886, and served in that office seventeen years, during ten of which he was chairman of the board He was not especially active in politics He was a Republican, and served the city as alderman during the administrations of Mayors Clark Jillson, Charles B Pratt and Frank H Kelley He attended the Congregational church, and contributed liberally to its charities He always took an interest in Berlin, his native place, and often expressed his affection for the town

Mr Sawyer died January 2, 1904, after a short illness The estimation in which he was held generally by his fellow citizens is perhaps best expressed by extracts from the formal actions of the various boards of which he was a member The trustees of the Worcester Five Cents Savings Bank in their memorial said "His long business life of over fifty years in this city made him familiar with most of its leading business men, and his good judgment as to the value of property eminently fitted him for usefulness in this bank He carried the burden of his years with the vigor of a much younger man and was rarely absent from the stated meetings of the bank" In the memorial of the Mechanics' National Bank the following statement was made "He was a director for thirty-seven years During that time he has taken an active interest in its affairs, and has been constant in his attendance at its meetings While he was always careful and conservative in his views on the various questions that might arise, and in his judgment of men, he was at the same time willing to lend assistance and credit to those whom he felt were entitled to receive it He exhibited the same traits in his own affairs, and from a small beginning he built up a strong and substantial business He was a gentleman of the old school and his pleasant manners and genial ways made friends of those who met him or were associated with him" The directors of the Worcester Mutual Fire Insurance Company expressed their appreciation of Mr Sawyer as follows "His business experience in Worcester, covered a period of about sixty years, during which Worcester grew from a town of some 6000 inhabitants to a city of multiform activities, with a population of nearly 130 000, and he had much to do as a public-spirited citizen in furthering its growth and prosperity We record our high appreciation of his loyalty to duty, his upright character, his pure mindedness, his thorough integrity, his uniform kindness, his honest purpose to serve well his fellow men, and his rare example of carrying to ripe years the cheerfulness, courage and hope which pertains to young manhood"

He married Lucy Fairbanks Sawyer, daughter of Deacon Oliver Sawyer, granddaughter of William Sawyer, the son of Deacon Josiah Sawyer, whose family is given in this sketch She died December 29 1847 He married (second) Mary W Bigelow, Worcester, December 2, 1857 His children were 1 Lucy Fairbanks (by first marriage), born December 29, 1847, resides in Worcester, unmarried The children by the second marriage were 2 Mary Sophia, born at Worcester, November 1, 1858, died March 9, 1859 3 Harriet Louise, born in Worcester, September 26, 1862, died March 19, 1868 4 Stephen, born October 29, 1868 5 Grace May, born in Worcester, March 6, 1871, resides with her mother and brother Stephen at 31 Chestnut street, Worcester

(VIII) Stephen Sawyer, Jr, son of Stephen Sawyer (7), was born in Worcester, Massachusetts, October 29 1868 He attended the public schools of his native city, and graduated in due course from the Worcester high school with the class of 1887 He immediately went into the Clark, Sawyer & Company store to learn the business and was soon afterward admitted to partnership The firm was incorporated in 1890 under the laws of Massachusetts, with a capital of $100 000 During the latter years of his father's life the son assumed his share of the work in the store The present officers of the company are President, Charles A Fletcher, treasurer, George Richardson, secretary, Stephen Sawyer Mr Sawyer has devoted his attention to business exclusively In politics he is a Republican He is a member of Quinsigamond Lodge, F and A M, and of Eureka Chapter, R A M, and of the Tatassit Canoe Club

(V) William Sawyer, ancestor of Mrs Stephen Sawyer son of Deacon Josiah Sawyer (4), born March 5 1740, married Hannah Barrett daughter of Lieut Oliver and Hannah (Hunt) Barrett of Bolton January 10, 1764 The Barrett family has always been prominent in Bolton William Sawyer settled on part of his father's homestead in Berlin now or lately owned by M Reed Tyler known as Lakeside He died February 28, 1822 aged eighty years, she died February 8 1830 aged eighty-eight years He was in the revolutionary war in Captain Benjamin Hastings' company Col John Whitcomb's regiment 1775 and possibly also in the Continental army in 1776 The children of William and Hannah (Barrett) Sawyer were 1 Abigail, born May 5, 1765 married Cotton Newton 2 William born February 6 1767 3 Amos born March 17 1769 4 Mary born February 8 1771, married September 26 1792 Rufus Howe, of Berlin, son of Joseph Howe, of Gates Pond, resided at Marlboro, Vermont 5 Oliver born April 17, 1774 6 Asa born August 2 1775 settled in Jaffray New Hampshire 1803 to 1817 7 Uriah born May 24, 1778 married, February 2 1803, Sally Spofford, resided at Jaffray New Hampshire and in Ohio 8 Polly born 1780 married Rufus Howe, who died in Marlboro, Vermont, she returned to Berlin 9 Hannah, born January 6, 1781, married Robert Fosgate, resided at Winchester, New Hampshire, died there, 1871, aged ninety years 10 Levi born 1784 died young

(VI) Deacon Oliver Sawyer, son of William Sawyer (5), born in Berlin, Massachusetts, April 17, 1774, married Lucy Fairbanks, of Northboro, who died April 22, 1810, aged twenty-three years He married (second) Sophia Rice of Northboro He succeeded to the homestead on Sawyer Hill in Berlin, and built the house that was burned there while owned later by Madame Rudersdorff, the mother of Richard Mansfield, the famous actor Deacon Oliver Sawyer was prominent in the town as well as the church He was a town officer, and highly respected by his fellow citizens He died April 15, 1851 his wife Sophia, died September 1, 1841 Their children were 1 Lewis, born February 2, 1813, died on the homestead, February 8, 1856 unmarried 2 Oliver Barrett, born June 5, 1816 3 Lucy Fairbanks (twin), born September 9, 1819, married Stephen Sawyer, of Worcester, January 8, 1845, died in Worcester, December 29, 1847 4 Sophia (twin), born September 9, 1819, died on the homestead October 24, 1873, unmarried

BIGELOW FAMILY John Bigelow (1), the common ancestor of the Worcester families of the same surname, was the progenitor of Mary Woodbury Bigelow, who married Stephen Sawyer of Worcester

John Bigelow is believed to have come from England, but the variations in spelling at the time of his emigration to New England make it difficult to trace this name, which was spelled according to the fancy of the writers He was born in 1617 and came to America before 1642 The first mention of his name on the records is found in Watertown, Massachusetts, where, September 30, 1642, he married Mary daughter of John and Margaret Warren, and said to have been born in England She died October 19, 1691 He took the oath of fidelity at Watertown in 1652, and was made a freeman April 18 1690 He was a blacksmith by trade and was allowed certain timber for the building of his forge by the town He was highway surveyor 1652 and 1660, constable 1663 and one of the selectmen 1665, 1670 and 1671 His homestead consisted of six acres He married (second) October 2, 1694, Sarah, daughter of Joseph Bemis, of Watertown (See Bemis) He died July 14, 1703, aged eighty-six His will was dated January 4, 1703, and proved July 23, 1703 The children of John and Mary (Warren) Bigelow were 1 John, born October 27, 1643, married Rebecca Olmstead, lived in Hartford Connecticut 2 Mary, born March 14 1648, married June 3 1674 Michael Flagg son of Thomas and Mary Flagg, he was born March 23 1651 and died about 1711, she died before, as he married (second) Mary Earle 4 Daniel born December 1, 1650 married Abigail Pratt, lived in Framingham, Massachusetts 5 Samuel born October 28 1653 married Mary Flagg, lived in Watertown 6 Joshua born November 5 1655 married Elizabeth Flagg, lived in Watertown and Westminster 7 Elizabeth born June 15 1657, married Lieut John Stearns, and lived in Billerica Massachusetts where they had a large family of children she died April 18 1694 8 Sary, born September 29, 1659 married July 23 1679, Isaac Learned son of Isaac and Mary (Stearns) Learned He was born October 5 1655 They moved to Framingham near the Sherborn line He was selectman of Framingham in 1711 9 James, married thrice resided in Watertown 10 Martha, born April 1, 1662, married twice, her second husband was Obadiah Woods, of East Hartford Connecticut; he died April 11, 1712 11 Abigail, born February 4, 1664 married December 10, 1684, Benjamin Harrington 12 Hannah, born March 4, 1666, died March 8, 1666 13 A son, born and died December 18, 1667

(II) Samuel Bigelow son of John Bigelow (1), born October 28, 1653, married, June 3, 1674, at the same time that his sister Mary was married, Mary Flagg, daughter of Thomas and Mary Flagg She was born January 14, 1658, and died September 7, 1720 He was a prominent man in Watertown, an innholder 1702-16, and represented the town in the general court 1708, 1709 and 1710 His will, dated September 30, 1720 proved February 21, 1731, mentioned his sons John, Samuel, Thomas and Isaac, daughters Mercy Garfield, Abigail Cutler and Deliverance Stearns, sons-in-law Thomas Read, Josiah Howe and Daniel Warren, grandchildren David Bruce Nathaniel Read Isaac Read, Thomas Read, Catherine Read, Phinehas Howe, Abraham Howe, Rachel Howe, Samuel Warren, Daniel Warren and Hannah Warren The children of Samuel and Mary (Flagg) Bigelow were 1 John, born May 9, 1675, married Jerusha Garfield lived in Marlboro 2 Mary, born September 12, 1677, married, February 2, 1700 David Bruce, of Marlboro, married (second) Thomas Read, Jr, of Sudbury 3 Samuel, born September 18, 1679, married Ruth Warren, lived in Marlboro 4 Sarah, born October 1, 1681, married, December 11, 1706, Josiah Howe, of Marlboro, a grandson of John Howe, the first settler (See Howe) 5 Thomas, born October 24 1683, married Mary Livermore, of Watertown 6 Mercy, born April 4, 1686 (recorded Martha), married January 2 1707, Lieut Thomas Garfield (See Garfield), she died February 23, 1745, and he died February 4, 1752 7 Abigail, born May 7, 1687, married, August 1, 1710, Jonathan Cutler, of Killingly, Connecticut, resided at Colchester, Connecticut 8 Hannah, born May 24 1711, married Daniel Warren and they lived in Westboro, Shrewsbury, he was a soldier in the French and Indian war, and was taken prisoner to Canada 9 Isaac, born May 19, 1691, married Mary Bond and lived in Colchester, Connecticut 10 Deliverance born September 22 1695, married August 10, 1715, John Stearns of Lexington, Massachusetts, resided in Worcester, where many descendants have lived

(III) Samuel Bigelow son of Samuel Bigelow (2), born Watertown, Massachusetts, September 18, 1679, married in Watertown March 28 1705, Ruth Warren of Watertown They removed to Marlboro, where she died April 12 1716 He married (second) December 4, 1716 Mary Gleason daughter of Joseph and Martha Gleason, of Sudbury She was born October 6 1682, and died in Shrewsbury, May 14 1752 He died in Marlboro The children of Samuel and Ruth (Warren) Bigelow were 1 Mary, born December 17, 1705 married, December 10, 1727 Daniel Ward son of Joseph and Abiah (Wheelock) Ward, of Marlboro he was born April 14 1701 2 Samuel born October 16 1707, married Jedidah Hathorn lived in Shrewsbury 3 Cornelius born November 24, 1710 married Mary Graves lived in Westboro 4 Jedediah born February 8 1714 married Thamazin Nurse, lived in Douglas Massachusetts 5 Ruth, born April 10, 1716, died July 25 1716 6 Jason born April 11, 1718 married Abigail Witt lived in Brookfield, Massachusetts 7 Ruth born December 30 1719, married June 7, 1743 Daniel Hemmway, of Framingham, and moved to Sherborn in 1745, she died

November 15, 1794 8 Amariah, born September 14, 1722 married Lydia Brigham, lived in Shrewsbury 9 Martha, born October 21, 1724 married December 14 1749, Ezekiel Brigham, of Marlboro and Grafton, Massachusetts

(IV) Samuel Bigelow, son of Samuel Bigelow (3), born in Marlboro, October 16, 1707, married, November 28, 1729, Jedidah Hathorn, and moved to Shrewsbury, where he settled in the south part of the town, near the Grafton town line She died, and he married (second) May 7, 1770, Mrs Abigail Hastings, widow of Moses Hastings and daughter of William Taylor His will dated April 14, 1795 mentions wife Abigail daughters Dorcas Leland and Jedidah Wheeler, children of Samuel (deceased), child of daughter Sarah Smith (deceased), sons Solomon and Ithamar, who were appointed executors The children of Samuel and Jedidah (Hathorn) Bigelow were 1 Samuel born June 24, 1731, married Phebe Rand 2 Jedidah, born March 21, 1733, married April 30, 1760, John Wheeler, of Shrewsbury 3 Dorcas, born July 6, 1735, married, December 1, 1768, Seth Swan, of Paxton 4 Solomon, born July 25, 1767, died October 25, 1742 5 Silas born October 10 1739, married Sarah Hall, resided at Paxton 6 Solomon, born July 1, 1742, married Sarah Newton 7 Ithamar, born July 30, 1745, married Persis Barrett 8 Sarah, born September 10, 1747, married June 8, 1767, Ephraim Smith of Grafton Massachusetts

(V) Samuel Bigelow, son of Samuel Bigelow (4), born Shrewsbury, Massachusetts, June 24, 1731, married, at Shrewsbury, July 1, 1755, Phebe Rand, daughter of Daniel Rand She died June 10, 1770 He married (second) 1770, Anna Winchester, of Grafton He died in 1787 The children of Samuel and Phebe (Rand) Bigelow were 1 Levinan, born February 1, 1756, married, November 5, 1776, Samuel Whitney, of Westboro 2 Mary, born April 13, 1757 3 Vashti, born May 19, 1758, married, February 26 1777 James Wheeler, son of Ebenezer Wheeler, of Grafton 4 Lucretia, born June 1, 1760, married, August 14 1781 Adam Harrington of Shrewsbury 5 Humphrey, born September 4, 1761, married Mary Underwood 6 Serena, born March 16 1765 married, November 13, 1786, Benjamin Jennings of Brookfield

(VI) Humphrey Bigelow son of Samuel Bigelow (5) was born in Shrewsbury, Massachusetts, September 4, 1761 He married, December 20, 1786, Mary Underwood of Westford, Massachusetts She died in Shrewsbury, October 6 1789 He married (second), October 26, 1791, Hannah Whipple, of Grafton She was born October 5, 1771, and died in Worcester, January 5 1848 They lived in Shrewsbury until 1804 when they removed to Charlton, Massachusetts where they lived several years Later they lived in Sutton and Westford and then moved back to Shrewsbury He died October 2 1842 Children of Humphrey and Mary (Underwood) Bigelow 1 John born August 12 1787, married Mary Jones 2 Samuel born August 1 1789, died October 1789 The children of Humphrey and Hannah (Whipple) Bigelow 3 Samuel born July 2, 1793, married Cynthia Forbush 4 Catherine born August 12 1795 married November 2, 1818, Joel Fay, of Sutton 5 Hannah, born October 2 1797, married Samuel Lamb, resided at Charlton, married (second) Daniel Richardson married (third) Pardon Aldrich of Grafton 6 Mary, born August 4 1799 died December 25 1819 unmarried 7 Silas born August 10, 1801, married Silence Pierce 8 Moses born July 23 —— married Amanda Smith 9 Susan Whipple, born September 1, 1806, married, November 30, 1826, Owen W Allen, of Shrewsbury, moved to Ohio 10 Miriam, born September 6, 1809 married June 12, 1833 Joel Fay, late husband of her deceased sister, she died August 15, 1837 11 Whipple, born February 16, 1812, married Amy Chase 12 John, born November 27, 1814, married Lucinda M Slocumb

(VII) Silas Bigelow, son of Humphrey Bigelow (7), was born in Shrewsbury, Massachusetts, August 10, 1801 He married, November 20, 1823, Silence Pierce She was born February 6, 1803, daughter of Amos and Anna (Hicks) Pierce of Sutton He died in Worcester, October 12, 1883, she died there August 12, 1886 He went to Sutton before he was married, and carried on a boot and shoe manufacturing business in addition to conducting his farm He removed to Worcester in 1847, and continued in the shoe manufacturing business there until 1860 All their children were born in Sutton, viz 1 Silence Adaline born August 9 1824, married, June 1 1846, Curtis B Greene, she died June 30, 1902, their only child, Jennie A, married Frank E Kimball resides at 8 John street, he is with E T Smith Co, wholesale grocers 2 Harriet Ann born February 14 1826 married December 13, 1864 Albert G Mann, of Worcester (see Mann) 3 Mary Woodbury, born July 5, 1828, married, December 2, 1857, Stephen Sawyer (see Sawyer) 4 Edward H (twin), born at Northbridge, Massachusetts, July 5, 1830, married April 21, 1852, Mary S, daughter of Samuel and Martha Patterson, resided in Worcester, where he died September 10, 1867, Louisa Carrie, their only child, born June 19, 1853, married, December 25, 1882, Luther Baker, and died 1905 5 Emily (twin), born July 5 1830, died February 19 1834 6 Silas Austin, born October 22, 1832, died March 26 1844 7 Charles Amos, born October 3, 1834 in Sutton, married February 14 1856, Mary Caroline Patch (born in Worcester, September 10, 1836, died August 10, 1883), lived several years in Texas, then engaged in the wholesale grocery business with E T Smith, he died in Worcester, April 23 1885 His children were 1 Charles Frederick born in Worcester September 9 1857, married Mabel E Hewitt, November 4, 1885, lieutenant in Battery B, engaged in the business of E T Smith Co, died November 4, 1900, ii Frank A Bigelow, born in Belton, Texas, January 2, 1861, resided at New York city, iii Mary Ella, born in Salado, Texas, September 20, 1866, married Frank Green of Gardner, resides in Brooklyn 8 Luther Henry, born December 30 1836, in Sutton, married C Helen Lovell, daughter of A Beaman Lovell, resided in Worcester, where he died November 22 1871, his two children died in infancy He entered the book store of Jonathan Grout when a boy, later became a partner under the name of Grout & Bigelow (now Davis & Banister), he was in Company C, 51st Regiment Massachusetts Volunteer Militia in the civil war, with rank of lieutenant 9 James Whipple, born September 8, 1839 married October 24 1877, Mrs C Helen (Lowell) Bigelow widow of his deceased brother, Lieut Luther H Bigelow he was a partner of Walker Armington in the grocery business in Worcester, he died November 30, 1901, she died December 9 1882

(VIII) Mary Woodbury Bigelow, daughter of Silas Bigelow (7), was born July 5 1828 She married December 2 1857, Stephen Sawyer, of Worcester (See Sawyer)

DOLLIVER FAMILY Robert Dolliver or Dalliber (1), as it was then generally spelled in the English records was the progenitor in England of the Dolliver family of Essex and Worcester counties, Massachusetts ancestor of Edward B Dolliver, a business man of Worcester, and Henry W Dolliver postmaster of Whitinsville, Massachusetts Robert Dolliver lived in the parish of Stoke Abbot Dorset county England The name is said to be of Welsh origin and the earliest location of the English branch was at North Junterice in Wales Robert Dolliver was a yeoman He died in 1633, and his will, dated March 20, 1632 proved March 27, 1633, gives much information of his family He directed that he should 'be buried in the churchyard of Stoke Abbot before the church porch there, near the place where my father was buried" indicating thereby that the family had been located there for some time, and giving a clue to the English ancestry 'And my will and desire is" the will declares "that I may have a tomb set over me and towards that charge I give 13 shillings four pence" He remembered the poor and the church in his will (See pages 128 Genealogical Register 1894) 1 Robert, Jr Eldest' was executor 2 Samuel, left fifty pounds in father's will, see forward 3 Tristram baptized 1598 May 28, at Stoke Abbot, came to Salem before 1641 and was in the fishing business at Marblehead and Gloucester, returned to Stoke Abbot—whence he wrote, April 20, 1648, to John Balch about accounts due him in New England asked for the date of death of his wife from the records gave power of attorney to his brother Samuel Dolliver of Marblehead for collection of money from John Whitt of Wenham he came again to Massachusetts, he married (first) Mary —— who died July 3 1644, and (second), at Stoke Abbot, August 31, 1657, Sarah Peavie, he died at Gloucester July 3 1664 4 Joseph married Rachel —— and settled at Greenwich, Rhode Island 5 Mary 6 Sarah 7 Rebecca 8 Daughter married Walter Burt 9 Daughter, married John Lestry and had three sons, John, Edward and William Lestry

(II) Samuel Dolliver, son of Robert Dolliver (1) was baptized at Stoke Abbot England February 5 1608 He settled in Marblehead, Massachusetts about 1642 and was probably in Salem for a time before that He was admitted a proprietor of the town and elected to various town offices He bought of Thomas Millrad, of Newbury, Massachusetts his farm of forty acres of tillage and ten acres of marsh at Fresh Water Cove, Gloucester He died at Gloucester, July 22 1683 leaving an estate valued on inventory dated September, 1683 at 113 pounds The division of the estate was made to the eldest son Joseph sons Richard William and John daughters Mary, wife of Richard Babson, Sarah Dolliver (Dalliber as it was then spelled), to son-in-law Richard Dike, to Mary his widow who was then the wife of James Gardner The heirs receipted for their portions at various dates from 1684 to 1696 Samuel Dolliver had the unusually large herd of ten cows at the time of his death He married (first) ————, and (second) August 1654 Mary Elwell daughter of Robert Elwell The children of the first marriage were 1 Joseph, born 1629 "the eldest" see forward 2 Dorothy married at Marblehead November, 1653 John Waldron 3 Rebecca married Richard Dike, at Gloucester and had many children The children of Samuel and Mary Dolliver were 4 Captain William born August 16, 1656 married Anne Higginson daughter of Rev John Higginson she was accused of witchcraft marriage was unfortunate 5 Samuel born July 9 1658 6 Mary born March 26 1662 married Richard Babson 7 Richard, born April 18 1665 6 Sarah, born December 24 1667, married Joseph Killum 9 John, born September 2, 1671 married Susanna Marriner, November, 1700; she died February 26, 1705, married (second), February 11, 1706, Elizabeth Wood, had eight children removed to North Falmouth Maine

(III) Joseph Dolliver, son of Samuel Dolliver (2), was born in 1629, in England He gave his age as forty in 1669 He was among the early proprietors of Marblehead He is said to have been early of Salem, also but he was settled in 1648 in Marblehead where he lived the remainder of his life, and died there in 1688 He was a constable of Marblehead in 1660 He married Lucy ——— and among their children were 1 Joseph Jr, see forward 2 Abigail, born 1685, baptized December 13, 1685

(IV) Joseph Dolliver son of Joseph Dolliver (3), was born about 1665, in Marblehead Massachusetts He settled in his native town and seems to have had three wives all named Mary He married (first), January 16, 1689-90 Mary Pousland, (second) Mary Furnace October 19, 1704 and (third) April 10 1707, Mary Salmon all at Marblehead The children of Joseph and his wives were 1 Peter died young 2 Samuel, baptized March 8 1690-91 3 John, Jr," see forward 4 Thomas, baptized September 27 1696, died May 11 1760, aged sixty-two years, six months 5 Peter, born 1701 see forward 6 Joseph, married January 27, 1736-37 Lucy Merritt

(V) John Dolliver (called Jr because of an elder John of Marblehead, according to the prevailing custom), son of Joseph Dolliver (4), was baptized at Marblehead Massachusetts May 19, 1695 He settled in Marblehead and all his five children were born there He married January 2, 1715-16 at Marblehead Mary Tierry She died at Marblehead 1751, aged fifty-six years Their children 1 John baptized June 23 1723 2 Mary, baptized July 12, 1726 3 Sarah baptized June 22, 1729 4 Annice (Agnes) baptized May 20, 1733 5 Richard baptized November 2, 1735

(V) Peter Dolliver son of Joseph Dolliver (4), was baptized at Marblehead when probably less than a month old November 30, 1701 He married December 29 1724 Mary Dennis, and their children all born in Marblehead were 1 Peter born 1726, baptized March 6, 1725-26 2 Hannah baptized November 5 1727 3 Mary, born February 25, 1732-33 4 Joseph baptized April 6 1735 5 Thomas baptized March 20 1736 6 John baptized June 10 1739 7 Sarah baptized July 29 1744

(VI) Richard Dolliver son of John Dolliver (5), was baptized November 2 1735 He married Sarah Coffin October 2 1759 and settled at Marblehead, where their children were born viz 1 Sarah baptized September 6 1761 2 Richard baptized January 5 1764 died young 3 Mary, baptized December 15 1765 4 Richard baptized June 28 1767 5 William baptized April 29 1770 6 Joseph baptized February 24 1771 7 John, baptized May 8, 1774 see forward

(VI) Thomas Dolliver son of Peter Dolliver (5) was baptized at Marblehead March 20, 1736-37 He settled in Marblehead and was a soldier in the revolutionary war He married, August 7 1759, Sarah Bowdoin and their children were 1 Thomas, born October 24 1762 2 Samuel baptized October 7 1764 3 Mary, baptized November 2 1766 4 Peter baptized November 6 1768 5 William baptized 1770 died young 6 Mary, baptized November 1 1772 7 John, baptized August 8 1773 8 Sarah baptized April 2 1775 9 John baptized December 8 1776, see forward 10 Thomas baptized July 5 1778 11 Sally baptized December 26 1779 12 Sarah, baptized September 17, 1780 13 William baptized July 28 1782 14 Thomas, baptized June 15, 1783 15 Isaac, baptized December 12, 1784 16 Isaac baptized November 5, 1786 17 Polly baptized September 24 1786 18 Benjamin baptized July 11, 1790 19 Benjamin Stone, baptized April 27, 1794 20 Hannah, baptized February 9, 1800 21 Mary Green, baptized January 26 1812

(VII) John Dolliver, son of Richard Dolliver (6), born 1774, baptized at Marblehead, May 8, 1774, or son of Thomas Dolliver (6), and baptized December 8, 1776, descendant unquestionably from Joseph Dolliver (4), was born and brought up in Marblehead, where so many generations of his ancestors had lived He learned the trade of shoemaker He removed to Worcester and bought a lot of land of Joseph Searl He removed to Grafton in the thirties and bought land there of Elijah Brooks, Samuel Wood and Jonathan Warren, of Grafton six acres with the house, etc He became a manufacturer of shoes and at his death bequeathed his half-interest in the shoe factory at Grafton to his son Joseph He died January 7, 1863 John Dolliver lived at Lynn for some time before coming to Worcester and some of his children were born there He removed to Worcester, where his wife was born and the remainder of the children were born in that town He married at Worcester November 11, 1802 Mary or Mercy Barber, daughter of Joseph and Elizabeth Barber, and she was born in Worcester, May 20, 1779 Joseph was the son of Robert and Sarah Barber and was born at Worcester, April 25, 1738 The children of John and Mercy Dolliver were 1 Mercy, born at Lynn, May 13 1804 2 Betsey, born at Lynn November 17, 1805, died at Worcester April 25 1826 3 John B born at Lynn December 17 1807 died before his father, left children Ellen McKenzie, Caroline Augusta Aspinwall Mary Eliza Dolliver and Annie E Dolliver all born in Worcester 4 Samuel Varnum (took the middle name B) born at Lynn, September 20, 1810 see forward 5 Martha, born at Worcester July 8, 1813 married Benjamin Goddard of Worcester 6 Joseph born at Worcester May 22 1816, married, April 12, 1842, Zurviah Mason, resided at Grafton 7 Horatio, born at Worcester, July 12, 1819, resided at South Reading, Massachusetts

(VIII) Samuel B Dolliver (recorded at Lynn as Samuel Varnum Dolliver), son of John Dolliver (7), was born at Lynn Massachusetts September 20 1810 and died at Grafton Massachusetts, July 18 1880 He followed his father's trade of shoemaker and shoe manufacturer most of his life For a few years late in life he was employed by the Worcester Machine Screw Company He was a leading citizen of the town of Grafton In politics he was a Democrat He served the town of Grafton as assessor and selectman He married (first), July 29 1834, Delia E Blake, born in Shrewsbury, Massachusetts June 18 1814 She died at Grafton, February 7, 1863 He married (second) Nancy G ——— who survived him The children of Samuel B and Delia E Dolliver were 1 Edward S born in Grafton, June 4 1835, died March 26, 1840 2 Mary E, born in Grafton February 12, 1841, died July 10, 1849 3 Maria E born in Grafton, May 16 1843, married A W Gifford of Worcester 4 Edward B, born in Grafton September 1, 1848, see forward 5 Henry W born in Grafton, December 29 1854, see forward

(IX) Henry W Dolliver son of Samuel B Dolliver (8), was born in Grafton Massachusetts, December 29 1854 He was educated in the public and high schools of his native town Like his father and grandfather he learned the trade of shoemaker, and worked in the shoe factory of J H Brigham, at Worcester, four years, and for his brother-in-law, A W Gifford of Worcester He then took the position of clerk of the Quinsigamond Hotel at North Grafton After six months he suffered an accident while hunting that nearly cost him his right hand, and laid him up for a year He began work again as clerk in the market of G B Brooks, Grafton In 1879 he removed to Whitinsville Massachusetts, a village in the adjoining town of Northbridge He was assistant postmaster for four years under D P Gray, at Whitinsville, was bookkeeper three years for J V Prentice, and again was under Postmaster Gray for seven years or until his death, when Mr Dolliver was appointed to succeed him March 1, 1905 He is a member of the Whitinsville Lodge of Odd Fellows In politics he is a Republican, and has been clerk of the Northbridge board of selectmen from 1896 to 1900

He married October 6, 1876, Clara F Gray Their children are 1 Maud L, graduate of the Whitinsville high school 2 Jessie L member of the class of 1908, Whitinsville high school 3 Harold G

EDWARD B DOLLIVER, one of the successful business men of Worcester, was born in Grafton Worcester county, Massachusetts September 1, 1848, son of Samuel B and Delia E (Blake) Dolliver, and grandson of John and Mary or Mercy (Barber) Dolliver who were the parents of five children John Joseph, Horatio, Samuel B and Martha John Dolliver (grandfather) was born in Marblehead Massachusetts was a shoemaker by trade, and died in Grafton, Massachusetts, about 1860

Samuel B Dolliver (father) was born in Lynn Massachusetts, September 20, 1810 He followed his trade of shoemaker up to about 1870 when he entered the employ of the Worcester Machine Screw Company, remaining with them for a number of years He was a Democrat in politics, and held the offices of selectman and assessor in the town of Grafton, Massachusetts He married Delia E Blake, born in Shrewsbury Massachusetts, June 18 1814, and their children were 1 Edward S, born in Grafton, June 4 1835 died March 25, 1840 2 Mary A born in Grafton February 12 1841, died July 10, 1849 3 Maria E born in Grafton May 16 1843, wife of A W Gifford of Worcester 4 Edward B (see forward) 5 Henry W, born in Grafton, December 29 1854 postmaster at Whitinsville Massachusetts married Clara Gray and they are the parents of three children Maud Jessie and Harold Samuel B Dolliver (father) died in Grafton, July 18, 1880, and his wife also passed away in the same town February 7, 1863

Edward B Dolliver acquired his education in the common schools of Grafton and at the age of fourteen having completed his studies, entered into his first regular employment in the shoemaking business with his father He continued along the same lines until he was twenty-one years old and then engaged in clerking in the Quinsigamond House, in North Grafton remaining for about two years He then clerked in the Waverly House in Worcester until the spring of 1872, when he removed to Boston there acting as clerk in the Warwick House, where he remained until September, 1872 He was then employed in a restaurant, in which his father held an interest and in 1873 he purchased his father's interest, and conducted the establishment until September 1876, when he sold out to his partners Messrs Dolliver and Currier Two months later Mr Dolliver removed to Worcester, where he found employment in the Worcester Machine Screw Company, serving about three years as a workman in the factory. In the spring of 1879 when Mr Gifford purchased the interest of his two partners, becoming sole owner of the establishment Mr Dolliver was placed in charge of the office, which position he retained until April, 1900, discharging the responsible duties with efficiency and credit. In 1900 Mr Gifford sold his business to the Standard Screw Company, and Mr Dolliver was elected manager of this branch of the company, and is also treasurer and one of the directors of the company. His career as a business man has been one of success and prosperity, and his is an example that might well be followed by the rising generation. Thrown upon his own resources at the tender age of fourteen, with no capital but those success-bringing qualities—energy, industry and perseverance—he has attained an enviable place in the business world. He is a member of the Worcester Continentals in which he has held membership for about twenty years, and has held the positions of first lieutenant quartermaster, sergeant and quartermaster having been appointed by Colonel Hopkins. He is a member of the Worcester Mechanics Association, and was a director in the same during the years 1901-02-03. He is a member of the board of trade, serving on the membership committee. He is a member of Quinsigamond Lodge, Free and Accepted Masons, joining January 20, 1880 and has served his lodge as worshipful master from 1887 to 1889, and is now a trustee of the permanent fund and treasurer of the board of trustees of the charity fund. He is also a member of Eureka Chapter, Royal Arch Masons, Hiram Council, Royal Select Masters, Worcester County Commandery, Knights Templar, Worcester Lodge of Perfection, and the Tatassit Canoe Club.

He married May 6 1875 Augusta O Pratt, born in Grafton Massachusetts, July 5, 1852, a graduate of the Grafton high school, daughter of Chandler M and Olivia (Fisher) Pratt, who were the parents of two other children, as follows: Julius F, born in Grafton Massachusetts, April 15 1845, died in Scotland July 7 1900, and Clarence M, born in Grafton, Massachusetts, January 28, 1850, died May 22, 1879. Chandler M Pratt was born in Thompson Connecticut, September 23 1802, died May 7, 1864 in Grafton, Massachusetts. His wife, Olivia (Fisher) Pratt, was born in Medway, Massachusetts October 23, 1807, died February 7, 1855 in Grafton Massachusetts. The children born to Mr and Mrs Dolliver were: Winifred O, born June 8 1884 obtained her education in the public and high schools of Worcester, graduating from the latter in the class of 1903 after which she attended Bradford Academy for one year. She is a teacher in the Sunday school of Old South Congregational Church. Clarence E, born August 21, 1885, died December 14, 1904.

HENRY ALBERT MACGOWAN of Worcester Massachusetts was born in Greenville, New Hampshire May 2 1864. On the maternal side he is a descendant of William Basset who came from England to Massachusetts between 1620 and 1630. Colonel William Basset a relative was a successor of Captain Miles Standish in the office of marshal of Plymouth county. Daniel Basset a great-great-grandson of William Basset the pioneer ancestor, served as a lieutenant in Colonel Gamaliel Bradford's Regiment in the Continental army in the war of the revolution. Lieutenant Daniel Bassett was accompanied in this service by his son Joseph who was one of the last of the revolutionary pensioners of the town of Barnstable, Massachusetts, dying July 7, 1855 at the advanced age of ninety-three years. He was a sea captain and school master by occupation.

The paternal grandfather of Henry A Macgowan, came to this country from Scotland, in 1842. Soon after locating here, he superintended the fitting out of the first mill at Highbridge, New Hampshire, and lived to see five large mills erected along the same stream within a distance of three miles, with the operation of which he was for many years connected. His son, Joseph, father of the subject of this sketch, succeeded him in his position in connection with these mills. In 1872 Joseph removed to Clinton, Massachusetts, where for over thirty years he has been the proprietor of a large grocery business. For many years he has been a deacon of the First Congregational Church of Clinton, Massachusetts. In social, business and church life he has enjoyed a merited reputation for absolute integrity, sound judgment, business sagacity and public-spirited citizenship. He married Clementine Baxter, daughter of Ansel and Octavia (Bassett) Baxter, and granddaughter of Joseph Bassett mentioned above.

As a boy, Henry A Macgowan attended the public schools in Clinton, Massachusetts, graduating from the high school of that place as valedictorian of the class of 1882. The same year he entered Amherst College became a member of the Chi Phi fraternity, and was graduated in 1886 with the degree of Bachelor of Arts, having been previously elected a member of the Phi Beta Kappa Society. He afterwards attended Andover Theological Seminary for one year, but failure of health compelled the abandonment of theological study. The following year having partially regained his health, he turned his attention to the vocation of teaching. From 1888 to 1890 he served as principal of the Sterling (Massachusetts) high school, from 1890 to 1892 of the Scituate (Massachusetts) high school, and from 1892 to 1897 of the Marblehead (Massachusetts) high school and academy. In the spring of 1897 Mr Macgowan resigned his position at Marblehead and engaged with his brother in the insurance business in Worcester the firm becoming managing agents for Central Massachusetts of the Mutual Benefit Life Insurance Company of Newark, New Jersey, and in addition doing a general insurance business, including surety bonding.

Mr Macgowan has always affiliated with the Republican party in state and national politics. He has been a member of the Church of the Unity in Worcester, and has served the same in various official capacities. He is also actively interested in the Masonic fraternity, holding membership in a large number of the bodies. He has served as an officer of Athelstan Lodge, A F and A M, Worcester County Commandery of Knights Templar, and Aletheia Grotto of M O V P. He is a member of the Twentieth Century Club, an honorary member of the Worcester Continentals and has served as president of the Amherst College Club of Central Massachusetts. Mr Macgowan is the author of "The New Century Outline Maps which are widely used in the public schools.

June 26 1889 in Sterling Massachusetts Mr Macgowan was married to Grace R Butterick, daughter of James and Mary (Rugg) Butterick, of Sterling. On both sides of Mrs Macgowan's family the ancestry dates back to the founders of Massachusetts and to revolutionary soldiers. On the maternal side Mrs Macgowan is a direct descendant of four founders of colonies, Samuel Hagar, one of the founders of Westminster, and John Prescott,

Geo Sessions

Thomas Sawyer, and John Rugg, founders of Lancaster The children of Mr and Mrs Macgowan are Marjorie Butterick, born May 14, 1890, Mary Josephine, born January 25, 1892, and Eleanor Butterick, born August 30, 1893

GEORGE SESSIONS Samuel Sessions (1), the emigrant ancestor of the late George Sessions, of Worcester, came from England to America in 1630 He had a son Alexander

(II) Alexander Sessions, son of Samuel Sessions (1), was born about 1645 He was living in Andover Massachusetts, in 1669, and died there February 26, 1688-9 He married Elizabeth Spofford, of Rowley, Massachusetts, April 24, 1672 Both Mr and Mrs Sessions were members of the Andover church in 1686 They had a son Nathaniel

(III) Nathaniel Sessions, son of Alexander Sessions, (2), was born at Andover, Massachusetts, August 8, 1681, and died in Pomfret, Connecticut, in 1771 He married Johanna Miller They had a son, Amasa, born August 13, 1715

(IV) Amasa Sessions, son of Nathaniel Sessions (3), was born August 13, 1715, and died April 17, 1799 He married Hannah Miller He was a captain in the revolutionary war in Colonel Backus' regiment of Connecticut He had a son Samuel, born November 26, 1746

(V) Samuel Sessions, son of Amasa Sessions (4), was born November 26, 1746 He resided at Union and Westford, Connecticut, and died in 1818 He married Abigail Ruggles, of Pomfret, Connecticut, October 11, 1767, and settled in Heath, Massachusetts He was in the revolutionary war, a lieutenant in Captain Grant's company, Colonel Johnson's regiment in 1781, and was at West Point in 1781 in Colonel Canfield s regiment He had a son George, baptized at Union, Connecticut, in 1771

(VI) George Sessions, son of Samuel Sessions (5), was born at Union, Connecticut, and baptized there in 1771 He married February 20, 1800, Lucina Lumbard, at Brimfield, Massachusetts She was born October 13, 1781, and was the daughter of Joseph, Jr and Mary Lumbard (Joseph Lumbard and Joseph, Jr were both in the revolutionary war) He settled at Heath, Massachusetts, and had a son George, born October 23, 1814

(VII) George Sessions, son of George Sessions (6), was born at Heath, October 23, 1814, and died at Worcester, Massachusetts November 8, 1901 He married Mary Groves Mirick, daughter of Tilley and Persis (Moore) Mirick

George Sessions left his home at the age of seventeen to make his own way in the world He came to Worcester and worked first as a farm hand Then for twelve years he was employed at the State Lunatic Asylum on Summer street His first business venture was with a partner named Howe in the manufacture of tools for shoemakers The firm was Howe and Sessions, and the business was successfully conducted for ten years, when he sold to his partner, who continued for many years under the name of John Howe Mr Sessions was appointed city undertaker in 1850, and immediately started in the business which for nearly fifty years he conducted with remarkable success, taking the lead in his business, and maintaining his firm far in advance of all his competitors His appointment, which gave him the opportunity to make use of his natural ability for the difficult duties of his vocation was from Levi Lincoln, then mayor of Worcester, afterward governor of Massachusetts When he began he had charge of all the interments in the city During part of the two first years he was in partnership with Danforth B Cummings, In 1852 he formed partnership with Horace G Mirick, which continued for seven years, subsequently he took his sons into partnership with him As his business grew with the city's growth, he increased his facilities, and added a wholesale department to his undertaking business He held his position as city undertaker until 1886 when he resigned He turned over to his sons, Waldo E and Frank E, who had been in partnership with their father for many years, the management of the business The business has been carried on under the firm name of George Sessions and Sons Mr Sessions lived to see his business more than fifty years old He died November 8, 1901, at his home in Worcester

During his long career in Worcester Mr Sessions had charge of the funerals of many thousands of all classes, and of some very prominent men During the civil war he frequently showed his charity for the widows and orphans of soldiers who gave their lives to their country, and many soldiers were buried at the expense of George Sessions

Mr Sessions married Mary G Mirick, of Holden, Massachusetts (See sketch of her family herewith) They celebrated their golden wedding anniversary in 1888 Three weeks afterward, October 21, 188, Mrs Sessions died Their children were Waldo E, born at Heath, Massachusetts, February 12, 1843, Frank E, born at Worcester, Massachusetts, May 22, 1852, Mary L, born at Worcester, August 23, 1858

(VII) Waldo E Sessions, son of George Sessions (7), was born at Heath, Massachusetts, February 12, 1843 He married Josephine Ufford, October 19, 1869 She was the daughter of Dixon De Forest and Harriet (Gould) Ufford He has been the senior partner of the firm of George Sessions and Sons since the retirement of his father in 1886, and has been identified with it and active in its management for about forty years He is also a member of the wholesale firm of Frank E Sessions and Company Mr Sessions is one of the best known men in the Masonic fraternity in this vicinity, having taken the thirty-two degrees and belonging to the lodge, chapter, council, commandery and other Masonic bodies

The office and ware-rooms of George Sessions and Sons are in a large brick building recently erected at Nos 5 and 9 Trumbull street The wholesale factory of Frank E Sessions and Company is at Nos 7 to 18 Eaton place The firm is still the city sexton and undertaker, and manufactures coffins, broadcloth caskets, and undertakers' supplies

Mr Sessions had three children Laura J, born August 24 1875 married Burton W Grout assistant treasurer of the Worcester Five Cents Savings Bank, February 1, 1899, at Worcester, he died July 4 1905 Mary E born March 20, 1877, lives with her parents Waldo E, Jr, born February 3, 1882, married Marie G Webb daughter of George D Webb, of Worcester They have two daughters Katharine born May 6 1903, at Worcester, and Josephine Ufford born May 13, 1905

(VIII) Frank E Sessions, son of George Sessions (7), was born at Worcester, May 22, 1852 He married Anna Josephine Scranton, daughter of Crawford and Annie (Montgomery) Scranton, April 22, 1874, at Providence Rhode Island He is a partner with his brother Waldo in the firm of George Sessions and Sons also with F E Sessions and Company His children are George, born in 1875, died in the same year, Florence born June 26, 1876, married Edmund A Garland, October 6, 1899, at Worcester, Ethel born December 25, 1880, George, born August 12, 1886 died in 1888 Mr Sessions has been an active Mason for many years, is past master of Athelstan Lodge, has filled all the chairs, and since 1887 has held the office of treasurer continually, all but the three years when he was going through the chairs He has taken thirty-two degrees

(VIII) Mary L. Sessions, daughter of George Sessions (7), was born at Worcester, August 23, 1858 She married Charles G Warren, son of Samuel Warren, October 12 1879 Their children are George Sessions, born September 21, 1881 at Worcester, Charles G, Jr born at Worcester, August 18 1888, Arthur, born at Worcester, December 5, 1880 Philip, born at Worcester, July 12, 1893

THE MIRICK FAMILY (1) John Mirick was the emigrant ancestor of Mrs George Sessions, late of Worcester, Massachusetts He was the son of the Rev William Mirick, of Saint Davids, Wales, Pembrokeshire, and was born in England in 1614, and settled in Charlestown, Massachusetts, where he took the freeman's oath in 1641, and where he pursued his occupation of cooper and blockmaker He married in Charlestown in 1641, Hopestill ——— They had a son John

(II) John Mirick was born at Charlestown, Massachusetts, in 1655 He married Elizabeth Trowbridge February 9, 1682 at Newton, Massachusetts She was the daughter of Deacon James Trowbridge (1636-1717), and granddaughter of Thomas Trowbridge, of Taunton, England, who settled in Dorchester about 1634, went to New Haven, Connecticut, and back to England where he died in 1672 John Mirick was a tanner by trade He was admitted a freeman of Watertown July 21 1685 His will is dated April 29 1706, and he died in July, 1706 One report says he was killed by the Indians at Groton, Massachusetts, July 21, 1706, another that he died July 11 His wife died in 1734 at Newton, Massachusetts aged seventy-four years One of his sons was James born October 26, 1696, at Newton

(III) James Mirick, son of John Mirick (2), was born at Newton, Massachusetts October 26, 1696, and married, October 20, 1725, Mary Woolson She died at Templeton, Massachusetts, September 13, 1780 James was dismissed from Groton church to Weston June 24 1724, and died in Boston, October 26, 1774 He had a son Elisha, born September 13, 1735

(IV) Elisha Mirick son of James Mirick (3), was born at Weston Massachusetts September 13, 1735, and married January 6 1762, at Rutland, Massachusetts Persis Moore, daughter of Lieutenant Paul and Hannah (Hubbard) Moore She was born September 16, 1740, at Rutland and died January 31, 1810 Paul Moore was a soldier in the revolutionary war Elisha Mirick was a housewright and a sergeant in the revolution, in Captain Paul Raymond's company First Worcester Regiment He had a son Tilley, born May 26 1772

(IV) Tilley Mirick son of Elisha Mirick (4), was born at Holden, Massachusetts May 26 1772, married, November 12, 1799, at Holden, Polly Turner who died February 22 1854 Tilley Mirick died September 21, 1832 His daughter Mary Groves Mirick born May 20, 1815, married George Sessions (7), of Worcester, Massachusetts (See sketch of Sessions above)

JAMES A ATHY John Athy (1) father of Andrew Athy and grandfather of James A Athy of Worcester was obliged to leave his native home in Galway Ireland, in 1848, on account of political troubles, during which he had rendered himself obnoxious to the British government by his out-spoken opposition to the laws then in force, both in public speeches and as a leader and agitator among his own people The Athy family was of ancient Irish origin One of the first of the name in Galway erected the first castle in the town, where for many centuries the family has been conspicuous William de Athy was treasurer of Connaught in 1388 and in the charter of Galway given by James II the name of Andrew Athy appears William Athy and Edmond Athy were bailiffs in 1512 and 1514, and Francis Athy was sheriff in 1631 John Athy came to Boston in 1848 with a family of motherless children, his wife having died in Ireland, in 1846 Andrew Athy was left in Boston while John Athy and his son Philip went west They did not return until many years later, and not long afterward the Boston brother with whom Andrew was left also went west.

(II) Andrew Athy, son of John Athy (1), was not only the most prominent man of his race in Worcester, but in his day he was the best known Irish-American citizen in the state He was born January 1, 1832, in Galway, Ireland, and came to Boston with his father in 1848 When his uncle also went west Andrew Athy was left to look out for himself He went to work first in Westboro, where he was employed for a time by the father of Captain J Everts Greene, late postmaster of Worcester In 1850 Mr Athy came to Worcester and from that time until his death was a resident of that city He went to work for the firm of J Walker & Co, in which Hon Joseph H Walker was made a partner in 1851 He learned the trade of shoemaker and for many years worked in the factory of Congressman Walker, holding the position of foreman during a large part of the time In later years curiously enough he twice defeated Mr Walker his former employer as candidate for representative to the general court Although Mr Athy devoted to the shoe business about twenty-five years of his life, he is best known and remembered as the leading undertaker of this section among the Catholic people He went into business in 1875 as undertaker and followed that business the remainder of his life During his later years he took his son into partnership and thus was relieved from some of the burdens of business, which was located first at 16 Green street

Mr Athy never sought public office yet the instances are rare in the history of Worcester where public office so often sought the man A friend wrote of him "Public life had no attraction for him, as he was a better thinker than speaker, and the platform and legislative hall were to him almost places of torture" Yet he served the city in the common council in 1865-66-67-69-70-71-72-73-74-75-76-77-78-78-78-80 No man was more prominent and influential during all those years He represented the city in the general court in 1874-75, having as colleagues Hon W W Rice Samuel R Heywood Colonel J E Estabrook Enoch H Towne and Osgood Bradley He had important committee assignments in the legislature He served in the city council as an alderman in 1881-82-83-85-86 He was the chairman of the street lighting committee when electric lights superseded gas in illuminating the city streets He served on the most important committees Although usually among the minority Mr Athy's long experience and good judgment were always appreciated in the city government, and partisanship did not interfere to any extent with his work in the city government He lived to see the old prejudices against his race die out and his good example had much to do with the promotion of good feeling on the part of his own people He was the candidate for mayor of the Democratic party in 1886 at the close of Mayor Samuel Winslow's first term and although he consented to run only two days before the election he received more votes than the successful candidate the year before

In a Republican city his showing was very creditable to his personal popularity He was chairman of the Democratic city committee in 1891-92-93 When President Cleveland was elected he was prominently mentioned for the position of postmaster, but Captain Greene was re-appointed Mr Athy was a delegate to the Democratic National Convention in 1896 He was appointed one of the three members of the commission to supervise the erection of the new City Hall and attended to his duties on this board, in which he took great interest and satisfaction to the last The very last time he ever left his home was to attend a meeting of the commissioners on the occasion of the delivery of the keys by the contractors

The Spy said of him at the time of his death "Andrew Athy was an American of Americans and yet there has never lived in all America a warmer lover of his native Ireland than he was Every movement that was ever started since he reached the years of manhood having for its object the restoration of Ireland's independence or the amelioration of the condition of her people commanded always his active co-operation and material aid He was a member of the Jackson Guards when that organization was disbanded by Governor Gardner and later he took part in the organization of the Emmet Guards and went to the front with his company immediately after the breaking out of the civil war Such heroes as O'Neill, McConville, McCafferty, Daly and others whose names are on the soldiers' monument were his comrades and personal friends" He was a member of Alhambra Council, Knights of Columbus He was chief marshal of the parade on several St Patrick days Formerly March 17 was the greatest day of the year for the Irish-Americans When the Ancient Order of Hibernians was organized he became a charter member and held every office in the organization He was a charter member of the Irish Catholic Benevolent Society He was head centre of the Fenian Brotherhood from the first when it was in its prime When the Parnell movement started he was elected president of the local branch of the National Land League and served as delegate to several of the national conventions He was honorary member of the American-Irish Historical Society At the time of his death he was president of the Irish Centennial Society of '98 He was a member of the Worcester Board of Trade one of the founders of the Bay State Savings Bank and trustee of the People's Savings Bank In 1870 he was one of the state leaders in the strike of the Knights of St Crispin He went from city to city to present the cause of the strikers and raise funds A prominent shoe manufacturer of Worcester offered him an interest in his business if he would give up abetting the strikers and enter his employ Needless to say Mr Athy refused the offer

At the time of his death *The Spy* said of his knowledge of the theatre "If Andrew Athy had one leaning stronger than another in his nature it was towards the theatre and the stage He loved the play but only in its higher forms for there was no more fastidious theatre-goer in Worcester than he He not only loved the play, but he loved to talk with his friends about his observations of great players he had seen His analysis of the respective abilities of both the Booths, of Lawrence Barrett, of Barry Sullivan, of Henry Irving, Jefferson, Florence and other great actors was at all times interesting and intelligent as it was indeed remarkable As has well been said of him 'He was a dictionary of theatrical reminiscences'"

Mr Athy died May 15 1898 All the newspaper comment in obituary and editorial notices was in line with the following from the records of the city government "There was not a flaw in his armor of principle, integrity and zeal for his fellowmen There was no blemish to mar, no stain to dim the lustre of his character The life of such a man is an inspiration, his death a bereavement to the community" One who knew him well said "For the meagre opportunities that he had he was a wonderful man He was one of the best-read men in Worcester, his library was very extensive He possessed a wonderful memory Whatever he read he never forgot A mass of dates and statistics which would throw the ordinary mind into a chaotic state was with him always arranged for practical and immediate use"

He married Jane Duffy, who died July 8, 1894 His children were 1 Mary, married John J Horgan 2 Frances, a graduate of the high and normal schools in Worcester, and a teacher in the public schools 3 James A see forward 4 Nettie, a well known singer married Dr J J Rafferty 5 Annie, an actress who has been successful in her profession, married Dr P W Heffern, of Boston

Mr Athy's brother, Philip R Athy, who went west with his father was chief of police of Memphis, Tennessee, during the yellow fever epidemic of 1878, he was afterwards sheriff of the county He died there in 1882 at the age of forty-four years

(III) James Andrew Athy son of Andrew Athy (2), was born in Worcester, Massachusetts, January 15 1860 He received his early education in the Worcester public schools After two years in the high school he was appointed a page in the house of representatives of Massachusetts and he held this position in the years 1876-77-78-79, gaining by this experience in the state house a knowledge of men and affairs and a very practical education that has served him in good stead all his life He came back to Worcester to give all his time to his father's business and soon relieved his father of many of the cares and burdens of the same He was associated with him in partnership during most of his business career Andrew Athy established the business in 1875 and from the first James A Athy was familiar with the details After his father's death James A Athy bought out the other heirs and since May 26, 1900 has been the sole owner The office and ware-rooms were removed from Green street to the present location on Trumbull street, July 25, 1900, when the business had been established twenty-five years Mr Athy has been successful in business and stands high in the esteem of all his associates both in the business and social world He is a member of the Knights of Columbus Washington Club, Division 3, A O H, Worcester Lodge of Elks, O'Connel Associates Court Quinsigamond, Order of Forresters, the Frohsinns Wachusett Boat Club, honorary member of the Emmet Guards and George H Ward Post No 10 G A R, veteran member of the Worcester Light Infantry, in which he served in the years 1882-83-84

Mr Athy married (first) in Worcester, July 8, 1885 Mary Cannon daughter of Anthony and Mary (Grady) Cannon She was born in Elgin Illinois and died in Worcester November 8 1889 She was a sister of Tony Hart the famous comedian and minstrel They had one child Anthony Andrew Athy, born July 25 1888 called Tony Hart for his great-uncle he is a student at Holy Cross College, class of 1909 Mr Athy married (second) April 9 1896, Mary Rosa Lee daughter of Peter and Mary (Carrington) Lee, of Worcester

THE McGAULEY FAMILY of Worcester is descended from the McAuley or Macauley family of Scotland and Ireland, having been prominent in Scotland before history began and for many generations in Ireland. The clan Macauley, according to Anderson, belongs to the race MacAlpin of Rossshire and Argyleshire a surname held by a branch of the Rossshire of native Gael. and supposed to have been adopted from the Albanich the first known inhabitants of Scotland. The general denomination, Siel or Cinel (race of), Alpin includes several clans, descendants of the race to which Kenneth McAlpin, under whom the Scots and Picts were united belonged, namely, the clan Gregor, the clan Grant, the Mackinnons, the MacNabs, the MacDuffies or MacFies, the MacQuarries, and the MacAulays. The latter family belongs in Dumbartonshire. There was a laird there of this name in 1608. About that time the family emigrated with thousands of Scotch and English to the northern counties of Ireland. There were in 1890 some four thousand of the family Macauley in the two counties of Antrim and Donegal.

(I) Thomas Macauley, the first ancestor of whom there is any record in the family from which Thomas F. and Walter McGauley, of Worcester, descended lived in the parish and town of Dunleer, county Louth, Ireland, and his descendants still live in that and adjoining towns. He was a cattle dealer and it is believed that the family for some generations before had been engaged in raising and dealing in cattle.

(II) Thomas Macauley, son of Thomas Macauley (1), the preceding, was born and lived in Dunleer, and followed his father's vocation. He was appointed the agent of the cattle raisers and all shipments to the markets were made through him. This office has been held in the family for three generations.

(III) Thomas Macauley, the third of the name, son of Thomas Macauley (2), was the grandfather of the subjects of this sketch. He was born in Drogheda adjoining Dunleer, county Louth, Ireland, in 1809 or 1810. He was a cattle dealer and agent for the shipping of all the cattle of the section. He lived in Dunleer where his children were born. He married 1828-9 Elizabeth Morgan, born in 1806, daughter of C. G. P. Morgan and his wife Fanny Bellow. The children of Thomas and Elizabeth (Morgan) Macauley were: Thomas, of whom later. succeeded his father in office and was succeeded by his son John. Peter, born 1833. Patrick, 1834. Mary, 1836, married ——— Quinn, and died in New Hampshire. Matthew, 1838, lived in France. Margaret, 1840, died young. Elizabeth, 1842, married Thomas Maney, formerly a grocer of Worcester, he acquired a competence, his family resides on Cambridge street. Michael, 1854, resided on Cambridge street where his family now lives. Anne, 1848, married Thomas Nolan, their children reside in Worcester.

(IV) Thomas McGauley, son of Thomas Macauley or McAulay, was the first to adopt the present spelling of the surname in this country. He was born in Dunleer in 1829-30. He came to America when a young man and settled in Uxbridge, Massachusetts. There he married, May 19, 1853, Sarah Gardner, daughter of Walter Gardner, chief of constabulary of county Limerick. The Gardner family came originally from England and were staunch Episcopalians or Church of England in religious faith, but Mrs. Gardner was a Roman Catholic and her daughters followed her while the sons followed the father in church affiliations. The McGauley family came from stern old Scotch covenanters and were largely Presbyterian. Of Walter Gardner's sons: James Gardner became a bandmaster in the Union army during the civil war, Patrick was captain of a company in the First Minnesota Regiment in the civil war, representative and senator in the Minnesota legislature and sheriff of the county, Michael was chief on the Queen's staff with the rank of colonel when General Grant visited Ireland during his tour of the world, John was a policeman in Uxbridge and died there.

Thomas McGauley followed his trade of shoemaker in Uxbridge in the early fifties. He removed in 1858 to the adjoining town of Hopkinton, Massachusetts, where he worked in shoe factories, making boots and shoes by hand. At that time nearly every man in Hopkinton, Uxbridge and other Massachusetts towns known as shoe towns was a skillful shoemaker. In 1863 Mr. McGauley removed to Worcester. He worked in the boot factory of Walker & Brown, and was foreman for Timothy Stone & Sons, boot manufacturers. He died in Worcester, January 31, 1904. His wife died July 14, 1882.

The children of Thomas and Sarah (Gardner) McGauley were: Elizabeth, born February 19, 1855, died young. Thomas Francis, of whom later. Catherine, May 26, 1859, died young. Walter John, June 6, 1861, of whom later. Mary, June 16, 1865, married William B. Gallagher, of Worcester. Sarah, December 21, 1874, unmarried, lives with her brother Walter. Michael, August 28, 1878, died young.

(V) Thomas Francis McGauley, son of Thomas McGauley (4), was born in Uxbridge, Massachusetts, November 4, 1856. His early education was obtained in the public schools of Worcester, whither his parents moved when he was quite young. But his school days were brief, he went to work in the shoe factory under his father when he was twelve years old and continued until twenty-one. Those were the palmy days of the shoe business, and when a boy of fourteen he earned fifteen dollars a week. Compared with the wages in some other trades this was large and it is evidence of the capacity for hard work that has always characterized Mr. McGauley. He was employed by the firm for which his father had worked and later was foreman for Walker & Brown and H. B. Fay, who were prominent boot and shoe manufacturers of Worcester. When Mr. Fay went out of business in 1886, Mr. McGauley determined to make a venture in business on his own account. In December of that year he opened a grocery store at the corner of Cambridge and Douglas streets. Later he removed to his present location at the corner of Cambridge and Camp streets, near the former store. He does business under the name of the Cambridge Market Co. Mr. McGauley has been successful in his business, which has grown constantly from a modest beginning.

He was formerly a director in the Equity Coöperative Bank of Worcester. He is a member of the Worcester Agricultural Society. He was first lieutenant in the Emmet Guards just before that militia company became a part of the regular state militia. Mr. McGauley is best known for his services to the Republican party, of which he has been a staunch supporter and leader for many years. Since 1900 he has represented one of the two Worcester senatorial districts on the Republican state committee and has proved one of the most active, alert and faithful representatives that the committee has had from Worcester. For some twenty years he has served the party as delegate to various conventions. He has been on the Republican county and on the congressional committees. He is a member of the Republican Club. In all these years he has declined to run for office himself. He has given freely of his time and money to strengthen the party in which he believed and to which he belonged. He has the tact and good judgment necessary to make a successful political leader and few men in the city have a wider influence Mr McGauley is free from any obligations that money can create in the political world He believed in helping friends who have been faithful, but in the main his political interests have been centered where he thought the Republican party would be most strengthened He is absolutely trusted by his associates

Mr McGauley and his wife and family attend St Peter's Roman Catholic Parish since his removal to his present residence on Tirrell street With ancestors of Catholic, Presbyterian, Puritan and Church of England beliefs it is not remarkable that Mr McGauley is a man of toleration in religion as well as in politics He abhors bigotry of all kinds

He married, September 23, 1886 Elizabeth T Maloney, daughter of James and Margaret (Deveney) Maloney, of Worcester Their children are Thomas Francis, Jr, born October 17, 1887, James M, July 31 1889, Sarah L, April 10, 1891, Frank, April 26, 1893, Margaret, October 17, 1895, Leo, March 6 1897, Robert August 14, 1899, died young, Arthur, December 1, 1901, Edward, November 24, 1905

(V) Walter John McGauley, son of Thomas McGauley (4), was born in Hopkinton, Massachusetts, June 6, 1861 He followed the boot and shoe business like his father and brother He worked at the boot business in shop of Samuel Brown, corner of Front street and Bartlett place, Worcester for six years, and then he went to West Medway, Massachusetts, and worked for Fogg, Houghton & Coolidge for six months and then was engaged by H B Fay, of Worcester where he changed the system of handling the goods Instead of handling the boots, in course of manufacturing, five times, Mr McGauley did the same work by handling the goods only three times, thereby saving time and expense, and the boots had a better sale besides Mr McGauley remained with H B Fay for eleven years or until he went out of the business After leaving H B Fay he engaged in the grocery business at the corner of Cambridge and Douglas streets, Worcester, which was the beginning of the present business now owned by his brother, Thomas F, and known as the Cambridge Market After conducting the business for a year he sold out to his brother Owing to ill health he was advised by his physician to do outdoor work, and in April, 1888, he was appointed a letter carrier in the Worcester postoffice, in which capacity he is now serving

He married Susan A Littleton daughter of Stephen and Catherine (Hastings) Littleton, who were born in county Clare, Ireland, and who were married in Worcester, Thanksgiving Day, 1853, at St John's Church by Rev Father Gibson W J McGauley and Susan A Littleton were married in Worcester, November 28, 1883 by Rev Thomas J Conaty, at the Church of the Sacred Heart Their children are Susan A born September 17 1884, Sadie H October 3, 1886, Thomas J, September 28, 1887 Anne C, September 18, 1890 Walter Gardner, November 13 1891 Robert Morgan, July 3, 1893, Francis Hastings, June 22, 1897

ALONZO RAY WELLS Thomas Wells (1), who settled in Ipswich among the pioneers, was the emigrant ancestor of Alonzo Ray Wells, of Worcester He was born in England in 1605 and came in the spring of 1635 on the ship "Susan and Ellen" from London with young Richard Saltonstall He settled in Ipswich while his brother, Deacon Richard Wells, settled at Salisbury, Massachusetts, not far away Some writers think that Nathaniel Wells, of Rhode Island, was another brother Thomas was the founder of the Wells family in this country He married Abigail Warner His house lot was No 35 He drew other land afterward He was admitted a freeman May 17, 1637 He was a husbandman

He died October 26, 1666 His will was dated July 31, and proved November 15, 1666 His widow Abigail died July 22, 1671 Her will was made July 22 and proved September 26 1671 Their children were all born in Ipswich, Massachusetts, viz Nathaniel, married, October 29, 1661, Lydia Thurley, John, married, 1665, Sarah Littlefield, Sarah, married John Massie, Abigail, born June 19, 1661, married Nathaniel Treadwell, Thomas, see forward, Elizabeth, married John Burnham, June 9, 1669, Hannah, Lydia, married, March 25, 1669, John Ropes

(II) Rev Thomas Wells, fifth child of Deacon Thomas Wells (1), was born in Ipswich, Massachusetts, 1647 He married, January 10, 1669-70, Mary Perkins When the settlement was made at Wells, Maine, by his brother Nathaniel, he bought land there and he was living in Wells, in December, 1669, as a deed states He was preaching in Kittery and the Isle of Shoals, however, in 1670 He appears to have been a member of the class of 1669, and his father left a provision in his will for his education at Harvard College, but he did not graduate He probably went into the ministry early, as he was the first man honored by Harvard College with the degree of Master of Arts, honorary He appears as of the class of 1703, when the degree was given In 1672 or 1673 he became the first settled minister of Amesbury, Massachusetts He became a leading spirit of the town for some fifty years The history of Amesbury reveals much that is interesting of this good old Puritan minister He died July 10, 1734 His will was dated August 7, 1728, and proved July 29, 1734 His wife Mary died January 26, 1726-7

Their children were Thomas, born October 30, 1670, John, February 2, 1672-3, Luke, March 19, 1673-4, Titus, see forward, a son, who left descendants Abigail, married, February 6, 1704, Samuel Bartlet, Jr, Mary, marrried July 15 1702, John Martin, Eliezer, June 10, 1686, Elizabeth, December 17, 1688, John, October 9, 1692, whose son Thomas removed to Chester, New Hampshire, before 1768

(III) Titus Wells, fourth child of Rev Thomas Wells (2), was born in Amesbury, Massachusetts, March 14 1675-6 He settled in the West Parish in 1726, but always lived in Amesbury He died after 1736 He married Joanna Rowell The children of Titus and Joanna (Rowell) Wells were Sarah, born July 30, 1698 Thomas see forward, Mary, March 11, 1702, Timothy, April 16 1704, Titus and Hannah (twins), February 5 1705-6, he was for a time in Chester New Hampshire, with his brothers, Philemon, September 3, 1708, Jacob, August 28, 1710, went to Chester, New Hampshire, Philip, April 7, 1713, died February 2, 1714-5 Elizabeth March 11, 1716 Abigail December 18 1718

(IV) Lieutenant Thomas Wells, second child of Titus Wells (3), was born in Amesbury, Massachusetts March 4, 1699-1700 He married (first), December 15, 1720, Sarah Hadley, daughter of Samuel and Jane (Martin) Hadley, and granddaughter of the emigrant George Hadley He married (second), about 1738, Elizabeth Ingalls, daughter of Captain Samuel and Mary (Watts) Ingalls She was his eldest daughter and heir, he died in 1760 Captain Ingalls was from Andover, Massachusetts, and was born there May 7, 1683 Elizabeth was born September 18, 1709

Lieutenant Wells was in the service in the Indian wars He became a man of note in Chester, New Hampshire, where he moved in 1729, buying his farm of Eldad Ingalls, some relative of his second wife The lot was No 61 Lieutenant Wells died March, 1769 His will was allowed May 7, 1683 In it he names nine children, all by his second wife except Winthrop

The children were born at Chester, but are recorded at New Chester, (Bristol) New Hampshire except Winthrop They were Winthrop, born probably in Chester about 1730, married Dolly, daughter of William Healy, settled in Candia and Plymouth, New Hampshire, Sarah, December 2, 1739, married ——— Carr, Thomas, January 19, 1741, said to have been killed by John Tolford, December 27, 1773, Henry, March 24, 1743, settled at Sandown, Reuben, see forward, Samuel, August 24, 1749, revolutionary soldier, had homestead at Chester, removed to New Chester, Peter, July 26, 1752, soldier in the revolution, Ebenezer, May 3, 1754, married Sarah Favor, settled in Hill, New Hampshire, Phebe, October 14, 1757, Peter, January 20, 1762, revolutionary soldier, Timothy, May 10, 1765

(V) Reuben Wells, fifth child of Lieutenant Wells (4), was born in Chester, New Hampshire, August 28, 1746 He married Molly ——— He went with his father to New Chester, New Hampshire, now Bristol and Hill His father owned one hundred acres at Chester, one hundred and seventy acres at Goffstown and four hundred acres at New Chester, when he died He removed to New Chester with his six sons, among whom was Reuben, shortly before his death in 1769 Reuben's farm was lot No 61 fourth division in what is now Hill, New Hampshire He was living there in 1774 He died April 3, 1804, at Hill, aged fifty-seven years, seven months, five days, according to the records He was a soldier in 1777 in Captain Samuel McConnel's company, Colonel Thomas Stickney, General John Stark's regiment at Bennington

The children of Reuben and Molly Wells, all born in New Chester or Hill, New Hampshire, were Reuben, born April 3, 1770, see forward, Thomas, August 14, 1771, married Betty Bean, Hannah, January 16, 1777, married Ephraim Quimby, John, December 19, 1778, married Judith Favor, Samuel, September 29, 1780, married Rebecca Carleton, Henry, April 22, 1783 died June 26, 1800, Molly, November 5, 1784, Ebenezer, February 17, 1787, Peter, May 17, 1789, Joanna, January 24, 1792, married Samuel Hoyt, Sarah, October 27, 1793, died August 18, 1795 (There is an interesting letter from Reuben Wells relating to the enlistment of his brother Peter in the revolution on file at the state archives, Concord, New Hampshire, and printed in the state papers It refers to Lieutenant Thomas, his father and other members of the family It seems that Peter did service for other members of the family in the revolution when it was inconvenient for them to go Brother Peter was in charge of Reuben after his father's death)

(VI) Reuben Wells, eldest son of Reuben Wells (5), was born in New Chester, now Hill, New Hampshire, April 3, 1770 He married Priscilla Sanborn He was a farmer at Hill, where his children were born He died August 4, 1808 His wife died March 10 1807 Their children were Moses, see forward, Reuben, born April 22 1795, married Mahala ———, died March 22, 1819, in twenty-fifth year, leaving one child Lucy, November 8, 1797 married Moses Sanborn Sanborn, October 12, 1801, lived and died in Londonderry, had no children Sherburn, born July 31, 1805 married, September 28, 1828, Martha Washington Chase, who was born in Hill, November 15, 1802, located at Bristol in 1838, was custom carder and cloth dresser, played bass viol in the church, died at Bristol, November 16, 1874, wife died July 24, 1889 Their daughter, Martha A, born August 10, 1829, married William G Gould, and died September 4, 1857, leaving Francis Leroy Gould, now of Chicago, their son, Fletcher Chase, born July 15, 1831, married, September 3, 1857, Sarah S Drake, he died June 20, 1872, leaving Frank Fletcher Wells, born at New Hampton, May 22, 1858, now of Chicago, and Martha Ann, born at Bristol, July 20, 1860, married George P Everleth, a printer of 18 Goulding street, Worcester They have a daughter, Minnie Sadie, born in Bristol, September 19, 1881, married, September 24, 1902, Albert H Austin, and they have Chester Eveleth, born in Worcester, March 25, 1884 (The Austins reside at 18 Goulding street with the Everleths)

(VII) Moses Wells, eldest child of Reuben Wells (6), was born at Bristol, or Hill, New Hampshire, September 19, 1792 He married Elizabeth Ray, daughter of John Ray, of Manchester, New Hampshire She was born in Derryfield, New Hampshire, in 1795 Moses lived in Londonderry, New Hampshire, and Charlestown, Massachusetts John Ray was a revolutionary soldier and served under General Stark at Bunker Hill and Bennington He owned a large farm in the northern part of Derryfield and was active in the movement to change the name to Manchester He was a prominent citizen He was a friend and neighbor of General Stark

The children of Moses and Elizabeth (Ray) Wells were Amos, resided in Malden, Massachusetts, and Manchester, New Hampshire, where he kept a store, died there, left sons Horace and Sherburn Priscilla, married Josiah Sawyer, Elizabeth, married Josiah Sawyer (husband of sister Priscilla also), Mary, married John Fosdick, they resided in Lowell, Massachusetts, and Manchester, New Hampshire, their son, Sylvester Fosdick, resides in South Boston, Massachusetts, Alonzo Ray, see forward

(VIII) Alonzo Ray Wells, youngest son of Moses Wells (7), was born in Charleston, New Hampshire, May 1, 1842 He received a common school education Mr Wells enlisted 11 August, 1862, as a wagoner in Company A, Tenth New Hampshire Volunteers He was promoted first as forage master, then assistant wagon master and later wagon master, and had charge of the ammunition train in Butler's advance up the James in 1864 In 1865, after the close of the war, he was stationed in Richmond and used his teams in returning the refugees to their homes, leaving Richmond every Monday morning with sixty wagons and twenty ambulances loaded with refugees and their goods It usually took a week to make a trip and Mr Wells had many sad as well as laughable experiences He was discharged in 1865 with his regiment Soon after his discharge he entered the railroad service, became a locomotive engineer, and continued till 1887 He is now living retired at 9 Arbor Vitae street, Worcester

Mr Wells is a Free Mason and a member of the order of Elks He belongs to the Frohsinns, a social club, the George H. Ward Post, No 10, G A R, of Worcester, Worcester Driving Club and the Cottage Club and Improvement Society of Falmouth, Massachusetts, where he has a summer residence He is a Congregationalist in religious preferences and Republican in politics

He married (first) Emily Harris, daughter of C M and Emily (Dean) Harris She was born December 6, 1846, died March, 1891, in Worcester

He married (second) March 12, 1896, Eva Irene Bruso, daughter of Charles and Emily J Bruso, of Worcester She was born there November 3, 1874 She was educated in the Worcester schools, and is a graduate of the Worcester high school The only child of Mr Wells was by the first marriage Ray Dean, born in Worcester, April 29, 1890 He is at present a student in the Worcester high school

ALEXANDER COLE MUNROE, one of the most prominent citizens of Worcester, Massachusetts, and who has been actively identified with the steamship, railroad, insurance and musical interests of that city, traces his descent to a family that has had a distinguished record ever since the days of the pioneer settlers of the state of Massachusetts

(I) William Munroe, one of the first settlers of Lexington, Massachusetts, was the ancestor of most of those bearing this name in New England Some members of the family spell the name Monroe, and in the early history of the family in this country (and probably the the same practice was observed elsewhere) the first syllable "Mun" was omitted, and the name was variously spelled 'Roe," 'Row" and "Rowe" William Munroe was born in Scotland, in 1625, and belonged to the famous clan bearing that name He came to America in 1652, probably a prisoner of war taken by Cromwell at the battle of Worcester, or soon afterward, and sold in service to an American proprietor It is on record that in 1651 Robert Munroe, Hugh Munroe, John Munroe and another of the same family name, were among those consigned to Thomas Kemble, of Boston, and obliged to work for a certain period of time for those who had bought their services from the government William Munroe worked out his time and acquired property in Cambridge as early as 1657 He settled in Cambridge Farms (now Lexington) in 1660, near the Woburn line, his farm being on Woburn street, on or near the farm now or lately owned by Hugh Graham His sons lived with him after they had attained manhood, and it is related by his descendants that he made so many additions to his dwelling house, to accommodate the families of his sons, that the place resembled a ropewalk, it was so long He was admitted a freeman in 1690, and subscribed to the building fund for the first meetinghouse He was married three times, and though he was forty years old at the time of his first marriage, raised a family of thirteen children He died January 27, 1717, and his will, dated November 14, 1716, mentions sons—John, George, Daniel, Joseph and Benjamin—and daughters—Eleanor Burgess, Martha Comee, Hannah Peirce, Elizabeth Rugg, and Mary Fassett

He married (first), 1655, Martha ———, and their children were John, of whom later, Martha, born November 2, 1667, married, January 21, 1688, John Comee, of Concord, resided at Lexington, died, April 13, 1729, William, born October 10, 1669, married Mary Cutler, George, married Sarah ——— William Munroe married (second), 1672, Mary ———, born in 1651, died August, 1692 Their children were Daniel, born August 12, 1673, married Dorothy ———, Hannah, married, December 21, 1692, Joseph Peirce, and had eight children Joseph Peirce's first wife was Ruth Holland, and his third, Beriah Child, widow of Daniel Child, Elizabeth, married Thomas Rugg and had eleven children, Mary, born June 24, 1678, married about 1700, Joseph Fassett, lived on the Page place in Bedford, from thence moved to Lexington, David, born October 6, 1680, not mentioned in the will of his father, Eleanor, born February 24, 1683, married, August 21, 1707, William Burgess, of Charlestown, had four children, Sarah, born March 18, 1685, married George Blanchard, about 1707, Joseph, born August 16, 1687, married Elizabeth ———, Benjamin, born August 16, 1690, married twice William Munroe married (third) Elizabeth Wyer, widow of Edward Wyer, of Charlestown, she died December 14, 1715, in her eightieth year

(II) John Munroe, eldest child of William (1), and Martha Munroe, was born May 10, 1666 He was admitted to the church, February 1, 1699, together with his father, and his sisters, Martha Comee, Elizabeth Rugg, and Hannah Peirce He subscribed to the building fund of the meetinghouse in 1692, and was on the tax list of 1693 He became a very prominent citizen, serving the town as assessor in 1699, 1714 and 1720, constable in 1700, selectman in 1718-9 and 1726, and treasurer of the town in 1718-19-20 He held many positions of trust and honor He was lieutenant of the militia there He received a grant of nine hundred acres of land for his services in the battle with the Indians at Lamprey river, June 6, 1690 In addition to his many other offices and duties, he was sexton of the church and rang the bell for years in the first church in Lexington to call the worshipers to service His death occurred September 14, 1753 He married Hannah ———, who died April 14, 1716 Their children were John, born in Lexington, baptized 1699, probably married Rachel ———, Hannah, baptized 1699, died April 14, 1716, Constance, baptized 1699, Jonathan baptized March 12 1699 died August 20, 1724, William, baptized February 1, 1701, married twice, Elizabeth, baptized March 5, 1703, Susannah, baptized July 1, 1705, married, June 16, 1724, Ebenezer Nichols, Jonas, of whom later, Martha, born December 6, 1710, Marrett, born December 6 1713 married, April 17, 1737, Deliverance Parker

(III) Jonas Munroe, fourth son and eighth child of John (2), and Hannah Munroe, was born in Lexington, Massachusetts, November 22, 1707 He was a lieutenant of the Lexington Militia Company He married (first), June 3, 1734, Joanna Locke, born February 2, 1713 died September 17, 1748, daughter of Joseph and Mary (Mead) Locke Their children were Jonas, born November 2, 1735, died June 3, 1760, John, of whom later, Stephen born October 25, 1739, married, July 8, 1766, Nancy Perry, of Woburn, Massachusetts, Jonathan, born May 25 1742, married Abigail Kendall, of Woburn, Joanna, born April 12 1747, married, July 9, 1777, John Adams Jonas Munroe married (second), 1750, Rebecca Watts, of Chelsea He died November 9 1765, and his widow married, April 19, 1773, John Muzzy, of Lexington grandson of the first settler and his second wife The children of Jonas and Rebecca (Watts) Munroe were Ebenezer, born April 29 1752, he was a settler at Ashburnham, where other members of the family also located He was an officer in the revolutionary war, a prominent citizen and left many descendants He married, May 10, 1782 Lucy Simonds, of Woburn Rebecca, born June 17, 1755, married, May 22, 1777, John Muzzy Jr Martha, born September 12, 1758, died at Ashburnham, 1793, unmarried

(IV) John Munroe, second son and child of Jonas (3) and Joanna (Locke) Munroe, was born in Lexington, Massachusetts February 1 1737 He was a member of the Lexington Company of Militia in the battle of Lexington, and marched to Cambridge, June 17 1775 He probably rendered other services to his country The names of his children were obtained from a deed in which his heirs assign their rights to his real estate in Princeton to Jonathan Page, of Charlestown This Page married Lydia a daughter of John Munroe The deed bears date of February 23, 1805 One record gives the name of his first wife as Anna, and their children as Sarah, baptized July 12, 1767, probably died young, Anna, born November 18, 1759, baptized July 12, 1767, probably died young He married (second), April 13, 1762, Lydia Bemis, of Weston, Massachusetts, daughter of John and Hannah Bemis Their children were Lydia, born at Lexington, Massachusetts, May 9, 1767, baptized May 17, 1767, married, January 16, 1783, Jonathan Page, of Lincoln, Massachusetts, later of Charlestown, Massachusetts, where he kept a tavern of note He was colonel in the militia, and was stationed in Boston harbor, in 1812, to superintend the erection of some fortifications there He bought out the interests of the other heirs of John Munroe at Princeton Polly (Mary), married Nathaniel Brackett (intentions dated December 31, 1805) John Lucy, married John Stone (intentions dated February 7, 1802) Sally, born 1782, died June 28, 1836, at Princeton Massachusetts Nathan, of whom sketch follows

(V) Nathan Munroe, second son and sixth and youngest child of John (4) and Lydia (Bemis) Munroe, was born in Lexington or Newton, Massachusetts, June, 1773 He lived for a time in Newton, and then bought a lot in Rutland, June 3, 1801, and settled there He bought another lot, adjoining his farm, two years later He was living in Rutland in 1805 when he deeded his interest in the estate of his father, in Princeton, to his brother-in-law, Jonathan Page He sold a piece of land in Rutland, December 3, 1817, a tract of land, to Jesse Pitts, of Oakham, Massachusetts About that time he went to Pennsylvania on business, on his return he was taken sick, and died suddenly at Dana (Hardwick or Rutland before 1801), in 1818 He married Deidamia Wheeler, June 2, 1799, and their children were Charles, of whom later Isabella, born in Rutland, Massachusetts, November 24, 1802, died August 31, 1844 John, born in Rutland, Massachusetts, July 7, 1805, married Mary Epps, lived in Concord, New Hampshire, father of Hon John P Munroe, of Worcester, died February 21, 1896 George, born in Rutland, Massachusetts, April 3, 1807, died July, 1831 Cyrus, born in Rutland, Massachusetts, December 27, 1811, died December 12, 1864 Nathan, born in Rutland, Massachusetts, August 31, 1814, died February 8, 1839 Abigail, born in Rutland, Massachusetts, October 3, 1817, died June 14, 1818

(VI) Charles Munroe, eldest child of Nathan (5) and Deidamia (Wheeler) Munroe, was born in Newton, Massachusetts, March 6, 1800, died June 5, 1891 He married Mary Cole, of Millbury, June 26, 1828 Their children were Ruby Ann, born in Worcester, July 16, 1829, Alexander Cole, of whom later, Lyman Cole, born in Worcester, October 16 1838, died September 6, 1904

(VII) Alexander Cole Munroe, second child and eldest son of Charles (6) and Mary (Cole) Munroe, was born in Millbury, Massachusetts, August 22, 1831 Shortly afterward he removed with his parents to Worcester, where his youth was spent He attended the little white wooden and the brick schoolhouse, formerly on the common, with Caroline Corbett as teacher and Sarah Joyce as assistant Many of the boys who attended this school have made their mark in the world Later he attended the "English" school at the corner of Thomas and Summer streets, under the tuition of Warren Lazell His parents removed to Lowell, Massachusetts, in 1846, and he went with them He accepted a position in the Lowell postoffice, in 1850, and had charge of the mailing department for three years He was then for six years in the employ of the Boston & Lowell railroad, in the freight and ticket departments, being superintendent of transportation at Lowell for the two months prior to its consolidation with the Nashua and Lowell railroad While living here Mr Munroe took an active part in the work of the High Street Congregational Church, being for several years its treasurer, collector and librarian of the Sunday school

He finally left Lowell to accept a position as station agent for the Providence & Worcester Railroad, at Woonsocket, Rhode Island, in 1859, and remained there until his appointment, in 1861, as general agent for New England of the Providence & Worcester Railroad and Providence & New York Steamship Company, with headquarters at Worcester, Massachusetts The competition at that time for New York freight to and from Worcester and the north was very strong The combination between the steamship line and the railroad was made in 1858, and the monopoly previously enjoyed by the Norwich line was seriously disturbed When Mr Munroe accepted this position the competition was at its height Mr Munroe entered eagerly on this work, glad also to return to the city in which his boyhood had been spent His work was successful and satisfactory to the companies In spite of the fact that there were nine radical changes in the management of the companies during the twelve years he held this position, he retained his place undisturbed He handled all the freight of both corporations and also all freight by the Neptune line from Worcester, and points north and east to New York, the south and west, amounting in through billing to more than two hundred thousand dollars annually

Having purchased the insurance agency of General George A Washburn, of Worcester, in February, 1873, Mr Munroe took up with alacrity the new line of work with which he has since been identified He retained the management of the transportation business, at the request of the railroad and steamship companies interested, until October 1, 1873, when, finding the double duties burdensome, he resigned as general agent He largely extended the business of the fire insurance agency, he purchased, and has for many years been in the foremost ranks of fire insurance men in the state He has been president of the Worcester board of fire underwriters for four years, and at the present time (1906) is president of the Worcester protective department, of which he has been for thirty years a director On account of the increased scope of the business Mr Munroe decided to take a partner and on January 1, 1903, invited Edward P Ingraham to become his business associate, the firm name being A C Munroe & Ingraham Mr Ingraham is an expert in fire insurance, having been for fourteen years secretary of the board of underwriters of Worcester, and an energetic business man The efforts of the new firm have resulted in even greater gains than before, Mr Munroe calculating recently that the agency had earned about four hundred thousand dollars above the losses during the time he had been in the business The firm now represents the following companies Liverpool and London and Globe Insurance Company, Atlas Assurance Company of London Franklin Fire Insurance Company of Philadelphia, Spring Garden Insurance Company and Philadelphia Underwriters of Philadelphia Williamsburgh City Fire Insurance Company of New York, Newark Fire Insurance Company of Newark, New Jersey, Buffalo German Insurance Company and Buffalo Commercial Insurance Company of Buffalo, New York, Albany Insurance Company of New York, India Insurance Company of Boston, Camden Fire Insurance Association of New Jersey, Insurance Company of the State of Pennsylvania, Worcester Mutual Fire Insurance Company, the Merchants' and Farmers' Mutual Fire Insurance Company, The Abingdon Mutual Fire Insurance Company, The Dorchester Mutual Fire Insurance Company, Standard Life and Accident Insurance Company of Detroit, and the Columbia Insurance Company of New Jersey The A C Munroe & Ingraham agency is located in the Clark building on Main street, nearly opposite City Hall Mr Munroe has for many years been the leader in his line of business in the city of Worcester His judgment in insurance is sought by the business men of Worcester and implicitly followed In one case Mr Munroe had a million dollar insurance risk to place in a single day

He comes of a musical family, and has been interested in musical work ever since he took up his residence in Worcester He was at one time chairman of the board of trustees of the Worcester Mozart Society, treasurer of the Beethoven Society, afterward president of the Worcester Choral Union For thirty-four years he has been a member of the Worcester Musical Festival Chorus, and for thirty-three years of this time was executive officer of the association, having been secretary twenty-three years, vice-president eight years and president two years He was basso of the quartette choir of the Union Church for four years, and for twenty-three years basso and director of the choir of the Old South Church When he resigned from that position in 1888 he was substantially reminded of the good will of the congregation Many believe that the uniformly good music at the Old South Church is due to the faithful and constant efforts of Mr Munroe, and that this accounts for the growth and leadership of that church in music over many other churches in the city

During his official connection with the festivals, they advanced from small and modest efforts until they rivalled anything of the kind in this country or Europe and have made the name of Worcester famous in musical circles the world over

He has not lost his interest in the association, being still one of the most earnest and persistent workers for the success of the annual festivals While he was secretary much of the routine work and the burden of correspondence fell upon his shoulders In an article about Mr Munroe, *Worcester Light* says "Mr Munroe has requested *Light* not to say much about his services in connection with the Festivals, claiming that the marked success achieved is due to the unselfish devotion of a splendid body of choir leaders and teachers forming the board of government during his connection with it—to the location of the Festival in a region noted for a century for its love of music—to the teaching of music in the public schools—to the growth of the city itself—and to the undoubtedly high average intelligence of the population Admitting these facts, *Light* still believes that the work of Mr Munroe has been of so conspicuous a character in connection with the Festivals, that the general public will insist upon giving him a larger amount of commendation for the results attained, than he is at present inclined to receive"

Mr Munroe is a member of the Board of Trade, the Worcester Mechanics' Association, the Old South Church, the Congregational Club, of which he was formerly treasurer He is an honorary member of the Worcester Continentals He has been a member of the Worcester Society of Antiquity, and of the Commonwealth Club His executive ability and remarkable tact have been proven by the position he has held in musical circles, requiring probably more tact and judgment than any other position man is called upon to fill He has a very attractive personality, and all his acquaintances are drawn into the circle of his friendship He is quick to perceive and decide, but conciliatory in manner and speech, and although respecting the opinions of others, is not inclined to yield his own convictions He is one of the best examples of the gentleman in business, of exemplary character, refined and considerate of others, appreciating his duty as a citizen, loving art and music, yet thoroughly enjoying his business career

Mr Munroe married, October 19, 1859, Helen Augusta Hill, born in Whitefield, New Hampshire, March 23, 1834, daughter of Peter W and Hannah (Johnson) Hill At an early age she removed with her parents to Lowell, Massachusetts Mrs Munroe has had an unusual musical career She is an artist with much more than a local reputation, having been a leading member of quartette choirs for thirty-four years For twenty-eight years she was a member of the same choir as her husband, sustaining the soprano part for twelve years, and the contralto for sixteen years, her voice being of so extended a compass (from G below low C, to C in alt three octaves and three notes) that she was able to sing either part with remarkable success At the age of fourteen years she was engaged as the leading alto singer of the Worthen Street Methodist Church Choir, in Lowell, and until 1861, when she came to Worcester, sang constantly in Methodist, Unitarian, Episcopal and Congregational choirs in Lowell and its vicinity, as well as at public concerts of importance and social functions On coming to Worcester she was at once secured as contralto for the Union Church Quartette, Mr B D Allen being the organist and director She continued to be the leading attraction at concerts for many years, notably those given by the Hamilton," the Mozart" and "Beethoven" Societies, and the Worcester "Choral Union" For fourteen years prior to 1873 she was the leading contralto soloist of the Worcester Music Festivals, and then declined the position During these years Mrs Munroe filled engagements with many associations elsewhere, in concerts musical conventions and festivals in Boston Providence, Springfield, Greenfield, Fitchburg Brooklyn, New York, Bridgeton, New Jersey, and many other cities She has always been of a retiring disposition, modest and diffident, and, while enjoying church positions, disliked the notoriety of public concert work Possessed of a remarkable voice, which renders her at the present day a highly prized member of the "Home Music Club,' of which association she was a charter member, she was, when quite young, offered the opportunity to visit Europe and study for the operatic field Great success was prophesied for her, competent judges said of her voice that it was only equalled by that of the great Alboni Possessed of a fine stage presence, she would undoubtedly have been successful but she shrank from publicity, and at the advice of the friend whom she afterward married remained in America Mrs Munroe's grandfather, Asa Johnson, of Whitefield New Hampshire, was a teacher of music and singing schools, an excellent violin player, and well known throughout northern New Hampshire He was also a prosperous farmer His eight children—Simeon, James, David, William, Catherine, Joanna, Sarah and Hannah—were all musical, and it was said that the Johnson girls could "sing down anything in Coos county" Hannah, the mother of Mrs Munroe, could sing the "C in alt," (or high C,") while her husband, Peter W Hill, could as easily sing the "low C," it would thus appear that Mrs Munroe came very naturally by her unusual voice, and her musical ability The Hill family was a large one, and all the members were musical, the choir of the church in Whitefield, New Hampshire, was composed entirely of members of the Hill and Johnson families, under the charge of Asa Johnson, and was for years a very noted one Mrs Munroe has always been interested in religious and charitable work, having been for four years president of the Old South Benevolent Society, and for thirteen years president of the Women's Auxiliary to the Young Men's Christian Association

DANIEL AUSTIN HOWE John How or Howe (1), the immigrant ancestor of Daniel Austin Howe, of Worcester, Massachusetts, was an early settler at Watertown, Massachusetts He was born in Warwickshire, England, it is believed, the son of John Howe, who is supposed to be a descendant of John Howe, of Hodinhall, connected with Sir Charles Howe, of Lancaster, during the reign of Charles I

John Howe made his home in Sudbury with settlers from Watertown, then the adjoining town He was there in 1639 or earlier He was admitted a freeman in 1640 In 1642 he was one of the Sudbury selectmen According to tradition he was the first white inhabitant who settled in the Sudbury New Grant, as it was called He built his cabin a little to the eastward of the Indian plantation, and in this vicinity many of his descendants have lived and are living still His house was about one thousand rods from the Spring Hill Meeting House, a little to the east of the present road from Spring Hill to Feltonville, lately owned by Edward Rice

Howe was a man of dignity and universally respected, even by his Indian neighbors In 1655 he was appointed "to see to the restraining of the youth on the Lord's Day" Boys were boys even in the Puritan town of Sudbury in the days of Cromwell He was brought into contact often with his Indian neighbors and he won their confidence and good will and often he became an arbiter in case of differences between them The story is told of a pumpkin grown on the land of one Indian, but on a vine belonging to another Both claimed the pumpkin Howe was asked to decide the ownership of the pumpkin He cut it in two and gave a half to each From 1657 till his death in 1680 he lived in Marlboro, and was the founder of most of the families of this surname in Middlesex and Worcester counties

Descendants of Abraham Howe, another emigrant settler, also settled in Marlboro, however In 1662 he and Goodman Rice were appointed to make a grant of land to Thomas Danforth, or rather determine the size of a grant made by the general court in payment of services John Howe opened the first public house in Marlboro He petitioned the general court September 30, 1662, to be excused from training because he was aged, thick of hearing and maintained three soldiers in his family He died in Marlboro, May 28, 1680 His will was dated May 24, 1680, and proved June 15, 1680 He made bequests to his wife, Mary, and children Samuel, Isaac, Thomas, Eleazer, Sarah Ward, Mary Wetherby, grandchild, John, son of John He gave Thomas "the horse he troops on"

His children were John, born 1640, married, January 22, 1662, Elizabeth Woolson, was killed by the Indians, Samuel, October 20, 1642, married June 5, 1663, at Sudbury, Martha Bent, Sarah, September 25, 1644, married, June, 1667, Samuel Ward, died young, Mary, August 8, 1648, Isaac, August 8, 1648, married, June 17, 1671, Frances Wood, Josiah, married March 18, 1671, Mary Haynes, of Sudbury, Mary, June 18, 1654, married, September 18, 1672, John Wetherby, Thomas, June 12, 1656, married Sarah Hosmer, married (second) Mary Barron, Daniel, June 3, 1658, died 1661, Alexander, December 29, 1661, died January, 1662, Eleazer, January 18, 1662, married, 1683, Hannah Howe, daughter of Abraham Howe, of Marlboro

(II) Colonel Samuel Howe, son of John Howe (1), was born October 20, 1642, in Sudbury, Massachusetts He married, June 5, 1663, Martha Bent, daughter of John Bent, of Sudbury, and settled in his native town He was admitted a freeman in Sudbury in 1671 He married (second) Sarah Clapp, September 18, 1685, and had other children He was an important man in his day He was colonel of the regiment made up of companies from the towns in the vicinity He was a town officer

The children of Samuel and Martha (Bent) Howe were John, born July 24, 1664, Mary, March 2, 1665, Lydia, Samuel, May 19, 1668, Martha, October 9, 1669, Daniel, November 2, 1674, David, November 2, 1674, Hannah, April 6, 1677 The children of Colonel Samuel and Sarah (Clapp) Howe were Daniel, February 24, 1689, (probably) Moses, about 1695, Micagah, August 22, 1700

(III) David Howe, son of Colonel Samuel Howe (2), was born in Sudbury, Massachusetts, November 2, 1674 He married, December 25, 170-- (probably 1702, record torn) He built and conducted the Wayside Inn He received from his father, Samuel Howe, in 1702, the farm on which it is located It was part of one hundred and thirty acres in the New Grant territory, either lot 48 or 49 The tavern was built a few years after David Howe acquired the land The Indians were threatening during the first decade of the eighteenth century, and the workmen engaged in building it had to resort at night to the Parmenter garrison half a mile away It was opened as a public house It was not until 1746 that it became known as the Red Horse Tavern In that year Colonel Ezekiel Howe, David's son and successor as tavern keeper, put up as a sign a red horse, a time honored custom of the early taverns, being to designate for the benefit of the unlettered the house by some picture or sign by which one who could not read might identify the house In later years it became known as the Wayside Inn from the Tales of the Wayside Inn written by Longfellow Of course, the old tavern cannot claim all that Longfellow ascribed to it, but no more fitting country tavern could have been selected for his purpose It is a fine specimen of early architecture, plain, but spacious and interesting

During the revolutionary war, when it was conducted by Colonel Ezekiel Howe, the Red Horse Inn was the centre of revolutionary activity After the death of the famous old colonel his son, Adam Howe, conducted the hotel for forty years Then came the railroads and the paths of travel changed Lyman Howe was the last Howe in the direct line to run the hotel He sold it in 1866 The Wayside Inn has been at times since then run as a road house It is much frequented by lovers of Longfellow At present the old house is an attractive spot for automobile owners who are interested in colonial history and antiquities The quiet dignity of the old tavern is very charming, much different is the scene there today from the bustle and activity of nearly two hundred years ago when the tavern was one of the best on the road from Boston to the colonies to the westward It was a stopping place for settlers on their way to their new homes It was a halting place for troops during all the Indian wars and the revolution The farmers on their way to and from the market in Boston stopped there The stages to and from Boston passed there Washington and other celebrated men have slept in the old inn It would be of great historic interest even if Longfellow had not immortalized it The region round about corresponds well with the character of the building It is on the edge of a plain in what is called the Peckham district at the foot of Nobscot Hill Close to the inn runs a little brook known as Hop brook The hotel stands at the side of the broad road, looking today much as it did probably a hundred and seventy-five years ago David Howe died August 3, 1759, at Sudbury

The children of David and Hepsibah (Death) Howe were Thankful, born December 15, 1703, married Peter Howe, April 9, 1723, Hepsibah, October 1, 1706, Eliphalet, June 3, 1710, settled in Rutland, Israel, May 6, 1712, settled in Rutland, Ruth, February 23, 1714-5, David, June 13, 1717, Ezekiel, April 5, 1720, settled in Sudbury, owned the tavern there

(IV) Ezekiel Howe, son of David Howe (3), was born in Sudbury, Massachusetts, April 5, 1720 He married Bathsheba ———, January 19, 1743-4, and about the time of his marriage succeeded his father in the ownership of the tavern It was in 1746 that he named it the Red Horse Tavern He was chosen lieutenant-colonel of Colonel Henry Gardner's fourth Middlesex regiment, and commissioned February 15, 1776, but he declined to serve He was chosen colonel of the same regiment and commissioned May 10, 1776 He marched with his regiment at the Lexington alarm and served most of the time during the revolution until ill health compelled him to resign in a letter dated January 26, 1779 The resignation was accepted February 4, 1779 He was in some of the New York campaigns

Colonel Ezekiel Howe was probably the most prominent citizen of Sudbury and the vicinity at the period of the revolution He was honored and respected by his fellow citizen, a man of property and influence He held town offices and various positions of honor

The children of Colonel Ezekiel and Bathsheba Howe were Ruth, born May 2, 1745, Ann, January 8, 1746-7, (one record gives 1747-8), Hepsibah, April 27, 1749, Bathsheba, January 10, 1752, Molly, August 13, 1754, Ezekiel, May 19, 1756, Olive, July 19, 1758, Eliphalet March 23, 1761, Adam, May 15, 1763

(V) Eliphalet Howe, son of Colonel Ezekiel Howe (4), was born in Sudbury, Massachusetts, March 23, 1761 He married Hannah Henry, June 19, 1788 She died September 23, 1822 He died December 7, 1834 He settled in Barre, near Rutland, where his Uncle Eliphalet was one of the early settlers on Walnut Hill The history of Rutland mentions the uncle among the first settlers The name was spelled How in practically all the early records of Sudbury and Rutland, while another family named Howe was living in the same towns The distinction of the families ceased when practically all the Howe family added the final "e" The Howe family is one of the most prominent and numerous of all the early families in Worcester county Eliphalet Howe's place was in Barre and there his descendants still live

The children of Eliphalet and Hannah Howe were Adam, born April 8, 1789, drowned June 13, 1806, Hannah, May 5, 1791, married Moses Lawrence, Jr, of Hardwick, February 18, 1819, Artemas, born July 3, 1796, married (intentions dated December 18,) 1822, Sophia M Wetherell, of Petersham, Asenath, February 24, 1798, married John W Weston December 29, 1819, Submit, October 9, 1799, Charlotte, June 18, 1802, married Stillman Clark, of Hardwick (intentions dated April 22,) 1842, Eliphalet, February 18, 1804

(VI) Eliphalet Howe, Jr, son of Eliphalet Howe (5), was born in Barre, Massachusetts, February 18, 1804 He married Keziah Kinsman, June 28 1833 She was born January 1, 1802 He was a farmer living in Barre where all his children were born The children of Eliphalet and Keziah Howe were Samuel Austin, born May 6, 1834, Mercy Ellen, December 25, 1836, married Franklin Babbitt, died August 1, 1885, Augustus Elliott, born in Barre, October 23, 1837, Maria, October 23, 1839, Christina, May 4, 1843, Mary Elizabeth, November 1, 1847 died January 17, 1848, Frank

(VII) Samuel Austin Howe, son of Eliphalet Howe (6), was born in Barre, Massachusetts, May 6, 1834 He died in Barre, February 12, 1905 He married, December 29, 1858, Lucy Jane Warner, who was born June 15, 1835, at Hardwick, Massachusetts, of the well known Warner family She died October 18, 1887 They lived in Barre and Westboro, where Mr Howe carried on a farm and conducted a large milk route

The children of Samuel A and Lucy J Howe were Ella J, born December 19, 1859, married William A Reed, June 18, 1879, has two children William C, born April 4 1880, and Vera, August 7, 1889, Daniel Austin, January 17, 1862, married Florence G Tenney, December 5, 1899, Walter Eliphalet, Westboro, January 15, 1868, married Mary Ballou Upton, and had Maud, Daniel W, James Weston, Westboro, June 20, 1873, married Carrie Delano, and had one child, Madeline

(VIII) Daniel Austin Howe, son of Samuel Austin Howe (7), was born in Barre, Massachusetts, January 17, 1862 His father moved from Barre to Westboro when he was six years old, and he attended the public schools of Westboro, working on his father's farm in the summers until he was seventeen years of age He attended Bryan & Stratton's Commercial College in Boston At the age of seventeen he went to work as bookkeeper for Chickering & Boynton, of Westboro Four years later he bought the store, but sold it immediately and came to Worcester to locate With George E Stearns he bought the tea and coffee business of Alfred Holden, of Worcester This business had been established in 1857 by Mr Holden and had been in successful operation for twenty-seven years The firm of Stearns & Howe began business in 1883 After a short time Mr Howe bought out his partner and has since that time been in business alone at the same location next the Bay State House on Main street, Worcester When he bought the business it was retail and later he added the wholesale department Now two-thirds of the business is wholesale Mr Howe deals in spices, canned goods and groceries The house is known all over New England and Mr Howe's salesmen cover most of New England in their regular trips Mr Howe has been a successful business man, and at the same time he has found time to own and conduct a stock farm at Barre, the home of his ancestors The farm is Mr Howe's summer home

Mr Howe was formerly a member of Anchoria Lodge of Odd Fellows, the Hancock Club, Utopia Rebekah Lodge, No 107, Worcester Grange, Patrons of Husbandry He is a member of the Worcester

Board of Trade Worcester Agricultural Society and the Worcester County Horticultural Society He is a Republican in politics He is an active member of Central Congregational Church and Sunday school, and his been auditor of the church

He married, December 5 1899, Florence Gray Tenney She was born at Auburndale, Massachusetts, August 5, 1877, the daughter of Arthur Burton and Harriet Elizabeth (Gray) Tenney Her father was born at Newport, New Hampshire, May, 1846 Her mother was born at Waterford, Connecticut, September, 1844 She attended the Worcester schools and was graduated from the Worcester high school in the class of 1896 They reside at 8 Burncoat street, Worcester The children of Daniel Austin and Florence Gray (Tenney) Howe are Mildred Gray, born February 24, 1901, Frank Warner, October 27, 1902, Daniel Austin, Jr, November 24, 1903, Florence Ella, September 1, 1905

THE TENNEY FAMILY Thomas Tenney, the emigrant ancestor of Mrs Daniel Austin Howe, (Florence Gray Tenney) was a member of Rev Ezekiel Rogers's company of colonists from Yorkshire, England They arrived in Salem, Massachusetts, December 1, 1638, and settled at Rowley, Massachusetts, in April, 1639 He was one of the proprietors in 1643 He testified that he was sixty-six years old May 4, 1680, hence he was born in 1614 He was twenty-four years old when with his wife Ann he came to this country She died and was buried September 26, 1657 He married (second), 1658, Elizabeth Parratt, of Rowley She received a bequest of ten pounds from Rev Ezekiel Rogers when he died in 1660-1 Thomas Tenney's home lot is now or was lately owned and occupied by the Prime family, next south of house of George B Blodget, now or formerly Tenney had grants of land in 1661-67-70-73-74 He was ensign in the militia company He was town marshal in 1653-4 to 1666 He gave the official warning of town meetings in 1650-53-60-61-66 He was overseer of the poor in 1656-64-71 He was selectman in 1660-61-70 He was viewer of fences highways and chimneys in 1669, constable in 1656 tithingman in 1680 His services were evidently in constant demand by his fellow citizens

The children of Thomas and Ann Tenney were John born December 11 1640 Hannah March 15, 1642, Mary, June 17 1644, Thomas July 16 1648, James, August 15 1650, Sarah, April 15 1652, died April 10, 1653, Daniel, July 6, 1653

(II) Deacon John Tenney, son of Thomas Tenney (1), was born in Rowley Massachusetts December 14 1640 He married, in Rowley December 14 1663 Mercy Parrat daughter of Francis and Elizabeth Parrat, of Rowley She was born July 23, 1646, and died November 27 1667 He married (second) in Merrimac now Bradford Massachusetts, December 2, 1668, Susannah Woodbury daughter of Humphrey and Elizabeth Woodbury of Beverly, Massachusetts

John Tenney settled at Rowley, later at Bradford Susannah, his wife was born February 4 1648 She was dismissed from the Beverly church to the First Church at Bradford in 1682-3 She died April 9 1716 He bought one hundred acres of land of Edward Hazen of Rowley May 20, 1661 He was moderator of the first town meeting ever held in the town of Bradford, Massachusetts, February 2 1668 In 1668 he was clerk of writs and in 1669 selectman He was on the school committee and on the first list of deacons of the church, dated December 13, 1702 He was one of a committee to hire the minister June 28, 1705, and on an important committee appointed to heal differences in the church, showing that he must have been a person of tact and discretion He was one of the committee that invited Rev Thomas Symmes to become the Bradford pastor, June 14, 1708 John Tenney made a large number of real estate deals at Rowley He died April 13, 1722 Of his children there are records only of two Sarah, born October 17, 1665, baptized January 8, 1666, Samuel, November 20, 1667, baptized November 23, 1687

(III) Deacon Samuel Tenney, son of John Tenney (2), was born in Bradford Massachusetts, November 20, 1667 He married Abigail Bailey, daughter of Deacon Joseph Bailey She died at Bradford, November 2, 1689 He married (second), in Bradford, December 18, 1690, Sarah Boynton, daughter of Captain Joseph and Sarah (Swan) Boynton, of Bradford She was born January 11, 1671-2, and joined the church in full communion August 4, 1691, at Bradford She died April 3, 1709 He married (third) Hannah Moody, of Newbury, January 26 1710-11 She joined the church July 1, 1716 She died October 29, 1745 at Bradford, now Groveland, Massachusetts

His home lot was near or at the place of T H Finney, now or formerly, (1891) He joined the church January 23, 1687. He was chosen elder March 28, 1718 He was a shorthand writer, then a rare accomplishment, and used to take down the sermons for practice He was a gifted singer and led the church service for twenty-five years He was altogether one of the most distinguished men of his time He repeatedly held most of the offices of trust and honor within the gift of his fellow citizens He was a lieutenant in the provincial troops and member of the colonial assembly of 1725 He was one of the few who voted against the King's charter in the assembly He died February 3, 1747-8, in his eighty-first year A stone suitably inscribed marks his grave in the Groveland burying ground His will was dated October 23, 1735

The child of Samuel and Abigail (Bailey) Tenney was Abigail, born November 22, 1689 The children of Samuel and Sarah Boynton (Tenney) were Mercy, October 23, 1691, John, December 8, 1692, Susanna, February 5, 1694-5, married John Bailey, Sarah, March 29, 1696, Samuel, December 17, 1697, Joseph, March 16, 1698, Ann, September 24, 1700, Daniel, February 14, 1702, Jonathan, December 8, 1703, Dorothy, December 20, 1704, Philip, December 16, 1706

(IV) Daniel Tenney son of Samuel Tenney (3), was born in Bradford, Massachusetts, now Groveland, February 14, 1702 He married Sarah Kimball, who died August 31, 1732, aged twenty-seven years He married (second), May 18, 1733, Ann Coleman, of Newburyport, Massachusetts He settled in Bradford, where he joined the church June 26, 1720 He died May 7, 1751, and his son Thomas was appointed administrator of his estate His widow died June 28, 1768, aged sixty-eight years, and was buried in the Groveland graveyard

The children of Daniel and Sarah (Kimball) Tenney were Deborah, born June 30, 1726, Daniel, (twin) July 26, 1730, died young, Thomas (twin), July 26, 1730 The children of Daniel and Ann (Coleman) Tenney were Daniel, March 16, 1734, Jonathan, January 29, 1735-6, Sarah, July 29, 1737, Shubael, January 5, 1739-40

(V) Daniel Tenney, son of Daniel Tenney (4), was born in Bradford, Massachusetts, March 16, 1734 He married, June 25 1761, Joanna Cheney They settled in Bradford The children of Daniel and Ann (Coleman) Tenney were Daniel, born April 4, 1762, Eldad, April 20, 1764, Rhoda, August 25, 1766, Moses, April 16, 1769, Thomas, September 21, 1771, Aaron, July 11, 1774, Joanna, March 8, 1776, Paul, September 12, or 24, 1781, M D, was graduated at Dartmouth College in 1803 with A M degree, married, August 12, 1804, Anna Hoyt, daughter of Samuel Hoyt, of Poplin, New Hampshire, resided at Bedford Hills, Wilmot, New Hampshire, removed to Williamsburg, Ohio, died September 29, 1844

(VI) Thomas Tenney, son of Daniel Tenney (5), was born at Bradford, Massachusetts, September 21, 1771 He married Hannah Long, of Hopkinton, New Hampshire He married (second) Susan Cheney In 1796 he removed to Newport, New Hampshire, and occupied first the Hiall Call farm, later and for many years he lived on the place now or formerly of H F Pike He was a carpenter by trade He died in Newport, 1841

The children of Thomas Tenney were Joshua, born December 2, 1795, Mary, December 3, 1798, Hannah, September 6, 1800, Temperance, July 20, 1808, Susan, June 10, 1807, Abijah W, November 25, 1810, Isaac C, July 11, 1814, Daniel W, October 17, 1816

(VII) Abijah W Tenney, son of Thomas Tenney (6), was born in Newport, New Hampshire, November 25, 1810 He married, August 9, 1840, Hannah Stevens Jenks, daughter of Captain Bela W and Mary (Stevens) Jenks She was born November 26, 1816, and died September 12, 1848 He married (second), June 15, 1849, Emily Baker, daughter of James and Sophia (Chapin) Baker She was born April 22, 1823 He lived at Southville in Newport, New Hampshire He was a man of very genial nature, yet just to all with whom he dealt, and exacting justice and honesty in return Living an earnest, Christian life, trusted and honored by all who knew him, he exemplified the Golden Rule from day to day He had very strict ideas in regard to temperance and his entire family was brought up in accordance with them In politics he was a stanch Republican Although very much interested in town as well as national affairs, and enjoying the esteem of his fellow-townsmen, yet he would never hold any public office as he disliked heartily the many disputes and controversies in which a man of public affairs must be concerned Besides the farm which he always carried on, he was for many years engaged at his trade as a millwright He was always considered a very good mechanic and was skilled at various trades

The children of Abijah W and Hannah Stevens (Jenks) Tenney were Abijah Wallace, born September 9, 1841, died September 22, 1844, Mary Jenks, May 18, 1845, married Thomas Adelbert Montague Arthur Burton, May 22, 1846, George Hubbard, July 26, 1848, died December 11, 1866

(VIII) Arthur Burton Tenney, son of Abijah W Tenney, (7), was born at Newport, New Hampshire, May 22, 1846 He received his education here at the district schools and until nineteen years old worked with his father Then wishing to follow the carpenter's trade he left Newport, finally coming to Worcester He returned to Newport where for a short time he was engaged in building Soon he moved to Auburndale, Massachusetts, and there he took up the building business in company with Mr Soule He took his family next to Holyoke, Massachusetts, where they were settled for several years while he was engaged in New York and many of the nearer cities and towns until he finally came to Worcester, where he was connected with the erection of many of the large buildings of the city, the Knowles Loom Works being the last one While living in Worcester he superintended the construction of several large buildings in Providence, Rhode Island, among them being that of the Rhode Island Hospital Trust Co, and the B H Gladding Co' After the death of his wife, which occurred in 1893, he settled in Pawtucket, Rhode Island, where he lived until 1900 Then, owing to poor health, he went to Los Angeles, California, where he is at present successfully engaged in architecture and building

He married (first), at Worcester, September 17, 1868, Harriet Elizabeth Gray, who was born at Waterford, Connecticut, September 25, 1844

The children of Arthur Burton and Harriet Elizabeth (Gray) Tenney were Louis Burton, born December 18, 1872, married Mary Gould, of Pawtucket, July 3, 1900, has one child, Florence G, Florence Gray August 5, 1877, Estelle Palmer, October 1, 1882, died in Providence, Rhode Island, March 18, 1892 Mr Tenney married (second), 1897, Martha A Sheldon, of Pawtucket, Rhode Island

(IX) Florence Gray Tenney, daughter of Arthur Burton Tenney (8), was born August 5, 1877, at Auburndale, Massachusetts She married Daniel Austin Howe, December 5, 1899, at Worcester, Massachusetts (See sketch of Daniel A Howe and family)

FRED WENDELL WHITE Thomas White (1), of Weymouth, was the pioneer ancestor of Fred Wendell White, city treasurer of Worcester, Massachusetts

He came from his home in England in 1624 or soon after, and settled in Weymouth He was admitted a freeman March 3, 1636, and was a deputy to the general court in 1636 and 1637, 1657 and 1670 He was a proprietor of the town as early as 1643 According to the deposition to the will of Anne Looman, made October 21, 1659, he was born in England in 1599 or 1600 He was a carpenter by trade He died August, 1679 His will was dated July 5, 1679, and proved August 28, of that year He mentioned the children named below, grandchildren Lydia, Mary and Ebenezer White, Pastor Samuel Torrey and Elder Edward Bates Thomas Dyer, who witnessed the will, was of Mendon later

The children of Thomas White were Joseph, see forward, Samuel, born 1642, admitted a freeman 1666, married Mary Dyer, son of Thomas Dyer, named above, Thomas, admitted a freeman 1681, married Mary Pratt, of Braintree, Hannah, married June 24, 1660, John Baxter, Ebenezer, (Lieutenant), married Hannah Phillips, daughter of Nicholas, settled in Weymouth

(II) Captain Joseph White, son of Thomas White (1), was born about 1640 in Weymouth He married, September 9, 1660, Lydia Rogers, daughter of John Rogers, of Weymouth, one of the pioneers there Captain White died March 23, 1706, his wife Lydia died May 8, 1727 He settled in Nipmuc or Mendon in 1663, and was formally accepted on the list of ten men from Weymouth, and thirteen from Braintree who constituted the first settlers of the town His was one of the first fifteen families located in Mendon in 1662 and 1663 He was the largest taxpayer in the town for many years He held many offices and served on special committees for the new town Several of his children were born in Weymouth before he went to Mendon, several of them were born while the family was away from Mendon during King Philip's war Savage gives eleven children The Mendon records seem to give four children to Captain Joseph and Lydia, not mentioned by Savage, possibly belonging to Joseph, Jr

The children of Joseph and Lydia were Joseph, born at Weymouth, December 16, 1662, Samuel, February 14, 1667, at Mendon, John, Ebenezer, Thomas, Ann married a Mr Trask, Mary, married a Mr Hill, Experience, born in Mendon, December 5, 1680, Hannah, November 29, 1681, at Mendon, Joseph, October 19, 1683, see forward, Lydia, May 10, 1686, married a Mr Cook, Hannah, December 9, 1691, Abigail, November 10, 1693, William, and Benjamin, March 28, 1701

(III) Joseph White, son of Joseph White (2), was born in Mendon, Massachusetts, October 19, 1683, and died there October 28, 1757 He married, about 1711, Prudence ——— Their children, all born at Mendon, were Joseph, Jr, born September 22, 1712, see forward, Peter, December 6, 1714, Aaron, May 22, 1717, Moses, August 31, 1721

(IV) Joseph White, Jr, son of Joseph White (3), was born in Mendon, September 22, 1712, and settled in that part of Mendon, later Uxbridge, Massachusetts He married, December 4, 1734, Judith Clark, of Uxbridge, Rev Nathan Webb officiating They had thirteen children Sarah, born September 4, 1735, died September, 1747, Lyral, May 8, 1737, married, November 25, 1756, Abner Taft, at Uxbridge, Lois, August 25, 1739, married, January 6, 1757, Edward Seagraves, at Uxbridge, Eunice, November 1, 1741, Joseph, May 4, 1744 died September 8, 1747, Judith, December 1, 1746, died September, 1747, Amos, October 26, 1748, married May 17, 1770, Azubah Taft, at Uxbridge, he died in the Revolutionary army Joel, October 4, 1751, died at Northbridge, Massachusetts, July 22, 1835, Jesse, see forward, Obadiah, September 8, 1753, Edward, June 5, 1756, died June 14, 1756, Abner, April 5, 1758, died April 5, 1758, Moses, August 3, 1759, died August 8, 1759

(V) Jesse White, ninth child of Joseph White (4), was born in Uxbridge Massachusetts, June 12, 1754, married, March 28 1777, in Uxbridge, Anna Mason, of Uxbridge (published March 10, 1777, in Northbridge) He was educated and learned his trade as blacksmith at Uxbridge He was a farmer as well as a blacksmith He settled in Northbridge From him the elder Paul Whitney learned his trade

He was deacon in the Baptist church of some neighboring town, perhaps Grafton He held various town offices He was a revolutionary soldier, enlisting as a private in Captain Josiah Wood's company which marched from Northbridge to Roxbury April 19, 1775, on the Lexington alarm He was sergeant in Captain David Batcheller's company, Lieutenant Colonel Nathan Tyler's regiment which marched December 8, 1776, on the alarm to Providence He was sergeant in Captain David Batcheller's company, Colonel Nathan Tyler's regiment, which marched on the alarm to Rhode Island July 28, 1780 He was chosen by the town of Northbridge, July 29, 1779, one of a committee to hire men to enlist in the Continental army and was rated to pay for that service, six pounds, March 1, 1780, and one hundred and twenty pounds in old currency, March 12, 1781

He married Anna Mason, as stated above, and had eleven children Lucy, born May 5 1778 married Dr Artemas Bullard, Noah, February 21, 1780, Amos see forward, Jesse, June 13 1783 Alden, March 21, 1785, Anna, January 4 1787, died February 14, 1795, Joel, January 5, 1789, Eunice, March 4, 1791, Sally, May 6, 1793 died May 19, 1793, Mason, May 14, 1791, Washington, May 19, 1796 Jesse White, father of these children, died at Northbridge, March 2, 1830, and is buried there in what is known as the Cooper graveyard

(VI) Amos White, third child of Jesse White (5), was born in Northbridge, Massachusetts, September 19, 1781 He followed his father's trade of blacksmith, and had a blacksmith shop of his own later He manufactured edge tools, chiefly for boot and shoe makers, also axes

Mr White was a Methodist and was connected with that denomination until late in life when he attended the Congregational church He was captain of the Northbridge Militia Company, and was always known afterward as Captain White

He married, September 1, 1803, Hepzibath Aldrich, of Northbridge, who was born May 21, 1780, and died October 27, 1865 Both are buried in the Cooper graveyard Their children were Lowell, see forward, Jefferson, born June 18, 1805, Otis, October 12, 1806, Amos, June 3, 1809, Lydia, May 15, 1813, Lucy Bullard, September 30, 1814, Laura, November 24, 1817, Perry, August 29, 1820, died April 28, 1821, Luke, January 7, 1822, died July 16, 1882 Amos White, father of these children, died March 11, 1853

(VII) Lowell White, son of Amos White (6), was born in West Sutton, Massachusetts, May 20, 1804 At an early age he moved to Northbridge with his parents He received his early education in the common schools of Northbridge, working on his father's farm up to the age of fourteen years, when he was apprenticed to Cheney Taft, a grocer, with whom he remained for about three years He helped his father for a time on the home farm and then went to work in Levi Fuller's shoe shop and later in Warren Adams' shoe shop, some three years in all, and then for Deacon Joel Batcheller, manufacturing shoes until October, 1847, when he moved to Grafton and accepted a position in Captain John W Slocumb's shop He continued in the shoe business until within a year of his death He worked in Westboro for some time while living in Grafton

He was prominent in town affairs at Grafton, and served on the board of selectmen He was a Republican He was a member of the Congregational church and of the Grafton Lodge of Odd Fellows

He married, October 5, 1828, at Northbridge, (by Rev John Crane) Miranda Dodge, who was born February 19 1808 the daughter of Abner and Rhoda (Adams) Dodge, of Northbridge Mr Dodge was prominent in military affairs and had the rank of captain in the militia

The children of Lowell and Miranda White were Catherine Augusta, born February 6, 1830, Merrick Dodge (see forward), Sarah Frances born October 1835 died October 9 1836, Ann Maria (twin) born July 23, 1840, Jane Sophia (twin), born July 23, 1840 Lowell White, father of these children died February 12, 1875

(VIII) Merrick Dodge White, second child of Lowell White and father of Fred W White, was born in Northbridge Massachusetts, September 16, 1834 He attended the Northbridge public schools until he was thirteen years of age and helped his father make shoes When the family moved to Grafton in October, 1847, he went to work in the shoe factory of Captain John W Slocumb He worked there until December 25 1858, when he took a position as cutter in the shoe shop of John Hayes, at Dover, New Hampshire He returned in 1861 and worked for a year in Worcester for J W Brigham Southbridge street, and for two years at South Framingham in the Charles Prentice shop, and for a year in the shops of Augustus Forbush and H C Green-

E. Warner

wood, in Grafton He was clerk in the Sherman House, Natick, two years and a half, and later was engaged in the restaurant business in Westboro and Grafton, conducting a business in the last named town on his own account After more experience in the hotel business he returned to shoe making for C H Tilton, Ashland, where he worked for five years In 1889 he began work for his brother-in-law, Samuel A Prescott, in the manufacture of shoddy He was in this business for eleven years when he lost his arm in an accident and had to retire He is at present living with his sister, Mrs Prescott In politics he is a Democrat, and while in Natick was delegate to various party conventions He attends the Congregational church He served five years in the Grafton Military Company He married Emma Adelaide Wendell (intentions dated August 18, 1860), at Dover, New Hampshire She was a daughter of George Washington and Prudence (Jenness) Wendell, of Dover New Hampshire She died August 18, 1889 Their children were. Harry Lowell, born at Dover, New Hampshire, January 24, 1861, Fred Wendell, see forward, Clinton Sutton, born at Grafton, June 2, 1864

(IX) Fred Wendell White, son of Merrick Dodge White (8), was born at Dover, New Hampshire, March 16, 1862 In the fall of 1866 he moved with his parents to Grafton, Massachusetts, where he entered the common schools of that town After completing two terms in the high school he went to Worcester to take a position, April 7, 1879, as assistant cashier at the store of Barnard & Sumner He remained in that position until March 8, 1880, when he entered the employ of W H Morse & Company, bankers, as assistant cashier He became assistant bookkeeper at the First National Bank October 11, 1880, of the same year, and continued in various positions, advancing to the positions of paying and receiving teller, in all some seventeen years, when he resigned to accept a position with Mr Barton He was appointed assistant city treasurer by William S Barton, then the city treasurer, September 24, 1897 Upon the retirement of Mr Barton owing to failing health, January 2, 1899, he was elected treasurer of the city and has been re-elected to the position at every election since The position is one of great responsibility The city treasurer receives all of the taxes and assessments and disburses all the money of the city Millions of dollars are handled every year in his office Mr White has given the utmost satisfaction to the city officers and the taxpayers

He is a member of the Adams Square Congregational church, is its treasurer, and member of the music committee In politics he is a Republican He is a prominent Free Mason, member of Montacute Lodge, of Worcester Royal Arch Chapter and of Hiram Council He is a member of Worcester Lodge, No 56, Odd Fellows, of the Hancock Club, of the Worcester Automobile Club, of the Worcester County Mechanics' Association, of the Sons of the American Revolution, Worcester Congregational Club, the Economic Club, and Worcester County Horticultural Society He was formerly a member of Company G. Sixth Regiment, Massachusetts Volunteer Militia, from 1880 to 1884 inclusive, and belongs to the Veteran Association

He married, April 22, 1886, Mabel Josephine Boyd, who was born October 19, 1864, the daughter of John T and Elizabeth W (Butts) Boyd, of Boston Mr Boyd was a sailmaker at Charlestown Navy Yard, a veteran and lieutenant colonel in the Fifth Massachusetts Infantry in the civil war

The children of Fred Wendell and Mabel Josephine (Boyd) White were Marion Winter, born April 17, 1889, Frances Lowell, born January 31, 1892, died September 9, 1903, Eloise Boyd, born August 16, 1900

EMERSON WARNER, M D (I) William Warner, the emigrant ancestor of the Warner family of Barre, and of Dr Emerson Warner, of Worcester, is believed to be a son of Samuel Warner, of Boxted, Essex, England, and was doubtless born in England about 1590 William Warner was one of the pioneers at Ipswich, Massachusetts, was one of the proprietors as early as 1635, and his name appears on a list of proprietors dated 1637 He was admitted a freeman, May 2, 1638 The date of his death is unknown but he was living October 29, 1654 Records exist in this country of three of his children namely Daniel, John, born about 1616 in England, and a daughter, born in England, became the wife of Thomas Wells, and died July, 1671

(II) John Warner, son of William Warner, was born in England about the year 1616 He was reared in his native land and came to the Ipswich Colony, Massachusetts Bay either shortly before or after the remainder of the family He was a passenger from London on the ship 'Increase" in 1635, when he gave his age of twenty years He removed from Ipswich to Brookfield in 1670, was one of three men there who took the Indian deed for the town of Brookfield December 19, 1673, and was one of the principal inhabitants there When the town was destroyed by the Indians in 1675 he retreated with his younger children to Hadley, Massachusetts, whither Mark Warner an elder son, and other children had gone to settle He probably died at the home of some of his children, 1692

John Warner married (first) ——— ——— He married (second) Pricilla Symonds, daughter of Mark Symonds, about 1655 The children of John Warner and his first wife were Samuel, born about 1640, John, born about 1643, died at Springfield, Massachusetts, January 21 1724, Mark, born 1646, died at Northampton, Massachusetts, May 31, 1738, aged ninety-two years, Nathaniel, born about 1650, was a resident of Brookfield in 1673, died in Hadley, Massachusetts, January 15, 1714, Daniel, born about 1653 died in Ipswich, Massachusetts, June 8, 1659 The children of John and Priscilla (Symonds) Warner were Joseph born August 15 1657, died June 18, 1658, Mehitable, born April 16, 1659, died at Hadley Massachusetts, June 12, 1678, Daniel, born April 16, 1661 died 1688, Eleazer, born November 13, 1662, died at Hadley, Massachusetts, May 8, 1729, Priscilla, born 1664, married Thomas Cummings, of Dunstable, Massachusetts, December 19, 1688

(III) Samuel Warner son of John Warner, was born in Ipswich Massachusetts, about 1640 He was in Brookfield in 1673, but his family was not with him He was one of the petitioners for the incorporation of the town of Brookfield, and possibly was there two years later when the town was destroyed He testified March 26, 1678 describing himself as thirty-eight years old and that he formerly owned land in Brookfield He became one of the pioneers in Dunstable Massachusetts, now Nashua, New Hampshire was one of the fourteen proprietors residing there November 30 1682 and was one of the seven male members of the first church which was organized December 16 1685 He purchased a farm in Groton Massachusetts the adjoining town, October 14, 1689, and probably died there about 1703

He married (first) in Ipswich, Massachusetts, October 21, 1662, Mercy Swan, who died in Dunstable, Massachusetts, April 3, 1683 Their children were Priscilla, born September 25, 1666, died young, Samuel, born July 5, 1668, settled at Pomfret, Connecticut, John, born August 2, 1670, died July 14, 1671, Dorothy, born June 2, 1672, Sarah, born May 28 1674, Richard, born August 13, 1676, at Groton, died 1767, aged ninety-one years, his will dated June 10, 1763, was proved October 15, 1767 Samuel Warner married (second), May 4, 1684 Mary Swallow, and their children were. Eleazer, born January 27, 1686, Priscilla The children of his first wife were probably all born in Ipswich, and the children of his second wife were born in Dunstable

(IV) Eleazer Warner, son of Samuel Warner, was born in Dunstable, Massachusetts, January 27, 1686 When a young man he devoted several years to the military service He was assigned to duty on the frontier and for many years was stationed with the military company at Brookfield the scene of his grandfather's disaster in King Philip's war He enlisted as a private and rose in rank from time to time through the grades of sergeant, ensign and lieutenant of the company commanded by Captain Samuel Wright of Rutland Later he became captain of the military company at Hardwick and New Braintree and retained the office until 1756, when he was seventy years old He evidently liked the military service and enjoyed a vigorous old age He is the hero of the only Indian tale related of Hardwick settlers In 1830, while he was in the military service, he removed his family from their residence in Groton or Dunstable to Hardwick, now New Braintree His land was near Ditch meadow, and his farm included part of the old Indian fort at Winnimisset Shortly afterward he had to go to Canada to effect an exchange of prisoners and while he was there an Indian became offended at him and followed him home

According to family tradition the Indian lurked about for several days for a chance to take a shot at Warner One day Captain Warner went into the forest with his musket and came across his enemy The Indian jumped behind a tree, and Warner dropped behind a log Placing his hat on a stick Warner raised it above the edge of the log, and the Indian was deceived by the old trick and let fire at the empty hat The captain sprang up and the Indian rushed forward with his scalping knife only to meet the contents of the white man's gun His body was thrown in the lily pond between the road and river, half a mile east of Old Furnace After his marriage Captain Warner went to live on the west side of the road from New Braintree to Warren, on the south side of the brook, at the head of Ditch meadow, then Brookfield, now New Braintree About 1730 he removed to a farm which he sold to Perez Cobb, May 4 1764, and which was for many years known as the Perez Cobb farm It was located on the road to Rutland about a mile east of Furnace village already mentioned Mr Warner became one of the most active and honored citizens of the new town of New Braintree, was selectman for six years assessor for a similar period of time, was often chosen moderator of the town meetings, and was one of twelve man who formed the first church there

Captain Eleazer Warner married, December 4, 1722 when thirty-six years old Prudence Barnes, daughter of Thomas Barnes, of Brookfield Their children were Mary, born April 21, 1724 married Thomas Robinson, November 23, 1744 died August 7 1812, Phineas born October 11, 1726, married Martha Nash, Warham, born November 1 1730, (November 2 in New Braintree records) resided at New Braintree and died there December 4, 1817, leaving a large family, Eleazer, born February 26, 1733-34, was a soldier in the French war, died in the service November 20, 1755, Martin, born September 2, 1735 settled in Norwich, Silas, born May 21, 1737, died of wounds received in French war, August 24, 1760, Samuel, born October 7, 1739, lived at New Braintree, married Unity Ware, April 19, 1769, Noah, born February 9, 1741-42, killed in battle in the French war, 1760, Prudence, born June 14, 1744, married Daniel Eldridge, February 10 1767. Eleazer Warner, father of these children, died in New Braintree, February 28, 1776, aged ninety years He survived his wife several years, she passing away in New Braintree February 25, 1770, aged sixty-six years Seven sons of this old warrior, Captain Warner, entered the military service during the French war, and three lost their lives

(V) Phineas Warner, son of Captain Eleazer Warner, was born October 11, 1726, at New Braintree, then Brookfield Massachusetts He was deacon of the church in New Braintree, and a man of distinction He married Martha Nash, of Hatfield, Massachusetts, February 11, 1752, and their children were Eleazer, born 1756, died November 17, 1758, aged seventeen months, Phineas born 1759 died May 6, 1762 aged two years, eight months, Martha, born 1767 died September 4, 1778, aged seventeen years, Phineas, born November 2, 1763, died at New Braintree July 24, 1841, and perhaps others Deacon Phineas Warner died March 25, 1795, at New Braintree, and his wife passed away at the same place October 23 1811

(VI) Phineas Warner, son of Phineas Warner, was born in New Braintree, Massachusetts, November 2 1763, and died there July 24, 1841 He was an ensign in the army He married Mary Pollard She died 1841 Their children were Patty, born November 7, 1784 Daniel, born August 28, 1786, Eli, born June 22, 1788, Betsey, born April 8, 1790, Amory P, born July 9, 1805, died April 28, 1880

(VII) Amory P Warner, son of Phineas Warner, was born in New Braintree, Massachusetts, July 9 1805 died at Worcester, Massachusetts, April 28 1880 He was reared on a farm in New Braintree, educated in the public schools of his native town and was a farmer by occupation He was a member of the Methodist church He was a Republican in politics He married, March 12, 1829, Cemira C Haskins, born in Prescott Massachusetts, September 13 1811, died February 6, 1881 They were the parents of one child Emerson born April 30, 1831, at New Braintree, Massachusetts

(VIII) Emerson Warner, son of Amory P Warner, was born in New Braintree Massachusetts, April 30, 1831 He attended the district schools of New Braintree, Wilbraham Academy, Wesleyan University at Middletown Connecticut, which he entered in 1852, graduated therefrom in 1856, and received the degree of Master of Arts in 1859 For a few years thereafter he taught in Wilbraham Academy He received his degree of Doctor of Medicine from Harvard Medical School in 1863, began to practice in Shrewsbury, but removed to Worcester, January 1, 1866, and led a very busy professional life there for twenty years In 1872 and 1873 he visited many of the leading medical institutions in Europe Since 1886, when his career was interrupted by illness, he has not been in active practice, but has traveled extensively in Asia, Africa, South America, North America and Europe, accompanied by Mrs Warner They have passed several winters in the Azores and the south because of the modified climate Dr Warner has been across the country many times in every direction, visiting most of the states and important cities in the United States and Canada, and he has been around the world twice by different routes In these nineteen years Dr Warner has acquired a cosmopolitan knowledge of the world, its geography and its people such as few men are fortunate enough to possess

When Dr Warner came to Worcester he took possession of the house on Main street erected in 1793 by the Rev Dr Austin, then pastor of the Old South Church A portion of that landmark is still standing near the Crompton & Knowles loom works, whither it was moved in order to make room for the present Warner block, a four story building, extending from 570 to 576 Main street, where he now resides Dr Warner was in regular attendance at the opening of the Worcester Dispensary, and for seventeen years was on the staff at the Worcester City Hospital He has been consulting surgeon at the Memorial Hospital since it was established was president of the Worcester District Medical Society, and for many years was a councilor of the Massachusetts Medical Society In politics he is a Republican He was a member of school boards in the cities in which he resided prior to taking up his residence in Worcester, and was a member of the Worcester school board for twenty years He represented Worcester in the general court in 1884 and 1885, and as chairman of the committee on public health did important work in sanitary legislation He is an active member of the Methodist Episcopal church, and was delegate to the general conference in 1880 He has been interested in the Worcester Associated Charities, and belongs to the Worcester Art Museum Corporation

Dr Warner married (first), July 18, 1851, L Angeline Cleveland, of Hardwick, Massachusetts, and the two children born of this union died young Mrs Warner died September 20, 1854 Dr Warner married (second), May 24, 1856, Isabelle H Andrews, of Glastonbury, Connecticut, daughter of David and Honoria (Sparks) Andrews, and granddaughter of David and Rebecca (Stratton) Andrews Her father was born July 3, 1791, was a farmer in Glastonbury, and represented that town in the Connecticut legislature in 1842 and 1843 He married, December 25 1819, Honoria Sparks, born June 3, 1802, died September 14 1879, and his death occurred March 23, 1858 The children of Dr Emerson and Isabelle H (Andrews) Warner were Effie L, born September 7, 1865 died September 30, 1884 Isabel, born November 20, 1860, educated in the Worcester schools, married, October 30, 1887, Dean S Ellis, M D, born in Vermontville, Franklin county New York August 28, 1856, son of Samuel and Emily M (Towne) Ellis Dr Ellis obtained his preliminary education in the public schools of Worcester and at New Salem Academy, where he pursued a four years course He then entered Jefferson Medical College, graduating in the class of 1883, and immediately thereafter began practice in Worcester where he at once became popular with all classes He is skilled as a general practitioner, ranks well among his fellow-physicians, and is recognized as one of the leading practicing physicians of Worcester He is medical examiner for eight insurance companies, surgeon to eleven local societies, and a fellow of the Massachusetts Medical Society, American Medical Association, and the Worcester Medical Association In 1904 Dr Ellis purchased the granite block, 578 and 580 Main street, remodeled the entire building, and at the present time it is one of the best in the city He is a lover of fine horses, and always drives animals of splendid breed and fine mettle Dr and Mrs Ellis have traveled quite extensively both in this country and abroad Their children are Ruth, born December 17, 1889, Ralph Warner, born November 16, 1891, Ethel, born July 29, 1894, Myrtle Isabel, born August 8, 1896, died September 7, 1901, and Dean Emerson, born July 5, 1903

STEPHEN P STREETER Stephen Streeter (1), first of Gloucester Massachusetts, in 1642, was the emigrant ancestor of Stephen P Streeter, of Worcester He is believed to have come to New England before 1640 He may have preceded the settlers of 1642 in Gloucester, as Blynman's grant as that time included a lot primarily given to Streeter He had a house in Gloucester, but did not remain long there after its permanent settlement In 1644 he was in Charlestown recorded as a householder, and he took the freeman's oath there May 29, 1644 He and his wife Ursula joined the church there March 21 1652 The family genealogists think the proof conclusive that Stephen Streeter came from the Streeter family in Goudherst, England The tradition in some branches of the American family is that the emigrant came from Surrey while Goudherst is in Kent, but there are representatives in both counties now and have been for centuries

Stephen Streeter's will was made June 10, 1652 He was a shoemaker by trade His wife Ursula is said to have been the daughter of Henry Adams, of Braintree, but the relationship is not proved After Streeter's death his widow married, October 13, 1656 or 7, in Charlestown, Massachusetts, Samuel Hosier, of Watertown He died July 29, 1665 His widow married, about 1666, William Robinson, of Dorchester, whose name first appears in Dorchester records in 1636 He was killed July 6, 1668, being caught in the wheel of his mill and torn in pieces His widow married Griffin Crafts, of Roxbury She died before 1690 The children of Stephen and Ursula Streeter were Stephen, Sarah, who was under eighteen when her father's will was made in 1652, Samuel, John, a soldier in King Philip's war, 1675, Hannah, born November 10, 1644, Rebecca, Mary, (posthumous) born about 1652

(II) Stephen Streeter, son of Stephen Streeter (1), was probably born in England and died in Cambridge, Massachusetts, 1689 He lived in Charlestown, Watertown, Brookline and Cambridge, Massachusetts He sold half of the homestead in Charlestown, inherited from his father, in 1679, and other land in 1681 His wife Deborah was admitted to the church at Cambridge in full communion July 13, 1701, and after her husband's death she married, August 10, 1704, Samuel Sears, of Wrentham Massachusetts

The children of Stephen and Deborah Streeter were Stephen, born June 20, 1667, at Watertown; Sarah born October 2 1669 in Watertown, Samuel, John, born probably at Brookline, Rebecca, born September 3, 1683, at Cambridge, Deborah, born September 25, 1685, died April 7, 1689 at Cambridge, Joseph born September 18, 1687, Benjamin, born November 25, 1689, died April 23, 1690

(III) Samuel Streeter, son of Stephen Streeter (2), was born probably at Brookline, Massachusetts, and died at Framingham, Massachusetts, 1752 He probably removed from Cambridge to Attleboro, Massachusetts, about 1706, where he bought land on several occasions, but later he was again in Framingham, Massachusetts His will is dated April 23, 1751, and probated September 16, following

He married (first) Deborah ———, who died November 13 1708, and (second) Mercy ———, who was probably a widow Howe The children of Samuel and Deborah Streeter were Mary, baptized February 2, 1696-7, Sarah, baptized February 2, 1696-7, Stephen, baptized in 1698, died in Douglas, Massachusetts, September 22, 1756, Samuel, baptized January 7, 1699-1700, died in Charlton, Massachusetts, June 7, 1763, Mercy, baptized May 14, 1704, Susanna, baptized April 28, 1706, in Cambridge, Joseph, born May 10, 1708, Deborah, married Jedediah Belknap, of Framingham, Elizabeth, married Ebenezer Frizzell, of Framingham

(IV) Stephen Streeter, son of Samuel Streeter (3), was baptized September 4, 1698 He settled in Framingham and removed to Douglas, Massachusetts, where he died September 22, 1756 He was a yeoman He bought a one hundred and sixty acre farm at Douglas, December 14, 1744 He married Catherine Adams, and they joined the church in full communion at Framingham, February 7, 1725 Seven of their children were born in Framingham The children of Stephen and Catherine (Adams) Streeter were Esther, born January 13, 1724-5, married Josiah Haven, of Framingham, Stephen, born February 14, 1726-7, Abigail, born January 15, 1728-9, Elizabeth, born January 9, 1729-30, John, born February 14, 1731-2, Ursula, born November 9, 1733, Adams, born December 31, 1735, Zebulon, born March 24, 1739, Naphtali, born March 6, 1741, in Douglas, owned land in Royalston, Massachusetts, Samuel, born January 16, 1743, in Douglas, Mary, born April 1, 1747, probably married Benjamin Green, of Spencer, Massachusetts

(V) Zebulon Streeter, son of Stephen Streeter (4), was born in Douglas, Massachusetts, March 24, 1739 He settled in Surrey, New Hampshire, where he died October 14, 1808 He and his brother, Adams Streeter, were two of the leading ministers of the Universalist denomination in their day His will was made December 3, 1807, and proved October 26, 1808

He married, July 16, 1760, at Oxford, Massachusetts, Tabitha Harvey, who was born 1736 and died in Surrey, New Hampshire, January 25, 1813, aged seventy-six years Their first three children were born in Douglas, the others in Winchester, New Hampshire The children of Rev Zebulon and Tabitha (Harvey) Streeter were Benjamin, born April 21, 1762, Daniel, born June 23, 1764, Benoni, born June 22, 1766, Hannah, married Samuel Hudson, Lucy, born January, 1771, Jesse, born October 25, 1773, Elijah, born July 3, 1775, David, Tabitha, married ——— Smith, of Grafton, Vermont, Eliab, born 1774, died 1806, unmarried

(VI) David Streeter, son of Zebulon Streeter (5), was born in Winchester, New Hampshire, December 2, 1777 He removed early to Concord, Vermont, where he took the freeman's oath, March 4, 1799, and was on the tax list as a voter and property owner in 1802 He married, July 18, 1803, at Concord, Vermont, Anna Winslow, of Wendell, Massachusetts

The children of David and Anna (Winslow) Streeter, all born in Concord, Vermont, were Phebe, born May 23, 1806, David, born January 14, 1808, Zebulon, born October 19, 1809, died March 15, 1810, Anna or Nancy, born December 25, 1810, married ——— Howard, Susanna, born September 14, 1812

(VII) David Streeter, son of David Streeter (6), was born in Concorn, Vermont, January 14, 1808, and died there He married, December 6, 1832, Mercy Row, at Concord, Massachusetts All their children were born at Concord, viz Jane W, born September 8, 1833, Anna L, born February 23, 1835, Chester P, born May 12, 1837, died February 25, 1882, married, March 28, 1858, Eliza Boutwell, Prescott B

(VIII) Prescott B Streeter, son of David Streeter (7), was born in Concord, Vermont, May 12, 1837 He married, February 8, 1865, Georgianna Boutwell They settled in Concord, Vermont, where their children were born, viz Adelbert D, born April 18, 1866, William P, born May 27, 1868, Elmira E born May 11, 1870, Stephen P, born April 13, 1872, Dene F, born March 19, 1874, Alice M, born April 27, 1877, Henry P, born June 8, 1882, Carrie E, born February 1, 1885

(IX) Stephen Streeter, son of Prescott B Streeter (8), is the subject of this sketch

Stephen P Streeter was born in Concord, Vermont, April 13, 1872 The public and high schools of his native town gave him the foundation of his education He took a course in the State Normal School of Vermont and at Oberlin College, Oberlin, Ohio After graduating from college Mr Streeter taught for a year and a half in the Vermont Industrial School, where he learned by experience the excellencies and defects of the various systems of teaching boys schools He taught in the public schools also He is a natural teacher and from the first showed himself able to transfer his thoughts to his pupils and also to inspire in them self-confidence and self-reliance, characteristics that are essential in any attempt to educate In 1896 Mr Streeter accepted the position of teacher and assistant superintendent of the Worcester County Truant School at Oakdale He remained there for about two years, the results being unusually good, and won the esteem and praise of the officers of that institution In 1898 he became the master of the congregate department of the Boston Parental School

When Edwin F Northrup resigned as superintendent of the Worcester Boys' Club in April, 1900, the executive committee selected Mr Streeter to fill the position and neither Mr Streeter nor the managers of the club have ever had any occasion to regret the choice His experience and natural ability made him especially adapted to the peculiar work demanded of the administrative officer of an institution of this kind To the technical and industrial side of the Boys' Club Mr Streeter brought a mind richly stored with facts of value to him in his work He had kept closely in touch with scientifiec and technical education in school and in private study When Superintendent Streeter commenced his duties in Worcester there were no organized classes, no systematic way of visiting the house, the dormitory was unfurnished, there was no reading room and the manual training department was not in existence He made provision for all these needs and deficiencies and provided a library and reading room He organized the business classes also, and established the gymnasium

The Boys' Club was established in 1889, although the real beginning of its usefulness was in 1893, when it was incorporated The chief departments of the club in past years have been the savings bank, wherein small sums several hundred dollars are on deposit with the club, the manual training classes, the civil government and business classes In the manual training department there are classes in carpentry, carving and printing The boys show great interest of course in the gymnasium where they are given some instruction and encouraged to take systematic exercises There are classes in music and in basketry There are of course various games for recreation and the reading room is well patronized The police court is one of the newer departments of the club Some of thhe rougher members are turned over to a lady probation officer, who gets them to join the classes, visits them in their homes and tries to get them interested in study or useful occupations It is the purpose of the club to prevent crime among boys by getting them away from evil companionship and idleness and keep them usefully employed or interested in harmless play and sports

The membership fee is one cent In previous years it has been free Each member when he pays his dues is presented with a membership ticket, and if he loses it he has to pay two cents for a duplicate The money is used to buy games for the club Superintendent Streeter reserves the right to take up a boy's ticket, but that is seldom necessary If a member violates the rules he is fined a nickel In 1905 there were classes in manual training, printing, pyrography, and they had an orchestra, Sunshine Club, Checker Club, Ping Pong Club, Athletic Club, Dramatic Club, Music Club and Glee Club About fifteen hundred boys are enrolled as members and there is an average nightly attendance of two hundred and twenty The club is supported by voluntary subscriptions Enrolled on the list of contributors are the names of a majority of the merchants, manufacturers, bankers, capitalists and citizens, who realize the importance of organized action in educating the boys The present officers of the club are President, George T Dewey, vice-president, W S B Hopkins, secretary, Florence A Rider, executive committee, Henry L Miller, James Taylor, Jr, Lewis C Muzzy, Mrs David F O'Connell, U Waldo Cutler and M Adelaide Mellen

The secret of Superintendent Streeter's success is in his character, his intense earnestness and enthusiasm for his work, his appreciation of its meaning and vast importance to the boys themselves as well as the community, and above all his personal magnetism, which is always in evidence notwithstanding his quiet manners and unobtrusive ways His work is not confined to the limits of the club He was the author of the bill introduced in the last legislature by Representative Arthur M Taft, of Worcester, and passed, providing for indeterminate sentences up to sixteen years of age for boys committed to truant schools, instead of the old sentence of from forty days to two years at the discretion of the court

Mr Streeter is a member of the Piedmont Congregational Church and is superintendent of its Sunday school and member of the standing committee He is a member of Boylston Lodge, A F and A M of West Boylston, U S Grant Lodge, Knights of Malta, Beulah Sisterhood of Daughters of Malta, the National Association of Charities and Corrections, the Massachusetts Civic League, the National Conference of Boys Clubs' Superintendents, treasurer of the Knights of Malta, member of the Twentieth Century Club, the Worcester Sportsmen's Club, the National Conference on Education of Backward, Truant and Delinquent Children Mr Streeter is unmarried

JAMES MILES James Miles (1), was the father of James Miles, a prominent builder and contractor of Worcester He married Jane French They lived in Oxfordshire, England He died when a comparatively young man The children of James and Jane (Franch) Miles were 1 Eliza, married in England Thomas Larke, they are now living in Woonsocket, Rhode Island, have no children 2 William, came to America and settled in Blackstone, Massachusetts, and became associated with his brother James in business In 1885 he settled in South Dakota, where he and his children are living, viz · William, Millie, Albert, Arthur 3 Emma, married James Collett, they are living in Blackstone Massachusetts 4 James

(II) James Miles, son of James Miles (1), was born in Oxfordshire, England, May 24, 1847 His father died when he was a young boy He left school to learn the mason's trade in London He worked there at his trade until 1869 His brother and one sister were already in America He came over in 1869 and his mother and other sister soon followed He worked at his trade in Woonsocket, Rhode Island, for three months, coming then to Worcester, where he worked for several years He returned to Woonsocket to enter into partnership with his brother, William Miles, as masons and contractors under the firm name of Miles Brothers They soon developed a large business Among other large buildings erected by this firm were the mills of the Woonsocket Rubber Co, one of the first large brick buildings in that city, the Conant thread works, No 5 mill at Pawtucket, Rhode Island, and numerous other mills in Rhode Island cities He retired from business on account of his wife's health and from 1881 to 1886 conducted a farm, which he bought at Grafton, Massachusetts

Mr Miles started in business again in 1886 in Worcester under his own name Besides taking large contracts he has built and sold buildings in Worcester to the value of $250,000 or more He has been one of the leading builders of brick buildings in Worcester Among the buildings he has erected are The hotel building on Main street now occupied by the Worcester market, Hotel Adams at the corner of Pleasant and High streets, owned by Dr Wesley Davis, the Forrest building, corner of Main and Austin streets for R C Taylor At this time his son became associated with him and they built a factory for Lafayette Robbins on Lagrange street, The Buckingham and The Kensington, apartment houses on Murray avenue, The Victoria, an apartment house on Orange street, a large shop for the Crompton & Thayer loom works, Cambridge street, the Abbott street school house for the city, a repair shop for the school department, two large shops for Abraham Israel on Water street In late years the business has been conducted under the name of James Miles & Son, his son having been admitted to partnership

Mr Miles married, in Blackstone, Massachusetts, April 14, 1872, Ella Elizabeth Boyden, daughter of William Wesley Boyden Mr Boyden was a carpenter by trade, born in Mendon, Massachusetts, in what is now Blackstone, September 7, 1835 William Wesley Boyden was son of Joel and Mercy (Briggs) Boyden and grandson of Amos and Sally (Benson) Boyden Joel Boyden was born July 7, 1803, in old Mendon He married, November 28, 1833, Mercy Briggs Amos Boyden was the son of David and Abigail (Carrol) Boyden He was born May 31, 1766 He married Sally Benson, September 30, 1790 The children of James and Elizabeth (Boyden) Miles were Walter James, Grace Ella, born in Grafton, Massachusetts

(III) Walter James Miles, son of James Miles (2), was born in Northbridge, Massachusetts He married, March 15, 1898, Phoebe A Blanchard, daughter of Daniel Blanchard, of Adams, Massachusetts He was educated in the Worcester schools He learned his father's trade and since leaving school has been associated with him He is now a member of the firm of James Miles & Son He resides at the corner of Pleasant street and Richmond avenue on Richmond Heights The children of Walter J and Phoebe A (Blanchard) Miles are Dorothy, Marjorie, born July 29, 1902, Priscilla, born June 19, 1905

SAMUEL GUSTAVUS CURTIS Henry Curtis (1) was the immigrant ancestor of the Curtis family of Worcester, prominent from the first settler to the present day One of his most prominent and best known descendants of the present generation is Samuel Gustavus Curtis, of Worcester

Henry Curtis came from England at the age of twenty-seven, in the ship 'Elizabeth and Ann,' in the year 1635, and settled in Watertown, New England He was a proprietor of that town in 1636 Soon afterward he removed to the adjoining town of Sudbury, of which he was, in 1639, a proprietor His house and barn were burned during King Philip's war just before his death He died May 8, 1678, and the estate was administered by his son Joseph His homestead was on the north street of the settlement, probably where the old Curtis house stood His sister, Joan Parker, of St Saviour's parish, Southwark, England, bequeathed to Henry Curtis of Sudbury, a silver tankard and six silver spoons, and to his wife and three sons, Ephraim, John and Joseph, with him, twenty shillings apiece

He married Mary Guy, daughter of Nicholas Guy, who died in Sudbury She died there December 3, 1682 Their children were 1 Ephraim, born in Sudbury, mentioned below 2 John, born 1644 3 Joseph, born 1647, married at Sudbury, February 5, 1678, Abigail C Grout of Sudbury, daughter of Captain John Grout, settled in Shrewsbury

(II) Ephraim Curtis, son of Henry Curtis (1), born in Sudbury, Massachusetts, March 31, 1642, was the first white settler of the present city of Worcester In the fall of 1673, according to the judgment of Caleb A Wall, as nearly as he could fix the date, Ephraim Curtis left his home in Sudbury with a pack on his back, a long, light Spanish gun and his axe Two days later he camped on the very spot which was owned and occupied by him and his descendants for many generations The principal reason for his selecting this locality to settle was his belief that there was mineral wealth in the soil, from the report that a valuable lead mine had been discovered by the Indians, who had a sort of rendezvous on Wigwam hill while on hunting and fishing excursions He settled down to clear the land and make a home in the wilderness, and for two years remained there, working alone He used to confess in later years that when he sat down and turned his face toward old Sudbury, where his family was, he could not always restrain his tears But he persisted Such was the self-denial and pertinacity of the pioneers For a time Curtis laid claim to the whole township of Worcester, but he had to be content with about two hundred acres near upper Plantation street, and another lot near Grafton gore, granted by the general court as his share of the town

The Indian war drove him away from his forest home in 1675 He was a brave soldier and served on the committee to confer with the Indian sachems before the war broke out He was a lieutenant in the militia company He was at Brookfield at the time of the massacre It was he who crept from the garrison house, under cover of the night, eluded the Indians, intercepted the Lancaster company of forty-six men, under Major Willard and Captain Parker, who were going in another direction, and brought relief to Brookfield He was of a sturdy, ventersome nature, a frontiersman, soldier and scout, used to the customs of his Indian adversaries, and familiar with the camp fire and the ambuscade

His two sons were 1 John, born 1707, was a captain, inherited the homestead, commanded a company in the French and Indian war in 1757, died June 29, 1797, aged ninety years, married Elizabeth Prentice, daughter of Rev John Prentice, of Lancaster 2 Ephraim, mentioned below

(III) Ephraim Curtis, Jr, son of Ephraim Curtis (2), was born about 1710 He inherited from his father a farm of two hundred and fifty acres near the line between Auburn, Millbury and Worcester He married Mary Rice, of Sudbury, Massachusetts, December 23, 1729 Their children, born in or near Worcester, were 1 Samuel, (see forward) 2 Judith, born September 6 (or 26) (twin) 1730 3 Mary, born March 5, 1732 4 Abigail, born June 21 1734 5 Ephraim, born September 6, 1736 6 Oliver, born January 29, 1740, resided on that part of his father's farm lying near the present location of Holy Cross College

(IV) Samuel Curtis, son of Ephraim Curtis (3), born in Worcester, Massachusetts, September 26, 1730, died at Auburn, Massachusetts, October 18, 1814, aged eighty-four years He resided on the Auburn homestead of this branch of the family During the revolution he was one of the most prominent patriots of the town He served on various committees One who knew him wrote of him "His patriotism and valuable qualities always insured the confidence and esteem of his townsmen Gifted by nature with a strong mind he cultivated and improved it by observation and reflection, and as a reward of his merit he was repeatedly promoted to the highest offices of the town As selectman, representative to the general court, his integrity was always conspicuous and his usefulness always apparent"

He married, March 3, 1757, Mary Ward, daughter of Major Daniel Ward, she was born in 1736, and died June 3, 1830, aged ninety-four years Their children were all born in Worcester, viz 1 Samuel, born 1759, baptized January 21, 1759, died young 2 Mary, born February 10, 1760 3 Samuel, born October 11, 1761, mentioned below 4 Ephraim, born 1763, baptized April 3, 1763, had the homestead, left no children 5 Sarah, baptized June 23, 1765 6 Levi, baptized October 4, 1767 7 Lecretia, baptized May 27, 1770 8 Lydia, born July 26, 1772 9 Azubah, baptized January 22, 1775 10 Lydia, born August 13, 1780

(V) Samuel Curtis, Jr, son of Samuel Curtis (4), was born in Worcester and baptized there April 3, 1763 He resided on the Curtis farm on Plantation street on the estate adjoining Colonel Benjamin Flagg's, afterwards owned by his son Benjamin F Curtis, and later by E B and G Dana He was captain of the Worcester Artillery company

He married (first), August 20, 1785, Eunice Flagg, of Uxbridge He married (second) Eunice (Taft) Stowell, daughter of Josiah Taft and widow of Stowell She was a member of the Old South Congregational Church She died in 1861 He died before his father, January 29, 1811 Children of Samuel and Eunice (Flagg) Curtis were 1 Sarah, born November 25, 1785, married Ebenezer Reed, their daughter was Mrs Sumner Pratt 2 Abigail, born February 23, 1788 3 Aaron, born March 5, 1790, father of Charles F Curtis, of Auburn 4 Samuel, born April, 1792 5 Ephraim, born April 8, 1794 6 Lydia, born March 22, 1796 7 John, born April 29, 1798 8 Benjamin F, mentioned below 9 Albert, born July 13, 1807, died July 18, 1898, aged ninety-one years, founder of Curtis & Marble and other large manufacturing concerns of Worcester, one of the most successful of the pioneer manufacturers to whom the city of Worcester owes much, married Sarah K G Houghton 10 William, born 1809, married Caroline Tompkins, of

New York 11 Eunice, baptized October 21, 1810, married Charles P Bancroft, died 1893 at Brookline, Massachuestts

(VI) Benjamin Franklin Curtis, eighth child of Samuel Curtis (5), born in Worcester, September 7, 1800, bought the Plantation street homestead and was a farmer, died there in 1858 He married, April 4, 1831, at Auburn, Massachusetts, Hannah S Wakefield, who was born in Vermont, the daughter of Henry Stone Wakefield, of Montpelier, Vermont Children were 1 Sarah Maria, born January 25, 1832, died young 2 Ellen Olivia, born August 21, 1835, unmarried 3 Samuel Gustavus, mentioned below 4 Charles F, enlisted in Company H, Twenty-fifth Massachusetts Regiment, and died in the service in 1864, at Newbern, North Carolina 5 Albert W, mentioned below

(VII) Samuel Gustavus Curtis, third child of Benjamin Franklin Curtis (6), born in Worcester June 10, 1838, on the old Plantation street homestead in Worcester, which is situated about a quarter of a mile from Belmont street and is near the Insane hospital He married, April 15, 1873, Mary Elizabeth Harrington, daughter of Benjamin Harrington, of Worcester, an uncle of ex-Mayor Francis A Harrington, of Worcester She was born January 25, 1836 He lives at 370 Plantation street on the homestead which he has carried on for many years, and is one of the most prosperous farmers of the city He is a member of the Union Congregational Church He has never cared for public office nor been interested in fraternal societies Their only child is Mabel, who resides with her parents at the homestead They had a daughter, Sarah Edith, who died young

(VII) Albert W Curtis, fifth and youngest child of Benjamin Franklin Curtis (6), was born in Worcester, May 26, 1848 He was educated there in the public and high schools and at Yale College, from which he was graduated in 1871 He studied law under Judge Thomas L Nelson, of Worcester, and at the Harvard law school, and was admitted to the bar in 1874 Two years later he opened an office in Spencer, where he has made his home since As local magistrate he is generally known as Judge Curtis He is a trustee of the public library and the Spencer Savings Bank He has been town clerk since 1877, and member of the board of selectmen for a number of years He is a prominent Republican, and a man of considerable influence in the community He a Past Grand Master of Good Will Lodge of Odd Fellows

He married Mary R Morse, of Spencer They had five children Anna S, L Edith, Alice W, Charles Samuel, Helen M

HENRY MELLEN Richard Mellen (1), the immigrant ancestor of Henry Mellen, was one of the early settlers of Charlestown, Massachusetts He was admitted a freeman September 7, 1639, and had doubtless been in the colony for several years before that He removed to Weymouth in 1642 or 1643, and probably did not live long afterward Savage calls attention to the difficulty of tracing the name because of the great variety of spelling found in the records It is found spelled Mellins, Mullins, Mallins, Melling, Melen, and even Meles He had a land grant in Weymouth in 1642 and 1644 on the back side of Kingoak Hill, but removed from there or died soon after, as his name does not appear again on the records Some of his children were James, born in Charlestown, June 3, 1642, Sarah, born April 4, 1643, at Weymouth, Mary, married at Charlestown, 1662, Daniel Whittemore Simon, perhaps born in England, mentioned below

(II) Simon Mellen, son of Richard Mellen (1), born about 1644, in New England, or before 1639 in Old England, married Mary ——— and settled in the southern part of Framingham, Massachusetts, in 1687 He had civil privileges in Sherborn, and left descendants there He died December 19, 1694, and when his estate was settled in 1695 all his children were mentioned His widow died in Framingham, Massachusetts, June 1, 1709, aged seventy years Their children Simon, born at Winnemesit, Boston, September 25, 1665, (and at Malden), Thomas, mentioned below, Richard, born January 2, 1671-2, married, December 6, 1695, Mary Gleason, daughter of Thomas Gleason, of Framingham, James, born 1681, John, born January 29, 1685-6

(III) Thomas Mellen, second child of Simon Mellen (2), was born in Malden, Massachusetts, August, 1668 He married Elizabeth ——— and they settled in Framingham He was elected tythingman there in 1704 The children of Thomas and Elizabeth Mellen were Henry, born August 12, 1691, mentioned below, Thomas, born August 12, 1693, at Sherborn, died February 4, 1711-2, Lydia, born at Sherborn, April 12, 1695 Sarah, born March 22, 1697, at Framingham, Mary, born October 16, 1699, Richard, born November 10, 1701, Tabitha, born January 4, 1703-4, married Mark Whitney, of Hopkinton, 1727

(IV) Henry Mellen, eldest son of Thomas Mellen, (3), was born August 12, 1691, married, March 24, 1711-2, Abigail Pratt He lived at Framingham until 1725, when he removed to Hopkinton About that time a colony of Scotch-Irish settled in Hopkinton and a number of Henry Mellen's children married into these families Henry Mellen with his wife was admitted to the Framingham church, March 11, 1720, they were dismissed to the Hopkinton church, December 27, 1724, and received there January 3d, following He was deacon of the Hopkinton church in 1732 He died there May 3, 1767, aged seventy-five years His widow Abigail died July 30, 1781, aged eighty-eight years Their children, born in Framingham were Thomas, mentioned below, Daniel, born March 6, 1714-5, Sybilla, born July 20, 1717, Abigail, born November 20, 1719, John, baptized June 3, 1722, graduate of Harvard College, 1741, teacher at Sudbury, ordained as minister at Sterling, December 19, 1744, later at Hanover, was a distinguished man, Mary, baptized June 26, 1724, married John Jones, of Hopkinton, 1749 The children born at Hopkinton, were as follows Lydia, born April 20, 1726, married, 1747, Jacob Chamberlain, Joseph, born May 20, 1728, married Ruhamah Butler, 1747, Elizabeth (twin), born July 1, 1730 married James Nutt, 1747, at Hopkinton, Martha (twin), born July 1, 1730, married Samuel Chamberlain, James, baptized 1732

(V) Thomas Mellen, eldest son of Henry Mellen (4), was born at Framingham, May 15, 1713 He married Elizabeth ——— and they had nine children He married (second) Widow Wilson He died in Hopkinton in 1782 The children of Thomas and Elizabeth were Henry, baptized 1735, died 1813, Elizabeth, born May 25, 1737, James, born June 10, 1739, mentioned below, Mary, born 1742, Sarah, born 1744, Lucy, born September 11, 1746, married Abner Stone, removed to Fitzwilliam, New Hampshire, Sarah, born May 25, 1749, Mehitable, born September 7, 1751, Thomas, born February 25, 1754, major in the revolution, died 1805 The only child of Thomas and his second wife was Joseph, settled in Milford, Massachusetts

(VI) Colonel James Mellen third child of Thomas Mellen (5), was born in Hopkinton, Massachusetts, June 10, 1739 He married Elizabeth Russell, daughter of James Russell, of Holliston, a man of distinction Her brother, Jonathan was a noted man, ambassador to Sweden, and holding other important positions Colonel Mellen went into the revolutionary war a private and was mustered out a colonel He marched in Captain Jesse Eames company from Framingham to Lexington and fought during the day, April 19, 1775 He was captain of a company in Colonel Ward's regiment at the battle of Bunker Hill He soon afterward entered the Continental line and was major, commanding the Twenty-first Regiment in 1776 He was promoted lieutenant-colonel in Colonel James Wesson's regiment in January, 1777, and was stationed at Hudson river, New York, and served faithfully in various responsible positions as lieutenant-colonel for four years He was discharged January 1, 1781 He served on Washington's staff and became a friend, dining often with the general He was officer of the day October 2, 1780, when Andre was hanged for a spy He carried Andre's message to Washington, asking that he be shot instead of hanged Washington's reply "The laws of War forbid it," must have been taken to the condemned man by Colonel Mellen Another important service was in taking two hundred men and supplies safely to Fort Schuyler previous to the attack of Burgoyne

Like most of the Continental officers Colonel Mellen returned home worn out in health, poor in property and cheered only by wordy honors and promises of compensation never fulfilled It is hard to realize the truth in some of these cases He finally lost heart and broke down completely during the last years of his life, mentally as well as physically He lived fourteen years at Milford and fourteen at Mendon, where he died September 27, 1812, aged seventy-three years His widow Elizabeth died June 19, 1830, aged ninety years They are both buried at Mendon and their graves are suitably marked Their children, all born at Hopkinton, were David, born August 17, 1763, settled at Nassau, New York, William, born May 20, 1766, married Lucretia Marsh, Mary, born January 10, 1768, married Samuel Warren, Jr, 1797, Betsey, born April 14, 1770, married Rev John Fiske, Abigail, born June 12, 1775, married Samuel Penniman, 1804, James, mentioned below

(VII) James Mellen, son and youngest child of Colonel James Mellen (6), was born in Hopkinton, October 28, 1780 Married (first), February 12, 1801, Submit Wheelock, daughter of Jesse and Phebe Wheelock She was born January 18, 1782 James Mellen was a farmer and traveling merchant. His homestead was at the north end of Caleb's Hill or Inman's Hill in Mendon His wife Submit died January 29, 1823, and he removed to Spofford, New York, where he married (second) Maria McKnight, of Spofford, and they had one child Mr Mellen died at Orange, Massachuestts, at the home of his son Nathaniel The children of James and Submit Mellen all born in Mendon, were Nathaniel R, born August 19, 1801, married Ruth C Wales, resided at North Orange, February 14, 1824, David, born July 1, 1803, died young, Leonard, born April 10 1806, married Elizabeth S Mayo, March, 1834, William, born December 12, 1811, married (first) Elizabeth Odell (second) Charlotte Jackson, Mary W, born November 5, 1813, married Robert B Shepard, of New Orleans, a child born December 30, 1815, died young, James, born November 23, 1817, died young

(VIII) Leonard Mellen, third child of James Mellen, Jr, (7), was born in Mendon, April 10, 1806 He received a common school education there and became a farmer In 1840 he removed to Hardwick, Massachusetts, where he bought a farm In early life he was a Whig, later a Republican He was an active member of the Congregational church and very strict in his views In early life he was connected with the Mendon Light Infantry He died January 20, 1873 He married Elizabeth S Mayo, twin daughter of Captain Peter Mayo, a sea captain, of Harwich She was born October 24, 1810, died February 22, 1897 Their children Edward, born 1830, was a farmer in Rutland, married Abigail Bemis (see sketch of Dr Bemis and family), Mary Warren, lives at Hardwick, unmarried, Henry, died young, Henry, mentioned below, Hannah, lives at Hardwick, unmarried, James Franklin, born January 31, 1845, unmarried

(IX) Henry Mellen, fourth child of Leonard Mellen (8), was born in Hardwick, Massachusetts, February 4, 1840 He attended the district schools there until he was sixteen He came to Worcester August 29, 1856, as an apprentice for Alvin T Burgess, mason and builder He served four years, for which he received his board and $40 the first year, $50 the second year, $60 the third year and $70 the fourth year He remained with Mr Burgess for several years and was his foreman the last year he worked for him at the then generous wages of five dollars a day He learned all kinds of mason's work, brick, stone and plaster When he left Mr Burgess he began in business for himself in a small way, but met with uniform success, and in a few years was reckoned among the leading masons of the city He began in business in partnership with Sylvester W Dearborn under the firm name of Dearborn & Mellen After three years he sold his interests to his partenr and was alone until he admitted his son, Walter L Mellen, to partnership in 1890, when the firm name was changed to Henry Mellen & Son Mr Mellen was the mason and contractor for all of the buildings of Jonas G Clark, except the stone work on his residence He built the Clark blocks on Main and Front streets, and the buildings at Clark University erected by Mr Clark He had the contract for building the Worcester City Hospital He built the Chadwick building, the Armsby, Main street, the residences of Dr Workman, Elm street, William H Sawyer, 66 Lincoln street, Charles E Thwing, Elm street, and many other of the fine residences of the city For the city he built school houses at Adams square, New Worcester, Union Hill, Adams street He has constructed the mills and other buildings for F E Reed, a tack shop on Lagrange street for D E Somers and a large addition to the Bowler brewery He built the Quincy high school house, the Brookfield Town Hall, and many other buildings in the country He went to New Bedford in 1877 on a contract and remained three years on that and other work offered him He built there Robeson's block with nine stores, the Masonic block, Waite's building, the Thayer & Judd candle works and the first factory of the famous Pierpont Manufacturing Co, silver-smiths

Mr Mellen was in Company A, of the City Guards, Captain A B R Sprague company, Major Charles Devens's regiment He enlisted in 1861 In the following year he re-enlisted in Company E, Forty-second Regiment, and was detailed as orderly at brigade headquarters with the rank of first corporal He was mustered out in 1863 He was a member of the common council from ward eight in 1885 and 1886, and has always taken an active part in public affairs He is a Republican He was formerly a member of the Board of Trade, he is a member and was for three years a trustee of the Worcester County Mechanics' Association He is a member of the Plymouth (Congregational) parish

He married, August 29, 1862, Mary Adelaide Felt, daughter of Elijah and Hannah (Lawrence) Felt She was born at Templeton, Massachusetts, July 6, 1843 Their children are Walter Leslie, mentioned below Bessie Frances, born March 5, 1876, died April 3, 1891

Elijah Felt was born November 11, 1799, died March 19, 1849 Married Hannah Lawrence, daughter of Josiah and Tabitha Lawrence, born February 17, 1807 Elijah was the son of Samuel Felt, who was born March 17, 1788, died June 26, 1826, was a private in Captain John Bacheller's company, Colonel Ebenezer Bridge's regiment on the Lexington Alarm, April 19, 1775 Later he served in Captain Jonathan Brooking's company, Colonel Enoch Hale's regiment Samuel married Naomi Woods Samuel Felt's father was Aaron Felt, who married Mary Wyatt Moses, the father of Aaron Felt, was born in 1651, married Lydia Felt His father, George Felt, was the immigrant, and was born in England in 1601 The name was also spelled Felch George Felt was a mason by trade and came to Charlestown, in New England, as early as 1633, he resided on the Malden side in 1640, he removed to Casco Bay, but returned to Malden He married Elizabeth Wilkinson, daughter of Widow Prudence Wilkinson He died in 1693, his widow in 1694. Mrs Mellen is a member of the Worcester Woman's Club and of Colonel Timothy Bigelow Chapter, Daughters of the American Revolution

(X) Walter Leslie Mellen, only son of Henry Mellen (9), was born in Worcester, January 10, 1868 He attended the public schools there and graduated in 1887 from the Classical high school He went to work for his father and in 1890 was admitted to partnership in the business under the firm name of Henry Mellen & Son Some of the work done since he became connected with the business is mentioned above in the account of the business He is a prominent Free Mason, a member of the Morning Star Lodge, Hiram Council, Eureka Chapter and the Worcester County Commandery of Worcester, he has taken the eighteenth degree in the Scottish Rite and belongs to Aleppo Temple in Boston Mr Mellen is a member of the Commonwealth Club He is a Republican in politics and a Congregationalist in religion, being a member of Plymouth Church

He married Carrie E Fisher, of Fisherville, Massachusetts, a village of Grafton named for her grandfather, who established a mill there His name was Erastus Fisher Her parents were Albert Laban and Ellen Agnes (Hill) Fisher Her father had a grocery store at Fisherville for many years The children of Walter and Carrie E (Fisher) Mellen are Albert Fisher, born July 29, 1893, Dorothy, born December 29, 1894 They reside at 41 Queen street, in a double house, with Mr Mellen's parents

JAMES HUNT, well known throughout Worcester county as deputy sheriff and for his prominence in political life, was born January 27, 1833, in Gloucestershire, England He was the son of William and Harriet (Hodges) Hunt

He attended private schools in his native place In 1850, at the age of seventeen, he came to America He learned the trade of boot and shoe manufacturing and worked at his trade in New Braintree, Massachusetts, and Stafford, Connecticut In 1861 he moved to Rockville, Connecticut, and learned the trade of wool dyer at the Leeds mill He became boss dyer later at the Windermere mill at Ellington, Connecticut, and the Thomas Lewis mill at Naugatuck, Connecticut In 1865 he went to Meriden, Connecticut, and engaged in the retail boot and shoe business, where he remained until 1873, when he removed to Worcester He worked at his trade of shoemaker for a number of years First he worked for D G Rawson & Co, shoe manufacturers, afterwards the firm of Goddard, Fay & Stone He worked also for S R Heywood He was appointed for one year on the police force by Mayor Samuel E Hildreth, but at the end of the year took up his trade again He worked in the shoe factory of C C Houghton In 1886 he was appointed a constable for civil cases by Mayor Francis A Harrington He has since then devoted his time to the duties of that office and of deputy sheriff combined with the real estate business He was appointed deputy sheriff first in February, 1893, by Sheriff Robert A Cham- the vicinity of Webster square, Worcester, and on Union Hill For the past twenty years Mr Hunt has been occupied chiefly with the business of constable and deputy sheriff His office is in the Walker building In a position requiring the utmost tact and descretion, has has been uniformly successful

Mr Hunt has always been a Republican and taken his part in the work of the organization He has shown his interest by constant activity He served the city in the common council in 1897-98-99 He was on the committees on police, public buildings, education, legislative matters and bills in the second reading He represented ward six In 1899 and 1900 he was elected representative to the general court from ward six He was on the committees on cities, and on parishes and religious societies He was elected an overseer of the poor in 1899 for a three-year term, and in 1901 was re-elected He has been favorably mentioned as candidate for senator in his district

He has the unique distinction of being the senior member of the order of Knights of Pythias in Worcester He took the degrees of this order in 1868 at Meriden, Connecticut, in Myrtle Lodge, No 4 The order was at that time enjoying a period of very rapid growth In 1885 Mr Hunt transferred his membership to Regulus Lodge of Worcester, and since that time has been one of the most active and prominent members of the order in Worcester Mr Hunt has seen the order grow from nothing to a membership of about a thousand in thirty years in Worcester He is a member of Montacute Lodge of Free Masons He is a member of U S Grant Commandery, Knights of Malta, and of Prince Consort Lodge, Sons of St George He belongs to the Webster Square Methodist Episcopal Church and is one of the trustees He is a trustee and president of the board of trustees of the Sterling Methodist Camp Meeting Association, which owns the grounds at Sterling Junction

He married (first) Sarah L Russell She was born in Stafford, Connecticut, January 21, 1838, died May 28, 1894 He married (second) Mrs Annie Turner, widow of William C Turner, born in St John, New Brunswick He has no children

THE CARY FAMILY in England is one of the oldest as it is one of the most illustrious and honored in the kingdom of Great Britain The name existed in England before the Conquest and must have been as old as the time of the Saxons

(I) Adam de Kari (Cary) was lord of the

Castle Kari in 1198 according to Sir William Pole He was born about 1170 and married Ann, daughter of Sir William Trevett, Knight The castle no longer exists but the town is called Castle Cary still It is in Somersetshire During the reign of King Stephen the Lord of Cari was opposed to him, the king assaulted and took the castle, in 1153 it was again besieged and nearly ruined The site of the old castle is very interesting to antiquarians

(II) John de Kary, son of Adam (1), was born about 1200, married Elizabeth, daughter of Sir Richard Stapleton, Knight

(III) William de Kary or Karry, son of Sir John (2), was born about 1230, married Alice, daughter of Sir William Beaumont, Knight

(IV) John de Karry, of Castle Karry son of William (3), was born about 1270, married Phillippa, daughter of Sir Warren Archdeacon, Knight Sometimes the "de" was used, sometimes not

(V) Sir John Cary son of John (4), was born about 1300 married Margaret Bozon or Bozume, of Clovelly in Devon

(VI) Sir John Cary, Knight, son of William (5), was born about 1325, married Agnes, daughter of Lord Stafford, and (second) Jane, daughter of Sir Guy de Bryen, Knight Since the reign of Edward II the spelling has been Cary

(VII) Sir John Cary Knight, son of John (6), was born in 1350 at Holway in northwest Devon, married Margaret Holway, was very noted, chief Baron of the Exchequer, judge After the king (Richard II) was put to death by Henry IV, Sir John was banished and all his goods and lands confiscated to the crown He died in Waterford, Ireland, four years later, 1404

(VIII) Sir Robert Cary, son of Sir John (7), was born about 1375 He married Elizabeth, daughter of Philip Courtenay, Knight He married (second) Jane daughter of Sir William Hanchford, Knight He defeated in single combat a Knight of Arragon, for which Henry V restored unto him a good part of his father's lands, and at the same time Robert took the coat of arms of his opponent, which he and his successors have since borne: Argent, on bend sable three roses argent Before that the arms were "Gules, chevron entre three swans argent" The motto is Virtute Excerptae

(IX) Sir Philip Cary, son of Sir Robert (8), was born about 1400 He married Christian Orchard He died 1437

(X) Sir William Cary, Knight son of Philip (9), was born in 1437 He married Elizabeth Paulett He was known as the Knight of Cockington He took part in the War of the Roses on the Lancaster side His side suffered defeat at the Battle of Tewksbury May 4, 1471 and Cary with others took refuge in the Abbey Church a sanctuary where, according to the custom of the times, they could not be molested They were enticed out on promise of pardon and two days later were beheaded His property was confiscated but Henry VII restored it to his son later William left two sons Robert, born 1460, Thomas born 1465

(XI) Robert Cary, son of William (10), was born about 1460 He inherited Clovelly from his father He married (first) Jane Carew, daughter of Nicholas Carew and they had two sons, John de Cary born about 1485 and Thomas de Cary born about 1495 Robert Cary married (second) Agnes daughter of Sir William Hody and they had one son William born about 1500 He married (third) Margaret Fulkeram who bore him a son Robert, about 1510 Robert Cary died in 1540 and has a monument in the Clovelly Church

(XII) William Cary, son of Robert (11) and Agnes (Hody) Cary, was born about 1500 He was sheriff of Somersetshire in 1532, residing at Bristol He was mayor of that city in 1546 He died March 28, 1572

(XIII) Robert Cary, eldest son of William Cary (12) was born in Bristol in 1525 and died 1570

(XIV) William Cary, eldest son of Robert Cary (13), was born October 3, 1560 He was sheriff of Bristol in 1599 and mayor 1611 He had eight sons, three of whom came to America in 1634, 1635 and 1640 respectively

THE AMERICAN LINE

(XV) John Cary, son of William Cary (14), was born in Bristol, Somersetshire, England He came to New England about 1634 His brother James settled in Charlestown and his brother Miles near Jamestown, Virginia A family record made by one of his grandsons states that when a youth the immigrant, John Cary, was sent by his father to France to perfect his education and that while he was absent his father died On returning home to Somersetshire he differed with his brothers in the settlement of their father's estate, finally compromising by taking one hundred pounds as his share and immediately sailed for America John Cary was among the original settlers of Duxbury and Bridgewater, and his name is in the original grant as well as in the subsequent Indian deed He was elected constable of Bridgewater in 1656, the first and only officer elected in the town that year, the first after its incorporation He was elected the first town clerk and held the office until 1681 In 1656 he was one of the ten freemen of the town In 1677 Deacon Willis and John Cary were appointed "to take in all the charges of the late war (King Philip's) since last June and the expenses of the scouts before and since June"

He married, 1644, Elizabeth Godfrey, daughter of Francis Godfrey, one of the first settlers of Bridgewater He died in 1681 The children of John and Elizabeth Cary were John, born 1645, Francis, 1647, Elizabeth, 1649, married William Britt James, 1652, Mary 1654, Jonathan 1656, see forward, David 1658, Hannah, 1661, died unmarried, Joseph, 1663, Rebecca, 1665, married Samuel Allen, Sarah, 1667

(XVI) Jonathan Cary, son of John Cary immigrant (15), was born in Bridgewater, Massachusetts, 1656 He married Sarah Allen daughter of Samuel Allen He died before middle life, 1695, at Bridgewater Their children Recompence, born about 1688 see forward, John, born about 1690, Jonathan, born about 1692

(XVII) Recompence Cary son of Jonathan Cary (16), was born in Bridgewater Massachusetts, 1688 He married Mary Crossman in Bridgewater 1711, and resided there during his whole life, a man of influence and character He died 1719 Their children Seth, born 1714, died unmarried 1742, Ichabod, 1715, Ebenezer, 1717 died unmarried, Saran, 1718, married Benjamin Haywood, 1742, and had a large family Simeon, 1719, Zebulon 1721, Jonathan, 1723, Josiah, 1724, died unmarried 1743, Mary 1726, married Joseph Crossman of Easton, Abigail 1729

(XVIII) Jonathan Cary, son of Recompence Cary (17), was born in Bridgewater, Massachusetts, 1723 He "was remarkable for his probity and Christian character" He was a member of the Congregational church in Bridgewater for seventy years, deacon for sixty years He lived with the wife of his youth for a period of sixty-five years, and died February 2 1813, aged ninety years He married Mary Curtis, daughter of Captain Joseph Curtis of Stoughton, in 1747 She died at the age of ninety-five years

Their children were Moses, born November 20, 1748, Mary, born 1750, died 1768, Dorothy, born December 17, 1752 died unmarried, Jonathan, born February 14, 1757, Huldah, born 1759 died 1763, Alpheus, born April 21, 1761, Huldah, born August 4 1763, died 1775, Sarah, married (first) Daniel Alden, 1786, (second) L A Beal, 1809, James, born 1766

(XIX) Jonathan Cary, son of Jonathan Cary (18), was born in Bridgewater, Massachusetts, February 14 1757 He was a soldier in the revolution and during his declining years drew a pension He died December 25, 1852, aged ninety-five years He married 1784 Abigail Perkins, daughter of Jonathan Perkins Their children were Huldah, born 1785, married Darius Howard, Caleb, 1788, Jonathan, 1791, Luther, 1794, Martin, 1795 Abigail, born about 1797, married Isaac Dunham, Sally, born about 1799, married Zibot Keith, Mary, born about 1800 married James Littlefield, Aurelia, born about 1802 died in infancy, Nancy, 1804, died in infancy

(XX) Luther Cary, son of Jonathan Cary (19), was born in Bridgewater, Massachusetts 1794 He removed when young to East Machias, Maine, and settled finally in Cooper, Maine He died there He was a farmer He married, 1818 Eliza W Foster Their children were James Webber born August 1819 Eliza A, born April, 1822, died May, 1827, George Williams, August, 1824, Mary L, November, 1826, died July, 1827, Delia F, June, 1828, married Stephen J Getchel, of Cooper, October, 1853, and had three children, Charlotte A, December, 1830, married Henry L Foster, 1858, and resided in Providence Rhode Island, Mary E, March, 1834, married Charles Cary, of East Machias, Maine, and had two children, Martin L, September, 1836 was a soldier in civil war, Martha E, April, 1838, lived at Providence, Hiram Foster, August, 1842, see forward

(XXI) Hiram Foster Cary, son of Luther Cary (20), was born at Cooper, Maine, August, 1842 He received a common school education and worked during his youth on his father's farm He enlisted, 1862, in the civil war in the Ninth Rhode Island Cavalry, and served with credit throughout the war

He left Maine when sixteen years old, went to Providence, Rhode Island, and was apprenticed in the stucco business After the war he want to Boston and engaged in the manufacturing of paper collars and cuffs About 1876 went to Ballston Spa, New York, and engaged in some business About six years later went to Saratoga, New York, and engaged in the spring mattress business He left there and returned to his wife's old home, Millbury, Massachusetts, twelve years later, where he still resides

He married Frances J Harrington at Jamaica Plain, Massachusetts now Boston She was born May 24, 1843 the daughter of Thomas J Harrington, (born at Worcester, January 26, 1804 and Eliza J (Waters) Harrington, who was born May 21, 1798, and died December 22, 1876 The children of Thomas J and Eliza J Harrington were 1 Fidelia, born June 5 1838, died November 19, 1848 2 Sophia, born March 3, 1841 unmarried 3 Frances J, born May 24, 1843, mentioned above Noah Harrington was the father of Thomas J Harrington

The only child of Hiram Foster and Frances Cary was Foster Harrington, born August 3, 1874, mentioned above

(XXII) Dr Foster Harrington Cary, son of Hiram Foster Cary (21), was born at Jamaica Plain, Boston Massachusetts, August 3, 1874 His parents removed to Ballston Spa, New York, when he was quite young, and he attended the public schools there He attended the Saratoga high school, at Saratoga, New York and the Worcester Academy, Worcester, Massachusetts, where he was graduated in 1894 He was active in athletics and won distinction on the relay team and other field events At graduation he was the class historian From 1894 to 1898 he was a student at Harvard Medical School He received his degree of M D in 1898 and received a house appointment in the Boston City Hospital, serving there until July, 1900, when he took a place on the staff of the Boston Lying-in-Hospital In 1902 he began to practice his profession in Worcester with his office at 130 Main street, removing after a few years to 11 Elm street He is a member of the Massachusetts Medical Society, the Worcester District Society, the American Medical Association He is a Free Mason, a member of Olive Branch Lodge Since coming to Worcester, he has been appointed visiting obstetrician at the Worcester City Hospital, visiting gynecologist at the City and Memorial Hospitals, out-patient departments He is a member of the Quinsigamond Boat Club and of the Winter Club

PEVEY FAMILY George Abbot (1) was the pioneer ancestor of the Pevey family of Worcester His identity has been established by record discovered since the genealogy was published He may have come with his adult sons He was a proprietor of Rowley in 1643 The general court referred his will to the Salem court, November 11, 1647 The inventory was taken August 30, 1649, showing houses and lands some of which were at Newbury, thirty books, household effects

We learn of his family from the will of his son Thomas, of Rowley This will, made September 5, 1659, and proved September 27, bequeathed to wife Dorothy, father-in-law Richard Swan brothers George, Nehemiah and Thomas (sic) Abbot The three brothers, George of Andover mentioned below Nehemiah of Ipswich, and Thomas of Concord, sold November 25, 1659, land at Rowley, formerly belonging to their father, George Abbot, deceased, subject to the life interest of the widow, Dorothy Abbot The children of George and Dorothy Abbot were George, mentioned below, Nehemiah, mentioned above, Thomas, mentioned above

(II) George Abbot, son of George Abbot (1), the pioneer ancestor of the Pevey family of Worcester, emigrated from Yorkshire to New England in 1640 in the same vessel with Hannah Chandler, whom he afterward married He was one of the first settlers of the town of Andover Massachusetts, in 1643, and was one of the proprietors He lived and died on a farm in Andover, that is now or was recently in the possession of his descendants His house before his death and long afterward was used as a garrison house He married Hannah Chandler, who was the daughter of William and Annis Chandler Her brother, Thomas Chandler, was among the first settlers

George Abbot died December 24 1681 aged sixty-six years His widow married Rev Francis Dane, who died February, 1697, aged eighty-one years, and his widow died July 11 1711, aged eighty-two years The children of George and Hannah Abbot were John born March 2, 1648 died March 19, 1721; Joseph born March 11 1649, died June 24, 1650 (the first death record in the town), Hannah, born June 9, 1650, died March 2, 1740, Joseph, born March 30, 1652, died April 8, 1676 killed, first of the Andover victims of King Philip's war, George, born June 7, 1655, died February 27, 1736, William, born November 18, 1657, died October 24, 1713, Sarah, born November 14, 1659, died June 28, 1711, Benjamin, mentioned below, Timothy, born November 17, 1663 died September 9, 1730, Thomas born May 6, 1666 died April 28, 1728, Edward, died young, Nathaniel, born July 4, 1671, died December, 1749, Elizabeth, born February 9, 1673, died May 4, 1750

(III) Benjamin Abbot, son of George Abbot (2), was born in Andover, Massachusetts, December 20, 1661, and died there March 30, 1703 He married, 1685, Sarah Farnum, daughter of Ralph Farnum, cleared a farm near Shawshene river, where his descendants now or lately lived on the same place He was an active, enterprising and respectable citizen The children of Benjamin and Sarah (Farnum) Abbot were Benjamin, mentioned below, Jonathan, born September, 1687, David, January 29, 1689, Samuel, May 19, 1694

(IV) Benjamin Abbot, son of Benjamin Abbot (3), was born in Andover, Massachusetts, July 11, 1686, and died December 8, 1748 He assisted his brothers in clearing their farms and was an active, upright man He married Elizabeth Abbot, daughter of George Abbot She died 1718 and he married (second), 1722, Mary Carlton, who died January, 1726 He married (third), 1729, Abigail Abbot, daughter of Deacon Nehemiah Abbot She died December 8, 1753, aged fifty-four years The Abbot family is one of the most distinguished as a family in New England It has produced many noted clergymen, authors and public men Many of the descendants of other surnames were equally prominent In this family of Benjamin four of his daughters had eleven sons graduate at college and eighteen grandsons The child of Benjamin and Elizabeth Abbot was Sarah, born August 13, 1718 The children of Benjamin and Mary were Benjamin, born November 1, 1723, Daniel, January 9, 1726 The children of Benjamin and Abigail were Abigail, April 8, 1730, Mary, August 1, 1731, Abigail, January 24, 1734, Abiel, August 4, 1735, Jacob, February 13 1737, died in the army at Albany, February, 1760, Elizabeth mentioned below, Anna, October 23, 1739, Joel, November 6, 1742, Dorcas, August 12, 1744

(V) Elizabeth Abbot, daughter of Benjamin Abbot (4), was born in North Andover, Massachusetts November 8, 1738 and died October 12, 1789 He married, 1758, Ebenezer Cummings, of Hollis and (second) Thomas Merrill, of Conway, New Hampshire She died in 1788, aged sixty-six years The children of Ebenezer and Elizabeth (Abbot) Cummings were Elizabeth, born November 23, 1759, Ebenezer, September 15, 1761, Abigail, July 1, 1763, Bridget, July 15, 1765, Lucy, July 9, 1767, mentioned below, Mary, October 22, 1770, Jacob Abbot, November 2, 1772, Sarah, January 28, 1775 The children of Thomas and Elizabeth (Abbot) (Cummings) Merrill were John, March 2 1782, Benjamin March 15 1784 (H U 1804 LL D)

(V) Lucy Cummings, daughter of Elizabeth (Abbot) Cummings (4), was born in Hollis, Massachusetts, July 9 1767 She married, April 8, 1787, Peter Pevey, mentioned below

The first records discovered of the Pevey family in America are at Hampton, New Hampshire About 1720 three of this name appeared in the vicinity, probably from England Peter settled in Hampton Edward in Dover, Joseph in Dover The name seems to be correctly spelled Pevey, although several generations and some of the present generation spell the name Peavey Edward Pevey was baptized in the Dover New Hampshire, church, January 12, 1724 Mary, wife of Edward Pevey, was dismissed to the Berwick church, August 11, 1727, from the Dover church Joseph Pevey and child Esther were baptized in the Dover church, April 7, 1728

(I) Peter Pevey, the first ancestor of this surname of the Worcester family of the same name, was born in 1697, presumably in England, he died November 23, 1756, in Andover, Massachusetts He married, July 15, 1720, at Andover, Esther Barker, of that town They settled in Hampton New Hampshire, after their marriage and lived there until 1724 or 1725 The two eldest children were born there and the four eldest were baptized there The children of Peter and Esther (Barker) Pevey were Hannah, born in Hampton, July 14, 1721, married, March 28, 1758, William Bent, Mary, born in Hampton, March 22, 1723 married, May 5, 1748, Eliakim Wardwell Rachel, born in Andover, Massachusetts, February 18, 1726, baptized at Hampton May 23, 1726, Esther, born at Andover, April 23, 1728 baptized June 2, at Hampton, Peter, born in Andover, October 17, 1731, died there unmarried August 3, 1754, Thomas, mentioned below

(II) Thomas Pevey, youngest child of Peter Pevey (1), was born in Andover, Massachusetts, March 14, 1736 He married, March 22, 1758, Dorcas Holt They settled in Andover Their children Peter, born April 14, 1762, mentioned below, Hannah, born at Andover, married there Peter Johnson, September 10, 1795 Probably other children

(III) Major Peter Pevey, son of Thomas Pevey (2), ancestor of the Pevey family of Worcester, was born April 14, 1762 During the revolutionary war he was living in Andover Massachusetts At the age of fifteen in fact just before he was fifteen, he enlisted April 7, 1777, as a private in Captain Abbot's company, Colonel Tupper's regiment and served in the army until December 31, 1779 He is also reported as of Captain Benjamin Farnum s company, Colonel Ebenezer Francis's regiment in 1777 and 1778 He was with the army at the surrender of General Burgoyne Soon after the revolution he went to Wilton New Hampshire, and conducted the mills at the French place He began the settlement in the south part of Greenfield and built himself a log house there In the spring of 1789 he started with a yoke of oxen to take his furniture to his cabin His wife whom he married two years before, rode horseback with a bundle lashed to the saddle and her baby in her arms She was first to arrive at the new home Mr Pevey was prominent in military affairs and was major of the Twenty-sixth New Hampshire regiment He was one of the founders of Greenfield He married, April 8, 1787, Lucy Cummings, who was born July 9, 1767, and died October 15, 1854 Her brother, J A Cummings, was the author of a spelling book and geography used extensively in the early part of the nineteenth century The children of Peter and Lucy Pevey were Peter, born July 29 1788, resided in Greenfield deacon of the church there, married at Wilton, New Hampshire, June 22 1819 Dorcas Holt, married (second), April 9, 1857 Tamazin Holt, Sally, born July 11, 1790 married, June 2, 1855, William Wright, Lucy Cummings, born July 3 1792 married July 11, 1816, Farnham Holt, Benjamin Abbot, mentioned below, Jacob, born December 1796, married, November 2 1824 Susan Campbell, married (second), March 26, 1840 Sarah Marsh, Abiel, born March 27 1799, died November 29 1799, Dorcas, born October 8, 1801, married March 2 1824, Edward Pratt married (second) April 27 1847 William Sheldon, Elizabeth, born April 6, 1803, died November 5, 1803, Eliza-

E P Perry

beth, born August 30 1804, married, June 4, 1833, Nehemiah Lowe, Abiel, born January 17, 1807, married, December 4, 1832, Louisa Stone, John Merrill, born November 30, 1809 died December 2, 1809, Merrill Cummings, born August 7, 1812, married, June 3 1841, Elizabeth Stone

(VII) Benjamin Abbott Pevey, son of Peter Pevey and grandson of Elizabeth Abbott (Abbot) (5) was born in Greenfield, New Hampshire, September 25, 1794 died November 16, 1864 He resided in Greenfield and Bennington, New Hampshire, and Schaghticoke, New York In the fall of 1853 one of his sons bought of John A Putnam the mill that was built by Philip Putnam and carried it on for several years

Benjamin Abbott Pevey married, May 13 1820, Clarissa Whittemore, daughter of Amos Whittemore who was born December 11, 1799, died May 19, 1871 Their children were Amos Whittemore, born April 6, 1821, died September 27, 1821, Clarissa Livonia born January 28, 1823, unmarried, resided with Dr Benjamin Pevey at 80 Pleasant street, Worcester, until her death January 21, 1903, Lucy Cummings, born March 18, 1825, married, 1851, George S Russell, they are living (1906) in Wellesley, Massachusetts, Amos Abbot, born July 6, 1827, mentioned below, Benjamin Merrill, born March 26, 1831, died September 17, 1832, Franklin Merrill, born at Bennington New Hampshire, May 2, 1833, mentioned below, Edward Payson, mentioned below, Benjamin Merrill, born in Schaghticoke, June 6, 1838, mentioned below, Mary Elizabeth, born in Schaghticoke, February 7, 1844, married, October 17, 1866, Simeon Thompson, married (second), July 4 1871, Richard Henry French, who died in 1903, Charles Kimball, born in Schaghticoke, January 25, 1844, mentioned below The first four of the preceding were born in Greenfield, the next three in Hancock, New Hampshire and the last three in Schaghticoke, New York

(VIII) Amos Abbot Pevey, fourth child of Benjamin Abbot Pevey (7), was born in Greenfield, New Hampshire He received a common school education and then studied dentistry with a well-known and able practitioner Diligent and painstaking, he soon acquired proficiency in his profession and, when ready to open an office of his own, located in Clinton, Massachusetts He soon proved his skill as a dentist and developed a large practice After some years he decided to remove to Woonsocket Rhode Island, where he was even more successful For many years he was recognized as one of the most prominent men of his profession in the state

He helped to establish three of his brothers in the same profession They learned the business in his office in Clinton and at one time all four were dentists at the same time in Clinton His brother Frank practiced for many years in Boston, but the two other brothers subsequently located and practiced in Worcester Each built up a substantial business Dr Pevey was a prominent member of the Rhode Island Dental Association

Dr Pevey married, October 9, 1854, Ellen F Judd, daughter of Lucian Judd, who removed from Waterbury Connecticut, to Clinton, Massachusetts Mr Judd was a soldier in the war of 1812 and his father was in the revolution He is a descendant of Thomas Judd, who was in Cambridge in 1634 or 1635, and removed thence to Farmington Connecticut and thence to Northampton, Massachusetts Of his six sons, Thomas Jr and Philip settled in Waterbury, Connecticut Dr Pevey's widow resides at 13 Hammond street Worcester Their children Edward, born November 10, 1857, died September 20, 1861, Helen Augusta, born October 1864, now Mrs Fred Ashley married (first) George Lyford Gould, one son, George Lyford Gould, Jr, they reside at 13 Hammond street, Worcester Dr Amos Abbot Pevey died March 6, 1889, in Worcester

(VIII) Franklin Merrill Pevey, sixth child of Benjamin Abbot Pevey (7), was born in Bennington, New Hampshire May 2, 1833 When he was three years old his parents removed to New York state, where he lived until he was eighteen years old He then went to Clinton, Massachusetts, to study dentistry in his brother's office From 1854 to 1857 he had an office in New Ipswich, New Hampshire Since his marriage he has lived in Wilton, New Hampshire, and practiced his profession He was interested extensively in real estate He was one of the committee in charge of the building of the town house, and the bell was a gift to the town from him He died in Wilton May 1, 1901 Dr Pevey married, December 26, 1858, Nancy B Sheldon, daughter of Uzziel and Eliza (Barrett) Sheldon They had no children She died September 27, 1903

(VIII) Edward Payson Pevey, seventh child of Benjamin Abbot Pevey (7), was born in Greenfield, New Hampshire, February 27, 1836, died December 20, 1903, at Richmond, Virginia He was a young boy when the family removed to Schaghticoke, New York, a small town situated a few miles above Troy where his father had a saw mill He received a common school education in the district schools of New Hampshire and New York, his opportunities for school being limited When he was a young man he returned to Wilton, New Hampshire, where he worked in his father's saw mill From there he went to Lowell, to work for his uncle, Abiel Pevey, whose son Gilbert A A Pevey, became a distinguished lawyer in Boston He removed in a short time to Boston, where he conducted a restaurant and later was the proprietor of a stall in the famous old Faneuil Hall Market From there he removed to Marlboro, Massachusetts, and was there proprietor of a restaurant

Mr Pevey came to Worcester following the civil war and established a meat market at 39 Exchange street He built up a large business there He was the first of the family to locate in Worcester A few years later Dr B M Pevey and Dr Charles K Pevey started in business as Pevey Brothers, dentists at 244 Main street Mr Pevey removed his market to Southbridge street but about 1870 became connected with the firm of White, Houghton & Co, 16 Front street In 1874 the firm of White Pevey & Dexter, pork packers, was organized, the original members being Rollin G White, Mr Pevey and Edwin C Dexter, now the only survivor A sketch of Mr White appears elsewhere in this work The firm was very successful in business and their trade extended all over New England The first store was on Front street opposite the old city hall and the abbatoir was on the Grafton road The business was afterward moved further down Front street to A B Hall's block, now the Commonwealth Hotel, where the company was located for a number of years In 1800 they moved to the present location on Bridge street The abbatoir at present is located on Putnam lane and is one of the largest and best of the kind in New England The company was incorporated in 1890 and a few years later sold to the firm of Swift & Co, of Chicago Mr Pevey retired from active business at the time of the sale, and made his home at the Bay State Hotel His wife died February 3, 1886 He died of heart trouble when in the south on a pleasure trip with his daughter Mrs Charles M Booth

Mr Pevey's business ability and common sense, integrity and good nature won for him a leading position among the business men of the city He was universally liked and esteemed He was an active Mason and well known in the Masonic fraternity of the state He was a member of Montacute Lodge, Eureka Royal Arch Chapter, the Worcester County Commandery, Knights Templar, of which for twenty-six years he was the standard bearer He was a charter member of the Worcester Continentals and was on the colonel's staff as commissary sergeant He belonged to the Commonwealth Club He attended Piedmont Congregational Church In politics he was an active and earnest Republican He enlisted, September 6, 1862, and served until September 2, 1863, in Company I, Fifty-third Regiment Massachusetts Volunteer Militia He was a member of Post No 10, G A R

He married, September 25, 1858, Martha Jane Buell, daughter of Daniel and Abigail (Holden) Buell, of Newport, New Hampshire Their children were Nellie Florence, born November 20, 1859, mentioned below, Frank B, born July 21, 1873, died January 22 1874

(IX) Nellie Florence Pevey, daughter of Edward Payson Pevey (8), was born in Wilton, New Hampshire, November 20, 1859 She married in Worcester, November 16, 1881, Charles Matthew Booth who was born January 28, 1859, the son of Benjamin and Betsey (Charnley) Booth, both natives of England Mr Booth was for forty years superintendent of the Quinsigamond wire mill of Washburn & Moen He retired a few years before his death Benjamin Booth died May 19, 1901, his wife died November 14, 1905 Their children were. George Jones, born April 1, 1855, died April 5, 1882, Olina Elizabeth, born 1657, at Lowell, married William H McClure, superintendent of the Worcester fire alarm system, resides at 26 Kingsbury street, Worcester, Charles Matthew, mentioned above

Charles M Booth was educated in the public and high schools of Worcester He began in business as clerk in Kinnicutt's hardware store In August, 1884, he entered Washburn & Moen's offices and rose through various positions to sales agent and head of the flat wire and specialty department of the American Steel and Wire Company He is a member of Montacute Lodge of Free Masons, Hiram Council, Eureka Chapter and Worcester County Commandery, the Tatassit Canoe Club, the Automobile Club He is a Republican He resides at 284 Highland street, Worcester The children of Charles M and Nellie Florence (Pevey) Booth are Edith Florence, born in Worcester, December 12, 1884, died August 2, 1885, Martha Pevey, born in Worcester, December 23, 1890, a student in the Worcester high school

(VIII) Benjamin Merrill Pevey, eighth child of Benjamin Abbot Pevey (7), was born in Shagticoke, New York, June 6, 1838 He studied dentistry in the office of his brother, Dr Amos A Pevey, at Clinton He practiced first at Clinton, then removed to Worcester with his brother, Dr Charles K Pevey In recent years his office has been at his residence, 80 Pleasant street He is a prominent Free Mason, a member of Worcester County Commandery, Knights Templar He attends Union Church He married November 19, 1870, Ella Fisk, who died in 1873 Their only child, Frank Fisk died in infancy

(VIII) Mary Elizabeth Pevey daughter of Benjamin Abbot Pevey (7), was born in Schaghticoke, New York, February 7, 1841 She married (first), October 17, 1866, Simeon Thompson and had one son Simeon E, who has a livery stable at Corona, California, is married and has two sons and two daughters She married (second), July 4, 1871, Richard Henry French, and had three children Sanger Eames and Edith Bradford (twins), born July 6, 1872, Henry, born June 8, 1874, of whom Sanger E French alone survives He is a stable keeper, is married but has no children Mrs French resides with her son, Simeon E Thompson, at Corona

(VIII) Dr Charles Kimball Pevey, youngest child of Benjamin A Pevey (7), was born in Schaghticoke, New York, June 6, 1848 He studied dentist He also learned his profession with his brother, Dr Amos A Pevey, at Clinton, and was formerly in partnership with his brother, Dr Benjamin M Pevey, in Worcester His present offices are at 438 Main street He is a Knight Templar and prominent in the Masonic fraternity He is unmarried

(VIII) Lucy Cummings Pevey, third child of Benjamin Abbot Pevey (7), was born in Greenfield, New Hampshire, March 18, 1825, and married, 1851, George S Russell, a farmer They are now living at Wellesley, Massachusetts Their children are George, born 1852, died 1852, William Tolman, born September 20, 1854, Mary Claretta, born December 19, 1857, George Amey, born December 24, 1859, died July 22, 1906

EBENEZER BUTTERICK, inventor of the celebrated and useful "Butterick Patterns," was born in Sterling Worcester county, Massachusetts, May 29, 1826 He was the son of Francis and Ruhamah (Buss) Butterick, grandson of Jonathan and Hannah (Sawyer) Buttrick, great-grandson of Francis and Hannah (Gilson) Buttrick, great-great-grandson of John and Elizabeth (Falkner) Buttrick, great-great-great-grandson of John and Mary (Blood) Buttrick The father of the last name John was a son of William and Sarah (Bateman) Buttrick, and grandson of William Buttrick, who was born in England in 1616, came to America from Kingston-on-Thames in 1635, and died in Concord, Massachusetts, June 30, 1698 Ebenezer Butterick's father was a farmer and carpenter, an active and leading citizen, and the principal founder of a Universalist Society in Sterling, a proof of the intellectual courage which he never lacked, and which his son inherited and enlarged

The son was educated in the common schools of Sterling and in the Leicester Academy, an ancient and still flourishing school in Leicester Massachusetts The best business habits of his life he credited to his clerkship in his brother's village store, the firm Butterick and Bartlett Still a youth, he began the business of tailoring as an apprentice in Worcester, Massachusetts Careful application soon made him expert and enabled him to establish himself as a merchant tailor of taste and skill in Sterling, Leominster, and finally in Fitchburg, Massachusetts In 1850 he married Ellen Augusta Pollard, of his native town, who died in 1879 leaving a daughter, Mary Ellen Butterick, a son having died in infancy

In the conduct of his business, Mr Butterick was much annoyed by the waste of time in cutting children's garments and conceived the idea that a set of graded patterns would be a great advantage to him and to other tailors, and especially to mothers making clothes for their own children It was during a period of recuperation from disabling sickness and anxiety that his meditative mind conceived this idea It was highly characteristic that a benevolent impulse and an interest in little children were fundamental to the invention which is now so intimately and honorably associated with his name In June, 1863, he astonished his wife by telling her

Ebenezer Butterick

that he was going to set about the making of patterns as a new business, and her deterrent caution did not avail to check his enthusiastic confidence that he was on the track of a useful and profitable invention. Having made convincing experiments in Sterling, he cut the first salable patterns on an extension table in the sitting room of his Fitchburg house, 41 Grove street. They were patterns for boys' clothing and the boy who furnished the first measurements was Clarence Buttrick, a nephew of Mr E Butterick, then four years old and now, as then, living in Sterling, Massachusetts. The first positive success was with the "Butterick Shirt Pattern," but an equal success with patterns for boys' and girls' clothing soon followed. The first patterns were folded by members of the family, his own and his wife's relatives. They were packed in boxes containing each one hundred patterns, and were sold at a wholesale price of $10 for each box, $25 retail. The first small purchases were made in Shirley, Massachusetts and the purchasers of the first box were James Tuttle & Co of South Acton. Mr Butterick never spent the ten dollar bill which he personally got for this box of patterns, but kept it as an interesting reminder of the day of small things.

In September following the start in June, rooms were taken in a house near Mr Butterick's, and five girls and women were employed to do the folding under the direction of Mrs Butterick's sister. A Mr Curtis, of Fitchburg, did the first printing, and Mr A L Howard of Fitchburg was the first traveling salesman. Another salesman John Roach, traveling through New Hampshire, Maine and Nova Scotia in the fall of 1863 was successful to a degree that was decidedly encouraging. A device for "trimmed patterns" answered a good purpose till the introduction of cuts and drawings on the pattern labels superseded it. In the spring of 1864 the work was taken to the old Academy building in Fitchburg, and during the same season Mr Butterick issued his first fashion-plate, a small one, showing what he could do in the line of children's garments. Later in the year he began publishing gentlemen's fashion plates, accompanied by cut patterns, which did away with the labor of tracing and cutting out patterns from diagrams as had been previously necessary.

Some months in advance of these improvements, Mr Butterick had introduced his patterns in New York. In or about October, 1863 he had taken two upper rooms at 192 Broadway. Almost literally he "took up his bed and walked," for he brought a bedstead of his own invention from Sterling for the back room where, using it by night by day it could be folded back against the wall. His inventive genius was always seeking and finding new avenues of expression. Shortly Mr Abner W Pollard, later for a long time a partner in the business, came to New York to assist Mr Butterick, his brother-in-law, and he also lodged in the back room, which b day was store-room and work-shop, in the front room Mr Butterick meeting his customers. Factory and home were removed to Brooklyn in 1865, December 7th, a day of national thanksgiving for the return of peace. The home gathered in seven persons who had assisted in the work in Fitchburg while for the factory a second story in a dwelling house was at first sufficient room. From time to time a room was added then a larger building was taken, and finally a commodious building on the corner of Throop and Lafayette avenues, which has until now (1904) been equal to the manufacturing requirements of the business. It was Mr Butterick's habit to go to the manufactory in its humble stage every morning before breakfast and sweep the rooms and make the fires after breakfast going to the New York office. In 1867 Mr Butterick associated with himself J W Wilder, his general agent, and A W Pollard, his secretary, in the firm of E Butterick & Co, and the business throve apace until 1875, when particular circumstances conspired with the financial depression of the time to cripple it seriously. It soon rallied in response to the heroic efforts put forth by Mr Butterick, his partners assisting to maintain an enterprise in which he had unfailing confidence and pride. The Butterick Publishing Company was organized in 1881. In the meantime subsidiary offices had been established in all important centres in this country and abroad, and the praise of the Butterick patterns was everywhere heard, especially as, since 1866, their most significant appeal has been to women, whose convenience and economy and taste they had preeminently served.

In 1883 Mr Butterick's health suffered a serious collapse. It rallied slowly, but never completely, during the remainder of his life, during which, still interested and influential in the conduct of the business, he lived in a quiet meditative fashion, spending nearly or quite half the year in the town where he was born, and where he made himself a commodious but simple home on a large farm, and endeared himself to all the neighborhood by his cordial friendliness. His participation in the business ceased in 1899 but never his interest in this creation of his mind and heart. Of his physical disabilities he made mental opportunities. His liberal means took nothing from the simplicity of his character and tastes. To gentle manners he united an inflexible will and a sense of justice that was an immovable rock. Of a deeply religious nature, he cherished a most comfortable faith in the openness to each other of this life and the life beyond. He was formally associated with the Metropolitan Art Museum, the Brooklyn Institute of Arts and Sciences the Brooklyn Guild, and the American Unitarian Association. In the welfare of poor children he had special interest and a generous appreciation of their needs. No man was ever less injured by good fortune or less convinced that mere money-getting is the chief end of life. After a short illness he died March 31 1903 and was buried in Leominster, Massachusetts, a town adjoining the pleasant town where he was born.

DANIEL EDWARD DENNY. Robert Denny (1), to whom the line of Daniel Edward Denny, of Worcester, Massachusetts has been traced, was living in England in 1590. His children were: Edmund born probably at Combs Suffolk county, England married Johan ——, he was buried at Combs May 11, 1609. Robert married Margaret ——, he was buried at Combs, February 1, 1624, she was buried there February 7, 1609.

(II) Edmund Denny son of Robert Denny (1), married Johan ——. He was buried at Combs, May 11, 1609. The children of Edmund and Johan Denny were: Edmund born at Combs, baptized there 1575. Johan married —— Wade.

(III) Edmund Denny, son of Edmund Denny (2) was baptized at Combs 1575. He married Agnes Castard, of Battysford May 1601. Among their children was a son, Edmund born March 31, 1681.

(IV) Edmund Denny son of Edmund Denny (3), was buried March 31 1681. He married Dorothea Moore of Rattlesden, 1627. She died October 1637. He married (second) Susan Syer (Sawyer). His child by first wife was Edmund, died 1707 His children by second wife were Thomas, buried November 22, 1717, John, died unmarried 1684 or 5, Samuel, buried October 7, 1727, married Amy —— who died in 1733, Susannah, married Ralph Weeler, Deborah, married Thomas Granger, of Ipswich, died about 1685

(V) Thomas Denny, son of Edmund Denny (4), was born in England and died there November, (buried November 22,) 1717 He married Grace Cook, about 1686 She was born in March, 1655, and was buried December 19, 1741 See sketch of Denny family of Leicester for further details The children of Thomas and Grace (Cook) Denny were Edmund, died December 18, 1731, Thomas, born at Combs, buried there February 17, 1772, Samuel, born 1689, landed in America, July 20, 1717, died June 2, 1772, Daniel, born November 30, 1694, died April 16, 1760, Sarah, married William Green, of Battisford, married (second) —— Pierson, Deborah, born 1699, died June 1, 1766

(VI) Daniel Denny, son of Thomas Denny (5), was born at Combs, England, November 30, 1694, died April 16, 1760 He was the emigrant ancestor He left England in June, 1715, and arrived at Boston, September 12, 1715 He settled in Leicester, March, 1717 He married Rebecca Jones, of Worcester, December, 1722 She died December 20, 1740, aged forty years For a more extended account of the pioneer in Leicester see sketch of the Denny Family of Leicester in this work The children of Daniel and Rebecca (Jones) Denny were 1 A child who died young 2 Thomas, born March 19, 1725, died October 23, 1774, he married Tabitha Cutler, of Grafton, June 25, 1752, she died August 8, 1753, and he married (second), October 21, 1755, Mary (Chaplin) Storrs, widow, of Pomfret, Connecticut, he was a member of the first Provincial congress in 1774, he has been called 'most active and zealous of those who in 1770 were in opposition to parliament, he died while a member of the Provincial congress 3 Mary, born April 22, 1727, died August 8, 1822, married Nathan Sargent 4 Rebecca, born April 10, 1729, married John Lynde, married (second) Asa Stowers 5 Samuel, born May 20, 1731 6 Sarah, born January, 1778, married (first) Thomas Sargent, married (second) Hon Seth Washburn 7 Daniel, born October, 1736, died November 17, 1742 8 Isaac, born August, 1739, died 1743

(VII) Colonel Samuel Denny, son of Daniel Denny (6), was born in Leicester, Massachusetts, May 20, 1731 He died September 20, 1817 He married Elizabeth Henshaw, September 29, 1757 She was born September 29, 1737, died December 7 1787 She was a descendant of Joshua Henshaw John Alden, the Pilgrim of Plymouth, was another ancestor See Henshaw family elsewhere in this work Samuel Denny was lieutenant-colonel of Colonel William Henshaw's regiment of minutemen which marched upon the Lexington alarm April 19, 1775 February 21, 1776, he was elected colonel of the first regiment in the county of Worcester, and in November he was stationed with the army at Tarrytown, New York He was colonel of the Second Regiment, which was engaged October 21 1779 He was a representative in the general court in 1778, and was a member of the convention called to act upon the ratification of the Constitution of the United States in January, 1788 He lived on Moose Hill in the northwest part of the town

The children of Colonel Samuel and Elizabeth (Henshaw) Denny were Daniel, born August 6, 1758, died in Worcester, April, 1822, married Nancy Watson, Elizabeth, born March 1, 1760, died November 18, 1846, married Thomas Walter Ward, of Shrewsbury Samuel born April 21, 1762, married Desire Boyden, June 2, 1812, David, born January 7, 1764 married Betsey Spooner, Isaac, born November 27, 1765, married Grace Tidd, William, born September 17 1767, married Patty Smith, Sarah, born May 23, 1769, married Stephen Harris, Thomas (afterwards Nathaniel Paine), born July 22, 1771, married Sally Swan, married (second) Mary Denny, of Worcester, Harvard, 1797, studied law under Hon Nathaniel Paine and by act of the legislature took his name, was seven years a representative in the general Court, and in 1823 and 1824 was in the senate, he was president of the Leicester Bank, Polly, born August 21, 1773, died October, 1852, married, May 1, 1798, Rev John Miles, of Grafton, Joseph, born April 2, 1777, married (first) Phebe Henshaw, married (second) Lucinda Henshaw, sister of his first wife, and his cousin

(VIII) Isaac Denny, son of Colonel Samuel Denny (7), was born in Leicester, Massachusetts, November 27, 1765 He was a soldier in the revolution at the age of sixteen He married May 16, 1703, Grace Tidd descended from an old Lexington family The emigrant John Tidd was a tailor He came early and was settled in Charlestown, Massachusetts, and proprietor of the town in 1637 He removed to Woburn, the adjoining town, in 1640 He was a town officer there Isaac Denny died at Hardwick, Vermont, March 19, 1813 His widow, Grace (Tidd) Denny, married in 1818, John Sargent, and died in Leicester, Massachusetts, April 16, 1859, aged eighty-five years Isaac Denny was a farmer He removed to Hardwick Vermont, after the revolution and settled there Washburn's History of Leicester says of his military record "In July 1781, seven men from Leicester enlisted into the Continental service for the term of three months, viz Jotham Smith, Isaac Denny, Ebenezer Upham, Asa Green, Marshall Newton, John Hapgood Howe Some of these were not quite sixteen years of age"

The children of Isaac and Grace (Tidd) Denny were Harriet, born February 14 1794 died June 29, 1870, married, April 16, 1816, Elisha P Mathews, who died March 10, 1861, Gratia, born October 18, 1795, died October 22, 1860, married, March 31, 1829, Ebenezer Williams of Brimfield, Massachusetts, where Mrs Williams died, Maria, born December 3 1797, married, November 22, 1826, Elizabeth Henshaw, born January 29, 1801, lived in Newburyport, Massachusetts, unmarried, died September 25 1886 Isaac born March 8, 1805, died November 24, 1831, unmarried, Laura Amelia, born September 3, 1807, married, June 17, 1834, John Balch of Newburyport, who died July 11, 1871, she died July 17 1886 Edwards Whipple born June 9, 1810, died February 11, 1865, at Worcester, Massachusetts

(IX) Edwards Whipple Denny, son of Isaac Denny (8) was born in Hardwick, Vermont He was a deaf mute but notwithstanding this handicap was entirely successful in business He was educated at the American Asylum at Hartford, Connecticut He married May 4, 1837, Elizabeth D Stone, who was also a deaf mute She was born in Eden, Vermont, but both were pupils at Hartford among the first of the pupils of Rev Thomas Gallaudet, the principal who accomplished so much for the deaf and dumb during his lifetime Dr Gallaudet's own wife was a deaf mute and he went to Europe to learn the methods of teaching the deaf mutes and to learn how to talk with his fingers Mr Denny learned the carpenter's trade and was a skilled wood worker He came to Worcester when it was a small village and bought a large estate on Highland estate, which has become very valuable during the past thirty years The residence of Daniel E Denny on West street stands on a portion of the old place The children of Edwards Whipple and Elizabeth D (Stone) Denny, both born in Worcester, were Ann Elizabeth, February 4, 1841, died December 20, 1857 Daniel Edward, born July 14, 1845

(X) Daniel Edward Denny, son of Edwards Whipple Denny (9), was born in Worcester, Massachusetts, July 14, 1845 He attended the public schools of Worcester and Worcester Academy He learned the trade of machinist in the shops of Lucius W Pond and worked for twenty years at his trade, principally for Mr Pond and at the Washburn shops of the Worcester Polytechnic Institute He was a skillful mechanic, and perhaps should be cited in a history of Worcester county as a fine example of the combination of brains and mechanical skill in the workshops of Worcester that have built up the city and attracted new enterprises here After twenty years of labor at the lathe and drill Mr Denny accepted a position in the railway mail service He was promoted step by step till he was 'clerk-in-charge" He retired at the end of twenty years to enter the real estate and fire and accident insurance business Since 1902, when Mr Denny went into business for himself, he has been in public life and has served the city creditably in several capacities

He served the city in the common council in 1904 and 1905 He was elected from ward one for a two years term In his second year he was elected president of the board, one of the highest honors in the city government Some matters of great public importance have been acted upon since Mr Denny has been in the city council He has been on the committees on streets, sewers and on military affairs The making of a boulevard out of Shrewsbury street from the railroad station to Lake Quinsigamond has been carried into effect The Greenwood Street Park has been acquired and the magnificent Green Hill estate has been acquired at a nominal figure from the heirs The water works have been extended along the Asnebumskit brook in Paxton The city has been redistricted, making ten wards instead of eight He was a member of redistricting committee Mr Denny has been an active and efficient councilman His good record in the city government was recognized by his constituents, and by a flattering vote he was elected to the general court for 1906, from ward one, the fifteenth district

Mr Denny is known best from his brilliant career at the head of George H Ward Post, No 10, G A R, of Worcester Mr Denny entered the service at the age of nineteen in Company E, Forty-second Regiment, Massachusetts Volunteer Militia He joined the Worcester Grand Army Post in 1869, and has since then been an active member and held various offices from time to time He has been the commander in 1904 and 1905 During those two years this post made a remarkable gain in membership Forty years after the civil war and over forty after the military service of most of the men began, this post added to its membership one hundred and twenty-six members, bringing the total membership to seven hundred and sixty-eight, and putting the post in the first place in the country in point of numbers Those who know the men believe that this post stands at the head also in the character and standing of the members, in their records as soldiers and as citizens The auxiliary associates of this post number nearly four hundred, and that also is the largest auxiliary of any post The head of the post deserves some share of the credit for the strength and gains made in the membership His earnestness and executive ability have helped materially in putting the post at the head and maintaining the lead

Mr Denny is known all over the state among the Knights of Pythias He was a charter member of Regulus Lodge of Worcester, No 71, K P and was first master-at-arms of that body He served through the various offices and was elected chancellor commander in 1887 He was admitted to the grand lodge the year following under the administration of P G C Charles B Newton and was appointed grand master-at-arms, in 1891 he was elected grand prelate by a handsome vote The year following he was chosen grand vice-chancellor, and in 1893 was given a unanimous election as the twenty-second grand chancellor of the Grand Lodge of Massachusetts When the parade and field day sports of the Knights of Pythias of the state were held in Worcester he was grand marshal, a position for which his military training and physique admirably fitted him Mr Denny is a Free Mason of high standing He belongs to Morning Star Lodge, Eureka Royal Arch Chapter, Hiram Council and to Worcester County Commandery, Knights Templar He is also a member of the Worcester County Mechanics Association and has recently been elected a trustee He was formerly a member of the Royal Arcanum He has attended Central church since a young boy

He married, April 17, 1867, Martha Alice Fisher, daughter of Robert D and Alice (Russell) Fisher She was born in Northbridge, Massachusetts, October 8, 1844 They were married in Worcester Their children are 1 Frank Edward, born September 9, 1869, died May 16, 1872 2 Alice Elizabeth, born March 27, 1871, a graduate of the Worcester Classical high school, 1890, and afterwards a teacher in the same school for four years, married Peter Robinson Culbert, who is a newsdealer at 334 Main street, Worcester, January 11, 1900, they have one child, Janet Denny Culbert, born December 7, 1904 3 Edward Arthur, born in Worcester, December 16, 1872, graduate of the Worcester Classical high school, 1892, married Bertha J Griswold, September 17, 1901, at Worcester, he has been with the State Mutual Life Assurance Company for ten years and is at present assistant cashier 4 Florence Isabel, born November 11, 1881, graduate of the Worcester Classical high school, class of 1900, now employed at the Worcester County Registry of Deeds

WARREN CARLTON JEWETT Edward Jewett (1), of Bradford, England, father of the emigrants of the name, Maximilian and Joseph Jewett, was ancestor of Warren Carlton Jewett, of Worcester Edward Jewett was a clothier in Bradford in the West Riding of Yorkshire, England He was descended from Henry de Juatt, a knight of the First Crusade Edward Jewett married, October 1, 1604, Mary Taylor, daughter of William Taylor He lived and died at Bradford His will was dated February 2, 1614, and proved July 12 1615, his wife Mary being executor The will mentions sons William, Joseph and Maximilian, daughter Sarah, and father-in-law William Taylor His children, baptized at Bradford were William, September 15, 1605, Maximilian, October 4, 1607, Joseph, December 31 1609 came with Maximilian to Rowley and became a prominent man there, proprietor deputy to the general court, died February, 1660, Sarah, and perhaps others

(II) Maximilian Jewett son of Edward Jewett (1), was born in Bradford, England, and was baptized there October 4, 1607 He came to this country with Rev Ezekiel Rogers in 1639 He settled at Rowley, Massachusetts, and was admitted a freeman May 13, 1640 He was very early a deacon of the church and always known as Deacon Jewett, even on the town records He was for many years selectman and a deputy to the general court His wife Ann, whom he married in England, died November 1667, buried November 9 He died October 19, 1684 He drew his home lot at Rowley, January 10, 1643-4, on Bradford street, named for his home in England It consisted of two acres and was alongside the home lot of his brother Joseph, part west and part east of the street He drew many lots of land in later years In 1652 he and Thomas Dickerman the two largest taxpayers of Rowley, each had six cows, but Dickerman's stock was valued by the assessors at a slightly larger amount Jewett's assessed property was valued at one hundred and five pounds, eight shillings, four pence He married (second), August 30, 1671, Ellen Boynton, widow of John Boynton His widow married (third), in Ipswich, June 1, 1686, Daniel Warner, Sr, of Ipswich She died August 5, 1689

The children of Maximilian and Ann Jewett were Ezekiel, born March 5 1643, married Faith Parrat Anna born February 26, 1644-5, married, December 5, 1666, Barzilla Barker, Mary, born February 18 1646-7, married, in Merrimac Village, now Bradford, named from the birthplace of the Jewetts in England, November 26 1668, David Haseltine, Elizabeth, born May 22 1650, married, in Bradford, July 21, 1680, Robert Haseltine, Faith, born October 8, 1652, married Samuel Dowse, of Charlestown, Joseph, born about 1655 married Rebecca Law, Sarah, born March 17, 1658-9, buried June 19, 1660, Sarah born about 1660 married, May 13, 1689, Jeremiah Ellsworth, Priscilla, born May 19, 1664, buried September 4 1664

(III) Ezekiel Jewett son of Maximilian Jewett (2) was born in Rowley Massachusetts, March 5, 1643-4 He was chosen to succeed his father as deacon of the church at Rowley and ordained there October 24, 1686 He married, February 26, 1663-4, Faith Parrat, daughter of Francis Parrat She died October 15, 1715 in her seventh-fourth year He married (second) October 23 1716 Elizabeth Jewett, widow of John Jewett Ezekiel died September 2 1723, in his eighty-first year His will was dated February 16, 1722-3 and was proved November 4, 1723 He left land at Boxford to his sons Ezekiel and Thomas in Bradford to his son Francis His widow married (fourth), December 2 1723, Ensign Andrew Stickney, son of William Stickney

The children of Ezekiel and Faith Jewett were Francis born March 15, 1664-5, married Sarah Hardy, Thomas born September 20 baptized October 28 1666 married Hannah Swan Ezekiel, Jr born July 24 baptized September 6, 1668 died young, Ezekiel Jr born October 25 1669 was in the expedition against Canada in 1690, settled at Boxford and had a large family there married Martha ——, Maximilian born February 5, baptized October 11, 1671-2 married Sarah ——, Ann born September 29, 1673 died September 11, 1689 Sarah born November 24 1675, married January 30, 1707-8 Jonathan Bailey, Elizabeth born March 29 1678 married November 30, 1704 Isaac Platts married (second), June 6, 1716, Francis Nelson Nathaniel born February 12, 1681, married Mary Gage Stephen, born February 23, 1682-3 married Priscilla Jewett

(IV) Francis Jewett, son of Ezekiel Jewett (3), was born in Rowley, Massachusetts, March 15, 1664-5. He married, in Bradford, Massachusetts, June 20, 1693, Sarah Hardy, daughter of John Hardy, of Bradford She was born there March 25, 1672, died there February 3, 1744, in her seventy-second year Her grave is in Groveland as that part of Bradford in which they lived, East Bradford, is now known He died at Bradford, September 19, 1751, in his eighty-seventh year, and was buried in the graveyard at Groveland His will was dated September 18, 1751, and proved December 9 1751 The children of Francis and Mary (Hardy) Jewett were Samuel, born April 26, 1694, married, in Bradford, October 23 1718, Ruth Hardy, of Bradford, James, born April 16, 1696, died young, Ann, born September 24, 1698 married, at Bradford, April 16, 1737 Ephraim Pemberton, of Amesbury, Massachusetts, Mary, born July 6, 1702, died young, Ezekiel, born April, 1704, died October 4, 1727, buried in Groveland Mary, born October 20, 1706, Sarah, born October 5, 1708, Nathaniel, born November 20, 1710, baptized December 3, 1710, married, in Bradford December 25, 1734 Susanna Gooden (Gooding), of Bradford, James, born April 26, 1713, not mentioned in father's will, 1751, Esther, born December 9, 1719, died July 13, 1720

(V) Deacon Nathaniel Jewett son of Francis Jewett (4), was born in Rowley, Massachusetts, November 20, 1710, baptized December 10 1710 He married, in Bradford, Massachusetts, December 25, 1734, Susan Gooden, of Bradford, Massachusetts He was a soldier in the revolution at the age of sixty-six He was at Ticonderoga He removed to Hollis, New Hampshire, where he died October 5, 1791, at the age of eighty-one years The children of Deacon Nathaniel and Susan (Gooding) Jewett were Mary, born 1740, died December 12, 1747; Lieutenant Ebenezer, born 1743, and others born at Hollis New Hampshire

(VI) Ebenezer Jewett, son of Deacon Nathaniel Jewett (5), was born in Rowley probably, possibly Bradford in 1743 He enlisted in June, 1777, in Captain Emerson's company on the Ticonderoga Alarm and again in 1780 he was lieutenant in Captain Barron's company, Colonel Nichols' regiment at the defence of West Point He was selectman of Hollis, New Hampshire, in 1782 He married Mary Rideout, March 15, 1792, and settled at Hollis, New Hampshire He died October 6, 1826, at the age of eighty-three years The children of Lieutenant Ebenezer and Mary (Rideout) Jewett were Ebenezer, born February 13, 1793, Polly born September, 1794, Nathaniel born July 21 1796, James born March 29, 1799, Francis born May 26, 1801, Susannah born December 16, 1803 Lydia, born April 26, 1806

(VII) Ebenezer Jewett son of Ebenezer Jewett (6), was born in Hollis, New Hampshire, February 13 1793, and spent his early life there He lived for some years in Quincy and his children were all born there He came to Worcester where he died April 1870 He married Elizabeth Walker His estate was administered by his son, Eben Jewett The children of Ebenezer Jewett were Eben, Elizabeth, married Edward A Spear of Quincy, Massachusetts Joseph, lived in Hubbardston, Mary, married Joseph W Carlton, of Boston

(VIII) Eben Jewett, son of Ebenezer Jewett, Jr (7), was born in Quincy, New Hampshire He came to Worcester with his father and settled on the farm on the corner of Holden and Chester streets, where he has since lived He was a successful farmer He married Emily Jane Knowlton, daughter of Jeremiah and Emily Knowlton, born June 21 1836 The children of Eben and Emily Jane (Knowlton) Jewett were Warren Carlton, born

January 28, 1855, J Henry, born in Worcester, November 10 1857

(IX) Warren Carlton Jewett, son of Eben Jewett (8), was born in Worcester, Massachusetts, January 28, 1855 He was born and brought up on the Jewett farm at the corner of Holden road and Chester street, Worcester He attended the Worcester common and high schools He worked with his father after leaving school and has remained there since owning and running the farm in late years He has developed the property until he has one of the most productive and profitable farms in this section

He was elected to the common council from ward one in 1887 and served three years In the city election of 1890 he was elected a member of the board of aldermen and served four years He was president of the board in 1894, when the new city charter went into effect He established a reputation for thorough and faithful work in the interests of the city when in the city council He has also served the city for the past four years in the general court He was on the committees on cities and on agriculture

He has been prominent in the Grange He was secretary of the Massachusetts State Grange for six years, and was master for four years He was for two years president of the Worcester Agricultural Society He is a member of the State Board of Agriculture by appointment of the governor, and is serving his second term of three years He is unquestionably one of the best known farmers in the state He has held offices of honor and trust for the past twenty years and invariably filled them satisfactorily He has been prominently mentioned as a Republican candidate for the senate in his district Mr Jewett in his capacity of master of the State Grange and on the State Board of Agriculture has been in great demand as a speaker and is considered an authority on agricultural matters in New England He has a wide acquaintance among the leading farmers and public men of the country

He married Mary Elizabeth Vaughan, of Thetford, Vermont They have one daughter, Jennie Warren, born April 5, 1884

BROWN FAMILY Nicholas Brown (1), the pioneer ancestor in America of the late William O Brown county commissioner for a number of years, and Edward Augustus Brown treasurer of Worcester county, Massachusetts, was the son of Edward Brown and Jane Side, daughter of Thomas Side The father lived and died in the parish of Inkbarrow, Worcestershire, England, and the son, Nicholas, was doubtless born there

Nicholas Brown was in Lynn in New England before 1638 His son John's name appears in the Indian deed of Lynn as "ye Worshipful Mr Brown" He sent this son John to England in 1660 to look after the property of his father-in-law, which as next heir to the Side estate, he had inherited Nicholas Brown was a mariner in his early days He settled in Lynn at the northwest of Saddlers' Rock in what is now Saugus He had two hundred and ten acres of land there, granted by the town, situated on the river His neighbors were Boniface Buxton on the south, Lieutenant Thomas Marshall and Jeremiah Swain on the west North of his land was the Wigwams meadow He owned two hundred acres in Reading and three hundred and twenty-seven acres on the north-side of Ipswich river He was admitted a freeman September 7, 1638, and was a deputy to the general court from Lynn in 1641 Mr Brown was a leading citizen in the town of Reading where he lived after the town was incorporated from Lynn in 1644 He was appointed commissioner to hear small causes in 1640, the title of the local magistrate at that time He was deputy to the general court in 1655-56-61, and was also selectman during those years

Nicholas Brown, his wife and children were dismissed from the Lynn church to the Reading church February 6, 1663 She died November 1, 1674 He died April 5, 1673 His will was dated March 9, 1673 and proved June 17, 1673 He bequeathed to children John, Josiah, Edward Joseph, Cornelius and Elizabeth, and to wife Elizabeth The children of Nicholas and Elizabeth Brown were John; Josiah, both born in England probably, Edward, born August 15, 1640 Joseph, December 10, 1647, Cornelius, Sarah June 6, 1650, Elizabeth

(II) Joseph Brown son of Nicholas Brown (1), was born in Reading Massachusetts, December 10, 1647 He married, May 26, 1674 Elizabeth Bancroft She was the daughter of Lieutenant Thomas and Elizabeth (Metcalf) Bancroft and was born in Reading, December 7, 1653 Lieutenant Thomas Brown was born in England in 1622, perhaps at Cheadle Stafford county, where a Thomas Bancroft was baptized February 10, 1622 The first wife of Thomas Bancroft, Alice Bacon, had one child who died young (For further details of Thomas Bancroft, see Bancroft family elsewhere in this work) Joseph Brown died at Reading, October 16, 1723 and Elizabeth Brown, who died there December 31, 1732 may have been his widow

Michael Metcalf father of Thomas Bancroft's second wife, Elizabeth, was born in Tatterford, county of Norfolk, England in 1586 He was a Dornix weaver, that is weaver of a kind of stuff used for carpets and curtains He lived in Norwich in Norfolk county He married Sarah Ellwyn, who was born June 17, 1593, in the adjoining town of Waynham of Wymondham, where they were married October 13, 1616 Their seven eldest children were born in St Benedict's, Norwich, and four younger at St Edmondsbury

On his way to America Michael Metcalf wrote a letter to "All the true professors of Christ's Gospel within the city of Norwich," saying, "I was persecuted in the land of my father's sepulchres for not bowing at the name of Jesus, and observing other ceremonies in religion, forced upon me at the instance of Bishop Wren of Norwich and his chancellor, Dr Corbett, whose violent measures troubled me in the Bishop's court, and returned me into the High Commissioners Court Suffering many times for the cause of religion I was forced for the sake of the liberty of my conscience to flee from my wife and my children, to go into New England taking ship for the voyage at London Sept 17, 1636 being by tempests tossed up and down the seas till the Christmas following, then veering about to Plymouth in Old England in which time I met with many sore afflictions Leaving the ship I went down to Yarmouth in Norfolk County, whence I shipped myself and family to come to New England and sailed April 15 1637 " Michael Metcalf settled at Dedham where he was admitted a freeman May 13, 1640 He was town officer and schoolmaster He died December 27 1664 and his will dated December 27 1664 mentions his wife and children

(III) Nicholas Brown son of Joseph Brown (2), was born in Reading Massachusetts, September 22, 1677 He married May 28 1700, Rebecca Nichols, who was born August 10 1684 daughter of Captain Thomas and Rebecca (Eaton) Nichols After the death of Nicholas Brown his widow married (second) Deacon Jonathan Barrett as his second wife Her father, Captain William Nichols, married December 1, 1680, in Reading, Rebecca, daughter of John and Elizabeth (Kendall) Eaton John Eaton was born in Staple, county Kent, December 20, 1635, his father, William Eaton, was born about 1604-5, they settled in Watertown, Massachusetts, and Reading, where William died May 13, 1673, and Martha, his widow, November 14, 1680 John Eaton died in 1691 in Reading also Elizabeth Kendall, who married John Eaton, was daughter of Thomas Kendall of Reading, brother of Francis Kendall, of Woburn (See sketch of Kendall family in this work) Rebecca Kendall, widow of Deacon Thomas Kendall, died July 17, 1703, aged eighty-five years Her epitaph is famous "Here lyeth the mother of ten who had 175 grand and great grand children" But her descendants were all by her daughters, those of the name Kendall are as a rule descended from Francis Kendall Nicholas Brown, clerk, died September 2, 1713, aged thirty-six years, at Reading, where he had lived He was buried in the old graveyard at South Reading, as was also his wife Bebecca, widow of Deacon Barrett She died March 18, 1765, aged eighty-five years

(IV) Deacon Benjamin Brown, son of Nicholas Brown (3), was born at Reading, Massachusetts, February 21, 1702, died at Reading, April 1, 1768 He married Susannah ——

(V) General Benjamin Brown son of Deacon Benjamin Brown (4), was born in Reading, Massachusetts, March 22, 1728 died there January 4, 1801, aged seventy-three years He married (first), June 20, 1749, in Reading, Hannah Swain, who was born August 26, 1731, in Reading He married (second) Elizabeth Wiley, February 20, 1772

Hannah Swain was the daughter of Thomas Swain, whose father was Lieutenant Benjamin Swain, a doctor, whose father was Jeremiah Swain Major Jeremiah Swain, the last mentioned, was son of Jeremiah, who was born in England, and settled at Charlestown, Massachusetts, in 1638, probably the year in which he emigrated, settled in 1640 in Reading, married Mary ——, died 1658

Major and Doctor Jeremiah Swain (2) fought in King Philip's war and was wounded at Ft Narragansett He was captain in 1676, in 1689 he was in command of the forces sent against the Indians, he was selectman of Reading eight years, representative to the general court ten years and governor's assistant in 1690 and 1696, he married, 1664, Mary Smith, daughter of Francis Smith, one of the pioneer settlers

Benjamin Swain, son of Major Jeremiah Swain, was also a physician He was for many years selectman of Reading and died in 1747, he married (first) Margaret ———, by whom he had nine children, in 1714 he married Elizabeth Boutwell, widow of James Boutwell, by whom he had one child, his son, Thomas Swain, was the father of Hannah Swain, who married General Benjamin Brown as stated above

Hannah (Swain) Brown died June 12, 1771, aged forty years Thomas Swain was a private in Captain John Walton's company, Colonel David Green's regiment, and marched with the company on the Lexington call He was appointed by the general court lieutenant-colonel in Colonel Jonathan Fox's regiment of Middlesex county, and was commissioned in council February 12, 1776 In 1777 he was lieutenant-colonel in Colonel Samuel Bullard's Massachusetts regiment He was present at the surrender of Burgoyne He was at Ticonderoga with General Gates in 1776, and an interesting letter written to his wife is printed in Eaton's History of Reading Massachusetts He was a general of the militia after the war

(VI) William Brown son of General Benjamin Brown (5), was born in Reading, Massachusetts, April 1, 1758 He married Martha Richardson, who was probably born in Lynnfield, Massachusetts She used to talk of that place and of Lynn, Saugus and Reading to her grandchildren He was a soldier in the revolution and marched with his father on the Lexington call in the Reading company He was also in the Train Band under John Walton, captain, May 13, 1775 He settled in Royalston Massachusetts, on the Prouty place as it is now called He was a tanner by trade and he built a tannery in Royalston He then bought of Elder Whitman Jacobs the farm south of and adjoining Newton's, where as is supposed Abel Whitney first settled In several purchases he annexed to his farm the Thomas Heminway place farther south and became a large landed proprietor In his later years he settled his son, Colonel Benjamin Brown, with him

Colonel Brown commanded the Royalston Grenadiers when they marched for the defence of Boston in the last war with Great Britain It should be added here that the farm passed to Colonel Benjamin Brown's son, Lieutenant Benjamin H Brown and the farm has remained in the possession of his descendants to the present time

William Brown died in Royalston, December 23, 1830 His widow died there January 16, 1851, aged ninety years, nine months, seven days The children of William and Martha (Richardson) Brown, of Reading and Royalston, were William born April 15, 1784, died aged nineteen years, Benjamin of whom later, Otis, born September 11, 1793, died August 19, 1796 Hannah, born December 13, 1795, died July 12 1886

(VII) Col Benjamin Brown second child of William Brown (6), was born at Reading, Massachusetts, May 16, 1787, and came to Royalston with his parents He was captain of a company which went from Royalston in the war of 1812 He married Betsy Reed, daughter of Nathan Reed, of Rutland, Massachusetts, later of Royalston Betsey's sister, Lois Reed, married W R Sargent, and lived to an advanced age in Shrewsbury, Massachusetts Nathan Reed was born in Rutland, Massachusetts, May 31, 1761 He married Lois Maynard and settled in Royalston He married (second), September 14, 1783, Lois Maynard, who was born December 20, 1764, the daughter of Moses and Tabitha (Moore) Maynard of Rutland At the age of sixty-seven Moses Maynard tipped the scales at four hundred and fifty-one pounds He died December, 1796 His ancestry was Moses Maynard, born about 1697, died March 26, 1782, Zachery Maynard, born in Sudbury, June 7, 1647 died 1724, John Maynard, the emigrant, was of Sudbury 1639, married, June 14 1646, Mary Axtell, daughter of Comfort Starr (See sketch of Comfort Starr elsewhere in this work)

Lois (Maynard) Reed died December 24 1846, and Nathan Reed died May 6, 1850 He was a brother of Deacon Jonas Reed, who wrote the history of Rutland Their father Deacon Jonas Reed, of Littleton was born June 7 1722, and married Elizabeth Wright, of Concord April 17 1746 The father of Deacon Jonas Reed was Major Benjamin Reed, who removed from Lexington, Massachusetts, where he was born October 22 1696, to Littleton He married Rebecca Stone sister of Deacon John Stone Benjamin died July 13 1789 aged ninety-three years and his first wife died November 1718 aged fifty-two years

The father of Benjamin Reed was William Reed captain, who was born September 22 1662, and who married Abigail Kendall, his father's cousin,

Wm O. Brown

May 24, 1686 She had the Kendall peculiarity that has been noted for centuries of extra toes and fingers Captain Reed settled in Cambridge Farms, now Lexington, and was a great landholder in Cambridge Farms, Woburn and Billerica He was justice of the peace and captain of the military company He was one of the first board of selectmen chosen after the incorporation of Lexington in 1713, and died there May 12, 1718 His widow died October 12, 1734, and both were buried in Lexington

The father of Captain William Reed was George Reed, who was born in England, in 1629, and bought a farm in Woburn, November 7, 1651, from Rebecca Terrace He married Elizabeth Jennings or Jennison, of Watertown, Massachusetts, August 4 1651, and he bought land in Weymouth, April 16, 1665 He married (second) Hannah Rockwell, of Charlestown, November 9, 1665, having eight children by the first marriage and five by the second The farm of George Reed is now or was lately owned by Nathan Blanchard, and it is within the limits of the town of Burlington He was wealthy and influential and deacon of the Woburn church He died February 21, 1706, aged seventy-seven years

The father of George Reed was the emigrant, William Reed, of Woburn William Reed or Reade is believed to be the son of Thomas and Mary Reade, of Brocket Hall, Hertfordshire, England, and was born in 1587 He sailed from London in the ship Defence' in July, 1635, and arrived at Boston, October 6, 1635, with his wife, who was Mabel Kendall, born in 1605 (See Reade family for further details)

Elizabeth J Jennison, who married George Reed, as stated above, born April 12, 1637, in Woburn, Massachusetts, was the daughter of Robert Jennison, of Watertown, and her birth is the earliest record we have of the family Robert Jennison was admitted a freeman in May, 1645 His wife, Elizabeth Jennison, died October 30, 1638, aged thirty, and he married (second) Grace ——, who died November 26, 1686, he died July 4, 1690 His will mentions his son-in-law, George Reed

The first wife of Benjamin Reed, mentioned above was Rebecca Stone, who was born November 19, 1696, died November 30, 1748, they married about 1718, and they lived at Lexington, Massachusetts She was the daughter of Samuel and Dorcas (Jones) Stone Samuel Stone was born October 1, 1656, and died June 17, 1743, aged eighty-seven They were married June 12, 1679, and lived in Lexington where he and his father before were deacons of the church Dorcas Stone died September 24, 1746, aged eighty-seven

Samuel Stone was the son of Samuel and Sarah (Stearns) Stone, of Cambridge Farms, born 1635, and was a prominent man, town officer and deacon He died September 27, 1715, aged eighty years, seven months His wife, Sarah Stone, died October 4, 1700, and he married (second) Abigail ——, who died in Woburn, 1728, aged seventy-one

The father of Samuel Stone, Sr, was the emigrant, Gregory Stone, who came in 1635 and settled in Cambridge He was deacon of the first church He married Lydia Cooper, widow, who had two children by her first marriage and six by the second He was a deputy to the general court He died November 30, 1672 aged eighty-two, and Lydia died June 24, 1674 His father was a dissenting minister in Sudbury, Suffolk county, England, where Gregory was born about 1590 The father, Rev Samuel Stone, allowed four sons to emigrate in order to enjoy religious freedom The wife of Samuel Stone, Sr, was Sarah Stearns wife of Isaac Stearns, the emigrant (See sketch of Stearns family) The wife of Samuel Stone, 2d, Dorcas Jones, is believed to have been daughter of John and Dorcas Jones, of Concord

Betsey Reed's father, Nathan Reed, was the son of Jonas and Elizabeth (Wright) Reed Elizabeth Wright was the daughter of Joseph and Elizabeth Wright Samuel Wright, his father, settled in Sudbury, Massachusetts, where he was born April 9, 1670 He removed to Rutland and was prominent in town and military affairs He died January 15, 1740, and his wife, Mary, daughter of Cyprian Stevens, died May 18, 1739 (See Stevens Family)

Samuel Wright was the son of Edward Wright, captain and pioneer in Sudbury, who died there August 7, 1703 Captain Edward married, June 18, 1659, Hannah Axtell, who died May 18, 1708 He was probably the son of Dorothy Wright, widow, an early settler in Sudbury, who married (second) John Blandford, Hannah Axtell was the daughter of Thomas Axtell He was buried in Sudbury, March 8, 1646, leaving a widow Mary, who married (second) John Goodnow

Colonel Benjamin Brown (VII), was prominent among the early settlers in Royalston He became a colonel in the militia, and served two terms in the general court, served in the town in all the important offices, and was many years selectman He was a prosperous farmer His two brothers, William and Otis, died young His sister Hannah married William Pierce, of Royalston, and (second) Samuel Dadmun, of Fitchburg, and lived in Fitchburg The children of Benjamin and Betsey (Reed) Brown were William Otis, born March 30, 1815, died January 29, 1890, of whom later, Isabella R, May 3, 1818, married John Forrester Brooks, the well known proprietor of the Massasoit House, Barre, Eliza Morse, October 18, 1820, unmarried, resides in Royalston and Fitchburg, Mary Richardson, December 27, 1822, died January 10, 1823, Benjamin Hammond, July 31, 1824, farmer at Rayalston, Massachusetts, married Nancy L Wood, he was a soldier in the civil war, Edward Augustus, August 7, 1827, married Bessie Maria Harding, served his regiment in the civil war as quartermaster,-has for many years been treasurer of the county of Worcester, resides in Worcester, Moses Reed, born April 1, 1830, died January 27, 1864, unmarried, Elizabeth Reed, March 22, 1833, resides in Chicago, Illinois, where she was a school teacher about forty years and is now enjoying a teachers' pension for length of service

(VIII) William Otis Brown, eldest child of Benjamin Brown (7), was born in Royalston, Massachusetts, March 30, 1815, died January 30, 1890 He was brought up in Royalston and received his early education in the district schools there He worked at mechanical trades when a young man in his native town In 1854 he removed to Fitchburg, a neighboring town and started in business as a dealer in grain and flour with his brother, Edward A Brown, the present county treasurer, and W A Crehore under the firm name of Brown, Crehore & Co In 1857 he formed a partnership with ex-Mayor H A Blood Their grain store was in the building on Water street opposite the Union Station until 1861 He enlisted as quartermaster in the Twenty-fifth Massachusetts Regiment, and was mustered into the service with the rank of first lieutenant September 20 1864 Soon after the capture of Newbern North Carolina, he was appointed first commissary at that important point

The historian of the Twenty-fifth Regiment, Captain J W Denny, wrote, wrote of him 'Lieutenant William O Brown was esteemed by all as a most capable and efficient officer Indeed, it was often remarked that his department was the best managed one in the service ' Near the close of his time of service yellow fever broke out at Newbern, and one of the first victims was a clerk in his department The disease was not at first recognized by the army surgeons who were not familiar with it Mr Brown had a severe attack which nearly proved fatal and doubtless left its mark on his naturally vigorous constitution After the close of the war he held a responsible position at the construction of the Hoosac tunnel, which was then being excavated under state management, and remained in that position until the contract for the completion of the tunnel was let to the Shanleys in 1869

Mr Brown had a long record of faithful service in town and county, and was highly esteemed as a discreet, conservative and thoroughly honest official He was selectman of Fitchburg from 1857 until 1861, and after his return from the service in 1865-66-70 He represented ward three in the board of aldermen in 1888, and served on the committees on police, highways, city property and buildings He was elected county commissioner of Worcester county in 1868 and re-elected six times He completed his twenty-first year of continuous service at the close of 1889, only a few months before his death, when failing health obliged him to decline a re-election In January, 1877, he succeeded J Warren Bigelow as chairman of the board, a position which he held during the remainder of his term of service He had had the direct oversight of the erection of the court house, of that part of the jail built after the fire in Fitchburg, and the extension of the jail in 1888 His successive elections were proof of his ability and fidelity to the duties of his position

He was one of the incorporators of the Wachusett National Bank of Fitchburg, Massachusetts, which began business June 1, 1875, and was a director to the time of his death and vice-president since January 9, 1877 For several years he was treasurer of the Walter Heywood Chair Manufacturing Company He was director of the Fitchburg Mutual Fire Insurance Company from 1865 to 1868, and from July 7, 1870, until his death

He was an entertaining companion and during his long and varied experience had acquired a large fund of anecdotes which he could effectively relate He had a deep love for children and was often seen leading or entertaining them, and no citizen had more friends among the little folks

He married Hannah G Heywood, of Royalston, Massachusetts She died October, 1868 She bore him two sons, George and Charles, who died at the ages of thirteen and nine years, respectively Mr Brown married (second), October 4, 1870, Rosa Heywood, daughter of Walter and Nancy (Foster) Heywood, of Gardner, Massachusetts They had no children Mrs Brown resides at the homestead on Main street, Fitchburg, where she is highly esteemed She is active in church and charitable work

(VIII) Edward Augustus Brown, son of Colonel Benjamin Brown (7), was born at Royalston, Massachusetts, August 7 1827 He was educated in the public schools of Royalston and at the Westminster Academy in a neighboring town After leaving home he was employed first by Captain Ephraim Murdock of Winchendon in his wooden ware establishment for two years or more In 1854 he went to Fitchburg and worked as clerk in the store of Brown Crehore & Company, dealers in groceries, butter, etc In the year following he went west and located in Beloit, Wisconsin, as a dealer in furniture, and remained there until the fall of 1859, when he returned to Fitchburg and was employed in the flour and grain store of Blood & Brown for whom he worked until he enlisted

Although he lost the sight of one eye through an accident in childhood and could not have been drafted as a soldier, he was accepted when he volunteered having demonstrated that he had an excellent vision, nothwithstanding the defect When President Lincoln called for volunteers in the spring of 1861 Mr Brown was a member of the Fitchburg Fusiliers, then commanded by General John W Kimball, and the company was offered as a whole, but was not accepted He joined the Twenty-fifth Massachusetts Regiment when it organized and was made quartermaster-sergeant The regiment went into camp September 20, 1861 It was in the Burnside expedition to Roanoke Island and Newbern, North Carolina, in the fall of 1862, he was appointed first lieutenant and quartermaster of the Fifty-third Massachusetts Volunteers and he went with the regiment to Louisiana, where he was stationed during the remainder of his service with that regiment After the nine months of his enlistment had expired and he was mustered out, he returned to Newbern and worked in the commissary department until the summer of 1864 when he received from President Lincoln a commission as commissary of subsistence with the rank of captain, and remained in the service until the surrender at Appomattox Court House and the close of the war He was also breveted major by President A Johnson and discharged as such He was mustered out October 2, 1865, after more than four years of service

He returned to his father's home at Royalston and assisted him until his father died in February, 1866 On the first of May following he was appointed general passenger and ticket agent of the Boston, Clinton & Fitchburg Railroad, with central offices in Fitchburg, a position that he filled with credit He resigned January 20, 1876, to accept the appointment of county treasurer to fill an unexpired term of Charles A Chase, resigned He has been re-elected at the expiration of each of his three year terms of office, and has (1906) already served continuously over thirty years Mr Brown has the honor of serving for the longest period of any treasurer of Worcester county In the meantime the duties of the office have greatly multiplied, the population of the county has become vastly greater and amount of money and the number of accounts handled by the treasurer greatly increased Yet the administration of Mr Brown's office has been above criticism The expense, compared with some other counties in New York and New England, is remarkably small Mr Brown has been a most useful public servant As he served the government and the railroad company, so he has served the county, with the same regard for economy and scrupulous regard for the treasury He could not be more conscientious and painstaking in any business, private or public

Mr Brown removed from Fitchburg to Worcester in 1877 to be nearer the office of the county treasurer He has resided for many years at 31 Harvard street In politics he is a Republican in 1875 he was a member of the common council of Fitchburg but he has never cared for party politics or for political contests He attends Plymouth Congregational Church to which his family belongs He is a member of E B Sumner Post, Grand Army, of Fitchburg

He married September 13, 1869 Bessie Maria Harding daughter of Theodore and Nancy (Clark) Harding of East Medway, Massachusetts Her

Edward A. Brown

father was a farmer there She was born April 14, 1841, and died at Worcester, August 15, 1903 The children of Edward Augustus and Bessie Maria Brown are 1 Anna Grace, born at Fitchburg, February 5, 1872, married, December 25 1899, Clifford Raymond Harris, graduate of the Worcester Polytechnic Institute, 1897, manager at present of the Standard Plunger Elevator Company of Worcester, residing at 61 Beachmont street, they have two children Edward Augustus Harris, born March 8, 1902, Joseph Harris, born April 26, 1905 2 Sarah Abbie, born February 22, 1875, resides at home with her father 3 Mary Alice, born August 30, 1879, resides at home with her father

BALDWIN FAMILY Richard Baldwin (1), ancestor of John S Baldwin and Charles C Baldwin, of Worcester, held the Manor of Dunbridge, in Aston-Clinton, Buckinghamshire, England, early in the sixteenth century His will was proved in 1552-53 His heir was Henry Baldwin

(II) Henry Baldwin, son of Richard Baldwin (1), was heir to the Manor at Aston-Clinton, which is in the Hundred of Aylesbury and Deanery of Wendover, four miles from Aylesbury east on the road from London through Tring Dundridge and the Chapel farm of the Baldwins were in that part of Aston-Clinton called St Leonards Dundridge remained in the Baldwin family until 1748 when it was sold by the heir of J M Baldwin, Esq, to Edward Darrell, Esq

Henry Baldwin married Alice King and had eight children, four sons and four daughters His will, dated January 2, 1599, mentions his children as follows Agnes, Jane, married James Bonus, Mary, married Richard Salter, Richard, who inherited the Manor, John, Robert, and Sylvester (see forward)

(III) Sylvester Baldwin, son of Henry Baldwin (2), was born at the Manor of Dundridge about 1765 He married Jane Welles in 1590 He died previous to 1632 His children were Harry, buried in 1594, John, not living in 1632, Henry, inherited Dundridge, Richard, William, Sylvester, married Sarah Bryan in 1620 These sons were born between 1590 and 1600

(IV) Sylvester Baldwin, son of Sylvester Baldwin (3), was born about 1600 at Aston-Clinton He lived at St Leonards in Aston-Clinton near Dundridge, where he owned the Chapel farm He was the executor of the will of his uncle, Richard Baldwin, who died without issue in 1636, leaving the Manor to Henry Baldwin, son of Sylvester Baldwin (3) and brother of Sylvester Baldwin (4), who was the residuary legatee, as well as the executor

Sylvester Baldwin was the emigrant ancestor In July 1638, with his wife Sarah and six children, he sailed for America in the ship "Martin" They belonged to the New Haven Company

Sylvester Baldwin died in mid-ocean July 21, 1638 When the ship arrived in Boston Mrs Baldwin and her son Richard were appointed executors of the will by the Court of Assistants He left a large estate The widow and six children decided to remain in America and settled as they had intended at New Haven In 1643 the Mrs Baldwin was rated as one of the wealthiest proprietors After 1643 she married (second) Captain Astwood and removed to Milford, Connecticut, where she died in 1669 Captain Astwood died in London in 1654

Sylvester Baldwin married Sarah Bryan in 1620 Their children, all born and baptized at Aston-Clinton were 1 Sarah, baptized April 22 1621, married 1638 Benjamin Fenn, of Milford, Connecticut 2 Richard baptized August 25, 1622 married, 1642, Elizabeth Alsop, of New Haven, he lived at Derby and Milford was town clerk of Milford and deputy to the general court, he his many descendants 3 Mary, baptized February 28, 1624, died in 1624 4 Mary, baptized February 19 1625, married, 1640, Robert Plum of Milford 5 Martha, baptized April 20, 1628 6 Ruth, born in 1630 7 Samuel, baptized January, 1632, died in 1632 8 Elizabeth, baptized January 25, 1633, died 1633 9 John, born in 1635 (see forward)

(V) John Baldwin son of Sylvester Baldwin (4), was born in Aston-Clinton, England, in 1635, and died August 19, 1683 The maiden name of his first wife is unknown It is conjectured that she was a daughter of Captain John Astwood, his step-father They were married in 1656 and a house lot was assigned to them in Milford, Connecticut, and later he received other grants of land in that town His wife died in 1657 soon after the birth of her only child, John In 1664 John Baldwin settled in New London Connecticut He married (second), July 24, 1672 Rebecca Palmer, widow of Elisha Chesebro, and daughter of Walter Palmer (I) of Stonington, Connecticut They settled permanently in Stonington where she owned an extensive tract of land She died May 2, 1713

The children of John Baldwin were 1 John, born April 13, 1657, died in 1676, in England 2 Rebecca May 20, 1673, married Elnathan, son of Deacon Manasseh Minor, town clerk of Stonington 3 Mary, February 24, 1675, married John Randall, of Stonington 4 Sylvester, March 4, 1677, received a bequest in 1702 from the estate of his grandmother, Sarah (Bryan) (Baldwin) Astwood, he married Lydia Minor and Elizabeth Avery 5 Sarah, 1680, died unmarried 6 Jane, 1681 died before 1692 7 Theophilus, 1683, married Priscilla Mason, (see forward)

(VI) Theophilus Baldwin son of John Baldwin (5), was born in Stonington, Connecticut, June, 1683 He settled there He married (first) Priscilla Mason, daughter of Daniel Mason, May 25, 1710 She was the granddaughter of Captain John Mason, the Indian fighter, and of Rev Peter Hobart, of Hingham, Massachusetts, whose daughter Rebecca was Daniel Mason's second wife

The children were born by the first wife He married (second), May 1, 1724, Jemima Powers, who died in 1733, and he married (third) Elizabeth Hascall, widow, of Norwich He was the first deacon of the church organized in 1727 in what is now North Stonington In many ways he was a man of mark in the town, having character, ability, wealth and a remarkably sunny temper

The children of Theophilus and Priscilla (Mason) Baldwin were 1 John, born July 12, 1711, (see forward) 2 Priscilla, November 17, 1713, married Daniel Caulkins 3 Theophilus, October 23, 1716 married (first), February 5, 1738, Sarah Lamb, and (second), January 20 1764 Elizabeth Billings of Stonington 4 Sylvester, March, 1719, married (first) Anna ——— and (second) Bridget Chesebro, of Stonington, and had ten children

(VII) Captain John Baldwin, son of Theophilus Baldwin (6), was born July 12, 1711 at Stonington, Connecticut He married, February 6, 1736 Mary Clarke She died January 24 1737 four weeks after the birth of her son John He married (second) Eunice Spaulding of Plainfield, Connecticut, twin daughter of Thomas Spaulding She was born July 28 1720 He died in 1762 He held a commission as captain in the militia His widow married (second) November 1 1764 Isaac Williams, who died September 22 1788 She died January, 1819, aged ninety-eight years and six months

The children of John Baldwin were 1 John, born December 27, 1736, died January 8, 1737 2 Mary, February 9, 1741, married Stephen Frink 3 Priscilla, May 20, 1743, married Hubbard Borroughs, Jr, and died in 1771 4 Elizabeth, June 23, 1745, married November 24, 1765, Jesse Swan of Stonington 5 Eunice, October 25, 1747, died August 23, 1761 6 Thomas, April 6, 1751, died April 10 1751 7 John May 12 1752, (see forward) 8 Ziba, February 16, 1755, married, July 20, 1775 Amy Brown, of Preston Connecticut, died September 27, 1803

(VIII) Major John Baldwin, son of John Baldwin (7) was born May 12, 1752 in Stonington, Connecticut He was a thrifty, forcible and influential man He married, January 23, 1772, Sarah Denison of Stonington She was the daughter of John and the granddaughter of Daniel Denison, who was the son of Colonel George Denison, the emigrant ancestor She was born May 3 1752

Major Baldwin settled on the homestead in Stonington Mrs Baldwin died June 19, 1813, he died August 3, 1814 Their children were 1 John, born October 28, 1772, married, January 31, 1796, Abigail Boardman, of Griswold, and (second) in 1825, Anner Rose a widow, he died in 1858 2 Eunice, March 16, 1775, married, January 17, 1793, Stephen Tucker of Griswold, Connecticut 3 Denison, March 25, 1778, died unmarried 4 Andrew December 15, 1780, married, November 22, 1801, Mary Boardman 5 Daniel, May 21, 1783, married (first) Eunice Frink, (second) Lucy Boardman, and (third) Hannah Stanton by whom he had nine children 6 Polly, February 1, 1786, married Stephen Frink 7 George Washington, July 21, 1788 married November 16 1809, Mary C Kinney, of Griswold died in St Louis in 1846 8 Sarah in 1790, married 1815, Thomas Holmes died in Fall River, 1853 9 Nancy, in 1793 died in 1834 unmarried

(IX) Daniel Baldwin son of John Baldwin (8) was born May 21, 1783 He married (first) April 22, 1804 Eunice Frink, who died childless, May 1 1805 He married (second), January 22, 1806, Lucy Boardman, who died childless, August 17, 1806 He married (third) April 21, 1808, Hannah Stanton who bore him nine children She was the daughter of Captain Nathaniel Stanton, of Groton, Connecticut, whose descent was Nathaniel (4) his father Joseph (3), Captain John (2), Thomas (1) the first settler Her mother was a lineal descendant of the first James Avery, of Groton Massachusetts, through his son Captain James Avery

Daniel Baldwin settled first in North Stonington, Connecticut, where their first four children were born After 1816 they lived seven years in Chenango county New York where their next four children were born Then they returned to North Stonington where their youngest child was born

Daniel Baldwin died October 28 1855 His widow who was born March 11, 1786 died March 19 1877, at the age of ninety-one Their children are 1 John Denison born September 28, 1809, (see forward) 2 Daniel Avery July 2, 1811, married (first), May 23 1835 Betsey Rogers of Lyme Connecticut who died April 17, 1851, he married (second) May 22, 1853 Amanda Colgrove, of Voluntown Connecticut, he was a shipmaster of New London Connecticut He had ten children 3 Sally Adaline July 17, 1813, died young 4 Nancy Adeline April 27, 1815 married, December 3, 1839, Frederick P Frink of Salisbury, Connecticut, and died childless in New London October 31 1869 5 Andrew born and died April 1817 6 Mary Ann, May 8 1818 married November 1 1837, Charles D Smith, of Woodstock, resided at Worcester and had two children Ebenezer Smith November 7, 1839, Hannah Amelia September 16, 1845, married Samuel Woodward, who did business in Quincy Market, Boston They have one child Charles Smith Woodward, born September 16, 1868 7 Hannah, October 9, 1820, died young 8 Robert Stanton August 21, 1822, drowned June 3, 1838, in Norwich 9 Amy Avery, September 9, 1825, married, October 4, 1847, James Boardman, of Norwich, and died childless July 30, 1866

(X) John Denison Baldwin, son of Daniel Baldwin (9), was born in North Stonington, Connecticut, September 28 1809 He died at Worcester, Massachusetts, July 8, 1883, aged seventy-three years, nine months and ten days

When he was seven years old the family moved from his native town to Chenango county, New York, which at that time was wilderness, and for seven years the son labored with his father and other members of the family to subdue the soil, as their ancestors had done in New England nearly two hundred years before He learned to shoot straight and to love nature Those years in the New York forests strengthened his character as well as his muscles and developed the poetical side of his nature When the family returned to live in Stonington, he was fourteen years old He attended school and studied diligently during the next three years. At the age of seventeen he began to teach school He entered Yale College and pursued his course from time to time, as his other duties permitted He did not graduate in regular course He began the study of law, but soon abandoned it for theology. He preached for a short time to a Methodist congregation, but later entered the Divinity School at Yale College and was graduated in 1834 In 1839 he received his degree of Master of Arts out of regular course

He was ordained September 3, 1834 and was pastor of the Congregational church at West Woodstock, Connecticut until July 25, 1837 From January 17, 1838 to May, 1845 he was pastor of the church at North Brandford Connecticut, and at North Killingly from April 29, 1846, to September 17, 1849 He made his mark as a preacher and as a man of sagacity and public spirit He took his part in public affairs He was elected to the Connecticut legislature from North Killingly by the Free Soil party As chairman of the committee on education he reported a bill for the establishment of normal schools and in 1850 his bill was passed He was on the board of trustees upon whom he devolved the selection of a site The normal school was built at New Britain At that time the normal school was an innovation in the educational system and it required no little agitation and earnest efforts to establish in Connecticut the schools for the proper training of public school teachers now deemed essential to the public school system everywhere As a member of the legislature he became more than ever interested in the Free Soil party and the anti-slavery movement He sought a larger field of usefulness in order to advance the reforms in which he was interested He turned from preaching to journalism He became editor of the *Free Soil* newspaper, the *Charter Oak* published weekly at Hartford, later called the *Republican* Editorial work he found to his liking and his pen became recognized as one of the political forces to be reckoned with In 1852 he went to the larger field in Boston as joint owner of the *Daily Commonwealth* with William Claflin John B Alley, Dr Samuel G Howe, and William Spooner Mr Baldwin was the editor and manager He established close connections with the leaders of the Free Soil and Republican party and gave substantial aid through his paper to the organization of the Republican party Charles Sumner, Henry Wilson and Theodore Parker were almost daily visitors at his office and the friendships formed then were continued through life The *Commonwealth* became the *Daily Telegraph* later and was consolidated with the *Traveler* eventually

Mr Baldwin bought the *Cambridge Chronicle* and edited it for a few months only In 1859 he came to Worcester With his two sons, John Stanton Baldwin and Charles Clinton Baldwin he bought the *Worcester Spy* The *Spy* was founded in Boston by Isaiah Thomas in 1770, and removed to Worcester in 1775 where the first issue was printed May 3 1775, just after the Battle of Lexington The daily edition was established in 1845 When Mr Baldwin took charge of *The Spy* the paper had had some lean years though it was fairly prosperous The memorable election of 1860 and the subsequent events that culminated in the Civil war made new demands on the publishers of daily newspapers Mr Baldwin and his sons took advantage of the opportunity Better facilities were secured The telegraphic news came into use and the editorial page of the newspaper was looked upon as the political guide of the Republicans The friends of *The Spy* used to call it the 'Worcester County Bible', its political opponents expressed their dissent from the editorial opinions of the paper by calling it 'The Lying Spy"

As the newspaper grew in circulation and prestige it became a very profitable business enterprise Mr Baldwin and his sons acquired competences A brick building was built on Main street opposite the City Hall for a home for the newspaper Mr Baldwin had not only the efficient help of his sons, whose knowledge of the printing business and conduct of the counting room relieved him of a large share of detail to devote his attention to editorial work and his literary and political interests, but he surrounded himself with capable newspaper men The late Captain J Everts Greene was perhaps the best known among his assistants

Mr Baldwin was the head of his paper until his death, though he was not able to do office work during the last few years He was a thorough newspaper man of the old school He was a shrewd business man as well as a clear and forcible writer farsighted and uncompromising

He entered political life to further the principles that he advocated in his newspapers His leadership was recognized by his Republican associates in Worcester county when he was selected the year after he came to Worcester as a delegate to the Republican National Convention of 1860 His influence at the convention was felt and it was at his suggestion that Hannibal Hamlin of Maine was nominated for vice-president At the next Congressional election in 1862, Mr Baldwin was elected a representative by a large majority He was re-elected in 1864 and 1868 by even greater majorities His successor was George Frisbie Hoar, late United States Senator

In Congress he served on the Committees on Expenditures, on Public Buildings, on the District of Columbia on Printing and on the Library He was not a frequent speaker but many of his speeches were notable efforts He spoke March 5, 1864, on state sovereignty and treason, the House being in Committee of the Whole He made a brilliant speech April 7, 1866 on congress and reconstruction in the house, and again January 11, 1868 in reply to Hon James Brooks, of New York, on the negro race, he made a memorable speech Some of his speeches were published He was active and influential in committee work He made an effort to secure an international copyright act during his last term, and his speeches and reports entitle him to stand among the benefactors of American literature

Mr Baldwin will be remembered not only for his achievements in the political world and as a congressman not only as one of the great editors of the civil war period of Massachusetts but as an author and student At the close of his life he wrote in his autobiography that he had been a close student all his life and he had never known a time when it was not a pleasure for him to study This autobiography, which, with his portrait painted by the late William Willard, was left to his grandson, Robert S Baldwin, is an important contribution to the history of the eventful period in which he lived It gives his political and religious views as well as his part in the activities of life

After he was a preacher he acquired the French and German languages He made a special study of archeology He was interested in science and was one of the first to take up the process of making portraits by the daguerreotype process and some pictures of his family and others that he took have been preserved While in congress he had an opportunity for archeological research His book on Prehistoric Nations was published by Harpers in 1869 In 1872 he published Ancient America, which had a large sale and attracted much attention In 1880 he published his genealogy of the Descendants of John Baldwin, of Stonington, Connecticut In 1881 in collaboration with Rev William Clift he published a Record of the Descendants of Captain George Denison of Stonington In 1882 he published a partial genealogy of the descendants of Thomas Stanton, of Stonington In 1847 he published a collection of his poems entitled "The Story of Raymond Hill and Other Poems" The book reveals both the poetical temperament of the author and skillful use of English in verse as well as prose The last time Mr Baldwin appeared in a public assembly as a speaker was in Mechanics' Hall, June 24 1878, at the exercises attending the re-interment of the remains of Isaiah Thomas when he read a very interesting account of the labors of Mr Thomas in the revolution

Mr Baldwin was a member of the American Oriental Society of New Haven, established in 1843 He was elected a member of the New England Historic-Genealogical Society April 22, 1868 of the American Antiquarian Society, October 21 1869 and an honorary member of the Worcester Society of Antiquity, January 2, 1877

One who knew him intimately wrote the following at the time of his death "Mr Baldwin was a man of imposing stature, much exceeding six feet in height of large frame and great muscular strength In his early manhood, his massive head erect figure and stalwart proportions, indicative of activity and power gave an aspect of uncommon force and dignity His mind like his body was large and vigorous His political sagacity was highly esteemed by those who had long been associated with him Though so much of a recluse especially in later years, he knew human nature well and could foresee with great accuracy the political effect of any measure or event His election forecasts were in general singularly near the truth and his judgment of men their character capabilities and popularity was rarely at fault His advice in political matters was often sought and highly valued It was delivered confidently but without arrogance and more than once those who had refused to be guided by it at an important juncture had cause to regret that it had been rejected As a writer Mr Baldwin was direct, clear and forcible His style had no ornament It was sometimes rugged, but always strong and sincere His wide range of reading and retentive memory gave him a vast store of facts, and his knowledge of political history was especially large and accurate But though his profession of journalism kept his mind occupied much with such subjects, his favorite pursuit was the study of antiquity, both the dim past of which authentic history gives only hints and suggestions, and the less remote but almost as difficult, field of family genealogy to which most of his later years, while his health allowed, was devoted"

Mr Baldwin married, April 3 1832 Lemira Hathaway, daughter of Captain Ebenezer and Betsey (Crane) Hathaway, of Dighton, Massachusetts Captain Hathaway, born in 1779 was the son of Stephen Hathaway, born in 1745, and the grandson of Nicholas Hathaway, born in 1722 His mother's maiden name was Hope Pierce Lemira Hathaway was born March 6 1813 and died April 2, 1904

The children of John Denison and Lemira (Hathaway) Baldwin were 1 Ellen Frances, born in Dighton Massachusetts, January 19, 1853, died in New Orleans, March 1854 ("She had made it certain," her father wrote of her "that, if she had lived, she would have won a brilliant reputation in literature") 2 John Stanton, born in New Haven, Connecticut, January 6 1834, (see forward) 3 Charles Clinton, born in Woodstock, Connecticut, May 4 1835, (see forward) 4 Mary Jane, born in Woodstock, Connecticut, May 6, 1836, died in Hartford Connecticut, December 29 1850 ("She was bright vigorous and promising," her father wrote of her, "and had seemed sure of a long life")

(XI) John Stanton Baldwin son of John Denison Baldwin (10) was born in New Haven, Connecticut, January 6, 1834 He was educated in the public schools and his was one of the first classes graduated from the State Normal School of Connecticut at New Britain He learned the art of printing in the newspaper offices with which his father was connected in Hartford and Boston At Hartford the Republican office had a job printing department Mr Baldwin learned the printing business thoroughly in all departments, and when he came to Worcester with his father was well equipped to conduct the mechanical and business departments of the newspaper as well as the editorial department During the larger part of the time that *The Spy* was owned by the Baldwin family, from 1859 until 1898, he was the active and responsible head of the paper After his father's death in 1883 the firm of John D Baldwin & Sons continued for five years to run the paper with Mr Baldwin at the head The Spy Publishing Company was organized April 23, 1887, under the corporation law of Massachusetts John S Baldwin was president Charles C Baldwin his brother, treasurer, and Robert S Baldwin his son, secretary In 1892 when Charles C Baldwin withdrew from the company John S Baldwin became president and treasurer, and his son, John D Baldwin became a director

Mr Baldwin served in the Civil war as captain of Company F, Fifty-first Massachusetts Regiment He is a member of Post 10, G A R, and of the Loyal Legion He was a representative to the general court in 1871 and he has served the city of Worcester as a member of the board of license commissioners, the school board and the common council Since Mr Baldwin retired from the newspaper business in 1898 he has devoted a large part of his time to his summer place at Marion Massachusetts on Buzzards Bay

He married October 19 1863 Emily Brown, of Worcester, daughter of Albert and Mary (Eaton) Brown (See sketch of Edwin Brown and the Brown Family) The children of John Stanton and Emily (Brown) Baldwin were 1 Mary Eleanor, born November 25 1864, was a teacher in the Worcester high school, married Professor Frederick Dunlap teacher of chemistry at University of Michigan She has a daughter Roselee, born 1903 2 Robert Stanton, December 17, 1865, graduated at Harvard University in 1891, was one of the editors and directors of *The Worcester Spy* until 1898, has been teacher since then in the Worcester Normal School, 3 Alice Hathaway, November 26, 1867, married, 1897 Miron L Foster lumber merchant of Worcester, their children were Marcella, December 21, 1898, Alicia, December 8, 1899 Ellen F, born August 9, 1900 4 John Denison, May 26, 1871, graduated at Harvard University in 1893, was director and business manager of *The Worcester Spy* until 1898 has since been in the life insurance business in Worcester married, 1898, Mary, daughter of Thomas B Eaton, of Worcester, they have two children Charlotte, born March 20, 1899, and John Denison, born in 1903 5 Emily Brown, March 27, 1873, died May 24, 1874 6 Rosamond, September 24, 1874 died September 2, 1876 7 Henry Brown, August 9, 1877, lives with parents 8 Emily Clinton January 28, 1884.

(XI) Charles Clinton Baldwin son of John Denison Baldwin (10), was born in Woodstock Connecticut, May 4, 1835 He was educated in the public schools and in the course of newspaper work He learned the business from typesetting to bookkeeping on the newspapers edited at Hartford and Boston by his father When he came to Worcester he had charge of the counting room and for more than thirty years he performed the duties of treasurer of *The Worcester Spy* He resigned as treasurer of The Spy Publishing Company in November, 1892, and retired from active business

Mr Baldwin is highly esteemed among all his acquaintances He has no taste for public life He prefers his study and home life He is a member of the Worcester Club He has a decided taste for genealogy and is a member of the Worcester Society of Antiquity He belongs to the Worcester Horticultural Society He and his wife are members of All Saints Episcopal Church They reside at a beautiful home at 11 Cedar street He is a Republican

Mr Baldwin married, October 1 1868 Ella L T Peckham, daughter of Dr F H Peckham, of Providence (See sketch of the Peckham Family for her ancestry)

Their children are 1 Katherine Torrey, born July 17, 1869 married April 29 1887, Lynde Sullivan son of Dr John Langdon Sullivan, of Malden he is a lawyer graduate of Harvard College and Law School living at Malden, practicing law in Boston has one child John Langdon Sullivan, born March 12 1903 2 Edith Ella, November 19, 1870 3 Grace Peckham May 16 1874 4 Rose Danielson October 22, 1882, died November 8 1893

(I) John Peckham was the emigrant ancestor of Mrs Charles C Baldwin of Worcester, of her sister Dr Grace Peckham Murray, of New York, and of the widow of George Whitman Danielson, late editor of Providence Rhode Island, another sister

John Peckham was admitted an inhabitant of the island of Aquidneck (Rhode Island) March 20, 1638 He was made a freeman of Newport March 16 1641 He was one of the ten male members in full communion of the First Baptist Church in 1648 and one of its founders in 1644 He was a resident of that part of Newport which became Middletown, where he was made a freeman in 1655 He married (first) Mary Clarke, who died in 1648 He married (second) Eleanor ——— His children were John William Stephen, (see forward), Thomas, James, Clement Sarah Rebecca, Deborah, Phebe Elizabeth and Susannah

(II) Stephen Peckham, son of John Peckham (1), was one of the earliest settlers of Dartmouth, Massachusetts He had a grant of land in Narragansett in 1679, but probably never went there to live He also purchased land in Dartmouth in 1679, and was a substantial farmer in that part of Dartmouth now included in the city limits of New Bedford He died April 23, 1724 His estate in round numbers amounted to 1,800 pounds His wife's name was Mary and their children were Stephen, born February 23, 1683, Samuel, August 17 1684, Eleanor, January 12, 1686, William, October 27, 1688, Mary, August 17, 1690, Hannah, January 28, 1692, John, January 15, 1697, Deborah, June, 1699, married, January 19, 1727, Thomas Nye, Joseph, February 2 1701, Jean, January 23, 1703, married, April 4, 1729 Thomas Delano, Isaiah September 14, 1705, married April 19, 1736, Ruth Morton

(III) Stephen Peckham son of Stephen Peckham (2), was born in Middleton, Massachusetts, February 23, 1683, and died June, 1764, leaving an estate valued at 512 pounds His father left him in his will the northerly part of the homestead which he had divided into four parts for his four sons The children of Stephen and Content Peckham were 1 James, born October 4 1716 2 Stephen, September 14 1718 3 Seth November 29, 1723, probably died young The children of Stephen and Keturah (Arthur) Peckham were 4 Elizabeth, July 5, 1741 5 Eunice, December 6, 1742 6 Richard, December 16, 1744

(IV) Stephen Peckham son of Stephen Peckham (3) was born September 14, 1718 He married (first) about 1739, Sarah Boss, who was born July 5, 1724 and died December 12, 1768 He married (second) Elizabeth White, who was born December 22, 1740 He bought and inherited from his father, portions of the old homestead so that he finally owned half of the entire farm, his brother Richard inheriting the other half His wife Elizabeth died April 12 1791

The children of Stephen and Sarah (Boss) Peckham were Elizabeth, born December 22, 1740, Peleg, September 27 1744, Mercy, February 23, 1746, Stephen, April 6, 1748, Seth, October 31, 1750, (see forward), Jonathan, February 8, 1753, married Hannah Soule, widow, daughter of Peleg White, James, May 11, 1756; Sarah, June 9, 1758, Lydia, January 9, 1761, Amy, February 18, 1763, Joseph, January 27, 1766 Of these Stephen and Seth moved to the town of Gloucester, Providence county, Rhode Island

(V) Seth Peckham son of Stephen Peckham (4), was born in Dartmouth, Massachusetts, October 31, 1750 He married January 26, 1775, Mercy Smith, daughter of Captain John and Sarah (Hopkins) Smith Sarah Hopkins was the daughter of the famous Thomas Hopkins, of Rhode Island Mr Peckham lived on a farm in Gloucester, and was probably a farmer During the revolution he was in Captain Joseph Kimball's company in which his brother-in-law was a lieutenant He died in 1826 His children were 1 Hazael, born November 16, 1777 (see forward) 2 Thomas January 10 1780, married Anna Sweet 3 Sarah June 20 1782, married Chad Taylor 4 Seth October, 1784, married Deborah Keach and lived in Gloucester 5 Mercy, 1787 married in 1807, Josiah Wescott of Scituate, Rhode Island 6 John, 1793, married in 1820, Hannah Smith, daughter of Gideon Smith, of Scituate

(VI) Dr Hazael Peckham, son of Seth Peckham (5), was born in Gloucester, November 16, 1777, married in 1797, Susannah Thornton, who was born October 8, 1776, daughter of Jeremiah Thornton, of Burrillville, and his wife, Esther Wright, of Providence Their children were 1 Paris, born in 1798 2 Smith 1800, died in 1878 3 Amey, 1801, married William Day, 4 Susan, 1809, married Dr Justin Hammond 5 Hazael, 1810, died in 1888 6 Pamelia, 1816, married Rhodes Hopkins, and died in 1886 7 Fenner Harris 1817, (see forward)

(VII) Dr Fenner Harris Peckham, son of Dr Hazael Peckham (6), was born in Killingly, Connecticut, January 27, 1817 He studied medicine in the office of Dr Justin Hammond a physician of Windham county, Connecticut, and Professors Knight and Hooker of New Haven He was graduated from the Yale Medical College in 1842 He practiced first at East Killingly but soon removed to what is now known as Putnam Heights, where he continued until 1852, having an extensive practice In 1852 he removed to Providence where he lived and practiced the rest of his life He was one of the best known physicians in the state While in Connecticut he was a member of the State Medical Society, and when he removed to Rhode Island he became a member of the Rhode Island Medical Society, and was twice its president He was for many years physician and surgeon of the Marine Hospital at Providence, and was a member of the medical board of the Economical Life Insurance Company He wrote a monograph on Hydrophobia, and another on the Topographical Geological Condition of the Second District of Rhode Island

When the civil war broke out Dr Peckham volunteered his services, and was commissioned surgeon of the Third Rhode Island Heavy Artillery, August 15, 1861 He had first been assigned to duty with the Second Rhode Island Volunteers at Washington, and had charge of the medical department of Camp Sprague after the first Battle of Bull Run He joined the Third Regiment after the command had reached and taken possession of Port Royal, South Carolina, but ill health caused by the climate caused him to resign in February, 1862 In April, 1863, he was appointed surgeon for the board of enrollment of the second district of Rhode Island, and at the request of Gen J Y Smith, officially visited Fortress Monroe, continuing his efficient services with the board to the end of the war He died February 17, 1887, and was buried in Swan Point Cemetery

He married Catherine Davis, daughter of Captain William Torrey Their children were 1 Katherine Fenner, born February, 1841, graduate of Mount Holyoke and Woman's Medical College, Philadelphia, with the degree of M D resides at Putnam Heights, Connecticut, practiced her profession in Boston, is life member of Colonel Timothy Bigelow Chapter, D A R of Worcester 2 Rosa Frances October 28, 1842, (see forward) 3 Dr Fenner H, February 11 1844 4 Ella Lois Torrey, September 12, 1846 5 Grace October 16 1848 6 Mary Davis, February 10, 1853, died February 10, 1853

(VIII) Rosa Frances Peckham daughter of Dr Fenner Harris Peckham (7) was born October 28, 1842 She graduated in 1862 from the Providence high school She studied art and painting for ten years in Paris She has pictures exhibited in the Salon at Paris In later years she has painted miniatures and has done some excellent work

She married January 25, 1881, George Whitman Danielson of Providence He was a former publisher and editor of the *Providence Journal* He died March 25 1884 She is one of the founders and charter members of the Providence Art Club She is a life member of Colonel Timothy Bigelow Chapter, D A R of Worcester Her children are Whitman, born December 17, 1881, a graduate at Harvard, and Rosamond, born November 6. 1884, graduate of Bryn Mawr College, Pennsylvania, class of 1904

(VIII) Dr Fenner Harris Peckham son of Dr Fenner H Peckham (7), was born in East Killingly, Connecticut, February 11, 1844 He graduated from Yale Medical School in 1866 and became associated with his father, after whose death he continued the practice alone He has now virtually retired, and has been succeeded by his son, Dr Charles F Peckham He served in the Civil war as lieutenant in the Twelfth Rhode Island Volunteers

He married, October 29, 1867, in Providence, Mary H Olney, daughter of Elam and Helen (Fuller) Olney Their children are 1 Charles Fenner, graduated at Columbia in 1890 with the degree of M D, he was surgeon to the Rhode Island Naval Reserves in the Spanish American war with the rank of lieutenant 2 Alice, lives at home 3 William Torrey graduated at Brown in 1897, married Alice Hetherington Dike, October 22, 1901

Dr Fenner H Peckham is a Free Mason, a member of Whatcheer Lodge He is also a member of the Massachusetts Commandery, Loyal Legion, Rodman Post, G A R, the Squantum Club, the University Club, the West Side Club, the Central Club, the Agawam Hunt Club, and the Long Meadow Golf Club He is State Commissioner of Birds He is a member of the Rhode Island Medical Society, and the American Medical Association and is United States pension examining surgeon He is president of the Hope Webbing Company, vice-president of the Providence Telephone Company, director of the Narragansett Electric Lighting Company, Mechanics National Bank, Free Masons Hall Company, Providence & Springfield Railroad Company and Wood River Branch Railroad Company He is trustee of the Mechanics Savings Bank

(VIII) Dr Grace Peckham Murray, daughter of Dr Fenner Harris Peckham (7), graduated from Mount Holyoke College in 1867 She graduated in 1882 from the Woman's Medical College of the New York Infirmary After having obtained her degree she was interne and resident physician of the New York Infirmary for Women and Children for three years, after which she commenced her private practice in New York city, in which she has since been engaged For many years she was attending physician to the hospital, and was engaged in the college and dispensary of that institution In 1902 she was appointed professor of women's diseases at the New York Post Graduate School, which position she now holds

For three years she was sent as a delegate to the New York State Medical Society by the New York County Medical Society, of which she is a member She also belongs to the New York Academy of Medicine the New York Neurological and the Women's Medical Association of New York, of which she was president four years She is vice-president of the National Social Science Association She has been on the editorial staff of the *New York Medical Record* and has contributed many medical articles to the current medical literature of the day She is associate editor of the *Women's Medical Journal* She is a frequent and regular contributor to *The Delineator* and other magazines She is a member of the National Arts Club, the Wednesday Afternoon Club, the Barnard Club, the New England Society, and the Manhattan Chapter, D A R She married, 1893 Hon Charles H Murray, who is a prominent Republican and lawyer

(VIII) Ella Lois Torrey Peckham, daughter of Dr Fenner H Peckham (7), was educated in the public schools of Providence and in Mount Holyoke College, South Hadley, Massachusetts, where she was graduated in 1867 She organized the Worcester County Mount Holyoke Alumni Association, and filled the office of president for twelve years She founded the Fortnightly Club of Worcester She is a very active member of the Worcester Woman's Club, and was president in 1896, 1897 and 1898 She is a member of the building committee of the club house, and director of its corporation She has been an active member and vice-president of the Massachusetts State Federation of Women's Clubs She belongs also to the Worcester Art Society and Public School Art League She is a charter member of Colonel Timothy Bigelow Chapter D A R She was married to Charles C Baldwin in 1868 (See sketch of Baldwin family) Her daughter, Katherine Torrey, studied art in Paris and has exhibited her work in the Paris Salon Edith Ella Baldwin was also educated in Paris in art Her work has been exhibited in the Champs de Mars Salon of Paris and at the Society of American Artists in New York Grace Peckham Baldwin was educated at Bryn Mawr College and at the Drexel Institute Library School, Philadelphia

TORREY ANCESTRY OF MRS BALDWIN

William Torrey (1) who settled in Weymouth, Massachusetts, in 1640, was the emigrant ancestor of Mrs Charles C Baldwin through her mother's line He was born in Combe, St Nicholas, Somersetshire, England, in 1608, son of Philip Torrey (2), and his wife Alice, a lineal descendant in the fifth generation of William Torrey, who died at Combe, St Nicholas in 1657 leaving a wife Thomasine, and two sons The line in England was William (1), Philip (2), William (3), Philip (4), and William (5), the emigrant, designated above as William Torrey (1) His brothers James, Philip and Joseph also came to New England in 1640

William Torrey (1) served many years as clerk of the general court and was captain of the militia

(II) Captain William Torrey, son of William Torrey (1), commanded the Weymouth Company in King Philip's war He married Deborah Green

(III) Joseph Torrey, son of Captain William Torrey (2) was a merchant at Weymouth He married Elizabeth Symmes

(IV) Rev Joseph Torrey, son of Joseph Torrey (3), settled at South Kingston, Rhode Island He married Elizabeth Fiske

(V) Captain William Torrey, son of Rev Joseph Torrey (4) settled at Killingly Connecticut He married Zilpah Davison daughter of Daniel and Catherine (Davis) Davison He was born in 1763, and died in 1847 His children were 1 Zilpah, married William Harris of Scituate Massachusetts, and one of her eight children is Dr William T Harris United States Commissioner of Education 2 Catherine Davis Torrey, born in 1819, married Dr Fenner Harris Peckham

(VI) Catherine Davis Torrey daughter of Captain William Torrey (5), married Dr Fenner H Peckham They had one son and five daughters (See Peckham Family sketch)

(VII) Ella Lois Torrey Peckham daughter of Dr Fenner H Peckham, married Charles C Baldwin

ANDREW HILL HAMMOND was born in Alton, New Hampshire, August 3, 1830 During

A H Hammond

his infancy his parents removed to Gilmanton, New Hampshire, where his early years were spent on a farm His father was a Baptist minister, but combined with his pastoral duties the occupation of a farmer, after the custom of the early days He attended the district school in Gilmanton At the age of nine he went to live with his grandparents in the Gore district of his native town, and while there was for several years under the tuition of his maternal uncle, Jonathan Prescott Hill, who was a surveyor, mathematician and school teacher of note in that region Mr Hill was grandson of Dr Jonathan Hill, who married Mercy Prescott

Mr Hammond s experience as a pupil of Mr Hill was of great benefit in after years, as it gave him a love of books and study that attended him through life, and gave him a place among the self-educated as well as the self-made men of his day and generation After he returned to Gilmanton to his father's home, he attended the academy there, and also worked on the farm At the age of eighteen he went to Manchester, New Hampshire, and learned the trade of an iron moulder, and was employed in Laconia, New Hampshire, at that occupation until 1851, when he came to Worcester and found a position in the malleable iron works of Waite, Chadsey and Company Later he was employed in the foundries of Goddard Rice and Company, and William A Wheeler

He had musical gifts which he cultivated while working in the foundries, studying under such well known instructors as S R Leland, founder of the firm that still bears his name, Albert S Allen and E S Nason, and became a proficient teacher of singing One of his early experiences was a trip west to teach singing schools, travelling down the Ohio valley and up the Mississippi, returning through the town of Chicago, then a small but growing village He continued to study music and obtained a position in the organ reed factory owned by Augustus Rice and Edwin Harrington, beginning on wages of seventy-five cents a day, but his mechanical skill, his inventive genius and musical ability soon made him a force in the business He originated new methods and appliances which increased the quantity and improved the quality of the product, and was soon in charge of the manufacturing department Subsequently the firm became Redding and Harrington, and they made a contract with Mr Hammond to give him the benefit of all inventions and improvements that he should introduce, that would be of benefit to the firm In a short time they found it advisable to give him a third interest in the business Later he purchased their interest and became the sole owner, and continued in business under his own name

In 1868 Mr Hammond built his first factory on the present location on May street, and added to it from time to time until it was the largest organ reed factory in the world, a position it held for a number of years It is equipped with special machinery devised by Mr Hammond for the purposes of the business The Hammond organ reeds are known as a standard product all over the world The making of organ reeds is a distinct business from the manufacture of organs, and is confined practically to factories in Chicago and Worcester The great success of his business has been due not only to the machinery that he has devised, and the excellent goods that he has been able to produce, but to the tact and judgment he has shown in business dealings Although Mr Hammond has had few interests outside of his business, he has always been a reader and student, and has a very large and valued library in his beautiful home on Claremont street, Worcester After his son Richard Hill Hammond, left school he was taken into business by his father, and later became its manager Under his direction the affairs of the business have continued to grow and prosper In 1892 the Hammond Reed Company was incorporated Since then Andrew Hill Hammond has been president and treasurer, Richard Hill Hammond has been general manager and assistant treasurer and Alice B Hammond and Mabel F Hammond, two daughters of Mr Hammond, directors

Andrew H Hammond married, 1860, R Maria Barber, daughter of Benjamin Barber, of Worcester She was a woman of rare accomplishments and ability To her Mr Hammond attributes much of his material success She died May 21, 1891 Their children were Charles Warren, died in infancy, Nellie Prescott, born April 26, 1866, a graduate of Oxford University, England, and teacher of Chicago University, Alice Barber, born January 16, 1868, married Clarence B Shirley, of Boston, Robert, died young, Richard Hill, born January 6, 1871, the business manager, Mabel Florence, student at Radcliffe College, Cambridge, Massachusetts

Mr Hammond was a strong anti-slavery man He joined the Free Soil party when it was formed, and later became a Republican, with which party he has since acted politically, giving it his hearty support He never cared for public office, although always ready to do his duty as a Republican and citizen But to his business he devoted the energy of his life, and made it a success He died at his home in Worcester, March 1, 1906

(VIII) Richard Hill Hammond, son of Andrew Hill Hammond (7), was born in Worcester, Massachusetts He attended the Worcester schools including the high school and the Worcester Polytechnic Institute, and went from the college into his father s business, where he soon became manager, and for several years the entire care and management of the concern has been on his shoulders, and it is to his credit to say that the business has in no way suffered at his hands, but on the contrary there has been a steady improvement, and since the death of his father Mr Hammond has devoted himself entirely to business, thus early displaying the same characteristics and aptitude that made his father successful He has never been in politics, and is unmarried

Andrew Hill Hammond, mentioned at the head of this sketch, is a direct descendant from William Ham (1), an emigrant from England to Exeter, New Hampshire, in 1646, Andrew Hill Hammond having when a young man legally changed his name fram Ham to Hammond William Ham removed from Exeter to Portsmouth New Hampshire, in 1652, having there a grant of fifty acres of land on Freeman s point, just above Portsmouth bridge He had at least two children Matthew, who had one grant of land from the town in 1654 and another in 1660, Elizabeth, who married ——— Cotton William Ham died in 1672, and his will is at Concord, New Hampshire, originally proved at Exeter His son Matthew was dead, and he bequeathed his property to his daughter Elizabeth (Cotton) and grandsons William, John and Thomas Ham

(II) John Ham, grandson of William Ham (1), the emigrant, was born in 1649, and was on the tax list of Cocheco (Dover) in 1665 He married Mary Heart, daughter of John Heart, of Dover, 1669 His first homestead was at "Tolend" near the second falls of the Cocheco Later he removed to a farm on Garrison hill, at Dover, was a juryman in 1688, and a lieutenant was town clerk in 1694 His wife died in 1706, and he died in 1727 His will, proved at Exeter, named the following children Mary, born October 2, 1668, married John Waldron, John, 1671, Samuel, Joseph, born June 3, 1678, Elizabeth, born January 2, 1781, married Jeremiah Rollins, Priphena, married John Tucker, who was captured by the Indians in 1696, but soon found his way back to Dover, New Hampshire, he had a grant of land from the town of Dover at Scatterwit, Sarah, married Thomas Downes, Mercy, married Richard Nason, Benjamin, born 1693

(III) Benjamin Ham, son of John Ham (2), was born in Dover, New Hampshire, 1693 He married Patience Hartford, daughter of Nicholas Hartford, in 1720 He inherited his father's farm near Garrison's hill, where the last days of John Ham, his father, were spent He was constable in 1731, and had one full share in the common lands in 1732 His wife joined the First Church in 1737 He was surveyor of highways in 1738, and voted in 1757 with twelve others against building the new meeting house at Pine Hill, Dover He died in 1781 The farm on which he lived was purchased of Peter Coffin in 1690 The original deed and part of the farm are now, or were lately, owned by John T W Ham, a descendant His children were William, born November 25, 1722, Mary, October 8, 1723, baptized October 23, 1737, married ——— Young, John, 1736, Patience, 1737, baptized March 25, 1739, Elizabeth, 1739, baptized December 10, 1749, married Jenness ———

(IV) William Ham, son of Benjamin Ham (3), was born at Dover, New Hampshire, November 25, 1722 and joined the First Church of Dover, January 3, 1742, removed to Rochester, New Hampshire, and died there in 1800 His children were Charity, married Job Allard, Benjamin, born 1753, married Mary Waldron, removed to Farmington, New Hampshire, where he died 1846, William, May 8, 1757, Francis, May 3, 1763, married Experience Knowles, removed to Albany, New Hampshire, Ephraim, died unmarried, Eleanor, married Samuel Twombley

(V) William Ham, son of William Ham (4), was born in Dover, New Hampshire, May 8, 1757 He was a soldier in the revolutionary war He settled at Gilmanton, New Hampshire He married Anne Meader He died in 1843 His children were Miriam, married Francis Elliot, Sarah, married Ezekiel Hayes, Eli, Ezra

(VI) Rev Ezra Ham, son of William Ham (5), was born in Gilmanton, New Hampshire He married Mercy Prescott Hill, daughter of Andrew W and Mary P (Ham) Hill, in 1824, and granddaughter of Dr Jonathan and Mary (Prescott) Hill He became a Free Will Baptist clergyman, and farmer in Lower Gilmanton, New Hampshire The children of Ezra Ham and Mercy (Prescott) Hill were George Edward, resides on Silver street, Worcester, works for Grompton and Knowles loom works, James C, Lemuel M, Mercy Elizabeth, Mary A, Enos H, Otis F, William Andrew Hill, born at Alton, New Hampshire, August 3, 1830, changed his name to Hammond

HENRY A DESPER, of Worcester, is descended on his father's side from French stock The immigrant, who was his great-great-grandfather, in coming to this country was shipwrecked somewhere on the coast of Massachusetts It is known that he was born in France, but the family records are lost and the writer cannot give any details of his ancestry, even to his given name, further than to state that he settled here in Massachusetts, and a son of his was named Edward Dispeaux, which surname has since been changed to Despeaux and Dispeau and is generally spelled Desper by the present generation Mr Desper comes of Pilgrim stock on his mother's side and is descended from several of the "Mayflower" passengers, John Alden, Priscilla Molines and her parents, James and Susannah Chilton, Francis Cook, besides a number of the Puritan fathers of Massachusetts Bay colony, as given below

(II) Edward Dispeaux, son of the immigrant ancestor, referred to above, settled in Massachusetts, but his wife's name is unknown His descendants are scattered up and down the Blackstone Valley from Grafton to Providence, Rhode Island, as well as in other sections and states He had nineteen children, it is said He gave all the sons names commencing with "J"

(III) James Desper, son of the preceding Edward Dispeaux (2), was born May 25, 1789 He married, August 25, 1811, Anna Cheney, who was born in Auburn, Massachusetts, June 11, 1790, and died January 29, 1842 He died November, 1872 They had nine children, only five of whom lived to grow up, viz James H, Jason, Miranda, William E, mentioned below, Mary Ann

(IV) William E Desper, son of the preceding James Desper (3), was born in Auburn, Massachusetts, April 20, 1824, and died October 3, 1902, aged seventy-eight years, five months, thirteen days He married, March 29, 1847, Elvira Orcutt, who was born in Stafford, Connecticut, March 4, 1823, died August 4, 1897, aged seventy-four years, five months Mr Desper was a machinist by trade and a manufacturer of water meters in Worcester, Massachusetts He was a Republican in politics, and was a member of the Second Adventist Church William E and Alvira (Orcutt) Desper had five children, three of whom lived to grow up, viz Henry A, Wilton H, Ernest W Desper

ANCESTRY OF ELVIRA (ORCUTT) DESPER

William Molines and John Alden, both of whom came to Plymouth on the "Mayflower," were ancestors of Elvira (Orcutt) Desper, of Worcester Both signed the Mayflower compact at Provincetown, November 15, 1620 William and Alice Molines were of the Walloon Huguenot contingent

(I) John Alden was born in England, 1599, he married in Plymouth, New England, Priscilla Molines, daughter of William and Alice Molines, mentioned above Her parents and brother Joseph died during the "first sickness" Longfellow has made John Alden and his bride the best known of the younger Pilgrims They lived at Plymouth a few years and then removed to Duxbury John Alden was also one of the original proprietors of Bridgewater, Massachusetts He died at Duxbury, September 19, 1687 His wife died February 5, 1688 They had ten children

(II) Joseph Alden, son of John Alden (1), was born in 1627 He married Mary Simmons

(III) Joseph Alden, son of Joseph Alden (2), was born in 1667 He was deacon of the church He married in 1690, Hannah Dunham, daughter of Daniel Dunham He died December 22, 1747, and his wife died January 13, 1748

(IV) Mary Alden, daughter of Deacon Joseph Alden (3), was born in Bridgewater, Massachusetts, April 10, 1699 She married, 1719, Timothy Edson, son of Joseph Edson, and she died at Stafford, Connecticut, 1782 Timothy was born in 1689, they had six children, they resided at Stafford, Connecticut

(V) Timothy Edson, son of Timothy and Mary (Alden) Edson (4), was born in 1722, he married Lydia Joy, of Hingham who was born October 5, 1725, and died at Randolph, Vermont, August 23, 1806 They had eleven children

(V) Mary Edson, daughter of Timothy and

Lydia (Joy) Edson (4), was born June 22, 1767 She married Ebenezer Johnson

(VI) Selenda Johnson, daughter of Ebenezer and Mary (Edson) Johnson (5), married, 1816, Warren Orcutt They had nine children, all daughters, and all except one lived to be seventy years of age or more except the youngest, who is now (1906) sixty-five years old

(VII) Elvira Orcutt, daughter of Warren and Selenda (Johnson) Orcutt (6), was born March 4, 1823, married William E Desper, March 29, 1847

(VIII) Henry A Desper, son of William E and Elvira (Orcutt) Desper (8), is the subject of this sketch, mentioned below

(I) James Chilton, another Mayflower ancestor of Henry A Desper, mentioned above, also signed the compact He brought with him his wife Mary, who died within a few months after the landing He died December 6, 1620

(II) Mary Chilton, daughter of James Chilton (1), married John Winslow, in 1627

John Winslow, brother of Governor Edward Winslow, and son of Edward Winslow, of Droitwich, Worcestershire, England, was baptized there April 18, 1597 He came to Plymouth in the "Fortune" in 1621 and in 1655 removed to Boston, where he bought the mansion of the late Antipas Boice, September 19, 1671 His wife Mary came with him to Plymouth He married Mary Chilton before 1627 She is said to have been the first woman to land from the "Mayflower" His will was dated March 12, 1673, and proved May 21, 1674 He bequeathed to wife Mary, sons Benjamin, Edward, and John, to William Payne, son of his daughter Sarah Meddlecott, and numerous other relatives His wife died about 1676 Their daughter Sarah married in Boston, July 19, 1660, Myles Standish, Jr

(III) Susannah Winslow, daughter of John and Mary (Chilton) Winslow (2), married Robert Latham, son of William Latham, the emigrant, in 1649, and settled in East Bridgewater before 1667 Their children were Mercy, born 1650, at Plymouth, James Chilton, Joseph, Elizabeth, Hannah, Sarah

(IV) Mercy Latham, daughter of Robert and Susannah (Winslow) Latham (3), was born in 1650, married Isaac Harris, son of Arthur and Martha Harris (He married (second) Mary Dunbar, daughter of Robert Dunbar, of Hingham and sister of Peter Dunbar He and his wife both died in 1707) The children of Isaac and Mercy (Latham) Harris were Arthur, Isaac, Samuel, Desire, Jane, Susana, Mary, Mercy, born 1680

(V) Mary Harris, daughter of Isaac and Mercy (Latham) Harris (4), married, 1713, Daniel Packard, son of Samuel and Elizabeth (Lathrop) Packard Their children were Sarah, born 1714, Mary, 1716, Susanna, 1718, Martha, 1720, Daniel, 1722, Isaac, 1724, Nehemiah, 1727

(VI) Susannah Packard, daughter of Daniel and Mary (Harris) Packard (5), was born 1718, married, 1734 David Orcutt, and had three sons Daniel, mentioned below, Stephen, David, Jr

(VII) Daniel Orcutt, son of David and Susannah (Packard) Orcutt (6), was born 1734, married (first) Lydia Cushman, who was mother of his children, and (second) Mary Hurlburt His children were Lydia, born 1756, married Edward Bisby, Stephen, May 13, 1757, mentioned below, Mary, 1759, married Uriah Clough, Susie, married Timothy Clough, Betsey, married Pember Howard Sally, married John Clough, Daniel, Jr, married Betsey Wood, Joseph O, born 1772, married Polly Clough and Ruth Gould, Abigail

(VII) Stephen Orcutt, son of Daniel and Lydia (Cushman) Orcutt (7), was born May 13, 1757, married, 1782, Molly Washburn, and had James, born April 28, 1783, married Polly Hitchcock, January, 1805, Horace, May 14, 1785, married, May 14, 1807, Polly Howe, Stephen, Jr, August 14, 1787, married, May 30, 1813, Phillip, January 22, 1790, married November 25, 1813, Persis Talmadge, Warren, mentioned below, John, October 16, 1795, married, 1821, Minerva Bradley married, 1857, Fidelia Case, Julia, March 12, 1798, married, March 6, 1817, William Rogers, Laura, September 23, 1801, married Abraham Francis, August 28, 1823, Polly, March 12, 1804, died May 8, 1877

Polly Clough, sister of Stephen Orcutt (8), who married Uriah Clough as stated above, had nine children, one of whom, Mordecai Clough, married Lucy Case and had six children Of the latter, Sarah Clough married Naaman Grant, and one of their three children is Rev Roland D Grant, the noted lecturer

(IX) Warren Orcutt, fifth child of Stephen Orcutt (8), was born October 6, 1792, married, 1816, Selenda Johnson, mentioned above Their children were Marietta, born February 27, 1817, married Austin Warren, 1842, Delina Augusta, July 12, 1819, died January 12, 1822, Elvira, mentioned below, Charlotte, January 2, 1826, Amelia Miranda, February 16, 1828, married Isaiah Merrit Babcock in 1852, and Miner Fenton in 1858, Laura Emeline, February 22, 1830, married, 1853, Ashbel Burnham Studley, Elizabeth Cornelia, July 1, 1833, married Josiah Converse, in 1862, Maria Celenda, October 5, 1837, married Charles Franklin Pasco, in 1859, and Orrin Lincoln Fletcher in 1865, Aurelia Frances, July 20, 1841, married Julius Perry Maine, in 1865

(X) Elvira Orcutt, daughter of Warren Orcutt (9), was born March 4, 1823, married William E. Desper, March 29, 1847

(XI) Henry A Desper, son of William E and Elvira (Orcutt) Desper (10), is the subject of this sketch

(I) Francis Cook, another Mayflower ancestor of Mr Desper, also signed the compact He brought with him his son John His wife Hester, a Walloon, a member of the church, came in the "Anne" in 1623 with other of his children He settled in Plymouth where he was admitted a freeman in 1633 He died April 7, 1663 His will was dated December 7, 1659, and proved June 5, 1633 His children were John, Jacob, James, Hester, Mary, Jane, mentioned below.

(II) Jane Cook, daughter of Francis Cook (1), married Experience Mitchell

(III) Elizabeth Mitchell, daughter of Experience and Jane (Cook) Mitchell (2), married, 1645, John Washburn, Jr

(IV) Jane Washburn, daughter of John Jr and Elizabeth (Mitchell) Washburn, married William Orcutt, Jr

(V) Martha Orcutt, daughter of William, Jr., and Jane (Washburn) Orcutt, married Solomon Washburn, 1732

(VI) Molly Washburn, daughter of Solomon and Martha (Orcutt) Washburn (5), married Stephen Orcutt, 1782, as stated above

(VII) Warren Orcutt son of the preceding, married Selenda Johnson, 1816

(VIII) Elvira Orcutt, daughter of the preceding, married 1847 William E Desper

(IX) Henry A Desper, son of the preceding, is the subject of this sketch

(I) Thomas Joy, one of the Puritan progenitors of Henry A Desper, was a carpenter by trade He was a proprietor of the town of Boston in 1636 He and Bartholomew Bernard, August 1, 1657 were awarded the contract to build the first town house of Boston, which marks him as the master builder of the colony and links his name forever with an interesting and historic edifice This was the first capitol or state house of Massachusetts and it stood until 1711, when it was destroyed by fire, and on its site was erected the present building known as the old state house at the corner of Washington and State streets, one of the most venerated monuments of colonial Boston Thomas Joy was arrested in 1646 for helping to get signers to the petition for enlarged franchise, and for questioning the general court s authority in arresting him He was soon released He removed to Hingham, where in 1650 he owned a tide-mill and other property He married Joan Gallop, daughter of John Gallop and his wife Christabel, she was born in England and died in Hingham, March 20, 1690, he died in Hingham, October 21, 1678, in the sixty-ninth year of his age

(II) Ensign Joseph Joy, son of Thomas Joy (1), was born April 1, 1645, married Mary Prince

(III) Joseph Joy, son of Ensign Joseph Joy (2), was born July 30, 1668, and married, May 22, 1690, Elizabeth Andrews, daughter of Thomas and Ruth Andrews He died in Hingham, April 29, 1716, and his gravestone with the inscription still legible in the Hingham graveyard is the oldest gravestone of the Joy family in America

(IV) John Joy, son of Joseph Joy (3), was born February 7, 1695, married Lydia Lincoln, December 19, 1724

(V) Lydia Joy, daughter of John Joy (4), was born October 5, 1725, married Timothy Edson, as mentioned above

(VI) Mary Edson, daughter of the preceding, born June 22, 1767, married Ebenezer Johnson

(VII) Selenda Johnson, daughter of Ebenezer and Mary (Edson) Johnson (6), married Warren Orcutt, as stated above

(VIII) Elvira Orcutt, daughter of Warren Orcutt (7), married William E Desper

(IX) Henry A Desper, son of the preceding, is the subject of this sketch

(I) Deacon Samuel Edson, emigrant ancestor of Mr Desper, was born in 1612 in England He was living in Salem in New England in 1639 and later removed to Bridgewater, one of the first settlers there He built and owned the first mill, was a member of the council of war He married, about 1637, Susanna Orcutt and they had nine children Samuel, Joseph, Josiah, Susanna, Elizabeth, Mary, Sarah, Bethiah, Benjamin

(II) Joseph Edson, son of Deacon Samuel Edson (1), was born in 1649, married (first) Experience Field and (second) Mary Turner He had seven children

(III) Timothy Edson, son of Joseph Edson (2), was born in 1689, married Mary Alden, February 10, 1719, and had five children

(IV) Timothy Edson, son of Timothy Edson (3), was born in 1722, married Lydia Joy He was an ancestor of Admiral George Dewey and of Calvin Edson, the famous living skeleton" His daughter Mary Edson, born 1767, married Ebenezer Johnson, as stated above Their daughter, Selenda Johnson, married Waren Orcutt, father of Mrs William E and grandfather of Henry A Desper

(IV) Henry A Desper, son of William E Desper (3), and Elvira Orcutt (X), his wife, was born in Worcester, Massachusetts, at 37 Shelby street, July 14, 1851 He has always lived either at 37 or 40 Shelby street He attended the public schools of Worcester until he was fifteen years old, when he went to Worcester Academy for a year He then went to work for Marcus Moore, builder, to learn the carpenter s trade He followed this trade for five years in Worcester, Martha s Vineyard and other places He made patterns for his father and assisted him in the manufacture and sale of water meters In 1873 he invented a new kind of water meter and began to manufacture it In 1875, for about six months, he was engaged on a line of plumbing work in Boston He returned and entered into partnership with his father in the water meter business, also doing some plumbing business In 1892 he bought out his father and has since carried on the business under his own name At one time he carried on an extensive plumbing business The Desper business was located for twenty-five years at 22 Cypress street and while there was burned out six times, having a serious loss three times In 1900 Mr Desper moved his business to 194 Union street, his present location He is at present manufacturing elevator registers, plumbing specialties, hydraulic valves and water meters He makes a specialty of large hydraulic valves for water works, etc In 1857-8 he was superintendent of a small water works and he can fairly claim to be one of the oldest superintendents of water works in the country

Mr Desper is a Republican, but has had no time for public office He has been a member of the Worcester County Mechanics' Association since 1868, is a member of the National Association of Master Plumbers, the Massachusetts State Association of Master Plumbers, the New England Water Works Association, and has been a member of the order of American Mechanics and also the Good Templars

He married, March 13, 1876, in Chelsea, Mary Abby Frances Drawbridge, daughter of George D and Abby (Littlefield) Drawbridge She was for several years engaged with some of the large department stores in Boston Her father was foreman of the paper hanging and decorating department of the Clark Sawyer Company from 1870 to 1874 Subsequently he removed to New Hampshire, where he held the office of selectman, postmaster, etc George D Drawbridge was the son of David Drawbridge, who came to America in 1846 from England, where he was an upholsterer and decorator He was collector of taxes in the old country He married Elizabeth Doebell, in England, and their oldest son, George, was born there in 1835 David Drawbridge settled first in Chelsea, later in Wells and Kennebunk, Maine, where some of his descendants still live The Drawbridge family came to England from Holland with William of Orange There are branches of the family in Maryland and Delaware descended, it is said, from one of four brothers in England The immigrant returned to England to claim his inheritance after fighting with the colonists against the British, and found his share confiscated

George Doebell Drawbridge married, in Kennebunk, Maine, Abby Littlefield, daughter of Robert and Rebecca (Houston) Littlefield The Littlefields were among the original settlers of Kennebunk, then a part of Wells, and the father of Robert Littlefield, who owned two hundred acres of land at the old falls" on the Mousam river where the power house of the Sanford & Cape Porpoise railroad now stands One of the women was scalped by the Indians and left for dead at the "Old Falls," but she recovered and lived to be an old woman, always wearing a cap to hide the disfigurement

The children of Henry A and Mary Abby Frances (Drawbridge) Desper are Arthur Merrit, born January 6, 1877, died December 1, 1884, Flora Winifred, October 25, 1881, bookkeeper in her father's office, Alice Genevieve, April 30, 1889, student in the English high school, Worcester, Mabel Irene, December 23, 1892, Charles Warren, March 14, 1895, Myrtice Vivian, April 10, 1899

DAVIS FAMILY Dolor Davis (1), who was the immigrant ancestor of the larger part of the Worcester county branches of the Davis families, was the progenitor of John W Davis, of Worcester Dolor Davis came from England and settled in Cambridge before August 4, 1634, when he received a grant of land in that town He lived later in Concord and Barnstable, Massachusetts He was a carpenter and builder He was born in England and died at Barnstable, Massachusetts, June, 1673 His wife and children came over in 1635 with his brother-in-law, Simon Willard, of Horsemonden, Kent county, who was one of the founders of Concord

Dolor Davis was admitted a freeman at Duxbury, August 5, 1638-9, and had a grant of land there in 1640 He was admitted a freeman at Barnstable, June 2, 1646, after living there three years He and his wife were dismissed from the Duxbury church to Barnstable, August 27, 1648 He was surveyor of highways, constable and on various committees of Barnstable In 1655 he left Plymouth colony and returned to Massachusetts, where he bought at Concord one hundred and fifty acres and a house In 1666 he went back to Barnstable and died there

He married (first), March 29, 1624, Margery Willard, who was baptized at Horsemonden, Kent, November 7, 1602, and died prior to 1667 She was the daughter of Richard Willard, yeoman, and sister of the famous Major Simon Willard, mentioned above The children of Dolor Davis were John, born in England about 1626, inherited the Concord homestead, Mary, born in England about 1631, Elizabeth, born in England, Lieutenant Simon, born in Concord, mentioned in sketch of Samuel E Davis family, Samuel, mentioned below, Ruth, born in Barnstable, March 24, 1645

(II) Samuel Davis, son of Dolor Davis (1), was born probably in Concord, married, at Lynn, January 11, 1665-6, Mary Mead or Meddowes, who died at Concord, October 3, 1710 He married (second), October 18, 1711, Ruth Taylor, who died August 6, 1720 Samuel was admitted a freeman March 21, 1689-90 He settled in Concord, Massachusetts, in that part which became Bedford, and his homestead is now or was lately still owned by his descendants It was on the road from Concord to Bedford, on the edge of the river meadow, and the old well which is still in use is believed to have been dug by Samuel He was a farmer He was living in 1714, the date of his death is not recorded The children of Samuel and Mary were Mary, born October 27, 1666, died December 18, 1667, Samuel, June 21, 1669, married at Concord, March Law, resided at Bedford, Daniel, March 16 or 26, 1673, resided at Bedford, Mary, August 12, 1677, 2, 1697-8, Abigail Read, married (second) Mary Eleazer, July 26, 1680, resided at Bedford, Simon lieutenant, mentioned below, Stephen, March 30, 1686, resided at Bedford

(III) Lieutenant Simon Davis, son of Samuel Davis (2), was born at Concord, August 9, 1683, died 1763 He married Dorothy Hale in 1713 He removed to Rutland, Massachusetts, about 1720, to what has been known lately as the 'Old King Farm" containing seventy-six acres on Muschopauge pond He became one of the most prominent citizens He was one of the first board of selectmen When he cleared his farm there was no road and he had to carry his plow on his shoulder to reach his fields before the road was built He escaped from the Indians at the time Rev Mr Willard and the sons of Deacon Stevens were killed, as he happened to return home by a different route and earlier than usual The Indians were lying in wait for him His wife Dorothy died July 21, 1776, in her eighty-fourth year, both are buried in lot 6, in the Holden burying ground Their last days were spent in Holden with their son Eleazer

The children of Lieutenant Simon and Dorothy Davis were 1 Simon, born May 17, 1714, died April 9, 1754, married Hannah Gates, settled in Rutland, his son Isaac, born February 27, 1749, was the father of Governor John Davis, born January 13, 1787 2 Israel, born August 31, 1717, died 1791, married Mary Hurlburt, resided at Holden and had ten children 3 Rev Joseph, born July 16, 1720 (H C 1740), minister at Holden, 1742-1773, died March 4, 1799 4 Eleazer, mentioned below The preceding were born in Concord or Bedford, the following in Rutland 5 Martha, baptized July 27, 1729, married ——— Smith and resided in Holden 6 Oliver, baptized April 16, 1732, married Mary Read, resided in Princeton 7 Azybah, baptized December 2, 1739 8 Dolly, married ——— Brown, settled in Maine

(IV) Eleazer Davis, fourth child of Lieutenant Simon Davis (3), was born in Concord or Bedford about 1725, married Sarah Ward, July 27, 1748, at Holden, Massachusetts, and settled there There is no record of service, but he enlisted in the revolutionary army, 1775, in Captain David Hawes' company, Colonel Samuel Holden's tenth regiment The children of Eleazer and Sarah Davis were Asahel, born March 5, 1749, Eleazer, Jr, March 22, 1751, Bela, April 12, 1753, a son, Lucretia, June 4, 1758, Sarah, May 10, 1760, Dorothy, October 7, 1762, Molly, August 11, 1764, Jonathan, April 22, 1767, Lydia, August 28, 1769, James, see forward, Lucy, March 18, 1777

(V) James Davis (2d), son of Eleazer Davis (4), was born in Holden, Massachusetts, June 22, 1772 He married Ruhamah Smith, of Worcester, in that town, November 26, 1801 She was the daughter of Elisha, Jr, and Persis Smith, and was born March 1, 1779 James Davis was a farmer at Holden The children of James and Ruhamah, all born at Holden, were Walter Hull, see forward, Charlotte Threcy (Theresa), May 17, 1804, Jane Catherine, March 13, 1807, James Sullivan Madison, June 30, 1810, Ruhamah Lusanna, January 16, 1815, Persis Smith, May 7, 1818

(VI) Walter Hull Davis, eldest child of James Davis (5), was born on the old homestead at Holden, now the town farm, originally six hundred acres in extent At the age of twenty he removed to Worcester and for thirty or forty years engaged in farming He invested his savings in tenement buildings, and at length devoted all his time to building and caring for his property At the time of his death he owned sixty tenements in Worcester He died February 28, 1882

He married Roxanna Adams, of Harvard, Massachusetts Their children were 1 John Walter, see forward 2 Francis A, born March 11, 1827, a carpenter and builder, married Harriet D Boyden, of Holden, and had two sons Walter, who resides in Providence, and Charles, who resides in Connecticut 3 Sarah, born January, 1831, married Samuel L Mitchell, a farmer on Long Island, New York, both are deceased, they had children Jane E Mitchell, unmarried, resides in Worcester, Marion E Mitchell, married A Q Thayer, a baker, of Worcester formerly for twenty-five years a policeman of Worcester and their children are Jennie E Thayer, Clifton Thayer, and Lottie M Thayer

(VII) John Walter Davis, son of Walter Howe

Davis (6), was born in Worcester, Massachusetts, August 21, 1829, died August 17, 1906 Married, November 29, 1849, Myra W Kilburn, of Holden, daughter of William and Nancy Kilburn The latter died at the age of one hundred and three at the residence of her son-in-law, William Kilburn, a carpenter and builder J Walter Davis, as he was generally known, came to Worcester and started in the manufacture of refrigerators, a business he followed successfully for twenty-five years He was a builder and contractor also for many years He was a member of the Masonic fraternity The children of John Walter and Myra W Davis were William L, of whom later, Mary A, born March 11, 1850, married John A Sears, son of Alden Sears, president of the Walker Ice Company, had one son who died in infancy, Harry

(VIII) William L Davis, son of John Walter Davis (7), was born in Worcester He was educated in the public schools of Worcester He went to work as clerk in the drug store of Fairbanks, Harlan & Co, then located on Southbridge street at the corner of Myrtle street He started in business for himself on the present site of the Federal building, between Southbridge and Main streets, in 1880 When the building was sold by the owner, Ransom C Taylor, for the postoffice, the present store at 602 Main street was built for him Mr Davis is a member of Athelstan Lodge of Free Masons, Eureka Chapter, Royal Arch Masons, Hiram Council and Worcester County Commandery, Knights Templar, Worcester Lodge of Perfection, Goddard Council, Lawrence Chapter of Rose Croix He has been at the head of the last four bodies as presiding officer He is a member of the Massachusetts Consistory and of other Masonic bodies

He married Annette Steadman, of Bristol, Vermont, daughter of Oliver C and Maria Steadman Her father was a farmer at Bristol The children of William L and Annette Davis are Herbert E, born February 17, 1878, Florence M (twin), born May 20, 1889, Grace M (twin), born May 20, 1889

CHAMBERLAIN FAMILY William (1), Count Tankerville, of Tankerville Castle in Normandy, who came to England with William, the Conqueror, was the progenitor of the Chamberlain family in England He himself returned to Normandy, but his descendants remained in England on the land granted to him

(II) John De Tankerville, son of the former earl, was lord chamberlain to King Henry I, and assumed his title as a surname (III) Richard, son of John (2), was also chamberlain to King Stephen, and the surname Chamberlain has since his day been that of his family (IV) William Chamberlain, son of Richard (3) (V) Robert Chamberlain was son of William (4) (VI) Sir Richard Chamberlain was son of Robert (5) (VII) Sir Robert Chamberlain, was son of Robert (6) The line continues Sir Richard (IX), John (X), Thomas (XI), John (XII), William Chamberlain (XIII) The American family, of which William Chamberlain was the immigrant ancestor, doubtless belongs to this family, though the line of ancestry is not traced The Chamberlain coat of arms Gules an in escutcheon argent between eight mullets in orle, or Quartering Gules, a chevron between three escallops or Motto Virtuti Nihil Invium Seat Duns-Tew in Oxfordshire, England.

(I) William Chamberlain, the immigrant ancestor of General Robert Horace Chamberlain, of Worcester, was born in England about 1620 His brother, Thomas Chamberlain, was one of the three original purchasers of the Dudley farm at Billerica, but he settled at Chelmsford, Massachusetts Another brother, Edmund, settled first in Woburn, then removed to Chelmsford before 1656, when he sold land at Billerica Savage says that Edmund finally settled in Woodstock

William Chamberlain was admitted an inhabitant of Woburn, January 6, 1648, and permitted to buy land there He removed to Billerica in 1654, about the time his brothers left that town, and spent the remainder of his life there He died May 31, 1706, aged eighty-six years His house in Shawshin (Billerica) was on the farm, probably near the Woburn road, in the southwest part of the village His name appears first on the records October, 1654, on a petition to enlarge the bounds of the town and to change the name to Billerica (Billerikey in the original paper) A little later, when the committee on militia ordered Sergeant Hills' house to be a garrison, William Chamberlain's family was one of those assigned to it He married Rebecca ———, who died September 26, 1692, in the prison at Cambridge, where she was held on the preposterous charge of witchcraft The children of William and Rebecca Chamberlain were Timothy, born at Concord, Massachusetts, August 13, 1649-50, Isaac, born at Concord, October 1, 1650, died July 20, 1681, John, died March 3, 1652, Sarah, born at Billerica, May 20, 1655-56, married John Shedd, Jacob, born January 18, 1657-58, see forward And these also at Billerica Thomas, born February 20, 1659, Edmund, born July 15, 1660, married Mary Abbott, Rebecca, born February 25, 1662, married Thomas Stearns, Abraham, born January 6, 1664, Ann, born March 3, 1665-66, Clement, born May 30, 1669, Daniel, born September 27, 1671, Isaac, born January 20, 1681

(II) Jacob Chamberlain, son of William Chamberlain (1), was born at Billerica, Massachusetts, January 18, 1657-58 He resided at Roxbury and Brookline (Muddy River, part of Boston) He should not be confused with Jacob Chamberlain, who married Experience, and lived in Newton and vicinity, for both Jacob and Experience belonged to a generation earlier, nor with Jacob Chamberlain, of Boston and Newton, whose wife's name was also Susanna The latter Jacob may have been a son of Edmund Chamberlain, mentioned above Jacob, son of William Chamberlain, was admitted a freeman in 1690 He removed to Newton in 1700 or shortly before that date, but died at Brookline His will mentions the names of his four children He married, January 24, 1685, Mary Child, daughter of Benjamin Child Their children were Jacob, born March 7, 1686, see forward, John, born at Roxbury, August 1, 1687, Mary, married Samuel Davis, Elizabeth, married Joseph Weld

(III) Jacob Chamberlain, Jr, son of Jacob Chamberlain (2), was born March 7, 1686, and died at Newton, Massachusetts, July 28, 1771 He came to Newton with his father from Brookline about 1700. His name is among those on a protest dated May 20 1720 against having but one school house in the town He was selectman in 1746 He married about 1718, Susannah Stone, who was born at Groton, October 23, 1694, the daughter of Deacon Simon and Sarah Stone, of Groton Their children, all born at Newton, were Jacob, Jr, born November 28, 1719 see forward, Josiah, born November 13, 1721, died in French war about 1755, Susanna born September 27, 1724 died February 22, 1748-49, Isaac born April 6, 1728, William, born September 22, 1730 died December 9 1760, of smallpox married, June 20, 1754, Ann Hyde, Sarah, born September 19, 1733, died September 5, 1796, Margaret, born September 20, 1736, Simon, born August 10, 1739, married, 1763, Rebecca Cleveland

(IV) Jacob Chamberlain, eldest son of Jacob Chamberlain (3), was born at Oak Hill, Newton, Massachusetts, November 28, 1719 Early in 1742 he removed to Worcester, where he bought a tract of land of Richard Flagg on Salisbury street, February 28, 1742 (See Worcester Registry of Deeds) This land was handed down to his son John and from him seventy-two acres were handed down to his son Thomas, since inherited by his sons Robert H and Thomas, Jr, who are the present owners of the property Jacob Chamberlain was a farmer by occupation He held the office of selectman in Worcester in 1761 In 1774 he was a Tory protestor, numbered among the internal enemies by the committee of correspondence in 1775, and disarmed by that committee Again, June 16, 1777, he was reported among others that the selectmen deemed enemies to the "Common Cause" (See Worcester Book, No 354) He was deacon of the old first church on the common from 1775 to 1790 He left the church August 8, 1779, on account of the innovation in singing (See Lincoln's history of Worcester by Franklin P Rice, page 153)

He died March 17, 1790, and was buried on the common and his headstone with the others there was taken down and placed under the sod The stone bears the following inscription 'Sacred to the memory of Deacon Chamberlain who departed this life March 17, 1790, in the 71st year of his age Who fulfilled the office of deacon in the Church of Christ in Worcester for about 28 years with satisfaction to the church and honor to himself He was possessed of good natural abilities useful in society of which he was a member Instructive and entertaining in conversation Compassionate to the afflicted Given to hospitality, sound in faith And now, we trust, has entered into his eternal rest"

After coming to Worcester he married, at Newton, June 7, 1744, Lydia Stone, born May 4, 1724, the daughter of John and Abigail (Stratton) Stone, of Newton Their children were John, born July 22, 1745, see forward Sarah, born January 26, 1746-47, died December 5, 1833, married Joseph Howard, of Holden, September 13, 1770 Thaddeus, born November 17, 1748, married Judith Barnard, January 27, 1774 Susannah, born June 10, 1751, died young Jacob, born September 19, 1753, married (first) Lydia Buck, of Sutton, March 18, 1784, (second) Mrs Esther Kingsbury, February 3 1824 Lydia, born October 8, 1755, died October 5, 1841, married Tyler Curtis, September 5, 1776 Susannah, born November 22, 1757, died December 16, 1845, married Benjamin Butman, October 22, 1786 Abigail, born September 16, 1760, died February 2, 1829, married Abel Heywood Jr, April 27, 1780 Mary, born July 13, 1763, died November 21, 1802, married Nathan Heywood, of Shrewsbury, July 1, 1793 William, born July 25, 1767 died May 6, 1853, married (first) Betsey Curtis, January 10, 1791, (second) Dolly Chadwick, October 11, 1810 The child of Jacob and his second wife, Mrs Anna Heywood, whom he married June 3, 1769, was Anna, born July 21, 1770, died February 1, 1838 Anna Heywood was born at Brookline, Massachusetts, widow of Abel Heywood, Sr, son of Major Daniel Heywood, of Worcester, of Indian war fame

(V) John Chamberlain, eldest son of Jacob Chamberlain (4), was born at Worcester, July 22, 1745 He received the education common to the farmer boy of those days and worked with his father on the farm, which later came to him He dealt extensively in real estate and owned considerable property Seventy-two acres of the old homestead was handed down to his son Thomas by will dated June 5, 1806 In May, 1775, he was disarmed by the committee of safety and correspondence, he being in accord with his father's principles of loyalty to the Crown He was a selectman during the years 1785 to 1795, inclusive, 1797, 1798, 1801, 1802 He was deacon of the First Parish Church twenty-two years, succeeding his father in 1791 He died in 1813

He married, at Worcester, June 27, 1771, Mary Curtis, born October 14, 1747, daughter of Captain John and Elizabeth (Prentice) Curtis, of Worcester The children of John and Mary Chamberlain were John Curtis, born June 5, 1772, died December 8, 1834, a lawyer of note in Charlestown, New Hampshire, was member of congress from his district Elizabeth Prentice, born November 8, 1774 Henry Vassall, born January 11, 1777, a lawyer of some note who settled in Mobile, Alabama, and became a judge Mary, born April 8 1779, married Daniel Greenleaf, April 3, 1800 Thomas, see forward Elizabeth, born May 25, 1785, died young Levi born May 14, 1788, a lawyer of Keene, New Hampshire, where he died Dolly, born January 16, 1792, died unmarried

(VI) Thomas Chamberlain, son of John Chamberlain (5), was born at Worcester, March 6, 1783 He received his education in the common schools of this town In early life and also after he was married he taught school Among others in his charge were the schools at Tatnuck and Quinsigamond He conducted the farm formerly owned by his father and grandfather in what was known as the Chamberlain district His purpose of advancing the science and encouraging and improving the art of horticulture was widened by the fact that he was one of the founders and first trustees of the Worcester Horticultural Society in 1840 His portrait may be seen on the wall of Horticultural Hall, Front street, Worcester He was crier of the Worcester court for seventeen years He was a member and first president of the common council of the city of Worcester after incorporation, and all of his public duties he discharged with ability and faithfulness He filled most of the offices of the state militia, from corporal to brigadier-general, with highest honor to himself and satisfaction to those under his command He was originally a Whig in politics, later a Republican He attended the Old South Church

He married (first), May 30, 1810, Nancy Woods, of Groton, born February 19, 1718, the daughter of Colonel Sampson Woods She died July 25, 1831 He married (second), October 30, 1832, Hannah Blair, born February 19, 1793, died August 23, 1873, daughter of Robert and Elizabeth (Harrington) Blair, of Worcester He died September 5, 1855 Children of Thomas and Nancy Chamberlain were. Charles Thomas, born May 30, 1811, died July 4, 1867, married Sarah E Hathaway, September 21, 1841 Nancy Woods, born June 16, 1813, died May 20, 1891, married, June 3, 1839, A Watson Grant George Alexander, born September 24, 1815 died July 22, 1866, married Martha W Barnes, May 8, 1858 John Curtis, born October 7, 1817, died July 23, 1884, married, at Mobile, Alabama, Hannah Elizabeth Chamberlain Mary Elizabeth, born July 25, 1819, died July 25, 1886, married (first) Andrew Kettell Hunt, December 7, 1843, married (second) Herbert Curtis Francis Henry, born September 5, 1821, died August 10, 1888, married Lucy Parker Sarah Jane, born July 1, 1824, died December 4, 1891, married Massena Parker, of Mobile, Alabama.

Caroline Maria, born October 26, 1826, died April 27, 1854, married James P Lowe, of Washington, D C The children of Thomas and Hannah (Blair) Chamberlain were Dolly Curtis, born February 10, 1834, died October 4, 1872 Thomas, Jr, born June 4, 1835, married Augusta Hovey, August 31, 1858 Robert Horace, see forward

(VII) General Robert Horace Chamberlain, youngest son of Thomas Chamberlain (6), was born at Worcester, Massachusetts, June 16, 1838 He was educated in the public schools of Worcester, followed by a course in Worcester Academy At the age of eighteen he began an apprenticeship with Ball & Ballard, machinists, School street, where he remained until the civil war He enlisted in Company A, Fifty-first Regiment, Massachusetts Volunteer Militia, September 25, 1862, for nine months, and was appointed a sergeant of his company He was in the campaign in North Carolina, taking part in the engagements of Goldsboro, Whitehall and Kingston, and was afterwards at Fortress Monroe, White House, Baltimore, Harper's Ferry and with the Army of the Potomac after Gettysburg in pursuit of Lee He was mustered out July 27, 1863 He enlisted again July 20, 1864, in Company F, Sixtieth Regiment, and received a lieutenant's commission He was subsequently promoted a captain The regiment was assigned to Indianapolis, Indiana, on special guard duty at a camp of five thousand Confederate prisoners He was mustered out November 30, 1864 He then returned to Worcester and worked at his trade of machinist until 1870, when he was appointed by Mayor Blake superintendent of sewers He held this position for eighteen years, from 1870 to 1888, during which time the system was developed and widely extended In 1888 he was appointed master of the House of Correction, and in 1892 was elected to his present position of high sheriff of Worcester county

For twelve years after the war he was active in the state militia In 1865 he re-organized the Worcester City Guards and was the first captain of that company for two years He also re-organized a battery of artillery in Worcester and it was called the Chamberlain Light Battery He received the commission of major and afterwards of colonel of the Tenth Regiment and was made brigadier-general of the Third Brigade, December 31, 1868 He resigned and retired from the service in 1876 Before he was superintendent of sewers, General Chamberlain had served from 1867 to 1870 in the common council of the city He is a Republican in politics He is a member of Union Congregational Church General Chamberlain is a prominent Free Mason He became a member of Montacute Lodge, A F and A M, September 9, 1862, of Worcester Chapter of Royal Arch Masons, May 6, 1864, of Hiram Council of Royal and Select Masters, March 23, 1865 He received the Templar degrees in Worcester County Commandery, Knights Templar, December 1, 1865 In 1892 he was elected grand commander of the Grard Commandery of Massachusetts and Rhode Island He is a member of Massachusetts Consistory, Thirty-second degree, of Scottich Rite Masonry He is at present treasurer of the board of trustees of the Masonic fraternity and has been for twenty years, also of the Masonic Mutual Relief Association He is a charter member of George H Ward Post, No 10, Grand Army of the Republic, and a member of the Loyal Legion, Boston He is a member of the Hancock Club and of the Worcester Board of Trade

He married, January 10, 1865, Esther Browning, born July 12, 1841, daughter of Joshua and Lavinia (Morse) Browning, of Hubbardston, Massachusetts Her father was a carpenter and captain of a company of artillery The children of Robert Horace and Esther Browning Chamberlain are Flora Browning, born August 16, 1868, married Charles B Weatherby, June 12, 1894, and their children are—Esther Sherman Weatherby, born July 16, 1898, Olive Benedict Weatherby, born August 21, 1902, Jean Chamberlain Weatherby, born December 31, 1904 Mabel Susan, born at Worcester, March 15, 1872, resides with her parents

GEORGE H RICE Edmund Rice (1), the immigrant ancestor of George H Rice, of Worcester, and of all the Rice families, in fact, of that vicinity, was one of the principal settlers of the old town of Sudbury, Massachusetts He was born in England in 1594 and settled in Sudbury before 1639, when he was proprietor and selectman there He was admitted a freeman May 13, 1642, and was deputy to the general court in 1643 He was a member of the committee to convey lands at Whip Sufferage in 1657 He was deacon of the church in 1648 He became a proprietor of Marlborough, Massachusetts, and moved there Thomas, Samuel and Joseph Rice, his sons, and he were among the petitioners for church privileges in Marlborough He sold land to his sons, Edward and Henry Rice, February 20, 1654 He died May, 1663 The petition for the division of his estate was signed June 16, 1663, by the widow, Mercy, eight elder and two younger children While there were five other immigrants in Massachusetts from England of this surname before 1650 most of the name can trace their ancestry to Edmund, of Sudbury

He married, in England, Tamazin ———, who died in Sudbury, June 13, 1654 He married (second) Mercy (Heard) Brigham, widow of Thomas Brigham, March 1, 1655 The children of Edmund and Tamazin Rice were Henry, born in England, 1616, of whom later, Edward, born in England, 1618, married Anna ———, Thomas, married Mary ———, Mathew, married Martha Lamson, Samuel, married Elizabeth King, Jacob, born 1637, married Mercy King, Lydia, married Hugh Drury, Daniel Edmund, Jr, Benjamin, born May 31, 1640 The children of Edmund and Mercy Rice were Ruth, born September 29, 1659, Ann, born November 19, 1661, Mary These are probably not in the correct order of birth

(II) Henry Rice, eldest child of Edmund Rice (1), was born in England in 1616 and came to America with his father He married at Sudbury, February 1, 1643, Elizabeth Moore, daughter of another of the Sudbury pioneers, John Moore (See sketch of Moore family in this work) Henry Rice took the oath of fidelity July 9, 1645 His first grant of land was in 1643 on the southern part of Mr Dunster's farm He was admitted a freeman in 1658 He received from his father in 1659 the deed of a tract of land in the wilderness at what was called "New Trouble" and also about the same time land south of the Cochituate brook confirmed later by Indian deeds dated March 10, 1672-3 In 1679 his brother, Benjamin Rice, conveyed to him land near his house Henry lived at what was called Rice's End in the adjoining town of Framingham, and he bequeathed his house there to his son Jonathan Henry died February 10, 1710, and being older than his brother Edward, must have been about ninety-three years of age His will was proved in Middlesex county His wife Elizabeth died at Framingham, August 3, 1705 Their children were Mary, born September 9, 1646, Elizabeth, August 4, 1648, married John Brewer, Jonathan, July 3, 1654, Abigail, June 17, 1657, married Thomas Smith, David,

ROBERT H. CHAMBERLAIN

December 27, 1659, Tamasin, February 2, 1661, married Benjamin Parmenter, Rachel, May 10, 1664, Lydia, June 4, 1668, Mercy, January 1, 1670, Hannah

(III) David Rice, son of Henry Rice (2), was born in Sudbury, Massachusetts, December 27, 1659 He was one of the original members and one of the first deacons of the Framingham Church He was selectman of Framingham four years, town treasurer two years, and was a leading citizen His homestead was probably near that of the late Deacon Luther Havens He died October 16, 1723, at Framingham His heirs divided the property by mutual agreement He married, April 7, 1687, Hannah Walker, who died December 18, 1704 Their children were Elizabeth, born September 8, 1689, married Samuel Frost, February 1, 1710-11, Hannah, January 5, 1691-2, married John Bent, Bezaleel, of whom later, Josiah, August 19, 1701

(IV) Bezaleel Rice, third child of David Rice (3), was born in Framingham, Massachusetts He married Sarah Buckminster, June 23, 1720, and owned the covenant with his wife February 19, 1721 She was admitted to the church May 5, 1722 He was a physican His homestead was in the old red house near the late Elisha Belknap's house He was a selectman in 1742 He was a soldier in the revolution, being a private in Captain Clark's company from Framingham Their children were Bezaleel, of whom later, David, September 17, 1723, Sarah, September 21, 1725, married David Stone, died at Petersham, October 22, 1815, aged ninety years, Zerviah, February 14, 1727-8, died March 4, 1739-40, Josiah, November 23, 1734, Martha, July 9, 1737, married ——— Drury, and lived in Shrewsbury

(V) Bezaleel Rice, eldest child of Bezaleel Rice (4), was born in Framingham, May 19, 1721 He married (first) Susanna Jennings, daughter of Stephen and Susanna (Bigelow) Jennings and granddaughter of Stephen and Hannah (Stanhope) Jennings, of Sudbury His wife Susannah died September 15, 1750 He married (second) Sarah Bent, March 13, 1751, and she was admitted to the Framingham church, January 13, 1754 She was the daughter of David and Mary (Drury) Bent He lived in the house at Framingham lately owned by Joseph Goodnow He died March 13, 1806, aged eighty-five years He spent his last years with his son Samuel The children of Bezaleel and Susannah Rice were Bezaleel, born April 11, 1744, died August 10, 1748, Hezekiah, of whom later, Susanna, July 6, 1748, married Ezra Twitchell, Sarah September 5, 1750 The children of Bezaleel and Sarah Rice were Bezaleel, December 5, 1751, died unmarried, John, February 9, 1754, Nathan, August 1, 1756, Mary, baptized March 28, 1762, Samuel, born 1764, baptized September 23, 1764

(VI) Hezekiah Rice, second child of Bezaleel Rice (5), was born in Framingham, October 2, 1745 He married Abigail Eames, of Hopkinton, in 1773 Both owned the covenant April 10, 1774 He married (second) Elizabeth Eames, of Hopkinton, Massachusetts, 1775 He removed to Dublin, New Hampshire, but returned to Framingham He was a soldier in the revolution He removed to Hopkinton, an adjoining town, in August, 1793, and was received in the church there He was sometimes called Hezekiah Rice, Jr, because there was another Hezekiah Rice older than he in the same town He lost three children in an epidemic of canker rash The children surviving were Ruth, baptized April 17, 1774, John, of whom later, Hannah, born about 1778

(VIII) Dexter Rice, son of John Rice (7), was Dexter, the grandfather of George H Rice, of born in Framingham, Massachusetts, about 1780 He settled in Hopkinton Among his children was Worcester

(VII) John Rice, son of Hezekiah Rice (6), was born in Hopkinton, Massachusetts, about 1800 He married Mary Ann Adams, daughter of John Adams, of Hopkinton She was a descendant of Henry Adams, of Braintree, the ancestor of President John Adams and most of that surname in this county He was a carpenter and builder He also conducted a farm and during part of his life was a shoe manufacturer The twelve children of Dexter and Mary Ann (Adams) Rice were John A, resides at 5 Gates street, Worcester, is a carpenter by trade, Alfred D, Marie Annie, George H, of whom later, Lewis W, of whom later, Marilla, Alice B, Abbott B, Henry W, Minnie died young, Sarah B, Wilbur C All living but Minnie and Henry W

(IX) George H Rice, son of Dexter Rice (8), was born in Hopkinton, Massachusetts, August 10, 1854 He was educated there in the public schools He began his business career as a clerk in a grocery store, where he worked for a year He worked another year in the ice business, then learned the trade of carpenter in Hopkinton He began business there as carpenter and builder in 1876 and was a general contractor and builder in Hopkinton for about thirteen years In June, 1889, he removed to Worcester, where he carried on the same business He has built many residences and business blocks since coming to Worcester He built the James A Colvin machine shop on Lagrange street, the Beaver block on Main street, James Kindred's apartment house on Oread street, the Smith block in South Framingham, the largest building in that town, containing stores, offices and the Masonic Hall He superintended the erection of a $100,000 building for T M Walker in Springfield, Massachusetts His own contracts in Worcester amounted to over $300,000 In 1894 he began to build tenement houses for investment in Worcester in partnership with his brother, Louis W Rice, under the firm name of George H and L W Rice They have at present seven large, modern brick buildings, containing apartments Mr Rice is a Free Mason In politics he is a Republican and is at present serving his second term on the school board of Worcester

Mr Rice married Frances Delia Clapp, daughter of Emory Pierce and Cynthia Jane (Woods) Clapp, August 29, 1877 Mrs Rice was born October 19, 1856, in Barrington, Illinois, where her father was a contractor in the oil well supply business He removed later to Michigan and later to the oil regions in Pennsylvania He returned to his old home in Hopkinton and manufactured shoes He enlisted in Company C, in the Fortieth New York Regiment, in 1861, being one of the first men to enlist from Hopkinton He died in Westboro October 28, 1899 Mr Rice's home is at 4 Lowell street and his office is there also The children of George H Rice are Florence Pearl born July 10, 1879, Bertha C, January 15 1882; Freda F, April 3, 1894

(IX) Lewis W Rice son of Dexter Rice (8), was born in Hopkinton, Massachusetts, April 2, 1856 He was educated in his native town in the public schools He worked on a farm after leaving school and later engaged in the meat business with Frank Chandler under the firm name of Rice and Chandler, on Main street, Westboro Massachusetts, for several years Later he sold out his meat business and worked in a boot factory at Hopkinton, Massachusetts, for several years He learned the carpenter's trade and worked at it in Hopkinton and vicinity In 1894 he went into partnership with his brother, George H Rice, in building and renting tenements in Worcester He married, September 22, 1880, Annie Amelia Stebbins, daughter of George H and Caroline Antoinette (Knowlton) Stebbins Their children are Edward Dexter born July 8, 1881, Nettie M, October 21, 1882, Blanche Maria, October 26, 1886

EDWARD M DODGE Richard Dodge (1), the emigrant ancestor of Edward M Dodge, of Worcester, Massachusetts, came to Salem, Massachusetts, in 1638 He was the son of Richard Dodge, of East Coker, Somersetshire England After he came to America he lived for a short time with his brother William Dodge, who had already established his home at Salem Richard settled in what is now North Beverly, and the locality is called Dodge Row It is near Wenham Lake He and his wife Edith were members of the Wenham church before 1648 His name was first on a list of twenty-one subscribers to Harvard College and he gave the largest amount He was probably born in 1602 He died late in 1670 or early in 1671 His widow died probably in 1677

Their children were John, baptized December 29 1631 in England lived in North Beverly, died October 11, 1711 Mary, born 1632, married, 1653, Zachary Herrick, died August 18, 1710 Sarah baptized 1644, died 1726, married Peter Woodbury, who was born 1640, and died 1704, Richard, born 1643, lived at Wenham, Massachusetts, died April 13, 1705 Samuel born 1645, died December 4, 1705, Edward born at North Beverly died February 13, 1721, Joseph, born 1651, at North Beverly, died August 10, 1716

(II) Samuel Dodge, son of Richard Dodge (1), was born at Beverly 1645, died December 4, 1705, he married Mary daughter of Thomas Parker, of Reading His wife died August 6, 1717 He was a farmer at Ipswich, and was well-to-do In his will proved December 24, 1705, he left property valued at one thousand and fifty-one pounds The house he lived in was left to his son Antipas The graves of both Samuel and his wife are marked by stones in the burying ground at Dodge Row Their children were Samuel born January 22, 1668 at Ipswich died young, Joseph, February 14 1670, married Martha White, of Wenham, Annamah, born January 9, 1672, was a tailor in Boston, Ann, born December 20 1674 married John Edwards, Antipas, (see forward), Mary, born June 6, 1680, married Rice Knowlton Amy, born August 27, 1682 died 1719 Deborah born April 1685 Jabez born March 22, 1686 married Margery Knowlton lived at Ipswich, Manchester, and Shrewsbury, Massachusetts, died October 1774 at Shrewsbury, Parker, married Mary Choate, lived at Ipswich, died September, 1742, Samuel born December 11, 1692, married Susannah Bishop

(III) Antipas Dodge son of Samuel Dodge (2), born September 7 1677 married Joanna Low in 1699 and settled in Ipswich on the old homestead, of which he inherited a fifth in 1705 He died soon afterward In May 1707 his wife was appointed his administratrix The estate was valued at two hundred and five pounds The widow married Joseph Hale, of Boxford published September 19 1708, and he was appointed guardian of Joshua Dodge her minor son The children of Antipas Dodge were Joshua, born February 1 1701, Joanna born July 15, 1702, married Ambrose Hale of Boxford, who was born February 10 1698-9 son of Joseph and Mary (Watson) Hale, David, born 1704, married Martha Esgate in Haverhill

(IV) Joshua Dodge son of Antipas Dodge (3) was born February 1, 1701, in Ipswich, Massachusetts He was brought up by his step-father who was appointed his guardian He went to Boston and worked at his trade of cordwainer He was elected sealer of leather in Boston 1729 and 1735 Joshua Dodge bought of Timothy Brown, of Brookfield, seventy-five acres of land on the west side of the township of Brookfield, August 12, 1734 He bought land extensively He gave half the homestead to his son Josiah June 24, 1760, and willed the other half to him His will was dated November 13, 1706, and proved July 2, 1793 His children were Joshua, Jr, born probably at Boston, Caleb, born probably at Boston, Josiah, born probably at Boston, Elizabeth, Sarah, married ——— Peabody, Samuel, of Londonderry, New Hampshire

(V) Joshua Dodge, son of Joshua Dodge (4), was born in Boston 1723-7 His father removed from Boston about 1740, and was a cordwainer at Marlborough, Massachusetts, in 1742 In 1743 the family was living at Brookfield, Massachusetts He married Thankful Morse She died November 1, 1797 He died at West Brookfield, Massachusetts, February 24, 1796 His will dated February 22, 1796, and proved April 26, 1796, mentions his wife Thankful five sons and other heirs All the children were probably born at Brookfield They were Lydia, born July 9, 1749 married, June 5, 1775, David Smith, of Brookfield, Moses, born October 23, 1750, married Betsey Parker, of Shrewsbury, 1773, Jonas born August 27, 1752, Nathaniel lived on the old Dexter Forbes place, Rufus, Thaddeus, born June 18, 1758, married Susan Holloway, of Ipswich published December 10, 1781, Artemas, born July, 1765, died March 9, 1845, Eunice, married Joshua Dodge, of New London Connecticut

(VI) Thaddeus Dodge, son of Joshua Dodge (5), born at Brookfield, Massachusetts, June 18, 1758, married (published December 10, 1781). Susan Holloway, of Ipswich, she died May 20, 1812, married (second), May 21 1815 Esther Tyler of West Brookfield He died February 18, 1837 She married (second), May 12 1840 Ephraim Dewing The children of Thaddeus Dodge were Lewis, born 1782, Darius born March 18, 1784 died September 8, 1854, Rebecca married ——— Wright, Susan married ——— Sly, Pliny (see forward) Fanny, born September 30, 1794, married December 30 1813 Reuben Stoddard, of North Brookfield, she died November 24, 1871, Harriet, Betsey

(VII) Pliny Dodge, son of Thaddeus Dodge (6), born June 11, 1791, in Brookfield He married December 9 1821, Cynthia Converse, of North Brookfield She was born in Spencer, Massachusetts 1799, and died in Warren August 15, 1883 He died June 11, 1869 Their children were Luke Converse, born April 23, 1822 married Minerva Adams daughter of Amos and Eliza (Sanborn) Adams, of Lowell, Massachusetts, Henry H born August 11, 1823, married Elvira M Pratt and Jane Chambers, Edwin L, born April 10, 1825 married Lucy A Haven, of Worcester Charles, born April 29, 1826, married July 8, 1849, Lauretta E Ainsworth, of Sturbridge, Massachusetts, died March 10 1883 at Worcester, Warren F, born May 9 1827, married, March 7, 1867 Rebecca A Stout of Topsham Maine died at Earlville, Illinois October 5 1884 Thomas W, born September 10, 1829 at Spencer, Massachusetts John Q, born July 28, 1832, Pamelia C, born May 26, 1836, at Warren Massachusetts married July 21, 1864 Celia M Wheeler, of West Brookfield, who died at Fitzwilliam New Hampshire, December 22, 1877, Anna E born September 22, 1840, Theodore O born May 24 1843

(VIII) Henry H Dodge son of Pliny Dodge (7), born August 11, 1823 died at Bureau county,

J. P. Grosvenor

Illinois, about June 6 1887, married Elvira M Pratt, of Worcester, September 22, 1844 Divorced He married (second), June 29, 1859, Jane Chambers Elvira married (second) Dr J Marcus Rice, surgeon for the Twenty-fifth Massachusetts Regiment in the civil war She accompanied him and acted as a nurse with the Twenty-fifth Massachusetts Regiment She died January 28, 1893 Henry H and Elvira Dodge had Edward H Dodge, born November 26 1845

(IX) Edward H Dodge, son of Henry H Dodge (8), born in Worcester, November 26, 1845, married June 19, 1872, Ella A Hubbard He served in the commissary department of the Twenty-fifth Regiment, Massachusetts Volunteer Militia, during the civil war He was an expert accountant and bookkeeper by profession He died at Worcester May 11, 1897 They had but one child Edward M, born at Worcester, July 20, 1873

(X) Edward M Dodge, son of Edward H Dodge (9), was born at Worcester, July 20, 1873 He attended the Worcester public schools, and graduated from the English high school in 1893 He was a member of the Sumner Club and treasurer of the class of '93 He was with George H Clemence, the architect, at his office in the Walker building, for five years He then formed a partnership with William Estabrook to carry on the business of fire insurance January 1 1906, Mr Estabrook withdrew from the firm and Mr Dodge is still in business He has been an active member of the Church of the Unity in Worcester He was secretary and assistant superintendent of the Sunday school for six years, resigning in 1903 He is well known in Unitarian circles in the city and county He is a member of the Worcester County Mechanics' Association, of the Worcester Board of Underwriters, the Commercial Travellers' Association, the Worcester Grange, Patrons of Husbandry

He married, September 23, 1903, Helen Esther Fletcher, daughter of Charles A Fletcher, of Worcester She was born in Fitchburg, Massachusetts, May 21, 1876 She was educated in the Worcester schools and at Miss E A Kimball's School for Girls, Worcester

JONATHAN PRESCOTT GROSVENOR

John Grosvenor (1) was the emigrant ancestor of Jonathan Prescott Grosvenor, of Worcester He was born in England, and came to America probably when a young man The family tradition makes him a nobleman's son and a relative of Queen Elizabeth At any rate he brought the Grosvenor coat-of-arms and used it and it is inscribed on his gravestone at Roxbury, Massachusetts He married Esther Clark, born in 1651, died at Pomfret, Connecticut, June 15 1738 He died at Roxbury, September 27, 1691 Among their children was Ebenezer Grosvenor

(II) Ebenezer Grosvenor, son of John Grosvenor (1), was born in Roxbury, Massachusetts October 9 1684. He married at Pomfret, Connecticut, Ann Marcy, born 1687, died July 30, 1743 He died September 20, 1730 Among their children was Ebenezer Jr, born at Pomfret, where they settled

(III) Ebenezer Grosvenor, son of Ebenezer Grosvenor (2), was born at Pomfret, Connecticut December, 1713 He married Lucy Cheney, and among their children was Daniel

(IV) Rev Daniel Grosvenor, son of Ebenezer Grosvenor (3), was born at Pomfret, Connecticut, 1749 He was graduated from Yale College, 1769, was ordained at Grafton, Massachusetts, October 19 1774, and dismissed January 1, 1788, on account of failure of health He was installed at Paxton, November 5, 1794, and dismissed November 17, 1802 He was a trustee of Leicester Academy from July 4, 1785, to 1815, when he resigned At the Lexington alarm, April 19, 1775, he shouldered his musket and marched with the minutemen to Cambridge He was an affable and able pastor, but gave up preaching because of bronchial trouble, and removed to Petersham, Massachusetts, where he died July 22, 1834

He married in Sutton, May 9, 1776, Deborah Hall, born in Sutton, Massachusetts March 5, 1756, daughter of Rev David Hall, of Sutton, who was the pastor of a church in Sutton for nearly sixty years, and who died May 8, 1789 Rev David Hall was the son of Joseph and Hannah (Miller) Hall, the latter named having been a daughter of Rev John Miller Rev David Hall married, June 24, 1731, Elizabeth, daughter of Dr Jonathan Prescott, of Concord, who was a son of Jonathan and Elizabeth (Hoar) Prescott, the latter named having been a daughter of Hon John Hoar of Concord Jonathan Prescott was descended from John Prescott, first settler of Worcester county at Lancaster, Massachusetts to whom the wife of the late Governor Roger Wolcott has erected a memorial stone, he being an ancestor of hers Dr Jonathan Prescott married Rebecca, daughter of Hon Peter Bulkeley, Jr, born in Concord, 1642 was graduated from Harvard, 1660 He married Rebecca Wheeler, April 16, 1667 His father, Rev Peter Bulkeley, first minister of Concord was born at Woodhill, Bedfordshire, England, January 31, 1583 He was the tenth generation in direct line of descent from Robert Bulkeley, one of the barons at the time of the death of King John, 1216 The names of lineal descendants 1 Robert 2 William 3 Robert 4 Peter, married Nicholsus Biard, of Haughton 5 John, married Andryne, daughter and heir of John Colley of Ward, and died 1450 6 Hugh, married Helen Wilbraham, of Woodley 7 Humphrey, married Cyle, daughter and heir of John Mutten 8 William married Beatryce, daughter and heir of William of Bulansdale 9 Thomas married Elizabeth daughter of Randelle Grosvenor 10 Edward, D D, of Woodhill, married Olive Irlby, of Lincolnshire 11 Peter, of Corcord

The Bulkeleys and Grosvenors intermarried in England and America The Rev Peter Bulkeley, father of the Rev Edward Bulkeley, who was a cousin of Queen Elizabeth, was a faithful minister of the gospel, under whose directions his son received a learned and religious education, suited to his distinguished rank About the age of sixteen he was admitted a member of St John's College at Cambridge of which he was afterwards chosen fellow and from which he received the degree of Bachelor of Divinity He succeeded his father in the ministry of his native town, where he was a zealous preacher of evangelical truth about twenty years and for the most part of the time lived an unmolested nonconformist At length, his preaching meeting with distinguished success, and his church being very much increased, complaints were entered against him by Archbishop Laud, and he was silenced for his nonconformity to the requirements of the English church This circumstance induced him to emigrate to New England, where he might enjoy liberty of conscience He arrived in Cambridge, 1634 and was the leader of those resolute men and self-denying Christians, who soon after went further up into the woods and settled Concord Mr Bulkley was remarkable for his benevolence and here he expended most of his estate for the benefit of his people He was a thorough scholar, an elevated, devotional Christian, laborious in his profession and as a preacher, evangelical faithful, and of remarkably energetic, powerful and persuasive eloquence Two of Mr Bulkeley's manuscripts are preserved in the library of the American Antiquarian Society He gave a part of his library and some other donations to Harvard College After a laborious and useful life, he died March 9, 1659, in his seventy-seventh year He married for his first wife Jane daughter of Sir Thomas Allen, of Goldington, whose nephew was Lord Mayor of London By her he had nine sons and two daughters Eight years after her death he married Grace, daughter of Sir Richard Chitwood by whom he had three sons and one daughter From his son, Rev Edward Bulkeley, who succeeded his father in the ministry at Concord, is descended Ralph Waldo Emerson

(V) Jonathan Prescott Grosvenor, son of Rev Daniel Grosvenor (4), was born at Grafton, Massachusetts, November 30, 1779 He married, April 23, 1804, Bethia, born at Holden, Massachusetts, October 13, 1781, daughter of Rev Joseph and Mary (Allen) Avery Rev Joseph Avery was born at Dedham, Massachusetts, October 14 1751, son of Deacon William and Bethia (Metcalf) Avery Dr William very, who came to Dedham, 1650, was the emigrant ancestor He built his house almost under the boughs of the Avery oak History says that this tree was an ancient tree more than two hundred and fifty years ago, when the town was settled The top has been much twisted and torn by the storms of centuries, but the tree shows all signs of life and vigor, apparently sufficient to weather storms for centuries to come It measures sixteen feet in circumference five feet from the ground It is owned by the Historical Society The Fairbanks house, where some of his ancestors lived, is still there, it was built in 1636 Rev Joseph Avery entered Harvard before the close of his sixteenth year During the four years of his college life he was an uncommonly exemplary and conscientious student He has been heard to remark that one time he was the only undergraduate of the university not addicted to the use of tobacco He was graduated in the class of 1771 with much honor He was ordained and settled over the church in Holden, December 1774 He married Mary Allen, an aunt of Judge Charles Allen, of Worcester Her mother was Mary Adams a sister of Hon Samuel Adams, "Father of the American Revolution," governor of the commonwealth and cousin to President John Adams Mary Allen was born in Boston, February 8, 1755, died April 1, 1842 Rev Joseph Avery died in Holden, March 5, 1824, having been pastor there about fifty years

(VI) Charles William Grosvenor, 'son of Jonathan Prescott Grosvenor (5), born at Paxton, February 14, 1827, married at Holden, March 21, 1848, Nancy, daughter of David and Nancy (Davis) Clapp, the latter named having been born June 1, 1828, died at Leicester, May 10, 1888 Thomas Clapp, son of Richard Clapp was the emigrant ancestor The line of descent was Thomas 1, Thomas 2, Joshua 3, Seth 4, Seth 5 David 6 Mrs Clapp's emigrant ancestor was Dolar Davis, who married Margery, sister of Simon Willard emigrant ancestor of Frances E Willard The line of descent was Dolar (1), Simon (2), James (3), Thomas (4), Captain E James (5), captain of company of state militia in the revolutionary war, Edmond (6), a revolutionary soldier, Nancy (7), Nancy (8)

Children of Charles William and Nancy (Clapp) Grosvenor were 1 Ella Elizabeth, born December 27 1848 at Paxton married, December 21, 1880, Henry H Kingsbury of Spencer 2 Samuel Avery, born at Leicester, November 30, 1850, married, March 4, 1875, Eva L McIntire 3 Jonathan Prescott born April 24, 1853 4 Clarence William, born in Paxton, September 11, 1855, married (first), December, 1880, H Maria Bottomly, (second) October 20, 1898, Cora E Bancroft, of Worcester 5 David Clapp, born in Paxton, March 1, 1858, married, August 27, 1885, Anna M Wilson 6 Adeline Maria, born in Leicester, September 1, 1860 7 Herbert Wright, born in Leicester, December 16, 1863, died June 6 1872 8 Edith Marion, born February 9, 1868, died May 30, 1872

(VII) Jonathan Prescott Grosvenor, son of Charles William Grosvenor (6), born at Paxton, April 24, 1853, attended the public schools of his native town, completing his education at Leicester Academy, one of the leading educational institutions for preparing students for college After graduating he entered the office of Childs & Manning Bros, jobbers of boots and shoes in Worcester, and learned the business He became traveling salesman for the firm covering the state of New York In 1884 he went into business for himself, establishing the Worcester Slipper Company, which proved a success from the first and has grown steadily For twelve years the business was located at 13 Mechanic street, in August, 1898, he removed the factory to Park avenue, occupying a spacious four-story brick building, one hundred and twenty by forty-five feet three hundred feet in length, formerly occupied by the E H Stark Company shoe manufactory The building is well equipped with the latest devices for fire protection He gives employment to two hundred and fifty hands To the business of ladies' slippers Mr Grosvenor then added the manufacture of ladies' shoes, and the innovation again proved profitable The Grosvenor factory is well built and arranged for its purposes, and is one of the best equipped in the state The latest tools and machinery are installed and the business kept right up-to-date The product of the factory is sold direct to jobbers, and the reputation of the Worcester Slipper Company is said to be unsurpassed for reliable and stylish goods The name of the company is a synonym for Mr Grosvenor, who has made it from the start his personal business and built it up step by step to its present proportions, giving employment to a couple of hundred hands and producing every week goods worth many thousand dollars In politics Mr Grosvenor is a Republican He is a member of Plymouth Church

He married August 25 1881, Delia S Gardner, of Richville St Lawrence county, New York Their children Pauline Le Rose born March 21, 1891, died March 9, 1892, Evelyn C, born September 4, 1894

ALBERT WILLARD ANDREWS Robert Andrews (1), the emigrant ancestor of Albert Willard Andrews, of Boylston and Worcester, Massachusetts, was a native of Boxford, England He may have been a relative of Robert Andrews, of Ipswich but the relationship is not known

Robert Andrews or Andros (1), as the name was commonly spelled by the first generation emigrated from Boxford, England to New England about 1656 with six children and settled in Boxford Massachusetts He bought two hundred acres of land of John Lambert, of Rowley The sale was confirmed by the government in July 1661 The farm was situated on the west side of Pye brook in the vicinity of the farm now or lately owned by Joseph H Janes He erected his house on the land and cleared part of it He bought several other tracts of land in Boxford and in the neighboring village of Topsfield He bought of Zaccheus Gould a lot on Fish brook His house was in some way destroyed before 1668, when this lot was called the cellar lot and he erected a new house The second house, built in 1668, was probably the old Andrews house which was below the lot of Nathaniel Smith on the same road He left this house and the homestead lot to his son Thomas, the eldest, and the ancestor of the Worcester family It had been supposed until lately that the Worcester branch was descended from John, another son

Robert Andrews was an extensive cultivator of the soil When he died in May, 1668, he had twenty-five acres of corn planted Among the things mentioned in the inventory of his estate were a ship saw and other carpenter's tools, indicating that he was a mechanic and carpenter as well as a farmer He died May 29, 1668 His will was dated May 16, 1668, and proved July 1, 1668

He married in England Grace ——— She died December 25, 1700, at Boxford Her will was dated September 4, 1699, and was proved January 4, 1702-3 Both were probably buried at Topsfield Their children were Mary, born about 1638 in England, married Isaac Cummings, of Topsfield, November 27, 1659, Hannah, born about 1642 in England, married Captain John Peabody, one of the pioneer settlers of Boxford, Elizabeth, born in England about 1643, married Samuel Symonds, a pioneer settler of Boxford, Thomas, born about 1646 in England, John, born 1648, married Sarah Dickinson, daughter of James and Rebecca Dickinson, of Rowley, April 18, 1683-4, admitted a freeman October, 1690, settled in Boxford, had eight children James, Hannah, John, Joshua, Lydia, Josiah, Oliver and Rebecca There is no evidence that he had a son Robert as indicated by the Shrewsbury history Robert, born about 1651, probably died unmarried, will dated December 6, 1675, Rebecca, born about 1654, married Samuel Marble, Joseph, born September 18, 1657, married (first) Sarah Perley February 1, 1681, she died January 15, 1693-4, and he married (second) Mary Dickinson, of Rowley, Massachusetts, March 29, 1695, she died February 25, 1700, resided at Boxford He was the great-great-grandfather of John A Andrew, famous as "the War Governor" of Massachusetts Sarah, born 1658, married Daniel Wood, Ruth, born May 27, 1664, married Edward Phelps, son of Edward and Elizabeth Phelps, of Andover, May 19, 1683

(II) Thomas Andrews, son of Robert Andrews (1), was born about 1645 in England He inherited the Andrews homestead and settled in Boxford He was admitted a freeman May 2, 1689-90 He was a prominent man in his day He was selectman in 1688-91-96-97-1704 and held other positions of honor and trust

He married (first) Martha Antrum, of Ipswich, widow of Obadiah Antrum, June 22, 1670 He married (second) Mary Belcher, February 9, 1681, married (third) Rebecca ——— The children of Thomas and Martha Andrews were Elizabeth, born January 16, 1671, married William Wilson, of Ipswich, April 19, 1693, Martha, born December 25, 1673 The children of Thomas and Mary (Belcher) Andrews were Rebecca, born April 14, 1686, ———, born October 1, 1688, Patience, born March 29, 1689-90, Esther, born February 16, 1692-3, married John Bixby, of Boxford, May 8, 1722, Thomas, born December 18, 1694, married, March 1, 1722, Ruth Bixby, had eight children, resided at Boxford, Robert, born May 16, (about 1696)

(III) Robert Andrews, son of Thomas Andrews (2), was born in Boxford, Massachusetts, on the old homestead, about 1696, on May 16 He inherited the homestead of his father and grandfather in Boxford He married, March 10, 1719-20, Deborah Fries, at Andover, Massachusetts He died at Boxford, April 14, 1751

The history of Boxford, page 26, shows that this Robert Andrews, undoubtedly father of Robert Andrews, who settled in Shrewsbury, was son of Thomas, not of John Andrews, as stated in Ward's History of Shrewsbury, while there is no record that John Andrews ever had a son Robert The homestead went to Robert's son, Nathan Andrews Robert was selectman in Boxford in 1726-32-38-39-41-42-43-44

The children of Robert Andrews were Lieutenant James, born March 19, 1721, married Ruth Wood, February 18, 1747-8, she died August 7, 1764, and he married (second) Elizabeth Bryant, April 16, 1765, resided at Boxford, died there 1794, aged seventy-five years Robert, November 8, 1722, Nathan, May 25, 1726, married Mehitable Foster, of Andover, April 23, 1751, married (second) Sarah Symonds, widow, February 6, 1764, Samuel, 1731

(IV) Robert Andrews, son of Robert Andrews (3), was born in Boxford, Massachusetts, November 8, 1722 He married Lucy Bradstreet, of Topsfield, May 19, 1746-7 She was a daughter of Simon, who was grandson of Governor Simon Bradstreet, for many years governor of the Massachusetts Bay colony Lucy Bradstreet was also great-great-granddaughter of Governor Dudley Soon after his marriage he removed to Brookfield, but in 1747 or 1748 settled in the north parish of Shrewsbury, now Boylston He bought several small farms, about three hundred acres in all, which remained the family homestead for one hundred and fifty years, the greater part of this land is now beneath the waters of the Metropolitan Water Basin

He was captain of the Shrewsbury Second Precinct Militia Company and served in the revolution in 1775 He was a selectman of Shrewsbury in 1774-75-76-79 He was accidentally killed at Boylston, November 11, 1789, aged sixty-seven years His widow died December 22, 1815, aged ninety-one years

Their children were Robert, born January 8, 1748, married Dorothy Goodenow, of Princeton, died July 13, 1835, aged eighty-seven, of their seven children, one was Dr John Andrews, born March 31, 1793 Samuel, September 14, 1750, married Judith Flagg, daughter of Stephen Flagg, July 10, 1777, married (second) Annis Morse, daughter of Rev Ebenezer Morse Daniel, July 22, 1752, married Dinah Bigelow, daughter of Joseph Bigelow, Jr, 1781, he died March 12, 1826, aged seventy-four, killed by an unruly bull Elizabeth, February 17, 1755, died September 29 1757 John March 29, 1757, married Margaret Parker, of Holden, December 4, 1794, died February 13, 1822, aged sixty-five Lucy, married Jonathan Bond, Jr Asa, May 11, 1762, graduate of Harvard, 1783, settled in Ipswich, appointed by President George Washington collector of the port of Ipswich in 1796 and held the office thirty years, he married, October 12, 1788, Joanna Heard, daughter of Hon John Heard, of Ipswich, she died July 12, 1797, he married (second) Hannah Farley, October 25, 1798, she died January 9, 1807, aged thirty-six, he married (third) Sarah Farley, July 3, 1807 The son of Robert and Joanna Heard, John Dudley, graduated at Harvard in 1810, Edward also in 1810, daughter Elizabeth married Hon Sidney Willard, professor at Harvard Jotham, December 18, 1766, died young Theodore and Charlotte were the children of the second wife

(V) John Andrews, son of Robert Andrews (4), was born in Shrewsbury now Boylston, Massachusetts, May 29, 1757 He married Margaret Parker, of Holden, December 4, 1794, and settled upon the homestead He was selectman in Boylston in 1798-1801-03-04-05-12-13 He was a prominent man in town affairs for many years He died February 13, 1822, aged sixty-five years

Their children were Mary Parker, born June 26, 1795, married Jonathan Flagg, March 27, 1817, Robert, March 22, 1797, died 1798, Willard October 6, 1798, Lucy Bradstreet, March 6, 1800, died 1801, John, March 2, 1802, married Mary E Dunton, November 3, 1831, Robert, January 2, 1805 Married Caroline Wilder, Thomas Denny, September 29, 1806, died October 1, 1833

(VI) Willard Andrews, son of John Andrews (5), was born in Boylston, Massachusetts, October 6, 1798 He married, Dolly Houghton, June 18, 1829 He had the homestead Willard Andrews was a prominent man in town affairs, he was assessor for nine years He died April 23, 1874, his widow died December, 1888

The children, all born in Boylston, were Albert Willard, born July 19, 1831, Theodore, January 11 1833, town treasurer, 1865, died March 1, 1888, Julia A, May 30, 1835, married Samuel I Rice, of Northboro, Ferdinand, December 13, 1838, served three years in the civil war, corporal of Company D, Twenty-fifth Regiment, Massachusetts Volunteers, died November 24, 1864, William, November 20, 1840, died 1841, Emma E, March 13, 1846, married John A Ware

(VII) Albert Willard Andrews, son of Willard Andrews (6), was born in Boylston, Massachusetts, July 19, 1831 He was brought up on the old homstead where the family had lived for several generations He attended the public schools of his native town, the West Boylston high school and the Worcester Academy He remained at home on the farm, teaching school during the winter seasons six or seven years, until he married, January 12, 1860, Elizabeth Wright Bond, daughter of Thomas and Harriet (Slocomb) Bond, of Boylston She was born in Shrewsbury, Massachusetts, September 12, 1837, and also comes from a prominent and patriotic ancestry

His grandfather, Captain John Bond, who was born in Westboro, Massachusetts, was in the sixth generation from William Bond, who came from Bury St Edmunds, England, to Watertown, Massachusetts, when a mere lad, apparently only six years old, in company with relatives He was the third son of Thomas Bond of Bury St Edmunds, a maltster William was in Watertown as early as 1631 He married, February 7, 1649-50, Sarah, daughter of Nathaniel Bisco, (see Bisco Family sketch in this work) "the rich tanner," and became one of the leading citizens of the colony and the province, filling various positions of public trust Lieutenant Bond, father of Captain John, was first lieutenant in Captain Edmund Brigham's company that marched for Lexington on the alarm, April 19, 1775, and was commissioned lieutenant April 5, 1776, and marched to re-enforce the northern army under General Gates Lieutenant Thomas Bond's father, Jonathan, was a soldier in the French and Indian war, serving as lieutenant in Captain Benjamin Woods' company in 1755, and in Captain Benjamin Flagg's company in 1756

After his marriage Albert Willard Andrews owned a farm and saw mill in Boylston for a few years Then he removed to Worcester, where he lived for over twenty years on Catherine street, engaged in the business of carpenter and builder He is still a member of the Congregational church at Boylston He was the town treasurer there in 1859-60-61 He was assessor there in 1863-64 and for six years a member of the school committee He is a Republican He is well known in the building trades as a carpenter and contractor of high reputation for good and honest work He built a large number of houses in Worcester and the vicinity, and for the past twelve years has resided on Lincoln street

The children of Albert and Elizabeth Wright (Bond) Andrews were Harriet Bond, born March 4, 1862, attended Worcester high school, graduate of Normal School at Worcester, 1881, Normal Art School, Boston, 1893, studied at Worcester Art Museum, formerly teacher of drawing in Worcester public schools, now teacher of drawing in Holden high school and Bancroft school, Worcester, lives at home with her parents, Ferdinand, born June 30, 1867, graduate of the Worcester high school, 1885, Worcester Polytechnic Institute, 1889, was for five years assistant chemist in lead works at Carnegie, Pennsylvania, now head chemist in Raritan Copper Works at Perth Amboy, New Jersey, married, June 17, 1896, Esther Garbart, daughter of John Garbart, Pittsburg, Pennsylvania, lives at Perth Amboy, has son, John Willard, born February 13, 1899 Arthur Willard, born May 9, 1869, attended the Worcester high school and the Worcester Polytechnic Institute, formerly draughtsman for N E Telephone & Telegraph Company, Boston, now inspector of the American Telephone & Telegraph Company in New York City, married, August, 1899, Margaret Bingham, daughter of John Bingham, of Boston, they have one child, Grace, born June 30, 1902

ALBERT A SPAULDING Edward Spaulding (1), the emigrant ancestor of Albert A Spaulding of Worcester, was a pioneer settler in Braintree, Massachusetts It is believed that he came from England about 1630 He was a proprietor of Braintree in 1640, was admitted a freeman May 13, 1640, and was a juryman in 1648 He removed first to Wenham and later to Chelmsford, Massachusetts, where he was one of the proprietors in 1655 He sold his house and lands in Wenham, August 18, 1648, his wife Rachel, consenting He was a town officer of Chelmsford He married (first) Margaret, she died in 1640 He married (second) Rachel He died February 26, 1670 His will was dated February 13, 1666, and proved April 5, 1670 He made bequests to his wife, to sons Edward, John, and Andrew, and daughter, Dinah

Children of Edward and Margaret Spaulding were 1 John, born about 1633, died 1721, married Hannah Hale, freeman at Chelmsford, 1690 2 Lieutenant Edward born about 1635, died January, 1708, married (first) Priscilla Underwood, married (second) Margaret Barrett, November 22, 1681, she died May 25, 1748 3 Grace, died May, 1641 Children of Edward and Rachel were 4 Benjamin, born April 7, 1643 in Braintree, died before May 25, 1708, married Olive Farwell, October 30, 1668, daughter of Henry and Olive Farwell 5 Joseph, born October 25, 1646, died April 3, 1740, aged ninety-six, at Plainfield, Connecticut, married Mercy Jewell, December 9, 1670 6 Dinah, born March 14, 1649 7 Andrew, born November 19, 1652, died May 5, 1713, married Hannah Jefes, daughter of Henry Jefes, of Billerica, April 30, 1674

(II) Benjamin Spaulding, son of Edward

Spaulding (1), born in Braintree, Massachusetts, April 7, 1643, died before 1708, married Olive Farwell, daughter of Henry and Olive Farwell, first of Concord, then of Chelmsford, Massachusetts, October 30, 1668 Benjamin was admitted a freeman in 1689. He was mentioned in his father's will, having previously received his portion of the estate He purchased a large tract of land in the north part of Canterbury, Windham county, Connecticut, now the town of Brooklyn His homestead there descended to his son, Edward, and grandson Ebenezer, son of Edward

Children of Benjamin and Olive (Farwell) Spaulding were 1 Sarah, born January 4, 1669, married John Merriam 2 Edward, (see forward) 3 Benjamin, born July 6, 1685, in Chelmsford, died September 17, 1712, married Sarah Hall, daughter of Stephen Hall, she married (second) William Blodgett, August 18, 1714 4 Elizabeth, married Ephraim Wheeler 5 Mary, married Isaac Morgan

(III) Edward Spaulding, son of Benjamin Spaulding (2), born in Chelmsford, Massachusetts, June 18, 1672, died November 29, 1740, aged sixty-seven years The Canterbury record gives the date 1739 He married Mary Adams, who died September 20, 1754, aged seventy-eight years They belonged to the First church in Chelmsford and to the Canterbury church They settled in Canterbury, Connecticut, on the Spaulding homestead, and he died there He was the third settler within the present limits of Brooklyn, Connecticut He bought land north of Canterbury bounds, at the foot of Tadwich, in 1707 He was with Joseph Adams and Henry Smith on the first committee of the Religious Society organized in 1731

Children were 1 Benjamin, born July 20, 1696 2 Elizabeth, born August 15, 1698, married William Darbe 3 Ephraim, (see forward) 4 Jonathan, born April 15, 1704 5 Ezekiel, born September 8, 1706 6 Ruth, born September 28, 1710, married John Bacon 7 Abigail, born March 10, 1713, married Banajah Douglass 8 Ebenezer, born August 7, 1719 9 John, born December 1, 1721

(IV) Ephraim Spaulding, son of Edward Spaulding (3), born in Canterbury, Connecticut, April 3, 1700, married Abigail Bullard, of Plainfield, Connecticut, and settled there His children were 1 John, born August 8, 1724, died May 29, 1768, removed to Plainfield, New Hampshire 2 Phineas, born March 25, 1726, died August 31, 1785 3 Reuben, born February 26, 1728 4 Josiah, born December 7, 1729 5 Ezekiel, born September 30, 1731 6 Palatiah, born March 19, 1734, died October 3, 1750 7 Abigail, born March 16, 1736, married Captain Samuel Hall, May 19, 1756 8 Oliver, born September 30, 1739 9 Mary, born May 16, 1744, married John Larrabee, December 16, 1662 10 Ephraim, (see forward)

(V) Ephraim Spaulding, son of Ephraim Spaulding (4), born in Plainfield, Connecticut, May 24, 1747, died in 1811 He married (first) Esther Snow, May 20, 1773 She died July 17, 1806, in her sixty-first year, married (second) Hannah Stowell, September 1, 1808 She died March 9, 1823, in her sixty-fifth year They resided at Ashford, Connecticut He was a soldier in the revolution and served in Captain Jonathan Parker's company, Colonel Comfort Sage's regiment, in 1776 His company was in the campaign in New York and Long Island, and the battle of White Plains He was in the same company, in Colonel Webb's regiment, in 1780, and apparently served during the war

Children of Ephraim and Ether (Snow) Spaulding were 1 Alva born May 30, 1773, died April 27, 1796, unmarried 2 Betsey, born September 2, 1775, married Nicholas Aldrich in 1800, they settled in Tolland, Connecticut, he died at Maltonville, New York 3 Lena, born September 29, 1780, married Edward Holton or Houghton, and lived at Antwerp, New York 4 Dua, (see forward) 5 Edmund, born September 27, 1784

(VI) Dua Spaulding, son of Ephraim Spaulding (5), born September 26, 1782, died January 23, 1863, at Eastford, Connecticut, married Mercy Warren, April 30, 1807 She was born February 29, 1788 Children were 1 Warner, born March 18, 1808, died March, 1828 2 Erastus, born April 23, 1809 3 John Warren, born May 25, 1811 4 Eliza, born April 12, 1813, married Nelson Whitford, resided in Wilmington, Connecticut 5 Lyman, born March 25, 1815 6 Nelson, born February, 1817 7 Augustus, (see forward) 8 Gilbert, born July 3, 1821 9 Ephraim, born December 26, 1822 10 Edmund, born October 18, 1824 11 Mary Ann, born April 8, 1827, died unmarried

(VII) Augustus Spaulding, son of Dua Spaulding (6), was born in Eastford, Connecticut, settled in Eastford, married Abigail Catherine Richards, November 7, 1843 She was the daughter of Ebenezer and Catherine (Newell) Richards, of Dedham, born November 12, 1824, died July 25, 1905 He died August 17, 1898 Children were 1 Albert Augustus, (see forward) 2 George Richards, born April 2, 1857 3 Carrie Newell, born September 23 1862

(VIII) Albert Augustus Spaulding, son of Augustus Spaulding (7), born in Ashford, Connecticut, October 14, 1853 He was educated in the public schools of his native town and came to Worcester, Massachusetts, September 19, 1870, when seventeen years of age, his capital then consisting of seven dollars He accepted a position as clerk for Charles B Eaton, a dealer in dry goods, whose store stood where the State Mutual building now stands, and served in that capacity three years The following seven years he was an employe of Denholm & McKay in the Boston store, a department store located then on the corner of Main and Mechanic streets In 1881 he became associated with John C MacInnes, a dry goods dealer, whose business was established in 1873, at No 462 Main street, Worcester, in the Gross & Strauss building The business increased rapidly both in volume and importance, and is now (1906) one of the three largest department stores in Worcester, occupying several blocks on Main street, opposite the common The present corporation was formed in 1892, when Mr Spaulding was elected vice president The other officers of the company are President, John C MacInnes the founder of the business, clerk, Charles A Homer, and director, with the other officers, Alexander T Moir The capital stock is $100 000 Mr Spaulding has been very active in the development of the business, possessing a thorough knowledge of the details of the same and deserves a full share of the credit for the prosperity of the house

Mr Spaulding is in every respect what is termed a self-made man Beginning life humbly, without capital and unaided by influential friends, he attained a position of honor and usefulness solely through his own ability, and the exercise of energy and unconquerable determination At every stage of his effort he faithfully met every requirement with entire loyalty and trustworthy devotion, and his advancement from time to time came to him as the fruit of his own conduct In all his business relations he is integrity personified, and in his personal character is an earnest, christian man He is a Republican in politics, but has never sought or held office, preferring to devote his leisure time to his home and family, in which he takes great pride He is a consistent member of the Adams Square Congregational Church, takes an active part in the work thereof, serving as a member of the standing committee since 1898 He is a member of the Independent Order of Odd Fellows, Worcester Board of Trade, and the Worcester Automobile Club A man of pleasing personality, genial in disposition, a good entertainer, and a lover of out-door sports He married, June 1, 1880, Helen Fraser, born February 22, 1856, daughter of James and Mary (McPherson) Fraser

James Fraser was born in Wigtown, Scotland, 1823, died in Worcester, Massachusetts, 1885 When a young man he came to America, and later located and lived for a time at Halifax, Nova Scotia, where he was united in marriage to Mary McPherson, of Scotch descent, born 1822, died in Worcester, Massachusetts, 1879 They were the parents of six children Bessie, deceased, Hannah, deceased, Susan, Mary Ann, deceased, Helen, wife of Albert A Spaulding, Cora, deceased James Fraser was a carpenter and cabinet maker by trade, a Master Mason, and a member of Plymouth Church, Worcester, Massachusetts

The children of Albert A and Helen (Fraser) Spaulding are 1 Cora Fraser, born January 18, 1881, graduate of Worcester high school, married, June 26, 1905, Harry C Rose, of Worcester, resides at No 299 Lincoln street 2 Edith M, born December 25, 1885, graduate of the Worcester high school, a student in Pratt Institute, Brooklyn, New York 3 Paul W, born September 14, 1893, attending city school

Mr Spaulding has been an extensive traveler and in this way has broadened his views and ideas of men and places In 1900 accompanied by his eldest daughter, Cora Fraser Spaulding, he took a trip to Europe, visiting many of the principal cities of the old world, and in 1904 he and his wife spent the winter in California, and also visited all of the important points in the West, places of interest and note The family reside in a beautiful colonial home on Marie avenue, Worcester, and enjoy the acquaintance of a wide circle of friends

ROLLIN G WHITE, for many years an enterprising and prominent business man of Worcester, Massachusetts, and a well-known philanthropic citizen of that town, born December 17, 1823, in Newfane, Windham county, Vermont, son of Phineas and Susan (Tyler) White, died November 19, 1905

Phineas White (father) was born in Southbridge, Massachusetts, June 27, 1781, son of Cyrus White, also a native of Southbridge, Massachusetts Phineas White was in his early days a merchant in Boston, and later moved to Vermont, where he followed farming He married in Charlestown, Massachusetts, May 19, 1809, Susan Tyler, born April 20, 1790, in Woburn, Massachusetts The following named children were born to them Susan Putnam, born in Boston, July 18, 1811, deceased, James Lawrence, born August 23, 1813, in Boston, died in Warren, Massachusetts, June 11, 1900, Thomas Cyrus, born December 8, 1815, in Boston, died in Minnesota, about 1895, George Tyler, born August 1, 1817, in Dover, Vermont, died in Baltimore June 14, 1903, Charles Augustus, born November 8, 1818, in Dover, died about 1890 in Baltimore, Catherine Lewis, born in Dover, May 1, 1820, died in Boston January 10, 1900, Sallie Tyler, born in Newfane, Vermont, April 11, 1822, died in Troy, October 12, 1857, Rollin G, of whom later, Cordelia E, born June 23, 1825, in Newfane, Vermont died in West Wardsboro, Vermont, June 12, 1861, Mary A, born November 19, 1827, in Newfane, Vermont, died in Leroy, New York, March 19, 1897, Artemisia, born May 13, 1829, in Newfane, died in Brattleboro, Vermont, Rhoda Ann, born June 26, 1832, resides at Auburndale, Middlesex county, Massachusetts, in the Woodland Park Hotel, and has a son Frederick M Gooding The father of these children died January 2, 1864, at Wardsboro, Vermont, and Mrs White died in West Wardsboro, January 4, 1874

Rollin G White, eighth child and fifth son of Phineas and Susan (Tyler) White, obtained his education at Wardsboro, Vermont At the age of twenty-one he removed to Worcester, Massachusetts, and entered into his first regular employment in a livery stable with G S Switzer and remained some five years, receiving for his services twelve dollars a month He then went into the retail meat business with Stowell Maynard, under the firm name of Maynard & White In 1857 he engaged in the wholesale meat business in the Agricultural building on Front street He conducted this business with considerable success for about ten years, when he established himself in the pork packing business, associated with a Mr Pevey and Mr Dexter, and conducting business under the firm name of White, Pevey & Dexter This firm carried on a most extensive and profitable business, and in 1893 sold their plant to the firm of Swift & Company, Chicago, Illinois From the outset Mr White's business career was successful and prosperous, owing in a great part to the straightforward methods and general fair dealing that always characterized his business transactions

Politically Mr White was a stanch Republican, and while he never aspired to public office was untiring in his efforts to promote the welfare of that organization He attended the Old South Church for a number of years, and later became a member of the Union Church of Worcester, contributing five thousand dollars to the building fund and five thousand dollars to help pay off the debt of this church

Rollin G White was married three times First to Sarah B Mann, daughter of Jason and Sarah (Bond) Mann, of Holden, Massachusetts She died about five years after her marriage, and Mr White married for his second wife Lusanna T Spear, daughter of Luther and Hanna (Conant) Spear, of Oakham, Massachusetts Of this union the following named children were born Alice and Susan, both deceased, Lucy A, wife of Ralph H Brigham, of Southbridge, Massachusetts, and has one son, Rollin White Brigham, born August 11, 1893 Mr White married for his third wife, November 5, 1896, Mary E (Parker) Reed, who was born in Rutland, Massachusetts, December 13, 1837, the daughter of Emory and Sarah (Estey) Parker, and widow of James G Reed, of Rutland, Massachusetts, a farmer, who died in June, 1885

CHARLES STEARNS HALL John Hall, the grandfather of Charles S Hall, deceased, for many years a citizen of Worcester, Massachusetts, was born 1779, died 1857 He married Nancy Moore, who was born in Leicester, Massachusetts, 1780, died 1860 Following are the children of John and Nancy Hall, Lucy, John, Fidelia, John, Elbridge Gerry, Nancy, William Gray, Willard Moore, Nancy Hall

Elbridge Gerry Hall, father of Charles S Hall, married Elizabeth T, daughter of Stephen and Deborah Putnam Stearns, of Worcester She was born April 19, 1814 Stephen Stearns was one of

Charles S. Hall

the largest real estate owners in Worcester and a man of prominence His farm included Columbus Park and extended south to Hope cemetery Deborah Putnam Stearns was a niece of General Israel Putnam The children of Mr and Mrs Hall were Ann Elizabeth, born August 7, 1843, died March 7, 1896, Charles Stearns Hall, born April 26, 1847, died June 18, 1905

Charles Stearns Hall spent his youth in Worcester, attending the public schools, and after graduating from the high school pursued his studies at Howe's Business College He then entered the employ of the Washburn & Moen Manufacturing Company, at the South Worcester plant, as shipping clerk When this branch was destroyed by fire Mr Hall was transferred to the main works at Grove street, where he became assistant quartermaster and then quarter-master His next position was assistant to Superintendent Charles H Morgan, with the title of assistant manufacturer, the superintendent looking out for the construction and maintenance of buildings and machinery, and Mr Hall being charged with the manufacture and development of the wire making art After a connection of thirty-four years with this company, Mr Hall resigned on July 1, 1901, and engaged in business for himself as a manufacturer at North Brookfield This business he conducted successfully for four years, or up to the time of his death He was also a member of a real estate company, conducting business under the firm name of Davis & Hall Mr Hall was a Republican in politics, but never held office, having no taste for public life He was a member of the Second Advent Church, and served on the official board and as teacher in the Sunday school He was a life member of the Worcester Mechanics' Association, and for a time a director of the Worcester Co-Operative Bank Mr Hall was of a retiring nature, devoted to his home and friends His sympathies were broad and tender, and almost every unfortunate who came to him found a friend

Mr Hall married, June 17, 1880, Emma Goddard, born November 25, 1859, daughter of Dorrance S Goddard Their children, born in Worcester, Massachusetts, were as follows Winthrop Goddard, born April 1 1881, Raymond Stearns, born December 12, 1884, Annie Gertrude, born June 29, 1888, Marjorie Williams, born February 2, 1891, Roderick Chesley, born April 13, 1893, Elizabeth Putnam, born June 17, 1896 Mr Hall died at his home in Worcester, Massachusetts, June 18, 1905

GEORGE H MILLS Samuel Mills (1), the pioneer ancestor of George H Mills, of Worcester, is believed to have come from Lancashire, England He came to New England before 1640, and was at Weymouth, working for Henry Waltham March 11, 1640 He deposed then that he was twenty-one years old, making his date of birth 1619 He removed to Dedham, where he settled and spent the remainder of his days He was a townsman there January 1, 1644-5, and a member of the Dedham church before 1646 He married (first) Frances —— and (second) Mary —— The latter died October 30, 1694 He died January 16, 1695

Children were 1 Samuel, baptized March 29, 1646, died April, 1646 2 Samuel, died December 15 1649 3 Benjamin, (see forward) 4 Elizabeth, born December 5 1652 5 Stephen, died December 3, 1653 6 Sarah, born November 5, 1654 7 Rebecca, born April 10, 1657

(II) Benjamin Mills, son of Samuel Mills (1), born in Dedham, Massachusetts, April 13, 1651, married Mary ——, and settled in Dedham His children as recorded at Dedham, were 1 Benjamin, born June 7, 1675 2 Mary, April 25, 1677 3 Samuel, March 7, 1677-8 4 William, (see forward)

(III) William Mills, youngest child of Benjamin Mills (2), born in Dedham, Massachusetts, May 2, 1682 He removed to the adjoining town of Needham, or was living in that part of Dedham when it was set off He was one of the original members of the First church at Needham He died at Needham July 9, 1759 His wife died October 3, 1759 Among their children, was William Mills, Jr, probably the eldest son

(IV) William Mills, Jr, probably the eldest son of William Mills, Sr, born in Needham, Massachusetts, about 1725, married (first) Hannah ——, who died at Needham, February 23, 1758, second ———, and (third) Eunice Eddy, at Oxford, March 4, 1772 He seems to have had a distinguished record as soldier and officer in the revolutionary war Children of William and Hannah Mills were 1 James (see forward) 2 Esther, December 10, 1751 Children by the second wife were 3 Enoch, born May 27, 1759 4 Rhoda, born January 2, 1761

(V) James Mills, eldest child of William Mills, Jr (4), born in Needham, Massachusetts, January 30, 1750 He served in the revolutionary war in Captain Nathaniel Heath's company, Colonel Jonathan Reed's detachment of guards, in 1778 He served in 1779 with the guards at Cambridge and elsewhere about Boston Nehemiah Mills, of Needham, supposed to be a relative, was in the same company Philip Mills who was with James Mills, later at Dublin, New Hampshire, served in a Needham company also under Captain Robert Smith and Colonel William Heath in 1775 James Mills settled before the war was over at Dublin, New Hampshire, where Philip Mills went the year before (See history of Dublin, New Hampshire, and Bethel, Maine) He married a Dublin girl and lived there about four years, when with others from Dublin, including relatives of his wife, he removed to Bethel, Maine Philip and his wife Anna remained in Dublin until 1797 It should be mentioned that Philip and his wife were dismissed to the Dublin church, although just after they arrived they had been warned, after the ancient custom of New England (January, 1780)

James Mills married February 7, 1782, Hannah Mason daughter of Moses Mason They removed to Bethel in 1785, and settled on a farm on Grove Hill In 1790 he was killed by a falling tree while cutting wood He left a widow and five young children The widow married (second) September 10, 1792 Elijah Grover He died in 1805

Hannah Mason was the sixth child of Moses Mason born in Dublin, New Hampshire, May 4, 1762 Moses Mason was a great-grandson of Captain Hugh and Esther Mason (See sketch of Mason family) Captain Hugh Mason was a settler at Watertown, a tanner by trade, captain of the Watertown company, Indian fighter, magistrate, and deputy to the general court, born in England in 1606, sailed April 30 1634, with wife Esther in ship "Francis of Ipswich" The line is through Captain Hugh (1), John (2), Daniel (3) Moses Mason (4) was the youngest son of Daniel (3) and Experience He married Lydia Knapp daughter of Jesse and Mary Knapp, of Boston who settled in Dublin New Hampshire The Mason family removed to Bethel, Maine, in 1799

The Grover family was closely allied by marriage with the Mills family They are very numerous and highly respectable They are descended from

Thomas Grover (1), the emigrant, who came from England and settled in Charlestown, Massachusetts, in 1642 He removed to Malden later

Thomas Grover, son of the emigrant, married Sarah Chadwick, daughter of John Chadwick, and had three sons Thomas (3), Andrew (3), and Ephraim (3) In 1702 he settled in that part of Norton, Massachusetts, known as the Taunton West Purchase, afterwards incorporated as Norton, later as Mansfield (1770) Andrew Grover (3), and Mary, had Jonas, born September 7, 1699 He married Sarah Austin Their son, James, Jr (5), born August 15, 1729, married April 8, 1754, Sarah Wellman James Grover (5), moved from Mansfield, Massachusetts, to Peckersfield, now Nelson, New Hampshire, and later went to Bethel, Maine. His son Elijah married Mrs Hannah (Mason) Mills

Children of James and Hannah (Mason) Mills were 1 John, born July 31, 1783, at Dublin, New Hampshire, married Asenath Cummings 2 James 3 Hannah, born in Dublin, January 9, 1786 4 Deborah, born at Bethel, January 27, 1786 5 Cyrus (see forward)

(VI) Cyrus Mills, youngest child of James Mills (5), born in Bethel, Maine, April 28, 1790, settled in Bethel, Maine, later removed to the Fryeburg Academy grant, now Mason, Maine, adjoining Bethel In 1816 he and his brother John were living in Bethel, and a road was laid out by the town from their houses to that of their mother, Widow Grover Cyrus married Abiah Bean, daughter of Daniel and Margaret (Shaw) Bean, born December 31, 1792 Margaret Shaw was the daughter of Ebenezer and Anna (Philbrick) Shaw, of Standish Maine Daniel Bean was a revolutionary soldier and late in life drew a pension He was the son of Jonathan Bean, of Kingston, or the adjacent town of Brentwood, New Hampshire, who with his wife Abigail removed to Sudbury, Canada, he died in 1800, aged forty-three, married in 1780 and had thirteen children He was born in Kingstonton, or Brentwood, New Hampshire, resided at Chester, New Hampshire, and was a descendant of John Bean, a native of Scotland, who settled in Exeter, New Hampshire He removed to Standish, Maine, and later to Bethel, where he bought a farm near that of his brother-in-law, Eleazer Twichell

Children of Cyrus and Abiah (Bean) Mills were 1 William Dexter born September 18, 1816, in Bethel 2 Daniel, born April 10, 1818, Bethel 3 Nelson September 20, 1819, in Bethel 4 Mary Bean, born April 5, 1822, in Mason, Maine 5 Charlotte, born 1823 6 Nathan Grover, born February 20, 1824 7 Cyrus, Jr, born 1826 8 O'Neal R, born 1828 9 Betsey S born 1830 10 J Mason born 1832 11 George H (see forward) 12 Elijah G, born January 9, 1835 13 Stephen, died when one and a half years of age

(VII) George Horace Mills, son of Cyrus Mills (6) next to the youngest of the children, was born March 31, 1833 in Fryeburg Academy grant now the town of Mason, Maine He received a common school education in the schools of his native town He removed to Charlestown, Massachusetts, when a young man, and there learned his trade of carpenter He came to Worcester to take the position of foreman for Henry W Eddy, the contractor and builder, with whom he has been associated during most of his residence in Worcester One of the early triumphs of building in Worcester was the freight house of the Boston & Maine Railroad the roof of which 65x400 feet, was the largest in the country, built up to that time without supports or pillars Mr Mills had a notable career in the civil war He enlisted in Company C, Thirty-sixth Regiment, a company raised by P Emory Aldrich, later justice of the superior court, within six days from the beginning, until one hundred and ten men were secured A A Goodell was the captain He served from August 8, 1862, until June 8, 1865 He was in the first battle of Fredericksburg The story of his service is that of his regiment, until he was taken prisoner From Virginia the regiment went to Jamestown, Kentucky, and thence to Vicksburg, Mississippi The next move was to Jackson, whence they returned to Kentucky They served at Campello Station and at the siege of Knoxville, at Blaine's Crossroads, in East Tennessee, and at Strawberry Plain in the same section In 1864 the regiment left Tennessee, in April, and in May took part in the battle of the Wilderness, and Spottsylvania Court House, where they suffered heavy losses May 21, they marched to North Anna river, continually skirmishing At Cold Harbor, Mr Mills was made first corporal of the company for his services in taking a line of rifle pits from the enemy The march from this point to White House Landing, was made in forty-eight successive hours, a distance of sixty miles The regiment arrived at Harrison Landing June 15, 1864 The regiment made a gallant record at Petersburg, taking two forts, four stands of colors and five hundred and sixteen prisoners, and then settled down to besiege Petersburg Mr Mills was taken prisoner at Dr Basan's house, and taken to the prison first in Petersburg, then to Libby prison, in Richmond, where he was kept from October 5 to 9, when he was taken to the parole camp and detained until May, 1865 Although he was mustered out at Alexandria Virginia, June 8, the regiment proceeded to Readville Massachusetts, to be paid off and discharged, and he was the last to do guard duty, being detailed to guard the arms to be turned over to the United States government there He is a member of George H Ward Post 10, Grand Army of the Republic, of Worcester In politics he is a Republican He is a member of the Methodist Episcopal church He married Mary Jane Prescott, daughter of Harvey and Mary (Stuart) Prescott, of West Boylston, Massachusetts They were married at Clinton Massachusetts, February 14 1857 Mrs Mills numbers among her ancestors Colonel Jonathan Prescott of revolutionary fame In the Grover family her great-grandfather, also, was a soldier in the revolution

Children of George Horace and Mary Jane (Prescott) Mills were 1 George Lyman, born December 15 1857, married Emma Viola Ryan, no children 2 Arthur Goodell, born January 23, 1863, was a member of the city guards served through the Spanish war in Company A, Second Massachusetts Volunteers, married Myrtie Merriam, they have a son, Harold Leroy, born November 29, 1903 3 Harvey Prescott, born August 10, 1867, died October 16, 1899, unmarried 4 Grace Mabel born September 29, 1869, married James Henry Burke of Prince Edwards Island November 23, 1903 they have one daughter, Ada Mills Burke, born October 1 1904, he is an expert solderer for the Hamblen & Russell Manufacturing Company Worcester 5 John Stuart, born October 17, 1878 died January 18, 1892

BANCROFT FAMILY John Bancroft (1), was the pioneer ancestor of the Bancroft families, of Auburn and Worcester He was the progenitor of Bertram A Bancroft, of Worcester John and his wife, Jane Bancroft came to New England on the ship "James" sailing from London in 1632 They settled at Lynn where John died in 1637 In 1638 the widow received a grant of land in Lynn Her son, John, went to Connecticut early, and is the founder of the Connecticut branch of the family There is a family tradition that she went to live with him, and died in Connecticut Children of John and Jane Bancroft, all born in England, were Amos, John, settled in Connecticut, Thomas (see forward), Samuel, and probably William

(II) Thomas Bancroft, son of John Bancroft (1), was born in England in 1622 He became a townsman of Dedham in 1648 In 1653 or earlier he removed to Reading, Massachusetts, and settled there He had land at Lynnfield and lived there for a time, and perhaps in West Reading He married (first) March 31, 1647, Alice Bacon, daughter of Michael Bacon, of Dedham She died March 29, 1648 He married (second) July 15, 1648, Elizabeth Metcalf, daughter of Michael and Sarah Metcalf She was admitted to the Dedham church December 14, 1651, and dismissed to the Reading church November 22, 1669 He was in the service with the rank of lieutenant He died at Lynn, August 19, 1691 His widow died May 1, 1711 Children of Thomas Bancroft were Thomas, born and died in 1648, Thomas (see forward), Elizabeth, born 1653, married Joseph Brown, John, born 1658, Sarah, born 1660 died 1661, Raham, born 1662, died 1683, Sarah, born 1665 married John Woodward, Ebenezer, 1667, Mary, 1670

(III) Deacon Thomas Bancroft, son of Lieutenant Thomas Bancroft (2), born in Dedham, Massachusetts, in 1649, married in 1673, Sarah Poole He was an officer in King Philip's war, and was selectman of Reading for several years He built the fourth house in the west parish, near the Abraham Temple house, generally known as the ancient Bancroft homestead Children of Deacon Thomas and Sarah (Poole) Bancroft, all born in Reading, Massachusetts, were Thomas, born in 1673, Jonathan, born and died 1675, Sarah, born 1676, married Abraham Bryant (2), of Reading and Sudbury, Massachusetts, Mehitable, born 1678, married ——— Parker, Jonathan, born 1681, married Sarah ——, Raham or Rayham (see forward) Judith, born 1688, married —— Parker, Samuel, born 1691, died 1692, Samuel, born 1693, Elizabeth born 1698, married, 1713, John Lampson

(IV) Deacon Rayham Bancroft, sixth child of Deacon Thomas Bancroft (3), born in Reading, Massachusetts, in 1684, married (first) Abigail Eaton, of a prominent Reading family, daughter of Jonas and Hannah (Mason) Eaton She died 1728, aged forty years He married (second), 1730, Ruth Kendall, daughter of Samuel and Mary Kendall She died 1758 aged fifty-six years He died 1758, aged seventy-four years Rev Mr Hobby called him "That good man, my friend Deacon Bancroft" Children of Deacon Rayham and Abigail (Eaton) Bancroft were Joshua, born 1712, Abigail born 1716, David (see forward), James, born 1729, died young, Ruth, born 1731, Abigail, born 1733, died 1750, Judith, born 1735, James, born 1739, married (first), 1757, Sarah Pearson, (second) Sarah Parker, revolutionary soldier, selectman representative to general court, died 1831, aged ninety-two years

(V) David Bancroft, third child of Deacon Rayham Bancroft (4), born in Reading Massachusetts, August 2, 1718, removed to Worcester and settled in the southern part of the town in what was later Ward, now Auburn, Massachusetts The births of his children are recorded in Worcester, except the eldest Eunice He came to Worcester about 1742 His first wife was Eunice She died October 15, 1777, aged fifty-nine years, and is buried in Auburn He married (second) Ruth Stone, widow, at Ward, October 14, 1779 She died August 2, 1809, aged ninety-four years David died at Auburn, April 16, 1782, aged sixty-three years His will dated December 15, 1781, and allowed May 6, 1782, mentioned land at Auburn (Ward) and Winchendon, church, pew, books, etc His grave at Auburn is marked by a stone suitably inscribed Children of David and Eunice Bancroft were Eunice, born, probably at Reading, 1742, David, born at Worcester May 6, 1743, Jonas, October 26, 1744, John, December 10, 1745-6, Ebenezer, September 19, 1748, Jonathan, May 25, 1750, Mary, May 4, 1752, Ruth, March 24, 1754, Hannah, March 1, 1756, Nathaniel, March 18, 1758, Timothy, December 1, 1760 (see forward)

(VI) Timothy Bancroft, youngest child and son of David Bancroft (5), born in that part of Worcester, now Auburn, December 1, 1760, married Mary Rice, June 13, 1782, died March, 1834, aged seventy-three years He was a farmer and settled in Auburn, where all the children were born Children were Comfort (daughter), born January 11, 1786, married —— Chapin and had children Lucy, Mary, Elizabeth, Benjamin, Peter, died October 26, 1786, Peter M, Timothy Rice, May 19, 1794, died March 21, 1795, Harvey, November 11, 1796, inherited the homestead in Auburn, Timothy, Jr, May 26, 1798 (see forward), Rominah, July 24, 1801 Mary, widow of Timothy, died October 10, 1844 aged eighty-four years

(VII) Timothy Bancroft, Jr, son of Timothy Bancroft (6), born in Auburn, Massachusetts, May 26, 1798, married Mary Clark, June 6, 1820, at Auburn, and settled there on a farm Their children, born in Auburn, were Mary Smith, born June 3, 1821, died January 3, 1823, Samuel Clark, December 9, 1822, died December 21, 1838, Mary S, married ——— Elliott, Almira Salina, April 16, 1826, married ——— Burrill, Laura, March 25, 1828, died February 19 1846, Nelson T, June 14, 1830, Malissa, April 23, 1832, married —— Walker, Erastus, July 16, 1834, Eliza J, married —— Pond, Martha J, married J Lovelin, Enoch (see forward), Roswell S Nine of the children were named in the will Timothy Bancroft was evidently a man of property and education He bequeathed a desk, books and bookcases to his son Enoch, the residuary legatee

(VIII) Enoch Bancroft, son of Timothy Bancroft, Jr (7), was born in Auburn, Massachusetts His father left him his farm and all his real estate in Auburn land bought of George W Rugg, wood lot in Leicester, wood lots in Shrewsbury, his desk, Bible, books bookcases family effects and heirlooms, and he had to pay some $4 500 in cash bequests to the other heirs He sold the farm in Auburn and bought one on Lincoln street in Worcester, where he died in 1875 in the prime of life He married Mary Prime His children were W E A P, Bertram A (see forward), two who died young, Mary L, married A L Haven, of Worcester

(IX) Bertram A Bancroft, son of Enoch Bancroft (8), born in Worcester, Massachusetts, January 15 1867 His father died when he was a young boy He attended the Worcester schools and has always lived in his native city The growth of the city has brought the Bancroft farm within the suburbs, and recently it has been placed on the market in building lots, under the title of the Bancroft Investment Company Since he discontinued running the farm, he has been in the teaming business and is a successful business man His integrity and many attractive qualities have made for him a host of friends He stands as well socially as in the business world He married Susan A (Mason) Rice, widow of William Rice, of Holden, born in West Boylston, Massachusetts, November 12, 1858, and had one child by her first marriage, Andrew Jackson Rice, born May 8, 1881

Mrs Bancroft is the daughter of William H and Mary (Howe) Mason William H Mason was born March 3, 1833 Mary S Howe was born January 11, 1838, and died January 11, 1905 They had eight children, of whom six are living (1905) Mrs Bancroft s great-grandfather was Samuel Mason, and his wife, her great-grandmother, was Hannah Whitney, daughter of William Whitney, said to be the first settler in what is now the town of West Boylston, Massachuestts He was a descendant of John Whitney, of Watertown, the emigrant (See Whitney family) Their son, William Mason, married Relief Henry, and they had Hannah, Esther, Samuel, Sarah A, Mary A, William, H, (see forward) Children of William H and Mary S (Howe) Mason were Susan, born November 12, 1858, D Waldo, October 27, 1860, Julia L, 1862, married William E Bancroft, of Worcester, farmer and milk dealer, Willie H, born 1864, Mary E, born 1866, Lucy E, born 1868, died July 29, 1903, Samuel F, born 1873, George G, born 1875

The only child of Bertram E and Susan A (Mason) Bancroft is Ralph Enoch Bancroft, born at Worcester, November 11, 1893, student in the public schools of Worcester He is the fourth generation of Bancrofts who have lived in this home Mr Bancroft s home is on the old homestead, 334 Lincoln street, Worcester

Samuel Mason, born in Lexington, Massachusetts, great-grandfather of Mrs Bancroft, mentioned above, was in Captain Solomon Stuart's company, Colonel Josiah Whitney's regiment, in 1777, and marched on the Bennington call

DR FELIX D FONTAINE has practiced in Worcester, largely among the French speaking citizens, for nearly thirty years He was born in St Hugues, Quebec, Canada, December 14 1832 He comes from early French stock that came from old France to New France early in the eighteenth century His great-grandfather Fontaine, who lived to the remarkable age of one hundred and thirteen years, settled at Vercheres, near Montreal, and his grandfather Felix, for whom he was named, was born there and died there at the age of ninety years, nine months, about 1855 His father, Louis Fontaine, was also born at Vercheres, but settled at St Hugues

Felix D Fontaine spent his boyhood on his father's farm and attended the parish schools of his native place In 1846 he was sent to the college at St Hyacinthe, and here he took the seven year course, graduating with the degree of A B, in 1853 He then took up the study of medicine at Montreal in what was then known as the Medical School of Canada, now Victoria University Medical School He received his degree of M D from the Ontario University He had hospital practice in Montreal He began the practice of medicine at St Jude, near St Hyacinthe, where he remained until 1860 March, 1860, he settled at St Barnaby Yamachiche near Three Rivers, Quebec, where he was engaged in general practice for sixteen years In 1876 he removed to Nicolet, Quebec, but after eighteen months there removed to Worcester, where he has practiced ever since He came to Worcester, October 15, 1877, and opened an office in Primeau s drug store, 54 Front street Four years later he moved his office to Salem square, and finally in July, 1885, to 16 Portland street, having purchased the property there Excepting Dr Napoleon Jacques he was the first French physician to build up a practice in Worcester, and, excepting Dr Jacques, is the oldest practicing physician among the French speaking population in and about Worcester He is a member of the Massachusetts Medical Society, of Union St Jean Baptiste d Amerique, and of St Joseph's Union of Worcester In politics he is a Democrat He is a member of Notre Dame Roman Catholic Church

He married (first) May 23, 1860, Emma Regnault of St Pierre, Canada She was born in France She had seven children, only one of whom survived She died October 20, 1867 He married (second) May 24, 1874, Mary Cresse, of Nicolet, who bore him children, all but one of whom are living She died in Worcester, October 10, 1898 Among his children were Albert, born at St Barnaby, Canada, 1867, Joseph Didyme Steven, born at St Barnaby, June 4, 1875, Marie Flora Albertine, born at St Barnaby, May 4, 1876, Marie Laura Camelia, born at Nicolet, Canada, July 21, 1877, Marie Ida, born August 8, 1879, in Worcester, Marie Hortense Eva, born in Worcester, October 18, 1881, Marie Rose Eveline, born March, 1883, Joseph Arthur Steven, born in Worcester, May 25, 1884, Joseph Robert Emil, born in Worcester, September 2, 1886, Joseph Dona Rudolph, born in Worcester, December 11, 1887, Marie Blanche Rebecca Alexandrine, born April 7, 1890, Joseph Arthur Henry, born in Worcester, November 11, 1891, Joseph Philip Auguste, born in Worcester, January 15, 1893, Joseph Anatole Oscar, born April 11, 1895, died December 23, 1895 Six of the elder children died in infancy or in early life

CHARLES A HOMER Homer is an old Saxon surname, derived it is said from the Manor Homere, now called Hummer, in Somerset county England The earliest records containing the surname in England are the Inquisitiones Post Mortem in the reign of Richard II, 1381-2 In these ancient books the name is spelled invariably Homere and it occurs repeatedly The old Manor House in Somerset is gone, it was built of wood, and was very ancient when it was torn down

The first nobleman of the name was Thomas de Homere, Lord of the Manor of Homere, to whom lands in the neighboring county of Dorset were granted in 1338 by Lord Maltravers A family tradition holds that the Homer family in Staffordshire left this manor in Dorset on account of a duel, in which presumably his adversary got the worst of the encounter, and settled at Ettingshall, where the family has been located since the fourteenth century The old Manor Hall at Ettingshall was taken down in 1868, it dated back to Elizabethan times A pew is still preserved that was built in the church attended by the Homers of Ettingshall in 1626, built as the inscription states by Edward Homer The church is in the parish of Sedgley The name appears first in the Sedgley parish register in 1560, but some of the family removed to Worcester, England, in 1552 The records at Ettingshall give Richard Homer, married October, 1565, Margaret Wright, and was buried in 1606 at Ettingshall He was probably grandfather of the following Edward Homer, from whom the line is traced with apparent correctness to the Worcester (England) family

(I) Edward Homer progenitor of Charles A Homer, of Worcester, Massachusetts, lived at Ettingshall, England He married, July 8, 1628, Eliza-

Félix D. Fontaine M.D.

beth Wilkes He was buried December 19, 1681, under the name of "Old Edward Homer" of Ettingshall His wife Elizabeth was buried February 22, 1685 Their children were Edward, baptized November 5, 1634, see forward, Thomas, baptized June 15, 1637, buried July 2, 1637, Simon, baptized March 10, 1639, Richard, baptized January 23, 1642

(II) Edward Homer, son of the preceding Edward Homer (1), and probably great-grandson of Richard, named above, was born in Ettingshall and baptized there July 8, 1628 He married, July 16 1656, Anne Gibbins She was buried May 12, 1675, and he married (second) Jane—— His children born at Ettingshall were Joseph, died young, buried February 9, 1660, Anne, baptized January 7, 1661, Edward, baptized November 8, 1664, probably died young, Captain John, baptized March 20, 1665, see forward, Edward, baptized February 9, 1668, Mary, buried July 25, 1672, Francis, baptized September 11, 1673, Rebecca, Benjamin, baptized November 23, 1682, married Mary Palmer

(III) Captain John Homer, the immigrant, son of the preceding Edward Homer (2), was baptized at Ettingshall, England, March 20, 1665 He appears to have resigned his rights to the succession to a younger brother and was perhaps well paid for doing so, as he was owner of the vessel of which he was the captain He came to New England to live about 1690 He settled at Yarmouth, though he lived in Boston for a time He married, July 13, 1693, Margery Stevens He died November 1, 1717, aged fifty-two years She died at Yarmouth, 1762, aged ninety-six or ninety-eight years The children of Captain John and Margery (Stevens) Homer were John, born August 8, 1694, administrator of his father's estate, Mary, born 1696, died young, Benjamin, born May 8, 1698; see forward, William, born June 29, 1701, Michael, born September 26, 1703, Robert, born May 29, 1706, merchant in Honduras, Central America, sent his sons to Boston to be educated, sold out his goods and started with part of his gold on one ship while his wife took the rest of it by another, but both were lost, probably victims of pirates, Thomas, born 1707, Mary, born 1708

(IV) Benjamin Homer, son of Captain John Homer (3), was born in Boston, Massachusetts, May 8, 1698 He removed to Yarmouth and built a house, which is or was lately standing He died at Yarmouth, October 24, 1776, aged seventy-eight years He married Elizabeth Crowe or Crowell, daughter of John and Bethia (Sears) Crowell and granddaughter of John Crowell, one the three original grantees of Yarmouth Massachusetts Benjamin Homer was a prominent citizen, a magistrate and deputy to the general court The children of Benjamin and Elizabeth (Crowell) Homer were Bethia, born March 18, 1722, married Benjamin Cobbs, of Boston, John, born September 28, 1724 married September 28, 1749, Abigail Osborn, of Nantucket, removed to Boston and became a ship owner and merchant, was one of the fifteen who organized the famous patriotic society—the Sons of Liberty—but later when the break came he remained loyal to England, and removed to Nova Scotia, where his descendants have been prominent, Margery, born June 13, 1727, married, January 3, 1765, William Sears, of Harwich, William, born July 14, 1729, was a loyalist, removed to Barrington, Nova Scotia, and died on a voyage from Barbadoes to Boston, Benjamin, born August 5, 1731, removed to Boston, Stephen, born April 15, 1734, married Elizabeth Chapman, of Yarmouth, Thomas, see forward, Elizabeth, born November 18, 1738, married David Knowles, of Eastham, Robert, born January 28, 1742, married (first) Jerusha Sears, married (second) widow of John Thatcher

(V) Thomas Homer, seventh child of Benjamin Homer (4), was born in Yarmouth, Massachusetts, March 21, 1736 He settled there and probably his children were born there He married, November 21, 1765, Elizabeth Sears One record states that he went to Vermont, but a deed in the Worcester county records shows that Thomas Homer, of Barnstable, bought a homestead at Rutland, Massachusetts, of William Caldwell, of Rutland, July 20, 1789 The land was south side of John Rice's meadow and there were other lots besides the home lot He lived in Rutland about twenty years, and several generations have lived on the old homestead since his death He died at Rutland, November 21, 1812, aged seventy-six years His widow Elizabeth died August 19 or 20, 1819, aged seventy-two years She was a lineal descendant of Richard Sears (See the Sears family sketch in this work) The will of Thomas Homer was made October 17, 1807, and filed November 24, 1812 It names the six children as given below and wife Elizabeth He left the real estate to his three sons, Thomas, Benjamin and William Thomas settled in Virgil, Cortland county, New York, Benjamin in Spofford, Onondaga county, and their shares in the property were purchased by William, who remained on the old homestead in Rutland, for one hundred and forty dollars The deed is dated September 9, 1813 The children of Thomas and Elizabeth (Sears) Homer were Mary, married —— Stewart, Bethiah, married Almond Coleman, Desire, married —— Smith and had a son Francis, mentioned in the will of Thomas Homer, Sr, Thomas, married Lydia Glazier, of New Braintree, in 1800 and they had Edmund, born May 9, 1801, Benjamin, born March 8, 1804, Thomas Stacy, born July 1, 1802, and probably others after he removed to Virgil, Courtland county, New York, Benjamin, settled in Spofford, Onandaga county, New York, William, see forward

(VI) William Homer, son of Thomas Homer (5), was born in Barnstable, in 1784, and came to Rutland when very young He died at Rutland, March 3, 1841, aged fifty-seven years He married Experience Reed, October 24, 1813 They had eleven children born in Rutland, viz Lyman Homer, see forward, Cyrus, born December 2, 1816, married in 1849, Julia K Lackey, he died July 24, 1881, Samuel Read, born July 22, 1818, died May 26, 1852, William Sears, born September 16, 1820, died September 5 or 6, 1847, Elizabeth, born January 16, 1822, married in 1842, Amos Hosmer, of Sterling, she died July 2, 1905, George Washington, born January 16, 1824, married Elsie Holden Rogers, April, 1863, died May 10, 1899, Sophronia Relief, born March 11, 1826, married William Green, of Hubbardston, April 13, 1847, Amasa Craft, born July 30, 1828, married Myra Holden, of Rutland, and died February 4, 1906, Mary, born December 9, 1830, died October 14, 1901, she married Addison Green of Hubbardston, Eunice Phylinda, born September 20, 1833, died December 21, 1893, she married Theodore Cook, of Leominster, Sarah Eveline, born March 24, 1838, died May 9 1897, she married Henry Cook, of Leominster, Massachusetts

(VII) Lyman Homer, eldest child of William Homer (6), was born in Rutland, Massachusetts, March 13, 1814, and died in Worcester, August 6, 1879, aged sixty-five years He married Adeline Russell, April 29, 1840, at Rutland The children of Lyman and Adeline (Russell) Homer were Agnes M, and Charles A, see forward

(VIII) Charles A Homer, only son of Lyman Homer (7), of Rutland, was born in Rutland He went to school in Rutland and Syracuse, New York, and attended Wilbraham Academy After leaving school he went to work in the store of Walter E Forbes & Co, dealers in fancy goods, 204 Main street, Worcester He learned the business thoroughly and remained with this concern about eight years He formed the firm of Homer & Freeman, which purchased the business of Rufus L Smith, dealer in fancy goods, at 180 Main street, Worcester After three years the partnership was dissolved Since 1889 he has been connected with the John C MacInnes Company department store, first as one of the heads of departments and since the incorporation as a director and secretary of the company Since his connection with this business it has become one of the largest and most prosperous stores of the kind in this section The business was established by Mr MacInnes in 1873 at 462 Main street The company was formed in 1892 with the same officers that are in charge at present John C MacInnes, president and treasurer, Albert A Spaulding, vice-president, Charles A Homer, secretary, Alexander J Moir and the other officers and directors The store has been enlarged by adding new departments and more room until at present they have an entire four story building at 462 Main street with a large frontage, opposite the City Hall, and the Gorman block on the north and the Buttrick and Whipple building on the south are used by the company Mr Homer has paid especial attention to the gloves, hosiery and underwear departments In addition to his other duties he is assistant treasurer of the corporation Mr Homer has always devoted himself to business and especially for the past twenty years He enjoys travel and has made a number trips across the continent, spending several winters in California In politics he is a Republican He is a member of the First Universalist parish He is a member of the Worcester Board of Trade, the Worcester County Mechanics' Association the Worcester Antiquarian Society, the Worcester Grange, the Quinsigamond Lodge and Wachusett Encampment of Odd Fellows He has recently built a residence on Richmond Heights

Mr Homer married, May 30, 1886, Susie H Ham, of San Francisco, California, daughter of Israel Hayes Ham, descendant of the the Ham family of Dover, New Hampshire, a sketch of which has been written for this work They have one child Adeline Grace, born in Worcester, September 19, 1889, a student in the Classical high school, Worcester, class of 1907

ALEXANDER MAXWELL David Maxwell (1), the immigrant ancestor of Alexander Maxwell, of Worcester and of the Maxwell families of Wells, Maine, Industry, Maine, and other towns in that vicinity, is said to have come from Scotland and settled about 1690 at Wenham, Massachusetts He drew land there in 1705, but little is known of him One of his daughters married Luke Morgan and resided in New Gloucester Another married a Mr Pulsifer and settled in Poland, Maine One son settled in Nantucket and another in New Jersey

Another branch of the family descended from Hugh Maxwell a Scotch-Irish settler in western Massachusetts and has many distinguished men among its numbers Another well known family in New Jersey is possibly related to the Wenham settler John Maxwell son of John, settled in Greenwich Sussex county, New Jersey, when a young man He was born in county Tyrone, Ireland, of Scotch parents, in 1701, and died in Greenwich, August 19, 1786 He was a descendant of Thomas Maxwell, who at the capitulation of Limerick, Ireland, 1601, settled in Tyrone

(II) Gershom Maxwell, son of David Maxwell (1), was born at Wenham in 1696 He was baptized March 13, 1720, on profession of faith at Wells, Maine, where he settled, and with eight others of his family was received in full communion January 10, 1742, during a great revival season His children were Abigail, born March, 1720, died unmarried, John, born March, 1722, baptized March 18, 1722, David, born June 24, 1724, of whom later, Miriam, born March, 1729, baptized March 2, 1729, married Abel Gatchell, Barak, born January, 1732, baptized April 9, 1732, Susanna, born March, 1734, baptized March 2, 1734, married —— Littlefield, Martha, born April, 1736, baptized April 18, 1736, married Benjamin Brown, Gershom born March, 1740, baptized March 30, 1740

(III) David Maxwell, third child of Gershom Maxwell (2), was born in Wells, Maine, June, 1724, and baptized there June 17, 1724 He married Abigail Morrison and settled in Wells, where their children were born, viz Daniel, born May, 1747, died young, Alexander, December 5, 1748, David, December, 1750, married Abigail Gilkey, no children (David Maxwell was a settler in Industry, Maine, October 1, 1802, on Lot No 3, a near neighbor of James Thompson), Abigail December, 1750, twin of David, married James Rankin, Mary, November, 1753, married Theodore Rounds, and resided at Shapleigh, Maine, Sarah, November 1757, married Elisha Littlefield, Susannah, December, 1760, married Nathaniel Edwards, Eleanor, August 17, 1762, married Joseph Maxwell, son of Barak Maxwell (III), resided in Gorham, Maine, Gershom, of whom later, Benjamin, March, 1766, married —— Weed, Martha, June, 1768 married Nathaniel Kimball, and lived in Kennebunk, Maine

(IV) Gershom Maxwell, ninth child of David Maxwell (3), was born in Wells, Maine, August, 1764 He settled in Industry, Maine, where his children were born He married Eunice Sawyer Their children Gershom, of whom later, David, Alexander, Mary

(V) Gershom Maxwell, son of Gershom Maxwell (4), was born in Industry, Maine, about 1790 He married Sally Taylor, who was born in Stark, Maine He was a farmer at Industry Among their children was Roswell, the father of Alexander Maxwell, of Worcester

(VI) Roswell Maxwell, son of Gershom Maxwell (5), was born about 1810 at Industry, Maine He was a farmer at Industry He married Sally Fish He lived most of his life in Industry, but late in life removed to Mercer, where he died Their children Rosina, married Philip Welsh, and resided at New Portland, Maine, Lydia, married Seth Fletcher, and resided at Skowhegan, Maine, Howard, married Euphrata Merrow, and resided in Lewiston Maine, Alexander married Mary R Curtis, of whom later, Sarah, married Samuel Blethen, and resided at Madison, Maine, Hannah, married Marcellus Ward, and resided at Madison, Maine, Lorenzo, married, resides in St Paul, Minnesota

(VII) Alexander Maxwell, fourth child of Roswell Maxwell (6), was born in Industry, Maine, August 22, 1838 He received a common school education there He learned the butcher's trade and when a young man went into business for himself, having a slaughter house at Mercer, Maine He bought cattle and shipped beef to Boston markets He conducted a successful business until he retired in 1891 He removed to Worcester in September 1891, in order to live nearer his son who was located in that city He has invested extensively in real estate in that city, and is occupied in the care of his tenements He resided several years at 9 Elizabeth street, for the last eleven years he has lived at 55 Orchard street Mr Maxwell is a member of no fraternal or religious organizations

He married, August 27, 1865, Margaret Curtis She was born in Mercer, Maine, the daughter of Stephen and Elmira (Works) Curtis Her father was born December 5 1800, and died August 12, 1882 Her mother was born December 6, 1806, and died July 22, 1865, she was the daughter of Joel and Hannah (Partridge) Works, whose children were Selden, Joel, Almon, Elmira, mentioned above, Sabra

The children of Stephen and Elmira (Works) Curtis were Mary, born at Mercer, 1829, died 1841 Sabra, born at Mercer May 20, 1833, died December 23, 1881, at Mercer, Margaret, mentioned above, married Alexander Maxwell The father of Stephen Curtis was John Curtis, who came from an old Massachusetts family of this name, removing from Bradford, Massachusetts, to Mercer when a young man His wife was Margaret Robinson Their children were Eliza Betsey, Sally, Reuben, Margaret, John, Stephen Curtis mentioned above Both John Curtis and his wife lived to the advanced age of ninety-two years

The two children of Alexander and Margaret (Curtis) Maxwell are Arthur Leroy, born July 14, 1867, of whom later, and Mabel Vester, born January 6, 1875 died at the age of two years and a half Mrs Maxwell was a member of the Congregational church at Mercer Maine, but has not joined any church since removing to Worcester

(VIII) Arthur Leroy Maxwell, only living child of Alexander Maxwell (7), was born in Mercer, Maine, July 14, 1867 He was educated in the public schools of his native town When twenty-one years old he came to Worcester and went to work for the G Henry Whitcomb Envelope Company, where he remained for nine years Since February, 1899, he has been with the Sherman Envelope Company, one of the office staff He is a Republican He resides at 55 Orchard street in the same house with his parents

He married Cora (Dakin) Vaughn, a widow, who has a daughter by her first marriage Florence B Vaughn born July 2, 1882 The child of Arthur and Cora Maxwell is Arthur Leroy, Jr, born February 3, 1892

THE CUTHBERTSON FAMILY from which Mrs Jane (Cuthbertson) Pike, of Worcester, descends is of Scotch origin Her father, Alexander Cuthbertson, lived in Glasgow, Scotland He married Annie Robertson of Glasgow She had a brother James and a sister Agnes (Robertson) Davison, who died in Lawrence Massachusetts The Cuthbertsons came to America in 1848 and settled first in Phenix, Rhode Island, later in Farnhamville Massachusetts, and later in Holden, where the mother died March 14, 1885, and the father died March 1 1887, in Worcester, where he had made his home with Mrs Pike after the death of his wife

The children of Alexander and Anne Cuthbertson were Jane, born in Glasgow, Scotland, November 12 1841, see forward, Alexander born 1843, in Johnston, Scotland, see forward Jeanette, born at Glasgow, Scotland 1846, Edward born at Jackson, Rhode Island died June 1905, Mary Ann, born at Burrillville Rhode Island, died June, 1902, Elizabeth born at Worcester, see forward

(II) Jane Cuthbertson, born in Glasgow, Scotland November 12, 1841 She came to America in 1848 with her parents and was educated in the public schools here She married Cyril Pike, of Worcester, who was a well known grocer and provision dealer of that city whose place of business for many years was at 33 Liberty street He was a very successful business man and was in every respect self-made and highly respected He was born in St Hyacinthe, Canada, and died in Worcester, March 14 1890 He was a Baptist in religion and a Democrat in politics He was for some years a member of the Worcester Democratic city committee Mrs Pike is an active member of the home and foreign missionary societies of the Lincoln Square Baptist Church, to which she belongs and of which she is a generous supporter She was for ten years previously a member of the Church of Christ, Worcester She resides at 5 Carroll street

(II) Alexander Cuthbertson, Jr, son of Alexander Cuthbertson (1), was born in Johnston Scotland, 1843 and died January 6 1906 He came to America with his parents when a young boy and was educated here He married Addie Thompson and their children are Lola M bookkeeper, Effie Maud, born at Fitchburg, graduate of the public and high schools there and of the Worcester Normal School, now teaching in Fitchburg, Jeanette, married Andrew Keogh, of Holden and their children are James Alexander Keogh, salesman, married Edith Eames Mary Jane Keogh, married Augustus Ferrier, salesman Charlotte, married Randall M Whitney commercial traveler Jennie Keogh, deceased

(II) Mary Ann Cuthbertson, daughter of Alexander Cuthbertson (1), was born in Burrillville, Rhode Island, about 1850 She married John Crawshaw and their children were Lillie Maud born at Holden, married Russell Foote November 29, 1904, and have one child Veara Maud, John Edward, born in Worcester, April 19 1880, graduate of the Worcester high school attended Colby College, Maine, graduated at Worcester Polytechnic Institute in 1902, making a specialty of chemistry, now with the Dupont Powder Company in its great eastern laboratory New Jersey Cyril Pike born July 16 1889, graduate of the Classical high school, Worcester, 1906

(II) Elizabeth Cuthbertson, daughter of Alexander Cuthbertson (1), was born in Worcester and died there March 28, 1901 Was bookkeeper for Cyril Pike She was an active member of Lincoln Square Baptist Church and teacher in the Sunday school

PUTNAM FAMILY In the history of the early settlement of Sutton are found the names of seven persons by the name of Putnam, whose immediate relationship cannot be traced but it is confidently believed that they are descended from John Putnam who came from Buckinghamshire, England in 1634 and settled in Salem He was admitted as a freeman in 1647 and died in 1663 Three sons came with him—Thomas Nathaniel, and John Hence in tracing the genealogy of this family John Putnam is taken as the ancestor of the family in America

(II) Thomas Putnam son of John (1) was admitted as a freeman in 1642 and to the church in Salem in 1643 In August of the same year he married Prudence Holyoke from Tamworth, England the daughter of Edward Holyoke who settled in Lynn in 1630 Their children were three sons and five daughters The names of the sons only can be traced—Thomas Joseph and Edward

(III) Thomas Putnam, eldest son of Thomas (2),

married Ann Carr, September 25, 1678. They had one son and four daughters, whose names are not given in the records.

(III) Edward Putnam, youngest son of Thomas (2), married Mary Hale in 1681. Their children were: Edward, born 1682; Holyoke, 1683, killed by the Indians; Elisha, 1685, settled in Sutton; Joseph, 1687; Nehemiah, 1694; Ezra, 1696; Isaac, 1698, settled in Sutton.

(IV) Edward Putnam, eldest son of Edward (3), was married, and his children were: Holyoke, born 1705, settled in Sutton; Edward, 1711, died February, 1800; Miles, 1725.

(V) Holyoke Putnam, eldest son of Edward (4), first married Eunice ——, and (second) Esther Lovell, in 1742. Their children were: Sarah, born 1735, married E. Bateman; Ebenezer, 1738, married Hannah Dike, January, 1766; Hannah, 1741; Martha, 1743; Eunice, 1745; Susanna, 1747; Joseph, 1749; Ezra, 1751; Thomas, 1754; Mary, 1758.

(VI) Ezra Putnam, eighth child and third son of Holyoke (5), married Rebekah Dike, December, 1780. Their children were: Daniel, born 1781; Charlotte, June, 1783.

(V) Edward Putnam, second son of Edward (4), came to Sutton in 1737 and lived and died where Peter H. Putnam lived later on. He married Ruth Fuller, of Middleton, and their children were: John, born August, 1735, died 1809; Stephen, 1739, died in the French and Indian war; Ruth, June, 1741, married Samuel Rich, Jr., March, 1761; Archelaus, February, 1743, died 1809; Phoebe, November, 1745, married Nathaniel, son of Elisha Rich; Sarah, March, 1747, married Paul, son of Jonathan Sibley, December, 1766; Molly, baptized 1750, married Bartholomew Putnam; David, July, 1752, married Phoebe Woodbury, July, 1776; Caleb, October, 1754, married Judith Sibley; Peter, 1757; Lucy, 1760, married Henry Phelps, Jr., August, 1777; Asa, 1763.

(VI) John Putnam, eldest son of Edward (5), was a captain in the revolutionary war, and a colonel in the militia. He married Mary, daughter of Rev. David Hall, D. D., in 1758. Their children were: Joseph, born 1758, died in the revolution; Stephen, 1761, removed to Vermont; Elizabeth, 1763, married Thomas Eddy, 1784; John, 1766, was a physician; Charles, 1768; Mary, 1771, married Aaron Putnam, 1790; Deborah, 1773, died 1789; Rebekah Hall, baptized 1776, died young; Sarah, 1778, married Rufus Marble, 1798; Joseph Hall, 1780; Rebekah Prescott, 1783, married Solomon Putnam, 1805.

(VII) Charles Putnam, fifth child and fourth son of John (6), married Rhoda Stone, and their children were: Polly, born 1794, married Captain Charles Chase; Sally, 1796; Matilda, 1798; Rhoda, 1801, died same year; Betsy, 1802, married Otis Pratt, 1828; Charles Prescott, 1804, married Mary E. Marble, 1843; Sumner, twins, June 26, 1807.

(VII) Joseph Hall Putnam, tenth child and fifth son of John (6), married Nancy Blandon, in 1805, and (second) Watty Black. Their children were: Brooksey, born 1806; Sullivan, 1808; Sumner, 1809, died 1876; Pearley, 1815; Nancy, 1824, married Joseph Jones, 1846; Emeline, 1828, married Joshua Lackey.

(VIII) Sullivan Putnam, second child of Joseph (7), married Millia R. Draper, and their children were: Alfred, born 1842, married Abbie M. Putnam, 1867; Joseph Hall, February, 1849.

(IX) Joseph Hall Putnam, youngest child of Sullivan (8), married Anna L. Whipple, by whom one child was born—Millia, who died when a mere child.

(VIII) Sumner Putnam, third child of Joseph (7), married Susan Dudley in 1840. Their children: Louisa, born 1846, married F. Everett Burdon, October, 1867, and died August, 1869; Joseph Edward, December 19, 1848, died June 7, 1862.

(VIII) Pearley Putnam, fourth child of Joseph (7), married Julia A. Walker, in 1841, and their children were: Clarence D., born 1846; an infant daughter, born July 22, 1850, died September 13, same year; Mary E. W., August 13, 1860, married Lovell W. Putnam, October 9, 1878.

(VI) Archelaus Putnam, son of Edward (5), married Sarah Putnam, 1765. Their children were: Aaron, born July 13, 1766; Archelaus, August 17, 1768, died February 9, 1854; Sarah, December 26, 1770, married Isaac King, November 27, 1788; Andrew, September 24, 1773; Ruth, March 22, 1776, married Adonijah Bartlett, who died in the army, she then married Abner Putnam, March 13, 1799; Betsy, September 14, 1781, married Captain Cyrus Carpenter.

(VII) Aaron Putnam, eldest child of Archelaus (6), married Mary Putnam, May 18, 1790. Their children were: Polly, born 1790, married Jason Morse, 1812; Caleb, October 18, 1792, unmarried; Charles, December 12, 1794; Willard, March 29, 1798; Rebekah, October 13, 1802, married Samuel Waters; Betsey, August 15, 1804; Jason, September 4, 1807; Palmer, October 10, 1814.

(VII) Archelaus, second of the sons and children of Archelaus (6), married Phoebe Hicks, March 14, 1792. Their children were: Silence, born May 22, 1793; Tyler, November 8, 1795, died September 9, 1849; Julia, May 30, 1798, married John Leland, April, 1821; Nancy, February 17, 1805, married (first) Simon Tenney, February 6, 1828, (second) Dr. David Hall.

(VIII) Tyler Putnam, second son of Archelaus (7), in 1820 married Phoebe Woodbury. Their children were: Mary Ann, born November 17, 1821, married Andrew W. Pierce; Alvan, October 18, 1824; John E., married Nancy A. Merriam, he removed to Big Lake, Minnesota; Julia L., September 3, 1828, died March 26, 1851; Emily Jane, December 9, 1830, married John B. Pratt, of Oxford; Henry Tyler, November 18, 1832, married Caroline P. Newton; Susan F., October 8, 1834, died April 6, 1836.

(IX) Alvan Woodbury Putnam, second child and eldest son of Tyler (8), married Mary Lovell Knight, by whom ten children were born, as follows: Elwin Tyler, April 29, 1849; Edgar Eugene, March 6, 1852; Irving Wilbur, December, 1853; Lovell Woodbury, November, 1856, married Mary E. W. Putnam, October 9, 1878; Milton Knight, May 20, 1859; Jennie Frances, July 14, 1862, died February 8, 1863; Elmer Julius, May 27, 1864; Edward Pratt and Edward Pierce, twins, May 13, 1867, died same day; Emma Carrie, November 14, 1868.

(IV) Elisha Putnam, son of Edward (3), lived on and near the place known as the James Freeland farm. He probably came to Sutton as early as 1725, was admitted to the church in 1730, and chosen a deacon in 1731. He was town clerk for many years, and also town treasurer. His children were: Elisha, born December, 1715, died in 1758; Nehemiah, March 22, 1719, died November 27, 1791; Jonathan, July 19, 1721; Hannah, married Jonathan Dudley, Esq.; Susannah, married (first) Timothy Holton, February 24, 1742, and (second) John Whipple; Mary, June 12, 1725, died April 22, 1736; Stephen, April, 1728; Amos, July 22, 1730, died September 17, 1811; Eunice, July 6, 1732, died at Windham unmarried; Huldah, May 25, 1734, married a Matthews; Rufus, April 7, 1738.

(V) Elisha, eldest son and child of Elisha (4), was a soldier in the French and Indian war, and died at or near Crown Point about 1758. He married, March 3, 1742, ——— ——— Their children were Andrew, born May 2, 1742, married Lucy Park, January 10, 1764, Elisha, December 4, 1745, died May 25, 1784, Antipas, July 24, 1747, Jokton, May 1, 1750, removed to Sutton, Vermont, Luke, October 5, 1755, was a revolutionary soldier, William, January 7, 1758

(VI) Elisha Putnam, second son of Elisha (5), married Abigail Chamberlain, April 2, 1765 Their children were Molly, born February 23, 1766, married Moses Sibley, Vashti, January 28, 1768, married a Wheelock, Hannah and Deborah, twins, January 20, 1770, Deborah, died February 6, 1770, Elisha, August, 1772, married Levina Ellis, Abraham, January 19 1775, died April 14, 1777, Abner, March 28 1777, married a Stearns, Lucy, November 16, 1779 married Oliver Sibley

(VI) Luke Putnam, son of Elisha (5), married Mary Putnam, November 23, 1786, and their only child was Tyler, born September 11, 1791

(V) Nehemiah Putnam, second son of Elisha (4), married Sarah Manning, October 5, 1742 Their children were Aaron, born March 23, 1744, Sarah, March 10 1746, Hannah, July 26, 1748, married Jonathan Willard, November 25, 1773, Rachel, April 17 1750 Susanna, January 19 1752, married John Fuller March 26, 1771, Eunice, December 4, 1753, married Benjamin Shumway, April 4, 1773, Reuben, April 9 1757 Joseph and Benjamin, twins, September 20 1760, Benjamin married Patty Mason

(VI) Aaron Putnam, son of Nehemiah (5), married and his children were Calvin, Franklin, and Luther the last named of whom died young

(VII) Calvin Putnam, eldest son of Aaron (6), married Abigail Davidson, December 3, 1799 Two children were born to them Samuel and Hannah

(VI) Reuben Putnam son of Nehemiah (5), married Elizabeth Mason Their children were Aaron, born August 29, 1781, died February, 1854, Jonas, March 5 1783, Mason December 20, 1784, Manning April 12, 1787, Rufus Austin, November 18 1791 Polycarp (afterward changed to John Milton) February 26, 1794, John O, July 26, 1796

(VI) Joseph Putnam, son of Nehemiah (5), married Tamar Towne and their children were Tamar born July 8, 1786, John Towne, September 24 1787, Daniel, August 30, 1789

(V) Jonathan Putnam, son of Elisha (4), married Mrs Anne (Chase) Stockwell, November 8, 1743 Their children were Adonijah, born October 9 1744 married Mary Wilkins, November, 1766, Mary, December 25, 1755, married Luke Putnam, November 23, 1786, Francis, September 24, 1758, Jonathan Follansbee, May 9, 1763, died October 30, 1858

(VI) Francis Putnam, son of Jonathan (5), married Joanna Leland, December 11 1783 Their children were Nancy born February 8, 1784, married Charles Rich April 9 1800 Phebe February 7, 1786, Silas October 15, 1788, Royal April 16, 1791 married Mary Ann Seaver, Olive, May 27, 1794 Maria, June 28 1796 married Aaron Elliot Prudy February 28, 1799, married Simon L Marble June 16 1822 Pliny February 15, 1801, married Olive Ersy Fanny May 28, 1804

(VII) Silas Putnam son of Francis (6) married Sarah daughter of Captain Levi Ludden a descendant of George Soule one of the Pilgrims who came from England in the "Mayflower" Their children were Syra Leland, born September 18, 1824 Annette Soule April 24 1826, William Pitt, March 10 1828 Walter Tell, August 11, 1829, Rosetta Aseneth, July 24, 1831, Ada Freeman, May 11, 1833

(VI) Jonathan Follansbee Putnam, son of Jonathan (5), married Philana Leland, July 6, 1786 Their children were Jonathan F, born May 6, 1787, Philana, November 1, 1789, married Major Rufus Burdon, ——, born July 11, 1795, died June 13, 1855

(VII) Jonathan Follansbee Putnam, son of Jonathan (6) married Harriet Hall Their children were Denney Sumner, born March 13, 1817, Harriet Ward.

(VII) Jim Putnam, son of Jonathan (6), married Roxana Burdon Their children were Estes, born December 2, 1819, Roxana, July 5, 1821

(VIII) Estes Putnam, son of Jim (7), married Sarah P King in 1840 Their children were Sarah R, married Joseph Bodo, Hannah E, born January 30, 1848, married Artemas Pickering, Albert F, January 19, 1860

(VIII) Sumner Putnam, son of Jim (7), married Laura E Lowe Their children were Sarah Elizabeth, born March 14, 1857, married Frank Walden, James Selah, October 17, 1858, Jennie Josephine, February 24, 1861, George Decatur, November 21, 1862, Hattie Estella, September 5, 1866, John E L B, October 1, 1870, Fred Thurston, October 7, 1872

(V) Stephen Putnam, son of Elisha (4), married Mary Gibbs, March 14, 1755 Their children were Solomon, born July 17, 1755, Mary, June 8, 1757, Rhoda, July 2, 1759 This family moved to Hampshire county

(V) Amos Putnam, son of Elisha (4), married Sarah Swift, June 26, 1700 Their children were Eliphal, born July 8, 1762, died September 25, 1845, Lucretia, September 6, 1764, died January, 1852, Rebekah, February 18, 1767, died December 29, 1854, Paul, March 4, 1769, died 1779, Susannah, died in childhood Elizabeth, October 22, 1772, married Ebenezer Newton, Polly, 1775, died 1851 Martha October 25, 1781 died 1851, Martha, October 25, 1781, married Silas Livermore, died October 3, 1852

(V) Rufus Putnam, son of Elisha (4), married (first) Persis Rice Their children were Elizabeth, born November 19, 1765, Persis, June 6, 1767, Susannah August, 1768, Abigail August 7, 1770, William Rufus, December 12, 1771, Franklin, May 27, 1774, died April, 1776, Edwin, January 19, 1776, Patty, November 25, 1777, Catherine, October 17, 1780, Agnes

(IV) Isaac Putnam, the fourth in line of descent from John Putnam, the American ancestor, settled in Sutton about 1722 on the farm which in later years was owned by Oliver Hall and Robert Luther He was admitted to the church in February, 1730 His name is not found on the records after 1740 He died in the fifty-ninth year of his age No one of his posterity is known to be living in Sutton at the present time Deacon Palmer Marble, Mrs James Freeland and the children of John Waters, deceased, are his great-grand children His children: Phineas, born October 1, 1722, Asaph, September 11, 1724, Ann, July 27 1726, Susannah, August 20 1728, married John Saddler, of Upton January, 1746 Nathan October 24 1730, Edward, February 5, 1733, Isaac, November 4, 1734, Lydia October 20, 1736, Daniel, March 28, 1739, married Ann daughter of Hon Samuel Chase, removed to Corinth, New Hampshire

(V) Phineas Putnam, son of Isaac (4), married and his children were Levi, who settled at Whittingham Vermont, Enoch, Daniel, Betty, Huldah, Eunice

(VI) Daniel Putnam son of Phineas (5), married Phebe Walker, of Upton Their child was Austin, born March 16, 1796

(V) Asaph Putnam, son of Isaac (4), married Sarah Park, in 1743 The church records show that they had the following family Abijah, baptized October 21, 1744, Asaph, baptized June 18, 1749, Jonas, baptized August 16, 1752, Ephraim, baptized July 7, 1756, Park, baptized July 7, 1756

(V) Nathan Putnam, son of Isaac (4), married Betty —— Their children were Zadock, born December 29, 1752, married Abigail Elliot, Micah, April 8, 1754, James, November 26 1755, married Betsey Willard, settled in Grafton, Betty, January 12, 1758, married Lieutenant Stephen Marble November 14 1776, Lydia, December 31 1759, married Stephen Fuller, November 7, 1777, Nathan May 16, 1761, Hannah, March 13 1763, married John Waters, Jr December 15 1790 Abner, March 17 1765 married Abigail Waters, Sally, February 27, 1767, married Jesse Marble, February 26 1790, Tamar, October 23 1768, married John King, Jr, March 17, 1785, Polly April 1, 1770, married Amos Waters, July 4 1791, John September 3, 1771, Oliver, July 9, 1773 married Betsey Newton, December 15, 1796, George W, died without issue, Abigail, married a Mr Rawson

(II) Nathaniel Putnam, son of John (1) married and was the father of five children Samuel, John, Joseph, Nathaniel, Benjamin, born July 11, 1764

(III) Benjamin Putnam, grandson of the ancestor in America, married Sarah Holton, August 25, 1686 They had seven sons and one daughter Among the sons were Tarrant born April 12, 1688, Cornelius, September 3, 1702

(IV) Tarrant Putnam, son of Benjamin (3), married ————, and their children were Tarrant born April 3 1716, Israel, Samuel Gideon

(V) Tarrant Putnam, son of Tarrant (4), married Priscilla Baker, December 9, 1742 Their children were Tarrant, born April 24 1744, died December 7, 1770 Elijah January 23, 1747, graduated at Harvard College in 1766, Elizabeth May 30, 1749 married Abraham Brown, March 2, 1773, Priscilla, August 22, 1751, married Adam Brown, December 3, 1772, Sarah, August 4, 1753, married Timothy Merriam, June 21, 1775, Martha, July 15, 1775, married David Copeland, September 1, 1778, Rebekah, May 5, 1759, married Aaron Marble November 16 1784, Lydia, July 27, 1761, Molly, November 15 1763, Israel May 22, 1767

(VI) Israel Putnam, son of Tarrant (5), married Hannah Woodbury, January 30 1795 She died September, 1795 He married (second) Hannah Le Baron April 24 1796 Their children were Hannah Le Baron, born March 10 1797, married Jabez Hull October 22, 1821, Le Baron, August 19, 1799, Tarrant, May 18, 1801, Mary Le Baron, November 7, 1803 married Dr Leonard Pierce, November 15 1831, Israel December 25 1805, Edwin January 9 1808, Frederick William August 3 1810, Frederick Augustus May 30, 1813, Theodore Elijah, September 12 1815, Caroline Priscilla, August 3 1818 married (first) Dr N C Sibley, November 29 1838

(VII) Le Baron Putnam son of Israel (6) married Ann Braman daughter of Dr Amasa Braman, of Millbury Their children were Henry, born January 3 1824 George Frederick, August 20, 1826 Edward Francis December 28 1828

(VII) Tarrant Putnam son of Israel (6) married Cornelia Titus Van Nortwick of New York, October 4 1828 Their children were William Bruce born July 29 1829, Emma Le Baron, March 27 1831 Caroline Monroe, October 7 1832

(VII) Israel Putnam, son of Israel (6) married Sarah Frost, of Maine He graduated at Brown University, he was a physician and practiced his profession in Wales and afterwards at Bath, Maine. One child was born of this union William Le Baron 1835

(IV) Cornelius Putnam son of Benjamin (3), married Sarah —— She died June 9, 1741 His second marriage was to Elizabeth Perkins, of Salem, November 12, 1741 His children were Sarah, born January 3, 1726, died May 30, 1738, Bertha, December 18, 1728, Cornelius, May 23, 1730, married Elizabeth Perkins, August 1753, Benjamin, May 13, 1732, Nathaniel, May 3, 1734, Tarrant, March 28, 1736, Bartholomew April 19, 1739, died young, David and Sarah (twins), May 31, 1741, Sarah, March 18, 1743 married Captain Archelaus Putnam, October 16, 1765, Bartholomew, April 21, 1745, David May 14 1747, Elizabeth, September 28, 1749, Anna November 21 1754

(V) Nathaniel Putnam, son of Cornelius (4), married Deborah Towne, November 23, 1756 Their children were Moses, born January 23, 1758, Molly, February 25, 1759, married Jennison, January 29, 1778, Hannah, May 11, 1761, married Tarrant Dibley, April 22, 1779, Stephen, January 17, 1764 died July, 1779

(VI) Moses Putnam, son of Nathaniel (5), married Mary Allen, June 24, 1779 Their children were Deborah born June 26, 1780, Polly, September 25, 1781, Stephen, December 24, 1782, Nathaniel, February 13, 1785 Elijah, October 9, 1786, died December 31, 1788, Moses, August 17, 1788, Elijah, July 16 1790, Sally, July 14 1792, married Abraham Howard, April 3, 1811, Stillman January 15 1797, died August 17, 1798, Suky, June 13, 1799, died August 22, 1803

(VII) Stephen Putnam, son of Moses (6), married Mrs Betsey Goddard, June 27, 1810 Their children were Fayette, born March 24, 1811, died August, 1813, Eliza, April 13, 1813, Mary Allen, April 18, 1816, Fayette, July 29, 1819, Marsilla, October 11, 1820, Emila Sarah, July 22 1824

(VII) Stephen Putnam, son of Moses (6), married Charlotte, daughter of Joshua Morse Their children were Susan, November 18, 1805, Stillman, July 13, 1807, Emily R October 5, 1810, died July 13, 1813, Hannah W, March 7, 1820

(V) Bartholomew Putnam, son of Cornelius (4), married (first) Mary Putnam, and (second) Hannah Axtell Their children were Bartholomew, born July 13, 1774, Lucy, July 18, 1779, Edward, January 26, 1782 Prudence, November 13, 1784, married Daniel Hathaway, Phebe, October 10, 1787, married Captain Elijah Bigelow, Lewis, July 15, 1796, Cynthia, August 27, 1804

(VI) Bartholomew, son of Bartholomew (5), married Hannah Tarrant Sibley, September 4, 1801 Their children were Russell, born February 3, 1802, Polly April 4 1804 married Bethel Leonard, August 8, 1826, Clark, February 18, 1806, Prudence, February 19, 1808, Leonard, April 26, 1810, Zilpha, April 8 1812

(VII) Russell Putnam, son of Bartholomew (6), married Adeline ———— Their children were Russell Bartholomew, born April 4, 1825, Lucien July 24, 1827, Silas, July 19, 1830, Leonard, March 27, 1833

(V) David Putnam, son of Cornelius (4), married Elizabeth Woodbury, April 12, 1770 Their children were David, born April 30, 1771 died young Betty April 14 1773 married Aaron Elliot, Abner, May 14 1775, died June 25, 1859, Cyrus, August 21 1777, Jerusha December 13, 1779 married Thomas Bigelow, August 28, 1803, Cornelius, January 28 1782, Sally, July 28 1784 married Samuel Bigelow, December 27, 1806, Lucy, September

8, 1787, married, June 1, 1805, Simeon, son of Deacon Aaron Elliott, Joseph, February 23, 1790

(VI) Abner Putnam, son of David (5), married Amy, daughter of Captain Archelaus Putnam, March 13, 1799 Their children were Ruth, born June 12, 1800, Sally, April 29, 1802, married (first) Darius Putnam (second) Tourtellott Inman, Harvey, November 29, 1804, Anna, November 3, 1806, married Charles H Newton, October 23, 1831, Archelaus, December 3, 1808, Willard, February 7, 1811, Dexter, November 11 1813, married Ruby T Torrey, March 16, 1840, Louisa, October 14, 1816, Lawson, September 18, 1820

(VII) Harvey Putnam, son of Abner (6), married Rebekah Lee, January 7, 1829 Their children were Elias Merriam, born October 7, 1829, Susan Ann November 7, 1830, married Salem J Shaw, February 18, 1851, Ann Janette

(VII) Archelaus Putnam, son of Abner (6), married Laura Nichols Their children were Francis, born February 16, 1833, Gilbert, Willard, Addison, Laura

(VII) Lawson Putnam, son of Abner (6), first married Martha M Inman, March 1, 1847 She died July 11, 1858 He married for his second wife Sarah R S Johnson, February 29, 1860 Their children were Milo Herbert, born December 19, 1849, died May 30, 1853, Wilmet S, September 20, 1852, Arthur L, April 18, 1862, Sarah E, August 7, 1864, Effie R, September 27, 1866, Amasa S, December 5, 1870

(VI) Cyrus Putnam, son of David (5), married Lucinda Hathaway, May 17, 1800 Their children were Salmon, born December 29, 1800, David, February 6, 1803, Prudence, December 20, 1804, died December 28, 1804, Lucinda, October 5, 1806, married Merritt Cook, died January 14, 1845, Horace, February 16, 1809, Mary Reid, October 2, 1811, died January 15, 1812, Philander and Leander (twins), March 10, 1815

(VII) Salmon Putnam, son of Cyrus (6), married Tryphena Bigelow, February 24, 1824 Their children were Henry, Otis E, Samuel, Mary Lucinda, Persis Jane

(VII) David Putnam, son of Cyrus (6), married (first) Polly Titus, 1825, she died 1829 In the latter named year he married Almy Hicks, she died in 1842 In the same year he married Susan Williams, who died in 1846 The following year he married Rebekah Church His children were Waterman born October, 1826, died February, 1828, Mary, December 13, 1828, Serentha, June 21, 1832, died July 19, 1842, Philander, December 30, 1833, Cyrus, October 5, 1844, Albra, July 28, 1846

(VII) Horace Putnam, son of Cyrus (6), married Clarinda Boyce Their children were Maria, Jane, Silas, William, Ann, Julia, Emma

(VII) Philander Putnam, son of Cyrus (6), married Harriet Prentice, October, 1838 The children by this union were Marcus, born November 10, 1839, Wheelock, September 9, 1841, Edward, July 14, 1843, Emma Jane, June 28, 1847

(VII) Leander Putnam, son of Cyrus (6), married Eunice Lackey, June 1, 1837 She died March, 1852 He married (secondly) Mrs Martha A Bower, March 28, 1853 His children were Dorcas Ann Lackey, born December 29, 1838, married Reuben A Usher, Emerlaide, February 6, 1843, married Franklin Howard, Jerome, died March 26, 1852, Franklin L, born March 28, 1853

(VI) Cornelius Putnam, son of David (5), married Abigail Bigelow, by whom the following children were born Polly, June 1 1804, Darius, September 30, 1806, Lucy, September 3, 1808, Alver Abigail, January 18, 1811, married Nathan Waters, December 2, 1832, Harrison Bigelow, April 18, 1813

(VI) Joseph Putnam, son of David (5), married Polly Putnam, December 26, 1813, he married for his second wife, Fanny Whittemore His children were Maria Louisa, born January 4, 1815, Palmer, May 1, 1817, Mary Elizabeth, July 3, 1819, Simeon, November 17, 1821, Alexander, June 29, 1824, George Whittemore, August 11, 1827, Charles Vernon, July 6, 1829, Porter Franklin, July 21, 1831

(II) John Putnam, son of John (1), the ancestor, born about 1630, was a military officer, a representative of Salem during the years 1680-86-90-91 He was admitted as a freeman in 1665 He married Rebekah Prince, by whom four sons and four daughters were born The name of only one is given in the records, Ebenezer, born 1665

(III) Ebenezer Putnam, son of John Putnam (2), married Hannah Brown They had three sons and two daughters Among the sons was Jeptha, born August 24, 1699

(IV) Jeptha Putnam, son of Ebenezer (3), married (first) Ruth Ray, (second) Mrs Ruth Hayward, of Beverley, January 8, 1746 Their children were Benjamin, born August 27, 1725, Samuel, May 10, 1727, Hannah, August 13, 1728, married Benjamin Woodbury, May, 1746, Ebenezer, February 22, 1730, died March 5, 1730, Fuller, January 13, 1731, Ruth, October 18, 1732, married Stephen Halman, November 5, 1751, John, July 27, 1738, Mary, October 23, 1741, Benajah, September 7, 1747, Gideon

(V) Samuel Putnam, son of Jeptha (4), married Kezia Hayward, September 22, 1757 They had one son who enlisted in the army of the revolution and was killed in battle

(V) Fuller Putnam, son of Jeptha (4), married (first) Mary Cummings, December, 1752, (second) Eunice Haywood, November 23, 1756 Their children were David, born January 26, 1753, Eli, September 27, 1754, Ruth, December 4, 1757, John, July 8, 1760, Jeptha, September 24, 1762, Sarah, July 20, 1765, married Nathan Putnam, Jr, March 31, 1785, Lucy, February 16, 1768, married Tyler Marsh, May 9, 1781, Ruby, September 20, 1770, Prudy, July 20, 1774, married Caleb Dibley, January 1, 1794

(VI) David Putnam, son of Fuller (6), married Martha Waters, January 15, 1781 There is no record of their children, but their names were Rufus, who married Sally Sibley 1805, Patty, who married Captain Peter Putnam, Eli, who married Elizabeth Harback

(VI) John Putnam, son of Fuller (5), married (first) Huldah Waters, August 22, 1781 He married (second) Anne Powers He married (third) Dorcas Sylvanus His children were John, Sylvanus, Harry, Ruth, born March, 1820, Esther, born October 28, 1822, married Freeman Sibley

(VII) John Putnam, son of John (6), married Nancy, daughter of Abner Cummings Their children were Dulceva, born December 12, 1813, died July 20, 1816, Harriet, March 20, 1815, died July 20, 1816, Jane, November 1, 1816, married Waters Putnam, John Perry, March 27, 1818, Ira, November 15, 1819, died May 12, 1821, Ephraim Lughton, April 30, 1821, died December 3, 1822

(VIII) John Perry Putnam, son of John (7), married Harriett M Ward January 26 1850 Their children were John Walter, born September 13, 1852, Emma Jane, born March 19, 1854

(IX) John W Putnam, son of John P (8), married Adora L Putnam One child was born to them, Lucy Harriet, February 12, 1876

(VII) Sylvanus Putnam, son of John (6), married (first) Betsey Elliott, (second) Persia Harback, July 31, 1839 Their children were Ira Sylvanus, born August 14, 1827, Mary Elizabeth, June 8, 1829, died July 26, 1844, Julia Ann, January 12, 1833, married the Rev Joseph Barber, Sarah Maria, March 24, 1835, married Franklin Sibley

(V) John Putnam, son of Jeptha (4), married Mary Cumming, April 9, 1761 Their children were Rebekah, born September 13, 1763, Jacob, November 20, 1764, John, March 8, 1766, Olive, August 28, 1767, Simeon, August 10, 1769, married Martha Batchellor

(V) Benajah Putnam, son of Jeptha (4), in 1770, married Mrs Sarah Fitts Their children were Sarah, born July 5, 1771, married Peter Stockwell, September 30, 1803, Phebe, November 26, 1773, married Samuel Dudley, February 15, 1795, Mehitable, April 25, 1775, married Captain Samuel Marble, Anne, May 11, 1777, Abijah, July 30, 1779, Eunice, June 17, 1782, Molly, May 2, 1784, married Andrew Sibley, James, November 2, 1786, Sylvester

(VI) Abijah Putnam, son of Benajah (5), married Betsey Burdon, May 15, 1803 Their children were Sally, born 1803, Melona, June 4, 1805, married Nichols Woodward, Vilota, June 26, 1807, Luther February 16, 1809, Jason, February 14, 1811, Lyman, January 28, 1813, James, February 7, 1816, Emory, July 16, 1818, Sylvester, September 12, 1821, married Ann M Lynch, March, 1820, Sally, November 26, 1823, Rufus, November 19, 1827

(VII) Lyman Putnam son of Abijah (6), married Eliza J Brigham Their children were Sarah J, born January 4, 1840, Julia M, December 31, 1846, Laura D, April 12, 1848, Orason L, December 17, 1850, died September 19, 1870, Emma A, November 27, 1859

(VII) James Putnam, son of Abijah (6), married Phebe P Sloan, November 9, 1836 Their children were Jane Elizabeth, born November 11, 1837, Henry Clinton, July 6, 1839, George Emory, January 9, 1841, Abbie Melissa, December 3, 1844, married Alfred A Putnam, December 3, 1867

(VIII) Henry Clinton Putnam, son of James (7), married Harriet M Fuller Their children were Flora L, born July 20, 1860, George Henry, February 11, 1865

(VII) Emory Putnam, son of Abijah (6), married (first) Martha E Muller, (second) Jane Miranda Miller He was the father of one child, Martha Jane, born June 13, 1852, married Lewis Pratt

(VII) Rufus Putnam, son of Abijah (6), married Hannah J Graver Two children were born to them Ella Frances, born May 22, 1871, Walter Edwin

(V) Gideon Putnam, son of Jeptha (4), married Abigail Holton, November 28, 1775 Their children were Gideon, born 1776, Nabby, April 23, 1778, Artemas May 31, 1780 He removed with his family to Calais, Vermont

(VIII) Otis Earle Putnam son of Salmon and Tryphena (Bigelow) Putnam (7), was born in Leicester, Massachusetts, February 20, 1831 After a residence in Boston of some seven years his parents came to Worcester, Massachusett, and since he was fourteen years old Mr Putnam's home has been in that city He received his education in the common and high schools of Worcester, and in 1847, at the age of sixteen years began his career as clerk in the store of John B Wyman, who in 1850 sold his business to H H Chamberlain Mr Putnam remained in the employ of H H Chamberlain & Company and the succeeding firm, Chamberlain, Barnard & Company, until 1857, when he was admitted to the firm, then Barnard & Sumner, and later Barnard, Sumner & Putnam In 1892 the business was transferred to a corporation under the laws of Massachusetts Mr Putnam was successively treasurer and vice-president of the company and finally president, the position he still holds In short, Mr Putnam has risen from the position of a junior clerk to the head of one of the best known and most prosperous and thoroughly reliable department stores in New England The business of the Barnard, Sumner & Putnam Company has shown a steady and healthful growth from the beginning, when Worcester was a mere village In 1891 the facilities of the company were enormously increased by the erection of a six story addition to the spacious Main street building, extending to Waldo street in the rear Many new departments were added to the store

Mr Putnam is connected with various social and financial institutions of the city He is a director of the Worcester Electric Light Company, the Sherman Envelope Company the Eastern Bridge and Structural Company, the Worcester & Holden Street Railway Company, and trustee of the Worcester Five Cent Savings Bank, and of the Worcester Music Hall Association He was a director of the City National Bank and of the Worcester and Marlboro Street Railway Company before the consolidation He is a member of the Worcester Club, the Commonwealth Club, the Board of Trade, and honorary member of the Worcester Light Infantry, Battery B, and the Worcester Continentals Mr Putnam has been in the front ranks of the mercantile men of Worcester He has always affiliated with the Republican party in politics, but his interest in municipal affairs particularly has not been narrowed by partisanship He has always declined to accept public office

Mr Putnam married (first) Harriet E Waite, of Worcester, who died in 1863 He married (second) in 1866, Louisa Davis, of Lowell, who died March 25, 1892 They had one son, Arthur Davis, mentioned hereinafter Mr Putnam married (third) Florence Mace, of Baltimore, Maryland

(IX) Davis Putnam, son of Otis Earle and Louisa (Davis) Putnam (8) was born at Worcester, Massachusetts, February 16 1868 He attended the common schools of the city, and for a short period of time prior to attaining his twentieth year was a student in the high school of that city He then entered the employ of Barnard & Sumner, beginning in the position of clerk behind the counter, and learning the business thoroughly in each and every department Finally through the exercise of energy and determination, he advanced to the position of assistant treasurer, in which capacity he served the firm until the severance of his connection therewith in 1903 From that time until the early part of 1905 he took no active interest in business, then becoming connected with the Pepperell Card & Paper Company from which he retired after serving a few months Mr Putnam was formerly a director of the Barnard Sumner & Putnam Company He is an attendant of Plymouth Congregational Church of Worcester, and served as its assessor for a period of six years His political inclinations are strongly Republican He is not affiliated with any orders, but is a strong spirit of good fellowship at the Commonwealth Club where he takes a great interest having served on several committees

Mr Putnam married, May 21, 1890 Lou Frances Sartelle daughter of Francis K and Deborah (March) Sartelle of Worcester Francis K Sartelle was master mechanic of Washburn & Moen Manufac-

Otis E. Putnam

turing Company for years and their Canadian representative until his death. Their children are: Ethel Davis, born April 18, 1891; Otis Francis, January 18, 1893; Arthur Davis, June 21, 1898, died August 25, 1899; and Louise Davis, May 20, 1903.

PAINE FAMILY. Stephen Paine, the founder of the Paine family in New England, came from Great Ellingham, county Norfolk, England, 1638, with a large company of emigrants from the neighborhood of Hingham, bringing his wife, three children and four servants, in the ship "Diligent," of Ipswich. He settled first in Hingham, Massachusetts, but about 1643 removed to Rehoboth, of which town he was the founder. He possessed large estates in that and adjoining towns, was prominent in the affairs of the church and colony, and was representative to the general court for many successive years and until his death in August, 1679. His wife, "Neele," died at Rehoboth, January 20, 1660, after which he married Alice, widow of William Parker, of Taunton; she died December 5, 1682. Of his children, authentic records have been preserved of the sons, Stephen and Nathaniel. The third child mentioned as coming with the family from England probably died young. The first son, Stephen, had a very large family. Nathaniel, the second son, was the progenitor of the Worcester Paines.

(II) Nathaniel Paine, son of Stephen Paine (1), settled in Rehoboth, Massachusetts, where he became a man of much influence and importance. He died in Boston, 1678, leaving a wife, Elizabeth, and one son, Nathaniel.

(III) Nathaniel Paine, son of Nathaniel Paine (2), born at Rehoboth, October 18, 1661, married Dorothy, daughter of Jonathan Rainsford, of Boston. He was a judge of the court of common pleas, judge of probate, and a councillor of Massachusetts Bay. He died February 28, 1723. He had eleven children, Nathaniel, the fourth, being the progenitor of the Worcester Paines. There seems but little doubt that this was the Nathaniel Paine who in 1706 was appointed by the council of Massachusetts Bay as one of a committee to consider the expediency of resettling the town of Worcester, and the building of the fort there, in accordance with the request of owners of land in that settlement. The request was not granted by the general court, as the disturbed condition of the times rendered the enterprise too dangerous to be sanctioned by the legislature. The children of Nathaniel Paine and Dorothy, his wife, were: 1. Elizabeth, born November 6, 1681, married Samuel Vernon. 2. Mary, born June 8, 1682, married Simeon Drown. 3. Hannah, born April 20, 1685, married Lieut. Charles Church. 4. Nathaniel, born March 9, 1688, married Sarah Clark. He was the immediate progenitor of the Worcester Paines. 5. Edward, born October 7, 1690, died young. 6. Jonathan, born April 18, 1695, died young. 7. Alathea, born August 28, 1697, married Timothy Fales. 8. Sarah, born May 5, 1699, died in August same year. 9. Stephen, born 1701, graduated at Harvard College in 1721. He was register of probate for Bristol county in 1721-49, judge of inferior court of common pleas for Bristol county, 1745 and until his death in 1749. 10 and 11. Dorothy and Sarah, twins, born March 19, 1706. Dorothy married John Williams, of Boston, October 13, 1726, and died in 1774. Sarah married Joseph Russell, of Barnstable, and died in 1764. Mr. Paine died at Bristol, Rhode Island, February 28, 1723, and his wife, Dorothy (Rainsford) Paine, in January, 1755.

(IV) Nathaniel Paine, the fourth child of Nathaniel (3), of Bristol, Massachusetts (now Rhode Island), and his wife Dorothy, was born in Bristol, March 9, 1688. He was an active man, holding many town offices, and was also representative for five years. In 1723 he was a member of a court of admiralty specially commissioned for the trial of pirates, of which William Drummer was president. In 1724 he was appointed judge of the inferior court of common pleas for Bristol county, and remained in office until his death. He married, June 25, 1713, Sarah, daughter of Timothy Clark, of Boston, by whom he had seven children: 1. Edward, born in Boston, April 18, 1714, married, February, 1739, Mary Bosworth, daughter of Benjamin Bosworth, of Bristol. 2. Sarah, born August 17, 1716, married Thomas Drowne, March 24, 1736. They had a son, Nathaniel Paine Drowne, graduated at Harvard College in 1764. 3. Nathaniel, born June 17, 1719. 4. Dorothy, born January 20, 1723, married Hon. John Chandler, of Worcester, who was a loyalist, and one of six citizens of Worcester who in 1775 were banished from the country for giving aid and comfort to the enemy. 5. Samuel, born September 3, 1725, died young. 6. Samuel Clark, born February 11, 1727; he was a captain of a company at the reduction of Ticonderoga and Crown Point. 7. Timothy, born July 8, 1730, at Bristol. Nathaniel Paine died at Bristol, 1729. His widow married John Chandler and removed to Worcester, where she died, 1780.

(V) Timothy Paine, son of Nathaniel (4), of Bristol, and Sarah Clark, his wife, was born at Bristol, July 8, 1730, a short time after the death of his father. He lived in Bristol until the marriage of his mother, in 1739, to John Chandler, of Worcester, when he removed there and remained a citizen of that place until his death. He stood fifth in his class at Harvard College when he graduated in 1748. After his college days he returned to Worcester and became one of the most active and influential citizens. In 1751 he was appointed clerk of the court for Worcester county, remaining in that office until 1774. He was register of probate from April, 1757, to 1767, register of deeds, 1761-77, special justice of the supreme court in 1771, and one of His Majesty's council from 1763-68. He was town clerk, 1754-64, one of the selectmen of Worcester, 1754-64, and 1766-73, and representative of the general court, 1755-57, 1759-62, 1788-89. In 1789 he was a candidate for congress, but his opponents made use of the fact that he had been appointed one of the mandamus councillors before the revolutionary war, and this, with the general charge of loyalty to the English government, was pressed with such force by the newspapers that he lost his election, although a man of recognized ability and unblemished character. He was a real estate owner at Worcester as early as 1751, and by 1767 became owner of a large tract of land on the "great road to Boston," now Lincoln street. He was prominent in forming the second Congregational parish in Worcester (Unitarian) in 1785, under the pastorate of the Rev. Aaron Bancroft, father of George Bancroft, the historian.

In 1749 Timothy Paine married Sarah, daughter of Hon. John Chandler and Hannah Gardner. His wife, Madame Paine, was a most zealous loyalist. The Timothy Paine house is still standing (1905) on the west side of Lincoln street, a short distance from Lincoln square. She died at Worcester, 1811, aged eighty-five years. He died July 17, 1793, and was buried in the old burying ground on Mechanic street, Worcester, but later the remains were removed to Rural Cemetery. The children of Timothy and Sarah Paine were: 1. William, born June 5,

1750 2 Timothy, born January 3, 1752, at Worcester died December 29, 1775 unmarried 3 Samuel, born at Worcester August 23, 1753 graduated Harvard College 1721, and like his father and brother was a warm supporter of the Royal government The Paines and Chandlers had long held office under the Crown and therefore felt in duty bound to do so 4 Hannah, born July 22, 1755, married 1772, Ebenezer Bradish of Cambridge, Massachusetts 5 Nathaniel, born July 22, 1755, died December 25, 1757 6 Nathaniel, born January 5 1759 died October 7, 1840 7 Anthony, born November 13, 1760, died July 8 1788 was in the apothecary business at the corner of Main and Elm streets 8 John, born July 25 1762, died unmarried, December 23, 1835 9 Sarah, born March 28 1764, married, January, 1786, James Perkins Jr of Boston and died in that city December 1841 10 Elizabeth, born January 12 1766 married, February, 1786 Dr Joseph Trumbull she died in Worcester, July 10, 1832, leaving one son George Augustus

(VI) William Paine, the first child of Timothy (5) and Sarah Paine, was born June 5, 1750 at Worcester, Massachusetts He graduated at Harvard College in the class of 1768, his name standing second in the catalogue, according to the dignity of families He studied medicine with Dr Edward A Holyoke, a physician of Salem One of his instructors before entering college was John Adams, afterward president of the United States, who taught in the Worcester school while studying law with Hon James Putnam, a lawyer of great ability He commenced his practice in Worcester in 1771, in connection with the business of an apothecary In 1772, with Dr Levi Shepard and Ebenezer Hunt, of Northampton, he opened the first apothecary store in Worcester county Like his father and brother Samuel he was very friendly to the Crown, and took an active part in the politics of his day In the spring of 1774 there was great excitment in Worcester owing to the objectionable acts of parliament then lately passed especially at the report of an effort to have the general court offer indemnity for the tea destroyed in Boston harbor The loyalists of the town were much excited at what they considered the treasonable action of the Whigs in opposing the acts of parliament, and finally a protest signed by over fifty of them was presented at a town meeting held in June, 1774 This protest, which was the joint production of Hon James Putnam and Dr Paine, was quite lengthy, and complained bitterly of the outrages perpetrated by the Whigs, alluding especially to "the teas of immense value lately belonging to the East India Co not long since scandalously destroyed in Boston," and also protesting against the committee of correspondence then being formed and ending thus 'It is by these committees also, that papers have been lately published and are now circulating through the province, inviting, and wickedly tempting all persons These and all such enormities we detest and abhor, and the authors of them we esteem enemies to our King and country violaters of all law and civil liberty, the malevolent disturbers of the peace of society, subscribers of the established constitution and enemies of mankind" These resolutions were spread upon the town records of Worcester and when the opposition found it out trouble ensued they demanding of the selectmen that the clerk be ordered to strike and erase the same from the public records The selectmen voted to so order the record erased and thereupon the clerk, in open town meeting, with his pen defaced the pages on which the obnoxious record was made, but this not proving satisfactory to the patriotic voters there assembled, he was made to dip his fingers into the ink and draw them across the records, so effectually accomplishing the object that the words have been utterly illegible as may be seen by inspection of the volume in the hands of the city clerk of Worcester, at this late date

Soon after this Dr Paine went to England, where he remained until the spring of 1775, but as the war came on he was denounced as a loyalist, and, as he could not return to his family and home, he at once sailed for Liverpool, deigning to avail himself of the advantages and means of improvement afforded by foreign institutions, until the war should terminate After a year's attendance in hospitals, and having received the degree of M D from Marischal College, at Aberdeen, he was appointed to the office of apothecary to the English forces in America Later he was admitted to the Royal College of Physicians of London He returned to America in 1782, landing in New York in March, and in October of the same year was appointed by Sir Guy Carleton physician of the army He was ordered to Halifax and remained there on duty until the troops were reduced in 1783, when he was discharged on half pay All of this is found in Lincoln's "History of Worcester" In the summer of 1784 Dr William Paine took possession of La Tete, an island in Passamaquoddy Bay, granted him by the English government for his "service in war" He wrote to his brother Nathaniel, in June, 1784 "I am going to move, bag and baggage, to Passamaquoddy I have already erected a house on the island, which is the spot upon which I intend to reside" But on account of poor society, lack of schools, etc, he removed from that point in 1785 to St John, where he began to practice his chosen profession again He was appointed by Governor Thomas Carleton one of the first board of aldermen of St John, and in 1786 was unanimously elected alderman from Sidney ward He was elected to a seat in the assembly of New Brunswick, and was appointed clerk of the house He was afterward chosen speaker of the assembly but as he soon after left the province retained the office but a short time In October, 1785, he was appointed "Surveyor-General of Woods in the Province of Nova Scotia, all other His Majesties Territories in America," by Sir John Wentworth, with orders to "carefully survey and diligently make and register such white pine trees as may now or hereafter be fit for the use of the Royal Navy" He retained this position until the summer of 1787, when the act of banishment having been repealed, he by permission of the war office, went to Salem, Massachusetts After the death of his father, in 1793, he returned to Worcester and occupied the paternal estate until his death Until 1812 he was on half pay as a British officer, when he was called upon by the British government for service, but rather than act against his countrymen he resigned his commission In June of the last named year he petitioned the legislature of Massachusetts for consent to his being naturalized as a citizen of the United States Dr Paine was one of the founders of the American Antiquarian Society, and its first vice-president He died in Worcester, April 19, 1833, the anniversary of the fight at Lexington

Dr Paine was married September 22 1773, by Paine Wingate to Lois Orne of Salem by license of his friend, Sir John Wentworth Their children were 1 Esther Orne born August 18 1774 2 Harriet born November 13 1778, died December 20 1778 3 Harriet born November 21, 1779 4 William, born November 2, 1783, died, unmarried,

July 21, 1834 at Batavia 5 Elizabeth Putnam, born at St John, New Brunswick June 26, 1786, died at Worcester Massachusetts 6 Frederick William born at Salem, Massachusetts, May 23 1788

(VI) Nathaniel Paine, sixth son of Timothy (5) and Sarah (Chandler) Paine, was born in Worcester, August 5, 1759 He graduated at Harvard College in 1775 read law with Hon John Sprague, of Lancaster Massachusetts, and was admitted to the bar of Worcester county in 1781 After five years practice in Groton, Massachusetts he returned to Worcester He was a representative of the general court 1798-1800, county attorney for a similar period of time, and was appointed judge of probate, January 24, 1804, holding the office thirty-five years, resigning in 1836 on account of failing health He was one of the founders and a councillor of the American Antiquarian Society The late Governor Levi Lincoln in a paper read before the Worcester Fire Society of which Mr Paine was one of the founders in 1793 says of him 'He was of bland and courteous manners, an inquiring and observant habit, rare colloquial powers and a memory so singularly retentive as to become a perfect storehouse of historic fact and personal anecdote, he was a most instructive and delightful companion"

He married, December 18, 1785 Elizabeth, daughter of Gardiner Chandler of Worcester Judge Paine died at Worcester, October 7, 1840 Their children were 1 Nancy Leonard, born November 25 1786 died January 8, 1802 2 Charlotte, born in old Paine house in Worcester, August 9, 1788 3 Nathaniel Anthony, born November 19 1791, died February 9, 1819, unmarried 4 Sarah Chandler, born November 29, 1794, died Worcester, October 15 1840 5 Gardiner, born May 23 1799 6 Henry, born August 12, 1804 entered Yale College 1820, but left on account of failing health 7 Charles, born August 12, 1804

(VII) Frederick William Paine, the sixth child of Dr William Paine, removed to Worcester with his father in 1793 He entered Harvard College in 1803, but left after a stay of nine months to engage in commercial pursuits In 1806 and again in 1809 he made a voyage around the world, visiting China and the northwest coast of America In 1818 he went to Europe remaining there about four years, during which time he was connected with the commercial house of James and Thomas H Perkins He finally became a permanent resident of Worcester about 1816, and for the remainder of his life was actively interested in the local affairs of the place He was a member of the General Court of Massachusetts in 1829 one of the selectmen of Worcester 1827-31, and most of the time from 1838 to 1849, at which time the town was chartered as a city He was an assessor of taxes for the town most of the time from 1829 to 1848, and his judgment as to the value of real estate was much esteemed He early manifested an interest in horticulture, his garden on Lincoln street being noted for its flowers and fruit For many years he was an active and influential member of the Worcester County Horticultural Society, serving most of the time as treasurer He was a valuable member of the American Antiquarian Society, contributing largely to its library also serving as one of its councillors Mr Paine was a man of literary tastes spending much of his time in reading His library, at the time of his death was considered as among the largest private collections in the state numbering several thousand volumes, representing every branch of literature When but fourteen years of age he was employed to correct the proofsheets of the first Greek Testament published in North America and issued from the pen of Isaiah Thomas, "the patriot printer of the Revolution" Mr Paine died at Worcester September 16 1869 He was married May 5 1822 to Ann Cushing Sturgis, daughter of Hon Russell Sturgis Their children were 1 William Russell born January 26, 1823 2 Elizabeth Orne, born March 27, 1826 3 James Perkins, born Worcester, December 16 1827 4 Mary Pickard, born March 13, 1830 5 George Sturgis, born June 4 1833 6 Annie Cushing Sturgis, born March 5, 1836 died November 19 1873

(VII) Esther Orne Paine, born August 28, 1774, married (first) Joseph Cabot, of Salem September, 1795, married (second) Ichabod Tucker, of Worcester, November 5 1811 Two children were born to them Joseph S and William Paine Cabot

(VII) Harriet Paine, born at Newport Rhode Island November 21, 1779 married March 7, 1802 Joseph Warner Rose and died June 20 1860 They had nine children, among whom were Harriet, born February 5, 1804, married John C Lee, of Salem, Josephine born February 13, 1815, married, May 4 1842 George Chandler

(VII) Charlotte Paine second child of Nathaniel and Elizabeth Paine, was born August 9 1788 She married September 25, 1818, Timothy Paine Bradish of Natchez Mississippi She died at Worcester, December 3, 1866 They had one child, Walter Burling who died without issue

(VII) Gardiner Paine, fifth child of Nathaniel and Elizabeth Paine, was born May 23, 1799 He married October 11, 1831, Emily Baker, of Dedham, Massachusetts Two children were born to them Nathaniel and Anne Elizabeth In 1826 Mr Paine was major of the Sixth Regiment, First Brigade, Massachusetts Militia under Col Samuel Ward, of Worcester, and was in command of a regiment at the laying of the corner stone of Bunker Hill monument He was in business for several years in partnership with Daniel Heywood in a dry goods and general store located on the west side of Main street, about halfway between Pearl and Pleasant streets Worcester He died January 27 1854

(VIII) George Chandler and Josephine (Rose) Paine had two daughters that attained years of womanhood 1 Mary, born at Concord, New Hampshire, February 17 1845, she married, October 4, 1871, A George Bullock, of Worcester, and had issue Chandler born August 24 1872, Alexander Hamilton born November 7 1874, Augustus G, born April 20, 1880 died April 20, 1880, Rockwood, born —— 2 Fanny, born Worcester, Massachusetts, January 5, 1852 she married Waldo Lincoln, of Worcester and had issue Merrick, born May 25 1875, and Josephine Rose, born February 28, 1878

(VIII) William Russell was born July 26 1823 He married, April 12 1855, Frances Thomas Choeker, of Taunton They had five children—four daughters and one son, Frederick William, born February 22, 1866

(VIII) James Perkins was born in Worcester, December 16 1827 He married, May 11 1865, Sarah Turner of Boston They had four children—three daughters and one son, Russell Sturgis, born June 6 1874

(VIII) Mary Pickard was born March 13 1830 She married May 3 1851 Allyn Weston of Duxbury One child, a daughter, was born to them

(VIII) Nathaniel Paine son of Gardiner and Emily (Baker) Paine was born at Worcester, Massachusetts August 6 1832 He was educated in the public schools and academy of his native city By the above family history it will be observed that he came of ancestors of prominence in revolutionary days in town affairs, and that his grandfather was many years judge of probate in Worcester county. When seventeen years of age, having clerked for a time in a leather store, he entered the Mechanics' Bank as a clerk. In 1854 he was made the assistant cashier of the City Bank, and three years later was promoted to cashier, which office he held until December 12, 1898, when he was elected president. When the banks were merged into the Worcester Trust Company, a short time since, he became vice-president and still holds the position. He has been connected with many of the financial concerns of Worcester. He was vice-president of the Worcester Five Cent Savings Bank, and chairman of the Clearing Association. The honorary degree of Master of Arts was conferred upon him by Harvard College in 1898. He was from young manhood possessed of a literary taste, and is especially fond of history and art. He has written much of local history, and many articles from his pen have appeared in different publications. Among the papers prepared by Mr Paine were "Early Paper Currency of Massachusetts," "Historical Notes on the Town of Worcester," "The Drama in Worcester," and "Early American Imprints in the Library of the American Antiquarian Society." He also edited with notes the "Diary of Christopher Columbus Baldwin, Librarian of the Antiquarian Society." He is also connected with many other societies. He was one of the founders of the Worcester Art Society and has been its president, and is director of the Art Museum Corporation, also was a director of the Free Public Library for eighteen years. He served in the common council one term. He is a great lover of good books, and possesses a fine library. The following list will explain his prominence in society matters: Treasurer American Antiquarian Society, treasurer Worcester County Horticultural Society, treasurer Home for Aged Men, treasurer Devens Monument Association, president Worcester Lyceum, president Worcester Natural History Association, director Free Library, and secretary for more than a dozen years and director of the Worcester Art Museum. He holds membership in the Massachusetts Historical Society, New England Historic and Genealogical Society, American Society of Advancement of Science, Colonial Society of Massachusetts, American Historical Association, Folk-Lore Society of Massachusetts, Bunker Hill Monument Association, Worcester Society of Antiquity, Worcester Art Society, honorary member of the Pennsylvania Historical Society. He is also a corresponding member of the Long Island Historical Society, Numismatic and Antiquarian Society of Philadelphia, La Societie Numismatique of Montreal, Canada, Numismatic and Antiquarian Society of Melrose, Scotland, and the Georgia Historical Society. He was one of the original members of the Club of Odd Volumes of Boston. His has been a busy life and many public institutions have felt the touch of his literary influence.

Mr Paine was married June 14, 1865, to Susan M Barnes.

JUDGE HENRY CHAPIN, son of Elisha and Sarah (Wood) Chapin, was born in Upton, Massachusetts, May 13, 1811. Soon after entering his teens his father died and the boy Henry was forced thus early to care for himself. Having improved the opportunities granted by the public schools of his native village he began to learn the trade of a carpenter, but a brief trial at that occupation proved to his own mind he was not intended for a carpenter. He then turned his attention to study, and fitting for college entered Brown University and graduated from that institution in 1835.

After teaching school for a time in Upton he began the study of law with the late Emery Washburn, and also at Cambridge. He was admitted to the bar in 1838, and at once began the practice of his profession in the town of Uxbridge. Eight years later he removed to Worcester and became a partner of the late Rejoice Newton. In that city he grew rapidly into popularity, and his legal practice became extensive. He was industrious, faithful and efficient, consequently highly successful in his professional undertakings, and within three years of his coming to Worcester the people felt such confidence in his integrity and ability that they elected him to the office of chief magistrate of the city, re-electing him in 1850 but he declined a third nomination. In 1858 the courts of probate and insolvency, hitherto distinct, were united, and Mr Chapin was appointed to preside over the new court, a position which he held at the time of his death. It has been said that during the twenty years he held the office of judge of probate and insolvency more than half the estates in Worcester county passed under his jurisdiction in one or the other side of his court, and that he was brought into official relations with a larger number of persons in all conditions of life than any other public officer of the county. His patience, fidelity and impartialty have been universally admitted, and his kindly nature, courteous manner and keen perception of justice to all parties gained for him the confidence and respect of the people of the county.

Judge Chapin was not an aspirant for political office, and although entertaining firm political convictions was not an offensive partisan. He represented the town of Uxbridge in the general court in 1845 and received the nomination for congress in 1856 by the Republican convention, but declined the honor. In 1870 although he had served as mayor of the city of Worcester two terms, he accepted the office again when chosen by the council to fill a vacancy caused by the death of Mayor James B Blake, but retired after serving a few months, as soon as a successor could be provided by a popular election. In 1848 he was appointed by Governor Briggs commissioner of insolvency, and in 1855 by Governor Gardner commissioner under the "personal liberty law" of Massachusetts designed for the protection of persons charged with being fugitive slaves. For many years he was a member of the state board of education and for fifteen years one of the trustees of the Worcester Lunatic Hospital. He was for many years president of the People's Fire Insurance Company, a director of the City National Bank, vice-president of the Worcester County Institution for Savings, and for thirty years served as a director of the Providence and Worcester Railroad. Judge Chapin was possessed of a kindly and highly sympathetic nature, always ready to do a benevolent act, and was active in helping to organize institutions through which charity could be wisely dispensed to the unfortunate and the needy. The Old Men's Home of Worcester was one of the institutions conceived and aided by him.

In religious belief Judge Chapin was a conservative Unitarian and was an active influential member of the Church of the Unity in Worcester, in which for many years he served as superintendent of the Sabbath school. After resigning the office of superintendent he joined the Bible class and thus continued his connection with the school until failing health prevented his attendance. He was an active, strong man in the Unitarian denomination and for many years took a prominent position in it. He was twice elected president of the American Unitarian Association, and for four years was a mem-

J. Fred Humes

ber of the council of the national conference of Unitarian churches Judge Chapin was a man of varied gifts that made him successful, he was a good business man, an able lawyer, an upright judge, an honored and respected citizen, a man of the people, for with all his accomplishments and the great esteem in which he was held by those who came in contact with him, he never displayed any taint of egotism As a speaker on public occasions he was in great demand His wholesome wit and characteristic presentation of anecdotes, interspersed with flashes of oratory, gave him a reputation as a good after dinner speaker, and the people of Worcester county were always pleased and instructed as they listened to the voice of Judge Chapin at their annual gatherings given under the auspices of the various agricultural societies Although he claimed no right to be classed as a poet, yet many of his productions are highly prized by his friends During the days of the anti-slavery agitation he spoke frequently and effectively in behalf of the Free Soil and Republican parties but after his acceptance of a judicial office he though it unbecoming to take a conspicuous part in political controversies He was interested in historical research and a prominent member of the American Antiquarian Society, serving as its treasurer for many years

Mr Chapin was twice married First on October 8 1839, to Sarah, daughter of Joseph Thayer, Esq, of Uxbridge She died April 30, 1869, and their only child a son, died at the age of seven years and ten months He married (second), May 23, 1871, Louisa Thayer a sister of his former wife, by whom he had one child, Margaret, born 1874, married William Bazeley, two children Louisa Thayer, born 1900, Margaret Ley, born 1905, they reside in Uxbridge, Massachusetts

The progenitor of this Chapin family was

(I) Samuel Chapin, who came from England with his wife Cicely and several children in the year 1636, and first settled in Roxbury, Massachusetts, but later removed to Springfield

(II) Josiah Chapin, a son of Samuel Chapin, settled in Braintree, was an active, enterprising man and a land surveyor He removed to Mendon about the year 1682 and became quite a distinguished man He was representative to the general court, and gained the prominent title then of esquire He had sixteen children

(III) Captain Seth Chapin, son of Josiah Chapin, Esq, was born in Braintree, Massachusetts, August 4, 1668, and was the seventh child in his father's family He married (first) Mary Read, married (second) Bethiah Thurston He is said to have been a man of talent and of considerable wealth He had fourteen children He died in 1746, aged seventy-eight years

(IV) Seth Chapin son of Captain Seth Chapin, born in Medfield, July 2, 1692, was the eldest of fourteen children He married, February 5, 1713, Abigail Adams aunt of John Adams, second president of the United States His home place was in that part of Mendon now Hopedale, where he was a large land holder He died April 1, 1737, leaving ten children

(V) Moses Chapin the youngest child of Seth Chapin was born in 1736 He married December 9 1756, Lydia Atwood daughter of Eldad and Martha Atwood They lived in what is now Hopedale He died June 9, 1802 She died February 8, 1813 Their children were David born 1757, Jerusha, born 1760, Elizabeth, born 1762, Nathan, born 1765, Henry, born 1767 died young, Lydia, born 1770 Olive, born 1772, Anna

(VI) David Chapin, son of Moses Chapin, married (first) July 4, 1777, Judith Thayer, daughter of Seth and Judith Thayer She died and he married (second), February 12, 1784, Martha Bates, of Mendon and settled in the territory now known as Upton He was a farmer He died February 6, 1814, aged fifty-six She died May 3 1846, aged eighty-one Their children were Elisha, born April 10, 1778, by first wife, Judith, born March 21, 1785, Sarah, born October 14, 1788, Lydia, born February 17, 1791, Joseph Bates, born April 25, 1793, David, born July 2, 1795

(VII) Elisha Chapin, son of David Chapin, born April 10, 1778, married Sarah Wood, July 8, 1802, in Upton, where they lived and died He died June 13, 1826 Their children were Experience, born September 24, 1803, Sarah Ann, born May 11, 1807 Henry, born May 13, 1811, subject of this sketch

JOHN FRED HUMES Notwithstanding the handicap of poor health for several years John Fred Humes, or as he is better known J Fred Humes, has made in recent years rapid progress in his profession He is in touch with important litigation, especially in the office of the city solicitor to whom he is assistant Mr Humes was born in Sutton, where his family has been prominent for several generations He is the son of John R and Sarah (Putnam) Humes of Sutton His youth was spent in his native town and he graduated from the high school in 1883 He attended Worcester Academy the following year and graduated with the class of 1884 He matriculated at Brown University and studied there for three years and a half, but owing to a long illness in his junior year and poor health following he abandoned college without his degree He undertook first the study of law in the office of Frank B Goulding After six months his health again gave out, and it was six years before he was fully restored to health Then he entered the offices of Henry F Harris and Charles M Thayer After two years and a half he was admitted to the bar In June, 1897, he began his career as an attorney He remained with Mr Harris and Mr Thayer for three years In 1900 he opened an office at 532 State Mutual building In August, 1904, he moved to his present offices in the building of the Five Cents Savings Bank In November, 1903, he was appointed assistant city solicitor to succeed Ernest I Morgan, and is the second incumbent of the office Mr Morgan was appointed in 1899, when the position was created Mr Humes is secretary and treasurer of the Bar Association of Worcester County

Until his marriage Mr Humes resided at Sutton with his parents He has since made his home in Worcester He married, June 22, 1898, Susan A Main daughter of John and Ella (Reed) Main, of Gloucester She was born in Gloucester, August 4, 1869 The Main family is one of the old families of Gloucester Their children are Warren Main, born July 5, 1899, Raymond Putnam, born April 4, 1901

(I) Amos Humes settled at Douglas Massachusetts, where his son Warren was born July, 1802

(II) Warren Humes, son of Amos Humes (1), was born probably in Douglas July, 1802 The history of Douglas says that he possessed in a great degree the ability that characterized his father, who was evidently a man of mark in Douglas Warren had limited opportunity for an education, but was self-educated to an unusual degree and exerted all his life a powerful influence in local affairs He was endowed with a remarkable memory, being able the Douglas history says, to retain and correctly impart a vast amount of general information He began the practice of his profession of civil engineer and surveyor at the age of twenty-five, and was later acknowledged to be one of the best in the southern part of the county He became an authority on real estate law He had a large share of the business of conveyancing in his locality He was a justice of the peace He was intensely interested in politics For thirty years he was at the head of the Democratic party in Douglas, and controlled the town on all important matters His one great failure to control is the exception that proves the rule He opposed the purchase of a town poor farm, and after a bitter contest was defeated in town meeting, whereat the joy of the public was expressed by a sort of Fourth of July celebration The wife of Warren Humes was Phebe Rich, daughter of Samuel Rich, Jr, of Sutton Samuel Rich, Sr of Douglas, married Elizabeth ———, who died March 20, 1803 Their children were Samuel born July 30 1735, Benjamin, born July 20, 1737, married Rebekah Daggett, July 15, 1762, Hannah, born April 16, 1738, Elizabeth, born July 29, 1741, Sarah, born April 3, 1743, David, born March 7 1744, Jonathan, born July 20 1747, Reuben born May 10, 1752, Amos, born September 4, 1757

Samuel Rich, Jr, son of Samuel Rich, was born July 30, 1735 He married Ruth Putnam, November 18, 1761 She died December 28, 1811 Their children were Stephen, born January 3, 1762, Elijah, born April 4 1764, Ruth, born July 31, 1766, Samuel, born February 26, 1769, Elizabeth born January 23, 1772, Phebe, married Warren Humes The children of Warren and Phebe Humes were John R, born February 22, 1834, Amos A, born April 14 1835, Milton, born April 13 1840, Maria, L, born June 13, 1846 George W, born February 17, 1837, died October 28, 1863, Juliet A, born January 19 1850

(III) John R Humes, son of Warren (2) and Phebe (Rich) Humes, was born in Douglas, February 22, 1834 He resides in Sutton, where he runs a farm and deals in lumber He has held the offices of selectman and assessor in Sutton He married Sarah M Putnam Their children are George M, born May 30, 1860, married Lottie E Wheeler, and resides in Auburn, John Fred, born October 10, 1866 (see sketch), Nancy Evelyn, born December 24, 1868 married James Cranska, of Sutton, bookkeeper at Manchaug, and has two daughters and a son Frank Edwin, born September 14, 1872, resides with parents at Sutton

BARNARD FAMILY The late Dr Rebecca Barnard, of Worcester, Massachusetts, was a descendant in the eighth generation from Robert Barnard, of Andover, Massachusetts The line is as follows

(I) Robert Barnard, called of Andover, Massachusetts He was in Salisbury in 1642, Andover 1644 and Nantucket 1663 He was one of the founders of the church in Andover, and several of his descendants were ministers and physicians He died about 1682 Administration on his estate was granted his grandson, Robert Barnard February 1, 1714-15, more than thirty years after the senior Robert's death who by wife Joanna ——— who died March 31, 1705, had the following children John Stephen, born 1648-49

(II) Stephen Barnard second son of Robert and Joanna Barnard married in Andover, Rebecca How, May 1, 1671 and resided in that town Had sons Nathaniel James Robert and Stephen

(III) Robert Barnard, third son of Stephen and Rebecca (How) Barnard, born in Andover, March 28, 1689, married (first) Rebecca Osgood, at Andover, September 14 1710, and she died July 29, 1727 He married (second) Elizabeth Bailey, May 15, 1729 In 1723 he purchased of Jeremiah Barstow, of Marlboro, three hundred and fifty acres of land on which there was a mill and other buildings, and removed from Andover to Marlboro where he was known as a miller and also kept a public house Their children were Robert, born August 30 1714, Benjamin, born February 14, 1715-16, Martha, Rebecca, Elizabeth, born June 3 1730, Joel, born July 14, 1732, Abigail, born April 28, 1734, Solomon, born December 27, 1735, Martha, born April 26, 1740, John, born May 19, 1743 This John was a physician and settled in Sterling, Massachusetts

(IV) Benjamin Barnard, second son of Robert and Rebecca (Osgood) Barnard, born February 14, 1715-16, married (first) Lucy Bush, of Marlboro She died and he married (second), in Harvard, Mary Hunt, February 22, 1759 Mr Barnard lived in Marlboro until 1743, when he purchased the home place of Stephen Houghton in Harvard and removed there, where he died October 24, 1794 He was prominent in the church, and held the office of selectman His children were Benjamin, born August 13 1738, Jonathan born June 18, 1740, died 1742, Lucy born November 13, 1742, died January 24 1752, Jonathan, born February 24 1745, Ephraim born May 3 1747, Moses born May 7, 1749, Jonathan, born September 22, 1751 died September 27, 1756, David, born January 18 1754 At least three of the above sons of Benjamin and Lucy (Bush) Barnard served in the war of the revolution Benjamin, the eldest, served in Isaac Gates company, the Fourth, Colonel Asa Whitcomb's regiment, April 19, 1775, eight and a half days at Cambridge He also was paid mileage from Harvard to Danbury December 17 1776 He also marched in Captain Samuel Hill's company, Colonel Josiah Whitney's regiment, on alarm at Bennington, August 19, 1777, and again in October of the same year Moses, the sixth child, was a graduate of Harvard College 1773, a physician served as surgeon's mate to Dr Dinsmore, Colonel Asa Whitcomb's regiment, service two months and fourteen days Also in Captain Fuller's company, Colonel Whitcomb's Worcester county regiment, in August and September, 1775 Again as surgeon on sloop "Republic" commanded by Captain John F Williams, engaged August 20, 1776, and discharged November 18, 1776. (See Massachusetts Soldiers and Sailors in Revolutionary War, Vol 1)

(V) Jonathan Barnard, third son of Benjamin and Lucy (Bush) Barnard, born February 24, 1745, married Lucy ——— He served in Captain James Burt's company, Colonel Asa Whitcomb's regiment, in response to the alarm, April 19, 1775 He settled in Harvard on the home place, which at present writing still remains in the Barnard family A fact worth recording is that for sixty years there was not a death in this family His children were: Jacob, born April 16, 1769, Jonathan, January 27, 1771, Lucy September 26 1774, Benjamin, June 12 1777, Sabra, July 24 1779 Calvin, July 25, 1781, Sarah, February 3, 1784, Esther, June 1, 1786, Levi, April 20, 1789, Joel and Joab (twins), May 12, 1793

(VI) Benjamin Barnard, third son of Jonathan and Lucy Barnard, born June 12, 1777 married (first) Rebecca Keep He married (second) Jemima Whitcomb of Boxboro His children were Franklin born May 17, 1809 Granville born January 1, 1812 died September 15, 1895, Rebecca, born May 8, 1814, died November 5, 1817, Josiah, born May 1, 1816, died June 20, 1858, Benjamin K, born December 17, 1818, died January 14, 1900, Levi, born

John R. Back.

March 22 1822, died December 25, 1886, Abner, born February 14, 1832

(VII) Dr Franklin Barnard, eldest son of Benjamin and Jemima (Whitcomb) Barnard born May 17, 1809, married, March 3 1833, Maria Ann Plummer, of Andover, Massachusetts daughter of Hezekiah Smith Plummer and his wife Betsey Stimpson Poor who were married April 3, 1806 Her great-grandmother, Lovejoy Poor, purchased in Salem, Massachusetts a negro child whom she called Salem Poor It is related in the history of Essex county that Dr Barnard displayed unusual courage as a soldier, and on one occasion shot an English general He studied with Dr Samuel Thompson in Boston He died in Worcester November 29 1889, and his wife died March 1, 1885 Their children were Anna M, born in Andover, May 13, 1835, Dr Rebecca, born April 29, 1837, Esther, born in Harvard August 24, 1839, Caroline born in Worcester November 19, 1842

(VIII) Dr Rebecca Barnard, second daughter of Dr Franklin and Maria Ann (Plummer) Barnard, was born in Andover, April 29, 1837 She came to Worcester, Massachusetts a child in her father s family in the year 1840 Her early education was attained in the public schools of Worcester and at the Baptist Academy, after which for more than fifteen years she was a teacher in the city schools, during which engagement she was not absent from her duties in her school room a single day As a teacher she gave most excellent satisfaction the personal interest she took in her pupils and the kindly assistance rendered them was the means of creating many lasting attachments between teacher and scholar which was only terminated by her death Her medical studies were pursued at the College of the New York Infirmary New York city After serving as an interne at the hospital connected with that institution, she began the practice of her chosen profession in Worcester In the city directory for 1879 her name appears as physician with office at 49 Pearl street As she was very generally and favorably known throughout the city, she found a fertile field in which to locate, and a large and lucrative practice was soon obtained and attended with remarkable success professionally As the years came and went her practice increased, severely taxing her physical strength yet her interest in educational institutions led her to accept a position on the school board, to which she was elected, serving six years Her practical knowledge on educational matters proved of considerable assistance to the board She was a member of various medical societies among them the Boston, New England Hospital, and the Worcester District Medical Society For many years her residence and of late her office was at the northerly end of Main street, in what has been known as the Baldwin Eaton house, one of the old time landmarks, built in 1760, and purchased by Dr Rebecca Barnard in 1879 Miss Sarah Eaton, from whom the purchase was made, remained in the house until her death in 1887, in the same room in which she was born July 3 1800 Dr Rebecca Barnard died unmarried September 9, 1905

HJALMAR S ANDERSON Erik Anderson, the father of Hjalmar S Anderson, of Worcester of the firm of Robinson & Anderson, jewelers, was born October 10, 1841, in Smedjebaken Dalarne, Sweden He was the son of Anders and Greta (Carlson) Anderson He married Charlotte E Hallvorson who died in Worcester, November 6, 1901 He removed to Worcester Massachusetts, November 20, 1881 Their children are Hjalmar M, see forward, Knut H, Arthur E Gustav E, Ernst, Minnie E Francis Two children died in infancy

Hjalmar Anderson son of Erik Anderson, was born in Ramnas Westmanland, Sweden, December 13 1870, and came to this country when quite young with his parents He was educated in the Worcester public schools When he was twelve years old he went to work as office boy in the Palmer wire mill He returned to school for a time, then became a weigher in the wire mill at Palmer where the family was then living They moved to Worcester and he entered the employ of the Taber Organ Company He worked for a time also for the Washburn & Moen Company in the wire mill At the age of seventeen he began to learn the jewelry trade of A L Burbank & Company He remained with the firm and its successors and since the recent death of William H Robinson is the head and sole owner of the business The present name of the firm under which he is doing business is Robinson & Anderson, and the store is at 375 Main street He is a Republican in politics and member of Thule Lodge, No 239, I O O F, Worcester, Massachusetts

He married, December 3 1892, Elizabeth Fisk, who was born in Rotneros, Wermland Sweden January 30, 1869, and educated in Sweden She came to America in 1887 Their children are Hjalmar S, Jr, born August 18, 1893, Irving E L, born March 30, 1900, Wendall, born October 21, 1903

JOHN RICHARD BACK Jacob Back (1), the grandfather of John R Back, of Worcester, settled in Twerton, a village in Somersetshire, England, half way between Bristol and Bath He married Sophia Frances, by whom he had two sons, Arthur and William He died when a comparatively young man His widow married again and had a daughter, Mary Francis The latter came to America some years ago, but returned to her native place and married John Hill

While the English ancestry of Jacob Back is not traced it is known that the surname belongs to an old English family One branch of the Back family came early to Connecticut but the connection, if any, with the Worcester family is not known Judah Back, to whom the Connecticut family trace their ancestry, was born September 21, 1765, in that portion of Windham, Connecticut, now the town of Chaplin He died September 21, 1828 in Holland, Massachusetts It is likely that the father of Judah Back was the emigrant from England No other branch of this family is known in this country

The children of Jacob and Sophia (Francis) Back were 1 William, of whom later 2 Arthur, who came to Worcester, Massachusetts about 1840, and was interested in business before 1850 with L W Pond, later he moved to Susquehanna Pennsylvania, where he spent the remainder of his days and where his children settled, he was master mechanic there in the railroad shops of the Erie Railroad, the children of Arthur Back were 1 Arthur, 2 Mary, resided at Binghamton, New York, 3 Sarah 4 Charlotte 5 Josephine

(II) William Back, son of Jacob Back (1), was born in Twerton, England, August 22, 1818 He was educated in his native town and learned his trade there He became a very expert finisher of woolen goods In fact the goods that took the prize at the Crystal Palace Fair in England in 1850 were made in the mill where he was employed as the finisher But when in 1851 he came to Worcester with his wife and child he made a change in his occupation because he wished to give his two sons a mechanical education He came to Worcester because his brother was located here, and he went to work in the Pond machine shop A number of other English families came to Worcester at the same time that Mr Back came There was an urgent call at that time for skilled mechanics The industries of the state of Massachusetts were at an important stage of their development, especially the woolen mills Some of the best mechanics in the English woolen mills were induced to come to New England These English families came from the prosperous middle classes They were ambitious, skillful in their trades, God-fearing and worthy people A group of these English families settled in Worcester in what was then called Oregon" on the west side Neighbors in the old country they remained neighbors in Worcester

He married in England Sarah Silcox, who died in Worcester at the age of eighty-two He died there in 1893 at the age of seventy-five Their children were 1 Arthur John, born in 1843 in Twerton, England, was brought up in Worcester, he was killed in 1864 on the Erie Railroad in a wreck at Callicoon 2 William Thomas, born May 24, 1846, in Twerton, England, came to Worcester with his parents when five years old, was educated in Worcester public schools and learned the machinist's trade, for twenty-two years, since 1883, he has been a foreman for F E Reed, manufacturer of machine tools in Worcester, he is a prominent Odd Fellow, he married Ella Russell, of Worcester, and they have two sons Arthur John, clerk at the F E Reed Company shop, married, and resides on Maywood street, William Russell, inspector at the F E Reed Company shop, resides with his parents at 52 Florence street 3 John Richard, of whom later

(III) John Richard Back, son of William Back (2), was born in Worcester, Massachusetts, April 24 1851, about a month after his father and mother came to Worcester to live He received in the public schools of that city his early education At the age of thirteen, however, he went to work in George Crompton's loom works, Green street, and remained there for two years He tried mercantile business for a time and worked as clerk in several stores He returned to manufacturing and served a regular three year apprenticeship with Wood & Light, makers of machine tools He was promoted to a foremanship, and remained thirteen years with the firm, working, in fact, until the firm went out of business About 1886 he began to work as a contractor for F E Reed Two years later the contract system was done away with and the Reed shop reorganized Mr Back became the superintendent, a position that he has held ever since Meanwhile, of course, the Reed business has greatly increased At first he had but fifteen men under him, and now he has three hundred The F E Reed Company is described at some length in the sketch of Mr Reed It is the largest concern in its line of work in Worcester and in its special field of engine lathes produces more than any other shop in the country The Reed lathes are known all over the world The company has a large export trade The business has grown constantly Mr Reed and Mr Back have worked together in the development of this industry, Mr Reed in charge of the selling and Mr Back in charge of the manufacturing end Since the corporation was formed in 1894 Mr Back has been a stockholder and director of the company, and has been granted several patents on engine lathes

Mr Back is a member of the board of trade and served one term as a director He is serving his second three-year term as director of the Worcester County Mechanics' Association, and he served two terms as director of the Young Men's Christian Association of Worcester He is a Republican in politics He served the city of Worcester in the common council from ward six in 1896-97-98 He was an alderman in 1899 and 1900 In 1896 he was on the committees on education, legislative matters, in 1897 on public buildings, education and legislative matters, in 1898 on education, legislative matters and public buildings, in 1899 and 1900 on finance, police, education, public claims and public buildings, and chairman of the last two He devoted himself particularly to the work of the committee on education and claims In 1898 he was a member of the grade crossing commission appointed to solve the problem of abolishing the crossings at grade of highways and steam railroads Mr Back retired from the city council in 1900 at the end of his term He was appointed license commissioner by Mayor W. H Blodget with James F Carberry and Captain John S Baldwin for the year 1904 He was elected chairman of the board He was reappointed and again served in 1905 as commissioner Under the present charter of the city of Worcester the chief duty of the three license commissioners consists in deciding between the various applicants for licenses to sell intoxicating liquors and to grant the licenses to the number permitted by law The purpose of the license commission is to eliminate the influence of the saloons in municipal politics by taking the granting of licenses out of the hands of the aldermen

In every public position in which Mr Back has served he has completely won and held the public confidence, he has devoted himself unreservedly to the duties of the office Few men having the heavy business responsibilities of Mr Back can be found with the public spirit necessary to fill municipal offices properly, if they are willing to take them at all Although still a young man Mr Back is to be reckoned among the founders of the great industries of Worcester Surely the men who create industries and develop machinery for which a demand exists is entitled to a large measure of public gratitude An establishment like the Reed shop benefits not only the three hundred employees and their families, but every taxpayer in the city, every merchant and many other manufacturing industries Mr Back is a member of the South Baptist Church and has been on the board of trustees since 1897 He is a member of no fraternal or secret order

He married, November 15, 1877 Frances Lorena Parker, born in Boston, daughter of Charles Parker, of Worcester Their home is at 24 Oread street Their children are Sadie May, born in Worcester, April 23, 1881, married Herbert Sumner Ramsdell, of Worcester, a clerk of the Duncan-Goodell Company hardware store, Worcester, they have a son, Herbert Francis, born January, 1904 Lorena Frances, born January 12, 1890, a student in the Worcester high school

WILLIAM HENRY GOULDING Peter Goulding (1), emigrant ancestor of the Goulding family of Worcester was the progenitor of William Henry Goulding of Worcester There were a number of emigrants to New England in the middle of the seventeenth century, but none of them appear to have left descendants by the name of Goulding except Peter He came from England, probably from Shipdam, six miles from Norwich He was a descendant of Rev Thomas Goulding, who was co-executor to the Bishop of Norwich He was a saddler by trade, but seems to have been an attorney at law with a considerable practice in the courts He was not a Puritan, never took the oath of fidelity, nor joined the church He was a man of morality, as his Puritan critics described his virtues, of talent and rare enterprise and courage By marriage he was connected with the aristocratic families of the colony He was in Virginia in 1667 He is said to have become one of the earliest anti-slavery men of Massachusetts, after visiting his brother in the south He was in 1670 attorney for Joseph Deakin, of Boston, in a suit against Thomas Jenner, mariner, for the recovery of a negro slave, to the sale of whom three years before in Virginia he testified His writing is mentioned as beautiful, and as more than a generation in advance of his New England contemporaries He had a serious difference with the Suffolk county court and was prosecuted and fined 'for charges that he divulged against the court and clerk of Suffolk county" In consequence, October 18, 1681, he addressed a complaint and petition to the general court, but instead of sustaining his appeal the general court sentenced him to make public acknowledgment of his fault, to satisfy the court, or pay a fine of twenty pounds to the treasurer of the colony But the general court accepted a very ambiguous and dubious acknowledgment, and the fine was remitted He bought of Isaac Negus April 11, 1682, two hundred acres of land north of the Merrimac river, on Beaver Brook creek He was also interested in the second attempt to settle Worcester in 1683, and bought the town rights of Thomas Hall He probably took up his residence there until the settlement was the second time broken up He had several grants of land in Worcester, and his son Palmer revived his claim to one hundred and fifty-seven acres when the third settlement was made in 1713, and the claim was allowed The family has been prominent in Worcester ever since Goulding was the owner also of three thousand and twenty acres in Hassanamesset (Grafton), which at that time was included in the south part of Worcester In 1694, when he left Worcester at the time the settlement was abandoned, he went to Sudbury, where he died in 1703, eleven years before the successful settlement of Worcester He was only a sojourner in Sudbury, expecting to return some time to Worcester He was a cordwainer as well as a farmer Peter Goulding married Jane ———, who was the mother of three and probably five of his children He married (second) Sarah Palmer, sister of Hon Thomas Palmer, of Boston, and in succeeding generations Palmer was a common name for the sons His children 1 Peter, recorded in Boston in list 1665 died young 2 Mary, born January 21, 1665-6, died young 3 Francis, born February 22, 1667-8, probably died young 4 Martha, born probably in Virginia, married John Smith, of Hadley 5 Elizabeth, born October 6, 1773, married William Jenison, of Charlestown, settled in Sudbury and Worcester 6 Winsor, born March 3, 1674-5 7 Thomas, born January 2, 1677 8 Sarah, born August 19 1679 9 John (captain), born probably near Merrimac, Massachusetts, 1682, married, 1705, Abigail Curtis 10 Jane, born at Boston, January 16, 1683-4 11 Mercy, born at Boston, September 8, 1786 12 Peter, born probably at Worcester 13 Abigail, born probably at Worcester 14 Arabella, born at Sudbury or Worcester 15 Captain Palmer, see forward

(II) Captain Palmer Goulding son of Peter Goulding (1), probably born in Sudbury, 1695, died February 11, 1777, married, at Concord, Massachusetts, December 4, 1722, Abigail Rice, who died at Holden, February 17, 1722, aged seventy He is buried on the Worcester common, then the burying ground of the town He removed from Sudbury to Worcester in 1728 He sold some land here in 1722, and October 1, 1723, bought twelve hundred and six acres in the southern part of Worcester He built his house where the Fourth Congregational Church stood later, near Front street, and carried on a varied and extensive business as tanner, shoemaker, curer of hams, maltster, etc His house was used in 1732 as a school, Richard Rogers, teacher He was on the committee to seat the meeting, an important duty then He was constable 1726-27-28-29, selectman 1730-31-37, treasurer 1738, assessor 1732-33-34 He dealt in land extensively in Worcester He had a fine military record He was at the capture of Louisburg, June 17, 1745, in command of a company February 24, 1750, he and William Johnson bought one hundred and thirty-seven acres on the shore of Lake Quinsigamond Children of Captain Palmer Goulding 1 Palmer, born February 18, 1722-3, died January 30, 1792, married Abigail Haywood 2 Abigail, born September 24, 1724, died May 17, 1736 3 Colonel John, born October 3, 1726, died November 22 1791, married Lucy Brooks 4 Millicent, born November 12 or 25, 1728, died unmarried August 9, 1813, talented teacher, once a Shaker 5 Zurvilla (or Trovilla), born December 25 1730 married Cornelius Stowell 6 Winsor, born December 4, 1732, married Elizabeth Rice 7 Ignatius, born September 6, 1734 died November 5, 1814, married Elizabeth Goodwin 8 Peter, see forward 9 Abel, born March 4 1738, died December 6, 1817, married Keziah Johnson, of Shrewsbury 10 Elizabeth, born May 1, 1741, died unmarried 11 Patty, married John Miller

(III) Peter Goulding, son of Captain Palmer Goulding (2), born in Worcester, December 30, 1736, died July 17, 1790, married Lucy Brewer He was a carpenter by trade, and was killed by a fall, July 17, 1790 His children 1 Levi, born March 15, 1767, died June 8, 1767 2 Clark, see forward 3 Lucy, born April 10, 1770, married Nathan Gates 4 Patty, born March 11, 1772, married, 1791, Charles Johnson 5 Lucinda, born February 23, 1774, married Timothy Johnson, 1792, resided in Worcester 6 Peter, born May 15, 1776 7 Sally, born April 28, 1778 died June 27, 1778 8 Sally, born April 18, 1780, married Reuben Scott 9 Zervilla, born September 21, 1781 10 Nabby, born December 23, 1783, died February 25, 1799 11 Levi, born September 11, 1787, married, April 18, 1809, Sally Harrington

(IV) Clark Goulding, son of Peter Goulding (3), born September 2? 1768, in Worcester, died there August 14, 1829, married Prudence Rice, born April 9, 1776, married 1795, and died April 13, 1849 Their children 1 Mary, born October 23 1795, died 1837, married, 1834, Arthur Keyes, of Boylston 2 Lewis, born August 18, 1797, died May 8, 1847, married, 1825 Luvy Adams, resided at Gardner, Maine 3 Abigail, born June 21, 1799, married, 1823, Elisha Chaffin, of Worcester 4 Harriet, born February 22, 1801, married, 1841, Ebenezer Dana 5 Henry see forward 6 Eli born August 12, 1804 married Martha Alexander, of Deerfield, 1833 7 Clark, born March 31, 1806, died at De Kalb Junction, New Hampshire, January 29, 1894 8. Lucy, born October 15, 1807, married, 1844 Jason Chapin 9 Peter, born March 30, 1810, died March, 1896, married Malinda Hubbard 10 Emelia, born March 15, 1812, died April 17, 1812 11 Frederick, born December 12, 1813, died February 8, 1814 12 Hannah born June 15 1815, married 1832, H P Dunham 13 Fanny, born August 2, 1816, married, 1837, Gardner Childs 14 Frederic, born July 19, 1823 married, 1852, Calista Perkins, he died 1893

(V) Henry Goulding, son of Clark Goulding (4), born December 13, 1802, died January 30,

1866, in Worcester He married, 1829, Sarah Rice, and lived in Worcester He was a man of considerable property He built the mansion at 26 Harvard street in which his son, William H Goulding, has lived for many years He was a manufacturer of woolen machinery, one of the first, and retired from business in 1851 He served as selectman, was one of the founders and president of the Mechanics Bank, a member of the fire department in 1840 In politics he was originally a Whig, and afterward a Republican His children 1 Sarah Rice, born January 1, 1830, married Henry O Clark, lived in Worcester 2 William Henry, see forward 3 Sewall Foster, born July 17, 1836, died June 3, 1840

(VI) William Henry Goulding, son of Henry Goulding (5), was born in Worcester, Massachusetts, May 23, 1833 He attended the public schools of his native town, and in 1850 was graduated from the high school He took a course also at Leicester Academy He went to work in Boston as salesman first for the wholesale firm of Pierce, Howe & Co After a year in their store he went into partnership in the tailoring business with Henry Chaffin, under the firm name of Chaffin & Goulding After a period of eight years, Mr Goulding sold his interests to his partner and returned to Worcester Here he decided to make his home, and founded the drug store at present known as Buffington's, in 1859 The store has always been on the spot now occupied, except during the time the present building was being constructed after the fire He carried on the drug store for eight years, and in 1866 sold it to Elisha D Buffington, whose estate still owns the business, as the Buffington Pharmacy Company At that time the large property interests of Mr Goulding kept him busy, and since then he has had no other business than the management of his real estate and other property interests He enjoys travel, and spends only a part of the year at his home, 26 Harvard street He has a cottage in Cottage City at the sea shore, and in winter prefers the climate of Florida to that of New England He is a member of the Commonwealth Club, and attends Plymouth Church He married first, October 6, 1862, Florence Berry, daughter of Scotto and Mary (Lovett) Berry, of Douglas and Worcester She died April 25, 1870 He married (second), November 18, 1891, Rose T Ford, daughter of Joseph T and Henrietta W (Womrath) Ford, of Philadelphia, where they were married Three children were born of the first marriage, all in Worcester, 1 Mary Sarah, born December 13, 1865, married Charles H Curtis, of Boston, their children Herman Goulding Curtis, born October 26, 1890, Philip Goulding Curtis, born July 8, 1893, Amy Goulding Curtis, born May 1, 1898, Charles Goulding Curtis, born July 26 1902 2 Harry Scotto, born June 16, 1867, lives with his parents at home 3 Louis Rice, born April 7, 1870, married Minnie Whitney, and resides in Boston, where he has a store, Beacon street, and conducts a business of interior decorating To Mr Goulding was born, of his second marriage, a son, William Ford, September 4, 1893, a student in the Bancroft School

THE HORNE FAMILY was an early one in Maine and many of them were engaged in the lumbering business and were sturdy, thrifty people Of the branch of this family represented in Worcester county Ichabod Horne (1), who was engaged in lumber cutting and rafting throughout his active life, was indeed very successful He married and among his children, who were born at his home place, near where he was, at Bingham, Maine, was one named Ichabod, Jr, who became the father of the gentleman for whom this personal memoir is written

(II) Ichabod Horne was borne October 7, 1829 He was educated at the common schools of his native county and upon ending his school days began farming, but later in life saw greater possibilities in the business of his ancestors and began lumbering, in which he was eminently successful He died in 1902 He was a stanch Democrat in political views, but never aspired to office and belonged to no secret society He married Olive Gleason, who died in 1873 She was the daughter of Bryant and Elizabeth (Corson) Gleason, of Maine, and became the mother of the following children Frederick J, born October 10, 1856, Florence E, March 31, 1858, died November, 1887 Charles F, August 15, 1859, Sherman, January, 1862, Thomas, of whom later, Flora M, July 19, 1866, died July 1883

(III) Thomas Horne was born on the old homestead at Bingham, Maine, August 22, 1864 He was educated in the common schools in Clinton, Pittsfield and Canaan, Maine, which had greatly improved since the days of his father's and grandfather's school days, and after obtaining the average education came to Worcester, where he held a clerical position for one year He then went to Wisconsin, where for a time he embarked in the lumbering business But the old Pine Tree State still had charms for him, and we next find him in his native state, where for three years he was engaged in buying hay It was in 1887 that he again came to Worcester, accepting a position with the Washburn-Moen Wire Company, where he remained seventeen years He was faithful to every duty imposed upon him and rose to the position of assistant superintendent of their great works In 1903 he was elected by the city council to the office of assessor, and has held the position ever since, filling it with much credit to himself and satisfaction to the tax payers He was re-elected in 1906 for three years

He is a thoroughgoing, genial business man and willing to do his share in any project for the general advancement of his adopted city and county Like many another enterprising modern business character, he is identified with the Odd Fellows and Masonic fraternities He belongs to the Blue Lodge of Free and Accepted Masons

He married, May 15, 1888, Georgia A Drew, a daughter of Albert and Helen Maine Drew The father was a merchant of Pittsfield, Maine By this union two sons were born Roland D, March 14, 1895, and Evart J, January 26, 1903, both still living at home

HON WILLIAM TROWBRIDGE FORBES Daniel Forbes (1), the immigrant ancestor of William Trowbridge Forbes, judge of probate of Worcester county, was probably born at Kinellar, Scotland, about 1620 It is thought that he was one of the Scotch prisoners of war taken at the battle of Dunbar, September 3, 1650 eight thousand of whom were sent to the English colonies In the early town records his name and that of his descendants is spelled variously Forbes, Farrabas, Farrowbush Forbush, Furbish Farebush, etc, and the name Forbes is still pronounced in Scotland with two syllables In Burke's Heraldry it is stated that the surname of Forbes was assumed from the lands of Forbes county Aberdeen Scotland, granted by Alexander II in 1249 to the progenitor of this noble family Daniel Forbes was in the employ of Edmund Angier to whom he conveyed land granted him by the town of Cambridge, Massachusetts He removed from Cambridge to Concord and thence to Marlboro, where

E. T. Forbes.

he died October, 1687 He married at Cambridge, March 26 or 27, 1660, Rebecca Perriman, supposed to have been a sister of Thomas Perriman, of Weymouth, and of Frances Perriman, who married, 1654, Isaac Andrew, of Cambridge His first wife died May 3, 1677, and he married (second), May 23, 1679, Deborah, of Concord, born 1652, daughter of John and Ann Rediat of Sudbury She married (second) Alexander Stewart He had eight children Daniel, Thomas, Elizabeth, Rebecca, Samuel, John, Isaac, Jonathan

(II) Deacon Jonathan Forbes, son of Daniel (1), born in Marlborough, Massachusetts, March 12, 1684, died at Westborough, an adjoining town, March 24, 1768 He was prosperous, owning a sawmill and large tracts of land, was constable, moderator of town meetings and selectman of the town, and deacon of Westboro church He married, January 2, 1706, Hannah Holloway, daughter of Adam and Hannah (Hayward) (Farrar) Holloway, of Marlboro Their children Mary, Dinah, Daniel, Thankful, Jonathan, mentioned below, Abigail, Patience, Phinehas, Eli

(III) Deacon Jonathan Forbes, Jr, son of Deacon Jonathan Forbes (2), born February 3, 1715, in that part of Marlboro subsequently incorporated as Westboro, died November, 1756 He married, in Westboro, November 23, 1738, Joanna Tainter, their children John, Jonathan mentioned below, Phinehas, Mehitable, Joanna, died young, Joanna, died young, Sarah, died young, Hannah, died young

(IV) Deacon Jonathan Forbes, son of Deacon Jonathan Forbes (3), born in Westboro, March 1, 1746, died there June 5, 1805 He married, July 2, 1772, Sarah Brigham, born April 18, 1751, died August 20, 1827, bequeathing to each of her forty-five grandchildren a Bible Their children Moses, Jonathan mentioned below, Holland, Ephraim, Sarah, Elias, Nancy, Achsah, all these children attained maturity and married

(V) Captain Jonathan Forbes, son of Deacon Jonathan Forbes (4), born December 6, 1775, at the Forbes homestead, West Main street, Westboro, where he always resided, and where he died, January 5, 1861 He taught school when a young man He was captain in the militia as early as 1813, and in that year was also elected deacon of the Evangelical church, holding the latter office forty-eight years, the fourth of the name in direct line holding the office of deacon in the Westboro church He held most of the town offices and was a leader in town affairs, it is said that he was chairman of every committee on which he served He married, January 17, 1802, Esther, daughter of Ebenezer and Esther Chamberlain, a niece of Judge Edmund Trowbridge Their children 1 Sarah Brigham, born April 16, 1803, married Rev Charles Forbush, of Upton, and died August 22, 1851, he died 1838 2 Julia Miranda, born June 25, 1804, married Rev John Wilde, who died in Alexandria, Virginia, 1868 3 Jonathan, born November 26, 1806, died January 24, 1820 4 Daniel H, born September 13, 1809, married Jane Jemima Baker, second, Mary Avery White 5 Esther Louise, born June 22, 1810, died October 3, 1812 6 Moses, born September 25, 1812, married Eliza L Southwick 7 Ephraim, mentioned below 8 Sophia, born January 7, 1821, died unmarried, August 14, 1881

(VI) Deacon Ephraim Trowbridge Forbes, son of Captain Jonathan Forbes (5), and father of Judge Forbes, was born at Westboro, March 25, 1815 He received his education in the common schools and at Phillips Academy, Andover, Massachusetts He taught school in Westboro and Southboro, and for many years was on the Westboro school committee He was active in the Evangelical church, and for many years deacon He resided on the farm formerly owned by his father and grandfather, at the junction of West Main street and the road to North Grafton He died August 2, 1863 He married, 1842 Catharine White, born July 25, 1815, daughter of William and Nancy (Avery) White, of Westboro, formerly of Roxbury, Massachusetts, and great-great-granddaughter of Captain Samuel Adams, father of Governor Samuel Adams, of Massachusetts, descendant of Henry Adams, of Braintree, the immigrant Children of Deacon Ephraim T and Catherine Forbes 1 Catharine Salome, born September 12, 1845, married, March 12, 1867, Charles Brigham Kittridge, resides at Seattle, Washington 2 Esther Louise, born June 17, 1847, resides in Westboro 3 William T, mentioned below 4 Francis White, born May 1, 1852, married first, Jane A Nason, (second) Fannie E Hooker 5 Susan Eliza, born September 20, 1854, died December 30, 1860

(VII) Hon William Trowbridge Forbes, third child of Deacon Ephraim Trowbridge Forbes (6), was born in Westboro, on the old homestead, May 24, 1850 He fitted for college in the public schools, the Allen Classical School at West Newton, Massachusetts, and under the private instruction of Rev James Tufts, of Monson, Massachusetts At Amherst College, where he was graduated in the class of 1871, he received first prize in mathematics in his second year, and a German scholarship in his third year He was historian of his class, and one of the editors of *The Amherst Student* He rowed in his class crew in the regatta of 1870 on the Connecticut river On leaving college he went to Constantinople, Turkey, and for three years was instructor of mathematics in Robert College there He made a geological survey of the vicinity of Constantinople with Dr George Washburn, president of the college, collecting about two thousand specimens of fossils, many of them new varieties which were exhibited at the Vienna Exposition

He returned to Worcester to study law in the office of Hopkins & Bacon, and for three years was standing justice of the First district court of Eastern Worcester He resigned in 1879, and practiced law in Westboro until he was appointed in 1888 to his present position as judge of the courts of probate and insolvency for Worcester county Judge Forbes held many of the town offices of Westboro He was representative to general court 1881-82 and state senator from his district 1886-87 He served on the committees on liquor law, being house chairman, and on the judiciary, probate insolvency, and election laws In 1887 he prepared and carried through the legislature laws abolishing taxation for church purposes, and providing for the incorporation of churches without a parish or religious society He has taken much interest in local history, and wrote the history of Westboro in Lewis's 'History of Worcester County,' and co-operated in the preparation of the town history published in 1891 He is a Congregationalist in religion, and has been president of the Worcester Congregational Club

He married, February 5, 1884 in Worcester, Harriette Merrifield, daughter of William T and Maria C (Brigham) Merrifield, of Worcester (See Trowbridge and Merrifield families) Their children 1 William Trowbridge Merrifield, born April 23, 1885, graduate of Amherst College, and instructor in Robert College, Constantinople 2 Allan White born June 20, 1886 a junior in Amherst College 3 Cornelia Brigham, born July 14, 1888, a sophomore in

Vassar College 4 Katherine Maria, born September 23, 1889 5 Esther Louise, born June 28, 1891 6 Malcolm Stuart, born November 22, 1892, died February 4, 1893

MERRIFIELD FAMILY Thomas Merrifield was an ancestor of Harriette (Merrifield) Forbes, wife of Hon William Trowbridge Forbes, of Worcester, Massachusetts His ancestry is not fully proved It is possible that he was that Thomas born in Boston August 8, 1708, son of Joseph and Margaret (Warden) Merrifield Joseph, born June 8, 1675, was son of John and Sarah (Goad) Merrifield, John being the eldest son of Henry Merrifield, of Dorchester, and his wife Margaret, the original immigrants in this country

The name of Merrifield has always been common in the south of England, especially in Devon, from which county Henry Merrifield is supposed to have come As far as is known he was the only one of the name to come to New England until the eighteenth century, and probably all of the name who figure in the early New England records descended from him Thomas was a popular name in the family, and possibly some other Thomas may have been the one who was in Dedham, rather than this son of Joseph

Thomas Merrifield lived in Dedham certainly from 1736 to 1752, the dates of birth of the first and last of his children recorded on the town records No record of his death has been found He married, in Groton, Massachusetts, July 12, 1732, Mary, born in Watertown August 29, 1711, daughter of John and Rebecca (Waight) Anderson Her father was a Scotchman, her mother a daughter of John and Mary (Woodward) Waight, descended respectively from Richard Waite (1) and George Woodward (Richard 1), both of Watertown Among the children of Thomas and Mary (Anderson) Merrifield was Timothy, mentioned below

(II) Timothy Merrifield, son of Thomas Merrifield (4), born in Dedham, Massachusetts, January 4, 1739 He owned land there in 1765, when he deeded four acres to Ephraim Bacon, which bounded southerly on his own land There is, however, no recorded deed showing when he bought his Dedham farm In Sherborn he purchased a hundred-acre farm on the road leading from Morse's farm to Daniel Whitney's, in 1778, and a few months afterward deeded one-half of it to his brother Asaph, and probably they lived here together until 1784, when they bought of Jonathan Amory, of Boston, one hundred and twenty-seven acres in what was then the easterly part of Holden, now West Boylston Their old house is still standing, now occupied by J Lambert, and is evidently very old, probably built about 1739, when the land was purchased by Joseph Woolley from Benjamin Flagg, Jr It is very low-studded, with heavy timbers, wide floor boards, and large square bricks in the hearths It had at the time of his purchase been recently the home of Paul Raymond Asaph Merrifield lived here the rest of his life, and after his death the house acquired the curious reputation that old houses in the country sometimes did, of being haunted Queer things happened to the passersby, wheels came off their carts, etc, and thirty cats were known to be kept in one of the front rooms It has, however, outlived these superstitions and looks strong and solid for another century of existence In 1780 Timothy Merrifield sold his half of the Holden farm to Joseph Dwelly, and bought of him the farm on the old turnpike, now Mountain street, Worcester, afterward known as the Merrifield farm, where he lived the rest of his life, dying in 1806 His life was uneventful, with the exception of his serving as a private in the revolution He married, 1766, Lydia Cheney, died in 1770 Her two children also died He married (second), June 10, 1772, in Sherborn, Mercy Perry, who was mother of all his children that grew to maturity She was daughter of John and Mercy (Nelson) Perry, and was born in Sherborn, 1742 Her father was descended from John Perry of Roxbury, through John (3), and Samuel (2) Mercy Nelson was the daughter of Francis Nelson of Rowley, and granddaughter of Thomas Nelson (1) Children of Timothy and Mercy Merrifield Alpheus, mentioned below, Caroline, Chloe

(III) Alpheus Merrifield, son of Timothy Merrifield (2), was born in Sherborn, Massachusetts, November 19, 1779 At the age of twenty-five he commenced his public career by holding that curious office, hog-reeve, to which it was the custom of the time to elect young men immediately after their marriage In 1810 he was town constable and collector of public taxes, serving for six years In 1812 and afterward he served on the school committee of Worcester, he was also highway surveyor, assessor, overseer of the poor many years, and selectman five years, also a member of many important town committees, and was prominent in the First Unitarian Church, being deacon for twenty years The early part of his married life was spent on the Mountain street farm, inherited from his father He became a contractor and builder, carrying on business not only at home but in South Carolina He moved to Summer street, where he died January 3, 1852 He married, November 12, 1804, Mary Trowbridge, daughter of William and Sarah (Rice) Trowbridge They had eight children

(IV) William Trowbridge Merrifield, eldest son of Alpheus Merrifield (3), was born at the Mountain street farm, April 10, 1807 At fifteen he commenced to learn the carpenter's trade and served a seven year apprenticeship with his father At twenty-one he entered into business for himself as contractor and builder, and built many of the important buildings in Worcester, including the main structure of Worcester Academy, the Lancaster Mills, and many houses In 1839 he purchased the lot on Union and Exchange streets, where he erected for renting purposes brick buildings, four stories high, covering about two acres These were burned in 1854 and the present Merrifield buildings took their place They were designed to furnish room and power to small manufacturers, and here Deacon Washburn laid the foundation of the wire industry, Knowles and Crompton founded the loom works, and hundreds of other successful manufacturers were attracted to Worcester because it was possible to begin in a small way with little outlay of capital These were the first buildings in Worcester of this nature, and they gave an impetus to the mechanical growth of the city which did much to determine her future Mr Merrifield was one of the founders of Union Church He was always active in the agricultural and horticultural societies Although not caring for public life, he served in the city government, being a member of the first city council, was also in the state legislature, for ten years was trustee of the State Lunatic Hospital, and was president for a number of years of the Worcester County Mechanics' Association He died December 26, 1895, aged eighty-eight He had had only one illness in his life When in town, as he almost always was, he never failed to go to his office He stayed at home the day before his death because it was Christmas Day, and not because he was ready to give up his work He was twice married, first,

April 27, 1830, to Margaret, daughter of Jabez and Nancy (Kingsbury) Brigham Two children of this marriage survive 1 William Frederic, born in Worcester, August 30, 1837, resides in Brookline, Massachusetts 2 Henry Kingsbury, born July 21, 1840, resides in Worcester A grandson of his daughter Catherine, Guy Merrifield French, is living in Ottawa, Canada He married (second), March 9, 1847, Maria Caroline, daughter of Charles and Susannah (Baylies) Brigham, of Grafton One of their children is living Harriette, wife of William Trowbridge Forbes, judge of probate for Worcester county, mentioned above Mrs Forbes was educated at the Oread Institute She is interested in local history and genealogy, and has written many papers on historical subjects She wrote "The Hundredth Town," sketches of the town of Westborough, and edited the "Journal of the Rev Ebenezer Parkman" She has been regent of Colonel Timothy Bigelow Chapter, D A R, and is now a member of the State Council of the Massachusetts D A R

TROWBRIDGE FAMILY Thomas Trowbridge (1), of Taunton, England, the immigrant ancestor of both Judge and Mrs Forbes, is the progenitor of all of the name in New England He married Elizabeth Marshall

(II) James Trowbridge, youngest son of Thomas Trowbridge (1), was an early settler in Charlestown, was lieutenant, selectman, clerk of writs, deputy to general court, commissioner, and deacon

(III) William Trowbridge, son of Lieutenant James Trowbridge (2), born November 19, 1684, married Sarah Ward

(IV) James Trowbridge, son of William Trowbridge (3), born at Newton, Massachusetts, April 21, 1717, married, 1740, Jerusha, daughter of Richard and Sarah (Fuller) Park He was the first settler of the name in Worcester He was a turner by trade He came to Worcester in 1739 and bought of Matthew Clark his farm of sixty acres and his house on Tatnuck Hill This farm is now the property of the Tatnuck Country Club He lived there until 1747, when he sold it to Richard Flagg and bought near the Auburn line the farm which was for many years in the possession of himself and his son, the central part of which is now called Trowbridgeville His old house stood until a few years ago He also owned the mill privilege where he had a corn and a saw mill He died July 21, 1806 Of his nine children only one seems to have remained in Worcester, William

(V) William Trowbridge, son of James Trowbridge (4), was born in the Trowbridgeville homestead, Worcester, March 20, 1751 He served as corporal in the early days of the revolution, and also on the committees of correspondence He was deacon of the First Unitarian Church for twenty years He held numerous town offices, being constable, warden, collector of highway taxes, serving on the school committee and on various other town committees His mansion house, still standing at Trowbridgeville, was built 1798-9, and was then considered one of the handsomest in Worcester This reputation was owing, perhaps, to the wainscoting and interior finish, rather than to any special features of the exterior William Trowbridge died in the home of his daughter, Mrs Lewis Chapin, just over the line in Auburn, September 30, 1838 He was buried in the Mechanics street burying ground, Worcester, and when Foster street was continued to the Union Station and the bodies removed from that ground, his body and those of his family were taken back to his old farm and reinterred in that part of it which is now Hope Cemetery He married, December 12, 1776, Sarah, daughter of Thomas and Judith (Stearns) Rice They were the parents of Mary, who married Alpheus Merrifield, mentioned above

HON ALFRED S PINKERTON A citizen of Worcester since early youth, self-educated and self-made and prominent as a member of the Worcester bar, a former president of the Massachusetts senate and one of the honored councillors of the Republican state organization, a national figure in the Odd Fellows brotherhood, a gifted orator Hon Alfred S Pinkerton stands high in the estimation of his fellow citizens not only of Worcester but to an unusual degree to others, near and far He is one of the men that high honors make modest and retiring

Mr Pinkerton's father was a merchant at Lancaster, Pennsylvania, dealing in hardware, iron and steel He died when Alfred was a boy of fourteen and his mother came to Worcester to live, bringing her two children, a son and a daughter His school days were short He had to become a bread winner when a mere child He gathered his education as many good Americans have done without the aid of the school teacher He was clerk in several Worcester stores and manufacturing enterprises, thus acquiring a thorough mercantile training But he turned his attention to the law and decided to make it his profession He studied in the office of the late Peter C Bacon, of Worcester, was admitted to the bar in 1881, when he was twenty-five, and has ever since been engaged in the active practice of his profession

He was a member of the Massachusetts house of representatives, representing ward two, in 1887-88-89 Upon his first entrance to the house in 1887 he was appointed by Speaker Charles J Noyes chairman of the committee on towns, a position which that year was a particularly conspicuous one by reason of several vigorous and hotly contested town division cases involving questions of unusual legal popular interest These contests were heard in the first instance by this committee and later by the legislature, he was the spokesman of his committee on the floor and successful in maintaining its contention This was the year of the famous Beverly division contest and the spirited debates that marked this long struggle, as well as the Medford division issue that followed, which are memorable in the annals of the legislature and of the literature of town divisions

In 1888 he was a member of the committee on the judiciary and of that on constitutional amendments, and was also a member of a special committee to represent the state in connection with the celebrations commemorative of the settlement of the Northwest Territory In 1890 he was elected to represent the fourth Worcester district, which included the wards of Worcester, the city of Fitchburg and a number of towns, in the senate, and was that year chairman of the committee on constitutional amendments, and member of the committee on the judiciary, probate and insolvency, and of the special committee to which was referred the first contested election arising under the new Australian ballot law The report of the last named committee has been followed as a precedent in cases involving the construction of the law In 1891 he was chairman of the committee on the judiciary and by virtue of that position leader of the senate He was also member of the committee on probate and insolvency and chairman of a joint special committee to consider state commissions and their relation to state governments.

The last named committee was one of great importance under the circumstances. The then Democratic governor, William E. Russell, had made in his inaugural address a violent attack upon the system of state commissions and contended for a greater degree of executive authority. In consequence of his inaugural address the general subject of state commissions, their powers, duties, authority and relation to the state government, were referred to this special committee, of which Mr. Pinkerton was chairman and of which Josiah Quincy, late mayor of Boston, was a member. The committee held numerous hearings, and was allowed to sit in recess, and made an elaborate report prepared by Mr. Pinkerton to the legislature the following year. The Democratic members made minority report upon certain phases of the situation. This report, following a campaign in which commissions were freely discussed, formed the basis of future legislation on the subject of commissions. Its suggestions and recommendations are worth the attention and study of those interested in the uses of commissions as an auxiliary of state administration.

The senate of 1891 was tied politically between the Republican and Democratic members. Mr. Pinkerton was chairman of the Republican steering committee and spokesman of the Republican side, a position requiring much tact and parliamentary skill, but so well was the work done that in 1892 he was elected president of the senate by the unanimous vote of both Republican and Democratic members, and the same compliment was given him the year following. During his occupancy of the chair he was made chairman of a special committee to sit during the recess and consider the laws relative to corporations other than municipal, the report of this committee drafted largely by him is exhaustive and comprehensive. It has been the basis of much subsequent legislation to prevent the watering of stock and otherwise to guard the interests of the stockholders. As a result of this investigation and report, the private investor is protected by law, probably as much as the law can protect him, from loss and depreciation of stocks while by later legislation great progress has been made in regulating the public service corporations.

In 1895 he was chairman of the committee to revise the rules of the legislature. He declined a renomination in the following year and has since been engaged in the practice of law, giving freely of his time to party interests and public affairs. As a presiding officer he won an enviable reputation as a parliamentarian and for impartiality. While he was the president of the senate a number of close parliamentary questions came to him for decision, and his rulings have since been followed as precedents. He seldom reserved his decision on points of order and questions to be decided, but almost invariably decided them forthwith. It is a proof of his knowledge of parliamentary law and practice as well as of his judicial mind to note that in every instance his rulings were sustained. He is and for several years has been the chairman of the executive committee of the Republican state committee, and has declined election as chairman of the committee. He has been secretary and is now chairman of the Republican county committee of Worcester county. He is vice-president of the Middlesex Club, a famous organization of men prominent in business and politics. He has been one of the prominent campaign speakers of the Republican party for many years and has been the orator on many occasions of public interest. He was for several years director of the Public Library.

He is also known for his leadership and honors in fraternal and secret orders. He is past master of Athelstan Lodge of Masons, a member of Eureka Royal Arch Chapter, Hiram Council and Worcester County Commandery of Knights Templar.

He became a member of the Worcester Lodge of Odd Fellows in 1878, and was noble grand of the lodge in 1881. He was elected grand master of Massachusetts for the year beginning August, 1888, and was the youngest man ever chosen to fill the position. He was elected to the sovereign grand lodge the following year, but resigned before taking his seat, entering that body as representative in 1890 and was continued as a member until his election as deputy grand sire at Dallas, Texas, and as grand sire in 1898 at Boston. During his service as grand sire, at the head of the Odd Fellows of the United States and of the world, he devoted a large part of his time to the order. The good results of his labor are apparent in the prosperity that is attending the organization. He had the satisfaction of having all his acts and one hundred and sixty-four decisions approved. As an attorney Colonel Pinkerton, to use the title by which he is generally known, has had to do with some very important and noted cases. At present his time is almost exclusively given to the practice of his profession.

Mr. Pinkerton was born at Lancaster, Pennsylvania, the son of William Cooper and Maria (Fiske) Pinkerton, March 19, 1856. His mother was a daughter of Samuel Fiske, of Lexington, Massachusetts, a lineal descendant of one of the emigrants who founded the commonwealth of Massachusetts in 1630-40. His paternal grandfather was Henry Pinkerton, of Lancaster, Pennsylvania, who married into the well known Atlee family of Pennsylvania. The Pinkertons were early settlers of Pennsylvania, coming from England. His father died at Scranton, Pennsylvania, December 28, 1871; his mother died while visiting her sister at Cambridge, Massachusetts, in 1886. The children of William C. and Maria Pinkerton were: 1. Alfred S., born March 19, 1856, married, August 18, 1904, Betsy Howe Chapin, daughter of Willard and Lydia Chapin, of Malden, Massachusetts. 2. Ella, born June 28, 1858, married A. M. Weeks, of Princeton, Massachusetts, in 1877, and has two children: Alice E. Weeks, born December 7, 1877, married Harry Alexander, of Upton, Massachusetts; William J. Weeks, of Princeton, born July 26, 1882.

Maria Fiske, mother of Colonel Pinkerton, was born at Lexington, Massachusetts. Her father's family follows: Samuel Fiske came to Lexington when a child and lived with John Chandler, who had him baptized at Lexington, May 29, 1803. He was born at Salem, Massachusetts, September 30, 1789. He married, January 25, 1818, Cordelia L. Tufts, of Charlestown, who was born January 7, 1795. She died April 15, 1833. He removed from Lexington to Shirley and later to Worcester, where he died October 25, 1844. He was a representative in the general court from Lexington in 1828-29-30. Their children were: 1. Lucy Ann, born at Kinderhook, New York, May 7, 1819, married, October 12, 1841, Joseph P. Hale, of Bernardston. 2. Ammi R., born at Charlestown (now Boston), Massachusetts, September 28, 1820, married December 28, 1846, Phebe James, of Newburyport, Massachusetts. 3. Augusta, born at Lexington, December 31, 1822, married, September 3, 1848, Timothy W. Wellington; moved to Shirley, Massachusetts, thence to Worcester. 4. Lucretia, born July 12, 1825, married, October 19, 1845, William Hudson, of Lexington, who was a soldier in the civil war, was in the signal corps in Burnside's expedition to North Carolina, died of disease, August 20, 1862, leaving John A Hudson, born December 26, 1846, and William F Hudson, born October 3, 1848 5 Ardelia L, born April 20, 1827, married, April 20, 1847, Lucius W Pond, who became one of the most prominent manufacturers of his day in Worcester 6 Maria, born December 20 1828 married, April 21, 1853, William C Pinkerton, of Lancaster, Pennsylvania (See parents of Hon A S Pinkerton) 7 Lydia, born July 27, 1830 8 Samuel, born March 23, 1833, went to Lancaster, Pennsylvania, married Amanda Stoddard, of Philadelphia

HARRINGTON FAMILY Chauncey Goodrich Harrington was born in Worcester, June 30, 1826, in a house that stood on the west corner of Park and Salem streets, which at that time was occupied as a public house, his father, William Harrington, being the landlord His early education was obtained in the public schools of his native town, and after passing through the various grades he found employment with a maker of spectacles, then a Worcester industry He later worked in a factory in Millbury, where carpenters' and gardeners' tools were made

In the fall of 1850, the Harrington block, corner of Main and Front streets, was built by his father, and Chauncey G Harrington, in company with Edward Bemis, opened here a store for the sale of boots and shoes, the style of the firm being Bemis & Co, the location No 2 Harrington corner Although the firm name was subsequently changed to Bemis & Company, Mr Harrington continued a member of the firm until the spring of 1873 During the summer of that year he, accompanied by his wife, made a trip to Niagara Falls, Toronto, and down the River St Lawrence to Montreal, thence to the White Mountains, where on June 11, while making a tour by coach from the Crawford House, and on the way from Bethlehem to the Profile House, a most thrilling accident occurred in which Mr Harrington met with a narrow escape from death Two coaches each drawn by six horses left the Crawford House in the morning, both well laden with passengers and their baggage The ride to the town of Bethlehem was one of special pleasure Here a short stop was made to allow the passengers to partake of light refreshments and stretch their limbs At the appointed time, when the signal was given, each one of the jolly party clambered into their proper places and the two coaches with their precious human freight started from the Sinclair House at a rapid clip amid the waving of handkerchiefs and cheers from the patrons of the hotel, responded to by the passengers with songs of music, the swinging of hats and waving adieus as they whirled along over the smooth road in the direction of the Profile House The second coach carried eighteen passengers, nine including Mr Harrington on the top and nine including Mrs Harrington on the inside There were also upon the top of the coach several heavy trunks, making the vehicle rather topheavy For some distance the two coaches traveled within easy communication of each other, but on reaching a certain house the driver of the rear coach halted for a few minutes when on again mounting the box the forward coach was out of sight The driver as well as the horses being apparently eager to overtake their leader, and the road for a considerable distance being descending, the coach was soon proceeding at a fearful speed and as the attempt was made to pass a curve in the road near the foot of Whitcomb hill, was overturned throwing the nine persons and the trunks that were on top of the coach in a heap by the road side Three of the passengers who were sitting near Mr Harrington when the coach went over were killed and all of the others were more or less injured Mr Harrington's injuries confined him in the house in Bethlehem to which he was removed from the scene of the accident for about three weeks Mrs Harrington came from the wreck unharmed, although her lady companion in the coach received a broken arm Of late years Mr Harrington has occupied his time in caring for a valuable property, the accumulation of many years Harrington block at the corner of Main and Front streets is considered one of the best locations for business purposes in the city of Worcester He attends the Main Street Baptist Church, and is a member of the Commonwealth Club, and also of the Worcester Society of Antiquity

He married (first) Lois Ann Harrington, of Millbury She died, and he married (second) Harriet Elizabeth Bemis, June 20, 1867 She was daughter of William and Catherine (Eveleth) Bemis, of Spencer, where she was born October 8, 1831 During her childhood her parents removed to Worcester, where she received her early education in the public schools and the Oread Collegiate Institute, later becoming a teacher of music in that institution, continuing from 1854 to 1857

Mrs Harrington is a lineal descendant of John Bemis, who was born in Dedham, Essex county, England, as early as 1550, and at his death left a will proved June 28, 1604, by which we learn that he had by wife Anne the following children Isaac, Luke, Neary, James, Susan, Abraham, and Joseph This last named Joseph Bemis married, lived and died in England, leaving 1 son Joseph, born in England, 1619, who came to New England and settled in Watertown, Massachusetts, as early as 1640, where he died August 7, 1684, having had by wife Sarah, nine children The widow Sarah died about 1712

John, born 1657, the youngest son of this Joseph, the farmer and blacksmith, married Mary Harrington in 1680, lived in Watertown and had fourteen children Their sixth child, Samuel, born 1690, married, April 12, 1715, Sarah Barnard, and had eight children William, the third child born in Sudbury, November 1, 1722, married Rebecca White, July 5, 1750, and had Jesse, 1751, Sarah, 1753, David, 1755, Sibbilah, 1758, Rebecca, 1761, Persis, 1764, William, August 18, 1766, Silas, 1770 He died March 23, 1801, and his widow Rebecca died March 17, 1819 William Bemis, born August 18 1766, married Lucretia Mirick, of Princeton, the intention of marriage is dated February 3, 1802 She died January 5, 1814 He married (second) Catherine Eveleth, also of Princeton, June 1, 1814 Children were Charles, born July 6, 1805, Dexter, August 5, 1806, Jesse, March 12, 1808, Elizabeth, March 17, 1811, David, August 3, 1812, Lucretia Mirick, May 12, 1815, William, December 14, 1816, George July 25, 1818, Horace, June 25, 1821, Edward, July 27, 1824, and Harriet Elizabeth, October 8, 1826

(I) The ancestral line of Chauncey Goodrich Harrington has been traced from Robert who was born in England in 1616 He embarked from there in the ship 'Elizabeth,' April 10, 1634 and on arriving in Massachusetts settled in Watertown, where his name appears among the list of proprietors in 1642 and 1644 He married, October 1, 1648 Susanna George, daughter of John George of Watertown then deceased as was also her mother, the widow of Henry Goldstone being her guardian Robert was admitted freeman March 27, 1663, and died May 11 1707 aged ninety-one years His will, dated January 1, 1704-05, mentions sons John, Daniel,

Benjamin, Samuel, Thomas, and Edward To the latter he gave his homestead His will also mentions daughters, Susanna Beers, Sarah Winship, and Mary Bemis, showing thus early a union between the Harrington family in New England with the Bemis family The inventory of Robert's estate mentioned six hundred and forty-seven and one-half acres of land and included a house and mill all appraised at seven hundred and seventeen pounds

(II) Edward Harrington, born March 2, 1668-69, the youngest son to grow to manhood of Robert and Susanna (George) Harrington, married (first), March 30, 1692, Mary Occington She died and he married (second) Anna, widow of Jonathan Bullard, of Weston, Massachusetts He was selectman of Watertown 1716-30-31 Their children were Mary, born 1692, William, 1694, Mindwell, 1697, Joanna, 1699, Edward, 1702, Samuel, August 3, 1704, Nathaniel, June 25, 1706, was a graduate of Harvard College 1728, and known as "Master Harrington", Francis, June 11, 1709, Susanna, September 9, 1711

(III) Samuel Harrington, born August 3, 1704, married, October 19 1725, Sarah Warren He was called of Waltham They had Samuel, baptized May 19, 1728, Mary, baptized same day

(IV) Samuel Harrington, baptized May 19, 1728, was called of Worcester in 1776, at which time his daughter Hannah married Daniel Maynard, of Shrewsbury, and may have been in Worcester prior to April 19, 1775, when his son Samuel marched from Worcester in Captain Timothy Bigelow's company for Lexington His children were Samuel, born 1754, married Silance Robinson, he died 1838, aged eighty-four years, Hannah, born 1757, married Daniel Maynard, and lived in Shrewsbury, Noah, born February 2, 1760, married Lois Kingsley, Joshua, and Jubal

(V) Noah Harrington born February 2, 1760, was matross in Colonel Thomas Craft's artillery regiment, 1775, William Todd's eighth Massachusetts company, February 1 to May 8, 1776, three months and seven days in service He may also have served in Captain Sibley's company, Colonel Keyes' regiment, mustered August 18, ——, and in Captain Joseph Sibley's company, Colonel Danforth Keyes' regiment, enlisted July 20, 1777, and again from December 1, 1777, to January 2, 1778, and under Captain Dex for Rutland, afterward enlisting for three years

He married, July 27, 1784 Lois, daughter of Enoch Kingsley She was born September 12, 1760, and died October 11, 1820 Their first home was in Shrewsbury where three of their children were born They removed to Worcester about 1792, and lived on the road to Grafton where it passes quite near the Boston & Albany Railroad tracks He with his brother Samuel, kept a tavern in Boston on the site of the present Adams House His children were Lydia, born December 25, 1784, William, 1786, died in infancy, Hannah, September 23, 1792, died young, Samuel, died young, William, February 25, 1788, Luke, September 12, 1789, died November 1855, Samuel, 1797, died April 4, 1855, Eliza 1800, married a Mr Shay, died July 17, 1869, Thomas J, January 27, 1804, died July 5, 1888, Hannah, July 17, 1809, married Henry Tower, and died March 23, 1853

(VI) William Harrington, born February 25, 1788, married Abigail Adaline, daughter of Peter and Elizabeth Stowell She was born March 15, 1799 Her father and his brother Ebenezer, in company with their father, Cornelius Stowell, were manufacturers of woolen goods, making a specialty of weaving carpets, dyeing and dressing woolen goods, and printing calicoes They made the first carpets used in the present state house in Boston

Mr Harrington passed his boyhood days upon his father's farm and attending the common schools, when a young man sought to learn the trade of a mason and bricklayer, and during the construction of the old Exchange building on Main street, near Exchange, when the brick walls were nearing their full height, the staging on which Mr Harrington and others were at work gave way, and the workmen with their bricks and mortar fell to the ground, several of the men being severely injured Mr Harrington was taken up for dead and carried to the opposite side of Main street near the corner of Walnut street, and laid in Mr Hamilton's yard Mrs. Hamilton detected some signs of life and efforts were made to revive him, which proved successful In the fall his knee had been crushed That with his other light injuries confined him to the house nearly five years, when the limb was amputated by Dr John Green As soon as he recovered from the operation he attended the Leicester Academy where he fitted for a teacher, and taught school in the Central Worcester district He later kept a store on Main street on the site now occupied by the Piper block, and also was engaged in keeping a tavern at corner of Salem and Park streets He died February 12, 1871, aged eighty-two years, eleven months and seventeen days His children were Frances A, born October 4, 1821, William Henry, April 29, 1824, Chauncey Goodrich, June 30, 1826

HILTON FAMILY The immigrant ancestor of most of the New England family of Hilton was William Hilton, who came from England to America in the ship "Fortune" to Plymouth, November, 1621 His wife and children came in 1623 in the ship "Anne" Land was assigned to the family at Plymouth in 1623 He removed to Newbury, Massachusetts, where he was living in 1635 He was admitted a freeman May 19, 1642 He was a deputy to the general court in 1642 and 1643 He removed again to New Hampshire His children were Sarah, born June, 1641, evidently of a second marriage, Charles, July, 1643, Ann, February 12, 1648, Elizabeth, November 6, 1650, William, June 28, 1663

Page Hilton, a descendant of William Hilton, mentioned above, was born in Maine and died in Bath, Maine He married Mary Ann Caton He was the father of Charles Fowle Hilton and grandfather of Charles Eugene Hilton, of Worcester

William Hilton, brother of Page Hilton, was born in Salisbury, Massachusetts, November 28, 1813, and died at Hotel Brunswick, Boston, December 25, 1887 He started in business as a country storekeeper at Frye village, Andover, Massachusetts His education was limited in his early years but he was eventually a well-educated man with a bright, open and inquiring mind and wide experience in public affairs He began buying wool of the farmers who then kept sheep generally About 1843 he removed to Boston to extend his operations in the wool market and produce In the successive firms of Hilton & Gore, Williams, Hilton & Company and in Hilton, Weston & Company this energetic man rose to the rank of the greatest wool merchant in Boston, well known in all the markets of that staple throughout the world Every year, in the interests of his house, he spent considerable time in London Eminently successful as a merchant, public-spirited, just and sagacious, he enjoyed the esteem of the best people of the city Mr Hilton was rated as a millionaire

E. C. Bigelow

He married Esther A ———, and they have one daughter—Mrs Catherine (Hilton) Fiske, who survived him In his will Mr Hilton provided for the eventual distribution of $540,000 among fifteen religious societies, colleges and charities

Charles Fowle Hilton, son of Page Hilton and nephew of William Hilton, was a resident of Whitefield, Maine He married Charlotte Roe Chapman, daughter of Benjamin and Lydia Ann (Turnbull) Chapman He died in Freeport, Maine Charles Fowle Hilton was a lumberman by occupation, also a farmer He married (second) Eliza Spratt, of Lewiston, Maine, by whom he had eight children, five of whom are living Charles F Hilton was a leading citizen of Castle Hill Plantation, in Aroostook county, Maine The children of Charles Fowle and Charlotte Roe (Chapman) Hilton were Frances Caroline, Charles Eugene, of whom later, Mary Enez, Lydia Ann, Frank Ellsworth The children of Charles Fowle and Eliza (Spratt) Hilton were Laban Page, Mary, Abigail, William, and several others

Charles Eugene Hilton, son of Charles Fowle Hilton, was born in Whitefield, Maine He attended the public schools at Castle Hill, Maine, and later in Worcester, Massachusetts He worked at farming, having charge of the Heywood farm, Worcester, for ten years He then bought his present estate, the old Allen place, and opened a stone quarry His farm on both sides of Grafton street, the buildings on Woodland place Mr Hilton has been very successful in contract work, excavating cellars and furnishing stone for foundations, building highways, driveways, etc He is a Free Mason, a member of Athelstan Lodge of Worcester, of Worcester Royal Arch Chapter, of the Republican Club and other organizations The former owner of the Hilton place was Major Allen, who sold it to Edward I Bliss, of the New York banking firm of Bliss, Morton & Company Mr Hilton bought the farm of Mr Bliss's widow

Mr Hilton married Rose May Rich, daughter of Henry V Rich, of Worcester Her mother was Deborah Sprague, of Rhode Island, a descendant of the well-known Sprague family of that section Their children are Benjamin Charles, born April 13, 1891, Irving Henry, February 27, 1893

GEORGE CONVERSE BIGELOW John Bigelow (I), the ancestor of the late George Converse Bigelow, of Worcester, was an early settler in Watertown being a descendant, according to the pedigree of Bigelow by the late H G Somerby, who spent considerable time in searching the English records, viz the Herald's visitations, deeds, charters, wills, parish registers and other original documents, of Richard de Baguley, Lord of Baguley, in the county of Chester, England 1243, since whose time the name has had many variations of spelling, the present one having been accepted by nearly all the later generations Some of the descendants spell the name Bagley, however Not to occupy too much space, we will take the direct line of descent to John Bigelow, of Watertown, from Richard de Baguley, Lord of Baguley, above mentioned, who married Alice daughter of Ralph de Vernon, and had a son

(II) Ralph de Baguley, who married a daughter of Hamon Massey Baron of Dunham Massey He had lands in Baguley and Ollerton in the parish of Knutsford He had three sons

(III) Hamon de Baguley, third son of Ralph, and Lord of the Manor of Ollerton Hall in the parish of Knutsford in the county of Chester, left many descendants in Ollerton

(IV) Ralph de Baguley, of Ollerton Hall, a descendant of Hamon de Baguley, made his will and died in 1540, and left two sons Randall and Nicholas

(V) Randall de Baguley, of Ollerton Hall, married Eleanor ———, and died 1556, he left two sons. Philip and Robert

(VI) Robert de Baguley, of Ollerton, was buried at Knutsford, November 4, 1582, leaving two sons Randall and John

(VII) Randall Baguley son of Robert, of Ollerton married Jane ———, died at Wrentham, county of Suffolk and was buried May 17, 1626 They had at Wrentham Persis, Susan, William, Margaret, John

(VIII) John, above named, is said by Mr Somerby to be the John Biglo or Bigelow, of Watertown He was a proprietor there as early as 1642 He bought a house and land there in 1649 and took the oath of fidelity at Watertown in 1652, and was admitted a freeman April 18, 1690 He was a blacksmith and planter in the colony, was chosen a surveyor of highways, 1652 and 1660, a constable, 1663, and one of "the seven men" (selectmen) in 1665-70-71 His homestead was bounded north by Richard Ambler and William Parker, east by Thomas Straight south by the highway and on the west by Miles Ives He married (first), August 30, 1642, Mary Warren, a daughter of John and Margaret Warren, and theirs was the first marriage recorded in Watertown She died October 19, 1691 He married (second), October 2, 1694, Sarah Bemis daughter of Joseph Bemis, of Watertown He died July 14 1703, at the age of eighty-six His will dated January 4, 1703, was proved July 23, 1703 The children of John and Mary (Warren) Bigelow were John, born March 14 1643 Jonathan, born December 11, 1646, Mary, born March 14 1648, married Michael Flagg, ancestor of the Worcester county Flaggs, Daniel, born December 1 1650, resided in Framingham Samuel, born October 28, 1653, Joshua, born November 5, 1655, resided in Watertown and Weston, married Elizabeth Flagg, he was a soldier in King Philip's war in Captain Ling's company, was wounded, and in consideration of his service the general court gave him a grant of land in Narragansett, Elizabeth, born June 15, 1657, married Lieutenant John Stearns, Sarah, born September 29, 1659, married Isaac Learned of Sherborn near Framingham, James lived in Watertown; Martha, born April 1 1662, Abigail, born February 4 1664, married Benjamin Harrington, Hannah, born March 4, 1666, died young, a son born and died December 18 1667

By his first marriage with Mary Warren the Bigelows are connected by descent with the Warren family Mary Warren's father, John Warren, was on the list of one hundred and eighteen freeman at Watertown, May 18 1631 He was selected as one to lay out the highways and see that they be sufficiently repaired and was selectman from 1636 to 1640 In a very elaborate genealogy of the Warren family, Professor John C Warren traced the descent of John Warren from William the Conqueror, and gives the direct line is extended back to the Saxon incursion into England in A D, 495, as also back through the royal lines of France, Germany and Italy It will be seen from tables given that the blood of the royal lines of England France, Germany and Italy flows in the veins of the Bigelows and Warrens William de Warren, the first of the name was one of the Norman barons who fought at the battle of Hastings

Samuel Bigelow, fifth child of John Bigelow, was born in Watertown Massachusetts, October 28, 1653 He married Mary Flagg, daughter of Thomas and

Mary Flagg who was born January 14, 1658, and died September 7 1720 He was a prominent citizen of Watertown He was an innholder from 1702 to 1716 He represented the town in the general court in 1708-09-10 His will, dated September 30 1720, mentions his children, as given below, and also some of his grandchildren John born May 9 1675, Mary, born September 12, 1677, Samuel, born September 18, 1679, Sarah born October 1, 1681, married Josiah Howe, Thomas of whom later, Mercy, born April 4, 1686, (also given Martha) married Lieutenant Thomas Garfield son of Captain Benjamin Garfield, Abigail born May 7, 1687 married August 1 1710, Jonathan Cutler, of Killingly, Connecticut, Hannah, born May 24, 1711, married Daniel Warren, a soldier in the French war, taken prisoner by the Indians and carried to Canada. Isaac born May 19, 1691, married Mary Bond and lived at Colchester, Connecticut, Deliverance, born September 22, 1695, married August 10, 1715. John Stern es

Thomas Bigelow, fifth child of Samuel Bigelow, was born in Watertown, October 24 1683, married, July 12 1705 Mary Livermore, of Watertown He removed to Marlboro Massachusetts, where he resided until 1720 when he removed to Waltham, where he died October 6, 1755 His wife died August 14 1753 Their children Thomas, born April 26 1706 resided in Marlboro, Mary, born September 2 1707 Grace, born February 7, 1709, Uriah, born July 13 1711, killed in an acident at Marlboro, March 5 1734 unmarried Abraham born March 5, 1713 resided at Weston, Isaac, born September 1, 1716 Jacob born September, 1717, Sarah, born May 15 1720, married Lieutenant Elisha Livermore, prominent in Waltham. Josiah, born July 30, 1730

Lieutenant Josiah Bigelow, youngest child of Thomas Bigelow was born in Waltham, July 30, 1730 married July 27, 1749, Mary Harrington, daughter of Jonas and Abigail (Stearns) Harrington She was born March 8 1730 Like his brothers Jacob and Abraham he was prominent in town affairs and in military service He was lieutenant of the Weston Artillery Company on the Lexington alarm April 10 1775 He died at Waltham July 15, 1810 aged eighty years His children, all born in Waltham were 1 William, born in Weston, October 1? 1749 was the original character described by Harriet Beecher Stowe in the story of "Old Town Folks" as 'Deacon Badger" his wife Hepsibah is described as 'Grandmother Badger" and those who remember them say their characters were most accurately depicted William, the eldest son is described as "Uncle Bill" Hepsibah, the mother of Professor Calvin E Stowe, was known as 'Susy," while Eunice figured as "Aunt Lois" and Abigail as 'Aunt Keziah" Professor Stowe was the author of many theological works 2 Anna, born August 23 1751 3 Uriah born November 30, 1753 4 Converse born January 20 1755, of whom later 5 Mary born March 3 1756 6 Alpheus, born November 2 1757 7 Eunice married April 24 1788, Joseph Morse and settled in Templeton Massachusetts and Eaton New York had eight children 8 Uriah born March 15 1766 9 Thomas, born August 11 1768 10 Sarah born July 31, 1773, married July 8 1790 Hezekiah Morse

Converse Bigelow fourth child of Lieutenant Josiah Bigelow was born at Waltham January 20, 1755 married October 8 1778 Anna Parks, who was born in Brighton Massachusetts February 5, 1756 and died at Sherborn September 9 1843 aged eighty-seven years He removed early to Templeton where his first three children were born then to Sherborn where he lived the remainder of his days and died April 23, 1829 He served in the revolutionary war from Weston in Captain Samuel Lawson's company, April 19, 1775, also in Captain Asahel Wheeler's company, Colonel John Robinson's regiment, in 1776, also corporal in Captain Charles Miles company, Colonel Jonathan Reed's regiment, at Ticonderoga in 1777 Their children were Betsey, born July 31, 1779, married, May 27, 1806, John Goulding, of Sherborn, had six children, Anne, born March 21, 1781, died unmarried December 26, 1871, aged ninety years, John, born January 26, 1783 married Hannah Partridge and settled in Sherborn, died December 8, 1839, she died August 27, 1840, Converse, Jr, born November 20, 1784, married Mary Viles, Elijah, born August 31, 1786, married Rebecca Fish, Calvin, born June 30, 1790, married Elizabeth Adams Sukey born April 17, 1792 married Josiah Battelle, Sally, born February 4 1794, married Nathaniel Stearns, resided in Acton, Josiah, born March 22, 1796, married Harriet Swain, Amos born March 17 1798 died July, 1798, Moses, born June 29 1801, of whom later

Amos Bigelow, youngest child of Converse Bigelow, was born in Sherborn Massachusetts, June 29, 1801, married, May 27 1827, Lucy Stowe born in Stow, Massachusetts July 27, 1809, died in Sherborn, August 29 1885 He was a farmer and for many years carried on the Bigelow homestead there, but late in life retired, bought a place in the village and sold the old farm He was interested in the family history and contributed much to the Bigelow genealogy Their children were 1 George Converse of whom later 2 Amos Elbridge, born May 10, 1830, married Mary Pratt Green, April 4, 1860 and their children are Irving Elbridge, Grace Hawley and Mary Eleanor 3 Henry, born November 25, 1833, married May 10, 1863 Catharine Pierce born May 10, 1839, died March 13, 1878, he married (second), April 27 1886, Mary Cockell. Henry came to Worcester in 1864 and engaged in the retail boot and shoe business, and about 1873 engaged in the real estate business and appraising property for banks, insurance companies etc 4 Edmund Dowse, born December 5 1838, married Alzina E Jenkins, born in Nantucket, and settled in Baltimore, Maryland, where he resided many years in ship chandlers' business, afterwards removing to Kansas City, where he now resides, their children, born in Baltimore, Maryland are Edmund Sprague Lucy Stowe and Florence E He enlisted in the Forty-second Massachusetts Regiment His military services consisted of duty in defense of Washington, D C, until April, 1863, expedition to Mills Cross Roads, Virginia, after Stuart's Cavalry December 28-29, 1862, duty on Columbia Pike, February 12, to March 30 1863, and at Vienna until April 11, moved to Norfolk thence to Suffolk Virginia, April 15-16, siege of Suffolk April 17-May 4 Nansemond River, May 3, Siege of Suffolk raised May 4 moved to West Point, May 5 thence to Yorktown May 31, raid to Jamestown Island June 10-13, Dix s Peninsula Campaign, June 12-July 10, action at Baltimore Cross Roads, July 2 moved to Washington D C, July 10-11, march in pursuit of Lee to Berlin Maryland, July 13-21 moved to Alexandria August 6 thence sailed to Folly Island, South Carolina August 7-13, siege operations on Morris Island, South Carolina, against Forts Wagner and Gregg, and on Morris and Folly Islands against Fort Sumter and Charleston, August 15 to November 13, expedition to Seabrook Island, November 13-15 resigned and honorably discharged from service on surgeon's certificate of disability, December 12 1863 5 Lucy Ann born May 7, 1840, died June 29, 1874 unmarried 6 Wesley, born November 16, 1847, manufacturer of decorative furniture in New York, unmarried

George Converse Bigelow, eldest child of Amos and Lucy (Stowe) Bigelow, was born in Sherborn, Massachusetts, March 11, 1828, where his boyhood was passed acquiring a good public school and practical education After a short residence in Dover, where he learned the trade of carpenter and builder, building the residence of Hon Henry Wilson in Natick, he removed to Worcester, the city of his adoption, in 1851, and there spent the remainder of his life He had much native ability and push and soon became a well known contractor and builder, and enjoyed the esteem and confidence of his fellow citizens The first important work on his own account was the direction of the construction of the Congregational Church in his native town In 1860 he formed a partnership with his brother, Amos E Bigelow, which continued until about 1886 under the firm name of G C and A E Bigelow, carpenters and builders During this period they erected a large number of buildings in Worcester and vicinity In partnership with Silas E Batchelder, Beacon street the firm built Piedmont Congregational Church, corner of Main and Piedmont streets Among other buildings constructed by the Bigelow firm were St John's Episcopal Church, Lincoln street, the Armenian Church, Laurel street, Baptist Church Lutheran Church, Mulberry street, shops for F E Reed, various additions to the Taylor and Farley organ factory Hanover street, most of the residences on Mt Pleasant street, a block of residences on Oread street, a residence on Main street, all the blocks of residences on Oread place, three residences on Benefit street, one on Benefit terrace, a block of two houses on Austin street, a business block on Front street, stores on Main street, &c, were built for the senior partner Many handsome buildings were built by them in different sections of the city The firm always enjoyed the highest reputation for business integrity and thorough work and never met with a failure After Mr Bigelow retired from the firm he took the contract for the Knowles building, corner of Main and Chatham streets, one of the finest office buildings in the city at the time of its erection He was never active in politics, though interested and did not aspire to public office, but was essentially a home man, where there was shown the radiance of love in his heart for those who were near and dear to him Mr Bigelow was an active member of Piedmont Church for seventeen or eighteen years After a long and painful illness, which he fought bravely, without a murmur he submitted to the inevitable April 13, 1892, leaving wife and daughter Alice J, born August 8 1856 educated at Oread Collegiate Institute, married, October 2, 1879 Frank P Knowles, of the Crompton & Knowles loom works They have children George Francis, born in Worcester, October 19, 1881, Alice Marian, born in Worcester, February 2, 1886, and Lillian, born in Worcester, August 26, 1888

George Converse Bigelow married, at Worcester, November 29, 1855, Eleanor J Doane born in Spencer, June 8, 1834, daughter of Cheney and Lorinda (Green) Doane After finishing her education at Wesleyan Academy, Wilbraham, Massachusetts and the Oread Collegiate Institute, Worcester she became a teacher in the public schools of Worcester, where she has been a resident for more than fifty years She has been an active member of Piedmont Church since its first organization, interested and helpful in all charitable and educational work, liberal and fair-minded kind and free to help others even at the expense of her own interests cheerful and appreciative of kindness, enterprising and energetic with a nature susceptible and responsive to noble influences, and thus thought and life were strengthened with her years She was also a member of the Woman's Club of Worcester

History tells us that Deacon John Done, or Doane as the name is now spelled the progenitor of the Doane family in all its branches in this country, came from England with his wife about 1629, when history also informs us that thirty-five of the Leyden Company with their families arrived at Plymouth He no doubt was one of these and a member of Mr Robinson's church While it is not definitely known from what part of the kingdom originally came the founder of the Doane family in America, we are fortunate in having our notes on the English family from the pen of Mrs Sarah Cash of Delamere, Cheshire, England a writer well known to the genealogical magazines of her country Mrs Cash's home is within the limits of the ancient Delamere Forest, of which for many years the Dones were Chief Foresters, and during the past few years she has contributed to 'Chester Notes and Queries" a series of highly interesting articles on the Dones of Utkinton It is supposed the earliest settlement of Dones at Utkinton was in King John's reign, 1199-1216, as in the old histories at a very early period is given a marriage between a Done and a Kingsley, formerly spelled Kyngslie, and when, as appeared the ancient Manor of that name had just passed from a Saxon ownership The office of forestship or Rangers of the Forest, by any nobleman holding such post, the same is held figuratively speaking by the "tenure of a horn," which particular horn in this case had been held by the Dones through transcending generations Frequent intermarriages of the Dones with other great families in Cheshire took place as a natural consequence to their relative associations and possessions This family is allied to one of the notably older families of the county, the Venables of Utkinton, a race spoken of as a race of warriors

The first and chief residence of the Done family appears to have been at the old Hall of Utkinton, county Chester Tradition still speaks of the hospitalities of Utkinton Hall during the occupancy of Sir John Doane the last possessor of the ancient line His lady, Dorothy Doane was possessed of such amiableness of temper and excellency of character, that when a Cheshire man would express excellency in the fair sex, he will say, "as fair as Lady Done," or 'there's a Lady Done for you," both of which are well known proverbs to this day in Cheshire The Dones monuments still to be seen in Tarporley church are very striking examples of fine arts; sculptured in marble they retain in a great degree their purity and whiteness, while in the evident care and truthfulness of execution they show excellent workmanship and artistic skill The medallion wall piece of Sir John Doane in Tarporley Church represents him in the costume of the reign of King James I his left hand resting upon the hilt of his sword, and with the Done motto 'Omnia Mei Dona Dei' The portrait reproduction of Sir John and Lady Done has been photographed from an ancient painting now hanging in Maple Hall near Stockport There is a similar portrait of Sir John Done at Arderne Hall the property of the Earl of Haddington The picture is well preserved, though dark in tone and the figure appears to have been depicted as wearing the Bugle Horn This Sir John Doane, Knight born 1576 knighted by James I, at Utkinton, 1617 died April 13, 1629 and was buried at Tarporley 1629 He married Dorothy daughter of Thomas Wilbraham, Esq, of Woodhey, and with his youthful bride went to reside for some time, according to the desire of his father-in-law, in the house of the celebrated John Bruen, of Stapleford, in order to be schooled in the principles and habits of Puritanism It is very probable that Deacon John Doane, of Plymouth, was a descendant of Sir John Done Knight in England

John Doane must have been known to the Pilgrims previous to his coming to Plymouth He was a strong man The Pilgrims were very careful to give no titles where they were not due The late Amos Otis, genealogist of "Early Barnstable Families," says In the Plymouth Colony the governor, deputy governor magistrates and assistants, ministers of the church, schoolmasters, officers in the militia, men of great wealth or connected with the gentry or nobility, were entitled to be called 'Mister" and their wives "Mistress" This rule was rigidly enforced in earlier Colonial times and in all lists of names it was almost the universal custom to commence with those who stood highest in rank and to follow that order to the end His associates and the offices he was bidden to undertake by the governor, the court, and by the suffrages of his townsmen show him to have been a man of superior qualities The names of the Freemen of the incorporation of Plymouth in New England in 1633 were Edward Wynslow, governor, Captain Miles Standish, William Bradford, John Howland John Alden John Done Stephen Hopkins William Gilson, Plymouth Colony Record, vol 1, page 3, council January 2, 1633-34, at this court Mr John Doane being formally chosen to the office of a deacon in the church, rather than an assistant to the governor in the affairs of the colony, resigned His position would suggest that he deemed the offices inconsistent one with the other The question of the day was " Separation and Independence" Hence we can slightly appreciate his course of thought in deciding Nevertheless Mr Doane henceforth was frequently summoned to act upon committees for the welfare of the community

In 1636 Elder Brewster, Pastor Smith and Deacons Doane and Jenney, of Plymouth Jonathan Brewster and Christopher Wadsworth of Duxbury, James and Anthony Annable, of Scituate, were joined to the governor and council for the preparation of a regular system of laws They began with the declaration of the Mayflower Compact, &c Until now, 1636, there was no law establishing the offices of governor, councillors or constables By general consent for fifteen years they were chosen annually Goodwin's 'Pilgrim Republic" page 401 They assembled according to the order and having read the combination made at Cape Cod, the 11th of November, 1620 on board the "Mayflower," they performed the important work for which they were appointed This was the first revision of the laws of the colony and to be appointed one of the committee for this work was a mark of distinction showing that Deacon Doane was respected for his wisdom and integrity Pratt's History of Eastham, page 16 March 3 1644-45 It is ordered that Mr Miles Standish, Mr John Doane and John Dunham shall take the accounts of Mr Thomas Prence for his treasurership of its receipts and payments and certifye the Court thereof, Plymouth Colony Record vol II, page 82 '

In 1644 there was a movement toward a new settlement at Nauset but the final removal was in 1645 The leaders in the enterprise were ex-Governor Thomas Prence, Deacon John Doane, Nicholas Snow Josiah Cook, Richard Higgins, John Smalley and Edward Bangs It is noted in Plymouth Colony Record, vol XII, that Mr John Doane sold his home in Plymouth in 1645 to Mr William Hanbury The territory of Nauset, purchased by the Indians, embraced the greater part of the present town of Orleans, Eastham and Wellfleet Our forefather gave the name of Nauset to the whole purchase and it was so called until 1651, when the court of Plymouth promulgated an order that henceforth Nauset should be called Eastham Deacon Doane had about two hundred acres of land, at various times having land granted him by court as well as by the town afterwards In Eastham town affairs Mr John Doane was an important man He was appointed by the court, June 1, 1663, to solemnize marriages and to administer oaths to witnesses. He was a deacon of the First Church there, and served the town as selectman for many years In 1649-50-51-53-59 he was a deputy to the colony court for Eastham, as he had been in 1642-43 for the town of Plymouth He died February 21, 1685, aged about ninety-five In his will his wife's name appears as Abigail His children were

1 John 2 Lydia, who was probably born before her parents came to Plymouth, she married Samuel Hicks, who came to Plymouth with his mother, younger brother, and sisters in the Ann" in 1623 His father Robert Hicks, came over in the Fortune' in 1621, and was one of the foremost of the Pilgrim fathers Abigail 2 (John I) born January 13, 1631 in Plymouth, married, 1690, Samuel Lothrop, born in England, second son of Rev John Lothrop, died at Norwich, Connecticut, January 23, 1734-35 John 2, born at Plymouth, 1635, died at Eastham March 15, 1708, married (first), April 30, 1662, Hannah, daughter of Edward Bangs, who came over to Plymouth in the "Ann" in July, 1623, married (second) January 14, 1694 Rebecca Pettee, whom he outlived He went with his father's family to Eastham, where he was a man of prominence and was for many years in public service He was a large landholder and was quite extensively engaged in farming He was a member of the First Church of Eastham His children were John 3, born March 20, 1663, died May 15, 1663, John, born May 29, 1664, Ann, born July 25, 1666, died at Orleans, July 12 1745, Rebecca born May 12, 1668, Hannah born May 12, 1669, died June 6, 1765, married February 12, 1701-02, John Collins, born at Eastham, December 18, 1674, died May 24, 1765, son of Joseph Collins From them descended the Hon Enos Collins a distinguished merchant of Liverpool, Nova Scotia, who married a daughter of Sir Brenton Halliburton, chief justice of Nova Scotia, and who died at Liverpool, in 1871, aged ninety-seven years Isaac, born June 2, 1670, Samuel, born March 2 1673, David, born about 1674, died November 18 1748, of whom later Daniel 2 born about 1636 died December 20, 1712 He was an extensive landholder and a prominent man in Eastham Ephraim 2, born at Plymouth removed to Eastham, died 1700 He married (first) Mercy Knowles the daughter of Richard and Ruth (Bower) Knowles, married (second), after 1692, Mary Snow, who was born in Barnstable December 11 1647 died at Eastham, 1703

David Doane 3 youngest son of John Doane, Jr 2, born at Eastham about 1674, died November 18 1748 Married, September 30, 1701, Dorothy Horton, and in his will in 1738 names his wife Sarah He was a juryman 1708-09-13-14-15-19-20-28-30, and a constable 1711-12 Besides being a farmer it is understood that he was a physician, and that he had a lucrative practice is evident He had seven sons viz Jonathan, John, Nathan, Eleazer, Joshua David and Enoch Daughters Hannah, married Samuel Atwood, married (second) ——

Higgins, Keziah, married Isaac Bacon, married (second) Dr John Duncain, Abigail, married Prince Collins, Rachel, married —— Higgins

Jonathan Doane 4, born July 7 1703, at Eastham, died January 24, 1780, married, August 8, 1723, Martha Higgins, and settled in Eastham He was a representative to the general court, a justice of the peace, town assessor, &c

Elisha Doane 5, eldest child of Jonathan Doane, born November 24, 1724, at Eastham, Massachusetts, died at Spencer, Massachusetts, about 1810 He was commissioned captain of Sixth (Second Eastham) Company, Second Barnstable Regiment of Massachusetts Militia, April 20, 1776 His widow Martha drew a pension for his revolutionary services and spent her last days at the home of her grandson in Spencer, she died November 10, 1837, aged eighty-eight years Their children were Oliver, born at Eastham, about 1754, Amos, born at Eastham 1758, Nathan, born Eastham, Elisha, born Eastham, January 7, 1770, Martha, Lucy, married Samuel Flagg

Nathan Doane 6, born Eastham, died at Brookfield about 1840, married, May 21, 1785, Betsey Smalley, who died August 7, 1834 He was a soldier in the war of 1812 His children were eight sons and two daughters, the youngest, John, born December 12, 1803, was drowned December 7 1816

Cheney Doane 7, youngest living son of Nathan Doane, born at Brookfield, Massachusetts, April 15, 1802 died April 2, 1866 Married Lorinda Green, of Spencer, born May 7 1812, died June 9, 1890 Children Eleanor J, born at Spencer June 8, 1834, married G C Bigelow, Elbridge, born February 2, 1840 was a soldier in the war of the rebellion enlisting in the Fifteenth Massachusetts Regiment Infantry, Company F, the last of June 1861 was mustered into the United States army July 12 1861, and was discharged at Worcester, Massachusetts, July 28, 1864 He was engaged in the battles of Balls' Bluff, Fredericksburg and Gettysburg He was taken prisoner in the first battle in which he fought and was wounded in the battle of Gettysburg, which caused his absence from his regiment for several months, and in consequence of which his health was so depleted that he was put on the list of pensioners He married Julia Barber, of Esmond South Dakota had one daughter, Alma, born February 28 1892 Lorenzo F, born August 13, 1842, died at St Louis Missouri He enlisted in the Twenty-fourth Regiment Massachusetts Infantry, Company I, and was promoted to corporal He was in all the battles fought by the Twenty-fourth Regiment during his term of service and was duly discharged He married, July 26, 1903, Mary R Jones, born at Falmouth, Massachusetts, March 10 1856, daughter of Captain Silas and Harriet B (Robinson) Jones Children Bertha Leigh, born at Pawtucket, Rhode Island, July 29, 1878, Joseph Robinson, born Kansas City, Missouri, October 2, 1882, Mary Dorothy born at Clear Lake Iowa, July 22, 1886, Paul, born at Denver, Colorado, October 12, 1887 Anna Izette, born October 2, 1847, married Rimmon Colton Fay, of Brookfield, February 22, 1870 Children Walter Chapman born Hartford, Connecticut, April 28, 1872 died April 29, 1872, Ralph Warren born Lincoln, Rhode Island, July 28 1873, died September 7, 1874, Elsie Florence born Brookfield Massachusetts March 21, 1875, teacher in Friends' School, Frankford, Philadelphia, Pennsylvania, Arthur Colton born Pawtucket, Rhode Island, April 18, 1877, George Lucius, born Lincoln, Rhode Island, August 15, 1879 Rimmon Wesley, born Milford Massachusetts, November 22, 1881, Frank Homer, born Milford, Massachusetts, February 14, 1883, Alice Eleanor, born Milford, Massachusetts September 1, 1884 died January 10, 1885, Pauline Ruby, born Hopedale, Massachusetts, September 7, 1887, Dorothy Izette, born Ilion, New York, January 12 1892

Thomas Doane, a descendant of Deacon John Doane, of Plymouth, in a direct line from Samuel Doane, brother of David, sons of John, Jr, who was born at Orleans, Massachusetts, September 20, 1821 died October 22, 1879, was one of the first civil engineers of his time, having done very extensive and important work from Massachusetts to Dakota He was an active member of the Boston Society of Civil Engineers, and was elected president shortly after its organization in 1879 and was nine times re-elected to that position He became a member of the American Society of Civil Engineers in 1882 From 1869 to 1873, while a resident of Nebraska, he was instrumental in founding Doane College" situated in Crete, on the "Big Blue" river, twenty miles west of Lincoln, and one of the leading educational institutions of that state, and of which David Brainard Perry, son of Deacon Samuel Perry of Worcester, is president, and who married Mr Doane's eldest daughter, Helen, July 3, 1876 Mr Doane resided for many years at No 8 Pearl street, in one of the oldest houses in Charlestown It was at one time owned by Oliver Holden, the composer of the famous hymn 'Coronation," who lived there for many years and died in one of the upper rooms

In 1863 Mr Doane was appointed chief engineer of the Hoosac tunnel, and located the line of the tunnel, built the dam in the Deerfield river to furnish water power and in this work introduced nitroglycerine and electric blasting for the first time in this country He also introduced compressed air, and invented the machinery for it, and had a large share in inventing the pneumatic drills used there On the opening of the tunnel in 1875 he run the first engine, the 'N C Munson" through it In 1869 he went to Nebraska and built two hundred and forty miles of railroad on the extension of the Chicago, Burlington & Quincy Railroad and located and named nearly all the towns on the extension Completing his work in Nebraska in 1873 he returned to Charlestown, and soon afterwards was appointed consulting engineer of the Hoosac tunnel and had charge of the reconstruction of the Troy and Greenfield Railway and of the tunnel He finished his duties in this direction in 1877, and two years later was appointed consulting and acting chief engineer of the Northern Pacific Railroad for one year During that time he located the Pend d' Oreille division across the Columbia Plains in Washington Territory, and parts of the Missouri division in Dakota Mr Doane was at one time employed as consulting engineer of the West End Street Railway, Boston and in the winter of 1877-78 in company with other officials of the railway, visited a number of western cities for the purpose of examining cable systems A large part of the engineering for the city of Charlestown was done by Mr Doane previous to that city becoming a part of Boston in 1874 Mr Doane has at one time or another been connected with all the railroads running out of Boston, but particularly with the Boston & Maine In company with his brother, John Doane Jr he opened an office at No 21 City Square under the firm name of T and J Doane, Jr, for the general practice of civil engineering and surveying an office which was maintained until his death in 1897

WILLIAM HOWE BLISS, son of Harrison and Sarah (Howe) Bliss, was born September 23,

1850, at Worcester, Massachusetts His mother was the daughter of William and Sarah (Hayden) Howe, of Worcester He attended the public schools and Highland Military Academy He entered Worcester Academy but did not complete his course He began his business life in the jewelry business in 1870 Later he was superintendent of the Boston, Clinton & Fitchburg Railroad at New Bedford, a position he filled for two years For a year he was at Tiffin, Ohio, engaged in the manufacture of staves for oil and flour barrels Since the death of his father his time has been occupied in the care of the real estate and property He was formerly a member of the Tatnuck Country Club and of the Hancock Club He is a member of the Worcester Society of Antiquity He married (first) May 31, 1883, Nellie J Winch, daughter of Martin Winch He married (second), April 15, 1891, Florence E W Weston, daughter of David and Almira Weston, of Fort Fairfield Maine Almira Weston was the daughter of Rev Amos and Mary (Watson) Parmer an English clergyman who came to New Brunswick as a missionary Mrs Bliss was born at Fort Fairfield, Aroostook county, Maine The children of these two marriages were Elizabeth Howe, born January 11 1886, now at Smith College, class of 1908, Sarah, June 7, 1893, died August 22, 1894, Florence, May 22, 1895, and Dorothea, November 17, 1898

(I) Thomas Bliss, was the last English ancestor of the Bliss family of Worcester He resided at Belstone and was a man of property He was a Puritan and his wealth and prominence perhaps invited the persecution he suffered and through which he lost both his wealth and his health He was imprisoned for his religious and political views His children of whom Thomas and George emigrated to America to escape persecution, were Jonathan, died 1635-36 Thomas, died in 1640, Elizabeth, married Sir John Calcliffe of Belstone, George born 1591, died August 31, 1667, and Mary (Polly)

(II) Jonathan Bliss, son of Thomas Bliss (1), of Belstone, was born about 1580 at Belstone On account of his non-conformist views he was persecuted and virtually driven out of England, suffering heavy fines and eventualy dying at an early age from a fever contracted in prison Four children are said to have died in infancy, two grew up They were Thomas, died in 1649, and Mary

(III) Thomas Bliss of Rehoboth, Massachusetts, son of Jonathan Bliss, of Belstone, England, was born in Belstone, and on the death of his father in 1636 he removed to Boston, thence to Braintree, thence to Hartford, Connecticut, thence back to Weymouth, Massachusetts, and in 1643, with others he helped make the settlement at Rehoboth He was a freeman at Cambridge, May 18, 1642, and in Plymouth colony January 4, 1645 In June, 1645, of that year he drew a lot of land at the Great Plain, Seekonk In 1646 he was fence viewer, in 1647 the surveyor of highways, two important offices in the colonial days He died at Rehoboth, June, 1649, and is buried in the graveyard at Seekonk, Massachusetts, now Rumford, East Providence, Rhode Island His will was proved June 8, 1649 Their children were Jonathan, born about 1625 died about 1687, ————, married Thomas Williams, Mary, married Nathaniel Harmon of Braintree, Nathaniel possibly of Springfield, seems to have left no descendants in male line (See Chapin Genealogy)

(IV) Jonathan Bliss, son of Thomas (3) and Mistress Ide Bliss, born in England about 1625, was made a freeman of the Plymouth colony 1655 He was "way warden" at the town meeting in Rehoboth May 24, 1652, and May 17, 1655, was on the grand jury He was a blacksmith He was made a freeman in Rehoboth, February 22, 1658, and drew land June 22, 1658 He was one of the eighty who made what is called the North Purchase He married, 1647-48, Miriam Harmon (probably a sister of his sister's husband) He died 1687 The inventory of his estate was sworn to May 23, 1687 The magistrate was the famous governor, Sir Edmund Andros Their children were 1 Ephraim, born 1649 2 Rachel, December 1, 1651, married, October 28, 1674, Thomas Manning, of Swansea, Massachusetts 3 Jonathan, March 4, 1653, died 1653 4 Mary, September 31 (sic), 1655 5 Elizabeth, January 29, 1657, married June 25, 1684, James Thurber 6 Samuel, June 24, 1660, died August 28, 1720 7 Martha, April, 1663 8 Jonathan, (sometimes recorded Timothy) September 17, 1666, died October 16, 1719 9 Dorothy, January 27, 1668, married, June 26, 1690, James Carpenter 10 Bethia, August 1671, married, April 15, 1695, Daniel Carpenter, died February 27, 1702-03 Her husband was son of William Carpenter and Miriam Searles, of Rehoboth, born October 8, 1669

(V) Ephraim Bliss, son of Jonathan (4) and Miriam Bliss, was born at Rehoboth, February 5, 1649 He resided at Braintree, Quincy, Scituate, Rehoboth and Providence, Rhode Island Their children were Jonathan, born at Braintree about 1672-73, Mary, Thomas, Ephraim, married Mary ——, resided at Rehoboth (she was born 1702, died November 14, 1730), and Daniel

(VI) Jonathan Bliss, son of Ephraim (5) and —— Bliss, was born at Rehoboth, 1672-73 All his children died young without issue except John They were Hannah, Thomas, Mary, John, born 1711, died June, 1752, Nathaniel, and Ephraim

(VII) John Bliss, son of Jonathan (6), was born at Rehoboth, 1711 He married on Thanksgiving Day, 1735, Rebecca ——, a very capable and energetic manager, history tells us, who with great prudence and thrift cared for her property after the death of her husband He died 1752 Their children were Nathan born December 19, 1736, died December 3 1820, Elizabeth, April 5, 1738, Anne, April 1, 1740, William, June 6, 1742, died 1822, Rebecca, December 20, 1744, John, August 21, 1747, died March 12, 1825, Abigail, April 28, 1750, Keziah born November 26, 1752, died 1793-94

(VIII) Nathan Bliss, son of John (7) and Rebecca Bliss, was born at Rehoboth, December 19, 1736 He was a farmer at Rehoboth He married, December 26, 1760, Joanna Bowen, who died March 10, 1823 He died December 3, 1820 Their children were 1 Nathan born December 19, 1761, died January 31, 1852 2 Abel, December 22, 1763 was a farmer at Rehoboth captain in the militia, married Olive Briggs, of Dighton, who died May 17, 1823, he married (second) Hannah Horton, died without issue, November 13, 1843 (she died March 7, 1859, aged sixty-six years) 3 Olive, October 2, 1765, married, January 4, 1786, Samuel Goff 4 Joanna, July 25, 1767, married, January 18, 1787, Shubael Horton and —— Payne 5 Sylvanus, July 9, 1769, died June 23, 1859 6 Rebecca, July 12, 1771, married May 23, 1793, Sylvester Goff, of Rehoboth 7 John, born September 1, 1773, died August 29, 1859 8 Thomas, October 17, 1775, died 1855 9 Anna, September 17, 1777 10 Cromwell, March 17, 1779, died February 7, 1848 11 Ezra, June 17, 1780 died May 11, 1857

(IX) Nathan Bliss, son of Nathan (8) and Joanna Bliss, was born at Rehoboth, December 19, 1761 He removed to Royalston, Massachusetts, between 1770 and 1775, and married Ruth Briggs, at Dighton, Massachusetts, who died at Royalston, November 28, 1862 She was born at Dighton, December 22, 1765 He died at Royalston, January 31, 1852 He was a farmer Their children were Annie living at Royalston, unmarried, Abel born August 23, 1785, died July 4, 1852, Ruth 1795, married James Buffum, who lived in Keene, New Hampshire She died 1856, Sally, born 1806, married Benjamin Buffum, of Royalston

(X) Abel Ballou Bliss, son of Nathan Bliss, Jr (9), was born at Royalston, August 23, 1785 He was a shoemaker He married Nicena Ballou, who was born March 6, 1788, and died April 7, 1847 He died July 4, 1852 Their children were Nathan, born September, 1808, married Emily Lovett, 1832, Abel Ballou, February 21, 1811, died August 4, 1852, Harrison, October 9, 1812, married Sarah H Howe, Russell, December 5, 1815, married Mary May, March 8, 1835, died June 15, 1852, James July 16, 1818, married Julia Drury, died January 16, 1842, Nicena J, December 12, 1823, died January 7, 1845, unmarried, Olive Lucian, July 3, 1825, married May 9, 1847, Charles C Balch, carpenter, resided at Shirley, Massachusetts

(XI) Harrison Bliss, son of Abel (10) and Nicena Ballou Bliss of Royalston, was born at Royalston, October 9, 1812 What education he got in school was obtained in his native place He started out at the age of eighteen to make his own living He landed in Worcester, as he used to say with just seventeen cents in his pockets

He went to work first at the very place where he afterward bought one of the finest houses in the city, where his son, William H Bliss, now lives His employer was Dr Oliver Fiske That was in 1830 He worked for four years in the Worcester Post Office when Deacon James Wilson was postmaster in the present Union Block, and under Jubal Harrington in the old Central Exchange Building He went into business with Deacon Alexander Harris in the Salisbury Block in Lincoln Square, dealing in groceries and in flour Later he took Joseph E Gregory as partner He sold his interest in this store in 1850 and later opened a flour store in partnership with T and J Sutton under the name of Bliss, Sutton & Co, on Mechanic street, and in 1857 sold out to his partners From that time to his death he was occupied with his real estate and banking business He started Hon H A Blood, of Fitchburg, in business Mr Blood was in his employ in his store in Worcester

Mr Bliss was president of the New Bedford and Taunton branch of the Boston, Clinton & Fitchburg Railroad Company, and vice-president of the Framingham and Lowell branch, both of which are now operated by the New York, New Haven & Hartford Railroad Company

Mr Bliss and the late Hon Francis H Dewey founded the Mechanics National Bank in 1848 He was president from 1860 to his death in 1882 He was interested in the Mechanics' Savings Bank from its organization in 1851 He was on the board of investment He was president from 1864 to his death He was largely interested in the old Music Hall Company, the successor of which owns the Worcester Theatre He was interested largely in the Bay State House corporation He was a representative to the general court in 1855, 1865 and 1874 He was an Alderman in 1861, 1863, 1864, 1865, 1875 and 1876 He was chief owner of the Oriental Powder Company, manufacturing gun powder near Portland, Maine During the Franco-Prussian war he made a snug sum of money selling powder to the belligerents The house in which his son-in-law, Francis H Dewey lives, he said was built from the profits of the sale of powder at that time He sold out to advantage later He married Sarah H Howe, April 5 1836 daughter of William Howe, of Worcester (See Howe family) A brother of his wife, Rev William Howe, of Cambridge, Massachusetts, is still living (1905), and will be one hundred years old May, 1906 Her father was a contractor He had the contract for the building of the Worcester Turnpike over which for some distance the cars of the Boston & Worcester Electric Railroad run He lost money and was ruined by the contract Mrs Bliss died July 24, 1882, a few weeks after her husband She was a very capable woman and famous for her charities He died July 7, 1882 Their children were 1 Harrison, Jr, born July 30, 1843, married Amy Brown, of Dighton, November 6, 1864 died May 12, 1868 2 Sarah, September 22, 1845, died November 18, 1849 3 William Howe, September 23, 1850 4 Pamelia Washburn, May 21, 1854, died September 9, 1854 5 Lizzie Davis, March 12, 1856, married Francis H Dewey, December 12, 1878, at Worcester They have one son and one daughter (See Dewey family and Bullock family)

The mother of Harrison Bliss (11), was Nicena Ballou She married Abel Bliss, in Richmond, New Hampshire She was born March 6, 1788, in Richmond, he was born August 23, 1785, at Rehoboth, and when six weeks old was carried on horse back in his mother's arms from Rehoboth to their new home in Royalston The Ballou family is widely scattered but many Worcester county families are related to the Ballous

(I) Maturin Ballou, the emigrant ancestor, married Hannah Pike, daughter of Robert and Catherine Pike, probably of Providence, Rhode Island 1646 to 1649 He died February 24, 1661, to January 31, 1663 Their children were John, born 1650, married Hannah Garrett, James, born probably at Providence, 1652, married Susanna Whitman, 1683, Peter, 1654, married Barbary ——, Hannah, 1656, died unmarried, Nathaniel, 1658, died young, Samuel, 1660, drowned June 10, 1669

(II) James Ballou, son of Maturin (1), was born at Providence, Rhode Island, 1652 He married Susanna Whitman daughter of Valentine and Mary Whitman (or Wightman), who was born in Providence, February 28, 1658, married July 25, 1683 James was a large owner of land With what he inherited and bought he had fully a thousand acres Their children were James, born November 1, 1684 married Catherine Arnold, January 25, 1714, Nathaniel, April 9, 1687, married Mary Lovell, December 7, 1716, Obadiah, September 6 1689, married Damaris Bartlett, January 5, 1717, second —— Salisbury, Samuel, January 23, 1692, married Susannah Arnold, second Mary Smith, Susanna, January 3, 1695, married John Inman, and Richard Sayles, Bathsheba, February 15 1698, married Daniel Arnold October 16, 1720, Nehemiah January 20, 1702, married Mary Holt and Abigail Perry

(III) James Ballou, son of James (2) and Susanna Ballou, was born in Providence afterward called Smithfield, now Lincoln, Rhode Island November 1, 1684 He married Catherine Arnold daughter of Elisha and Susanna (Carpenter) Arnold, in Providence January 25 1713 She was born in Wrentham later called Cumberland, Rhode Island, February 28 1690 He was one of three pioneers to cross the Blackstone river and settle Cumberland The Cooks and Ballous, two of these families often intermarried They were Baptists of the Roger Williams sort The little church built in or about 1745, still standing at Cumberland, was known as the "Elder Ballou Meeting House" James Ballou died February 10, 1764 Their children were Sarah, born November 15, 1713, married Uriah Jillson, 1733, Ariel, November 18, 1715, married Jerusha Slack, 1740, Bathsheba, November 26, 1717, married Michael Keith and Elisha Newell, Martha, October 6, 1720, married Elder Nathaniel Cook, January 27, 1742, James, December 10, 1723, married Tamasin Cook, June 7, 1744, Elisha, November 15, 1726, married Hepsibah Thayer, November 30, 1748, Priscilla, November 6, 1731, married William Cook, 1753

(IV) James Ballou, son of James (3) and Catherine Ballou, was born in Wrentham, near Cumberland, Rhode Island, December 10, 1723, married Tamasin Cook (Daniel (3), Nicholas (2), Walter (1)), born June 16, 1725, married June 7, 1744 He was made a freeman of Cumberland April 19, 1749 In 1774 he moved to Richmond, New Hampshire, with other Rhode Island associates He and other Ballous settled on what has since been known as Ballou Hill The town was divided in factions later owing to a schism in the Baptist church caused by "the New Lights," in which James was interested but later abandoned His wife Tamasin, died April 25, 1804, and he married, second, Huldah Carpenter, widow of Joseph Carpenter, June 19, 1806 He died January 21, 1812 His children were 1 Seth, born February 20, 1748, married Margaret Hilton 2 Olive, May 13, 1751, married Preserved Whipple 3 Silas, February 24, 1753, married Hannah Hilton, April 17, 1774 4 Susannah, June 16, 1755, married Nathan Harkness, June 4 1775 5 Ozicl, July 11 1757, married Hannah Robinson, December 7, 1790 6 Tamasin, June 29, 1759, married Ebenezer Swan, February 15, 1778 7 James, April 25, 1761, married Mehitable Ingalls, November 5, 1786 8 Russell, July 11, 1763, married Henrietta Aldrich and —— 9 Aaron, September 25 1766, married Catherine Bowen, September 8, 1786 10 Daniel, May 26, 1768, married Mary Hix, April 8, 1787 11 Priscilla, January 3, 1772, married Nathan Bullock, February 28, 1790

(V) Russell Ballou, son of James (4) and Tamasin, was born at Cumberland, July 11, 1763, He married Henrietta Aldrich, daughter of Jonathan and Patience Aldrich, of Cambridge, Massachusetts, who was born August 20, 1764, certified, (married) February 23, 1783 All their children were born at Richmond, New Hampshire He removed in 1804, to Royalston, Massachusetts His wife Henrietta died June 8, 1827, aged sixty-seven, and he married, second, Mrs Beebe Mellen, of Swansea, New Hampshire, widow of Joel Mellen, April 16, 1827 He died at Swansea, New Hampshire, November 10, 1847, she died 1854 His children were Betsey, born October 6, 1783, married Royal Blanding, November 18, 1802, Amey, October 27, 1785 married Stephen Parks, Nicena, March 6, 1788, married Abel Bliss, 1806 (see Bliss Family), Asquire May 8, 1792 maried Arathusa Maynard, May 29, 1816, Russell, September 9, 1794, married Lucy D Norton, January 29, 1816, Luther, September 7 1797, married Clarissa Davis, December 3, 1818, Priscilla June 25, 1800, died unmarried, May 8, 1814, Olive, born August 29 1803, married Jacob Boyce, 1829, Russell, died in infancy

HOWE FAMILY Ezekiel Howe, son of Thomas Howe (3), grandson of Thomas, and great-grandson of John Howe, of Sudbury, was born in Marlboro Massachusetts, January 29, 1720 He married Elizabeth Rice, of that town, May 10, 1740, and their first child Patience was born in Marlboro, but recorded also at Worcester whither the father moved about 1742 Their children were Patience, born June 10, 1742, Elizabeth, February 12, 1744, Ebenezer, November 4, 1746, Joel, November 2, 1748, Jotham, June 17, 1750, Lucy, April 20, 1752, Rebecah, April 3, 1754, Ezekiel, March 20, 1756

(V) Ezekiel Howe, son of Ezekiel (4) and Elizabeth Howe, was born at Worcester, March 20, 1756 He married December 21, 1773, Mary Young She was born in Worcester, May 14, 1757 William died in 1820 Their children were William, baptized July 20, 1783, Mary, baptized July 20, 1783, Asa, baptized July 20, 1783, Ezekiel, baptized September 28, 1783 These records are from the Old South Church They were born between 1774 and 1783

(VI) William Howe, son of Ezekiel, Jr (5) and Mary Howe, was born at Worcester about 1780, and died in 1820 He married Sarah Gould, December 22, 1805 Their children were William, born March 25, 1806, now living (1905), John, born August 7, 1808, Rufus, born July 27, 1812, Sarah H, born June 30, 1814 married Harrison Bliss (See W H Bliss, Bliss Family)

(VII) William Howe son of William Howe (6), was born May 25, 1806, so if he lives till his next birthday he will be one hundred years old He is the oldest clergyman living in the United States Although always in close touch with the members of his family in Worcester, he has made his home in Cambridge, Massachuestts In appearance Dr Howe is no older than he has been for the past ten years His sight and hearing have failed but his intellect is clear and his memory excellent

His youth in Worcester at the home of his parents, town of Holden, and Market street, Worcester, is rich with anecdotes that after nearly a century are full of interest At that time Worcester was a country village around the court house, and except for a few stores even Main street was the location of farms It is a marvelous thing to remember events a hundred years ago When he was fourteen his father died and his mother had the care of three younger than he She managed her affairs which were somewhat tangled at the time of her husband's death in a way to win praise from the most astute financiers of the town who knew the problems that she had to meet William was fitted for college and entered Waterville (now Colby) College, which is a favorite Baptist institution There were thirteen men in his class, nine of whom graduated Needless to say he is the oldest living graduate of Colby He was educated for the ministry at Newton Theological Seminary, and it was while he was there that he began the work that he continued for over half a century, that resulted in the establishment of four Baptist parishes growing out of his mission work This work he began in Boston as city missionary, walking to Boston from Newton, some ten miles every Saturday and Monday to carry on the work In a sail loft on Charlestown street he started the first mission and Sunday school that grew into the present Merrimac Street Union Baptist Church He established seven others and carried on the eight missions simultaneously From a Commercial Street Sunday school grew the Baptist Bethel Church on Hanover street' The Union Baptist Church united with the Tremont Temple Church, and has become the most important Baptist church in Boston and probably the best known in the country From another Sunday school developed the Harvard Street Church, and from still another the Bowdoin Square

Church Dr Howe himself was the first pastor of the Merrimac Street Church, the building being dedicated in 1846, and he remained pastor till 1858 when the union with Tremont Temple took place

In 1863 Dr Howe accepted the pastorate of a chapel on Harvard street, Cambridge, and under his hands this chapel grew into the parish of the Broadway Baptist Church Since he was seventy he has been living in retirement at 910 Massachusetts avenue, Cambridge, Massachusetts He married in 1832, Angeline Ammidon, of Boston She was one the first women to form an anti-slavery society when the abolition movement began in Massachusetts She died in 1883 They had no children He was one of the founders of the Associated Charities of Boston, and was at one time a member of the Boston school board He knew personally Daniel Webster, Henry Clay, John C Calhoun, Rufus Choate, and other famous men long since dead He has always been interested in the Spellman seminary for colored girls at Atlanta, Georgia, and in that city he has erected a memorial chapel to his wife

JOHN E BRADLEY Among the most important factors in the industrial world is recognized the Bradley family, whose name is particularly identified with railway development in the United States, and as pioneers in the great business of building stage coaches and subsequently the manufacture of steam and electric railway cars

(I) The Bradley family in America was founded by Daniel Bradley, who sailed from England, April 28 1635, and settled at Haverhill, Massachusetts, later resided at Ipswich He married Elizabeth Ayer and they had sons, Daniel and Joseph He was killed by Indians, August 13, 1689

(II) Joseph Bradley, son of Daniel (1), married Hannah Heath, April 4, 1691, and their children were Mehitable, Joseph, Martha, Sarah, David, Nehemiah, Samuel and William

(III) William Bradley, son of Joseph (2), married Mehitable Emerson Their children were Susan, Sarah, Abigail, Hannah, Mehitable, Joseph, Jonathan, William, Moses and Nancy

(IV) Jonathan Bradley married Sarah Osgood, of North Andover, June 17, 1773 Their children were Thomas Osgood, born September 28, 1774, Sarah Mary, William, Elizabeth, and Jonathan

(V) Thomas Osgood Bradley, son of Jonathan, married Mehitable Carlton, and had children Osgood, born January 15, 1800, died May 11, 1884, John and Frederick

(VI) Osgood Bradley son of Thomas (5), was born January 15, 1800 He received a high school education, and early entered upon an active career His life affords a striking example of the great results attainable through industry and well directed effort Beginning as a carriage maker, he prosecuted his labors with such success that at the time of his death he was held in honor as the oldest of the pioneer car builders in America He learned the carriage-making trade in Framingham, coming in 1822 to Worcester, where he began the making of coaches and carriages in an old wooden building in the rear of the 'Green Store," but subsequently removed to other and larger quarters as business expanded In 1826 he began the making of coaches for the large stage line operators in New York and New England, and for years built the majority of those in use in that region At the dawn of the railway era in 1835 he turned his attention to the building of railway coaches, and in 1837 sold out his carriage business to become exclusively a railway coach builder, constructing the pioneer cars for many of the early eastern roads, maintaining one manufacturing location for a full half century For a decade prior to 1849 he was associated in business with Edward B Rice During the civil war Mr Bradley entered into large contracts with the government for the construction of gun carriages for field, sea-coast artillery fully maintaining the high reputation of the Bradley works and receiving the cordial appreciation of the War and Navy departments

Mr Bradley was a splendid representative of his residential city Progressive and enterprising, he was a leading factor in its upbuilding, and used his influence and means without stint for its advancement in moral and intellectual as well as in material affairs He was a man of great nobility of character, of strict integrity and the highest moral worth, and was held in esteem by the entire community He was prominently connected with the Plymouth Congregational Church, and aided efficiently in promoting its interests and usefulness In 1845 he bought the fine mansion which stood on the site of the present Chase building, where he lived for many years, and where he died, May 11, 1884 in his eighty-fifth year Nearly ten years before his demise (on January 15, 1875) he there celebrated his seventy-fifth birthday This was one of the notable events of the day, being the occasion of a remarkable gathering of men whose heads had become whitened with the frosts of many a winter, among the number being many railway magnates from various sections of the country

His first wife was Fanny Sanger, by whom were born 1 Elizabeth Mehitable born September 11, 1824, married George A Hamilton 2 Maria Sanger, September 29, 1826, married John B Wyman, in 1843, he became a prominent military man in the civil war period 3 Henry Osgood see forward 4 John, April 10, 1831 5 Daniel Sanger, February 9 1834 6 Osgood, December 26, 1836 7 Sarah Olivia November 2, 1839 Mr Bradley, after his first wife's death, married Sarah J Makepeace, by whom was born one child, A Jeannie, who resides in Worcester and is unmarried

(VII) Henry Osgood Bradley, third child and eldest son of Osgood (6), was born September 17, 1828 He received a liberal education, and early in life became associated with his father in business affairs becoming the office manager and general accountant of the Bradley works, and displaying the same sterling qualities which characterized the sire He was a man of unusually broad information his mind well expanded not only through liberal reading but by much travel He was just of age (in 1849) when the California gold-seeking voyagers set out, and he went on the first vessel sailing from Boston, remaining away a year He became familiarly acquainted with the United States and twice made a tour of Europe, visiting the industrial and art centres solely for purposes of recreation and mind improvement With quiet domestic tastes, he was devoted to his family, and would attach himself to no societies whatever He bore a full share in promoting every community interest, but with entire want of personal ambition and would not enter upon any public career He supported the principles of the Democratic party

Mr Bradley married (first) Sarah L Stockbridge, of Hanover Massachusetts, and of this marriage were born two children Fanny Sawyer and John Erving Mrs Bradley died November 22, 1867 For his second wife Mr Bradley married Alice Wetherell, of Providence Rhode Island who died in February, 1895 Mr Bradley survived her until October, 1901

(VIII) John Erving Bradley, only son of Henry Osgood and Sarah L (Stockbridge) Bradley, was born February 26, 1860 He received academical instruction in the high school of Worcester, and studied for one year in Amherst College At the early age of eighteen years he entered upon an independent career taking employment with the old Jerome Marble Company of Worcester, manufacturer of paints, oils, and mill supplies He remained with the firm for four years, acquiring a familiar knowledge of all developments of the business including all the manufacturing processes, and was about to enter upon a traveling engagement in the interests of the establishment when (in March, 1882) he entered the employ of Osgood Bradley & Sons After the death of the uncle in 1896 he became general manager of Osgood Bradley & Sons' business, and was so occupied for five years and until the death of his father, when he became full owner Under his management the high reputation of the house has been fully maintained, and the scope of its business considerably enlarged, while its worth to the community is manifested by the employment it affords to a company of nearly three hundred operatives, the majority being men of family His deep interest in industrial affairs is evidenced by his connection with various important bodies,—the National Association of Manufacturers, the Master Car Builders' Association of America, the American Railroad Appliance Association, the New England Steam Railroad Club, the New England Street Car Railroad Club, in which he is a member of the executive board, and the Worcester Metal Trade Association He is also a member of the Worcester Club, and of its membership committee, the Tatnuck Country Golf and Tennis Club, the Tatassit Canoe Club, of which he is commodore, and the Up-Town Club, of which he is president He served for three years in the Worcester Light Infantry, and is a member of its Veteran Association, and of the membership committee of that body His political affiliations are with the Republican party He has been frequently solicited to enter upon active political life, and to become a candidate for various offices, but his deep interest in business concerns and in the commercial and social bodies to which he is attached would not permit him to accept proffers which were at once sincere and importunate

Mr Bradley married, October, 1887, Emma L D Dingley daughter of Hon John B and Maria M (Kinney) Dingley, both of whom are deceased Her father was a prominent business man of Gardiner, Maine, and was the first mayor of the city, occupying the position for several terms through various re-elections Two children have been born to Mr and Mrs Bradley—Helen, June, 1888, and Katherine, April, 1895

BENJAMIN ALLEN BARBER has been one of the leaders in musical affairs in Worcester for fully twenty-five years He was born December 23, 1855 in Worcester, and has spent his whole life there He is a son of Benjamin and Ann Maria (Collins) Barber His father was born in the little town of Wardsboro Vermont, in 1804 died in Worcester in 1867 His mother was of the Collins family of Southboro Massachusetts where she was born July 6 1816 She was a daughter of Daniel and Polly (Chamberlin) Collins She died at Worcester in 1904 Benjamin Barber was a stone cutter by trade After he came to Worcester about 1830, he followed his trade and soon began to take contracts, having at first David Woodward as his partner He built many substantial buildings in Worcester He was the contractor for the mason work of the old city hall He married Ann Maria Collins of Southboro, November 20, 1838 Their children were Rhoda Maria, born September 5, 1840, Warren, died young, Emery Perry, born August 20 1846, resides in Boston, retired, unmarried, Linda Frances, born August 12, 1851, married Albert E Peirce and resides at Evanston, Illinois, they have a son and daughter, Benjamin Allen, born December 23, 1855

Benjamin Allen Barber, son of Benjamin and Ann Maria (Collins) Barber, married Georgie Lee, daughter of Benjamin Franklin Lee, of Worcester, April 17, 1883 They have one child, Edith Louise, born October 14, 1884 Mrs Barber's mother was Louise Bramhall Hammond, daughter of John and Adeline Hammond, of Worcester, and Mr Barber has charge of the extensive estate of the late John Hammond, who was one of the leading men of the city in his day and owner of much real estate His handsome old mansion on Highland street is the one now occupied by Colonel William A Gile

Benjamin Allen Barber obtained his early education in the Worcester schools and passed the examinations for entrance to the high school which at that time was in the small building on Walnut street opposite the present classical high school He went to work first for F A Clapp, who was a dealer in men's furnishing goods, the predecessor of E B Clapp, his brother The store was then where the R J Healey shoe store now is After two years and a half experience as clerk and salesman he entered the employ of Jerome Marble & Co, then and now the largest dealers in paints, oils, chemicals and drugs in this section The present name of the firm is J Russel Marble & Co Mr Barber has been with the firm since 1872, a period of thirty-three years, and has occupied close confidential relations with the owners as the cashier

Mr Barber has taken a high place in the Masonic fraternity He took eighteen of the degrees in Worcester and the remainder, including the thirty-second, in Boston He belongs to Quinsigamond Lodge, Eureka Chapter, the Worcester County Commandery, Hiram Council He is interested in athletics, being a member of the Boston Athletic Association and of the Worcester Golf Club He has always taken an interest in amateur theatricals, and has helped many amateur performances in a city where amateurs have developed unusual talent He is best known, however, as a singer He has sung bass in most of the Protestant churches having quartettes in Worcester He has been one or more seasons in the quartette at Old South Congregational Church, the First Baptist Church, Piedmont Congregational Church Central Congregational Church, First Unitarian Church and at the Church of the Unity He is the only surviving member of the original Schumann Quartette, and he still sings first bass in the present Schumann Quartette It has been Mr Barber's custom to entertain during the week of the Worcester Festival the visiting artists At the festival of 1904, for instance, over a hundred and fifty lovers of music gathered at his invitation at his house to meet some of the Festival soloists Mr Barber is personally a charming man He is popular in the social circles of the city and has one of the largest lists of acquaintances and friends Mr Barber has a beautiful home at 31 Germain street, Worcester

CHARLES ALBERT ALLEN The name of Allen occupies a conspicuous place in the history of Worcester county, Massachusetts It is found not only in the industrial but in the professional life of the people who have stood for all that is noblest and best Persons in the United States bearing

Charles A. Allen

this surname find many lines to follow in reaching the progenitor, for there are now at least twenty persons of the name of Allen who came to these American shores prior to 1640 But to James, who settled in Dedham and removed to Medfield, a considerable number can trace their ancestry, among them Charles Albert Allen, who was born in Worcester, son of Albert S Allen

He attended the schools of his native town, passing up through the various grades, after which he took a full course in the Worcester Academy, acquiring the profession of a civil engineer For several years he found employment at his profession in Worcester and vicinity, a considerable portion of the time being engaged in making important surveys for the W & N R R During this period he designed and constructed the railroad viaduct at Worcester, also constructed the State Lunatic Hospital at the lake, the railroad bridges on Southbridge street, and other important works In the year 1877 he was elected by the city council to succeed Percy Daniels as civil engineer for the city of Worcester, and was annually re-elected until the year 1893 During the fifteen years that he was at the head of the engineering department of the city there were, aside from the natural and rapid growth of the city, various special instances when the department was seriously taxed with responsibility, namely the construction of the new dam for the storage of the water, known as the Tatnuck brook supply, and the disposal of the sewage of the city, both of which was handled with professional skill and sound judgment Mr Allen has given much time to the study of sewage disposal for cities and towns and has personally investigated various systems both in this country and in Europe When Worcester was compelled by an act of the legislature to purify her sewage before turning it into the Blackstone river, Mr Allen, after careful investigation, recommended a system which was finally put in use to the acceptance of all interested parties Since Mr Allen's retirement from the city government he has been engaged in expert work, as consulting engineer, special engineer, or commissioner in various parts of New England and in the south and middle west Within the past ten years fully one hundred different cases have come under his attention and service, many of them of unusual importance and public interest such as the abolition of grade crossings, he having been appointed by the superior court on forty-three grade crossing commissions, questions of supplying cities and towns with pure water, disposal of sewage water power development and attendance before the courts or commissions to give evidence as an expert engineer He was appointed by Governor Greenhalge a member of the Metropolitan water board, but was obliged to decline serving on account of other engagements consuming his time Mr Allen belongs to the American Society of Civil Engineers, the Boston Society of Civil Engineers, the Worcester County Society of Civil Engineers the New England Water Works Association, the Massachusetts Highway Association, Commonwealth Club of which he is president the Tatnuck Country Club, the Quinsigamond Boat Club, and the Boston Club of Boston He is also a member of Quinsigamond Lodge, A F and A M In politics he is a Republican

As has been stated Mr Allen traces his descent back through the following ancestral lines to

(I) James Allen who came to America and settled in Dedham Massachusetts, in 1637, married Annie Guild, the sixteenth day of the first month in 1638 He was a proprietor there in 1642, and five years later took the oath of a freeman He removed with the first thirteen settlers to establish the town of Medfield, and drew his house lot on South street and was living there in 1660, and may have died there, September 27, 1676 His wife died March 29, 1672-73 Their children were John born December 4, 1639, Mary and Martha, twins, born 1641, Mary married Joseph Clark, Martha married William Sabin, Sarah, born 1644, married Domingo White, James, born 1646, married Lydia Adams, Nathaniel, born 1648, married (first) Mary Sabin (second) Mary Frizzell, Joseph, born 1652, married Hannah Sabin, of Seaconk

(II) Joseph Allen married Hannah Sabin, in 1673, and took his house lot in the north part of Medfield, since known as the "Allen peace" He was a cooper by trade, and at the time of the sacking of Medfield by the Indians, during Philip's war, all the houses were burned except Joseph Allen's He died January 14, 1703-04 She died 1730 Their children were Joseph, born December 19, 1676, married Miriam Wight, Hannah, born June 23, 1679, married Benoni Twichell in 1705, Daniel, born April 21, 1681, settled in Pomfret, Connecticut, David, born 1683, settled in Ashford, Connecticut, Noah born April 21, 1685, Eleazer, born August 25, 1688, married Mary Battle in 1712, Jeremiah, born August 5 1690 Hezekiah, born November 3, 1692, married Mary Draper Abigail born October 24, 1694, married Ebenezer Battle, Nehemiah, born April 22, 1699 married Mary Parker, Thankful, Mary

(III) Joseph Allen, born December 19, 1676, married Miriam Wight, of Medfield, November 4, 1701 She was a daughter of Ephraim Wight, of that town, and was born August 22, 1675, she was a granddaughter of Thomas Wight who came from the Isle of Wight and was in Watertown, Massachusetts, 1636 Joseph Allen died May 25, 1727, in Medfield His children were Joseph born August 16, 1702, Miriam, born May 27, 1704, died March 3 1727-28, Moses, born September 20, 1708, Lydia, born 1714, Aaron, born March 11, 1715, married Hannah ——

(IV) Aaron Allen, born March 11 1715, married (first) Hannah ——, who died August 17, 1778 He married (second), January 4, 1779 Deborah, widow of Colonel Daniel Plimpton She died February 20, 1787 He married (third) widow Catharine Smith, August 9, 1787 He died May 3, 1794, in Sturbridge This Mr Allen with his brothers, Joseph and Moses, about the year 1736 removed to Sturbridge, Massachusetts Joseph and Moses were chosen town officers the year following the incorporation of that town, 1738 The children of Aaron were Aaron, born August 22 1739 married Abigail Allen, daughter of Nehemiah, Simeon born June 26, 1741, married Sarah Puffer, Elizabeth born March 29, 1743, married John Allen, Thankful, born June 29, 1745, died May 3, 1759 Prudence, born December 1, 1747, married March Stacy, Reuben born November 12, 1749, died November 5 1754, Ithmar, born October 9 1751, married Dolly Pincheon Joel, born October 26, 1753 died August 27, 1754, Caleb born June 25, 1755, married Rhoda Allen Amosa born September 27, 1757, died October 26, 1759, Elisha, born November 20 1759 married Cylinda ——, Hannah, born September 29 1762 died October 27, 1762

At least four of the above named sons served in the war of the revolution Aaron marched to reenforce General Gates at the north ward enlisted September 26 1777 discharged October 18, was in Lieutenant Benjamin Freeman's company, Colonel Jonathan Holeman's regiment He also enlisted July 30, 1780 in Captain Abel Mason's company Colonel Jacob Davis's regiment, serving twelve days in Rhode Island Ithmar also served in Lieutenant Benjamin

Freeman's company on the same expedition to re-enforce General Gates Caleb evidently served in several campaigns, was sergeant in Captain Joseph Sibley's company, Colonel Glenforth Key's regiment, enlisted July 8, 1777, discharged January 3, 1778 He was a revolutionary war pensioner, August 15, 1833 He died August 22, 1839

(V) Elisha Allen, born November 20, 1759, married Cylinda —— He evidently enlisted December 10, 1776 and served in Captain Abel Mason's company, Colonel Jonathan Holeman's regiment, discharged January 20, 1777, he was stationed at Providence Rhode Island He very likely served at other periods during the revolutionary war He was a farmer and resided at Sturbridge having received by will from his father Aaron Allen all his Personal and Real Estate not before given or shall hereafter be given in this will, he paying all my just debts and personal charges, the Legacies in this will and erecting a proper monument over my grave" In order to correct errors in former published accounts of this Allen family we quote further from this will, which may be found in Worcester county probate records, volume twenty-six, page ninety-eight, filed May 21, 1794, allowed October 28 1794

'I give to my beloved son Aaron Allen Jr, Simeon, Ithmar & Caleb, each the sum of fourteen pounds to be paid in silver money or Indian corn at three shillings per bushel I give my beloved daughter the wife of John Allen the sum of four pounds To my beloved daughter Prudence the wife of Mark Stacy, four pounds My son Elisha to be executor"

The will appears to have been signed January 3 1794 although perhaps drawn August 24, 1791, the will does not give the name of his wife But Elisha, in settling the estate, took a receipt from Catharine Allen (his mother-in-law) for the amount agreed upon for her legacy, July 5 1794 Elisha died January 30, 1818 His children were Oren, born April 10, 1786, died January 31, 1814, Walter, born March 22, 1788, married Harriet Holbrook, Thankful, born July 22, 1790, Cylinda, born April 6, 1792, died October 5, 1826, Calesta, born November 10, 1795, married Pardon Thompson, Alvan, born November 13, 1798, married Lucy Salisbury, Martha, born December 20, 1800, married Alfred Hitchcock, Elisha Dwight, born March 27, 1804, married Orril Merrick

(VI) Alvan Allen married Lucy Salisbury, daughter of Benjamin and Catharine Salisbury, who died in Brimfield, Massachusetts He died in 1841, Catharine in 1850 For some years Mr Allen resided in his native town, Sturbridge, Massachusetts, but in the year 1836 removed to Worcester, and with Ginery Twichell, Simeon Burt, and Frederick Billings became interested in establishing various stage lines for the transportation of passengers and the United States mail He visited Washington at intervals, securing government contracts for carrying the mail, and while the N & W R R was in process of construction he held a contract for carrying passengers from the end of the road to the wharf where they took steamboat for the city of New York In 1845 he engaged in the grocery business and three years later opened a store for the sale of pianofortes securing about the year 1848 the sole agency in Worcester for the sale of Chickering piano and this agency he retained until his death In 1849 1850 and 1858 he represented ward four in the city council In 1853 he was assistant assessor and also city marshal Five years later he was chosen to serve on the school committee He was a member of the Massachusetts state militia and held the office of major On November 29, 1859 while passing from Front to Mechanic street over the location of the N & W R R tracks, he was accidentally struck by a passing train and killed Their children were Albert S, born October 2, 1827, married Eliza A Cole, Benjamine D, born February 10, 1831, married Eliza F White

(VII) Albert S Allen married Eliza A Cole, daughter of James and Eliza (Prouty) Cole Elizabeth Prouty was the daughter of Joel and Elizabeth or 'Betsey" (Gates) Prouty of Boston, Massachusetts Elizabeth Gates was the daughter of Sylvanus Gates, of Rutland and Spencer, and Elizabeth Graham, his wife, whose mother was Jane Thompson, granddaughter of Lord Craig Joel Prouty was son of Asa and Lydia (Livermore) Prouty, of Leicester, and grandson of David Prouty, senior, of that town Mr Allen was a teacher of music as early as 1847, he opened rooms in Pains New Block Main street, Worcester, where he gave instruction on the pianoforte, and from that time until his death he continued as organist in various churches and teacher of music, with the exception of the time spent in the service of his country during the civil war as a member of Company A, Fifty-seventh Regiment, Massachusetts Volunteer Militia He served through the Wilderness campaign, and was there on duty at Camp Distribution at Baltimore, Maryland, until the close of the war He died in Worcester April 25, 1895 Eliza Ann Cole, wife of Albert S Allen, died February 2, 1885 Their children were Charles Albert, born January 27, 1852, Mary Salisbury, born November 23, 1853, Frank L born August 8, 1862

(VIII) Charles Albert Allen, whose name heads this sketch married Grace T Chase, daughter of Joseph Chase, for many years a woolen manufacturer in Blackstone Lowell and Worcester, Massachusetts Their children were Robert Chase, born March 8, 1878 graduate from the Worcester Polytechnic Institute, Charles Albert, Jr, died May 2, 1884, Chester Salisbury, born November 25, 1881, was educated in the public schools Worcester Academy, and Brown University, Mary Harville, born March 10, 1886, graduated from the high school, and is now in St Margaret's School for Girls Waterbury Connecticut, Grace Walker, born February 26, 1889, now a student in the high school. Robert Chase and Chester Salisbury are civil engineers Robert Chase Allen married Florence Akens Taylor April 14, 1903, and they are the parents of two children Donald Taylor, born February 29, 1904, and Charles Albert, second, born August 14, 1905

REV FREDERIC W BAILEY Benoni Bailey (I), the pioneer ancestor of the Rev Frederic W Bailey, was an early settler of Danbury, Connecticut, at a place called 'Wild Cat" in the present town of Bethel The destruction of the early town records by the British during the revolution has prevented any fuller knowledge of him except that in his family bible, now possessed by Mr Joseph T Bailey, of Philadelphia, his age is mentioned as ninety-six at his death in 1793 In the absence of any definite information, indications have pointed to the Bailey family of Massachuestts as the probable original

He married Lydia, daughter of Solomon Ferry, of Danbury, descendant of Charles Ferry, of Springfield, Massachusetts Their children were Samuel, Rebecca and Sarah who married Ebenezer Munson

(II) Samuel Bailey, eldest son of Benoni, born 1728 died 1808 He inherited the old farm in Danbury and lived there throughout his life Was appointed lieutenant of the Ninth Company Train Band in the Sixteenth Regiment of Connecticut by Act of Assembly, May, 1776, and served in the revolutionary war He married Lydia Beebe, a great-granddaughter of Captain James Beebe, of Danbury, and Sarah Benedict, daughter of Thomas, of Norwalk The children of Samuel and Lydia Bailey were Ebenezer (see forward), Lydia, born May 8, 1769, married Edmund Beebe, Samuel, married Huldah Hoyt, Benjamin, born December 9, 1756, married Hannah Dibble, Lemuel, born November 2, 1779, married Abbey Gregory

(III) Ebenezer Bailey, son of Samuel (2), was born in Danbury, 1760, and died March 31, 1801 He married, December 7, 1778, at Danbury, Ann, daughter of Samuel Starr, of Danbury, fourth in descent from Dr Comfort Starr, of Cambridge, Massachusetts The children of Ebenezer and Ann Bailey were 1 Clara (Beebe), born May 27, 1779 2 Lucy (Benedict) (Comstock), April 2, 1782 3 Zoe (Hitchcock), July 13, 1784 4 Lydia, June 11, 1788 5 Noah Starr, (see forward) 6 Ebenezer Gould, February 7, 1795 7 Samuel P, December 24, 1797

(IV) Noah Starr Bailey, fifth child of Ebenezer Bailey (3), was born in Danbury, July 16, 1790, and died in Norwalk, October 26, 1853 Brought up to the trade of a tailor, he later developed into a candy manufacturer and dealer at Norfolk, a business which was continued both there and at St Louis, Missouri, by his son Samuel

Noah Starr Bailey married Angeline, daughter of Clausen Holley, or Hawley, and wife Sarah Dibble, of Danbury She was born June 17, 1790 The children of Noah Starr and Angeline Bailey were Mary Louisa, born June 9, 1815, William Egbert, (see forward), Samuel Henry, born March 16, 1820, Sarah Ann (Terry), born March 20, 1823, and Frederick Starr, of Springfield, born May 24, 1825

(V) William Egbert Bailey, second child of Noah Starr Bailey, was born at Norwalk, Connecticut, October 31, 1817, and died in Brooklyn, New York, 1893 He early entered upon a mercantile career in New York city being for some years with the clothing house of Taylor, Ryno & Company, with a branch office at New Orleans After his marriage he became a resident of Brooklyn, Eastern District, where most of his life was passed William E Bailey, married, December 25, 1839, in New York, Jane, a daughter of John Sharpe or Scherp, and Marcy Higbie, daughter of Aaron and granddaughter of Samuel and Jean Higbie, of Jamaica, Long Island Jane Sharpe, born in Brooklyn, New York, March 19, 1814, was a granddaughter of Jacob Hendrick Sharpe, of New York, and Francina Schaats, a descendant of Rev Gideon Skaats first pastor of the Dutch church at Albany, New York, and great-granddaughter of Jacob Sharpe or Scherp, the Palatine of Germantown, New York, and his wife Anna Maria Bomper, daughter of Lodewick Bomper, of New York

The children of William E and Jane (Sharpe) Bailey were Peter Sharpe, of Springfield, Massachusetts, born May 31, 1841, captain of Company D, Twenty-seventh Infantry, Massachusetts, in civil war, William Starr, born February 14 1845 member of Ninth New York Volunteers, killed in battle of Fredericksburg, December 21, 1862, John Henry born February 14 1849, Sarah Louise, born June 1, 1851, Emma Jane, born February 3, 1855, Frederic William, born January 31, 1858, Mary Angeline, born December 25, 1859, died October 19, 1895

(VI) The Rev Frederic W Bailey, son of William Egbert and Jane S Bailey, was born in Brooklyn, New York, January 31, 1858 Graduating from the public schools he was for a time with H J Baker & Brother, wholesale druggists of New York Under the pastoral care of Rev Dr Almon Gunnison, then pastor of All Souls Church, Brooklyn, he was led to think of the ministry as his vocation He graduated from St Lawrence University, Canton, New York, in 1878, with the degree of B D, and after serving in pastorates at East Jaffrey, New Hampshire, and Hightstown, New Jersey, and persuing a course of study at the Boston School of Oratory under Professor Moses True Brown, he received a call from the new All Souls' Universalist Church on Kilby street, Worcester, as its first pastor For some three years he served thus, in which time the land at the corner of Woodland and Norwood streets was secured and plans for a new brown stone church were drawn after designs prepared by Mr James A Norcross, who was greatly interested in the enterprise At this period Mr Bailey found himself little in sympathy with the prevailing thought of the Universalist denomination, and in January, 1889, promptly withdrew therefrom to seek orders in the Episcopal church He was confirmed at St James' Church, Cambridge, and after a special course at the General Theological Seminary, New York was ordained Deacon by the Rt Rev B H Paddock, D D, Bishop of Massachusetts, at Christ Church, Brooklyn, Eastern District, in 1889, and a priest in St Paul's Church, Natick, in 1890 Of this parish he remained in charge till 1891, establishing during that time the St Andrew's Church in Wellesley, which became part of his parish In 1891 he returned to Worcester as the rector's assistant at All Saints Church, and in 1893 was called to the rectorship of the Church of the Ascension in New Haven, Connecticut In 1898 he was chosen Secretary of the Commission on Parochial Archives, diocese of Connecticut, and copyist, and did much to preserve the old church records and papers there Since 1901 he has resided at 33 Harvard street, Worcester, and is serving as a missionary of the diocese of Western Massachusetts, under his former associate, Bishop Vinton. He had charge of Christ Church, Rochdale, in 1903, re-opened and renovated the dormant Grace Church, Oxford, and in 1905 established the Holy Trinity Church at Southbridge

Mr Bailey is widely known as a genealogist and historian, especially such as pertains to early Connecticut He has himself published seven books of early Connecticut marriages, all taken from church records, and two books of early Massachusetts marriages all of which have had wide circulation and have been of great service in establishing old family connections In 1892 he copyrighted and patented a book for the keeping of family records and tracing ancestry which is in such favor that a fourth edition is now contemplated, greatly enlarged and improved He is a member of the New England Historic Genealogical Society in Boston, the New Haven Colony Historical Society, and the Massachusetts Society of the Sons of the American Revolution

On January 14 1891, Mr Bailey married at Worcester, Lena Olive Marble daughter of Jerome and Susan Emeline (Blanchard) Marble Her father was born at Charlton, September 10, 1824, and died in Worcester, February 14 1906 He married, March 21, 1849, Susan Emeline, daughter of William K Blanchard, of Charlton (son of Isaac) and Susanna Boomer, who descended through her father, Rev James Boomer from Matthew Boomer, an original settler of Freetown, Massachusetts The children of Jerome and Susan E Marble were Estella and Lena Olive, as mentioned above Jerome

Marble was for years the leading wholesale dealer in paints and oils of Worcester, having also a branch at Boston.

John Putnam Marble, the father of Jerome, was born in Charlton, October 1, 1802, and died in Worcester, January 23, 1901, at 33 Harvard street, where he had for some years resided. He married, November 30, 1823, Ruth Ann, daughter of William P. Ryder, a great-grandson of Eleazer Ryder, of Sherborn, and of his wife Elizabeth, daughter of Major General Salem Towne, of Oxford, who descended from William Towne, an original settler of Salem, Massachusetts. They had two children: Thaddeus, who died single in 1852, and Jerome, mentioned above.

Thaddeus Marble, father of John Putnam Marble, was born in Sutton, February 24, 1758, and died in Charlton, March 19, 1817. He was a scythe maker. He married Olive, daughter of John Putnam, of Sutton, son of Jeptha, who was great-grandson of John Putnam, an original settler of Salem, Massachusetts, in 1634. (See sketch of the Putnam family of Sutton, Massachusetts, in this work.)

Enoch Marble, father of Thaddeus, was a son of Fregrace Marble the pioneer of the family at Sutton, and a son of Samuel, of Andover. (See the Marble family elsewhere in this work.)

The children of Rev. Frederic William and Lena Olive (Marble) Bailey are: John Marble, born October 17, 1891, at Worcester; Nella May, August 25, 1897, at New Haven, Connecticut; Frederic Starr, October 18, 1900, at New Haven, Connecticut.

GEORGE W. CARR, president of the George W. Carr Company of Worcester, was born in St. Johns, New Brunswick, May 24, 1853, a son of Charles and Eliza (Smith) Carr, natives of London and Hull, England, respectively. Charles Carr (father), a sailmaker by trade, came to St. Johns, New Brunswick, from England, in early manhood, and was there united in marriage to Eliza Smith.

George W. Carr was educated in the public schools of St. Johns. He began his business life as clerk in a men's furnishing goods, boot and shoe store, acquiring thereby a thorough knowledge of the duties of that position and performing the same in a highly creditable manner. He came to Worcester, Massachusetts, in September, 1873. After working a short time at harness making and carriage trimming, he engaged in business in partnership with Eugene Curtis, under the firm name of Curtis & Carr, in the construction of concrete roofs and walks. Later he was in partnership with Charles O. Richardson in the same business. The firms with which Mr. Carr has been connected have conducted a large and profitable business in Worcester and vicinity, especially in gravel roofs and artificial stone, granolithic and concrete construction. In 1901 the firm was incorporated under the name of the George W. Carr Company with George W. Carr as president, H. C. Wilson as treasurer, and A. H. Carr as superintendent of the work in Worcester and vicinity. In 1906 this firm assumed the interests of the Carr and Anderson corporation of Boston, and Mr. J. Fred Carr became the manager of the Boston office.

Among the more important contracts for concrete work of extensive proportions are the following: The New Home Sewing Machine Company works at Orange, Massachusetts; Saunders cotton mill at Saundersville; Paul Whitin Manufacturing Company at Northbridge; Draper Machine Company at Hopedale; Chapel Mills Manufacturing Company at Cherry Valley, Leicester; L. S. Starrett Company mill at Athol; Bayard Thayer's stable at Lancaster (granolithic); Harry Payne Whitney's stable at Manhasset, Long Island; Art Museum building at Pittsfield; Zenas Crane's place at Pittsfield; Hon. L. D. Apsley's place at Hudson; railroad station for the New York, New Haven & Hartford Company at Marlboro; C. K. G. Billings' place, New York city; new City Hall, Worcester, (granolithic); residence of Henry C. Pratt on Burncoat street, Worcester; residence of Luther C. Brown on Cedar street, Worcester; driveway and wall of residence of George F. Hutchins, Ripley street, Worcester; sidewalks of Westland street, Vernon street and Stoneland road; sidewalk of Conservatory of Music, Boston; sidewalk and interior of Horticultural Hall, Boston; East Boston Drainage (concrete) of the Boston & Albany Railroad; retaining walls, steps, paving and yard of the Roger Wolcoot school, Dorchester; granolithic floors and sidewalks of Motor Mart, Boston; waterproofing floors and basement of Eden Jordan's stable, Boston; granolithic floor of Anglier building, Brockton, and tar concrete work of car shop, Portland, Maine.

George W. Carr married, August, 1885, Georgianna Kindred, daughter of Amos and Sarah (Ketch) Kindred, of New Brunswick, natives of England and New Brunswick, respectively, and one child was born to them, Ella L. Carr. Mr. Carr is a member of the Independent Order of Odd Fellows and Knights of Pythias.

FREDERICK WILLIAM BLACKMER. William Blackmer, or Blackmore (I), as it was sometimes spelled, was the emigrant ancestor of Frederick W. Blackmer, of Worcester. He came from England in 1665 to Scituate to live with his uncle, Peter Collamore, who had made him one of his heirs. Mr. Collamore came to Scituate early. He was a proprietor in 1640, was able to bear arms 1643, and was a town officer in 1650. He lived about twenty years after his nephew came to New England, and the nephew had a family and had been dead about eight years when the uncle died in 1664. Mr. Collamore made his will January 16, 1683. It was probated June 4, 1664. It mentioned his wife Mary; and various relatives among then the four children of William Blackmer, Peter, John, Phebe and William Blackmer.

A farm was laid out to William Blackmer at Scituate by the freemen. It was located where the late Captain Elijah Curtis resided. He married, July 17, 1666, Elizabeth Bankes. In 1669 he was freed from military duty on account of the loss of an eye, yet he must have volunteered when King Philip's war desolated the colonies, for he was killed by the Indians, April 21, 1676. On January 24, 1677, his widow married Jacob Bumpas, who was born March 28, 1644, at Duxbury, son of Edward Bumpas (originally Bonrepos), of Plymouth, who came on the "Fortune" in 1621. Jacob and Elizabeth Bumpas had two sons and other children and left many descendants in Middletown and Rochester, Massachusetts, where they settled later.

The children of William Blackmer were: Peter, baptized July 7, 1667; John, baptized May 29, 1670, married Anna Branch, December 19, 1700, resided at Marshfield, Massachusetts; Phebe, baptized September 22, 1672, married Ebenezer Holmes; William, baptized April 11, 1675, was an infant only a few days old when his father was killed, died 1698, unmarried, leaving his property to his brothers and their children.

(II) Peter Blackmer, son of William Blackmer (I), was born May 25, 1667, at Scituate, Massachusetts, and died at Rochester, Massachusetts, August 1, 1717 He married Elizabeth ——, and became one of the pioneers and first settlers of Rochester, Massachusetts He married (second) at Rochester Sarah Edwards, daughter of Samuel Edwards, October 24, 1711 All but the last two children, Samuel (2d) and Mary, were by his first wife, and all but Peter were born at Rochester

The children of Peter Blackmer were Peter, born probably at Scituate, died 1692, John, born September 25, 1690, Jane, born December 8, 1693, Jemima, born November 16, 1695, Joseph born September 4, 1697, William, born October 11 1699, Peter, born March 21, 1702, Stephen, born July 27, 1704, Samuel, born April 12 1705, died young, Samuel, born July 20, 1712, Mary, born November 5, 1714

(III) Peter Blackmer, son of Peter Blackmer (2), was born at Rochester, Massachusetts, March 21, 1702 He and his older brother, John Blackmer, settled in Warren and Palmer, Massachusetts John Blackmer raised a family at Rochester He married Mercy Brickett, March 5, 1711-12, and had Nathaniel, born July 3 1712, Elizabeth, born March 12 1713-14, Susannah born July 8, 1716, John, born March 21, 1717-18, Mary, born March 8 1719-20 John drew sixty-three acres in the second division of Palmer in 1746 on John Patterson's right, and Peter in 1743 drew thirty acres in the first division of the common lands on Joseph Brooks' right in Palmer Peter Blackmer of Palmer was in Captain Buckminster's company at Fort Dummer, August 6 to 20, 1748 in the French and Indian war He later settled at Warren Massachusetts John Blackmer who fought against the Indians in 1758, in this vicinity, was probably a son of Peter The names of his children have not been found He had a son Peter, Jr, born 1729

(IV) Peter Blackmer, son of Peter Blackmer (3), was born near Warren or Palmer, Massachusetts, in 1729 He moved to Greenwich about 1760 and was one of the prominent men of that town He married Esther Sheppard, who died October 17, 1801, aged seventy-two years He was a farmer His place is now or was recently owned by George Wheeler Their children were born from about 1760 to 1790 Not all the dates have been preserved Their children were Rolen or Roland, engaged in Shay's Rebellion, went to Pelham, was treasurer and selectman of that town had Mary, David, Peter, Susan, Esther Thankful, Amos Asa, Moses, Mary, married Archibald Lammon, David, married Louise Stebbins, Peter, born 1781, died July 2, 1838, married Betsey Stebbins Susan married Abner Strone, Esther, married Bethens Huck Thankful, married Barnabas Sears, Asia, married Sally Stebbins, Amos, born November 1 1769 died April 18, 1823, married Margaret Gray who died March 7, 1853, aged seventy-three years, Moses, married Mary Vaughan

(V) Amos Blackmer, son of Peter Blackmer (4), was born at Greenwich, November 1, 1769 He married (intentions March 7), 1802, Margaret Gray daughter of Daniel Gray, of Pelham They settled in Prescott Massachusetts, on the farm of Daniel Gray Amos died April 18, 1823 his wife died March 7 1853 Their children, all born at Greenwich, Massachusetts, were Mary D, born 1805, died young, Daniel Gray, born 1809, married Adeline Sears, of Prescott, Massachusetts, Peter, born October 31, 1811 died February 27, 1882, he never married, William H, born April 14 1814, died November 15, 1885, moved from Prescott to Hardwick in 1858, Esther Shepard, born May 12, 1821, died in North Brookfield, December 18, 1885, Amos Harvey born November 12, 1817 married Lydia E Sanger, of Westboro, Massachusetts residing at Greenwich, where he died January 17, 1901

(VI) William Hack Blackmer, born at Prescott, Massachusetts, April 14, 1814 married Harriet Newell Howe, at Worcester, April 14, 1839, he died November 15, 1885 He settled in Hardwick Massachusetts, in 1858, on the Petersham road He was a farmer and his widow is now living at No 150 Lincoln street, Worcester, Massachusetts She was born July 16, 1817 The children of William Hack and Harriet N Blackmer were Francis Thaxter, born in Worcester, March 30 1844, died in Washington, D C, January 15, 1884, Daniel Gray, born in Prescott, January 3 1846, died in Worcester, November 30, 1872, William born in Prescott, July 10, 1847, died July 26, 1847, Mary Anjeannette born in Prescott, September 18, 1848, died in Hardwick, December 24 1869, Edwin Augustus born in Prescott, November 9 1850 died in Worcester, November 30, 1882, Charles Henry, born in Prescott, November 23 1852, died in Hardwick, December 1, 1869, Emory Washburn, born in Prescott, May 24, 1854, died in Hardwick December 24 1869, Hattie Adaline born in Prescott, June 29, 1856, died March 30, 1857, Frederick William, born in Hardwick, April 10, 1858, George Albert, born in Hardwick, March 26, 1860 died in Colorado Springs, Colorado, April 25, 1889, Herbert Theodore, born in Hardwick, February 11, 1862, died in Worcester, July 14 1902

(VII) Francis T Blackmer, son of William H (6), was born in Worcester Massachusetts, 1844 but spent his boyhood in Prescott and Hardwick, where his parents lived He was educated in the district schools and at Wilbraham Academy When twenty years of age he returned to Worcester to enter the law office of the late Hon William W Rice He was admitted to the bar in 1867, but he continued in the employ of Mr Rice until he was admitted to partnership In 1875 he was elected city solicitor of Worcester, and he continued in this office until 1881, when he resigned to take the place as district attorney of Judge Staples, who was at that time promoted to the bench In both of these important public offices he was distinguished for faithful and able service In 1883 his health failed so that he was obliged to give up work He tried by rest and travel to regain his health but the struggle was vain and in January, 1884, he died at Washington, D C at the very beginning of one of the most promising legal careers and with remarkable attainments for a lawyer only forty years old He was particularly successful as a trial lawyer He was very effective in persuading juries to his way of thinking His familiarity with Yankee character and his easy confidence-winning mannerisms commanded the attention of rural jurors as nobody else could He probably became known to more persons in the course of his career as a lawyer and district attorney than any other lawyer in the county In the examination of witnesses he had no peer among his contemporaries He was always in control of his temper and composed under the greatest stress

(VII) Frederick William Blackmer son of William H Blackmer (6) was born April 10, 1858, at Hardwick Massachusetts He attended the common schools in towns where his parents lived and fitted for college at Barre Academy and the Hitchcock high school at Brimfield, Massachusetts He came to Worcester in 1880 to enter the office of Francis T Blackmer his brother and take a course at the law school He had hardly become familiar with the details of his brother's practice when his brother was taken sick, retired and died The business needed him and his legal education was gained by hard work in actual practice He had to give up the plan to go to the law school In 1883 he was admitted to the bar at Fitchburg Shortly after his brother's death he formed a partnership with Ernest H Vaughan In March, 1884, the new firm opened offices in the old postoffice building on Pearl street After a year they moved to the Walker building, and on the completion of the State Mutual building they took the corner suite No 801-804, where they are at present For about ten years Blackmer & Vaughan have ranked as the oldest firm of lawyers in Worcester They have been extremely successful in their practice for over twenty years They have made a specialty of corporation cases, especially bankruptcy proceedings, and settlements of financial embarrassments They have organized hundreds of corporations and are regular counsel for over fifty different corporations Their most notable achievement in court perhaps was in the famous Kettle Brook litigation They won some one hundred and twenty suits for damages against the city of Worcester on account of the taking of water for city uses The damages amounted to about $680,000 in all

Mr Blackmer is a member of the Commonwealth Club and the Worcester Golf Club He and his family attend the Central Congregational Church He enjoys travel and has made frequent trips to the south and west He is familiar with every city in California and with most of the cities of the northwest He resides in a very attractive new home on Massachusetts avenue

He married in 1883 Maggie Osgood Whitney, daughter of Lovell and Hannah (Moore) Whitney, of Boylston, Massachusetts, and a descendant of John Whitney, who came to Watertown in April, 1635 Their children are Ralph Fred, born in 1885, graduated from Worcester Academy in the class of 1904, Albert Whitney, born in 1887, graduated from Worcester Academy in the class of 1905, and now a member of the class of 1909 in Amherst College, Waldo Harvey, born in 1890, and Bernice, born in 1893

ALBERT GEARY MANN Richard Mann (I), who was in the town of Scituate Massachusetts, before 1644, was the emigrant ancestor of the late Albert Geary Mann of Worcester, and his family He took the oath of fidelity there January 15, 1644 He was one of the twenty-six partners in the celebrated Conihassett grant in 1646 He was drowned February 16 1655 while crossing the ice on the pond near his house John Hoar, who subsequently went to Concord Massachusetts was his near neighbor and was on the jury that held an inquest after the death The verdict shows that with the vain attempts of those present to help him he struggled for an hour and finally succumbed to the cold and was drowned It is supposed that Rebecca Mann who married John Cowen in 1656 was the widow of Richard Mann The name of Richard's wife was Rebecca Richard Mann was a farmer or planter, and one of the original proprietors His farm was beautifully located His neighbor on the south was John Hoar, who early removed to Concord Massachusetts On the east was the sea and on the north was Musquascut pond, in which the drowning accident happened

The children of Richard and Rebecca Mann were Nathaniel born September 23, 1646 died July 20, 1688 Thomas born August 15 1650 married Sarah, died 1732 Richard born February 5 1652 married Elizabeth Sutton Josiah born December 10, 1654, probably died young, though he may be the Josiah who was in Boston 1674-5-6

(II) Richard Mann, son of Richard Mann (1), was born February 5, 1652, at Scituate, Massachusetts He married Elizabeth Sutton, who was born in 1662 She was the eldest daughter of John Sutton, of Scituate, and granddaughter of Elder Nathaniel Tilden, who was a wealthy citizen and emigrated from Tenterden, in Kent, England, before 1628 and settled in Scituate, Massachusetts Richard Mann was three years old at the time of his father's death, and four when his mother married John Cowen When eleven he was apprenticed to Governor Thomas Hinckley, of Barnstable, for a term of ten years He was a soldier in King Philip's war and received his portion of land for services, especially at the Narragansett sortie fight, so-called This tract of land was at Hebron, Connecticut, and was deeded later by him to his son Nathaniel In 1703 he sold his farm at Scituate to his brother Thomas, and about the same time deeded a tract of Connihasset land to Gershom Ewell April 13, 1703, he bought a farm of three thousand acres at Middleboro, Massachusetts, of John Allen Soon afterward he settled at Lebanon, Connecticut, where he spent the remainder of his days All his children, except the youngest, Elisha, were born before the family left Scituate

The children were 1 John, born April 7, 1684, was in Lebanon, Connecticut, 1719, but removed to western Massachusetts or to New Hampshire, where he raised a family 2 Rebecca, born March 22, 1686, married Isaac Tilden, of Lebanon, June 4, 1716, and had six children 3 Hannah, born April 13, 1689 4 Nathaniel, born October 27, 1693, married (first) Mary Root 5 Richard, born March 10, 1694, married probably Mary Culver, July 23, 1719, settled at Lebanon, Connecticut, and had Esther, born December 18, 1721, removed to New Hampshire or Massachusetts 6 Elizabeth, born August 27, 1696 7 Abigail, born February 23, 1698-9, probably married at Lebanon, April 6, 1721, Simon Baxter 8 Elisha, resided for a time at Lebanon

(III) Nathaniel Mann, son of Richard Mann (2), was born at Scituate, Massachusetts, October 27, 1693 He removed early with his parents to Lebanon, Connecticut, about 1704 He married (first) Mary Root, of Hebron, Connecticut, February 1, 1713 She died May 19, 1728 He married (second) Mary Sprague, March 4, 1729 She died October 15, 1735 He married (third) Patience Role, September 5, 1736 He had six children by his first wife and two by his second, according to the records of Hebron, Connecticut, where they were born Mary Root was the daughter of Jacob Root, son of John Root, one of the first settlers of Hartford, Connecticut Jacob Root was one of the first settlers of Northampton Massachusetts, removed to Hebron, Connecticut, 1705, and was one of those chosen to run the bounds between Colchester and Hebron in 1710 He died August 9, 1731, aged about seventy Mary was born at Northampton, November 24, 1689

The children of Nathaniel Mann were Joseph, born April 5, 1713 (probably 1714), Nathaniel, born June 16, 1715-16 married Deborah Tillotson, June 5, 1739, Benjamin, born March 3, 1717, John, born November 20, 1721, married (first) Margaret Peters; Mary, born June 5, 1723, Nathan, born June 20, 1727, married Elizabeth Skinner, February 12, 1752, and had five children, Abigail, born February 14, 1730-31, Abijah, born August 7, 1734, married Sarah Porter

(IV) John Mann, son of Nathaniel Mann (3), was born at Hebron, Connecticut, November 20, 1720, died June 4 1806 The Mann farm at Hebron

ALBERT G. MANN

contains about two hundred and fifty acres The present house was built in 1782 by Andrew Mann and is in good repair (1884) The place was never sold after Nathaniel Mann bought it until within a few years John Mann married Margaret Peters, of Hebron, aunt of Governor Peters, of Hebron She was born August, 1724, died June 2, 1789 He married (second), about 1790, Hannah Kellogg, widow of Samuel Kellogg, of Marlboro All his children were by the first wife They are 1 Mary or Margaret, born April 14, 1742, married ——— Cross, and settled at Montreal, Canada, had two sons 2 John, born December 25, 1743, died 1828, married (first) Lydia Porter 3 Mary, born February 25, 1745-6, died May 18, 1817, married, October 16, 1768, Jacob Loomis, who was born at Andover, Connecticut, May 20, 1745, died May 9, 1813, had three children 4 Hannah, born 1747 5 Mercy, born March 5 or 16, 1749, married Joel Mann 6 Elijah, born August 9, 1751, married (first), August 20, 1771, Mary Perkins, who died 1781; he married (second), November 14, 1782, Widow Baxter, of Lebanon, Connecticut, had four children 7 Andrew, captain, born March 18, 1755, married Harriet Phelps 8 Dr Nathaniel, born August 11, 1757, educated at Dartmouth College and in England as a physician married a Miss Owen, of Hebron, May 6, 1787, removed to Georgia, where he practiced medicine, had two daughters 9 Phebe, born August 6, 1763 (or 68), probably married ——— Buel 10 Hannah, born June 5, 1772, married Theophilus Baldwin, who was born August 25, 1769, lived for a time at Bradford, Connecticut, removed to Holland Erie county, New York, where they died, had four or more children

(V) John Mann, son of John Mann (4), was born at Hebron, Connecticut, December 25, 1743 He married in 1765, Lydia Porter, of Hebron, Connecticut She was born March 17, 1746, daughter of John Porter, of Hebron He removed with her on horseback to Orford, New Hampshire, in October, 1765 and settled on a tract of land given him by his father They arrived in the wilderness October 24, 1765, and passed the winter with a family that was already located there, in a hut covered with bark That family moved away so that Mr Mann and his wife were the first abiding settlers of the town After the arrival of other settlers and much clearing had been done, Mr Mann bought other lots, making a large farm, and built his house in what is now the centre of a thriving village He died at Orford, New Hampshire, May 9, 1828 A handsome monument erected to his memory is to be seen in the village grave yard His wife Lydia died March 5, 1805 It is said that late in life he married (second) a Widow Barber He had fifteen children by his wife Lydia, born at Orford, New Hampshire all of whom except the two youngest lived to marry and have children They were John, born May 21, 1766 married (first) Lydia Dutton, Solomon, born August 19, 1768, married ——— Parkhurst, Jared, born November 6, 1770, married Mindwell Hale, Ira born September 8 1772, married (first) ——— Bailey, Aaron, born July 21, 1774, married (first) Sally Melvin, Lydia born September 17, 1776, died at Littleton, New Hampshire December 29, 1851, married Joseph Pratt and had four children, Sarah, born June 4, 1778, died at Orford, New Hampshire, November 5 1864, married Dr Rogers, had one child Nathaniel born December 29, 1779 married Mary Mason Benning (judge), born November 25, 1781, married Phebe Mann, Asaph, born September 30, 1783 married Mary Barker, Cyrus (Rev), born April 3 1785 married Nancy Sweetser, Phebe, born March 7, 1787, died November 25, 1871, married Samuel Sargent, had seven children, Joel (Rev), born February 7, 1789, married Catherine Vernon, Abijah, born April 3, 1791, died March 8, 1809, a son who died in infancy

(VI) Aaron Mann, son of John Mann (5), wsa born at Orford, New Hampshire, July 21, 1774, died in Elgin, Illinois, in 1851 having moved there and settled with his family in 1838 He married (first) Sally Melvin, (second) Sally Ingraham Captain Mann, as he was called, had sixteen children, eight by each wife They were Sally born at Orford, married Reuben Roberts, resided at Fisherville, New Hampshire, Aaron, born February 28, 1799, married Eliza Weld, Harriet, married Francis Weld, Philoxa, born 1803, died October 20, 1831, at Elbridge, New York, married, September 12, 1827, Peter Clark, graduate of Union College, president of Washington College Kent county, Maryland, had one son, Eliphalet Kimball, born in New Hampshire, went to Elgin, Illinois about 1833, died in Chicago about 1880, Isaac, Cyrus, Adin, William, Leonard, Benning, Munroe, Charles, Eunice, Maria, died young, and an infant that was buried with his mother

(VII) Aaron Mann, son of Aaron Mann (6), was born February 28, 1799, at Orford, New Hampshire, died March 10, 1854 He resided in the easterly part of Orford and was a farmer and dealer in lumber He married Eliza Weld, at Orford, New Hampshire She was born April 15, 1800, died August 9, 1876 Their children were 1 Caroline, born January 17, 1825, married Oliver Chase, of Paxton, Massachusetts, married (second) Calvin Proctor, of Claremont, New Hampshire, has a son, Henry Chase, now or lately of Worcester, Massachusetts 2 Albert Geary, born July 19, 1827, married (first) Julia Maria Sanborn, of Orford, New Hampshire, married (second) Harriet A Bigelow, of Worcester, Massachusetts 3 Henry A, born September 1, 1832, died January 9, 1835 4 Louisa, born October 8, 1836, died February 9, 1859, married, January 14, 1857, John E Spaulding, of Worcester has no children

(VIII) Albert Geary Mann, son of Aaron Mann (7), was born at Orford, New Hampshire, July 17, 1827 He was brought up on the New Hampshire farm During a part of the year he was engaged in burning lime, a business that his father carried on at times, and in this occupation he learned the rudiments of the business which he followed later in life He attended the district schools of his native town, but like most of the successful men who started life under similar conditions, was taught to understand that school furnishes a man only a slight start in his education At the age of eighteen he left home and went to Leicester, Massachusetts, to work He was back and forth between Orford, Leicester and Worcester for several years In 1847 he was employed for about three months by David Wodward the leading stone mason in Worcester at that time, and he cut most of the window caps and sills for the Warren block, then building on Pearl street

In 1851 Mr Mann located himself in Worcester, and two years later entered into partnership with David Damon, they having a stone yard on School street In 1857 the firm was dissolved and he continued alone He bought some property on Southbridge street and established there the extensive stone business which he conducted for many years He enlarged the stone yard several times by the purchase of adjoining property For twenty-five years he carried on the largest stone business in Worcester, employing at times as many as eighty stone cutters and masons In 1868 he bought the granite quarry at Marlborough, New Hampshire, where most of his stone was secured He sold the city much of the block paving He furnished all the stone for the ashlar work on the Union station and Plymouth Church In 1888 he was the contractor for the granite in Jonas G Clark's building, opposite the City Hall, the largest and best block at that time in the city Much of his work was for cemeteries, such as tombs, headstones and monuments In the course of his business life Mr Mann made many inventions and improvements, such as the hardening of the heads of the tools used in cutting stone and alterations in the derricks used in the quarries and on construction of buildings In 1876, in consequence of the threatened withdrawal of railroad facilities, Mr Mann removed his stone yard to Crescent street, and in 1885 he sold his entire business, including the New Hampshire quarry, to George D Webb, who has continued the business with marked success since then After the sale of his business Mr Mann occasionally served on building committees and places where his knowledge and experience were invaluable He was on the building committee of the Young Men's Christian Association and also of Central Church Mr Mann had a handsome residence on Harvard street overlooking the town, so much of which he had taken part in building He was an excellent business man with a reputation for square dealing and uprightness, and personally he was simple, sincere and courteous He was a member of the Society of Antiquity and of the Worcester County Mechanics' Association

He married (first) Julia Maria Sanborn, of Orford, New Hampshire, and (second), December 13, 1864, Harriet A Bigelow, of Worcester who survives him They had no children Mr Mann died June 9, 1899, after an illness lasting about a month

SILAS EMERSON HARTHAN William Harthan (1) (spelled Harthborne, Hawthorn and various other ways in the early records) was the emigrant ancestor of Silas Emerson Harthan, of Worcester, Massachusetts He was also the progenitor of Nathaniel Hawthorne, who changed the spelling of his name from Hathorne Following is the line of descent of Nathaniel Hawthorne, the author 1 William Hathorne 2 John Hathorne and wife Ruth Gardner 3 Joseph Hathorne and wife Sarah Bowditch 4 Daniel Hathorne and wife Rachel Phelps 5 Nathaniel Hathorne and wife Elizabeth Clark Manning 6 Nathaniel Hathorne and wife Sophia Peabody, married July 4 1804 He changed his name to Hawthorne, died at Plymouth, New Hampshire, May 19, 1864

William Hathorne, the emigrant, is the ancestor of most of the families of Harthan and Hathorn and other variations of the spelling He and his brother John were the only emigrants of colonial days of this name Both lived in Salem and it is difficult to distinguish between the two families

William and John Hathorne were sons of William and Sarah Hathorne, of Binfield, Berkshire county, England William was born in 1607 and came with Governor Winthrop in the "Arabella" in 1630 He settled in Dorchester, where he was a proprietor He was admitted a freeman May 14, 1634 He was a town officer there He removed to Salem in 1636 He represented Dorchester in the general court 1635 and 1637, and Salem many years after his removal He was elected speaker of the house of deputies in 1644 and re-elected a number of times He had a grant of land of six hundred and forty acres September 6, 1676, for extra services to the state This was the first grant in Townsend, Massachusetts, and is probably the land occupied by his sons and grandsons in Stow, Marlboro and Townsend later He was elected assistant to the governor in 1662 and served until 1679 He was one of the most able, energetic and widely influential men in New England He was at the great training in Boston in 1639 He was captain of the Salem military company appointed May 1, 1646, commissioned major 1656 He was narrow and bigoted arbitrary and intolerant in church and state, judged by present standards, but he was a zealous and fearless advocate of personal rights against the encroachments of the royal agents He had letters from his brother, Robert Hathorne, of Bray, England, April 1 1653, with a message to his brother John, who has been mentioned above

A list of his children written by his own hand has been preserved He died in 1681, in his seventy-fourth year His will was dated February 17, 1679-80 and an inventory is dated June 10, 1681 His wife Ann was executor He bequeathed to his wife, to William, Samuel and Abigail, children of his deceased son Eleazer, to son John, to Sarah, widow of deceased son William, to grandchildren Jervice Helwyde, land at Groton if he came over from "Urop" to enjoy it, to daughter Sarah Coaker's two eldest sons by her husband Coaker, to the rest of his grandchildren The estate was settled by his sons, John Hathorne and Israel Porter The children of William and Anne Hathorne were Sarah, born March 11, 1634-5, married Joseph Coker, of Newbury, Massachusetts, Eleazer, born August 1, 1637, married Abigail Curwen, daughter of George Curwen, Nathaniel, born August 11, 1639, John, born August 5, 1641, married Ruth Gardner, daughter of George Gardner, Anna, born December 12, 1643, married Joseph Porter, William, born April 1, 1645, married Sarah ———, Elizabeth, born 1649, married Israel Porter, Mary, baptized May 1, 1653

(II) John Hathorne, son of William Hathorne (1), was born August 5, 1641, in Salem, Massachusetts He was distinguished in civil and military life He was a captain in the war with the eastern Indians, later colonel of his regiment and chief in command of the expedition in 1696 against the Indians He was a magistrate, except during the brief administration of Sir Edmund Andros, and was a most cruel and intolerant judge during the witchcraft delusion He married Ruth Gardner Their children were John, Nathaniel, Ebenezer, Joseph, baptized June, 1691, married Sarah Bowditch, Ruth, Benjamin There is some doubt whether the Ebenezer and Nathaniel Hathorne, who settled in Marlboro, Massachusetts, about 1720, were sons of John (II) or Nathaniel, but there is more reason to think that they were the sons of Nathaniel

(II) Nathaniel Hathorne, son of William Hathorne (1), was born in Salem, Massachusetts, August 11, 1639 He settled in Lynn, Massachusetts Among his children the historian of Marlboro evidently believes were the two settlers, viz Ebenezer and Nathaniel, though the Marlboro settlers may have been sons of Ebenezer Hathorne (III), the son of Nathaniel (II) The children of Nathaniel Hathorne (II) were Ebenezer, married, 1683, Esther Witt, probably daughter of Jonathan and Mary Witt, she was born 1665, Nathaniel, born in Lynn, Massachusetts

(III) Ebenezer Hathorne, son of Nathaniel Hethorne (2), was probably father of Nathaniel and Ebenezer Hathorne, of Marlboro There is no doubt that the Marlboro line is connected with the Salem family and probably in one of the ways indicated Ebenezer Hathorne married a Witt and the Witt and Hathorne families came to Marlboro together from Lynn and Salem

(IV) Nathaniel Hathorne, son of Ebenezer Hathorne (3), was born in Lynn or Salem about 1690

He is brother of the ancestor of Silas E Harthan, and came with his brother to Marlboro He married (first) Martha ——— and had several children He married (second), 1728, Sarah Stevens, probably of Stow, where the Hathornes seemed to have settled before coming to Marlboro He settled on what is now the Marlboro town farm The children of Nathaniel and Martha Hathorne were Nathaniel, baptized August 11, 1723, died young, Martha, baptized December 23, 1726, Nathaniel, born December 23, 1726 The children by the second marriage were Ebenezer, born June 30, 1734, married, May 6, 1757, Rhoda Howe, Mary, born 1730, married, November 5, 1754, Amasa Cranston, Deliverance, married, March 1, 1764, John Cutler, of Shrewsbury

(IV) Ebenezer Hathorne, probably son of Ebenezer Hathorne (3), was born in Salem or Lynn about 1690 He came to Stow and later to Marlboro with his brother, Nathaniel Hathorne, about 1720 He married, 1730, Elizabeth Goodale, daughter of Benjamin Goodale The Goodales were settlers in Salem also So were the Stevens family, into which his brother married The children of Ebenezer and Elizabeth (Goodale) Hathorne were Lucy, born February 28, 1730, Silas, born December 22, 1732, was in French war, 1759, afterwards lived in Shrewsbury, Micah, born March 31, 1735, Solomon, born February 24, 1738, married, 1761, Mary Gates, and had Ebenezer, born April 8, 1763, and Eunice, born April 1, 1765

(V) Micah Harthan, as he usually spelled it, son of Ebenezer Hathorne (4), was born in Marlboro, Massachusetts, March 31, 1735 He was a soldier in the French and Indian war in 1757 He was in Captain Samuel Howe's company at the fall of Fort William Henry in the relief expedition He was also a soldier in the revolution at the Bennington alarm He enlisted in Captain Solomon Stuart's company and Colonel Josiah Whitney's regiment, August 21, 1777 The powder horn carried by Micah Harthan in the French and Indian war has been preserved and is in the possession of Silas E Harthan

Micah Harthan came from Marlboro to the north district of Shrewsbury, now located in West Boylston, in 1761 He married Sarah Jones, of Marlboro, November 26, 1761, recorded in Shrewsbury She was born March 8, 1734, died 1820, aged eighty-six years He died in 1803, aged sixty-eight years The widow declined to administer the estate and Jonas Temple, who married his daughter Lois, was appointed, the other heirs consenting The children of Micah and Sarah (Jones) Harthan were Caty, married Samuel Straw, of Peterboro, January 27, 1801, David, born January 15, 1764 married Prudence Winn Smith, Eunice, married, November 20, 1794, Lois, married Jonas Temple, December 27, 1791, Lucy, married Benjamin Pollard, of Greenfield, New Hampshire, February 2, 1796, Lydia, married Thomas Keyes, Jr, March 26, 1791, Olive, married Hiram Howe, of Holden, January 6, 1800

(VI) David Harthan, son of Micah Harthan (5), was born in Shrewsbury, now West Boylston, Massachusetts, January 15, 1764 He married, July 15 1786, Prudence Winn Smith, widow, born in 1764, daughter of Jacob Winn He was the founder of the well known Harthan Mills in West Boylston, Massachusetts His home was about fifty rods north of the present railroad station at West Boylston The children of David and Prudence (Winn) Harthan were Antipas Smith, born in West Boylston, October 3, 1788, Silas, born in West Boylston, November 28, 1791, Lois, born November 19, 1793, Dennis, born November 17, 1796, Ward Boylston, born July 28, 1804

(VII) Antipas Smith Harthan, son of David Harthan (6), was born in West Boylston, Massachusetts, October 2, 1788 He married Cynthia Fairbanks, born in West Boylston, Massachusetts, July 10, 1784 She was a descendant of Jonathan Fairbank, of Dedham (See Fairbanks Family sketch elsewhere in this work) This branch of the family settled Lancaster and is that from which the vice president of the United States, Charles W Fairbanks, is descended Antipas Smith Harthan died in 1815 The children of Antipas Smith and Cynthia (Fairbanks) Harthan were Silas Smith, born in West Boylston, Massachusetts, August 7, 1814, Prudence Maria

(VIII) Silas Smith Harthan, son of Antipas Smith Harthan (7), was born in West Boylston, Massachusetts, August 7, 1814 When eighteen years of age he learned the trade of cabinet maker and carpenter He had a common school education He settled in Sterling, but in 1844 removed to Worcester and lived in the old Dan Tucker house on Pleasant street, opposite High street, where the Brunswick block now stands, the house at that time being the first one on the street coming from Main street In 1845 he built and occupied the house on Chatham street, then called Division street, corner of Clinton street, now occupied by General Josiah Pickett Afterwards he removed to Guilford, Connecticut, Sterling and West Boylston, Massachusetts His home at West Boylston was taken by the Metropolitan water board during the construction of the reservoir there, and the last few months of his life were spent on the old homestead in West Boylston, where he was born eighty-eight years before He died September 18, 1902 He was a member of Quinsigamond Lodge, I O O F, when in Worcester In politics he was a Republican He was a Congregationalist and belonged formerly to the Old South Church, Worcester, of which his wife was also a member

He married, January 6, 1836, Mary Ann Ross, born in Sterling, Massachusetts. January 22, 1817, the daughter of Peter and Polly (Burpee) Ross She was the mother of thirteen children, of whom Silas E Harthan was the second She attended the old Redstone school in Sterling, the very school attended by Mary Sawyer, of whom the verses "Mary Had a Little Lamb" were written many years ago Mrs Harthan was reared in the strict Orthodox faith of her ancestors and she brought up her own children in the same way She died December 6 1902 A sister of Mrs Harthan, Mrs Olive Ross Burbank, was the mother of Luther Burbank, of Santa Rosa, California, known throughout the world as "The Wizard of Horticulture" Mr Burbank and Silas E Harthan are first cousins

(IX) Silas Emerson Harthan, son of Silas Smith Harthan (8), was born in West Boylston, Massachusetts, March 5, 1838 He attended the same little district school that his mother before him had attended, the Redstone Hill school in Sterling Massachusetts After the family removed to Worcester he attended the school house formerly on the Common and the old Thomas street school He attended the academy at Guilford, Connecticut When a small boy he sold the *Daily Spy* and the *Daily Telegraph* in Worcester In 1848-49-50 he sold the Worcester Directory, then only twelve and a half cents a copy While in the academy at Guilford he began to learn the machinist's trade When seventeen years of age he was given charge of the department making dies for tin toys and tinware About that time he constructed his first steamboat It was twenty-one feet in length and he made the boiler, engine, patterns, castings and all himself Afterwards he built a side wheeler used in the passenger trade on the Providence river and at Martha's Vineyard In 1873 he built the steamboats "Addie" and Little Favorite," and later four other steamboats used on Lake Quinsigamond These were the first steamboats on the lake He has built more than fifty steamboats The last boat the Mr Harthan built was the "Sterling," now in commission on Lake Waushacum, Sterling, Massachusetts

Mr Harthan came to Worcester in 1860 and went to work for the Cleveland Machine Company on contract work He was also superintendent there for a time He worked for the Gilbert loom works also on contract work In 1869 he became master mechanic for the Bay State Shoe and Leather Company, of which H H Bigelow was the general manager Mr Harthan invented the Bigelow Heeling Machine, an ingenious machine for compressing scraps of leather into heels, shaping the heel and driving the nails part way through, ready for use Each machine had a capacity of three thousand heels a day, and each machine produced about four thousand five hundred dollars a year in royalties The perfecting of this machine brought about the consolidation of the Bigelow Heeling Company and the McKay Company He also invented other machines used in the manufacture of boots and shoes The Armsby property at 44, 46 and 48 Central street was purchased and rebuilt for use in making these heel machines Many of these machines are still in use by the Bay State Shoe and Leather Company at 68 High street

In 1879 Mr Harthan became the manager of the first electric light company and later the first electric railway, the first electric power, the first storage battery, operated in Worcester The first arc lamps used in Worcester were in the Skating Rink on Foster street during the New England Fair in September, 1879 The next were installed at Union Station When the Denholm & McKay Company moved into their present quarters opposite the Common in 1881, the department store was fitted with electric lights The announcement that the store was to be lighted by electricity awakened the fears of some good old citizens There was quite a public demonstration against the innovation A meeting of the city government was hurriedly called as a last resort to prevent the use of the new-fangled lights on the opening night of the Boston Store, but they failed to locate the management of the light in time Denholm & McKay's big Boston Store was lighted with electricity on the opening night of course, in spite of the clamor, and it was not long before many stores in the city were lighted with electric lamps The dynamos then in use were in the brick station on the old Skating Rink grounds There were very few instruments for measuring electricity at that time Lighting was done by thumb rule at first, but the old rule that necessity is the mother of invention was again demonstrated in the simplicity and reliability of the modern electric light plant In 1883 the electric light business was sold to the Worcester Electric Light Company The Worcester Electric Power Company was organized by a Boston company with Mr Harthan as manager It was sold to H H Bigelow in 1887

A number of electrical exhibitions were held in the Skating Rink under the direction of S E Harthan and H H Bigelow to demonstrate to the public the usefulness of electricity in the industrial world The public was made familiar in this way with the uses that could be made from the same electrical circuit, such as operating street railways, furnishing power for running machinery, for both arc and incandescent lighting, for heating, cooking ranges, for sad irons, etc An electric railroad for carrying passengers was in operation in the skating rink during these exhibitions This was the first electric railway in Worcester, if not in Massachusetts Soon after, in 1889, the cars on the dummy railroad owned by H H Bigelow, connecting Lake Quinsigamond with the business centre of Worcester, were operated by a trolley electric system The Foster Street Electric Railway was built in 1890 and later the North End Street Railway Both of these street railways were operated from the station on the Skating Rink grounds In 1897 the Worcester Electric Power Company was adopted by the Worcester Electric Light Company

In 1897 Mr Harthan was employed by some capitalists to re-open the old coal mine near Lake Quinsigamond after it had been abandoned for about seventy years He found the mine about forty feet deep and full of water After pumping out two hundred thousand gallons of water some fifteen or twenty tons of coal were taken out and experimented with Mr Harthan burned some of the coal in his furnace, as did others, and it was found to be of too poor a quality to pay to operate the mine The coal was mixed with graphite and other foreign matter Mr Harthan retired in 1898 after selling his shop fittings and tools He has devoted his time since then to the care of his real estate and to the operation of the steamboat "Sterling" on Lake Waushacum, Sterling, running during the season from the Methodist Camp Grounds at Sterling Junction to the Waushacum Park Picnic Grounds, a tract of land about thirty acres in extent owned by a company in which Mr Harthan is a partner These picnic grounds are the only grounds in the state used exclusively for church and society picnics They have been open since 1878

Mr Harthan married, January 15, 1860, Mary Elizabeth Tufts, born in Lancaster, May 19, 1838, died September 11, 1877 She was the daughter of Albert Tufts, of Medford, Massachusetts, of the family that founded Tufts College in Medford Her mother was Mary Louise Newhall, of Lancaster, daughter of Albert Newhall, of Lancaster, an eminent teacher and composer of music Mr Harthan married (second) Maria Carpenter Buker, born in Stonington, Connecticut, daughter of Nelson Carpenter, later of Putnam Heights, Connecticut Her mother was Mercy Randall Brayton, of the old Brayton family of Rhode Island She was a direct descendant of Roger Williams

The children of Silas Emerson Harthan were 1 Frank Ellsworth, died in infancy in 1863 2 Charles Emerson, born in Worcester, educated in the public schools and at the Polytechnic Institute, is associated with the General Electric Company at Lynn, Massachusetts, as electrical engineer and at the head of the entire arc light department, in 1905 was made designing engineer of the whole General Electric Company, he has made for the General Electric Company a number of valuable inventions He married, June 21, 1888, Annie Hinks Dow, of Lynn, Massachusetts, and has one child Lewis Emerson, born September 30, 1891, who has unusual musical talents 3 Addie Maria, born in Worcester; educated in the Worcester public schools and the State Normal school at Worcester, has been a teacher in the Worcester public schools for the past fourteen years 4 Herbert Miller, born in Worcester, educated in the public schools there, was of marked mechanical ability, married, February 22, 1900, Harriet Allerton Purinton, a direct descendant of the Allertons who came on the "Mayflower", he was injured in the factory where he was employed and died three days later, June 28, 1900, aged thirty-one years

THE PARSONS FAMILY is of English descent, and are found at a very early date in New England Whether in the domains of England or on the New England shores they have borne an honorable part in all that has been for the upbuilding of refined society and good forms of government As a family they have been prominent both in England and the United States Whether as soldiers, jurists, scholars, physicians, or clergymen, the name stands for loyalty and high-minded living Mrs M E Schieffelin, a descendant, says "The Parsons family is of the same descent as the Earl of Rosse, of Parsonstown, Ireland The Parsons went from England to Ireland Their coat-of-arms is similar to ours, and the form and face of the members of the two branches have a striking resemblance"

(II) Joseph Parsons, on July 4 1635, sailed with his brother Benjamin and others of the family from Gravesend, England, in the bark "Transport," bound for America He was born in Great Torrington, near Exeter, Devonshire, England, and is supposed to have descended from Sir Thomas Parsons, of Milton Royal, who was knighted by Charles II, 1634. The record states that "His brother Benjamin Parsons was a grandson of Thomas Parsons, of Great Milton, Oxfordshire, England, who died in 1597" Joseph Parsons married, November 26, 1646, Mary, daughter of Thomas and Margaret (Ford) Bliss, of Hartford, Connecticut She was born in England, 1620, and died January 29, 1712 He died October 9, 1683, at Springfield, Massachusetts He was a man of much prominence in his day, and was one of the witnesses to the Indian deed of the territory of Springfield, given to William Pyncheon and others for a consideration of eighteen yards of wampum, eighteen hatchets, eighteen knives, July 15, 1636 In 1642 he removed to Northampton, and was among the first purchasers from the Indians in 1645 For fifty years he was the leading business man of the Connecticut Valley He was a fur trader, and had a monopoly on the beaver trade in Connecticut, for which he paid annually the sum of twelve pounds He left a large estate, part of which is still held by the heirs He was styled 'Cornet," indicating that he had been an officer in a British cavalry regiment The children of Joseph and Margaret Parsons 1 Joseph, born at Springfield, November, 1647, died November, 1729 2 John, born 1649, married Sarah Clarke, at Northampton, December 23, 1675 3 Samuel, born 1652, he settled at Durham, Connecticut, 1706 4 Ebenezer, born 1655, killed by Indians in King Philip's war, September 8, 1675 5 Jonathan, born June, 1657, died October, 1684 6 David, born April, 1659 7 Mary, born June, 1661 8 Hannah, born 1663 9 Abigail, born September, 1666 10 Hester, born 1672, married Joseph Smith, of Greenwich, Connecticut

(II) Joseph Parsons and wife Elizabeth had ten children Joseph, John, Ebenezer, Elizabeth, David, Josiah Daniel Moses, Abigail, Noah

(II) Samuel Parsons and wife, settled at Durham, Connecticut, had children Timothy, Simeon, Phineas. Aaron, Ithamar

(III) Joseph Parsons, grandson of the ancestor, married Elizabeth Thompson, and had children Joseph, Samuel, William, Elizabeth, John

(IV) Joseph Parsons, great-grandson of the American ancestor married Frances Usher, their children Frances Elizabeth, Joseph, Thomas, Samuel, Dr John, William, Sarah, Edward

(IV) Samuel Parsons and Mary his wife had children Mary, Joseph, Hannah, Betsey

(IV) William Parsons married Sarah Burnham, their children Sarah, William, Elizabeth, John, Joseph, Ebenezer

(III) Rev David Parsons and wife Sarah (Stebbings) Parsons had one child, David, and his children were Ezekial, Williams, David, Prudence, Thomas, Harriet, Francis, Mary, Caroline, Sophia, William, James

(IV) Israel Parsons, born 1715, died 1767, married Hannah Waite, and for his second wife Lois Wiley His children Hannah, Sarah, Deborah, Israel, Ebenezer, James, Ruth

(V) Israel Parsons, son of Israel (4), lived in Hatfield, and married Nancy Parmlee Their children Nancy, Lucina, Harriet, Israel, Epaphroditus, Susan, Hannah

(IV) Dr Solomon Parsons married Elizabeth Taylor, their children Jerusha, Elizabeth, Phebe, Solomon

(V) Solomon Parsons, fourth son of Dr Solomon Parsons (4), born August 29, 1757, died May 11, 1831 He married, 1789, Rebecca Coburn Wesson, of Shrewsbury, Massachusetts, a native of that place, born 1726, died in Worcester, 1836 He removed from Leicester to Worcester in 1812 He enlisted in the army during the revolution, in March, 1777, being only nineteen years old at the time He was present at the surrender of Burgoyne, and afterward at the battle of Monmouth, June 28, 1778, where he was severely wounded and left to die on the field but in a most wonderful manner survived and lived for more than half a century His own graphic story of his service in that engagement appears in the history of the Parsons family, and illustrates the sterling virtues of the brave soldier and Christian man His children Samuel, Elizabeth, Sally, Bloomfield, Maria, Solomon

It is noteworthy that Bloomfield, fourth son of Solomon Parsons, was named in honor of the surgeon who attended him when he was wounded at the battle of Monmouth The following is the verbatim statement of Solomon Parsons relative to his service in the revolutionary war

"I Solomon Parsons, of Leicester, listed March 9, 1777, during the war, and was at the taking of Burgoyne, then marched to the southward and was in the battle of Monmouth where I endeavored to act well my part until I received a ball which broke my thigh Our men being on the retreat I fell into the enemies hands where I was stabbed with a bayonette three times, one through my arm and one on my shoulder and knee, and received a blow from the ramrod of the artillery on my head which rendered me senseless After the battle I was carried to Princeton College where I had my wounds dressed I was then carried to Trenton My father came with the solicitations of my friends to return home if possible before I breathed my last which all expected soon I received a pass Sept 30. and went home with my father and was confined seven years on my friends and my own expense In 1780 General Washington ordered all sick absentees to be returned deserters unless they returned or made a return of themselves I being unable my father got a return made out signed by the Selectmen of the Town and sent it on to Camp It not being carried up through a neglect I lost all my arrears of pay and clothing and the hundred acres of land At the close of seven years our Representative sent for me to go to Boston with him In the year 1785 the Commissary gave me a Pention of twenty shillings per month In the year 1816 I received $6 per month My fractured thigh continues to be a running sore and very painful when it stops running until it is lanced anew, which frequently occurs This I labor under with the inconveniences of a stiff knee which this wound occasioned But I have now the consolation of seeing this country in its Glory, which partly compensates me

"(Signed) SOLOMON PARSONS"

(VI) Solomon Parsons, son of Solomon, of revolutionary fame, was born October 18, 1800, less than a year after the death of Washington Born on a New England farm, Mr Parsons's long life was devoted to the cultivation of the soil, an occupation in which he took delight In 1812 his father bought the farm near Valley Falls, in Worcester Here the elder Parsons and his son spent the remainder of their days, and the latter's son, Samuel B Parsons, still occupies the place Solomon Parsons married, April 16, 1828, Sarah Hasey Child, of Cambridge, Massachusetts She died 1876 During the last years of his life, Mr Parsons had a strong aversion to war and all connected with it, but in his veins ran patriotic blood that has never failed to manifest itself in every generation of this good old Worcester family Among the family keepsakes is a ribbon badge, worn in 1824, when he acted as military guard in escorting General Lafayette through Worcester It bears a fine likeness of Lafayette and the outline of Bunker Hill monument Solomon Parsons was one of the founders of the First Methodist Episcopal Church of Worcester, One of his peculiarities was the fact of his being a consistent vegetarian, and he attributed his robust constitution and long life to the fact of his not being a meat eater He was a strong advocate of the anti-slavery movement, and, when the civil war came on, he gave up his son, named after him, to the service of his country He was fond of travel, in 1865 he sailed for the West Indies, and in 1869-70 made a journey to the Holy Land and traversed the section once so familiar to the feet of Christ and his apostles In 1877, when long past three score and ten, he made an ocean trip to South America But time finally caused his earthly travels to cease, and December 16, 1893, he died on the old homestead He lived to pass his ninety-third birthday, surviving nearly all who began life's race with him 'Uncle Solomon", as he was called by many both in and outside the family, loved peace and loathed passion He loved and prayed, and when his mission ended his mortal remains were placed in the finest shades of Hope cemetery, where he sleeps by the side of his wife and son His children were 1 Sarah Frances, born January 24, 1829, married, July 4, 1849, Samuel H T Bennett, of Pepperell, Massachusetts 2 Solomon, born June 9, 1830, married, April 21, 1856, Mary Smith Gilbert, of Windsor, Connecticut He entered the Union army as a member of Company F, Fifty-first Massachusetts Regiment, and died January 18, 1863 They had one son Albert Gilbert, born June 7, 1857, died April 13, 1882 3 Samuel Bloomfield, born February 24, 1832, married Elizabeth L Gibbs, December 11, 1861 4 Mary Elizabeth, born October 1, 1833, married, March 29, 1853, Elmer Woodward, of Orange, Massachusetts 5 William Augustine, born October 30, 1836, died July 2, 1850 6 Lucy Mason born July 19, 1840, married Nathaniel H Bryant, of Boston 7 Anna Eliza, born June 21, 1843, married Angus Henderson, of Provincetown, Massachusetts He died December 21, 1897

(VII) Samuel B Parsons, son of Solomon and Sarah Hasey (Child) Parsons (6), born February 24, 1832, in Worcester county, where he was reared and educated He has served as justice of the peace for thirty-five years After finishing his education at the Leicester Academy, he took up civil engineering and has followed it for more than fifty years He married Elizabeth L Gibbs, of Boylston, December 11, 1861 Their children 1 Anna Gibbs, born November 2, 1862 2 Norman Bloomfield, September 28, 1865 3 Irene Elizabeth, December 8, 1867 4 Nellie Merriam, September 18, 1870, died August 25, 1871

(VIII) Norman Bloomfield Parsons, son of Samuel B, as above, born September 28, 1865, was educated at the Worcester high school, and for a number of years had charge of the old home farm which has belonged to the Parsons family since 1812 In 1902 he was elected as a commissioner from the seventh ward in Worcester, and re-elected in 1904 by twelve hundred majority He has been treasurer of the Republican Club for seven years, taking a lively interest in all political matters

WALTER HEYWARD FISKE Symon Fiske (1), to whom the ancestry of Walter H Fiske, of Upton, is traced was Lord of the Manor of Stadhaugh parish of Laxfield, county of Suffolk, England He married (first) Susannah Smyth and (second) Katherine ——— His will was dated December 22, 1463, and proved at Norwich, February 26, 1463-4 He died in February, 1464 His children were William, Jeffrey, John, Edmund, Margaret

(II) William Fiske, son of Sir Symond Fiske (1), was born at Stadhaugh, England He married Joan Lynne, of Norfolk His widow made her will July 15, 1504, proved February 28, 1505 He died about 1504 Their children were Thomas, William, Augustine, Simon, Robert, John, Margery, Margaret

(III) Simon Fiske, son of William Fiske (2), was born in Laxfield He married Elizabeth ———, who died in Halesworth, in June, 1558 His will was dated July 10, 1536 and proved July 13, 1538 He died June, 1538 His children were Simon, William, Robert Joan, Jeffrey, Gelyne, Agnes, Thomas, Elizabeth, John

(IV) Simon Fiske, son of Simon Fiske (3), was born in Laxfield His will was dated January 25 1505, and he died that year His children were Robert, John, George, Nicholas, Jeffrey, Jeremy, William, Richard, married Agnes Crispe, Joan, Gelyne, Agnes

(V) Robert Fiske son of Simon Fiske (4), was born at Stadhaugh, England, about 1525 He married Mrs Sybil (Gould) Barber For some time he was of the parish of St James, South Elmham, England Sybil, wife of Robert, was in great danger in the time of the religious persecution, 1553-8, as was her sister Isabella born Gould, who was confined in the castle of Norwich and escaped death only through the intercession of her brothers Robert himself fled for the sake of his religious beliefs to Geneva during the reign of Bloody Mary He died in 1600 and his will was proved July 28, 1600 The progeny of his three sons William Jeffrey and Thomas settled in New England His children were William, born 1566, Jeffrey Thomas, Eleazer died in England, 1615, s p, Elizabeth, married Robert Bernard

(VI) Thomas Fiske, son of Robert Fiske (5), was born in Laxfield England He married Margery ——— His will is dated February 20, 1610, and proved February 28, 1610 He died February, 1610 He lived at Fressingfield, England His children were Thomas, settled in Madfield, Massachusetts, James, Phinehas, born 1610, Elizabeth, Mary

(VII) Captain Phinehas Fiske, son of Thomas

Fiske (6), was born in Laxfield, England He married there in 1638, Sarah ———, who died September 10, 1659 He married (second) in Wenham, Massachusetts, June 4, 1660, Elizabeth Easterick He was admitted a freeman in Wenham, Massachusetts, 1642, and in fact was one of the first settlers of the town and a leading citizen He was captain of the militia company He was constable in 1644, deputy to the general court in 1653, magistrate to end small causes in 1654 His will was dated March, 1673, and proved in June of that year He died June 7 His children, all by the first wife, were. James, born in England, John, Thomas, born in England, 1632, married Peggy ———

(VIII) Hon John Fiske, son of Phinehas Fiske (7), was born in England He married, December 10, 1651, Remember ——— She married (second) Deacon William Goodhue, of Ipswich She was his fourth wife and she died February 16, 1702 John Fiske was admitted a freeman in 1649, was a constable in 1654 and representative in 1669 and 1682 He died intestate in 1683 He was in King Philip's war in Captain William Turner's company, and in the Falls fight he was wounded In consideration of the wound which disabled him he was permitted to keep a public house He died October 27, 1682-3, at Wenham, Massachusetts, where he had lived Children of John and Remember Fiske were John, born December 12, 1654, married Hannah Baldwin, Samuel, born 1660, Noah, born November 14, 1662, Elizabeth, born March 8, 1673, Remember, Waite (Genealogy gives Jonathan, born in December 12, 1688, after father's death, obviously an error of some kind)

(IX) Dr John Fiske, son of John Fiske (8), was born at Wenham, Massachusetts, December 12, 1654 He married January 17, 1682, Hannah Baldwin, daughter of John Baldwin, of Milford, Connecticut, and wife Mary Bowen, born November 20, 663 John Fiske was admitted a freeman in 1685 He practiced medicine and surgery in Wenham and also in Milford, Connecticut, whither he removed with his family in 1694 and joined the church there He sold his property in Wenham, November 15, 1693 He was a prominent physician in his day and he was a man of wealth He was a soldier in the Indian wars and on account of a wound received in the war was released by the court from the payment of country rates He died about 1715 18 Children of Dr John and Hannah (Baldwin) Fiske were Phinehas, born December 4, 1682, Benjamin born 1683, Ebenezer, born 1689, married Mehitable ———, and Rebecca Trowbridge, John, born 1693, Hannah, married, August 20, 1713, Jeremiah Peck

(X) Benjamin Fiske, son of Dr John Fiske (9), was born in 1683 and baptized in Milford, Connecticut March, 1696 He married, July 24, 1701, Abigail Bowen, of Rehoboth, Massachusetts She was the daughter of Obadiah and Abigail (Bullock) Bowen, of Rehoboth After Benjamin removed to Rhode Island he was justice of the peace for years at Scituate He resided at Swansey, Massachusetts, also He died February 14, 1765 Children of Benjamin and Abigail (Bowen) Fiske were Mary, born April 28, 1702, Hezekiah, June 11, 1704, Benjamin, March 8, 1706, Elizabeth, May 9, 1708, Daniel, December 16, 1709, Job, 1711, John, January 11, 1713, Freelove, March 29, 1716, Noah 1722 Abigail

(XI) Daniel Fiske, son of Benjamin Fiske (10), was born in Rehoboth Massachusetts, December 16, 1709 He married, December 24, 1732, Freelove Williams daughter of Peleg and Elizabeth (Carpenter) Williams, granddaughter of Daniel Williams, and great-granddaughter of Rev Roger Williams At the time of his marriage Daniel Fiske lived in Scituate His wife was born November 13, 1713, died April 20, 1791 Mrs Fiske's grandfather was murdered by the Indians while hoeing his corn His wife was watching him from the cabin door when she saw the Indian throw the tomahawk and scalp his victim Daniel Fiske died June 27, 1804 He lived at Scituate, Rhode Island Children of Daniel and Freelove (Williams) Fiske were Eunice, born April 5, 1736, Joseph April 23, 1738, Waite, February 23, 1740, Rhoda, January 16, 1751, Daniel, April 28, 1753

(XII) Daniel Fiske, son of Daniel Fiske (11), was born at Rehoboth, Massachusetts April 28, 1753 He married, in Cranston, April 13, 1785, Freelove Knight, daughter of Stephen and Mary (Manchester) Knight She was born January 21, 1766 She married (second) ——— Thomas, and she died May 20, 1819 He was a member of the Rhode Island legislature He lived at Scituate, Rhode Island, and died there, May 5, 1810 Children of Daniel and Freelove (Knight) Fiske were Rhoda, born November 20, 1786, died unmarried 1872, Celia, February 17, 1788, married Stephen Burlingame, Stephen K, April 26, 1789, Isaac, March 4, 1792, Hardin March 4 1795, Betsey, July 7, 1798, died February 27 1819, Arnold, July 26, 1802, married Susan R Miller

(XIII) Stephen Knight Fiske, son of Daniel Fiske (12) was born in Scituate, Rhode Island, April 26, 1789 He married, in Scituate, March 2, 1817, Mercey Burlingame, of Clemence She was born April 8, 1800, died July 19 1857 His father died when he was twenty-one He carried on the farm with the help of some of his younger brothers and supported the family At the age of twenty-eight he and a brother bought the farm His wife died in 1857 He gave part of his farm to his youngest son Almond, and made his home with him for many years, then went to live with another son at whose home he died, August 18, 1871, in Scituate He was eighty-three years old and had his health until his last illness which was brief He was held in high esteem by his fellow citizens He was representative to the state legislature two years town councilman for many years, held many other positions of trust and settled many important estates

Children of Stephen Knight and Mercey (Burlingame) Fiske were Almond W, born August 23, 1830, married Amy Cahoon, Daniel, May 27, 1817, married Ruth Burlingame, Clarinda Ann, March 23, 1818 married, February, 1838, Zephaniah Ramsdell, he died January 26, 1885, she died January 26 1885, Stephen, June 21, 1819 married Cynthia Colvin, Ebenezer, August 31 1821 married Amy Colvin, Cynthia, August 30, 1824, died July 22, 1828, Elizabeth, September 3, 1828, died July 14, 1844

(XIV) Daniel Fiske son of Stephen Knight Fiske (13), was born in Scituate, May 27 1817 He married at East Killingly, Connecticut July 3, 1842, Ruth Burlingame She was born June 20 1820 He attended the country schools and worked on the farm during his boyhood By studying at home he fitted himself for the high school After his course in the South Scituate high school he taught school in the village of Hope in Scituate At the age of twenty-five he moved with his father to the village of Hope and was married the following summer He and his father carried on the farm together In February, 1848, he bought a good farm of one hundred and fifty acres in Brookfield, Massachusetts, and went there with wife and three children to make his home In 1876 he gave up business and removed to 56 Coral street' Worcester, Massachusetts, where he spent the remainder of his days He died

March 19 1897 He was a justice of the peace in Rhode Island

Children of Daniel and Ruth (Burlingame) Fiske were Julia Ann born August 13 1844 married, November 15 1865 George R Hamant, of North Brookfield, Mary Elizabeth, born January 10, 1846, married, November 16 1865, Moses Hobbs, of North Brookfield, Massachusetts, Susan Maria, resides in Worcester, Stephen Burlingame, born October 30 1849 married Alice N Stebbins, Celia Jane, born April 7, 1854, resided lately at 56 Coral street, Worcester, Charles Daniel, born March 13 1856 married Melinda Brooks, Sarah Frances, born December 15 1858 married, June 1, 1887, John Charles Hawkins, of Fiskville, Rhode Island

(XV) Stephen Burlingame Fiske, son of Daniel Fiske (14), was born in Brookfield, Massachusetts, October 30, 1849 He married, at North Brookfield Massachusetts, March 3, 1873, Alice N Stebbins born July 23 1852 Mr Fiske was educated in the public schools of Brookfield He assisted his father for some time on the farm before he was twenty Afterwards he served an apprenticeship of three years in the drug business in Woonsocket, Rhode Island, and he was for one year a member of the firm of G R Hamant, of North Brookfield Massachusetts For the next five years he kept a drug store in East Jaffrey, New Hampshire In 1879 he came to Upton Massachusetts, and succeeded to the drug business formerly carried on there by James S Le Sure at the corner of North Main and Milford streets He had no opposition in his line and he built up a large and successful business A few years ago he built near the old location a new business block, where he has a main salesroom thirty by seventy-six feet, with office, prescription department and laboratory in the rear About three thousand square feet of floor space is devoted to the business Mr Fiske was not only the town apothecary, but he was the advisor and business confident of half the town He was most accommodating and helpful to those needing advice and assistance, and no man in the vicinity had the confidence and esteem of the community more completely

Mr Fiske was a Republican in politics and was intensely interested in public affairs His business ability as well as his high standing in the community have called him often into the public service After he had declined the office of town treasurer, when he had been a resident of the town only three years, he was in 1884 induced to accept the position and he held it to the satisfaction of all concerned until his death except for two years He was a member of the committee to construct the school house and was a member of the library committee for several years He was chief engineer of the fire department, was a notary public and justice of the peace As a magistrate he was particularly helpful to the veterans in putting their pension papers in shape He was an active member of a number of fraternal orders

He invested largely in Upton real estate and industries and in every way possible helped in the development of his town He built a handsome residence on Nelson hill known as Maple Terrace Since the death of Mr Fiske, his widow has lived with her son in the building over the drug store in the village square Mr Fiske died April 1, 1904, after a long illness

He married March 3 1873 Alice N Stebbins, of a prominent North Brookfield family Their children were Charles Norman, born at East Jaffrey, New Hampshire April 22 1876 Harry Austin, born at Upton June 12 1880 died there April 10, 1897, Walter Heyward, born January 3 1882

(XVI) Dr Charles Norman Fiske, son of Stephen Burlingame Fiske (15), was born in East Jaffrey, New Hampshire, April 22, 1876 He received his early school training in the Upton schools graduating from the high school 1892 He then studied a year at Phillips (Exeter) Academy, graduating 1893, and entered Harvard College He decided to try for the office of surgeon in the navy, and accordingly left college to enter the Harvard Medical School, from which he was graduated in 1900 He entered the navy and is now (1905) a past assistant surgeon, attached to the Marblehead, now undergoing alterations and repairs in the Mare Island navy yard San Francisco He married, September 25 1902, Helen Tucker Hawke, daughter of Admiral James T Hawke, who is living since his retirement at Sonoma California They have one child, John Norman born November 15, 1903

(XVI) Walter Heyward Fiske, son of Stephen Burlingame Fiske (15) was born in Upton, Massachusetts, January 3, 1882 He attended the common schools of his native town and graduated from the Upton high school, 1899 He studied at Phillips (Exeter) Academy one year and took a course in Becker's Business College in Worcester He came into the store as soon as he left school and assisted his father in the business The entire management of the business soon devolved on him by reason of his father's ill health He was virtually the town treasurer also during the last illness of his father Since the death of his father, in 1904, Mr Fiske has held the position of treasurer He is a member of the Republican town committee In a way he has taken his father's place in the town as well as in the business Those who had learned to trust the father have reposed equal confidence in the son, and he is popular with all his fellow citizens He is a member of the Milford Lodge, No 223 Independent Order of Odd Fellows, also Master Mason of Montgomery Lodge, Milford Massachusetts, Benevolent and Protective Order Elks Milford Lodge, No 628, Court Upton Foresters of America No 195

He married October 22 1902, Ernestine Saunders, daughter of Milton Saunders of Milford, Massachusetts They have one child, Helen, born in Upton April 24, 1904

CALVIN LYON HARTSHORN No name has been more prominent in the history of the development of agriculture and horticulture in Worcester county than that of Hartshorn Three generations of them have pursued the vocation of farming in the city of Worcester with success They have each kept ahead of their times and have led rather than kept pace The three representatives of these generations are Calvin Lyon Hartshorn, his father Jonas and his son Arthur E They are descended from the Hartshorns of Reading, Dedham Walpole, Sherborn Boylston and Worcester

(I) Thomas Hartshorn, the founder of the family of the name in America settled in Reading in the Massachusetts Bay colony His original farm has been occupied continuously by lineal descendants to the present time He was born in England in 1614 The Hartshorns in England took their name from an ancient parish of this name in Litchfield diocese, Derby county It is believed that the parish was named from its geographical resemblance to a hart's horn The family was well established, as the records show, as far back as the thirteenth century Henry de Hertishorn and others are mentioned as residing in Derby county They bore arms The coat of arms contains three bucks' heads and the crest is a buck's head The design obviously refers to the name's significance Thomas Hartshorn took the freeman's oath at Reading, May 10, 1648 He was a prominent and influential citizen, serving his fellow colonists as selectman and in other positions of trust and honor He died about May 18, 1683

His wife, Susannah, died March 18, 1659-60 He married (second) Hannah ———, who was received from the church in Ipswich 6 (2) 1663 She died July 20, 1673 He married (third) Sarah widow of William Lamson, of Ipswich His children were Thomas, born October 30, 1646, died young, Thomas, born September 30, 1648, John, born May 6, 1650, Joseph, born July 2, 1652, Benjamin, born 1654, Jonathan, born August 20, 1656, David, born 1657, Susannah, born March 2, 1659, Timothy, born February 3, 1661, Mary, born August 19, 1672

(II) Joseph Hartshorn, son of Thomas (1), and Susannah Hartshorn, was born July 2, 1652, at Reading, Massachusetts, died July 30, 1727, at Walpole He resided at Reading and Dedham, and was a soldier in King Philip's war He married Sarah ———, and their children were Susanna, born 1677, Sarah, born 1679 married Samuel Guild, of Dedham, January 8, 1700-1, Mary, born 1681, married Jonathan Fairbank February 3, 1702, Abigail, born 1686, Joseph, born 1688, Tabitha, born 1690, Rebeka, born December 7, 1693, Thomas, born May 8, 1695, Ebenezer, born July 10, 1697, married Rebekah ——— Dedham, Martha, born July 2, 1700

(III) Joseph Hartshorn son of Joseph (2) and Sarah Hartshorn, was born at Reading, 1688, died at Walpole, December 22 1758 He married Rachel ———, of Sherborn, March 17, 1709, and she died November 14, 1769 They lived at Walpole and Sherborn Some of their children were Joseph, born March 12, 1710, a daughter born September 25, 1712, Sarah, born May 28 1726

(IV) Joseph Hartshorn Jr, son of Joseph (3) and Rachel Hartshorn, was born March 12, 1710, at Walpole He married Hannah Foster, December 29 1721 and their children, all born at Walpole, were Joseph, born October 15, 1732, Samuel, born April 22, 1734, died September 9, 1747, Joseph and Hannah, twins, born January 9, 1735-6, Jacob, born November 27, 1737, Mary, born January 11, 1742-3, Ebenezer, born January 12, 1745-6, ———, born March 31, 1747, Samuel, born April 30, 1749, Sibbel, born October 5, 1751

(V) Deacon Ebenezer Hartshorn, son of Joseph, Jr (4) and Hannah (Foster) Hartshorn, was born January 12, 1745-6, married Thankful ———, who died November 24 1796 He married (second) Betty, daughter of Jonas and Sarah Greenwood, August 30, 1798, at Walpole Ebenezer Hartshorn was a farmer and also a carpenter He moved from Walpole to Boylston, Massachusetts, soon after 1790 He died May 27, 1813, at Boylston His children were Jacob born August 17, 1769, ———, September 23, 1771, Daniel, February 7, 1774, Ebenezer June 13, 1778, Nancy, January 23 1781, at Stoughtenham, Warren June 13, 1783, Grata, October 27, 1788, Jonas, June 1802 Calvin, March 6, 1804 died November 8, 1889, Susan August 19, 1806, died September 25, 1881, married William Kendall, December 25, 1828, Sarah February 16, 1811, married Simeon Partridge of Boylston

(VI) Calvin Hartshorn, son of Ebenezer (5) and Betty Hartshorn was born March 6 1804 He remained at Walpole following his vocation of millwright He married, November 19, 1832, Maria Ann Guild, born at Walpole October 7, 1807 Their children were 1 Anna Maria, born September 12, 1833, married Luther Swan Leech of Stoughton, Massachusetts who died April 11, 1875, leaving his widow and a son, Joseph Swan Leech, born November 14, 1860 2 Calvin Guild, born February 23, 1840 at Walpole 3 Edwin Curtis, born September 28 1844 died April 21, 1849

(VI) Deacon Jonas Hartshorn, son of Ebenezer (5) and Betty Hartshorn, was born at Sherborn, Massachusetts, June, 1802 His father died when he was a mere child and his mother apprenticed him to a man named Temple at Boylston, with whom he served his seven years He came to Worcester and for a time was guard and turnkey at the county jail He bought a farm on Mountain street, but in 1839 sold it and bought of Joseph and William W Patch, two brothers, half of their farm of about two hundred acres The other half was retained by William W Patch This new farm is the present Hartshorn estate The new owner set out orchards and shade trees built the present barn and dwelling house vastly improving the property

Jonas Hartshorn married (first) Eunice Patch, April 1, 1828 She died October 2, 1834, at the age of thirty years He married (second) Laura Ann Patch, September 22, 1835 She died August 15, 1847, at the age of thirty years He married (third) Abigail Whitney, August 10, 1848 She died March 23, 1862, at the age of forty-nine years He married (fourth) Lydia W Bray, March 15, 1864 Following are the children John Clark, born January 20, 1829 died November 26, 1831, Nathan Greenwood born June 23 1831, died November 26 1831, Calvin Lyon, born December 25, 1832, Caroline Elizabeth, born November 9 1836, died December 25, 1839, John Warren born September 9, 1839, Ann Eliza, born October 15, 1842, died August 22, 1845, Emma Jane, born May 15, 1845, died August 30, 1845, Laura Ann, born August 3, 1847, died August 15, 1847

(VI) Susan Hartshorn, daughter of Ebenezer (5) and Betty Hartshorn, was born August 19, 1806, died September 25 1881 She married William Sanford Kendall, a miller of Templeton, Massachusetts, December 25, 1828 He was born in Boylston, August 9, 1803 died in South Royalston, February 23, 1879 Their children were 1 William Sanford, born at Templeton, October 18, 1829, died in Templeton, March 25, 1835 2 Albert Warren, born September 8, 1832, died May 9, 1900, aged sixty-seven years He was a gate tender at one of the crossings on the Boston & Maine Railroad in Gardner He married (first), January 7, 1854, Charlotte Barrett Tyler born in Hinsdale, New Hampshire, October 17, 1832, died in South Royalston, Massachusetts, May 23, 1856 He married (second), May 8, 1862, at Three Oaks, Michigan, Nellie Gilligan, born in Joliet, Illinois January 17, 1840 died in South Royalston February 5, 1878 He married (third), November 25 1885, in South Royalston Lucy Hill born in Boston August 7 1860 His children were Arthur Clarence, born in Momence Illinois June 27, 1863, a chairmaker in South Royalston married in Gardner, October 25 1888 Emma Elizabeth Woffenden, born in South Royalston November 29 1859 Mary Arabella, born July 24 1865, died September 19, 1899 aged thirty-four years Charles Edward, born South Royalston, October 15 1869 died September 11 1873, Blanche Evelyn born January 18, 1875, resides at Somerville, Massachusetts unmarried Ruth Lilla, born June 5, 1887, 3 Charles Augustus, born in Templeton December 15, 1834 died May 23 1902 aged sixty-seven years he was a bookkeeper in Somerville married October 18, 1870, Lydia Clifford born in Edgecomb Maine 4 and 5 Sarah Sophia and Susan Maria (twins), born October 20 1837. Sarah S died October 7 1896 aged fifty-eight years Susan M married November 27 1856 Jeremiah Atkins Rich born April 11, 1825, a chair maker in South Royalston

Susan M Rich died December 12, 1903, aged sixty-six years 6 William Sanford, born December 8, 1839, a miller in Athol Centre, Massachusetts, married, September 8 1868 Adelaide Smith, born in Athol, July 20, 1836, died October 29, 1896, their children were Leila Gertrude, born in South Royalston May 14 1869, died in Lynn, Massachusetts, August 29, 1873, William Webster, born October 26 1870, a sash and blind maker in Athol, married, March 8 1893, Blanche Elsie Dennis, born in Athol, November 10, 1876 having two children Lelia Blanche, born 1893, and Gladys Lenora, born April 6, 1896, Elwood Lynde, born in Glenville, Connecticut September 19, 1879, Goodman, born in East Port Chester, Connecticut, September 9, 1880, died September 26 1881 7 Edward, born in South Royalston November 27, 1843, died January 5, 1845 8 Edward Hartshorn, born March 30, 1847, died June 13, 1850

(VI) Sarah Hartshorn, daughter of Ebenezer (5) and Betty Hartshorn, was born February 16 1811 died August, 1890 She married, November 27 1837 Simeon Partridge, born July 6, 1799, died 1866 He was a farmer at Boylston Their children were 1 Mary Keyes, born July 9, 1839 married, June, 1866, Henry Harlow, born in Shrewsbury, Massachusetts, where he resides on a farm, they had Hiram Edward, born January 12, 1869, is a farmer on the home farm in Shrewsbury, being of the fourth generation on that farm, Arthur John, born January 16, 1871, married Annie Kershaw, born England June 3, 1904, he is a farmer, Edith Maria, born March 27, 1873, is a teacher in the public schools of Worcester, Ruth Alice, born October 2, 1875 resides on the home farm Helen Elmira, born January 29, 1879, married Charles Edward Allen son of Romeo Allen, of Shrewsbury December 25, 1902 and resides in Shrewsbury, Robert Henry, born December 11, 1882 owns a milk route in the city of Worcester he boards in his father's family in Shrewsbury 2 Caroline Elizabeth, born November 5, 1841, married, April 6 1869, John William Warren, born in Princeton and is on the Worcester police force (1898) They had Herbert Anson born March 14, 1870, a civil engineer in New York city, married, March 6 1895, Maude Sophia Bosworth, of Worcester and they had three children, among whom were Edwin Taylor, born April 27, 1896 and Barbara Bosworth born March 24 1898, Thaddeus Chenery, born September 18, 1871, an electrician in Worcester, married, September 19, 1895 Adaline E Stearns Susie Greenwood, born August 29 1876 clerk at the Worcester Insane Asylum, John Partridge, born February 24 1878, assistant superintendent at the salesrooms of the White Automobile Company in New York city Sara Maria, born November 3 1880 resides in New Rochelle, New York, Philip Hamilton, born January 17 1882, graduated June 1905 at the Lowell Textile School, and is now in New Rochelle, New York 3 Ruth Ellen, born January 15, 1844, resides in Worcester 4 Susan Abigail born April 14 1847, for twenty-five years a teacher in the public schools of Worcester resides in Worcester

(VII) John Warren Hartshorn son of Jonas (6) and Laura Hartshorn, was born September 19, 1839, married Emma J Lyon December 16 1869 She was born December 10 1846 at New London Connecticut, died October 29 1895 He is an insurance agent at New London, Connecticut Their children were Albert Lyon born January 17, 1871, Laura Ann born April 16 1873, Grace Evelyn, born June 8, 1883

(I) Thomas Greenwood was the emigrant ancestor of Betty Greenwood who married into the Hartshorn family He came to Boston in 1665 He was born in England in 1643 and learned the trade of weaver there He settled in Cambridge, now Newton, and was first town clerk there In 1667 he was constable and for four years selectman He married (first) Hannah Ward, July 16, 1690, and (second) Abigail Spring, and had children by both His children were Thomas, born January 22, 1671, Thomas (Rev), born July 15, 1673, graduate at Harvard College, 1690, John, James born December 19, 1687, William born October 14, 1689 Thomas died September 11, 1693

(II) William Greenwood, son of Thomas (1) and Abigail Greenwood, was born October 14, 1689 He was deacon of the church He removed from Newton to Sherborn It is related in the history of Sherborn that Greenwood was the first man in the town to receive potatoes, which were introduced in New England in 1720 by the Scotch-Irish Their use spread slowly He tried his first mess in 1730 and after testing them declared that "after freezing and thawing a few times they would be good" He was a farmer and was always active in church and town affairs For twenty-four years he was the town clerk and for six years selectman In 1747 he was representative to the general court at Boston He married Abigail Woodward, and their children were Abigail, born June 2, 1716, Dorcas born July 17 1717, William, born November 4, 1721, Caleb, born September 9, 1724 died February 4, 1800, Jonas, born April 25, 1727, died May 28 1802, Samuel, born March 21, 1729, John born December 16, 1730, Daniel, born July 22, 1732, Joseph, born June 10, 1734, Abigail, born August 10 1737

(III) Jonas Greenwood son of William (2) and Abigail Greenwood, was born April 25, 1727, died May 28, 1802 He married Sarah ———, and their children were 1 Jonathan, born November 12, 1755 married Sybil ———, and had Alvin, born April 3, 1781, and Sybil, born January 2, 1785, at Sherborn 2 Mary, born March 16 1758 3 Belle, born April 4 1760 married Mary Babcock, July 10, 1783 4 Betty, born January 23 1765 5 Betty, born August ' 1767, married Ebenezer Hartshorn at Walpole August 30, 1798 See Ebenezer (V) Hartshorn for genealogy She died February, 1815 6 Reuben, born January 9, 1770 married —— Cate, and had five children 7 Susannah, born July 4, 1772 8 Jonas born July 19, 1775 married Polly Stratton, and had Aaron born October 30, 1799, and Sally Stratton, born October 13, 1811 9 Achsah, born December 16, 1778

(IV) Betty Greenwood, daughter of Jonas (3) and Sarah Greenwood, married Ebenezer Hartshorn See Hartshorn (V)

(VII) Calvin Lyon Hartshorn, son of Jonas (6) and Eunice Hartshorn was born in Worcester, Christmas Day, 1832 He was educated in the Worcester public schools at Worcester Academy and Essex Seminary (now Essex Academy) at Essex, Connecticut His early years when not in school were spent on his father's farm When he began for himself he bought a milk route, which is remarkable for its long continued prosperity It was established in 1838 by his father and has been conducted without interruption to the present time It is the oldest in the city Later he returned home and conducted his father's farm He began the raising of early vegetables with a few small hot beds, and as he found it profitable he extended the business until he has on the farm at present over four hundred hotbed sash and two modern green-houses, each one hundred and seventy-five feet in length About thirty hands are employed on the place in summer and fifteen in winter Mr Hartshorn has remodeled the farm-house and built other buildings He has laid out part of the farm, which is at the corner of May and June streets in a rapidly growing and very attractive suburban section of Worcester, and has sold some of the property for building lots Such important city streets as Courtland, Walworth, Lovell, June, May and Chandler cross the farm He has built a brick machine shop on Chandler street, first occupied by the Wright Machine Company and now owned by Bay State Stamping Company A new house on the farm is occupied by his son, Arthur E Hartshorn, who for several years has taken up the active management of the business The farm is generally known as the Walnut Hill Farm The fruits and vegetables raised here are prize winners at all the horticultural and agricultural exhibitions in this vicinity

Mr Hartshorn has been prominent all his life in city affairs He and his wife were charter members of Worcester Grange, Patrons of Husbandry, which has developed into an exceedingly strong and successful organization For five years he was the master of the Grange His prominence among the men of his own business is shown best perhaps by his service in the Agricultural and Horticultural societies and in the public offices he has held in which special knowledge and training in agriculture are requisite He has been for many years trustee and vice president of the Worcester Agricultural Society He is also a trustee and vice-president of the Worcester County Horticultural Society For twelve years he was a member of the State Board of Agriculture, for six years a member of the Dairy Bureau of Massachusetts, for six years a member of the executive committee of the State Board of Agriculture, for four years a director of the state experimental station at the Massachusetts Agricultural College at Amherst, Massachusetts In his own business his word is taken as authority Mr Hartshorn is a member of the Dewey Street Baptist Church

He has had a very creditable career in the city government Men of his sterling honesty and common sense are the kind needed in the public service perhaps more today than formerly because of the tendency of active and successful business men to avoid public life Mr Hartshorn was in the common council from 1870 to 1874 Through his efforts mainly the fire department was extended to give better protection to the residence section on the West Side He assisted the project of constructing the boulevard which at that time was looked upon by some of the people as a wild extravagant and useless expense Time has shown the wisdom of the construction of this great thoroughfare As a public officer he had the gift of foresight as well as regard for the present economies He made an admirable servant on the board of overseers of the poor on which he served for twelve years He was appointed a park commissioner and the duties were congenial, but after one year he was obliged to resign on account of the pressure of other business He served Worcester as representative in the general court, as his ancestors had done before him He represented the twenty-fourth district in 1879 and 1880 He was nominated for mayor, but refused to run against the late Mayor E B Stoddard Notwithstanding his announced withdrawal he received a very handsome complimentary vote in the annual election of 1881, receiving 1571 votes

Although retired from the active management of his business, he has spent the past few years in travel and special work of various sorts in which he was interested His personal qualities have attracted a large circle of friends in all parts of the state He seems to be universally popular not only in this city but throughout the length and breadth of the commonwealth

He married, September 30, 1858, Helen Marcelia Marcy, of Charlton, born November 29, 1831, died February 25, 1902 She was the daughter of Andrew and Clarentine (Towne) Marcy Their children were 1 Annie Maud, born October 18, 1860, married William K Stanley, of Fitchburg, Massachusetts, October 18, 1881 He was born October 9, 1857 At present he occupies a responsible position with the Barnard, Sumner & Putnam Company, one of the leading department stores of Worcester Their children are Helen Maud Stanley, born October 19 1882, married William Irving Whiting, of Worcester, and had Stanley Hartshorn Whiting, born March 27, 1905, Grace Hartshorn Stanley, born June 16, 1884 2 Arthur Ernest, born February 10, 1867

(VIII) Arthur Ernest Hartshorn, son of Calvin Lyon (7) and Helen Marcelia (Marcy) Hartshorn, was born February 10, 1867, married September 17, 1890, Annie Maria, daughter of Thomas and Ann (Buckley) Williams She was a born at Worcester, December 10, 1869 Her father was a manufacturer Arthur E Hartshorn was educated in the Worcester public schools and graduated at Hinman s Business College At present he is the manager of the Walnut Hill Farm and is conducting its business along the most progressive and scientific lines

ALFRED SEELYE ROE, who has achieved an extended reputation as a teacher, writer and lecturer, and who has read many papers before the historical societies of the various states, is descended from the old colonial families who settled in Massachusetts in the seventeenth century

(I) John Roe, or Rowe, as the name is variously spelled, it being Rowe on his tombstone, but his descendants invariably using the former form, was born in Ireland in 1628, but was of English extraction He emigrated to America in 1655, settled in Lynn, Massachusetts, but soon afterward went to Easthampton, Long Island, New York Thence he removed to Setauket, now (1906) Port Jefferson, Brookhaven township, and was one of the first, if not the very first, settler in that place The house erected by him in 1690 is still standing and in good condition, and is in use at the present time He was one of the constitutent members of the Presbyterian church of Setauket and in his will he calls himself a "cordwainer" The original burying place has been destroyed by the laying out of new streets, and his tombstone is now to be found with those of his descendants in the public cemetery of Port Jefferson Family tradition states that John Roe met Hannah Purrier, a descendant of an English family on ship board, and they were married Among their children was a son, Nathaniel

(II) Nathaniel Roe, son of John (1) and Hannah (Purrier) Roe, married Hannah Reeve, of Long Island, and many of their descendants are prominent in Long Island today especially in Port Jefferson, Patchogue and Huntington

(III) John Roe, son of Nathaniel (2) and Hannah (Reeve) Roe, married a widow, Joanna (Miller) (Helme) whose first husband Thomas Helme, was killed while felling a tree, and left one son, Thomas, who became a prominent citizen of Long Island, and was a member of the committee of safety during the revolution John and Joanna (Miller) (Helme) Roe had eight children, of whom the fourth was Daniel

(IV) Daniel Roe, fourth child of John (3) and Joanna (Miller) (Helme) Roe, was a man of prominence and influence in his day He was captain in the Second Regiment of the New York troops during the war of the revolution, and was also a member of the original committee of safety in Brookhaven township His family suffered greatly at the hands of the enemy, and were obliged to flee to Connecticut, where the last four of his children were born He married Deborah Brewster, fifth in line of descent from Elder Brewster of the "Mayflower" Among their children was a son, Austin

(V) Austin Roe, youngest child of Daniel (4) and Deborah (Brewster) Roe, was born in Woodbury, Connecticut, in 1782 He married his first cousin, Sally Roe, of Brookhaven township, Long Island, and among their children was a son, Austin Marinus

(VI) Rev Austin Marinus, son of Austin (5) and Sally (Roe) Roe, was born in Brookhaven, Long Island, September 27, 1823 With his parents he removed to Rose, Wayne county, New York, in 1833, and was there reared on a farm In his early days he acquired as good an education as the public schools of that time afforded, and in his later teens was a student at Red Creek Academy for a time He entered the ministry of the Methodist Episcopal denomination, and from 1850 until the present time has been a clergyman in that church He has been retired from active service for the past twenty years, having his home in Fulton, New York He is a member of the Northern New York formerly the Black River Conference As a young man he was a Democrat, casting his first presidential vote for James K Polk, in 1844 He next voted the first Free Soil ticket, and remained faithful to this party until 1856, when he voted for Fremont, and was a firm upholder of the tenets of the Republican party, until of late, when he began casting his vote for Prohibition candidates He married, more than sixty years ago, Polly Catharine Seelye, born August 29, 1827, daughter of Colonel George and Polly Catharine (Shepard) Seelye, the latter being seventh in descent from Dr Edward Fuller, of the "Mayflower" company Colonel Seelye was an officer in the New York state militia, and his commissions bear the signatures of Governors William L Marcy and William H Seward Her paternal ancestry descends from Watertown, Massachusetts, New Milford and Danbury, Connecticut, and Washington county, New York, in which latter place her great-grandfather, Nehemiah Seelye, was a captain in the revolutionary army and was in action at Saratoga His home in Kingsbury was destroyed by the forces of Burgoyne in their march from Canada The Shepards also came from Watertown, Massachusetts, and after a time were found in Litchfield county, Connecticut, whence Aaron Shepard and family went by means of ox teams to the wilderness of the Genessee district in 1812 Among the children of Rev Austin Marinus and Polly Catharine (Seelye) Roe is a son Alfred S Roe, the particular subject of this sketch

(VIII) Alfred Seelye Roe, son of Rev Austin Marinus (6) and Polly Catharine (Seelye) Roe, was born in Rose, Wayne county, New York, June 8, 1844 He was a pupil in the public schools of his locality until he had attained the age of sixteen years when he became a student at the Falley Seminary in Fulton New York where he received his preparatory training for college, expecting to enter an institution of learning of that class in 1864 He took a course in army tactics first, however, and matriculated at the Wesleyan University, Middletown, Connecticut, in 1866 and was graduated from this institution in 1870 He is a member of the Phi Beta Kappa He officiated as principal of the high school in Ashland, Massachusetts, until 1875, and until 1890 in the high school of Worcester, being principal during the last ten years Since that time he has been engaged in writing and lecturing, and has also served his country in the legislature In politics he is a stanch Republican, and in the campaigns has always been an eloquent and convincing speaker in behalf of that party He represented ward one of Worcester from 1892 to 1895, inclusive, in the Massachusetts legislature, and was senator from the Second Worcester district from 1896 to 1898, inclusive, during nearly all of this time being chairman of the committee on education He was instrumental in the passage of a number of acts which were greatly for the public benefit, among them being The act which today renders secondary education in the state possible to the people of the poorest and most remote towns, an act exempting the property of invalid soldiers from taxation, and the veteran's preference bill At present he is supervisor of the evening schools of Worcester He enlisted in Company A, Ninth New York Heavy Artillery, January 21, 1864, and served until October 17, 1865 His regiment helped build and man the defences of Washington, and in the spring of 1864 joined the Sixth Army Corps, sharing its fortunes until the surrender of Lee He was captured at Monocacy Junction, Maryland, July 9, 1864, and was a prisoner for almost eight months in Danville, Virginia He has been a member of the George H Ward Post, No 10, Grand Army of the Republic, more than twenty-five years, was its commander two years, and is now (1906) the junior vice-commander, Department of Massachusetts He has frequently represented Post No 10 in department encampments, and in 1883 and 1892 was delegated to national encampments In 1895 and 1896 he was an aide on the staff of Commander Derby, was inspector-general for Commanders Blackmar and Judd, an aide for Commander Field in 1905, and in 1905 was a member of the council of administration He was reared in the creed of the Methodist Episcopal church, of which his family have been members for more than a century, and has been an official member of Grace Church, Worcester He is a lay preacher in that denomination, but speaks frequently in other houses of worship on subjects pertinent to the place and time He was president of the Red Cross organization during the Spanish-American war He is also connected with the following organizations Rose Lodge, No 590, Free and Accepted Masons, of Rose, New York, Worcester Society of Antiquity, before which he has read many papers, New England Methodist Historical Society He is an honorary member of Rhode Island Soldiers' and Sailors' Historical Society, Kansas Historical Society, Old Colony Historical Society, and the Westboro Historical Society He is also a member of the Massachusetts Society and is president of the Worcester Chapter of the Sons of the American Revolution

For many years he has been a forcible speaker in the cause of temperance, and has been a prolific writer, for the political, religious and educational press Among his books may be mentioned "History of the Worcester Classical and English High School," "History of Rose, Wayne County, New York, "History of the Ninth New York Heavy Artillery," "History of the Worcester Young Men's Christian Association," "History of the Twenty-fourth Regiment, Massachusetts Volunteers," "History of Worcester in the Spanish War," "Diary of Captain Daniel Roe," and many others

He married, June 22, 1874 in Ashland, Massachusetts, Nora Ardelia Metcalf, daughter of Alvah and Harriet Hannah (Vose) Metcalf Alvah Metcalf was born in Appleton, Maine, though many generations of his family had lived in Massachusetts He was the seventh in descent from Michael Metcalf, the first schoolmaster of Dedham, Massachusetts, and his wife, Mary Fairbanks, whose girlhood home stills stands in Dedham, the oldest dwelling house in continuous use in America, but it is in excellent preservation and is still in use as a dwelling Harriet Hannah Vose, mother of Mrs Roe, was the daughter of Alexander and Malinda Myra (Weeks) Vose, and was the seventh in a direct line of descent from John Alden and Priscilla, of "Mayflower" history Mrs Roe had the advantage of an excellent public school education, and for many years has been a contributor to the press, especially that of the Methodist church She is the author of "Three Little Street Singers," published by Lee & Shepard, of Boston Mr and Mrs Alfred S Roe have had children 1 Adelaide Estelle, born April 6, 1875, died February 24, 1878 2 Annabel Catherine, born September 3, 1879, was graduated from Mount Holyoke College in 1901, and is a teacher in the public schools of Worcester 3 Delos Metcalf, born January 8, 1883 died May 28, 1892 4 Harriet Eudora, born June 5 1885, is in her senior year in Mount Holyoke College

EDGAR EUGENE BUCK William Buck (1) was the emigrant ancestor of Edgar Eugene Buck, of Worcester, and of a branch of the Buck family that settled in Connecticut William Buck came to New England on the "Increase," sailing in April, 1635, from England and landing a month later at Boston, Massachusetts He gave his age as fifty years and accordingly was born in 1585 His son Roger was with him, and his age was given as eighteen He settled at Cambridge, Massachusetts In 1652 he had a grant of land, twenty acres, lot No 91 in the Cambridge Survey, so-called Here he built a new home for his family It was in what was called the west field, northeast from Garden street, on what is now Raymond street He died intestate January 24, 1658, and was buried in the old cemetery at Cambridge, Massachusetts His son Roger was administrator and it does not appear that there were any other children William Buck was a plough-wright

(II) Roger Buck, son of William Buck (1), was born in England, 1617 He emigrated to New England on the Increase," April 15, 1635, Captain Le Master, with his father, William Buck His mother was probably dead It is generally supposed that Enoch Buck and Emanuel Buck, who settled at Wethersfield, Connecticut were relatives, possibly older sons of William Buck, who was fifty when he came over He was a plough-wright and farmer He settled at Cambridge near his father On the death of his wife Susannah he moved to Woburn, where some of his children lived He died there November 10, 1693

The children of Roger and Susannah were Mary, born January 23, 1648, died unmarried August 31, 1669, Ruth, born November 6 1653, died September 21, 1682, married Thomas Bathrick or Baverick, Elizabeth, born July 5, 1657, married August 20, 1678, Joshua Wood, Lydia, married, November 3, 1672, Henry Smith, John, born September 3, 1644, died unmarried, Samuel born March 16, 1669, married Rachel Levin or Leven settled in West Cambridge (Menotomy) where he died September 21, 1690, his wife Rachel died 1694 and his estate was divided among his children (Samuel has many descendants), Ephraim, born July 26, 1646, married, January 1, 1671, Sarah Brooks, of Woburn, Massachusetts

(III) Ephraim Buck, son of Roger Buck (2), was born at Cambridge, Massachusetts, July 26, 1646 He married, January 1, 1671, Sarah Brooks, daughter of John and Eunice (Mousall) Brooks, of Woburn He settled there probably a few years earlier, as he is mentioned in the will of John Mousall, whose granddaughter he married Mr Mousall died March 27, 1665 He also left a bequest to John Brooks Ephraim Buck became a man of distinction he was the local magistrate appointed to try small causes by the general court He was a farmer His grandson, Jonathan Buck, son of Ebenezer, was the founder of the town of Bucksport, Maine, and he has thousands of descendants in Maine and northern New England, through this son, Ebenezer (See the Bangor Historical Register) He died January, 1721 at Woburn, Massachusetts The children of Ephraim and Sarah (Brooks) Buck were Sarah, born January 11, 1673, married Thomas Grover, Ephraim, born July 13, 1676, married Esther Wagget, John, born January 11, 1678-9, died young, John, born February 7 1679 80, married Priscilla ———, Samuel, born November 13, 1682, married Hannah ———, Eunice, born July 7, 1685, Ebenezer, born May 20, 1689, married Lydia Eames, Mary, born October 28, 1691, married (first) Nathaniel Pike or Spike, married (second) Samuel Bigsbee

(IV) Samuel Buck, son of Ephraim (3), was born at Woburn, Massachusetts, November 13, 1682 He married Hannah ——— about 1708 He was a farmer He settled in Woburn, Massachusetts The children of Samuel and Hannah Buck were Hannah, born February 1, 1710, Samuel, born May 7, 1711, Sarah, born April 16, 1716, Zebediah, born August 29 1719

(V) Samuel Buck, son of Samuel Buck (4), was born at Woburn, Massachusetts, May 7, 1711, died December, 1765, at Killingly, Connecticut, according to the old church records From somewhat meagre and unsatisfactory records in Connecticut the establishment of the family at Thompson and its connection with that at Woburn is ascertained Samuel Buck went with other Woburn, Lexington and Watertown families or followed them to Killingly and Thompson, Connecticut, where this branch of the Buck family lived Eleazer Bateman joined the Killingly Church September 15, 1715 He was from Woburn Richard Blosse, of West Watertown, joined the church May 23, 1716, George and Sarah Blanchard, of Lexington, October 18, 1715, and the stream of emigration continued to Thompson from Woburn for a number of years In 1729 James Wilson and Ivory Upham, who had just come from Woburn, joined the church In the thirties probably Samuel Buck, of Woburn, came with or followed relatives There is a record of the marriage of Robert Buck, of Killingly, in 1715, but nothing else about him He may have been one of the Wethersfield family

He was one of the heads of families who on November 19, 1745 signed the covenant and called Rev Perley Howe, of Dudley, Massachusetts, to settle as the minister at Killingly He bought a farm in 1756 on Killingly Hill of Ebenezer Adams and settled on it The Rev Mr Howe kept no church records and information about Samuel Buck's family is difficult to find He was deacon of the church for many years He was succeeded by Lieutenant Benjamin Levens, who may have been a relative of Samuel Buck from Woburn, Massachusetts The son of Samuel Samuel, Jr, married a Miss Bloss whose grandparents came from Watertown, Massachusetts The following are believed to be some of Samuel's children 1 Zerviah, married

Giles Roberts, April 3, 1754 2 David, married Anna Russell, June 22, 1756 One account of his line says he was born in Massachusetts and came to Putnam, part of Thompson or Killingly townships, Connecticut He was a joiner and farmer His children were David, Jonathan, Aaron, Mrs Josiah Dean, Mrs Benjamin Cutler By second wife, David, Eliza, married Henry Adams Aaron, son of David Buck, was born at Killingly and lived on the old homestead He married Annie, daughter of Asa Lawrence, of Killingly His children were Lucy, married Calvin Leffingwell, Rosamond, married Calvin Boyden, Mary, married Jesse Herenden, Anne married Caleb Howe, Erastus, Elisha, Augustus, George, born October 13, 1810 There are many descendants of David Buck (VI) in the vicinity of Thompson and Killingly, Connecticut 3 Samuel, married Martha Bloss, January 1, 1760 4 Jonathan, was in the revolutionary war, second lieutenant, killed at the battle of Harlem, New York, September 15, 1776, he was one of those who gave to the fund to buy the Killingly common in 1775, no record of his marriage or children 5 Aaron, died August 24, 1755 6 Child, died October 5, 1756 7 Reuben, married Elizabeth, joined the church 1769 Some of the above may not be the children of Samuel but there seems to be good reason to think all are, some certainly are

(VI) Samuel Buck, son of Samuel Buck (5) was born at Killingly, Connecticut, about 1740 He settled in that part of the town called Putnam He married Martha Bloss, January, 1760 He and his wife joined the church April 2, 1764 The records of his family are found in part in the records of the old church at Putnam Heights, the second church built east of Quinebaug in a parish formed in Windham, Connecticut Some of the children of Samuel and Martha Buck were Mary, baptized February 26, 1764, Hannah, baptized February 26, 1764, Johannah, baptized February 26, 1764, Joseph, baptized June 1, 1766, Simeon, baptized May 28, 1773

(VII) Joseph Buck, son of Samuel Buck (6), was born in Putnam or Killingly, Connecticut, in 1766, baptized June 1, 1766 He is mentioned as prominent in 1793 among the early Methodists of Thompson, Connecticut and vicinity He was blind for many years He settled at Thompson, Connecticut, where his four children were born, as follows Richard, who was a soldier in the war of 1812 was in Captain Solomon Sikes company stationed at New London, Amy, Barney and Aaron (twins), Barney married Amy Sprague, of Thompson, Connecticut

(VIII) Barney Buck son of Joseph Buck (7), was born at Thompson, Connecticut, about 1790 He was in Captain John Joslin's company at New London in the war of 1812 He married Amy Sprague, of Thompson The children of Barney and Amy (Sprague) Buck were Warren, married Sophia ———, went to Michigan to live, Hiram, married Cynthia Brown, Henry, married Sophronia Sheldon, married (second) Sophia Anderson, Aaron, married Emiline Randall, Barney, married Almeda Conian, William L, married Martha Maddox, Abbie, married Sidney Bolton, Caroline, married Liberty Brown

(IX) William L Buck son of Barney Buck (8), was born in New York state, died July 13, 1893 at Woodstock Connecticut He married Martha Maddox, July 25, 1847 She was the daughter of William and Jane (Moran) Maddox, of Union, Maine He died at Appleton, Maine Mrs Buck is living in Worcester The children of William L and Martha (Maddox) Buck were 1 William Henry, born August 20, 1848, at Thompson, Connecticut, married, 1867, Ellen White, at Killingly, Connecticut, and had two children Marcus, born 1871, and Elmer White, born 1873, both of whom reside in Worcester, Massachusetts 2 Rosalie M, born May 19, 1850, at Thompson, Connecticut, died September 13, 1851 3 Lewis Franklin, born November 11, 1851, died at North Grafton, Massachusetts, August 10, 1856 4 George L., born December 11, 1853, at Thompson, Connecticut, died October 3, 1885 5 Mary Jane, born October 28, 1855, at Plainfield, Connecticut, married Frank F Clark, January 26, 1877, had Ada Frances, born October 30, 1877, and Florence Edna Clark, born July 23, 1884, resides at Coral street, Worcester, Massachusetts 6 Charles Warren, born January 27, 1858, at Plainfield, Connecticut, married Anna Taft, April 16, 1884 7 Edgar Eugene, born February 10, 1860, at Putnam, Connecticut 8 Frederick Lorenzo, born August 27, 1864, at Plainfield, Connecticut, died April 16, 1865

(X) Edgar Eugene Buck, son of William L Buck (9), was born at Putnam, Connecticut, February 10, 1860 The family moved frequently while he was a boy and he lived at various times at Woodstock, Danielson, Putnam, Moosup His father was employed in cotton mills He finished his early education in the Putnam schools While a mere boy he went into business on his own account as a truckman After four or five years he went to work in the shoe manufacturing business as a cutter He was employed at Webster, Grafton, Nashua, and Worcester He became proficient in the art of cutting leather economically and was made foreman of the cutting departments first at S R Heywood's factory, then at Whitcomb & Miles' About ten years ago he began the manufacture of novelties in quarters in the Bowker building, Washington square Two years later he bought the business of P A Thompson & Co, leather dealers Later he took into partnership Arthur Davis and his son The name of the firm is the E E Buck Leather Company, and their present location is on Main street in Franklin spuare The business has been extended and enlarged Mr Buck is a thorough business man and has won his way in life by hard work and his own energy He has been a member of the Gideons, the Christian Commercial Travelers, the order of United American Mechanics, the Knights of Honor He is a member of the Dewey Street Baptist Church In politics he has voted with the Republicans

He married, April 17, 1883, Addie Josephine Herindene, of Woodstock, Connecticut She is a descendant of Laben Herindene, who came from Rhode Island to Woodstock when young He married Mary Marcy, who was born in Woodstock, Connecticut Laben Herindene was born 1770 died 1850 Their children were Laben, Simeon, Wilbur, Levi, Hannah, Mary

Wilbur Herindene, son of Laben Herindene, settled at Woodstock, Connecticut He married Mary Estabrook He was born 1795, at Woodstock, died April 5, 1851 His wife died January 28, 1862 Their children were Wilbur, Alfred, Fidelia, Sarah Jane, Nelson, Mary Ann, Hannah, Emeline, James, Levi

James Herindene or Herindeen, son of Wilbur Herindene, was born at Providence, Rhode Island, May 16, 1823 He married Emily Chamberlain, May 30, 1847 She was born at Woodstock, October 12, 1824 He died January 15, 1894 He was a life member of the local grange He was captain of a militia company He settled at Woodstock, Connecticut Their daughter, Addie Josephine Herindeen, married Edgar Eugene Buck, of Worcester, Massachusetts James Lester Buck, son of Edgar

E and Addie Buck, was born in Worcester, August 31, 1885, married, May 17, 1905, Jessie Evlyn Hubbard, of Holden

WELLINGTON FAMILY Fred W Wellington, of Worcester, comes of the Wellington family, headed by Roger Wellington, a planter, born about 1609, and became one of the early proprietors of Watertown, Massachusetts He removed from Boston to that place He has a record at Watertown in 1642 He was admitted as a freeman in 1690 He married Mary, eldest daughter of Dr Richard, of Charlestown He died March 11, 1698 His will mentions sons John, Benjamin, Oliver, Palgrave

To take up the genealogical line of the family let Roger, the planter, born 1609, be known as Roger Wellington (1)

(II) Benjamin Wellington, son of Roger (1), was admitted as a freeman, 1677, and in 1671 was married to Elizabeth Sweetman He died January 8, 1710

(III) Benjamin Wellington, son of Benjamin (2), was born January 21, 1676, died at Lexington, November 15, 1738 He married Lydia Brown, and settled in Lexington, Massachusetts, where they were admitted to the church, June 10, 1705 She died May 13, 1711, and he married (second), December 25, 1712, Elizabeth Phelps She died January 7, 1730, aged fifty-four years, and he then married Mary Whitney He was for many years one of the most popular men of the town, having been elected as assessor, serving sixteen years, town clerk, fifteen years, treasurer, three years, and representative, three years Of his seven children one was

(IV) Timothy Wellington, son of Benjamin (3), was born July 27, 1719, and died previous to 1760 He married Rebecca Stone, born January 22, 1721, daughter of Jonathan and Chary (Adams) Stone, of Lexington, Massachusetts They have five children Benjamin, born August 7, 1743, married Martha Ball, Chary, born July 12, 1745, Timothy, born April 15, 1747, died April, 1809, Abigail, born March 14, 1749, married, December 29, 1768, Danieal Cotting, of Waltham, Rushman, born September 4, 1751

(V) Captain Timothy Wellington, son of Timothy (4), born April 15, 1747, died April, 1809 He was a member of Captain Parker's company, and on the way to Lexington was taken prisoner, being the first prisoner taken in the revolutionary war He was paroled, but he stole through the woods and joined his company and fought that day He married Hannah W Abbott, May 1, 1776

(VI) Nehemiah Wellington, son of Timothy (5), was born January 1, 1780, and was the grandfather of General Fred W Wellington He married Nancy Stearns, May 16, 1805, a daughter of Joshua Stearns, of Waltham He died May 11, 1857 He served as a representative, 1836-38, assessor, 1840, and selectman, 1841 They had nine children Anna Eliza, born March 2, 1806, died October 3, 1822, Augustus, born January 15, 1807, Hannah Maria, born November 17, 1809, married Samuel Bridge, in 1835, Timothy W, born July 4, 1811, mentioned in the following paragraph, Sullivan, born November 8 1813, Jonas Clarke, born November 30, 1815, married, October 17, 1839 Harriet Bosworth, of Attleboro, Horatio, born September 6, 1817, married, December 16, 1841, Mary Bowman Tell, Avis M, born June 27, 1819, married Emory Abbott Mulliken, Joseph A, born June 12, 1812, married Ellen A Smith

(VII) Timothy W Wellington, son of Nehemiah (6), was born July 4, 1811 He married (first) Susan Ray, November 4, 1835, by whom he had seven children, four of whom are as follows Edward W, born September 20, 1840 In the civil war or war of the rebellion he enlisted in 1861 as a private in the Twenty-fifth Regiment, Massachusetts Volunteers, was promoted to lieutenant in the Second Massachusetts Cavalry, served in the Army of the Potomac, but on account of failing health was obliged to resign Frank W, born November 13, 1842 He also enlisted as a private in the same company, same regiment, same date as did his brother Edward, was detailed to the commissary department at Newberne, North Carolina, and served until the close of the war in 1865 George, born April 12, 1847, enlisted (first) in the Forty-second Massachusetts Regiment of Infantry, when but seventeen years of age, and went to New Orleans, and (second) in the Second Massachusetts Heavy Artillery, was taken prisoner at Plymouth, North Carolina, and sent to Andersonville prison, where he died the following year Charles, a twin brother of George, elisted in the navy, serving fifteen months under Admiral Farragut at New Orleans The mother of these children died April 28, 1847 Mr Wellington married (second), September 5, 1848, Augusta Tufts Fiske, daughter of Samuel and Adelia L Fiske, born December 31, 1822, died at Worcester April 2, 1906, being over eighty-three years of age By this marriage two children were born Fred W, and Delia Maria, who died September 18, 1871, being then a bright girl of fourteen years In 1855 Timothy W Wellington moved to Worcester from Shirley At the opening of the war of the rebellion he took an active part in sustaining the Union, in addition to sending four sons to the front He provided at his own expense a hospital at Worcester for sick and disabled soldiers, which he supported about five months and dispensed favors to more than sixty soldiers In 1864 he represented the twenty-seventh Worcester district in the legislature The Worcester Society of Antiquity has many valuable war relics given it by Mr Wellington He died at Alburgh Springs, Vermont, August 26, 1884, aged seventy-three years His widow has since died at Worcester, Massachusetts

(VIII) General Fred W Wellington, subject of this memoir, son of Timothy (7), was born May 31, 1851, in Shirley, Massachusetts The family moved to Worcester in 1855 Fred W attended the schools of Worcester, also studied two years in France and Germany Handed down from ancestry, his military likings were strong, and in his youth he was a drummer boy from 1861 to 1865 for the old state guard In 1868 he took a position in the First National Bank of Worcester as a bookkeeper, remaining until August, 1870, and from that date to 1871 was in charge of the coal yard at Southbridge street, belonging to T W Wellington & Company The following year was spent in the sunny land of California In April, 1872, he returned and entered into partnership with T W Wellington & Company, of which firm he was the junior member, conducting a wholesale and retail coal business He continued in that line until May, 1874 At that time he associated himself with James S Rogers and Arthur A Goodell, coal merchants, the firm name being J S Rogers & Company, in 1876 he became a member of the firm and in 1877 the name of the firm changed to A A Goodell & Company, Mr Rogers retiring It was on January 1, 1878, that General Wellington leased the coal yard at the corner of Canterbury and Hammond streets and engaged in the wholesale and retail coal trade under the firm name of Fred W Wellington & Company, and for thirty (30) years he has been the sole owner In 1880 he purchased the present location, corner of

Southbridge and Hammond streets, more than twenty-nine (29) years, where he has conducted the same business Among other enterprises with which he is associated is the American Car Sprinkler Company, organized for the purpose of watering streets by electric power, and he has been the president of this company since its organization in 1894 In 1888 he in addition to his other business, accepted the treasurer's position and became general manager of the Arthur C Wellington Coal Company, where he remained until 1896, when the company was dissolved

It was in 1882 that General Wellington joined the militia, being elected and receiving his commission as second lieutenant in Battery B, Light Artillery, unattached, First Brigade, Massachusetts Volunteer Militia In January, 1883 he was elected first lieutenant and soon became recognized as a model military man, being very popular with his command September 29, 1884, he was elected captain, commanding the battery, in which position he served until January 1, 1886, when he was appointed assistant inspector-general on the staff of Governor Ames, with rank of colonel, which position he resigned in 1889 He was re-appointed to the same position by Governor Brackett in 1890 and 1891, when he again resigned, and in the latter year he enlisted as a private in Battery B, his old command He was re-appointed as colonel to the same place on the staff of Governor Greenhalge, 1894, and was re-appointed by him in 1895, (the year of the death of Governor Greenhalge) and he was then appointed by Acting Governor Wolcott, who continued Colonel Wellington in the same position by successive annual re-appointments up to 1900 In January of that year he was appointed commissary general by Governor Crane, with rank of colonel, and in May of the same year was given the rank of brigadier-general by the legislature He was continued in the position of commissary general by Governor Crane during 1901-2 and was re-appointed commissary general by Governor Bates in 1903-04 In the latter year he was placed on the retired list at his own request with rank of brigadier-general The Wellington Rifles, Company H, Second Regiment of Infantry, Massachusetts Volunteer Militia, was named in honor of General Wellington

Very naturally such a gentleman finds his place of prominence in the civic societies Among such connections it may be stated that he is a thirty-second degree Mason, being a member of the Boston Consistory He also belongs to the Worcester County Commandery, Knights Templar In 1892 he was captain-general of that body Politically he is a Republican, believing that this party best serves the interests of the rank and file of the American people He served on the Republican State Central Committee in 1887-88-89, and again in 1893-94-95-96 and served as a member of the executive committee from 1887 to 1896

General Wellington married, September 4 1883, Lydia A, widow of General Arthur A Goodell, of the Thirty-sixth Massachusetts Regiment, war of the rebellion

PLINY MOORE John Moore (1), of Sudbury, Massachusetts, was the first ancestor of Pliny Moore and probably hundreds of other Worcester men and women Moore was a proprietor as early as 1640 He was a farmer His eldest son, John was also a proprietor of that town, but later made his home in Lancaster and is the progenitor of a large branch of the family, some of whom are in the city and more in the various towns of the county The wife of John Moore was Elizabeth, daughter of Philemon Whale The Whale family came from Colchester, England, where a brother died in 1609 Elizabeth, wife of Philemon, and mother of Mrs Moore, died April 20, 1647 He married (second) Sarah, widow of Thomas Cakebread, and (third) Elizabeth ———, who died November 8, 1688 He died February 22, 1675, leaving his property to his widow and the children of his daughter, Elizabeth Moore John Moore died in 1674, his will being proved April 7, 1674 His wife Elizabeth died June 6, 1664 Their children were John, of Lancaster, William, Lydia, born at Sudbury, June 24, 1643, married (first) Samuel Wright, (second) James Cutler, Jacob, born at Sudbury, April 28, 1645, Joseph, Benjamin, Elizabeth, born January 10, 1649, married Henry Rice, Mary, married Daniel Stone

(II) Jacob Moore, son of John and Elizabeth Moore (1), was born at Sudbury, April 28, 1645 He married Elizabth Loker, May 29, 1667 He was a captain in the Indian wars He died March 23, 1715-16 Their children as recorded at Sudbury were Richard, born September 12, 1670, see forward, John, born December 13, 1673, Elizabeth, born February 4, 1675, Nathaniel, born June 21, 1678, see forward, Hannah, born July 18, 1680, Jacob, born 1680

(III) Richard Moore, son of Jacob (2) and Elizabeth Moore, was born at Sudbury, September 12, 1670, and resided there, but he seems to have resided at Cambridge later in life He married Mary ——— Their children as recorded at Sudbury were Sebella, born September 2, 1694, Collins, born October 17, 1698, settled in Worcester (See Wall's History), Isaac, born June 11, 1700, settled in Worcester, Abijah, born December 22, 1705, Richard, born January 10, 1707-08, Mary, born May 15, 1710, Lydia, baptized March 17, 1712-13

(IV) Isaac Moore, son of Richard (3) and Mary Moore, was born at Sudbury, June 11 1700 He came to Worcester at an early age with his brother Collins, and Nathaniel, his uncle, his father's youngest brother (See Nathaniel Moore) He was a proprietor in 1726 He married Hannah ——— His children, born and recorded in Worcester, were Hannah, born March 31, 1725, Thomas, May 1, 1727, David, October 21, 1729, Jonathan, January 10, 1732, Samuel, May 5, 1736, Phebe, November 28 1738, John and Isaac, (twins) March 11, 1741, Mary, May 19, 1743, Sarah, November 9, 1744, Susanna, March 22, 1747

(III) Nathaniel Moore, son of Jacob (2), was born at Sudbury, June 21, 1678 He married Grace Rice, a sister of Jonas Rice, of Sudbury, who was the first settler of the town of Worcester Nathaniel Moore is reckoned as the third settler, coming there in 1715, with others of the family, James and Comfort, and Collins and Isaac, sons of his brother Richard He was a deacon of the church He died November 25, 1761, his wife died 1768, at the age of ninety-four years (See Sketch of Jonas Rice) Children of Nathaniel and Grace Moore have many Worcester descendants They were Mary, born December 20, 1702, Sarah, July 2, 1704, Henry, January 10, 1705-06, Judith February 12, 1708, Grace, July 7, 1709-10, Elizabeth, June 23, 1711, Eleanor, February 16, 1713, Nathaniel, January 31, 1714-15

(V) John Moore, son of Isaac (4) and Hannah Moore, was born in Worcester, November 28, 1738 John Moore bought a farm near Tatnuck and built there in 1763 the house which has been occupied since by his descendants He married, September 11, 1760, Esther Bigelow who lived on a farm near Lake Quinsigamond Their children were William, born April 19, 1761, Lydia, October 7, 1763,

Matilda, February 5 1768, Esther April 26, 1769, Tyler, March 10, 1771, Joshua, November 20, 1772, Willard, October 12, 1775

(VI) Willard Moore, son of John (5) and Esther Moore, was born October 12, 1775, in the house at Tatnuck in Worcester He followed farming as a calling, but was an invalid and recluse He married, January 1, 1798, Mary Curtis, born February 2, 1776 Their children were Seraph, born December 11, 1798, Nathaniel Curtis, October 11, 1800, Alexander, October 10, 1802, Sybil, September 25 1804, Peregrine Craig, October 23, 1806, John Bisco, August 7, 1809, Winthrop, January 25, 1812, Ephraim Curtis, February 15, 1815, Harrison, May 14, 1818

(VII) Nathaniel Curtis Moore, son of Willard (6) and Mary Curtis Moore, was born October 11, 1800, at Tatnuck, Worcester He lived at home until he was fifteen, then came to Worcester and worked on a farm He married, December 20, 1825, Sarah Childs, daughter of Moses N Childs, of Worcester, who lived in the house built in 1763 in which Pliny Moore now lives Nathaniel was captain of an independent cavalry company of Worcester Sarah (Childs) Moore died January 4, 1832, and left three children 1 Calvin, born December 1, 1826, he and his wife moved to Jacmel, Hayti, February, 1865, and both died there a few months after 2 Curtis, born May 30, 1828, he died in Holyoke, Massachusetts, April 20, 1902 3 Luther, born April 9, 1830, he died in Worcester, January 9, 1901 Nathaniel C Moore married for his second wife, March 13, 1833, Patty Moore, daughter of Jonathan Moore, of Holden Their children 1 Sarah (now living in Iowa), born December 9, 1833 2 Martha, born May 30, 1835, died October 11, 1835 3 Infant, born May 20, 1836, died unnamed 4 Seraph, born October 25, 1838, resides with her brother Pliny in Worcester 5 Eunice, born April 7, 1841, resides in Worcester 6 Baxter, born November 16, 1842, resides in Dudley, Massachusetts 7 Pliny, born October 7, 1847

(VIII) Pliny Moore, son of Nathaniel Curtis (7) and Patty Moore, was born at Worcester, October 7, 1847, and has lived all his life in the house where he was born He is one of the best known farmers in Worcester He belongs to Worcester Grange, Patrons of Husbandry For twelve years he was secretary of the Chamberlain District Farmers' Club, a flourishing and influential organization of Worcester farmers, started in 1873 He has been chairman for many years and is at present the head of the club He is a member of the Worcester Agricultural Society

(VIII) Baxter Moore, son of Nathaniel C Moore (7), was born at Worcester, November 16, 1842 Until nineteen he attended the public schools of the city and Worcester Academy Then he joined the quartermaster's department of Burnside's Division of the Union army, stationed at Camp Nelson, in Kentucky, subsequently he followed various occupations, part of the time farming, also working at mechanical business for several years until the year 1877, when he bought the Walnut Grove farm, where he now resides In 1882 he conducted the farm at the Highland Military Academy, in 1883 and 1884 he was farm manager of the Buffum farm in Oxford, Massachusetts, but since 1884 he has run the Walnut Grove farm successfully He is a trustee of the Worcester South Agricultural Society, a member of Dudley Grange, Patrons of Husbandry, for six years He was a member of the Worcester City Guards in the sixties and declined a commission He is naturally of a retiring disposition and has taken no active part in politics He is a Congregationalist

He married, May 5, 1868, Jennie E Mayers, daughter of Francis R and Harriet (Gowen) Mayers, of Worcester Their children were Herbert Francis, born January 22, 1869, died at birth, Harry Lawton, born December 20, 1872, married, December 9, 1898, Florence A Bisco, of Worcester, she died July 8, 1899, Marian Jennie, born January 21, 1878, married, November 14, 1899, George L Penniman, of Dudley, and their children are George Forest, born October 9, 1900, Earl Anson, born February 28, 1903, died September 6, 1904, and Wesley Moore Penniman, born December 7, 1905

CHARLES GREENWOOD is city forester of Worcester, which office he has held since 1898, a prominent citizen of the city, to which he removed February 14, 1875, and since April 1, 1886, a resident on the Patch farm, one of the oldest in Worcester, was born in the town of Hubbardston, Worcester county, Massachusetts, November 21, 1849

Moses Greenwood, great-grandfather of Charles Greenwood, born in 1752, settled with his two brothers—Abijah and Levi—in the town of Holden Moses Greenwood married Betsy Dunlap, March 22, 1778, she was born in Cherry Valley, New York, in 1756 When four years of age she was rescued from the Indians, who had murdered her parents and burned their dwelling She died December 9, 1826, aged seventy years She was survived by her husband who passed away at the age of seventy-five years, March 8, 1827 Their children were 1 Ethan A, born May 27, 1779, married Mrs Caroline Warren, of Roxbury, who died January 20, 1875, he died May 3, 1856 He graduated at Dartmouth College, and studied law for a short period of time He became a successful portrait painter, and proprietor of the New England museum in Boston He also painted a large silk banner for the military companies of the town He acquired a large property in Boston and Hubbardston 2 Aaron, born March 22, 1781, married Eliza Thatcher, removed to Pennsylvania and died there in the year 1807 3 Sally, born May 6, 1783, married Abel Warren, of Northboro, June 4, 1805 Their deaths occurred in the town of Northboro 4 Moses, born November 4, 1785 (see forward) 5 Betsey, born December 12, 1787, died April 24 1797 6 James, born September 4, 1792, married (first) Sally Hunting, March 3, 1814, she died October 17, 1818, married (second) Betsey Rice May 1, 1819, removed to Pennsylvania and there died His children were Lucy, born December 1, 1814, died at Harford, Pennsylvania, Stephen, born August 23, 1817, died April 22, 1818, and Asa Willard, born November 4, 1819 7 Cynthia, born October 1, 1794, was drowned May 15, 1808 (Cynthia Greenwood with two other young people went to the mill-pond of Major Greenwood's estate in Hubbardston, built a raft and started to cross the pond but the raft parted and they were drowned) 8 Betsey, born May 20, 1799, married Elisha Whittemore

Moses Greenwood, grandfather of Charles Greenwood, was born in Hubbardston, Massachusetts, November 4, 1785, died September 26, 1828 He was a prosperous farmer, and owned a sawmill, where he manufactured lumber On January 9, 1806, he was married to Polly Brown, born in Hubbardston May 16, 1780, died January 14, 1859 Their children were 1 Lyman, born June 13, 1806, married Augusta Marean November 19, 1829, and died October 5, 1880 Their children were Milo, born

March 4, 1831, removed South, and died in the war of the rebellion, Moses, born October 9, 1832, married Adelaide Wright, January 1, 1857, was the father of one child, Helen Mabel, born July 9, 1862, and resided in Cambridge, died in Ashburnham, Massachusetts, in 1904, Ann Elizabeth, born September 16, 1834, married Lyman Woodward, Joseph L, born June 10, 1836, removed to Abington, Asa Morrill, born December 22, 1839, married Mary E Nichols, April 12, 1865, died in Leominster, 1904, Helen A, born May 29, 1843, married James H Gleason, Mary Alice, born March 21, 1847, married Thomas B Grimes, Frank B, born November 25, 1851 2 Moses, born May 23, 1808, married Adeline Ayers, of North Brookfield, resides in Louisiana 3 Aaron (see forward) 4 Cynthia, born February 20, 1812, married William Joslin, a farmer of Hubbardston She died when about seventy years of age, leaving three daughters and two sons

Aaron Greenwood, father of Charles Greenwood, was born May 23, 1808, in Hubbardston, Massachusetts He was for many years a selectman of Hubbardston, and for one year represented that town and Templeton in the general court He removed to Worcester a short time prior to his death, August 3, 1878 On April 14, 1831, he married Adeline Rice, a native of Hubbardston, daughter of William and Rebecca (Allen) Rice, the former named having been born May 17, 1788, died November 13, 1831, and the latter born in 1790, died when eighty-three years of age Mrs Adeline Greenwood died in 1883 She was the mother of nine children, as follows 1 Celia Jane, born February 28, 1832, married Lorenzo Barnes 2 Sarah Rebecca, born January 5, 1834, married William H Earle 3 Lucy Agnes, born January 31, 1836, died April 17, 1843 4 Charlotte, born May 15, 1838, married George P Earle 5 Aaron Holbert, born January 21, 1841, enlisted June 29, 1861, Company D, Thirteenth Massachusetts Regiment, wounded at Antietam, September 17, 1862, discharged February 14, 1863, died at Alexandria, Virginia, soon afterward 6 George, born May 11, 1843, enlisted August 7, 1862, Company I, Twenty-fifth Massachusetts Regiment, died of wounds received at Point of Rocks, Virginia, May 10, 1864 7 Lucy Addie, born April 3, 1845, married William H Earle, (second wife) 8 Chester, born June 22, 1847 9 Charles, born November 21, 1849, (of whom later)

Charles Greenwood attended the public schools regularly until fourteen years of age, continuing thereafter during the winters for several years At the age of twenty-two he took up his residence in Fitchburg, and there gained his first experience in market gardening as a means of livelihood, continuing that occupation for two and a half years On February 14, 1875, he removed to Worcester and, in 1886, purchased the Patch farm, consisting of one hundred and four acres, but subsequently disposed of all but fifteen acres, on which he resides He was a member of the Worcester common council for two years, and in the spring of 1898 was appointed to his present position of city forester by the board of park commissioners He is a Republican in politics He was for two years master, and is now (1906) treasurer, for a term of seven years, to Worcester Grange He married, December 10, 1873, Ella E Grimes, daughter of Joseph and Augusta (Maynard) Grimes, and their children are Burt W, born March 18, 1881, graduated from the Worcester high school in 1900, and from Harvard University in 1904 He is now connected with the Worcester Trust Company, and resides in the family homestead Harold J, born May 7, 1884, studied designing in the Eric Pape school of art, Boston, where he won high honors, being a prize winner in the competition of 1905, and a student of general artistic ability He resides at home Mrs Greenwood is a member of the Union Congregational Church

Joseph Grimes, father of Mrs Greenwood, conducted a farm for a number of years, and also was employed in a chair factory at Gardner He died in 1894, aged seventy-four years His wife, Augusta (Maynard) Grimes, was a native of Sterling, and died in 1899, at the age of seventy-five years They were the parents of eight children, one son, Frederick W Grimes, a resident of Jamaica Plains, and seven daughters, all of whom attained years of maturity

JAMES PRESCOTT HAMILTON John Hamilton, (1), the immigrant ancestor of James Prescott Hamilton, president of the Worcester National Bank, was born in England or Scotland The name was frequently spelt Hambleton on the early records The first record of John Hamilton is found in Charlestown, Massachusetts, in 1658 He was then owner of four acres of woodland and three of commons He removed to Concord, Massachusetts, before 1667, and in 1671 is said to have removed to Marlborough, but King Philip's war in 1675 caused the settlers there to abandon their homes and he probably removed to some town near Boston Indeed, his son Joseph seems to have been an innkeeper in Boston later His wife's name is spelt Christian in the Concord records Their children John, see forward, Joseph, born at Concord, January 9, 1671

(II) John Hamilton, son of John Hamilton (1), was born in Concord, Massachusetts, March 1, 1667-68 He was maltster by trade He settled in Brookfield about 1700 He sold his house, barn and land at Concord, January 25, 1702, after moving to Brookfield It was not until March 18, 1708, that he sold the homestead at Concord The purchaser was Obadiah Wheeler He had a grant of land at Brookfield, November, 1701, comprising fifty acres of upland, formerly of James Hosmer, on the county road east of Joseph Bannister's land He had a special grant of land from the town of Brookfield to encourage him to set up his trade as maltster there He married (first) Sarah ——, (second) Hannah —— Two of his children were born at Concord Children Joseph, born at Concord, September 5, 1697, resided at Brookfield, married Sarah ——, John, see forward, Hannah, married, January 8, 1724, William Ayres, Dorothy, born December 4, 1725, married Josiah Wood, Jonah, Nathan, Amos

(III) John Hamilton, son of John Hamilton (2), was born in Concord, Massachusetts, August 26, 1699 He resided in Brookfield He married, January 8, 1725, Mary Wheeler Their children Reuben, born November 6, 1726, John, December 18, 1728, removed to Palmer, Massachusetts, Levi, December 25, 1730, Hannah, December 10, 1733, married, March 11, 1756, Nathaniel Wolcott, Silas, February 10, 1736, removed to Whitingham, Vermont, Mary, November 4, 1739, married —— Goodrich, of Hadley, Massachusetts, Mercy, June 11, 1743

(IV) Reuben Hamilton, son of John Hamilton (3), born November 6, 1726, was for many years a deacon of the second precinct church, Brookfield He removed to Worcester, where he died in 1790 The administrator's bond is dated July 14, 1790 His son Asa settled the estate Deacon Reuben Hamilton married, April, 1756, Lucretia Hubbard,

of Brookfield She married (second) Captain Jonathan Fay, of Westborough, Massachusetts, (intentions dated March 30, 1798) and she died in 1805 Children of Reuben and Lucretia Hamilton 1 Reuben, born April 13, 1757, married, March 9, 1780, Elizabeth Woodbury, of Leverett, Massachusetts, resided in Dublin, New Hampshire, and Canada 2 Lucretia, born October 23, 1758, married, November 22, 1778, Joseph Bartlett, of Brookfield 3 Hannah, born May 30, 1760, married, January 8, 1783, Elijah Allen, removed to Craftsbury, Vermont Silas, born August 16, 1762, married and moved to Hanover, Massachusetts, sailed from Boston and was never heard of 5 Asa, see forward 6 Lydia, born June 1, 1767, died October 23, 1768 7 Mary, born August 26, 1768, married Byfield Pierce, of Worcester, removed to Craftsbury, Vermont 8 Dr Samuel, born November 5, 1770, died 1847, married, October 23, 1793, Mehitable Bemis, of Worcester, went to Dublin, New Hampshire, was clerk of the Social Library, 1794, representative in the legislature, selectman, prosperous merchant, removed to Canandaigua and Rochester, New York, children—i Ashley, born February 24, 1794, married Clarissa Chamberlain, ii Eliza, born August 9, 1796, removed to Rochester, New York, wife of Silas Ball, iii Rebecca, born June 16, 1798, iv Harriet, born August 3, 1800, v Mary, born November 7, 1802 9 Dorothy, born May 23, 1772, married, 1796, Asahel Washburn, of Leicester, she died May, 1849 10 Luke, born March 29, 1775 11 Betsey, born March 27, 1778, married Reuben Muzzy, of Dublin, removed to Athens, Pennsylvania 12 Eli, born April 19, 1781, married Mary Woodward, resided in Dublin, died March 24, 1852

(V) Asa Hamilton, son of Reuben Hamilton (4), was born in Brookfield, Massachusetts, November 28, 1763 He made his home in Worcester before he was of age, and in 1793 opened a tavern on the old Post road from Worcester to Lancaster, three miles from Worcester common, in a house occupied later by Solomon Parsons, and conducted it until 1800, when he bought a store on the west side of Main street He carried on this store, dealing chiefly in dry goods, the remainder of his days He is credited with a month and a third service in the revolution for the town of Brookfield He remained in the militia after the war and rose to the rank of captain He was admitted to the Worcester Fire Society, July 5, 1802 He was prominent in public affairs and held many offices of trust and responsibility At the time of his death he was town treasurer. In personal appearance he was straight and erect, a fine-looking gentleman, very neat and polite, and a great favorite with the women who bought goods at his store He died suddenly at his residence on Main street, December 14, 1831 He married, August 28, 1788, Elizabeth Blair, who died July 17, 1834 Their children Sewall, see forward; Charles Augustus, see forward

(VI) Sewall Hamilton, son of Asa Hamilton (5), was born in Worcester, March 1, 1789, married, October 11, 1810, Nancy Howard Fullerton He died December 10, 1824, in his thirty-sixth year Their children 1 Mary Lucretia, born December 26, 1810 2 Alexander Sewall (changed to Edward), see forward 3 Elizabeth Blair, born September 12, 1814, married, October 23, 1839, William Coe, who died August 24, 1850, leaving five children 4 Martha Sanders, born May 31, 1816, married, November 11, 1839, Hiram Gould, he died October 27, 1846, leaving children—i Martha Cornelia Gould, born August 19, 1840, married W H Balcom, ii Sarah Goddard Gould, born August 4, 1846, married, December 6, 1866, Captain John N Coe and they had Arthur Hamilton Coe, born July 14, 1867 5 George Augustus, born March 25, 1823, married, April 2, 1845, Elizabeth M Bradley, daughter of Osgood Bradley, the car manufacturer, resided in St Paul, Minnesota, and had—i Fanny S B, born 1847, ii Edward Fullerton, born November, 1858

(VI) Charles Augustus Hamilton, son of Asa Hamilton (5), was born in Worcester, May 11, 1805, died there October 30, 1879 He received his education in the common schools of his native town, beginning his business career as clerk in the book store of George A Trumbull, in 1821 In 1823 was clerk in a Boston store, the following years in his father's store in Worcester, and in 1826 went into partnership with his father In 1829 he was in the office of the clerk of courts of Worcester county, and during the next two years held various public offices, 'deputy sheriff, constable, auctioneer, collector of taxes, treasurer of the school district, assessor of the second parish, and took care of a reading room in Paine's Building," to quote from his diary This variety of work was excellent preparation for his career as a banker It gave him a thorough knowledge of business, a wide acquaintance with men, valuable legal training and self-confidence He was made cashier of the Quinsigamond Bank when it was organized in 1833 He resigned this position in 1853 to become treasurer of the Worcester County Institute for Savings, a position he filled with conspicuous ability and success until his death This bank has from the start held the lead among the savings banks of Worcester county

Mr Hamilton was the first city clerk of Worcester He was town clerk from 1836 until the city was organized in 1848 He resigned as city clerk in 1855, a period of twenty years in charge of the public records He was notary public from 1835 to 1839 and justice of the peace from 1844 to 1864 He was much attached to his church, the second parish, now known as the First Unitarian Church, of which he was elected deacon in 1847 He was actively engaged in Sunday school work, and in 1881 became a life member of the American Unitarian Association At the time of his death he was the oldest survivor of the Worcester Light Infantry, which he joined in the autumn of 1821 He was made corporal in 1822, sergeant and clerk in 1824, lieutenant in 1826 and captain in 1828 He resigned in 1831 He was first president of the Veteran Association of the Light Infantry

He married, March 7, 1826, Eliza Abbott Porter, daughter of Oliver and Sarah (Abbott) Porter, of Boston She was born October 29, 1803, and died July 8, 1840 He married (second), April 13, 1843, Hannah Maria Prescott born January 18, 1811, died October 26, 1864, daughter of James and Hannah (Champney) Prescott Mr Hamilton died at Worcester, October 30, 1879 Children of Charles A and Eliza A Hamilton 1 Sarah Abbott born March 22, 1827, married, April 10, 1850, William Cross, son of William and Sophia A (Thompson) Cross, children—i Eliza Hamilton Cross, born January 26, 1851, died May 5, 1865, ii Mary Stacy Cross, born April 17, 1854 died July 27, 1855 2 Frances Towne, born July 25, 1828, married, October 4, 1853, Joseph Trumbull, of Worcester, son of George A and Louisa (Clapp) Trumbull, she died January 25 1859, children—i Helen Carnes Trumbull, born December 27, 1856, ii Frances Hamilton Trumbull, born January 17, 1859, died in Philadelphia, March 28, 1885 3 Calvin Willard, born January 12, 1833, see sketch elsewhere in this work

Children of Charles A and Hannah M Hamilton 4 James Prescott, see forward 5 Edward Bangs, born April 13, 1846, died November 2, 1897

(VII) Edward Hamilton, son of Sewall Hamilton (6), was born in Worcester, January 6, 1812 His name was originally Alexander Sewall, but was changed after his marriage by legal process to Edward He was a teacher of music by profession and prominent in musical circles He was assistant treasurer of the Worcester County Institution for Savings He married, June 5, 1841, Mary Coe, who died August 4, 1863, daughter of John Coe, of Worcester He married (second), April 15, 1865, Sarah Cornelia Moore Perkins, of Holliston, Massachusetts He died in Worcester, January 2, 1870 The only child of Edward and Sarah C Hamilton was George Howard, born December 14, 1868

(VII) James Prescott Hamilton, son of Charles Augustus Hamilton (6), was born in Worcester, March 10, 1844 After receiving the education afforded by the common and high schools of his native city, at the age of seventeen, he began his career as clerk in the Worcester County Institution for Savings, of which his father was treasurer He remained in this bank for several years, and acquired an excellent training for his profession In January, 1865, he entered the National Park Bank of New York city, and during the next three years filled several important positions in the several departments of this great institution He left New York in May, 1868, to accept the position of assistant cashier of the Worcester National Bank, and his life since that time has been identified with the banking interests of his native city He was immediately promoted to the position of cashier The "Old Worcester Bank" (as his bank is familiarly known) is the oldest in the city, having rounded out a century of existence in 1904 It is and always has been the largest bank in the city, unless trust companies be included in the comparison In the past thirty-seven years during which he has been cashier, the business has grown steadily In January, 1904, Mr Hamilton was given increased responsibility, being promoted to the vice-presidency of the bank The assistant cashier, Samuel D Spurr, was made cashier, and Frederick M Hedden assistant cashier, to fill the vacancies caused by his promotion The president until his death in 1905 was Stephen Salisbury, whose father, also Stephen Salisbury was president until his death In 1906 Mr Hamilton was elected president of the bank An idea of the present business of the institution may be obtained form the exhibit of deposits, which in March 1905, amounted to $3,356,381 12 The capital stock is $250,000 The growth of the business has obliged the bank to plan for larger quarters, and the alterations are now (1906) being made in the bank building on Foster street Mr Hamilton is one of three executors of Mr Salisbury's will

Mr Hamilton is also treasurer of the Worcester Gas Light Company, trustee of the People's Savings Bank, and was formerly vice-president until the enactment of the present law forbidding national bank officers holding executive offices in savings banks He is also auditor of the State Mutual Life Assurance Company, and president of the Worcester Clearing House Association He is executor of the will of Josiah H Clarke He is also auditor of Clark University, and was an executor of the will of Jonas G Clark, its founder, and later of his widow's estate Under Mr Clark's will Mr Hamilton became custodian of certain funds, and the following clause from the will explains the duty he had to perform, and indirectly testifies to the confidence reposed in him by the distinguished philanthropist

"I think it proper to provide and do accordingly direct my executors to appoint Mr James P Hamilton one of their number, as treasurer, to hold and have charge of such of the funds as are directed to be kept separate from the general endowment fund of the University for the space of five years after the probate of this instrument, in order that my purpose to keep these funds intact and independent of said general fund may not fail"

Mr Hamilton was one of the forty charter members of the Worcester Art Museum He is a member of the Worcester Club, the Quinsigamond Boat Club, the Tatnuck Country Club, the Worcester Fire Society, and was a member of the Commonwealth Club He is a regular attendant of the First Unitarian Church, has served as its treasurer, and is now chairman of its parish committee In politics he is a Republican

Mr Hamilton married, September 24, 1874, Sarah Antoinette, daughter of George A and Sarah A (Hadwen) Kimball Their children are 1 Edith, born October 23, 1875, graduated at Radcliffe, 1904, taught school at St Agnes, Albany, same year 2 Charles Augustus, born July 15, 1877, graduated Harvard University, 1899, entered the law offices of Charles M Thayer, and was admitted to the bar 1902, and has since practiced having offices with Mr Thayer 3 Mary, born March 12, 1882, graduated Smith College, 1904

(VII) Calvin Willard Hamilton, son of Charles Augustus (6), was born in Worcester, January 12, 1833, and was educated there in the public and high schools He began his mercantile career in Boston as clerk in a dry goods establishment and learned the business there He started in business in Worcester in the firm of Jenkins, Hamilton & Company, dry goods dealers, succeeding B L Hardon, in the store on Main street between Walnut and Maple street During the civil war he entered partnership with Charles Fox, his wife's brother, under the firm name of C W Hamilton & Company, and manufactured army cloth in the old Fox mills Worcester After this firm was dissolved Mr Hamilton started in the manufacture of tapes and narrow fabrics, and continued for many years with marked success The business was located at 83 Water street and went under the name of Hamilton Flock Company He manufactured all kinds of flocks, woolen yarns, etc, and was a dealer in shear and gig flocks, woolen waste, etc After giving up his manufacturing business about 1885 he was connected with George Upton, glue manufacturer of Boston, as traveling salesman, and later with the American Glue Company in same business up to the time of his death, October 3, 1901

Mr Hamilton had few interests outside his home and business He was a member of the First Unitarian church and a Republican in politics He was of a social nature and made friends readily He won the confidence as well as the esteem of his friends He made his home at 37 Oak avenue, Worcester, opposite the residence of Senator Hoar who counted him as one of his friends and neighbors His family are living there at present The house is filled with antique furniture and treasures that have been inherited in the family

Mr Hamilton married, October 27, 1859, Eliza Fox, born March 23, 1834 (See Fox family sketch with Dr L Fox Woodward's sketch) She resides at the homestead, 37 Oak avenue The only child of Calvin W and Eliza Hamilton was Fanny Maria, born at Worcester, March 9, 1865, educated

T. S. Johnson

in private schools and at the Worcester State Normal school, and is now teacher of kindergarten at the Elizabeth street school, Worcester

COLONEL THEODORE S JOHNSON, former trial justice for Blackstone, and at present and for many years previous clerk of the courts of Worcester county, Massachusetts, is a man whose high ideals and executive ability render him in an eminent degree an interesting and influential citizen in the community in which he lives He traces his descent back through a number of generations

(I) *Solomon Johnson*, the founder of the Johnson family in America, came to this country prior to 1639, for in that year he was one of the proprietors of and settled in Sudbury, Massachusetts He brought with him his wife and several children It appears from the records of Watertown, Massachusetts, which bordered on Sudbury in the early days, that Solomon was born in 1615, that he was appointed to have charge of the public cowpen (pound) near the Sudbury line, March 31, 1651, and that he continued there until 1660, when he removed to Marlboro He sold land in Sudbury in 1653, and was one of the selectmen of Marlboro from 1661 to 1666, inclusive, being a leader among the pioneers of that town He was very active in King Philip's war, as all Marlboro men had to be in order to protect their families and themselves from the Indians He had some difficulty with the town of Watertown about the payment of church rates after his removal to Marlboro, and the selectmen of Watertown ordered a suit brought to compel him and his son John to pay balance of ministry rates Solomon Johnson made his will March 28, 1686, and he died the following year, for his will was proved October 6, 1687 This will makes mention of his children, Nathaniel and John, of his grandsons, the children of Nathaniel, and of his son-in-law, John Barnes No mention is made of any other of his descendants living at this time He was a tailor by trade, and was also a farmer Solomon Johnson was married three times His first wife, Elinor, came to this country at the same time as he did He married (second), about 1650, Hannah ———, by whom he had three children, and who died at Sudbury, June 4, 1685 He married (third), February 1, 1686-87, at Watertown, Massachusetts, Hannah Crafts The record of his children is as follows John, born probably in England 1635 to 1637, married in Sudbury, Massachusetts, Deborah Ward, 1657, resided at Marlboro, Nathaniel (twin), born February 3, 1639-40, of whom later, Joseph (twin), born February 3, 1639-40, married Susannah ———, at Marlboro, November 19, 1667, and died in 1668, Johanna, born February 16, 1641, Mary, born February 23, 1643, Caleb, born February 1, 1645, was shot and killed near Watertown line by accident, May 4, 1654, Solomon, born 1646, was at Marlboro at the opening of King Philip's war, and probably died July 28, 1690 (He may have been the Solomon who married Abigail Goodnow of Sudbury, Massachusetts, June 6, 1716, and had Hepsebath, born October 12, 1716, and John, born October 17, 1718, in Sudbury, but it is not likely if he were born as early as some authorities think he was), Jonathan, born (probably) 1646 his wife died December 28, 1728, and they had three children, Samuel, born March 6, 1654, Hannah, born April 27, 1656, married George Parmenter, of Sudbury, Caleb, born October 31, 1658, married Agnes Bent July 9, 1684, who died June 4, 1729, Caleb died December 1, 1715

(II) Nathaniel Johnson, second son and child of Solomon Jonhson (1), was born February 3, 1639-40, at Sudbury, Massachusetts He went to Marlboro, Massachusetts, in 1660, and settled there He and his brothers, John and Jonathan, were especially active at the time of King Philip's war In 1675 he was at the meeting when plans were made to defend the town When the town was garrisoned about 1711, he was in Captain Kerby's garrison near his dwelling house on the road to Southboro The Johnson families may have left the town for a short time during these Indian troubles, but in the main they remained at their posts Nathaniel Johnson died July 24, 1718 He married, November 16, 1671, Mary Plympton, who died November 27, 1736 The children of this marriage were Joseph, born October 6, 1672, married, January 9, 1705, Sarah Maynard, Samuel, born August 28, 1674, died 1740, Mary, born February, 1675, John, of whom later, Joanna, born November 7, 1682, Dorothy, born April 26, 1685, Jane, born March 22, 1687, died 1688, Abigail, born 1691, died 1693

(III) John Johnson, third son and fourth child of Nathaniel (2) and Mary (Plympton) Johnson, was born March 24, 1679, at Marlboro, Massachusetts He was a farmer, and married, February 25, 1707, Mary Plimpton, who died July 19, 1720 He died February 15, 1758 Their children were Abraham, born June 13, 1709, Abigail, born September 1, 1711, died February 10, 1760, unmarried, Elizabeth, born July 30, 1713, died October 30, 1756, unmarried, John, born May 29, 1715, was in the French wars in 1756, Mary, born December 8, 1716, Nathaniel, of whom sketch follows

(IV) Nathaniel Johnson, third son and sixth and youngest child of John (3) and Mary (Plympton) Johnson, was born at Marlboro, March 18, 1718, He resided in Marlboro, but in 1763 moved to Hardwick, Massachusetts, where he died November 3, 1790 He married, December 31, 1740, Sarah Forbush, of Westboro, Massachusetts, and they had children as follows Joel, born October 31, 1743, Silas, April 21, 1746, Sarah, July 26, 1748, Stephen, June 6, 1751, Catherine, April 25, 1753, Mary, October 15, 1755, Susanna, July 5, 1758, died April 16, 1761, Persis, May 2, 1760, Nathaniel January 12, 1762, Aaron, May 10, 1763, Tryphena, September 15, 1764, married Sylvanus Brimhall, September 14, 1783. All the children were born in Marlboro, except the youngest, who was born in Hardwick, Massachusetts

(V) Silas Johnson, second son and child of Nathaniel (4) and Sarah (Forbush) Johnson, was born at Marlboro, Massachusetts, April 21, 1746, died July 12, 1822 November 27, 1766, he married Patience Walker, of Petersham, who died October 18, 1813, at the age of sixty-nine years Their children were as follows Silas, of whom a sketch follows, Susanna, born April 15, 1770

(VI) Silas Johnson, eldest child and only son of Silas (5) and Patience (Walker) Johnson, was born November 27, 1767 He married (first), Hannah Nye, December 15, 1785, and after her death he married (second), Celia Howard February 24, 1799 He died March 19, 1840, and his widow married (second), John Peckham of Petersham, April 20 1741 The children of Silas Johnson (6) are as follows Silas Nye, born September 3, 1799, died at Dana, Massachusetts, April 1, 1879, Alanson, born November 9, 1800, Hiram, September 3, 1892, Gardner, October 25, 1804, Nehemiah Howard, May 26, 1807, resides in Illinois, September 21, 1841, when he married Eunice Randall, Ranslure, July 15, 1809, Theodore Wilder, of whom a sketch follows

(VII) Theodore Wilder, seventh and youngest son and child of Silas (7) and Celia (Howard) Johnson, was born June 3, 1820, at Hardwick, Massachusetts He married, April, 1842, Emily Sears Mellen, of Prescott, Massachusetts Mrs Johnson died at Worcester, Massachusetts, January 5, 1902 She was of Scotch Presbyterian ancestry Theodore Wilder Johnson died at Worcester, Massachusetts, January 10, 1890 He and his wife were the parents of the following named children Colonel Theodore S, of whom later, Emily Helen, born at Dana, Massachusetts, Charles Rensselaer, born at Dana, Massachusetts, Samuel Howard, born at Dana, Massachusetts, died in the same town, March 23, 1857

(VIII) Colonel Theodore S Johnson, eldest child of Theodore Wilder (7) and Emily S (Miller) Johnson, was born at Dana, Massachusetts, July 1, 1843 His youth was spent on the old place in his native town He attended the Dana schools and after graduating from the high school went to Wilbraham Academy In 1864 he came to Worcester, Massachusetts, to study law He entered the office of Dewey & Williams, one of the leading law firms of the county He was admitted to the bar in 1866 and immediately opened an office and began the practice of law at Blackstone, Massachusetts In 1867 he was appointed a trial justice for Blackstone by Governor Bullock This office under the Massachusetts statutes provides a magistrate for large towns similar in jurisdiction to the district courts The trial justice has jurisdiction of minor civil causes and criminal cases that are not serious enough to go before the grand jury Colonel Johnson was the local judge for about four years, when he resigned to take the position of clerk of the district court in the city of Worcester Hon Hartley Williams, of Dewey & Williams, with whom Mr Johnson had studied law, was the justice and he naturally turned to Mr Johnson as a man having the necessary experience, executive ability and dignity for the office Mr Johnson held this office for ten years to the entire satisfaction of the members of the bar and other authorities with whom he had relations In the civil and criminal branches of a municipal court, in a city as large and cosmopolitan as Worcester, there is a natural demand for the highest ability on the part of the clerk to keep the machinery of the court in good order The high reputation of this court during the time that Colonel Johnson was its administrative officer, was a test of his ability, and won him promotion to his present position as clerk of courts of Worcester county He was elected in November, 1881, and re-elected in 1886-91-96 and 1901 He is serving his twentieth year and through all this period he has given the utmost satisfaction The details of his office are too many and perhaps too technical to be enumerated here, and it is difficult to explain to others than lawyers what are the elements of Mr Johnson's success and popularity However, the public realizes that he is efficient The machinery of the courts at Fitchburg and Worcester always runs smoothly, the records of his office are always up to date, and lawyers go out of their way to show their appreciation of the administration of Colonel Johnson Perhaps his tact and courtesy have much to do with the success of his department He never hesitates to accommodate those having business with his office, even at considerable personal sacrifice At times the duties of his position require him to turn night into day to keep up with the volume of business to be transacted He has chosen an excellent corps of assistants to whom he gives much of the credit of the efficiency of his office, but, as in all such cases, the credit belongs to the chief, because he had the sagacity to choose the right persons and the wisdom to keep forces well organized and disciplined

The county of Worcester has had through all its history a reputation for having in its clerks of court men of high character and pronounced ability The office of clerk of courts requires exact legal knowledge almost as extensive as that of the bench itself It requires great personal dignity, modified by a proper sense of the fitness of things and the occasion It often requires the practical ability to cut the Gordian knot of legal red tape to get results If there is one thing more than another that Colonel Johnson likes to do it is to have the court get results, to solve the problems brought to it and end litigation rather than to continue it indefinitely Since the incorporation of the county of Worcester in 1731, there have been but eleven different persons holding this office It has attracted men who have been in congress, and who have held other high offices, because of the liberal reward allowed by the county and because of the importance and honor of the place Yet it is universally conceded by men familiar with the conditions and competent to judge, that the present clerk is the most competent as well as the most successful No matter what standard may be applied, Colonel Johnson must be deemed the best clerk of courts that Worcester county has ever had His success in life must be measured by his work as clerk, for that has been his chief occupation

He has always been interested as a citizen in municipal politics, and has at times been very active in the Republican organization He was captain and advocate general on the staff of the Third Brigade Massachusetts Volunteer Militia from 1874 to 1876, inclusive He was appointed in 1878 by Governor Talbot as colonel and aide-de-camp on his staff, whence the title by which he is generally known He represented the city of Worcester on the Republican state central committee in 1881-2-3 and 1884 In 1883 he was elected director of the Quinsigamond National Bank and was an active factor in the management of that bank until its liquidation Is at present a director of the Merchants' National Bank He has been connected with various local corporations as director, and his business ability and common sense have made him particularly useful in the companies in which he has been an investor He is also a member of a number of social organizations He married, in April, 1873, Amanda M Allen, of Blackstone, Massachusetts

(VIII) Charles Rensselaer Johnson, second son and third child of Theodore Wilder (7) and Emily Sears (Miller) Johnson, was born in Dana, Massachusetts, December 28, 1852 He attended school in his native town and in 1865 removed with his parents to Worcester, and was graduated from the Worcester high school in 1871 He entered Harvard University and graduated from there in 1875 He then entered the law office of Rice & Blackmer and studied under their personal supervision, being admitted to the bar in 1878, and has since practiced law in Worcester His office is in the State Mutual building For many years he shared offices with the late David Manning Mr Johnson has made a special study of divorce, probate and chancery cases He became interested in the public schools and for twenty years or more has been the most influential figure in the administration of the schools Much of the high reputation of these schools is due to the wise judgment and unfailing interest that Mr Johnson has taken as chairman of the board He has been a member of the school board since

1877, with the exception of a period from 1879 to 1892, and has been zealous at all times for the advancement and development of the great public schools system of Worcester No citizen of this town has shown a more continuous and unselfish interest in this matter, and Mr Johnson's long experience and familiarity with the schools and school buildings, with the conditions of the past as well as of the present, furnish a fund of information that is invaluable to the city and that could not be bought for money It is services like those rendered by Mr Johnson that have made New England what it is—an educational model for the world

Mr Johnson was a member of the Republican city committee in 1880-81 He has been a master in chancery since 1882, and is a notary public He is a member of various fraternal orders and was a member of the supreme council Royal Arcanum, in 1899 He is a life member of the Worcester Society of Antiquity, and corresponding member of the Western Reserve Historical Society He is interested in local and family history and has written various articles on historical subjects He is also a member of the state board of charity, having been appointed by Governor Bates in 1904 He represented the seventh ward of Worcester in the legislature in 1898-99, was on the committee on probate and insolvency in the house in 1898 and chairman of the committee on constitutional amendments (house chairman) and member of the committee on judiciary in 1899

Mr Johnson married, August 8, 1882, Mary McGann, of Maynard, who died at Worcester, Massachusetts, December 6, 1887, leaving one daughter, Florence Emily, born at Maynard July 19, 1883 He married (second), May 29, 1889, Susie Serry, of Davenport, Iowa, and they have two sons Charles Ward, born at Worcester, Massachusetts, March 8, 1894, Theodore Howard born at Worcester, Massachusetts, October 24, 1896

WILLIAM WATSON McKIBBEN, M D The McKibben family of America is of Scotch-Irish origin The progenitor came to Pennsylvania during the great emigration from 1720 to 1750 from the northern province of Ireland, which gave to Pennsylvania its sturdiest and best stock

The variations in spelling the name make it somewhat difficult to trace The family settled in the counties of Down and Antrim in the province of Ulster, Ireland, and are to be found nowhere else in the old country The name is rare in Scotland, as at present spelled The family was Presbyterian in religion and intermarried with the other Scotch families in Down and Ulster It is possible that a careful research would connect the Pennsylvania progenitor of the McKibbins or McKibbens with the family of Knockhashum, mentioned in the genealogy of the family of James Orr of Ballyblack, who died in 1627 and whose wife, Janet McClement died in 1636 The pedigree also mentions the McKibbins of Haw Descendants of the Orr family of Scotch-Irish came to New Hampshire and Pennsylvania with the early Scotch-Irish settlers

In Pennsylvania Rev J McMillan mentions John McKibben in his diary under date of 1775 as his host when he preached at Dunlap's creek, probably in Washington county

William McKibben son probably of the first settler of the name, was great-grandfather of Dr W W McKibben, of Worcester, and was born probably about 1760 in Pennsylvania

James McKibben, Jr, grandfather of Dr W W McKibben of Worcester, was born at Cedar Run in what is now Clinton county Pennsylvania, about nine miles southeast of Lockhaven, Pennsylvania, about 1800 He married Catherine Lamb, daughter of Hugh and —— (Allison) McManigal Her mother was the daughter of Daniel Allison, and was an aunt of United States Senator W B Allison She was born June 11, 1807, in Centre county, Pennsylvania and died September 5, 1855 He died July 28 1858 Their children were Frank Reed, see forward, David A, resides in Leavenworth, Kansas, and is president of the Home-Riverside Coal Mining Company of Leavenworth, Joseph, Lucetta, and James A

Frank Reed McKibben, father of Dr W W McKibben was born at Caroline, Seneca county, Ohio, December 2, 1843 He was the fifth child of a family of six children He received a common school education, but was largely self educated At the death of his father in 1858 he went to live with Henry Isabel, at Plymouth, Ohio, where he took up the trade of carriage trimmer He worked with Mr Isabel also at Mansfield and Shenandoah Ohio, working at his trade until after the civil war broke out

He enlisted in November, 1861, in Company A, Major William McLoughlin's Squadron, First Ohio Independent Cavalry, which was soon afterward attached to the famous brigade of General W T Sherman The company proceeded from Mansfield to the Big Sandy valley in Eastern Kentucky serving under Colonel (afterwards President) James A Garfield in the campaign against Brigadier-General Humphrey Marshall, of the Confederate forces Mr McKibben was in the battle of Kernstown Virginia March 23 1862, against Stonewall Jackson In the summer of 1863 his squadron was transferred to Burnside's command in the Army of the Potomac, and he was in the battles of Knoxville September 3 1863, at Cumberland Gap, Morristown, Strawberry Plains and in many skirmishes and minor engagements At Smoky Mountain he was wounded in the breast and leg and carried back to the city of Knoxville in an ambulance, and remained for many weeks in the hospital He was later transferred to General Sherman's command at Buzzard's Roost, in northern Georgia, and was in the famous March to the Sea He finally rode back to Nashville where he was mustered out in 1865

After the war he located for a short time at Plymouth Ohio and Leavenworth, Kansas, and finally settled at Fort Smith, Arkansas, in the dry goods business, as clerk for his brother, David A McKibben He had a tobacco store of his own for a time, but eventually bought a farm which he carried on working in his brother's store in the winter season and on his farm in the summer In 1870 he was superintendent of the Shaw-Cotton Plantation on the Arkansas river for about a year He removed to Van Buren, Arkansas where he opened a general store which he carried on for about seven years alone then took into partnership his brother-in-law, Henry Pape, under the firm name of McKibben & Pape In 1893 he sold out his interests and the business was continued by the firm of H F and C A Pape

He bought a stock ranch of 6,000 acres five miles from Wagoner, Indian Territory on the reservation of the Creek Indians In addition to his ranch he carried on a general store there His store was burned and he lost heavily After four years he returned to Van Buren and became the General Agent of the Union Central Life Insurance Company of Cincinnati Ohio He became interested in real estate in Kansas City and had property there valued at $60,000 In 1900 he was appointed United States jailer at Fort Smith in the Federal Jail He built and owned the McKibben Opera House at Van Buren and was an extensive land owner there

He was a Republican in politics and was a delegate to the Republican National Convention at Minneapolis in 1892 He was a member of Van Buren Lodge of Free Masons, No 6, at Van Buren, Arkansas He was also an Odd Fellow He was director of the Crawford Company National Bank at Van Buren, also of the Van Buren Canning Company, the Van Buren Ice Company and the Van Buren Cotton Compress Company He attended the Methodist church and was a liberal contributor to its charities

He married at Fort Smith, Arkansas, September 7 1870, Elizabeth Pape, who was born in Cincinnati, Ohio, January 16, 1851, the daughter of Henry Pape who was born in Berlin, Germany, in 1828, and his wife, Elizabeth Ziegenbein born in the province of Hanover Germany, 1827 Her father was a contractor and builder before and after coming to America, he and his wife located in Cincinnati Ohio about 1848 They were attracted thither, as were many other Germans, by a book which was circulated in Germany telling about the grape industry which began as follows

"A little before the middle of the ninteenth century the culture of the grape was introduced into the neighborhood of Cincinnati and for many years it was thought that Hamilton county was destined to be a great wine country Nicholas Longworth is principally entitled to the credit for the endeavor to add this attractive product to the list of those successfully harvested in this county He had for many years given much attention to the cultivation of the grape with the view of making wine His first efforts were confined to the acclimatization of foreign vines He tried about forty varieties before the idea occurred to him of testing our indigenous grapes He met with such success that he withdrew from the practice of law and commenced experimenting more elaborately upon the production of wine from the native grapes Two of these varieties, the Catawba and the Isabella, seemed to him to possess the best qualities for wine and to be best adapted to the climate and soil He soon cultivated large vineyards and built extensive wine vaults where he stored the wine manufactured from his own grapes as well as those purchased from others As a result Cincinnati became world famous as the center of a wine region, and thousands of vine growers flocked to it, causing the vine-clad hills to become famous the world over In 1851 Mr Longworth had one hundred and fifteen acres in grapes, almost exclusively Catawba and he bottled during the season 75,000 bottles" From about 1859 on, the vine growers began to have trouble with their vines and soon it became apparent that the vine culture was no longer adapted to the locality of Cincinnati and "the vine-clad hills along the banks of the beautiful river, have long since become a thing of the past"

The children of Frank Reed and Elizabeth (Pape) McKibben were Frank Pape born November 13, 1871, see forward, William Watson, see forward, Bertha Lucetta born January 29 1887, unmarried, has lived at Newton Centre, Massachusetts, since 1902, Minnie Vera, born December 13, 1888 died at Van Buren January 7 1893 Frank Reed McKibben died at Duncan, Indian Territory, May 11, 1901

Frank Pape McKibben son of Frank Reed McKibben and brother of Dr William Watson McKibben, was born at Fort Smith, Arkansas, November 13 1871 He received his education in the common schools of Van Buren, Arkansas, whither he moved with his parents when he was an infant He studied three years at the Arkansas Industrial University of Fayetteville, Arkansas He then took a year's preparatory course for West Point but failed on his physical tests In 1890 he entered the Massachusetts Institute of Technology, graduating as civil engineer in 1894 He became a teacher of bridge engineering at the institute and is at present associate professor of civil engineering there He has designed and superintended the building of several important bridges and has designed some of the structures of the Boston Elevated Railway

He is the assistant engineer of the Massachusetts Railroad Commissioners, appointed September 30, 1901 He is a member of the American Society of Civil Engineers, of the Boston Society of Civil Engineers, of the American Society for Testing Materials, of the Society for the Promotion of Engineering Education He has been librarian of the Boston Society of Civil Engineers for several years He is a Republican in politics and is actively interested in the work of the Young Men's Christian Association, for which he has lectured and worked on various occasions He is a member of the Congregational church, at Newton Center, where he is at present living

He married, January 26, 1899, Arabelle Almy, at New Bedford She was a teacher in the New Bedford training school She is a daughter of Warren W and Sarah (Gray) Almy Her father is a farmer of Tiverton Four Corners, Rhode Island The only child of Frank Pape and Arabella McKibben is Elliott Spencer, born March 23, 1902

William Watson McKibben, son of Frank Reed McKibben, was born in Fort Smith, Arkansas, August 22, 1874 When he was two years old his parents moved to Van Buren, an adjacent town, where he attended the common schools after he was six years old and graduated from the high school at the age of thirteen He entered the Arkansas Industrial University, taking a two-year preparatory course and then entered the collegiate department, where he studied civil engineering for a year Finding himself disinclined for this profession he left college and entered the office of the Adams Express Company as billing clerk In 1891 he came to Boston and entered the Berkeley School (Chauncey Hall) where in one year he prepared for Harvard University, entering September 26, 1892 He graduated with the degree of A B in 1896 and entered the Harvard Medical School from which he was graduated in 1900 with the degree of M D In the summers of 1899 and 1900 he served in the Boston Floating Hospital for children He was house surgeon previously in the Free Hospital for Women at Brookline He came to the Worcester City Hospital as house officer September 5, 1900, and remained fourteen months

He opened an office and began to practice medicine at 662 Main street, Worcester, where he remained until July 1 1903 when he entered the South Department of the Boston City Hospital as assistant resident physician giving up his Worcester practice for the time being, in order to make a special study of children's diseases In April 1904, he went to London and Paris where he studied pediatrics, or children's diseases after which he traveled in Switzerland and Germany, returning to Worcester September 1, 1904 and resuming his practice at the old stand In July, 1905 he removed to 738 Main street, where he now resides and has his office

Dr McKibben is a member of Piedmont Congregational Church, and is at present a teacher in the Sunday school In politics he is a Republican He is a member of Quinsigamond Lodge of Free Masons, Worcester, of Quinsigamond Tribe of Red Men, of Court Cunningham Foresters of America, of the Delta Upsilon fraternity of Harvard, of the Twentieth Century Club, the Congregational Club, the Economic Club the Massachusetts Associated Boards of Health, the Boston Society of Medical Sciences, the Massachusetts Medical Society, and the Worcester Medical Society He is an honorary member of the Stationary Engineers He is a member and physician of the Junior Order of American Mechanics He received military instruction at the college in Arkansas under Colonel Fletcher, U S A

He married, September 11, 1905, Olive Beatrice Flint, daughter of Charles W and Cora (Flint) Flint, of Worcester

DANIEL WEBSTER ELLINWOOD Ralph Ellinwood (1) was the emigrant ancestor of the Ellinwood and Ellenwood families of America He sailed from England September, 1635 at the age of twenty-eight years in the ship "Truelove" He settled in Salem Massachusetts, where he was living in 1637 He was a planter He removed to the new town of Beverly nearby According to a deposition made in 1669 he was aged about sixty years He was admitted to the church March 21, 1647, and his wife was admitted August 13, 1648 He married (second) March 14 1655, Ellen Lyn He died 1673-4 His will was dated January 7, 1673, and proved August 3, 1674 He bequeathed to his wife Ellen ("Helen") and children Ralph, John, Joseph, Benjamin David, Mary and Elizabeth The widow signed her name Eleanor, which was probably the correct way of spelling it

Children of Ralph Ellinwood by the first marriage were 1 Josiah, baptized May 26, 1644, and probably others Children of Ralph and Eleanor (Lyn) Ellinwood were 2 Stephen, baptized March 16, 1656 3 Ralph, baptized April 26, 1657 4 Ralph, born March 18, 1658 John, August 2, 1659 6 Joseph, May 12, 1662 7 Mary, April 3, 1664 8 Elizabeth, born June 27, 1666 9 Sarah, baptized August 7 1666 10 Benjamin, born April 1, 1668 11 David, born July 6, 1670

(II) John Ellinwood, son of Ralph Ellinwood (1) was born in Beverly, Massachusetts, August 2, 1659 married (first) Elizabeth Rawlinson, second Sarah Morrill The widow of John Ellinwood presumably Sarah, died at Beverly, Massachusetts, 1764 at the age of ninety-eight years

Children of John and Elizabeth (Rawlinson) Ellinwood were 1 John baptized February 9, 1666 2 Joseph, probably settled at Amherst, New Hampshire, where other members of the family went 3 Dorothy 4 Elizabeth 5 David, born August 16, 1696 6 Jonathan (not on records available) Child of John and Sarah (Morrill) Ellinwood was Anna, February 6, 1704 Benjamin Ellinwood (2) also lived in Beverly and had seven or more children Ralph Ellinwood (2) had by his wife Ellen Lyn two or more children at Beverly

(III) Jonathan Ellinwood, presumed to be son of the preceding grandson of Ralph Ellinwood (1), was born in Beverly Massachusetts, about 1690 With a party from Roxbury and some from Beverly and Essex county he removed to Woodstock which was in Connecticut some of the time, and in Massachusetts at other times The Trasks and Wallis families of Beverly were neighbors of Ellinwood in Woodstock, and perhaps relatives Jonathan Ellinwood was a blacksmith by trade, although he owned considerable land and doubtless always conducted a farm He was a soldier in the Cape Breton expedition when Louisburg was captured June 17, 1745, but died or was killed in the service In the papers relating to his estate at the Probate office in Worcester is a charge by his administrator "To a journey to Worcester to settle with Colonel Willard and Captain Stearns about Cape Breton" That was in 1753 though Ellinwood died in 1745 There was on the same account another charge for "a trip to Beverly, Massachusetts to discharge two obligations given by the deceased to maintain his mother" That establishes beyond question the family to which he belonged, although it does not name his father Joannah Ellinwood, his widow, married, about 1746, Zebulon Dodge, who thus became one of the administrators of Jonathan Ellinwood s estate He then sold for forty pounds twenty acres in Woodstock to Hezekiah Goff, as directed by an order of the court John Peake, as mortgagee, joined in the deed

Jonathan Ellinwood bought, September 9, 1740, land of a company of which Robert Hale and others of Beverly were members, the property being at Woodstock He bought land there March 30, 1738, of John Kathan, and September 7, 1740, an adjoining lot of John Peake, who took a mortgage on the land, as stated above John Peake was guardian of the minor children of Jonathan Ellinwood, with Jabez Lyon as surety Peake was surety on the widow's bond with Joseph Wright

Children of Jonathan were 1 Thomas mentioned in the settlement of the estate apparently the only son of age during the father's life 2 Ephraim, born 1735, settled in Woodstock 3 Joanna, born 1739 4 Mary, born 1741

(IV) Thomas Ellinwood, son of Jonathan Ellinwood (3) was probably born in Beverly before his father came to Woodstock, about 1710 He bought land in Woodstock October 23, 1730, of Jabez Lyons of Woodstock, half of lots 82 and 83 He bought more land March 20, 1734-5, of Benjamin Childs He bought lots 86 and 87 of Ichabod Davis and William Davis of Brookline, Massachusetts, January 5 1740 and more land originally laid out to Samuel Lyon of Roxbury February 17 1742, bought of Edward Sumner, of Roxbury He sold out about 1745 and removed with a colony of Woodstock families to Brimfield, Massachusetts He sold land in the first division fourth range lots 85 86 and 87 to Jabez Lyon, who had helped settle Jonathan's estate He was not married when this deed was passed He was a joiner or carpenter by trade At Brimfield where he went in 1746 or 1747 he was a very prominent citizen He was selectman and assessor in Brimfield in 1748, when his name first appears in the town history He was selectman also in 1769 and 1775 He was also assessor in 1766-67-73-74-75-76-80-81-84

He married, probably for his second wife, Rebecca Livermore, widow of Edmund Livermore of Sturbridge Massachusetts which adjoined the old home town of the Ellinwoods in Woodstock In 1760 one of her two Livermore children was already married to Eliphalet brother of Nehemiah Allen, who was guardian of the two children, and who bought the real estate of Edmund Livermore sold by order of the court He paid one hundred and thirty-two pounds for the fifty-acre homestead at auction

Children of Thomas Ellinwood were 1 Hananiah soldier in the revolution 2 Dr Daniel (see forward) 3 Thomas Jr, born about 1760, died in

Athol in 1840, leaving sons Frederick, Thomas, and George Benjamin and relatives Austin and Benjamin who owed him money, he married Persis 4 Jonathan soldier in the revolution from Brimfield

(V) Dr Daniel Ellinwood son of Thomas Ellinwood (4), was brought up in Brimfield, Massachusetts He was born there about 1746 and educated in the schools there He studied medicine under Dr Israel Trask one of the noted physicians of his day When Dr Ellinwood looked about for a place to practice he decided on Athol, Massachusetts Dr Trask was the son of Benjamin Trask Dr Trask sold land in Athol to Dr Ellinwood March 29 1779, and Dr Ellinwood settled there He married Lucy Children were born probably in Athol, Massachusetts Dr Ellinwood died at Athol in 1794 The inventory of his estate was filed December 3, 1779 Six of his children were under age at the time of his death

Children of Dr Daniel and Lucy Ellinwood were 1 Daniel, born about 1775 2 Senaca 3 James (see forward) 4 Justus settled in Hubbardston in 1812 married Sophia McClenathan, July 14 1814, he died September 4 1844, she died September 21, 1851, they had six children Lucy married Artemis Wilder, of Petersham (intentions dated February 21) 1808 6 Abigail, married Dr Chaplin of Athol Massachusetts

(VI) James Ellinwood son of Dr Daniel Ellinwood (5) was born at Athol, Massachusetts about 1780 He is buried in Athol where he died He was a carpenter by trade and a skillful mechanic He worked at his trade in Boston for a number of years He married Rebecca Higgins of Mount Desert Maine (See sketch of M P Higgins for a sketch of her ancestors) After his marriage he removed to Athol, Massachusetts, and settled on the farm on the border of Phillipston, where he lived the rest of his days

Children of James and Rebecca (Higgins) Ellinwood were 1 Elvira 2 Cynthia 3 Horatio N 4 Eliza 5 Daniel (see forward) 6 Edwin O 7 Eucevia 8 Tilden 9 Lucy

(VII) Daniel Ellinwood, fifth child of James Ellinwood (6) was born in Athol Massachusetts, September 13 1814 He attended the district schools of his native town He was apprenticed to his brother, Captain Benjamin Twitchell, of Athol, at the mason's trade He followed his trade all his life He was known as a workman of unusual skill, and he was known far and wide for his stucco work He finally came to Worcester, where he remained for two years, working at his trade He left Worcester to go to Michigan, where he had decided to locate with his family, but returned sick after the household goods were packed for the trip He had to give up the change and settled again in Athol in 1850 Shortly afterward he bought a farm which he conducted in addition to his work as a mason He died there March 16, 1870

He was an active member of the Methodist Episcopal church and with Asa Waite and Mr Estey was one of the founders of the Trinity Methodist Church which was at first located in Park street He was for many years a member of the Second Advent Christian church at Athol He was a charter member of that organization and for many years a deacon of the church He was a man of exemplary character highly esteemed in both church and civil life He was a Republican in politics but never an office seeker He was a member of Worcester Lodge, No 56, of Odd Fellows He married October 6 1835 Dulcinia Chase, daughter of Moses and Miriam (Twitchell) Chase, of Athol Massachusetts Moses Chase was a blacksmith in Athol many years.

Children of Daniel and Dulcinia (Chase) Ellinwood were 1 Leroy Sunderland, born August 21, 1837, died April 18, 1839 2 Miriam, born January 17, 1839, married Franklin Sawtelle, of Athol, and they have two children Jennie and Albert 3 Leroy, born December 4, 1840, married Emily Homer, of Westboro, Massachusetts and they have five children Flora, Ada, Daniel, Edith, and Alphonzo 4 Sarah, born January 17, 1842, married Samuel F Parsons, of Woodstock, New Brunswick, and had four children, all deceased 5 Hannah Maria, born July 30, 1843, married Eliphas S Gage, of Worcester (See sketch) 6 Edwin, born March 29, 1845, married Clara Webster, of Athol, and they have six children Cora-Mabelle, Edwin-Clyde Daniel-Webster, Henry-Orvil, Arthur-Winired (deceased), and Eva-Gladys 7 Daniel Webster, born February 21, 1847 (mentioned below) 8 Eugene, born May 21, 1851 9 Eva Rebecca, born February 8, 1854, married Harry M Leland, of Worcester, and they have three children Ernest, Maud-Helen and Stanley

(VIII) Daniel Webster Ellinwood son of Daniel Ellinwood (7), was born in Athol Massachusetts, February 21, 1847 He received his education in the common schools of Athol up to the age of eighteen, when he came to Worcester and served an apprenticeship with A T Burgess, a mason and contractor, serving the customary three years He remained another year in the employ of Mr Burgess In 1869 he entered in business for himself, in partnership with Anthony Potter The partnership was dissolved after six months, and since then Mr Ellinwood has been in business alone His office is at his home, 10 Winslow street He has been the mason and contractor for many notable buildings Among those for which he was the mason are the Salisbury street school house, the Abbott street school house, several brick buildings on Pleasant street the Millbury street school house large business blocks for John E Day, also for G Henry Whitcomb of Worcester, and the Heywoods, of Gardner, Massachusetts

He attends the Second Advent church, Piedmont and Chandler streets, Worcester In politics he is a Republican He is a member of Damascus Lodge, Knights of Pythias of Worcester

He married, April 29, 1869, Anna Eliza Withington, daughter of Josiah Muzzy and Isabella Babcock (Smith) Withington, of Harvard, Massachusetts Her father was a farmer Their children are 1 Hattie Dulcema, born February 24, 1870, unmarried, lives with her parents 2 George Francis, born March 30, 1873, married Lois M Magoon, of Bristol, Vermont, daughter of Rev John B Magoon they reside at Thomaston, Connecticut, where Mr Ellinwood is principal of the high school, and also superintendent of the schools of the town, they have one child, Leonard Webster Ellinwood, born February 13, 1905

(VIII) Dr Eugene Ellinwood, son of Daniel Ellinwood (7), and brother of the preceding was born in Athol Massachusetts, May 29, 1851 He received his early education in the district schools of his native town At the age of seventeen he attended the New Salem Academy, where many noted Worcester county men received part of their training

He entered the dental office of Dr James Hemenway, of Athol, to learn dentistry After two years of study and experience he went to Woodstock, New Brunswick where he practiced for a year, but wishing to study further he went to Philadelphia and entered the Pennsylvania College of Dental Surgery, graduating from there in 1872 with the degree of D D S He opened an office in Clinton and resumed practice About eighteen months later he had an opportunity to buy the practice of Dr J B Walker, whose office was at the corner of Main and Elm streets, in Worcester Since buying this business Dr Ellinwood has continued in the same offices to the present time He has met with constant success in the practice of his profession He built a residence in 1876 at 14 Winslow street, and seven years later sold it to his brother, D W Ellinwood, and built his present home at 47 Piedmont street He attends the Park Congregational Church In politics he is a Republican and has frequently served his party as delegate to senatorial and other conventions He was the organizer and director of the Fraternal Aid Society that was afterwards called the Massachusetts Benefit Association He was treasurer and director of the Single Tax Club of Worcester, and organizer and assistant treasurer of the Basin Mining and Milling Company, of Portland, Maine He is a member of the Massachusetts Dental Society, formerly a member of the Connecticut Valley Dental Association up to the time it was merged into the Massachusetts Dental Society He has been a member of the Worcester County Mechanics' Association, and is a member of Quinsigamond Lodge of Odd Fellows, Worcester

He married Abbie Priest, February 3, 1876, daughter of Ira and Sarah Jane (Brocklebank) Priest, of Lancaster, Massachusetts Her father was an official of the Massachusetts state prison for many years The only child of Dr Eugene and Abbie (Priest) Ellinwood is Ralph Waldo, born Febraury 21, 1883, now a student in Harvard University

GAGE FAMILY Robert Gage (1), the progenitor of Eliphas S Gage, of Worcester was born about 1690 He lived in Weston, formerly Watertown, Massachusetts, where his children were born His widow Mary died in Lincoln, Massachusetts, March 14, 1777, at an advanced age Their children 1 Robert, Jr, born April 14, 1720, married, April 3, 1747, Susanna Smith, of Waltham 2 Isaac, born September 26, 1721, estate administered November 8, 1751 3 Philip, born August 11, 1723, married March 7, 1744-45, Anne Priest, settled in Sturbridge, Massachusetts 4 Rachel, born July 23, 1725, admitted in full communion in the Watertown church, December, 1742, died January 19, 1746 5 Jonathan, mentioned below 6 Lydia 7 Alice, born 1732

(II) Jonathan Gage, son of Robert Gage (1), was born probably in Weston, 1725 He married Ruth Underwood (published April 4, 1752) They had a son, Jonathan, born in Lincoln, Massachusetts, October 6, 1755, mentioned below

(III) Jonathan Gage, son of Jonathan Gage (2), was born in Lincoln Massachusetts, October 6, 1755 He was a soldier in the revolution, taking active part in the fighting April 19, 1775, a private in Captain William Smith's company of Minute Men, Colonel Abijah Pierce's regiment, corporal later in 1775 in Captain Nathan Fuller's company, Lieutenant-Colonel William Bond's (Thirty-seventh) regiment He was a corporal in the Continental army for three years—1777 to 1780—in Captain Abijah Child's company, Colonel John Greaton s regiment He lived during the revolution in Lincoln and Weston, but removed later to Berlin He bought land at Leicester, while a resident of Berlin, of John Brigham, of Northboro, April 30, 1785 He settled finally on the old Dr Parsons place in the northwest part of Leicester on the road leading to Zolva Green's The old house has long since been torn down He married Mary Brigham Their children, born in Leicester, were 1 Levi, born August 9, 1786, see forward 2 Silas, born April 13, 1788 3 Mary (Polly), born April 15, 1790 4 Brigham, born November 17, 1793

(IV) Levi Gage, son of Jonathan Gage (3), was born in Leicester, Massachusetts, August 9, 1786 He was a farmer by occupation He married Nancy Barnes Children Levi, Anson, mentioned below, Marian Brigham, Silas, Willard Hervey and Nancy, all deceased but Hervey and Nancy Levi Gage taught school in his younger days, as did his wife, Nancy Barnes

(V) Anson Gage, son of Levi Gage (4), was born August 25, 1815 He married Rhoda Fidelia Chapin in November, 1840 He died September, 1889 The mother died December 10, 1891, in Worcester at the home of our subject, both are buried at Northfield, Massachusetts Among their children was Eliphas S, mentioned below Isabelle Ellen died an infant Edward A born February 8, 1843, and died in 1857 Elliot Chapin born July 3, 1847, resides in Worcester Anson Gage, the father, was in politics a Republican and prominent in the Advent church

(VI) Eliphas Samuel Gage son of Anson Gage (5), was born in Northfield, Massachusetts, September 15, 1841 He was educated in the public schools of his native town When a young man he was employed for some two years in piano manufactories at Montague and Irving, Massachusetts He came to Worcester in 1866 where he learned the trade of paper hanging and followed it until his health failed him and he took up the real estate business which he has since followed In politics is a Republican, being on the Republican Central Committee some five years, was justice of the peace in Worcester over twenty-one years, is a member of the Advent Christian church belongs to A F & A M, Royal Arch Chapter, Hiram Council

He married, April 11, 1865, Hannah Maria Ellinwood, daughter of Daniel and Dulcinia (Chase) Ellinwood Their children are 1 Minnie Isabel, born September 24 1866 graduate of the Worcester schools and the Worcester State Normal school in 1888 she taught one year in Spencer public schools and has since except for two years in mission work in the south taught in the Worcester schools being at present a teacher in the Salisbury street school, member of the Advent Christian church of Worcester, and for several years a member of the Woman s Mission board of the Advent Christian denomination, taking a very active part and spending two years in the south, as before mentioned 2 Edward Anson, born June 4, 1869 graduate of the Worcester high school and of the Worcester Polytechnic Institute, class of 1893, now assistant inspector of ordnance in the United States navy, stationed at Quincy Massachusetts, married, June 15 1896 Edith Newton, children—Donald Newton and Sydney Vernon 3 Frederick Eugene, born July 22, 1873, educated in the public and high schools of Worcester and an Indiana Business College, now assistant foreman of the operating department of the American Steel and Wire Company Worcester member of Plymouth Congregational church, married Mary L Frisbie, child Marjorie Chase 4 Arthur Chase born May 23 1880, educated in the Worcester public and high schools, now traveling salesman for the Plunger Elevator Company of Worcester, unmarried

DR CHARLES CLINTON SCOTT William Scott (1), of Hatfield in New England, was probably the son of Benjamin Scott, the immigrant, of New Braintree Benjamin and Hannah Scott were inhabitants of Braintree in 1643 Their children were Hannah married Christopher Webb, February 18, 1654-55, John, born December 25 1640, Peter, born March 6, 1643, Benjamin, died 1683 Benjamin Scott's widow Hannah married, September 21, 1647, John Harbor

William Scott married January 28, 1670, Hannah Ellis (or Allis), of Braintree, the daughter of William Ellis, who settled in Braintree in 1639 was admitted a freeman May 18, 1640, was a deacon of the church, removed to Hadley, then to Hatfield, was lieutenant, assistant of the court in 1676, died September, 1678 Very little is known of William Scott His children were Josiah, see forward, Richard, born February 22, 1673, William, November 24, 1676, Hannah, August 11, 1679, Joseph, March 21, 1682, John, July 6, 1684, died February 8, 1692, Mary, 1686, Mehitable, September 9, 1687, died September 18, 1687, Jonathan, November 1, 1688, died young, Abigail, November 28, 1689

(II) Josiah Scott, eldest child of William Scott (1), was born in Hatfield He was one of the proprietors of Bernardston, Massachusetts He married Sarah Berrett Their children Josiah, born November 29, 1699, settled in Whately, Sarah, September 9, 1701, Hannah, May 30, 1704, Benjamin, May 31, 1708, married Jemima ——, and settled in Whately, died 1792, Mehitable, May 4, 1711, Moses, see forward, Ruth, November 25, 1715

(III) Moses Scott, sixth child of Josiah Scott (2), was born in Hatfield, Massachusetts, February 3, 1713 He settled on his father's grant of land in Bernardston, and as these grants were to the men engaged in the fall fight in King Philip's war in May, 1676, William Scott (1) was undoubtedly one of the soldiers Moses Scott was a selectman in 1761 He built a bridge near his saw mill in 1760 Moses Scott was captured with Sergeant Hawks, August 20, 1746, with his wife and two sons, one of whom died in captivity He returned from Canada and served again in the last French war with Captain Clesson He died at Bernardston, July 23, 1799 aged eighty-six years He married, August 24, 1742, Miriam Nash, daughter of Ebenezer Nash, of Hadley Their children Ebenezer, born 1743, was the first white male born in Bernardston, see forward, Moses, Jr, born 1745 died in Canada, February 11, 1747

(IV) Ebenezer Scott, elder son of Moses Scott (3), was born in Bernardston, the first male child of white parents, in 1743 When two or three years old, he was captured by the Indians and taken to Canada, where he was sold to the French He returned to Bernardston with his father He served in the revolutionary war and drew a pension late in life He removed to the adjoining town of Vernon, Vermont where he died in 1826 The names of his children have not been secured, some of them were Eleazer, born 1788, married Sarah Strickland, of Gill, settled in Vernon, Robert, see forward, Lemuel, settled in Fletcher, an adjacent town

(V) Robert Scott, son of Ebenezer Scott (4), was born probably in Bernardston Massachusetts, or a town in that vicinity in Massachusetts or southern Vermont, in 1763-64 He died in Bakersfield, Vermont in 1833, aged sixty-nine years He was brought up in Vernon Vermont He lived for a time after his marriage in various towns in the vicinity He settled first in Townshend He removed to Bakersfield, an adjoining town, in 1804, and his descendants are living there at present He was the first of the name in that town He had a farm but his regular occupation was carrying the freight from Bakersfield to Boston and return

He married Hannah Hesseltine, about 1690 Her sister, Judith Hesseltine, married, 1782, Ebenezer Brigham, who was born March 3, 1761, in Sutton, Massachusetts The mother of Hannah Hesseltine married (second) Silas Whitney

One of Robert Scott's children was named for Ebenezer Brigham Both Robert and his wife are buried in the Bakersfield cemetery Children of Robert and Hannah (Hesseltine) Scott were Thomas Woodburn, born about 1792, in Townshend, married Jerusha Shattuck, their son, Hamblet H Scott, inherited the homestead and still lives on the original farm of Robert Scott, Nancy, born about 1794, married Solomon Hull, is buried at North Fairfield, Vermont, Russell, died at the age of twenty-six years and is buried at North Fairfield, Ebenezer Brigham, see forward, Nahum, removed to Palmyra, New York

(VI) Ebenezer Brigham Scott, generally called Brigham son of Robert Scott (5) was born in Townshend, Vermont, 1797 He removed with his parents to Bakersfield in 1804 and went to school there The opportunities in those new towns in Vermont for good schools were not favorable He was a soldier from Bakersfield in the war of 1812 Though he was under age at the time of his enlistment he was of unusual size and was accepted He removed to Oakham, Massachusetts, in 1832, and worked for a traveling merchant Later in life he settled in Spencer and conducted a farm He died in Spencer in 1860

He married (first), 1815, Caroline Potter, whose ancestry is given herewith They were divorced and she married (second) Levi Janes, of Bakersfield, and had three children Marther Baker, Charles Wesley and Caroline Potter Janes E Brigham Scott also married (second), April 28, 1838, at Oakham, Ann Thompson, of Spencer, Massachusetts Children of Ebenezer Brigham and Caroline (Potter) Scott were Whitney, born January 14, 1816, died 1830, Ebenezer Woodburn, see forward, Nancy Caroline, born January 22, 1821, married (first), July 7, 1844, Josiah Lyon, son of Aaron and Betsey Lyon, he was born 1817 and died 1863, she married (second) Willard Howe, son of Aaron and Elizabeth Howe, he was born 1815 and died 1888, she married (third) —— Rowell, they lived in Paxton, Mrs Rowell is living with her daughter, Mrs Partridge, (1906) at 423 Pleasant street, Worcester Luke Cullin, born July 4 1824 married, November, 1846, Lizzie Ball Joseph Barker, born November 27, 1826, married, January, 1856, Amanda E Young, born 1838, daughter of Francis and Sarah Young, he was a soldier in the Mexican war and never came north afterward, but settled at Dade, Bastrop county, Texas, where he was living in 1903

(VII) Ebenezer Woodburn Scott son of Ebenezer Brigham Scott (6), was born in Bakersfield, Vermont, January 20, 1818 in the log cabin on his father's farm The opportunities for education were scarce The Bakersfield school at that time was in a log house and school was kept but a few weeks each year When he was fourteen years old his mother died and his father decided to come to Massachusetts They traveled on foot nearly two hundred miles to Oakham, where his father and he both were employed by a traveling merchant He was paid $7 per month and his father $15 per month, and he used to say that the wandering life was rather pleasant After three years he went to work in the slaughter house of John Corey at

Watertown, and in the course of four years had become an important factor in the business He and Mr Corey's son were partners in a livery stable business for a time In 1852 Mr Scott came to Rutland with his six children and settled on the Charles Spooner farm on the Paxton road, where he lived for twenty-three years In June, 1877, he removed to his late home, the former parsonage of the Congregational church In politics he was a Democrat He was a highway surveyor and member of the school committee He cast his first vote for Van Buren in 1840 and voted the Democratic ticket until 1896, when he was against the free silver Democratic candidates He attended the Congregational church In his younger days he belonged to an artillery company and to a fire engine company He died July 27, 1902, at the age of eighty-four years

He married Sarepta White, of Sturbridge, who died October 4, 1888 Their children Mary, married C B Linton, of Brooklyn, New York, and has three sons, Caroline, married H J Davis, of Rutland, and has six children, Ebenezer Woodburn, Jr resides in Philadelphia, Pennsylvania, a milk dealer, was in the Forty-second Massachusetts Regiment in the civil war, Elizabeth A, married the late Denny E Mason, she resides in Rutland, Charles Potter, born in Watertown, Massachusetts, July 24, 1849, a farmer of Holden, has a son Harry and daughter, Della, Etta, married Warren W Bryant and they have two sons and a daughter, their home is in Princeton, Massachusetts, Clinton Brigham, see forward, Adelia Maria, died when fourteen years old

(VIII) Clinton Brigham Scott, seventh child of Ebenezer Woodburn Scott (7), was born in Rutland Massachusetts, and when a young boy was brought up on a farm there He went to the Rutland schools Soon after he was married he removed to Worcester and worked for several years in the meat market of Aaron Hammond, on Main street He worked later in Prentice's market, Southbridge street, and Ring's market at the corner of Coral and Grafton streets He went into business for himself in 1889 at 42 Chandler street and met with gratifying success His market became one of the largest in the city at that time He retired from business in 1895 and went to live on the homestead in Rutland Mr Scott is a member of Quinsigamond Lodge of Odd Fellows and of Worcester Lodge, Ancient Order of United Workmen In politics he is a Democrat

He married, at Paxton, Clara A Marsh, daughter of Luther and Augusta Marsh She died December 25, 1890, in Worcester Their children Charles Clinton, see forward, Clarence Nelson, born in Worcester, February 4, 1887, student of dentistry in his brother's office, Edith Clara, born in Worcester, December 18, 1890, lives with her father at Rutland

(IX) Charles Clinton Scott, eldest child of Clinton Brigham Scott (8), was born in Paxton, June 28, 1878 His parents moved to Worcester with him when he was eighteen months old He attended the public schools of Worcester, leaving the high school at the end of his second year He entered the dental offices of Dr F H Kendrick, where he remained for six months In 1895 he entered the Dental School of the University of Pennsylvania at Philadelphia He won his degree at the end of his first year by crowding three years work into one In the summer of 1896, after graduating, he entered the office of Dr W H Sears, Worcester, where he practiced for three years From 1899 to the fall of 1904 he was associated with Dr H H Gabler, of Worcester Since then he has been practicing at 578 Main street, where he has elaborately appointed offices and employs an operator and assistant He is a member of Anchoria Lodge of Odd Fellows, of the Massachusetts Dental Society and has been a member of the Hancock Club He is a Republican and attends Piedmont Congregational church He married, June 14, 1905, Bessie Bonker, daughter of Harry L and Caroline (Haring) Bonker, of Worcester Her father is at present an inspector of locomotives for the New York Central & Hudson River Railroad and lives in Worcester

(I) Nicholas Potter was the pioneer ancestor of Dr Charles C Scott, through Caroline Scott, who married Brigham Scott, mentioned above He was a settler in Lynn as early as 1638, a bricklayer by trade He married (first) Eunice ——— He married (second) Alice Weeks and (third) Mary Gedney, daughter of John Gedney His children Mary, born and died 1659, Hannah, baptized March 25, 1661, Sarah, born October 4, 1662, Mary, born November 10, 1663, Samuel, baptized March 10, 1664-66, died March 10 1664--66, Hannah, baptized April 8, 1666, Lydia, baptized February 10, 1666-67, died 1668, Bethiah, baptized July 12, 1668, Samuel, baptized April 25, 1669, Lydia, baptized July 17, 1670, Robert, Elizabeth Benjamin

(II) Robert Potter, son of Nicholas Potter (1), was born in Lynn, New England, married Ruth Driver and lived in Lynn

(III) Robert Potter, son of Robert Patter (2), was born March 18 1661, married, January 9, 1682, Martha Hale and they lived in Lynn

(IV) Ephraim Potter, son of Robert Potter (3), was born in Lynn, Massachusetts, February 5, 1683, and settled in Marlboro, Massachusetts He married, November 23, 1708, Sarah Witt and their children all born in Marlboro, were Mary, September 11, 1709, Martha, September 1, 1711, Joseph, February 3, 1713, Persis, August 29, 1715; Ephraim, March 5, 1718, Sarah, January 26, 1721; Theophilus, see forward, Elizabeth, January 25, 1728

(V) Theophilus Potter, seventh child of Ephraim Potter (4), was born January 26, 1725, and settled in Brookfield, Massachusetts, where he died September 13, 1814 He married in 1748 Lois Walker, of Sudbury Of their children, the first four were born in Marlboro, the other eight in North Brookfield Their children Silas, born June 17, 1749, Barnabas, June 15, 1751, Ephraim, July 31, 1752, Hannah, December 17, 1755, Thomas, November 16, 1757, Abijah January 23, 1760, Lois, January 30, 1762, married Thomas Knight, Thaddeus, May 18, 1764, Esther, January 15, 1767, Elizabeth, July 17 1770, died young, Luke, see forward, Aaron, March 29, 1776

(VI) Luke Potter, eleventh child of Theophilus Potter (5), was born in North Brookfield, April 28, 1772 and died October 19, 1812 He married Lydia Baker the daughter of Joseph Baker, the first settler and proprietor of Bakersfield Vermont, for whom that town was named She died in North Brookfield, January 28 1810 Their children: Lydia, born 1794, died at Palmer in 1813, Nancy, born July 26 1796 Roswell, born 1798, died at Stockholm New York, Caroline, see forward, Luke, born 1802, died in Canada about 1878, married Elvira Page of Waterville, New York

(VII) Caroline Potter, fourth child of Luke Potter (6), was born in North Brookfield, 1800 She died at Bakersfield Vermont She married Ebenezer Brigham Scott, mentioned above

HORACE WYMAN. The name of Wyman is beyond doubt of Saxon origin, and in common with family names of the earliest period, appears in various different forms, as Wyman, Wiman, Wymant, Wymond, Wimond, etc. It is estimated that there are now in the United States about eight thousand persons who appear under one or another form of the name.

It was discovered by Henry F. Waters, A. M., of London, in the record of a will made by Francis Wyman, farmer, of the parish of West Mill, county of Herts (Hertfordshire), England, that he was the father of Francis and John Wyman, the emigrant ancestors of the American branch of the family. The family estate in England was inherited by their elder brother Thomas. The names of John and Francis Wyman first appear in Woburn, Massachusetts, in 1640, as signers of town orders. They had farm houses near the town site of Woburn; that of John was demolished many years ago, but that built by Francis, in 1664, is yet standing. It was used for defensive purposes during King Philip's war, and the loop-holes for the rifles of its defenders are still visible. It is now owned by the "Wyman Associates," and the descendants of the family have an annual re-union there. The brothers also owned houses in the village, opposite the park, at the junction of Main and Wyman streets. Their tannery was located nearby, and the vats yet exist, but are buried beneath several feet of earth. The ancient gravestone of Francis Wyman is still plainly discernable, but its inscription is wellnigh obliterated:

"Here lies ye bdy of Francis Wyman, aged about 82 years, died Nov. 28, 1699. The memory of ye just is blessed."

The line of descent of the Horace Wyman family of Worcester, is as follows:

(I) John Wyman, born in West Mill, Herts county, England, in 1621, emigrated to this country in 1640, and was one of the first settlers of the town of Woburn, Massachusetts. He married Sarah Nutt, in 1644. He was a man of enterprise and marked independence. He, with others, was prosecuted before the courts in December, 1671, some "for publicly manifesting contempt for the ordinance of infant baptism as administered in the church of Woburn," others for withdrawing from the worship of that church. Some of those prosecuted received public admonition, and others were fined. That he bore a prominent part in the Indian difficulties is established by documentary evidence.

(1) Sewell's "History of Woburn" says of the fifty-eight persons enlisted from that place in 1675 in King Philip's war, that one of the number, Simpson, was apparently a Scotchman, one of those who, for espousing the cause of Charles II was sent over to this country by Cromwell after he had defeated them at the battle at Dunbar, 1650, or of Worcester, 1651, to be sold, and being a tanner by trade, was bought by Lieutenant John Wyman, tanner, of Woburn, "on purpose for the management of his tanyard." (By "sale" is meant indenture for a term, in payment of the ship passage of Simpson.—Ed.). "Mr. Wyman, his master, (having had his son slain in the fight at Narragansett) petitioned the general court May 16, 1676, that his servant Simpson might be returned," etc. This document is contained in the papers of the Massachusetts Historical Society, and is as follows:

To the Honorable Govers: ye Council now Sitting in Boston

The Petition of John Wyman

Humbly Sheweth that yore Petitioner Hath beene often out in the service of ye Country against the Indians: his sone also was out and slaine by the enemy: and his servants hath beene long out in the warrs and now being reduced to greate wants for clotheing: desires liberty to come downe from Hadly where he now remains a garrison souldier: and he is a taner by traid and yore Petitioner bought him on purpose for that management of his tan yard: and himselfe being unexperienced in that calling doth humbly request that favore of your honors to consider the premisses and to grant his said servant Robert Simpson a dismission from this present service that so his lether now in the fatts may not be spoyled but yore Petitioner be ever engaged to pray &c. Jno. Wyman.

THE WYMAN HOMESTEAD
Birthplace of Horace Wyman

(II) Jonathan Wyman, son of John (1), born 1661, married Hannah Fowle, 1690.

(III) Jonathan Wyman, son of Jonathan (2), born 1704, married Martha Thompson. He served in the war of the revolution.

(IV) Jonathan Wyman, son of Jonathan (3), born 1734, married Abigail Wright.

(V) Jonathan Wyman, son of Jonathan (4), born 1763, married Ruby Richardson. Their children were: Jonathan, born 1787; Abel, 1793; Abigail, 1795; Sylvester, Joseph, Stephen, Ray, Ruby, and Ipps.

(VI) Abel Wyman, second son and child of Jonathan (5) and Ruby (Richardson) Wyman, was born in 1793, and died in 1864. He was a boot and shoe manufacturer, and was noted for his integrity, tact and sagacity in business relations, and was of strong moral character. He married Maria Wade, in 1817. Their children were: Charles Austin, born 1817; Ward, 1819; Winthrop, 1821; Nancy Maria, 1823; Horace, 1827.

Maria (Wade) Wyman was the

Horace Wyman

daughter of Ebenezer (5) and Leah Wade whose other children were Nancy and Harriet Her ancestry is traced back as follows

(I) Jonathan Wade a native of England, emigrated to America from Denver, near Donnham Market Norfolk county, in 1632 in the ship "Lion" He first settled in Ipswich Massachusetts and afterwards removed to Medford and was elected the first town clerk there in 1674 He was a prominent person in the town and the largest owner of land there and paid the highest tax for many years He gave a public landing place for boats and shipping on the Mystic river upon which the town is situated

(II) Major Nathaniel Wade, son of Jonathan (1) married Mercy Bradstreet, daughter of Governor Simon and Anne Bradstreet, and granddaughter of Governor Thomas Bradley (2)

Governor Bradstreet made an affidavit relative to this marriage, which is curious for its quaint phrasing as well as for the subject matter It is quoted as follows from "Genealogy of the Dudley Family" vol II, pp 1031-1033

When Mr Jonathan Wade of Ipswich came first to my house att Andvar | yeare—72—to make a motion of marriage betwixt his son Nathaniel and | my daughter Mercy hee freely of himself told me what he would | give to his son viz one halfe of his ffarme att Mistic and one third pt of his | land in England when he Dyed and that he should have liberty to make | use of pt of impved and broken upp ground upon the sd ffarme till | hee could gett some broken upp for him selfe upon his own pt and like wise | that hee should live in and have the use of halfe the house &c till he had one | of his owne blt upon his part of the ffarme I was willing to accept of his | offer or at least sd nothing against it but ppounded that hee would make his sd son a deede of guift of that third pt of his land in England to enjoy to | him and his heired after his death—this he was not free to do but sd it was | as sure for he had soe putt it into his will that his 3 sons should have | that in England equally devyded betwixt them vz each a pt I objected | hee might alter his will when hee pleased & his wife might dye & hee marry | again and have othr children wch hee thought a vaine obiecon much othr discourse there was about the stock on the ffarme &c but remayning unwilling | to give a deed for that in England saying hee might have to spend it and often | repeating hee had soe ordered it in his will as aforesd wch hee should never alter without | great necessity or words to that purpos so wee pted for that time leaving | that matter to further considracon | after hee came home hee told sevall of my | ffriends and others they informed me that he had pfferd them 1000 L and I would not accept of it the next tyme he came to my howse after some | discourse about the premsis and pceiveing his resolucon as formly I consented | to accept of wt hee had formly ingaged and left it to him to ad wt he pleased | towards the building of him a howse &c and soe agreed that the young psons | might pceede in marriage with both o consent wch accordingly they did

S BRADSTREET

The Hon ble Simon Bradstreet Esq r | made oath to the truth of the above written | (Sept 21, 1683) | before SAMLL NOWELL, ASSISTT |

(III) Captain Samuel Wade, son of Nathaniel (2)

(IV) Nathaniel Wade, son of Samuel (3)

(V) Ebenezer Wade son of Nathaniel (4)

(VI) Ebenezer Wade, son of Ebenezer (5) He served in the French and Indian war, and also the revolutionary war

(VII) Maria Wade, daughter of Ebenezer (6), married Abel Wyman

Horace Wyman youngest child of Abel and Maria (Wade) Wyman, was born in Woburn November 27, 1827 He was educated at the Woburn and Francestown (New Hampshire) Academies He commenced his business career in 1846 as machinist in the Amoskeag Manufacturing Company in New Hampshire and afterwards in the Lowell Machine Shop and in the Hinckley Locomotive Works in Boston He then entered into the employ of the Holyoke Water Power Company as a draughtsman, and in 1860 became associated with George Crompton, of Worcester, as superintendent and manager of his Loom Works He is noted for his mechanical ability and inventive genius particularly in the line of loom and factory machinery

The records of the United States Patent Office disclose the fact that he has taken out over one hundred and fifty patents the great majority of them relating to textile machinery, many of his machines being in use in the principal mills throughout the country with the result of improved goods, in greater quantities in a given time, and at a reduced cost of production From time to time he has been associated with others, but the principal machines with which his name is connected were altogether conceived in his own brain and wrought out by his own masterly mechanical skill The Crompton Loom Works of Worcester owed much of their success to improvements of his designing and introduction When George Crompton died in 1886, the business was reorganized by incorporation, with Mr Wyman as vice-president and manager, and when that corporation was merged into the Crompton and Knowles Loom Works in 1897 he became its consulting mechanical engineer

While Mr Wyman has been thus busily engaged along lines which seemingly would tax the ability of one man to the utmost, he has at the same time been actively interested in various other enterprises entering into the commercial and financial life of the city, serving as president of the Worcester Storage Company a director in the Quinsigamond Bank the People's Savings Bank and the Uxbridge & Blackstone Street Railway Company He has also served as a member of the board of aldermen He is an active member of the American Society of Mechanical Engineers the Worcester County Mechanics' Association the Worcester Society of Antiquity and of the board of managers of the Old Men's Home He is also affiliated with local bodies of the Masonic fraternity In politics he is a Republican and his religious connection is with the Unitarian faith Of studious habits and cultivated tastes he has read and traveled much He is familiarly acquainted with nearly all regions of the United States and he has several times visited Europe at times on business, and again solely for recreation and mental improvement He has made much careful study of genealogical subjects and has published two works involving a great amount of careful and patient research The Wyman Families of Great and Little Hormead Herts county England " 1895 and "Some Account of the Wyman Genealogy and Wyman Families in Herts county England " 1897

In 1869 Mr Wyman married Louisa B Horton of Orleans Massachusetts who died in 1894 She was of English extraction a daughter of Sparrow and Betsey (Deane) Horton, and a descendant of John Doane who was born in 1590 He arrived at Plymouth Massachusetts in 1630 and was assistant to Governor Thomas Prince in 1633 Of this marriage were born four children

(I) Horace Winfield Wyman, born May 30, 1861, died October 11 1905 He was educated in Worcester—in the public schools the Worcester Academy, and the Polytechnic Institute In 1883 at the age of twenty-two, he formed a partnership with Lyman F Gordon, a classmate at all the above named schools, and engaged in the manufacture of iron and steel drop forgings an industry then in its comparative infancy This business they built up and developed, until it has become one of the foremost in the world its product reaching all parts of the United States and every foreign market open to American commerce Mr Wyman possessed in marked degree the mechanical taste and ability, as well as the inventive genius which characterize his father and much of the efficiency and success of the great works with which he was identified, was due to his mechanical ability joined to a keen business judgment He was treasurer of the Worcester Storage Company a trustee of the Worcester County Institute for Savings and has been twice president of the Alumni Association of the Polytechnic Institute He was a member of the International Iron and Steel Institute, the American Society of Mechanical Engineers and of prominent clubs in Boston, New York and Cleveland as well as of Worcester In politics he was a Republican but he never aspired to public office In 1889 he married Mary Wills Haskill of Atchison Kansas, and their children are Aurelia, Horace and Louise

(II) Maria Louise born in 1864

(III) Josie Horton born in 1867 died in 1868

(IV) Adelaide Richards, born 1870 married in 1898 Ernest Wood of the firm of C G Wood & Company woolen manufacturers of Worcester

THOMAS ARMIT PELLETT Thomas Pellett (1) the immigrant ancestor of Thomas Armit Pellett, of Worcester settled in Concord Massachusetts where he married, March 5, 1660 Mary Dane or Deane of Concord He was a farmer Their children, all born in Concord were Mary born August 27, 1662 Thomas born April 18 1666 Daniel born August 1, 1668 Samuel, born March 28 1671 Richard, mentioned below John, born November 9 1675, Elizabeth, born April 8 1679 Jonathan born April 18, 1682 Sarah born September 5 1685 Susanna born January 18 1690

(II) Richard Pellett, eighth child of Thomas Pellett (1), was born in Concord, Massachusetts April 23 1673 He settled at Canterbury Connecticut and died there June 15, 1758 He married, April 2, 1703 Ann Brooks of Canterbury She died October 25, 1756 Their children all born in Canterbury were Jonathan mentioned below Thomas born September 9, 1706 married March 18, 1730, Martha Tibbets Samuel born March 7, 1709 married (first) Margaret —— who died February 28 1748 (second) July 1752 Hannah Underwood Hezekiah born April 28, 1712 married March 5 1738 Abigail Brown John born April 4 1715, Ephraim born June 21 1718 married Hannah ——, Patience and Ann (twins) born August 8 1721

(III) Jonathan Pellett, eldest child of Richard Pellett (2) was born in Canterbury Connecticut, March 2 1704 married February 20 1733 Jerusha Bradford who died June 15 1788 She was a direct descendant of Elder William Bradford who came in the Mayflower to Plymouth in 1620 The line is through William Bradford (1) who married (first) Alice Richards (second) Widow Wiswell (third) Widow Mary Holmes Thomas Bradford (II) son of William Bradford (I), settled in Norwich, Connecticut, married (first) Anna Fitch, daughter of Rev James Fitch, married (second) Priscilla Mason, daughter of Major John Mason, the hero of the Pequot war James Bradford (III), son of Thomas Bradford (II), was the father of Jerusha Bradford born June 27 1716 Her sister Mary married William Pellett The children of Jonathan and Jerusha (Bradford) Pellett were all born in Canterbury viz Jonathan born June 20, 1734, died young, Edith, born March 25, 1735, died young, James born February 9, 1737, died young, Jonathan, born October 19, 1739 died young Thomas born November 20, 1742 Jerusha born June 6 1744, Joseph, born March 18 1748 David born February 21, 1750, *Jonathan born July 12, 1753*, *Hepzibah*, born February 25, 1757 Rufus mentioned below

(IV) Rufus Pellett, youngest child of Jonathan Pellett (3), was born at Canterbury, May 25 1760 He also was a farmer at Canterbury, where he died in 1806 He married Drusilla Wheeler Their children all born at Canterbury were Rufus born November 4 1781 John born July 4 1783, graduate of Harvard College (M D) died at Salem, Massachusetts 1809 Eunice born October 26 1784 married Joseph Graves of Canterbury Esther born December 9 1786 Jonathan died young Timothy, born May 4 1791 Jonathan born August 17 1792; Archibald died young Chester, mentioned below, Maria born April 22 1800 resided in Canterbury to advanced age Marian born March 25 1803, married Aaron Stearns, of North Brookfield removed to Whitely Heman born September 1805 died young

(V) Chester Pellett ninth child of Rufus Pellett (4) was born in Canterbury Connecticut May, 1797 He was raised in his native town but removed to Wales Massachusetts Among his children was the father of Thomas Armit Pellett John C Pellett

(V) John C Pellett son of Chester Pellett (5) was *born in Canterbury Connecticut* He resided at North Brookfield and Wales Massachusetts He married January 28, 1849, Sarah Harwood who was born June 15 1820, the daughter of Thomas Armit Harwood

John C Pellett was a railroad man a section boss on the New London & Northern Railroad and later on the Vermont Central Railroad He served two years in the civil war He was color sergeant of the Eleventh Vermont Regiment and he lost his right arm in a skirmish during the campaign in the Shenandoah Valley He died at Brattleboro Vermont in 1897 The children of John C and Sarah (Harwood)) Pellett were 1 Mary, married Andrew Thomas, of Claremont, New Hampshire, and they have a son Leon Andrew, and a daughter Genevieve Louise, both born in Brattleboro, Vermont 2 John C Jr married Grace Doubleday of Binghamton New York married (second) Lizette Winslow resides at 6 Jaques avenue Worcester, is a mason and contractor, at present engaged in Brattleboro Vermont He has three children by the first wife Charles Arnold, Louise, John 3 Thomas A, mentioned below

Thomas Armit Harwood son of Captain Peter Harwood was born in Spencer, Massachusetts, February 6 1789 married (first), May 24, 1818, Hannah Palmer Pellett of North Brookfield, who died September 1, 1830, married (second), June 15 1831, Ann Mead of North Brookfield who died August 30 1870 aged eighty years he died April 4 1880 aged ninety-one years He was a soldier in the war of 1812 They had a large family of children Thomas Armit Harwood Jr was in the British service had a very adventurous life all over the world, in 1879 was living in India under the name of Francis Hudson

Peter Harwood, grandfather of Mrs John C Pellett, was the son of Major Peter Harwood, born in North Brookfield, September 16, 1765 He was a tavern keeper and farmer He served three years in the revolutionary army with his father who was captain of the North Brookfield company He succeeded Captain Aaron Forbes as captain of the company and was himself succeeded by his brother, Captain Abel Harwood He was selectman and assessor He married, in Dover, New Hampshire, about 1788, Elizabeth Armit, who was born in Scotland (North Brookfield history says London, England) and came to America when she was three years old Captain Peter died in Spencer, April 17, 1836 Their eldest child was Thomas Armit Harwood, mentioned above

Major Peter Harwood, great-grandfather of Mrs John C Pellett, son of Ebenezer Harwood, was born in Littleton, Massachusetts, May 10, 1740 He was a millwright and farmer He married, May 26, 1763, Phebe Prouty, of Spencer, who was born August 3, 1744, died February 13, 1811, he died in Delaware, January 14, 1805 He was an officer in the revolutionary army—brave, daring and impetuous He was court-martialled for disobedience of orders to abandon and destroy a bridge at White Plains, then being held by the American army, in attempting to hold it he was captured, the result of the court-martial was in his favor and he retained his rank and was further promoted After the war he built a brick house, the most expensive one in town He had nine children

Ebenezer Harwood father of Major Peter Harwood and son of Peter Harwood, was born in Concord, Massachusetts, February 22, 1714 He married Dorothy Hubbard, who died in Brookfield August 15, 1809 He removed from Concord to Littleton in 1737 with his father and brother Joseph, and thence to North Brookfield in 1743-4 In April, 1745, he joined the secret expedition against Louisburg in Captain Olmstead's company under Sir William Pepperell and was killed during the siege June 17, 1745 His widow drew his prize money at Boston, February 15 1748 She married (second) at Worcester, July 5, 1750, Nathaniel Bartlett, of North Brookfield

Peter Harwood, father of Ebenezer Harwood and son of Nathaniel Harwood, was born in Concord, Massachusetts, January 12, 1671 He married, November 7, 1700 Mary Fox, of Concord, and died at Littleton in 1740 He had seven children

Nathaniel Harwood, the immigrant ancestor of Mrs John C Pellett and her descendants, father of Peter Harwood, was first in Boston, then in Concord between 1665 and 1667 In 1665 he signed a declaration of non-freemen of Boston as to their satisfaction with the government He married Elizabeth ——, who died April 25, 1715 He died February 7, 1716

(VII) Thomas Armit Pellett, son of John C Pellett (6), was born in Wales, Massachusetts, May 19, 1850 He attended the public schools in Brattleboro, Vermont, whither his parents moved when he was only four years old He learned the mason's trade in Brattleboro In 1874 the contractor for the Worcester Insane Hospital at Bloomingdale, Worcester, J D Plummer sub-let the contract for the brick work to Mr Pellett This contract took three years during the warm months and took thirteen million bricks Mr Pellett next superintended the building of the Mount Hermon Boys' School at Gill, Massachusetts, for Rev Dwight L Moody, for about a year and a half In partnership with Mr Plummer, under the firm name of Pellett & Plummer, his firm built a school house at Saxtons river and a paper mill in Bellows Falls, the Amherst hat shop and two stores at Amherst In partnership with his brother, John C Pellett, under the name of Pellett Brothers, he built the high school building in Brattleboro, Vermont, the Canal street school house, the Hooker block, the railroad station and the engine house, all at Brattleboro In company with J M Boswell he built an addition to the Worcester Insane Hospital, comprising two large wings This firm also executed important contracts at the gas works, Worcester, and built Lamb's block on Front street

Again he went into partnership with his brother as T A and J C Pellett This firm had the contract for the tower on St Paul's Church In 1903 the firm was dissolved, J C having important contracts in Brattleboro, Vermont, where he has been working since then, while Thomas A Pellett has remained in business in Worcester under his own name In 1896 the firm was associated with John H Pickford in building the Standish Hotel, additions to Bowler Brothers' brewery, additions to the gas house, The Aurora, Main street, for Charles F Stevens, the foundations of Bicknell block and two tenement buildings for Rice Brothers Pellett Brothers also built the Worcester Society of Antiquity building, Mr Shell's residence Northfield, Massachusetts, the Free Will Baptist Church, the German Lutheran Church, Worcester, the old Ethan Allen factory on Jackson street Some of the buildings constructed by Mr Pellett, when he was not in partnership were The Methodist Church at Brattleboro, engine house and barn at North Brookfield, stable for Charles Bush, engine house for the town of North Brookfield, a fine residence at St John, New Brunswick

He married April 2, 1878, Emily Barrett, of Wardsboro, Vermont Her father, Emerson Barrett, was a wood-worker by trade Their children are: Arthur, born August 26, 1880, Annie, born February 24, 1882, Bradford, born June 15, 1889, Marion, born April 6, 1901

FRANK LUCIUS MURDOCK *The name* Murdock (Murdoch or Murtogh) is of Gaelic origin and signifies Admiral, Sea Leader or Sea Power The Murdock *coat of arms* is thus described Argent, two ravens hanging paleways (sable) transfixed by an arrow through their heads fess ways *The family motto is* "Omnia Pro Bono" (All Things for the Good) The C of A was registered by Murdock of Camlodden in 1672 and has never been reduced *The crest* is a raven rising, shot through the breast by an arrow

Murdoch is the Scotch way of spelling the surname, which in England and America is spelled Murdock The name has been common in Scotland for centuries, especially in Ayrshire At the same time branches of the family are found over the line in England Henry Murdac who died in 1153, was a famous archbishop of York He came of a wealthy and important family in Yorkshire He joined the Cistercian order of Monks at Clairvaux He was enthroned at York, January 25 1151 The second Duke of Albany was Murdac or Murdoch

John Murdoch, born in Ayr, in 1747, died there 1824, was a distinguished writer and friend of Robert Burns Another famous Scotch author was Patrick Murdoch who died in 1774 educated at Edinburgh, a native of Dumfries Perhaps the best known member of the family was William Murdoch, the inventor of coal-gas lighting He was born in Ayrshire at Bellow Mill near Old Cumnock, the second son of John Murdock, millwright, August 21, 1754, died in 1839 His father and grandfather were both gunners in the royal artillery After Murdoch removed to England he spelled his name Murdock At the present time Rev Alexander Murdoch is Canon of Edinburgh, an office he has held since 1883 He has been rector of All Saints Church, Edinburgh, since 1867

(I) Robert Murdock, the first American ancestor of Frank L. Murdock, of Worcester, Massachusetts, was born in Scotland about 1665 He and his brother, John Murdock, came to America about 1688 and settled in Plymouth colony in New England John remained there and is the ancestor of a numerous branch of the family Robert stayed about four years in Plymouth In 1692 he removed to Roxbury, Massachusetts On the early records the name is spelled Murdo and Murdow as well as Murdock His was the only name of this family on the Roxbury records before 1700 He married, at Roxbury, April 28, 1692, Hannah Stedman, born in 1667, daughter of Thomas and Mary Stedman, of Cambridge Robert Murdock and his family removed from Roxbury to Newton in 1703 and bought a house and one hundred and twenty acres of land there for ninety pounds of Jonathan Hyde and John Woodward The farm was west of the school lot and the Dedham road north of Jacob Chamberlain's farm, and east of John Hyde's Later he owned the place called the Captain Jeremiah Wiswall place

His wife Hannah died 1727, aged sixty He married (second) Abigail —— He died April, 1754, aged eighty-nine years Children of Robert and Hannah (Stedman) Murdock were Hannah, born January 22, 1693, Lt Robert, February 11, 1695, married Abigail Hyde, daughter of Samuel Hyde, November 5, 1719, and his only son settled in Hubbardston with his cousin, Robert ancestor of the Worcester branch, Lieutenant Robert was seclectman, representative to the general court, etc, John, May 25, 1696, ancestor of the Uxbridge, Massachusetts, and Windham county, Connecticut, branches of the family, see forward, Samuel, March 24 1698 Benjamin, March 4, 1701, married, 1725, Mary Hyde, Hannah, born at Newton, May 22, 1705

(II) John Murdock, third child of Robert Murdock (1) was born in Roxbury, Massachusetts, May 25, 1696 He married, in 1722, Sarah —— He bought twenty-two acres of land in Newton in 1721 of William Hyde for two hundred pounds His place was on the west side of the road His neighbors were on the north James Prentice and on the south Daniel Hyde He died March, 1744, aged forty-eight years His wife died 1779 aged seventy-six years Children of John and Sarah Murdock were Hannah, born July 17, 1723, died young, Abiel, February 21, 1724-25, went to Brookfield, Massachusetts, thence to Hubbardston, married Rebecca Watson, who died June 3, 1772 aged seventy-five years, he died January 20, 1834, aged ninety years, John, December 24, 1727, founder of the Uxbridge branch, Ephraim, April 18, 1729, died young, Amos, August 7, 1730, founder of the Windham Connecticut, branch, Elisha, August 25, 1732, died 1749, Aaron, August 28, 1735, Ephraim, March 19, 1737, married, 1761 Sarah Sever, and 1768 Charity Davis lived at Roxbury deacon, James, March 15, 1738, married Deborah Williams, October 10, 1765, Robert, see forward, Sarah, September 17, 1741 Hannah, February 21, 1744, married Nathaniel Sparhawk, 1768

(III) Robert Murdock, tenth child of John Murdock (2) was born in Newton, Massachusetts September, 1739 He was a soldier in the revolution He was in Captain William Marean's company, Colonel Doolittle's regiment, at Lexington, April 19, 1775 He was second lieutenant in Captain William Marean's company, Colonel Nathan Sparhawk's (Seventh Worcester) regiment He was commissioned as lieutenant April 6, 1776 Lieutenant Robert Murdock removed from Newton to Hubbardston, Massachusetts, about 1765 He married Margaret Cheney, of Newton He died October 1, 1819, she died March 11, 1826, aged eighty-four years Children of Robert and Margaret (Cheney) Murdock were Margaret, born 1768, in Hubbardston, married Luther Goodspeed, Ebenezer 1771, Robert, see forward, Sarah, November 14, 1779, died September 24, 1798, Hannah, July 8, 1782, married Ebenezer Stowe

(IV) Robert Murdock third child of Robert Murdock (3), was born in Hubbardston, Massachusetts, August 31, 1773 He settled in his native town and his children were all born there He married Sally Nichols, March 15, 1804 He died April 27, 1852; she died September 5, 1855 Children of Robert and Sally (Nichols) Murdock were William, born January 27, 1805, married Sarah Wheelock February, 1833, he died at Wendell, June 4, 1860, and she died October 14, 1863, aged fifty-six, they had nine children, Mary, August 10, 1806 married, March 1, 1832, Joshua P Pillsbury and lived in Washington, D C, died April 30, 1892, Ebenezer, September 27, 1808 married Betsey Wheeler, March 2, 1836, died July 6, 1845, their daughter Ellen married, June 3, 1863, John D Williams, Sumner, July 28, 1810, married Charlotte W Howe, January 23, 1833, and had four children among whom were Charles W, Henry L, Clara E, married Albert Mason, of Gardner, Joseph Cheney, November 30, 1812, died December 14, 1882, married Julia Greenwood, January 5 1838, and had six children Julia Ann, Leander L, Willie C, Alfred C Abby L, John G, Elisha, see forward, Sarah, July 31, 1818, married Richard Leonard, died December, 1900

(V) Elisha Murdock, sixth son of Robert Murdock (4), was born in Hubbardston, Massachusetts, June 21, 1815 He married Nancy Temple, daughter of Thomas Temple, January 17, 1837 She died September 2, 1853 He married (second) Abigail A (Clark) Young, May 24 1855 She died February 17 1875 He married (third) Mrs Martha J Evans, of Royalston, Massachusetts, April 9, 1877 He resided all his life in Hubbardston and was a highly respected and esteemed citizen of that town Children of Elisha and Nancy (Temple) Murdock were Lucius Adelbert, see forward, Elwin, died young, George Elwin August 7, 1840, resided in Worcester Child of Elisha and Abigail A, (Clark) Murdock was Nancy Ella born March 16, 1857

(VI) Lucius Adelbert Murdock, son of Elisha Murdock (5), was born in Hubbardston, Massachusetts August 28, 1837 He attended the public schools of his native town until eleven years old. At that age he left home with fifty cents in his pocket and hired out to William Joslin He earned sixteen dollars in the first month of working out and he saved as well as earned money At the age of fifteen he bought a farm in Hubbardston, which has since been known as the Murdock Farm, and in three years he had cut off wood enough, so that with his savings he had the property free of debt His ambition led him finally to leave Hubbardston He sold the farm to good advantage and went to East Templeton as engineer for the Derby Chair Company He was there but a short time when he had an opportunity to make some money by handling winnowing machines His thrift and energy interested William Smith, a manufacturer of tinware in Templeton Centre, and Mr Murdock accepted a position offered him by Mr Smith In

1861 Mr Smith moved his business to Worcester and took Mr Murdock into partnership The firm name was Smith & Murdock and their place of business was 174 Main street, near Lincoln square The firm manufactured and dealt in silver and tin ware In 1873 the firm was dissolved and Mr Murdock went into business with his son, Frank L Murdock, dealing in wool stock at Bigelow court

In 1880 he was appointed general agent of the Penn Mutual Life Insurance Company of Philadelphia, Pennsylvania, with offices in Boston, and he withdrew from business in Worcester For twenty-five years he was actively engaged in the duties of his position with the Penn company He was well known throughout New England among insurance men and took a high standing among them He enjoyed the complete confidence of his company, and under his management the business grew to large proportions Mr Murdock made his home at 21 Highland street He attended the Plymouth Congregational Church, Pearl street, and was one of its founders In politics he was a Republican He was a charter member of the Brookline Lodge of Elks at Brookline Massachusetts, where he lived during his later years He was a member of the Home Market Club of Boston He was always interested in public affairs and was well posted in current events He was an authority on insurance matters He died January 29, 1905, at Worcester

He married, November 25, 1858, Ellen Hager, daughter of Charles White and Lydia Parkhurst (Whipple) Hager, of Hubbardston, Massachusetts Charles W Hager was a farmer there Children of Lucius A and Ellen (Hager) Murdock were Frank Lucius, see forward, William Herbert, born July 10, 1863, died August 24, 1864, Mary Boyden, born March 17, 1870, married Charles Crompton, son of George Crompton, of Worcester June 6, 1892

(VII) Frank Lucius Murdock, eldest child of Lucius A Murdock (6), was born in East Templeton, Massachusetts, February 29, 1860 His parents removed to Worcester when he was a year old At the age of five he began to attend the public schools in Worcester He took a two years' course in the high school and left to enter upon a business career In 1876 he entered into business with his father, dealing in wool stock He was in the firm of Lucius A Murdock for four years, when his father went into the life insurance business and he became connected with Tower, Wing & Co, of Lawrence, Massachusetts, manufacturers in wool stock and commission merchants He remained with this firm until 1892, when he became vice-president of the Basch & Greenfield Company, of Newark, New Jersey He resides at 714 Pleasant street, Worcester He and his family attend the First Universalist Church In politics Mr Murdock is a Republican He is a member of the Worcester Automobile Club, and the Home Market Club of Boston He was from 1877 to 1880 a member of Company C, Worcester Light Infantry, Second Regiment, Massachusetts Volunteer Militia

He married, January 1, 1880, Inez Estelle Budding, daughter of Benjamin Quincy and Lucy Ann (Fessenden) Budding, of Worcester Mrs Murdock is a member of the Home Club of Worcester, Timothy Bigelow Chapter, Daughters of the American Revolution Their only child is Alice Camille, born March 22, 1881, who lives with her parents Mrs Murdock's father, Benjamin Quincy Budding, was a well known inventor of shoe machinery

JOSEPH RICE TORREY In all parts of the world, wherever razors and razor strops are used, the name of Torrey is known, and that for a reason to be seen farther on in this brief memoir of one of the enterprising manufacturers of the city of Worcester

Joseph Rice Torrey was born August 23, 1828, at New Salem, Massachusetts When but two years of age his father died and his mother moved to Barre, Massachusetts, where he attended the common schools and subsequently his his own efforts the Wesleyan Academy at Wilbraham, Massachusetts, and also took a course at the Leicester Academy, where he early showed in a marked degree the physical strength and power of endurance of an athlete which has served him so well in the hard and constant work of later years At the age of seventeen he taught school, teaching for two years in Barre and Leicester, and then became an apprentice to the trade of stone-cutting, at which he worked for about four years

Being considered an expert penman he took up the teaching of penmanship at Leicester and Westminster academies and other places in Worcester county, finally locating in the city of Worcester in 1852, where he engaged as bookkeeper with William H Dexter, then in the flour and grain business While occupying this position he originated a system of accounts which was approved by Mr Dexter, and adopted by several large dealers in the same line of business We next find him in the grocery trade, conducting a large retail business under the firm name of Eddy & Torrey, this partnership was dissolved in 1858 Feeling that he had not yet discovered his favorite calling he decided, after carefully following out a line of investigation in which he had been much interested for some time, to engage in the manufacture of razor strops His grocery business not having proved financially successful owing to the great trade depression culminating in the disastrous year of 1857, he began his new venture without capital depending solely upon his own labor for the support of his family, but by untiring industry nights as well as days he soon established a reputation for making goods superior to any other in this his newly chosen line Year by year he continued to expand this business and enlarge his territory for trade Commencing in a small way in 1858, by 1880 he owned the largest industry of the kind in existence During the year 1880 he added the manufacture of razors and organized with Joseph Turner, a skilled expert in that line of cutlery, the J R Torrey Razor Company, with Mr Turner as president and himself as treasurer They were as conservative in this venture as Mr Torrey had been in the strop business, but with the passing years of steady growth, the razor business has increased until now this firm is by far the largest exclusive manufacturers of razors in this country, if not in the world, and wherever men shave their faces the "Torrey" brand is known and appreciated for its exceedingly fine temper and keen cutting qualities

There had been several previous attempts to manufacture razors in the United States Some of them on quite an extensive scale, bringing from England experienced workmen, and in one instance barrels of water were imported in which to harden the blades, under the singular delusion that the water in this country was not suitable for that purpose But all these attempts proved failures, and it remained for the J R Torrey Razor Company to establish the first successful manufactory for that article in America

Joseph Rice Torrey was never above his business and never shirked his personal duty He learned to creep before he tried to walk He first made by hand the razor strops which he sold upon the streets of Worcester, New York and other cities, until the people who used such articles became acquainted with the superior quality of his goods, and dealers sought after them Reputation thus gained became his capital and earned for him the handsome reward he now enjoys Let his record stand out boldly as an example to the rising young man who would make a success of life

In 1870 he was elected to represent Worcester in the state legislature, being re-elected in 1871 He is a stanch Republican in his political views and at one time wielded an influence in the councils of his party second to none in the county He served on city, county and congressional committees in many hotly contested campaigns He has always been a strong advocate of temperance and always practiced total abstinence as the only consistent and safe manner of living In his social relations he is numbered among the Masonic fraternity, Worcester Board of Trade, Massachusetts Club of Boston He belongs to the Old South Congregational Church He is an associate member of the Grand Army, George H Ward Post, No 10, of Worcester

In 1852 he married Ann Adelia Lewis, daughter of John Lewis, of Westminster, Massachusetts Two children blessed this union Frank William who died at the age of sixteen years, and Lewis Hamilton who is now associated with his father as a member of the firm of J R Torrey & Company, and is also a director in the Torrey Razor Company Mrs Torrey died in 1869 and in 1877 he married Eliza Rice, of Barre, Massachusetts, by whom he has one daughter, Annie Louise

The following regarding the ancestry of Joseph Rice Torrey is of interest

(I) William Torrey, one of the American immigrant ancestors of the Torrey family in Massachusetts, was born at Combe St Nicholas Somersetshire, England, about 1590, he was descended from an eminent family of that county, received a good classical education and came to Massachusetts with his brother James about 1640 James settled at Scituate, and William at Weymouth, where he became a magistrate and captain of the trainband of the colony (the highest military rank of the time), and was many years a representative from Weymouth in the general court Being a good penman he was frequently chosen clerk of that body He was prominent in all committee work where they had to do with literary and educational questions He died at Weymouth about 1675

His son Samuel, born in England, graduated at Harvard College, and became an eminent minister at Weymouth Preached the "Election Sermon" three times and twice declined the presidency of Harvard College He was born about 1631, and died in 1707

Ebenezer Torrey, the grandfather of Joseph Rice Torrey, born in 1771, at Weymouth, Massachusetts, when a young man moved to New Salem, Massachusetts He married a Miss Day of that place by whom he had two sons Sumner and William Ebenezer Torrey was very active politically and prominent in the state militia In 1810 was commissioned captain by Governor Gore He served as a member of the Massachusetts legislature from 1831 to 1833 and was earnestly interested in securing the charter for the first line of railway from Boston to Worcester He died in 1863 and was buried at New Salem, Massachusetts

William Torrey, son of Ebenezer Torrey, was born at New Salem, in 1799 married Clarissa Rice, daughter of Joseph Rice, of Barre, December 1, 1825 she being of the fourth generation from Gershom Rice one of the first settlers of Worcester Their only child was Joseph Rice Torrey, whose father, William Torrey, died in 1830, aged thirty-one years and was buried in New Salem, that part of which is now in the town of Orange

CRAWFORD FAMILY While the Crawford family was well established in Scotland before 1200 we are told that it is of Anglo-Norman origin some two centuries earlier and the Crawfords of Scotland trace their ancestry to a Norman noble of the days of William, the Conqueror The name is spelled sometimes Crawfurd in the early Scotch records, while Crauford was the ordinary spelling until later days A list of the heads of important Scotch families in 1291 has been preserved It is known to historians as the Ragman's Roll On this list are the names of five Crawfords John de Crauford, of Ayrshire John de Crauford, tenant le Roi, Ayrshire, Renaud de Crawford, of Ayrshire, Roger de Crauford and William de Crauford The records show families in Lanarkshire, Renfrewshire and Stirlingshire as well as Ayrshire, before the year 1200 The titles held in Scotland by this family were The Viscountcy of Mount Crawford and Garnock The Earldom of Crawford belonged to the Lindsey family A number of Crawfords were amoung the Scotch given grants of land in the province of Ulster, Ireland in 1610 and later by King James I The first settler in Tyrone, whence came the American immigrant of the branch of the family under consideration was George Crawford Nicholas Pynnar who made a survey of the Scotch Irish settlements in 1619, reported that in the precinct of Mountjoy county Tyrone, George Crawford had transferred his thousand acre grant to Alexander Sanderson The name is common in the Protestant districts of Antrim, Down, Londonderry and Tyrone at the present time

(I) Aaron Crawford, the pioneer ancestor in America of William H Crawford, of Worcester, was born in county Tyrone in 1677 If George Crawford were his ancestor, the family had been there some sixty years when he was born and George would have been his grandfather or great-grandfather He came to New England with his family in 1713 some five years before the first extensive emigration of the Scotch-Irish began He arrived in Boston in the spring or summer of 1713 and lived there probably until he settled in Rutland, Massachusetts, soon afterward The grant of what is now Rutland was confirmed to the children of Major Simon Willard, of Lancaster, and others by order of the general court, February 23, 1713 It is said that the first clearing was made in 1716 and that the settlers began moving there in September, 1719 The town was incorporated May 13, 1722, and the first meeting of the settlers under the act of incorporation was held on the last Monday of July 1722 As one of the Crawford family was elected to a town office at the first meeting it is believed that Aaron Crawford was one of the earliest settlers

Aaron Crawford married Agnes Wilson in the parish of Capy county Tyrone, Ireland She was born in 1678 Three sons Samuel, John and Alexander born in Ireland, in this parish of Capy were brought over by the parents, also Martha Alexander was less than a year old when the family arrived in Boston Aaron and his wife both died at Rutland and are buried in the graveyard in the centre of the town He died August 6, 1754, she died December 10 1760 Their children, Samuel, born 1705 in Ireland died October 17, 1760, married Margaret Montgomery and had no children Martha born 1706 died September 20 1795 in Rutland, married, May 24 1733, James Bell, of Ireland, who died March 25, 1793, they had Molly, William, Martha, James, John, Aaron, Abraham, Agnes, Samuel, Simson and Sarah Bell John, born in Ireland, settled in Palmer, Massachusetts, died there unmarried Alexander, born 1713 in Ireland, see forward Isabella, died young Mary, born in Rutland, April 15, 1721, married, April 15, 1745, William McCobb and they had Elizabeth, Isabella, Aaron, Margaret, Nancy, Fanny, John, Molly, Martha, and Samuel McCobb Moses, died unmarried in Rutland, where he settled

(II) Alexander Crawford, son of Aaron Crawford (1), was born in the county of Tyrone, Ireland, in 1713, probably early in the year He was an infant less than a year old when the family came to America in 1713 He went to Rutland with the family in 1719 and helped his father clear the farm during his youth He settled in Rutland and followed the life of a pioneer farmer until 1750, when he removed to Rutland West Wing, now Oakham, where he died October 11, 1793, in his eightieth year

He married Elizabeth Crawford, probably a distant relative, February 5, 1735-36 She died April 27, 1774, aged sixty-two years, doubtless also born in Ireland, in Londonderry county, emigrating with several brothers and sisters from Magherafelt, of that county, and settling in New Jersey, Pennsylvania, and Virginia Their children William, died in infancy John, born January 7, 1739, was captain in the revolution, married, February 9, 1759, Rachel Henderson and had Elizabeth, born March 14, 1760, married Robert Wilson, John, born May 2, 1762, drowned, unmarried, aged thirty-five, a school teacher Alexander, born February 12, 1765, married Bethia Willis and had eight children, Samuel, born July 16, 1767, Samuel, born August 9, 1769, married Huldah Burden and had ten children, Calvin, born October 18, 1770, married Catherine Bence and had several children removed to New York state, Rachel, born April 2, 1773, married —— Stimpson, of Vermont, Josiah, born April 25, 1776, Patty (twin), born December 11, 1778, Polly (twin), born December 11, 1778 Infant, died young Aaron, married, January 31, 1768, Gilles Gill and had six sons and three daughters, removed to Canada William, born October 23, 1745, see forward

(III) William Crawford, son of Alexander Crawford (2), was born in Rutland, Massachusetts, October 23, 1745 He removed to Oakham with his parents when five years of age and was brought up on the farm, getting a meagre education in the common schools He learned the trade of clock-making and became one of the most skilful and famous mechanics in his line His home was in the eastern part of the town He was a soldier in the revolution and sergeant in Captain John Crawford's company, Colonel James Converse's regiment, enlisting July 22, 1777, and was discharged July 26, 1777, serving in the Rhode Island campaign He was under the same officers on the Bennington Alarm, from August 20, 1777, to August 23, 1777 He was short of stature and somewhat lame in consequence of a fever sore He became captain of his company in the militia and was afterward always called Captain Crawford

He married Mary Henderson, who was born July 30, 1748, died November 26, 1838, of old age She was the daughter of James and Sarah Henderson, of Rutland Their children Elizabeth, born February 10, 1774 died February 3, 1838, married, September 1815 Jonathan King, who died April 1, 1827 James born August 11, 1775, see forward Lucy, born February 7, 1778 William, born February 25, 1780, died March 30, 1781 Sarah, born January 30, 1782, died February 1, 1798 William, born January 30, 1782, died February 1, 1798 William, born October 5, 1780, was representative to the general court 1813-23-35-41-46, to the state senate 1825 and 1826, and was county commissioner from 1836 to 1850 inclusive, graduate of Dartmouth and prominent school teacher, a giant mentally as well as physically, general in the state militia Rufus, born November 13, 1785, married, January 16, 1820, (intentions dated) Clarissa Cunningham, of Spencer, and had Laura del Rosetta, born March 5, 1826, married, May 10, 1846, Edwin Fuller and had one child Edward L Fuller, Amanda Malvina, born November 30, 1834 Molly, born October 6, 1787, married, June 27, 1812, Samuel Tenney and had Paul, born October 12, 1822, Lucy Maria, born May 3, 1814, Martha Rice, born November 30, 1816, Mary Chandler, born July 5, 1819, Rufus Oswell, born May 7, 1821, Laura Hazen, born November 30, 1822, Ellen Elizabeth, born July 27, 1825, Isabella, born February 24 1796, died November 16, 1845 Alexander, born April 16, 1792, married, September 6, 1813, Mary Henderson and had Emeline Mariah, born September 30, 1814, Anson Alexander, born January 17, 1817, William Amory, born October 7, 1820 Harriet, born March 10, 1795, died March 19, 1795

(IV) James Crawford, son of William Crawford (3), was born at Oakham, Massachusetts, August 11, 1775 He received his education in the public schools of his native town and helped his father on the farm In early manhood he learned the trade of gunsmith, following it through life He died at Albany, New York, February 5, 1814 He had been employed in the government arsenal there He was an active and robust man, fully six feet in height

He married March, 1800 Molly Butler, born at Oakham, Massachusetts, October 17, 1780, died January 31, 1825, daughter of John and Grace Butler, of Oakham Their children Laureston Faulkner, born October 8, 1801, married October 8, 1829, Caroline R Cummings, of Hardwick born 1809, died August 29, 1838, leaving son Joseph, born 1830, daughter Mary Reed, born June 4 1832, and daughter Emily Augusta, born January 29, 1834 Algernon Sidney, born April 27, 1805, died July 1846, at Puebla, Mexico, of yellow fever during the Mexican war, married (first) Eliza Gay and had son James, (second) Lucy Stone, of Rutland, and had daughters Jane and Ann William Theron, born April 2, 1807, see forward

(V) William Theron Crawford son of James Crawford (4), was born at Oakham, Massachusetts, April 8 1807 He received his education in the common schools of that town He became a wheelwright by trade and while a young man and unmarried worked at Rochester, New York He married Almira Clark at Barre Massachusetts and lived for a year or more in Rutland Massachusetts, but settled shortly in Barre where he bought the farm where his wife's ancestors for several generations had lived He lived there until his death, January 8 1858 He attended the Congregational church regularly all his life but was never a member In politics he was a Whig until the organization of the Republican party, with which he affiliated in his last years He was selectman in Barre in 1845

He married according to the family records, November 6 1831, Almira Clark daughter of Thomas and Sarah (Demond) Clark descendant of one of the oldest families of Massachusetts, her immigrant ancestor being one of the first settlers Their children 1 Charles, born May 11, 1833, married

Louise Blakeman, at Minneapolis, Minnesota, November 2, 1866, died at Chicago, Illinois, May 31, 1905, was paymaster of the United States Volunteers from 1861 to 1865, stationed at Fort Leavenworth, Kansas, and Denver, Colorado, made brevet lieutenant colonel at close of the war, his children were—Charles, Jr and Marion 2 William, born January 3, 1835, at Barre married Judith Perkins Cochran, daughter of Rev Joseph Gallup and Deborah Plumb Cochran, missionaries at Mount Seir, Persia, at Buffalo, New York, May 31, 1880, educated in Barre schools, Leicester Academy, Amherst College and Andover Theological Seminary, he had pastorates at Central City, Colorado, Green Bay, Sparta, and Mazomanie, Wisconsin, received degree of Doctor of Divinity from Amherst College in 1893, his children—William Wilberforce, born at Washington, Connecticut June 30 1882, educated at Beloit College, Wisconsin, and Oberlin College, Ohio, married at South Milwaukee Wisconsin September 5, 1905, journalist in Chicago Illinois, Arthur Whipple, born at Sparta March 5, 1885, graduated at Beloit College Wisconsin, 1906, Dora Judith born at Sparta, April 24, 1888 3 Henry, born March 5, 1839, died February 17, 1843 4 Sidney, see forward 5 Sarah Clark, born in Barre, May 22, 1843 died there December 26, 1861 6 Ellen Almira, born in Barre, April 4, 1846, died in Barre, April 27, 1873 7 Joseph Bowman born in Barre, February 11, 1848, died in Barre, December 20, 1851 8 Frederick Bowman, born in Barre, September 12, 1854, was educated at Sheffield Scientific School in Yale University, was in business at Baltimore and Philadelphia until his death, October 7, 1894 He married Jame Campbell, October 14, 1880, children—Bessie, Frederick Campbell and Mary Helmsworth

(VI) Sidney Crawford, son of William Theron Crawford (5), was born in Barre, Massachusetts, January 31, 1841 He received his early education in the public schools of Barre, fitting for college in the high school of that town and at Monson Academy He entered Amherst College in 1857 and graduated in 1861 From 1861 to 1864 he was principal of Walton Academy, Delaware county, New York He was for one year assistant paymaster in the United States Volunteers at Leavenworth, Kansas, and Denver, Colorado Then he studied theology at Andover Seminary graduating in the class of 1870 He has had pastorates in Fairhaven, Vermont, Lyons, Iowa, Tampa, Florida, Rutland, Massachusetts, and Provincetown, Massachusetts During his residence in Florida he was a member of the board of trustees of Rollins College at Winter Park He is author of "Historic Sketch of First Congregational Church, Lyons, Iowa" and of "Rufus Putnam, and his Pioneer Life in the Northwest," printed in the proceedings of the American Antiquarian Society 1899 He united first with the Congregational church in Andover Seminary and since then has kept his connection with the church of which he was pastor In politics he has always been a Republican He belongs to two college fraternities, the Alpha Delta Phi and the Phi Beta Kappa

He married, at Green Bay, Wisconsin, 1875, Harriet Phinney Peak, daughter of Dr James Madison and Celestia Benjamin Peak, of Cooperstown New York Mrs Crawford died in Tampa, Florida, 1888. He married (second), 1901, in Provincetown, Massachusetts, Edith Small daughter of Josiah F and Adelaide L Small The children of Rev Sidney and Harriet Phinney (Peak) Crawford were 1 Frederick Stuart born in 1876 at Lyons, Iowa graduated at Amherst College 1897, since then he has been on the staff of the *New York Tribune*, New York city, married, 1902, Mabel Rosemond McLean, of Elmira, New York, their two children are: Frederic Stuart Crawford, Jr, born 1903, Sidney Peak, born 1905 2 Paul Peak, born 1879, died young 3 Marjorie Peak, born 1881, died young

(V) Elias Butler Crawford, son of James Crawford (4), was born in Oakham, Massachusetts, November 19, 1810, and was educated there in the common schools When he was about twenty-one he left home and went to New England, village of Grafton, Massachusetts, and was engaged in the thread business, he remained there until 1835, when he removed to Oxford, Massachusetts, and for a time manufactured spools Later he manufactured thread, and this business was continued under the firm name of DeWitt, Campbell & Company, Alexander DeWitt being agent until after May, 1836, when he was succeeded by Benjamin F Campbell, who continued until May 25 1842, when the mill was burned and the business discontinued On September 20, 1842, Stearns DeWitt conveyed to Elias B Crawford three-fourths of the estate of Buffumville, including lands called Pierpont together with the remnant of the plant of the old thread company not destroyed, and Mr Crawford continued the manufacture of thread in a shop near the site of the mill and had his home on this property Mr Crawford acquired the other quarter interest in the property April 24, 1845, from the Samuel Dowse estate, and he began the building of the present mill of brick and had it nearly completed, when he sold it to Charles L Harding, who fitted it up for making broadcloths and doeskins In 1854 Mr Crawford occupied the basement of the Sigourney mill in the manufacture of twine Elias B Crawford bought of H G Otis and Asa B Taft, April 16, 1853, the old Jacob Marble place on Rocky Hill, and the Crawfords lived there until April, 1860, when they sold to Francis Coughlin, of Rhode Island Mr Crawford removed to Putnam, Connecticut, and for a time manufactured cotton goods Later he manufactured woolen goods at Stafford, Connecticut, finally coming to Wilkinsonville, Massachusetts, where he owned a mill and manufactured woolen goods at what was known as Woodbury Village His market was mostly in New York city He sold out finally to Moses Taft, of Uxbridge, in 1888, and retired from active business, making his home in Worcester with his daughter, Mrs Caleb Colvin He died there January 29, 1890 In politics he was a Republican and in 1855 held the office of assessor in the town of Oxford, and at one time highway commissioner

He married at Grafton (intention dated) March 8, 1834, Jane Thankful Taft, who died January 10, 1876, daughter of Otis granddaughter of Silas, descendant of Robert Taft, the immigrant, through his son Robert (See sketch of Taft families) Their children 1 Eliza Jane, born January 18, 1836, married June 26, 1860, Albert H Appleby of Oxford Massachusetts and had Elmira Harris, born September 8, 1861, Marian born February 17, 1864, married David Glass of Oxford, Nettie Louise, born October 5 1867, Addie Eliza born October 9, 1869, Elias Butler, born August 23, 1875 2 Ellen Minerva, born November 11, 1837, died February 25, 1901, married, October 8, 1877, Caleb Colvin, a prominent Worcester manufacturer, 3 William Henry, see forward 4 Annette born September 21, 1850, died January 22, 1905, married Albert Harry Stone, of Worcester, and they had—Nellie Crawford Stone, born August 24, 1880, Arthur Stone, born July 11, 1888

(VI) William Henry Crawford, son of Elias B.

Crawford (5), was born at Oxford, Massachusetts, May 7, 1840 He received his early education in the public schools At the age of eighteen years he went to Schrawlenburg New Jersey, where he taught school for two years In 1860 he went to Worcester and entered the employ of Sumner Pratt, a prominent dealer in mill supplies, and spent his first year in the business with which he has been connected all of the time since After his first year he took a course at Wesleyan Academy at Wilbraham, Massachusetts, and then returned to the employ of Mr Pratt He was a clerk in the concern until 1870, when he was admitted a partner by Mr Pratt under the firm name of Sumner Pratt & Company The store was at 22 Front street and the stock consisted of manufacturers' supplies for the cotton and woolen industries The firm continued until December 1, 1896, when Mr Crawford became the senior partner and John T Brierly was admitted to the firm The present name of Crawford & Company was then assumed The business was moved to 15 and 17 Mechanic street April 1, 1900, where it remained until burned out March 17, 1905 Since then the firm has occupied handsome and spacious quarters at 663 and 665 Main street, in the Bellmar block scarcely a month elapsing from the time of the fire until the firm was able to supply its trade from the new store The firm does a prosperous business with mills in all parts of New England, New York, New Jersey, Canada and other sections

Mr Crawford is an attendant of the Plymouth Congregational Church, and has been on the board of assessors of the parish three years In politics he is a Republican and had frequently taken part in county, councillor, senatorial and congressional conventions of his party as delegate He was a member of the Worcester common council in 1884 and 1885, and of the school board three years He has been a member of Montacute Lodge of Free Masons since October 14, 1872 He was a director of the Citizens' National Bank for several years Mr Crawford has an elegant residence at 11 Massachusetts avenue

He married, June 8, 1865, at Palmer Massachusetts, Mary Ann Moore, daughter of Henry A and Elmira (Ruggles) Moore, of Palmer Her father was a scythe maker Their children 1 Lillian Moore, born May 4, 1868, teacher in the Classical high school, Worcester 2 Mabel Jane born October 17, 1870, married Dr Frank H Howland, of Worcester, one of the leading dentists of the city, and they have Mabel Gladys Howland, born March 4, 1904 3 Anna Cutler, born June 3, 1873, resides at home with parents 4 Harry Colvin, born September 23 1883, graduate of Amherst, 1906, and is with the firm of Crawford & Company

FROST FAMILY Elder Edmund Frost (1) the immigrant ancestor of Frederick E Frost, of Worcester, Massachusetts, was born in England about 1610 He settled in Cambridge, Massachusetts, where he was during his life ruling elder of the Cambridge church He was admitted a freeman March 3, 1635-36, and was a proprietor of the town as early as 1636 He bought land of Thomas Blodgett in 1639 on the west side of Dunster street, between Harvard square and Mt Auburn street He sold this place to Catherine Haddon and bought a house on the west side of Garden street, near Mason street He sold land to Richard Eccles in 1646 He seems to have owned the land on the west side of Kirkland street from Divinity Hall avenue to Francis avenue His descendants owned it until recently He married (first) in England Thomasin (Tamasin) ———, and (second) Reana Daniels, who was the widow successively of ——— James, William Andrew and Robert Daniel He died July 12, 1672 His will was dated April 16, and proved October 1, 1671 He bequeathed to wife Reana, to sons Ephraim, Thomas, John and Joseph, to his two daughters, Sarah and Mary, to Jacob French and his wife and the children of Golden More, to Harvard College and to Mr Alcock's son there The inventory of the estate of the widow was dated January 3, 1675-76 The children John, born and baptized in England, Thomas, born April, 1637, died young, Samuel, born February, 1638, Joseph, born January 13, 1639, James, born April 9, 1640, Mary, born July 24, 1645, Ephraim, see forward, Thomas, Sarah, born 1653

(II) Ephraim Frost, son of Edmund Frost (1), was born in Watertown, Massachusetts, in 1646, died there January 2, 1717-18 He settled in Cambridge, and married Hepsibath ——— Their children Edmund, born March 14, 1679-80, Ephraim, born September 23, 1682, Thomas, born 1688, Ebenezer, born in Cambridge, baptized January 17, 1696-97, see forward, Sarah, married, May 17, 1720, Nathaniel Patten

(III) Ebenezer Frost, son of Ephraim Frost (2), was born in Cambridge, Massachusetts, and baptized there January 17, 1696-97 He married, July 2, 1723, Deborah Martin In 1730 he bought a lot on the east side of North (now Massachusetts) avenue, Cambridge He seems to have lived in Charlestown also and his children may have been born there, or some of them He was taxed there in 1741, 1745 to 1766 He sold Gideon Frost four acres, late of John Cooper Frost was a currier by trade He died in 1768 His will was dated April 16, 1768, and proved June 28, 1768 The children Abraham, born March 7, 1723-24, married, June 8, 1747, Mary Oliver, Ebenezer, baptized August 22, 1725, see forward, James, born March 2, 1731-32, married Elizabeth Roby, daughter of Dr Ebenezer Roby

(IV) Ebenezer Frost, son of Ebenezer Frost (3), was born in Cambridge, Massachusetts, and baptized there August 22, 1725 He removed to Rutland, Massachusttts, after his second marriage in 1761 He bought a farm of one hundred and four acres including house and barn at Rutland of Joseph Bartlett, of that town The land was bounded by land of William Allen, Captain Samuel Brown, Samuel Mansland and Israel How The deed is dated December 19, 1760

He married Naomi Dana, daughter of Thomas Dana, April 21, 1748 He married (second) Ruth Wright, of Woburn (published February 24, 1761) He was appointed guardian of his four children of his first wife July 13, 1761 His wife Ruth died at Rutland, July 20, 1789, aged eighty-nine years according to the inscription on her gravestone He was a soldier in the revolution a private in Captain David Bent's company, Colonel Nathan Sparhawk's regiment, and marched at the Bennington alarm The children of Ebenezer and Naomi Frost Ebenezer, born in Cambridge or Charlestown, baptized February 19, 1748-49, see forward, Mary, baptized February 24, 1750-51, David, baptized June 9 1754, Deborah, baptized February 12, 1758 Children of Ebenezer and Ruth Frost Ruth, born August 4, 1762, Joseph, baptized December 29, 1765, married, November 20, 1784, Adonijah Bartlett, Jonathan, baptized December 13, 1767, Dana, born 1769, died May 28 1843, Stephen, baptized April 8, 1770, married Polly Kendall, August 5, 1790

Ebenezer Frost, son of Ebenezer Frost (4), was born in Cambridge or Charlestown, Massachusetts, and baptized in Cambridge, February 19, 1748-49 He settled for a short time in Southborough, but sold his land there September 5, 1771, to his father, Ebenezer Frost, of Rutland, and went to Norwich, New London county, Connecticut He kept a tavern there with good success He also followed his trade of stone mason until incapacitated by an accident while laying a stone wall He was an extensive dealer in horses, many of which he sold in Cuba There is a deed in the Worcester registry in which Ebenezer Frost, of Norwich, county of New London, conveys to Thomas Read, of Parkstown, Massachusetts, for twenty pounds all his right to the real estate of his father, Ebenezer Frost, late of Rutland, Massachusetts, as set off to 'my mother, Mrs Ruth Frost, as her dower' The deed is dated May 17, 1799, ten years after the death of the Widow Frost Ebenezer Frost married Luthena Cady, a native of France Their children Ebenezer, Henry, Joseph, born 1792, see forward, Polly Luthena, married ——— Peckham, and lived at Hartford, Connecticut

(VI) Joseph Frost, son of Ebenezer Frost (5), was born at Norwich, Massachusetts, February 17, 1792 He was educated in the district schools of this locality, and in early manhood went to Woodstock, Connecticut, to learn the trade of cabinet maker After a few years he went to Greenfield, Massachusetts, where he followed his trade and made carriages in the employ of one Clay After his marriage, five years later, he removed to Stratton, Vermont, worked at his trade there two years, then came back to Greenfield and worked for one Bancroft and for Miles & Lyon He remained in Greenfield until 1860, when he removed to Waterbury, Connecticut, and worked there as carpenter and cabinet maker for the next ten years He spent the last two years of his life in Lunenburg, Massachusetts, living with George Washburn Frost, his son Mr Frost was an Episcopalian in early life, later a Unitarian He was a Whig until the Republican party came into being, when he became a firm supporter of the new organization and remained so until his death He was a member of the state militia in his youth

He married at Greenfield, Massachusetts, December 2, 1819, Susanna Waite Guellow, born September 30, 1801 Their children Joseph Warren, born at Stratton, Vermont, November 14 1820, married, March 17, 1845, Harriet Buck, of Brattleboro, Vermont, and had children—Webb Warren, born February 4, 1846, married December 20, 1866, Celia N Armstrong, Hallie Eliza, born February 22, 1848, married, 1866, Sidney J Enson and had one son, Clarence, born June 20, 1869, Rush Stanhope, born October 17, 1757, married S Elmor Davies and and have Clarence Stanley, born November 26, 1884, Herbert Leslie, born September 26, 1886, Rush Raymond, born August 11, 1890, Howard Davies, born January 25, 1893, Marjorie Adelaide born May 27, 1906 Daniel Webb, born May 11, 1822, at Greenfield, Massachusetts, married, January 14, 1847, Louisa Cook, of Windsor, Connecticut, died August 19, 1903, they had children—Henry, born April 22, 1848, died August 19, 1904, Jennie Louise, born 1832, died 1859, S Otis, born January 17, 1858, Charles H, born December 10, 1859 Luthena Cady, born at Greenfield Massachusetts, April 28, 1824, married, July 3, 1843, Samuel Azaro Corser, of Greenfield, born December 6, 1823, and they had children—George Albert, born September 23 1845, died in civil war, unmarried, Ida Luthena born at Fitchburg, Massachusetts, April 28, 1848, married, August 2, 1866, Waterman D Bristol, of Waterbury, Connecticut, Ada, born May 25, 1850, died February 19, 1883, unmarried Charles Henry, born in Millbury, died young, Elizabeth, born November 23, 1855, married, April, 1889, George Hawley and have a son, George William Hawley, Susan Jane, born at Worcester, 1857, died young, Hezekiah Stone, born in Greenfield, February 15, 1826, died April 26, 1898, married, March 13, 1845, Mary Esther Munsell, born November 27, 1827, died December 25, 1895, and they had children—Mary Elizabeth, born February 8, 1847, married, October 28, 1902, Joseph Bowers, of Chicago, Ella Augusta, born June 29 1848, married, June 27, 1869, Edward B Beals, of Springfield, Massachusetts, and had Alfred Tennyson, born April 21, 1870, Grace Frost, born October 23, 1871, Nellie Elizabeth, born September 28, 1873, Edna Winifred, born October 18, 1876, Joseph Frost, born March 1, 1850, died September, 1851 George Washburn, born at Greenfield, July 2, 1828, died August 20, 1830 George Washburn, born April 18, 1831, see forward Elizabeth, born May 16, 1833, married, January 3, 1853, Noble Terrill, of Hamden, Connecticut, and had children—Joseph Henry, born June 17, 1855, died February 1, 1875, Ida Louise, born February 15, 1858, married, July 2, 1877, Noyes E Bassett and have—Raymond E, Louise H, Leon N, Jennie Lusina, born April 22, 1867, married, June 6, 1888, Octave Petitjean, and they have Mabel T, Clifford O, Hazel J, Jessie Evelina, born May 9 1875, died August 10, 1875 Charles Henry, born March 24, 1835, married Eliza Cook, of Windsor, Connecticut, had no issue Joseph Frost married (second), October, 1856, at Greenfield, Maria (Andrews) Abbott, mother of George Washburn Frost's wife They had no children

(VII) George Washburn Frost, son of Joseph Frost (6), was born at Greenfield, Massachusetts, April 18, 1831 He was educated in the common schools of that town He went to work first at the age of eleven years and when not in school was employed in the factory of the Russell Cutlery Company He then went to Fitchburg, Massachusetts, and learned the trade of iron molder of Asher Green, remaining with him four years when he removed to Worcester and entered the employ of William A Wheeler, in whose foundry he worked for nine years He worked also at his trade for the Fall River Iron Works at Fall River, Massachusetts, for the Holmes Iron Foundry at Providence and for the Whitin Machine Works at Whitinsville He went to Springfield about 1857, and two years later returned to Fitchburg, where for ten years he was employed in the foundry of Page & Smith and for ten years by the Putnam Machine Company, residing in Fitchburg and Lunenburg for twenty years About 1881 he went again to Worcester and worked in the foundry of Caleb Colvin and for other foundries for a number of years He is at present associated with his son, Frederick E Frost, at 505 Main street He resides on Piedmont street He is an Episcopalian in religion and a Republican in politics He has served at various times as delegate to nominating conventions of his party He was a member of the Molders' Union of Fitchburg from 1873 to 1878

He married, March 20, 1856, Mary Ellen Abbott, born January 22, 1840, daughter of Jonathan Wood Abbott born at Shapleigh, New Hampshire, April 17, 1789, and Maria (Andrews) Abbott, born at Machias, Maine, June 9, 1798 Her father was a custom tailor Their children Joseph, born at Springfield, August 11, 1857, died at Lunenburg, February 8, 1875, Willard Francis born at Fitchburg September 13, 1860, unmarried, George Albert, born at Fitchburg, July 25, 1866, died July 1, 1868, George Henry, born at Fitchburg, March 1, 1864, died August 12, 1864, Frederick Eugene, born at Fitchburg, March 13, 1869 see forward, Emma Luella, born at Lunenburg, October 10, 1872, died June 16, 1873, Harry Lincoln, born at Lunenburg, June 12, 1877, died December 15, 1879

(VIII) Frederick Eugene Frost, son of George Washburn Frost (7), was born in Fitchburg, Massachusetts, March 13, 1869 He received his early education in the public schools there At the age of thirteen he came to Worcester with his parents and attended the public and high schools He was graduated from the Classical high school in 1888 He entered the employ of Perkins & Butler, dealers in paper, twine, etc, as clerk, and remained two years He then started in business for himself at 554 Main street in the manufacture and sale of rubber stamps A year later he removed to 535 Main street, upstairs, where he was located for a year He was then at 537 Main street for a year In the spring of 1898 he bought of William L Lewis the old established stationery store, formerly owned by C B Eaton, at 505 Main street, where he has since been located He has made a specialty of typewriters, stamps and stencils, in which he does a large business as well as in the regular lines of stationery, office supplies, etc He manufactures seals, door plates, badges and incidentally has a large business in soda, confectionery and cigars He owns a fine residence at 33 Newbury street He attends the First Universalist Church In politics he is a Republican He is a member of Morning Star Lodge of Free Masons, joining June 19, 1906 He became a member of Worcester Chapter of Royal Arch Masons He is also a member of Quinsigamond Lodge, No 43, Odd Fellows, and of the Worcester Automobile Club

He married, November 1, 1890, Edith Emily Cook, daughter of Benjamin Munroe and Susan B (Walden) Cook, of Worcester Her father is a machinist in the Crompton & Knowles Loom Works, a veteran of the civil war Their children Raymond Harrison, Mabel Sophia, Harold Lincoln

HARRINGTON FAMILY The ship "Elizabeth" which sailed from England, April 10, 1634, had as one of its passengers Robert Harrington, born in England, 1616 He settled in Watertown, Massachusetts, where he was given a "homestall" by Deacon Thomas Hastings, probably a relative Harrington's name appears last on the list of proprietors of Watertown, made 1642 to 1644, at which time he owned the above named "homestall" October 1, 1648, he married Susan, (or Susanna) George, daughter of John George, of Watertown She was at that time an orphan, the widow of Henry Goldstone being her guardian She died July 6, 1694 He was admitted freeman May 27, 1663, and died May 11, 1707, aged ninety-one years His will, dated January 1, 1704, mentions sons—John, Daniel, Benjamin, Samuel, Thomas and Edward To Edward he gave the homestead His will also mentions daughters, Susanna Beers, Mary Bemis, Sarah Winship, his grandson, Joseph, son of Joseph, deceased, and daughter-in-law, Joanna Ward, late wife of his deceased son Joseph His inventory mentions sixteen lots of land amounting to six hundred and forty-seven and one-half acres, appraised at seven hundred and seventeen pounds The estate included house and mill, valued at one hundred and twenty pounds The children of Robert and Susan (George) Harrington were Susanna, born August 18, 1649, married, February 9, 1671, John Cutting, John, August 24, 1651, died August 24, 1741, Robert, August 31, 1653, died young, George, November 24, 1655, was in Captain Samuel Wadsworth's company and was killed by Indians at Lancaster, February, 1675, Daniel, November 1, 1657, died April 19, 1728, Joseph, December 28, 1659, Benjamin, January 26, 1661, died 1724, Mary, January 12, 1663, married John Bemis, Thomas, April 20, 1665, died March 29, 1712, Samuel, December 18, 1666, Edward, March, 1668, Sarah, March 10, 1670, married Joseph Winship, Jr, November 24, 1687, and died November 28, 1710, David, June 1, 1673, died March 11, 1675

(II) Edward Harrington, son of the ancestor Robert, married (first), March 30, 1692, Mary Ocington, and (second), May 24, 1727, Anna, widow of Jonathan Bullard, of Weston, Massachusetts He was selectman of Watertown, 1716-30-31 Their children were Mary, born January 2, 1692, married Daniel Rogers, December 7, 1710, William, November 11, 1694, died February 27, 1751, Mindwell, June 19, 1697, died October 14, 1700, Joanna, August 16, 1699, married John Taintor, May 25, 1720, Edward, June 27, 1702, died December 6, 1792, Samuel, August 3, 1704, Nathaniel, June 25, 1706, known as Master Harrington', Francis, June 11, 1709, married Prudence Stearns, Susanna, born September 9, 1711, married Samuel Barnard, her son Samuel was one of the Boston tea party, and a major in the revolutionary war

(III) Samuel Harrington, son of Edward and Mary Harrington, was born August 3, 1704 He married, October 19, 1725, Sarah Warren He was called "of Walthams" and had children Samuel, baptized May 19, 1728, Mary, baptized May 19, 1728, Elijah, born 1734, probably another son, was in Worcester prior to 1768 ——

(IV) Samuel Harrington, was called "of Worcester" in 1776, at which time his daughter Hannah married Daniel Maynard, of Shrewsbury He very likely was here prior to April, 1775, when his son Samuel marched from Worcester in Captain Timothy Bigelow's company for Lexington His children were Samuel, born 1754, married Silence Robinson, he died 1838, aged eighty-four years, Hannah, born 1757, married Daniel Maynard, Noah, born February 2, 1760, married Lois Kingsley

(V) Samuel Harrington, fifth in line from the ancestor Richard, married November 19 1782, Mrs Silence Robinson, at Dorchester, Massachusetts, where they first settled and there all but one of their children were born He marched from Worcester on the alarm at Lexington, April 19, 1775, in Captain Bigelow's company of Worcester men, and served twenty-three days in Colonel Artemas Ward's regiment He came with his family to Worcester about the year 1796, and here his youngest son was born, September 1, that year Their children were Susanna, born February 12, 1783 married Abel Flagg, October 31, 1802, Samuel, October 3, 1784, married Nancy White, April 23, 1812, Lucretia, August 21, 1786, married John Baird, December 25, 1800, James, June 23, 1788, married Esther Flagg, April 25, 1821, Sarah April 12, 1790, married John Gleason, and Peter White, Ebenezer, September 22, 1792, Mary, August 24, 1794, married Samuel Perry, Austin, September 1, 1796

(V) Noah Harrington, son of Samuel Harrington (4), was born February 2, 1760, and died July 18, 1832, aged seventy-two years He served as matross in Colonel Timothy Craft's regiment of artillery He was also in Captain Joseph Sibley's company in 1777, and served in other capacities in the revolutionary struggle He is described as five feet, eleven inches tall and of light complexion He married, July 27, 1784 Lois Kingsley, born September 12, 1760, died October 11, 1820, aged fifty-four years They first settled in Shrewsbury, where three children were born to them They came to

Worcester about 1792, and lived on the Grafton road, where it passes near the Boston & Albany Railway tracks He, with his brother Samuel, kept a tavern in Boston on the site of the present Adams House Their children were Lydia, born December 25, 1784, William, 1786, died in infancy, Hannah, 1792, died young, Samuel, died young, William, February 25, 1788, died February 12, 1871, Luke, September 12, 1789, died November 1, 1855, Samuel, 1797, died April 4, 1855, Eliza, 1800, married Mr Shay, and died July 17, 1869, Thomas J, January 27, 1804, died July 5, 1888, Hannah, July 17, 1809, married Henry Tower, and died March 23, 1853

(VI) William Harrington, son of Noah (5), was born February 25, 1788, died February 12, 1871 He married Abigail Adaline Stowell, daughter of Peter and Elizabeth Stowell She was born March 15, 1799 Mr Harrington passed his youthful days on his father's farm, and when a young man attempted to master the trade of a mason While at work on the original Exchange building on Main street, Worcester, the staging on which he and others were at work gave way and all were thrown to the ground Young Harrington was picked up for dead and carried to Mr Hampilton's residence In a few moments Mrs Hampilton discovered signs of life, when every effort was put forth in his behalf His knee was crushed in the fall, and after a confinement lasting five years the limb was finally amputated by Dr John Green He then fitted himself for a teacher and taught in the Central Worcester district Charles Stiles, George Bancroft, Stephen Salisbury and Henry W Miller attended his school Later he conducted a store and a tavern The second time he embarked in mercantile business, he located at what has come to be known as Harrington s corner Flour sold in 1812 here at twenty-five dollars per barrel He resided on Park street, near Salem street He died in 1871, aged eighty-two years, eleven months and seventeen days His children were Frances A, born October 4, 1821, William Henry, April 29, 1824, Chauncy Goodrich, June 30, 1826

(VII) William Henry Harrington was born April 29, 1824 He married Lucy Forbes, of Millbury, and had one son to reach mature years, William Harrington, now of Worcester After the death of his first wife he married Mrs Bemis Mr Harrington was a manufacturer, and many years operated the plant known as the Berlin mills, where woolens are manufactured Prior to this he made wrenches About 1855 he bought out the business of Calvin Witherbee in Millbury, where he continued making monkey-wrenches, chisels and drawing knives After the beginning of the civil war he made bayonets for the government A Mr Heald was interested with him in starting in business at the Berlin mills, and also the Atlanta mills in Millbury

(III) Josiah Harrington, son of John Harrington, an elder brother of Edward, the father of Francis, was born June 12, 1709 He married, May 20, 1730, Dinah Flagg, youngest child of Allen Flagg He bought land in Worcester of Cornelius Durant May, 1754, he was 'of Walthams, Massachusetts" Their children were Huldah, baptized September 25, 1731, Dinah, baptized May 20, 1733, died September 30, 1759, was the wife of Elijah Livermore, Elijah, baptized November 17, 1734 Tabitha, baptized September 11, 1737, Elizabeth, baptized April 15, 1739, Josiah, baptized May 11, 1740, married Mary Jones, January 10, 1764, Hannah, baptized November 22, 1741, Jemima, baptized July 29, 1744, Sarah, baptized May 11, 1746, Jemima, baptized January 24, 1748, Anna, baptized July 2, 1749, Mary, baptized September 15, 1751, Silas, baptized May 21, 1752, married, November 25, 1773, Mindwell Wellington, she died October 27, 1808, aged fifty-seven years Silas Harrington married Abigail Thorp, February 1, 1809 He died in Worcester, June 15, 1831 His children were Olive, born 1775, Lyda, 1778, Jeremiah, 1779, Josiah, 1781, Clarissa, 1784, Silas, 1786, Mindwell Wellington, 1810, Hannah Bucklin, 1812, Clarissa Harlan, 1815, Mary, 1817, Silas Flagg, 1820

(IV) Elijah Harrington, son of Josiah and Dinah (Flagg) Harrington, married Azubah Rice, February 8, 1758 She died in April, 1768, aged thirty-four years He married (second) Mehitable Draper, in 1769 He died February 3, 1811, aged seventy-seven years Their children were Ephraim, baptized June 29, 1760, Azubah, baptized April 11, 1761, died in infancy, Azubah, baptized March 24, 1762, Mehitable, baptized May 24, 1770, Abigail, baptized July 14, 1773, Tamesin, baptized June 7, 1776, Fanny, baptized August 14, 1777, Elijah, baptized August 2, 1779

(III) Francis Harrington, eighth child of Edward (2) and grandson of Robert the American ancestor, was born June 11, 1709 He married Prudence Stearns, of Watertown, Massachusetts, in 1736 She was born April 27, 1713, and died at Worcester, August, 1751, aged about thirty-eight years He married (second) Deborah Brigham, in Westboro, November 14, 1752 She died in Worcester, April 20, 1799, aged eighty-four years He died July 18, 1793, aged eighty-four years At the date of his marriage with Prudence Stearns he was called 'of Grafton" Thither he took his young wife and established his home, and there their eldest child Francis, Jr, was born In the Spring of 1741 he purchased of Joseph Dana and Mary Dana, his wife, of Pomfret, Connecticut, the farm in Worcester that was to become his future home He no doubt took possession of the purchase just named as soon as Charles Davenport (then on the land) could easily vacate the premises, and Harrington was the first of his name to settle in Worcester, as evidenced by the town records, the name of Francis Harrington appearing in the list of "persons qualified to serve as jurymen agreeable to law" This list was laid before the selectmen at the meeting held July 19, 1742, and soon public honors and responsibilities came to him, for at the next meeting he was chosen field driver, and was re-elected the next year The record shows that at a meeting held May 16, 1743, it was voted that in consideration of great sickness in Francis Harrington's family, his tax for the last year be repaid to him, being one pound, three shillings, and August 29, the town voted him seventy-two shillings for 'two birds two tails" In March, 1748, he was chosen constable For four years, 1754 to 1777 inclusive, he was chosen to serve on committee to provide schoolmasters for his district His chief service, however, was given to the office of surveyor of highways and collector of highway taxes, having been first chosen to that office in 1750, and re-elected in 1758-63-68-72-83

The children of Francis and Prudence (Stearns) Harrington were Francis, born in Grafton, 1737, died in Worcester, April 6, 1768, Nathaniel, born in Worcester, 1742, married Ruth Stone, Mary, born in Worcester, December 16, 1753, married Jonathan Stone, Jr, February, 1777, Prudence, born April 20, 1755, married Jonah Perry, July 6, 1780, William, born November 18, 1756, married Mary Perry, May 29, 1781

(IV) Nathaniel Harrington, son of Francis and Prudence Harrington, was born in Worcester, 1742

D. A. Harrington

Francis H. Harrington.

He married Ruth Stone, July 2, 1776, who was born in 1748, and died August 24, 1817, aged sixty-nine years Mr Harrington was born and reared on the Harrington homestead, and when the alarm was sounded calling for men to assist in defending the rights and liberties of the colony, he responded, going out as sergeant in Captain Timothy Bigelow's company of minute-men, Colonel Artemas Ward's regiment, which marched on the alarm of April 19, 1775 He signed, with others, order for advance pay in June, 1775 He was also first lieutenant in Captain Joshua Whitney's company, Fifth Worcester County Regiment of Massachusetts militia Mr Harrington's introduction into public office in his native town was March 11, 1777, when at town meeting he was chosen, with seven others, to serve as "hog reeves" Two years later his name appears on the jury list, and in 1780 also as assessor, and the following year as one to provide schooling in his district In 1788-94 Mr Harrington was chosen surveyor of highways and collector of highway taxes He served on the school committee from 1790 to 1808, and was chosen on committee for building public schoolhouses in 1797-99 For more than twenty-five years from 1798 he was paid by the town for boarding and nursing Kezia Morse, a poor person In 1799 he was fence viewer, and he served as a selectman from 1803 to 1809 inclusive About the last public service rendered the town was in running the boundary line between Worcester and Shrewsbury In 1808 he, with the other members of the board, signed a letter to the selectmen of Boston declining their request that the citizens of Worcester be assembled in town meeting to concur with the sentiments expressed by the inhabitants of Boston in a petition addressed to President Jefferson, praying for the suspension of the embargo act He died February 28, 1831, aged eighty-nine years His children were Francis, born May 15, 1777, died October 17, 1841, Jonathan, October 31, 1779, married Mary Flagg, Sarah, August 14, 1786

(V) Captain Francis Harrington married Lydia Perry, May 13, 1801 He remained on the old homestead He was captain of the militia of the Worcester South Company Although not prominent in public affairs, he was honored more or less with responsible positions by the town, such as school committeeman, surveyor of highways and collector of highway taxes In 1816 he was chosen with William Trowbridge, Thaddeas Chapin, Benjamin Thaxter and Ebenezer Mower to report at a future meeting on the claim made by Isaiah Thomas, Esq, "for work, etc, done at the bridge near Mr Salisbury's, etc" His children were Daniel, born October 4, 1802, married Clarissa Gray, Mary, March 20, 1804, married Captain and Deacon Samuel Perry, Hannah, February 12, 1806 died July 14, 1823, Joseph, February 27, 1808, died April 13, 1812, Francis, August 11, 1811, married (first) Harriet W Robbinson, (second) Frances J Moore, he was an alderman in 1860, Lydia, December 12, 1814, married Nahum Flagg

(V) Jonathan Harrington, son of Nathaniel (4), was born October 31, 1779 He married Molly (or Mary) Flagg, 1804, and resided on a portion of the original homestead Their only child was Benjamin, born April 8, 1805, died August 15, 1873 His home was at Harrington Court, near his cousin, Daniel Harrington He married Lucretia Flagg, March 18, 1834 Their children Mary Elizabeth, born January 25, 1836, married Samuel G Curtis, Benjamin F, September 2, 1838, married Harriet W Harrington, Hannah Flagg, November 12, 1842, died April 11, 1845, Henry Augustus, September 8, 1846, married Delia M Griggs, he was a member of overseers of the poor, 1888 to 1896, and a member of the board of aldermen, 1900-01, Sarah A, married Gonzalo Buxton

(VI) Captain Daniel Harrington, son of Captain Francis Harrington (5), was born October 4, 1802, and died September 11, 1863 He married Clarissa Gray, born August 23, 1809, and died June 6, 1885 He succeeded to the home estate, and in 1831 his name appears on the jury list Subsequently he was called to fill the position of fence viewer, school committee and highway surveyor He served in the common council, 1849-1850, and board of aldermen, 1851 Their children were

1 Joseph A Harrington, born October 26, 1829, died December 4, 1875, a soldier in Fifty-first Regiment, Massachusetts Volunteer Infantry, in civil war for nine months, married Zelia M Pierce

2 Emily A Harrington, born October 23, 1831, married George S Battelle, died 1883

3 Charles A Harrington, born May 20, 1834, died October 16, 1905 He married (first) Lucy Goulding, (second) Margaret Patch He served in the city council, 1882-1883 His children were Elmer W, Herbert H

4 Henry M Harrington, born March 20, 1836, died August 6, 1837

5 Delia A Harrington, born March 21, 1841, married George B Andrews, 1863, residence Clinton, Massachusetts

6 Maria A Harrington, born September 2, 1843, married Edward W Wellington, son of T W Wellington, coal dealer at Worcester, Mr Wellington enlisted in the civil war, serving as lieutenant His two children were Delia M, Frank E

7 Hon Francis Alfred Harrington, born November 17, 1846, married (first) Roxanna M Grout, who died December 24, 1900, (second) Mrs Lillia (Dudley) Leighton He was born and reared at the old homestead, the farm purchased in 1741, which he now owns He is a prominent Odd Fellow and Free Mason, and also active in Grange organizations, having been treasurer of the State Grange for twenty years He was elected as alderman to represent ward three in the city government, serving during the years 1887-88-89 in the board of aldermen The following year he was elected mayor, and was twice re-elected His administration covered a period from 1890 to 1893, and proved one of economy and success, for all there were many difficult problems to solve He was then called higher and represented the Second Worcester senatorial district in the legislature for the years 1899-1900-01 He is past eminent commander of the Worcester County Commandery, Knights Templar, and past master of Athelstan Lodge of Master Masons

The children of Hon Francis Alfred Harrington are Charles A, married Luella B Crook, of Columbus, Ohio, he was a teacher in the Worcester high school, now engaged in the insurance business, he is commander of the Worcester County Commandery, Knights Templar, past master of Athelstan Lodge, Ancient, Free and Accepted Masons, and master of the Worcester Grange, Patrons of Husbandry Their children are Ruth Anna and Mildred Elizabeth Frank C, married Leora Leighton and they have Frank L, Robert Dudley, Lillia L, and Anna G, he is the secretary of the Callahan Supply Company of Worcester, and is past master of Athelstan Lodge, Ancient Free and Accepted Masons May E, married James P Gray

8 George A Harrington, born July 8, 1849, died 1883

9 Daniel A Harrington, born May 8, 1851, was educated at the Worcester public schools and academy, also graduated at Howes Business College,

Worcester, in 1867 He resided on the old Harrington homestead, farming and contracting in the dairy business until 1876, when he became identified with the livery business, in which he has been engaged for twenty-eight years His barns are models of up-to-date liveries He is also president and treasurer of the Harrington Automobile Station He is a member of the Independent Order Odd Fellows and in 1903 was elected brigadier-general of the Second Brigade of Patriarchs Militant of Independent Order Odd Fellows He served two terms on the board of aldermen, and was a member of the board when the vote was passed to build the new city hall of Worcester, that now so beautifully adorns the Common Among other things he had the honor of being chairman of the committee that induced the trustees to locate the State Odd Fellows Home in Worcester, and was chief marshal of the immense parade when the corner stone of that institution was laid in 1892

Mr Harrington married Jennie A Spiers, by whom the following children were born Clara A, a teacher in the Worcester schools Josie A, married Herbert Linnell, a graduate of the Worcester Polytechnic Institute, who is now holding a position as resident engineer of the city of Colon at the Isthmus of Panama His was the first family to reside there, from this country, after our government took possession of that territory Mr and Mrs Linnell have two sons—Herbert H, born 1898, and Phillip, born 1900 John S Harrington, married Mabel M Clark, by whom two sons were born—John S, Jr, October 27, 1903, and William Clark, June 28, 1905

(VI) Mary Harrington, daughter of Captain Francis Harrington, married Captain and Deacon Samuel Perry, and they settled on the old Harrington homestead, Vernon street, Worcester Their children were Hannah Harrington, born October 8, 1824, Mary Stone, November 8, 1826, Joseph Stone, November 3, 1828, Julia Maria, October 13, 1830, Nathan Fiske, March 10, 1833, Lydia Almira, February 27, 1835, Harriet Newell, February 28, 1837, David Brainard, March 7, 1839, Samuel Payson, March 18, 1841, Moses, July 15, 1843

HOPKINS FAMILY This surname was spelled Hopkyns in England in the sixteenth century It is an ancient English family of Oxford county John Hopkyns was a civic officer in Coventry, Oxfordshire, in 1567 From the strong resemblance of the armorial bearings of the Wykehams of Swelcliffe Oxford county, and of Hopkins of Oving, it is conjectured by Burke that in early times some bond of connection existed between these families In confirmation of this surmise there is in Sibford Gower in Swalcliffe Parish a small estate which is charged with a quit-rent of a hundred pence that tradition has assigned to the late owners as the nineteenth John Hopkins who has successively and lineally inherited it without the intervention of any other Christian name than John It belonged some fifty years ago to Mr D D Hopkins, who had then in his possession a deed of the ninth year of Elizabeth's reign when the name was written Hopkyns As this estate joins immediately to Warwickshire, it may fairly be assumed that the family of Hopkins in Coventry and Swalcliffe derive from a common ancestor Following is the ancestry of the Coventry family

(I) William Hopkins, chosen to preside over the city of Coventry His sons William, the heir, Richard, sheriff of Coventry 1554, Nicholas, sheriff of Coventry 1561

(II) William Hopkins, son of William (1), was sheriff of Coventry 1557, mayor 1564, was presented for heresy, married Agnes Riley, daughter of Thomas Riley

(III) Richard Hopkins, son of William Hopkins (2), was also of Coventry His sons Samuson, William, proprietor of Shortley

(IV) Sampson Hopkins, son of Richard Hopkins (3), was mayor of Coventry 1609, represented the city in parliament He died 1622 Children Sir Richard, Sampson, mayor 1640, Ann, married Matthew Babbington, Esq, of Rothby Temple, county Leicester, died 1648, aged thirty-three years

(V) Sir Richard Hopkins, son of Sampson Hopkins (4), was steward of Coventry, represented the city in Parliament, married Sarah Burton, the daughter and co-heir of John and Mary (Jesson) Burton, of Buckland, Hampshire Mary Jesson's father, William Jesson, was mayor of Coventry in 1631 Children Richard, Thomas, Sarah, married Sir John Goodricke

The American ancestor it is fair to assume was connected with this family of Coventry, though actual proof has not been found The Hopkins coat of arms Sa a chev arg charged with three roses gu between three matchlocks, or

(I) Thomas Hopkins, the immigrant ancestor of many of the numerous families bearing the name of Hopkins, especially in Rhode Island and Massachusetts, was the progenitor of Frederick Ferdinand Hopkins, of Worcester He was the son of William and Joanna (Arnold) Hopkins, and was born in England, April 7, 1616, died in Providence prior to December 27, 1792 His mother was a daughter of Thomas and Alice (Gully) Arnold Joanna Arnold was baptized November 30, 1577, her brother, William Arnold, was born June 24, 1587, the father of Bendict Arnold, not the traitor but the first governor of Rhode Island under the royal charter of 1643 and ancestor of the Arnolds of Warwick Her half-brother, Thomas Arnold, is progenitor of the Arnold families of northern Rhode Island The wife of Thomas Hopkins is believed to be Elizabeth Arnold, daughter of William Arnold, and sister to Governor Benedict Arnold, a cousin Thomas Hopkins was a deputy to the general assembly from Providence for the years 1652-59-60-66-67, a member of the town council for 1667-72 Children William, see forward, Thomas, Jr, died April 1, 1718

(II) Major William Hopkins, son of Thomas Hopkins (1), was born about 1650 He was admitted a freeman April 30, 1672, and married, about 1680, Abigail Dexter, widow of Stephen Dexter, son of Rev Gregory Dexter, daughter of John and Sarah Whipple, early settlers in Providence, removing from Dorchester about 1659 Major Hopkins was a man of marked ability, serving the colony in both civil and military offices to an advanced age He was noted as a surveyor of lands throughout the colony and numerous accounts of his labors in this profession are found in the records His home at the time of his death and probably for a long time previous was at Massapauge, a portion of Providence that was included in the part set off to make the town of Cranston in 1754 He died July 8 1723, leaving a large property, the bulk of which he bequeathed to his grandson William His widow died 1725 The only child of Major William and Abigail Hopkins was William, see forward

(III) William Hopkins, son of William Hopkins (2), was born about 1682, and died in Scituate in 1738 He married early in life Ruth Wilkinson, daughter of Samuel and Plaine (Wickenden) Wilkinson Samuel was a son of Lawrence Wilkinson, an early settler in Providence, and Plaine was a daughter of Rev William Wickenden, who succeeded Rev Gregory Dexter as pastor of the First Baptist Church in Providence The will of William Hopkins was made June 11, 1738, and proved October 9, 1738 The children William, born probably at Cranston about 1705, died in Providence, February 17, 1755, Stephen, born March 7, 1707, see forward, Rufus, John, born about 1710, died February 1, 1755, Hope, born March 3, 1717, died July 20, 1803, Esek, born April 26, 1718, died February 26, 1802, Samuel, died September, 1744, Abigail, born 1727, died January 30, 1772, Susanna, born 1728, died November 8, 1745

(IV) Governor Stephen Hopkins, son of William Hopkins (3), was born in Cranston, Rhode Island, March 7, 1707, as is shown by a record of his family made by himself February 3, 1754, which sets at rest the oft-repeated account of Scituate being his birthplace He was elected the first moderator of the town of Scituate in 1730, and in 1731 was town clerk He was first elected to the general assembly in 1732 In 1742 he removed to Providence After that he represented Providence in the general assembly for many years and was several times the speaker He was for ten years chief justice of the superior court In 1755 he was elected governor of Rhode Island and held that office nine years In 1774 he was elected member of the continental congress and he was one of the signers of the Declaration of Independence At that time he was suffering from a nervous affliction that made writing very difficult For a number of years previous to 1776 it is stated on the authority of his friend and associate, Moses Brown, that when he wrote at all he was compelled to guide his right hand with his left This accounts for the poor appearance of his signature on the Declaration of Independence In early life he wrote a beautiful hand, as shown in his town records written when town clerk of Scituate

Stephen Hopkins did not confine himself to politics and the holding of office He took an intelligent and active share in building the commerce of Providence, and the Brown family, then already prominent among the great mercantile and shipping houses of New England, found in the rising judge and statesman an energetic and practical coadjutor in their efforts to increase the facilities for traffic and commercial intercourse Such necessary public works as bridging the rivers met with strenuous opposition, and every improvement of a public nature had to be fought for in those days A system of insurance policies for the benefit of merchants and chiefly if not entirely marine, appears to have been instituted by Governor Hopkins as early as 1756, although the first insurance corporation, the Providence Insurance Company, was incorporated February 3, 1799, and is still in existence, the oldest in New England He began to write a history of Rhode Island, but was interrupted by the revolutionary war and the difficulties preceding it, so that only the first chapter, published in the *Providence Gazette* and *Country Journal*, was ever written Governor Hopkins, more than any other man, was responsible for the national sentiment that developed slowly in Rhode Island, but which finally triumphed and brought the state into the Union He was for a life time an advocate of co-operation among the colonies, of independence even if force were necessary, as it was found necessary, and of a policy leading up to a national government "Next perhaps to Samuel Adams and Thomas Jefferson, he was," says his biographer, William E Foster, "most active in developing the system of committees of correspondence It was he who may well be called the father of the Congress of 1774, and whose commanding influence in that Congress led to the formation of a powerful sentiment in favor of separation from the home government, the member who introduced, advocated and carried through the Second Congress those measures creating an independent postal service, and an American naval armament, which did so much to commit the still reluctant colonies to the exercise of the national functions"

In a paper read before the Rhode Island Historical Society, Mr Foster thus summed up the character and service of Governor Hopkins "Father of the commercial development and ever-increasing prosperity of Providence, distinguished among the founders of this college (Brown), the founder of the first public library in Providence, the first Rhode Island man to make the name and influence of the colony a power outside of its limits, the very first delegate ever nominated and elected to the very first Congress of the United States, the governor of the colony for a greater number of years than any other of its Eighteenth Century governors, with two exceptions,—yet the strongest of his claims to distinction is associated with the creation and growth of a national sentiment in Rhode Island Rhode Island has had few names more worthy of honor, few historic characters more worthy of careful study, than that of Stephen Hopkins"

The *Providence Journal*, June 23, 1884, says of Hopkins "Stephen Hopkins lived to see the states independent, he did not live to see them a united nation He died July 13, 1785, in his own house on Towne street in Providence and was followed to his grave by the judges of the courts, the President, Corporation and students of the college and in the language of the *Providence Gazette* by 'a prodigious concourse of respectable citizens' The state and the nation, and more especially the people of Providence, whose particular champion he was in all the struggles of party, owe to him a debt of immortal gratitude, and his name will be remembered in Rhode Island while Point Judith repulses the assaults of the Atlantic, and Prospect Hill looks down upon our city of homes"

Governor Hopkins married (first), October 9 1726, Sarah Scott, born June 25, 1707, died September 9, 1753, daughter of Sylvanus and Joanna (Jenckes) Scott, and granddaughter of John Scott, son of Richard Scott, said to have been the first Quaker to settle in Providence He married (second), January, 2, 1755, Anne Smith, widow of Benjamin Smith, and daughter of a man of the same name She had by Benjamin Smith four children, one of whom, Benjamin, born October 14, 1744 was the father of thirteen children, whose home was at Quinsnaket in the Arnold neighborhood, in what is now the town of Lincoln The children of Stephen and Sarah Hopkins Rufus, see forward, John, born November 6, 1728, died July 20, 1753, Ruth, born October 3, 1731, died April 2, 1735, Lydia, born January 6, 1733, died June 29 1793, Silvanus, born October 19 1734, died April 23, 1753, Simon, born August 26 1736, died April 2, 1744, George, born January 11, 1739, died 1775

(V) Rufus Hopkins son of Governor Stephen Hopkins (4), was born in Cranston, Rhode Island, February 10, 1727, died in Scituate, November 13, 1812 He entered early upon a distinguished career in business and public life His early life was spent in maritime pursuits in which he attained high rank as a nautical commander He held many offices of trust and honor He was for several years a judge of the court of common pleas for Providence county and for a season justice of the superior court of the state, was repeatedly elected to represent

Scituate in the general assembly, a trustee of Brown University from 1782 to his death About 1766 he was associated with his father and Messrs Nicholas, Joseph, John and Moses Brown and Jabez Bowen in a project to utilize a bed of iron ore found in Cranston and the building of Hope Furnace in which was cast, among other articles, cannon for use of the army in the revolution The bell now in use in the steeple of the First Baptist Church was broken in 1787 and recast at Hope Furnace It was at Scituate and Rufus Hopkins was in charge

He married (first), October 13, 1747, Abigail Angell, who died July 21, 1758, aged twenty-seven years, eleven days, daughter of John Angell He married (second), November 11, 1759, Sarah Olney, daughter of Captain Joseph Olney, and sister of Colonel Jeremiah Olney She was born March 31, 1732, died October 2, 1785 The children of Rufus and Abigail Hopkins John, born October 11, 1750, died September 2, 1754, a daughter, born and died April 5, 1753, Silvanus, born September 17, 1756, died August 21, 1757 The children of Rufus and Sarah Hopkins Stephen, born January 1, 1762, died June 2, 1830, Silvanus, born June 25, 1764 see forward, Rufus, born November 15, 1771, died August 29, 1773, Joseph Olney, born March 20, 1774 died January 5, 1792

(VI) Colonel Silvanus Hopkins, son of Rufus Hopkins (5), was born June 25, 1764, died August 18, 1824 He was for many years a resident of Scituate, Rhode Island, and engaged in the manufacture of cotton goods He stood high socially as well as in business, and rose to the rank of colonel in the military service About 1819 he removed to Washington Village, Coventry, Rhode Island, and became cashier of the Bank of Kent located there Subsequently he removed again to Norwich, Connecticut, where he died August 18, 1824, and his widow August 28th of the same year He married Mary Wanton, daughter of Captain Peter and Elizabeth (Gardner) Wanton, of a distinguished Rhode Island family The children of Colonel Silvanus and Mary Hopkins Sarah Olney, died June 1, 1821, in her twenty-ninth year, Joseph Olney, born January 22, 1794 died December 1 1841, William Wanton, died November 24, 1824, aged twenty-six years, Samuel Stow, died October 16, 1826, aged twenty-six years, Edward A, born July 4, 1802, died September 16, 1836, George Silvanus, see forward

(VII) George Silvanus Hopkins, son of Colonel Silvanus Hopkins (6), was born in Scituate, Rhode Island December 3 1804 died December 12, 1863, at Colchester, Connecticut, aged fifty-nine years

George Silvanus Hopkins received his education in the common schools of his native town At the age of fifteen he removed with his parents to Coventry, Rhode Island In early manhood he learned the trade of machinist, which he followed through life He was master mechanic for a time at the Naumkeag Mills Salem, Massachusetts, and for another mill in New Hampshire He was master mechanic at the Heywood Rubber Company at Colchester, Connecticut, for a number of years, and at Unionville, Connecticut At one time he was in the machine business at Norwich, Connecticut, in partnership with Joseph Hopkins, his brother He was a Methodist in religion In politics he was a Whig until the Republican party was organized and afterward a Republican He was a member of the Masonic fraternity at Norwich

He married September 15 1832, Esther (Rose) Cooley, who died January 23, 1838, aged twenty-nine years He married (second), September 1, 1843, Dianthia Robinson, who died December 7, 1850, aged forty-eight years The children of George S and Esther Hopkins William W, born October 1, 1833, died August 7, 1850, Frederick Ferdinand, born February 17, 1836, see forward, Mary Esther, born December 25, 1837 The only child of George Silvanus and Dianthia Hopkins was George Warren, born April 1, 1845

(VIII) Frederick Ferdinand Hopkins, son of George Silvanus Hopkins (7), was born at Norwich, Connecticut, February 17, 1836 He attended the common schools of his native place until about seventeen years old In 1854 he came to Worcester and entered the employ of Allen & Thurber, manufacturers of fire arms Mr Hopkins continued with the firm about three years He worked for a short time in a firearms factory at Newark, New Jersey He was an expert machinist and skilled in the making of fire arms From 1858 to 1869 he did contract work for Frank Wesson, brother of Daniel B Wesson, late of Springfield (of the famous firm of Smith & Wesson) In 1870 Mr Hopkins began as solicitor of business for the State Mutual Life Assurance Company He was promoted finally to the position which he still occupies, as general agent of the company He formerly attended the old Salem Street Congregational Church, but has been a member of Piedmont Congregational Church since its organization, and was for sixteen years secretary and treasurer of the Sunday school He is a member of the Worcester Congregational Club He is an honorary member of the Worcester Continentals and was formerly an active member He is an associate member of George H Ward Post, No 10, Grand Army of the Republic

He married, January 1, 1857, Sarah Maria Lewis, born in Norwich, Connecticut, December 16, 1836, daughter of Joseph B and Deborah (Rathbun) Lewis Their children Herbert Perry, see forward, Edward Earle, see forward, Marion A, born June 16, 1862, died August 5, 1864, Frederick Sylvanus, see forward

(IX) Herbert Perry Hopkins, son of Frederick Ferdinand Hopkins (8), was born at Norwich, Connecticut, June 25, 1858 He removed with his parents to Worcester when a young boy and was educated there in the public schools, and the Classical high school In 1878 he entered the employ of the Boston, Barre & Gardner Railroad as an express driver, was soon made express messenger, and was appointed baggage master within a short time A year later he became clerk in the general offices of the company, and in 1880 was made a conductor of passenger trains, a position he held for six years He resigned to become associated with his father, who was general agent of the State Mutual Life Assurance Company, with offices at 240 Main street, later in the Burnside building and finally to the present quarters in the new State Mutual building He remained with his father until his death, December 28, 1904 He was elected treasurer of the Worcester Association of Life Underwriters, a position he held to the time of his death He attended All Saints Protestant Church, Worcester He was a Republican in politics He was made a member of Quinsigamond Lodge, Free Masons, April 12, 1889, Eureka Chapter, Royal Arch Masons, June 4, 1889, Worcester County Commandery, Knights Templar, September 20, 1889 He was a member of Company C, Second Regiment, Massachusetts Volunteer Militia, Worcester Light Infantry, from December 2, 1879, to December, 1882 He was at one time a member of the Arling

F. F. Hopkins

ton Social Club and for a number of years its president He also belonged to the Latassit Canoe Club and the Uptown Club

He married, October 5, 1893, and had one child, Sarah M, born in Worcester, May 14, 1901 Mr Hopkins died in the very prime of life, cutting short a promising career in business He had the natural ability and the personal magnetism that makes a man especially successful in the insurance business He attracted friends by his voice and manners, was social, sympathetic and generous, and his death was universally regretted

(IX) Edward Earle Hopkins, son of Frederick Ferdinand Hopkins (8), was born at Colchester, Connecticut, August 26, 1860 He received his early education in the Worcester public schools, graduating from the Classical high school in 1878 While still in school he began the study of dentistry In 1880 he entered the Harvard Dental School, Boston, and was graduated in 1882 with the degree of D M D In the fall of that year he began to practice in Boston His offices were at 85 Newbury street, where he was located for fifteen years He purchased the estate at 175 Newbury street, Boston, in 1879, and has been located there since that time He was for seven years after graduating an instructor in operative dentistry and had charge of the crown and bridge work in Harvard Dental School He resides at 355 Newtonville avenue, Newtonville, Massachusetts He and his family attend the Newtonville Congregational Church In politics Dr Hopkins is a Republican He is a member of the Newton Social Club, the American Academy of Dental Science, the Harvard Dental Alumni Association and was formerly a member of the Harvard Odontological Society

He married, August 4, 1886, Annie Louise Tullock, born April 7, 1861, daughter of Arthur and Emily C (Preble) Tullock, of Whitefield, Maine Their children Helen, born July 29, 1887, Stephen Tullock, born March 19, 1892, named for Governor Stephen Hopkins (IV), mentioned above

(IX) Frederick Sylvanus Hopkins, son of Frederick Ferdinand Hopkins (8), was born in Worcester, December 11, 1864 He was educated in the Worcester public schools and the Classical high school In 1883 he became clerk in the Worcester National Bank Two years later he accepted a position in the office of Norcross Brothers In the fall of 1886 he entered Harvard Dental School, from which he was graduated in 1889 with the degree of D M D He started at once to practice in offices at 2 Park Square, Boston After two years he removed his offices to 159 Newbury street and later to 161 Newbury street, his present location From 1889 to 1893 he was instructor of operative dentistry in the Harvard Dental School He resides in Worcester Dr Hopkins and family attend Piedmont Congregational Church He is a Republican in politics He is a member of the Harvard Odontological Society, the Harvard Dental Alumni Association, the Boston Chapter, Sons of the Revolution, and the Tatnuck Country Club at Worcester He was formerly a member of the Commonwealth Club and of the Worcester Light Infantry, Company C, Second Regiment, Massachusetts Volunteer Militia, from 1885 to 1887

He married, August 23, 1892, at Plymouth, Massachusetts, Etta May Holbrook, born May 22, 1865, daughter of Eliphalet and Harriet (Rice) Holbrook, of Worcester, Massachusetts Their children Esther, born August 6, 1894, in Plymouth, Massachusetts, Robert Holbrook, born in Worcester, Massachusetts, March 22, 1902, Frederick Sylvanus, Jr, born in Worcester, Massachusetts, September 27, 1903, died May 24, 1905

WARD FAMILY William Ward (1) was the immigrant ancestor of Edward Dickinson Ward, of Worcester, Massachusetts, and of most of the branches of the Ward family in Worcester county He was probably from York county, England One of the captains under William the Conqueror was named Ward, of whom there is a record dated 1066 In 1175 William de la Ward resided in Chester The family was numerous and well scattered over England at the time of the settlement of the American colonies The ancient coat of arms of this family was Az a cross baton pr Crest Wolf's head erased

The first record of William Ward is found in Sudbury in 1639 He may have been there several years He was admitted a freeman May 10, 1643, and for many years was one of the chief men of the town He was a deputy to the general court from Sudbury in 1644, for many years was a selectman and most of the time chairman of the board He was the local magistrate—the commissioner to end small causes He deposed October 4 1664, that he was about sixty-one years old, fixing the year of his birth as 1603 He was one of the nine Sudbury men who petitioned for the grant subsequently known as Marlboro, and including originally not only the present city of Marlboro, but the towns of Westboro, Northboro and Southboro In 1660, the year of incorporation Ward settled in the new town where his descendants have been numerous and distinguished He was chosen the first deacon of the Marlboro church He drew fifty acres, the largest size of house lot granted by the proprietors These home lots varied, according to the importance of the individual proprietor, from fifteen to fifty acres His house was on the south side of the road nearly opposite the meeting house, and his land extended to what was then called Belcher's pond, near which the tavern of his son-in-law, Abraham Williams, was located Ward suffered the usual hardships and losses of the pioneer and especially during King Philip's war he lost heavily His buildings were burned, his cattle destroyed and one son slain He died at Marlboro, August 10, 1687, aged eighty-five years His will was dated April 6, 1686 He bequeathed to his wife Elizabeth, children John and Increase, the children of sons Richard and Eleazer, deceased, son-in-law Abraham Williams, to all his children by former wife and present wife The widow died December 9, 1700, in her eighty-seventh year Their children were John, born about 1626, married Hannah Jackson, Joanna, born 1628, married Abraham Williams, Obadiah, born 1632, see forward, Richard, born 1635, married Mary Moore, Deborah, born 1637, married John Johnson Hannah, born 1639, married Abraham How William, born January 22, 1640, married Hannah Eames, Samuel, born September 24 1641, married Sarah How, Elizabeth, born April 14, 1643, Increase, born February 22, 1644, married ——— Record, Hopestill, born February 24 1646, married James Woods Mary, born about 1647, married Daniel Stone, William, born February 12, 1648-49, Eleazer, married Hannah Rice, Bethia, born 1658, married Daniel Price

(II) Obadiah Ward, son of William Ward (1), was born in 1632, died in Marlborough, Massachusetts January 5 1718 aged eighty-six years He had lands assigned him in Sudbury in 1653 and house lot of twenty-one acres with the after divisions in Marlboro in 1660, and he moved there soon after He was a deputy to the general court in 1689 from Marlboro He married, November 13, 1667, Mary ———, who died August 22, 1706, at Marlboro He married (second) Joanna Mixer, daughter of Isaac Mixer, of Watertown Joanna was born December 14 1666 Children of Obadiah and Mary Ward were Alice, born November 14, 1668, William, born January 7, 1670, see forward, Obadiah, born September 18 1672, married Elizabeth ——— Bethia, born 1674, died same year, Mary, born May 4, 1676 Jane born 1677, Edmund, born January 21, 1679, Sarah born January 29, 1681, married Samuel Bartlett, Richard, born April 26, 1683, Elizabeth born December 4, 1685, died unmarried, January 21, 1730, Hannah, born January 3, 1688, Eleazer, born November 2, 1689, Prudence, born 1691

(III) William Ward, son of Obadiah Ward (2), was born in Marlboro Massachusetts, January 7, 1676 He resided in Marlboro, where all the children were born, and in 1711 sold out to Samuel Morris and removed to Ashford, Connecticut, where he purchased land in 1715 and where his son William bought land in 1720 Jacob Ward another son, received a gift of lands there in 1726 William Ward removed to Union, Connecticut, where he died January 8, 1731, aged sixty-one years His death was the first in the town of Union His wife Judith died in Union, January 21, 1746 Their children were William, born June 9, 1691, Jemima, born July 5, 1693 Gamaliel, born October 2, 1694, married Damaris ———, Jacob, born March 9, 1696-97, married Hannah ———, Judith, born March 6, 1699-1700, Keziah, born June 4, 1703, Dinah, born October 2, 1704

(IV) William Ward, son of William Ward (3), was born at Marlboro Massachusetts, June 9, 1691 He resided in Union Connecticut, where he became a very prominent citizen, as appears from the town records He was a large land owner and conducted several farms There is a large rock on the old place with the letters "W W" roughly hewed on the surface and it is said that they were cut by William Ward. His will was dated August 12, 1772 and was proved October 2, 1780 Children of William and Rachel Ward were Uriah born February 24 1715 married Elizabeth Ingraham, John, born November 9 1716 see forward, Ebenezer born April 9 1719 married Anna Peache, Moses born September 16 1622, married Eunice Rood, Obadiah, born February 9 1725 married Esther Ruggles, Rachel, born April 23, 1727, married Joseph Enos, Jesse, born August 6 1729 married Elizabeth Abbe, Benjamin born February, 1731, died October 19, 1741, Sarah, died January 13, 1740, William, died April 23, 1735

(V) John Ward, son of William Ward (4), was born at Union Connecticut November 9 1716, and resided there He removed in 1740 to Belchertown, Massachusetts, with his family Five children were born in Union the remainder in Belchertown He married (first at Union October 10 1739 Abigail Walker he married (second) Abigail Heath, of Tolland Connecticut March 27 1748, and she died at Belchertown February 21 1813 aged eighty-two years He died there in 1800, aged eighty-four years Children of John and Abigail (Walker) Ward were Sarah born about 1740 married Jonathan Drade Dorcas born June 24 1742 died December 4 1748, Eunice, born December 15 1744, married Captain Shearman of Brimfield where he died without issue John Jr born January 1, 1747 died June 20 1747 Children of John and Abigail (Heath) Ward were Aaron born October 11 1748, died November 1 1748 John born about 1749 married Bethia Fuller Benjamin born 1751, married Mary Clough, Tirzah, born 1753, married Richard Lull, Zeruiah, born November 27, 17—, married Samuel Ward, Sybil, born December 7, 1756, married Benjamin Clough, Mehitable, born February 6, 1759, married John Pease, Ruth, born April 21, 1761, married Guild Wilson, of Belchertown, June, 1780, and resided at Hebron, New York, Hepzibah, born June 1, 1765 see forward, Beulah born August 20, 1767, married Samuel White, of Pelham, February 20, 1787, at Madison, New York, Moses, born October 29 1769, married Rachel Convers, Ebenezer, born July 19, 1773, see forward

(VI) Ebenezer Ward, son of John Ward (5), was born at Belchertown Massachusetts, July 19, 1773 He also settled at Belchertown, probably in that part of the town set off as Enfield He married, July 7, 1796, Rebecca Randall, of Belchertown Their children, all born at Belchertown, were Israel, born February 8, 1797, married Rachel Thayer, Alvah, born September 17, 1798, married Louisa Shaw, John, born May 19, 1800, married Sylvia H Shaw, Mercy, born September 10, 1801, married Samuel Tinkham, Abigail, born May 8, 1803, married Alvah Thayer, Zerviah, born July 23, 1804, Elizabeth, born February 25 1807, Benjamin, born April 24, 1809, married Elizabeth W Hawks, Mary, (twin) born April 23, 1811, married Oromel Walker, Sarah, (twin), born April 23, 1811, Estes, born May 3, 1815.

(VII) John Ward, son of Ebenezer Ward (6), was born at Belchertown, Massachusetts He lived in Enfield Massachusetts formerly part of Belchertown, and other towns of the vicinity He married Sylvia H Shaw daughter of Asa Shaw, of Enfield, and his wife Abigail Hanks, who died November 15 1839, in her fifty-third year, the mother of ten children Sylvia was born March 6, 1807 The father of Abigail was Ebenezer Hanks, of Belchertown, who married Hepsibah Ward, April 12, 1785 He was a soldier in the revolution they had eight children Hepsibah was the daughter of John Ward (V), the thirteenth child Children of John and Sylvia H Ward all born at Enfield Massachusetts, were Charles Rockwood, born April 27, 1834 see forward Verona A born April 1, 1839 Caroline F born April 1 1839, Proctor L, born May 23, 1841 Henry W, born August 19 1847

(VIII) Charles Rockwood Ward son of John Ward (7) was born at Enfield, Massachusetts, April 27, 1834 He was educated in the public schools of his native town He was a carpenter by trade He married Julia Reed He died October 26, 1901

The children of Charles Rockwood and Julia Ward were Abbie J born March 19, 1861, married Simon A Norcross and resides at 728 Main street, Worcester, Cora L born November 27, 1862, died when five years old Edward Dickinson see forward Nellie A, born December 16 1866, married F A Abbott, of Worcester, John Waldo born March 11, 1868, a carpenter married Ida Hacker, died in Worcester, Delbert E, born April 5 1870, carpenter resides in Worcester, Carrie B, born November 3, 1873, Albert E born February 13, 1875, a boat builder resides in New York city Frederick, born November 3, 1878, died young

(IX) Edward Dickinson Ward, son of Charles Rockwood Ward (8), was born in Enfield Massachusetts March 6, 1864 He was educated in the public and high schools of his native town He learned the carpenter's trade of his father and worked for some years as a journeyman in Worcester and other places He started in business for himself in Worcester in company with W F Blanding After a few years the partnership was dissolved and Mr Ward continued on his own account He has

Albert A. Barker.

built many of the finest residences and public buildings of Worcester in the past ten years, and ranks among the leading contractors and builders of the city He resides at 46 Alvarado avenue and has his office and shop at 48 Alvarado avenue In politics Mr Ward is a Republican He married, December 9, 1891, Miss Mabel E Kibbe of Worcester, daughter of Eugene H and Mary Kibbe Their children are Mildred May, born July 4 1893, Ethel Mabel, born March 30, 1896, Irene Belle, born September 12, 1898

ALBERT AUGUSTUS BARKER Richard Barker (1), the only man known to have been in Andover, Massachusetts, before 1643, was the progenitor of Albert Augustus Barker, late of Worcester, Massachusetts For more than fifty years he was one one of the leading citizens The Essex county records show that he bought stock and produce of William Hughes in 1643 He was called a husbandman in the early records His home lot in Andover was near that of John Osgood on the north side of the Cochichaucke pond, and his family and descendants have owned the land almost surrounding Great Pond as it is now called He was one of those who organized the first church October 24, 1645 He was entrusted with the administration of many estates His will was dated April 7, 1688, and proved March 28, 1693 It mentions eight children, granddaughters, Priscilla, Hester and Sarah, children of his deceased daughter Hannah The children of Richard and Joanna Barker were 1 John, died in 1722 of small-pox, deacon of North church, Indian fighter 2 William, born 1646, died 1718 3 Ebenezer, born March 12, 1651, died 1747, aged ninety-five 4 Richard, born April 10, 1654 5 Stephen, see forward 6 Benjamin, born February 28, 1663, married Hannah Marston, died 1750 7 Sarah, married, November 17, 1673, John Abbott 8 Hester married John Stevens 9 Hannah, born October 21, 1665, married, May 27, 1680, Christopher Osgood

(II) Stephen Barker, fifth child of Richard Barker (1), was born July 6, 1659 in Andover, Massachusetts He settled in Haverhill where he was active in securing the incorporation of Methuen Atkinson, where his sons lived, was originally part of Haverhill, Massachusetts The children of Stephen Barker were Stephen, Zebediah, see forward, James and perhaps others

(III) Zebediah Barker, son of Stephen Barker (2), was born in Andover, Massachusetts, probably about 1700-10 He settled in Andover and Haverhill where he loaned the town money August 14 1777 He married Deborah Merrill and they settled at Atkinson New Hampshire Among their children were 1 Peter, see forward 2 Abijah, born 1760, married Susannah Wood, settled in Antrim, New Hampshire in 1787, was a soldier in the revolution, his wife was a sister of Peter Barker's wife 3 Zebediah Jr who was a soldier in Captain Samuel Johnson's Company, Andover, 1777

(IV) Peter Barker, son of Zebediah Barker (3), was born in Atkinson, New Hampshire, in 1755 He married Sally Wood, daughter of Samuel Wood, of Methuen, sister of Susannah Wood who married his brother Abijah, who came to Antrim, New Hampshire, with him to make a home there Peter probably was in Antrim earlier, but he had his family there early in 1789 He bought the place now, or lately, of Levi Curtis, but later exchanged with his brother-in-law Charles Wood, for the place that was known as the Moody Barker place Peter Barker was captain of the alarm list He was a soldier in the revolutionary war He died May 23, 1829, aged seventy-four His wife died in 1843, aged eighty-eight years Their children were. Samuel, born in Atkinson, died in Oppenheim, New York, Hannah, born in Atkinson, married Daniel McIlvane, Peter, born in Antrim, March 14, 1789, died in Cleveland, Ohio, Isaac, July 2, 1791, Thomas, 1793, Captain Moody Morse, see forward, Sally, January 26, 1797, married Deacon Asa Bond

(V) Captain Moody Morse Barker, son of Captain Peter Barker (4), was born in Antrim, New Hampshire, May 24, 1795 He received a common school education in his native town He inherited the homestead and early in life he devoted himself to farming, and was a prosperous man He was a strict Presbyterian and stood high in the estimation of his associates in the church and his fellow citizens In politics he was a Whig, but later in life became a Democrat, adhering strongly to his political views He was for some years captain of the militia company in Antrim, though never in the service He married Nancy Bixby, of Hillsboro, New Hampshire, in 1821 They lived together until March 24, 1873, when he died She died two days later Their children were 1 John Bixby, see forward 2 Emily, born in 1824, married Samuel Brown, of Wilton, New Hampshire, had no children 3 Adeline, born September 12, 1829 married, July 3, 1854, Charles Woods, of Hillsboro, New Hampshire, and had two children Charles Woods, who married —— Downs of Francestown, New Hampshire, and had three children He died July, 1905, Adeline Woods, who married Mark Woodbury, of Antrim, and has sons Mark and Valentine 4 Miles C, born 1832, married Sarah J Carr, of Hillsboro, New Hampshire resides in Nashua, New Hampshire, and has two daughters Carrie C, unmarried, Jennie Hatch, married Arthur Jefferson, of Conway, New Hampshire, and has two children 5 Henry Martin born August 24, 1838, married, November 30, 1864, Mary Jane Colburn, they live in Staatsburg, New York, and have three sons Herbert Luther, M D born August 27 1866 married Luella J Herrick of Staatsburg, New York, and has one son, Robert Herrick Barker, Harry Colburn (Lawyer), born March 31, 1870, married Marion Hughes, of Staatsburg, New York, Fred Martin born May 4, 1871 married Grace Barnes, of Rhinebeck, New York and has a son, Clifford V Barker

(VI) John Bixby Barker, eldest son of Captain Moody Morse Barker (5), was born in Antrim, New Hampshire, November 13, 1822 He was educated in the common schools of Antrim, and worked on his father's farm there Later he removed to Bennington New Hampshire where he remained for about six years, two of which he was engaged in making sand paper He also learned the art of paper making in the mills at Bennington In 1850 he was induced by his brother-in-law, Frederick A Newton of Bennington, to accept a position in a paper mill situated in Guadalajara Mexico, under the control of Grant and Warren of Boston, Massachusetts Soon after he became familiar with the plant he was made the superintendent with a handsome salary He remained there six years, then went to Southern California where he invested in wheat growing He lost money owing to a long drought, and returned to his old position in Mexico where he remained until his death two years later, November 22, 1860 He was the first American buried in the cemetery of that Mexican city, the permit being obtained through the intercession of the American consul

In his younger days Mr Barker was a Presbyterian, but he became more liberal in his religious views and later joined the Universalist church During the short time he was in this country after the formation of the Republican party he was an earnest supporter of the new political faith His early death cut short a very promising career He married, October 10 1848, Harriet Elizabeth Newton, daughter of Luther and Harriet Elizabeth (Griswold) Newton, of Bennington, New Hampshire Luther Newton was a paper manufacturer and learned his trade of the Cranes in Dalton, Massachusetts He was a Republican He was a member of the paper making firm of Newton & Tufts, of Alstead New Hampshire The children of John Bixby and Harriet Elizabeth (Newton) Barker were Albert Augustus, see forward, Mary Frances, born in Guadalajara, Mexico, April 19, 1855, never married, has lived in Worcester with her mother and brother and is a teacher in the Oxford street public school, Adelaida Elizabeth born in Guadalajara, August 6, 1859, died October 22, 1860

(VII) Albert Augustus Barker, eldest child of John Bixby Barker (6), was born in Guadalajara, Mexico November 20, 1852 After his father's death, when eight years of age, he came with his family to Bennington, New Hampshire where he lived five years In 1865 he came to Worcester where he attended the public schools After leaving school he entered the office of Elbridge Boyden, one of the oldest and best known architects of Worcester During the time he was with Mr Boyden he was frequently employed by Thomas H Dodge, one of the most successful patent attorneys in the country in his day from whom he received instruction as patent solicitor He started in business for himself March 1 1879 forming a partnership with Walter B Nourse, under the firm name of Barker & Nourse, as architects and solicitors of patents January 1, 1904, the partnership was dissolved, and during the last year of his life Mr Barker was in business alone He was instructor in the evening drawing schools of the city of Worcester, having charge of the architectural department and was supervisor of drawing in the Worcester County Mechanics' Association evening schools As an architect he enjoyed a wide fame, and many public and private buildings erected from his plans, and under his personal supervision, are a monument to his ability Among some of the more conspicuous buildings are The Society of Antiquity, the Odd Fellows Home, the Winslow Surgery at the City Hospital, the English High School, the Day Building, the Aurora Hotel all of Worcester, the Gardner High School, the Uxbridge High School, the West Boylston High School the Princeton High School the Shrewsbury Public Library, the Johnsonio Hotel at Fitchburg

Mr Barker was a Unitarian in religious faith, and since 1865 a member of the Church of the Unity on Elm street He was chairman of the Parish Committee at the time of his death, and supervising architect of the recent remodelling of the church He was a member of no secret orders He belonged to the Society of Antiquity, the Worcester Board of Trade Builders' Exchange Worcester Chapter of the American Institute of Architects, Worcester County Mechanics' Association, Royal Arcanum and the Hancock Club He was always a Republican but never sought or held office He married October 24 1877, Eacyetta Boyd, daughter of George and Rebecca (MacGerigle) Boyd, of Worcester, Massachusetts Mr Boyd was overseer in a boot manufactory He was also engaged in woolen industry He was of Scotch-Irish stock born in Londonderry, Ireland He was a citizen of Worcester for sixty years As early as 1840 he was a member of the Worcester Fire Company, and was on duty at the great Merrifield Fire He was a Republican The children of Albert Augustus and Eacyetta (Boyd) Barker were 1 Everett Newton, born in Worcester, Massachusetts June 4 1881, succeeded his father in business, as patent solicitor and architect and resides at the homestead, 88 Chatham street 2 Robert Stuart born in Worcester, Massachusetts, April 3, 1884, is in the mercantile business, and is also at the homestead

Mr Barker was cut off in his prime June 9, 1905 A wide circle of friends will always hold him in kindly remembrance, for he was an upright, courteous gentleman, winning the love and respect of all who knew him

ALONZO WILTON WHITCOMB John Whitcomb (1), the first of the Whitcomb family to settle permanently in this country, was the ancestor of Alonzo Wilton Whitcomb, of Worcester He appeared in Dorchester as early as 1633 He joined the church there in 1635 and his youngest son Josiah was born in Dorchester It had been supposed for a long time that he was the son of Symon Whitcomb or Whetcombe, who was one of the original patentees of the old Massachusetts Bay colony, but the will of Symon's father shows this belief absolutely wrong He may have been the brother The belief is gaining ground among those who have studied the records that the emigrant, John Whitcomb, was the second son of John and Anne (Harper) Whitcomb of London John Harper, whose daughter was the mother of John Whitcomb, was a member of the East India Company June 16 1620, and it is recorded that he gave John Whitcomb who married his daughter Anne, a share in Virginia viz America

In 1640 John Whitcomb removed from Dorchester to settle in Scituate Massachusetts, where he already owned land During his residence in Scituate he was made constable He was on the list of those able to bear arms in 1643 He was admitted a freeman June 3 1652 In 1654 he removed to Lancaster, Massachusetts where in 1652, when the town was laid out, he had invested some money Not all his children accompanied him to Lancaster His daughter Catherine was settled in Scituate, where in 1644 she married Rodolphus Ellmes, who came in 1635 on the "Planter" aged fifteen Robert Whitcomb remained in Scituate James Whitcomb settled in Boston

John Whitcomb and his son John, Jr, were among the founders of the town of Lancaster After some thirty years of pioneer life in the colony John Whitcomb died September 24 1662, aged about seventy-four years He was buried in the old graveyard at Lancaster, but there is no stone

He married in England Frances ——, and there his elder children were born He had certainly five sons perhaps six and three daughters He died intestate and the widow and children mutually agreed upon a division of his estate, which was approved by the court His widow, Frances, made her will May 12 1671, and died at Lancaster, May 17, 1671 She named her youngest daughter Mary as executrix The children of John Whitcomb were 1 Catherine, married 1644 Rodolphus Ellmes, of Scituate, resided there and had nine children 2 James, born in England, settled in Boston, may have remained in Dorchester and Boston when his father removed to Scituate not mentioned in his father's will, owned a place of five acres opposite the Boston Common died in Boston November 23, 1686 married twice, Rebecca and Elizabeth had ten children 3 John born in England may have been the oldest son, was most closely associated with his father

(Their signatures are found together in several places—once as early as 1652 when they both signed the town covenant of Lancaster, and in 1654-5 both are among the twenty families named in a petition for a township drawn up by John Whitcomb, Sr) Married May 19 1669 or January 16 1671, probably on the latter date, which is given by Savage, he died April 7, 1683, accidentally drowned, leaving wife Mary and two daughters 4 Robert remained at Scituate when his father went to Lancaster, married 1660 by a Quaker preacher, in Rhode Island, to Mary Cudworth, daughter of General James Cudworth, but this marriage being pronounced unlawful by the Puritan authorities he was remarried March 9 1660 (She was born July 23, 1637) The preacher was Henry Hobson, of Rhode Island Robert Whitcomb was the first to settle at "Beechwood" in the Beeches, the family place at Scituate where several generations of Whitcombs have lived He had seven children 5 Jonathan, was on the jury at the inquest upon the death of Richard Mann of Scituate, Massachusetts February 16, 1655 with his brother-in-law Rodolphus Ellmes, John Hoar and others (See Mann Family Sketch) He removed from Scituate to Lancaster married November 25, 1667, Hannah ——, died February 1690, July 18, 1692, his widow Hannah was killed by the Indians at the house of Peter Joslin, in Lancaster He had eleven children One of his descendants is G Henry Whitcomb the envelope manufacturer, of Worcester 6 Abigail no record 7 Job was a surveyor at Lancaster, married May 19, 1669, Mary —— He did not return to Lancaster after King Philip's war, but settled at Wethersfield, Connecticut He died 1683 He had six children and has many descendants in Connecticut 8 Josiah (see forward) 9 Mary married John Moore, August 13, 1663, son of John and Anna (Smith) Moore

(II) Josiah Whitcomb, son of John Whitcomb (1) was born in Dorchester, Massachusetts, in 1638, and is believed to be the youngest son He accompanied his father's family from Scituate to Lancaster in 1654 and his name appears variously in the records of Lancaster In 1688 he received a bounty for killing a wolf He was named in an action for damages for killing swine belonging to Stephen Gates He married January 4, 1664, in Lancaster Rebecca Waters, daughter of Lawrence and Ann (Linton) Waters, of Watertown, Lancaster and Charlestown She was born February, 1640 During Queen Anne's war (1702-17) he was allowed a garrison for protection against the Indians This garrison was situated in what is now called Bolton, set off from Lancaster in 1738 He lived in the southeastern part of Bolton He was commander of the garrison In 1705 he was selectman and in 1708 he and twenty-nine others signed the church covenant In 1710 he was elected deputy to the general court He died in 1718 In his will made March 20, 1718, he gave to each of his children one-eighth part of his right to land in Littleton His widow died in 1726 His posterity is very numerous thought to be the most numerous of the sons of John Whitcomb Their is a gravestone in the Bolton graveyard marking his burial place His children were 1 Josiah born November 12, 1665, died same day 2 Josiah born January 7, 1667, married (first) 1690 Mary ——, second Elizabeth ——, he died April 12, 1718, widow married (second), March 25 1719, Jabez Fairbanks, of Lancaster, Massachusetts 3 David (see forward) 4 Rebecca, born November 12 1671, married Jacob Houghton, 1704 5 Johannah born March 8 1674 married, December 26, 1708 Peter Joslin died September 24, 1717 6 Hezekiah born September 14, 1681, married Hannah ——, lived in Bolton, where he was prominent in the church, died previous to June 20 1732 had eight children 7 Deborah, born December 26 1683, probably died young 8 Damaris, married in Marlboro Nathaniel Wilder 9 Mary, named in father's will 10 Abigail, born March 13, 1687-8, married Josiah White, June 26, 1706 11 Eunice

(III) David Whitcomb, son of Josiah Whitcomb (2) born February 20 1668, married May 31 1700, in Concord, Massachusetts Widow Mary (Hayward) Fairbanks who was descended from Resolved White who came over in the "Mayflower" with his parents Her husband Jonathan Fairbanks was killed by the Indians at Lancaster, Massachusetts, September 4, 1697, she was taken a captive, but was returned January 17 1699, on the Province Galley from Casco Bay While in captivity she acquired a knowledge of herbs and afterward she dispensed medicines and was called Doctress They lived in the southeastern part of Bolton, where they kept a tavern He died intestate April 11 1730, and his wife Mary died January 5 1734, in the sixty-seventh year of her age

The children of David and Mary (Hayward) (Fairbanks) Whitcomb were 1 David, married in Lancaster, Massachusetts, January 13 1730-1, Betty White, joined the Lancaster church July 18, 1736 and in 1741 was dismissed to the Bolton church, was called Deacon will probated December 5, 1786, mentions ten children 2 Jonathan, born at Lancaster Massachusetts married Rachel Woods, December 12, 1722, died October 7, 1743 3 Joseph, born at Lancaster 4 Rebecca, baptized 1708, married Ezra Sawyer January 16 1725-6 5 Benjamin, born in Lancaster, baptized October or November 26, 1710, lived in Lunenburg in 1735, removed thence to northerly part of Leominster, Massachusetts, where he was elected deacon of the church December 2, 1747, married Dorothy White daughter of Captain John and Eunice (Wilder) White, he died October, 1778 6 Simon, born in Lancaster, baptized there March 7 1713-4, married Thankful Houghton, of Lancaster July 12, 1733, had eleven children Order of birth unknown

(IV) Joseph Whitcomb son of David Whitcomb (3), born in Lancaster, married Damaris Priest, daughter of John and Anna (Houghton) Priest of Lancaster January 20, 1725 and the births of their children are recorded in Lancaster About 1760 the family moved to West Swanzey, New Hampshire where Joseph Whitcomb built a saw mill and a grist mill making the mill privilege on which now stands the Stratton mills and the Box and Bucket shops He owned an extensive tract of land He was about sixty when he went to Swanzey He died November 1792 at the age of ninety-two years, and was buried in Swanzey His wife died November 12 1770 In the expedition which laid siege to Louisburg in 1745 Joseph Whitcomb was lieutenant in company four of which John Warner was captain and Samuel Willard colonel He was also a lieutenant in the Crown Point Expedition in 1755 In the conquest of Canada in 1758 Joseph Whitcomb was captain in Colonel Timothy Ruggles' regiment His five sons took a very prominent part in the revolution One gained the title of general, two of colonel, one of lieutenant

The children of Joseph and Damaris Whitcomb were 1 Abigail, born April 13 1726, married —— Derby 2 Elizabeth born December 3, 1728 3 Joseph born March 15 1731-2, married December 16 or 18 1754 Elizabeth Wheelock of Leominster, Massachusetts was lieutenant in the revolutionary army at Ticonderoga according to town records, also other service, removed to Grafton, Vermont, in 1790 or 1792 4 Benjamin, born September 1 1735 died young 5 Damaris, born January 7, 1737, died young 6 Benjamin, born September 29, 1738 7 Jonathan Priest (see forward) 8 Elisha (twin) born October 18, 1742 had the military title of major, was eleven months and eight days in Canada in 1776, was in service also in 1777, called colonel afterward on records, was at the battle of Bunker Hill, married Joanna Whitcomb, of Leominster, Massachusetts prominent citizen of Swanzey, state senator seven years, died September 17, 1814, widow died December 17, 1835, had thirteen children 9 Elizabeth (twin), born October 18 1742 10 Damaris born May 21, 1746 married April 3, 1765, Jonathan Carter, she died July 6, 1820 11 Philemon, born October 29, 1748, had the military title of general in the revolution, had a saw mill and a trip hammer, married (first) Martha Sawyer, of Lunenburg (intentions March 23, 1770), married (second) Mrs Anna Aldrich, widow of Amasa Aldrich, died January 10 1824 12 Abijah, born June 25 or 27, 1751, built a saw and grist mill on the west side of the river at West Swanzey, New Hampshire, and later with his brother Philemon built a saw mill at what is now Sprague ville, New Hampshire, was in the battle of Bunker Hill, was a pensioner, served in Captain Jonathan Whitcomb's company Colonel Reed's regiment, of New Hampshire, married (first), November 6, 1786, Mary Seaver, daughter of Shubael Seaver married (second) Susanna Warner daughter of Daniel Warner 13 Anna, born 1755, married June 19, 1775, John Carter

(V) Jonathan Priest Whitcomb, son of Joseph Whitcomb (4), born January 14 1740, at Leominster, Massachusetts married September 5, 1764 Dorothy Carter She was born March 9, 1746, died October 22, 1827 He settled in Swanzey, New Hampshire, and kept the first store and the first tavern in the town He served in the revolutionary war and was paid for eight and one-half months service at Cambridge Massachusetts during the siege of Boston in 1775 He was captain of the largest company in Colonel James Reid's regiment at Lexington, April 10 1775 and at Bunker Hill June 17, 1775 His company encamped on Winter Hill, numbering about seventy men from Keene New Hampshire, and Swanzey He was promoted to the rank of colonel in 1775 He had a difficulty with a Captain Marcy, who accused him of cowardice but a clean and gallant war record was sustained by the court of inquiry Colonel and Mrs Whitcomb used to make horseback trips to Boston to buy goods and on one occasion brought home some lilacs the first they ever saw which were planted on the old homestead Colonel Jonathan died June 13, 1792, and his old regiment attended the funeral His widow died at the home of her son Nathan (Where the dates in this family are double it is due to a conflict between the dates of the Swanzey history and the Carter Genealogy)

The children of Colonel Jonathan Priest and Dorothy (Carter) Whitcomb were 1 Dorothy, born March 3 or May 23, 1765, died May 2, 1825, married Nathan Capron and had four daughters 2 Jonathan born September 20, 1766, or 67, married May 11 1786 Miriam Willard, he died December 13 1811 resided at Swanzey 3 John, born March 22 1768 died October 17 1770 4 Nathan (see forward) 5 John, born March 9 1772, married May 7 1795 Esther Morse, of Swanzey, daughter of Henry Morse, removed to Grafton Vermont, and Saxton's River Vermont, where in 1830 he bought the old Judge Baxter place, died 1875 6 Ephraim, born June 4 or 9, 1774, died August 15, 1777 7 Damaris born April 29, 1777, died June, 1784 8 Anna, born April 9, 1779, died June 17, 1784 9 Ephraim, born February 26, 1782, married (first), in 1798, Dorothy Chamberlain, married (second) her sister, Charlotte Chamberlain, in 1817, he died March, 1869, was a saddle-maker by trade 10 Salome, born March 3, 1784, died March or May 30, 1785 11 Salome born April 25, 1786, married Amos Bailey

(VI) Nathan Whitcomb, son of Colonel Jonathan Priest Whitcomb (5) was born May 14 1770 He settled at Swanzey and died there He married, October 23, 1791, Penelope White, of Milford, Massachusetts She was born in 1771, died March 15, 1850 Their children were 1 Leonard, born January 26, 1793, married Betsey Woodward, daughter of Josiah Woodward, February 9, 1819, died at West Swanzey in 1866, aged seventy-four years 2 Carter (see forward) 3 Otis, born September, 1796, married July 22, 1818, Esther Osgood, daughter of Ezekiel Osgood He died March 18, 1882 He had eighteen children His wife was born October 17, 1799, died April 20, 1867 He was called captain and always took great interest in military matters He has been made famous by Denman Thompson's play "Joshua Whitcomb" The character of Joshua was a combination of Joshua Holbrook and Otis Whitcomb Mr Thompson, the playwright was a native of Swanzey, and very fond of Mr Whitcomb, and often had him at performances Four or more sons were in the civil war 4 Nathan, died in Fitchburg Massachusetts 5 Alva born about 1800, married Almira, daughter of Ezekiel Osgood September 21, 1820, removed to Pennsylvania where he died 1850 6 Lyman, born April 22 1804 married September 26 1837, Eliza Curtis, daughter of Oliver and Elizabeth Curtis of Sharon, Massachusetts 7 Eliza born at Swanzey married May 12 1839 Rev James W Bailey 8 Son, born 1812, died from scald, March 9, 1814 9 Infant 10 Infant died young

(VII) Carter Whitcomb, son of Nathan Whitcomb (6), was born at Swanzey, New Hampshire, February 9 1794 married December 26, 1815 to Lucy Baker daughter of Jonidab Baker of Marlboro, New Hampshire She was born February 4, 1794 died October 3 1890, aged ninety-six years He died May 1 1879 He was a merchant and manufacturer of woolen goods from 1815 to 1837 in Saxton's River village Vermont, in partnership with Clement Godfrey He took an active interest in military and town affairs and was colonel of a Vermont regiment In 1837 he returned to Swanzey and spent the remainder of his life there, on his farm Except the youngest his children were born in Saxton's River His children were 1 Alonzo (see forward) 2 Carter born May 27, 1820 married Emily Augusta Spring of Worcester Massachusetts, who was born December 11, 1827 in Uxbridge He was in active business with his brother Alonzo until 1871 His death occurred December 1, 1880 in Worcester His children were Ida Francena born April 29, 1851, married Walter G Beal, Carrie Jane born January 13, 1853, died February 4 1856 Henry Carter, born August 29, 1857 resides in New York city, Franklin Luther, born March 5, 1862, at Worcester, married in Pittsburg Pennsylvania November 15, 1893, Mary Piatt Parry is a manufacturer of car-wheels in Chicago, where he lives has three children Carter Parry, born January 9 1895 at Detroit Michigan Franklin Luther born June 15 1896 at Chicago, Pemberton, born December 22 1900, at Chicago 3 Jonidab Baker, born October 2, 1823, married Cynthia A

Cutter, of Grafton, Vermont April 5, 1855, settled in Berkley, California, compiled "Ancestry and Descendants of Colonel Jonathan Priest Whitcomb," died January 22, 1890 4 Byron born April 17, 1826, married January 12 1858, Eliza V Lott, of Flatlands, Long Island, New York, learned machinist's trade at Worcester and removed to Fall River, Massachusetts, went to California in 1849; went with brother Jonidab Baker to the Yuba river at Foster's Bar from 1858 to 1868 lived at Young Hill in Yuba county, removed then to Worcester, where he went into business for a few years finally settled at Flatlands, Long Island, has five children 5 Clement Godfrey, born December 12, 1828, died April 1, 1893, at San Francisco, unmarried 6 Lucy Jane, born May 9 1834, married George Carpenter, of Swanzey, New Hampshire 7 Henry Homer, born May 13 1837, unmarried, died September 12, 1899

(VIII) Alonzo Whitcomb, son of Colonel Carter Whitcomb (7), was born at Saxton's River, Vermont, April 30 1818 He came to Worcester in 1845 and was employed in the machine shops of S C Coombs & Company until 1849 when, with his brother Carter Whitcomb (q v) he purchased the copying-press business of George C Taft, on Union street, in the old Howe & Goddard shop In a few years they had developed this business largely and the firm, then known as C Whitcomb & Co, moved in 1852, to secure larger quarters, into the Merrifield building at the corner of Exchange and Union streets, where it remained until burned out in the great fire of 1854 After the fire the Junction shop was occupied temporarily then the firm moved into the new Merrifield building at the corner of Exchange and Cypress streets In addition to the manufacture of copying presses the firm also took up the manufacture of metal-working machine tools soon after its first establishment in the Merrifield building and this branch soon became the most important part of the business

In 1871 Carter Whitcomb retired from the firm and the name was changed to The Whitcomb Manufacturing Company In 1872 Mr Whitcomb moved to the Estabrook shop at the Junction, and later in 1877 to the Rice & Griffin shop on Gold street Here he had another disastrous fire, having a $45,000 loss with only $5 000 insurance, but the business suffered no interruption In 1892 he built the shop at the corner of Sargent and Gold streets, since occupied by his business From 1866 to 1881 he was a partner in the firm of Rice & Whitcomb with Augustus Rice in the business established by Timothy F Taft, manufacturing metal shears and presses Upon the retirement of Mr Rice this business was united with the other Mr Whitcomb being sole owner of both He was one of the founders of the Kabley Foundry His partners in that concern were Frederick E Reed and Arnold Kabley Before the death of Mr Whitcomb that business had been incorporated and the officers were President Arnold Kabley, treasurer, Alonzo Whitcomb, director, F E Reed The foundry is located at 56 Gold street In spite of times of financial depression when it was the common thing for shops to shut down, Mr Whitcomb always kept a certain number of men at work, preferring to suffer loss of profits himself to depriving men who had been faithful in their work for many years of their much needed wages,

Mr Whitcomb died March 28 1900 after an active business career of over fifty years When over eighty he continued to do his work and was remarkably active He was of a quiet and retiring nature He preferred his home life to public affairs and social activity He owned the famous old Governor John Davis house on Lincoln street Dickens, Thackeray and other famous men have been guests in this house, which is one of the most interesting in the city It is now the home of his son Alonzo Wilton

Mr Whitcomb married in 1857 Sybell (Heald) Clary, who was born in Troy, Maine, October 17, 1820 Mrs Whitcomb and her daughter, Camilla Gertrude, reside at 35 Oxford street, the home built by Mr Whitcomb in 1860 The children of Alonzo and Sybell (Heald) (Clary) Whitcomb were Lucy Stella, married J F Browning, Camilla Gertrude, Alonzo Wilton

(IX) Alonzo Wilton Whitcomb, son of Alonzo Whitcomb (8), was born in Worcester, Massachusetts, April 11, 1862 He attended the Worcester schools and graduated in 1880 from the Worcester high school He went to Amherst College where he graduated in 1884 He came directly into his father's business and worked in all the departments until thoroughly familiar with all its details and machinery He was associated with his father in partnership until his death in 1900, and during most of the time in active management of the large interests of the firm Upon the death of Alonzo Whitcomb the business was incorporated with Mrs Sybell H Whitcomb, president, Alonzo Wilton Whitcomb, treasurer, Samuel H Clary, clerk and director The stock of Mr Reed and Mr Kabley in the Kabley Foundry was purchased, and the same officers chosen for the Kabley corporation In 1905 a further consolidation took place by the union of the P Blaisdell Machine Co and Whitcomb Manufacturing Company, in one Massachusetts corporation, with a capital of $200,000 This consolidation gives the new company a foundry and two large machine shops, each having a large and prosperous business The officers of the new corporation are President A W Whitcomb, vice-president and treasurer, Charles E Hildreth, directors William A Blaisdell, Samuel H Clary and Camilla G Whitcomb The company now makes a specialty of metal planers, engine lathes and upright drills The ordinary force employed is three hundred and twenty-five The name of the new corporation is the Whitcomb-Blaisdell Machine Tool Company

Mr Whitcomb is a member of Quinsigamond Lodge of Free Masons and of the Commonwealth Club He is a trustee of the Worcester County Mechanics' Association and on the Executive Council of the Worcester Metal Trades Association He is a member of the Worcester Board of Trade

He married April 4 1894 Gertrude Coffey, who was born in Worcester, April 11, 1871 Their children are Dorothy, born January 2, 1895, Preston born May 30, 1897, Wilton Alonzo, born April 4, 1900

HENRY AUGUSTUS GREEN Bartholomew Green was a soldier in the revolutionary war serving in Captain Samuel Dexter's company Colonel Learned's regiment The company return is dated Roxbury Camp, January, 1776 This company was raised in New Braintree Hardwick and Oakham, he being credited to the latter town We find him also associated with the companies of Captain Barnabas Sears and Captain Ralph Earll Colonel Danforth Keyes' regiment, enlisting in the latter company July 2 1777 discharged January 4 1778, roll dated Providence and sworn to in Worcester county (Vol VI, p 795, Mass Soldiers and Sailors War of Revolution)

Records seem to be wanting to connect this Bartholomew with other branches of the Green family but it is perhaps a significant fact that one Joel Green, of Spencer, Massachusetts, also Jeduthan

Green, of same town served in Colonel Learned's regiment and it is also a fact that children of both Bartholomew and Jeduthan made their homes in Rutland Massachusetts, which fact at least is an intimation that there was a family relationship existing between them Jeduthan Green was son of William and Rebecca (Tucker) Green, and lived on the Charlton road in Leicester, born October 27, 1744 Jeduthan enlisted from Spencer, and after the revolutionary war settled in Barre William, father of Jeduthan, was born of Captain William and Sarah (Sprague) Green, his father was son of Thomas Green, of Malden, Massachusetts

Bartholomew, the revolutionary soldier married (as it would appear) rather late in life in Barre, April 11, 1804, Hannah daughter of Skelton Felton, born September 2, 1778 Her mother was Silance Hale, born in Bolton, Massachusetts, February, 1776 Skelton Felton was in the fifth generation descent from Nathaniel Felton, who was born about 1615, came from Great Yarmouth county of Norfolk, England to Salem Massachusetts in 1633, where he lived and died July 30 1705, aged ninety years, leaving ten children His son Nathaniel, born August 15 1655 by wife Ann Horn, had eight children, among whom was Skelton, born about 1680, married, May, 1712, Hepsibah Sheldon, among their seven children was Joseph, baptized August 14 1715, married Mary Trask, of Salem, in 1736, and had thirteen children, the seventh being Skelton born December 21, 1750 and married Silance Hale Children of Bartholomew Green, who died in Barre, January 8 1835 and his wife Hannah, who died in Holden Massachusetts in 1846 Elbridge Gerry, James Sullivan, Josiah Martin, Bartholomew, Mary, Lydia, and Silance No dates of their births appear on the town records of Barre

James Sullivan Green was born 1807, in Barre, where he received his early education in the common schools, and in early life worked on the farm that was the property of his grandfather, Skelton Felton, of Barre, under the direction of his uncle, Captain Benjamin Felton, his mother's brother, who after the death of the father, July 9, 1822, administered on the estate Captain Benjamin Felton died in Worcester, April 6 1875, aged eighty-two years After a number of years farm work Mr Green removed to Grafton where for several years he kept the hotel now known as the Kirby House He then went to Millbury, and conducted the Tourtelotte House, which for many years enjoyed an enjoyable reputation as a popular hostelry September 12, 1837, Mr Green married Abigail Martin, of Shrewsbury daughter of John and Sarah (Fay) Brigham At the time of this marriage Mr Green was a resident of Grafton He died in Millbury, November 21, 1844 aged thirty-seven years and three months His children James Oscar Henry Augustus see forward, Marion Augusta, Sarah Abigail, born May 7 1843 in Millbury

Henry Augustus Green was born in Grafton, September 7, 1842 After the death of his father, the mother removed with her children to Shrewsbury where the subject of this sketch attended the public schools and when a young man secured employment in the store of Mr Boutelle, where he remained until September 25, 1862, when he enlisted in Company A, Fifty-first Massachusetts Infantry, serving with the Eighteenth Army Corps, in Captain E A Wood's company, in the General Foster expedition He was at New Berne Kingston, White Hall and Goldsboro North Carolina being among the nine months men and was honorably discharged July 27 1862 On his return home he entered the employ of F T Smith in the wholesale grocery trade in Worcester, Massachusetts Here he remained until 1870, when he opened a store on Shrewsbury street for the sale of groceries on his own account, later taking Jesse Smith into partnership, the style of the firm being Smith & Green, dealing in groceries and provisions, lime and cement, their store being on the corner of Shrewsbury and Mulbury streets, and there the business was continued up to the time of Mr Green's death, November 26, 1893 Mr Green was an attendant at the Universalist church and was a Republican in politics He received his Master Mason degree in Montacute Lodge, his Royal Arch degree in Eureka Chapter, his Knight Templar degree in Worcester County Commandery, No 5 He was a member of George H Ward Post, No 10, G A R He married, January, 1868, Frances Maria Gates, born March 20, 1846, in Worcester, daughter of Ephraim Gates, born in Worcester, October 27 1815 Her mother Maria (Campbell) Gates, was born in Worcester, February, 1822 Children of Henry Augustus and Frances M Green 1 Walter James, born February, 1870, died February 8, 1871 2 Alice Elizabeth, born December 12, 1872 3 Albert Henry, born July 27, 1875, married Edith Wood Armington, of Worcester, children Richard Henry, Bradford, and Frances, born March 20, 1895 4 Marion Frances, born October 6, 1880, married Frederick E Goulding, of Worcester 5 Florence Lillian, born October 25, 1882 6 Cora Helen, born September 18, 1885

THE HEYWOOD FAMILY OF WORCESTER The surname Heywood is distinct from Haywood, Hayward and Howard, although the spelling of each in every possible way makes it difficult not to confuse the families, especially where Heywards, Howards and Heywoods were living in the same town

The derivation of the name Heywood is given in a pedigree prepared by Peter John Heywood of Whitehaven, England 1781, and published in "Hunter's Life and Times of Oliver Heywood," who was a non-conformist clergyman of note in the days of Charles I The pedigree runs back to the year 1164, a period when surnames were beginning to come into use in the mother country Often some local feature of a man's place of residence was employed to distinguish him from others bearing the same Christian name The earliest authentic document containing the name of Heywood or its prototype is a title deed still preserved for a tract of land in Lancashire, from one Adame de Burgo or de Bury, who held the knight's fee to a large section of territory in the vicinity to Peter de Ey-wood, that is "of wooded island" The latter was the reputed founder of the Heywood family in England, from which the American family is descended This estate remained in the possession of the descendants of Peter Heywood more than five hundred years, or until 1717 when Robert Heywood sold it to John Starkey, of Rochdale, whose grandson, James Starkey, dying intestate, allowed the place to pass into the hands of the Crown It is now an attractive public park, having been donated for the purpose by Queen Victoria While the English line is traced in an unbroken line from this Peter Heywood, the ancestry of the emigrants to America had not at last accounts been discovered James and John Heywood, both about twenty-two years old, presumably brothers came together in the ship "Planter" in 1635 They were both certified from Stepney Parish London James Heywood settled in Charlestown and Woburn where he died November 20, 1642 John Heywood is the ancestor of the Worcester and Gardner families of this name

Amos M. Eaton

(I) John Heywood, mentioned above, settled in Concord, Massachusetts, and was probably born in London, England, about 1620 He married (first), August 17, 1656, Rebecca Atkinson, daughter of Thomas Atkinson She was probably not his first wife unless his age is estimated wrongly She died 1665 He married (second), August 5, 1665, Sarah Simonds He married (third) Priscilla ——, who survived him He was admitted a freeman in 1670

The children of John and Rebecca (Atkinson) Heywood, born in Concord, were Rebecca, born September 9, 1657, died young, Rebecca, May 13, 1660, John, Jr (Deacon), mentioned below, Persis, April 11, 1664, Benoni, July 31, 1665, died young, The children of John and Sarah (Simonds) Heywood were Sarah, born August 30, 1666, Judith, January 3, 1667, Mary, November 3, 1669, Abigail, April 9, 1672, William, April 17, 1674, Huldah, September 17, 1676, James, January 27, 1678-79, Joseph, January 3, 1680-81, Benjamin, March 17, 1682-83

(II) Deacon John Heywood, third child of John Heywood (1), was born in Concord, Massachusetts, April 5, 1662, where he also settled and lived, and where, January 2, 1718, he died In 1676 he was a constable He was keeper of an ordinary at Concord in his later years He married Sarah —— Their children were 1 Sarah 2 Thomas, born July 16, 1686 3 Samuel, October 11, 1687, married Elizabeth Hubbard in 1710, was deacon and town officer, died October 28, 1750, had thirteen children 4 Edmund, July 31, 1689 5 Josiah, November 15, 1691 6 Daniel, April 15, 1694, removed to Worcester and is ancestor of a large number of the Worcester family, married Hannah, daughter of Obadiah Ward, another pioneer at Worcester, he lived and kept an inn on the site of the Bay State House, and his son and grandson maintained the tavern there for over a hundred years 7 Eleazer, August 3, 1696 8 Nathan, September 24 1698. 9 Sarah, January 18, 1700-01 10 John, March 14, 1703, settled in Lunenburg 11 Mary, March 23, 1704 12 Phinehas, mentioned below 13 Benjamin, October 25, 1709

(III) Phinehas Heywood, twelfth child of Deacon John Heywood (2), was born in Concord, Massachusetts, July 18, 1707 He settled in Shrewsbury in 1739, in the northwest part near the Worcester line His descendants have been and are very numerous in Worcester, Shrewsbury, Gardner, and other sections of Worcester county He was a prominent man, being a selectman of Shrewsbury, representative to the general court, delegate to the provincial congress, committee of safety and correspondence 1774 and 1775 He was concerned in one of the first overt acts of rebellion against the crown just a year before the battle of Lexington Together with fourteen other Worcester county men, among whom was Colonel Timothy Bigelow and Joshua Bigelow, he was on the grand jury that signed the famous protest against Chief Justice Oliver who had been impeached by the general court for accepting pay from the king in addition to his salary from the province This protest presented to the judges of the superior court of judicature at Worcester, stated the purpose of the jurors to decline to act if the chief justice were present on the bench "because we apprehend it would be highly injurious to subject a fellow-countryman to a trial at a bar where one of the judges is convicted in the minds of the people more heinous in all probability than any that might come before him" The protest was read publicly by the clerk, considered by the four judges present who at length stated that it was not probable that the chief justice would attend the session No attempt was made to discipline the rebellious jurors Although greatly interested in the events that led up to the revolutionary war, he died at the very beginning of the conflict, March 6, 1776

He married Elizabeth Moore, daughter of Deacon Nathaniel Moore, of another of the important pioneer families of Worcester She died June 20, 1797, aged eighty-six years Their children, all born in Shrewsbury, were 1 Elizabeth, born May 15, 1755, married John Curtis, Jr of another pioneer Worcester family 2 Mary, married Samuel Jennison, an early Worcester family 3 Seth 4 Timothy, born February 11, 1740, died at Westminster, 1825, aged eighty-five 5 Keziah, April 30, 1742, married Bezaleel Howe, of Marlboro 6 Phinehas, July 29, 1744 7 Benjamin, October 25, 1746 (judge), father of Dr Benjamin F, grandfather of John G Heywood 8 Nathaniel, baptized November 13, 1748, mentioned below 9 John, born April 25, 1751 10 Levi, May 12, 1753, settled in Gardner

(IV) Nathaniel Heywood, eighth child of Phinehas Heywood (3), was born in Shrewsbury and baptized November 13, 1748 He married (first), April 23, 1778, and lived on the homestead at Shrewsbury His wife died May 25, 1792, aged thirty-five He married (second), July 1, 1793, Mary Chamberlain, daughter of Deacon Jacob Chamberlain She died November 21, 1802, aged thirty-nine He died November 18, 1834, aged eighty-six

He was a corporal in Captain Timothy Bigelow's company, Colonel Artemas Ward's regiment, April 19, 1775, at Lexington, and also in Captain Jonas Hubbard's company, Colonel Ward's regiment, in 1775 He was lieutenant under Captain William Gates, in 1777, and served in New York

The children of Nathaniel and Hannah (Curtis) Heywood were 1 Levi, born September 21, 1777, died September 17, 1804 2 Nathaniel, February 6, 1780, died October 4, 1836 3 Benjamin, March 29, 1782 4 John, August 24, 1784, died August 16, 1833, at Shrewsbury 5 Phinehas, May 4, 1788 6 Daniel, November 17, 1790, died December 20, 1802 The children of Nathaniel and Mary (Chamberlain) Heywood were 7 Hannah, February 9, 1794 8 Daniel, mentioned below 9 Marietta, May 9, 1802, married Elijah Stow, of Grafton

(V) Daniel Heywood, eighth child of Lieutenant Nathaniel Heywood (4), was born March 9, 1796, at Shrewsbury He married, October 21, 1824, Maria Brooks, of Princeton He settled in Shrewsbury and his children were born there, viz John Brooks, born August 8, 1825, George Chamberlain, June 18, 1827, died November 12, 1829, Charles Leland, mentioned below, George Chamberlain, June 17, 1832, Edwin Chapin, September 27, 1836, Henry Adams, June 23, 1842 The baptisms of the children are recorded in the second parish, Worcester

(VI) Charles Leland Heywood third child of Daniel Heywood (5), of Shrewsbury and Worcester, Massachusetts, was born in Shrewsbury, October 21, 1828

(VII) Charles H Heywood, son of Charles Leland Heywood (6), was born in Worcester, Massachusetts He married, November 22, 1886, Cora Maria Eaton, daughter of Amos Madison and Eliza Maria (Kelley) Eaton of Worcester Their children are Muriel Clio, Vincey Eaton, and Charles Errol

AMOS MADISON EATON John Eaton (1) was the emigrant ancestor of Amos Madison Eaton of Worcester He was the son of Nicholas and Katherine (Marston) Eaton, and was baptized in England August 21, 1611 Nicholas Eaton was a curate and church warden John Eaton received a bequest of ten pounds from his step-mother's will dated April 10, 1635

John Eaton is believed to have come with others of the family on the ship Elizabeth and Ann in April, 1635. He settled first in Watertown, Massachusetts, where he was a proprietor, and where May 25, 1636, he was admitted a freeman. He removed to Dedham a year later and was a proprietor there in 1637. He had grants of land at Watertown, July, 1636, and February 28, 1636-37-38. He joined the Dedham church in 1641 and signed the famous Covenant there. He bought the rights of Thomas Hastings when he went to Dedham May 11, 1637. He was first present at the Dedham town meeting, November 28, 1637, although he was one of a committee in 1637 to cut pines for the meeting house. He helped build the first foot-bridge across the Charles river. He was on a committee to lay out land for settlers and survey highways. He was wood reeve for several years. He had the delicate task in 1647 of deciding who were behind on the highway work. In 1650 he was on the committee to repair the foot-bridge. He had numerous grants of land

He married in England, Abigail Damon, or Dammant, who had two children, John and Jane, by her previous marriage. He died November 17, 1658. His will was made November 2, 1658, and proved December 16, 1658. The children of John and Abigail Eaton were: 1 Mary, baptized in Dover, England, March 20, 1630-31, married, May 5, 1651, John Mason. 2 John, baptized in Dover, England, October 1, 1633, buried there January 27, 1734. 3 Thomas, born in England, 1634, died in Dedham, September 10, 1649. 4 John, born in Watertown, (see forward). 5 Abigail, born in Dedham, January 6, 1640, married Robert Mason, of Medfield. 6 Jacob, born in Dedham, June 8, 1642, died March 20, 1646

(II) John Eaton, fourth child of John Eaton (1), was born probably in 1636 in Watertown, Massachusetts. He inherited the homestead at Dedham. He married Alice ——, who died May 8, 1694

The children of John and Alice Eaton were: John, born July 15, 1665, died October 15, 1665, John, September 17, 1671, Thomas, July 23, 1675, William, August 11, 1677, Judith, September 17, 1679, died April 26, 1780, Jonathan, (see forward), David, March 8, 1683, died March 28, 1683, Ebenezer, May 3, 1687, died May 23, 1688

(III) Jonathan Eaton, son of John Eaton (2), was born in Dedham, Massachusetts, September 3, 1681. He went to Connecticut in 1703, and bought land in Woodstock in the part now Putnam, Connecticut. In 1702 he paid taxes in Dedham, in 1704 in Woodstock. In 1705 he paid in Dedham only, being "eased from all rates" in Woodstock by special vote of the town. He attended church at Woodstock until the establishment of a church at Killingly, January 28, 1730, of which he was chosen the first deacon. This church is now the North Society of Thompson, Connecticut. He married the second daughter of Comfort and Mary Starr, of Dedham. Comfort Starr was the son of John and the grandson of Dr Comfort Starr, of Dedham, Massachusetts. Abiah (Starr) Eaton was born February 8, 1687-88. Although her name was Abiah she was baptized Lydia, June 17, 1688. Her sister, Mary Starr, married her husband's brother, William Eaton. Deacon Jonathan Eaton died June 25, 1748, aged sixty-seven years. His wife died March 4, 1751

The children of Deacon Jonathan and Abiah (Starr) Eaton, all recorded at Woodstock, were: Lydia, born November 5, 1707, married Philemon Chandler, Keziah, May 24, 1710, Alice, November 28, 1712, Susannah, April 8, 1715, Jerusha, April 16, 1717, Hannah, August 17, 1719, Jonathan, November 10, 1721, John, May 18, 1724, settled at Adams, Massachusetts, Penelope, March 21, 1727, Comfort, September 25, 1729, Marston, October 21, 1731, died May 3, 1776, (see forward). (See Dedham Reg Vol 11.) The gravestone of Jonathan is at Putnam, Connecticut

(IV) Marston Eaton, youngest child of Jonathan Eaton (3), was born in Killingly, Connecticut, in the section now Thompson. He married Elizabeth Lyon, of Woodstock, January 7, 1762. He removed to Belchertown, Massachusetts, in 1776, and shortly after his arrival there he died, May 3, 1776. He and his brother Comfort operated a mill on the Quinebaug river on land given them by their father. The children of Marston and Elizabeth (Lyon) Eaton were: Comfort, and Marston, see forward

(V) Marston Eaton, second child of Marston Eaton (4), was born at Killingly, Connecticut, April 13, 1767. When a young boy he moved with his parents in 1776 to Belchertown, Massachusetts, where he attended the public schools. He also lived and went to school in the adjoining town of Pelham, Massachusetts. He moved to Amherst, Massachusetts, in 1804 and established a store there, removing to Pelham in 1806. He was prosperous and had what was for his day and location a fortune. The loss of $10,000 of convention money embarrassed him, and he finally retired to his farm where he spent the later years of his life. His farm was in Pelham, where, October 10, 1845, he was accidently killed by a tree which he cut and which fell upon him. He was a member of the Universalist Church. He was a Whig in politics and influential in town affairs. He was collector of taxes in Pelham for many years and held other town offices. He was a Free Mason. At the time of Shays's Rebellion he and other citizens in that vicinity started for Worcester to join the ranks of the malcontents, but he failed to carry out his purpose and went to Connecticut until the trouble was at an end

He married Charlotte Dutton, of Ludlow, Massachusetts, December 22, 1793. Their children were: 1 Rufus, born in Belchertown, Massachusetts, May 1, 1794, married Fannie Holden. 2 Mary, born in Belchertown, December 29, 1796, married David Abercrombie, of Pelham, and had seven children. 3 De Marcus, September 10, 1798, married Ora Austin, of Canterbury, Connecticut. Their children were: Phebe A, married Charles Ray, of Canterbury, Fayette, married Fannie Lester, of Canterbury, and had Elmer Ellsworth and Sarah, Calvin, married —— Payne, of Providence, Rhode Island, and had Charles H and one daughter, Mary Hannah, unmarried, lives in Canterbury, Connecticut, and Lutheria. 4 Lily, June 29, 1800, married Asa Briggs, of North Adams, Massachusetts, and had eight children. 5 Walter, July 24, 1802, married Jerusha Austin, of Canterbury, Connecticut. 6 Jefferson, June 26, 1804. 7 Marston, see forward. 8 Hannah, September 25, 1808, died at age of three. 9 Madison, August 23, 1811, died October 19, 1836, married Orinda Hall of Shutesbury, Massachusetts. 10 Calvin Dutton, October 20, 1814, married Harriet Dudley, of Dudley, Massachusetts, and had five children: Heman, Homer, Julia, Cornelia and Ellen. 11 Monroe, July 24, 1817, married Clarissa Boyden and had three children: Morton Monroe, Frank Lapierre, and Augusta, who lives in Hancock, Iowa

(VI) Marston Eaton, seventh child of Marston Eaton (5), was born in Pelham, Massachusetts, May 26, 1806 He received his early education in the district schools of his native town, but he was a self-educated man in the proper sense of the word He was a life-long student He began to teach school when he was about nineteen years old, working at home on his father's farm during the summer seasons For about fifteen years he was a school teacher in Pelham, Amherst and vicinity During this time he worked two summers for his brother DeMarcus, in Canterbury, Connecticut, in his axe factory He then returned to his home and resumed teaching and farming for two or three years In 1847 he came to Worcester with his family and settled near Millstone Hill Later he bought a farm in Holden and lived there for six or seven years, during which time he had charge of the quarries at Millstone Hill He finally exchanged his Holden property for a farm at the corner of Belmont and Elizabeth streets, as the location is now known He built two dwelling houses there He lived there and in other parts of the city In 1869 he retired from active business and went to Shrewsbury where he bought another farm on which he spent the remainder of his days and where he died January 3, 1873 He was a member of the Baptist church He was a Republican in politics He served in the militia in his younger days and was drummer of the Pelham Company, being very expert with the drumsticks

Marston Eaton married (first), May 23 1829 in Millbury, Massachusetts, Betsey, daughter of Sylvanus and Alice (Sprague) Joslyn, of Douglas, Massachusetts Sylvanus Joslyn was a farmer He was drowned in a pond on his own farm Marston Eaton married (second) Sarah Whitney, of Boylston, Massachusetts He married (third) Abigail Winter, of West Boylston He married (fourth) Angeline L Bond, of Worcester The children of Marston and Betsey (Joslyn) Eaton were 1 Rufus Joslyn, born in Pelham, Massachusetts, 1831 married Julia Sampson, of Brookfield, Massachusetts, who died February, 1905 They had four children Charles Henry, lives in Dallas, Texas, and has four children, Carrie Augusta, deceased, married Henry Boatmer, of Dallas, Texas, and had one child, James W Boatmer, Grace, died young, Mary Louise, married Henry W Fobes, of New Braintree, Massachusetts, lives in Dallas Rufus Joslyn died in Dallas in 1896 2 Amos Madison, see forward 3 Marston Monroe, born in Worcester, June 14, 1836, married (first) Emily Thayer, of Barre, Massachusetts They had two children Bessie, who died young, Emma Viola, deceased He married (second) Marietta Knowlton, of Springville, New York They had two children Bessie, who was burned to death at the age of eighteen, Marston Monroe, Jr, of Deer Lodge, Montana, a Methodist clergyman, has four children Marston Monroe, Jr, Mary Harriet, Pauline and Lois 4 Calvin Jefferson, born in Worcester, June 3, 1839, killed at Gettysburg battle July 4, 1863, he was in Company B, Fifteenth Massachusetts Infantry 5 Elizabeth Dimmis, born in Worcester, April 14, 1841 died in 1873, married Augustus D A Guild, of Worcester, who was killed in the battle of Spottsylvania, married, Thanksgiving Day, 1858, and had one child, Marston Augustus Guild, deceased, who married Ella Boutelle, of Aztalan, Wisconsin They had four daughters Bernice Alvira, Elizabeth Eaton, Cora Eaton, and Beulah 6 Mary Harriet born in Holden, Massachusetts, March 7, 1847, lives at 24 Maywood street, Worcester, unmarried 7 Orinda, born in Holden, Massachusetts, April 6, 1849, married Benjamin T Marsh, of Worcester The children of Marston and Angeline L (Bond) Eaton were 8 Walter Fayette, died young 9 Lily Luthera, married Edward A Bartlett, of Shrewsbury, Massachusetts They have five children Henry A, Edith, Gladys, Herbert, and Everett 10 Annie Eliza, married Charles A Bacon, of Worcester, and they have five children Hazel Irene, Eunice Evelyn, Arthur Charles, Ruth Belle, and Marston Eaton Bacon 11 Carrie Belle, married William T Pratt, of Shrewsbury, Massachusetts 12 Annie Frances, married Fred C Pratt, of Shrewsbury, and had one child Carlisle Clifton Pratt Annie Frances Pratt died December 25, 1901

(VII) Amos Madison Eaton, second son of Marston Eaton (6), was born in Pelham, Massachusetts, October 21, 1833 At the age of ten or twelve years he came to Worcester with his father's family who soon afterward went to Holden where he attended the district schools After receiving a common school education he attended the Claremont (New Hampshire) Academy His first employment was driving a baker's cart for George T King, of Orange street, Worcester Then, after a year or two in the bakery business, he went into partnership with Oran A Kelley, on School street, in the retail grocery business After two years he bought out his partner and for twenty-five years he carried on the business there, at 19 School street After retiring from the grocery business he carried on a real estate business for about thirteen years and cared for his own real estate interests He was also in the sand business for a few years and died while engaged in that line of business, July 4, 1895, at his home in Worcester, 807 Main street

Mr Eaton had a kindly social disposition that won him many friends He was a man of uprightness and integrity He won the esteem of his friends by his frankness, honesty and good nature He was a member of the Unitarian church In politics he was a Republican

He married Eliza Maria Kelley, daughter of Oran A Kelley of Worcester (See sketch of Oran A Kelley's family in this work)

The only child of Amos Madison and Eliza Maria (Kelley) Eaton was Cora Maria, who married Charles H Heywood of Worcester November 22, 1886 He is an inventor of envelope machinery, and is a stockholder in the United States Envelope Company Their home is in the west

The children of Charles H and Cora Maria (Eaton) Heywood are Muriel Clio, Vincey Eaton and Charles Errol

HENRY WARD BATES The family of Bates, Bate or Batt as it was variously spelled in ancient times is an ancient name in England, and many members of the family in England as well as America have been distinguished The Bates coat of arms in England is a lion's head erased go The name is a form of Bertelot (Bartlett) derived from the ancient name Bartholomew when surnames came into vogue Five generations of the family are traced in England in the direct line of ancestry of Clement Bates, Hingham, the emigrant ancestor

(I) Thomas Bates the ancestor of Henry Ward Bates, of Worcester, lived in Lydd, parish of All Hallows county Kent, England, and died there in 1485

(II) John Bates son of the preceding Thomas Bates (1) died in 1522

(III) Andrew Bates, son of the preceding John Bates (2) had four sons, he died in 1533 at Lydd

(IV) John Bates son of the preceding Andrew Bates (3), died at Lydd in 1580, leaving three sons

(V) James Bates, son of the preceding John Bates (4), died at Lydd in 1614 Among his children authorities give the three American pioneers of this name Clement, of Hingham, Edward, of Weymouth, and James, of Dorchester, Massachusetts

(VI) Clement Bates, son of the preceding James Bates (5), was born in Hingham, county Kent, England, in 1595 At the age of forty he embarked with his wife Anna of the same age April 6, 1635, on the ship "Elizabeth," William Stagg, master He had with him also five children He settled at Hingham Massachusetts, about the same time that Rev Peter Hobart s company arrived in September, 1635, and had a homestead of five acres on Town street, near South street, and the original house was lately standing and owned by descendants of the emigrant

Anna Bates died in Hingham, October 1, 1669, aged seventy-four years, Clement died September 17, 1671, aged seventy-six years In his will dated at Hingham, October 12, 1669, he gives land to sons, Joseph, Benjamin and Samuel The children of Clement and Anna Bates were James, born 1621, Clement, 1623, Rachel 1627, died June, 1647, Joseph, 1630, Benjamin, 1633, Samuel, baptized in Hingham, March 24, 1639

(VII) Joseph Bates, son of Clement Bates (6), was born in county Kent, England, about 1630, married in Hingham, Massachusetts, January 9, 1657-8, Esther Hilliard, daughter of William Hilliard She died June 3, 1709 Joseph died April 30, 1706, aged seventy-six years In his will of April 24, 1706, he mentions and provides for his wife Esther, also for four sons and for daughters He was a bricklayer by trade, and undoubtedly a brickmaker as well He was constable from 1675 to 1678, inclusive He was selectman 1671-77-84-92, he was appointed sexton of the parish in 1673 and served in that office until the new meetinghouse was erected He resided on the old homestead, South street

The children of Joseph were Joseph, born September 28 1660, Esther, August 29, 1663, married Richard Cobb, Caleb, March 30, 1666, Hannah, October 31, 1668, Joshua, August 14, 1671, Bathsheba, January 26, 1673-4, Clement, September 22 1676, drowned June 29, 1706, in thirtieth year, Eleanor, August 29, 1679, died September, 1679, Abigail, October 16, 1680, married, June 12, 1704, John Chubbuck

(VIII) Joshua Bates, son of Joseph Bates (7), was born in Hingham, Massachusetts August 14, 1671, married, January 15 1695-6, Rachel Tower daughter of Ibrook and Margaret (Hardin) Tower She was born in Hingham, March 16, 1674-5 Their children, all born in Hingham, were Rachel, July 14, 1696, Joshua, June 15, 1698, Bathsheba, February 9, 1699-1700, Elizabeth, November 23 1703, Solomon, April 13, 1706, Isaac, March 3, 1707-8, Jacob, August 20, 1710, of whom later

(IX) Jacob Bates, son of Joshua Bates (8), was born in Hingham, August 20, 1710 He married, November 19, 1730, Mary Clark, daughter of John and Rebecca (Lincoln) Clark He resided in the second precinct of Hingham and in 1745 was constable Late in life he removed to Attleboro, Massachusetts and later to Dudley, where he died at an advanced age, July 6, 1795 The children of Jacob and Mary (Clark) Bates were Mary born July 9, 1732, Simeon, March 21, 1737-8, Obadiah, May ·, 1741, James, April 19, 1743, Lydia, July 10, 1744, Elijah, December 2, 1746, John, December 4, 1748, of whom later, Jacob, April 15, 1751, Israel, April 5, 1753, Elizabeth, baptized May 8, 1761

(X) John Bates, son of Jacob Bates (9), was born in Hingham, December 4, 1748, died December 12, 1834, aged eighty-six years He married Chloe Fuller, who was born August 6, 1747, died July 11, 1825, aged seventy-nine years She was the daughter of Ensign Noah Fuller, who was born October 18, 1714, and died August 10, 1786, an ensign in the militia Her mother, Mary Cushman, was a descendant of Mayflower stock He was a soldier in the revolution and was paid for services at the battle of Bunker Hill, he was in Captain Ide s company, Colonel Daggett s regiment He was also in the service in Rhode Island in 1776 and later In 1775 he was in Attleboro and he went from there to Bellingham, where other relatives lived Later he settled in Dudley, Massachusetts, now a part of Webster, where he spent the remainder of his life He was a farmer and large landowner

His children were Captain Alanson, born January 30, 1772, in Attleboro, Massachusetts, died August 22, 1842, married twice, John, born 1780, of whom later, Subil, married ——— Joslin, resided at Thompson, Connecticut

(XI) Captain John Bates, son of John Bates (10) was born 1780 and died 1863, aged eighty-three years He married (first) Patty ———, born 1786, died August 9, 1844, aged fifty-eight He settled in Thompson, Connecticut He had only one child, John Wakefield Bates, born about 1800 Captain John Bates was a man of wealth and influence in his day

(XII) John Wakefield Bates, son of Captain John Bates (11), was born about 1800 He was brought up in Thompson, Connecticut, and went to school there He learned the weaver's trade, at which he worked for several years He removed to Webster, Massachusetts, when a young man and went to work in the Slater mill After a couple of years he bought a farm at Rochdale, Massachusetts, known as the Bridges farm and became a farmer for the remainder of his life When a young man he was a school teacher for a time in the common schools in and about Thompson He was a member of the Baptist church In politics he was a Republican He died September 25, 1881, at Rochdale

He married Alma Perry, who was a native of Connecticut, she died August 20, 1881 Their children were John Franklin, died unmarried, Henry Thompson, of whom later, Alma Jane, died May 5, 1867, married Washington Hill Merritt, of Warren Massachusetts, and their only child, Blanche, died young, Emery F, died January 4, 1864, unmarried

(XIII) Dr Henry Thompson Bates, son of John Wakefield Bates (12), was born in Webster, Massachusetts, November 12, 1832 At an early age he removed with his parents to Rochdale, and was educated in the public schools of that town He also attended Leicester Academy, and was graduated at the age of eighteen He then came to Worcester as a clerk in the drug establishment of William Bush (now Brewer & Co's), Front street He began to study medicine there and after two years entered the Worcester Medical College on Providence street, where the old Worcester Academy now is He studied there under Dr Newton and Dr A Jackson Howe He subsequently went to the College of Medicine at Cincinnati, Ohio, and received his degree of M D there

He bought the practice of Dr Hall, of Lowell, and practiced his profession there for three years Then he disposed of his business there and removed to Brookfield, Massachusetts, where he practiced for ten years with gratifying success But his health became impaired and he removed to Norwich, Connecticut, where he resided for a year and then came to Worcester, where he spent the remainder of his life He never recovered his health and was able to practice but little after leaving Brookfield During the last two years he was a hopeless invalid He died April 4, 1870 He was a Congregationalist and while in Brookfield was the clerk of the parish In politics he was a Republican He was on the school committee in Brookfield when the school committee had to run the schools and give them personal attention He was a member of Hayden Lodge of Free Masons of Brookfield and of the Worcester District Medical Society.

He married, August 4, 1857, Charlotte Howe Bush, daughter of Eleazer and Sarah (Howe) Bush, of North Brookfield Eleazer Bush was a farmer and prominent in the militia The children of Dr and Charlotte Howe (Bush) Bates were Grace Alma, born October 1, 1860, resides at 58 Wachusett street, Worcester, unmarried, Henry Ward, born February 13, 1863, of whom later

(XIV) Henry Ward Bates, son of Dr Henry Thompson Bates (13), was born at Brookfield, Massachusetts, February 13, 1863 He began his early education in his native town, but soon removed to Norwich, Connecticut, where he went to school for a time He removed with the family to Worcester and attended the public and high schools In 1879 he took the place of one of John D Washburn's clerks who had resigned on account of illness He showed an aptitude for the insurance business, and has been connected with this firm as clerk and later as partner ever since He was admitted to partnership in 1896 and the firm name became John D Washburn, Willis, Green & Bates This agency is one of the largest as well as one of the oldest in the county

Mr Bates attends Central Congregational Church and has been on its board of assessors three years, part of the time as chairman He has been a member of the Worcester Congregational Club for eleven years and is at present the treasurer He is treasurer and clerk of the Worcester Board of Trade, first vice-president of the Worcester Board of Underwriters, member of the corporation of the Worcester County Institution for Savings, member of the Massachusetts Association of Local Fire Insurance Agents, the Worcester County Mechanics' Association, the Tatassit Canoe Club, the Automobile Club, and other social organizations In politics he is a Republican Mr Bates served four years in the militia and was second sergeant of the Worcester Light Infantry, Company C, Second Regiment, Massachusetts Volunteer Militia

He married, October 15, 1895, Mabel Washburn Jenkins, who was born February 25, 1871, the daughter of James E Jenkins, of Vernon, New York The children of Henry Ward and Mabel Washburn (Jenkins) Bates were Rachel, born in Worcester, September 10, 1896, Hester, born in Worcester, June 9, 1900

General James E Jenkins, father of Mrs Henry Ward Bates, was the son of L Whipple Jenkins, and was born in Vernon, New York, in 1842 His father was one of the ablest lawyers in the state in his day His father's brother, Hon Timothy Jenkins, of Oneida Castle, was a congressman for several years He attended the schools of his native village and afterwards prepared himself for college He was a student at Hamilton College when the civil war broke out, and left at once to enlist He helped to raise a company of which he was to be the captain, but after the company was raised there was a long and costly delay in mustering them in, so the men were scattered Mr Jenkins then became first lieutenant of the Oneida Cavalry Company, which went to the front in September, 1861, and was made headquarters guard for the Army of the Potomac and remained on this duty till the end of the war, being mustered out September, 1865 In March, 1863, Lieutenant Jenkins was transferred with the same rank to the One Hundred and Forty-sixth New York Infantry, known as the Fifth Oneida The lieutenant colonel of this regiment was David T Jenkins, his brother Lieutenant Jenkins was soon made a captain and was brevetted for special bravery at the battle of Spottsylvania He was terribly wounded at Gettysburg, shot through the neck by a musket ball and at the same time his back was badly torn by an exploding shell He was nursed back to health by his mother, who took him to her home in Vernon as soon as he could be moved His brother, Colonel Jenkins, was killed in the battle of the Wilderness while he was recovering from his wounds In September, 1864, Captain Jenkins, re-enlisted in the Oneida Cavalry Company and retained his command until mustered out a year later

After the war Captain Jenkins engaged in business in Worcester, Massachusetts, but in 1871 removed to New York, where he remained for about ten years He never recovered from the wounds and exposures of army life, and in 1881 had to retire from business He went to Florida, then to South Dakota, and in 1882 decided to locate there He pre-empted a homestead in Brule county, near Chamberlain, removing his family there the following year His health improved and he became prominent in his new home In 1883 he was elected treasurer of the county for three years, and in 1886 was re-elected In 1887 he was appointed by Governor Church adjutant general of Dakota, and thus became known as General Jenkins Had his life been spared he gave promise of becoming one of the distinguished men of the territory

Mr A P Case wrote of him at the time of his death 'Brave and manly as a boy, brave on the battle field, brave in his last struggle with his last antagonist death In the field he did not seem to know what fear was Always cool and collected, a model commander, quick to see, prompt to act, he only wanted a larger field of action to have become distinguished as an officer Himself friendly, he always made friends, and was a favorite with his playmates, his college chums, his army comrades, and with the far western people among whom he finally cast his lot But with his friendliness he always kept his stately, courteous manner, his self-respect, his positive, determined character, thus compelling the respect of others In these respects, as well as in personal appearance and dignity, he often reminded his friends of his uncle, the late Hon Timothy Jenkins, of Oneida Castle His vigorous youth and erect form promised a long life, but four years of army life hardships sapped it beyond recovery "

He married Lizzie Learned Pierce, of Spencer, Massachusetts They had six children Mabel W, Mrs Henry W Bates, David T, resides in Minneapolis, Alice S, at home, Bessie, deceased, Marshall P, at home, Gennette E, resides with Mrs Bates

GEORGE HENRY SHERMAN The name Sherman had a German origin, but the family in England is very ancient

(I) Henry Sherman, the first English progenitor to whom the line of George Henry Sherman, of Worcester, can be traced, lived in Dedham, Essex county, England, married Agnes ——, died in 1589 Their children were 1 Henry, see forward 2 Edmond 3 Judith 4 John 5 Robert

(II) Henry Sherman, son of Henry Sherman (1), married Susan Hills He died in Dedham in 1610 His children were 1 Henry, born 1571, died 1645 2 Samuel (see forward) 3 Susan 4 Edward 5 Nathaniel, died young 6 Nathaniel 7 John 8 Elizabeth 9 Ezekiel 10 Mary 11 Daniel

(III) Samuel Sherman, son of Henry Sherman (2), born 1573, in Dedham, England married Phillippa ——, died in England 1615 Their children were 1 Mary born 1599 2 Samuel, died in Boston, Massachusetts, and 3 Henry (twins), died young 4 Henry, born June 25 1603 5 Martha January 24 1604 6 Sarah, February 12, 1606, died December 12, 1612 7 Philip (see forward)

(IV) Hon Philip Sherman, son of Samuel Sherman (3) born in Dedham England, February 5, 1610, died in Portsmouth Rhode Island, 1687 married Sarah Odding daughter of Mrs John Porter He came to New England in 1634 and settled first at Roxbury, Massachusetts He became interested in the doctrines and opinions of Anne Hutchinson, and when she was exiled he, with others left Massachusetts Bay colony and went to Rhode Island Here by advice of Roger Williams, they bought the island of Aquetnet, now Rhode Island, March 24, 1638 The government was established July, 1639, with William Coddington as governor, and Sherman secretary He often held offices afterward He was a man of intelligence, wealth and influence The early records of Portsmouth Rhode Island, are in his handwriting which shows an unusual degree of education He was a neat and skilful penman After settling in Rhode Island Sherman became a Quaker, and many of his descendants have been Quakers also Hon John Sherman and his brother, General William T Sherman were descended from Philip's brother Edmund Sherman, who settled in Watertown Massachusetts

Children of Hon Philip and Sarah Sherman were 1 Eber (see forward) 2 Sarah, born 1636, married Thomas Mumford of South Kingston, Rhode Island 3 Peleg, born in Portsmouth, Rhode Island 4 Mary, died young 5 Edmund born 1641 6 Samson born 1642, died 1720 7 William died young 8 John, born 1644, died 1734 9 Mary, married Samuel Wilbor, of Swansea 10 Hannah married William Chase, of Swansea 11 Samuel, born 1648, died 1717 12 Benjamin, born 1650, married December 3 1674, Hannah Marcy His son Jonathan had son Jonathan and grandson Benajah who lived in Exeter (no record available of Benajah's children) He was born in 1723 died 1785 13 Philip, born October 1, 1652, married —— Hathaway

(V) Eber Sherman, eldest son of Philip Sherman (4), born in Roxbury Massachusetts, 1634, settled at North Kingston and died there in 1706 North Kingston formerly included Exeter, Rhode Island Children of Eber Sherman were 1 Eber, married Martha Remington, and resided at North Kingston 2 Stephen, farmer of North Kingston 3 William, married May 12 1681, Martha Wilbor 4 Peleg (see forward) 5 Elisha resided in North Kingston 6 Samuel, died 1744, unmarried

(VI) Peleg Sherman fourth child of Eber Sherman (5) born in North Kingston Rhode Island resided there on the farm now in the limits of Exeter Rhode Island now or lately owned by Othniel Sherman Children were 1 Ichabod born December 3 1715 2 Lydia 1717 married William Sweet 3 Elizabeth 1719 4 Moses (see forward) 5 Mary born June 27 1725

(VII) Moses Sherman, fourth child of Peleg Sherman (6), born in North Kingston, July 8 1723, settled in that part of the town now Exeter, perhaps on the homestead He married (first), March 31, 1745, Sarah Austin, (second) Mary Tarbox, July 13, 1758 Children of Moses and Sarah (Austin) Sherman were 1 Mellicent, born July 20, 1747 2 Elizabeth, October 4, 1749 3 Hannah, February 26, 1752 4 Moses, March 7, 1756 Children of Moses and Mary (Tarbox) Sherman were 5 Rufus January 28 1759 6 Sarah, January 15 1761 7 Abiel, February 15 1767 8 Benajah (see forward) (not in printed records) 9 Samuel married Mary Niles of West Greenwich, January 18, 1794 (Birth not recorded of Samuel, see marriage record)

(VIII) Benajah Sherman son of Moses Sherman (7), born in Exeter, Rhode Island, April 16, 1774 was the father of Peleg Brown Sherman, born October 11 1798

(IX) Peleg Brown Sherman son of Benajah Sherman (8), born in Exeter Rhode Island October 11, 1798 was the grandfather of George H Sherman, of Worcester, and father of Hazard Sherman, born January 14, 1821 His wife was Elsie Dawley and they had fourteen children Harriet, Mary, Hazard Susan, Peleg, Martha and Ruth (twins), George, Robert, was in the navy during the civil war, Elsie, Alford, Hannah, Emily and one who died young He was killed by an accident, his horse running away He was a merchant

(X) Hazard Sherman, son of Peleg Brown Sherman (9) and grandson of Benajah Sherman was born January 14, 1821, in Exeter, Rhode Island, where the family lived for many generations The town of Exeter was set off from North Kingston, where the family located about 1660 His father was born there October 11, 1798, and his grandfather, Benajah Sherman, was born on the same farm in North Kingston April 16 1744 Hazard Sherman settled in Lonsdale, Rhode Island where he kept a general store and was postmaster, was also a carpenter and contractor He was a member and captain of the old Rough and Ready fire company, of Pawtucket, Rhode Island He was a man of influence, and much esteemed by his fellow citizens For a number of years he served in the town council He was a Free Mason and Knight Templar, and a charter member of Unity Lodge of Lonsdale He removed from Pawtucket to Lonsdale later in life He attended and supported all churches liberally He married Susan B Follett of Massachusetts daughter of James Follett and their children were 1 Hazard B 2 Fred A 3 George Henry (see forward) 4 Frank P 5 Charles J 6 Susan E 7 Cora J He died in Lonsdale about 1882 She is still living (1906) and resides at Pawtucket Rhode Island

(XI) George Henry Sherman, son of Hazard Sherman (10) born in Pawtucket Rhode Island, March 24 1850 attended school in his native town and in Lonsdale, and was graduated from the Lonsdale high school in 1867 He went to work in his father's store, and for a time, while clerking there was assistant postmaster He was in the store six years He then started in business for himself in Lonsdale, but after a short time removed to Florida where he opened a general store, first in Micanopy where he remained a year, then in Gainesville He made a specialty there of dealing in Sea Island cotton He was in business in Florida in all five years In 1880 he accepted a position with the American Supply Company, of Providence dealers in mill supplies for cotton and woolen mills, as commercial traveler, and has been with this house ever since He is well known to the mill owners of New England He lived in Valley Falls, Rhode

Island, for six years and in Pawtucket nine years In 1897 he came to Worcester, and a few years later built an attractive home at 690 Pleasant street, opposite Newton Hill He is a Free Mason, a member of Union Lodge of Pawtucket, Pawtucket Royal Arch Chapter, Holy Sepulchre Commandery, Knights Templar, Palestine Temple, Mystic Shrine of Providence, and Tatassit Canoe Club, of Worcester He was in the Pawtucket Light Guards in 1867-68 He is a Republican and in 1877 served in the common council of Gainesville, Florida He and family attend the Universalist Church Worcester

He married October 30, 1871, Harriet E Cook, born August 20 1851, the daughter of Olney M and Harriet E (Arnold) Cook Olney M Cook died January, 1876, he was a farmer and merchant, born and died in Cumberland, Rhode Island His wife died February, 1896 Their children were 1 Sarah 2 Mary 3 Davis 4 Charles 5 George O Cook Her grandparents were Amos and Olive (Darling) Cook, whose children were 1 Ellis 2 Eliza 3 Arnold 4 Sarah 5 Olive and 6 Olney (twins) 7 Levi 8 Barton 9 Davis 10 Albertis 11 Amos 12 Edmund Amos Cook lived in Cumberland and was a tavern-keeper

Mrs Sherman's mother was the daughter of Simon and Lydia (Sheldon) Arnold Their five children were 1 Edmund married Virginia Chapin 2 Harriet married Olney M Cook 3 Henry, married Abbie Chapin 4 Hetty, married Asa Carpenter 5 Rosa, married Flavel Carr The Arnolds lived in Pawtucket

The children of George Henry and Harriet E (Cook) Sherman are 1 Lola Gertrude, born August 19 1873 graduate of the Pawtucket high school, married William B Hay, November 10, 1898, he is manager of advertising of the Burroughs Screen Company of Partland, Maine, he is son of Henry H and Eleanor Hay of Portland, they have a son, Sherman Hay, born June 7, 1905 2 Harrie Hazard, born October 19, 1879, graduate of the Pawtucket high school in 1897, graduate of the Worcester Polytechnic Institute, 1901, is assistant manager of the Webb Pink Granite Company of Milford Massachusetts, married June 9, 1902, Juliet Jennie Webb and they have two children 1 Webb Hazard, born December 1 1903 2 Harrie Hazard, Jr, born September 14 1905

EDWIN BUTCHER, son of Edwin and Mary Ann (Perks) Butcher, was born in Kidderminster, England, March 28, 1848 His parents were born in Kidderminster, which is in the midst of the great carpet manufacturing district of Great Britain

When Edwin Butcher, Jr, was a year old he was deprived by death of his father, and consequently at the early age of eight was set to work in a carpet mill His time was divided between school and the mill work, half a day at his books and half among the looms He naturally became a weaver and followed his trade in England until 1879, when he came to America seeking a chance to better himself He sailed on the ship Ohio' of the White Star line, landing at Philadalphia, November 1, 1879 He secured work at his trade in that city but the following year moved to Thompsonville, Connecticut and in 1882 came to Worcester, Massachusetts He began work in a very small way in a wood shed at the back door of his house moving later to the attic of his residence at No 13 Cheever street, and subsequently to the cellar He came near abandoning the business, owing to the low prices which he was receiving for his goods, but he received an order from M J Whittall, the carpet manufacturer of Worcester, for ten thousand at an advanced price which enabled him to manufacture at a profit Thus the business began to grow, and he sold large quantities in the United States, Canada and England In 1902, after working twenty years at his trade in Worcester, he was forced to abandon weaving on account of trouble with his eyesight He is now engaged in the manufacture of heddles for carpet looms having secured valuable patents in the United States and England One was granted to him August 3, 1897, and another November 29, 1904, they are for certain new and useful improvements in heddles for Jacquard looms for carpet manufacturing In the first year of manufacturing this device he sold one hundred thousand His shop is now located at No 4 Cheever street, Worcester

Mr Butcher has accumulated considerable property through thrift and careful investment He owns large apartment houses in Worcester, believing in the solid value of such real estate He is an excellent example of adopted citizenship He has overcome the disadvantages of poverty and realized the reward of the man who honors his trade and has contributed something to improve it He is an active and influential Republican He is a member of the Congregational church, and of the Foresters

Mr Butcher married (first) Eliza Burns, daughter of Jasper Burns, of Kidderminster, England She was born in 1844 and died on Easter Sunday, 1900 He married (second) Mary Follows, daughter of John and Ann Roslyn (Badlands) Follows She was born in Kidderminster England, February 4, 1857 coming to America with her parents when two years old Her family came to Worcester in 1870 Her father died in 1883, aged sixty-three, and her mother in 1861, aged thirty-nine No children were born to either union

ALEXANDER DE WITT John Witt (1), who came from Holland to Lynn, Massachusetts, about 1630 and settled there, was the ancestor of Alexander De Witt of Worcester, Massachusetts The prefix De was added by later generations and is doubtless properly part of the surname He married Sarah ———, and is said to have had two wives He died at Lynn, December 2, 1675 His children were John, married Elizabeth Baker, Jonathan, married, March 23, 1663, Mary Dimond, of Lynn, probably daughter of John Dimond, Ann, married ——— Barnes, Elizabeth, Sarah, Mary, Martha, born at Lynn, March 5, 1659, Thomas, born at Lynn, July 25 1661, married, February 26, 1685, Bethia Potter daughter of Nicholas Potter, Ebenezer, born April 6, 1665 died young

(II) John Witt, son of John Witt (1), was born probably about 1650 in Lynn He married January 14, 1676 Elizabeth Baker They resided in Lynn, where all their children were born, not all being recorded The children shown by the Lynn records were Elizabeth, born August 9, 1677, John, born June 3, 1679 married Mary Dane, Mary, born August 14, 1681, Jonathan married in Marlboro, Lydia Mathews, Abigail born February 10, 1687 Samuel born at Lynn October 20 1691, married (first) Elizabeth Breed, of Lynn, (second) Susanna Pierce Ebenezer born August 8, 1693, Thomas, born February 18, 1696, married Mary Ivory, Persis born May 2, 1698

(III) John Witt, son of John Witt (2), was born at Lynn, Massachusetts, June 3, 1679 He married Mary Dane They settled in Marlborough, Massachusetts, about 1707 He died there in 1743 His will was made March 6, 1741, and proved May 16, 1743 It mentions his wife Mary, sons, William, Elias, Joseph, John and Ebenezer, daughters, Mary

Dike and Elizabeth, granddaughter, Rebecca Goodell He settled on the Indian plantation in the northeast part of the town where his descendants have since lived The children of John and Mary (Dane) Witt were William, born May 13, 1708, Mary, born July 29, 1710, Elias, born June 30, 1714, married, March 31, 1742, Elizabeth Marble, Rebecca, born 1715, married, January 17, 1733, Eleazer Goodale, of Sutton, David, born April 11, 1720, married Sarah ——, and had Thomas, born April 11, 1745, Ebenezer, born 1722, baptized June 22, 1722, married Lydia Woodbury, Elizabeth, married Benoni Bailey, John, see forward

John Witt, son of John Witt (3), was born at Marlborough, Massachusetts, about 1720 He was a nephew of Captain Ebenezer Witt, of Brookfield, and he came to North Brookfield to settle as early as 1744 with his wife Sarah They lived on what is lately known as the Cheever place John Witt sold his farm to Samuel Cheever, July 19, 1769 He was one of the forty-eight charter members of the Second Church, formed May 28, 1752 He was a lieutenant in the militia in the Indian wars Four of his children only are recorded at North Brookfield, as follows Benjamin, born August 15, 1750, Ivory, October 20, 1752, Stephen, August 15, 1754, Joseph, January 3, 1757

(V) Benjamin Witt, son of John Witt (4), was born at North Brookfield, Massachusetts, August 15, 1750 He removed to New Braintree He married Olivia Campbell, daughter of Duncan Campbell, and settled at Oxford Massachusetts He was a soldier in the revolutionary war In 1794 he removed again to New Braintree, where he died April 17, 1818 His widow married Daniel Bacon, of Charlton, Massachusetts, and died February 5, 1848, at Oxford, Massachusetts Their children were 1 Stearns, born December 22, 1787 (named for his maternal grandmother, Elizabeth Stearns This name in England has always been "Stern" and Captain De Witt early discarded the "A" and wrote his name Sterns") 2 Sophia, born April 22, 1789, married, August 14, 1808, William Earle, resided at New Braintree, Oxford, Franklin and Boston where he died August 27, 1867, she died January 3, 1885 Their children were Olivier S, born 1812, William, 1814, Samuel H, 1816, Benjamin A, 1818, Paul, 1821, Henry A, 1824, Mary M, 1829, Nancy S, 1831 3 Polly, born March 22, 1791 married Amos Thompson, 1810 4 Hollis, born December 22, 1792 5 Archibald, born October 27, 1794, married Martha Fisher, daughter of A F Fisher, of Franklin, where they settled, he died May, 1759 His children were George Alexander, William, Martha and Horace 6 Susan, born August 17, 1796, married Rufus Harris 7 Alexander, born April 2, 1798 8 Nancy, born March 29, 1800, married Horace Smith 9 Elizabeth, born February 17, 1803, married Jonas Bacon

(VI) Nancy De Witt, daughter of Benjamin Witt, was born March 29, 1800, at New Braintree Massachusetts She married Horace Smith, of Leicester, his second wife She died September 24, 1830, and her two children were adopted by her brother, Colonel Alexander De Witt, who was childless The children were Eliza L, born at Leicester, May 2, 1825, married Dr William Newton, Horace De Witt, name changed to Horace Smith De Witt, born at Leicester, Massachusetts, October 2, 1828, married, March 29, 1852, Sarah Jane Phelps, daughter of James Phelps, of Sutton

(VII) Horace Smith De Witt, son of Horace and Nancy De Witt Smith (6), was born at Leicester, Massachusetts, October 2, 1828 He married March 29, 1852, Sarah Jane Phelps, daughter of James Phelps, of Sutton, Massachusetts He died May 4, 1859 They settled at Pepperell, Massachusetts, where their only son was born Alexander, March 7, 1854

(VI) Colonel Alexander De Witt, son of Benjamin Witt (5), born April 2, 1798, at New Braintree, Massachusetts He was great-uncle of Alexander De Witt, of Worcester, his namesake He was the next oldest brother of Nancy De Witt Ammidown says of him "He was emphatically what is termed a self-made man Self-reliance was his motto and from this resource he rose to whatsoever position he sustained in either public or private life" He went to work at the age of fifteen in the store of the Merino Manufacturing Company at Dudley, Massachusetts, and remained in that position four years, travelling some of the time to sell goods In 1818 he went to Franklin and engaged in manufacturing cotton thread in partnership with Dr Miller Next year he started a mill and country store at Oxford, selling the thread he made from his wagon After he married he manufactured thread at Franklin with his father-in-law until 1824, when he entered a partnership with his three brothers, Sterns, Archibald and Hollis, and they began a small business at what is now Buffum village in Oxford They continued but a few years As his means increased he became interested in cotton and wool manufacturing elsewhere He resided in Oxford all his life except from 1837 to 1840, when he was a partner in a commercial house in Boston and lived in that city, and in 1848 and 1849, when for about a year he resided in Worcester He became wealthy and held investments in railroads, insurance companies and many different industrial concerns

He was for twenty-six years a director of the Worcester Mechanics' and Farmers' Insurance Company, for twenty-seven years director of the State Mutual Life Assurance Company of Worcester, for twenty years with the Mechanics' Savings Bank of Worcester as trustee and president, director and for nine years president of the Mechanics' National Bank of Worcester, for five years president of the Oxford Bank, three years president of the Worcester & Nashua Railroad, for seventeen years director of the Providence & Worcester Railroad, for twenty-five years director of the Norwich & Worcester Railroad He was often moderator of the Oxford town meetings He was representative in the general court five years, state senator in 1842-44-50-51 He was a delegate to the constitutional convention in 1853 He was elected to congress in 1852 over the Whig and Democratic nominees from the ninth congressional district, and re-elected in 1854 He gave freely to charitable objects and was the largest contributor in the town to religious institutions He left a legacy to the Oxford Congregational Church He is described as a large, florid, handsome man, jovial and hearty in his manner and very attractive personally He married, June 5, 1820, Mary Makepeace, of Franklin, Massachusetts He died January 13, 1879, she died April 6, 1887, at the age of eighty-nine They had no children, but adopted the children of his sister, Nancy (De Witt) Smith

(VIII) Alexander De Witt, son of Horace De Witt (7), was born at Pepperell, Massachusetts, March 7, 1854 He received his education in the public schools at Sutton, Oxford, and Leicester Academy, and in 1871 came to Worcester to live He began his business career in the office of Kinnicutt & Co, hardware merchants, Main street The firm was composed of F H Kinnicutt, Samuel Woodward and L N Kinnicutt He remained with this firm until 1881 He was then associated

Edward F. Fletcher

with J and J Murdock, of Lester, until 1883 He entered the banking business in partnership with Lincoln N Kinnicutt, in 1884, and continued until January, 1906 They were interested with others in the successful purchase and re-organization of the Worcester Safe Deposit & Trust Company, now the Worcester Trust Company, of which Mr De Witt is a director He is also trustee of the People's Savings Bank He married, September 21, 1880, Caroline Murdock, daughter of Joshua Murdock, of Leicester, Massachusetts

HON EDWARD FOSTER FLETCHER The surname Fletcher is derived from the occupation of arrow maker, or maker of bows and arrows, from the Anglo-Saxon "fledge," an allusion to the feathering of an arrow The family is ancient, coming, it is said, from Burgundy, now the Canton de Vaud, in Switzerland The first Fletcher came to England with the Normans at the time of the Conquest The ancient coat-of-arms of the Fletchers was Sable, a cross flory between four scallop shells, argent.

Moses Fletcher came in the "Mayflower," signed the Compact, and died soon after arriving There were three other prominent immigrants to New England Edward, from Badgeden, county Gloucester, returned to England, Robert, of Concord, mentioned below, and William, of Concord No proof of relationship between them has been found

(I) Robert Fletcher, the progenitor of Hon Edward Foster Fletcher, ex-mayor of Worcester was born in England in 1592 The family tradition has it that he came from Yorkshire, and the name is common in the north of England Robert settled in Concord, in New England, in 1630, and became wealthy and prominent, he was appointed by the general court a constable November 2, 1637 He removed to Chelmsford, he joined with William Fletcher and others in 1654 in inviting Mr John Fiske and the Wenham church to remove to Chelmsford in a body He died at Concord, April 3, 1677, aged eighty-five years His will was made February 4, 1672, aged about four score years, in it he commits his wife to the care of his son Francis and wife, bequeathed to sons Francis, William and Samuel The inventory is dated May 12, 1677 His children 1 Luke, born in England, died May 21, 1665, unmarried 2 William, mentioned below 3 Caroline, married ——— Kebby 4 Samuel, born 1632 5 Francis, born 1630, married Elizabeth Wheeler

(II) William Fletcher, son of Robert Fletcher (1), born in England, 1622, came with his father to Concord when eight years old He was admitted a freeman May 10, 1643, was selectman 1655, the first public meeting, November 22, 1654, being held at his house, in 1673 was appointed a commissioner for Chelmsford He was the owner of a tract of land embracing what is now the city of Lowell A part of the original lot, near the meeting house at Chelmsford, has been occupied more than two hundred years by his descendants He died November 6, 1677, his wife Lydia died October 12, 1704 He married Lydia Bates, of Concord, October 7, 1645 Their children 1 Lydia, born January 30, 1647, married Rev John Fiske 2 Joshua, mentioned below 3 Paul, married, April 12, 1705, Deliverance Stevens 4 Sarah 5 William, born in Chelmsford, February 21, 1657 6 Mary, born in Chelmsford, October 4, 1658 7 Esther, born at Chelmsford, April 12, 1664 8 Samuel, born July 23, 1664

(III) Joshua Fletcher, son of William Fletcher (2), was born at Concord, March 20, 1648, and admitted a freeman March 11, 1689 He married, May 4, 1668, Grissies Jewell, who died January, 1682, and (second) Sarah Willey, July 18, 1682 He died November 21, 1713 The only child on record of Joshua and Grissies Fletcher was Joshua, born about 1669, married about 1700, Dorothy Hale Children of Joshua and Sarah 2 Paul, born 1683, resided at Chelmsford, belonged to the Snow Shoe company of soldiers in the Indian war 1724, was town treasurer 3 Rachel, born June 27, 1683 4 Timothy, born October, 1685, died March 2, 1705 5 John, born at Chelmsford May 7, 1687, married Hannah Phelps 6 Joseph, mentioned below 7 Sarah, born January 21, 1690, married Thomas Reed 8 Jonathan, married, May 5, 1735, Jane Chamberlain, and settled in Westford, his widow lived to be a hundred years old 9 Elizabeth, born June 10, 1698, married Samuel Hartwell 10 Jonas, born 1694

(IV) Captain Joseph Fletcher, sixth child of Joshua Fletcher (3), born in Chelmsford, June 10, 1689, married Sarah Adams, of Concord, November 17, 1712 She was born 1691 and died April 24, 1761, he died October 4, 1772 They settled and lived in Westford, adjoining Chelmsford, on the place known as the E Tower place, where all the children were born Their children 1 Joseph, born July 6, 1713 2 Benjamin, born August 8, 1716, married twice 3 Timothy, born April 12, 1719 4 Thomas, born March 10, 1721 5 Sarah 6 Edith, born April 8, 1725, married Benjamin Carver 7 Pelatiah, mentioned below 8 Joshua, born November 20, 1731 9 Ruth, born August 28, 1733 10 Mary, born August 29, 1735, married, January 16, 1755, Eleazer Fletcher

(V) Captain Pelatiah Fletcher, seventh child of Captain Joseph Fletcher (4), born in Chelmsford, May 3, 1727, married Dorothy, daughter of James Hildreth, January 13, 1757 She was born August 26, 1736, died June 14, 1784 He married (second) Widow Betty Keyes, born in Hartwell, October 13, 1782 He was sent as a delegate from Westford to the convention of committees from the towns held at Dracut, November 26, 1776 He died February 23, 1807 Children 1 Betsey, born December 15, 1757 2 Dorothy, born December 21, 1759, married Sampson Fletcher 3 Joseph, born November 6, 1761, died December 25, 1765 4. Sarah, born August 12, 1763, died August 22, 1783 5 Lucy, born November 14, 1765, died July 1, 1766 6 Pelatiah, mentioned below 7 Joseph, born May 13, 1769, married Frances (Grant) Keyes 8 Lucy, born February 12, 1771, married Joseph Rockwood, of Groton 9 Adams, born March 10, 1773, died September 27, 1775 10 Ezra, born October 9 1774 11 Polly, born August 11, 1776, married Abram Prescott 12 Adams, born August 17, 1779

(VI) Pelatiah Fletcher, sixth child of Pelatiah Fletcher (5), born April 4, 1767, married Patty Keyes, December 5, 1785 She died December 9, 1786, he married (second) Sally Woodward, September 22, 1788, (third) Mrs Buelah Heywood, of Concord, June 23, 1803, she died May, 1814 He died May 7, 1811 Children of Pelatiah and Patty Fletcher 1 Joel, born at Westford, 1786, married Abigail Dinsmore, in Anson, Maine, seven children Children of Pelatiah and Sarah 2-3 Sally and Patty, twins, born in Ashburnham, June 28, 1789, Sally married Richard Adams, December 9, 1806, Patty married, April 9, 1807, Jacob Osgood, of Westford, born March 13, 1787, died 1857, and had a large family 4 Wiley, born at Groton, February 7, 1791, married Elizabeth Lyman of Sandlake, New York, removed to Albany, New York 5 Samuel, born at Ashburnham, March 21, 1792, married, April 13, 1813, Buelah Heywood, of

Westford; he died February 25, 1860. 6. Timothy, born at Groton, November 28, 1795; married, January 25, 1825, Elizabeth Ann Edes; he was county commissioner several years. 8. Harriet, born at Groton, July 31, 1800; married Nathan S. Hamlin, of Westford, November, 1829. 9. Mary, born at Westford, January 25, 1803; married Thomas Richardson, January 23, 1840; died March 22, 1877. Children of Pelatiah and Buelah: 10. Pelatiah, born in Westford, June 27, 1804, married, May 13, 1830, Susan Hamlin, born August 29, 1808, died April 15, 1850; settled in Pepperell. 11. Lucy, born at Westford, September 10, 1806, married Abel Stevens, of Fitchburg, Massachusetts.

(VII) Calvin Fletcher, seventh child of Pelatiah Fletcher (6), born in Groton, Massachusetts, February 20, 1797. He was a farmer in Groton and dealt also extensively in lumber. He served the town as selectman, representative to general court, and in other positions of trust and honor. He was one of the prominent men of his day. At the time of his death he owned a large amount of land at Ayer Junction. He was well educated, and in his younger days was a school teacher. He married, October 10, 1819, Nancy Reed, daughter of Samuel Reed. Their children: 1. Nancy E., born at Westford, 1820; married William Sawtelle, of Shirley. 2. Calvin J., born at Westford, 1822, died December 24, 1905; married Elizabeth Whitney, of Stowe, 1848, who died December 24, 1905; three children: Emma C., born 1849; Mary F., 1851; Helen B., 1861. 3. Rufus R., mentioned below. 4. Samuel W., born 1826, died 1845, unmarried. 5. Pelatiah, born 1827, died 1833. 6. Mary F., born 1829; married Frederick W. Pope, 1853; three children: Nellie F., born 1854; Frank F., 1859; William F., Pope, died October 21, 1906. 7. Martha P., born 1833, married Jacob W. Cooper, 1853; had Ida S. Cooper, born 1854. 8. Pelatiah, born 1836, died. 9. Joseph, born 1837, died; married, 1862, Sarah J. Stone, and had: Calvin, born 1863; Charles S., born 1867. 10. Albert Francis, born 1840, died March 14, 1906; married, 1889; two children—Robert and Edwin. Sarah J. Stone died August 6, 1905.

(VIII) Rufus Reed Fletcher, third child of Calvin Fletcher (7), born at Westford, July 2, 1823, died April 16, 1906. He was brought up and went to the public schools in his native town. He became a nurseryman and florist in early life, and followed that occupation during his active life, over fifty years, and at the time of his death was living at Rutland, Vermont. When a young man he owned some valuable inventions and travelled extensively in the west and south. He was an active member of the Unitarian church in Ayer, where he resided until recently. He was at various times trustee, collector and treasurer of the church. Mr. Fletcher was a gifted conversationalist. He had a fund of good stories and good nature that attracted everybody who knew him. He made friends everywhere, and few men were more fortunate in winning the good-will and esteem of a multitude. He married first, 1848, Sarah Marble Whitney, born November 3, 1819, died September 17, 1892. He married (second) Mrs. Mary E. Hayward, of South Acton, Massachusetts. Children of Rufus Reed and Sarah Marble (Whitney) Fletcher: 1. Harriet Josephine, born August 25, 1849, resides in Worcester, unmarried. 2. Sarah Elizabeth, born October 5, 1850, married Charles B. Felch, a printer, of Ayer, Massachusetts, who died 1881; she resides in Worcester; they had one son, Percy Fletcher Felch, born March 5, 1878, died July 8, 1900. He attended the city schools of Worcester and then entered the Massachusetts Agricultural College at Amherst, and graduated in 1901, well advanced in his class. He was very popular among his classmates; he was persuaded to remain after graduation for a few days with his friends, and two days later, while bathing, was drowned. He possessed marked musical talent. His death was a severe blow not only to his widowed mother, but also to his numerous friends, who revered and esteemed him for his many noble characteristics, which shone forth clearly in his daily walk and conversation. 3. Daniel Whitney, born February 1, 1852, resides at Ayer; president Middlesex Northwest Savings Bank of Ayer, and vice-president Ayer National Bank; is owner of Fletcher block; a dealer in men's clothing, furnishings, shoes, etc., and has his two sons in business with him. He married Emma Phelps, and has five children: Ethel A., Howard P., Frank W., Dorris, Hazel died June, 1894. 4. Edward Foster mentioned below. 5 Samuel Wyley, born May 28, 1857; was engaged in the clothing business at Nashua, but March 1, 1906, sold this and associated himself with his brother, Edward Foster, in business in Worcester. He married Susan Fletcher; two children. 1. Mary M., a teacher in the kindergarten at Nashua, New Hampshire; she has a fine contralto voice and sings in public, thus furnishing pleasure for many people; she is noted for her many acts of charity among the poor and deserving. 2. Nina G., the well known violinist, who has been heard with favor in Boston Symphony Concerts and many recitals, and gives promise of a brilliant career.

(IX) Edward Foster Fletcher, fourth child of Rufus Reed Fletcher (8), was born in Littleton, Massachusetts, June 17, 1854. When he was four years of age his parents removed with him to Ayer, and he attended the public schools of Ayer and Lawrence Academy, at Groton, Massachusetts. At the age of twenty-one he entered into the boot and shoe business in Ayer, where he continued for six years, and then formed a connection with the Oakdale Shoe Company, at Oakdale, Massachusetts. Two years later he formed a partnership with Gilbert G. Bemis, and began business in Worcester in the Crompton block, on Mechanic street, 1883, under the name of the Waverly Shoe Company. The rapid growth of the business necessitated its removal in 1886 to larger quarters on Front street, where the firm continued for five years, when, having again outgrown their quarters, they removed to the large factory building in the rear of 560-62 Main street. The Waverly Shoe Company was one of the most prosperous shoe concerns making shoes in Worcester. In 1895 the firm was dissolved and Mr. Fletcher sold his interests to his partner. Mr. Bemis moved the business to Laconia, New Hampshire. Mr. Fletcher retained for ten years a special partnership in the company. In 1896 Mr. Fletcher formed the Lincoln Shoe Company, and built up an extensive business as jobber and wholesaler of shoes. George F. Leavitt and P. E. Bassett had an interest in this corporation. In 1904 Mr. Fletcher disposed of his stock in the Lincoln Shoe Company to the White Shoe and Rubber Company, of Worcester, Franklin White, president, Front street, Worcester. The companies were consolidated and at present are conducted by Mr. White under the name of White Shoe & Rubber Company and Lincoln Shoe Company, Consolidated.

Mr. Fletcher had become interested in the Hough Shade Corporation at Janesville, Wisconsin, and since disposing of his shoe business has devoted much time to this business, which is in a very prosperous condition. He is vice-president of the company, which has a capital stock of two hundred thousand dollars, employs one hundred and fifty hands, and owns large brick and stone factories covering seventy-four thousand square feet of land More recently Mr Fletcher purchased the patents of the Criss-Cross tube cleaner, and is now engaged in the manufacture and sale of this very useful contrivance His office and factory are at 26 Southbridge street The device for cleaning tubes is the best known for use in boilers gun barrels, etc It is a metallic spring arrangement that will adjust itself to the variations of size and shape in the tube and yet effectively cut the dirt and deposits to be removed The factory is rushed with orders from all parts of the country Mr Fletcher is doing business under the name of the Reversible Tube Cleaner Company He has secured additional valuable patents since buying the original in 1905 He has salesmen on the road in Canada and England as well as in this country He is director and active in the management of the Tharston Wrench Company, a rapidly growing concern with a very valuable patented wrench The factory is on Hermon street With these business interests and the care of his real estate, Mr Fletcher is a busy man He is not only successful in the various lines of business he has undertaken, but his methods have been fair and honorable, and he has the respect and friendship of even his active rivals in trade He is a Republican His personal popularity and success in business brought to him requests to run for office, which in most cases he declined He served the city as member of common council in 1892, however, and again in 1893 When the city had elected a Democratic major through dissensions in the Republican party, and the city seemed to be about to continue the administration then in power, a conference of leaders was held and Mr Fletcher selected as the man best fitted in the city to bring harmony in the party and redeem the city for the Republicans, as well as to give a thoroughly capable business administration He was consulted and reluctantly consented to run At the city convention next day the nomination was made, and Mr Fletch er s election followed He was mayor of Worcester in 1902, and re-elected for the following year by an increased majority He gave the city a clean, honest and business-like administration, the tax rate was reduced, waste in various departments cut off and less money borrowed, he paved Main, Mechanic and School streets and made many important improvements in the highways of the city He became interested in the City Hospital and great improvements have been effected in that institution The coal strike occurred while he was mayor, and he organized the Fuel League, contributing one thousand dollars of his own money to buy Welsh coal to be sold to the people at cost The day the coal arrived in Boston, Worcester dealers dropped their price from fifteen dollars a ton to twelve, and the day the Fuel League began to sell at eight dollars and a quarter a ton Worcester dealers dropped their price to eight dollars and a quarter, while coal was selling elsewhere in the state as high as twelve dollars a ton He made a strong effort to establish a consumptives' home, or hospital, and though the movement has not yet resulted in building, he organized a cornoration, of which he was the first president, for the purpose of holding the funds collected and raising more for the purpose In a word, Mr Fletcher gave the city a business administration of its municipal affairs Mr Fletcher is a member of Montacute Lodge, F and A M, Quinsigamond Tribe of Red Men, the Worcester County Agricultural Society, and the Worcester Board of Trade He is president of the board of trustees of All Souls Universalist Church He has been a director of the Worcester County Mechanics' Association

A statement issued December 3, 1901, by a committee of twenty-five Republicans, contained this summary of Mr Fletcher's character "He is a successful business man, in the vigor of manhood, trained and fitted by previous service in the city government to manage its affairs He has not sought the office, but the office has sought him He stands as the type of honest, independent, clear-headed, vigorous and successful since Worcester needs these qualities in her mayor in the coming year" James Logan, general manager of the United States Envelope Company, was chairman of this committee

He married (first), June 17, 1880 Mary E Milant, of Boston, one child, Charles Edward, died August 23, 1881 Mrs Fletcher died August 8, 1881 He married (second), February 18, 1887, Helen Bassett, born February 17, 1860, died December 22, 1893, daughter of Hon William Bassett, of Berlin The children of Edward F and Helen (Bassett) Fletcher were Raymond Bassett, born April 16, 1890, a student in the Worcester high school, and Earle Whitney, born February 11, 1892, died March 10, 1894 Mr Fletcher married (third), July 7, 1897, Florence M Bassett, a sister of his second wife Mr Fletcher resides at No 2 Tirrell street and has a summer home at Berlin, Massachusetts

GEORGE JENNISON The Jennings family and the Jennison family are descended from the same immigrant ancestor Two brothers, Robert and William Jennings, came to New England in 1630 or before They came from Colchester, England One of the descendants of Robert Jennison was prominent among the pioneers of the town of Worcester None of the founders was more prominent

William Jennison was a settler in Charlestown and built his house there in 1630 He sold out and removed to Watertown, where Robert Jennison settled August 16, 1631 He held the rank of captain He was admitted a freeman May 18, 1631 He was formerly a partner of Richard Spitty of Grey's Inn, London He was one of the first selectmen, was deputy to the general court, went for a pilot in the ship Thunder' to Bermuda, October 17, 1633, and reported improved conditions there on his return, commanded a company against the Pequot Indians in the war in 1636, was called to court in July, 1644, for a slight difference of opinion on the question between Parliament and the king proved to be most loyal to the colony and commonwealth, was employed by the Earl of Warwick to see to his vessel at Boston, June 27, 1646, returned to Colchester, England He was ensign August 16, 1631, captain March 9, 1636-7, captain of the Trainband 1638, selectman 1635-42-44, deputy to the general court 1637-42-45

(I) Robert Jennison, brother of the preceding, settled at Watertown in New England and was appointed ensign to Captain Patrick in the military company August 16, 1631 He was a proprietor of Watertown and was admitted a freeman in May, 1645 As attorney for his brother William, formerly of Watertown, then of Colchester, England, he sold land in 1657 His wife Elizabeth died October 30, 1638, aged thirty years He married (second) Grace ———, and she died November 26, 1686 He died July 4 1690 His will was dated September 15, 1688, with a codicil April 21, 1689, proved October 7, 1690, it mentions his wife, daughter, Michal Warren, son-in-law, George Reed, son

Samuel, executor, grandsons, William and Robert Jennison

His children were 1 Elizabeth, born April 12, 1637, married, in Woburn, October 4, 1652, Deacon George Reed, who was born 1629, son of William and Mabel Reed, of Woburn 2 Michal, born December 17, 1640, married, February 10, 1657-8, Richard Bloys, who died August 7, 1665, she married (second) John Warren, Jr, she died July 14, 1713 3 Samuel, of whom later

(II) Ensign Samuel Jennison, son of Robert Jennison (1), was born at Watertown, Massachusetts, December 15, 1642 He married, October 30, 1666, Judith Macomber, who died March 1, 1722-3 Their children were Judith, born August 13, 1667, Mercy, January 23, 1669-70, Rachel, October 8, 1671, Samuel, of whom later, William, October 17, 1676, settled in Worcester, one of the founders, judge of the court, died in Worcester, September 19, 1741, Elizabeth, twin of the preceding, born October 17, 1676, Grace, February 11, 1678, Peter, October 1, 1681, Robert, July 24, 1684, Lydia May 18, 1688

(III) Samuel Jennison, son of Ensign Samuel Jennison (2), was born October 12, 1673 He married Mary Stearns, daughter of Samuel and Hannah (Manning) Stearns He lived in Watertown or Newton Their children were Mary, born August 17, 1700, Hannah, July 17, 1702, Samuel, of whom later, William, February 9, 1706-7 (H C 1724), Nathaniel, April 5, 1709, settled in Watertown, later in Weston, married, October 23, 1729, Abigail Mead, John, February 19, 1710-11, married in Lunenburg, July 21, 1740, Mary Hubbard, Lydia, April 2, 1712, Abigail, April 22, 1715, married in Lunenburg September 24, 1739, Jonathan Hubbard, Jr, Mercy, March 11, 1717-18, Sarah, died November 11, 1720, Eunice, born 1721-2, married, July 11, 1739, Joshua Richardson, of Woburn

(IV) Samuel Jennison, third child of Samuel Jennison (3), was born September 26, 1704, married, February 13, 1733-4, Abigail Holden, of Watertown The children of Samuel and Abigail were Samuel, born November 6, 1734, Abigail, October 7, 1736, Mary, June 27, 1741, Phinehas of whom later, Lucy, baptized April 20, 1746, Sarah, June 8, 1748, William, baptized September 23, 1750, Joshua, baptized April 22, 1753, Mercy or Mary, baptized April 22, 1753

(V) Phinehas Jennison, fourth child of Samuel Jennison (4), was born in Watertown, September 27, 1743, married, August 28, 1767, Susan Newton, married (second), August 27, 1792, Sarah Whitney, who died in 1815 at the age of seventy-two years Phinehas Jennison removed from Watertown to the adjoining town of Newton in 1795 and died there February 11, 1825, aged eighty-two years His children were Phinehas, baptized January 14 1770, Susan, baptized January 14, 1770, Elias, baptized April 26, 1772, died 1842, married Sally Tallman and had twelve children, Benjamin, baptized October 23, 1774, of whom later, Phineas, baptized September 30, 1781, Josiah, baptized September 30, 1781, settled in Holden, Massachusetts, William, baptized 1784, died unmarried, Fanny, born in Newton

(VI) Benjamin Jennison, fourth child of Phinehas Jennison (5), was born in Watertown, Massachusetts, and baptized October 23, 1774 He settled in Newton and was for many years an undertaker at West Newton He was a leading citizen He attended the Congregational church He married, 1804, Mary Tolman, who died March 7, 1842, aged sixty years (Records of marriage give name Sukey Gravestone gives the name Mary and age fifty-six) The children of Benjamin and Mary Jennison were Joel, married Lucy Trowbridge, November 10, 1831, George, Albert, married Elizabeth Wilton, Edwin, Matilda, Mary

(VII) George Jennison, second child of Benjamin Jennison (6), was born in Newton, Massachusetts He handled the freight in the early days of the Boston & Worcester Railroad at the first depot in Worcester He was a member of the Congregational church In politics he was a Whig He married Nancy Fiske Their children were George, of whom later, Mary Jane, born May 25, 1838, at Worcester, married Curtis E Robinson, of Framingham, and had one child, Fred N Robinson, born at Holyoke, Massachusetts, Martha Sophia, born February 25, 1840, in Worcester, died there, married William H Richardson, of Poultney, Vermont, and had one child, George William Richardson

(VIII) George Jennison, eldest child of George Jennison (7), was born January 6, 1836, at Worcester, Massachusetts His father died when he was only four years old and he went to live with his grandfather, Benjamin Jennison, at West Newton He went to school there until he was thirteen, when he removed to Millbury, Massachusetts, and worked for a year on the farm of Charles A Smith He then came to Worcester and started to learn the trade of tin, sheet iron and copper worker in the shop of his brother-in-law, Isaiah D Russell, on Front street After his four years of apprenticeship was out he worked two years for various concerns, and four years for George R Peckham making condenser rolls for carding machines He made copper pumps for N G Tucker, Pleasant street, for several years He finally changed his occupation and became clerk in the fish market of G P Cobb & Co, on Front street, and about eighteen months later opened a store on his own account at 24 Green street The business was prosperous and he acquired a competence, retiring in February, 1903, when he sold out to George W Barker

Mr Jennison attends the First Universalist Church He is a Republican and has been somewhat active in politics, having represented his party in municipal, councillor, senatorial and state conventions, and received the nomination for representative to the general court He is a member of Athelstan Lodge of Free Masons, Eureka Chapter of Royal Arch Masons, Hiram Council and is a fourteenth, sixteenth and eighteenth degree Scottish Rite Mason He is a member of Quinsigamond Lodge, No 43, Odd Fellows, of Blake Lodge, Knights of Pythias, of the Worcester Veteran Firemen's Association, having been a member of the fire department twenty-five years, of which he has been the president, and of the Worcester County Mechanics' Association

He married, December 26, 1861, Caroline Blanchard, born January 26, 1840, in Lyndeboro, New Hampshire, daughter of Asa and Elizabeth Blanchard, of Lyndeboro, New Hampshire Her father was a farmer The children of George and Caroline Jennison, all born in Worcester, were Alice Marian, born September 13, 1863, died February 25, 1864, Benjamin Fiske, born August 21, 1869, Mabel Blanchard, born May 27, 1872, Grace Goodwin, born April 28, 1875, works at the City Hall, Walter Russell, born September 14, 1877, is in the grocery business at Edison, Washington, Harry Irving, born August 6, 1880, died October 23, 1882

EDWARD A COWEE James Cowee (1), was the first ancestor of the Cowee family in this country He is the progenitor of Edward A Cowee, of Worcester, Massachusetts

James Cowee or Cohee, as the name was sometimes spelled, was born in 1726 or 1727 in the north part of Ireland of Scotch Presbyterian stock His mother died when he was a young lad and his father took a second wife She did not take kindly to her stepchildren, James and his brother Bartholomew, and neglected and abused them As they grew to manhood the father decided to send them to America, where he believed they would have a better chance than they would in the old country Accordingly, he made arrangements with a sea captain, whom he knew, to take the boys as passengers Bartholomew, the youngest boy, died on the voyage The captain of the ship proved himself a scoundrel by keeping the money that the boys' father had entrusted to him to be given to the boys when they reached their destination in America, and by selling James into temporary service in accordance with an evil custom of those days He was taken to a frontier settlement and when his term of service expired he worked his way back among the settlements of eastern Massachusetts He was at Chocksett (now Sterling) for a time He came to Narragansett No 2, later the town of Westminster, Massachusetts, where he eventually settled He bought of Rev Elisha Marsh lot No 96, in the north part of the town, and proceeded to turn a section of the wilderness into a farm He bought his place October 1, 1750 It is now or was recently owned by Isaac N Smith of Westminster By the following July he had six acres cleared, his orchard set, and a good house built with cellar The site of the house may be discovered near the road, a few rods below the present commodious dwelling house on the old place

James Cowee was an industrious man, and he became a skillful shrewd and prosperous farmer He was a man of much independence and force of character He became one of the largest land-holders in the town, and at the time of the federal tax levy in 1798 owned one of the most valuable residences there

While he was working in Sterling he became acquainted with Mary Pearson (probably a daughter of John Pearson) of Rowley, Massachusetts They were married March 3, 1757, and had a large family of children He died April 29, 1801, aged seventy-four years She died March 11, 1813, aged eighty-three years Their children were 1 John, born July 20 1758, married Mary Rand and settled at Chittenden, Vermont 2 Sarah, born October 12, 1759, married Zeeb Green, settled in Westminster 3 Mehitable born March 2, 1761, married Nathan Wood, settled in Westminster 4 David, born March 2, 1763, married Mellicent Jackson, settled in Westminster 5 James, born February 21, 1765, married Susannah Baldwin, resided in Westminster and Gardner, Massachusetts, and had fifteen children 6 Mary, born January 17, 1767, married John Bigelow, had no children, died March 7, 1819 7 Rebecca, born September 14, 1768, married (first) Jonathan Eager, married (second) John Bigelow 8 Nathan, born June 19 1770, died unmarried, April 21, 1813 9 Rhoda, born April 30, 1772, married William Sawin, had two children, died April 29, 1823 10 Joel, born February 15, 1774, died young 11 Pearson, born October 9, 1775, married Susannah Upton, resided at Westminster, died August 29, 1850

(II) James Cowee, son of James Cowee (1), born at Westminster Massachusetts, February 21, 1765 married Susannah Baldwin, daughter of Josiah and Susannah (Green) Baldwin, February 17, 1783 They settled in Westminster, but after ten years they removed to Gardner, Massachusetts, where they spent the remainder of their lives, and where many of their descendants have lived Their farm at Gardner is known as the Eli Keyes, now or lately the property of B P Hill The site of the dwelling house may be easily recognized in what is called the Cowee pasture Of their fifteen children six were born in Westminster and all the others in Gardner except the last, Reuel G, who was born at Ashby, Massachusetts The Cowee place at Gardner was where Hezekiah Corey afterwards lived It was made a part of Ashburnham by act of the legislature in 1814 at the request of Mr Corey The children of James and Susannah (Baldwin) Cowee were 1 Persis 2 Joel, married Bridget Glazier, resided in Gardner and had seven children 3 Rebecca 4 Susannah 5 Betsey 6 Mehitable 7 Sally, born April 15, 1794 8 Lucinda, born December 14, 1795 9 Pearson, born October 6, 1797, married Sarah J Glazier 10 George W, born September 3, 1799, married (first) Leonora Greenwood and had six children, married (second) Sarah Wilcox and had five more 11 Aaron, born August 1, 1801, married Susan Spaulding and settled in Emden 12 James, born December 28, 1802 13 William born February 12, 1805 14 John, born June 9, 1807, was the first maker of cane seated chairs at Gardner, which is now a great centre of the chair manufacturing business 15 Reuel G (see forward)

(III) Reuel G Cowee, son of James Cowee (2), born at Ashby, Massachusetts, about 1809 He was the first to engage in the manufacture of chairs by machinery in Gardner, which is now one of the great centres of chair manufacturing in the East He sold his Gardner business and moved to West Boylston, Massachusetts, in 1850 Here he bought a mill privilege and operated a grist mill His son Aaron Cowee and his son-in-law George F Hildreth were later associated with him in the mill and feed business His grandson Edward A Cowee is at present conducting the business that he established He died in West Boylston in 1880 at the age of seventy-one years He married Lucy Ann Severy and settled in Gardner They had only two children They were' Aaron (see forward), Mary, (see forward)

(IV) Aaron Cowee, son of Reuel G Cowee (3), born at Gardner, Massachusetts, June 10, 1836, married Sarah Winter They had one son Edward A Cowee, born July 23, 1857 Aaron Cowee owned a mill at West Boylston, Massachusetts

(V) Edward A Cowee son of Aaron Cowee (4), was born at West Boylston, Massachusetts, July 23, 1857 He was educated in the schools of his native place and after graduating from the grammar school entered the business of his father, who had a grist mill, and dealt in grain and other supplies for farmers Not only his father but his grandfather and great-grandfather were millers Mr Cowee has an inherited liking and aptitude for his business Edward A Cowee started in for himself in the grain and feed business when twenty-one years of age with M H Bosworth for two years and then with R G Cowee, his grandfather, and remained with him until the death of the latter when he took the business alone and continued the business at the old mill until driven out by the Metropolitan Water Board and at the present writing the buildings are torn down and land covered with water, there having been a mill on the property about one hundred and fifty years At the present time he is running a mill and elevator at 193 Summer street, Worcester, with stores in different parts of the city and one in Jefferson and one in Rutland and one in Auburn He has a livery stable at 14 Market street, Worcester Mr Cowee has been an active Republican all his life and a leader in his district He represented the eleventh Worcester representative district in the general court in 1896 and the thirteenth district in 1897 He has been urged to become a candidate for senator in his district and at this writing seems to be the probable Republican candidate in 1905 For the past few years he has resided at 25 Shaffner street, Worcester, although he has large interests in West Boylston where he lived for so many years His mother lives with him

He married October 1, 1882, Hattie L Cutler, daughter of Oliver B and Harriett R (Cutting) Cutler They have two children Howard born November 10, 1884 Marjorie, born November 21, 1890

(IV) Mary Cowee, daughter of Reuel G Cowee (3), born at Gardner Massachusetts November 18, 1839 married in 1861 George F Hildreth, born in Sterling January 22 1836 son of James D and Betsey F (Winn) Hildreth His paternal grandfather, Timothy Hildreth and wife were both natives of Sterling and died there They were members of the Sterling Baptist church Timothy Hildreth was a farmer

James D Hildreth, son of Timothy Hildreth, of Sterling, was born in Sterling, and there and in West Boylston spent the greater part of his life He grew up on his father's farm, and attended the schools of his native town He subsequently transported various kinds of freight on wagons before the day of steam railroads He carried goods between Leominster and Boston, Gardner and Boston, Sterling and Boston and Providence and Gardner He died at the age of fifty-eight, and his wife in 1894 at the age of ninety-three Their children were James N George F Charles E, Sarah A wife of Alonzo Smith Georgia A, married Alphonso Smith, twin brother of Alonzo, whom her sister Sarah married Two children died young

George F Hildreth son of James D Hildreth, attended the Sterling schools when a boy and worked on the farm until he was twenty-one He then went to Worcester where he worked for the city for two years In 1859 he removed to West Boylston, and for the next twenty years was engaged in the grain business there He entered the employ of Reuel G Cowee and became the manager of Mr Cowee's grist mill later entering partnership with Mr Cowee, whose daughter he married shortly after moving to West Boylston He was an assessor of West Boylston trustee of the West Boylston cemetery, and superintendent until his removal to Worcester in 1897, where he has made his home since at 5 Newton avenue

Mrs Hildreth is the last survivor of her father's family She is greatly interested in the Sunday school work of her church both at West Boylston and Worcester Mr and Mrs Hildreth are Congregationalists Mr Hildreth served for twenty-five years on the parish committee of the West Boylston church

HENRY AUGUSTUS SKINNER Thomas Skinner (1) the emigrant ancestor of Henry A Skinner of Worcester was an early settler at Malden Massachusetts He was born in England in 1617 and came from Chichester England some time between 1649 and 1652 He settled at Malden where he kept a tavern He had two sons, both of whom came to this country with him He was admitted a freeman of Malden May 18 1653 He was married in England to Mary ——— who came with him to Malden She died April 9 1671 He married (second) Lydia Ball who died March 2 1704 His children were Thomas born July 25 1645, Abraham, September 29 1649, married Hannah ———, who died January 14, 1725-26

(II) Thomas Skinner, son of Thomas Skinner (1), was born in Subdeanerie parish, Chichester, England, July 25, 1645 He married Mary Pratt, daughter of Richard and Mary Pratt, of Malden, Essex county, England Richard Pratt was baptized there June 29, 1615, died 1691 Deacon Thomas Skinner removed with his family consisting of his wife, his sons Richard, Benjamin, Ebenezer, Nathaniel and daughter Abigail to Colchester, Connecticut, where he was one of the original proprietors His name and that of his son Ebenezer frequently occur in the early records He held various town offices and served on important committees He and his son Benjamin were granted lots January 21, 1702, and in May, 1702, he drew his house lot The diary of his son Thomas has been preserved and gives many interesting details of family history All the children were born in Malden His wife died March 26, 1704 Their children were Mary, born November 3 1666 Thomas, November 3, 1668, removed to Norton Massachusetts Abiah June 16, 1761, John April 5, 1673 settled at Norton with his brother Thomas they were among the earliest settlers have many descendants in and about Norton Richard, June 2 1675, married Hannah Pratt and had six children Joseph, January 13, 1678, died January 18 1725 Hannah, died October 21, 1728, Benjamin January 30 1681, died at Hebron, Connecticut June 2 1750, Ebenezer April 23 1684, Nathaniel January 27 1686, married June 13 1706, Mary Gillett had eleven children, Abigail February 17 1691 married July 13 1708-09, Ebenezer Mudge born at Northampton, Massachusetts, February 26, 1683 died at Sharon, Connecticut, April 21, 1758 she died at Sharon

(III) Benjamin Skinner, son of Thomas Skinner (2) was born January 30, 1681 at Hebron Connecticut He married Elizabeth ——— who died December 1 1753 at Hebron Connecticut, where all their children were born viz Martha December 19, 1713, Richard, March 2 1716-17, Benjamin, October 5 1718 Hannah February 17, 1720-21; Joseph June 3 1723 married December 31 1741, Ruth Strong and had five children, Jeremiah March 17 1725 Thomas May 5 1731, married August 14 1751 Martha Wright and had six children

(IV) Benjamin Skinner son of Benjamin Skinner (3) was born at Hebron Connecticut October 5 1718 married May 2 1739, Rebecca Gott She was born 1725 and died April 27 1774 Their children were Benjamin born May 1750, married Mehitable Root David February 23 1752 married (first) September 18 1780 Lydia Perkins who died June 22 1781 he married (second) October 17, 1782 Ruth Chapell Lydia, September 30 1754, John, April 18 1759, died same day Daniel August 3 1761 Oliver April 20, 1764 married November 26 1792, Sibyl Root Aaron, July 8 1767, married, February 16 1794 Elizabeth Austin of Lyme Connecticut and had a large family

(V) Benjamin Skinner, son of Benjamin Skinner (4) was born in Hebron Connecticut, May 2, 1750 He married Mehitable Root He settled in New Hampshire probably Among his children was Benjamin the grandfather of Henry A Skinner, of Worcester

(VI) Benjamin Skinner son of Benjamin Skinner (5) was born probably in New Hampshire Among his children was Otis Skinner, see forward

(VII) Otis Skinner, son of Benjamin Skinner (6) was born in Dana, Massachusetts February 3, 1813 He married Hannah Putnam Nourse, born in Littleton New Hampshire, November 17, 1816

He worked on a farm and attended the common schools when a boy He learned the trade of carpenter and became a maker of piano legs At North Dana he had a grist mill He was a man of exceptional mechanical skill He died May 18 1893 in New Haven, Connecticut, and is buried at North Dana Massachusetts His wife died May 13 1874, at Worcester, aged fifty-seven years Her father was John W Nourse His children were Sherman born October 1 1814 died at Grafton New Hampshire, about 1895, aged eighty years, Hannah Putnam born November 17, 1816, died May 13, 1874 married Otis Skinner, April 10, 1837, Vashti, born April 27, 1819, died at Whitefield, New Hampshire October 16, 1901, Polly, born April 29, 1821, died at Littleton, New Hampshire, October 8 1822, John W, born February 3, 1823, died at Whitefield, New Hampshire, April 24, 1903, Cynthia, born April 24, 1825 died at Patch Grove, Wisconsin, 1899, Eunice born July 12, 1827, died at Littleton, an infant, William born July 5, 1830, died in Boston, 1852, Ezra, enlisted in 1863 was wounded in battle, discharged and returned home, upon his recovery he returned to the war and was never heard from afterward by his family John Nourse grandfather of the above family of children was born near Boscawen, New Hampshire, and died April 11, 1846, aged eighty-four years, ten months and fourteen days His wife died May 5, 1814, aged fifty-one years, one month and three days John W Nourse father of the above children, died May 6 1876 aged eighty-eight years two months and twenty-five days His wife died December 24, 1864 aged seventy-six years twenty days They were married November 11, 1813

Children of Otis and Hannah Putnam (Nourse) Skinner were 1 Polly Williams, born at Bethlehem New Hampshire January 25 1838, died in Dana, Massachusetts September 20, 1839 John W, born at Stratford, New Hampshire, November 27, 1856 died at Worcester, July 21 1900 Sherman Franklin born at Dana Massachusetts, February 24 1840, died in Dana August 9 1842 Sarah Addie, born June 22 1842 resided at New Haven, removed to New Jersey married (first) Stillman Briggs (second) Charles Magaffey, by whom she had one son Harry (third) William B Collier, living 1905 in New Jersey Lydia Lenura born at Phillipston, Massachusetts December 22, 1844 died in Dana, October 10 1862 unmarried Henry Augustus born at Bethlehem New Hampshire, April 20 1847 see forward Lois V born at Littleton New Hampshire, July 2 1849 died August 22 1895 in Springfield, married John T Wright had one daughter Edith, born in April 1872, died June 10 1879, has son George who resides in Bridgeport and son Lewis who resides in Springfield Benjamin Elias, born at Littleton New Hampshire, March 16 1851 Charles E, born at Littleton, New Hampshire, June 1 1853

(II) Henry Augustus Skinner was born at Bethlehem New Hampshire April 20 1847 He attended the North Dana (Massachusetts) public schools His father was a carpenter and maker of piano legs He learned his father's trade and worked at it until twenty years old when he took a trip west and south to see the country When he returned he worked for a time at Orange, Massachusetts, for the New Home Sewing Machine Company In 1868 he returned to Worcester to live He worked for N P Malloy, gunsmith and locksmith at 394 Main street, for J B Lincoln in his repair shop Foster street, and for G Henry Whitcomb repairing envelope machinery at the envelope factory on Front street He returned for a time to sewing machine work for S L Shaffer In the meantime he had been experimenting and had several inventions which he sold to a Springfield man, and he went there to manufacture the goods for him After three years in Springfield he spent some time in Providence, resided thirty-nine years in Worcester, and in November, 1905 moved to Malden where he now (1906) resides He came with the Massachusetts Oilless Bearing Company

He started in business at 17 Hermon street in the manufacture of patterns, experimenting and building experimental machinery At present the business is incorporated under the name of the Worcester Pattern and Novelty Company Mr Skinner is president, John M Sawyer is treasurer and J Walter Smith clerk They are the owners of the stock and the directors of the company Mr Skinner has some valuable inventions One is a buzz planer which does the work of two ordinary planers and never requires oil, having the new oilless bearings Another invention is a band saw also with the new bearings He has an ingenious printing machine that does the work of four machines He has a window fastener that keeps the window locked while open any distance desired The Security Blind Fastener, which he invented has been on the market and in steady demand for thirty-two years He invented the Security Broom Holder, and has a new device for blind hinges to secure the blinds against the wind The latter is not yet on the market An electric device of Mr Skinner for indicating the height of water in a reservoir is in successful use at Readsboro, Vermont He has patented a switch for street cars to be operated by the motorman with his foot without leaving the car He has a patented device for automatically shutting off water to prevent freezing of pipes in cold weather He invented the automatic car coupler and sold it to the Boston & Albany and the Boston & Maine Railroads a few years ago He secured fourteen patents which were pending at the same time in the patent office Mr Skinner is one of the most ingenious and versatile inventors in a city remarkable for the number and value of its patents He is as active as ever in the study of mechanical devices and his inventions which now number over five hundred, are of a widely different kind He has not been limited to the industrial field nor to labor-saving domestic contrivances He has turned a natural mechanical genius loose wherever he saw a chance for improvement in devices or machines in use He has been a very busy worker and has spent most of his time in his shop He is a member of the order of the Golden Star

He married, January 22 1872, Zilpha Lavinia Vance of Barnet, Vermont She was the daughter of Richard West and Lydia M (Prouty) Vance He died November 1886 His wife Lydia Morgan Vance died in 1876, aged fifty-eight years, at New Bedford Massachusetts The day of his death is not known, for he wandered away from his home, 23 Prospect street, and was found dead the day after Thanksgiving Children of Henry Augustus and Zilpha Lavinia Skinner are Mabel Luella born July 22 1874 married Walter W Green of Providence Rhode Island Walter Arthur, born February 28 1877 married Nellie Price, of London, England now of Lowell Massachusetts, where they reside Charles Alton born in Springfield Massachusetts June 20 1879 has been in the photograph business under the name of the Worcester View Company for the past ten years has made a collection of old and new views of the city of Worcester and vicinity, resided with his parents at 61 Piedmont street Worcester, but in November, 1905, moved with his parents to Malden, Massachusetts, and has opened a photograph studio at 56 Pleasant street

CLOUGH FAMILY John Clough (1) the immigrant ancestor of that branch of the Clough family to which Dr Benjamin F Clough of Worcester belongs, was born in England in 1613 He was twenty-two years old in 1635, when he sailed for America in the ship "Elizabeth" The date of sailing is given as April 11 The name for many generations has been spelled variously Clow Clough, (pronounced to rhyme with "how") and Cluff and Cluffe, pronounced as written The established spelling Clough seems to be the proper way

John Clough deposed in 1691 that his age was seventy-seven years, thus substantiating the approximate date of his birth obtained from his age at emigration He may have lived at Boston for a time, but it is difficult to prove whether John Clough of the Boston records is John of Watertown or John of Salisbury John of Watertown was a tailor The John Clough of this pedigree settled in Salisbury, was a proprietor there as early as 1639, and a house carpenter by trade He had a second grant of land 1640 and others later He was admitted a freeman May 18, 1642, and took the oath of fidelity 1650, and was a commoner and taxpayer 1650 The general court granted to John Clough then of Boston, a lot of land at Salisbury (see Hoyt's Families) March 13, 1638-9, the record stating that he had served his master four years, indicating that he was either apprenticed to learn his trade of carpenter or was bound out for a term—a common way of paying passage money Or he may have been a prisoner of war It seems most likely that he was apprenticed at Boston in some family that he knew in England and with whom he came to this country He must have been counted a desirable citizen even as a young man, or he would not have been granted land by the general court He died July 26, 1691, and his will was proved November 3d, following He made bequests to his wife Martha, sons John, Samuel and Thomas, son-in-law Daniel Merrill; daughters Elizabeth Horne and Sarah Merrill, the children of daughter Martha, wife of Cornelius Page, late of Andover and other grandchildren He married (first) Jane ——, died January 16, 1679 He married (second) January 15, 1686, Martha Cilley, or Sibley Children of John and Jane Clough 1 Elizabeth, born December 16, 1642, married —— Horne 2 Mary, born July 30, 1644, died before her father 3 Sarah, born June 28, 1646, married May 14, 1667, Daniel, son of Nathaniel Merrill 4 John, born March 9, 1648-9, married November 13, 1674, Mercy Page, was eldest son in 1691 5 Thomas, mentioned below 6 Martha, born March 22, 1654, married November 13, 1674 Cornelius Day 7 Samuel, born February 20, 1656-7, married August 31, 1679, Elizabeth Brown

(II) Thomas Clough son of John Clough (1), was born at Salisbury Massachusetts May 29, 1651 He took the oath of fidelity and allegiance 1677 He was a farmer or yeoman 1730 and probably all his life He and his wife joined the church in Salisbury, July 27, 1718 He married first March 10, 1680 Hannah, daughter of Samuel Gile She died December 22 or January 22, 1683 He married (second) 1687, Ruth, daughter of Cornelius Connor Their children born in Salisbury were 1 Samuel, born December 5, 1680, mentioned below 2 Thomas, Jr, born December 9, 1681, cordwainer by trade 3 Jeremiah, born June 21 1688 4 Ebenezer, born July 5, 1690 died young 5 Ebenezer, born April 27, 1691 6 Zaccheus, born February 17, 1693 (?) 7 Isaac, born January 24, 1693-4 8 Rebecca, born June 3, 1696, baptized, an adult, 1716 9 Hannah, born September 25, 1698, died February 3, 1715 10 Judith, born October 1, 1700 11. Martha born February 25, 1702-3

(III) Samuel Clough, son of Thomas Clough (2), born at Salisbury, Massachusetts, December 5, 1686, also settled in Salisbury He married Sarah —— She administered his estate, receiving her appointment as administratrix in 1728. Their children 1 Theophilus, born 1703 2 Eliphalet, died 1706 3 Samuel, mentioned below 4 Daniel, born 1716 5 Anna, married Abraham Morrill 6 Abigail, married Benjamin Morrill, of Kingston 7 Sarah, married Daniel Marston Hampton 8 Mehitable 9 Miriam All were living in 1728, except Eliphalet

(IV) Samuel Clough, son of Thomas Clough (3), was born about 1708 at Salisbury or vicinity He removed thence to the adjacent town of Kittery, now in Maine, and married, February 14, 1736-7, Hannah Hutchins, of one of the old families of that section Two of their children and perhaps more were born at Kittery He removed to Arundel, now Kennebunkport, Maine, about 1758 Four or more of their sons were soldiers in the revolution Children of Samuel and Hannah Clough 1 Joseph, born at Kittery, February 21, 1742-3, was a revolutionary soldier, married Elvira Hutchins and after the war removed to Hollis, New Hampshire 2 Thomas, married Hannah Goodnow 3 Samuel, married Lucy Wakefield. 4 Enoch, a soldier in the revolution, died at sea 5 Noah, mentioned below 6 Joel, married Dorothy Hutchins 7 Rhoda, born at Kittery, May 2, 1745, married Paul March 8 Martha, married Thomas Huff 9 Lydia, married Silas Abbot

(V) Noah Clough son of Samuel Clough (4), was born in Arundel now Kennebunkport, 1754 He was a soldier in the old French war in the sixties and again in the revolution He was in the battle of Bunker Hill He was wounded in the attack on Quebec, was captured and kept a prisoner, was in other service as stated below after he was exchanged, and had a pension granted him after the war on account of his health, he was then an invalid His war service in detail was Private in Captain Jesse Dorman's company, Colonel James Scammon's regiment, enlisting May 8, 1715, went into Continental army 1778 for six months, was a private in Captain Abel Moulton's company, Colonel Jonathan Titcomb's regiment 1777, Rhode Island campaign, in Captain Joshua Nason's company, Colonel Storer's regiment, at Queman's Heights, served in same company in Northern army 1777, mustered in for six months October 25, 1780 The revolutionary war rolls describe his personal appearance thus Age twenty-six years height, five feet, ten inches, dark complexion His children David, mentioned below Obed Shadrach

(VI) David Clough, son of Noah Clough (5) was born in Kennebunkport Maine, November 16, 1780, and died March 16, 1864 He settled in Kennebunkport where he was a farmer all his life His children Melville, Horace, Arthur, mentioned below Lois, Phebe, Charles W

(VII) Arthur Clough, son of David Clough (6), was born in Kennebunkport, Maine, April 16, 1811 He received his education there in the public schools and worked during his minority on his father's farm He also became a farmer He bought a large farm on the road from Kennebunkport to Saco church, and lived there during his active life All of his children were born there His farm yielded excellent clay, and he made bricks in large quanti-

Dr. B. F. Clough

ties to supply the demand in and about Kennebunkport He sold out his farm and brickyards in later life and bought a house in the village of Kennebunk, where he lived the rest of his life without the care of farm or business He died there February 17, 1886 Early in life he was a Methodist, but in later years he belonged to an Orthodox Congregational church In politics he was a Republican He married, May 7, 1837, Harriet Gilpatrick, of Kennebunkport, Maine, born June 11, 1809 Their children 1 Dr Benjamin Franklin, mentioned below 2 George Sylvester, born May 2, 1839, married January 5, 1865, Mercy Stone March, of Saco, Maine, one child, Hattie, died young, he married (second) March 7, 1874, Sarah Jane, of Kennebunkport, Maine, born May 31, 1845, daughter of Thomas Cleaves and Olive Littlefield (Hatch) Worth, their children John Arthur, born December 22, 1874, attorney at law, Worcester, Cora Belle, born December 1, 1877, resides with mother and brother at 1 Merrick street, George S Clough was a prominent carpenter and builder, member of the school board of Worcester three years, common council, general court 1891-92, prominent in the Masonic fraternity 3 John Hill, born November 7, 1846, settled in Worcester, was a school teacher, died March 23, 1871, married Abbie Elizabeth Redding of Worcester, January 14, 1869 4 Arthur Howard, born June 24, 1852, died August 8, 1852

(VIII) Dr Benjamin Franklin Clough, son of Arthur Clough (7), was born at Kennebunkport, Maine, February 4, 1838 He attended the common schools there and supplemented his schooling with a course at Berwick Academy, at South Berwick, Maine, where he was fitted for Harvard College To prepare himself for his medical studies he entered the drug store of Alexander Warren at Kennebunk, Maine, as an apprentice November 6, 1856, and remained there until March, 1858, when he accepted a clerkship in Biddeford, Maine, where he remained until November 6, 1860 He took a short vacation and then came to Boston to work in the drug store at the corner of Tremont and Boylston streets, April 12, 1861 He remained in that position until October 16, 1863, when he received an appointment as surgeon's steward in the United States navy He proceeded to Cairo, Illinois, to report to Admiral Porter on his flagship "Black Hawk," began his new duties October 23d, and served on that ship during the Red River campaign and other engagements The "Black Hawk" was destroyed by fire April 22, 1865, and he was transferred to the hospital ship "Red Rover," where he served until the close of the war He was mustered out August 12, 1865

He returned to Boston and accepted a clerkship in the old drug store, corner of Tremont and Boylston streets, remaining until the fall of 1866, when he entered Harvard Medical School He was graduated with the degree of M D in 1869, and started to practice in Worcester His office was at 2 Myrtle street until September 14, 1886, when he removed to 46 Austin street, where he practiced to the time of his death, May 8, 1899 He enjoyed a large general practice and was accounted a wise and successful physician He ranked high in citizenship as well as in his profession He was an active member of Trinity Methodist Church and of the Epworth League He was a Republican in politics He was prominent in the Masonic fraternity, a life member of Montacute Lodge, being raised November 13 1893 made a member of Eureka Royal Arch Chapter February 6, 1894, was a member of Hiram Council of Royal and Select Masters, and of Stella Chapter, Order of the Eastern Star He was a member of Charles Devens Council, American Mechanics He was one of the most interested members of the Grand Army of the Republic He joined George H Ward Post No 10 during the first year of his residence in Worcester, and was mustered in by Captain Amos M Parker in May, 1869 He was elected post surgeon to succeed Dr Albert Wood, December, 1891, and re-elected December, 1892, serving up to the time of his death Hon A S Roe calls him the "most devoted surgeon Post 10, G A R., ever had" He was also president of the board of trustees of Post 10, having charge of the relief work of that organization He was an active member of Farragut Association (Naval) of Philadelphia, Pennsylvania He was a member of the Massachusetts Medical Society, the Worcester District Medical Society, and the Harvard Alumni Medical Society He married August 15, 1871, Adelia Jane, born September 13, 1845, daughter of John and Catherine (Sweetzer) Perkins, of Lynnfield, Massachusetts Her father was a farmer and late in life was occupied largely with the settlement of estates, was twenty-one years town clerk, captain of the militia, and representative to general court The only child of Dr Benjamin Franklin and Adelia Jane Clough was Bertha Frances, born August 1, 1873, died November 16, 1884

HOLLAND JOSEPH ADAMS Henry Adams (1), of Braintree, the immigrant ancestor of Holland Joseph Adams, of Worcester, was probably born in Braintree, Essex county, England The Adams family in England is very ancient, but the exact pedigree of Henry Adams is still in doubt He arrived in Boston in 1632 or 1633 accompanied by his wife, eight sons and one daughter He was allotted land at Mount Wollaston, later the town of Braintree, where many of his descendants have lived The name of his wife is unknown, and it is thought that she and her daughter, possibly also her son John, returned to England Henry Adams died in Braintree June 8, 1647

His children were 1 Lieutenant Henry, born 1604, married in Braintree, Elizabeth Paine, daughter of Moses Paine, he was deputy to the general court, lieutenant of the military company, was killed by the Indians while standing in the doorway of his home at Medfield, and his sick wife was accidentally killed the same day 2 Lieutenant Thomas, born 1612, married Mary Blackmer or Blackmore, was town clerk, selectman, and deputy to the general court, he settled in Concord, Massachusetts 3 Captain Samuel, born 1617 married (first) Rebecca Graves, married (second) Esther Sparhawk, was prominent in civil and military life 4 Deacon Jonathan, born 1619, married (first) Elizabeth Fussell, married (second) Mary ——, settled in Medfield with several brothers and had his house burned by the Indians there in 1676 5 Peter, born 1622, married Rachel ——, and had his house burned by Indians, 1676, at Medfield, where he settled 6 John, born about 1624, possibly John of Cambridge 7 Joseph born 1626, maltster, selectman, married Abigail Baxter 8 Ensign Edward, (see forward) 9 Ursula, daughter

(II) Ensign Edward Adams, youngest son of Henry Adams (1), born in England in 1630, married (first) Lydia Rockwood, daughter of Richard and Agnes (Bicknell) Rockwood, who died March 3, 1676, married (second) 1678, Widow Abigail (Craft) Ruggles, of Roxbury, Massachusetts, (or Abigail Day) who died 1707 married (third) January 6 1709-10, Sarah Taylor He settled, with three other brothers, in Medfield, Massachusetts and was ensign in the military company, selectman of the town, and deputy to the general court in 1689-92, and 1702. He died in Medfield, November 12, 1716, the last of the original settlers.

Children of Ensign Edward and Lydia Adams, all born in Medfield, were: Lydia, born July 12, 1653, married twice; Captain Jonathan, April 4, 1655, married twice; John (see forward); Eliashib, February 18, 1658-9, married a great-granddaughter of Captain Miles Standish and settled in Bristol, Rhode Island; Sarah, May 29, 1660, married John Turner, who fought in Captain Moseley's company; Lieutenant James, January 4, 1661-2, settled in Bristol, now Barrington, Rhode Island; Henry, October 29, 1663, settled in Providence, Rhode Island, and Canterbury, Connecticut; Mehitable, born March 30, 1665, married Josiah Faxon, of a well known Braintree family; Elisha, born August 25, 1666, settled in Bristol; Edward, Jr., born June 29, 1668; settled in Bristol and left children; Bethia, born April 12, 1670; died 1672; Bethia, born August 18, 1672, died young; Abigail, born June 25, 1675, died young; Miriam, born February 26, 1676, died young.

(III) John Adams, son of Ensign Edward Adams (2), born in Medfield, Massachusetts, February 18, 1657; married (first), 1682, Deborah Partridge, daughter of John and Magdalen (Bullard) Partridge, born 1662; died before 1695; married (second) Susanna Breck, daughter of Thomas and Mary (Hill) Breck, born in Sherborn, Massachusetts, May 10, 1667, died May 28, 1744, at Medway. John Adams inherited the homestead at Medfield and lived on it. He died there March 1, 1751.

Children of John and Deborah Adams were: Edward, born January 13, 1682; John, Jr., born in Medway, December 22, 1684, settled on the homestead of his grandfather in Medfield; Daniel, born January 12, 1686; Eleazer, born September 22, 1687, was a prominent man in West Medway; Obadiah, born January 20, 1689; Jonathan, born 1692, settled on the homestead in Medway. The children of John and Susanna Adams were: Thomas (see forward); Susanna, born July 30, 1697; Jeremiah, born July 3, 1699, settled in Brookfield; Abraham, born August 1, 1701, settled in Brookfield; Bethia, born June 1702; Phineas, born May 19, 1705; Hannah, born March 29, 1707; Esther, born November 15, 1708.

(IV) Thomas Adams, seventh child of John Adams (3), born in Medway, Massachusetts, February 11, 1695-6, married October 26, 1720, Abigail Fisher, daughter of Jonathan and Rachel (Fairbanks) Fisher. She was probably born in 1701. He settled in Ashford, Connecticut, going thither from Amherst, Massachusetts, in 1737; died in Amherst, near Leverett, 1743-5. Children were: Isaiah, born in Ashford, Connecticut, 1726, died in Amherst, Massachusetts, 1810, unmarried, aged eighty-four years; Asa, born in Ashford, April 4, 1729, a pioneer settler of Shutesbury, Massachusetts; died there aged ninety-eight years; Nathan, born at Ashford, July 1, 1731, died young; John, born in Ashford, 1732; lived in Amherst and Rowe, Massachusetts; Abner (see forward); Nathan, born in Ashford, May 16, 1736; was soldier in French and Indian war, 1757; settled in Sunderland; Elizabeth, born in Amherst, Massachusetts; married Bezaleel Wilder, Jr., of Shutesbury.

(V) Abner Adams, fifth child of Thomas Adams (4), born in Ashford, Connecticut, August 10, 1733; married May 9, 1754, Dorothy Murray, daughter of General William and Hannah (Dickinson) Murray, of Amherst, born August 11, 1729; died in Marlboro, Vermont, January 16, 1809. He was in Amherst until 1792, but removed to Marlboro, Vermont, before 1795; died there after a long illness which affected his mind, 1828-9. He was a private in Captain Noah Dickinson's company, Colonel Elisha Porter's regiment in 1777, and marched to New Providence. Children were: Dorothy, born in North Amherst, Massachusetts, baptized April 10, 1757; settled in Pittsfield, Monroe county, New York; Thomas (see forward); Naomi, born in North Amherst, October 17, 1759; David, born in North Amherst, was a soldier in the revolution; Reuben, born in North Amherst, July 8, 1770, fell into a well and died in Genesee county, New York, unmarried.

(VI) Thomas Adams, second child of Abner Adams (5), born in North Amherst, Massachusetts, October 21, 1758; married, 1783, Lucy Perkins, born in Bridgewater, Massachusetts, December 1, 1757; died in Marlboro, Vermont, January 26, 1854-6. He was a soldier in the revolution. He settled in Marlboro, Vermont, in 1795. Late in life he removed to Halifax, Vermont, with his son-in-law Isaac Worden, and died there April 14, 1858, aged ninety-nine years. Children were: David, born in Amherst, Massachusetts, May 22, 1785, married, October 22, 1807, Susan Warren, daughter of Captain Jonathan Warren; Zebina, born in Amherst, August 1, 1787, married Clarissa Wheeler; Sally, born in Amherst, June or August 17, 1790, married Jonathan Warren; Chester (see forward); Roswell, born in Marlboro, Vermont, December 27, 1795, died from a fall at Watertown, New York, June 28, 1817, unmarried; Orinda, born in Marlboro, December 27, 1797-1800, married Captain Isaac Worden, of Halifax, Vermont.

(VII) Chester Adams, fourth child of Thomas Adams (6), born in Amherst, Massachusetts, January 14, 1793; married June, 1824, Lana Spear, of Wilmington, Vermont, daughter of Francis B. Spear; she died June 22, 1858, aged sixty-one years. He died January 22, 1852. He was a prosperous farmer at Marlboro, Vermont. Children, all born at Marlboro, Vermont, were: 1. Samuel, born January 29, 1826, died February 7, 1826. 2. Francis Chester, born March 24, 1829, died November, 1905, married Mrs. Hannah (King) Powers; resided at Newfane, Vermont, and had two children: Herbert, married Mrs. Worden, and they have two children; Nellie, married Leslie Stratton, and has two children. 3. Lana Marana, born September 18, 1830, married, November 20, 1851, Alonzo H. Brewer, of Bennington, Vermont, had two children. 4. Infant, died September 8, 1832. 5. Lucy Ann, born December 3, 1833, married, November 15, 1856, James Bennett, of Brattleboro, Vermont; had two boys. 6. Winthrop Hart, born August 21, 1836, married, September 17, 1858, Mary Ann Eames, daughter of John Eames, of Dover, Vermont; has one daughter who married Charles Jones; resided at Brattleboro, Vermont, since 1870. 7. Holland Joseph (see forward).

(VIII) Holland Joseph Adams, seventh and youngest child of Chester Adams (7), was born in Marlboro, Vermont, October 11, 1839. He received his early education in the common schools of his native town. He left school at the age of thirteen, and for six years worked on the farm at home. He then settled on a farm at Dover, Vermont, where he remained until 1867. He removed to Fitchburg, Massachusetts, in 1870, and took charge of the farm of J. B. Fisher for a year. After another year in Fitchburg, working for Joseph Cushion, dealer in flour and grain, he removed to Worcester and started in business for himself, manufacturing trunks, April, 1872, under the firm name of Brown & Adams. After two years he went into the fruit business with Samuel Burbank, and later became a partner in the firm of Hiram H. Ames & Company, dealers in furniture, remaining two years. He then withdrew and purchased the confectionery business of Eugene C Akers at 506 Main street where the Clark-Sawyer Company is now located Three years afterward he removed to Front street and later to his present location 24 Pleasant street He has for a number of years made a specialty of ice cream for the trade He is the largest manufacturer of ice cream in the city He provides ices and ice cream for parties, fairs, and families as well as in wholesale quantities to other dealers He is a Republican in politics and a member of the Universalist church and of Anchoria Lodge of Odd Fellows, and Naomi Lodge of the Rebekahs He resides at 4 Dewey street, Worcester He married Mariama Asquith Knight daughter of John and Diana (Brown) Knight, December 31, 1866 Her father lived at Dover, Vermont Their children are 1 Emma Adelia, born at Worcester, June 25 1871, married, February 6, 1890 Charles Augustus Piper, of Worcester, and they have two children Carl Adams, born April 15, 1891 Raymond Hendrick born August 9, 1896 2 Charles Holland, born in Worcester, August 11, 1875, married Ella L Green, of Colbrooke, Massachusetts, and they have Chester Green, born May 28, 1894

JOHN T BRIERLY, *son of James and Hannah* Brierly (born Barrett) was born at Millbury, Massachusetts James Brierly was a cotton manufacturer at Millbury John T Brierly received his early education in the Millbury schools After graduating from the high school he went into his father's cotton mill to learn the business But finding that the dust in the cotton seriously affected his health he gave up his intention to follow cotton manufacturing He accepted a position as bookkeeper in the woolen mill of Ashworth & Jones at Valley Falls, in Worcester, near the Leicester line, and found there an opportunity to learn the business He put on jumper and overalls and worked in the mill beginning at the job of wool-sorting, working in every department in the mill ending with the cloth finishing department He left Ashworth & Jones to take a position as superintendent of the Brick City mill in Cherry Valley owned by Edward D Thayer Two years later Sumner Pratt & Company made him a very favorable proposition to come to them in the machinery supply business at 22 Front street He accepted the offer and has since been identified with that business It was established in 1847 by Sumner Pratt Mr Pratt was born in Oxford Massachusetts, September 30, 1809 He came to Worcester in 1843, transferring the machinery from Woonsocket to a mill in New Worcester and manufactured cotton thread finally selling the business to Albert Curtis in 1845, and soon afterward starting the business of selling cotton and woolen machinery and mill supplies The store at 22 Front street was established in 1847, and the business gradually extended to reach manufacturers in distant parts of the country When Mr Brierly went to the business it was of large proportions and very profitable Mr Pratt died January 6 1887 The present head of the firm William H Crawford went to work for Mr Pratt in 1860 In 1870 Mr Crawford was taken into partnership by Mr Pratt with his sons Frederick S and Edward Pratt Edward Pratt died later A few years before his death Mr Sumner Pratt retired from the business

The firm of Sumner Pratt & Company became Crawford & Company in 1898 The partners were, and at present are, William H Crawford and John T Brierly Crawford & Company had spacious stores at 17 Mechanic street until March 17 1905, when the fire in the Crompton building compelled them to vacate The firm located in May, 1905, at 673 Main street, where they have a very large and well stocked store

Mr Brierly is also a partner in the Whitaker Reed Company With Charles A Geer he owns and manages this industry The Whitaker Reed Company was established in 1869 by John Whitaker, who was born in Lowell, Massachusetts, July 5, 1839 His father was a silk printer in that city In 1849 his father went to California to dig gold and was never heard from The boy was thrown upon his own resources when very young He was sent to Worcester to school He learned the machinist's trade at Brown's shop on Mechanic street As soon as he was thirty years of age he began the manufacture of loom-reeds on his own account, and continued in this business until his death He was very successful and made a fortune in the business He died March 3 1897 The Whitaker reeds are adapted to all varieties of looms, cotton, woolen and wire cloth, and are made of the finest steel The Whitaker shop was at 184 Front street, and continued there until the founder's death The administrator of his estate sold the business to John McIntosh, who continued in the same shop until 1900, when he sold out to Mr Brierly and Mr Geer Before Mr Whitaker began to make reeds they were produced by hand labor He applied machinery to the manufacture of reeds and kept constantly making improvements in the process The present company has maintained the high standards that he established, and manifested the same spirit of progress The shops were moved to 84 Austin street a few years ago, and larger quarters secured Mr Geer came to Worcester from Connecticut, where he had worked in a woolen mill and acquired a practical knowledge of the machinery used, and the needs of the manufacturers Besides the reeds the firm makes ring travelers for cotton, woolen and worsted mills The manufacture of these rings is a unique industry in Worcester The work is done at the Whitaker Reed Company shops

Mr Brierly is a member of Anchoria Lodge, Independent Order Odd Fellows, Regulus Lodge, Knights of Pythias, and Pilgrim Congregational Church, also one of the directors of the Worcester Collateral Loan Association

WALTER SCOTT CHASE Joseph Chase (1), great-grandfather of Walter Scott Chase, of Worcester, was born on Cape Cod and lived there all his life He was a farmer He was descended from Aquila Chase, mariner, who was at Hampton, Massachusetts, in 1640, and removed to Newbury Massachusetts, where he was a proprietor in 1646 He was born in England about 1618, died December 27, 1670 His widow Anne married (second) June 14 1672, Daniel Mussilway She died April 21 1687 The second generation of the Chase family settled in the Plymouth Colony towns and has left a numerous posterity on Cape Cod and vicinity

Joseph Chase married Isabelle Thomas, of Newport, Rhode Island She was niece (or cousin) of General John Thomas, one of the first four generals commanding under Washington He was born at Marshfield Massachusetts in 1725 He was a practicing physician and surgeon, and was the surgeon for the provincial army sent to Nova Scotia in 1746 He was on General Shirley's medical staff in 1747 and 1759 colonel of a provincial regiment He commanded a regiment under Generals Amherst and Haviland in 1760 in the capture of Montreal Colonel Thomas was one of the most active Sons of Liberty in Massachusetts before the revolution He was appointed brigadier-general by Congress in 1775 He commanded a brigade at the siege of

Boston After the evacuation he was sent to take command of the American troops in Canada He joined the army before Quebec, May 1, 1776, but fell a victim to smallpox a month later He died at Chamblay, June 2, 1776

(II) John Chase, son of Joseph Chase (1), was born at Douglas, Massachusetts, in 1804 He was engaged in the manufacture of woolen goods from 1835 to the time of his death in 1871 By his wife, Elizabeth, who was a native of Pascoag, he had three children Oscar F, Mariette, Frederick T

(III) Oscar Francis Chase, son of John Chase (2), married Catherine Brown Howard He was a woolen manufacturer in Dudley, North Oxford and Wilsonville, Connecticut He made his home in later years at Webster, Massachusetts They had one son Walter Scott Chase, born in Thompson, Connecticut

(IV) Walter Scott Chase, son of Oscar Francis Chase (3), was educated in the public schools and then went to work in the woolen mills of John Chase & Sons, established by his grandfather at Wilsonville, Connecticut, at North Oxford and Webster, Massachusetts These mills have since been incorporated with the American Woolen Company Mr Chase left the woolen mill to learn the trade of steam fitting, and he studied the subject of heating and lighting houses in a scientific way He has become an expert in his business He makes a specialty of heating apparatus, high or low pressure steam, and hot water heaters He installs ventilating machinery and steam power plants, also gas-piping, bronzing and pipe covering He has been engaged in the business for twenty years His headquarters are at 10 Westfield street, Worcester He had the contract for the residence of Dr George E Adams, corner of Stafford and Ludlow street, for the residence of W E Turple, at 919 Pleasant street, Albert E Sanders at 19 Alvarado avenue, M H Pettigrew at 3 Fairfield street, some twenty houses for J B Scrimgeour, the real estate dealer, four for James H Howland, real estate dealer, for John D Cummings, foreman for Crompton & Knowles, at 5 Woodbine street, for George Warden, at Auburn, Massachusetts, for the shop of George L Brownell, Union street, for the Coes Wrench shops to heat with exhaust steam without back pressure on the engine

He is a member of the Independent Order of Odd Fellows, Anchoria Lodge Mr Chase has studied six years in the International Correspondence School of Scranton, Pennsylvania, an institution that has all the time some fifteen hundred students in Worcester county, studying engineering of the various trades for which technical knowledge is required He married Stella Maud Buckley, of North Grosvenordale, Connecticut They have two sons Walter Minot, born May 12, 1889, and Hyram Howard, born June 16, 1905

(III) Frederick T Chase, son of John Chase (2), was born at Pascoag, Rhode Island, November 22, 1844 He was educated in the schools of his native town In 1860 he came to Webster, Massachusetts, with his parents He went into the woolen mill of his father at Webster and learned the business thoroughly His brother Oscar F and he became associated with his father and owned several mills under the firm name of John Chase & Sons After his father's death he acquired the business and became sole proprietor In 1879 he found it necessary to enlarge the mill, and later made further additions until it had three times its original capacity The mill eventually was sold to the American Woolen Company Mr Chase had always been interested in politics He was a Republican and had repeatedly served the town as selectman He was chairman of the board for five years He represented his district in the general court in 1876, and was chairman of the committee on manufactures He was a member of the Webster Lodge of Free Masons, of the Worcester County Commandery, and has taken all the degrees of the Scottish Rite He attended the Universalist church, he died January 16, 1898 He married Jennie S Alton, daughter of S and Emby Alton His children were John F, Frederick T, Jr, Bessie F

ELEAZER D JORJORIAN The emigrants from Europe in the last half century have been largely from countries where English was an unknown tongue Most of the emigrants have been deficient in early education, so that they have been seriously handicapped in learning the language of this country Under the circumstances the Americanizing of the emigrants of recent years has proceeded with amazing rapidity and most gratifying completeness The American government has no more loyal supporters, no more conservative and sincere citizens than men from Italy, Russia, Syria, Hungary, and the Scandinavian countries which have sent such a numerous and excellent colony to Worcester

Among the business men of foreign birth Eleazer D Jorjorian is one of the best examples of success won in a new country, against all obstacles that fortune seemed to have put in his way He was born in Turkey in the state of Harpoot He was the son of Stephen and Margaret (Tashjgaian) Jorjorian His father and ancestors were tillers of the soil He was born August 24, 1870, and is still a young man at the beginning of a promising business career He came to this country in 1888 and immediately took advantage of the Worcester evening schools to get a knowledge of English, and some general education While he was studying at night he was working by day in the electro-type foundry of A B Brunell Besides making electro-types Mr Brunell also did all kinds of electro-plating Mr Jorjorian was in the employ of Mr Brunell for several years and learned his trade thoroughly He could have had no better opportunity, nor served under no better craftsman He was ambitious to be something more than a skillful mechanic and operative, and made the most of his opportunities He left Worcester to work in the largest silver plating shops in the country, at New Britain, Connecticut He worked later in the silver manufacturing concerns at Meriden and at Hartford, for four or five years He gained a varied experience in all branches of his trade He returned to Worcester in 1894, to start his own shop at 13 Mechanic street He sold out this business and bought out J N Massoit's business on Hermon street, known as the Acme Plating Company In 1897 he changed the name of the business to The New Acme Plating Company, and in 1904 he removed his shop to 54 Hermon street, where he has been conducting a prosperous and growing business His company does all kinds of electro-plating and has a large demand for its work from the varied manufacturing industries of Worcester In fact the product of Mr Jorjorian's shop goes all over the world in connection with the machinery produced in Worcester He has been a careful and prudent business man He has acquired considerable property, some of which is invested in Worcester real estate He owns the block on Beacon and on Wellington streets, and two other tenement houses on Beacon street

Mr Jorjorian takes an active interest in public

Scott T. Peirce

affairs and is a leader among the Turkish people in this community His influence as a good citizen has often been used in political campaigns He married, August 7, 1897, Zabelle M Thomanjero, in Worcester His wife is also a native of Turkey, daughter of Th and Yaesa Thomanjero They have one son Leon E, born in Worcester

SCOTT THEODORE PIERCE Thomas Pierce (1), immigrant ancestor of Scott Theodore Pierce, of Worcester, Massachusetts, was born in England in 1583-84 Many of the descendants of Thomas Pierce spell the surname Peirce, although the pronunciation is uniformly *purse* in Massachusetts The genealogy of the family gives as the coat of arms Three ravens rising, sable Fesse hummette Crest Dove with olive branch in beak Motto "Dixit et Fecit"

Thomas Pierce came from England in 1633 or 1634 with his wife Elizabeth and settled in Charlestown, Massachusetts His wife Elizabeth was admitted to the church January 10, 1634, and he was admitted February 21, 1634-35 He was admitted a freeman May 6, 1635 He was one of the twenty-one commissioners appointed September 27, 1642, "to see that salt peter heaps were made by the farmers of the colony" He removed to Woburn and was a proprietor there in 1643 and was elected to town offices His wife Elizabeth was born in England, 1595-96 She stated her age as seventy-one in 1667 He died October 7, 1666 His will was dated November 7, 1665, aged about eighty-two years He bequeathed to wife Elizabeth, grandchildren Mary Bridge and Elizabeth Jeffs now dwelling with him, to all grandchildren, to Harvard College The widow deposed to the inventory March 22, 1666-67, aged seventy-one years The children John, mariner, admitted to church at Charlestown, 1652, Samuel, married Mary ———, Thomas, Jr, see forward, Robert, married, February 18, 1657, Sarah Eyre, Mary, married Peter Jeffs and had Elizabeth, Elizabeth, married ——— Randall and ——— Nichols, Persis, married William Bridge and had child Mary, married (second) John Harrison, she was admitted to the church at Charlestown November 30, 1643, Abigail, born June 17, 1639

(II) Thomas Pierce, Jr, son of Thomas Pierce (1), was born in England in 1608, married, May 6, 1635, Elizabeth Cole, who died March 5, 1688 He died November 6, 1683 They resided in Charlestown in the part now Woburn He is called sergeant in the records, indicating military prominence He was the progenitor of President Franklin Pierce, viz Franklin (VII), Benjamin (VI), Benjamin (V), Stephen (IV), Stephen (III), Thomas (II) Thomas (I) Sergeant Thomas Pierce was admitted to the Charlestown Church February 21, 1634 He was an inhabitant of Woburn as early as 1643 He was selectman in 1660, and served on the committee to divide the common lands He was one of the "Right Proprietors" elected March 28, 1667, and also of the committee of the general court appointed 1668 to divide lands, etc The children Abigail, born August 17, 1639, John, March 7, 1643, married, July 5, 1663, Deborah Converse, Thomas, June 21, 1645, married, 1680, Rachel Bacon, Elizabeth, December 25, 1646, married, November 9, 1666, Thomas Whittemore, and died March 10, 1670, Joseph, September 22, 1646, died February 27, 1649, Stephen, July 16, 1651, married, November 18, 1676, Tabitha Parker, Samuel, February 20, 1654, died October 27, 1655, Samuel, April 7, 1656, see forward William March 20, 1658, married, April 8, 1690, Abigail Sommers, nee Warren, James, May 7, 1659, married Elizabeth Kendall, Abigail, November 20, 1660, married February 18, 1684, George Reed, Jr, Benjamin, married Mary Reed

(III) Samuel Pierce, son of Thomas Pierce (2), was born April 7, 1656, at Woburn, Massachusetts He married, December 9, 1680, Lydia Bacon, who was born March 6, 1656, and died December 5, 1717 They resided at Woburn, where he died July 5, 1721 His son Samuel, Jr, was appointed administrator of the estate July 28, 1721 The agreement to settle the estate was signed July 17, 1721, by Peter Waite as guardian of his two children, by Hannah P, by Tabitha P, by Isaac, Timothy and Abraham Hill The children, born at Woburn, were Samuel, Jr, see forward, Lydia born March 25, 1683, married Tomothy Snow, Joseph, born March 28, 1685, died young, Isaac, born March 22, 1687, married Grace Tucker, May 5, 1708, Abigail, born February 27, 1689, married May 22, 1718, Peter White, Sarah, born June 22, 1691, married Peter Waite, Ruth, born February 14, 1693 married Abraham Hill, Tabitha born August 28, 1797, died September 30, 1797, Tabitha, born March 10, 1700

(IV) Samuel Pierce, son of Samuel Pierce (3), was born at Woburn, Massachusetts, November 25, 1681 He resided at Wilmington and Woburn, Massachusetts, and Mansfield, Connecticut He married, June 14, 1705, Abigail Johnson, died March 16, 1787 The children Samuel, born June 3, 1706, married Abigail ———, Josiah, born July 13, 1708, married Miriam Cook, Abigail, born February 28, 1711, married Zephaniah Wyman, Esther, born February 7, 1715 married Shubael ———, Seth, born November 30, 1716, married Elizabeth Nye; Enoch, born March 22, 1719, married Mary Mason

(V) Seth Pierce son of Samuel Pierce (4), was born in Woburn, Massachusetts, or at Mansfield Connecticut, after his parents removed, November 30, 1716 He married Elizabeth Nye, of Tolland, Connecticut, who was born 1680 and died May 14, 1749 Seth settled in Mansfield, Connecticut, where the children were born, viz Seth, born September 12, 1744, see forward, Elizabeth, born June 2, 1748, married Bennett Fields, Enoch, Daniel married ——— Nye, of Montpelier, Vermont

(VI) Seth Pierce, son of Seth Pierce (5) was born in Mansfield, Connecticut He was a captain in the revolution in the Connecticut regiment commanded by Major Smith on the New Haven Alarm, 1779 He married, April 17, 1767, Bethia Fields, who was born in 1745 and died September 18, 1807 He married (second), 1813, Patty Rindge He died at Homer, New York, in 1835, at an advanced age The children Sarah, born November 20, 1767, married Royal Storrs, Lucinda, born September 14, 1769 married, November 27, 1788, Thomas Welch and had a large family, Bennett, born September 12, 1771, died March 17, 1773, Gordon, born August 31, 1773, married, 1796, Thirza Smalley, Bennett, born July 14, 1775, Samuel born May 23, 1777, died August 26, 1778, Samuel, born May 20, 1779, married Persis Barrows, Elijah, born April 27, 1781, married, February 8, 1801, Patty Moulton, Seth, born February 17, 1784, Daniel, born March 16, 1786, Elizabeth, born September 12, 1788, married Chester Collins Bela, born April 13 1792

(VII) Samuel Pierce, son of Seth Pierce (6), was born May 20, 1779 He married, 1800, Persis Barrows, who was born October, 1783, and died February 5, 1858 He died August 17, 1858 They resided in Brimfiled and Hardwick, Massachusetts The house of Samuel Pierce was on the boundary line between Hardwick and Ware, and it is related that he slept in two towns and two counties every night, his head in Ware, Hampshire county, and his feet in Hardwick, Worcester county Their children Seth, born May 15 1802 married, September 22, 1831, Fidelia Bassett Chester, born June 20, 1803, married, March 15, 1831, Abigail Marsh Eliza born February 7, 1805, married, February 10, 1825, William Pepper and had Caroline W, born March 4, 1828, married George F Tyler, Samuel J, born November 2, 1829, married Sarah Torrey, Abbie F, born June 24, 1832, married D A Sampson, William A, born June 25, 1834, Ashbell, born April 7, 1838, married Martha Sibley, Elijah, born April 27, 1840, Austin, born January 23, 1845, married Eva Burnett Granger, born 1806, see forward S Austin, born October 6, 1808, married January 28, 1831, Roxanne Harwood William, born March 4, 1810, married Sarah Witherell Brigham, born 1812, married Mrs Cook Mandly, born October 31, 1817, married, May 3, 1842, Emily Thomas Octavia, born December 18, 1819, married, December 15, 1844, Byram H Hervey, resided in New Braintree

(VIII) Granger Pierce, son of Samuel Pierce (7), was born in Hatfield, Massachusetts, November 7, 1806 At an early age he removed with his parents to Hardwick, Massachusetts, where he was educated in the common schools, working also at home on the farm He began to work out on various farms in that locality until his marriage in 1822, when he settled in New Braintree, Massachusetts He bought there the old Warner place near the Winimmisett brook, where Warner killed the Indian Eleazer Warner was the leading settler before incorporation of the town Here was formerly an Indian town of considerable importance, the headquarters and chief rendezvous of the Indians when Brookfield was destroyed in King Philip's war In 1865 Pierce came to Worcester and bought the old Reed farm on Holden street, a place of historic interest, and continued there farming until his death, March 17, 1886 He was a Congregationalist in religion and attended the Central Church, Worcester He was in his early days a Whig and Democrat, but in later years a Republican He belonged to the famous old Horse Thief Detecting Society at New Braintree and to the Worcester West Agricultural Society at Barre, Massachusetts He was a member of the Hardwick militia company at one time

He married, February 16, 1832, at Hardwick, Mercy Stockwell of Prescott, Massachusetts, a neighboring town She was the daughter of Simon and Dolly Stockwell Their children Rufus Judson, born January 12, 1839, see forward, Scott Theodore, born June, 1841, was a member of the Fifty-third Massachusetts Regiment and died in the service during the civil war

(IX) Rufus Judson Pierce, son of Granger Pierce (8), was born in New Braintree, Massachusetts, January 12, 1839 While a mere lad he worked with his father on the farm, going to school in his native town and later at New Salem Academy and the Deerfield Academy at Deerfield, Massachusetts At the age of twenty he began to give all his time to his father's farm In 1865 his father and he went to Worcester and bought the Rogers farm, known also as the old Reed farm, Holden street, where Scott T Pierce now lives The farm originally consisted of sixty acres Rufus Pierce continued in the management of the farm until his father's death, March 17, 1886, when he became the owner Though he sold off some of the farm he continued to carry on the place until shortly before his death, when he turned the management over to his son Scott He died February 5, 1903 at his home He was a Universalist in religion and attended the First Universalist Church, Worcester In politics he was a Republican He was a member of Worcester Grange, Patrons of Husbandry, No 22, and of the North Worcester Aid Society

He married, April 18, 1860, Sarah E Nye, who was born September 25, 1834 daughter of Hosea W and Emily (Bartlett) Nye, of Hardwick, Massachusetts, her father was a blacksmith The only child was Scott Theodore, born December 23, 1864 see forward

(X) Scott Theodore Pierce, son of Rufus Judson Pierce (9), was born at New Braintree, Massachusetts, December 23, 1864 He removed when a year old to Worcester with his parents and was educated there in the public schools and at Foster's Business College, where he graduated For a number of years he assisted his father on the farm In 1888 he started a retail milk business, selling the milk from his father's dairy He gradually took charge of the farm He sold out his milk business January 1, 1901 At the death of his father, February 5, 1903, he inherited the farm and has continued to run it since then In June, 1903, he erected the present modern residence on a sightly spot some distance from the main road, commanding a picturesque view of Indian lake It is one of the most attractive residences in that section of the city Mr Pierce makes a specialty of market gardening and cider, having a cider mill on the farm The present area of the farm is about fifty acres Mr Pierce is a member of the First Universalist Church In politics he is a Republican He is a member of Quinsigamond Lodge of Odd Fellows, No 43 of Worcester, of Worcester Grange, Patrons of Husbandry, No 22, of the Worcester Yacht Club and of the Worcester Agricultural Society He is an active member and director of the North Worcester Aid Company, a charitable organization

He married, October 15, 1890, Nancy Davis Chamberlain, who was born at Holden, October 12, 1866, the daughter of Sumner and Cynthia (Clapp) Chamberlain of Holden They have one child, Ralph Chamberlain, born at Worcester, August 20, 1891

EARLE FAMILY Ralph Earle (1), who was in Newport, Rhode Island, as early as 1638, was the emigrant ancestor in the paternal line of Mrs Emily D Richardson, of Worcester, Massachusetts He married Joan Savage, who was born in England 1594 or 1595 Ralph Earle was born in 1606 and they were doubtless married in England Ralph Earle was one of fifty-nine persons admitted, October 1, 1638, freemen of the Island of Aquecdneck (Newport) He bought and sold land frequently for many years in various parts of Rhode Island In 1655 and 1669 he served on the grand jury On May 25th, he was appointed by the court of commissioners to keep a house of entertainment He joined a company of horse August 10, 1667, and later was chosen captain On June 7, 1671, he was on a special jury to try two Indians Ralph claimed the lands of the Dutch House of Good Hope, now Hartford, Connecticut, and commenced a lawsuit to establish his claim against Richard Lord and James Richard, possessors of the Dutch land about 1667 Earle affirmed that he purchased the land of Underhill in August, 1653 and paid him twenty pounds sterling for it, but Underhill protested against the claim of Earle It is not improbable that the claim was well founded

The children of Ralph and Joan Earle were Ralph, married Dorcas Sparague, William, married (first) Mary Walker, (second) Prudence ——,

Mary, married William Cory, Martha, married William Wood, Sarah, married Thomas Cornell

(II) William Earle, son of Ralph Earle (1), was born in England The first known record of William Earle is dated April 2, 1634, when he and his wife Mary sold to James Sands their interest in fourteen acres that came by right of the late Widow Walker, the land having come by marriage of Mary Walker, daughter of the widow, to William Earle He was admitted a freeman at Bristol, Rhode Island, May 11, 1658, and on May 18th he was admitted a freeman of the colony at the general court held at Warwick On June 8th, in the same year, he was chosen to represent Bristol in the general court of trials at Newport He was given a grant of land in partnership with William Cory May 1, 1665, provided they maintain a windmill for the use of the town In 1668 the windmill had been erected William Earle removed to Dartmouth about 1670, and stayed there several years, his interests there being large He owned more than two thousand acres from his claims in the original division of the land

The general assembly for Rhode Island and Providence plantations, for the election of general officers for the colony, was held May 6, 1691, at the house of William Earle, it being removed from Newport by reason of the distemper He was a deputy from Portsmouth to the general assemblies held at Providence, October 25, 1704, and at Newport May 1, 1706, and July 3, 1706 He made a will November 13, 1713, mentioning various legatees He died January 15, 1715 The children of William Earle were Mary, born 1655, married John Borden, William, born at Portsmouth, Rhode Island, married Elizabeth ——, Ralph (see forward), Thomas, married Mary Taber, Caleb, married Mary ——, John, born at Portsmouth, married Mary Wait, Prudence, married Benjamin Durfee

(III) Ralph Earle, son of William Earle (2), born in 1660, married Mary (Carr) Hicks, widow of John Hicks, and daughter of Robert Carr, of Newport, Rhode Island She died the same year that he died, 1757, at Leicester, Massachusetts, and both are buried in the Friends' burying ground at Leicester, where the graves of no less than six generations of their descendants are The earliest known record of Ralph Earle is to the effect that he had taken the freeman's oath prior to March 24, 1686 In 1688 his father gave to him and his wife the land adjoining the "fall river" at Pocasset, in Freetown, His removal to and occupancy of this land must have occurred soon afterward He lived there between twenty-five and thirty years, the site of this house being on what is now Bedford street, about ten rods northeast of the northeast corner of the market, which was standing in 1860 The house had a gambrel roof and was destroyed about 1848 He was surveyor of Highways in 1690-92-96, constable in 1699, and grand juryman in 1700 and 1715 He had the military title of ensign

In 1716 he went through Providence, Rhode Island, into the interior of Massachusetts, as far as what is now Leicester On the way, at Grafton, he hired an Indian, named Moses Printer, as guide Over part of the way there was no path and they blazed their way in order to find the track back again In 1717 he removed with part of his family to Leicester and purchased of the original proprietors of the town two tracts of land, containing in the aggregate five hundred and fifty acres One of the tracts included the Mulberry Grove, now or lately owned by George and Billings Mann, and the other was on the west side of Asnebumskit Hill, in what is now town of Paxton Its westerly boundary appears to have been the road leading northerly from the Penniman place, a mile east of Paxton Centre His dwelling house was built about one and one-half miles northeasterly from the present village of Leicester, on Mulberry street, and very near the site of the residence now or lately owned by Benjamin Wilson It was a one story house with a gambrel roof and was torn down in 1846 In 1721 he was a member of the church that is the Congregational church of Leicester Within a year a Society of Friends, commonly called Quakers, was organized in the town and he joined it In 1732 he and his sons William and Robert, with four other men, asked to be released from paying any part of the tax for the support of the minister or ministers established by the laws of this province, alleging that they as Quakers with a conscientious scruple against paying such a tax The Quaker meeting house was erected upon land taken from the farm of Ralph Earle and that of his neighbor, Nathaniel Potter, both of whose graves are within a few feet of the site of the old church Ralph Earle's interest in the society was so great that he made a trip to Philadelphia to visit William Penn, the best known Quaker in the country Penn at the time was building a house at Pennsburg and it is said told Earle that he would put his initials on the chimney

He still retained the confidence of his fellow-citizen for he was chosen March 22, 1736, to perambulate the line between Leicester and Worcester, with the committee from the other town, for which the town paid the munificent sum of four shillings It is said that Earle once owned Mount Hope, Rhode Island, but no deed of it can be found on record

His will was made May 25, 1750 Among the bequests to his wife is the negro boy Sharp, and he directs that if the negro be faithful and well behaved, he should have his freedom at her decease; if not, he may be sold But before Earle died he himself manumitted the slave and April 6, 1756, gave him thirty acres of land on the southern declivity of Asnebumskit The negro took the name of Freeborn as a surname later

Children of Ralph and Mary (Hicks) Earle were. William, born November 12, 1690, married Anna Howard, John, born April 24, 1692, married Widow Sarah Borden, Mary, born October 24, 1693, married —— Sheffield, Elizabeth, born December 24, 1696, married Robert Lawson, Sarah, born January 18, 1698, married Stephen Manchester, Martha, born December 21, 1700, Patience, born November 24, 1702, married Benjamin Richardson, Ralph, born March 14, 1704, Robert, (see forward), Mercy, born March 13, 1708, married Jotham Rice, Benjamin, born March 14, 1711, married (first) Abigail Newhall, (second) Deborah (Buffum) Slade

(IV) Robert Earle, son of Ralph Earle (3), born March 2, 1706, in Freetown, Massachusetts, married (first) Mary Newhall, born November 5, 1704, daughter of Thomas Newhall, of Leicester, formerly of Malden, Massachusetts, by whom he had ten children He married (second), March 23, 1756, Hepsibah Johnson, of Worcester, Massachusetts He died in 1796 He was eleven years old when his father moved to Leicester, Massachusetts When he was of age his father gave him two tracts of land, on one of which he erected his house at the corner of Earle and Mulberry streets, and resided there during all his married life He sold the place to his grandsons, Pliny and Jonah Earle, for three thousand pounds, April 11, 1792 In the following year Pliny removed the old dwelling house to the opposite side of the road and erected upon the old site a new house, which with some changes and additions is still standing Here Robert Earle passed the remainder of his days with the family of his grandson Pliny He had a remarkable constitution and retained his vigor and activity to almost the close of his long life After the ninetieth anniversary of his birth he went alone on horseback to visit his sons at Chester, Vermont On his return he arrived home at night, having ridden fifty miles during the day Once at least when at this extreme age he rode, in one day, to Providence, Rhode Island to attend the yearly meeting of the Society of Friends, to which he belonged Some years before his death he was injured by a fall from his horse, and was afterward somewhat lame from the effects of the injury received

The wife of Robert Earle, Mary Newhall, was the granddaughter of Thomas Newhall, the first white child born in Lynn, Massachusetts He was the son of Thomas Newhall, who died at Lynn, May 25, 1674, and Mary Newhall, who died September 25, 1665 Both were emigrants from England Children of Robert Earle were Martha, born November 3, 1726, married (first) David Earle, (second) Hezekiah Ward, Nathan, born May 12, 1728, married Elizabeth Richardson, Mary, born August 10, 1730, married Jonathan Sargent, Elizabeth, born October 18, 1732, married John Whittemore, George, born March 3, 1735, married Mary Baker, Thomas, August 27, 1737, married Hannah Wait, Esek, born February 10, 1741, married Mehitable Snow, Robert born October 10, 1743, married Sarah Hunt, Lydia, born August 15, 1746, married (first) John Wilson, (second) Micah Johnson, (third) Jonas Newton, Marmaduke, (see forward), Phebe, born December 22, 1756, married Francis Flagg, Timothy, born March 13 1759, died in the Unites States army, November 3, 1777

(V) Marmaduke Earle, son of Robert Earle (4), born in Leicester, Massachusetts, March 8, 1749, married, 1772, Elizabeth Newton, daughter of Jonas and Rebecca (Richardson) Newton, of Paxton Massachusetts She was born June 22, 1755, died November 3, 1840, he died May 29, 1839 He was a farmer and his homestead was on the road to Barre, about a mile northwest of Paxton Centre He and his wife retained their membership in the Society of Friends during life and were buried in the Friends' burying ground, at Leicester None of the children were Quakers Children were Lucretia, born February 25, 1773, married Samuel Brown, Catherine, born March 3, 1775, married Francis Washburn, Winthrop, born May 5, 1777, died, unmarried in Paxton, January 15, 1836, Deliverance, born November 10, 1779, married Jonathan Cunningham, Samuel, born December 26, 1781, died June 21, 1787, Amasa, born March 11, 1784 married Lucy Howe, Philip, born April 10, 1786, married Patty Barton, Rebecca, born July 21, 1788, married James Thompson, Emory, born September 10, 1790, married Eunice Smith, Candace, born November 3 1792, married William Boynton, Persis, born December 18, 1794 married William H Scott, Phebe, born June 22, 1797, married Moses Parkhurst, Elmer, (see forward), Homer, born May 6 1802, died August 30, 1804

(VI) Elmer Earle, son of Marmaduke Earle (5), born January 6 1800, in Paxton Massachusetts, married Sally Bellows daughter of Jonas and Martha (Bridges) Bellows born April 19 1804, died March 30, 1881 They lived in Worcester Massachusetts, where he died September 2, 1869 Their children were Louisa, born February 9, 1825, died September 26, 1827, Adeline A, born October 26, 1827, married Charles Newton, Emily D (see forward); Charles G, born April 22, 1833, married Louisa M Starkweather, Susan M (see forward), Henry M, born July 23, 1841 died September 4, 1845

(VII) Emily Davis Earle, daughter of Elmer Earle (6), born at Leicester, Massachusetts, August 31, 1830, married July 9, 1851, Seneca M Richardson, of whom later (See Richardson Family under William A Richardson sketch elsewhere in this work)

(VII) Susan M Earle, daughter of Elmer Earle (6), born in North Brookfield, Massachusetts, August 24, 1838, married Gilbert J Rugg, of Lancaster, Massachusetts October 20, 1858, at Worcester

(VIII) Seneca Merrill Richardson, son of Wyman Richardson (7) was born in Corinth, Vermont, December 5 1830 For the ancestry of Mr Richardson see sketch of his brother, William A Richardson He was educated in the schools at Smithville, where his parents were living during his boyhood He learned the machinist's trade as his brother and ancestors had done Both father and grandfather on the Richardson side were expert blacksmiths and machinists His father worked in various places He was at Athol, Barre, Petersham and Boston, filling positions where his skill and experience as a mechanic and superintendent were needed

Seneca Richardson came to Worcester to work for Willard Williams & Company manufacturers of wood-working machinery, in their machine shop He went to Fitchburg and worked there in the manufacture of cane goods for five years Then he took the position of superintendent of the E C Cleveland Machine Co manufacturers of woolen machinery, in the so-called Junction shop This firm was composed of J M Bassett, one of the veteran manufacturers of Worcester, and J C Mason also a well known name in Worcester industrial history In 1864 he went into business for himself in the firm of Witherby, Rugg & Richardson, to manufacture wood-working machinery His partners were Luke B Witherby and Gilbert J Rugg, both men who had worked in the shops, manufacturing wood-working machinery such as the new firm began to make They began in a shop in the Armsby building, at the corner of Central and Union streets with twenty men Later they moved to the building on Salisbury street which was built by the older firm of wood-working machine makers Ball & Williams in 1865 The firm of Ball & Williams formerly employed all three of the partners in the firm of Witherby, Rugg & Richardson It was founded in 1839 by Thomas E Daniels in the Court Mills, sold to Deacon Richard Ball and Thomas Rice, who were succeeded by the firm of Ball & Ballard This firm became later Ball & Williams the partners being Richard Ball and Warren Williams, his son-in-law Mr Williams retired from business in 1865 The business of Witherby, Rugg & Richardson prospered for nearly thirty years when the death of Mr Witherby and Mr Richardson left the business in the hands of Mr Rugg It was incorporated in 1901 and Mr Rugg was elected president of the company—the Witherby, Rugg & Richardson Company—and managed the business until March 1, 1903, when the entire capital stock of the corporation was sold to the Hobbs Manufacturing Company of Worcester Mr Rugg then retired from the business, which has since been conducted by the Hobbs Manufacturing Company as part of their business Mr Richardson was highly esteemed as a citizen He ranked high as a business man, and was acknowledged to be one of the best mechanical experts in his line of business He died August 15, 1899 He was a well known Mason, being a member of the

Worcester County Commandery, Knights Templar He was a charter member of Quinsigamond Lodge, Ancient Free and Accepted Masons He was a Republican and thoroughly posted in public matters, and interested in public affairs He represented Ward One for two years in the board of aldermen He and his wife were life members of the Unitarian Association and were leaders, both being delegates to different conventions and active in the councils of the association He married, July 9, 1851 Emily Davis Earle, daughter of Elmer and Sally (Bellows) Earle (See sketch of Earle family) Her father was born in Paxton Massachusetts, January 6, 1800, the son of Marmaduke and Elizabeth (Newton) Earle Her mother was born in West Boylston, Massachusetts Mr and Mrs Richardson had one child Hattie Collins, born November 18, 1856, married May 15, 1879 William Henry Brigham and they have three children William Seneca, Bertha Emily, Katharine

Mrs Richardson lives in an attractive home at 134 Paine street, Worcester, Massachusetts

She is a descendant of Ralph Earle, the emigrant, who settled in Rhode Island among the early colonists, and of his grandson, Ralph Earle the Quaker, who was among the early settlers of Leicester Massachusetts (See sketch of the Earle Family in this work)

JOHN OTIS HALE Oliver Hale, of Leominster, was probably the son of one of the Hales or their descendants who settled in various places in Massachusetts, the most prominent of which was Thomas Hale, of Newbury He was probably a descendant of Robert Hale, of Charlestown, a carpenter by trade who was admitted a freeman on May 14 1634, joined the Charlestown church in 1630 and was a deacon thereof, also a town officer of Charlestown and an ensign in the militia Subsequently he took up his residence in Malden, Massachusetts His wife, Joan Hale, bore him the following children John, born June 3 1636, admitted to the church, August 22, 1658, and became a minister of the Beverly church Mary, born May 17, 1639 Zachariah born April 3, 1641 died 1643 Samuel, born April 9 1644 Joanna Zachariah 2d Robert Hale died July 16 1659 and in his will he mentions wife and children His widow married Richard Jacobs Oliver Hale Leominster, born January 1, 1720, in Stowe, Massachusetts, was married twice His first wife, Hannah (Frost) Hale, bore him several children His second wife, Catherine (Boutwell) Hale, born in Sudbury, Massachusetts, October 7, 1732 a member of the same family as the late ex-Governor Boutwell bore him the following children Thomas, Daniel, Oliver, Calvin Luther, Hannah Catherine, Sarah Betty Oliver Hale died May 7 1799 he was survived by his wife, who passed away July 16, 1821

Luther Hale, son of Oliver and Catherine (Boutwell) Hale, of Leominster, Massachusetts removed from that town about 1788 and settled in Hubbardston, where his descendants have since resided He was born about 1765 He married (first), January 16 1787, Joanna Carter, who died July 30, 1803, at the age of thirty-three years He married (second), April 8 1804 Phebe Wyman, who died July 23 1826 aged forty-seven years He married (third) October 23, 1834 Phebe (Kimball) Upham who died March 8 1846 aged eighty-two years He died February 7, 1845 aged seventy-eight years His children were John born June 24 1787, died January 7 1850 Lucy, born August 23 1789, died May 3, 1805 Clara born June 12, 1791, died January 14, 1860 Otis, born March 16, 1793, died April 13, 1822 Luther, born January 19 1795 married Melinda Goodspeed, January, 1823, removed to Vermont Roland, born December 28, 1796, married Clarissa Rice, of Templeton, June 13 1833, died July 29, 1861 Esther born February 17, 1799 died about the year 1885, she married James Newton, and removed to Greenfield, Massachusetts Laura, born January 1, 1801, died June 1, 1815 Oliver, born September 28, 1804, was drowned on the voyage to California, February 16 1853, he married March 18 1830, Sarah D Parker who died May 3, 1891 Thomas, born July 6 1808 married, March 20, 1831, Mary Pond, died April 2, 1861 Lucy, born February 13 1810 died about the year 1883, she married Daniel Wilkinson, of Templeton, July 11, 1833 Joanna born March 11, 1812 died about 1886, she married Benjamin W Fletcher of Worcester Susan, born April 2, 1814 died 1891, she married Amasa Hyde and removed to Shrewsbury, Massachusetts Charles born September 5, 1816, died December 30, 1818 Luke, born August 21 1818 died 1896 he married Sophronia Wyman, of Winchendon, Massachusetts, and resided there Thomas above mentioned and his wife Mary (Pond) Hale, were the parents of the following children Louisa Minerva born September 30 1832 died February 13 1854 Thomas Irving, born October 9 1838, married (first) Martha A (Thompson) Hale, November 29 1865 married (second) Helen D Pond, January 16, 1878 Luther Hobart, born February 11, 1841, married Martha A Thompson March 28 1862 enlisted September 3 1862 in Company H Fifty-third Regiment Massachusetts Volunteer Militia and died at Cleveland, September 12 1863 on his way home from the hospital Merrill born November 25, 1845 Luke, born July 15 1850, died October 3, 1862

Oliver Hale son of Luther Hale was born at Hubbardston, Massachusetts, September 28, 1804 He resided in Hubbardston until the gold fever of 1849 and was drowned on the voyage to California, February 16, 1853 He married, March 18, 1830, Sarah D Parker, and their children were John Otis born April 2 1831, see forward Sarah Maria, born August 3 1833, died August 2, 1898, she married Luke Davis, of Boston, August 31, 1862, and his death occurred August 31, 1883 they resided at Newton Massachusetts Minerva Florilla, born June 27 1837 resides in West Newton Massachusetts Catherine Swan, born June 8 1841 Clara, twin of Catherine Swan, born June 8, 1841, resides in West Newton Seth P H, born February 12, 1846, married, December 2 1867 Abby Bennett who died March 8, 1888, leaving one son, William B, born May 14, 1871 he married (second), February 12, 1894 H Gertrude Powers and they are the parents of one daughter Gladys born December 26, 1899 Seth P H enlisted in Company G, Fourth Massachusetts Cavalry, January 4 1864, and was honorably discharged from the service on June 7, 1865

John Otis Hale, son of Oliver and Sarah D (Parker) Hale was born at Hubbardston Massachusetts April 2, 1831 He settled in his native town and was a manufacturer of chair stock and chair seats in Williamsville a village of Hubbardston He was a capable energetic man and was chosen to represent the district in the general court during the years 1868 and 1869 John O Hale and J D Williams were instrumental in getting the Ware River Railroad through Williamsville, they authorized costly surveys to be made at their own expense and created so great an interest that the Burnshirt Valley line was adopted Construction was begun on this road in Hubbardston, November,

1870 and passenger trains commenced running upon the entire road in November, 1873 only a few days prior to the death of Mr Hale Mr Hale was also instrumental in securing the valley road from Templeton to Barre He was a Free Mason and a Knight Templar Mr Hale married, November 7 1860 Lucy Browning daughter of Joshua and Laura (Morse) Browning of Hubbardston and sister of Mrs Robert H Chamberlain, of Worcester, and Mrs Wheelock A Cheney, who resides at No 15 Bowdoin street, Worcester Their children are Abby Calista born July 21, 1862 died May 1 1899 Oliver, born December 12, 1863 Joshua Browning born June 14 1865, married, August, 1890 Nellie M Lewis and their children are Robert B, born June 13, 1891, and Roger W L, born December 29, 1902 the family reside in Providence John Otis born December 1, 1866 Lucy Dorritt, born August 18, 1868 John O Hale the father of these children died December 8, 1873 His wife died January 28, 1878

John Otis Hale, son of John Otis and Lucy (Browning) Hale, was born at Williamsville, Hubbardston Massachusetts, December 1, 1866 His father died when he was only seven years old He was educated in the public schools of Hubbardston, and during his early life worked on a farm At the age of eighteen he accepted a position as steward of an institution at Barre Massachusetts, and was there employed for about five years He then came to Worcester, Massachusetts, entered into partnership with his brother in the manufacture of chains, and at the expiration of four years purchased his brother's interest in the business This enterprise was started in a shop at No 65 Beacon street, but the steady growth of the business necessitated its removal in 1901 to the present location at No 42 Lagrange street The business was incorporated January 1, 1905, as Hale Bros Company John Otis Hale being the chief owner and president of the company The product of their plant consists of jack and ladder chains which they manufacture in a variety of styles of all sizes, and their trade extends throughout all the states of the Union Mr Hale is a member of the First Universalist Church

Mr Hale married, April 26 1904 Josephine Ann Aldus, of Belfast Maine, daughter of William S and Jane (Robinson) Aldus

THOMAS F EAGAN, a successful hardware manufacturer of Worcester, was born in county Kerry Ireland March 25 1850, and came with his parents to America in 1853

His childhood was spent in Worcester where his father settled He was educated in the public schools He went to work first for Salem Copeland a manufacturer of firearms, and learned the trade of machinist After three years he accepted a place with the firm of Amesbury & Harrington, makers of the Union Mowing Machine After three years he went to the machine shop of L W Pond and there served a regular apprenticeship to perfect himself in his trade He next was employed by the Knifflin Mowing Machine Company in Worcester, and for nearly twenty years remained in various capacities with this company In 1892 he bought the business of the owner, Charles W Chamberlin, of Worcester A year later he bought the Copeland Hardware Manufacturing Company of Worcester His business for nine years remained in the old location in the N A Lombard building In 1901 he moved to Blithewood avenue, where he built a shop for his use Mr Eagan has a well equipped machine shop, in which he carries on the manufacture of Copeland's and Cook's extension dividers, window springs, storm window fasteners, calipers, and of late years has carried as a side line the agency of the Walter A Wood harvesting machinery with a repair shop designed to handle mowing machines and in fact all kinds of harvesting machines

He married September 14, 1881, Catherine I Devine daughter of Daniel and Ellen Devine, formerly of Auburn, Massachusetts The children are as follows Edward D, born September 1, 1882, Nellie G, born July 20, 1884, Thomas F, born September 25 1886 John J, deceased, born March 16, 1888, Charles H, born October 29, 1890, Isabella C deceased, born December 14, 1893, and Mary E, deceased, born November 20, 1896

THE HARLOW FAMILY

By Major William T Harlow

In a book on Derivation of Family Names, by Rev William Arthur, it is said that the name Harlow is derived from the town of Harlow in England The modern town of Harlow is situate on the east bank of the river Stort in the county of Essex, twenty-three miles north of London, on the high road to Newcastle, and is a station of the Great Eastern Railway Territorially, the town is only a small fraction of, and nominally it is the last surviving relic of, a much larger tract of land, once called the Half Hundred of Harlow, or Dimidium de Herloua and by the latter name many times mentioned in Domesday Book It extended twelve miles from north to south, and six miles in width, along the east side of the river Stort, and contained seventy-two square miles As to the identity of the Dimidium of Domesday with the Half Hundred and of the names of Herloua and Harlow my authority is Morant's History of the County of Essex,—an elaborate work in two ponderous volumes, wherein the learned author traces everything in the county back to Saxon origins The Half Hundred of Harlow contained eleven parishes, of which one was called the Parish of Harlow, which parish included six manors (landed estates), of which one was named Harlowbury The term hundred, originally used by the ancient Saxons to mean one hundred men, assigned with their families, under a quasi military form of organization, to occupy a large tract of land in time became the name of the tract itself, and later came to signify an intermediate territorial division, now obsolete, between town and county

Mr Arthur classifies Harlow with names of local origin, i e names derived from places and leaves his derivation of the name from the town of Harlow to rest on unsupported assertion This is not the place to discuss at length the learned opinions of accepted authorities But I beg to suggest, what in the absence of proof to the contrary seems to me the more probable supposition that Harlow was originally the name of a man of whom the *town* is the namesake Towns, always the products of men, not infrequently take their names from those of men, of which one may recall very numerous instances, capable historically of easy proof As to the reverse derivation of English family names from those of towns, I make bold to challenge proof of a single instance I limit my challenge to English names, in which I do not include *titles* of rank nor names with the prefix De, or its equivalent But my purpose in referring to the origin of our family name is to show its high antiquity and to suggest to others where with time and opportunity for foreign research which the present scribe hath not they may look for light upon our earlier family history.

(I) William Harlow, the first comer of the Harlow name from England to New England was unaccompanied by wife, parents or kindred of any degree His name appears here first in a list of residents (1629-1700) of Lynn, Massachusetts In 1637 ten men of Lynn, originally called Saugus, had leave granted them to take up and settle land in Sandwich, and nine of the ten, with forty-six others, of whom William Harlow was one, removed from Lynn to Sandwich and settled there The same year one Thomas Hampton, of Sandwich, not one of the new comers from Lynn, died without family or kindred leaving a will, of which William Harlow was both an attesting witness and legatee, colony law allowing such attesting The same year also he was fined ten shillings for keeping "3 hogges unwringed" In 1639 he was proposed for admission as a freeman and took the preliminary oath of fidelity In 1640 he had assigned to him at a town meeting of Sandwich four acres of meadow I mention these rather unimportant items because of their bearing upon the question of how old he then was, to which I shall recur again

William Harlow removed to Plymouth later He was a cooper by trade He built several houses in Plymouth, of which one, built in 1667 on a lot granted him by the town and described as a 'little knoll or parcel, lying near his now dwelling house on the westerly side of the road to sett a new house upon," still stands where it was built on the road to Sandwich (now named Sandwich street), about a quarter of a mile southerly from Plymouth postoffice Another house built by him in 1660, referred to in the above description, called the Doten House, stood on the easterly side of the same road a few rods further south till 1898, when it was taken down The house, still standing, was framed out of old timbers of the Pilgrim Fort on Burial Hill in Plymouth As sergeant of the South Company William Harlow had had charge of the old fort for many years and after King Philip's war (1675-6), he bought it of the town and used the old timbers in the construction of his new house In 1882, when some repairs were being made on this house a ponderous iron hinge of the Fort Gate, attached to a timber was discovered, and may now be seen with other Pilgrim relics in Pilgrim Hall

Sergeant Harlow, so-called in many records of the time still preserved, did military duty at a period when the Home Guards were not a laughing stock, ready day and night without compulsion or compensation to defend home and country against the savage foe No details of his military service are preserved, but there can be no doubt of his employment in the Indian warfare of his time, of which the chief event was the great Narragansett fight, when both the Plymouth companies were present under the command of Major William Bradford Doubtless, Sergeant Harlow was with his company when every able-bodied man in the colony was there

In civil affairs, William Harlow, having been admitted as a freeman (1654), served as juror or grand juror every year, was rater (assessor) and excise man many years, deputy to the general court two sessions (Josiah Winslow being then governor), a member of the board of selectmen fifteen years and its chairman at the time of his death He was also active in the church affairs, and his name is of very frequent occurrence in the records of the colony, town and church

The inventory of his estate real and personal, foots up to 234 pounds, 16 shillings, 11 pence, and it was "ordered by the court that his four sons have all his lands, the eldest to have a double portion according to our law saving to the widow her thirds, the remainder to be divided among the seven daughters '

What was William Harlow's age at his death? According to the town records he died August 26, 1691, aged sixty-seven years This would fix his birth in 1624 and his age at thirteen years when he removed from Lynn to Sandwich and witnessed Hampton's will, and was mulcted for keeping swine contrary to law, and at fifteen when he applied for admission as freeman, and took the oath of fidelity, and at sixteen when he had a parcel of land assigned to him by public authority And still earlier he must have crossed the sea without care of parents or other kindred Everywhere apparently treated as a man after his appearance here, we can have little doubt that he was at least twenty-one years old when he left England and that he must have been at least seventy-five years old when he died

He married, at Plymouth, December 30, 1649, Rebecca Bartlett, who bore him four children and died 1657, aged twenty-eight years He married (second), July 15, 1658 Mary Faunce, who bore him four children and died October 4, 1664 He married (third), January 15, 1665 Mary Shelley, who bore him five children and survived him Of his thirteen children, all but the first born, lived to grow up The children of the first wife were William, born and died 1650, Samuel, see forward, Rebecca born June 12, 1655, William, born June 2, 1657 The children by the second wife were Mary, born May 9, 1659, Repentance born November 22, 1660, John, born October 19 1662, Nathaniel born September 30, 1664 The children by his third wife were Hannah, born October 28, 1665, Bathsheba, born April 21, 1667, Joanna, born March 24, 1669, Mehitable, born October 4 1672, Judith, born August 2, 1676

William Harlow's first wife was a daughter of Robert and Mary (Warren) Bartlett, and granddaughter of Richard Warren, the Pilgrim The name of her grandmother (Warren's wife) was Elizabeth Juat Marsh, and she was, when she married Warren the widow of one Marsh, Juat being her maiden name She did not come over in the 'Mayflower" in 1620 with her husband, but later in 1623 in the ship 'Ann," in which at the same time came Bartlett and Mary Warren, not then married and two other daughters of the Pilgrim and his wife

(II) Samuel Harlow son of William (1) and Rebecca (Bartlett) Harlow, was born in Plymouth, January 27, 1652 He followed his father's calling of cooper and received as his double portion of his father's estate the house built out of the old fort timbers and lived in it during the remainder of his life He was admitted a freeman in 1689 and held divers minor offices Like his father he bore the prefix of sergeant, having succeeded him as orderly in the South Company At the time of King Philip's war Samuel was twenty-three years old and it is more than probable that he took part in the Narragansett fight

He married (first) Priscilla —— and (second) Hannah —— whose parentage and surnames are unknown Their Christian names were common among the Pilgrims and that Samuel's wives were both of Pilgrim descent is little short of certain, considering that in his time there were few Plymouth families without at least one "Mayflower" ancestor He died March 2 1734 aged eighty-two years His second wife survived him His children, by his first wife, were Rebecca, born January 27 1678 by his second wife John, born December 19, 1685, Hannah, born November 15, 1688, Samuel, born August 14 1690, William, born July

26 1692 Eleazer, see forward. Priscilla, born October 3. 1695.

(III) Eleazer Harlow youngest son of Samuel (2) and Hannah Harlow was born April 18 1694 and lived in Plymouth, though not in the house built by his grandfather that having passed to his older brother John Eleazer died suddenly in 1728, aged thirty-four years, but his grave has not been found His brothers, John and William, each have good headstones on Burial Hill, Plymouth that of William who died April 11 1751, being the earliest stone with the Harlow name upon it on the hill I have counted the names of eighty-eight Harlows on stones mostly in the vicinity of the Cushman monument, all doubtless descendants of the first William At the time of his death the hill was already in use as a place of burial The earliest date on any original stone on the hill is 1681, that of Edward Gray Elder Cushman's original stone gives as the date of his death 1691 The hill was used until the close of King Philip's war for military observation and fortification but it doubtless began to be used for a burial place soon after the war So there can be little doubt that Eleazer Harlow his father Samuel and his grandfather William are all buried there, though no visible memorials mark their graves

Eleazer Harlow married October 5 1715, Hannah Delano daughter of Dr Benoni Delano and granddaughter of Dr Thomas Delano, both of Duxbury She died October 1719 Eleazer married (second), 1720 Hannah Pratt who survived him Dr Thomas Delano was the son of Philip Delano (De la Noye), the Huguenot Pilgrim, so-called, who came over from Holland to Plymouth in the ship 'Fortune' in 1621, and settled on a forty-acre lot by Mill Brook in Duxbury and there lived the remainder of his life The wife of Philip Delano and mother of Dr Thomas was Hester Dewsbury, supposed to have come from England with the Quakers and to have been of their persuasion The wife of Dr Thomas and mother of Dr Benoni Delano was Mary Alden, daughter of John and Priscilla (Mullens) Alden, and granddaughter of William and Alice Mullens, all 'Mayflower" Pilgrims Nothing is known of Dr Benoni's wife, not even her given name The children of Eleazer and Hannah (Delano) Harlow were Eliphas, born March 5 1716 Lemuel, born November 29, 1717, Eleazer, see forward The children of Eleazer and Hannah (Pratt) Harlow were Elizabeth born October 21, 1721, Patience, born October 1 1722

(IV) Eleazer Harlow Jr, son of Eleazer (3) and Hannah (Delano) Harlow, was born at Plymouth October 17 1719 Left an orphan at an early age his mother dying shortly after his birth and his father when he was only nine years old, he was brought up by his grandfather, Dr Benoni Delano who evidently designing him to be his successor, began early to teach him the healing art But the doctor died April 5 1738, before his pupil was out of his teens Nevertheless having come by inheritance into possession of his granfather's medical and surgical effects, books drugs recipes, panaceas lancets forceps, old mare and saddle bags all and singular and no rival putting in an appearance to dispute his title to inherit also his grandfather's patients young Doctor Harlow married a wife three years younger and started out as his grandfather's successor about fifteen months after his death In due course of time, the young doctor succeeded to the old doctor's place in the confidence and patronage of the people of Duxbury In 1765 his house in the village of Millbrook Duxbury was burned and two children, his own daughter Abigail aged thirteen years and his step-daughter, Polly Dabney, aged eleven years, perished in the flames His wife, mother of Polly saved herself by jumping from a chamber window The doctor had another house on or near the same site burned in 1797, after which, being seventy-eight years old, he gave up his medical practice and went to live with his son Gideon at Crooked Lane near Marshfield line, and died there August 5 1812, aged ninety-two years, seven months, eighteen days In his last years his eyesight failed and he became entirely blind, though he retained his memory and mental faculties to the end of life

The estate of Dr Harlow, valued at $3994 85 in the inventory, was settled by his son Asaph, then living in Cambridge The graves of the doctor and his third wife, marked by large headstones with well cut inscriptions, are in an old and much neglected graveyard, about a mile from his son Gideon's farm at Crooked Lane The grave of his first wife is at Cedar Grove in Marshfield near the Congregational church, with those of her father's family The site of Dr Harlow's burned houses was near 'Ford's Store" in Millbrook village which is partly within the forty-acre farm settled by Philip Delano Here also lived and died Philip's son, Dr Thomas, and his grandson, Dr Benoni Delano Dr Harlow was their lineal descendant and successor and the united terms of the trio as practitioners in Duxbury extends from Pilgrim times to within the memory of the writer's father who was in his fourteenth year at the death of Dr Harlow, his great-grandfather

He married (first) November 9. 1739 Abigail Thomas, daughter of Gideon and Abigail (Baker) Thomas, of Marshfield The bride's age on her wedding day was sixteen years eleven months, five days and the groom's age was twenty years and twenty-two days She died November 24 1743 He married (second), September 11, 1745 Abigail Clark, of Plymouth and (third), about 1760, Mrs Elizabeth Dabney, widow of Charles Dabney, of Boston The only child of Dr Eleazer and Abigail (Thomas) Harlow was Gideon see forward The children of Dr Eleazer and Abigail (Clark) Harlow were Asaph Thomas Abigail, William, Arunah, Hannah, Elizabeth, Patience

(V) Gideon Harlow son of Dr Eleazer (4) and Abigail (Thomas) Harlow, was born in Duxbury, October 28 1743 He was brought up by his mother's parents Gideon Thomas and wife, who lived in Marshfield very near the line between that town and Duxbury His mother, Abigail, was the eldest of their seven daughters and, after her death, her son seems to have taken her place in the hearts of her parents The Gideon Thomas homestead has never passed out of the possession of his descendants and is now the property of his great-great-great-grandson P Foster White, of Worcester Through his grandmother Thomas Gideon Harlow was descended from Governor William Bradford, the Pilgrim and also from Ellen Newton another of the English exiles in Holland who followed the Mayflower' two years later in the ship "Ann" and rejoined their fellows at New Plymouth in 1623 His grandmother Thomas was the daughter of Kenelm and Sarah (Bradford) Baker granddaughter of Major William Bradford and great-granddaughter of the Pilgrim governor by his second wife, widow Alice (Carpenter) Southworth, who was also a passenger of the "Ann" Kenelm Baker was the son of Samuel and Ellen (Winslow) Baker and grandson of Ellen Newton by her second husband, Kenelm Winslow, who was a brother of Edward and Gilbert Winslow the Pilgrims Kenelm came over in 1629 from Droitwich near Worcester, England,

and settled in Marshfield where the house that he built and lived in with his wife Ellen is still standing.

Gideon Harlow has the addition of 'housewright' in the deed of his farm, but except building a house on his own farm, he did not to much extent follow that trade. His house is still standing, though not on its original site, an excellent example of old colony architecture and handicraft. It contains ornamental work of no mean order, and lumber of choice character such as one might now ransack all the forests of Massachusetts in vain to find. The great pines and oaks such as were wrought into that house are not growing now anywhere in the commonwealth.

He was a revolutionary soldier, serving first as a minute man at the Lexington alarm. He served several years as assessor and as selectman of Duxbury. His church relations, however, were with the Marshfield church, of which he was a regular attendant all his life and many years a deacon. He was a prosperous and well-to-do farmer. He married January 4, 1770 Patience Ford Eames, widow of Abner Eames of Marshfield. Gideon and his wife were both descendants of the widow Martha Ford, and of her son William who came over in the 'Fortune' in 1621, and of John Thomas, who came in the ship 'Hopewell' in 1634. For more than a hundred years the Fords and Thomases of Marshfield and Duxbury had been intermarrying and their descendants of the third, fourth and later generations were all cousins of some degree.

The Ford line of descent from the widow Martha to Patience was by the widow's son William, grandson Michael, great-grandson Thomas and great-great-grandson Thomas Ford Jr, who was the father and whose wife Jane Thomas (daughter of Israel and granddaughter of John Thomas) was the mother of Patience. Gideon Harlow's grandfather, Gideon Thomas, was son of Samuel and grandson of John Thomas. The wife of Samuel and mother of Gideon Thomas was Mercy Ford daughter of William Ford, Jr granddaughter of the first William, and great-granddaughter of the widow Martha.

Gideon Harlow died a year and four months before his father, April 9, 1811, aged sixty-seven years, five months, and thirteen days. His wife long survived him and died December 22, 1840, aged ninety-seven years six months and twelve days. His sons Abner and Eleazer settled his estate valued in the inventory at $19 105 49. The graves of Gideon and his wife are with those of his father and stepmother at the neglected old yard in Duxbury, before referred to and are marked by good headstones. Children of Gideon and Patience (Ford) Harlow were: Abigail, born November 26, 1771, Arunah, born January 29, 1773, Thomas, see forward, Lydia, born May 4, 1777, Elizabeth, born May 10, 1779, Abner, born February 1, 1782, Eleazer, born November 4, 1784, Gideon, born April 10, 1786. All of them except Lydia, who died in infancy, lived to ages beyond the average of human life.

(VI) Thomas Harlow, son of Gideon Harlow (5), was born May 17, 1775. He learned the tanner's trade at Weymouth by a term of regular apprenticeship (seven years), which expired March 16, 1796. The very next morning, which was that of his twenty-first birthday, he made an early start to go on foot to Shrewsbury—fifty miles—for the purpose of buying the tannery of one Seth Pratt, who welcomed his customer on the evening of the same day that he left Weymouth* and sold him the tannery for $1 000. A house and twenty-one acres of land went with the tannery, of which no vestige now remains but the house which Pratt built in 1775 is still standing, and the land was the nucleus of the farm now owned by Henry Harlow, grandson of Thomas. There Thomas Harlow followed his calling about forty years and invested his gains therefrom in land, until he came to own at one time nearly three hundred acres. The only civil office that he ever held was, that of highway surveyor, to which he was elected in accordance with an understanding in his highway district, that the taxpayers should each serve in rotation. Though a public-spirited man and regular attendant and voter at elections and town meetings, he never sought or desired public office. In the Congregational Church of Shrewsbury, of which he was a member, the office of deacon was thrust upon him and he served as such many years. He was a great reader of the Bible and was accounted high authority on all Bible questions.

He married May 17, 1798, Thankful Banister, daughter of Nathan and Sarah (Whitney) Banister of the North Parish of Shrewsbury, now Boylston. Nathan was born in Brookfield, removing in 1775 to Shrewsbury to live with his wife's father and mother on their farm in the southwest part of the North Parish. His father was Joseph Banister, son of Christopher, who came from Marlboro to settle in Brookfield, and grandson of Nathan, Jr, whose parents, Nathan and Mary Banister, came from England in or before 1669 and settled in Charlestown. The first mentioned Nathan Banister, Thankful's father, was a blacksmith by trade, and a soldier in the revolutionary war. Two of Thomas Harlow's brothers followed him later to Shrewsbury and settled there—Arunah (whose grandson, George H Harlow, is the present register of probate for Worcester county) in 1798 and Abner in 1812. And most of the Harlows now living in Worcester county are lineal descendants of the three who a century ago came here from Duxbury. Thomas Harlow died November 20, 1865, aged ninety years, his wife Thankful died January 5, 1847, aged seventy-three years. Their children were: Gideon, see forward, Nancy, born July 25, 1802, died in infancy, Elmira, born April 23, 1805, Abigail born April 25, 1810.

(VII) Giedon Harlow, son of Thomas Harlow (6), was born in Shrewsbury, February 17, 1799. He succeeded his father under the latter's will as owner of the home farm. He built the brick house now standing on the farm and occupied it with his family during his life, his father and mother continuing to occupy the older house built by Seth Pratt. Like his father, Gideon Harlow served his term as highway surveyor, and he was selectman several years, also assessor and member of the school committee. He was elected deacon of the Congregational church, but declined to serve. He did not like the tanner's trade in which he was brought up, and devoted his life with untiring energy and application to improvement of the homestead by good culture and the planting of fruit trees. There was

*The writer well remembers how if any one expressed astonishment at grandfather Harlow's great walking feat he would immediately tell a still more wonderful tale of his nephew, Joshua Ford who was sent up from Pembroke by his parents to learn the tanner's trade with him at Shrewsbury and got so homesick that he had to go home and ran all the way back (sixty miles) in a single day.

Many years afterwards I asked Joshua's sister Mrs Benjamin F Gleason of Worcester (nee Mary Ann Ford) about her brother's great day's journey on foot. She said there was no doubt at all about it. She was then a girl and late in the evening when her father's family were about going to bed Josh took them all by surprise opening the door and coming into the room where they were. And so ashamed was he of his return that he did not tell them that he left his uncle's house in Shrewsbury in the morning. Nor did they know it till receipt of a letter from Uncle Thomas about it.

a great quantity of wood and timber on the farm which he cut off and marketed chiefly in Worcester, where demand for firewood, telegraph poles, railroad sleepers and lumber for building purposes in his time always seemed to exceed supply. Many years before his death, his father had by will devised the farm to him, and ever afterwards, with his father's consent and approval, he made the same use of it as if the fee simple of it were already his.

No man ever did or could, with more persistent self-denial and conscientiousness than Gideon Harlow, devote himself to the welfare of his family. That his children should have opportunity by education and every other way to do better in life than he had himself, was the mainspring of all his conduct. Often did he say in the presence of his children: "I had rather lose a day in haytime than have a child of mine lose a day in school." The writer often recalls with gratitude his father's reply, now nearly sixty years ago, to the request of some friends for leave to start a movement in Shrewsbury to nominate him for representative to the general court. He thanked them, but instantly added: "No, I have so many things to do this coming winter that I cannot attend to it." One of the things he had to do was to haul to market in Worcester a lot of wood to pay his son's expenses in college.

He married, January 1, 1828, Harriet Howe, daughter of Nathan and Mary (Parker) Howe. Her father was the son of Captain Nathan and Hepzibah (Taylor) Howe, and grandson of Daniel Howe, who, with William Taylor, Hepzibah's father, and several others, came from Marlboro to Shrewsbury and settled there in 1717. Daniel Howe was the son of Josiah and grandson of John Howe, who was in Sudbury in 1638, when, or very shortly before, he is supposed to have come over from England. Mary Parker, wife of Nathan Howe, Jr., was the daughter of Simon Parker, who came to Shrewsbury from Groton in 1742, and was the son of Samuel and grandson of James Parker, both also of Groton. Simon Parker and both the Nathan Howes were soldiers in the revolutionary war. Of Nathan, senior, Ward says in his history of Shrewsbury: "He was an officer in the (British) service at Lake George in the French war and aided in the building of Fort William Henry. In 1776 he commanded a company in throwing up works at Dorchester Heights during the night (March 4-5). From an illness taken there he never recovered."

Nathan Howe, Jr., only fourteen years old in 1776, was not permitted by his father to enter the United States service until after the fatal nature of his own illness had unmistakably developed.

Captain Howe died March 21, 1781, aged fifty-one years, of a lingering consumption. His original commission as captain, dated February 5, 1776, at Watertown, and signed not by Royal Governor Gage, who was then over in Boston with the Redcoats, but by William Sever, of Kingston, and fourteen others "Major Part of the Council of the Massachusetts Bay in New England," is in the possession of the writer.

Gideon Harlow, of Shrewsbury, died October 26, 1877, aged seventy-eight years and six months. His wife Harriet died March 15, 1870, aged seventy years and seven months. The children of Gideon and Harriet (Howe) Harlow were: William Taylor, see forward; Thomas, born August 18, 1830; Henry, born October 13, 1833; Hiram, born November 27, 1839, died October 5, 1858; Harriet Ann, born December 4, 1841, died April 2, 1883.

MAJOR WILLIAM T. HARLOW

By Charles Nutt

(VIII) William Taylor Harlow, son of Gideon Harlow (7), was born in Shrewsbury, October 3, 1828. He was named for his great-great-grandfather, William Taylor, one of the first settlers of the town of Shrewsbury, and donor to the town of the site of the Congregational meeting house, originally fifteen acres of land, old style measure. His American ancestry on the Harlow side, down to his grandfather, all belonged to Plymouth colony and included six "Mayflower" pilgrims and eight other exiles, three in the "Fortune," 1621, and five in the "Ann," 1623, who followed the pioneers of 1620 to New Plymouth, as appears in greater detail in the foregoing sketch of the family. His four great-grandfathers and one of his grandfathers were soldiers of the American revolution, and brief mention of their service has been made above.

He received his early education in the district schools of his native town, supplemented by a few terms of private schools. When not attending school he worked with his father and brothers on the homestead. He continued his studies at home, and was prepared for college chiefly by himself without a teacher. He attended Monson Academy one term in the spring and summer of 1848 under the instruction of Principal Charles Hammond, and upon his recommendation was admitted to the sophomore class of Yale College in 1848, where he was graduated in 1851. He studied law with Thomas and Foster of Worcester (Benjamin F. Thomas and Dwight Foster, both afterwards justices of the supreme court of Massachusetts) and was admitted to the bar at the March term of the court of common pleas, 1853. He opened an office for the practice of law, first in Worcester, but in less than a year removed to Spencer, where he practiced until the civil war.

He entered the United States service as first lieutenant of Company C, Twenty-first Regiment, Massachusetts Volunteers, in August, 1861, having been occupied since the war began in April, mainly in recruiting and drilling recruits, first at Spencer and later at Camp Lincoln, Worcester. He took part in the engagements of 1862—at Roanoke Island, February 8, at Newbern, March 14 and at Camden Court House, April 19, in North Carolina, at the second battle of Bull Run, August 28-31, and at Chantilly, September 1, in Virginia, at South Mountain, September 14, and at Antietam, September 17, in Maryland, and at Fredericksburg, December 12-15, also in Virginia. He was detailed and acted as regimental quartermaster after the battle of Newbern for about three months and was promoted captain July 29, 1862. The losses of his company by wounds, disease and death in the campaigns of 1862 were such that he had in his company only nine men left for duty. One of his lieutenants was killed at Chantilly and the other at Antietam. Though so fortunate himself as to escape serious wounds, he suffered much from malaria. As the other companies of this regiment had suffered similar losses to those of Company C, the colonel and several other officers of whom Captain Harlow was one, resigned with the expectation that the Twenty-first would soon be consolidated with some other regiment. He received another commission, as major of the Fifty-seventh Veteran Regiment, and assisted in recruiting it, but did not go with it to service in the field.

He returned to the practice of law in Worcester in October, 1863, and continued it there until January, 1866, when he went to California with a view

Wm. T. Harlow.

to locate there. At Red Bluff in the Sacramento Valley, (head of river navigation,) where his brother Thomas had been living for several years, and was then extensively engaged in wheat raising, Major Harlow remained nearly two years. Soon after his arrival there he received appointments as county surveyor (Tehama county) and assistant assessor of United States internal revenue. With these offices and practice of law he did not lack employment, but suffered much from malaria contracted during the war, more, in fact, than he had ever suffered in the river valleys of the Neuse and Rappahannock. He finally on account of health decided to return to Massachusetts, reluctantly giving up his business in California, for he said that like opportunity for doing well in the law and most other kinds of business he had never found elsewhere.

He was appointed, June 22, 1869, assessor of internal revenue for the eighth Massachusetts district, identical territorially with the eighth congressional district, then represented in congress by Hon. George F. Hoar, through whose kindness he received the appointment. He held the office until it was abolished. It was laborious and responsible, but with the aid of assistant assessors and clerks, its duties were performed by him to the satisfaction of the government at Washington and to the taxpayers of the district. The four years employment, during which he held this position, is said by Major Harlow to have been the most agreeable and remunerative of any of his life.

He again returned to the practice of law in Worcester, and continued in practice there until January, 1877, when he was appointed by the justices of the supreme judicial court assistant clerk of the courts for the county of Worcester for a three-year term, and held the office by successive re-appointments until January 1, 1904, when, pursuant to an intention of long standing to retire at the age of seventy-five years, and thereafter to take *cum otio* what of life might remain to him, he declined another appointment.

On retiring, he was surprised by his brethren of the Worcester bar by the tender of a banquet, whereat he was overwhelmed with expressions of their esteem, friendship and good will. And he has received not only from the bar, but from the justices of the courts, and the county commissioners of Worcester county cumulative assurances of their satisfaction with his discharge of his clerical duties.

Major Harlow spent the summer of 1904 abroad with his daughter. He is a member of the First Unitarian church of Worcester. In politics he is a Republican. He served on the school committee of Spencer and later at Worcester on the school board and as a director of the Free Public Library. He is a comrade of the George H. Ward Post, No. 10, Grand Army of the Republic, and a companion of the Military Order of the Loyal Legion of the United States, Massachusetts Commandery.

After his return form the war, at Spencer, May 31, 1863, Major Harlow married Jeannette Bemis, daughter of Lewis and Maria (Stearns) Bemis. Her father, a farmer, merchant and manufacturer, was born, lived and died in Spencer. He was the son of Joshua, grandson of another Joshua and great-grandson of Samuel Bemis, the second settler in Spencer, who came there from Watertown in 1721. Maria, wife of Lewis and mother of Jeannette Bemis, was the daughter of Charles and Elizabeth (McFarland) Stearns, of Worcester. Children of Major Harlow and wife, all born in Worcester, were: Frederick Bemis, see forward; Gideon, died in infancy; Margaret, see forward.

(IX) Frederick Bemis Harlow, son of Major Harlow (8), and named after his uncle First Lieutenant Frederick A. Bemis, of the Twenty-first Regiment, Massachusetts Volunteers, who was killed September 1, 1862, at Cantilly, Virginia, was fitted for college at the Worcester high school and entered Williams in 1881. After remaining there two years he entered Amherst (junior class) and was graduated there in 1885. He studied law, and was admitted to the Worcester bar in the superior court, February 24, 1888. He opened an office in Worcester and remained there in practice until May, 1900, when he removed to Paris, France, where he has since been practicing his profession.

(IX) Margaret Harlow, daughter of Major Harlow (8), graduated from the Worcester high school in 1891. She then went abroad and spent most of the next two years in the study of the German and French languages. Returning to Worcester she taught German in the Worcester high school until her mother's death, when she resigned her place as teacher to become her father's housekeeper.

Mrs. Harlow died January 11, 1901. Younger than her husband by nearly eight years, he had not expected to survive her. A true helpmeet to him in life, her death, sudden and unexpected, by apoplectic stroke, was to him an irreparable loss.

"Her children rise up, and call her blessed.
Her husband also, and he praiseth her, saying:
Many daughters have done virtuously,
But thou excellcth them all." *

HARLOW FAMILY. George Herbert Harlow, the present efficient and popular Register of Probate and Insolvency for Worcester county, is a descendant from William Harlow, who came to Massachusetts, and was proprietor in Sandwich, March, 1637, and removed to Plymouth, where he was a proprietor 1653. The line has been traced from this William through Arunah Harlow, of the sixth generation to the subject of this sketch. (See sketch of Major William Taylor Harlow.)

(VI) Arunah Harlow, son of Gideon Harlow (5), grandfather of George Herbert Harlow, of Worcester, was born in Duxbury, Massachusetts, January 29, 1773. He removed to Shrewsbury, Massachusetts, in 1798, where his brother had settled and where he became a prominent and highly respected citizen. He was a carpenter by trade and built the house, wherein he spent his remaining days, upon the lines of the Duxbury homestead. He married June 27, 1799 Sarah Banister, who died September 14, 1841, the daughter of Nathan and Sarah (Whitney) Banister, of Boylston, Massachusetts. Their children were: Sarah, born September 20, 1800, married September 9, 1824, Nathan Pratt, Jr. Eliza, born March 26, 1802, married May 4, 1826, Samuel A. Knox. Patience, born March 1, 1804, married, March 18, 1834, John Barnes, of Boylston, Massachusetts. Nancy, born August 7, 1806. Nathan Bannister, born September 2, 1808, married (intentions dated April 20) 1844, Louisa D. Kendall, of Warwick, Massachusetts. Clarissa, born May 2, 1811, married Christopher C. Doty. Arunah, Jr., born April 17, 1813, married, November 7, 1839, Maria C. Adams. Cleora Eager, born August 15, 1815, married Samuel G. Reed, of Worcester. John Thomas, born May 29, 1818, married Laura J. Wood. George Henry, born June 18, 1820, see forward.

(VII) George Henry Harlow, son of Arunah

*Prov. XXXI. 28 and 29, Revised Version

Harlow (6), was born at Shrewsbury, Massachusetts, June 18, 1820. He received his education in the common schools of that town and at the Worcester Academy and the State Normal school at Barre, and became a popular and successful school teacher in several towns of Worcester county. He settled in Worcester in 1850 where he was a merchant and fire insurance agent, his place of business being on Front street in the block afterward owned by Dr Frank H Kelly just east of William Bush's drug store, where Brewer & Company are now located. He continued in this store until 1861 when he returned to Shrewsbury and purchased the farm formerly belonging to his wife's father and known as the Dr Edward Flint place situated near the centre of the village, on the old Worcester turnpike. The house was built in 1752, in 1768 was owned by Dr Edward Flint and is at present owned by George Herbert Harlow, of Worcester. On this farm George Henry Harlow spent the remainder of his days, and died May 7, 1891. Aside from his merchant and farm interests he carried on a fire insurance business upwards of forty years representing the Merchants & Farmers Worcester Mutual Companies of Worcester and others.

He was a member of the Shrewsbury Congregational church. In politics he was a Republican from the organization of the party. Active earnest and steadfast prominent in the councils of the party and interested alike in town, state and national affairs, he was frequently elected delegate to important nominating conventions but never sought office for himself. He served on the school board of Worcester from ward four in 1855 and from ward six in 1856. After removing from Worcester to Shrewsbury he represented the district composed of that town and Grafton in the general court of 1873, being elected by the largest majority ever given a candidate for that office in the district. He was trusted by all men, regardless of political beliefs. For more than twenty-four years he was president of the Farmers and Mechanics Club of Shrewsbury, and was for many years a trustee of the Worcester Agricultural Society. He was widely known among Worcester county farmers, who held him in high esteem, and his enthusiasm for the work of the Farmers Club was characteristic, he had the nature of a leader and organizer and stirred others to action by his energy and example, and his influence was shown particularly in the annual fairs of the Farmers' Club.

He married Jane Flint, who was baptized December 22, 1822, the daughter of Major Josiah Flint who was born December 15, 1775 and his wife, Mary (Stone) Flint, daughter of Luther Stone, of Southboro, Massachusetts. Jane Flint was a granddaughter of Dr Edward Flint, who came from Concord Massachusetts to Shrewsbury in 1758 and bought the old homestead of eighty acres in 1768. She was a lineal descendant of Hon Thomas Flint, who came from Mattock Derbyshire England, to Concord in 1638 and died there October 3, 1653. Dr Edward Flint, grandson of the immigrant, Thomas Flint was surgeon in the expedition to Canada in the French and Indian war in 1758, and served with the Massachusetts Troops at Cambridge in 1775 in the revolution. He died November 13, 1813, aged eighty-five years. The only child of George Henry and Jane (Flint) Harlow is George Herbert, see forward.

(VIII) George Herbert Harlow, son of George Henry Harlow (7), was born in Worcester Massachusetts, educated there in the public schools, and at Shrewsbury and Worcester high schools. When a young man he entered the internal revenue office as clerk for Major William T Harlow, then assessor. He afterward became deputy collector of internal revenue under General Augustus B R Sprague, of Worcester, and Judge Adin Thayer. He was appointed assistant register of probate and insolvency for Worcester county, June 1, 1886, by Judge Adin Thayer, a position that he held until January 3, 1894, when he was elected the register, his present position. The high reputation of the Worcester county probate office for system neatness, accuracy and efficiency, speaks for his ability and his attention to the details of his position. In politics Mr Harlow is a Republican.

He is an active member in the Masonic order, was made a Master Mason February 12, 1892, in Quinsigamond Lodge of Worcester, became a member of Eureka Chapter of Royal Arch Masons April 26, 1892, of Hiram Council Royal and Select Masters May 3, 1892, of Worcester County Commandery, Knights Templar, June 23, 1892. Is a member of Worcester Lodge of Perfection, Goddard Council Princes of Jerusalem and Lawrence Chapter of Rose Croix, A and A S Rite. In 1876 he became one of the early members of the Worcester Continentals an independent military organization, organized that year in memory of the fathers of our country, for the purpose of preserving the customs and ideals of the Minute Men of Revolutionary days, a kindred organization of though not so old as the Ancient and Honorable Artillery Company of Boston, Mr Harlow was elected clerk of the company with rank of sergeant in 1878, and in 1891 was made first lieutenant and clerk upon the staff of Lieutenant-Colonel Aaron S Taft. He was elected to the command of the organization February 10, 1905, with the rank of lieutenant-colonel. He was for some years a member and secretary of the Hancock Club. He is a member of the Commonwealth Club and of the Tatassit Canoe Club, both of Worcester.

He married Ella Eliza Walker daughter of Appleton and Zibah (Beaman) Walker, of Worcester. She is a member of the Worcester Home Club, the Worcester Woman's Club and of the Colonel Timothy Bigelow Chapter, Daughters of the American Revolution.

PORTER FAMILY. Richard Porter, who settled in Weymouth, Massachusetts, in 1635, embarked at Weymouth, England, before March 20, 1635. He was a farmer, and a man of unusual activity and prominence in the colony. He was admitted a freeman May 18, 1653, and held several important offices. He died in 1689. His will was dated December 25, 1685 and proved December 26, 1689, bequeathing to Thomas only son of deceased son Thomas, to son John, to grandchildren Ruth Richards and Samuel Bayly, and to daughter Mary Bicknell. He married Ruth, daughter of Mary Bicknell. Their children: 1 John, mentioned below. 2 Ruth, born October 3, 1639, married September 19, 1660, Thomas Bailey, Jr. 3 Thomas, married Sarah Vining. 4 Mary, married January 2, 1659, John Bicknell.

(II) John Porter, son of Richard Porter (1), was like his father prominent in the affairs of Weymouth. He gave the Common to the town, built the first saw mill, and held various town offices and had a large estate. He married Deliverance, daughter of Nicholas and Martha (Shaw) Byram. He died September 8, 1717, she died September 30, 1720. Children: 1 Mary, born October 12, 1663, married William Pittee. 2 Susannah, born June 2, 1665, married Matthew Pratt. 3 John, born July 2, 1667. 4 Samuel, born 1670, mentioned below 5 Nicholas, married Bathsheba Reed 6 Ruth, married September 18, 1776, Nathaniel Willis 7 Thomas, married Susanna Pratt 8 Ebenezer, married Sarah Humphrey 9 Sarah, married John Dingley

(III) Samuel Porter, son of John Porter (2), was born about 1670, in Weymouth, and died August 31, 1725 He also lived in his native town, and held town offices there About 1705 he removed to Abington, where he lived the rest of his life He was a schoolmaster as well as a shoemaker and farmer He was assessor of Abington in 1716, selectman 1714, 1715, 1716, 1717 He was an original member of the Abington Church He married, 1698, Mary Nash, daughter of Jacob and Abigail (Dyer) Nash Children 1 Samuel, born May 14, 1699, mentioned below 2 Mary, born October 5, 1701 3 David, born 1702 4 Jacob, born August 10, 1704 5 Hannah, born December 16, 1712 6 John, died young 7 John, born February 2, 1716 8 Abigail, born June 23, 1719

(IV) Samuel Porter, son of Samuel Porter (3), was born at Abington, May 14, 1699 He settled in Bridgewater, and married Sarah Joslyn, daughter of Joseph and Sarah (Ford) Joslyn Children 1 Sarah, born May 26, 1723 2 Mary, born February 9, 1725 3 Samuel, born October 12, 1727 4 Joseph, born February 27, 1730, mentioned below 5 Ebenezer, born September 15, 1731 6 Mary, born August 3, 1733 7 Adam, born February 24, 1735 8 Hannah, born February 18, 1736 9 Bettina, born September 23, 1737 10 Noah, born May 13, 1740 11 Jonathan, born August 27, 1741, married Mary Chipman, 1763 12 Deliverance, born July 19, 1742 13 Abigail, born July 7, 1743 14 Tabitha, born 1744, married Samuel Brown, Jr 15 Sarah, born 1757, married Noah Tinkham

(V) Joseph Porter, son of Samuel Porter (4), was born in Abington, February 27, 1730 and died at Canton, Massachusetts, in 1803 He resided at East Bridgewater and Stoughton, now Canton He was a lieutenant of his company in the Massachusetts troops in the revolution He married Elizabeth, daughter of Samuel and Content (Whitcomb) Burrill Their first seven children were born at Bridgewater, the others at Canton His wife and daughters were women of remarkable beauty Children 1 Elizabeth, born November 8, 1753 2 Joseph, born June 10, 1754 3 Hannah, born July 21, 1758 4 Robert, born March 30, 1762 5 Isaac, born February 23, 1765 6 Content, born February 5, 1767 7 Mehitable, born April 15, 1769 8 Libbeus, born at Stoughton April 22, 1771 9 Cyrus, born at Stoughton December 23, 1774

(VI) Colonel Cyrus Porter, son of Joseph Porter (5), was born December 23, 1774 and died May 29, 1856 He married (intention dated November 30), 1799, Rebecca French, born at Canton, May 4, 1782, daughter of William and Mary (Perkins) French He married (second), September 8, 1835, Martha Alden, widow of Calvin Alden, daughter of Ebenezer Hayden They resided in Stoughton, where he was a prominent citizen He was a farmer He rose to the command of his regiment Children 1 Oliver, born October 16, 1800, married Caleb Copeland, Jr 2 Ahira, born November 9, 1801, mentioned below 3 Rebecca, born November 11, 1803, died May 25, 1804 4 Rebecca born 1805, married Marcus Copeland 5 Cyrus, born June 12, 1807, married Eliza J Dunbar 6 Mehitable, born December 3 1808, married Ezra Churchill 7 Eliza Ann, married, April 5, 1829, William Hall 8 Luther, born December 18, 1814, married Lucy Talbot 9 William French, born January 23, 1823 The order of birth is not known exactly

(VII) Ahira Porter, son of Cyrus Porter (6), was born in Stoughton, November 9, 1807, died December 6, 1863 He was a mechanic residing in Stoughton, married, 1826, Rachel D Swan, who died November 4, 1861 Children 1 Ahira Swan, born January 30, 1827 2 Rachel D, born December 27, 1827 3 William, born August 30, 1831 4 Samuel, born June 27, 1833, mentioned below 5 James, born October 4, 1835 6 George N, born January 30, 1843

(VIII) Samuel Porter, son of Ahira Porter (7), was born at Stoughton, June 27, 1833 He spent his youth in his native town and attended school there When a young man he came to Worcester and engaged in the wood working business, but later turned his entire attention to the manufacture of lasts for shoe manufacturers, and established the industry with which his name is associated in the business world His son succeeded him in the business

Mr Porter was a member of the Masonic order He was a Republican in politics and a member of the Universalist Church He married, first, November 26, 1857, Sarah Chamberlin, daughter of Benjamin and Patience Chamberlin, of Marion, Massachusetts She died May 18, 1865 He married (second), June 1, 1870, Helen Frances Kendall, of Portland, Maine He married (third) Emma G Putnam, nee Wingate, daughter of Aaron and Phoebe I (Lamos) Wingate She married (first) E J Putnam, of North Grafton, Massachusetts, he died August 28, 1891 She married (second) Samuel Porter, as stated above, July 4 1894, he died February 16, 1904 The children of Aaron and Phoebe Wingate, her parents, were Sarah, died 1828, Anne Susan, born January 12, 1830, George, born July 12, 1832, Edward P and Ann Martha, died in infancy, Elizabeth C, born May 31, 1841, Emma G, born January 6, 1844 The children by the two wives of Samuel Porter were Addie Lester, born July 9, 1859, died September 24, 1865, Walter Chamberlin, May 13, 1865, Marian Kendall, September 28, 1874

(IX) Walter Chamberlin Porter, son of the late Samuel (8) and Sarah (Chamberlin) Porter, was born in Worcester, May 13, 1865 He married Louisa Phillips, of Worcester, who died January 4, 1905 He has succeeded to his father's business of last making with W E Bigelow, conducting business under the old name of Samuel Porter & Co, at 25 Union street He resides at 10 Lenox street His children are Helen Irene, born June 24 1889, Oscar Stanley, November 3, 1892

HILDRETH FAMILY Richard Hildreth (1) was the emigrant ancestor of the well known Hildreth family of Worcester county, to which Charles H Hildreth, 1, Charles H Hildreth, 2, and George F Hildreth, of Worcester, belong Richard Hildreth was an early settler in Cambridge and Woburn He was admitted a freeman May 10 1643 He was one of the founders of Chelmsford, Massachusetts, and had a special grant of land in 1663 on account of having lost his right hand A full account of the emigrant is given in the sketch of Andrew G Hildreth elsewhere in this work The children of Richard Hildreth were James, Joseph born April 16 1658, Persis, born February 8, 1659, Thomas, born February 1, 1664, Isaac, born July, 1663, Ephraim

(II) Joseph Hildreth, son of Sergeant Richard Hildreth (1), was born at Chelmsford, Massachusetts, April 16, 1658 He married Abigail Wilson, of Woburn, Massachusetts, December 12, 1683 He died January 28, 1706 Among his children were Joseph, born November 30, 1695, Ephraim, born at Chelmsford, settled at Westford, Massachusetts, and had twelve children there

(III) Joseph Hildreth, son of Joseph Hildreth (2), was born November 30, 1695, died in 1780 in Westford, where he settled, aged eighty-five years in 1780 He lived in what is known as Minot's Corner He married (first) Deliverance —— He married (second) Abigail Hill, of Billerica The children of Joseph and Deliverance Hildreth were Ephraim, born 1718, Jonathan, 1722, Phineas, born 1725, Hannah, born 1726, William, born 1728, Wilson, born 1731, Hannah, born 1738 The children of Joseph and Abigail (Hill) Hildreth were Ezekiel, born 1744, died young, Hosea, born 1744-5, Timothy, born 1746, died young, Abigail, born 1747, Hannah, born 1750, Ezekiel, born 1753, Timothy (2), born 1756

(IV) Timothy Hildreth, son of Joseph Hildreth (3), was born in Westford, Massachusetts, December 31, 1756 He married Hannah Hildreth Richard Hildreth, the historian, who was his grandson, said of him "My grandfather emigrated to Cavendish Vermont, and there cut out for himself a farm in the woods, but he soon returned to Massachusetts and passed the greater part of his life on a farm in Sterling He had ten children Hosea, his third son, was my father" Timothy Hildreth responded to the call to arms April 19, 1775, and went to Boston with the Westford company After the battle of Bunker Hill he was ordered to drive a yoke of oxen hauling fascines for the American breastworks at Nooks Hill on the peninsular The work required great patience and endurance as it had to be done at night over bad roads The drivers could not even speak to the oxen In after years he admitted that he shed youthful tears of vexation over the hardships of his work there At the same time he expressed the greatest indignation at the transformation of Faneuil Hall by the British soldiers into a theatre for amateur performances and the use of Old South Church for a riding school After his service he returned to Westford, where he married Hannah Hildreth She was descended from Richard Hildreth (1) also as follows

(II) Ephraim Hildreth, son of Richard Hildreth (1), and great-grandfather of Hannah Hildreth, who married Timothy Hildreth, was born in Chelmsford, Massachusetts He moved to Dracut in 1710 He owned land near the Providence Meadows in Westford, Massachusetts He was a grantee of Concord, New Hampshire He married Anna Moore, of Lancaster, Massachusetts His children were Joseph, born 1688, Abigail, born 1691, James, born 1692, died young, Ebenezer, born 1696, James born 1698, Anna, born 1703, Thomas, born 1707, Jacob, born 1709, David, born 1711, Josiah

(III) James Hildreth, son of Ephraim Hildreth (2), was born 1698, in Westford, Massachusetts He settled there and married Dorothy —— He lived on the place lately owned by J Boynton Reed His children were Rebecca, Zechariah, born 1728, Amos born 1730, Dorothy, born 1732, died 1735, Dorothy, born 1736, married Pelatiah Fletcher, Lucy, born 1742, Samuel, born 1744, died 1748

(IV) Zechariah Hildreth, son of James Hildreth (3), was born in Westford, Massachusetts, 1728 He married 1753, Elizabeth Prescott, daughter of Jonas and Elizabeth Prescott Their children were Zechariah born 1754, at Westford, Elizabeth, born 1755 at Westford, Hannah, born at Westford 1758, Timothy, born at Westford, 1760, James, born at Westford, 1762, Lucy, born at Westford, 1764, Jonas, born at Westford, 1766, Ruth, born at Westford, 1768, Ed, born at Westford, 1771, Jesse, born at Westford, 1773, Hita, born 1775

(V) Hannah Hildreth, daughter of Zechariah Hildreth (IV), was born in Westford, Massachusetts, 1758 She married Timothy Hildreth

Timothy Hildreth settled in West Boylston, Massachusetts, about 1800, after his return from Vermont In 1803 he removed to the town of Sterling and spent the remainder of his days there He made his will April 29, 1816, and it was proved May 20, 1817 His wife Hannah was made his legatee and executor and all the heirs consented in writing to the probate of the will The names of the heirs were Richard Hildreth, Timothy Hildreth, Hosea Hildreth, Abel F Hildreth, Nabby Hildreth, Joseph Hildreth, Sophia (Hildreth) Robinson and her husband, Winthrop Robinson, Hannah Patten and her husband James P Patten Ezekiel was probably out west and did not sign The children of Timothy and Hannah Hildreth were Timothy, lived at Sterling, Hosea, father of Richard Hildreth, the historian was an instructor in Philips Exeter Academy, graduated at Harvard College in 1805, settled minister at Gloucester, Massachusetts, Ezekial, graduated at Harvard in 1814 taught school at Wheeling, Virginia, married —— Zane, of the family for which Zanesville, Ohio, was named, Abel Fletcher, graduated at Harvard in 1818, was a teacher in the Riverside Academy Auburndale, Massachusetts, Nabby (sic), Joseph Sophia, married Winthrop Robinson, Hannah, married James P Patten, Richard, an infant, Sarah, probably

(V) Timothy Hildreth, son of Timothy Hildreth (1), was born at Westford Massachusetts or Cavendish Vermont, about 1780 He was a farmer and settled at Sterling, Massachusetts, where he came with his father in 1803 He married Eunice Sawyer, of Sterling They had six children Thomas, James Dwight, born June 8, 1808, George, married Sophia Howe had no children, John, never married, Sarah, never married, Sophia, married Samuel Howe, of Sterling, Massachusetts, Mrs Howe was living in 1905, her husband was a blacksmith by trade, their children were Samuel, never married John, his two children, William, unmarried, Martha, widow of —— Ryder

(VI) James Dwight Hildreth, son of Timothy Hildreth (5), was born in Sterling Massachusetts, June 8, 1808, died December 16, 1865 He married Betsey E Weston, a widow born Winn, September 8 1801 She had one daughter, Elizabeth Jane Weston, by her first marriage who married E W Johnson, of West Boylston Massachusetts, and is living in West Boylston Betsey E Hildreth died November 23 1894 at the age of ninety-three years, having made her home with her son, George F Hildreth for thirty-two years The children of James Dwight and Betsey E Hildreth were James Nelson born August 13 1833 in West Boylston, Massachusetts George Francis, born in Sterling, January 22 1836, Charles Henry, born in West Boylston November 5 1837, John Harvard born June 2 1839, in West Boylston, died in Grafton, Massachusetts, January 11, 1894, Henrietta Sophia, born in Rutland Massachusetts July 12, 1841, died in Worcester May 5 1863, Sarah Ann, born in Rutland April 22, 1844 married June 30, 1867, Alonzo Smith, Georgianna Elizabeth, born in Rutland June 23 1846, married, June, 1870, Alphonso Smith

James Dwight Hildreth spent most of his life in West Boylston and Sterling He was on his

Bertha A Thomas

Carl. C. T. Thomas.

father's farm until seventeen years old He was well known as the driver of a six-horse team from Leominster to Boston and various other points in New England in the days when freight was transported in that way He carried chairs and farm produce from Leominster to Boston and on the return trip brought dry goods and West India goods Later he owned his own team and drove from Sterling to Boston He at various times drove teams from Gardner to Boston and Gardner to Providence He was noted as a skillful horseman and whip and for his knowledge of horses

(VII) James Nelson Hildreth, son of James Dwight Hildreth (6), was born in West Boylston, Massachusetts August 13, 1833 He married Mary Frances Meaghan They had seven children Charles Henry, Everett died young, Frederick Albert, Effie, married Charles Poole of Worcester, Nettie, married Fred Fisher, bookkeeper, of Worcester and their children are Harry Woodbury, and Clayton Fay Fisher Clifford W, Maud

(VII) George Francis Hildreth, son of James Dwight Hildreth (6), was born in Sterling, Massachusetts, January 22, 1836 He attended the common schools of his native town and worked at home until twenty-one He then went to Worcester and for two years worked for the city In 1859 he engaged in the grain business in West Boylston but at the end of twenty years sold out and retired from active business After a year, during which time he was in charge of the grist mill of Reuel G Cowee, he became a partner The business was one of the largest in the vicinity The mill and grain business at West Boylston were destroyed by the building of the Metropolitan water basin at West Boylston Mr Hildreth for the past few years has lived in Worcester at 5 Newton avenue He was a trustee of the West Boylston cemetery and until 1897 superintendent Mr and Mrs Hildreth are member of the West Boylston Congregational church, and Mr Hildreth served for twenty-five years on the parish committee He married, May 1, 1861, Mary Cowee, daughter of Reuel Green Cowee, with whom he was in partnership, the grandfather of E A Cowee, who is now proprietor of the grain business conducted by his father and grandfather (See sketch of the Cowee Family in this work)

(VIII) Charles H Hildreth, son of James Nelson Hildreth (7) was born in West Boylston, Massachusetts October 2, 1857 He attended school at West Boylston but came to Worcester when a young boy He went into business with Charles H Hildreth, first, in a livery stable business on Market street, Worcester In 1890 Mr Hildreth established the stable at 10 Sever street, which he has since conducted successfully He was for four years in the city council in 1895-96 was in the common council and in 1897-98 in the board of aldermen In the council he did good work for the city on the street committee and in the board of aldermen was on the street water, legislature committees and the special committee on grade crossings He is prominent in the Republican organization He is a Free Mason He married (first) Ada Elizabeth Rockwood, of Leicester, Massachusetts, and (second) Addie Elizabeth Kennon, of Worcester He has no children

(VIII) Frederick Albert Hildreth brother of C H Hildreth, Jr married Elise Lord, of Worcester and their children are Charles H, Harold, Everett and Randolph Lord Hildreth

(VII) Charles Henry Hildreth, son of James Dwight Hildreth (6), was born in West Boylston, Massachusetts, November 5 1837 He has always been in the sale stable and livery business For many years he had a stable at Newton square, Worcester He is at present the superintendent of the city stables of Worcester He is a veteran of the civil war He married Sarah Luce, a widow, who was a native of Maine, but her parents moved when she was very young to West Boylston They have an adopted daughter Lillian Hildreth

(VII) John Harvard Hildreth, son of James Dwight Hildreth (6), was born June 2, 1839, in West Boylston, Massachusetts He married Ruth Lincoln They have two children Herbert H, and Etta E John H Hildreth died at Grafton, Massachusetts January 11, 1894

(VII) Sarah Ann Hildreth, daughter of James Dwight Hildreth (6), was born in Rutland, Massachusetts, April 22 1844 She married, June 30, 1867, Alonzo Smith, who is in the express business in Worcester, Massachusetts They have no children

(VII) Georgianna Elizabeth Hildreth, daughter of James Dwight Hildreth (6), was born in Rutland, Massachusetts, June 23, 1846 She married, June, 1870, Alphonso Smith, who is with the Worcester Hardware Company, 556 Main street, Worcester They have several children

AUGUST E DICK, the surviving partner of the well known firm of Thomas & Co, cabinet makers and carvers, manufacturers of church furniture with shops at 110 Exchange street and 151 Union street, was born in Saxony, Germany, March 13, 1858 He is the son of A F Dick, a weaver by trade

Mr Dick started for America, July 1, 1872, with his parents They settled at Lawrence, Massachusetts He worked in the Washington mills there, and at the age of nineteen learned the trade of carpenter He came to Worcester to work for Cutting & Bishop, contractors and builders, and worked steadily for that firm for eleven years Then he accepted a position with Thomas & Co which was established in the seventies, at No 47 Foster street, of which later he became a partner and is now the only surviving member of the firm He is a member of the Worcester Social Turn Verein He married Annie O Behrmann, of Lawrence, in that city Their children are Minnie H, born August 21, 1887, Annie, born in Worcester, May 8, 1889, George, born in Worcester, February 9, 1891, August, born in Worcester, October 23, 1892

CARL C T THOMAS Frederick Carl Thomas, father of the late Carl C T Thomas, of Worcester, was a native of Mecklenberg, Germany He married Mary Frederika Sass a native of Sweden and they made their home in Pomerania, Prussia He was a wheelwright by trade His wife died in 1849 and he married again He was employed by a nobleman, Herr Wehard Von Heiden A conversation between the employer and the workman made a strong impression on Carl when a boy of about twelve When asked what Carl was going to do when he was grown up Mr Thomas said that he expected the boy to learn his trade of wheelwright Then the shrewd German gave him this advice "Whatever trade he learns, let him be familiar with the use of the tools that he makes" That is good advice for any maker of tools or machines to follow

In 1853 the father started for America with his wife her baby, and the three children of the first marriage He died on shipboard and when the unfortunate little family reached New York, the mother and infant were sent to Ward's Island The child died soon afterward and the mother left the island and was never heard of again by her stepchildren The other children Carl C T, John, and Mary Christine, were sent to the Five Points Mission House of Industry Carl soon found work in New York, and after a time the other two children were sent to Marblehead Massachusetts, where John was employed in a hotel rowing a small boat from the shore to an island hotel in Salem harbor When the civil war broke out John enlisted in the Forty-fourth Massachusetts Regiment, and served nine months in the vicinity of Newbern, North Carolina When he returned from the service he went to work for Edward Hixon of Cambridgeport, Massachusetts, for whom he had worked before enlisting He became an expert cabinet maker He died unmarried

Mary Christine was brought up by a Marblehead family She married Charles Ewell, of Abington, Massachusetts, and resided in Worcester Massachusetts, and Chicago, Illinois Both are dead They had a son Carl Ewell, born 1889 who survives them

Carl C T Thomas, son of Frederick Carl Thomas, before mentioned, born in Pomerania, Prussia, June 22, 1838, died in Worcester, May 31, 1905 He started in life under the most depressing conditions, being left alone in a strange country with a younger brother and sister unprovided for He knew something of the wood-working business and found employment in the cabinet shop of Shaeffer & Suckow, manufacturers of fine furniture He and Anton Burckel who was afterwards his partner in business, learned the trade together The shop was at 127 Anthony street, later on Mulberry street, New York

In 1859 he removed to Beverly, Massachusetts, in order to be with his brother and sister, and he contributed to their support He enlisted in July 1861, in Company D, Fourteenth Massachusetts Regiment, and served three years He was wounded June 19, 1864 in the battle of Spottsylvania, and sent home by way of Fredericksburg His regiment was in the Second Army Corps, in General Birney's division General Mott's brigade, General Hancock commanding Anton Burckel was in the same company and both were transferred to the heavy artillery After the war he worked at his trade in Beverly, Boston and Cambridge, Massachusetts, and finally decided to locate in Worcester He worked first for William G Anderson & Company, cabinet makers, corner of Union and Exchange streets for a short time He did wood carving for various furniture makers and builders In the early seventies he formed a partnership with Elisha Witherell under the firm name of Thomas & Company, and established his business as cabinet maker A year later his partner died In 1873 his old friend and comrade Anton Burckel became his partner, the firm name remaining the same Their shop was then at 91 Exchange street and they made a specialty of wood-carving and machine work, later they removed to the Baker building where they carried on cabinet making on a larger scale After Mr Burckel left the business, Mr Thomas took another partner, Edward Minault who was a member of the firm for two years After that he was alone in business until his son was old enough to join the firm This son John Thomas, died July 11 1893 again leaving the senior partner the sole proprietor His shop was then at 110 Exchange street He took in November 1897 as his last and surviving partner, August E Dick who now conducts the business (See sketch of Mr Dick)

The firm of Thomas & Company has done the finest interior wood-work, such as church altars and pews, in the churches of Worcester, and in fact, all over New England The firm always prospered and never met with failure in business Mr. Thomas was a member of George H Ward Post, Grand Army, Athelstan Lodge of Free Masons, Encampment 83, Union Veterans, Stella Chapter, Order of the Eastern Star He was a man of kindly, sympathetic nature, who made many friends His generous care of his orphan brother and sister, to whom he took the place of father and mother, was but an instance of his character

He married December 11, 1865, Louise D Allen, daughter of Samuel Allen (3) (mentioned below in the Allen family sketch) She was born September 4, 1839, and resides at the home 66 Jaques avenue Their children were 1 John Carl, born January 1, 1868, educated in Worcester, was his father's partner, died July 11, 1896 2 Louisa Augusta, born October 3, 1870, married Charles Amos Black January 23, 1895, their children are—Arline Mildred born August 15, 1897 Harold Everett, born October 27, 1899 3 Bertha Allen, born September 9, 1872, was educated in the Worcester public schools and was prominent in the Old South church died at Pine Bluff, North Carolina, March 30, 1906, buried in Worcester 4 Talbot and 5 Susan Anna, born August 9 1877 (twins) died April 6 1890 All of the children were born in Worcester, Massachusetts, with the exception of the eldest, who was born at Beverly, Massachusetts

ALLEN FAMILY (I) William Allen the immigrant ancestor of Mrs Carl C T Thomas, of Worcester, Massachusetts, was born in Manchester, England, about 1602, according to a deposition made November 30, 1664 He was one of the Dorchester company on Cape Ann in 1623, and he went to Salem with Roger Conant in 1626 He applied for freemanship October 19 1630, and was admitted May 18 1631 He served on the jury in 1637 and was one of the grantees of Jeffreys Creek in 1640, but was not then a resident Jeffreys Creek is that part of Salem now the town of Manchester He removed to Jeffreys Creek before it was incorporated as a town May 14 1645, and was one of the petitioners for the division of the town He sold his house and land in Salem in 1652, but was one of the first board of selectmen of Manchester He was called an influential and enterprising citizen, was a carpenter by trade When he deposed in 1664 that he had lived in Salem for thirty-eight years he must have included his residence in Manchester as being formerly Salem

He married (first) Alice ——, who died March 8, 1631-2, and (second) Elizabeth Bradley who probably survived him He and his wife Elizabeth were among the early members of the Salem church He made his will June 7, 1678 (?) and it was proved June 26 1679 He died May 10 1679 Children of William and Alice Allen were 1 Persis, born and died 1630 2 Samuel, mentioned below The children of William and Elizabeth Allen were 3 Elizabeth, born September, 1634 4 Deborah, born April 1637 5 Bethia, baptized January 16 1630-40 6 Onesiphorus born June 30, 1642 7 William baptized March 31 1646 8 Jonathan, baptized July 29, 1649, probably died young

(II) Samuel Allen son of William Allen (1), born in Salem, January 8 1631-2 Like his father he was a housewright or carpenter, and became a man of property and standing He was a selectman in 1676-77-88-93 in the town of Manchester and held other positions of trust He married Sarah —— who was living in 1695 His will dated

November 21, 1702, was disallowed December 5, 1709 Children of Samuel and Sarah Allen were 1 Samuel, born August 2, 1663 2 John, born February 12, 1666 3 Sarah, born March 12, 1668 4 William, born March 18, 1670 5 Joseph, born June 26, 1672 6 Alice, born September 20, 1674 7 Rachel, born February 19, 1677 8 Elizabeth, born March 18, 1679 9 Benjamin, born June 4, 1681 10. Jonathan, born September 4, 1684

(III) Samuel Allen, eldest child of Samuel Allen (2), born in Manchester, Massachusetts, August 4, 1663, was a fisherman in his younger days and later a trader, residing in Manchester He married Abigail Williams, at Marblehead, March 17, 1687 She was living in 1720, and administration was granted on his estate February 4, 1744 Children, all born in Manchester, were 1 Sarah, born July 4, 1687 2 Abigail born June 10, 1690 3 Samuel, mentioned below 4 Hannah, born May 22, 1695 5 Rachel, born October 1, 1698 6 Daniel, born August 1, 1701 7 Martha born January 26, 1706-7 8 Jerusha, born January 24, 1712

(IV) Samuel Allen, son of Samuel Allen (3), born in Manchester, October 7, 1692, was a fisherman and farmer, and lived in his native town He was the town clerk there in 1740, and a selectman in 1753 He married Sarah Tuck, May 1, 1717 She was living in 1754 and he in 1758 Their children were 1 Sarah, baptized in Manchester Church May 31, 1719 2 Hannah, born April 29, 1721 3 Samuel, mentioned below 4 Ambrose, born December 27, 1724 5 Jeremiah, born April 16, 1727 6 Jerusha, born August 24, 1729 7 William, born June 9, 1731 8 John, born July 30, 1733 9 Abigail, born April 29 1737 10 Joseph, born December 3, 1738 11 Dorcas, born August 3, 1740 12 Michael, born August 22, 1742 13 Mary, born March 23, 1745

(V) Samuel Allen, third child of Samuel Allen (4), born in Manchester, March 4, 1722-3, was farmer, fisherman and trader at different periods, residing in Manchester He married February 20, 1750-1, Sarah Marsters, of Manchester, who died February 27, 1815, at the age of eighty-six years He died December 12, 1814, aged ninety-one years Their children were 1 and 2 Twins, born and died 1752, unnamed 3 Benjamin Marsters, born May 1, 1753 4 Ruth, born July 25, 1755 5 Samuel, born September 25 1757 6 Ede, born December 11, 1761 7 Nathaniel Marsters, born November 3, 1767, mentioned below

(VII) Nathaniel Marsters Allen, youngest child of Samuel Allen (6), born in Manchester November 3, 1767, resided in Manchester and married there Elizabeth Lee, of that town, December 10, 1789 She died February 28, 1847, aged eighty years and he died January 31, 1855, aged eighty-nine years Their children, all born in Manchester, were 1 Sarah, born February 22 1791 2 Elizabeth, born January 22, 1793 3 Nathaniel, born May 14, 1795 4 Samuel born February 7, 1799, mentioned below 5 Lydia, born December 18, 1801 6 Benjamin, born April 8, 1803

(VIII) Samuel Allen, fourth child of Samuel Marsters Allen (7), born in Manchester, February 7, 1799, married Nabby Smith, of Beverly Their children were 1 Elizabeth Allen born August 6, 1829 2 Mary T, born January 26, 1831 3 Sarah M, born December 5, 1833 4 Abby S, born February 9, 1835 5 Lydia S, born March 24, 1837 6 Augusta W (twin), born September 4, 1839 7 Louise D (twin), born September 4, 1839, mentioned above in sketch of Carl C T Thomas, her husband 8 Eva, born January 4,

1842 9 Samuel L, born April 22, 1844 10 Susan, born September 6, 1847

WINSLOW HARLAND ROBINSON John Robinson (1), the emigrant ancestor of Winslow Harland Robinson, of Worcester, Massachusetts, is believed to have been born in Buoytown, Scotland, about 1770 He certainly was of Scottish birth He came to America when a young man and settled on Tinkers Island, Mt Desert, Maine He married Betsey Fogg, probably at Mt Desert, and afterward settled at Machiasport He was a man of extraordinary physique, and at the age of ninety-nine years or thereabouts, in 1869, rowed from Machiasport to Jonesport to shoot ducks He must have been taken ill after he landed on Fisherman's Island, for there he was found by two men, nearly frozen to death By his side were six ducks that he had shot He was taken to the mainland and nursed, but did not survive the exposure He died the following day His wife lived until after 1856 The children of John and Betsey (Fogg) Robinson were James, married Harriet Small, Stephen, William, married Jane Sanborn, Hiram, lost at sea, Rachel, married a Mr Callaghan, Louise, married a Mr Merritt, Lucy married a Mr Robbins, Eleanor, married John Huntley, Clara, Julia, married Stephen Huntley

(II) James Robinson, son of John Robinson (1), was born in Machiasport, Maine, in 1811, and died there in 1898 He married Harriet Small He was a seafaring man, and became a captain His death at the age of eighty-seven was due to an accident The children of James and Harriet (Small) Robinson were Edgar, born at Machiasport, married Lorena Smith, Elenor, born in Machiasport, married Charles Holmes, Fred born in Machiasport, married Maggie Hay, was lost at sea, Flora, born in Machiasport, unmarried, Rosa, born in Machiasport, married Lee Pike, Winslow H, born at Machiasport, April 17, 1861, Frank, born in Machiasport, married Annie Small

(III) Winslow Harland Robinson, son of James Robinson (2), was born Machiasport, Maine, April 17, 1861 He was sent to the district schools of his native town until he was seventeen, when he left home to learn the ship caulker's trade He had some experience as a mariner, having sailed on his father's ship He came to Worcester in 1882, when he was twenty-one He went to work for W O Wilder, who had a tin shop at 153 Front street, and was a dealer in stoves, furnaces, etc, and learned his trade there When Mr Wilder sold out next year to T B Foss, Mr Robinson was employed by his successor with whom he remained for five years In 1889 Mr Robinson engaged in business for himself, dealing in furnaces and steam and hot water heaters. His first store was at 20 Lincoln square Two years later he removed to 47 and 49 Main street, near Lincoln square, where he was located for nine years Then he removed to his present quarters, 1 Lincoln square, at 3 Prescott street, in the rear of the old Salisbury mansion He has made a specialty of hot air furnace work, tin copper, sheet iron work He has installed in Worcester alone over six hundred furnaces He has been successful in business and stands well among the business men of the city

Mr Robinson is a well known Free Mason, having taken all the thirty-two degrees of Masonry He is also a member of the Odd Fellows order He is a member of Adams Square Congregational Church He resides at 7 Lyford street, near Brittan square

He married Ida May Smith, daughter of Charles

B Smith, a farmer, of Denmark Maine Mr and Mrs Robinson have a cottage at Denmark, where they spend their summer vacations Their children are Paul W, born October 25, 1894, Ruth M, born in Worcester, September 2, 1896, Marion B, born in Worcester, February 14, 1898, Stanley S born in Worcester, March 5, 1901

ANDREW GARDNER HILDRETH Richard Hildreth (1) was the emigrant ancestor of Andrew Gardner Hildreth, of Worcester, Massachusetts He settled first at Cambridge, Massachusetts, where he was admitted a freeman May 10, 1643 He was a town officer in Cambridge in 1645 He removed to Woburn, Massachusetts He signed the petition dated May 10, 1653, with twenty-eight others, for the town subsequently named Chelmsford He was before that a petitioner for Woburn and Concord The Chelmsford town records show that Sergeant Hildreth received prior to March 3, 1663, from the general court, grants of eight separate lots of land amounting to one hundred and five acres In 1664 the general court allowed him one hundred and fifty acres additional, on account of his having lost his right hand

It is believed that Richard Hildreth and his son James were the ancestors from which all the Hildreth families of the country are descended Richard Hildreth died in 1688, aged eighty-three years Elizabeth, wife of Richard died at Malden, August 3, 1693 aged sixty-eight

Sergeant Hildreth made his will February 9, 1686, in which he mentions his wife Elizabeth and various children The children of Sergeant Hildreth were 1 James, born 1631 (by the first wife of Sergeant Richard Hildreth) 2 Elizabeth, born September 21, 1646 3 Sarah, born August 8 1648 4 Joseph born April 16 1658, married Abigail Wilson, December 12, 1683, he died January 28, 1706 5 Persis, born February 8, 1659-60 6 Thomas, born February 1, 1661-2 7 Isaac, born July, 1663 8 Abigail, married Moses Parker, of Chelmsford 9 (Probably one of the eldest—mentioned as "natural" in the will) Ephraim, of Stowe to whom the Chelmsford homestead was beqeauthed

(II) James Hildreth son of Sergeant Richard Hildreth (1), was probably born in England in 1631, according to an affidavit made September 30, 1651, to be found in the Middlesex files This affidavit establishes the fact that Richard was his father He was a freeman in 1665

He died intestate The estate was administered by his son-in-law, Israel Proctor The division of the estate in 1695 names the children then living in the order of birth James Hildreth married Margaret Ward, June 1 1659 He died April 14, 1695 Children were Richard the eldest son Margaret, married Israel Proctor, Abigail, Dorothy, Ephraim

(III) Major Ephraim Hildreth, son of James Hildreth (2) born in Chelmsford Massachusetts, January 9 1680, died in Dracut formerly part of Chelmsford September 26, 1740 married Mercy (Parish) Richardson in 1707 She was the daughter of Lieutenant Josiah and Mercy (Parish) Richardson was born January 9 1688 in Chelmsford died December 25 1743 in Dracut Mercy Parish, her mother was the daughter of Robert and Elizabeth (Blanchard) Parish of Groton, Massachusetts Lieutenant Josiah Richardson was son of Captain Josiah and Remembrance (Underwood) Richardson Captain Josiah Richardson was the son of Ezekiel and Susannah Richardson of Woburn (See Richardson Family)

Ephraim seems to have been a surveyor and was repeatedly employed by the town During his early life he was a resident of Chelmsford, and after the part of the town in which he lived became Dracut he became identified with the history of the new town He was town clerk of Dracut most of the time from 1713 to his death in 1740, and was succeeded as clerk by his son Ephraim It is rather remarkable that the succession continued through four generations After Ephraim, Jr, came William and William, Jr, in direct line On March 3, 1800, Lieutenant Israel Hildreth was chosen town clerk, making the fifth Hildreth in successive generations to hold the position

Major Hildreth was a commissioner September 3, 1734 from Dracut to other neighboring towns concerning a new county, of which Chelmsford was to be the county seat He was sergeant in 1712 He was assessor, surveyor of highways, tithingman, town treasurer, trustee and selectman of the town of Dracut at various times He served on many special committees for the town He became captain about 1722 and major about 1736 His will was proved in 1740 It mentions his children by name Children were 1 Ephraim, Jr, born July 18, 1708, died in Dracut, Massachusetts, August 5, 1769, was very prominent in Dracut, town clerk, selectman, ensign and many other offices, married Mary Clark of Chelmsford, February 11, 1735 2 Josiah, born February 14, 1710 died in Dracut, August 7 1754, married Rebecca Wright, of Dracut, December 20, 1740, was town clerk in 1747 3 Robert (see forward) 4 Mercy or Mary, born January 27, 1715, died in Dracut Massachusetts, December 10, 1720 5 Zachariah, born September 26, 1718, died in Dracut, January 10, 1745

(IV) Robert Hildreth, son of Ephraim Hildreth (3) born at Dracut, Massachusetts, May 18 1713, married Sarah Abbott of Andover Massachusetts, November 15, 1734 Robert Hildreth settled in Dracut He was elected deer reeve March 5 1749 His wife was school teacher for a time in Dracut He served on various committees for the town Children were 1 Sarah, born in Dracut, August 31, 1735, married Simeon Wood, of Dracut, November 16 1754 2 Bridget born at Dracut, May 16, 1737, married Eliezer Colburn, of Dracut November 1 1760 3 Robert, born at Dracut March 7 1739 died there August 17, 1741 4 Robert, Jr, born at Dracut, February 23, 1740 5 Paul (see forward 6 Susanna born in Dracut, December 5, 1748 7 Benjamin, born January 23, 1754

(V) Paul Hildreth son of Robert Hildreth (4), was born at Dracut, Massachusetts, October 5 1746 He was the first white settler at what is now Lewiston Maine He was a hunter He built a log house there in 1770, and was a resident of the village in 1788 and was there when the place was incorporated on February 18 1795 The route by which he went to Lewiston from Dracut was down the Merrimac river to the sea in a boat He was towed by a sailing vessel to Harraseket, now Freeport, Maine Thence he went by portages through the forest to Royalstown, now Durham where he again put out in his boat and eventually arrived at Twenty Mile falls in safety He was joined in 1771 by David Pettingill and one of the Dracut Varnums and one other from New Gloucester Before he was married he had his cabin on the island in the river above the falls The light in his cabin by which he frequently read late at night was a beacon to guide the Indians who were not afraid of the rapids On one occasion an Indian girl warned him of a plot to murder him at night The Indians were jealous of his success in killing otter Paul shifted the beacon putting his lantern in his boat anchored in such a place that if the Indians came and mis-

A. G. Hildreth

took the light for the cabin where it usually shone, they would be swept over the falls and lost. The trick was successful and the Indians, who never discovered the trick, left him alone afterward, believing that he had a charmed life.

He married Hannah Merrill. The record of their children here is incomplete. Two of them were: 1. David, born November 9, 1770, died at Gardiner, Maine, July 12, 1848, aged seventy-seven years, eight months. He married April 22, 1792, Esther Moody, daughter, probably, of Samuel and Esther Moody, who were early settlers of Industry, Maine. She was born in Waterboro, Maine, May 16, 1770. David Hildreth settled in Industry, Maine, in 1804, on the place now or lately owned by Charles S. Rackliff. He removed later to Gardiner, Maine, where he owned a saw mill. He was captain of the Industry militia company. His wife died in Gardiner, February 15, 1842. They had ten children, the two eldest of which were born in Lewiston, Maine, where Paul Hildreth lived and where David was born. 2. Robert (see forward).

(VI) Robert Hildreth, son of Paul Hildreth (5), born probably in Lewiston about 1780, married Phebe Marston, of West Gardiner, Maine. He died at West Gardiner, October 20, 1833, his wife died there February 4, 1871. Children, born in West Gardiner, were: 1. Emma Jane, born December 22, 1814, died April, 1902. 2. William, born November 16, 1816, died October 28, 1898, unmarried. 3. Daniel, born September 1, 1818, living at West Gardiner, Maine, unmarried (1905). 4. Mehitable, born October 12, 1822, died May 16, 1883, unmarried. 5. Robert Gardner (see forward). 6. Thaddeus, born May 17, 1826, died young. 7. Esther, born September 28, 1829, died young. 8. Hannah, born May 4, 1832, living at Farmingdale, Maine.

(VII) Robert Gardner Hildreth, son of Robert Hildreth (6), born at West Gardiner, Maine, September 24, 1824, was killed in the civil war July 29, 1863. He was a farmer. He married January 3, 1856, Hulda Hodgton, of Framingdale, Maine, born October 17, 1838, died in Portland, Maine. He enlisted in Company E, Twenty-fourth Maine Infantry, in the fall of 1861 for nine months service, and his time had expired at the time he was killed. Children were: 1. Charles Albert, born November 18, 1856, married Carrie E. Chamel (?), of Lewiston, Maine, November 18, 1876; he is a manufacturer of overalls, etc., at Lewiston, Maine. 2. Andrew Gardner (see forward). 3. Walter Thaddeus, born February 17, 1861, died April 17, 1885, unmarried. 4. William Clinton, born May 10, 1863, married Jane Weymouth, of Webster, Maine. His daughter Myra Orissa, born March 26, 1884, is living in Worcester, Massachusetts. His son Herbert Leroy, born April 29, 1886, is living in Lewiston, Maine. He went to sea and has not been heard from for some years.

(VIII) Andrew Gardner Hildreth, son of Robert Gardner Hildreth (7), was born at West Gardiner, Maine, December 20, 1858. He was but four years old when his father was killed in the civil war, and the family was broken up. His mother married again but lived only a few years. So Mr. Hildreth began life under adverse conditions. When a mere child he worked on the farms of those who were keeping him, attending the district and village schools in the winter terms only. The physical fatigue, the loneliness and the plain living of a New England farm life forty years ago either made a boy ambitious to do better or ground the very heart out of him. Sometimes the work developed the boy into a man of great physical strength, of a philosophy that met every difficulty in business with patience and determination, of a strength of character that sternness alone develops. Worcester county has thousands of examples of successful men developed under similar conditions to those of Mr. Hildreth's boyhood.

At the age of sixteen he went to work in the Kennebec Wire Works at Hallowell, a town near his native place. He remained in this position until 1882, when he came to Worcester. He had arranged to enter partnership with his brother Walter Hildreth as soon as the volume of business was large enough to need two of them. But his brother died soon afterward, and although the firm was known as Hildreth Brothers in 1883, when the business was established, and for some years afterward, Mr. Hildreth was really alone in the business until 1890, when he formed a partnership with W. J. Hall, under the firm name of A. G. Hildreth & Co. Twelve years later, in 1902, Mr. Hall retired from the firm, and since then Mr. Hildreth has done business under his own name. The first shop was at 558 Main street. From there Mr. Hildreth moved to the Stevens building, Southbridge street. The factory was moved in August, 1904, to the present location, 25 Hermon street. In April he bought the land and buildings which he occupies. The floor space used at present is about 15,000 feet. The regular force employed in the factory is 110. Since 1898 the product has been doubled, and every year the business has shown a large percentage of increase over the year preceding. In 1904 Mr. Hildreth made 45,370 dozens of garments and sold 44,438 dozen garments. Besides the making of overalls, Mr. Hildreth manufactures shirts, frocks, etc. Among well known specialties are his mechanic overalls and outing shirts. His trade extends all over the country. He has the best of machinery for the work; everything is made in the factory under his direct supervision. Mr. Hildreth is a member of Ridgeley Lodge, Independent Order Odd Fellows.

He married Emma Augusta Hovey, September 12, 1880. She is a daughter of Eben Hovey, of Hallowell, Maine, born April 12, 1859, in Hallowell, Maine. Their children are: 1. Pearl C., born October 1, 1881, died October 13, 1881. 2. Walter Hallowell, born July 25, 1886, attended the Worcester high school. (In 1902 when Mr. Hall retired and sold his interest to Mr. Hildreth, Walter H., his son, entered his father's shop to learn the business and assist as salesman. He is at present associated with his father in the business but not as a partner.) 3. Margaret Ina, born January 29, 1890, lives at home. 4. Bessie Andrews, born October 26, 1892, lives at home.

BOYCE FAMILY. Joseph Boyes (1), the immigrant ancestor of Franklin James Boyce, of Worcester, was born in England about 1615. The name is also spelled Boyce and Boyse. It is of French origin meaning Wood, and probably dates back to the Norman conquest. Du Bois is still a common name in France. In Scotland, whence came most of the Boyes families of America either directly or from the branches settled in Ulster province, Ireland, the family home is in Forfarshire. Joseph Boyes, who came to America, was a tanner by trade. He settled in Salem, where he was a proprietor in 1639. He was admitted to the church there April 7, 1640, and was made a freeman May 18, 1642. He sold his house and land in 1657. But little is known of him. His will was dated November 4, 1684, and proved February 18, 1694-5, bequeathing to his wife Eleanor, son Joseph, daughters Mary Southick, Hester ——, and

Elizabeth Hanson, to Joseph's children, Joseph and Benjamin

The children of Joseph and Eleanor Boyes were Hester, baptized February 21, 1640, Eliza or Elizabeth, baptized at Salem, March 6, 1642, married —— Hanson, Joseph, of whom later, Benjamin, baptized May 16, 1647, died before 1684, Mary married —— Southick

(II) Joseph Boyce, son of Joseph Boyce or Boyes (1), was born March, 1644, baptized at Salem, March 31, 1644 He lived in Salem until about the time of his father's death He married, February 4, 1667-8 Only the first child is recorded at Salem Their children Sarah, born December 4, 1668, Joseph, mentioned in grandfather's will, 1684, Benjamin, mentioned in will aforesaid, William, born about 1690, of whom later

(III) William Boyce, believed to be the son of Joseph Boyce (2), was born about 1690, perhaps in Rhode Island The first records relating to William Boyes are found at Mendon, Massachusetts, when he was hired as school teacher Under date of August 20, 1718, we find 'Having settled with Thomas Sabford, town treasurer, for ye years 1716 and 1718, the selectmen then agreed with William Boyce to be ye town's School Master from ye day of ye date until ye 4th day of March next to keep said school at ye direction of ye selectmen and that ye selectmen pay ye sd Boyce after ye rate of 28 pounds a year and likewise after that rate for the time ye said Boyce has kept school in ye said town of Mendon from ye 12 day of May last to ye day of date hereof, ye sd Boyce giving account to ye selectmen what time he hath lost" One writer gives the date of his coming to Mendon as 1717, but from this record it appears that he began May 12, 1718 He must have been well educated to have filled the position He was already a man of family and had probably taught elsewhere in the colonies The fact that he came to Mendon at the time the first Scotch-Irish emigration began to come makes it worth while to consider whether he could not have been one of these immigrants It seems out of the question to think that old Mendon would hire a Presbyterian Scotchman for a school teacher under any circumstances, such was the feeling in evidence against the Scotch-Irish who came into the colonies He proved satisfactory as a school teacher and citizen He continued to teach until 1728, when he was succeeded by Grindal Rawson, son of Rev Grindal Rawson, and the first person living in Mendon to graduate at the college Mr Boyce's contract in 1721 contained the curious provision that he should keep a 'Reading and wrighting school during the year, unless the town shall be presented (by the grand jury) for want of a grammar school, when he was to cease teaching at ye selectmen's orders" His salary was twenty-eight pounds unless "Moving when he should receive thirty pounds He taught most of the time one quarter each year in four different sections of the town—at the school house, at the south end, at Mill river and at Great river (Uxbridge) He gained in favor rapidly He was a selectman in 1723-24 He bought the lands and rights of Obadiah Wheelock, and December 5, 1719, the town of Mendon laid out to William Boyce fifty acres of the seventh division, and forty acres of Obadiah Wheelock on the south of Wigwam Hill He bought more land of John Rawson January 25 1719-20, in Mendon, and another piece the same day of William Hayward He bought other land in Mendon January 13, 1723-4, of Woodward Thompson, November 15, 1726, of Nathaniel Woodbury, and four parcels February 6, 1738-9, one of Obadiah Wheelock, one of James Heath, one of Joseph Dorr and the other of Jonathan Hayward

He died in 1733 in Mendon Guardians were appointed for his nine children February 7, 1734-5, giving their approximate ages The names of the other children are to be found in the administration papers of Jonathan, son of William Boyce The children of William Boyce were 1 William, Jr, born 1714, died 1738 Benjamin, born 1719, resided in Abington in 1742, probably the one who died at Mendon, 1787, John, of whom later, Samuel, born in 1721, resided in Medfield in 1742, Jonathan, born 1723, resided in Uxbridge in 1747, died that year, administrator appointed May 14, 1747, Bethia, born 1726, Margaret, born 1726 Daniel Boyce, who drew land in Mendon in 1733, may belong in this list of William's children, but if so, he died before the settlement of his brother's estate in 1747

(IV) John Boyce, son of William Boyce (3), was born in 1718, in Mendon, Massachusetts He probably settled about the time of his marriage in Uxbridge, formerly part of Mendon, where he owned land in 1739 He sold part of the house lot of his father, William Boyce, to Edmund Nurse, of Mendon, July 30, 1739 His brother William died in 1738, leaving a wife Lydia and four brothers His brother Jonathan, blacksmith, died 1747 John was administrator of his estate By deed dated February 15, 1747, he bought of his two surviving brothers their interests in the estates of the two deceased brothers, William Boyce, late of Mendon, and Jonathan Boyce, late of Uxbridge The brothers were Samuel Boyce, of Medfield, blacksmith, Benjamin Boyce, of Abington, cordwainer Benjamin died in 1787, leaving four children—Jonathan, who died without issue, Lucius, Asa, who left no sons, Phebe, and in his will mentions the children of his daughter, Lydia Going It follows that John Boyce, of Rutland, if he belonged to this family, was son of Samuel or of John Boyce Samuel was last heard of in Medfield, while John removed to Oxford Gore, while John of Rutland was living in Rutland John Boyce sold out in Mendon, January 22, 1781, to Benjamin Read and to his brother, Benjamin Boyce, who returned from Abington This land was that of his father and brothers and a lot bought of John Legg, May 30, 1751 He sold a lot of land in Oxford South Gore, thirty-two acres, July 10, 1786, to Benoni Benson

He married Sarah —— who survived him He died at Oxford South Gore in 1791, intestate In the administration of his estate the names of Priscilla Amphas and Asenath are mentioned Cenia lived there at the time John of Rutland must have been son or nephew

(V) John Boyce son of nephew or John Boyce (4) was born in 1736 He bought land in Rutland of William and Sarah Phillips of Boston, January 19 1767 He had been living there since his marriage in 1763 and for some time previously He sold a lot of land in Rutland, February 14, 1769, to John Smith who married his wife's sister His place was in the southern part of the town The history of Rutland says of him "John Boyce had land in Dublin originally laid out to William Fenton on which he lived many years He bought land in Rutland, April 16 1777, of William Whittaker and February 8 1775, land at Paxton of Hollen Maynard, of Northboro He sold land at Barre May 21, 1782 to Joseph Robinson, of Barre, and February 18, 1784, one hundred and seven acres at Barre to the same man John Boyce and his son Thomas sold out their interests in Rutland to Joseph Sweetser, of Paxton, December 14, 1813 On the same day he deeded various lots to his son, John, Jr, who remained at Rutland He deeded a farm of sixty-one acres to John, Jr, June 20, 1794, at the time he gave an undivided half of the homestead to Thomas

He married (first), April 7, 1763, at Rutland, Martha Dickee or Dickey, who died April 19, 1810 He married (second), July 23, 1812, at Rutland, Mrs Anna Oliver, widow of James Oliver, of Barre She died November 8, 1828, aged eighty years, at Barre He died at Barre, May, 1817, aged eighty years or more The children of John and Martha Boyce were 1 Thomas, baptized November 3, 1765, married, February 18, 1790, Patty Reed, who died April 30, 1810, married (second) (intentions dated January 3), 1811, Widow Margaret Thompson, of Princeton Thomas had twelve children born at Rutland 2 Jane, born October 4, 1767, married Elijah Stearns, Jr (Intentions dated June 25), 1785 3 Martha, born at Rutland, baptized June 25, 1769 4 Isabel, born in Rutland, baptized September 1, 1771, married Darius Bent (intentions dated January 28, 1797) 5 John, Jr, born April 28, 1773, settled in Rutland, of whom later

(VI) John Boyce, son of John Boyce (5), was born at Rutland, Massachusetts, April 28, 1773 He received a common school education and worked during his youth for his father on the farm After his marriage he purchased a farm which he worked until 1819, when he removed to Worcester and bought the old Bigsbee farm, which is now owned in part by the heirs, his grandson, John Richard Boyce, located on Webster street Although during his last years he was retired he continued to live there until his death He was a Whig in politics and an Episcopalian in religion He was in his younger days a member of the state militia

He married (first), May 28, 1794, Ruth Thompson, who was born December, 1768 He married (second), May, 1812, Polly Bond, of Leicester, who died March 8, 1813 He married (third), June 29, 1815, Lucy H Prouty, of Brookfield, who was born February 24, 1782, and died November 3, 1827 He married (fourth) Hannah D Fuller, of Worcester The children of John and Ruth Boyce were James Thompson, born March 1, 1795, Martha Patty, born December 1, 1796, John Frazier, born November 12, 1798, Ruth, born May 22, 1801, Clarinda, born March 18, 1804, Witness, born October 21, 1811, died November 24, 1811 The children of John and Polly Boyce were Mary Eliza, born March 3, 1813 died January 31, 1814 The children of John and Lucy were Lucy J, born March 14, 1819, Samuel Dexter, born September 24, 1825 The children of John and Hannah were George Washington, born January 7, 1830, Louisa Elizabeth, born July 13, 1831, William W, born June 14, 1834, died August 20, 1839

(VII) John Frazier Boyce, third child of John Boyce (6), was born at Rutland, Massachusetts, November 12, 1798, died August 18, 1878 He received his education in the district schools of his native town and worked afterward with his father on the farm until the family removed to Worcester in 1819 He came to Worcester with the family and learned the trade of dyer at Rochdale in the woolen mill there, and worked there for a number of years He removed to Millbury and worked at his trade there He drew a quarter section of land (one hundred and sixty acres) from the government at Franklinville, Cattaraugus county, New York, and for three years worked upon it from spring to fall Then he exchanged it for the farm of Elliott Boyce, his cousin, at Spencer Later he sold the Spencer property to good advantage, and took charge of his father's farm on Webster street, Worcester He bought the place and carried on the farm profitably until his death He was orthodox in religion and attended the Old South Church, then on the Worcester common He was a Republican in politics and served on the school committee for many years He was in the militia in his younger days

He married (first), at Barre, March 6, 1838 Adeline Adams, of Barre, no children He married (second), at Heath, Massachusetts, April 23, 1840, Sophia Temple, who was born March 6, 1810, daughter of Richard and Caroline (Christie) Temple Her father was a farmer The children of John Frazier and Sophia Temple Boyce were 1 Adaline Adams born March 26, 1841, died May 10, 1860 2 Eunice Jennette, born January 5, 1843, married Otis H Bancroft, May 15, 1862, and they have four children—Adaline Jennette, born May 15, 1863, Cora Eliza, born March 22, 1865, Nettie Louisa, Clara May, born July 23, 1873 3 Emma Sophia, born December 27, 1845, died unmarried February 1, 1905 4 John Richard, born February 2, 1848, died February 18, 1901, married Lizzie Cora Rockwell, and they have had two children—Bernice Marion, born April 29, 1892, Raymond John, born February 12, 1894 5 Franklin James, born March 4, 1850 6 William Charles, born July 10, 1852, died July 15, 1889

(VIII) Franklin James Boyce, fifth child of John Frazier Boyce (7), was born at Worcester, Massachusetts, March 4, 1850 He received his education in the common schools, taking also two terms in Howe's Business College, Worcester At the age of twenty years he entered the employ of Rice & Griffin, manufacturers of doors, sash, blinds, etc, at the corner of Union and Exchange streets, where he was located for four years, when he and his brother, William C, took charge of the farm until the father's death, when it was willed to the three brothers, John R, Franklin James and William Charles, and the two sisters His early experience on the farm proved useful to him when he and his brother John took charge of the paternal farm So well did the partnership with his brother succeed that it was continued after the father's death, when they became the joint owners of the property with their brother William After the death of William in 1889 without issue, the two brothers, John R and Franklin James, continued the same equal division of the property in joint ownership with their two sisters As the city grew the farm land became more and more valuable Finally in 1889 Mr Boyce and his brother began to build houses on the property and more than forty have been erected and sold since then Mr Boyce built his residence at 284 Webster street in 1874 He also owns land in Auburn, a part of his present farm When the father died the farm contained one hundred and forty-four acres, the brothers added to until they owned over three hundred acres

In religion Mr Boyce is liberal, formerly attending the Universalist church, now the Bethany Congregational church In politics he is a Republican He is a Free Mason, member of the Morning Star Lodge, of Worcester Royal Arch Chapter, Hiram Council and of Worcester County Commandery, Knights Templar, Worcester Lodge of Perfection Goddard Council, Lawrence Chapter of Rose Croix the Massachusetts Consistory and of the Aleppo Temple Order of Mystic Shrine He is a member of the Worcester Agricultural Society and of the New England Fair Association

He married, December 28, 1881, Josephine E Buck, who was born April 2, 1858, the daughter of

Ezra and Louisa (Boyce) Buck, of Machias, New York. Her father is a farmer. The children of Franklin James and Josephine E Boyce are 1 Eugene Franklin, born December 20, 1883, a student in Clark College 2 Mabel Louise, born October 6, 1885, married Albert Stevens Allen, of Auburn, Massachusetts 3 Gladys Myrtle, born July 1, 1888 Hazel Emma, born February 10, 1891

THE BELISLE FAMILY Alexander Belisle (I), first of the name in Worcester, was born in St Damase, Canada, December 28, 1831, son of Antoine Levasseur and Marguerite (Delage) Belisle At the age of eighteen he emigrated alone to this country, and in the spring of 1847 found employment in the shoe factory of Captain Wood at West Millbury He resided in St Marcel, Canada, for a few years, then returned to Worcester county, and during most of his life followed his trade of shoemaker in the various factories of Worcester He died in Worcester, March 14, 1903, aged seventy-two years

He married, in Millbury, July 10, 1853, Marie Dorval, who was born in St Ours, Canada, 1832, the daughter of Louis and Marie (Benoit) Dorval Her parents removed to Millbury in 1835 She died in Worcester, January 31, 1906, aged seventy-four years Of the fifteen children of Alexander and Marie Belisle, six died in infancy Those who grew to maturity were Josephine, married Gaspard Dupuis, of of Sutton, Massachusetts, Elmire, died 1897, married Andre G Lajoie, a well known grocer of Worcester, Alexander, Jr, of whom later, Felix A, of whom later, Eugene L, of whom later, George E, a lawyer, of whom later, Charles Edmond, managing editor of *L'Opinion Publique* of Worcester, of whom later, Hector L, graduate of Harvard teacher, of whom later, Anna, a music teacher, resides at the homestead, 69 Salem street, Worcester

(II) Alexander Belisle, Jr, son of Alexander Belisle (I), was born at Ste Victoire, Canada, September 4, 1856 His father had returned to Canada on account of a long illness, returning to Worcester, December 31, 1862 Alexander, Jr, attended the public schools of Worcester and learned the trade of shoemaker with his father He left the shoe business at the age of twenty-two to become business manager of *Le Travailleur*, a French newspaper, published in Worcester by the late Edward Gagnon In 1887 he entered the insurance office of the late Colonel John D Washburn, where he is still employed He has taken an active part in politics and was the first Franco-American elected to the common council of his city, serving four years, 1888 to 1891 He is at present a director of the Free Public Library, and one of the best known men among the Franco-Americans of the county

An interesting fact concerning his education was brought to mind by the death of Miss Carrie A George recently When a young man Alexander, Jr, attended with his father the evening school in Worcester then in charge of Miss George Later she was the teacher at Cambridge street school when his sons went there, and all of them were in her class at various times Thus she taught three generations of the same family Mr Belisle is a member of several Franco-American societies, the Worcester County Mechanics' Association since 1882, and the Worcester Society of Antiquity

He married at the age of twenty-one, 1877, Albina Boulay, who was born at La Presentation, Canada March 21 1854, daughter of Narcisse and Hedwidge (Laviolette) Boulay, of Acton, Canada Of their eight children, all of whom were born in Worcester, four sons are living, viz Narcisse A, born October 14, 1878, a clerk at present in the Worcester postoffice, Emilio H, April 21, 1881, graduate of Holy Cross College, 1906, Ferdinand J, August 20, 1883, graduate of Clark College, 1906, Eugene S, September 3, 1891, student in the Classical high school

(II) Felix A Belisle, son of Alexander Belisle (I), was born in St Marcel, Richelieu, Quebec, October 22, 1857 He came to Worcester when a boy of five years with the family, and was educated there in the public schools and in Foster's Business College For some years he worked at the trade of shoemaking with his father Then he engaged in newspaper work on the *Patrie Nouvelle* of Cohoes, New York, and later on *Le Travailleur* of Worcester with the late Ferdinand Gagnon In 1885 he made up his mind to study law and gave up newspaper work to enter a law office in Lowell He completed his preparation as a lawyer in Worcester in the office of Henry L Parker and was admitted to the bar in 1887 He entered immediately upon the practice of his profession, in which he was eminently successful There was need for a capable French speaking attorney in Worcester county where the French speaking population is already large and has been growing rapidly He had a very promising career before him cut short by his death, April 13, 1905 He was taken ill in the fall of 1904 after his return from a visit to the St Louis fair He was twice operated upon in St Vincent's hospital and his ultimate recovery had been expected He died in an attack of heart failure At the time of his death Mr Belisle was president of L'Alliance Francaise of Worcester, a member of the St Jean Baptiste Society, the Casino Club and of the Bar Association of Worcester County He married Agnes C Smith, who survives him They had no children

(II) Eugene L Belisle, son of Alexander Belisle (I), was born in St Marcel, Canada, March 10, 1859 He came to Worcester with the family December 31, 1862, and was educated in the public schools there He also learned the shoemaker's trade of his father In the early eighties he was an athlete of some note and was widely known as one of the best polo players on roller skates in New England He started in business for himself as a grocer with a store on Hanover street, Worcester He gave up this business to became the business manager and part owner of *L'Opinion Publique*, a daily newspaper in the French language printed in Worcester In politics he is a Republican and has been prominent in public affairs for a number of years He was twice elected to the common council of the city of Worcester, serving in 1893-94-95, and he was also a trustee of the City Hospital In 1905 he traveled extensively in Europe, and in April, 1906, on recommendation of Congressman Rockwood Hoar and of Senators Lodge and Crane, he was appointed consul at Limoges, France He is unmarried

(II) George E Belisle, son of Alexander Belisle (I), was born in Worcester, July 7, 1867 He attended the public schools there and was graduated from Holy Cross College in 1888 He worked seven years in the Worcester postoffice and ten years in the postoffice department in Washington While in Washington he used his spare time as many department clerks with ambition have done and are doing, attending the law school of Georgetown University He completed the course and was admitted to the bar He was an active and prominent member of Carroll Institute, the Catholic Club of the National Capital He succeeded to the law practice of his brother, Felix A Belisle, who died in 1905 He is unmarried

(II) Charles Edmond Belisle, son of Alexander Belisle (1), was born in Worcester, March 22, 1869, and was educated there in the public schools and in Foster's Business College He learned the trade of printer under Charles R Stobbs, of Worcester, then went to New York as journeyman and became a department foreman in the great printing establishment of the city printer, Martin B Brown In January, 1893, he returned to Worcester and in partnership with four of his brothers founded *L'Opinion Publique*, now a Franco-American daily newspaper, of which he is the managing editor and which he has been very successful in its field The Belisles have built up also a large book and job printing business and have a large printing plant Mr Belisle is a member of several Franco-American societies He married, July 19, 1897, Josephine M Perreault, daughter of the well known foundryman, Presbey Pero (Perreault originally), of Worcester She died February 3, 1900 They had no children

(II) Hector L Belisle, son of Alexander Belisle (1), was born in Worcester, October 8, 1874. He attended the public schools and graduated in 1896 from the Classical high school, one of the honor men He composed the music of the class song at graduation He entered Harvard the same year and was graduated *cum laude* in 1900 He became at once teacher of French and history in the high school of Lawrence, Massachusetts In the year following he was elected principal of the John R Rollins grammar school of that city, a position he has held for the past six years He married, June 20, 1905, Grace Mildred Potter, of Boston, a teacher in the Dorchester high school, Boston They have a son, George Edmond, born April 1 1906

MICHAEL PHILIP McGRATH, of Worcester, a railroad builder and contractor, was born in the town in which he now resides, November 15, 1860, a son of Michael and Johanna (Powers) McGrath

Michael McGrath (father) was born in county Waterford, Ireland, about 1825 He married, about 1849 or 1850, Johanna Powers, also a native of county Waterford, Ireland, born about 1825, and the following day they sailed for America, landing in Boston, Massachusetts, and going direct to Worcester, where he devoted his time and attention to the business of a contractor About three decades ago he erected a house at No 2 Woodland street, Worcester, the same in which his son, Michael P, now resides, and there spent the remainder of his days He died in 1877, and his widow passed away at her home in Worcester in 1893 They were the parents of nine children, one of whom died in infancy, and the names of the others were as follows Richard Desmond, William, who is employed by his brother, Michael P, Mary, wife of the late James E Fay, of Worcester, Johanna, wife of Frank E Reynolds, of Worcester, Patrick Desmond, Michael P, (see forward), Margaret F, deceased, and John J, a resident of Worcester, and a prominent member of the Catholic church

The public schools of Worcester, Massachusetts, afforded Michael P McGrath the means of obtaining a practical, English education Upon the completion of his studies he went to Clinton, Massachusetts, where he secured employment with the Lancaster Gingham Company Later he went to Kansas, and while a resident of that state had charge of gangs of men who were engaged in laying water pipes made by R D Wood & Co, of Philadelphia, manufacturers of iron pipes, who were also the contractors for the work Upon his return to his native city, Worcester, he began the contracting business on his own account, and his first piece of work was the building of the Millbury line of electric railway He also was awarded the contract to build the electric line from Rochester, New York, to Buffalo, seventy-eight miles, and one from Malden, Massachusetts, to Haverhill, sixty miles He equips the roads complete, all ready for the cars, power houses, barns, etc He has built about forty railroads, electric and steam, throughout various sections of the United States His latest contract is for the building of three hundred and fifty miles of railroad line for the Ottawa River Railway Company of Canada, of which Colonel Edgar McMullen, of Boston, is president, the project involving an expenditure of more than ten million dollars, exclusive of equipment The line will be from Montreal to Ottawa, one hundred and six miles, thence to Midland, Ontario, on the Georgian Bay, where connection will be made with the vessels which ply the great lakes It is a steam road, and will run through a strip of territory between eighty and one hundred miles wide, between the Grand Trunk and the Canadian Pacific railroads, and, with a terminus at Midland, it will be in a position to communicate with any port on Lakes Superior, Michigan and Huron Later this is to be an electric road

The introduction of electrically propelled equipment for passenger and freight service will be an innovation in Canada, and the outcome of the movement, which the projectors believe is beyond the experimental stage, even so far as stiff grades are concerned, will be watched with interest by railroad men and the general public in the Dominion The Ottawa River Railway is the western extension of the Atlantic & Lake Superior Railroad, running along the south shore of the St Lawrence river, between Baie des Chaleurs, Quebec, and Montreal, where it has communication with ocean-going steamships The terminal stations are to be built at Montreal, Ottawa and Midland, in addition to the smaller stations along the line The company will join with American and Canadian roads in a union station to be in the heart of the uptown business district in Montreal, the entrance being by tunnel The station is to be modern in every respect Mr McGrath has also the contract to equip the company's system The total contracts involve an expenditure of fourteen million dollars, the road is to be in operation in three years

Mr McGrath serves in the capacity of general manager of the Northampton Traction Company, and chairman of its executive board, general manager of the Lansdale & Norristown Electric Railroad, which he built in 1902, and purchased May 27, 1905, general manager of the St Lawrence International Electric Railroad running from Redwood to Alexandria Bay, New York which he built in 1892, and a stockholder in two banks, several railroads, and a number of manufacturing concerns, the principal one being the Fibre Pail Manufacturing Company of Stockton, Pennsylvania He is an advocate of Democratic principles, but not a strong partisan, as in local affairs he casts his vote for the candidates who in his opinion are best qualified for office He holds membership in the Knights of Columbus In 1898 he took a trip to Europe, visiting the places of note and interest in the Old World, including the home of his parents in Ireland He married, January 20 1886 Ellen Frances Walsh, daughter of Michael and Margaret (Power) Walsh, late of Worcester, Massachusetts, whose family consisted of eight children, as follows Bridget, wife of Patrick Roach, of Worcester, John, deceased, Mary, deceased, Michael P, Thomas J, Edmund A, Ellen Frances, wife of Michael P McGrath, and Margaret, deceased Michael Walsh was born in county Waterford, Ireland, about 1828, emigrated to the United States about 1849, and for many years was employed by the old Norwich & Worcester Railroad About the year 1850 Mr Walsh married Margaret Power, born in county Waterford, Ireland, died in 1874 He died in 1891 Mr Walsh and family were members of the Catholic church Three children were born to Mr and Mrs McGrath Michael J, who is a student at the Norwich University, Vermont, Mary Eleanor, a student at the Worcester high school, and Edmund Mr McGrath and his family are members of the Catholic church

FAYETTE ASARYL AMIDON Roger Amidon (1) was the emigrant ancestor of Fayette A Amidon, manager and proprietor of the Worcester Market, Worcester, Massachusetts, and of perhaps all in this country of the name of Amidon The name has been spelled variously Ammidon, Ammidown, Amadon Roger Amidon was in Salem, Massachusetts, before 1637, when he was mentioned as the owner of half an acre of meadow There seems to be no evidence that he was a French Huguenot, except that some of his descendants mingled with the Huguenots and perhaps intermarried with them at Oxford He removed to Weymouth in 1640, and was in Boston in 1643 He settled finally at Seekonk, in Rehoboth, Massachusetts His house was at the northeasterly end of the semicircle of houses comprising the original village of Seekonk, and was about a mile north of the church in the present town He drew his house lot July 18, 1648, and drew other lots June 3, 1662, June 7, 1665, in 1668 and 1671 He was one of the original proprietors of Rehoboth, and was there probably as early as 1645, when it was incorporated He married first, Sarah ———, who died at Rehoboth, June 20, 1668 He married (second) Joanna, daughter of George and Jane Harwood She died July 1, 1711 He was buried November 13, 1673 There were suspicions at the time that his death was not natural, and an inquest was held He had four children by his first wife and three by the second His estate was divided March 4, 1674, among his widow Joanna, son Ebenezer, by his representative, John Cobleeh, of Swansea, daughter Hannah, wife of Jeremiah Wheaton John Harrod, of Patucksett, brother of the widow, gave advice in the settlement of the estate The children of Roger Amidon 1 Ebenezer, mentioned in settlement of estate, 1674, was in Rehoboth 1689, advanced money in King Philip's war, 1675 2 Sarah, born December 6, 1640, Weymouth 3 Lydia, born February 27, 1643, Boston 4 Hannah, born September 20, 1652, married Jeremiah Wheaton, of Rehoboth, had eight children, died at Rehoboth, September 13, 1719 5 Philip, see forward 6 Henry, born at Rehoboth, January 24 1671, was on list of inhabitants of Rehoboth 1689 7 Mehitable, born at Rehoboth, August 27, 1672, married, December 23, 1709, John Thompson of Rehoboth

(II) Philip Amidon, son of Roger Amidon (1), born at Rehoboth, January 26 1670, resided there until the death of his first wife, when he removed to Mendon In 1717 he removed to Oxford, Massachusetts, where many French Huguenots settled about that time, and died there March 15, 1747 He was a farmer and cooper He and his wife joined the Oxford church in 1720 He was a selectman 1730, constable 1735 His will was proved May 12, 1747 Of his old homestead three-fourths belongs to the farm now or recently owned by Franklin H Clark, and the other quarter belonged recently to Lucinda Morse He married first, at Rehoboth, May 27, 1698, Mehitable, daughter of Samuel and Mary (Willard) Perry, born April 30, 1680 She had one child and died at Rehoboth, July 4, 1699, aged nineteen He went to Mendon about 1700 and married (second), September 16, 1700, Ithamar Warfield, who survived him She was born March 28, 1676, daughter of Deacon John W and Hannah (Randall) Warfield, of Mendon His will was proved May 12, 1747 His children 1 Henry A, see forward 2 Roger, born February 6, 1702 3 Ichabod, born May, 1704 4 Mary, born March 30, 1706, married, July 18, 1728, Benjamin Chamberlain resided at Oxford 5 Philip born 1708, resided in that part of Oxford set off as Charlton, and left many descendants 6 Ephraim, born 1710 7 Ithamar, born April 25, 1712 8 John, born May 19, 1713 9 Hannah, born February 2, 1717, married Samuel Wheelock, of Hardwick Their daughter Mary, born 1738, married Caleb Cheney, of Mendon They resided at Milford, where he was town clerk, selectman and lieutenant in the revolutionary army They had twelve children, one of whom was an ancestor of General A B Underwood, U S A

(III) Henry A Amidon, son of Philip Amidon (2), born at Rehoboth, February 8, 1699, married, at Mendon, March 31, 1718, Meltiah, daughter of Joseph and Hannah (Thurston) Cheney, born October 14, 1690, died May 17, 1780 He was a farmer at Oxford and Dudley until 1744, when he removed to Ashford, Connecticut, where he died March 5, 1778 His children 1 Jacob, born February 28, 1720 2 Mehitable, born January 15, 1723, married, December 12, 1742, William Curtis, of Dudley, had James, Henry and other children 3 Joseph, born February, 1725 4 Henry, born May 3, 1727

(IV) Captain Henry Amidon, son of Henry (3), born at Oxford, Massachusetts, May 3, 1727, was a farmer He settled at Pomfret, Connecticut, in 1752 removed to Willington, Connecticut, where he died He answered the Lexington call to arms in 1775 as a private from Willington He was appointed by Governor Trumbull captain of Third company, Twenty-second regiment, March 21, 1777, and served at New London and other places He married, at Pomfret, Connecticut, September 25, 1751, Sarah Doubledee (Doubleday), who died at Willington, January 8, 1794 His children 1 Jedediah, born May 15, 1752, died August 11, 1752 2 Jedediah, born 1753 3 Moses, born 1756 4 Jonathan, born 1757 5 Mary, born 1762, married Jonathan Flint, lived at Braintree, Vermont, where he died August 26, 1840, had Asaryl, born 1785, Elisha, 1788, Joseph, 1789, Augustus, 1792, Anna, 1794, Sally, 1796, Polly, 1798 6 Jacob, born March 5, 1764 7 William, born January 30, 1767 8 Henry, born February 9, 1769 9 Asaryl, see forward 10 Sarah, born February 9, 1774, married Shubael Hall, removed to Orange county, New York, 1799, died there March 27, 1841 His children were Shubael, born 1796, Sallie, 1800, George, 1805, married Ruth West

(V) Asaryl Amidon, son of Henry Amidon (4), was born at Willington, Connecticut, July 20, 1771 He served in the war of 1812 He removed to Belchertown, Massachusetts, where he settled, and died there February 7, 1853 He married, November 20 1799, Alethia Perry, born February 28, 1773, died August 13, 1757 His children 1 Asaryl, see forward 2 Alethia, born July 23, 1802, died June, 1886 3 Bridget born July 28, 1804 died December 11, 1822 Sally, born August 4, 1807, married Porter

C A Amidon

Edwards, and died in Willington, Connecticut, November 23, 1845, leaving daughter, Sarah E, born November 7, 1845, died April 6, 1861 5 Samuel, born May 29, 1809, married, April, 1835, Harriet, daughter of Martin and Sally (King) Sedgwick, born June 29, 1827, died July 12, 1889, resided at Belchertown Samuel died May 14, 1858, and widow removed to Springfield, Massachusetts They had no children, but adopted George Franklin Amidon, who lives at Springfield, and has a son George Samuel Amidon 6 Polly, born November 9, 1811, died January 12, 1824

(VI) Asaryl Amidon, son of Asaryl Amidon (5), born September 26, 1800, at Mansfield, Connecticut, married, October 11, 1830, Aurelia McIntire, born April 9, 1809, at Thetford, Vermont He died at Belchertown, February 4, 1847 His widow married Foster Edwards She died 1871, at Belchertown Children of Asaryl 1 Samuel Gillett, born October 16, 1833 2 Edward Perry, see forward 3 John Alvin, born September 1, 1845, died November 24, 1847

(VII) Edward Perry Amidon, son of Asaryl Amidon (6), born at Belchertown, September 4, 1837, married, May 10, 1860, Sophia Olive, daughter of Asa and Orlinda Shumway, born March 7, 1840, at Palmer, Massachusetts He died at Belchertown, November 12, 1874 She resides with her only son, Fayette Asaryl Amidon

(VIII) Fayette Asaryl Amidon, son of Edward Perry Amidon (7), was born at Belchertown, Massachusetts, July 13, 1862 He attended school in his native town until the age of seventeen In 1880 he removed with his mother to New Haven, Connecticut, where he went to work in a large pork-packing establishment Later he worked five years in a department meat store Then he went into business for himself, dealing in butter and eggs His health failed, and he had to give up business for a time He resided at Springfield and Gilbertville, Massachusetts He resumed business in Manchester, New Hampshire, in charge of the butter and egg department in a large provision store, and remained there four years He then entered into partnership with Oscar Swanson, Gustaf T Malmstead and George H Pettis, to start the well known Providence Market in Providence, a department market carrying groceries as well as all kinds of meat, fruit and vegetables, on a more extensive scale than had been done hitherto, and the venture was an instant success The firm started a similar department store at Worcester, Massachusetts in October, 1894, and Mr Amidon took personal charge of it He moved to Worcester soon after the store was opened, and has a handsome home on Germain street It is generally conceded that the Worcester Market, as their store is called, is by far the largest and most profitable market and grocery in the county The credit for the remarkable success of the house is given in large measure to the business astuteness and personal attention of Mr Amidon A self-made man, he stands high in the estimation of other business men of the city He is a member of Trinity Church, and of its finance committee, and is a Republican in politics, but has never aspired to office He is a member of the Board of Trade, and president of the Speedway Club, being an owner and admirer of good horses

Mr Amidon married, June 16, 1895, Lucy Ella Higgins, of Providence, Rhode Island, daughter of Charles and Lucy (Watson) Higgins Her father died in East Greenwich, Rhode Island, in 1874, at the age of fifty-eight years Her mother died in 1881, aged fifty-seven, at Saylorsville, Rhode Island She was one of nine children born to her parents, eight of whom lived to maturity Mrs Amidon is a graduate of the high school

CHARLES WALTER KING William King, Esq (1), the emigrant ancestor of Charles Walter King, of Worcester, was a Puritan emigrant from England, sailing before March 20, 1635, from Weymouth, Dorsetshire, England The records show that he was aged forty, his wife Dorothy thirty-four, and they had with them five children Mary, aged twelve, Katheryn aged ten, William, aged eight, Hannah, aged six, Samuel, aged two They settled at Salem, Massachusetts He was admitted a freeman there May 25, 1636 He had grants of land of forty acres on Jeffrey's Creek, now Manchester-by-the-Sea, thirty acres at Royal-side at the head of Bass river, now Beverly, and he located his homestead there He was a grand juror in 1637 He was a member of the First church at Salem, but in 1637 joined the Antinomians and came under the ban of the Salem authorities He was requested to sever his connection with the new church or have his arms taken away from him He remained with the new faith and gave up his gun to Lieutenant Danforth Later he was banished for a time for sheltering the persecuted Quakers He died in 1650-51 and his estate was administered by his widow Dorothy and son William

He married Dorothy Hayne, born in England about 1601 and died in Southold, Suffolk county, New York, where her daughters Hannah, wife of Richard Browne, Sr, and Deliverance, wife of John Tuthill, were living The widow of William King bought a dwelling house and land at Salem of John Swasey She sold it in 1653, and removed to Long Island She sold the homestead to her son, William King The records at Sherburne, England, show that William King and Dorothy Hayne were married February 17, 1616-17 The parish of Sherburne is in Dorsetshire

Children of William and Dorothy King were 1 William, of Royal-side, Salem, born about 1627-28 in England was persecuted as a Quaker, he married Katharine Shaflin, daughter of Michael Shaflin of Salem 2 Samuel, of Southold, Long Island born in England about 1633-34 removed from Salem to Southold, where he owned some four hundred acres of land in 1658, died November 29, 1721, aged eighty-eight, married Abigail, daughter of William Ludlaw 3 John, of Salem, baptized there November 11, 1638, in 1706 he gave deed of land in Salem to son Samuel, died before 1719 4 Mary, born about 1623 in England, married probably, 1646, John Scudder son of Thomas Scudder 5 Katherine, born about 1625, in England, married John Swasey of Salem removed to Southold, Long Island 1658 6 Hannah born in England about 1629, married Lieutenant Richard Browne, Sr, of Southold, Long Island, admitted freeman 1662, died 1686-87 7 Mehitable born about 1635, baptized in Salem, December 25 1636, probably died young 8 Deliverance baptized in Salem, October 31, 1636, married at Southold, Long Island, February 7, 1657, died there January 25, 1688-89 aged forty-nine married John Tuthill, Sr, justice of the peace, member the colonial assembly, 1695-98, descendant of John Tuthill, of Saxlingham, England

(II) John King, son of William King (1), was baptized November 11, 1638, in Salem, Massachusetts In 1682 he was called son-in-law in the will of Thomas Goldthwait In 1699 with his wife Elizabeth he gave a deed to Caleb Buftam, and in 1706 he gave a deed of land in Salem to his son Samuel King He died before 1719

He married Elizabeth Goldthwait, daughter of

Thomas and Rachel Goldthwait, of Salem She was baptized November 20 1647, and married, September, 1660 Thomas Goldthwait was in Roxbury in 1631 and was admitted a freeman of Salem in 1634 and was member of the church there His will was proved at Salem March 6 1719 Children of John and Elizabeth (Goldthwait) King were 1 John, born October 1662 2 Samuel, born in Salem, May, 1664, married Elizabeth Marsh, daughter of Zachary and Mary (Silsbee) Marsh, of Salem, and granddaughter of John Marsh who settled 1636-37 with his wife Susan (Skelton) Marsh, daughter of Rev Samuel Skelton, among their children was Ebenezer, who settled in Rutland 3 Captain William, born at Salem, 1669 signed deed for partition of land left his father by Thomas Goldthwait, his grandfather, settled in Sutton, Massachusetts, with his brother Jonathan, and was one of the most prominent and wealthy men there, bought land at Charlton, died November, 1748, married Hannah Cooke, daughter of Isaac and Elizabeth (Buxton) Cooke, June 4, 1695, married (second) Rebecca Littlefield, of Wells Maine, daughter of Edmund and Agnes Littlefield, who came to Boston from England in 1641 and removed to Wells 4 Elizabeth, born February 16, 1671, married Nathaniel Aters, December 12, 1690 5 Jonathan, born February 16, 1674, of whom later 6 Thomas, born February, 1677, died October, 1680 7 Hannah, born April, 1681, married, June 24, 1709, Benjamin Marsh 8 Mary, born May, 1687

(III) Jonathan King, son of John King (2), was born February 1674 at Salem, and about 1717 settled in Sutton At first he was not a proprietor but he bought a farm of his brother, William King, and his brother-in-law Benjamin Marsh, a fifteenth of 3000 acres in deed dated August 14, 1715 His house was situate a few rods east of the one now or lately of Solomon Severy Subsequently he built another on the spot where the Severy house stands At first his mother lived with him, and he was over fifty when he married He married, February 2, 1726 in Salem Alice Verry After his death his farm was divided and his son John later bought out the other heirs and had the homestead, and the other children moved out of town Children of Jonathan and Alice were 1 Desire born at Sutton June 22, 1729, married Amos Gould, October 31, 1749 and removed to Charlton, she died in New at the home of her son, Amos Gould 2 Sarah, born March 11 1731 married, December 26, 1755, Eliphalet Rowell, and settled in Great Barrington 3 Jonathan Jr, born September 31, 1734, of whom later 4 John born January 19, 1837, married, January 10 1758, Elizabeth Town

(IV) Jonathan King, Jr, son of Jonathan King (3), was born in Sutton, Massachusetts, September 3 1734 He settled in that part of Petersham which became Dana, Massachusetts, in 1801 He lived in Sutton for some time before his removal to Petersham and his house was on the road from Eight Lots School house to Millbury, nearly opposite what is now called the Harwood place on the west side of the road He was a soldier in the revolution and late in life a pensioner His widow drew a pension after his death until her death about 1850 He married (first) April 10, 1755, and (second) at Petersham April 25, 1787, Rachel Claflin Children of Jonathan, Jr and Elizabeth were 1 Mary, married December 14 1780 Benjamin Davidson, settled in Spencer, grandparents of John C Davidson of Worcester 2 John 3 Stephen, of whom later and perhaps others

(V) Stephen King son of Jonathan King (4), was born in Sutton, Massachusetts, about 1765 At the age of sixteen he ran away from home in order to enlist in the American army in the revolution The story that he used to tell himself as to the effect of being under fire for the first time is given in the Sutton history His hair stood up with fright and he had to pull his hat down several times after it had been lifted from his head by the scare He soon got over this feeling however, and made a good soldier Stephen King enlisted, according to the revolutionary archives in the state house at Boston, when he was sixteen years old One record gives his age as fifteen and a half He enlisted in the Continental army agreeable to the resolve of the general court of December 2, 1780, as returned by the enlisting officer Seth Washburn, supervisor He was in Captain Elliot's company, Colonel Davis's regiment The records give his stature as five feet two inches (also as five feet, three inches), complexion light and his occupation as farmer He was born in Sutton and engaged for the town of Sutton enlisting December 25 1780 Later he was in Captain Remick's company the First Massachusetts Regiment, for a term of three years This company, in which he served to the end of the war, was in the regiment of Colonel Joseph Vose (First) His name is on a muster roll dated at Garrison, West Point April, 1781 he was at Camp Phillipsburg in May June and July, 1781 In October and November, 1781, he was at York Hutts He is on a list of men tried by court martial subsequent to 1781 King was tried December 6, 1781, by regimental court martial, Captain William, president, on the charge of stealing grain, the charge was not supported and King was acquitted He was at York Hutts January and February, 1782 His father deeded him a farm in Petersham (later Dana) by deed dated December 1, 1793 He sold land in Dana April 8, 1802, to Joel Amsden, the land deeded to Stephen by his father lying north of the farm of Jonathan A few months later Stephen and his wife Mehitable sold their farm of sixty-five acres on the southeast corner "of my father Jonathan's farm, land in Dana to Elisha Woodward of Petersham Stephen King died at Dana, September, 1827 His widow Mehitable administered the estate Children of Stephen and Mehitable King were 1. Stephen Jr, of whom later, 2 Betsey 3 John

(VI) Stephen King Jr, son of Stephen King (5) was born in Petersham now Dana about 1790 He resided in the north part of the town of Dana and died there He was a farmer He married Sophia Dunham, of Brimfield, Massachusetts Their children all born at Dana, were John born May 20 1821, of whom later, Jesse Woodward, born 1824 of whom later, George married Lucy Jane Barnes Stephen married Esther Richardson and their daughter Belle married Addison Marsh; Mary Ann, married Thomas McGrath and they had —Eugene Ada George, Abbie Herbert, Melvin, and Edmund McGrath Charlotte, married James Gleason, and their children were James and Frank Gleason

(VII) John King son of Stephen King (6), was born at Dana, Massachusetts May 20, 1821 He settled in Greenwich village in the adjoining town and is at present living there with his son He has seven children, nineteen grandchildren and nine great-grandchildren, all living in 1906 He has six four-generation pictures, the fourth generation in each group representing a different family

Mr King married at Hardwick in the fall of 1844 Mary J Richardson daughter of Seth and Alice (Johnson) Richardson, and their children are: 1 Jane Elvira, born May 1 1845, at Dana married Orville L Johnson and had two children—Eldora

E Johnson born June 15. 1869, Bertha Ella Johnson, born June 22, 1871 married Louis F Conkey and their children are Annie E Conkey, born July 29, 1891, and James O Conkey born August 5, 1898 2 Alfred C, now residing at Greenwich village, born December 7 1846 married Sarah E Hall, of Hardwich, and they have five children—John Houghton King, resides at Greenwich village, born July 3 1874, married Mrs Hattie (Johnson) Rollins, January 6, 1903, and have one child—Charles Hermon King, born January 23, 1904, Arthur Willard King, born October 2, 1879, resides in Greenwich village, Walter Austin King, born September 10, 1882, resides at Springfield, Massachusetts, married Winifred W Gray and they have one child—Austin W King, born March 31, 1904, Sara M King born March 31, 1884, resides in Greenwich village, Louise E King, born June 9, 1886, lives in Springfield, Massachusetts 3 Sarah Eveline King, born January 10, 1848, married Lucius E Sears and they have three children—Lillie Eveline Sears, born April 14, 1867, married William K Clute, and have one child, Donald Sears Clute, born July 3, 1892, Minnie Eliza Sears, born January 26, 1869 married W Erle Lemon, Mabel Edna Sears, born August 13, 1871, all the Sears family are living in Michigan 4 Edward T King, born November 13, 1850, married Mary J Robinson, resides in Greenwich village, and have children—Nellie M King, born May 2, 1872, married Frank Parker and they have two children—Lowell Parker born October 18 1895 and Doris Parker, born April 2, 1900, Willia Robinson King, born August 13, 1875 married, December 19, 1895, Bertha L Gray, who died in 1897, married (second), 1898, Lena Reed and have two children—Stanwood King, born September 16, 1899, and Raymond King, born December 14 1900, they reside at Greenwich village, Edward Grafield King, born November 2, 1880, married Nellie M Nevins, resides in Ware, Massachusetts, Oscar Asa King, born October 1, 1883, resides at Greenwich, Harry Lucius King, born September 18, 1886 Lawrence Taylor King, born October 16 1895 5 Harvey Walker King, born August 16, 1852, married Mrs Helen Cleveland and they have one daughter—Maude E King, who married Walter Burgess, resides in Somerville, Massachusetts 6 Della E King, born February 8, 1857, married Ira Howe, died June 1900 7 Marshall J King born February 20, 1859, resides in California 8 Albert K King, born September 30, 1862, resides in Oklahoma, married Ida Foster and they have two children—Dow King, born March 9, 1893 Alice King, born July 25, 1895

(VII) Jesse Woodward King, son of Stephen King (6), was born in Danna 1824, and died December 3 1865, aged thirty-one years He married, October 21, 1848, Huldah M Barnes daughter of Amos Barnes She married (second) Billings Cummings, November 22, 1859 She died December 10, 1868 aged thirty-eight years Children of Jesse Woodward and Huldah M King were Charles Walter born November 12, 1849

(VIII) Charles Walter King son of Jesse Woodward King (7), was born in Hardwick, Massachusetts November 12, 1849 He was educated in the public schools of Hardwick, Massachusetts, and worked at farming until he came of age He went to Athol, Massachusetts, October 26 1871, and engaged in the trucking business He added the ice and coal business and had the contract for sprinkling the streets of the town He was successful in his various ventures In 1884, however, he decided to enter a larger field and came to Worcester, buying the livery stable at the rear of Piedmont Court In May of that year he began business there and has continued in the same line, though on a larger scale, ever since In 1886 he purchased the property at 13 Piedmont street and added another stable to his holdings He added also to his business the stable at 59 High street formerly conducted by Dr Charles H Perry The premises there were remodeled and extensively improved and enlarged Mr King has won a prominent place among the business men of the city and is counted among the leaders in his line He is an excellent judgeg of horse flesh, a careful buyer and has a liking only for handling the best stock His stable is thoroughly modern The personal attention he gives to details is largely responsible for the growth of the business

Mr King is a member of Ridgeley Lodge, No 112 Independent Order of Odd Fellows, Worcester Lodge, No 56, Ancient Order of United Workmen, of which he was one of the organizers, Helping Hand Lodge, and of Charles Devens Council, American Mechanics In political faith Mr King is a Republican His residence is at 13 Piedmont street

He married March 29, 1872 Lora E King and they have one child, Jesse Walter King, born in Athol, March 21, 1879 now associated in business with his father, married, 1905, Mabel Sanborn, widow of Worcester

(III) Samuel King son of John King (2), mentioned above, was the ancestor of Lora E King, who married Charles W King Samuel was born in Salem, Massachusetts, May, 1664 In 1716 he gave a deed of land in Salem to Benjamin Lynde and others In 1719, as the eldest son, he was one of the signers of a deed of partition of his father's estate He died before 1738, when his sons signed a deed of partition recorded in Salem, 1754

He married Elizabeth Marsh, daughter of Zachery and Mary (Silsbee) Marsh, of Salem, granddaughter of John Marsh, who settled 1636-37 with his wife Susan Skelton daughter of Rev Samuel Skelton Children of Samuel and Elizabeth King were 1 Lieutenant Samuel, lived in that part of the town that became Danvers and had many descendants there 2 Zachariah, married Hannah Southwick daughter of John and Mary (Trask) Southwick, in 1739 he joined his brother Ebenezer King, in a deed to Joseph Goldthwait of rights in the common lands in Salem died about 1771, wife Hannah administrator 3 Ebenezer, born 1700, of whom later

(IV) Ebenezer King son of Samuel King (3), bought 120 acres of land in Rutland. August 5, 1754 though he may have lived there some time before that He bought his farm of Joseph and Hepsibah Felton and added to his holdings land in Barre and Petersham The Rutland history says of him "Ebenezer King and wife Mary with their children were from Danvers He bought the Simon Davis farm, where he and his son for many years kept a tavern As early as 1724 there was an orchard on this farm and some of the trees were standing until lately King was a town officer at Danvers before he moved and was prominent also at Rutland He deeded his property to his sons before his death The deed to his son William of Rutland District (Barre) was "on account of fatherly love and affection" and included several parcels of land, one in Petersham one in Barre containing fifty acres, part of Farm No 22 and was dated March 20 1770 Ebenezer King died in 1786, and his estate was divided finally May 15, 1789 Children of Ebenezer and Mary King were 1 Joseph, married November 22, 1778 Mary Church, daughter of Ephraim Church, married (second) Esther ——— was lieutenant in revolution 2 William, of whom later 3 a daughter married ——— Parlin and left children Lemuel and Hannah Parlin 4 Hannah, married Thomas Stimpson

(V) William King, son of Ebenezer King (4), was born in Danvers, Massachusetts, about 1750 He came to Rutland with his parents He married Sarah ———, and they settled in Barre probably on land of his father's He had extensive dealings in real estate He bought land in 1795 of Ebenezer Rice at Barre and in 1795 of Samuel Bullard, also of William Russell in 1790 a farm of seventy-two acres and buildings In 1788 he bought land and buildings on the road from Rutland to Barre He was in Barre as early as 1771 when he bought five acres of Moses Boyden As late as 1804 he bought land in Barre of Micah Hamilton William King was a soldier in the revolution, a private in Captain Benjamin Nye's company, Colonel Nathan Sparhawk's regiment enlisting August 21, 1777 and marched to reinforce General Stark He died March 17 1813 aged seventy-nine years His wife Sarah died February 3 1846, at the age of eighty-nine years Children of William and Sarah King were Sarah, born 1777, died in Barre, April 17, 1793, Samuel, born August 25, 1778, of whom later, Hannah married December 27 1810 Luther Freeman, of Hardwick. William, born in Barre, October 12, 1782, married Hannah Fiske, December 11, 1816, John, born in Barre about 1798 Samuel Lee was his guardian after his father died appointed February 1, 1814, married, May 15, 1816 Hannah, daughter of Daniel and Eunice (Clark) Parlin

(VI) Samuel King, son of William King (5), was born at Barre, Massachusetts, August 25, 1778, and settled there He married November 20 1801, Sophia Clark of Hardwick She was born March 10, 1784 Their children were Mary, born June 16, 1802 died March 5 1810, Anna P, born December 25, 1803, married Elliott B Trow of Hardwick, March 27 1831, Sarah born February 6, 1806, William Putnam, born October 24, 1808, married Caroline Morgan, of Brimfield, 1831, Harriet, born August 25 1810, married, June 23 1831, Sylvanus N Atwood Jennison Clark, born October 2 1811, married, May 26, 1833, Cynthia Carruth, Charles, born December 7, 1813, Charlotte born May 1, 1816, married December 22 1836 W B Blodgett Samuel, born July 12 1818, married 1840, Sybil Raymond of Hardwick, Mary, born November 26 1821, married December 8, 1840 Charles M Flagg, Joseph born May 28, 1824, of whom later, Jane, born March 17, 1820

(VII) Joseph King son of Samuel King (6), was born in Barre, Massachusetts, May 28, 1824 He married Irene Burroughs, of Dover, New Hampshire and they had seven children, viz Elias F, born in Barre, January 28, 1847, married Mary Bemas of Oakham, Massachusetts, Julia Maria, born in Barre December 25 1849, married James Brown, of Dana, and had—Ida, Alice Arthur Brown Lora of whom later, Anna, married George W Bishop, of Claremont, Frank, had children—Lyman Elias, Mary, Jennie married Clarence ∖ Charles of Dana Charles, married Florence Needham of Coldbrook and had Irene and Ruth King

(VIII) Lora King daughter of Joseph King (7), was born in Barre Massachusetts She is the wife of Charles Walter King whose name heads this sketch

GEORGE PEIRCE Abraham Peirce (1) one of the "purchasers or old-comers' at Plymouth was the emigrant ancestor of George Peirce, of Worcester Abraham Peirce was born in England and was the first actual settler of that surname in America He was a taxpayer in Plymouth Colony as early as 1623, and he shared in a division of the common cattle in 1627 In the same year he exchanged two shares he owned in a red cow for a ewe lamb owned by Captain Miles Standish In 1629 he sold some land abutting on Hobbs Hole to Thomas Clark for thirty pounds of tobacco He was admitted a freeman in 1633, was a taxpayer in 1634, a house holder in 1637 and in 1639 and 1640 had more land granted him He served as a soldier in 1643 under the famous Captain Miles Standish In 1645 he was one of the original purchasers of ancient Bridgewater, Massachusetts He married Rebecca ———, and settled at Duxbury His daughter Alice was taken to Barnstable for baptism by his wife's sister, Goody Scudder, and baptized July 21, 1650 He died 1673, and his son Abraham was appointed administrator June 3 1673 His children were 1 Abraham, born in Plymouth, January, 1638, married, October 29, 1695, Hannah Glass of Duxbury, he died in Duxbury, January 1718 2 Rebecca, married ——— Wills died Marshfield, March 30, 1724 3 Mary, married ——— Baker 4 Alice, baptized July 21, 1650, married ——— Parker, died at Duxbury, 1673 5 Isaac, born about 1661, married Alice ———, he died in Middleboro, now Lakeville, February 28, 1732, was a soldier in King Philip's war

(II) Isaac Peirce, son of Abraham Peirce (1), was born about 1661 in Duxbury, Massachusetts Tradition says that he had two thumbs on one hand He married Alice ——— He died at Middleboro, now Lakeville, Massachusetts February 28, 1732 His will was dated 1722 His children were Isaac, Jr, Thomas, married, April 16, 1714, Naomi Booth, of Middleboro Mary, married ——— Saunders Lydia married (first), July 3, 1706, John Heyford of Bridgewater, married (second), January 12, 1725 Aaron Seckel, Mercy, married, May 15, 1707, Joseph Trouant of Bridgewater, Sarah married ——— Macomber, Rebecca married Samuel Hoar, of Middleboro, she died July 12, 1765, he died February 13 1746

Isaac Peirce, Sr, was left an orphan at the age of thirteen and at the age of sixteen served in the army in King Philip's war For his services his heirs received a grant of land in township No 4, in New Hampshire This was exchanged later for land at Greenwich, Massachusetts, then known as Quabbin His wife was said by tradition to be Alice Chartley, whose fare from Scotland Isaac paid upon her arrival and forthwith married her

(III) Isaac Peirce Jr, son of Isaac Peirce (2), was born about 1680 He married (first), 1703, Judith Booth youngest daughter of John Booth, of Scituate She was born March 13 1680 They were married contrary to the law of the colony, according to the Quaker form Isaac Peirce was a member of the Society of Friends He was persecuted to the extent that he was fined for not conforming to the law regulating marriage He pleaded guilty was fined and seems to have been let alone afterward whereas many of the Quakers had their homes broken up by the religious fanatics then in control of affairs in the colonies Many Baptists suffered the same way later The curious ignorance shown by the genealogist of the Peirce family in reporting this court record requires this explanation here

John Booth the father of Mrs Peirce was at Scituate in 1656 His son Benjamin was a partner of Isaac Peirce Jr his brother-in-law, in the purchase of a tract of land at Middleboro and Taunton in 1700 Judith (Booth) Peirce died May 4 1733 He married (second) 1736 Abigail ——— In his will made 1756 he bequeaths a negro slave Jack He died January 17, 1757 He was called a very

Wm. A. Richardson

uncompromising man and he "suffered great disquietude because his children, except one, left the Quakers and became Calvinist Baptists" Accordingly he left to his Quaker son, the youngest, who had been "willing and obedient" the lion s share of his property His children were 1 Ebenezer, born 1704, married, December 13, 1728, Mary Hoskins, daughter of Henry Hoskins and granddaughter of William Hoskins, Ebenezer died August 14, 1796, his wife died October 5, 1768 2 Isaac, born 1705, married, May 5, 1735 Deliverance Holloway, of Middleboro 3 Elisha, married, November 10, 1738, Margaret Paine, of Freetown, daughter of John Paine and Rebecca Davis 4 Abigail, married, October 28, 1736 John Howland, of Middleboro, she died 1756, he died 1790, aged eighty 5 Judith, born July 4, 1709, married, December 2, 1736, Lieutenant Thomas Nelson, Jr, of Middleboro, who was twelve years selectman fourteen years in general court, lieutenant of Fourth Company of which Isaac Peirce was ensign, she died January 22, 1792 6 Elkanah, married, March 2, 1742, Hannah Eddy, they were Quakers

(IV) Isaac Peirce, son of Isaac Peirce (3), was born about 1705 He married, May 5, 1735, Deliverance Holloway, of Middleboro He was commissioned ensign 1762 in the Fourth Company of militia The captain was Joseph Leonard, lieutenant, Thomas Nelson, colonel, George Watson, of Plymouth Ensign Peirce died September 18, 1782 His wife died October 11, 1801, aged eighty-seven years Their children were George, born October 16, 1735, married September 14, 1757, Sarah Peirce, daughter of Shadrach Peirce and a relative, he died July 17, 1774, she died April 20, 1778 2 An infant 3 Enos, born September 30, 1739, married, December 28, 1785, Ruth Durfee, of Freetown, he died July 29, 1794, she died October 9, 1811, aged fifty-two 4 David, born March 20, 1741, married, July, 1764, Abigail Hathaway, daughter of Ensign Hathaway, of Freetown, David was ensign of the first militia company of Freetown, served in the revolution and was accidentally killed March 9, 1779, by the fall of a tree while cutting timber, his widow married Joshua Howard, of Freetown, March 3, 1789 5 Silas, born July 25, 1744 6 Lucy, born May 28, 1755, married, November 30, 1775, Captain Samuel French, soldier, deputy sheriff of Bristol county, died March 26, 1830, she died April 26, 1845, they resided at Berkeley Tavern, Berkeley, Massachusetts

(V) Silas Peirce, son of Isaac Peirce (4), was born July 25, 1744 He married Anna Hathaway, of Taunton, October 31, 1771 She was the daughter of Melatiah and Anna (Hoskins) Hathaway Silas was for nine months a private in the revolutionary army under Captain Amos Washburn, of Middleboro He died May 1, 1816 and was buried in East Freetown, Massachusetts The children of Silas and Anne (Hathaway) Peirce were 1 Hope, born February 2, 1772, married Simeon Peirce of Taunton, she died May 6, 1857, he died November 17, 1859 2 David, born October 12, 1773, died April 7 1809 3 Lucy, born March 31, 1776, married Levi Peirce, of Middleboro, removed to Worcester county 4 Anna, born April 28, 1778, married Oliver Peirce, Esq of Middleboro, she died February 12, 1847, he died August 17, 1860 5 George, born August 24 1780, married Eunice Tinkham, of Rochester, Massachusetts, she died June 22, 1827, aged forty-five 6 Isaac, born February 10, 1786, married Deliverance Sherman, daughter of Nehemiah and Deborah (Peirce) Sherman, Isaac died 1868 he was a private soldier in the war of 1812 in the coast guard near Plymouth 7 Judith, born April 20, 1788, married William E Ellis, of Rochester, Massachusetts she died May, 1861, resided at Rochester 8 Deliverance, born March 4, 1790 9 Meletiah H, born October 7, 1792, married Sally White

(VI) Meletiah Peirce, son of Silas Peirce (5), was born October 7, 1792 He was a ship carpenter by trade He married Sally White, of Fairhaven, Massachusetts His children were Benjamin, Philip Judith, Laura, Samuel, John M

(VII) Benjamin Peirce, son of Meletiah Peirce (6), was born in New Bedford, Massachusetts He was a carpenter He married Mary A Vail, and their children were George, born in New Bedford, July 19 1845, Benjamin Franklin, lives in the west, a child who died at age of two years

(VIII) George Peirce, son of Benjamin Peirce (7), was born in New Bedford, Massachusetts, July 19, 1845 He attended the public schools of his native place and worked on a farm during his youth He was only fifteen years old, however, when he enlisted in the Twenty-ninth Massachusetts Infantry and was sent from New Bedford to Newport News, Virginia, where he saw the famous encounter of the Merrimac and Monitor He was in the company of Captain Willard Tripp, of Taunton Company F, Twenty-ninth Massachusetts Volunteer Militia, Colonel Ebenezer Peirce He served three years and seven months and was in twenty-three battles He was discharged July 29, 1865, and mustered out in August Among the engagements in which he took part with his company were Hamilton Roads, Virginia, Gaines Mills, Peach Orchard, Savage Station, Shady Grove, Virginia, Cold Harbor, Virginia, Petersburg, Virginia, Licks Station, Popular Grove, Virginia, Fort Stedman, Virginia He was wounded at Cold Harbor and was taken prisoner at Fort Stedman He fought in White Oak Swamp, Glendale, Malvern Hill, on the seven days retreat with General McClellan, Second Bull's Run, Antietam, Vicksburg, Mississippi, Jackson, Mississippi, Blue Springs Tennessee, Campbell's Station, Tennessee, Fort Saunders, Tennessee, and Totopotomoy, Virginia, he was at Petersburg in 1865

After the war he followed his trade as a carpenter at Springfield, Illinois After two years he removed to Walpole Massachusetts He worked at Boston and Foxboro, Massachusetts, also In 1872, soon after his marriage at Foxboro, he came to Worcester and settled He began in business for himself as a contractor and builder, and in the past thirty years has built many dwelling houses and business blocks in Worcester Among the contracts he had was for the New Park Hotel, the Bellmar Hotel and part of the Standish Apartment Hotel He is a member of Montacute Lodge, A F and A M, of Post 10, G A R, A O U W, and the American Order of Fraternal Helpers

He married, in Foxboro, Massachusetts, Isabella D Hatch, daughter of William Hatch She died in Worcester in 1884. He married (second) Sophia G Hatch, sister of his first wife He married (third) Mary A Cummings, of North Brookfield She was the daughter of Benjamin Cummings, Jr, a farmer of North Brookfield Her grandfather, Benjamin Cummings, also of North Brookfield, married Mary Ann Mead The family was prominent in the history of Brookfield and is one of the old Worcester county families Mr Peirce has no children He resides at 131 Pleasant street, Worcester, Massachusetts

WILLIAM A RICHARDSON Samuel Richardson (1) was the first ancestor in this country of William A Richardson, of Worcester Three brothers Ezekiel, Samuel and Thomas Richardson settled in Woburn, Massachusetts Samuel was born about 1610 and the first record of his name was in 1636 The three brothers and four others were the founders of Woburn, all coming from Charlestown A street in Woburn, where they located, is still known as Richardson's Row Samuel was selectman in 1644-45-46-49-50-51, the largest taxpayer in 1645 His wife joined the church at Charlestown, September 9, 1639 He died March 23, 1658. Their children were 1 Mary, baptized February 25, 1637-38, married Thomas Mousall, son of Deacon John Mousall, one of the founders 2 John, baptized November 12, 1639, married Elizabeth Bacon Mary Pierson, Margaret Willing 3 Hannah and the following were born in Woburn, she was born March 8 1641-2, died April 8, 1642 4 Joseph, born July 27, 1643, married Hannah Green 5 Samuel, born May 22, 1646, married Martha ———, Hannah Kingsbury, Phebe Baldwinn Sarah Hayward 6 Stephen (see forward) 7 Thomas, born December 31, 1651, died September 27, 1657 8 Elizabeth, born 1665

(II) Stephen Richardson son of Samuel (1) and Joanna Richardson, born at Woburn August 15 1649, married January 2 1674-5 at Billerica, Abigail (Read) Wyman He took the freeman's oath 1690, died March 22 1717-18 His widow died September 17 1720 Their children were 1 Stephen, born February 20, 1675-6, married Susanna Wilson 2 Francis, January 19 1677-8, died January 27 1677-8 3 William, December 14, 1678, married Rebecca Vinton 4 Francis, January 15, 1680-1, married Sarah Houghton 5 Timothy, December 6 1682 died January 18, 1683 6 Abigail, November 14, 1683, married John Vinton 7 Prudence January 17, 1685-6 married Samuel Kendall 8 Timothy January 24, 1687-8, married Susanna Holden 9 Seth, January 16, 1689-90, married Mary Brown 10 Daniel October 16 1691, married Joanna Mousall 11 Mary May 3, 1696 12 Rebecca, June 10 1698, died December 6 1711 13 Solomon, March 27, 1702 married Abigail Evans, of Reading

(III) William Richardson, son of Stephen (2) and Abigail Richardson born at Woburn December 14 1678, married September 15 1703, Rebecca Vinton born March 26 1683 daughter of John and Hannah (Green) Vinton of Woburn They removed to Stoneham in 1710, and to Attleboro in 1718 Their children were 1 Rebecca born August 4 1704 died unmarried 2 Hannah born October 28, 1706 3 Abigail born April 18 1709, married John Shepard 4 William, born April 17, 1712 5 Stephen born September 7 1714, died unmarried November 11 1797 6 John (see forward) 7 Joanna born September 17, 1722

(IV) John Richardson son of William (3) and Rebecca Richardson born at Attleboro, November 27 1719 married Elizabeth Wilmarth April 19, 1742 Their children were 1 Lucy, born December 5 1742 2 John born May 24 1744 married Ruth Woodcock 3 Wyman (see forward) 4 Betsey born April 4, 1748 5 Joel born October 10, 1750 married Sarah Wyman 6 Henry, born August 7 1752 married Olive Blackinton

(V) Wyman Richardson, son of John (4) and Elizabeth Richardson born at Attleboro May 13, 1746 married October 31 1771 Ruth Lane, born at Norton Massachusetts December 1 1752 They removed to Swanzey New Hampshire October 1779 His wife died at Acworth, New Hampshire, January 2 1835 He died October 11 1839 at the age of ninety-three years Their children were 1 Ruth and 2 Orra (twins), born August 8, 1772, 3 Azubah, February 8 1775, died at Acworth New Hampshire, August, 1838 4. Wyman (see forward) 5 Elkanah, July 9, 1780, died at Stow, Ohio, January 8, 1836 6 Stephen, June 4, 1783 7 Luna, May 10, 1785, died July 11, 1824. 8 Ruth, September 18, 1787 9 Calvin, July 17, 1790, died at Wolcott, Vermont, July 12, 1828 10 Lucy, ——— 14, 1793, died at Newfane, Vermont, May, 1830 11 Sophia, July 8, 1796, died at Swanzey, New Hampshire, September 25, 1813 12 Esther, April 27, 1799, died at Newfane, May 12, 1833

(VI) Wyman Richardson, son of Wyman (5) and Ruth Richardson, born at Attleboro, June 10, 1777, married at Richmond, New Hampshire, October 22, 1802, Deliverance Bolles, daughter of Elder Nathaniel Bolles, of Rochester and Richmond, New Hampshire, born at Richmond, July 23, 1782 Wyman Richardson learned the blacksmith's trade from his father, who was also a proficient cooper, and worked at both trades He died February 26, 1868, aged ninety years His wife died August 11, 1870 Their children were 1 Wyman (see forward) 2 Nathaniel, born December 21, 1804, married Eurelia Young 3 Delia, born April 23, 1807, married Hiram Boardman 4 Luna Bolles, born December 27, 1809, married Mary Kimball 5 Thankful born January 17, 1813, married Ethan Lord and had five children 6 Almira, born October 16, 1817, married Jonathan Goodell and had one son, Jonathan 7 Nathan Henry, born May 31, 1823, married Martha Ann Barber 8 Phebe Sophia, born April 19, 1826, married Lorenzo N Hewes and had seven children

(VII) Wyman Richardson, son of Wyman (6) and Deliverance grandson of Wyman (5) and great-grandson of John (4), and father of William A, born at Swanzey, New Hampshire, March 5, 1803, married at Athol Massachusetts, August 13, 1827, Arethusa Southwick (Lee), born at Shutesbury Massachusetts, March 6, 1809 They settled at Corinth, Vermont, where the three eldest children were born then removed to Athol and Fitchburg Massachusetts They resided at Barre, Petersham and Boston At Petersham he was the superintendent of a button factory which was burned in 1847, when the family moved to a part of Barre known as Smithville, from the name of the mill owner, John Smith whose machinery Richardson was put in charge of, after being employed first as a machine hand In 1850 David J Foster one of the proprietors of the button factory that was burned at Petersham, opened a new shop in Boston and Richardson, together with his sons moved thither to work for him After a few years in Boston Richardson moved to Fitchburg and went into business as a rattan manufacturer, his sons working for him Their children were 1 Solon Oscar, born July 3, 1828 married Nancy Nichols Fairbanks died March 31, 1872 2 Seneca Merrill born December 5, 1829, married Emily D Earle, of Worcester, and was partner in the manufacturing firm of Wetherbee, Rugg & Richardson had a daughter Harriet 3 Lyman Collins, born November 26 1831 never married, located on Pacific coast, was in British service 4 William Augustus, December 20 1833 married Mary Ann Cowen, daughter of Captain Robert Cowen of Plymouth, Massachusetts 5 Charles Oswald, born November 13, 1839, died at Athol September 26 1840

(VIII) William Augustus Richardson, son of Wyman (7) and Arethusa Richardson, was born at Athol Massachusetts, December 20, 1833 When the family moved to Barre William was seven years old and there he obtained most of his schooling, though for a time he attended school at Petersham His first work was in the mill at Smithville as a machine hand He worked at the various branches of the machinist's trade with and for his father, becoming a mechanic of extraordinary skill He went with his father to Foster's button factory, in Boston and was with him in his rattan factory at Fitchburg In 1860 he went to Waltham as an expert machinist for the American Watch Company In 1863 he started in business for himself in New York, manufacturing rattan goods but after one year gave it up and entered the employ of Ball & Williams, gun manufacturers at Worcester Later he went into the factory of Frank Wesson, at Worcester, to manufacture pistols under the patents of Gilbert H Harrington, who subsequently became a partner of Mr Richardson, and whom he met there for the first time In 1874 the foundation of the Harrington & Richardson Arms Company was made, in a partnership between William A Richardson and Gilbert H Harrington, to manufacture guns They started in quarters at 18 Manchester street, but these soon were too small and they moved to 31 Hermon street, where they continued until March 1, 1894, enlarging their factory from time to time as business grew The firm of Harrington & Richardson were the exclusive manufacturers of the celebrated Anson & Deeley hammerless gun the first of its kind to be made in this country from 1880 to 1887 They secured a patent in April, 1887, for the safety hammerless gun and in the same year in October patented the cylinder catch which is still used They took out a design patent in 1889 applying to stocks and in 1895 a patent applying to lever springs They own other valuable patents In January, 1888 the firm was incorporated as The Harrington & Richardson Arms Company The capital is $75000 Mr Harrington was president, Mr Richardson treasurer and George F Brooks secretary Since the death of the two partners Mr Brooks has been the manager The present handsome building was built in 1893-4 It is a five story brick structure situated at the corner of the Boulevard and Chandler street In 1900 and 1901 large additions were made to the factory It now covers 100000 square feet and about five hundred hands are employed No more attractive building, architecturally has been built for manufacturing in this city of many mills and factories No more prosperous and well-ordered business is to be found in New England It is one of the shops to which Worcester people point with pride, and it constitutes perhaps the most substantial and enduring monument to the mechanical skill and business sagacity of Mr Richardson and his partner Mr Richardson's skill and love for the mechanics must have been largely inherited from his ancestors who were blacksmiths and machinists He was conceded to be one of the most skillful machinists in the state Personally Mr Richardson was a careful unostentatious man generous with his wealth, but preferring domestic life above all things He was a member of no societies or clubs He was a member and trustee of the First Universalist Church and was liberal in his gifts to churches and charities He gave a large sum to All Souls' Church Since his death his wife has continued to donate as she thinks he would have done had his life been spared She recently gave to St Lawrence University, of which the Rev Dr Gunnison formerly pastor of the First Universalist Church, is the president a gift of $10000 He was a Republican in politics The dominant characteristic of Mr Richardson was that of most self-made men it was untiring energy and tenacity He stuck to an idea, and followed up a project to the end He took an honorable satisfaction in the knowledge that his success in life had come without outside aid His only capital was his skilful hands at the start He never would accept his wife's fortune to aid him He married Mary Ann Cowen, daughter of Captain Robert and Ann (Tilden) Cowen Her father was a ship master at Plymouth, Massachusetts They had no children but reared several Mr Richardson died November 21, 1897 Mrs Richardson lives at their handsome home, 921 Main street, Worcester

EDWIN HAWES Edward Hawes (1), one of the early settlers of Dedham, Massachusetts, was the emigrant ancestor of Edwin Hawes, of Worcester He was a mason by trade He came from England and was in Dedham as early as 1648, when the records show that he was engaged to plaster the meeting house there He died June 28, 1686 He married, April 15, 1648, at Dedham, Eliony Lumber or Lombard (See sketch in this work of Manson D Hawes) Children of Edward Hawes were 1 Lydia, born January 26, 1649, married ——— Gay 2 Mary, born November 4, 1650 3 Daniel (see forward) 4 Hannah, born February 1, 1654-5 married January 5, 1676, John Mason 5 John, born December 17, 1657, died February 21, 1731-2 6 Nathaniel, born August 14, 1660, died October 16, 1714 7 Abigail, born October 2, 1662, married John Fales 8 Joseph, born August 9, 1664 9 Deborah, born September 1, 1666, married (first) Ephraim Pond, married (second) ——— Bacon

(II) Daniel Hawes, son of Edward Hawes (1), born February 10, 1652, at Dedham, Massachusetts, married, February 11, 1677, Abial Gay, born April 23, 1649, daughter of John and Joanna Gay John Gay came to Watertown from England before 1635 and removed to Dedham in 1636 He was admitted a freeman May 6, 1635 He was a town officer of Dedham His wife Joanna was admitted to the Dedham church, July 25 1639, and John Balducke her son by a former husband was baptized August 8, 1639 John Gay died March 4, 1688, and his will was proved December 17, 1689 The children of John and Joanna Gay were 1 Samuel, born March 10 1639 2 Hezekiah, born July 3, 1640 3 Nathaniel born February 11, 1642-3 4 Joanna, born March 23 1644, married John Ware 5 Eliezer, born June 25 1647 6 Abial (twin) born April 23, 1649 married Daniel Hawes 7 Judith (twin), born April 23 1649 married John Ware 8 John born May, 1651 9 Jonathan, born August 1, 1653 10 Hannah born October 16 1656 11 probably Elizabeth, who married Richard Martin at Salem in 1660 (Lydia Hawes married one of the sons, probably)

Daniel Hawes died March 16, 1737-8, aged eighty-six years His children were 1 Mary, born September 17 1679 married Eleazer Ware 2 Abigail, born November 15, 1681, married Thomas Mann 3 Daniel (see forward) 4 Josiah, born April 6, 1686 5 Hezekiah, born November 22, 1688 married Esther Ware 6 Ruth, born July 9, 1691 married Nathaniel Wright 7 Benjamin, born March 14, 1696, married Abigail Fales

(III) Daniel Hawes son of Daniel Hawes (2), born in Dedham March 30 1684, died January 15, 1763 He settled in Wrentham, Massachusetts, in what is now Franklin He married December 20 1710 Beriah Mann Their children were 1 Daniel born October 21 1711 2 Samuel, born January 7, 1713 3 Peletiah born October 8 1714 married Judith Peck 4 Moses, born August 28, 1716 5 Aaron, born April 13 1718 6 Ichabod, born September 18 1720 7 Timothy born June 21 1722, married Mary Ware 8 Beriah (twin), born March 30 1724 9 Josiah (see forward) 10 Mary, born February 11 1725-6 married Ebenezer Lawrence 11 Joseph born March 21, 1727-8

(IV) Josiah Hawes, son of Daniel Hawes (3), born in Wrentham, Massachusetts, March 30, 1724, died February 28, 1804 He settled in Franklin, Massachusetts, and married, December 18, 1751, Maria Lyon, who died August 28, 1779 Their children were 1 Abijah, born August 31, (September 11, new style) 1752, at Wrentham, died January 10 1839, at Wrentham, settled at Union, Maine, married, December, 1782, second cousin, Margaret Hawes, born May 9, 1756, died May 24, 1833, had five children 2 Mary, born October 27, 1753, died August 8, 1785 3 Mathias (see forward) 4 Jemima born January 28, 1761, died April 26, 1835, married, November 23, 1782, Eliab Wright or Wight, of Bellingham 5 Beriah, born April 17, 1762, died October 20, 1818 6 Levi, born May 22, 1765, died September 4, 1839, married January 1, 1793, Permelia Clark, who died September 4, 1839 The old house in which Josiah Hawes, of Franklin, lived, built about two hundred years ago, is standing, or was until recently

(V) Mathias Hawes, son of Josiah Hawes (4), born at Franklin, Massachusetts (then Wrentham), October 6, 1754, died November 4, 1828, married, January 1, 1783, in Warren, Maine, Sarah Payson, daughter of Captain Samuel Payson, who subsequently moved from Warren to Hope, Maine, where he died Their children were Sarah or Sally, born April 5, 1784, died December 10, 1850, married William Brown, son of James and Ruth Brown, and left many descendants 2 James, born November 11, 1785, died November 23, or 24, 1793, of throat distemper 3 Mary, born June 17, 1787, married, August 14, 1808, Simon Barrett, born at Concord, Massachusetts, September 24, 1765, resided at Hope, Maine, died at Augusta, Maine, April 20, 1845, and left many descendants 4 Sukey (twin of Mary), born June 17, 1787, died of throat distemper December 20, 1793 5 Oliver, born March 8, 1789, died March 11, 1789 6 Hermon (twin), born January 6, died January 17, 1790 7 Pliny (twin), born January 6, died January 17, 1790 8 Meletiah, born April 21, 1791, married, June 2, 1825, David Crabtree, born February 26, 1781, resided at Hope, Maine 9 Otis (see forward) 10 Austin, born September 22, 1794 died April 5 1795 11 Noyes Payson, born February 4, 1796, married, October 25, 1827, Abigail Richardson, daughter of John Wilkes Richardson, of Franklin, Massachusetts, resided at Boston 12 July, born November 17, 1797 13 Silas, born August 1 1799 14 Lavinia Anthony, born September 20 1800, married Vinal Ware 15 Galen born April 13, 1802, lived on the old homestead in Union died August 4, 1834, married, January 6, 1831 Harriet Lindley, daughter of Captain John W Lindley, widow married (second) Elias Blake, of Bangor, Maine 16 Levi, born December 24 1804, died August 12, 1805 17 Child, stillborn, July, 1806 18 Child stillborn, August, 1807 19 Madison, born March 24, 1809, printer resided in California, married, May 1, 1854 Nancy Nelson Dam

(VI) Otis Hawes, son of Mathias Hawes (5), born at Union, Maine, January 21 or 31, 1793, married, September 20, 1818, Elsie Davis, daughter of John Davis of Appleton, Maine Their children were 1 Sarah, born April 9, 1820, died September 23 1838 2 Silas (see forward) 3 Roxanna Nott, born December 18, 1823 married 1843, Isaac C Hovey and had Arthur M and Carrie E 4 Lavinia A, born July 20, 1825, married Rev Albert Thurston 5 Philander, born September 22, 1827 6 Julia, born December 17, 1829 7 Cyrene J, born February 9 1833 resides in Union, Maine, unmarried 8 Laurinda, born July 19, 1835, married Augustus Vaughan 9 Edwin, born November 3, 1839 10. Charles Barrett, born November 26, 1841

(VII) Silas Hawes, son of Otis Hawes (6), born at Union, Maine, December 26, 1821, married, September 10, 1848, Margaret Hills, daughter of Sarah B Hills (See Hills Family sketch) He resided at Union, Maine, where he owned a farm. Children were 1 Emma F, born December 20, 1849, married Levi Daniels, resides at South Union in the town of Union, Maine, and has one son, Nathan S, who married Mabel N Moody He works with his father on the farm 2 Anna Florence, born July 11, 1852, resides at Union, Maine; unmarried 3 William, born at Union, Maine, December 20, 1854, owns the old Hills homestead at Union, Maine 4 Edwin (see forward)

(VIII) Edwin Hawes, son of Silas Hawes (7), was born at Union, Maine, January 23, 1857 He spent his boyhood in his native town He attended the district and village schools of Union and worked on the farm At the age of seventeen he left home and entered the shops of the Walworth Manufacturing Company, in Boston This company was engaged in the steam-heating business, together with steam fitting, etc Within a year a business depression caused Mr Hawes to leave this position, and he went to work next for Morey & Rogers, at Hollis-ton, manufacturing straw hats After leaving the business he went to the shop of H O Bernard & Co, straw manufacturers, at Westborough, Massachusetts, where for nine years he was employed as a blocker In 1885 he returned to the steam-heating business and became shop foreman for the firm of Braman, Dow & Company, Washington Square Worcester This is the oldest house of its kind in the city The firm is in business still having its headquarters in Boston, and a very prosperous store and shop in Worcester

Mr Hawes went into business on his own account in the same line, June 1, 1893, in a small shop on Canal street, near the corner of Front street He was successful in his venture and soon took the store at 246 Main street, where he remained until Flint & Barker took a lease on the building and he had to seek a new location In 1898 he removed his store and shop to 185 Front street, where he was located for about three years In 1900 he removed to his present location at 17 Vine street The business was incorporated under the laws of Massachusetts in 1905 The officers of the company are President, Edwin Hawes, secretary and treasurer, James E L Todd Mr Hawes is also treasurer of the Eddy Manufacturing Company, which makes razor strops at 42 Southbridge street, Worcester He is a director of the company also He is a member of Anchoria Lodge Independent Order of Odd Fellows the Hancock Club and the board of trade In politics he is a staunch Republican He belongs to Trinity Methodist Episcopal Church He married November 10, 1884, Hattie L Richardson, daughter of Duquesnel H Richardson, of West Brookfield, Massachusetts They have one son Herbert Richardson, born in Worcester, May 30, 1887, graduate of the Worcester classical high school, 1905 and a member of the class of 1909, Dartmouth College

HILLS FAMILY Joseph Hills (1), the emigrant, ancestor of Edwin Hawes through his mother's line, was born in the parish of Great Burstead, Billericay, Essex county, England He was baptized there March, 1602, son of George Hills, who married Mary Simonds, of Billericay, widow of the late William Symonds, of Billericay, tanner The marriage license was dated October 13, 1596, at which time Joseph Hills did not use the final "s" in his surname. It appears first February, 1608, probably through a change in the vicar who kept the records.

Joseph Hills married Rose Clarke, at Great Burstead, July 22, 1624, and the elder children were born there. Not later than March, 1632, he and his family removed to Maldon, a place in Essex county, England, which was the birthplace of their sons John and Stephen, and daughter Sarah. In 1638 he was an "undertaker" or stockholder in the voyage of the "Susan and Ellen," which arrived July 17, 1638, at Boston, with him and his family. They made their first abiding place in Charlestown, Massachusetts, near the Market place, but soon removed to a farm on the Mystic side. He was one of the founders of the town of Malden. He was the first deputy to the general court, and continuously represented the town in the legislature until 1664. It was he who gave the name to the town, after the name of his last place of residence in England, Maldon. He was selectman of Malden in 1644 and speaker of the house of deputies in 1647. He was captain of the Trainband, and willed his buff coat to his son Samuel, and his back sword to Henry Lunt, his step-son. He was one of the most prominent legislators of his day. In 1666, when he retired from public life, he was succeeded by his son-in-law, John Waite, who filled the position of deputy for nineteen years, being speaker in 1684 and nominated as a magistrate in 1683.

In 1645 Joseph Hills was named by the general court to set out the lots to settlers in the Nashaway plantation. In 1650 he was second on a committee, of which the governor was the chairman, to draw up instructions for the Massachusetts delegates to a gathering of commissioners of all the colonies. In 1653 he served on a commission to consider the question as to whether the United Colonies have power by the articles of agreement to engage the colonies in war. In 1654 with Captain Hawthorne, Captain Johnson and the treasurer of the colony, he was on a committee to frame an answer to the home government, which had demanded an explanation of certain acts. He was on a committee to audit the treasury accounts in 1650-53-61. He framed the first code of laws in the colony, and was for many years engaged in the revision of the statutes. In 1648 he was one of the committee that reported the first codification of the laws of the colony, and it was he who compiled the laws, prepared the copy for the printer and supervised the printing. He was voted as extra compensation for his work five hundred acres of land on the Nashua river and remission of taxes in his old age. He was appointed more times to edit the laws than even Governor Bellingham.

His wife died in Malden, March 24, 1650, and he married (second), June 21, 1651, Hannah (Smith) Mellows, widow of Edward Mellows, of Charlestown, who died 1655. In January, 1656, he married (third) Helen, Ellen or Eleanor Atkinson. She died January 6, 1663. In one of his marriages Mr. Hills acted the part of magistrate as well as groom, and married himself. The law required marriages to be solemnized by magistrates. Governor Bellingham set Mr. Hills an example by marrying himself to Penelope Pelham. He was called upon to come down and plead to a complaint against him for the act, but he refused to do so. Joseph Hills, being a magistrate to end small causes, followed the example of the governor, January, 1656, and was presented to the grand jury for marrying himself contrary to the laws of the colony. The records show that he freely acknowledged his offense therein and his misunderstanding the grounds whereon he went, which he now confesseth to be unwarrantable. And he was admonished by the court. (Middlesex county records.) He married (fourth) at Newbury, Massachusetts, Ann Lunt, widow of Henry Lunt, and made his home at Newbury his residence thereafter. He became blind in 1678. He died at Newbury, Massachusetts, February 5, 1688. His children were: 1. Mary, baptized at Great Burstead, England, November 13, 1625, died at Malden, November 25, 1674. 2. Elizabeth, born in Great Burstead, baptized October 21, 1627, died at Malden. 3. Joseph, born at Great Burstead, August 2, 1629, died at Malden, April 19, 1674. 4. James, born at Maldon, England, March 6, 1631, died young. 5. John, born in Maldon, England, March 21, 1632, died at Malden, July 28, 1652. 6. Rebecca, born April 20, 1634, died at Malden, Massachusetts, June 16, 1674. 7. Steven, born May 1, 1636, died at Maldon before 1638. 8. Sarah, born at Maldon, baptized August 14, 1637, died there August 14, 1637. 9. Gershom, born at Charlestown, July 27, 1639, died in Malden, Massachusetts, between 1710 and 1721. 10. Mehitable, born at Malden, Massachusetts, January 1, 1641, died there July, 1652. 11. Samuel, (see forward). 12. Nathaniel, born at Malden, Massachusetts, December 19, 1653, died there 1664. 13. Hannah, born at Malden. 14. Deborah, born at Malden, Massachusetts, March, 1657, died at Malden, October, 1662. 15. Abigail, born at Malden, October 6, 1658, died there October 9, 1662.

(II) Samuel Hills, son of Joseph Hills (1), was born at Malden, July, 1652, died at Newbury, Massachusetts, August 18, 1732. He was a sergeant in the service during King Philip's war, and was in the battle of Bloody Brook, September 18, 1675, and Narragansett, December 19, 1675. He married at Newbury, Massachusetts, May 20, 1677, Abigail Wheeler, who died April 13, 1742, daughter of David and Sarah (Wise) Wheeler, of Newbury, Massachusetts. David Wheeler was the son of John Wheeler, who was born in Salisbury, Wiltshire, England, 1625, and came over in the "Confidence" in 1638. He married Sarah Wise, May 11, 1650. Children of Samuel and Abigail (Wheeler) Hills were: 1. Samuel, born at Newbury, Massachusetts, February 16, 1680, died at Rehoboth, July 17, 1748. 2. Joseph, born at Newbury, July 21, 1681, died at Newbury, November 6, 1745. 3. Nathaniel, born at Newbury, February 9, 1683, died at Hudson, New Hampshire, April 12, 1748. 4. Benjamin, (see forward). 5. Abigail, born at Newbury, September 2, 1686, died there August 11, 1688. 6. Henry, born at Newbury, April 23, 1688, died at Hudson, New Hampshire, August 20, 1757. 7. William, born at Newbury, October 8, 1689, died there before January 20, 1724. 8. Josiah, born at Newbury, July 27, 1691, died there April 26, 1726. 9. John, born at Newbury, September 20, 1693, died after 1734. 10. Abigail, born at Newbury, June 27, 1695. 11. James, (twin) born at Newbury, February 26, 1697. 12. Hannah, (twin) born at Newbury, February 26, 1697. 13. Daniel, born at Newbury, December 8, 1700, removed to Nottingham west, then to Nova Scotia about 1754. 14. Smith, born at Newbury, April 10, 1706, died at Leominster, Massachusetts, August 23, 1786.

(III) Benjamin Hills, son of Samuel Hills (2), born at Newbury, Massachusetts, October 16, 1684, died at Chester, New Hampshire, November 3, 1762, married November 7, 1709, Rebecca Ordway, daughter of Hananiah and Abigail Ordway. Hananiah was the son of James Ordway. Rebecca was born December 22, 1690, died September 4,

1769 His children, all born at Newbury, Massachusetts, were 1 Samuel, (see forward) 2 Abigail born November 3, 1713, married Isaac Bailey 4 Joannah, born March 15, 1717, married Thomas Haseltine 5 Ruth, born March 15 1719, married Nathan Mason 6 Benjamin, born March 12, 1721, died at Chester, New Hampshire, May 6, 1801 7 Abner, born February 13, 1723, died at Chester, October 3, 1794 8 Hannah, born November 10, 1724 died October 5, 1806 9 Prudence, born February 12, 1726, died 1773 10 Moses, born February 9, 1728

(IV) Samuel Hills, son of Benjamin Hills (3), born at Newbury, Massachusetts, August 10, 1710, died at Chester, New Hampshire, February 2, 1762, married (first), January 28, 1735, Rebecca Thurston of Newbury She died May 21, 1743, married (second), November 18, 1743, Elizabeth Swain, of Newbury She died July 31, 1793 She married (second) Ebenezer Dearborn, after the death of Samuel Hills He had three children by the first and ten by the second marriage His children were 1 Edmund, born in Newbury, December 7, 1735 2 John born May 25, 1738, died February 22, 1818 3 Samuel, born May 17, 1743 4 Isaac, born August 31, 1744, died at Chester, September 24, 1824 5 Stephen, born at Chester, March 29, 1746, died at Amesbury, Massachusetts, January 31, 1831 6 Elizabeth, born at Chester, January 4, 1747, died 1778 7 Hannah, born at Chester, June 5, 1750 8 Reuben, (see forward) 9 Rachel, born at Chester, August 6 1754 10 Rebecca, born at Chester, August 6, 1756 11 Josiah, born at Chester, October 30, 1760, died at Chester, September 22, 1790 13 Rachel born at Chester, May 12, 1762

(V) Reuben Hills, son of Samuel Hills (4), was born at Chester, New Hampshire, August 14, 1752 He removed to Hawke now Danville, New Hampshire, thence to Union, Maine He was a soldier in the revolution He was prominent in the Methodist church, but late in life became a Quaker He married, January 18, 1779, Sarah Currier, daughter of Gideon Currier She died at Union, Maine, November 1, 1835 He died there September 28, 1828 Their children, ten of whom were born in Danville, New Hampshire, and two in Union, Maine, were 1 Samuel (see forward) 2 Sarah, born January 27, 1781, died at Searsmont Maine, May 3, 1862, married John Dickey January 20, 1803, resided at Searsmont 3 Nathan, born July 17, 1784 died at Union Maine, August 28, 1858 4 Reuben, born March 2, 1786, died at Lincolnville, Maine, October 3, 1874 5 Josiah born April 2, 1788 died in Union, Maine, March 28, 1875 6 Isaac born February 12, 1790 died at Lincolnville, Maine, January 7, 1840 7 Nancy, born January 29, 1793 died at Union, Maine, May 25 1862, married, January 16 1817 Jonathan Eastman 8 Betsey, born March 2 1795 died May 8, 1796, in Union, Maine 9 Dr Cyrus, born January 16, 1797, died at Cushing Maine October 26 1860 10 Alden, born July 14 1801, drowned at Union, Maine, July 17, 1807 11 Charlotte, born June 29, 1802, died 1804 12 Louisa, born July 6 1804 died in Union, Maine, June 11 1850, married, February 14, 1822, George Silloway

(VI) Samuel Hills, son of Reuben Hills (5), was born at Danville New Hampshire, November 18 1779 died at Union May 16, 1853 He was a farmer and settled at Union He should not be confused with a distant relative, Samuel Hills living in Union at the same time, whose son, Joel Hills, married Abigail Hawes, daughter of Levi and Pamelia Hawes, of this same line of the Hawes family into which the daughter Margaret of the first named Samuel Hills (6) married Samuel Hills married, January 11, 1816, Sarah B Rogers, who died October, 1836 Children were 1 Edward, married Almena Drake, had ten children, resided at Thomaston, Maine and was high sheriff of the county 2 Israel, resided at Appleton, Maine 3 Benjamin B, born February 18, 1821, married at Union, Amelia H Oxton, of Appleton, March 11, 1849, went to Warren and built a house on the Patterson road 4 Emeline, married John Walton, resides at Union 5 Margaret, married Silas Hawes 6 Samuel, Jr, married and resided at New Orleans, Louisiana 7 Sarah, born at Union, married Nathaniel Thurston, resides at Union

(VII) Margaret Hills, daughter of Samuel Hills (6), was born in Union, Maine, married Silas Hawes, before mentioned

DR EMIL SAUER, a well established general practitioner of Worcester, and who has attained distinction in certain special fields of his profession, is a native of the city named, and comes from an excellent German family

Wendel Sauer, his paternal grandfather, was a resident of Hesse Darmstadt, and a shoemaker by trade Prior to 1812 he entered the French army as a substitute He died at the age of sixty-one years, and his wife at the age of fifty-one years They were the parents of six children, only one of whom, Joseph, came to the United States

Joseph Sauer, son of Wendel Sauer, was born in Hesse Darmstadt, Germany, January 29, 1839 He was educated in the schools of his native village, and at the age of fifteen years came to America, landing in New York after a passage of thirty-two days For a time he worked in a woolen mill in Broad Brook, Connecticut, and in 1859, located in Worcester, Massachusetts There he found employment in the Allen & Wheelock pistol factory, afterward in the Crompton loom works, and still later in the carbine factory of the Ballards, with whom he remained until they removed their works to Newburyport, Massachusetts Early in the civil war period he enlisted as a musician in the Fifteenth Regiment, Massachusetts Volunteers, and during a portion of his term of service performed hospital duty After the war closed he opened a restaurant on Front street, Worcester subsequently expanding his business to a hotel, and from which business he retired in 1903 He married, August 13, 1864 Caroline Meyer, born in Wittenberg Germany, April 25, 1841, who came to the United States with her parents when she was seven years old, her father, Francis Meyer, died at the age of sixty-five years Their children were Carrie, married Julius Ehlers, of Hartford, Connecticut, and they have two sons, Minnie, married Herman Klingle, of Worcester, and they have two daughters, Emil, to be further mentioned

Emil, youngest child and only son of Joseph and Caroline (Meyer) Sauer, was born in Worcester, Massachusetts, March 14 1881 He was educated in the public schools of that city and after leaving the high school in 1899, at the age of eighteen years, he entered the Jefferson Medical College of Philadalphia, completed the four year course, and was graduated with the degree of Doctor of Medicine in 1903 He was for some time associated with the eminent Philadelphia specialist in gynecology and surgery, Professor Fisher, and subsequently went abroad to further study professional specialties For six months he attended the Vienna General Hospital, having among other instructors the noted surgeon Dr Lorenz For a like period he was a student in Berlin, and during his sojourn there was a

C. E. Hunt

member of the Anglo-American Medical Association of Berlin In 1902 he made a previous trip to Europe, with his bride, and during this time observed methods in the Strasburg hospitals In 1904 he entered upon general practice in his native city, making a specialty of diseases of women and children, for which he had prepared himself by his particular study of gynecology and pediatrics From the first he met with unusual success Dr Sauer is connected with various leading fraternal and social organizations—Morning Star Lodge, F and A M, Iroquois Lodge, Improved Order of Red Men, the order of the Eagles, the Frohsinns, and the Socialer Turn Verein He is a Republican in politics In 1904 he was presented in the Republican primary in ward seven for the nomination for school committeeman, and was defeated by the narrow margin of forty-three votes, and in 1905 was elected to the two year term which he is now serving Dr Sauer married, June 11, 1902, Ethel S Jordan, daughter of the late John W Jordan, a member of John W Jordan & Company, dealers in stoves, ranges and furnaces Their children are Caroline Frances, born May 2, 1904, and Helen Louise, born July 5, 1905

Mrs Ethel S (Jordan) Sauer is descended from Samuel Jordan, a native of England, who came to this country in young manhood and married, in 1805 Sarah Rogers, born in 1786, said to have been a descendant of John Rogers, who 'for heresy' was burned at the stake in 1555 under Bloody Queen Mary ' Of their children two daughters and three sons grew to maturity, and one of the former died in Michigan at an advanced age

John Rogers, son of Samuel and Sarah (Rogers) Jordan, was born in Philadalphia, Pennsylvania, February 28, 1806 His mother being left a widow, he was early thrown upon his own resources When about ten years old he was sent to New Hampshire to live upon a farm He learned the trade of stone mason, and became owner of an excellent quarry at Lynn, Massachusetts, where he settled He was a man of character and ability, and an influential member of the community He was actively interested in public affairs, served in both branches of the city council, was a captain of militia, and was a member of the Masonic fraternity He was a man of fine physique and handsome features He reared an interesting family of nine children, by his first wife, who was Susan Darling, one of a family of seventeen children, whom he married in Mason, New Hampshire His wife died in 1877, and he had one child by his second marriage His children were John W, see forward, Susan Elizabeth, married Ebenezer Harris, and resided in Fitchburg, Massachusetts, Mary A, married Warren Bailey, of Lynn, Massachusetts, Sarah, married J Wilson, of the same city, Lucy A, married a Russell, also of Lynn, Alexander, resides in Somerville, Massachusetts, Samuel, who enlisted before he was eighteen years old, at Lowell, Massachusetts, to serve in the Mexican war, and died at Fort Jessup, New Mexico, while en route to the front, Oliver Hazard Perry, born 1830, died in Worcester in 1863 leaving wife, son and three daughters, Edward Darling, served in the civil war in Company G, Fifteenth Massachusetts Infantry Regiment, he was wounded in the leg at the battle of Antietam, and died a few days afterward at Sharpsburg, and was buried in Worcester, Henry Harrison, died young

John Warren, eldest child of John Rogers and Susan (Darling) Jordan, was born in Mason, New Hampshire, October 1, 1826 At the age of eight years he went to live with the family of Thomas Kidder—the same among whom his father had been brought up He lived there for five years, during that time attending the district school only during two short terms When thirteen he went to work as a bobbin boy in a mill, and in four years had been advanced to overseer of a room He subsequently learned the tinsmith trade at Manchester. In August, 1845, he arrived in Worcester, his entire capital amounting to twenty-five cents, but he unexpectedly found old New Hampshire friends and soon procured employment He enlisted for the Mexican war at Governor's Island, Boston Harbor In 1852 he established in Worcester the business with which his name has been associated for more than a half century, which he conducted until his death, in 1902—the oldest firm in Worcester in the hardware and plumbing business Since the death of Mr Jordan the managing company has had for its head his son, Frederick B Jordan Mr Jordan was not only a successful man of affairs, but an honored and useful member of the community He served in the common council in 1859 and 1861, and in the board of aldermen in 1870 and 1871 He was affiliated with Montacute Lodge, Free and Accepted Masons, in which he was a past master, and he had attained the thirty-second degree, Scottish Rite Mr Jordan and his family were members of Piedmont Congregational Church

Mr Jordan married, in November, 1847, Caroline C Loring, of Townsend, Massachusetts, daughter of Elmer and Mary (Hastings) Loring, and one of a family of twelve children She bore to her husband four children, of whom but one came to maturity—Genevieve H, who became the wife of D E Forrest, of Medford, Massachusetts Mrs Jordan died December 12, 1869, and Mr Jordan married (second), November 24, 1870, Lydia Almira Perry, daughter of Joseph S Perry The children of Mr Jordan by his second marriage were Lillie May, born March, 1872, died young, Annie Rogers, born June 4, 1873, died February, 1879, John Warren, born June 14, 1874, Frederick B, born August 15, 1875, married Bessie Edwards, and they have two sons—Fred and Leslie, Ethel S, born July 27, 1881, who became the wife of Dr Emil Sauer

CHARLES EDWARD HUNT William Hunt (1) was the emigrant ancestor of Charles Edward Hunt of Worcester It is believed that William Hunt was born in 1605 in England He came to New England and settled before 1640 in Concord, Massachusetts He was admitted a freeman June 2, 1641 He was a witness to the will of a neighbor in Concord, William Bowstred, October 23, 1642 He was a farmer He married (first) Elizabeth Best She died 1661 He married (second) Mercy (Hurd) Rice widow of Edmund Rice 1664 He removed to Marlboro where he died October 1667 He made his will October 23, 1667 leaving an estate valued at 596 pounds He bequeathed to wife Mary, sons Samuel Nehemiah and Isaac, and daughter Elizabeth Barnes His children were Nehemiah married Mary Toole 1663 and settled at Concord, Massachusetts, Isaac see forward, William, Elizabeth, married ——— Barnes, Hannah, Samuel

(II) Isaac Hunt, son of William Hunt (1), was born in 1647 in Concord, Massachusetts He married Mary Stone May 14 1667 He died at Concord, 1681 His estate was appraised April 5, 1681, and his wife Mary Hunt was appointed administratrix Their children were Isaac, born January 12 1668, died June, 1669, Hannah, June 5, 1670, married

——— Fletcher (see Fletcher sketch), Samuel, October 26, 1672, Isaac, November 18, 1675, Ebenezer, July 12, 1677

(III) Isaac Hunt, fourth child of Isaac Hunt (2), was born in Concord, Massachusetts, November 18, 1675 He settled in Sudbury He married Mary Willard She was admitted to the Sudbury church January 20, 1717-8 He left a large estate, having lands at Lancaster and Rutland The inventory of his estate amounted to 1,477 pounds The children of Isaac and Mary (Willard) Hunt of Sudbury, all born there, were Isaac, Thomas, August 20 1701 Mary, Ebenezer, Samuel, January 11, 1709, John see forward, Simon, April 20, 1713, Henry, March 10, 1715, Abidah, July 31, 1717

(IV) John Hunt, sixth child of Isaac Hunt (3), was born in Sudbury, Massachusetts, February 12, 1711 He removed to what is now Hardwick, Massachusetts, and was one of the earliest settlers He lived for a short time at Grafton after leaving Sudbury He married Mary ——— His farm and homestead was about three-quarters of a mile north of the common in Hardwick where Willis Tavern stood He was a tavern keeper as well as farmer During the revolutionary war his inn was a stopping place for soldiers, and as there was an epidemic of small pox in various places Mr Hunt went to the pest house at New Braintree to be inoculated with virus He died of the disease and was buried in the orchard at the angle of the road to New Braintree, a few rods south of the former residence of Colonel Stephen Fay The children of John and Mary Hunt of Hardwick were Samuel, born September 27, 1736, Moses December 18, 1738, died June 20, 1747, Hannah, March 18, 1744, Mary, October 13 1746, John, January 31, 1749-50, Moses, October 28 1756, Joseph, December 8, 1759 married Elizabeth Fay and removed to Bennington, Vermont

(V) Moses Hunt seventh son of John Hunt (4) was born in Hardwick, Massachusetts, October 28 1756 He married Esther Jenney, daughter of John Jenney, December 10, 1778 He was a farmer His homestead was in the northern part of Hardwick He died there July 10, 1822 He was a revolutionary soldier in Captain Samuel Dexter's company, 1776, Colonel Leonard's regiment, also Captain Hodges' company, Colonel Job Cushing, in 1777, at the Bennington call The children of Moses and Esther (Jenney) Hunt were Sophia, born October 2, 1779 married Joseph Dexter, Moses, August 27, 1781 Abigail, September 23 1786, John, June 26, 1788, married Mabel Hopkins, January 4, 1816, settled in Hadley, Massachusetts, Mary Palmer, April 19, 1790 Esther Jenney, February 10, 1792, Zephaniah August 4, 1793 settler in Barre, Orsamus, see forward, Horace or Hiram April 15, 1799 died January 15 1803, William, June 27, 1800, died January 11 1803 Hammond, July 8 1802, died May 20 1803, William, September 6 1804

(VI) Orsamus Hunt, eighth child of Moses Hunt (5), was born in Hardwick, Massachusetts, February 16, 1797 He married (first) Laura Newton daughter of Silas Newton, January 7, 1821 She died at Granby, Massachusetts January 14 1851, aged fifty-six years He married (second) her sister Caroline Newton He died at Shrewsbury, Massachusetts, May 25, 1864 He was a mason by trade also a contractor and builder and lived in various towns as his employment demanded He was in Stockbridge after he left Hardwick for several years He removed to Lee, Massachusetts an adjacent town, where he resided for seven years The family lived in Amherst for a year and thence removed to Granby, where he was living in 1851 when his wife died F B Knowles, founder of the Knowles loom works, married a sister of Mrs Hunt. The children of Orsamus and Laura (Newton) Hunt were 1 Addison Augustus, born in Hardwick, June 20, 1822, married Clarissa E Thomas, March 16, 1852, was a school teacher, died 1892 2 Calvin Newton, born June 8, 1825, died May 21, 1830 3 Charles Edward see forward 4 Edwin Newton, born in Lee, Massachusetts, December 14, 1834, was a soldier and died at the age of sixty years

(VII) Charles Edward Hunt, third child of Orsamus Hunt (6), was born in Stockbridge, Massachusetts, May 21, 1830 He was educated in the common schools in the towns where his parents lived during his boyhood, in Lee, Berkshire county, Massachusetts, Amherst and Granby in the same vicinity At the age of fifteen he came to Worcester as an apprentice in the composing room of the old *Worcester County Gazette* At that time the paper was a weekly owned by Estey & Evans Political feeling was strong Abolition was an absorbing topic of political conversation and action Even the boys who carried the paper to subscribers realized the depth of feeling when some good citizen, angered by a political editorial in the *Gazette*, would not only stop his paper but would vent his feelings by chasing the paper boy away from the house when he came to deliver the offending sheet While in the *Gazette* office Mr Hunt used to deliver papers Tuesday night and Wednesday morning after publication There has been some change in the business of printing newspapers since then, not only in putting stereotype presses in place of Washington hand presses and Mergenthaler linotype machines in place of the compositor, but in hours of labor and wages paid Mr Hunt received his board for his work during the first year He was to receive his board and ten dollars the second year It is the custom to pay boys a dollar a day for the first year and from $8 to $10 the second year in Worcester newspaper composing rooms, while the scale of wages for journeymen is $18 a week for day work, and eight hours per day instead of ten Among other boys in the *Gazette* office at the time was Hezekiah Conant, who later built the big mills at Pawtucket, Rhode Island, and became very wealthy

Mr Hunt left the *Gazette* office after a year and a half to return to Granby, where he worked during the fall and winter He worked the next year or two for H S Taylor of Springfield who established the first book and job office in Springfield, Massachusetts When he was nineteen he went to Greenfield, Massachusetts and worked for one season on a hand press in a printing office He attended school for a time at Easthampton and later taught school at Belchertown, Massachusetts In the spring of 1851 he went to work in a printing office at New London Connecticut on what was then a new and up-to-date press In 1852 he was assistant teacher with his brother Addison at Ware, Massachusetts In the spring of 1852 he went to Springfield, Massachusetts to do the power press work on the *Springfield Republican* After a year and a half he went into the job printing department of the *Republican* office but a few months later took charge of the job press room as foreman The publishers of the *Republican* at that time were Samuel Bowles Dr Holland and Clark W Bryan the business manager The firm name was Samuel Bowles & Co When the panic and hard times came just before the civil war Mr Bryan had to reduce the force and cut salaries Mr Hunt declined to have his salary cut, and in 1858 left the printing office again for the old farm at Granby which his father bought in 1839 and which was left to the sons at the death of their mother, January 14, 1851 He conducted the farm for four years and then returned to Springfield to work for Joshua F Tannett, who had a small printing office, and there worked two years when the business was sold He was offered his old position of foreman of the press room in the *Republican* office at twenty-one dollars per week and accepted the place During the civil war the modern newspaper was developed The telegraph service became a necessity, and faster and better presses were demanded Mr Hunt was in the *Republican* office during this important period of development, at the time that the reputation of the *Republican* was established He left the paper May 1, 1869, and again returned to the farm at Granby, where he remained until 1872, when he bought out the interests of the other owners and settled down on the farm until he sold it in 1887

Mr Hunt took an active part in town affairs at Granby He was elected superintendent of the Sunday school before he had removed to the town, and in 1870 was elected deacon of the church He declined to accept either of these honors at the time, but later became deacon He was elected secretary of the Town Mutual Fire Insurance Company, a position he held for ten years He was for eight years a member of the school committee and declined re-election The district schools were still in vogue there and the day of the superintendent had not arrived In his report for the year ending March 1, 1881 Mr Hunt advocated the grading of the schools and concentrating them at the centre of the town His views have since been adopted, but at the time they caused great commotion among the old farmers and hurt his prestige as a safe and sane man His friends saw to it that he was re-elected, however, without his making an effort The public system of which Massachusetts is so proud to-day was the product of some struggles, and it developed and is developing slowly The struggle in which Mr Hunt was a leader in his town went on for years throughout the state The graded school displaced the district school only after the proof of its superiority became overwhelming from actual experience

Mr Hunt declined to run for selectman, but was drafted into the office of assessor Of his experience in this office, he says "I did not prove successful, for when I found the lands of the rich farmers that cut two crops of hay each season assessed at $20 an acre while that of some of the poor struggling fellows that was not so good, assessed at $30 and in at least one case $45, I insisted that there should be a square deal One old fellow, rich in mortgages, who had for several years paid only a poll tax, was brought to book when we found he had $4,000 on a building in Holyoke The rate was one per cent and he was taxed on the full amount, making his bill $42 in all As I was the tax collector that year I had the fun of collecting it" He was not re-elected assessor for obvious reasons It is a well known fact that no department of municipal affairs, even in the smallest towns is so corrupt and unjustly administered as the assessment for purposes of taxation A co-operative society or Grange was formed in Granby in the seventies by twelve farmers Mr Hunt was secretary They met once a week to transact business in rooms fitted up for the purpose They had discussions of public questions, lectures etc They bought their groceries by wholesale in Boston and saved hundreds of dollars during the four years that the society lasted Mr Hunt sold his farm at Granby in 1887 and came to Millbury, Massachusetts to manage a country place and stock farm for his cousin F B Knowles, the loom manufacturer The farm was sold in 1894 In 1895 Mr Hunt took charge of the country place of Frank P Knowles, son of F B Knowles, at Pacachoag Hill, Auburn, where a beautiful country home has been built and a magnificent stock farm equipped and developed Mr Hunt was in charge of the work until 1897, when he resigned Since then Mr Hunt has resided in Worcester and been engaged in the real estate business His home is at 62 Dewey street He is a member of the Old South Congregational Church, Worcester

He married, September 4, 1855, Laura Warner, of Springfield, Massachusetts Their children are 1 Hattie Maria, born March 21, 1858, at home, she taught school seven years at Granby and Waltham 2 Frank, born March, 1862, married Lucy Cathon, and has two children Francis and Ruth G, they reside in Allston 3 Samuel, born April 12, 1868, married Cordelia Mathers two children Gertrude and Charles, they reside in Allston 4 Fred, born September, 1870, unmarried, remained with his father until 1897, when he learned the trade of moulder and is now employed in Detroit, Michigan, as instructor

BIRNEY ASHER ROBINSON Thomas Robinson (I) was the emigrant ancestor of Birney Asher Robinson, of Worcester He was a proprietor of Roxbury about 1636, and his wife Silence was a member of the church there He removed to Boston It was not until November 11, 1662, however, that he disposed of all his land at Roxbury He was a mariner and sold the ship "Speedwell," in which many emigrants came to this country, to Thomas Witherly of Southwark, county Surrey, July 27, 1640 Then he appears to have gone to Scituate where, in 1640, he bought land of William Gilson He bought house and lands there in 1642 He represented Scituate in the general court in 1643 He was elected deacon of the second church of Scituate He was a juryman at Scituate in 1644, and took the oath of fidelity March 3, 1644-5 He was proposed for freeman and probably admitted 1650 In August and September 1654, he bought two estates in Boston, adjoining each other, on the west side of Washington street, opposite the Old South church The lots were two hundred and seventy feet deep He lived there some of the time, though his children were taken to Scituate to be baptized, perhaps because he was a deacon there All were baptized there except James Isaac Robinson, unquestionably a son of Rev John Robinson, pastor of the Pilgrims in Holland, settled in Scituate at the time that Thomas went there, and some believe that he also was a son of Rev John Robinson, but proof is lacking

He made his will March 17, 1665 and it was proved April 27, 1666 He made bequests to his wife, to children, Thomas, James, Joseph, and Mary, son John supposed to be in England, to brother Joseph Rocke After his first wife Silence died, he married (second) Mary (Cogan) Woody, of Boston, in that town January 11, 1652-3 She was the widow of John Woody and the daughter of John Cogan, of Boston She died October 26 1661 He married (third) Elizabeth Sherman, widow of Richard Sherman Her will was dated August 21, 1666 and was proved November 16, 1667 Thomas Robinson died March 23, 1665-6 Children of Thomas and Silence (probably) were 1 John, merchant, supposed to be in England at the time of his father's death was administrator of brother Samuel's estate October 28, 1662 2 Samuel, merchant, died unmarried January 16 1661-2 aged twenty-four years 3 Josiah, apprenticed to Joseph Rocke, who was named in father's will, died April 17, 1660 4. Ephraim, born in Scituate probably, died September 22 1661 Children of Thomas and Mary (Cogan) Robinson were 5 Thomas (see forward) 6 James, born in Boston, March 14, 1654-5, died September, 1676 7 Joseph baptized March 8 1656-7, married Sarah ——, died April, 1713 8 Mary baptized February 28, 1657-8 died young 9 Mary, baptized November 6, 1659, married Jacob Green, Jr, of Charlestown Joseph Rocke, before mentioned, married Elizabeth sister of Mary Cogan, second wife of Thomas Robinson

(II) Thomas Robinson, son of Thomas Robinson (1), born probably in Boston, but baptized in Scituate March 5, 1653-4, married Sarah Dennison, daughter of Edward Dennison, of Roxbury He inherited part of the Robinson homestead, where he resided, and also his grandfather Cogan's house and store on the corner of Washington and State streets He was a cordwainer or shoemaker by trade He died June, 1700 His wife Sarah died in Roxbury November 15, 1710 aged fifty-three years Their children were 1 Thomas born November 5 1677 married Sarah Beswick, June 26, 1707 died (s p) February 15, 1729-30 2 Sarah, baptized December 28, 1679, married (first) John Ingoldsbury, May 4 1704 married (second) John Perry, May 27 1707 3 Joseph baptized November 20 1681 died young 4 Elizabeth born September 26 1686, died young 5 James, born March 15 1689-90

(III) James Robinson, son of Thomas Robinson (2) was born March 15, 1689-90, at Roxbury (?) He married at Roxbury, Patience Ruggles daughter of Captain Samuel Ruggles, of Roxbury He was a housewright The homestead of his grandfather on Washington street, Boston, he sold February 7, 1711-12 He bought a house on the south side of Boylston street which he sold April 12 1714, and removed to Rochester, Massachusetts, where Rev Timothy Ruggles, his wife's brother, was settled He lived there until the Spring of 1757, when he exchanged his farm in Rochester for one in Hardwick Massachusetts, where several of his children were already settled Of his eight children Dorothy alone remained in Rochester all the others settling in Barre and Hardwick in Worcester county His farm was on the road to Ware marked on the R map 'Mr Leonard' He died shortly before March 11 1762 when the will was proved His wife Patience died January, 1768, aged seventy-eight years Their children were 1 James born March 1 1711-12 married Elizabeth Smith settled on the River Road from Hardwick to Barre in the then wilderness 2 Thomas, born September 15, 1713 died young 3 Samuel born November 1, 1715 4 Thomas, born April 20 1718 5 Sarah born July 2 1720 married Ebenezer Spooner of Rochester, 1746 6 Dorothy, born March 10 1722-3 married David Peckham October 27, 1743 and Major Elnathan Haskell November 26 1749, died at Rochester, September 25 1810 7 Dennison born July 16 1725 8 Joseph, born September 13 1727 9 Hannah born November 16 1730, married Benjamin Green August 31 1764

(IV) Joseph Robinson, son of James Robinson (3) born September 13 1727 married Martha Hedge in 1753 and they settled in Barre Six of their twelve children are recorded as born in Barre Some of their children were 1 Mary, born June 3 1754 2 Dorothy, born February 23 1756 3 Lemuel, born January 4 1758, his son Lemuel Jr, and probably others settled in Bennington, Vermont 4 Martha born November 23 1759 5 Samuel Hedge, born January 25, 1761 6 Levi, baptized May 20 1770

(V) Levi Robinson, son of Joseph Robinson (4), was born in Barre, Massachusetts, and baptized in the First church there, May 20, 1770, married September 30, 1798, Betsey Nye, of Hardwick, in that town They settled in Westford, Vermont Their children, born at Westford, were 1 Nye, born March 14 1799 had three children 2 Annis, born 1800, taught school at Westford Vermont, 1820, died unmarried, 1821 3 Charles had two children 4 Lucinda married Ira Graves and had two children 5 Levi, born February 23 1808, at Westford, Vermont, had eight children, died October 16 1877 6 Joseph, born November 28, 1809 7 Stephen Pearl, born March 16, 1808, lived at Westford

(VI) Joseph Robinson, son of Levi Robinson (5), born in Westford Vermont, November 28 1809, married Aurelia Cross, October 17, 1833 They settled in Fairfax and Underhill, Vermont Their children were 1 Sarah E, born August 18 1834, at Fairfax, Vermont died September 18, 1834 2 Sophronia L, born October 2, 1836, died at Fairfax June 7, 1843 3 Asher C, born February 15, 1839 at Fairfax 4 Lucinda A, born July 13, 1841, at Fairfax, died August 1, 1858 5 Sophronia (twin), born March 26, 1845, at Fairfax, died August 8, 1845 6 Malona (twin), born March 26 1845 died July 9 1847 7 Fillmore Joseph born October 27, 1849 at Underhill, Vermont 8 Fayette H, born March 17, 1854 at Underhill, died April 7, 1854

(VII) Asher C Robinson son of Joseph Robinson (6), born in Fairfax, Vermont February 15, 1839, married Euretta Stevens, of Richmond Vermont, March 22, 1860 She was the daughter of Rufus and Ann Stevens and was born in Richmond, Vermont, August 20, 1838 died May 27, 1903 He represented the town of Westford in the Legislature in 1874-5 and Chittenden county in the Senate in 1880-81 Their children were 1 George C, born December 28, 1860, at Clifton, Michigan, resides at West Rutland, Vermont 2 Mortimer C, born March 2, 1862, at Richmond, Vermont 3 Adelle born at Underhill, September 9, 1863 4 Ermine born in Underhill, May 16, 1865 5 Birney A (twin), born August 24 1869, at Westford Vermont (see forward) 6 Bertha (twin), born August 24 1869, at Westford Vermont 7 Fanny L, born June 12 1874, at Westford, Vermont, died January 1 1888

(VIII) Birney Asher Robinson son of Asher C (7) and Euretta (Stevens) Robinson, was born at Westford Vermont August 24, 1869 His boyhood was spent in his native town and he attended the public schools there Later he attended St Johnsbury Academy at St Johnsbury Vermont His first business experience was with Swift & Company, the meat dealers and packers of Chicago Illinois, where he worked as salesman in one of the Chicago branches of the concern He left this company to accept a position in the office of the Vermont Marble Company, of which Senator Proctor, of Vermont, is the head, at Proctor, Vermont Later he was sent to St Louis to the branch office in that city In 1896 he spent most of the year in St Johnsbury, Vermont, coming to Worcester Massachusetts, to live in 1897. After an extensive foreign trip he returned to Worcester and started on his own account in the automobile business in Worcester When he opened his first place at the corner of Clinton and Pleasant streets he was the first to venture in this line of trade in Worcester and has perhaps been the most successful As the demand for the machines increased he was obliged to enlarge his quarters He moved first from Pleasant street to the Bellmar block on Main street In August, 1904 he removed again to a large building on Church place, at the rear of the First Universalist Church on Pleasant street. Here he conducts a general business in automobiles and supplies in connection with the garage, boarding and renting machines as well as dealing in them. He has also a repair shop a not unimportant part of the business. Mr. Robinson deals in a number of the leading styles of automobiles and has sold a large proportion of the machines owned in Worcester.

He is a member of the Worcester Automobile Club, the Worcester Continentals, the Commonwealth Club and the American Automobile Association. In politics he is a Republican. He and his family attend the Plymouth Congregational Church. He married October 23, 1895, Mabel Fairbanks, daughter of William P. Fairbanks of the famous Fairbanks Scale Company, of St. Johnsbury, Vermont. Her mother was Rebecca Pike. She (Mabel) was born at St. Johnsbury August 14, 1871. Their children are: 1. Bertha, born November 9, 1896. 2. Clifton Fairbanks, born July 13, 1901. 3. Winfield Fairbanks, born September 28, 1902.

FAIRBANKS FAMILY (I) Jonathan Fairbanks of Dedham, one of the most famous of the pioneers on account of his large and distinguished posterity, and perhaps also because his home in Dedham is still preserved and has always been occupied by his family and descendants, is the emigrant ancestor of Mrs. Birney A. Robinson of Worcester, and of many others to whom reference is made in this work.

Jonathan Fairebanke (Fairbank, Fairbanks) came from 'Sowerby, in the West Riding of Yorkshire, England, to Boston, Massachusetts, in the year 1633, and in 1636 settled in Dedham, Massachusetts, where he built the noted old "Fairbanks House" which is still standing and is to be indefinitely preserved by the family which, through the Fairbanks Association, has purchased it. This house is an object of great interest to the visitors to Dedham. It is claimed that the oldest part of the house was built in 1636. The house as it stands to-day was probably complete as early as 1654. Jonathan Fairbanks signed the famous Dedham Covenant which regulated the future conduct of the town. Among the one hundred and twenty-five signers were his sons John, George and Jonathan Fairbanks, Jr. Jonathan Fairbanks was admitted a freeman March 23, 1637-8. John was admitted a freeman as early as 1642, George about 1651 and Jonathan, Jr., in 1654. Jonathan received numerous grants of land. He joined the church August 14, 1646.

His will was made June 4, 1668. He evidently believed in the old English law of primogeniture, for he bequeathed the homestead to his eldest son, John. The house has since been occupied successively by John, Joseph, Joseph 2d, Ebenezer, Ebenezer 2d, Prudence, Sarah (Sally), Nancy and Rebecca. In July, 1892, the house was struck by lightning and damaged and Rebecca Fairbanks removed for a time to Boston but later returned and occupied it until 1904, when the Fairbanks Family Association took possession.

Of the immediate English ancestors of Jonathan Fairbanks little is known. He was evidently not of the ignorant lower classes but had a fair education and was, as tradition says, a man of strong common-sense, sound judgment and good executive ability. His name appears frequently in the town records, though he held only minor town offices. There are good grounds for the inference that he had more ample means than the average pioneer. He built a better house and seems to have lived in better style than most of his neighbors. And he left considerable property. He was born about 1600 in England, died in Dedham December 5, 1668. His wife was Grace Lee. She died December 28, 1673, or May 19, 1676.

Their children, all born in England, were: 1. John, married Sarah Fiske in 1641, held offices and various commissions to explore the Charles river, Deerfield, etc., inherited the homestead, joined the church May 4, 1651, died November 13, 1684, wife died November 26, 1683, had nine children. 2. Captain George (see forward). 3. Mary, born April 18, 1622, died May 10, 1676, or June 4, 1684, married Michael Metcalf April 2, 1644 (born in England August 29, 1620, died March 25, 1654); married (second) August 2, 1654, Christopher Smith; among their descendants was Judge Theron Metcalf, of the Massachusetts supreme court. 4. Susan, married Ralph Day, of Dedham, a mason; she died July 8, 1659, and he married (second) November 15, 1659, Abigail Craft, daughter of Griffith Craft, of Roxbury, and widow of John Ruggles; he died November 28, 1677; had six children. 5. Jonas, ancester of Hon. Charles W. Fairbanks, vice-president of the United States, removed to Lancaster, Massachusetts, in 1657, signed the Covenant March 7, 1659, and was called one of the "fathers of the town"; he was a farmer and believed to be also a carpenter; in 1652 he was fined for wearing great boots before he was worth two hundred pounds, which was contrary to a statute of 1651; he and his son Joshua were killed by the Indians February 10, 1676, during a raid in King Philip's war; he married May 28, 1658, Lydia Prescott, daughter of John Prescott, who came from Sowerby Parish of Halifax, England. She was born in Watertown, Massachusetts, August 15, 1641, and after the death of Jonas she married (second) Elias Barron, of Watertown, afterwards of Groton and Lancaster. Jonas had seven children. 6. Jonathan, born in England, admitted townsman in Dedham, January 1, 1654-5, and signed the Covenant, resided at Dedham, died January 28, 1711-12, was a soldier in King Philip's war, serving in the first or Mount Hope campaign in 1675 and in several subsequent campaigns, married Deborah Shepard, of Cambridge, daughter of Edward Shepard, who came from England with her May 10, 1643; she died September 7, 1705; had thirteen children.

(II) George Fairbanks, son of Jonathan Fairbanks (1), came with his father from England and resided in Dedham until about 1657, when he removed to the southern part of Sherborn, afterwards East Medway, now the town of Millis. He was one of the first settlers there and was an esteemed citizen. His homestead in Medfield remained in the family for four generations. The stone house originally occupied by him was the garrison house built by the settlers on the Bogistow Farms on the borders of Bogistow Pond as a place of refuge and defence in time of Indian troubles. It was sixty-five or seventy feet long and two stories high. The walls were built of flat stones laid in mortar. It had a double row of port holes on all sides and was lined with heavy planks of oak. The Medway Historical Society has marked the site, the building having been long since removed. In 1662 he signed the first petition for the town of Sherborn, and again in 1674 he signed the successful petition, becoming one of the proprietors of Sherborn, including the present towns of Sherborn, Holliston and parts of Framingham and Ashland. He was four years selectman of Sherborn, and was on the committee to engage and settle a minister. His sudden death by drowning in 1682 was a severe loss to the new settlement He was a member of the Ancient and Honorable Artillery Company of Boston He died January 10, 1682

He married October 26, 1646, Mary Adams, of Dedham, who died August 11, 1711, in Mendon Massachusetts, probably at the home of her son-in-law William Holbrook Their children were 1 Mary born November 10, 1647, married January 16 1665-6, Deacon Joseph Daniels, son of Robert and Elizabeth Daniels, freeman of Medfield, she died August 9, 1682, he died June 23 1715, had nine children 2 George born May 26, 1650, in Medfield, Massachusetts inherited south part of father's farm, died 1737, was principal inhabitant of the new town of Medway, October 14, 1713, married Rachel Adams daughter of Peter and Rachel Adams in 1671, she died May 12, 1678, and he married Susanna —— and Sarah ——, had ten children 3 Samuel, born October 28 1652, died November 20, 1676 4. Eliesur, born June 8, 1655 5 Jonas born March 23, 1656-7, died November 28 1676 6 Jonathan born in Medway, May 1, 1662 resided in Sherborn, afterwards set off as Medway probably in the old stone garrison house near Bogistow Pond, was the first physician in Sherborn selectman for several years and town clerk drowned December 19, 1719, by falling through the ice while crossing the river from Medfield in the night married Sarah ———, who died July 9 1713, married (second) Annie ——, had six children 7 Margaret born June 27 1664, married William Holbrook of Mendon, will proved December 16, 1714, had three children

(III) Eliesur Fairbanks son of George Fairbanks (2) born June 8, 1655, settled in Sherborn, Massachusetts He drew a home lot of eighteen acres on the main street of Sherborn adjoining Peters Hill, he was selectman in 1703 He married Martha —— Their children were 1 Mary born October 31, 1678 married May 8, 1700 Isaac Woods of Sudbury second wife, he died July 18, 1720, had seven children 2 Martha born January 22, 1680, married Oliver Death April 17, 1697, he died March 3 1704-5 and she married (second) Ebenezer Leland January 9 1708, he planted the magnificent elms to be see on the old Leland place about 1708, had six children 3 Lydia, born March 8 1682, married May 25 1702 Edward Rice of Marlboro (born June 20, 1672 died July 20, 1741), she died September 13 1755, had ten children 4 Margaret, born December 19, 1684, died in 1698 5 Mercy, born October 18 1688, married (first) Lieutenant Joshua Underwood of Sherborn January 13 1708, married (second) Joshua Fairbanks July 26 1732, she died September 11 1742, had seven children 6 Eleasur born December 29 1690

(IV) Captain Eleasur Fairbanks, son of Eliesur Fairbanks (3) born in Sherborn, December 29, 1690 resided there died September 19, 1741 He married Martha Bullard, daughter of Captain Samuel Bullard December 25 1712 She married (second) John Phips, December 22 1743 and removed to Brookfield, Massachusetts Their children were 1 Eleazer, born July 23, 1716 removed to Plainfield, Connecticut where he was admitted to the Congregational church May 24 1753, removed to Killingly Connecticut, married Prudence Cary, was a preacher, had seven children 2 Joseph, born September 17 1718, was commissioned Lieutenant of Foot by General William Shirley Captain General of his Majesty's Governors of Massachusetts Bay under George II in 1755 was at the siege of Louisburg and after its capture went to Halifax, where he was one of the earliest settlers, was a member of the first House of Assembly, which was convened by Governor Lawrence in 1758 with nineteen members, became a wealthy and influential man and with the most prominent people there was identified with the growth and prosperity of Halifax, married (second) Lydia Blagden, daughter of Samuel and Ann Blagden, and sister of Colonel Samuel Blagden of the American revolutionary army, died 1790 without issue 3 Deborah, born November 12, 1719, married Joseph Twitchell, Esq, June 28, 1739, was captain of the militia, commissary for the army in 1776, town clerk, representative and magistrate, and the leading man of the town until succeeded by his junior half-brother Hon Daniel Whitney, had fourteen children, all born in Sherborn 4 Moses, born August 14, 1721, was in the colonial wars from April 2, 1759 to September 29, 1760 5 Sarah, born August 2, 1724, married September 28, 1741, Benjamin Mason, son of Joseph and Mary (Monck) Mason, who was born in Watertown, Massachusetts, July 14, 1717, died July 5, 1801, she died in Sullivan, New Hampshire. February 4, 1815, they settled in Dublin, New Hampshire, one of their descendants is the author, Alice Morse Earle of Worcester, Massachusetts, and Brooklyn, New York 7 Abel, born November 28, 1726 8 Abigail born August 18, 1728, died young 9 David, born February 2, 1731 10 Abigail, born May 5 1732 11 Ebenezer, born June 1, 1734 12 Mary, married in 1757, Captain Samuel Sanger, and died without issue

(V) Deacon Ebenezer Fairbanks, son of Eleazer Fairbanks (4), was born in Sherborn, Massachusetts, June 1, 1734 He removed to Brimfield, Massachusetts, and settled on a farm in the northeast part of the town He was an esteemed citizen, and a deacon in the Congregational church there He died June 6, 1812 He was one of the minute men who responded to the Lexington Alarm, April 19, 1775, with the rank of lieutenant He also served as a private later in the war He married July 2, 1761, Elizabeth Dearth, who was born September 24, 1743 and died at Monson, Massachusetts, June 15, 1818 Their children were 1 Asa, born March 4, 1762, removed to Dublin, New Hampshire, in 1784, and died there July 26, 1819, enlisted in the revolution service at the age of fourteen and served on guard duty in Sherborn, at Rhode Island and West Point, married April 28, 1784, Hepzibah Adams, daughter of Captain Moses Adams, she was born in Sherborn, December 8, 1761, had four children 2 Joseph, (see forward) 3 Betsey born August 23, 1766, died September 22 1767 4 Ebenezer, born December 15, 1768, died October 26, 1796 5 Henry, born December 21, 1770, at Brimfield, died July 20, 1827, married October 29 1795, Margaret Bliss, born March 5, 1773, died June 4, 1843, aged seventy years, two months, twenty-nine days, had six children 6 Thaddeus, born March 13, 1773, was graduated at Yale College in 1796, licensed to preach in 1800, preached as a licentiate apparently for some years, but was not ordained, preached at Canterbury, Connecticut, for a time, married Pamelia Burt, died at Monson, Massachusetts, December 21, 1815, had three children 7 Elizabeth, born January 3 1775, married Roswell Merrick, died at Dayton, Ohio, January, 1855, aged eighty years, had ten children 8 Levi, born August 24 1778 at Sherborn, Massachusetts settled in Brimfield Massachusetts, died there about 1850, married Betsey Smith and Mrs E Howard, had one child by each

(VI) Joseph Fairbanks, son of Ebenezer Fairbanks (5) was born in Sherborn, November 1, 1763 When he was twenty years old, his uncle Joseph, who had received a lot of land in Halifax, Nova Scotia, in recognition of his services under the Government of Massachusetts in reducing the Island of Cape Breton, sent for him to go and live with him The vessel in which he took passage from Boston was forced to turn back for repairs and, as the winter was coming on, he returned home In the spring he decided to go to Brimfield with his father instead of going to Halifax His cousin Rufus Fairbanks went in his stead At Brimfield he bought a farm and also worked at the carpenter's trade Having Mr and Mrs Paddock, his wife's parents, in the family through many years of expensive illness, he had slow work paying for his farm, but was finally successful In 1815 he sold out his place at Brimfield and removed to St Johnsbury, Vermont, where his son, Erastus Fairbanks, was already established with his uncle, Mrs Joseph Fairbanks' brother, Judge Paddock He purchased a small water-power and timber, with which he and his son built a dam, a saw mill, a grist mill and a wagon shop The family endured the hardships of pioneer life, together with the special and unusual discomfort of snow storms or frosts every month in the year The growing prosperity afterwards was due to his great energy and ability as well as that of his sons He was a man of sterling character, of the best New England type, influential among his neighbors and highly respected

He died suddenly September 27, 1846 His wife, to whom not less than to himself his sons owed their strength of character died at the advanced age of ninety-three years He married October 21, 1790, Phebe Paddock, daughter of James and Ann Paddock, of Holland, Massachusetts, whose emigrant ancestor came to this country with Governor Carver She was born September 6, 1760, died May 5 1853 The Paddock family gave many honored citizens to Vermont

The children of Joseph and Phebe (Paddock) Fairbanks were 1 Erastus, born October 28, 1792, at Brimfield, Massachusetts in the little red house near the Sturbridge line, he died November 20, 1864, he came to St Johnsbury alone in 1812 and for ten years afterward struggled against difficulties and reverses, and acquired early maturity of habits and purpose, frugality, industry, persistence, knowledge of men and of business, following the invention of the platform scale by his brother Thaddeus, he became the head of the firm of E & T Fairbanks & Co, a position which he held for thirty years during which time, under his energetic and skillful management, the business grew to large proportions and well established fame, in 1836 he was sent to the State Legislature, where from the first he was a leader, especially active in the interests of temperance and educational measures, he was a presidential elector of the Whig party in 1848, and about that time was actively pushing the construction of the Passumpsic Railroad, of which he was president from White River to St Johnsbury, at which terminus he greeted the first engine in November, 1850, two years later he was elected governor of Vermont and among other important legislative acts he had the satisfaction of affixing his signature to the Prohibitory Liquor Law, in 1860 he was elected governor again and became the war governor of Vermont and at the close of his service, in acknowledgment of his delicate, laborious and successful official acts, the Senate and House passed joint resolutions of the most appreciative and complimentary sort, and it was found that "the salary to which he was entitled was never touched, and it remains in the treasury of the state, another evidence of his generous love for Vermont whose interests were dearer to him than his own, and an honor to both people and Executive," he was for fifty years active in the Congregational church, and in later life an officer and member of many benevolent boards; he married Lois Crossman, daughter of Samuel and Lois (Chamberlain) Crossman, born November 13, 1792, died May 15, 1866, had nine children 2 Thaddeus, born January 17, 1796, at Brimfield, Massachusetts, died in St Johnsbury, Vermont, April 12, 1886 As a child he was slender and delicate in health, nervous and diffident and, indeed, he never enjoyed good health Much of his early education was received at home from his mother He learned the use of tools early in life Moving to Vermont with his father in 1815, after building their mills, he first made wagons, then in 1823 established a small iron foundry, doing much of the work with his own hands, and being joined by his brother Erastus, went on under the name of E & T Fairbanks His parlor stove and his patented cooking stove sold well, where only the open fire had been used before, and he invented and introduced the plow with cast iron mold board, now universally used, its novelty being attested by the patent he received on it

In 1829 he built hemp dressing machines and as manager of the hemp mills had to weigh what he bought To fill this need he invented the platform scale The first scales were for weighing wagons and their loads, but he soon extended the principle to all kinds and styles of scales until several hundreds of varieties were on the market He obtained thirty-two patents in this country on scales alone, besides patents for a hemp machine, stoves, plow, a device for creating draughts, a steam-heater, a feed-water heater, which was patented on his ninetieth birthday, and a refrigerator which he gave away at a time when he lacked the means to develop it, which has proved to be worth more than a million dollars to its owners The Fairbanks Scales have won prizes at all the World's Expositions In 1842 he and his brothers established St Johnsbury Academy, and he gave liberally to educational and charitable organizations He married January 17, 1820, Lucy Peck Barker, a native of St Johnsbury, whose father Barnabas Barker came with his father John and were the first settlers of the town Both John and Barnabas Barker were revolutionary soldiers, and were in the battle of Bunker Hill She was born April 29, 1799, died in St Johnsbury, December 29, 1866 she had two children 3 Joseph Paddock, born November 26 1806

(VII) Joseph Paddock Fairbanks, son of Joseph Fairbanks (6), was born in Brimfield, Massachusetts, November 26, 1806, died in St Johnsbury, Vermont, May 15, 1855 He began life as a lawyer, but joined his two brothers in the scale manufacturing business, and was in partnership with them twenty-two years to the time of his death His business abilities were of the very first order Much of the early success of the enterprise was due to his sagacity, minute attention to details and facility in dealing with men and with business difficulties and problems His mind was strong, capacious alert and remarkably well balanced He took broad views of everything was deeply religious and unsparing in his efforts for the good of men He was intelligently familiar with law theology science, history, and literature He was averse to public life while at the same time in more ways than men ever knew, he was influencing public opinion and pushing needed reforms He was influential in the Legislature especially in securing the passage of the Prohibitory Law and acts to improve the school system He sent out hundreds of pages of letters and press articles on almost every theme of current interest

He was literally a leader of thought in his day He was a man of strong individuality, though never alienating the love and respect of those from whom he differed He was benevolent and generous He was only forty-eight years old when he died

He married in Derry New Hampshire, June 11, 1835 Almira Taylor, daughter of James and Persis (Hemphill) Taylor She was born October 12 1811 She married (second) September 4, 1857 Rev W W Thayer of St Johnsbury, and died there January 20 1883 The children of Joseph Paddock and Almira (Taylor) Fairbanks were 1 Edward Taylor, born May 12, 1836 at St Johnsbury Vermont He was educated at Yale College, class of 1859 and at Andover Theological Seminary He spent two years and a half abroad in study and travel He was ordained January 1, 1868, as pastor of the Congregational Church in St Johnsbury, and since January 1874 has held his pastorate there He wrote the history of St Johnsbury and many pamphlets He is connected with many educational and religious organizations He received the honorary degree of D D from the University of Vermont in 1893 He married in Derry New Hampshire July 9 1862, Emma Cornelia Taplin daughter of Guy Carleton and Sally Malvina (Cady) Taplin, of Montpelier, Vermont where she was born March 11 1844 They have one child Cornelia Taylor, born June 25, 1876 2 William Paddock, born July 27, 1840

(VIII) William Paddock Fairbanks son of Joseph Paddock Fairbanks (7), was born at St Johnsbury Vermont July 27, 1840 He entered Dartmouth College in 1858 but left before completing the course to engage in business He was for several years in the office of E & T Fairbanks and a member of that firm Upon its incorporation in 1874 he was made secretary and treasurer He held the same office in the St Johnsbury and Lake Champlain Railroad Company and offices of trust in other corporations

While in Michigan he was a member of Governor Pingree's staff and ably represented his native town in the Legislature in 1884-85-86 In 1888 he went to New York as secretary of the Fairbanks Company of the city where he remained until his death which occurred suddenly December 15 1895 He was a man of force and strong personality wise, careful and accurate in business dealings, of quiet tastes benevolent and generous He married in St Johnsbury, Vermont April 18 1861, Rebecca Pike, daughter of Dennison and Huldah (Johnson) Pike of Waterford Vermont where she was born November 8, 1841 Their children were 1 Almira Taylor, born February 12, 1865, married January 17, 1888 Herbert W Blodgett of St Johnsbury, has one child, Donald F Blodgett, born June 6 1895 2 Mabel, born August 14, 1871 3 Joseph, born December 12, 1881

(IX) Mabel Fairbanks, daughter of Colonel William Paddock Fairbanks was born at St Johnsbury, Vermont August 14 1871 She married October 23, 1895 Birney A Robinson of Westford, Vermont (See sketch of Birney A Robinson)

CARL ELWOOD BURLINGAME Sheldon F Burlingame (1), son of Harris and Sarah Avis (Warren) Burlingame was born at East Killingly, Connecticut March 30, 1851 He was educated in the public schools of his native town His father was a carpenter and all the family had an inheritance of unusual manual dexterity and mechanical ingenuity Sheldon was set to work to learn the machinist's trade in Worcester, in the shop of Abraham Burlingame on Cypress street In years past the steam engines made by A Burlingame & Co were among the best, and many of them are in use in Worcester giving the utmost satisfaction After Sheldon Burlingame learned his trade he went to Philadelphia where he worked for several years He worked at his trade in New Jersey for a time, but when he was prepared to enter business for himself he returned to Worcester and opened a shop on Central street, where he built steam engines and did repairing

After a few years he removed to Florida where he was employed by Governor Drew, of that state, as master mechanic in the New Branford mills He followed his trade for several years in the South, living at New Branford, Live Oak, High Springs, Columbia City and other towns He returned North and worked for a short time for his brother, Abraham Burlingame Early in the nineties he turned his attention to gas and gasoline engines believing that these were the coming engines for small plants The development of the gasoline engine for use in the automobile has exceeded all predictions of the most sanguine Meanwhile Mr Burlingame has established an exceedingly busy little shop at Greendale where he has for ten years been making an excellent machine, and his business is rapidly growing The gasoline engine to-day is in demand on every up-to-date farm as well as in small manufacturing plants The name of Mr Burlingame's firm is the Greendale Gas Engine Company His son Carl E a skillful mechanic also, is in business with him as partner The factory is at 416 West Boylston street, at the end of the Greendale car line

The Greendale engine is wonderfully simple compared to the mechanisms called gas engines fifteen or twenty years ago This engine is started with crank such as those used on automobiles, and the operation of starting the machine, which was formerly difficult and trying, and not always successful even when undertaken by an expert is now very simple The gasoline tank is in the base of the machine out of sight It seems beyond belief to the man who operated the old style gas engine that this machine has only two valves, one for inlet, the other for exhaust The inlet valve works by suction the exhaust valve is water-jacketed The cylinder is of one casting and jacketed All parts are made interchangeable after the custom now prevailing in all the best manufactories The engines leave the Greendale factory set up and in running order after a thorough test The makers have no fear of trouble or accident when sending them to the most inexperienced owners or the most difficult positions, such as for use to run portable saw mills; dragged about the country on a cart in all sorts of weather, exposed to rain and having often very little attention from the operator The machines are run by unskillful farm hands to cut feed, to saw wood to run threshing machines to operate electric light plants to pump water for private reservoirs, and for a thousand purposes formerly requiring manual labor The result offsets the growing scarcity of help on the farm, and saves the life and strength of the farmer and his family, making the disagreeable and discouraging features of agriculture far less numerous Mr Burlingame understands the revolution that he is helping to effect with his machinery in agricultural conditions One of his engines has been run three weeks day and night without a stop Another five horse-power engine was used eighteen months on a truck for sawing wood in constant use with a total repair bill of thirty-five cents That shows the usefulness and

perfection of the modern gas engine Four sizes are made three and a half, five, seven, and fifteen horse-power the cost ranging from $175 to $360 Several hundred of these machines operated either by gas or gasoline are in use in and about Worcester county and giving universal satisfaction The company does not hesitate to print the entire list of those to whom machines have been sold The modern gas engine is a machine that sells itself Each customer makes others Mr Burlingame is a Free Mason, having joined a southern lodge He was formerly a member of the Worcester County Mechanics' Association

He married November 26, 1872, Ida F Chase, daughter of Israel and Polly (Young) Chase, of Killingly, Connecticut, born in Killingly, September 10 1855 Their children are Carl Elwood (see forward) Maud S, born May 19, 1881, married Robert C Sweetser, instructor in chemistry at the Worcester Polytechnic Institute and has one child, Sedric Sheldon, resides at 2 Randall street Worcester, Juniata born in New Branford Florida, August 5 1888 Marion Pearle, born in Worcester, December 24, 1896

Carl Elwood Burlingame, son of Sheldon F Burlingame was born at East Killingly, Connecticut, September 1, 1876 His education was obtained in the schools of the various towns in Massachusetts and Florida where his parents made their home during his youth He graduated from Branford Academy at Branford, Florida, in 1893 He learned the machinist s trade and worked for the A Burlingame Co, engine manufacturers, for the Wheelock Engine Company and for the Marcus Mason Company, builders of coffee machinery He entered partnership with his father when the Greendale factory was built, and has had a large share in building up the business of the company His business ability, mechanical skill and persistent energy have shown good results in the business He is generally regarded as one of the very promising young manufacturers of the city He is unmarried He is a member of the order of Knights of Pythias and was formerly a member of the Worcester County Mechanics' Association He is a member of the Congregational church at Greendale

FRANK H HAMBLIN, manufacturer of wire goods Worcester, Worcester county, Massachusetts, was born in East Boston, August 23, 1853 a son of Joseph G and Elizabeth (Hartwell) Hamblin

Joseph G Hamblin was one of the earliest settlers of East Boston, and a builder and real estate operator having built over one hundred houses on his own property During the latter part of his life he was an assistant United States Assessor

Frank H Hamblin obtained his education in the public schools of Boston, and afterwards studied for a professional career Deciding to go into business however, he was variously employed until 1883 when he removed to Worcester and engaged in the manufacture of wire goods The following year he incorporated the firm known as the Ayres Manufacturing Company the name being changed in 1887 to Hamblin & Russell Manufacturing Company, Mr Hamblin becoming its treasurer which office he continues to hold When this business was commenced Mr Hamblin employed only five or six hands in a building on Front street, which is now the Commonwealth hotel Owing to the rapidly increasing business the firm were forced to seek larger quarters, and accordingly removed their establishment into the boot and shoe factory of J H Walker on Water street which was subsequently purchased by the firm The enterprise has been one of the greatest success, and three hundred hands are now employed in the factory They make the largest variety of household utensils of any like concern in the country also hardware specialties The firm occupies about 80,000 square feet of floor space Mr Hamblin is a member of the Worcester Board of Trade, Commonwealth and Congregational clubs He married in 1889 Mercy P Sturtevant, who bore him one child Howard Parker After the death of his first wife, Mr Hamblin married Nellie Tucker of Worcester, in 1891, and they have three children Louis Tucker, Marion Laurette and Robert Hartwell

EDWIN RUTHVEN MORSE No family has ranked higher in eastern Massachusetts for the past two hundred and fifty years than the descendants of Samuel Morse, of Dedham The family has had many distinguished members, not the least of whom is Samuel F B Morse, to whom the world owes so much for the telegraph

(I) Samuel Morse was born in England in 1586 He sailed for New England in the ship Increase," April 15 1635, and settled at Dedham He was admitted a freeman there October 8, 1640 and later removed to the adjoining new town of Medfield, where many of his descendants have lived He was a town officer of Dedham and one of the proprietors He died April 5, 1654, and his will was proved January 30 1654 His widow died June 20 1655 He married in England Elizabeth ——, who was forty-eight years old when she emigrated born therefore about 1587 Their children were A son John, born 1611, died November 16, 1657 Daniel born 1613 Joseph, mentioned below Abigail married Daniel Fisher of Dedham, Mary, married Samuel Bullen, Jeremiah went east

(II) Joseph Morse son of Samuel Morse (1), the immigrant, also a progenitor of Edwin Ruthven Morse of Worcester was born in England in 1615 He settled first in Watertown but in 1637, after his father came, removed to Dedham He married in 1638 Hannah Phillips While he was clearing the land at Medfield and preparing the house for his family they lived at Dorchester, but he died before he had his new home ready and the growing corn and unfinished log house were left for his children to care for The widow married in 1658 Thomas Boyden who died in Boston in 1676 at the home of her eldest daughter The children of Joseph and Hannah (Phillips) Morse were Samuel, born 1639, mentioned below Hannah 1640, Sarah 1643, Dorcas 1645 died 1725 Elizabeth 1647 died 1715, Joseph, 1649, died 1718 settled in Sherborn, Jeremiah 1651 A child, who died young

(III) Samuel Morse, eldest child of Joseph Morse (2), was born in Dedham, Massachusetts 1639 He inherited part of his father's and grandfather's estate His house built in 1663 on the knoll east of Main and Pound streets junction was burned by the Indians in 1676 and was not rebuilt on that site, where the old cellar hole is or was lately visible He built his second house near that lately of John Ord Jr, and the old well is still in use In 1705 he was a lieutenant of militia and teacher of the school at Medfield In 1706 he obtained leave to flow the land "near the cowpens" for a fulling mill, which was built on the site of the stone mill lately owned by Crehore Samuel Morse was selectman six years and deputy to the general court in 1707 He married 1665, Elizabeth Wood who died in 1682 He married (second), 1684 Sarah Thurston, who died in 1688 He died in 1718 The children of Samuel and Elizabeth (Wood) Morse were Samuel, born 1665, Elizabeth, March 21, 1668, Hannah,

August 31, 1669, died young, Ruth, March 21, 1672, Joseph 1674, Joshua, April 2, 1677, mentioned below, Eleazer, August 10, 1680, Benoni, June 19, 1682 died 1704 Children of Samuel and Sarah (Thurston) Morse were Solomon, born 1684 died 1704, Sarah, 1686, married Isaac Bullard, of Sherborn

(IV) Joshua Morse, sixth child of Samuel Morse (3), was born on the homestead at Medfield, Massachusetts, April 2, 1677 He inherited part of the farm of his father in Medfield and bought much land on his own account He was an innholder and owned a grist mill and saw mill He built the house now or lately on the Jeremiah Johnston place He married, 1699, Elizabeth Penniman, daughter of Samuel Penniman of Braintree, born 1675 died 1705 He married (second) Widow Mary Paine, of Braintree who died in 1747 He was largely interested in the settlement of Sturbridge, Massachusetts, and the first meetings were held at his tavern to organize the proprietors He was deputy to the general court six years He died in 1749 The children of Joshua and Elizabeth (Penniman) Morse were Elizabeth born 1701, Zipporah April 20 1702, Samuel, May 4, 1703, settled in Uxbridge, Mary 1707, settled in Worcester, married —— Lovell Jemima, 1709 Joshua, December 28 1710 Eliakim, 1712, Lydia, October 27, 1714, Ruth, October 6 1716, Ebenezer mentioned below, Joseph, November 30, 1721 married Olive Mason, and settled in Nova Scotia

(V) Rev Ebenezer Morse son of Joshua Morse (4), was born in Medfield, Massachusetts, March 2, 1717-8 He graduated at Harvard College in 1737 and was settled as minister of Shrewsbury North District now Boylston Massachusetts, December 26, 1743 His relations with his parish were pleasant until just before the revolution when political feeling was intense He was summarily dismissed June 1775 and excluded from his pulpit for "toryism," confined to the town limits and later re-dismissed by advice of an ecclesiastical council He then practiced medicine during the remainder of his active days He died in 1802, at the age of eighty-four He married Persis Bush, daughter of John Bush, November 27 1745 He married (second) Rebecca Symmes widow of Thomas Symmes, who died in the revolution The children of Rev Ebenezer and Persis (Bush) Morse were Dr John, mentioned below Mary, born December 24 1747 Eliakim, March 8 1750, died 1758, Joshua, March 8, 1752, mentioned below, Ebenezer, June 11, 1754, died young Ebenezer, July 10 1755, Joseph January, 1757, married Sophia Bigelow Amherst, November 11 1760, Annis, May 19, 1764, Mary, August 12, 1767

(VI) Dr John Morse, eldest son of Rev Ebenezer Morse (5), was born in Shrewsbury (now Boylston) July 15, 1746 married May 11, 1769, Elizabeth Andrews mentioned below of Boylston They removed to Newfane Vermont and settled on the farm late of Elwin Ingram, June 1774 Theirs was the twentieth family to settle He was the first physician and for many years the only one in the town his services were of inestimable value to the pioneers He died April 7 1822 on the farm which he had cleared and on which he had lived half a century His children were Elizabeth, born March 2 1770 at Boylston John January 15 1773, at Boylston Ebenezer, July 14 1775, at Newfane, Jonathan January 9 1778 Mary September 10, 1782 Thomas Andrews mentioned below

(VII) Thomas Andrews Morse youngest child of Dr John Morse (6) born March 13 1786 He married Lucinda Wood He was a man of great industry and excellent character He died July 29, 1840 His children were Caroline, born November 28, 1810, Elizabeth A (VIII), married Austin J. Morse (VIII) mentioned below, Frederick J, October 23, 1814, Franklin B, September 20, 1817, Ann W June 8, 1822, Andrews T, October 17, 1824

(VI) Joshua Morse, fourth child of Rev Ebenezer Morse (5), was born in Shrewsbury North District (Boylston), March 8, 1752 He married Levinah Holland, of Boylston, daughter of Ephraim Holland, sister of the wife of Luke Knowlton, who came to Newfane, Vermont, with him in 1773 and settled on the farm lately owned by Welcome Allen, then removed to the Dr Olds place on Newfane Hill and subsequently to the farm later owned by Sabine Morse He died October 1, 1828 The children of Joshua and Levinah Morse were Tabitha, born in Boylston September 8, 1773, died unmarried 1817, Amherst, mentioned below, Ephraim, May 23, 1778, Joseph, September 16, 1780, died January 26, 1792, Luke, February 6, 1783, Persis, January 17 1785, Eunice March 28, 1787, Eunice, August 30, 1789, Windsor, January 7, 1793, Sewall, April 12, 1795, died 1795; Betsey, August 24, 1796

(VII) Amherst Morse, second child of Joshua Morse (6), was born in Newfane Vermont, April 25, 1776 He married Abigail Holden, February 11, 1800 and settled on the farm now or late of Marshall Houghton in Newfane, afterwards removing to his father's farm on Newfane Hill, where he lived until his death July 20, 1842 The children of Amherst and Abigail Morse were Maria, born May 4, 1804, married Nathaniel Cheney, of Wardsboro, Vermont, October 27, 1825, removed to Brattleboro, Abigail H, born May 20, 1807 married Huntington Fitch, April 23, 1832, removed to Columbus, Ohio, Austin J, mentioned above and below, Sabin P, March 15, 1817, married Sarah C Fitts, September 12, 1839 owned the homestead

(VIII) Austin J Morse, third child of Amherst Morse (7) was born in Newfane, Vermont, November 11, 1812 He married, April 9, 1835, Elizabeth A Morse (VIII), mentioned above, the daughter of Thomas Andrews Morse (VII) Married (second) Catherine Miller March 18, 1847 He resided at Newfane many years and also at Fayetteville, Vermont He was an extensive farmer and cattle drover He was a representative in the legislature in 1863 and 1864, a delegate to the constitutional convention in 1870 He removed to Brattleboro, where he died April 18, 1895 The children of Austin J and Elizabeth A (Morse) Morse were: Edwin Ruthven mentioned below, Amherst, who was a soldier in the civil war, a prisoner in Libby and died from its effects The children of Austin J and Catherine (Miller) Morse were Ellen, Mrs. M J Reed of Vermont Allie F, unmarried

BRADSTREET FAMILY (I) Governor Simon Bradstreet was an ancestor of Edwin Ruthven Morse, of Worcester He was born in Hobling Lincoln, England, in 1603, received his A B at Cambridge in 1620 A M in 1624, was appointed assistant to the Massachusetts Bay colony March 18 1630, and came with Governor Winthrop in 1630 He was secretary of the colony from August 23, 1630, to 1636 deputy governor 1673-8 governor 1679-86, again after the rising against Sir Edmond Andros 1689-92 He died March 27, 1697, aged ninety-four He married Ann Dudley, daughter of Governor Thomas Dudley, who was born in Northampton, England, in 1576 came to Massachusetts in 1638 with the commission of deputy governor, was governor from 1634 to 1640 was one of the signers of the charter of Harvard College Anne Dudley was the first poetess of note in New England, one of her brothers was later governor of the colony and a nephew was chief justice She died September 16, 1672, and Governor Bradstreet married (second) Ann Gardner widow of Joseph Gardner, daughter of Emanuel Downing, she died 1683 The children of Governor Simon and Ann (Dudley) Bradstreet were Samuel (H C 1653), Dorothy, married Rev Seaborn Cotton, Simon, born September 28, 1643, Hannah, Mercy, 1647, Dudley, 1648, John, born July 22, 1652

(II) John Bradstreet, son of Governor Simon Bradstreet (1), was born at Andover, Massachusetts, July 22, 1652, married June 11, 1677, Sarah Perkins daughter of Rev William Perkins, of Topsfield He was living in Salem in 1681, but most of his life was spent in Topsfield Their children were Simon, mentioned below, John, born January 30, 1693, Mary, November 27, 1696, Samuel, August 4, 1699

(III) Simon Bradstreet eldest child of John Bradstreet (2), was born in Topsfield, Massachusetts, April 14, 1682, married Elizabeth Capen, October 12, 1711 Their children, all born in Topsfield were Elizabeth, born August 28, 1712, Simon, April 21, 1714, Dudley May 27, 1716, John, March 2, 1717-8, Margaret, born April 24, 1720, married Thomas Andrews mentioned below, Priscilla, September 27, 1722, Lucy, November 25, 1724, Joseph, May 13, 1727, Mercy November 27, 1728, Mary, May 10, 1731

(IV) Margaret Bradstreet, daughter of the preceding (See Andrews)

ANDREWS FAMILY (I) Robert Andrews was the immigrant ancestor of Edwin Ruthven Morse, of Worcester, through Elizabeth Andrews, who married Dr John Morse (VI), as given above The mother of Elizabeth Andrews was Margaret (Bradstreet), mentioned above Robert Andrews was a native of Boxford, England, who settled in Boxford Massachusetts, in 1656, bringing with him six children and settling on a one hundred acre farm bought of John Lambert, of Rowley He bought other land later He died May 29, 1668 His will was made May 16, 1668, and proved July 1, 1668 His widow was Grace Andrews, died December 25, 1700, and her will made September 4, 1699 was proved January 4, 1702-3 Both are buried at Topsfield Their children, born there, were Mary 1638, Hannah, 1642, Elizabeth, 1645, married Samuel Simonds (see sketch of the Simonds family), Thomas, 1645 resided at Boxford, John 1648, settled in Boxford mentioned below, Robert 1651, Rebecca, married Samuel Marble, Joseph, September 18, 1657, great-great-grandfather of Governor John A Andrew Sarah, 1658, Ruth, May 27, 1664

(II) John Andrews, son of Robert Andrews (1), was born 1648 married, July 9, 1713 Patience Andrews, married (second) Hannah Kimball April 28 1724 They settled at Boxford The children of John and Patience were Hannah, born April 28, 1715, Thomas mentioned below, Mary, May 25, 1720 The children of John and Hannah were Samuel, baptized May 28 1727, Jeremiah, born August 7, 1727 Daniel December 27, 1729

(III) Thomas Andrews second child of John Andrews (2), was born in Boxford Massachusetts, September 4, 1717, married, at Topsfield, November 27, 1739 Margaret Bradstreet, daughter of Simon Bradstreet, whose ancestry is given above Her sister Lucy married Robert Andrews and both Robert and Thomas removed to the North District of Shrewsbury, later called Boylston, Massachusetts Thomas Andrews died at Newfane, Vermont in 1760 His eldest children were David, Jonathan, died unmarried, Elizabeth, who married Dr John Morse (Stated above)

(IV) Elizabeth Andrews, daughter of Thomas Andrews (2), married Dr John Morse (See sketch above)

(IX) Edwin Ruthven Morse, son of Austin J Morse (8), was born in Newfane, Vermont, February 24, 1843, and died in Worcester, August 30, 1887 Mr Morse was for many years a provision dealer with a store at 145 Main street, Worcester, a man of high standing in business and successful He was well known in Masonic circles, being a member of Montacute Lodge, Worcester Royal Arch Chapter, the Worcester County Commandery and in the Scottish Rite had taken all the degrees including the thirty-second In politics he was a Republican, but never sought public office

He married Martha E Osgood, of Minneapolis, Minnesota, March 16, 1869 She was born in Newfane, Vermont daughter of Willard Emory and Hannah (Park) Osgood and granddaughter of Deacon Jonathan Park, who was an officer in the revolutionary war and fought in the battle of Bennington She was educated at Wesleyan Seminary and was a teacher in the public schools of Minneapolis before her marriage Their only child was Lulu Mabel, born in Worcester, February 24, 1884, educated in the Worcester public schools and at a business college

HOMER RISING KING John Alden (1), made famous by Longfellow in the poem "Courtship of Miles Standish," was an ancestor of Homer Rising King, of Worcester, Massachusetts, and of others named elsewhere in this work

John Alden was born in England in 1599 He joined the Pilgrims on the "Mayflower" at Southampton as the ship was on its way to America When the ship stopped there for supplies he was hired as the cooper He had not been with them at Leyden and was probably not a member of the Independent church, but soon joined He cast his fortunes with the Pilgrims after enduring the hardships of that first terrible winter at Plymouth, when so many died He was doubtless influenced in this decision by his love for Priscilla Mullens, the story of which, with some embellishment, is told in "The Courtship of Miles Standish" She was the daughter of William Mullens, who came on the "Mayflower" with his family John and Priscilla were married in the spring of 1621 When the common property of the colony was divided in 1627 Alden went with Captain Standish, Elder Brewster, John Howland, Francis Eaton and Peter Brown to Mattakeeset, the Indian name of the territory now included in Duxbury, Marshfield, Pembroke, Hanson and Bridgewater, Massachusetts For several years they were obliged to return to Plymouth during the winter season to combine all their forces against the possible Indian attack that was always dreaded and not unexpected The residents in Plymouth in winter also gave then an opportunity to attend worship and the records show a written agreement of Alden and others in 1632 to remove their families to Plymouth in the winter

In 1633 Alden was appointed assistant to the governor, an office which he held for nearly the whole of the remainder of his life, serving with Edward Winslow, Josiah Winslow, Bradford, Prince and Thomas Hinckley From 1666 until his death he held the office of first assistant, was often called the deputy governor, and was many times acting-governor in the absence of the governor From 1640 to 1650 he was also deputy to the colonial council from Duxbury Winslow's history of Duxbury says of him "Holding offices of the highest trust, no important measure was proposed, or any responsible agency ordered in which he had not a part He was one of the council of war, many times an arbitrator, a surveyor of lands for the government as well as for individuals and on several important occasions was authorized to act as agent or attorney for the colony He was possessed of a sound judgment and of talents which, though not brilliant, were by no means ordinary Writers who mention him bear ample testimony to his industry, integrity and exemplary piety, and he has been represented as a worthy and useful man of great humility and eminent for sanctity of life, decided, ardent, resolute and persevering, indifferent to danger, stern austere and unyielding, and of incorruptible integrity He was always a firm supporter of the church, and everything of an innovating nature received determined opposition" From the Puritan point of view Alden was a model if the description of his virtues is truthful He took his part in making the life of the Quakers at Plymouth colony intolerable

On the Alden farm there stands the house built by John Alden's son Jonathan having been occupied by eight generations of Aldens in direct line It is the oldest house in New England with three exceptions the old Fort at Medford, built in 1634, the Fairbanks house at Dedham, built in 1636, and the old stone house at Guilford, Connecticut, built in 1640 Here Alden spent his declining years He died in Duxbury, September 12, 1686, aged eighty-seven, the last of the famous band of Pilgrim Fathers, and the last of the "Mayflower" company except only Mary Allerton, who died in 1699, aged ninety

John Alden had eleven children, only eight of whom are known These were 1 John, born at Plymouth about 1622, Freeman, 1648, at Boston, died May 14, 1702, aged eighty-nine years, married, April 1 1660 Elizabeth Everell, widow, daughter of William Phillips 2 Joseph, (see forward) 3 Elizabeth, born 1625, died at Little Compton, Rhode Island, aged ninety-three, married William Peabody 4 Jonathan, born about 1627, captain, married, December 10, Abigail Hallett 5 Sarah, married Alexander Standish, son of Captain Miles Standish 6 Ruth, married John Bass, of Braintree, from whom the Presidents Adams descended 7 Mary married Thomas Delano, of Duxbury son of Philip Delano, who came in the "Fortune" in 1621 8 David, prominent man of Duxbury

(II) Joseph Alden, son of John Alden (1), born in Plymouth, Massachusetts, in 1624, died February 8, 1697 He inherited land at Bridgewater, where he settled and also at Middleboro Massachusetts He was admitted a freeman 1659 He married Mary Simmons, daughter of Moses Simmons, Jr, who came in the "Fortune" in 1621 and settled at Duxbury Joseph Alden's will was dated December 14, 1696, and proved March 10, 1697 His children were 1 Isaac, born at Bridgewater, married (second) Mehitable Allen December 2 1685 2 Joseph (see forward) 3 John, born at West Bridgewater died September 29 1730, aged fifty-six, married Hannah White, daughter of Ebenezer White, of Weymouth 4 Elizabeth, married, 1691, Benjamin Snow 5 Mary married, 1700, Samuel Allen

(III) Joseph Alden, son of Joseph Alden (2), born at Bridgewater, Massachusetts, 1667, died January 22, 1747 He was deacon of the church there and a prominent man His will was dated November 12, 1743 He lived at South Bridgewater He married, 1690, Hannah Dunham, daughter of Daniel Dunham, of Plymouth She died January 13 1748, aged seventy-eight Their children were 1 Daniel, born January 29, 1691, married, 1717, Abigail Shaw and settled in Stafford, Connecticut 2 Joseph, born August 26, 1693, died December 9, 1695 3 Eleazer, born September 27, 1694, married, 1720, Martha Shaw, he died January 30, 1773 4 Hannah, born 1696, married (first) Joseph Alden, married (second), 1722, Mark Lothrop, of Easton 5 Mary, born April 10, 1699, married, second, 1719, Timothy Edson 6 Joseph, born September 5, 1700, died October 5, 1700 7 Jonathan, born December 3, 1703, died November 10, 1704 8 Samuel, (see forward) 9 Mehitable, born October 18, 1707, died April 11, 1737 10 Seth, born July 6, 1710, died September 6, 1784, married Mehitable Carver, settled at Bridgewater

(IV) Samuel Alden, son of Joseph Alden (3), born at South Bridgewater, Massachusetts, August 20, 1705, died 1785, married 1728, Abiah Edson, daughter of Captain Joseph Edson, and settled at Titicut Their children were 1 Abiah born 1729, married Seth Harris, lived at North Bridgewater 2 Mehitable, born 1732, married Joshua Packard, lived in Maine 3 Sarah, born 1734, married Timothy Packard 4 Samuel, born 1736, died 1816, married Hannah Williams 5 Josiah, (see forward) 6 Simeon, born 1740, settled at Bridgewater and Titicut, married, 1763, Mary Packard 7 Silas, died aged twenty-one 8 Mary 9 Hosea, killed by kick of horse, married two daughters of Josiah Washburn

(V) Josiah Alden, son of Samuel Alden (4), born in Bridgewater, Massachusetts, 1738, settled in his native town later in Wales, Massachusetts He married 1761, Bathsheba Jones of Raynham, Massachusetts Their children were 1 Elijah, settled at Brimfield and Ludlow was soldier in revolution married Rebecca Fuller 2 Azel (son), born 1770 died 1854, married 1791 Bethany Wilbur 3 Abiah married Benjamin Winchester 4 Bathsheba 5 Charity, married Peter Trask, of Randolph Vermont 6 Josiah (see forward) 7 Lucy, married Amos Fletcher 8 Rebecca, married Benjamin Snoe, settled in Belchertown, Massachusetts 9 Benjamin, married Polly Hodges

(VI) Josiah Alden, son of Josiah Alden (5), born 1773, died September 3, 1833, married (first) Olive Brown, married (second) Widow Bates Children of Josiah and Olive (Brown) Alden were 1 Azel (son) born August 12 1792, died October 22 1860 married Mary Brainard 2 Justus, born September 15 1793, died September 30 1831 married Betsey Porter 3 Zenas born November 1, 1795 died January 1, 1840 married Betsey Taylor 4 Charity born June 5 1797, died August 11, 1829 5 Washington Brown, born July 14 1799, died August 5, 1859, married Hannah B Bartlett 6 Charles, born December 6 1803 died May 22, 1862, married Margaret Moore and Louisa Paine 7 John, married Huldah Wright, June 17 1827 8 Orsamus, born June 5 1808 married, June 28 1842 Eliza Ann Lehman 9 Mary Needham born September 13, 1810 married, October 27, 1831, Henry Fuller 10 Eunice Brown (see forward)

(VII) Eunice Brown Alden, daughter of Josiah Alden (6) born at Ludlow Massachusetts December 23 1813 married March 24 1833 Marvin King, of Longmeadow, Massachusetts They settled at Ludlow where he had a farm He died in Ludlow, January 1, 1903 aged ninety-five years His wife died 1863 Their children were 1 Mary Madelia, born February 9 1834 married, November 26, 1852, Justus Alden 2 Marvin Henry, born April 5, 1835

3 Ann Frances, born February 28, 1837, married Charles Henry Knapp, of Northampton 4 Samuel Alden born December 15 1838, magistrate, sergeant in civil war 5 Julia Isadora, born March 22, 1841 6 Arthur Delano, born May 13 1843, corporal in civil war 7 Homer Washington born December 8 1844 died September 5, 1846 8 Homer Rising, born June 4 1846 9 Olive Eugenie, born May 14, 1848 10 Frank E, born May 26, 1850, died October 1 1852 11 Frederick Augustus, born November 17 1852 12 Lelia Imogene, born December 23, 1854

(VIII) Homer Rising King, son of Marvin (7) and Eunice Brown (Alden) King, was born in Ludlow, Hampton county, Massachusetts June 4, 1846 He attended the district schools of his native town and worked on his father's farm until the age of seventeen when he enlisted in Company I, Twenty-seventh Massachusetts Infantry, Captain Henry A Hubbard Colonel Horace C Lee, of Springfield, Massachusetts, under whom he served two years He was with his regiment in the following battles Wallhollow Junction, Virginia, Fairfield church, Virginia Cold Harbor, Petersburg, Bermuda Hundred, and in the battles in front of Richmond up to 1864 He was mustered out at the end of the civil war He returned to Ludlow and entered the grocery and provision business In March, 1866, he gave up his store and went to Colorado He travelled on foot from Atchison, Kansas, to Fairplay and South Park, Colorado, a distance of seven hundred miles He engaged in placer-mining and in the provision business for four years He was elected trial justice and deputy county clerk for Jefferson county, Colorado, for three years In 1870 he came east and with his brother, Arthur D King, started in the grocery and provision business in Wilbraham Massachusetts Three years later he removed to Worcester, where he followed the same business dealing also in cattle He has for many years been in the wholesale business only, dealing in meats and cattle In 1880 he bought the farm of one hundred and forty acres at Tatnuck, in Worcester It is well equipped for his business of dealing in cattle and slaughtering purposes

Mr King has been repeatedly honored with public office He was for three years alderman in 1893-94-95, and served on the committees of water and highways, being the chairman He was a member of the common council also in 1890-91-92, and chairman of the same committees for three years He represented the eighth ward district in the general court He was on the water supply committee two years and served on the special committee that dedicated the Massachusetts monument at Andersonville Georgia in 1901 He is a life member of Athelstan Lodge of Free Masons, Worcester Lodge of Perfection and Eureka Chapter He is a member of the State Grange, Patrons of Husbandry, of Commonwealth Lodge, United Order of American Mechanics and of Post 10, Grand Army

He married December 9, 1869 Hattie L Ward, daughter of E L Ward, of Worcester, sister of Mrs H M Tompkins (See sketch of Tompkins Family) They have one child Mabel L King, born February 9, 1876

THE MOONEY FAMILY, represented in the present generation by Nicholas Joseph Mooney, Richard Henry Mooney, A M, and John Francis Henry Mooney residents of Worcester, Massachusetts, was founded in this country by Patrick Mooney, farmer who came from Carrick-Beg, county of Waterford Ireland, 1842, and settled in Worcester, Massachusetts, where a number of his descendants are now to be found He was accompanied by his daughter and son-in-law, Mr and Mrs John Blade, and his two sons, Richard and Nicholas, his wife, Nancy (Hagerty) Mooney, having died in Ireland Patrick Mooney, accompanied by Mr and Mrs John Blade, went to Wisconsin, where he engaged in farming, and subsequently became the owner of one of the largest and most productive farms in his region which he cultivated and improved, and resided on up to the time of his death Nicholas Mooney aforementioned, died in Worcester Massachusetts, June 12, 1848, and was the first person buried in St John s cemetery

Richard Mooney, son of Patrick and Nancy (Hagerty) Mooney, was born in Ireland, from whence he came to the United States with his father He was a builder and contractor, learning his trade in Ireland, where he served an apprenticeship of seven years becoming at the same time a practical surveyor and architect He was continuously engaged in his business and built a large number of houses in Worcester By prudent and careful management he acquired considerable landed property, and was one of the most prominent men of his day, taking an active part in all town and municipal affairs Being among the earliest Irish residents of Worcester, and a man of education and business ability his assistance and advice was often sought by his countrymen His home was a center of information for the Irish people, and he not only received their letters but often wrote their replies

Richard Mooney was married in 1845 at St John's Church, Worcester, Massachusetts by the Rev Matthew W Gibson to Margaret Doyle, a native of the county of Waterford, Ireland Their children are Julia A married James H Mellen, had seven children, William R John F H, Annie T Catharine James, deceased, Francis, deceased, and Richard F Mellen Nicholas Joseph, mentioned hereinafter Annie Statia, died September 24 1874 Richard Henry mentioned hereinafter John Francis Henry, mentioned hereinafter Margaret Elizabeth married John J Foley, who was for many years organist at St Anne's Church, he died in 1902 leaving five children Margaret, Catherine, Anna Elizabeth, and John J Foley Richard Mooney father of these children, died February 16, 1860, aged forty years, as the result of an accident, caused by the giving away of a scaffolding His widow Margaret (Doyle) Mooney, died at her home, 78 Madison street Worcester, December 19, 1905 aged eighty years The funeral services were conducted in St Paul s Church, of which she was a benefactor At the time of her death, she was the oldest Irish Catholic in Worcester, in point of residence She located in Worcester in 1842, when the city was only a town She was one of the attendants at the laying of the corner stone of the College of the Holy Cross in 1843 and was one of the original members of St John's parish, being present at the exercises of the laying of the corner-stone of that church in 1846 Mrs Mooney is survived by three sons—Nicholas J Richard H and John F H—and one daughter, Mrs Margaret M Foley Another daughter, Mrs James H Mellen died May 9 1885

Nicholas Joseph Mooney, son of Richard and Margaret (Doyle) Mooney, was born in Worcester, Massachusetts, October 10, 1848 He attended the public schools of his native city, and after completing his studies worked as a carpenter, machinist and boot crimper In 1877 he was appointed a member of the police force of Worcester, Massachusetts by Hon Charles B Pratt, mayor After a service of fifteen years on the force, he resigned therefrom, and later engaged in the fire insurance business, beginning as an agent for the Germania Fire Insurance Company of New York In 1902 he became general local manager of the company, which he still represents He also represents the Reliance, of Philadelphia, Commercial Union, of New York, American Insurance, of Boston, the Worcester Mutual, and the Merchants and Farmers In the insurance business Mr Mooney has been successful in an eminent degree, building up one of the largest and best known offices in this line in Worcester His advice is considered safe and sound in all financial matters, and is often sought in estimating the value of real estate and in investments He is one of the original incorporators of the Bay State Savings Bank, and a member of its investment committee

Mr Mooney has always taken an active interest in all public and municipal affairs, laboring efficiently in forwarding every material and moral interest He was a member of the common council for two terms, serving on important committees and always on the finance committee During the famous strike of the Knights of Saint Crispin, in 1870, Mr Mooney was secretary of the organization and was a prominent factor in the management and directing of the same during that troublous time He is a member of the Ancient Order of Hibernians, and of the Father Matthew Total Abstinence and Mutual Benefit Society, of which he was president for five consecutive terms, and was serving in that capacity when the society presented a testimonial to the late Hon George Frisbie Hoar, in recognition of his public services, and he was appointed to make the presentation speech He is a charter member of the Police Relief Association of Worcester In politics he is a sterling Democrat

In 1885 Mr Mooney married Joanna M Healey, of Cambridge, Massachusetts Their children are Frances C, John J, Richard J, died March 25, 1905 Rachel Annie and Julia

Richard Henry Mooney, A M, son of Richard and Margaret (Doyle) Mooney, was born in Worcester, Massachusetts, and has always lived there He attended the public schools of his native city, and entered the College of the Holy Cross, Worcester from which he was graduated in the class of 1879, with the degree of Bachelor of Arts During his college course he took a very high rank in his class, gaining prizes in English composition, elocution, mathematics and physics Having decided to make teaching his profession he entered the theological and pedagogical department of the Laval University of Montreal, Canada, where he pursued a special course in theology, moral and dogmatic, sacred Scripture and history of sacred writings, literature, ancient, medieval and modern history, history of education, psychology and philosophy He then became a special student in the State Normal school, at Worcester, under the direction and supervision of Professor E Harlow Russell, principal of the school, a recognized authority in pedagogy and child study In June 1881, he received his diploma from the State Normal school, and his degree of Master of Arts from his alma mater

In September, 1881, he began his work of teaching in the Adams Square school, Worcester, which was then an ungraded school where he taught everything from the alphabet to algebra In September 1882 he was appointed by the school committee principal of the Quinsigamond school over which he still presides In the growth and development of this school Mr Mooney takes pardonable pride, and the entire village of Quinsigamond, which is the largest and most thriving of the many suburbs of Worcester, the location of the South works, so-called, of the American Steel and Wire Company, is contributory to this educational institution When Mr Mooney first took charge of the school there were five teachers in charge of about two hundred pupils, but at the present time (1906) there are twenty-five teachers in charge of over one thousand pupils The graduates of this school are now engaged in the various active pursuits of life, in the shop, office, store, in the army and navy, in public service in different departments of the city and county, in the legislative department of the state government, and the customs department of the United States It has always been the constant aim of Mr Mooney in training the pupils under his charge to thoroughly qualify them for the duties of life He does not leave them on the threshold of the school-room, but meets them out in the world in the various walks of business, professional, and social life, and cheers them on in their undertakings In his career as a teacher he has manifested diligence, industry, executive ability of a very high order, decision, energy, and a careful preparation of every detail in school organization, discipline, and teaching In school economy, methods of culture and history of education—in all that goes to make a thorough and practical master of pedagogy, and in the science and art of education, he holds high rank Many of the methods and devices occasionally put forward by lecturers at school conventions as new and original, have been in vogue in the Quinsigamond school for many years Especially is this so in regard to promotions, individual work with pupils special attention to defective and backward pupils, small classes, continuous and generous use of the blackboards by pupils and teachers, and in many other aids devices methods, and principles of teaching

Mr Mooney's collateral work has always been along the lines of educational thought, activity and philanthropy He has interested himself very much in the organization of societies which he foresaw would or might do some good In 1887 he was elected secretary of the Alumni Association of the College of the Holy Cross, his alma mater, and he has built up that organization to its present prosperous condition In 1899 he organized the Young Ladies' Lyceum of the Church of the Sacred Heart, Worcester over which the Right Rev Thomas J Conaty now Bishop of Los Angeles, California, presided, and was appointed its first president In 1890 he organized the Worcester County Total Abstinence Union, comprising the active total abstinence societies in the towns and cities of the county, and was appointed its lecturer He has also organized many total abstinence societies for young men and young ladies throughout Worcester county and has lectured on temperance in many cities and towns in New England He was one of the incorporators of the St Vincent Hospital, House of Providence, and of St Joseph's Industrial Home, Millbury, Massachusetts

Mr Mooney has published several books as aids in the work of teaching In 1891 he published "One Thousand Questions and Answers on United States History Civil Government Literature and Finance," also One Hundred Questions and Answers on Alcohol" In 1892 he published historical papers, containing with notes the "Declaration of Independence" the "Articles of Confederation" the "Constitution of the United States" "Washington's Farewell Address" and "A Table of the Presidents" In 1892 by vote of the Worcester County Teachers' Association in convention assembled, he prepared a classified list of books for supplementary reading by grades for the public schools In 1893 he published "Patriotic Prose and Poetry" All of these books have had an extended circulation Mr Mooney has now in preparation "A Short History of Ireland," and Elementary Algebra, and a Problem Book in Arithmetic

During the winters of 1886-87-88-89-90 Mr Mooney lectured before the pupils of the various evening schools on historical, scientific and other subjects He has spoken before many local audiences, teachers' associations and societies in adjacent cities and towns on literary, educational and patriotic subjects He is often introduced by presiding officers as 'the silver-tongued orator" In 1895, while serving as president of the Worcester County Teachers' Association, he presided over the largest convention of that association ever held up to that time He is a member of the Massachusetts Teachers' Association On Memorial Day, 1895, Mr Mooney was the orator on behalf of the Grand Army of the Republic and the citizens in general at the soldiers' monument on the common, where he delivered one of the most eloquent and patriotic addresses ever heard there In May, 1899, he spoke under the auspices of the Men's Union of the Trinity Methodist Episcopal Church on the Catholic Religion In 1895 Mr Mooney was chairman of the committee which organized the Schoolmasters' Club of Worcester county, of which G Stanley Hall president of Clark University, was the first president, and Mr Mooney held that office in 1899 Mr Mooney presided at the first dinner given by that club Mr Mooney is an associate member—a life member—of the George H Ward Post, No 10, Grand Army of the Republic, and is always a welcome speaker at its gatherings He was a member of the committee of fifteen, chosen at a meeting of citizens, to arrange for the reception and dinner in honor of the soldiers who returned from the Spanish-American war In 1896 he was chairman of the committee which inaugurated the first course of lectures for teachers ever given in Worcester In September of that year, as editor and proprietor, he began the publication of the School Register," a monthly paper devoted to the interests of education

Mr Mooney takes an active interest in public and civic affairs and is always ready to perform his duty as a citizen He believes that a quiet, conservative intercourse between the world and the school is of mutual benefit In 1885 he was appointed by the executive of the commonwealth to the office of justice of the peace, which commission he still holds, a period of twenty-one years, which is an eloquent testimonial to his ability as an adjudicator as well as of his sterling integrity He is a member of the board of trade and serves on the committee on municipal affairs As president of the Quinsigamond Improvement Society, he has been instrumental in securing many improvements for the village in the way of better roads, sidewalks electric lights, shade trees electric car service, and finally, after years of agitation and hearings before different committees of the city government a public play ground for the youth of the village called Greenwood Park

In 1892 Mr Mooney married Edith Genevieve Loring of Westborough Massachusetts daughter of Willard Loring of that town Mrs Mooney was graduated from the Westborough high school and from the State Normal school at Worcester, and previous to her marriage was a teacher in the public schools of Worcester Their children are Margaret Loring, Richard Henry Jr, Miles, and Edith Loring Mooney The family home is on Vernon street in the southern part of the city of Worcester, and is surrounded by a spacious lawn and four acres of land The estate is dotted with many fruit and ornamental trees

Mr Mooney is a member of no organization or society not connected with his profession of teaching Everything is subordinated with him to the great work of turning out good, intelligent and patriotic citizens In religion he is a Catholic, in politics a Republican

John Francis Henry Mooney, A B, son of Richard and Margaret (Doyle) Mooney, was born in Worcester, Massachusetts After his graduation from the public schools he entered the College of the Holy Cross, where he was graduated in 1879, with the degree of Bachelor of Arts He immediately took up journalism and for twenty years was connected with the *Worcester Evening Gazette* as reporter and was also the local daily correspondent of the *Boston Globe* He is now (1906) engaged in the insurance business with his brother Nicholas J Mooney In 1884 he was elected a member of the house of representatives in the state legislature from ward 5 and served on the committee on education which reported the free text book bill, which was passed that year He served six years as a member of the Worcester Light Infantry, in which he attained the rank of sergeant He is a member of the Ancient Order of Hibernians and was for a long time president of his division He is a member of the Independent Order of Elks Mr Mooney is one of the best known men in Worcester, meeting in his work for a number of years men of all conditions and in all walks of life He is a sterling Democrat

JOHN J POWER William Power, father of Alderman John J Power, of Worcester, Massachusetts, was born in Waterford, Ireland, about 1850 He belonged to a well known and numerous family of this surname, among whom there were many men of distinction in Ireland He came to America in 1860 when a young man, and made his home in Worcester He had learned the carpenter's trade thoroughly in the old country and was a skilful mechanic For the first year he worked for John P McDonald, carpenter and builder, of Worcester In 1870 he started in business for himself, and soon became one of the leading carpenters of the city, in the course of his career he built over three hundred houses in Worcester He had many contracts also outside of the city, and continued actively in business until his death January 29, 1894 He was a member of the Ancient Order of Hibernians, and of St John's Roman Catholic Church His home was always in the fourth ward where he was highly esteemed and had considerable influence among his fellow citizens He owned a number of houses in that ward He married Nora Ahassey in St John's Church Worcester Their children are Alice G resides at home, John J (see forward), M Agnes, resides at home, William H, George A, student in the Harvard Medical school James T student at Worcester Polytechnic Institute, Thomas F student at Amherst College Henry R, student in the Worcester Classical high school orator of the class of 1906

John J Power, son of William Power was born in Worcester, Massachusetts, October 31 1876 He received his education in the public schools of Worcester and at Holy Cross College He became associated in business with his father while still in school His father died when he was less than eighteen years old and he succeeded to the business and care of the estate being the eldest son He continued the business successfully, and has since carried on a general contracting and building business He is a member of the builders' exchange and of the board of trade He belongs to the Washington Club In politics he is a Democrat, and he has taken a strong interest in public affairs He was elected from ward four, a member of the common council for the years 1901-2-3-4, and of the board of aldermen for 1905 6 He has served on all the important committees of the city council and is, notwithstanding his youth, one of the veterans of the city council, an efficient and faithful official Alderman Power resides in a handsome new residence at No 1 Granite street He built the house for his own use He married, October 31, 1905, Hannah M Kehoe, daughter of Michael and Mary Kehoe, of Worcester

ROBERT LYONS GOLBERT, for many years identified with the business interests of Worcester, in which city he has spent the greater part of his life was born in Boston, Massachusetts, July 2, 1837, a son of Robert Lyons and Rebecca (Stevens) Golbert, of Boston, whose family consisted of four other children, namely George, who died while serving in the Army of the Potomac during the civil war, Benjamin B, who died in 1903, was a soldier in the Ninth Company of Massachusetts Volunteer Infantry, Elizabeth died in infancy, and William Robert Lyons Golbert (father) was probably a native of Boston, was of German descent, and followed the trade of a sail maker His wife, Rebecca (Stevens) Golbert was a native of Boston, Massachusetts, and a descendant of an English family who were for many years residents of Boston

Robert Lyons Golbert attended school in Boston until twelve years of age when his father died, and he then went to live at Hanson, Massachusetts At the age of seventeen he returned to Boston and secured employment in the last factory of John Armstrong, where he thoroughly mastered all the details of the trade In 1856 he came to Worcester and entered the employ of Samuel Mawhinney, the well known last manufacturer and in 1869 was admitted to partnership with his employer This connection continued until Mr Mawhinney moved his business to Brockton Massachusetts, and Mr Golbert continued to manufacture lasts in Worcester until February, 1905 when the business was incorporated as the Golbert Last Company, his associates being A B Taylor and Louis A Wheeler Mr Golbert is a member of Athelstan Lodge, Eureka Chapter, Worcester County Commandery and Grand Lodge of Perfection Free and Accepted Masons He is also a member of the Worcester Board of Trade Worcester Mechanics Association, and the Hancock Club He is a Republican in politics Mr Golbert married Mary Elizabeth Field, of Nantucket, Massachusetts and they are the parents of one daughter Sadie Golbert

JOSIAH H CLARKE Joseph Clarke (1), the emigrant ancestor of the late Josiah Howe Clarke, of Worcester, was one of the pioneer settlers in Dedham Massachusetts He was a proprietor in Dedham September 28 1640 He was one of the first thirteen settlers of Medfield Massachusetts He was admitted a freeman there May 18 1653 His homestead was on the south side of South street, Medfield and the old cellar hole near the corner of Oak street still indicates the location of his house He was selectman in 1660 but was seldom in office He died in 1684 His wife Alice whom he probably married in England, died in 1710 Their children were Joseph born July 27, 1642 Benjamin, see forward, Ephraim, born February 9, 1644, Daniel, born September 29, 1647, died in 1676 of wounds received from the Indians during the attack and burning of Medfield, Mary, born March 12, 1649 married, 1673, John Boyden, Sarah, born February 20, 1651, died 1704, John, born 1652, died 1720, Nathaniel, born 1658, Rebecca, born 1660, died 1739

(II) Benjamin Clarke, second child of Joseph Clarke (1), was born in Dedham, Massachusetts, February 9, 1644 He married, 1665, Dorcas Morse He had a grant of land in Medfield, "near the way as you go to Nantasket" His house was on Main street, opposite Pound street The original well is said to be still in use His house was burned by the Indians in 1676, and he built again on the same spot What is known as the Peak House in Medfield is an addition subsequently made to his second house in or about 1762 After the old part decayed and was torn down, the present structure was moved to its present location Its unique shape has attracted much attention and is even believed to be one of the houses left from the burning in King Philip's war Benjamin Clarke was a very prominent citizen He was for seventeen years selectman of the town and two years deputy to the general court He died in 1724 and his widow in 1725 Their children were Hannah, born October 22, 1666, died 1757, Benjamin, born November 20, 1668, died at the Eastward, Theophilus, see forward, Tabitha, born December 10, 1672, Timothy, born December 19, 1674, died 1676, Timothy, born May 12, 1677, Edward, born November 11, 1679 died 1746, at Medway, Ebenezer, born 1682, died 1683, Rebecca, born 1684, died 1687, Seth born 1687

(III) Theophilus Clarke, third child of Benjamin Clarke (2), was born in Medfield, Massachusetts, September 25, 1670 He married Rachel ——— They settled in Medfield, where he lived until after her death, December 1, 1717 He married (second) Elizabeth Cutler, of Reading Massachusetts February 24, 1718 Thereafter he lived in Medway He had twelve children by the first marriage and three by the second The children of Theophilus and Rachel, all born in Medfield, were Ebenezer, born January 21, 1690 died 1700, Rachel, December 13 1692, James, March 7 1693-4, Rebecca January 21 1694-5, Benjamin, Theophilus born April 16, 1698, died August 28, 1716, Deborah October 12, 1701, Zebiah, November 1, 1703, Caleb, (see forward), Dorcas, March 13, 1706-7, Mary, May 5 1710, Abigail, April 20 1712 The children of Theophilus and Elizabeth (Cutler) Clarke Esther, January 1, 1719, Lieutenant Theophilus, April 19, 1722, died in service 1760, Benjamin, March 17, 1724

(IV) Caleb Clarke, ninth child of Theophilus Clarke (3) of Medfield, and Medway was born in Medfield Massachusetts September 24, 1705 He married Phebe —— They were living in Framingham in 1734, when he appears among the taxpayers In 1735 he was in Sudbury, the adjoining town His brother Theophilus settled in Holliston, which adjoins Framingham on the other side They had ten children born in Sudbury and perhaps others before they settled there The children of Caleb and Phebe Clarke were Phebe born August 26, 1735, Rebecca, March 28 1737 Rachel October 7, 1738, Abigail March 19, 1740-1 died March 20, 1741, Benjamin, see forward Seth, June 29 1746, Calvin August 26, 1735 a soldier in the revolution, married Martha Hunt Jonas (twin), born June 15, 1751, Abigail (twin) born June 15 1751, Zebiah, February 12 1753, named for her aunt her father's sister Caleb Jr was probably his eldest son

(V) Benjamin Clarke, son of Caleb Clarke (4), and his fifth child, was born in Sudbury, Massa-

Josiah H. Clarke

chusetts July 17, 1744 He seems to have been a soldier in the revolution credited to Framingham He married October 19, 1768, Abigail Hunt daughter of William and Mary Hunt She was born in Sudbury December 17, 1750, and married there She died February 11, 1830, in Marlboro, aged seventy-nine years He died April 15, 1829 aged eighty-six years They settled in Marlboro which was a colony of Sudbury Some of their children were born in Sudbury, however They probably moved in 1776 The children of Benjamin and Abigail (Hunt) Clarke were Mary, born in Sudbury, December 18, 1769, married, August 29, 1787, Simon Eames, Abigail, born in Sudbury, March 22, 1772, Sarah or Sally March 30, 1774, died young, Benjamin see forward, Sally, May 4, 1780, married, September 11, 1798 Jonathan Weeks, Nancy, March 5, 1782 Betsey October 10, 1784, married, February 20, 1805 Levi Colby

(VI) Benjamin Clarke, fourth child of Benjamin Clarke (5), was born in Marlboro, April 2, 1778 He married in 1800, Catherine Eustis and they had sixteen children, among whom was Benjamin, born about 1801 He settled in Marlboro and all his children were born there He was a farmer

(VII) Benjamin Clarke, eldest son of Benjamin Clarke (6), was born in Marlboro, Massachusetts about 1801 He married Lucy Howe, of Marlboro, born November 1 1794, the daughter of Josiah and Molly (Adams) Howe (married February 24, 1770) Josiah Howe was the son of Josiah and Mary (Goodale) Howe (married August 12 1741) Mary Goodale was the daughter of Benjamin and Hannah Goodale Josiah was born December 22, 1720 He was the son of Josiah and Sarah (Bigelow) Howe (married June 14, 1706) and he died June 14 1766 The latter Josiah Howe was born in 1678 and was the son of Josiah and Mary (Haynes) Howe who were married March 18, 1672 The last named Josiah was the son of John Howe (1) (See Howe Family elsewhere in this work for John Howe (1) of Sudbury) Benjamin Clarke was a prosperous farmer of Marlboro Massachusetts Three of his children came to Worcester to live John B, who was associated with his brother Josiah H in the dry goods business, Dr Henry, see forward, Josiah Howe see forward

(VIII) Dr Henry Clarke son of Benjamin Clarke (7), was born in Marlboro Massachusetts, October 3, 1824 He attended the schools of his native town and spent several years at the academies in Leicester and Marlboro He began his professional studies in the office of Dr Henry Sargent, of Worcester in 1847 In 1848 he entered the Harvard Medical School, where he distinguished himself and won the Boylston prize He was graduated in 1850 and after a year spent in the hospitals of Paris and Vienna began to practice medicine in Worcester To his practice he devoted himself with a zeal and industry that often overtaxed his physical strength never very robust, and in 1861-67 he went to Europe for rest and study During the civil war he was for several months, in 1862, at the front as a volunteer surgeon He was for several years in the fifties city physician He was a member of the school board and for fourteen years physician to the county jail He was one of the original trustees of Memorial Hospital under the will of Ichabod Washburn and was surgeon at the City Hospital from the first He died after a short illness April 17 1880 aged fifty-five years Though at his death he had barely passed middle life and in aspect and manner appeared younger than his years he stood in the very first rank of Massachusets surgeons and physicians As a surgeon he was remarkable bold and skilful He was often called in difficult cases

(VIII) Josiah Howe Clarke, son of Benjamin Clarke (7), was born in Marlborough, Massachusetts, December 26, 1827 He received his early education in the public schools of his native town He also attended Leicester Academy At the age of twenty he engaged in the retail dry goods business in Marlboro as a member of the firm of Bucklin, Clarke & Co About two years later he removed to Worcester (in 1850), where he worked for his brother's firm, Newcomb, Thayer & Clarke, established in 1846 In 1851 his brother, John B. Clarke, became the sole owner In 1853 he sold the store to Josiah, who was for more than forty-four years identified with the business In 1864 Thomas B Eaton entered the firm with Mr Clarke under the name of J H Clarke & Co In 1882 Mr Eaton withdrew and Mr Clarke admitted Hannibal A Johnson and Charles H Carpenter as partners Mr Carpenter had been connected with the business for some time Mr Johnson came from Jordan, Marsh & Co, Boston In 1897 Mr Clarke withdrew from the firm, selling to his partners Thomas F Knight was admitted as a partner and for a time the old name was retained Mr Knight withdrew and the firm became Johnson, Carpenter & Co The firm went out of business January 1, 1906, on account of the illness of Mr Johnson

For some years Mr Clarke's store was located in the Partridge block, opposite the Central Exchange on Main street, but for thirty odd years it was located at the last location, 353 Main street in the American House block The business has always been conducted as a legitimate dry goods store Two floors were occupied and some thirty clerks and assistants employed Mr Clarke made a fortune in this business and none stood higher in Worcester among business men At the time he sold out his interests in the store he had large financial interests requiring his attention He was for many years a director of the Worcester National Bank He was a trustee and member of the finance committee of the State Mutual Life Assurance Company, a director of the Norwich & Worcester Railroad Company, the Worcester & Shrewsbury Railroad, now part of the consolidated system, the Worcester Gaslight Company, the State Safe Deposit Company the McKay Shoe Machinery Company of Boston the Union Trimmer Company of Boston, director and vice-president of the Shermin Envelope Company and trustee of the Worcester County Institution for Savings He was an active member and vestryman of All Saints Protestant Episcopal Church for more than thirty years He was a member of the common council in Worcester in 1862 He was a Republican in politics Mr Clarke was fond of travel and in 1865 made a voyage around the world, remaining some time at Foo Choo with his brother, Adason L. Clarke who was consul at that port He went west and to Europe several times and in 1898 travelled to the far east, including Greece Turkey, Egypt and the Nile

Mr Clarke married in 1858 Frances C Ayres, daughter of Horace and Mary (Woodworth) Ayres She was born in Worcester, March 18 1836 She died in Worcester July 11 1840 aged thirty years Her father married (second), November 19 1844, Caroline Corbett By the first marriage they had Julia Anne born 1833, died 1839 William J born and died 1858, Frances C, wife of Josiah H Clarke By the second marriage Mr Ayers had one son, Horace C Ayers born 1850 died 1896 Mr Clarke died in Worcester, May 30, 1904 The children of Josiah Howe and Frances (Ayers) Clarke were.

Mary Woodworth, born January 8, 1862, resides at home with her mother at 50 Elm street, Frances Ayres, born July 4, 1868, married Leonard P Kinnicutt professor in the Worcester Polytechnic Institute (see Kinnicutt Family in this work), Grace Howe, born September 29, 1869, died June 10, 1870, Josiah Howe, Jr, born August 13, 1872, died April 19, 1895

FRANK EUGENE POWERS, a well known citizen of Worcester, Massachusetts, prominently identified with the coal and lumber industries of the state is descended from an old and honored family of England He is a representative of the eighth generation in this country

The family name of Powers, or Power, as it was originally, is from the old Norman name le Poer," and was known in England in the time of William the Conqueror, one of whose officers, at the battle of Hastings bore that name, as appears on the roll of survivors in Battle Abbey From that time onward the name has occupied an honored place in the history of England In the Herald's College a curious incident is related of Richard le Poer, high sheriff of Gloucestershire 1187, that he was killed while defending the Lord's day When King Henry II invaded Ireland 1171, an important command seems to have been given to Sir Roger le Poer an "English knight" and "for his distinguished services rendered," large tracts of land were bestowed upon him by the crown Haverty's history says, the county of Waterford and the British parliament have had many members in their ranks from his descendants, from whom, and from the native Celts who took the name of the estates to which they were attached, the name has become very common in that country

In this country the name can be traced back to several people In 1643 the name of John Power appears in the Farmers Genealogy of New England, and about the same time Nicholas Power appeared in Massachusetts, but made his permanent home in Rhode Island where he married and had one son, Nicholas He was followed by several generations, each having one son the last having no male issue, and the name of this branch of the family became extinct By records in the town of Charlestown we find that the wife of John Power was authorized to make sale of the house and lands of her absent husband He is referred to as John Power, "hosier" and it is likely that not finding his business profitable in the new country he returned to Europe and then sent for his family A writer in the "New England History and Genealogical Register Volume XXII says the early settlers bearing the name of Powers in New England, came originally from Essex England The fact is that the names of Walter and William Power were common there and Walter seems to have settled with other families from that part of England a daughter of one of which families he married That the town where he settled was named for Lord Littleton member of parliament for Essex and other similar circumstances, would lead to the conclusion that he came from that district

(I) Walter Power the direct ancestor of Frank Eugene Powers was born 1630, died February 22, 1708 He appears on the Middlesex county records in 1654 as a boy of about fourteen Little is known of him He probably had no great educational advantages and depended upon the strength of his body and sterling common-sense to establish a home for himself and family He settled on a tract of land in or near Concord which took the name of Concord village, now the town of Littleton, and adjoining the Indian town of Nashobe, about the year 1661 He bought of Thomas Waban and other Indians in 1694, one-fourth of the township of Nashobe His remains were doubtless buried in the old "Powers' burying ground," which was on the Concord road about two miles from the common, in a southeasterly direction He married, March 11, 1661, Trail Sheppard, daughter of Deacon Ralph and Thankes Sheppard, of Malden She seems to have been a woman of considerable education, and from the position which his sons later took in the community, we may take it for granted that they were well educated for the times The sons seem, at various times, to have added the final "s" to the name

(II) Daniel Powers fourth son of Walter (1) and Trail (Sheppard) Power, seems to have been the first to add the final "s" to the family name He was born May 10 1669 Married (first), April 8, 1702 Elizabeth Whitcomb married (second) Martha Bates He settled in Littleton, and his children were all born in Nashobe or Littleton, although some are found recorded in Groton

(III) Peter Powers, fourth son of Daniel (2) and Elizabeth (Whitcomb) Powers born in 1707, died August 27 1757 His early youth was spent on the farm of his father After his marriage he removed to that part of Dunstable now known as Nashua, during the summer and fall of 1730, he built the first house in Hollis, New Hampshire and in January, 1730, removed, with his young wife and two children through the primeval forest to his new home They were the first settlers in that now thriving town Here their first daughter was born, she being the first child of English descent born in the town There were forty families within the town limits in 1738, and he with others, petitioned for a town charter He was prominent in the official business of the town, and particularly so in devising ways and means for the building of a meeting house, and in maintaining a preacher While living in Dunstable he had received a commission as captain of militia from Governor Wentworth He was sent by the government at the head of an exploring party through the Connecticut river valley in 1754 but the news of renewed hostilities between the English and French armies, produced such a commotion that his report was never published and was finally deposited in the rooms of the Connecticut Historical Society, in Hartford Captain Powers raised a company of men mostly residents of Hollis in 1755, to march under Colonel Joseph Blanchard, against the French at Crown Point, on the shores of Lake Champlain In this company were enrolled Jonathan Powers and Levi Stephen and Whitcomb Powers the last three named being sons of Captain Peter, who died shortly after this undertaking He was one of the most prominent men in the community He married Anna Keyes in 1728

(IV) Stephen Powers second son of Captain Peter (3) and Anna (Keys) Powers was born, presumably in Dunstable October 28 1729 He married July 15 1775 in Hollis, New Hampshire

(V) William Powers son of Stephen (4) married Pamelia Wright, of Pepperell

(VI) Jonathan Jackson Powers son of William (5) and Pamelia (Wright) Powers was born in Pepperell July 20 1807 and died in Worcester, Massachusetts June 7, 1870 He resided in Pepperell and Shirley where for a time he kept a store of general supplies He was a cooper by trade but turned his attention to various other occupations, being gifted naturally as a mechanic, and able to take advantage of any opportunity which presented itself He spent the last ten or twelve years of his life in Grafton, Massachusetts

He married, October 12, 1825, Priscilla E Reid, who died October 9, 1864 Their children were 1 Pamelia Emily, born January 23, 1827, married Elbridge Farnsworth 2 Caroline Augusta, November 27 1828, married Nathan B Chandler 3 John Jackson, of whom later 4 Charles Barron, June 19 1832, married Sarah Hemphill 5 Lucy Anne, October 9 1833, married Jabez J Harnden 6 Hannah Elizabeth, June 8, 1835, married Charles A Longley 7 William Henry, February 7, 1837 8 Albert Louis, November 19, 1838, died November 8, 1839 9 Marcius Marton, September 14 1840, died January 29, 1859 10 Martin Van Buren, January 8 1843 11 Harriet Lewis, August 24, 1844, married Alonzo Wessen, died in Nebraska 1876 12 Perlina Parker, September 18, 1846, married Charles Bohannan of Hollis, New Hampshire 13 Martha Chloe, January 27 1850, married (first) Henry Bohannan, of Hollis, New Hampshire, married, (second) John Hildreth, of Townsend, Massachusetts

(VII) John Jackson Powers, third child and eldest son of Jonathan Jackson (6) and Priscilla E (Reid) Powers, was born in Pepperell, Massachusetts September 1, 1830 His education was acquired in the schools of his native town When still quite a lad he worked for Major Longley, a prominent citizen of Shirley, who desired to adopt him having no son of his own At the age of nineteen he commenced working for the Old Colony Railroad, now a part of the New Haven system, and later for the Worcester & Nashua Railroad, now a part of the Boston & Maine system He was division master on the Worcester & Nashua, and his brother-in-law succeeded him when he resigned in order to take a similar position with the Providence & Worcester Railroad Eventually he became roadmaster, a position of great responsibility He resigned from railroad work after thirty-five years of continuous active work in various positions He was known among the railroad men of the state as an expert in practical railroad matters, having been actively engaged during the important period of introduction early growth, and development of the railroads of the country The contrast between the railroads of 1849, when he began and those of 1884, when he retired from this field of activity, is one of the most remarkable and sensational demonstration of American prosperity and progress In the early seventies he started in the coal business in Millbury, while his son Frank was still a boy attending school In this he met with unusual and immediate success Later, in partnership with his son established a coal business in Worcester Massachusetts, under the firm name of J J & F E Powers This also was successful from the very beginning, and Mr Powers demonstrated great business ability in the years that followed His career was cut short by sudden death while he was with his men in the field on his farm, at Grafton, June 19 1893 He was an honored and valued citizen, and had filled, very acceptably, several town offices He was a strict temperance man and a Republican

He married, May 18 1852 Anna Maria Stevens, born September 26, 1833, died March 31, 1897, daughter of Seth Stevens of Townsend, Massachusetts Her direct ancestor, Solomon Stevens was one of the pioneer Baptists of Townsend in 1769, when the church was weak and small his home was the headquarters of the preachers His son John Stevens, was one of the founders of the Baptist College in Granville, Ohio, now Denison University, and he was president of this institution until he was more than eighty years of age Dr John Steven's eldest son, William A Stevens, is now professor of the New Testament Interpretation in the Rochester Theological school

Children of John Jackson and Anna Maria (Stevens) Powers are 1 Edgar Norton, born July 2, 1853, died July 26 1853 2 Cora Isabelle, March 7, 1856 Attended the public schools of her native town, and for several years was a student at the Oread Institute a school for young girls, which existed from 1854 until 1881, and which enjoyed an excellent reputation It was located in the southern part of the city of Worcester in a building called "Oread Castle" She married, December 7 1887, in Grafton Frederick A Dodge, of Sutton He operated a grain mill at Saundersville, Massachusetts, and also conducted a retail and wholesale business, at No 362 Social street Woonsocket, Rhode Island He was lay reader in St John's Episcopal Church He died April 11 1906 Mrs Dodge is a member of the Congregational church in Grafton, the St John's guild, and the Woman's Club, of Millbury Their children are 1 Chester A Dodge, born in Grafton August 21, 1890, is now (1906) a junior in the Grafton high school 2 Leslie Powers Dodge, born in Grafton, June 24, 1894 3 Frank Eugene (see forward)

(VIII) Frank Eugene Powers, only surviving son and youngest child of John Jackson (7) and Anna Maria (Stevens) Powers was born in Grafton, Massachusetts July 17, 1858 He acquired a good education in the public schools of his native town, and attended the high school for a time When he removed to Worcester he took a course in the commercial school there He was but seventeen years of age when he took charge of the business interests of his father in Millbury In 1879 he bought out his father's interest in this business, and continued it alone for some time adding building materials and lumber to the coal business Business increased in volume and he was busily engaged until 1890 when he sold out to H M Goddard In the meantime, in 1886 the business in Worcester had been commenced, and he devoted more time to this This was located on Southbridge street, and having a chance to secure land on Southgate street, which was much better suited to the requirements of the business they moved to this location which has been the home of the concern since that time Mr Powers bought out the interest of his father in Worcester in 1891 and since the death of the latter, in 1893 has conducted the business under his own name During the past twenty years he has won a high standing for himself in the commercial circles of the city He is a quiet man and devotes himself strictly to business affairs, rarely taking a vacation He and his family have resided since removing from Millbury, at No 38 Maywood street, Worcester, Massachusetts They are members and attendants at the Piedmont Congregational Church and devote much time to charitable undertakings He is a member of the Commonwealth Club of Worcester, a director of the Millbury National Bank a trustee and a vice-president of the Millbury Savings Bank

He married June 15 1882, Laura Belle Lincoln, daughter of Dr W H Lincoln of Millbury Mrs Powers was educated at Millbury, Massachusetts, and is a graduate of Mount Holyoke She is a member of the Woman's Club of Worcester Their children are 1 Frank Lincoln born in Millbury, June 12 1883 now associated with his father in the business in Southgate street 2 Hiram Stevens, in Millbury, September 29, 1884, now a junior in Harvard College 3 Gladys, born in Worcester June 13, 1892, is attending the public schools in that city

CHARLES ARCHIBALD MIDDLEMAS Peter Middlemas (1), grandfather of Charles Archibald Middlemas, of Worcester, Massachusetts, was born in Scotland He settled in Nova Scotia He was a millwright by trade He learned his trade in the old country and followed it in Nova Scotia

(II) John S Middlemas, son of Peter Middlemas (1), was born in Nova Scotia He married Rebecca Parker He was a contractor and builder They had seven children, five sons and two daughters

(III) Charles Archibald Middlemas, son of John S Middlemas (2), was born in Middleton, Annapolis county, Nova Scotia, November 11, 1859 He attended the common schools of his native town He worked with his father as a carpenter and in the general store owned by his brother-in-law He also learned the plumber s trade He came to Worcester in 1882 and bought the business of J D Sisson & Co at 33 Southbridge street, corner of Allen court The business was originally on the site of the present Federal building He has built up a large business and reputation for skill and reliable work Among the contracts for plumbing that he has had during the past few years are the Windsor, the Boynton buildings, the City Hospital, Rawson & Gibbs building, Main street, the Standish Apartment Hotel, the Royal Worcester corset factory, the City Farm, the Bellmar, the Brunswick, the State Insane Asylum at Medfield, Massachusetts In recent years he has been heavily interested in street railway enterprises He built the Worcester & Webster Street Railway in 1899 He built the Gardner & Templeton line and the St Albans, Vermont Street Railway, of which he is the treasurer Mr Middlemas is now engaged in the hay grain and feed business at No 258 Park avenue, Worcester, in a building which he erected for the purpose He began business November 25, 1905 He is a Free Mason, a member of the Worcester County Commandery, Knights Templar He is also a member of the Independent Order of Odd Fellows

He married, November 11, 1885, Clark J Prouty, daughter of Frank and Josephine (Hitt) Prouty, of Spencer They have one daughter, Sybil Frances, born January 15, 1896

ERNEST AUGUSTUS TIMME was born in Hatzberg, Germany, a city in Hanover, October 20, 1821 He was educated in his native place and learned the trade of engraver At the age of twenty-six years in the year 1847 he came to America He worked the first winter in New York city and the following spring went to Worcester Massachusetts, to work for Mr Wheelock in Allen's pistol factory After several years he went to work for J B Knox, who carried on business as a steel letter cutter and die sinker While working there Mr Timme added steel letter cutting to the business

Mr Timme started in business on his own account with a partner, J P Bailey, at 144 South Clark street, Chicago, making steel dies and similar goods Mr Timme bought out his partner and conducted the business alone for some years Then he returned during the civil war and worked for various manufacturers of firearms, in which he was an expert mechanic He was employed by Colt, of Hartford He returned to Worcester in 1864 to his former employer, J B Knox, who was in partnership with Mr Lang in the manufacture of dies, seals, steel stamps, etc Mr Knox established this business in Worcester in 1854 Mr Timme bought the interest of Mr Lang and eventually became sole owner of the business The shop was at Harrington, corner of Main and Front streets, for many years It is now located at 554 Main street In his line of work Mr Timme had few equals He was a good business man and prospered In 1869 he bought a country place in Holden, Massachusetts, a town adjoining Worcester, where he enjoyed the pleasures of agriculture as a diversion from the cares of his shop and business He died March 26, 1890 During the last few years of his life he had as partner his son, Augustus F Timme, and the firm name was Ernst A Timme & Son

Mr Timme married (first) Rebecca Read, of Worcester He married (second), in 1862, at Hartford, Connecticut, Henrietta Anna Albinus, a native of Hamburg, Germany, who died at Worcester, February 20, 1890 The children of Ernst Augustus and Rebecca Timme were A son who died in infancy, Carrie R, died November 7, 1905 The children of Ernst Augustus and Henrietta A A Timme were Agnes L, married Henry C. Meyer, of Worcester, and they have two children, Ernst H, and Anna Meyer Augustus F, unmarried, mentioned below, Hannah H, married Louis Gilbert, of Milford, Massachusetts, and they have two children Emil and Alton (twins), Louise C, married William Fisher, a farmer of Holden, and they have five children Charles, George, Millard, Edna, Albert, Ernst, died at the age of four years, Albert S, resides in Boston, unmarried, Minnie C, a trained nurse

Augustus F Timme, son of Ernst Augustus Timme, was born in Worcester, October 5, 1865 He was educated in the public schools and learned the trade of die sinking and engraving with his father He was taken into partnership by his father and the firm became E A Timme & Son. After his father's death in 1890 he became the sole owner, but the name of the firm was continued unchanged Mr Timme manufactures dies, steel stamps, stencils, seal presses, seals, brands, door plates, checks, embossing dies, etc, does all kinds of engraving on metal, also manufactures rubber stamps for the trade His shop is at 554 Main street He is unmarried

GEORGE WILLIAM HOUCK, son of John T. and Annie (Phebus) Houck, was born in Frederick City, Maryland, January 29, 1864 On the paternal side his ancestors were of German origin

He was educated in his native town in the public schools At the age of seventeen he left home and located in Massachusetts After working on a Shrewsbury farm for some months he decided to learn the trade of mason He served his apprenticeship under William F Dearborn, the well known contractor and mason, of Worcester, and worked for him afterward as a journeyman But at the age of twenty-two years he started in business for himself, and for twenty years has conducted a successful business Excepting for a few years in the early nineties he has been alone in business At that time he was in partnership with James Miles of Worcester under the firm name of Miles & Houck Mr Houck has built a large number of substantial brick and stone structures in the city and county of Worcester In later years he has invested heavily in Worcester real estate He has a ten tenement apartment house at 89 Pleasant street, the Whittier block, corner of Fruit and Pleasant street, a large block on Crown street and he is building a new apartment house on Chatham street He has built mostly on his own account lately

In addition to his building contracts he has taken a number of large railroad contracts He had the contract and built the Worcester and Clinton Electric Railway He built a portion of the electric lines at Milford He constructed the Buffalo, Hamburg & Aurora Railroad in 1901 He built another railroad at Penn Yan, New York

Mr Houck is a member of Montacute Lodge of Free Masons, Worcester, and of Worcester Chapter, Royal Arch Masons In politics he is a Republican

He married, October 5, 1884, Annie Margaret Whittier, daughter of Elias and Charlotte (Curtis) Whittier She was born in Enfield, Maine, March 24, 1866 The children of George William and Annie M Houck were 1 Harvey Arfue, born at Worcester June 11, 1886, graduate of the Classical High School, Worcester, 1905, at present a collector of the New England Telephone Company 2 Charlotte Annie, born at Worcester, December 21, 1887, graduate of the Classical High School bookkeeper in the auditing department of the New England Telephone Company Among the buildings contracted are Gray block, corner Summer and Thomas streets, Day block, 306 Main street, Higgins block, Main street, Forest block, corner Main and Austin streets, nine on upper High and Summer streets, ten for the insane colony at Medfield, Jane Chase block in Hudson, and many others

PHILIP M PFAFFMANN Martin Pfaffmann (1), the father of Philip M Pfaffmann, of Worcester, was born in Germany He was a gardener and florist He was educated and learned his trade in his native land He came to America in 1848 when a young man and settled on Long Island, New York, and later removed to South Marshfield, Massachusetts, where he was employed by Colonel Fletcher Webster as head gardener Colonel Fletcher Webster was the son of Daniel Webster At that time he was living on what is now known as the Caswell place, about two miles from his father's farm Mr Pfaffmann worked there until the death of his employer's father, in 1852, when he became head gardener on the Webster homestead He filled this position for Colonel Fletcher Webster until 1870, when he purchased a nursery at Quincy, Massachusetts, started in business on his own account, and has since then continued in that business He married, at South Marshfield, Margaret Lawley Two of their children died in infancy The others are Charlotte, Philip M, see forward, Catherine, Caroline, Sibylla, George, see forward, Adeline

(II) Philip M Pfaffmann, second child of Martin Pfaffman (1), was born in South Marshfield, Massachusetts, November 18, 1855 He was educated in the public schools of Marshfield He learned the trade of carpenter In 1885 he came to Worcester to work at his trade for his father-in-law, Lucien Bonaparte Butler, manufacturer of satinets, at 1469 Main street He learned the business incidentally from the ground up and became useful to the owner in the management of the business He purchased the business of Mr Butler in 1899 and has since carried it on successfully Mr Pfaffmann is is a member of the Independent Order of Odd Fellows, of the lodge, encampment and the Patriarchs Militant, Grand Canton He is also a member of the Royal Arcanum

He married, November 22, 1883, Helen Butler, daughter of Lucien Bonaparte Butler Mr Butler was born in Rhode Island, and married Elizabeth O Ingalls, a native of New York state He began life as a mill hand and worked his way up to the position of proprietor He is counted among the substantial men of affairs of the city He is an Odd Fellow and belongs to the Commonwealth Club He resides at 1404 Main street The children of Philip M and Helen (Butler) Pfaffmann were. Ethel May, Maude, Gladys, Philip M, Jr

(II) George Pfaffman, son of Martin Pfaffmann (1), was born in South Marshfield, Massachusetts He married Mabel Shaw, daughter of John Shaw, former president of the Home Market Club, the head of the firm of John Shaw & Co, dealers in chemicals and dye stuffs at India Wharf, Boston George Pfaffman is a member of the firm His home is in Quincy, Massachusetts The children of George and Mabel (Shaw) Pfaffmann are John and Carl

GEORGE MASON RICHARDSON Samuel H Richardson (1), father of George Mason and Charles C Richardson, of Worcester, was born December 16, 1811, in Dana, Massachusetts, formerly Hardwick, Massachusetts He was in his early years a merchant, later a farmer He formerly lived on what was later the town farm of Hardwick He then bought a farm near the line between Hardwick and Petersham in the northeast part of Dana, where he lived for many years Shortly before his death in 1895 he removed to Dana Centre Mr. Richardson was a delegate to the constitutional convention from Dana in 1853

He married, March 31, 1836, Caroline Chipman (intentions dated at Petersham, March 4 1836) She was born December 10, 1811, six days after his birth, and she died January 31, 1895 one day before his death They were buried in the same grave They had lived together as man and wife for fifty-nine years

The children of Samuel H and Caroline (Chipman) Richardson were 1 George M, of whom later, Charles C, born March 30, 1840 married Sarah Lloyd, of Canada, resided first at Dana, now at the corner of Highland and Dover streets, Worcester, he is superintendent of a department of the Royal Worcester Corset Company and in charge of the machinery, he is a machinist by trade, Martha J, born September 25, 1841, was a school teacher for many years in Petersham Phillipston, Barre, Athol, Orange, Dana and Hardwick, after she retired from teaching she was elected on the Dana school committee, she died February 8, 1901, Ella L, born June 20, 1850, was a school teacher until recently, now residing in Ware, Massachusetts, Mary C, born February 12, 1856, married George Joslin of Dana and has one daughter

(II) George Mason Richardson, son of Samuel Mason Richardson, was born at Hardwick Massachusetts He attended the public schools and New Salem Academy, and graduated at Wilbraham, Massachusetts He learned the trade of machinist at Barre, Massachusetts, and followed it in various positions since He worked in Worcester for a year, then for five years he was in charge of sewing machines used in the Knowlton shops in West Upton He made a specialty of the machinery used in hat manufacture and worked in the hat shop at Medway, Milford and Fishkill on Hudson New York and in New York, where for seven years he had charge of machinery used in the sewing and making of mens hats He returned to his native state and for a time worked for a hat manufactory at Westboro For the past twelve or thirteen years he has been an expert machinist for the Royal Worcester Corset Company of Worcester

He resides at 14 Dover street In politics Mr. Richardson is a Republican

He married (first), September 26 1865, Alice Cutting Hastings, of Petersham, who was born July 6, 1838, and died September 12, 1870 They had one child, Alice Gertrude, born June 3, 1870, deceased Mr Richardson married (second), April 21, 1874, Lucy A Moore, of whom later

(I) John Moore, the pioneer ancestor of Lucy A (Moore) Richardson, wife of George Mason Richardson, of Worcester, came from England to Sudbury before 1642 when he appears as proprietor there His son John was of age and was also proprietor in 1642 John, Sr, bought a house of Edmund Rice, the progenitor of the Rice Family of Worcester This house was in the east part of the town in the south part of what is now Wayland He was admitted a freeman in Sudbury, July 9, 1645 Later he bought land of John Stone and a house in Sudbury He signed the Lancaster covenant March 11, 1653, and drew forty acres of land there November 30, 1653 His son John settled there and possibly other sons and daughters He stayed in Sudbury and became a prominent man there He was a prosperous farmer His will was dated August 25, 1668, and proved April 7, 1674 He mentioned his sons and daughters

He married Elizabeth Whale, daughter of Philemon Whale Their children were Elizabeth, married Henry Rice, Mary, married, September 8, 1661, Richard Ward, he was drowned, she married (second) Deacon David Stone, Lydia, born June 24, 1643, married Samuel Wright, John, married Ann Smith daughter of John Smith, the pioneer, William, Jacob, born April 28 1645, Joseph, born 1647, married Lydia Hayward, Benjamin, of whom later

(II) Benjamin Moore, youngest son of John Moore (1), was born in Sudbury, Massachusetts, December 13, 1648 He married, November 11, 1686, Dorothy Wright, who died October 20, 1717 They lived in Sudbury In 1726 he divided his land between his sons, William, Edward, Hezekiah, Uriah and Peter The children of Benjamin and Dorothy (Wright) Moore were Dorothy, born September 18, 1687, Abigail, December 2, 1688, Prudence, July 4, 1690, died young, William, Peter, Edward, Hezekiah, September 13, 1696, Uriah, of whom later, Comfort, July 22 1704, Benjamin

(III) Dr Uriah Moore, eighth child of Benjamin Moore (2), was born in Sudbury, Massachusetts, about 1700 He married, October 5, 1721, Abigail Haynes, daughter of David and Tabitha Haynes, who was born in Sudbury, March 8, 1700-1, and died October 16, 1729 He married (second) Mary ———, who died October 19, 1741 He married (third), January 2, 1742, Parnel Parker, who died in 1746, as his widow administered his estate She was probably the daughter of Thomas Britnall He had two sons David, of whom later, Uriah

(IV) Ensign David Moore, son of Uriah Moore (3), was born in Sudbury, Massachusetts, January 21, 1722 He married, December 22, 1743, Hannah Parker, daughter of his father's third wife He was a soldier in the revolution He was lieutenant in Captain John Nixon's company, Colonel Abijah Pierce's regiment, April 19 1775 He was later captain in Colonel John Nixon's regiment, June 5, 1775 and also in Colonel Whitney's regiment, (the Second Worcester) He died in 1808 and his will was proved at Cambridge, his oldest son, William was named executor

The children of David and Hannah (Parker) Moore were 1 Uriah born July 3 1744 died April 27, 1746 Abigail October 25 1745, died March 27, 1751, William of whom later, Susanna December, 1747, Uriah, September, 1751, was a soldier in the revolution, David, March 2, 1754, was a soldier in Captain Haynes' company, Thaddeus, November 9, 1758, Timothy, January 9, 1761, married, April 2, 1780, Hepzibah Nixon, daughter of General Nixon, revolutionary soldier, Reuben, November 21, 1762, was in the revolution in 1781, Abigail, November 12, 1764, married, April 8, 1784, Joshua Bacon, of Lincoln

(V) William Moore, third child of David Moore (4), was born in Sudbury, October, 1747 He was a corporal in Captain John Nixon's company, Colonel Abijah Pierce's regiment, April 19, 1775, and also in the army in 1777 He married Abigail Wheeler, October 12, 1769 He died March 29, 1836

The children of William and Abigail (Wheeler) Moore as recorded in their native town, Sudbury, were Elisha, born January 7, 1770, died young, Caleb, November 2, 1771, may have been the Caleb who bought land in Bolton in 1791 of John Richardson, though other branches of the family settled there, Uriah, December 20, 1773, died young, Uriah, April 4, 1776, may have gone to Salem (David Moore, of Salem, of the Sudbury family, was guardian of the children of Uriah in 1821 and sold land in Worcester county to Enoch Wiswall and John Hunting), David, of whom later, Mary December 26, 1780, William, December 14, 1782, Abigail, February 13, 1785, Sarah, May 19, 1787, Elisha, August 7, 1792, was given a lot of land in Hubbardston in Worcester county by his father, William Moore, of Sudbury, in 1813, Wheeler, April 24, 1795, Hannah, August 29, 178--

(VI) David Moore, fifth child of William Moore (5), was born in Sudbury, Massachusetts Family tradition has it that he lived for a time in Salem Members of his father's family went to Salem, unquestionably, and also to Boylston Uriah Moore, probably his father's brother, sold land in Boylston to Abijah Moore, perhaps his son, in Boylston in 1791 Uriah lived in Bolyston Abijah died in 1796, leaving young children, for whom Henry Powers, of Berlin, was guardian There was also in Boylston before David Moore a Hugh Moore, who left land in New Salem to his son Hugh He was possibly of the Salem family also

David Moore probably came to Boylston to live with relatives, for in 1805 he married a Boylston girl As mentioned above David Moore, of Salem, was guardian of Uriah Moore and other children of Uriah Moore, and sold land in Worcester county in 1821 This David, of Salem, was born in Sudbury, according to his son, David Moore, who was born in 1817 and was living in 1904 in Salem He was very likely a son of one of David Moore's (Boylston) uncles

He married (first), April 26, 1804, Fanny Tilton, who died December 10, 1806 She was the daughter of Joseph and Elizabeth Tilton, of Boylston Most of the children were born in Hamilton, near Salem, Massachusetts Some were born in Princeton, where Uriah Moore, uncle of David Moore, settled and where he and his wife died Abijah Moore, born October 1, 1757, at Princeton, son of Abijah and Eunice Moore, who was born in Princeton and came to Boylston to settle the estate of David Moore He probably knew his wife as a girl in Princeton, Hamilton or Ipswich

The children of Joseph and Elizabeth Tilton were Fanny, born January 14, 1782, at Hamilton, Nathan, born at Hamilton, September 11, 1783, Joseph Tilton July 16, 1785, died October 20, 1802, Dolly Tilton, September 2 1786, Oliver Tilton, September 14, 1788, Aaron Tilton, July 17, 1792, died December 2, 1793, Ann Tilton, September 2, 1794, Betsey Tilton, December 28, 1796, Aaron Tilton,

Lucy A. Richardson -

May 1, 1799 The last three were born at Princeton Joseph Tilton died March 6 or 7, 1847, aged eighty-seven years, six months His widow, November 19, 1841, aged eighty David Moore's wife Fanny died December 10, 1806, after having one child, David Tilton Moore, born August 14, 1806, of whom later, who was raised in his mother's family

David Moore married (second) Dolly Hastings, April 6, 1809, in Boylton Members of this family also came to Princeton and Boylston to settle She was born September 2, 1786 David Moore removed about 1817 with his children by the second wife to Athens, Ohio, where he died He was a carpenter and had a mill at Boylston at one time The children of David and Dolly (Hastings) Moore were Fanny, born September 4, 1809, died April 5, 1810, Chandler Carter, January 22, 1811, Eliakim Hastings, June 19, 1812 (His son is Bishop David Hastings Moore, of the Methodist Episcopal church, formerly of Ohio, now living in Portland, Oregon, he served his church four years in China, Japan and Corea), Eliakim, died at Athens, Ohio, April 4, 1900, Joseph, February 8, 1814, Elizabeth Upton, January 28, 1816, died 1816, Lorinda, born in Athens, 1818, Solomon, Patience, Lorenzo

(VII) David Tilton Moore, eldest son of David Moore (6), was born in Boylston, Massachusetts, August 14, 1806 His mother died when he was only a few months old and he was brought up by his grandmother Tilton He inherited the Tilton homestead at Boylston He succeeded his grandfather and carried on the farm during the active years of his life and left a competence when he died in 1879

The following tribute was written by a fellow townsman "Mr Moore was a life-long resident of this town (Boylston) His brother, E H Moore, was a representative in Congress from Ohio, to which state his father early removed Mr Moore was a very prosperous farmer and in connection with his sons at the time of his death owned and occupied one of the largest and finest farms in this section

"Mr Moore throughout his active life and until within a few years of his death when compelled by failing health to relinquish all care and anxiety, was an honored and useful citizen, deeply identifying himself with every enterprise that had for its object the promotion of the prosperity of the town and the social and moral elevation of its people He was frequently called upon to act in official positions of honor and trust, and he served the town of Boylston upon the boards of selectmen and assessors, much of the time in association with the late Capt Andrews whom in death he so quickly followed

In early life he took a deep interest in educational matters and served for many years upon the Boylston school committee Possessed of abundant means, ever kind and courteous in his bearing, always acting under a sense of his duty in every department of life in which he was called, he exhibited a firm and dignified course, carefully seeking and zealously guarding the rights of himself and others Of a vigorous mind and rare and discriminating judgment, success was always sure to follow in whatever he undertook He had long been a leading and perhaps one might more truthfully and unostentatiously say the leading member of the Congregational Church and Society which he was ever ready to assist, and to his wise counsel and generous hand the church was indebted more than to anything else for its financial prosperity and by his associates in the church he will long be revered as a faithful Christian member, a wise and true counsellor and ever ready friend "

He married Sally Wellington, daughter of John and Elizabeth (Temple) Wellington and granddaughter of John and Mary Gould (Hurd) Wellington Her grandfather, John Wellington, married (first) Mary Gould Hurd, a sister of General Hurd, of the revolution, and settled in Michigan They had four children John, of whom later, Ebenezer, Priscilla and Sally He married (second) Priscilla Cutting, and had one child, Jonathan Wellington

The son, John Wellington, born 1765, died 1825, married Elizabeth Temple The Wellingtons settled in Old Boylston after the revolution The children of John Wellington were Polly, married David Kendall, late of Worcester, (see Kendall sketch in this work), Betsey, Eben, September 23, 1805, John, April 25, 1806, Lucy Andrews, November 16, 1807, died 1865, Thomas Hurd, November 12, 1809, Sally, April 24, 1811, died September 10, 1886, wife of David Tilton Moore, Judith,, September 4, 1812, William, November 6, 1814, deceased, Asa, December 14, 1816, died May 10, 1892, Lydia Brooks, August 11, 1819 (or August 10), Agnes or Annis, April 14, 1821, died November 19, 1902, Eunice, February 26, 1823, died August 16, 1903

The children of David Tilton and Sally (Wellington) Moore were William Alfred, Sarah Elizabeth, born July 22, 1836, George Harris, July 29, 1838, Olive Kendall, February 20, 1841, Lucy Ann, married George Mason Richardson mentioned above, Charles Walter, October 5, 1847, Harriet Fanny, January 11, 1850, Jennie Mar, October 6, 1857

(VIII) Lucy Ann Moore, fifth child of David Tilton Moore (7), was born in Boylston, Massachusetts, January 4, 1843 (not January 7, as given in the Boylston records) She attended the public schools in her native town Having developed an aptitude for drawing and painting she studied art under Mrs Kellogg, corner of Fourteenth street and Fifth avenue, New York She studied also under Miss Edgar at Newburgh, New York Miss Edgar studied in Rome and Florence for fifteen or sixteen years She then took lessons in sketching of Joseph Greenwood, the famous artist She has developed talent for painting and has devoted a large part of her time to her profession She is known among Worcester artists for her clever work and her constant interest in art The following is a partial list of the pictures painted by Lucy A Richardson A scene on the Charles River, Edge of the Wood, Mirror Lake, The Christ Child, copied from the original paintings in Rome, Beatrice Cenci by Guido Reni, one of the old masters, by Miss L Edgar, A Summer Morning, owned by Dr W F Ball, city, Under the Oak owned by Mr O S Kendall, Jr 15 Fruit street, city A Wood Interior, owned by Mrs C E Sawyer Brooklyn, New York At Close of Day, owned by Mrs C Goddard, Grafton, Poppies, owned by Mrs Arthur Rockwell, Westboro Summer Morning owned by Westminster Library, Bancroft Tower, owned by Miss L E Case, Osaka Japan

Alice G Richardson, daughter of George Mason Richardson was educated in the public schools at Mt Beacon Academy and at the State Normal school at Albany She taught schools at Fishkill-on-Hudson New York, for two years, at Attleboro and Milford Massachusetts Then she attended Becker's Business College as a student, taking the full course She then taught in the evening high school in Worcester one year She died at the very beginning of a promising career, May 22, 1899

CHARLES HENRY KNAPP. William Knapp (1), the emigrant ancestor of Charles Henry Knapp, of Worcester, was in Watertown as early as 1630, as he is referred to in the Colonial records of November 3, 1630. He died August 30, 1659, aged about eighty years, and accordingly his birth must have occurred about 1579, and he was over fifty years of age when he emigrated to New England. Nicholas Knapp also settled at Watertown in 1630, and the presumption seems warrantable that they came together from England prior to the month of March, 1630. If Nicholas was his brother he was much younger; he was not his son.

William Knapp was a carpenter by trade. He was one of the proprietors of Watertown in 1636, and in 1655 he made a deed of gift to his son, John Knapp. The will of William Knapp mentions his wife Priscilla, who was the widow of Thomas Akers, also children: William, Jr., married Mary ———, died September 25, 1676; John, born 1624; James, born 1627, married Elizabeth Warren; Mary, married Thomas Smith; Judith, married Michael Cady, of Watertown; Anne, married Thomas Philbrick; her death occurred prior to the death of her father; Elizabeth, widow of ——— ———, of St. Mary, Suffolk county, England; she sent power of attorney, December 27, 1660, for collection of her dues. Most of the estate was bought up by Nathaniel Coolidge.

(II) John Knapp, son of William Knapp (1), was born in England, possibly at Bury St. Mary's, in Suffolk county, where his sister lived, in 1624. He was also a carpenter by trade. He was admitted a freeman in 1652. He sold land to John Fiske in 1666, and a very large number of real estate transactions of his are on the records. He married, May 25, 1660, Sarah Young, and their children were: John, born May 4, 1661; Sarah, born September 5, 1662; Henry, Isaac, Daniel and Abigail. His will was dated January 22, 1695-96, and proved April 27, 1696. His estate was administered by his brother-in-law, Henry Young. It mentions his wife Sarah, and children, Henry, Isaac, John, Daniel and Abigail.

(III) John Knapp, son of John Knapp (2), was born May 4, 1661, in Watertown, Massachusetts. He settled in Newton, Massachusetts, the adjoining town. He married, August 4, 1686, Sarah Parks, and their children were: John, born in Newton, December 11, 1688, died 1730; he married (first), July 13, 1713, Mary Whitney, of Watertown, and married (second) Sarah ———, who died in 1736. James, born February 4, 1690. John Knapp (III) died 1733; his wife died 1727.

(IV) James Knapp, son of John Knapp (3), was born in Newton, Massachusetts, February 4, 1690-91. He married, April 2, 1714, Elizabeth Bond, who died January 12, 1715-16, and their child was Jonathan, born October 23, 1714. He married (second), October 10, 1716, Mary Fiske, and their children were: James, born in Watertown or Waltham, baptized November 24, 1723; Elizabeth, born at Watertown, May 15, 1729; John, born October 31, 1731. James Knapp (IV) died about 1748, and his son James had a guardian appointed in Worcester; the guardian was Benjamin Flagg. The Flaggs and Kings intermarried and there was some relationship between the lad and his guardian. The names on the bond of James Knapp were: James Moore, John Chandler and Moses Marcy, of Worcester, Massachusetts.

(V) John Knapp, son of James Knapp (4), was born in Waltham or Watertown, October 31, 1731. His father died in 1748, when he was about sixteen years of age. The probate records at Worcester show that on May 17, 1748, Benjamin Flagg, of Worcester, was appointed his guardian. He was described as John Knapp, son of James Knapp, late of Waltham, aged about sixteen years. The sureties and witnesses were James Moore, John Chandler and Moses Marcy, of Worcester. John Knapp married (first), about 1760, Anna ———, and settled in Petersham, Massachusetts, where their seven children were born, namely: Lydia, April 10, 1761; Levi, May 16, 1763; Jazaniah, October 1, 1765; James, May 20, 1767; Anna, September 22, 1770; Lucy, January 31, 1773; Molly, June 24, 1775. John Knapp married (second) Elizabeth Felton, of Templeton. Intentions dated January 2, 1779.

(VI) Jazaniah Knapp, son of John Knapp (5), was born in Petersham, Massachusetts, October 1, 1765. He married, October 25, 1798, Elizabeth Howe, of Petersham, and they settled in that town. Elizabeth, or Betsey, as the name is given on the town records, was born July 4, 1773, daughter of Asa and Mary Howe, of Petersham. Their children were: Eliza, born September 21, 1799, died February 15, 1801; Lucy, born June 12, 1801, married Erastus Swan, died at Athol, June 28, 1877; Levi, born May 13, 1804; Mary H., born October 6, 1807, died March 8, 1813; Mehitable, born in Petersham, March 31, 1810, married Seth Cole, died at Geneseo, Henry county, Illinois, April 20, 1864. Jazaniah Knapp (VI) died March 21, 1812; his wife died September 17, 1835.

(VII) Levi Knapp, son of Jazaniah Knapp (6), was born in Petersham, Massachusetts, May 13, 1804, and died there June 7, 1888. He married Fidelia Ballou, and they settled in Petersham. Their children were: George, never married; John, enlisted in Company H, Fourth Regiment, Heavy Artillery, August 10, 1864, and was discharged June 17, 1865, at Fort Richardson, Virginia, at the close of the war; he married Mrs. Morgan, widow, resides in Petersham; Caroline Elizabeth, married Jerome Lord, of Athol, and has a son, Palmer J. Lord; Mary Jane, born in Petersham, October 19, 1844; Charles Henry, born in Petersham, August 12, 1846; Harry Taft, born in Phillipston, married Mrs. Carrie Adele Jackson, widow, December 31, 1884, and their children were: Grace Adele, born November 25, 1885; Florence Lillian, born September 26, 1887; Edwin LeRoy, born July 14, 1889; Elsie Mildred, born December 28, 1893; Annie Laura, born September 2, 1897.

(VIII) Mary Jane Knapp, daughter of Levi Knapp (7), was born in Petersham, Massachusetts, October 19, 1844. She married, September 27, 1868, William Henry Damon, then of South Hampton, Massachusetts, born in Chesterfield, Massachusetts, February 10, 1842. When only a year old William H. Damon was taken by his parents to Worthington, Massachusetts, where he lived until he was fourteen. He went to work in a Northampton store, and after remaining there four years went to Springfield and worked as a clerk in a store until he enlisted in the civil war, remaining in the service for three years. He married (first) Sarah A. Elliott, of Southampton, Massachusetts, March 10, 1866; she died at Springfield, Massachusetts, March 12, 1867. Immediately after his marriage to Mary Jane Knapp, Mr. Damon settled in Easthampton, Massachusetts, on a farm, and the first four children were born there. After living there for seven years they removed to Northampton and there resided for four years. They then moved to Old Hadley, Massachusetts, thence to West Brookfield, then to Barre, where they remained three years, then to North

Brookfield, where they remained one year, and for the past three years has resided at New Braintree, Massachusetts

The children of William Henry and Mary Jane (Knapp) Damon were Lillian Augusta, born December 21, 1869, in East Hampton, Massachusetts, died there August 31, 1870, Minnie Jane, born March 6, 1871, married Albert L Woodis, February 11, 1892, in North Brookfield, Massachusetts, where he was born, and they have one child, Annie Augusta, born in Easthampton, July 19, 1873, Charles Henry, born in Easthampton, December 3, 1875, Bennie W, born in Northampton, March 8, 1879, Lizzie Carrie, born in Old Hadley, March 26, 1883

(VIII) Charles Henry Knapp, son of Levi Knapp (7), was born in Petersham, Massachusetts, August 12, 1846 He was educated in the Petersham schools After the age of twelve he worked for wages on a farm, and during the school term in the winter he worked for his board A sample of the work imposed upon young children by the hard conditions existing as lately as fifty years ago is shown by a story told by Mr Knapp The town shoemaker offered him a pair of cowhide boots, when he was only thirteen years old, in payment for sawing four cords of wood for the church He sawed the wood and secured the boots It must be said that the shoe business would be very dull, if each pair cost the sawing of a big woodpile like that That incident showed the determination and grit of the boy He left Petersham to seek a larger field in Worcester, being then twenty years old His first employment was in the wood working department of the Ames Plow Company, and during his two years connection with this company had considerable experience in the machinist trade as well as in wood working For a short time thereafter he worked at his trade in Worcester, and then engaged in business for himself as a contractor and builder

Mr Knapp performed a large part of the building for H H Bigelow at the time when Mr Bigelow was very actively engaged in building, erecting a block containing seventy-two rooms for him, also the buildings for the dummy railroad which that gentleman constructed to make Lake Quinsigamond accessible to the people of Worcester Mr Knapp built the Lakeside Boat Club-house, the Dodge Pavilion, and fine residences for Edwin Ames, Louis Dean, Frank Gray, and E D Cheney He also built about forty dwelling houses at Lake View The larger part of his work has been the construction of dwelling houses in Worcester, he having built ten or twelve yearly, and in all has been the contractor or builder for nearly two hundred houses in the city He made a specialty, as many other Worcester builders have done, of building houses to sell when he had the opportunity Mr Knapp resides at No 17 Baker street, Worcester, and attends to business at his home He is an attendant of the First Universalist Church He belongs to the Worcester County Mechanics' Association and to the Worcester Agricultural Society

Mr Knapp married (first), April 23, 1874 Elizabeth S, daughter of Levi Miles, of Hubbardston, Massachusetts She died in Worcester, November 3, 1895 He married (second), February 3 1897, Annie Elizabeth, daughter of Captain Merrick Houghton

John Houghton (1), the emigant ancestor of Mrs Charles Henry (Houghton) Knapp, was born in England in 1631 He came to New England in the ship "Abigail" in June, 1635, when he was only four years old He came from Eaton Bray, Bedford county, England, and may have been born there He resided in Dedham until after his marriage to Beatrix ———, about 1658-59, and then settled in Lancaster, Massachusetts His will was proved in 1684 His cousin, Ralph Houghton, was one of the early settlers in Lancaster, Massachusetts It is believed that he was in Lancaster as early as 1652

(II) Jonas Houghton, son of John Houghton (1), was born in Lancaster (probably) in 1660 He married, February 16, 1681, Mary Berbeame (or Berban), of Woburn, while the family was staying there on account of the Indian troubles Woburn records say that she was born there and married in Lancaster After his father's death he settled in Bolton on his father's land on Vaughn's Hill Jonas Houghton served in Queen Anne's war

(III) James Houghton, son of Jonas Houghton (2), was born in Woburn or Lancaster, 1700, baptized August 3, 1718 He served in the Indian war under Captain John Lovewell and Captain John White in 1724-35 He also had power of attorney to represent Jonathan Parlin, of Concord, who for the same service was to draw land He sold Jonathan Parlin's right to Josiah Richardson, October 5, 1733, and his own to William Richardson, of Lancaster, October 30, 1733 His wife Mary is mentioned in the deed He married, October 8, 1725, Mary Jones, of Concord He died in Lancaster, August 9, 1770

(IV) Nathaniel Houghton, son of James Houghton (3), was born in Lancaster, September 5, 1729 He married Mary ———, and they settled in that part of Lancaster, now Sterling, or Bolton, Massachusetts The children of Nathaniel and Mary Houghton were Nathaniel, born in Lancaster, July 16, 1759, Ephraim, March 28, 1761, Stephen, May 8, 1765, Josiah, November 20, 1768, Manasseh, April 18, 1771, Mary, November 30, 1773, Tilly, March 20, 1776, Jonas, July 25, 1778

(V) Manasseh Houghton, son of Nathaniel Houghton (4), was born in Lancaster, April 18, 1771 He settled in Sterling, Massachusetts The children of Manasseh Houghton were Nancy, born December 20, 1798, Heman, October 31, 1800, Eunice, December 17, 1802, Manasseh, October 6, 1804, Eli, January 21, 1807, Merrick, December 24, 1809, Susan, April 15, 1811, Torry, July 3, 1813, James February 18, 1816

(VI) Merrick Houghton, son of Manasseh Houghton (5), was born in Sterling, December 24, 1809 came to Worcester in 1865 and spent the remainder of his life there The children of Captain Merrick Houghton were Mary Caroline, born February 25, 1838, George Merrick, January 20, 1840, Hattie Kendall, April 1, 1842, Annie Elizabeth February 19, 1845 aforementioned as the wife of Charles Henry Knapp, Sarah Enselin, March 21, 1847, and John Lynds, August 23, 1849

THOMAS ASA SHAW Abraham Shaw (1), the immigrant ancestor of Thomas Asa Shaw, of Worcester, came from Halifax York county, England and settled in Dedham, Massachusetts before 1636 In that year he signed the famous Dedham Covenant In the old country he was a clothier and a man of some property He was a planter at Dedham When he first came to America he went to Watertown, Massachusetts, where he was a proprietor in 1636, his house was burned in October of that year, whereupon he seems to have removed to Dedham, where he was a constable in 1636-37-38 and was admitted a freeman March 9, 1637 He removed to Cambridge and was a town officer there in 1640 He was owner of coal mines in Halifax and November 2, 1637, shortly before his death, he received a grant of half the coal and iron he might find in the common lands He was given a permit to erect a corn mill February 12, 1637 Mary, supposed to be his wife, was admitted to the church at Charlestown, July 1, 1646 He died in 1638, and his will, made November of that year, was proved before the end of the year He mentions Joseph, John, Mary and Martha, his children, and Nicholas Byram, son-in-law Of the children Joseph removed to Weymouth, John is mentioned below, Mary was born about 1638, Martha born about ———, Susanna married Nicholas Byram before 1638

(II) John Shaw, son of Abraham Shaw (1), was born about 1625-30 He married Alice Phillips, of Weymouth, where they settled and where their eleven children were born, viz John, about 1655, Elizabeth, February 26, 1656, Abraham, October 10, 1657, Mary, May 24, 1660, Nicholas, March 23, 1662, Joseph, April 15, 1664, Alice, July 6, 1666, Hannah, April 7, 1668, Benjamin, June 16, 1670, Abigail, July 15, 1672, Ebenezer, April 24, 1674

(III) John Shaw, eldest son of John Shaw (2), was born about 1655, in Weymouth, Massachusetts He married Hannah ———, and their children, born in Weymouth, were Hannah, born December 16, 1679, probably died young, Abraham, born February 14, 1685, Hannah, born April 26, 1687, John, born January 20, 1690, Mary, born May 5, 1691, Benjamin, born July 25, 1693, mentioned below

(IV) Benjamin Shaw, youngest son of John Shaw (3), was born July 25, 1693 The records of him are meagre He married Hannah Rogers, of Abington His children Benjamin, born 1728, William, mentioned below

(V) William Shaw, son of Benjamin and Hannah Shaw (4), was born in Abington, February 22, 1730 He was a tanner and shoemaker by trade He removed to the North Parish in 1734 and settled there He was an excellent moral and religious character and of very industrious habits" He married, 1754, Hannah West, who died November 9, 1772 He married (second) Dorcas Smith, June 24, 1773, she died July 23, 1797, aged sixty-four years He died January 17, 1809, aged seventy-nine years The children of William and Hannah Shaw were Hannah, born March 26, 1755, William, born January 14, 1757, Dan, mentioned below, Isaiah, born October 19, 1760, died November 19, 1760, Rhoda, born August 1, 1762, Napthali, born June 20, 1764, was a revolutionary soldier, graduated at Dartmouth in 1790, taught school in Boston, studied theology and settled at Kensington, New Hampshire, and remained twenty-one years, bought a farm in Bradford, Vermont, near his brother Dan, had four children by wife, Mary Crafts, Betsey, born June 12, 1766, Michael, born September 25, 1768, Patience, born August 28, 1770, Molly, born November 4, 1772 The only child of William and Dorcas was Abigail, born January 29, 1775

(VI) Colonel Dan Shaw, third child of William Shaw (5), was born in Bridgewater, Massachusetts, November 15, 1758 He was a tanner and currier by trade He married in March, 1780, Joanna Perkins, daughter of Deacon Isaac Perkins, of Middleboro Massachusetts She was born January 5, 1761 They came immediately to Lyme, New Hampshire, to make their home He established a tannery there, the first in that section, and a bark mill, became a leading citizen, was selectman, and held other positions of trust and honor He had much to do with maintaining the efficiency of the state militia, rose from the ranks to the command of his regiment, and was for many years prominent in military circles To his energy and enterprise is due the building of the county road from where he lived to Lyme Plain He joined the orthodox church when sixteen years old and later was deacon He became liberal in his views later in life, and even published a pamphlet dissenting from doctrine preached by Rev William Conant, and advocating more liberal views About 1805 he left Lyme and bought a farm in Bradford, Vermont, his place being on the west side of the River road, where later Amos Clement lived He preached often in his later years along the lines of universal salvation, and became morbidly interested in religion, so much so that it undermined his health, mentally and physically His wife Joanna died at Lyme, November 22, 1803, and he married (second) Mary Bliss He died at Bradford, November 14, 1814, and she married (second) Colonel Freeman, of Hanover, New Hampshire

The children of Colonel Dan and Joanna Shaw were Nancy P, born December 16, 1780, married Joshua Balch, of Lyme, June 15, 1800, and died there January 24, 1850, Dan, Jr, born October 13, 1782, died May 4, 1805, Samuel, born November 12, 1784, died March 31, 1803, Joanna, born April 3, 1787, married Abel Kent, Jr, of Lyme, January 1, 1806, died November 4, 1856, Asa, mentioned below, Abraham Perkins, born June 20, 1813, married Mary Jenkins, daughter of Joseph Jenkins, of Bradford, June 20, 1813, they resided at Bradford, he was a cabinet maker, Naphthali, born May 20, 1793, married, January 21, 1817, Hannah Worthern, of Bradford, she died August 16, 1844, he died September 3, 1861, Pollycarpus, born February 25, 1797, went to Indiana, died February 1, 1849, Mandana, born April 9, 1799, died June 6, 1801, at Lyme

(VII) Asa Shaw, son of Colonel Dan Shaw (6), was born February 20, 1789 He married Eliza T Slade, of Hanover, born November 14, 1801, daughter of Thomas and Elizabeth (Thurston) Slade Her father was born September 29, 1776, and her mother July 22, 1780, and they were married February 22, 1801 Her mother died November 25, 1801, and her father married (second) Polly Thurston her mother's sister, February 12 1807 They had a daughter, Polly Thurston Slade, December 3, 1807, and the mother died September 27, 1808, aged twenty-two years The grandfather, Samuel Slade, was born September 15, 1747, married, November 28, 1773, Sarah Durkee, born November 18, 1755, and they had thirteen children Isaac Davis, born November 30, 1774, Thomas, mentioned above, Esther born June 13, 1778, Samuel, born October 12, 1780, Sally (twin) born September 16, 1782, Polly, (twin) born September 16, 1782, died October 4, 1784, Polly, born November 27, 1784, Harry, born May 19, 1787, Becca, born May 19, 1789, Susa, born May 2, 1791, Elizabeth, born August 31, 1793, Eunice, born September 15, 1795, Lavinia, born August 29, 1797, died August 3, 1800

Asa Shaw was a merchant, senior partner of the firm of Shaw, Hewes & Perkins, of Lyme Plain Later the firm was Shaw & Churchill He was the leading citizen of the town for many years, postmaster, town clerk for thirty-seven years, a member of the legislature in 1832 and 1833 For more than forty years he was a member of the Congregational church at Lyme, and his life was that of an exemplary Christian He was a Free Mason He died July 4, 1861, and his widow removed to Worcester, where she died at the home of her son Their children were Thomas Asa, mentioned below Eliza, born 1824, died unmarried, 1884, at Lyme

(VIII) Thomas Asa Shaw, only son of Asa Shaw (7), was born in Lyme, New Hampshire, April 27, 1827 He attended the district schools of his native town, and Thetford and Hebron Academies, Vermont He served in his father's store, and was clerk in a general store in Buffalo, New York, and Newark, Ohio, for several years In 1864 he came to Hartford, Connecticut, and established a flour and grain store, which he conducted with marked success for thirty-three years He had several partners in his early days in business, one after another, but only for a short time, preferring to do business alone He built up one of the largest stores of its kind in that section, and was prudent and successful in business All the years of his business in Hartford he was at 542 Main street, and at a store nearly opposite, near the corner of Trumbull street He was a Democrat in politics, but never cared for public office He was devoted to business exclusively, and belonged to no clubs or social orders He attended the Congregational church, but was not a member In 1884 he made arrangements to remove his store to Worcester, and he bought his present residence at that time, 24 King street, but decided to remain in Hartford, and although he lived in Worcester and had his family here, he continued in business in Hartford until December 1, 1897, when he retired and has since lived quietly at his home on King street He married, October 11, 1865, Marie Persis Bond, daughter of Thomas Bond (For her ancestry see the Bond Family, sketch of Oran A Kelly in this work) Their only child was Dr Thomas Bond Shaw

(IX) Dr Thomas Bond Shaw, only son of Thomas Asa Shaw (8), was born at Worcester, Massachusetts, December 3, 1866 He attended public and high schools of Hartford, Connecticut, but took his last year and was graduated from the Worcester Classical high school in 1886, and was graduated at Yale University in 1890 He attended the New York College of Physicians and Surgeons in 1891 and 1892, then entered Dartmouth Medical College, where he was graduated in 1893 He received hospital training in the Roosevelt and other New York city hospitals In 1894 he was surgeon on a Ward line mail steamer to Cuba and Mexico For two years (1895-96) he took instruction in the Allgemeine Krankenhaus, Vienna, and the Hotel Dieu, Paris He located in Worcester, in 1897, opening an office at 47 Pleasant street, and has built up an extensive practice, and made for himself an excellent reputation as a physician and surgeon He is a member of leading professional bodies—the Massachusetts Medical Society, Worcester District Society and American Academy of Medicine, and of the Life Insurance Examiners He is staff surgeon of the Second Regiment Infantry, Massachusetts Volunteer Militia He is a member of the Union Congregational Church and of its parish He is a member of the following societies and clubs Secretary and treasurer of the Yale Alumni Association of Central and Western Massachusetts, Dartmouth College Alumni Association, Alumni Association of Kings County Hospital, Brooklyn, Hancock Club, Automobile Club, Tatassit Canoe Club, Commonwealth Club, Uptown Club, Lakeside Boat Club, and Worcester Continentals Dr Shaw resides with his parents at 24 King street, Worcester

WALTER H RICHARDSON, D D S Edward Eugene Richardson, father of Walter H Richardson, and son of Heman Richardson, was born at Holden, Massachusetts, October 23, 1845 He received his education in the common schools of Holden, working on the farm when not in school He became an attendant in the State Lunatic Asylum, Worcester, where he worked two or three years Then he served an apprenticeship in the machinist's trade in the shop of R Ball & Co, Worcester He was employed by this firm for about ten years, until it went out of business, when he took a position with the N A Lombard concern, corner of Union and School streets, and worked there more than fifteen years He worked for Davis & Nelson for two years and for the North Emery Wheel Company about the same length of time About 1901 he entered the employ of Wehinger & Co, where he remained a year and a half He then took up farming at the old place in the west part of Holden, on Muschopauge street His father left the farm to him and his brother Isaac, whom he bought out about 1886, and has since carried on the farm there He attends the Holden Congregational church In politics he is a Republican He is a life member of the Worcester County Mechanics' Association of Worcester

He married, October 1, 1868, Victoria Augusta Bolton, born April 18, 1840, daughter of Ransom and Fidelia (Traverse) Bolton, of Gardner, Massachusetts Her father was a farmer Their children Edith August, born April 29, 1869, married, October 17, 1888, Joseph Hildreth Hadley, of Princeton, Massachusetts, and they have—Helen Augusta Hadley, born February 3, 1889, Ruth Hildreth Hadley, born March 15, 1891, Maud Esther Hadley, born November 22, 1895, Edith Richardson Hadley, born January 4, 1897, Alice, born October 5, 1900, died June 24, 1901, Joseph Hildreth, born July 9, 1903 Elmer Eugene, born June 29, 1872, married, June 15, 1889, Sarah May Keyes and they have—May Eugenie, born December 14, 1900, Arthur Edwin, born May 11, 1903, Edward Eugene, born June 18, 1904 Walter Herbert, see forward

Walter Herbert Richardson, son of Edward Eugene Richardson, was born in Holden, Massachusetts, November 22, 1874 His parents moved to Worcester when he was two years old, and he received his early education there in the public schools The family returned to Holden to live when he was eleven years old, and he was graduated from the Holden high school He then took the full course at Hinman's Business College, graduating in 1890 He entered the employ of the Worcester Corset Company as bookkeeper and remained two years He was bookkeeper for the Singer Sewing Machine Company two years He decided to study dentistry for a profession and entered the University of Pennsylvania, where he was graduated in 1897 with the degree of D D S In the fall he opened an office at 520 State Mutual building, Worcester, where he practiced for three years He left to associate himself with Dr John F Adams, at 4 Elm street, where he was located six years In June, 1906, Dr Adams retired and Dr Richardson removed from the old office, which was one of the buildings torn down to make way for the new Slater building, to his present quarters at 11 Elm street Dr Richardson enjoys a large and select practice many of his patients coming from a distance He resides at 303 Lincoln street, Worcester In politics he is a Republican He belongs to Quinsigamond Lodge of Free Masons, Worcester, since January 15, 1904, to Eureka Chapter of Royal Arch Masons since May 24, 1904, and to Worcester County Commandery, No 5 Knights Templar, since September 27, 1906, belongs also to Worcester Lodge of Perfection, fourteenth degree, Goddard Council Princes of Jerusalem, sixteenth degree, Lawrence Chapter, Rose Croix, eighteenth degree, since February 23 1905 all Scottish Rite Masonry He is a member of Tatassit Canoe Club, the Uptown Club, and Leicester Country Club He was a charter member of the Worcester Golf Club He is a member of the National Dental Association, Massachusetts Dental Society, the Central District Dental Association the Northeastern Dental Association, the National Federation of Dentists While at University of Pennsylvania was a member of the college society He rowed with the University of Pennsylvania (Freshman Varsity) crew in 1894 Was also a member of the Huston Club of Philadelphia, Pennsylvania, of Delta Sigma Delta fraternity, and of the Sophomore Society Theta Nu Epsilon He was manager in 1895 of the Dental Football Team He served three years in the Worcester Light Infantry in Company C Second Regiment, Massachusetts Volunteer Militia

He married, October 12, 1897, Mary Silence Warren, born January 24 1875. daughter of Berthier Warren and Eunice Chace (Boyden) Warren (See sketch of the Warren family of Holden) Their only child is Berthier Warren Richardson, born August 20, 1900

HERMAN S HASTINGS was born February 2, 1873, at Berlin, Massachusetts He is the son of Samuel H and Harriet (Barnes) Hastings His paternal grandfather was Henry Hastings, born and reared at Roxbury, Massachusetts He was a farmer His great-grandfather was Captain Henry Hastings, a soldier in the revolutionary war, also an officer in the militia He was a man of much means and a prosperous farmer The maternal grandfather of Herman S Hastings was Daniel Barnes, an influential farmer in Berlin, Massachusetts, where he spent the better part of his life The father of Herman S was a contractor and builder of much eminence He had four children Matilda, married George H Hastings, Nettie L, who married R W McOrmand, Leo L., Herman S

Herman S Hastings was educated at the public graded schools of Worcester, and later attended the Boston University Law School At eighteen he graduated from the Foster Business College of Worcester For a time he followed bookkeeping, but later became secretary of the Worcester Republican committee during which period he was associated as a lawyer with Frank L Dean, of Worcester, and devoted much of his time to the adjustment of estates In 1901 he was elected secretary of the Worcester Agricultural Society, the oldest and wealthiest organization of its kind in the United States Two years later he was appointed secretary of the Worcester Metal Trades Aassociation a manufacturers' association, which place he still fills with much credit to all concerned Politically he is an active worker in the Republican party He has held all the offices of the Worcester Republican Club, which has a membership of five hundred As an accountant and bookkeeper he stands at the head among his profession in Worcester

ROGER FREEMAN UPHAM John Upham (1) probably of Somersetshire in England, came to America in the company with Rev Joseph Hull known as the Hull colony in 1635 With him were his wife Elizabeth aged thirty-two, Sarah Upham, probably his sister aged twenty-six and his children, John Jr aged seven, Nathaniel aged five Elizabeth aged three His wife was probably Elizabeth Webb These emigrants made their home at Weymouth where John Upham was made a freeman September 2 1635 at the same time that Rev Mr Hull acquired his citizenship in the colonies in the same way In 1636 Mr Upham drew land at Weymouth and from time to time afterward added by purchase and drawing He was a prominent figure in the colony from the outset He was one of the six who treated with the Indians for lands at Weymouth He was appointed a commissioner to try small cases He was selectman in 1645-46-47, and was a deputy to the general court He removed to Malden, about 1648, and was elected selectman there in 1651-52-53 He was commissioner also for Malden In August, 1671, he married ——— Hollie, probably Katheryn widow of Angell Holland He was moderator of the town meetings in Malden in 1678-79-80 He was a deacon of the church for twenty-four years He and his son were interested in the settlement of Worcester at the time of King Philip's war He died February 25, 1681, aged eighty-four years

His children were 1 Nathaniel, born May 23, 1629-30 in England, married Elizabeth Steadman, March 5, 1661-2, died March 20, 1661-2, leaving no children, widow married Henry Thompson, 1669 2 Elizabeth, born 1632, married Thomas Welch, had thirteen children died January 12, 1705-6 3 Phineas born probably 1635 4 Mary, married John Whittemore, died June 27, 1677 5 Priscilla, born 1672, married Thomas Crosswell, died 1717, she had twelve children, she died December 8, 1717

(II) Lieutenant Phineas Upham, son of John (1) Upham, of Malden, was born in 1635 at Weymouth or during the voyage from England He married Ruth Wood, April 14, 1658 He bought land in Malden in 1663 and resided there In 1673 he surveyed a road from Malden to Cambridge In the year 1672 he first became interested in the settlement of Worcester together with other Malden men He drew a lot of fifty acres July 8, 1673, in consideration of his services in promoting the colony The grant was confirmed in April, 1675 The breaking out of Philip's war at this junction turned the attention of the lieutenant from real estate to the battlefield He was commissioned as lieutenant in the little army of the colonies as early as September of the year 1675 The forces under General Winslow met the Indians in battle December 19, 1675 In this fight which is known as the storming of Ft Canonicus or the battle at the Great Swamp Fort, he was mortally wounded With other wounded he was carried to Wickford from the field of battle H was sent to Rhode Island, January 6, 1675-6, and later was borne to his home at Malden The march from Rhode Island is called the Hungry March There was much suffering from lack of food and the horses were killed and eaten on the way In October, 1676, he died The general court made a special appropriation to pay the cost of his long illness and gave the widow ten pounds as she was left with seven small children to support The wife was Ruth widow of Edward Wood, who died in Charlestown, August 20, 1642 She died January 18 1696-7 at the age of sixty years The Upham Genealogy says of him "In battle Lieutenant Upham exhibited the character of a brave man and patriot purchasing with mortal wounds the palm of victory and the government was not unmindful of his great sacrifice but bore testimony upon the records to the long and good services he did to the country and the great loss sustained by his friends in his death" His children were Phineas, born May 22 1659 Nathaniel born 1661, Ruth born 1664 died December 8 1676 John born December 9 1666 married Abigail Hayward (or Howard), Elizabeth married Samuel Green, October 28 1691, Thomas born 1668 Richard born 1675

(III) Nathaniel Upham son of Lieutenant Phineas Upham (2), of Malden was born at Malden, 1661 He married Sarah Floyd, who died aged fifty-three, October 14, 1715 He died November

Roger F. Upham.

11, 1717, and left by will his property to his children His gravestone is to be seen at the old burying ground at Malden He had the rank of sergeant in the militia His children were Nathaniel born 1685-6, Sarah, born 1688-9, married Samuel Samuel Grover, 1713, Ruth, born 1691, married Nathaniel Nichols, 1716-7, Dorothy, married John Coleman, 1723, died 1734-5, at the age of forty-two, Noah born 1696, Joanna, born 1699, married Samuel Wesson, 1717, Lois, born 1701, married James Hill, 1727, Eunice, born 1707, married Benjamin Wesson, April 18, 1726

(IV) Noah Upham, son of Nathaniel Upham (3), of Malden, Massachusetts, was born at Malden, 1694 married Lydia Jenkins, daughter of Obadiah and Mary Jenkins and widow of Joseph Lewis, of Swanzey She died October 14, 1762 He lived at Malden until he was thirty-three years old when he removed to Pomfret, Connecticut, and bought a farm of one hundred and three acres with buildings, fences, etc, built, for Joseph and Elizabeth Sessions for five hundred pounds The date of the deed 1727 is probably the date of their removal from the old home in Malden In 1748 he was living in Pomfret, Connecticut He died February 8, 1766 His children were Noah born at Malden 1720, married Hannah ——, Benjamin, born April 10, 1723 married Ann Wood, Lydia, born January 3 1725 at Malden, Mary, born October 22, 1730, at Pomfret, died at Mansfield, October 31, 1745

(V) Noah Upham, son of Noah Upham (4), of Malden and Promfret, Connecticut, was born at Malden, Massachusetts, 1720 He married Hannah —— who was the administratrix of his estate October 2, 1750 He died September 16 1750, only thirty years old His father was appointed guardian of his minor children Their children were Joseph, born March 30, 1748, married Mary Fletcher, resided at Mansfield, Connecticut, Noah born December 18, 1749, married Rebecca Freeman and settled in Marathon, New York, Mary married Aaron Blackman, of Windham, Connecticut

(VI) Roger Upham son of Noah Upham (5), was born at Mansfield or Pomfret Connecticut, December 18, 1749 He married Rebecca Freeman, March 26, 1771 She was a daughter of Prince Freeman and born June 14 1749 She was a sister of Experience Freeman, who married Jane Upham, January 17, 1781 He married (second) after the death of Rebecca, Widow (Newell) Solace He moved from Mansfield, Connecticut, to Hanover, New Hampshire, and thence to Monson, Massachusetts In 1808 he went to Marathon, New York He died in Cincinnatus, New York, February 17, 1817 Their children were John born November 22, 1772, lived and died in Woodstock, Connecticut, had a son Freeman, Roger Freeman, born January 3 1777, married Anna Howard, Clarissa, born March 18 1785 in Hanover New Hampshire married, May 14 1807 Spencer Keep of Monson, New York and died there May 6, 1829, Newell Noah born August 5, 1793, married Isabella Green, died September 10, 1878

(VII) Roger Freeman Upham son of Roger Upham (6), was born in Mansfield, Connecticut, January 3, 1777 He married November 25 1802, Anna Howard at Woodstock Connecticut She was born at Ashfield Connecticut December 27, 1779, died at Belchertown, October 14, 1857 He removed from Connecticut to Belchertown Massachusetts in 1812 He died in Belchertown, March 14 1858 Their children were Howard born December 17, 1803 married Cynthia Freeman Childs resided at Belchertown, Freeman, born April 1, 1805, married Elizabeth Livermore, Lucius, born July 7, 1807, died December 12, 1855, married no children, Amos, born August 2 1809 married Eloisa Leonard, resided at Castile, New York, Anna, born February 25 1811 died at Enfield, Massachusetts unmarried Newell, born September 6, 1812 married twice, Whitman, born December 6, 1814, died January 22, 1825 Lathrop born January 1, 1816, married Calista Livermore, Hannah born December 17, 1817, married Abijah Child, September 24, 1840, Porter, born October 1, 1820, died April 17, 1872, unmarried, Martha, born November 18 1822, married George L Washburn, of Castile, New York, Emily, born August 25 1825 married April 7, 1847, Gilbert McKenny died January 8, 1883

(VIII) Freeman Upham, son of Roger Freeman Upham (7), was born at Mansfield Connecticut, April 1, 1805 He married Elizabeth Livermore, daughter of David Livermore, of Spencer Massachusetts who was born June 18, 1809 They settled in Worcester, Massachusetts He was a prominent contractor and builder He died February 1, 1876 They had one child, Roger Freeman, born at Worcester, September 13 1848

(IX) Roger Freeman Upham son of Freeman Upham (8), was born at Worcester September 13, 1848 The other lines of Mr Upham's ancestry are not less interesting A prominent ancestor on his mother's side was Oliver Watson of Leicester a revolutionary soldier His mother was a Livermore, a lineal descendant of John Livermore, who settled in Watertown in 1638, and of his son, John Livermore who was a lieutenant in the King Philip war fighting in the same troops with which Lieutenant Phineas Upham served The great-grandfather of Roger Upham David Livermore was a soldier in the revolution He was in Captain Ebenezer Mason's company from Spencer, which marched to Lexington at the Lexington alarm and joined the regiment commanded by Colonel Jonathan Warner

Roger Freeman Upham was educated in the public schools of his native city He was the salutatorian of the class of 1866 at the Worcester high school Immediately after graduation he entered the office of the People's Fire Insurance Company of Worcester as entry clerk and was soon advanced to the position of bookkeeper In a few years he had become assistant secretary a position that he occupied when the great Boston fire of 1872 which ruined so many fire insurance companies caused the failure of the People's Company Mr Upham soon afterward entered the office of the Worcester Mutual Fire Insurance Company, with which he has been associated ever since

The Worcester Mutual Fire Insurance, of which Mr Upham has been secretary for twenty-five years and of which he is also the treasurer is the oldest mutual fire insurance conducting business in the state of Massachusetts It was organized in 1823 and its first president was Levi Lincoln, who resigned within a year to become the governor of the Commonwealth The presidents have been among the most prominent men of their day—Rejoice Newton Frederick William Paine Anthony Chase, Ebenezer Torrey, John A Fayerweather Mr Upham has been president of the Massachusetts Mutual Fire Insurance Union an organization composed of the managers of the various fire insurance companies of the state Mr Upham is a vice-president of the Worcester Five Cents Savings Bank trustee of the Rural Cemetery Corporation and secretary of the Home for Aged Men He is interested in other social and charitable organizations in the city He is a Republican in politics

He married, June 16, 1873, Clara C Story, daughter of Simeon N Story She was born April 2, 1850 They have one child, Edith Story, born September 21, 1882

WATSON FAMILY The surname Watson is derived from 'Wat,' the familiar form for Walter, with the termination "son," signifying therefore, son of Walter It is of English origin, though the family for some generations before coming to America lived near Londonderry in the northern part of Ireland and intermarried with the Scotch-Irish people there The Watson family of England bore arms and members of the family were Barons of Rockingham To this branch of the family it is believed that the American family's descent may be traced

Edward Watson, of Lydington, Rutland county, had fifteen children His eldest son and heir died in 1530, leaving a son Edward of Rockingham Castle, county Northampton His son, the second Baron of Rockingham, married Lady Anne Wentworth, eldest daughter of the Earl of Stafford, and had two sons Lewis who became the Baron of Rockingham, and Thomas, who took his mother's name, Wentworth The son of this Thomas (Watson) Wentworth became Earl of Malton and later also the heir of the barony of Rochester The arms of the family brought to America by the first emigrant are Parted Pr Pale first argent on Chevron Azure three crescents or between three martletts sable (See the Watson Family of Leicester, printed for the family)

(I) Matthew Watson, the immigrant ancestor, was from Londonderry, coming to Boston in 1718 with his wife Mary Orr Her father was a victim of the Catholic soldiers at the time of the siege of Londonderry He was not only killed but his head was severed from the body and borne on a pike A branch of this Orr family settled in New Hampshire, where the largest number of the Scotch-Irish immigrants in 1718 settled The Watsons spent the first season in Framingham Massachusetts and in 1720 settled in Leicester and built their home in that year Mr Watson introduced the potato in that section Before the year closed he was killed by a falling tree, and his widow and children had to take up the task of carrying on the farm In Ireland Mr Watson had been a manufacturer and dealer in linens and cloth He married there in 1695 and eight of their nine children were born in Ireland, the youngest being born on shipboard on the way over

The children Matthew, born March 1696, died at Barrington, Rhode Island, January 17 1803 aged one hundred and seven years, married Bethia Reed, had a remarkable career left an estate worth $80,000, a fortune in his day, Samuel born 1698 died at Leicester March 19 1776 Patrick born 1706, Robert William, Elizabeth born 1700 died December 1 1815 Margaret, married a Mr McNeal John, born November 1716 died at Palmer, November 9 1795 Oliver of whom later

(II) Oliver Watson son of Matthew Watson (1) was born in 1718 on the voyage to America spent his early life in Leicester He bought 2000 acres of land there from Joel Whittemore at the time of the incorporation of Spencer May 14 1753 his place was included in the new town it is the first farm over the line on the old post road from Leicester to Spencer He became one of the leading citizens In 1771 he was third in point of wealth he was selectman in 1755 1756 1757 1760 to 1767 inclusive 1771-1778 town treasurer 1757 to 1768 inclusive, assessor 1755, 1756 1757 1760 to 1767 inclusive, 1771, 1778, four years in the general court He was a patriot before and during the revolution, he was a delegate to the provincial congress in Watertown in 1775 and was also a member of the committee of safety and correspondence of that year He was deacon of the Spencer church Three of his sons served in the revolutionary army He died December 20, 1804, aged eighty-six years

He married (first) Elizabeth Blair, of Worcester, December 4, 1742 She died December 4 1779, aged fifty-five years He married (second) Hannah Peters, of Brookfield, November, 1782 She died March 6, 1808, aged eighty-four years The children of Oliver and Elizabeth Watson all born in Spencer, were Oliver, born November 18, 1743, Robert of whom later Elizabeth, born January 1, 1748, Mary born April 30, 1752 James, born July 20 1754 Abigail born November 27, 1759, married Reuben Whittemore Martha, born June 18, 1763, married Benjamin Green David, born March 17, 1766

(III) Robert Watson, second child of Oliver Watson (2) was born in Spencer, May 28, 1746, married 1777 Tamer Whittemore, who was born June 12 1757 and died October 9 1836 He died January 20 1806 He was a Minute Man in Captain Eben Mason's company from Spencer in 1775 and marched to Lexington He inherited the homestead and always lived in Spencer His children Amos born March 2, 1778 married Polly Wood, Betsey October 28 1779, An infant, born October 13 1781, died next day, Jeremiah, of whom later Charles October 15, 1784 Robert, October 16, 1787, married Lydia Watson, who died April 11 1889 aged one hundred and two years, Sally, July 18, 1788 married Simeon Sibley, Aaron born 1800, died October 28 1813, Tamer married, September 4 1816, Josiah Green she died October 13 1820, Polly, married Jonathan Ryan, of Charlton, A child born April 4 1796 died young A child born October 27, 1797, died young, Sibilla, born February 24 1799 married William Mouley, Ashtabula, Ohio

(IV) Jeremiah Watson fourth child of Robert Watson (3) was born December 14 1782 in Spencer married Chloe Sprague daughter of James and Chloe (Baldwin) Sprague Sr July 6, 1809 She was born December 30 1786 and died 1860 He died January 2 1856 Their children Lodicea Amanda, born April 5 1810 married Horace Waite of Leicester, Lory Sprague of whom later, Emily born July 14 1817 married Thomas Hersey, Roswell born July 31 1819 died November 6, 1820, Roswell S, born February 26 1822, died December 1876, George Henry born April 29, 1828 died October 30 1828

(V) Lory Sprague Watson, second child of Jeremiah Watson (4) was born in Spencer, May 4 1814 He obtained his education in the common schools and while living with his father helped on the farm and learned the carpenter's trade, at which he worked in Spencer for a short time In 1842 he removed to Leicester and in company with his brother-in-law Horace Waite under the firm name of Waite & Watson began the manufacture of hand cars and stripping cards In 1845 Mr Watson purchased his parner's interests and continued alone adding to the business the manufacture of wire heddles His business constantly grew and he had to increase his facilities from time to time The business was incorporated in 1890 with Mr Watson as president, a position he continued to fill until his death His son Edwin L Watson was associated with him in the business as secretary and treasurer of the company and after his death he became the president The name of the corporation is the L S Watson Manufacturing Co

Mr Watson took a leading part in public affairs

Henry C Hall

in Leicester He was for several years in succession selectman and assessor, in 1868 and 1870 he represented the town in the general court, serving on important committees The handsome public library building of Leicester was his gift to the town, it is a standing monument to his generosity and public spirit In politics Mr Watson was an active and loyal Republican He was a director of the Leicester National Bank and president of the Leicester Savings Bank He was an active member of the Congregational church, and a liberal contributor to the building fund and to the various departments of the church His interests were thoroughly identified with those of the town, and no man in his day was more generally respected and esteemed by his fellow-citizens

He married, February 23 1837, Mehitable Luther, who was born April 22, 1811, and died October 19, 1885, the daughter of Sylvester and Catherine (Howe) Luther, of Spencer He married (second), June 16, 1887, Mrs Hannah (Grout) Watson, widow of Roswell S Watson, his brother She was born November 27, 1825, the daughter of Joel Grout Lory S Watson died May 21 1898 The children of Lory Sprague and Mehitable Watson were Edwin Lucius, of whom later, Henry Luther, of whom later

(VI) Edwin Lucius Watson, eldest child of Lory Sprague Watson (5), was born in Spencer, Massachusetts, January 22, 1841 He is at present living in Worcester He was educated in the public schools of Leicester and in Wilbraham and Leicester Academies He became early in life associated with his father in the manufacture of hand cards, and when the business was incorporated in 1890 he became the secretary and treasurer of the corporation For many years the burden of the business has been on his shoulders Since the retirement of his father he has been the president of the L S Watson Manufacturing Company At present the company manufactures improved cotton and wool hand cards of every description Hand stripping cards are made of all lengths from eight to fifty inches of hardened and tempered steel wire The patent heddles of the company have a high reputation among manufacturers They are made on machinery specially designed for the purpose The company also manufactures shuttles, pickers and lug straps and is agent for the Endless Steel Tempered Tinned Wire Heddle Mr Watson was a director of the Leicester National Bank now in liquidation He is a Republican, but has declined to accept public office He is a member of the Congregational church Mr Watson was active in getting the electric railway built to connect Worcester, Leicester and Spencer, and was president of the Worcester, Leicester & Spencer Street Railway Company

He married June 10, 1869 Lottesa M Cogswell, daughter of John D and Fanny H (Leonard) Cogswell, of Leicester She was born July 15, 1846, and died March 3 1893 He married (second), September 12 1896 Rhoda M Lawson His only child was Walter Cogswell, of whom later

(VI) *Henry Luther Watson*, youngest child of Lory Sprague Watson (5), was born in Leicester July 12, 1845 He was educated in the schools of his native town and Wilbraham Academy In 1867 he removed to Minnesota and entered the woolen manufacturing business In 1873 he returned to Leicester and was interested in the card manufacturing business He was a soldier in the civil war For ten years he was trustee of the town library

He married November 21 1867 Amelia Maria Brown, daughter of Hugh C and Sarah (Young) Brown of Leicester She was born March 30, 1848, and died December 27, 1873 He married (second), May 16, 1876 Gertrude Moore Ray, daughter of Trask and Mary (Davis) Ray, of Templeton, Massachusetts She was born June 18, 1854 The children of Henry Luther and Amelia M Watson were: Edwin R, born August 20, 1868, Amelia B, born December 6, 1873, died August 27, 1882 The children of Henry Luther and Gertrude were Henry Ray, born February 27, 1885, Gertrude, born May 24, 1892

(VII) Walter Cogswell Watson, only child of Edwin Lucius Watson (6), was born in Leicester, May 21, 1870 His education was received in the public schools and at the famous old Leicester Academy of his native town He became connected with the L S Watson Manufacturing Co, established in 1842 by his grandfather, and at the present time (1906) is the manager of the company and director of the corporation He has served the town of Leicester for five years as town treasurer He is a trustee of the public library, of which his grandfather was the founder and in which the Watson family has always been interested He is an active Republican, and takes an interest in the affairs of the town and state He is a member of the Leicester Congregational Society of which he is at the present time the treasurer

He married, December 6, 1893, Lelia Blanche Jordan, daughter of John Quincy and Mary S. (Lane) Jordan, of Leicester She was born in Lewiston Maine, February 25 1872 Their children are: Wilbur Lory and Clifton Edwin

AMOS A GOULD, who is now leading a retired life at his home in Leicester, surrounded with peace and plenty, and realizing to the full that there is no reward so satisfactory as the consciousness of a life well spent, was born in Douglas, Massachusetts, August 28, 1841, one of fourteen children born to Sylvester and Julia A (Aldrich) Gould, the former named being for many years a prominent resident of Douglas, Massachusetts

At the early age of three years Amos A Gould was brought by his parents to the town of Sutton, where he resided six years, after which he located in Oxford, remaining there two years, from thence he removed to Charlton, and after a residence of ten years there came to Leicester, where he resides at the present time (1905) He devoted his time and attention to box making, which line of business he successfully conducted up to his retirement from active pursuits The esteem in which he is held by his fellow-citizens is evidenced by the fact that he was chosen to fill various offices of trust and responsibility, among them being tax collector, in which he served ten years, constable, in which he served fourteen years, assessor, in which he served two years, and water commissioner, in which he served six years He adheres to the principles of the Republican party Mr Gould married Charlotte E Kent, a daughter of Emerson and Sophronia (Ayers) Kent, of Leicester, Massachusetts, and one child was the issue of this union Sarah S, deceased Mrs Gould passed away August 26, 1900

HENRY CLAY HALL John Hall (1) the emigrant ancestor of Henry Clay Hall late of Millbury, Massachusetts, was born in England about 1605 The English ancestry has been traced and the surname has been common for many centuries in England originating, it is said, in Saxony John Hall came to America in 1633 He was in the Pequot war in 1637, was made a freeman of the Massachuetts colony as early as 1634 and probably lived in Boston until 1639, when he removed to New Haven, Connecticut He married Jane Woolen, of Boston, who had lived in the family of William Wilkes, of Boston, and probably came with his family, for he paid her fare After her marriage she had to bring suit against him for unpaid wages for services in his household John Hall became one of the early proprietors of Wallingford, Connecticut, and he and his descendants have been conspicuous in the history of that fine old town ever since its settlement The first list of proprietors contains the names of John Hall, David Hall and Dr Hall, the latter being Isaac Hall, son of Francis Hall, of Fairfield, Connecticut In 1669 Samuel Hall and John Hall signed the first covenant of planters at Wallingford Just before his death John Hall and his son, John, Jr, were on a committee together In his sixtieth year he was freed from military service by order of the general court, dated 1665 He served the town of Wallingford as selectman in 1675 and in many other important commissions He died March 3, 1676, making an oral will on his deathbed Children of John and Jane (Woolen) Hall 1-2 John and Sarah, twins baptized August 1646 3 Richard, baptized July 11, 1645, (his daughter married Governor Thomas Fitch) 4 Samuel, born May 21, 1646 5 Daniel, about 1647-8 6 Thomas, March 25, 1649 7 Jonathan, April 5, 1651 8 David, March 17, 1652

(II) John Hall, son of John Hall (1), born probably in Wallingford, 1641, baptized August 9, 1646, died at the age of seventy-six, September 2, 1721 He married, December 6, 1666, Mary, daughter of Edward Parker, of New Haven She died September 22, 1725 John Hall became the first deacon of the church at Wallingford, was selectman and deputy to general court 1687, and held other positions of trust Rev Aaron Hall, formerly minister at Keene, New Hampshire had one of the silver spoons of John Hall, marked John and Mary Hall He and his son John and brother Samuel Hall were on a committee to treat with Rev Mr Whittelsy and offer to buy him a home lot on Deacon John Hall's land if he would come to Wallingford John, Samuel, Thomas and David Hall had land in Meriden in 1689 John Hall had numerous other land grants Children of Deacon John and Mary (Parker) Hall 1 Elizabeth born August 1670, New Haven 2 Daniel, born July 26, 1672 Mary, June 23, 1675 4 Nathaniel, February 8, 1677 5 John, March 14, 1681 6 Lydia January 1683 7 Samuel, December 24, 1686 died young Esther, born August 30, 1692 9 Caleb, September 14 1697

(III) John Hall, son of Deacon John Hall (2), born in Wallingford, March 14, 1681, married, June 1707, Elizabeth Royce who died September 2, 1755, aged sixty-six years He died April 27, 1766, aged eighty-five years They resided at Wallingford where he was a prominent citizen Children of John and Elizabeth (Royce) Hall 1-2 Isaac and Peter, twins, born July 22, 1709 3 John, December 28, 1712 4 Abel 5 Asahel born January 1717 6 Royce, December 26 1718 (Yale 1735) died May 29 1752 7 Abigail, born March 7, 1723 Elizabeth July 9, 1725 9 Benjamin, April 4 1728 10 Elisha, September 15, 1730 11 Sarah, August 25 1732

(IV) Asahel Hall, son of John Hall (3), born Wallingford June 19 1717 died November 11 1795 married, July 29 17—, Sarah Goldsmith, died February 25 1784 Their children 1 Catherine, born August 6 1739 2 Joel, May 21, 1741 3 Sarah March 5 1743, died young 4 Asahel, born May 15, 1745, died young 5 Jerusha, born August 31, 1746, died young 6 Sarah, born June 9, 1748, died young 7 Asahel, born July 16, 1750, died young 8 Mehitable, born March 13, 1753 9 Aaron, born July 28, 1755, died October 6, 1759 10 Charles, born November 12, 1757 11 Asahel, born January 14, 1759 12 Aaron, born November 4, 1760

(V) Aaron Hall, son of Asahel Hall (4), born in Wallingford, November 4, 1760, died September 30, 1839, aged seventy-nine years He married, May 24, 1781, Elizabeth Cook, married (second), December 11, 1820, Sarah widow of Charles Hall, married (third), June 18, 1827, Anna Brooks He was a soldier in the revolution, and was with Washington in the New Jersey campaign, he served from 1777 to 1781 Children of Aaron and Elizabeth (Cook) Hall 1 Benjamin Atwater, born April 6, 1782 2 Elizabeth, October 23, 1783 3 Electa, September 9, 1785 4 Aaron C, November 11, 1787 5 Mary, January 20, 1790 6 Asahel, April 6, 1792 7 Salmon August 12, 1793 8 Anna, January 6, 1796 9 Caroline, December 21, 1798 10 Kirtland, July 4, 1805

(VI) Dr Asahel (or Asa, as he was generally called) Hall, son of Aaron Hall (5), was born in Wallingford, April 6, 1792 He was studying to be a physician when the war of 1812 broke out, and he entered the service when only about twenty years old as an army surgeon, and was stationed at Fort Griswold, Connecticut After the war he located in Dutchess county New York, and lived at Rhinebeck, Fishkill and Poughkeepsie During the last twenty years of his life he lived in Poughkeepsie, and practiced there He married Catherine (Vanderberg) Toffie, of Rhinebeck, widow, descendant of one of the ancient Dutch families of New York Dr Hall died in Poughkeepsie in 1877, and his wife in 1880, at the age of eighty-eight years Children of Dr Asa and Catherine Vanderberg Hall 1 Henry Clay 2 George Vanderberg, resides in New York city 3 Anna, married Silas Woodell, lived and died in Poughkeepsie 4 Dewitt Clinton, resides in New York city

(VII) Henry Clay Hall, son of Dr Asahel Hall (6), born in Dutchess county, New York, August 17, 1820 died in Millbury, Massachusetts, October 29 1901 He was for nearly thirty consecutive years in the consular and diplomatic service of the United States in Cuba and Central America His public life was remarkable and brilliant He served in the foreign field under eight presidents from Buchanan to Cleveland and his long and honorable career is believed to be without parallel in the history of the consular or diplomatic service

After leaving school he went to Mexico as agent for a cotton mill and remained there nine years, holding this position during the Mexican war, when few Americans cared to remain in Mexico He returned to his home in Fishkill New York where he was engaged in commercial business until 1853 In the fifties he went to Cuba His first appointment was consular agent for the United States at Matanzas He was promoted to vice-consul March 18 1864 his appointment signed by President Abraham Lincoln He did effective work for his government during the civil war in detecting blockade runners which were often equipped in Cuba He was appointed vice-consul general at Matanzas February 27, 1869 and consul general January 15 1872 He was appointed vice-consul general at Havana, December 8 1873, and consul general December 24 1879 He was appointed, April 17 1882, minister resident in Central America and July 13 1882 received a new commission from President Arthur as envoy extraordinary and minister plenipotentiary to the Central American Republics He resided from 1882 to 1889 at Guatemala and represented the United States in five of the Central American States At present this district has been divided in two parts For many years Mr Hall held the position of dean to the diplomatic corps, and retained his position when Cleveland was president He remained in the service until 1892 during Harrison's administration After leaving the consular service he became interested in the Nicaragua Canal, and he drafted the original treaty which provided for its building It was a great disappointment to him when the plan which seemed to be in a fair way to be executed failed at last Doubtless the more recent coup d'etat in Panama would have been even more distressing to Mr Hall when it seemed finally decided that the United States would build over the Nicaragua route Mr Hall's health compelled him to relinquish his duties in Central America, being afflicted with rheumatism He made his home in Millbury near the residence of the mother of Secretary Taft, and there spent his last days, and died October 29, 1901 and is interred at Poughkeepsie, New York

He never lost interest in public affairs He kept himself well informed, and followed closely the great public questions of national importance Although so much of his life was passed on foreign shores he was always thoroughly American in his ideas He was an interesting talker on the events of his life and times but extremely modest and professionally reticent too modest to speak much of his own work It is a remarkable fact that Mr Hall was seventy-six years old when he cast his first vote, for he was out of the country so much that he had not acquired a legal residence in the United States until he came to Millbury after he retired from public life His services in behalf of Central America are gratefully remembered there where he was generally known as the "Father of the Nicaragua Canal"

Mr Hall was a Mason, initiated in Sylvan Grove Lodge, No 275, of New York city, March 25, 1856 He was a member of some local societies and clubs in Cuba and Central America He appreciated the value of the Masonic order and occasionally told an incident in the life of his wife's father Antonio Echeverria who was an eminent merchant of Cuba in his day Before the youthful American Republic sent its warships to the Mediterranean to destroy the pirates, American shipping suffered constantly Mr Echeverria was once on his own ship on the way from Africa to Cuba, when taken by pirates It was the custom then to make the captured sailors and passengers walk the plank over the side of the vessel into the sea to suffer death by drowning Some of the prisoners were ready for the fatal step and all had resigned themselves to their fate when the pirate chief was recognized as a fellow Mason by Mr Echeverria, and remained faithful to his Masonic pledges even at that critical moment The lives of the prisoners were saved and the Cuban merchant loaded with costly gifts before they parted company Mrs Hall remembers many of the articles that her father brought from this remarkable adventure The secretary of the lodge wrote to Mrs Hall after the death of her husband "In his death this lodge has lost one of its oldest members an upright and true Mason, an honor to the fraternity and this Lodge"

During his official life he was the means of destroying the coolie trade in Cuba and perhaps took more satisfaction in this act of humanity than in any other experience He was appointed a representative of the Chinese government at the suggestion of the Washington authorities of the Chinese and American governments and was able to put such evidence in the way of the Chinese government that Chinese laborers were forbidden and prohibited from engaging in the voluntary slavery which had disgraced China and all those countries engaged in the cruel business When a Chinese coolie was sold by the Spanish government to a Cuban planter for about $300 for eight years of service, the Chinaman was practically doomed to slavery for life as the pittance he received would not help to give him a start in life

Mr Hall's services in the interests of the American nation were during some critical times, when it took a man of iron will and cool brain to stand firmly at his post and defend his country's honor He was in Havana during the civil war, holding the post of consul general in the days of the civil war, and his conduct of affairs in those perilous times when his life was in constant danger, attracted the attention and admiration of diplomats the world over, and won for him the highest praise and approval of President Lincoln and his cabinet For thirty years he was the trusted servant of his country in foreign lands In many respects his career was unique

Mr Hall married, March 27, 1856, at Wilmington Delaware, Leila Echeverria, daughter of Antonio and Sarah (Newell) Echeverria Her father was born in Florence, Italy, but lived nearly all his life in Cuba, where he was a leading merchant in the foreign trade Her mother came of the Newell family of Marblehead, Massachusetts, where she was born This family is one of the oldest and best known of Essex county Leila was born in Matanzas Cuba, July 15 1828, and was educated there and in the United States She is a remarkably well preserved woman cultivated and charming in manners, bright and entertaining in conversation She resides part of the year in her Millbury home She has no children

ALDEN E BACON, a lifelong resident of the town of Leicester born October 3, 1872, is a son of Frank A and Emily (Bond) Bacon Frank A Bacon (father) was born in Paxton, Worcester county, Massachusetts from whence in later life he removed to Leicester He was identified with the Baptist church, and was a Republican in politics By his marriage to Emily Bond of Leicester, the following named children were born George F, conductor of street railway resides in Worcester, Massachusetts, is married, but no children have been born to this union, Charles A a resident of Shrewsbury, Massachusetts, married Annie Eaton, of that town, and they have four children Ruth, Haezl Arthur and Eunice Bacon Mary E resides with her mother at Leicester Alden E, see forward

The educational advantages enjoyed by Alden E Bacon were obtained at Leicester Academy, from which institution he was graduated Throughout his active career he has followed the quiet but useful calling of agriculture, and by industry and good management his land yields abundant harvests which well repay him for the labor expended thereon He has served his town in the capacity of overseer of the poor and superintendent of streets, his incumbency of office being noted for efficiency and capability He holds membership in the Congregational church, and his political affiliations are with the Republican party, the principles of which he firmly advocates and upholds Mr Bacon married, October 30, 1894, Cynthia Anna Gilman, a resident of Connellsville, Pennsylvania No children have been born of this marriage

MILO BOLTON, a well known and esteemed citizen of Leicester, in which town he has resided for more than half a century, is a native of Vermont He is engaged in the card clothing business, from which he derives an income that is ample to supply his family with the necessaries and some of the comforts of life He is a member of the Congregational church, and a Republican in politics

Mr Bolton married Mary A Loring, born in Leicester, Massachusetts, in 1833, a daughter of John and Eliza (Ayers) Loring, who were the parents of four children John Loring was born in Spencer, December 10, 1795 The death of his wife occurred January 26, 1837 Mr Loring married (second), May 12, 1839, Clarinda Reed, born at Rutland, Massachusetts, December 4 1806, died March 7, 1884, leaving three children Four children were born to Mr and Mrs Bolton, namely Walter E, married Jennie Tilden, of Hyde Park, Massachusetts, and one son was the issue, Milo Oscar Bolton, Herbert L, Oscar, Fred Augustus, a farmer by occupation, married Dora Brown, and resides at Monroe, New Hampshire Mrs Bolton, the mother of these children, received her education at the academy in Leicester, and prior to her mariage taught school in that town for eight years, including one winter in Cherry Valley

ESTABROOK FAMILY. Joseph Estabrook (1), the pioneer ancestor of the Estabrook family, of Worcester county, and of James E Estabrook and Arthur E Estabrook, of Worcester, was born in Enfield, Middlesex county, England He came to New England in 1660 He entered Harvard college and graduated there in 1664 He was ordained soon afterward as the colleague of Rev Edward Bulkeley, of Concord, Massachusetts, and on the death of the pastor in 1696, succeeded him, filling the position with honor to himself and his people until his death, September 16, 1711 He was succeeded by Rev Joseph Whiting (H C 1661) Joseph Estabrook was admitted a freeman May 3 1665 His biographer tells us that as a preacher he was plain, practical and persuasive In his intercourse with his people he was grave, affectionate and greatly beloved In fact, he was generally known as "The Apostle" He was invited to take a church in Boston and urged to go to a larger field by friends who knew his powers But great things have originated in the little town of Concord, the greatest men of America history have been born there, and lived there—men like Estabrook, who helped frame the characters of the early generations there men of his spirit and pride in his own town, though its population was small and its business future unpromising, His salary at Concord was only forty pounds a year in money, and forty in farm produce of various kinds The *Boston News Letter* said of him at the time of his death "He was eminent for his skill in the Hebrew language, and a most orthodox, learned and worthy divine, of excellent principles in religion indefatigably laborious in the ministry, and of holy life and conversation" He was chaplain of the Massachusetts legislature He married, May 20 1668 at Watertown, Mary Mason, daughter of Captain Hugh Mason, the Indian fighter, and his wife, Esther Mason (See Mason sketch) She was born December 18 1640 The children of Rev Joseph and Mary (Mason) Estabrook were Joseph born at Concord Massachusetts May 6 1669 Benjamin, February 24 1670-1, (H C 1690) first minister at Lexington, Massachusetts, installed October 16, 1696, died July 22, 1697, married Abigail Willard, and had two children His widow married (second) Rev Samuel Treat, and had three children, one of whom was the mother of Robert Treat Paine, signer of the Declaration of Independence, attorney-general, and supreme court justice Mary, born at Concord, October 28, 1672, married Jonathan Green, April 30, 1700 Samuel, born Concord, June 7, 1674 (H C 1696), taught grammar school at Concord 1706-10, and assisted his father in the ministry, was ordained June 13, 1711, as the first pastor of Canterbury, Connecticut, where he served until his death, June 26, 1727 He married, March 3, 1713, Rebecca Hobart (same family as Hubbard), daughter of Rev Nehemiah and Sarah (Jackson) Hobart, of Newton, Massachusetts Daniel, born February 14, 1676, married at Concord, November 21, 1701, Abigail Flint, born January 11, 1675, daughter of John and Mary (Oakes) Flint, removed to Weston, thence to Sudbury, died January 7, 1735 Ann, born December 30, 1677, married, January 26, 1709, Joshua Haynes, of Sudbury

(II) Joseph Estabrook, son of Rev Joseph Estabrook (1), born Concord, Massachusetts, May 6, 1669 He settled first in Hingham, and in 1710 moved to Lexington, Massachusetts He was the eldest deacon there in 1716, and held the office until his death, September 23, 1733 He was highly respected, and filled almost every town office, including town clerk, terasurer, selectman, assessor and representative to the general court He was captain of the military company and school teacher He was often employed as surveyor He died September 23, 1733

He married, December 31, 1689, Millicent Woodis, daughter of Henry W Woodis She died March 26, 1692 He married (second), August 25, 1693, Hannah Loring, of Hingham, daughter of John Leavitt and widow of Joseph Loring The child of Joseph and Millicent Estabrook was Joseph, born October 10, 1690, died August 19 1740 The children of Joseph and Hannah Estabrook were John, born July 28, 1694, married, October 27, 1720, Prudence Harrington, Solomon, born December 22, 1696, died July 7, 1697, Hannah, March 2 1698, married, May 23, 1717, Joseph Frost, Millicent, March 21, 1700, married (first) Jonathan Rand and (second) in 1764 John Chamberlain, Elijah, August 25, 1703, married, 1733, in Sherborn, Hannah ——

(III) Joseph Estabrook son of Joseph Estabrook (2), born Hingham, Massachusetts, October 10, 1690 He married at Lexington July 8 1713, his step-sister, Submit Loring They had two children She died March 31, 1718, and he married (second) March 26, 1719, Hannah Bowman He succeeded his father as a leading citizen in all the walks of life He became captain of the military company and deacon of the church He was town clerk, assessor, treasurer, and selectman at various times He bought the Estabrook farm, in Holden, of Gershom Rice, five shares, July 29, 1724 so that the Estabrook family dates back to the very settlement of Worcester He died August 19, 1740 and his widow married, July 19, 1753 Captain Benjamin Reed, of Lexington She died April 15 1771 aged seventy-two years

Children of Joseph and Submit (Loring) Estabrook Joseph born June 27, 1714 died July 17, 1714 Joseph, March 16, 1717-8, died March 18, 1717-8 The children of Joseph and Hannah (Bowman) Estabrook Joseph April, 1720, died December 7 1747, Hannah, September 26, 1725, died September 29, 1728, Benjamin, born October 9 1727,

James E. Estabrook

died December 29, 1728, Hannah, born October 9, 1727, died December 29, 1728, (probably one of the two foregoing is an error of record—Ed), Benjamin, born December, 1729, married Hannah Hubbard, May 9, 1757, was revolutionary soldier, Hannah, born October 6, 1731, married Ebenezer Hubbard, Solomon, born June 10, 1733, died October 1, 1733, Samuel, born June 16, 1735, entered Harvard College, died July 25, 1754, Millicent, born July 25, 1738, married James Barrett, Ebenezer (posthumous), born September 21, 1740, married Ruth Reed

(IV) Ebenezer Estabrook, son of Joseph Estabrook (3), born Lexington, Massachusetts, September 21, 1740 He married, December 13, 1759, Ruth Reed, the daughter of Captain Isaac and Rebecca Reed, born November 7, 1741 Soon after they were married they removed to Holden, about 1760, probably, and made their home there, where so many of their descendants have since lived He was an influential citizen of Holden, was selectman twelve years, and representative to general court four years He died June 29, 1811 She died June 9, 1782 Children of Ebenezer and Ruth (Reed) Estabrook 1 Molly, born February 27, 1760, married Solomon C Cheney 2 Hannah, born February 27, 1762 3 Ebenezer, born February 19, 1764 4 Jonathan, born April 4, 1766 5 James, born May 16, 1768 6 Joseph, born August 1, 1770 7 John, born January 11, 1773 8 Rhoda, born March 19, 1775

(V) James Estabrook, son of Ebenezer Estabrook (4), born May 16, 1768, at Holden, Massachusetts He married December 15, 1795, Betsey Lovell at Holden She was born July 28, 1775 He died at Holden November 26, 1825 She died February 22, 1826 They lived in Holden, and all their children were born there He was prominent in town affairs In 1821 he was elected selectman, and served in that capacity in 1822-23-24 The other members of the board in 1821 were, Samuel Damon, Silas Flagg, Abner Perry, John Davis, all prominent men, whose descendants have been honored in the city of Worcester as well as the town of Holden It would be dificult to find five men of their day who have had a more illustrious ancestry in Massachusetts, or have been followed by more distinguished posterity Children of James and Betsey (Lovell) Estabrook 1 James, born September 4, 1796, married November 15, 1822, Almira Read, of Rutland. Massachusetts 2 Benjamin, born July 2, 1798 3 Betsey, born December 18, 1800 4 Millie, born March 24, 1803, married Rev John Davis Pierce 5 Simon Read, born December 31, 1805, married, 1828, Frances A Scarborough, daughter of Philip Scarborough, of Brooklyn, Connecticut She died June, 1834, and he married (second), March 2, 1836, Mary Bushnell, daughter of General Andrew Bushnell, of Hartford, Ohio, born April 29, 1815, removed to Warren, Ohio in 1837, and lived there until killed by the cars on a railroad July 7, 1871, she died October 20, 1879 6 Eliza Barrett, born September 17, 1809, married July 2, 1834, John Crowell of Warren, Ohio

(VI) Colonel James Estabrook, son of James Estabrook (5), was born in Holden, Massachusetts, September 4, 1796 Although known generally as a Worcester man, he never forgot his native town He was raised in Holden and attended school there, and the Leicester academy He got his start in life there Colonel James Estabrook, as he was always called, obtained the title as the commander of the last regiment of cavalry maintained in the county, He led his regiment, in 1824, at the reception to Lafayette in Worcester, having the right of line as escort He was not only prominent as an officer of the town, and as a military man at an early age, but as a Free Mason In 1825 the Worcester County Commandery, Knights Templar, was organized, at Holden, with Colonel Estabrook as the Eminent Commander Some of the ceremonies were held on the Holden common He married Almira Read of Rutland, in 1822 and removed to that town for a time In 1828 he came to Worcester to live, and, with the exception of a few years spent in Boston, his life was identified with the town and city of Worcester, and he played an important part in its development and prosperity In 1829 he began business in Worcester in the retail grocery trade, with Gen Nathaniel Heard as partner, in the old Green store, as it was called, but soon removed to Boston Upon his return to Worcester he again opened a grocery store His second location was in Lincoln square, in the Salisbury block He was not only a successful merchant, but became interested in real estate and various manufacturing enterprises He was for many years one of the most active business men of the city, a leading citizen in every sense of the term He was sheriff of the county when the coalition of the Democrats and Free Soilers defeated the old Whig party, and put Governor Boutwell in office The Whigs temporarily recovered power, and he lost the place after two years He was an officer in the custom house, Boston, for a time But usually he affiliated with the minority party and, therefore, held few offices He was one of the eight men who voted for Andrew Jackson It must be admitted that his prestige in his party all over the state would have placed within his reach almost any office, had his party been in the ascendancy He was self-educated but well-educated, for he had a shrewd and conscientious teacher He was the only man elected to the Worcester Fire Society, then and now the most exclusive, and one of the oldest, organizations in Worcester He was evidently welcomed, when he first came to Worcester, as a man of importance He was active in the Old South Church and later in Union Church He died in Worcester, 1874

In 1841 he sent a characteristic greeting to Holden on the occasion of the centennial celebration there It was "The Early Settlers of Holden Distinguished for their love of order, peace and sobriety, and piously devoted to the cause of civil and religious liberty, may we, their descendants, cherish their virtues and not prove recreant sons by neglecting to do all in our power to hand them unimpaired to those who shall come after us ' The late Hon John D Washburn wrote of him In stature he was below middle height His complexion was very dark His manner quick, his eye bright and intelligent * * He was courteous to his opponents, reframed from the imputation of unworthy motives, and carried none of the bitterness of party contest into the relations of private life"

The old homestead was located where the Norwich & Worcester freight station is now He married Almira Read, of Rutland, Massachusetts, 1822 Children of James and Almira (Read) Estabrook 1 Almira Rowena Julietta, born July 31, 1824 2 James E, born October 29, 1829, at Worcester 3 Arthur Edgar, born in Boston, August 11, 1832 4 Francis Albert, born April 22, 1835, in Boston 5 Willis Herbert, born in Worcester, November 29, 1843 died December 4, 1844

(VII) James E Estabrook, son of Colonel James Estabrook (6), was born in Worcester, Massachusetts, October 29, 1829 He attended the Worcester public schools and fitted for college in the

Worcester high school He was graduated from Yale College in 1851 He then studied law with Judge Benjamin F Thomas, in Worcester, attended the Harvard law school and was admitted to the bar in the autumn of 1853, at the age of twenty-three Later he became the law partner of Dwight Foster, late justice of the Massachusetts supreme court, and practiced law until the outbreak of the civil war

Colonel Estabrook, as he is generally called by his friends, responded promptly to the call for arms, although politically he had acted with the Democratic party His example was of particular value to the Union cause at that time He was assigned to duty on the staff of General Charles Devens, and later served on the staff of General Benjamin F Butler, in the Department of the Gulf Compelled to resign from the service by sickness, he returned to Worcester His father left a large estate, and the increase in real estate values added to it materially Mr Estabrook found his private interests sufficient to engross his attention and abilities, and since the war he has not actively practiced law He has been active in politics, however, and has been a leader of the Democratic party in this section for fifty years Not only in Worcester and Massachusetts but in national affairs he has been an influence in shaping history He has been a delegate to almost every national convention of the Democratic party since the close of the civil war He has been chairman of the Democratic state central committee of Massachusetts, as well as the county, district, congressional, and city committees of his party Even his political opponents have given him respect and esteem Judge Adin Thayer, who for many years was leader of the dominant Republican party in Worcester county, was a close personal friend of Colonel Estabrook They knew how to retain their friendship even in the exigencies of political controversy, because both played fair and both deserved the respect and confidence of their followers and the people It was the natural and graceful thing for the Democratic leaders to induce President Cleveland to appoint Colonel Estabrook postmaster, when a Democratic administration came into power He served with credit during his term of office He was succeeded by the late J Everts Greene for many years the associate editor of the *Worcester Spy*, when the Democratic administration was ended Colonel Estabrook served the city of Worcester on the school board He was president of the common council in 1861 and served in the legislature in 1874 He represented the city for some time in the general court He has been a director of the free public library, a position most congenial to him He has one of the best private libraries in the city and has always been fonder of books than of any other recreation or amusement He never married He has made his home with his brother for many years in his handsome residence, 8 Lagrange street, Worcester

(VII) Arthur Edgar Estabrook, son of Colonel James Estabrook (6) was born in Boston, August 11, 1832, but came to Worcester with his parents when very young Except for two years 1851 to 1853 he has lived in Worcester He was educated in the Worcester schools His life has largely been associated with that of his father whom he assisted, until his death, in his various business enterprises, and since then in the care and management of the estate He and his brother, James E Estabrook, have been associated together in their business interests He is an officer of the Union Congregational society He is considered a man of sagacity and high business principles by the business leaders of the city He married November 15, 1873, Emily H Hickox at Cleveland, Ohio She was educated in the public schools of Akron, Ohio She died in 1882 Children of Arthur Edgar and Emily H (Hickox) Estabrook 1 Millicent Barrett, born in Worcester, October 20, 1874, tutored by Miss Williams for ten years, graduated at Smith College in 1895 2 Jane D, born in Worcester, September 14, 1876, educated by Miss Williams, her tutor, graduated at Smith College in 1896 She married Dr Arthur Errell September 6, 1905 He is a professor in the Worcester Polytechnic Institute

NELSON FAMILY Thomas Nelson (1), the immigrant ancestor of the Nelson family of Grafton, to which Charles H Nelson belonged, was the wealthiest of the Yorkshiremen who founded Rowley, Massachusetts He was given the prefix "Mr" in the early records, signifying a man of high station He came first to Boston and was one of the twenty families that emigrated with the Rev Ezekiel Rogers from Rowley, England, in December, 1638 They probably spent the winter in Salem and vicinity, and Nelson went with them in the spring to a place between Ipswich and Newbury, called at first Mr Rogers's Plantation In the following September the general court gave it the name Rowley Nelson lent money on mortgage to Richard Evered, of Cambridge, showing that he had money to invest when he came over Thomas Nelson was admitted a freeman May 23, 1639, was deputy to general court 1640 and 1641, and commissioner of the court In 1643 he was chairman of a committee to make a survey of the town and lay out and register lots In October, 1644, he was appointed magistrate with power to perform marriages He built mills in 1640-42 In January 1644, the town granted him thirty-six acres on the mill field, ten of which were to encourage him in building a mill The Nelson mill was built just above tide water on Mill river, where there have been mills down to the present time, now owned by Nathaniel N Dummer, a descendant of the family to which the wife of the immigrant Nelson belonged Nelson's grist mill was leased in 1643 to John Pearson He went to England on business and died there He made his will here, adding to it when about to start for home, December 4 1645 and August 6, 1648 It was proved February 21 1650 He bequeathed to his son Phillip a double portion to sons Thomas and Samuel and daughter Mercy He refers to his aunt Katherine Witham and to a legacy she had left to his eldest son Phillip Richard Bellingham and Richard Dummer were executors and had charge of the education of the three youngest children He left to his wife Joan his mill mill house and lands at Rowley for her life the reversion to his children The commissioners of the estate found in Mr Dummer's hands 1 685 pounds The division of the houses and lands was agreed upon September 16, 1676 by the sons Philip and Thomas Nelson and John Stocke, who married their sister Mercy his attorney, Benjamin Alford acting for him The probate account shows that the administrator went to York and Hull to collect moneys due the estate, proved the will, and had it recorded in England He married first —— who came with him and died soon He married (second), contract dated February 15, 1641-2 Joan daughter of Thomas Dummer, niece of the famous Richard Dummer Thomas Dummer was from Chicknell North Stoneham, county Hants England, and came in the "Bevis," May 1638 with daughter Joan aged nineteen years, settled at Rowley, Newbury and

Salisbury His will was proved in England, November 9, 1650 In it he mentions his eldest daughter Jane Nelson Children of Thomas and Joan (Dummer) Nelson 1 Phillip born in England, 1636, died August 19 1691 2 Thomas born in England, 1638, died April 6, 1712 3 Mercy born at Rowley, February 26, 1643-4, married John Stork 4 Samuel, born 1646 at Rowley 5 Mary, born December 21, 1648, at Rowley

(II) Sergeant Thomas Nelson, second son of Thomas Nelson (1), born in England, 1638 died April 6, 1712 He married Ann, daughter of Francis Lambert, the immigrant settler She died January 2, 1678 He married (second), May 18 1680, Mary Lunt, of Newburg, died May 28 1688 He married (third), April 9, 1690, Philippa Platts, of Rowley, died October 10, 1709 He was admitted a freeman May 3 1665 The gravestone of Thomas Nelson at Rowley has the following inscription "Here Lyes buried Mr Thomas Nelson, who died April ye 5th, 1712

Who lived a saintlike harmless life
I oved all good books but no bad strife
Who dyed a quiet easie death
And to Christ resigned his breath
So live, my sons my Christ O seek
And when you die like Christ be meek "

The children of Thomas and Ann Nelson were 1 Thomas, mentioned below 2 Dorothy, born February 14 1662 3 Hannah, born June 22, 1665 4 Jonathan, born November 20, 1667, died 1690 5 Elizabeth, born February 25 1669, died December 31, 1688 6 Gershom, born July 11, 1672, removed to Mendon, died there September 15 1727 7 Francis born February 19 1675 Children of Thomas and Mary Nelson 8 Ephraim, born March 23, 1681

(III) Thomas Nelson, eldest child of Thomas Nelson (2), born March 16, 1661, died May 20, 1719, aged fifty-nine years He married Hannah ——, 1690 They resided at Rowley, and there their children were born 1 Samuel, born February 14 1691, married September 3 1721, Hannah Palmer, removed to Upton about 1728, where Hannah, his wife, died November 13 1788 aged ninety-two years 2 Hannah, born December 17, 1693, removed to Upton Massachusetts with her brother 3 Abigail born February 4 1696 died May 12, 1716 4 Lieutenant Jonathan mentioned below 5 Dorothy, born Rowley. 1701 died at Upton, 1794, resided with brother Jonathan never married 6 Elizabeth, born in Rowley, October 5 1704, married Joseph Aspinwall, June 5 1728

(IV) Lieutenant Jonathan Nelson son of Thomas Nelson (3), was born in Rowley, December, 1698, died at Upton August 29 1792 aged ninety-four years He settled in Upton He married first Mary ——, died February 16 1730 He married (second), 1732, Sarah Ames died March 6, 1740 He married third (intentions dated November 27) 1742, Anna Jones died May 7, 1780 Children of Jonathan and Sarah Nelson 1 Jonathan, born 1732, died September 16, 1732 2 Nathan, born October 7, 1733, died young 3 Mary, born February 6, 1735-6, died April 15 1736 4 David mentioned below 5 Jonathan born January 26 1739-40 died March 10 1740 Children of Jonathan and Anna below 5 Jonathan born January 26 1739-40 died March 8 1743-4 7 Sarah born 1741, married Stephen Williams of Uxbridge Massachusetts 8 Mary, born August 14 1745 died May 24 1826, aged eighty-one years, married Grindall Wood of Mendon who died June 29 1825 one son and four daughters 9 Hannah born June 5 1749, married Thomas Barden, 1770, joined Shaker settlement at Harvard, one son, Shadrach 10 Lois, born March 19 1752, married —— White, of Gorham, Massachusetts 11 Isaac, born October 16, 1755, died December 30, 1812 from injuries received from falling tree, married Hannah Fisk, of Upton

(V) David Nelson, son of Lieutenant Jonathan Nelson (4), born June 4, 1737, in Shrewsbury, Massachusetts He married first, 1761, Susannah Bachelder, of Upton second, Susannah, daughter of John Brigham November 24, 1785 He died March 30, 1830 aged ninety-three years His widow died March 12, 1830 aged eighty-five years Children of David and Susannah (Bachelder) Nelson 1 Abijah born at Shrewsbury, March 28, 1762, married Sarah daughter of Asa Mixer, 1791 2 Susannah, born December 30 1764, married Captain Peter Salter, 1784, removed to western New York, three sons and two daughters 3 Thankful born September 21 1766 4 David, Jr, born May 23, 1769, married Lucy Adams, of Northbridge nine daughters 5 Solomon, born August 10 1771 married Elizabeth Dunn of Northbridge, removed to Ohio four sons and three daughters 6 Jonathan, born July 6 1773, married Eunice Stone, March 8, 1798 7 Daniel born December 15 1775, removed to Ohio married Sarah Smith, of Orange, Vermont 8 Josiah mentioned below 9 Amasa, born October 2 1780 married a daughter of Daniel Mixter 10 Sarah, born March 20, 1783, married 1806, Isaac Newton four sons and two daughters

(VI) Josiah Nelson son of David Nelson (5), was born in Shrewsbury, Massachusetts February 15 1778 He lived on the homestead of his fathers in his native town He married Sophia Goddard, June 28 1812, at Shrewsbury Their children 1 James Horace born October 29, 1814, died February, 1815 2 Luther Goddard, born March 31 1816, married Sarah Newton 3 Henry Harrison, born January 23 1818 4 Henry born February 20 1819, married Susan Vickers two sons 5 Jasper Stone, mentioned below

(VII) Jasper Stone Nelson son of Josiah Nelson (6) was born in Shrewsbury, Massachusetts, June 2 1822, on the old homestead that has been in the Nelson family since revolutionary days He attended the district school of his native town and worked on the farm after the fashion of the farmer's boy of his day until he was eighteen years old He finished his education with one term at Worcester Academy He learned the trade of shoemaker from his elder brother and until about twenty-three years old he divided his time between the farm and the bench In 1845 his career as a shoe manufacturer began in Shrewsbury The shop in which his first shoes were made was a plain wooden building ten by thirteen feet situated only a few rods from the house in which he was born His business prospered and he doubled the size of his little shop He and his brother worked together They selected the leather and other stock, prepared it themselves for the shoemakers most of whom sewed and treed and lasted the boots and shoes in their own little shops on their farms The Nelson brothers were also their own salesmen They managed to produce satisfactory goods and their business prospered In 1848 Mr Nelson removed to what is now North Grafton and became associated with James S Stone of Boston a native and former resident of Grafton In 1850 Stone & Nelson purchased a tract of land near the Boston & Albany station and with it a building which forms part of the present establishment Mr Nelson bought out his partner November 1 1857 and carried on the business in his own name until January 1 1860, when George H Rugg a former employe became his partner In 1873 Charles H Nelson, his only son also became a partner Four years later Mr Rugg retired, January 1, 1877, and the firm during the rest of its existence was known as J S Nelson & Son The factory, which was originally thirty by forty feet two stories high has been enlarged from time to time to meet the requirements of steadily growing business, until at the time of Mr Nelson's death the buildings were 30 by 264 feet, four stories high and the firm employed two hundred hands

During the civil war he was on a special committee chosen by the town to co-operate with the selectmen in charge of the military affairs of the town and he was foremost in the work of relief for those left destitute by the soldiers at the front or bereaved by their death He led the movement to give aid and encouragement to the troops in every way He was on the board of selectmen two years and a representative to general court in 1870-71 He was a stanch Republican in politics

Mr Nelson was an ideal employer, never losing the knowledge that he himself gained as a shoemaker at the bench nor his sympathy and understanding of the men who worked for him He was just and honorable in dealing with his hands In turn the men loved and respected him He was an earnest supporter of the temperance movement a man of law and order loving justice and righteousness He was an active member of the Baptist church, and a liberal contributor to its various funds One who knew Mr Nelson wrote of him "To known Mr Nelson at his best was to know him as a friend, and those thus favored—and there were many, for he was a man to attract others—found in him at all times and under all circumstances the courteous gentleman the genial companion and sympathetic helper He was a man of strong attachments loyal to his friends and eminently domestic in his habits, he loved his home and was not easily enticed away from its luxury and comforts" In person Mr Nelson was a man of fine physique and commanding presence blessed with a vigorous constitution, and until the closing year of his life he enjoyed excellent health He died October 22 1884 while yet upon the rising tide of a prosperous business career beloved and mourned by all who knew him He married October 31 1848, Mary E Wheelock, daughter of Gardner Wheelock She was born January 1 1825 and died June 26 1896 Their children 1 Emma Elizabeth born July 31 1849 died December 3 1865 2 Charles Horatio mentioned below 3 Carrie Gilman born September 24, 1855, died July 9 1869

(VIII) Charles Horatio Nelson son of Jasper Stone Nelson (7) was born in Grafton Massachusetts January 9 1852 He was educated in the public schools of his native town and at an early age became familiar with the various departments of his father's factory He became a partner at the age of twenty-one and the firm name became J S Nelson & Son He acted successively as salesman buyer and manager of the concern and for twenty years after his father's death he conducted the business The change from firm to a corporation affected the name slightly The J S Nelson Shoe Company succeeded J S Nelson & Son Mr Nelson was principal owner and president of the concern He increased the business improved the plant with new machinery and continued its history of prosperity and growth up to the time of his last illness The line of footwear produced in late years by this factory was used exclusively by the high-class retail trade in all parts of the United States before this the company had only manufactured the plainest kind of goods Although not an old man when he died, Mr Nelson was a veteran among shoe manufacturers He had taken part in the revolution of ways and means of making shoes, and had the intelligence and foresight to profit instead of losing by the changes He was an example of progress and enterprise in this line of business About a year before his death his health failed and he had to withdraw from active business Owing to his continued illness the business was wound up, the corporation dissolved, and the factory that had so long been the centre of an important industry became silent and empty The *Boot and Shoe Recorder* said of him at the time of his death "He was for many years a leading representative of the New England shoe manufacturing business having been first associated with his father in the production of men's and women's plain shoes at North Grafton, and in later years becoming the head of the business * * * His social qualities endeared him to a large circle of friends in and out of the trade In Boston he was among the best known of the many shoe manufacturers who visited the city frequently His erect figure and quick alert step made him conspicuous at all times, while his hearty greeting was invariably forthcoming"

The following tribute from the pen of a close personal friend was published in the *Boston Herald*: "Of the typical virtues of a high-minded and upright New England manufacturer even those who knew him only casually could readily bear witness His energy resourcefulness, integrity and courage here could be seen toward his employes who depended on him his liberality toward any that stood in need of him—these though obviously visible to only a limited circle, could also not be hidden But the fine poise of his intellect his stern, uncompromising with wrong his delicate perception of true beauty in art, going straight to the core thereof with keen discernment his truly classic enthusiasm, as distinguishing from the fancy of the faddists, for nature's flowers in nature's own seasons, in nature's own surroundings, his democratic wholeheartedness withal in everything that appealed to him from whatever field of letters and life, and only the best did appeal to him—these qualities stamping him as they do as one of nature's own noblemen, were of necessity, visible only to the few He had ample means to satisfy his love for flowers, to have them within his own reach at all seasons of the year But instead, he had the poet boy's joy in going himself into nature's own hidden recesses to gather them there with his own hands even if he had to walk miles and into regions where nature exacts her tribute of discomfort to the flesh before yielding up her treasures In spite of his four and fifty years Charles Horatio Nelson was a young man young to the last in his energy, young in his feeling young in his enthusiasms young above all, in his devotion to loved ones He was liked by all, loved by not a few and he inspired with a passionate devotion to himself those who were entitled to passionate devotion from him In Charles H Nelson his townsmen in Grafton, where he was born, where he had lived all his days lose not only a great industrial force which will henceforth be missed there even materially but they lose also a most valued citizen who never shrank from the performance of a public duty even if it involved consequences disagreeable to himself But his friends mourn in him a soul the like of which is only rarely met and the void created in their hearts by his departure they feel to be one that cannot be filled" (I P)

To the town of Grafton he was a large and frequent benefactor More than one public gift serves

Lucian A. Taylor

as a memorial to him and his lamented father In politics Mr Nelson was a Republican, but was too busy to take public office He was a member of the Republican town committee He served the town from 1886 to 1890 as selectman and declined a re-election He was a charter member of the Algonquin Club of Boston a member of the Commonwealth Club of Worcester and of the Tatassit Canoe Club also of Worcester He married, January 2, 1897, Annie Boleyn Brown at Providence, Rhode Island, who survives him She is the daughter of James Brown, a native of Pictou, Nova Scotia, of English ancestry Her mother was Candace A (Wheelock) Brown daughter of L S Wheelock, a descendant of Ralph Wheelock one of the pioneers of New England Her grandfather was Robert Brown Mr Nelson died December 30, 1905

FRANCIS A RICHARDSON, deceased, for forty years a resident of the town of Leicester, was born in Shrewsbury, Massachusetts, September 16 1834, and died at his home in Leicester, Massachusetts, May 31, 1889 He was educated in the schools of his native town, and then removed to Millbury, residing there until he was fifteen years of age, when he took up his residence in Leicesfer He devoted his entire attention to the card clothing trade and this line of business enabled him to provide a comfortable home for his family In religion he was a Congregationalist and in politics a Republican

Mr Richardson married, August 13, 1856, Sarah A Knowles, born October 4, 1834, in the old Washburn mansion at Leicester, Massachusetts, where she now (1905) resides and which was built in 1789, it being one of the oldest houses in that town She was educated at a select school in Leicester Two children were the issue of this marriage May A, born July 26 1862, in Leicester, died August 1, 1862, and Edward, born December 5 1865, died September 11, 1866 Mrs Richardson is a member of the Congregational church Edward Knowles, father of Mrs Sarah A Richardson, was born in Hardwick Massachusetts, September 13 1799 He was educated in the schools of that town, and later learned the trade of carpenter which he followed for a number of years in the town of Leicester, Massachusetts He attended the Congregational church, and was a Republican in politics By his marriage to Sarah Bigelow, of Spencer, a daughter of John Bigelow, who came to that town from Framingham the following named children were born Dennis Wright, born October 5, 1829, died 1833 Sarah A born October 4 1834, widow of Francis A Richardson, George F, born February 19 1836 died 1871, and John B, born June 3, 1837, died March 17, 1850

JOHN EDWARD BACON, a merchant of Spencer Worcester county, Massachusetts, was there born July 11, 1837 He was the son of Berthier and Cynthia Ann (Wilson) Bacon His father is a tanner by trade and his mother Cynthia Ann Wilson was the daughter of Jacob and Lydia Wilson of Spencer Massachusetts

John Edward Bacon received his first educational training in the common schools of Charlton and at the age of sixteen years went to Leicester Academy, later to Quabog Seminary of Warren Massachusetts, and then to the high school at Spencer, Massachusetts After leaving the school room he started in the boot manufacturing business In 1865 he entered the Charles & George Watson Boot Manufacturing Company, and in 1866 the firm name was changed to George Watson & Co, Mr Bacon then becoming a member of the firm One year later he took hold of the business himself and conducted an establishment under the firm name of Kent & Bacon for eight years In 1875 his business consolidated with that of Bush & Grout, and continued that way for two years From 1877 to 1880 the firm was known as Bacon & Co, and for the next thirteen years as Bacon Kent & Co From that time, 1889, he conducted the business alone for the remainder of his life During middle life Mr Bacon engaged in school teaching, and also in the grocery and provision business with Asa Lamb

Mr Bacon's political sympathies lie with the Republican party, and he served in the legislature in 1893 and 1894, on the State House and agriculture committee being chairman of the latter in 1894 He was school committeeman of Spencer for a number of years He was also on the board of selectmen for a number of years In religious affairs he affiliated with the Universalist faith, and was very active in organizing the Universalist church of Spencer Mr Bacon was very fond of music, and had charge of the church choir for a number of years He was a member of the Masonic Order

On January 1, 1867, he married Mary J Hersey, of Spencer, Massachusetts Miss Hersey is a daughter of Nathan Hersey, who was born January 11, 1809 and the granddaughter of Elijah Hersey, who was born 1750 and died 1850 Her father, Nathan Hersey was sheriff of Worcester county He married Harriet Lamb, of Spencer April 18, 1838 Their children were Lucinda Ann, born 1840, died 1842 Harriet Newhall, born May 3 1842, and Mary Jane born September 2, 1845 Nathan Hersey died November 6 1895, and his wife died October 20, 1849 The children born to Mr and Mrs John E Bacon were Linus Hersey, born October 22, 1872, married June 28 1899 Edith Florence Howland, who was born in Oxford July 8 1871 Their children are Rachel, born September 11, 1900, and Mary, September 21 1902 William E, born October 8, 1874 married August 3, 1897 Sarah Antoinette Carpenter born August 16 1875 They have one child, Gertrude Louise, born January 22, 1899 Mr Bacon passed away February 4, 1898

LUCIAN A TAYLOR Robert Taylor (1) the immigrant ancestor of Lucian A Taylor of Worcester Massachusetts was born in England about 1620 He resided at Scituate Massachusetts, and at Newport Rhode Island He was a rope maker by trade He was admitted a freeman in 1655, served on the jury October 21, 1673 at Newport was prison keeper appointed October 29 1673, by the general assembly He died at Newport January 13 1688 He married, November, 1646 Mary Hodges Their children were Mary born November 1647 married 1664 George Hulate Ann, February 12 1650 Margaret January 30 1652 Robert, October 4 1653 died June 12 1707, married Deborah Peckham John of whom later Peter July, 1661, died 1736 James, died October 7, 1690, married Catherine ——

(II) John Taylor, son of Robert Taylor (1), was born in Newport Rhode Island June, 1657, died June 9 1747 at Little Compton, Rhode Island He settled at Little Compton His will was dated April 24 1745 and proved 1747 John and Robert Taylor executors He married (first) Abigail ——, who died September 16 1720 He married (second) Sarah ——, who died 1764 Her will was dated October 27 1756, and proved August 7, 1764 The children of John and Abigail Taylor were Mary, born October 25 1682 Anna September, 1686, Margaret, July, 1688, Lydia, April, 1691, John,

January 7, 1694, of whom later, Robert, December, 1695, Philip, May 13, 1697

(III) John Taylor, son of John Taylor (2), was born in Little Compton Rhode Island, January 7, 1694 He settled at Providence and married Neomy or Naomi —— Their children were John, born August 6, 1716, of whom later, Elizabeth, January 3 1717, Benjamin, January 27, 1719, Charity, May 10 1721

(IV) John Taylor, son of John Taylor (3), was born in Providence, Rhode Island, August 6, 1716

(V) Richard Taylor, the son of John Taylor (4) was born in Providence about 1750 He married Susannah, who died May 20, 1830 aged seventy-eight years, making her birth in 1752 Some of their children were William born November 4 1783, died April 17, 1816, married, February 14, 1808, Ruth Smith, Richard, Jr, born about 1775 of whom later Stephen, of whom later

(VI) Stephen Taylor, son of Richard Taylor (5), was born about 1770 in Rhode Island, and died 1810, aged forty years He married Freelove Harris Among their children was Jared Taylor, of whom later

(VII) Jared Taylor, son of Stephen Taylor (6), was born in Scituate, Rhode Island He lived at Woodstock Connecticut, where he died and was buried He was a farmer He married Catherine Truesdell, and their children were Henry Fenner, John Erstine, Sophia Truesdell Elizabeth Elvira, Andrew Harris Lucian A, of whom later, a boy who died in infancy

(VIII) Lucian A Taylor, son of Jared Taylor (7) was born in Burrillville, Rhode Island, June 20 1846 He obtained his early education there and at Woodstock, Connecticut, whither the family removed when he was twelve years old At Woodstock he went to school in the building his grandfather built for the town When he was sixteen he enlisted in the Eighteenth Connecticut Volunteer Regiment and served three years in the civil war Before he was seventeen years old he was captured at the battle of Winchester and imprisoned at Belle Isle and Libby prisons He was exchanged later after undergoing great suffering from want of proper food and clothing He served in various campaigns under Generals Milroy Sigel Hunter Crook, and Sheridan He was at Lynchburg and in the Shenandoah valley campaign He was mustered out in June, 1865 He returned to Woodstock and resumed his studies at Woodstock Academy and Howe's Business College Worcester

In April 1867 he entered the office of the city engineer of Worcester the first assistant employed in the office He was connected with the city engineering department for seventeen years He was in charge of work for the sewer and water departments In 1884 he was elected water commissioner and served also in 1885 and part of 1886 He resigned to accept a position in Boston In 1888 his employer died and he went into business for himself as general consulting engineer He made a specialty of public works such as reservoirs dams water works and sewer systems He has had his headquarters in Boston He has had charge of the construction of the water works of many of the principal cities of New England and has also been engineer of construction and consulting engineer for many cities and towns in Massachusetts He has often been called as an expert in litigation over water works and has often served as appraiser in condemning land property for water works, etc He has designed many water works for towns and villages Mr Taylor is a member of the American Society of Civil Engineers, the Boston Society of Civil Engineers, the Connecticut Society of Civil Engineers, the New England Water Works Association, George H Ward Post, No 10, Grand Army of the Republic and the Worcester County Mechanics Association

He married, August 29 1868 Jennette Arnold, of Putnam Connecticut She was the daughter of Alexander and Nancy (Bellows) Arnold Their children are Edwin A, graduate of the Worcester Polytechnic Institute, Civil Engineer, employed by the Atlantic Coast Railway, has two children, Eva M, lives at home with parents, at 8 Dean street

LEVI HUBBARD HOWE John How (1), the English progenitor of Levi Hubbard Howe, of Holden, Massachusetts, was descended from an ancient and distinguished family His immediate family descent we are told is from the Hows of Hodinhall Very little is known of the English ancestry beyond the name and that John How lived in Warwickshire and was the father of John How, the immigrant ancestor, of whom later

(II) John Howe son of John How (1), came to New England when a young man and is said to have been at Watertown for a short time He settled in Sudbury in 1639 and lived there nearly twenty years In 1642 he was selectman, and in 1655 was appointed by the minister and selectmen to "see to restraining the youth on the Lord's Day" He was admitted a freeman May 13, 1640 He was one of the Sudbury petitioners to the general court in 1657 for the grant of land which constituted Marlboro and he was the first white man to settle in what is now the flourishing city of Marlboro He has had a host of descendants in that town and the vicinity though some of the families of this name are descended from another early settler in Marlboro, Abraham Howe, who came there from Roxbury Edward Howe, of Watertown, Massachusetts was some relation of John Howe John Howe settled about a hundred rods from Spring Hill meeting house a little east of the present road from Spring Hill to Feltonville He was a neighbor and friend of the Indians until the war broke out in 1675, and was often an arbitrator and advisor He was selectman of Marlboro He petitioned the general court September 30, 1662 to be excused from training because he was "aged thick of hearing and maintained three soldiers in the family" It is likely that these three sons fought in King Philip's war He kept the first public house in Marlboro

He died at Marlboro May 28, 1680 His will was made May 24 1680 and proved June 15 following He bequeathed to his wife Mary, children Samuel Isaac Josiah Thomas Eleazer Sarah Ward, Mary Witherby grandchild John, son of John The children of John and Mary Howe were John, Jr born August 24, 1640 married January 22, 1662, Elizabeth —— he was killed by the Indians Samuel born October 20 1642 married, June 5, 1663, Martha Bent Sarah born September 25, 1644 married June 1667 Samuel Ward, Mary, born June 18 1646 died 1647 Isaac born August 8, 1648, married June 17 1671 Francis Wood, Josiah married March 18 1671 Mary Haynes of Sudbury, Mary born January 18 1654 married, September 18 1672 John Witherby Thomas born June 12, 1656 see forward Daniel born June 3 1658 died 1661 Alexander born December 29, 1661, died January following Eleazer born January 18 1662, married 1683 Hannah How daughter of Abraham How the immigrant

(III) Thomas Howe son of John Howe (2),

was born in Sudbury, Massachusetts, June 12, 1656 He became one of the most prominent citizens of his day in Marlboro He held the principal town offices, assessor, selectman etc, and was deputy to the general court He doubtless fought in King Philip's war and afterward he took part in a severe engagement with Indians at Lancaster, he became colonel of his regiment and was the most prominent military man of his section He was one of His Majesty's justices of the peace He kept a public house at Marlboro in 1696 He married (first), June 8, 1681 Sarah Hosmer She died April 7, 1724, and he married (second), December 24, 1724, Mary Barron He died February 16, 1733 aged seventy-seven years Children of Colonel Thomas and Sarah Howe were Tabitha born March 29, 1684, married, April 2, 1713, James Eager, James, born June 27, 1685, married Margaret Gates, Jonathan, born April 23, 1687, married, April 5, 1711, Lydia Brigham, Prudence, born August 2, 1678, married, January 5, 1715, Abraham Williams, Thomas, born June 16, 1692, see forward, Sarah, born August 16, 1697

(IV) Thomas Howe, son of Colonel Thomas Howe (3), was born in Marlboro, Massachusetts, June 16, 1692 He settled in Marlboro also He married Rebecca ——, who died July 3, 1797 He died at Marlboro, April 2, 1777 Their children, all born at Marlboro were Thomas born June 20, 1710, Mary, June 30, 1718, Ezekiel, June 29, 1720, see forward, Simon, October 28, 1722, married Lydia Baker, of Littleton Massachusetts, Sarah, July 4, 1725, married 1746, Benjamin Hoar, Rebecca August 16, 1727

(V) Ezekiel Howe, son of Thomas Howe (4), was born in Marlboro, Massachusetts, January 29, 1720 He was brought up at Marlboro and married there Elizabeth Rice, daughter of Samuel and Abigail (Clapp) Rice, descendant of Edmund Rice, the immigrant, a sketch of whom is given elsewhere in this work Ezekiel Howe removed to Worcester about 1743 and is the ancestor of many of this surname in Worcester county Children of Ezekiel and Elizabeth Howe were Patience, born June 10, 1742, at Marlboro, Elizabeth, born at Worcester, February 12, 1744 Ebenezer, born November 4, 1746, settled in Winchendon, Massachusetts, Joel, born November 2 1748 Jotham, see forward, Lucy, born April 20 1752, Rebecca, born April 3, 1754, Ezekiel, Jr born March 20, 1756

(VI) Jotham Howe son of Ezekiel Howe (5), was born at Worcester, Massachusetts, June 17, 1754 His name appears in a list of revolutionary soldiers that were enlisted for active service in Captain Samuel Thomson's company, Major Asa Baldwin's division of Colonel Denny's regiment, September 26 1777 to reinforce the northern department of the Continental army He lived at Winchendon a few years, where his brother Ebenezer settled He bought a farm in Holden, February 25, 1773 of Moses Stickney, formerly Colonel Hatch's

He married July 2, 1770 Dorothy Smith, at Worcester She was born in Holden, March 1, 1751, daughter of Isaac and Martha (Davis) Smith He settled in Holden in 1773 He was a farmer He and his wife belonged to the Congregational church until November 15 1784 when at their own request they were dismissed and recommended to Mr Gair's, of Medfield, evidently a Baptist society, for the church record states "the objections offered against the church were admitting persons without a verbal relation of a work of grace on the heart, and baptizing infants without warrant from the word of God"

Children of Jotham and Dorothy Howe, all born in Holden, were 1 Dolly, born November 11, 1770 2 Patty, born May 25, 1779, married, August 7, 1797, Isaac Fuller, of Holden, and had Amasa 3 Dorothy, born September 12, 1780, married, November 28 1799, Aaron Holt, of Holden, and they had—Joel, born March 30, 1803, Jotham How, born born February 22, 1805 4 Jotham, Jr, born April 17, 1783, see forward 5 Thomas, born August 19, 1785, married Sally Walker, September 25, 1806, at Holden and they had Amasa, born November 13, 1807, Lyman, born December 13, 1811, William, born June 1, 1814 Thomas, born April 8, 1816, Joel, born May 11 1818

(VII) Jotham Howe, son of Jotham Howe (6), was born at Holden, Massachusetts, April 17, 1782 He was a farmer and cooper by trade, and he followed his trade to some extent besides conducting his farm, which was situated in the northeast part of the town He joined the Baptist Society of Templeton, March 13, 1805 and was exempted from being taxed to pay the Congregational church expenses He was later a constituent member of the Holden Baptist church

He married (intentions dated June 29) 1807, Elmor Henry of Princeton Their children were. Almira, born at Holden, September 27, 1808, died January 1832 Jotham, Jr, born May 23 1810, Sukey, born September 30, 1813, Silas, see forward, Harriet Newell, born July 13, 1827, died July 6, 1833

(VIII) Silas Howe, son of Jotham Howe (7), was born in Holden, Massachusetts, October 5 1814 He was educated in the common schools of his native town and during his youth assisted his father on the farm Then he worked in the saw mill at the North woods, and during the busy seasons used to work nights and half the days as well putting in eighteen hours out of twenty-four in the mill When he was twenty-two years of age, he went to live on the homestead of his wife's father, Benjamin Hubbard, in the northern part of the town and later he bought the farm, which contained some one hundred and ten acres He carried on this farm for a period of forty years or more In his younger days he taught school for several terms He did an extensive teaming business and burned charcoal for the market before the days of anthracite and bituminous coal He cut timber and sold lumber and fire wood besides his general farm work He was a man of great activity and energy, and used to say that he did not know what it was to be tired His physical endurance must have been remarkable and it was tested almost daily through a long life of hard labor He was thrifty saving and shrewd in making investments, and acquired a competence He invested largely in government bonds at a time when financial support was appreciated by friends of the Union He used to answer those who questioned the wisdom of his course by saying that, which ever way the war went he stood as good a chance as anyone In this case he combined shrewdness and patriotism He was a close student of public affairs a well-read man on many subjects a man of independent judgment, common sense and self-reliance In religion he was a Baptist and in politics a Republican He served on the district school committee, was overseer of the poor and highway surveyor He died at Holden October 29 1891

He married, April 24 1838 Persis Walker Hubbard, born September 24, 1815 daughter of Benjamin and Polly (Walker) Hubbard of Holden Her father was a farmer, and one of the charter members of the Baptist church Children of Silas and Persis W Howe were Augustus Franklin, born

April 19, 1839, died October 25 1879, Charles Nelson, born January 27, 1841, Levi Hubbard, born August 23, 1845, see forward, Mary Chandler (twin), born October 10, 1847, died February 5, 1869, Joseph Leander (twin), born October 10, 1847, Hervey Newton, born June 4, 1849, died September 27, 1849, Silas A, born September 18, 1856, died August 6, 1878, Frances N

(IX) Levi Hubbard Howe son of Silas Howe (8), was born at Holden, Massachusetts, August 23, 1845 He began his school life rather early and attended the public schools of Holden until he was fifteen years old, working at the same time on his father's farm At the age of sixteen years and until he was twenty-five, he carted wood from Holden to Worcester, bringing back groceries, coal and general merchandise for the Holden merchants In 1871 he removed to Princeton, where he bought of his uncle, Warren Hubbard, an eighty-five acre farm in the south part of the town, and conducted a dairy farm, selling his milk and eggs in Worcester, largely to private customers In 1894 he returned to Holden to take charge of the homestead and he remained there eleven years In 1892 shortly after his father's death, he bought his present farm of twenty-four acres at Holden Centre of Thomas W Gleason It was known as the Ethan Davis place at that time He has been especially successful with his dairy and has a large herd of cows His residence is one of the finest in the town

Mr Howe is a member of the Baptist church and one of the executive committee, of which he has been the chairman In politics he is a Republican and has been delegate to various nominating conventions of that party He was tax collector of Holden 1895-96, and is at present (1906) the president of the Cemetery Commission He served as road commissioner while in Princeton He is a member of Anchoria Lodge, No 42, Odd Fellows, of Worcester He is also a member of the Worcester Agricultural Society, of the Farmers' and Mechanics' Association of Holden the Worcester County Bee Association, and the Harvest Club of Holden

He married, May 3, 1871, Angelina Rouett Moore, born March 11, 1848, daughter of William and Angeline (Chaffin) Moore of Holden Her father was a farmer, was prominent in town affairs He was an active member of the Holden Rifle Club of Massachusetts Volunteers Children of Levi Hubbard and Angelina R all born in Holden, were 1 William Josephine born August 1, 1874 married, September 2 1896, George C Johnson of Holden, and they have Robert Howe, born November 19, 1898 Raymond Walker, born July 14, 1902, Benjamin Hubbard, born December 14, 1904 2 Edith Georgia born December 22, 1875, resides with parents 3 Clara Persis, born June 16, 1877 married June 18, 1902 Edward Franklin Drawbridge, of Brookline 4 Olive Angeline, born February 2, 1880 married November 26, 1903, George Herbert Marsh of Holden

EDWARD MARVIN WOOD comes of Colonial ancestors The progenitor of the family was John Wood alias Atwood who settled in Plymouth, Massachusetts as early as 1636, and died leaving a will probated March 7, 1675 which mentioned sons John, Nathaniel, Isaac, and six daughters For many generations their descendants have paid tribute to the old historic Plymouth Colony

Among the early settlers of Stafford Hartford county, Connecticut, were the families of Wood, Alden Fuller, Foster and others from Plymouth county, Massachusetts Thomas Wood, of Bridgewater, a blacksmith by trade, bought of James Lindsley, January 4, 1742-43, for one hundred and thirty pounds current money, fifty acres of land in Stafford, the deed having been recorded January 24, 1742-43 After making this purchase, he seems to have returned to Bridgewater where, February 23, 1744, was recorded the intention of his marriage to Dinah Perry Having taken Dinah to wife, they returned to Stafford where, May 30, 1748, he purchased twenty-five acres of land of James Blodgett, deed recorded July 19, 1748, and states that both the parties were of Stafford The children of Thomas and Dinah (Perry) Wood, as recorded at Stafford, were Joshua, born January 26, 1747-48, John, January 20 1749, Nathan, March 16, 1752 next child record was torn, name not readable, Ruth August 15 1756, Lydia, August 22, 1758

Nathan Wood, born March 16, 1752, married Anne Bixby, November 30, 1780, and died August 28, 1806 Their children were born in Stafford, but on account of the condition of the record the names and dates cannot all be deciphered They had a daughter ———, Celinda, died May 3, 1793, Nathan Marble, Abijah, and Homer John, born April 2, 1794, through whom the ancestral line is continued

Homer John Wood, the grandfather of Edward M Wood, was born in Stafford, Connecticut, April 2, 1794, his father, Nathan Wood, dying when he was twelve years of age At the age of eighteen, Homer J Wood entered the employ of the United States government at the armory in Springfield, remaining there continuously for fifty years, living to the age of seventy-four years, and died October 15, 1868 A part of the land now occupied by the Springfield Armory was formerly owned by him

Corbin O Wood, father of Edward M Wood, born August 25, 1821, invented and patented several improvements in guns He was first employed at the United States armory in Springfield, but in 1852 entered the employ of the late Ethan Allen, of Worcester, as a contractor, and employing as contractor twenty-five men in the making of guns He was a skillful straightener of rifle barrels, an art which at that time was confined to comparatively a few men He retired from active business in the year 1883 to enjoy in tranquility the fruits of his previous years of skillful labor and success In early life he was somewhat of a musician, playing the violin in the church choir After having retired from business, he made violins as a recreation, duplicating by actual measurement the celebrated violins of Guanarius and Stradivarius and producing some really fine instruments He was a man of natural intelligence, a great reader of books, of progressive ideas and mechanical ingenuity

May 18, 1843, he married Eunice A daughter of Marvin Kirkland of Agawam She died December 3, 1890 having been the mother of two children, Sarah C and Edward M He died in the year 1904 at the age of eighty-three, leaving an honorable record

Edward M Wood, a resident of Worcester, was for over twenty years a manufacturer of edge tools at Millbury He was born in Springfield Massachusetts January 27, 1851, attended the public schools of Worcester and the Wesleyan Academy at Wilbraham He strove to become broad-minded by good reading and the liberal education which association with the men of the Commonwealth inspires With a desire to acquire a thorough knowledge of mechanical processes by actual labor under proper instructions he was taught in the machine shop of Ethan Allen mechanical drawing pattern making, and the operation of various machine tools, as lathes, planers, milling machines, etc Turning his

Edward M. Wood

attention to the commercial side of manufacturing, after serving an apprenticeship in the hardware store of White & Conant, he, at the age of twenty-one, with a partner, opened a hardware store on Main street near Franklin square, in Worcester, and buying out his partner in 1879 he continued the business successfully until 1884, when he disposed of the same to W H Willard & Co, who are at the present time (1906) continuing the business at the same place In 1884 he became connected with the Buck Brothers Riverlin Works, edge tool manufactory in Millbury, and was for a number of years the senior member of the firm This enterprise is a fair representation of an old Sheffield industry, transplanted to this country and firmly established, and is the culmination of efforts of three generations of skillful edge tool makers The Riverlin works were established in 1853 and occupy a substantial brick building erected for the manufacture of edge tools, which is surrounded by neat cottages, forming an attractive little village The product of this firm is of a high order of excellence, enjoying an enviable reputation, and consignments are sent on orders to nearly all parts of the world The tools made here are adopted as samples by the United States government

While not claiming to be an inventor, Mr Wood has by inheritance and training acquired an inclination toward things mechanical, and his knowledge in that direction has enabled him to contrive devices for greatly facilitating and improving the process of the manufacture of the output which has in turn contributed materially to the success and enlargement of the Riverlin works He retired from this firm, and from active business in 1905 He has made several foreign trips, believes in out-door recreation and is connected with several social clubs, being a member of the Society of Antiquity, the Worcester Club, the Tatnuck Country Club, and was for many years a member of the Art Students Club He is an enthusiastic automobilist, being among the first to take up that form of recreation having been interested as far back as 1894, when he visited the shop of one of the first makers of automobiles in Paris long before they came into general use

Mr Wood married, May 27, 1879, Annie M Buck, of Millbury, and two children were born to them, Bessie, March 24, 1882, died April 10, 1892, and Helen Frances, February 18, 1888 Mr Wood is by profession a Congregationalist and a member of Piedmont church, as are also his wife and daughterer The family resides at Nd 6 Ripley street, Worcester, Massachusetts

STONE FAMILY Gregory Stone (I), the immigrant ancestor of Lyman T Stone, of Boylston, Massachusetts, was baptized in Great Bromley, Essex county England, April 19, 1592 According to his own deposition made September 18, 1658, he was born 1591 or 1592 his age being about sixty-seven years His age at death November 30, 1672, was given as eighty-two years He was probably born therefore, in 1591 He was the son of David and Ursula Stone, and grandson of Simon and Agnes Stone, all of England He had a brother Simon Stone, who also emigrated to America sailing in the ship "Increase," April 15, 1635 settled in Watertown, was admitted freeman May 25, 1636 town officer and deacon, died September 22, 1665 Various other immigrant settlers have been erroneously supposed to be brothers of Gregory, Rev Samuel Stone of Hartford was not a brother Gregory Stone was admitted a freeman with his brother Simon, May 25, 1636 He was a proprietor of Watertown but resided most of his life in Cambridge He had some famous orchards for his day His farm was on the present site of the Botanic Gardens of Harvard University He was one of the most prominent men of his day, a deputy to the general court, was elected deacon of Shepard Mitchell's church, and served thirty-four years, being the last survivor of the original membership, was a civil magistrate, and one of the governor's deputies His will, proved December 14, 1672, mentions his wife Lydia and her children by her former husband—John Cooper and Lydia Fiske, his sons Daniel, David, John and Samuel, daughter Elizabeth Porter, daughter Sarah, wife of David Miriam, grandson John, son of David Stone He married in England July 20, 1617, Margaret Garrad, born December 5, 1597, died August, 1626, in England He married (second) Lydia Cooper, widow, who died June 24, 1674 Her son by her former husband was John, married Anne Sparhawk, her daughter Lydia married David Fiske Children of Gregory and Margaret Stone 1 John, mentioned below 2 Daniel, baptized July 15, 1620, settled in Cambridge, married Mary ——, was a physician 3 David, baptized September 22, 1622, resided at Cambridge, married three times—Elizabeth, Dorcas and Hannah 4 Elizabeth, baptized October 3 1624, buried in Nayland, England Children of Gregory and Lydia Stone 5 Elizabeth, baptized March 6, 1628, married Anthony Porter 6 Samuel, baptized February 4, 1630, died September 27, 1715, resided at Lexington, married first. Sarah Stearns, of Watertown, married (second), June 7, 1655, Abigail —— 7 Sarah, baptized February 8, 1632, died 1677, married July 12, 1653, Joseph Merriam (Miriam) These children were baptized at Nayland, England

(II) John Stone son of Gregory Stone (I), baptized at Nayland England July 31, 1618, died at Cambridge, Massachusetts, May 5, 1683 He removed to Sudbury with the early settlers, was a proprietor there, and shared in three divisions of land He bought of the Indians at Natick, May 15, 1656, ten acres of land on the south side of the river at Sudbury and his purchase was confirmed by general court 1656 together with a grant of fifty acres of land for services, etc He added to the tract he already owned in what is now the village of Saxonville, in the town of Framingham, until he owned a very large stretch of land He built his house where the present railroad station is located in Saxonville He built the first house in what is now the village of Cochituate, in the present town of Wayland then Sudbury He built in all six houses in Sudbury and Framingham and built the first mill in Framingham, in 1659 at the falls now known as Stone's Mills a corn mill, and his son Daniel built there the first saw mill He was appointed fence viewer 1654 town clerk 1655 and was admitted a freeman 1665 In 1645 he sold his house in Sudbury to John Moore He was the first to build his house in Framingham He located, without having a grant at Otter Neck, on the west side of Sudbury in 1646 7 He married 1638 Anne born in England, daughter of Elder Edward and Margaret Howe, natives of England Children of John and Annie Stone 1 Hannah born June 6, 1640 married July 1 1658 John Bent 2 Mary, married Isaac Hunt second April 30 1681, Eliphalet Fox 3 Daniel born August 31, 1644, mentioned below 4 David born October 31, 1646, married Susanna 5 Elizabeth, born 1650 married 1678 Samuel Stow 6 Margaret born October 22, 1653 married William Brown January 11 1605 7 Tabitha born May 20, 1655 married November 3, 1674, John Rice 8 Sarah born September 22, 1654, married Jacob Hill 9 Nathaniel born May 11 1660, married Sarah Wayt of Malden April 25 1684 10 John, non compos mentis 11 ——, died young 12 ——, died young

(III) Daniel Stone, son of John Stone (2), born August 31 1644, died 1719, aged seventy-five years He had the mill, and May 22, 1711, sold a quarter interest in the water privilege to Samuel How, Sr, of Sudbury, but bought it back February 15, 1714 The mills remained in the Stone family until 1824, when the business was incorporated Daniel settled in one of his father's houses near his father's residence He was one of the first board of selectmen of the town of Framingham in 1700, and was for two years deacon of the Sudbury church before that He married, November 2, 1667, Mary (Moore) Ward widow, a school teacher in 1693-4 in Sudbury died June 10 1703, in Framingham He married (second) February 6, 1704, Abigail Wheeler, died October 28, 1711 He married (third) November 18, 1712 Ruth Haynes, of Sudbury His son John administered the estate Children of Daniel and Mary Stone 1 Daniel, mentioned below 2 Anne, born January 15, 1670 3 Tabitha, born May 4 1673, married David Haynes 4 Sarah born February 14 1675, married James Rice 5 Mary, born August 10, 1677, married Jonas Rice 6 Elizabeth, born November 9, 1678, married Joseph Livermore 7 Abigail born February 13, 1680, married Dr John Sherman 8 John, married Anne Tileston of Dorchester, January 31 1706-7, died November 26, 1710, she died March 25 1733

(IV) Daniel Stone, Jr, son of Daniel Stone (3), born in Sudbury Massachusetts, November 22, 1668, died at Framingham, December 22, 1702, aged thirty-four years Although a young man when he died, he was selectman and town treasurer of Framingham in 1702 and served in the expedition to Canada under Phipps in 1690 with the Sudbury company He married Patience Brown, who died November 13, 1722 at Framingham She married (second) Nathaniel Rice Children of Daniel and Patience Stone 1 Priscilla married James Fox, of Dorchester 2 Beulah born August 23, 1695, married January 14, 1719 Josiah Brown of Sudbury, (second) Colonel Timothy Minot of Concord 3 Keziah born July 20 1697 married March 5, 1728 Eliab Moore 4 Micah mentioned below 5 Lois born November 21, 1701 married Moses Maynard, of Sudbury, March 18 1723-4

(V) Micah Stone, son of Daniel Stone, Jr (4), born on "The Island," Sudbury, now Wayland, March 11, 1699, died October 13 1738 of small pox, at the age of thirty-nine years He resided in Framingham and was selectman there 1732 until his death deputy 1734 and 1735 He married, April 2 1724 Abigail Stone, of Lexington She married (second) January 22, 1752, Colonel Joseph Perry and she died October 4, 1796, at an advanced age Children of Micah and Abigail Stone 1 Josiah born December 23, 1724 married Anne Haven, February 24, 1746-7, died April 2 1785 2 Daniel mentioned below 3 Micah, born May 30, 1729 married Rachel Haynes of Sudbury, October 11, 1748 married (second) Sarah Bacheller widow of Grafton 4 John born March 28, 1731, died in army, December 6 1755 5 Moses, born June 26 1734 married Hannah Moore, of Sudbury November 14 1754 died in Framingham July 13 1813 6 Eliab born May 5 1737, married October 17 1765 Sarah Hubbard of Concord, died August 31 1822 graduate of Harvard 1758, teacher at Sudbury ordained minister at Reading, May 20, 1761

(VI) Daniel Stone son of Micah Stone (5), born at Framingham Massachusetts April 11 1727, died April 3 1813 aged eighty-six years He was selectman 1767-68 His house was burned in 1766 He and his wife are buried in the Church Hill cemetery at Framingham Centre, near the middle of the yard, in a lot enclosed by iron fence He married 1749, Persis Haynes born 1728 and died May 7 1804 aged seventy-six years Their children 1 Persis, born July 17, 1750, died March 1, 1752 2 Nahum, born November 25, 1752, married Hannah Haven, died at Grafton, 1805 3 John, mentioned below 4 Daniel born September 5, 1760, married Sally Buckminster, born 1770, died April 9, 1845 he died November 9, 1834 5 Persis, born August 15, 1762, married Buckley Adams, February, 1785

(VII) John Stone, son of Daniel Stone (6), born at Framingham, February 17 1757, died at Cambridge, August 18, 1844 His occupation was hotel keeping, at which he was popular and successful At one time he worked for Governor Livingston at Livingston Manor, New York, and his son, Peter Royal Stone, was named for the governor John Stone had hotels at various times in Wayland and Sudbury He finally bought a farm at Cambridge, where he and his daughter Abigail lived after the death of his wife He married June 25, 1778, Ann Hunt, born 1760 died October 20 1829 Their children 1 John, Jr, born 1779, died December 16 1807, at Washington, Vermont 2 Peter R married Lavinia Winship, of Lexington, died May, 1875, buried at Mt Auburn 3 Daniel, married Mary Jackson, of Boston, died at Newton, 1860 4 Walter, born January 13 1796, died August 22, 1869, married Jane Merriam born July 13 1797, died May 23 1873 5 William, mentioned below 6 Nancy, married —— Hatch of New York 7 Mary, married Daniel Learned 8 Hannah married Reuben Hastings, of Northboro 9 Abigail, died unmarried 10 Persis, married Coolidge Jones, and died of consumption soon after her marriage

(VIII) William Stone son of John Stone (7), born at Sudbury May 13 1787 died there March 10 1862 He followed his father's business of keeping hotel and was proprietor of taverns at Wayland Sudbury and Stow He was an earnest worker and became well-to-do He married October 25, 1805 Sukey Cutter, born February 6, 1786 at Sudbury and died there January 18 1871 Their children 1 Dana mentioned below 2 Emeline Susan, born October 16, 1808, married Abel Dakin of Wayland and (second) Walter Rogers of Sudbury, July 10, 1855 3 William born December 2 1810, unmarried died at sea on whaling voyage and buried in Indian Ocean 4 John born November 8 1812, at Stow, died April 15, 1892 5 George W, born January 23 1815 died September 30 1871, married Maria Dudley, born at Wayland 1835 died July 10 1889 6 Albina born September 5 1817, married Warren Barker Hale June 29 1834

(IX) Dana Stone, son of William Stone (8), born at Stow Massachusetts, February 19 1806 He attended the common schools at Sudbury He worked at farming at Marlboro and Wayland, and also engaged in stage driving After his first wife's death he settled in Northboro He died June 1883 He married first Mary A Whitney a native of Weston Massachusetts and descendant of John Whitney of Watertown the immigrant ancestor of most of the Massachusetts families of Whitney He died June 1883 In his younger days he was in the state militia and trained for many years He was at one time road commissioner of the town of Northboro He was first a Whig in politics later a Democrat He attended the Unitarian church He married (second) Mary Newton of Northboro (third) Lois Newton of the same town and (fourth) Mrs Nancy Rogers also of Northboro Children of Dana and Mary A (Whitney) Stone 1 George Dana, born November 10 1833 resided in Northboro 2 Mary Ann born October 1, 1835, married Emery Coolidge who held a position on a transatlantic steamship and crossed the ocean over a hundred times, both died at Northboro 3 John Alphonzo, born December 25, 1836 resided in Hudson, Massachusetts 4 Susan Ellen, born October 27, 1838, died a young lady 5 William, born November 11, 1839, died when about thirty years old 6 Louise, born October 17, 1841 married Albert Wheelock, and resided in Shrewsbury 7 Lyman T mentioned below 8 Lavinia, born May 25, 1846, married Joseph Fairbanks, and resides in Worcester

(IX) Lyman T Stone, son of Dana Stone (8), was born in Northboro, Massachusetts, April 23, 1843 and attended the public schools there He began life on a farm, but when a young man learned the trade of butcher When the civil war broke out he enlisted in Company A, Fifty-first Regiment Massachusetts Volunteer Infantry, with which he served for a period of eleven months, and was honorably discharged at the end of his term of enlistment He returned to Massachusetts and settled in Boylston, where he bought a farm and combined with farming the business of butcher and dealer in meats and provisions, and he has acquired a competence In politics he is a Republican, and he has served the town very acceptably as highway commissioner He attends the Unitarian church He married October 1 1867 Mary E, daughter of Henry Southwick, a native of Connecticut Their children 1 Theodore H, born July 4, 1868, died November 2, 1901 married Bernice Peckham, and had one son, Ernest W 2 Louis C, born February 13, 1870, married Amy Taylor 3 Lois M, born November 25 1871 4 Carrie E, born February 26, 1873, married Ernest Doty, and had one daughter, Clarissa 5 Alfred A, born March 20 1876 6 Herman H, born May 30, 1878, enlisted in Twenty-second Regiment United States Infantry, afterwards in the Twelfth Infantry, killed in the Phillipine Islands, October 27, 1899 7 Angie B, born March 20, 1888 married George Bruseau 8 Laura A, born June 28, 1884, married Rupert Smith, and they have two children Bernard R and Ethel Irene

EDWARD FOSTER BISCO Edward Bisco(1), is the first known ancestor of Edward Foster Bisco, of Worcester, and the Bisco family of Worcester county, Massachusetts The usual form of the name is Biscoe Edward Bisco lived at Little Missenden in Bucks county, England He died in May, 1563, and was buried June 1 1563 His wife was probably Ann, who was buried at Little Missenden, April 22, 1561 Their children were 1 Thomas, of Little Missenden, tanner, buried there December 3, 1594, died without issue, married November 25, 1565 Lettice Randall, daughter of John Randall of Little Missenden, and wife Joyce, she died February, 1598-9, both left wills 2 Robert, settled in Wendover, Bucks county, and was a tanner 3 Elizabeth born at Missenden buried there February 17, 1597-8, married Hugh Venables, July 6, 1567, at Little Missenden 4 Agnes, buried at Amersham, September 2, 1596, will dated July 30, 1596, married Thomas Webbe of Agmondesham, Bucks county, September 16, 1567 5 John, married Joan Randall

(II) John Bisco, son of Edward Bisco (1), lived at Little Missenden He was a yeoman He died June 3, 1606, his will was dated May 27, 1606, and was proved July 8 1606 He owned lands at Agmondesham from his mother's estate He married Joan Randall, July 18 1567, at Little Missenden Her will is dated March 13 1617-8, and was proved 1622 Children of John and Joan (Randall) Bisco were 1 Edward, baptized at Little Missenden, July 31, 1569 married Alice Taylor 2 Richard, baptized Little Missenden, March 2, 1567 3 Robert, baptized Little Missenden, February 2, 1571-2, died September 16, 1630, will dated September 14, 1630, proved October 25, 1630, lived at High Wycombe, Bucks county, was gentleman and sometime alderman, married Joan Hell, widow, at Little Missenden, August 11, 1596, married (second) Susan, daughter of Thomas Lane, of Northdeane, parish of Hughenden, Bucks county yeoman, who died in 1615, Agnes Lane, his wife, died 1636, Susan (Lane) Bisco's will was dated April 9, 1648, proved May 17, 1648 4 John, baptized Little Missenden, January 30, 1574-5, buried there March 13, following 5 Richard, baptized Little Missenden, May 6, 1576 6 John, baptized Little Missenden, September 21, 1578, buried there August 17, 1615, will made August 7, proved September 27, 1615, married Elizabeth —— 7 Jane, baptized Little Missenden, January 29, 1581-2, married there October 12, 1601, Henry Edlyn, both living May 27, 1606 8 Joan, baptized Little Missenden, 1583, buried there November 12, 1583 9 Elizabeth, baptized Little Missenden July 31, 1587

(III) Edward Bisco, son of John Bisco (2), baptized Little Missenden, July 31, 1569, resided in Agmondesham, Buckshire, England, buried at Amersham, October 26, 1605, will dated October 18, 1605, proved January 20, 1605-6, married Alice, daughter of Henry Taylor, he was buried at Little Missenden, July 3, 1610, she married (second) John Randall, at Little Missenden, March 3, between 1603 and 1606 Children of Edward and Alice (Taylor) Bisco 1 Nathaniel, baptized Little Missenden November 16, 1595, emigrated to New England 1639, and was in Watertown 1643, returned to England about the end of 1651, married October 21, 1615, Elizabeth, daughter of Henry Honor, yeoman (who was buried at Little Missenden, April 23, 1623), Elizabeth died at Watertown, buried there November 20, 1642 2 Sarah, baptized Amersham, February 26, 1597-8 3 Rebecca, twin sister of preceding, baptized Amersham, February 26, 1597-8, buried there March 19 same year 4 Rebecca, baptized Amersham, September 21, 1602 5 John, baptized April 27, 1600, resided St Margaret's, Westminster, London, citizen and apothecary of London, buried November 14, 1644, married Elizabeth, daughter of Thomas Gabriell, November 14, 1626, she married (second) Christopher Thomlinson citizen and draper of London, who was buried at Bunhill Fields, 1680-1 6 Phebe, born 1594, Little Missenden, died young 7 Walter, baptized Amersham, December 16, 1604, buried there February 27, 1604-5

(IV) Nathaniel Bisco, son of Edward Bisco (3), baptized Little Missenden, England, November 16, 1595, emigrated to New England 1639 In 1642 he wrote and circulated privately a pamphlet against the way of supporting ministers" that gave great offense, and for which he was fined ten pounds In that year his barn with leather and corn to the value of two hundred pounds was destroyed by fire He was so dissatisfied with the prevailing religious intolerance that he returned to England about the end of 1651 He sold to John Wincol, October 2 1651, the forty-six acres of land that he had bought of the town His son, Nathaniel Bisco, Jr was one of the witnesses on the deed He wrote a letter, dated London, September 7, 1652, which fell into the hands of the government and produced some excitement at the time In that letter he mentions his uncle, Richard Bisco (or Briscoe, as he usually spelled the name) who died a little before the date of the letter Nathaniel left his four grown children in Massachusetts when he returned to England, and from them have descended the American Bisco families His wife died at Watertown, and was buried there November 20, 1642 He was commonly known both in England and America as 'the Rich Tanner" His children were 1 Nathaniel, baptized Little Missenden, May 18, 1629, mentioned in his father's letter and by Governor Winthrop as a gentleman born, was the first usher of Nathaniel Eaton, the first person who had charge of the institution" (i e Harvard College) 2 Mary, married Thomas Broughton, one of the witnesses to the deed of sale of the elder Nathaniel Bisco's property when he returned to England (Broughton first settled, but in 1650 removed to Boston, where he died November 12, 1700, aged eighty-seven, had nine children) Mary was baptized in Little Missenden, England, September 16, 1619, Thomas Broughton was the son of Edward Broughton of London 3 John, born 1622, baptized June 13, 1623 4 Sarah, baptized Little Missenden, May 7, 1626, married William Bond, Esq, from whom Dr Henry Bond, the genealogist and historian, is descended, they had nine children, she died February, 1692-3

(V) John Bisco, son of Nathaniel Bisco (4), the emigrant, baptized June 23, 1623, at Little Missended, came to New England in 1639 with his father and mother He learned his father's trade of tanner He was admitted a freeman of Watertown, Massachusetts, April 18, 1650 He married, December 13, 1650, Elizabeth Bidleston, she died August 18, 1685, and he died October 18, 1690 His will, dated October 15, 1690, and proved November 21st, following, appointed his sons-in-law, Abraham Jackson and Edward Goffe, executors He was selectman several times between 1650 and 1680, and was designated as Mr Bisco when the term Mr indicated a class distinction Children of John and Elizabeth (Bidleston) Bisco 1 John, born October 5, 1651, died young 2 Elizabeth, born December 18, 1653, married, November 20, 1679, Abraham Jackson (born 1655, died 1739, son of Deacon Edward Jackson), had eleven children 3 Thomas, born April 1, 1655 4 Mary, born November 22, 1658, married Edward Goffe (born November 28, 1658, son of Samuel and Hannah (Barnard) Goffe of Cambridge, tanner, died about 1691 5 Sarah, born March 14, 1661, died 1669

(VI) Thomas Bisco, son of John Bisco (5), born Watertown, Massachusetts, April 1, 1655, died previous to October 15, 1690 He married, December 24, 1684, Hannah, daughter of Samuel and Hannah (Manning) Stearns Hannah Manning was eldest daughter of William and Dorothy Manning of Cambridge, and was born June 21, 1642 Hannah Stearns was born December 8, 1666 Samuel Stearns was the sixth child of Isaac and Mary Stearns, and was born April 24, 1638, died August 3, 1683 Isaac was from Stoke Nayland, Suffolk county, was a freeman of Watertown May 18, 1631, town officer, tailor by trade, married Mary, daughter of John Barker, of Stoke Nayland He died 1693, and Hannah Biscoe, his widow, took out letters of administration January 1, 1693-4 She married (second), September 28, 1708, Samuel Gookin, Esq, high sheriff of Middlesex Children of Thomas and Hannah (Stearns) Bisco 1 John born October 22, 1685 2 Elizabeth, baptized July 17, 1687 3 Thomas, baptized May, 1689

(VII) John Bisco, son of Thomas Bisco (6), born Watertown Massachusetts, October 22 1685, he married, in Cambridge Massachusetts February 1, 1710-11, Sarah Remington His will is dated September 6 1714 and proved January 8, 1714-5 After the birth of his first child he removed to Cambridge, where he was living at the time of his death His children 1 Thomas, born Watertown, November 11, 1711 2 Name unknown 3 Elizabeth, born 1713, June 3, 1734, chose for her guardian Samuel Danforth, she resided in Reading in 1738

(VIII) Thomas Bisco, son of John Bisco (7), born Watertown, November 11, 1711, married, June 14, 1737, Abigail Mason, born in Watertown, October 10 1715, daughter of Joseph and Mary (Monk) Mason Joseph first settled in Boston and later at Watertown, where he was justice of the peace, town clerk, representative 1733 and 1734 Mary Monk was daughter of Elias and Hope Monk, of that part of Dorchester now called Stoughton Joseph Mason was son of Joseph Mason and his wife, Mary Fiske, and was born October 2, 1688 Mary Fiske, born July 5, 1661, was daughter of John Fiske, born 1619 John Fiske was born in England, married December 11 1651, Sarah Wyeth, eldest child of Nicholas Wyeth of Cambridge, Massachusetts Joseph Mason, Sr, was son of Capt Hugh Mason, one of the first settlers of Watertown, Massachusetts, and most prominent among the pioneers, deputy to general court ten years, selectman twenty-nine years, made captain May 5, 1652, died October 10, 1678, aged seventy-three, wife Esther died May 1, 1692 Children of Thomas and Abigail (Mason) Bisco 1 John born Watertown, April 10, 1738 2 Josiah, born July 18, 1740, settled at Watertown, married, September 30, 1765, Grace Whitney, she died April 30, 1773, and he married Mary, daughter of Joseph and Grace (Bond) Mason, December 1762 he returned from Woodstock, Connecticut to Watertown

(IX) John Bisco, son of Thomas Bisco (8), born Watertown, April 10, 1738 He was a soldier at Lake George, 1756-7 He removed to Spencer, Massachusetts 1763 He married, May 10, 1764, Deborah Prouty, born October 19, 1742, daughter of Jacob and Ann (Capen) Prouty, of Spencer She died December 22 1795 and he married (second), November 1795 Mrs Esther Moore of Worcester He died November 15, 1808 He settled in the central part of the town on the farm still known as the Bisco farm The history of Spencer says He was a gentleman of good education, sound judgment and unblemished character" He had the respect and confidence of his townsmen to an unusual degree He held the highest offices of honor and trust From 1767 until his death he was town clerk, selectman, assessor or treasurer He was representative in general court 1777, 1780, 1781 and member of state constitutional convention 1779 He was appointed justice of the peace, with the duties of magistrate by Governor John Hancock in March, 1781 He was deacon of the Spencer church "As a magistrate he was correct faithful and impartial, as a churchman he was devout, pious and exemplary as a citizen and man he was honest, dignified and patriotic" (From the inscription on his gravestone) Children of Deacon John and Deborah (Prouty) Bisco 1 John, born May 29, 1765 died May, 1812 unmarried 2 Elizabeth born October 9 1767 married July 15, 1690, Enoch Mason son of Capt Ebenezer Mason who removed from Watertown to Spencer she died in Nelson New York 3 Abijah born February 7 1770, graduated Dartmouth College 1798, candidate for ministry but died 1801 before he was settled 4 Jacob born June 12, 1772 married January 1 1700 Sarah daughter of Capt John Draper 5 Abigail, born July 25 1777, married November 7 1799 David Prouty, Jr son of Major David Prouty she died April 22 1846 6 Anne born March 8, 1780 married December 13, 1807 George W Harwood son of Maj Peter Harwood, of Brookfield, Massachusetts

Dwight Bisco

(X) Jacob Bisco, son of John Bisco (9), born Spencer, Massachusetts June 12, 1772, married Sarah, daughter of Capt John Draper He inherited his father's homestead, and lived and died in Spencer He died April 7, 1837, aged sixty-five years His wife Sarah died May 27, 1855 Children of Jacob Bisco 1 Dwight, see forward 2 Chloe, born August 20, 1800, married, August 18, 1818, Spencer Prouty, son of Reuben and Sally (Bartlett) Prouty He was born at Marlboro, Vermont, September 20, 1796 She died February 22, 1823, at Spencer 3 Adeline, born November 16, 1801 married, May 18, 1817, Abiathar Johnson son of Abiathar and Meribah (Fuller) Johnson, he was born at Weston, Massachusetts, September 30, 1795, died at Worcester, November 6, 1863, she died at North Brookfield, Massachusetts, September 14, 1827 4 Foster, born July 10, 1803 (died at Spencer, June 18, 1881), married, September 16, 1830 Eunice Whipple Rice, daughter of Jonas and Esther (Bixby) Rice, of Worcester, she was born at Worcester, December 25, 1802, died at Spencer, January 17, 1863, he married (second), October 27, 1864, Mrs Eliza Wallis, of Cherry Valley, Leicester, who was born June 2, 1813, and died at Spencer, March 24 1877, he married (third), June 26, 1877, Martha Cecilia Rising daughter of Julius and Statia Rising, she was born at West Suffield Connecticut, November 11, 1832 5 Emily, born September 10, 1804, married, 1827, Liberty Prouty, son of Eli and Rebekah (Browning) Prouty, he was born at Spencer, July 1, 1800, died at Spencer, February 27, 1854, she died at Spencer, April 6, 1857 6 Alden born October 25, 1806, married, August 17, 1833, Selinda Martin, of Oxford, Massachusetts, she was born February 24, 1810, died at Melrose Massachusetts, May 19, 1874, he died at Leicester, January 11, 1843 7 John, born October 9 1808, married, November 25, 1835, Letitia Moore Lee, of Woodbridge, New Jersey she was born December 30, 1816, died in New York city, March 18, 1892, he died at New York city February 7, 1895 8 Hull, born November 10, 1810 died unmarried at Spencer, April 23 1836 9 Roswell, born April 16 1813, married, August 9, 1838, Abigail Watson Whittemore, daughter of Daniel and Fanny (Prouty) Whittemore, she was born in Spencer October 13 1818, died May 10, 1886, he died May 5, 1896 10 Lavinia Bisco born August 16 1815, married, May 10, 1838, Reuben Randall Hills, son of Nathaniel and Mary (Randall) Hills, he was born at Richmond, New Hampshire, March 5, 1812, died at Leicester, April 5, 1893, she died at Leicester, April 30, 1901, they celebrated their golden wedding May 10, 1888 11 Jacob born October 8, 1817, married April 15, 1849, Emeline Statia Rising, daughter of Julius and Statia Rising she was born at West Suffield Connecticut, June 7, 1827 he died at Dudley, Massachusetts, March 25, 1896

(XI) Dwight Bisco son of Jacob Bisco (10), was born at Spencer, Massachusetts, April 27, 1799 For sixty years he was one of the leading citizens and business men of the town of Leicester, which adjoins Spencer, his native place He was raised in Spencer and worked on his father's farm until twenty-two years of age, when with a silver dollar (as his biographer Rev Samuel May put it) as his only money capital, he came to Leicester and went to work for Cheney Hatch manufacturer of card clothing—a business of which at that time Leicester had almost a monopoly "Bringing with him" Mr May says, "good character, intelligence habits of industry and self-control and not afraid of work, he steadily acquired skill in this intricate and difficult manufacture" In 1826 he associated himself as partner with Isaac Southgate, Joshua Lamb, John Stone and Joseph A Denny (See Denny Family), another house in the same business In 1843 Mr Denny and he bought the interests of the other partners and continued the business under the name of Bisco & Denny until Mr Denny's death in 1875 It was then passed on by Mr Bisco into the hands of his sons and of Mr Denny's only son, he continuing to occupy himself in the factory until February, 1882, when he withdrew entirely He was then in his eighty-third year In middle life he had invested the chief part of his savings in the Leicester Boot Company It was unfortunate, and was brought to end by the burning of the company's buildings and stock The investment was a total loss Mr May says that with quiet courage he applied himself again to business as closely as in his youth, and was enabled in a few years to make good his loss and to present to his eight children at a Thanksgiving dinner table, $500 each He was a leader in town affairs repeatedly a selectman of the town, a member of the state legislature in 1847 and 1848, director of the Leicester Bank for eleven years and treasurer of the Pine Grove Cemetery Company for forty years, deacon of the Unitarian Congregational church, and for forty years the treasurer

He married, at Leicester, Massachusetts Ruth Woodcock, daughter of John Woodcock, Sr, and sister of John, Josephus and Lucius Woodcock, January 8, 1826, and they lived together more than fifty years when they celebrated their golden wedding, January 8, 1876 "we saw them," says Rev Mr Coolidge, "standing together a spectacle rarely witnessed, an unbroken family"—parents, children and grandchildren—a circle which death had then never entered But in September of that year Mrs Bisco died She was born in Rutland, Massachusetts, December 13, 1802, and died in Leicester, September 20, 1876 Mr Bisco died December 7, 1882 In a notice of him in the *Christian Register*, Abraham Firth wrote of his public life, of "his marked faithfulness in all these relations and in every sphere of life in which he moved He was always found on the side of virtue and of political and spiritual freedom Brought up under the teaching of Calvinism, it never satisfied him" One who was long in daily business association with him wrote in the *Worcester Spy* "he was known among his associates as an honest, upright man, of superior sense and judgment" His pastor, during his later years, wrote of him, "I have never known a truer man, nor one of greater strength of character" A memorial book of Mr and Mrs Dwight Bisco has been published

The children of Dwight and Ruth (Woodcock) Bisco were 1 Emily Avesta, born April 11, 1826, married, August 29, 1848, Josiah Quincy Lamb, son of Liberty and Harriet (Stone) Lamb, of Oxford; she died at Webster, February 4, 1895, he was born at Oxford May 9 1823, died at Webster, February 23, 1886, their children Clara Adeline Lamb, born at Webster, October 7, 1849, married William Morris, and had Alice Josephine, born June 2, 1877, Ruth Anna Lamb, born March 26, 1855, married, January 22, 1884, Charles Herman Klebart, son of Henry and Johanna Dorothy (Lippold) Klebart, who was born in Reitherback, Germany, December 25, 1841, and their children are Arthur Herman Klebart born at Webster, February 10, 1885, Leroy Elmer, born at Webster August 5, 1886, died August 25, 1886, Marion Emily, born March 15 1888, Louise Frances, born June 10, 1893 2 Charles Dwight, see forward 3 George, born November

8, 1830. married, November 24 1853, Ellen Josephine Hill, daughter of Stephen and Charlotte (Lamb) Hill, she was born in Portsmouth, New Hampshire, July 6, 1835, they resided in Manchester, New Hampshire, where they celebrated their golden wedding November 26, 1903, their only child, Charles Edwin, born July 31 1856, resides at Manchester John Waldo, born July 10, 1834, married, July 0, 1857, Ellen Maria Eames, daughter of William A and Hannah Park (Waite) Eames, she was born t Worcester, December 30, 1837, he resided in Worcester and there died December 1, 1904, their only hild, Annie Louise born June 15, 1862, married, une 20, 1882, Joseph Bradford Sargent (See Sarent sketch) 5 William, see forward 6 Henry, see forward 7 Edward F, see forward 8 Fred Alden, born February 25, 1847, married, June 6 1881, Abbie Eliza Hodges daughter of Ira and ane Hodges, she was born in Winslow, Maine, anuary 28, 1859, he died in Leicester, June 5, 1891, hey had two children Frederick Raymond, born t Leicester, January 19. 1883, died October 31, 1905, aura Rosamond, born in Leicester, May 28, 1884

(XII) Charles Dwight Bisco. second child of Dwight Bisco (11), was born in Leicester, January , 1828 He married November 29, 1853, Elizabeth Ann Outley, at St Louis, she was born in Dublin, reland August 15 1833 died at New Orleans, Lousiana, December 6, 1880 He died at Newark, New ersey, December 3, 1895 Their children were 1 Harry Dwight, born at St Louis, October 26, 1854, arried, April 26, 1876, Libby Carpenter, of Troy, New York, daughter of William O Carpenter, he ied at New York city, September 27, 1890 2 oseph Outley, born March 24, 1858 3 Agnes Louise. born June 25 1866, married, December 25, 886 Horace Hurlburt Mitchell, one child, Marguerite Frances Mitchell, born in Newark, New ersey July 22, 1888

(XI) William Bisco, fifth child of Dwight Bisco 11), was born in Leicester, February 21, 1839 He received a common school education in his native town At the age of sixteen he began his apprenticeship in he card clothing manufactory of his father at Leicester He became a skilful card machine operator and continued in this occupation until the business was sold in 1890 to the American Card Clothing Company William and in fact all his brothers xcept Edward learned the trade of their father, erving a three years apprenticeship Mr Bisco ever married He was a quiet studious disposition nd a love of nature that has been like an avocation o him He is a skilful painter in oil and water olors and is especially fond of painting flowers Mr Bisco is also interested in genealogy and local istory He is the family historian and has collected a vast amount of material about the family, nd also incidentally about matters of local interst He has some very valuable scrap-books for ny student of Leicester history He lives in the ouse in which he was born in Leicester with his rother, Henry Bisco The homestead is full of reasures of antique furniture, plate and china anded down for many generations Mr Bisco has mong other articles of family interest the Bisco oat-of-arms painted in colors on parchment The rms are Az three greyhounds courant sa seizng a hare ppr The family motto is "Grata sume manu" He is a member of the Young Men's Chrisian Association of Worcester, and of the First Congregational Church of Leicester In politics he is a Republican

(XII) Henry Bisco, sixth child of Dwight Bisco (11), was born in Leicester, March 19, 1841 He attended the public schools of his native town and also Leicester Academy in 1859 and 1860 At the age of sixteen he was apprenticed for three years, and except for the three months in winter while school kept he worked at his trade until he enlisted He earned fifty dollars the first year, seventy-five dollars the second and one hundred and twenty-five dollars the third year He served in the civil war in Company F of the Forty-second Massachusetts Volunteer Infantry, under Captain John D Cogswell and Colonel Isaac Burrill When he was mustered out of the service he went back to Leicester and has worked at his trade ever since He is an expert card machine operator He continued with the American Card Clothing Company after his father's business was absorbed by that concern in 1890 He worked in the central factory in Leicester until March 1905, since then he has worked in the Worcester factory Mr Bisco lives in the Bisco homestead and has inherited many rare specimens of antique colonial furniture, china, pewter, etc He is a member of Quinsigamond Lodge of Free Masons of Worcester, and has been president of the Leicester Masonic Association He is at present quartermaster sergeant of George H Thomas Post, No 10, Grand Army of the Republic, and has filled about all the chairs He was for seven years the commander In politics he is an independent and in religion a Unitarian He has for some years been treasurer of the Unitarian church at Leicester He organized the relief corps connected with the Grand Army post while he was the commander, and his wife was the first president It is called George H Thomas Relief Corps, No 152

He married (first), at Ware, Massachusetts, August 29, 1864, Laura Melvinia Stowe, daughter of John T and Lavinia Stowe She was born in Grafton, July 31, 1846, died at Leicester, September 29, 1884 He married (second), at Worcester, June 16, 1887, Moselle Olmstead, daughter of Sylvanus Eaton and Anna R (Dean) Olmstead She was born in New Braintree November 20 1858 The children of Henry and Laura M Bisco were Alice Maria, born August 6, 1868, Herbert Henry, born at Leicester, October 8, 1876

(XII) Edward Foster Bisco son of Dwight Bisco (11), was born in Leicester, Massachusetts, February 19, 1844 He was brought up in his native town and attended the public schools there He graduated from the high school in 1862, and went into the Leicester Bank (later the Leicester National Bank) to learn the banking business In October 1865, he took a position in the National Park Bank of New York city, where he gained valuable metropolitan experience filling various positions there until July 1, 1872, when he was elected secretary of the Worcester Safe Deposit and Trust Company to succeed the late Samuel T Bigelow He came to Worcester at that time, and has since made his home there He was secretary of this trust company until October, 1891, when he was elected president In 1903 there was a revolution in the banking business of Worcester The controlling interests in the Worcester Safe Deposit and Trust Company changed hands, and in February the Trust Company absorbed two of the largest and most prosperous national banks of the city—the Central National Bank and the City National Bank Later in the year two more banks were absorbed—the First National Bank and the Citizens' National Bank of Worcester The name was changed later to the simpler form of Worcester Trust Company When Mr Bisco became an officer of the bank in 1872 the deposits amounted to about $1 200,000 When the consolidation took place the deposits amounted to $3,300,000 After the consolidation the deposits aggregated $9,000,000 The shrewd and prudent management of Mr Bisco had much to do with bringing his bank to the foremost position among the banks and trust companies of Massachusetts, the largest outside of Boston He was called to the presidency of the Washington Trust Company of Boston, October 1, 1904 The banking rooms of this company are at 20 Milk street, Boston Mr Bisco stands in the front rank of the successful bankers of the state He has attained this position through much natural ability and constant devotion to his profession He began at the lowest round of the ladder with a salary of $100 a year, and has thoroughly deserved all the success that he has won in life Mr Bisco continues to reside at 11 Irving street, Worcester He is a member of the Commonwealth Club, and of the Tatassit Canoe Club, a trustee of the People's Savings Bank of Worcester, and commissioner under the city government of the Jacques Fund of the City Hospital He and his family attend the First Universalist Church He is a Republican He married, November 29 1866 Anna Eliza Sprague, daughter of Austin and Laura (Wilson) Sprague, of Leicester She is a descendant of William Sprague of Hingham, Massachusetts, who was a proprietor there in 1636 He was a brother of Richard Sprague and Ralph Sprague, both of Charlestown The only child of Edward Foster Bisco is Adelme Maud, who resides with her parents in Worcester

DRAPER FAMILY Thomas Draper (1), ancestor of Edward F Bisco, lived and died in Yorkshire, England, in the parish of Hempstontell and vicarage of Halifax He was a clothier by trade His children were Thomas, John, William, James, Mary, Martha, all except James died in England

(II) James Draper, son of Thomas Draper (1), born in Hempstontell England, 1618, came to Roxbury, Massachusetts, where he was a proprietor 1640-50 He was proprietor of Lancaster in 1654 He is generally known from his religious tendencies as James Draper, the Puritan His gravestone is to be seen in the West Roxbury graveyard He married ——— Stansfield, who came from the same parish in England He died July, 1691, aged seventy-seven years His children were James, John, Moses, Daniel, Jonathan

(III) James Draper, son of James Draper (2), was born about 1660 He married Abigail Whiting of Dedham He died April 30, 1698, aged forty-four years His wife died October 25 1721, aged fifty-nine Their children Nathaniel, William, James, Gideon, Ebenezer

(IV) James Draper, son of James Draper (3), born in Roxbury, Massachusetts, about 1694, married Rachel Aldrich who died early without issue He married (second) Abigail Child November 12, 1719 She was noted for musical gifts They lived in Dedham He was captain of the militia company there He died April, 1768, she died November 12, 1767 Their children 1 James born September 22, 1720, died Dedham, November 8, 1745 2 Abigail, born December 12, 1721, married Henry White 3 John, born June 16, 1723 4 Joshua, born December 25 1724 5 Josiah 6 Rachel 7 Mary 8 Abijah 9 Samuel and three others all by the second wife The first four came to Spencer, Massachusetts

(V) James Draper, son of James Draper (4), born Roxbury, Massachusetts, September 22, 1720, married Mehitable Whiting of Dedham, November 12, 1742, (second) Martha Ward widow of William Ward Jr of Southboro He died March 2, 1781 She died September, 1791 Their children were 1 Rebecca married Benjamin Bemis, Jr, November 17, 1768 2 John, born November 16, 1745 3 James, born July 24, 1747, was in the revolution 4 Ira, born February 14, 1753 5 Mehitable, born August 29, 1756, married Noah Forbush, of Brookfield, November 9, 1779

(VI) John Draper, son of James Draper (5), married Rebecca, daughter of Deacon John Muzzy December 24 1770 He died December 22, 1822 aged seventy-seven years His wife Rebecca died April 29, 1818 Their children were born in Spencer He was a private in Captain Ebenezer Mason's company of minute men, Colonel Jonathan Warner's regiment, which marched on the Lexington alarm April 19, 1775 He was sergeant in Captain Joel Green's company, Col Ebenezer Learned's regiment enlisted May 3 1775, was in Capt Josiah White's company 'Lt Col Benjamin Flagg's division, Col Samuel Denny's regiment 1777, and in Capt David Prouty's company, September 25, 1777, which marched to reinforce the Northern army The children of John Draper 1 Zenas, born May 31, 1772 married Jemima, daughter of Israel Allen 2 Olive born January 30, 1774 married Elias Hatch, November 10, 1791 3 Sarah, born August 8 1779, married Jacob Bisco (X), 1799 4 Charles, married Thomas Loring, September 28, 1803 5 Nancy, born October 28, 1783, married Samuel Gleason, February 3, 1811 6 Becca, born April 10, 1786, married January 18, 1817, Willard Prouty 7 John born July 22 1788, married Lavinia daughter of Eli Prouty, December 4 1817 8 Rhoda born July 10, 1791, married, 1817 Ebenezer Cogswell 9 Eleazer Bradshaw, born August 26, 1795, married, May 15, 1821, Louisa Prouty

(VI) Sarah Draper (or Sally), daughter of John Draper (6), born Spencer, Massachusetts, August 8 1779, married 1799, Jacob Bisco (X), grandfather of Edward F Bisco

JONATHAN NELSON FLAGG Thomas Flagg (1), immigrant ancestor of Jonathan Nelson Flagg, of Worcester is the progenitor of all the colonial families of this name in Massachusetts He was born doubtless in England, and came to America in April, 1637, in the service of Richard Carver, of Skratby England, where Flagg may have come from also Flagg was twenty-one years old, hence his year of birth was 1616 He settled at Watertown Massachusetts, and was yeoman, lieutenant, proprietor and town officer there and selectman in 1671 1674 1675 1676, and 1678 He lost his left eye by a gunshort wound previous to 1659 He died February 6, 1697-8 His will dated March 5, 1697 and proved February 16, 1697-8, bequeaths to wife Mary, sons Michael, Thomas, Eleazer, Allen and Benjamin, daughters Mary and Elizabeth Bigelow and Rebecca Cooke, grandchildren John Flagg and heirs of deceased son Gershom The widow Mary born 1619, made will December 30, 1702 proved April 21 1703 names children Mary and Elizabeth Bigelow Rebecca Cook and Benjamin Flagg Children of Thomas and Mary Flagg 1 Gershom, born April 16, 1641 2 John, born June 14, 1643 died February 6 1696-7 3 Bartholomew, born February 23 1644-5 4 Thomas, born April 28 1645 5 Michael, born March 23 1650-1, died October 16, 1711, was one of the earliest proprietors of Worcester at the first attempt to settle 6 Eleazer born May 14, 1653 ancestor of many Worcester county families 7 Elizabeth, born March 22, 1654-5, died August 9, 1729, married Joshua Bigelow, settled at Worcester and Westminster 8 Mary born June 14, 1657, died September 7, 1720 9 Rebecca, born

September 5, 1660, married Deacon Stephen Cook 10 Benjamin, mentioned below 11 Allen, born May 16, 1665, died November 17, 1711

(II) Benjamin Flagg, son of Thomas Flagg (1), was born June 25, 1662 He removed to Worcester and settled there as one of the early proprietors, was admitted a freeman April 19, 1690, and died there May 3, 1741 He married, September 26, 1690, Experience, daughter of Richard Child, of Watertown She died at Worcester, 1747 Children of Benjamin Flagg and wife Experience 1 Benjamin, born August 25 1691, died at Worcester June 12, 1751, selectman, captain, sheriff 2 Experience, born May 5, 1693, married, October 26, 1713, Caleb Ball, of Concord 3 Abigail, born April 16, 1694-5 4 Bartholomew, born November 16, 1697, mariner of Bristol 5 Elizabeth, born December 28, 1699, married Peter King 6 Gershom, mentioned below 7 Mary, baptized April 9, 1704 8 Ebenezer, born January 21, 1705-6 9 Richard, born May 30, 1708, lieutenant Holden company, died November 12, 1799, aged ninety-two years, he settled in Holden, and his son was Colonel Samuel, who was selectman of Worcester 1790-1808, owned 240 acres on Green street

(III) Gershom Flagg son of Benjamin Flagg (2), born in Watertown, Massachusetts, July 11, 1702, removed to Worcester with his father and settled in the adjoining town of Shrewsbury He had lot No 36 in Shrewsbury in 1729 He married Hannah daughter of Captain John Keyes, January 6, 1725 Their children all born in Shrewsbury, were 1 Persis, born June 8, 1726 2 Stephen, mentioned below 3 Jotham born July 30, 1730, married Rebecca Kendall 4 Solomon, born March 6, 1733 5 Gershom, Jr, born January 1, 1735 6 Thankful, born January 21, 1739

(IV) Stephen Flagg, son of Gershom Flagg (3), born in Shrewsbury, Massachusetts, July 22, 1728, settled there and married December 6, 1750 Judith, daughter of Eleazer Taylor She died in Boylston, February 21, 1810, aged eighty years Their children all born at Shrewsbury, were 1 John, October 4, 1751 2 Solomon, August 13, 1753 died 1756 3 Stephen, March 23 1755, died 1758 4 Judith, March 6, 1757, married 1777 Samuel Andrews 5 Stephen mentioned below 6 John, December 21, 1760, died January 30, 1785 7 Solomon, April 21, 1764, died July 5, 1810, married, October 17, 1789, Rebecca Dakin 8 Benjamin, May 25, 1766 9 Lucretia, June 2, 1768 10 Gershom, September 2, 1770

(V) Stephen Flagg, Jr, son of Stephen Flagg (4) born June 8 1759, at Shrewsbury, died at Boylston May 25, 1828, aged sixty-nine years He settled in Boylston, formerly Shrewsbury, North District He was a soldier in the revolution, in Captain Asa Rice's company Colonel Job Cushing's regiment, in 1777, at the Bennington Alarm, also in Captain Joseph Warren's company, Lieutenant-Colonel Wheelock's regiment, with the rank of corporal, 1777, also in Captain David Moore's company, Colonel John Jacob's regiment Light Infantry, in Rhode Island campaign 1779 He married Betsey ——, who died April 1, 1838, aged seventy-seven years Their children were 1 Abijah, mentioned below 2 John, born May 9, 1790 3 David February 17, 1794 4 Stephen, March 14, 1796, died August 30, 1849 at Boylston 5 Mary (Polly), February 19, 1783 married —— Gough, who was the father of John B Gough the great temperance orator 6 Betty, March 17, 1787 7 Sally, November 22, 1789 8 Dolly October 18 1788 9 Lydia, April 27, 1792, married Benjamin Fassett

(VI) Deacon Abijah Flagg, son of Stephen Flagg (5), born in Boylston, Massachusetts, August 27, 1784 died there December, 1850 He was a farmer through his active life A man of strong religious views, he served the First Congregational Church at Boylston as deacon His farm is at present occupied by Montraville Flagg In politics he was a Whig He trained with the militia company of Boylston He married Mary, born February 18, 1786, died March 3, 1863, aged seventy-six years, daughter of James Longley, a very prominent citizen, representative to general court thirteen years, town treasurer, selectman eighteen years, and chairman of the board thirteen years, assessor seventeen years and chairman twelve member of school committee, justice of the peace (See Longley family) Children of Deacon Abijah and Mary Flagg 1 William Frederick, born at Boylston, April 2, 1808, and had children Sarah, Fanny, Edward 2 Montraville, born at Boylston January 31, 1810, died February 17, 1888, married Parney Houghton, of Boylston 3 Nahum, mentioned below 4 John Dexter, born August 3 1815, married Elizabeth Davenport, children—John Nathaniel, George Abijah, Estella V, Harriet F, Mary Maria 5 Mary, married —— Stewart 6 Israel, died aged eighteen years

(VII) Nahum Flagg, son of Deacon Abijah Flagg (6), was born at Boylston, Massachusetts, July 15, 1811 and died April 1 1862 He was educated in the common schools of his native town and began life on his father's farm He followed farming through his active life on the part of the homestead which he inherited He purchased large tracts of woodland which he cut off at various times and sold to good advantage The farm was divided before the father's death between Nahum and his brother Montraville, each working his part separately He was a member of the Boylston Congregational church and served on the parish committee In politics he was a Republican He served the town as highway surveyor In early life he was in the militia He married, at Worcester, Hannah Brackett Nelson, born June 13 1812, daughter of Jonathan and Hannah (Nelson) Nelson, of Upton, Massachusetts Their children 1 Jonathan Nelson, born May 3, 1840 mentioned below 2 Emma Elizabeth, born September 27, 1842

(VIII) Jonathan Nelson Flagg, son of Nahum Flagg (7), was born at Boylston May 3 1840 He was educated in the common schools of that town and at the Worcester Academy He then taught school at Lonsdale, Rhode Island, for two winters, working at home on his father's farm in the summers In 1860 and 1861 he taught school at Rutland Massachusetts, and later at Boylston until he was twenty-six years old After his father's death he carried on the homestead until 1867, when he sold it He bought another farm at West Boylston and conducted it two years August 23, 1870, he entered the employ of the United States and Canada Express Company at Worcester as messenger, a position that he filled for seventeen years In July 1887, he accepted the position of janitor of the Worcester County Mechanics' Association in charge of Mechanics' Hall, Worcester and has filled that position to the present time He is a member of Central Congregational Church, Worcester In politics he is a Republican, and has frequently been elected delegate to various nominating conventions He was collector of taxes in Boylston two years, and member of the school committee there for five years He is a member of Worcester Lodge, No 56, I O O F, and of Wachusett Encampment, No 10, of which he has been an officer, and of the Worcester County Mechanics' Association He married first, September

7, 1867, M Edna Andrews, born in Boylston, July 7, 1842, daughter of Robert and Martha (Toombs) Andrews Her father was a farmer He married (second) June 4 1879, Anna Belle daughter of John and Olive (Hobbs) Drew, of Somersworth, New Hampshire Her father was a foreman in machine works there, and later at the navy yard at Porthmouth, New Hampshire Children of Jonathan Nelson and M Edna Flagg 1 Robert Nelson, born July 9, 1870 2 Lucy Edna, August 16, 1871, died March 20, 1872

GEORGE A FLAGG of the same family, traces his line to Benjamin Flagg (5), son of Stephen Flagg (4), who was born May 25, 1766, at Shrewsbury, Massachusetts He settled in the north precinct of Shrewsbury, now Boylston He married August 26, 1787, Persis Dakin, at Boylston, and she died March 24 1848 aged seventy-nine years, at Boylston Their children were Lucretia, born November 24, 1787, Joseph, of whom later, Hepzibah December 13, 1791, Benjamin, January 2, 1794, Judith, March 13, 1796, Levi, April 21, 1798, Seth, July 15, 1800, Sally, February 19, 1803, Persis, March 5, 1809

(VI) Joseph Flagg, son of Benjamin Flagg (5), was born at Boylston Massachusetts, October 22, 1789 He settled in his native town and was a farmer He was a highly respected citizen He married Patty Hastings, December 26, 1815 Their children, all born at Boylston, were Persis, December 23 1816, Levi Lincoln, of whom later Mary Martha March 23, 1820, Edward Whipple June 7, 1822, Ezra Hastings, November 1, 1823, Seth Alden, December 22, 1825, Henry Martin, August 19, 1830, Cleora Maria, August 1, 1833

(VII) Levi Lincoln Flagg son of Joseph Flagg (6), was born in Boylston, Massachusetts, September 20, 1818 He attended the district schools of his native town and of Shrewsbury and then went to work in the good old way, as a farm hand For the first two years he worked for neighboring farmers for the sum of eight dollars per month with board His next position brought him one hundred and sixty dollars per year With money saved by frugal management from this small income, he bought the homestead of his father and thereafter he divided his time between the farm and the live-stock business in both of which he was successful financially He is living on his farm at Boylston, at present, active in spite of his advanced age

He is a Republican in politics and has always been active in public affairs He was assessor for twenty-five years, representative to the general court and for a period of thirty years was on the board of selectmen of the town of Boylston a remarkable tribute on the part of his fellow-townsmen to his ability and good judgment, such as few men in any town of the Commonwealth have ever received A service of thirty years is sometimes found in the offices of town clerk or town treasurer, but the instances of such long service as that of Mr Flagg in the office of selectman are very rare in the past as well as in the present generation

He married 1847, Caroline Barnes, who died in 1872 Their children are Elmer E married Preston P Lane, and they have two children, Christopher L, Arthur, married Elizabeth Blackman and they have two children, Joseph Walter, married Isabel Whitten, George A, of whom later, Alice J married George Hazzard, and died, leaving four children, Jennie L, Mary M married Merritt Stewart and they have seven children

(VIII) George A Flagg, son of Levi Lincoln Flagg (7), was born in Boylston, Massachusetts, June 14, 1855 He was educated in the public schools of his native town For three years he remained at home after his schooling was ended and assisted his father on the farm Then he bought a farm in Boylston and conducted it on his own account In addition to his farm he has dealt to a considerable extent in cattle He is counted among the most successful and prosperous farmers of the town

Mr Flagg has invested largely in local electric railway companies, which have given such an enormous advance in the value of suburban farm property In politics Mr Flagg is a Republican and has been honored by his fellow-citizens with many positions of responsibility and trust He has served as collector of taxes, assessor, and town treasurer of Boylston He and his family attend the Congregational church

Mr Flagg married February 21, 1888 Mary L Bruseau, daughter of Joseph and Mary (Hawsville) Bruseau, of Worcester Their nine children are: Mabel, born May 4, 1888, Levi Lincoln April 16, 1890, Frank E, January 21 1892, Caroline Elizabeth, August 10, 1893, died December 1, 1900, Gertrude Elizabeth August 24, 1895, Augustus, July 21, 1897 died January 4, 1901, J Walter, July 16, 1899 George A, September 21, 1901, Henry M, October 28 1904

JOHN NATHANIEL FLAGG of the same family, is a son of John Dexter and Elizabeth (Davenport) Flagg, the former of whom was born in Boylston, August 3, 1815 Provided with a good education which was completed at Philips (Andover) Academy, he adopted agricultural as an occupation and followed it in Worcester, Westboro, Millsbury and Spencer successively John Dexter Flagg died December 23, 1893 In early life he was a member of the state militia Politically he acted with the Republican party, but never aspired to office He was an active member of the Congregational church His wife Elizabeth, who is also deceased, became the mother of six children, namely George A, Estelle V, Harriet E, Mary, Maria and John Nathaniel, the principal subject of this sketch

John Nathaniel Flagg was born in Boylston, October 12, 1854 He pursued the primary branches of his education in the public schools of his native town and completed his studies at a private school in Boston When a young man he engaged in teaming but subsequently turned his attention exclusively to agriculture in Boylston which he is now following with profit In politics he is a Republican and has served with ability as road commissioner He is a member of the local grange Patrons of Husbandry His religious affiliations are with the Congregational church Mr Flagg married January 8, 1879, Abbie Frances Ball, daughter of James Emerson Ball, a prosperous farmer of Boylston Mr and Mrs Flagg have no children

FRANK EUGENE DUNTON a manufacturer of Spencer Massachusetts, was there born August 28 1846 a son of Warren Hamilton and Eliza (Jones) Dunton, and grandson of Abner Dunton His grandfather Abner Dunton lived in Brookfield for a number of years and in March, 1807, was united in marriage to Mary Dickerman in Boston, Massachusetts His son Warren Hamilton Dunton, father of Frank E Dunton, was born in Brookfield, Massachusetts December 11 1820 He married Eliza Jones (See Erastus Jones), of Spencer, and their children were Henry Asa born 1844 died in infancy, Frank Eugene born 1846 Mary Lucy, born 1849 married Arthur M Stone, of Worcester, Massachusetts September 7, 1860 Angelina Powers born 1853 died in infancy Warren Hamilton Dunton died August 15, 1853 at the age of thirty-three years

Frank E Dunton, second son of Warren H Dunton, acquired his early education in the common schools of his native place, and later attended high school . After leaving the school room, he learned the boot manufacturing business with E Jones & Co, and in 1867 in conjunction with D A Drury, established a boot factory at Spencer in the old C & G Watson shop under the firm name of D A Drury & Co This association continued for three years, when Mr Dunton sold his interest in the business He then entered the firm of E Jones & Company, then consisting of Erastus Jones, H P Starr and F E Dunton Since Mr Starr's retiracy from the firm in 1889 the business has been conducted by Erastus Jones and F E Dunton Politically Mr Dunton is a Republican, and in religious affairs affiliates with the Congregational church, of which he was treasurer for twenty-one years He was one of the founders of Spencer National Bank and is one of its board of directors He was instrumental in establishing the Savings Bank and kept its first set of books

On June 20, 1871, Mr Dunton married Jennie L Prouty, daughter of Isaac Prouty, (See Prouty Family) and their children were Lewis W, born November 3, 1872, married June 28, 1905, Grace D Taylor, of Rockland, Maine, Charles Erastus, born December 25, 1876, married Cora M Watson, of Spencer Massachusetts, October 11, 1898, (Mrs Cora (Watson) Dunton is a daughter of Frank Boice Watson, who was a provision merchant of Spencer, Massachusetts), Florence Prouty, born September 14, 1880 Messrs Lewis W and Charles Erastus Dunton are associated with the E Jones Co, of Spencer

ABRAHAM CAPEN, for many years a well-known merchant of Spencer, Massachusetts, was born in South Spencer, November 20, 1825 son of Abraham and Lydia (Mason) Capen, of Spencer, and grandson of James Capen, a farmer of Spencer, Massachusetts His father, Abraham Capen, was a farmer of Spencer, he married for his first wife, Polly Hinds After the decease of his first wife, he married Anna Bemis, and their children were Alfred, Aurelia, Alonzo and Annie Mrs Capen died, and Mr Capen took for his third wife Lydia Mason, of Spencer and the following children were born Abraham, Mary, Eliza, Ebenezer, James and Susan

Abraham Capen, the eldest son of Abraham and Lydia (Mason) Capen, was educated in the Pine Wood school house of Spencer, and after leaving the school room worked first at farming, and then entered into the meat business, in which occupation he was engaged for twenty-three years Then the ice and coal business took up his attention for about fifteen years and he subsequently returned to farming Politically Mr Capen affiliated with the Republican party, and he was a member of the board of selectmen for ten years, also overseer of the poor He was a member of the Grange In religious affairs he accorded with the Congregational faith

Mr Capen married, September 18, 1859 Sarah L Craig of Leicester, Massachusetts the daughter of Nathan and Dulcina (Huntington) Craig The following children were born to Mr and Mrs Capen Wallace A deceased Nathan Craig, 1861, superintendent of streets of Spencer and also stock farmer of Leicester Stella Maria deceased, married Benjamin Choate Richardson, of Vermont, Clarence A, deceased

ERASTUS JONES Lewis Jones (1), the immigrant ancestor of Erastus Jones, of Spencer, Massachusetts, came from England and settled in Roxbury in New England before 1640 He was a member of the church there in 1640 He lived in Roxbury until about 1650, when he removed to Watertown, where many of his descendants have made their homes He owned land near Fresh Pond and in other parts of Watertown He died April 11, 1684, and the inventory of his estate is dated April 20, 1684 His will is dated January 7, 1678-9, and was proved June 14, 1684 The children of Lewis and Anna Jones were Josiah, born 1643, of whom later, Phebe, born at Roxbury, January 21, 1645, died there 1650, Lydia, married Jonathan Whitney, Shubael, born July 1, 1651

(II) Josiah Jones, son of Lewis Jones (1), was born in 1643 He was admitted a freeman April 18, 1690 He settled in that part of Watertown now Weston, was a charter member of the Weston Church and was elected deacon January 4, 1709-10 He was captain of one of the Watertown companies, and about 1690 the town was divided into the districts of Weston, Watertown and Waltham, of which the officers in command of the military companies were respectively Lieutenant Jones, Captain Garfield and Captain Bond Later Josiah Jones was made captain He was selectman of Watertown in 1685-86-87-90-1702 to 1709 inclusive Among his real estate was a farm of one hundred and twenty-four acres purchased of John and Sarah Stone, situated on the north side of the Sudbury highway, about two miles from Sudbury He died October, 1714

He married, October 2, 1667, Lydia Treadway, who died September 17, 1743, aged ninety-four years Their children Lydia, born August 25, 1668, married Nathaniel Coolidge, Josiah, born October 20, 1670, Mary, born December 10, 1672, Nathaniel, of whom later, Samuel, born July 9, 1677, died January 17, 1717-8, James, born September 4, 1679, Sarah, born February 6, 1681, married John Warren, Anna, born June 28, 1684, married Deacon Joseph Mixer, John, born March 19, 1686-7, Isaac, baptized May 25, 1690, settled at Bolton, Connecticut

(III) Nathaniel Jones, fourth child of Josiah Jones (2), was born in Watertown, December 31, 1674 He became a prominent citizen of Watertown, was one of the first settlers of Worcester, and later in life went to Falmouth, York county, Maine, and settled there He was a captain of the Weston company In 1719 he drew forty acres in the first division and was one of the third and permanent colony to settle Worcester He was selectman of Worcester in 1722-23, and representive to the general court in 1727 He left Worcester about 1730 and settled in Falmouth, now the state of Maine He was in Falmouth in 1731 when he deeded land in Sutton, though in 1729 when he deeded land there to his son, Nathaniel Jones, Jr, he was still of Worcester An extra grant of land on account of an error in a previous grant was made to Captain Nathaniel Jones in Worcester, March 17, 1735 Captain Jones had land in Oxford which he sold in 1737 While in Worcester Captain Jones kept a tavern on the road to Leicester, about a mile beyond New Worcester, and for a century afterward it was known as the Jones Tavern

He married (first) Mary Cook, and they had eleven children, five of whom were born in Worcester He married (second) Mary Flagg, and had three more children, the youngest of whom was born in Falmouth, Maine He died in Falmouth, November, 1745 The children of Nathaniel Jones were 1 Phinehas, born February 28, 1704-5, died November 3, 1743, settled in Portland or Falmouth (?), had three daughters 2 Nathaniel, of

Erastus Jones

whom later 3 Stephen, born August 17, 1709, married, July 31, 1735, Lydia Jones, settled in Falmouth near his brother Phinehas, was captain of a company in the Quebec expedition in 1746 and was killed during an attack by the French January 7, 1746, he left two sons and two daughters 4 Noah, born November 26, 1711, married Rebecca Heywood, (?) of Worcester 5 Jonas, born April 22, 1715, married, September 6, 1763 6 Ichabod, baptized May 26, 1717, married ——— Coffin, of Newbury, Massachusetts, settled in Boston 7 Isaac, born in Worcester, October 14, 1722, married a Nantucket girl and died in the West Indies 8 Sarah 9 Mary, born August 10, 1719 10 Eunice, born November 21, 1724 (twin) 11 Lucy, born November 21, 1724 (twin) 12 Moses, had one daughter 13 Lydia 14 Jabez, inherited the farm at Falmouth, had three wives

(IV) Nathaniel Jones, Jr, second child of Captain Nathaniel Jones (3), was born April 5, 1707, at Weston, Massachusetts He lived in Sutton, Leicester and Charlton He married, according to Bond, four times, but the writer found records of only three of the marriages The first wife had seven children, of whom Enos and Asa alone were living at the time of the father's death in 1795 Nathaniel was living in Leicester in 1742 In 1858 or before he removed to the Country Gore as Charlton was then called He was a Baptist and belonged to the Sutton Baptist Church He filed a certificate with others at Charlton in 1761 to secure exemption from paying rates for the support of the Charlton church or parish His third son, Daniel, was killed by the French at the attack on Ticonderoga in 1758

The children of the first marriage were 1 Enos, born about 1730, perhaps in Sutton, married Amphas ——— before 1750, settled in Charlton 2 Asa, born about 1735, married (intentions dated November 6) 1762, Dorcas Wade, of Gloucester 3 Daniel, killed in 1758 at Ticonderoga Child of Nathaniel and Hannah 4 Mary, born at Leicester, August 12, 1742, married in 1761, at Charlton, Daniel Streeter No children recorded of Nathaniel and Elizabeth Butler (intentions filed at Leicester, both recorded as of the Country Gore) The children of Nathaniel and Eleanor (Woodward) Jones She was of Newton, Massachusetts, intentions dated April 10, 1758 5 Eli, born June 5, 1759 6 Hannah, born September 28, 1760 7 Phinehas, born February 7, 1762, was a soldier in the revolution 8 Eleanor, born December 26, 1764 All the eight children just named were mentioned in the will of the father made in 1795, except Daniel, who was deceased

(V) Eli Jones, son of Nathaniel Jones Jr, (4), was born in Charlton, Massachusetts, June 5, 1759 He was a private in Captain Abijah Lamb's Charlton company, Colonel Jonathan Holman's regiment, in 1776 and 1777 He settled at Charlton, married there, April 21, 1786, Lydia Lamb, and died there February 13, 1812 Lydia (Lamb) Jones died May 27, 1848 Their children Dr Asa, of whom later, Eli, born April 16 (1789, Susannah, January 20, 1792, Ebenezer, May 15, 1794, Lydia, May 21, 1796, Erastus, March 31, 1800, Hannah, June 24, 1806

(VI) Dr Asa Jones, eldest son of Eli Jones (5), was born in Charlton, Massachusetts, February 20, 1787 He studied medicine for a number of years and settled in Spencer, where he practiced his profession during all the active years of his life He was only forty-four years old when he died, October 22, 1831 He married, December 22, 1814, Lucy Dunbar, the daughter of Thomas and Lucretia (Smith) Dunbar, of Leicester, she died at Spencer, July 27, 1844, aged fifty-four years Their children Mary White, born September 9, 1817, at Spencer, married Rev Gideon Johnson, of Haverhill, Eliza, born May 7, 1819, married Warren H Dunton, May 9, 1844, Asa Thomas, born August 17, 1820, founder of the shoe factory in Spencer, Erastus, of whom later, Lucy Dunbar, born August 2, 1828

(VII) Erastus Jones, fourth child of Dr Asa Jones (6), was born in Spencer, Massachusetts, September 11, 1825 He was educated in the public schools of Spencer, completing his course of study at the high school He spent several years in the employ of his brother, Asa Thomas Jones, who was a shoe manufacturer in Spencer Asa T Jones began to make boots and shoes in 1841 in the old Livermore house at the corner of Main and North streets When Erastus was of age he was admitted to partnership by his brother and the firm name became A T & E Jones This partnership continued until 1862, when the senior member of the firm retired and Hezekiah P Starr was admitted The style of the firm then became E Jones & Co, a name that has been familiar to the shoe trade of the country as well as to all the people of the vicinity for forty years or more The present Jones factory was built in 1860, but has been enlarged to several times its original capacity, and the firm has almost constantly given employmet to several hundred hands The factory is a five-story structure, eighty feet long, with two ells of like dimensions, and has a capacity of more than twenty-five hundred pairs of shoes a day The firm has been very successful While all the latest machinery has been adopted and advanced ideas in production sought for, the management has avoided speculation and risks of all kinds

Mr Jones has been president of the Spencer National Bank since its organization in 1875, and for about twenty-five years was the president, trustee and member of the board of investment of the Spencer Savings Bank He was town treasurer of Spencer for a number of years and also town clerk In 1874 he was representative to the general court, and in 1896-97 was state senator from the fourth Worcester senatorial district During his first term in the senate he was on the committee on banks and banking, and chairman of the joint standing committee on liquor laws During his second year he was chairman of the committee on banks and banking, also a member of the committee on taxation and on printing He is an earnest and consistent Republican in politics

Mr Jones and his wife are members of the Congregational church of Spencer The Spencer *Sun* said of Mr Jones not long ago "Mr Jones is a man of marked characteristics, in both his business and private life, and his generous disposition through long years of intercourse has endeared him to his business associates and numerous employees They have found him a man of few words, but yet enough to convey an unmistakable meaning He is quiet to a fault, if that be possible, nevertheless there is an energy in his quietness which has made his business life a success * * * His life from the beginning of his business career has been one of untiring industry" Mr Jones has been a generous contributor to various charities and public objects

He married, June 5, 1850, Mary I Starr, daughter of John B H Starr, of Thomaston, Maine They have four children Lucy I, born July 3, 1852, married Charles L Kingsbury, of Boston, Massachusetts, Julia F, born January 5, 1856, Mary P, born July 31, 1866, married, June 4, 1891, Albert Sauveur, of Boston, a member of Harvard College faculty, Everett Starr, of whom later

(VIII) Everett Starr Jones, youngest child of Erastus Jones (7), was born in Spencer, Massachusetts, November 28, 1864 He was graduated at Harvard University in the class of 1890 He was employed actively for several years in the factory of his father's firm and became the general superintendent of the factory For about two years he was with the American Ballot Company, engaged in the manufacture of election apparatus In the spring of 1897 he left this company and in the fall sailed for Germany, spending a year and a half at the universities of Leipsic and Berlin Upon his return he accepted a position as teacher of German in the Providence Classical high school In the fall of 1899 he was appointed an instructor in the department of modern languages at Tome Institute, Port Deposit Maryland, where he has ever since been engaged

He married, July 8, 1897, Anna Arnold Hunt, of Boston They have three children David Everett, born in Charlottenburg, Germany, November 12, 1898, Sheldon Starr Jones, born at Fort Deposit, Maryland, June 2, 1900, Erastus, born 1905

LONGLEY FAMILY John Longley (1), father of the immigrant ancestor of the Longley family of Shirley, Massachusetts, and of Charles I Longley, of Boylston, was a resident of Frisby, Lincoln county, England He was a clerk Shortly after his son and heir William went to America, John Longley died, and August 8, 1638, William, his son, made a letter of attorney (power of attorney) to Thomas Meeke, of Wynflete, St Mary, Lincoln county, to sell and rent lands, goods and legacies descended to him from his father Owing to an error in the records at Lynn in the name of William when his land was granted to him, Savage and others were led to believe that Richard Longley was the father of William It is doubtful if any Richard Longley ever lived in Lynn in the early days If so, William knew him not William seems to be the only son who emigrated to America

(II) William Longley, son of John Longley (1), was born in Frisbie, Lincoln county, England, in 1614 He came to Lynn as early as 1638, and was admitted a freeman March 4, 1639 He resided in Lynn twenty-two years, and was a prominent citizen and office holder there He removed to Groton about 1659 His name appears first on the Groton records in 1663, and in 1665 he was elected selectman William Longley had to go to the courts to correct the title to his lands at Lynn which he drew in 1638, and on which he had lived over twenty years It seems that through a clerical error William's name was entered as Richard Longley on the proprietors' book, and the court records give ample proof that no Richard Longley existed, so the title was cured and doubtless William was able to deed his land to the purchaser when he went to Groton to live He had to leave Groton, of course, in 1675, on account of King Philip's war, and he went to Charlestown to live during the hostilities He served at one time as clerk of writs, indicating that he was well educated He died November 29, 1680 His will, made November 3, 1680, was recorded April 10, 1681, bequeathing to wife Joanna, sons John and William, daughters, Mary Lemmond, Hannah Tarbell, Lydia Nutting, and Sarah Rand, and their children specified

He married, in England, Joanna Goffe, sister of Thomas Goffe, who was deputy governor of the Massachusetts Bay Company that received a grant from the Crown, March 19, 1628 Goffe was a member of both Plymouth and Massachusetts Bay companies, was a merchant of London, lost money on the business of chartering ships for the colonists of Governor Winthrop and others His widow married (second), Benjamin Crispe, and she died in 1698 The children of William and Joanna (Goffe) Longley were 1 John 2 Mary, married, 1666, Samuel M Lemont 3 Sarah, born October 15, 1660, married June 17, 1679, Thomas Rand, father of Robert Rand, to whom a grant of a thousand acres of land was given by the general court in what is now New Hampshire, on account of the losses suffered by Governor Goffe, his great-uncle 4 Lydia, married James Nutting 5 William, Jr, mentioned below 6 Hannah married Thomas Tarbell, Jr 7 Ann 8 Elizabeth, married James Blood

(III) William Longley, Jr son of William Longley (2), was born about 1640, at Lynn, Massachusetts, and removed with his father to Groton in 1661, or earlier He was well educated, and stood well among his townsmen He was town clerk from 1666 to the time of his death in 1694, when he and his family were victims of an Indian raid All were slain except three of the children, who were carried into captivity The house was rifled and burned Near where it stood the mutilated bodies were buried by the neighbors and the spot marked by a small stone A few years ago a more suitable monument was erected to mark the site of the massacre and locate the graves of the victims It is said in Butler's History that the daughter Jemima, who had been tomahawked and scalped with the others, was found alive sitting upon a rock, that she recovered, married and raised a family Those who were captured were Betty, Lydia and John Betty died of starvation Lydia was sold to the French in Canada, became a Catholic, entered a convent and became very zealous and bigoted She wrote letters to her brother John, expressing her sorrow that he should remain under the influence of a heretical faith through which none could attain salvation John, who was about twelve years old when he was captured, told the Indians that his father's sheep were shut up in a barn and would starve unless they would permit him to go back and let them out He promised to return if they would let him go back, they consented and he kept his word and apparently won their admiration and confidence at the same time He made the best of his predicament and often said in after years that he liked the wild life he led among them and hoped he should never have to return to civilization And when the government finally ransomed him after five years, he had to be taken with force But soon after his return to Groton he entered upon his duties as a citizen with interest and zeal He was well educated and a man of uncommon ability

William Longley, Jr, married Lydia ——— He married (second) May 15, 1672, Deliverance Pease His children Betty, died in captivity, Jemima, scalped, but lived, Lydia, the nun, William, born February 17, 1675, John, mentioned above and also below, Joseph, born January 6, 1687

(IV) John Longley, son of William Longley, Jr, (3) was born in 1683, at Groton, Massachusetts He was captured by the Indians, July 27, 1694 and lived with them until ransomed in 1699 After he was brought back by force and educated, he became a leading citizen He was town clerk six years, deacon of the church from 1722 to the time of his death, 1750, town treasurer and parish treasurer and deputy to the general court, for three terms He was called a good man and an exemplary Christian He died May 25, 1750, aged sixty-seven years He married (first) Sarah Prescott, of Groton, who died March 8, 1718 He married (second) about 1720, Deborah Houghton, who died November 7, 1763 His first wife was a sister of Hon Benjamin Prescott, father of Colonel William Prescott, of Bunker Hill fame, of Colonel James and of Dr Oliver Prescott, of Groton The children of John and Sarah were Sarah, born March 28, 1706, William, February 13, 1708, John, January 6, 1710, Jonas, January 22, 1712, Lydia, June 26, 1716, married Amos Farnsworth Among the children of John and Deborah Longley were Zachary, born August 30, 1721, Joseph, September 12, 1724, died of wounds in the revolutionary army at Greenbush, New York, 1758, Jonathan, November 18, 1726, Zachariah, June 7, 1729, Nathaniel, September 6, 1731, Robert, March 11, 1733-4

(V) William Longley, son of John Longley (4), was born in Groton, Massachusetts, February 7, 1708 He settled in what is now the South Village of Groton, and his house was on the north side of the Catacunemaug on the side of the hill about half way between the river and the present location of the Fitchburg Railroad He and Samuel Hazen built the first grist mill in Shirley, and later added a saw mill The mills tood on the north side of the river His brothers Jonas and William also settled in what is now the town of Shirley, then Groton, in 1751, thirty years after the first settlement there, and two years before it was incorporated as a district of Groton The Shirley history contains an interesting account of the removal of the three Longley families through the wilderness to their new homes in Shirley The trip took three days, though only about ten miles as the crow flies William Longley died at Shirley, May 15, 1788 He married, January 4, 1734, Mary Parker, of Groton Their children were 1 William, born at Groton, died young 2 Mary, born at Groton, October 13, 1736, died in 1749 3 William, born at Groton, May 23, 1738, was a miller, left numerous descendants in Shirley 4 Sarah, born at Groton, February 18, 1740, married (first) James Willard, (second) a Mr Hall, of Swansea 5 Anna, born at Groton, March 10, 1742, married Samuel Bartlett 6 Lydia, born at Groton, December 31, 1743, married Thomas Bennett, of Lancaster 7 Israel, born at Groton, October 12, 1745, progenitor through his son Israel, of a large family of the name in Nova Scotia and vicinity 8 Nehemiah, born at Groton, September 4 1747, married Miriam Sawtell, of Shirley 9 Mary, born at Groton, November 4, 1749, married John Priest, of Lancaster 10 Joshua, born at Groton, July 23, 1751, married Bridget Melvin, of Concord 11 James, mentioned below 12 Abigail, born at Shirley, December 1, 1755, died October, 1758

(VI) James Longley, son of William Longley (5), was born at Shirley, Massachusetts, November 4, 1753 He married Molly Bartlett, of Northborough, who died August 27, 1831 He resided in Boylston during his active life, and died there January 14, 1837 He had to begin early in life to earn his own living He was bound out to Samuel Gamble, of Northborough, a carpenter by trade, and received rather shabby treatment that would not be allowed under modern conditions The boy was not properly fed nor clothed, and received no schooling He completed his apprenticeship according to the terms of his father's agreement As soon as he became of age he obtained work in a hotel at Northboro and arranged with a private teacher to assist him in acquiring a knowledge of the alphabet and the first principles of education He learned rapidly and soon mastered all that was taught in his day in the public schools He was a student all his life He became captain of the military company He was for nearly half a century a justice of the peace, an office that formerly possessed the importance of local magistrate For many years he was assessor and selectman and deputy to the general court He was a soldier in the revolution First he served as mariner under Commodore Moody, and made several successful cruises He afterward joined the land forces, and was with the army under General Sullivan in the famous retreat after the Battle of Long Island He was in the campaign that ended with the surrender of General Burgoyne He settled in Boylston, Massachusetts, shortly before the end of the war During his declining years he enjoyed a pension He was loyal to the new government at the time of Shay's Rebellion, and held a commission for its suppression He was in that night march from Hadley to Petersham through a blinding storm of snow

The children of James and Molly Longley were 1 Otis, born December 8, 1784, married Lydia Patch, of Worcester, had six children, all born in Boylston 2 Mary, born in Boylston, February 18, 1786, married, February 18, 1808, Deacon Abijah Flagg, who died December 22, 1850, they had seven children 3 Jonas, born November 11, 1787, married, December 22, 1812, Susan Smith, of Northboro, he died at Westborough, January 31, 1866, they had four children 4 Jonathan, born June 21, 1789, graduate of Harvard, a preacher of distinction, never married, died January 26, 1850 5 James, born June 22, 1791, died June 10, 1793 6 Israel, born November 21, 1792, died June 6, 1793 7 James, born September 3, 1794, married Sally Eustice, of Boston, July 3, 1838, he was an alderman of Boston 8 Israel, born November 8, 1795, died November 30, 1812 9 Betsey, born May 28, 1799, married Daniel Barnes, of Berlin, they had ten children, all born in Boylston 10 Parker, mentioned below 11 Lois, born May 26, 1805, married, April 29, 1829, Joseph Dudley

(VII) Parker Longley, son of James Longley (6), was born in Shirley, November 22, 1800 He married, April 3, 1832, Lydia D Green, of Northboro He was never possessed of firm health, and was obliged to go abroad in his youth, following the sea for a number of years and visiting Nova Scotia, where he had relatives, and various other places He was a man of kindly and generous nature, and was highly esteemed by all who knew him He followed farming through life In politics he was a Whig, and in his last years a Republican He attended the Congregational church His wife, Lydia Davis, the daughter of Aaron and Lydia (Goddard) Green, of Northboro, died at Boylston, October 9, 1877 Their children were 1 Edwin, born October 3, 1833, died October 17, 1833 2 Edwin Franklin, born August 29, 1834, married Emily Stephenson, of Northboro January 19, 1856 They have three children Nellie Anna, born September 4, 1857, Edwin Franklin, born November 19, 1858, died February 17, 1859, Charles Herbert, born December 28, 1860 3 Charles Israel, mentioned below 4 Asahel Parker, born November 11, 1840, resided at Marlborough

(VIII) Charles Israel Longley, son of Parker Longley (7), was born in Boylston, Massachusetts, April 12, 1837, and was educated there in the public schools He went to work first for his brother, Edwin F Longley, Marlboro, who was a large manufacturer of boots and shoes, later of shoe boxes After four years in this business, he returned to Boylston, purchased the interests of his brothers in the homestead, and conducted it the rest of his life He took a lively interest in public affairs He was a Republican in politics, and active in the party organization, serving frequently as delegate to senatorial and other conventions He was for seven years on the board of assessors, and for two years collector of taxes He was one of the trustees and clerk of the Boylston Social Library for nearly twenty years, and was among those who helped organized and promote the Boylston Public Library which was the successor of the Social Library, and he was on the first board of trustees In his early days he was a member of the militia company He was an active member of the Congregational church, and served on the Parish Committee He was interested in music and had a well trained voice For many years he was the leader of the church choir Few men in Boylston had a larger sphere of influence in his day, and none was more highly respected and loved than Mr Longley He died September 5, 1900, having been an invalid for eighteen years previous to his death

Mr Longley married, June 4, 1864, Olive Esther Stratton, daughter of Jonathan and Laura (Wickwire) Stratton, born October 12, 1840 Her father was a farmer and wheelwright Their children, all born in Boylston, were 1 George Henry, born February 5, 1867, married Lena Walker, of Boylston, and has one child—Harriet Walker, born September 7, 1903 2 Walter Stratton, born September 29, 1870, married Jennie B Lancourt, of Worcester, and has one child, Henry Wright, born September 2, 1900 3 Levi Parker, born January 5, 1873, married Sallie N Miller, of Hagerstown, Maryland, and has one child, Bertha Miller, born September 9, 1902 4 Charles Frederick, born February 12, 1876 5 James Edwin, born February 22, 1880

WALTER EVERETT MYRICK, of Spencer, Massachusetts, was born March 26, 1872, the son of Charles Willis and Catherine (Woodhead) Myrick, and grandson of Nathaniel Myrick, who was born in East Dennis, but lived in Spencer the greater part of his life, engaged in the wire manufacturing business, one of the leading industries of Spencer, of which he was one of the founders in conjunction with Richard Sugden W E Myrick's father, Charles Willis Myrick, was a boot and shoe manufacturer of Spencer, Massachusetts, with Edward Kent, under the firm name of Kent & Myrick, and his wife, Catherine Woodhead, was a native of England

Walter E Myrick received his early education in the common schools of his native place, and later attended high school, thus acquiring a good, general English education After leaving school he first engaged in the cranberry business for four years, and later for about eighteen months he was engaged in boot and shoe manufacturing business, as stockholder of the Tyler Moulton Shoe Company of Brookfield He subsequently returned to the cranberry business, in which he is at present engaged, conducting a profitable and extensive business, and is the owner of bogs in Wareham and Carver in the cape He holds the offices of president and manager of the Chandler Bog Company and the Myrick Bog Company, both of Plymouth county Mr Myrick's political sympathies lie with the Republican party, and he is a member of Spencer Lodge, F and A M, Worcester Chapter, R A M, and I O O F In religious affairs he accords with the Universalist faith

Mr Myrick married Fanny Chandler Packard, of Wareham, Massachusetts, the daughter of Freeman G Packard, a wheelwright, and Sarah Abby Packard Nathaniel W, a younger son of the late Charles Willis Myrick, married Helen Fairchild, of Los Angeles, California, where Mr Myrick is treasurer of Consolidated Iron and Pipe Company

FRANK ADAMS DRURY, a member of the banking firm of Drury & Bonney, of Worcester, and also actively interested and identified with other financial enterprises, was born in Spencer, Worcester county, Massachusetts, July 12, 1868, a son of Franklin and Caroline H (Bemis) Drury, grandson of ——— Drury, of Spencer, a prosperous farmer, and great-grandson of ——— Drury, who located in Spencer from Boston early in the eighteenth century Franklin Drury (father) was a boot manufacturer of Spencer, and he and his wife were the parents of four children Angenette, wife of Edward G Desoe, of Springfield, Massachusetts, and mother of two children Roland and Harold, Carrie, wife of Abner C Clark, of Spencer, and mother of three children Edith, Mabel, and Earle, Sadie, wife of A G Lamb, of Worceser, and mother of two children Miriam and Gladys, and Frank Adams Drury

In 1884, after completing a common and high school education, Frank Drury became connected with the Spencer National Bank, assumed the position of cashier in 1889 and held the same until his resignation in 1901 He then came to Worcester and engaged in the banking business under the name of Drury & Bonney, which has continued to the present time (1906) He was largely instrumental in the organization of the Merchants' National Bank of Worcester, and is a director and vice-president of the Spencer National Bank He holds membership in the Worcester, Commonwealth and Congregational Clubs He gives his political support to the candidates of the Republican party, the principles of which he firmly believes to be for the best form of government

Mr Drury married, June 4, 1891, Ellen S Prouty, daughter of Lewis Prouty, a boot manufacturer, who was a son of Isaac Prouty, of Spencer (See Prouty family) They are the parents of one child Percival Prouty Drury, born August 9, 1895. Mr and Mrs Drury are members of Plymouth Congregational Church of Worcester

ARTHUR NEWTON BOOTH Edward Booth (1), the great-grandfather of Arthur Newton Booth, of Worcester, was born in England, about 1775 He came to America when a young man and settled in Otter Creek, Wallingford, Vermont He married ——— Hill He was a farmer He met his death accidentally about 1812 from the overturning of a wagon in which he was riding After his death his widow and family removed to Potsdam New York, and later to Parishville, New York His children, all born in Wallingford, Vermont, were Ludwick, who was a shoemaker by trade, Norman, who was a tanner, Edward Skinner, see forward, Lavina, married Ira Sayles, a farmer

(II) Edward Skinner Booth, son of Edward Booth (1), was born about 1808, in Otter Creek, Wallingford, Vermont He settled in Parishville, New York, and was a prosperous farmer there. Among his children was John Hill Booth, of Worcester, see forward

(III) John Hill Booth, son of Edward Skinner Booth (2), was born in Parishville, New York, January 16, 1839 He attended school there and then learned the trade of painter At the age of twenty-three, August 18, 1862, he enlisted in Company A, Fifty-third Massachusetts Regiment, and served one year He was in the battle of Port Hudson and at Fort Bisland in Louisiana Returning

A. N. Booth

H. P. Starr

from his service in the civil war, Mr Booth went to Illinois and later to Michigan, where he engaged in farming He returned after a time to New York, however, and worked at his trade of house painting in Hornellsville He removed to Fitchburg, Massachusetts, where he worked at his trade He was also employed at Lowell for a time He came to Worcester, May 30, 1887, and was soon afterward appointed night janitor of the old city hall When the new city hall was built he retained his position and holds it at the present time He is a member of George H Ward Post, No 10, Grand Army, the Ancient Order of United Workmen, Victor Lodge, and a member of the Laurel Street Methodist Church

He married (first) Charlotte Sophia May, daughter of Nathan and Sophia Powers May, of Sterling, Massachusetts, and they had one child He married (second), March 6, 1865, Maria Lucy Parks, daughter of Aaron Parks Her parents were both born in Vermont He married (third) Semira Augusta Wheeler, daughter of Lorenzo and Jane (Spofford) Wheeler There were three children by the second wife, none by the third

The only child of John Hill and Charlotte Sophia May Booth, Jennie L, died in infancy The children of John Hill and Maria Lucy Booth were Lottie May, died in infancy, Volney Harvey, born August 23, 1867, married Nora Moore, resides in Springfield, Massachusetts, Arthur Newton, see forward, Clayton O, born November 25, 1872, died July 26, 1890

(IV) Arthur Newton Booth, son of John Hill Booth (3), was born in Gardner, Illinois, June 5, 1869 He attended the public schools at Hornellsville, New York, Fitchburg and Worcester, Massachusetts After completing his education he began to learn the carpenter's trade under M L Hall, for whom he worked three years, then for about seven years for Charles A Vaughan, the builder and contractor, becoming foreman for Mr Vaughan on important and difficult work In 1896 he started in business for himself, and achieved success from the first He is known as one of the most reliable and responsible builders in the city, with a thorough practical knowledge of his business As a workman is known by his chips, the following buildings among those Mr Booth built in the past ten years testify to his skill and ability as a builder The residence of Frank L Coes, Coes Square, N S Liscomb, a large double house, the first built on the Merrifield estate, Thomas Brown's, Germain street, Edwain Hall's, Oberlin street, Edward McCabe's, and J F Healy's, Forrest street, Arthur Ballard's, Louis E Booth's, Dean street, near Highland, Deacon H H Merriam's at Shrewsbury Mr Booth built the handsome residence, 18 Schussler road, in which he lives He has had the contracts for many of the tenement houses in Worcester He built school houses at Northville and Trowbridgeville for the city and the Highland Street Church of Christ Mr Booth has a wood-working shop at 51 Hermon street, where he gets out his own finish and cabinet work He is a member of Worcester Lodge of Odd Fellows, of Wachusetts Encampment, Canton, Worcester, No 3, Athelstan Lodge of Free Masons and Eureka Royal Arch Chapter

He married, November 25, 1891, Annie T Holland, daughter of Thomas and Ellen (Curran) Holland Her father was born in England and her mother in Ireland Their children are Clayton Thomas, died young, Ethel May, born May 11, 1893, Mildred Evelyn, born February 14, 1896

HEZEKIAH PRINCE STARR, who is now leading a retired life at his home in Spencer, surrounded with peace and plenty, and realizing to the full that there is no reward so satisfactory as the consciousness of a life well spent, was born in Thomaston, Maine, January 14, 1832, a son of John Bentley and Isabella (Prince) Starr, of Thomaston, Maine, and grandson of Richard Starr, a Baptist minister of Maine The family of which Hezekiah P Starr is a member consists of two other children John B, and Mary Isabella, wife of Erastus Jones, of Spencer, whose personal history and genealogy are contained in this publication

The educational advantages enjoyed by Hezekiah P Starr were obtained in the common schools of Thomaston, Maine, and the grammar school at Bath, Maine He then served an apprenticeship at the trade of tin and sheet iron worker, which line of business he continued for five years In 1854 he located in Spencer, where in the following year he entered the employ of A T and E Jones, boot and shoe manufacturers, with whom he continued to be associated up to 1862, when the senior member of the firm retired from the company and Mr Starr became a member of the company thereafter known as E Jones & Co Mr Starr retired from business in 1888 Mr Starr was one of the founders of Spencer Savings Bank and also one of its board of trustees A Republican politically he served as member of board of selectmen, and in earlier years was especially actively interested in Spencer's fire department He was a member of Commonwealth Club, of Worcester, Massachusetts

In January, 1857, Mr Starr married Ellen Smith Prouty, daughter of Isaac Prouty, who died January 7, 1860 One child was the issue of this union. Ellen Prouty Starr, born January 4, 1858, died May 22, 1898, she was the wife of Chester I Linley, and mother of three children Helen Frances, born May 2, 1890, Isabella Prince, born November 1, 1892, and Richard Starr, born October 26, 1896 On April 23, 1867, Mr Starr married Ellen E Lamson, of Worcester, daughter of Eli B Lamson, and her death occurred March 22, 1894 The children of this marriage are as follows Sarah Lamson, born January 31, 1868, died January 15, 1900, she became the wife of Ralph B Stone, of Spencer, April 23, 1891, and their children were Gerald Starr, born March 9, 1897, and Marjorie Adele, born February 14, 1899 Erastus Jones Starr, born December 19, 1869, married, August 1, 1893, Flora Elizabeth Bemis, of Spencer, and their children are Conant Lamson, born February 16, 1895, Ellen Bemis, born August 2, 1896, and Hezekiah Prince, born July 27, 1899

BOND FAMILY Jonas Bond (1), progenitor of the Bond family of Worcester county, Massachusetts, lived in Bury St Edmunds, Suffolk county, England He moved there about 1590, after the birth of his second child, and was buried there August 5, 1601 He belongs to an ancient English family He married Rose Wood and their children were 1 Oliver 2 John, elder of the name, two being given the same name, both living 3 John, the younger, baptized December 26, 1591, married, June 28, 1612, Lydia Tixtott and had eight children 4 Bartholomew, born in Bury St Edmunds, mentioned in father's will 5 William, baptized December 28, 1595 6 Thomas, baptized September 8, 1597, maltster, of Bury St Edmunds 7 Elizabeth, baptized March 12, 1599, married (second), February 8, 1625, Deacon Ephraim Child, of Water-own, Massachusetts 8 Margaret, baptized December 10, 1600.

(II) Thomas Bond, son of Jonas Bond (1), was amily and resided in the Plymouth colony born in Bury St Edmunds, England 1597, and baptized September 8, 1597 He settled there, married and had children 1 Thomas, baptized September 2, 1622 2 John, baptized February 5, 1624 3 William, mentioned below 4 Henry, baptized April , 1628 5 Elizabeth, baptized March 12, 1630 6 Thomas, baptized May 31, 1632 7 Mary, baptized January 31, 1636 8 Jonas, baptized August 5, 1638, grocer at Bury St Edmunds

(III) William Bond, son of Thomas Bond (2), was the immigrant ancestor He was born at Bury St Edmunds, 1625, and baptized there September , 1625 He probably came to New England in 1630 with Deacon Ephraim Child, whose wife Elizabeth was sister of Bond's father He settled on what is lately known as John P Cushing's place, in Watertown, and was an ancestor of the historian, Dr Bond William Bond became one of the foremost men of his day, was town clerk, justice of the peace, captain of the Watertown military company, on the council of safety in 1689, was a deputy to the general court, first speaker under the new charter uniting Plymouth with Massachusetts Bay Colony, and presided in 1691, 1693 and 1695 He was admitted a freeman 1682, and joined the church in full communion March 27, 1687 He served with Captain Prentice and Deacon John Stone on the committee to rebuild Lancaster after King Philip's war He died December 14, 1695 An agreement for the division of his estate was made January 23d following between sons William, Thomas, Nathaniel, and Elizabeth Barsham and Richard and Mary Coolidge He married, February 7, 1649-50, Sarah, daughter of Nathaniel Bisco, the rich tanner (See Bisco family) She died February, 1692-3, and he married (second), 1695, Elizabeth, widow of John Nevinson Children of William and Sarah Bond 1 William, born December 1, 1650, lieutenant and deacon 2 John, December, 1652, freeman April 18, 1690, housewright and sergeant 3 Thomas, mentioned below 4 Elizabeth, born November 30, 1656, married Captain Nathaniel Barsham 5 Nathaniel, born January 19, 1658-9, died young 6 Nathaniel, born January 9, 1659-60 lieutenant, admitted freeman April 18, 1690 7 Sarah, born July 27, 1661, married Dr Palgrave Wellington 8 Jonas, born July 3, 1664, lieutenant colonel and justice of the peace, died April 21, 1727 9 Mary, married, June 22, 1693, Richard Coolidge

(IV) Thomas Bond, son of William Bond (3), born in Watertown, December 23, 1654, died December 17, 1704 He settled in that part of Watertown now Weston He married, September 30, 1680, Sarah, born 1661, daughter of Thomas Woolson, of Newton Bond died 1704 and administration on his estate was granted to his widow Sarah and son Thomas, January 22, 1704-5 Their children 1 Thomas, mentioned below 2 Sarah, born December 2, 1685, married, February 12, 1701-2, James Tredway 3 William, born February 1, 1687-8 4 Mary, baptized December 7, 1690, married, December 29, 1709, Isaac Bigelow 5 John, born July 14, 1695 6 Isaac, born July 22, 1698, cordwainer, resided in Sherborn, Natick and Sudbury

(V) Thomas Bond, son of Thomas Bond (4) born at Watertown, April 29, 1683, married, August 25, 1706, Lydia Spring, he died May 17, 1737, his widow married, June 20, 1744, Deacon John Warren, of Weston Children of Thomas and Lydia Bond 1 Thomas, born May 3 1708, settled in Newton 2 Jonathan, mentioned below 3 Henry, born September 6, 1712 4 Amos, born August 23, 1714, died September 29, 1762 5 Thaddeus, born January 15, 1716-7, married in Marlborough, March 24, 1740, Mary Rice, married (second), April 11, 1745, Prudence Warren, of Weston 6 Lydia, born May 21, 1718, married, March 21, 1744-5, Samuel Fiske 7 Phinehas, born January 8, 1724-5 8 Abijah, born November 28, 1727

(VI) Deacon Jonathan Bond, son of Thomas Bond (5), was born at Watertown, November 7, 1710 He resided at Waltham, Mendon and Westborough He married, April 13, 1732, at Watertown, Mary Harrington and settled in the West Precinct of Waltham, whence he moved to Mendon in 1743, and thence to Westborough in 1750 He served in Captain Benjamin Woods' company as lieutenant in 1755 in the French war, and in Captain Flagg's company in 1757 He was dismissed from the Watertown church to that of Westborough, September 29, 1757, and was for many years deacon of it He died January 11, 1789 Children of Deacon Jonathan and Mary Bond 1 Mary, born at Watertown, December 2, 1732, married Aaron Warner, of Upton, and settled in Westborough 2 Jonathan, born April 22, 1736, mentioned below 3 Thomas, born January 30, 1737 4 Eunice, born at Waltham, February 18, 1742, married ——— Newton, of Westborough 5 Joseph, born at Mendon, July 6, 1744, married Hepsibah Pratt, and settled in Westborough, removed to Bondstown, now Hampton, Ohio 6 Lydia, born at Mendon, January 12, 1747, married Moses Wheelock 7 Elizabeth, born at Westborough, March 28, 1752, died 1756 6 Lucy, born June 22, 1755

(VII) Jonathan Bond, son of Deacon Jonathan Bond (6), was born at Watertown, April 22, 1736 He settled in Boylston, Massachusetts, was deacon of the church there, and died there 1794 His will was dated November 1, 1793 and his son John was executor He married Ruth Tyler, who died at North Brookfield April 26, 1814 After the death of Deacon Bond she went to live with her son, Deacon Jonathan Bond, and married (second) October 11, 1809, Robert Bruce, of North Brookfield Children of Deacon Jonathan and Ruth Bond 1 Jonathan, born at Sturbridge, March 17, 1760 2 Joseph, born March 8, 1762, died October 16, 1781 3 Solomon born May 9, 1764 4 Mary, born at Brookfield, August 27, 17— 5 Sarah, born May 14, 1771, married Abijah Pierce, of Boylston 6 Ruth, born March 14, 1771, married John Bond, of Boylston, and died soon, leaving son Tyler 7 Eunice, born August 13 1775, at Boylston, married John Gates, of Stratford

(VIII) Jonathan Bond, Jr, son of Jonathan Bond (7), was born at Sturbridge, Massachusetts, March 17, 1760 He settled at Boylston, and married, 1784 Lucy, daughter of Robert Andrews, Sr She died October 14, 1817, aged fifty-eight years, five months, eighteen days He married (second) Mrs Mary Cobb, December 3 1818, he died at Boylston, September 3, 1821, aged sixty-one years, six months He was deacon of the church at Boylston and representative to general court Children of Jonathan and Lucy Bond 1 Joseph, born November 20, 1784, mentioned below 2 Lucy, born December 8, 1786 3 Lucinda, May 5, 1790 4 Joanna Hurd, January 11, 1792 5 Eli, May 28, 1794 6 Elliott, June 29, 1797 7 Ruth Tyler, November 10, 1801

(IX) Joseph Bond, son of Jonathan Bond (8), was born in Boylston, Massachusetts, November 20, 1784 He was educated in the public schools He kept a general store in his native town until 1832, when he bought the farm on Lincoln street where

THE SAWYER MEMORIAL LIBRARY
BOYLSTON, MASSACHUSETTS.

his grandson, Charles Elliott Bond, now lives, about half way between Worcester and Boylston, and is a very productive and valuable estate He lived there the rest of his life He was a prominent member of the Second Parish (First Unitarian) Church, and an active religious worker In politics he was a Whig until that party disbanded, when he joined the Republican party He died in 1863, and left his farm to his son, Joseph Elliott Bond He married (published September 2) 1814, Sophia, daughter of Moses Smith, of Sterling Their children Sophia, born at Boylston November 9, 1815, Joseph Elliott, born at Boylston June 20, 1820

(X) Joseph Elliott Bond, son of Joseph Bond (9), was born in Boylston, June 20, 1820 He was educated in the public schools of Boylston and Worcester and at Worcester Academy As the only son he was associated with his father in conducting the farm, and at the death of his father he succeeded to the ownership of the homestead He was a Unitarian in religion, and was one of the original members of the Republican party in Worcester He married Julia Ann, daughter of Silas and Hannah (Stowell) Barber, who resided in the vicinity of Barber's Crossing, Worcester Children of Joseph Elliott and Julia Ann Bond, all born in Worcester 1 Elizabeth Sophia, July 21, 1847 2 Mary Chapin, January 23, 1850 3 Florence Amelia, January 15, 1857 4 Charles Elliott

(XI) Charles Elliott Bond, son of Joseph Elliott Bond (10), was born in Worcester, October 3, 1851 He attended the public schools of his native town and took the course of study at the old Worcester Academy, then located at Lincoln Square He also took a commercial course in Howe's Business College, Worcester He assisted his father on the homestead, and lated succeeded his father in the ownership of the farm Mr Bond has lived all his life in the house on Lincoln street, and is one of the best known citizens of that locality He is an active Republican, and has frequently served his party as delegate to nominating conventions He is a member of Worcester Grange, Patrons of Husbandry, and Quinsigamond Lodge of Odd Fellows He is a Unitarian in religion, but usually attends the First Universalist Church He married, November 17, 1880, Fanny Louise, born in Chelsea, Massachusetts, December 26, 1850, daughter of George Francis Kingman and Lydia (Loring) Kingman Her father was a prominent sail maker of Chelsea They have no children

EVERETT KENDALL Francis Kendall (1), the immigrant ancestor of Everett Kendall, of Boylston, Massachusetts, born in England ih 1620, gave his age as about thirty-eight years in a deposition December, 1658 He settled in Woburn, Massachusetts, in 1640, or earlier, and was one of the thirty-two men of Charlestown who signed the town orders for Woburn He was on the Woburn tax list in 1645 with his brother, Thomas Kendall, and was admitted freeman May 26, 1647 When he married, December 24, 1644, Mary Tidd, his name was recorded "Francis Kendall, alias Miles," and the family tradition explains this alias by the fact that he was said to have left England without the consent of his parents His brother Thomas seems never to have used any other name Francis Kendall served the town at different times eighteen years on the board of selectmen, and often on important committees, such as the laying out of lots to the proprietors and the building of the meeting house He was tithing man in 1676 He got into trouble with the Puritan church because he did not believe very much in infant baptism, failed to attend communion, and was even found guilty of attending Anabaptist meetings He was also fined for being late once at a selectmen's meeting He died 1708, and his wife died 1705 His will was dated May 9, 1706 He was a miller, and left his corn mill to sons John, Thomas and Samuel This old mill was in the ownership of the family for six generations The present mill, known as Kendall's Mill, was built by Samuel Kendall shortly after 1700 Children of Francis and Mary Kendall 1 John, born July 2, 1646 2 Thomas, January 10, 1648-9 3 Mary, January 20, 1650-1, married Israel Reed 4 Elizabeth, born January 15, 1652-3, married first, Ephraim Winship, second, James Pierce 5 Hannah, born January 26, 1654-5, married William Green, Jr, as his second wife 6 Rebecca, born March 2, 1657, married Joshua Eaton, December, 1706 7 Samuel, mentioned below 8 Jacob, born January 25, 1660-1 9 Abigail, born April 6, 1666, married William Reed, May 24, 1686

(II) Samuel Kendall, son of Francis Kendall (1), born in Woburn, Massachusetts, March 8, 1659, settled about 1742 in Lancaster, Massachusetts, and is the progenitor of the Sterling family as well as that of Boylston and others of the vicinity His will was made December 6, 1742, and proved 1749 He died about 1749, when he was ninety years old He married, November 13, 1683, Rebecca, daughter of Isaac Mixer She died October 25, 1691 He married (second), March 3, 1692, Mary, daughter of William Locke Children of Samuel and Rebecca Kendall were 1 Samuel, mentioned below 2 Isaac, born September 13, 1686, married, October 9, 1706, Hannah Walker, and settled in Ashford, Connecticut 3 Joshua, born March, 1689, married, March 25, 1710, Susannah Harrington, resided at Watertown, Massachusetts, and Ashford, Connecticut 4 Rebecca, born July 6, 1691, died November 25, 1691 5 Mary, born February 3, 1692-3, died August 14, 1727 6 Rebecca, born January 26 1694-5, married Samuel Russell 7 Abigail, born March 3, 1697, married William Nichols, of Reading, 1719-20 8 Ebenezer, born May 16, 1700, married Hannah ——— 9 Ruth, born April 23, 1703 married Bancroft 10 Tabitha, born January 22 1706-7, married, 1729, Nathan Richardson

(III) Samuel Kendall, son of Samuel Kendal (II), was born August 13, 1684 He married Prudence ——— about 1710 Their children were 1 Samuel, mentioned below 2 Rebecca, bor August 27, 1714 3 Stephen, born March 10, 171

(IV) Samuel Kendall, son of Samuel Kenda (III), was born September 4, 1711 He settled i Sterling, Massachusetts, and married Phebe Brin tain September 23, 1736 Sterling then was know as Chocksett, part of Lancaster These children c Samuel and Phebe were baptized in Sterling b Rev Mr Mellen 1 Samuel, baptized Februar 17, 1745 2 Rebecca, baptized February 17, 174 3 Abigail, baptized July 20, 1746 4 Caleb, bap tized May 15, 1748 5 Bartholomew, baptized Feb ruary 18, 1749 6 Caleb, baptized March 24, 175 7 Bartholomew, baptized February 28, 1753 8 Wil iam, baptized October 13, 1754 9 Phebe, baptiz July 3, 1757 10 Lucy, baptized February 10, 176 11 Lucinda, baptized November 14, 1762

(V) Caleb Kendall, son of Samuel Kendall (4 born 1750, baptized in Sterling (Chocksett) Churc March 24, 1750, settled in Boylston He marrie first, Priscilla Savory, who bore him four childre He married (second), April 15, 1788, Mrs Lu (Baldwin) Kendall, widow of Thomas Kendall S died at Boylston, November 22, 1845, aged eighty-fi years Children of Caleb and Priscilla 1 Priscill 2 Zipporah 3 Caleb, Jr, married, June 24, 18

Dolly Sawyer 4 Joshua, mentioned below Children of Caleb and Lucy 5 Lucy, married Joseph Sawyer 6 David, born March 12, 1791 7 Samuel, born October, 1792 8 Hannah, married Phineas Moore 9 Elmira, married Jotham Howe 10 Emily, married James Hastings 11 William, married Susan Hartshorn

(VI) Joshua Kendall, son of Caleb Kendall (5), born at Boylston (Shrewsbury, North Precinct) May 1, 1781, died there September 22, 1813, aged thirty-two years, four months and twenty-one days He was, according to an account we have of him, "a veritable giant in his day, whom no single man would care to meet in any contest, yet his kindly nature and amiable disposition made him a choice companion among his associates" He resided in the house now or lately owned by Mr Lynch He married at Boylston, May 25, 1807, Patty Sawyer Their children 1 Oliver Sawyer, mentioned below 2 Charles Sheldon, born August 19, 1809, married Mary Andrews 3 Horace Hastings, died young

(VII) Oliver Sawyer Kendall, son of Joshua Kendall (6), was born at Boylston, April 30, 1808 He resided on the Oliver Sawyer farm at Boylston, where he died July 26, 1881 His educational opportunities in youth were limited, but largely by his own efforts was a man of excellent education In early manhood he engaged in the lumber business, which he followed successfully for many years He was a prominent man in local affairs, serving the town as assessor for several terms, selectman from 1853-6 and was representative to general court 1854 In politics he was originally a Whig, but with the majority of his party associates joined the Republican party at the time of its organization He married, December 13, 1836, Mindwell (called "Minday"), daughter of Nathaniel Lamson, of Boylston Their children, all born in Boylston 1 Nathaniel Lamson, born June 27, 1841 2 Everett, born July 17, 1845, mentioned below 3 Oliver Sawyer, Jr, born July 30, 1848, married Hattie Moore, 1871, and resides in Worcester (the founder of the well known house of Oliver S Kendall & Son, dealers in stoves, furnaces, steam heaters, gas and electric fittings, mantels, etc He was in partnership with his son, Oliver S Kendall, Jr

(IX) Everett Kendall, son of Oliver Sawyer Kendall (8), was born in Boylston, Massachusetts, July 17, 1844 He attended the public schools of his native town and the New Ipswich (New Hampshire) Academy For some years he was employed by his father in the lumber and firewood business Then for some time he was engaged in farming After his marriage he removed to Worcester and entered the grain and feed business, but after his father's death he resumed farming on the homestead at Boylston in company with his brother Nathaniel, and has ever since resided there The Kendall farm is one of the most desirable in the town Mr Kendall was at one time actively interested in the local grange, Patrons of Husbandry He was formerly a member of the Sunday school class of John B Gough, the famous temperance orator, whose home was in Boylston In politics Mr Kendall is a Republican He has been on the board of assessors of the town of Boylston He married, January 9, 1872, in Sterling, Mary Frances daughter of Asa and Lucy Walker (Hubbard) Keyes Her father was a prosperous farmer, selectman of Sterling, and representative to general court 1872 Mr and Mrs Kendall have no children

DARLING FAMILY Dennis Darling (1), the immigrant ancestor of the Darling family of Mendon, to which the late Albert Newbury Darling belonged, was a pioneer at Braintree and Mendon, Massachusetts He had an older brother, George Darling, who settled in Salem, Massachusetts, about 1647 and resided also at Lynn and Marblehead Another brother, John, came with Dennis Darling to Braintree and also to Mendon John Darling settled in what is now Blackstone and south Bellingham Dennis located at first near the town seat, but his children located more in the south parish He removed to Mendon just after the close of King Philip's war in 1677 or 1678 He signed a pathetic petition of the inhabitants of old Mendon, in 1681, asking aid and church privileges of the general court His name appears on the tax list for 1685

He was married, May 3, 1662, by Peter Brackett, at Braintree, to Hannah Francis They seem to have had six children in Braintree and four in Mendon, viz Cornelius, born June 1, 1663, at Braintree, John, born 1664-5, see forward, A child, born August 18, 1667, died next day, Sarah, born January 26 1669-70, Cornelius, born March 23, 1675 Hannah, born June 14 1677 Ebenezer, Daniel, born at Mendon, Elizabeth, Benjamin, born at Mendon

(II) John Darling, son of Dennis Darling (1), was born at Braintree, September 2, 1664, died at Bellingham, May 29, 1753, in his ninetieth year Captain John Darling became a great business man and landed proprietor He headed the petition for the setting off of the town of Bellingham which was incorporated in 1719 and he owned land in Mendon in 1718 As one of the heirs of Samuel Shepherd, in 1691, he gave a quitclaim deed and again in 1706 . Land was laid out to John Darling in Mendon June 7, 1700, and he served on committees to lay out land there

He married (first) Elizabeth Thompson who died 1687 He married (second) Ann —— 1689 She died 1690 He married (third) Elizabeth Morse The only child by first marriage was John, see forward, by the second marriage was Ann The children of John and Elizabeth (Morse) Darling were Elizabeth Samuel, born March 18, 1693-4, Ruth Hannah, Margaret, Ebenezer, ancestor of the Oxford and Sutton families, Mary, Martha, Abigail, Deborah

(III) John Darling Jr, son of John Darling (2) was born in Mendon Massachusetts, April 1, 1687 He is first mentioned on the Mendon records in 1718, when he received a five acre home lot in the sixth division The place was located on Caleb hill, south of the common and adjoining lands of Benjamin Wheelock and Thomas Thayer and his own land He had many grants after that, in 1718-22-23-29 He is called Junior as lately as 1740, when his father apparently became identified with Bellingham where he died in 1753 Among his children was Pelatiah, born in Mendon, see forward

(IV) Pelatiah Darling, son of John Darling (3), was born in 1720 at Mendon, Massachusetts He is first mentioned on the Mendon records in 1746, when land was laid out to him adjoining his other land, probably inherited or deeded to him by his father He drew four acres April 17, 1757, in the eleventh division He must have been in the militia and served in the revolution as he was called ensign on the records He was a private in Captain William Henry's company in 1779 at Castle and Governor's Island in Boston harbor He was also in Captain B Beard's company, commanded by Lieutenant John Benson He was in Captain Philip Ammidon's company, Colonel Dean's regiment, in 1781 He was called lieutenant on some records He was on the Mendon school committee (11th

ALBERT N. DARLING

district) in 1780 He was moderator of the proprietors' meeting, April 3, 1792 He deeded a farm to his eldest son John in 1787, another to Pelatiah, Jr, in 1797 He died in 1798, and his estate was in process of settlement in July, 1798

He married (intentions dated November 4), 1743, Elizabeth Darling Their children were John, settled in Mendon, Pelatiah, settled in Mendon, see forward, Abigail, Joshua Mary, Ruth, Phinehas, Elizabeth The foregoing are probably not in the correct order of birth

(V) Pelatiah Darling, Jr, son of Pelatiah Darling (4), was born at Mendon, Massachusetts, April, 1760, and was a soldier in the revolution, serving in Captain Peter Penniman's company, Lieutenant Colonel Nathan Tyler's regiment, in 1776 and 1777 He deeded his farm to Pelatiah Darling, Jr, in 1831 He married, July 22, 1790, Phila Taft, born January 4 1772, died September 6, 1841 He died April 3, 1839 Their children were Newton, born August 22, 1791, Maria, born March 22, 1794, Newbury, born September 18, 1797, see forward, Phila, born September 4 1800, Pelatiah, Jr, had the old homestead, Cyrus, Willis, Hannah

(VI) Newbury Darling, son of Pelatiah Darling, Jr (5), was born at Millville, Massachusetts, September 18, 1797 He became a manufacturer of scythes at Easthampton, Connecticut, and at Millville Massachusetts During the latter part of his life he lived on a farm He married, August 17, 1824, Olive Kelley, born December 11, 1806 died November 4, 1867, the daughter of Wing and Diama Kelley Her father was born May 15 1773, died December 17, 1836, her mother Diama Daniels, was born March 14 1774, died February 14, 1842 The children of Wing and Joanna (Fowler) Kelley (Joanna born August 22, 1774 died October 12, 1797) were Nancy, Lydia Abigail The children of Wing and Diama (Daniels) Kelley were Joanna, born December 1, 1802, Ruth, born November 4, 1804, Olive, mentioned above, Diama born October 14 1808, Abby, born January 15, 1811, Albert, born March 30 1813 Marguerita Lucy, born September 15 1817 The children of Newbury and Olive (Kelley)) Darling were Isadora, born February 20, 1826, Albert Newbury see forward, Ellen M, born June 21, 1829, Eva, born November 13, 1829 died December 29, 1830, Homer Wing see forward, Susan Caroline, born January 2, 1834, at Easthampton Connecticut died February 1900, Newton, born June 15, 1840, at Easthampton, see forward, Warren Pollard, born December 10, 1843, died July 25 1844

(VII) Albert Newbury Darling, son of Newbury Darling (6), was born at Easthampton, Connecticut, August 31, 1827, died at Mendon, Massachusetts, December 22, 1902 He received a common school education at Easthampton, supplemented by instruction in a private school He became associated with his father in the manufacture of scythes at Millville, Massachusetts After giving up this business he was engaged in various enterprises, among which was a grocery store in Millville, Massachusetts In 1869 he went to Brooklyn as treasurer of the Brooklyn Watch Case Company, and there resided until 1888, when he retired from active business and went to Mendon to live Mr Darling was a large owner of stock in the Fahy's Watch Case Company and the Brooklyn Watch Case Company He was a Republican in politics, but devoted his attention almost exclusively during his active life to his business and acquired a large competence

He married (first), June 21, 1852, at Millville, Julia A Wilson, who died June 13, 1853 He married (second), November 19, 1855, at Johnston, Rhode Island Frances M Potter, who was born in 1833 and died February 14, 1860 He married (third), at Worcester, April 3, 1861, Harriet E Field, who was born at Coldbrook, Massachusetts, September 23, 1833 She resides at the homestead in Mendon The children of Albert Newbury and Frances (Potter) Darling were Julia Frances, born at Millville, Massachusetts, February 27, 1857, resides at Mendon and is an active member of the Unitarian church, Bert, born April 2, 1858, at Burrillville, Rhode Island, died August 30, 1859 The children of Albert Newbury and Harriet E (Field) Darling were Albert W, born August 3, 1862, at Millville, Massachusetts, died at Warren, Rhode Island, June 24, 1903, married, May, 1887, in Hopedale, Abbie Dudley, who was born May, 1867, in Mendon, Florence, born July 2, 1867, at Providence, Henry Field, born at Providence, September 4, 1869, died at Brooklyn, July 3, 1870, Justin, born at Brooklyn, New York, February 27, 1871, died same day, Everett F, born March 3, 1875, married, February 3, 1905, Bertha Ehlers, born September 11, 1875, in Trinidad, and they have—Ruth Ehlers Darling, born February 1, 1906, at New Rochelle, New York

(VII) Ellen M Darling, daughter of Newbury Darling (6), was born at Easthampton, June 21, 1824, died 1887 She married Edward Thayer Their children were Albert S, Edward D, Ellen O, Ernest L Thayer

(VII) Homer Wing Darling, son of Newbury Darling (6), was born at Easthampton, Connecticut, January 8, 1832, died December 11, 1892 He was a farmer during the greater part of his life He married, April 7, 1857, at Uxbridge, Abbie Cook, who was born at Uxbridge, November 11, 1839 Their children were 1 Emily, born March 28, 1858, at Burrillville, Rhode Island, married, May 2, 1876, Samuel Bennett, their children are Edith, born at Mendon, June 13, 1878, married, August 1, 1896, Timothy Raymond Scott, and their children are Florence, born October 17, 1897, at Providence, Robert, born June 8, 1902, Florence, born August 21, 1882, at Mendon 2 George Homer, born February 7, 1860, at Uxbridge, married, January 24, 1883, Annie Parkinson, and their children are Ida Olive, born December 19, 1883, at Mendon, Abbie M, born August 13, 1887, Homer, born September 16, 1893 3 Grace, born July 14, 1872, at Mendon, married, February 16, 1898, Fred Platt, and their children are Infant son, born December 27, 1898, at Lynn, Marjorie Platt, born December 31, 1899, at Saugus, Doris Platt, born September 24, 1900, at Saugus, Gertrude Platt, born October 24, 1902, at Saugus

(VII) Newton Darling, son of Newbury Darling (6), was born at Easthampton, Connecticut, June 15, 1840, died January 31, 1895 He was in various lines of business in early life, but for many years was interested in the Brooklyn Watch Case Company, of which his brother was treasurer for many years He married, at Mendon, October 10, 1867 Mary Hastings Their children were Clare, Christine, Clarence

WILLIAM HENRY HASTINGS The Hastings family of Boylston are the descendants of Thomas Hastings, who came from Ipswich, England, as a stowaway on a ship which arrived in Massachusetts Bay, April 10, 1634 He settled in Scituate, where he married, and many of his descendants are to be found in this commonwealth

Nathaniel Hastings, William Hastings' grandfather, was a lifelong resident of Boylston, and a prosperous farmer of his day He served in the local militia company Eli Hastings, father of William H Hastings, was born in Boylston, April 29, 1831 In his earlier years he was a noted cattle dealer in that section, but the active period of his life has, for the most part, been devoted to tilling the soil He formerly took an interest in civic affairs, serving as road commissioner for a number of terms, and died May 25, 1906 Eli Hastings married Adeline Maynard, daughter of Asa and Adelaide (Minter) Maynard She died about 1884

William Henry Hastings, the principal subject of this sketch, was born in Boylston, January 27, 1860 He acquired his education in the Boylston public schools When a young man he engaged in the live-stock business, which he followed with gratifying success for a number of years, or until unable to compete with the western cattle shippers, and he then engaged in farming exclusively For two years he served as an assessor, and is at the present time chairman of the overseers of the poor In politics he is a Republican He is heartily in sympathy with all movements relative to the general improvement of the community, and is an active member of the local grange, Patrons of Husbandry In his religious belief he is a Congregationalist

In 1885 Mr Hastings married (first) Arvilla Snow, a native of Eastford Midway, Nova Scotia The children of this union are Eli Leigh, born in 1887, and William Earle, born in 1889 His present wife, who was, before marriage, Melinda Anastasia Tumbling, daughter of John Austin and Elizabeth (Miener) Tumbling of Lahave, Nova Scotia, is the mother of one son, Calvin Raymond Hastings, born October 27, 1900 Since retiring from the cattle business Mr Hastings has engaged extensively in market gardening and the growing of apples, also conducts quite an extensive dairy farm

DAVID CARROLL, one of the early Irish settlers of Worcester, was born in Bruree, county Limerick, Ireland, August 15, 1814, son of David and Ellen (Fitzgerald) Carroll, natives of Ballingarry, county Limerick, Ireland, whose family consisted of four other children namely James, John, Mary and Anne The Carrolls were well-to-do farmers, and belonged to the powerful and ancient Irish sept of the O'Carrolls To this sept also belongs the ancestors of Charles Carroll, of Carrollton a signer of the Declaration of Independence

David Carroll, of this review, learned the trade of a cabinet maker in early manhood He and his brother James and sister Mary left their native townland of Rockhill, Bruree parish, in April, 1840, and after a voyage of about thirty days landed in Mirimichi, on the northeast coast of New Brunswick, where they remained for about four months, David and James being employed at shipbuilding and the sister as a domestic In October of that year they came to Boston, Massachusetts, and late in the following month came to Worcester, David and James being employed, in the meantime repairing bridges on the old Boston & Worcester Railroad As early as 1842 David Carroll paid a real estate tax in the city of Worcester, but later he took a notion to try farming, and in 1856 moved to Charlton, having purchased a large farm in that town upon which he lived until 1873, when he returned to Worcester In 1875 he purchased the house at No 128 Central street, in which he has resided ever since

Mr Carroll and his wife were among the first (Miener) Tumbling, of Lahave, Nova Scotia, is contributors to the fund to build St John's Church They were members of Christ's Church, the first Catholic church that was built in Worcester, occupying the site now covered by St John's Church For more than thirty years Mr Carroll has been a communicant at St Anne's Church He contributed his labor as a carpenter, free for sixty days to erect the first St Anne's church on Shrewsbury street, which was abandoned when the new St Anne's Church was built In 1846 Mr Carroll was selected by Rev M W Gibson, then pastor of St John's Church, to purchase a site for a Catholic cemetery in some central location, the Catholic burying ground at Tatnuck, from which the bodies were removed this year (1906), being considered too far out of the way He purchased a tract of land for the cemetery from old 'Deacon" Brooks, south of Cambridge street between the old Norwich & Worcester and the Providence & Worcester railroads After the price had been agreed upon, however, the good "Deacon" found out that this land was to be used as a Catholic cemetery, and accordingly refused to give the deed Mr Carroll then purchased a tract of sixteen acres from the Hon Eli Thayer for one hundred dollars an acre, it being stipulated in the agreement that four hundred dollars should be paid down That tract formed the nucleus of St John's cemetery, which at present covers an area several times the size of the original tract

David Carroll married, October 6, 1842, Margaret Purcell, born near Limerick, Ireland, daughter of James and Mary (Quinn) Purcell the former named having been an uncle of Archbishop Purcell Their children are Thomas Edward, born December 23, 1845, married Bridget Butler, of Oxford, Massachusetts, January, 1873, and their children are Addie, Florence, Gertrude, Julia Cecelia Charles, Edward Thomas, David Chester, Margaret and Mildred John, born May, 1855, married Mary Weisman, of Millbury, Massachusetts Margaret, born August 26, 1856 Mary Jane, born August 13, 1858 Julia, born August 3, 1860, married Eugene M Moriarty, of Worcester, Massachusetts

LEANDER SIBLEY, who for many years prior to his death, April 7, 1890, led a retired life at his home in Spencer, Massachusetts, surrounded with peace and plenty, and realizing to the full that there is no reward so satisfactory as the consciousness of a life well spent, was born in Hardwick, Massachusetts, July 10, 1838, son of Sardius and Mary (Johnson) Sibley

John Sibley, the founder of the American branch of the Sibley family, was a native of England, from whence he emigrated in 1629, took freeman's oath at Old Salem, and settled in Sutton, Massachusetts The line of descent from this pioneer ancestor is as follows Samuel Sibley, who came to Sutton, 1652, and his wife Sarah (Leland) Sibley, born in England 1625, also took up her residence in that town the same year Even Sibley, who came to Sutton in 1680 James Sibley Moses Sibley Sarah Sibley, who was born in Sutton, 1755, died 1842 Charles Sibley who married Huldah Harwood, of Barre, Massachusetts Sardius Sibley, father of Leander Sibley, was born in Barre, Massachusetts, 1804 He married Betsey Johnson, of Barre, Massachusetts, and their children were Huldah, born 1827 wife of the Rev Benjamin Stevenson, and Sardius J, born 1829 On April 4, 1831, Mr Sibley married for his second wife Mary Johnson, who bore him the following children Betsey, born in Barre, 1834, became the wife of Roland Oakes, of Holyoke Mary Jane, born in Hardwick, 1836, became the wife of Joseph Perce, of Worcester Leander, born in Hardwick 1838 Charlotte Ellen, born 1840, became the wife of Orlando Remington,

Leander Sibley

of Fitchburg. Julia M., born 1842, became the wife of Samuel S. Dennis, of Hardwick. Emily L., born 1844.

Leander Sibley was deprived of a father's care at the age of four years, his mother being left with six children to rear and educate, but, being a woman of strength of character and experience, she was equal to the task and guided her children in such a way that they all became useful and active members of society. During his boyhood he depended partly on his own exertion, and his education was acquired in the public schools of Hardwick and the academy at New Salem. At the age of nineteen he had an illness which left him a cripple for the remainder of his life, but notwithstanding this he led a useful and industrious life. For seventeen years he taught school in Hardwick, a profession for which he was well qualified. In 1873 he removed to Spencer, Massachusetts, and opened a news and variety store, thereby earning a comfortable livelihood, and in 1885 he disposed of the business and retired from active labor. During his residence in Hardwick, Mr. Sibley served as a member of the board of assessors, and he also filled a similar office in Spencer, in addition to serving as a member of the school committee, commissioner of public parks, and commissioner of roads. He was an active and consistent member of the Universalist church, and donated generously toward the building of a new structure for that denomination a year prior to his death. He was a Republican in politics and aided to the best of his ability toward the success of the measures adopted by that party and to the election of its candidates.

On October 24, 1876, Mr. Sibley married Henrietta E. Fales, daughter of Charles Fales, a boot manufacturer of Brookfield, and granddaughter of Daniel Fales. No children were born of this marriage.

INDEX

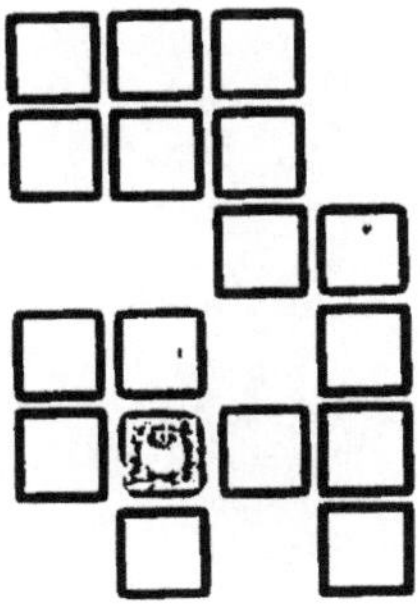

CPSIA information can be obtained
at www.ICGtesting.com
Printed in the USA
LVHW010135261218
601652LV00018B/812/P

9 781363 257416